✓ Y0-CBA-830

THE OFFICIAL®

1997 PRICE GUIDE TO

BASEBALL CARDS

BY
DR. JAMES BECKETT

SIXTEENTH EDITION

HOUSE OF COLLECTIBLES • NEW YORK

© 1996 by James Beckett III

All rights reserved under International and Pan-American Copyright Conventions.

 This is a registered trademark of Random House, Inc.

Published by:
House of Collectibles
201 East 50th Street
New York, New York 10022

Distributed by Ballantine Books, a division of Random House, Inc., New York, and simultaneously in Canada by Random House of Canada Limited, Toronto.

Manufactured in the United States of America

ISSN: 1062-7138

ISBN: 0-676-60003-4

Sixteenth Edition: April 1996

10 9 8 7 6 5 4 3 2 1

Table of Contents

Advertisers

About the Author

Jim Beckett, the leading authority on sport card values in the United States, maintains a wide range of activities in the world of sports. He possesses one of the finest collections of sports cards and autographs in the world, has made numerous appearances on radio and television, and has been frequently cited in many national publications. He was awarded the first "Special Achievement Award" for Contributions to the Hobby by the National Sports Collectors Convention in 1980, the "Jock-Jaspersen Award" for Hobby Dedication in 1983, and the "Buck Barker, Spirit of the Hobby" Award in 1991.

Dr. Beckett is the author of *Beckett Baseball Card Price Guide, The Official Price Guide to Baseball Cards, The Sport Americana Price Guide to Baseball Collectibles, The Sport Americana Baseball Memorabilia and Autograph Price Guide, Beckett Football Card Price Guide, The Official Price Guide to Football Cards, Beckett Hockey Card Price Guide, The Official Price Guide to Hockey Cards, Beckett Basketball Card Price Guide, The Official Price Guide to Basketball Cards,* and *The Sport Americana Baseball Card Alphabetical Checklist.* In addition, he is the founder, publisher, and editor of *Beckett Baseball Card Monthly, Beckett Basketball Monthly, Beckett Football Card Monthly, Beckett Hockey Monthly, Beckett Future Stars, Beckett Racing Monthly,* and *Beckett Tribute* magazines.

Jim Beckett received his Ph.D. in Statistics from Southern Methodist University in 1975. Prior to starting Beckett Publications in 1984, Dr. Beckett served as an Associate Professor of Statistics at Bowling Green State University and as a vice president of a consulting firm in Dallas, Texas. He currently resides in Dallas with his wife, Patti, and their daughters, Christina, Rebecca, and Melissa.

How to Use This Book

Isn't it great? Every year this book gets bigger and bigger with all the new sets coming out. But even more exciting is that every year there are more collectors, more shows, more stores, and more interest in the cards we love so much. This edition has been enhanced and expanded from the previous edition. The cards you collect — who appears on them, what they look like, where they are from, and (most important to most of you) what their current values are — are enumerated within. Many of the features contained in the other *Beckett Price Guides* have been incorporated into this volume since condition grading, terminology, and many other aspects of collecting are common to the card hobby in general. We hope you find the book both interesting and useful in your collecting pursuits.

The *Beckett Guide* has been successful where other attempts have failed because it is complete, current, and valid. This Price Guide contains not just one, but three prices by condition for all the baseball cards listed. The prices were added to the card lists just prior to printing and reflect not the author's opinions or desires but the going retail prices for each card, based on the marketplace (sports memorabilia conventions and shows, sports card shops, hobby papers, current mail-order catalogs, local club meetings, auction results, and other firsthand reportings of actually realized prices).

What is the best price guide available on the market today? Of course, card sellers prefer the price guide with the highest prices, while card buyers naturally prefer the one with the lowest prices. Accuracy, however, is the true test. Use the price guide trusted by more collectors and dealers than all the others combined. Look for the *Beckett®* name. I won't put my name on any-

Complete Baseball Card Sets

Topps Sets

1996 Series 1 (220 cards)	$ 15.00
1996 Series 2 (220 cards)	15.00
1995 (660)	50.00
1994 (792)	45.00
1993 (825)	35.00
1992, 1991, 1990, 1989, 1988, or 1987 (792 cards each set)	ea. 25.00
1986 (792)	40.00
1985 (792)	70.00
1984 (792)	70.00

Topps Traded Sets

1995 (165 cards)	25.00
1994 (140)	45.00
1993 (132)	13.00
1992 (132)	15.00
1991 (132)	8.00
1990 (132)	7.00
1989 (132)	8.00
1988 (132)	14.00
1987 (132)	8.00
1986 (132)	15.00
1985 (132)	20.00

Other Topps Sets

1996 Mantle Reprint (19 cards)	120.00
1996 Mantle Finest (19 cards)	140.00
1996 Master of the Game (20)	30.00
1996 Profiles (40)	45.00
1996 Wrecking Crew (15)	30.00
1993 Finest (199)	250.00
1993 Black Gold (44)	50.00
1993 Stadium Club Murphy (212)	30.00
1992 Stadium Club Dome (200)	25.00
1991 '90 Major League Debut (171)	20.00
1990 '89 Major League Debut (152)	15.00

Donruss Sets

1996 (550 cards)	40.00
1995 (550)	40.00
1994 (660)	50.00
1993 (792)	30.00
1992 (788)	15.00
1991 (796)	15.00
1990 (728)	10.00
1989 (672)	15.00
1991 Rookies (56)	5.00
1990 Rookies (56)	5.00
1988 Rookies (56)	16.00
1987 Opening Day (272)	15.00

Fleer Sets

1996 (600 cards)	50.00
1995 (600)	50.00
1994 (720)	50.00
1993 (720)	45.00
1992 (720)	25.00
1991 (732)	12.00
1990 (672)	12.00
1989 (672)	18.00
1988 (672)	25.00
1987 (672)	60.00
1986 (660)	100.00

Fleer Update Sets

1995 (200 cards)	20.00
1994 (210)	20.00
1993 Final Edition (310)	12.00
1991, 1990, 1989(132 each)	ea. 7.00
1988 (132)	12.00
1987 (132)	15.00
1986 (132)	15.00
1985 (132)	20.00

Upper Deck Sets

1996 Series 1 (240 cards)	30.00
1995 (450)	50.00
1994 (550)	50.00
1993 (840)	45.00
1992 (800)	25.00
1991 (800)	20.00
1990 (800)	$ 25.00
1989 (800)	110.00

Other Upper Deck Sets

1995 Checklists (10)	15.00
1995 Steal of a Deal (15)	75.00
1995 Electric Diamond (450)	100.00
1994 Collector's Choice (675)	32.00
1992, 1991, or 1990 High Nos. (100 per)	ea. 4.00
1991 Final Edition (100)	5.00
1989 High Numbers (100)	10.00

Score Sets

1996 (517 cards)	30.00
1995 (605)	25.00
1994 (660)	30.00
1993 (660)	40.00
1992 (910)	25.00
1991 (900)	20.00
1990 (704)	15.00
1989 or 1988 (660 each)	ea. 12.00

Other Score Sets

1992 Pinnacle Rookies (30)	6.00
1991 Rookie/Traded (110)	4.00
1990 Rookie/Traded (110)	10.00
1990 Young Superstars (84)	8.00
1989 Young Superstars (84)	8.00
1989 Rookie/Traded (110)	8.00
1988 Rookie/Traded (110)	50.00
1988 Young Superstars (80)	8.00

Supplies

Soft Sleeves (100 per pack)

10 packs for	10.00
20 packs for	18.00
100 packs for	45.00

Hard Card Holders

100 for	15.00
200 for	27.00
500 for	50.00

Ultra Pro 9 Pocket Sheets

250 sheets for	32.50
500 sheets for	60.00
1,000 sheets for	110.00

3" x 5" Screwdown Holders

20 holders for	17.00
50 holders for	35.00

Cardsaver II's

400 holders for	28.00
1,000 holders for	55.00

We also carry unopened boxes: base-ball, football, basketball and hockey. Call or write for prices.

All orders $25.00 and over include shipping.
Under $25.00, add $3.00 for shipping.

VISA and MASTERCARD accepted.

Please provide adequate street address for U.P.S. delivery
U.S. funds only
Alaska and Hawaii add 15% postage
Foreign add 25% postage
All prices subject to change

Send Orders To:

BILL DODGE
P.O. BOX 40154
Bay Village, OH 44140
Phone: (216) 899-9901

Eighteen years of quality mail order service

thing I won't stake my reputation on. Not the lowest and not the highest — but the most accurate, with integrity.

To facilitate your use of this book, read the complete introductory section on the following pages before going to the pricing pages. Every collectible field has its own terminology; we've tried to capture most of these terms and definitions in our glossary. Please read carefully the section on grading and the condition of your cards, as you cannot determine which price column is appropriate for a given card without first knowing its condition.

Welcome to the world of baseball cards.

How to Collect

Each collection is personal and reflects the individuality of its owner. There are no set rules on how to collect cards. Since card collecting is a hobby or leisure pastime, what you collect, how much you collect, and how much time and money you spend collecting are entirely up to you. The funds you have available for collecting and your own personal taste should determine how you collect. Information and ideas presented here are intended to help you get the most enjoyment from this hobby.

It is impossible to collect every card ever produced. Therefore, beginners as well as intermediate and advanced collectors usually specialize in some way. One of the reasons this hobby is popular is that individual collectors can define and tailor their collecting methods to match their own tastes. To give you some ideas of the various approaches to collecting, we will list some of the more popular areas of specialization.

Many collectors select complete sets from particular years. For example, they may concentrate on assembling complete sets from all the years since their birth or since they became avid sports fans. They may try to collect a card for every player during that specified period of time.

Many others wish to acquire only certain players. Usually such players are the superstars of the sport, but occasionally collectors will specialize in all the cards of players who attended a particular college or came from a certain town. Some collectors are only interested in the first cards or Rookie Cards of certain players. A handy guide for collectors interested in pursuing the hobby this way is the *Sport Americana Baseball Card Alphabetical Checklist*.

Another fun way to collect cards is by team. Most fans have a favorite team, and it is natural for that loyalty to be translated into a desire for cards of the players on that favorite team. For most of the recent years, team sets (all the cards from a given team for that year) are readily available at a reasonable price. *The Sport Americana Team Baseball Card Checklist* will open up this field to the collector.

Obtaining Cards

Several avenues are open to card collectors. Cards still can be purchased in the traditional way: by the pack at the local candy, grocery, drug or major discount stores.

But there are also thousands of card shops across the country that specialize in selling cards individually or by the pack, box, or set. Another alternative is the thousands of card shows held each month around the country, which feature anywhere from eight to 800 tables of sports cards and memorabilia for sale.

For many years, it has been possible to purchase complete sets of baseball cards through mail-order advertisers found in traditional sports media pub-

lications, such as *The Sporting News, Baseball Digest, Street & Smith* year-books, and others. These sets also are advertised in the card collecting period-icals. Many collectors will begin by subscribing to at least one of the hobby periodicals, all with good up-to-date information. In fact, subscription offers can be found in the advertising section of this book.

Most serious card collectors obtain old (and new) cards from one or more of several main sources: (1) trading or buying from other collectors or dealers; (2) responding to sale or auction ads in the hobby publications; (3) buying at a local hobby store; and/or (4) attending sports collectibles shows or conventions.

We advise that you try all four methods since each has its own distinct advantages: (1) trading is a great way to make new friends; (2) hobby periodicals help you keep up with what's going on in the hobby (including when and where the conventions are happening); (3) stores provide the opportunity to enjoy personalized service and consider a great diversity of material in a relaxed sports-oriented atmosphere; and (4) shows allow you to choose from multiple dealers and thousands of cards under one roof in a competitive situation.

Preserving Your Cards

Cards are fragile. They must be handled properly in order to retain their value. Careless handling can easily result in creased or bent cards. It is, however, not recommended that tweezers or tongs be used to pick up your cards since such utensils might mar or indent card surfaces and thus reduce those cards' conditions and values.

In general, your cards should be handled directly as little as possible. This is sometimes easier to say than to do.

Although there are still many who use custom boxes, storage trays, or even shoe boxes, plastic sheets are the preferred method of many collectors for storing cards.

A collection stored in plastic pages in a three-ring album allows you to view your collection at any time without the need to touch the card itself. Cards can also be kept in single holders (of various types and thickness) designed for the enjoyment of each card individually.

For a large collection, some collectors may use a combination of the above methods. When purchasing plastic sheets for your cards, be sure that you find the pocket size that fits the cards snugly. Don't put your 1951 Bowman in a sheet designed to fit 1981 Topps.

Most hobby and collectibles shops and virtually all collectors' conventions will have these plastic pages available in quantity for the various sizes offered, or you can purchase them directly from the advertisers in this book.

Also, remember that pocket size isn't the only factor to consider when looking for plastic sheets. Other factors such as safety, economy, appearance, availability, or personal preference also may indicate which types of sheets a collector may want to buy.

Damp, sunny and/or hot conditions — no, this is not a weather forecast — are three elements to avoid in extremes if you are interested in preserving your collection. Too much (or too little) humidity can cause the gradual deterioration of a card. Direct, bright sun (or fluorescent light) over time will bleach out the color of a card. Extreme heat accelerates the decomposition of the card. On the other hand, many cards have lasted more than 75 years without much scientific intervention. So be cautious, even if the above factors typically present a problem only when present in the extreme. It never hurts to be prudent.

Collecting vs. Investing

Collecting individual players and collecting complete sets are both popular vehicles for investment and speculation.

Most investors and speculators stock up on complete sets or on quantities of players they think have good investment potential.

There is obviously no guarantee in this book, or anywhere else for that matter, that cards will outperform the stock market or other investment alternatives in the future. After all, baseball cards do not pay quarterly dividends and cards cannot be sold at their "current values" as easily as stocks or bonds.

Nevertheless, investors have noticed a favorable long-term trend in the past performance of baseball and other sports collectibles, and certain cards and sets have outperformed just about any other investment in some years.

Many hobbyists maintain that the best investment is and always will be the building of a collection, which traditionally has held up better than outright speculation.

Some of the obvious questions are: Which cards? When to buy? When to sell? The best investment you can make is in your own education.

The more you know about your collection and the hobby, the more informed the decisions you will be able to make. We're not selling investment tips. We're selling information about the current value of baseball cards. It's up to you to use that information to your best advantage.

Terminology

Each hobby has its own language to describe its area of interest. The nomenclature traditionally used for trading cards is derived from the American Card Catalog, published in 1960 by Nostalgia Press. That catalog, written by Jefferson Burdick (who is called the "Father of Card Collecting" for his pioneering work), uses letter and number designations for each separate set of cards. The letter used in the ACC designation refers to the generic type of card. While both sport and non-sport issues are classified in the ACC, we shall confine ourselves to the sport issues. The following list defines the letters and their meanings as used by the American Card Catalog.

(none) or N - 19th Century U.S. Tobacco
B - Blankets
D - Bakery Inserts Including Bread
E - Early Candy and Gum
F - Food Inserts
H - Advertising
M - Periodicals
PC - Postcards
R - Candy and Gum since 1930

Following the letter prefix and an optional hyphen are one-, two-, or three-digit numbers, R(-)999. These typically represent the company or entity issuing the cards. In several cases, the ACC number is extended by an additional hyphen and another one- or two-digit numerical suffix. For example, the 1957 Topps regular-series baseball card issue carries an ACC designation of R414-11. The "R" indicates a Candy or Gum card produced since 1930. The "414" is the ACC designation for Topps Chewing Gum baseball card issues, and the "11" is the ACC designation for the 1957 regular issue (Topps' eleventh baseball set). Like other traditional methods of identification, this system provides order to the process of cataloging cards; however, most serious collectors learn the ACC designation of the popular sets by repetition and familiarity, rather than by attempting to "figure out" what they might or should be. From 1948 forward, collectors and dealers commonly refer to all sets by their year, maker, type of issue, and any other distinguishing characteristic. For example, such a characteristic could be an unusual issue or one of several regular issues put out by a specific maker in a single year. Regional issues are usually referred to by year, maker, and sometimes by title or theme of the set.

Glossary/Legend

Our glossary defines terms used in the card collecting hobby and in this book. Many of these terms are also common to other types of sports memorabilia collecting. Some terms may have several meanings depending on use and context.

ACC - Acronym for American Card Catalog.

ACETATE - A transparent plastic.

ANN- Announcer.

AS - All-Star card. A card portraying an All-Star Player of the previous year that says "All-Star" on its face.

ATG - All-Time Great card.

ATL - All-Time Leaders card.

AU(TO) - Autographed card.

BC - Bonus Card.

BL - Blue letters.

BLANKET - A felt square (normally 5 to 6 inches) portraying a baseball player.

BOX CARD - Card issued on a box (i.e., 1987 Topps Box Bottoms).

BRICK - A group of 50 or more cards having common characteristics that is intended to be bought, sold or traded as a unit.

CABINETS - Popular and highly valuable photographs on thick card stock produced in the 19th and early 20th century.

CHECKLIST - A list of the cards contained in a particular set. The list is always in numerical order if the cards are numbered. Some unnumbered sets are artificially numbered in alphabetical order, by team and alphabetically within the team, or by uniform number for convenience.

CL - Checklist card. A card that lists in order the cards and players in the set or series. Older checklist cards in Mint condition that have not been marked are very desirable and command premiums.

CO - Coach.

COIN - A small disc of metal or plastic portraying a player in its center.

COLLECTOR ISSUE - A set produced for the sake of the card itself with no product or service sponsor. It derives its name from the fact that most of these sets are produced for sale directly to the hobby market.

COM - Card issued by the Post Cereal Company through their mail-in offer.

COMM - Commissioner.

COMMON CARD - The typical card of any set; it has no premium value accruing from subject matter, numerical scarcity, popular demand, or anomaly.

CONVENTION - A gathering of dealers and collectors at a single location for the purpose of buying, selling, and trading sports memorabilia items. Conventions are open to the public and sometimes feature autograph guests, door prizes, contests, seminars, etc. They are frequently referred to simply as "shows."

COOP - Cooperstown.

COR - Corrected card.

COUPON - See Tab.

CY - Cy Young Award.

DEALER - A person who engages in buying, selling, and trading sports collectibles or supplies. A dealer may also be a collector, but as a dealer, his main goal is to earn a profit.

DIE-CUT - A card with part of its stock partially cut, allowing one or more parts to be folded or removed. After removal or appropriate folding, the remaining part of the card can frequently be made to stand up.

DISC - A circular-shaped card.

DISPLAY CARD - A sheet, usually containing three to nine cards, that is printed and used by the manufacturer to advertise and/or display the packages containing his products and cards. The backs of display cards are blank or contain advertisements.

DK - Diamond King.

DL - Division Leaders.

DP - Double Print (a card that was printed in double the quantity compared to the other cards in the same series) or a Draft Pick card.

DUFEX - A method of card manufacturing technology patented by Pinnacle Brands, Inc. It involves a refractive quality to a card with a foil coating.

EMBOSSED - A raised surface; features of a card that are projected from a flat background.

ERA - Earned Run Average.

ERR - Error card. A card with erroneous information, spelling, or depiction on either side of the card. Most errors are not corrected by the producing card company.

ETCHED - Impressions within the surface of a card.

EXHIBIT - The generic name given to thick-stock, postcard-size cards with single color obverse pictures. The name is derived from the Exhibit Supply Co. of Chicago, the principal manufacturer of this type of card. These also are known as Arcade cards since they were found in many arcades.

FDP - First or First Round Draft Pick.

FOIL - Foil embossed stamp on card.

FOLD - Foldout.

FS - Father/son card.

FULL BLEED - A borderless card; a card containing a photo that encompasses the entire card.

FULL SHEET - A complete sheet of cards that has not been cut up into individual cards by the manufacturer. Also called an uncut sheet.

FUN - Fun Cards.

GL - Green letters.

GLOSS - A card with luster; a shiny finish as in a card with UV coating.

HIGH NUMBER - The cards in the last series of numbers in a year in which such higher-numbered cards were printed or distributed in significantly lesser amounts than the lower-numbered cards. The high-number designation refers to a scarcity of the high-numbered cards. Not all years have high numbers in terms of this definition.

HL - Highlight card.

HOF - Hall of Fame, or a card that portrays a Hall of Famer (HOFer).

HOLOGRAM - A three-dimensional photographic image.

HOR - Horizontal pose on card as opposed to the standard vertical orientation found on most cards.

IA - In Action card.

IF - Infielder.

INSERT - A card of a different type or any other sports collectible (typically a poster or sticker) contained and sold in the same package along with a card or cards of a major set. An insert card is either unnumbered or not numbered in the same sequence as the major set. Sometimes the inserts are randomly distributed and are not found in every pack.

INTERACTIVE - A concept that involves collector participation.

ISSUE - Synonymous with set, but usually used in conjunction with a manufacturer, e.g., a Topps issue.

KARAT - A unit of measure for the fineness of gold; i.e. 24K.

LAYERING - The separation or peeling of one or more layers of the card stock, usually at the corner of the card.

LEGITIMATE ISSUE - A set produced to promote or boost sales of a product or service, e.g., bubblegum, cereal, cigarettes, etc. Most collector issues are not legitimate issues in this sense.

LHP - Lefthanded pitcher.

LID - A circular-shaped card (possibly with tab) that forms the top of the container for the product being promoted.

LL - League leaders or large letters on card.

MAJOR SET - A set produced by a national manufacturer of cards containing a large number of cards. Usually 100 or more different cards comprise a major set.

MEM - Memorial card. For example, the 1990 Donruss and Topps Bart Giamatti cards.

METALLIC - A glossy design method that enhances card features.

MG - Manager.

MINI - A small card; for example, a 1975 Topps card of identical design but smaller dimensions than the regular Topps issue of 1975.

ML - Major League.

MULTI-PLAYER CARD - A single card depicting two or more players (but not a team card).

MVP - Most Valuable Player.

NAU - No autograph on card.

NH - No-Hitter.

NNOF - No Name on Front.

NOF - Name on Front.

NON-SPORT CARD - A card from a set whose major theme is a subject other than a sports subject. A card of a sports figure or event that is part of a non-sport set is still a non-sport card, e.g., while the "Look 'N' See" non-sport card set contains a card of Babe Ruth, a sports figure, that card is a non-sport card.

NOTCHING - The grooving of the card, usually caused by fingernails, rubber bands, or bumping card edges against other objects.

OF - Outfield or Outfielder.

OLY - Olympics Card.

ORG - Organist.

P - Pitcher or Pitching pose.

P1 - First Printing.

P2 - Second Printing.

P3 - Third Printing.

PACKS - A means with which cards are issued in terms of pack type (wax, cello, foil, rack, etc.) and channels of distribution (hobby, retail, etc.).

PANEL - An extended card that is composed of two or more individual cards. Often the panel forms the back part of the container for the product being promoted, e.g., a Hostess panel, a Bazooka panel, an Esskay Meat panel.

PARALLEL- A card that is similar in design to its counterpart from a basic set, but offers a distinguishing quality.

PCL - Pacific Coast League.

PF - Profiles.

PLASTIC SHEET - A clear, plastic page that is punched for insertion into a binder (with standard three-ring spacing) containing pockets for displaying cards. Many different styles of sheets exist with pockets of varying sizes to hold the many differing card formats. Also called a display sheet or storage sheet.

PLATINUM - A metallic element used in the process of creating a glossy card.

PR - Printed name on back.

PREMIUM - A card, sometimes on photographic stock, that is purchased or obtained in conjunction with, or redemption for, another card or product. The premium is not packaged in the same unit as the primary item.

PRES - President.

PRISMATIC/PRISM - A glossy or bright design that refracts or disperses light.

PUZZLE CARD - A card whose back contains a part of a picture which, when joined correctly with other puzzle cards, forms the completed picture.

PUZZLE PIECE - A die-cut piece designed to interlock with similar pieces (e.g., early 1980's Donruss).

PVC - Polyvinyl Chloride, a substance used to make many of the popular card display protective sheets. Non-PVC sheets are considered preferable for long-term storage of cards by many.

RARE - A card or series of cards of very limited availability. Unfortunately, "rare" is a subjective term frequently used indiscriminately to hype value. "Rare" cards are harder to obtain than "scarce" cards.

RB - Record Breaker.

REDEMPTION - A program established by multiple card manufacturers that allows collectors to mail in a special card (usually a random insert) in return for special cards, sets or other prizes not available through conventional channels.

REFRACTORS - A card that features a design element which enhances (distorts) its color/appearance through deflecting light.

REGIONAL - A card or set of cards issued and distributed only in a limited geographical area of the country.

REPLICA - An identical copy or reproduction.

REV NEG - Reversed or flopped photo side of the card. This is a major type of error card, but only some are corrected.

RHP - Righthanded pitcher.

ROY - Rookie of the Year.

RP - Relief pitcher.

SA - Super Action card.

SASE - Self-Addressed, Stamped Envelope.

SB - Stolen Bases.

SCARCE - A card or series of cards of limited availability. This subjective term is sometimes used indiscriminately to hype value. "Scarce" cards are not as difficult to obtain as "rare" cards.

SCR - Script name on back.

SD - San Diego Padres.

SEMI-HIGH - A card from the next to last series of a sequentially issued set. It has more value than an average card and generally less value than a high number. A card is not called a semi-high unless the next to last series in which it exists has an additional premium attached to it.

SERIES - The entire set of cards issued by a particular producer in a particular year; e.g., the 1971 Topps series. Also, within a particular set, series can refer to a group of (consecutively numbered) cards printed at the same time; e.g., the first series of the 1957 Topps issue (#1 through #88).

SET - One each of the entire run of cards of the same type produced by a particular manufacturer during a single year. In other words, if you have a complete set of 1976 Topps then you have every card from #1 up to and including #660, i.e., all the different cards that were produced.

SF - Starflics.

SHEEN - Brightness or luster emitted by a card.

SKIP-NUMBERED - A set that has many unissued card numbers between the lowest number in the set and the highest number in the set; e.g., the 1948 Leaf baseball set contains 98 cards skip-numbered from #1 to #168. A major set in which a few numbers were not printed is not considered to be skip-numbered.

SP - Single or Short Print (a card which was printed in lesser quantity compared to the other cards in the same series; see also DP and TP).

SPECIAL CARD - A card that portrays something other than a single player or team; for example, a card that portrays the previous year's statistical leaders or the results from the previous year's World Series.

SS - Shortstop.

STAMP - Adhesive-backed papers depicting a player. The stamp may be individual or in a sheet of many stamps. Moisture must be applied to the adhesive in order for the stamp to be attached to another surface.

STANDARD SIZE - Most modern sports cards measure 2-1/2 by 3-1/2 inches. Exceptions are noted in card descriptions throughout this book.

STAR CARD - A card that portrays a player of some repute, usually determined by his ability, however, sometimes referring to sheer popularity.

STICKER - A card with a removable layer that can be affixed to (stuck onto) another surface.

STOCK - The cardboard or paper on which the card is printed.

STRIP CARDS - A sheet or strip of cards, particularly popular in the 1920s and 1930s, with the individual cards usually separated by broken or dotted lines.

SUPERIMPOSED - To be affixed on top of something, i.e., a player photo over a solid background.

SUPERSTAR CARD - A card that portrays a superstar; e.g., a Hall of Famer or player with strong Hall of Fame potential.

TAB - A card portion set off from the rest of the card, usually with perforations, that may be removed without damaging the central character or event depicted by the card.

TC - Team Checklist.

TEAM CARD - A card that depicts an entire team.

TEST SET - A set, usually containing a small number of cards, issued by a national card producer and distributed in a limited section or sections of the country. Presumably, the purpose of a test set is to test market appeal for a particular type of card.

THREE-DIMENSIONAL (3D) - A visual image that provides an illusion of depth and perspective.

TOPICAL - a subset or group of cards that have a common theme (e.g., MVP award winners).

TP - Triple Print (a card that was printed in triple the quantity compared to the other cards in the same series).

TRANSPARENT - Clear, see through.

TR - Trade reference on card.

TRIMMED - A card cut down from its original size. Trimmed cards are undesirable to most collectors.

UDCA - Upper Deck Classic Alumni.

UER - Uncorrected Error.

UMP - Umpire.

USA - Team USA.

UV - Ultraviolet, a glossy coating used in producing cards.

VAR - Variation card. One of two or more cards from the same series with the same number (or player with identical pose if the series is unnumbered) differing from one another by some aspect, the different feature stemming from the printing or stock of the card. This can be caused when the manufacturer of the cards notices an error in one or more of the cards, makes the changes, and then resumes the print run. In this case there will be two versions or variations of the same card. Sometimes one of the variations is relatively scarce.

VERT - Vertical pose on card.

WAS - Washington National League (1974 Topps).

WC - What's the Call?

WL - White letter on front.

WS - World Series card.

YL - Yellow letters on front

YT - Yellow team name on front.

* - to denote multi-sport sets.

Understanding Card Values

Determining Value

Why are some cards more valuable than others? Obviously, the economic laws of supply and demand are applicable to card collecting just as they are to any other field where a commodity is bought, sold or traded in a free, unregulated market.

Supply (the number of cards available on the market) is less than the total number of cards originally produced since attrition diminishes that original quantity. Each year a percentage of cards is typically thrown away, destroyed or otherwise lost to collectors. This percentage is much, much smaller today than it was in the past because more and more people have become increasingly aware of the value of their cards.

For those who collect only Mint condition cards, the supply of older cards can be quite small indeed. Until recently, collectors were not so conscious of the need to preserve the condition of their cards. For this reason, it is difficult to know exactly how many 1953 Topps are currently available, Mint or otherwise. It is generally accepted that there are fewer 1953 Topps available than 1963, 1973 or 1983 Topps cards. If demand were equal for each of these sets, the law of supply and demand would increase the price for the least available sets. Demand, however, is never equal for all sets, so price correlations can be complicated. The demand for a card is influenced by many factors. These include: (1) the age of the card; (2) the number of cards printed; (3) the player(s) portrayed on the card; (4) the attractiveness and popularity of the set; and (5) the physical condition of the card.

In general, (1) the older the card, (2) the fewer the number of the cards printed, (3) the more famous, popular and talented the player, (4) the more attractive and popular the set, and (5) the better the condition of the card, the higher the value of the card will be. There are exceptions to all but one of these factors: the condition of the card. Given two cards similar in all respects except condition, the one in the best condition will always be valued higher.

While those guidelines help to establish the value of a card, the countless exceptions and peculiarities make any simple, direct mathematical formula to determine card values impossible.

Regional Variation

Since the market varies from region to region, card prices of local players may be higher. This is known as a regional premium. How significant the premium is — and if there is any premium at all — depends on the local popularity of the team and the player.

The largest regional premiums usually do not apply to superstars, who often are so well-known nationwide that the prices of their key cards are too high for local dealers to realize a premium.

Lesser stars often command the strongest premiums. Their popularity is concentrated in their home region, creating local demand that greatly exceeds overall demand.

Regional premiums can apply to popular retired players and sometimes can be found in the areas where the players grew up or starred in college.

A regional discount is the converse of a regional premium. Regional discounts occur when a player has been so popular in his region for so long that local collectors and dealers have accumulated quantities of his key cards. The abundant supply may make the cards available in that area at the lowest prices anywhere.

Set Prices

A somewhat paradoxical situation exists in the price of a complete set vs. the combined cost of the individual cards in the set. In nearly every case, the sum of the prices for the individual cards is higher than the cost for the complete set. This is prevalent especially in the cards of the last few years. The reasons for this apparent anomaly stem from the habits of collectors and from the carrying costs to dealers. Today, each card in a set normally is produced in the same quantity as all other cards in its set.

Many collectors pick up only stars, superstars and particular teams. As a result, the dealer is left with a shortage of certain player cards and an abundance of others. He therefore incurs an expense in simply "carrying" these less desirable cards in stock. On the other hand, if he sells a complete set, he gets rid of large numbers of cards at one time. For this reason, he generally is willing to receive less money for a complete set. By doing this, he recovers all of his costs and also makes a profit.

The disparity between the price of the complete set and the sum of the individual cards also has been influenced by the fact that some of the major manufacturers now are pre-collating card sets. Since "pulling" individual cards from the sets involves a specific type of labor (and cost), the singles or star card market is not affected significantly by pre-collation.

Set prices also do not include rare card varieties, unless specifically stated. Of course, the prices for sets do include one example of each type for the given set, but this is the least expensive variety.

Scarce Series

Scarce series occur because cards issued before 1974 were made available to the public each year in several series of finite numbers of cards, rather than all cards of the set being available for purchase at one time. At some point during the year, usually toward the end of the baseball season, interest in current year baseball cards waned. Consequently, the manufacturers produced smaller numbers of these later-series cards.

Nearly all nationwide issues from post-World War II manufacturers (1948 to 1973) exhibit these series variations. In the past, Topps, for example, may have issued series consisting of many different numbers of cards, including 55, 66, 80, 88 and others. Recently, Topps has settled on what is now its standard sheet size of 132 cards, six of which comprise its 792-card set.

While the number of cards within a given series is usually the same as the number of cards on one printed sheet, this is not always the case. For example, Bowman used 36 cards on its standard printed sheets, but in 1948 substituted 12 cards during later print runs of that year's baseball cards. Twelve of the cards from the initial sheet of 36 were removed and replaced by 12 different cards giving, in effect, a first series of 36 cards and a second series of 12 new cards. This replacement produced a scarcity of 24 cards — the 12 cards removed from the original sheet and the 12 new cards added to the sheet. A full sheet of 1948 Bowman cards (second printing) shows that card numbers 37 through 48 have replaced 12 of the cards on the first printing sheet.

The Topps Company also has created scarcities and/or excesses of certain cards in many of its sets. Topps, however, has most frequently gone the other direction by double printing some of the cards. Double printing causes an abundance of cards of the players who are on the same sheet more than one time. During the years from 1978 to 1981, Topps double printed 66 cards out of their large 726-card set. The Topps practice of double printing cards in earlier years is the most logical explanation for the known scarcities of particular cards in some of these Topps sets.

From 1988 through 1990, Donruss short printed and double printed certain cards in its major sets. Ostensibly this was because of its addition of bonus team MVP cards in its regular-issue wax packs.

We are always looking for information or photographs of printing sheets of cards for research. Each year, we try to update the hobby's knowledge of distribution anomalies. Please let us know at the address in this book if you have first-hand knowledge that would be helpful in this pursuit.

Grading Your Cards

Each hobby has its own grading terminology — stamps, coins, comic books, record collecting, etc. Collectors of sports cards are no exception. The one invariable criterion for determining the value of a card is its condition: The better the condition of the card, the more valuable it is. Condition grading, however, is subjective. Individual card dealers and collectors differ in the strictness of their grading, but the stated condition of a card should be determined without regard to whether it is being bought or sold.

No allowance is made for age. A 1952 card is judged by the same standards as a 1992 card. But there are specific sets and cards that are condition sensitive (marked with "!" in the Price Guide) because of their border color, consistently poor centering, etc. Such cards and sets sometimes command premiums above the listed percentages in Mint condition.

Centering

Current centering terminology uses numbers representing the percentage of border on either side of the main design. Obviously, centering is dimin-

Centering

Well-centered

Slightly Off-centered

Off-centered

Badly Off-centered

Miscut

Corner Wear

The partial cards here have been photographed at 300%. This was done in order to magnify each card's corner wear to such a degree that differences could be shown on a printed page.

The 1962 Topps Mickey Mantle card definitely has a rounded corner. Some may say that this card is badly rounded, but that is a judgement call.

The 1962 Topps Hank Aaron card has a slightly rounded corner. Note that there is definite corner wear evident by the fraying and that there is no longer a sharp point to which the corner converges.

The 1962 Topps Gil Hodges card has corner wear; it is slightly better than the Aaron card above. Nevertheless, some collectors might classify this Hodges corner as slightly rounded.

The 1962 Topps Manager's Dream card showing Mantle and Mays has slight corner wear. This is not a fuzzy corner as very slight wear is noticeable on the card's photo surface.

The 1962 Topps Don Mossi card has very slight corner wear such that it might be called a fuzzy corner. A close look at the original card shows that the corner is not perfect, but almost. However, note that coner wear is somewhat academic on this card. As you can plainly see, the heavy crease going across his name breaks through the photo surface.

ished in importance for borderless cards such as Stadium Club.

Slightly Off-Center (60/40): A slightly off-center card is one that, upon close inspection, is found to have one border bigger than the opposite border. This degree once was offensive to only purists, but now some hobbyists try to avoid cards that are anything other than perfectly centered.

Off-Center (70/30): An off-center card has one border that is noticeably more than twice as wide as the opposite border.

Badly Off-Center (80/20 or worse): A badly off-center card has virtually no border on one side of the card.

Miscut: A miscut card actually shows part of the adjacent card in its larger border and consequently a corresponding amount of its card is cut off.

Corner Wear

Corner wear is the most scrutinized grading criteria in the hobby. These are the major categories of corner wear:

Corner with a slight touch of wear: The corner still is sharp, but there is a slight touch of wear showing. On a dark-bordered card, this shows as a dot of white.

Fuzzy corner: The corner still comes to a point, but the point has just begun to fray. A slightly "dinged" corner is considered the same as a fuzzy corner.

Slightly rounded corner: The fraying of the corner has increased to where there is only a hint of a point. Mild layering may be evident. A "dinged" corner is considered the same as a slightly rounded corner.

Rounded corner: The point is completely gone. Some layering is noticeable.

Badly rounded corner: The corner is completely round and rough. Severe layering is evident.

Creases

A third common defect is the crease. The degree of creasing in a card is difficult to show in a drawing or picture. On giving the specific condition of an expensive card for sale, the seller should note any creases additionally. Creases can be categorized as to severity according to the following scale:

Light Crease: A light crease is a crease that is barely noticeable upon close inspection. In fact, when cards are in plastic sheets or holders, a light crease may not be seen (until the card is taken out of the holder). A light crease on the front is much more serious than a light crease on the card back only.

Medium Crease: A medium crease is noticeable when held and studied at arm's length by the naked eye, but does not overly detract from the appearance of the card. It is an obvious crease, but not one that breaks the picture surface of the card.

Heavy Crease: A heavy crease is one that has torn or broken through the card's picture surface, e.g., puts a tear in the photo surface.

Alterations

Deceptive Trimming: This occurs when someone alters the card in order (1) to shave off edge wear, (2) to improve the sharpness of the corners, or (3) to improve centering — obviously their objective is to falsely increase the perceived value of the card to an unsuspecting buyer. The shrinkage usually is evident only if the trimmed card is compared to an adjacent full-sized card or if the trimmed card is itself measured.

Obvious Trimming: Obvious trimming is noticeable and unfortunate. It is usually performed by non-collectors who give no thought to the present or future value of their cards.

Deceptively Retouched Borders: This occurs when the borders (especially on those cards with dark borders) are touched up on the edges and corners with magic marker or crayons of appropriate color in order to make the card appear Mint.

Categorization of Defects—Miscellaneous Flaws

The following are common minor flaws that, depending on severity, lower a card's condition by one to four grades and often render it no better than Excellent-Mint: bubbles (lumps in surface), gum and wax stains, diamond cutting (slanted borders), notching, off-centered backs, paper wrinkles, scratched-off cartoons or puzzles on back, rubber band marks, scratches, surface impressions and warping.

The following are common serious flaws that, depending on severity, lower a card's condition at least four grades and often render it no better than Good: chemical or sun fading, erasure marks, mildew, miscutting (severe off-centering), holes, bleached or re-touched borders, tape marks, tears, trimming, water or coffee stains and writing.

Condition Guide

Grades

Mint (Mt) - A card with no flaws or wear. The card has four perfect corners, 60/40 or better centering from top to bottom and from left to right, original gloss, smooth edges and original color borders. A Mint card does not have print spots, color or focus imperfections.

Near Mint-Mint (NrMt-Mt) - A card with one minor flaw. Any one of the following would lower a Mint card to Near Mint-Mint: one corner with a slight touch of wear, barely noticeable print spots, color or focus imperfections. The card must have 60/40 or better centering in both directions, original gloss, smooth edges and original color borders.

Near Mint (NrMt) - A card with one minor flaw. Any one of the following would lower a Mint card to Near Mint: one fuzzy corner or two to four corners with slight touches of wear, 70/30 to 60/40 centering, slightly rough edges, minor print spots, color or focus imperfections. The card must have original gloss and original color borders.

Excellent-Mint (ExMt) - A card with two or three fuzzy, but not rounded, corners and centering no worse than 80/20. The card may have no more than two of the following: slightly rough edges, very slightly discolored borders, minor print spots, color or focus imperfections. The card must have original gloss.

Excellent (Ex) - A card with four fuzzy but definitely not rounded corners and centering no worse than 80/20. The card may have a small amount of original gloss lost, rough edges, slightly discolored borders and minor print spots, color or focus imperfections.

Very Good (Vg) - A card that has been handled but not abused: slightly rounded corners with slight layering, slight notching on edges, a significant amount of gloss lost from the surface but no scuffing and moderate discoloration of borders. The card may have a few light creases.

Good (G), Fair (F), Poor (P) - A well-worn, mishandled or abused card: badly rounded and layered corners, scuffing, most or all original gloss missing, seriously discolored borders, moderate or heavy creases, and one or more serious flaws. The grade of Good, Fair or Poor depends on the severity of wear and flaws. Good, Fair and Poor cards generally are used only as fillers.

The most widely used grades are defined above. Obviously, many cards will not perfectly fit one of the definitions.

Therefore, categories between the major grades known as in-between grades are used, such as Good to Very Good (G-Vg), Very Good to Excellent (VgEx), and Excellent-Mint to Near Mint (ExMt-NrMt). Such grades indicate a card with all qualities of the lower category but with at least a few qualities of the higher category.

The Official Price Guide to Baseball Cards lists each card and set in three grades, with the middle grade valued at about 40-45% of the top grade, and the bottom grade valued at about 10-15% of the top grade.

The value of cards that fall between the listed columns can also be calculated using a percentage of the top grade. For example, a card that falls between the top and middle grades (Ex, ExMt or NrMt in most cases) will generally be valued at anywhere from 50% to 90% of the top grade.

Similarly, a card that falls between the middle and bottom grades (G-Vg, Vg or VgEx in most cases) will generally be valued at anywhere from 20% to 40% of the top grade.

There are also cases where cards are in better condition than the top grade or worse than the bottom grade. Cards that grade worse than the lowest grade are generally valued at 5-10% of the top grade.

When a card exceeds the top grade by one — such as NrMt-Mt when the top grade is NrMt, or Mint when the top grade is NrMt-Mt — a premium of up to 50% is possible, with 10-20% the usual norm.

When a card exceeds the top grade by two — such as Mint when the top grade is NrMt, or NrMt-Mt when the top grade is ExMt — a premium of 25-50% is the usual norm. But certain condition sensitive cards or sets, particularly those from the pre-war era, can bring premiums of up to 100% or even more.

Unopened packs, boxes and factory-collated sets are considered Mint in their unknown (and presumed perfect) state. Once opened, however, each card can be graded (and valued) in its own right by taking into account any defects that may be present in spite of the fact that the card has never been handled.

Selling Your Cards

Just about every collector sells cards or will sell cards eventually. Someday you may be interested in selling your duplicates or maybe even your whole collection. You may sell to other collectors, friends or dealers. You may even sell cards you purchased from a certain dealer back to that same dealer. In any event, it helps to know some of the mechanics of the typical transaction between buyer and seller.

Dealers will buy cards in order to resell them to other collectors who are interested in the cards. Dealers will always pay a higher percentage for items that (in their opinion) can be resold quickly, and a much lower percentage for those items that are perceived as having low demand and hence are slow moving. In either case, dealers must buy at a price that allows for the expense of doing business and a margin for profit.

If you have cards for sale, the best advice we can give is that you get several offers for your cards — either from card shops or at a card show — and take the best offer, all things considered. Note, the "best" offer may not be the one for the highest amount. And remember, if a dealer really wants your cards, he won't let you get away without making his best competitive offer. Another alternative is to place your cards in an auction as one or several lots.

Many people think nothing of going into a department store and paying $15 for an item of clothing for which the store paid $5. But if you were selling your $15 card to a dealer and he offered you $5 for it, you might consider his mark-up unreasonable. To complete the analogy: Most department stores (and card dealers) that consistently pay $10 for $15 items eventually go out of business. An exception is when the dealer has lined up a willing buyer for the item(s) you are attempting to sell, or if the cards are so Hot that it's likely he'll likely have to hold the cards for just a short period of time.

In those cases, an offer of up to 75 percent of book value still will allow the dealer to make a reasonable profit considering the short time he will need to hold the merchandise. In general, however, most cards and collections will bring offers in the range of 25 to 50 percent of retail price. Also consider that most material from the last five to 10 years is plentiful. If that's what you're selling, don't be surprised if your best offer is well below that range.

Interesting Notes

The first card numerically of an issue is the single card most likely to obtain excessive wear.

Consequently, you typically will find the price on the #1 card (in NrMt or Mint condition) somewhat higher than might otherwise be the case.

Similarly, but to a lesser extent (because normally the less important, reverse side of the card is the one exposed), the last card numerically in an issue also is prone to abnormal wear. This extra wear and tear occurs because the first and last cards are exposed to the elements (human element included) more than any of the other cards. They are generally end cards in any brick formations, rubber bandings, stackings on wet surfaces and like activities.

Sports cards have no intrinsic value. The value of a card, like the value of other collectibles, can be determined only by you and your enjoyment in viewing and possessing these cardboard treasures.

Remember, the buyer ultimately determines the price of each baseball card. You are the determining price factor because you have the ability to say "No" to the price of any card by not exchanging your hard-earned money for a given issue. When the cost of a trading card exceeds the enjoyment you will receive from it, your answer should be "No." We assess and report the prices. You set them!

We are always interested in receiving the price input of collectors and dealers. We happily credit major contributors.

We welcome your opinions, since your contributions assist us in ensuring a better guide each year.

If you would like to join our survey list for the next editions of this book and others authored by Dr. Beckett, please send your name and address to Dr. James Beckett, 15850 Dallas Parkway, Dallas, TX 75248.

History of Baseball Cards

Today's version of the baseball card, with its colorful and oft times high-tech fronts and backs, is a far cry from its earliest predecessors. The issue remains cloudy as to which was the very first baseball card ever produced, but the institution of baseball cards dates from the latter half of the 19th century, more than 100 years ago. Early issues, generally printed on heavy cardboard, were of poor quality, with photographs, drawings, and printing far short of today's standards.

Goodwin & Co., of New York, makers of Gypsy Queen, Old Judge, and other cigarette brands, is considered by many to be the first issuer of baseball and other sports cards. Its issues, predominantly sized 1-1/2 by 2-1/2 inches, generally consisted of photographs of baseball players, boxers, wrestlers, and other subjects mounted on stiff cardboard. More than 2,000 different photos of baseball players alone have been identified. These "Old Judges," a collective name commonly used for the Goodwin & Co. cards, were issued from 1886 to 1890 and are treasured parts of many collections today.

Among the other cigarette companies that issued baseball cards still attracting attention today are Allen & Ginter, D. Buchner & Co. (Gold Coin Chewing Tobacco), and P.H. Mayo & Brother. Cards from the first two companies bear colored line drawings, while the Mayos are sepia photographs on black cardboard. In addition to the small-size cards from this era, several tobacco companies issued cabinet-size baseball cards. These "cabinets" were considerably larger than the small cards, usually about 4-1/4 by 6-1/2 inches, and were printed on heavy stock. Goodwin & Co.'s Old Judge cabinets and the National Tobacco Works' "Newsboy" baseball photos are two that remain popular today.

By 1895, the American Tobacco Company began to dominate its competition. They discontinued baseball card inserts in their cigarette packages (actually slide boxes in those days). The lack of competition in the cigarette market had made these inserts unnecessary. This marked the end of the first era of baseball cards. At the dawn of the 20th century, few baseball cards were being issued. But once again, it was the cigarette companies — particularly, the American Tobacco Company — followed to a lesser extent by the candy and gum makers that revived the practice of including baseball cards with their products. The bulk of these cards, identified in the American Card Catalog (designated hereafter as ACC) as T or E cards for 20th century "Tobacco" or "Early Candy and Gum" issues, respectively, were released from 1909 to 1915.

This romantic and popular era of baseball card collecting produced many desirable items. The most outstanding is the fabled T-206 Honus Wagner card. Other perennial favorites among collectors are the T-206 Eddie Plank card, and the T-206 Magee error card. The former was once the second most valuable card and only recently relinquished that position to a more distinctive and aesthetically pleasing Napoleon Lajoie card from the 1933-34 Goudey Gum series. The latter misspells the player's name as "Magie," the most famous and most valuable blooper card.

The ingenuity and distinctiveness of this era has yet to be surpassed. Highlights include:

• the T-202 Hassan triple-folders, one of the best looking and the most distinctive cards ever issued;

• the durable T-201 Mecca double-folders, one of the first sets with players' records on the reverse;

• the T-3 Turkey Reds, the hobby's most popular cabinet card;

• the E-145 Cracker Jacks, the only major set containing Federal League player cards;

• the T-204 Ramlys, with their distinctive black-and-white oval photos and ornate gold borders.

These are but a few of the varieties issued during this period.

Increasing Popularity

While the American Tobacco Company dominated the field, several other tobacco companies, as well as clothing manufacturers, newspapers and periodicals, game makers, and companies whose identities remain anonymous, also issued cards during this period. In fact, the Collins-McCarthy Candy Company, makers of Zeenuts Pacific Coast League baseball cards, issued cards yearly from 1911 to 1938. Its record for continuous annual card production has been exceeded only by the Topps Chewing Gum Company. The era of the tobacco card issues closed with the onset of World War I, with the exception of the Red Man chewing tobacco sets produced from 1952 to 1955.

The next flurry of card issues broke out in the roaring and prosperous 1920s, the era of the E card. The caramel companies (National Caramel, American Caramel, York Caramel) were the leading distributors of these E cards. In addition, the strip card, a continous strip with several cards divided by dotted lines or other sectioning features, flourished during this time. While the E cards and the strip cards generally are considered less imaginative than the T cards or the recent candy and gum issues, they still are pursued by many advanced collectors.

Another significant event of the 1920s was the introduction of the arcade card. Taking its designation from its issuer, the Exhibit Supply Company of Chicago, it is usually known as the "Exhibit" card. Once a trademark of the penny arcades, amusement parks and county fairs across the country, Exhibit machines dispensed nearly postcard-size photos on thick stock for one penny. These picture cards bore likenesses of a favorite cowboy, actor, actress or baseball player. Exhibit Supply and its associated companies produced baseball cards during a longer time span, although discontinuous, than any other manufacturer. Its first cards appeared in 1921, while its last issue was in 1966. In 1979, the Exhibit Supply Company was bought and somewhat revived by a collector/dealer who has since reprinted Exhibit photos of the past.

If the T card period, from 1909 to 1915, can be designated the "Golden Age" of baseball card collecting, then perhaps the "Silver Age" commenced with the introduction of the Big League Gum series of 239 cards in 1933 (a 240th card was added in 1934). These are the forerunners of today's baseball gum cards, and the Goudey Gum Company of Boston is responsible for their success. This era spanned the period from the Depression days of 1933 to America's formal involvement in World War II in 1941.

Goudey's attractive designs, with full-color line drawings on thick card stock, greatly influenced other cards being issued at that time. As a result, the most attractive and popular vintage cards in history were produced in this "Silver Age." The 1933 Goudey Big League Gum series also owes its popularity to the more than 40 Hall of Fame players in the set. These include four cards of Babe Ruth and two of Lou Gehrig. Goudey's reign continued in 1934, when it issued a 96-card set in color, together with the single remaining card from the 1933 series, #106, the Napoleon Lajoie card.

In addition to Goudey, several other bubblegum manufacturers issued baseball cards during this era. DeLong Gum Company issued an extremely attractive set in 1933. National Chicle Company's 192-card "Batter-Up" series of 1934-1936 became the largest die-cut set in card history. In addition, that company offered the popular "Diamond Stars" series during the same period. Other popular sets included the "Tattoo Orbit" set of 60 color cards issued in 1933 and Gum Products' 75-card "Double Play" set, featuring sepia depictions of two players per card.

In 1939, Gum Inc., which later became Bowman Gum, replaced Goudey Gum as the leading baseball card producer. In 1939 and the following year, it issued two important sets of black-and-white cards. In 1939, its "Play Ball America" set consisted of 162 cards. The larger, 240-card "Play Ball" set of 1940 still is considered by many to be the most attractive black-and-white cards ever produced. That firm introduced its only color set in 1941, consisting of 72 cards titled "Play Ball Sports Hall of Fame." Many of these were colored repeats of poses from the black-and-white 1940 series.

In addition to regular gum cards, many manufacturers distributed premium issues during the 1930s. These premiums were printed on paper or photographic stock, rather than card stock. They were much larger than the regular cards and were sold for a penny across the counter with gum (which was packaged separately from the premium). They often were redeemed at the store or through the mail in exchange for the wrappers of previously purchased gum cards, like proof-of-purchase box-top premiums today. The gum premiums are scarcer than the card issues of the 1930s and in most cases no manufacturer's name is present.

World War II brought an end to this popular era of card collecting when paper and rubber shortages curtailed the production of bubblegum baseball cards. They were resurrected again in 1948 by the Bowman Gum Company (the direct descendent of Gum, Inc.). This marked the beginning of the modern era of card collecting.

In 1948, Bowman Gum issued a 48-card set in black and white consisting of one card and one slab of gum in every 1 cent pack. That same year, the Leaf Gum Company also issued a set of cards. Although rather poor in quality, these cards were issued in color. A squabble over the rights to use players' pictures developed between Bowman and Leaf. Eventually Leaf dropped out of the card market, but not before it had left a lasting heritage to the hobby by issuing some of the rarest cards now in existence. Leaf's baseball card series of 1948-49 contained 98 cards, skip numbered to #168 (not all numbers were printed). Of these 98 cards, 49 are relatively plentiful; the other 49, however, are rare and quite valuable.

Bowman continued its production of cards in 1949 with a color series of 240 cards. Because there are many scarce "high numbers," this series remains the most difficult Bowman regular issue to complete. Although the set was printed in color and commands great interest due to its scarcity, it is considered aesthetically inferior to the Goudey and National Chicle issues of the 1930s. In addition to the regular issue of 1949, Bowman also produced a set of 36 Pacific Coast League players. While this was not a regular issue, it still is prized by collectors. In fact, it has become the most valuable Bowman series.

In 1950 (representing Bowman's one-year monopoly of the baseball card market), the company began a string of top quality cards that continued until its demise in 1955. The 1950 series was itself something of an oddity because the low numbers, rather than the traditional high numbers, were the more difficult cards to obtain.

The year 1951 marked the beginning of the most competitive and perhaps the highest quality period of baseball card production. In that year, Topps Chewing Gum Company of Brooklyn entered the market. Topps' 1951 series consisted of two sets of 52 cards each, one set with red backs and the other with blue backs. In addition, Topps also issued 31 insert cards, three of which remain the rarest Topps cards ("Current All-Stars" Konstanty, Roberts and Stanky). The 1951 Topps cards were unattractive and paled in comparison to the 1951 Bowman issues. They were successful, however, and Topps has continued to produce cards ever since.

Intensified Competition

Topps issued a larger and more attractive card set in 1952. This larger size became standard for the next five years. (Bowman followed with larger-size baseball cards in 1953.) This 1952 Topps set has become, like the 1933

Goudey series and the T-206 white border series, the classic set of its era. The 407-card set is a collector's dream of scarcities, rarities, errors and variations. It also contains the first Topps issues of Mickey Mantle and Willie Mays.

As with Bowman and Leaf in the late 1940s, competition over player rights arose. Ensuing court battles occurred between Topps and Bowman. The market split due to stiff competition, and in January 1956, Topps bought out Bowman. (Topps, using the Bowman name, resurrected Bowman as a later label in 1989.) Topps remained essentially unchallenged as the primary producer of baseball cards through 1980. So, the story of major baseball card sets from 1956 through 1980 is by and large the story of Topps' issues. Notable exceptions include the small sets produced by Fleer Gum in 1959, 1960, 1961 and 1963, and the Kellogg's Cereal and Hostess Cakes baseball cards issued to promote their products.

A court decision in 1980 paved the way for two other large gum companies to enter (or reenter, in Fleer's case) the baseball card arena. Fleer, which had last made photo cards in 1963, and the Donruss Company (then a division of General Mills) secured rights to produce baseball cards of current players, thus breaking Topps' monopoly. Each company issued major card sets in 1981 with bubblegum products.

Then a higher court decision in that year overturned the lower court ruling against Topps. It appeared that Topps had regained its sole position as a producer of baseball cards. Undaunted by the revocation ruling, Fleer and Donruss continued to issue cards in 1982 but without bubblegum or any other edible product. Fleer issued its current player baseball cards with "team logo stickers," while Donruss issued its cards with a piece of a baseball jigsaw puzzle.

Sharing the Pie

Since 1981, these three major baseball card producers all have thrived, sharing relatively equal recognition. Each has steadily increased its involvement in terms of numbers of issues per year. To the delight of collectors, their competition has generated novel, and in some cases exceptional, issues of current Major League Baseball players. Collectors also eagerly accepted the debut efforts of Score (1988) and Upper Deck (1989), the newest companies to enter the baseball card producing derby.

Upper Deck's successful entry into the market turned out to be very important. The company's card stock, photography, packaging and marketing gave baseball cards a new standard for quality, and began the "premium card" trend that continues today. The second premium baseball card set to be issued was the 1990 Leaf set, named for and issued by the parent company of Donruss. To gauge the significance of the premium card trend, one need only note that two of the most valuable post-1986 regular-issue cards in the hobby are the 1989 Upper Deck Ken Griffey Jr. and 1990 Leaf Frank Thomas Rookie Cards.

The impressive debut of Leaf in 1990 was followed by Studio, Ultra, and Stadium Club in 1991. Of those, Stadium Club made the biggest impact. In 1992, Bowman, and Pinnacle joined the premium fray. In 1992, Donruss and Fleer abandoned the traditional 50-cent pack market and instead produced premium sets comparable to (and presumably designed to compete against) Upper Deck's set. Those moves, combined with the almost instantaneous spread of premium cards to the other major team sports cards, serve as strong indicators that premium cards probably are here to stay. Bowman had been a lower-level product from 1989 to '91.

In 1993, Fleer, Topps and Upper Deck produced the first "superpremium" cards with Flair Finest SP. Judging by the success of both, the baseball card market is headed toward higher, not lower, price levels.

In 1994, the market swung even further toward high-end products with the introduction of Topps' Bowman's Best (a hybrid of prospect-oriented Bowman and the superpremium Finest) and Leaf Limited. Other 1994 debuts included Upper Deck's entry-level Collector's Choice, Fleer's oversized Extra Bases and Pinnacle's hobby-only Select.

Of course, the biggest news of 1994 was the strike that halted the season prematurely. While the baseball card hobby obviously suffered from the strike, there was no catastrophic market crash as some had feared. In fact, cards of standouts such as Ken Griffey Jr., Frank Thomas and Cal Ripken continued to sell well, and certain tough inserts such as Flair Hot Gloves and Upper Deck SP Holoview Die-Cuts experienced strong demand long after the strike.

Overall, inserts continued to dominate the hobby scene, although there were some market indications that collectors were tiring of the parallel chase cards first introduced by Topps in 1992.

By 1995, almost every major product had one or more accompanying parallel insert sets. Among the most popular of these were the Score Gold Rush cards, which could be "upgraded" by mail to Platinum cards once a team set was assembled, and the Select Artist's Proofs, which benefited from hobby-only, one-per-box scarcity. However, it could be argued that the high price tags on parallel cards (four Select Artist's Proofs had already reached the $300 plateau by year's end) were driving more current collectors out of the hobby than drawing new ones in.

This was just one facet of a larger industry problem: simply too many products for the market to bear. Two of the six major baseball card manufacturers, Pinnacle and Topps, produced seven different brands each -- many of them with multiple series. As recently as 1992, the total number of brands was only 12. The result? A buyer's market in which new products usually were available cheaper to the consumer than they originally cost the dealer from the factory. As the year came to a close, the hobby was facing this very complex problem with no easy solutions.

Finding Out More

The above has been a thumbnail sketch of card collecting from its inception in the 1880s to the present. It is difficult to tell the whole story in just a few pages — there are several other good sources of information. Serious collectors should subscribe to at least one of the excellent hobby periodicals. We also suggest that collectors visit their local card shop(s) and also attend a sports collectibles show in their area. Card collecting is still a young and informal hobby. You can learn more about it in either place. After all, smart dealers realize that spending a few minutes teaching beginners about the hobby often pays off in the long run.

Additional Reading

Each year Beckett Publications produces comprehensive annual price guides for each of the four major sports: *Beckett Baseball Card Price Guide*, *Beckett Football Card Price Guide*, *Beckett Basketball Card Price Guide*, and *Beckett Hockey Card Price Guide*. The aim of these annual guides is to provide information and accurate pricing on a wide array of sports cards, ranging from main issues by the major card manufacturers to various regional, promotional, and food issues. Also alphabetical checklists, such as *Sport Americana Baseball Card Alphabetical Checklist #6*, are published to assist the collector in identifying all the cards of any particular player. The seasoned collector will find these tools valuable sources of information that will enable him to pursue his hobby interests.

In addition, abridged editions of the Beckett Price Guides have been published for each of the four major sports as part of the House of Collectibles series: *The Official Price Guide to Baseball Cards*, *The Official Price Guide to Football Cards*, *The Official Price Guide to Basketball Cards*, and *The Official Price Guide to Hockey Cards*. Published in a convenient mass-market paperback format, these price guides provide information and accurate pricing on all the main issues by the major card manufacturers.

Advertising

Within this Price Guide you will find advertisements for sports memorabilia material, mail order, and retail sports collectibles establishments. All advertisements were accepted in good faith based on the reputation of the advertiser; however, neither the author, the publisher, the distributors, nor the other advertisers in this Price Guide accept any responsibility for any particular advertiser not complying with the terms of his or her ad.

Readers also should be aware that prices in advertisements are subject to change over the annual period before a new edition of this volume is issued each spring. When replying to an advertisement late in the baseball year, the reader should take this into account, and contact the dealer by phone or in writing for up-to-date price information. Should you come into contact with any of the advertisers in this guide as a result of their advertisement herein, please mention this source as your contact.

Prices in this Guide

Prices found in this guide reflect current retail rates just prior to the printing of this book. They do not reflect the FOR SALE prices of the author, the publisher, the distributors, the advertisers, or any card dealers associated with this guide. No one is obligated in any way to buy, sell or trade his or her cards based on these prices. The price listings were compiled by the author from actual buy/sell transactions at sports conventions, sports card shops, buy/sell advertisements in the hobby papers, for sale prices from dealer catalogs and price lists, and discussions with leading hobbyists in the U.S. and Canada. All prices are in U.S. dollars.

Acknowledgments

A great deal of diligence, hard work, and dedicated effort went into this year's volume. The high standards to which we hold ourselves, however, could not have been met without the expert input and generous amount of time contributed by many people. Our sincere thanks are extended to each and every one of you.

A complete list of these invaluable contributors appears after the Price Guide section.

1948 Bowman

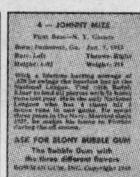

The 48-card Bowman set of 1948 was the first major set of the post-war period. Each 2 1/16" by 2 1/2" card had a black and white photo of a current player, with his biographical information printed in black ink on a gray back. Due to the printing process and the 36-card sheet size upon which Bowman was then printing, the 12 cards marked with an SP in the checklist are scarcer numerically, as they were removed from the printing sheet in order to make room for the 12 high numbers (37-48). Many cards are found with over-printed, transposed, or blank backs. The set features the Rookie Cards of Hall of Famers Yogi Berra, Ralph Kiner, Stan Musial, Red Schoendienst, and Warren Spahn. Half of the cards in the set feature New York players (Yankees or Giants).

	NRMT	VG-E	GOOD
COMPLETE SET (48)	3600.00	1600.00	450.00
COMMON CARD (1-36)	20.00	9.00	2.50
COMMON CARD (37-48)	30.00	13.50	3.70

		NRMT	VG-E	GOOD
☐ 1	Bob Elliott	80.00	12.00	4.00
☐ 2	Ewell Blackwell	40.00	18.00	5.00
☐ 3	Ralph Kiner	150.00	70.00	19.00
☐ 4	Johnny Mize	100.00	45.00	12.50
☐ 5	Bob Feller	225.00	100.00	28.00
☐ 6	Yogi Berra	500.00	220.00	60.00
☐ 7	Pete Reiser SP	80.00	36.00	10.00
☐ 8	Phil Rizzuto SP	300.00	135.00	38.00
☐ 9	Walker Cooper	20.00	9.00	2.50
☐ 10	Buddy Rosar	20.00	9.00	2.50
☐ 11	Johnny Lindell	22.50	10.00	2.80
☐ 12	Johnny Sain	55.00	25.00	7.00
☐ 13	Willard Marshall SP	40.00	18.00	5.00
☐ 14	Allie Reynolds	50.00	22.00	6.25
☐ 15	Eddie Joost	20.00	9.00	2.50
☐ 16	Jack Lohrke SP	40.00	18.00	5.00
☐ 17	Enos Slaughter	100.00	45.00	12.50
☐ 18	Warren Spahn	350.00	160.00	45.00
☐ 19	Tommy Henrich	40.00	18.00	5.00
☐ 20	Buddy Kerr SP	40.00	18.00	5.00
☐ 21	Ferris Fain	25.00	11.00	3.10
☐ 22	Floyd Bevens SP	45.00	20.00	5.50
☐ 23	Larry Jansen	20.00	9.00	2.50
☐ 24	Dutch Leonard SP	40.00	18.00	5.00
☐ 25	Barney McCosky	20.00	9.00	2.50
☐ 26	Frank Shea SP	45.00	20.00	5.50
☐ 27	Sid Gordon	20.00	9.00	2.50
☐ 28	Emil Verban SP	40.00	18.00	5.00
☐ 29	Joe Page SP	70.00	32.00	8.75
☐ 30	Whitey Lockman SP	50.00	22.00	6.25
☐ 31	Bill McCahan	20.00	9.00	2.50
☐ 32	Bill Rigney	20.00	9.00	2.50
☐ 33	Bill Johnson	22.50	10.00	2.80
☐ 34	Sheldon Jones SP	40.00	18.00	5.00
☐ 35	Snuffy Stirnweiss	20.00	9.00	2.50
☐ 36	Stan Musial	850.00	375.00	105.00
☐ 37	Clint Hartung	30.00	13.50	3.70
☐ 38	Red Schoendienst	150.00	70.00	19.00
☐ 39	Augie Galan	30.00	13.50	3.70
☐ 40	Marty Marion	75.00	34.00	9.50
☐ 41	Rex Barney	35.00	16.00	4.40
☐ 42	Ray Poat	30.00	13.50	3.70
☐ 43	Bruce Edwards	30.00	13.50	3.70
☐ 44	Johnny Wyrostek	30.00	13.50	3.70
☐ 45	Hank Sauer	50.00	22.00	6.25
☐ 46	Herman Wehmeier	30.00	13.50	3.70
☐ 47	Bobby Thomson	90.00	40.00	11.00
☐ 48	Dave Koslo	60.00	14.50	4.10

1949 Bowman

The cards in this 240-card set measure approximately 2 1/16" by 2 1/2". In 1949 Bowman took an intermediate step between black and white and full color with this set of tinted photos on colored backgrounds. Collectors should note the series price variations, which reflect some inconsistencies in the printing process. There are four major varieties in name printing, which are noted in the checklist below: NOF: name on front; NNOF: no name on front; PR: printed name on back; and SCR: script name on back. These variations resulted when Bowman used twelve of the lower numbers to fill out the last press sheet of 36 cards, adding to numbers 217-240. Cards 1-3 and 5-73 can be found with either gray or white backs. The set features the Rookie Cards of Hall of Famers Roy Campanella, Bob Lemon, Robin Roberts, Duke Snider, and Early Wynn as well as Rookie Cards of Richie Ashburn and Gil Hodges.

	NRMT	VG-E	GOOD
COMPLETE SET (240)	14000.00	6300.00	1800.00
COMMON CARD (1-144)	16.00	7.25	2.00
COMMON CARD (145-240)	50.00	22.00	6.25

		NRMT	VG-E	GOOD
☐ 1	Vern Bickford	80.00	16.00	4.80
☐ 2	Whitey Lockman	20.00	9.00	2.50
☐ 3	Bob Porterfield	20.00	9.00	2.50
☐ 4A	Jerry Priddy NNOF	16.00	7.25	2.00
☐ 4B	Jerry Priddy NOF	40.00	18.00	5.00
☐ 5	Hank Sauer	16.00	7.25	2.00

☐ 6	Phil Cavarretta	16.00	7.25	2.00	☐ 77	Ernie Bonham	16.00	7.25	2.00
☐ 7	Joe Dobson	16.00	7.25	2.00	☐ 78A	Sam Zoldak NNOF	16.00	7.25	2.00
☐ 8	Murry Dickson	16.00	7.25	2.00	☐ 78B	Sam Zoldak NOF	40.00	18.00	5.00
☐ 9	Ferris Fain	20.00	9.00	2.50	☐ 79	Ron Northey	16.00	7.25	2.00
☐ 10	Ted Gray	16.00	7.25	2.00	☐ 80	Bill McCahan	16.00	7.25	2.00
☐ 11	Lou Boudreau	60.00	27.00	7.50	☐ 81	Virgil Stallcup	16.00	7.25	2.00
☐ 12	Cass Michaels	16.00	7.25	2.00	☐ 82	Joe Page	16.00	7.25	2.00
☐ 13	Bob Chesnes	16.00	7.25	2.00	☐ 83A	Bob Scheffing NNOF	16.00	7.25	2.00
☐ 14	Curt Simmons	35.00	16.00	4.40	☐ 83B	Bob Scheffing NOF	40.00	18.00	5.00
☐ 15	Ned Garver	16.00	7.25	2.00	☐ 84	Roy Campanella	700.00	325.00	90.00
☐ 16	Al Kozar	16.00	7.25	2.00	☐ 85A	Johnny Mize NNOF	80.00	36.00	10.00
☐ 17	Earl Torgeson	16.00	7.25	2.00	☐ 85B	Johnny Mize NOF	150.00	70.00	19.00
☐ 18	Bobby Thomson	35.00	16.00	4.40	☐ 86	Johnny Pesky	30.00	13.50	3.70
☐ 19	Bobby Brown	35.00	16.00	4.40	☐ 87	Randy Gumpert	16.00	7.25	2.00
☐ 20	Gene Hermanski	16.00	7.25	2.00	☐ 88A	Bill Salkeld NNOF	16.00	7.25	2.00
☐ 21	Frank Baumholtz	20.00	9.00	2.50	☐ 88B	Bill Salkeld NOF	40.00	18.00	5.00
☐ 22	Peanuts Lowrey	16.00	7.25	2.00	☐ 89	Mizell Platt	16.00	7.25	2.00
☐ 23	Bobby Doerr	60.00	27.00	7.50	☐ 90	Gil Coan	16.00	7.25	2.00
☐ 24	Stan Musial	500.00	220.00	60.00	☐ 91	Dick Wakefield	16.00	7.25	2.00
☐ 25	Carl Scheib	16.00	7.25	2.00	☐ 92	Willie Jones	20.00	9.00	2.50
☐ 26	George Kell	55.00	25.00	7.00	☐ 93	Ed Stevens	16.00	7.25	2.00
☐ 27	Bob Feller	175.00	80.00	22.00	☐ 94	Mickey Vernon	35.00	16.00	4.40
☐ 28	Don Kolloway	16.00	7.25	2.00	☐ 95	Howie Pollet	16.00	7.25	2.00
☐ 29	Ralph Kiner	110.00	50.00	14.00	☐ 96	Taft Wright	16.00	7.25	2.00
☐ 30	Andy Seminick	20.00	9.00	2.50	☐ 97	Danny Litwhiler	16.00	7.25	2.00
☐ 31	Dick Kokos	16.00	7.25	2.00	☐ 98A	Phil Rizzuto NNOF	125.00	55.00	15.50
☐ 32	Eddie Yost	27.00	12.00	3.40	☐ 98B	Phil Rizzuto NOF	200.00	90.00	25.00
☐ 33	Warren Spahn	175.00	80.00	22.00	☐ 99	Frank Gustine	16.00	7.25	2.00
☐ 34	Dave Koslo	16.00	7.25	2.00	☐ 100	Gil Hodges	250.00	110.00	31.00
☐ 35	Vic Raschi	55.00	25.00	7.00	☐ 101	Sid Gordon	16.00	7.25	2.00
☐ 36	Pee Wee Reese	175.00	80.00	22.00	☐ 102	Stan Spence	16.00	7.25	2.00
☐ 37	Johnny Wyrostek	16.00	7.25	2.00	☐ 103	Joe Tipton	16.00	7.25	2.00
☐ 38	Emil Verban	16.00	7.25	2.00	☐ 104	Eddie Stanky	35.00	16.00	4.40
☐ 39	Billy Goodman	16.00	7.25	2.00	☐ 105	Bill Kennedy	16.00	7.25	2.00
☐ 40	Red Munger	16.00	7.25	2.00	☐ 106	Jake Early	16.00	7.25	2.00
☐ 41	Lou Brissie	16.00	7.25	2.00	☐ 107	Eddie Lake	16.00	7.25	2.00
☐ 42	Hoot Evers	16.00	7.25	2.00	☐ 108	Ken Heintzelman	16.00	7.25	2.00
☐ 43	Dale Mitchell	16.00	7.25	2.00	☐ 109A	Ed Fitzgerald SCR	16.00	7.25	2.00
☐ 44	Dave Philley	16.00	7.25	2.00	☐ 109B	Ed Fitzgerald PR	40.00	18.00	5.00
☐ 45	Wally Westlake	16.00	7.25	2.00	☐ 110	Early Wynn	110.00	50.00	14.00
☐ 46	Robin Roberts	225.00	100.00	28.00	☐ 111	Red Schoendienst	70.00	32.00	8.75
☐ 47	Johnny Sain	40.00	18.00	5.00	☐ 112	Sam Chapman	16.00	7.25	2.00
☐ 48	Willard Marshall	16.00	7.25	2.00	☐ 113	Ray LaManno	16.00	7.25	2.00
☐ 49	Frank Shea	20.00	9.00	2.50	☐ 114	Allie Reynolds	40.00	18.00	5.00
☐ 50	Jackie Robinson	900.00	400.00	110.00	☐ 115	Dutch Leonard	16.00	7.25	2.00
☐ 51	Herman Wehmeier	16.00	7.25	2.00	☐ 116	Joe Hatton	16.00	7.25	2.00
☐ 52	Johnny Schmitz	16.00	7.25	2.00	☐ 117	Walker Cooper	16.00	7.25	2.00
☐ 53	Jack Kramer	16.00	7.25	2.00	☐ 118	Sam Mele	16.00	7.25	2.00
☐ 54	Marty Marion	27.00	12.00	3.40	☐ 119	Floyd Baker	16.00	7.25	2.00
☐ 55	Eddie Joost	16.00	7.25	2.00	☐ 120	Cliff Fannin	16.00	7.25	2.00
☐ 56	Pat Mullin	16.00	7.25	2.00	☐ 121	Mark Christman	16.00	7.25	2.00
☐ 57	Gene Bearden	20.00	9.00	2.50	☐ 122	George Vico	16.00	7.25	2.00
☐ 58	Bob Elliott	20.00	9.00	2.50	☐ 123	Johnny Blatnick	16.00	7.25	2.00
☐ 59	Jack Lohrke	16.00	7.25	2.00	☐ 124A	Danny Murtaugh SCR	30.00	13.50	3.70
☐ 60	Yogi Berra	275.00	125.00	34.00	☐ 124B	Danny Murtaugh PR	45.00	20.00	5.50
☐ 61	Rex Barney	20.00	9.00	2.50	☐ 125	Ken Keltner	20.00	9.00	2.50
☐ 62	Grady Hatton	16.00	7.25	2.00	☐ 126A	Al Brazle SCR	16.00	7.25	2.00
☐ 63	Andy Pafko	16.00	7.25	2.00	☐ 126B	Al Brazle PR	40.00	18.00	5.00
☐ 64	Dom DiMaggio	35.00	16.00	4.40	☐ 127A	Hank Majeski SCR	16.00	7.25	2.00
☐ 65	Enos Slaughter	70.00	32.00	8.75	☐ 127B	Hank Majeski PR	40.00	18.00	5.00
☐ 66	Elmer Valo	16.00	7.25	2.00	☐ 128	Johnny VanderMeer	30.00	13.50	3.70
☐ 67	Alvin Dark	35.00	16.00	4.40	☐ 129	Bill Johnson	20.00	9.00	2.50
☐ 68	Sheldon Jones	16.00	7.25	2.00	☐ 130	Harry Walker	16.00	7.25	2.00
☐ 69	Tommy Henrich	35.00	16.00	4.40	☐ 131	Paul Lehner	16.00	7.25	2.00
☐ 70	Carl Furillo	80.00	36.00	10.00	☐ 132A	Al Evans SCR	16.00	7.25	2.00
☐ 71	Vern Stephens	16.00	7.25	2.00	☐ 132B	Al Evans PR	40.00	18.00	5.00
☐ 72	Tommy Holmes	20.00	9.00	2.50	☐ 133	Aaron Robinson	16.00	7.25	2.00
☐ 73	Billy Cox	35.00	16.00	4.40	☐ 134	Hank Borowy	16.00	7.25	2.00
☐ 74	Tom McBride	16.00	7.25	2.00	☐ 135	Stan Rojek	16.00	7.25	2.00
☐ 75	Eddie Mayo	16.00	7.25	2.00	☐ 136	Hank Edwards	16.00	7.25	2.00
☐ 76	Bill Nicholson	16.00	7.25	2.00	☐ 137	Ted Wilks	16.00	7.25	2.00

		NRMT	VG-E	GOOD
☐ 138	Buddy Rosar	16.00	7.25	2.00
☐ 139	Hank Arft	16.00	7.25	2.00
☐ 140	Ray Scarborough	16.00	7.25	2.00
☐ 141	Tony Lupien	16.00	7.25	2.00
☐ 142	Eddie Waitkus	16.00	7.25	2.00
☐ 143A	Bob Dillinger SCR	16.00	7.25	2.00
☐ 143B	Bob Dillinger PR	75.00	34.00	9.50
☐ 144	Mickey Haefner	16.00	7.25	2.00
☐ 145	Sylvester Donnelly	50.00	22.00	6.25
☐ 146	Mike McCormick	30.00	13.50	3.70
☐ 147	Bert Singleton	50.00	22.00	6.25
☐ 148	Bob Swift	50.00	22.00	6.25
☐ 149	Roy Partee	50.00	22.00	6.25
☐ 150	Allie Clark	50.00	22.00	6.25
☐ 151	Mickey Harris	50.00	22.00	6.25
☐ 152	Clarence Maddern	50.00	22.00	6.25
☐ 153	Phil Masi	50.00	22.00	6.25
☐ 154	Clint Hartung	30.00	13.50	3.70
☐ 155	Mickey Guerra	50.00	22.00	6.25
☐ 156	Al Zarilla	50.00	22.00	6.25
☐ 157	Walt Masterson	50.00	22.00	6.25
☐ 158	Harry Brecheen	50.00	22.00	6.25
☐ 159	Glen Moulder	50.00	22.00	6.25
☐ 160	Jim Blackburn	50.00	22.00	6.25
☐ 161	Jocko Thompson	50.00	22.00	6.25
☐ 162	Preacher Roe	125.00	55.00	15.50
☐ 163	Clyde McCullough	50.00	22.00	6.25
☐ 164	Vic Wertz	75.00	34.00	9.50
☐ 165	Snuffy Stirnweiss	30.00	13.50	3.70
☐ 166	Mike Tresh	50.00	22.00	6.25
☐ 167	Babe Martin	50.00	22.00	6.25
☐ 168	Doyle Lade	50.00	22.00	6.25
☐ 169	Jeff Heath	50.00	22.00	6.25
☐ 170	Bill Rigney	50.00	22.00	6.25
☐ 171	Dick Fowler	50.00	22.00	6.25
☐ 172	Eddie Pellagrini	50.00	22.00	6.25
☐ 173	Eddie Stewart	50.00	22.00	6.25
☐ 174	Terry Moore	100.00	45.00	12.50
☐ 175	Luke Appling	125.00	55.00	15.50
☐ 176	Ken Raffensberger	50.00	22.00	6.25
☐ 177	Stan Lopata	30.00	13.50	3.70
☐ 178	Tom Brown	30.00	13.50	3.70
☐ 179	Hugh Casey	30.00	13.50	3.70
☐ 180	Connie Berry	50.00	22.00	6.25
☐ 181	Gus Niarhos	50.00	22.00	6.25
☐ 182	Hal Peck	50.00	22.00	6.25
☐ 183	Lou Stringer	50.00	22.00	6.25
☐ 184	Bob Chipman	50.00	22.00	6.25
☐ 185	Pete Reiser	100.00	45.00	12.50
☐ 186	Buddy Kerr	50.00	22.00	6.25
☐ 187	Phil Marchildon	50.00	22.00	6.25
☐ 188	Karl Drews	50.00	22.00	6.25
☐ 189	Earl Wooten	50.00	22.00	6.25
☐ 190	Jim Hearn	50.00	22.00	6.25
☐ 191	Joe Haynes	50.00	22.00	6.25
☐ 192	Harry Gumbert	50.00	22.00	6.25
☐ 193	Ken Trinkle	50.00	22.00	6.25
☐ 194	Ralph Branca	100.00	45.00	12.50
☐ 195	Eddie Bockman	50.00	22.00	6.25
☐ 196	Fred Hutchinson	75.00	34.00	9.50
☐ 197	Johnny Lindell	30.00	13.50	3.70
☐ 198	Steve Gromek	50.00	22.00	6.25
☐ 199	Tex Hughson	50.00	22.00	6.25
☐ 200	Jess Dobernic	50.00	22.00	6.25
☐ 201	Sibby Sisti	50.00	22.00	6.25
☐ 202	Larry Jansen	50.00	22.00	6.25
☐ 203	Barney McCosky	50.00	22.00	6.25
☐ 204	Bob Savage	50.00	22.00	6.25
☐ 205	Dick Sisler	30.00	13.50	3.70
☐ 206	Bruce Edwards	50.00	22.00	6.25
☐ 207	Johnny Hopp	50.00	22.00	6.25
☐ 208	Dizzy Trout	50.00	22.00	6.25
☐ 209	Charlie Keller	100.00	45.00	12.50
☐ 210	Joe Gordon	100.00	45.00	12.50
☐ 211	Boo Ferriss	50.00	22.00	6.25
☐ 212	Ralph Hamner	50.00	22.00	6.25
☐ 213	Red Barrett	50.00	22.00	6.25
☐ 214	Richie Ashburn	550.00	250.00	70.00
☐ 215	Kirby Higbe	50.00	22.00	6.25
☐ 216	Schoolboy Rowe	30.00	13.50	3.70
☐ 217	Marino Pieretti	50.00	22.00	6.25
☐ 218	Dick Kryhoski	50.00	22.00	6.25
☐ 219	Virgil Fire Trucks	30.00	13.50	3.70
☐ 220	Johnny McCarthy	50.00	22.00	6.25
☐ 221	Bob Muncrief	50.00	22.00	6.25
☐ 222	Alex Kellner	50.00	22.00	6.25
☐ 223	Bobby Hofman	50.00	22.00	6.25
☐ 224	Satchell Paige	1100.00	500.00	140.00
☐ 225	Jerry Coleman	90.00	40.00	11.00
☐ 226	Duke Snider	900.00	400.00	110.00
☐ 227	Fritz Ostermueller	50.00	22.00	6.25
☐ 228	Jackie Mayo	50.00	22.00	6.25
☐ 229	Ed Lopat	125.00	55.00	15.50
☐ 230	Augie Galan	50.00	22.00	6.25
☐ 231	Earl Johnson	50.00	22.00	6.25
☐ 232	George McQuinn	50.00	22.00	6.25
☐ 233	Larry Doby	150.00	70.00	19.00
☐ 234	Rip Sewell	50.00	22.00	6.25
☐ 235	Jim Russell	50.00	22.00	6.25
☐ 236	Fred Sanford	50.00	22.00	6.25
☐ 237	Monte Kennedy	50.00	22.00	6.25
☐ 238	Bob Lemon	200.00	90.00	25.00
☐ 239	Frank McCormick	50.00	22.00	6.25
☐ 240	Babe Young UER (Photo actually Bobby Young)	100.00	22.00	6.25

1950 Bowman

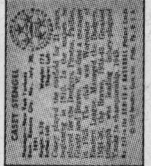

The cards in this 252-card set measure approximately 2 1/16" by 2 1/2". This set, marketed in 1950 by Bowman, represented a major improvement in terms of quality over their previous efforts. Each card was a beautifully colored line drawing developed from a simple photograph. The first 72 cards are the scarcest in the set, while the final 72 cards may be found with or without the copyright line. This was the only Bowman sports set to carry the famous "5-Star" logo. Key rookies in this set are Hank Bauer, Don Newcombe, and Al Rosen.

	NRMT	VG-E	GOOD
COMPLETE SET (252)	9500.00	4300.00	1200.00
COMMON CARD (1-72)	50.00	22.00	6.25
COMMON CARD (73-252)	18.00	8.00	2.20

1	Mel Parnell	150.00	30.00	9.00
2	Vern Stephens	55.00	25.00	7.00
3	Dom DiMaggio	65.00	29.00	8.00
4	Gus Zernial	60.00	27.00	7.50
5	Bob Kuzava	50.00	22.00	6.25
6	Bob Feller	225.00	100.00	28.00
7	Jim Hegan	55.00	25.00	7.00
8	George Kell	75.00	34.00	9.50
9	Vic Wertz	55.00	25.00	7.00
10	Tommy Henrich	65.00	29.00	8.00
11	Phil Rizzuto	225.00	100.00	28.00
12	Joe Page	50.00	22.00	6.25
13	Ferris Fain	55.00	25.00	7.00
14	Alex Kellner	50.00	22.00	6.25
15	Al Kozar	50.00	22.00	6.25
16	Roy Sievers	65.00	29.00	8.00
17	Sid Hudson	50.00	22.00	6.25
18	Eddie Robinson	50.00	22.00	6.25
19	Warren Spahn	225.00	100.00	28.00
20	Bob Elliott	55.00	25.00	7.00
21	Pee Wee Reese	225.00	100.00	28.00
22	Jackie Robinson	750.00	350.00	95.00
23	Don Newcombe	125.00	55.00	15.50
24	Johnny Schmitz	50.00	22.00	6.25
25	Hank Sauer	50.00	22.00	6.25
26	Grady Hatton	50.00	22.00	6.25
27	Herman Wehmeier	50.00	22.00	6.25
28	Bobby Thomson	65.00	29.00	8.00
29	Eddie Stanky	55.00	25.00	7.00
30	Eddie Waitkus	50.00	22.00	6.25
31	Del Ennis	65.00	29.00	8.00
32	Robin Roberts	150.00	70.00	19.00
33	Ralph Kiner	100.00	45.00	12.50
34	Murry Dickson	50.00	22.00	6.25
35	Enos Slaughter	100.00	45.00	12.50
36	Eddie Kazak	55.00	25.00	7.00
37	Luke Appling	75.00	34.00	9.50
38	Bill Wight	50.00	22.00	6.25
39	Larry Doby	65.00	29.00	8.00
40	Bob Lemon	75.00	34.00	9.50
41	Hoot Evers	50.00	22.00	6.25
42	Art Houtteman	50.00	22.00	6.25
43	Bobby Doerr	75.00	34.00	9.50
44	Joe Dobson	50.00	22.00	6.25
45	Al Zarilla	50.00	22.00	6.25
46	Yogi Berra	325.00	145.00	40.00
47	Jerry Coleman	60.00	27.00	7.50
48	Lou Brissie	50.00	22.00	6.25
49	Elmer Valo	50.00	22.00	6.25
50	Dick Kokos	50.00	22.00	6.25
51	Ned Garver	50.00	22.00	6.25
52	Sam Mele	50.00	22.00	6.25
53	Clyde Vollmer	50.00	22.00	6.25
54	Gil Coan	50.00	22.00	6.25
55	Buddy Kerr	50.00	22.00	6.25
56	Del Crandall	60.00	27.00	7.50
57	Vern Bickford	50.00	22.00	6.25
58	Carl Furillo	75.00	34.00	9.50
59	Ralph Branca	60.00	27.00	7.50
60	Andy Pafko	55.00	25.00	7.00
61	Bob Rush	50.00	22.00	6.25
62	Ted Kluszewski	100.00	45.00	12.50
63	Ewell Blackwell	50.00	22.00	6.25
64	Alvin Dark	60.00	27.00	7.50
65	Dave Koslo	50.00	22.00	6.25
66	Larry Jansen	55.00	25.00	7.00
67	Willie Jones	50.00	22.00	6.25
68	Curt Simmons	55.00	25.00	7.00
69	Wally Westlake	50.00	22.00	6.25
70	Bob Chesnes	50.00	22.00	6.25
71	Red Schoendienst	75.00	34.00	9.50
72	Howie Pollet	50.00	22.00	6.25
73	Willard Marshall	16.00	7.25	2.00
74	Johnny Antonelli	35.00	16.00	4.40
75	Roy Campanella	275.00	125.00	34.00
76	Rex Barney	20.00	9.00	2.50
77	Duke Snider	275.00	125.00	34.00
78	Mickey Owen	20.00	9.00	2.50
79	Johnny VanderMeer	25.00	11.00	3.10
80	Howard Fox	16.00	7.25	2.00
81	Ron Northey	16.00	7.25	2.00
82	Whitey Lockman	20.00	9.00	2.50
83	Sheldon Jones	16.00	7.25	2.00
84	Richie Ashburn	100.00	45.00	12.50
85	Ken Heintzelman	16.00	7.25	2.00
86	Stan Rojek	16.00	7.25	2.00
87	Bill Werle	16.00	7.25	2.00
88	Marty Marion	25.00	11.00	3.10
89	Red Munger	16.00	7.25	2.00
90	Harry Brecheen	20.00	9.00	2.50
91	Cass Michaels	16.00	7.25	2.00
92	Hank Majeski	16.00	7.25	2.00
93	Gene Bearden	20.00	9.00	2.50
94	Lou Boudreau	55.00	25.00	7.00
95	Aaron Robinson	16.00	7.25	2.00
96	Virgil Trucks	20.00	9.00	2.50
97	Maurice McDermott	16.00	7.25	2.00
98	Ted Williams	850.00	375.00	105.00
99	Billy Goodman	20.00	9.00	2.50
100	Vic Raschi	35.00	16.00	4.40
101	Bobby Brown	35.00	16.00	4.40
102	Billy Johnson	20.00	9.00	2.50
103	Eddie Joost	16.00	7.25	2.00
104	Sam Chapman	16.00	7.25	2.00
105	Bob Dillinger	16.00	7.25	2.00
106	Cliff Fannin	16.00	7.25	2.00
107	Sam Dente	16.00	7.25	2.00
108	Ray Scarborough	16.00	7.25	2.00
109	Sid Gordon	16.00	7.25	2.00
110	Tommy Holmes	20.00	9.00	2.50
111	Walker Cooper	16.00	7.25	2.00
112	Gil Hodges	100.00	45.00	12.50
113	Gene Hermanski	16.00	7.25	2.00
114	Wayne Terwilliger	16.00	7.25	2.00
115	Roy Smalley	16.00	7.25	2.00
116	Virgil Stallcup	16.00	7.25	2.00
117	Bill Rigney	16.00	7.25	2.00
118	Clint Hartung	16.00	7.25	2.00
119	Dick Sisler	20.00	9.00	2.50
120	John Thompson	16.00	7.25	2.00
121	Andy Seminick	16.00	7.25	2.00
122	Johnny Hopp	20.00	9.00	2.50
123	Dino Restelli	16.00	7.25	2.00
124	Clyde McCullough	16.00	7.25	2.00
125	Del Rice	16.00	7.25	2.00
126	Al Brazle	16.00	7.25	2.00
127	Dave Philley	16.00	7.25	2.00
128	Phil Masi	16.00	7.25	2.00
129	Joe Gordon	16.00	7.25	2.00
130	Dale Mitchell	20.00	9.00	2.50
131	Steve Gromek	16.00	7.25	2.00
132	Mickey Vernon	20.00	9.00	2.50
133	Don Kolloway	16.00	7.25	2.00
134	Paul Trout	16.00	7.25	2.00
135	Pat Mullin	16.00	7.25	2.00
136	Warren Rosar	16.00	7.25	2.00
137	Johnny Pesky	20.00	9.00	2.50
138	Allie Reynolds	35.00	16.00	4.40
139	Johnny Mize	75.00	34.00	9.50
140	Pete Suder	16.00	7.25	2.00
141	Joe Coleman	16.00	7.25	2.00
142	Sherm Lollar	25.00	11.00	3.10

☐ 143	Eddie Stewart	16.00	7.25	2.00
☐ 144	Al Evans	16.00	7.25	2.00
☐ 145	Jack Graham	16.00	7.25	2.00
☐ 146	Floyd Baker	16.00	7.25	2.00
☐ 147	Mike Garcia	30.00	13.50	3.70
☐ 148	Early Wynn	60.00	27.00	7.50
☐ 149	Bob Swift	16.00	7.25	2.00
☐ 150	George Vico	16.00	7.25	2.00
☐ 151	Fred Hutchinson	16.00	7.25	2.00
☐ 152	Ellis Kinder	16.00	7.25	2.00
☐ 153	Walt Masterson	16.00	7.25	2.00
☐ 154	Gus Niarhos	16.00	7.25	2.00
☐ 155	Frank Shea	20.00	9.00	2.50
☐ 156	Fred Sanford	20.00	9.00	2.50
☐ 157	Mike Guerra	16.00	7.25	2.00
☐ 158	Paul Lehner	16.00	7.25	2.00
☐ 159	Joe Tipton	16.00	7.25	2.00
☐ 160	Mickey Harris	16.00	7.25	2.00
☐ 161	Sherry Robertson	16.00	7.25	2.00
☐ 162	Eddie Yost	20.00	9.00	2.50
☐ 163	Earl Torgeson	16.00	7.25	2.00
☐ 164	Sibby Sisti	16.00	7.25	2.00
☐ 165	Bruce Edwards	16.00	7.25	2.00
☐ 166	Joe Hatton	16.00	7.25	2.00
☐ 167	Preacher Roe	35.00	16.00	4.40
☐ 168	Bob Scheffing	16.00	7.25	2.00
☐ 169	Hank Edwards	16.00	7.25	2.00
☐ 170	Dutch Leonard	16.00	7.25	2.00
☐ 171	Harry Gumbert	16.00	7.25	2.00
☐ 172	Peanuts Lowrey	16.00	7.25	2.00
☐ 173	Lloyd Merriman	16.00	7.25	2.00
☐ 174	Hank Thompson	25.00	11.00	3.10
☐ 175	Monte Kennedy	16.00	7.25	2.00
☐ 176	Sylvester Donnelly	16.00	7.25	2.00
☐ 177	Hank Borowy	16.00	7.25	2.00
☐ 178	Ed Fitzgerald	16.00	7.25	2.00
☐ 179	Chuck Diering	16.00	7.25	2.00
☐ 180	Harry Walker	16.00	7.25	2.00
☐ 181	Marino Pieretti	16.00	7.25	2.00
☐ 182	Sam Zoldak	16.00	7.25	2.00
☐ 183	Mickey Haefner	16.00	7.25	2.00
☐ 184	Randy Gumpert	16.00	7.25	2.00
☐ 185	Howie Judson	16.00	7.25	2.00
☐ 186	Ken Keltner	20.00	9.00	2.50
☐ 187	Lou Stringer	16.00	7.25	2.00
☐ 188	Earl Johnson	16.00	7.25	2.00
☐ 189	Owen Friend	16.00	7.25	2.00
☐ 190	Ken Wood	16.00	7.25	2.00
☐ 191	Dick Starr	16.00	7.25	2.00
☐ 192	Bob Chipman	16.00	7.25	2.00
☐ 193	Pete Reiser	25.00	11.00	3.10
☐ 194	Billy Cox	25.00	11.00	3.10
☐ 195	Phil Cavarretta	25.00	11.00	3.10
☐ 196	Doyle Lade	16.00	7.25	2.00
☐ 197	Johnny Wyrostek	16.00	7.25	2.00
☐ 198	Danny Litwhiler	16.00	7.25	2.00
☐ 199	Jack Kramer	16.00	7.25	2.00
☐ 200	Kirby Higbe	16.00	7.25	2.00
☐ 201	Pete Castiglione	16.00	7.25	2.00
☐ 202	Cliff Chambers	16.00	7.25	2.00
☐ 203	Danny Murtaugh	20.00	9.00	2.50
☐ 204	Granny Hamner	25.00	11.00	3.10
☐ 205	Mike Goliat	16.00	7.25	2.00
☐ 206	Stan Lopata	16.00	7.25	2.00
☐ 207	Max Lanier	16.00	7.25	2.00
☐ 208	Jim Hearn	16.00	7.25	2.00
☐ 209	Johnny Lindell	16.00	7.25	2.00
☐ 210	Ted Gray	16.00	7.25	2.00
☐ 211	Charlie Keller	20.00	9.00	2.50
☐ 212	Jerry Priddy	16.00	7.25	2.00
☐ 213	Carl Scheib	16.00	7.25	2.00

☐ 214	Dick Fowler	16.00	7.25	2.00
☐ 215	Ed Lopat	35.00	16.00	4.40
☐ 216	Bob Porterfield	20.00	9.00	2.50
☐ 217	Casey Stengel MG	100.00	45.00	12.50
☐ 218	Cliff Mapes	20.00	9.00	2.50
☐ 219	Hank Bauer	65.00	29.00	8.00
☐ 220	Leo Durocher MG	60.00	27.00	7.50
☐ 221	Don Mueller	30.00	13.50	3.70
☐ 222	Bobby Morgan	16.00	7.25	2.00
☐ 223	Jim Russell	16.00	7.25	2.00
☐ 224	Jack Banta	16.00	7.25	2.00
☐ 225	Eddie Sawyer MG	20.00	9.00	2.50
☐ 226	Jim Konstanty	40.00	18.00	5.00
☐ 227	Bob Miller	16.00	7.25	2.00
☐ 228	Bill Nicholson	20.00	9.00	2.50
☐ 229	Frank Frisch MG	40.00	18.00	5.00
☐ 230	Bill Serena	16.00	7.25	2.00
☐ 231	Preston Ward	16.00	7.25	2.00
☐ 232	Al Rosen	40.00	18.00	5.00
☐ 233	Allie Clark	16.00	7.25	2.00
☐ 234	Bobby Shantz	40.00	18.00	5.00
☐ 235	Harold Gilbert	16.00	7.25	2.00
☐ 236	Bob Cain	16.00	7.25	2.00
☐ 237	Bill Salkeld	16.00	7.25	2.00
☐ 238	Nippy Jones	16.00	7.25	2.00
☐ 239	Bill Howerton	16.00	7.25	2.00
☐ 240	Eddie Lake	16.00	7.25	2.00
☐ 241	Neil Berry	16.00	7.25	2.00
☐ 242	Dick Kryhoski	16.00	7.25	2.00
☐ 243	Johnny Groth	16.00	7.25	2.00
☐ 244	Dale Coogan	16.00	7.25	2.00
☐ 245	Al Papai	16.00	7.25	2.00
☐ 246	Walt Dropo	30.00	13.50	3.70
☐ 247	Irv Noren	20.00	9.00	2.50
☐ 248	Sam Jethroe	35.00	16.00	4.40
☐ 249	Snuffy Stirnweiss	20.00	9.00	2.50
☐ 250	Ray Coleman	16.00	7.25	2.00
☐ 251	John Moss	16.00	7.25	2.00
☐ 252	Billy DeMars	35.00	9.50	3.50

1951 Bowman

 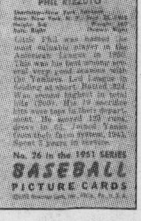

The cards in this 324-card set measure approximately 2 1/16" by 3 1/8". Many of the obverses of the cards appearing in the 1951 Bowman set are enlargements of those appearing in the previous year. The high number series (253-324) is highly valued and contains the true "Rookie" cards of Mickey Mantle and Willie Mays. Card number 195 depicts Paul Richards in caricature. George Kell's card (number 46) incorrectly *lists him as being in the "1941" Bowman series. Player names are found printed in a panel on the front of the card. These cards were supposedly also sold in sheets in variety stores in the Philadelphia area.*

		NRMT	VG-E	GOOD
	COMPLETE SET (324)	17000.00	7600.00	2100.00
	COMMON CARD (1-252)	18.00	8.00	2.20
	COMMON CARD (253-324)	50.00	22.00	6.25
☐ 1	Whitey Ford	800.00	200.00	65.00
☐ 2	Yogi Berra	300.00	135.00	38.00
☐ 3	Robin Roberts	75.00	34.00	9.50
☐ 4	Del Ennis	18.00	8.00	2.20
☐ 5	Dale Mitchell	22.00	10.00	2.70
☐ 6	Don Newcombe	40.00	18.00	5.00
☐ 7	Gil Hodges	75.00	34.00	9.50
☐ 8	Paul Lehner	18.00	8.00	2.20
☐ 9	Sam Chapman	18.00	8.00	2.20
☐ 10	Red Schoendienst	55.00	25.00	7.00
☐ 11	Red Munger	18.00	8.00	2.20
☐ 12	Hank Majeski	18.00	8.00	2.20
☐ 13	Eddie Stanky	18.00	8.00	2.20
☐ 14	Alvin Dark	30.00	13.50	3.70
☐ 15	Johnny Pesky	18.00	8.00	2.20
☐ 16	Maurice McDermott	18.00	8.00	2.20
☐ 17	Pete Castiglione	18.00	8.00	2.20
☐ 18	Gil Coan	18.00	8.00	2.20
☐ 19	Sid Gordon	18.00	8.00	2.20
☐ 20	Del Crandall UER	22.00	10.00	2.70
	(Misspelled Crandell on card)			
☐ 21	Snuffy Stirnweiss	22.00	10.00	2.70
☐ 22	Hank Sauer	18.00	8.00	2.20
☐ 23	Hoot Evers	18.00	8.00	2.20
☐ 24	Ewell Blackwell	25.00	11.00	3.10
☐ 25	Vic Raschi	35.00	16.00	4.40
☐ 26	Phil Rizzuto	125.00	55.00	15.50
☐ 27	Jim Konstanty	18.00	8.00	2.20
☐ 28	Eddie Waitkus	18.00	8.00	2.20
☐ 29	Allie Clark	18.00	8.00	2.20
☐ 30	Bob Feller	125.00	55.00	15.50
☐ 31	Roy Campanella	225.00	100.00	28.00
☐ 32	Duke Snider	225.00	100.00	28.00
☐ 33	Bob Hooper	18.00	8.00	2.20
☐ 34	Marty Marion	25.00	11.00	3.10
☐ 35	Al Zarilla	18.00	8.00	2.20
☐ 36	Joe Dobson	18.00	8.00	2.20
☐ 37	Whitey Lockman	25.00	11.00	3.10
☐ 38	Al Evans	18.00	8.00	2.20
☐ 39	Ray Scarborough	18.00	8.00	2.20
☐ 40	Gus Bell	35.00	16.00	4.40
☐ 41	Eddie Yost	22.00	10.00	2.70
☐ 42	Vern Bickford	18.00	8.00	2.20
☐ 43	Billy DeMars	18.00	8.00	2.20
☐ 44	Roy Smalley	18.00	8.00	2.20
☐ 45	Art Houtteman	18.00	8.00	2.20
☐ 46	George Kell 1941 UER	55.00	25.00	7.00
☐ 47	Grady Hatton	18.00	8.00	2.20
☐ 48	Ken Raffensberger	18.00	8.00	2.20
☐ 49	Jerry Coleman	25.00	11.00	3.10
☐ 50	Johnny Mize	55.00	25.00	7.00
☐ 51	Andy Seminick	18.00	8.00	2.20
☐ 52	Dick Sisler	25.00	11.00	3.10
☐ 53	Bob Lemon	55.00	25.00	7.00
☐ 54	Ray Boone	35.00	16.00	4.40
☐ 55	Gene Hermanski	18.00	8.00	2.20
☐ 56	Ralph Branca	30.00	13.50	3.70
☐ 57	Alex Kellner	18.00	8.00	2.20
☐ 58	Enos Slaughter	55.00	25.00	7.00
☐ 59	Randy Gumpert	18.00	8.00	2.20
☐ 60	Chico Carrasquel	25.00	11.00	3.10
☐ 61	Jim Hearn	22.00	10.00	2.70
☐ 62	Lou Boudreau	55.00	25.00	7.00
☐ 63	Bob Dillinger	18.00	8.00	2.20
☐ 64	Bill Werle	18.00	8.00	2.20
☐ 65	Mickey Vernon	25.00	11.00	3.10
☐ 66	Bob Elliott	22.00	10.00	2.70
☐ 67	Roy Sievers	22.00	10.00	2.70
☐ 68	Dick Kokos	18.00	8.00	2.20
☐ 69	Johnny Schmitz	18.00	8.00	2.20
☐ 70	Ron Northey	18.00	8.00	2.20
☐ 71	Jerry Priddy	18.00	8.00	2.20
☐ 72	Lloyd Merriman	18.00	8.00	2.20
☐ 73	Tommy Byrne	18.00	8.00	2.20
☐ 74	Billy Johnson	22.00	10.00	2.70
☐ 75	Russ Meyer	18.00	8.00	2.20
☐ 76	Stan Lopata	18.00	8.00	2.20
☐ 77	Mike Goliat	18.00	8.00	2.20
☐ 78	Early Wynn	55.00	25.00	7.00
☐ 79	Jim Hegan	22.00	10.00	2.70
☐ 80	Pee Wee Reese	150.00	70.00	19.00
☐ 81	Carl Furillo	40.00	18.00	5.00
☐ 82	Joe Tipton	18.00	8.00	2.20
☐ 83	Carl Scheib	18.00	8.00	2.20
☐ 84	Barney McCosky	18.00	8.00	2.20
☐ 85	Eddie Kazak	18.00	8.00	2.20
☐ 86	Harry Brecheen	22.00	10.00	2.70
☐ 87	Floyd Baker	18.00	8.00	2.20
☐ 88	Eddie Robinson	18.00	8.00	2.20
☐ 89	Hank Thompson	22.00	10.00	2.70
☐ 90	Dave Koslo	22.00	10.00	2.70
☐ 91	Clyde Vollmer	18.00	8.00	2.20
☐ 92	Vern Stephens	22.00	10.00	2.70
☐ 93	Danny O'Connell	18.00	8.00	2.20
☐ 94	Clyde McCullough	18.00	8.00	2.20
☐ 95	Sherry Robertson	18.00	8.00	2.20
☐ 96	Sandy Consuegra	18.00	8.00	2.20
☐ 97	Bob Kuzava	18.00	8.00	2.20
☐ 98	Willard Marshall	18.00	8.00	2.20
☐ 99	Earl Torgeson	18.00	8.00	2.20
☐ 100	Sherm Lollar	22.00	10.00	2.70
☐ 101	Owen Friend	18.00	8.00	2.20
☐ 102	Dutch Leonard	18.00	8.00	2.20
☐ 103	Andy Pafko	25.00	11.00	3.10
☐ 104	Virgil Trucks	22.00	10.00	2.70
☐ 105	Don Kolloway	18.00	8.00	2.20
☐ 106	Pat Mullin	18.00	8.00	2.20
☐ 107	Johnny Wyrostek	18.00	8.00	2.20
☐ 108	Virgil Stallcup	18.00	8.00	2.20
☐ 109	Allie Reynolds	35.00	16.00	4.40
☐ 110	Bobby Brown	28.00	12.50	3.50
☐ 111	Curt Simmons	18.00	8.00	2.20
☐ 112	Willie Jones	18.00	8.00	2.20
☐ 113	Bill Nicholson	22.00	10.00	2.70
☐ 114	Sam Zoldak	18.00	8.00	2.20
☐ 115	Steve Gromek	18.00	8.00	2.20
☐ 116	Bruce Edwards	18.00	8.00	2.20
☐ 117	Eddie Miksis	18.00	8.00	2.20
☐ 118	Preacher Roe	35.00	16.00	4.40
☐ 119	Eddie Joost	18.00	8.00	2.20
☐ 120	Joe Coleman	18.00	8.00	2.20
☐ 121	Jerry Staley	18.00	8.00	2.20
☐ 122	Joe Garagiola	75.00	34.00	9.50
☐ 123	Howie Judson	18.00	8.00	2.20
☐ 124	Gus Niarhos	18.00	8.00	2.20
☐ 125	Bill Rigney	22.00	10.00	2.70
☐ 126	Bobby Thomson	30.00	13.50	3.70
☐ 127	Sal Maglie	50.00	22.00	6.25
☐ 128	Ellis Kinder	18.00	8.00	2.20
☐ 129	Matt Batts	18.00	8.00	2.20

☐	130	Tom Saffell	18.00	8.00	2.20	☐	200	Jack Kramer	18.00	8.00	2.20

☐	130	Tom Saffell	18.00	8.00	2.20
☐	131	Cliff Chambers	18.00	8.00	2.20
☐	132	Cass Michaels	18.00	8.00	2.20
☐	133	Sam Dente	18.00	8.00	2.20
☐	134	Warren Spahn	125.00	55.00	15.50
☐	135	Walker Cooper	18.00	8.00	2.20
☐	136	Ray Coleman	18.00	8.00	2.20
☐	137	Dick Starr	18.00	8.00	2.20
☐	138	Phil Cavarretta	22.00	10.00	2.70
☐	139	Doyle Lade	18.00	8.00	2.20
☐	140	Eddie Lake	18.00	8.00	2.20
☐	141	Fred Hutchinson	18.00	8.00	2.20
☐	142	Aaron Robinson	18.00	8.00	2.20
☐	143	Ted Kluszewski	40.00	18.00	5.00
☐	144	Herman Wehmeier	18.00	8.00	2.20
☐	145	Fred Sanford	22.00	10.00	2.70
☐	146	Johnny Hopp	22.00	10.00	2.70
☐	147	Ken Heintzelman	18.00	8.00	2.20
☐	148	Granny Hamner	18.00	8.00	2.20
☐	149	Bubba Church	18.00	8.00	2.20
☐	150	Mike Garcia	22.00	10.00	2.70
☐	151	Larry Doby	30.00	13.50	3.70
☐	152	Cal Abrams	18.00	8.00	2.20
☐	153	Rex Barney	22.00	10.00	2.70
☐	154	Pete Suder	18.00	8.00	2.20
☐	155	Lou Brissie	18.00	8.00	2.20
☐	156	Del Rice	18.00	8.00	2.20
☐	157	Al Brazle	18.00	8.00	2.20
☐	158	Chuck Diering	18.00	8.00	2.20
☐	159	Eddie Stewart	18.00	8.00	2.20
☐	160	Phil Masi	18.00	8.00	2.20
☐	161	Wes Westrum	18.00	8.00	2.20
☐	162	Larry Jansen	22.00	10.00	2.70
☐	163	Monte Kennedy	18.00	8.00	2.20
☐	164	Bill Wight	18.00	8.00	2.20
☐	165	Ted Williams	725.00	325.00	90.00
☐	166	Stan Rojek	18.00	8.00	2.20
☐	167	Murry Dickson	18.00	8.00	2.20
☐	168	Sam Mele	18.00	8.00	2.20
☐	169	Sid Hudson	18.00	8.00	2.20
☐	170	Sibby Sisti	18.00	8.00	2.20
☐	171	Buddy Kerr	18.00	8.00	2.20
☐	172	Ned Garver	18.00	8.00	2.20
☐	173	Hank Arft	18.00	8.00	2.20
☐	174	Mickey Owen	22.00	10.00	2.70
☐	175	Wayne Terwilliger	18.00	8.00	2.20
☐	176	Vic Wertz	25.00	11.00	3.10
☐	177	Charlie Keller	22.00	10.00	2.70
☐	178	Ted Gray	18.00	8.00	2.20
☐	179	Danny Litwhiler	18.00	8.00	2.20
☐	180	Howie Fox	18.00	8.00	2.20
☐	181	Casey Stengel MG	75.00	34.00	9.50
☐	182	Tom Ferrick	18.00	8.00	2.20
☐	183	Hank Bauer	30.00	13.50	3.70
☐	184	Eddie Sawyer MG	22.00	10.00	2.70
☐	185	Jimmy Bloodworth	18.00	8.00	2.20
☐	186	Richie Ashburn	90.00	40.00	11.00
☐	187	Al Rosen	25.00	11.00	3.10
☐	188	Bobby Avila	18.00	8.00	2.20
☐	189	Erv Palica	18.00	8.00	2.20
☐	190	Joe Hatten	18.00	8.00	2.20
☐	191	Billy Hitchcock	18.00	8.00	2.20
☐	192	Hank Wyse	18.00	8.00	2.20
☐	193	Ted Wilks	18.00	8.00	2.20
☐	194	Peanuts Lowrey	18.00	8.00	2.20
☐	195	Paul Richards MG (Caricature)	22.00	10.00	2.70
☐	196	Billy Pierce	30.00	13.50	3.70
☐	197	Bob Cain	18.00	8.00	2.20
☐	198	Monte Irvin	100.00	45.00	12.50
☐	199	Sheldon Jones	18.00	8.00	2.20

☐	200	Jack Kramer	18.00	8.00	2.20
☐	201	Steve O'Neill MG	18.00	8.00	2.20
☐	202	Mike Guerra	18.00	8.00	2.20
☐	203	Vernon Law	30.00	13.50	3.70
☐	204	Vic Lombardi	18.00	8.00	2.20
☐	205	Mickey Grasso	18.00	8.00	2.20
☐	206	Conrado Marrero	18.00	8.00	2.20
☐	207	Billy Southworth MG	18.00	8.00	2.20
☐	208	Blix Donnelly	18.00	8.00	2.20
☐	209	Ken Wood	18.00	8.00	2.20
☐	210	Les Moss	18.00	8.00	2.20
☐	211	Hal Jeffcoat	18.00	8.00	2.20
☐	212	Bob Rush	18.00	8.00	2.20
☐	213	Neil Berry	18.00	8.00	2.20
☐	214	Bob Swift	18.00	8.00	2.20
☐	215	Ken Peterson	18.00	8.00	2.20
☐	216	Connie Ryan	18.00	8.00	2.20
☐	217	Joe Page	18.00	8.00	2.20
☐	218	Ed Lopat	35.00	16.00	4.40
☐	219	Gene Woodling	40.00	18.00	5.00
☐	220	Bob Miller	18.00	8.00	2.20
☐	221	Dick Whitman	18.00	8.00	2.20
☐	222	Thurman Tucker	18.00	8.00	2.20
☐	223	Johnny VanderMeer	25.00	11.00	3.10
☐	224	Billy Cox	18.00	8.00	2.20
☐	225	Dan Bankhead	22.00	10.00	2.70
☐	226	Jimmy Dykes MG	22.00	10.00	2.70
☐	227	Bobby Schantz UER (Sic, Shantz)	22.00	10.00	2.70
☐	228	Cloyd Boyer	22.00	10.00	2.70
☐	229	Bill Howerton	18.00	8.00	2.20
☐	230	Max Lanier	18.00	8.00	2.20
☐	231	Luis Aloma	18.00	8.00	2.20
☐	232	Nelson Fox	150.00	70.00	19.00
☐	233	Leo Durocher MG	60.00	27.00	7.50
☐	234	Clint Hartung	22.00	10.00	2.70
☐	235	Jack Lohrke	18.00	8.00	2.20
☐	236	Warren Rosar	18.00	8.00	2.20
☐	237	Billy Goodman	22.00	10.00	2.70
☐	238	Pete Reiser	22.00	10.00	2.70
☐	239	Bill MacDonald	18.00	8.00	2.20
☐	240	Joe Haynes	18.00	8.00	2.20
☐	241	Irv Noren	22.00	10.00	2.70
☐	242	Sam Jethroe	22.00	10.00	2.70
☐	243	Johnny Antonelli	22.00	10.00	2.70
☐	244	Cliff Fannin	18.00	8.00	2.20
☐	245	John Berardino	25.00	11.00	3.10
☐	246	Bill Serena	18.00	8.00	2.20
☐	247	Bob Ramazzotti	18.00	8.00	2.20
☐	248	Johnny Klippstein	18.00	8.00	2.20
☐	249	Johnny Groth	18.00	8.00	2.20
☐	250	Hank Borowy	18.00	8.00	2.20
☐	251	Willard Ramsdell	18.00	8.00	2.20
☐	252	Dixie Howell	18.00	8.00	2.20
☐	253	Mickey Mantle	8000.00	3600.00	1000.00
☐	254	Jackie Jensen	100.00	45.00	12.50
☐	255	Milo Candini	50.00	22.00	6.25
☐	256	Ken Sylvestri	50.00	22.00	6.25
☐	257	Birdie Tebbetts	60.00	27.00	7.50
☐	258	Luke Easter	60.00	27.00	7.50
☐	259	Chuck Dressen MG	60.00	27.00	7.50
☐	260	Carl Erskine	100.00	45.00	12.50
☐	261	Wally Moses	55.00	25.00	7.00
☐	262	Gus Zernial	60.00	27.00	7.50
☐	263	Howie Pollet	55.00	25.00	7.00
☐	264	Don Richmond	50.00	22.00	6.25
☐	265	Steve Bilko	55.00	25.00	7.00
☐	266	Harry Dorish	50.00	22.00	6.25
☐	267	Ken Holcombe	50.00	22.00	6.25
☐	268	Don Mueller	55.00	25.00	7.00
☐	269	Ray Noble	50.00	22.00	6.25

☐ 270	Willard Nixon	50.00	22.00	6.25
☐ 271	Tommy Wright	50.00	22.00	6.25
☐ 272	Billy Meyer MG	50.00	22.00	6.25
☐ 273	Danny Murtaugh	55.00	25.00	7.00
☐ 274	George Metkovich	50.00	22.00	6.25
☐ 275	Bucky Harris MG	55.00	25.00	7.00
☐ 276	Frank Quinn	50.00	22.00	6.25
☐ 277	Roy Hartsfield	50.00	22.00	6.25
☐ 278	Norman Roy	50.00	22.00	6.25
☐ 279	Jim Delsing	50.00	22.00	6.25
☐ 280	Frank Overmire	50.00	22.00	6.25
☐ 281	Al Widmar	50.00	22.00	6.25
☐ 282	Frank Frisch MG	75.00	34.00	9.50
☐ 283	Walt Dubiel	50.00	22.00	6.25
☐ 284	Gene Bearden	55.00	25.00	7.00
☐ 285	Johnny Lipon	50.00	22.00	6.25
☐ 286	Bob Usher	50.00	22.00	6.25
☐ 287	Jim Blackburn	50.00	22.00	6.25
☐ 288	Bobby Adams	50.00	22.00	6.25
☐ 289	Cliff Mapes	55.00	25.00	7.00
☐ 290	Bill Dickey CO	100.00	45.00	12.50
☐ 291	Tommy Henrich CO	60.00	27.00	7.50
☐ 292	Eddie Pellegrini	50.00	22.00	6.25
☐ 293	Ken Johnson	50.00	22.00	6.25
☐ 294	Jocko Thompson	50.00	22.00	6.25
☐ 295	Al Lopez MG	120.00	55.00	15.00
☐ 296	Bob Kennedy	55.00	25.00	7.00
☐ 297	Dave Philley	50.00	22.00	6.25
☐ 298	Joe Astroth	50.00	22.00	6.25
☐ 299	Clyde King	50.00	22.00	6.25
☐ 300	Hal Rice	50.00	22.00	6.25
☐ 301	Tommy Glaviano	50.00	22.00	6.25
☐ 302	Jim Busby	50.00	22.00	6.25
☐ 303	Marv Rotblatt	50.00	22.00	6.25
☐ 304	Al Gettell	50.00	22.00	6.25
☐ 305	Willie Mays	3500.00	1600.00	450.00
☐ 306	Jim Piersall	100.00	45.00	12.50
☐ 307	Walt Masterson	50.00	22.00	6.25
☐ 308	Ted Beard	50.00	22.00	6.25
☐ 309	Mel Queen	50.00	22.00	6.25
☐ 310	Erv Dusak	50.00	22.00	6.25
☐ 311	Mickey Harris	50.00	22.00	6.25
☐ 312	Gene Mauch	60.00	27.00	7.50
☐ 313	Ray Mueller	50.00	22.00	6.25
☐ 314	Johnny Sain	60.00	27.00	7.50
☐ 315	Zack Taylor MG	50.00	22.00	6.25
☐ 316	Duane Pillette	50.00	22.00	6.25
☐ 317	Smoky Burgess	75.00	34.00	9.50
☐ 318	Warren Hacker	50.00	22.00	6.25
☐ 319	Red Rolfe MG	55.00	25.00	7.00
☐ 320	Hal White	50.00	22.00	6.25
☐ 321	Earl Johnson	50.00	22.00	6.25
☐ 322	Luke Sewell MG	55.00	25.00	7.00
☐ 323	Joe Adcock	75.00	34.00	9.50
☐ 324	Johnny Pramesa	90.00	27.00	9.00

1952 Bowman

The cards in this 252-card set measure approximately 2 1/16" by 3 1/8". While the Bowman set of 1952 retained the card size introduced in 1951, it employed a modification of color tones from the two preceding years. The cards also appeared with a facsimile autograph on the front, and for the first time since 1949, premium advertising on the back. The 1952 set was apparently sold in sheets as well as in gum packs. Artwork for 15 cards that were never issued

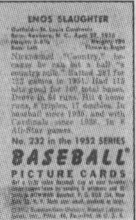

was discovered in the early 1980s. Notable Rookie Cards in this set are Lew Burdette, Gil McDougald, and Minnie Minoso.

	NRMT	VG-E	GOOD
COMPLETE SET (252)	8000.00	3600.00	1000.00
COMMON CARD (1-216)	18.00	8.00	2.20
COMMON CARD (217-252)	40.00	18.00	5.00

☐ 1	Yogi Berra	400.00	125.00	40.00
☐ 2	Bobby Thomson	35.00	16.00	4.40
☐ 3	Fred Hutchinson	18.00	8.00	2.20
☐ 4	Robin Roberts	60.00	27.00	7.50
☐ 5	Minnie Minoso	125.00	55.00	15.50
☐ 6	Virgil Stallcup	18.00	8.00	2.20
☐ 7	Mike Garcia	25.00	11.00	3.10
☐ 8	Pee Wee Reese	125.00	55.00	15.50
☐ 9	Vern Stephens	25.00	11.00	3.10
☐ 10	Bob Hooper	18.00	8.00	2.20
☐ 11	Ralph Kiner	50.00	22.00	6.25
☐ 12	Max Surkont	18.00	8.00	2.20
☐ 13	Cliff Mapes	18.00	8.00	2.20
☐ 14	Cliff Chambers	18.00	8.00	2.20
☐ 15	Sam Mele	18.00	8.00	2.20
☐ 16	Turk Lown	18.00	8.00	2.20
☐ 17	Ed Lopat	40.00	18.00	5.00
☐ 18	Don Mueller	25.00	11.00	3.10
☐ 19	Bob Cain	18.00	8.00	2.20
☐ 20	Willie Jones	18.00	8.00	2.20
☐ 21	Nellie Fox	60.00	27.00	7.50
☐ 22	Willard Ramsdell	18.00	8.00	2.20
☐ 23	Bob Lemon	50.00	22.00	6.25
☐ 24	Carl Furillo	35.00	16.00	4.40
☐ 25	Mickey McDermott	18.00	8.00	2.20
☐ 26	Eddie Joost	18.00	8.00	2.20
☐ 27	Joe Garagiola	50.00	22.00	6.25
☐ 28	Roy Hartsfield	18.00	8.00	2.20
☐ 29	Ned Garver	18.00	8.00	2.20
☐ 30	Red Schoendienst	50.00	22.00	6.25
☐ 31	Eddie Yost	25.00	11.00	3.10
☐ 32	Eddie Miksis	18.00	8.00	2.20
☐ 33	Gil McDougald	75.00	34.00	9.50
☐ 34	Alvin Dark	18.00	8.00	2.20
☐ 35	Granny Hamner	18.00	8.00	2.20
☐ 36	Cass Michaels	18.00	8.00	2.20
☐ 37	Vic Raschi	25.00	11.00	3.10
☐ 38	Whitey Lockman	25.00	11.00	3.10
☐ 39	Vic Wertz	25.00	11.00	3.10
☐ 40	Bubba Church	18.00	8.00	2.20
☐ 41	Chico Carrasquel	25.00	11.00	3.10
☐ 42	Johnny Wyrostek	18.00	8.00	2.20
☐ 43	Bob Feller	125.00	55.00	15.50
☐ 44	Roy Campanella	225.00	100.00	28.00
☐ 45	Johnny Pesky	18.00	8.00	2.20

☐	46	Carl Scheib	18.00	8.00	2.20	☐	117	Bill Wight	18.00	8.00	2.20

#	Name				#	Name			
46	Carl Scheib	18.00	8.00	2.20	117	Bill Wight	18.00	8.00	2.20
47	Pete Castiglione	18.00	8.00	2.20	118	Ray Murray	18.00	8.00	2.20
48	Vern Bickford	18.00	8.00	2.20	119	Bill Howerton	18.00	8.00	2.20
49	Jim Hearn	18.00	8.00	2.20	120	Chet Nichols	18.00	8.00	2.20
50	Jerry Staley	18.00	8.00	2.20	121	Al Corwin	18.00	8.00	2.20
51	Gil Coan	18.00	8.00	2.20	122	Billy Johnson	18.00	8.00	2.20
52	Phil Rizzuto	125.00	55.00	15.50	123	Sid Hudson	18.00	8.00	2.20
53	Richie Ashburn	90.00	40.00	11.00	124	Birdie Tebbetts	22.00	10.00	2.70
54	Billy Pierce	18.00	8.00	2.20	125	Howie Fox	18.00	8.00	2.20
55	Ken Raffensberger	18.00	8.00	2.20	126	Phil Cavarretta	22.00	10.00	2.70
56	Clyde King	25.00	11.00	3.10	127	Dick Sisler	18.00	8.00	2.20
57	Clyde Vollmer	18.00	8.00	2.20	128	Don Newcombe	30.00	13.50	3.70
58	Hank Majeski	18.00	8.00	2.20	129	Gus Niarhos	18.00	8.00	2.20
59	Murry Dickson	18.00	8.00	2.20	130	Allie Clark	18.00	8.00	2.20
60	Sid Gordon	18.00	8.00	2.20	131	Bob Swift	18.00	8.00	2.20
61	Tommy Byrne	18.00	8.00	2.20	132	Dave Cole	18.00	8.00	2.20
62	Joe Presko	18.00	8.00	2.20	133	Dick Kryhoski	18.00	8.00	2.20
63	Irv Noren	22.00	10.00	2.70	134	Al Brazle	18.00	8.00	2.20
64	Roy Smalley	18.00	8.00	2.20	135	Mickey Harris	18.00	8.00	2.20
65	Hank Bauer	25.00	11.00	3.10	136	Gene Hermanski	18.00	8.00	2.20
66	Sal Maglie	20.00	9.00	2.50	137	Stan Rojek	18.00	8.00	2.20
67	Johnny Groth	18.00	8.00	2.20	138	Ted Wilks	18.00	8.00	2.20
68	Jim Busby	18.00	8.00	2.20	139	Jerry Priddy	18.00	8.00	2.20
69	Joe Adcock	18.00	8.00	2.20	140	Ray Scarborough	18.00	8.00	2.20
70	Carl Erskine	30.00	13.50	3.70	141	Hank Edwards	18.00	8.00	2.20
71	Vernon Law	18.00	8.00	2.20	142	Early Wynn	50.00	22.00	6.25
72	Earl Torgeson	18.00	8.00	2.20	143	Sandy Consuegra	18.00	8.00	2.20
73	Jerry Coleman	20.00	9.00	2.50	144	Joe Hatton	18.00	8.00	2.20
74	Wes Westrum	22.00	10.00	2.70	145	Johnny Mize	50.00	22.00	6.25
75	George Kell	40.00	18.00	5.00	146	Leo Durocher MG	50.00	22.00	6.25
76	Del Ennis	18.00	8.00	2.20	147	Marlin Stuart	18.00	8.00	2.20
77	Eddie Robinson	18.00	8.00	2.20	148	Ken Heintzelman	18.00	8.00	2.20
78	Lloyd Merriman	18.00	8.00	2.20	149	Howie Judson	18.00	8.00	2.20
79	Lou Brissie	18.00	8.00	2.20	150	Herman Wehmeier	18.00	8.00	2.20
80	Gil Hodges	75.00	34.00	9.50	151	Al Rosen	25.00	11.00	3.10
81	Billy Goodman	22.00	10.00	2.70	152	Billy Cox	18.00	8.00	2.20
82	Gus Zernial	22.00	10.00	2.70	153	Fred Hatfield	18.00	8.00	2.20
83	Howie Pollet	18.00	8.00	2.20	154	Ferris Fain	22.00	10.00	2.70
84	Sam Jethroe	22.00	10.00	2.70	155	Billy Meyer MG	18.00	8.00	2.20
85	Marty Marion CO	25.00	11.00	3.10	156	Warren Spahn	125.00	55.00	15.50
86	Cal Abrams	22.00	10.00	2.70	157	Jim Delsing	18.00	8.00	2.20
87	Mickey Vernon	25.00	11.00	3.10	158	Bucky Harris MG	25.00	11.00	3.10
88	Bruce Edwards	18.00	8.00	2.20	159	Dutch Leonard	18.00	8.00	2.20
89	Billy Hitchcock	18.00	8.00	2.20	160	Eddie Stanky	25.00	11.00	3.10
90	Larry Jansen	22.00	10.00	2.70	161	Jackie Jensen	35.00	16.00	4.40
91	Don Kolloway	18.00	8.00	2.20	162	Monte Irvin	50.00	22.00	6.25
92	Eddie Waitkus	18.00	8.00	2.20	163	Johnny Lipon	18.00	8.00	2.20
93	Paul Richards MG	22.00	10.00	2.70	164	Connie Ryan	18.00	8.00	2.20
94	Luke Sewell MG	22.00	10.00	2.70	165	Saul Rogovin	18.00	8.00	2.20
95	Luke Easter	22.00	10.00	2.70	166	Bobby Adams	18.00	8.00	2.20
96	Ralph Branca	18.00	8.00	2.20	167	Bobby Avila	22.00	10.00	2.70
97	Willard Marshall	18.00	8.00	2.20	168	Preacher Roe	25.00	11.00	3.10
98	Jimmy Dykes MG	22.00	10.00	2.70	169	Walt Dropo	22.00	10.00	2.70
99	Clyde McCullough	18.00	8.00	2.20	170	Joe Astroth	18.00	8.00	2.20
100	Sibby Sisti	18.00	8.00	2.20	171	Mel Queen	18.00	8.00	2.20
101	Mickey Mantle	2500.00	1100.00	300.00	172	Ebba St.Claire	18.00	8.00	2.20
102	Peanuts Lowrey	18.00	8.00	2.20	173	Gene Bearden	18.00	8.00	2.20
103	Joe Haynes	18.00	8.00	2.20	174	Mickey Grasso	18.00	8.00	2.20
104	Hal Jeffcoat	18.00	8.00	2.20	175	Randy Jackson	18.00	8.00	2.20
105	Bobby Brown	25.00	11.00	3.10	176	Harry Brecheen	22.00	10.00	2.70
106	Randy Gumpert	18.00	8.00	2.20	177	Gene Woodling	22.00	10.00	2.70
107	Del Rice	18.00	8.00	2.20	178	Dave Williams	22.00	10.00	2.70
108	George Metkovich	22.00	10.00	2.70	179	Pete Suder	18.00	8.00	2.20
109	Tom Morgan	22.00	10.00	2.70	180	Ed Fitzgerald	18.00	8.00	2.20
110	Max Lanier	18.00	8.00	2.20	181	Joe Collins	22.00	10.00	2.70
111	Hoot Evers	18.00	8.00	2.20	182	Dave Koslo	18.00	8.00	2.20
112	Smoky Burgess	25.00	11.00	3.10	183	Pat Mullin	18.00	8.00	2.20
113	Al Zarilla	18.00	8.00	2.20	184	Curt Simmons	25.00	11.00	3.10
114	Frank Hiller	18.00	8.00	2.20	185	Eddie Stewart	18.00	8.00	2.20
115	Larry Doby	30.00	13.50	3.70	186	Frank Smith	18.00	8.00	2.20
116	Duke Snider	200.00	90.00	25.00	187	Jim Hegan	22.00	10.00	2.70

☐	188	Charlie Dressen MG.	25.00	11.00	3.10
☐	189	Jim Piersall	25.00	11.00	3.10
☐	190	Dick Fowler	18.00	8.00	2.20
☐	191	Bob Friend	40.00	18.00	5.00
☐	192	John Cusick	18.00	8.00	2.20
☐	193	Bobby Young	18.00	8.00	2.20
☐	194	Bob Porterfield	18.00	8.00	2.20
☐	195	Frank Baumholtz	18.00	8.00	2.20
☐	196	Stan Musial	600.00	275.00	75.00
☐	197	Charlie Silvera	18.00	8.00	2.20
☐	198	Chuck Diering	18.00	8.00	2.20
☐	199	Ted Gray	18.00	8.00	2.20
☐	200	Ken Silvestri	18.00	8.00	2.20
☐	201	Ray Coleman	18.00	8.00	2.20
☐	202	Harry Perkowski	18.00	8.00	2.20
☐	203	Steve Gromek	18.00	8.00	2.20
☐	204	Andy Pafko	22.00	10.00	2.70
☐	205	Walt Masterson	18.00	8.00	2.20
☐	206	Elmer Valo	18.00	8.00	2.20
☐	207	George Strickland	18.00	8.00	2.20
☐	208	Walker Cooper	18.00	8.00	2.20
☐	209	Dick Littlefield	18.00	8.00	2.20
☐	210	Archie Wilson	18.00	8.00	2.20
☐	211	Paul Minner	18.00	8.00	2.20
☐	212	Solly Hemus	18.00	8.00	2.20
☐	213	Monte Kennedy	18.00	8.00	2.20
☐	214	Ray Boone	22.00	10.00	2.70
☐	215	Sheldon Jones	18.00	8.00	2.20
☐	216	Matt Batts	18.00	8.00	2.20
☐	217	Casey Stengel MG.	125.00	55.00	15.50
☐	218	Willie Mays	1400.00	650.00	180.00
☐	219	Neil Berry	40.00	18.00	5.00
☐	220	Russ Meyer	40.00	18.00	5.00
☐	221	Lou Kretlow	40.00	18.00	5.00
☐	222	Dixie Howell	40.00	18.00	5.00
☐	223	Harry Simpson	40.00	18.00	5.00
☐	224	Johnny Schmitz	40.00	18.00	5.00
☐	225	Del Wilber	40.00	18.00	5.00
☐	226	Alex Kellner	40.00	18.00	5.00
☐	227	Clyde Sukeforth CO.	40.00	18.00	5.00
☐	228	Bob Chipman	40.00	18.00	5.00
☐	229	Hank Arft	40.00	18.00	5.00
☐	230	Frank Shea	40.00	18.00	5.00
☐	231	Dee Fondy	40.00	18.00	5.00
☐	232	Enos Slaughter	80.00	36.00	10.00
☐	233	Bob Kuzava	40.00	18.00	5.00
☐	234	Fred Fitzsimmons CO	40.00	18.00	5.00
☐	235	Steve Souchock	40.00	18.00	5.00
☐	236	Tommy Brown	40.00	18.00	5.00
☐	237	Sherm Lollar	50.00	22.00	6.25
☐	238	Roy McMillan	40.00	18.00	5.00
☐	239	Dale Mitchell	50.00	22.00	6.25
☐	240	Billy Loes	50.00	22.00	6.25
☐	241	Mel Parnell	50.00	22.00	6.25
☐	242	Everett Kell	40.00	18.00	5.00
☐	243	Red Munger	40.00	18.00	5.00
☐	244	Lew Burdette	55.00	25.00	7.00
☐	245	George Schmees	40.00	18.00	5.00
☐	246	Jerry Snyder	40.00	18.00	5.00
☐	247	Johnny Pramesa	40.00	18.00	5.00
☐	248	Bill Werle	40.00	18.00	5.00
☐	249	Hank Thompson	50.00	22.00	6.25
☐	250	Ike Delock	40.00	18.00	5.00
☐	251	Jack Lohrke	40.00	18.00	5.00
☐	252	Frank Crosetti CO	100.00	25.00	8.00

1953 Bowman B/W

The cards in this 64-card set measure approximately 2 1/2" by 3 3/4". Some col-

lectors believe that the high cost of producing the 1953 color series forced Bowman to issue this set in black and white, since the two sets are identical in design except for the element of color. This set was also produced in fewer numbers than its color counterpart, and is popular among collectors for the challenge involved in completing it. There are no key Rookie Cards in this set.

			NRMT	VG-E	GOOD
	COMPLETE SET (64)		2400.00	1100.00	300.00
	COMMON CARD (1-64)		30.00	13.50	3.70
☐	1	Gus Bell	110.00	22.00	8.75
☐	2	Willard Nixon	30.00	13.50	3.70
☐	3	Bill Rigney	30.00	13.50	3.70
☐	4	Pat Mullin	30.00	13.50	3.70
☐	5	Dee Fondy	30.00	13.50	3.70
☐	6	Ray Murray	30.00	13.50	3.70
☐	7	Andy Seminick	30.00	13.50	3.70
☐	8	Pete Suder	30.00	13.50	3.70
☐	9	Walt Masterson	30.00	13.50	3.70
☐	10	Dick Sisler	35.00	16.00	4.40
☐	11	Dick Gernert	30.00	13.50	3.70
☐	12	Randy Jackson	30.00	13.50	3.70
☐	13	Joe Tipton	30.00	13.50	3.70
☐	14	Bill Nicholson	35.00	16.00	4.40
☐	15	Johnny Mize	125.00	55.00	15.50
☐	16	Stu Miller	40.00	18.00	5.00
☐	17	Virgil Trucks	35.00	16.00	4.40
☐	18	Billy Hoeft	30.00	13.50	3.70
☐	19	Paul LaPalme	30.00	13.50	3.70
☐	20	Eddie Robinson	30.00	13.50	3.70
☐	21	Clarence Podbielan	30.00	13.50	3.70
☐	22	Matt Batts	30.00	13.50	3.70
☐	23	Wilmer Mizell	35.00	16.00	4.40
☐	24	Del Wilber	30.00	13.50	3.70
☐	25	Johnny Sain	50.00	22.00	6.25
☐	26	Preacher Roe	50.00	22.00	6.25
☐	27	Bob Lemon	125.00	55.00	15.50
☐	28	Hoyt Wilhelm	125.00	55.00	15.50
☐	29	Sid Hudson	30.00	13.50	3.70
☐	30	Walker Cooper	30.00	13.50	3.70
☐	31	Gene Woodling	50.00	22.00	6.25
☐	32	Rocky Bridges	30.00	13.50	3.70
☐	33	Bob Kuzava	30.00	13.50	3.70
☐	34	Ebba St.Claire	30.00	13.50	3.70
☐	35	Johnny Wyrostek	30.00	13.50	3.70
☐	36	Jim Piersall	50.00	22.00	6.25
☐	37	Hal Jeffcoat	30.00	13.50	3.70
☐	38	Dave Cole	30.00	13.50	3.70
☐	39	Casey Stengel MG.	300.00	135.00	38.00
☐	40	Larry Jansen	35.00	16.00	4.40
☐	41	Bob Ramazzotti	30.00	13.50	3.70

		NRMT	VG-E	GOOD
☐ 42	Howie Judson	30.00	13.50	3.70
☐ 43	Hal Bevan	30.00	13.50	3.70
☐ 44	Jim Delsing	30.00	13.50	3.70
☐ 45	Irv Noren	35.00	16.00	4.40
☐ 46	Bucky Harris MG	50.00	22.00	6.25
☐ 47	Jack Lohrke	30.00	13.50	3.70
☐ 48	Steve Ridzik	30.00	13.50	3.70
☐ 49	Floyd Baker	30.00	13.50	3.70
☐ 50	Dutch Leonard	30.00	13.50	3.70
☐ 51	Lou Burdette	50.00	22.00	6.25
☐ 52	Ralph Branca	35.00	16.00	4.40
☐ 53	Morrie Martin	30.00	13.50	3.70
☐ 54	Bill Miller	30.00	13.50	3.70
☐ 55	Don Johnson	30.00	13.50	3.70
☐ 56	Roy Smalley	30.00	13.50	3.70
☐ 57	Andy Pafko	35.00	16.00	4.40
☐ 58	Jim Konstanty	30.00	13.50	3.70
☐ 59	Duane Pillette	30.00	13.50	3.70
☐ 60	Billy Cox	40.00	18.00	5.00
☐ 61	Tom Gorman	30.00	13.50	3.70
☐ 62	Keith Thomas	30.00	13.50	3.70
☐ 63	Steve Gromek	30.00	13.50	3.70
☐ 64	Andy Hansen	50.00	15.00	3.70

1953 Bowman Color

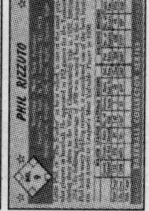

The cards in this 160-card set measure approximately 2 1/2" by 3 3/4". The 1953 Bowman Color set, considered by many to be the best looking set of the modern era, contains Kodachrome photographs with no names or facsimile autographs on the face. Numbers 113 to 160 are somewhat more difficult to obtain, with numbers 113 to 128 being the most difficult. There are two cards of Al Corwin (126 and 149). There are no key Rookie Cards in this set.

	NRMT	VG-E	GOOD
COMPLETE SET (160)	12000.00	5400.00	1500.00
COMMON CARD (1-112)	30.00	13.50	3.70
COMMON CARD (113-128)	70.00	32.00	8.75
COMMON CARD (129-160)	60.00	27.00	7.50

		NRMT	VG-E	GOOD
☐ 1	Dave Williams	100.00	20.00	6.00
☐ 2	Vic Wertz	35.00	16.00	4.40
☐ 3	Sam Jethroe	35.00	16.00	4.40
☐ 4	Art Houtteman	30.00	13.50	3.70
☐ 5	Sid Gordon	30.00	13.50	3.70
☐ 6	Joe Ginsberg	30.00	13.50	3.70
☐ 7	Harry Chiti	30.00	13.50	3.70
☐ 8	Al Rosen	40.00	18.00	5.00

		NRMT	VG-E	GOOD
☐ 9	Phil Rizzuto	160.00	70.00	20.00
☐ 10	Richie Ashburn	150.00	70.00	19.00
☐ 11	Bobby Shantz	35.00	16.00	4.40
☐ 12	Carl Erskine	40.00	18.00	5.00
☐ 13	Gus Zernial	35.00	16.00	4.40
☐ 14	Billy Loes	35.00	16.00	4.40
☐ 15	Jim Busby	30.00	13.50	3.70
☐ 16	Bob Friend	35.00	16.00	4.40
☐ 17	Gerry Staley	30.00	13.50	3.70
☐ 18	Nellie Fox	75.00	34.00	9.50
☐ 19	Alvin Dark	35.00	16.00	4.40
☐ 20	Don Lenhardt	30.00	13.50	3.70
☐ 21	Joe Garagiola	50.00	22.00	6.25
☐ 22	Bob Porterfield	30.00	13.50	3.70
☐ 23	Herman Wehmeier	30.00	13.50	3.70
☐ 24	Jackie Jensen	40.00	18.00	5.00
☐ 25	Hoot Evers	30.00	13.50	3.70
☐ 26	Roy McMillan	35.00	16.00	4.40
☐ 27	Vic Raschi	40.00	18.00	5.00
☐ 28	Smoky Burgess	35.00	16.00	4.40
☐ 29	Bobby Avila	35.00	16.00	4.40
☐ 30	Phil Cavarretta	35.00	16.00	4.40
☐ 31	Jimmy Dykes MG	35.00	16.00	4.40
☐ 32	Stan Musial	700.00	325.00	90.00
☐ 33	Pee Wee Reese HOR	800.00	350.00	100.00
☐ 34	Gil Coan	30.00	13.50	3.70
☐ 35	Maurice McDermott	30.00	13.50	3.70
☐ 36	Minnie Minoso	60.00	27.00	7.50
☐ 37	Jim Wilson	30.00	13.50	3.70
☐ 38	Harry Byrd	30.00	13.50	3.70
☐ 39	Paul Richards MG	35.00	16.00	4.40
☐ 40	Larry Doby	50.00	22.00	6.25
☐ 41	Sammy White	30.00	13.50	3.70
☐ 42	Tommy Brown	30.00	13.50	3.70
☐ 43	Mike Garcia	35.00	16.00	4.40
☐ 44	Yogi Berra / Hank Bauer / Mickey Mantle	675.00	300.00	85.00
☐ 45	Walt Dropo	35.00	16.00	4.40
☐ 46	Roy Campanella	275.00	125.00	34.00
☐ 47	Ned Garver	30.00	13.50	3.70
☐ 48	Hank Sauer	35.00	16.00	4.40
☐ 49	Eddie Stanky MG	35.00	16.00	4.40
☐ 50	Lou Kretlow	30.00	13.50	3.70
☐ 51	Monte Irvin	60.00	27.00	7.50
☐ 52	Marty Marion MG	40.00	18.00	5.00
☐ 53	Del Rice	30.00	13.50	3.70
☐ 54	Chico Carrasquel	30.00	13.50	3.70
☐ 55	Leo Durocher MG	70.00	32.00	8.75
☐ 56	Bob Cain	30.00	13.50	3.70
☐ 57	Lou Boudreau MG	50.00	22.00	6.25
☐ 58	Willard Marshall	30.00	13.50	3.70
☐ 59	Mickey Mantle	3000.00	1350.00	375.00
☐ 60	Granny Hamner	30.00	13.50	3.70
☐ 61	George Kell	60.00	27.00	7.50
☐ 62	Ted Kluszewski	60.00	27.00	7.50
☐ 63	Gil McDougald	60.00	27.00	7.50
☐ 64	Curt Simmons	35.00	16.00	4.40
☐ 65	Robin Roberts	90.00	40.00	11.00
☐ 66	Mel Parnell	35.00	16.00	4.40
☐ 67	Mel Clark	30.00	13.50	3.70
☐ 68	Allie Reynolds	40.00	18.00	5.00
☐ 69	Charlie Grimm MG	35.00	16.00	4.40
☐ 70	Clint Courtney	30.00	13.50	3.70
☐ 71	Paul Minner	30.00	13.50	3.70
☐ 72	Ted Gray	30.00	13.50	3.70
☐ 73	Billy Pierce	30.00	13.50	3.70
☐ 74	Don Mueller	35.00	16.00	4.40
☐ 75	Saul Rogovin	30.00	13.50	3.70
☐ 76	Jim Hearn	30.00	13.50	3.70
☐ 77	Mickey Grasso	30.00	13.50	3.70

		NRMT	VG-E	GOOD
☐ 78	Carl Furillo	40.00	18.00	5.00
☐ 79	Ray Boone	35.00	16.00	4.40
☐ 80	Ralph Kiner	70.00	32.00	8.75
☐ 81	Enos Slaughter	70.00	32.00	8.75
☐ 82	Joe Astroth	30.00	13.50	3.70
☐ 83	Jack Daniels	35.00	16.00	4.40
☐ 84	Hank Bauer	40.00	18.00	5.00
☐ 85	Solly Hemus	30.00	13.50	3.70
☐ 86	Harry Simpson	30.00	13.50	3.70
☐ 87	Harry Perkowski	30.00	13.50	3.70
☐ 88	Joe Dobson	30.00	13.50	3.70
☐ 89	Sandy Consuegra	30.00	13.50	3.70
☐ 90	Joe Nuxhall	40.00	18.00	5.00
☐ 91	Steve Souchock	30.00	13.50	3.70
☐ 92	Gil Hodges	160.00	70.00	20.00
☐ 93	Phil Rizzuto and Billy Martin	250.00	110.00	31.00
☐ 94	Bob Addis	30.00	13.50	3.70
☐ 95	Wally Moses CO	35.00	16.00	4.40
☐ 96	Sal Maglie	40.00	18.00	5.00
☐ 97	Eddie Mathews	250.00	110.00	31.00
☐ 98	Hector Rodriguez	30.00	13.50	3.70
☐ 99	Warren Spahn	225.00	100.00	28.00
☐ 100	Bill Wight	30.00	13.50	3.70
☐ 101	Red Schoendienst	70.00	32.00	8.75
☐ 102	Jim Hegan	35.00	16.00	4.40
☐ 103	Del Ennis	40.00	18.00	5.00
☐ 104	Luke Easter	40.00	18.00	5.00
☐ 105	Eddie Joost	30.00	13.50	3.70
☐ 106	Ken Raffensberger	30.00	13.50	3.70
☐ 107	Alex Kellner	30.00	13.50	3.70
☐ 108	Bobby Adams	30.00	13.50	3.70
☐ 109	Ken Wood	30.00	13.50	3.70
☐ 110	Bob Rush	30.00	13.50	3.70
☐ 111	Jim Dyck	30.00	13.50	3.70
☐ 112	Toby Atwell	30.00	13.50	3.70
☐ 113	Karl Drews	70.00	32.00	8.75
☐ 114	Bob Feller	300.00	135.00	38.00
☐ 115	Cloyd Boyer	70.00	32.00	8.75
☐ 116	Eddie Yost	75.00	34.00	9.50
☐ 117	Duke Snider	550.00	250.00	70.00
☐ 118	Billy Martin	275.00	125.00	34.00
☐ 119	Dale Mitchell	75.00	34.00	9.50
☐ 120	Marlin Stuart	70.00	32.00	8.75
☐ 121	Yogi Berra	575.00	250.00	70.00
☐ 122	Bill Serena	70.00	32.00	8.75
☐ 123	Johnny Lipon	70.00	32.00	8.75
☐ 124	Charlie Dressen MG	70.00	32.00	8.75
☐ 125	Fred Hatfield	70.00	32.00	8.75
☐ 126	Al Corwin	70.00	32.00	8.75
☐ 127	Dick Kryhoski	70.00	32.00	8.75
☐ 128	Whitey Lockman	70.00	32.00	8.75
☐ 129	Russ Meyer	60.00	27.00	7.50
☐ 130	Cass Michaels	60.00	27.00	7.50
☐ 131	Connie Ryan	60.00	27.00	7.50
☐ 132	Fred Hutchinson	75.00	34.00	9.50
☐ 133	Willie Jones	60.00	27.00	7.50
☐ 134	Johnny Pesky	75.00	34.00	9.50
☐ 135	Bobby Morgan	60.00	27.00	7.50
☐ 136	Jim Brideweser	60.00	27.00	7.50
☐ 137	Sam Dente	60.00	27.00	7.50
☐ 138	Bubba Church	60.00	27.00	7.50
☐ 139	Pete Runnels	75.00	34.00	9.50
☐ 140	Al Brazle	60.00	27.00	7.50
☐ 141	Frank Shea	60.00	27.00	7.50
☐ 142	Larry Miggins	60.00	27.00	7.50
☐ 143	Al Lopez MG	75.00	34.00	9.50
☐ 144	Warren Hacker	60.00	27.00	7.50
☐ 145	George Shuba	75.00	34.00	9.50
☐ 146	Early Wynn	120.00	55.00	15.00
☐ 147	Clem Koshorek	60.00	27.00	7.50

		NRMT	VG-E	GOOD
☐ 148	Billy Goodman	75.00	34.00	9.50
☐ 149	Al Corwin	60.00	27.00	7.50
☐ 150	Carl Scheib	60.00	27.00	7.50
☐ 151	Joe Adcock	75.00	34.00	9.50
☐ 152	Clyde Vollmer	60.00	27.00	7.50
☐ 153	Whitey Ford	500.00	220.00	60.00
☐ 154	Turk Lown	60.00	27.00	7.50
☐ 155	Allie Clark	60.00	27.00	7.50
☐ 156	Max Surkont	60.00	27.00	7.50
☐ 157	Sherm Lollar	75.00	34.00	9.50
☐ 158	Howard Fox	60.00	27.00	7.50
☐ 159	Mickey Vernon UER. (Photo actually Floyd Baker)	75.00	34.00	9.50
☐ 160	Cal Abrams	80.00	27.00	7.50

1954 Bowman

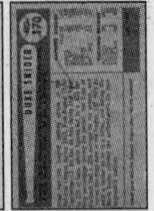

The cards in this 224-card set measure approximately 2 1/2" by 3 3/4". A contractual problem apparently resulted in the deletion of the number 66 Ted Williams card from this Bowman set, thereby creating a scarcity that is highly valued among collectors. The set price below does NOT include number 66 Williams but does include number 66 Jim Piersall, the apparent replacement for Williams in spite of the fact that Piersall was already number 210 to appear later in the set. Many errors in players' statistics exist (and some were corrected) while a few players' names were printed on the front, instead of appearing as a facsimile autograph. The notable Rookie Cards in this set are Harvey Kuenn and Don Larsen.

		NRMT	VG-E	GOOD
COMPLETE SET (224)		4000.00	1800.00	500.00
COMMON CARD (1-128)		10.00	4.50	1.25
COMMON CARD (129-224)		12.00	5.50	1.50
☐ 1	Phil Rizzuto	150.00	45.00	15.00
☐ 2	Jackie Jensen	12.00	5.50	1.50
☐ 3	Marion Fricano	10.00	4.50	1.25
☐ 4	Bob Hooper	10.00	4.50	1.25
☐ 5	Billy Hunter	10.00	4.50	1.25
☐ 6	Nellie Fox	30.00	13.50	3.70
☐ 7	Walt Dropo	12.00	5.50	1.50
☐ 8	Jim Busby	10.00	4.50	1.25
☐ 9	Dave Williams	10.00	4.50	1.25
☐ 10	Carl Erskine	12.00	5.50	1.50
☐ 11	Sid Gordon	10.00	4.50	1.25

☐ 12 Roy McMillan	12.00	5.50	1.50
☐ 13 Paul Minner	10.00	4.50	1.25
☐ 14 Jerry Staley	10.00	4.50	1.25
☐ 15 Richie Ashburn	75.00	34.00	9.50
☐ 16 Jim Wilson	10.00	4.50	1.25
☐ 17 Tom Gorman	10.00	4.50	1.25
☐ 18 Hoot Evers	10.00	4.50	1.25
☐ 19 Bobby Shantz	10.00	4.50	1.25
☐ 20 Art Houtteman	10.00	4.50	1.25
☐ 21 Vic Wertz	12.00	5.50	1.50
☐ 22 Sam Mele	10.00	4.50	1.25
☐ 23 Harvey Kuenn	35.00	16.00	4.40
☐ 24 Bob Porterfield	10.00	4.50	1.25
☐ 25 Wes Westrum	12.00	5.50	1.50
☐ 26 Billy Cox	10.00	4.50	1.25
☐ 27 Dick Cole	10.00	4.50	1.25
☐ 28 Jim Greengrass	10.00	4.50	1.25
☐ 29 Johnny Klippstein	10.00	4.50	1.25
☐ 30 Del Rice	10.00	4.50	1.25
☐ 31 Smoky Burgess	12.00	5.50	1.50
☐ 32 Del Crandall	12.00	5.50	1.50
☐ 33A Vic Raschi	20.00	9.00	2.50
(No mention of trade on back)			
☐ 33B Vic Raschi	35.00	16.00	4.40
(Traded to St.Louis)			
☐ 34 Sammy White	10.00	4.50	1.25
☐ 35 Eddie Joost	10.00	4.50	1.25
☐ 36 George Strickland	10.00	4.50	1.25
☐ 37 Dick Kokos	10.00	4.50	1.25
☐ 38 Minnie Minoso	20.00	9.00	2.50
☐ 39 Ned Garver	10.00	4.50	1.25
☐ 40 Gil Coan	10.00	4.50	1.25
☐ 41 Alvin Dark	10.00	4.50	1.25
☐ 42 Billy Loes	12.00	5.50	1.50
☐ 43 Bob Friend	12.00	5.50	1.50
☐ 44 Harry Perkowski	10.00	4.50	1.25
☐ 45 Ralph Kiner	35.00	16.00	4.40
☐ 46 Rip Repulski	10.00	4.50	1.25
☐ 47 Granny Hamner	10.00	4.50	1.25
☐ 48 Jack Dittmer	10.00	4.50	1.25
☐ 49 Harry Byrd	10.00	4.50	1.25
☐ 50 George Kell	25.00	11.00	3.10
☐ 51 Alex Kellner	10.00	4.50	1.25
☐ 52 Joe Ginsberg	10.00	4.50	1.25
☐ 53 Don Lenhardt	10.00	4.50	1.25
☐ 54 Chico Carrasquel	10.00	4.50	1.25
☐ 55 Jim Delsing	10.00	4.50	1.25
☐ 56 Maurice McDermott	10.00	4.50	1.25
☐ 57 Hoyt Wilhelm	25.00	11.00	3.10
☐ 58 Pee Wee Reese	75.00	34.00	9.50
☐ 59 Bob Schultz	10.00	4.50	1.25
☐ 60 Fred Baczewski	10.00	4.50	1.25
☐ 61 Eddie Miksis	10.00	4.50	1.25
☐ 62 Enos Slaughter	40.00	18.00	5.00
☐ 63 Earl Torgeson	10.00	4.50	1.25
☐ 64 Eddie Mathews	50.00	22.00	6.25
☐ 65 Mickey Mantle	1200.00	550.00	150.00
☐ 66A Ted Williams	4500.00	2000.00	550.00
☐ 66B Jim Piersall	75.00	34.00	9.50
☐ 67 Carl Scheib	10.00	4.50	1.25
☐ 68 Bobby Avila	12.00	5.50	1.50
☐ 69 Clint Courtney	10.00	4.50	1.25
☐ 70 Willard Marshall	10.00	4.50	1.25
☐ 71 Ted Gray	10.00	4.50	1.25
☐ 72 Eddie Yost	12.00	5.50	1.50
☐ 73 Don Mueller	12.00	5.50	1.50
☐ 74 Jim Gilliam	30.00	13.50	3.70
☐ 75 Max Surkont	10.00	4.50	1.25
☐ 76 Joe Nuxhall	12.00	5.50	1.50
☐ 77 Bob Rush	10.00	4.50	1.25

☐ 78 Sal Yvars	10.00	4.50	1.25
☐ 79 Curt Simmons	12.00	5.50	1.50
☐ 80 Johnny Logan	12.00	5.50	1.50
☐ 81 Jerry Coleman	12.00	5.50	1.50
☐ 82 Billy Goodman	12.00	5.50	1.50
☐ 83 Ray Murray	10.00	4.50	1.25
☐ 84 Larry Doby	20.00	9.00	2.50
☐ 85 Jim Dyck	10.00	4.50	1.25
☐ 86 Harry Dorish	10.00	4.50	1.25
☐ 87 Don Lund	10.00	4.50	1.25
☐ 88 Tom Umphlett	10.00	4.50	1.25
☐ 89 Willie Mays	425.00	190.00	52.50
☐ 90 Roy Campanella	175.00	80.00	22.00
☐ 91 Cal Abrams	10.00	4.50	1.25
☐ 92 Ken Raffensberger	10.00	4.50	1.25
☐ 93 Bill Serena	10.00	4.50	1.25
☐ 94 Solly Hemus	10.00	4.50	1.25
☐ 95 Robin Roberts	50.00	22.00	6.25
☐ 96 Joe Adcock	12.00	5.50	1.50
☐ 97 Gil McDougald	20.00	9.00	2.50
☐ 98 Ellis Kinder	10.00	4.50	1.25
☐ 99 Pete Suder	10.00	4.50	1.25
☐ 100 Mike Garcia	12.00	5.50	1.50
☐ 101 Don Larsen	50.00	22.00	6.25
☐ 102 Billy Pierce	10.00	4.50	1.25
☐ 103 Steve Souchock	10.00	4.50	1.25
☐ 104 Frank Shea	10.00	4.50	1.25
☐ 105 Sal Maglie	12.00	5.50	1.50
☐ 106 Clem Labine	12.00	5.50	1.50
☐ 107 Paul LaPalme	10.00	4.50	1.25
☐ 108 Bobby Adams	10.00	4.50	1.25
☐ 109 Roy Smalley	10.00	4.50	1.25
☐ 110 Red Schoendienst	30.00	13.50	3.70
☐ 111 Murry Dickson	10.00	4.50	1.25
☐ 112 Andy Pafko	12.00	5.50	1.50
☐ 113 Allie Reynolds	12.00	5.50	1.50
☐ 114 Willard Nixon	10.00	4.50	1.25
☐ 115 Don Bollweg	10.00	4.50	1.25
☐ 116 Luke Easter	12.00	5.50	1.50
☐ 117 Dick Kryhoski	10.00	4.50	1.25
☐ 118 Bob Boyd	10.00	4.50	1.25
☐ 119 Fred Hatfield	10.00	4.50	1.25
☐ 120 Mel Hoderlein	10.00	4.50	1.25
☐ 121 Ray Katt	10.00	4.50	1.25
☐ 122 Carl Furillo	20.00	9.00	2.50
☐ 123 Toby Atwell	10.00	4.50	1.25
☐ 124 Gus Bell	12.00	5.50	1.50
☐ 125 Warren Hacker	10.00	4.50	1.25
☐ 126 Cliff Chambers	10.00	4.50	1.25
☐ 127 Del Ennis	12.00	5.50	1.50
☐ 128 Ebba St.Claire	10.00	4.50	1.25
☐ 129 Hank Bauer	16.00	7.25	2.00
☐ 130 Milt Bolling	12.00	5.50	1.50
☐ 131 Joe Astroth	12.00	5.50	1.50
☐ 132 Bob Feller	75.00	34.00	9.50
☐ 133 Duane Pillette	12.00	5.50	1.50
☐ 134 Luis Aloma	12.00	5.50	1.50
☐ 135 Johnny Pesky	16.00	7.25	2.00
☐ 136 Clyde Vollmer	12.00	5.50	1.50
☐ 137 Al Corwin	12.00	5.50	1.50
☐ 138 Gil Hodges	75.00	34.00	9.50
☐ 139 Preston Ward	12.00	5.50	1.50
☐ 140 Saul Rogovin	12.00	5.50	1.50
☐ 141 Joe Garagiola	30.00	13.50	3.70
☐ 142 Al Brazle	12.00	5.50	1.50
☐ 143 Willie Jones	12.00	5.50	1.50
☐ 144 Ernie Johnson	25.00	11.00	3.10
☐ 145 Billy Martin	50.00	22.00	6.25
☐ 146 Dick Gernert	12.00	5.50	1.50
☐ 147 Joe DeMaestri	12.00	5.50	1.50
☐ 148 Dale Mitchell	16.00	7.25	2.00

☐ 149	Bob Young	12.00	5.50	1.50
☐ 150	Cass Michaels	12.00	5.50	1.50
☐ 151	Pat Mullin	12.00	5.50	1.50
☐ 152	Mickey Vernon	16.00	7.25	2.00
☐ 153	Whitey Lockman	16.00	7.25	2.00
☐ 154	Don Newcombe	25.00	11.00	3.10
☐ 155	Frank Thomas	20.00	9.00	2.50
☐ 156	Rocky Bridges	12.00	5.50	1.50
☐ 157	Turk Lown	12.00	5.50	1.50
☐ 158	Stu Miller	16.00	7.25	2.00
☐ 159	Johnny Lindell	12.00	5.50	1.50
☐ 160	Danny O'Connell	12.00	5.50	1.50
☐ 161	Yogi Berra	175.00	80.00	22.00
☐ 162	Ted Lepcio	12.00	5.50	1.50
☐ 163A	Dave Philley (No mention of trade on back)	20.00	9.00	2.50
☐ 163B	Dave Philley (Traded to Cleveland)	36.00	16.00	4.50
☐ 164	Early Wynn	50.00	22.00	6.25
☐ 165	Johnny Groth	12.00	5.50	1.50
☐ 166	Sandy Consuegra	12.00	5.50	1.50
☐ 167	Billy Hoeft	12.00	5.50	1.50
☐ 168	Ed Fitzgerald	12.00	5.50	1.50
☐ 169	Larry Jansen	16.00	7.25	2.00
☐ 170	Duke Snider	140.00	65.00	17.50
☐ 171	Carlos Bernier	12.00	5.50	1.50
☐ 172	Andy Seminick	12.00	5.50	1.50
☐ 173	Dee Fondy	12.00	5.50	1.50
☐ 174	Pete Castiglione	12.00	5.50	1.50
☐ 175	Mel Clark	12.00	5.50	1.50
☐ 176	Vern Bickford	12.00	5.50	1.50
☐ 177	Whitey Ford	90.00	40.00	11.00
☐ 178	Del Wilber	12.00	5.50	1.50
☐ 179	Morrie Martin	12.00	5.50	1.50
☐ 180	Joe Tipton	12.00	5.50	1.50
☐ 181	Les Moss	12.00	5.50	1.50
☐ 182	Sherm Lollar	16.00	7.25	2.00
☐ 183	Matt Batts	12.00	5.50	1.50
☐ 184	Mickey Grasso	12.00	5.50	1.50
☐ 185	Daryl Spencer	12.00	5.50	1.50
☐ 186	Russ Meyer	12.00	5.50	1.50
☐ 187	Vernon Law	16.00	7.25	2.00
☐ 188	Frank Smith	12.00	5.50	1.50
☐ 189	Randy Jackson	12.00	5.50	1.50
☐ 190	Joe Presko	12.00	5.50	1.50
☐ 191	Karl Drews	12.00	5.50	1.50
☐ 192	Lou Burdette	20.00	9.00	2.50
☐ 193	Eddie Robinson	12.00	5.50	1.50
☐ 194	Sid Hudson	12.00	5.50	1.50
☐ 195	Bob Cain	12.00	5.50	1.50
☐ 196	Bob Lemon	40.00	18.00	5.00
☐ 197	Lou Kretlow	12.00	5.50	1.50
☐ 198	Virgil Trucks	16.00	7.25	2.00
☐ 199	Steve Gromek	12.00	5.50	1.50
☐ 200	Conrado Marrero	12.00	5.50	1.50
☐ 201	Bobby Thomson	20.00	9.00	2.50
☐ 202	George Shuba	16.00	7.25	2.00
☐ 203	Vic Janowicz	16.00	7.25	2.00
☐ 204	Jack Collum	12.00	5.50	1.50
☐ 205	Hal Jeffcoat	12.00	5.50	1.50
☐ 206	Steve Bilko	12.00	5.50	1.50
☐ 207	Stan Lopata	12.00	5.50	1.50
☐ 208	Johnny Antonelli	12.00	5.50	1.50
☐ 209	Gene Woodling	12.00	5.50	1.50
☐ 210	Jim Piersall	20.00	9.00	2.50
☐ 211	Al Robertson	12.00	5.50	1.50
☐ 212	Owen Friend	12.00	5.50	1.50
☐ 213	Dick Littlefield	12.00	5.50	1.50
☐ 214	Ferris Fain	16.00	7.25	2.00
☐ 215	Johnny Bucha	12.00	5.50	1.50
☐ 216	Jerry Snyder	12.00	5.50	1.50
☐ 217	Hank Thompson	16.00	7.25	2.00
☐ 218	Preacher Roe	20.00	9.00	2.50
☐ 219	Hal Rice	12.00	5.50	1.50
☐ 220	Hobie Landrith	12.00	5.50	1.50
☐ 221	Frank Baumholtz	12.00	5.50	1.50
☐ 222	Memo Luna	12.00	5.50	1.50
☐ 223	Steve Ridzik	12.00	5.50	1.50
☐ 224	Bill Bruton	30.00	5.50	1.50

1955 Bowman

The cards in this 320-card set measure approximately 2 1/2" by 3 3/4". The Bowman set of 1955 is known as the "TV set" because each player photograph is cleverly shown within a television set design. The set contains umpire cards, some transposed pictures (e.g., Johnsons and Bollings), an incorrect spelling for Harvey Kuenn, and a traded line for Palica (all of which are noted in the checklist below). Some three-card advertising strips exist, the backs of these panels contain advertising for Bowman products. Advertising panels seen include Nellie Fox/Carl Furillo/Carl Erskine, Hank Aaron/Johnny Logan/Eddie Miksis, and a panel including Early Wynn and Pee Wee Reese. The notable Rookie Cards in this set are Elston Howard and Don Zimmer.

	NRMT	VG-E	GOOD
COMPLETE SET (320)	4800.00	2200.00	600.00
COMMON CARD (1-224)	8.00	3.60	1.00
COMMON CARD (225-320)	18.00	8.00	2.20

☐ 1	Hoyt Wilhelm	90.00	20.00	6.00
☐ 2	Alvin Dark	10.00	4.50	1.25
☐ 3	Joe Coleman	8.00	3.60	1.00
☐ 4	Eddie Waitkus	8.00	3.60	1.00
☐ 5	Jim Robertson	8.00	3.60	1.00
☐ 6	Pete Suder	8.00	3.60	1.00
☐ 7	Gene Baker	8.00	3.60	1.00
☐ 8	Warren Hacker	8.00	3.60	1.00
☐ 9	Gil McDougald	20.00	9.00	2.50
☐ 10	Phil Rizzuto	65.00	29.00	8.00
☐ 11	Bill Bruton	10.00	4.50	1.25
☐ 12	Andy Pafko	10.00	4.50	1.25
☐ 13	Clyde Vollmer	8.00	3.60	1.00
☐ 14	Gus Keriazakos	8.00	3.60	1.00

☐ 15	Frank Sullivan	8.00	3.60	1.00
☐ 16	Jim Piersall	10.00	4.50	1.25
☐ 17	Del Ennis	10.00	4.50	1.25
☐ 18	Stan Lopata	8.00	3.60	1.00
☐ 19	Bobby Avila	10.00	4.50	1.25
☐ 20	Al Smith	10.00	4.50	1.25
☐ 21	Don Hoak	8.00	3.60	1.00
☐ 22	Roy Campanella	125.00	55.00	15.50
☐ 23	Al Kaline	125.00	55.00	15.50
☐ 24	Al Aber	8.00	3.60	1.00
☐ 25	Minnie Minoso	20.00	9.00	2.50
☐ 26	Virgil Trucks	10.00	4.50	1.25
☐ 27	Preston Ward	8.00	3.60	1.00
☐ 28	Dick Cole	8.00	3.60	1.00
☐ 29	Red Schoendienst	25.00	11.00	3.10
☐ 30	Bill Sarni	8.00	3.60	1.00
☐ 31	Johnny Temple	10.00	4.50	1.25
☐ 32	Wally Post	8.00	3.60	1.00
☐ 33	Nellie Fox	20.00	9.00	2.50
☐ 34	Clint Courtney	8.00	3.60	1.00
☐ 35	Bill Tuttle	8.00	3.60	1.00
☐ 36	Wayne Belardi	8.00	3.60	1.00
☐ 37	Pee Wee Reese	65.00	29.00	8.00
☐ 38	Early Wynn	25.00	11.00	3.10
☐ 39	Bob Darnell	10.00	4.50	1.25
☐ 40	Vic Wertz	10.00	4.50	1.25
☐ 41	Mel Clark	8.00	3.60	1.00
☐ 42	Bob Greenwood	8.00	3.60	1.00
☐ 43	Bob Buhl	10.00	4.50	1.25
☐ 44	Danny O'Connell	8.00	3.60	1.00
☐ 45	Tom Umphlett	8.00	3.60	1.00
☐ 46	Mickey Vernon	10.00	4.50	1.25
☐ 47	Sammy White	8.00	3.60	1.00
☐ 48A	Milt Bolling ERR	10.00	4.50	1.25
	(Name on back is			
	Frank Bolling)			
☐ 48B	Milt Bolling COR	30.00	13.50	3.70
☐ 49	Jim Greengrass	8.00	3.60	1.00
☐ 50	Hobie Landrith	8.00	3.60	1.00
☐ 51	Elvin Tappe	8.00	3.60	1.00
☐ 52	Hal Rice	8.00	3.60	1.00
☐ 53	Alex Kellner	8.00	3.60	1.00
☐ 54	Don Bollweg	8.00	3.60	1.00
☐ 55	Cal Abrams	8.00	3.60	1.00
☐ 56	Billy Cox	10.00	4.50	1.25
☐ 57	Bob Friend	10.00	4.50	1.25
☐ 58	Frank Thomas	10.00	4.50	1.25
☐ 59	Whitey Ford	75.00	34.00	9.50
☐ 60	Enos Slaughter	25.00	11.00	3.10
☐ 61	Paul LaPalme	8.00	3.60	1.00
☐ 62	Royce Lint	8.00	3.60	1.00
☐ 63	Irv Noren	10.00	4.50	1.25
☐ 64	Curt Simmons	10.00	4.50	1.25
☐ 65	Don Zimmer	25.00	11.00	3.10
☐ 66	George Shuba	10.00	4.50	1.25
☐ 67	Don Larsen	20.00	9.00	2.50
☐ 68	Elston Howard	70.00	32.00	8.75
☐ 69	Billy Hunter	8.00	3.60	1.00
☐ 70	Lou Burdette	8.00	3.60	1.00
☐ 71	Dave Jolly	8.00	3.60	1.00
☐ 72	Chet Nichols	8.00	3.60	1.00
☐ 73	Eddie Yost	10.00	4.50	1.25
☐ 74	Jerry Snyder	8.00	3.60	1.00
☐ 75	Brooks Lawrence	8.00	3.60	1.00
☐ 76	Tom Poholsky	8.00	3.60	1.00
☐ 77	Jim McDonald	8.00	3.60	1.00
☐ 78	Gil Coan	8.00	3.60	1.00
☐ 79	Willie Miranda	8.00	3.60	1.00
☐ 80	Lou Limmer	8.00	3.60	1.00
☐ 81	Bobby Morgan	8.00	3.60	1.00
☐ 82	Lee Walls	8.00	3.60	1.00
☐ 83	Max Surkont	8.00	3.60	1.00
☐ 84	George Freese	8.00	3.60	1.00
☐ 85	Cass Michaels	8.00	3.60	1.00
☐ 86	Ted Gray	8.00	3.60	1.00
☐ 87	Randy Jackson	8.00	3.60	1.00
☐ 88	Steve Bilko	8.00	3.60	1.00
☐ 89	Lou Boudreau MG	25.00	11.00	3.10
☐ 90	Art Ditmar	8.00	3.60	1.00
☐ 91	Dick Marlowe	8.00	3.60	1.00
☐ 92	George Zuverink	8.00	3.60	1.00
☐ 93	Andy Seminick	8.00	3.60	1.00
☐ 94	Hank Thompson	10.00	4.50	1.25
☐ 95	Sal Maglie	10.00	4.50	1.25
☐ 96	Ray Narleski	8.00	3.60	1.00
☐ 97	Johnny Podres	20.00	9.00	2.50
☐ 98	Jim Gilliam	16.00	7.25	2.00
☐ 99	Jerry Coleman	10.00	4.50	1.25
☐ 100	Tom Morgan	8.00	3.60	1.00
☐ 101A	Don Johnson ERR	12.00	5.50	1.50
	(Photo actually			
	Ernie Johnson)			
☐ 101B	Don Johnson COR	30.00	13.50	3.70
☐ 102	Bobby Thomson	10.00	4.50	1.25
☐ 103	Eddie Mathews	40.00	18.00	5.00
☐ 104	Bob Porterfield	8.00	3.60	1.00
☐ 105	Johnny Schmitz	8.00	3.60	1.00
☐ 106	Del Rice	8.00	3.60	1.00
☐ 107	Solly Hemus	8.00	3.60	1.00
☐ 108	Lou Kretlow	8.00	3.60	1.00
☐ 109	Vern Stephens	10.00	4.50	1.25
☐ 110	Bob Miller	8.00	3.60	1.00
☐ 111	Steve Ridzik	8.00	3.60	1.00
☐ 112	Granny Hamner	8.00	3.60	1.00
☐ 113	Bob Hall	8.00	3.60	1.00
☐ 114	Vic Janowicz	10.00	4.50	1.25
☐ 115	Roger Bowman	8.00	3.60	1.00
☐ 116	Sandy Consuegra	8.00	3.60	1.00
☐ 117	Johnny Groth	8.00	3.60	1.00
☐ 118	Bobby Adams	8.00	3.60	1.00
☐ 119	Joe Astroth	8.00	3.60	1.00
☐ 120	Ed Burtschy	8.00	3.60	1.00
☐ 121	Rufus Crawford	8.00	3.60	1.00
☐ 122	Al Corwin	8.00	3.60	1.00
☐ 123	Marv Grissom	8.00	3.60	1.00
☐ 124	Johnny Antonelli	10.00	4.50	1.25
☐ 125	Paul Giel	10.00	4.50	1.25
☐ 126	Billy Goodman	10.00	4.50	1.25
☐ 127	Hank Majeski	8.00	3.60	1.00
☐ 128	Mike Garcia	10.00	4.50	1.25
☐ 129	Hal Naragon	8.00	3.60	1.00
☐ 130	Richie Ashburn	45.00	20.00	5.50
☐ 131	Willard Marshall	8.00	3.60	1.00
☐ 132A	Harvey Kueen ERR	12.50	5.50	1.55
	(Sic, Kuenn)			
☐ 132B	Harvey Kuenn COR	30.00	13.50	3.70
☐ 133	Charles King	8.00	3.60	1.00
☐ 134	Bob Feller	70.00	32.00	8.75
☐ 135	Lloyd Merriman	8.00	3.60	1.00
☐ 136	Rocky Bridges	8.00	3.60	1.00
☐ 137	Bob Talbot	8.00	3.60	1.00
☐ 138	Davey Williams	8.00	3.60	1.00
☐ 139	Shantz Brothers	10.00	4.50	1.25
	(Wilmer and Bobby)			
☐ 140	Bobby Shantz	10.00	4.50	1.25
☐ 141	Wes Westrum	10.00	4.50	1.25
☐ 142	Rudy Regalado	8.00	3.60	1.00
☐ 143	Don Newcombe	20.00	9.00	2.50
☐ 144	Art Houtteman	8.00	3.60	1.00
☐ 145	Bob Nieman	8.00	3.60	1.00
☐ 146	Don Liddle	8.00	3.60	1.00
☐ 147	Sam Mele	8.00	3.60	1.00

☐ 148	Bob Chakales	8.00	3.60	1.00	☐ 208	Ed Fitzgerald	8.00	3.60	1.00
☐ 149	Cloyd Boyer	8.00	3.60	1.00	☐ 209	Smoky Burgess	10.00	4.50	1.25
☐ 150	Billy Klaus	8.00	3.60	1.00	☐ 210	Earl Torgeson	8.00	3.60	1.00
☐ 151	Jim Brideweser	8.00	3.60	1.00	☐ 211	Sonny Dixon	8.00	3.60	1.00
☐ 152	Johnny Klippstein	8.00	3.60	1.00	☐ 212	Jack Dittmer	8.00	3.60	1.00
☐ 153	Eddie Robinson	8.00	3.60	1.00	☐ 213	George Kell	20.00	9.00	2.50
☐ 154	Frank Lary	10.00	4.50	1.25	☐ 214	Billy Pierce	8.00	3.60	1.00
☐ 155	Gerry Staley	8.00	3.60	1.00	☐ 215	Bob Kuzava	8.00	3.60	1.00
☐ 156	Jim Hughes	10.00	4.50	1.25	☐ 216	Preacher Roe	10.00	4.50	1.25
☐ 157A	Ernie Johnson ERR	10.00	4.50	1.25	☐ 217	Del Crandall	10.00	4.50	1.25
	(Photo actually				☐ 218	Joe Adcock	10.00	4.50	1.25
	Don Johnson)				☐ 219	Whitey Lockman	10.00	4.50	1.25
☐ 157B	Ernie Johnson COR	30.00	13.50	3.70	☐ 220	Jim Hearn	8.00	3.60	1.00
☐ 158	Gil Hodges	40.00	18.00	5.00	☐ 221	Hector Brown	8.00	3.60	1.00
☐ 159	Harry Byrd	8.00	3.60	1.00	☐ 222	Russ Kemmerer	8.00	3.60	1.00
☐ 160	Bill Skowron	25.00	11.00	3.10	☐ 223	Hal Jeffcoat	8.00	3.60	1.00
☐ 161	Matt Batts	8.00	3.60	1.00	☐ 224	Dee Fondy	8.00	3.60	1.00
☐ 162	Charlie Maxwell	10.00	4.50	1.25	☐ 225	Paul Richards MG	22.00	10.00	2.70
☐ 163	Sid Gordon	8.00	3.60	1.00	☐ 226	Bill McKinley UMP	25.00	11.00	3.10
☐ 164	Toby Atwell	8.00	3.60	1.00	☐ 227	Frank Baumholtz	18.00	8.00	2.20
☐ 165	Maurice McDermott	8.00	3.60	1.00	☐ 228	John Phillips	18.00	8.00	2.20
☐ 166	Jim Busby	8.00	3.60	1.00	☐ 229	Jim Brosnan	20.00	9.00	2.50
☐ 167	Bob Grim	15.00	6.75	1.85	☐ 230	Al Brazle	18.00	8.00	2.20
☐ 168	Yogi Berra	90.00	40.00	11.00	☐ 231	Jim Konstanty	22.00	10.00	2.70
☐ 169	Carl Furillo	18.00	8.00	2.20	☐ 232	Birdie Tebbetts MG	22.00	10.00	2.70
☐ 170	Carl Erskine	18.00	8.00	2.20	☐ 233	Bill Serena	18.00	8.00	2.20
☐ 171	Robin Roberts	35.00	16.00	4.40	☐ 234	Dick Bartell CO	18.00	8.00	2.20
☐ 172	Willie Jones	8.00	3.60	1.00	☐ 235	Joe Paparella UMP	25.00	11.00	3.10
☐ 173	Chico Carrasquel	8.00	3.60	1.00	☐ 236	Murry Dickson	18.00	8.00	2.20
☐ 174	Sherm Lollar	10.00	4.50	1.25	☐ 237	Johnny Wyrostek	18.00	8.00	2.20
☐ 175	Wilmer Shantz	8.00	3.60	1.00	☐ 238	Eddie Stanky MG	18.00	8.00	2.20
☐ 176	Joe DeMaestri	8.00	3.60	1.00	☐ 239	Edwin Rommel UMP	25.00	11.00	3.10
☐ 177	Willard Nixon	8.00	3.60	1.00	☐ 240	Billy Loes	22.00	10.00	2.70
☐ 178	Tom Brewer	8.00	3.60	1.00	☐ 241	Johnny Pesky CO	18.00	8.00	2.20
☐ 179	Hank Aaron	225.00	100.00	28.00	☐ 242	Ernie Banks	350.00	160.00	45.00
☐ 180	Johnny Logan	10.00	4.50	1.25	☐ 243	Gus Bell	22.00	10.00	2.70
☐ 181	Eddie Miksis	8.00	3.60	1.00	☐ 244	Duane Pillette	18.00	8.00	2.20
☐ 182	Bob Rush	8.00	3.60	1.00	☐ 245	Bill Miller	18.00	8.00	2.20
☐ 183	Ray Katt	8.00	3.60	1.00	☐ 246	Hank Bauer	25.00	11.00	3.10
☐ 184	Willie Mays	225.00	100.00	28.00	☐ 247	Dutch Leonard CO	18.00	8.00	2.20
☐ 185	Vic Raschi	8.00	3.60	1.00	☐ 248	Harry Dorish	18.00	8.00	2.20
☐ 186	Alex Grammas	8.00	3.60	1.00	☐ 249	Billy Gardner	22.00	10.00	2.70
☐ 187	Fred Hatfield	8.00	3.60	1.00	☐ 250	Larry Napp UMP	25.00	11.00	3.10
☐ 188	Ned Garver	8.00	3.60	1.00	☐ 251	Stan Jok	18.00	8.00	2.20
☐ 189	Jack Collum	8.00	3.60	1.00	☐ 252	Roy Smalley	18.00	8.00	2.20
☐ 190	Fred Baczewski	8.00	3.60	1.00	☐ 253	Jim Wilson	18.00	8.00	2.20
☐ 191	Bob Lemon	25.00	11.00	3.10	☐ 254	Bennett Flowers	18.00	8.00	2.20
☐ 192	George Strickland	8.00	3.60	1.00	☐ 255	Pete Runnels	22.00	10.00	2.70
☐ 193	Howie Judson	8.00	3.60	1.00	☐ 256	Owen Friend	18.00	8.00	2.20
☐ 194	Joe Nuxhall	10.00	4.50	1.25	☐ 257	Tom Alston	18.00	8.00	2.20
☐ 195A	Erv Palica	10.00	4.50	1.25	☐ 258	John Stevens UMP	25.00	11.00	3.10
	(Without trade)				☐ 259	Don Mossi	25.00	11.00	3.10
☐ 195B	Erv Palica	30.00	13.50	3.70	☐ 260	Edwin Hurley UMP	25.00	11.00	3.10
	(With trade)				☐ 261	Walt Moryn	22.00	10.00	2.70
☐ 196	Russ Meyer	10.00	4.50	1.25	☐ 262	Jim Lemon	18.00	8.00	2.20
☐ 197	Ralph Kiner	30.00	13.50	3.70	☐ 263	Eddie Joost	18.00	8.00	2.20
☐ 198	Dave Pope	8.00	3.60	1.00	☐ 264	Bill Henry	18.00	8.00	2.20
☐ 199	Vernon Law	10.00	4.50	1.25	☐ 265	Albert Barlick UMP	75.00	34.00	9.50
☐ 200	Dick Littlefield	8.00	3.60	1.00	☐ 266	Mike Fornieles	18.00	8.00	2.20
☐ 201	Allie Reynolds	10.00	4.50	1.25	☐ 267	Jim Honochick UMP	75.00	34.00	9.50
☐ 202	Mickey Mantle UER	800.00	350.00	100.00	☐ 268	Roy Lee Hawes	18.00	8.00	2.20
	Birthdate listed as 10/30/31				☐ 269	Joe Amalfitano	22.00	10.00	2.70
	Should be 10/20/31				☐ 270	Chico Fernandez	22.00	10.00	2.70
☐ 203	Steve Gromek	8.00	3.60	1.00	☐ 271	Bob Hooper	18.00	8.00	2.20
☐ 204A	Frank Bolling ERR	10.00	4.50	1.25	☐ 272	John Flaherty UMP	25.00	11.00	3.10
	(Name on back is				☐ 273	Bubba Church	18.00	8.00	2.20
	Milt Bolling)				☐ 274	Jim Delsing	18.00	8.00	2.20
☐ 204B	Frank Bolling COR	30.00	13.50	3.70	☐ 275	William Grieve UMP	25.00	11.00	3.10
☐ 205	Rip Repulski	8.00	3.60	1.00	☐ 276	Ike Delock	18.00	8.00	2.20
☐ 206	Ralph Beard	8.00	3.60	1.00	☐ 277	Ed Runge UMP	30.00	13.50	3.70
☐ 207	Frank Shea	8.00	3.60	1.00	☐ 278	Charlie Neal	35.00	16.00	4.40

		MINT	NRMT	EXC
☐ 279	Hank Soar UMP	25.00	11.00	3.10
☐ 280	Clyde McCullough	18.00	8.00	2.20
☐ 281	Charles Berry UMP	25.00	11.00	3.10
☐ 282	Phil Cavarretta	22.00	10.00	2.70
☐ 283	Nestor Chylak UMP	25.00	11.00	3.10
☐ 284	Bill Jackowski UMP	25.00	11.00	3.10
☐ 285	Walt Dropo	22.00	10.00	2.70
☐ 286	Frank Secory UMP	25.00	11.00	3.10
☐ 287	Ron Mrozinski	22.00	10.00	2.70
☐ 288	Dick Smith	22.00	10.00	2.70
☐ 289	Arthur Gore UMP	25.00	11.00	3.10
☐ 290	Hershell Freeman	22.00	10.00	2.70
☐ 291	Frank Dascoli UMP	25.00	11.00	3.10
☐ 292	Marv Blaylock	22.00	10.00	2.70
☐ 293	Thomas Gorman UMP	30.00	13.50	3.70
☐ 294	Wally Moses CO	22.00	10.00	2.70
☐ 295	Lee Ballanfant UMP	25.00	11.00	3.10
☐ 296	Bill Virdon	35.00	16.00	4.40
☐ 297	Dusty Boggess UMP	25.00	11.00	3.10
☐ 298	Charlie Grimm MG	22.00	10.00	2.70
☐ 299	Lon Warneke UMP	30.00	13.50	3.70
☐ 300	Tommy Byrne	22.00	10.00	2.70
☐ 301	William Engeln UMP	25.00	11.00	3.10
☐ 302	Frank Malzone	30.00	13.50	3.70
☐ 303	Jocko Conlan UMP	75.00	34.00	9.50
☐ 304	Harry Chiti	22.00	10.00	2.70
☐ 305	Frank Umont UMP	25.00	11.00	3.10
☐ 306	Bob Cerv	22.00	10.00	2.70
☐ 307	Babe Pinelli UMP	30.00	13.50	3.70
☐ 308	Al Lopez MG	50.00	22.00	6.25
☐ 309	Hal Dixon UMP	25.00	11.00	3.10
☐ 310	Ken Lehman	22.00	10.00	2.70
☐ 311	Lawrence Goetz UMP	25.00	11.00	3.10
☐ 312	Bill Wight	22.00	10.00	2.70
☐ 313	Augie Donatelli UMP	45.00	20.00	5.50
☐ 314	Dale Mitchell	22.00	10.00	2.70
☐ 315	Cal Hubbard UMP	75.00	34.00	9.50
☐ 316	Marion Fricano	22.00	10.00	2.70
☐ 317	William Summers UMP	30.00	13.50	3.70
☐ 318	Sid Hudson	22.00	10.00	2.70
☐ 319	Al Schroll	22.00	10.00	2.70
☐ 320	George Susce Jr.	45.00	10.00	2.70

1989 Bowman

 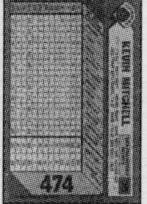

The 1989 Bowman set, which was actually produced by Topps, contains 484 cards measuring approximately 2 1/2" by 3 3/4". The fronts have white-bordered color photos with facsimile autographs and small Bowman logos. The backs are scarlet and feature charts detailing 1988 player perfor-mances vs. each team. The cards are checklisted below alphabetically according to teams in the AL and NL as follows: Baltimore Orioles (1-18), Boston Red Sox (19-36), California Angels (37-54), Chicago White Sox (55-72), Cleveland Indians (73-91), Detroit Tigers (92-109), Kansas City Royals (110-128), Milwaukee Brewers (129-146), Minnesota Twins (147-164), New York Yankees (165-183), Oakland Athletics (184-202), Seattle Mariners (203-220), Texas Rangers (221-238), Toronto Blue Jays (239-257), Atlanta Braves (262-279), Chicago Cubs (280-298), Cincinnati Reds (299-316), Houston Astros (317-334), Los Angeles Dodgers (335-352), Montreal Expos (353-370), New York Mets (371-389), Philadelphia Phillies (390-408), Pittsburgh Pirates (409-426), St. Louis Cardinals (427-444), San Diego Padres (445-462), and San Francisco Giants (463-480). Cards 258-261 form a father/son sub-set. The cards were released in midseason 1989 in wax, rack, and cello pack formats. Rookie Cards in this set include Jim Abbott, Steve Avery, Andy Benes, Rico Brogna, Royce Clayton, Ken Griffey Jr., Tino Martinez, Gary Sheffield, John Smoltz, Ed Sprague and Robin Ventura. Topps also produced a limited Bowman "Tiffany" set with reportedly only 6,000 sets being produced. This Tiffany version is valued approximately from five to eight times the values listed below.

	MINT	NRMT	EXC
COMPLETE SET (484)	12.00	5.50	1.50
COMPLETE FACT.SET (484)	12.00	5.50	1.50
COMMON CARD (1-484)	.05	.02	.01

☐ 1	Oswald Peraza	.05	.02	.01
☐ 2	Brian Holton	.05	.02	.01
☐ 3	Jose Bautista	.05	.02	.01
☐ 4	Pete Harnisch	.08	.04	.01
☐ 5	Dave Schmidt	.05	.02	.01
☐ 6	Gregg Olson	.08	.04	.01
☐ 7	Jeff Ballard	.05	.02	.01
☐ 8	Bob Melvin	.05	.02	.01
☐ 9	Cal Ripken	.75	.35	.09
☐ 10	Randy Milligan	.05	.02	.01
☐ 11	Juan Bell	.05	.02	.01
☐ 12	Billy Ripken	.05	.02	.01
☐ 13	Jim Traber	.05	.02	.01
☐ 14	Pete Stanicek	.05	.02	.01
☐ 15	Steve Finley	.20	.09	.03
☐ 16	Larry Sheets	.05	.02	.01
☐ 17	Phil Bradley	.05	.02	.01
☐ 18	Brady Anderson	.40	.18	.05
☐ 19	Lee Smith	.10	.05	.01
☐ 20	Tom Fischer	.05	.02	.01
☐ 21	Mike Boddicker	.05	.02	.01
☐ 22	Rob Murphy	.05	.02	.01
☐ 23	Wes Gardner	.05	.02	.01
☐ 24	John Dopson	.05	.02	.01
☐ 25	Bob Stanley	.05	.02	.01
☐ 26	Roger Clemens	.20	.09	.03
☐ 27	Rich Gedman	.05	.02	.01
☐ 28	Marty Barrett	.05	.02	.01
☐ 29	Luis Rivera	.05	.02	.01
☐ 30	Jody Reed	.05	.02	.01
☐ 31	Nick Esasky	.05	.02	.01

☐ 32 Wade Boggs	.15	.07	.02
☐ 33 Jim Rice	.10	.05	.01
☐ 34 Mike Greenwell	.08	.04	.01
☐ 35 Dwight Evans	.08	.04	.01
☐ 36 Ellis Burks	.10	.05	.01
☐ 37 Chuck Finley	.08	.04	.01
☐ 38 Kirk McCaskill	.05	.02	.01
☐ 39 Jim Abbott	.30	.14	.04
☐ 40 Bryan Harvey	.10	.05	.01
☐ 41 Bert Blyleven	.10	.05	.01
☐ 42 Mike Witt	.05	.02	.01
☐ 43 Bob McClure	.05	.02	.01
☐ 44 Bill Schroeder	.05	.02	.01
☐ 45 Lance Parrish	.08	.04	.01
☐ 46 Dick Schofield	.05	.02	.01
☐ 47 Wally Joyner	.08	.04	.01
☐ 48 Jack Howell	.05	.02	.01
☐ 49 Johnny Ray	.05	.02	.01
☐ 50 Chili Davis	.10	.05	.01
☐ 51 Tony Armas	.05	.02	.01
☐ 52 Claudell Washington	.05	.02	.01
☐ 53 Brian Downing	.05	.02	.01
☐ 54 Devon White	.10	.05	.01
☐ 55 Bobby Thigpen	.05	.02	.01
☐ 56 Bill Long	.05	.02	.01
☐ 57 Jerry Reuss	.05	.02	.01
☐ 58 Shawn Hillegas	.05	.02	.01
☐ 59 Melido Perez	.05	.02	.01
☐ 60 Jeff Bittiger	.05	.02	.01
☐ 61 Jack McDowell	.15	.07	.02
☐ 62 Carlton Fisk	.10	.05	.01
☐ 63 Steve Lyons	.05	.02	.01
☐ 64 Ozzie Guillen	.08	.04	.01
☐ 65 Robin Ventura	.50	.23	.06
☐ 66 Fred Manrique	.05	.02	.01
☐ 67 Dan Pasqua	.05	.02	.01
☐ 68 Ivan Calderon	.05	.02	.01
☐ 69 Ron Kittle	.05	.02	.01
☐ 70 Daryl Boston	.05	.02	.01
☐ 71 Dave Gallagher	.05	.02	.01
☐ 72 Harold Baines	.10	.05	.01
☐ 73 Charles Nagy	.50	.23	.06
☐ 74 John Farrell	.05	.02	.01
☐ 75 Kevin Wickander	.05	.02	.01
☐ 76 Greg Swindell	.08	.04	.01
☐ 77 Mike Walker	.05	.02	.01
☐ 78 Doug Jones	.08	.04	.01
☐ 79 Rich Yett	.05	.02	.01
☐ 80 Tom Candiotti	.05	.02	.01
☐ 81 Jesse Orosco	.05	.02	.01
☐ 82 Bud Black	.05	.02	.01
☐ 83 Andy Allanson	.05	.02	.01
☐ 84 Pete O'Brien	.05	.02	.01
☐ 85 Jerry Browne	.05	.02	.01
☐ 86 Brook Jacoby	.05	.02	.01
☐ 87 Mark Lewis	.05	.02	.01
☐ 88 Luis Aguayo	.05	.02	.01
☐ 89 Cory Snyder	.05	.02	.01
☐ 90 Oddibe McDowell	.05	.02	.01
☐ 91 Joe Carter	.15	.07	.02
☐ 92 Frank Tanana	.05	.02	.01
☐ 93 Jack Morris	.10	.05	.01
☐ 94 Doyle Alexander	.05	.02	.01
☐ 95 Steve Searcy	.05	.02	.01
☐ 96 Randy Bockus	.05	.02	.01
☐ 97 Jeff M. Robinson	.05	.02	.01
☐ 98 Mike Henneman	.08	.04	.01
☐ 99 Paul Gibson	.05	.02	.01
☐ 100 Frank Williams	.05	.02	.01
☐ 101 Matt Nokes	.05	.02	.01
☐ 102 Rico Brogna UER	.50	.23	.06

(Misspelled Ricco on card back)			
☐ 103 Lou Whitaker	.10	.05	.01
☐ 104 Al Pedrique	.05	.02	.01
☐ 105 Alan Trammell	.10	.05	.01
☐ 106 Chris Brown	.05	.02	.01
☐ 107 Pat Sheridan	.05	.02	.01
☐ 108 Chet Lemon	.05	.02	.01
☐ 109 Keith Moreland	.05	.02	.01
☐ 110 Mel Stottlemyre Jr.	.08	.04	.01
☐ 111 Bret Saberhagen	.10	.05	.01
☐ 112 Floyd Bannister	.05	.02	.01
☐ 113 Jeff Montgomery	.08	.04	.01
☐ 114 Steve Farr	.05	.02	.01
☐ 115 Tom Gordon UER	.15	.07	.02
(Front shows autograph of Don Gordon)			
☐ 116 Charlie Leibrandt	.05	.02	.01
☐ 117 Mark Gubicza	.05	.02	.01
☐ 118 Mike Macfarlane	.08	.04	.01
☐ 119 Bob Boone	.08	.04	.01
☐ 120 Kurt Stillwell	.05	.02	.01
☐ 121 George Brett	.40	.18	.05
☐ 122 Frank White	.08	.04	.01
☐ 123 Kevin Seitzer	.05	.02	.01
☐ 124 Willie Wilson	.05	.02	.01
☐ 125 Pat Tabler	.05	.02	.01
☐ 126 Bo Jackson	.15	.07	.02
☐ 127 Hugh Walker	.05	.02	.01
☐ 128 Danny Tartabull	.08	.04	.01
☐ 129 Teddy Higuera	.05	.02	.01
☐ 130 Don August	.05	.02	.01
☐ 131 Juan Nieves	.05	.02	.01
☐ 132 Mike Birkbeck	.05	.02	.01
☐ 133 Dan Plesac	.05	.02	.01
☐ 134 Chris Bosio	.05	.02	.01
☐ 135 Bill Wegman	.05	.02	.01
☐ 136 Chuck Crim	.05	.02	.01
☐ 137 B.J. Surhoff	.05	.02	.01
☐ 138 Joey Meyer	.05	.02	.01
☐ 139 Dale Sveum	.05	.02	.01
☐ 140 Paul Molitor	.15	.07	.02
☐ 141 Jim Gantner	.05	.02	.01
☐ 142 Gary Sheffield	.60	.25	.07
☐ 143 Greg Brock	.05	.02	.01
☐ 144 Robin Yount	.20	.09	.03
☐ 145 Glenn Braggs	.05	.02	.01
☐ 146 Rob Deer	.05	.02	.01
☐ 147 Fred Toliver	.05	.02	.01
☐ 148 Jeff Reardon	.10	.05	.01
☐ 149 Allan Anderson	.05	.02	.01
☐ 150 Frank Viola	.08	.04	.01
☐ 151 Shane Rawley	.05	.02	.01
☐ 152 Juan Berenguer	.05	.02	.01
☐ 153 Johnny Ard	.05	.02	.01
☐ 154 Tim Laudner	.05	.02	.01
☐ 155 Brian Harper	.08	.04	.01
☐ 156 Al Newman	.05	.02	.01
☐ 157 Kent Hrbek	.08	.04	.01
☐ 158 Gary Gaetti	.05	.02	.01
☐ 159 Wally Backman	.05	.02	.01
☐ 160 Gene Larkin	.05	.02	.01
☐ 161 Greg Gagne	.05	.02	.01
☐ 162 Kirby Puckett	.40	.18	.05
☐ 163 Dan Gladden	.05	.02	.01
☐ 164 Randy Bush	.05	.02	.01
☐ 165 Dave LaPoint	.05	.02	.01
☐ 166 Andy Hawkins	.05	.02	.01
☐ 167 Dave Righetti	.05	.02	.01
☐ 168 Lance McCullers	.05	.02	.01
☐ 169 Jimmy Jones	.05	.02	.01

□ 170 Al Leiter	.05	.02	.01
□ 171 John Candelaria	.05	.02	.01
□ 172 Don Slaught	.05	.02	.01
□ 173 Jamie Quirk	.05	.02	.01
□ 174 Rafael Santana	.05	.02	.01
□ 175 Mike Pagliarulo	.05	.02	.01
□ 176 Don Mattingly	.40	.18	.05
□ 177 Ken Phelps	.05	.02	.01
□ 178 Steve Sax	.05	.02	.01
□ 179 Dave Winfield	.15	.07	.02
□ 180 Stan Jefferson	.05	.02	.01
□ 181 Rickey Henderson	.15	.07	.02
□ 182 Bob Brower	.05	.02	.01
□ 183 Roberto Kelly	.08	.04	.01
□ 184 Curt Young	.05	.02	.01
□ 185 Gene Nelson	.05	.02	.01
□ 186 Bob Welch	.08	.04	.01
□ 187 Rick Honeycutt	.05	.02	.01
□ 188 Dave Stewart	.10	.05	.01
□ 189 Mike Moore	.05	.02	.01
□ 190 Dennis Eckersley	.15	.07	.02
□ 191 Eric Plunk	.05	.02	.01
□ 192 Storm Davis	.05	.02	.01
□ 193 Terry Steinbach	.08	.04	.01
□ 194 Ron Hassey	.05	.02	.01
□ 195 Stan Royer	.05	.02	.01
□ 196 Walt Weiss	.05	.02	.01
□ 197 Mark McGwire	.10	.05	.01
□ 198 Carney Lansford	.08	.04	.01
□ 199 Glenn Hubbard	.05	.02	.01
□ 200 Dave Henderson	.05	.02	.01
□ 201 Jose Canseco	.30	.14	.04
□ 202 Dave Parker	.10	.05	.01
□ 203 Scott Bankhead	.05	.02	.01
□ 204 Tom Niedenfuer	.05	.02	.01
□ 205 Mark Langston	.15	.07	.02
□ 206 Erik Hanson	.25	.11	.03
□ 207 Mike Jackson	.05	.02	.01
□ 208 Dave Valle	.05	.02	.01
□ 209 Scott Bradley	.05	.02	.01
□ 210 Harold Reynolds	.05	.02	.01
□ 211 Tino Martinez	.40	.18	.05
□ 212 Rich Renteria	.05	.02	.01
□ 213 Rey Quinones	.05	.02	.01
□ 214 Jim Presley	.05	.02	.01
□ 215 Alvin Davis	.05	.02	.01
□ 216 Edgar Martinez	.20	.09	.03
□ 217 Darnell Coles	.05	.02	.01
□ 218 Jeffrey Leonard	.05	.02	.01
□ 219 Jay Buhner	.15	.07	.02
□ 220 Ken Griffey Jr.	5.00	2.20	.60
□ 221 Drew Hall	.05	.02	.01
□ 222 Bobby Witt	.08	.04	.01
□ 223 Jamie Moyer	.05	.02	.01
□ 224 Charlie Hough	.08	.04	.01
□ 225 Nolan Ryan	.75	.35	.09
□ 226 Jeff Russell	.05	.02	.01
□ 227 Jim Sundberg	.05	.02	.01
□ 228 Julio Franco	.08	.04	.01
□ 229 Buddy Bell	.08	.04	.01
□ 230 Scott Fletcher	.05	.02	.01
□ 231 Jeff Kunkel	.05	.02	.01
□ 232 Steve Buechele	.05	.02	.01
□ 233 Monty Fariss	.05	.02	.01
□ 234 Rick Leach	.05	.02	.01
□ 235 Ruben Sierra	.15	.07	.02
□ 236 Cecil Espy	.05	.02	.01
□ 237 Rafael Palmeiro	.25	.11	.03
□ 238 Pete Incaviglia	.08	.04	.01
□ 239 Dave Stieb	.08	.04	.01
□ 240 Jeff Musselman	.05	.02	.01

□ 241 Mike Flanagan	.05	.02	.01
□ 242 Todd Stottlemyre	.08	.04	.01
□ 243 Jimmy Key	.10	.05	.01
□ 244 Tony Castillo	.05	.02	.01
□ 245 Alex Sanchez	.05	.02	.01
□ 246 Tom Henke	.08	.04	.01
□ 247 John Cerutti	.05	.02	.01
□ 248 Ernie Whitt	.05	.02	.01
□ 249 Bob Brenly	.05	.02	.01
□ 250 Rance Mulliniks	.05	.02	.01
□ 251 Kelly Gruber	.05	.02	.01
□ 252 Ed Sprague	.25	.11	.03
□ 253 Fred McGriff	.25	.11	.03
□ 254 Tony Fernandez	.08	.04	.01
□ 255 Tom Lawless	.05	.02	.01
□ 256 George Bell	.05	.02	.01
□ 257 Jesse Barfield	.05	.02	.01
□ 258 Roberto Alomar Sandy Alomar	.25	.11	.03
□ 259 Ken Griffey Jr. Ken Griffey Sr.	1.00	.45	.12
□ 260 Cal Ripken Jr. Cal Ripken Sr.	.30	.14	.04
□ 261 Mel Stottlemyre Jr. Mel Stottlemyre Sr.	.05	.02	.01
□ 262 Zane Smith	.05	.02	.01
□ 263 Charlie Puleo	.05	.02	.01
□ 264 Derek Lilliquist	.05	.02	.01
□ 265 Paul Assenmacher	.05	.02	.01
□ 266 John Smoltz	.40	.18	.05
□ 267 Tom Glavine	.40	.18	.05
□ 268 Steve Avery	.50	.23	.06
□ 269 Pete Smith	.05	.02	.01
□ 270 Jody Davis	.05	.02	.01
□ 271 Bruce Benedict	.05	.02	.01
□ 272 Andres Thomas	.05	.02	.01
□ 273 Gerald Perry	.05	.02	.01
□ 274 Ron Gant	.25	.11	.03
□ 275 Darrell Evans	.08	.04	.01
□ 276 Dale Murphy	.10	.05	.01
□ 277 Dion James	.05	.02	.01
□ 278 Lonnie Smith	.05	.02	.01
□ 279 Geronimo Berroa	.08	.04	.01
□ 280 Steve Wilson	.05	.02	.01
□ 281 Rick Sutcliffe	.08	.04	.01
□ 282 Kevin Coffman	.05	.02	.01
□ 283 Mitch Williams	.08	.04	.01
□ 284 Greg Maddux	.75	.35	.09
□ 285 Paul Kilgus	.05	.02	.01
□ 286 Mike Harkey	.05	.02	.01
□ 287 Lloyd McClendon	.05	.02	.01
□ 288 Damon Berryhill	.05	.02	.01
□ 289 Ty Griffin	.05	.02	.01
□ 290 Ryne Sandberg	.30	.14	.04
□ 291 Mark Grace	.15	.07	.02
□ 292 Curt Wilkerson	.05	.02	.01
□ 293 Vance Law	.05	.02	.01
□ 294 Shawon Dunston	.08	.04	.01
□ 295 Jerome Walton	.08	.04	.01
□ 296 Mitch Webster	.05	.02	.01
□ 297 Dwight Smith	.05	.02	.01
□ 298 Andre Dawson	.15	.07	.02
□ 299 Jeff Sellers	.05	.02	.01
□ 300 Jose Rijo	.10	.05	.01
□ 301 John Franco	.08	.04	.01
□ 302 Rick Mahler	.05	.02	.01
□ 303 Ron Robinson	.05	.02	.01
□ 304 Danny Jackson	.05	.02	.01
□ 305 Rob Dibble	.08	.04	.01
□ 306 Tom Browning	.05	.02	.01
□ 307 Bo Diaz	.05	.02	.01

□	308	Manny Trillo	.05	.02	.01
□	309	Chris Sabo	.08	.04	.01
□	310	Ron Oester	.05	.02	.01
□	311	Barry Larkin	.20	.09	.03
□	312	Todd Benzinger	.05	.02	.01
□	313	Paul O'Neill	.10	.05	.01
□	314	Kal Daniels	.05	.02	.01
□	315	Joel Youngblood	.05	.02	.01
□	316	Eric Davis	.08	.04	.01
□	317	Dave Smith	.05	.02	.01
□	318	Mark Portugal	.08	.04	.01
□	319	Brian Meyer	.05	.02	.01
□	320	Jim Deshaies	.05	.02	.01
□	321	Juan Agosto	.05	.02	.01
□	322	Mike Scott	.05	.02	.01
□	323	Rick Rhoden	.05	.02	.01
□	324	Jim Clancy	.05	.02	.01
□	325	Larry Andersen	.05	.02	.01
□	326	Alex Trevino	.05	.02	.01
□	327	Alan Ashby	.05	.02	.01
□	328	Craig Reynolds	.05	.02	.01
□	329	Bill Doran	.05	.02	.01
□	330	Rafael Ramirez	.05	.02	.01
□	331	Glenn Davis	.05	.02	.01
□	332	Willie Ansley	.05	.02	.01
□	333	Gerald Young	.05	.02	.01
□	334	Cameron Drew	.05	.02	.01
□	335	Jay Howell	.05	.02	.01
□	336	Tim Belcher	.05	.02	.01
□	337	Fernando Valenzuela	.05	.02	.01
□	338	Ricky Horton	.05	.02	.01
□	339	Tim Leary	.05	.02	.01
□	340	Bill Bene	.05	.02	.01
□	341	Orel Hershiser	.10	.05	.01
□	342	Mike Scioscia	.05	.02	.01
□	343	Rick Dempsey	.05	.02	.01
□	344	Willie Randolph	.08	.04	.01
□	345	Alfredo Griffin	.05	.02	.01
□	346	Eddie Murray	.20	.09	.03
□	347	Mickey Hatcher	.05	.02	.01
□	348	Mike Sharperson	.05	.02	.01
□	349	John Shelby	.05	.02	.01
□	350	Mike Marshall	.05	.02	.01
□	351	Kirk Gibson	.10	.05	.01
□	352	Mike Davis	.05	.02	.01
□	353	Bryn Smith	.05	.02	.01
□	354	Pascual Perez	.05	.02	.01
□	355	Kevin Gross	.05	.02	.01
□	356	Andy McGaffigan	.05	.02	.01
□	357	Brian Holman	.05	.02	.01
□	358	Dave Wainhouse	.05	.02	.01
□	359	Dennis Martinez	.08	.04	.01
□	360	Tim Burke	.05	.02	.01
□	361	Nelson Santovenia	.05	.02	.01
□	362	Tim Wallach	.05	.02	.01
□	363	Spike Owen	.05	.02	.01
□	364	Rex Hudler	.05	.02	.01
□	365	Andres Galarraga	.15	.07	.02
□	366	Otis Nixon	.05	.02	.01
□	367	Hubie Brooks	.05	.02	.01
□	368	Mike Aldrete	.05	.02	.01
□	369	Tim Raines	.15	.07	.02
□	370	Dave Martinez	.05	.02	.01
□	371	Bob Ojeda	.05	.02	.01
□	372	Ron Darling	.08	.04	.01
□	373	Wally Whitehurst	.05	.02	.01
□	374	Randy Myers	.10	.05	.01
□	375	David Cone	.15	.07	.02
□	376	Dwight Gooden	.08	.04	.01
□	377	Sid Fernandez	.08	.04	.01
□	378	Dave Proctor	.05	.02	.01
□	379	Gary Carter	.10	.05	.01
□	380	Keith Miller	.05	.02	.01
□	381	Gregg Jefferies	.20	.09	.03
□	382	Tim Teufel	.05	.02	.01
□	383	Kevin Elster	.05	.02	.01
□	384	Dave Magadan	.05	.02	.01
□	385	Keith Hernandez	.08	.04	.01
□	386	Mookie Wilson	.08	.04	.01
□	387	Darryl Strawberry	.10	.05	.01
□	388	Kevin McReynolds	.08	.04	.01
□	389	Mark Carreon	.05	.02	.01
□	390	Jeff Parrett	.05	.02	.01
□	391	Mike Maddux	.05	.02	.01
□	392	Don Carman	.05	.02	.01
□	393	Bruce Ruffin	.05	.02	.01
□	394	Ken Howell	.05	.02	.01
□	395	Steve Bedrosian	.05	.02	.01
□	396	Floyd Youmans	.05	.02	.01
□	397	Larry McWilliams	.05	.02	.01
□	398	Pat Combs	.05	.02	.01
□	399	Steve Lake	.05	.02	.01
□	400	Dickie Thon	.05	.02	.01
□	401	Ricky Jordan	.05	.02	.01
□	402	Mike Schmidt	.25	.11	.03
□	403	Tom Herr	.05	.02	.01
□	404	Chris James	.05	.02	.01
□	405	Juan Samuel	.05	.02	.01
□	406	Von Hayes	.05	.02	.01
□	407	Ron Jones	.05	.02	.01
□	408	Curt Ford	.05	.02	.01
□	409	Bob Walk	.05	.02	.01
□	410	Jeff D. Robinson	.05	.02	.01
□	411	Jim Gott	.05	.02	.01
□	412	Scott Medvin	.05	.02	.01
□	413	John Smiley	.05	.02	.01
□	414	Bob Kipper	.05	.02	.01
□	415	Brian Fisher	.05	.02	.01
□	416	Doug Drabek	.10	.05	.01
□	417	Mike LaValliere	.05	.02	.01
□	418	Ken Oberkfell	.05	.02	.01
□	419	Sid Bream	.05	.02	.01
□	420	Austin Manahan	.05	.02	.01
□	421	Jose Lind	.05	.02	.01
□	422	Bobby Bonilla	.15	.07	.02
□	423	Glenn Wilson	.05	.02	.01
□	424	Andy Van Slyke	.08	.04	.01
□	425	Gary Redus	.05	.02	.01
□	426	Barry Bonds	.40	.18	.05
□	427	Don Heinkel	.05	.02	.01
□	428	Ken Dayley	.05	.02	.01
□	429	Todd Worrell	.05	.02	.01
□	430	Brad DuVall	.05	.02	.01
□	431	Jose DeLeon	.05	.02	.01
□	432	Joe Magrane	.05	.02	.01
□	433	John Ericks	.05	.02	.01
□	434	Frank DiPino	.05	.02	.01
□	435	Tony Pena	.05	.02	.01
□	436	Ozzie Smith	.30	.14	.04
□	437	Terry Pendleton	.10	.05	.01
□	438	Jose Oquendo	.05	.02	.01
□	439	Tim Jones	.05	.02	.01
□	440	Pedro Guerrero	.08	.04	.01
□	441	Milt Thompson	.05	.02	.01
□	442	Willie McGee	.08	.04	.01
□	443	Vince Coleman	.08	.04	.01
□	444	Tom Brunansky	.05	.02	.01
□	445	Walt Terrell	.05	.02	.01
□	446	Eric Show	.05	.02	.01
□	447	Mark Davis	.05	.02	.01
□	448	Andy Benes	.25	.11	.03
□	449	Ed Whitson	.05	.02	.01

				MINT	NRMT	EXC
☐	450	Dennis Rasmussen	.05	.02	.01
☐	451	Bruce Hurst	.05	.02	.01
☐	452	Pat Clements	.05	.02	.01
☐	453	Benito Santiago	.08	.04	.01
☐	454	Sandy Alomar Jr.	.20	.09	.03
☐	455	Garry Templeton	.05	.02	.01
☐	456	Jack Clark	.08	.04	.01
☐	457	Tim Flannery	.05	.02	.01
☐	458	Roberto Alomar	.50	.23	.06
☐	459	Carmelo Martinez	.05	.02	.01
☐	460	John Kruk	.10	.05	.01
☐	461	Tony Gwynn	.30	.14	.04
☐	462	Jerald Clark	.05	.02	.01
☐	463	Don Robinson	.05	.02	.01
☐	464	Craig Lefferts	.05	.02	.01
☐	465	Kelly Downs	.05	.02	.01
☐	466	Rick Reuschel	.05	.02	.01
☐	467	Scott Garrelts	.05	.02	.01
☐	468	Wil Tejada	.05	.02	.01
☐	469	Kirt Manwaring	.05	.02	.01
☐	470	Terry Kennedy	.05	.02	.01
☐	471	Jose Uribe	.05	.02	.01
☐	472	Royce Clayton	.25	.11	.03
☐	473	Robby Thompson	.08	.04	.01
☐	474	Kevin Mitchell	.08	.04	.01
☐	475	Ernie Riles	.05	.02	.01
☐	476	Will Clark	.20	.09	.03
☐	477	Donell Nixon	.05	.02	.01
☐	478	Candy Maldonado	.05	.02	.01
☐	479	Tracy Jones	.05	.02	.01
☐	480	Brett Butler	.10	.05	.01
☐	481	Checklist 1-121	.05	.02	.01
☐	482	Checklist 122-242	.05	.02	.01
☐	483	Checklist 243-363	.05	.02	.01
☐	484	Checklist 364-484	.05	.02	.01

1990 Bowman

 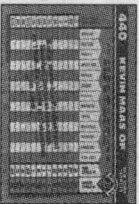

The 1990 Bowman set was issued in the standard card size of 2 1/2" by 3 1/2". This was the second issue by Topps using the Bowman name. The set consists of 528 cards, increased from 1989's edition of 484 cards. The cards feature a white border with the player's photo inside and the Bowman logo on top. Again, the Bowman cards were issued with the backs featuring team by team statistics. The card numbering is in team order with the teams themselves being ordered alphabetically within each league. The set numbering is as follows: Atlanta Braves (1-20), Chicago Cubs (21-40), Cincinnati Reds (41-60), Houston

Astros (61-81), Los Angeles Dodgers (82-101), Montreal Expos (102-121), New York Mets (122-142), Philadelphia Phillies (143-162), Pittsburgh Pirates (163-182), St. Louis Cardinals (183-202), San Diego Padres (203-222), San Francisco Giants (223-242), Baltimore Orioles (243-262), Boston Red Sox (263-282), California Angels (283-302), Chicago White Sox (303-322), Cleveland Indians (323-342), Detroit Tigers (343-362), Kansas City Royals (363-383), Milwaukee Brewers (384-404), Minnesota Twins (405-424), New York Yankees (425-444), Oakland A's (445-464), Seattle Mariners (465-484), Texas Rangers (485-503), and Toronto Blue Jays (504-524). Rookie Cards in this set include Moises Alou, Carlos Baerga, Scott Cooper, Delino DeShields, Cal Eldred, Travis Fryman, Leo Gomez, Juan Gonzalez, Tommy Greene, Marquis Grissom, Bob Hamelin, Chris Hoiles, Dave Hollins, Darryl Kile, Chuck Knoblauch, Ray Lankford, Kevin Maas, Ben McDonald, Jose Offerman, John Olerud, Sammy Sosa, Frank Thomas, Mo Vaughn, and Larry Walker. Topps also produced a Bowman Tiffany glossy set. Production of these Tiffany Bowmans was reported to be approximately 3,000 sets. These Tiffany versions are valued at approximately five to ten times the values listed below.

		MINT	NRMT	EXC
COMPLETE SET (528)		12.00	5.50	1.50
COMPLETE FACT.SET (528)		12.00	5.50	1.50
COMPLETE ART SET (11)		2.00	.90	.25
COMMON CARD (1-528)		.05	.02	.01

			MINT	NRMT	EXC
☐	1	Tommy Greene	.10	.05	.01
☐	2	Tom Glavine	.25	.11	.03
☐	3	Andy Nezelek	.05	.02	.01
☐	4	Mike Stanton	.05	.02	.01
☐	5	Rick Luecken	.05	.02	.01
☐	6	Kent Mercker	.20	.09	.03
☐	7	Derek Lilliquist	.05	.02	.01
☐	8	Charlie Leibrandt	.05	.02	.01
☐	9	Steve Avery	.20	.09	.03
☐	10	John Smoltz	.10	.05	.01
☐	11	Mark Lemke	.08	.04	.01
☐	12	Lonnie Smith	.05	.02	.01
☐	13	Oddibe McDowell	.05	.02	.01
☐	14	Tyler Houston	.05	.02	.01
☐	15	Jeff Blauser	.08	.04	.01
☐	16	Ernie Whitt	.05	.02	.01
☐	17	Alexis Infante	.05	.02	.01
☐	18	Jim Presley	.05	.02	.01
☐	19	Dale Murphy	.10	.05	.01
☐	20	Nick Esasky	.05	.02	.01
☐	21	Rick Sutcliffe	.08	.04	.01
☐	22	Mike Bielecki	.05	.02	.01
☐	23	Steve Wilson	.05	.02	.01
☐	24	Kevin Blankenship	.05	.02	.01
☐	25	Mitch Williams	.08	.04	.01
☐	26	Dean Wilkins	.05	.02	.01
☐	27	Greg Maddux	.60	.25	.07
☐	28	Mike Harkey	.05	.02	.01
☐	29	Mark Grace	.15	.07	.02
☐	30	Ryne Sandberg	.30	.14	.04
☐	31	Greg Smith	.05	.02	.01
☐	32	Dwight Smith	.05	.02	.01

☐ 33	Damon Berryhill	.05	.02	.01
☐ 34	Earl Cunningham UER	.05	.02	.01
	(Errant * by the			
	word "in")			
☐ 35	Jerome Walton	.05	.02	.01
☐ 36	Lloyd McClendon	.05	.02	.01
☐ 37	Ty Griffin	.05	.02	.01
☐ 38	Shawon Dunston	.05	.02	.01
☐ 39	Andre Dawson	.10	.05	.01
☐ 40	Luis Salazar	.05	.02	.01
☐ 41	Tim Layana	.05	.02	.01
☐ 42	Rob Dibble	.08	.04	.01
☐ 43	Tom Browning	.05	.02	.01
☐ 44	Danny Jackson	.05	.02	.01
☐ 45	Jose Rijo	.08	.04	.01
☐ 46	Scott Scudder	.05	.02	.01
☐ 47	Randy Myers UER	.10	.05	.01
	(Career ERA .274,			
	should be 2.74)			
☐ 48	Brian Lane	.05	.02	.01
☐ 49	Paul O'Neill	.10	.05	.01
☐ 50	Barry Larkin	.20	.09	.03
☐ 51	Reggie Jefferson	.05	.02	.01
☐ 52	Jeff Branson	.05	.02	.01
☐ 53	Chris Sabo	.05	.02	.01
☐ 54	Joe Oliver	.05	.02	.01
☐ 55	Todd Benzinger	.05	.02	.01
☐ 56	Rolando Roomes	.05	.02	.01
☐ 57	Hal Morris	.08	.04	.01
☐ 58	Eric Davis	.08	.04	.01
☐ 59	Scott Bryant	.05	.02	.01
☐ 60	Ken Griffey Sr.	.08	.04	.01
☐ 61	Darryl Kile	.08	.04	.01
☐ 62	Dave Smith	.05	.02	.01
☐ 63	Mark Portugal	.05	.02	.01
☐ 64	Jeff Juden	.05	.02	.01
☐ 65	Bill Gullickson	.05	.02	.01
☐ 66	Danny Darwin	.05	.02	.01
☐ 67	Larry Andersen	.05	.02	.01
☐ 68	Jose Cano	.05	.02	.01
☐ 69	Dan Schatzeder	.05	.02	.01
☐ 70	Jim Deshaies	.05	.02	.01
☐ 71	Mike Scott	.05	.02	.01
☐ 72	Gerald Young	.05	.02	.01
☐ 73	Ken Caminiti	.10	.05	.01
☐ 74	Ken Oberkfell	.05	.02	.01
☐ 75	Dave Rohde	.05	.02	.01
☐ 76	Bill Doran	.05	.02	.01
☐ 77	Andujar Cedeno	.08	.04	.01
☐ 78	Craig Biggio	.15	.07	.02
☐ 79	Karl Rhodes	.05	.02	.01
☐ 80	Glenn Davis	.05	.02	.01
☐ 81	Eric Anthony	.05	.02	.01
☐ 82	John Wetteland	.08	.04	.01
☐ 83	Jay Howell	.05	.02	.01
☐ 84	Orel Hershiser	.10	.05	.01
☐ 85	Tim Belcher	.05	.02	.01
☐ 86	Kiki Jones	.05	.02	.01
☐ 87	Mike Hartley	.05	.02	.01
☐ 88	Ramon Martinez	.10	.05	.01
☐ 89	Mike Scioscia	.05	.02	.01
☐ 90	Willie Randolph	.08	.04	.01
☐ 91	Juan Samuel	.05	.02	.01
☐ 92	Jose Offerman	.08	.04	.01
☐ 93	Dave Hansen	.05	.02	.01
☐ 94	Jeff Hamilton	.05	.02	.01
☐ 95	Alfredo Griffin	.05	.02	.01
☐ 96	Tom Goodwin	.15	.07	.02
☐ 97	Kirk Gibson	.10	.05	.01
☐ 98	Jose Vizcaino	.05	.02	.01
☐ 99	Kal Daniels	.05	.02	.01
☐ 100	Hubie Brooks	.05	.02	.01
☐ 101	Eddie Murray	.25	.11	.03
☐ 102	Dennis Boyd	.05	.02	.01
☐ 103	Tim Burke	.05	.02	.01
☐ 104	Bill Sampen	.05	.02	.01
☐ 105	Brett Gideon	.05	.02	.01
☐ 106	Mark Gardner	.05	.02	.01
☐ 107	Howard Farmer	.05	.02	.01
☐ 108	Mel Rojas	.08	.04	.01
☐ 109	Kevin Gross	.05	.02	.01
☐ 110	Dave Schmidt	.05	.02	.01
☐ 111	Denny Martinez	.08	.04	.01
☐ 112	Jerry Goff	.05	.02	.01
☐ 113	Andres Galarraga	.15	.07	.02
☐ 114	Tim Wallach	.05	.02	.01
☐ 115	Marquis Grissom	.60	.25	.07
☐ 116	Spike Owen	.05	.02	.01
☐ 117	Larry Walker	.75	.35	.09
☐ 118	Tim Raines	.15	.07	.02
☐ 119	Delino DeShields	.15	.07	.02
☐ 120	Tom Foley	.05	.02	.01
☐ 121	Dave Martinez	.05	.02	.01
☐ 122	Frank Viola UER	.08	.04	.01
	(Career ERA .384,			
	should be 3.84)			
☐ 123	Julio Valera	.05	.02	.01
☐ 124	Alejandro Pena	.05	.02	.01
☐ 125	David Cone	.10	.05	.01
☐ 126	Dwight Gooden	.05	.02	.01
☐ 127	Kevin D. Brown	.05	.02	.01
☐ 128	John Franco	.10	.05	.01
☐ 129	Terry Bross	.05	.02	.01
☐ 130	Blaine Beatty	.05	.02	.01
☐ 131	Sid Fernandez	.08	.04	.01
☐ 132	Mike Marshall	.05	.02	.01
☐ 133	Howard Johnson	.08	.04	.01
☐ 134	Jaime Roseboro	.05	.02	.01
☐ 135	Alan Zinter	.05	.02	.01
☐ 136	Keith Miller	.05	.02	.01
☐ 137	Kevin Elster	.05	.02	.01
☐ 138	Kevin McReynolds	.05	.02	.01
☐ 139	Barry Lyons	.05	.02	.01
☐ 140	Gregg Jefferies	.10	.05	.01
☐ 141	Darryl Strawberry	.08	.04	.01
☐ 142	Todd Hundley	.08	.04	.01
☐ 143	Scott Service	.05	.02	.01
☐ 144	Chuck Malone	.05	.02	.01
☐ 145	Steve Ontiveros	.05	.02	.01
☐ 146	Roger McDowell	.05	.02	.01
☐ 147	Ken Howell	.05	.02	.01
☐ 148	Pat Combs	.05	.02	.01
☐ 149	Jeff Parrett	.05	.02	.01
☐ 150	Chuck McElroy	.05	.02	.01
☐ 151	Jason Grimsley	.05	.02	.01
☐ 152	Len Dykstra	.15	.07	.02
☐ 153	Mickey Morandini	.08	.04	.01
☐ 154	John Kruk	.10	.05	.01
☐ 155	Dickie Thon	.05	.02	.01
☐ 156	Ricky Jordan	.05	.02	.01
☐ 157	Jeff Jackson	.05	.02	.01
☐ 158	Darren Daulton	.15	.07	.02
☐ 159	Tom Herr	.05	.02	.01
☐ 160	Von Hayes	.05	.02	.01
☐ 161	Dave Hollins	.10	.05	.01
☐ 162	Carmelo Martinez	.05	.02	.01
☐ 163	Bob Walk	.05	.02	.01
☐ 164	Doug Drabek	.08	.04	.01
☐ 165	Walt Terrell	.05	.02	.01
☐ 166	Bill Landrum	.05	.02	.01
☐ 167	Scott Ruskin	.05	.02	.01
☐ 168	Bob Patterson	.05	.02	.01

☐ 169	Bobby Bonilla	.15	.07	.02
☐ 170	Jose Lind	.05	.02	.01
☐ 171	Andy Van Slyke	.08	.04	.01
☐ 172	Mike LaValliere	.05	.02	.01
☐ 173	Willie Greene	.08	.04	.01
☐ 174	Jay Bell	.08	.04	.01
☐ 175	Sid Bream	.05	.02	.01
☐ 176	Tom Prince	.05	.02	.01
☐ 177	Wally Backman	.05	.02	.01
☐ 178	Moises Alou	.25	.11	.03
☐ 179	Steve Carter	.05	.02	.01
☐ 180	Gary Redus	.05	.02	.01
☐ 181	Barry Bonds	.30	.14	.04
☐ 182	Don Slaught UER	.05	.02	.01
	(Card back shows headings for a pitcher)			
☐ 183	Joe Magrane	.05	.02	.01
☐ 184	Bryn Smith	.05	.02	.01
☐ 185	Todd Worrell	.05	.02	.01
☐ 186	Jose DeLeon	.05	.02	.01
☐ 187	Frank DiPino	.05	.02	.01
☐ 188	John Tudor	.05	.02	.01
☐ 189	Howard Hilton	.05	.02	.01
☐ 190	John Ericks	.05	.02	.01
☐ 191	Ken Dayley	.05	.02	.01
☐ 192	Ray Lankford	.50	.23	.06
☐ 193	Todd Zeile	.08	.04	.01
☐ 194	Willie McGee	.08	.04	.01
☐ 195	Ozzie Smith	.20	.09	.03
☐ 196	Milt Thompson	.05	.02	.01
☐ 197	Terry Pendleton	.10	.05	.01
☐ 198	Vince Coleman	.08	.04	.01
☐ 199	Paul Coleman	.05	.02	.01
☐ 200	Jose Oquendo	.05	.02	.01
☐ 201	Pedro Guerrero	.08	.04	.01
☐ 202	Tom Brunansky	.05	.02	.01
☐ 203	Roger Smithberg	.05	.02	.01
☐ 204	Eddie Whitson	.05	.02	.01
☐ 205	Dennis Rasmussen	.05	.02	.01
☐ 206	Craig Lefferts	.05	.02	.01
☐ 207	Andy Benes	.08	.04	.01
☐ 208	Bruce Hurst	.05	.02	.01
☐ 209	Eric Show	.05	.02	.01
☐ 210	Rafael Valdez	.05	.02	.01
☐ 211	Joey Cora	.08	.04	.01
☐ 212	Thomas Howard	.05	.02	.01
☐ 213	Rob Nelson	.05	.02	.01
☐ 214	Jack Clark	.08	.04	.01
☐ 215	Garry Templeton	.05	.02	.01
☐ 216	Fred Lynn	.08	.04	.01
☐ 217	Tony Gwynn	.30	.14	.04
☐ 218	Benito Santiago	.08	.04	.01
☐ 219	Mike Pagliarulo	.05	.02	.01
☐ 220	Joe Carter	.15	.07	.02
☐ 221	Roberto Alomar	.30	.14	.04
☐ 222	Bip Roberts	.08	.04	.01
☐ 223	Rick Reuschel	.05	.02	.01
☐ 224	Russ Swan	.05	.02	.01
☐ 225	Eric Gunderson	.05	.02	.01
☐ 226	Steve Bedrosian	.05	.02	.01
☐ 227	Mike Remlinger	.05	.02	.01
☐ 228	Scott Garrelts	.05	.02	.01
☐ 229	Ernie Camacho	.05	.02	.01
☐ 230	Andres Santana	.05	.02	.01
☐ 231	Will Clark	.20	.09	.03
☐ 232	Kevin Mitchell	.08	.04	.01
☐ 233	Robby Thompson	.08	.04	.01
☐ 234	Bill Bathe	.05	.02	.01
☐ 235	Tony Perezchica	.05	.02	.01
☐ 236	Gary Carter	.10	.05	.01
☐ 237	Brett Butler	.10	.05	.01
☐ 238	Matt Williams	.30	.14	.04
☐ 239	Earnie Riles	.05	.02	.01
☐ 240	Kevin Bass	.05	.02	.01
☐ 241	Terry Kennedy	.05	.02	.01
☐ 242	Steve Hosey	.05	.02	.01
☐ 243	Ben McDonald	.15	.07	.02
☐ 244	Jeff Ballard	.05	.02	.01
☐ 245	Joe Price	.05	.02	.01
☐ 246	Curt Schilling	.08	.04	.01
☐ 247	Pete Harnisch	.08	.04	.01
☐ 248	Mark Williamson	.05	.02	.01
☐ 249	Gregg Olson	.05	.02	.01
☐ 250	Chris Myers	.05	.02	.01
☐ 251A	David Segui ERR	.05	.02	.01
	(Missing vital stats at top of card back under name)			
☐ 251B	David Segui COR	.05	.02	.01
☐ 252	Joe Orsulak	.05	.02	.01
☐ 253	Craig Worthington	.05	.02	.01
☐ 254	Mickey Tettleton	.08	.04	.01
☐ 255	Cal Ripken	.75	.35	.09
☐ 256	Billy Ripken	.05	.02	.01
☐ 257	Randy Milligan	.05	.02	.01
☐ 258	Brady Anderson	.08	.04	.01
☐ 259	Chris Hoiles UER	.15	.07	.02
	(Baltimore is spelled Balitmore)			
☐ 260	Mike Devereaux	.08	.04	.01
☐ 261	Phil Bradley	.05	.02	.01
☐ 262	Leo Gomez	.05	.02	.01
☐ 263	Lee Smith	.10	.05	.01
☐ 264	Mike Rochford	.05	.02	.01
☐ 265	Jeff Reardon	.10	.05	.01
☐ 266	Wes Gardner	.05	.02	.01
☐ 267	Mike Boddicker	.05	.02	.01
☐ 268	Roger Clemens	.15	.07	.02
☐ 269	Rob Murphy	.05	.02	.01
☐ 270	Mickey Pina	.05	.02	.01
☐ 271	Tony Pena	.05	.02	.01
☐ 272	Jody Reed	.05	.02	.01
☐ 273	Kevin Romine	.05	.02	.01
☐ 274	Mike Greenwell	.10	.05	.01
☐ 275	Maurice Vaughn	1.25	.55	.16
☐ 276	Danny Heep	.05	.02	.01
☐ 277	Scott Cooper	.10	.05	.01
☐ 278	Greg Blosser	.05	.02	.01
☐ 279	Dwight Evans UER	.08	.04	.01
	(* by "1990 Team Breakdown")			
☐ 280	Ellis Burks	.08	.04	.01
☐ 281	Wade Boggs	.15	.07	.02
☐ 282	Marty Barrett	.05	.02	.01
☐ 283	Kirk McCaskill	.05	.02	.01
☐ 284	Mark Langston	.08	.04	.01
☐ 285	Bert Blyleven	.10	.05	.01
☐ 286	Mike Fetters	.05	.02	.01
☐ 287	Kyle Abbott	.05	.02	.01
☐ 288	Jim Abbott	.10	.05	.01
☐ 289	Chuck Finley	.08	.04	.01
☐ 290	Gary DiSarcina	.15	.07	.02
☐ 291	Dick Schofield	.05	.02	.01
☐ 292	Devon White	.08	.04	.01
☐ 293	Bobby Rose	.05	.02	.01
☐ 294	Brian Downing	.05	.02	.01
☐ 295	Lance Parrish	.08	.04	.01
☐ 296	Jack Howell	.05	.02	.01
☐ 297	Claudell Washington	.05	.02	.01
☐ 298	John Orton	.05	.02	.01
☐ 299	Wally Joyner	.10	.05	.01
☐ 300	Lee Stevens	.05	.02	.01
☐ 301	Chili Davis	.10	.05	.01

☐	302	Johnny Ray	.05	.02	.01	☐	371	Frank White	.08	.04	.01
☐	303	Greg Hibbard	.05	.02	.01	☐	372	Brent Mayne	.05	.02	.01
☐	304	Eric King	.05	.02	.01	☐	373	Bob Boone	.08	.04	.01
☐	305	Jack McDowell	.15	.07	.02	☐	374	Jim Eisenreich	.05	.02	.01
☐	306	Bobby Thigpen	.05	.02	.01	☐	375	Danny Tartabull	.08	.04	.01
☐	307	Adam Peterson	.05	.02	.01	☐	376	Kurt Stillwell	.05	.02	.01
☐	308	Scott Radinsky	.05	.02	.01	☐	377	Bill Pecota	.05	.02	.01
☐	309	Wayne Edwards	.05	.02	.01	☐	378	Bo Jackson	.15	.07	.02
☐	310	Melido Perez	.05	.02	.01	☐	379	Bob Hamelin	.10	.05	.01
☐	311	Robin Ventura	.25	.11	.03	☐	380	Kevin Seitzer	.05	.02	.01
☐	312	Sammy Sosa	.75	.35	.09	☐	381	Rey Palacios	.05	.02	.01
☐	313	Dan Pasqua	.05	.02	.01	☐	382	George Brett	.40	.18	.05
☐	314	Carlton Fisk	.10	.05	.01	☐	383	Gerald Perry	.05	.02	.01
☐	315	Ozzie Guillen	.05	.02	.01	☐	384	Teddy Higuera	.05	.02	.01
☐	316	Ivan Calderon	.05	.02	.01	☐	385	Tom Filer	.05	.02	.01
☐	317	Daryl Boston	.05	.02	.01	☐	386	Dan Plesac	.05	.02	.01
☐	318	Craig Grebeck	.05	.02	.01	☐	387	Cal Eldred	.08	.04	.01
☐	319	Scott Fletcher	.05	.02	.01	☐	388	Jaime Navarro	.05	.02	.01
☐	320	Frank Thomas	4.00	1.80	.50	☐	389	Chris Bosio	.05	.02	.01
☐	321	Steve Lyons	.05	.02	.01	☐	390	Randy Veres	.05	.02	.01
☐	322	Carlos Martinez	.05	.02	.01	☐	391	Gary Sheffield	.20	.09	.03
☐	323	Joe Skalski	.05	.02	.01	☐	392	George Canale	.05	.02	.01
☐	324	Tom Candiotti	.05	.02	.01	☐	393	B.J. Surhoff	.05	.02	.01
☐	325	Greg Swindell	.08	.04	.01	☐	394	Tim McIntosh	.05	.02	.01
☐	326	Steve Olin	.08	.04	.01	☐	395	Greg Brock	.05	.02	.01
☐	327	Kevin Wickander	.05	.02	.01	☐	396	Greg Vaughn	.08	.04	.01
☐	328	Doug Jones	.05	.02	.01	☐	397	Darryl Hamilton	.05	.02	.01
☐	329	Jeff Shaw	.05	.02	.01	☐	398	Dave Parker	.10	.05	.01
☐	330	Kevin Bearse	.05	.02	.01	☐	399	Paul Molitor	.15	.07	.02
☐	331	Dion James	.05	.02	.01	☐	400	Jim Gantner	.05	.02	.01
☐	332	Jerry Browne	.05	.02	.01	☐	401	Rob Deer	.05	.02	.01
☐	333	Joey Belle	1.00	.45	.12	☐	402	Billy Spiers	.05	.02	.01
☐	334	Felix Fermin	.05	.02	.01	☐	403	Glenn Braggs	.05	.02	.01
☐	335	Candy Maldonado	.05	.02	.01	☐	404	Robin Yount	.20	.09	.03
☐	336	Cory Snyder	.05	.02	.01	☐	405	Rick Aguilera	.08	.04	.01
☐	337	Sandy Alomar Jr.	.08	.04	.01	☐	406	Johnny Ard	.05	.02	.01
☐	338	Mark Lewis	.05	.02	.01	☐	407	Kevin Tapani	.15	.07	.02
☐	339	Carlos Baerga	1.50	.70	.19	☐	408	Park Pittman	.05	.02	.01
☐	340	Chris James	.05	.02	.01	☐	409	Allan Anderson	.05	.02	.01
☐	341	Brook Jacoby	.05	.02	.01	☐	410	Juan Berenguer	.05	.02	.01
☐	342	Keith Hernandez	.08	.04	.01	☐	411	Willie Banks	.05	.02	.01
☐	343	Frank Tanana	.05	.02	.01	☐	412	Rich Yett	.05	.02	.01
☐	344	Scott Aldred	.05	.02	.01	☐	413	Dave West	.05	.02	.01
☐	345	Mike Henneman	.05	.02	.01	☐	414	Greg Gagne	.05	.02	.01
☐	346	Steve Wapnick	.05	.02	.01	☐	415	Chuck Knoblauch	.50	.23	.06
☐	347	Greg Gohr	.05	.02	.01	☐	416	Randy Bush	.05	.02	.01
☐	348	Eric Stone	.05	.02	.01	☐	417	Gary Gaetti	.05	.02	.01
☐	349	Brian DuBois	.05	.02	.01	☐	418	Kent Hrbek	.08	.04	.01
☐	350	Kevin Ritz	.05	.02	.01	☐	419	Al Newman	.05	.02	.01
☐	351	Rico Brogna	.25	.11	.03	☐	420	Danny Gladden	.05	.02	.01
☐	352	Mike Heath	.05	.02	.01	☐	421	Paul Sorrento	.20	.09	.03
☐	353	Alan Trammell	.10	.05	.01	☐	422	Derek Parks	.05	.02	.01
☐	354	Chet Lemon	.05	.02	.01	☐	423	Scott Leius	.05	.02	.01
☐	355	Dave Bergman	.05	.02	.01	☐	424	Kirby Puckett	.30	.14	.04
☐	356	Lou Whitaker	.10	.05	.01	☐	425	Willie Smith	.05	.02	.01
☐	357	Cecil Fielder UER	.15	.07	.02	☐	426	Dave Righetti	.05	.02	.01
		(* by "1990 Team				☐	427	Jeff D. Robinson	.05	.02	.01
		Breakdown")				☐	428	Alan Mills	.05	.02	.01
☐	358	Milt Cuyler	.05	.02	.01	☐	429	Tim Leary	.05	.02	.01
☐	359	Tony Phillips	.10	.05	.01	☐	430	Pascual Perez	.05	.02	.01
☐	360	Travis Fryman	.50	.23	.06	☐	431	Alvaro Espinoza	.05	.02	.01
☐	361	Ed Romero	.05	.02	.01	☐	432	Dave Winfield	.15	.07	.02
☐	362	Lloyd Moseby	.05	.02	.01	☐	433	Jesse Barfield	.05	.02	.01
☐	363	Mark Gubicza	.05	.02	.01	☐	434	Randy Velarde	.05	.02	.01
☐	364	Bret Saberhagen	.10	.05	.01	☐	435	Rick Cerone	.05	.02	.01
☐	365	Tom Gordon	.08	.04	.01	☐	436	Steve Balboni	.05	.02	.01
☐	366	Steve Farr	.05	.02	.01	☐	437	Mel Hall	.05	.02	.01
☐	367	Kevin Appier	.25	.11	.03	☐	438	Bob Geren	.05	.02	.01
☐	368	Storm Davis	.05	.02	.01	☐	439	Bernie Williams	.30	.14	.04
☐	369	Mark Davis	.05	.02	.01	☐	440	Kevin Maas	.05	.02	.01
☐	370	Jeff Montgomery	.08	.04	.01	☐	441	Mike Blowers	.20	.09	.03

☐ 442	Steve Sax	.05	.02	.01
☐ 443	Don Mattingly	.40	.18	.05
☐ 444	Roberto Kelly	.08	.04	.01
☐ 445	Mike Moore	.05	.02	.01
☐ 446	Reggie Harris	.05	.02	.01
☐ 447	Scott Sanderson	.05	.02	.01
☐ 448	Dave Otto	.05	.02	.01
☐ 449	Dave Stewart	.10	.05	.01
☐ 450	Rick Honeycutt	.05	.02	.01
☐ 451	Dennis Eckersley	.10	.05	.01
☐ 452	Carney Lansford	.08	.04	.01
☐ 453	Scott Hemond	.05	.02	.01
☐ 454	Mark McGwire	.15	.07	.02
☐ 455	Felix Jose	.05	.02	.01
☐ 456	Terry Steinbach	.08	.04	.01
☐ 457	Rickey Henderson	.15	.07	.02
☐ 458	Dave Henderson	.05	.02	.01
☐ 459	Mike Gallego	.05	.02	.01
☐ 460	Jose Canseco	.20	.09	.03
☐ 461	Walt Weiss	.05	.02	.01
☐ 462	Ken Phelps	.05	.02	.01
☐ 463	Darren Lewis	.15	.07	.02
☐ 464	Ron Hassey	.05	.02	.01
☐ 465	Roger Salkeld	.05	.02	.01
☐ 466	Scott Bankhead	.05	.02	.01
☐ 467	Keith Comstock	.05	.02	.01
☐ 468	Randy Johnson	.40	.18	.05
☐ 469	Erik Hanson	.08	.04	.01
☐ 470	Mike Schooler	.05	.02	.01
☐ 471	Gary Eave	.05	.02	.01
☐ 472	Jeffrey Leonard	.05	.02	.01
☐ 473	Dave Valle	.05	.02	.01
☐ 474	Omar Vizquel	.05	.02	.01
☐ 475	Pete O'Brien	.05	.02	.01
☐ 476	Henry Cotto	.05	.02	.01
☐ 477	Jay Buhner	.15	.07	.02
☐ 478	Harold Reynolds	.05	.02	.01
☐ 479	Alvin Davis	.05	.02	.01
☐ 480	Darnell Coles	.05	.02	.01
☐ 481	Ken Griffey Jr.	2.00	.90	.25
☐ 482	Greg Briley	.05	.02	.01
☐ 483	Scott Bradley	.05	.02	.01
☐ 484	Tino Martinez	.20	.09	.03
☐ 485	Jeff Russell	.05	.02	.01
☐ 486	Nolan Ryan	.75	.35	.09
☐ 487	Robb Nen	.08	.04	.01
☐ 488	Kevin Brown	.08	.04	.01
☐ 489	Brian Bohanon	.05	.02	.01
☐ 490	Ruben Sierra	.15	.07	.02
☐ 491	Pete Incaviglia	.05	.02	.01
☐ 492	Juan Gonzalez	1.25	.55	.16
☐ 493	Steve Buechele	.05	.02	.01
☐ 494	Scott Coolbaugh	.05	.02	.01
☐ 495	Geno Petralli	.05	.02	.01
☐ 496	Rafael Palmeiro	.15	.07	.02
☐ 497	Julio Franco	.08	.04	.01
☐ 498	Gary Pettis	.05	.02	.01
☐ 499	Donald Harris	.05	.02	.01
☐ 500	Monty Fariss	.05	.02	.01
☐ 501	Harold Baines	.10	.05	.01
☐ 502	Cecil Espy	.05	.02	.01
☐ 503	Jack Daugherty	.05	.02	.01
☐ 504	Willie Blair	.05	.02	.01
☐ 505	Dave Stieb	.08	.04	.01
☐ 506	Tom Henke	.08	.04	.01
☐ 507	John Cerutti	.05	.02	.01
☐ 508	Paul Kilgus	.05	.02	.01
☐ 509	Jimmy Key	.08	.04	.01
☐ 510	John Olerud	.20	.09	.03
☐ 511	Ed Sprague	.08	.04	.01
☐ 512	Manuel Lee	.05	.02	.01

☐ 513	Fred McGriff	.20	.09	.03
☐ 514	Glenallen Hill	.05	.02	.01
☐ 515	George Bell	.05	.02	.01
☐ 516	Mookie Wilson	.05	.02	.01
☐ 517	Luis Sojo	.05	.02	.01
☐ 518	Nelson Liriano	.05	.02	.01
☐ 519	Kelly Gruber	.05	.02	.01
☐ 520	Greg Myers	.05	.02	.01
☐ 521	Pat Borders	.05	.02	.01
☐ 522	Junior Felix	.05	.02	.01
☐ 523	Eddie Zosky	.05	.02	.01
☐ 524	Tony Fernandez	.08	.04	.01
☐ 525	Checklist 1-132 UER	.05	.02	.01
	(No copyright mark			
	on the back)			
☐ 526	Checklist 133-264	.05	.02	.01
☐ 527	Checklist 265-396	.05	.02	.01
☐ 528	Checklist 397-528	.05	.02	.01

1991 Bowman

This 704-card standard size (2 1/2" by 3 1/2") set marked the third straight year that Topps issued a set using the Bowman name. The cards are arranged in team order by division as follows: AL East, AL West, NL East, and NL West. Some of the specials in the set include cards made for all the 1990 MVP's in each minor league, the leader sluggers by position (Silver Sluggers), and special cards commemorating long-time baseball figure Jimmie Reese, General Colin Powell, newly inducted Hall of Famer Rod Carew and Rickey Henderson's 938th Stolen Base. The cards themselves are designed just like the 1990 Bowman set while the backs again feature the innovative team by team breakdown of how the player did the previous year against a green background. The set numbering is as follows: Toronto Blue Jays (6-30), Milwaukee Brewers (31-56), Cleveland Indians (57-82), Baltimore Orioles (83-106), Boston Red Sox (107-130), Detroit Tigers (131-154), New York Yankees (155-179), California Angels (187-211), Oakland Athletics (212-238), Seattle Mariners (239-264), Texas Rangers (265-290), Kansas City Royals (291-316), Minnesota Twins (317-341), Chicago White Sox (342-366), St. Louis Cardinals (385-409), Chicago Cubs (411-433), Montreal Expos (434-459), New York Mets (460-484), Philadelphia

Phillies (485-508), Pittsburgh Pirates (509-532), Houston Astros (539-565), Atlanta Braves (566-590), Los Angles Dodgers (591-615), San Fransico Giants (616-641), San Diego Padres (642-665), and Cincinnati Reds (666-691). Subsets include minor league MVP's (180-185/693-698), AL Silver Sluggers (367-375) and NL Silver Sluggers (376-384). There are two instances of misnumbering in the set; Ken Griffey (should be 255) and Ken Griffey Jr. are both numbered 246 and Donovan Osborne (should be 406) and Thomson/Branca share number 410. Rookie Cards in this set include Jeff Bagwell, Bret Boone, Jeromy Burnitz, Jeff Conine, Wil Cordero, Dave Fleming, Carlos Garcia, Pat Hentgen, Chipper Jones, Eric Karros, Steve Karsay, Ryan Klesko, Kenny Lofton, Javy Lopez, Sam Militello, Raul Mondesi, Mike Mussina, Marc Newfield, Donovan Osborne, Phil Plantier, Ivan Rodriguez, Tim Salmon, Reggie Sanders, Jim Thome, Todd Van Poppel, Rondell White, and Bob Wickman.

	MINT	NRMT	EXC
COMPLETE SET (704)	30.00	13.50	3.70
COMPLETE FACT.SET (704)	30.00	13.50	3.70
COMMON CARD (1-704)	.05	.02	.01

☐	1 Rod Carew I	.10	.05	.01
☐	2 Rod Carew II	.10	.05	.01
☐	3 Rod Carew III	.10	.05	.01
☐	4 Rod Carew IV	.10	.05	.01
☐	5 Rod Carew V	.10	.05	.01
☐	6 Willie Fraser	.05	.02	.01
☐	7 John Olerud	.08	.04	.01
☐	8 William Suero	.05	.02	.01
☐	9 Roberto Alomar	.25	.11	.03
☐	10 Todd Stottlemyre	.05	.02	.01
☐	11 Joe Carter	.15	.07	.02
☐	12 Steve Karsay	.08	.04	.01
☐	13 Mark Whiten	.08	.04	.01
☐	14 Pat Borders	.05	.02	.01
☐	15 Mike Timlin	.05	.02	.01
☐	16 Tom Henke	.08	.04	.01
☐	17 Eddie Zosky	.05	.02	.01
☐	18 Kelly Gruber	.05	.02	.01
☐	19 Jimmy Key	.08	.04	.01
☐	20 Jerry Schunk	.05	.02	.01
☐	21 Manuel Lee	.05	.02	.01
☐	22 Dave Stieb	.05	.02	.01
☐	23 Pat Hentgen	.15	.07	.02
☐	24 Glenallen Hill	.05	.02	.01
☐	25 Rene Gonzales	.05	.02	.01
☐	26 Ed Sprague	.05	.02	.01
☐	27 Ken Dayley	.05	.02	.01
☐	28 Pat Tabler	.05	.02	.01
☐	29 Denis Boucher	.05	.02	.01
☐	30 Devon White	.08	.04	.01
☐	31 Dante Bichette	.20	.09	.03
☐	32 Paul Molitor	.10	.05	.01
☐	33 Greg Vaughn	.08	.04	.01
☐	34 Dan Plesac	.05	.02	.01
☐	35 Chris George	.05	.02	.01
☐	36 Tim McIntosh	.05	.02	.01
☐	37 Franklin Stubbs	.05	.02	.01
☐	38 Bo Dodson	.05	.02	.01
☐	39 Ron Robinson	.05	.02	.01
☐	40 Ed Nunez	.05	.02	.01
☐	41 Greg Brock	.05	.02	.01
☐	42 Jaime Navarro	.05	.02	.01
☐	43 Chris Bosio	.05	.02	.01
☐	44 B.J. Surhoff	.05	.02	.01
☐	45 Chris Johnson	.05	.02	.01
☐	46 Willie Randolph	.08	.04	.01
☐	47 Narciso Elvira	.05	.02	.01
☐	48 Jim Gantner	.05	.02	.01
☐	49 Kevin Brown	.05	.02	.01
☐	50 Julio Machado	.05	.02	.01
☐	51 Chuck Crim	.05	.02	.01
☐	52 Gary Sheffield	.10	.05	.01
☐	53 Angel Miranda	.05	.02	.01
☐	54 Teddy Higuera	.05	.02	.01
☐	55 Robin Yount	.15	.07	.02
☐	56 Cal Eldred	.05	.02	.01
☐	57 Sandy Alomar Jr.	.08	.04	.01
☐	58 Greg Swindell	.05	.02	.01
☐	59 Brook Jacoby	.05	.02	.01
☐	60 Efrain Valdez	.05	.02	.01
☐	61 Ever Magallanes	.05	.02	.01
☐	62 Tom Candiotti	.05	.02	.01
☐	63 Eric King	.05	.02	.01
☐	64 Alex Cole	.05	.02	.01
☐	65 Charles Nagy	.08	.04	.01
☐	66 Mitch Webster	.05	.02	.01
☐	67 Chris James	.05	.02	.01
☐	68 Jim Thome	1.50	.70	.19
☐	69 Carlos Baerga	.40	.18	.05
☐	70 Mark Lewis	.05	.02	.01
☐	71 Jerry Browne	.05	.02	.01
☐	72 Jesse Orosco	.05	.02	.01
☐	73 Mike Huff	.05	.02	.01
☐	74 Jose Escobar	.05	.02	.01
☐	75 Jeff Manto	.05	.02	.01
☐	76 Turner Ward	.05	.02	.01
☐	77 Doug Jones	.05	.02	.01
☐	78 Bruce Egloff	.05	.02	.01
☐	79 Tim Costo	.05	.02	.01
☐	80 Beau Allred	.05	.02	.01
☐	81 Albert Belle	.50	.23	.06
☐	82 John Farrell	.05	.02	.01
☐	83 Glenn Davis	.05	.02	.01
☐	84 Joe Orsulak	.05	.02	.01
☐	85 Mark Williamson	.05	.02	.01
☐	86 Ben McDonald	.08	.04	.01
☐	87 Billy Ripken	.05	.02	.01
☐	88 Leo Gomez UER	.05	.02	.01
	Baltimore is spelled Balitmore			
☐	89 Bob Melvin	.05	.02	.01
☐	90 Jeff M. Robinson	.05	.02	.01
☐	91 Jose Mesa	.05	.02	.01
☐	92 Gregg Olson	.05	.02	.01
☐	93 Mike Devereaux	.08	.04	.01
☐	94 Luis Mercedes	.05	.02	.01
☐	95 Arthur Rhodes	.05	.02	.01
☐	96 Juan Bell	.05	.02	.01
☐	97 Mike Mussina	1.00	.45	.12
☐	98 Jeff Ballard	.05	.02	.01
☐	99 Chris Hoiles	.08	.04	.01
☐	100 Brady Anderson	.08	.04	.01
☐	101 Bob Milacki	.05	.02	.01
☐	102 David Segui	.05	.02	.01
☐	103 Dwight Evans	.08	.04	.01
☐	104 Cal Ripken	.75	.35	.09
☐	105 Mike Linskey	.05	.02	.01
☐	106 Jeff Tackett	.05	.02	.01
☐	107 Jeff Reardon	.08	.04	.01
☐	108 Dana Kiecker	.05	.02	.01
☐	109 Ellis Burks	.08	.04	.01
☐	110 Dave Owen	.05	.02	.01

☐ 111 Danny Darwin	.05	.02	.01
☐ 112 Mo Vaughn	.50	.23	.06
☐ 113 Jeff McNeely	.05	.02	.01
☐ 114 Tom Bolton	.05	.02	.01
☐ 115 Greg Blosser	.05	.02	.01
☐ 116 Mike Greenwell	.10	.05	.01
☐ 117 Phil Plantier	.15	.07	.02
☐ 118 Roger Clemens	.15	.07	.02
☐ 119 John Marzano	.05	.02	.01
☐ 120 Jody Reed	.05	.02	.01
☐ 121 Scott Taylor	.05	.02	.01
☐ 122 Jack Clark	.08	.04	.01
☐ 123 Derek Livernois	.05	.02	.01
☐ 124 Tony Pena	.05	.02	.01
☐ 125 Tom Brunansky	.05	.02	.01
☐ 126 Carlos Quintana	.05	.02	.01
☐ 127 Tim Naehring	.05	.02	.01
☐ 128 Matt Young	.05	.02	.01
☐ 129 Wade Boggs	.15	.07	.02
☐ 130 Kevin Morton	.05	.02	.01
☐ 131 Pete Incaviglia	.05	.02	.01
☐ 132 Rob Deer	.05	.02	.01
☐ 133 Bill Gullickson	.05	.02	.01
☐ 134 Rico Brogna	.08	.04	.01
☐ 135 Lloyd Moseby	.05	.02	.01
☐ 136 Cecil Fielder	.15	.07	.02
☐ 137 Tony Phillips	.10	.05	.01
☐ 138 Mark Leiter	.05	.02	.01
☐ 139 John Cerutti	.05	.02	.01
☐ 140 Mickey Tettleton	.08	.04	.01
☐ 141 Milt Cuyler	.05	.02	.01
☐ 142 Greg Gohr	.05	.02	.01
☐ 143 Tony Bernazard	.05	.02	.01
☐ 144 Dan Gakeler	.05	.02	.01
☐ 145 Travis Fryman	.20	.09	.03
☐ 146 Dan Petry	.05	.02	.01
☐ 147 Scott Aldred	.05	.02	.01
☐ 148 John DeSilva	.05	.02	.01
☐ 149 Rusty Meacham	.05	.02	.01
☐ 150 Lou Whitaker	.10	.05	.01
☐ 151 Dave Haas	.05	.02	.01
☐ 152 Luis de los Santos	.05	.02	.01
☐ 153 Ivan Cruz	.05	.02	.01
☐ 154 Alan Trammell	.10	.05	.01
☐ 155 Pat Kelly	.08	.04	.01
☐ 156 Carl Everett	.25	.11	.03
☐ 157 Greg Cadaret	.05	.02	.01
☐ 158 Kevin Maas	.05	.02	.01
☐ 159 Jeff Johnson	.05	.02	.01
☐ 160 Willie Smith	.05	.02	.01
☐ 161 Gerald Williams	.05	.02	.01
☐ 162 Mike Humphreys	.05	.02	.01
☐ 163 Alvaro Espinoza	.05	.02	.01
☐ 164 Matt Nokes	.05	.02	.01
☐ 165 Wade Taylor	.05	.02	.01
☐ 166 Roberto Kelly	.08	.04	.01
☐ 167 John Habyan	.05	.02	.01
☐ 168 Steve Farr	.05	.02	.01
☐ 169 Jesse Barfield	.05	.02	.01
☐ 170 Steve Sax	.05	.02	.01
☐ 171 Jim Leyritz	.05	.02	.01
☐ 172 Robert Eenhoorn	.05	.02	.01
☐ 173 Bernie Williams	.10	.05	.01
☐ 174 Scott Lusader	.05	.02	.01
☐ 175 Torey Lovullo	.05	.02	.01
☐ 176 Chuck Cary	.05	.02	.01
☐ 177 Scott Sanderson	.05	.02	.01
☐ 178 Don Mattingly	.40	.18	.05
☐ 179 Mel Hall	.05	.02	.01
☐ 180 Juan Gonzalez	.50	.23	.06
Minor League MVP			
☐ 181 Hensley Meulens	.05	.02	.01
Minor League MVP			
☐ 182 Jose Offerman	.08	.04	.01
Minor League MVP			
☐ 183 Jeff Bagwell	2.00	.90	.25
Minor League MVP			
☐ 184 Jeff Conine	.60	.25	.07
Minor League MVP			
☐ 185 Henry Rodriguez	.05	.02	.01
Minor League MVP			
☐ 186 Jimmie Reese CO.	.15	.07	.02
☐ 187 Kyle Abbott	.05	.02	.01
☐ 188 Lance Parrish	.08	.04	.01
☐ 189 Rafael Montalvo	.05	.02	.01
☐ 190 Floyd Bannister	.05	.02	.01
☐ 191 Dick Schofield	.05	.02	.01
☐ 192 Scott Lewis	.05	.02	.01
☐ 193 Jeff D. Robinson	.05	.02	.01
☐ 194 Kent Anderson	.05	.02	.01
☐ 195 Wally Joyner	.10	.05	.01
☐ 196 Chuck Finley	.08	.04	.01
☐ 197 Luis Sojo	.05	.02	.01
☐ 198 Jeff Richardson	.05	.02	.01
☐ 199 Dave Parker	.08	.04	.01
☐ 200 Jim Abbott	.10	.05	.01
☐ 201 Junior Felix	.05	.02	.01
☐ 202 Mark Langston	.10	.05	.01
☐ 203 Tim Salmon	1.50	.70	.19
☐ 204 Cliff Young	.05	.02	.01
☐ 205 Scott Bailes	.05	.02	.01
☐ 206 Bobby Rose	.05	.02	.01
☐ 207 Gary Gaetti	.05	.02	.01
☐ 208 Ruben Amaro	.05	.02	.01
☐ 209 Luis Polonia	.05	.02	.01
☐ 210 Dave Winfield	.15	.07	.02
☐ 211 Bryan Harvey	.05	.02	.01
☐ 212 Mike Moore	.05	.02	.01
☐ 213 Rickey Henderson	.15	.07	.02
☐ 214 Steve Chitren	.05	.02	.01
☐ 215 Bob Welch	.05	.02	.01
☐ 216 Terry Steinbach	.08	.04	.01
☐ 217 Earnest Riles	.05	.02	.01
☐ 218 Todd Van Poppel	.08	.04	.01
☐ 219 Mike Gallego	.05	.02	.01
☐ 220 Curt Young	.05	.02	.01
☐ 221 Todd Burns	.05	.02	.01
☐ 222 Vance Law	.05	.02	.01
☐ 223 Eric Show	.05	.02	.01
☐ 224 Don Peters	.05	.02	.01
☐ 225 Dave Stewart	.10	.05	.01
☐ 226 Dave Henderson	.05	.02	.01
☐ 227 Jose Canseco	.20	.09	.03
☐ 228 Walt Weiss	.05	.02	.01
☐ 229 Dann Howitt	.05	.02	.01
☐ 230 Willie Wilson	.05	.02	.01
☐ 231 Harold Baines	.10	.05	.01
☐ 232 Scott Hemond	.05	.02	.01
☐ 233 Joe Slusarski	.05	.02	.01
☐ 234 Mark McGwire	.15	.07	.02
☐ 235 Kirk Dressendorfer	.05	.02	.01
☐ 236 Craig Paquette	.05	.02	.01
☐ 237 Dennis Eckersley	.10	.05	.01
☐ 238 Dana Allison	.05	.02	.01
☐ 239 Scott Bradley	.05	.02	.01
☐ 240 Brian Holman	.05	.02	.01
☐ 241 Mike Schooler	.05	.02	.01
☐ 242 Rich DeLucia	.05	.02	.01
☐ 243 Edgar Martinez	.15	.07	.02
☐ 244 Henry Cotto	.05	.02	.01
☐ 245 Omar Vizquel	.05	.02	.01
☐ 246 Ken Griffey Jr.	1.50	.70	.19

(See also 255)
☐ 247 Jay Buhner	.15	.07	.02
☐ 248 Bill Krueger	.05	.02	.01
☐ 249 Dave Fleming	.05	.02	.01
☐ 250 Patrick Lennon	.05	.02	.01
☐ 251 Dave Valle	.05	.02	.01
☐ 252 Harold Reynolds	.05	.02	.01
☐ 253 Randy Johnson	.25	.11	.03
☐ 254 Scott Bankhead	.05	.02	.01
☐ 255 Ken Griffey Sr. UER	.08	.04	.01

(Card number is 246)
☐ 256 Greg Briley	.05	.02	.01
☐ 257 Tino Martinez	.10	.05	.01
☐ 258 Alvin Davis	.05	.02	.01
☐ 259 Pete O'Brien	.05	.02	.01
☐ 260 Erik Hanson	.05	.02	.01
☐ 261 Bret Boone	.50	.23	.06
☐ 262 Roger Salkeld	.05	.02	.01
☐ 263 Dave Burba	.05	.02	.01
☐ 264 Kerry Woodson	.05	.02	.01
☐ 265 Julio Franco	.08	.04	.01
☐ 266 Dan Peltier	.05	.02	.01
☐ 267 Jeff Russell	.05	.02	.01
☐ 268 Steve Buechele	.05	.02	.01
☐ 269 Donald Harris	.05	.02	.01
☐ 270 Robb Nen	.05	.02	.01
☐ 271 Rich Gossage	.08	.04	.01
☐ 272 Ivan Rodriguez	.50	.23	.06
☐ 273 Jeff Huson	.05	.02	.01
☐ 274 Kevin Brown	.08	.04	.01
☐ 275 Dan Smith	.05	.02	.01
☐ 276 Gary Pettis	.05	.02	.01
☐ 277 Jack Daugherty	.05	.02	.01
☐ 278 Mike Jeffcoat	.05	.02	.01
☐ 279 Brad Arnsberg	.05	.02	.01
☐ 280 Nolan Ryan	.75	.35	.09
☐ 281 Eric McCray	.05	.02	.01
☐ 282 Scott Chiamparino	.05	.02	.01
☐ 283 Ruben Sierra	.15	.07	.02
☐ 284 Geno Petralli	.05	.02	.01
☐ 285 Monty Fariss	.05	.02	.01
☐ 286 Rafael Palmeiro	.15	.07	.02
☐ 287 Bobby Witt	.05	.02	.01
☐ 288 Dean Palmer UER	.08	.04	.01

(Photo actually
Dan Peltier)
☐ 289 Tony Scruggs	.05	.02	.01
☐ 290 Kenny Rogers	.05	.02	.01
☐ 291 Bret Saberhagen	.10	.05	.01
☐ 292 Brian McRae	.30	.14	.04
☐ 293 Storm Davis	.05	.02	.01
☐ 294 Danny Tartabull	.08	.04	.01
☐ 295 David Howard	.05	.02	.01
☐ 296 Mike Boddicker	.05	.02	.01
☐ 297 Joel Johnston	.05	.02	.01
☐ 298 Tim Spehr	.05	.02	.01
☐ 299 Hector Wagner	.05	.02	.01
☐ 300 George Brett	.40	.18	.05
☐ 301 Mike Macfarlane	.05	.02	.01
☐ 302 Kirk Gibson	.10	.05	.01
☐ 303 Harvey Pulliam	.05	.02	.01
☐ 304 Jim Eisenreich	.05	.02	.01
☐ 305 Kevin Seitzer	.05	.02	.01
☐ 306 Mark Davis	.05	.02	.01
☐ 307 Kurt Stillwell	.05	.02	.01
☐ 308 Jeff Montgomery	.08	.04	.01
☐ 309 Kevin Appier	.08	.04	.01
☐ 310 Bob Hamelin	.08	.04	.01
☐ 311 Tom Gordon	.08	.04	.01
☐ 312 Kerwin Moore	.05	.02	.01
☐ 313 Hugh Walker	.05	.02	.01

☐ 314 Terry Shumpert	.05	.02	.01
☐ 315 Warren Cromartie	.05	.02	.01
☐ 316 Gary Thurman	.05	.02	.01
☐ 317 Steve Bedrosian	.05	.02	.01
☐ 318 Danny Gladden	.05	.02	.01
☐ 319 Jack Morris	.10	.05	.01
☐ 320 Kirby Puckett	.30	.14	.04
☐ 321 Kent Hrbek	.08	.04	.01
☐ 322 Kevin Tapani	.08	.04	.01
☐ 323 Denny Neagle	.20	.09	.03
☐ 324 Rich Garces	.05	.02	.01
☐ 325 Larry Casian	.05	.02	.01
☐ 326 Shane Mack	.05	.02	.01
☐ 327 Allan Anderson	.05	.02	.01
☐ 328 Junior Ortiz	.05	.02	.01
☐ 329 Paul Abbott	.05	.02	.01
☐ 330 Chuck Knoblauch	.25	.11	.03
☐ 331 Chili Davis	.10	.05	.01
☐ 332 Todd Ritchie	.05	.02	.01
☐ 333 Brian Harper	.05	.02	.01
☐ 334 Rick Aguilera	.08	.04	.01
☐ 335 Scott Erickson	.25	.11	.03
☐ 336 Pedro Munoz	.08	.04	.01
☐ 337 Scott Leius	.05	.02	.01
☐ 338 Greg Gagne	.05	.02	.01
☐ 339 Mike Pagliarulo	.05	.02	.01
☐ 340 Terry Leach	.05	.02	.01
☐ 341 Willie Banks	.05	.02	.01
☐ 342 Bobby Thigpen	.05	.02	.01
☐ 343 Roberto Hernandez	.15	.07	.02
☐ 344 Melido Perez	.05	.02	.01
☐ 345 Carlton Fisk	.10	.05	.01
☐ 346 Norberto Martin	.05	.02	.01
☐ 347 Johnny Ruffin	.05	.02	.01
☐ 348 Jeff Carter	.05	.02	.01
☐ 349 Lance Johnson	.05	.02	.01
☐ 350 Sammy Sosa	.25	.11	.03
☐ 351 Alex Fernandez	.10	.05	.01
☐ 352 Jack McDowell	.15	.07	.02
☐ 353 Bob Wickman	.05	.02	.01
☐ 354 Wilson Alvarez	.08	.04	.01
☐ 355 Charlie Hough	.08	.04	.01
☐ 356 Ozzie Guillen	.08	.04	.01
☐ 357 Cory Snyder	.05	.02	.01
☐ 358 Robin Ventura	.10	.05	.01
☐ 359 Scott Fletcher	.05	.02	.01
☐ 360 Cesar Bernhardt	.05	.02	.01
☐ 361 Dan Pasqua	.05	.02	.01
☐ 362 Tim Raines	.15	.07	.02
☐ 363 Brian Drahman	.05	.02	.01
☐ 364 Wayne Edwards	.05	.02	.01
☐ 365 Scott Radinsky	.05	.02	.01
☐ 366 Frank Thomas	2.00	.90	.25
☐ 367 Cecil Fielder SLUG	.10	.05	.01
☐ 368 Julio Franco SLUG	.08	.04	.01
☐ 369 Kelly Gruber SLUG	.05	.02	.01
☐ 370 Alan Trammell SLUG	.10	.05	.01
☐ 371 Rickey Henderson SLUG	.10	.05	.01
☐ 372 Jose Canseco SLUG	.10	.05	.01
☐ 373 Ellis Burks SLUG	.08	.04	.01
☐ 374 Lance Parrish SLUG	.05	.02	.01
☐ 375 Dave Parker SLUG	.05	.02	.01
☐ 376 Eddie Murray SLUG	.10	.05	.01
☐ 377 Ryne Sandberg SLUG	.15	.07	.02
☐ 378 Matt Williams SLUG	.10	.05	.01
☐ 379 Barry Larkin SLUG	.10	.05	.01
☐ 380 Barry Bonds SLUG	.15	.07	.02
☐ 381 Bobby Bonilla SLUG	.10	.05	.01
☐ 382 Darryl Strawberry SLUG	.08	.04	.01
☐ 383 Benny Santiago SLUG	.05	.02	.01
☐ 384 Don Robinson SLUG	.05	.02	.01

☐ 385	Paul Coleman	.05	.02	.01
☐ 386	Milt Thompson	.05	.02	.01
☐ 387	Lee Smith	.10	.05	.01
☐ 388	Ray Lankford	.10	.05	.01
☐ 389	Tom Pagnozzi	.05	.02	.01
☐ 390	Ken Hill	.10	.05	.01
☐ 391	Jamie Moyer	.05	.02	.01
☐ 392	Greg Carmona	.05	.02	.01
☐ 393	John Ericks	.05	.02	.01
☐ 394	Bob Tewksbury	.05	.02	.01
☐ 395	Jose Oquendo	.05	.02	.01
☐ 396	Rheal Cormier	.05	.02	.01
☐ 397	Mike Milchin	.05	.02	.01
☐ 398	Ozzie Smith	.20	.09	.03
☐ 399	Aaron Holbert	.05	.02	.01
☐ 400	Jose DeLeon	.05	.02	.01
☐ 401	Felix Jose	.05	.02	.01
☐ 402	Juan Agosto	.05	.02	.01
☐ 403	Pedro Guerrero	.08	.04	.01
☐ 404	Todd Zeile	.08	.04	.01
☐ 405	Gerald Perry	.05	.02	.01
☐ 406	Donovan Osborne UER	.05	.02	.01
	(Card number is 410)			
☐ 407	Bryn Smith	.05	.02	.01
☐ 408	Bernard Gilkey	.08	.04	.01
☐ 409	Rex Hudler	.05	.02	.01
☐ 410	Thomson/Branca Shot	.15	.07	.02
	Bobby Thomson			
	Ralph Branca			
	(See also 406)			
☐ 411	Lance Dickson	.05	.02	.01
☐ 412	Danny Jackson	.05	.02	.01
☐ 413	Jerome Walton	.05	.02	.01
☐ 414	Sean Cheetham	.05	.02	.01
☐ 415	Joe Girardi	.05	.02	.01
☐ 416	Ryne Sandberg	.30	.14	.04
☐ 417	Mike Harkey	.05	.02	.01
☐ 418	George Bell	.05	.02	.01
☐ 419	Rick Wilkins	.05	.02	.01
☐ 420	Earl Cunningham	.05	.02	.01
☐ 421	Heathcliff Slocumb	.15	.07	.02
☐ 422	Mike Bielecki	.05	.02	.01
☐ 423	Jessie Hollins	.05	.02	.01
☐ 424	Shawon Dunston	.05	.02	.01
☐ 425	Dave Smith	.05	.02	.01
☐ 426	Greg Maddux	.60	.25	.07
☐ 427	Jose Vizcaino	.05	.02	.01
☐ 428	Luis Salazar	.05	.02	.01
☐ 429	Andre Dawson	.10	.05	.01
☐ 430	Rick Sutcliffe	.08	.04	.01
☐ 431	Paul Assenmacher	.05	.02	.01
☐ 432	Erik Pappas	.05	.02	.01
☐ 433	Mark Grace	.15	.07	.02
☐ 434	Dennis Martinez	.08	.04	.01
☐ 435	Marquis Grissom	.20	.09	.03
☐ 436	Wil Cordero	.40	.18	.05
☐ 437	Tim Wallach	.05	.02	.01
☐ 438	Brian Barnes	.05	.02	.01
☐ 439	Barry Jones	.05	.02	.01
☐ 440	Ivan Calderon	.05	.02	.01
☐ 441	Stan Spencer	.05	.02	.01
☐ 442	Larry Walker	.25	.11	.03
☐ 443	Chris Haney	.05	.02	.01
☐ 444	Hector Rivera	.05	.02	.01
☐ 445	Delino DeShields	.08	.04	.01
☐ 446	Andres Galarraga	.15	.07	.02
☐ 447	Gilberto Reyes	.05	.02	.01
☐ 448	Willie Greene	.05	.02	.01
☐ 449	Greg Colbrunn	.20	.09	.03
☐ 450	Rondell White	1.00	.45	.12
☐ 451	Steve Frey	.05	.02	.01
☐ 452	Shane Andrews	.08	.04	.01
☐ 453	Mike Fitzgerald	.05	.02	.01
☐ 454	Spike Owen	.05	.02	.01
☐ 455	Dave Martinez	.05	.02	.01
☐ 456	Dennis Boyd	.05	.02	.01
☐ 457	Eric Bullock	.05	.02	.01
☐ 458	Reid Cornelius	.05	.02	.01
☐ 459	Chris Nabholz	.05	.02	.01
☐ 460	David Cone	.10	.05	.01
☐ 461	Hubie Brooks	.05	.02	.01
☐ 462	Sid Fernandez	.08	.04	.01
☐ 463	Doug Simons	.05	.02	.01
☐ 464	Howard Johnson	.05	.02	.01
☐ 465	Chris Donnels	.05	.02	.01
☐ 466	Anthony Young	.05	.02	.01
☐ 467	Todd Hundley	.08	.04	.01
☐ 468	Rick Cerone	.05	.02	.01
☐ 469	Kevin Elster	.05	.02	.01
☐ 470	Wally Whitehurst	.05	.02	.01
☐ 471	Vince Coleman	.05	.02	.01
☐ 472	Dwight Gooden	.05	.02	.01
☐ 473	Charlie O'Brien	.05	.02	.01
☐ 474	Jeromy Burnitz	.05	.02	.01
☐ 475	John Franco	.10	.05	.01
☐ 476	Daryl Boston	.05	.02	.01
☐ 477	Frank Viola	.08	.04	.01
☐ 478	D.J. Dozier	.05	.02	.01
☐ 479	Kevin McReynolds	.05	.02	.01
☐ 480	Tom Herr	.05	.02	.01
☐ 481	Gregg Jefferies	.10	.05	.01
☐ 482	Pete Schourek	.40	.18	.05
☐ 483	Ron Darling	.05	.02	.01
☐ 484	Dave Magadan	.05	.02	.01
☐ 485	Andy Ashby	.05	.02	.01
☐ 486	Dale Murphy	.10	.05	.01
☐ 487	Von Hayes	.05	.02	.01
☐ 488	Kim Batiste	.05	.02	.01
☐ 489	Tony Longmire	.05	.02	.01
☐ 490	Wally Backman	.05	.02	.01
☐ 491	Jeff Jackson	.05	.02	.01
☐ 492	Mickey Morandini	.05	.02	.01
☐ 493	Darrel Akerfelds	.05	.02	.01
☐ 494	Ricky Jordan	.05	.02	.01
☐ 495	Randy Ready	.05	.02	.01
☐ 496	Darrin Fletcher	.05	.02	.01
☐ 497	Chuck Malone	.05	.02	.01
☐ 498	Pat Combs	.05	.02	.01
☐ 499	Dickie Thon	.05	.02	.01
☐ 500	Roger McDowell	.05	.02	.01
☐ 501	Len Dykstra	.10	.05	.01
☐ 502	Joe Boever	.05	.02	.01
☐ 503	John Kruk	.10	.05	.01
☐ 504	Terry Mulholland	.05	.02	.01
☐ 505	Wes Chamberlain	.05	.02	.01
☐ 506	Mike Lieberthal	.08	.04	.01
☐ 507	Darren Daulton	.05	.02	.01
☐ 508	Charlie Hayes	.08	.04	.01
☐ 509	John Smiley	.05	.02	.01
☐ 510	Gary Varsho	.05	.02	.01
☐ 511	Curt Wilkerson	.05	.02	.01
☐ 512	Orlando Merced	.15	.07	.02
☐ 513	Barry Bonds	.30	.14	.04
☐ 514	Mike LaValliere	.05	.02	.01
☐ 515	Doug Drabek	.08	.04	.01
☐ 516	Gary Redus	.05	.02	.01
☐ 517	William Pennyfeather	.05	.02	.01
☐ 518	Randy Tomlin	.05	.02	.01
☐ 519	Mike Zimmerman	.05	.02	.01
☐ 520	Jeff King	.05	.02	.01
☐ 521	Kurt Miller	.05	.02	.01
☐ 522	Jay Bell	.08	.04	.01

☐ 523 Bill Landrum	.05	.02	.01
☐ 524 Zane Smith	.05	.02	.01
☐ 525 Bobby Bonilla	.15	.07	.02
☐ 526 Bob Walk	.05	.02	.01
☐ 527 Austin Manahan	.05	.02	.01
☐ 528 Joe Ausanio	.05	.02	.01
☐ 529 Andy Van Slyke	.08	.04	.01
☐ 530 Jose Lind	.05	.02	.01
☐ 531 Carlos Garcia	.15	.07	.02
☐ 532 Don Slaught	.05	.02	.01
☐ 533 Gen.Colin Powell	.75	.35	.09
☐ 534 Frank Bolick	.05	.02	.01
☐ 535 Gary Scott	.05	.02	.01
☐ 536 Nikco Riesgo	.05	.02	.01
☐ 537 Reggie Sanders	.60	.25	.07
☐ 538 Tim Howard	.05	.02	.01
☐ 539 Ryan Bowen	.05	.02	.01
☐ 540 Eric Anthony	.05	.02	.01
☐ 541 Jim Deshaies	.05	.02	.01
☐ 542 Tom Nevers	.05	.02	.01
☐ 543 Ken Caminiti	.10	.05	.01
☐ 544 Karl Rhodes	.05	.02	.01
☐ 545 Xavier Hernandez	.05	.02	.01
☐ 546 Mike Scott	.05	.02	.01
☐ 547 Jeff Juden	.05	.02	.01
☐ 548 Darryl Kile	.05	.02	.01
☐ 549 Willie Ansley	.05	.02	.01
☐ 550 Luis Gonzalez	.15	.07	.02
☐ 551 Mike Simms	.05	.02	.01
☐ 552 Mark Portugal	.05	.02	.01
☐ 553 Jimmy Jones	.05	.02	.01
☐ 554 Jim Clancy	.05	.02	.01
☐ 555 Pete Harnisch	.05	.02	.01
☐ 556 Craig Biggio	.10	.05	.01
☐ 557 Eric Yelding	.05	.02	.01
☐ 558 Dave Rohde	.05	.02	.01
☐ 559 Casey Candaele	.05	.02	.01
☐ 560 Curt Schilling	.05	.02	.01
☐ 561 Steve Finley	.05	.02	.01
☐ 562 Javier Ortiz	.05	.02	.01
☐ 563 Andujar Cedeno	.05	.02	.01
☐ 564 Rafael Ramirez	.05	.02	.01
☐ 565 Kenny Lofton	2.00	.90	.25
☐ 566 Steve Avery	.10	.05	.01
☐ 567 Lonnie Smith	.05	.02	.01
☐ 568 Kent Mercker	.05	.02	.01
☐ 569 Chipper Jones	3.00	1.35	.35
☐ 570 Terry Pendleton	.10	.05	.01
☐ 571 Otis Nixon	.05	.02	.01
☐ 572 Juan Berenguer	.05	.02	.01
☐ 573 Charlie Leibrandt	.05	.02	.01
☐ 574 David Justice	.20	.09	.03
☐ 575 Keith Mitchell	.05	.02	.01
☐ 576 Tom Glavine	.20	.09	.03
☐ 577 Greg Olson	.05	.02	.01
☐ 578 Rafael Belliard	.05	.02	.01
☐ 579 Ben Rivera	.05	.02	.01
☐ 580 John Smoltz	.10	.05	.01
☐ 581 Tyler Houston	.05	.02	.01
☐ 582 Mark Wohlers	.40	.18	.05
☐ 583 Ron Gant	.10	.05	.01
☐ 584 Ramon Caraballo	.05	.02	.01
☐ 585 Sid Bream	.05	.02	.01
☐ 586 Jeff Treadway	.05	.02	.01
☐ 587 Javier Lopez	1.25	.55	.16
☐ 588 Deion Sanders	.25	.11	.03
☐ 589 Mike Heath	.05	.02	.01
☐ 590 Ryan Klesko	1.50	.70	.19
☐ 591 Bob Ojeda	.05	.02	.01
☐ 592 Alfredo Griffin	.05	.02	.01
☐ 593 Raul Mondesi	2.00	.90	.25
☐ 594 Greg Smith	.05	.02	.01
☐ 595 Orel Hershiser	.10	.05	.01
☐ 596 Juan Samuel	.05	.02	.01
☐ 597 Brett Butler	.10	.05	.01
☐ 598 Gary Carter	.10	.05	.01
☐ 599 Stan Javier	.05	.02	.01
☐ 600 Kal Daniels	.05	.02	.01
☐ 601 Jamie McAndrew	.05	.02	.01
☐ 602 Mike Sharperson	.05	.02	.01
☐ 603 Jay Howell	.05	.02	.01
☐ 604 Eric Karros	.60	.25	.07
☐ 605 Tim Belcher	.05	.02	.01
☐ 606 Dan Opperman	.05	.02	.01
☐ 607 Lenny Harris	.05	.02	.01
☐ 608 Tom Goodwin	.08	.04	.01
☐ 609 Darryl Strawberry	.08	.04	.01
☐ 610 Ramon Martinez	.10	.05	.01
☐ 611 Kevin Gross	.05	.02	.01
☐ 612 Zakary Shinall	.05	.02	.01
☐ 613 Mike Scioscia	.05	.02	.01
☐ 614 Eddie Murray	.20	.09	.03
☐ 615 Ronnie Walden	.05	.02	.01
☐ 616 Will Clark	.15	.07	.02
☐ 617 Adam Hyzdu	.05	.02	.01
☐ 618 Matt Williams	.20	.09	.03
☐ 619 Don Robinson	.05	.02	.01
☐ 620 Jeff Brantley	.05	.02	.01
☐ 621 Greg Litton	.05	.02	.01
☐ 622 Steve Decker	.05	.02	.01
☐ 623 Robby Thompson	.05	.02	.01
☐ 624 Mark Leonard	.05	.02	.01
☐ 625 Kevin Bass	.05	.02	.01
☐ 626 Scott Garrelts	.05	.02	.01
☐ 627 Jose Uribe	.05	.02	.01
☐ 628 Eric Gunderson	.05	.02	.01
☐ 629 Steve Hosey	.05	.02	.01
☐ 630 Trevor Wilson	.05	.02	.01
☐ 631 Terry Kennedy	.05	.02	.01
☐ 632 Dave Righetti	.05	.02	.01
☐ 633 Kelly Downs	.05	.02	.01
☐ 634 Johnny Ard	.05	.02	.01
☐ 635 Eric Christopherson	.05	.02	.01
☐ 636 Kevin Mitchell	.08	.04	.01
☐ 637 John Burkett	.08	.04	.01
☐ 638 Kevin Rogers	.05	.02	.01
☐ 639 Bud Black	.05	.02	.01
☐ 640 Willie McGee	.08	.04	.01
☐ 641 Royce Clayton	.08	.04	.01
☐ 642 Tony Fernandez	.05	.02	.01
☐ 643 Ricky Bones	.08	.04	.01
☐ 644 Thomas Howard	.05	.02	.01
☐ 645 Dave Staton	.05	.02	.01
☐ 646 Jim Presley	.05	.02	.01
☐ 647 Tony Gwynn	.30	.14	.04
☐ 648 Marty Barrett	.05	.02	.01
☐ 649 Scott Coolbaugh	.05	.02	.01
☐ 650 Craig Lefferts	.05	.02	.01
☐ 651 Eddie Whitson	.05	.02	.01
☐ 652 Oscar Azocar	.05	.02	.01
☐ 653 Wes Gardner	.05	.02	.01
☐ 654 Bip Roberts	.08	.04	.01
☐ 655 Robbie Beckett	.05	.02	.01
☐ 656 Benito Santiago	.05	.02	.01
☐ 657 Greg W.Harris	.05	.02	.01
☐ 658 Jerald Clark	.05	.02	.01
☐ 659 Fred McGriff	.15	.07	.02
☐ 660 Larry Andersen	.05	.02	.01
☐ 661 Bruce Hurst	.05	.02	.01
☐ 662 Steve Martin UER	.05	.02	.01
Card said he pitched at Waterloo			
He's an outfielder			

☐ 663	Rafael Valdez	.05	.02	.01
☐ 664	Paul Faries	.05	.02	.01
☐ 665	Andy Benes	.08	.04	.01
☐ 666	Randy Myers	.10	.05	.01
☐ 667	Rob Dibble	.08	.04	.01
☐ 668	Glenn Sutko	.05	.02	.01
☐ 669	Glenn Braggs	.05	.02	.01
☐ 670	Billy Hatcher	.05	.02	.01
☐ 671	Joe Oliver	.05	.02	.01
☐ 672	Freddy Benavides	.05	.02	.01
☐ 673	Barry Larkin	.15	.07	.02
☐ 674	Chris Sabo	.05	.02	.01
☐ 675	Mariano Duncan	.05	.02	.01
☐ 676	Chris Jones	.05	.02	.01
☐ 677	Gino Minutelli	.05	.02	.01
☐ 678	Reggie Jefferson	.08	.04	.01
☐ 679	Jack Armstrong	.05	.02	.01
☐ 680	Chris Hammond	.05	.02	.01
☐ 681	Jose Rijo	.08	.04	.01
☐ 682	Bill Doran	.05	.02	.01
☐ 683	Terry Lee	.05	.02	.01
☐ 684	Tom Browning	.05	.02	.01
☐ 685	Paul O'Neill	.10	.05	.01
☐ 686	Eric Davis	.08	.04	.01
☐ 687	Dan Wilson	.05	.02	.01
☐ 688	Ted Power	.05	.02	.01
☐ 689	Tim Layana	.05	.02	.01
☐ 690	Norm Charlton	.05	.02	.01
☐ 691	Hal Morris	.08	.04	.01
☐ 692	Rickey Henderson	.10	.05	.01
☐ 693	Sam Militello	.05	.02	.01
	Minor League MVP			
☐ 694	Matt Mieske	.10	.05	.01
	Minor League MVP			
☐ 695	Paul Russo	.05	.02	.01
	Minor League MVP			
☐ 696	Domingo Mota	.05	.02	.01
	Minor League MVP			
☐ 697	Todd Guggiana	.05	.02	.01
	Minor League MVP			
☐ 698	Marc Newfield	.20	.09	.03
	Minor League MVP			
☐ 699	Checklist 1-122	.05	.02	.01
☐ 700	Checklist 123-244	.05	.02	.01
☐ 701	Checklist 245-366	.05	.02	.01
☐ 702	Checklist 367-471	.05	.02	.01
☐ 703	Checklist 472-593	.05	.02	.01
☐ 704	Checklist 594-704	.05	.02	.01

1992 Bowman

The cards in this 705-card set measure the standard size (2 1/2" by 3 1/2") and feature

posed and action color player photos on a UV-coated white card face. A gradated orange bar accented with black diagonal stripes carries the player's name at the bottom right corner. The backs display close-up color photos and biography on a burlap-textured background. Below the photo, statistical information appears in a yellow-and-white grid with the player's name in a red bar at the top of the grid. Interspersed throughout the set are 45 special cards with an identical front design except for a textured gold-foil border. Each foil card has an extremely slight variation in that the photos are cropped differently. There is no additional value to either version. The foil cards were inserted one per wax pack and two per jumbo (23 regular cards) pack. These foil cards feature past and present Team USA players and minor league POY Award winners. Their backs have the same burlap background but display one of three emblems: 1) U.S. Baseball Federation; 2) Topps Team USA 1992; or 3) National Association of Professional Baseball Leagues. The player's name and biography are shown in a blue-and-white box above these emblems. Some of the regular and special cards picture players in civilian clothing who are still in the farm system. The cards are numbered on the back. Rookie Cards in this set include Billy Ashley, Jason Bere, Carlos Delgado, Cliff Floyd, Alex Gonzalez, Bobby Jones, Pat Listach, David Nied, Melvin Nieves, Alex Ochoa, Jose Oliva, J.R. Phillips, Mike Piazza, Manny Ramirez, Scott Ruffcorn, Aaron Sele, Brien Taylor, Salomon Torres, Michael Tucker, Allen Watson, and Nigel Wilson.

	MINT	NRMT	EXC
COMPLETE SET (705)	325.00	145.00	40.00
COMMON CARD (1-705)	.15	.07	.02

☐ 1	Ivan Rodriguez	1.00	.45	.12
☐ 2	Kirk McCaskill	.15	.07	.02
☐ 3	Scott Livingstone	.15	.07	.02
☐ 4	Salomon Torres	.50	.23	.06
☐ 5	Carlos Hernandez	.15	.07	.02
☐ 6	Dave Hollins	.15	.07	.02
☐ 7	Scott Fletcher	.15	.07	.02
☐ 8	Jorge Fabregas	.50	.23	.06
☐ 9	Andujar Cedeno	.15	.07	.02
☐ 10	Howard Johnson	.15	.07	.02
☐ 11	Trevor Hoffman	1.00	.45	.12
☐ 12	Roberto Kelly	.20	.09	.03
☐ 13	Gregg Jefferies	.30	.14	.04
☐ 14	Marquis Grissom	1.00	.45	.12
☐ 15	Mike Ignasiak	.15	.07	.02
☐ 16	Jack Morris	.20	.09	.03
☐ 17	William Pennyfeather	.15	.07	.02
☐ 18	Todd Stottlemyre	.15	.07	.02
☐ 19	Chito Martinez	.15	.07	.02
☐ 20	Roberto Alomar	1.50	.70	.19
☐ 21	Sam Militello	.15	.07	.02
☐ 22	Hector Fajardo	.15	.07	.02
☐ 23	Paul Quantrill	.15	.07	.02
☐ 24	Chuck Knoblauch	1.25	.55	.16
☐ 25	Reggie Jefferson	.15	.07	.02
☐ 26	Jeremy McGarity	.15	.07	.02

☐ 27	Jerome Walton	.15	.07	.02
☐ 28	Chipper Jones	30.00	13.50	3.70
☐ 29	Brian Barber	.50	.23	.06
☐ 30	Ron Darling	.15	.07	.02
☐ 31	Roberto Petagine	.50	.23	.06
☐ 32	Chuck Finley	.15	.07	.02
☐ 33	Edgar Martinez	.60	.25	.07
☐ 34	Napoleon Robinson	.15	.07	.02
☐ 35	Andy Van Slyke	.20	.09	.03
☐ 36	Bobby Thigpen	.15	.07	.02
☐ 37	Travis Fryman	1.25	.55	.16
☐ 38	Eric Christopherson	.15	.07	.02
☐ 39	Terry Mulholland	.15	.07	.02
☐ 40	Darryl Strawberry	.20	.09	.03
☐ 41	Manny Alexander	.50	.23	.06
☐ 42	Tracy Sanders	.15	.07	.02
☐ 43	Pete Incaviglia	.15	.07	.02
☐ 44	Kim Batiste	.15	.07	.02
☐ 45	Frankie Rodriguez	1.00	.45	.12
☐ 46	Greg Swindell	.15	.07	.02
☐ 47	Delino DeShields	.30	.14	.04
☐ 48	John Ericks	.15	.07	.02
☐ 49	Franklin Stubbs	.15	.07	.02
☐ 50	Tony Gwynn	2.50	1.10	.30
☐ 51	Clifton Garrett	.15	.07	.02
☐ 52	Mike Gardella	.15	.07	.02
☐ 53	Scott Erickson	.15	.07	.02
☐ 54	Gary Caraballo	.15	.07	.02
☐ 55	Jose Oliva	.75	.35	.09
☐ 56	Brook Fordyce	.15	.07	.02
☐ 57	Mark Whiten	.20	.09	.03
☐ 58	Joe Slusarski	.15	.07	.02
☐ 59	J.R. Phillips	.75	.35	.09
☐ 60	Barry Bonds	2.00	.90	.25
☐ 61	Bob Milacki	.15	.07	.02
☐ 62	Keith Mitchell	.15	.07	.02
☐ 63	Angel Miranda	.15	.07	.02
☐ 64	Raul Mondesi	20.00	9.00	2.50
☐ 65	Brian Koelling	.15	.07	.02
☐ 66	Brian McRae	.30	.14	.04
☐ 67	John Patterson	.15	.07	.02
☐ 68	John Wetteland	.15	.07	.02
☐ 69	Wilson Alvarez	.20	.09	.03
☐ 70	Wade Boggs	.60	.25	.07
☐ 71	Darryl Ratliff	.15	.07	.02
☐ 72	Jeff Jackson	.15	.07	.02
☐ 73	Jeremy Hernandez	.15	.07	.02
☐ 74	Darryl Hamilton	.20	.09	.03
☐ 75	Rafael Belliard	.15	.07	.02
☐ 76	Rick Trlicek	.15	.07	.02
☐ 77	Felipe Crespo	.50	.23	.06
☐ 78	Carney Lansford	.20	.09	.03
☐ 79	Ryan Long	.15	.07	.02
☐ 80	Kirby Puckett	2.50	1.10	.30
☐ 81	Earl Cunningham	.15	.07	.02
☐ 82	Pedro Martinez	2.50	1.10	.30
☐ 83	Scott Hatteberg	.15	.07	.02
☐ 84	Juan Gonzalez UER	3.00	1.35	.35
	(65 doubles vs. Tigers)			
☐ 85	Robert Nutting	.15	.07	.02
☐ 86	Calvin Reese	2.00	.90	.25
☐ 87	Dave Silvestri	.15	.07	.02
☐ 88	Scott Ruffcorn	.50	.23	.06
☐ 89	Rick Aguilera	.20	.09	.03
☐ 90	Cecil Fielder	.40	.18	.05
☐ 91	Kirk Dressendorfer	.15	.07	.02
☐ 92	Jerry DiPoto	.15	.07	.02
☐ 93	Mike Felder	.15	.07	.02
☐ 94	Craig Paquette	.20	.09	.03
☐ 95	Elvin Paulino	.15	.07	.02
☐ 96	Donovan Osborne	.15	.07	.02
☐ 97	Hubie Brooks	.15	.07	.02
☐ 98	Derek Lowe	.20	.09	.03
☐ 99	David Zancanaro	.15	.07	.02
☐ 100	Ken Griffey Jr.	12.00	5.50	1.50
☐ 101	Todd Hundley	.15	.07	.02
☐ 102	Mike Trombley	.15	.07	.02
☐ 103	Ricky Gutierrez	.15	.07	.02
☐ 104	Braulio Castillo	.15	.07	.02
☐ 105	Craig Lefferts	.15	.07	.02
☐ 106	Rick Sutcliffe	.20	.09	.03
☐ 107	Dean Palmer	.20	.09	.03
☐ 108	Henry Rodriguez	.20	.09	.03
☐ 109	Mark Clark	.50	.23	.06
☐ 110	Kenny Lofton	12.00	5.50	1.50
☐ 111	Mark Carreon	.15	.07	.02
☐ 112	J.T. Bruett	.15	.07	.02
☐ 113	Gerald Williams	.20	.09	.03
☐ 114	Frank Thomas	12.00	5.50	1.50
☐ 115	Kevin Reimer	.15	.07	.02
☐ 116	Sammy Sosa	1.00	.45	.12
☐ 117	Mickey Tettleton	.20	.09	.03
☐ 118	Reggie Sanders	4.00	1.80	.50
☐ 119	Trevor Wilson	.15	.07	.02
☐ 120	Cliff Brantley	.15	.07	.02
☐ 121	Spike Owen	.15	.07	.02
☐ 122	Jeff Montgomery	.20	.09	.03
☐ 123	Alex Sutherland	.15	.07	.02
☐ 124	Brien Taylor	.50	.23	.06
☐ 125	Brian Williams	.15	.07	.02
☐ 126	Kevin Seitzer	.20	.09	.03
☐ 127	Carlos Delgado	8.00	3.60	1.00
☐ 128	Gary Scott	.15	.07	.02
☐ 129	Scott Cooper	.30	.14	.04
☐ 130	Domingo Jean	.15	.07	.02
☐ 131	Pat Mahomes	.20	.09	.03
☐ 132	Mike Boddicker	.15	.07	.02
☐ 133	Roberto Hernandez	.20	.09	.03
☐ 134	Dave Valle	.15	.07	.02
☐ 135	Kurt Stillwell	.15	.07	.02
☐ 136	Brad Pennington	.15	.07	.02
☐ 137	Jermaine Swinton	.15	.07	.02
☐ 138	Ryan Hawblitzel	.15	.07	.02
☐ 139	Tito Navarro	.15	.07	.02
☐ 140	Sandy Alomar	.20	.09	.03
☐ 141	Todd Benzinger	.15	.07	.02
☐ 142	Danny Jackson	.15	.07	.02
☐ 143	Melvin Nieves	2.00	.90	.25
☐ 144	Jim Campanis	.15	.07	.02
☐ 145	Luis Gonzalez	.20	.09	.03
☐ 146	Dave Doorneweerd	.15	.07	.02
☐ 147	Charlie Hayes	.20	.09	.03
☐ 148	Greg Maddux	6.00	2.70	.75
☐ 149	Brian Harper	.15	.07	.02
☐ 150	Brent Miller	.15	.07	.02
☐ 151	Shawn Estes	.50	.23	.06
☐ 152	Mike Williams	.15	.07	.02
☐ 153	Charlie Hough	.20	.09	.03
☐ 154	Randy Myers	.30	.14	.04
☐ 155	Kevin Young	.15	.07	.02
☐ 156	Rick Wilkins	.15	.07	.02
☐ 157	Terry Shumpert	.15	.07	.02
☐ 158	Steve Karsay	.20	.09	.03
☐ 159	Gary DiSarcina	.15	.07	.02
☐ 160	Deion Sanders	1.50	.70	.19
☐ 161	Tom Browning	.15	.07	.02
☐ 162	Dickie Thon	.15	.07	.02
☐ 163	Luis Mercedes	.15	.07	.02
☐ 164	Riccardo Ingram	.15	.07	.02
☐ 165	Tavo Alvarez	.20	.09	.03
☐ 166	Rickey Henderson	.60	.25	.07
☐ 167	Jaime Navarro	.15	.07	.02

☐ 168	Billy Ashley	3.00	1.35	.35
☐ 169	Phil Dauphin	.15	.07	.02
☐ 170	Ivan Cruz	.15	.07	.02
☐ 171	Harold Baines	.30	.14	.04
☐ 172	Bryan Harvey	.15	.07	.02
☐ 173	Alex Cole	.15	.07	.02
☐ 174	Curtis Shaw	.20	.09	.03
☐ 175	Matt Williams	1.50	.70	.19
☐ 176	Felix Jose	.15	.07	.02
☐ 177	Sam Horn	.15	.07	.02
☐ 178	Randy Johnson	2.00	.90	.25
☐ 179	Ivan Calderon	.15	.07	.02
☐ 180	Steve Avery	.50	.23	.06
☐ 181	William Suero	.15	.07	.02
☐ 182	Bill Swift	.15	.07	.02
☐ 183	Howard Battle	.50	.23	.06
☐ 184	Ruben Amaro	.15	.07	.02
☐ 185	Jim Abbott	.30	.14	.04
☐ 186	Mike Fitzgerald	.15	.07	.02
☐ 187	Bruce Hurst	.15	.07	.02
☐ 188	Jeff Juden	.15	.07	.02
☐ 189	Jeromy Burnitz	.15	.07	.02
☐ 190	Dave Burba	.15	.07	.02
☐ 191	Kevin Brown	.20	.09	.03
☐ 192	Patrick Lennon	.15	.07	.02
☐ 193	Jeff McNeely	.15	.07	.02
☐ 194	Wil Cordero	2.00	.90	.25
☐ 195	Chili Davis	.30	.14	.04
☐ 196	Milt Cuyler	.15	.07	.02
☐ 197	Von Hayes	.15	.07	.02
☐ 198	Todd Revenig	.15	.07	.02
☐ 199	Joel Johnston	.15	.07	.02
☐ 200	Jeff Bagwell	4.00	1.80	.50
☐ 201	Alex Fernandez	.30	.14	.04
☐ 202	Todd Jones	.50	.23	.06
☐ 203	Charles Nagy	.20	.09	.03
☐ 204	Tim Raines	.40	.18	.05
☐ 205	Kevin Maas	.15	.07	.02
☐ 206	Julio Franco	.20	.09	.03
☐ 207	Randy Velarde	.15	.07	.02
☐ 208	Lance Johnson	.15	.07	.02
☐ 209	Scott Leius	.15	.07	.02
☐ 210	Derek Lee	.15	.07	.02
☐ 211	Joe Sondrini	.15	.07	.02
☐ 212	Royce Clayton	.20	.09	.03
☐ 213	Chris George	.15	.07	.02
☐ 214	Gary Sheffield	.30	.14	.04
☐ 215	Mark Gubicza	.15	.07	.02
☐ 216	Mike Moore	.15	.07	.02
☐ 217	Rick Huisman	.15	.07	.02
☐ 218	Jeff Russell	.15	.07	.02
☐ 219	D.J. Dozier	.15	.07	.02
☐ 220	Dave Martinez	.15	.07	.02
☐ 221	Alan Newman	.15	.07	.02
☐ 222	Nolan Ryan	6.00	2.70	.75
☐ 223	Teddy Higuera	.15	.07	.02
☐ 224	Damon Buford	.50	.23	.06
☐ 225	Ruben Sierra	.40	.18	.05
☐ 226	Tom Nevers	.15	.07	.02
☐ 227	Tommy Greene	.15	.07	.02
☐ 228	Nigel Wilson	.50	.23	.06
☐ 229	John DeSilva	.15	.07	.02
☐ 230	Bobby Witt	.15	.07	.02
☐ 231	Greg Cadaret	.15	.07	.02
☐ 232	John Vander Wal	.15	.07	.02
☐ 233	Jack Clark	.20	.09	.03
☐ 234	Bill Doran	.15	.07	.02
☐ 235	Bobby Bonilla	.40	.18	.05
☐ 236	Steve Olin	.15	.07	.02
☐ 237	Derek Bell	1.50	.70	.19
☐ 238	David Cone	.30	.14	.04
☐ 239	Victor Cole	.15	.07	.02
☐ 240	Rod Bolton	.15	.07	.02
☐ 241	Tom Pagnozzi	.15	.07	.02
☐ 242	Rob Dibble	.15	.07	.02
☐ 243	Michael Carter	.15	.07	.02
☐ 244	Don Peters	.15	.07	.02
☐ 245	Mike LaValliere	.15	.07	.02
☐ 246	Joe Perona	.15	.07	.02
☐ 247	Mitch Williams	.20	.09	.03
☐ 248	Jay Buhner	.60	.25	.07
☐ 249	Andy Benes	.20	.09	.03
☐ 250	Alex Ochoa	4.00	1.80	.50
☐ 251	Greg Blosser	.15	.07	.02
☐ 252	Jack Armstrong	.15	.07	.02
☐ 253	Juan Samuel	.15	.07	.02
☐ 254	Terry Pendleton	.30	.14	.04
☐ 255	Ramon Martinez	.20	.09	.03
☐ 256	Rico Brogna	2.00	.90	.25
☐ 257	John Smiley	.15	.07	.02
☐ 258	Carl Everett	2.50	1.10	.30
☐ 259	Tim Salmon	10.00	4.50	1.25
☐ 260	Will Clark	1.00	.45	.12
☐ 261	Ugueth Urbina	.50	.23	.06
☐ 262	Jason Wood	.15	.07	.02
☐ 263	Dave Magadan	.15	.07	.02
☐ 264	Dante Bichette	1.00	.45	.12
☐ 265	Jose DeLeon	.15	.07	.02
☐ 266	Mike Neill	.15	.07	.02
☐ 267	Paul O'Neill	.30	.14	.04
☐ 268	Anthony Young	.15	.07	.02
☐ 269	Greg W. Harris	.15	.07	.02
☐ 270	Todd Van Poppel	.20	.09	.03
☐ 271	Pedro Castellano	.15	.07	.02
☐ 272	Tony Phillips	.30	.14	.04
☐ 273	Mike Gallego	.15	.07	.02
☐ 274	Steve Cooke	.20	.09	.03
☐ 275	Robin Ventura	.30	.14	.04
☐ 276	Kevin Mitchell	.20	.09	.03
☐ 277	Doug Linton	.15	.07	.02
☐ 278	Robert Eenhoorn	.15	.07	.02
☐ 279	Gabe White	.20	.09	.03
☐ 280	Dave Stewart	.20	.09	.03
☐ 281	Mo Sanford	.15	.07	.02
☐ 282	Greg Perschke	.15	.07	.02
☐ 283	Kevin Flora	.15	.07	.02
☐ 284	Jeff Williams	.15	.07	.02
☐ 285	Keith Miller	.15	.07	.02
☐ 286	Andy Ashby	.15	.07	.02
☐ 287	Doug Dascenzo	.15	.07	.02
☐ 288	Eric Karros	4.00	1.80	.50
☐ 289	Glenn Murray	.20	.09	.03
☐ 290	Troy Percival	.50	.23	.06
☐ 291	Orlando Merced	.20	.09	.03
☐ 292	Peter Hoy	.15	.07	.02
☐ 293	Tony Fernandez	.15	.07	.02
☐ 294	Juan Guzman	.20	.09	.03
☐ 295	Jesse Barfield	.15	.07	.02
☐ 296	Sid Fernandez	.20	.09	.03
☐ 297	Scott Cepicky	.15	.07	.02
☐ 298	Garret Anderson	12.00	5.50	1.50
☐ 299	Cal Eldred	.75	.35	.09
☐ 300	Ryne Sandberg	2.00	.90	.25
☐ 301	Jim Gantner	.15	.07	.02
☐ 302	Mariano Rivera	.50	.23	.06
☐ 303	Ron Lockett	.15	.07	.02
☐ 304	Jose Offerman	.15	.07	.02
☐ 305	Denny Martinez	.20	.09	.03
☐ 306	Luis Ortiz	.50	.23	.06
☐ 307	David Howard	.15	.07	.02
☐ 308	Russ Springer	.15	.07	.02
☐ 309	Chris Howard	.15	.07	.02

☐ 310	Kyle Abbott	.15	.07	.02
☐ 311	Aaron Sele	4.00	1.80	.50
☐ 312	David Justice	1.25	.55	.16
☐ 313	Pete O'Brien	.15	.07	.02
☐ 314	Greg Hansell	.15	.07	.02
☐ 315	Dave Winfield	.75	.35	.09
☐ 316	Lance Dickson	.15	.07	.02
☐ 317	Eric King	.15	.07	.02
☐ 318	Vaughn Eshelman	.50	.23	.06
☐ 319	Tim Belcher	.15	.07	.02
☐ 320	Andres Galarraga	.40	.18	.05
☐ 321	Scott Bullett	.15	.07	.02
☐ 322	Doug Strange	.15	.07	.02
☐ 323	Jerald Clark	.15	.07	.02
☐ 324	Dave Righetti	.15	.07	.02
☐ 325	Greg Hibbard	.15	.07	.02
☐ 326	Eric Hillman	.15	.07	.02
☐ 327	Shane Reynolds	1.50	.70	.19
☐ 328	Chris Hammond	.15	.07	.02
☐ 329	Albert Belle	4.00	1.80	.50
☐ 330	Rich Becker	.50	.23	.06
☐ 331	Eddie Williams	.15	.07	.02
☐ 332	Donald Harris	.15	.07	.02
☐ 333	Dave Smith	.15	.07	.02
☐ 334	Steve Fireovid	.15	.07	.02
☐ 335	Steve Buechele	.15	.07	.02
☐ 336	Mike Schooler	.15	.07	.02
☐ 337	Kevin McReynolds	.15	.07	.02
☐ 338	Hensley Meulens	.15	.07	.02
☐ 339	Benji Gil	2.00	.90	.25
☐ 340	Don Mattingly	4.00	1.80	.50
☐ 341	Alvin Davis	.15	.07	.02
☐ 342	Alan Mills	.15	.07	.02
☐ 343	Kelly Downs	.15	.07	.02
☐ 344	Leo Gomez	.15	.07	.02
☐ 345	Tarrik Brock	.15	.07	.02
☐ 346	Ryan Turner	.15	.07	.02
☐ 347	John Smoltz	.30	.14	.04
☐ 348	Bill Sampen	.15	.07	.02
☐ 349	Paul Byrd	.15	.07	.02
☐ 350	Mike Bordick	.15	.07	.02
☐ 351	Jose Lind	.15	.07	.02
☐ 352	David Wells	.15	.07	.02
☐ 353	Barry Larkin	1.00	.45	.12
☐ 354	Bruce Ruffin	.15	.07	.02
☐ 355	Luis Rivera	.15	.07	.02
☐ 356	Sid Bream	.15	.07	.02
☐ 357	Julian Vasquez	.15	.07	.02
☐ 358	Jason Bere	4.00	1.80	.50
☐ 359	Ben McDonald	.20	.09	.03
☐ 360	Scott Stahoviak	.50	.23	.06
☐ 361	Kirt Manwaring	.15	.07	.02
☐ 362	Jeff Johnson	.15	.07	.02
☐ 363	Rob Deer	.15	.07	.02
☐ 364	Tony Pena	.15	.07	.02
☐ 365	Melido Perez	.15	.07	.02
☐ 366	Clay Parker	.15	.07	.02
☐ 367	Dale Sveum	.15	.07	.02
☐ 368	Mike Scioscia	.15	.07	.02
☐ 369	Roger Salkeld	.15	.07	.02
☐ 370	Mike Stanley	.20	.09	.03
☐ 371	Jack McDowell	.30	.14	.04
☐ 372	Tim Wallach	.15	.07	.02
☐ 373	Billy Ripken	.15	.07	.02
☐ 374	Mike Christopher	.15	.07	.02
☐ 375	Paul Molitor	.75	.35	.09
☐ 376	Dave Stieb	.15	.07	.02
☐ 377	Pedro Guerrero	.15	.07	.02
☐ 378	Russ Swan	.15	.07	.02
☐ 379	Bob Ojeda	.15	.07	.02
☐ 380	Donn Pall	.15	.07	.02
☐ 381	Eddie Zosky	.15	.07	.02
☐ 382	Darnell Coles	.15	.07	.02
☐ 383	Tom Smith	.15	.07	.02
☐ 384	Mark McGwire	.75	.35	.09
☐ 385	Gary Carter	.30	.14	.04
☐ 386	Rich Amaral	.15	.07	.02
☐ 387	Alan Embree	.15	.07	.02
☐ 388	Jonathan Hurst	.15	.07	.02
☐ 389	Bobby Jones	4.00	1.80	.50
☐ 390	Rico Rossy	.15	.07	.02
☐ 391	Dan Smith	.15	.07	.02
☐ 392	Terry Steinbach	.15	.07	.02
☐ 393	Jon Farrell	.15	.07	.02
☐ 394	Dave Anderson	.15	.07	.02
☐ 395	Benny Santiago	.15	.07	.02
☐ 396	Mark Wohlers	1.25	.55	.16
☐ 397	Mo Vaughn	4.00	1.80	.50
☐ 398	Randy Kramer	.15	.07	.02
☐ 399	John Jaha	.50	.23	.06
☐ 400	Cal Ripken	8.00	3.60	1.00
☐ 401	Ryan Bowen	.15	.07	.02
☐ 402	Tim McIntosh	.15	.07	.02
☐ 403	Bernard Gilkey	.20	.09	.03
☐ 404	Junior Felix	.15	.07	.02
☐ 405	Cris Colon	.15	.07	.02
☐ 406	Marc Newfield	2.00	.90	.25
☐ 407	Bernie Williams	.30	.14	.04
☐ 408	Jay Howell	.15	.07	.02
☐ 409	Zane Smith	.15	.07	.02
☐ 410	Jeff Shaw	.15	.07	.02
☐ 411	Kerry Woodson	.15	.07	.02
☐ 412	Wes Chamberlain	.15	.07	.02
☐ 413	Dave Mlicki	.15	.07	.02
☐ 414	Benny Distefano	.15	.07	.02
☐ 415	Kevin Rogers	.15	.07	.02
☐ 416	Tim Naehring	.15	.07	.02
☐ 417	Clemente Nunez	1.00	.45	.12
☐ 418	Luis Sojo	.15	.07	.02
☐ 419	Kevin Ritz	.15	.07	.02
☐ 420	Omar Olivares	.15	.07	.02
☐ 421	Manuel Lee	.15	.07	.02
☐ 422	Julio Valera	.15	.07	.02
☐ 423	Omar Vizquel	.15	.07	.02
☐ 424	Darren Burton	.20	.09	.03
☐ 425	Mel Hall	.15	.07	.02
☐ 426	Dennis Powell	.15	.07	.02
☐ 427	Lee Stevens	.15	.07	.02
☐ 428	Glenn Davis	.15	.07	.02
☐ 429	Willie Greene	.20	.09	.03
☐ 430	Kevin Wickander	.15	.07	.02
☐ 431	Dennis Eckersley	.30	.14	.04
☐ 432	Joe Orsulak	.15	.07	.02
☐ 433	Eddie Murray	.75	.35	.09
☐ 434	Matt Stairs	.15	.07	.02
☐ 435	Wally Joyner	.20	.09	.03
☐ 436	Rondell White	8.00	3.60	1.00
☐ 437	Rob Maurer	.15	.07	.02
☐ 438	Joe Redfield	.15	.07	.02
☐ 439	Mark Lewis	.15	.07	.02
☐ 440	Darren Daulton	.30	.14	.04
☐ 441	Mike Henneman	.15	.07	.02
☐ 442	John Cangelosi	.15	.07	.02
☐ 443	Vince Moore	.20	.09	.03
☐ 444	John Wehner	.15	.07	.02
☐ 445	Kent Hrbek	.20	.09	.03
☐ 446	Mark McLemore	.15	.07	.02
☐ 447	Bill Wegman	.15	.07	.02
☐ 448	Robby Thompson	.15	.07	.02
☐ 449	Mark Anthony	.15	.07	.02
☐ 450	Archi Cianfrocco	.15	.07	.02
☐ 451	Johnny Ruffin	.15	.07	.02

□	452	Javier Lopez	10.00	4.50	1.25
□	453	Greg Gohr	.15	.07	.02
□	454	Tim Scott	.15	.07	.02
□	455	Stan Belinda	.15	.07	.02
□	456	Darrin Jackson	.15	.07	.02
□	457	Chris Gardner	.15	.07	.02
□	458	Esteban Beltre	.15	.07	.02
□	459	Phil Plantier	.30	.14	.04
□	460	Jim Thome	12.00	5.50	1.50
□	461	Mike Piazza	40.00	18.00	5.00
□	462	Matt Sinatro	.15	.07	.02
□	463	Scott Servais	.15	.07	.02
□	464	Brian Jordan	2.00	.90	.25
□	465	Doug Drabek	.20	.09	.03
□	466	Carl Willis	.15	.07	.02
□	467	Bret Barberie	.15	.07	.02
□	468	Hal Morris	.20	.09	.03
□	469	Steve Sax	.15	.07	.02
□	470	Jerry Willard	.15	.07	.02
□	471	Dan Wilson	.15	.07	.02
□	472	Chris Hoiles	.20	.09	.03
□	473	Rheal Cormier	.15	.07	.02
□	474	John Morris	.15	.07	.02
□	475	Jeff Reardon	.20	.09	.03
□	476	Mark Leiter	.15	.07	.02
□	477	Tom Gordon	.20	.09	.03
□	478	Kent Bottenfield	.15	.07	.02
□	479	Gene Larkin	.15	.07	.02
□	480	Dwight Gooden	.15	.07	.02
□	481	B.J. Surhoff	.15	.07	.02
□	482	Andy Stankiewicz	.15	.07	.02
□	483	Tino Martinez	.30	.14	.04
□	484	Craig Biggio	.50	.23	.06
□	485	Denny Neagle	.75	.35	.09
□	486	Rusty Meacham	.15	.07	.02
□	487	Kal Daniels	.15	.07	.02
□	488	Dave Henderson	.15	.07	.02
□	489	Tim Costo	.15	.07	.02
□	490	Doug Davis	.15	.07	.02
□	491	Frank Viola	.15	.07	.02
□	492	Cory Snyder	.15	.07	.02
□	493	Chris Martin	.15	.07	.02
□	494	Dion James	.15	.07	.02
□	495	Randy Tomlin	.15	.07	.02
□	496	Greg Vaughn	.20	.09	.03
□	497	Dennis Cook	.15	.07	.02
□	498	Rosario Rodriguez	.15	.07	.02
□	499	Dave Staton	.15	.07	.02
□	500	George Brett	3.00	1.35	.35
□	501	Brian Barnes	.15	.07	.02
□	502	Butch Henry	.15	.07	.02
□	503	Harold Reynolds	.15	.07	.02
□	504	David Nied	.50	.23	.06
□	505	Lee Smith	.30	.14	.04
□	506	Steve Chitren	.15	.07	.02
□	507	Ken Hill	.30	.14	.04
□	508	Robbie Beckett	.15	.07	.02
□	509	Troy Afenir	.15	.07	.02
□	510	Kelly Gruber	.15	.07	.02
□	511	Bret Boone	2.50	1.10	.30
□	512	Jeff Branson	.15	.07	.02
□	513	Mike Jackson	.15	.07	.02
□	514	Pete Harnisch	.15	.07	.02
□	515	Chad Kreuter	.15	.07	.02
□	516	Joe Vitko	.15	.07	.02
□	517	Orel Hershiser	.30	.14	.04
□	518	John Doherty	.15	.07	.02
□	519	Jay Bell	.20	.09	.03
□	520	Mark Langston	.30	.14	.04
□	521	Dann Howitt	.15	.07	.02
□	522	Bobby Reed	.15	.07	.02
□	523	Roberto Munoz	.15	.07	.02
□	524	Todd Ritchie	.20	.09	.03
□	525	Bip Roberts	.15	.07	.02
□	526	Pat Listach	.20	.09	.03
□	527	Scott Brosius	.15	.07	.02
□	528	John Roper	.50	.23	.06
□	529	Phil Hiatt	.20	.09	.03
□	530	Denny Walling	.15	.07	.02
□	531	Carlos Baerga	2.50	1.10	.30
□	532	Manny Ramirez	30.00	13.50	3.70
□	533	Pat Clements UER (Mistakenly numbered 553)	.15	.07	.02
□	534	Ron Gant	.60	.25	.07
□	535	Pat Kelly	.15	.07	.02
□	536	Billy Spiers	.15	.07	.02
□	537	Darren Reed	.15	.07	.02
□	538	Ken Caminiti	.30	.14	.04
□	539	Butch Huskey	2.00	.90	.25
□	540	Matt Nokes	.15	.07	.02
□	541	John Kruk	.30	.14	.04
□	542	John Jaha FOIL	.20	.09	.03
□	543	Justin Thompson	1.00	.45	.12
□	544	Steve Hosey	.15	.07	.02
□	545	Joe Kmak	.15	.07	.02
□	546	John Franco	.30	.14	.04
□	547	Devon White	.20	.09	.03
□	548	Elston Hansen FOIL	.15	.07	.02
□	549	Ryan Klesko	12.00	5.50	1.50
□	550	Danny Tartabull	.20	.09	.03
□	551	Frank Thomas FOIL	15.00	6.75	1.85
□	552	Kevin Tapani	.20	.09	.03
□	553	Willie Banks (See also 533)	.15	.07	.02
□	554	B.J. Wallace FOIL	.20	.09	.03
□	555	Orlando Miller	.50	.23	.06
□	556	Mark Smith	.20	.09	.03
□	557	Tim Wallach FOIL	.30	.14	.04
□	558	Bill Gullickson	.15	.07	.02
□	559	Derek Bell FOIL	.75	.35	.09
□	560	Joe Randa FOIL	.20	.09	.03
□	561	Frank Seminara	.15	.07	.02
□	562	Mark Gardner	.15	.07	.02
□	563	Rick Greene FOIL	.15	.07	.02
□	564	Gary Gaetti	.15	.07	.02
□	565	Ozzie Guillen	.20	.09	.03
□	566	Charles Nagy FOIL	.20	.09	.03
□	567	Mike Milchin	.15	.07	.02
□	568	Ben Shelton	.15	.07	.02
□	569	Chris Roberts FOIL	.20	.09	.03
□	570	Ellis Burks	.20	.09	.03
□	571	Scott Scudder	.15	.07	.02
□	572	Jim Abbott FOIL	.30	.14	.04
□	573	Joe Carter	.75	.35	.09
□	574	Steve Finley	.20	.09	.03
□	575	Jim Olander FOIL	.15	.07	.02
□	576	Carlos Garcia	.20	.09	.03
□	577	Gregg Olson	.15	.07	.02
□	578	Greg Swindell FOIL	.15	.07	.02
□	579	Matt Williams FOIL	1.50	.70	.19
□	580	Mark Grace	.40	.18	.05
□	581	Howard House FOIL	.15	.07	.02
□	582	Luis Polonia	.15	.07	.02
□	583	Erik Hanson	.15	.07	.02
□	584	Salomon Torres FOIL	.20	.09	.03
□	585	Carlton Fisk	.30	.14	.04
□	586	Bret Saberhagen	.30	.14	.04
□	587	Chad McConnell FOIL	.20	.09	.03
□	588	Jimmy Key	.20	.09	.03
□	589	Mike Macfarlane	.15	.07	.02
□	590	Barry Bonds FOIL	2.00	.90	.25
□	591	Jamie McAndrew	.15	.07	.02

☐ 592	Shane Mack	.15	.07	.02
☐ 593	Kerwin Moore	.15	.07	.02
☐ 594	Joe Oliver	.15	.07	.02
☐ 595	Chris Sabo	.15	.07	.02
☐ 596	Alex Gonzalez	4.00	1.80	.50
☐ 597	Brett Butler	.30	.14	.04
☐ 598	Mark Hutton	.15	.07	.02
☐ 599	Andy Benes FOIL	.20	.09	.03
☐ 600	Jose Canseco	1.25	.55	.16
☐ 601	Darryl Kile	.15	.07	.02
☐ 602	Matt Stairs FOIL	.15	.07	.02
☐ 603	Robert Butler FOIL	.20	.09	.03
☐ 604	Willie McGee	.20	.09	.03
☐ 605	Jack McDowell FOIL	.30	.14	.04
☐ 606	Tom Candiotti	.15	.07	.02
☐ 607	Ed Martel	.15	.07	.02
☐ 608	Matt Mieske FOIL	.20	.09	.03
☐ 609	Darrin Fletcher	.15	.07	.02
☐ 610	Rafael Palmeiro	.75	.35	.09
☐ 611	Bill Swift FOIL	.15	.07	.02
☐ 612	Mike Mussina	1.50	.70	.19
☐ 613	Vince Coleman	.15	.07	.02
☐ 614	Scott Cepicky FOIL UER (Bats: LEFLT)	.15	.07	.02
☐ 615	Mike Greenwell	.30	.14	.04
☐ 616	Kevin McGehee	.15	.07	.02
☐ 617	Jeffrey Hammonds FOIL	3.00	1.35	.35
☐ 618	Scott Taylor	.15	.07	.02
☐ 619	Dave Otto	.15	.07	.02
☐ 620	Mark McGwire FOIL	.75	.35	.09
☐ 621	Kevin Tatar	.15	.07	.02
☐ 622	Steve Farr	.15	.07	.02
☐ 623	Ryan Klesko FOIL	3.00	1.35	.35
☐ 624	Dave Fleming	.20	.09	.03
☐ 625	Andre Dawson	.30	.14	.04
☐ 626	Tino Martinez FOIL	.30	.14	.04
☐ 627	Chad Curtis	2.00	.90	.25
☐ 628	Mickey Morandini	.15	.07	.02
☐ 629	Gregg Olson FOIL	.15	.07	.02
☐ 630	Lou Whitaker	.30	.14	.04
☐ 631	Arthur Rhodes	.15	.07	.02
☐ 632	Brandon Wilson	.15	.07	.02
☐ 633	Lance Jennings	.15	.07	.02
☐ 634	Allen Watson	.50	.23	.06
☐ 635	Len Dykstra	.30	.14	.04
☐ 636	Joe Girardi	.15	.07	.02
☐ 637	Kiki Hernandez FOIL	.15	.07	.02
☐ 638	Mike Hampton	.75	.35	.09
☐ 639	Al Osuna	.15	.07	.02
☐ 640	Kevin Appier	1.00	.45	.12
☐ 641	Rick Helling FOIL	.20	.09	.03
☐ 642	Jody Reed	.15	.07	.02
☐ 643	Ray Lankford	1.25	.55	.16
☐ 644	John Olerud	.20	.09	.03
☐ 645	Paul Molitor FOIL	.75	.35	.09
☐ 646	Pat Borders	.15	.07	.02
☐ 647	Mike Morgan	.15	.07	.02
☐ 648	Larry Walker	1.25	.55	.16
☐ 649	Pedro Castellano FOIL	.15	.07	.02
☐ 650	Fred McGriff	1.00	.45	.12
☐ 651	Walt Weiss	.15	.07	.02
☐ 652	Calvin Murray FOIL	.20	.09	.03
☐ 653	Dave Nilsson	.60	.25	.07
☐ 654	Greg Pirkl	.20	.09	.03
☐ 655	Robin Ventura FOIL	.30	.14	.04
☐ 656	Mark Portugal	.15	.07	.02
☐ 657	Roger McDowell	.15	.07	.02
☐ 658	Rick Hirtensteiner FOIL	.15	.07	.02
☐ 659	Glenallen Hill	.15	.07	.02
☐ 660	Greg Gagne	.15	.07	.02
☐ 661	Charles Johnson FOIL	6.00	2.70	.75
☐ 662	Brian Hunter	.15	.07	.02
☐ 663	Mark Lemke	.15	.07	.02
☐ 664	Tim Belcher FOIL	.15	.07	.02
☐ 665	Rich DeLucia	.15	.07	.02
☐ 666	Bob Walk	.15	.07	.02
☐ 667	Joe Carter FOIL	.75	.35	.09
☐ 668	Jose Guzman	.15	.07	.02
☐ 669	Otis Nixon	.15	.07	.02
☐ 670	Phil Nevin FOIL	.30	.14	.04
☐ 671	Eric Davis	.20	.09	.03
☐ 672	Damion Easley	.75	.35	.09
☐ 673	Will Clark FOIL	1.00	.45	.12
☐ 674	Mark Kiefer	.15	.07	.02
☐ 675	Ozzie Smith	1.50	.70	.19
☐ 676	Manny Ramirez FOIL	8.00	3.60	1.00
☐ 677	Gregg Olson	.15	.07	.02
☐ 678	Cliff Floyd	5.00	2.20	.60
☐ 679	Duane Singleton	.50	.23	.06
☐ 680	Jose Rijo	.20	.09	.03
☐ 681	Willie Banks	.20	.09	.03
☐ 682	Michael Tucker FOIL	4.00	1.80	.50
☐ 683	Darren Lewis	.20	.09	.03
☐ 684	Dale Murphy	.30	.14	.04
☐ 685	Mike Pagliarulo	.15	.07	.02
☐ 686	Paul Miller	.15	.07	.02
☐ 687	Mike Robertson	.15	.07	.02
☐ 688	Mike Devereaux	.20	.09	.03
☐ 689	Pedro Astacio	.20	.09	.03
☐ 690	Alan Trammell	.30	.14	.04
☐ 691	Roger Clemens	1.25	.55	.16
☐ 692	Bud Black	.15	.07	.02
☐ 693	Turk Wendell	.20	.09	.03
☐ 694	Barry Larkin FOIL	1.00	.45	.12
☐ 695	Todd Zeile	.20	.09	.03
☐ 696	Pat Hentgen	.20	.09	.03
☐ 697	Eddie Taubensee	.15	.07	.02
☐ 698	Guillermo Velasquez	.15	.07	.02
☐ 699	Tom Glavine	.60	.25	.07
☐ 700	Robin Yount	1.00	.45	.12
☐ 701	Checklist 1-141	.15	.07	.02
☐ 702	Checklist 142-282	.15	.07	.02
☐ 703	Checklist 283-423	.15	.07	.02
☐ 704	Checklist 424-564	.15	.07	.02
☐ 705	Checklist 565-705	.15	.07	.02

1993 Bowman

This 708-card standard-size (2 1/2" by 3 1/2") set features white-bordered color action player photos on its fronts. The player's name appears in white lettering at the bottom right, with his last name printed on *an ocher rectangle. The horizontal backs carry the player's name in green lettering above another color player photo on the left side, which displays his positon within a yellow circle at its lower right. His team name appears vertically in yellow lettering within a black rectangle near the left edge. The player's biography, career highlights, and stats appear on the right side. A simulated wooden strip across the top accents the back and carries the card's number. The 48 foil subset cards (339-374 and 693-704) feature sixteen 1992 MVPs of the Minor Leagues plus top prospects. One foil card was inserted into every 14-card pack. Rookie Cards in this set include Rene Arocha, James Baldwin, Trey Beamon, Marshall Boze, Roger Cedeno, Tim Clark, Danny Clyburn, Marty Cordova, Midre Cummings, Russ Davis, Kenny Felder, Jimmy Haynes, Lee Heath, Sterling Hitchcock, Brian L. Hunter, Derek Jeter, Jason Kendall, Mike Lansing, James Malave, Ray McDavid, Greg McMichael, Chad Mottola, James Mouton, Jose Pett, Kevin Roberson, J.T. Snow, Paul Spoljaric, Larry Sutton, Tony Tarasco, Steve Trachsel, Darrell Whitmore, and Preston Wilson.*

	MINT	NRMT	EXC
COMPLETE SET (708)	75.00	34.00	9.50
COMMON CARD (1-708)	.10	.05	.01
☐ 1 Glenn Davis	.10	.05	.01
☐ 2 Hector Roa	.10	.05	.01
☐ 3 Ken Ryan	.10	.05	.01
☐ 4 Derek Wallace	.10	.05	.01
☐ 5 Jorge Fabregas	.20	.09	.03
☐ 6 Joe Oliver	.10	.05	.01
☐ 7 Brandon Wilson	.10	.05	.01
☐ 8 Mark Thompson	.20	.09	.03
☐ 9 Tracy Sanders	.10	.05	.01
☐ 10 Rich Renteria	.10	.05	.01
☐ 11 Lou Whitaker	.30	.14	.04
☐ 12 Brian Hunter	2.50	1.10	.30
☐ 13 Joe Vitiello	.30	.14	.04
☐ 14 Eric Karros	.30	.14	.04
☐ 15 Joe Kmak	.10	.05	.01
☐ 16 Tavo Alvarez	.20	.09	.03
☐ 17 Steve Dunn	.10	.05	.01
☐ 18 Tony Fernandez	.10	.05	.01
☐ 19 Melido Perez	.10	.05	.01
☐ 20 Mike Lieberthal	.10	.05	.01
☐ 21 Terry Steinbach	.20	.09	.03
☐ 22 Stan Belinda	.10	.05	.01
☐ 23 Jay Buhner	.30	.14	.04
☐ 24 Allen Watson	.20	.09	.03
☐ 25 Daryl Henderson	.10	.05	.01
☐ 26 Ray McDavid	.20	.09	.03
☐ 27 Shawn Green	2.00	.90	.25
☐ 28 Bud Black	.10	.05	.01
☐ 29 Sherman Obando	.20	.09	.03
☐ 30 Mike Hostetler	.10	.05	.01
☐ 31 Nate Minchey	.20	.09	.03
☐ 32 Randy Myers	.30	.14	.04
☐ 33 Brian Grebeck	.10	.05	.01
☐ 34 John Roper	.10	.05	.01
☐ 35 Larry Thomas	.10	.05	.01
☐ 36 Alex Cole	.10	.05	.01
☐ 37 Tom Kramer	.10	.05	.01
☐ 38 Matt Whisenant	.10	.05	.01
☐ 39 Chris Gomez	.25	.11	.03
☐ 40 Luis Gonzalez	.20	.09	.03
☐ 41 Kevin Appier	.30	.14	.04
☐ 42 Omar Daal	.20	.09	.03
☐ 43 Duane Singleton	.20	.09	.03
☐ 44 Bill Risley	.10	.05	.01
☐ 45 Pat Meares	.20	.09	.03
☐ 46 Butch Huskey	.20	.09	.03
☐ 47 Bobby Munoz	.10	.05	.01
☐ 48 Juan Bell	.10	.05	.01
☐ 49 Scott Lydy	.10	.05	.01
☐ 50 Dennis Moeller	.10	.05	.01
☐ 51 Marc Newfield	.20	.09	.03
☐ 52 Tripp Cromer	.10	.05	.01
☐ 53 Kurt Miller	.10	.05	.01
☐ 54 Jim Pena	.10	.05	.01
☐ 55 Juan Guzman	.10	.05	.01
☐ 56 Matt Williams	.50	.23	.06
☐ 57 Harold Reynolds	.10	.05	.01
☐ 58 Donnie Elliott	.10	.05	.01
☐ 59 Jon Shave	.10	.05	.01
☐ 60 Kevin Roberson	.10	.05	.01
☐ 61 Hilly Hathaway	.10	.05	.01
☐ 62 Jose Rijo	.20	.09	.03
☐ 63 Kerry Taylor	.10	.05	.01
☐ 64 Ryan Hawblitzel	.10	.05	.01
☐ 65 Glenallen Hill	.20	.09	.03
☐ 66 Ramon Martinez	.20	.09	.03
☐ 67 Travis Fryman	.30	.14	.04
☐ 68 Tom Nevers	.10	.05	.01
☐ 69 Phil Hiatt	.20	.09	.03
☐ 70 Tim Wallach	.20	.09	.03
☐ 71 B.J. Surhoff	.20	.09	.03
☐ 72 Rondell White	.75	.35	.09
☐ 73 Denny Hocking	.20	.09	.03
☐ 74 Mike Oquist	.10	.05	.01
☐ 75 Paul O'Neill	.20	.09	.03
☐ 76 Willie Banks	.10	.05	.01
☐ 77 Bob Welch	.20	.09	.03
☐ 78 Jose Sandoval	.10	.05	.01
☐ 79 Bill Haselman	.10	.05	.01
☐ 80 Rheal Cormier	.10	.05	.01
☐ 81 Dean Palmer	.20	.09	.03
☐ 82 Pat Gomez	.10	.05	.01
☐ 83 Steve Karsay	.20	.09	.03
☐ 84 Carl Hanselman	.10	.05	.01
☐ 85 T.R. Lewis	.10	.05	.01
☐ 86 Chipper Jones	3.00	1.35	.35
☐ 87 Scott Hatteberg	.10	.05	.01
☐ 88 Greg Hibbard	.10	.05	.01
☐ 89 Lance Painter	.10	.05	.01
☐ 90 Chad Mottola	.25	.11	.03
☐ 91 Jason Bere	.30	.14	.04
☐ 92 Dante Bichette	.40	.18	.05
☐ 93 Sandy Alomar Jr.	.20	.09	.03
☐ 94 Carl Everett	.20	.09	.03
☐ 95 Danny Bautista	.20	.09	.03
☐ 96 Steve Finley	.20	.09	.03
☐ 97 David Cone	.30	.14	.04
☐ 98 Todd Hollandsworth	1.25	.55	.16
☐ 99 Matt Mieske	.10	.05	.01
☐ 100 Larry Walker	.40	.18	.05
☐ 101 Shane Mack	.10	.05	.01
☐ 102 Aaron Ledesma	.10	.05	.01
☐ 103 Andy Pettitte	2.50	1.10	.30
☐ 104 Kevin Stocker	.20	.09	.03
☐ 105 Mike Mohler	.10	.05	.01
☐ 106 Tony Menendez	.10	.05	.01
☐ 107 Derek Lowe	.20	.09	.03
☐ 108 Basil Shabazz	.10	.05	.01

□	#	Player			
□	109	Dan Smith	.10	.05	.01
□	110	Scott Sanders	.25	.11	.03
□	111	Todd Stottlemyre	.20	.09	.03
□	112	Benji Simonton	.20	.09	.03
□	113	Rick Sutcliffe	.20	.09	.03
□	114	Lee Heath	.10	.05	.01
□	115	Jeff Russell	.10	.05	.01
□	116	Dave Stevens	.25	.11	.03
□	117	Mark Holzemer	.10	.05	.01
□	118	Tim Belcher	.10	.05	.01
□	119	Bobby Thigpen	.10	.05	.01
□	120	Roger Bailey	.20	.09	.03
□	121	Tony Mitchell	.20	.09	.03
□	122	Junior Felix	.10	.05	.01
□	123	Rich Robertson	.10	.05	.01
□	124	Andy Cook	.10	.05	.01
□	125	Brian Bevil	.20	.09	.03
□	126	Darryl Strawberry	.20	.09	.03
□	127	Cal Eldred	.20	.09	.03
□	128	Cliff Floyd	.30	.14	.04
□	129	Alan Newman	.10	.05	.01
□	130	Howard Johnson	.10	.05	.01
□	131	Jim Abbott	.30	.14	.04
□	132	Chad McConnell	.10	.05	.01
□	133	Miguel Jimenez	.20	.09	.03
□	134	Brett Backlund	.10	.05	.01
□	135	John Cummings	.20	.09	.03
□	136	Brian Barber	.20	.09	.03
□	137	Rafael Palmeiro	.30	.14	.04
□	138	Tim Worrell	.10	.05	.01
□	139	Jose Pett	.75	.35	.09
□	140	Barry Bonds	.75	.35	.09
□	141	Damon Buford	.10	.05	.01
□	142	Jeff Blauser	.20	.09	.03
□	143	Frankie Rodriguez	.20	.09	.03
□	144	Mike Morgan	.10	.05	.01
□	145	Gary DiSarcina	.10	.05	.01
□	146	Calvin Reese	.30	.14	.04
□	147	Johnny Ruffin	.10	.05	.01
□	148	David Nied	.10	.05	.01
□	149	Charles Nagy	.20	.09	.03
□	150	Mike Myers	.10	.05	.01
□	151	Kenny Carlyle	.10	.05	.01
□	152	Eric Anthony	.10	.05	.01
□	153	Jose Lind	.10	.05	.01
□	154	Pedro Martinez	.30	.14	.04
□	155	Mark Kiefer	.10	.05	.01
□	156	Tim Laker	.10	.05	.01
□	157	Pat Mahomes	.20	.09	.03
□	158	Bobby Bonilla	.30	.14	.04
□	159	Domingo Jean	.10	.05	.01
□	160	Darren Daulton	.30	.14	.04
□	161	Mark McGwire	.30	.14	.04
□	162	Jason Kendall	1.00	.45	.12
□	163	Desi Relaford	.20	.09	.03
□	164	Ozzie Canseco	.10	.05	.01
□	165	Rick Helling	.20	.09	.03
□	166	Steve Pegues	.10	.05	.01
□	167	Paul Molitor	.30	.14	.04
□	168	Larry Carter	.10	.05	.01
□	169	Arthur Rhodes	.20	.09	.03
□	170	Damon Hollins	1.00	.45	.12
□	171	Frank Viola	.20	.09	.03
□	172	Steve Trachsel	.20	.09	.03
□	173	J.T. Snow	1.00	.45	.12
□	174	Keith Gordon	.10	.05	.01
□	175	Carlton Fisk	.30	.14	.04
□	176	Jason Bates	.25	.11	.03
□	177	Mike Crosby	.10	.05	.01
□	178	Benny Santiago	.10	.05	.01
□	179	Mike Moore	.10	.05	.01
□	180	Jeff Juden	.10	.05	.01
□	181	Darren Burton	.10	.05	.01
□	182	Todd Williams	.10	.05	.01
□	183	John Jaha	.20	.09	.03
□	184	Mike Lansing	.20	.09	.03
□	185	Pedro Grifol	.10	.05	.01
□	186	Vince Coleman	.20	.09	.03
□	187	Pat Kelly	.10	.05	.01
□	188	Clemente Alvarez	.20	.09	.03
□	189	Ron Darling	.10	.05	.01
□	190	Orlando Merced	.20	.09	.03
□	191	Chris Bosio	.10	.05	.01
□	192	Steve Dixon	.10	.05	.01
□	193	Doug Dascenzo	.10	.05	.01
□	194	Ray Holbert	.20	.09	.03
□	195	Howard Battle	.20	.09	.03
□	196	Willie McGee	.20	.09	.03
□	197	John O'Donoghue	.10	.05	.01
□	198	Steve Avery	.30	.14	.04
□	199	Greg Blosser	.10	.05	.01
□	200	Ryne Sandberg	.75	.35	.09
□	201	Joe Grahe	.10	.05	.01
□	202	Dan Wilson	.10	.05	.01
□	203	Domingo Martinez	.10	.05	.01
□	204	Andres Galarraga	.30	.14	.04
□	205	Jamie Taylor	.10	.05	.01
□	206	Darrell Whitmore	.10	.05	.01
□	207	Ben Blomdahl	.10	.05	.01
□	208	Doug Drabek	.20	.09	.03
□	209	Keith Miller	.10	.05	.01
□	210	Billy Ashley	.30	.14	.04
□	211	Mike Farrell	.10	.05	.01
□	212	John Wetteland	.30	.14	.04
□	213	Randy Tomlin	.10	.05	.01
□	214	Sid Fernandez	.10	.05	.01
□	215	Quilvio Veras	.75	.35	.09
□	216	Dave Hollins	.10	.05	.01
□	217	Mike Neill	.10	.05	.01
□	218	Andy Van Slyke	.20	.09	.03
□	219	Bret Boone	.30	.14	.04
□	220	Tom Pagnozzi	.10	.05	.01
□	221	Mike Welch	.10	.05	.01
□	222	Frank Seminara	.10	.05	.01
□	223	Ron Villone	.20	.09	.03
□	224	D.J. Thielen	.10	.05	.01
□	225	Cal Ripken	3.00	1.35	.35
□	226	Pedro Borbon Jr.	.25	.11	.03
□	227	Carlos Quintana	.10	.05	.01
□	228	Tommy Shields	.10	.05	.01
□	229	Tim Salmon	1.00	.45	.12
□	230	John Smiley	.20	.09	.03
□	231	Ellis Burks	.20	.09	.03
□	232	Pedro Castellano	.10	.05	.01
□	233	Paul Byrd	.10	.05	.01
□	234	Bryan Harvey	.20	.09	.03
□	235	Scott Livingstone	.10	.05	.01
□	236	James Mouton	.25	.11	.03
□	237	Joe Randa	.20	.09	.03
□	238	Pedro Astacio	.20	.09	.03
□	239	Darryl Hamilton	.10	.05	.01
□	240	Joey Eischen	.20	.09	.03
□	241	Edgar Herrera	.25	.11	.03
□	242	Dwight Gooden	.20	.09	.03
□	243	Sam Militello	.10	.05	.01
□	244	Ron Blazier	.20	.09	.03
□	245	Ruben Sierra	.30	.14	.04
□	246	Al Martin	.20	.09	.03
□	247	Mike Felder	.10	.05	.01
□	248	Bob Tewksbury	.10	.05	.01
□	249	Craig Lefferts	.10	.05	.01
□	250	Luis Lopez	.20	.09	.03

☐ 251 Devon White	.20	.09	.03
☐ 252 Will Clark	.40	.18	.05
☐ 253 Mark Smith	.20	.09	.03
☐ 254 Terry Pendleton	.30	.14	.04
☐ 255 Aaron Sele	.30	.14	.04
☐ 256 Jose Viera	.20	.09	.03
☐ 257 Damion Easley	.20	.09	.03
☐ 258 Rod Lofton	.10	.05	.01
☐ 259 Chris Snopek	.75	.35	.09
☐ 260 Quinton McCracken	.20	.09	.03
☐ 261 Mike Matthews	.25	.11	.03
☐ 262 Hector Carrasco	.20	.09	.03
☐ 263 Rick Greene	.20	.09	.03
☐ 264 Chris Holt	.20	.09	.03
☐ 265 George Brett	1.25	.55	.16
☐ 266 Rick Gorecki	.25	.11	.03
☐ 267 Francisco Gamez	.10	.05	.01
☐ 268 Marquis Grissom	.30	.14	.04
☐ 269 Kevin Tapani UER	.10	.05	.01
(Misspelled Tapan			
on card front)			
☐ 270 Ryan Thompson	.20	.09	.03
☐ 271 Gerald Williams	.10	.05	.01
☐ 272 Paul Fletcher	.10	.05	.01
☐ 273 Lance Blankenship	.10	.05	.01
☐ 274 Marty Neff	.10	.05	.01
☐ 275 Shawn Estes	.20	.09	.03
☐ 276 Rene Arocha	.10	.05	.01
☐ 277 Scott Eyre	.10	.05	.01
☐ 278 Phil Plantier	.10	.05	.01
☐ 279 Paul Spoljaric	.10	.05	.01
☐ 280 Chris Gambs	.10	.05	.01
☐ 281 Harold Baines	.20	.09	.03
☐ 282 Jose Oliva	.20	.09	.03
☐ 283 Matt Whiteside	.10	.05	.01
☐ 284 Brant Brown	.10	.05	.01
☐ 285 Russ Springer	.10	.05	.01
☐ 286 Chris Sabo	.10	.05	.01
☐ 287 Ozzie Guillen	.10	.05	.01
☐ 288 Marcus Moore	.10	.05	.01
☐ 289 Chad Ogea	.20	.09	.03
☐ 290 Walt Weiss	.10	.05	.01
☐ 291 Brian Edmondson	.20	.09	.03
☐ 292 Jimmy Gonzalez	.10	.05	.01
☐ 293 Danny Miceli	.25	.11	.03
☐ 294 Jose Offerman	.10	.05	.01
☐ 295 Greg Vaughn	.10	.05	.01
☐ 296 Frank Bolick	.10	.05	.01
☐ 297 Mike Maksudian	.10	.05	.01
☐ 298 John Franco	.20	.09	.03
☐ 299 Danny Tartabull	.20	.09	.03
☐ 300 Len Dykstra	.30	.14	.04
☐ 301 Bobby Witt	.10	.05	.01
☐ 302 Trey Beamon	1.50	.70	.19
☐ 303 Tino Martinez	.20	.09	.03
☐ 304 Aaron Holbert	.20	.09	.03
☐ 305 Juan Gonzalez	.60	.25	.07
☐ 306 Billy Hall	.10	.05	.01
☐ 307 Duane Ward	.10	.05	.01
☐ 308 Rod Beck	.30	.14	.04
☐ 309 Jose Mercedes	.10	.05	.01
☐ 310 Otis Nixon	.10	.05	.01
☐ 311 Gettys Glaze	.10	.05	.01
☐ 312 Candy Maldonado	.10	.05	.01
☐ 313 Chad Curtis	.20	.09	.03
☐ 314 Tim Costo	.10	.05	.01
☐ 315 Mike Robertson	.10	.05	.01
☐ 316 Nigel Wilson	.10	.05	.01
☐ 317 Greg McMichael	.20	.09	.03
☐ 318 Scott Pose	.10	.05	.01
☐ 319 Ivan Cruz	.10	.05	.01

☐ 320 Greg Swindell	.10	.05	.01
☐ 321 Kevin McReynolds	.10	.05	.01
☐ 322 Tom Candiotti	.10	.05	.01
☐ 323 Rob Wishnevski	.10	.05	.01
☐ 324 Ken Hill	.20	.09	.03
☐ 325 Kirby Puckett	1.00	.45	.12
☐ 326 Tim Bogar	.10	.05	.01
☐ 327 Mariano Rivera	.20	.09	.03
☐ 328 Mitch Williams	.20	.09	.03
☐ 329 Craig Paquette	.20	.09	.03
☐ 330 Jay Bell	.20	.09	.03
☐ 331 Jose Martinez	.10	.05	.01
☐ 332 Rob Deer	.10	.05	.01
☐ 333 Brook Fordyce	.10	.05	.01
☐ 334 Matt Nokes	.10	.05	.01
☐ 335 Derek Lee	.10	.05	.01
☐ 336 Paul Ellis	.10	.05	.01
☐ 337 Desi Wilson	.10	.05	.01
☐ 338 Roberto Alomar	.60	.25	.07
☐ 339 Jim Tatum FOIL	.20	.09	.03
☐ 340 J.T. Snow FOIL	1.00	.45	.12
☐ 341 Tim Salmon FOIL	1.00	.45	.12
☐ 342 Russ Davis FOIL	.30	.14	.04
☐ 343 Javier Lopez FOIL	1.00	.45	.12
☐ 344 Troy O'Leary FOIL	.50	.23	.06
☐ 345 Marty Cordova FOIL	3.00	1.35	.35
☐ 346 Bubba Smith FOIL	.20	.09	.03
☐ 347 Chipper Jones FOIL	3.00	1.35	.35
☐ 348 Jessie Hollins FOIL	.20	.09	.03
☐ 349 Willie Greene FOIL	.20	.09	.03
☐ 350 Mark Thompson FOIL	.20	.09	.03
☐ 351 Nigel Wilson FOIL	.20	.09	.03
☐ 352 Todd Jones FOIL	.20	.09	.03
☐ 353 Raul Mondesi FOIL	2.00	.90	.25
☐ 354 Cliff Floyd FOIL	.30	.14	.04
☐ 355 Bobby Jones FOIL	.20	.09	.03
☐ 356 Kevin Stocker FOIL	.20	.09	.03
☐ 357 Midre Cummings FOIL	.50	.23	.06
☐ 358 Allen Watson FOIL	.20	.09	.03
☐ 359 Ray McDavid FOIL	.20	.09	.03
☐ 360 Steve Hosey FOIL	.20	.09	.03
☐ 361 Brad Pennington FOIL	.20	.09	.03
☐ 362 Frankie Rodriguez FOIL	.20	.09	.03
☐ 363 Troy Percival FOIL	.20	.09	.03
☐ 364 Jason Bere FOIL	.20	.09	.03
☐ 365 Manny Ramirez FOIL	2.50	1.10	.30
☐ 366 Justin Thompson FOIL	.20	.09	.03
☐ 367 Joe Vitiello FOIL	.30	.14	.04
☐ 368 Tyrone Hill FOIL	.20	.09	.03
☐ 369 David McCarty FOIL	.20	.09	.03
☐ 370 Brien Taylor FOIL	.20	.09	.03
☐ 371 Todd Van Poppel FOIL	.20	.09	.03
☐ 372 Marc Newfield FOIL	.20	.09	.03
☐ 373 Terrell Lowery FOIL	.20	.09	.03
☐ 374 Alex Gonzalez FOIL	.30	.14	.04
☐ 375 Ken Griffey Jr.	3.00	1.35	.35
☐ 376 Donovan Osborne	.10	.05	.01
☐ 377 Ritchie Moody	.10	.05	.01
☐ 378 Shane Andrews	.20	.09	.03
☐ 379 Carlos Delgado	.60	.25	.07
☐ 380 Bill Swift	.10	.05	.01
☐ 381 Leo Gomez	.10	.05	.01
☐ 382 Ron Gant	.30	.14	.04
☐ 383 Scott Fletcher	.10	.05	.01
☐ 384 Matt Walbeck	.20	.09	.03
☐ 385 Chuck Finley	.10	.05	.01
☐ 386 Kevin Mitchell	.20	.09	.03
☐ 387 Wilson Alvarez UER	.30	.14	.04
(Misspelled Alverez			
on card front)			
☐ 388 John Burke	.20	.09	.03

□	#	Player			
□	389	Alan Embree	.20	.09	.03
□	390	Trevor Hoffman	.20	.09	.03
□	391	Alan Trammell	.30	.14	.04
□	392	Todd Jones	.20	.09	.03
□	393	Felix Jose	.10	.05	.01
□	394	Orel Hershiser	.30	.14	.04
□	395	Pat Listach	.10	.05	.01
□	396	Gabe White	.20	.09	.03
□	397	Dan Serafini	.50	.23	.06
□	398	Todd Hundley	.30	.14	.04
□	399	Wade Boggs	.30	.14	.04
□	400	Tyler Green	.20	.09	.03
□	401	Mike Bordick	.10	.05	.01
□	402	Scott Bullett	.10	.05	.01
□	403	LaGrande Russell	.10	.05	.01
□	404	Ray Lankford	.30	.14	.04
□	405	Nolan Ryan	2.50	1.10	.30
□	406	Robbie Beckett	.10	.05	.01
□	407	Brent Bowers	.20	.09	.03
□	408	Adell Davenport	.10	.05	.01
□	409	Brady Anderson	.20	.09	.03
□	410	Tom Glavine	.30	.14	.04
□	411	Doug Hecker	.20	.09	.03
□	412	Jose Guzman	.10	.05	.01
□	413	Luis Polonia	.10	.05	.01
□	414	Brian Williams	.10	.05	.01
□	415	Bo Jackson	.30	.14	.04
□	416	Eric Young	.20	.09	.03
□	417	Kenny Lofton	1.25	.55	.16
□	418	Orestes Destrade	.10	.05	.01
□	419	Tony Phillips	.10	.05	.01
□	420	Jeff Bagwell	1.25	.55	.16
□	421	Mark Gardner	.10	.05	.01
□	422	Brett Butler	.20	.09	.03
□	423	Graeme Lloyd	.10	.05	.01
□	424	Delino DeShields	.20	.09	.03
□	425	Scott Erickson	.20	.09	.03
□	426	Jeff Kent	.30	.14	.04
□	427	Jimmy Key	.20	.09	.03
□	428	Mickey Morandini	.10	.05	.01
□	429	Marcos Armas	.10	.05	.01
□	430	Don Slaught	.10	.05	.01
□	431	Randy Johnson	.60	.25	.07
□	432	Omar Olivares	.10	.05	.01
□	433	Charlie Leibrandt	.10	.05	.01
□	434	Kurt Stillwell	.10	.05	.01
□	435	Scott Brow	.10	.05	.01
□	436	Robby Thompson	.10	.05	.01
□	437	Ben McDonald	.10	.05	.01
□	438	Deion Sanders	.60	.25	.07
□	439	Tony Pena	.10	.05	.01
□	440	Mark Grace	.30	.14	.04
□	441	Eduardo Perez	.20	.09	.03
□	442	Tim Pugh	.20	.09	.03
□	443	Scott Ruffcorn	.20	.09	.03
□	444	Jay Gainer	.10	.05	.01
□	445	Albert Belle	1.25	.55	.16
□	446	Bret Barberie	.10	.05	.01
□	447	Justin Mashore	.10	.05	.01
□	448	Pete Harnisch	.10	.05	.01
□	449	Greg Gagne	.10	.05	.01
□	450	Eric Davis	.10	.05	.01
□	451	Dave Mlicki	.10	.05	.01
□	452	Moises Alou	.30	.14	.04
□	453	Rick Aguilera	.20	.09	.03
□	454	Eddie Murray	.50	.23	.06
□	455	Bob Wickman	.10	.05	.01
□	456	Wes Chamberlain	.10	.05	.01
□	457	Brent Gates	.30	.14	.04
□	458	Paul Wagner	.20	.09	.03
□	459	Mike Hampton	.10	.05	.01
□	460	Ozzie Smith	.60	.25	.07
□	461	Tom Henke	.20	.09	.03
□	462	Ricky Gutierrez	.10	.05	.01
□	463	Jack Morris	.30	.14	.04
□	464	Joel Chimelis	.10	.05	.01
□	465	Gregg Olson	.10	.05	.01
□	466	Javier Lopez	1.00	.45	.12
□	467	Scott Cooper	.10	.05	.01
□	468	Willie Wilson	.10	.05	.01
□	469	Mark Langston	.30	.14	.04
□	470	Barry Larkin	.40	.18	.05
□	471	Rod Bolton	.10	.05	.01
□	472	Freddie Benavides	.10	.05	.01
□	473	Ken Ramos	.10	.05	.01
□	474	Chuck Carr	.10	.05	.01
□	475	Cecil Fielder	.30	.14	.04
□	476	Eddie Taubensee	.10	.05	.01
□	477	Chris Eddy	.10	.05	.01
□	478	Greg Hansell	.10	.05	.01
□	479	Kevin Reimer	.10	.05	.01
□	480	Denny Martinez	.20	.09	.03
□	481	Chuck Knoblauch	.30	.14	.04
□	482	Mike Draper	.10	.05	.01
□	483	Spike Owen	.10	.05	.01
□	484	Terry Mulholland	.10	.05	.01
□	485	Dennis Eckersley	.30	.14	.04
□	486	Blas Minor	.10	.05	.01
□	487	Dave Fleming	.10	.05	.01
□	488	Dan Cholowsky	.10	.05	.01
□	489	Ivan Rodriguez	.30	.14	.04
□	490	Gary Sheffield	.30	.14	.04
□	491	Ed Sprague	.10	.05	.01
□	492	Steve Hosey	.10	.05	.01
□	493	Jimmy Haynes	.75	.35	.09
□	494	John Smoltz	.20	.09	.03
□	495	Andre Dawson	.30	.14	.04
□	496	Rey Sanchez	.10	.05	.01
□	497	Ty Van Burkleo	.10	.05	.01
□	498	Bobby Ayala	.20	.09	.03
□	499	Tim Raines	.30	.14	.04
□	500	Charlie Hayes	.20	.09	.03
□	501	Paul Sorrento	.10	.05	.01
□	502	Richie Lewis	.10	.05	.01
□	503	Jason Pfaff	.10	.05	.01
□	504	Ken Caminiti	.20	.09	.03
□	505	Mike Macfarlane	.10	.05	.01
□	506	Jody Reed	.10	.05	.01
□	507	Bobby Hughes	.10	.05	.01
□	508	Wil Cordero	.20	.09	.03
□	509	George Tsamis	.10	.05	.01
□	510	Bret Saberhagen	.20	.09	.03
□	511	Derek Jeter	2.50	1.10	.30
□	512	Gene Schall	.20	.09	.03
□	513	Curtis Shaw	.10	.05	.01
□	514	Steve Cooke	.20	.09	.03
□	515	Edgar Martinez	.30	.14	.04
□	516	Mike Milchin	.10	.05	.01
□	517	Billy Ripken	.10	.05	.01
□	518	Andy Benes	.20	.09	.03
□	519	Juan de la Rosa	.10	.05	.01
□	520	John Burkett	.10	.05	.01
□	521	Alex Ochoa	.30	.14	.04
□	522	Tony Tarasco	.40	.18	.05
□	523	Luis Ortiz	.20	.09	.03
□	524	Rick Wilkins	.10	.05	.01
□	525	Chris Turner	.10	.05	.01
□	526	Rob Dibble	.10	.05	.01
□	527	Jack McDowell	.30	.14	.04
□	528	Daryl Boston	.10	.05	.01
□	529	Bill Wertz	.10	.05	.01
□	530	Charlie Hough	.20	.09	.03

#	Player			
☐ 531	Sean Bergman	.10	.05	.01
☐ 532	Doug Jones	.10	.05	.01
☐ 533	Jeff Montgomery	.20	.09	.03
☐ 534	Roger Cedeno	1.50	.70	.19
☐ 535	Robin Yount	.40	.18	.05
☐ 536	Mo Vaughn	.50	.23	.06
☐ 537	Brian Harper	.10	.05	.01
☐ 538	Juan Castillo	.10	.05	.01
☐ 539	Steve Farr	.10	.05	.01
☐ 540	John Kruk	.30	.14	.04
☐ 541	Troy Neel	.10	.05	.01
☐ 542	Danny Clyburn	.75	.35	.09
☐ 543	Jim Converse	.20	.09	.03
☐ 544	Gregg Jefferies	.30	.14	.04
☐ 545	Jose Canseco	.50	.23	.06
☐ 546	Julio Bruno	.10	.05	.01
☐ 547	Rob Butler	.20	.09	.03
☐ 548	Royce Clayton	.20	.09	.03
☐ 549	Chris Hoiles	.20	.09	.03
☐ 550	Greg Maddux	3.00	1.35	.35
☐ 551	Joe Ciccarella	.10	.05	.01
☐ 552	Ozzie Timmons	.30	.14	.04
☐ 553	Chili Davis	.20	.09	.03
☐ 554	Brian Koelling	.10	.05	.01
☐ 555	Frank Thomas	3.00	1.35	.35
☐ 556	Vinny Castilla	.30	.14	.04
☐ 557	Reggie Jefferson	.10	.05	.01
☐ 558	Rob Natal	.10	.05	.01
☐ 559	Mike Henneman	.10	.05	.01
☐ 560	Craig Biggio	.30	.14	.04
☐ 561	Billy Brewer	.10	.05	.01
☐ 562	Dan Melendez	.10	.05	.01
☐ 563	Kenny Felder	.20	.09	.03
☐ 564	Miguel Batista	.20	.09	.03
☐ 565	Dave Winfield	.30	.14	.04
☐ 566	Al Shirley	.20	.09	.03
☐ 567	Robert Eenhoorn	.10	.05	.01
☐ 568	Mike Williams	.10	.05	.01
☐ 569	Tanyon Sturtze	.20	.09	.03
☐ 570	Tim Wakefield	.30	.14	.04
☐ 571	Greg Pirkl	.20	.09	.03
☐ 572	Sean Lowe	.20	.09	.03
☐ 573	Terry Burrows	.10	.05	.01
☐ 574	Kevin Higgins	.10	.05	.01
☐ 575	Joe Carter	.30	.14	.04
☐ 576	Kevin Rogers	.10	.05	.01
☐ 577	Manny Alexander	.10	.05	.01
☐ 578	David Justice	.40	.18	.05
☐ 579	Brian Conroy	.10	.05	.01
☐ 580	Jessie Hollins	.10	.05	.01
☐ 581	Ron Watson	.10	.05	.01
☐ 582	Bip Roberts	.10	.05	.01
☐ 583	Tom Urbani	.10	.05	.01
☐ 584	Jason Hutchins	.10	.05	.01
☐ 585	Carlos Baerga	.60	.25	.07
☐ 586	Jeff Mutis	.10	.05	.01
☐ 587	Justin Thompson	.20	.09	.03
☐ 588	Orlando Miller	.20	.09	.03
☐ 589	Brian McRae	.30	.14	.04
☐ 590	Ramon Martinez	.30	.14	.04
☐ 591	Dave Nilsson	.20	.09	.03
☐ 592	Jose Vidro	.25	.11	.03
☐ 593	Rich Becker	.20	.09	.03
☐ 594	Preston Wilson	.50	.23	.06
☐ 595	Don Mattingly	1.50	.70	.19
☐ 596	Tony Longmire	.10	.05	.01
☐ 597	Kevin Seitzer	.10	.05	.01
☐ 598	Midre Cummings	.50	.23	.06
☐ 599	Omar Vizquel	.10	.05	.01
☐ 600	Lee Smith	.30	.14	.04
☐ 601	David Hulse	.10	.05	.01
☐ 602	Darrell Sherman	.10	.05	.01
☐ 603	Alex Gonzalez	.30	.14	.04
☐ 604	Geronimo Pena	.10	.05	.01
☐ 605	Mike Devereaux	.20	.09	.03
☐ 606	Sterling Hitchcock	.25	.11	.03
☐ 607	Mike Greenwell	.20	.09	.03
☐ 608	Steve Buechele	.10	.05	.01
☐ 609	Troy Percival	.20	.09	.03
☐ 610	Roberto Kelly	.20	.09	.03
☐ 611	James Baldwin	.40	.18	.05
☐ 612	Jerald Clark	.10	.05	.01
☐ 613	Albie Lopez	.25	.11	.03
☐ 614	Dave Magadan	.10	.05	.01
☐ 615	Mickey Tettleton	.20	.09	.03
☐ 616	Sean Runyan	.10	.05	.01
☐ 617	Bob Hamelin	.20	.09	.03
☐ 618	Raul Mondesi	2.00	.90	.25
☐ 619	Tyrone Hill	.20	.09	.03
☐ 620	Darrin Fletcher	.10	.05	.01
☐ 621	Mike Trombley	.10	.05	.01
☐ 622	Jeromy Burnitz	.10	.05	.01
☐ 623	Bernie Williams	.20	.09	.03
☐ 624	Mike Farmer	.10	.05	.01
☐ 625	Rickey Henderson	.30	.14	.04
☐ 626	Carlos Garcia	.20	.09	.03
☐ 627	Jeff Darwin	.10	.05	.01
☐ 628	Todd Zeile	.20	.09	.03
☐ 629	Benji Gil	.20	.09	.03
☐ 630	Tony Gwynn	1.00	.45	.12
☐ 631	Aaron Small	.10	.05	.01
☐ 632	Joe Rosselli	.25	.11	.03
☐ 633	Mike Mussina	.50	.23	.06
☐ 634	Ryan Klesko	1.50	.70	.19
☐ 635	Roger Clemens	.50	.23	.06
☐ 636	Sammy Sosa	.30	.14	.04
☐ 637	Orlando Palmeiro	.10	.05	.01
☐ 638	Willie Greene	.20	.09	.03
☐ 639	George Bell	.20	.09	.03
☐ 640	Garvin Alston	.10	.05	.01
☐ 641	Pete Janicki	.10	.05	.01
☐ 642	Chris Sheff	.10	.05	.01
☐ 643	Felipe Lira	.25	.11	.03
☐ 644	Roberto Petagine	.20	.09	.03
☐ 645	Wally Joyner	.20	.09	.03
☐ 646	Mike Piazza	2.50	1.10	.30
☐ 647	Jaime Navarro	.10	.05	.01
☐ 648	Jeff Hartsock	.10	.05	.01
☐ 649	David McCarty	.10	.05	.01
☐ 650	Bobby Jones	.20	.09	.03
☐ 651	Mark Hutton	.10	.05	.01
☐ 652	Kyle Abbott	.10	.05	.01
☐ 653	Steve Cox	1.00	.45	.12
☐ 654	Jeff King	.10	.05	.01
☐ 655	Norm Charlton	.10	.05	.01
☐ 656	Mike Gulan	.10	.05	.01
☐ 657	Julio Franco	.20	.09	.03
☐ 658	Cameron Cairncross	.10	.05	.01
☐ 659	John Olerud	.20	.09	.03
☐ 660	Salomon Torres	.20	.09	.03
☐ 661	Brad Pennington	.10	.05	.01
☐ 662	Melvin Nieves	.20	.09	.03
☐ 663	Ivan Calderon	.10	.05	.01
☐ 664	Turk Wendell	.20	.09	.03
☐ 665	Chris Pritchett	.10	.05	.01
☐ 666	Reggie Sanders	.30	.14	.04
☐ 667	Robin Ventura	.30	.14	.04
☐ 668	Joe Girardi	.10	.05	.01
☐ 669	Manny Ramirez	2.50	1.10	.30
☐ 670	Jeff Conine	.30	.14	.04
☐ 671	Greg Gohr	.10	.05	.01
☐ 672	Andujar Cedeno	.10	.05	.01

		MINT	NRMT	EXC
☐ 673	Les Norman	.10	.05	.01
☐ 674	Mike James	.10	.05	.01
☐ 675	Marshall Boze	.20	.09	.03
☐ 676	B.J. Wallace	.20	.09	.03
☐ 677	Kent Hrbek	.20	.09	.03
☐ 678	Jack Voigt	.10	.05	.01
☐ 679	Brien Taylor	.20	.09	.03
☐ 680	Curt Schilling	.10	.05	.01
☐ 681	Todd Van Poppel	.20	.09	.03
☐ 682	Kevin Young	.10	.05	.01
☐ 683	Tommy Adams	.10	.05	.01
☐ 684	Bernard Gilkey	.20	.09	.03
☐ 685	Kevin Brown	.10	.05	.01
☐ 686	Fred McGriff	.40	.18	.05
☐ 687	Pat Borders	.10	.05	.01
☐ 688	Kirt Manwaring	.10	.05	.01
☐ 689	Sid Bream	.10	.05	.01
☐ 690	John Valentin	.20	.09	.03
☐ 691	Steve Olsen	.10	.05	.01
☐ 692	Roberto Mejia	.20	.09	.03
☐ 693	Carlos Delgado FOIL	.60	.25	.07
☐ 694	Steve Gibralter FOIL	.50	.23	.06
☐ 695	Gary Mota FOIL	.20	.09	.03
☐ 696	Jose Malave FOIL	.40	.18	.05
☐ 697	Larry Sutton FOIL	.25	.11	.03
☐ 698	Dan Frye FOIL	.20	.09	.03
☐ 699	Tim Clark FOIL	.20	.09	.03
☐ 700	Brian Rupp FOIL	.20	.09	.03
☐ 701	Felipe Alou FOIL Moises Alou Father and Son	.20	.09	.03
☐ 702	Barry Bonds FOIL Bobby Bonds Father and Son	.40	.18	.05
☐ 703	Ken Griffey Sr. FOIL Ken Griffey Jr. Father and Son	1.00	.45	.12
☐ 704	Brian McRae FOIL Hal McRae Father and Son	.20	.09	.03
☐ 705	Checklist 1	.10	.05	.01
☐ 706	Checklist 2	.10	.05	.01
☐ 707	Checklist 3	.10	.05	.01
☐ 708	Checklist 4	.10	.05	.01

1994 Bowman

The 1994 Bowman set consists of 682 standard-size, full-bleed cards. In addition to a color photo on the front, there is a line of gold foil that runs up the far left side and across the bottom of the card. The player's name is also in gold foil at bottom and the Bowman logo at bottom left is enclosed in gold foil. Horizontal backs contain a player photo on the left and statistics and highlights on the right. There are 51 Foil cards (337-388) that include a number of top young stars and prospects. These foil cards were issued one per foil pack and two per jumbo. Rookie Cards include Brian Anderson, Alan Benes, John Hudek, Jason Jacome, Brooks Kieschnick, Chan Ho Park, Ruben Rivera and Will VanLandingham.

		MINT	NRMT	EXC
	COMPLETE SET (682)	110.00	50.00	14.00
	COMMON CARD (1-682)	.10	.05	.01
☐ 1	Joe Carter	.30	.14	.04
☐ 2	Marcus Moore	.10	.05	.01
☐ 3	Doug Creek	.10	.05	.01
☐ 4	Pedro Martinez	.30	.14	.04
☐ 5	Ken Griffey Jr.	3.00	1.35	.35
☐ 6	Greg Swindell	.10	.05	.01
☐ 7	J.J. Johnson	.10	.05	.01
☐ 8	Homer Bush	.20	.09	.03
☐ 9	Arquimedez Pozo	.40	.18	.05
☐ 10	Bryan Harvey	.10	.05	.01
☐ 11	J.T. Snow	.20	.09	.03
☐ 12	Alan Benes	1.00	.45	.12
☐ 13	Chad Kreuter	.10	.05	.01
☐ 14	Eric Karros	.20	.09	.03
☐ 15	Frank Thomas	3.00	1.35	.35
☐ 16	Bret Saberhagen	.20	.09	.03
☐ 17	Terrell Lowery	.10	.05	.01
☐ 18	Rod Bolton	.10	.05	.01
☐ 19	Harold Baines	.20	.09	.03
☐ 20	Matt Walbeck	.10	.05	.01
☐ 21	Tom Glavine	.30	.14	.04
☐ 22	Todd Jones	.10	.05	.01
☐ 23	Alberto Castillo	.20	.09	.03
☐ 24	Ruben Sierra	.30	.14	.04
☐ 25	Don Mattingly	1.50	.70	.19
☐ 26	Mike Morgan	.10	.05	.01
☐ 27	Jim Musselwhite	.20	.09	.03
☐ 28	Matt Brunson	.25	.11	.03
☐ 29	Adam Meinershagen	.25	.11	.03
☐ 30	Joe Girardi	.10	.05	.01
☐ 31	Shane Halter	.10	.05	.01
☐ 32	Jose Paniagua	.25	.11	.03
☐ 33	Paul Perkins	.10	.05	.01
☐ 34	John Hudek	.20	.09	.03
☐ 35	Frank Viola	.10	.05	.01
☐ 36	David Lamb	.30	.14	.04
☐ 37	Marshall Boze	.10	.05	.01
☐ 38	Jorge Posada	.10	.05	.01
☐ 39	Brian Anderson	.20	.09	.03
☐ 40	Mark Whiten	.10	.05	.01
☐ 41	Sean Bergman	.20	.09	.03
☐ 42	Jose Parra	.20	.09	.03
☐ 43	Mike Robertson	.10	.05	.01
☐ 44	Pete Walker	.10	.05	.01
☐ 45	Juan Gonzalez	.75	.35	.09
☐ 46	Cleveland Ladell	.20	.09	.03
☐ 47	Mark Smith	.20	.09	.03
☐ 48	Kevin Jarvis	.10	.05	.01
☐ 49	Amaury Telemaco	.50	.23	.06
☐ 50	Andy Van Slyke	.30	.14	.04
☐ 51	Rikkert Faneyte	.10	.05	.01
☐ 52	Curtis Shaw	.10	.05	.01
☐ 53	Matt Drews	.75	.35	.09
☐ 54	Wilson Alvarez	.30	.14	.04
☐ 55	Manny Ramirez	1.50	.70	.19
☐ 56	Bobby Munoz	.10	.05	.01
☐ 57	Ed Sprague	.10	.05	.01

☐ 58	Jamey Wright	.30	.14	.04
☐ 59	Jeff Montgomery	.20	.09	.03
☐ 60	Kirk Rueter	.20	.09	.03
☐ 61	Edgar Martinez	.30	.14	.04
☐ 62	Luis Gonzalez	.10	.05	.01
☐ 63	Tim Vanegmond	.10	.05	.01
☐ 64	Bip Roberts	.10	.05	.01
☐ 65	John Jaha	.10	.05	.01
☐ 66	Chuck Carr	.10	.05	.01
☐ 67	Chuck Finley	.10	.05	.01
☐ 68	Aaron Holbert	.20	.09	.03
☐ 69	Cecil Fielder	.30	.14	.04
☐ 70	Tom Engle	.10	.05	.01
☐ 71	Ron Karkovice	.10	.05	.01
☐ 72	Joe Orsulak	.10	.05	.01
☐ 73	Duff Brumley	.10	.05	.01
☐ 74	Craig Clayton	.10	.05	.01
☐ 75	Cal Ripken	3.00	1.35	.35
☐ 76	Brad Fulimer	.30	.14	.04
☐ 77	Tony Tarasco	.30	.14	.04
☐ 78	Terry Farrar	.10	.05	.01
☐ 79	Matt Williams	.50	.23	.06
☐ 80	Rickey Henderson	.30	.14	.04
☐ 81	Terry Mulholland	.10	.05	.01
☐ 82	Sammy Sosa	.30	.14	.04
☐ 83	Paul Sorrento	.10	.05	.01
☐ 84	Pete Incaviglia	.10	.05	.01
☐ 85	Darren Hall	.10	.05	.01
☐ 86	Scott Klingenbeck	.20	.09	.03
☐ 87	Dario Perez	.10	.05	.01
☐ 88	Ugueth Urbina	.20	.09	.03
☐ 89	Dave Vanhof	.25	.11	.03
☐ 90	Domingo Jean	.10	.05	.01
☐ 91	Otis Nixon	.10	.05	.01
☐ 92	Andres Berumen	.10	.05	.01
☐ 93	Jose Valentin	.10	.05	.01
☐ 94	Edgar Renteria	.50	.23	.06
☐ 95	Chris Turner	.10	.05	.01
☐ 96	Ray Lankford	.30	.14	.04
☐ 97	Danny Bautista	.10	.05	.01
☐ 98	Chan Ho Park	.30	.14	.04
☐ 99	Glenn DiSarcina	.20	.09	.03
☐ 100	Butch Huskey	.20	.09	.03
☐ 101	Ivan Rodriguez	.30	.14	.04
☐ 102	Johnny Ruffin	.10	.05	.01
☐ 103	Alex Ochoa	.20	.09	.03
☐ 104	Torii Hunter	.25	.11	.03
☐ 105	Ryan Klesko	.75	.35	.09
☐ 106	Jay Bell	.20	.09	.03
☐ 107	Kurt Peltzer	.10	.05	.01
☐ 108	Miguel Jimenez	.20	.09	.03
☐ 109	Russ Davis	.20	.09	.03
☐ 110	Derek Wallace	.10	.05	.01
☐ 111	Keith Lockhart	.10	.05	.01
☐ 112	Mike Lieberthal	.10	.05	.01
☐ 113	Dave Stewart	.20	.09	.03
☐ 114	Tom Schmidt	.10	.05	.01
☐ 115	Brian McRae	.20	.09	.03
☐ 116	Moises Alou	.30	.14	.04
☐ 117	Dave Fleming	.10	.05	.01
☐ 118	Jeff Bagwell	1.00	.45	.12
☐ 119	Luis Ortiz	.10	.05	.01
☐ 120	Tony Gwynn	1.00	.45	.12
☐ 121	Jaime Navarro	.10	.05	.01
☐ 122	Benny Santiago	.10	.05	.01
☐ 123	Darrell Whitmore	.10	.05	.01
☐ 124	John Mabry	.20	.09	.03
☐ 125	Mickey Tettleton	.20	.09	.03
☐ 126	Tom Candiotti	.10	.05	.01
☐ 127	Tim Raines	.30	.14	.04
☐ 128	Bobby Bonilla	.30	.14	.04
☐ 129	John Dettmer	.20	.09	.03
☐ 130	Hector Carrasco	.10	.05	.01
☐ 131	Chris Hoiles	.20	.09	.03
☐ 132	Rick Aguilera	.20	.09	.03
☐ 133	David Justice	.40	.18	.05
☐ 134	Esteban Loaiza	.30	.14	.04
☐ 135	Barry Bonds	.75	.35	.09
☐ 136	Bob Welch	.10	.05	.01
☐ 137	Mike Stanley	.10	.05	.01
☐ 138	Roberto Hernandez	.10	.05	.01
☐ 139	Sandy Alomar	.20	.09	.03
☐ 140	Darren Daulton	.30	.14	.04
☐ 141	Angel Martinez	.30	.14	.04
☐ 142	Howard Johnson	.10	.05	.01
☐ 143	Bob Hamelin	.10	.05	.01
☐ 144	J.J. Thobe	.10	.05	.01
☐ 145	Roger Salkeld	.10	.05	.01
☐ 146	Orlando Miller	.10	.05	.01
☐ 147	Dmitri Young	.20	.09	.03
☐ 148	Tim Hyers	.10	.05	.01
☐ 149	Mark Loretta	.25	.11	.03
☐ 150	Chris Hammond	.10	.05	.01
☐ 151	Joel Moore	.40	.18	.05
☐ 152	Todd Zeile	.20	.09	.03
☐ 153	Wil Cordero	.30	.14	.04
☐ 154	Chris Smith	.10	.05	.01
☐ 155	James Baldwin	.20	.09	.03
☐ 156	Edgardo Alfonzo	.75	.35	.09
☐ 157	Kym Ashworth	.40	.18	.05
☐ 158	Paul Bako	.20	.09	.03
☐ 159	Rick Krivda	.20	.09	.03
☐ 160	Pat Mahomes	.10	.05	.01
☐ 161	Damon Hollins	.10	.05	.01
☐ 162	Felix Martinez	.25	.11	.03
☐ 163	Jason Myers	.30	.14	.04
☐ 164	Izzy Molina	.20	.09	.03
☐ 165	Brien Taylor	.30	.14	.04
☐ 166	Kevin Orie	.25	.11	.03
☐ 167	Casey Whitten	.30	.14	.04
☐ 168	Tony Longmire	.10	.05	.01
☐ 169	John Olerud	.30	.14	.04
☐ 170	Mark Thompson	.10	.05	.01
☐ 171	Jorge Fabregas	.10	.05	.01
☐ 172	John Wetteland	.10	.05	.01
☐ 173	Dan Wilson	.10	.05	.01
☐ 174	Doug Drabek	.30	.14	.04
☐ 175	Jeffrey McNeely	.10	.05	.01
☐ 176	Melvin Nieves	.20	.09	.03
☐ 177	Doug Glanville	.20	.09	.03
☐ 178	Javier De La Hoya	.10	.05	.01
☐ 179	Chad Curtis	.20	.09	.03
☐ 180	Brian Barber	.20	.09	.03
☐ 181	Mike Henneman	.10	.05	.01
☐ 182	Jose Offerman	.10	.05	.01
☐ 183	Robert Ellis	.10	.05	.01
☐ 184	John Franco	.10	.05	.01
☐ 185	Benji Gil	.20	.09	.03
☐ 186	Hal Morris	.20	.09	.03
☐ 187	Chris Sabo	.10	.05	.01
☐ 188	Blaise Ilsley	.10	.05	.01
☐ 189	Steve Avery	.30	.14	.04
☐ 190	Rick White	.10	.05	.01
☐ 191	Rod Beck	.20	.09	.03
☐ 192	Mark McGwire UER	.30	.14	.04
	(No card number on back)			
☐ 193	Jim Abbott	.30	.14	.04
☐ 194	Randy Myers	.10	.05	.01
☐ 195	Kenny Lofton	1.00	.45	.12
☐ 196	Mariano Duncan	.10	.05	.01
☐ 197	Lee Daniels	.10	.05	.01
☐ 198	Armando Reynoso	.10	.05	.01

☐ 199	Joe Randa	.10	.05	.01	☐ 269	Tom Henke	.10	.05	.01
☐ 200	Cliff Floyd	.20	.09	.03	☐ 270	Calvin Reese	.20	.09	.03
☐ 201	Tim Harkrider	.10	.05	.01	☐ 271	Greg Zaun	.20	.09	.03
☐ 202	Kevin Gallaher	.10	.05	.01	☐ 272	Todd Ritchie	.10	.05	.01
☐ 203	Scott Cooper	.20	.09	.03	☐ 273	Javier Lopez	.50	.23	.06
☐ 204	Phil Stidham	.10	.05	.01	☐ 274	Kevin Young	.10	.05	.01
☐ 205	Jeff D'Amico	.75	.35	.09	☐ 275	Kirt Manwaring	.10	.05	.01
☐ 206	Matt Whisenant	.10	.05	.01	☐ 276	Bill Taylor	.10	.05	.01
☐ 207	De Shawn Warren	.20	.09	.03	☐ 277	Robert Eenhoorn	.10	.05	.01
☐ 208	Rene Arocha	.10	.05	.01	☐ 278	Jessie Hollins	.10	.05	.01
☐ 209	Tony Clark	.50	.23	.06	☐ 279	Julian Tavarez	.60	.25	.07
☐ 210	Jason Jacome	.25	.11	.03	☐ 280	Gene Schall	.20	.09	.03
☐ 211	Scott Christman	.10	.05	.01	☐ 281	Paul Molitor	.20	.09	.03
☐ 212	Bill Pulsipher	.50	.23	.06	☐ 282	Neifi Perez	.25	.11	.03
☐ 213	Dean Palmer	.20	.09	.03	☐ 283	Greg Gagne	.10	.05	.01
☐ 214	Chad Mottola	.20	.09	.03	☐ 284	Marquis Grissom	.30	.14	.04
☐ 215	Manny Alexander	.10	.05	.01	☐ 285	Randy Johnson	.60	.25	.07
☐ 216	Rich Becker	.20	.09	.03	☐ 286	Pete Harnisch	.10	.05	.01
☐ 217	Andre King	.25	.11	.03	☐ 287	Joel Bennett	.20	.09	.03
☐ 218	Carlos Garcia	.10	.05	.01	☐ 288	Derek Bell	.20	.09	.03
☐ 219	Ron Pezzoni	.10	.05	.01	☐ 289	Darryl Hamilton	.10	.05	.01
☐ 220	Steve Karsay	.10	.05	.01	☐ 290	Gary Sheffield	.30	.14	.04
☐ 221	Jose Musset	.10	.05	.01	☐ 291	Eduardo Perez	.10	.05	.01
☐ 222	Karl Rhodes	.10	.05	.01	☐ 292	Basil Shabazz	.10	.05	.01
☐ 223	Frank Cimorelli	.10	.05	.01	☐ 293	Eric Davis	.10	.05	.01
☐ 224	Kevin Jordan	.20	.09	.03	☐ 294	Pedro Astacio	.20	.09	.03
☐ 225	Duane Ward	.10	.05	.01	☐ 295	Robin Ventura	.20	.09	.03
☐ 226	John Burke	.20	.09	.03	☐ 296	Jeff Kent	.20	.09	.03
☐ 227	Mike Macfarlane	.10	.05	.01	☐ 297	Rick Helling	.10	.05	.01
☐ 228	Mike Lansing	.20	.09	.03	☐ 298	Joe Oliver	.10	.05	.01
☐ 229	Chuck Knoblauch	.30	.14	.04	☐ 299	Lee Smith	.30	.14	.04
☐ 230	Ken Caminiti	.20	.09	.03	☐ 300	Dave Winfield	.30	.14	.04
☐ 231	Gar Finnvold	.10	.05	.01	☐ 301	Deion Sanders	.60	.25	.07
☐ 232	Derrek Lee	1.25	.55	.16	☐ 302	Ravelo Manzanillo	.10	.05	.01
☐ 233	Brady Anderson	.20	.09	.03	☐ 303	Mark Portugal	.10	.05	.01
☐ 234	Vic Darensbourg	.20	.09	.03	☐ 304	Brent Gates	.20	.09	.03
☐ 235	Mark Langston	.30	.14	.04	☐ 305	Wade Boggs	.30	.14	.04
☐ 236	T.J. Mathews	.20	.09	.03	☐ 306	Rick Wilkins	.10	.05	.01
☐ 237	Lou Whitaker	.30	.14	.04	☐ 307	Carlos Baerga	.60	.25	.07
☐ 238	Roger Cedeno	.50	.23	.06	☐ 308	Curt Schilling	.20	.09	.03
☐ 239	Alex Fernandez	.30	.14	.04	☐ 309	Shannon Stewart	.20	.09	.03
☐ 240	Ryan Thompson	.20	.09	.03	☐ 310	Darren Holmes	.10	.05	.01
☐ 241	Kerry Lacy	.10	.05	.01	☐ 311	Robert Toth	.20	.09	.03
☐ 242	Reggie Sanders	.20	.09	.03	☐ 312	Gabe White	.20	.09	.03
☐ 243	Brad Pennington	.10	.05	.01	☐ 313	Mac Suzuki	.30	.14	.04
☐ 244	Bryan Eversgerd	.10	.05	.01	☐ 314	Alvin Morman	.10	.05	.01
☐ 245	Greg Maddux	3.00	1.35	.35	☐ 315	Mo Vaughn	.50	.23	.06
☐ 246	Jason Kendall	.30	.14	.04	☐ 316	Bryce Florie	.10	.05	.01
☐ 247	J.R. Phillips	.20	.09	.03	☐ 317	Gabby Martinez	.25	.11	.03
☐ 248	Bobby Witt	.10	.05	.01	☐ 318	Carl Everett	.20	.09	.03
☐ 249	Paul O'Neill	.20	.09	.03	☐ 319	Kerwin Moore	.10	.05	.01
☐ 250	Ryne Sandberg	.75	.35	.09	☐ 320	Tom Pagnozzi	.10	.05	.01
☐ 251	Charles Nagy	.20	.09	.03	☐ 321	Chris Gomez	.30	.14	.04
☐ 252	Kevin Stocker	.20	.09	.03	☐ 322	Todd Williams	.10	.05	.01
☐ 253	Shawn Green	.40	.18	.05	☐ 323	Pat Hentgen	.20	.09	.03
☐ 254	Charlie Hayes	.20	.09	.03	☐ 324	Kirk Presley	.30	.14	.04
☐ 255	Donnie Elliott	.10	.05	.01	☐ 325	Kevin Brown	.10	.05	.01
☐ 256	Rob Fitzpatrick	.10	.05	.01	☐ 326	Jason Isringhausen	6.00	2.70	.75
☐ 257	Tim Davis	.10	.05	.01	☐ 327	Rick Forney	.20	.09	.03
☐ 258	James Mouton	.20	.09	.03	☐ 328	Carlos Pulido	.20	.09	.03
☐ 259	Mike Greenwell	.20	.09	.03	☐ 329	Terrell Wade	.40	.18	.05
☐ 260	Ray McDavid	.10	.05	.01	☐ 330	Al Martin	.10	.05	.01
☐ 261	Mike Kelly	.20	.09	.03	☐ 331	Dan Carlson	.10	.05	.01
☐ 262	Andy Larkin	.30	.14	.04	☐ 332	Mark Acre	.10	.05	.01
☐ 263	Marquis Riley UER	.10	.05	.01	☐ 333	Sterling Hitchcock	.20	.09	.03
	(No card number on back)				☐ 334	Jon Ratliff	.20	.09	.03
☐ 264	Bob Tewksbury	.10	.05	.01	☐ 335	Alex Ramirez	.50	.23	.06
☐ 265	Brian Edmondson	.10	.05	.01	☐ 336	Phil Geisler	.10	.05	.01
☐ 266	Eduardo Lantigua	.20	.09	.03	☐ 337	Eddie Zambrano	.10	.05	.01
☐ 267	Brandon Wilson	.10	.05	.01	☐ 338	Jim Thome	.60	.25	.07
☐ 268	Mike Welch	.10	.05	.01	☐ 339	James Mouton	.20	.09	.03

☐ 340 Cliff Floyd	.20	.09	.03
☐ 341 Carlos Delgado	.20	.09	.03
☐ 342 Roberto Petagine	.20	.09	.03
☐ 343 Tim Clark	.10	.05	.01
☐ 344 Bubba Smith	.10	.05	.01
☐ 345 Randy Curtis	.20	.09	.03
☐ 346 Joe Biasucci	.20	.09	.03
☐ 347 D.J. Boston	.20	.09	.03
☐ 348 Ruben Rivera	10.00	4.50	1.25
☐ 349 Bryan Link	.10	.05	.01
☐ 350 Mike Bell	.25	.11	.03
☐ 351 Marty Watson	.10	.05	.01
☐ 352 Jason Myers	.30	.14	.04
☐ 353 Chipper Jones	1.50	.70	.19
☐ 354 Brooks Kieschnick	2.50	1.10	.30
☐ 355 Calvin Reese	.20	.09	.03
☐ 356 John Burke	.10	.05	.01
☐ 357 Kurt Miller	.10	.05	.01
☐ 358 Orlando Miller	.10	.05	.01
☐ 359 Todd Hollandsworth	.20	.09	.03
☐ 360 Rondell White	.20	.09	.03
☐ 361 Bill Pulsipher	.50	.23	.06
☐ 362 Tyler Green	.10	.05	.01
☐ 363 Midre Cummings	.20	.09	.03
☐ 364 Brian Barber	.20	.09	.03
☐ 365 Melvin Nieves	.20	.09	.03
☐ 366 Salomon Torres	.20	.09	.03
☐ 367 Alex Ochoa	.20	.09	.03
☐ 368 Frankie Rodriguez	.20	.09	.03
☐ 369 Brian Anderson	.20	.09	.03
☐ 370 James Baldwin	.30	.14	.04
☐ 371 Manny Ramirez	1.50	.70	.19
☐ 372 Justin Thompson	.20	.09	.03
☐ 373 Johnny Damon	1.50	.70	.19
☐ 374 Jeff D'Amico	.75	.35	.09
☐ 375 Rich Becker	.20	.09	.03
☐ 376 Derek Jeter	.75	.35	.09
☐ 377 Steve Karsay	.10	.05	.01
☐ 378 Mac Suzuki	.30	.14	.04
☐ 379 Benji Gil	.20	.09	.03
☐ 380 Alex Gonzalez	.20	.09	.03
☐ 381 Jason Bere	.20	.09	.03
☐ 382 Brett Butler	.20	.09	.03
☐ 383 Jeff Conine	.30	.14	.04
☐ 384 Darren Daulton	.30	.14	.04
☐ 385 Jeff Kent	.20	.09	.03
☐ 386 Don Mattingly	1.50	.70	.19
☐ 387 Mike Piazza	1.25	.55	.16
☐ 388 Ryne Sandberg	.75	.35	.09
☐ 389 Rich Amaral	.10	.05	.01
☐ 390 Craig Biggio	.20	.09	.03
☐ 391 Jeff Suppan	.50	.23	.06
☐ 392 Andy Benes	.20	.09	.03
☐ 393 Cal Eldred	.20	.09	.03
☐ 394 Jeff Conine	.30	.14	.04
☐ 395 Tim Salmon	.60	.25	.07
☐ 396 Ray Suplee	.10	.05	.01
☐ 397 Tony Phillips	.10	.05	.01
☐ 398 Ramon Martinez	.20	.09	.03
☐ 399 Julio Franco	.20	.09	.03
☐ 400 Dwight Wooden	.10	.05	.01
☐ 401 Kevin Lomon	.10	.05	.01
☐ 402 Jose Rijo	.20	.09	.03
☐ 403 Mike Devereaux	.20	.09	.03
☐ 404 Mike Zolecki	.10	.05	.01
☐ 405 Fred McGriff	.40	.18	.05
☐ 406 Danny Clyburn	.20	.09	.03
☐ 407 Robby Thompson	.10	.05	.01
☐ 408 Terry Steinbach	.20	.09	.03
☐ 409 Luis Polonia	.10	.05	.01
☐ 410 Mark Grace	.30	.14	.04

☐ 411 Albert Belle	1.25	.55	.16
☐ 412 John Kruk	.10	.05	.01
☐ 413 Scott Spiezio	.30	.14	.04
☐ 414 Ellis Burks UER	.20	.09	.03
(Name spelled Elkis on front)			
☐ 415 Joe Vitiello	.20	.09	.03
☐ 416 Tim Costo	.10	.05	.01
☐ 417 Marc Newfield	.20	.09	.03
☐ 418 Oscar Henriquez	.25	.11	.03
☐ 419 Matt Perisho	.25	.11	.03
☐ 420 Julio Bruno	.10	.05	.01
☐ 421 Kenny Felder	.10	.05	.01
☐ 422 Tyler Green	.20	.09	.03
☐ 423 Jim Edmonds	.50	.23	.06
☐ 424 Ozzie Smith	.60	.25	.07
☐ 425 Rick Greene	.10	.05	.01
☐ 426 Todd Hollandsworth	.20	.09	.03
☐ 427 Eddie Pearson	.30	.14	.04
☐ 428 Quilvio Veras	.20	.09	.03
☐ 429 Kenny Rogers	.10	.05	.01
☐ 430 Willie Greene	.10	.05	.01
☐ 431 Vaughn Eshelman	.20	.09	.03
☐ 432 Pat Meares	.10	.05	.01
☐ 433 Jermaine Dye	1.50	.70	.19
☐ 434 Steve Cooke	.10	.05	.01
☐ 435 Bill Swift	.10	.05	.01
☐ 436 Fausto Cruz	.20	.09	.03
☐ 437 Mark Hutton	.10	.05	.01
☐ 438 Brooks Kieschnick	2.50	1.10	.30
☐ 439 Yorkis Perez	.10	.05	.01
☐ 440 Len Dykstra	.30	.14	.04
☐ 441 Pat Borders	.10	.05	.01
☐ 442 Doug Walls	.25	.11	.03
☐ 443 Wally Joyner	.10	.05	.01
☐ 444 Ken Hill	.20	.09	.03
☐ 445 Eric Anthony	.10	.05	.01
☐ 446 Mitch Williams	.10	.05	.01
☐ 447 Cory Bailey	.10	.05	.01
☐ 448 Dave Staton	.10	.05	.01
☐ 449 Greg Vaughn	.20	.09	.03
☐ 450 Dave Magadan	.10	.05	.01
☐ 451 Chili Davis	.20	.09	.03
☐ 452 Gerald Santos	.10	.05	.01
☐ 453 Joe Perona	.10	.05	.01
☐ 454 Delino DeShields	.20	.09	.03
☐ 455 Jack McDowell	.20	.09	.03
☐ 456 Todd Hundley	.20	.09	.03
☐ 457 Ritchie Moody	.10	.05	.01
☐ 458 Bret Boone	.30	.14	.04
☐ 459 Ben McDonald	.20	.09	.03
☐ 460 Kirby Puckett	1.00	.45	.12
☐ 461 Gregg Olson	.10	.05	.01
☐ 462 Rich Aude	.20	.09	.03
☐ 463 John Burkett	.10	.05	.01
☐ 464 Troy Neel	.10	.05	.01
☐ 465 Jimmy Key	.20	.09	.03
☐ 466 Ozzie Timmons	.20	.09	.03
☐ 467 Eddie Murray	.40	.18	.05
☐ 468 Mark Tranberg	.10	.05	.01
☐ 469 Alex Gonzalez	.30	.14	.04
☐ 470 David Nied	.20	.09	.03
☐ 471 Barry Larkin	.40	.18	.05
☐ 472 Brian Looney	.10	.05	.01
☐ 473 Shawn Estes	.20	.09	.03
☐ 474 A.J. Sager	.10	.05	.01
☐ 475 Roger Clemens	.50	.23	.06
☐ 476 Vince Moore	.10	.05	.01
☐ 477 Scott Karl	.20	.09	.03
☐ 478 Kurt Miller	.10	.05	.01
☐ 479 Garret Anderson	1.00	.45	.12
☐ 480 Allen Watson	.10	.05	.01

☐	481 Jose Lima	.50	.23	.06	☐ 552 Ryan Karp	.20	.09	.03
☐	482 Rick Gorecki	.10	.05	.01	☐ 553 Juan Guzman	.10	.05	.01
☐	483 Jimmy Hurst	.30	.14	.04	☐ 554 Bryan Rekar	.40	.18	.05
☐	484 Preston Wilson	.20	.09	.03	☐ 555 Kevin Appier	.20	.09	.03
☐	485 Will Clark	.40	.18	.05	☐ 556 Chris Schwab	.25	.11	.03
☐	486 Mike Ferry	.10	.05	.01	☐ 557 Jay Buhner	.20	.09	.03
☐	487 Curtis Goodwin	.50	.23	.06	☐ 558 Andujar Cedeno	.10	.05	.01
☐	488 Mike Myers	.10	.05	.01	☐ 559 Ryan McGuire	.20	.09	.03
☐	489 Chipper Jones	1.50	.70	.19	☐ 560 Ricky Gutierrez	.10	.05	.01
☐	490 Jeff King	.10	.05	.01	☐ 561 Keith Kimsey	.10	.05	.01
☐	491 William VanLandingham	.30	.14	.04	☐ 562 Tim Clark	.10	.05	.01
☐	492 Carlos Reyes	.20	.09	.03	☐ 563 Damion Easley	.10	.05	.01
☐	493 Andy Pettitte	.75	.35	.09	☐ 564 Clint Davis	.10	.05	.01
☐	494 Brant Brown	.10	.05	.01	☐ 565 Mike Moore	.10	.05	.01
☐	495 Daron Kirkreit	.10	.05	.01	☐ 566 Orel Hershiser	.20	.09	.03
☐	496 Ricky Bottalico	.20	.09	.03	☐ 567 Jason Bere	.20	.09	.03
☐	497 Devon White	.10	.05	.01	☐ 568 Kevin McReynolds	.10	.05	.01
☐	498 Jason Johnson	.10	.05	.01	☐ 569 Leland Macon	.25	.11	.03
☐	499 Vince Coleman	.10	.05	.01	☐ 570 John Courtright	.10	.05	.01
☐	500 Larry Walker	.40	.18	.05	☐ 571 Sid Fernandez	.10	.05	.01
☐	501 Bobby Ayala	.10	.05	.01	☐ 572 Chad Roper	.10	.05	.01
☐	502 Steve Finley	.10	.05	.01	☐ 573 Terry Pendleton	.10	.05	.01
☐	503 Scott Fletcher	.10	.05	.01	☐ 574 Danny Miceli	.10	.05	.01
☐	504 Brad Ausmus	.10	.05	.01	☐ 575 Joe Rosselli	.10	.05	.01
☐	505 Scott Talanoa	.10	.05	.01	☐ 576 Mike Bordick	.10	.05	.01
☐	506 Orestes Destrade	.10	.05	.01	☐ 577 Danny Tartabull	.20	.09	.03
☐	507 Gary DiSarcina	.10	.05	.01	☐ 578 Jose Guzman	.10	.05	.01
☐	508 Willie Smith	.10	.05	.01	☐ 579 Omar Vizquel	.10	.05	.01
☐	509 Alan Trammell	.20	.09	.03	☐ 580 Tommy Greene	.10	.05	.01
☐	510 Mike Piazza	1.25	.55	.16	☐ 581 Paul Spoljaric	.10	.05	.01
☐	511 Ozzie Guillen	.10	.05	.01	☐ 582 Walt Weiss	.10	.05	.01
☐	512 Jeromy Burnitz	.10	.05	.01	☐ 583 Oscar Jimenez	.25	.11	.03
☐	513 Darren Oliver	.10	.05	.01	☐ 584 Rod Henderson	.20	.09	.03
☐	514 Kevin Mitchell	.20	.09	.03	☐ 585 Derek Lowe	.10	.05	.01
☐	515 Rafael Palmeiro	.30	.14	.04	☐ 586 Richard Hidalgo	.75	.35	.09
☐	516 David McCarty	.10	.05	.01	☐ 587 Shayne Bennett	.20	.09	.03
☐	517 Jeff Blauser	.20	.09	.03	☐ 588 Tim Belk	.20	.09	.03
☐	518 Trey Beamon	.40	.18	.05	☐ 589 Matt Mieske	.10	.05	.01
☐	519 Royce Clayton	.20	.09	.03	☐ 590 Nigel Wilson	.10	.05	.01
☐	520 Dennis Eckersley	.30	.14	.04	☐ 591 Jeff Knox	.20	.09	.03
☐	521 Bernie Williams	.30	.14	.04	☐ 592 Bernard Gilkey	.20	.09	.03
☐	522 Steve Buechele	.10	.05	.01	☐ 593 David Cone	.30	.14	.04
☐	523 Denny Martinez	.20	.09	.03	☐ 594 Paul LoDuca	.20	.09	.03
☐	524 Dave Hollins	.20	.09	.03	☐ 595 Scott Ruffcorn	.20	.09	.03
☐	525 Joey Hamilton	.20	.09	.03	☐ 596 Chris Roberts	.20	.09	.03
☐	526 Andres Galarraga	.30	.14	.04	☐ 597 Oscar Munoz	.10	.05	.01
☐	527 Jeff Granger	.20	.09	.03	☐ 598 Scott Sullivan	.20	.09	.03
☐	528 Joey Eischen	.20	.09	.03	☐ 599 Matt Jarvis	.10	.05	.01
☐	529 Desi Relaford	.20	.09	.03	☐ 600 Jose Canseco	.50	.23	.06
☐	530 Roberto Petagine	.20	.09	.03	☐ 601 Tony Graffanino	.20	.09	.03
☐	531 Andre Dawson	.30	.14	.04	☐ 602 Don Slaught	.10	.05	.01
☐	532 Ray Holbert	.10	.05	.01	☐ 603 Brett King	.20	.09	.03
☐	533 Duane Singleton	.10	.05	.01	☐ 604 Jose Herrera	.30	.14	.04
☐	534 Kurt Abbott	.25	.11	.03	☐ 605 Melido Perez	.10	.05	.01
☐	535 Bo Jackson	.30	.14	.04	☐ 606 Mike Hubbard	.10	.05	.01
☐	536 Gregg Jefferies	.30	.14	.04	☐ 607 Chad Ogea	.20	.09	.03
☐	537 David Mysel	.10	.05	.01	☐ 608 Wayne Gomes	.40	.18	.05
☐	538 Raul Mondesi	1.00	.45	.12	☐ 609 Roberto Alomar	.60	.25	.07
☐	539 Chris Snopek	.10	.05	.01	☐ 610 Angel Echevarria	.50	.23	.06
☐	540 Brook Fordyce	.10	.05	.01	☐ 611 Jose Lind	.10	.05	.01
☐	541 Ron Frazier	.10	.05	.01	☐ 612 Darrin Fletcher	.10	.05	.01
☐	542 Brian Koelling	.10	.05	.01	☐ 613 Chris Bosio	.10	.05	.01
☐	543 Jimmy Haynes	.20	.09	.03	☐ 614 Darryl Kile	.20	.09	.03
☐	544 Marty Cordova	1.00	.45	.12	☐ 615 Frankie Rodriguez	.30	.14	.04
☐	545 Jason Green	.25	.11	.03	☐ 616 Phil Plantier	.10	.05	.01
☐	546 Orlando Merced	.20	.09	.03	☐ 617 Pat Listach	.10	.05	.01
☐	547 Lou Pote	.10	.05	.01	☐ 618 Charlie Hough	.10	.05	.01
☐	548 Todd Van Poppel	.20	.09	.03	☐ 619 Ryan Hancock	.30	.14	.04
☐	549 Pat Kelly	.10	.05	.01	☐ 620 Darrel Deak	.10	.05	.01
☐	550 Turk Wendell	.10	.05	.01	☐ 621 Travis Fryman	.30	.14	.04
☐	551 Herbert Perry	.30	.14	.04	☐ 622 Brett Butler	.20	.09	.03

☐ 623 Lance Johnson	.10	.05	.01
☐ 624 Pete Smith	.10	.05	.01
☐ 625 James Hurst	.10	.05	.01
☐ 626 Roberto Kelly	.10	.05	.01
☐ 627 Mike Mussina	.40	.18	.05
☐ 628 Kevin Tapani	.10	.05	.01
☐ 629 John Smoltz	.20	.09	.03
☐ 630 Midre Cummings	.20	.09	.03
☐ 631 Salomon Torres	.20	.09	.03
☐ 632 Willie Adams	.10	.05	.01
☐ 633 Derek Jeter	.75	.35	.09
☐ 634 Steve Trachsel	.20	.09	.03
☐ 635 Albie Lopez	.20	.09	.03
☐ 636 Jason Moler	.10	.05	.01
☐ 637 Carlos Delgado	.20	.09	.03
☐ 638 Roberto Mejia	.10	.05	.01
☐ 639 Darren Burton	.10	.05	.01
☐ 640 B.J. Wallace	.10	.05	.01
☐ 641 Brad Clontz	.50	.23	.06
☐ 642 Billy Wagner	.60	.25	.07
☐ 643 Aaron Sele	.20	.09	.03
☐ 644 Cameron Cairncross	.10	.05	.01
☐ 645 Brian Harper	.10	.05	.01
☐ 646 Marc Valdes UER	.20	.09	.03
(No card number on back)			
☐ 647 Mark Ratekin	.10	.05	.01
☐ 648 Terry Bradshaw	.20	.09	.03
☐ 649 Justin Thompson	.20	.09	.03
☐ 650 Mike Busch	.20	.09	.03
☐ 651 Joe Hall	.10	.05	.01
☐ 652 Bobby Jones	.20	.09	.03
☐ 653 Kelly Stinnett	.10	.05	.01
☐ 654 Rod Steph	.10	.05	.01
☐ 655 Jay Powell	.30	.14	.04
☐ 656 Keith Garagozzo UER	.10	.05	.01
(No card number on back)			
☐ 657 Todd Dunn	.20	.09	.03
☐ 658 Charles Peterson	.50	.23	.06
☐ 659 Darren Lewis	.10	.05	.01
☐ 660 John Wasdin	.60	.25	.07
☐ 661 Tate Seefried	.20	.09	.03
☐ 662 Hector Trinidad	.25	.11	.03
☐ 663 John Carter	.10	.05	.01
☐ 664 Larry Mitchell	.10	.05	.01
☐ 665 David Catlett	.25	.11	.03
☐ 666 Dante Bichette	.40	.18	.05
☐ 667 Felix Jose	.10	.05	.01
☐ 668 Rondell White	.20	.09	.03
☐ 669 Tino Martinez	.30	.14	.04
☐ 670 Brian L. Hunter	.75	.35	.09
☐ 671 Jose Malave	.20	.09	.03
☐ 672 Archi Cianfrocco	.10	.05	.01
☐ 673 Mike Matheny	.10	.05	.01
☐ 674 Bret Barberie	.10	.05	.01
☐ 675 Andrew Lorraine	.25	.11	.03
☐ 676 Brian Jordan	.20	.09	.03
☐ 677 Tim Belcher	.10	.05	.01
☐ 678 Antonio Osuna	.25	.11	.03
☐ 679 Checklist	.10	.05	.01
☐ 680 Checklist	.10	.05	.01
☐ 681 Checklist	.10	.05	.01
☐ 682 Checklist	.10	.05	.01

1994 Bowman's Best

This 200-card standard-size set consists of 90 veteran stars, 90 rookies and prospects

and 20 Mirror Image cards. The veteran cards have red backs and are designated 1R-90R. The rookies and prospects cards have blue backs and are designated 1B-90B. The Mirror Image cards feature a veteran star and a prospect matched by position. These cards are numbered 91-110. Subsets featured are Super Vet (1R-6R), Super Rookie (82R-90R), and Blue Chip (1B-11B). Rookie Cards include Brooks Kieschnick and Chan Ho Park.

	MINT	NRMT	EXC
COMPLETE SET (200)	90.00	40.00	11.00
COMMON BLUE CARD (B1-B90)	.40	.18	.05
COMMON RED CARD (R1-R90)	.40	.18	.05
COMMON MIR. IMAGE (X91-X110)	.40	.18	.05

☐ B1 Chipper Jones	5.00	2.20	.60
☐ B2 Derek Jeter	2.50	1.10	.30
☐ B3 Bill Pulsipher	1.50	.70	.19
☐ B4 James Baldwin	.60	.25	.07
☐ B5 Brooks Kieschnick	6.00	2.70	.75
☐ B6 Justin Thompson	.40	.18	.05
☐ B7 Midre Cummings	.40	.18	.05
☐ B8 Joey Hamilton	.40	.18	.05
☐ B9 Calvin Reese	.60	.25	.07
☐ B10 Brian Barber	.40	.18	.05
☐ B11 John Burke	.40	.18	.05
☐ B12 DeShawn Warren	.60	.25	.07
☐ B13 Edgardo Alfonzo	2.00	.90	.25
☐ B14 Eddie Pearson	1.00	.45	.12
☐ B15 Jimmy Haynes	.60	.25	.07
☐ B16 Danny Bautista	.40	.18	.05
☐ B17 Roger Cedeno	1.25	.55	.16
☐ B18 Jon Lieber	.40	.18	.05
☐ B19 Billy Wagner	2.00	.90	.25
☐ B20 Tate Seefried	.60	.25	.07
☐ B21 Chad Mottola	.40	.18	.05
☐ B22 Jose Malave	.60	.25	.07
☐ B23 Terrell Wade	1.25	.55	.16
☐ B24 Shane Andrews	.60	.25	.07
☐ B25 Chan Ho Park	1.00	.45	.12
☐ B26 Kirk Presley	1.00	.45	.12
☐ B27 Robbie Beckett	.40	.18	.05
☐ B28 Orlando Miller	.40	.18	.05
☐ B29 Jorge Posada	.40	.18	.05
☐ B30 Frankie Rodriguez	.75	.35	.09
☐ B31 Brian L.Hunter	2.50	1.10	.30
☐ B32 Billy Ashley	.75	.35	.09
☐ B33 Rondell White	1.25	.55	.16
☐ B34 John Roper	.40	.18	.05
☐ B35 Marc Valdes	.60	.25	.07
☐ B36 Scott Ruffcorn	.60	.25	.07
☐ B37 Rod Henderson	.40	.18	.05
☐ B38 Curtis Goodwin	2.00	.90	.25

☐ B39 Russ Davis	.75	.35	.09	☐ R20 Steve Avery	.60	.25	.07
☐ B40 Rick Gorecki	.40	.18	.05	☐ R21 John Wetteland	.40	.18	.05
☐ B41 Johnny Damon	4.00	1.80	.50	☐ R22 Ben McDonald	.40	.18	.05
☐ B42 Roberto Petagine	.40	.18	.05	☐ R23 Jack McDowell	.60	.25	.07
☐ B43 Chris Snopek	.40	.18	.05	☐ R24 Jose Canseco	1.50	.70	.19
☐ B44 Mark Acre	.40	.18	.05	☐ R25 Tim Salmon	2.00	.90	.25
☐ B45 Todd Hollandsworth	.75	.35	.09	☐ R26 Wilson Alvarez	.60	.25	.07
☐ B46 Shawn Green	2.00	.90	.25	☐ R27 Gregg Jefferies	.75	.35	.09
☐ B47 John Carter	.40	.18	.05	☐ R28 John Burkett	.40	.18	.05
☐ B48 Jim Pittsley	1.25	.55	.16	☐ R29 Greg Vaughn	.60	.25	.07
☐ B49 John Wasdin	2.00	.90	.25	☐ R30 Robin Ventura	.60	.25	.07
☐ B50 D.J.Boston	.75	.35	.09	☐ R31 Paul O'Neill	.40	.18	.05
☐ B51 Tim Clark	.40	.18	.05	☐ R32 Cecil Fielder	.75	.35	.09
☐ B52 Alex Ochoa	.75	.35	.09	☐ R33 Kevin Mitchell	.40	.18	.05
☐ B53 Chad Roper	.40	.18	.05	☐ R34 Jeff Conine	.75	.35	.09
☐ B54 Mike Kelly	.40	.18	.05	☐ R35 Carlos Baerga	2.00	.90	.25
☐ B55 Brad Fullmer	1.00	.45	.12	☐ R36 Greg Maddux	10.00	4.50	1.25
☐ B56 Carl Everett	.75	.35	.09	☐ R37 Roger Clemens	1.50	.70	.19
☐ B57 Tim Belk	.60	.25	.07	☐ R38 Deion Sanders	2.00	.90	.25
☐ B58 Jimmy Hurst	1.00	.45	.12	☐ R39 Delino DeShields	.60	.25	.07
☐ B59 Mac Suzuki	1.00	.45	.12	☐ R40 Ken Griffey Jr.	10.00	4.50	1.25
☐ B60 Michael Moore	.40	.18	.05	☐ R41 Albert Belle	4.00	1.80	.50
☐ B61 Alan Benes	3.00	1.35	.35	☐ R42 Wade Boggs	.75	.35	.09
☐ B62 Tony Clark	1.50	.70	.19	☐ R43 Andres Galarraga	.75	.35	.09
☐ B63 Edgar Renteria	1.50	.70	.19	☐ R44 Aaron Sele	.75	.35	.09
☐ B64 Trey Beamon	1.25	.55	.16	☐ R45 Don Mattingly	5.00	2.20	.60
☐ B65 LaTroy Hawkins	1.00	.45	.12	☐ R46 David Cone	.75	.35	.09
☐ B66 Wayne Gomes	1.25	.55	.16	☐ R47 Len Dykstra	.75	.35	.09
☐ B67 Ray McDavid	.40	.18	.05	☐ R48 Brett Butler	.60	.25	.07
☐ B68 John Dettmer	.40	.18	.05	☐ R49 Bill Swift	.40	.18	.05
☐ B69 Willie Greene	.40	.18	.05	☐ R50 Bobby Bonilla	.60	.25	.07
☐ B70 Dave Stevens	.40	.18	.05	☐ R51 Rafael Palmeiro	.75	.35	.09
☐ B71 Kevin Orie	.75	.35	.09	☐ R52 Moises Alou	.60	.25	.07
☐ B72 Chad Ogea	.60	.25	.07	☐ R53 Jeff Bagwell	3.00	1.35	.35
☐ B73 Ben Van Ryn	.40	.18	.05	☐ R54 Mike Mussina	1.25	.55	.16
☐ B74 Kym Ashworth	1.25	.55	.16	☐ R55 Frank Thomas	10.00	4.50	1.25
☐ B75 Dmitri Young	.75	.35	.09	☐ R56 Jose Rijo	.60	.25	.07
☐ B76 Herbert Perry	1.00	.45	.12	☐ R57 Ruben Sierra	.60	.25	.07
☐ B77 Joey Eischen	.60	.25	.07	☐ R58 Randy Myers	.40	.18	.05
☐ B78 Arquimedez Pozo	1.25	.55	.16	☐ R59 Barry Bonds	2.00	.90	.25
☐ B79 Ugueth Urbina	.60	.25	.07	☐ R60 Jimmy Key	.40	.18	.05
☐ B80 Keith Williams	1.25	.55	.16	☐ R61 Travis Fryman	.75	.35	.09
☐ B81 John Frascatore	.40	.18	.05	☐ R62 John Olerud	.60	.25	.07
☐ B82 Garey Ingram	.40	.18	.05	☐ R63 David Justice	1.25	.55	.16
☐ B83 Aaron Small	.40	.18	.05	☐ R64 Ray Lankford	.75	.35	.09
☐ B84 Olmedo Saenz	.40	.18	.05	☐ R65 Bob Tewksbury	.40	.18	.05
☐ B85 Jesus Tavarez	.60	.25	.07	☐ R66 Chuck Carr	.40	.18	.05
☐ B86 Jose Silva	1.25	.55	.16	☐ R67 Jay Buhner	.60	.25	.07
☐ B87 Jay Witasick	.75	.35	.09	☐ R68 Kenny Lofton	3.00	1.35	.35
☐ B88 Jay Maldonado	.60	.25	.07	☐ R69 Marquis Grissom	.60	.25	.07
☐ B89 Keith Heberling	.60	.25	.07	☐ R70 Sammy Sosa	.75	.35	.09
☐ B90 Rusty Greer	1.25	.55	.16	☐ R71 Cal Ripken	10.00	4.50	1.25
☐ R1 Paul Molitor	.75	.35	.09	☐ R72 Ellis Burks	.40	.18	.05
☐ R2 Eddie Murray	1.25	.55	.16	☐ R73 Jeff Montgomery	.60	.25	.07
☐ R3 Ozzie Smith	2.00	.90	.25	☐ R74 Julio Franco	.60	.25	.07
☐ R4 Rickey Henderson	.75	.35	.09	☐ R75 Kirby Puckett	3.00	1.35	.35
☐ R5 Lee Smith	.60	.25	.07	☐ R76 Larry Walker	1.25	.55	.16
☐ R6 Dave Winfield	.75	.35	.09	☐ R77 Andy Van Slyke	.60	.25	.07
☐ R7 Roberto Alomar	2.00	.90	.25	☐ R78 Tony Gwynn	3.00	1.35	.35
☐ R8 Matt Williams	1.50	.70	.19	☐ R79 Will Clark	1.25	.55	.16
☐ R9 Mark Grace	.75	.35	.09	☐ R80 Mo Vaughn	1.50	.70	.19
☐ R10 Lance Johnson	.40	.18	.05	☐ R81 Mike Piazza	4.00	1.80	.50
☐ R11 Darren Daulton	.75	.35	.09	☐ R82 James Mouton	.60	.25	.07
☐ R12 Tom Glavine	.75	.35	.09	☐ R83 Carlos Delgado	.75	.35	.09
☐ R13 Gary Sheffield	.75	.35	.09	☐ R84 Ryan Klesko	2.50	1.10	.30
☐ R14 Rod Beck	.60	.25	.07	☐ R85 Javier Lopez	1.50	.70	.19
☐ R15 Fred McGriff	1.25	.55	.16	☐ R86 Raul Mondesi	3.00	1.35	.35
☐ R16 Joe Carter	.75	.35	.09	☐ R87 Cliff Floyd	.75	.35	.09
☐ R17 Dante Bichette	1.25	.55	.16	☐ R88 Manny Ramirez	5.00	2.20	.60
☐ R18 Danny Tartabull	.60	.25	.07	☐ R89 Hector Carrasco	.40	.18	.05
☐ R19 Juan Gonzalez	2.00	.90	.25	☐ R90 Jeff Granger	.60	.25	.07

☐ X91	Frank Thomas	5.00	2.20	.60
	Dmitri Young			
☐ X92	Fred McGriff	2.50	1.10	.30
	Brooks Kieschnick			
☐ X93	Matt Williams	.75	.35	.09
	Shane Andrews			
☐ X94	Cal Ripken	5.00	2.20	.60
	Kevin Orie			
☐ X95	Barry Larkin	1.25	.55	.16
	Derek Jeter			
☐ X96	Ken Griffey Jr.	6.00	2.70	.75
	Johnny Damon			
☐ X97	Barry Bonds	.75	.35	.09
	Rondell White			
☐ X98	Albert Belle	2.00	.90	.25
	Jimmy Hurst			
☐ X99	Raul Mondesi	10.00	4.50	1.25
	Ruben Rivera			
☐ X100	Roger Clemens	1.00	.45	.12
	Scott Ruffcorn			
☐ X101	Greg Maddux	5.00	2.20	.60
	John Wasdin			
☐ X102	Tim Salmon	1.00	.45	.12
	Chad Mottola			
☐ X103	Carlos Baerga	1.00	.45	.12
	Arquimedez Pozo			
☐ X104	Mike Piazza	2.00	.90	.25
	Bobby Hughes			
☐ X105	Carlos Delgado	.75	.35	.09
	Melvin Nieves			
☐ X106	Javier Lopez	1.00	.45	.12
	Jorge Posada			
☐ X107	Manny Ramirez	2.50	1.10	.30
	Jose Malave			
☐ X108	Travis Fryman	2.50	1.10	.30
	Chipper Jones			
☐ X109	Steve Avery	1.00	.45	.12
	Bill Pulsipher			
☐ X110	John Olerud	.75	.35	.09
	Shawn Green			

1994 Bowman's Best Refractors

This 200-card set is a parallel to the basic Bowman's Best issue. The cards were randomly inserted in packs at a rate of one in nine Bowman's Best packs. The only difference is the refractive finish that allows for a more glossy appearance. The cards are numbered with an "R" suffix.

	MINT	NRMT	EXC
COMPLETE SET (200)	1200.00	550.00	150.00
COMMON CARD	3.00	1.35	.35
*RED STARS: 6X to 12X BASIC CARDS			
*BLUE STARS: 4X to 8X BASIC CARDS			
*MIRROR IMAGE STARS:3X to 6X BASIC CARDS			

☐ B1	Chipper Jones	50.00	22.00	6.25
☐ B5	Brooks Kieschnick	30.00	13.50	3.70
☐ B41	Johnny Damon	30.00	13.50	3.70
☐ R36	Greg Maddux	100.00	45.00	12.50
☐ R40	Ken Griffey Jr.	100.00	45.00	12.50

☐ R41	Albert Belle	40.00	18.00	5.00
☐ R45	Don Mattingly	50.00	22.00	6.25
☐ R53	Jeff Bagwell	30.00	13.50	3.70
☐ R55	Frank Thomas	100.00	45.00	12.50
☐ R68	Kenny Lofton	30.00	13.50	3.70
☐ R71	Cal Ripken	120.00	55.00	15.00
☐ R75	Kirby Puckett	30.00	13.50	3.70
☐ R78	Tony Gwynn	30.00	13.50	3.70
☐ R81	Mike Piazza	40.00	18.00	5.00
☐ R86	Raul Mondesi	30.00	13.50	3.70
☐ R88	Manny Ramirez	50.00	22.00	6.25
☐ X99	Ruben Rivera	60.00	27.00	7.50
	Raul Mondesi			

1995 Bowman

This 439-card set includes 54 silver foil cards. The typical card front has the player name at bottom right with the last name in gold foil and team logo at bottom left. The Bowman logo at top right is done in red foil. The left border is a reversed negative of the photo. The backs are horizontally designed with a photo to the right and an analysis of how the player fared against each team. The foil subset, largely comprising of minor league stars, have embossed borders and are found one per pack. Rookie Cards include Hideo Nomo and Andruw Jones.

	MINT	NRMT	EXC
COMPLETE SET (439)	100.00	45.00	12.50
COMMON CARD (1-439)	.10	.05	.01
COMP. GOLD FOIL SET (54)	200.00	90.00	25.00
COMMON GOLD FOIL (221-274)	1.00	.45	.12
GOLD FOIL SEMISTARS	2.00	.90	.25
*STARS 5X REGULAR CARDS			

☐ 1	Billy Wagner	.20	.09	.03
☐ 2	Chris Widger	.10	.05	.01
☐ 3	Brent Bowers	.10	.05	.01
☐ 4	Bob Abreu	.75	.35	.09
☐ 5	Lou Collier	.25	.11	.03
☐ 6	Juan Acevedo	.10	.05	.01
☐ 7	Jason Kelley	.30	.14	.04
☐ 8	Brian Sackinsky	.10	.05	.01
☐ 9	Scott Christman	.10	.05	.01
☐ 10	Damon Hollins	.20	.09	.03
☐ 11	Willis Otanez	.25	.11	.03
☐ 12	Jason Ryan	.50	.23	.06
☐ 13	Jason Giambi	.10	.05	.01

☐ 14 Andy Taulbee	.20	.09	.03
☐ 15 Mark Thompson	.10	.05	.01
☐ 16 Hugo Pivaral	.40	.18	.05
☐ 17 Brien Taylor	.10	.05	.01
☐ 18 Antonio Osuna	.10	.05	.01
☐ 19 Edgardo Alfonzo	.20	.09	.03
☐ 20 Carl Everett	.10	.05	.01
☐ 21 Matt Drews	.20	.09	.03
☐ 22 Bartolo Colon	1.50	.70	.19
☐ 23 Andruw Jones	6.00	2.70	.75
☐ 24 Robert Person	.10	.05	.01
☐ 25 Derrek Lee	.30	.14	.04
☐ 26 John Ambrose	.30	.14	.04
☐ 27 Eric Knowles	.25	.11	.03
☐ 28 Chris Roberts	.10	.05	.01
☐ 29 Don Wengert	.10	.05	.01
☐ 30 Marcus Jensen	.25	.11	.03
☐ 31 Brian Barber	.10	.05	.01
☐ 32 Kevin Brown	.20	.09	.03
☐ 33 Benji Gil	.10	.05	.01
☐ 34 Mike Hubbard	.10	.05	.01
☐ 35 Bart Evans	.10	.05	.01
☐ 36 Enrique Wilson	.60	.25	.07
☐ 37 Brian Buchanan	.25	.11	.03
☐ 38 Ken Ray	.30	.14	.04
☐ 39 Micah Franklin	.60	.25	.07
☐ 40 Ricky Otero	.10	.05	.01
☐ 41 Jason Kendall	.20	.09	.03
☐ 42 Jimmy Hurst	.10	.05	.01
☐ 43 Jerry Wolak	.10	.05	.01
☐ 44 Jayson Peterson	.30	.14	.04
☐ 45 Allen Battle	.10	.05	.01
☐ 46 Scott Stahoviak	.10	.05	.01
☐ 47 Steve Schrenk	.10	.05	.01
☐ 48 Travis Miller	.30	.14	.04
☐ 49 Eddie Rios	.25	.11	.03
☐ 50 Mike Hampton	.10	.05	.01
☐ 51 Chad Frontera	.20	.09	.03
☐ 52 Tom Evans	.10	.05	.01
☐ 53 C.J. Nitkowski	.20	.09	.03
☐ 54 Clay Caruthers	.25	.11	.03
☐ 55 Shannon Stewart	.20	.09	.03
☐ 56 Jorge Posada	.10	.05	.01
☐ 57 Aaron Holbert	.10	.05	.01
☐ 58 Harry Berrios	.25	.11	.03
☐ 59 Steve Rodriguez	.10	.05	.01
☐ 60 Shane Andrews	.10	.05	.01
☐ 61 Will Cunnane	.40	.18	.05
☐ 62 Richard Hidalgo	.20	.09	.03
☐ 63 Bill Selby	.10	.05	.01
☐ 64 Jay Cranford	.10	.05	.01
☐ 65 Jeff Suppan	.20	.09	.03
☐ 66 Curtis Goodwin	.20	.09	.03
☐ 67 John Thomson	.30	.14	.04
☐ 68 Justin Thompsn	.20	.09	.03
☐ 69 Troy Percival	.10	.05	.01
☐ 70 Matt Wagner	.20	.09	.03
☐ 71 Terry Bradshaw	.10	.05	.01
☐ 72 Greg Hansell	.10	.05	.01
☐ 73 John Burke	.10	.05	.01
☐ 74 Jeff D'Amico	.20	.09	.03
☐ 75 Ernie Young	.10	.05	.01
☐ 76 Jason Bates	.10	.05	.01
☐ 77 Chris Stynes	.10	.05	.01
☐ 78 Cade Gaspar	.30	.14	.04
☐ 79 Melvin Nieves	.10	.05	.01
☐ 80 Rick Gorecki	.10	.05	.01
☐ 81 Felix Rodriguez	.20	.09	.03
☐ 82 Ryan Hancock	.10	.05	.01
☐ 83 Chris Carpenter	.30	.14	.04
☐ 84 Ray McDavid	.10	.05	.01
☐ 85 Chris Wimmer	.10	.05	.01
☐ 86 Doug Glanville	.10	.05	.01
☐ 87 DeShawn Warren	.10	.05	.01
☐ 88 Damian Moss	.50	.23	.06
☐ 89 Rafael Orellano	.50	.23	.06
☐ 90 Vladimir Guerrero	1.00	.45	.12
☐ 91 Raul Casanova	.75	.35	.09
☐ 92 Karim Garcia	2.50	1.10	.30
☐ 93 Bryce Florie	.10	.05	.01
☐ 94 Kevin Orie	.10	.05	.01
☐ 95 Ryan Nye	.40	.18	.05
☐ 96 Matt Sachse	.25	.11	.03
☐ 97 Ivan Arteaga	.20	.09	.03
☐ 98 Glenn Murray	.10	.05	.01
☐ 99 Stacy Hollins	.20	.09	.03
☐ 100 Jim Pittsley	.20	.09	.03
☐ 101 Craig Mattson	.20	.09	.03
☐ 102 Neifi Perez	.10	.05	.01
☐ 103 Keith Williams	.10	.05	.01
☐ 104 Roger Cedeno	.20	.09	.03
☐ 105 Tony Terry	.25	.11	.03
☐ 106 Jose Malave	.10	.05	.01
☐ 107 Joe Rosselli	.10	.05	.01
☐ 108 Kevin Jordan	.10	.05	.01
☐ 109 Sid Roberson	.10	.05	.01
☐ 110 Alan Embree	.10	.05	.01
☐ 111 Terrell Wade	.20	.09	.03
☐ 112 Bob Wolcott	.20	.09	.03
☐ 113 Carlos Perez	.75	.35	.09
☐ 114 Mike Bovee	.25	.11	.03
☐ 115 Tommy Davis	.40	.18	.05
☐ 116 Jeremey Kendall	.10	.05	.01
☐ 117 Rich Aude	.10	.05	.01
☐ 118 Rick Huisman	.10	.05	.01
☐ 119 Tim Belk	.10	.05	.01
☐ 120 Edgar Renteria	.20	.09	.03
☐ 121 Calvin Maduro	.30	.14	.04
☐ 122 Jerry Martin	.20	.09	.03
☐ 123 Ramon Fermin	.20	.09	.03
☐ 124 Kimera Bartee	.25	.11	.03
☐ 125 Mark Farris	.10	.05	.01
☐ 126 Frank Rodriguez	.10	.05	.01
☐ 127 Bobby Higginson	.30	.14	.04
☐ 128 Bret Wagner	.10	.05	.01
☐ 129 Edwin Diaz	.30	.14	.04
☐ 130 Jimmy Haynes	.10	.05	.01
☐ 131 Chris Weinke	.25	.11	.03
☐ 132 Damian Jackson	.40	.18	.05
☐ 133 Felix Martinez	.10	.05	.01
☐ 134 Edwin Hurtado	.10	.05	.01
☐ 135 Matt Raleigh	.10	.05	.01
☐ 136 Paul Wilson	.60	.25	.07
☐ 137 Ron Villone	.10	.05	.01
☐ 138 Eric Stuckenschneider	.10	.05	.01
☐ 139 Tate Seefried	.10	.05	.01
☐ 140 Rey Ordonez	.40	.18	.05
☐ 141 Eddie Pearson	.10	.05	.01
☐ 142 Kevin Gallaher	.10	.05	.01
☐ 143 Torii Hunter	.10	.05	.01
☐ 144 Daron Kirkreit	.10	.05	.01
☐ 145 Craig Wilson	.10	.05	.01
☐ 146 Ugueth Urbina	.10	.05	.01
☐ 147 Chris Snopek	.10	.05	.01
☐ 148 Kym Ashworth	.10	.05	.01
☐ 149 Wayne Gomes	.10	.05	.01
☐ 150 Mark Loretta	.10	.05	.01
☐ 151 Ramon Morel	.30	.14	.04
☐ 152 Trot Nixon	.10	.05	.01
☐ 153 Desi Relaford	.10	.05	.01
☐ 154 Scott Sullivan	.10	.05	.01
☐ 155 Marc Barcelo	.10	.05	.01

☐ 156	Willie Adams	.10	.05	.01	☐ 227 Todd Greene MVP	.50	.23	.06
☐ 157	Derrick Gibson	2.00	.90	.25	☐ 228 Larry Sutton MVP	.10	.05	.01
☐ 158	Brian Meadows	.25	.11	.03	☐ 229 Derek Jeter MVP	.40	.18	.05
☐ 159	Julian Tavarez	.10	.05	.01	☐ 230 Sal Fasano MVP	.30	.14	.04
☐ 160	Bryan Rekar	.10	.05	.01	☐ 231 Ruben Rivera MVP	2.00	.90	.25
☐ 161	Steve Gibralter	.10	.05	.01	☐ 232 Chris Truby MVP	.25	.11	.03
☐ 162	Esteban Loaiza	.10	.05	.01	☐ 233 John Donati MVP	.10	.05	.01
☐ 163	John Wasdin	.10	.05	.01	☐ 234 Decomba Conner MVP	.25	.11	.03
☐ 164	Kirk Presley	.10	.05	.01	☐ 235 Sergio Nunez MVP	.25	.11	.03
☐ 165	Mariano Rivera	.10	.05	.01	☐ 236 Ray Brown MVP	.60	.25	.07
☐ 166	Andy Larkin	.10	.05	.01	☐ 237 Juan Melo MVP	.30	.14	.04
☐ 167	Sean Whiteside	.10	.05	.01	☐ 238 Hideo Nomo FI	6.00	2.70	.75
☐ 168	Matt Apana	.10	.05	.01	☐ 239 Jamie Bluma FI	.20	.09	.03
☐ 169	Shawn Senior	.20	.09	.03	☐ 240 Jay Payton FI	2.00	.90	.25
☐ 170	Scott Gentile	.10	.05	.01	☐ 241 Paul Konerko FI	.20	.09	.03
☐ 171	Quilvio Veras	.10	.05	.01	☐ 242 Scott Elarton FI	.50	.23	.06
☐ 172	Eliezer Marrero	.25	.11	.03	☐ 243 Jeff Abbott FI	.75	.35	.09
☐ 173	Mendy Lopez	.30	.14	.04	☐ 244 Jim Brower FI	.20	.09	.03
☐ 174	Homer Bush	.10	.05	.01	☐ 245 Geoff Blum FI	.30	.14	.04
☐ 175	Brian Stephenson	.25	.11	.03	☐ 246 Aaron Boone FI	.60	.25	.07
☐ 176	Jon Nunnally	.10	.05	.01	☐ 247 J.R. Phillips TP	.10	.05	.01
☐ 177	Jose Herrera	.10	.05	.01	☐ 248 Alex Ochoa TP	.10	.05	.01
☐ 178	Corey Avrard	.20	.09	.03	☐ 249 Nomar Garciaparra TP	.30	.14	.04
☐ 179	David Bell	.10	.05	.01	☐ 250 Garret Anderson TP	.60	.25	.07
☐ 180	Jason Isringhausen	1.50	.70	.19	☐ 251 Ray Durham TP	.20	.09	.03
☐ 181	Jamey Wright	.10	.05	.01	☐ 252 Paul Shuey TP	.10	.05	.01
☐ 182	Lonell Roberts	.10	.05	.01	☐ 253 Tony Clark TP	.10	.05	.01
☐ 183	Marty Cordova	.50	.23	.06	☐ 254 Johnny Damon TP	1.00	.45	.12
☐ 184	Amaury Telemaco	.10	.05	.01	☐ 255 Duane Singleton TP	.10	.05	.01
☐ 185	John Mabry	.10	.05	.01	☐ 256 LaTroy Hawkins TP	.10	.05	.01
☐ 186	Andrew Vessel	.40	.18	.05	☐ 257 Andy Pettitte TP	.40	.18	.05
☐ 187	Jim Cole	.10	.05	.01	☐ 258 Ben Grieve TP	.75	.35	.09
☐ 188	Marquis Riley	.10	.05	.01	☐ 259 Marc Newfield TP	.10	.05	.01
☐ 189	Todd Dunn	.10	.05	.01	☐ 260 Terrell Lowery TP	.10	.05	.01
☐ 190	John Carter	.10	.05	.01	☐ 261 Shawn Green TP	.10	.05	.01
☐ 191	Donnie Sadler	.60	.25	.07	☐ 262 Chipper Jones TP	1.25	.55	.16
☐ 192	Mike Bell	.10	.05	.01	☐ 263 Brooks Kieschnick TP	.60	.25	.07
☐ 193	Chris Cumberland	.25	.11	.03	☐ 264 Calvin Reese TP	.10	.05	.01
☐ 194	Jason Schmidt	.20	.09	.03	☐ 265 Doug Million TP	.20	.09	.03
☐ 195	Matt Brunson	.10	.05	.01	☐ 266 Marc Valdes TP	.10	.05	.01
☐ 196	James Baldwin	.10	.05	.01	☐ 267 Brian Hunter TP	.40	.18	.05
☐ 197	Bill Simas	.10	.05	.01	☐ 268 Todd Hollandsworth TP	.10	.05	.01
☐ 198	Gus Gandarillas	.10	.05	.01	☐ 269 Rod Henderson TP	.10	.05	.01
☐ 199	Mac Suzuki	.10	.05	.01	☐ 270 Bill Pulsipher TP	.20	.09	.03
☐ 200	Rick Holifield	.10	.05	.01	☐ 271 Scott Rolen TP	.75	.35	.09
☐ 201	Fernando Lunar	.25	.11	.03	☐ 272 Trey Beamon TP	.10	.05	.01
☐ 202	Kevin Jarvis	.10	.05	.01	☐ 273 Alan Benes TP	.30	.14	.04
☐ 203	Everett Stull	.10	.05	.01	☐ 274 Dustin Hermanson TP	.10	.05	.01
☐ 204	Steve Wojciechowski	.10	.05	.01	☐ 275 Ricky Bottalico	.10	.05	.01
☐ 205	Shawn Estes	.10	.05	.01	☐ 276 Albert Belle	1.25	.55	.16
☐ 206	Jermaine Dye	.40	.18	.05	☐ 277 Deion Sanders	.60	.25	.07
☐ 207	Marc Kroon	.10	.05	.01	☐ 278 Matt Williams	.50	.23	.06
☐ 208	Peter Munro	.20	.09	.03	☐ 279 Jeff Bagwell	1.00	.45	.12
☐ 209	Pat Watkins	.20	.09	.03	☐ 280 Kirby Puckett	1.00	.45	.12
☐ 210	Matt Smith	.10	.05	.01	☐ 281 Dave Hollins	.10	.05	.01
☐ 211	Joe Vitiello	.10	.05	.01	☐ 282 Don Mattingly	1.50	.70	.19
☐ 212	Gerald Witasick Jr.	.10	.05	.01	☐ 283 Joey Hamilton	.10	.05	.01
☐ 213	Freddy Garcia	.20	.09	.03	☐ 284 Bobby Bonilla	.10	.05	.01
☐ 214	Glenn Dishman	.25	.11	.03	☐ 285 Moises Alou	.10	.05	.01
☐ 215	Jay Canizaro	.40	.18	.05	☐ 286 Tom Glavine	.10	.05	.01
☐ 216	Angel Martinez	.10	.05	.01	☐ 287 Brett Butler	.10	.05	.01
☐ 217	Yamil Benitez	.40	.18	.05	☐ 288 Chris Hoiles	.10	.05	.01
☐ 218	Fausto Macey	.30	.14	.04	☐ 289 Kenny Rogers	.10	.05	.01
☐ 219	Eric Owens	.10	.05	.01	☐ 290 Larry Walker	.40	.18	.05
☐ 220	Checklist	.10	.05	.01	☐ 291 Tim Raines	.10	.05	.01
☐ 221	Dwayne Hosey MVP	.10	.05	.01	☐ 292 Kevin Appier	.10	.05	.01
☐ 222	Brad Woodall MVP	.10	.05	.01	☐ 293 Roger Clemens	.50	.23	.06
☐ 223	Billy Ashley MVP	.10	.05	.01	☐ 294 Chuck Carr	.10	.05	.01
☐ 224	Mark Grudzielanek MVP	.20	.09	.03	☐ 295 Randy Myers	.10	.05	.01
☐ 225	Mark Johnson MVP	.10	.05	.01	☐ 296 Dave Nilsson	.10	.05	.01
☐ 226	Tim Unroe MVP	.25	.11	.03	☐ 297 Joe Carter	.30	.14	.04

☐ 298	Chuck Finley	.10	.05	.01
☐ 299	Ray Lankford	.20	.09	.03
☐ 300	Roberto Kelly	.10	.05	.01
☐ 301	Jon Lieber	.10	.05	.01
☐ 302	Travis Fryman	.20	.09	.03
☐ 303	Mark McGwire	.20	.09	.03
☐ 304	Tony Gwynn	1.00	.45	.12
☐ 305	Kenny Lofton	1.00	.45	.12
☐ 306	Mark Whiten	.10	.05	.01
☐ 307	Doug Drabek	.10	.05	.01
☐ 308	Terry Steinbach	.10	.05	.01
☐ 309	Ryan Klesko	.60	.25	.07
☐ 310	Mike Piazza	1.25	.55	.16
☐ 311	Ben McDonald	.10	.05	.01
☐ 312	Reggie Sanders	.20	.09	.03
☐ 313	Alex Fernandez	.10	.05	.01
☐ 314	Aaron Sele	.10	.05	.01
☐ 315	Gregg Jefferies	.10	.05	.01
☐ 316	Rickey Henderson	.10	.05	.01
☐ 317	Brian Anderson	.10	.05	.01
☐ 318	Jose Valentin	.10	.05	.01
☐ 319	Rod Beck	.10	.05	.01
☐ 320	Marquis Grissom	.10	.05	.01
☐ 321	Ken Griffey, Jr.	3.00	1.35	.35
☐ 322	Bret Saberhagen	.10	.05	.01
☐ 323	Juan Gonzalez	.75	.35	.09
☐ 324	Paul Molitor	.20	.09	.03
☐ 325	Gary Sheffield	.10	.05	.01
☐ 326	Darren Daulton	.10	.05	.01
☐ 327	Bill Swift	.10	.05	.01
☐ 328	Brian McRae	.10	.05	.01
☐ 329	Robin Ventura	.10	.05	.01
☐ 330	Lee Smith	.10	.05	.01
☐ 331	Fred McGriff	.40	.18	.05
☐ 332	Delino DeShields	.10	.05	.01
☐ 333	Edgar Martinez	.20	.09	.03
☐ 334	Mike Mussina	.40	.18	.05
☐ 335	Orlando Merced	.10	.05	.01
☐ 336	Carlos Baerga	.60	.25	.07
☐ 337	Wil Cordero	.10	.05	.01
☐ 338	Tom Pagnozzi	.10	.05	.01
☐ 339	Pat Hentgen	.10	.05	.01
☐ 340	Chad Curtis	.10	.05	.01
☐ 341	Darren Lewis	.10	.05	.01
☐ 342	Jeff Kent	.10	.05	.01
☐ 343	Bip Roberts	.10	.05	.01
☐ 344	Ivan Rodriguez	.10	.05	.01
☐ 345	Jeff Montgomery	.10	.05	.01
☐ 346	Hal Morris	.10	.05	.01
☐ 347	Danny Tartabull	.10	.05	.01
☐ 348	Raul Mondesi	.75	.35	.09
☐ 349	Ken Hill	.10	.05	.01
☐ 350	Pedro Martinez	.10	.05	.01
☐ 351	Frank Thomas	3.00	1.35	.35
☐ 352	Manny Ramirez	1.25	.55	.16
☐ 353	Tim Salmon	.50	.23	.06
☐ 354	W. VanLandingham	.10	.05	.01
☐ 355	Andres Galarraga	.10	.05	.01
☐ 356	Paul O'Neill	.10	.05	.01
☐ 357	Brady Anderson	.10	.05	.01
☐ 358	Ramon Martinez	.10	.05	.01
☐ 359	John Olerud	.10	.05	.01
☐ 360	Ruben Sierra	.10	.05	.01
☐ 361	Cal Eldred	.10	.05	.01
☐ 362	Jay Buhner	.20	.09	.03
☐ 363	Jay Bell	.10	.05	.01
☐ 364	Wally Joyner	.10	.05	.01
☐ 365	Chuck Knoblauch	.20	.09	.03
☐ 366	Len Dykstra	.10	.05	.01
☐ 367	John Wetteland	.10	.05	.01
☐ 368	Roberto Alomar	.60	.25	.07
☐ 369	Craig Biggio	.20	.09	.03
☐ 370	Ozzie Smith	.60	.25	.07
☐ 371	Terry Pendleton	.10	.05	.01
☐ 372	Sammy Sosa	.20	.09	.03
☐ 373	Carlos Garcia	.10	.05	.01
☐ 374	Jose Rijo	.10	.05	.01
☐ 375	Chris Gomez	.10	.05	.01
☐ 376	Barry Bonds	1.00	.45	.12
☐ 377	Steve Avery	.10	.05	.01
☐ 378	Rick Wilkins	.10	.05	.01
☐ 379	Pete Harnisch	.10	.05	.01
☐ 380	Dean Palmer	.10	.05	.01
☐ 381	Bob Hamelin	.10	.05	.01
☐ 382	Jason Bere	.20	.09	.03
☐ 383	Jimmy Key	.10	.05	.01
☐ 384	Dante Bichette	.40	.18	.05
☐ 385	Rafael Palmeiro	.20	.09	.03
☐ 386	David Justice	.40	.18	.05
☐ 387	Chili Davis	.10	.05	.01
☐ 388	Mike Greenwell	.10	.05	.01
☐ 389	Todd Zeile	.10	.05	.01
☐ 390	Jeff Conine	.20	.09	.03
☐ 391	Rick Aguilera	.10	.05	.01
☐ 392	Eddie Murray	.40	.18	.05
☐ 393	Mike Stanley	.10	.05	.01
☐ 394	Cliff Floyd	.20	.09	.03
☐ 395	Randy Johnson	.60	.25	.07
☐ 396	David Nied	.10	.05	.01
☐ 397	Devon White	.10	.05	.01
☐ 398	Royce Clayton	.10	.05	.01
☐ 399	Andy Benes	.10	.05	.01
☐ 400	John Hudek	.10	.05	.01
☐ 401	Bobby Jones	.10	.05	.01
☐ 402	Eric Karros	.20	.09	.03
☐ 403	Will Clark	.40	.18	.05
☐ 404	Mark Langston	.10	.05	.01
☐ 405	Kevin Brown	.10	.05	.01
☐ 406	Greg Maddux	3.00	1.35	.35
☐ 407	David Cone	.20	.09	.03
☐ 408	Wade Boggs	.10	.05	.01
☐ 409	Steve Trachsel	.10	.05	.01
☐ 410	Greg Vaughn	.10	.05	.01
☐ 411	Mo Vaughn	.50	.23	.06
☐ 412	Wilson Alvarez	.10	.05	.01
☐ 413	Cal Ripken	3.00	1.35	.35
☐ 414	Rico Brogna	.10	.05	.01
☐ 415	Barry Larkin	.40	.18	.05
☐ 416	Cecil Fielder	.20	.09	.03
☐ 417	Jose Canseco	.50	.23	.06
☐ 418	Jack McDowell	.10	.05	.01
☐ 419	Mike Lieberthal	.10	.05	.01
☐ 420	Andrew Lorraine	.10	.05	.01
☐ 421	Rich Becker	.10	.05	.01
☐ 422	Tony Phillips	.10	.05	.01
☐ 423	Scott Ruffcorn	.10	.05	.01
☐ 424	Jeff Granger	.10	.05	.01
☐ 425	Greg Pirkl	.10	.05	.01
☐ 426	Dennis Eckersley	.10	.05	.01
☐ 427	Jose Lima	.10	.05	.01
☐ 428	Russ Davis	.10	.05	.01
☐ 429	Armando Benitez	.10	.05	.01
☐ 430	Alex Gonzalez	.10	.05	.01
☐ 431	Carlos Delgado	.20	.09	.03
☐ 432	Chan Ho Park	.20	.09	.03
☐ 433	Mickey Tettleton	.10	.05	.01
☐ 434	Dave Winfield	.20	.09	.03
☐ 435	John Burkett	.10	.05	.01
☐ 436	Orlando Miller	.10	.05	.01
☐ 437	Rondell White	.20	.09	.03
☐ 438	Jose Oliva	.10	.05	.01
☐ 439	Checklist	.10	.05	.01

1995 Bowman's Best

This 195-card consists of 90 veteran stars, 90 rookies and prospects and 15 Mirror Image cards. The veteran cards have red backs and are designated R1-R90. Cards of rookies and prospects have blue backs and are designated B1-B90. The Mirror Image cards feature a veteran star and a prospect matched by position. These cards are numbered X1-X15. The fronts have an action photo with the background in silver-foil with the team names at the top and red or blue at the bottom corresponding to the back. The packs contain seven cards and the suggested retail price was $5. The backs have a head shot along with player statistics and information. Rookie Cards include Andruw Jones and Hideo Nomo.

	MINT	NRMT	EXC
COMPLETE SET (195)	85.00	38.00	10.50
COMMON BLUE CARD (B1-B90)	.30	.14	.04
COMMON RED CARD (R1-R90)	.30	.14	.04
COMMON CARD (X1-X15)	1.00	.45	.12

☐	B1 Derek Jeter	1.00	.45	.12
☐	B2 Vladimir Guerrero	1.50	.70	.19
☐	B3 Bob Abreu	1.25	.55	.16
☐	B4 Chan Ho Park	.30	.14	.04
☐	B5 Paul Wilson	1.25	.55	.16
☐	B6 Chad Ogea	.30	.14	.04
☐	B7 Andruw Jones	10.00	4.50	1.25
☐	B8 Brian Barber	.30	.14	.04
☐	B9 Andy Larkin	.30	.14	.04
☐	B10 Richie Sexson	2.00	.90	.25
☐	B11 Everett Stull	.30	.14	.04
☐	B12 Brooks Kieschnick	1.50	.70	.19
☐	B13 Matt Murray	.30	.14	.04
☐	B14 John Wasdin	.30	.14	.04
☐	B15 Shannon Stewart	.30	.14	.04
☐	B16 Luis Ortiz	.30	.14	.04
☐	B17 Marc Kroon	.30	.14	.04
☐	B18 Todd Greene	1.25	.55	.16
☐	B19 Juan Acevedo	.30	.14	.04
☐	B20 Tony Clark	.30	.14	.04
☐	B21 Jermaine Dye	1.00	.45	.12
☐	B22 Derrek Lee	.50	.23	.06
☐	B23 Pat Watkins	.50	.23	.06
☐	B24 Calvin Reese	.30	.14	.04
☐	B25 Ben Grieve	1.25	.55	.16
☐	B26 Julio Santana	.30	.14	.04
☐	B27 Felix Rodriguez	1.00	.45	.12
☐	B28 Paul Konerko	.50	.23	.06
☐	B29 Nomar Garciaparra	1.00	.45	.12
☐	B30 Pat Ahearne	.30	.14	.04
☐	B31 Jason Schmidt	.50	.23	.06
☐	B32 Billy Wagner	.50	.23	.06
☐	B33 Rey Ordonez	1.00	.45	.12
☐	B34 Curtis Goodwin	.30	.14	.04
☐	B35 Sergio Nunez	1.00	.45	.12
☐	B36 Tim Belk	.30	.14	.04
☐	B37 Scott Elarton	1.00	.45	.12
☐	B38 Jason Isringhausen	4.00	1.80	.50
☐	B39 Trot Nixon	.50	.23	.06
☐	B40 Sid Roberson	.30	.14	.04
☐	B41 Ron Villone	.30	.14	.04
☐	B42 Ruben Rivera	4.00	1.80	.50
☐	B43 Rick Huisman	.30	.14	.04
☐	B44 Todd Hollandsworth	.30	.14	.04
☐	B45 Johnny Damon	2.50	1.10	.30
☐	B46 Garret Anderson	1.50	.70	.19
☐	B47 Jeff D'Amico	.50	.23	.06
☐	B48 Dustin Hermanson	.30	.14	.04
☐	B49 Juan Encarnacion	1.50	.70	.19
☐	B50 Andy Pettitte	1.00	.45	.12
☐	B51 Chris Stynes	.30	.14	.04
☐	B52 Troy Percival	.30	.14	.04
☐	B53 LaTroy Hawkins	.30	.14	.04
☐	B54 Roger Cedeno	.50	.23	.06
☐	B55 Alan Benes	.75	.35	.09
☐	B56 Karim Garcia	4.00	1.80	.50
☐	B57 Andrew Lorraine	.30	.14	.04
☐	B58 Gary Rath	1.00	.45	.12
☐	B59 Bret Wagner	.50	.23	.06
☐	B60 Jeff Suppan	.50	.23	.06
☐	B61 Bill Pulsipher	.50	.23	.06
☐	B62 Jay Payton	4.00	1.80	.50
☐	B63 Alex Ochoa	.50	.23	.06
☐	B64 Ugueth Urbina	.30	.14	.04
☐	B65 Armando Benitez	.30	.14	.04
☐	B66 George Arias	1.00	.45	.12
☐	B67 Raul Casanova	1.25	.55	.16
☐	B68 Matt Drews	.50	.23	.06
☐	B69 Jimmy Haynes	.50	.23	.06
☐	B70 Jimmy Hurst	.30	.14	.04
☐	B71 C.J. Nitkowski	.30	.14	.04
☐	B72 Tommy Davis	1.00	.45	.12
☐	B73 Bartolo Colon	3.00	1.35	.35
☐	B74 Chris Carpenter	1.00	.45	.12
☐	B75 Trey Beamon	.50	.23	.06
☐	B76 Bryan Rekar	.30	.14	.04
☐	B77 James Baldwin	.30	.14	.04
☐	B78 Marc Valdes	.30	.14	.04
☐	B79 Tom Fordham	1.00	.45	.12
☐	B80 Marc Newfield	.30	.14	.04
☐	B81 Angel Martinez	.30	.14	.04
☐	B82 Brian L. Hunter	1.00	.45	.12
☐	B83 Jose Herrera	.30	.14	.04
☐	B84 Glenn Dishman	1.00	.45	.12
☐	B85 Jacob Cruz	1.50	.70	.19
☐	B86 Paul Shuey	.30	.14	.04
☐	B87 Scott Rolen	1.25	.55	.16
☐	B88 Doug Million	1.00	.45	.12
☐	B89 Desi Relaford	.30	.14	.04
☐	B90 Michael Tucker	.50	.23	.06
☐	R1 Randy Johnson	1.50	.70	.19
☐	R2 Joe Carter	.75	.35	.09
☐	R3 Chili Davis	.30	.14	.04
☐	R4 Moises Alou	.30	.14	.04
☐	R5 Gary Sheffield	.50	.23	.06
☐	R6 Kevin Appier	.30	.14	.04
☐	R7 Denny Neagle	.30	.14	.04

☐ R8	Ruben Sierra	.30	.14	.04
☐ R9	Darren Daulton	.50	.23	.06
☐ R10	Cal Ripken	8.00	3.60	1.00
☐ R11	Bobby Bonilla	.30	.14	.04
☐ R12	Manny Ramirez	3.00	1.35	.35
☐ R13	Barry Bonds	2.00	.90	.25
☐ R14	Eric Karros	.50	.23	.06
☐ R15	Greg Maddux	8.00	3.60	1.00
☐ R16	Jeff Bagwell	2.50	1.10	.30
☐ R17	Paul Molitor	.75	.35	.09
☐ R18	Ray Lankford	.50	.23	.06
☐ R19	Mark Grace	.30	.14	.04
☐ R20	Kenny Lofton	2.50	1.10	.30
☐ R21	Tony Gwynn	2.50	1.10	.30
☐ R22	Will Clark	1.00	.45	.12
☐ R23	Roger Clemens	1.25	.55	.16
☐ R24	Dante Bichette	1.00	.45	.12
☐ R25	Barry Larkin	1.00	.45	.12
☐ R26	Wade Boggs	.30	.14	.04
☐ R27	Kirby Puckett	2.50	1.10	.30
☐ R28	Cecil Fielder	.30	.14	.04
☐ R29	Jose Canseco	1.25	.55	.16
☐ R30	Juan Gonzalez	2.00	.90	.25
☐ R31	David Cone	.30	.14	.04
☐ R32	Craig Biggio	.30	.14	.04
☐ R33	Tim Salmon	1.25	.55	.16
☐ R34	David Justice	1.00	.45	.12
☐ R35	Sammy Sosa	.50	.23	.06
☐ R36	Mike Piazza	3.00	1.35	.35
☐ R37	Carlos Baerga	1.50	.70	.19
☐ R38	Jeff Conine	.50	.23	.06
☐ R39	Rafael Palmeiro	.50	.23	.06
☐ R40	Bret Saberhagen	.30	.14	.04
☐ R41	Len Dykstra	.50	.23	.06
☐ R42	Mo Vaughn	1.25	.55	.16
☐ R43	Wally Joyner	.30	.14	.04
☐ R44	Chuck Knoblauch	.50	.23	.06
☐ R45	Robin Ventura	.30	.14	.04
☐ R46	Don Mattingly	4.00	1.80	.50
☐ R47	Dave Hollins	.30	.14	.04
☐ R48	Andy Benes	.30	.14	.04
☐ R49	Ken Griffey Jr.	8.00	3.60	1.00
☐ R50	Albert Belle	3.00	1.35	.35
☐ R51	Matt Williams	1.25	.55	.16
☐ R52	Rondell White	.50	.23	.06
☐ R53	Raul Mondesi	1.50	.70	.19
☐ R54	Brian Jordan	.30	.14	.04
☐ R55	Greg Vaughn	.30	.14	.04
☐ R56	Fred McGriff	1.00	.45	.12
☐ R57	Roberto Alomar	1.50	.70	.19
☐ R58	Dennis Eckersley	.30	.14	.04
☐ R59	Lee Smith	.30	.14	.04
☐ R60	Eddie Murray	1.00	.45	.12
☐ R61	Kenny Rogers	.30	.14	.04
☐ R62	Ron Gant	.30	.14	.04
☐ R63	Larry Walker	1.00	.45	.12
☐ R64	Chad Curtis	.30	.14	.04
☐ R65	Frank Thomas	8.00	3.60	1.00
☐ R66	Paul O'Neill	.30	.14	.04
☐ R67	Kevin Seitzer	.30	.14	.04
☐ R68	Marquis Grissom	.30	.14	.04
☐ R69	Mark McGwire	.30	.14	.04
☐ R70	Travis Fryman	.50	.23	.06
☐ R71	Andres Gallarraga	.50	.23	.06
☐ R72	Carlos Perez	1.50	.70	.19
☐ R73	Tyler Green	.30	.14	.04
☐ R74	Marty Cordova	1.25	.55	.16
☐ R75	Shawn Green	.30	.14	.04
☐ R76	Vaughn Eshelman	.30	.14	.04
☐ R77	John Mabry	.30	.14	.04
☐ R78	Jason Bates	.30	.14	.04

☐ R79	Jon Nunnally	.30	.14	.04
☐ R80	Ray Durham	.30	.14	.04
☐ R81	Edgardo Alfonzo	.30	.14	.04
☐ R82	Esteban Loaiza	.30	.14	.04
☐ R83	Hideo Nomo	10.00	4.50	1.25
☐ R84	Orlando Miller	.30	.14	.04
☐ R85	Alex Gonzalez	.30	.14	.04
☐ R86	Mark Grudzielanek	.75	.35	.09
☐ R87	Julian Tavarez	.30	.14	.04
☐ R88	Benji Gil	.30	.14	.04
☐ R89	Quilvio Veras	.30	.14	.04
☐ R90	Ricky Bottalico	.30	.14	.04
☐ X1	Ben Davis Ivan Rodriguez	1.25	.55	.16
☐ X2	Mark Redman Manny Ramirez	1.25	.55	.16
☐ X3	Reggie Taylor Deion Sanders	1.50	.70	.19
☐ X4	Ryan Jaroncyk Shawn Green	1.25	.55	.16
☐ X5	Juan LeBron Juan Gonzalez	1.25	.55	.16
☐ X6	Toby McKnight Craig Biggio	1.25	.55	.16
☐ X7	Michael Barrett Travis Fryman	1.25	.55	.16
☐ X8	Corey Jenkins Mo Vaughn	2.50	1.10	.30
☐ X9	Ruben Rivera Frank Thomas	5.00	2.20	.60
☐ X10	Curtis Goodwin Kenny Lofton	1.25	.55	.16
☐ X11	Brian L. Hunter Tony Gwynn	1.50	.70	.19
☐ X12	Todd Greene Ken Griffey Jr.	4.00	1.80	.50
☐ X13	Karim Garcia Matt Williams	1.50	.70	.19
☐ X14	Billy Wagner Randy Johnson	1.00	.45	.12
☐ X15	Pat Watkins Jeff Bagwell	1.25	.55	.16

1995 Bowman's Best Refractors/Diffraction Foil

Randomly inserted at a rate of one in six packs, this set is a parallel to the basic Bowman's Best issue. As far as the refractive qualities, the final 15 Mirror Image cards (X1-X15) are considered diffractors which reflects light in a different manner than the typical refractor. Jumbo versions of the Albert Belle and Greg Maddux refractors were issued for retail distribution only; they are valued at one-fourth the listed price.

	MINT	NRMT	EXC
COMPLETE SET (195)	900.00	400.00	110.00
COMMON CARD	3.00	1.35	.35

*RED STARS: 7X to 12X BASIC CARDS
*BLUE STARS: 4X TO 8X BASIC CARDS
*MIRROR IMAGE DIFFRACTION: 2.5X TO 5X BASIC CARDS

☐ B7 Andruw Jones	75.00	34.00	9.50
☐ B42 Ruben Rivera	40.00	18.00	5.00
☐ R10 Cal Ripken	100.00	45.00	12.50
☐ R12 Manny Ramirez	40.00	18.00	5.00
☐ R15 Greg Maddux	100.00	45.00	12.50
☐ R16 Jeff Bagwell	30.00	13.50	3.70
☐ R20 Kenny Lofton	30.00	13.50	3.70
☐ R21 Tony Gwynn	30.00	13.50	3.70
☐ R27 Kirby Puckett	30.00	13.50	3.70
☐ R36 Mike Piazza	40.00	18.00	5.00
☐ R46 Don Mattingly	50.00	22.00	6.25
☐ R49 Ken Griffey Jr.	100.00	45.00	12.50
☐ R50 Albert Belle	40.00	18.00	5.00
☐ R65 Frank Thomas	100.00	45.00	12.50
☐ R83 Hideo Nomo	75.00	34.00	9.50
☐ X9 Ruben Rivera	25.00	11.00	3.10
Frank Thomas			
☐ X12 Todd Greene	20.00	9.00	2.50
Ken Griffey Jr.			

1994 Collector's Choice

Issued by Upper Deck, this 670 standard-size card set was issued in two series of 320 and 350. Factory sets contain five Gold Signature cards for a total of 675 cards. Card fronts feature color player action photos with white borders that are highlighted by vertical gray pinstripes. The player's name and team appear in white lettering at the bottom of the picture. The player's position appears within a black oval beneath an action player icon in a lower corner. The pinstripe border design reappears on the back, which carries another color player action photo in its upper portion. The player's name and position appear vertically within a team color-coded stripe along the photo's right side. A team logo appears at the lower left corner of the photo. Beneath the picture appear the player's biography and stats. Subsets include Rookie Class (1-20), First Draft Picks (21-30), Top Performers (306-315), Up Close (631-640)

and Future Foundation (641-650). Rookie Cards include Brian Anderson, Michael Jordan, Brooks Kieschnick, Derrek Lee, Alex Rodriguez, Jose Silva and Terrell Wade.

	MINT	NRMT	EXC
COMPLETE SET (670)	30.00	13.50	3.70
COMPLETE FACT.SET (675)	32.00	14.50	4.00
COMPLETE SERIES 1 (320)	12.00	5.50	1.50
COMPLETE SERIES 2 (350)	18.00	8.00	2.20
COMMON CARD (1-320)	.05	.02	.01
COMMON CARD (321-670)	.05	.02	.01
COMP. SILV SIG SET (670)	200.00	90.00	25.00
COMMON SILV. SIG (1-670)	.10	.05	.01
SILV. SIG. SEMISTARS	.20	.09	.03
SILV. SIG STARS	.30	.14	.04

*SILV SIG VETERAN STARS: 4X TO 8X BASIC CARDS
*SILV. SIG YOUNG STARS: 2.5X TO 5X BASIC CARDS
*SILV. SIG RC'S: 1.5X TO 3X BASIC CARDS

☐ 1	Rich Becker	.10	.05	.01
☐ 2	Greg Blosser	.05	.02	.01
☐ 3	Midre Cummings	.10	.05	.01
☐ 4	Carlos Delgado	.15	.07	.02
☐ 5	Steve Dreyer	.05	.02	.01
☐ 6	Carl Everett	.15	.07	.02
☐ 7	Cliff Floyd	.15	.07	.02
☐ 8	Alex Gonzalez	.15	.07	.02
☐ 9	Shawn Green	.25	.11	.03
☐ 10	Butch Huskey	.10	.05	.01
☐ 11	Mark Hutton	.05	.02	.01
☐ 12	Miguel Jimenez	.10	.05	.01
☐ 13	Steve Karsay	.05	.02	.01
☐ 14	Marc Newfield	.10	.05	.01
☐ 15	Luis Ortiz	.05	.02	.01
☐ 16	Manny Ramirez	1.00	.45	.12
☐ 17	Johnny Ruffin	.05	.02	.01
☐ 18	Scott Stahoviak	.05	.02	.01
☐ 19	Salomon Torres	.10	.05	.01
☐ 20	Gabe White	.05	.02	.01
☐ 21	Brian Anderson	.10	.05	.01
☐ 22	Wayne Gomes	.25	.11	.03
☐ 23	Jeff Granger	.10	.05	.01
☐ 24	Steve Soderstrom	.20	.09	.03
☐ 25	Trot Nixon	.50	.23	.06
☐ 26	Kirk Presley	.20	.09	.03
☐ 27	Matt Brunson	.15	.07	.02
☐ 28	Brooks Kieschnick	1.50	.70	.19
☐ 29	Billy Wagner	.40	.18	.05
☐ 30	Matt Drews	.50	.23	.06
☐ 31	Kurt Abbott	.15	.07	.02
☐ 32	Luis Alicea	.05	.02	.01
☐ 33	Roberto Alomar	.40	.18	.05
☐ 34	Sandy Alomar Jr.	.10	.05	.01
☐ 35	Moises Alou	.15	.07	.02
☐ 36	Wilson Alvarez	.15	.07	.02
☐ 37	Rich Amaral	.05	.02	.01
☐ 38	Eric Anthony	.05	.02	.01
☐ 39	Luis Aquino	.05	.02	.01
☐ 40	Jack Armstrong	.05	.02	.01
☐ 41	Rene Arocha	.10	.05	.01
☐ 42	Rich Aude	.10	.05	.01
☐ 43	Brad Ausmus	.05	.02	.01
☐ 44	Steve Avery	.15	.07	.02
☐ 45	Bob Ayrault	.05	.02	.01
☐ 46	Willie Banks	.05	.02	.01
☐ 47	Bret Barberie	.05	.02	.01
☐ 48	Kim Batiste	.05	.02	.01
☐ 49	Rod Beck	.10	.05	.01
☐ 50	Jason Bere	.15	.07	.02

□	51	Sean Berry	.05	.02	.01
□	52	Dante Bichette	.25	.11	.03
□	53	Jeff Blauser	.10	.05	.01
□	54	Mike Blowers	.15	.07	.02
□	55	Tim Bogar	.05	.02	.01
□	56	Tom Bolton	.05	.02	.01
□	57	Ricky Bones	.05	.02	.01
□	58	Bobby Bonilla	.15	.07	.02
□	59	Bret Boone	.15	.07	.02
□	60	Pat Borders	.05	.02	.01
□	61	Mike Bordick	.05	.02	.01
□	62	Daryl Boston	.05	.02	.01
□	63	Ryan Bowen	.05	.02	.01
□	64	Jeff Branson	.05	.02	.01
□	65	George Brett	.75	.35	.09
□	66	Steve Buechele	.05	.02	.01
□	67	Dave Burba	.05	.02	.01
□	68	John Burkett	.05	.02	.01
□	69	Jeromy Burnitz	.05	.02	.01
□	70	Brett Butler	.05	.02	.01
□	71	Rob Butler	.05	.02	.01
□	72	Ken Caminiti	.10	.05	.01
□	73	Cris Carpenter	.05	.02	.01
□	74	Vinny Castilla	.15	.07	.02
□	75	Andujar Cedeno	.05	.02	.01
□	76	Wes Chamberlain	.05	.02	.01
□	77	Archi Cianfrocco	.05	.02	.01
□	78	Dave Clark	.05	.02	.01
□	79	Jerald Clark	.05	.02	.01
□	80	Royce Clayton	.10	.05	.01
□	81	David Cone	.15	.07	.02
□	82	Jeff Conine	.15	.07	.02
□	83	Steve Cooke	.10	.05	.01
□	84	Scott Cooper	.10	.05	.01
□	85	Joey Cora	.05	.02	.01
□	86	Tim Costo	.05	.02	.01
□	87	Chad Curtis	.10	.05	.01
□	88	Ron Darling	.05	.02	.01
□	89	Danny Darwin	.05	.02	.01
□	90	Rob Deer	.05	.02	.01
□	91	Jim Deshaies	.05	.02	.01
□	92	Delino DeShields	.10	.05	.01
□	93	Rob Dibble	.05	.02	.01
□	94	Gary DiSarcina	.05	.02	.01
□	95	Doug Drabek	.15	.07	.02
□	96	Scott Erickson	.05	.02	.01
□	97	Rikkert Faneyte	.05	.02	.01
□	98	Jeff Fassero	.05	.02	.01
□	99	Alex Fernandez	.15	.07	.02
□	100	Cecil Fielder	.15	.07	.02
□	101	Dave Fleming	.05	.02	.01
□	102	Darrin Fletcher	.05	.02	.01
□	103	Scott Fletcher	.05	.02	.01
□	104	Mike Gallego	.05	.02	.01
□	105	Carlos Garcia	.05	.02	.01
□	106	Jeff Gardner	.05	.02	.01
□	107	Brent Gates	.10	.05	.01
□	108	Benji Gil	.10	.05	.01
□	109	Bernard Gilkey	.10	.05	.01
□	110	Chris Gomez	.10	.05	.01
□	111	Luis Gonzalez	.05	.02	.01
□	112	Tom Gordon	.05	.02	.01
□	113	Jim Gott	.05	.02	.01
□	114	Mark Grace	.15	.07	.02
□	115	Tommy Greene	.05	.02	.01
□	116	Willie Greene	.10	.05	.01
□	117	Ken Griffey Jr.	2.00	.90	.25
□	118	Bill Gullickson	.05	.02	.01
□	119	Ricky Gutierrez	.05	.02	.01
□	120	Juan Guzman	.10	.05	.01
□	121	Chris Gwynn	.05	.02	.01
□	122	Tony Gwynn	.60	.25	.07
□	123	Jeffrey Hammonds	.15	.07	.02
□	124	Erik Hanson	.05	.02	.01
□	125	Gene Harris	.05	.02	.01
□	126	Greg W. Harris	.05	.02	.01
□	127	Bryan Harvey	.10	.05	.01
□	128	Billy Hatcher	.05	.02	.01
□	129	Hilly Hathaway	.05	.02	.01
□	130	Charlie Hayes	.10	.05	.01
□	131	Rickey Henderson	.15	.07	.02
□	132	Mike Henneman	.05	.02	.01
□	133	Pat Hentgen	.10	.05	.01
□	134	Roberto Hernandez	.05	.02	.01
□	135	Orel Hershiser	.10	.05	.01
□	136	Phil Hiatt	.10	.05	.01
□	137	Glenallen Hill	.10	.05	.01
□	138	Ken Hill	.10	.05	.01
□	139	Eric Hillman	.05	.02	.01
□	140	Chris Hoiles	.10	.05	.01
□	141	Dave Hollins	.10	.05	.01
□	142	David Hulse	.05	.02	.01
□	143	Todd Hundley	.10	.05	.01
□	144	Pete Incaviglia	.05	.02	.01
□	145	Danny Jackson	.05	.02	.01
□	146	John Jaha	.05	.02	.01
□	147	Domingo Jean	.05	.02	.01
□	148	Gregg Jefferies	.15	.07	.02
□	149	Reggie Jefferson	.05	.02	.01
□	150	Lance Johnson	.05	.02	.01
□	151	Bobby Jones	.15	.07	.02
□	152	Chipper Jones	1.00	.45	.12
□	153	Todd Jones	.05	.02	.01
□	154	Brian Jordan	.10	.05	.01
□	155	Wally Joyner	.10	.05	.01
□	156	David Justice	.25	.11	.03
□	157	Ron Karkovice	.05	.02	.01
□	158	Eric Karros	.10	.05	.01
□	159	Jeff Kent	.10	.05	.01
□	160	Jimmy Key	.10	.05	.01
□	161	Mark Kiefer	.05	.02	.01
□	162	Darryl Kile	.10	.05	.01
□	163	Jeff King	.05	.02	.01
□	164	Wayne Kirby	.05	.02	.01
□	165	Ryan Klesko	.50	.23	.06
□	166	Chuck Knoblauch	.15	.07	.02
□	167	Chad Kreuter	.05	.02	.01
□	168	John Kruk	.10	.05	.01
□	169	Mark Langston	.15	.07	.02
□	170	Mike Lansing	.10	.05	.01
□	171	Barry Larkin	.25	.11	.03
□	172	Manuel Lee	.05	.02	.01
□	173	Phil Leftwich	.05	.02	.01
□	174	Darren Lewis	.05	.02	.01
□	175	Derek Lilliquist	.05	.02	.01
□	176	Jose Lind	.05	.02	.01
□	177	Albie Lopez	.10	.05	.01
□	178	Javier Lopez	.30	.14	.04
□	179	Torey Lovullo	.05	.02	.01
□	180	Scott Lydy	.10	.05	.01
□	181	Mike Macfarlane	.05	.02	.01
□	182	Shane Mack	.10	.05	.01
□	183	Greg Maddux	2.00	.90	.25
□	184	Dave Magadan	.05	.02	.01
□	185	Joe Magrane	.05	.02	.01
□	186	Kirk Manwaring	.05	.02	.01
□	187	Al Martin	.10	.05	.01
□	188	Pedro A. Martinez	.10	.05	.01
□	189	Pedro J. Martinez	.15	.07	.02
□	190	Ramon Martinez	.15	.07	.02
□	191	Tino Martinez	.15	.07	.02
□	192	Don Mattingly	1.00	.45	.12

☐	193 Derrick May	.05	.02	.01
☐	194 David McCarty	.10	.05	.01
☐	195 Ben McDonald	.10	.05	.01
☐	196 Roger McDowell	.05	.02	.01
☐	197 Fred McGriff UER (Stats on back have 73 stolen bases for 1989; should be 7)	.25	.11	.03
☐	198 Mark McLemore	.05	.02	.01
☐	199 Greg McMichael	.10	.05	.01
☐	200 Jeff McNeely	.05	.02	.01
☐	201 Brian McRae	.10	.05	.01
☐	202 Pat Meares	.05	.02	.01
☐	203 Roberto Mejia	.05	.02	.01
☐	204 Orlando Merced	.10	.05	.01
☐	205 Jose Mesa	.10	.05	.01
☐	206 Blas Minor	.05	.02	.01
☐	207 Angel Miranda	.05	.02	.01
☐	208 Paul Molitor	.15	.07	.02
☐	209 Raul Mondesi	.60	.25	.07
☐	210 Jeff Montgomery	.10	.05	.01
☐	211 Mickey Morandini	.05	.02	.01
☐	212 Mike Morgan	.05	.02	.01
☐	213 Jamie Moyer	.05	.02	.01
☐	214 Bobby Munoz	.05	.02	.01
☐	215 Troy Neel	.05	.02	.01
☐	216 Dave Nilsson	.05	.02	.01
☐	217 John O'Donoghue	.05	.02	.01
☐	218 Paul O'Neill	.10	.05	.01
☐	219 Jose Offerman	.05	.02	.01
☐	220 Joe Oliver	.05	.02	.01
☐	221 Greg Olson	.05	.02	.01
☐	222 Donovan Osborne	.05	.02	.01
☐	223 J. Owens	.05	.02	.01
☐	224 Mike Pagliarulo	.05	.02	.01
☐	225 Craig Paquette	.05	.02	.01
☐	226 Roger Pavlik	.05	.02	.01
☐	227 Brad Pennington	.05	.02	.01
☐	228 Eduardo Perez	.05	.02	.01
☐	229 Mike Perez	.05	.02	.01
☐	230 Tony Phillips	.10	.05	.01
☐	231 Hipolito Pichardo	.05	.02	.01
☐	232 Phil Plantier	.10	.05	.01
☐	233 Curtis Pride	.10	.05	.01
☐	234 Tim Pugh	.05	.02	.01
☐	235 Scott Radinsky	.05	.02	.01
☐	236 Pat Rapp	.05	.02	.01
☐	237 Kevin Reimer	.05	.02	.01
☐	238 Armando Reynoso	.05	.02	.01
☐	239 Jose Rijo	.10	.05	.01
☐	240 Cal Ripken	2.00	.90	.25
☐	241 Kevin Roberson	.05	.02	.01
☐	242 Kenny Rogers	.10	.05	.01
☐	243 Kevin Rogers	.05	.02	.01
☐	244 Mel Rojas	.05	.02	.01
☐	245 John Roper	.10	.05	.01
☐	246 Kirk Rueter	.05	.02	.01
☐	247 Scott Ruffcorn	.10	.05	.01
☐	248 Ken Ryan	.05	.02	.01
☐	249 Nolan Ryan	2.00	.90	.25
☐	250 Bret Saberhagen	.10	.05	.01
☐	251 Tim Salmon	.40	.18	.05
☐	252 Reggie Sanders	.10	.05	.01
☐	253 Curt Schilling	.05	.02	.01
☐	254 David Segui	.05	.02	.01
☐	255 Aaron Sele	.10	.05	.01
☐	256 Scott Servais	.05	.02	.01
☐	257 Gary Sheffield	.15	.07	.02
☐	258 Ruben Sierra	.15	.07	.02
☐	259 Don Slaught	.05	.02	.01
☐	260 Lee Smith	.10	.05	.01
☐	261 Cory Snyder	.05	.02	.01
☐	262 Paul Sorrento	.05	.02	.01
☐	263 Sammy Sosa	.15	.07	.02
☐	264 Bill Spiers	.05	.02	.01
☐	265 Mike Stanley	.05	.02	.01
☐	266 Dave Staton	.05	.02	.01
☐	267 Terry Steinbach	.10	.05	.01
☐	268 Kevin Stocker	.10	.05	.01
☐	269 Todd Stottlemyre	.10	.05	.01
☐	270 Doug Strange	.05	.02	.01
☐	271 Bill Swift	.05	.02	.01
☐	272 Kevin Tapani	.05	.02	.01
☐	273 Tony Tarasco	.15	.07	.02
☐	274 Julian Tavarez	.40	.18	.05
☐	275 Mickey Tettleton	.10	.05	.01
☐	276 Ryan Thompson	.10	.05	.01
☐	277 Chris Turner	.05	.02	.01
☐	278 John Valentin	.15	.07	.02
☐	279 Todd Van Poppel	.10	.05	.01
☐	280 Andy Van Slyke	.10	.05	.01
☐	281 Mo Vaughn	.30	.14	.04
☐	282 Robin Ventura	.10	.05	.01
☐	283 Frank Viola	.05	.02	.01
☐	284 Jose Vizcaino	.05	.02	.01
☐	285 Omar Vizquel	.05	.02	.01
☐	286 Larry Walker	.25	.11	.03
☐	287 Duane Ward	.10	.05	.01
☐	288 Allen Watson	.05	.02	.01
☐	289 Bill Wegman	.05	.02	.01
☐	290 Turk Wendell	.05	.02	.01
☐	291 Lou Whitaker	.15	.07	.02
☐	292 Devon White	.10	.05	.01
☐	293 Rondell White	.15	.07	.02
☐	294 Mark Whiten	.05	.02	.01
☐	295 Darrel Whitmore	.05	.02	.01
☐	296 Bob Wickman	.05	.02	.01
☐	297 Rick Wilkins	.05	.02	.01
☐	298 Bernie Williams	.15	.07	.02
☐	299 Matt Williams	.30	.14	.04
☐	300 Woody Williams	.05	.02	.01
☐	301 Nigel Wilson	.10	.05	.01
☐	302 Dave Winfield	.15	.07	.02
☐	303 Anthony Young	.05	.02	.01
☐	304 Eric Young	.10	.05	.01
☐	305 Todd Zeile	.10	.05	.01
☐	306 Jack McDowell TP John Burkett Tom Glavine	.10	.05	.01
☐	307 Randy Johnson TP	.15	.07	.02
☐	308 Randy Myers TP	.05	.02	.01
☐	309 Jack McDowell TP	.10	.05	.01
☐	310 Mike Piazza TP	.40	.18	.05
☐	311 Barry Bonds TP	.25	.11	.03
☐	312 Andres Galarraga TP	.15	.07	.02
☐	313 Juan Gonzalez TP Barry Bonds	.20	.09	.03
☐	314 Albert Belle TP	.40	.18	.05
☐	315 Kenny Lofton TP	.30	.14	.04
☐	316 Barry Bonds CL	.15	.07	.02
☐	317 Ken Griffey Jr. CL	.50	.23	.06
☐	318 Mike Piazza CL	.20	.09	.03
☐	319 Kirby Puckett CL	.15	.07	.02
☐	320 Nolan Ryan CL	.50	.23	.06
☐	321 Roberto Alomar CL	.10	.05	.01
☐	322 Roger Clemens CL	.10	.05	.01
☐	323 Juan Gonzalez CL	.10	.05	.01
☐	324 Ken Griffey Jr. CL	.50	.23	.06
☐	325 David Justice CL	.10	.05	.01
☐	326 John Kruk CL	.05	.02	.01
☐	327 Frank Thomas CL	.50	.23	.06
☐	328 Tim Salmon TC	.10	.05	.01

☐ 329	Jeff Bagwell TC	.30	.14	.04
☐ 330	Mark McGwire TC	.05	.02	.01
☐ 331	Roberto Alomar TC	.15	.07	.02
☐ 332	David Justice TC	.10	.05	.01
☐ 333	Pat Listach TC	.05	.02	.01
☐ 334	Ozzie Smith TC	.15	.07	.02
☐ 335	Ryne Sandberg TC	.25	.11	.03
☐ 336	Mike Piazza TC	.40	.18	.05
☐ 337	Cliff Floyd TC	.10	.05	.01
☐ 338	Barry Bonds TC	.25	.11	.03
☐ 339	Albert Belle TC	.40	.18	.05
☐ 340	Ken Griffey Jr. TC	1.00	.45	.12
☐ 341	Gary Sheffield TC	.05	.02	.01
☐ 342	Dwight Gooden TC	.05	.02	.01
☐ 343	Cal Ripken TC	1.00	.45	.12
☐ 344	Tony Gwynn TC	.30	.14	.04
☐ 345	Lenny Dykstra TC	.05	.02	.01
☐ 346	Andy Van Slyke TC	.05	.02	.01
☐ 347	Juan Gonzalez TC	.15	.07	.02
☐ 348	Roger Clemens TC	.10	.05	.01
☐ 349	Barry Larkin TC	.10	.05	.01
☐ 350	Andres Galarraga TC	.05	.02	.01
☐ 351	Kevin Appier TC	.05	.02	.01
☐ 352	Cecil Fielder TC	.05	.02	.01
☐ 353	Kirby Puckett TC	.30	.14	.04
☐ 354	Frank Thomas TC	1.00	.45	.12
☐ 355	Don Mattingly TC	.50	.23	.06
☐ 356	Bo Jackson	.15	.07	.02
☐ 357	Randy Johnson	.40	.18	.05
☐ 358	Darren Daulton	.15	.07	.02
☐ 359	Charlie Hough	.05	.02	.01
☐ 360	Andres Galarraga	.15	.07	.02
☐ 361	Mike Felder	.05	.02	.01
☐ 362	Chris Hammond	.05	.02	.01
☐ 363	Shawon Dunston	.05	.02	.01
☐ 364	Junior Felix	.05	.02	.01
☐ 365	Ray Lankford	.15	.07	.02
☐ 366	Darryl Strawberry	.10	.05	.01
☐ 367	Dave Magadan	.05	.02	.01
☐ 368	Gregg Olson	.05	.02	.01
☐ 369	Lenny Dykstra	.15	.07	.02
☐ 370	Darrin Jackson	.05	.02	.01
☐ 371	Dave Stewart	.10	.05	.01
☐ 372	Terry Pendleton	.05	.02	.01
☐ 373	Arthur Rhodes	.05	.02	.01
☐ 374	Benito Santiago	.05	.02	.01
☐ 375	Travis Fryman	.15	.07	.02
☐ 376	Scott Brosius	.05	.02	.01
☐ 377	Stan Belinda	.05	.02	.01
☐ 378	Derek Parks	.05	.02	.01
☐ 379	Kevin Seitzer	.05	.02	.01
☐ 380	Wade Boggs	.15	.07	.02
☐ 381	Wally Whitehurst	.05	.02	.01
☐ 382	Scott Leius	.05	.02	.01
☐ 383	Danny Tartabull	.10	.05	.01
☐ 384	Harold Reynolds	.05	.02	.01
☐ 385	Tim Raines	.15	.07	.02
☐ 386	Darryl Hamilton	.05	.02	.01
☐ 387	Felix Fermin	.05	.02	.01
☐ 388	Jim Eisenreich	.05	.02	.01
☐ 389	Kurt Abbott	.10	.05	.01
☐ 390	Kevin Appier	.10	.05	.01
☐ 391	Chris Bosio	.05	.02	.01
☐ 392	Randy Tomlin	.05	.02	.01
☐ 393	Bob Hamelin	.05	.02	.01
☐ 394	Kevin Gross	.05	.02	.01
☐ 395	Wil Cordero	.15	.07	.02
☐ 396	Joe Girardi	.05	.02	.01
☐ 397	Orestes Destrade	.05	.02	.01
☐ 398	Chris Haney	.05	.02	.01
☐ 399	Xavier Hernandez	.05	.02	.01
☐ 400	Mike Piazza	.75	.35	.09
☐ 401	Alex Arias	.05	.02	.01
☐ 402	Tom Candiotti	.05	.02	.01
☐ 403	Kirk Gibson	.10	.05	.01
☐ 404	Chuck Carr	.05	.02	.01
☐ 405	Brady Anderson	.10	.05	.01
☐ 406	Greg Gagne	.05	.02	.01
☐ 407	Bruce Ruffin	.05	.02	.01
☐ 408	Scott Hemond	.05	.02	.01
☐ 409	Keith Miller	.05	.02	.01
☐ 410	John Wetteland	.05	.02	.01
☐ 411	Eric Anthony	.05	.02	.01
☐ 412	Andre Dawson	.15	.07	.02
☐ 413	Doug Henry	.05	.02	.01
☐ 414	John Franco	.05	.02	.01
☐ 415	Julio Franco	.10	.05	.01
☐ 416	Dave Hansen	.05	.02	.01
☐ 417	Mike Harkey	.05	.02	.01
☐ 418	Jack Armstrong	.05	.02	.01
☐ 419	Joe Orsulak	.05	.02	.01
☐ 420	John Smoltz	.10	.05	.01
☐ 421	Scott Livingstone	.05	.02	.01
☐ 422	Darren Holmes	.05	.02	.01
☐ 423	Ed Sprague	.05	.02	.01
☐ 424	Jay Buhner	.10	.05	.01
☐ 425	Kirby Puckett	.60	.25	.07
☐ 426	Phil Clark	.05	.02	.01
☐ 427	Anthony Young	.05	.02	.01
☐ 428	Reggie Jefferson	.05	.02	.01
☐ 429	Mariano Duncan	.05	.02	.01
☐ 430	Tom Glavine	.15	.07	.02
☐ 431	Dave Henderson	.05	.02	.01
☐ 432	Melido Perez	.05	.02	.01
☐ 433	Paul Wagner	.05	.02	.01
☐ 434	Tim Worrell	.05	.02	.01
☐ 435	Ozzie Guillen	.05	.02	.01
☐ 436	Mike Butcher	.05	.02	.01
☐ 437	Jim Deshaies	.05	.02	.01
☐ 438	Kevin Young	.05	.02	.01
☐ 439	Tom Browning	.05	.02	.01
☐ 440	Mike Greenwell	.10	.05	.01
☐ 441	Mike Stanton	.05	.02	.01
☐ 442	John Doherty	.05	.02	.01
☐ 443	John Dopson	.05	.02	.01
☐ 444	Carlos Baerga	.40	.18	.05
☐ 445	Jack McDowell	.15	.07	.02
☐ 446	Kent Mercker	.05	.02	.01
☐ 447	Ricky Jordan	.05	.02	.01
☐ 448	Jerry Browne	.05	.02	.01
☐ 449	Fernando Vina	.05	.02	.01
☐ 450	Jim Abbott	.15	.07	.02
☐ 451	Teddy Higuera	.05	.02	.01
☐ 452	Tim Naehring	.10	.05	.01
☐ 453	Jim Leyritz	.05	.02	.01
☐ 454	Frank Castillo	.05	.02	.01
☐ 455	Joe Carter	.15	.07	.02
☐ 456	Craig Biggio	.10	.05	.01
☐ 457	Geronimo Pena	.05	.02	.01
☐ 458	Alejandro Pena	.05	.02	.01
☐ 459	Mike Moore	.05	.02	.01
☐ 460	Randy Myers	.05	.02	.01
☐ 461	Greg Myers	.05	.02	.01
☐ 462	Greg Hibbard	.05	.02	.01
☐ 463	Jose Guzman	.05	.02	.01
☐ 464	Tom Pagnozzi	.05	.02	.01
☐ 465	Marquis Grissom	.15	.07	.02
☐ 466	Tim Wallach	.05	.02	.01
☐ 467	Joe Grahe	.05	.02	.01
☐ 468	Bob Tewksbury	.05	.02	.01
☐ 469	B.J. Surhoff	.10	.05	.01
☐ 470	Kevin Mitchell	.10	.05	.01

#	Player			
☐ 471	Bobby Witt	.05	.02	.01
☐ 472	Milt Thompson	.05	.02	.01
☐ 473	John Smiley	.05	.02	.01
☐ 474	Alan Trammell	.10	.05	.01
☐ 475	Mike Mussina	.30	.14	.04
☐ 476	Rick Aguilera	.05	.02	.01
☐ 477	Jose Valentin	.05	.02	.01
☐ 478	Harold Baines	.10	.05	.01
☐ 479	Bip Roberts	.05	.02	.01
☐ 480	Edgar Martinez	.05	.02	.01
☐ 481	Rheal Cormier	.05	.02	.01
☐ 482	Hal Morris	.10	.05	.01
☐ 483	Pat Kelly	.05	.02	.01
☐ 484	Roberto Kelly	.05	.02	.01
☐ 485	Chris Sabo	.05	.02	.01
☐ 486	Kent Hrbek	.10	.05	.01
☐ 487	Scott Kamieniecki	.05	.02	.01
☐ 488	Walt Weiss	.05	.02	.01
☐ 489	Karl Rhodes	.05	.02	.01
☐ 490	Derek Bell	.10	.05	.01
☐ 491	Chili Davis	.10	.05	.01
☐ 492	Brian Harper	.05	.02	.01
☐ 493	Felix Jose	.05	.02	.01
☐ 494	Trevor Hoffman	.05	.02	.01
☐ 495	Dennis Eckersley	.15	.07	.02
☐ 496	Pedro Astacio	.10	.05	.01
☐ 497	Jay Bell	.10	.05	.01
☐ 498	Randy Velarde	.05	.02	.01
☐ 499	David Wells	.05	.02	.01
☐ 500	Frank Thomas	2.00	.90	.25
☐ 501	Mark Lemke	.05	.02	.01
☐ 502	Mike Devereaux	.10	.05	.01
☐ 503	Chuck McElroy	.05	.02	.01
☐ 504	Luis Polonia	.05	.02	.01
☐ 505	Damian Easley	.05	.02	.01
☐ 506	Greg A. Harris	.05	.02	.01
☐ 507	Chris James	.05	.02	.01
☐ 508	Terry Mulholland	.05	.02	.01
☐ 509	Pete Smith	.05	.02	.01
☐ 510	Rickey Henderson	.15	.07	.02
☐ 511	Sid Fernandez	.05	.02	.01
☐ 512	Al Leiter	.05	.02	.01
☐ 513	Doug Jones	.05	.02	.01
☐ 514	Steve Farr	.05	.02	.01
☐ 515	Chuck Finley	.05	.02	.01
☐ 516	Bobby Thigpen	.05	.02	.01
☐ 517	Jim Edmonds	.30	.14	.04
☐ 518	Graeme Lloyd	.05	.02	.01
☐ 519	Dwight Gooden	.05	.02	.01
☐ 520	Pat Listach	.05	.02	.01
☐ 521	Kevin Bass	.05	.02	.01
☐ 522	Willie Banks	.05	.02	.01
☐ 523	Steve Finley	.05	.02	.01
☐ 524	Delino DeShields	.10	.05	.01
☐ 525	Mark McGwire	.15	.07	.02
☐ 526	Greg Swindell	.05	.02	.01
☐ 527	Chris Nabholz	.05	.02	.01
☐ 528	Scott Sanders	.05	.02	.01
☐ 529	David Segui	.05	.02	.01
☐ 530	Howard Johnson	.05	.02	.01
☐ 531	Jaime Navarro	.05	.02	.01
☐ 532	Jose Vizcaino	.05	.02	.01
☐ 533	Mark Lewis	.05	.02	.01
☐ 534	Pete Harnisch	.05	.02	.01
☐ 535	Robby Thompson	.05	.02	.01
☐ 536	Marcus Moore	.05	.02	.01
☐ 537	Kevin Brown	.05	.02	.01
☐ 538	Mark Clark	.05	.02	.01
☐ 539	Sterling Hitchcock	.10	.05	.01
☐ 540	Will Clark	.25	.11	.03
☐ 541	Denis Boucher	.05	.02	.01
☐ 542	Jack Morris	.15	.07	.02
☐ 543	Pedro Munoz	.05	.02	.01
☐ 544	Bret Boone	.15	.07	.02
☐ 545	Ozzie Smith	.40	.18	.05
☐ 546	Dennis Martinez	.10	.05	.01
☐ 547	Dan Wilson	.05	.02	.01
☐ 548	Rick Sutcliffe	.10	.05	.01
☐ 549	Kevin McReynolds	.05	.02	.01
☐ 550	Roger Clemens	.30	.14	.04
☐ 551	Todd Benzinger	.05	.02	.01
☐ 552	Bill Haselman	.05	.02	.01
☐ 553	Bobby Munoz	.05	.02	.01
☐ 554	Ellis Burks	.10	.05	.01
☐ 555	Ryne Sandberg	.50	.23	.06
☐ 556	Lee Smith	.15	.07	.02
☐ 557	Danny Bautista	.10	.05	.01
☐ 558	Rey Sanchez	.05	.02	.01
☐ 559	Norm Charlton	.05	.02	.01
☐ 560	Jose Canseco	.30	.14	.04
☐ 561	Tim Belcher	.05	.02	.01
☐ 562	Denny Neagle	.05	.02	.01
☐ 563	Eric Davis	.05	.02	.01
☐ 564	Jody Reed	.05	.02	.01
☐ 565	Kenny Lofton	.60	.25	.07
☐ 566	Gary Gaetti	.05	.02	.01
☐ 567	Todd Worrell	.05	.02	.01
☐ 568	Mark Portugal	.05	.02	.01
☐ 569	Dick Schofield	.05	.02	.01
☐ 570	Andy Benes	.10	.05	.01
☐ 571	Zane Smith	.05	.02	.01
☐ 572	Bobby Ayala	.05	.02	.01
☐ 573	Chip Hale	.05	.02	.01
☐ 574	Bob Welch	.05	.02	.01
☐ 575	Deion Sanders	.40	.18	.05
☐ 576	Dave Nied	.15	.07	.02
☐ 577	Pat Mahomes	.05	.02	.01
☐ 578	Charles Nagy	.10	.05	.01
☐ 579	Otis Nixon	.05	.02	.01
☐ 580	Dean Palmer	.10	.05	.01
☐ 581	Roberto Petagine	.10	.05	.01
☐ 582	Dwight Smith	.05	.02	.01
☐ 583	Jeff Russell	.05	.02	.01
☐ 584	Mark Dewey	.05	.02	.01
☐ 585	Greg Vaughn	.10	.05	.01
☐ 586	Brian Hunter	.05	.02	.01
☐ 587	Willie McGee	.05	.02	.01
☐ 588	Pedro J. Martinez	.15	.07	.02
☐ 589	Roger Salkeld	.05	.02	.01
☐ 590	Jeff Bagwell	.60	.25	.07
☐ 591	Spike Owen	.05	.02	.01
☐ 592	Jeff Reardon	.10	.05	.01
☐ 593	Erik Pappas	.05	.02	.01
☐ 594	Brian Williams	.05	.02	.01
☐ 595	Eddie Murray	.25	.11	.03
☐ 596	Henry Rodriguez	.05	.02	.01
☐ 597	Erik Hanson	.05	.02	.01
☐ 598	Stan Javier	.05	.02	.01
☐ 599	Mitch Williams	.05	.02	.01
☐ 600	John Olerud	.15	.07	.02
☐ 601	Vince Coleman	.05	.02	.01
☐ 602	Damon Berryhill	.05	.02	.01
☐ 603	Tom Brunansky	.05	.02	.01
☐ 604	Robb Nen	.05	.02	.01
☐ 605	Rafael Palmeiro	.15	.07	.02
☐ 606	Cal Eldred	.10	.05	.01
☐ 607	Jeff Brantley	.05	.02	.01
☐ 608	Alan Mills	.05	.02	.01
☐ 609	Jeff Nelson	.05	.02	.01
☐ 610	Barry Bonds	.50	.23	.06
☐ 611	Carlos Pulido	.05	.02	.01
☐ 612	Tim Hyers	.05	.02	.01

☐ 613	Steve Hosey	.05	.02	.01
☐ 614	Brian Turang	.05	.02	.01
☐ 615	Leo Gomez	.05	.02	.01
☐ 616	Jesse Orosco	.05	.02	.01
☐ 617	Dan Pasqua	.05	.02	.01
☐ 618	Marvin Freeman	.05	.02	.01
☐ 619	Tony Fernandez	.05	.02	.01
☐ 620	Albert Belle	.75	.35	.09
☐ 621	Eddie Taubensee	.05	.02	.01
☐ 622	Mike Jackson	.05	.02	.01
☐ 623	Jose Bautista	.05	.02	.01
☐ 624	Jim Thome	.40	.18	.05
☐ 625	Ivan Rodriguez	.15	.07	.02
☐ 626	Ben Rivera	.05	.02	.01
☐ 627	Dave Valle	.05	.02	.01
☐ 628	Tom Henke	.05	.02	.01
☐ 629	Omar Vizquel	.05	.02	.01
☐ 630	Juan Gonzalez	.50	.23	.06
☐ 631	Roberto Alomar UP	.15	.07	.02
☐ 632	Barry Bonds UP	.25	.11	.03
☐ 633	Juan Gonzalez UP	.15	.07	.02
☐ 634	Ken Griffey Jr. UP	1.00	.45	.12
☐ 635	Michael Jordan UP	4.00	1.80	.50
☐ 636	David Justice UP	.15	.07	.02
☐ 637	Mike Piazza UP	.40	.18	.05
☐ 638	Kirby Puckett UP	.30	.14	.04
☐ 639	Tim Salmon UP	.15	.07	.02
☐ 640	Frank Thomas UP	1.00	.45	.12
☐ 641	Alan Benes FF	.60	.25	.07
☐ 642	Johnny Damon FF	1.00	.45	.12
☐ 643	Brad Fullmer FF	.20	.09	.03
☐ 644	Derek Jeter FF	.50	.23	.06
☐ 645	Derrek Lee FF	.75	.35	.09
☐ 646	Alex Ochoa FF	.15	.07	.02
☐ 647	Alex Rodriguez FF	1.50	.70	.19
☐ 648	Jose Silva FF	.25	.11	.03
☐ 649	Terrell Wade FF	.25	.11	.03
☐ 650	Preston Wilson FF	.15	.07	.02
☐ 651	Shane Andrews	.10	.05	.01
☐ 652	James Baldwin	.15	.07	.02
☐ 653	Ricky Bottalico	.05	.02	.01
☐ 654	Tavo Alvarez	.05	.02	.01
☐ 655	Donnie Elliott	.05	.02	.01
☐ 656	Joey Eischen	.10	.05	.01
☐ 657	Jason Giambi	.10	.05	.01
☐ 658	Todd Hollandsworth	.15	.07	.02
☐ 659	Brian L. Hunter	.50	.23	.06
☐ 660	Charles Johnson	.15	.07	.02
☐ 661	Michael Jordan	8.00	3.60	1.00
☐ 662	Jeff Juden	.05	.02	.01
☐ 663	Mike Kelly	.05	.02	.01
☐ 664	James Mouton	.10	.05	.01
☐ 665	Ray Holbert	.05	.02	.01
☐ 666	Pokey Reese	.10	.05	.01
☐ 667	Ruben Santana	.10	.05	.01
☐ 668	Paul Spoljaric	.05	.02	.01
☐ 669	Luis Lopez	.05	.02	.01
☐ 670	Matt Walbeck	.05	.02	.01

1994 Collector's Choice Gold Signature

The 670-card Gold Foil Signature set is a parallel to the basic Collector's Choice issue. These cards were randomly inserted at a rate of one in 36 1994 Upper Deck Collector's Choice 12-card packs (11 regular issue cards plus the Gold Foil Signature insert). The other packs each contained one card from the more plentiful Silver Foil Signature set. Gold cards were also issued five per factory set. Gold Foil Signature cards share the same photo as the corresponding regular issue cards, but the borders on the basic player cards are enhanced with a layer of gold foil. Each card is stamped with a gold replica autograph. Some subset cards feature borderless designs (unlike the basic player cards), thus their corresponding borderless Gold Foil Signature cards differ only by the gold foil replica autograph. The Jeffrey Hammonds card has the signature of Orioles General Manager Roland Hemond.

	MINT	NRMT	EXC
COMPLETE SET (670)	3600.00	1600.00	450.00
COMPLETE SERIES 1 (320)	1800.00	800.00	220.00
COMPLETE SERIES 2 (350)	1800.00	800.00	220.00
COMMON CARD (1-320)	2.00	.90	.25
COMMON CARD (321-670)	2.00	.90	.25
*VETERAN STARS: 50X to 75X BASIC CARDS			
*YOUNG STARS: 30X to 50X BASIC CARDS			
*RCs: 20X to 40X BASIC CARDS			

☐ 16	Manny Ramirez	60.00	27.00	7.50
☐ 28	Brooks Kieschnick FDP	40.00	18.00	5.00
☐ 65	George Brett	65.00	29.00	8.00
☐ 117	Ken Griffey Jr.	125.00	55.00	15.50
☐ 122	Tony Gwynn	40.00	18.00	5.00
☐ 152	Chipper Jones	60.00	27.00	7.50
☐ 183	Greg Maddux	125.00	55.00	15.50
☐ 192	Don Mattingly	60.00	27.00	7.50
☐ 209	Raul Mondesi	40.00	18.00	5.00
☐ 240	Cal Ripken	140.00	65.00	17.50
☐ 249	Nolan Ryan	125.00	55.00	15.50
☐ 340	Ken Griffey JR. TC	60.00	27.00	7.50
☐ 354	Frank Thomas TC	60.00	27.00	7.50
☐ 400	Mike Piazza	50.00	22.00	6.25
☐ 425	Kirby Puckett	40.00	18.00	5.00
☐ 500	Frank Thomas	125.00	55.00	15.50
☐ 565	Kenny Lofton	40.00	18.00	5.00
☐ 590	Jeff Bagwell	40.00	18.00	5.00
☐ 620	Albert Belle	50.00	22.00	6.25
☐ 634	Ken Griffey Jr. UP	60.00	27.00	7.50
☐ 635	Michael Jordan UP	80.00	36.00	10.00
☐ 640	Frank Thomas UP	60.00	27.00	7.50
☐ 647	Alex Rodriguez	50.00	22.00	6.25
☐ 661	Michael Jordan	160.00	70.00	20.00

1995 Collector's Choice

This set contains 530 cards issued in packs that were sold in 12-card foil hobby and retail foil-packs for a suggested price of 99 cents. There was also a mail-in offer with acks for a National Packtime card set. The

fronts have a color photo with a white bor
der and the player's last name at the bot
tom in his team's color. The backs have an
action photo at the top with statistics and
information at the bottom with a silver
Upper Deck hologram below that. Subsets
featured are: Rookie Class (1-27), Future
Foundation (28-45), Best of the '90s (51-
65) and What's the Call? (86-90).

	MINT	NRMT	EXC
COMPLETE SET (530)	20.00	9.00	2.50
COMPLETE FACT.SET (545)	28.00	12.50	3.50
COMMON CARD (1-530)	.05	.02	.01
COMP. SILV. SIG. SET (530)	75.00	34.00	9.50
SILV. SIG. COMMON(1-530)	.10	.05	.01
SILV. SIG. SEMISTARS	.20	.09	.03

*SILV. SIG. VETERAN STARS: 2X TO 4X BASIC CARDS
*SILV. SIG. YOUNG STARS: 1.5X TO 3X BASIC CARDS

☐ 1	Charles Johnson	.15	.07	.02
☐ 2	Scott Ruffcorn	.05	.02	.01
☐ 3	Ray Durham	.15	.07	.02
☐ 4	Armando Benitez	.05	.02	.01
☐ 5	Alex Rodriguez	.40	.18	.05
☐ 6	Julian Tavarez	.10	.05	.01
☐ 7	Chad Ogea	.10	.05	.01
☐ 8	Quilvio Veras	.10	.05	.01
☐ 9	Phil Nevin	.05	.02	.01
☐ 10	Michael Tucker	.10	.05	.01
☐ 11	Mark Thompson	.05	.02	.01
☐ 12	Rod Henderson	.05	.02	.01
☐ 13	Andrew Lorraine	.10	.05	.01
☐ 14	Joe Randa	.05	.02	.01
☐ 15	Derek Jeter	.30	.14	.04
☐ 16	Tony Clark	.05	.02	.01
☐ 17	Juan Castillo	.05	.02	.01
☐ 18	Mark Acre	.05	.02	.01
☐ 19	Orlando Miller	.10	.05	.01
☐ 20	Paul Wilson	.40	.18	.05
☐ 21	John Mabry	.10	.05	.01
☐ 22	Garey Ingram	.05	.02	.01
☐ 23	Garret Anderson	.40	.18	.05
☐ 24	Dave Stevens	.05	.02	.01
☐ 25	Dustin Hermanson	.10	.05	.01
☐ 26	Paul Shuey	.05	.02	.01
☐ 27	J.R. Phillips	.05	.02	.01
☐ 28	Ruben Rivera FF	1.25	.55	.16
☐ 29	Nomar Garciaparra FF	.15	.07	.02
☐ 30	John Wasdin FF	.15	.07	.02
☐ 31	Jim Pittsley FF	.15	.07	.02
☐ 32	Scott Elarton FF	.40	.18	.05
☐ 33	Raul Casanova FF	.50	.23	.06
☐ 34	Todd Greene FF	.30	.14	.04
☐ 35	Bill Pulsipher FF	.15	.07	.02
☐ 36	Trey Beamon FF	.15	.07	.02
☐ 37	Curtis Goodwin FF	.15	.07	.02
☐ 38	Doug Million FF	.30	.14	.04
☐ 39	Karim Garcia FF	1.50	.70	.19
☐ 40	Ben Grieve FF	.50	.23	.06
☐ 41	Mark Farris FF	.10	.05	.01
☐ 42	Juan Acevedo FF	.10	.05	.01
☐ 43	C.J. Nitkowski FF	.10	.05	.01
☐ 44	Travis Miller FF	.20	.09	.03
☐ 45	Reid Ryan FF	.15	.07	.02
☐ 46	Nolan Ryan	1.25	.55	.16
☐ 47	Robin Yount	.20	.09	.03
☐ 48	Ryne Sandberg	.40	.18	.05
☐ 49	George Brett	.50	.23	.06
☐ 50	Mike Schmidt	.30	.14	.04
☐ 51	Cecil Fielder B90	.10	.05	.01
☐ 52	Nolan Ryan B90	.60	.25	.07
☐ 53	Rickey Henderson B90	.10	.05	.01
☐ 54	Brett/Yount/Winfield B90	.40	.18	.05
☐ 55	Sid Bream B90	.05	.02	.01
☐ 56	Carlos Baerga B90	.10	.05	.01
☐ 57	Lee Smith B90	.05	.02	.01
☐ 58	Mark Whiten B90	.05	.02	.01
☐ 59	Joe Carter B90	.10	.05	.01
☐ 60	Barry Bonds B90	.25	.11	.03
☐ 61	Tony Gwynn B90	.30	.14	.04
☐ 62	Ken Griffey Jr. B90	1.00	.45	.12
☐ 63	Greg Maddux B90	1.00	.45	.12
☐ 64	Frank Thomas B90	1.00	.45	.12
☐ 65	Dennis Martinez B90 Kenny Rogers	.05	.02	.01
☐ 66	David Cone	.15	.07	.02
☐ 67	Greg Maddux	2.00	.90	.25
☐ 68	Jimmy Key	.10	.05	.01
☐ 69	Fred McGriff	.25	.11	.03
☐ 70	Ken Griffey Jr.	2.00	.90	.25
☐ 71	Matt Williams	.30	.14	.04
☐ 72	Paul O'Neill	.10	.05	.01
☐ 73	Tony Gwynn	.60	.25	.07
☐ 74	Randy Johnson	.40	.18	.05
☐ 75	Frank Thomas	2.00	.90	.25
☐ 76	Jeff Bagwell	.60	.25	.07
☐ 77	Kirby Puckett	.60	.25	.07
☐ 78	Bob Hamelin	.05	.02	.01
☐ 79	Raul Mondesi	.50	.23	.06
☐ 80	Mike Piazza	.75	.35	.09
☐ 81	Kenny Lofton	.60	.25	.07
☐ 82	Barry Bonds	.50	.23	.06
☐ 83	Albert Belle	.75	.35	.09
☐ 84	Juan Gonzalez	.50	.23	.06
☐ 85	Cal Ripken Jr.	2.00	.90	.25
☐ 86	Barry Bonds WC	.25	.11	.03
☐ 87	Mike Piazza WC	.40	.18	.05
☐ 88	Ken Griffey Jr. WC	1.00	.45	.12
☐ 89	Frank Thomas WC	1.00	.45	.12
☐ 90	Juan Gonzalez WC	.10	.05	.01
☐ 91	Jorge Fabregas	.05	.02	.01
☐ 92	J.T. Snow	.15	.07	.02
☐ 93	Spike Owen	.05	.02	.01
☐ 94	Eduardo Perez	.05	.02	.01
☐ 95	Bo Jackson	.15	.07	.02
☐ 96	Damion Easley	.05	.02	.01
☐ 97	Gary DiSarcina	.05	.02	.01
☐ 98	Jim Edmonds	.25	.11	.03
☐ 99	Chad Curtis	.10	.05	.01
☐ 100	Tim Salmon	.30	.14	.04
☐ 101	Chili Davis	.10	.05	.01
☐ 102	Chuck Finley	.10	.05	.01
☐ 103	Mark Langston	.10	.05	.01
☐ 104	Brian Anderson	.05	.02	.01

☐ 105	Lee Smith	.15	.07	.02	☐ 176	Jose Valentin	.05	.02	.01
☐ 106	Phil Leftwich	.05	.02	.01	☐ 177	Turner Ward	.05	.02	.01
☐ 107	Chris Donnels	.05	.02	.01	☐ 178	Darryl Hamilton	.05	.02	.01
☐ 108	John Hudek	.05	.02	.01	☐ 179	Pat Listach	.05	.02	.01
☐ 109	Craig Biggio	.15	.07	.02	☐ 180	Matt Mieske	.05	.02	.01
☐ 110	Luis Gonzalez	.10	.05	.01	☐ 181	Brian Harper	.05	.02	.01
☐ 111	Brian L. Hunter	.25	.11	.03	☐ 182	Dave Nilsson	.10	.05	.01
☐ 112	James Mouton	.10	.05	.01	☐ 183	Mike Fetters	.05	.02	.01
☐ 113	Scott Servais	.05	.02	.01	☐ 184	John Jaha	.05	.02	.01
☐ 114	Tony Eusebio	.05	.02	.01	☐ 185	Ricky Bones	.05	.02	.01
☐ 115	Derek Bell	.15	.07	.02	☐ 186	Geronimo Pena	.05	.02	.01
☐ 116	Doug Drabek	.10	.05	.01	☐ 187	Bob Tewksbury	.05	.02	.01
☐ 117	Shane Reynolds	.05	.02	.01	☐ 188	Todd Zeile	.10	.05	.01
☐ 118	Darryl Kile	.05	.02	.01	☐ 189	Danny Jackson	.05	.02	.01
☐ 119	Greg Swindell	.05	.02	.01	☐ 190	Ray Lankford	.15	.07	.02
☐ 120	Phil Plantier	.05	.02	.01	☐ 191	Bernard Gilkey	.10	.05	.01
☐ 121	Todd Jones	.05	.02	.01	☐ 192	Brian Jordan	.15	.07	.02
☐ 122	Steve Ontiveros	.05	.02	.01	☐ 193	Tom Pagnozzi	.05	.02	.01
☐ 123	Bobby Witt	.05	.02	.01	☐ 194	Rick Sutcliffe	.05	.02	.01
☐ 124	Brent Gates	.10	.05	.01	☐ 195	Mark Whiten	.10	.05	.01
☐ 125	Rickey Henderson	.15	.07	.02	☐ 196	Tom Henke	.10	.05	.01
☐ 126	Scott Brosius	.05	.02	.01	☐ 197	Rene Arocha	.05	.02	.01
☐ 127	Mike Bordick	.05	.02	.01	☐ 198	Allen Watson	.10	.05	.01
☐ 128	Fausto Cruz	.05	.02	.01	☐ 199	Mike Perez	.05	.02	.01
☐ 129	Stan Javier	.05	.02	.01	☐ 200	Ozzie Smith	.40	.18	.05
☐ 130	Mark McGwire	.15	.07	.02	☐ 201	Anthony Young	.05	.02	.01
☐ 131	Geronimo Berroa	.05	.02	.01	☐ 202	Rey Sanchez	.05	.02	.01
☐ 132	Terry Steinbach	.10	.05	.01	☐ 203	Steve Buechele	.05	.02	.01
☐ 133	Steve Karsay	.05	.02	.01	☐ 204	Shawon Dunston	.05	.02	.01
☐ 134	Dennis Eckersley	.15	.07	.02	☐ 205	Mark Grace	.15	.07	.02
☐ 135	Ruben Sierra	.15	.07	.02	☐ 206	Glenallen Hill	.10	.05	.01
☐ 136	Ron Darling	.05	.02	.01	☐ 207	Eddie Zambrano	.05	.02	.01
☐ 137	Todd Van Poppel	.05	.02	.01	☐ 208	Rick Wilkins	.05	.02	.01
☐ 138	Alex Gonzalez	.10	.05	.01	☐ 209	Derrick May	.10	.05	.01
☐ 139	John Olerud	.10	.05	.01	☐ 210	Sammy Sosa	.15	.07	.02
☐ 140	Roberto Alomar	.40	.18	.05	☐ 211	Kevin Roberson	.05	.02	.01
☐ 141	Darren Hall	.05	.02	.01	☐ 212	Steve Trachsel	.05	.02	.01
☐ 142	Ed Sprague	.05	.02	.01	☐ 213	Willie Banks	.05	.02	.01
☐ 143	Devon White	.10	.05	.01	☐ 214	Kevin Foster	.05	.02	.01
☐ 144	Shawn Green	.15	.07	.02	☐ 215	Randy Myers	.10	.05	.01
☐ 145	Paul Molitor	.15	.07	.02	☐ 216	Mike Morgan	.05	.02	.01
☐ 146	Pat Borders	.05	.02	.01	☐ 217	Rafael Bournigal	.05	.02	.01
☐ 147	Carlos Delgado	.15	.07	.02	☐ 218	Delino DeShields	.10	.05	.01
☐ 148	Juan Guzman	.10	.05	.01	☐ 219	Tim Wallach	.05	.02	.01
☐ 149	Pat Hentgen	.10	.05	.01	☐ 220	Eric Karros	.15	.07	.02
☐ 150	Joe Carter	.15	.07	.02	☐ 221	Jose Offerman	.05	.02	.01
☐ 151	Dave Stewart	.10	.05	.01	☐ 222	Tom Candiotti	.05	.02	.01
☐ 152	Todd Stottlemyre	.05	.02	.01	☐ 223	Ismael Valdes	.05	.02	.01
☐ 153	Dick Schofield	.05	.02	.01	☐ 224	Henry Rodriguez	.05	.02	.01
☐ 154	Chipper Jones	.75	.35	.09	☐ 225	Billy Ashley	.10	.05	.01
☐ 155	Ryan Klesko	.40	.18	.05	☐ 226	Darren Dreifort	.05	.02	.01
☐ 156	David Justice	.25	.11	.03	☐ 227	Ramon Martinez	.10	.05	.01
☐ 157	Mike Kelly	.10	.05	.01	☐ 228	Pedro Astacio	.05	.02	.01
☐ 158	Roberto Kelly	.05	.02	.01	☐ 229	Orel Hershiser	.10	.05	.01
☐ 159	Tony Tarasco	.10	.05	.01	☐ 230	Brett Butler	.10	.05	.01
☐ 160	Javier Lopez	.25	.11	.03	☐ 231	Todd Hollandsworth	.10	.05	.01
☐ 161	Steve Avery	.15	.07	.02	☐ 232	Chan Ho Park	.10	.05	.01
☐ 162	Greg McMichael	.05	.02	.01	☐ 233	Mike Lansing	.05	.02	.01
☐ 163	Kent Mercker	.05	.02	.01	☐ 234	Sean Berry	.10	.05	.01
☐ 164	Mark Lemke	.10	.05	.01	☐ 235	Rondell White	.15	.07	.02
☐ 165	Tom Glavine	.15	.07	.02	☐ 236	Ken Hill	.10	.05	.01
☐ 166	Jose Oliva	.05	.02	.01	☐ 237	Marquis Grissom	.15	.07	.02
☐ 167	John Smoltz	.10	.05	.01	☐ 238	Larry Walker	.25	.11	.03
☐ 168	Jeff Blauser	.10	.05	.01	☐ 239	John Wetteland	.10	.05	.01
☐ 169	Troy O'Leary	.10	.05	.01	☐ 240	Cliff Floyd	.10	.05	.01
☐ 170	Greg Vaughn	.05	.02	.01	☐ 241	Joey Eischen	.05	.02	.01
☐ 171	Jody Reed	.05	.02	.01	☐ 242	Lou Frazier	.05	.02	.01
☐ 172	Kevin Seitzer	.05	.02	.01	☐ 243	Darrin Fletcher	.05	.02	.01
☐ 173	Jeff Cirillo	.10	.05	.01	☐ 244	Pedro J. Martinez	.15	.07	.02
☐ 174	B.J. Surhoff	.10	.05	.01	☐ 245	Wil Cordero	.10	.05	.01
☐ 175	Cal Eldred	.05	.02	.01	☐ 246	Jeff Fassero	.10	.05	.01

	#	Player			
☐	247	Butch Henry	.05	.02	.01
☐	248	Mel Rojas	.10	.05	.01
☐	249	Kirk Rueter	.05	.02	.01
☐	250	Moises Alou	.10	.05	.01
☐	251	Rod Beck	.10	.05	.01
☐	252	John Patterson	.05	.02	.01
☐	253	Robby Thompson	.05	.02	.01
☐	254	Royce Clayton	.10	.05	.01
☐	255	Wm. VanLandingham	.10	.05	.01
☐	256	Darren Lewis	.05	.02	.01
☐	257	Kirt Manwaring	.05	.02	.01
☐	258	Mark Portugal	.05	.02	.01
☐	259	Bill Swift	.05	.02	.01
☐	260	Rikkert Faneyte	.05	.02	.01
☐	261	Mike Jackson	.05	.02	.01
☐	262	Todd Benzinger	.05	.02	.01
☐	263	Bud Black	.05	.02	.01
☐	264	Salomon Torres	.05	.02	.01
☐	265	Eddie Murray	.25	.11	.03
☐	266	Mark Clark	.05	.02	.01
☐	267	Paul Sorrento	.05	.02	.01
☐	268	Jim Thome	.30	.14	.04
☐	269	Omar Vizquel	.10	.05	.01
☐	270	Carlos Baerga	.40	.18	.05
☐	271	Jeff Russell	.05	.02	.01
☐	272	Herbert Perry	.10	.05	.01
☐	273	Sandy Alomar Jr.	.10	.05	.01
☐	274	Dennis Martinez	.10	.05	.01
☐	275	Manny Ramirez	.75	.35	.09
☐	276	Wayne Kirby	.05	.02	.01
☐	277	Charles Nagy	.10	.05	.01
☐	278	Albie Lopez	.10	.05	.01
☐	279	Jeromy Burnitz	.05	.02	.01
☐	280	Dave Winfield	.15	.07	.02
☐	281	Tim Davis	.05	.02	.01
☐	282	Marc Newfield	.10	.05	.01
☐	283	Tino Martinez	.15	.07	.02
☐	284	Mike Blowers	.05	.02	.01
☐	285	Goose Gossage	.15	.07	.02
☐	286	Luis Sojo	.05	.02	.01
☐	287	Edgar Martinez	.15	.07	.02
☐	288	Rich Amaral	.05	.02	.01
☐	289	Felix Fermin	.05	.02	.01
☐	290	Jay Buhner	.15	.07	.02
☐	291	Dan Wilson	.10	.05	.01
☐	292	Bobby Ayala	.05	.02	.01
☐	293	Dave Fleming	.05	.02	.01
☐	294	Greg Pirkl	.05	.02	.01
☐	295	Reggie Jefferson	.05	.02	.01
☐	296	Greg Hibbard	.05	.02	.01
☐	297	Yorkis Perez	.05	.02	.01
☐	298	Kurt Miller	.05	.02	.01
☐	299	Chuck Carr	.05	.02	.01
☐	300	Gary Sheffield	.15	.07	.02
☐	301	Jerry Browne	.05	.02	.01
☐	302	Dave Magadan	.05	.02	.01
☐	303	Kurt Abbott	.05	.02	.01
☐	304	Pat Rapp	.10	.05	.01
☐	305	Jeff Conine	.15	.07	.02
☐	306	Benito Santiago	.05	.02	.01
☐	307	Dave Weathers	.05	.02	.01
☐	308	Robb Nen	.10	.05	.01
☐	309	Chris Hammond	.05	.02	.01
☐	310	Bryan Harvey	.10	.05	.01
☐	311	Charlie Hough	.10	.05	.01
☐	312	Greg Colbrunn	.15	.07	.02
☐	313	David Segui	.05	.02	.01
☐	314	Rico Brogna	.10	.05	.01
☐	315	Jeff Kent	.10	.05	.01
☐	316	Jose Vizcaino	.05	.02	.01
☐	317	Jim Lindeman	.05	.02	.01
☐	318	Carl Everett	.10	.05	.01
☐	319	Ryan Thompson	.05	.02	.01
☐	320	Bobby Bonilla	.15	.07	.02
☐	321	Joe Orsulak	.05	.02	.01
☐	322	Pete Harnisch	.05	.02	.01
☐	323	Doug Linton	.05	.02	.01
☐	324	Todd Hundley	.10	.05	.01
☐	325	Bret Saberhagen	.10	.05	.01
☐	326	Kelly Stinnett	.05	.02	.01
☐	327	Jason Jacome	.05	.02	.01
☐	328	Bobby Jones	.10	.05	.01
☐	329	John Franco	.10	.05	.01
☐	330	Rafael Palmeiro	.15	.07	.02
☐	331	Chris Hoiles	.10	.05	.01
☐	332	Leo Gomez	.05	.02	.01
☐	333	Chris Sabo	.05	.02	.01
☐	334	Brady Anderson	.10	.05	.01
☐	335	Jeffrey Hammonds	.10	.05	.01
☐	336	Dwight Smith	.05	.02	.01
☐	337	Jack Voigt	.05	.02	.01
☐	338	Harold Baines	.10	.05	.01
☐	339	Ben McDonald	.10	.05	.01
☐	340	Mike Mussina	.25	.11	.03
☐	341	Bret Barberie	.05	.02	.01
☐	342	Jamie Moyer	.05	.02	.01
☐	343	Mike Oquist	.05	.02	.01
☐	344	Sid Fernandez	.05	.02	.01
☐	345	Eddie Williams	.05	.02	.01
☐	346	Joey Hamilton	.10	.05	.01
☐	347	Brian Williams	.05	.02	.01
☐	348	Luis Lopez	.05	.02	.01
☐	349	Steve Finley	.10	.05	.01
☐	350	Andy Benes	.10	.05	.01
☐	351	Andujar Cedeno	.05	.02	.01
☐	352	Bip Roberts	.05	.02	.01
☐	353	Ray McDavid	.10	.05	.01
☐	354	Ken Caminiti	.05	.02	.01
☐	355	Trevor Hoffman	.10	.05	.01
☐	356	Mel Nieves	.10	.05	.01
☐	357	Brad Ausmus	.05	.02	.01
☐	358	Andy Ashby	.05	.02	.01
☐	359	Scott Sanders	.05	.02	.01
☐	360	Gregg Jefferies	.15	.07	.02
☐	361	Mariano Duncan	.05	.02	.01
☐	362	Dave Hollins	.05	.02	.01
☐	363	Kevin Stocker	.05	.02	.01
☐	364	Fernando Valenzuela	.10	.05	.01
☐	365	Lenny Dykstra	.10	.05	.01
☐	366	Jim Eisenreich	.05	.02	.01
☐	367	Ricky Bottalico	.05	.02	.01
☐	368	Doug Jones	.05	.02	.01
☐	369	Ricky Jordan	.05	.02	.01
☐	370	Darren Daulton	.10	.05	.01
☐	371	Mike Lieberthal	.05	.02	.01
☐	372	Bobby Munoz	.05	.02	.01
☐	373	John Kruk	.10	.05	.01
☐	374	Curt Schilling	.05	.02	.01
☐	375	Orlando Merced	.10	.05	.01
☐	376	Carlos Garcia	.10	.05	.01
☐	377	Lance Parrish	.10	.05	.01
☐	378	Steve Cooke	.05	.02	.01
☐	379	Jeff King	.05	.02	.01
☐	380	Jay Bell	.10	.05	.01
☐	381	Al Martin	.10	.05	.01
☐	382	Paul Wagner	.05	.02	.01
☐	383	Rick White	.05	.02	.01
☐	384	Midre Cummings	.10	.05	.01
☐	385	Jon Lieber	.05	.02	.01
☐	386	Dave Clark	.05	.02	.01
☐	387	Don Slaught	.05	.02	.01
☐	388	Denny Neagle	.05	.02	.01

☐	389	Zane Smith	.05	.02	.01	☐	460	Brian McRae	.10	.05	.01
☐	390	Andy Van Slyke	.10	.05	.01	☐	461	Tom Gordon	.05	.02	.01
☐	391	Ivan Rodriguez	.15	.07	.02	☐	462	Kevin Appier	.10	.05	.01
☐	392	David Hulse	.05	.02	.01	☐	463	Billy Brewer	.05	.02	.01
☐	393	John Burkett	.05	.02	.01	☐	464	Mark Gubicza	.05	.02	.01
☐	394	Kevin Brown	.05	.02	.01	☐	465	Travis Fryman	.15	.07	.02
☐	395	Dean Palmer	.10	.05	.01	☐	466	Danny Bautista	.10	.05	.01
☐	396	Otis Nixon	.05	.02	.01	☐	467	Sean Bergman	.05	.02	.01
☐	397	Rick Helling	.05	.02	.01	☐	468	Mike Henneman	.05	.02	.01
☐	398	Kenny Rogers	.05	.02	.01	☐	469	Mike Moore	.05	.02	.01
☐	399	Darren Oliver	.05	.02	.01	☐	470	Cecil Fielder	.15	.07	.02
☐	400	Will Clark	.25	.11	.03	☐	471	Alan Trammell	.15	.07	.02
☐	401	Jeff Frye	.05	.02	.01	☐	472	Kirk Gibson	.10	.05	.01
☐	402	Kevin Gross	.05	.02	.01	☐	473	Tony Phillips	.05	.02	.01
☐	403	John Dettmer	.05	.02	.01	☐	474	Mickey Tettleton	.10	.05	.01
☐	404	Manny Lee	.05	.02	.01	☐	475	Lou Whitaker	.15	.07	.02
☐	405	Rusty Greer	.05	.02	.01	☐	476	Chris Gomez	.05	.02	.01
☐	406	Aaron Sele	.10	.05	.01	☐	477	John Doherty	.05	.02	.01
☐	407	Carlos Rodriguez	.05	.02	.01	☐	478	Greg Gohr	.05	.02	.01
☐	408	Scott Cooper	.05	.02	.01	☐	479	Bill Gullickson	.05	.02	.01
☐	409	John Valentin	.15	.07	.02	☐	480	Rick Aguilera	.10	.05	.01
☐	410	Roger Clemens	.30	.14	.04	☐	481	Matt Walbeck	.05	.02	.01
☐	411	Mike Greenwell	.10	.05	.01	☐	482	Kevin Tapani	.05	.02	.01
☐	412	Tim Vanegmond	.05	.02	.01	☐	483	Scott Erickson	.10	.05	.01
☐	413	Tom Brunansky	.05	.02	.01	☐	484	Steve Dunn	.05	.02	.01
☐	414	Steve Farr	.05	.02	.01	☐	485	David McCarty	.05	.02	.01
☐	415	Jose Canseco	.30	.14	.04	☐	486	Scott Leius	.05	.02	.01
☐	416	Joe Hesketh	.05	.02	.01	☐	487	Pat Meares	.05	.02	.01
☐	417	Ken Ryan	.05	.02	.01	☐	488	Jeff Reboulet	.05	.02	.01
☐	418	Tim Naehring	.10	.05	.01	☐	489	Pedro Munoz	.10	.05	.01
☐	419	Frank Viola	.05	.02	.01	☐	490	Chuck Knoblauch	.15	.07	.02
☐	420	Andre Dawson	.15	.07	.02	☐	491	Rich Becker	.10	.05	.01
☐	421	Mo Vaughn	.30	.14	.04	☐	492	Alex Cole	.05	.02	.01
☐	422	Jeff Brantley	.05	.02	.01	☐	493	Pat Mahomes	.05	.02	.01
☐	423	Pete Schourek	.15	.07	.02	☐	494	Ozzie Guillen	.05	.02	.01
☐	424	Hal Morris	.10	.05	.01	☐	495	Tim Raines	.15	.07	.02
☐	425	Deion Sanders	.40	.18	.05	☐	496	Kirk McCaskill	.05	.02	.01
☐	426	Brian R. Hunter	.05	.02	.01	☐	497	Olmedo Saenz	.05	.02	.01
☐	427	Bret Boone	.15	.07	.02	☐	498	Scott Sanderson	.05	.02	.01
☐	428	Willie Greene	.10	.05	.01	☐	499	Lance Johnson	.05	.02	.01
☐	429	Ron Gant	.15	.07	.02	☐	500	Michael Jordan	2.50	1.10	.30
☐	430	Barry Larkin	.25	.11	.03	☐	501	Warren Newson	.05	.02	.01
☐	431	Reggie Sanders	.15	.07	.02	☐	502	Ron Karkovice	.05	.02	.01
☐	432	Eddie Taubensee	.05	.02	.01	☐	503	Wilson Alvarez	.10	.05	.01
☐	433	Jack Morris	.15	.07	.02	☐	504	Jason Bere	.10	.05	.01
☐	434	Jose Rijo	.10	.05	.01	☐	505	Robin Ventura	.15	.07	.02
☐	435	Johnny Ruffin	.05	.02	.01	☐	506	Alex Fernandez	.10	.05	.01
☐	436	John Smiley	.05	.02	.01	☐	507	Roberto Hernandez	.10	.05	.01
☐	437	John Roper	.05	.02	.01	☐	508	Norberto Martin	.05	.02	.01
☐	438	Dave Nied	.05	.02	.01	☐	509	Bob Wickman	.05	.02	.01
☐	439	Roberto Mejia	.05	.02	.01	☐	510	Don Mattingly	1.00	.45	.12
☐	440	Andres Galarraga	.15	.07	.02	☐	511	Melido Perez	.05	.02	.01
☐	441	Mike Kingery	.05	.02	.01	☐	512	Pat Kelly	.05	.02	.01
☐	442	Curt Leskanic	.10	.05	.01	☐	513	Randy Velarde	.05	.02	.01
☐	443	Walt Weiss	.10	.05	.01	☐	514	Tony Fernandez	.05	.02	.01
☐	444	Marvin Freeman	.05	.02	.01	☐	515	Jack McDowell	.15	.07	.02
☐	445	Charlie Hayes	.10	.05	.01	☐	516	Luis Polonia	.05	.02	.01
☐	446	Eric Young	.10	.05	.01	☐	517	Bernie Williams	.10	.05	.01
☐	447	Ellis Burks	.10	.05	.01	☐	518	Danny Tartabull	.10	.05	.01
☐	448	Joe Girardi	.05	.02	.01	☐	519	Mike Stanley	.10	.05	.01
☐	449	Lance Painter	.05	.02	.01	☐	520	Wade Boggs	.15	.07	.02
☐	450	Dante Bichette	.25	.11	.03	☐	521	Jim Leyritz	.05	.02	.01
☐	451	Bruce Ruffin	.05	.02	.01	☐	522	Steve Howe	.05	.02	.01
☐	452	Jeff Granger	.05	.02	.01	☐	523	Scott Kamieniecki	.05	.02	.01
☐	453	Wally Joyner	.10	.05	.01	☐	524	Russ Davis	.10	.05	.01
☐	454	Jose Lind	.05	.02	.01	☐	525	Jim Abbott	.15	.07	.02
☐	455	Jeff Montgomery	.10	.05	.01	☐	526	Eddie Murray CL	.10	.05	.01
☐	456	Gary Gaetti	.10	.05	.01	☐	527	Alex Rodriguez CL	.10	.05	.01
☐	457	Greg Gagne	.05	.02	.01	☐	528	Jeff Bagwell CL	.30	.14	.04
☐	458	Vince Coleman	.05	.02	.01	☐	529	Joe Carter CL	.10	.05	.01
☐	459	Mike Macfarlane	.05	.02	.01	☐	530	Fred McGriff CL	.10	.05	.01

1995 Collector's Choice Gold Signature

This set is a parallel of the 530 regular cards from the Collector's Choice set and inserted one per 35 packs, 12 per gold super pack and 15 per factory set. The only difference between the sets is that this one has a gold signature at the bottom.

	MINT	NRMT	EXC
COMPLETE SET (530)	1200.00	550.00	150.00
COMMON CARD (1-530)	1.00	.45	.12
*VETERAN STARS: 25X to 40X BASIC CARDS			
*YOUNG STARS: 18X to 30X BASIC CARDS			

		MINT	NRMT	EXC
☐ 28	Ruben Rivera	20.00	9.00	2.50
☐ 46	Nolan Ryan	40.00	18.00	5.00
☐ 49	George Brett	20.00	9.00	2.50
☐ 52	Nolan Ryan B90	20.00	9.00	2.50
☐ 62	Ken Griffey Jr. B90	25.00	11.00	3.10
☐ 63	Greg Maddux B90	25.00	11.00	3.10
☐ 64	Frank Thomas B90	25.00	11.00	3.10
☐ 67	Greg Maddux	50.00	22.00	6.25
☐ 70	Ken Griffey Jr.	50.00	22.00	6.25
☐ 73	Tony Gwynn	15.00	6.75	1.85
☐ 75	Frank Thomas	50.00	22.00	6.25
☐ 76	Jeff Bagwell	15.00	6.75	1.85
☐ 77	Kirby Puckett	15.00	6.75	1.85
☐ 80	Mike Piazza	20.00	9.00	2.50
☐ 81	Kenny Lofton	15.00	6.75	1.85
☐ 83	Albert Belle	20.00	9.00	2.50
☐ 85	Cal Ripken	50.00	22.00	6.25
☐ 88	Ken Griffey Jr. WC	25.00	11.00	3.10
☐ 89	Frank Thomas WC	25.00	11.00	3.10
☐ 154	Chipper Jones	20.00	9.00	2.50
☐ 275	Manny Ramirez	20.00	9.00	2.50
☐ 500	Michael Jordan	60.00	27.00	7.50
☐ 510	Don Mattingly	25.00	11.00	3.10

1995 Collector's Choice SE

The 1995 Collector's Choice SE set consists of 265 standard-size cards. One in

every 216 packs was a Silver Super Pack, containing 12 silver signature cards. One in every 720 packs was a Gold Super Pack, containing 12 gold signature cards. The fronts feature color action player photos with blue borders. The player's name, position and the team name are printed on the bottom of the photo. The SE logo in blue-foil appears in a top corner. On a white background, the backs carry another color player photo with a short player biography, career stats and 1994 highlights. Subsets featured include Rookie Class (1-25), Record Pace (26-30), Stat Leaders (137-144), Fantasy Team (249-260).

	MINT	NRMT	EXC
COMPLETE SET (265)	20.00	9.00	2.50
COMMON CARD (1-265)	.10	.05	.01
COMP. SILV. SIG. SET (265) .	60.00	27.00	7.50
SILV. SIG. COMMON (1-265) ..	.20	.09	.03
SILV. SIG. SEMISTARS	.30	.14	.04
*SILV. SIG. VETERAN STARS: 2X TO 4X BASIC CARDS			
*SILV. SIG. YOUNG STARS: 1.5X TO 3X BASIC CARDS			

		MINT	NRMT	EXC
☐ 1	Alex Rodriguez................	.60	.25	.07
☐ 2	Derek Jeter...................	.50	.23	.06
☐ 3	Dustin Hermanson	.10	.05	.01
☐ 4	Bill Pulsipher.................	.30	.14	.04
☐ 5	Terrell Wade	.10	.05	.01
☐ 6	Darren Dreifort................	.10	.05	.01
☐ 7	LaTroy Hawkins	.10	.05	.01
☐ 8	Alex Ochoa	.30	.14	.04
☐ 9	Paul Wilson	.60	.25	.07
☐ 10	Rod Henderson..............	.10	.05	.01
☐ 11	Alan Benes	.30	.14	.04
☐ 12	Garret Anderson.............	.60	.25	.07
☐ 13	Armando Benitez.............	.10	.05	.01
☐ 14	Mark Thompson	.10	.05	.01
☐ 15	Andrew Lorraine	.20	.09	.03
☐ 16	Jose Silva	.10	.05	.01
☐ 17	Orlando Miller	.20	.09	.03
☐ 18	Russ Davis	.20	.09	.03
☐ 19	Jason Isringhausen.....	1.50	.70	.19
☐ 20	Ray McDavid.................	.20	.09	.03
☐ 21	Tim VanEgmond..............	.10	.05	.01
☐ 22	Paul Shuey..................	.10	.05	.01
☐ 23	Steve Dunn	.10	.05	.01
☐ 24	Mike Lieberthal.............	.10	.05	.01
☐ 25	Chan Ho Park...............	.20	.09	.03
☐ 26	Ken Griffey Jr. RP........	1.50	.70	.19
☐ 27	Tony Gwynn RP	.50	.23	.06
☐ 28	Chuck Knoblauch RP	.30	.14	.04
☐ 29	Frank Thomas RP	1.50	.70	.19
☐ 30	Matt Williams RP	.30	.14	.04
☐ 31	Chili Davis	.20	.09	.03
☐ 32	Chad Curtis	.20	.09	.03
☐ 33	Brian Anderson	.10	.05	.01
☐ 34	Chuck Finley	.20	.09	.03
☐ 35	Tim Salmon	.50	.23	.06
☐ 36	Bo Jackson	.30	.14	.04
☐ 37	Doug Drabek	.20	.09	.03
☐ 38	Craig Biggio.................	.30	.14	.04
☐ 39	Ken Caminiti	.20	.09	.03
☐ 40	Jeff Bagwell	1.00	.45	.12
☐ 41	Darryl Kile	.10	.05	.01
☐ 42	John Hudek.................	.10	.05	.01
☐ 43	Brian L. Hunter	.40	.18	.05
☐ 44	Dennis Eckersley...........	.30	.14	.04
☐ 45	Mark McGwire	.30	.14	.04
☐ 46	Brent Gates	.20	.09	.03

☐ 47	Steve Karsay	.10	.05	.01
☐ 48	Rickey Henderson	.30	.14	.04
☐ 49	Terry Steinbach	.20	.09	.03
☐ 50	Ruben Sierra	.30	.14	.04
☐ 51	Roberto Alomar	.60	.25	.07
☐ 52	Carlos Delgado	.20	.09	.03
☐ 53	Alex Gonzalez	.20	.09	.03
☐ 54	Joe Carter	.30	.14	.04
☐ 55	Paul Molitor	.30	.14	.04
☐ 56	Juan Guzman	.20	.09	.03
☐ 57	John Olerud	.20	.09	.03
☐ 58	Shawn Green	.30	.14	.04
☐ 59	Tom Glavine	.30	.14	.04
☐ 60	Greg Maddux	3.00	1.35	.35
☐ 61	Roberto Kelly	.20	.09	.03
☐ 62	Ryan Klesko	.60	.25	.07
☐ 63	Javier Lopez	.40	.18	.05
☐ 64	Jose Oliva	.10	.05	.01
☐ 65	Fred McGriff	.40	.18	.05
☐ 66	Steve Avery	.30	.14	.04
☐ 67	David Justice	.40	.18	.05
☐ 68	Ricky Bones	.10	.05	.01
☐ 69	Cal Eldred	.10	.05	.01
☐ 70	Greg Vaughn	.10	.05	.01
☐ 71	Dave Nilsson	.20	.09	.03
☐ 72	Jose Valentin	.10	.05	.01
☐ 73	Matt Mieske	.10	.05	.01
☐ 74	Todd Zeile	.20	.09	.03
☐ 75	Ozzie Smith	.60	.25	.07
☐ 76	Bernard Gilkey	.20	.09	.03
☐ 77	Ray Lankford	.30	.14	.04
☐ 78	Bob Tewksbury	.10	.05	.01
☐ 79	Mark Whiten	.20	.09	.03
☐ 80	Gregg Jefferies	.30	.14	.04
☐ 81	Randy Myers	.20	.09	.03
☐ 82	Shawon Dunston	.10	.05	.01
☐ 83	Mark Grace	.30	.14	.04
☐ 84	Derrick May	.20	.09	.03
☐ 85	Sammy Sosa	.30	.14	.04
☐ 86	Steve Trachsel	.10	.05	.01
☐ 87	Brett Butler	.20	.09	.03
☐ 88	Delino DeShields	.20	.09	.03
☐ 89	Orel Hershiser	.20	.09	.03
☐ 90	Mike Piazza	1.25	.55	.16
☐ 91	Todd Hollandsworth	.20	.09	.03
☐ 92	Eric Karros	.30	.14	.04
☐ 93	Ramon Martinez	.20	.09	.03
☐ 94	Tim Wallach	.10	.05	.01
☐ 95	Raul Mondesi	.75	.35	.09
☐ 96	Larry Walker	.40	.18	.05
☐ 97	Wil Cordero	.20	.09	.03
☐ 98	Marquis Grissom	.30	.14	.04
☐ 99	Ken Hill	.20	.09	.03
☐ 100	Cliff Floyd	.20	.09	.03
☐ 101	Pedro J. Martinez	.30	.14	.04
☐ 102	John Wetteland	.20	.09	.03
☐ 103	Rondell White	.30	.14	.04
☐ 104	Moises Alou	.20	.09	.03
☐ 105	Barry Bonds	.75	.35	.09
☐ 106	Darren Lewis	.10	.05	.01
☐ 107	Mark Portugal	.10	.05	.01
☐ 108	Matt Williams	.50	.23	.06
☐ 109	William VanLandingham	.20	.09	.03
☐ 110	Bill Swift	.10	.05	.01
☐ 111	Robby Thompson	.10	.05	.01
☐ 112	Rod Beck	.20	.09	.03
☐ 113	Darryl Strawberry	.20	.09	.03
☐ 114	Jim Thome	.50	.23	.06
☐ 115	Dave Winfield	.30	.14	.04
☐ 116	Eddie Murray	.40	.18	.05
☐ 117	Manny Ramirez	1.25	.55	.16
☐ 118	Carlos Baerga	.60	.25	.07
☐ 119	Kenny Lofton	1.00	.45	.12
☐ 120	Albert Belle	1.25	.55	.16
☐ 121	Mark Clark	.10	.05	.01
☐ 122	Dennis Martinez	.20	.09	.03
☐ 123	Randy Johnson	.60	.25	.07
☐ 124	Jay Buhner	.30	.14	.04
☐ 125	Ken Griffey Jr.	3.00	1.35	.35
☐ 126	Goose Gossage	.30	.14	.04
☐ 127	Tino Martinez	.30	.14	.04
☐ 128	Reggie Jefferson	.10	.05	.01
☐ 129	Edgar Martinez	.30	.14	.04
☐ 130	Gary Sheffield	.30	.14	.04
☐ 131	Pat Rapp	.20	.09	.03
☐ 132	Bret Barberie	.10	.05	.01
☐ 133	Chuck Carr	.10	.05	.01
☐ 134	Jeff Conine	.30	.14	.04
☐ 135	Charles Johnson	.30	.14	.04
☐ 136	Benito Santiago	.10	.05	.01
☐ 137	Matt Williams STL	.30	.14	.04
☐ 138	Jeff Bagwell STL	.50	.23	.06
☐ 139	Kenny Lofton STL	.50	.23	.06
☐ 140	Tony Gwynn STL	.50	.23	.06
☐ 141	Jimmy Key STL	.10	.05	.01
☐ 142	Greg Maddux STL	1.50	.70	.19
☐ 143	Randy Johnson STL	.30	.14	.04
☐ 144	Lee Smith STL	.20	.09	.03
☐ 145	Bobby Bonilla	.30	.14	.04
☐ 146	Jason Jacome	.10	.05	.01
☐ 147	Jeff Kent	.20	.09	.03
☐ 148	Ryan Thompson	.20	.09	.03
☐ 149	Bobby Jones	.20	.09	.03
☐ 150	Bret Saberhagen	.20	.09	.03
☐ 151	John Franco	.20	.09	.03
☐ 152	Lee Smith	.30	.14	.04
☐ 153	Rafael Palmeiro	.30	.14	.04
☐ 154	Brady Anderson	.20	.09	.03
☐ 155	Cal Ripken Jr.	3.00	1.35	.35
☐ 156	Jeffrey Hammonds	.20	.09	.03
☐ 157	Mike Mussina	.40	.18	.05
☐ 158	Chris Hoiles	.20	.09	.03
☐ 159	Ben McDonald	.10	.05	.01
☐ 160	Tony Gwynn	1.00	.45	.12
☐ 161	Joey Hamilton	.30	.14	.04
☐ 162	Andy Benes	.20	.09	.03
☐ 163	Trevor Hoffman	.20	.09	.03
☐ 164	Phil Plantier	.10	.05	.01
☐ 165	Derek Bell	.30	.14	.04
☐ 166	Bip Roberts	.10	.05	.01
☐ 167	Eddie Williams	.10	.05	.01
☐ 168	Fernando Valenzuela	.20	.09	.03
☐ 169	Mariano Duncan	.10	.05	.01
☐ 170	Lenny Dykstra	.30	.14	.04
☐ 171	Darren Daulton	.30	.14	.04
☐ 172	Danny Jackson	.10	.05	.01
☐ 173	Bobby Munoz	.10	.05	.01
☐ 174	Doug Jones	.10	.05	.01
☐ 175	Jay Bell	.20	.09	.03
☐ 176	Zane Smith	.10	.05	.01
☐ 177	Jon Lieber	.10	.05	.01
☐ 178	Carlos Garcia	.20	.09	.03
☐ 179	Orlando Merced	.20	.09	.03
☐ 180	Andy Van Slyke	.20	.09	.03
☐ 181	Rick Helling	.10	.05	.01
☐ 182	Rusty Greer	.20	.09	.03
☐ 183	Kenny Rogers	.10	.05	.01
☐ 184	Will Clark	.40	.18	.05
☐ 185	Jose Canseco	.50	.23	.06
☐ 186	Juan Gonzalez	.75	.35	.09
☐ 187	Dean Palmer	.20	.09	.03
☐ 188	Ivan Rodriguez	.30	.14	.04

☐	189	John Valentin	.30	.14	.04
☐	190	Roger Clemens	.50	.23	.06
☐	191	Aaron Sele	.20	.09	.03
☐	192	Scott Cooper	.10	.05	.01
☐	193	Mike Greenwell	.20	.09	.03
☐	194	Mo Vaughn	.50	.23	.06
☐	195	Andre Dawson	.30	.14	.04
☐	196	Ron Gant	.30	.14	.04
☐	197	Jose Rijo	.20	.09	.03
☐	198	Bret Boone	.30	.14	.04
☐	199	Deion Sanders	.60	.25	.07
☐	200	Barry Larkin	.40	.18	.05
☐	201	Hal Morris	.20	.09	.03
☐	202	Reggie Sanders	.30	.14	.04
☐	203	Kevin Mitchell	.20	.09	.03
☐	204	Marvin Freeman	.10	.05	.01
☐	205	Andres Galarraga	.30	.14	.04
☐	206	Walt Weiss	.20	.09	.03
☐	207	Charlie Hayes	.20	.09	.03
☐	208	Dave Nied	.20	.09	.03
☐	209	Dante Bichette	.40	.18	.05
☐	210	David Cone	.30	.14	.04
☐	211	Jeff Montgomery	.20	.09	.03
☐	212	Felix Jose	.10	.05	.01
☐	213	Mike Macfarlane	.10	.05	.01
☐	214	Wally Joyner	.20	.09	.03
☐	215	Bob Hamelin	.10	.05	.01
☐	216	Brian McRae	.20	.09	.03
☐	217	Kirk Gibson	.20	.09	.03
☐	218	Lou Whitaker	.30	.14	.04
☐	219	Chris Gomez	.20	.09	.03
☐	220	Cecil Fielder	.30	.14	.04
☐	221	Mickey Tettleton	.20	.09	.03
☐	222	Travis Fryman	.30	.14	.04
☐	223	Tony Phillips	.10	.05	.01
☐	224	Rick Aguilera	.20	.09	.03
☐	225	Scott Erickson	.20	.09	.03
☐	226	Chuck Knoblauch	.30	.14	.04
☐	227	Kent Hrbek	.20	.09	.03
☐	228	Shane Mack	.10	.05	.01
☐	229	Kevin Tapani	.10	.05	.01
☐	230	Kirby Puckett	1.00	.45	.12
☐	231	Julio Franco	.20	.09	.03
☐	232	Jack McDowell	.30	.14	.04
☐	233	Jason Bere	.20	.09	.03
☐	234	Alex Fernandez	.30	.14	.04
☐	235	Frank Thomas	3.00	1.35	.35
☐	236	Ozzie Guillen	.10	.05	.01
☐	237	Robin Ventura	.20	.09	.03
☐	238	Michael Jordan	4.00	1.80	.50
☐	239	Wilson Alvarez	.20	.09	.03
☐	240	Don Mattingly	1.50	.70	.19
☐	241	Jim Abbott	.30	.14	.04
☐	242	Jim Leyritz	.10	.05	.01
☐	243	Paul O'Neill	.20	.09	.03
☐	244	Melido Perez	.10	.05	.01
☐	245	Wade Boggs	.30	.14	.04
☐	246	Mike Stanley	.20	.09	.03
☐	247	Danny Tartabull	.20	.09	.03
☐	248	Jimmy Key	.20	.09	.03
☐	249	Greg Maddux FT	1.50	.70	.19
☐	250	Randy Johnson FT	.30	.14	.04
☐	251	Bret Saberhagen FT	.10	.05	.01
☐	252	John Wetteland FT	.10	.05	.01
☐	253	Mike Piazza FT	.60	.25	.07
☐	254	Jeff Bagwell FT	.50	.23	.06
☐	255	Craig Biggio FT	.20	.09	.03
☐	256	Matt Williams FT	.30	.14	.04
☐	257	Wil Cordero FT	.10	.05	.01
☐	258	Kenny Lofton FT	.50	.23	.06
☐	259	Barry Bonds FT	.40	.18	.05

☐	260	Dante Bichette FT	.30	.14	.04
☐	261	Ken Griffey Jr. CL	1.00	.45	.12
☐	262	Goose Gossage CL	.10	.05	.01
☐	263	Cal Ripken CL	1.25	.55	.16
☐	264	Kenny Rogers CL	.10	.05	.01
☐	265	John Valentin CL	.20	.09	.03

1995 Collector's Choice SE Gold Signature

A parallel to the basic 265-card Collector's Choice set, each card features a gold-foil replica signature on it. Inserted one in 35 packs, the fronts feature color action player photos with blue borders. The player's name, position and the team name are printed on the bottom of the photo. The SE logo in blue-foil appears in a top corner. On a white background, the backs carry another color player photo with a short player biography, career stats and 1994 highlights. Following subsets are included in this set: Rookie Class (1-25), Record Pace (26-30), Stat Leaders (137-144), Fantasy Team (249-260), and Checklists (261-265).

	MINT	NRMT	EXC
COMPLETE SET (265)	1800.00	800.00	220.00
COMMON CARD (1-265)	3.00	1.35	.35
*VETERAN STARS: 25X to 40X BASIC CARDS			
*YOUNG STARS: 18X to 30X BASIC CARDS			

☐	26	Ken Griffey Jr.	60.00	27.00	7.50
☐	29	Frank Thomas	60.00	27.00	7.50
☐	40	Jeff Bagwell	40.00	18.00	5.00
☐	60	Greg Maddux	125.00	55.00	15.50
☐	90	Mike Piazza	50.00	22.00	6.25
☐	117	Manny Ramirez	50.00	22.00	6.25
☐	119	Kenny Lofton	40.00	18.00	5.00
☐	120	Albert Belle	50.00	22.00	6.25
☐	125	Ken Griffey Jr	125.00	55.00	15.50
☐	142	Greg Maddux STL	60.00	27.00	7.50
☐	155	Cal Ripken Jr.	150.00	70.00	19.00
☐	160	Tony Gwynn	40.00	18.00	5.00
☐	230	Kirby Puckett	40.00	18.00	5.00
☐	235	Frank Thomas	125.00	55.00	15.50
☐	238	Michael Jordan	150.00	70.00	19.00
☐	240	Don Mattingly	60.00	27.00	7.50
☐	249	Greg Maddux FT	60.00	27.00	7.50
☐	261	Ken Griffey Jr. CL	40.00	18.00	5.00
☐	263	Cal Ripken CL	50.00	22.00	6.25

1996 Collector's Choice

This 365-card set was issued in 12-card packs with 36 packs per box and 20 boxes per case. Suggested retail price on these

packs was $0.99 cents. Trade cards for card sets from the Divisional Playoffs, League Championship Series and the World Series respectively were inserted one every 11 packs. These cards have an ordering deadline of May 13. The fronts of the regular set feature a player photo, his name and team logo. Super packs were made again in 1996. The backs feature another photo, vital stats and a baseball quiz. The set is broken down thusly: 1995 Stat Leaders (2-9), Rookie Class (10-39), Atlanta Braves (40-49), Baltimore Orioles (50-58), Boston Red Sox (59-68), California Angels (69-78), Chicago Cubs (79-88), Chicago White Sox (89-98), Cincinnati Reds (99, 109-117), Traditional Threads (100-108), Cleveland Indians (118-127), Colorado Rockies (128-137), Detroit Tigers (138-147), Florida Marlins (148-157), Houston Astros (158-167), Kansas City Royals (168-177), Los Angeles Dodgers (178-187), Milwaukee Brewers (188-197), Minnesota Twins (198-207), Montreal Expos (208-217), New York Mets (218-227), New York Yankees (228-237), Oakland A's (238-247), Philadelphia Phillies (248-257), Pittsburgh Pirates (258-267), Fantasy Team (268-279), St. Louis Cardinals (280-289), San Diego Padres (290-299), San Francisco Giants (300-309), Seattle Mariners (310-319), Texas Rangers (320-324, 343-347), International Flavor (325-342), Toronto Blue Jays (348-357), and Checklists (358-365). Rookie Cards in this set include Juan Castro.

	MINT	NRMT	EXC
COMPLETE SERIES 1 (365)	15.00	6.75	1.85
COMMON CARD (1-365)	.05	.02	.01
COMP.POST.TRADE SET (3)	2.00	.90	.25
COMP. SILV. SIG. SERIES 1 (365)	60.00	27.00	7.50
SILVER SIG. COMMON (1-365)	.10	.05	.01
SILV. SIG. SEMISTARS	.20	.09	.03

*SILV. SIG. VETERAN STARS: 2X TO 4X BASIC CARDS
*SILV. SIG. YOUNG STARS: 1.5X TO 3X BASIC CARDS

☐	1	Cal Ripken	2.00	.90	.25
☐	2	Edgar Martinez SL	.30	.14	.04
		Tony Gwynn			
☐	3	Albert Belle SL	.40	.18	.05
		Dante Bichette			
☐	4	Albert Belle SL	.40	.18	.05
		Mo Vaughn			
		Dante Bichette			
☐	5	Kenny Lofton SL	.30	.14	.04
		Quilvio Veras			
☐	6	Mike Mussina SL	.75	.35	.09
		Greg Maddux			
☐	7	Randy Johnson SL	.40	.18	.05
		Hideo Nomo			
☐	8	Randy Johnson SL	.75	.35	.09
		Greg Maddux			
☐	9	Jose Mesa SL	.05	.02	.01
		Randy Myers			
☐	10	Johnny Damon	.30	.14	.04
☐	11	Rick Krivda	.05	.02	.01
☐	12	Roger Cedeno	.15	.07	.02
☐	13	Angel Martinez	.10	.05	.01
☐	14	Ariel Prieto	.10	.05	.01
☐	15	John Wasdin	.10	.05	.01
☐	16	Edwin Hurtado	.05	.02	.01
☐	17	Lyle Mouton	.10	.05	.01
☐	18	Chris Snopek	.05	.02	.01
☐	19	Mariano Rivera	.10	.05	.01
☐	20	Ruben Rivera	.30	.14	.04
☐	21	Juan Castro	.25	.11	.03
☐	22	Jimmy Haynes	.15	.07	.02
☐	23	Bob Wolcott	.15	.07	.02
☐	24	Brian Barber	.10	.05	.01
☐	25	Frank Rodriguez	.10	.05	.01
☐	26	Jesus Tavarez	.10	.05	.01
☐	27	Glenn Dishman	.05	.02	.01
☐	28	Jose Herrera	.10	.05	.01
☐	29	Chan Ho Park	.15	.07	.02
☐	30	Jason Isringhausen	.25	.11	.03
☐	31	Doug Johns	.05	.02	.01
☐	32	Gene Schall	.05	.02	.01
☐	33	Kevin Jordan	.05	.02	.01
☐	34	Matt Lawton	.10	.05	.01
☐	35	Karim Garcia	.30	.14	.04
☐	36	George Williams	.05	.02	.01
☐	37	Orlando Palmeiro	.05	.02	.01
☐	38	Jamie Brewington	.10	.05	.01
☐	39	Robert Person	.05	.02	.01
☐	40	Greg Maddux	2.00	.90	.25
☐	41	Marquis Grissom	.15	.07	.02
☐	42	Chipper Jones	.75	.35	.09
☐	43	David Justice	.25	.11	.03
☐	44	Mark Lemke	.10	.05	.01
☐	45	Fred McGriff	.25	.11	.03
☐	46	Javier Lopez	.15	.07	.02
☐	47	Mark Wohlers	.10	.05	.01
☐	48	Jason Schmidt	.15	.07	.02
☐	49	John Smoltz	.10	.05	.01
☐	50	Curtis Goodwin	.05	.02	.01
☐	51	Greg Zaun	.05	.02	.01
☐	52	Armando Benitez	.05	.02	.01
☐	53	Manny Alexander	.05	.02	.01
☐	54	Chris Hoiles	.10	.05	.01
☐	55	Harold Baines	.10	.05	.01
☐	56	Ben McDonald	.05	.02	.01
☐	57	Scott Erickson	.10	.05	.01
☐	58	Jeff Manto	.05	.02	.01
☐	59	Luis Alicea	.05	.02	.01
☐	60	Roger Clemens	.30	.14	.04
☐	61	Rheal Cormier	.05	.02	.01
☐	62	Vaughn Eshelman	.05	.02	.01
☐	63	Zane Smith	.05	.02	.01
☐	64	Mike Macfarlane	.05	.02	.01
☐	65	Erik Hanson	.10	.05	.01
☐	66	Tim Naehring	.10	.05	.01
☐	67	Lee Tinsley	.05	.02	.01
☐	68	Troy O'Leary	.10	.05	.01
☐	69	Garret Anderson	.15	.07	.02
☐	70	Chili Davis	.10	.05	.01

#	Player			
☐ 71	Jim Edmonds	.15	.07	.02
☐ 72	Troy Percival	.10	.05	.01
☐ 73	Mark Langston	.05	.02	.01
☐ 74	Spike Owen	.05	.02	.01
☐ 75	Tim Salmon	.25	.11	.03
☐ 76	Brian Anderson	.05	.02	.01
☐ 77	Lee Smith	.15	.07	.02
☐ 78	Jim Abbott	.15	.07	.02
☐ 79	Jim Bullinger	.05	.02	.01
☐ 80	Mark Grace	.15	.07	.02
☐ 81	Todd Zeile	.05	.02	.01
☐ 82	Kevin Foster	.05	.02	.01
☐ 83	Howard Johnson	.05	.02	.01
☐ 84	Brian McRae	.10	.05	.01
☐ 85	Randy Myers	.10	.05	.01
☐ 86	Jaime Navarro	.05	.02	.01
☐ 87	Luis Gonzalez	.10	.05	.01
☐ 88	Ozzie Timmons	.10	.05	.01
☐ 89	Wilson Alvarez	.10	.05	.01
☐ 90	Frank Thomas	2.00	.90	.25
☐ 91	James Baldwin	.05	.02	.01
☐ 92	Ray Durham	.15	.07	.02
☐ 93	Alex Fernandez	.10	.05	.01
☐ 94	Ozzie Guillen	.05	.02	.01
☐ 95	Tim Raines	.15	.07	.02
☐ 96	Roberto Hernandez	.10	.05	.01
☐ 97	Lance Johnson	.05	.02	.01
☐ 98	John Kruk	.10	.05	.01
☐ 99	Mark Portugal	.05	.02	.01
☐ 100	Don Mattingly TT	.50	.23	.06
☐ 101	Roger Clemens TT	.15	.07	.02
☐ 102	Raul Mondesi TT	.10	.05	.01
☐ 103	Cecil Fielder TT	.10	.05	.01
☐ 104	Ozzie Smith TT	.15	.07	.02
☐ 105	Frank Thomas TT	1.00	.45	.12
☐ 106	Sammy Sosa TT	.10	.05	.01
☐ 107	Fred McGriff TT	.10	.05	.01
☐ 108	Barry Bonds TT	.05	.02	.01
☐ 109	Thomas Howard	.05	.02	.01
☐ 110	Ron Gant	.15	.07	.02
☐ 111	Eddie Taubensee	.05	.02	.01
☐ 112	Hal Morris	.05	.02	.01
☐ 113	Jose Rijo	.05	.02	.01
☐ 114	Pete Schourek	.15	.07	.02
☐ 115	Reggie Sanders	.15	.07	.02
☐ 116	Benito Santiago	.05	.02	.01
☐ 117	Jeff Brantley	.05	.02	.01
☐ 118	Julian Tavarez	.10	.05	.01
☐ 119	Carlos Baerga	.40	.18	.05
☐ 120	Jim Thome	.15	.07	.02
☐ 121	Jose Mesa	.10	.05	.01
☐ 122	Dennis Martinez	.10	.05	.01
☐ 123	Dave Winfield	.15	.07	.02
☐ 124	Eddie Murray	.25	.11	.03
☐ 125	Manny Ramirez	.75	.35	.09
☐ 126	Paul Sorrento	.05	.02	.01
☐ 127	Kenny Lofton	.60	.25	.07
☐ 128	Eric Young	.10	.05	.01
☐ 129	Jason Bates	.10	.05	.01
☐ 130	Bret Saberhagen	.10	.05	.01
☐ 131	Andres Galarraga	.15	.07	.02
☐ 132	Joe Girardi	.05	.02	.01
☐ 133	John VanderWal	.05	.02	.01
☐ 134	David Nied	.05	.02	.01
☐ 135	Dante Bichette	.25	.11	.03
☐ 136	Vinny Castilla	.15	.07	.02
☐ 137	Kevin Ritz	.05	.02	.01
☐ 138	Felipe Lira	.05	.02	.01
☐ 139	Joe Boever	.05	.02	.01
☐ 140	Cecil Fielder	.15	.07	.02
☐ 141	John Flaherty	.05	.02	.01
☐ 142	Kirk Gibson	.10	.05	.01
☐ 143	Brian Maxcy	.05	.02	.01
☐ 144	Lou Whitaker	.15	.07	.02
☐ 145	Alan Trammell	.15	.07	.02
☐ 146	Bobby Higginson	.15	.07	.02
☐ 147	Chad Curtis	.10	.05	.01
☐ 148	Quilvio Veras	.10	.05	.01
☐ 149	Jerry Browne	.05	.02	.01
☐ 150	Andre Dawson	.15	.07	.02
☐ 151	Robb Nen	.05	.05	.01
☐ 152	Greg Colbrunn	.15	.07	.02
☐ 153	Chris Hammond	.05	.02	.01
☐ 154	Kurt Abbott	.05	.02	.01
☐ 155	Charles Johnson	.10	.05	.01
☐ 156	Terry Pendleton	.10	.05	.01
☐ 157	Dave Weathers	.05	.02	.01
☐ 158	Mike Hampton	.05	.02	.01
☐ 159	Craig Biggio	.15	.07	.02
☐ 160	Jeff Bagwell	.60	.25	.07
☐ 161	Brian L.Hunter	.15	.07	.02
☐ 162	Mike Henneman	.05	.02	.01
☐ 163	Dave Magadan	.05	.02	.01
☐ 164	Shane Reynolds	.10	.05	.01
☐ 165	Derek Bell	.15	.07	.02
☐ 166	Orlando Miller	.10	.05	.01
☐ 167	James Mouton	.10	.05	.01
☐ 168	Melvin Bunch	.05	.02	.01
☐ 169	Tom Gordon	.05	.02	.01
☐ 170	Kevin Appier	.10	.05	.01
☐ 171	Tom Goodwin	.05	.02	.01
☐ 172	Greg Gagne	.05	.02	.01
☐ 173	Gary Gaetti	.10	.05	.01
☐ 174	Jeff Montgomery	.10	.05	.01
☐ 175	Jon Nunnally	.10	.05	.01
☐ 176	Michael Tucker	.10	.05	.01
☐ 177	Joe Vitiello	.10	.05	.01
☐ 178	Billy Ashley	.05	.02	.01
☐ 179	Tom Candiotti	.05	.02	.01
☐ 180	Hideo Nomo	1.00	.45	.12
☐ 181	Chad Fonville	.10	.05	.01
☐ 182	Todd Hollandsworth	.05	.02	.01
☐ 183	Eric Karros	.10	.05	.01
☐ 184	Roberto Kelly	.05	.02	.01
☐ 185	Mike Piazza	.75	.35	.09
☐ 186	Ramon Martinez	.10	.05	.01
☐ 187	Tim Wallach	.05	.02	.01
☐ 188	Jeff Cirillo	.10	.05	.01
☐ 189	Sid Roberson	.05	.02	.01
☐ 190	Kevin Seitzer	.05	.02	.01
☐ 191	Mike Fetters	.05	.02	.01
☐ 192	Steve Sparks	.05	.02	.01
☐ 193	Matt Mieske	.05	.02	.01
☐ 194	Joe Oliver	.05	.02	.01
☐ 195	B.J. Surhoff	.10	.05	.01
☐ 196	Alberto Reyes	.05	.02	.01
☐ 197	Fernando Vina	.05	.02	.01
☐ 198	LaTroy Hawkins	.05	.02	.01
☐ 199	Marty Cordova	.15	.07	.02
☐ 200	Kirby Puckett	.60	.25	.07
☐ 201	Brad Radke	.05	.02	.01
☐ 202	Pedro Munoz	.10	.05	.01
☐ 203	Scott Klingenbeck	.05	.02	.01
☐ 204	Pat Meares	.05	.02	.01
☐ 205	Chuck Knoblauch	.15	.07	.02
☐ 206	Scott Stahoviak	.05	.02	.01
☐ 207	Dave Stevens	.05	.02	.01
☐ 208	Shane Andrews	.05	.02	.01
☐ 209	Moises Alou	.10	.05	.01
☐ 210	David Segui	.05	.02	.01
☐ 211	Cliff Floyd	.10	.05	.01
☐ 212	Carlos Perez	.15	.07	.02

#	Player			
☐ 213	Mark Grudzielanek	.05	.02	.01
☐ 214	Butch Henry	.05	.02	.01
☐ 215	Rondell White	.15	.07	.02
☐ 216	Mel Rojas	.10	.05	.01
☐ 217	Ugueth Urbina	.10	.05	.01
☐ 218	Edgardo Alfonzo	.10	.05	.01
☐ 219	Carl Everett	.10	.05	.01
☐ 220	John Franco	.10	.05	.01
☐ 221	Todd Hundley	.10	.05	.01
☐ 222	Bobby Jones	.10	.05	.01
☐ 223	Bill Pulsipher	.15	.07	.02
☐ 224	Rico Brogna	.15	.07	.02
☐ 225	Jeff Kent	.10	.05	.01
☐ 226	Chris Jones	.05	.02	.01
☐ 227	Butch Huskey	.10	.05	.01
☐ 228	Robert Eenhoorn	.05	.02	.01
☐ 229	Sterling Hitchcock	.05	.02	.01
☐ 230	Wade Boggs	.15	.07	.02
☐ 231	Derek Jeter	.15	.07	.02
☐ 232	Tony Fernandez	.05	.02	.01
☐ 233	Jack McDowell	.15	.07	.02
☐ 234	Andy Pettitte	.15	.07	.02
☐ 235	David Cone	.15	.07	.02
☐ 236	Mike Stanley	.10	.05	.01
☐ 237	Don Mattingly	1.00	.45	.12
☐ 238	Geronimo Berroa	.05	.02	.01
☐ 239	Scott Brosius	.05	.02	.01
☐ 240	Rickey Henderson	.15	.07	.02
☐ 241	Terry Steinbach	.10	.05	.01
☐ 242	Mike Gallego	.05	.02	.01
☐ 243	Jason Giambi	.10	.05	.01
☐ 244	Steve Ontiveros	.05	.02	.01
☐ 245	Dennis Eckersley	.15	.07	.02
☐ 246	Dave Stewart	.05	.02	.01
☐ 247	Don Wengert	.05	.02	.01
☐ 248	Paul Quantrill	.05	.02	.01
☐ 249	Ricky Bottalico	.05	.02	.01
☐ 250	Kevin Stocker	.05	.02	.01
☐ 251	Lenny Dykstra	.10	.05	.01
☐ 252	Tony Longmire	.05	.02	.01
☐ 253	Tyler Green	.05	.02	.01
☐ 254	Mike Mimbs	.05	.02	.01
☐ 255	Charlie Hayes	.05	.02	.01
☐ 256	Mickey Morandini	.05	.02	.01
☐ 257	Heathcliff Slocumb	.05	.02	.01
☐ 258	Jeff King	.05	.02	.01
☐ 259	Midre Cummings	.10	.05	.01
☐ 260	Mark Johnson	.05	.02	.01
☐ 261	Freddy Garcia	.05	.02	.01
☐ 262	Jon Lieber	.05	.02	.01
☐ 263	Esteban Loaiza	.05	.02	.01
☐ 264	Dan Miceli	.05	.02	.01
☐ 265	Orlando Merced	.10	.05	.01
☐ 266	Denny Neagle	.05	.02	.01
☐ 267	Steve Parris	.05	.02	.01
☐ 268	Greg Maddux FT	1.00	.45	.12
☐ 269	Randy Johnson FT	.15	.07	.02
☐ 270	Hideo Nomo FT	.40	.18	.05
☐ 271	Jose Mesa FT	.05	.02	.01
☐ 272	Mike Piazza FT	.40	.18	.05
☐ 273	Mo Vaughn FT	.15	.07	.02
☐ 274	Craig Biggio FT	.05	.02	.01
☐ 275	Edgar Martinez FT	.05	.02	.01
☐ 276	Barry Larkin FT	.15	.07	.02
☐ 277	Sammy Sosa FT	.05	.02	.01
☐ 278	Dante Bichette FT	.10	.05	.01
☐ 279	Albert Belle FT	.40	.18	.05
☐ 280	Ozzie Smith	.40	.18	.05
☐ 281	Mark Sweeney	.05	.02	.01
☐ 282	Terry Bradshaw	.05	.02	.01
☐ 283	Allen Battle	.05	.02	.01
☐ 284	Danny Jackson	.05	.02	.01
☐ 285	Tom Henke	.10	.05	.01
☐ 286	Scott Cooper	.05	.02	.01
☐ 287	Tripp Cromer	.05	.02	.01
☐ 288	Bernard Gilkey	.05	.02	.01
☐ 289	Brian Jordan	.15	.07	.02
☐ 290	Tony Gwynn	.60	.25	.07
☐ 291	Brad Ausmus	.05	.02	.01
☐ 292	Bryce Florie	.05	.02	.01
☐ 293	Andres Berumen	.05	.02	.01
☐ 294	Ken Caminiti	.05	.02	.01
☐ 295	Bip Roberts	.05	.02	.01
☐ 296	Trevor Hoffman	.10	.05	.01
☐ 297	Roberto Petagine	.05	.02	.01
☐ 298	Jody Reed	.05	.02	.01
☐ 299	Fernando Valenzuela	.10	.05	.01
☐ 300	Barry Bonds	.50	.23	.06
☐ 301	Mark Leiter	.05	.02	.01
☐ 302	Mark Carreon	.05	.02	.01
☐ 303	Royce Clayton	.05	.02	.01
☐ 304	Kirt Manwaring	.05	.02	.01
☐ 305	Glenallen Hill	.05	.02	.01
☐ 306	Deion Sanders	.40	.18	.05
☐ 307	Joe Rosselli	.05	.02	.01
☐ 308	Robby Thompson	.05	.02	.01
☐ 309	W. VanLandingham	.05	.02	.01
☐ 310	Ken Griffey Jr.	2.00	.90	.25
☐ 311	Bobby Ayala	.05	.02	.01
☐ 312	Joey Cora	.05	.02	.01
☐ 313	Mike Blowers	.10	.05	.01
☐ 314	Darren Bragg	.05	.02	.01
☐ 315	Randy Johnson	.40	.18	.05
☐ 316	Alex Rodriguez	.15	.07	.02
☐ 317	Andy Benes	.10	.05	.01
☐ 318	Tino Martinez	.15	.07	.02
☐ 319	Dan Wilson	.05	.02	.01
☐ 320	Will Clark	.25	.11	.03
☐ 321	Jeff Frye	.05	.02	.01
☐ 322	Benji Gil	.05	.02	.01
☐ 323	Rick Helling	.05	.02	.01
☐ 324	Mark McLemore	.05	.02	.01
☐ 325	Dave Nilsson IF	.05	.02	.01
☐ 326	Larry Walker IF	.10	.05	.01
☐ 327	Jose Canseco IF	.15	.07	.02
☐ 328	Raul Mondesi IF	.10	.05	.01
☐ 329	Manny Ramirez IF	.40	.18	.05
☐ 330	Robert Eenhoorn IF	.05	.02	.01
☐ 331	Chili Davis IF	.05	.02	.01
☐ 332	Hideo Nomo IF	.40	.18	.05
☐ 333	Benji Gil IF	.05	.02	.01
☐ 334	Fernando Valenzuela IF	.05	.02	.01
☐ 335	Dennis Martinez IF	.05	.02	.01
☐ 336	Roberto Kelly IF	.05	.02	.01
☐ 337	Carlos Baerga IF	.15	.07	.02
☐ 338	Juan Gonzalez IF	.10	.05	.01
☐ 339	Roberto Alomar IF	.15	.07	.02
☐ 340	Chan Ho Park IF	.05	.02	.01
☐ 341	Andres Galarraga IF	.05	.02	.01
☐ 342	Midre Cummings IF	.05	.02	.01
☐ 343	Otis Nixon	.05	.02	.01
☐ 344	Jeff Russell	.05	.02	.01
☐ 345	Ivan Rodriguez	.15	.07	.02
☐ 346	Mickey Tettleton	.10	.05	.01
☐ 347	Bob Tewksbury	.05	.02	.01
☐ 348	Domingo Cedeno	.05	.02	.01
☐ 349	Lance Parrish	.10	.05	.01
☐ 350	Joe Carter	.15	.07	.02
☐ 351	Devon White	.05	.02	.01
☐ 352	Carlos Delgado	.05	.02	.01
☐ 353	Alex Gonzalez	.05	.02	.01
☐ 354	Darren Hall	.05	.02	.01

		MINT	NRMT	EXC
☐ 355	Paul Molitor	.15	.07	.02
☐ 356	Al Leiter	.05	.02	.01
☐ 357	Randy Knorr	.05	.02	.01
☐ 358	Ken Caminiti CL	.05	.02	.01
	Steve Finley			
	Brian Williams			
	Roberto Petagine			
	Andujar Cedeno			
	Phil Plantier			
	Derek Bell			
	Pedro A. Martinez			
	Doug Brocail			
	Craig Shipley			
	Ricky Gutierrez			
☐ 359	Hideo Nomo CL	.40	.18	.05
☐ 360	Ramon A.Martinez CL	.05	.02	.01
	Ramon J.Martinez			
☐ 361	Robin Ventura CL	.05	.02	.01
☐ 362	Cal Ripken CL	1.00	.45	.12
☐ 363	Ken Caminiti CL	.05	.02	.01
☐ 364	Albert Belle CL	.40	.18	.05
	Eddie Murray			
☐ 365	Randy Johnson CL	.15	.07	.02

1996 Collector's Choice Gold Signature

This 365-card set parallels the basic Collector's Choice issue. These cards were inserted approximately one every 35 packs. These cards are similar to the regular issue except they have gold borders and a fac-simile signature of the player is in gold foil.

		MINT	NRMT	EXC
COMPLETE SET (365)		900.00	400.00	110.00
COMMON CARD (1-365)		1.00	.45	.12
*VETERAN STARS: 18X TO 30X BASIC CARDS				
*YOUNG STARS: 12X TO 20X BASIC CARDS				

		MINT	NRMT	EXC
☐ 1	Cal Ripken	50.00	22.00	6.25
☐ 6	M.Mussina/G.Maddux SL	20.00	9.00	2.50
☐ 7	R.Johnson/H.Nomo SL	10.00	4.50	1.25
☐ 8	R.Johnson/G.Maddux SL	20.00	9.00	2.50
☐ 40	Greg Maddux	50.00	22.00	6.25
☐ 42	Chipper Jones	20.00	9.00	2.50
☐ 90	Frank Thomas	50.00	22.00	6.25
☐ 100	Don Mattingly TT	12.00	5.50	1.50
☐ 105	Frank Thomas TT	25.00	11.00	3.10
☐ 125	Manny Ramirez	20.00	9.00	2.50
☐ 127	Kenny Lofton	15.00	6.75	1.85
☐ 160	Jeff Bagwell	15.00	6.75	1.85
☐ 180	Hideo Nomo	20.00	9.00	2.50
☐ 185	Mike Piazza	20.00	9.00	2.50
☐ 200	Kirby Puckett	15.00	6.75	1.85
☐ 237	Don Mattingly	25.00	11.00	3.10
☐ 268	Greg Maddux FT	25.00	11.00	3.10
☐ 270	Hideo Nomo FT	10.00	4.50	1.25
☐ 272	Mike Piazza FT	10.00	4.50	1.25
☐ 279	Albert Belle FT	10.00	4.50	1.25
☐ 290	Tony Gwynn	15.00	6.75	1.85
☐ 310	Ken Griffey Jr.	50.00	22.00	6.25
☐ 332	Hideo Nomo IF	10.00	4.50	1.25

		MINT	NRMT	EXC
☐ 359	Hideo Nomo CL	10.00	4.50	1.25
☐ 362	Cal Ripken CL	25.00	11.00	3.10

1996 Collector's Choice Ripken

This five card set is the beginning of a con-tinuing series with each Upper Deck prod-uct. The first five cards are exclusive to Collector's Choice. The next seventeen cards will be issued in Upper Deck (both series), Collector Choice Series 2, SP and SP Championship Series packs. These five cards feature recent Cal Ripken highlights. The fronts feature a full-color shot covering most of the card. The back is dedicated to an event in Ripken's career as well as a lit-tle inset photo. The cards are numbered as "X" of 22 in the upper left.

	MINT	NRMT	EXC
COMPLETE SET (5)	15.00	6.75	1.85
COMMON RIPKEN (1-4)	4.00	1.80	.50
HEADER CARD (NNO)	4.00	1.80	.50

1996 Collector's Choice You Make the Play

This 45-card set was inserted one per pack. Dealers also were offered extra You Make

the Play cards depending on how many cases ordered. A dealer who ordered one case received two 12-card packs of these cards for a total of 24 cards. Meanwhile, a dealer who ordered two cases received six 12-card packs for a total of 72 packs. Customers could also receive a 12 of these cards by sending 10 wrappers and $2 to an a mail-in order. This offer expired on May 15, 1996. The cards measure just about the standard-size but have rounded corners. Each player has two results on each card but the value is the same for either result.

	MINT	NRMT	EXC
COMPLETE SET (90)	20.00	9.00	2.50
COMMON CARD (1-45)	.15	.07	.02
COMPLETE GOLD SIG SET (90)	300.00	135.00	38.00
GOLD SIGNATURE COMMON (1-45)	1.00	.45	.12
GOLD SIGNATURE SEMISTARS	2.50	1.10	.30
*GOLD SIG. VETERAN STARS: 9X TO 15X BASIC CARDS			
*GOLD SIG. YOUNG STARS: 5X TO 10X BASIC CARDS			

		MINT	NRMT	EXC
☐ 1	Kevin Appier	.15	.07	.02
☐ 2	Carlos Baerga	.40	.18	.05
☐ 3	Jeff Bagwell	.60	.25	.07
☐ 4	Jay Bell	.15	.07	.02
☐ 5	Albert Belle	.75	.35	.09
☐ 6	Craig Biggio	.15	.07	.02
☐ 7	Wade Boggs	.15	.07	.02
☐ 8	Barry Bonds	.50	.23	.06
☐ 9	Bobby Bonilla	.15	.07	.02
☐ 10	Jose Canseco	.30	.14	.04
☐ 11	Joe Carter	.15	.07	.02
☐ 12	Darren Daulton	.15	.07	.02
☐ 13	Cecil Fielder	.15	.07	.02
☐ 14	Ron Gant	.15	.07	.02
☐ 15	Juan Gonzalez	.30	.14	.04
☐ 16	Ken Griffey Jr.	2.00	.90	.25
☐ 17	Tony Gwynn	.60	.25	.07
☐ 18	Randy Johnson	.40	.18	.05
☐ 19	Chipper Jones	.75	.35	.09
☐ 20	Barry Larkin	.25	.11	.03
☐ 21	Kenny Lofton	.60	.25	.07
☐ 22	Greg Maddux	2.00	.90	.25
☐ 23	Don Mattingly	1.00	.45	.12
☐ 24	Fred McGriff	.25	.11	.03
☐ 25	Mark McGwire	.15	.07	.02
☐ 26	Paul Molitor	.15	.07	.02
☐ 27	Raul Mondesi	.40	.18	.05
☐ 28	Eddie Murray	.25	.11	.03
☐ 29	Hideo Nomo	.75	.35	.09
☐ 30	Jon Nunnally	.15	.07	.02
☐ 31	Mike Piazza	.75	.35	.09
☐ 32	Kirby Puckett	.60	.25	.07
☐ 33	Cal Ripken	2.00	.90	.25
☐ 34	Alex Rodriguez	.15	.07	.02
☐ 35	Tim Salmon	.25	.11	.03
☐ 36	Gary Sheffield	.15	.07	.02
☐ 37	Lee Smith	.15	.07	.02
☐ 38	Ozzie Smith	.40	.18	.05
☐ 39	Sammy Sosa	.15	.07	.02
☐ 40	Frank Thomas	2.00	.90	.25
☐ 41	Greg Vaughn	.15	.07	.02
☐ 42	Mo Vaughn	.30	.14	.04
☐ 43	Larry Walker	.25	.11	.03
☐ 44	Rondell White	.15	.07	.02
☐ 45	Matt Williams	.30	.14	.04

1981 Donruss

 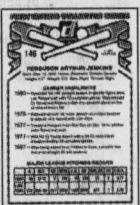

FERGUSON ARTHUR JENKINS

The cards in this 605-card set measure 2 1/2" by 3 1/2". In 1981 Donruss launched itself into the baseball card market with a set containing 600 numbered cards and five unnumbered checklists. Even though the five checklist cards are unnumbered, they are numbered below (601-605) for convenience in reference. The cards are printed on thin stock and more than one pose exists for several popular players. Numerous errors of the first print run were later corrected by the company. These are marked P1 and P2 in the checklist below. The key rookie cards in this set are Danny Ainge, Tim Raines, and Jeff Reardon.

		NRMT-MT	EXC	G-VG
COMPLETE SET (605)		40.00	18.00	5.00
COMMON CARD (1-605)		.10	.05	.01
☐ 1	Ozzie Smith	4.00	1.80	.50
☐ 2	Rollie Fingers	.40	.18	.05
☐ 3	Rick Wise	.10	.05	.01
☐ 4	Gene Richards	.10	.05	.01
☐ 5	Alan Trammell	1.50	.70	.19
☐ 6	Tom Brookens	.10	.05	.01
☐ 7A	Duffy Dyer P1 (1980 batting average has decimal point)	.20	.09	.03
☐ 7B	Duffy Dyer P2 (1980 batting average has no decimal point)	.10	.05	.01
☐ 8	Mark Fidrych	.20	.09	.03
☐ 9	Dave Rozema	.10	.05	.01
☐ 10	Ricky Peters	.10	.05	.01
☐ 11	Mike Schmidt	2.00	.90	.25
☐ 12	Willie Stargell	.75	.35	.09
☐ 13	Tim Foli	.10	.05	.01
☐ 14	Manny Sanguillen	.20	.09	.03
☐ 15	Grant Jackson	.10	.05	.01
☐ 16	Eddie Solomon	.10	.05	.01
☐ 17	Omar Moreno	.10	.05	.01
☐ 18	Joe Morgan	.75	.35	.09
☐ 19	Rafael Landestoy	.10	.05	.01
☐ 20	Bruce Bochy	.10	.05	.01
☐ 21	Joe Sambito	.10	.05	.01
☐ 22	Manny Trillo	.10	.05	.01
☐ 23A	Dave Smith P1 (Line box around stats is not complete)	.20	.09	.03
☐ 23B	Dave Smith P2 (Box totally encloses	.20	.09	.03

stats at top)

☐ 24 Terry Puhl	.10	.05	.01
☐ 25 Bump Wills	.10	.05	.01
☐ 26A John Ellis P1 ERR.	.20	.09	.03
(Photo on front shows Danny Walton)			
☐ 26B John Ellis P2 COR	.20	.09	.03
☐ 27 Jim Kern	.10	.05	.01
☐ 28 Richie Zisk	.10	.05	.01
☐ 29 John Mayberry	.10	.05	.01
☐ 30 Bob Davis	.10	.05	.01
☐ 31 Jackson Todd	.10	.05	.01
☐ 32 Alvis Woods	.10	.05	.01
☐ 33 Steve Carlton	1.00	.45	.12
☐ 34 Lee Mazzilli	.10	.05	.01
☐ 35 John Stearns	.10	.05	.01
☐ 36 Roy Lee Jackson	.10	.05	.01
☐ 37 Mike Scott	.10	.05	.01
☐ 38 Lamar Johnson	.10	.05	.01
☐ 39 Kevin Bell	.10	.05	.01
☐ 40 Ed Farmer	.10	.05	.01
☐ 41 Ross Baumgarten	.10	.05	.01
☐ 42 Leo Sutherland	.10	.05	.01
☐ 43 Dan Meyer	.10	.05	.01
☐ 44 Ron Reed	.10	.05	.01
☐ 45 Mario Mendoza	.10	.05	.01
☐ 46 Rick Honeycutt	.10	.05	.01
☐ 47 Glenn Abbott	.10	.05	.01
☐ 48 Leon Roberts	.10	.05	.01
☐ 49 Rod Carew	.75	.35	.09
☐ 50 Bert Campaneris	.20	.09	.03
☐ 51A Tom Donahue P1 ERR.	.20	.09	.03
(Name on front misspelled Donahue)			
☐ 51B Tom Donohue	.10	.05	.01
P2 COR			
☐ 52 Dave Frost	.10	.05	.01
☐ 53 Ed Halicki	.10	.05	.01
☐ 54 Dan Ford	.10	.05	.01
☐ 55 Garry Maddox	.10	.05	.01
☐ 56A Steve Garvey P1	.40	.18	.05
("Surpassed 25 HR")			
☐ 56B Steve Garvey P2	.40	.18	.05
("Surpassed 21 HR")			
☐ 57 Bill Russell	.20	.09	.03
☐ 58 Don Sutton	.40	.18	.05
☐ 59 Reggie Smith	.20	.09	.03
☐ 60 Rick Monday	.20	.09	.03
☐ 61 Ray Knight	.20	.09	.03
☐ 62 Johnny Bench	1.25	.55	.16
☐ 63 Mario Soto	.10	.05	.01
☐ 64 Doug Bair	.10	.05	.01
☐ 65 George Foster	.20	.09	.03
☐ 66 Jeff Burroughs	.10	.05	.01
☐ 67 Keith Hernandez	.40	.18	.05
☐ 68 Tom Herr	.20	.09	.03
☐ 69 Bob Forsch	.10	.05	.01
☐ 70 John Fulgham	.10	.05	.01
☐ 71A Bobby Bonds P1 ERR.	.40	.18	.05
(986 lifetime HR)			
☐ 71B Bobby Bonds P2 COR	.20	.09	.03
(326 lifetime HR)			
☐ 72A Rennie Stennett P1	.20	.09	.03
("Breaking broke leg")			
☐ 72B Rennie Stennett P2	.10	.05	.01
(Word "broke" deleted)			
☐ 73 Joe Strain	.10	.05	.01
☐ 74 Ed Whitson	.10	.05	.01
☐ 75 Tom Griffin	.10	.05	.01
☐ 76 Billy North	.10	.05	.01
☐ 77 Gene Garber	.10	.05	.01

☐ 78 Mike Hargrove	.20	.09	.03
☐ 79 Dave Rosello	.10	.05	.01
☐ 80 Ron Hassey	.10	.05	.01
☐ 81 Sid Monge	.10	.05	.01
☐ 82A Joe Charboneau P1	.20	.09	.03
('78 highlights, "For some reason")			
☐ 82B Joe Charboneau P2	.20	.09	.03
(Phrase "For some reason" deleted)			
☐ 83 Cecil Cooper	.20	.09	.03
☐ 84 Sal Bando	.20	.09	.03
☐ 85 Moose Haas	.10	.05	.01
☐ 86 Mike Caldwell	.10	.05	.01
☐ 87A Larry Hisle P1	.20	.09	.03
('77 highlights, line ends with "28 RBI")			
☐ 87B Larry Hisle P2	.10	.05	.01
(Correct line "28 HR")			
☐ 88 Luis Gomez	.10	.05	.01
☐ 89 Larry Parrish	.10	.05	.01
☐ 90 Gary Carter	.75	.35	.09
☐ 91 Bill Gullickson	.20	.09	.03
☐ 92 Fred Norman	.10	.05	.01
☐ 93 Tommy Hutton	.10	.05	.01
☐ 94 Carl Yastrzemski	1.00	.45	.12
☐ 95 Glenn Hoffman	.10	.05	.01
☐ 96 Dennis Eckersley	.75	.35	.09
☐ 97A Tom Burgmeier P1	.20	.09	.03
ERR (Throws: Right)			
☐ 97B Tom Burgmeier P2	.10	.05	.01
COR (Throws: Left)			
☐ 98 Win Remmerswaal	.10	.05	.01
☐ 99 Bob Horner	.20	.09	.03
☐ 100 George Brett	4.00	1.80	.50
☐ 101 Dave Chalk	.10	.05	.01
☐ 102 Dennis Leonard	.10	.05	.01
☐ 103 Renie Martin	.10	.05	.01
☐ 104 Amos Otis	.20	.09	.03
☐ 105 Graig Nettles	.20	.09	.03
☐ 106 Eric Soderholm	.10	.05	.01
☐ 107 Tommy John	.40	.18	.05
☐ 108 Tom Underwood	.10	.05	.01
☐ 109 Lou Piniella	.20	.09	.03
☐ 110 Mickey Klutts	.10	.05	.01
☐ 111 Bobby Murcer	.20	.09	.03
☐ 112 Eddie Murray	4.00	1.80	.50
☐ 113 Rick Dempsey	.20	.09	.03
☐ 114 Scott McGregor	.10	.05	.01
☐ 115 Ken Singleton	.20	.09	.03
☐ 116 Gary Roenicke	.10	.05	.01
☐ 117 Dave Revering	.10	.05	.01
☐ 118 Mike Norris	.10	.05	.01
☐ 119 Rickey Henderson	5.00	2.20	.60
☐ 120 Mike Heath	.10	.05	.01
☐ 121 Dave Cash	.10	.05	.01
☐ 122 Randy Jones	.10	.05	.01
☐ 123 Eric Rasmussen	.10	.05	.01
☐ 124 Jerry Mumphrey	.10	.05	.01
☐ 125 Richie Hebner	.10	.05	.01
☐ 126 Mark Wagner	.10	.05	.01
☐ 127 Jack Morris	.40	.18	.05
☐ 128 Dan Petry	.20	.09	.03
☐ 129 Bruce Robbins	.10	.05	.01
☐ 130 Champ Summers	.10	.05	.01
☐ 131A Pete Rose P1	2.00	.90	.25
(Last line ends with "see card 251")			
☐ 131B Pete Rose P2	2.00	.90	.25
(Last line corrected "see card 371")			

☐ 132 Willie Stargell	.75	.35	.09
☐ 133 Ed Ott	.10	.05	.01
☐ 134 Jim Bibby	.10	.05	.01
☐ 135 Bert Blyleven	.40	.18	.05
☐ 136 Dave Parker	.40	.18	.05
☐ 137 Bill Robinson	.20	.09	.03
☐ 138 Enos Cabell	.10	.05	.01
☐ 139 Dave Bergman	.10	.05	.01
☐ 140 J.R. Richard	.20	.09	.03
☐ 141 Ken Forsch	.10	.05	.01
☐ 142 Larry Bowa UER	.20	.09	.03
(Shortshop on front)			
☐ 143 Frank LaCorte UER	.10	.05	.01
(Photo actually			
Randy Niemann)			
☐ 144 Denny Walling	.10	.05	.01
☐ 145 Buddy Bell	.20	.09	.03
☐ 146 Ferguson Jenkins	.40	.18	.05
☐ 147 Dannny Darwin	.10	.05	.01
☐ 148 John Grubb	.10	.05	.01
☐ 149 Alfredo Griffin	.10	.05	.01
☐ 150 Jerry Garvin	.10	.05	.01
☐ 151 Paul Mirabella	.10	.05	.01
☐ 152 Rick Bosetti	.10	.05	.01
☐ 153 Dick Ruthven	.10	.05	.01
☐ 154 Frank Taveras	.10	.05	.01
☐ 155 Craig Swan	.10	.05	.01
☐ 156 Jeff Reardon	1.00	.45	.12
☐ 157 Steve Henderson	.10	.05	.01
☐ 158 Jim Morrison	.10	.05	.01
☐ 159 Glenn Borgmann	.10	.05	.01
☐ 160 LaMarr Hoyt	.20	.09	.03
☐ 161 Rich Wortham	.10	.05	.01
☐ 162 Thad Bosley	.10	.05	.01
☐ 163 Julio Cruz	.10	.05	.01
☐ 164A Del Unser P1	.20	.09	.03
(No "3B" heading)			
☐ 164B Del Unser P2	.10	.05	.01
(Batting record on back			
corrected ("3B")			
☐ 165 Jim Anderson	.10	.05	.01
☐ 166 Jim Beattie	.10	.05	.01
☐ 167 Shane Rawley	.10	.05	.01
☐ 168 Joe Simpson	.10	.05	.01
☐ 169 Rod Carew	.75	.35	.09
☐ 170 Fred Patek	.10	.05	.01
☐ 171 Frank Tanana	.20	.09	.03
☐ 172 Alfredo Martinez	.10	.05	.01
☐ 173 Chris Knapp	.10	.05	.01
☐ 174 Joe Rudi	.20	.09	.03
☐ 175 Greg Luzinski	.20	.09	.03
☐ 176 Steve Garvey	.40	.18	.05
☐ 177 Joe Ferguson	.10	.05	.01
☐ 178 Bob Welch	.20	.09	.03
☐ 179 Dusty Baker	.40	.18	.05
☐ 180 Rudy Law	.10	.05	.01
☐ 181 Dave Concepcion	.20	.09	.03
☐ 182 Johnny Bench	1.25	.55	.16
☐ 183 Mike LaCoss	.10	.05	.01
☐ 184 Ken Griffey	.20	.09	.03
☐ 185 Dave Collins	.10	.05	.01
☐ 186 Brian Asselstine	.10	.05	.01
☐ 187 Garry Templeton	.20	.09	.03
☐ 188 Mike Phillips	.10	.05	.01
☐ 189 Pete Vuckovich	.20	.09	.03
☐ 190 John Urrea	.10	.05	.01
☐ 191 Tony Scott	.10	.05	.01
☐ 192 Darrell Evans	.20	.09	.03
☐ 193 Milt May	.10	.05	.01
☐ 194 Bob Knepper	.10	.05	.01
☐ 195 Randy Moffitt	.10	.05	.01
☐ 196 Larry Herndon	.10	.05	.01
☐ 197 Rick Camp	.10	.05	.01
☐ 198 Andre Thornton	.20	.09	.03
☐ 199 Tom Veryzer	.10	.05	.01
☐ 200 Gary Alexander	.10	.05	.01
☐ 201 Rick Waits	.10	.05	.01
☐ 202 Rick Manning	.10	.05	.01
☐ 203 Paul Molitor	1.50	.70	.19
☐ 204 Jim Gantner	.20	.09	.03
☐ 205 Paul Mitchell	.10	.05	.01
☐ 206 Reggie Cleveland	.10	.05	.01
☐ 207 Sixto Lezcano	.10	.05	.01
☐ 208 Bruce Benedict	.10	.05	.01
☐ 209 Rodney Scott	.10	.05	.01
☐ 210 John Tamargo	.10	.05	.01
☐ 211 Bill Lee	.10	.05	.01
☐ 212 Andre Dawson UER	1.50	.70	.19
(Middle name Fernando,			
should be Nolan)			
☐ 213 Rowland Office	.10	.05	.01
☐ 214 Carl Yastrzemski	1.00	.45	.12
☐ 215 Jerry Remy	.10	.05	.01
☐ 216 Mike Torrez	.10	.05	.01
☐ 217 Skip Lockwood	.10	.05	.01
☐ 218 Fred Lynn	.20	.09	.03
☐ 219 Chris Chambliss	.20	.09	.03
☐ 220 Willie Aikens	.10	.05	.01
☐ 221 John Wathan	.10	.05	.01
☐ 222 Dan Quisenberry	.40	.18	.05
☐ 223 Willie Wilson	.10	.05	.01
☐ 224 Clint Hurdle	.10	.05	.01
☐ 225 Bob Watson	.20	.09	.03
☐ 226 Jim Spencer	.10	.05	.01
☐ 227 Ron Guidry	.20	.09	.03
☐ 228 Reggie Jackson	2.00	.90	.25
☐ 229 Oscar Gamble	.10	.05	.01
☐ 230 Jeff Cox	.10	.05	.01
☐ 231 Luis Tiant	.20	.09	.03
☐ 232 Rich Dauer	.10	.05	.01
☐ 233 Dan Graham	.10	.05	.01
☐ 234 Mike Flanagan	.20	.09	.03
☐ 235 John Lowenstein	.10	.05	.01
☐ 236 Benny Ayala	.10	.05	.01
☐ 237 Wayne Gross	.10	.05	.01
☐ 238 Rick Langford	.10	.05	.01
☐ 239 Tony Armas	.20	.09	.03
☐ 240A Bob Lacy P1 ERR	.40	.18	.05
(Name misspelled			
Bob "Lacy")			
☐ 240B Bob Lacey P2 COR	.10	.05	.01
☐ 241 Gene Tenace	.10	.05	.01
☐ 242 Bob Shirley	.10	.05	.01
☐ 243 Gary Lucas	.10	.05	.01
☐ 244 Jerry Turner	.10	.05	.01
☐ 245 John Wockenfuss	.10	.05	.01
☐ 246 Stan Papi	.10	.05	.01
☐ 247 Milt Wilcox	.10	.05	.01
☐ 248 Dan Schatzeder	.10	.05	.01
☐ 249 Steve Kemp	.10	.05	.01
☐ 250 Jim Lentine	.10	.05	.01
☐ 251 Pete Rose	2.00	.90	.25
☐ 252 Bill Madlock	.20	.09	.03
☐ 253 Dale Berra	.10	.05	.01
☐ 254 Kent Tekulve	.20	.09	.03
☐ 255 Enrique Romo	.10	.05	.01
☐ 256 Mike Easler	.10	.05	.01
☐ 257 Chuck Tanner MG	.20	.09	.03
☐ 258 Art Howe	.20	.09	.03
☐ 259 Alan Ashby	.10	.05	.01
☐ 260 Nolan Ryan	6.00	2.70	.75
☐ 261A Vern Ruhle P1 ERR	.20	.09	.03

(Photo on front
actually Ken Forsch)

261B	Vern Ruhle P2 COR	.20	.09	.03
262	Bob Boone	.20	.09	.03
263	Cesar Cedeno	.20	.09	.03
264	Jeff Leonard	.20	.09	.03
265	Pat Putnam	.10	.05	.01
266	Jon Matlack	.10	.05	.01
267	Dave Rajsich	.10	.05	.01
268	Billy Sample	.10	.05	.01
269	Damaso Garcia	.20	.09	.03
270	Tom Buskey	.10	.05	.01
271	Joey McLaughlin	.10	.05	.01
272	Barry Bonnell	.10	.05	.01
273	Tug McGraw	.20	.09	.03
274	Mike Jorgensen	.10	.05	.01
275	Pat Zachry	.10	.05	.01
276	Neil Allen	.10	.05	.01
277	Joel Youngblood	.10	.05	.01
278	Greg Pryor	.10	.05	.01
279	Britt Burns	.20	.09	.03
280	Rich Dotson	.20	.09	.03
281	Chet Lemon	.20	.09	.03
282	Rusty Kuntz	.10	.05	.01
283	Ted Cox	.10	.05	.01
284	Sparky Lyle	.20	.09	.03
285	Larry Cox	.10	.05	.01
286	Floyd Bannister	.10	.05	.01
287	Byron McLaughlin	.10	.05	.01
288	Rodney Craig	.10	.05	.01
289	Bobby Grich	.20	.09	.03
290	Dickie Thon	.20	.09	.03
291	Mark Clear	.10	.05	.01
292	Dave Lemanczyk	.10	.05	.01
293	Jason Thompson	.10	.05	.01
294	Rick Miller	.10	.05	.01
295	Lonnie Smith	.10	.05	.01
296	Ron Cey	.20	.09	.03
297	Steve Yeager	.10	.05	.01
298	Bobby Castillo	.10	.05	.01
299	Manny Mota	.20	.09	.03
300	Jay Johnstone	.20	.09	.03
301	Dan Driessen	.10	.05	.01
302	Joe Nolan	.10	.05	.01
303	Paul Householder	.10	.05	.01
304	Harry Spilman	.10	.05	.01
305	Cesar Geronimo	.10	.05	.01
306A	Gary Mathews P1 ERR	.40	.18	.05
	(Name misspelled)			
306B	Gary Matthews P2 COR	.20	.09	.03
307	Ken Reitz	.10	.05	.01
308	Ted Simmons	.20	.09	.03
309	John Littlefield	.10	.05	.01
310	George Frazier	.10	.05	.01
311	Dane Iorg	.10	.05	.01
312	Mike Ivie	.10	.05	.01
313	Dennis Littlejohn	.10	.05	.01
314	Gary Lavelle	.10	.05	.01
315	Jack Clark	.20	.09	.03
316	Jim Wohlford	.10	.05	.01
317	Rick Matula	.10	.05	.01
318	Toby Harrah	.20	.09	.03
319A	Dwane Kuiper P1 ERR	.20	.09	.03
	(Name misspelled)			
319B	Duane Kuiper P2 COR	.10	.05	.01
320	Len Barker	.10	.05	.01
321	Victor Cruz	.10	.05	.01
322	Dell Alston	.10	.05	.01
323	Robin Yount	2.00	.90	.25
324	Charlie Moore	.10	.05	.01
325	Lary Sorensen	.10	.05	.01
326A	Gorman Thomas P1	.40	.18	.05
	(2nd line on back: "30 HR mark 4th")			
326B	Gorman Thomas P2	.20	.09	.03
	("30 HR mark 3rd")			
327	Bob Rodgers MG	.10	.05	.01
328	Phil Niekro	.40	.18	.05
329	Chris Speier	.10	.05	.01
330A	Steve Rodgers P1	.40	.18	.05
	ERR (Name misspelled)			
330B	Steve Rogers P2 COR	.10	.05	.01
331	Woodie Fryman	.10	.05	.01
332	Warren Cromartie	.10	.05	.01
333	Jerry White	.10	.05	.01
334	Tony Perez	.40	.18	.05
335	Carlton Fisk	1.25	.55	.16
336	Dick Drago	.10	.05	.01
337	Steve Renko	.10	.05	.01
338	Jim Rice	.40	.18	.05
339	Jerry Royster	.10	.05	.01
340	Frank White	.20	.09	.03
341	Jamie Quirk	.10	.05	.01
342A	Paul Spittorff P1 ERR	.20	.09	.03
	(Name misspelled)			
342B	Paul Splittorff P2 COR	.10	.05	.01
343	Marty Pattin	.10	.05	.01
344	Pete LaCock	.10	.05	.01
345	Willie Randolph	.20	.09	.03
346	Rick Cerone	.10	.05	.01
347	Rich Gossage	.40	.18	.05
348	Reggie Jackson	2.00	.90	.25
349	Ruppert Jones	.10	.05	.01
350	Dave McKay	.10	.05	.01
351	Yogi Berra CO	.40	.18	.05
352	Doug DeCinces	.20	.09	.03
353	Jim Palmer	.75	.35	.09
354	Tippy Martinez	.10	.05	.01
355	Al Bumbry	.20	.09	.03
356	Earl Weaver MG	.20	.09	.03
357A	Bob Picciolo P1 ERR	.20	.09	.03
	(Name misspelled)			
357B	Rob Picciolo P2 COR	.10	.05	.01
358	Matt Keough	.10	.05	.01
359	Dwayne Murphy	.10	.05	.01
360	Brian Kingman	.10	.05	.01
361	Bill Fahey	.10	.05	.01
362	Steve Mura	.10	.05	.01
363	Dennis Kinney	.10	.05	.01
364	Dave Winfield	2.00	.90	.25
365	Lou Whitaker	1.00	.45	.12
366	Lance Parrish	.40	.18	.05
367	Tim Corcoran	.10	.05	.01
368	Pat Underwood	.10	.05	.01
369	Al Cowens	.10	.05	.01
370	Sparky Anderson MG	.20	.09	.03
371	Pete Rose	2.00	.90	.25
372	Phil Garner	.20	.09	.03
373	Steve Nicosia	.10	.05	.01
374	John Candelaria	.20	.09	.03
375	Don Robinson	.10	.05	.01
376	Lee Lacy	.10	.05	.01
377	John Milner	.10	.05	.01
378	Craig Reynolds	.10	.05	.01
379A	Luis Pujois P1 ERR	.20	.09	.03
	(Name misspelled)			
379B	Luis Pujols P2 COR	.10	.05	.01
380	Joe Niekro	.20	.09	.03
381	Joaquin Andujar	.20	.09	.03
382	Keith Moreland	.20	.09	.03

☐ 383 Jose Cruz	.20	.09	.03
☐ 384 Bill Virdon MG	.10	.05	.01
☐ 385 Jim Sundberg	.20	.09	.03
☐ 386 Doc Medich	.10	.05	.01
☐ 387 Al Oliver	.20	.09	.03
☐ 388 Jim Norris	.10	.05	.01
☐ 389 Bob Bailor	.10	.05	.01
☐ 390 Ernie Whitt	.10	.05	.01
☐ 391 Otto Velez	.10	.05	.01
☐ 392 Roy Howell	.10	.05	.01
☐ 393 Bob Walk	.20	.09	.03
☐ 394 Doug Flynn	.10	.05	.01
☐ 395 Pete Falcone	.10	.05	.01
☐ 396 Tom Hausman	.10	.05	.01
☐ 397 Elliott Maddox	.10	.05	.01
☐ 398 Mike Squires	.10	.05	.01
☐ 399 Marvis Foley	.10	.05	.01
☐ 400 Steve Trout	.10	.05	.01
☐ 401 Wayne Nordhagen	.10	.05	.01
☐ 402 Tony LaRussa MG	.20	.09	.03
☐ 403 Bruce Bochte	.10	.05	.01
☐ 404 Bake McBride	.10	.05	.01
☐ 405 Jerry Narron	.10	.05	.01
☐ 406 Rob Dressler	.10	.05	.01
☐ 407 Dave Heaverlo	.10	.05	.01
☐ 408 Tom Paciorek	.20	.09	.03
☐ 409 Carney Lansford	.20	.09	.03
☐ 410 Brian Downing	.20	.09	.03
☐ 411 Don Aase	.10	.05	.01
☐ 412 Jim Barr	.10	.05	.01
☐ 413 Don Baylor	.40	.18	.05
☐ 414 Jim Fregosi MG	.10	.05	.01
☐ 415 Dallas Green MG	.10	.05	.01
☐ 416 Dave Lopes	.20	.09	.03
☐ 417 Jerry Reuss	.20	.09	.03
☐ 418 Rick Sutcliffe	.40	.18	.05
☐ 419 Derrel Thomas	.10	.05	.01
☐ 420 Tom Lasorda MG	.20	.09	.03
☐ 421 Charles Leibrandt	.40	.18	.05
☐ 422 Tom Seaver	1.25	.55	.16
☐ 423 Ron Oester	.10	.05	.01
☐ 424 Junior Kennedy	.10	.05	.01
☐ 425 Tom Seaver	1.25	.55	.16
☐ 426 Bobby Cox MG	.10	.05	.01
☐ 427 Leon Durham	.20	.09	.03
☐ 428 Terry Kennedy	.10	.05	.01
☐ 429 Silvio Martinez	.10	.05	.01
☐ 430 George Hendrick	.20	.09	.03
☐ 431 Red Schoendienst MG	.10	.05	.01
☐ 432 Johnnie LeMaster	.10	.05	.01
☐ 433 Vida Blue	.20	.09	.03
☐ 434 John Montefusco	.10	.05	.01
☐ 435 Terry Whitfield	.10	.05	.01
☐ 436 Dave Bristol MG	.10	.05	.01
☐ 437 Dale Murphy	.75	.35	.09
☐ 438 Jerry Dybzinski	.10	.05	.01
☐ 439 Jorge Orta	.10	.05	.01
☐ 440 Wayne Garland	.10	.05	.01
☐ 441 Miguel Dilone	.10	.05	.01
☐ 442 Dave Garcia MG	.10	.05	.01
☐ 443 Don Money	.10	.05	.01
☐ 444A Buck Martinez P1 ERR	.20	.09	.03
(Reverse negative)			
☐ 444B Buck Martinez	.10	.05	.01
P2 COR			
☐ 445 Jerry Augustine	.10	.05	.01
☐ 446 Ben Oglivie	.20	.09	.03
☐ 447 Jim Slaton	.10	.05	.01
☐ 448 Doyle Alexander	.10	.05	.01
☐ 449 Tony Bernazard	.10	.05	.01
☐ 450 Scott Sanderson	.20	.09	.03
☐ 451 David Palmer	.10	.05	.01
☐ 452 Stan Bahnsen	.10	.05	.01
☐ 453 Dick Williams MG	.10	.05	.01
☐ 454 Rick Burleson	.10	.05	.01
☐ 455 Gary Allenson	.10	.05	.01
☐ 456 Bob Stanley	.10	.05	.01
☐ 457A John Tudor P1 ERR	.20	.09	.03
(Lifetime W-L "9.7")			
☐ 457B John Tudor P2 COR	.20	.09	.03
(Corrected "9-7")			
☐ 458 Dwight Evans	.40	.18	.05
☐ 459 Glenn Hubbard	.10	.05	.01
☐ 460 U.L. Washington	.10	.05	.01
☐ 461 Larry Gura	.10	.05	.01
☐ 462 Rich Gale	.10	.05	.01
☐ 463 Hal McRae	.40	.18	.05
☐ 464 Jim Frey MG	.10	.05	.01
☐ 465 Bucky Dent	.20	.09	.03
☐ 466 Dennis Werth	.10	.05	.01
☐ 467 Ron Davis	.10	.05	.01
☐ 468 Reggie Jackson UER	2.00	.90	.25
(32 HR in 1970,			
should be 23)			
☐ 469 Bobby Brown	.10	.05	.01
☐ 470 Mike Davis	.10	.05	.01
☐ 471 Gaylord Perry	.40	.18	.05
☐ 472 Mark Belanger	.20	.09	.03
☐ 473 Jim Palmer	.75	.35	.09
☐ 474 Sammy Stewart	.10	.05	.01
☐ 475 Tim Stoddard	.10	.05	.01
☐ 476 Steve Stone	.20	.09	.03
☐ 477 Jeff Newman	.10	.05	.01
☐ 478 Steve McCatty	.10	.05	.01
☐ 479 Billy Martin MG	.40	.18	.05
☐ 480 Mitchell Page	.10	.05	.01
☐ 481 Steve Carlton CY	1.00	.45	.12
☐ 482 Bill Buckner	.20	.09	.03
☐ 483A Ivan DeJesus P1 ERR	.20	.09	.03
(Lifetime hits "702")			
☐ 483B Ivan DeJesus P2 COR	.10	.05	.01
(Lifetime hits "642")			
☐ 484 Cliff Johnson	.10	.05	.01
☐ 485 Lenny Randle	.10	.05	.01
☐ 486 Larry Milbourne	.10	.05	.01
☐ 487 Roy Smalley	.10	.05	.01
☐ 488 John Castino	.10	.05	.01
☐ 489 Ron Jackson	.10	.05	.01
☐ 490A Dave Roberts P1	.20	.09	.03
(Career Highlights:			
"Showed pop in")			
☐ 490B Dave Roberts P2	.10	.05	.01
("Declared himself")			
☐ 491 George Brett MVP	2.50	1.10	.30
☐ 492 Mike Cubbage	.10	.05	.01
☐ 493 Rob Wilfong	.10	.05	.01
☐ 494 Danny Goodwin	.10	.05	.01
☐ 495 Jose Morales	.10	.05	.01
☐ 496 Mickey Rivers	.20	.09	.03
☐ 497 Mike Edwards	.10	.05	.01
☐ 498 Mike Sadek	.10	.05	.01
☐ 499 Lenn Sakata	.10	.05	.01
☐ 500 Gene Michael MG	.10	.05	.01
☐ 501 Dave Roberts	.10	.05	.01
☐ 502 Steve Dillard	.10	.05	.01
☐ 503 Jim Essian	.10	.05	.01
☐ 504 Rance Mulliniks	.10	.05	.01
☐ 505 Darrell Porter	.10	.05	.01
☐ 506 Joe Torre MG	.20	.09	.03
☐ 507 Terry Crowley	.10	.05	.01
☐ 508 Bill Travers	.10	.05	.01
☐ 509 Nelson Norman	.10	.05	.01

☐ 510	Bob McClure	.10	.05	.01
☐ 511	Steve Howe	.20	.09	.03
☐ 512	Dave Rader	.10	.05	.01
☐ 513	Mick Kelleher	.10	.05	.01
☐ 514	Kiko Garcia	.10	.05	.01
☐ 515	Larry Biittner	.10	.05	.01
☐ 516A	Willie Norwood P1	.20	.09	.03
	(Career Highlights: "Spent most of")			
☐ 516B	Willie Norwood P2	.10	.05	.01
	("Traded to Seattle")			
☐ 517	Bo Diaz	.10	.05	.01
☐ 518	Juan Beniquez	.10	.05	.01
☐ 519	Scot Thompson	.10	.05	.01
☐ 520	Jim Tracy	.10	.05	.01
☐ 521	Carlos Lezcano	.10	.05	.01
☐ 522	Joe Amalfitano MG	.10	.05	.01
☐ 523	Preston Hanna	.10	.05	.01
☐ 524A	Ray Burris P1	.20	.09	.03
	(Career Highlights: "Went on ...")			
☐ 524B	Ray Burris P2	.10	.05	.01
	("Drafted by ...")			
☐ 525	Broderick Perkins	.10	.05	.01
☐ 526	Mickey Hatcher	.10	.05	.01
☐ 527	John Goryl MG	.10	.05	.01
☐ 528	Dick Davis	.10	.05	.01
☐ 529	Butch Wynegar	.10	.05	.01
☐ 530	Sal Butera	.10	.05	.01
☐ 531	Jerry Koosman	.20	.09	.03
☐ 532A	Geoff Zahn P1	.20	.09	.03
	(Career Highlights: "Was 2nd in")			
☐ 532B	Geoff Zahn P2	.10	.05	.01
	("Signed a 3 year")			
☐ 533	Dennis Martinez	.20	.09	.03
☐ 534	Gary Thomasson	.10	.05	.01
☐ 535	Steve Macko	.10	.05	.01
☐ 536	Jim Kaat	.20	.09	.03
☐ 537	Best Hitters	2.50	1.10	.30
	George Brett Rod Carew			
☐ 538	Tim Raines	4.00	1.80	.50
☐ 539	Keith Smith	.10	.05	.01
☐ 540	Ken Macha	.10	.05	.01
☐ 541	Burt Hooton	.10	.05	.01
☐ 542	Butch Hobson	.20	.09	.03
☐ 543	Bill Stein	.10	.05	.01
☐ 544	Dave Stapleton	.10	.05	.01
☐ 545	Bob Pate	.10	.05	.01
☐ 546	Doug Corbett	.10	.05	.01
☐ 547	Darrell Jackson	.10	.05	.01
☐ 548	Pete Redfern	.10	.05	.01
☐ 549	Roger Erickson	.10	.05	.01
☐ 550	Al Hrabosky	.10	.05	.01
☐ 551	Dick Tidrow	.10	.05	.01
☐ 552	Dave Ford	.10	.05	.01
☐ 553	Dave Kingman	.20	.09	.03
☐ 554A	Mike Vail P1	.20	.09	.03
	(Career Highlights: "After two ...")			
☐ 554B	Mike Vail P2	.10	.05	.01
	("Traded to ...")			
☐ 555A	Jerry Martin P1	.20	.09	.03
	(Career Highlights: "Overcame a ...")			
☐ 555B	Jerry Martin P2	.10	.05	.01
	("Traded to ...")			
☐ 556A	Jesus Figueroa P1	.20	.09	.03
	(Career Highlights: "Had an ...")			
☐ 556B	Jesus Figueroa P2	.10	.05	.01
	("Traded to ...")			
☐ 557	Don Stanhouse	.10	.05	.01
☐ 558	Barry Foote	.10	.05	.01
☐ 559	Tim Blackwell	.10	.05	.01
☐ 560	Bruce Sutter	.20	.09	.03
☐ 561	Rick Reuschel	.20	.09	.03
☐ 562	Lynn McGlothen	.10	.05	.01
☐ 563A	Bob Owchinko P1	.10	.05	.01
	(Career Highlights: "Traded to ...")			
☐ 563B	Bob Owchinko P2	.10	.05	.01
	("Involved in a ...")			
☐ 564	John Verhoeven	.10	.05	.01
☐ 565	Ken Landreaux	.10	.05	.01
☐ 566A	Glen Adams P1 ERR	.20	.09	.03
	(Name misspelled)			
☐ 566B	Glenn Adams P2 COR	.10	.05	.01
☐ 567	Hosken Powell	.10	.05	.01
☐ 568	Dick Noles	.10	.05	.01
☐ 569	Danny Ainge	3.00	1.35	.35
☐ 570	Bobby Mattick MG	.10	.05	.01
☐ 571	Joe Lefebvre	.10	.05	.01
☐ 572	Bobby Clark	.10	.05	.01
☐ 573	Dennis Lamp	.10	.05	.01
☐ 574	Randy Lerch	.10	.05	.01
☐ 575	Mookie Wilson	.40	.18	.05
☐ 576	Ron LeFlore	.20	.09	.03
☐ 577	Jim Dwyer	.10	.05	.01
☐ 578	Bill Castro	.10	.05	.01
☐ 579	Greg Minton	.10	.05	.01
☐ 580	Mark Littell	.10	.05	.01
☐ 581	Andy Hassler	.10	.05	.01
☐ 582	Dave Stieb	.20	.09	.03
☐ 583	Ken Oberkfell	.10	.05	.01
☐ 584	Larry Bradford	.10	.05	.01
☐ 585	Fred Stanley	.10	.05	.01
☐ 586	Bill Caudill	.10	.05	.01
☐ 587	Doug Capilla	.10	.05	.01
☐ 588	George Riley	.10	.05	.01
☐ 589	Willie Hernandez	.20	.09	.03
☐ 590	Mike Schmidt MVP	1.50	.70	.19
☐ 591	Steve Stone CY	.10	.05	.01
☐ 592	Rick Sofield	.10	.05	.01
☐ 593	Bombo Rivera	.10	.05	.01
☐ 594	Gary Ward	.10	.05	.01
☐ 595A	Dave Edwards P1	.20	.09	.03
	(Career Highlights: "Sidelined the")			
☐ 595B	Dave Edwards P2	.10	.05	.01
	("Traded to ...")			
☐ 596	Mike Proly	.10	.05	.01
☐ 597	Tommy Boggs	.10	.05	.01
☐ 598	Greg Gross	.10	.05	.01
☐ 599	Elias Sosa	.10	.05	.01
☐ 600	Pat Kelly	.10	.05	.01
☐ 601A	Checklist 1-120 P1	.20	.09	.03
	ERR Unnumbered (51 Donahue)			
☐ 601B	Checklist 1-120 P2	.40	.18	.05
	COR Unnumbered (51 Donohue)			
☐ 602	Checklist 121-240	.20	.09	.03
	Unnumbered			
☐ 603A	Checklist 241-360 P1	.20	.09	.03
	ERR Unnumbered (306 Mathews)			
☐ 603B	Checklist 241-360 P2	.20	.09	.03
	COR Unnumbered (306 Matthews)			
☐ 604A	Checklist 361-480 P1	.20	.09	.03

ERR Unnumbered
(379 Pujois)
- [ ] 604B Checklist 361-480 P2 .20 .09 .03
COR Unnumbered
(379 Pujois)
- [ ] 605A Checklist 481-600 P1 .20 .09 .03
ERR Unnumbered
(566 Glen Adams)
- [ ] 605B Checklist 481-600 P2 .20 .09 .03
COR Unnumbered
(566 Glenn Adams)

1982 Donruss

 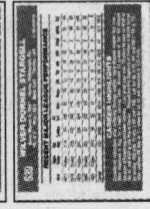

The 1982 Donruss set contains 653 numbered cards and the seven unnumbered checklists; each card measures 2 1/2" by 3 1/2". The first 26 cards of this set are entitled Donruss Diamond Kings (DK) and feature the artwork of Dick Perez of Perez-Steele Galleries. The set was marketed with puzzle pieces rather than bubble gum. There are 63 pieces to the puzzle, which, when put together, make a collage of Babe Ruth entitled "Hall of Fame Diamond King." The card stock in this year's Donruss cards is considerably thicker than that of the 1981 cards. The seven unnumbered checklist cards are arbitrarily assigned numbers 654 through 660 and are listed at the end of the list below. Rookie Cards in this set include George Bell, Brett Butler, Kent Hrbek, Cal Ripken Jr., Steve Sax, Lee Smith, and Dave Stewart.

	NRMT-MT	EXC	G-VG
COMPLETE SET (660)	70.00	32.00	8.75
COMPLETE FACT.SET (660)	80.00	36.00	10.00
COMMON CARD (1-660)	.10	.05	.01
[ ] 1 Pete Rose DK	2.00	.90	.25
[ ] 2 Gary Carter DK	.40	.18	.05
[ ] 3 Steve Garvey DK	.20	.09	.03
[ ] 4 Vida Blue DK	.15	.07	.02
[ ] 5A Alan Trammel DK ERR.	1.00	.45	.12
(Name misspelled)			
[ ] 5B Alan Trammell DK	.50	.23	.06
COR			
[ ] 6 Len Barker DK	.15	.07	.02
[ ] 7 Dwight Evans DK	.20	.09	.03
[ ] 8 Rod Carew DK	.60	.25	.07
[ ] 9 George Hendrick DK	.15	.07	.02
[ ] 10 Phil Niekro DK	.20	.09	.03
[ ] 11 Richie Zisk DK	.15	.07	.02
[ ] 12 Dave Parker DK	.20	.09	.03
[ ] 13 Nolan Ryan DK	4.00	1.80	.50
[ ] 14 Ivan DeJesus DK	.15	.07	.02
[ ] 15 George Brett DK	2.00	.90	.25
[ ] 16 Tom Seaver DK	.75	.35	.09
[ ] 17 Dave Kingman DK	.15	.07	.02
[ ] 18 Dave Winfield DK	1.50	.70	.19
[ ] 19 Mike Norris DK	.15	.07	.02
[ ] 20 Carlton Fisk DK	.40	.18	.05
[ ] 21 Ozzie Smith DK	2.00	.90	.25
[ ] 22 Roy Smalley DK	.15	.07	.02
[ ] 23 Buddy Bell DK	.15	.07	.02
[ ] 24 Ken Singleton DK	.15	.07	.02
[ ] 25 John Mayberry DK	.15	.07	.02
[ ] 26 Gorman Thomas DK	.15	.07	.02
[ ] 27 Earl Weaver MG	.15	.07	.02
[ ] 28 Rollie Fingers	.40	.18	.05
[ ] 29 Sparky Anderson MG	.15	.07	.02
[ ] 30 Dennis Eckersley	.60	.25	.07
[ ] 31 Dave Winfield	1.50	.70	.19
[ ] 32 Burt Hooton	.10	.05	.01
[ ] 33 Rick Waits	.10	.05	.01
[ ] 34 George Brett	3.50	1.55	.45
[ ] 35 Steve McCatty	.10	.05	.01
[ ] 36 Steve Rogers	.10	.05	.01
[ ] 37 Bill Stein	.10	.05	.01
[ ] 38 Steve Renko	.10	.05	.01
[ ] 39 Mike Squires	.10	.05	.01
[ ] 40 George Hendrick	.15	.07	.02
[ ] 41 Bob Knepper	.10	.05	.01
[ ] 42 Steve Carlton	.75	.35	.09
[ ] 43 Larry Biittner	.10	.05	.01
[ ] 44 Chris Welsh	.10	.05	.01
[ ] 45 Steve Nicosia	.10	.05	.01
[ ] 46 Jack Clark	.15	.07	.02
[ ] 47 Chris Chambliss	.15	.07	.02
[ ] 48 Ivan DeJesus	.10	.05	.01
[ ] 49 Lee Mazzilli	.10	.05	.01
[ ] 50 Julio Cruz	.10	.05	.01
[ ] 51 Pete Redfern	.10	.05	.01
[ ] 52 Dave Stieb	.15	.07	.02
[ ] 53 Doug Corbett	.10	.05	.01
[ ] 54 Jorge Bell	.75	.35	.09
[ ] 55 Joe Simpson	.10	.05	.01
[ ] 56 Rusty Staub	.15	.07	.02
[ ] 57 Hector Cruz	.10	.05	.01
[ ] 58 Claudell Washington	.10	.05	.01
[ ] 59 Enrique Romo	.10	.05	.01
[ ] 60 Gary Lavelle	.10	.05	.01
[ ] 61 Tim Flannery	.10	.05	.01
[ ] 62 Joe Nolan	.10	.05	.01
[ ] 63 Larry Bowa	.15	.07	.02
[ ] 64 Sixto Lezcano	.10	.05	.01
[ ] 65 Joe Sambito	.10	.05	.01
[ ] 66 Bruce Kison	.10	.05	.01
[ ] 67 Wayne Nordhagen	.10	.05	.01
[ ] 68 Woodie Fryman	.10	.05	.01
[ ] 69 Billy Sample	.10	.05	.01
[ ] 70 Amos Otis	.15	.07	.02
[ ] 71 Matt Keough	.10	.05	.01
[ ] 72 Toby Harrah	.15	.07	.02
[ ] 73 Dave Righetti	.40	.18	.05
[ ] 74 Carl Yastrzemski	.75	.35	.09
[ ] 75 Bob Welch	.15	.07	.02
[ ] 76A Alan Trammell ERR	1.50	.70	.19
(Name misspelled)			
[ ] 76B Alan Trammell COR	1.00	.45	.12
[ ] 77 Rick Dempsey	.15	.07	.02
[ ] 78 Paul Molitor	1.00	.45	.12
[ ] 79 Dennis Martinez	.15	.07	.02
[ ] 80 Jim Slaton	.10	.05	.01
[ ] 81 Champ Summers	.10	.05	.01

☐ 82	Carney Lansford	.15	.07	.02
☐ 83	Barry Foote	.10	.05	.01
☐ 84	Steve Garvey	.40	.18	.05
☐ 85	Rick Manning	.10	.05	.01
☐ 86	John Wathan	.10	.05	.01
☐ 87	Brian Kingman	.10	.05	.01
☐ 88	Andre Dawson UER	1.00	.45	.12
	(Middle name Fernando, should be Nolan)			
☐ 89	Jim Kern	.10	.05	.01
☐ 90	Bobby Grich	.15	.07	.02
☐ 91	Bob Forsch	.10	.05	.01
☐ 92	Art Howe	.10	.05	.01
☐ 93	Marty Bystrom	.10	.05	.01
☐ 94	Ozzie Smith	3.00	1.35	.35
☐ 95	Dave Parker	.20	.09	.03
☐ 96	Doyle Alexander	.10	.05	.01
☐ 97	Al Hrabosky	.10	.05	.01
☐ 98	Frank Taveras	.10	.05	.01
☐ 99	Tim Blackwell	.10	.05	.01
☐ 100	Floyd Bannister	.10	.05	.01
☐ 101	Alfredo Griffin	.10	.05	.01
☐ 102	Dave Engle	.10	.05	.01
☐ 103	Mario Soto	.10	.05	.01
☐ 104	Ross Baumgarten	.10	.05	.01
☐ 105	Ken Singleton	.15	.07	.02
☐ 106	Ted Simmons	.15	.07	.02
☐ 107	Jack Morris	.40	.18	.05
☐ 108	Bob Watson	.15	.07	.02
☐ 109	Dwight Evans	.20	.09	.03
☐ 110	Tom Lasorda MG	.15	.07	.02
☐ 111	Bert Blyleven	.20	.09	.03
☐ 112	Dan Quisenberry	.15	.07	.02
☐ 113	Rickey Henderson	3.00	1.35	.35
☐ 114	Gary Carter	.50	.23	.06
☐ 115	Brian Downing	.15	.07	.02
☐ 116	Al Oliver	.15	.07	.02
☐ 117	LaMarr Hoyt	.10	.05	.01
☐ 118	Cesar Cedeno	.15	.07	.02
☐ 119	Keith Moreland	.10	.05	.01
☐ 120	Bob Shirley	.10	.05	.01
☐ 121	Terry Kennedy	.10	.05	.01
☐ 122	Frank Pastore	.10	.05	.01
☐ 123	Gene Garber	.10	.05	.01
☐ 124	Tony Pena	.15	.07	.02
☐ 125	Allen Ripley	.10	.05	.01
☐ 126	Randy Martz	.10	.05	.01
☐ 127	Richie Zisk	.10	.05	.01
☐ 128	Mike Scott	.15	.07	.02
☐ 129	Lloyd Moseby	.10	.05	.01
☐ 130	Rob Wilfong	.10	.05	.01
☐ 131	Tim Stoddard	.10	.05	.01
☐ 132	Gorman Thomas	.15	.07	.02
☐ 133	Dan Petry	.10	.05	.01
☐ 134	Bob Stanley	.10	.05	.01
☐ 135	Lou Piniella	.15	.07	.02
☐ 136	Pedro Guerrero	.15	.07	.02
☐ 137	Len Barker	.10	.05	.01
☐ 138	Rich Gale	.10	.05	.01
☐ 139	Wayne Gross	.10	.05	.01
☐ 140	Tim Wallach	.75	.35	.09
☐ 141	Gene Mauch MG	.10	.05	.01
☐ 142	Doc Medich	.10	.05	.01
☐ 143	Tony Bernazard	.10	.05	.01
☐ 144	Bill Virdon MG	.10	.05	.01
☐ 145	John Littlefield	.10	.05	.01
☐ 146	Dave Bergman	.10	.05	.01
☐ 147	Dick Davis	.10	.05	.01
☐ 148	Tom Seaver	.75	.35	.09
☐ 149	Matt Sinatro	.10	.05	.01
☐ 150	Chuck Tanner MG	.10	.05	.01
☐ 151	Leon Durham	.10	.05	.01
☐ 152	Gene Tenace	.10	.05	.01
☐ 153	Al Bumbry	.15	.07	.02
☐ 154	Mark Brouhard	.10	.05	.01
☐ 155	Rick Peters	.10	.05	.01
☐ 156	Jerry Remy	.10	.05	.01
☐ 157	Rick Reuschel	.15	.07	.02
☐ 158	Steve Howe	.10	.05	.01
☐ 159	Alan Bannister	.10	.05	.01
☐ 160	U.L. Washington	.10	.05	.01
☐ 161	Rick Langford	.10	.05	.01
☐ 162	Bill Gullickson	.15	.07	.02
☐ 163	Mark Wagner	.10	.05	.01
☐ 164	Geoff Zahn	.10	.05	.01
☐ 165	Ron LeFlore	.15	.07	.02
☐ 166	Dane Iorg	.10	.05	.01
☐ 167	Joe Niekro	.15	.07	.02
☐ 168	Pete Rose	1.50	.70	.19
☐ 169	Dave Collins	.10	.05	.01
☐ 170	Rick Wise	.10	.05	.01
☐ 171	Jim Bibby	.10	.05	.01
☐ 172	Larry Herndon	.10	.05	.01
☐ 173	Bob Horner	.15	.07	.02
☐ 174	Steve Dillard	.10	.05	.01
☐ 175	Mookie Wilson	.15	.07	.02
☐ 176	Dan Meyer	.10	.05	.01
☐ 177	Fernando Arroyo	.10	.05	.01
☐ 178	Jackson Todd	.10	.05	.01
☐ 179	Darrell Jackson	.10	.05	.01
☐ 180	Alvis Woods	.10	.05	.01
☐ 181	Jim Anderson	.10	.05	.01
☐ 182	Dave Kingman	.15	.07	.02
☐ 183	Steve Henderson	.10	.05	.01
☐ 184	Brian Asselstine	.10	.05	.01
☐ 185	Rod Scurry	.10	.05	.01
☐ 186	Fred Breining	.10	.05	.01
☐ 187	Danny Boone	.10	.05	.01
☐ 188	Junior Kennedy	.10	.05	.01
☐ 189	Sparky Lyle	.15	.07	.02
☐ 190	Whitey Herzog MG	.15	.07	.02
☐ 191	Dave Smith	.10	.05	.01
☐ 192	Ed Ott	.10	.05	.01
☐ 193	Greg Luzinski	.15	.07	.02
☐ 194	Bill Lee	.10	.05	.01
☐ 195	Don Zimmer MG	.10	.05	.01
☐ 196	Hal McRae	.20	.09	.03
☐ 197	Mike Norris	.10	.05	.01
☐ 198	Duane Kuiper	.10	.05	.01
☐ 199	Rick Cerone	.10	.05	.01
☐ 200	Jim Rice	.20	.09	.03
☐ 201	Steve Yeager	.10	.05	.01
☐ 202	Tom Brookens	.10	.05	.01
☐ 203	Jose Morales	.10	.05	.01
☐ 204	Roy Howell	.10	.05	.01
☐ 205	Tippy Martinez	.10	.05	.01
☐ 206	Moose Haas	.10	.05	.01
☐ 207	Al Cowens	.10	.05	.01
☐ 208	Dave Stapleton	.10	.05	.01
☐ 209	Bucky Dent	.15	.07	.02
☐ 210	Ron Cey	.15	.07	.02
☐ 211	Jorge Orta	.10	.05	.01
☐ 212	Jamie Quirk	.10	.05	.01
☐ 213	Jeff Jones	.10	.05	.01
☐ 214	Tim Raines	2.00	.90	.25
☐ 215	Jon Matlack	.10	.05	.01
☐ 216	Rod Carew	.75	.35	.09
☐ 217	Jim Kaat	.15	.07	.02
☐ 218	Joe Pittman	.10	.05	.01
☐ 219	Larry Christenson	.10	.05	.01
☐ 220	Juan Bonilla	.10	.05	.01
☐ 221	Mike Easler	.10	.05	.01

☐ 222	Vida Blue	.15	.07	.02
☐ 223	Rick Camp	.10	.05	.01
☐ 224	Mike Jorgensen	.10	.05	.01
☐ 225	Jody Davis	.10	.05	.01
☐ 226	Mike Parrott	.10	.05	.01
☐ 227	Jim Clancy	.10	.05	.01
☐ 228	Hosken Powell	.10	.05	.01
☐ 229	Tom Hume	.10	.05	.01
☐ 230	Britt Burns	.10	.05	.01
☐ 231	Jim Palmer	.60	.25	.07
☐ 232	Bob Rodgers MG	.10	.05	.01
☐ 233	Milt Wilcox	.10	.05	.01
☐ 234	Dave Revering	.10	.05	.01
☐ 235	Mike Torrez	.10	.05	.01
☐ 236	Robert Castillo	.10	.05	.01
☐ 237	Von Hayes	.15	.07	.02
☐ 238	Renie Martin	.10	.05	.01
☐ 239	Dwayne Murphy	.10	.05	.01
☐ 240	Rodney Scott	.10	.05	.01
☐ 241	Fred Patek	.10	.05	.01
☐ 242	Mickey Rivers	.10	.05	.01
☐ 243	Steve Trout	.10	.05	.01
☐ 244	Jose Cruz	.15	.07	.02
☐ 245	Manny Trillo	.10	.05	.01
☐ 246	Lary Sorensen	.10	.05	.01
☐ 247	Dave Edwards	.10	.05	.01
☐ 248	Dan Driessen	.10	.05	.01
☐ 249	Tommy Boggs	.10	.05	.01
☐ 250	Dale Berra	.10	.05	.01
☐ 251	Ed Whitson	.10	.05	.01
☐ 252	Lee Smith	6.00	2.70	.75
☐ 253	Tom Paciorek	.15	.07	.02
☐ 254	Pat Zachry	.10	.05	.01
☐ 255	Luis Leal	.10	.05	.01
☐ 256	John Castino	.10	.05	.01
☐ 257	Rich Dauer	.10	.05	.01
☐ 258	Cecil Cooper	.15	.07	.02
☐ 259	Dave Rozema	.10	.05	.01
☐ 260	John Tudor	.15	.07	.02
☐ 261	Jerry Mumphrey	.10	.05	.01
☐ 262	Jay Johnstone	.15	.07	.02
☐ 263	Bo Diaz	.10	.05	.01
☐ 264	Dennis Leonard	.10	.05	.01
☐ 265	Jim Spencer	.10	.05	.01
☐ 266	John Milner	.10	.05	.01
☐ 267	Don Aase	.10	.05	.01
☐ 268	Jim Sundberg	.15	.07	.02
☐ 269	Lamar Johnson	.10	.05	.01
☐ 270	Frank LaCorte	.10	.05	.01
☐ 271	Barry Evans	.10	.05	.01
☐ 272	Enos Cabell	.10	.05	.01
☐ 273	Del Unser	.10	.05	.01
☐ 274	George Foster	.15	.07	.02
☐ 275	Brett Butler	2.00	.90	.25
☐ 276	Lee Lacy	.10	.05	.01
☐ 277	Ken Reitz	.10	.05	.01
☐ 278	Keith Hernandez	.20	.09	.03
☐ 279	Doug DeCinces	.15	.07	.02
☐ 280	Charlie Moore	.10	.05	.01
☐ 281	Lance Parrish	.20	.09	.03
☐ 282	Ralph Houk MG	.10	.05	.01
☐ 283	Rich Gossage	.20	.09	.03
☐ 284	Jerry Reuss	.10	.05	.01
☐ 285	Mike Stanton	.10	.05	.01
☐ 286	Frank White	.15	.07	.02
☐ 287	Bob Owchinko	.10	.05	.01
☐ 288	Scott Sanderson	.15	.07	.02
☐ 289	Bump Wills	.10	.05	.01
☐ 290	Dave Frost	.10	.05	.01
☐ 291	Chet Lemon	.10	.05	.01
☐ 292	Tito Landrum	.10	.05	.01
☐ 293	Vern Ruhle	.10	.05	.01
☐ 294	Mike Schmidt	2.00	.90	.25
☐ 295	Sam Mejias	.10	.05	.01
☐ 296	Gary Lucas	.10	.05	.01
☐ 297	John Candelaria	.10	.05	.01
☐ 298	Jerry Martin	.10	.05	.01
☐ 299	Dale Murphy	.60	.25	.07
☐ 300	Mike Lum	.10	.05	.01
☐ 301	Tom Hausman	.10	.05	.01
☐ 302	Glenn Abbott	.10	.05	.01
☐ 303	Roger Erickson	.10	.05	.01
☐ 304	Otto Velez	.10	.05	.01
☐ 305	Danny Goodwin	.10	.05	.01
☐ 306	John Mayberry	.10	.05	.01
☐ 307	Lenny Randle	.10	.05	.01
☐ 308	Bob Bailor	.10	.05	.01
☐ 309	Jerry Morales	.10	.05	.01
☐ 310	Rufino Linares	.10	.05	.01
☐ 311	Kent Tekulve	.15	.07	.02
☐ 312	Joe Morgan	.60	.25	.07
☐ 313	John Urrea	.10	.05	.01
☐ 314	Paul Householder	.10	.05	.01
☐ 315	Garry Maddox	.10	.05	.01
☐ 316	Mike Ramsey	.10	.05	.01
☐ 317	Alan Ashby	.10	.05	.01
☐ 318	Bob Clark	.10	.05	.01
☐ 319	Tony LaRussa MG	.15	.07	.02
☐ 320	Charlie Lea	.10	.05	.01
☐ 321	Danny Darwin	.10	.05	.01
☐ 322	Cesar Geronimo	.10	.05	.01
☐ 323	Tom Underwood	.10	.05	.01
☐ 324	Andre Thornton	.10	.05	.01
☐ 325	Rudy May	.10	.05	.01
☐ 326	Frank Tanana	.15	.07	.02
☐ 327	Dave Lopes	.15	.07	.02
☐ 328	Richie Hebner	.10	.05	.01
☐ 329	Mike Flanagan	.15	.07	.02
☐ 330	Mike Caldwell	.10	.05	.01
☐ 331	Scott McGregor	.10	.05	.01
☐ 332	Jerry Augustine	.10	.05	.01
☐ 333	Stan Papi	.10	.05	.01
☐ 334	Rick Miller	.10	.05	.01
☐ 335	Graig Nettles	.15	.07	.02
☐ 336	Dusty Baker	.20	.09	.03
☐ 337	Dave Garcia MG	.10	.05	.01
☐ 338	Larry Gura	.10	.05	.01
☐ 339	Cliff Johnson	.10	.05	.01
☐ 340	Warren Cromartie	.10	.05	.01
☐ 341	Steve Comer	.10	.05	.01
☐ 342	Rick Burleson	.10	.05	.01
☐ 343	John Martin	.10	.05	.01
☐ 344	Craig Reynolds	.10	.05	.01
☐ 345	Mike Proly	.10	.05	.01
☐ 346	Ruppert Jones	.10	.05	.01
☐ 347	Omar Moreno	.10	.05	.01
☐ 348	Greg Minton	.10	.05	.01
☐ 349	Rick Mahler	.10	.05	.01
☐ 350	Alex Trevino	.10	.05	.01
☐ 351	Mike Krukow	.10	.05	.01
☐ 352A	Shane Rawley ERR (Photo actually Jim Anderson)	.20	.09	.03
☐ 352B	Shane Rawley COR	.10	.05	.01
☐ 353	Garth Iorg	.10	.05	.01
☐ 354	Pete Mackanin	.10	.05	.01
☐ 355	Paul Moskau	.10	.05	.01
☐ 356	Richard Dotson	.10	.05	.01
☐ 357	Steve Stone	.15	.07	.02
☐ 358	Larry Hisle	.10	.05	.01
☐ 359	Aurelio Lopez	.10	.05	.01
☐ 360	Oscar Gamble	.10	.05	.01

☐ 361 Tom Burgmeier	.10	.05	.01
☐ 362 Terry Forster	.10	.05	.01
☐ 363 Joe Charboneau	.10	.05	.01
☐ 364 Ken Brett	.10	.05	.01
☐ 365 Tony Armas	.10	.05	.01
☐ 366 Chris Speier	.10	.05	.01
☐ 367 Fred Lynn	.15	.07	.02
☐ 368 Buddy Bell	.15	.07	.02
☐ 369 Jim Essian	.10	.05	.01
☐ 370 Terry Puhl	.10	.05	.01
☐ 371 Greg Gross	.10	.05	.01
☐ 372 Bruce Sutter	.15	.07	.02
☐ 373 Joe Lefebvre	.10	.05	.01
☐ 374 Ray Knight	.15	.07	.02
☐ 375 Bruce Benedict	.10	.05	.01
☐ 376 Tim Foli	.10	.05	.01
☐ 377 Al Holland	.10	.05	.01
☐ 378 Ken Kravec	.10	.05	.01
☐ 379 Jeff Burroughs	.10	.05	.01
☐ 380 Pete Falcone	.10	.05	.01
☐ 381 Ernie Whitt	.10	.05	.01
☐ 382 Brad Havens	.10	.05	.01
☐ 383 Terry Crowley	.10	.05	.01
☐ 384 Don Money	.10	.05	.01
☐ 385 Dan Schatzeder	.10	.05	.01
☐ 386 Gary Allenson	.10	.05	.01
☐ 387 Yogi Berra CO	.40	.18	.05
☐ 388 Ken Landreaux	.10	.05	.01
☐ 389 Mike Hargrove	.15	.07	.02
☐ 390 Darryl Motley	.10	.05	.01
☐ 391 Dave McKay	.10	.05	.01
☐ 392 Stan Bahnsen	.10	.05	.01
☐ 393 Ken Forsch	.10	.05	.01
☐ 394 Mario Mendoza	.10	.05	.01
☐ 395 Jim Morrison	.10	.05	.01
☐ 396 Mike Ivie	.10	.05	.01
☐ 397 Broderick Perkins	.10	.05	.01
☐ 398 Darrell Evans	.15	.07	.02
☐ 399 Ron Reed	.10	.05	.01
☐ 400 Johnny Bench	.75	.35	.09
☐ 401 Steve Bedrosian	.20	.09	.03
☐ 402 Bill Robinson	.15	.07	.02
☐ 403 Bill Buckner	.15	.07	.02
☐ 404 Ken Oberkfell	.10	.05	.01
☐ 405 Cal Ripken Jr.	55.00	25.00	7.00
☐ 406 Jim Gantner	.15	.07	.02
☐ 407 Kirk Gibson	.75	.35	.09
☐ 408 Tony Perez	.40	.18	.05
☐ 409 Tommy John UER (Text says 52-56 as Yankee, should be 52-26)	.20	.09	.03
☐ 410 Dave Stewart	1.50	.70	.19
☐ 411 Dan Spillner	.10	.05	.01
☐ 412 Willie Aikens	.10	.05	.01
☐ 413 Mike Heath	.10	.05	.01
☐ 414 Ray Burris	.10	.05	.01
☐ 415 Leon Roberts	.10	.05	.01
☐ 416 Mike Witt	.15	.07	.02
☐ 417 Bob Molinaro	.10	.05	.01
☐ 418 Steve Braun	.10	.05	.01
☐ 419 Nolan Ryan UER (Nisnumbering of Nolan's no-hitters on card back)	6.00	2.70	.75
☐ 420 Tug McGraw	.15	.07	.02
☐ 421 Dave Concepcion	.15	.07	.02
☐ 422A Juan Eichelberger ERR (Photo actually Gary Lucas)	.20	.09	.03
☐ 422B Juan Eichelberger	.10	.05	.01
COR			
☐ 423 Rick Rhoden	.10	.05	.01
☐ 424 Frank Robinson MG	.20	.09	.03
☐ 425 Eddie Miller	.10	.05	.01
☐ 426 Bill Caudill	.10	.05	.01
☐ 427 Doug Flynn	.10	.05	.01
☐ 428 Larry Andersen UER (Misspelled Anderson on card front)	.10	.05	.01
☐ 429 Al Williams	.10	.05	.01
☐ 430 Jerry Garvin	.10	.05	.01
☐ 431 Glenn Adams	.10	.05	.01
☐ 432 Barry Bonnell	.10	.05	.01
☐ 433 Jerry Narron	.10	.05	.01
☐ 434 John Stearns	.10	.05	.01
☐ 435 Mike Tyson	.10	.05	.01
☐ 436 Glenn Hubbard	.10	.05	.01
☐ 437 Eddie Solomon	.10	.05	.01
☐ 438 Jeff Leonard	.10	.05	.01
☐ 439 Randy Bass	.40	.18	.05
☐ 440 Mike LaCoss	.10	.05	.01
☐ 441 Gary Matthews	.15	.07	.02
☐ 442 Mark Littell	.10	.05	.01
☐ 443 Don Sutton	.40	.18	.05
☐ 444 John Harris	.10	.05	.01
☐ 445 Vada Pinson CO	.15	.07	.02
☐ 446 Elias Sosa	.10	.05	.01
☐ 447 Charlie Hough	.15	.07	.02
☐ 448 Willie Wilson	.15	.07	.02
☐ 449 Fred Stanley	.10	.05	.01
☐ 450 Tom Veryzer	.10	.05	.01
☐ 451 Ron Davis	.10	.05	.01
☐ 452 Mark Clear	.10	.05	.01
☐ 453 Bill Russell	.15	.07	.02
☐ 454 Lou Whitaker	.50	.23	.06
☐ 455 Dan Graham	.10	.05	.01
☐ 456 Reggie Cleveland	.10	.05	.01
☐ 457 Sammy Stewart	.10	.05	.01
☐ 458 Pete Vuckovich	.15	.07	.02
☐ 459 John Wockenfuss	.10	.05	.01
☐ 460 Glenn Hoffman	.10	.05	.01
☐ 461 Willie Randolph	.15	.07	.02
☐ 462 Fernando Valenzuela	.20	.09	.03
☐ 463 Ron Hassey	.10	.05	.01
☐ 464 Paul Splittorff	.10	.05	.01
☐ 465 Rob Picciolo	.10	.05	.01
☐ 466 Larry Parrish	.10	.05	.01
☐ 467 Johnny Grubb	.10	.05	.01
☐ 468 Dan Ford	.10	.05	.01
☐ 469 Silvio Martinez	.10	.05	.01
☐ 470 Kiko Garcia	.10	.05	.01
☐ 471 Bob Boone	.15	.07	.02
☐ 472 Luis Salazar	.10	.05	.01
☐ 473 Randy Niemann	.10	.05	.01
☐ 474 Tom Griffin	.10	.05	.01
☐ 475 Phil Niekro	.40	.18	.05
☐ 476 Hubie Brooks	.15	.07	.02
☐ 477 Dick Tidrow	.10	.05	.01
☐ 478 Jim Beattie	.10	.05	.01
☐ 479 Damaso Garcia	.10	.05	.01
☐ 480 Mickey Hatcher	.10	.05	.01
☐ 481 Joe Price	.10	.05	.01
☐ 482 Ed Farmer	.10	.05	.01
☐ 483 Eddie Murray	2.00	.90	.25
☐ 484 Ben Oglivie	.15	.07	.02
☐ 485 Kevin Saucier	.10	.05	.01
☐ 486 Bobby Murcer	.15	.07	.02
☐ 487 Bill Campbell	.10	.05	.01
☐ 488 Reggie Smith	.15	.07	.02
☐ 489 Wayne Garland	.10	.05	.01
☐ 490 Jim Wright	.10	.05	.01

☐ 491 Billy Martin MG	.15	.07	.02
☐ 492 Jim Fanning MG	.10	.05	.01
☐ 493 Don Baylor	.20	.09	.03
☐ 494 Rick Honeycutt	.10	.05	.01
☐ 495 Carlton Fisk	.75	.35	.09
☐ 496 Denny Walling	.10	.05	.01
☐ 497 Bake McBride	.10	.05	.01
☐ 498 Darrell Porter	.10	.05	.01
☐ 499 Gene Richards	.10	.05	.01
☐ 500 Ron Oester	.10	.05	.01
☐ 501 Ken Dayley	.10	.05	.01
☐ 502 Jason Thompson	.10	.05	.01
☐ 503 Milt May	.10	.05	.01
☐ 504 Doug Bird	.10	.05	.01
☐ 505 Bruce Bochte	.10	.05	.01
☐ 506 Neil Allen	.10	.05	.01
☐ 507 Joey McLaughlin	.10	.05	.01
☐ 508 Butch Wynegar	.10	.05	.01
☐ 509 Gary Roenicke	.10	.05	.01
☐ 510 Robin Yount	1.50	.70	.19
☐ 511 Dave Tobik	.10	.05	.01
☐ 512 Rich Gedman	.10	.05	.01
☐ 513 Gene Nelson	.10	.05	.01
☐ 514 Rick Monday	.10	.05	.01
☐ 515 Miguel Dilone	.10	.05	.01
☐ 516 Clint Hurdle	.10	.05	.01
☐ 517 Jeff Newman	.10	.05	.01
☐ 518 Grant Jackson	.10	.05	.01
☐ 519 Andy Hassler	.10	.05	.01
☐ 520 Pat Putnam	.10	.05	.01
☐ 521 Greg Pryor	.10	.05	.01
☐ 522 Tony Scott	.10	.05	.01
☐ 523 Steve Mura	.10	.05	.01
☐ 524 Johnnie LeMaster	.10	.05	.01
☐ 525 Dick Ruthven	.10	.05	.01
☐ 526 John McNamara MG	.10	.05	.01
☐ 527 Larry McWilliams	.10	.05	.01
☐ 528 Johnny Ray	.10	.05	.01
☐ 529 Pat Tabler	.15	.07	.02
☐ 530 Tom Herr	.15	.07	.02
☐ 531A San Diego Chicken	.75	.35	.09
COR (With TM)			
☐ 531B San Diego Chicken	.75	.35	.09
ERR (Without TM)			
☐ 532 Sal Butera	.10	.05	.01
☐ 533 Mike Griffin	.10	.05	.01
☐ 534 Kelvin Moore	.10	.05	.01
☐ 535 Reggie Jackson	1.00	.45	.12
☐ 536 Ed Romero	.10	.05	.01
☐ 537 Derrel Thomas	.10	.05	.01
☐ 538 Mike O'Berry	.10	.05	.01
☐ 539 Jack O'Connor	.10	.05	.01
☐ 540 Bob Ojeda	.20	.09	.03
☐ 541 Roy Lee Jackson	.10	.05	.01
☐ 542 Lynn Jones	.10	.05	.01
☐ 543 Gaylord Perry ERR	.40	.18	.05
☐ 544A Phil Garner ERR	.20	.09	.03
(Reverse negative)			
☐ 544B Phil Garner COR	.15	.07	.02
☐ 545 Garry Templeton	.15	.07	.02
☐ 546 Rafael Ramirez	.10	.05	.01
☐ 547 Jeff Reardon	.40	.18	.05
☐ 548 Ron Guidry	.15	.07	.02
☐ 549 Tim Laudner	.10	.05	.01
☐ 550 John Henry Johnson	.10	.05	.01
☐ 551 Chris Bando	.10	.05	.01
☐ 552 Bobby Brown	.10	.05	.01
☐ 553 Larry Bradford	.10	.05	.01
☐ 554 Scott Fletcher	.20	.09	.03
☐ 555 Jerry Royster	.10	.05	.01
☐ 556 Shooty Babitt UER	.10	.05	.01
(Spelled Babbitt			
on front)			
☐ 557 Kent Hrbek	1.00	.45	.12
☐ 558 Yankee Winners	.15	.07	.02
Ron Guidry			
Tommy John			
☐ 559 Mark Bomback	.10	.05	.01
☐ 560 Julio Valdez	.10	.05	.01
☐ 561 Buck Martinez	.10	.05	.01
☐ 562 Mike A. Marshall	.15	.07	.02
☐ 563 Rennie Stennett	.10	.05	.01
☐ 564 Steve Crawford	.10	.05	.01
☐ 565 Bob Babcock	.10	.05	.01
☐ 566 Johnny Podres CO	.15	.07	.02
☐ 567 Paul Serna	.10	.05	.01
☐ 568 Harold Baines	.75	.35	.09
☐ 569 Dave LaRoche	.10	.05	.01
☐ 570 Lee May	.15	.07	.02
☐ 571 Gary Ward	.10	.05	.01
☐ 572 John Denny	.10	.05	.01
☐ 573 Roy Smalley	.10	.05	.01
☐ 574 Bob Brenly	.10	.05	.01
☐ 575 Bronx Bombers	1.50	.70	.19
Reggie Jackson			
Dave Winfield			
☐ 576 Luis Pujols	.10	.05	.01
☐ 577 Butch Hobson	.15	.07	.02
☐ 578 Harvey Kuenn MG	.15	.07	.02
☐ 579 Cal Ripken Sr. CO	.15	.07	.02
☐ 580 Juan Berenguer	.10	.05	.01
☐ 581 Benny Ayala	.10	.05	.01
☐ 582 Vance Law	.10	.05	.01
☐ 583 Rick Leach	.10	.05	.01
☐ 584 George Frazier	.10	.05	.01
☐ 585 Phillies Finest	1.50	.70	.19
Pete Rose			
Mike Schmidt			
☐ 586 Joe Rudi	.10	.05	.01
☐ 587 Juan Beniquez	.10	.05	.01
☐ 588 Luis DeLeon	.10	.05	.01
☐ 589 Craig Swan	.10	.05	.01
☐ 590 Dave Chalk	.10	.05	.01
☐ 591 Billy Gardner MG	.10	.05	.01
☐ 592 Sal Bando	.15	.07	.02
☐ 593 Bert Campaneris	.15	.07	.02
☐ 594 Steve Kemp	.10	.05	.01
☐ 595A Randy Lerch ERR	.20	.09	.03
(Braves)			
☐ 595B Randy Lerch COR	.10	.05	.01
(Brewers)			
☐ 596 Bryan Clark	.10	.05	.01
☐ 597 Dave Ford	.10	.05	.01
☐ 598 Mike Scioscia	.15	.07	.02
☐ 599 John Lowenstein	.10	.05	.01
☐ 600 Rene Lachemann MG	.10	.05	.01
☐ 601 Mick Kelleher	.10	.05	.01
☐ 602 Ron Jackson	.10	.05	.01
☐ 603 Jerry Koosman	.15	.07	.02
☐ 604 Dave Goltz	.10	.05	.01
☐ 605 Ellis Valentine	.10	.05	.01
☐ 606 Lonnie Smith	.15	.07	.02
☐ 607 Joaquin Andujar	.15	.07	.02
☐ 608 Garry Hancock	.10	.05	.01
☐ 609 Jerry Turner	.10	.05	.01
☐ 610 Bob Bonner	.10	.05	.01
☐ 611 Jim Dwyer	.10	.05	.01
☐ 612 Terry Bulling	.10	.05	.01
☐ 613 Joel Youngblood	.10	.05	.01
☐ 614 Larry Milbourne	.10	.05	.01
☐ 615 Gene Roof UER	.10	.05	.01
(Name on front			

is Phil Roof)

		NRMT-MT	EXC	G-VG
☐ 616	Keith Drumwright	.10	.05	.01
☐ 617	Dave Rosello	.10	.05	.01
☐ 618	Rickey Keeton	.10	.05	.01
☐ 619	Dennis Lamp	.10	.05	.01
☐ 620	Sid Monge	.10	.05	.01
☐ 621	Jerry White	.10	.05	.01
☐ 622	Luis Aguayo	.10	.05	.01
☐ 623	Jamie Easterly	.10	.05	.01
☐ 624	Steve Sax	.50	.23	.06
☐ 625	Dave Roberts	.10	.05	.01
☐ 626	Rick Bosetti	.10	.05	.01
☐ 627	Terry Francona	.10	.05	.01
☐ 628	Pride of Reds	1.00	.45	.12
	Tom Seaver			
	Johnny Bench			
☐ 629	Paul Mirabella	.10	.05	.01
☐ 630	Rance Mulliniks	.10	.05	.01
☐ 631	Kevin Hickey	.10	.05	.01
☐ 632	Reid Nichols	.10	.05	.01
☐ 633	Dave Geisel	.10	.05	.01
☐ 634	Ken Griffey	.10	.05	.01
☐ 635	Bob Lemon MG	.15	.07	.02
☐ 636	Orlando Sanchez	.10	.05	.01
☐ 637	Bill Almon	.10	.05	.01
☐ 638	Danny Ainge	1.00	.45	.12
☐ 639	Willie Stargell	.50	.23	.06
☐ 640	Bob Sykes	.10	.05	.01
☐ 641	Ed Lynch	.10	.05	.01
☐ 642	John Ellis	.10	.05	.01
☐ 643	Ferguson Jenkins	.40	.18	.05
☐ 644	Lenn Sakata	.10	.05	.01
☐ 645	Julio Gonzalez	.10	.05	.01
☐ 646	Jesse Orosco	.10	.05	.01
☐ 647	Jerry Dybzinski	.10	.05	.01
☐ 648	Tommy Davis CO	.15	.07	.02
☐ 649	Ron Gardenhire	.10	.05	.01
☐ 650	Felipe Alou CO	.15	.07	.02
☐ 651	Harvey Haddix CO	.15	.07	.02
☐ 652	Willie Upshaw	.10	.05	.01
☐ 653	Bill Madlock	.15	.07	.02
☐ 654A	DK Checklist 1-26	.20	.09	.03
	ERR (Unnumbered)			
	(With Trammel)			
☐ 654B	DK Checklist 1-26	.15	.07	.02
	COR (Unnumbered)			
	(With Trammell)			
☐ 655	Checklist 27-130	.15	.07	.02
	(Unnumbered)			
☐ 656	Checklist 131-234	.15	.07	.02
	(Unnumbered)			
☐ 657	Checklist 235-338	.15	.07	.02
	(Unnumbered)			
☐ 658	Checklist 339-442	.15	.07	.02
	(Unnumbered)			
☐ 659	Checklist 443-544	.15	.07	.02
	(Unnumbered)			
☐ 660	Checklist 545-653	.15	.07	.02
	(Unnumbered)			

1983 Donruss

The cards in this 660-card set measure 2 1/2" by 3 1/2". The 1983 Donruss baseball set, issued with a 63-piece Diamond King puzzle, again leads off with a 26-card Diamond Kings (DK) series. Of the remaining 634 cards, two are combination cards, one portrays the San Diego Chicken, one

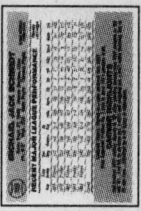

shows the completed Ty Cobb puzzle, and seven are unnumbered checklist cards. The seven unnumbered checklist cards are arbitrarily assigned numbers 654 through 660 and are listed at the end of the list below. The Donruss logo and the year of issue are shown in the upper left corner of the obverse. The card backs have black print on yellow and white and are numbered on a small ball design. The complete set price below includes only the more common of each variation pair. The key Rookie Cards in this set are Wade Boggs, Julio Franco, Tony Gwynn, Howard Johnson, Willie McGee, Ryne Sandberg, and Frank Viola.

	NRMT-MT	EXC	G-VG
COMPLETE SET (660)	90.00	40.00	11.00
COMPLETE FACT.SET (660)	100.00	45.00	12.50
COMMON CARD (1-660)	.10	.05	.01
☐ 1 Fernando Valenzuela DK	.30	.14	.04
☐ 2 Rollie Fingers DK	.30	.14	.04
☐ 3 Reggie Jackson DK	.75	.35	.09
☐ 4 Jim Palmer DK	.50	.23	.06
☐ 5 Jack Morris DK	.30	.14	.04
☐ 6 George Foster DK	.20	.09	.03
☐ 7 Jim Sundberg DK	.20	.09	.03
☐ 8 Willie Stargell DK	.30	.14	.04
☐ 9 Dave Stieb DK	.20	.09	.03
☐ 10 Joe Niekro DK	.20	.09	.03
☐ 11 Rickey Henderson DK	1.25	.55	.16
☐ 12 Dale Murphy DK	.35	.16	.04
☐ 13 Toby Harrah DK	.20	.09	.03
☐ 14 Bill Buckner DK	.20	.09	.03
☐ 15 Willie Wilson DK	.20	.09	.03
☐ 16 Steve Carlton DK	.50	.23	.06
☐ 17 Ron Guidry DK	.20	.09	.03
☐ 18 Steve Rogers DK	.20	.09	.03
☐ 19 Kent Hrbek DK	.20	.09	.03
☐ 20 Keith Hernandez DK	.20	.09	.03
☐ 21 Floyd Bannister DK	.20	.09	.03
☐ 22 Johnny Bench DK	.50	.23	.06
☐ 23 Britt Burns DK	.20	.09	.03
☐ 24 Joe Morgan DK	.35	.16	.04
☐ 25 Carl Yastrzemski DK	.50	.23	.06
☐ 26 Terry Kennedy DK	.20	.09	.03
☐ 27 Gary Roenicke	.10	.05	.01
☐ 28 Dwight Bernard	.10	.05	.01
☐ 29 Pat Underwood	.10	.05	.01
☐ 30 Gary Allenson	.10	.05	.01
☐ 31 Ron Guidry	.20	.09	.03
☐ 32 Burt Hooton	.10	.05	.01
☐ 33 Chris Bando	.10	.05	.01

□	#	Name			
□	34	Vida Blue	.20	.09	.03
□	35	Rickey Henderson	2.00	.90	.25
□	36	Ray Burris	.10	.05	.01
□	37	John Butcher	.10	.05	.01
□	38	Don Aase	.10	.05	.01
□	39	Jerry Koosman	.20	.09	.03
□	40	Bruce Sutter	.20	.09	.03
□	41	Jose Cruz	.20	.09	.03
□	42	Pete Rose	1.50	.70	.19
□	43	Cesar Cedeno	.20	.09	.03
□	44	Floyd Chiffer	.10	.05	.01
□	45	Larry McWilliams	.10	.05	.01
□	46	Alan Fowlkes	.10	.05	.01
□	47	Dale Murphy	.50	.23	.06
□	48	Doug Bird	.10	.05	.01
□	49	Hubie Brooks	.20	.09	.03
□	50	Floyd Bannister	.10	.05	.01
□	51	Jack O'Connor	.10	.05	.01
□	52	Steve Senteney	.10	.05	.01
□	53	Gary Gaetti	.75	.35	.09
□	54	Damaso Garcia	.10	.05	.01
□	55	Gene Nelson	.10	.05	.01
□	56	Mookie Wilson	.20	.09	.03
□	57	Allen Ripley	.10	.05	.01
□	58	Bob Horner	.20	.09	.03
□	59	Tony Pena	.20	.09	.03
□	60	Gary Lavelle	.10	.05	.01
□	61	Tim Lollar	.10	.05	.01
□	62	Frank Pastore	.10	.05	.01
□	63	Garry Maddox	.10	.05	.01
□	64	Bob Forsch	.10	.05	.01
□	65	Harry Spilman	.10	.05	.01
□	66	Geoff Zahn	.10	.05	.01
□	67	Salome Barojas	.10	.05	.01
□	68	David Palmer	.10	.05	.01
□	69	Charlie Hough	.20	.09	.03
□	70	Dan Quisenberry	.20	.09	.03
□	71	Tony Armas	.10	.05	.01
□	72	Rick Sutcliffe	.20	.09	.03
□	73	Steve Balboni	.10	.05	.01
□	74	Jerry Remy	.10	.05	.01
□	75	Mike Scioscia	.20	.09	.03
□	76	John Wockenfuss	.10	.05	.01
□	77	Jim Palmer	.60	.25	.07
□	78	Rollie Fingers	.30	.14	.04
□	79	Joe Nolan	.10	.05	.01
□	80	Pete Vuckovich	.10	.05	.01
□	81	Rick Leach	.10	.05	.01
□	82	Rick Miller	.10	.05	.01
□	83	Graig Nettles	.20	.09	.03
□	84	Ron Cey	.20	.09	.03
□	85	Miguel Dilone	.10	.05	.01
□	86	John Wathan	.10	.05	.01
□	87	Kelvin Moore	.10	.05	.01
□	88A	Byrn Smith ERR (Sic, Bryn)	.20	.09	.03
□	88B	Bryn Smith COR	.30	.14	.04
□	89	Dave Hostetler	.10	.05	.01
□	90	Rod Carew	.60	.25	.07
□	91	Lonnie Smith	.20	.09	.03
□	92	Bob Knepper	.10	.05	.01
□	93	Marty Bystrom	.10	.05	.01
□	94	Chris Welsh	.10	.05	.01
□	95	Jason Thompson	.10	.05	.01
□	96	Tom O'Malley	.10	.05	.01
□	97	Phil Niekro	.30	.14	.04
□	98	Neil Allen	.10	.05	.01
□	99	Bill Buckner	.20	.09	.03
□	100	Ed VandeBerg	.10	.05	.01
□	101	Jim Clancy	.10	.05	.01
□	102	Robert Castillo	.10	.05	.01
□	103	Bruce Berenyi	.10	.05	.01
□	104	Carlton Fisk	.75	.35	.09
□	105	Mike Flanagan	.20	.09	.03
□	106	Cecil Cooper	.20	.09	.03
□	107	Jack Morris	.30	.14	.04
□	108	Mike Morgan	.10	.05	.01
□	109	Luis Aponte	.10	.05	.01
□	110	Pedro Guerrero	.20	.09	.03
□	111	Len Barker	.10	.05	.01
□	112	Willie Wilson	.20	.09	.03
□	113	Dave Beard	.10	.05	.01
□	114	Mike Gates	.10	.05	.01
□	115	Reggie Jackson	1.25	.55	.16
□	116	George Wright	.10	.05	.01
□	117	Vance Law	.10	.05	.01
□	118	Nolan Ryan	5.00	2.20	.60
□	119	Mike Krukow	.10	.05	.01
□	120	Ozzie Smith	2.00	.90	.25
□	121	Broderick Perkins	.10	.05	.01
□	122	Tom Seaver	.75	.35	.09
□	123	Chris Chambliss	.20	.09	.03
□	124	Chuck Tanner MG	.10	.05	.01
□	125	Johnnie LeMaster	.10	.05	.01
□	126	Mel Hall	.20	.09	.03
□	127	Bruce Bochte	.10	.05	.01
□	128	Charlie Puleo	.10	.05	.01
□	129	Luis Leal	.10	.05	.01
□	130	John Pacella	.10	.05	.01
□	131	Glenn Gulliver	.10	.05	.01
□	132	Don Money	.10	.05	.01
□	133	Dave Rozema	.10	.05	.01
□	134	Bruce Hurst	.10	.05	.01
□	135	Rudy May	.10	.05	.01
□	136	Tom Lasorda MG	.20	.09	.03
□	137	Dan Spillner UER (Photo actually Ed Whitson)	.10	.05	.01
□	138	Jerry Martin	.10	.05	.01
□	139	Mike Norris	.10	.05	.01
□	140	Al Oliver	.20	.09	.03
□	141	Daryl Sconiers	.10	.05	.01
□	142	Lamar Johnson	.10	.05	.01
□	143	Harold Baines	.30	.14	.04
□	144	Alan Ashby	.10	.05	.01
□	145	Garry Templeton	.10	.05	.01
□	146	Al Holland	.10	.05	.01
□	147	Bo Diaz	.10	.05	.01
□	148	Dave Concepcion	.20	.09	.03
□	149	Rick Camp	.10	.05	.01
□	150	Jim Morrison	.10	.05	.01
□	151	Randy Martz	.10	.05	.01
□	152	Keith Hernandez	.30	.14	.04
□	153	John Lowenstein	.10	.05	.01
□	154	Mike Caldwell	.10	.05	.01
□	155	Milt Wilcox	.10	.05	.01
□	156	Rich Gedman	.10	.05	.01
□	157	Rich Gossage	.30	.14	.04
□	158	Jerry Reuss	.10	.05	.01
□	159	Ron Hassey	.10	.05	.01
□	160	Larry Gura	.10	.05	.01
□	161	Dwayne Murphy	.10	.05	.01
□	162	Woodie Fryman	.10	.05	.01
□	163	Steve Comer	.10	.05	.01
□	164	Ken Forsch	.10	.05	.01
□	165	Dennis Lamp	.10	.05	.01
□	166	David Green	.10	.05	.01
□	167	Terry Puhl	.10	.05	.01
□	168	Mike Schmidt (Wearing 37 rather than 20)	1.50	.70	.19
□	169	Eddie Milner	.10	.05	.01

☐ 170	John Curtis	.10	.05	.01
☐ 171	Don Robinson	.10	.05	.01
☐ 172	Rich Gale	.10	.05	.01
☐ 173	Steve Bedrosian	.20	.09	.03
☐ 174	Willie Hernandez	.20	.09	.03
☐ 175	Ron Gardenhire	.10	.05	.01
☐ 176	Jim Beattie	.10	.05	.01
☐ 177	Tim Laudner	.10	.05	.01
☐ 178	Buck Martinez	.10	.05	.01
☐ 179	Kent Hrbek	.30	.14	.04
☐ 180	Alfredo Griffin	.10	.05	.01
☐ 181	Larry Andersen	.10	.05	.01
☐ 182	Pete Falcone	.10	.05	.01
☐ 183	Jody Davis	.10	.05	.01
☐ 184	Glenn Hubbard	.10	.05	.01
☐ 185	Dale Berra	.10	.05	.01
☐ 186	Greg Minton	.10	.05	.01
☐ 187	Gary Lucas	.10	.05	.01
☐ 188	Dave Van Gorder	.10	.05	.01
☐ 189	Bob Dernier	.10	.05	.01
☐ 190	Willie McGee	.75	.35	.09
☐ 191	Dickie Thon	.10	.05	.01
☐ 192	Bob Boone	.20	.09	.03
☐ 193	Britt Burns	.10	.05	.01
☐ 194	Jeff Reardon	.20	.09	.03
☐ 195	Jon Matlack	.10	.05	.01
☐ 196	Don Slaught	.50	.23	.06
☐ 197	Fred Stanley	.10	.05	.01
☐ 198	Rick Manning	.10	.05	.01
☐ 199	Dave Righetti	.20	.09	.03
☐ 200	Dave Stapleton	.10	.05	.01
☐ 201	Steve Yeager	.10	.05	.01
☐ 202	Enos Cabell	.10	.05	.01
☐ 203	Sammy Stewart	.10	.05	.01
☐ 204	Moose Haas	.10	.05	.01
☐ 205	Lenn Sakata	.10	.05	.01
☐ 206	Charlie Moore	.10	.05	.01
☐ 207	Alan Trammell	.75	.35	.09
☐ 208	Jim Rice	.30	.14	.04
☐ 209	Roy Smalley	.10	.05	.01
☐ 210	Bill Russell	.20	.09	.03
☐ 211	Andre Thornton	.10	.05	.01
☐ 212	Willie Aikens	.10	.05	.01
☐ 213	Dave McKay	.10	.05	.01
☐ 214	Tim Blackwell	.10	.05	.01
☐ 215	Buddy Bell	.20	.09	.03
☐ 216	Doug DeCinces	.20	.09	.03
☐ 217	Tom Herr	.20	.09	.03
☐ 218	Frank LaCorte	.10	.05	.01
☐ 219	Steve Carlton	.75	.35	.09
☐ 220	Terry Kennedy	.10	.05	.01
☐ 221	Mike Easler	.10	.05	.01
☐ 222	Jack Clark	.20	.09	.03
☐ 223	Gene Garber	.10	.05	.01
☐ 224	Scott Holman	.10	.05	.01
☐ 225	Mike Proly	.10	.05	.01
☐ 226	Terry Bulling	.10	.05	.01
☐ 227	Jerry Garvin	.10	.05	.01
☐ 228	Ron Davis	.10	.05	.01
☐ 229	Tom Hume	.10	.05	.01
☐ 230	Marc Hill	.10	.05	.01
☐ 231	Dennis Martinez	.20	.09	.03
☐ 232	Jim Gantner	.20	.09	.03
☐ 233	Larry Pashnick	.10	.05	.01
☐ 234	Dave Collins	.10	.05	.01
☐ 235	Tom Burgmeier	.10	.05	.01
☐ 236	Ken Landreaux	.10	.05	.01
☐ 237	John Denny	.10	.05	.01
☐ 238	Hal McRae	.30	.14	.04
☐ 239	Matt Keough	.10	.05	.01
☐ 240	Doug Flynn	.10	.05	.01
☐ 241	Fred Lynn	.20	.09	.03
☐ 242	Billy Sample	.10	.05	.01
☐ 243	Tom Paciorek	.20	.09	.03
☐ 244	Joe Sambito	.10	.05	.01
☐ 245	Sid Monge	.10	.05	.01
☐ 246	Ken Oberkfell	.10	.05	.01
☐ 247	Joe Pittman UER (Photo actually Juan Eichelberger)	.10	.05	.01
☐ 248	Mario Soto	.10	.05	.01
☐ 249	Claudell Washington	.10	.05	.01
☐ 250	Rick Rhoden	.10	.05	.01
☐ 251	Darrell Evans	.20	.09	.03
☐ 252	Steve Henderson	.10	.05	.01
☐ 253	Manny Castillo	.10	.05	.01
☐ 254	Craig Swan	.10	.05	.01
☐ 255	Joey McLaughlin	.10	.05	.01
☐ 256	Pete Redfern	.10	.05	.01
☐ 257	Ken Singleton	.20	.09	.03
☐ 258	Robin Yount	1.50	.70	.19
☐ 259	Elias Sosa	.10	.05	.01
☐ 260	Bob Ojeda	.10	.05	.01
☐ 261	Bobby Murcer	.20	.09	.03
☐ 262	Candy Maldonado	.20	.09	.03
☐ 263	Rick Waits	.10	.05	.01
☐ 264	Greg Pryor	.10	.05	.01
☐ 265	Bob Owchinko	.10	.05	.01
☐ 266	Chris Speier	.10	.05	.01
☐ 267	Bruce Kison	.10	.05	.01
☐ 268	Mark Wagner	.10	.05	.01
☐ 269	Steve Kemp	.10	.05	.01
☐ 270	Phil Garner	.20	.09	.03
☐ 271	Gene Richards	.10	.05	.01
☐ 272	Renie Martin	.10	.05	.01
☐ 273	Dave Roberts	.10	.05	.01
☐ 274	Dan Driessen	.10	.05	.01
☐ 275	Rufino Linares	.10	.05	.01
☐ 276	Lee Lacy	.10	.05	.01
☐ 277	Ryne Sandberg	20.00	9.00	2.50
☐ 278	Darrell Porter	.10	.05	.01
☐ 279	Cal Ripken	16.00	7.25	2.00
☐ 280	Jamie Easterly	.10	.05	.01
☐ 281	Bill Fahey	.10	.05	.01
☐ 282	Glenn Hoffman	.10	.05	.01
☐ 283	Willie Randolph	.20	.09	.03
☐ 284	Fernando Valenzuela	.20	.09	.03
☐ 285	Alan Bannister	.10	.05	.01
☐ 286	Paul Splittorff	.10	.05	.01
☐ 287	Joe Rudi	.10	.05	.01
☐ 288	Bill Gullickson	.20	.09	.03
☐ 289	Danny Darwin	.10	.05	.01
☐ 290	Andy Hassler	.10	.05	.01
☐ 291	Ernesto Escarrega	.10	.05	.01
☐ 292	Steve Mura	.10	.05	.01
☐ 293	Tony Scott	.10	.05	.01
☐ 294	Manny Trillo	.10	.05	.01
☐ 295	Greg Harris	.10	.05	.01
☐ 296	Luis DeLeon	.10	.05	.01
☐ 297	Kent Tekulve	.20	.09	.03
☐ 298	Atlee Hammaker	.10	.05	.01
☐ 299	Bruce Benedict	.10	.05	.01
☐ 300	Fergie Jenkins	.30	.14	.04
☐ 301	Dave Kingman	.20	.09	.03
☐ 302	Bill Caudill	.10	.05	.01
☐ 303	John Castino	.10	.05	.01
☐ 304	Ernie Whitt	.10	.05	.01
☐ 305	Randy Johnson	.10	.05	.01
☐ 306	Garth Iorg	.10	.05	.01
☐ 307	Gaylord Perry	.30	.14	.04
☐ 308	Ed Lynch	.10	.05	.01
☐ 309	Keith Moreland	.10	.05	.01

□	#	Name			
□	310	Rafael Ramirez	.10	.05	.01
□	311	Bill Madlock	.20	.09	.03
□	312	Milt May	.10	.05	.01
□	313	John Montefusco	.10	.05	.01
□	314	Wayne Krenchicki	.10	.05	.01
□	315	George Vukovich	.10	.05	.01
□	316	Joaquin Andujar	.10	.05	.01
□	317	Craig Reynolds	.10	.05	.01
□	318	Rick Burleson	.10	.05	.01
□	319	Richard Dotson	.10	.05	.01
□	320	Steve Rogers	.10	.05	.01
□	321	Dave Schmidt	.10	.05	.01
□	322	Bud Black	.20	.09	.03
□	323	Jeff Burroughs	.10	.05	.01
□	324	Von Hayes	.20	.09	.03
□	325	Butch Wynegar	.10	.05	.01
□	326	Carl Yastrzemski	.75	.35	.09
□	327	Ron Roenicke	.10	.05	.01
□	328	Howard Johnson	.75	.35	.09
□	329	Rick Dempsey UER	.20	.09	.03
		(Posing as a left-handed batter)			
□	330A	Jim Slaton	.10	.05	.01
		(Bio printed black on white)			
□	330B	Jim Slaton	.10	.05	.01
		(Bio printed black on yellow)			
□	331	Benny Ayala	.10	.05	.01
□	332	Ted Simmons	.20	.09	.03
□	333	Lou Whitaker	.50	.23	.06
□	334	Chuck Rainey	.10	.05	.01
□	335	Lou Piniella	.20	.09	.03
□	336	Steve Sax	.20	.09	.03
□	337	Toby Harrah	.10	.05	.01
□	338	George Brett	3.00	1.35	.35
□	339	Dave Lopes	.20	.09	.03
□	340	Gary Carter	.30	.14	.04
□	341	John Grubb	.10	.05	.01
□	342	Tim Foli	.10	.05	.01
□	343	Jim Kaat	.20	.09	.03
□	344	Mike LaCoss	.10	.05	.01
□	345	Larry Christenson	.10	.05	.01
□	346	Juan Bonilla	.10	.05	.01
□	347	Omar Moreno	.10	.05	.01
□	348	Chili Davis	.75	.35	.09
□	349	Tommy Boggs	.10	.05	.01
□	350	Rusty Staub	.20	.09	.03
□	351	Bump Wills	.10	.05	.01
□	352	Rick Sweet	.10	.05	.01
□	353	Jim Gott	.20	.09	.03
□	354	Terry Felton	.10	.05	.01
□	355	Jim Kern	.10	.05	.01
□	356	Bill Almon UER	.10	.05	.01
		(Expos/Mets in 1983, not Padres/Mets)			
□	357	Tippy Martinez	.10	.05	.01
□	358	Roy Howell	.10	.05	.01
□	359	Dan Petry	.10	.05	.01
□	360	Jerry Mumphrey	.10	.05	.01
□	361	Mark Clear	.10	.05	.01
□	362	Mike Marshall	.10	.05	.01
□	363	Lary Sorensen	.10	.05	.01
□	364	Amos Otis	.20	.09	.03
□	365	Rick Langford	.10	.05	.01
□	366	Brad Mills	.10	.05	.01
□	367	Brian Downing	.20	.09	.03
□	368	Mike Richardt	.10	.05	.01
□	369	Aurelio Rodriguez	.10	.05	.01
□	370	Dave Smith	.10	.05	.01
□	371	Tug McGraw	.20	.09	.03
□	372	Doug Bair	.10	.05	.01
□	373	Ruppert Jones	.10	.05	.01
□	374	Alex Trevino	.10	.05	.01
□	375	Ken Dayley	.10	.05	.01
□	376	Rod Scurry	.10	.05	.01
□	377	Bob Brenly	.10	.05	.01
□	378	Scot Thompson	.10	.05	.01
□	379	Julio Cruz	.10	.05	.01
□	380	John Stearns	.10	.05	.01
□	381	Dale Murray	.10	.05	.01
□	382	Frank Viola	.60	.25	.07
□	383	Al Bumbry	.20	.09	.03
□	384	Ben Oglivie	.10	.05	.01
□	385	Dave Tobik	.10	.05	.01
□	386	Bob Stanley	.10	.05	.01
□	387	Andre Robertson	.10	.05	.01
□	388	Jorge Orta	.10	.05	.01
□	389	Ed Whitson	.10	.05	.01
□	390	Don Hood	.10	.05	.01
□	391	Tom Underwood	.10	.05	.01
□	392	Tim Wallach	.30	.14	.04
□	393	Steve Renko	.10	.05	.01
□	394	Mickey Rivers	.10	.05	.01
□	395	Greg Luzinski	.20	.09	.03
□	396	Art Howe	.10	.05	.01
□	397	Alan Wiggins	.10	.05	.01
□	398	Jim Barr	.10	.05	.01
□	399	Ivan DeJesus	.10	.05	.01
□	400	Tom Lawless	.10	.05	.01
□	401	Bob Walk	.10	.05	.01
□	402	Jimmy Smith	.10	.05	.01
□	403	Lee Smith	2.00	.90	.25
□	404	George Hendrick	.20	.09	.03
□	405	Eddie Murray	2.00	.90	.25
□	406	Marshall Edwards	.10	.05	.01
□	407	Lance Parrish	.20	.09	.03
□	408	Carney Lansford	.20	.09	.03
□	409	Dave Winfield	1.50	.70	.19
□	410	Bob Welch	.20	.09	.03
□	411	Larry Milbourne	.10	.05	.01
□	412	Dennis Leonard	.10	.05	.01
□	413	Dan Meyer	.10	.05	.01
□	414	Charlie Lea	.10	.05	.01
□	415	Rick Honeycutt	.10	.05	.01
□	416	Mike Witt	.10	.05	.01
□	417	Steve Trout	.10	.05	.01
□	418	Glenn Brummer	.10	.05	.01
□	419	Denny Walling	.10	.05	.01
□	420	Gary Matthews	.20	.09	.03
□	421	Charlie Leibrandt UER	.20	.09	.03
		(Liebrandt on front of card)			
□	422	Juan Eichelberger UER	.10	.05	.01
		(Photo actually Joe Pittman)			
□	423	Cecilio Guante UER	.20	.09	.03
		(Listed as Matt on card)			
□	424	Bill Laskey	.10	.05	.01
□	425	Jerry Royster	.10	.05	.01
□	426	Dickie Noles	.10	.05	.01
□	427	George Foster	.20	.09	.03
□	428	Mike Moore	.20	.09	.03
□	429	Gary Ward	.10	.05	.01
□	430	Barry Bonnell	.10	.05	.01
□	431	Ron Washington	.10	.05	.01
□	432	Rance Mulliniks	.10	.05	.01
□	433	Mike Stanton	.10	.05	.01
□	434	Jesse Orosco	.10	.05	.01
□	435	Larry Bowa	.20	.09	.03
□	436	Biff Pocoroba	.10	.05	.01

☐ 437	Johnny Ray	.10	.05	.01
☐ 438	Joe Morgan	.50	.23	.06
☐ 439	Eric Show	.20	.09	.03
☐ 440	Larry Biittner	.10	.05	.01
☐ 441	Greg Gross	.10	.05	.01
☐ 442	Gene Tenace	.10	.05	.01
☐ 443	Danny Heep	.10	.05	.01
☐ 444	Bobby Clark	.10	.05	.01
☐ 445	Kevin Hickey	.10	.05	.01
☐ 446	Scott Sanderson	.10	.05	.01
☐ 447	Frank Tanana	.20	.09	.03
☐ 448	Cesar Geronimo	.10	.05	.01
☐ 449	Jimmy Sexton	.10	.05	.01
☐ 450	Mike Hargrove	.20	.09	.03
☐ 451	Doyle Alexander	.10	.05	.01
☐ 452	Dwight Evans	.20	.09	.03
☐ 453	Terry Forster	.10	.05	.01
☐ 454	Tom Brookens	.10	.05	.01
☐ 455	Rich Dauer	.10	.05	.01
☐ 456	Rob Picciolo	.10	.05	.01
☐ 457	Terry Crowley	.10	.05	.01
☐ 458	Ned Yost	.10	.05	.01
☐ 459	Kirk Gibson	.60	.25	.07
☐ 460	Reid Nichols	.10	.05	.01
☐ 461	Oscar Gamble	.10	.05	.01
☐ 462	Dusty Baker	.30	.14	.04
☐ 463	Jack Perconte	.10	.05	.01
☐ 464	Frank White	.20	.09	.03
☐ 465	Mickey Klutts	.10	.05	.01
☐ 466	Warren Cromartie	.10	.05	.01
☐ 467	Larry Parrish	.10	.05	.01
☐ 468	Bobby Grich	.20	.09	.03
☐ 469	Dane Iorg	.10	.05	.01
☐ 470	Joe Niekro	.20	.09	.03
☐ 471	Ed Farmer	.10	.05	.01
☐ 472	Tim Flannery	.10	.05	.01
☐ 473	Dave Parker	.30	.14	.04
☐ 474	Jeff Leonard	.10	.05	.01
☐ 475	Al Hrabosky	.10	.05	.01
☐ 476	Ron Hodges	.10	.05	.01
☐ 477	Leon Durham	.10	.05	.01
☐ 478	Jim Essian	.10	.05	.01
☐ 479	Roy Lee Jackson	.10	.05	.01
☐ 480	Brad Havens	.10	.05	.01
☐ 481	Joe Price	.10	.05	.01
☐ 482	Tony Bernazard	.10	.05	.01
☐ 483	Scott McGregor	.10	.05	.01
☐ 484	Paul Molitor	.75	.35	.09
☐ 485	Mike Ivie	.10	.05	.01
☐ 486	Ken Griffey	.20	.09	.03
☐ 487	Dennis Eckersley	.50	.23	.06
☐ 488	Steve Garvey	.30	.14	.04
☐ 489	Mike Fischlin	.10	.05	.01
☐ 490	U.L. Washington	.10	.05	.01
☐ 491	Steve McCatty	.10	.05	.01
☐ 492	Roy Johnson	.10	.05	.01
☐ 493	Don Baylor	.30	.14	.04
☐ 494	Bobby Johnson	.10	.05	.01
☐ 495	Mike Squires	.10	.05	.01
☐ 496	Bert Roberge	.10	.05	.01
☐ 497	Dick Ruthven	.10	.05	.01
☐ 498	Tito Landrum	.10	.05	.01
☐ 499	Sixto Lezcano	.10	.05	.01
☐ 500	Johnny Bench	.75	.35	.09
☐ 501	Larry Whisenton	.10	.05	.01
☐ 502	Manny Sarmiento	.10	.05	.01
☐ 503	Fred Breining	.10	.05	.01
☐ 504	Bill Campbell	.10	.05	.01
☐ 505	Todd Cruz	.10	.05	.01
☐ 506	Bob Bailor	.10	.05	.01
☐ 507	Dave Stieb	.20	.09	.03

☐ 508	Al Williams	.10	.05	.01
☐ 509	Dan Ford	.10	.05	.01
☐ 510	Gorman Thomas	.10	.05	.01
☐ 511	Chet Lemon	.10	.05	.01
☐ 512	Mike Torrez	.10	.05	.01
☐ 513	Shane Rawley	.10	.05	.01
☐ 514	Mark Belanger	.10	.05	.01
☐ 515	Rodney Craig	.10	.05	.01
☐ 516	Onix Concepcion	.10	.05	.01
☐ 517	Mike Heath	.10	.05	.01
☐ 518	Andre Dawson UER	.75	.35	.09
	(Middle name Fernando, should be Nolan)			
☐ 519	Luis Sanchez	.10	.05	.01
☐ 520	Terry Bogener	.10	.05	.01
☐ 521	Rudy Law	.10	.05	.01
☐ 522	Ray Knight	.20	.09	.03
☐ 523	Joe Lefebvre	.10	.05	.01
☐ 524	Jim Wohlford	.10	.05	.01
☐ 525	Julio Franco	2.00	.90	.25
☐ 526	Ron Oester	.10	.05	.01
☐ 527	Rick Mahler	.10	.05	.01
☐ 528	Steve Nicosia	.10	.05	.01
☐ 529	Junior Kennedy	.10	.05	.01
☐ 530A	Whitey Herzog MG	.20	.09	.03
	(Bio printed black on white)			
☐ 530B	Whitey Herzog MG	.20	.09	.03
	(Bio printed black on yellow)			
☐ 531A	Don Sutton	.30	.14	.04
	(Blue border on photo)			
☐ 531B	Don Sutton	.30	.14	.04
	(Green border on photo)			
☐ 532	Mark Brouhard	.10	.05	.01
☐ 533A	Sparky Anderson MG.	.20	.09	.03
	(Bio printed black on white)			
☐ 533B	Sparky Anderson MG.	.20	.09	.03
	(Bio printed black on yellow)			
☐ 534	Roger LaFrancois	.10	.05	.01
☐ 535	George Frazier	.10	.05	.01
☐ 536	Tom Niedenfuer	.10	.05	.01
☐ 537	Ed Glynn	.10	.05	.01
☐ 538	Lee May	.20	.09	.03
☐ 539	Bob Kearney	.10	.05	.01
☐ 540	Tim Raines	.60	.25	.07
☐ 541	Paul Mirabella	.10	.05	.01
☐ 542	Luis Tiant	.20	.09	.03
☐ 543	Ron LeFlore	.20	.09	.03
☐ 544	Dave LaPoint	.10	.05	.01
☐ 545	Randy Moffitt	.10	.05	.01
☐ 546	Luis Aguayo	.10	.05	.01
☐ 547	Brad Lesley	.10	.05	.01
☐ 548	Luis Salazar	.10	.05	.01
☐ 549	John Candelaria	.10	.05	.01
☐ 550	Dave Bergman	.10	.05	.01
☐ 551	Bob Watson	.20	.09	.03
☐ 552	Pat Tabler	.10	.05	.01
☐ 553	Brent Gaff	.10	.05	.01
☐ 554	Al Cowens	.10	.05	.01
☐ 555	Tom Brunansky	.20	.09	.03
☐ 556	Lloyd Moseby	.10	.05	.01
☐ 557A	Pascual Perez ERR	2.00	.90	.25
	(Twins in glove)			
☐ 557B	Pascual Perez COR	.10	.05	.01
	(Braves in glove)			
☐ 558	Willie Upshaw	.10	.05	.01

☐ 559	Richie Zisk	.10	.05	.01
☐ 560	Pat Zachry	.10	.05	.01
☐ 561	Jay Johnstone	.20	.09	.03
☐ 562	Carlos Diaz	.10	.05	.01
☐ 563	John Tudor	.20	.09	.03
☐ 564	Frank Robinson MG	.30	.14	.04
☐ 565	Dave Edwards	.10	.05	.01
☐ 566	Paul Householder	.10	.05	.01
☐ 567	Ron Reed	.10	.05	.01
☐ 568	Mike Ramsey	.10	.05	.01
☐ 569	Kiko Garcia	.10	.05	.01
☐ 570	Tommy John	.30	.14	.04
☐ 571	Tony LaRussa MG	.20	.09	.03
☐ 572	Joel Youngblood	.10	.05	.01
☐ 573	Wayne Tolleson	.10	.05	.01
☐ 574	Keith Creel	.10	.05	.01
☐ 575	Billy Martin MG	.20	.09	.03
☐ 576	Jerry Dybzinski	.10	.05	.01
☐ 577	Rick Cerone	.10	.05	.01
☐ 578	Tony Perez	.30	.14	.04
☐ 579	Greg Brock	.10	.05	.01
☐ 580	Glenn Wilson	.20	.09	.03
☐ 581	Tim Stoddard	.10	.05	.01
☐ 582	Bob McClure	.10	.05	.01
☐ 583	Jim Dwyer	.10	.05	.01
☐ 584	Ed Romero	.10	.05	.01
☐ 585	Larry Herndon	.10	.05	.01
☐ 586	Wade Boggs	15.00	6.75	1.85
☐ 587	Jay Howell	.20	.09	.03
☐ 588	Dave Stewart	.50	.23	.06
☐ 589	Bert Blyleven	.30	.14	.04
☐ 590	Dick Howser MG	.20	.09	.03
☐ 591	Wayne Gross	.10	.05	.01
☐ 592	Terry Francona	.10	.05	.01
☐ 593	Don Werner	.10	.05	.01
☐ 594	Bill Stein	.10	.05	.01
☐ 595	Jesse Barfield	.20	.09	.03
☐ 596	Bob Molinaro	.10	.05	.01
☐ 597	Mike Vail	.10	.05	.01
☐ 598	Tony Gwynn	20.00	9.00	2.50
☐ 599	Gary Rajsich	.10	.05	.01
☐ 600	Jerry Ujdur	.10	.05	.01
☐ 601	Cliff Johnson	.10	.05	.01
☐ 602	Jerry White	.10	.05	.01
☐ 603	Bryan Clark	.10	.05	.01
☐ 604	Joe Ferguson	.10	.05	.01
☐ 605	Guy Sularz	.10	.05	.01
☐ 606A	Ozzie Virgil (Green border on photo)	.20	.09	.03
☐ 606B	Ozzie Virgil (Orange border on photo)	.20	.09	.03
☐ 607	Terry Harper	.10	.05	.01
☐ 608	Harvey Kuenn MG	.20	.09	.03
☐ 609	Jim Sundberg	.20	.09	.03
☐ 610	Willie Stargell	.30	.14	.04
☐ 611	Reggie Smith	.20	.09	.03
☐ 612	Rob Wilfong	.10	.05	.01
☐ 613	The Niekro Brothers Joe Niekro Phil Niekro	.30	.14	.04
☐ 614	Lee Elia MG	.10	.05	.01
☐ 615	Mickey Hatcher	.10	.05	.01
☐ 616	Jerry Hairston	.10	.05	.01
☐ 617	John Martin	.10	.05	.01
☐ 618	Wally Backman	.10	.05	.01
☐ 619	Storm Davis	.10	.05	.01
☐ 620	Alan Knicely	.10	.05	.01
☐ 621	John Stuper	.10	.05	.01
☐ 622	Matt Sinatro	.10	.05	.01

☐ 623	Geno Petralli	.20	.09	.03
☐ 624	Duane Walker	.10	.05	.01
☐ 625	Dick Williams MG	.10	.05	.01
☐ 626	Pat Corrales MG	.10	.05	.01
☐ 627	Vern Ruhle	.10	.05	.01
☐ 628	Joe Torre MG	.20	.09	.03
☐ 629	Anthony Johnson	.10	.05	.01
☐ 630	Steve Howe	.10	.05	.01
☐ 631	Gary Woods	.10	.05	.01
☐ 632	LaMarr Hoyt	.10	.05	.01
☐ 633	Steve Swisher	.10	.05	.01
☐ 634	Terry Leach	.10	.05	.01
☐ 635	Jeff Newman	.10	.05	.01
☐ 636	Brett Butler	.50	.23	.06
☐ 637	Gary Gray	.10	.05	.01
☐ 638	Lee Mazzilli	.10	.05	.01
☐ 639A	Ron Jackson ERR (A's in glove)	10.00	4.50	1.25
☐ 639B	Ron Jackson COR (Angels in glove, red border on photo)	.10	.05	.01
☐ 639C	Ron Jackson COR (Angels in glove, green border on photo)	.30	.14	.04
☐ 640	Juan Beniquez	.10	.05	.01
☐ 641	Dave Rucker	.10	.05	.01
☐ 642	Luis Pujols	.10	.05	.01
☐ 643	Rick Monday	.10	.05	.01
☐ 644	Hosken Powell	.10	.05	.01
☐ 645	The Chicken	.30	.14	.04
☐ 646	Dave Engle	.10	.05	.01
☐ 647	Dick Davis	.10	.05	.01
☐ 648	Frank Robinson Vida Blue Joe Morgan	.20	.09	.03
☐ 649	Al Chambers	.10	.05	.01
☐ 650	Jesus Vega	.10	.05	.01
☐ 651	Jeff Jones	.10	.05	.01
☐ 652	Marvis Foley	.10	.05	.01
☐ 653	Ty Cobb Puzzle Card	.30	.14	.04
☐ 654A	Dick Perez/Diamond King Checklist 1-26 (Unnumbered) ERR (Word "checklist" omitted from back)	.30	.14	.04
☐ 654B	Dick Perez/Diamond King Checklist 1-26 (Unnumbered) COR (Word "checklist" is on back)	.30	.14	.04
☐ 655	Checklist 27-130 (Unnumbered)	.20	.09	.03
☐ 656	Checklist 131-234 (Unnumbered)	.20	.09	.03
☐ 657	Checklist 235-338 (Unnumbered)	.20	.09	.03
☐ 658	Checklist 339-442 (Unnumbered)	.20	.09	.03
☐ 659	Checklist 443-544 (Unnumbered)	.20	.09	.03
☐ 660	Checklist 545-653 (Unnumbered)	.20	.09	.03

1984 Donruss

The 1984 Donruss set contains a total of 660 cards, each measuring 2 1/2" by 3 1/2";

 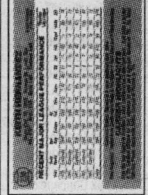

KEITH HERNANDEZ

however, only 658 are numbered. The first 26 cards in the set are again Diamond Kings (DK), although the drawings this year were styled differently and are easily differentiated from other DK issues. A new feature, Rated Rookies (RR), was introduced with this set with Bill Madden's 20 selections comprising numbers 27 through 46. Two "Living Legend" cards designated A (featuring Gaylord Perry and Rollie Fingers) and B (featuring Johnny Bench and Carl Yastrzemski) were issued as bonus cards in wax packs, but were not issued in the vending sets sold to hobby dealers. The seven unnumbered checklist cards are arbitrarily assigned numbers 652 through 658 and are listed at the end of the list below. The designs on the fronts of the Donruss cards changed considerably from the past two years. The backs contain statistics and are printed in green and black ink. The cards were distributed with a 63-piece puzzle of Duke Snider. There are no extra variation cards included in the complete set price below. The variation cards apparently resulted from a different printing for the factory sets as the Darling and Stenhouse no number variations as well as the Perez-Steel errors were corrected in the factory sets which were released later in the year. The key Rookie Cards in this set are Joe Carter, Ron Darling, Sid Fernandez, Tony Fernandez, Brian Harper, Tom Henke, Don Mattingly, Kevin McReynolds, Tony Phillips, Darryl Strawberry, and Andy Van Slyke.

	NRMT-MT	EXC	G-VG
COMPLETE SET (660)	225.00	100.00	28.00
COMPLETE FACT.SET (658)	275.00	125.00	34.00
COMMON CARD (1-658)	.30	.14	.04
☐ 1A Robin Yount DK ERR... (Perez Steel)	4.00	1.80	.50
☐ 1B Robin Yount DK COR... (Perez Steel)	5.00	2.20	.60
☐ 2A Dave Concepcion DK... ERR (Perez Steel)	.50	.23	.06
☐ 2B Dave Concepcion DK... COR	.75	.35	.09
☐ 3A Dwayne Murphy DK... ERR (Perez Steel)	.30	.14	.04
☐ 3B Dwayne Murphy DK.......	.40	.18	.05
☐ 4A John Castino DK ERR... (Perez Steel)	.30	.14	.04
☐ 4B John Castino DK COR....	.40	.18	.05

☐ 5A Leon Durham DK ERR... (Perez Steel)	.30	.14	.04
☐ 5B Leon Durham DK COR... (Perez Steel)	.40	.18	.05
☐ 6A Rusty Staub DK ERR..... (Perez Steel)	.40	.18	.05
☐ 6B Rusty Staub DK COR.....	.50	.23	.06
☐ 7A Jack Clark DK ERR........ (Perez Steel)	.40	.18	.05
☐ 7B Jack Clark DK COR........	.50	.23	.06
☐ 8A Dave Dravecky DK....... ERR (Perez Steel)	.40	.18	.05
☐ 8B Dave Dravecky DK......... COR	.50	.23	.06
☐ 9A Al Oliver DK ERR.......... (Perez Steel)	.40	.18	.05
☐ 9B Al Oliver DK COR..........	.50	.23	.06
☐ 10A Dave Righetti DK......... ERR (Perez Steel)	.40	.18	.05
☐ 10B Dave Righetti DK......... COR	.50	.23	.06
☐ 11A Hal McRae DK ERR......	.40	.18	.05
☐ 11B Hal McRae DK COR......	.50	.23	.06
☐ 12A Ray Knight DK ERR...... (Perez Steel)	.40	.18	.05
☐ 12B Ray Knight DK COR......	.50	.23	.06
☐ 13A Bruce Sutter DK ERR... (Perez Steel)	.40	.18	.05
☐ 13B Bruce Sutter DK COR...	.50	.23	.06
☐ 14A Bob Horner DK ERR..... (Perez Steel)	.40	.18	.05
☐ 14B Bob Horner DK COR.....	.50	.23	.06
☐ 15A Lance Parrish DK........ ERR (Perez Steel)	.50	.23	.06
☐ 15B Lance Parrish DK........ COR	.75	.35	.09
☐ 16A Matt Young DK ERR..... (Perez Steel)	.30	.14	.04
☐ 16B Matt Young DK COR.....	.40	.18	.05
☐ 17A Fred Lynn DK ERR....... (Perez Steel) (A's logo on back)	.40	.18	.05
☐ 17B Fred Lynn DK COR.......	.50	.23	.06
☐ 18A Ron Kittle DK ERR....... (Perez Steel)	.30	.14	.04
☐ 18B Ron Kittle DK COR.......	.40	.18	.05
☐ 19A Jim Clancy DK ERR...... (Perez Steel)	.30	.14	.04
☐ 19B Jim Clancy DK COR......	.40	.18	.05
☐ 20A Bill Madlock DK ERR.... (Perez Steel)	.40	.18	.05
☐ 20B Bill Madlock DK COR....	.50	.23	.06
☐ 21A Larry Parrish DK.......... ERR (Perez Steel)	.30	.14	.04
☐ 21B Larry Parrish DK.......... COR	.40	.18	.05
☐ 22A Eddie Murray DK ERR	2.50	1.10	.30
☐ 22B Eddie Murray DK COR	3.00	1.35	.35
☐ 23A Mike Schmidt DK ERR	4.00	1.80	.50
☐ 23B Mike Schmidt DK COR	5.00	2.20	.60
☐ 24A Pedro Guerrero DK...... ERR (Perez Steel)	.40	.18	.05
☐ 24B Pedro Guerrero DK...... COR	.50	.23	.06
☐ 25A Andre Thornton DK...... ERR (Perez Steel)	.40	.18	.05
☐ 25B Andre Thornton DK...... COR	.50	.23	.06
☐ 26A Wade Boggs DK ERR.	3.00	1.35	.35

(Perez Steel)

☐ 26B	Wade Boggs DK COR	3.50	1.55	.45
☐ 27	Joel Skinner RR	.30	.14	.04
☐ 28	Tommy Dunbar RR	.30	.14	.04
☐ 29A	Mike Stenhouse RR ERR (No number on back)	.30	.14	.04
☐ 29B	Mike Stenhouse RR COR (Numbered on back)	2.00	.90	.25
☐ 30A	Ron Darling RR ERR.. (No number on back)	1.25	.55	.16
☐ 30B	Ron Darling RR COR . (Numbered on back)	4.00	1.80	.50
☐ 31	Dion James RR	.40	.18	.05
☐ 32	Tony Fernandez RR....	2.00	.90	.25
☐ 33	Angel Salazar RR	.30	.14	.04
☐ 34	Kevin McReynolds RR ...	.75	.35	.09
☐ 35	Dick Schofield RR	.40	.18	.05
☐ 36	Brad Komminsk RR	.30	.14	.04
☐ 37	Tim Teufel RR	.30	.14	.04
☐ 38	Doug Frobel RR	.30	.14	.04
☐ 39	Greg Gagne RR	.75	.35	.09
☐ 40	Mike Fuentes RR	.30	.14	.04
☐ 41	Joe Carter RR	50.00	22.00	6.25
☐ 42	Mike Brown RR (Angels OF)	.30	.14	.04
☐ 43	Mike Jeffcoat RR	.30	.14	.04
☐ 44	Sid Fernandez RR	2.00	.90	.25
☐ 45	Brian Dayett RR	.30	.14	.04
☐ 46	Chris Smith RR	.30	.14	.04
☐ 47	Eddie Murray	8.00	3.60	1.00
☐ 48	Robin Yount	5.00	2.20	.60
☐ 49	Lance Parrish	.40	.18	.05
☐ 50	Jim Rice	.50	.23	.06
☐ 51	Dave Winfield	5.00	2.20	.60
☐ 52	Fernando Valenzuela	.40	.18	.05
☐ 53	George Brett	10.00	4.50	1.25
☐ 54	Rickey Henderson	5.00	2.20	.60
☐ 55	Gary Carter	1.25	.55	.16
☐ 56	Buddy Bell	.40	.18	.05
☐ 57	Reggie Jackson	4.00	1.80	.50
☐ 58	Harold Baines	.75	.35	.09
☐ 59	Ozzie Smith	7.00	3.10	.85
☐ 60	Nolan Ryan UER (Text on back refers to 1972 as the year he struck out 383; the year was 1973)	30.00	13.50	3.70
☐ 61	Pete Rose	5.00	2.20	.60
☐ 62	Ron Oester	.30	.14	.04
☐ 63	Steve Garvey	.75	.35	.09
☐ 64	Jason Thompson	.30	.14	.04
☐ 65	Jack Clark	.40	.18	.05
☐ 66	Dale Murphy	1.50	.70	.19
☐ 67	Leon Durham	.30	.14	.04
☐ 68	Darryl Strawberry	6.00	2.70	.75
☐ 69	Richie Zisk	.30	.14	.04
☐ 70	Kent Hrbek	.75	.35	.09
☐ 71	Dave Stieb	.40	.18	.05
☐ 72	Ken Schrom	.30	.14	.04
☐ 73	George Bell	.40	.18	.05
☐ 74	John Moses	.30	.14	.04
☐ 75	Ed Lynch	.30	.14	.04
☐ 76	Chuck Rainey	.30	.14	.04
☐ 77	Biff Pocoroba	.30	.14	.04
☐ 78	Cecilio Guante	.30	.14	.04
☐ 79	Jim Barr	.30	.14	.04
☐ 80	Kurt Bevacqua	.30	.14	.04
☐ 81	Tom Foley	.30	.14	.04
☐ 82	Joe Lefebvre	.30	.14	.04
☐ 83	Andy Van Slyke	3.00	1.35	.35

☐ 84	Bob Lillis MG	.30	.14	.04
☐ 85	Ricky Adams	.30	.14	.04
☐ 86	Jerry Hairston	.30	.14	.04
☐ 87	Bob James	.30	.14	.04
☐ 88	Joe Altobelli MG	.30	.14	.04
☐ 89	Ed Romero	.30	.14	.04
☐ 90	John Grubb	.30	.14	.04
☐ 91	John Henry Johnson	.30	.14	.04
☐ 92	Juan Espino	.30	.14	.04
☐ 93	Candy Maldonado	.30	.14	.04
☐ 94	Andre Thornton	.30	.14	.04
☐ 95	Onix Concepcion	.30	.14	.04
☐ 96	Donnie Hill UER (Listed as P, should be 2B)	.40	.18	.05
☐ 97	Andre Dawson UER (Wrong middle name, should be Nolan)	4.00	1.80	.50
☐ 98	Frank Tanana	.40	.18	.05
☐ 99	Curt Wilkerson	.30	.14	.04
☐ 100	Larry Gura	.30	.14	.04
☐ 101	Dwayne Murphy	.30	.14	.04
☐ 102	Tom Brennan	.30	.14	.04
☐ 103	Dave Righetti	.40	.18	.05
☐ 104	Steve Sax	.40	.18	.05
☐ 105	Dan Petry	.40	.18	.05
☐ 106	Cal Ripken	40.00	18.00	5.00
☐ 107	Paul Molitor UER ('83 stats should say .270 BA, 608 AB, and 164 hits)	4.00	1.80	.50
☐ 108	Fred Lynn	.40	.18	.05
☐ 109	Neil Allen	.30	.14	.04
☐ 110	Joe Niekro	.40	.18	.05
☐ 111	Steve Carlton	3.00	1.35	.35
☐ 112	Terry Kennedy	.30	.14	.04
☐ 113	Bill Madlock	.40	.18	.05
☐ 114	Chili Davis	.75	.35	.09
☐ 115	Jim Gantner	.40	.18	.05
☐ 116	Tom Seaver	4.00	1.80	.50
☐ 117	Bill Buckner	.40	.18	.05
☐ 118	Bill Caudill	.30	.14	.04
☐ 119	Jim Clancy	.30	.14	.04
☐ 120	John Castino	.30	.14	.04
☐ 121	Dave Concepcion	.40	.18	.05
☐ 122	Greg Luzinski	.40	.18	.05
☐ 123	Mike Boddicker	.30	.14	.04
☐ 124	Pete Ladd	.30	.14	.04
☐ 125	Juan Berenguer	.30	.14	.04
☐ 126	John Montefusco	.30	.14	.04
☐ 127	Ed Jurak	.30	.14	.04
☐ 128	Tom Niedenfuer	.30	.14	.04
☐ 129	Bert Blyleven	.50	.23	.06
☐ 130	Bud Black	.30	.14	.04
☐ 131	Gorman Heimueller	.30	.14	.04
☐ 132	Dan Schatzeder	.30	.14	.04
☐ 133	Ron Jackson	.30	.14	.04
☐ 134	Tom Henke	1.25	.55	.16
☐ 135	Kevin Hickey	.30	.14	.04
☐ 136	Mike Scott	.40	.18	.05
☐ 137	Bo Diaz	.30	.14	.04
☐ 138	Glenn Brummer	.30	.14	.04
☐ 139	Sid Monge	.30	.14	.04
☐ 140	Rich Gale	.30	.14	.04
☐ 141	Brett Butler	.75	.35	.09
☐ 142	Brian Harper	1.00	.45	.12
☐ 143	John Rabb	.30	.14	.04
☐ 144	Gary Woods	.30	.14	.04
☐ 145	Pat Putnam	.30	.14	.04
☐ 146	Jim Acker	.30	.14	.04
☐ 147	Mickey Hatcher	.30	.14	.04

☐ 148	Todd Cruz	.30	.14	.04
☐ 149	Tom Tellmann	.30	.14	.04
☐ 150	John Wockenfuss	.30	.14	.04
☐ 151	Wade Boggs UER	7.00	3.10	.85
	1983 runs 10; should be 100			
☐ 152	Don Baylor	.50	.23	.06
☐ 153	Bob Welch	.40	.18	.05
☐ 154	Alan Bannister	.30	.14	.04
☐ 155	Willie Aikens	.30	.14	.04
☐ 156	Jeff Burroughs	.30	.14	.04
☐ 157	Bryan Little	.30	.14	.04
☐ 158	Bob Boone	.40	.18	.05
☐ 159	Dave Hostetler	.30	.14	.04
☐ 160	Jerry Dybzinski	.30	.14	.04
☐ 161	Mike Madden	.30	.14	.04
☐ 162	Luis DeLeon	.30	.14	.04
☐ 163	Willie Hernandez	.40	.18	.05
☐ 164	Frank Pastore	.30	.14	.04
☐ 165	Rick Camp	.30	.14	.04
☐ 166	Lee Mazzilli	.30	.14	.04
☐ 167	Scot Thompson	.30	.14	.04
☐ 168	Bob Forsch	.30	.14	.04
☐ 169	Mike Flanagan	.30	.14	.04
☐ 170	Rick Manning	.30	.14	.04
☐ 171	Chet Lemon	.40	.18	.05
☐ 172	Jerry Remy	.30	.14	.04
☐ 173	Ron Guidry	.40	.18	.05
☐ 174	Pedro Guerrero	.40	.18	.05
☐ 175	Willie Wilson	.40	.18	.05
☐ 176	Carney Lansford	.40	.18	.05
☐ 177	Al Oliver	.40	.18	.05
☐ 178	Jim Sundberg	.40	.18	.05
☐ 179	Bobby Grich	.40	.18	.05
☐ 180	Rich Dotson	.30	.14	.04
☐ 181	Joaquin Andujar	.30	.14	.04
☐ 182	Jose Cruz	.40	.18	.05
☐ 183	Mike Schmidt	8.00	3.60	1.00
☐ 184	Gary Redus	.30	.14	.04
☐ 185	Garry Templeton	.30	.14	.04
☐ 186	Tony Pena	.40	.18	.05
☐ 187	Greg Minton	.30	.14	.04
☐ 188	Phil Niekro	.75	.35	.09
☐ 189	Ferguson Jenkins	.75	.35	.09
☐ 190	Mookie Wilson	.40	.18	.05
☐ 191	Jim Beattie	.30	.14	.04
☐ 192	Gary Ward	.30	.14	.04
☐ 193	Jesse Barfield	.40	.18	.05
☐ 194	Pete Filson	.30	.14	.04
☐ 195	Roy Lee Jackson	.30	.14	.04
☐ 196	Rick Sweet	.30	.14	.04
☐ 197	Jesse Orosco	.30	.14	.04
☐ 198	Steve Lake	.30	.14	.04
☐ 199	Ken Dayley	.30	.14	.04
☐ 200	Manny Sarmiento	.30	.14	.04
☐ 201	Mark Davis	.30	.14	.04
☐ 202	Tim Flannery	.30	.14	.04
☐ 203	Bill Scherrer	.30	.14	.04
☐ 204	Al Holland	.30	.14	.04
☐ 205	Dave Von Ohlen	.30	.14	.04
☐ 206	Mike LaCoss	.30	.14	.04
☐ 207	Juan Beniquez	.30	.14	.04
☐ 208	Juan Agosto	.30	.14	.04
☐ 209	Bobby Ramos	.30	.14	.04
☐ 210	Al Bumbry	.40	.18	.05
☐ 211	Mark Brouhard	.30	.14	.04
☐ 212	Howard Bailey	.30	.14	.04
☐ 213	Bruce Hurst	.40	.18	.05
☐ 214	Bob Shirley	.30	.14	.04
☐ 215	Pat Zachry	.30	.14	.04
☐ 216	Julio Franco	1.00	.45	.12
☐ 217	Mike Armstrong	.30	.14	.04
☐ 218	Dave Beard	.30	.14	.04
☐ 219	Steve Rogers	.30	.14	.04
☐ 220	John Butcher	.30	.14	.04
☐ 221	Mike Smithson	.30	.14	.04
☐ 222	Frank White	.40	.18	.05
☐ 223	Mike Heath	.30	.14	.04
☐ 224	Chris Bando	.30	.14	.04
☐ 225	Roy Smalley	.30	.14	.04
☐ 226	Dusty Baker	.50	.23	.06
☐ 227	Lou Whitaker	2.00	.90	.25
☐ 228	John Lowenstein	.30	.14	.04
☐ 229	Ben Oglivie	.30	.14	.04
☐ 230	Doug DeCinces	.30	.14	.04
☐ 231	Lonnie Smith	.40	.18	.05
☐ 232	Ray Knight	.40	.18	.05
☐ 233	Gary Matthews	.40	.18	.05
☐ 234	Juan Bonilla	.30	.14	.04
☐ 235	Rod Scurry	.30	.14	.04
☐ 236	Atlee Hammaker	.30	.14	.04
☐ 237	Mike Caldwell	.30	.14	.04
☐ 238	Keith Hernandez	.50	.23	.06
☐ 239	Larry Bowa	.40	.18	.05
☐ 240	Tony Bernazard	.30	.14	.04
☐ 241	Damaso Garcia	.30	.14	.04
☐ 242	Tom Brunansky	.40	.18	.05
☐ 243	Dan Driessen	.30	.14	.04
☐ 244	Ron Kittle	.30	.14	.04
☐ 245	Tim Stoddard	.30	.14	.04
☐ 246	Bob L. Gibson	.30	.14	.04
	(Brewers Pitcher)			
☐ 247	Marty Castillo	.30	.14	.04
☐ 248	Don Mattingly UER	50.00	22.00	6.25
	("Traiing" on back)			
☐ 249	Jeff Newman	.30	.14	.04
☐ 250	Alejandro Pena	.40	.18	.05
☐ 251	Toby Harrah	.30	.14	.04
☐ 252	Cesar Geronimo	.30	.14	.04
☐ 253	Tom Underwood	.30	.14	.04
☐ 254	Doug Flynn	.30	.14	.04
☐ 255	Andy Hassler	.30	.14	.04
☐ 256	Odell Jones	.30	.14	.04
☐ 257	Rudy Law	.30	.14	.04
☐ 258	Harry Spilman	.30	.14	.04
☐ 259	Marty Bystrom	.30	.14	.04
☐ 260	Dave Rucker	.30	.14	.04
☐ 261	Ruppert Jones	.30	.14	.04
☐ 262	Jeff R. Jones	.30	.14	.04
	(Reds OF)			
☐ 263	Gerald Perry	.40	.18	.05
☐ 264	Gene Tenace	.30	.14	.04
☐ 265	Brad Wellman	.30	.14	.04
☐ 266	Dickie Noles	.30	.14	.04
☐ 267	Jamie Allen	.30	.14	.04
☐ 268	Jim Gott	.30	.14	.04
☐ 269	Ron Davis	.30	.14	.04
☐ 270	Benny Ayala	.30	.14	.04
☐ 271	Ned Yost	.30	.14	.04
☐ 272	Dave Rozema	.30	.14	.04
☐ 273	Dave Stapleton	.30	.14	.04
☐ 274	Lou Piniella	.40	.18	.05
☐ 275	Jose Morales	.30	.14	.04
☐ 276	Broderick Perkins	.30	.14	.04
☐ 277	Butch Davis	.30	.14	.04
☐ 278	Tony Phillips	4.00	1.80	.50
☐ 279	Jeff Reardon	.50	.23	.06
☐ 280	Ken Forsch	.30	.14	.04
☐ 281	Pete O'Brien	.40	.18	.05
☐ 282	Tom Paciorek	.40	.18	.05
☐ 283	Frank LaCorte	.30	.14	.04
☐ 284	Tim Lollar	.30	.14	.04
☐ 285	Greg Gross	.30	.14	.04

☐ 286	Alex Trevino	.30	.14	.04
☐ 287	Gene Garber	.30	.14	.04
☐ 288	Dave Parker	.50	.23	.06
☐ 289	Lee Smith	2.00	.90	.25
☐ 290	Dave LaPoint	.30	.14	.04
☐ 291	John Shelby	.30	.14	.04
☐ 292	Charlie Moore	.30	.14	.04
☐ 293	Alan Trammell	2.00	.90	.25
☐ 294	Tony Armas	.30	.14	.04
☐ 295	Shane Rawley	.30	.14	.04
☐ 296	Greg Brock	.30	.14	.04
☐ 297	Hal McRae	.50	.23	.06
☐ 298	Mike Davis	.30	.14	.04
☐ 299	Tim Raines	2.00	.90	.25
☐ 300	Bucky Dent	.40	.18	.05
☐ 301	Tommy John	.50	.23	.06
☐ 302	Carlton Fisk	3.00	1.35	.35
☐ 303	Darrell Porter	.30	.14	.04
☐ 304	Dickie Thon	.30	.14	.04
☐ 305	Garry Maddox	.30	.14	.04
☐ 306	Cesar Cedeno	.40	.18	.05
☐ 307	Gary Lucas	.30	.14	.04
☐ 308	Johnny Ray	.30	.14	.04
☐ 309	Andy McGaffigan	.30	.14	.04
☐ 310	Claudell Washington	.30	.14	.04
☐ 311	Ryne Sandberg	20.00	9.00	2.50
☐ 312	George Foster	.40	.18	.05
☐ 313	Spike Owen	.40	.18	.05
☐ 314	Gary Gaetti	.40	.18	.05
☐ 315	Willie Upshaw	.30	.14	.04
☐ 316	Al Williams	.30	.14	.04
☐ 317	Jorge Orta	.30	.14	.04
☐ 318	Orlando Mercado	.30	.14	.04
☐ 319	Junior Ortiz	.30	.14	.04
☐ 320	Mike Proly	.30	.14	.04
☐ 321	Randy Johnson UER	.30	.14	.04
	('72-'82 stats are from Twins' Randy Johnson, '83 stats are from Braves' Randy Johnson)			
☐ 322	Jim Morrison	.30	.14	.04
☐ 323	Max Venable	.30	.14	.04
☐ 324	Tony Gwynn	20.00	9.00	2.50
☐ 325	Duane Walker	.30	.14	.04
☐ 326	Ozzie Virgil	.30	.14	.04
☐ 327	Jeff Lahti	.30	.14	.04
☐ 328	Bill Dawley	.30	.14	.04
☐ 329	Rob Wilfong	.30	.14	.04
☐ 330	Marc Hill	.30	.14	.04
☐ 331	Ray Burris	.30	.14	.04
☐ 332	Allan Ramirez	.30	.14	.04
☐ 333	Chuck Porter	.30	.14	.04
☐ 334	Wayne Krenchicki	.30	.14	.04
☐ 335	Gary Allenson	.30	.14	.04
☐ 336	Bobby Meacham	.30	.14	.04
☐ 337	Joe Beckwith	.30	.14	.04
☐ 338	Rick Sutcliffe	.40	.18	.05
☐ 339	Mark Huismann	.30	.14	.04
☐ 340	Tim Conroy	.30	.14	.04
☐ 341	Scott Sanderson	.30	.14	.04
☐ 342	Larry Biittner	.30	.14	.04
☐ 343	Dave Stewart	.50	.23	.06
☐ 344	Darryl Motley	.30	.14	.04
☐ 345	Chris Codiroli	.30	.14	.04
☐ 346	Rich Behenna	.30	.14	.04
☐ 347	Andre Robertson	.30	.14	.04
☐ 348	Mike Marshall	.30	.14	.04
☐ 349	Larry Herndon	.40	.18	.05
☐ 350	Rich Dauer	.30	.14	.04
☐ 351	Cecil Cooper	.40	.18	.05
☐ 352	Rod Carew	2.00	.90	.25
☐ 353	Willie McGee	.40	.18	.05
☐ 354	Phil Garner	.40	.18	.05
☐ 355	Joe Morgan	1.25	.55	.16
☐ 356	Luis Salazar	.30	.14	.04
☐ 357	John Candelaria	.40	.18	.05
☐ 358	Bill Laskey	.30	.14	.04
☐ 359	Bob McClure	.30	.14	.04
☐ 360	Dave Kingman	.40	.18	.05
☐ 361	Ron Cey	.40	.18	.05
☐ 362	Matt Young	.30	.14	.04
☐ 363	Lloyd Moseby	.30	.14	.04
☐ 364	Frank Viola	.50	.23	.06
☐ 365	Eddie Milner	.30	.14	.04
☐ 366	Floyd Bannister	.30	.14	.04
☐ 367	Dan Ford	.30	.14	.04
☐ 368	Moose Haas	.30	.14	.04
☐ 369	Doug Bair	.30	.14	.04
☐ 370	Ray Fontenot	.30	.14	.04
☐ 371	Luis Aponte	.30	.14	.04
☐ 372	Jack Fimple	.30	.14	.04
☐ 373	Neal Heaton	.40	.18	.05
☐ 374	Greg Pryor	.30	.14	.04
☐ 375	Wayne Gross	.30	.14	.04
☐ 376	Charlie Lea	.30	.14	.04
☐ 377	Steve Lubratich	.30	.14	.04
☐ 378	Jon Matlack	.30	.14	.04
☐ 379	Julio Cruz	.30	.14	.04
☐ 380	John Mizerock	.30	.14	.04
☐ 381	Kevin Gross	.40	.18	.05
☐ 382	Mike Ramsey	.30	.14	.04
☐ 383	Doug Gwosdz	.30	.14	.04
☐ 384	Kelly Paris	.30	.14	.04
☐ 385	Pete Falcone	.30	.14	.04
☐ 386	Milt May	.30	.14	.04
☐ 387	Fred Breining	.30	.14	.04
☐ 388	Craig Lefferts	.30	.14	.04
☐ 389	Steve Henderson	.30	.14	.04
☐ 390	Randy Moffitt	.30	.14	.04
☐ 391	Ron Washington	.30	.14	.04
☐ 392	Gary Roenicke	.30	.14	.04
☐ 393	Tom Candiotti	.75	.35	.09
☐ 394	Larry Pashnick	.30	.14	.04
☐ 395	Dwight Evans	.40	.18	.05
☐ 396	Goose Gossage	.50	.23	.06
☐ 397	Derrel Thomas	.30	.14	.04
☐ 398	Juan Eichelberger	.30	.14	.04
☐ 399	Leon Roberts	.30	.14	.04
☐ 400	Dave Lopes	.40	.18	.05
☐ 401	Bill Gullickson	.40	.18	.05
☐ 402	Geoff Zahn	.30	.14	.04
☐ 403	Billy Sample	.30	.14	.04
☐ 404	Mike Squires	.30	.14	.04
☐ 405	Craig Reynolds	.30	.14	.04
☐ 406	Eric Show	.30	.14	.04
☐ 407	John Denny	.30	.14	.04
☐ 408	Dann Bilardello	.30	.14	.04
☐ 409	Bruce Benedict	.30	.14	.04
☐ 410	Kent Tekulve	.40	.18	.05
☐ 411	Mel Hall	.40	.18	.05
☐ 412	John Stuper	.30	.14	.04
☐ 413	Rick Dempsey	.40	.18	.05
☐ 414	Don Sutton	.75	.35	.09
☐ 415	Jack Morris	.75	.35	.09
☐ 416	John Tudor	.40	.18	.05
☐ 417	Willie Randolph	.40	.18	.05
☐ 418	Jerry Reuss	.30	.14	.04
☐ 419	Don Slaught	.40	.18	.05
☐ 420	Steve McCatty	.30	.14	.04
☐ 421	Tim Wallach	.40	.18	.05
☐ 422	Larry Parrish	.30	.14	.04
☐ 423	Brian Downing	.40	.18	.05

☐ 424 Britt Burns	.30	.14	.04	
☐ 425 David Green	.30	.14	.04	
☐ 426 Jerry Mumphrey	.30	.14	.04	
☐ 427 Ivan DeJesus	.30	.14	.04	
☐ 428 Mario Soto	.30	.14	.04	
☐ 429 Gene Richards	.30	.14	.04	
☐ 430 Dale Berra	.30	.14	.04	
☐ 431 Darrell Evans	.40	.18	.05	
☐ 432 Glenn Hubbard	.30	.14	.04	
☐ 433 Jody Davis	.30	.14	.04	
☐ 434 Danny Heep	.30	.14	.04	
☐ 435 Ed Nunez	.30	.14	.04	
☐ 436 Bobby Castillo	.30	.14	.04	
☐ 437 Ernie Whitt	.30	.14	.04	
☐ 438 Scott Ullger	.30	.14	.04	
☐ 439 Doyle Alexander	.30	.14	.04	
☐ 440 Domingo Ramos	.30	.14	.04	
☐ 441 Craig Swan	.30	.14	.04	
☐ 442 Warren Brusstar	.30	.14	.04	
☐ 443 Len Barker	.30	.14	.04	
☐ 444 Mike Easler	.30	.14	.04	
☐ 445 Renie Martin	.30	.14	.04	
☐ 446 Dennis Rasmussen	.30	.14	.04	
☐ 447 Ted Power	.30	.14	.04	
☐ 448 Charles Hudson	.30	.14	.04	
☐ 449 Danny Cox	.40	.18	.05	
☐ 450 Kevin Bass	.30	.14	.04	
☐ 451 Daryl Sconiers	.30	.14	.04	
☐ 452 Scott Fletcher	.30	.14	.04	
☐ 453 Bryn Smith	.30	.14	.04	
☐ 454 Jim Dwyer	.30	.14	.04	
☐ 455 Rob Picciolo	.30	.14	.04	
☐ 456 Enos Cabell	.30	.14	.04	
☐ 457 Dennis Boyd	.40	.18	.05	
☐ 458 Butch Wynegar	.30	.14	.04	
☐ 459 Burt Hooton	.30	.14	.04	
☐ 460 Ron Hassey	.30	.14	.04	
☐ 461 Danny Jackson	1.00	.45	.12	
☐ 462 Bob Kearney	.30	.14	.04	
☐ 463 Terry Francona	.30	.14	.04	
☐ 464 Wayne Tolleson	.30	.14	.04	
☐ 465 Mickey Rivers	.30	.14	.04	
☐ 466 John Wathan	.30	.14	.04	
☐ 467 Bill Almon	.30	.14	.04	
☐ 468 George Vukovich	.30	.14	.04	
☐ 469 Steve Kemp	.30	.14	.04	
☐ 470 Ken Landreaux	.30	.14	.04	
☐ 471 Milt Wilcox	.30	.14	.04	
☐ 472 Tippy Martinez	.30	.14	.04	
☐ 473 Ted Simmons	.40	.18	.05	
☐ 474 Tim Foli	.30	.14	.04	
☐ 475 George Hendrick	.30	.14	.04	
☐ 476 Terry Puhl	.30	.14	.04	
☐ 477 Von Hayes	.30	.14	.04	
☐ 478 Bobby Brown	.30	.14	.04	
☐ 479 Lee Lacy	.30	.14	.04	
☐ 480 Joel Youngblood	.30	.14	.04	
☐ 481 Jim Slaton	.30	.14	.04	
☐ 482 Mike Fitzgerald	.30	.14	.04	
☐ 483 Keith Moreland	.30	.14	.04	
☐ 484 Ron Roenicke	.30	.14	.04	
☐ 485 Luis Leal	.30	.14	.04	
☐ 486 Bryan Oelkers	.30	.14	.04	
☐ 487 Bruce Berenyi	.30	.14	.04	
☐ 488 LaMarr Hoyt	.30	.14	.04	
☐ 489 Joe Nolan	.30	.14	.04	
☐ 490 Marshall Edwards	.30	.14	.04	
☐ 491 Mike Laga	.30	.14	.04	
☐ 492 Rick Cerone	.30	.14	.04	
☐ 493 Rick Miller UER	.30	.14	.04	
(Listed as Mike				

on card front)			
☐ 494 Rick Honeycutt	.30	.14	.04
☐ 495 Mike Hargrove	.40	.18	.05
☐ 496 Joe Simpson	.30	.14	.04
☐ 497 Keith Atherton	.30	.14	.04
☐ 498 Chris Welsh	.30	.14	.04
☐ 499 Bruce Kison	.30	.14	.04
☐ 500 Bobby Johnson	.30	.14	.04
☐ 501 Jerry Koosman	.40	.18	.05
☐ 502 Frank DiPino	.30	.14	.04
☐ 503 Tony Perez	.75	.35	.09
☐ 504 Ken Oberkfell	.30	.14	.04
☐ 505 Mark Thurmond	.30	.14	.04
☐ 506 Joe Price	.30	.14	.04
☐ 507 Pascual Perez	.30	.14	.04
☐ 508 Marvell Wynne	.30	.14	.04
☐ 509 Mike Krukow	.30	.14	.04
☐ 510 Dick Ruthven	.30	.14	.04
☐ 511 Al Cowens	.30	.14	.04
☐ 512 Cliff Johnson	.30	.14	.04
☐ 513 Randy Bush	.30	.14	.04
☐ 514 Sammy Stewart	.30	.14	.04
☐ 515 Bill Schroeder	.30	.14	.04
☐ 516 Aurelio Lopez	.40	.18	.05
☐ 517 Mike G. Brown	.30	.14	.04
☐ 518 Graig Nettles	.40	.18	.05
☐ 519 Dave Sax	.30	.14	.04
☐ 520 Jerry Willard	.30	.14	.04
☐ 521 Paul Splittorff	.30	.14	.04
☐ 522 Tom Burgmeier	.30	.14	.04
☐ 523 Chris Speier	.30	.14	.04
☐ 524 Bobby Clark	.30	.14	.04
☐ 525 George Wright	.30	.14	.04
☐ 526 Dennis Lamp	.30	.14	.04
☐ 527 Tony Scott	.30	.14	.04
☐ 528 Ed Whitson	.30	.14	.04
☐ 529 Ron Reed	.30	.14	.04
☐ 530 Charlie Puleo	.30	.14	.04
☐ 531 Jerry Royster	.30	.14	.04
☐ 532 Don Robinson	.30	.14	.04
☐ 533 Steve Trout	.30	.14	.04
☐ 534 Bruce Sutter	.40	.18	.05
☐ 535 Bob Horner	.40	.18	.05
☐ 536 Pat Tabler	.30	.14	.04
☐ 537 Chris Chambliss	.40	.18	.05
☐ 538 Bob Ojeda	.40	.18	.05
☐ 539 Alan Ashby	.30	.14	.04
☐ 540 Jay Johnstone	.40	.18	.05
☐ 541 Bob Dernier	.30	.14	.04
☐ 542 Brook Jacoby	.40	.18	.05
☐ 543 U.L. Washington	.30	.14	.04
☐ 544 Danny Darwin	.30	.14	.04
☐ 545 Kiko Garcia	.30	.14	.04
☐ 546 Vance Law UER	.30	.14	.04
(Listed as P			
on card front)			
☐ 547 Tug McGraw	.40	.18	.05
☐ 548 Dave Smith	.30	.14	.04
☐ 549 Len Matuszek	.30	.14	.04
☐ 550 Tom Hume	.30	.14	.04
☐ 551 Dave Dravecky	.40	.18	.05
☐ 552 Rick Rhoden	.30	.14	.04
☐ 553 Duane Kuiper	.30	.14	.04
☐ 554 Rusty Staub	.40	.18	.05
☐ 555 Bill Campbell	.30	.14	.04
☐ 556 Mike Torrez	.30	.14	.04
☐ 557 Dave Henderson	.40	.18	.05
☐ 558 Len Whitehouse	.30	.14	.04
☐ 559 Barry Bonnell	.30	.14	.04
☐ 560 Rick Lysander	.30	.14	.04
☐ 561 Garth Iorg	.30	.14	.04

☐ 562	Bryan Clark	.30	.14	.04
☐ 563	Brian Giles	.30	.14	.04
☐ 564	Vern Ruhle	.30	.14	.04
☐ 565	Steve Bedrosian	.40	.18	.05
☐ 566	Larry McWilliams	.30	.14	.04
☐ 567	Jeff Leonard UER	.30	.14	.04
	(Listed as P			
	on card front)			
☐ 568	Alan Wiggins	.30	.14	.04
☐ 569	Jeff Russell	.50	.23	.06
☐ 570	Salome Barojas	.30	.14	.04
☐ 571	Dane Iorg	.30	.14	.04
☐ 572	Bob Knepper	.30	.14	.04
☐ 573	Gary Lavelle	.30	.14	.04
☐ 574	Gorman Thomas	.30	.14	.04
☐ 575	Manny Trillo	.30	.14	.04
☐ 576	Jim Palmer	2.00	.90	.25
☐ 577	Dale Murray	.30	.14	.04
☐ 578	Tom Brookens	.40	.18	.05
☐ 579	Rich Gedman	.30	.14	.04
☐ 580	Bill Doran	.40	.18	.05
☐ 581	Steve Yeager	.30	.14	.04
☐ 582	Dan Spillner	.30	.14	.04
☐ 583	Dan Quisenberry	.40	.18	.05
☐ 584	Rance Mulliniks	.30	.14	.04
☐ 585	Storm Davis	.40	.18	.05
☐ 586	Dave Schmidt	.30	.14	.04
☐ 587	Bill Russell	.30	.14	.04
☐ 588	Pat Sheridan	.30	.14	.04
☐ 589	Rafael Ramirez	.30	.14	.04
	UER (A's on front)			
☐ 590	Bud Anderson	.30	.14	.04
☐ 591	George Frazier	.30	.14	.04
☐ 592	Lee Tunnell	.30	.14	.04
☐ 593	Kirk Gibson	1.25	.55	.16
☐ 594	Scott McGregor	.30	.14	.04
☐ 595	Bob Bailor	.30	.14	.04
☐ 596	Tommy Herr	.40	.18	.05
☐ 597	Luis Sanchez	.30	.14	.04
☐ 598	Dave Engle	.30	.14	.04
☐ 599	Craig McMurtry	.30	.14	.04
☐ 600	Carlos Diaz	.30	.14	.04
☐ 601	Tom O'Malley	.30	.14	.04
☐ 602	Nick Esasky	.30	.14	.04
☐ 603	Ron Hodges	.30	.14	.04
☐ 604	Ed VandeBerg	.30	.14	.04
☐ 605	Alfredo Griffin	.30	.14	.04
☐ 606	Glenn Hoffman	.30	.14	.04
☐ 607	Hubie Brooks	.40	.18	.05
☐ 608	Richard Barnes UER	.30	.14	.04
	(Photo actually			
	Neal Heaton)			
☐ 609	Greg Walker	.30	.14	.04
☐ 610	Ken Singleton	.40	.18	.05
☐ 611	Mark Clear	.30	.14	.04
☐ 612	Buck Martinez	.30	.14	.04
☐ 613	Ken Griffey	.40	.18	.05
☐ 614	Reid Nichols	.30	.14	.04
☐ 615	Doug Sisk	.30	.14	.04
☐ 616	Bob Brenly	.30	.14	.04
☐ 617	Joey McLaughlin	.30	.14	.04
☐ 618	Glenn Wilson	.40	.18	.05
☐ 619	Bob Stoddard	.30	.14	.04
☐ 620	Lenn Sakata UER	.30	.14	.04
	(Listed as Len			
	on card front)			
☐ 621	Mike Young	.30	.14	.04
☐ 622	John Stefero	.30	.14	.04
☐ 623	Carmelo Martinez	.30	.14	.04
☐ 624	Dave Bergman	.30	.14	.04
☐ 625	Runnin' Reds UER	1.50	.70	.19
	(Sic, Redbirds)			
	David Green			
	Willie McGee			
	Lonnie Smith			
	Ozzie Smith			
☐ 626	Rudy May	.30	.14	.04
☐ 627	Matt Keough	.30	.14	.04
☐ 628	Jose DeLeon	.40	.18	.04
☐ 629	Jim Essian	.30	.14	.04
☐ 630	Darnell Coles	.30	.14	.04
☐ 631	Mike Warren	.30	.14	.04
☐ 632	Del Crandall MG	.30	.14	.04
☐ 633	Dennis Martinez	.40	.18	.05
☐ 634	Mike Moore	.40	.18	.05
☐ 635	Lary Sorensen	.30	.14	.04
☐ 636	Ricky Nelson	.30	.14	.04
☐ 637	Omar Moreno	.30	.14	.04
☐ 638	Charlie Hough	.40	.18	.05
☐ 639	Dennis Eckersley	2.50	1.10	.30
☐ 640	Walt Terrell	.30	.14	.04
☐ 641	Denny Walling	.30	.14	.04
☐ 642	Dave Anderson	.30	.14	.04
☐ 643	Jose Oquendo	.40	.18	.05
☐ 644	Bob Stanley	.30	.14	.04
☐ 645	Dave Geisel	.30	.14	.04
☐ 646	Scott Garrelts	.40	.18	.05
☐ 647	Gary Pettis	.30	.14	.04
☐ 648	Duke Snider	.50	.23	.06
	Puzzle Card			
☐ 649	Johnnie LeMaster	.30	.14	.04
☐ 650	Dave Collins	.30	.14	.04
☐ 651	The Chicken	.50	.23	.06
☐ 652	DK Checklist 1-26	.40	.18	.05
	(Unnumbered)			
☐ 653	Checklist 27-130	.40	.18	.05
	(Unnumbered)			
☐ 654	Checklist 131-234	.40	.18	.05
	(Unnumbered)			
☐ 655	Checklist 235-338	.40	.18	.05
	(Unnumbered)			
☐ 656	Checklist 339-442	.40	.18	.05
	(Unnumbered)			
☐ 657	Checklist 443-546	.40	.18	.05
	(Unnumbered)			
☐ 658	Checklist 547-651	.40	.18	.05
	(Unnumbered)			
☐ A	Living Legends A	4.00	1.80	.50
	Gaylord Perry			
	Rollie Fingers			
☐ B	Living Legends B	8.00	3.60	1.00
	Carl Yastrzemski			
	Johnny Bench			

1985 Donruss

*The cards in this 660-card set measure 2
1/2" by 3 1/2". The 1985 Donruss regular
issue cards have fronts that feature jet
black borders on which orange lines have
been placed. The fronts contain the standard team logo, player's name, position,
and Donruss logo. The cards were distributed with puzzle pieces from a Dick Perez
rendition of Lou Gehrig. The first 26 cards
of the set feature Diamond Kings (DK), for
the fourth year in a row; the artwork on the
Diamond Kings was again produced by the
Perez-Steele Galleries. The jumbo (5 by 7*

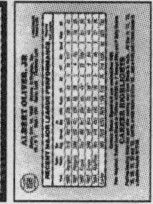

inch) versions of the 1985 Diamond Kings are valued equally to their standard-size counterparts. Cards 27-46 feature Rated Rookies (RR). The unnumbered checklist cards are arbitrarily numbered below as numbers 654 through 660. Rookie Cards in this set include Roger Clemens, Alvin Davis, Eric Davis, Shawon Dunston, Dwight Gooden, Orel Hershiser, Jimmy Key, Mark Langston, Terry Pendleton, Kirby Puckett, Jose Rijo, Bret Saberhagen, and Danny Tartabull.

	NRMT-MT	EXC	G-VG
COMPLETE SET (660)	120.00	55.00	15.00
COMPLETE FACT.SET (660)	150.00	70.00	19.00
COMMON CARD (1-660)	.10	.05	.01

☐ 1	Ryne Sandberg DK	3.00	1.35	.35
☐ 2	Doug DeCinces DK	.10	.05	.01
☐ 3	Richard Dotson DK	.10	.05	.01
☐ 4	Bert Blyleven DK	.20	.09	.03
☐ 5	Lou Whitaker DK	.40	.18	.05
☐ 6	Dan Quisenberry DK	.10	.05	.01
☐ 7	Don Mattingly DK	4.00	1.80	.50
☐ 8	Carney Lansford DK	.10	.05	.01
☐ 9	Frank Tanana DK	.10	.05	.01
☐ 10	Willie Upshaw DK	.10	.05	.01
☐ 11	Claudell Washington DK	.10	.05	.01
☐ 12	Mike Marshall DK	.10	.05	.01
☐ 13	Joaquin Andujar DK	.10	.05	.01
☐ 14	Cal Ripken DK	5.00	2.20	.60
☐ 15	Jim Rice DK	.20	.09	.03
☐ 16	Don Sutton DK	.20	.09	.03
☐ 17	Frank Viola DK	.20	.09	.03
☐ 18	Alvin Davis DK	.10	.05	.01
☐ 19	Mario Soto DK	.10	.05	.01
☐ 20	Jose Cruz DK	.10	.05	.01
☐ 21	Charlie Lea DK	.10	.05	.01
☐ 22	Jesse Orosco DK	.10	.05	.01
☐ 23	Juan Samuel DK	.10	.05	.01
☐ 24	Tony Pena DK	.10	.05	.01
☐ 25	Tony Gwynn DK	3.00	1.35	.35
☐ 26	Bob Brenly DK	.10	.05	.01
☐ 27	Danny Tartabull RR	1.50	.70	.19
☐ 28	Mike Bielecki RR	.10	.05	.01
☐ 29	Steve Lyons RR	.10	.05	.01
☐ 30	Jeff Reed RR	.10	.05	.01
☐ 31	Tony Brewer RR	.10	.05	.01
☐ 32	John Morris RR	.10	.05	.01
☐ 33	Daryl Boston RR	.10	.05	.01
☐ 34	Al Pulido RR	.10	.05	.01
☐ 35	Steve Kiefer RR	.10	.05	.01
☐ 36	Larry Sheets RR	.10	.05	.01
☐ 37	Scott Bradley RR	.10	.05	.01
☐ 38	Calvin Schiraldi RR	.10	.05	.01
☐ 39	Shawon Dunston RR	1.25	.55	.16
☐ 40	Charlie Mitchell RR	.10	.05	.01
☐ 41	Billy Hatcher RR	.30	.14	.04
☐ 42	Russ Stephans RR	.10	.05	.01
☐ 43	Alejandro Sanchez RR	.10	.05	.01
☐ 44	Steve Jeltz RR	.10	.05	.01
☐ 45	Jim Traber RR	.10	.05	.01
☐ 46	Doug Loman RR	.10	.05	.01
☐ 47	Eddie Murray	2.50	1.10	.30
☐ 48	Robin Yount	2.00	.90	.25
☐ 49	Lance Parrish	.20	.09	.03
☐ 50	Jim Rice	.30	.14	.04
☐ 51	Dave Winfield	1.50	.70	.19
☐ 52	Fernando Valenzuela	.20	.09	.03
☐ 53	George Brett	4.00	1.80	.50
☐ 54	Dave Kingman	.20	.09	.03
☐ 55	Gary Carter	.40	.18	.05
☐ 56	Buddy Bell	.20	.09	.03
☐ 57	Reggie Jackson	1.50	.70	.19
☐ 58	Harold Baines	.30	.14	.04
☐ 59	Ozzie Smith	2.50	1.10	.30
☐ 60	Nolan Ryan UER	10.00	4.50	1.25
	(Set strikeout record in 1973, not 1972)			
☐ 61	Mike Schmidt	3.00	1.35	.35
☐ 62	Dave Parker	.30	.14	.04
☐ 63	Tony Gwynn	6.00	2.70	.75
☐ 64	Tony Pena	.10	.05	.01
☐ 65	Jack Clark	.20	.09	.03
☐ 66	Dale Murphy	.40	.18	.05
☐ 67	Ryne Sandberg	6.00	2.70	.75
☐ 68	Keith Hernandez	.30	.14	.04
☐ 69	Alvin Davis	.20	.09	.03
☐ 70	Kent Hrbek	.20	.09	.03
☐ 71	Willie Upshaw	.10	.05	.01
☐ 72	Dave Engle	.10	.05	.01
☐ 73	Alfredo Griffin	.10	.05	.01
☐ 74A	Jack Perconte	.10	.05	.01
	(Career Highlights takes four lines)			
☐ 74B	Jack Perconte	.10	.05	.01
	(Career Highlights takes three lines)			
☐ 75	Jesse Orosco	.10	.05	.01
☐ 76	Jody Davis	.10	.05	.01
☐ 77	Bob Horner	.10	.05	.01
☐ 78	Larry McWilliams	.10	.05	.01
☐ 79	Joel Youngblood	.10	.05	.01
☐ 80	Alan Wiggins	.10	.05	.01
☐ 81	Ron Oester	.10	.05	.01
☐ 82	Ozzie Virgil	.10	.05	.01
☐ 83	Ricky Horton	.10	.05	.01
☐ 84	Bill Doran	.10	.05	.01
☐ 85	Rod Carew	.60	.25	.07
☐ 86	LaMarr Hoyt	.10	.05	.01
☐ 87	Tim Wallach	.20	.09	.03
☐ 88	Mike Flanagan	.10	.05	.01
☐ 89	Jim Sundberg	.20	.09	.03
☐ 90	Chet Lemon	.10	.05	.01
☐ 91	Bob Stanley	.10	.05	.01
☐ 92	Willie Randolph	.20	.09	.03
☐ 93	Bill Russell	.20	.09	.03
☐ 94	Julio Franco	.30	.14	.04
☐ 95	Dan Quisenberry	.20	.09	.03
☐ 96	Bill Caudill	.10	.05	.01
☐ 97	Bill Gullickson	.20	.09	.03
☐ 98	Danny Darwin	.10	.05	.01
☐ 99	Curtis Wilkerson	.10	.05	.01
☐ 100	Bud Black	.10	.05	.01
☐ 101	Tony Phillips	.30	.14	.04
☐ 102	Tony Bernazard	.10	.05	.01

☐ 103	Jay Howell	.20	.09	.03
☐ 104	Burt Hooton	.10	.05	.01
☐ 105	Milt Wilcox	.10	.05	.01
☐ 106	Rich Dauer	.10	.05	.01
☐ 107	Don Sutton	.30	.14	.04
☐ 108	Mike Witt	.10	.05	.01
☐ 109	Bruce Sutter	.20	.09	.03
☐ 110	Enos Cabell	.10	.05	.01
☐ 111	John Denny	.10	.05	.01
☐ 112	Dave Dravecky	.20	.09	.03
☐ 113	Marvell Wynne	.10	.05	.01
☐ 114	Johnnie LeMaster	.10	.05	.01
☐ 115	Chuck Porter	.10	.05	.01
☐ 116	John Gibbons	.10	.05	.01
☐ 117	Keith Moreland	.10	.05	.01
☐ 118	Darnell Coles	.10	.05	.01
☐ 119	Dennis Lamp	.10	.05	.01
☐ 120	Ron Davis	.10	.05	.01
☐ 121	Nick Esasky	.10	.05	.01
☐ 122	Vance Law	.10	.05	.01
☐ 123	Gary Roenicke	.10	.05	.01
☐ 124	Bill Schroeder	.10	.05	.01
☐ 125	Dave Rozema	.10	.05	.01
☐ 126	Bobby Meacham	.10	.05	.01
☐ 127	Marty Barrett	.10	.05	.01
☐ 128	R.J. Reynolds	.10	.05	.01
☐ 129	Ernie Camacho UER	.10	.05	.01
	(Photo actually			
	Rich Thompson)			
☐ 130	Jorge Orta	.10	.05	.01
☐ 131	Lary Sorensen	.10	.05	.01
☐ 132	Terry Francona	.10	.05	.01
☐ 133	Fred Lynn	.20	.09	.03
☐ 134	Bob Jones	.10	.05	.01
☐ 135	Jerry Hairston	.10	.05	.01
☐ 136	Kevin Bass	.10	.05	.01
☐ 137	Garry Maddox	.10	.05	.01
☐ 138	Dave LaPoint	.10	.05	.01
☐ 139	Kevin McReynolds	.20	.09	.03
☐ 140	Wayne Krenchicki	.10	.05	.01
☐ 141	Rafael Ramirez	.10	.05	.01
☐ 142	Rod Scurry	.10	.05	.01
☐ 143	Greg Minton	.10	.05	.01
☐ 144	Tim Stoddard	.10	.05	.01
☐ 145	Steve Henderson	.10	.05	.01
☐ 146	George Bell	.30	.14	.04
☐ 147	Dave Meier	.10	.05	.01
☐ 148	Sammy Stewart	.10	.05	.01
☐ 149	Mark Brouhard	.10	.05	.01
☐ 150	Larry Herndon	.10	.05	.01
☐ 151	Oil Can Boyd	.10	.05	.01
☐ 152	Brian Dayett	.10	.05	.01
☐ 153	Tom Niedenfuer	.10	.05	.01
☐ 154	Brook Jacoby	.10	.05	.01
☐ 155	Onix Concepcion	.10	.05	.01
☐ 156	Tim Conroy	.10	.05	.01
☐ 157	Joe Hesketh	.10	.05	.01
☐ 158	Brian Downing	.20	.09	.03
☐ 159	Tommy Dunbar	.10	.05	.01
☐ 160	Marc Hill	.10	.05	.01
☐ 161	Phil Garner	.20	.09	.03
☐ 162	Jerry Davis	.10	.05	.01
☐ 163	Bill Campbell	.10	.05	.01
☐ 164	John Franco	1.25	.55	.16
☐ 165	Len Barker	.10	.05	.01
☐ 166	Benny Distefano	.10	.05	.01
☐ 167	George Frazier	.10	.05	.01
☐ 168	Tito Landrum	.10	.05	.01
☐ 169	Cal Ripken	8.00	3.60	1.00
☐ 170	Cecil Cooper	.20	.09	.03
☐ 171	Alan Trammell	.75	.35	.09

☐ 172	Wade Boggs	2.50	1.10	.30
☐ 173	Don Baylor	.30	.14	.04
☐ 174	Pedro Guerrero	.20	.09	.03
☐ 175	Frank White	.20	.09	.03
☐ 176	Rickey Henderson	1.50	.70	.19
☐ 177	Charlie Lea	.10	.05	.01
☐ 178	Pete O'Brien	.20	.09	.03
☐ 179	Doug DeCinces	.10	.05	.01
☐ 180	Ron Kittle	.10	.05	.01
☐ 181	George Hendrick	.10	.05	.01
☐ 182	Joe Niekro	.20	.09	.03
☐ 183	Juan Samuel	.10	.05	.01
☐ 184	Mario Soto	.10	.05	.01
☐ 185	Goose Gossage	.30	.14	.04
☐ 186	Johnny Ray	.10	.05	.01
☐ 187	Bob Brenly	.10	.05	.01
☐ 188	Craig McMurtry	.10	.05	.01
☐ 189	Leon Durham	.10	.05	.01
☐ 190	Dwight Gooden	1.00	.45	.12
☐ 191	Barry Bonnell	.10	.05	.01
☐ 192	Tim Teufel	.10	.05	.01
☐ 193	Dave Stieb	.20	.09	.03
☐ 194	Mickey Hatcher	.10	.05	.01
☐ 195	Jesse Barfield	.10	.05	.01
☐ 196	Al Cowens	.10	.05	.01
☐ 197	Hubie Brooks	.20	.09	.03
☐ 198	Steve Trout	.10	.05	.01
☐ 199	Glenn Hubbard	.10	.05	.01
☐ 200	Bill Madlock	.20	.09	.03
☐ 201	Jeff D. Robinson	.10	.05	.01
☐ 202	Eric Show	.10	.05	.01
☐ 203	Dave Concepcion	.20	.09	.03
☐ 204	Ivan DeJesus	.10	.05	.01
☐ 205	Neil Allen	.10	.05	.01
☐ 206	Jerry Mumphrey	.10	.05	.01
☐ 207	Mike C. Brown	.10	.05	.01
☐ 208	Carlton Fisk	.75	.35	.09
☐ 209	Bryn Smith	.10	.05	.01
☐ 210	Tippy Martinez	.10	.05	.01
☐ 211	Dion James	.10	.05	.01
☐ 212	Willie Hernandez	.10	.05	.01
☐ 213	Mike Easler	.10	.05	.01
☐ 214	Ron Guidry	.20	.09	.03
☐ 215	Rick Honeycutt	.10	.05	.01
☐ 216	Brett Butler	.30	.14	.04
☐ 217	Larry Gura	.10	.05	.01
☐ 218	Ray Burris	.10	.05	.01
☐ 219	Steve Rogers	.10	.05	.01
☐ 220	Frank Tanana	.20	.09	.03
	(Bats Left listed			
	twice on card back)			
☐ 221	Ned Yost	.10	.05	.01
☐ 222	Bret Saberhagen UER	4.00	1.80	.50
	(18 career IP on back)			
☐ 223	Mike Davis	.10	.05	.01
☐ 224	Bert Blyleven	.30	.14	.04
☐ 225	Steve Kemp	.10	.05	.01
☐ 226	Jerry Reuss	.10	.05	.01
☐ 227	Darrell Evans UER	.20	.09	.03
	(80 homers in 1980)			
☐ 228	Wayne Gross	.10	.05	.01
☐ 229	Jim Gantner	.10	.05	.01
☐ 230	Bob Boone	.20	.09	.03
☐ 231	Lonnie Smith	.10	.05	.01
☐ 232	Frank DiPino	.10	.05	.01
☐ 233	Jerry Koosman	.20	.09	.03
☐ 234	Graig Nettles	.20	.09	.03
☐ 235	John Tudor	.20	.09	.03
☐ 236	John Rabb	.10	.05	.01
☐ 237	Rick Manning	.10	.05	.01
☐ 238	Mike Fitzgerald	.10	.05	.01

☐ 239	Gary Matthews	.10	.05	.01
☐ 240	Jim Presley	.10	.05	.01
☐ 241	Dave Collins	.10	.05	.01
☐ 242	Gary Gaetti	.20	.09	.03
☐ 243	Dann Bilardello	.10	.05	.01
☐ 244	Rudy Law	.10	.05	.01
☐ 245	John Lowenstein	.10	.05	.01
☐ 246	Tom Tellmann	.10	.05	.01
☐ 247	Howard Johnson	.20	.09	.03
☐ 248	Ray Fontenot	.10	.05	.01
☐ 249	Tony Armas	.10	.05	.01
☐ 250	Candy Maldonado	.10	.05	.01
☐ 251	Mike Jeffcoat	.10	.05	.01
☐ 252	Dane Iorg	.10	.05	.01
☐ 253	Bruce Bochte	.10	.05	.01
☐ 254	Pete Rose	2.00	.90	.25
☐ 255	Don Aase	.10	.05	.01
☐ 256	George Wright	.10	.05	.01
☐ 257	Britt Burns	.10	.05	.01
☐ 258	Mike Scott	.20	.09	.03
☐ 259	Len Matuszek	.10	.05	.01
☐ 260	Dave Rucker	.10	.05	.01
☐ 261	Craig Lefferts	.20	.09	.03
☐ 262	Jay Tibbs	.10	.05	.01
☐ 263	Bruce Benedict	.10	.05	.01
☐ 264	Don Robinson	.10	.05	.01
☐ 265	Gary Lavelle	.10	.05	.01
☐ 266	Scott Sanderson	.10	.05	.01
☐ 267	Matt Young	.10	.05	.01
☐ 268	Ernie Whitt	.10	.05	.01
☐ 269	Houston Jimenez	.10	.05	.01
☐ 270	Ken Dixon	.10	.05	.01
☐ 271	Pete Ladd	.10	.05	.01
☐ 272	Juan Berenguer	.10	.05	.01
☐ 273	Roger Clemens	20.00	9.00	2.50
☐ 274	Rick Cerone	.10	.05	.01
☐ 275	Dave Anderson	.10	.05	.01
☐ 276	George Vukovich	.10	.05	.01
☐ 277	Greg Pryor	.10	.05	.01
☐ 278	Mike Warren	.10	.05	.01
☐ 279	Bob James	.10	.05	.01
☐ 280	Bobby Grich	.20	.09	.03
☐ 281	Mike Mason	.10	.05	.01
☐ 282	Ron Reed	.10	.05	.01
☐ 283	Alan Ashby	.10	.05	.01
☐ 284	Mark Thurmond	.10	.05	.01
☐ 285	Joe Lefebvre	.10	.05	.01
☐ 286	Ted Power	.10	.05	.01
☐ 287	Chris Chambliss	.20	.09	.03
☐ 288	Lee Tunnell	.10	.05	.01
☐ 289	Rich Bordi	.10	.05	.01
☐ 290	Glenn Brummer	.10	.05	.01
☐ 291	Mike Boddicker	.10	.05	.01
☐ 292	Rollie Fingers	.30	.14	.04
☐ 293	Lou Whitaker	.60	.25	.07
☐ 294	Dwight Evans	.20	.09	.03
☐ 295	Don Mattingly	8.00	3.60	1.00
☐ 296	Mike Marshall	.10	.05	.01
☐ 297	Willie Wilson	.20	.09	.03
☐ 298	Mike Heath	.10	.05	.01
☐ 299	Tim Raines	.40	.18	.05
☐ 300	Larry Parrish	.10	.05	.01
☐ 301	Geoff Zahn	.10	.05	.01
☐ 302	Rich Dotson	.10	.05	.01
☐ 303	David Green	.10	.05	.01
☐ 304	Jose Cruz	.20	.09	.03
☐ 305	Steve Carlton	.75	.35	.09
☐ 306	Gary Redus	.10	.05	.01
☐ 307	Steve Garvey	.30	.14	.04
☐ 308	Jose DeLeon	.10	.05	.01
☐ 309	Randy Lerch	.10	.05	.01
☐ 310	Claudell Washington	.10	.05	.01
☐ 311	Lee Smith	1.00	.45	.12
☐ 312	Darryl Strawberry	.75	.35	.09
☐ 313	Jim Beattie	.10	.05	.01
☐ 314	John Butcher	.10	.05	.01
☐ 315	Damaso Garcia	.10	.05	.01
☐ 316	Mike Smithson	.10	.05	.01
☐ 317	Luis Leal	.10	.05	.01
☐ 318	Ken Phelps	.10	.05	.01
☐ 319	Wally Backman	.10	.05	.01
☐ 320	Ron Cey	.20	.09	.03
☐ 321	Brad Komminsk	.10	.05	.01
☐ 322	Jason Thompson	.10	.05	.01
☐ 323	Frank Williams	.10	.05	.01
☐ 324	Tim Lollar	.10	.05	.01
☐ 325	Eric Davis	1.00	.45	.12
☐ 326	Von Hayes	.10	.05	.01
☐ 327	Andy Van Slyke	.60	.25	.07
☐ 328	Craig Reynolds	.10	.05	.01
☐ 329	Dick Schofield	.10	.05	.01
☐ 330	Scott Fletcher	.10	.05	.01
☐ 331	Jeff Reardon	.30	.14	.04
☐ 332	Rick Dempsey	.10	.05	.01
☐ 333	Ben Oglivie	.10	.05	.01
☐ 334	Dan Petry	.10	.05	.01
☐ 335	Jackie Gutierrez	.10	.05	.01
☐ 336	Dave Righetti	.20	.09	.03
☐ 337	Alejandro Pena	.10	.05	.01
☐ 338	Mel Hall	.10	.05	.01
☐ 339	Pat Sheridan	.10	.05	.01
☐ 340	Keith Atherton	.10	.05	.01
☐ 341	David Palmer	.10	.05	.01
☐ 342	Gary Ward	.10	.05	.01
☐ 343	Dave Stewart	.30	.14	.04
☐ 344	Mark Gubicza	.30	.14	.04
☐ 345	Carney Lansford	.20	.09	.03
☐ 346	Jerry Willard	.10	.05	.01
☐ 347	Ken Griffey	.20	.09	.03
☐ 348	Franklin Stubbs	.10	.05	.01
☐ 349	Aurelio Lopez	.10	.05	.01
☐ 350	Al Bumbry	.20	.09	.03
☐ 351	Charlie Moore	.10	.05	.01
☐ 352	Luis Sanchez	.10	.05	.01
☐ 353	Darrell Porter	.10	.05	.01
☐ 354	Bill Dawley	.10	.05	.01
☐ 355	Charles Hudson	.10	.05	.01
☐ 356	Garry Templeton	.10	.05	.01
☐ 357	Cecilio Guante	.10	.05	.01
☐ 358	Jeff Leonard	.10	.05	.01
☐ 359	Paul Molitor	1.50	.70	.19
☐ 360	Ron Gardenhire	.10	.05	.01
☐ 361	Larry Bowa	.20	.09	.03
☐ 362	Bob Kearney	.10	.05	.01
☐ 363	Garth Iorg	.10	.05	.01
☐ 364	Tom Brunansky	.20	.09	.03
☐ 365	Brad Gulden	.10	.05	.01
☐ 366	Greg Walker	.10	.05	.01
☐ 367	Mike Young	.10	.05	.01
☐ 368	Rick Waits	.10	.05	.01
☐ 369	Doug Bair	.10	.05	.01
☐ 370	Bob Shirley	.10	.05	.01
☐ 371	Bob Ojeda	.20	.09	.03
☐ 372	Bob Welch	.20	.09	.03
☐ 373	Neal Heaton	.10	.05	.01
☐ 374	Danny Jackson UER	.20	.09	.03
	(Photo actually Frank Wills)			
☐ 375	Donnie Hill	.10	.05	.01
☐ 376	Mike Stenhouse	.10	.05	.01
☐ 377	Bruce Kison	.10	.05	.01
☐ 378	Wayne Tolleson	.10	.05	.01

☐ 379 Floyd Bannister	.10	.05	.01
☐ 380 Vern Ruhle	.10	.05	.01
☐ 381 Tim Corcoran	.10	.05	.01
☐ 382 Kurt Kepshire	.10	.05	.01
☐ 383 Bobby Brown	.10	.05	.01
☐ 384 Dave Van Gorder	.10	.05	.01
☐ 385 Rick Mahler	.10	.05	.01
☐ 386 Lee Mazzilli	.10	.05	.01
☐ 387 Bill Laskey	.10	.05	.01
☐ 388 Thad Bosley	.10	.05	.01
☐ 389 Al Chambers	.10	.05	.01
☐ 390 Tony Fernandez	.20	.09	.03
☐ 391 Ron Washington	.10	.05	.01
☐ 392 Bill Swaggerty	.10	.05	.01
☐ 393 Bob L. Gibson	.10	.05	.01
☐ 394 Marty Castillo	.10	.05	.01
☐ 395 Steve Crawford	.10	.05	.01
☐ 396 Clay Christiansen	.10	.05	.01
☐ 397 Bob Bailor	.10	.05	.01
☐ 398 Mike Hargrove	.20	.09	.03
☐ 399 Charlie Leibrandt	.10	.05	.01
☐ 400 Tom Burgmeier	.10	.05	.01
☐ 401 Razor Shines	.10	.05	.01
☐ 402 Rob Wilfong	.10	.05	.01
☐ 403 Tom Henke	.30	.14	.04
☐ 404 Al Jones	.10	.05	.01
☐ 405 Mike LaCoss	.10	.05	.01
☐ 406 Luis DeLeon	.10	.05	.01
☐ 407 Greg Gross	.10	.05	.01
☐ 408 Tom Hume	.10	.05	.01
☐ 409 Rick Camp	.10	.05	.01
☐ 410 Milt May	.10	.05	.01
☐ 411 Henry Cotto	.10	.05	.01
☐ 412 David Von Ohlen	.10	.05	.01
☐ 413 Scott McGregor	.10	.05	.01
☐ 414 Ted Simmons	.20	.09	.03
☐ 415 Jack Morris	.40	.18	.05
☐ 416 Bill Buckner	.20	.09	.03
☐ 417 Butch Wynegar	.10	.05	.01
☐ 418 Steve Sax	.20	.09	.03
☐ 419 Steve Balboni	.10	.05	.01
☐ 420 Dwayne Murphy	.10	.05	.01
☐ 421 Andre Dawson	1.50	.70	.19
☐ 422 Charlie Hough	.20	.09	.03
☐ 423 Tommy John	.30	.14	.04
☐ 424A Tom Seaver ERR	1.25	.55	.16
(Photo actually Floyd Bannister)			
☐ 424B Tom Seaver COR	25.00	11.00	3.10
☐ 425 Tommy Herr	.20	.09	.03
☐ 426 Terry Puhl	.10	.05	.01
☐ 427 Al Holland	.10	.05	.01
☐ 428 Eddie Milner	.10	.05	.01
☐ 429 Terry Kennedy	.10	.05	.01
☐ 430 John Candelaria	.10	.05	.01
☐ 431 Manny Trillo	.10	.05	.01
☐ 432 Ken Oberkfell	.10	.05	.01
☐ 433 Rick Sutcliffe	.20	.09	.03
☐ 434 Ron Darling	.20	.09	.03
☐ 435 Spike Owen	.10	.05	.01
☐ 436 Frank Viola	.20	.09	.03
☐ 437 Lloyd Moseby	.10	.05	.01
☐ 438 Kirby Puckett	30.00	13.50	3.70
☐ 439 Jim Clancy	.10	.05	.01
☐ 440 Mike Moore	.20	.09	.03
☐ 441 Doug Sisk	.10	.05	.01
☐ 442 Dennis Eckersley	.40	.18	.05
☐ 443 Gerald Perry	.10	.05	.01
☐ 444 Dale Berra	.10	.05	.01
☐ 445 Dusty Baker	.30	.14	.04
☐ 446 Ed Whitson	.10	.05	.01
☐ 447 Cesar Cedeno	.20	.09	.03
☐ 448 Rick Schu	.10	.05	.01
☐ 449 Joaquin Andujar	.10	.05	.01
☐ 450 Mark Bailey	.10	.05	.01
☐ 451 Ron Romanick	.10	.05	.01
☐ 452 Julio Cruz	.10	.05	.01
☐ 453 Miguel Dilone	.10	.05	.01
☐ 454 Storm Davis	.10	.05	.01
☐ 455 Jaime Cocanower	.10	.05	.01
☐ 456 Barbaro Garbey	.10	.05	.01
☐ 457 Rich Gedman	.10	.05	.01
☐ 458 Phil Niekro	.30	.14	.04
☐ 459 Mike Scioscia	.10	.05	.01
☐ 460 Pat Tabler	.10	.05	.01
☐ 461 Darryl Motley	.10	.05	.01
☐ 462 Chris Codiroli	.10	.05	.01
☐ 463 Doug Flynn	.10	.05	.01
☐ 464 Billy Sample	.10	.05	.01
☐ 465 Mickey Rivers	.10	.05	.01
☐ 466 John Wathan	.10	.05	.01
☐ 467 Bill Krueger	.10	.05	.01
☐ 468 Andre Thornton	.10	.05	.01
☐ 469 Rex Hudler	.10	.05	.01
☐ 470 Sid Bream	.30	.14	.04
☐ 471 Kirk Gibson	.30	.14	.04
☐ 472 John Shelby	.10	.05	.01
☐ 473 Moose Haas	.10	.05	.01
☐ 474 Doug Corbett	.10	.05	.01
☐ 475 Willie McGee	.20	.09	.03
☐ 476 Bob Knepper	.10	.05	.01
☐ 477 Kevin Gross	.10	.05	.01
☐ 478 Carmelo Martinez	.10	.05	.01
☐ 479 Kent Tekulve	.10	.05	.01
☐ 480 Chili Davis	.20	.09	.03
☐ 481 Bobby Clark	.10	.05	.01
☐ 482 Mookie Wilson	.20	.09	.03
☐ 483 Dave Owen	.10	.05	.01
☐ 484 Ed Nunez	.10	.05	.01
☐ 485 Rance Mulliniks	.10	.05	.01
☐ 486 Ken Schrom	.10	.05	.01
☐ 487 Jeff Russell	.20	.09	.03
☐ 488 Tom Paciorek	.20	.09	.03
☐ 489 Dan Ford	.10	.05	.01
☐ 490 Mike Caldwell	.10	.05	.01
☐ 491 Scottie Earl	.10	.05	.01
☐ 492 Jose Rijo	2.00	.90	.25
☐ 493 Bruce Hurst	.20	.09	.03
☐ 494 Ken Landreaux	.10	.05	.01
☐ 495 Mike Fischlin	.10	.05	.01
☐ 496 Don Slaught	.10	.05	.01
☐ 497 Steve McCatty	.10	.05	.01
☐ 498 Gary Lucas	.10	.05	.01
☐ 499 Gary Pettis	.10	.05	.01
☐ 500 Marvis Foley	.10	.05	.01
☐ 501 Mike Squires	.10	.05	.01
☐ 502 Jim Pankovits	.10	.05	.01
☐ 503 Luis Aguayo	.10	.05	.01
☐ 504 Ralph Citarella	.10	.05	.01
☐ 505 Bruce Bochy	.10	.05	.01
☐ 506 Bob Owchinko	.10	.05	.01
☐ 507 Pascual Perez	.10	.05	.01
☐ 508 Lee Lacy	.10	.05	.01
☐ 509 Atlee Hammaker	.10	.05	.01
☐ 510 Bob Dernier	.10	.05	.01
☐ 511 Ed VandeBerg	.10	.05	.01
☐ 512 Cliff Johnson	.10	.05	.01
☐ 513 Len Whitehouse	.10	.05	.01
☐ 514 Dennis Martinez	.20	.09	.03
☐ 515 Ed Romero	.10	.05	.01
☐ 516 Rusty Kuntz	.10	.05	.01
☐ 517 Rick Miller	.10	.05	.01

518	Dennis Rasmussen	.10	.05	.01
519	Steve Yeager	.10	.05	.01
520	Chris Bando	.10	.05	.01
521	U.L. Washington	.10	.05	.01
522	Curt Young	.10	.05	.01
523	Angel Salazar	.10	.05	.01
524	Curt Kaufman	.10	.05	.01
525	Odell Jones	.10	.05	.01
526	Juan Agosto	.10	.05	.01
527	Denny Walling	.10	.05	.01
528	Andy Hawkins	.10	.05	.01
529	Sixto Lezcano	.10	.05	.01
530	Skeeter Barnes	.10	.05	.01
531	Randy Johnson	.10	.05	.01
532	Jim Morrison	.10	.05	.01
533	Warren Brusstar	.10	.05	.01
534A	Jeff Pendleton ERR..	2.00	.90	.25
	(Wrong first name)			
534B	Terry Pendleton COR	10.00	4.50	1.25
535	Vic Rodriguez	.10	.05	.01
536	Bob McClure	.10	.05	.01
537	Dave Bergman	.10	.05	.01
538	Mark Clear	.10	.05	.01
539	Mike Pagliarulo	.10	.05	.01
540	Terry Whitfield	.10	.05	.01
541	Joe Beckwith	.10	.05	.01
542	Jeff Burroughs	.10	.05	.01
543	Dan Schatzeder	.10	.05	.01
544	Donnie Scott	.10	.05	.01
545	Jim Slaton	.10	.05	.01
546	Greg Luzinski	.20	.09	.03
547	Mark Salas	.10	.05	.01
548	Dave Smith	.10	.05	.01
549	John Wockenfuss	.10	.05	.01
550	Frank Pastore	.10	.05	.01
551	Tim Flannery	.10	.05	.01
552	Rick Rhoden	.10	.05	.01
553	Mark Davis	.10	.05	.01
554	Jeff Dedmon	.10	.05	.01
555	Gary Woods	.10	.05	.01
556	Danny Heep	.10	.05	.01
557	Mark Langston	3.00	1.35	.35
558	Darrell Brown	.10	.05	.01
559	Jimmy Key	1.50	.70	.19
560	Rick Lysander	.10	.05	.01
561	Doyle Alexander	.10	.05	.01
562	Mike Stanton	.10	.05	.01
563	Sid Fernandez	.30	.14	.04
564	Richie Hebner	.10	.05	.01
565	Alex Trevino	.10	.05	.01
566	Brian Harper	.20	.09	.03
567	Dan Gladden	.20	.09	.03
568	Luis Salazar	.10	.05	.01
569	Tom Foley	.10	.05	.01
570	Larry Andersen	.10	.05	.01
571	Danny Cox	.10	.05	.01
572	Joe Sambito	.10	.05	.01
573	Juan Beniquez	.10	.05	.01
574	Joel Skinner	.10	.05	.01
575	Randy St.Claire	.10	.05	.01
576	Floyd Rayford	.10	.05	.01
577	Roy Howell	.10	.05	.01
578	John Grubb	.10	.05	.01
579	Ed Jurak	.10	.05	.01
580	John Montefusco	.10	.05	.01
581	Orel Hershiser	4.00	1.80	.50
582	Tom Waddell	.10	.05	.01
583	Mark Huismann	.10	.05	.01
584	Joe Morgan	.50	.23	.06
585	Jim Wohlford	.10	.05	.01
586	Dave Schmidt	.10	.05	.01
587	Jeff Kunkel	.10	.05	.01
588	Hal McRae	.30	.14	.04
589	Bill Almon	.10	.05	.01
590	Carmen Castillo	.10	.05	.01
591	Omar Moreno	.10	.05	.01
592	Ken Howell	.10	.05	.01
593	Tom Brookens	.10	.05	.01
594	Joe Nolan	.10	.05	.01
595	Willie Lozado	.10	.05	.01
596	Tom Nieto	.10	.05	.01
597	Walt Terrell	.10	.05	.01
598	Al Oliver	.20	.09	.03
599	Shane Rawley	.10	.05	.01
600	Denny Gonzalez	.10	.05	.01
601	Mark Grant	.10	.05	.01
602	Mike Armstrong	.10	.05	.01
603	George Foster	.20	.09	.03
604	Dave Lopes	.20	.09	.03
605	Salome Barojas	.10	.05	.01
606	Roy Lee Jackson	.10	.05	.01
607	Pete Filson	.10	.05	.01
608	Duane Walker	.10	.05	.01
609	Glenn Wilson	.10	.05	.01
610	Rafael Santana	.10	.05	.01
611	Roy Smith	.10	.05	.01
612	Ruppert Jones	.10	.05	.01
613	Joe Cowley	.10	.05	.01
614	Al Nipper UER	.10	.05	.01
	(Photo actually			
	Mike Brown)			
615	Gene Nelson	.10	.05	.01
616	Joe Carter	6.00	2.70	.75
617	Ray Knight	.20	.09	.03
618	Chuck Rainey	.10	.05	.01
619	Dan Driessen	.10	.05	.01
620	Daryl Sconiers	.10	.05	.01
621	Bill Stein	.10	.05	.01
622	Roy Smalley	.10	.05	.01
623	Ed Lynch	.10	.05	.01
624	Jeff Stone	.10	.05	.01
625	Bruce Berenyi	.10	.05	.01
626	Kelvin Chapman	.10	.05	.01
627	Joe Price	.10	.05	.01
628	Steve Bedrosian	.10	.05	.01
629	Vic Mata	.10	.05	.01
630	Mike Krukow	.10	.05	.01
631	Phil Bradley	.20	.09	.03
632	Jim Gott	.10	.05	.01
633	Randy Bush	.10	.05	.01
634	Tom Browning	.30	.14	.04
635	Lou Gehrig	.50	.23	.06
	Puzzle Card			
636	Reid Nichols	.10	.05	.01
637	Dan Pasqua	.20	.09	.03
638	German Rivera	.10	.05	.01
639	Don Schulze	.10	.05	.01
640A	Mike Jones	.10	.05	.01
	(Career Highlights,			
	takes five lines)			
640B	Mike Jones	.10	.05	.01
	(Career Highlights,			
	takes four lines)			
641	Pete Rose	2.50	1.10	.30
642	Wade Rowdon	.10	.05	.01
643	Jerry Narron	.10	.05	.01
644	Darrell Miller	.10	.05	.01
645	Tim Hulett	.10	.05	.01
646	Andy McGaffigan	.10	.05	.01
647	Kurt Bevacqua	.10	.05	.01
648	John Russell	.10	.05	.01
649	Ron Robinson	.10	.05	.01

		MINT	NRMT	EXC
☐ 650	Donnie Moore .10	.05	.01
☐ 651A	Two for the Title ...... 3.00 Dave Winfield Don Mattingly (Yellow letters)	1.35	.35
☐ 651B	Two for the Title ...... 8.00 Dave Winfield Don Mattingly (White letters)	3.60	1.00
☐ 652	Tim Laudner .10	.05	.01
☐ 653	Steve Farr .20	.09	.03
☐ 654	DK Checklist 1-26 .20 (Unnumbered)	.09	.03
☐ 655	Checklist 27-130 .20 (Unnumbered)	.09	.03
☐ 656	Checklist 131-234 .20 (Unnumbered)	.09	.03
☐ 657	Checklist 235-338 .20 (Unnumbered)	.09	.03
☐ 658	Checklist 339-442 .20 (Unnumbered)	.09	.03
☐ 659	Checklist 443-546 .20 (Unnumbered)	.09	.03
☐ 660	Checklist 547-653 .20 (Unnumbered)	.09	.03

1986 Donruss

The cards in this 660-card set measure 2 1/2" by 3 1/2". The 1986 Donruss regular issue cards have fronts that feature blue borders. The fronts contain the standard team logo, player's name, position, and Donruss logo. The cards were distributed with puzzle pieces from a Dick Perez rendition of Hank Aaron. The first 26 cards of the set are Diamond Kings (DK), for the fifth year in a row; the artwork on the Diamond Kings was again produced by the Perez-Steele Galleries. The jumbo (5 by 7 inch) versions of the 1986 Diamond Kings are valued about five times their standard-size counterparts. Cards 27-46 again feature Rated Rookies (RR); Danny Tartabull is included in this subset for the second year in a row. The unnumbered checklist cards are arbitrarily numbered below as numbers 654 through 660. Rookie Cards in this set include Rick Aguilera, Jose Canseco, Vince Coleman, Darren Daulton, Len Dykstra, Cecil Fielder, Andres Galarraga, Fred McGriff, Paul O'Neill, and Mickey Tettleton.

			MINT	NRMT	EXC
	COMPLETE SET (660)		70.00	32.00	8.75
	COMPLETE FACT.SET (660) ..		80.00	36.00	10.00
	COMMON CARD (1-660)		.10	.05	.01
☐ 1	Kirk Gibson DK	.30	.14	.04
☐ 2	Goose Gossage DK	.30	.14	.04
☐ 3	Willie McGee DK	.20	.09	.03
☐ 4	George Bell DK	.10	.05	.01
☐ 5	Tony Armas DK	.10	.05	.01
☐ 6	Chili Davis DK	.30	.14	.04
☐ 7	Cecil Cooper DK	.10	.05	.01
☐ 8	Mike Boddicker DK	.10	.05	.01
☐ 9	Dave Lopes DK	.10	.05	.01
☐ 10	Bill Doran DK	.10	.05	.01
☐ 11	Bret Saberhagen DK	.30	.14	.04
☐ 12	Brett Butler DK	.20	.09	.03
☐ 13	Harold Baines DK	.30	.14	.04
☐ 14	Mike Davis DK	.10	.05	.01
☐ 15	Tony Perez DK	.30	.14	.04
☐ 16	Willie Randolph DK	.20	.09	.03
☐ 17	Bob Boone DK	.20	.09	.03
☐ 18	Orel Hershiser DK	.30	.14	.04
☐ 19	Johnny Ray DK	.10	.05	.01
☐ 20	Gary Ward DK	.10	.05	.01
☐ 21	Rick Mahler DK	.10	.05	.01
☐ 22	Phil Bradley DK	.10	.05	.01
☐ 23	Jerry Koosman DK	.20	.09	.03
☐ 24	Tom Brunansky DK	.10	.05	.01
☐ 25	Andre Dawson DK	.30	.14	.04
☐ 26	Dwight Gooden DK	.20	.09	.03
☐ 27	Kal Daniels DK	.10	.05	.01
☐ 28	Fred McGriff RR	16.00	7.25	2.00
☐ 29	Cory Snyder RR	.10	.05	.01
☐ 30	Jose Guzman RR	.20	.09	.03
☐ 31	Ty Gainey RR	.10	.05	.01
☐ 32	Johnny Abrego RR	.10	.05	.01
☐ 33A	Andres Galarraga RR . 5.00 (No accent)	2.20	.60
☐ 33B	Andre's Galarraga RR 5.00 (Accent over e)	2.20	.60
☐ 34	Dave Shipanoff RR	.10	.05	.01
☐ 35	Mark McLemore RR	.60	.25	.07
☐ 36	Marty Clary RR	.10	.05	.01
☐ 37	Paul O'Neill RR	2.50	1.10	.30
☐ 38	Danny Tartabull RR	.30	.14	.04
☐ 39	Jose Canseco RR	20.00	9.00	2.50
☐ 40	Juan Nieves RR	.10	.05	.01
☐ 41	Lance McCullers RR	.10	.05	.01
☐ 42	Rick Surhoff RR	.10	.05	.01
☐ 43	Todd Worrell RR	.30	.14	.04
☐ 44	Bob Kipper RR	.10	.05	.01
☐ 45	John Habyan RR	.10	.05	.01
☐ 46	Mike Woodard RR	.10	.05	.01
☐ 47	Mike Boddicker	.10	.05	.01
☐ 48	Robin Yount	1.00	.45	.12
☐ 49	Lou Whitaker	.30	.14	.04
☐ 50	Oil Can Boyd	.10	.05	.01
☐ 51	Rickey Henderson	.75	.35	.09
☐ 52	Mike Marshall	.10	.05	.01
☐ 53	George Brett	2.50	1.10	.30
☐ 54	Dave Kingman	.20	.09	.03
☐ 55	Hubie Brooks	.10	.05	.01
☐ 56	Oddibe McDowell	.10	.05	.01
☐ 57	Doug DeCinces	.10	.05	.01
☐ 58	Britt Burns	.10	.05	.01
☐ 59	Ozzie Smith	1.25	.55	.16
☐ 60	Jose Cruz	.10	.05	.01
☐ 61	Mike Schmidt	1.00	.45	.12
☐ 62	Pete Rose	1.00	.45	.12
☐ 63	Steve Garvey	.30	.14	.04

☐ 64 Tony Pena	.10	.05	.01
☐ 65 Chili Davis	.30	.14	.04
☐ 66 Dale Murphy	.30	.14	.04
☐ 67 Ryne Sandberg	2.50	1.10	.30
☐ 68 Gary Carter	.30	.14	.04
☐ 69 Alvin Davis	.10	.05	.01
☐ 70 Kent Hrbek	.20	.09	.03
☐ 71 George Bell	.20	.09	.03
☐ 72 Kirby Puckett	5.00	2.20	.60
☐ 73 Lloyd Moseby	.10	.05	.01
☐ 74 Bob Kearney	.10	.05	.01
☐ 75 Dwight Gooden	.30	.14	.04
☐ 76 Gary Matthews	.10	.05	.01
☐ 77 Rick Mahler	.10	.05	.01
☐ 78 Benny Distefano	.10	.05	.01
☐ 79 Jeff Leonard	.10	.05	.01
☐ 80 Kevin McReynolds	.20	.09	.03
☐ 81 Ron Oester	.10	.05	.01
☐ 82 John Russell	.10	.05	.01
☐ 83 Tommy Herr	.10	.05	.01
☐ 84 Jerry Mumphrey	.10	.05	.01
☐ 85 Ron Romanick	.10	.05	.01
☐ 86 Daryl Boston	.10	.05	.01
☐ 87 Andre Dawson	.50	.23	.06
☐ 88 Eddie Murray	1.00	.45	.12
☐ 89 Dion James	.10	.05	.01
☐ 90 Chet Lemon	.10	.05	.01
☐ 91 Bob Stanley	.10	.05	.01
☐ 92 Willie Randolph	.20	.09	.03
☐ 93 Mike Scioscia	.10	.05	.01
☐ 94 Tom Waddell	.10	.05	.01
☐ 95 Danny Jackson	.20	.09	.03
☐ 96 Mike Davis	.10	.05	.01
☐ 97 Mike Fitzgerald	.10	.05	.01
☐ 98 Gary Ward	.10	.05	.01
☐ 99 Pete O'Brien	.10	.05	.01
☐ 100 Bret Saberhagen	.50	.23	.06
☐ 101 Alfredo Griffin	.10	.05	.01
☐ 102 Brett Butler	.20	.09	.03
☐ 103 Ron Guidry	.20	.09	.03
☐ 104 Jerry Reuss	.10	.05	.01
☐ 105 Jack Morris	.20	.09	.03
☐ 106 Rick Dempsey	.10	.05	.01
☐ 107 Ray Burris	.10	.05	.01
☐ 108 Brian Downing	.20	.09	.03
☐ 109 Willie McGee	.20	.09	.03
☐ 110 Bill Doran	.10	.05	.01
☐ 111 Kent Tekulve	.10	.05	.01
☐ 112 Tony Gwynn	2.50	1.10	.30
☐ 113 Marvell Wynne	.10	.05	.01
☐ 114 David Green	.10	.05	.01
☐ 115 Jim Gantner	.10	.05	.01
☐ 116 George Foster	.20	.09	.03
☐ 117 Steve Trout	.10	.05	.01
☐ 118 Mark Langston	.50	.23	.06
☐ 119 Tony Fernandez	.20	.09	.03
☐ 120 John Butcher	.10	.05	.01
☐ 121 Ron Robinson	.10	.05	.01
☐ 122 Dan Spillner	.10	.05	.01
☐ 123 Mike Young	.10	.05	.01
☐ 124 Paul Molitor	.50	.23	.06
☐ 125 Kirk Gibson	.30	.14	.04
☐ 126 Ken Griffey	.20	.09	.03
☐ 127 Tony Armas	.10	.05	.01
☐ 128 Mariano Duncan	.30	.14	.04
☐ 129 Pat Tabler	.10	.05	.01
☐ 130 Frank White	.20	.09	.03
☐ 131 Carney Lansford	.20	.09	.03
☐ 132 Vance Law	.10	.05	.01
☐ 133 Dick Schofield	.10	.05	.01
☐ 134 Wayne Tolleson	.10	.05	.01
☐ 135 Greg Walker	.10	.05	.01
☐ 136 Denny Walling	.10	.05	.01
☐ 137 Ozzie Virgil	.10	.05	.01
☐ 138 Ricky Horton	.10	.05	.01
☐ 139 LaMarr Hoyt	.10	.05	.01
☐ 140 Wayne Krenchicki	.10	.05	.01
☐ 141 Glenn Hubbard	.10	.05	.01
☐ 142 Cecilio Guante	.10	.05	.01
☐ 143 Mike Krukow	.10	.05	.01
☐ 144 Lee Smith	.30	.14	.04
☐ 145 Edwin Nunez	.10	.05	.01
☐ 146 Dave Stieb	.20	.09	.03
☐ 147 Mike Smithson	.10	.05	.01
☐ 148 Ken Dixon	.10	.05	.01
☐ 149 Danny Darwin	.10	.05	.01
☐ 150 Chris Pittaro	.10	.05	.01
☐ 151 Bill Buckner	.20	.09	.03
☐ 152 Mike Pagliarulo	.10	.05	.01
☐ 153 Bill Russell	.20	.09	.03
☐ 154 Brook Jacoby	.10	.05	.01
☐ 155 Pat Sheridan	.10	.05	.01
☐ 156 Mike Gallego	.20	.09	.03
☐ 157 Jim Wohlford	.10	.05	.01
☐ 158 Gary Pettis	.10	.05	.01
☐ 159 Toby Harrah	.10	.05	.01
☐ 160 Richard Dotson	.10	.05	.01
☐ 161 Bob Knepper	.10	.05	.01
☐ 162 Dave Dravecky	.20	.09	.03
☐ 163 Greg Gross	.10	.05	.01
☐ 164 Eric Davis	.20	.09	.03
☐ 165 Gerald Perry	.10	.05	.01
☐ 166 Rick Rhoden	.10	.05	.01
☐ 167 Keith Moreland	.10	.05	.01
☐ 168 Jack Clark	.20	.09	.03
☐ 169 Storm Davis	.10	.05	.01
☐ 170 Cecil Cooper	.20	.09	.03
☐ 171 Alan Trammell	.30	.14	.04
☐ 172 Roger Clemens	2.50	1.10	.30
☐ 173 Don Mattingly	3.00	1.35	.35
☐ 174 Pedro Guerrero	.20	.09	.03
☐ 175 Willie Wilson	.10	.05	.01
☐ 176 Dwayne Murphy	.10	.05	.01
☐ 177 Tim Raines	.30	.14	.04
☐ 178 Larry Parrish	.10	.05	.01
☐ 179 Mike Witt	.10	.05	.01
☐ 180 Harold Baines	.30	.14	.04
☐ 181 Vince Coleman UER	.60	.25	.07
(BA 2.67 on back)			
☐ 182 Jeff Heathcock	.10	.05	.01
☐ 183 Steve Carlton	.50	.23	.06
☐ 184 Mario Soto	.10	.05	.01
☐ 185 Goose Gossage	.20	.09	.03
☐ 186 Johnny Ray	.10	.05	.01
☐ 187 Dan Gladden	.10	.05	.01
☐ 188 Bob Horner	.10	.05	.01
☐ 189 Rick Sutcliffe	.20	.09	.03
☐ 190 Keith Hernandez	.20	.09	.03
☐ 191 Phil Bradley	.10	.05	.01
☐ 192 Tom Brunansky	.10	.05	.01
☐ 193 Jesse Barfield	.10	.05	.01
☐ 194 Frank Viola	.20	.09	.03
☐ 195 Willie Upshaw	.10	.05	.01
☐ 196 Jim Beattie	.10	.05	.01
☐ 197 Darryl Strawberry	.30	.14	.04
☐ 198 Ron Cey	.20	.09	.03
☐ 199 Steve Bedrosian	.10	.05	.01
☐ 200 Steve Kemp	.10	.05	.01
☐ 201 Manny Trillo	.10	.05	.01
☐ 202 Garry Templeton	.10	.05	.01
☐ 203 Dave Parker	.30	.14	.04
☐ 204 John Denny	.10	.05	.01

☐ 205	Terry Pendleton	.30	.14	.04
☐ 206	Terry Puhl	.10	.05	.01
☐ 207	Bobby Grich	.20	.09	.03
☐ 208	Ozzie Guillen	.75	.35	.09
☐ 209	Jeff Reardon	.30	.14	.04
☐ 210	Cal Ripken	5.00	2.20	.60
☐ 211	Bill Schroeder	.10	.05	.01
☐ 212	Dan Petry	.10	.05	.01
☐ 213	Jim Rice	.30	.14	.04
☐ 214	Dave Righetti	.20	.09	.03
☐ 215	Fernando Valenzuela	.20	.09	.03
☐ 216	Julio Franco	.30	.14	.04
☐ 217	Darryl Motley	.10	.05	.01
☐ 218	Dave Collins	.10	.05	.01
☐ 219	Tim Wallach	.20	.09	.03
☐ 220	George Wright	.10	.05	.01
☐ 221	Tommy Dunbar	.10	.05	.01
☐ 222	Steve Balboni	.10	.05	.01
☐ 223	Jay Howell	.10	.05	.01
☐ 224	Joe Carter	2.50	1.10	.30
☐ 225	Ed Whitson	.10	.05	.01
☐ 226	Orel Hershiser	.60	.25	.07
☐ 227	Willie Hernandez	.10	.05	.01
☐ 228	Lee Lacy	.10	.05	.01
☐ 229	Rollie Fingers	.30	.14	.04
☐ 230	Bob Boone	.20	.09	.03
☐ 231	Joaquin Andujar	.10	.05	.01
☐ 232	Craig Reynolds	.10	.05	.01
☐ 233	Shane Rawley	.10	.05	.01
☐ 234	Eric Show	.10	.05	.01
☐ 235	Jose DeLeon	.10	.05	.01
☐ 236	Jose Uribe	.10	.05	.01
☐ 237	Moose Haas	.10	.05	.01
☐ 238	Wally Backman	.10	.05	.01
☐ 239	Dennis Eckersley	.30	.14	.04
☐ 240	Mike Moore	.10	.05	.01
☐ 241	Damaso Garcia	.10	.05	.01
☐ 242	Tim Teufel	.10	.05	.01
☐ 243	Dave Concepcion	.20	.09	.03
☐ 244	Floyd Bannister	.10	.05	.01
☐ 245	Fred Lynn	.20	.09	.03
☐ 246	Charlie Moore	.10	.05	.01
☐ 247	Walt Terrell	.10	.05	.01
☐ 248	Dave Winfield	.75	.35	.09
☐ 249	Dwight Evans	.20	.09	.03
☐ 250	Dennis Powell	.10	.05	.01
☐ 251	Andre Thornton	.10	.05	.01
☐ 252	Onix Concepcion	.10	.05	.01
☐ 253	Mike Heath	.10	.05	.01
☐ 254A	David Palmer ERR (Position 2B)	.10	.05	.01
☐ 254B	David Palmer COR (Position P)	.10	.05	.01
☐ 255	Donnie Moore	.10	.05	.01
☐ 256	Curtis Wilkerson	.10	.05	.01
☐ 257	Julio Cruz	.10	.05	.01
☐ 258	Nolan Ryan	5.00	2.20	.60
☐ 259	Jeff Stone	.10	.05	.01
☐ 260	John Tudor	.20	.09	.03
☐ 261	Mark Thurmond	.10	.05	.01
☐ 262	Jay Tibbs	.10	.05	.01
☐ 263	Rafael Ramirez	.10	.05	.01
☐ 264	Larry McWilliams	.10	.05	.01
☐ 265	Mark Davis	.10	.05	.01
☐ 266	Bob Dernier	.10	.05	.01
☐ 267	Matt Young	.10	.05	.01
☐ 268	Jim Clancy	.10	.05	.01
☐ 269	Mickey Hatcher	.10	.05	.01
☐ 270	Sammy Stewart	.10	.05	.01
☐ 271	Bob L. Gibson	.10	.05	.01
☐ 272	Nelson Simmons	.10	.05	.01
☐ 273	Rich Gedman	.10	.05	.01
☐ 274	Butch Wynegar	.10	.05	.01
☐ 275	Ken Howell	.10	.05	.01
☐ 276	Mel Hall	.10	.05	.01
☐ 277	Jim Sundberg	.10	.05	.01
☐ 278	Chris Codiroli	.10	.05	.01
☐ 279	Herm Winningham	.10	.05	.01
☐ 280	Rod Carew	.50	.23	.06
☐ 281	Don Slaught	.10	.05	.01
☐ 282	Scott Fletcher	.10	.05	.01
☐ 283	Bill Dawley	.10	.05	.01
☐ 284	Andy Hawkins	.10	.05	.01
☐ 285	Glenn Wilson	.10	.05	.01
☐ 286	Nick Esasky	.10	.05	.01
☐ 287	Claudell Washington	.10	.05	.01
☐ 288	Lee Mazzilli	.10	.05	.01
☐ 289	Jody Davis	.10	.05	.01
☐ 290	Darrell Porter	.10	.05	.01
☐ 291	Scott McGregor	.10	.05	.01
☐ 292	Ted Simmons	.20	.09	.03
☐ 293	Aurelio Lopez	.10	.05	.01
☐ 294	Marty Barrett	.10	.05	.01
☐ 295	Dale Berra	.10	.05	.01
☐ 296	Greg Brock	.10	.05	.01
☐ 297	Charlie Leibrandt	.10	.05	.01
☐ 298	Bill Krueger	.10	.05	.01
☐ 299	Bryn Smith	.10	.05	.01
☐ 300	Burt Hooton	.10	.05	.01
☐ 301	Stu Cliburn	.10	.05	.01
☐ 302	Luis Salazar	.10	.05	.01
☐ 303	Ken Dayley	.10	.05	.01
☐ 304	Frank DiPino	.10	.05	.01
☐ 305	Von Hayes	.10	.05	.01
☐ 306	Gary Redus	.10	.05	.01
☐ 307	Craig Lefferts	.10	.05	.01
☐ 308	Sammy Khalifa	.10	.05	.01
☐ 309	Scott Garrelts	.10	.05	.01
☐ 310	Rick Cerone	.10	.05	.01
☐ 311	Shawon Dunston	.20	.09	.03
☐ 312	Howard Johnson	.20	.09	.03
☐ 313	Jim Presley	.10	.05	.01
☐ 314	Gary Gaetti	.10	.05	.01
☐ 315	Luis Leal	.10	.05	.01
☐ 316	Mark Salas	.10	.05	.01
☐ 317	Bill Caudill	.10	.05	.01
☐ 318	Dave Henderson	.10	.05	.01
☐ 319	Rafael Santana	.10	.05	.01
☐ 320	Leon Durham	.10	.05	.01
☐ 321	Bruce Sutter	.20	.09	.03
☐ 322	Jason Thompson	.10	.05	.01
☐ 323	Bob Brenly	.10	.05	.01
☐ 324	Carmelo Martinez	.10	.05	.01
☐ 325	Eddie Milner	.10	.05	.01
☐ 326	Juan Samuel	.10	.05	.01
☐ 327	Tom Nieto	.10	.05	.01
☐ 328	Dave Smith	.10	.05	.01
☐ 329	Urbano Lugo	.10	.05	.01
☐ 330	Joel Skinner	.10	.05	.01
☐ 331	Bill Gullickson	.20	.09	.03
☐ 332	Floyd Rayford	.10	.05	.01
☐ 333	Ben Oglivie	.10	.05	.01
☐ 334	Lance Parrish	.20	.09	.03
☐ 335	Jackie Gutierrez	.10	.05	.01
☐ 336	Dennis Rasmussen	.10	.05	.01
☐ 337	Terry Whitfield	.10	.05	.01
☐ 338	Neal Heaton	.10	.05	.01
☐ 339	Jorge Orta	.10	.05	.01
☐ 340	Donnie Hill	.10	.05	.01
☐ 341	Joe Hesketh	.10	.05	.01
☐ 342	Charlie Hough	.10	.05	.01
☐ 343	Dave Rozema	.10	.05	.01

☐ 344 Greg Pryor	.10	.05	.01
☐ 345 Mickey Tettleton	2.00	.90	.25
☐ 346 George Vukovich	.10	.05	.01
☐ 347 Don Baylor	.30	.14	.04
☐ 348 Carlos Diaz	.10	.05	.01
☐ 349 Barbaro Garbey	.10	.05	.01
☐ 350 Larry Sheets	.10	.05	.01
☐ 351 Ted Higuera	.10	.05	.01
☐ 352 Juan Beniquez	.10	.05	.01
☐ 353 Bob Forsch	.10	.05	.01
☐ 354 Mark Bailey	.10	.05	.01
☐ 355 Larry Andersen	.10	.05	.01
☐ 356 Terry Kennedy	.10	.05	.01
☐ 357 Don Robinson	.10	.05	.01
☐ 358 Jim Gott	.10	.05	.01
☐ 359 Earnie Riles	.10	.05	.01
☐ 360 John Christensen	.10	.05	.01
☐ 361 Ray Fontenot	.10	.05	.01
☐ 362 Spike Owen	.10	.05	.01
☐ 363 Jim Acker	.10	.05	.01
☐ 364 Ron Davis	.10	.05	.01
☐ 365 Tom Hume	.10	.05	.01
☐ 366 Carlton Fisk	.50	.23	.06
☐ 367 Nate Snell	.10	.05	.01
☐ 368 Rick Manning	.10	.05	.01
☐ 369 Darrell Evans	.20	.09	.03
☐ 370 Ron Hassey	.10	.05	.01
☐ 371 Wade Boggs	1.00	.45	.12
☐ 372 Rick Honeycutt	.10	.05	.01
☐ 373 Chris Bando	.10	.05	.01
☐ 374 Bud Black	.10	.05	.01
☐ 375 Steve Henderson	.10	.05	.01
☐ 376 Charlie Lea	.10	.05	.01
☐ 377 Reggie Jackson	.75	.35	.09
☐ 378 Dave Schmidt	.10	.05	.01
☐ 379 Bob James	.10	.05	.01
☐ 380 Glenn Davis	.10	.05	.01
☐ 381 Tim Corcoran	.10	.05	.01
☐ 382 Danny Cox	.10	.05	.01
☐ 383 Tim Flannery	.10	.05	.01
☐ 384 Tom Browning	.20	.09	.03
☐ 385 Rick Camp	.10	.05	.01
☐ 386 Jim Morrison	.10	.05	.01
☐ 387 Dave LaPoint	.10	.05	.01
☐ 388 Dave Lopes	.20	.09	.03
☐ 389 Al Cowens	.10	.05	.01
☐ 390 Doyle Alexander	.10	.05	.01
☐ 391 Tim Laudner	.10	.05	.01
☐ 392 Don Aase	.10	.05	.01
☐ 393 Jaime Cocanower	.10	.05	.01
☐ 394 Randy O'Neal	.10	.05	.01
☐ 395 Mike Easler	.10	.05	.01
☐ 396 Scott Bradley	.10	.05	.01
☐ 397 Tom Niedenfuer	.10	.05	.01
☐ 398 Jerry Willard	.10	.05	.01
☐ 399 Lonnie Smith	.10	.05	.01
☐ 400 Bruce Bochte	.10	.05	.01
☐ 401 Terry Francona	.10	.05	.01
☐ 402 Jim Slaton	.10	.05	.01
☐ 403 Bill Stein	.10	.05	.01
☐ 404 Tim Hulett	.10	.05	.01
☐ 405 Alan Ashby	.10	.05	.01
☐ 406 Tim Stoddard	.10	.05	.01
☐ 407 Garry Maddox	.10	.05	.01
☐ 408 Ted Power	.10	.05	.01
☐ 409 Len Barker	.10	.05	.01
☐ 410 Denny Gonzalez	.10	.05	.01
☐ 411 George Frazier	.10	.05	.01
☐ 412 Andy Van Slyke	.20	.09	.03
☐ 413 Jim Dwyer	.10	.05	.01
☐ 414 Paul Householder	.10	.05	.01
☐ 415 Alejandro Sanchez	.10	.05	.01
☐ 416 Steve Crawford	.10	.05	.01
☐ 417 Dan Pasqua	.10	.05	.01
☐ 418 Enos Cabell	.10	.05	.01
☐ 419 Mike Jones	.10	.05	.01
☐ 420 Steve Kiefer	.10	.05	.01
☐ 421 Tim Burke	.10	.05	.01
☐ 422 Mike Mason	.10	.05	.01
☐ 423 Ruppert Jones	.10	.05	.01
☐ 424 Jerry Hairston	.10	.05	.01
☐ 425 Tito Landrum	.10	.05	.01
☐ 426 Jeff Calhoun	.10	.05	.01
☐ 427 Don Carman	.10	.05	.01
☐ 428 Tony Perez	.30	.14	.04
☐ 429 Jerry Davis	.10	.05	.01
☐ 430 Bob Walk	.10	.05	.01
☐ 431 Brad Wellman	.10	.05	.01
☐ 432 Terry Forster	.10	.05	.01
☐ 433 Billy Hatcher	.20	.09	.03
☐ 434 Clint Hurdle	.10	.05	.01
☐ 435 Ivan Calderon	.20	.09	.03
☐ 436 Pete Filson	.10	.05	.01
☐ 437 Tom Henke	.20	.09	.03
☐ 438 Dave Engle	.10	.05	.01
☐ 439 Tom Filer	.10	.05	.01
☐ 440 Gorman Thomas	.10	.05	.01
☐ 441 Rick Aguilera	1.00	.45	.12
☐ 442 Scott Sanderson	.10	.05	.01
☐ 443 Jeff Dedmon	.10	.05	.01
☐ 444 Joe Orsulak	.20	.09	.03
☐ 445 Atlee Hammaker	.10	.05	.01
☐ 446 Jerry Royster	.10	.05	.01
☐ 447 Buddy Bell	.20	.09	.03
☐ 448 Dave Rucker	.10	.05	.01
☐ 449 Ivan DeJesus	.10	.05	.01
☐ 450 Jim Pankovits	.10	.05	.01
☐ 451 Jerry Narron	.10	.05	.01
☐ 452 Bryan Little	.10	.05	.01
☐ 453 Gary Lucas	.10	.05	.01
☐ 454 Dennis Martinez	.20	.09	.03
☐ 455 Ed Romero	.10	.05	.01
☐ 456 Bob Melvin	.10	.05	.01
☐ 457 Glenn Hoffman	.10	.05	.01
☐ 458 Bob Shirley	.10	.05	.01
☐ 459 Bob Welch	.20	.09	.03
☐ 460 Carmen Castillo	.10	.05	.01
☐ 461 Dave Leeper OF	.10	.05	.01
☐ 462 Tim Birtsas	.10	.05	.01
☐ 463 Randy St.Claire	.10	.05	.01
☐ 464 Chris Welsh	.10	.05	.01
☐ 465 Greg Harris	.10	.05	.01
☐ 466 Lynn Jones	.10	.05	.01
☐ 467 Dusty Baker	.30	.14	.04
☐ 468 Roy Smith	.10	.05	.01
☐ 469 Andre Robertson	.10	.05	.01
☐ 470 Ken Landreaux	.10	.05	.01
☐ 471 Dave Bergman	.10	.05	.01
☐ 472 Gary Roenicke	.10	.05	.01
☐ 473 Pete Vuckovich	.10	.05	.01
☐ 474 Kirk McCaskill	.20	.09	.03
☐ 475 Jeff Lahti	.10	.05	.01
☐ 476 Mike Scott	.10	.05	.01
☐ 477 Darren Daulton	3.00	1.35	.35
☐ 478 Graig Nettles	.20	.09	.03
☐ 479 Bill Almon	.10	.05	.01
☐ 480 Greg Minton	.10	.05	.01
☐ 481 Randy Ready	.10	.05	.01
☐ 482 Len Dykstra	2.00	.90	.25
☐ 483 Thad Bosley	.10	.05	.01
☐ 484 Harold Reynolds	.20	.09	.03
☐ 485 Al Oliver	.20	.09	.03

☐ 486 Roy Smalley	.10	.05	.01	
☐ 487 John Franco	.20	.09	.03	
☐ 488 Juan Agosto	.10	.05	.01	
☐ 489 Al Pardo	.10	.05	.01	
☐ 490 Bill Wegman	.10	.05	.01	
☐ 491 Frank Tanana	.20	.09	.03	
☐ 492 Brian Fisher	.10	.05	.01	
☐ 493 Mark Clear	.10	.05	.01	
☐ 494 Len Matuszek	.10	.05	.01	
☐ 495 Ramon Romero	.10	.05	.01	
☐ 496 John Wathan	.10	.05	.01	
☐ 497 Rob Picciolo	.10	.05	.01	
☐ 498 U.L. Washington	.10	.05	.01	
☐ 499 John Candelaria	.10	.05	.01	
☐ 500 Duane Walker	.10	.05	.01	
☐ 501 Gene Nelson	.10	.05	.01	
☐ 502 John Mizerock	.10	.05	.01	
☐ 503 Luis Aguayo	.10	.05	.01	
☐ 504 Kurt Kepshire	.10	.05	.01	
☐ 505 Ed Wojna	.10	.05	.01	
☐ 506 Joe Price	.10	.05	.01	
☐ 507 Milt Thompson	.20	.09	.03	
☐ 508 Junior Ortiz	.10	.05	.01	
☐ 509 Vida Blue	.20	.09	.03	
☐ 510 Steve Engel	.10	.05	.01	
☐ 511 Karl Best	.10	.05	.01	
☐ 512 Cecil Fielder	8.00	3.60	1.00	
☐ 513 Frank Eufemia	.10	.05	.01	
☐ 514 Tippy Martinez	.10	.05	.01	
☐ 515 Billy Joe Robidoux	.10	.05	.01	
☐ 516 Bill Scherrer	.10	.05	.01	
☐ 517 Bruce Hurst	.20	.09	.03	
☐ 518 Rich Bordi	.10	.05	.01	
☐ 519 Steve Yeager	.10	.05	.01	
☐ 520 Tony Bernazard	.10	.05	.01	
☐ 521 Hal McRae	.30	.14	.04	
☐ 522 Jose Rijo	.50	.23	.06	
☐ 523 Mitch Webster	.10	.05	.01	
☐ 524 Jack Howell	.10	.05	.01	
☐ 525 Alan Bannister	.10	.05	.01	
☐ 526 Ron Kittle	.10	.05	.01	
☐ 527 Phil Garner	.20	.09	.03	
☐ 528 Kurt Bevacqua	.10	.05	.01	
☐ 529 Kevin Gross	.10	.05	.01	
☐ 530 Bo Diaz	.10	.05	.01	
☐ 531 Ken Oberkfell	.10	.05	.01	
☐ 532 Rick Reuschel	.10	.05	.01	
☐ 533 Ron Meridith	.10	.05	.01	
☐ 534 Steve Braun	.10	.05	.01	
☐ 535 Wayne Gross	.10	.05	.01	
☐ 536 Ray Searage	.10	.05	.01	
☐ 537 Tom Brookens	.10	.05	.01	
☐ 538 Al Nipper	.10	.05	.01	
☐ 539 Billy Sample	.10	.05	.01	
☐ 540 Steve Sax	.20	.09	.03	
☐ 541 Dan Quisenberry	.20	.09	.03	
☐ 542 Tony Phillips	.30	.14	.04	
☐ 543 Floyd Youmans	.10	.05	.01	
☐ 544 Steve Buechele	.20	.09	.03	
☐ 545 Craig Gerber	.10	.05	.01	
☐ 546 Joe DeSa	.10	.05	.01	
☐ 547 Brian Harper	.20	.09	.03	
☐ 548 Kevin Bass	.10	.05	.01	
☐ 549 Tom Foley	.10	.05	.01	
☐ 550 Dave Van Gorder	.10	.05	.01	
☐ 551 Bruce Bochy	.10	.05	.01	
☐ 552 R.J. Reynolds	.10	.05	.01	
☐ 553 Chris Brown	.10	.05	.01	
☐ 554 Bruce Benedict	.10	.05	.01	
☐ 555 Warren Brusstar	.10	.05	.01	
☐ 556 Danny Heep	.10	.05	.01	

☐ 557 Darnell Coles	.10	.05	.01	
☐ 558 Greg Gagne	.20	.09	.03	
☐ 559 Ernie Whitt	.10	.05	.01	
☐ 560 Ron Washington	.10	.05	.01	
☐ 561 Jimmy Key	.30	.14	.04	
☐ 562 Billy Swift	.20	.09	.03	
☐ 563 Ron Darling	.20	.09	.03	
☐ 564 Dick Ruthven	.10	.05	.01	
☐ 565 Zane Smith	.10	.05	.01	
☐ 566 Sid Bream	.20	.09	.03	
☐ 567A Joel Youngblood ERR	.10	.05	.01	
(Position P)				
☐ 567B Joel Youngblood COR	.10	.05	.01	
(Position IF)				
☐ 568 Mario Ramirez	.10	.05	.01	
☐ 569 Tom Runnells	.10	.05	.01	
☐ 570 Rick Schu	.10	.05	.01	
☐ 571 Bill Campbell	.10	.05	.01	
☐ 572 Dickie Thon	.10	.05	.01	
☐ 573 Al Holland	.10	.05	.01	
☐ 574 Reid Nichols	.10	.05	.01	
☐ 575 Bert Roberge	.10	.05	.01	
☐ 576 Mike Flanagan	.10	.05	.01	
☐ 577 Tim Leary	.10	.05	.01	
☐ 578 Mike Laga	.10	.05	.01	
☐ 579 Steve Lyons	.10	.05	.01	
☐ 580 Phil Niekro	.30	.14	.04	
☐ 581 Gilberto Reyes	.10	.05	.01	
☐ 582 Jamie Easterly	.10	.05	.01	
☐ 583 Mark Gubicza	.20	.09	.03	
☐ 584 Stan Javier	.20	.09	.03	
☐ 585 Bill Laskey	.10	.05	.01	
☐ 586 Jeff Russell	.10	.05	.01	
☐ 587 Dickie Noles	.10	.05	.01	
☐ 588 Steve Farr	.20	.09	.03	
☐ 589 Steve Ontiveros	.50	.23	.06	
☐ 590 Mike Hargrove	.20	.09	.03	
☐ 591 Marty Bystrom	.10	.05	.01	
☐ 592 Franklin Stubbs	.10	.05	.01	
☐ 593 Larry Herndon	.10	.05	.01	
☐ 594 Bill Swaggerty	.10	.05	.01	
☐ 595 Carlos Ponce	.10	.05	.01	
☐ 596 Pat Perry	.10	.05	.01	
☐ 597 Ray Knight	.20	.09	.03	
☐ 598 Steve Lombardozzi	.10	.05	.01	
☐ 599 Brad Havens	.10	.05	.01	
☐ 600 Pat Clements	.10	.05	.01	
☐ 601 Joe Niekro	.20	.09	.03	
☐ 602 Hank Aaron	.30	.14	.04	
Puzzle Card				
☐ 603 Dwayne Henry	.10	.05	.01	
☐ 604 Mookie Wilson	.20	.09	.03	
☐ 605 Buddy Biancalana	.10	.05	.01	
☐ 606 Rance Mulliniks	.10	.05	.01	
☐ 607 Alan Wiggins	.10	.05	.01	
☐ 608 Joe Cowley	.10	.05	.01	
☐ 609A Tom Seaver	.50	.23	.06	
(Green borders				
on name)				
☐ 609B Tom Seaver	2.00	.90	.25	
(Yellow borders				
on name)				
☐ 610 Neil Allen	.10	.05	.01	
☐ 611 Don Sutton	.30	.14	.04	
☐ 612 Fred Toliver	.10	.05	.01	
☐ 613 Jay Baller	.10	.05	.01	
☐ 614 Marc Sullivan	.10	.05	.01	
☐ 615 John Grubb	.10	.05	.01	
☐ 616 Bruce Kison	.10	.05	.01	
☐ 617 Bill Madlock	.20	.09	.03	
☐ 618 Chris Chambliss	.20	.09	.03	

			MINT	NRMT	EXC
☐ 619	Dave Stewart	.30	.14	.04
☐ 620	Tim Lollar	.10	.05	.01
☐ 621	Gary Lavelle	.10	.05	.01
☐ 622	Charles Hudson	.10	.05	.01
☐ 623	Joel Davis	.10	.05	.01
☐ 624	Joe Johnson	.10	.05	.01
☐ 625	Sid Fernandez	.20	.09	.03
☐ 626	Dennis Lamp	.10	.05	.01
☐ 627	Terry Harper	.10	.05	.01
☐ 628	Jack Lazorko	.10	.05	.01
☐ 629	Roger McDowell	.20	.09	.03
☐ 630	Mark Funderburk	.10	.05	.01
☐ 631	Ed Lynch	.10	.05	.01
☐ 632	Rudy Law	.10	.05	.01
☐ 633	Roger Mason	.10	.05	.01
☐ 634	Mike Felder	.10	.05	.01
☐ 635	Ken Schrom	.10	.05	.01
☐ 636	Bob Ojeda	.20	.09	.03
☐ 637	Ed VandeBerg	.10	.05	.01
☐ 638	Bobby Meacham	.10	.05	.01
☐ 639	Cliff Johnson	.10	.05	.01
☐ 640	Garth Iorg	.10	.05	.01
☐ 641	Dan Driessen	.10	.05	.01
☐ 642	Mike Brown OF	.10	.05	.01
☐ 643	John Shelby	.10	.05	.01
☐ 644	Pete Rose	.60	.25	.07
	(Ty-Breaking)			
☐ 645	The Knuckle Brothers...	.20	.09	.03
	Phil Niekro			
	Joe Niekro			
☐ 646	Jesse Orosco	.10	.05	.01
☐ 647	Billy Beane	.10	.05	.01
☐ 648	Cesar Cedeno	.20	.09	.03
☐ 649	Bert Blyleven	.30	.14	.04
☐ 650	Max Venable	.10	.05	.01
☐ 651	Fleet Feet	.20	.09	.03
	Vince Coleman			
	Willie McGee			
☐ 652	Calvin Schiraldi	.10	.05	.01
☐ 653	King of Kings	1.00	.45	.12
	(Pete Rose)			
☐ 654	Diamond Kings CL 1-26	.20	.09	.03
	(Unnumbered)			
☐ 655A	CL 1: 27-130	.20	.09	.03
	(Unnumbered)			
	(45 Beane ERR)			
☐ 655B	CL 1: 27-130	.20	.09	.03
	(Unnumbered)			
	(45 Habyan COR)			
☐ 656	CL 2: 131-234	.20	.09	.03
	(Unnumbered)			
☐ 657	CL 3: 235-338	.20	.09	.03
	(Unnumbered)			
☐ 658	CL 4: 339-442	.20	.09	.03
	(Unnumbered)			
☐ 659	CL 5: 443-546	.20	.09	.03
	(Unnumbered)			
☐ 660	CL 6: 547-653	.20	.09	.03
	(Unnumbered)			

1986 Donruss Rookies

The 1986 Donruss "The Rookies" set features 56 cards plus a 15-piece puzzle of Hank Aaron. Cards are in full color and are

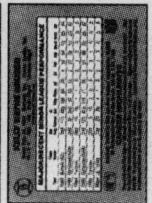

standard size, 2 1/2" by 3 1/2". The set was distributed in a small green box with gold lettering. Although the set was wrapped in cellophane, the top card was number 1 Joyner, resulting in a percentage of the Joyner cards arriving in less than perfect condition. Donruss fixed the problem after it was called to their attention and even went so far as to include a customer service phone number in their second printing. Card fronts are similar in design to the 1986 Donruss regular issue except for the presence of "The Rookies" logo in the lower left corner and a bluish green border instead of a blue border. The key (extended) Rookie Cards in this set are Barry Bonds, Bobby Bonilla, Will Clark, Bo Jackson, Wally Joyner, John Kruk, Kevin Mitchell, and Ruben Sierra.

	MINT	NRMT	EXC
COMPLETE FACT.SET (56)	25.00	11.00	3.10
COMMON CARD (1-56)	.10	.05	.01

		MINT	NRMT	EXC
☐ 1	Wally Joyner	1.00	.45	.12
☐ 2	Tracy Jones	.10	.05	.01
☐ 3	Allan Anderson	.10	.05	.01
☐ 4	Ed Correa	.10	.05	.01
☐ 5	Reggie Williams	.10	.05	.01
☐ 6	Charlie Kerfeld	.10	.05	.01
☐ 7	Andres Galarraga	3.00	1.35	.35
☐ 8	Bob Tewksbury	.15	.07	.02
☐ 9	Al Newman	.10	.05	.01
☐ 10	Andres Thomas	.10	.05	.01
☐ 11	Barry Bonds	7.00	3.10	.85
☐ 12	Juan Nieves	.10	.05	.01
☐ 13	Mark Eichhorn	.10	.05	.01
☐ 14	Dan Plesac	.10	.05	.01
☐ 15	Cory Snyder	.10	.05	.01
☐ 16	Kelly Gruber	.10	.05	.01
☐ 17	Kevin Mitchell	.50	.23	.06
☐ 18	Steve Lombardozzi	.10	.05	.01
☐ 19	Mitch Williams	.15	.07	.02
☐ 20	John Cerutti	.10	.05	.01
☐ 21	Todd Worrell	.15	.07	.02
☐ 22	Jose Canseco	4.00	1.80	.50
☐ 23	Pete Incaviglia	.30	.14	.04
☐ 24	Jose Guzman	.10	.05	.01
☐ 25	Scott Bailes	.10	.05	.01
☐ 26	Greg Mathews	.10	.05	.01
☐ 27	Eric King	.10	.05	.01
☐ 28	Paul Assenmacher	.10	.05	.01
☐ 29	Jeff Sellers	.10	.05	.01
☐ 30	Bobby Bonilla	2.00	.90	.25
☐ 31	Doug Drabek	.75	.35	.09
☐ 32	Will Clark UER	4.00	1.80	.50

			MINT	NRMT	EXC
(Listed as throwing right, should be left)					
☐ 33 Bip Roberts	.50	.23	.06
☐ 34 Jim Deshaies	.10	.05	.01
☐ 35 Mike LaValliere	.10	.05	.01
☐ 36 Scott Bankhead	.10	.05	.01
☐ 37 Dale Sveum	.10	.05	.01
☐ 38 Bo Jackson	2.00	.90	.25
☐ 39 Robby Thompson	.30	.14	.04
☐ 40 Eric Plunk	.10	.05	.01
☐ 41 Bill Bathe	.10	.05	.01
☐ 42 John Kruk	1.00	.45	.12
☐ 43 Andy Allanson	.10	.05	.01
☐ 44 Mark Portugal	.50	.23	.06
☐ 45 Danny Tartabull	.30	.14	.04
☐ 46 Bob Kipper	.10	.05	.01
☐ 47 Gene Walter	.10	.05	.01
☐ 48 Rey Quinones UER	.10	.05	.01
(Misspelled Quinonez)			
☐ 49 Bobby Witt	.15	.07	.02
☐ 50 Bill Mooneyham	.10	.05	.01
☐ 51 John Cangelosi	.10	.05	.01
☐ 52 Ruben Sierra	3.00	1.35	.35
☐ 53 Rob Woodward	.10	.05	.01
☐ 54 Ed Hearn	.10	.05	.01
☐ 55 Joel McKeon	.10	.05	.01
☐ 56 Checklist 1-56	.10	.05	.01

1987 Donruss

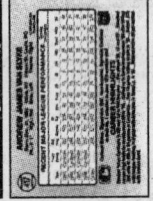

This 660-card set was distributed along with a puzzle of Roberto Clemente. The checklist cards are numbered throughout the set as multiples of 100. The wax pack boxes again contain four separate cards printed on the bottom of the box. Cards measure 2 1/2" by 3 1/2" and feature a black and gold border on the front; the backs are also done in black and gold on white card stock. The popular Diamond King subset returns for the sixth consecutive year. Some of the Diamond King (1-26) selections are repeats from prior years; Perez-Steele Galleries has indicated that a five-year rotation will be maintained in order to avoid depleting the pool of available worthy "kings" on some of the teams. The jumbo (5 by 7 inch) versions of the 1987 Diamond Kings are valued about five times their standard-size counterparts. Three of the Diamond Kings have a variation (on the reverse) where the yellow strip behind the words "Donruss Diamond Kings" is not printed and, hence, the background is white. Rookie Cards in this set include Barry Bonds, Bobby Bonilla, Kevin Brown, Will Clark, David Cone, Chuck Finley, Mike Greenwell, Bo Jackson, Wally Joyner, Barry Larkin, Greg Maddux, Dave Magadan, Kevin Mitchell, Rafael Palmeiro, Ruben Sierra, and Devon White. The backs of the cards in the factory sets are oriented differently than cards taken from wax packs, giving the appearance that one version or the other is upside down when sorting from the card backs.

		MINT	NRMT	EXC
COMPLETE SET (660)		30.00	13.50	3.70
COMPLETE FACT.SET (660)		30.00	13.50	3.70
COMMON CARD (1-660)		.05	.02	.01
☐ 1 Wally Joyner DK	.10	.05	.01
☐ 2 Roger Clemens DK	.30	.14	.04
☐ 3 Dale Murphy DK	.10	.05	.01
☐ 4 Darryl Strawberry DK	.10	.05	.01
☐ 5 Ozzie Smith DK	.30	.14	.04
☐ 6 Jose Canseco DK	.50	.23	.06
☐ 7 Charlie Hough DK	.05	.02	.01
☐ 8 Brook Jacoby DK	.05	.02	.01
☐ 9 Fred Lynn DK	.10	.05	.01
☐ 10 Rick Rhoden DK	.05	.02	.01
☐ 11 Chris Brown DK	.05	.02	.01
☐ 12 Von Hayes DK	.05	.02	.01
☐ 13 Jack Morris DK	.10	.05	.01
☐ 14A Kevin McReynolds DK ERR (Yellow strip missing on back)	.10	.05	.01
☐ 14B Kevin McReynolds DK COR	.05	.02	.01
☐ 15 George Brett DK	.40	.18	.05
☐ 16 Ted Higuera DK	.05	.02	.01
☐ 17 Hubie Brooks DK	.05	.02	.01
☐ 18 Mike Scott DK	.05	.02	.01
☐ 19 Kirby Puckett DK	.75	.35	.09
☐ 20 Dave Winfield DK	.15	.07	.02
☐ 21 Lloyd Moseby DK	.05	.02	.01
☐ 22A Eric Davis DK ERR (Yellow strip missing on back)	.10	.05	.01
☐ 22B Eric Davis DK COR	.10	.05	.01
☐ 23 Jim Presley DK	.05	.02	.01
☐ 24 Keith Moreland DK	.05	.02	.01
☐ 25A Greg Walker DK ERR (Yellow strip missing on back)	.05	.02	.01
☐ 25B Greg Walker DK COR	.05	.02	.01
☐ 26 Steve Sax DK	.05	.02	.01
☐ 27 DK Checklist 1-26	.10	.05	.01
☐ 28 B.J. Surhoff RR	.40	.18	.05
☐ 29 Randy Myers RR	.50	.23	.06
☐ 30 Ken Gerhart RR	.05	.02	.01
☐ 31 Benito Santiago RR	.10	.05	.01
☐ 32 Greg Swindell RR	.30	.14	.04
☐ 33 Mike Birkbeck RR	.05	.02	.01
☐ 34 Terry Steinbach RR	.30	.14	.04
☐ 35 Bo Jackson RR	1.00	.45	.12
☐ 36 Greg Maddux RR	18.00	8.00	2.20
☐ 37 Jim Lindeman RR	.05	.02	.01
☐ 38 Devon White RR	.75	.35	.09
☐ 39 Eric Bell RR	.05	.02	.01
☐ 40 Willie Fraser RR	.05	.02	.01
☐ 41 Jerry Browne RR	.10	.05	.01
☐ 42 Chris James RR	.05	.02	.01

☐ 43	Rafael Palmeiro RR	2.50	1.10	.30	☐ 112 Bob Knepper	.05	.02	.01
☐ 44	Pat Dodson RR	.05	.02	.01	☐ 113 Von Hayes	.05	.02	.01
☐ 45	Duane Ward RR	.15	.07	.02	☐ 114 Bip Roberts	.30	.14	.04
☐ 46	Mark McGwire RR	1.50	.70	.19	☐ 115 Tony Pena	.05	.02	.01
☐ 47	Bruce Fields RR UER	.05	.02	.01	☐ 116 Scott Garrelts	.05	.02	.01
	(Photo actually				☐ 117 Paul Molitor	.30	.14	.04
	Darnell Coles)				☐ 118 Darryl Strawberry	.15	.07	.02
☐ 48	Eddie Murray	.50	.23	.06	☐ 119 Shawon Dunston	.10	.05	.01
☐ 49	Ted Higuera	.05	.02	.01	☐ 120 Jim Presley	.05	.02	.01
☐ 50	Kirk Gibson	.15	.07	.02	☐ 121 Jesse Barfield	.05	.02	.01
☐ 51	Oil Can Boyd	.05	.02	.01	☐ 122 Gary Gaetti	.05	.02	.01
☐ 52	Don Mattingly	1.00	.45	.12	☐ 123 Kurt Stillwell	.05	.02	.01
☐ 53	Pedro Guerrero	.10	.05	.01	☐ 124 Joel Davis	.05	.02	.01
☐ 54	George Brett	1.00	.45	.12	☐ 125 Mike Boddicker	.05	.02	.01
☐ 55	Jose Rijo	.15	.07	.02	☐ 126 Robin Yount	.30	.14	.04
☐ 56	Tim Raines	.15	.07	.02	☐ 127 Alan Trammell	.15	.07	.02
☐ 57	Ed Correa	.05	.02	.01	☐ 128 Dave Righetti	.10	.05	.01
☐ 58	Mike Witt	.05	.02	.01	☐ 129 Dwight Evans	.10	.05	.01
☐ 59	Greg Walker	.05	.02	.01	☐ 130 Mike Scioscia	.05	.02	.01
☐ 60	Ozzie Smith	.60	.25	.07	☐ 131 Julio Franco	.10	.05	.01
☐ 61	Glenn Davis	.05	.02	.01	☐ 132 Bret Saberhagen	.15	.07	.02
☐ 62	Glenn Wilson	.05	.02	.01	☐ 133 Mike Davis	.05	.02	.01
☐ 63	Tom Browning	.05	.02	.01	☐ 134 Joe Hesketh	.05	.02	.01
☐ 64	Tony Gwynn	1.00	.45	.12	☐ 135 Wally Joyner	.50	.23	.06
☐ 65	R.J. Reynolds	.05	.02	.01	☐ 136 Don Slaught	.05	.02	.01
☐ 66	Will Clark	2.50	1.10	.30	☐ 137 Daryl Boston	.05	.02	.01
☐ 67	Ozzie Virgil	.05	.02	.01	☐ 138 Nolan Ryan	1.50	.70	.19
☐ 68	Rick Sutcliffe	.10	.05	.01	☐ 139 Mike Schmidt	.40	.18	.05
☐ 69	Gary Carter	.15	.07	.02	☐ 140 Tommy Herr	.05	.02	.01
☐ 70	Mike Moore	.05	.02	.01	☐ 141 Garry Templeton	.05	.02	.01
☐ 71	Bert Blyleven	.15	.07	.02	☐ 142 Kal Daniels	.05	.02	.01
☐ 72	Tony Fernandez	.10	.05	.01	☐ 143 Billy Sample	.05	.02	.01
☐ 73	Kent Hrbek	.15	.07	.02	☐ 144 Johnny Ray	.05	.02	.01
☐ 74	Lloyd Moseby	.05	.02	.01	☐ 145 Rob Thompson	.15	.07	.02
☐ 75	Alvin Davis	.05	.02	.01	☐ 146 Bob Dernier	.05	.02	.01
☐ 76	Keith Hernandez	.10	.05	.01	☐ 147 Danny Tartabull	.10	.05	.01
☐ 77	Ryne Sandberg	1.00	.45	.12	☐ 148 Ernie Whitt	.05	.02	.01
☐ 78	Dale Murphy	.15	.07	.02	☐ 149 Kirby Puckett	1.50	.70	.19
☐ 79	Sid Bream	.05	.02	.01	☐ 150 Mike Young	.05	.02	.01
☐ 80	Chris Brown	.05	.02	.01	☐ 151 Ernest Riles	.05	.02	.01
☐ 81	Steve Garvey	.15	.07	.02	☐ 152 Frank Tanana	.05	.02	.01
☐ 82	Mario Soto	.05	.02	.01	☐ 153 Rich Gedman	.05	.02	.01
☐ 83	Shane Rawley	.05	.02	.01	☐ 154 Willie Randolph	.10	.05	.01
☐ 84	Willie McGee	.10	.05	.01	☐ 155 Bill Madlock	.10	.05	.01
☐ 85	Jose Cruz	.05	.02	.01	☐ 156 Joe Carter	.60	.25	.07
☐ 86	Brian Downing	.05	.02	.01	☐ 157 Danny Jackson	.10	.05	.01
☐ 87	Ozzie Guillen	.15	.07	.02	☐ 158 Carney Lansford	.10	.05	.01
☐ 88	Hubie Brooks	.05	.02	.01	☐ 159 Bryn Smith	.05	.02	.01
☐ 89	Cal Ripken	2.00	.90	.25	☐ 160 Gary Pettis	.05	.02	.01
☐ 90	Juan Nieves	.05	.02	.01	☐ 161 Oddibe McDowell	.05	.02	.01
☐ 91	Lance Parrish	.10	.05	.01	☐ 162 John Cangelosi	.05	.02	.01
☐ 92	Jim Rice	.15	.07	.02	☐ 163 Mike Scott	.05	.02	.01
☐ 93	Ron Guidry	.10	.05	.01	☐ 164 Eric Show	.05	.02	.01
☐ 94	Fernando Valenzuela	.05	.02	.01	☐ 165 Juan Samuel	.05	.02	.01
☐ 95	Andy Allanson	.05	.02	.01	☐ 166 Nick Esasky	.05	.02	.01
☐ 96	Willie Wilson	.05	.02	.01	☐ 167 Zane Smith	.05	.02	.01
☐ 97	Jose Canseco	1.50	.70	.19	☐ 168 Mike C. Brown OF	.05	.02	.01
☐ 98	Jeff Reardon	.15	.07	.02	☐ 169 Keith Moreland	.05	.02	.01
☐ 99	Bobby Witt	.10	.05	.01	☐ 170 John Tudor	.05	.02	.01
☐ 100	Checklist 28-133	.10	.05	.01	☐ 171 Ken Dixon	.05	.02	.01
☐ 101	Jose Guzman	.05	.02	.01	☐ 172 Jim Gantner	.05	.02	.01
☐ 102	Steve Balboni	.05	.02	.01	☐ 173 Jack Morris	.15	.07	.02
☐ 103	Tony Phillips	.15	.07	.02	☐ 174 Bruce Hurst	.05	.02	.01
☐ 104	Brook Jacoby	.05	.02	.01	☐ 175 Dennis Rasmussen	.05	.02	.01
☐ 105	Dave Winfield	.20	.09	.03	☐ 176 Mike Marshall	.05	.02	.01
☐ 106	Orel Hershiser	.15	.07	.02	☐ 177 Dan Quisenberry	.10	.05	.01
☐ 107	Lou Whitaker	.15	.07	.02	☐ 178 Eric Plunk	.05	.02	.01
☐ 108	Fred Lynn	.10	.05	.01	☐ 179 Tim Wallach	.10	.05	.01
☐ 109	Bill Wegman	.05	.02	.01	☐ 180 Steve Buechele	.05	.02	.01
☐ 110	Donnie Moore	.05	.02	.01	☐ 181 Don Sutton	.15	.07	.02
☐ 111	Jack Clark	.10	.05	.01	☐ 182 Dave Schmidt	.05	.02	.01

☐ 183	Terry Pendleton	.15	.07	.02			
☐ 184	Jim Deshaies	.05	.02	.01			
☐ 185	Steve Bedrosian	.05	.02	.01			
☐ 186	Pete Rose	.50	.23	.06			
☐ 187	Dave Dravecky	.10	.05	.01			
☐ 188	Rick Reuschel	.05	.02	.01			
☐ 189	Dan Gladden	.05	.02	.01			
☐ 190	Rick Mahler	.05	.02	.01			
☐ 191	Thad Bosley	.05	.02	.01			
☐ 192	Ron Darling	.10	.05	.01			
☐ 193	Matt Young	.05	.02	.01			
☐ 194	Tom Brunansky	.05	.02	.01			
☐ 195	Dave Stieb	.10	.05	.01			
☐ 196	Frank Viola	.10	.05	.01			
☐ 197	Tom Henke	.10	.05	.01			
☐ 198	Karl Best	.05	.02	.01			
☐ 199	Dwight Gooden	.15	.07	.02			
☐ 200	Checklist 134-239	.10	.05	.01			
☐ 201	Steve Trout	.05	.02	.01			
☐ 202	Rafael Ramirez	.05	.02	.01			
☐ 203	Bob Walk	.05	.02	.01			
☐ 204	Roger Mason	.05	.02	.01			
☐ 205	Terry Kennedy	.05	.02	.01			
☐ 206	Ron Oester	.05	.02	.01			
☐ 207	John Russell	.05	.02	.01			
☐ 208	Greg Mathews	.05	.02	.01			
☐ 209	Charlie Kerfeld	.05	.02	.01			
☐ 210	Reggie Jackson	.40	.18	.05			
☐ 211	Floyd Bannister	.05	.02	.01			
☐ 212	Vance Law	.05	.02	.01			
☐ 213	Rich Bordi	.05	.02	.01			
☐ 214	Dan Plesac	.05	.02	.01			
☐ 215	Dave Collins	.05	.02	.01			
☐ 216	Bob Stanley	.05	.02	.01			
☐ 217	Joe Niekro	.10	.05	.01			
☐ 218	Tom Niedenfuer	.05	.02	.01			
☐ 219	Brett Butler	.15	.07	.02			
☐ 220	Charlie Leibrandt	.05	.02	.01			
☐ 221	Steve Ontiveros	.05	.02	.01			
☐ 222	Tim Burke	.05	.02	.01			
☐ 223	Curtis Wilkerson	.05	.02	.01			
☐ 224	Pete Incaviglia	.15	.07	.02			
☐ 225	Lonnie Smith	.05	.02	.01			
☐ 226	Chris Codiroli	.05	.02	.01			
☐ 227	Scott Bailes	.05	.02	.01			
☐ 228	Rickey Henderson	.30	.14	.04			
☐ 229	Ken Howell	.05	.02	.01			
☐ 230	Darnell Coles	.05	.02	.01			
☐ 231	Don Aase	.05	.02	.01			
☐ 232	Tim Leary	.05	.02	.01			
☐ 233	Bob Boone	.10	.05	.01			
☐ 234	Ricky Horton	.05	.02	.01			
☐ 235	Mark Bailey	.05	.02	.01			
☐ 236	Kevin Gross	.05	.02	.01			
☐ 237	Lance McCullers	.05	.02	.01			
☐ 238	Cecilio Guante	.05	.02	.01			
☐ 239	Bob Melvin	.05	.02	.01			
☐ 240	Billy Joe Robidoux	.05	.02	.01			
☐ 241	Roger McDowell	.05	.02	.01			
☐ 242	Leon Durham	.05	.02	.01			
☐ 243	Ed Nunez	.05	.02	.01			
☐ 244	Jimmy Key	.15	.07	.02			
☐ 245	Mike Smithson	.05	.02	.01			
☐ 246	Bo Diaz	.05	.02	.01			
☐ 247	Carlton Fisk	.25	.11	.03			
☐ 248	Larry Sheets	.05	.02	.01			
☐ 249	Juan Castillo	.05	.02	.01			
☐ 250	Eric King	.05	.02	.01			
☐ 251	Doug Drabek	.50	.23	.06			
☐ 252	Wade Boggs	.40	.18	.05			
☐ 253	Mariano Duncan	.05	.02	.01			
☐ 254	Pat Tabler	.05	.02	.01			
☐ 255	Frank White	.10	.05	.01			
☐ 256	Alfredo Griffin	.05	.02	.01			
☐ 257	Floyd Youmans	.05	.02	.01			
☐ 258	Rob Wilfong	.05	.02	.01			
☐ 259	Pete O'Brien	.05	.02	.01			
☐ 260	Tim Hulett	.05	.02	.01			
☐ 261	Dickie Thon	.05	.02	.01			
☐ 262	Darren Daulton	.15	.07	.02			
☐ 263	Vince Coleman	.10	.05	.01			
☐ 264	Andy Hawkins	.05	.02	.01			
☐ 265	Eric Davis	.10	.05	.01			
☐ 266	Andres Thomas	.05	.02	.01			
☐ 267	Mike Diaz	.05	.02	.01			
☐ 268	Chili Davis	.15	.07	.02			
☐ 269	Jody Davis	.05	.02	.01			
☐ 270	Phil Bradley	.05	.02	.01			
☐ 271	George Bell	.05	.02	.01			
☐ 272	Keith Atherton	.05	.02	.01			
☐ 273	Storm Davis	.05	.02	.01			
☐ 274	Rob Deer	.05	.02	.01			
☐ 275	Walt Terrell	.05	.02	.01			
☐ 276	Roger Clemens	.75	.35	.09			
☐ 277	Mike Easler	.05	.02	.01			
☐ 278	Steve Sax	.05	.02	.01			
☐ 279	Andre Thornton	.05	.02	.01			
☐ 280	Jim Sundberg	.05	.02	.01			
☐ 281	Bill Bathe	.05	.02	.01			
☐ 282	Jay Tibbs	.05	.02	.01			
☐ 283	Dick Schofield	.05	.02	.01			
☐ 284	Mike Mason	.05	.02	.01			
☐ 285	Jerry Hairston	.05	.02	.01			
☐ 286	Bill Doran	.05	.02	.01			
☐ 287	Tim Flannery	.05	.02	.01			
☐ 288	Gary Redus	.05	.02	.01			
☐ 289	John Franco	.10	.05	.01			
☐ 290	Paul Assenmacher	.05	.02	.01			
☐ 291	Joe Orsulak	.05	.02	.01			
☐ 292	Lee Smith	.15	.07	.02			
☐ 293	Mike Laga	.05	.02	.01			
☐ 294	Rick Dempsey	.05	.02	.01			
☐ 295	Mike Felder	.05	.02	.01			
☐ 296	Tom Brookens	.05	.02	.01			
☐ 297	Al Nipper	.05	.02	.01			
☐ 298	Mike Pagliarulo	.05	.02	.01			
☐ 299	Franklin Stubbs	.05	.02	.01			
☐ 300	Checklist 240-345	.10	.05	.01			
☐ 301	Steve Farr	.05	.02	.01			
☐ 302	Bill Mooneyham	.05	.02	.01			
☐ 303	Andres Galarraga	.40	.18	.05			
☐ 304	Scott Fletcher	.05	.02	.01			
☐ 305	Jack Howell	.05	.02	.01			
☐ 306	Russ Morman	.05	.02	.01			
☐ 307	Todd Worrell	.10	.05	.01			
☐ 308	Dave Smith	.05	.02	.01			
☐ 309	Jeff Stone	.05	.02	.01			
☐ 310	Ron Robinson	.05	.02	.01			
☐ 311	Bruce Bochy	.05	.02	.01			
☐ 312	Jim Winn	.05	.02	.01			
☐ 313	Mark Davis	.05	.02	.01			
☐ 314	Jeff Dedmon	.05	.02	.01			
☐ 315	Jamie Moyer	.10	.05	.01			
☐ 316	Wally Backman	.05	.02	.01			
☐ 317	Ken Phelps	.05	.02	.01			
☐ 318	Steve Lombardozzi	.05	.02	.01			
☐ 319	Rance Mulliniks	.05	.02	.01			
☐ 320	Tim Laudner	.05	.02	.01			
☐ 321	Mark Eichhorn	.05	.02	.01			
☐ 322	Lee Guetterman	.05	.02	.01			
☐ 323	Sid Fernandez	.10	.05	.01			
☐ 324	Jerry Mumphrey	.05	.02	.01			

□	#	Name			
□	325	David Palmer	.05	.02	.01
□	326	Bill Almon	.05	.02	.01
□	327	Candy Maldonado	.05	.02	.01
□	328	John Kruk	.50	.23	.06
□	329	John Denny	.05	.02	.01
□	330	Milt Thompson	.05	.02	.01
□	331	Mike LaValliere	.05	.02	.01
□	332	Alan Ashby	.05	.02	.01
□	333	Doug Corbett	.05	.02	.01
□	334	Ron Karkovice	.10	.05	.01
□	335	Mitch Webster	.05	.02	.01
□	336	Lee Lacy	.05	.02	.01
□	337	Glenn Braggs	.05	.02	.01
□	338	Dwight Lowry	.05	.02	.01
□	339	Don Baylor	.15	.07	.02
□	340	Brian Fisher	.05	.02	.01
□	341	Reggie Williams	.05	.02	.01
□	342	Tom Candiotti	.10	.05	.01
□	343	Rudy Law	.05	.02	.01
□	344	Curt Young	.05	.02	.01
□	345	Mike Fitzgerald	.05	.02	.01
□	346	Ruben Sierra	1.50	.70	.19
□	347	Mitch Williams	.10	.05	.01
□	348	Jorge Orta	.05	.02	.01
□	349	Mickey Tettleton	.10	.05	.01
□	350	Ernie Camacho	.05	.02	.01
□	351	Ron Kittle	.05	.02	.01
□	352	Ken Landreaux	.05	.02	.01
□	353	Chet Lemon	.05	.02	.01
□	354	John Shelby	.05	.02	.01
□	355	Mark Clear	.05	.02	.01
□	356	Doug DeCinces	.05	.02	.01
□	357	Ken Dayley	.05	.02	.01
□	358	Phil Garner	.10	.05	.01
□	359	Steve Jeltz	.05	.02	.01
□	360	Ed Whitson	.05	.02	.01
□	361	Barry Bonds	4.00	1.80	.50
□	362	Vida Blue	.10	.05	.01
□	363	Cecil Cooper	.10	.05	.01
□	364	Bob Ojeda	.05	.02	.01
□	365	Dennis Eckersley	.15	.07	.02
□	366	Mike Morgan	.05	.02	.01
□	367	Willie Upshaw	.05	.02	.01
□	368	Allan Anderson	.05	.02	.01
□	369	Bill Gullickson	.05	.02	.01
□	370	Bobby Thigpen	.05	.02	.01
□	371	Juan Beniquez	.05	.02	.01
□	372	Charlie Moore	.05	.02	.01
□	373	Dan Petry	.05	.02	.01
□	374	Rod Scurry	.05	.02	.01
□	375	Tom Seaver	.25	.11	.03
□	376	Ed VandeBerg	.05	.02	.01
□	377	Tony Bernazard	.05	.02	.01
□	378	Greg Pryor	.05	.02	.01
□	379	Dwayne Murphy	.05	.02	.01
□	380	Andy McGaffigan	.05	.02	.01
□	381	Kirk McCaskill	.05	.02	.01
□	382	Greg Harris	.05	.02	.01
□	383	Rich Dotson	.05	.02	.01
□	384	Craig Reynolds	.05	.02	.01
□	385	Greg Gross	.05	.02	.01
□	386	Tito Landrum	.05	.02	.01
□	387	Craig Lefferts	.05	.02	.01
□	388	Dave Parker	.15	.07	.02
□	389	Bob Horner	.05	.02	.01
□	390	Pat Clements	.05	.02	.01
□	391	Jeff Leonard	.05	.02	.01
□	392	Chris Speier	.05	.02	.01
□	393	John Moses	.05	.02	.01
□	394	Garth Iorg	.05	.02	.01
□	395	Greg Gagne	.10	.05	.01
□	396	Nate Snell	.05	.02	.01
□	397	Bryan Clutterbuck	.05	.02	.01
□	398	Darrell Evans	.10	.05	.01
□	399	Steve Crawford	.05	.02	.01
□	400	Checklist 346-451	.10	.05	.01
□	401	Phil Lombardi	.05	.02	.01
□	402	Rick Honeycutt	.05	.02	.01
□	403	Ken Schrom	.05	.02	.01
□	404	Bud Black	.05	.02	.01
□	405	Donnie Hill	.05	.02	.01
□	406	Wayne Krenchicki	.05	.02	.01
□	407	Chuck Finley	.30	.14	.04
□	408	Toby Harrah	.05	.02	.01
□	409	Steve Lyons	.05	.02	.01
□	410	Kevin Bass	.05	.02	.01
□	411	Marvell Wynne	.05	.02	.01
□	412	Ron Roenicke	.05	.02	.01
□	413	Tracy Jones	.05	.02	.01
□	414	Gene Garber	.05	.02	.01
□	415	Mike Bielecki	.05	.02	.01
□	416	Frank DiPino	.05	.02	.01
□	417	Andy Van Slyke	.10	.05	.01
□	418	Jim Dwyer	.05	.02	.01
□	419	Ben Oglivie	.05	.02	.01
□	420	Dave Bergman	.05	.02	.01
□	421	Joe Sambito	.05	.02	.01
□	422	Bob Tewksbury	.10	.05	.01
□	423	Len Matuszek	.05	.02	.01
□	424	Mike Kingery	.25	.11	.03
□	425	Dave Kingman	.10	.05	.01
□	426	Al Newman	.05	.02	.01
□	427	Gary Ward	.05	.02	.01
□	428	Ruppert Jones	.05	.02	.01
□	429	Harold Baines	.15	.07	.02
□	430	Pat Perry	.05	.02	.01
□	431	Terry Puhl	.05	.02	.01
□	432	Don Carman	.05	.02	.01
□	433	Eddie Milner	.05	.02	.01
□	434	LaMarr Hoyt	.05	.02	.01
□	435	Rick Rhoden	.05	.02	.01
□	436	Jose Uribe	.05	.02	.01
□	437	Ken Oberkfell	.05	.02	.01
□	438	Ron Davis	.05	.02	.01
□	439	Jesse Orosco	.05	.02	.01
□	440	Scott Bradley	.05	.02	.01
□	441	Randy Bush	.05	.02	.01
□	442	John Cerutti	.05	.02	.01
□	443	Roy Smalley	.05	.02	.01
□	444	Kelly Gruber	.05	.02	.01
□	445	Bob Kearney	.05	.02	.01
□	446	Ed Hearn	.05	.02	.01
□	447	Scott Sanderson	.05	.02	.01
□	448	Bruce Benedict	.05	.02	.01
□	449	Junior Ortiz	.05	.02	.01
□	450	Mike Aldrete	.05	.02	.01
□	451	Kevin McReynolds	.10	.05	.01
□	452	Rob Murphy	.05	.02	.01
□	453	Kent Tekulve	.05	.02	.01
□	454	Curt Ford	.05	.02	.01
□	455	Dave Lopes	.10	.05	.01
□	456	Bob Grich	.10	.05	.01
□	457	Jose DeLeon	.05	.02	.01
□	458	Andre Dawson	.15	.07	.02
□	459	Mike Flanagan	.05	.02	.01
□	460	Joey Meyer	.05	.02	.01
□	461	Chuck Cary	.05	.02	.01
□	462	Bill Buckner	.10	.05	.01
□	463	Bob Shirley	.05	.02	.01
□	464	Jeff Hamilton	.05	.02	.01
□	465	Phil Niekro	.15	.07	.02
□	466	Mark Gubicza	.05	.02	.01

☐ 467 Jerry Willard	.05	.02	.01
☐ 468 Bob Sebra	.05	.02	.01
☐ 469 Larry Parrish	.05	.02	.01
☐ 470 Charlie Hough	.10	.05	.01
☐ 471 Hal McRae	.15	.07	.02
☐ 472 Dave Leiper	.05	.02	.01
☐ 473 Mel Hall	.05	.02	.01
☐ 474 Dan Pasqua	.05	.02	.01
☐ 475 Bob Welch	.10	.05	.01
☐ 476 Johnny Grubb	.05	.02	.01
☐ 477 Jim Traber	.05	.02	.01
☐ 478 Chris Bosio	.20	.09	.03
☐ 479 Mark McLemore	.05	.02	.01
☐ 480 John Morris	.05	.02	.01
☐ 481 Billy Hatcher	.05	.02	.01
☐ 482 Dan Schatzeder	.05	.02	.01
☐ 483 Rich Gossage	.15	.07	.02
☐ 484 Jim Morrison	.05	.02	.01
☐ 485 Bob Brenly	.05	.02	.01
☐ 486 Bill Schroeder	.05	.02	.01
☐ 487 Mookie Wilson	.10	.05	.01
☐ 488 Dave Martinez	.10	.05	.01
☐ 489 Harold Reynolds	.05	.02	.01
☐ 490 Jeff Hearron	.05	.02	.01
☐ 491 Mickey Hatcher	.05	.02	.01
☐ 492 Barry Larkin	2.50	1.10	.30
☐ 493 Bob James	.05	.02	.01
☐ 494 John Habyan	.05	.02	.01
☐ 495 Jim Adduci	.05	.02	.01
☐ 496 Mike Heath	.05	.02	.01
☐ 497 Tim Stoddard	.05	.02	.01
☐ 498 Tony Armas	.05	.02	.01
☐ 499 Dennis Powell	.05	.02	.01
☐ 500 Checklist 452-557	.10	.05	.01
☐ 501 Chris Bando	.05	.02	.01
☐ 502 David Cone	2.00	.90	.25
☐ 503 Jay Howell	.05	.02	.01
☐ 504 Tom Foley	.05	.02	.01
☐ 505 Ray Chadwick	.05	.02	.01
☐ 506 Mike Loynd	.05	.02	.01
☐ 507 Neil Allen	.05	.02	.01
☐ 508 Danny Darwin	.05	.02	.01
☐ 509 Rick Schu	.05	.02	.01
☐ 510 Jose Oquendo	.05	.02	.01
☐ 511 Gene Walter	.05	.02	.01
☐ 512 Terry McGriff	.05	.02	.01
☐ 513 Ken Griffey	.10	.05	.01
☐ 514 Benny Distefano	.05	.02	.01
☐ 515 Terry Mulholland	.10	.05	.01
☐ 516 Ed Lynch	.05	.02	.01
☐ 517 Bill Swift	.10	.05	.01
☐ 518 Manny Lee	.05	.02	.01
☐ 519 Andre David	.05	.02	.01
☐ 520 Scott McGregor	.05	.02	.01
☐ 521 Rick Manning	.05	.02	.01
☐ 522 Willie Hernandez	.05	.02	.01
☐ 523 Marty Barrett	.05	.02	.01
☐ 524 Wayne Tolleson	.05	.02	.01
☐ 525 Jose Gonzalez	.05	.02	.01
☐ 526 Cory Snyder	.05	.02	.01
☐ 527 Buddy Biancalana	.05	.02	.01
☐ 528 Moose Haas	.05	.02	.01
☐ 529 Wilfredo Tejada	.05	.02	.01
☐ 530 Stu Cliburn	.05	.02	.01
☐ 531 Dale Mohorcic	.05	.02	.01
☐ 532 Ron Hassey	.05	.02	.01
☐ 533 Ty Gainey	.05	.02	.01
☐ 534 Jerry Royster	.05	.02	.01
☐ 535 Mike Maddux	.05	.02	.01
☐ 536 Ted Power	.05	.02	.01
☐ 537 Ted Simmons	.10	.05	.01
☐ 538 Rafael Belliard	.05	.02	.01
☐ 539 Chico Walker	.05	.02	.01
☐ 540 Bob Forsch	.05	.02	.01
☐ 541 John Stefero	.05	.02	.01
☐ 542 Dale Sveum	.05	.02	.01
☐ 543 Mark Thurmond	.05	.02	.01
☐ 544 Jeff Sellers	.05	.02	.01
☐ 545 Joel Skinner	.05	.02	.01
☐ 546 Alex Trevino	.05	.02	.01
☐ 547 Randy Kutcher	.05	.02	.01
☐ 548 Joaquin Andujar	.05	.02	.01
☐ 549 Casey Candaele	.05	.02	.01
☐ 550 Jeff Russell	.05	.02	.01
☐ 551 John Candelaria	.05	.02	.01
☐ 552 Joe Cowley	.05	.02	.01
☐ 553 Danny Cox	.05	.02	.01
☐ 554 Denny Walling	.05	.02	.01
☐ 555 Bruce Ruffin	.10	.05	.01
☐ 556 Buddy Bell	.10	.05	.01
☐ 557 Jimmy Jones	.05	.02	.01
☐ 558 Bobby Bonilla	1.00	.45	.12
☐ 559 Jeff D. Robinson	.05	.02	.01
☐ 560 Ed Olwine	.05	.02	.01
☐ 561 Glenallen Hill	.50	.23	.06
☐ 562 Lee Mazzilli	.05	.02	.01
☐ 563 Mike G. Brown P	.05	.02	.01
☐ 564 George Frazier	.05	.02	.01
☐ 565 Mike Sharperson	.05	.02	.01
☐ 566 Mark Portugal	.25	.11	.03
☐ 567 Rick Leach	.05	.02	.01
☐ 568 Mark Langston	.15	.07	.02
☐ 569 Rafael Santana	.05	.02	.01
☐ 570 Manny Trillo	.05	.02	.01
☐ 571 Cliff Speck	.05	.02	.01
☐ 572 Bob Kipper	.05	.02	.01
☐ 573 Kelly Downs	.05	.02	.01
☐ 574 Randy Asadoor	.05	.02	.01
☐ 575 Dave Magadan	.10	.05	.01
☐ 576 Marvin Freeman	.10	.05	.01
☐ 577 Jeff Lahti	.05	.02	.01
☐ 578 Jeff Calhoun	.05	.02	.01
☐ 579 Gus Polidor	.05	.02	.01
☐ 580 Gene Nelson	.05	.02	.01
☐ 581 Tim Teufel	.05	.02	.01
☐ 582 Odell Jones	.05	.02	.01
☐ 583 Mark Ryal	.05	.02	.01
☐ 584 Randy O'Neal	.05	.02	.01
☐ 585 Mike Greenwell	.50	.23	.06
☐ 586 Ray Knight	.10	.05	.01
☐ 587 Ralph Bryant	.10	.05	.01
☐ 588 Carmen Castillo	.05	.02	.01
☐ 589 Ed Wojna	.05	.02	.01
☐ 590 Stan Javier	.05	.02	.01
☐ 591 Jeff Musselman	.05	.02	.01
☐ 592 Mike Stanley	.25	.11	.03
☐ 593 Darrell Porter	.05	.02	.01
☐ 594 Drew Hall	.05	.02	.01
☐ 595 Rob Nelson	.05	.02	.01
☐ 596 Bryan Oelkers	.05	.02	.01
☐ 597 Scott Nielsen	.05	.02	.01
☐ 598 Brian Holton	.05	.02	.01
☐ 599 Kevin Mitchell	.25	.11	.03
☐ 600 Checklist 558-660	.10	.05	.01
☐ 601 Jackie Gutierrez	.05	.02	.01
☐ 602 Barry Jones	.05	.02	.01
☐ 603 Jerry Narron	.05	.02	.01
☐ 604 Steve Lake	.05	.02	.01
☐ 605 Jim Pankovits	.05	.02	.01
☐ 606 Ed Romero	.05	.02	.01
☐ 607 Dave LaPoint	.05	.02	.01
☐ 608 Don Robinson	.05	.02	.01

☐ 609	Mike Krukow	.05	.02	.01
☐ 610	Dave Valle	.05	.02	.01
☐ 611	Len Dykstra	.15	.07	.02
☐ 612	Roberto Clemente PUZ	.35	.16	.04
☐ 613	Mike Trujillo	.05	.02	.01
☐ 614	Damaso Garcia	.05	.02	.01
☐ 615	Neal Heaton	.05	.02	.01
☐ 616	Juan Berenguer	.05	.02	.01
☐ 617	Steve Carlton	.15	.07	.02
☐ 618	Gary Lucas	.05	.02	.01
☐ 619	Geno Petralli	.05	.02	.01
☐ 620	Rick Aguilera	.15	.07	.02
☐ 621	Fred McGriff	1.50	.70	.19
☐ 622	Dave Henderson	.05	.02	.01
☐ 623	Dave Clark	.10	.05	.01
☐ 624	Angel Salazar	.05	.02	.01
☐ 625	Randy Hunt	.05	.02	.01
☐ 626	John Gibbons	.05	.02	.01
☐ 627	Kevin Brown	.40	.18	.05
☐ 628	Bill Dawley	.05	.02	.01
☐ 629	Aurelio Lopez	.05	.02	.01
☐ 630	Charles Hudson	.05	.02	.01
☐ 631	Ray Soff	.05	.02	.01
☐ 632	Ray Hayward	.05	.02	.01
☐ 633	Spike Owen	.05	.02	.01
☐ 634	Glenn Hubbard	.05	.02	.01
☐ 635	Kevin Elster	.05	.02	.01
☐ 636	Mike LaCoss	.05	.02	.01
☐ 637	Dwayne Henry	.05	.02	.01
☐ 638	Rey Quinones	.05	.02	.01
☐ 639	Jim Clancy	.05	.02	.01
☐ 640	Larry Andersen	.05	.02	.01
☐ 641	Calvin Schiraldi	.05	.02	.01
☐ 642	Stan Jefferson	.05	.02	.01
☐ 643	Marc Sullivan	.05	.02	.01
☐ 644	Mark Grant	.05	.02	.01
☐ 645	Cliff Johnson	.05	.02	.01
☐ 646	Howard Johnson	.10	.05	.01
☐ 647	Dave Sax	.05	.02	.01
☐ 648	Dave Stewart	.15	.07	.02
☐ 649	Danny Heep	.05	.02	.01
☐ 650	Joe Johnson	.05	.02	.01
☐ 651	Bob Brower	.05	.02	.01
☐ 652	Rob Woodward	.05	.02	.01
☐ 653	John Mizerock	.05	.02	.01
☐ 654	Tim Pyznarski	.05	.02	.01
☐ 655	Luis Aquino	.05	.02	.01
☐ 656	Mickey Brantley	.05	.02	.01
☐ 657	Doyle Alexander	.05	.02	.01
☐ 658	Sammy Stewart	.05	.02	.01
☐ 659	Jim Acker	.05	.02	.01
☐ 660	Pete Ladd	.05	.02	.01

1987 Donruss Rookies

The 1987 Donruss "The Rookies" set features 56 cards plus a 15-piece puzzle of Roberto Clemente. Cards are in full color and are standard size, 2 1/2" by 3 1/2". The set was distributed in a small green and black box with gold lettering. Card fronts are similar in design to the 1987 Donruss regular issue except for the presence of "The Rookies" logo in the lower left corner and a green border instead of a black bor-

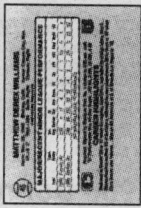

der. The key (extended) Rookie Cards in this set are Ellis Burks, Shane Mack, Luis Polonia, John Smiley, and Matt Williams.

	MINT	NRMT	EXC
COMPLETE FACT.SET (56)	20.00	9.00	2.50
COMMON CARD (1-56)	.08	.04	.01

☐ 1	Mark McGwire	1.50	.70	.19
☐ 2	Eric Bell	.08	.04	.01
☐ 3	Mark Williamson	.08	.04	.01
☐ 4	Mike Greenwell	.50	.23	.06
☐ 5	Ellis Burks	.75	.35	.09
☐ 6	DeWayne Buice	.08	.04	.01
☐ 7	Mark McLemore	.08	.04	.01
☐ 8	Devon White	.60	.25	.07
☐ 9	Willie Fraser	.08	.04	.01
☐ 10	Les Lancaster	.08	.04	.01
☐ 11	Ken Williams	.08	.04	.01
☐ 12	Matt Nokes	.15	.07	.02
☐ 13	Jeff M. Robinson	.08	.04	.01
☐ 14	Bo Jackson	1.00	.45	.12
☐ 15	Kevin Seitzer	.25	.11	.03
☐ 16	Billy Ripken	.08	.04	.01
☐ 17	B.J. Surhoff	.20	.09	.03
☐ 18	Chuck Crim	.08	.04	.01
☐ 19	Mike Birkbeck	.08	.04	.01
☐ 20	Chris Bosio	.15	.07	.02
☐ 21	Les Straker	.08	.04	.01
☐ 22	Mark Davidson	.08	.04	.01
☐ 23	Gene Larkin	.15	.07	.02
☐ 24	Ken Gerhart	.08	.04	.01
☐ 25	Luis Polonia	.40	.18	.05
☐ 26	Terry Steinbach	.20	.09	.03
☐ 27	Mickey Brantley	.08	.04	.01
☐ 28	Mike Stanley	.25	.11	.03
☐ 29	Jerry Browne	.08	.04	.01
☐ 30	Todd Benzinger	.08	.04	.01
☐ 31	Fred McGriff	2.50	1.10	.30
☐ 32	Mike Henneman	.25	.11	.03
☐ 33	Casey Candaele	.08	.04	.01
☐ 34	Dave Magadan	.15	.07	.02
☐ 35	David Cone	2.00	.90	.25
☐ 36	Mike Jackson	.15	.07	.02
☐ 37	John Mitchell	.08	.04	.01
☐ 38	Mike Dunne	.08	.04	.01
☐ 39	John Smiley	.25	.11	.03
☐ 40	Joe Magrane	.08	.04	.01
☐ 41	Jim Lindeman	.08	.04	.01
☐ 42	Shane Mack	.20	.09	.03
☐ 43	Stan Jefferson	.08	.04	.01
☐ 44	Benito Santiago	.15	.07	.02
☐ 45	Matt Williams	5.00	2.20	.60
☐ 46	Dave Meads	.08	.04	.01
☐ 47	Rafael Palmeiro	2.50	1.10	.30
☐ 48	Bill Long	.08	.04	.01

		MINT	NRMT	EXC
☐ 49	Bob Brower	.08	.04	.01
☐ 50	James Steels	.08	.04	.01
☐ 51	Paul Noce	.08	.04	.01
☐ 52	Greg Maddux	12.00	5.50	1.50
☐ 53	Jeff Musselman	.08	.04	.01
☐ 54	Brian Holton	.08	.04	.01
☐ 55	Chuck Jackson	.08	.04	.01
☐ 56	Checklist 1-56	.08	.04	.01

1988 Donruss

This 660-card set was distributed along with a puzzle of Stan Musial. The six regular checklist cards are numbered throughout the set as multiples of 100. Cards measure 2 1/2" by 3 1/2" and feature a distinctive black and blue border on the front. The popular Diamond King subset returns for the seventh consecutive year. The jumbo (5 by 7 inch) versions of the 1988 Diamond Kings are valued about 10 times their standard-size counterparts. Rated Rookies are featured again as cards 28-47. Cards marked as SP (short printed) from 648-660 are more difficult to find than the other 13 SP's in the lower 600s. These 26 cards listed as SP were apparently pulled from the printing sheet to make room for the 26 Bonus MVP cards. Numbered with the prefix "BC" for bonus card, this 26-card set featuring the most valuable player from each of the 26 teams was randomly inserted in the wax and rack packs. The cards are distinguished by the MVP logo in the upper left corner of the obverse, and cards BC14-BC26 are considered to be more difficult to find than cards BC1-BC13. Six of the checklist cards were done two different ways to reflect the inclusion or exclusion of the Bonus MVP cards in the wax packs. In the checklist below, the A variations (for the checklist cards) are from the wax packs and the B variations are from the factory-collated sets. The key Rookie Cards in this set are Roberto Alomar, Jay Bell, Jeff Blauser, Jay Buhner, Ellis Burks, Mike Devereaux, Ron Gant, Tom Glavine, Mark Grace, Gregg Jefferies, Roberto Kelly, Jack McDowell, and Matt Williams. There was also a Kirby Puckett card issued as the package back of Donruss blister packs; it uses a different photo from both of Kirby's regular and Bonus MVP cards and is

unnumbered on the back. The design pattern of the factory set card fronts is oriented differently from that of the regular wax pack cards.

		MINT	NRMT	EXC
	COMPLETE SET (660)	10.00	4.50	1.25
	COMPLETE FACT.SET (660)	10.00	4.50	1.25
	COMPLETE MVP SET (26)	3.00	1.35	.35
	COMMON CARD (1-647)	.05	.02	.01
	COMMON CARD SP (648-660)	.07	.03	.01
☐ 1	Mark McGwire DK	.25	.11	.03
☐ 2	Tim Raines DK	.10	.05	.01
☐ 3	Benito Santiago DK	.05	.02	.01
☐ 4	Alan Trammell DK	.10	.05	.01
☐ 5	Danny Tartabull DK	.10	.05	.01
☐ 6	Ron Darling DK	.05	.02	.01
☐ 7	Paul Molitor DK	.10	.05	.01
☐ 8	Devon White DK	.10	.05	.01
☐ 9	Andre Dawson DK	.10	.05	.01
☐ 10	Julio Franco DK	.10	.05	.01
☐ 11	Scott Fletcher DK	.05	.02	.01
☐ 12	Tony Fernandez DK	.05	.02	.01
☐ 13	Shane Rawley DK	.05	.02	.01
☐ 14	Kal Daniels DK	.05	.02	.01
☐ 15	Jack Clark DK	.05	.02	.01
☐ 16	Dwight Evans DK	.10	.05	.01
☐ 17	Tommy John DK	.10	.05	.01
☐ 18	Andy Van Slyke DK	.05	.02	.01
☐ 19	Gary Gaetti DK	.10	.05	.01
☐ 20	Mark Langston DK	.10	.05	.01
☐ 21	Will Clark DK	.20	.09	.03
☐ 22	Glenn Hubbard DK	.05	.02	.01
☐ 23	Billy Hatcher DK	.05	.02	.01
☐ 24	Bob Welch DK	.05	.02	.01
☐ 25	Ivan Calderon DK	.05	.02	.01
☐ 26	Cal Ripken DK	.40	.18	.05
☐ 27	DK Checklist 1-26	.10	.05	.01
☐ 28	Mackey Sasser RR	.05	.02	.01
☐ 29	Jeff Treadway RR	.05	.02	.01
☐ 30	Mike Campbell RR	.05	.02	.01
☐ 31	Lance Johnson RR	.20	.09	.03
☐ 32	Nelson Liriano RR	.05	.02	.01
☐ 33	Shawn Abner RR	.05	.02	.01
☐ 34	Roberto Alomar RR	2.00	.90	.25
☐ 35	Shawn Hillegas RR	.05	.02	.01
☐ 36	Joey Meyer RR	.05	.02	.01
☐ 37	Kevin Elster RR	.05	.02	.01
☐ 38	Jose Lind RR	.05	.02	.01
☐ 39	Kirt Manwaring RR	.10	.05	.01
☐ 40	Mark Grace RR	.50	.23	.06
☐ 41	Jody Reed RR	.10	.05	.01
☐ 42	John Farrell RR	.05	.02	.01
☐ 43	Al Leiter RR	.10	.05	.01
☐ 44	Gary Thurman RR	.05	.02	.01
☐ 45	Vicente Palacios RR	.05	.02	.01
☐ 46	Eddie Williams RR	.10	.05	.01
☐ 47	Jack McDowell RR	.40	.18	.05
☐ 48	Ken Dixon	.05	.02	.01
☐ 49	Mike Birkbeck	.05	.02	.01
☐ 50	Eric King	.05	.02	.01
☐ 51	Roger Clemens	.20	.09	.03
☐ 52	Pat Clements	.05	.02	.01
☐ 53	Fernando Valenzuela	.05	.02	.01
☐ 54	Mark Gubicza	.05	.02	.01
☐ 55	Jay Howell	.05	.02	.01
☐ 56	Floyd Youmans	.05	.02	.01
☐ 57	Ed Correa	.05	.02	.01
☐ 58	DeWayne Buice	.05	.02	.01
☐ 59	Jose DeLeon	.05	.02	.01

☐	60	Danny Cox	.05	.02	.01
☐	61	Nolan Ryan	.75	.35	.09
☐	62	Steve Bedrosian	.05	.02	.01
☐	63	Tom Browning	.05	.02	.01
☐	64	Mark Davis	.05	.02	.01
☐	65	R.J. Reynolds	.05	.02	.01
☐	66	Kevin Mitchell	.10	.05	.01
☐	67	Ken Oberkfell	.05	.02	.01
☐	68	Rick Sutcliffe	.10	.05	.01
☐	69	Dwight Gooden	.10	.05	.01
☐	70	Scott Bankhead	.05	.02	.01
☐	71	Bert Blyleven	.15	.07	.02
☐	72	Jimmy Key	.15	.07	.02
☐	73	Les Straker	.05	.02	.01
☐	74	Jim Clancy	.05	.02	.01
☐	75	Mike Moore	.05	.02	.01
☐	76	Ron Darling	.10	.05	.01
☐	77	Ed Lynch	.05	.02	.01
☐	78	Dale Murphy	.15	.07	.02
☐	79	Doug Drabek	.15	.07	.02
☐	80	Scott Garrelts	.05	.02	.01
☐	81	Ed Whitson	.05	.02	.01
☐	82	Rob Murphy	.05	.02	.01
☐	83	Shane Rawley	.05	.02	.01
☐	84	Greg Mathews	.05	.02	.01
☐	85	Jim Deshaies	.05	.02	.01
☐	86	Mike Witt	.05	.02	.01
☐	87	Donnie Hill	.05	.02	.01
☐	88	Jeff Reed	.05	.02	.01
☐	89	Mike Boddicker	.05	.02	.01
☐	90	Ted Higuera	.05	.02	.01
☐	91	Walt Terrell	.05	.02	.01
☐	92	Bob Stanley	.05	.02	.01
☐	93	Dave Righetti	.05	.02	.01
☐	94	Orel Hershiser	.10	.05	.01
☐	95	Chris Bando	.05	.02	.01
☐	96	Bret Saberhagen	.15	.07	.02
☐	97	Curt Young	.05	.02	.01
☐	98	Tim Burke	.05	.02	.01
☐	99	Charlie Hough	.10	.05	.01
☐	100A	Checklist 28-137	.10	.05	.01
☐	100B	Checklist 28-133	.10	.05	.01
☐	101	Bobby Witt	.10	.05	.01
☐	102	George Brett	.40	.18	.05
☐	103	Mickey Tettleton	.10	.05	.01
☐	104	Scott Bailes	.05	.02	.01
☐	105	Mike Pagliarulo	.05	.02	.01
☐	106	Mike Scioscia	.05	.02	.01
☐	107	Tom Brookens	.05	.02	.01
☐	108	Ray Knight	.10	.05	.01
☐	109	Dan Plesac	.05	.02	.01
☐	110	Wally Joyner	.10	.05	.01
☐	111	Bob Forsch	.05	.02	.01
☐	112	Mike Scott	.05	.02	.01
☐	113	Kevin Gross	.05	.02	.01
☐	114	Benito Santiago	.10	.05	.01
☐	115	Bob Kipper	.05	.02	.01
☐	116	Mike Krukow	.05	.02	.01
☐	117	Chris Bosio	.10	.05	.01
☐	118	Sid Fernandez	.10	.05	.01
☐	119	Jody Davis	.05	.02	.01
☐	120	Mike Morgan	.05	.02	.01
☐	121	Mark Eichhorn	.05	.02	.01
☐	122	Jeff Reardon	.15	.07	.02
☐	123	John Franco	.10	.05	.01
☐	124	Richard Dotson	.05	.02	.01
☐	125	Eric Bell	.05	.02	.01
☐	126	Juan Nieves	.05	.02	.01
☐	127	Jack Morris	.15	.07	.02
☐	128	Rick Rhoden	.05	.02	.01
☐	129	Rich Gedman	.05	.02	.01
☐	130	Ken Howell	.05	.02	.01
☐	131	Brook Jacoby	.05	.02	.01
☐	132	Danny Jackson	.05	.02	.01
☐	133	Gene Nelson	.05	.02	.01
☐	134	Neal Heaton	.05	.02	.01
☐	135	Willie Fraser	.05	.02	.01
☐	136	Jose Guzman	.05	.02	.01
☐	137	Ozzie Guillen	.10	.05	.01
☐	138	Bob Knepper	.05	.02	.01
☐	139	Mike Jackson	.10	.05	.01
☐	140	Joe Magrane	.05	.02	.01
☐	141	Jimmy Jones	.05	.02	.01
☐	142	Ted Power	.05	.02	.01
☐	143	Ozzie Virgil	.05	.02	.01
☐	144	Felix Fermin	.05	.02	.01
☐	145	Kelly Downs	.05	.02	.01
☐	146	Shawon Dunston	.10	.05	.01
☐	147	Scott Bradley	.05	.02	.01
☐	148	Dave Stieb	.10	.05	.01
☐	149	Frank Viola	.10	.05	.01
☐	150	Terry Kennedy	.05	.02	.01
☐	151	Bill Wegman	.05	.02	.01
☐	152	Matt Nokes	.05	.02	.01
☐	153	Wade Boggs	.15	.07	.02
☐	154	Wayne Tolleson	.05	.02	.01
☐	155	Mariano Duncan	.05	.02	.01
☐	156	Julio Franco	.10	.05	.01
☐	157	Charlie Leibrandt	.05	.02	.01
☐	158	Terry Steinbach	.10	.05	.01
☐	159	Mike Fitzgerald	.05	.02	.01
☐	160	Jack Lazorko	.05	.02	.01
☐	161	Mitch Williams	.10	.05	.01
☐	162	Greg Walker	.05	.02	.01
☐	163	Alan Ashby	.05	.02	.01
☐	164	Tony Gwynn	.30	.14	.04
☐	165	Bruce Ruffin	.05	.02	.01
☐	166	Ron Robinson	.05	.02	.01
☐	167	Zane Smith	.05	.02	.01
☐	168	Junior Ortiz	.05	.02	.01
☐	169	Jamie Moyer	.05	.02	.01
☐	170	Tony Pena	.05	.02	.01
☐	171	Cal Ripken	.75	.35	.09
☐	172	B.J. Surhoff	.10	.05	.01
☐	173	Lou Whitaker	.15	.07	.02
☐	174	Ellis Burks	.15	.07	.02
☐	175	Ron Guidry	.10	.05	.01
☐	176	Steve Sax	.05	.02	.01
☐	177	Danny Tartabull	.10	.05	.01
☐	178	Carney Lansford	.10	.05	.01
☐	179	Casey Candaele	.05	.02	.01
☐	180	Scott Fletcher	.05	.02	.01
☐	181	Mark McLemore	.05	.02	.01
☐	182	Ivan Calderon	.05	.02	.01
☐	183	Jack Clark	.10	.05	.01
☐	184	Glenn Davis	.05	.02	.01
☐	185	Luis Aguayo	.05	.02	.01
☐	186	Bo Diaz	.05	.02	.01
☐	187	Stan Jefferson	.05	.02	.01
☐	188	Sid Bream	.05	.02	.01
☐	189	Bob Brenly	.05	.02	.01
☐	190	Dion James	.05	.02	.01
☐	191	Leon Durham	.05	.02	.01
☐	192	Jesse Orosco	.05	.02	.01
☐	193	Alvin Davis	.05	.02	.01
☐	194	Gary Gaetti	.05	.02	.01
☐	195	Fred McGriff	.40	.18	.05
☐	196	Steve Lombardozzi	.05	.02	.01
☐	197	Rance Mulliniks	.05	.02	.01
☐	198	Rey Quinones	.05	.02	.01
☐	199	Gary Carter	.15	.07	.02
☐	200A	Checklist 138-247	.10	.05	.01

□	200B	Checklist 134-239	.10	.05	.01
□	201	Keith Moreland	.05	.02	.01
□	202	Ken Griffey	.10	.05	.01
□	203	Tommy Gregg	.05	.02	.01
□	204	Will Clark	.30	.14	.04
□	205	John Kruk	.15	.07	.02
□	206	Buddy Bell	.10	.05	.01
□	207	Von Hayes	.05	.02	.01
□	208	Tommy Herr	.05	.02	.01
□	209	Craig Reynolds	.05	.02	.01
□	210	Gary Pettis	.05	.02	.01
□	211	Harold Baines	.15	.07	.02
□	212	Vance Law	.05	.02	.01
□	213	Ken Gerhart	.05	.02	.01
□	214	Jim Gantner	.05	.02	.01
□	215	Chet Lemon	.05	.02	.01
□	216	Dwight Evans	.10	.05	.01
□	217	Don Mattingly	.40	.18	.05
□	218	Franklin Stubbs	.05	.02	.01
□	219	Pat Tabler	.05	.02	.01
□	220	Bo Jackson	.25	.11	.03
□	221	Tony Phillips	.15	.07	.02
□	222	Tim Wallach	.10	.05	.01
□	223	Ruben Sierra	.25	.11	.03
□	224	Steve Buechele	.05	.02	.01
□	225	Frank White	.10	.05	.01
□	226	Alfredo Griffin	.05	.02	.01
□	227	Greg Swindell	.10	.05	.01
□	228	Willie Randolph	.10	.05	.01
□	229	Mike Marshall	.05	.02	.01
□	230	Alan Trammell	.15	.07	.02
□	231	Eddie Murray	.25	.11	.03
□	232	Dale Sveum	.05	.02	.01
□	233	Dick Schofield	.05	.02	.01
□	234	Jose Oquendo	.05	.02	.01
□	235	Bill Doran	.05	.02	.01
□	236	Milt Thompson	.05	.02	.01
□	237	Marvell Wynne	.05	.02	.01
□	238	Bobby Bonilla	.15	.07	.02
□	239	Chris Speier	.05	.02	.01
□	240	Glenn Braggs	.05	.02	.01
□	241	Wally Backman	.05	.02	.01
□	242	Ryne Sandberg	.30	.14	.04
□	243	Phil Bradley	.05	.02	.01
□	244	Kelly Gruber	.05	.02	.01
□	245	Tom Brunansky	.05	.02	.01
□	246	Ron Oester	.05	.02	.01
□	247	Bobby Thigpen	.05	.02	.01
□	248	Fred Lynn	.10	.05	.01
□	249	Paul Molitor	.15	.07	.02
□	250	Darrell Evans	.10	.05	.01
□	251	Gary Ward	.05	.02	.01
□	252	Bruce Hurst	.05	.02	.01
□	253	Bob Welch	.10	.05	.01
□	254	Joe Carter	.15	.07	.02
□	255	Willie Wilson	.05	.02	.01
□	256	Mark McGwire	.50	.23	.06
□	257	Mitch Webster	.05	.02	.01
□	258	Brian Downing	.05	.02	.01
□	259	Mike Stanley	.10	.05	.01
□	260	Carlton Fisk	.15	.07	.02
□	261	Billy Hatcher	.05	.02	.01
□	262	Glenn Wilson	.05	.02	.01
□	263	Ozzie Smith	.30	.14	.04
□	264	Randy Ready	.05	.02	.01
□	265	Kurt Stillwell	.05	.02	.01
□	266	David Palmer	.05	.02	.01
□	267	Mike Diaz	.05	.02	.01
□	268	Robby Thompson	.10	.05	.01
□	269	Andre Dawson	.15	.07	.02
□	270	Lee Guetterman	.05	.02	.01
□	271	Willie Upshaw	.05	.02	.01
□	272	Randy Bush	.05	.02	.01
□	273	Larry Sheets	.05	.02	.01
□	274	Rob Deer	.05	.02	.01
□	275	Kirk Gibson	.15	.07	.02
□	276	Marty Barrett	.05	.02	.01
□	277	Rickey Henderson	.15	.07	.02
□	278	Pedro Guerrero	.10	.05	.01
□	279	Brett Butler	.15	.07	.02
□	280	Kevin Seitzer	.10	.05	.01
□	281	Mike Davis	.05	.02	.01
□	282	Andres Galarraga	.15	.07	.02
□	283	Devon White	.15	.07	.02
□	284	Pete O'Brien	.05	.02	.01
□	285	Jerry Hairston	.05	.02	.01
□	286	Kevin Bass	.05	.02	.01
□	287	Carmelo Martinez	.05	.02	.01
□	288	Juan Samuel	.05	.02	.01
□	289	Kal Daniels	.05	.02	.01
□	290	Albert Hall	.05	.02	.01
□	291	Andy Van Slyke	.10	.05	.01
□	292	Lee Smith	.15	.07	.02
□	293	Vince Coleman	.10	.05	.01
□	294	Tom Niedenfuer	.05	.02	.01
□	295	Robin Yount	.15	.07	.02
□	296	Jeff M. Robinson	.05	.02	.01
□	297	Todd Benzinger	.05	.02	.01
□	298	Dave Winfield	.15	.07	.02
□	299	Mickey Hatcher	.05	.02	.01
□	300A	Checklist 248-357	.10	.05	.01
□	300B	Checklist 240-345	.10	.05	.01
□	301	Bud Black	.05	.02	.01
□	302	Jose Canseco	.50	.23	.06
□	303	Tom Foley	.05	.02	.01
□	304	Pete Incaviglia	.10	.05	.01
□	305	Bob Boone	.10	.05	.01
□	306	Bill Long	.05	.02	.01
□	307	Willie McGee	.10	.05	.01
□	308	Ken Caminiti	.50	.23	.06
□	309	Darren Daulton	.15	.07	.02
□	310	Tracy Jones	.05	.02	.01
□	311	Greg Booker	.05	.02	.01
□	312	Mike LaValliere	.05	.02	.01
□	313	Chili Davis	.15	.07	.02
□	314	Glenn Hubbard	.05	.02	.01
□	315	Paul Noce	.05	.02	.01
□	316	Keith Hernandez	.10	.05	.01
□	317	Mark Langston	.15	.07	.02
□	318	Keith Atherton	.05	.02	.01
□	319	Tony Fernandez	.10	.05	.01
□	320	Kent Hrbek	.10	.05	.01
□	321	John Cerutti	.05	.02	.01
□	322	Mike Kingery	.05	.02	.01
□	323	Dave Magadan	.10	.05	.01
□	324	Rafael Palmeiro	.50	.23	.06
□	325	Jeff Dedmon	.05	.02	.01
□	326	Barry Bonds	.60	.25	.07
□	327	Jeffrey Leonard	.05	.02	.01
□	328	Tim Flannery	.05	.02	.01
□	329	Dave Concepcion	.10	.05	.01
□	330	Mike Schmidt	.25	.11	.03
□	331	Bill Dawley	.05	.02	.01
□	332	Larry Andersen	.05	.02	.01
□	333	Jack Howell	.05	.02	.01
□	334	Ken Williams	.05	.02	.01
□	335	Bryn Smith	.05	.02	.01
□	336	Billy Ripken	.05	.02	.01
□	337	Greg Brock	.05	.02	.01
□	338	Mike Heath	.05	.02	.01
□	339	Mike Greenwell	.15	.07	.02
□	340	Claudell Washington	.05	.02	.01

☐ 341	Jose Gonzalez	.05	.02	.01	☐ 411	Shane Mack	.10	.05	.01
☐ 342	Mel Hall	.05	.02	.01	☐ 412	Greg Gross	.05	.02	.01
☐ 343	Jim Eisenreich	.10	.05	.01	☐ 413	Nick Esasky	.05	.02	.01
☐ 344	Tony Bernazard	.05	.02	.01	☐ 414	Damaso Garcia	.05	.02	.01
☐ 345	Tim Raines	.15	.07	.02	☐ 415	Brian Fisher	.05	.02	.01
☐ 346	Bob Brower	.05	.02	.01	☐ 416	Brian Dayett	.05	.02	.01
☐ 347	Larry Parrish	.05	.02	.01	☐ 417	Curt Ford	.05	.02	.01
☐ 348	Thad Bosley	.05	.02	.01	☐ 418	Mark Williamson	.05	.02	.01
☐ 349	Dennis Eckersley	.15	.07	.02	☐ 419	Bill Schroeder	.05	.02	.01
☐ 350	Cory Snyder	.05	.02	.01	☐ 420	Mike Henneman	.15	.07	.02
☐ 351	Rick Cerone	.05	.02	.01	☐ 421	John Marzano	.05	.02	.01
☐ 352	John Shelby	.05	.02	.01	☐ 422	Ron Kittle	.05	.02	.01
☐ 353	Larry Herndon	.05	.02	.01	☐ 423	Matt Young	.05	.02	.01
☐ 354	John Habyan	.05	.02	.01	☐ 424	Steve Balboni	.05	.02	.01
☐ 355	Chuck Crim	.05	.02	.01	☐ 425	Luis Polonia	.20	.09	.03
☐ 356	Gus Polidor	.05	.02	.01	☐ 426	Randy St.Claire	.05	.02	.01
☐ 357	Ken Dayley	.05	.02	.01	☐ 427	Greg Harris	.05	.02	.01
☐ 358	Danny Darwin	.05	.02	.01	☐ 428	Johnny Ray	.05	.02	.01
☐ 359	Lance Parrish	.10	.05	.01	☐ 429	Ray Searage	.05	.02	.01
☐ 360	James Steels	.05	.02	.01	☐ 430	Ricky Horton	.05	.02	.01
☐ 361	Al Pedrique	.05	.02	.01	☐ 431	Gerald Young	.05	.02	.01
☐ 362	Mike Aldrete	.05	.02	.01	☐ 432	Rick Schu	.05	.02	.01
☐ 363	Juan Castillo	.05	.02	.01	☐ 433	Paul O'Neill	.15	.07	.02
☐ 364	Len Dykstra	.15	.07	.02	☐ 434	Rich Gossage	.15	.07	.02
☐ 365	Luis Quinones	.05	.02	.01	☐ 435	John Cangelosi	.05	.02	.01
☐ 366	Jim Presley	.05	.02	.01	☐ 436	Mike LaCoss	.05	.02	.01
☐ 367	Lloyd Moseby	.05	.02	.01	☐ 437	Gerald Perry	.05	.02	.01
☐ 368	Kirby Puckett	.40	.18	.05	☐ 438	Dave Martinez	.05	.02	.01
☐ 369	Eric Davis	.10	.05	.01	☐ 439	Darryl Strawberry	.15	.07	.02
☐ 370	Gary Redus	.05	.02	.01	☐ 440	John Moses	.05	.02	.01
☐ 371	Dave Schmidt	.05	.02	.01	☐ 441	Greg Gagne	.05	.02	.01
☐ 372	Mark Clear	.05	.02	.01	☐ 442	Jesse Barfield	.05	.02	.01
☐ 373	Dave Bergman	.05	.02	.01	☐ 443	George Frazier	.05	.02	.01
☐ 374	Charles Hudson	.05	.02	.01	☐ 444	Garth Iorg	.05	.02	.01
☐ 375	Calvin Schiraldi	.05	.02	.01	☐ 445	Ed Nunez	.05	.02	.01
☐ 376	Alex Trevino	.05	.02	.01	☐ 446	Rick Aguilera	.10	.05	.01
☐ 377	Tom Candiotti	.05	.02	.01	☐ 447	Jerry Mumphrey	.05	.02	.01
☐ 378	Steve Farr	.05	.02	.01	☐ 448	Rafael Ramirez	.05	.02	.01
☐ 379	Mike Gallego	.05	.02	.01	☐ 449	John Smiley	.20	.09	.03
☐ 380	Andy McGaffigan	.05	.02	.01	☐ 450	Atlee Hammaker	.05	.02	.01
☐ 381	Kirk McCaskill	.05	.02	.01	☐ 451	Lance McCullers	.05	.02	.01
☐ 382	Oddibe McDowell	.05	.02	.01	☐ 452	Guy Hoffman	.05	.02	.01
☐ 383	Floyd Bannister	.05	.02	.01	☐ 453	Chris James	.05	.02	.01
☐ 384	Denny Walling	.05	.02	.01	☐ 454	Terry Pendleton	.15	.07	.02
☐ 385	Don Carman	.05	.02	.01	☐ 455	Dave Meads	.05	.02	.01
☐ 386	Todd Worrell	.05	.02	.01	☐ 456	Bill Buckner	.10	.05	.01
☐ 387	Eric Show	.05	.02	.01	☐ 457	John Pawlowski	.05	.02	.01
☐ 388	Dave Parker	.15	.07	.02	☐ 458	Bob Sebra	.05	.02	.01
☐ 389	Rick Mahler	.05	.02	.01	☐ 459	Jim Dwyer	.05	.02	.01
☐ 390	Mike Dunne	.05	.02	.01	☐ 460	Jay Aldrich	.05	.02	.01
☐ 391	Candy Maldonado	.05	.02	.01	☐ 461	Frank Tanana	.05	.02	.01
☐ 392	Bob Dernier	.05	.02	.01	☐ 462	Oil Can Boyd	.05	.02	.01
☐ 393	Dave Valle	.05	.02	.01	☐ 463	Dan Pasqua	.05	.02	.01
☐ 394	Ernie Whitt	.05	.02	.01	☐ 464	Tim Crews	.10	.05	.01
☐ 395	Juan Berenguer	.05	.02	.01	☐ 465	Andy Allanson	.05	.02	.01
☐ 396	Mike Young	.05	.02	.01	☐ 466	Bill Pecota	.05	.02	.01
☐ 397	Mike Felder	.05	.02	.01	☐ 467	Steve Ontiveros	.05	.02	.01
☐ 398	Willie Hernandez	.05	.02	.01	☐ 468	Hubie Brooks	.05	.02	.01
☐ 399	Jim Rice	.15	.07	.02	☐ 469	Paul Kilgus	.05	.02	.01
☐ 400A	Checklist 358-467	.10	.05	.01	☐ 470	Dale Mohorcic	.05	.02	.01
☐ 400B	Checklist 346-451	.10	.05	.01	☐ 471	Dan Quisenberry	.10	.05	.01
☐ 401	Tommy John	.15	.07	.02	☐ 472	Dave Stewart	.10	.05	.01
☐ 402	Brian Holton	.05	.02	.01	☐ 473	Dave Clark	.05	.02	.01
☐ 403	Carmen Castillo	.05	.02	.01	☐ 474	Joel Skinner	.05	.02	.01
☐ 404	Jamie Quirk	.05	.02	.01	☐ 475	Dave Anderson	.05	.02	.01
☐ 405	Dwayne Murphy	.05	.02	.01	☐ 476	Dan Petry	.05	.02	.01
☐ 406	Jeff Parrett	.05	.02	.01	☐ 477	Carl Nichols	.05	.02	.01
☐ 407	Don Sutton	.15	.07	.02	☐ 478	Ernest Riles	.05	.02	.01
☐ 408	Jerry Browne	.05	.02	.01	☐ 479	George Hendrick	.05	.02	.01
☐ 409	Jim Winn	.05	.02	.01	☐ 480	John Morris	.05	.02	.01
☐ 410	Dave Smith	.05	.02	.01	☐ 481	Manny Hernandez	.05	.02	.01

☐ 482	Jeff Stone	.05	.02	.01
☐ 483	Chris Brown	.05	.02	.01
☐ 484	Mike Bielecki	.05	.02	.01
☐ 485	Dave Dravecky	.10	.05	.01
☐ 486	Rick Manning	.05	.02	.01
☐ 487	Bill Almon	.05	.02	.01
☐ 488	Jim Sundberg	.05	.02	.01
☐ 489	Ken Phelps	.05	.02	.01
☐ 490	Tom Henke	.10	.05	.01
☐ 491	Dan Gladden	.05	.02	.01
☐ 492	Barry Larkin	.30	.14	.04
☐ 493	Fred Manrique	.05	.02	.01
☐ 494	Mike Griffin	.05	.02	.01
☐ 495	Mark Knudson	.05	.02	.01
☐ 496	Bill Madlock	.10	.05	.01
☐ 497	Tim Stoddard	.05	.02	.01
☐ 498	Sam Horn	.05	.02	.01
☐ 499	Tracy Woodson	.05	.02	.01
☐ 500A	Checklist 468-577	.10	.05	.01
☐ 500B	Checklist 452-557	.10	.05	.01
☐ 501	Ken Schrom	.05	.02	.01
☐ 502	Angel Salazar	.05	.02	.01
☐ 503	Eric Plunk	.05	.02	.01
☐ 504	Joe Hesketh	.05	.02	.01
☐ 505	Greg Minton	.05	.02	.01
☐ 506	Geno Petralli	.05	.02	.01
☐ 507	Bob James	.05	.02	.01
☐ 508	Robbie Wine	.05	.02	.01
☐ 509	Jeff Calhoun	.05	.02	.01
☐ 510	Steve Lake	.05	.02	.01
☐ 511	Mark Grant	.05	.02	.01
☐ 512	Frank Williams	.05	.02	.01
☐ 513	Jeff Blauser	.15	.07	.02
☐ 514	Bob Walk	.05	.02	.01
☐ 515	Craig Lefferts	.05	.02	.01
☐ 516	Manny Trillo	.05	.02	.01
☐ 517	Jerry Reed	.05	.02	.01
☐ 518	Rick Leach	.05	.02	.01
☐ 519	Mark Davidson	.05	.02	.01
☐ 520	Jeff Ballard	.05	.02	.01
☐ 521	Dave Stapleton	.05	.02	.01
☐ 522	Pat Sheridan	.05	.02	.01
☐ 523	Al Nipper	.05	.02	.01
☐ 524	Steve Trout	.05	.02	.01
☐ 525	Jeff Hamilton	.05	.02	.01
☐ 526	Tommy Hinzo	.05	.02	.01
☐ 527	Lonnie Smith	.05	.02	.01
☐ 528	Greg Cadaret	.05	.02	.01
☐ 529	Bob McClure UER	.05	.02	.01
	("Rob" on front)			
☐ 530	Chuck Finley	.10	.05	.01
☐ 531	Jeff Russell	.05	.02	.01
☐ 532	Steve Lyons	.05	.02	.01
☐ 533	Terry Puhl	.05	.02	.01
☐ 534	Eric Nolte	.05	.02	.01
☐ 535	Kent Tekulve	.05	.02	.01
☐ 536	Pat Pacillo	.05	.02	.01
☐ 537	Charlie Puleo	.05	.02	.01
☐ 538	Tom Prince	.05	.02	.01
☐ 539	Greg Maddux	1.25	.55	.16
☐ 540	Jim Lindeman	.05	.02	.01
☐ 541	Pete Stanicek	.05	.02	.01
☐ 542	Steve Kiefer	.05	.02	.01
☐ 543A	Jim Morrison ERR	.05	.02	.01
	(No decimal before			
	lifetime average)			
☐ 543B	Jim Morrison COR	.05	.02	.01
☐ 544	Spike Owen	.05	.02	.01
☐ 545	Jay Buhner	.60	.25	.07
☐ 546	Mike Devereaux	.20	.09	.03
☐ 547	Jerry Don Gleaton	.05	.02	.01
☐ 548	Jose Rijo	.15	.07	.02
☐ 549	Dennis Martinez	.10	.05	.01
☐ 550	Mike Loynd	.05	.02	.01
☐ 551	Darrell Miller	.05	.02	.01
☐ 552	Dave LaPoint	.05	.02	.01
☐ 553	John Tudor	.05	.02	.01
☐ 554	Rocky Childress	.05	.02	.01
☐ 555	Wally Ritchie	.05	.02	.01
☐ 556	Terry McGriff	.05	.02	.01
☐ 557	Dave Leiper	.05	.02	.01
☐ 558	Jeff D. Robinson	.05	.02	.01
☐ 559	Jose Uribe	.05	.02	.01
☐ 560	Ted Simmons	.10	.05	.01
☐ 561	Les Lancaster	.05	.02	.01
☐ 562	Keith A. Miller	.05	.02	.01
☐ 563	Harold Reynolds	.05	.02	.01
☐ 564	Gene Larkin	.05	.02	.01
☐ 565	Cecil Fielder	.15	.07	.02
☐ 566	Roy Smalley	.05	.02	.01
☐ 567	Duane Ward	.10	.05	.01
☐ 568	Bill Wilkinson	.05	.02	.01
☐ 569	Howard Johnson	.10	.05	.01
☐ 570	Frank DiPino	.05	.02	.01
☐ 571	Pete Smith	.05	.02	.01
☐ 572	Darnell Coles	.05	.02	.01
☐ 573	Don Robinson	.05	.02	.01
☐ 574	Rob Nelson UER	.05	.02	.01
	(Career 0 RBI,			
	but 1 RBI in '87)			
☐ 575	Dennis Rasmussen	.05	.02	.01
☐ 576	Steve Jeltz UER	.05	.02	.01
	(Photo actually Juan			
	Samuel; Samuel noted			
	for one batting glove			
	and black bat)			
☐ 577	Tom Pagnozzi	.10	.05	.01
☐ 578	Ty Gainey	.05	.02	.01
☐ 579	Gary Lucas	.05	.02	.01
☐ 580	Ron Hassey	.05	.02	.01
☐ 581	Herm Winningham	.05	.02	.01
☐ 582	Rene Gonzales	.05	.02	.01
☐ 583	Brad Komminsk	.05	.02	.01
☐ 584	Doyle Alexander	.05	.02	.01
☐ 585	Jeff Sellers	.05	.02	.01
☐ 586	Bill Gullickson	.05	.02	.01
☐ 587	Tim Belcher	.10	.05	.01
☐ 588	Doug Jones	.15	.07	.02
☐ 589	Melido Perez	.10	.05	.01
☐ 590	Rick Honeycutt	.05	.02	.01
☐ 591	Pascual Perez	.05	.02	.01
☐ 592	Curt Wilkerson	.05	.02	.01
☐ 593	Steve Howe	.05	.02	.01
☐ 594	John Davis	.05	.02	.01
☐ 595	Storm Davis	.05	.02	.01
☐ 596	Sammy Stewart	.05	.02	.01
☐ 597	Neil Allen	.05	.02	.01
☐ 598	Alejandro Pena	.05	.02	.01
☐ 599	Mark Thurmond	.05	.02	.01
☐ 600A	Check. 578-660/BC1-BC26	.10	.05	.01
☐ 600B	Checklist 558-660	.10	.05	.01
☐ 601	Jose Mesa	.40	.18	.05
☐ 602	Don August	.05	.02	.01
☐ 603	Terry Leach SP	.07	.03	.01
☐ 604	Tom Newell	.05	.02	.01
☐ 605	Randall Byers SP	.07	.03	.01
☐ 606	Jim Gott	.05	.02	.01
☐ 607	Harry Spilman	.05	.02	.01
☐ 608	John Candelaria	.05	.02	.01
☐ 609	Mike Brumley	.05	.02	.01
☐ 610	Mickey Brantley	.05	.02	.01
☐ 611	Jose Nunez	.07	.03	.01

☐	612 Tom Nieto	.05	.02	.01
☐	613 Rick Reuschel	.05	.02	.01
☐	614 Lee Mazzilli SP	.07	.03	.01
☐	615 Scott Lusader	.05	.02	.01
☐	616 Bobby Meacham	.05	.02	.01
☐	617 Kevin McReynolds SP..	.07	.03	.01
☐	618 Gene Garber	.05	.02	.01
☐	619 Barry Lyons SP	.07	.03	.01
☐	620 Randy Myers	.15	.07	.02
☐	621 Donnie Moore	.05	.02	.01
☐	622 Domingo Ramos	.05	.02	.01
☐	623 Ed Romero	.05	.02	.01
☐	624 Greg Myers	.05	.02	.01
☐	625 Ripken Family	.40	.18	.05
	Cal Ripken Sr.			
	Cal Ripken Jr.			
	Billy Ripken			
☐	626 Pat Perry	.05	.02	.01
☐	627 Andres Thomas SP	.07	.03	.01
☐	628 Matt Williams SP	1.50	.70	.19
☐	629 Dave Hengel	.05	.02	.01
☐	630 Jeff Musselman SP	.07	.03	.01
☐	631 Tim Laudner	.05	.02	.01
☐	632 Bob Ojeda SP	.07	.03	.01
☐	633 Rafael Santana	.05	.02	.01
☐	634 Wes Gardner	.05	.02	.01
☐	635 Roberto Kelly SP	.30	.14	.04
☐	636 Mike Flanagan SP	.07	.03	.01
☐	637 Jay Bell	.30	.14	.04
☐	638 Bob Melvin	.05	.02	.01
☐	639 Damon Berryhill UER	.05	.02	.01
	(Bats: Switch)			
☐	640 David Wells SP	.25	.11	.03
☐	641 Stan Musial PUZ	.10	.05	.01
☐	642 Doug Sisk	.05	.02	.01
☐	643 Keith Hughes	.05	.02	.01
☐	644 Tom Glavine	1.25	.55	.16
☐	645 Al Newman	.05	.02	.01
☐	646 Scott Sanderson	.05	.02	.01
☐	647 Scott Terry	.05	.02	.01
☐	648 Tim Teufel SP	.07	.03	.01
☐	649 Garry Templeton SP....	.07	.03	.01
☐	650 Manny Lee SP	.07	.03	.01
☐	651 Roger McDowell SP	.07	.03	.01
☐	652 Mookie Wilson SP	.10	.05	.01
☐	653 David Cone SP	.50	.23	.06
☐	654 Ron Gant SP	1.25	.55	.16
☐	655 Joe Price SP	.07	.03	.01
☐	656 George Bell SP	.15	.07	.02
☐	657 Gregg Jefferies SP	1.00	.45	.12
☐	658 Todd Stottlemyre SP	.30	.14	.04
☐	659 Geronimo Berroa SP	.30	.14	.04
☐	660 Jerry Royster SP	.07	.03	.01

1988 Donruss Rookies

The 1988 Donruss "The Rookies" set features 56 standard-size full-color cards plus
a 15-piece puzzle of Stan Musial. The set
was distributed in a small green and black
box with gold lettering. Card fronts are similar in design to the 1988 Donruss regular
issue except for the presence of "The
Rookies" logo in the lower right corner and
a green and black border instead of a blue

and black border on the fronts. Extended
Rookie Cards in this set include Chris
Sabo, Walt Weiss, Brady Anderson, Bryan
Harvey, and Edgar Martinez.

	MINT	NRMT	EXC
COMPLETE FACT.SET (56)	14.00	6.25	1.75
COMMON CARD (1-56)	.07	.03	.01

☐	1 Mark Grace	1.50	.70	.19
☐	2 Mike Campbell	.07	.03	.01
☐	3 Todd Frohwirth	.07	.03	.01
☐	4 Dave Stapleton	.07	.03	.01
☐	5 Shawn Abner	.07	.03	.01
☐	6 Jose Cecena	.07	.03	.01
☐	7 Dave Gallagher	.07	.03	.01
☐	8 Mark Parent	.07	.03	.01
☐	9 Cecil Espy	.07	.03	.01
☐	10 Pete Smith	.07	.03	.01
☐	11 Jay Buhner	1.25	.55	.16
☐	12 Pat Borders	.10	.05	.01
☐	13 Doug Jennings	.07	.03	.01
☐	14 Brady Anderson	1.00	.45	.12
☐	15 Pete Stanicek	.07	.03	.01
☐	16 Roberto Kelly	.15	.07	.02
☐	17 Jeff Treadway	.07	.03	.01
☐	18 Walt Weiss	.15	.07	.02
☐	19 Paul Gibson	.07	.03	.01
☐	20 Tim Crews	.10	.05	.01
☐	21 Melido Perez	.10	.05	.01
☐	22 Steve Peters	.07	.03	.01
☐	23 Craig Worthington	.07	.03	.01
☐	24 John Trautwein	.07	.03	.01
☐	25 DeWayne Vaughn	.07	.03	.01
☐	26 David Wells	.10	.05	.01
☐	27 Al Leiter	.10	.05	.01
☐	28 Tim Belcher	.07	.03	.01
☐	29 Johnny Paredes	.07	.03	.01
☐	30 Chris Sabo	.10	.05	.01
☐	31 Damon Berryhill	.07	.03	.01
☐	32 Randy Milligan	.07	.03	.01
☐	33 Gary Thurman	.07	.03	.01
☐	34 Kevin Elster	.07	.03	.01
☐	35 Roberto Alomar	5.00	2.20	.60
☐	36 Edgar Martinez UER	1.50	.70	.19
	(Photo actually			
	Edwin Nunez)			
☐	37 Todd Stottlemyre	.50	.23	.06
☐	38 Joey Meyer	.07	.03	.01
☐	39 Carl Nichols	.07	.03	.01
☐	40 Jack McDowell	1.00	.45	.12
☐	41 Jose Bautista	.07	.03	.01
☐	42 Sil Campusano	.07	.03	.01
☐	43 John Dopson	.07	.03	.01
☐	44 Jody Reed	.10	.05	.01

☐ 45 Darrin Jackson	.07	.03	.01
☐ 46 Mike Capel	.07	.03	.01
☐ 47 Ron Gant	2.00	.90	.25
☐ 48 John Davis	.07	.03	.01
☐ 49 Kevin Coffman	.07	.03	.01
☐ 50 Cris Carpenter	.07	.03	.01
☐ 51 Mackey Sasser	.07	.03	.01
☐ 52 Luis Alicea	.07	.03	.01
☐ 53 Bryan Harvey	.15	.07	.02
☐ 54 Steve Ellsworth	.07	.03	.01
☐ 55 Mike Macfarlane	.30	.14	.04
☐ 56 Checklist 1-56	.07	.03	.01

1989 Donruss

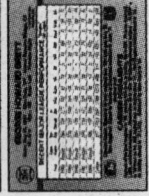

This 660-card set was distributed along with a puzzle of Warren Spahn. The six regular checklist cards are numbered throughout the set as multiples of 100. Cards measure 2 1/2" by 3 1/2" and feature a distinctive black side border with an alternating coating. The popular Diamond King subset returns for the eighth consecutive year. The jumbo (5 by 7 inch) versions of the 1989 Diamond Kings are valued about 10 times their standard-size counterparts. Rated Rookies are featured again as cards 28-47. The Donruss '89 logo appears in the lower left corner of every obverse. There are two variations that occur throughout most of the set. On the card backs "Denotes Led League" can be found with one asterisk to the left or with an asterisk on each side. On the card fronts the horizontal lines on the left and right borders can be glossy or non-glossy. Since both of these variation types are relatively minor and seem equally common, there is no premium value for either type. Rather than short-printing 26 cards in order to make room for printing the Bonus MVP's this year, Donruss apparently chose to double print 106 cards. These double prints are listed below by DP. Numbered with the prefix "BC" for bonus card, the 26-card set featuring the most valuable player from each of the 26 teams was randomly inserted in the wax and rack packs. These cards are distinguished by the bold MVP logo in the upper left background of the obverse, and the four doubleprinted cards are denoted by "DP" in the checklist below. Rookie Cards in this set include Sandy Alomar Jr., Brady

Anderson, Dante Bichette, Craig Biggio, Ken Griffey Jr., Randy Johnson, Felix Jose, Ramon Martinez, Hal Morris, Curt Schilling, Gary Sheffield, and John Smoltz.

	MINT	NRMT	EXC
COMPLETE SET (660)	10.00	4.50	1.25
COMPLETE FACT.SET (672)	12.00	5.50	1.50
COMP. GRANDSLAMMERS (12)	2.00	.90	.25
COMPLETE MVP SET (26)	1.50	.70	.19
COMMON CARD (1-660)	.05	.02	.01

☐ 1	Mike Greenwell DK	.10	.05	.01
☐ 2	Bobby Bonilla DP	.10	.05	.01
☐ 3	Pete Incaviglia DK	.05	.02	.01
☐ 4	Chris Sabo DK DP	.10	.05	.01
☐ 5	Robin Yount DK	.10	.05	.01
☐ 6	Tony Gwynn DK DP	.10	.05	.01
☐ 7	Carlton Fisk DK UER	.10	.05	.01
	(OF on back)			
☐ 8	Cory Snyder DK	.05	.02	.01
☐ 9	David Cone DK UER	.10	.05	.01
	(Sic, "hurdlers")			
☐ 10	Kevin Seitzer DK	.10	.05	.01
☐ 11	Rick Reuschel DK	.05	.02	.01
☐ 12	Johnny Ray DK	.05	.02	.01
☐ 13	Dave Schmidt DK	.05	.02	.01
☐ 14	Andres Galarraga DK	.10	.05	.01
☐ 15	Kirk Gibson DK	.10	.05	.01
☐ 16	Fred McGriff DK	.10	.05	.01
☐ 17	Mark Grace DK	.10	.05	.01
☐ 18	Jeff M. Robinson DK	.05	.02	.01
☐ 19	Vince Coleman DK DP	.10	.05	.01
☐ 20	Dave Henderson DK	.05	.02	.01
☐ 21	Harold Reynolds DK	.05	.02	.01
☐ 22	Gerald Perry DK	.05	.02	.01
☐ 23	Frank Viola DK	.10	.05	.01
☐ 24	Steve Bedrosian DK	.05	.02	.01
☐ 25	Glenn Davis DK	.05	.02	.01
☐ 26	Don Mattingly DK UER	.25	.11	.03
	(Doesn't mention Don's previous DK in 1985)			
☐ 27	DK Checklist 1-26 DP	.05	.02	.01
☐ 28	Sandy Alomar Jr. RR	.20	.09	.03
☐ 29	Steve Searcy RR	.05	.02	.01
☐ 30	Cameron Drew RR	.05	.02	.01
☐ 31	Gary Sheffield RR	.60	.25	.07
☐ 32	Erik Hanson RR	.25	.11	.03
☐ 33	Ken Griffey Jr. RR	5.00	2.20	.60
☐ 34	Greg W. Harris RR	.05	.02	.01
☐ 35	Gregg Jefferies RR	.20	.09	.03
☐ 36	Luis Medina RR	.05	.02	.01
☐ 37	Carlos Quintana RR	.05	.02	.01
☐ 38	Felix Jose RR	.05	.02	.01
☐ 39	Cris Carpenter RR	.05	.02	.01
☐ 40	Ron Jones RR	.05	.02	.01
☐ 41	Dave West RR	.10	.05	.01
☐ 42	Randy Johnson RR UER	1.00	.45	.12
	Card says born in 1964 he was born in 1963			
☐ 43	Mike Harkey RR	.05	.02	.01
☐ 44	Pete Harnisch RR DP	.10	.05	.01
☐ 45	Tom Gordon RR DP	.15	.07	.02
☐ 46	Gregg Olson RR DP	.05	.02	.01
☐ 47	Alex Sanchez RR DP	.05	.02	.01
☐ 48	Ruben Sierra	.15	.07	.02
☐ 49	Rafael Palmeiro	.25	.11	.03
☐ 50	Ron Gant	.25	.11	.03
☐ 51	Cal Ripken	.75	.35	.09
☐ 52	Wally Joyner	.10	.05	.01
☐ 53	Gary Carter	.15	.07	.02

54	Andy Van Slyke	.10	.05	.01
55	Robin Yount	.20	.09	.03
56	Pete Incaviglia	.10	.05	.01
57	Greg Brock	.05	.02	.01
58	Melido Perez	.05	.02	.01
59	Craig Lefferts	.05	.02	.01
60	Gary Pettis	.05	.02	.01
61	Danny Tartabull	.10	.05	.01
62	Guillermo Hernandez	.05	.02	.01
63	Ozzie Smith	.30	.14	.04
64	Gary Gaetti	.05	.02	.01
65	Mark Davis	.05	.02	.01
66	Lee Smith	.15	.07	.02
67	Dennis Eckersley	.15	.07	.02
68	Wade Boggs	.15	.07	.02
69	Mike Scott	.05	.02	.01
70	Fred McGriff	.25	.11	.03
71	Tom Browning	.05	.02	.01
72	Claudell Washington	.05	.02	.01
73	Mel Hall	.05	.02	.01
74	Don Mattingly	.40	.18	.05
75	Steve Bedrosian	.05	.02	.01
76	Juan Samuel	.05	.02	.01
77	Mike Scioscia	.05	.02	.01
78	Dave Righetti	.05	.02	.01
79	Alfredo Griffin	.05	.02	.01
80	Eric Davis UER	.10	.05	.01
	(165 games in 1988, should be 135)			
81	Juan Berenguer	.05	.02	.01
82	Todd Worrell	.05	.02	.01
83	Joe Carter	.20	.09	.03
84	Steve Sax	.05	.02	.01
85	Frank White	.10	.05	.01
86	John Kruk	.15	.07	.02
87	Rance Mulliniks	.05	.02	.01
88	Alan Ashby	.05	.02	.01
89	Charlie Leibrandt	.05	.02	.01
90	Frank Tanana	.05	.02	.01
91	Jose Canseco	.30	.14	.04
92	Barry Bonds	.40	.18	.05
93	Harold Reynolds	.05	.02	.01
94	Mark McLemore	.05	.02	.01
95	Mark McGwire	.15	.07	.02
96	Eddie Murray	.20	.09	.03
97	Tim Raines	.15	.07	.02
98	Robby Thompson	.10	.05	.01
99	Kevin McReynolds	.05	.02	.01
100	Checklist 28-137	.05	.02	.01
101	Carlton Fisk	.15	.07	.02
102	Dave Martinez	.05	.02	.01
103	Glenn Braggs	.05	.02	.01
104	Dale Murphy	.15	.07	.02
105	Ryne Sandberg	.30	.14	.04
106	Dennis Martinez	.10	.05	.01
107	Pete O'Brien	.05	.02	.01
108	Dick Schofield	.05	.02	.01
109	Henry Cotto	.05	.02	.01
110	Mike Marshall	.05	.02	.01
111	Keith Moreland	.05	.02	.01
112	Tom Brunansky	.05	.02	.01
113	Kelly Gruber UER	.05	.02	.01
	(Wrong birthdate)			
114	Brook Jacoby	.05	.02	.01
115	Keith Brown	.05	.02	.01
116	Matt Nokes	.05	.02	.01
117	Keith Hernandez	.10	.05	.01
118	Bob Forsch	.05	.02	.01
119	Bert Blyleven UER	.15	.07	.02
	(... 3000 strikeouts in 1987, should be 1986)			
120	Willie Wilson	.05	.02	.01
121	Tommy Gregg	.05	.02	.01
122	Jim Rice	.15	.07	.02
123	Bob Knepper	.05	.02	.01
124	Danny Jackson	.05	.02	.01
125	Eric Plunk	.05	.02	.01
126	Brian Fisher	.05	.02	.01
127	Mike Pagliarulo	.05	.02	.01
128	Tony Gwynn	.30	.14	.04
129	Lance McCullers	.05	.02	.01
130	Andres Galarraga	.15	.07	.02
131	Jose Uribe	.05	.02	.01
132	Kirk Gibson UER	.15	.07	.02
	(Wrong birthdate)			
133	David Palmer	.05	.02	.01
134	R.J. Reynolds	.05	.02	.01
135	Greg Walker	.05	.02	.01
136	Kirk McCaskill UER	.05	.02	.01
	(Wrong birthdate)			
137	Shawon Dunston	.10	.05	.01
138	Andy Allanson	.05	.02	.01
139	Rob Murphy	.05	.02	.01
140	Mike Aldrete	.05	.02	.01
141	Terry Kennedy	.05	.02	.01
142	Scott Fletcher	.05	.02	.01
143	Steve Balboni	.05	.02	.01
144	Bret Saberhagen	.15	.07	.02
145	Ozzie Virgil	.05	.02	.01
146	Dale Sveum	.05	.02	.01
147	Darryl Strawberry	.15	.07	.02
148	Harold Baines	.15	.07	.02
149	George Bell	.05	.02	.01
150	Dave Parker	.15	.07	.02
151	Bobby Bonilla	.15	.07	.02
152	Mookie Wilson	.10	.05	.01
153	Ted Power	.05	.02	.01
154	Nolan Ryan	.75	.35	.09
155	Jeff Reardon	.15	.07	.02
156	Tim Wallach	.05	.02	.01
157	Jamie Moyer	.05	.02	.01
158	Rich Gossage	.15	.07	.02
159	Dave Winfield	.15	.07	.02
160	Von Hayes	.05	.02	.01
161	Willie McGee	.10	.05	.01
162	Rich Gedman	.05	.02	.01
163	Tony Pena	.05	.02	.01
164	Mike Morgan	.05	.02	.01
165	Charlie Hough	.10	.05	.01
166	Mike Stanley	.10	.05	.01
167	Andre Dawson	.15	.07	.02
168	Joe Boever	.05	.02	.01
169	Pete Stanicek	.05	.02	.01
170	Bob Boone	.10	.05	.01
171	Ron Darling	.10	.05	.01
172	Bob Walk	.05	.02	.01
173	Rob Deer	.05	.02	.01
174	Steve Buechele	.05	.02	.01
175	Ted Higuera	.05	.02	.01
176	Ozzie Guillen	.10	.05	.01
177	Candy Maldonado	.05	.02	.01
178	Doyle Alexander	.05	.02	.01
179	Mark Gubicza	.05	.02	.01
180	Alan Trammell	.15	.07	.02
181	Vince Coleman	.10	.05	.01
182	Kirby Puckett	.40	.18	.05
183	Chris Brown	.05	.02	.01
184	Marty Barrett	.05	.02	.01
185	Stan Javier	.05	.02	.01
186	Mike Greenwell	.10	.05	.01
187	Billy Hatcher	.05	.02	.01
188	Jimmy Key	.15	.07	.02

☐ 189	Nick Esasky	.05	.02	.01
☐ 190	Don Slaught	.05	.02	.01
☐ 191	Cory Snyder	.05	.02	.01
☐ 192	John Candelaria	.05	.02	.01
☐ 193	Mike Schmidt	.25	.11	.03
☐ 194	Kevin Gross	.05	.02	.01
☐ 195	John Tudor	.05	.02	.01
☐ 196	Neil Allen	.05	.02	.01
☐ 197	Orel Hershiser	.15	.07	.02
☐ 198	Kal Daniels	.05	.02	.01
☐ 199	Kent Hrbek	.10	.05	.01
☐ 200	Checklist 138-247	.05	.02	.01
☐ 201	Joe Magrane	.05	.02	.01
☐ 202	Scott Bailes	.05	.02	.01
☐ 203	Tim Belcher	.05	.02	.01
☐ 204	George Brett	.40	.18	.05
☐ 205	Benito Santiago	.10	.05	.01
☐ 206	Tony Fernandez	.10	.05	.01
☐ 207	Gerald Young	.05	.02	.01
☐ 208	Bo Jackson	.15	.07	.02
☐ 209	Chet Lemon	.05	.02	.01
☐ 210	Storm Davis	.05	.02	.01
☐ 211	Doug Drabek	.15	.07	.02
☐ 212	Mickey Brantley UER (Photo actually Nelson Simmons)	.05	.02	.01
☐ 213	Devon White	.15	.07	.02
☐ 214	Dave Stewart	.15	.07	.02
☐ 215	Dave Schmidt	.05	.02	.01
☐ 216	Bryn Smith	.05	.02	.01
☐ 217	Brett Butler	.15	.07	.02
☐ 218	Bob Ojeda	.05	.02	.01
☐ 219	Steve Rosenberg	.05	.02	.01
☐ 220	Hubie Brooks	.05	.02	.01
☐ 221	B.J. Surhoff	.10	.05	.01
☐ 222	Rick Mahler	.05	.02	.01
☐ 223	Rick Sutcliffe	.10	.05	.01
☐ 224	Neal Heaton	.05	.02	.01
☐ 225	Mitch Williams	.10	.05	.01
☐ 226	Chuck Finley	.10	.05	.01
☐ 227	Mark Langston	.15	.07	.02
☐ 228	Jesse Orosco	.05	.02	.01
☐ 229	Ed Whitson	.05	.02	.01
☐ 230	Terry Pendleton	.15	.07	.02
☐ 231	Lloyd Moseby	.05	.02	.01
☐ 232	Greg Swindell	.10	.05	.01
☐ 233	John Franco	.10	.05	.01
☐ 234	Jack Morris	.15	.07	.02
☐ 235	Howard Johnson	.10	.05	.01
☐ 236	Glenn Davis	.05	.02	.01
☐ 237	Frank Viola	.10	.05	.01
☐ 238	Kevin Seitzer	.05	.02	.01
☐ 239	Gerald Perry	.05	.02	.01
☐ 240	Dwight Evans	.10	.05	.01
☐ 241	Jim Deshaies	.05	.02	.01
☐ 242	Bo Diaz	.05	.02	.01
☐ 243	Carney Lansford	.10	.05	.01
☐ 244	Mike LaValliere	.05	.02	.01
☐ 245	Rickey Henderson	.15	.07	.02
☐ 246	Roberto Alomar	.50	.23	.06
☐ 247	Jimmy Jones	.05	.02	.01
☐ 248	Pascual Perez	.05	.02	.01
☐ 249	Will Clark	.20	.09	.03
☐ 250	Fernando Valenzuela	.05	.02	.01
☐ 251	Shane Rawley	.05	.02	.01
☐ 252	Sid Bream	.05	.02	.01
☐ 253	Steve Lyons	.05	.02	.01
☐ 254	Brian Downing	.05	.02	.01
☐ 255	Mark Grace	.15	.07	.02
☐ 256	Tom Candiotti	.05	.02	.01
☐ 257	Barry Larkin	.20	.09	.03
☐ 258	Mike Krukow	.05	.02	.01
☐ 259	Billy Ripken	.05	.02	.01
☐ 260	Cecilio Guante	.05	.02	.01
☐ 261	Scott Bradley	.05	.02	.01
☐ 262	Floyd Bannister	.05	.02	.01
☐ 263	Pete Smith	.05	.02	.01
☐ 264	Jim Gantner UER (Wrong birthdate)	.05	.02	.01
☐ 265	Roger McDowell	.05	.02	.01
☐ 266	Bobby Thigpen	.05	.02	.01
☐ 267	Jim Clancy	.05	.02	.01
☐ 268	Terry Steinbach	.10	.05	.01
☐ 269	Mike Dunne	.05	.02	.01
☐ 270	Dwight Gooden	.10	.05	.01
☐ 271	Mike Heath	.05	.02	.01
☐ 272	Dave Smith	.05	.02	.01
☐ 273	Keith Atherton	.05	.02	.01
☐ 274	Tim Burke	.05	.02	.01
☐ 275	Damon Berryhill	.05	.02	.01
☐ 276	Vance Law	.05	.02	.01
☐ 277	Rich Dotson	.05	.02	.01
☐ 278	Lance Parrish	.10	.05	.01
☐ 279	Denny Walling	.05	.02	.01
☐ 280	Roger Clemens	.20	.09	.03
☐ 281	Greg Mathews	.05	.02	.01
☐ 282	Tom Niedenfuer	.05	.02	.01
☐ 283	Paul Kilgus	.05	.02	.01
☐ 284	Jose Guzman	.10	.05	.01
☐ 285	Calvin Schiraldi	.05	.02	.01
☐ 286	Charlie Puleo UER (Career ERA 4.24, should be 4.23)	.05	.02	.01
☐ 287	Joe Orsulak	.05	.02	.01
☐ 288	Jack Howell	.05	.02	.01
☐ 289	Kevin Elster	.05	.02	.01
☐ 290	Jose Lind	.05	.02	.01
☐ 291	Paul Molitor	.15	.07	.02
☐ 292	Cecil Espy	.05	.02	.01
☐ 293	Bill Wegman	.05	.02	.01
☐ 294	Dan Pasqua	.05	.02	.01
☐ 295	Scott Garrelts UER (Wrong birthdate)	.05	.02	.01
☐ 296	Walt Terrell	.05	.02	.01
☐ 297	Ed Hearn	.05	.02	.01
☐ 298	Lou Whitaker	.15	.07	.02
☐ 299	Ken Dayley	.05	.02	.01
☐ 300	Checklist 248-357	.05	.02	.01
☐ 301	Tommy Herr	.05	.02	.01
☐ 302	Mike Brumley	.05	.02	.01
☐ 303	Ellis Burks	.15	.07	.02
☐ 304	Curt Young UER (Wrong birthdate)	.05	.02	.01
☐ 305	Jody Reed	.05	.02	.01
☐ 306	Bill Doran	.05	.02	.01
☐ 307	David Wells	.05	.02	.01
☐ 308	Ron Robinson	.05	.02	.01
☐ 309	Rafael Santana	.05	.02	.01
☐ 310	Julio Franco	.10	.05	.01
☐ 311	Jack Clark	.10	.05	.01
☐ 312	Chris James	.05	.02	.01
☐ 313	Milt Thompson	.05	.02	.01
☐ 314	John Shelby	.05	.02	.01
☐ 315	Al Leiter	.05	.02	.01
☐ 316	Mike Davis	.05	.02	.01
☐ 317	Chris Sabo	.10	.05	.01
☐ 318	Greg Gagne	.05	.02	.01
☐ 319	Jose Oquendo	.05	.02	.01
☐ 320	John Farrell	.05	.02	.01
☐ 321	Franklin Stubbs	.05	.02	.01
☐ 322	Kurt Stillwell	.05	.02	.01
☐ 323	Shawn Abner	.05	.02	.01

☐ 324	Mike Flanagan	.05	.02	.01
☐ 325	Kevin Bass	.05	.02	.01
☐ 326	Pat Tabler	.05	.02	.01
☐ 327	Mike Henneman	.10	.05	.01
☐ 328	Rick Honeycutt	.05	.02	.01
☐ 329	John Smiley	.05	.02	.01
☐ 330	Rey Quinones	.05	.02	.01
☐ 331	Johnny Ray	.05	.02	.01
☐ 332	Bob Welch	.10	.05	.01
☐ 333	Larry Sheets	.05	.02	.01
☐ 334	Jeff Parrett	.05	.02	.01
☐ 335	Rick Reuschel UER (For Don Robinson, should be Jeff)	.05	.02	.01
☐ 336	Randy Myers	.15	.07	.02
☐ 337	Ken Williams	.05	.02	.01
☐ 338	Andy McGaffigan	.05	.02	.01
☐ 339	Joey Meyer	.05	.02	.01
☐ 340	Dion James	.05	.02	.01
☐ 341	Les Lancaster	.05	.02	.01
☐ 342	Tom Foley	.05	.02	.01
☐ 343	Geno Petralli	.05	.02	.01
☐ 344	Dan Petry	.05	.02	.01
☐ 345	Alvin Davis	.05	.02	.01
☐ 346	Mickey Hatcher	.05	.02	.01
☐ 347	Marvell Wynne	.05	.02	.01
☐ 348	Danny Cox	.05	.02	.01
☐ 349	Dave Stieb	.10	.05	.01
☐ 350	Jay Bell	.15	.07	.02
☐ 351	Jeff Treadway	.05	.02	.01
☐ 352	Luis Salazar	.05	.02	.01
☐ 353	Len Dykstra	.15	.07	.02
☐ 354	Juan Agosto	.05	.02	.01
☐ 355	Gene Larkin	.05	.02	.01
☐ 356	Steve Farr	.05	.02	.01
☐ 357	Paul Assenmacher	.05	.02	.01
☐ 358	Todd Benzinger	.05	.02	.01
☐ 359	Larry Andersen	.05	.02	.01
☐ 360	Paul O'Neill	.15	.07	.02
☐ 361	Ron Hassey	.05	.02	.01
☐ 362	Jim Gott	.05	.02	.01
☐ 363	Ken Phelps	.05	.02	.01
☐ 364	Tim Flannery	.05	.02	.01
☐ 365	Randy Ready	.05	.02	.01
☐ 366	Nelson Santovenia	.05	.02	.01
☐ 367	Kelly Downs	.05	.02	.01
☐ 368	Danny Heep	.05	.02	.01
☐ 369	Phil Bradley	.05	.02	.01
☐ 370	Jeff D. Robinson	.05	.02	.01
☐ 371	Ivan Calderon	.05	.02	.01
☐ 372	Mike Witt	.05	.02	.01
☐ 373	Greg Maddux	.75	.35	.09
☐ 374	Carmen Castillo	.05	.02	.01
☐ 375	Jose Rijo	.15	.07	.02
☐ 376	Joe Price	.05	.02	.01
☐ 377	Rene Gonzales	.05	.02	.01
☐ 378	Oddibe McDowell	.05	.02	.01
☐ 379	Jim Presley	.05	.02	.01
☐ 380	Brad Wellman	.05	.02	.01
☐ 381	Tom Glavine	.40	.18	.05
☐ 382	Dan Plesac	.05	.02	.01
☐ 383	Wally Backman	.05	.02	.01
☐ 384	Dave Gallagher	.05	.02	.01
☐ 385	Tom Henke	.10	.05	.01
☐ 386	Luis Polonia	.10	.05	.01
☐ 387	Junior Ortiz	.05	.02	.01
☐ 388	David Cone	.15	.07	.02
☐ 389	Dave Bergman	.05	.02	.01
☐ 390	Danny Darwin	.05	.02	.01
☐ 391	Dan Gladden	.05	.02	.01
☐ 392	John Dopson	.05	.02	.01
☐ 393	Frank DiPino	.05	.02	.01
☐ 394	Al Nipper	.05	.02	.01
☐ 395	Willie Randolph	.10	.05	.01
☐ 396	Don Carman	.05	.02	.01
☐ 397	Scott Terry	.05	.02	.01
☐ 398	Rick Cerone	.05	.02	.01
☐ 399	Tom Pagnozzi	.05	.02	.01
☐ 400	Checklist 358-467	.05	.02	.01
☐ 401	Mickey Tettleton	.10	.05	.01
☐ 402	Curtis Wilkerson	.05	.02	.01
☐ 403	Jeff Russell	.05	.02	.01
☐ 404	Pat Perry	.05	.02	.01
☐ 405	Jose Alvarez	.05	.02	.01
☐ 406	Rick Schu	.05	.02	.01
☐ 407	Sherman Corbett	.05	.02	.01
☐ 408	Dave Magadan	.05	.02	.01
☐ 409	Bob Kipper	.05	.02	.01
☐ 410	Don August	.05	.02	.01
☐ 411	Bob Brower	.05	.02	.01
☐ 412	Chris Bosio	.05	.02	.01
☐ 413	Jerry Reuss	.05	.02	.01
☐ 414	Atlee Hammaker	.05	.02	.01
☐ 415	Jim Walewander	.05	.02	.01
☐ 416	Mike Macfarlane	.10	.05	.01
☐ 417	Pat Sheridan	.05	.02	.01
☐ 418	Pedro Guerrero	.10	.05	.01
☐ 419	Allan Anderson	.05	.02	.01
☐ 420	Mark Parent	.05	.02	.01
☐ 421	Bob Stanley	.05	.02	.01
☐ 422	Mike Gallego	.05	.02	.01
☐ 423	Bruce Hurst	.05	.02	.01
☐ 424	Dave Meads	.05	.02	.01
☐ 425	Jesse Barfield	.05	.02	.01
☐ 426	Rob Dibble	.10	.05	.01
☐ 427	Joel Skinner	.05	.02	.01
☐ 428	Ron Kittle	.05	.02	.01
☐ 429	Rick Rhoden	.05	.02	.01
☐ 430	Bob Dernier	.05	.02	.01
☐ 431	Steve Jeltz	.05	.02	.01
☐ 432	Rick Dempsey	.05	.02	.01
☐ 433	Roberto Kelly	.10	.05	.01
☐ 434	Dave Anderson	.05	.02	.01
☐ 435	Herm Winningham	.05	.02	.01
☐ 436	Al Newman	.05	.02	.01
☐ 437	Jose DeLeon	.05	.02	.01
☐ 438	Doug Jones	.10	.05	.01
☐ 439	Brian Holton	.05	.02	.01
☐ 440	Jeff Montgomery	.10	.05	.01
☐ 441	Dickie Thon	.05	.02	.01
☐ 442	Cecil Fielder	.15	.07	.02
☐ 443	John Fishel	.05	.02	.01
☐ 444	Jerry Don Gleaton	.05	.02	.01
☐ 445	Paul Gibson	.05	.02	.01
☐ 446	Walt Weiss	.05	.02	.01
☐ 447	Glenn Wilson	.05	.02	.01
☐ 448	Mike Moore	.05	.02	.01
☐ 449	Chili Davis	.15	.07	.02
☐ 450	Dave Henderson	.05	.02	.01
☐ 451	Jose Bautista	.05	.02	.01
☐ 452	Rex Hudler	.05	.02	.01
☐ 453	Bob Brenly	.05	.02	.01
☐ 454	Mackey Sasser	.05	.02	.01
☐ 455	Daryl Boston	.05	.02	.01
☐ 456	Mike R. Fitzgerald	.05	.02	.01
☐ 457	Jeffrey Leonard	.05	.02	.01
☐ 458	Bruce Sutter	.10	.05	.01
☐ 459	Mitch Webster	.05	.02	.01
☐ 460	Joe Hesketh	.05	.02	.01
☐ 461	Bobby Witt	.10	.05	.01
☐ 462	Stew Cliburn	.05	.02	.01
☐ 463	Scott Bankhead	.05	.02	.01

☐ 464 Ramon Martinez	.30	.14	.04
☐ 465 Dave Leiper	.05	.02	.01
☐ 466 Luis Alicea	.05	.02	.01
☐ 467 John Cerutti	.05	.02	.01
☐ 468 Ron Washington	.05	.02	.01
☐ 469 Jeff Reed	.05	.02	.01
☐ 470 Jeff M. Robinson	.05	.02	.01
☐ 471 Sid Fernandez	.10	.05	.01
☐ 472 Terry Puhl	.05	.02	.01
☐ 473 Charlie Lea	.05	.02	.01
☐ 474 Israel Sanchez	.05	.02	.01
☐ 475 Bruce Benedict	.05	.02	.01
☐ 476 Oil Can Boyd	.05	.02	.01
☐ 477 Craig Reynolds	.05	.02	.01
☐ 478 Frank Williams	.05	.02	.01
☐ 479 Greg Cadaret	.05	.02	.01
☐ 480 Randy Kramer	.05	.02	.01
☐ 481 Dave Eiland	.05	.02	.01
☐ 482 Eric Show	.05	.02	.01
☐ 483 Garry Templeton	.05	.02	.01
☐ 484 Wallace Johnson	.05	.02	.01
☐ 485 Kevin Mitchell	.15	.07	.02
☐ 486 Tim Crews	.05	.02	.01
☐ 487 Mike Maddux	.05	.02	.01
☐ 488 Dave LaPoint	.05	.02	.01
☐ 489 Fred Manrique	.05	.02	.01
☐ 490 Greg Minton	.05	.02	.01
☐ 491 Doug Dascenzo UER	.05	.02	.01
(Photo actually Damon Berryhill)			
☐ 492 Willie Upshaw	.05	.02	.01
☐ 493 Jack Armstrong	.05	.02	.01
☐ 494 Kirt Manwaring	.05	.02	.01
☐ 495 Jeff Ballard	.05	.02	.01
☐ 496 Jeff Kunkel	.05	.02	.01
☐ 497 Mike Campbell	.05	.02	.01
☐ 498 Gary Thurman	.05	.02	.01
☐ 499 Zane Smith	.05	.02	.01
☐ 500 Checklist 468-577 DP	.05	.02	.01
☐ 501 Mike Birkbeck	.05	.02	.01
☐ 502 Terry Leach	.05	.02	.01
☐ 503 Shawn Hillegas	.05	.02	.01
☐ 504 Manny Lee	.05	.02	.01
☐ 505 Doug Jennings	.05	.02	.01
☐ 506 Ken Oberkfell	.05	.02	.01
☐ 507 Tim Teufel	.05	.02	.01
☐ 508 Tom Brookens	.05	.02	.01
☐ 509 Rafael Ramirez	.05	.02	.01
☐ 510 Fred Toliver	.05	.02	.01
☐ 511 Brian Holman	.05	.02	.01
☐ 512 Mike Bielecki	.05	.02	.01
☐ 513 Jeff Pico	.05	.02	.01
☐ 514 Charles Hudson	.05	.02	.01
☐ 515 Bruce Ruffin	.05	.02	.01
☐ 516 Larry McWilliams UER	.05	.02	.01
(New Richland, should be North Richland)			
☐ 517 Jeff Sellers	.05	.02	.01
☐ 518 John Costello	.05	.02	.01
☐ 519 Brady Anderson	.40	.18	.05
☐ 520 Craig McMurtry	.05	.02	.01
☐ 521 Ray Hayward	.05	.02	.01
☐ 522 Drew Hall DP	.05	.02	.01
☐ 523 Mark Lemke DP	.10	.05	.01
☐ 524 Oswald Peraza DP	.05	.02	.01
☐ 525 Bryan Harvey DP	.10	.05	.01
☐ 526 Rick Aguilera DP	.15	.07	.02
☐ 527 Tom Prince DP	.05	.02	.01
☐ 528 Mark Clear DP	.05	.02	.01
☐ 529 Jerry Browne DP	.05	.02	.01
☐ 530 Juan Castillo DP	.05	.02	.01
☐ 531 Jack McDowell DP	.15	.07	.02
☐ 532 Chris Speier DP	.05	.02	.01
☐ 533 Darrell Evans DP	.10	.05	.01
☐ 534 Luis Aquino DP	.05	.02	.01
☐ 535 Eric King DP	.05	.02	.01
☐ 536 Ken Hill DP	.50	.23	.06
☐ 537 Randy Bush DP	.05	.02	.01
☐ 538 Shane Mack DP	.10	.05	.01
☐ 539 Tom Bolton DP	.05	.02	.01
☐ 540 Gene Nelson DP	.05	.02	.01
☐ 541 Wes Gardner DP	.05	.02	.01
☐ 542 Ken Caminiti DP	.15	.07	.02
☐ 543 Duane Ward DP	.10	.05	.01
☐ 544 Norm Charlton DP	.10	.05	.01
☐ 545 Hal Morris DP	.15	.07	.02
☐ 546 Rich Yett DP	.05	.02	.01
☐ 547 Hensley Meulens DP	.05	.02	.01
☐ 548 Greg A. Harris DP	.05	.02	.01
☐ 549 Darren Daulton DP	.15	.07	.02
(Posing as right-handed hitter)			
☐ 550 Jeff Hamilton DP	.05	.02	.01
☐ 551 Luis Aguayo DP	.05	.02	.01
☐ 552 Tim Leary DP	.05	.02	.01
(Resembles M.Marshall)			
☐ 553 Ron Oester DP	.05	.02	.01
☐ 554 Steve Lombardozzi DP	.05	.02	.01
☐ 555 Tim Jones DP	.05	.02	.01
☐ 556 Bud Black DP	.05	.02	.01
☐ 557 Alejandro Pena DP	.05	.02	.01
☐ 558 Jose DeJesus DP	.05	.02	.01
☐ 559 Dennis Rasmussen DP	.05	.02	.01
☐ 560 Pat Borders DP	.10	.05	.01
☐ 561 Craig Biggio DP	.60	.25	.07
☐ 562 Luis DeLosSantos DP	.05	.02	.01
☐ 563 Fred Lynn DP	.10	.05	.01
☐ 564 Todd Burns DP	.05	.02	.01
☐ 565 Felix Fermin DP	.05	.02	.01
☐ 566 Darnell Coles DP	.05	.02	.01
☐ 567 Willie Fraser DP	.05	.02	.01
☐ 568 Glenn Hubbard DP	.05	.02	.01
☐ 569 Craig Worthington DP	.05	.02	.01
☐ 570 Johnny Paredes DP	.05	.02	.01
☐ 571 Don Robinson DP	.05	.02	.01
☐ 572 Barry Lyons DP	.05	.02	.01
☐ 573 Bill Long DP	.05	.02	.01
☐ 574 Tracy Jones DP	.05	.02	.01
☐ 575 Juan Nieves DP	.05	.02	.01
☐ 576 Andres Thomas DP	.05	.02	.01
☐ 577 Rolando Roomes DP	.05	.02	.01
☐ 578 Luis Rivera UER DP	.05	.02	.01
(Wrong birthdate)			
☐ 579 Chad Kreuter DP	.05	.02	.01
☐ 580 Tony Armas DP	.05	.02	.01
☐ 581 Jay Buhner DP	.15	.07	.02
☐ 582 Ricky Horton DP	.05	.02	.01
☐ 583 Andy Hawkins DP	.05	.02	.01
☐ 584 Sil Campusano	.05	.02	.01
☐ 585 Dave Clark	.05	.02	.01
☐ 586 Van Snider DP	.05	.02	.01
☐ 587 Todd Frohwirth DP	.05	.02	.01
☐ 588 Warren Spahn DP PUZ	.10	.05	.01
☐ 589 William Brennan	.05	.02	.01
☐ 590 German Gonzalez	.05	.02	.01
☐ 591 Ernie Whitt DP	.05	.02	.01
☐ 592 Jeff Blauser	.15	.07	.02
☐ 593 Spike Owen DP	.05	.02	.01
☐ 594 Matt Williams	.50	.23	.06
☐ 595 Lloyd McClendon DP	.05	.02	.01
☐ 596 Steve Ontiveros	.05	.02	.01
☐ 597 Scott Medvin	.05	.02	.01

□ 598 Hipolito Pena DP	.05	.02	.01
□ 599 Jerald Clark DP	.05	.02	.01
□ 600A Checklist 578-660 DP	.05	.02	.01
(635 Kurt Schilling)			
□ 600B Checklist 578-660 DP	.05	.02	.01
(635 Curt Schilling;			
MVP's not listed			
on checklist card)			
□ 600C Checklist 578-660 DP	.05	.02	.01
(635 Curt Schilling;			
MVP's listed			
following 660)			
□ 601 Carmelo Martinez DP	.05	.02	.01
□ 602 Mike LaCoss	.05	.02	.01
□ 603 Mike Devereaux	.10	.05	.01
□ 604 Alex Madrid DP	.05	.02	.01
□ 605 Gary Redus DP	.05	.02	.01
□ 606 Lance Johnson	.10	.05	.01
□ 607 Terry Valle DP	.05	.02	.01
□ 608 Manny Trillo DP	.05	.02	.01
□ 609 Scott Jordan	.05	.02	.01
□ 610 Jay Howell DP	.05	.02	.01
□ 611 Francisco Melendez	.05	.02	.01
□ 612 Mike Boddicker	.05	.02	.01
□ 613 Kevin Brown DP	.10	.05	.01
□ 614 Dave Valle	.05	.02	.01
□ 615 Tim Laudner DP	.05	.02	.01
□ 616 Andy Nezelek UER	.05	.02	.01
(Wrong birthdate)			
□ 617 Chuck Crim	.05	.02	.01
□ 618 Jack Savage DP	.05	.02	.01
□ 619 Adam Peterson	.05	.02	.01
□ 620 Todd Stottlemyre	.10	.05	.01
□ 621 Lance Blankenship	.05	.02	.01
□ 622 Miguel Garcia DP	.05	.02	.01
□ 623 Keith A. Miller DP	.05	.02	.01
□ 624 Ricky Jordan DP	.05	.02	.01
□ 625 Ernest Riles DP	.05	.02	.01
□ 626 John Moses DP	.05	.02	.01
□ 627 Nelson Liriano DP	.05	.02	.01
□ 628 Mike Smithson DP	.05	.02	.01
□ 629 Scott Sanderson	.05	.02	.01
□ 630 Dale Mohorcic	.05	.02	.01
□ 631 Marvin Freeman DP	.05	.02	.01
□ 632 Mike Young DP	.05	.02	.01
□ 633 Dennis Lamp	.05	.02	.01
□ 634 Dante Bichette DP	.75	.35	.09
□ 635 Curt Schilling DP	.15	.07	.02
□ 636 Scott May DP	.05	.02	.01
□ 637 Mike Schooler	.05	.02	.01
□ 638 Rick Leach	.05	.02	.01
□ 639 Tom Lampkin UER	.05	.02	.01
(Throws Left, should			
be Throws Right)			
□ 640 Brian Meyer	.05	.02	.01
□ 641 Brian Harper	.10	.05	.01
□ 642 John Smoltz	.40	.18	.05
□ 643 Jose Canseco	.15	.07	.02
(40/40 Club)			
□ 644 Bill Schroeder	.05	.02	.01
□ 645 Edgar Martinez	.20	.09	.03
□ 646 Dennis Cook	.05	.02	.01
□ 647 Barry Jones	.05	.02	.01
□ 648 Orel Hershiser	.10	.05	.01
(59 and Counting)			
□ 649 Rod Nichols	.05	.02	.01
□ 650 Jody Davis	.05	.02	.01
□ 651 Bob Milacki	.05	.02	.01
□ 652 Mike Jackson	.05	.02	.01
□ 653 Derek Lilliquist	.05	.02	.01
□ 654 Paul Mirabella	.05	.02	.01
□ 655 Mike Diaz	.05	.02	.01
□ 656 Jeff Musselman	.05	.02	.01
□ 657 Jerry Reed	.05	.02	.01
□ 658 Kevin Blankenship	.05	.02	.01
□ 659 Wayne Tolleson	.05	.02	.01
□ 660 Eric Hetzel	.05	.02	.01

1989 Donruss Rookies

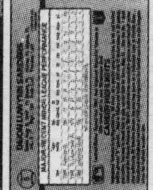

The 1989 Donruss Rookies set contains 56 standard-size (2 1/2" by 3 1/2") cards. The fronts have green and black borders; the backs are green and feature career highlights. The cards were distributed as a boxed set through the Donruss Dealer Network. Rookie Cards in this set include Jim Abbott, Junior Felix, Steve Finley, Deion Sanders, and Jerome Walton.

	MINT	NRMT	EXC
COMPLETE FACT.SET (56)	8.00	3.60	1.00
COMMON CARD (1-56)	.05	.02	.01
□ 1 Gary Sheffield	.60	.25	.07
□ 2 Gregg Jefferies	.20	.09	.03
□ 3 Ken Griffey Jr.	5.00	2.20	.60
□ 4 Tom Gordon	.10	.05	.01
□ 5 Billy Spiers	.05	.02	.01
□ 6 Deion Sanders	1.50	.70	.19
□ 7 Donn Pall	.05	.02	.01
□ 8 Steve Carter	.05	.02	.01
□ 9 Francisco Oliveras	.05	.02	.01
□ 10 Steve Wilson	.05	.02	.01
□ 11 Bob Geren	.05	.02	.01
□ 12 Tony Castillo	.05	.02	.01
□ 13 Kenny Rogers	.40	.18	.05
□ 14 Carlos Martinez	.05	.02	.01
□ 15 Edgar Martinez	.25	.11	.03
□ 16 Jim Abbott	.25	.11	.03
□ 17 Torey Lovullo	.05	.02	.01
□ 18 Mark Carreon	.05	.02	.01
□ 19 Geronimo Berroa	.10	.05	.01
□ 20 Luis Medina	.05	.02	.01
□ 21 Sandy Alomar Jr.	.10	.05	.01
□ 22 Bob Milacki	.05	.02	.01
□ 23 Joe Girardi	.10	.05	.01
□ 24 German Gonzalez	.05	.02	.01
□ 25 Craig Worthington	.05	.02	.01
□ 26 Jerome Walton	.05	.02	.01
□ 27 Gary Wayne	.05	.02	.01

☐ 28	Tim Jones	.05	.02	.01
☐ 29	Dante Bichette	.75	.35	.09
☐ 30	Alexis Infante	.05	.02	.01
☐ 31	Ken Hill	.50	.23	.06
☐ 32	Dwight Smith	.05	.02	.01
☐ 33	Luis de los Santos	.05	.02	.01
☐ 34	Eric Yelding	.05	.02	.01
☐ 35	Gregg Olson	.05	.02	.01
☐ 36	Phil Stephenson	.05	.02	.01
☐ 37	Ken Patterson	.05	.02	.01
☐ 38	Rick Wrona	.05	.02	.01
☐ 39	Mike Brumley	.05	.02	.01
☐ 40	Cris Carpenter	.05	.02	.01
☐ 41	Jeff Brantley	.05	.02	.01
☐ 42	Ron Jones	.05	.02	.01
☐ 43	Randy Johnson	1.00	.45	.12
☐ 44	Kevin Brown	.10	.05	.01
☐ 45	Ramon Martinez	.30	.14	.04
☐ 46	Greg W.Harris	.05	.02	.01
☐ 47	Steve Finley	.20	.09	.03
☐ 48	Randy Kramer	.05	.02	.01
☐ 49	Erik Hanson	.10	.05	.01
☐ 50	Matt Merullo	.05	.02	.01
☐ 51	Mike Devereaux	.10	.05	.01
☐ 52	Clay Parker	.05	.02	.01
☐ 53	Omar Vizquel	.25	.11	.03
☐ 54	Derek Lilliquist	.05	.02	.01
☐ 55	Junior Felix	.10	.05	.01
☐ 56	Checklist 1-56	.05	.02	.01

1990 Donruss

 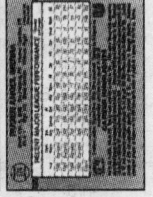

The 1990 Donruss set contains 716 standard-size (2 1/2" by 3 1/2") cards. The front borders are bright red. The horizontally oriented backs are amber. Cards numbered 1-26 are Diamond Kings; cards numbered 28-47 are Rated Rookies (RR). The jumbo (5 by 7 inch) versions of the 1990 Diamond Kings are valued about five times their standard-size counterparts. Numbered with the prefix "BC" for bonus card, a 26-card set featuring the most valuable player from each of the 26 teams was randomly inserted in all 1990 Donruss unopened pack formats. Card number 716 was added to the set shortly after the set's initial production, necessitating the checklist variation on card number 700. The set was the largest ever produced by Donruss, unfortunately it also had a large number of errors which were corrected after the cards were released. Every All-Star selection in the set has two

versions, the statistical heading on the back is either "Recent Major League Performance" or "All-Star Game Performance." There are a number of cards that have been discovered to have minor printing flaws, which are insignificant variations, that collectors have found unworthy of price differentials. These very minor variations include numbers 1, 18, 154, 168, 206, 270, 321, 347, 405, 408, 425, 583, 585, 619, 637, 639, 699, 701, and 716. The factory sets were distributed without the Bonus Cards; thus there were again new checklist cards printed to reflect the exclusion of the Bonus Cards. These factory set checklist cards are the B variations below (except for 700C). Rookie Cards in this set include Delino DeShields, Juan Gonzalez, Tommy Greene, Marquis Grissom, Dave Justice, Ben McDonald, John Olerud, Dean Palmer, Sammy Sosa, and Larry Walker. The unusual number of cards in the set (716 plus 26 BC's, i.e., not divisible by 132) apparently led to 50 double-printed numbers, which are indicated in the checklists below (1990 Donruss and 1990 Donruss Bonus MVP's) by DP.

	MINT	NRMT	EXC
COMPLETE SET (716)	8.00	3.60	1.00
COMPLETE FACT.SET (728)	8.00	3.60	1.00
COMPLETE MVP SET (26)	1.50	.70	.19
COMP.GRANDSLAMMERS SET	1.50	.70	.19
COMMON CARD (1-716)	.05	.02	.01

☐ 1	Bo Jackson DK	.15	.07	.02
☐ 2	Steve Sax DK	.05	.02	.01
☐ 3A	Ruben Sierra DK ERR (No small line on top border on card back)	.20	.09	.03
☐ 3B	Ruben Sierra DK COR	.15	.07	.02
☐ 4	Ken Griffey Jr. DK	1.00	.45	.12
☐ 5	Mickey Tettleton DK	.05	.02	.01
☐ 6	Dave Stewart DK	.10	.05	.01
☐ 7	Jim Deshaies DK DP	.05	.02	.01
☐ 8	John Smoltz DK	.10	.05	.01
☐ 9	Mike Bielecki DK	.05	.02	.01
☐ 10A	Brian Downing DK ERR (Reverse negative on card front)	.20	.09	.03
☐ 10B	Brian Downing DK COR	.05	.02	.01
☐ 11	Kevin Mitchell DK	.10	.05	.01
☐ 12	Kelly Gruber DK	.05	.02	.01
☐ 13	Joe Magrane DK	.05	.02	.01
☐ 14	John Franco DK	.10	.05	.01
☐ 15	Ozzie Guillen DK	.05	.02	.01
☐ 16	Lou Whitaker DK	.10	.05	.01
☐ 17	John Smiley DK	.05	.02	.01
☐ 18	Howard Johnson DK	.05	.02	.01
☐ 19	Willie Randolph DK	.05	.02	.01
☐ 20	Chris Bosio DK	.05	.02	.01
☐ 21	Tommy Herr DK DP	.05	.02	.01
☐ 22	Dan Gladden DK	.05	.02	.01
☐ 23	Ellis Burks DK	.10	.05	.01
☐ 24	Pete O'Brien DK	.05	.02	.01
☐ 25	Bryn Smith DK	.05	.02	.01
☐ 26	Ed Whitson DK DP	.05	.02	.01
☐ 27	DK Checklist 1-27 DP (Comments on Perez-Steele on back)	.05	.02	.01

28	Robin Ventura RR	.25	.11	.03
29	Todd Zeile RR	.10	.05	.01
30	Sandy Alomar Jr. RR	.10	.05	.01
31	Kent Mercker RR	.20	.09	.03
32	Ben McDonald RR UER	.15	.07	.02
	(Middle name Benard, not Benjamin)			
33A	Juan Gonzalez RR ERR	4.00	1.80	.50
	(Reverse negative)			
33B	Juan Gonzalez RR COR	1.25	.55	.16
34	Eric Anthony RR	.05	.02	.01
35	Mike Fetters RR	.05	.02	.01
36	Marquis Grissom RR	.60	.25	.07
37	Greg Vaughn RR	.10	.05	.01
38	Brian DuBois RR	.05	.02	.01
39	Steve Avery RR UER	.20	.09	.03
	(Born in MI, not NJ)			
40	Mark Gardner RR	.05	.02	.01
41	Andy Benes RR	.10	.05	.01
42	Delino DeShields RR	.15	.07	.02
43	Scott Coolbaugh RR	.05	.02	.01
44	Pat Combs RR DP	.05	.02	.01
45	Alex Sanchez RR DP	.05	.02	.01
46	Kelly Mann RR DP	.05	.02	.01
47	Julio Machado RR DP	.05	.02	.01
48	Pete Incaviglia	.05	.02	.01
49	Shawon Dunston	.05	.02	.01
50	Jeff Treadway	.05	.02	.01
51	Jeff Ballard	.05	.02	.01
52	Claudell Washington	.05	.02	.01
53	Juan Samuel	.05	.02	.01
54	John Smiley	.05	.02	.01
55	Rob Deer	.05	.02	.01
56	Geno Petralli	.05	.02	.01
57	Chris Bosio	.05	.02	.01
58	Carlton Fisk	.15	.07	.02
59	Kirt Manwaring	.05	.02	.01
60	Chet Lemon	.05	.02	.01
61	Bo Jackson	.15	.07	.02
62	Doyle Alexander	.05	.02	.01
63	Pedro Guerrero	.10	.05	.01
64	Allan Anderson	.05	.02	.01
65	Greg W. Harris	.05	.02	.01
66	Mike Greenwell	.15	.07	.02
67	Walt Weiss	.05	.02	.01
68	Wade Boggs	.15	.07	.02
69	Jim Clancy	.05	.02	.01
70	Junior Felix	.05	.02	.01
71	Barry Larkin	.20	.09	.03
72	Dave LaPoint	.05	.02	.01
73	Joel Skinner	.05	.02	.01
74	Jesse Barfield	.05	.02	.01
75	Tommy Herr	.05	.02	.01
76	Ricky Jordan	.05	.02	.01
77	Eddie Murray	.25	.11	.03
78	Steve Sax	.05	.02	.01
79	Tim Belcher	.05	.02	.01
80	Danny Jackson	.05	.02	.01
81	Kent Hrbek	.10	.05	.01
82	Milt Thompson	.05	.02	.01
83	Brook Jacoby	.05	.02	.01
84	Mike Marshall	.05	.02	.01
85	Kevin Seitzer	.05	.02	.01
86	Tony Gwynn	.30	.14	.04
87	Dave Stieb	.10	.05	.01
88	Dave Smith	.05	.02	.01
89	Bret Saberhagen	.15	.07	.02
90	Alan Trammell	.15	.07	.02
91	Tony Phillips	.15	.07	.02
92	Doug Drabek	.10	.05	.01
93	Jeffrey Leonard	.05	.02	.01
94	Wally Joyner	.15	.07	.02
95	Carney Lansford	.10	.05	.01
96	Cal Ripken	.75	.35	.09
97	Andres Galarraga	.15	.07	.02
98	Kevin Mitchell	.10	.05	.01
99	Howard Johnson	.10	.05	.01
100A	Checklist 28-129	.05	.02	.01
100B	Checklist 28-125	.05	.02	.01
101	Melido Perez	.05	.02	.01
102	Spike Owen	.05	.02	.01
103	Paul Molitor	.15	.07	.02
104	Geronimo Berroa	.10	.05	.01
105	Ryne Sandberg	.30	.14	.04
106	Bryn Smith	.05	.02	.01
107	Steve Buechele	.05	.02	.01
108	Jim Abbott	.15	.07	.02
109	Alvin Davis	.05	.02	.01
110	Lee Smith	.15	.07	.02
111	Roberto Alomar	.30	.14	.04
112	Rick Reuschel	.05	.02	.01
113A	Kelly Gruber ERR	.05	.02	.01
	(Born 2/22)			
113B	Kelly Gruber COR	.05	.02	.01
	(Born 2/26; corrected in factory sets)			
114	Joe Carter	.15	.07	.02
115	Jose Rijo	.10	.05	.01
116	Greg Minton	.05	.02	.01
117	Bob Ojeda	.05	.02	.01
118	Glenn Davis	.05	.02	.01
119	Jeff Reardon	.15	.07	.02
120	Kurt Stillwell	.05	.02	.01
121	John Smoltz	.15	.07	.02
122	Dwight Evans	.10	.05	.01
123	Eric Yelding	.05	.02	.01
124	John Franco	.15	.07	.02
125	Jose Canseco	.20	.09	.03
126	Barry Bonds	.30	.14	.04
127	Lee Guetterman	.05	.02	.01
128	Jack Clark	.10	.05	.01
129	Dave Valle	.05	.02	.01
130	Hubie Brooks	.05	.02	.01
131	Ernest Riles	.05	.02	.01
132	Mike Morgan	.05	.02	.01
133	Steve Jeltz	.05	.02	.01
134	Jeff D. Robinson	.05	.02	.01
135	Ozzie Guillen	.10	.05	.01
136	Chili Davis	.15	.07	.02
137	Mitch Webster	.05	.02	.01
138	Jerry Browne	.05	.02	.01
139	Bo Diaz	.05	.02	.01
140	Robby Thompson	.10	.05	.01
141	Craig Worthington	.05	.02	.01
142	Julio Franco	.10	.05	.01
143	Brian Holman	.05	.02	.01
144	George Brett	.40	.18	.05
145	Tom Glavine	.25	.11	.03
146	Robin Yount	.20	.09	.03
147	Gary Carter	.15	.07	.02
148	Ron Kittle	.05	.02	.01
149	Tony Fernandez	.10	.05	.01
150	Dave Stewart	.15	.07	.02
151	Gary Gaetti	.05	.02	.01
152	Kevin Elster	.05	.02	.01
153	Gerald Perry	.05	.02	.01
154	Jesse Orosco	.05	.02	.01
155	Wally Backman	.05	.02	.01
156	Dennis Martinez	.10	.05	.01
157	Rick Sutcliffe	.10	.05	.01
158	Greg Maddux	.60	.25	.07
159	Andy Hawkins	.05	.02	.01

☐ 160	John Kruk	.15	.07	.02	☐ 219 Dave Gallagher	.05	.02	.01
☐ 161	Jose Oquendo	.05	.02	.01	☐ 220 Tim Wallach	.05	.02	.01
☐ 162	John Dopson	.05	.02	.01	☐ 221 Chuck Crim	.05	.02	.01
☐ 163	Joe Magrane	.05	.02	.01	☐ 222 Lonnie Smith	.05	.02	.01
☐ 164	Bill Ripken	.05	.02	.01	☐ 223 Andre Dawson	.15	.07	.02
☐ 165	Fred Manrique	.05	.02	.01	☐ 224 Nelson Santovenia	.05	.02	.01
☐ 166	Nolan Ryan UER	.75	.35	.09	☐ 225 Rafael Palmeiro	.15	.07	.02
	(Did not lead NL in				☐ 226 Devon White	.10	.05	.01
	K's in '89 as he was				☐ 227 Harold Reynolds	.05	.02	.01
	in AL in '89)				☐ 228 Ellis Burks	.10	.05	.01
☐ 167	Damon Berryhill	.05	.02	.01	☐ 229 Mark Parent	.05	.02	.01
☐ 168	Dale Murphy	.15	.07	.02	☐ 230 Will Clark	.20	.09	.03
☐ 169	Mickey Tettleton	.10	.05	.01	☐ 231 Jimmy Key	.10	.05	.01
☐ 170A	Kirk McCaskill ERR	.05	.02	.01	☐ 232 John Farrell	.05	.02	.01
	(Born 4/19)				☐ 233 Eric Davis	.10	.05	.01
☐ 170B	Kirk McCaskill COR	.05	.02	.01	☐ 234 Johnny Ray	.05	.02	.01
	(Born 4/9; corrected				☐ 235 Darryl Strawberry	.10	.05	.01
	in factory sets)				☐ 236 Bill Doran	.05	.02	.01
☐ 171	Dwight Gooden	.05	.02	.01	☐ 237 Greg Gagne	.05	.02	.01
☐ 172	Jose Lind	.05	.02	.01	☐ 238 Jim Eisenreich	.05	.02	.01
☐ 173	B.J. Surhoff	.05	.02	.01	☐ 239 Tommy Gregg	.05	.02	.01
☐ 174	Ruben Sierra	.15	.07	.02	☐ 240 Marty Barrett	.05	.02	.01
☐ 175	Dan Plesac	.05	.02	.01	☐ 241 Rafael Ramirez	.05	.02	.01
☐ 176	Dan Pasqua	.05	.02	.01	☐ 242 Chris Sabo	.05	.02	.01
☐ 177	Kelly Downs	.05	.02	.01	☐ 243 Dave Henderson	.05	.02	.01
☐ 178	Matt Nokes	.05	.02	.01	☐ 244 Andy Van Slyke	.10	.05	.01
☐ 179	Luis Aquino	.05	.02	.01	☐ 245 Alvaro Espinoza	.05	.02	.01
☐ 180	Frank Tanana	.05	.02	.01	☐ 246 Garry Templeton	.05	.02	.01
☐ 181	Tony Pena	.05	.02	.01	☐ 247 Gene Harris	.05	.02	.01
☐ 182	Dan Gladden	.05	.02	.01	☐ 248 Kevin Gross	.05	.02	.01
☐ 183	Bruce Hurst	.05	.02	.01	☐ 249 Brett Butler	.15	.07	.02
☐ 184	Roger Clemens	.15	.07	.02	☐ 250 Willie Randolph	.10	.05	.01
☐ 185	Mark McGwire	.15	.07	.02	☐ 251 Roger McDowell	.05	.02	.01
☐ 186	Rob Murphy	.05	.02	.01	☐ 252 Rafael Belliard	.05	.02	.01
☐ 187	Jim Deshaies	.05	.02	.01	☐ 253 Steve Rosenberg	.05	.02	.01
☐ 188	Fred McGriff	.20	.09	.03	☐ 254 Jack Howell	.05	.02	.01
☐ 189	Rob Dibble	.10	.05	.01	☐ 255 Marvell Wynne	.05	.02	.01
☐ 190	Don Mattingly	.40	.18	.05	☐ 256 Tom Candiotti	.05	.02	.01
☐ 191	Felix Fermin	.05	.02	.01	☐ 257 Todd Benzinger	.05	.02	.01
☐ 192	Roberto Kelly	.10	.05	.01	☐ 258 Don Robinson	.05	.02	.01
☐ 193	Dennis Cook	.05	.02	.01	☐ 259 Phil Bradley	.05	.02	.01
☐ 194	Darren Daulton	.15	.07	.02	☐ 260 Cecil Espy	.05	.02	.01
☐ 195	Alfredo Griffin	.05	.02	.01	☐ 261 Scott Bankhead	.05	.02	.01
☐ 196	Eric Plunk	.05	.02	.01	☐ 262 Frank White	.10	.05	.01
☐ 197	Orel Hershiser	.15	.07	.02	☐ 263 Andres Thomas	.05	.02	.01
☐ 198	Paul O'Neill	.15	.07	.02	☐ 264 Glenn Braggs	.05	.02	.01
☐ 199	Randy Bush	.05	.02	.01	☐ 265 David Cone	.15	.07	.02
☐ 200A	Checklist 130-231	.05	.02	.01	☐ 266 Bobby Thigpen	.05	.02	.01
☐ 200B	Checklist 126-223	.05	.02	.01	☐ 267 Nelson Liriano	.05	.02	.01
☐ 201	Ozzie Smith	.20	.09	.03	☐ 268 Terry Steinbach	.10	.05	.01
☐ 202	Pete O'Brien	.05	.02	.01	☐ 269 Kirby Puckett UER	.30	.14	.04
☐ 203	Jay Howell	.05	.02	.01		(Back doesn't consider			
☐ 204	Mark Gubicza	.05	.02	.01		Joe Torre's .363 in '71)			
☐ 205	Ed Whitson	.05	.02	.01	☐ 270 Gregg Jefferies	.15	.07	.02
☐ 206	George Bell	.05	.02	.01	☐ 271 Jeff Blauser	.10	.05	.01
☐ 207	Mike Scott	.05	.02	.01	☐ 272 Cory Snyder	.05	.02	.01
☐ 208	Charlie Leibrandt	.05	.02	.01	☐ 273 Roy Smith	.05	.02	.01
☐ 209	Mike Heath	.05	.02	.01	☐ 274 Tom Foley	.05	.02	.01
☐ 210	Dennis Eckersley	.15	.07	.02	☐ 275 Mitch Williams	.10	.05	.01
☐ 211	Mike LaValliere	.05	.02	.01	☐ 276 Paul Kilgus	.05	.02	.01
☐ 212	Darnell Coles	.05	.02	.01	☐ 277 Don Slaught	.05	.02	.01
☐ 213	Lance Parrish	.10	.05	.01	☐ 278 Von Hayes	.05	.02	.01
☐ 214	Mike Moore	.05	.02	.01	☐ 279 Vince Coleman	.10	.05	.01
☐ 215	Steve Finley	.10	.05	.01	☐ 280 Mike Boddicker	.05	.02	.01
☐ 216	Tim Raines	.15	.07	.02	☐ 281 Ken Dayley	.05	.02	.01
☐ 217A	Scott Garrelts ERR	.05	.02	.01	☐ 282 Mike Devereaux	.10	.05	.01
	(Born 10/20)				☐ 283 Kenny Rogers	.05	.02	.01
☐ 217B	Scott Garrelts COR	.05	.02	.01	☐ 284 Jeff Russell	.05	.02	.01
	(Born 10/30; corrected				☐ 285 Jerome Walton	.05	.02	.01
	in factory sets)				☐ 286 Derek Lilliquist	.05	.02	.01
☐ 218	Kevin McReynolds	.05	.02	.01	☐ 287 Joe Orsulak	.05	.02	.01

☐ 288 Dick Schofield	.05	.02	.01
☐ 289 Ron Darling	.05	.02	.01
☐ 290 Bobby Bonilla	.15	.07	.02
☐ 291 Jim Gantner	.05	.02	.01
☐ 292 Bobby Witt	.05	.02	.01
☐ 293 Greg Brock	.05	.02	.01
☐ 294 Ivan Calderon	.05	.02	.01
☐ 295 Steve Bedrosian	.05	.02	.01
☐ 296 Mike Henneman	.05	.02	.01
☐ 297 Tom Gordon	.10	.05	.01
☐ 298 Lou Whitaker	.15	.07	.02
☐ 299 Terry Pendleton	.15	.07	.02
☐ 300A Checklist 232-333	.05	.02	.01
☐ 300B Checklist 224-321	.05	.02	.01
☐ 301 Juan Berenguer	.05	.02	.01
☐ 302 Mark Davis	.05	.02	.01
☐ 303 Nick Esasky	.05	.02	.01
☐ 304 Rickey Henderson	.15	.07	.02
☐ 305 Rick Cerone	.05	.02	.01
☐ 306 Craig Biggio	.15	.07	.02
☐ 307 Duane Ward	.05	.02	.01
☐ 308 Tom Browning	.05	.02	.01
☐ 309 Walt Terrell	.05	.02	.01
☐ 310 Greg Swindell	.10	.05	.01
☐ 311 Dave Righetti	.05	.02	.01
☐ 312 Mike Maddux	.05	.02	.01
☐ 313 Len Dykstra	.15	.07	.02
☐ 314 Jose Gonzalez	.05	.02	.01
☐ 315 Steve Balboni	.05	.02	.01
☐ 316 Mike Scioscia	.05	.02	.01
☐ 317 Ron Oester	.05	.02	.01
☐ 318 Gary Wayne	.05	.02	.01
☐ 319 Todd Worrell	.05	.02	.01
☐ 320 Doug Jones	.05	.02	.01
☐ 321 Jeff Hamilton	.05	.02	.01
☐ 322 Danny Tartabull	.10	.05	.01
☐ 323 Chris James	.05	.02	.01
☐ 324 Mike Flanagan	.05	.02	.01
☐ 325 Gerald Young	.05	.02	.01
☐ 326 Bob Boone	.10	.05	.01
☐ 327 Frank Williams	.05	.02	.01
☐ 328 Dave Parker	.10	.05	.01
☐ 329 Sid Bream	.05	.02	.01
☐ 330 Mike Schooler	.05	.02	.01
☐ 331 Bert Blyleven	.15	.07	.02
☐ 332 Bob Welch	.05	.02	.01
☐ 333 Bob Milacki	.05	.02	.01
☐ 334 Tim Burke	.05	.02	.01
☐ 335 Jose Uribe	.05	.02	.01
☐ 336 Randy Myers	.15	.07	.02
☐ 337 Eric King	.05	.02	.01
☐ 338 Mark Langston	.15	.07	.02
☐ 339 Teddy Higuera	.05	.02	.01
☐ 340 Oddibe McDowell	.05	.02	.01
☐ 341 Lloyd McClendon	.05	.02	.01
☐ 342 Pascual Perez	.05	.02	.01
☐ 343 Kevin Brown UER	.10	.05	.01
(Signed is misspelled			
as signeed on back)			
☐ 344 Chuck Finley	.10	.05	.01
☐ 345 Erik Hanson	.10	.05	.01
☐ 346 Rich Gedman	.05	.02	.01
☐ 347 Bip Roberts	.10	.05	.01
☐ 348 Matt Williams	.30	.14	.04
☐ 349 Tom Henke	.10	.05	.01
☐ 350 Brad Komminsk	.05	.02	.01
☐ 351 Jeff Reed	.05	.02	.01
☐ 352 Brian Downing	.05	.02	.01
☐ 353 Frank Viola	.10	.05	.01
☐ 354 Terry Puhl	.05	.02	.01
☐ 355 Brian Harper	.05	.02	.01
☐ 356 Steve Farr	.05	.02	.01
☐ 357 Joe Boever	.05	.02	.01
☐ 358 Danny Heep	.05	.02	.01
☐ 359 Larry Andersen	.05	.02	.01
☐ 360 Rolando Roomes	.05	.02	.01
☐ 361 Mike Gallego	.05	.02	.01
☐ 362 Bob Kipper	.05	.02	.01
☐ 363 Clay Parker	.05	.02	.01
☐ 364 Mike Pagliarulo	.05	.02	.01
☐ 365 Ken Griffey Jr. UER	2.00	.90	.25
(Signed through 1990,			
should be 1991)			
☐ 366 Rex Hudler	.05	.02	.01
☐ 367 Pat Sheridan	.05	.02	.01
☐ 368 Kirk Gibson	.15	.07	.02
☐ 369 Jeff Parrett	.05	.02	.01
☐ 370 Bob Walk	.05	.02	.01
☐ 371 Ken Patterson	.05	.02	.01
☐ 372 Bryan Harvey	.10	.05	.01
☐ 373 Mike Bielecki	.05	.02	.01
☐ 374 Tom Magrann	.05	.02	.01
☐ 375 Rick Mahler	.05	.02	.01
☐ 376 Craig Lefferts	.05	.02	.01
☐ 377 Gregg Olson	.05	.02	.01
☐ 378 Jamie Moyer	.05	.02	.01
☐ 379 Randy Johnson	.40	.18	.05
☐ 380 Jeff Montgomery	.10	.05	.01
☐ 381 Marty Clary	.05	.02	.01
☐ 382 Bill Spiers	.05	.02	.01
☐ 383 Dave Magadan	.05	.02	.01
☐ 384 Greg Hibbard	.05	.02	.01
☐ 385 Ernie Whitt	.05	.02	.01
☐ 386 Rick Honeycutt	.05	.02	.01
☐ 387 Dave West	.05	.02	.01
☐ 388 Keith Hernandez	.10	.05	.01
☐ 389 Jose Alvarez	.05	.02	.01
☐ 390 Joey Belle	1.00	.45	.12
☐ 391 Rick Aguilera	.10	.05	.01
☐ 392 Mike Fitzgerald	.05	.02	.01
☐ 393 Dwight Smith	.05	.02	.01
☐ 394 Steve Wilson	.05	.02	.01
☐ 395 Bob Geren	.05	.02	.01
☐ 396 Randy Ready	.05	.02	.01
☐ 397 Ken Hill	.15	.07	.02
☐ 398 Jody Reed	.05	.02	.01
☐ 399 Tom Brunansky	.05	.02	.01
☐ 400A Checklist 334-435	.05	.02	.01
☐ 400B Checklist 322-419	.05	.02	.01
☐ 401 Rene Gonzales	.05	.02	.01
☐ 402 Harold Baines	.15	.07	.02
☐ 403 Cecilio Guante	.05	.02	.01
☐ 404 Joe Girardi	.05	.02	.01
☐ 405A Sergio Valdez ERR	.05	.02	.01
(Card front shows			
black line crossing			
S in Sergio)			
☐ 405B Sergio Valdez COR	.05	.02	.01
☐ 406 Mark Williamson	.05	.02	.01
☐ 407 Glenn Hoffman	.05	.02	.01
☐ 408 Jeff Innis	.05	.02	.01
☐ 409 Randy Kramer	.05	.02	.01
☐ 410 Charlie O'Brien	.05	.02	.01
☐ 411 Charlie Hough	.05	.02	.01
☐ 412 Gus Polidor	.05	.02	.01
☐ 413 Ron Karkovice	.05	.02	.01
☐ 414 Trevor Wilson	.05	.02	.01
☐ 415 Kevin Ritz	.05	.02	.01
☐ 416 Gary Thurman	.05	.02	.01
☐ 417 Jeff M. Robinson	.05	.02	.01
☐ 418 Scott Terry	.05	.02	.01
☐ 419 Tim Laudner	.05	.02	.01

☐ 420	Dennis Rasmussen	.05	.02	.01	☐ 491	Domingo Ramos	.05	.02	.01
☐ 421	Luis Rivera	.05	.02	.01	☐ 492	Dave Clark	.05	.02	.01
☐ 422	Jim Corsi	.05	.02	.01	☐ 493	Tim Birtsas	.05	.02	.01
☐ 423	Dennis Lamp	.05	.02	.01	☐ 494	Ken Oberkfell	.05	.02	.01
☐ 424	Ken Caminiti	.15	.07	.02	☐ 495	Larry Sheets	.05	.02	.01
☐ 425	David Wells	.05	.02	.01	☐ 496	Jeff Kunkel	.05	.02	.01
☐ 426	Norm Charlton	.10	.05	.01	☐ 497	Jim Presley	.05	.02	.01
☐ 427	Deion Sanders	.50	.23	.06	☐ 498	Mike Macfarlane	.05	.02	.01
☐ 428	Dion James	.05	.02	.01	☐ 499	Pete Smith	.05	.02	.01
☐ 429	Chuck Cary	.05	.02	.01	☐ 500A	Checklist 436-537 DP	.05	.02	.01
☐ 430	Ken Howell	.05	.02	.01	☐ 500B	Checklist 420-517	.05	.02	.01
☐ 431	Steve Lake	.05	.02	.01	☐ 501	Gary Sheffield	.20	.09	.03
☐ 432	Kal Daniels	.05	.02	.01	☐ 502	Terry Bross	.05	.02	.01
☐ 433	Lance McCullers	.05	.02	.01	☐ 503	Jerry Kutzler	.05	.02	.01
☐ 434	Lenny Harris	.05	.02	.01	☐ 504	Lloyd Moseby	.05	.02	.01
☐ 435	Scott Scudder	.05	.02	.01	☐ 505	Curt Young	.05	.02	.01
☐ 436	Gene Larkin	.05	.02	.01	☐ 506	Al Newman	.05	.02	.01
☐ 437	Dan Quisenberry	.05	.02	.01	☐ 507	Keith Miller	.05	.02	.01
☐ 438	Steve Olin	.10	.05	.01	☐ 508	Mike Stanton	.05	.02	.01
☐ 439	Mickey Hatcher	.05	.02	.01	☐ 509	Rich Yett	.05	.02	.01
☐ 440	Willie Wilson	.05	.02	.01	☐ 510	Tim Drummond	.05	.02	.01
☐ 441	Mark Grant	.05	.02	.01	☐ 511	Joe Hesketh	.05	.02	.01
☐ 442	Mookie Wilson	.05	.02	.01	☐ 512	Rick Wrona	.05	.02	.01
☐ 443	Alex Trevino	.05	.02	.01	☐ 513	Luis Salazar	.05	.02	.01
☐ 444	Pat Tabler	.05	.02	.01	☐ 514	Hal Morris	.10	.05	.01
☐ 445	Dave Bergman	.05	.02	.01	☐ 515	Terry Mulholland	.10	.05	.01
☐ 446	Todd Burns	.05	.02	.01	☐ 516	John Morris	.05	.02	.01
☐ 447	R.J. Reynolds	.05	.02	.01	☐ 517	Carlos Quintana	.05	.02	.01
☐ 448	Jay Buhner	.15	.07	.02	☐ 518	Frank DiPino	.05	.02	.01
☐ 449	Lee Stevens	.05	.02	.01	☐ 519	Randy Milligan	.05	.02	.01
☐ 450	Ron Hassey	.05	.02	.01	☐ 520	Chad Kreuter	.05	.02	.01
☐ 451	Bob Melvin	.05	.02	.01	☐ 521	Mike Jeffcoat	.05	.02	.01
☐ 452	Dave Martinez	.05	.02	.01	☐ 522	Mike Harkey	.05	.02	.01
☐ 453	Greg Litton	.05	.02	.01	☐ 523A	Andy Nezelek ERR	.05	.02	.01
☐ 454	Mark Carreon	.05	.02	.01		(Wrong birth year)			
☐ 455	Scott Fletcher	.05	.02	.01	☐ 523B	Andy Nezelek COR	.05	.02	.01
☐ 456	Otis Nixon	.05	.02	.01		(Finally corrected			
☐ 457	Tony Fossas	.05	.02	.01		in factory sets)			
☐ 458	John Russell	.05	.02	.01	☐ 524	Dave Schmidt	.05	.02	.01
☐ 459	Paul Assenmacher	.05	.02	.01	☐ 525	Tony Armas	.05	.02	.01
☐ 460	Zane Smith	.05	.02	.01	☐ 526	Barry Lyons	.05	.02	.01
☐ 461	Jack Daugherty	.05	.02	.01	☐ 527	Rick Reed	.05	.02	.01
☐ 462	Rich Monteleone	.05	.02	.01	☐ 528	Jerry Reuss	.05	.02	.01
☐ 463	Greg Briley	.05	.02	.01	☐ 529	Dean Palmer	.20	.09	.03
☐ 464	Mike Smithson	.05	.02	.01	☐ 530	Jeff Peterek	.05	.02	.01
☐ 465	Benito Santiago	.10	.05	.01	☐ 531	Carlos Martinez	.05	.02	.01
☐ 466	Jeff Brantley	.05	.02	.01	☐ 532	Atlee Hammaker	.05	.02	.01
☐ 467	Jose Nunez	.05	.02	.01	☐ 533	Mike Brumley	.05	.02	.01
☐ 468	Scott Bailes	.05	.02	.01	☐ 534	Terry Leach	.05	.02	.01
☐ 469	Ken Griffey Sr.	.10	.05	.01	☐ 535	Doug Strange	.05	.02	.01
☐ 470	Bob McClure	.05	.02	.01	☐ 536	Jose DeLeon	.05	.02	.01
☐ 471	Mackey Sasser	.05	.02	.01	☐ 537	Shane Rawley	.05	.02	.01
☐ 472	Glenn Wilson	.05	.02	.01	☐ 538	Joey Cora	.10	.05	.01
☐ 473	Kevin Tapani	.15	.07	.02	☐ 539	Eric Hetzel	.05	.02	.01
☐ 474	Bill Buckner	.10	.05	.01	☐ 540	Gene Nelson	.05	.02	.01
☐ 475	Ron Gant	.15	.07	.02	☐ 541	Wes Gardner	.05	.02	.01
☐ 476	Kevin Romine	.05	.02	.01	☐ 542	Mark Portugal	.05	.02	.01
☐ 477	Juan Agosto	.05	.02	.01	☐ 543	Al Leiter	.05	.02	.01
☐ 478	Herm Winningham	.05	.02	.01	☐ 544	Jack Armstrong	.05	.02	.01
☐ 479	Storm Davis	.05	.02	.01	☐ 545	Greg Cadaret	.05	.02	.01
☐ 480	Jeff King	.10	.05	.01	☐ 546	Rod Nichols	.05	.02	.01
☐ 481	Kevin Mmahat	.05	.02	.01	☐ 547	Luis Polonia	.10	.05	.01
☐ 482	Carmelo Martinez	.05	.02	.01	☐ 548	Charlie Hayes	.10	.05	.01
☐ 483	Omar Vizquel	.05	.02	.01	☐ 549	Dickie Thon	.05	.02	.01
☐ 484	Jim Dwyer	.05	.02	.01	☐ 550	Tim Crews	.05	.02	.01
☐ 485	Bob Knepper	.05	.02	.01	☐ 551	Dave Winfield	.15	.07	.02
☐ 486	Dave Anderson	.05	.02	.01	☐ 552	Mike Davis	.05	.02	.01
☐ 487	Ron Jones	.05	.02	.01	☐ 553	Ron Robinson	.05	.02	.01
☐ 488	Jay Bell	.10	.05	.01	☐ 554	Carmen Castillo	.05	.02	.01
☐ 489	Sammy Sosa	.75	.35	.09	☐ 555	John Costello	.05	.02	.01
☐ 490	Kent Anderson	.05	.02	.01	☐ 556	Bud Black	.05	.02	.01

☐ 557 Rick Dempsey	.05	.02	.01
☐ 558 Jim Acker	.05	.02	.01
☐ 559 Eric Show	.05	.02	.01
☐ 560 Pat Borders	.05	.02	.01
☐ 561 Danny Darwin	.05	.02	.01
☐ 562 Rick Luecken	.05	.02	.01
☐ 563 Edwin Nunez	.05	.02	.01
☐ 564 Felix Jose	.05	.02	.01
☐ 565 John Cangelosi	.05	.02	.01
☐ 566 Bill Swift	.05	.02	.01
☐ 567 Bill Schroeder	.05	.02	.01
☐ 568 Stan Javier	.05	.02	.01
☐ 569 Jim Traber	.05	.02	.01
☐ 570 Wallace Johnson	.05	.02	.01
☐ 571 Donell Nixon	.05	.02	.01
☐ 572 Sid Fernandez	.10	.05	.01
☐ 573 Lance Johnson	.10	.05	.01
☐ 574 Andy McGaffigan	.05	.02	.01
☐ 575 Mark Knudson	.05	.02	.01
☐ 576 Tommy Greene	.15	.07	.02
☐ 577 Mark Grace	.15	.07	.02
☐ 578 Larry Walker	.75	.35	.09
☐ 579 Mike Stanley	.10	.05	.01
☐ 580 Mike Witt DP	.05	.02	.01
☐ 581 Scott Bradley	.05	.02	.01
☐ 582 Greg A. Harris	.05	.02	.01
☐ 583A Kevin Hickey ERR	.05	.02	.01
☐ 583B Kevin Hickey COR	.05	.02	.01
☐ 584 Lee Mazzilli	.05	.02	.01
☐ 585 Jeff Pico	.05	.02	.01
☐ 586 Joe Oliver	.05	.02	.01
☐ 587 Willie Fraser DP	.05	.02	.01
☐ 588 Carl Yastrzemski	.10	.05	.01
Puzzle Card DP			
☐ 589 Kevin Bass DP	.05	.02	.01
☐ 590 John Moses DP	.05	.02	.01
☐ 591 Tom Pagnozzi DP	.05	.02	.01
☐ 592 Tony Castillo DP	.05	.02	.01
☐ 593 Jerald Clark DP	.05	.02	.01
☐ 594 Dan Schatzeder	.05	.02	.01
☐ 595 Luis Quinones DP	.05	.02	.01
☐ 596 Pete Harnisch DP	.10	.05	.01
☐ 597 Gary Redus	.05	.02	.01
☐ 598 Mel Hall	.05	.02	.01
☐ 599 Rick Schu	.05	.02	.01
☐ 600A Checklist 538-639	.05	.02	.01
☐ 600B Checklist 518-617	.05	.02	.01
☐ 601 Mike Kingery DP	.05	.02	.01
☐ 602 Terry Kennedy DP	.05	.02	.01
☐ 603 Mike Sharperson DP	.05	.02	.01
☐ 604 Don Carman DP	.05	.02	.01
☐ 605 Jim Gott	.05	.02	.01
☐ 606 Donn Pall DP	.05	.02	.01
☐ 607 Rance Mulliniks	.05	.02	.01
☐ 608 Curt Wilkerson DP	.05	.02	.01
☐ 609 Mike Felder DP	.05	.02	.01
☐ 610 Guillermo Hernandez DP	.05	.02	.01
☐ 611 Candy Maldonado DP	.05	.02	.01
☐ 612 Mark Thurmond DP	.05	.02	.01
☐ 613 Rick Leach DP	.05	.02	.01
☐ 614 Jerry Reed DP	.05	.02	.01
☐ 615 Franklin Stubbs	.05	.02	.01
☐ 616 Billy Hatcher DP	.05	.02	.01
☐ 617 Don August DP	.05	.02	.01
☐ 618 Tim Teufel	.05	.02	.01
☐ 619 Shawn Hillegas DP	.05	.02	.01
☐ 620 Manny Lee	.05	.02	.01
☐ 621 Gary Ward DP	.05	.02	.01
☐ 622 Mark Guthrie DP	.05	.02	.01
☐ 623 Jeff Musselman DP	.05	.02	.01
☐ 624 Mark Lemke DP	.10	.05	.01

☐ 625 Fernando Valenzuela	.05	.02	.01
☐ 626 Paul Sorrento DP	.20	.09	.03
☐ 627 Glenallen Hill DP	.05	.02	.01
☐ 628 Les Lancaster DP	.05	.02	.01
☐ 629 Vance Law DP	.05	.02	.01
☐ 630 Randy Velarde DP	.05	.02	.01
☐ 631 Todd Frohwirth DP	.05	.02	.01
☐ 632 Willie McGee	.10	.05	.01
☐ 633 Dennis Boyd DP	.05	.02	.01
☐ 634 Cris Carpenter DP	.05	.02	.01
☐ 635 Brian Holton	.05	.02	.01
☐ 636 Tracy Jones DP	.05	.02	.01
☐ 637A Terry Steinbach AS	.08	.04	.01
(Recent Major			
League Performance)			
☐ 637B Terry Steinbach AS	.08	.04	.01
(All-Star Game			
Performance)			
☐ 638 Brady Anderson	.10	.05	.01
☐ 639A Jack Morris ERR	.10	.05	.01
(Card front shows			
black line crossing			
J in Jack)			
☐ 639B Jack Morris COR	.10	.05	.01
☐ 640 Jaime Navarro	.05	.02	.01
☐ 641 Darrin Jackson	.05	.02	.01
☐ 642 Mike Dyer	.05	.02	.01
☐ 643 Mike Schmidt	.25	.11	.03
☐ 644 Henry Cotto	.05	.02	.01
☐ 645 John Cerutti	.05	.02	.01
☐ 646 Francisco Cabrera	.05	.02	.01
☐ 647 Scott Sanderson	.05	.02	.01
☐ 648 Brian Meyer	.05	.02	.01
☐ 649 Ray Searage	.05	.02	.01
☐ 650A Bo Jackson AS	.15	.07	.02
(Recent Major			
League Performance)			
☐ 650B Bo Jackson AS	.15	.07	.02
(All-Star Game			
Performance)			
☐ 651 Steve Lyons	.05	.02	.01
☐ 652 Mike LaCoss	.05	.02	.01
☐ 653 Ted Power	.05	.02	.01
☐ 654A Howard Johnson AS	.05	.02	.01
(Recent Major			
League Performance)			
☐ 654B Howard Johnson AS	.05	.02	.01
(All-Star Game			
Performance)			
☐ 655 Mauro Gozzo	.05	.02	.01
☐ 656 Mike Blowers	.20	.09	.03
☐ 657 Paul Gibson	.05	.02	.01
☐ 658 Neal Heaton	.05	.02	.01
☐ 659A Nolan Ryan 5000K	1.50	.70	.19
(665 King of			
Kings back) ERR			
☐ 659B Nolan Ryan 5000K	.40	.18	.05
COR (Still an error as			
Ryan did not lead AL			
in K's in '75)			
☐ 660A Harold Baines AS	.75	.35	.09
(Black line through			
star on front;			
Recent Major			
League Performance)			
☐ 660B Harold Baines AS	1.00	.45	.12
(Black line through			
star on front;			
All-Star Game			
Performance)			
☐ 660C Harold Baines AS	.20	.09	.03

	(Black line behind star on front; Recent Major League Performance)		
☐ 660D	Harold Baines AS	.05	.02	.01
	(Black line behind star on front; All-Star Game Performance)		
☐ 661	Gary Pettis	.05	.02	.01
☐ 662	Clint Zavaras	.05	.02	.01
☐ 663A	Rick Reuschel AS	.05	.02	.01
	(Recent Major League Performance)		
☐ 663B	Rick Reuschel AS	.05	.02	.01
	(All-Star Game Performance)		
☐ 664	Alejandro Pena	.05	.02	.01
☐ 665A	Nolan Ryan KING	1.50	.70	.19
	(659 5000 K back) ERR		
☐ 665B	Nolan Ryan KING COR	.40	.18	.05
☐ 665C	Nolan Ryan KING ERR	.75	.35	.09
	(No number on back; in factory sets)		
☐ 666	Ricky Horton	.05	.02	.01
☐ 667	Curt Schilling	.10	.05	.01
☐ 668	Bill Landrum	.05	.02	.01
☐ 669	Todd Stottlemyre	.10	.05	.01
☐ 670	Tim Leary	.05	.02	.01
☐ 671	John Wetteland	.10	.05	.01
☐ 672	Calvin Schiraldi	.05	.02	.01
☐ 673A	Ruben Sierra AS	.10	.05	.01
	(Recent Major League Performance)		
☐ 673B	Ruben Sierra AS	.10	.05	.01
	(All-Star Game Performance)		
☐ 674A	Pedro Guerrero AS	.05	.02	.01
	(Recent Major League Performance)		
☐ 674B	Pedro Guerrero AS	.05	.02	.01
	(All-Star Game Performance)		
☐ 675	Ken Phelps	.05	.02	.01
☐ 676A	Cal Ripken AS	.75	.35	.09
	(Recent Major League Performance)		
☐ 676B	Cal Ripken AS	.40	.18	.05
	(All-Star Game Performance)		
☐ 677	Denny Walling	.05	.02	.01
☐ 678	Goose Gossage	.10	.05	.01
☐ 679	Gary Mielke	.05	.02	.01
☐ 680	Bill Bathe	.05	.02	.01
☐ 681	Tom Lawless	.05	.02	.01
☐ 682	Xavier Hernandez	.05	.02	.01
☐ 683A	Kirby Puckett AS	.30	.14	.04
	(Recent Major League Performance)		
☐ 683B	Kirby Puckett AS	.15	.07	.02
	(All-Star Game Performance)		
☐ 684	Mariano Duncan	.05	.02	.01
☐ 685	Ramon Martinez	.15	.07	.02
☐ 686	Tim Jones	.05	.02	.01
☐ 687	Tom Filer	.05	.02	.01
☐ 688	Steve Lombardozzi	.05	.02	.01
☐ 689	Bernie Williams	.30	.14	.04
☐ 690	Chip Hale	.05	.02	.01
☐ 691	Beau Allred	.05	.02	.01

☐ 692A	Ryne Sandberg AS	.30	.14	.04
	(Recent Major League Performance)		
☐ 692B	Ryne Sandberg AS	.15	.07	.02
	(All-Star Game Performance)		
☐ 693	Jeff Huson	.05	.02	.01
☐ 694	Curt Ford	.05	.02	.01
☐ 695A	Eric Davis AS	.05	.02	.01
	(Recent Major League Performance)		
☐ 695B	Eric Davis AS	.05	.02	.01
	(All-Star Game Performance)		
☐ 696	Scott Lusader	.05	.02	.01
☐ 697A	Mark McGwire AS	.15	.07	.02
	(Recent Major League Performance)		
☐ 697B	Mark McGwire AS	.15	.07	.02
	(All-Star Game Performance)		
☐ 698	Steve Cummings	.05	.02	.01
☐ 699	George Canale	.05	.02	.01
☐ 700A	Checklist 640-715 and BC1-BC26	.05	.02	.01
☐ 700B	Checklist 640-716 and BC1-BC26	.05	.02	.01
☐ 700C	Checklist 618-716	.05	.02	.01
☐ 701A	Julio Franco AS	.10	.05	.01
	(Recent Major League Performance)		
☐ 701B	Julio Franco AS	.10	.05	.01
	(All-Star Game Performance)		
☐ 702	Dave Johnson (P)	.05	.02	.01
☐ 703A	Dave Stewart AS	.10	.05	.01
	(Recent Major League Performance)		
☐ 703B	Dave Stewart AS	.10	.05	.01
	(All-Star Game Performance)		
☐ 704	Dave Justice	.75	.35	.09
☐ 705A	Tony Gwynn AS	.30	.14	.04
	(Recent Major League Performance)		
☐ 705B	Tony Gwynn AS	.15	.07	.02
	(All-Star Game Performance)		
☐ 706	Greg Myers	.05	.02	.01
☐ 707A	Will Clark AS	.20	.09	.03
	(Recent Major League Performance)		
☐ 707B	Will Clark AS	.15	.07	.02
	(All-Star Game Performance)		
☐ 708A	Benito Santiago AS	.05	.02	.01
	(Recent Major League Performance)		
☐ 708B	Benito Santiago AS	.05	.02	.01
	(All-Star Game Performance)		
☐ 709	Larry McWilliams	.05	.02	.01
☐ 710A	Ozzie Smith AS	.20	.09	.03
	(Recent Major League Performance)		
☐ 710B	Ozzie Smith AS	.20	.09	.03
	(All-Star Game Performance)		
☐ 711	John Olerud	.20	.09	.03
☐ 712A	Wade Boggs AS	.10	.05	.01
	(Recent Major		

	MINT	NRMT	EXC
League Performance)			
☐ 712B Wade Boggs AS	.10	.05	.01
(All-Star Game Performance)			
☐ 713 Gary Eave	.05	.02	.01
☐ 714 Bob Tewksbury	.05	.02	.01
☐ 715A Kevin Mitchell AS	.05	.02	.01
(Recent Major League Performance)			
☐ 715B Kevin Mitchell AS	.05	.02	.01
(All-Star Game Performance)			
☐ 716 Bart Giamatti COMM	.20	.09	.03
(In Memoriam)			

1990 Donruss Rookies

The 1990 Donruss Rookies set marked the fifth consecutive year that Donruss issued a boxed set honoring the best rookies of the season. This set, which used the 1990 Donruss design but featured a green border, was issued exclusively through the Donruss dealer network to hobby dealers. This 56-card, standard size, 2 1/2" by 3 1/2" set came in its own box and the words "The Rookies" are featured prominently on the front of the cards. The key Rookie Cards in this set are Carlos Baerga and Dave Hollins.

	MINT	NRMT	EXC
COMPLETE FACT.SET (56)	3.00	1.35	.35
COMMON CARD (1-56)	.05	.02	.01
☐ 1 Sandy Alomar Jr. UER	.10	.05	.01
(No stitches on baseball on Donruss logo on card front)			
☐ 2 John Olerud	.20	.09	.03
☐ 3 Pat Combs	.05	.02	.01
☐ 4 Brian DuBois	.05	.02	.01
☐ 5 Felix Jose	.05	.02	.01
☐ 6 Delino DeShields	.15	.07	.02
☐ 7 Mike Stanton	.05	.02	.01
☐ 8 Mike Munoz	.05	.02	.01
☐ 9 Craig Grebeck	.05	.02	.01
☐ 10 Joe Kraemer	.05	.02	.01
☐ 11 Jeff Huson	.05	.02	.01
☐ 12 Bill Sampen	.05	.02	.01

	MINT	NRMT	EXC
☐ 13 Brian Bohanon	.05	.02	.01
☐ 14 Dave Justice	.75	.35	.09
☐ 15 Robin Ventura	.25	.11	.03
☐ 16 Greg Vaughn	.05	.02	.01
☐ 17 Wayne Edwards	.05	.02	.01
☐ 18 Shawn Boskie	.05	.02	.01
☐ 19 Carlos Baerga	1.50	.70	.19
☐ 20 Mark Gardner	.05	.02	.01
☐ 21 Kevin Appier	.25	.11	.03
☐ 22 Mike Harkey	.05	.02	.01
☐ 23 Tim Layana	.05	.02	.01
☐ 24 Glenallen Hill	.10	.05	.01
☐ 25 Jerry Kutzler	.05	.02	.01
☐ 26 Mike Blowers	.15	.07	.02
☐ 27 Scott Ruskin	.05	.02	.01
☐ 28 Dana Kiecker	.05	.02	.01
☐ 29 Willie Blair	.05	.02	.01
☐ 30 Ben McDonald	.10	.05	.01
☐ 31 Todd Zeile	.15	.07	.02
☐ 32 Scott Coolbaugh	.05	.02	.01
☐ 33 Xavier Hernandez	.05	.02	.01
☐ 34 Mike Hartley	.05	.02	.01
☐ 35 Kevin Tapani	.10	.05	.01
☐ 36 Kevin Wickander	.05	.02	.01
☐ 37 Carlos Hernandez	.05	.02	.01
☐ 38 Brian Traxler	.05	.02	.01
☐ 39 Marty Brown	.05	.02	.01
☐ 40 Scott Radinsky	.05	.02	.01
☐ 41 Julio Machado	.05	.02	.01
☐ 42 Steve Avery	.20	.09	.03
☐ 43 Mark Lemke	.10	.05	.01
☐ 44 Alan Mills	.05	.02	.01
☐ 45 Marquis Grissom	.60	.25	.07
☐ 46 Greg Olson	.05	.02	.01
☐ 47 Dave Hollins	.05	.02	.01
☐ 48 Jerald Clark	.05	.02	.01
☐ 49 Eric Anthony	.05	.02	.01
☐ 50 Tim Drummond	.05	.02	.01
☐ 51 John Burkett	.10	.05	.01
☐ 52 Brent Knackert	.05	.02	.01
☐ 53 Jeff Shaw	.05	.02	.01
☐ 54 John Orton	.05	.02	.01
☐ 55 Terry Shumpert	.05	.02	.01
☐ 56 Checklist 1-56	.05	.02	.01

1991 Donruss

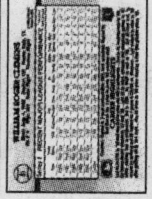

The 1991 Donruss set was issued in two series of 386 and 384 for of 770 cards. Twenty-two bonus cards, which can be considered part of the set, were randomly inserted in packs for a total of 792 cards. This set marked the first time Donruss issued cards in multiple series. First series cards feature a blue borders and second series green borders with some stripes and the players name in white against a red background. The cards measure the standard size of 2 1/2" by 3 1/2". The first 26 cards again feature the artwork of Dick Perez drawing each team's Diamond King. The jumbo (5 by 7 inch) versions of the 1991 Diamond Kings are valued about 10 times their standard-size counterparts. The first series also contains 20 Rated Rookie (RR) cards and nine All-Star cards (the AS cards are all American Leaguers in this first series). On cards 60, 70, 127, 182, 239, 294, 355, 368, and 377, the border stripes are red and yellow. As a separate promotion, wax packs were also given away with six and 12-packs of Coke and Diet Coke. Rookie Cards in the set include Wes Chamberlain, Jeff Conine, Luis Gonzalez, Brian McRae, Pedro Munoz, and Phil Plantier. The second series was issued approximately three months after the first series was issued. This series features the 26 MVP cards which Donruss had issued for the three previous years as their Bonus Cards, twenty more rated rookie cards and nine All-Star Cards (National Leaguers in this series). There were also special cards to honor the award winners and the heroes of the World Series.

	MINT	NRMT	EXC
COMPLETE SET (792)	8.00	3.60	1.00
COMPLETE W/4 LEAF PRVWS	12.00	5.50	1.50
COMPLETE W/4 STUDIO PRVWS	12.00	5.50	1.50
COMP.BONUS CARDS SET (22)	1.50	.70	.19
COMP.GRANDSLAMMERS SET (14)	2.00	.90	.25
COMMON CARD (1-386)	.05	.02	.01
COMMON CARD (387-770)	.05	.02	.01

☐ 1	Dave Stieb DK	.05	.02	.01
☐ 2	Craig Biggio DK	.05	.02	.01
☐ 3	Cecil Fielder DK	.10	.05	.01
☐ 4	Barry Bonds DK	.15	.07	.02
☐ 5	Barry Larkin DK	.15	.07	.02
☐ 6	Dave Parker DK	.05	.02	.01
☐ 7	Len Dykstra DK	.10	.05	.01
☐ 8	Bobby Thigpen DK	.05	.02	.01
☐ 9	Roger Clemens DK	.15	.07	.02
☐ 10	Ron Gant DK UER	.05	.02	.01
	(No trademark on team logo on back)			
☐ 11	Delino DeShields DK	.10	.05	.01
☐ 12	Roberto Alomar DK UER	.15	.07	.02
	(No trademark on team logo on back)			
☐ 13	Sandy Alomar Jr. DK	.05	.02	.01
☐ 14	Ryne Sandberg DK UER	.15	.07	.02
	(Was DK in '85, not '83 as shown)			
☐ 15	Ramon Martinez DK	.05	.02	.01
☐ 16	Edgar Martinez DK	.05	.02	.01
☐ 17	Dave Magadan DK	.05	.02	.01
☐ 18	Matt Williams DK	.15	.07	.02
☐ 19	Rafael Palmeiro DK UER	.15	.07	.02
	(No trademark on team logo on back)			
☐ 20	Bob Welch DK	.05	.02	.01
☐ 21	Dave Righetti DK	.05	.02	.01
☐ 22	Brian Harper DK	.05	.02	.01
☐ 23	Gregg Olson DK	.05	.02	.01
☐ 24	Kurt Stillwell DK	.05	.02	.01
☐ 25	Pedro Guerrero DK UER	.05	.02	.01
	(No trademark on team logo on back)			
☐ 26	Chuck Finley DK UER	.05	.02	.01
	(No trademark on team logo on back)			
☐ 27	DK Checklist 1-27	.05	.02	.01
☐ 28	Tino Martinez RR	.15	.07	.02
☐ 29	Mark Lewis RR	.05	.02	.01
☐ 30	Bernard Gilkey RR	.10	.05	.01
☐ 31	Hensley Meulens RR	.05	.02	.01
☐ 32	Derek Bell RR	.15	.07	.02
☐ 33	Jose Offerman RR	.10	.05	.01
☐ 34	Terry Bross RR	.05	.02	.01
☐ 35	Leo Gomez RR	.05	.02	.01
☐ 36	Derrick May RR	.10	.05	.01
☐ 37	Kevin Morton RR	.05	.02	.01
☐ 38	Moises Alou RR	.15	.07	.02
☐ 39	Julio Valera RR	.05	.02	.01
☐ 40	Milt Cuyler RR	.05	.02	.01
☐ 41	Phil Plantier RR	.15	.07	.02
☐ 42	Scott Chiamparino RR	.05	.02	.01
☐ 43	Ray Lankford RR	.20	.09	.03
☐ 44	Mickey Morandini RR	.05	.02	.01
☐ 45	Dave Hansen RR	.05	.02	.01
☐ 46	Kevin Belcher RR	.05	.02	.01
☐ 47	Darrin Fletcher RR	.05	.02	.01
☐ 48	Steve Sax AS	.05	.02	.01
☐ 49	Ken Griffey Jr. AS	.75	.35	.09
☐ 50A	Jose Canseco AS ERR	.15	.07	.02
	(Team in stat box should be AL, not A's)			
☐ 50B	Jose Canseco AS COR	.75	.35	.09
☐ 51	Sandy Alomar Jr. AS	.05	.02	.01
☐ 52	Cal Ripken AS	.40	.18	.05
☐ 53	Rickey Henderson AS	.15	.07	.02
☐ 54	Bob Welch AS	.05	.02	.01
☐ 55	Wade Boggs AS	.15	.07	.02
☐ 56	Mark McGwire AS	.15	.07	.02
☐ 57A	Jack McDowell ERR	.15	.07	.02
	(Career stats do not include 1990)			
☐ 57B	Jack McDowell COR	.25	.11	.03
	(Career stats do not include 1990)			
☐ 58	Jose Lind	.05	.02	.01
☐ 59	Alex Fernandez	.15	.07	.02
☐ 60	Pat Combs	.05	.02	.01
☐ 61	Mike Walker	.05	.02	.01
☐ 62	Juan Samuel	.05	.02	.01
☐ 63	Mike Blowers UER	.05	.02	.01
	(Last line has aseball, not baseball)			
☐ 64	Mark Guthrie	.05	.02	.01
☐ 65	Mark Salas	.05	.02	.01
☐ 66	Tim Jones	.05	.02	.01
☐ 67	Tim Leary	.05	.02	.01
☐ 68	Andres Galarraga	.15	.07	.02
☐ 69	Bob Milacki	.05	.02	.01
☐ 70	Tim Belcher	.05	.02	.01
☐ 71	Todd Zeile	.10	.05	.01
☐ 72	Jerome Walton	.05	.02	.01
☐ 73	Kevin Seitzer	.05	.02	.01
☐ 74	Jerald Clark	.05	.02	.01
☐ 75	John Smoltz UER	.15	.07	.02
	(Born in Detroit, not Warren)			
☐ 76	Mike Henneman	.05	.02	.01

☐ 77	Ken Griffey Jr.	1.50	.70	.19
☐ 78	Jim Abbott	.15	.07	.02
☐ 79	Gregg Jefferies	.15	.07	.02
☐ 80	Kevin Reimer	.05	.02	.01
☐ 81	Roger Clemens	.15	.07	.02
☐ 82	Mike Fitzgerald	.05	.02	.01
☐ 83	Bruce Hurst UER	.05	.02	.01
	(Middle name is Lee, not Vee)			
☐ 84	Eric Davis	.10	.05	.01
☐ 85	Paul Molitor	.15	.07	.02
☐ 86	Will Clark	.15	.07	.02
☐ 87	Mike Bielecki	.05	.02	.01
☐ 88	Bret Saberhagen	.15	.07	.02
☐ 89	Nolan Ryan	.75	.35	.09
☐ 90	Bobby Thigpen	.05	.02	.01
☐ 91	Dickie Thon	.05	.02	.01
☐ 92	Duane Ward	.05	.02	.01
☐ 93	Luis Polonia	.05	.02	.01
☐ 94	Terry Kennedy	.05	.02	.01
☐ 95	Kent Hrbek	.10	.05	.01
☐ 96	Danny Jackson	.05	.02	.01
☐ 97	Sid Fernandez	.10	.05	.01
☐ 98	Jimmy Key	.10	.05	.01
☐ 99	Franklin Stubbs	.05	.02	.01
☐ 100	Checklist 28-103	.05	.02	.01
☐ 101	R.J. Reynolds	.05	.02	.01
☐ 102	Dave Stewart	.15	.07	.02
☐ 103	Dan Pasqua	.05	.02	.01
☐ 104	Dan Plesac	.05	.02	.01
☐ 105	Mark McGwire	.15	.07	.02
☐ 106	John Farrell	.05	.02	.01
☐ 107	Don Mattingly	.40	.18	.05
☐ 108	Carlton Fisk	.15	.07	.02
☐ 109	Ken Oberkfell	.05	.02	.01
☐ 110	Darrel Akerfelds	.05	.02	.01
☐ 111	Gregg Olson	.05	.02	.01
☐ 112	Mike Scioscia	.05	.02	.01
☐ 113	Bryn Smith	.05	.02	.01
☐ 114	Bob Geren	.05	.02	.01
☐ 115	Tom Candiotti	.05	.02	.01
☐ 116	Kevin Tapani	.10	.05	.01
☐ 117	Jeff Treadway	.05	.02	.01
☐ 118	Alan Trammell	.15	.07	.02
☐ 119	Pete O'Brien	.05	.02	.01
	(Blue shading goes through stats)			
☐ 120	Joel Skinner	.05	.02	.01
☐ 121	Mike LaValliere	.05	.02	.01
☐ 122	Dwight Evans	.10	.05	.01
☐ 123	Jody Reed	.05	.02	.01
☐ 124	Lee Guetterman	.05	.02	.01
☐ 125	Tim Burke	.05	.02	.01
☐ 126	Dave Johnson	.05	.02	.01
☐ 127	Fernando Valenzuela	.05	.02	.01
	(Lower large stripe in yellow instead of blue) UER			
☐ 128	Jose DeLeon	.05	.02	.01
☐ 129	Andre Dawson	.15	.07	.02
☐ 130	Gerald Perry	.05	.02	.01
☐ 131	Greg W. Harris	.05	.02	.01
☐ 132	Tom Glavine	.20	.09	.03
☐ 133	Lance McCullers	.05	.02	.01
☐ 134	Randy Johnson	.25	.11	.03
☐ 135	Lance Parrish UER	.10	.05	.01
	(Born in McKeesport, not Clairton)			
☐ 136	Mackey Sasser	.05	.02	.01
☐ 137	Geno Petralli	.05	.02	.01
☐ 138	Dennis Lamp	.05	.02	.01
☐ 139	Dennis Martinez	.10	.05	.01
☐ 140	Mike Pagliarulo	.05	.02	.01
☐ 141	Hal Morris	.10	.05	.01
☐ 142	Dave Parker	.10	.05	.01
☐ 143	Brett Butler	.15	.07	.02
☐ 144	Paul Assenmacher	.05	.02	.01
☐ 145	Mark Gubicza	.05	.02	.01
☐ 146	Charlie Hough	.10	.05	.01
☐ 147	Sammy Sosa	.25	.11	.03
☐ 148	Randy Ready	.05	.02	.01
☐ 149	Kelly Gruber	.05	.02	.01
☐ 150	Devon White	.10	.05	.01
☐ 151	Gary Carter	.15	.07	.02
☐ 152	Gene Larkin	.05	.02	.01
☐ 153	Chris Sabo	.05	.02	.01
☐ 154	David Cone	.15	.07	.02
☐ 155	Todd Stottlemyre	.05	.02	.01
☐ 156	Glenn Wilson	.05	.02	.01
☐ 157	Bob Walk	.05	.02	.01
☐ 158	Mike Gallego	.05	.02	.01
☐ 159	Greg Hibbard	.05	.02	.01
☐ 160	Chris Bosio	.05	.02	.01
☐ 161	Mike Moore	.05	.02	.01
☐ 162	Jerry Browne UER	.05	.02	.01
	(Born Christiansted, should be St. Croix)			
☐ 163	Steve Sax UER	.05	.02	.01
	(No asterisk next to his 1989 At Bats)			
☐ 164	Melido Perez	.05	.02	.01
☐ 165	Danny Darwin	.05	.02	.01
☐ 166	Roger McDowell	.05	.02	.01
☐ 167	Bill Ripken	.05	.02	.01
☐ 168	Mike Sharperson	.05	.02	.01
☐ 169	Lee Smith	.15	.07	.02
☐ 170	Matt Nokes	.05	.02	.01
☐ 171	Jesse Orosco	.05	.02	.01
☐ 172	Rick Aguilera	.10	.05	.01
☐ 173	Jim Presley	.05	.02	.01
☐ 174	Lou Whitaker	.15	.07	.02
☐ 175	Harold Reynolds	.05	.02	.01
☐ 176	Brook Jacoby	.05	.02	.01
☐ 177	Wally Backman	.05	.02	.01
☐ 178	Wade Boggs	.15	.07	.02
☐ 179	Chuck Cary	.05	.02	.01
	(Comma after DOB, not on other cards)			
☐ 180	Tom Foley	.05	.02	.01
☐ 181	Pete Harnisch	.10	.05	.01
☐ 182	Mike Morgan	.05	.02	.01
☐ 183	Bob Tewksbury	.05	.02	.01
☐ 184	Joe Girardi	.05	.02	.01
☐ 185	Storm Davis	.05	.02	.01
☐ 186	Ed Whitson	.05	.02	.01
☐ 187	Steve Avery UER	.15	.07	.02
	(Born in New Jersey, should be Michigan)			
☐ 188	Lloyd Moseby	.05	.02	.01
☐ 189	Scott Bankhead	.05	.02	.01
☐ 190	Mark Langston	.15	.07	.02
☐ 191	Kevin McReynolds	.05	.02	.01
☐ 192	Julio Franco	.10	.05	.01
☐ 193	John Dopson	.05	.02	.01
☐ 194	Dennis Boyd	.05	.02	.01
☐ 195	Bip Roberts	.10	.05	.01
☐ 196	Billy Hatcher	.05	.02	.01
☐ 197	Edgar Diaz	.05	.02	.01
☐ 198	Greg Litton	.05	.02	.01
☐ 199	Mark Grace	.15	.07	.02
☐ 200	Checklist 104-179	.05	.02	.01
☐ 201	George Brett	.40	.18	.05

□	#	Name			
□	202	Jeff Russell	.05	.02	.01
□	203	Ivan Calderon	.05	.02	.01
□	204	Ken Howell	.05	.02	.01
□	205	Tom Henke	.10	.05	.01
□	206	Bryan Harvey	.05	.02	.01
□	207	Steve Bedrosian	.05	.02	.01
□	208	Al Newman	.05	.02	.01
□	209	Randy Myers	.15	.07	.02
□	210	Daryl Boston	.05	.02	.01
□	211	Manny Lee	.05	.02	.01
□	212	Dave Smith	.05	.02	.01
□	213	Don Slaught	.05	.02	.01
□	214	Walt Weiss	.05	.02	.01
□	215	Donn Pall	.05	.02	.01
□	216	Jaime Navarro	.05	.02	.01
□	217	Willie Randolph	.10	.05	.01
□	218	Rudy Seanez	.05	.02	.01
□	219	Jim Leyritz	.05	.02	.01
□	220	Ron Karkovice	.05	.02	.01
□	221	Ken Caminiti	.15	.07	.02
□	222	Von Hayes	.05	.02	.01
□	223	Cal Ripken	.75	.35	.09
□	224	Lenny Harris	.05	.02	.01
□	225	Milt Thompson	.05	.02	.01
□	226	Alvaro Espinoza	.05	.02	.01
□	227	Chris James	.05	.02	.01
□	228	Dan Gladden	.05	.02	.01
□	229	Jeff Blauser	.10	.05	.01
□	230	Mike Heath	.05	.02	.01
□	231	Omar Vizquel	.05	.02	.01
□	232	Doug Jones	.05	.02	.01
□	233	Jeff King	.05	.02	.01
□	234	Luis Rivera	.05	.02	.01
□	235	Ellis Burks	.10	.05	.01
□	236	Greg Cadaret	.05	.02	.01
□	237	Dave Martinez	.05	.02	.01
□	238	Mark Williamson	.05	.02	.01
□	239	Stan Javier	.05	.02	.01
□	240	Ozzie Smith	.20	.09	.03
□	241	Shawn Boskie	.05	.02	.01
□	242	Tom Gordon	.10	.05	.01
□	243	Tony Gwynn	.30	.14	.04
□	244	Tommy Gregg	.05	.02	.01
□	245	Jeff M. Robinson	.05	.02	.01
□	246	Keith Comstock	.05	.02	.01
□	247	Jack Howell	.05	.02	.01
□	248	Keith Miller	.05	.02	.01
□	249	Bobby Witt	.05	.02	.01
□	250	Rob Murphy UER	.05	.02	.01
		(Shown as on Reds in '89 stats, should be Red Sox)			
□	251	Spike Owen	.05	.02	.01
□	252	Garry Templeton	.05	.02	.01
□	253	Glenn Braggs	.05	.02	.01
□	254	Ron Robinson	.05	.02	.01
□	255	Kevin Mitchell	.10	.05	.01
□	256	Les Lancaster	.05	.02	.01
□	257	Mel Stottlemyre Jr.	.05	.02	.01
□	258	Kenny Rogers UER	.05	.02	.01
		(IP listed as 171, should be 172)			
□	259	Lance Johnson	.05	.02	.01
□	260	John Kruk	.15	.07	.02
□	261	Fred McGriff	.15	.07	.02
□	262	Dick Schofield	.05	.02	.01
□	263	Trevor Wilson	.05	.02	.01
□	264	David West	.05	.02	.01
□	265	Scott Scudder	.05	.02	.01
□	266	Dwight Gooden	.05	.02	.01
□	267	Willie Blair	.05	.02	.01
□	268	Mark Portugal	.05	.02	.01
□	269	Doug Drabek	.10	.05	.01
□	270	Dennis Eckersley	.15	.07	.02
□	271	Eric King	.05	.02	.01
□	272	Robin Yount	.15	.07	.02
□	273	Carney Lansford	.10	.05	.01
□	274	Carlos Baerga	.40	.18	.05
□	275	Dave Righetti	.05	.02	.01
□	276	Scott Fletcher	.05	.02	.01
□	277	Eric Yelding	.05	.02	.01
□	278	Charlie Hayes	.10	.05	.01
□	279	Jeff Ballard	.05	.02	.01
□	280	Orel Hershiser	.15	.07	.02
□	281	Jose Oquendo	.05	.02	.01
□	282	Mike Witt	.05	.02	.01
□	283	Mitch Webster	.05	.02	.01
□	284	Greg Gagne	.05	.02	.01
□	285	Greg Olson	.05	.02	.01
□	286	Tony Phillips UER	.15	.07	.02
		(Born 4/15, should be 4/25)			
□	287	Scott Bradley	.05	.02	.01
□	288	Cory Snyder UER	.05	.02	.01
		(In text, led is repeated and Inglewood is misspelled as Englewood)			
□	289	Jay Bell UER	.10	.05	.01
		(Born in Pensacola, not Eglin AFB)			
□	290	Kevin Romine	.05	.02	.01
□	291	Jeff D. Robinson	.05	.02	.01
□	292	Steve Frey UER	.05	.02	.01
		(Bats left, should be right)			
□	293	Craig Worthington	.05	.02	.01
□	294	Tim Crews	.05	.02	.01
□	295	Joe Magrane	.05	.02	.01
□	296	Hector Villanueva	.05	.02	.01
□	297	Terry Shumpert	.05	.02	.01
□	298	Joe Carter	.15	.07	.02
□	299	Kent Mercker UER	.05	.02	.01
		(IP listed as 53, should be 52)			
□	300	Checklist 180-255	.05	.02	.01
□	301	Chet Lemon	.05	.02	.01
□	302	Mike Schooler	.05	.02	.01
□	303	Dante Bichette	.20	.09	.03
□	304	Kevin Elster	.05	.02	.01
□	305	Jeff Huson	.05	.02	.01
□	306	Greg A. Harris	.05	.02	.01
□	307	Marquis Grissom UER	.20	.09	.03
		(Middle name Deon, should be Dean)			
□	308	Calvin Schiraldi	.05	.02	.01
□	309	Mariano Duncan	.05	.02	.01
□	310	Bill Spiers	.05	.02	.01
□	311	Scott Garrelts	.05	.02	.01
□	312	Mitch Williams	.10	.05	.01
□	313	Mike Macfarlane	.05	.02	.01
□	314	Kevin Brown	.10	.05	.01
□	315	Robin Ventura	.20	.09	.03
□	316	Darren Daulton	.15	.07	.02
□	317	Pat Borders	.05	.02	.01
□	318	Mark Eichhorn	.05	.02	.01
□	319	Jeff Brantley	.05	.02	.01
□	320	Shane Mack	.05	.02	.01
□	321	Rob Dibble	.10	.05	.01
□	322	John Franco	.15	.07	.02
□	323	Junior Felix	.05	.02	.01
□	324	Casey Candaele	.05	.02	.01
□	325	Bobby Bonilla	.15	.07	.02

□	#	Player			
□	326	Dave Henderson	.05	.02	.01
□	327	Wayne Edwards	.05	.02	.01
□	328	Mark Knudson	.05	.02	.01
□	329	Terry Steinbach	.10	.05	.01
□	330	Colby Ward UER (No comma between city and state)	.05	.02	.01
□	331	Oscar Azocar	.05	.02	.01
□	332	Scott Radinsky	.05	.02	.01
□	333	Eric Anthony	.05	.02	.01
□	334	Steve Lake	.05	.02	.01
□	335	Bob Melvin	.05	.02	.01
□	336	Kal Daniels	.05	.02	.01
□	337	Tom Pagnozzi	.05	.02	.01
□	338	Alan Mills	.05	.02	.01
□	339	Steve Olin	.05	.02	.01
□	340	Juan Berenguer	.05	.02	.01
□	341	Francisco Cabrera	.05	.02	.01
□	342	Dave Bergman	.05	.02	.01
□	343	Henry Cotto	.05	.02	.01
□	344	Sergio Valdez	.05	.02	.01
□	345	Bob Patterson	.05	.02	.01
□	346	John Marzano	.05	.02	.01
□	347	Dana Kiecker	.05	.02	.01
□	348	Dion James	.05	.02	.01
□	349	Hubie Brooks	.05	.02	.01
□	350	Bill Landrum	.05	.02	.01
□	351	Bill Sampen	.05	.02	.01
□	352	Greg Briley	.05	.02	.01
□	353	Paul Gibson	.05	.02	.01
□	354	Dave Eiland	.05	.02	.01
□	355	Steve Finley	.05	.02	.01
□	356	Bob Boone	.10	.05	.01
□	357	Steve Buechele	.05	.02	.01
□	358	Chris Hoiles	.10	.05	.01
□	359	Larry Walker	.25	.11	.03
□	360	Frank DiPino	.05	.02	.01
□	361	Mark Grant	.05	.02	.01
□	362	Dave Magadan	.05	.02	.01
□	363	Robby Thompson	.05	.02	.01
□	364	Lonnie Smith	.05	.02	.01
□	365	Steve Farr	.05	.02	.01
□	366	Dave Valle	.05	.02	.01
□	367	Tim Naehring	.05	.02	.01
□	368	Jim Acker	.05	.02	.01
□	369	Jeff Reardon UER (Born in Pittsfield, not Dalton)	.15	.07	.02
□	370	Tim Teufel	.05	.02	.01
□	371	Juan Gonzalez	.50	.23	.06
□	372	Luis Salazar	.05	.02	.01
□	373	Rick Honeycutt	.05	.02	.01
□	374	Greg Maddux	.60	.25	.07
□	375	Jose Uribe UER (Middle name Elta, should be Alta)	.05	.02	.01
□	376	Donnie Hill	.05	.02	.01
□	377	Don Carman	.05	.02	.01
□	378	Craig Grebeck	.05	.02	.01
□	379	Willie Fraser	.05	.02	.01
□	380	Glenallen Hill	.05	.02	.01
□	381	Joe Oliver	.05	.02	.01
□	382	Randy Bush	.05	.02	.01
□	383	Alex Cole	.05	.02	.01
□	384	Norm Charlton	.05	.02	.01
□	385	Gene Nelson	.05	.02	.01
□	386	Checklist 256-331	.05	.02	.01
□	387	Rickey Henderson MVP	.15	.07	.02
□	388	Lance Parrish MVP	.05	.02	.01
□	389	Fred McGriff MVP	.10	.05	.01
□	390	Dave Parker MVP	.05	.02	.01
□	391	Candy Maldonado MVP	.05	.02	.01
□	392	Ken Griffey Jr. MVP	.75	.35	.09
□	393	Gregg Olson MVP	.05	.02	.01
□	394	Rafael Palmeiro MVP	.15	.07	.02
□	395	Roger Clemens MVP	.15	.07	.02
□	396	George Brett MVP	.20	.09	.03
□	397	Cecil Fielder MVP	.10	.05	.01
□	398	Brian Harper MVP UER (Major League Performance, should be Career)	.05	.02	.01
□	399	Bobby Thigpen MVP	.05	.02	.01
□	400	Roberto Kelly MVP UER (Second Base on front and OF on back)	.15	.07	.02
□	401	Danny Darwin MVP	.05	.02	.01
□	402	Dave Justice MVP	.10	.05	.01
□	403	Lee Smith MVP	.10	.05	.01
□	404	Ryne Sandberg MVP	.15	.07	.02
□	405	Eddie Murray MVP	.15	.07	.02
□	406	Tim Wallach MVP	.05	.02	.01
□	407	Kevin Mitchell MVP	.05	.02	.01
□	408	Darryl Strawberry MVP	.05	.02	.01
□	409	Joe Carter MVP	.10	.05	.01
□	410	Len Dykstra MVP	.10	.05	.01
□	411	Doug Drabek MVP	.05	.02	.01
□	412	Chris Sabo MVP	.05	.02	.01
□	413	Paul Marak RR	.05	.02	.01
□	414	Tim McIntosh RR	.05	.02	.01
□	415	Brian Barnes RR	.05	.02	.01
□	416	Eric Gunderson RR	.05	.02	.01
□	417	Mike Gardiner RR	.05	.02	.01
□	418	Steve Carter RR	.05	.02	.01
□	419	Gerald Alexander RR	.05	.02	.01
□	420	Rich Garces RR	.05	.02	.01
□	421	Chuck Knoblauch RR	.25	.11	.03
□	422	Scott Aldred RR	.05	.02	.01
□	423	Wes Chamberlain RR	.05	.02	.01
□	424	Lance Dickson RR	.05	.02	.01
□	425	Greg Colbrunn RR	.20	.09	.03
□	426	Rich DeLucia RR UER (Misspelled Delucia on card)	.05	.02	.01
□	427	Jeff Conine RR	.60	.25	.07
□	428	Steve Decker RR	.05	.02	.01
□	429	Turner Ward RR	.05	.02	.01
□	430	Mo Vaughn RR	.50	.23	.06
□	431	Steve Chitren RR	.05	.02	.01
□	432	Mike Benjamin RR	.05	.02	.01
□	433	Ryne Sandberg AS	.15	.07	.02
□	434	Len Dykstra AS	.10	.05	.01
□	435	Andre Dawson AS	.10	.05	.01
□	436A	Mike Scioscia AS (White star by name)	.05	.02	.01
□	436B	Mike Scioscia AS (Yellow star by name)	.05	.02	.01
□	437	Ozzie Smith AS	.15	.07	.02
□	438	Kevin Mitchell AS	.05	.02	.01
□	439	Jack Armstrong AS	.05	.02	.01
□	440	Chris Sabo AS	.05	.02	.01
□	441	Will Clark AS	.15	.07	.02
□	442	Mel Hall	.05	.02	.01
□	443	Mark Gardner	.05	.02	.01
□	444	Mike Devereaux	.10	.05	.01
□	445	Kirk Gibson	.15	.07	.02
□	446	Terry Pendleton	.15	.07	.02
□	447	Mike Harkey	.05	.02	.01
□	448	Jim Eisenreich	.05	.02	.01
□	449	Benito Santiago	.05	.02	.01
□	450	Oddibe McDowell	.05	.02	.01
□	451	Cecil Fielder	.15	.07	.02

☐ 452 Ken Griffey Sr.	.10	.05	.01
☐ 453 Bert Blyleven	.15	.07	.02
☐ 454 Howard Johnson	.05	.02	.01
☐ 455 Monty Fariss UER	.05	.02	.01
(Misspelled Farris			
on card)			
☐ 456 Tony Pena	.05	.02	.01
☐ 457 Tim Raines	.15	.07	.02
☐ 458 Dennis Rasmussen	.05	.02	.01
☐ 459 Luis Quinones	.05	.02	.01
☐ 460 B.J. Surhoff	.05	.02	.01
☐ 461 Ernest Riles	.05	.02	.01
☐ 462 Rick Sutcliffe	.10	.05	.01
☐ 463 Danny Tartabull	.10	.05	.01
☐ 464 Pete Incaviglia	.05	.02	.01
☐ 465 Carlos Martinez	.05	.02	.01
☐ 466 Ricky Jordan	.05	.02	.01
☐ 467 John Cerutti	.05	.02	.01
☐ 468 Dave Winfield	.15	.07	.02
☐ 469 Francisco Oliveras	.05	.02	.01
☐ 470 Roy Smith	.05	.02	.01
☐ 471 Barry Larkin	.15	.07	.02
☐ 472 Ron Darling	.05	.02	.01
☐ 473 David Wells	.05	.02	.01
☐ 474 Glenn Davis	.05	.02	.01
☐ 475 Neal Heaton	.05	.02	.01
☐ 476 Ron Hassey	.05	.02	.01
☐ 477 Frank Thomas	2.00	.90	.25
☐ 478 Greg Vaughn	.10	.05	.01
☐ 479 Todd Burns	.05	.02	.01
☐ 480 Candy Maldonado	.05	.02	.01
☐ 481 Dave LaPoint	.05	.02	.01
☐ 482 Alvin Davis	.05	.02	.01
☐ 483 Mike Scott	.05	.02	.01
☐ 484 Dale Murphy	.15	.07	.02
☐ 485 Ben McDonald	.10	.05	.01
☐ 486 Jay Howell	.05	.02	.01
☐ 487 Vince Coleman	.05	.02	.01
☐ 488 Alfredo Griffin	.05	.02	.01
☐ 489 Sandy Alomar Jr.	.10	.05	.01
☐ 490 Kirby Puckett	.30	.14	.04
☐ 491 Andres Thomas	.05	.02	.01
☐ 492 Jack Morris	.15	.07	.02
☐ 493 Matt Young	.05	.02	.01
☐ 494 Greg Myers	.05	.02	.01
☐ 495 Barry Bonds	.30	.14	.04
☐ 496 Scott Cooper UER	.10	.05	.01
(No BA for 1990			
and career)			
☐ 497 Dan Schatzeder	.05	.02	.01
☐ 498 Jesse Barfield	.05	.02	.01
☐ 499 Jerry Goff	.05	.02	.01
☐ 500 Checklist 332-408	.05	.02	.01
☐ 501 Anthony Telford	.05	.02	.01
☐ 502 Eddie Murray	.20	.09	.03
☐ 503 Omar Olivares	.05	.02	.01
☐ 504 Ryne Sandberg	.30	.14	.04
☐ 505 Jeff Montgomery	.10	.05	.01
☐ 506 Mark Parent	.05	.02	.01
☐ 507 Ron Gant	.15	.07	.02
☐ 508 Frank Tanana	.05	.02	.01
☐ 509 Jay Buhner	.15	.07	.02
☐ 510 Max Venable	.05	.02	.01
☐ 511 Wally Whitehurst	.05	.02	.01
☐ 512 Gary Pettis	.05	.02	.01
☐ 513 Tom Brunansky	.05	.02	.01
☐ 514 Tim Wallach	.05	.02	.01
☐ 515 Craig Lefferts	.05	.02	.01
☐ 516 Tim Layana	.05	.02	.01
☐ 517 Darryl Hamilton	.10	.05	.01
☐ 518 Rick Reuschel	.05	.02	.01
☐ 519 Steve Wilson	.05	.02	.01
☐ 520 Kurt Stillwell	.05	.02	.01
☐ 521 Rafael Palmeiro	.15	.07	.02
☐ 522 Ken Patterson	.05	.02	.01
☐ 523 Len Dykstra	.15	.07	.02
☐ 524 Tony Fernandez	.05	.02	.01
☐ 525 Kent Anderson	.05	.02	.01
☐ 526 Mark Leonard	.05	.02	.01
☐ 527 Allan Anderson	.05	.02	.01
☐ 528 Tom Browning	.05	.02	.01
☐ 529 Frank Viola	.10	.05	.01
☐ 530 John Olerud	.10	.05	.01
☐ 531 Juan Agosto	.05	.02	.01
☐ 532 Zane Smith	.05	.02	.01
☐ 533 Scott Sanderson	.05	.02	.01
☐ 534 Barry Jones	.05	.02	.01
☐ 535 Mike Felder	.05	.02	.01
☐ 536 Jose Canseco	.20	.09	.03
☐ 537 Felix Fermin	.05	.02	.01
☐ 538 Roberto Kelly	.10	.05	.01
☐ 539 Brian Holman	.05	.02	.01
☐ 540 Mark Davidson	.05	.02	.01
☐ 541 Terry Mulholland	.05	.02	.01
☐ 542 Randy Milligan	.05	.02	.01
☐ 543 Jose Gonzalez	.05	.02	.01
☐ 544 Craig Wilson	.05	.02	.01
☐ 545 Mike Hartley	.05	.02	.01
☐ 546 Greg Swindell	.05	.02	.01
☐ 547 Gary Gaetti	.05	.02	.01
☐ 548 Dave Justice	.20	.09	.03
☐ 549 Steve Searcy	.05	.02	.01
☐ 550 Erik Hanson	.05	.02	.01
☐ 551 Dave Stieb	.05	.02	.01
☐ 552 Andy Van Slyke	.10	.05	.01
☐ 553 Mike Greenwell	.15	.07	.02
☐ 554 Kevin Maas	.05	.02	.01
☐ 555 Delino DeShields	.10	.05	.01
☐ 556 Curt Schilling	.05	.02	.01
☐ 557 Ramon Martinez	.15	.07	.02
☐ 558 Pedro Guerrero	.05	.02	.01
☐ 559 Dwight Smith	.05	.02	.01
☐ 560 Mark Davis	.05	.02	.01
☐ 561 Shawn Abner	.05	.02	.01
☐ 562 Charlie Leibrandt	.05	.02	.01
☐ 563 John Shelby	.05	.02	.01
☐ 564 Bill Swift	.05	.02	.01
☐ 565 Mike Fetters	.05	.02	.01
☐ 566 Alejandro Pena	.05	.02	.01
☐ 567 Ruben Sierra	.15	.07	.02
☐ 568 Carlos Quintana	.05	.02	.01
☐ 569 Kevin Gross	.05	.02	.01
☐ 570 Derek Lilliquist	.05	.02	.01
☐ 571 Jack Armstrong	.05	.02	.01
☐ 572 Greg Brock	.05	.02	.01
☐ 573 Mike Kingery	.05	.02	.01
☐ 574 Greg Smith	.05	.02	.01
☐ 575 Brian McRae	.30	.14	.04
☐ 576 Jack Daugherty	.05	.02	.01
☐ 577 Ozzie Guillen	.10	.05	.01
☐ 578 Joe Boever	.05	.02	.01
☐ 579 Luis Sojo	.05	.02	.01
☐ 580 Chili Davis	.15	.07	.02
☐ 581 Don Robinson	.05	.02	.01
☐ 582 Brian Harper	.05	.02	.01
☐ 583 Paul O'Neill	.15	.07	.02
☐ 584 Bob Ojeda	.05	.02	.01
☐ 585 Mookie Wilson	.05	.02	.01
☐ 586 Rafael Ramirez	.05	.02	.01
☐ 587 Gary Redus	.05	.02	.01
☐ 588 Jamie Quirk	.05	.02	.01
☐ 589 Shawn Hillegas	.05	.02	.01

☐ 590	Tom Edens	.05	.02	.01
☐ 591	Joe Klink	.05	.02	.01
☐ 592	Charles Nagy	.10	.05	.01
☐ 593	Eric Plunk	.05	.02	.01
☐ 594	Tracy Jones	.05	.02	.01
☐ 595	Craig Biggio	.15	.07	.02
☐ 596	Jose DeJesus	.05	.02	.01
☐ 597	Mickey Tettleton	.10	.05	.01
☐ 598	Chris Gwynn	.05	.02	.01
☐ 599	Rex Hudler	.05	.02	.01
☐ 600	Checklist 409-506	.05	.02	.01
☐ 601	Jim Gott	.05	.02	.01
☐ 602	Jeff Manto	.05	.02	.01
☐ 603	Nelson Liriano	.05	.02	.01
☐ 604	Mark Lemke	.05	.02	.01
☐ 605	Clay Parker	.05	.02	.01
☐ 606	Edgar Martinez	.15	.07	.02
☐ 607	Mark Whiten	.10	.05	.01
☐ 608	Ted Power	.05	.02	.01
☐ 609	Tom Bolton	.05	.02	.01
☐ 610	Tom Herr	.05	.02	.01
☐ 611	Andy Hawkins UER	.05	.02	.01
	(Pitched No-Hitter on 7/1, not 7/2)			
☐ 612	Scott Ruskin	.05	.02	.01
☐ 613	Ron Kittle	.05	.02	.01
☐ 614	John Wetteland	.10	.05	.01
☐ 615	Mike Perez	.05	.02	.01
☐ 616	Dave Clark	.05	.02	.01
☐ 617	Brent Mayne	.05	.02	.01
☐ 618	Jack Clark	.10	.05	.01
☐ 619	Marvin Freeman	.05	.02	.01
☐ 620	Edwin Nunez	.05	.02	.01
☐ 621	Russ Swan	.05	.02	.01
☐ 622	Johnny Ray	.05	.02	.01
☐ 623	Charlie O'Brien	.05	.02	.01
☐ 624	Joe Bitker	.05	.02	.01
☐ 625	Mike Marshall	.05	.02	.01
☐ 626	Otis Nixon	.05	.02	.01
☐ 627	Andy Benes	.10	.05	.01
☐ 628	Ron Oester	.05	.02	.01
☐ 629	Ted Higuera	.05	.02	.01
☐ 630	Kevin Bass	.05	.02	.01
☐ 631	Damon Berryhill	.05	.02	.01
☐ 632	Bo Jackson	.15	.07	.02
☐ 633	Brad Arnsberg	.05	.02	.01
☐ 634	Jerry Willard	.05	.02	.01
☐ 635	Tommy Greene	.10	.05	.01
☐ 636	Bob MacDonald	.05	.02	.01
☐ 637	Kirk McCaskill	.05	.02	.01
☐ 638	John Burkett	.10	.05	.01
☐ 639	Paul Abbott	.05	.02	.01
☐ 640	Todd Benzinger	.05	.02	.01
☐ 641	Todd Hundley	.10	.05	.01
☐ 642	George Bell	.05	.02	.01
☐ 643	Javier Ortiz	.05	.02	.01
☐ 644	Sid Bream	.05	.02	.01
☐ 645	Bob Welch	.05	.02	.01
☐ 646	Phil Bradley	.05	.02	.01
☐ 647	Bill Krueger	.05	.02	.01
☐ 648	Rickey Henderson	.15	.07	.02
☐ 649	Kevin Wickander	.05	.02	.01
☐ 650	Steve Balboni	.05	.02	.01
☐ 651	Gene Harris	.05	.02	.01
☐ 652	Jim Deshaies	.05	.02	.01
☐ 653	Jason Grimsley	.05	.02	.01
☐ 654	Joe Orsulak	.05	.02	.01
☐ 655	Jim Poole	.05	.02	.01
☐ 656	Felix Jose	.05	.02	.01
☐ 657	Denis Cook	.05	.02	.01
☐ 658	Tom Brookens	.05	.02	.01
☐ 659	Junior Ortiz	.05	.02	.01
☐ 660	Jeff Parrett	.05	.02	.01
☐ 661	Jerry Don Gleaton	.05	.02	.01
☐ 662	Brent Knackert	.05	.02	.01
☐ 663	Rance Mulliniks	.05	.02	.01
☐ 664	John Smiley	.05	.02	.01
☐ 665	Larry Andersen	.05	.02	.01
☐ 666	Willie McGee	.10	.05	.01
☐ 667	Chris Nabholz	.05	.02	.01
☐ 668	Brady Anderson	.10	.05	.01
☐ 669	Darren Holmes UER	.05	.02	.01
	(19 CG's, should be 0)			
☐ 670	Ken Hill	.15	.07	.02
☐ 671	Gary Varsho	.05	.02	.01
☐ 672	Bill Pecota	.05	.02	.01
☐ 673	Fred Lynn	.10	.05	.01
☐ 674	Kevin D. Brown	.05	.02	.01
☐ 675	Dan Petry	.05	.02	.01
☐ 676	Mike Jackson	.05	.02	.01
☐ 677	Wally Joyner	.15	.07	.02
☐ 678	Danny Jackson	.05	.02	.01
☐ 679	Bill Haselman	.05	.02	.01
☐ 680	Mike Boddicker	.05	.02	.01
☐ 681	Mel Rojas	.05	.02	.01
☐ 682	Roberto Alomar	.25	.11	.03
☐ 683	Dave Justice ROY	.15	.07	.02
☐ 684	Chuck Crim	.05	.02	.01
☐ 685	Matt Williams	.20	.09	.03
☐ 686	Shawon Dunston	.05	.02	.01
☐ 687	Jeff Schulz	.05	.02	.01
☐ 688	John Barfield	.05	.02	.01
☐ 689	Gerald Young	.05	.02	.01
☐ 690	Luis Gonzalez	.15	.07	.02
☐ 691	Frank Wills	.05	.02	.01
☐ 692	Chuck Finley	.10	.05	.01
☐ 693	Sandy Alomar Jr. ROY	.05	.02	.01
☐ 694	Tim Drummond	.05	.02	.01
☐ 695	Herm Winningham	.05	.02	.01
☐ 696	Darryl Strawberry	.10	.05	.01
☐ 697	Al Leiter	.05	.02	.01
☐ 698	Karl Rhodes	.05	.02	.01
☐ 699	Stan Belinda	.05	.02	.01
☐ 700	Checklist 507-604	.05	.02	.01
☐ 701	Lance Blankenship	.05	.02	.01
☐ 702	Willie Stargell PUZ	.05	.02	.01
☐ 703	Jim Gantner	.05	.02	.01
☐ 704	Reggie Harris	.05	.02	.01
☐ 705	Rob Ducey	.05	.02	.01
☐ 706	Tim Hulett	.05	.02	.01
☐ 707	Atlee Hammaker	.05	.02	.01
☐ 708	Xavier Hernandez	.05	.02	.01
☐ 709	Chuck McElroy	.05	.02	.01
☐ 710	John Mitchell	.05	.02	.01
☐ 711	Carlos Hernandez	.05	.02	.01
☐ 712	Geronimo Pena	.05	.02	.01
☐ 713	Jim Neidlinger	.05	.02	.01
☐ 714	John Orton	.05	.02	.01
☐ 715	Terry Leach	.05	.02	.01
☐ 716	Mike Stanton	.05	.02	.01
☐ 717	Walt Terrell	.05	.02	.01
☐ 718	Luis Aquino	.05	.02	.01
☐ 719	Bud Black	.05	.02	.01
	(Blue Jays uniform, but Giants logo)			
☐ 720	Bob Kipper	.05	.02	.01
☐ 721	Jeff Gray	.05	.02	.01
☐ 722	Jose Rijo	.10	.05	.01
☐ 723	Curt Young	.05	.02	.01
☐ 724	Jose Vizcaino	.05	.02	.01
☐ 725	Randy Tomlin	.05	.02	.01
☐ 726	Junior Noboa	.05	.02	.01

☐ 727	Bob Welch CY	.05	.02	.01
☐ 728	Gary Ward	.05	.02	.01
☐ 729	Rob Deer	.05	.02	.01
	(Brewers uniform, but Tigers logo)			
☐ 730	David Segui	.05	.02	.01
☐ 731	Mark Carreon	.05	.02	.01
☐ 732	Vicente Palacios	.05	.02	.01
☐ 733	Sam Horn	.05	.02	.01
☐ 734	Howard Farmer	.05	.02	.01
☐ 735	Ken Dayley	.05	.02	.01
	(Cardinals uniform, but Blue Jays logo)			
☐ 736	Kelly Mann	.05	.02	.01
☐ 737	Joe Grahe	.05	.02	.01
☐ 738	Kelly Downs	.05	.02	.01
☐ 739	Jimmy Kremers	.05	.02	.01
☐ 740	Kevin Appier	.10	.05	.01
☐ 741	Jeff Reed	.05	.02	.01
☐ 742	Jose Rijo WS	.10	.05	.01
☐ 743	Dave Rohde	.05	.02	.01
☐ 744	Dr.Dirt/Mr.Clean	.10	.05	.01
	Len Dykstra Dale Murphy UER (No '91 Donruss logo on card front)			
☐ 745	Paul Sorrento	.10	.05	.01
☐ 746	Thomas Howard	.05	.02	.01
☐ 747	Matt Stark	.05	.02	.01
☐ 748	Harold Baines	.15	.07	.02
☐ 749	Doug Dascenzo	.05	.02	.01
☐ 750	Doug Drabek CY	.10	.05	.01
☐ 751	Gary Sheffield	.15	.07	.02
☐ 752	Terry Lee	.05	.02	.01
☐ 753	Jim Vatcher	.05	.02	.01
☐ 754	Lee Stevens	.05	.02	.01
☐ 755	Randy Veres	.05	.02	.01
☐ 756	Bill Doran	.05	.02	.01
☐ 757	Gary Wayne	.05	.02	.01
☐ 758	Pedro Munoz	.10	.05	.01
☐ 759	Chris Hammond	.05	.02	.01
☐ 760	Checklist 605-702	.05	.02	.01
☐ 761	Rickey Henderson MVP	.15	.07	.02
☐ 762	Barry Bonds MVP	.15	.07	.02
☐ 763	Billy Hatcher WS	.05	.02	.01
	UER (Line 13, on should be one)			
☐ 764	Julio Machado	.05	.02	.01
☐ 765	Jose Mesa	.05	.02	.01
☐ 766	Willie Randolph WS	.05	.02	.01
☐ 767	Scott Erickson	.05	.02	.01
☐ 768	Travis Fryman	.20	.09	.03
☐ 769	Rich Rodriguez	.05	.02	.01
☐ 770	Checklist 703-770 and BC1-BC22	.05	.02	.01

1991 Donruss Elite

These special cards were inserted in the 1991 Donruss first and second series wax packs. Production was limited to a maximum of 10,000 cards for each card in the Elite series, and lesser production for the Sandberg Signature (5,000) and Ryan Legend (7,500) cards. The regular Elite cards are photos enclosed in a bronze marble borders which surround an evenly squared photo of the players. The Sandberg Signature card has a green marble border and is signed in a blue sharpie. The Nolan Ryan Legend card is a Dick Perez drawing with silver borders. The cards are all numbered on the back, 1 out of 10,000, etc. All of these special cards measure the standard, 2 1/2" by 3 1/2".

		MINT	NRMT	EXC
	COMPLETE SET (10)	1000.00	450.00	125.00
	COMMON CARD (1-8)	20.00	9.00	2.50
☐ 1	Barry Bonds	70.00	32.00	8.75
☐ 2	George Brett	120.00	55.00	15.00
☐ 3	Jose Canseco	60.00	27.00	7.50
☐ 4	Andre Dawson	40.00	18.00	5.00
☐ 5	Doug Drabek	20.00	9.00	2.50
☐ 6	Cecil Fielder	40.00	18.00	5.00
☐ 7	Rickey Henderson	40.00	18.00	5.00
☐ 8	Matt Williams	70.00	32.00	8.75
☐ L1	Nolan Ryan (Legend)	250.00	110.00	31.00
☐ S1	Ryne Sandberg (Signature Series)	350.00	160.00	45.00

1991 Donruss Rookies

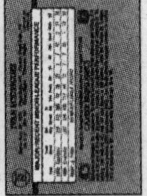

The 1991 Donruss Rookies set is a boxed set issued to honor the best rookies of the season. The cards measure the standard size (2 1/2" by 3 1/2"), and a mini puzzle featuring Hall of Famer Willie Stargell was included with the set. The fronts feature color action player photos, with white and red borders. Yellow and green stripes cut across the bottom of the card face, present-

ing the player's name and position. The words "The Rookies" and a baseball icon appear in the lower left corner of the picture. The horizontally oriented backs are printed in black on a green and white background, and present biography, statistics, and career highlights. The cards are numbered on the back. Rookie Cards showcased in this set include Jeff Bagwell, Chito Martinez, Orlando Merced, Dean Palmer, Ivan Rodriguez, Todd Van Poppel, and Rick Wilkins.

	MINT	NRMT	EXC
COMPLETE FACT.SET (56)	4.00	1.80	.50
COMMON CARD (1-56)	.05	.02	.01
☐ 1 Pat Kelly	.10	.05	.01
☐ 2 Rich DeLucia	.05	.02	.01
☐ 3 Wes Chamberlain	.05	.02	.01
☐ 4 Scott Leius	.05	.02	.01
☐ 5 Darryl Kile	.05	.02	.01
☐ 6 Milt Cuyler	.05	.02	.01
☐ 7 Todd Van Poppel	.10	.05	.01
☐ 8 Ray Lankford	.15	.07	.02
☐ 9 Brian R. Hunter	.05	.02	.01
☐ 10 Tony Perezchica	.05	.02	.01
☐ 11 Ced Landrum	.05	.02	.01
☐ 12 Dave Burba	.05	.02	.01
☐ 13 Ramon Garcia	.05	.02	.01
☐ 14 Ed Sprague	.05	.02	.01
☐ 15 Warren Newson	.05	.02	.01
☐ 16 Paul Faries	.05	.02	.01
☐ 17 Luis Gonzalez	.10	.05	.01
☐ 18 Charles Nagy	.15	.07	.02
☐ 19 Chris Hammond	.05	.02	.01
☐ 20 Frank Castillo	.05	.02	.01
☐ 21 Pedro Munoz	.15	.07	.02
☐ 22 Orlando Merced	.15	.07	.02
☐ 23 Jose Melendez	.05	.02	.01
☐ 24 Kirk Dressendorfer	.05	.02	.01
☐ 25 Heathcliff Slocumb	.15	.07	.02
☐ 26 Doug Simons	.05	.02	.01
☐ 27 Mike Timlin	.05	.02	.01
☐ 28 Jeff Fassero	.10	.05	.01
☐ 29 Mark Leiter	.05	.02	.01
☐ 30 Jeff Bagwell	2.00	.90	.25
☐ 31 Brian McRae	.15	.07	.02
☐ 32 Mark Whiten	.05	.02	.01
☐ 33 Ivan Rodriguez	.50	.23	.06
☐ 34 Wade Taylor	.05	.02	.01
☐ 35 Darren Lewis	.10	.05	.01
☐ 36 Mo Vaughn	.50	.23	.06
☐ 37 Mike Remlinger	.05	.02	.01
☐ 38 Rick Wilkins	.05	.02	.01
☐ 39 Chuck Knoblauch	.25	.11	.03
☐ 40 Kevin Morton	.05	.02	.01
☐ 41 Carlos Rodriguez	.05	.02	.01
☐ 42 Mark Lewis	.10	.05	.01
☐ 43 Brent Mayne	.05	.02	.01
☐ 44 Chris Haney	.05	.02	.01
☐ 45 Denis Boucher	.05	.02	.01
☐ 46 Mike Gardiner	.05	.02	.01
☐ 47 Jeff Johnson	.05	.02	.01
☐ 48 Dean Palmer	.10	.05	.01
☐ 49 Chuck McElroy	.05	.02	.01
☐ 50 Chris Jones	.05	.02	.01
☐ 51 Scott Kamieniecki	.05	.02	.01
☐ 52 Al Osuna	.05	.02	.01
☐ 53 Rusty Meacham	.05	.02	.01
☐ 54 Chito Martinez	.05	.02	.01
☐ 55 Reggie Jefferson	.10	.05	.01
☐ 56 Checklist 1-56	.05	.02	.01

1992 Donruss

The 1992 Donruss set contains 784 standard-size card. The front design features glossy color player photos with white borders. Two-toned blue stripes overlay the top and bottom of the picture, with the player's name printed in silver-and-black lettering above the bottom stripe. The horizontally oriented backs have a color headshot of the player (except on subset cards listed below), biography, career highlights, and recent Major League performance statistics (no earlier than 1987). The set includes Rated Rookies (1-20), AL All-Stars (21-30), Highlights (33, 94, 154, 215, 276), Rated Rookies (397-421), NL All-Stars (422-431), Highlights (434, 495, 555, 616, 677) and a puzzle of Hall of Famer Rod Carew. The cards are numbered on the back and checklisted below accordingly. Thirteen Diamond Kings cards featuring the artwork of Dick Perez were randomly inserted in first series foil packs and 13 more Diamond Kings were randomly inserted in second series foil packs. Inserted in both series foil and rack packs are 5,000 Cal Ripken Signature autographed cards, 7,500 Legend cards of Rickey Henderson, and 10,000 Elite cards each of Wade Boggs, Joe Carter, Will Clark, Dwight Gooden, Ken Griffey Jr., Tony Gwynn, Howard Johnson, Terry Pendleton, Kirby Puckett, and Frank Thomas. Rookie Cards in the set include Rod Beck, John Jaha, Pat Mahomes, Brian Williams, and Bob Zupcic.

	MINT	NRMT	EXC
COMPLETE SET (784)	12.00	5.50	1.50
COMPLETE HOBBY SET (788)	15.00	6.75	1.85
COMPLETE RETAIL SET (788)	25.00	11.00	3.10
COMPLETE SERIES 1 (396)	6.00	2.70	.75
COMPLETE SERIES 2 (388)	6.00	2.70	.75
COMP.BONUS CARDS (8)	2.00	.90	.25
COMMON CARD (1-784)	.05	.02	.01
☐ 1 Mark Wohlers RR	.10	.05	.01
☐ 2 Wil Cordero RR	.10	.05	.01
☐ 3 Kyle Abbott RR	.05	.02	.01
☐ 4 Dave Nilsson RR	.05	.02	.01

□ 5	Kenny Lofton RR	1.00	.45	.12
□ 6	Luis Mercedes RR	.05	.02	.01
□ 7	Roger Salkeld RR	.05	.02	.01
□ 8	Eddie Zosky RR	.05	.02	.01
□ 9	Todd Van Poppel RR	.10	.05	.01
□ 10	Frank Seminara RR	.05	.02	.01
□ 11	Andy Ashby RR	.05	.02	.01
□ 12	Reggie Jefferson RR	.05	.02	.01
□ 13	Ryan Klesko RR	.75	.35	.09
□ 14	Carlos Garcia RR	.10	.05	.01
□ 15	John Ramos RR	.05	.02	.01
□ 16	Eric Karros RR	.20	.09	.03
□ 17	Patrick Lennon RR	.05	.02	.01
□ 18	Eddie Taubensee RR	.05	.02	.01
□ 19	Roberto Hernandez RR	.10	.05	.01
□ 20	D.J. Dozier RR	.05	.02	.01
□ 21	Dave Henderson AS	.05	.02	.01
□ 22	Cal Ripken AS	.50	.23	.06
□ 23	Wade Boggs AS	.10	.05	.01
□ 24	Ken Griffey Jr. AS	.75	.35	.09
□ 25	Jack Morris AS	.10	.05	.01
□ 26	Danny Tartabull AS	.10	.05	.01
□ 27	Cecil Fielder AS	.10	.05	.01
□ 28	Roberto Alomar AS	.15	.07	.02
□ 29	Sandy Alomar Jr. AS	.05	.02	.01
□ 30	Rickey Henderson AS	.15	.07	.02
□ 31	Ken Hill	.15	.07	.02
□ 32	John Habyan	.05	.02	.01
□ 33	Otis Nixon HL	.05	.02	.01
□ 34	Tim Wallach	.05	.02	.01
□ 35	Cal Ripken	1.00	.45	.12
□ 36	Gary Carter	.15	.07	.02
□ 37	Juan Agosto	.05	.02	.01
□ 38	Doug Dascenzo	.05	.02	.01
□ 39	Kirk Gibson	.15	.07	.02
□ 40	Benito Santiago	.05	.02	.01
□ 41	Otis Nixon	.05	.02	.01
□ 42	Andy Allanson	.05	.02	.01
□ 43	Brian Holman	.05	.02	.01
□ 44	Dick Schofield	.05	.02	.01
□ 45	Dave Magadan	.05	.02	.01
□ 46	Rafael Palmeiro	.15	.07	.02
□ 47	Jody Reed	.05	.02	.01
□ 48	Ivan Calderon	.05	.02	.01
□ 49	Greg W. Harris	.05	.02	.01
□ 50	Chris Sabo	.05	.02	.01
□ 51	Paul Molitor	.15	.07	.02
□ 52	Robby Thompson	.05	.02	.01
□ 53	Dave Smith	.05	.02	.01
□ 54	Mark Davis	.05	.02	.01
□ 55	Kevin Brown	.10	.05	.01
□ 56	Donn Pall	.05	.02	.01
□ 57	Len Dykstra	.15	.07	.02
□ 58	Roberto Alomar	.20	.09	.03
□ 59	Jeff D. Robinson	.05	.02	.01
□ 60	Willie McGee	.10	.05	.01
□ 61	Jay Buhner	.15	.07	.02
□ 62	Mike Pagliarulo	.05	.02	.01
□ 63	Paul O'Neill	.15	.07	.02
□ 64	Hubie Brooks	.05	.02	.01
□ 65	Kelly Gruber	.05	.02	.01
□ 66	Ken Caminiti	.15	.07	.02
□ 67	Gary Redus	.05	.02	.01
□ 68	Harold Baines	.15	.07	.02
□ 69	Charlie Hough	.10	.05	.01
□ 70	B.J. Surhoff	.05	.02	.01
□ 71	Walt Weiss	.05	.02	.01
□ 72	Shawn Hillegas	.05	.02	.01
□ 73	Roberto Kelly	.10	.05	.01
□ 74	Jeff Ballard	.05	.02	.01
□ 75	Craig Biggio	.15	.07	.02
□ 76	Pat Combs	.05	.02	.01
□ 77	Jeff M. Robinson	.05	.02	.01
□ 78	Tim Belcher	.05	.02	.01
□ 79	Cris Carpenter	.05	.02	.01
□ 80	Checklist 1-79	.05	.02	.01
□ 81	Steve Avery	.15	.07	.02
□ 82	Chris James	.05	.02	.01
□ 83	Brian Harper	.05	.02	.01
□ 84	Charlie Leibrandt	.05	.02	.01
□ 85	Mickey Tettleton	.10	.05	.01
□ 86	Pete O'Brien	.05	.02	.01
□ 87	Danny Darwin	.05	.02	.01
□ 88	Bob Walk	.05	.02	.01
□ 89	Jeff Reardon	.10	.05	.01
□ 90	Bobby Rose	.05	.02	.01
□ 91	Danny Jackson	.05	.02	.01
□ 92	John Morris	.05	.02	.01
□ 93	Bud Black	.05	.02	.01
□ 94	Tommy Greene HL	.05	.02	.01
□ 95	Rick Aguilera	.10	.05	.01
□ 96	Gary Gaetti	.05	.02	.01
□ 97	David Cone	.15	.07	.02
□ 98	John Olerud	.10	.05	.01
□ 99	Joel Skinner	.05	.02	.01
□ 100	Jay Bell	.10	.05	.01
□ 101	Bob Milacki	.05	.02	.01
□ 102	Norm Charlton	.05	.02	.01
□ 103	Chuck Crim	.05	.02	.01
□ 104	Terry Steinbach	.10	.05	.01
□ 105	Juan Samuel	.05	.02	.01
□ 106	Steve Howe	.05	.02	.01
□ 107	Rafael Belliard	.05	.02	.01
□ 108	Joey Cora	.05	.02	.01
□ 109	Tommy Greene	.05	.02	.01
□ 110	Gregg Olson	.05	.02	.01
□ 111	Frank Tanana	.05	.02	.01
□ 112	Lee Smith	.15	.07	.02
□ 113	Greg A. Harris	.05	.02	.01
□ 114	Dwayne Henry	.05	.02	.01
□ 115	Chili Davis	.15	.07	.02
□ 116	Kent Mercker	.05	.02	.01
□ 117	Brian Barnes	.05	.02	.01
□ 118	Rich DeLucia	.05	.02	.01
□ 119	Andre Dawson	.15	.07	.02
□ 120	Carlos Baerga	.30	.14	.04
□ 121	Mike LaValliere	.05	.02	.01
□ 122	Jeff Gray	.05	.02	.01
□ 123	Bruce Hurst	.05	.02	.01
□ 124	Alvin Davis	.05	.02	.01
□ 125	John Candelaria	.05	.02	.01
□ 126	Matt Nokes	.05	.02	.01
□ 127	George Bell	.10	.05	.01
□ 128	Bret Saberhagen	.15	.07	.02
□ 129	Jeff Russell	.05	.02	.01
□ 130	Jim Abbott	.15	.07	.02
□ 131	Bill Gullickson	.05	.02	.01
□ 132	Todd Zeile	.10	.05	.01
□ 133	Dave Winfield	.15	.07	.02
□ 134	Wally Whitehurst	.05	.02	.01
□ 135	Matt Williams	.20	.09	.03
□ 136	Tom Browning	.05	.02	.01
□ 137	Marquis Grissom	.15	.07	.02
□ 138	Erik Hanson	.05	.02	.01
□ 139	Rob Dibble	.05	.02	.01
□ 140	Don August	.05	.02	.01
□ 141	Tom Henke	.10	.05	.01
□ 142	Dan Pasqua	.05	.02	.01
□ 143	George Brett	.40	.18	.05
□ 144	Jerald Clark	.05	.02	.01
□ 145	Robin Ventura	.15	.07	.02
□ 146	Dale Murphy	.15	.07	.02

☐	147	Dennis Eckersley	.15	.07	.02			
☐	148	Eric Yelding	.05	.02	.01			
☐	149	Mario Diaz	.05	.02	.01			
☐	150	Casey Candaele	.05	.02	.01			
☐	151	Steve Olin	.05	.02	.01			
☐	152	Luis Salazar	.05	.02	.01			
☐	153	Kevin Maas	.05	.02	.01			
☐	154	Nolan Ryan HL	.40	.18	.05			
☐	155	Barry Jones	.05	.02	.01			
☐	156	Chris Hoiles	.10	.05	.01			
☐	157	Bobby Ojeda	.05	.02	.01			
☐	158	Pedro Guerrero	.05	.02	.01			
☐	159	Paul Assenmacher	.05	.02	.01			
☐	160	Checklist 80-157	.05	.02	.01			
☐	161	Mike Macfarlane	.05	.02	.01			
☐	162	Craig Lefferts	.05	.02	.01			
☐	163	Brian Hunter	.05	.02	.01			
☐	164	Alan Trammell	.15	.07	.02			
☐	165	Ken Griffey Jr.	1.50	.70	.19			
☐	166	Lance Parrish	.10	.05	.01			
☐	167	Brian Downing	.05	.02	.01			
☐	168	John Barfield	.05	.02	.01			
☐	169	Jack Clark	.10	.05	.01			
☐	170	Chris Nabholz	.05	.02	.01			
☐	171	Tim Teufel	.05	.02	.01			
☐	172	Chris Hammond	.05	.02	.01			
☐	173	Robin Yount	.15	.07	.02			
☐	174	Dave Righetti	.05	.02	.01			
☐	175	Joe Girardi	.05	.02	.01			
☐	176	Mike Boddicker	.05	.02	.01			
☐	177	Dean Palmer	.10	.05	.01			
☐	178	Greg Hibbard	.05	.02	.01			
☐	179	Randy Ready	.05	.02	.01			
☐	180	Devon White	.10	.05	.01			
☐	181	Mark Eichhorn	.05	.02	.01			
☐	182	Mike Felder	.05	.02	.01			
☐	183	Joe Klink	.05	.02	.01			
☐	184	Steve Bedrosian	.05	.02	.01			
☐	185	Barry Larkin	.15	.07	.02			
☐	186	John Franco	.15	.07	.02			
☐	187	Ed Sprague	.10	.05	.01			
☐	188	Mark Portugal	.05	.02	.01			
☐	189	Jose Lind	.05	.02	.01			
☐	190	Bob Welch	.05	.02	.01			
☐	191	Alex Fernandez	.15	.07	.02			
☐	192	Gary Sheffield	.15	.07	.02			
☐	193	Rickey Henderson	.15	.07	.02			
☐	194	Rod Nichols	.05	.02	.01			
☐	195	Scott Kamieniecki	.05	.02	.01			
☐	196	Mike Flanagan	.05	.02	.01			
☐	197	Steve Finley	.10	.05	.01			
☐	198	Darren Daulton	.15	.07	.02			
☐	199	Leo Gomez	.05	.02	.01			
☐	200	Mike Morgan	.05	.02	.01			
☐	201	Bob Tewksbury	.05	.02	.01			
☐	202	Sid Bream	.05	.02	.01			
☐	203	Sandy Alomar Jr.	.10	.05	.01			
☐	204	Greg Gagne	.05	.02	.01			
☐	205	Juan Berenguer	.05	.02	.01			
☐	206	Cecil Fielder	.15	.07	.02			
☐	207	Randy Johnson	.25	.11	.03			
☐	208	Tony Pena	.05	.02	.01			
☐	209	Doug Drabek	.10	.05	.01			
☐	210	Wade Boggs	.15	.07	.02			
☐	211	Bryan Harvey	.10	.05	.01			
☐	212	Jose Vizcaino	.05	.02	.01			
☐	213	Alonzo Powell	.05	.02	.01			
☐	214	Will Clark	.15	.07	.02			
☐	215	Rickey Henderson HL	.15	.07	.02			
☐	216	Jack Morris	.15	.07	.02			
☐	217	Junior Felix	.05	.02	.01			
☐	218	Vince Coleman	.05	.02	.01			
☐	219	Jimmy Key	.10	.05	.01			
☐	220	Alex Cole	.05	.02	.01			
☐	221	Bill Landrum	.05	.02	.01			
☐	222	Randy Milligan	.05	.02	.01			
☐	223	Jose Rijo	.10	.05	.01			
☐	224	Greg Vaughn	.10	.05	.01			
☐	225	Dave Stewart	.15	.07	.02			
☐	226	Lenny Harris	.05	.02	.01			
☐	227	Scott Sanderson	.05	.02	.01			
☐	228	Jeff Blauser	.10	.05	.01			
☐	229	Ozzie Guillen	.10	.05	.01			
☐	230	John Kruk	.15	.07	.02			
☐	231	Bob Melvin	.05	.02	.01			
☐	232	Milt Cuyler	.05	.02	.01			
☐	233	Felix Jose	.05	.02	.01			
☐	234	Ellis Burks	.10	.05	.01			
☐	235	Pete Harnisch	.05	.02	.01			
☐	236	Kevin Tapani	.05	.02	.01			
☐	237	Terry Pendleton	.15	.07	.02			
☐	238	Mark Gardner	.05	.02	.01			
☐	239	Harold Reynolds	.05	.02	.01			
☐	240	Checklist 158-237	.05	.02	.01			
☐	241	Mike Harkey	.05	.02	.01			
☐	242	Felix Fermin	.05	.02	.01			
☐	243	Barry Bonds	.25	.11	.03			
☐	244	Roger Clemens	.15	.07	.02			
☐	245	Dennis Rasmussen	.05	.02	.01			
☐	246	Jose DeLeon	.05	.02	.01			
☐	247	Orel Hershiser	.15	.07	.02			
☐	248	Mel Hall	.05	.02	.01			
☐	249	Rick Wilkins	.05	.02	.01			
☐	250	Tom Gordon	.05	.02	.01			
☐	251	Kevin Reimer	.05	.02	.01			
☐	252	Luis Polonia	.05	.02	.01			
☐	253	Mike Henneman	.05	.02	.01			
☐	254	Tom Pagnozzi	.05	.02	.01			
☐	255	Chuck Finley	.05	.02	.01			
☐	256	Mackey Sasser	.05	.02	.01			
☐	257	John Burkett	.10	.05	.01			
☐	258	Hal Morris	.10	.05	.01			
☐	259	Larry Walker	.15	.07	.02			
☐	260	Billy Swift	.05	.02	.01			
☐	261	Joe Oliver	.05	.02	.01			
☐	262	Julio Machado	.05	.02	.01			
☐	263	Todd Stottlemyre	.05	.02	.01			
☐	264	Matt Merullo	.05	.02	.01			
☐	265	Brent Mayne	.05	.02	.01			
☐	266	Thomas Howard	.05	.02	.01			
☐	267	Lance Johnson	.05	.02	.01			
☐	268	Terry Mulholland	.05	.02	.01			
☐	269	Rick Honeycutt	.05	.02	.01			
☐	270	Luis Gonzalez	.10	.05	.01			
☐	271	Jose Guzman	.05	.02	.01			
☐	272	Jimmy Jones	.05	.02	.01			
☐	273	Mark Lewis	.05	.02	.01			
☐	274	Rene Gonzales	.05	.02	.01			
☐	275	Jeff Johnson	.05	.02	.01			
☐	276	Dennis Martinez HL	.05	.02	.01			
☐	277	Delino DeShields	.10	.05	.01			
☐	278	Sam Horn	.05	.02	.01			
☐	279	Kevin Gross	.05	.02	.01			
☐	280	Jose Oquendo	.05	.02	.01			
☐	281	Mark Grace	.15	.07	.02			
☐	282	Mark Gubicza	.05	.02	.01			
☐	283	Fred McGriff	.15	.07	.02			
☐	284	Ron Gant	.15	.07	.02			
☐	285	Lou Whitaker	.15	.07	.02			
☐	286	Edgar Martinez	.15	.07	.02			
☐	287	Ron Tingley	.05	.02	.01			
☐	288	Kevin McReynolds	.05	.02	.01			

☐ 289	Ivan Rodriguez	.15	.07	.02	☐ 360	Zane Smith	.05	.02	.01
☐ 290	Mike Gardiner	.05	.02	.01	☐ 361	Bill Pecota	.05	.02	.01
☐ 291	Chris Haney	.05	.02	.01	☐ 362	Tony Fernandez	.05	.02	.01
☐ 292	Darrin Jackson	.05	.02	.01	☐ 363	Glenn Braggs	.05	.02	.01
☐ 293	Bill Doran	.05	.02	.01	☐ 364	Bill Spiers	.05	.02	.01
☐ 294	Ted Higuera	.05	.02	.01	☐ 365	Vicente Palacios	.05	.02	.01
☐ 295	Jeff Brantley	.05	.02	.01	☐ 366	Tim Burke	.05	.02	.01
☐ 296	Les Lancaster	.05	.02	.01	☐ 367	Randy Tomlin	.05	.02	.01
☐ 297	Jim Eisenreich	.05	.02	.01	☐ 368	Kenny Rogers	.10	.05	.01
☐ 298	Ruben Sierra	.15	.07	.02	☐ 369	Brett Butler	.15	.07	.02
☐ 299	Scott Radinsky	.05	.02	.01	☐ 370	Pat Kelly	.05	.02	.01
☐ 300	Jose DeJesus	.05	.02	.01	☐ 371	Bip Roberts	.05	.02	.01
☐ 301	Mike Timlin	.05	.02	.01	☐ 372	Gregg Jefferies	.15	.07	.02
☐ 302	Luis Sojo	.05	.02	.01	☐ 373	Kevin Bass	.05	.02	.01
☐ 303	Kelly Downs	.05	.02	.01	☐ 374	Ron Karkovice	.05	.02	.01
☐ 304	Scott Bankhead	.05	.02	.01	☐ 375	Paul Gibson	.05	.02	.01
☐ 305	Pedro Munoz	.10	.05	.01	☐ 376	Bernard Gilkey	.10	.05	.01
☐ 306	Scott Scudder	.05	.02	.01	☐ 377	Dave Gallagher	.05	.02	.01
☐ 307	Kevin Elster	.05	.02	.01	☐ 378	Bill Wegman	.05	.02	.01
☐ 308	Duane Ward	.05	.02	.01	☐ 379	Pat Borders	.05	.02	.01
☐ 309	Darryl Kile	.05	.02	.01	☐ 380	Ed Whitson	.05	.02	.01
☐ 310	Orlando Merced	.05	.02	.01	☐ 381	Gilberto Reyes	.05	.02	.01
☐ 311	Dave Henderson	.05	.02	.01	☐ 382	Russ Swan	.05	.02	.01
☐ 312	Tim Raines	.15	.07	.02	☐ 383	Andy Van Slyke	.10	.05	.01
☐ 313	Mark Lee	.05	.02	.01	☐ 384	Wes Chamberlain	.05	.02	.01
☐ 314	Mike Gallego	.05	.02	.01	☐ 385	Steve Chitren	.05	.02	.01
☐ 315	Charles Nagy	.10	.05	.01	☐ 386	Greg Olson	.05	.02	.01
☐ 316	Jesse Barfield	.05	.02	.01	☐ 387	Brian McRae	.15	.07	.02
☐ 317	Todd Frohwirth	.05	.02	.01	☐ 388	Rich Rodriguez	.05	.02	.01
☐ 318	Al Osuna	.05	.02	.01	☐ 389	Steve Decker	.05	.02	.01
☐ 319	Darrin Fletcher	.05	.02	.01	☐ 390	Chuck Knoblauch	.15	.07	.02
☐ 320	Checklist 238-316	.05	.02	.01	☐ 391	Bobby Witt	.05	.02	.01
☐ 321	David Segui	.05	.02	.01	☐ 392	Eddie Murray	.15	.07	.02
☐ 322	Stan Javier	.05	.02	.01	☐ 393	Juan Gonzalez	.40	.18	.05
☐ 323	Bryn Smith	.05	.02	.01	☐ 394	Scott Ruskin	.05	.02	.01
☐ 324	Jeff Treadway	.05	.02	.01	☐ 395	Jay Howell	.05	.02	.01
☐ 325	Mark Whiten	.10	.05	.01	☐ 396	Checklist 317-396	.05	.02	.01
☐ 326	Kent Hrbek	.10	.05	.01	☐ 397	Royce Clayton RR	.10	.05	.01
☐ 327	Dave Justice	.15	.07	.02	☐ 398	John Jaha RR	.15	.07	.02
☐ 328	Tony Phillips	.15	.07	.02	☐ 399	Dan Wilson RR	.05	.02	.01
☐ 329	Rob Murphy	.05	.02	.01	☐ 400	Archie Corbin RR	.05	.02	.01
☐ 330	Kevin Morton	.05	.02	.01	☐ 401	Barry Manuel RR	.05	.02	.01
☐ 331	John Smiley	.05	.02	.01	☐ 402	Kim Batiste RR	.05	.02	.01
☐ 332	Luis Rivera	.05	.02	.01	☐ 403	Pat Mahomes RR	.05	.02	.01
☐ 333	Wally Joyner	.10	.05	.01	☐ 404	Dave Fleming RR	.05	.02	.01
☐ 334	Heathcliff Slocumb	.10	.05	.01	☐ 405	Jeff Juden RR	.05	.02	.01
☐ 335	Rick Cerone	.05	.02	.01	☐ 406	Jim Thome RR	.75	.35	.09
☐ 336	Mike Remlinger	.05	.02	.01	☐ 407	Sam Militello RR	.05	.02	.01
☐ 337	Mike Moore	.05	.02	.01	☐ 408	Jeff Nelson RR	.05	.02	.01
☐ 338	Lloyd McClendon	.05	.02	.01	☐ 409	Anthony Young RR	.05	.02	.01
☐ 339	Al Newman	.05	.02	.01	☐ 410	Tino Martinez RR	.15	.07	.02
☐ 340	Kirk McCaskill	.05	.02	.01	☐ 411	Jeff Mutis RR	.05	.02	.01
☐ 341	Howard Johnson	.05	.02	.01	☐ 412	Rey Sanchez RR	.05	.02	.01
☐ 342	Greg Myers	.05	.02	.01	☐ 413	Chris Gardner RR	.05	.02	.01
☐ 343	Kal Daniels	.05	.02	.01	☐ 414	John Vander Wal RR	.05	.02	.01
☐ 344	Bernie Williams	.15	.07	.02	☐ 415	Reggie Sanders	.20	.09	.03
☐ 345	Shane Mack	.05	.02	.01	☐ 416	Brian Williams RR	.05	.02	.01
☐ 346	Gary Thurman	.05	.02	.01	☐ 417	Mo Sanford RR	.05	.02	.01
☐ 347	Dante Bichette	.20	.09	.03	☐ 418	David Weathers RR	.05	.02	.01
☐ 348	Mark McGwire	.15	.07	.02	☐ 419	Hector Fajardo RR	.05	.02	.01
☐ 349	Travis Fryman	.15	.07	.02	☐ 420	Steve Foster RR	.05	.02	.01
☐ 350	Ray Lankford	.10	.05	.01	☐ 421	Lance Dickson RR	.05	.02	.01
☐ 351	Mike Jeffcoat	.05	.02	.01	☐ 422	Andre Dawson AS	.10	.05	.01
☐ 352	Jack McDowell	.15	.07	.02	☐ 423	Ozzie Smith AS	.15	.07	.02
☐ 353	Mitch Williams	.10	.05	.01	☐ 424	Chris Sabo AS	.05	.02	.01
☐ 354	Mike Devereaux	.10	.05	.01	☐ 425	Tony Gwynn AS	.15	.07	.02
☐ 355	Andres Galarraga	.15	.07	.02	☐ 426	Tom Glavine AS	.10	.05	.01
☐ 356	Henry Cotto	.05	.02	.01	☐ 427	Bobby Bonilla AS	.10	.05	.01
☐ 357	Scott Bailes	.05	.02	.01	☐ 428	Will Clark AS	.15	.07	.02
☐ 358	Jeff Bagwell	.50	.23	.06	☐ 429	Ryne Sandberg AS	.15	.07	.02
☐ 359	Scott Leius	.05	.02	.01	☐ 430	Benito Santiago AS	.05	.02	.01

☐ 431 Ivan Calderon AS	.05	.02	.01
☐ 432 Ozzie Smith	.20	.09	.03
☐ 433 Tim Leary	.05	.02	.01
☐ 434 Bret Saberhagen HL	.10	.05	.01
☐ 435 Mel Rojas	.05	.02	.01
☐ 436 Ben McDonald	.10	.05	.01
☐ 437 Tim Crews	.05	.02	.01
☐ 438 Rex Hudler	.05	.02	.01
☐ 439 Chico Walker	.05	.02	.01
☐ 440 Kurt Stillwell	.05	.02	.01
☐ 441 Tony Gwynn	.30	.14	.04
☐ 442 John Smoltz	.15	.07	.02
☐ 443 Lloyd Moseby	.05	.02	.01
☐ 444 Mike Schooler	.05	.02	.01
☐ 445 Joe Grahe	.05	.02	.01
☐ 446 Dwight Gooden	.05	.02	.01
☐ 447 Oil Can Boyd	.05	.02	.01
☐ 448 John Marzano	.05	.02	.01
☐ 449 Bret Barberie	.05	.02	.01
☐ 450 Mike Maddux	.05	.02	.01
☐ 451 Jeff Reed	.05	.02	.01
☐ 452 Dale Sveum	.05	.02	.01
☐ 453 Jose Uribe	.05	.02	.01
☐ 454 Bob Scanlan	.05	.02	.01
☐ 455 Kevin Appier	.10	.05	.01
☐ 456 Jeff Huson	.05	.02	.01
☐ 457 Ken Patterson	.05	.02	.01
☐ 458 Ricky Jordan	.05	.02	.01
☐ 459 Tom Candiotti	.05	.02	.01
☐ 460 Lee Stevens	.05	.02	.01
☐ 461 Rod Beck	.25	.11	.03
☐ 462 Dave Valle	.05	.02	.01
☐ 463 Scott Erickson	.05	.02	.01
☐ 464 Chris Jones	.05	.02	.01
☐ 465 Mark Carreon	.05	.02	.01
☐ 466 Rob Ducey	.05	.02	.01
☐ 467 Jim Corsi	.05	.02	.01
☐ 468 Jeff King	.05	.02	.01
☐ 469 Curt Young	.05	.02	.01
☐ 470 Bo Jackson	.15	.07	.02
☐ 471 Chris Bosio	.05	.02	.01
☐ 472 Jamie Quirk	.05	.02	.01
☐ 473 Jesse Orosco	.05	.02	.01
☐ 474 Alvaro Espinoza	.05	.02	.01
☐ 475 Joe Orsulak	.05	.02	.01
☐ 476 Checklist 397-477	.05	.02	.01
☐ 477 Gerald Young	.05	.02	.01
☐ 478 Wally Backman	.05	.02	.01
☐ 479 Juan Bell	.05	.02	.01
☐ 480 Mike Scioscia	.05	.02	.01
☐ 481 Omar Olivares	.05	.02	.01
☐ 482 Francisco Cabrera	.05	.02	.01
☐ 483 Greg Swindell UER	.05	.02	.01
(Shown on Indians, but listed on Reds)			
☐ 484 Terry Leach	.05	.02	.01
☐ 485 Tommy Gregg	.05	.02	.01
☐ 486 Scott Aldred	.05	.02	.01
☐ 487 Greg Briley	.05	.02	.01
☐ 488 Phil Plantier	.10	.05	.01
☐ 489 Curtis Wilkerson	.05	.02	.01
☐ 490 Tom Brunansky	.05	.02	.01
☐ 491 Mike Fetters	.05	.02	.01
☐ 492 Frank Castillo	.05	.02	.01
☐ 493 Joe Boever	.05	.02	.01
☐ 494 Kirt Manwaring	.05	.02	.01
☐ 495 Wilson Alvarez HL	.10	.05	.01
☐ 496 Gene Larkin	.05	.02	.01
☐ 497 Gary DiSarcina	.05	.02	.01
☐ 498 Frank Viola	.05	.02	.01
☐ 499 Manuel Lee	.05	.02	.01
☐ 500 Albert Belle	.50	.23	.06
☐ 501 Stan Belinda	.05	.02	.01
☐ 502 Dwight Evans	.10	.05	.01
☐ 503 Eric Davis	.10	.05	.01
☐ 504 Darren Holmes	.05	.02	.01
☐ 505 Mike Bordick	.05	.02	.01
☐ 506 Dave Hansen	.05	.02	.01
☐ 507 Lee Guetterman	.05	.02	.01
☐ 508 Keith Mitchell	.05	.02	.01
☐ 509 Melido Perez	.05	.02	.01
☐ 510 Dickie Thon	.05	.02	.01
☐ 511 Mark Williamson	.05	.02	.01
☐ 512 Mark Salas	.05	.02	.01
☐ 513 Milt Thompson	.05	.02	.01
☐ 514 Mo Vaughn	.40	.18	.05
☐ 515 Jim Deshaies	.05	.02	.01
☐ 516 Rich Garces	.05	.02	.01
☐ 517 Lonnie Smith	.05	.02	.01
☐ 518 Spike Owen	.05	.02	.01
☐ 519 Tracy Jones	.05	.02	.01
☐ 520 Greg Maddux	.75	.35	.09
☐ 521 Carlos Martinez	.05	.02	.01
☐ 522 Neal Heaton	.05	.02	.01
☐ 523 Mike Greenwell	.15	.07	.02
☐ 524 Andy Benes	.10	.05	.01
☐ 525 Jeff Schaefer UER	.05	.02	.01
(Photo actually Tino Martinez)			
☐ 526 Mike Sharperson	.05	.02	.01
☐ 527 Wade Taylor	.05	.02	.01
☐ 528 Jerome Walton	.05	.02	.01
☐ 529 Storm Davis	.05	.02	.01
☐ 530 Jose Hernandez	.05	.02	.01
☐ 531 Mark Langston	.15	.07	.02
☐ 532 Rob Deer	.05	.02	.01
☐ 533 Geronimo Pena	.05	.02	.01
☐ 534 Juan Guzman	.10	.05	.01
☐ 535 Pete Schourek	.10	.05	.01
☐ 536 Todd Benzinger	.05	.02	.01
☐ 537 Billy Hatcher	.05	.02	.01
☐ 538 Tom Foley	.05	.02	.01
☐ 539 Dave Cochrane	.05	.02	.01
☐ 540 Mariano Duncan	.05	.02	.01
☐ 541 Edwin Nunez	.05	.02	.01
☐ 542 Rance Mulliniks	.05	.02	.01
☐ 543 Carlton Fisk	.15	.07	.02
☐ 544 Luis Aquino	.05	.02	.01
☐ 545 Ricky Bones	.05	.02	.01
☐ 546 Craig Grebeck	.05	.02	.01
☐ 547 Charlie Hayes	.10	.05	.01
☐ 548 Jose Canseco	.15	.07	.02
☐ 549 Andujar Cedeno	.05	.02	.01
☐ 550 Geno Petralli	.05	.02	.01
☐ 551 Javier Ortiz	.05	.02	.01
☐ 552 Rudy Seanez	.05	.02	.01
☐ 553 Rich Gedman	.05	.02	.01
☐ 554 Eric Plunk	.05	.02	.01
☐ 555 Nolan Ryan HL	.25	.11	.03
(With Rich Gossage)			
☐ 556 Checklist 478-555	.05	.02	.01
☐ 557 Greg Colbrunn	.10	.05	.01
☐ 558 Chito Martinez	.05	.02	.01
☐ 559 Darryl Strawberry	.10	.05	.01
☐ 560 Luis Alicea	.05	.02	.01
☐ 561 Dwight Smith	.05	.02	.01
☐ 562 Terry Shumpert	.05	.02	.01
☐ 563 Jim Vatcher	.05	.02	.01
☐ 564 Deion Sanders	.20	.09	.03
☐ 565 Walt Terrell	.05	.02	.01
☐ 566 Dave Burba	.05	.02	.01
☐ 567 Dave Howard	.05	.02	.01

☐ 568 Todd Hundley	.05	.02	.01
☐ 569 Jack Daugherty	.05	.02	.01
☐ 570 Scott Cooper	.10	.05	.01
☐ 571 Bill Sampen	.05	.02	.01
☐ 572 Jose Melendez	.05	.02	.01
☐ 573 Freddie Benavides	.05	.02	.01
☐ 574 Jim Gantner	.05	.02	.01
☐ 575 Trevor Wilson	.05	.02	.01
☐ 576 Ryne Sandberg	.25	.11	.03
☐ 577 Kevin Seitzer	.05	.02	.01
☐ 578 Gerald Alexander	.05	.02	.01
☐ 579 Mike Huff	.05	.02	.01
☐ 580 Von Hayes	.05	.02	.01
☐ 581 Derek Bell	.10	.05	.01
☐ 582 Mike Stanley	.10	.05	.01
☐ 583 Kevin Mitchell	.10	.05	.01
☐ 584 Mike Jackson	.05	.02	.01
☐ 585 Dan Gladden	.05	.02	.01
☐ 586 Ted Power UER	.05	.02	.01
(Wrong year given for signing with Reds)			
☐ 587 Jeff Innis	.05	.02	.01
☐ 588 Bob MacDonald	.05	.02	.01
☐ 589 Jose Tolentino	.05	.02	.01
☐ 590 Bob Patterson	.05	.02	.01
☐ 591 Scott Brosius	.05	.02	.01
☐ 592 Frank Thomas	1.50	.70	.19
☐ 593 Darryl Hamilton	.10	.05	.01
☐ 594 Kirk Dressendorfer	.05	.02	.01
☐ 595 Jeff Shaw	.05	.02	.01
☐ 596 Don Mattingly	.50	.23	.06
☐ 597 Glenn Davis	.05	.02	.01
☐ 598 Andy Mota	.05	.02	.01
☐ 599 Jason Grimsley	.05	.02	.01
☐ 600 Jimmy Poole	.05	.02	.01
☐ 601 Jim Gott	.05	.02	.01
☐ 602 Stan Royer	.05	.02	.01
☐ 603 Marvin Freeman	.05	.02	.01
☐ 604 Denis Boucher	.05	.02	.01
☐ 605 Denny Neagle	.05	.02	.01
☐ 606 Mark Lemke	.05	.02	.01
☐ 607 Jerry Don Gleaton	.05	.02	.01
☐ 608 Brent Knackert	.05	.02	.01
☐ 609 Carlos Quintana	.05	.02	.01
☐ 610 Bobby Bonilla	.15	.07	.02
☐ 611 Joe Hesketh	.05	.02	.01
☐ 612 Daryl Boston	.05	.02	.01
☐ 613 Shawon Dunston	.05	.02	.01
☐ 614 Danny Cox	.05	.02	.01
☐ 615 Darren Lewis	.10	.05	.01
☐ 616 Braves No-Hitter UER	.05	.02	.01
Kent Mercker (Misspelled Merker on card front) Alejandro Pena Mark Wohlers			
☐ 617 Kirby Puckett	.30	.14	.04
☐ 618 Franklin Stubbs	.05	.02	.01
☐ 619 Chris Donnels	.05	.02	.01
☐ 620 David Wells UER	.05	.02	.01
(Career Highlights in black not red)			
☐ 621 Mike Aldrete	.05	.02	.01
☐ 622 Bob Kipper	.05	.02	.01
☐ 623 Anthony Telford	.05	.02	.01
☐ 624 Randy Myers	.15	.07	.02
☐ 625 Willie Randolph	.10	.05	.01
☐ 626 Joe Slusarski	.05	.02	.01
☐ 627 John Wetteland	.05	.02	.01
☐ 628 Greg Cadaret	.05	.02	.01
☐ 629 Tom Glavine	.15	.07	.02
☐ 630 Wilson Alvarez	.15	.07	.02
☐ 631 Wally Ritchie	.05	.02	.01
☐ 632 Mike Mussina	.25	.11	.03
☐ 633 Mark Leiter	.05	.02	.01
☐ 634 Gerald Perry	.05	.02	.01
☐ 635 Matt Young	.05	.02	.01
☐ 636 Checklist 556-635	.05	.02	.01
☐ 637 Scott Hemond	.05	.02	.01
☐ 638 David West	.05	.02	.01
☐ 639 Jim Clancy	.05	.02	.01
☐ 640 Doug Piatt UER	.05	.02	.01
(Not born in 1955 as on card; incorrect info on How Acquired)			
☐ 641 Omar Vizquel	.05	.02	.01
☐ 642 Rick Sutcliffe	.10	.05	.01
☐ 643 Glenallen Hill	.05	.02	.01
☐ 644 Gary Varsho	.05	.02	.01
☐ 645 Tony Fossas	.05	.02	.01
☐ 646 Jack Howell	.05	.02	.01
☐ 647 Jim Campanis	.05	.02	.01
☐ 648 Chris Gwynn	.05	.02	.01
☐ 649 Jim Leyritz	.05	.02	.01
☐ 650 Chuck McElroy	.05	.02	.01
☐ 651 Sean Berry	.10	.05	.01
☐ 652 Donald Harris	.05	.02	.01
☐ 653 Don Slaught	.05	.02	.01
☐ 654 Rusty Meacham	.05	.02	.01
☐ 655 Scott Terry	.05	.02	.01
☐ 656 Ramon Martinez	.15	.07	.02
☐ 657 Keith Miller	.05	.02	.01
☐ 658 Ramon Garcia	.05	.02	.01
☐ 659 Milt Hill	.05	.02	.01
☐ 660 Steve Frey	.05	.02	.01
☐ 661 Bob McClure	.05	.02	.01
☐ 662 Ced Landrum	.05	.02	.01
☐ 663 Doug Henry	.05	.02	.01
☐ 664 Candy Maldonado	.05	.02	.01
☐ 665 Carl Willis	.05	.02	.01
☐ 666 Jeff Montgomery	.10	.05	.01
☐ 667 Craig Shipley	.05	.02	.01
☐ 668 Warren Newson	.05	.02	.01
☐ 669 Mickey Morandini	.05	.02	.01
☐ 670 Brook Jacoby	.05	.02	.01
☐ 671 Ryan Bowen	.05	.02	.01
☐ 672 Bill Krueger	.05	.02	.01
☐ 673 Rob Mallicoat	.05	.02	.01
☐ 674 Doug Jones	.05	.02	.01
☐ 675 Scott Livingstone	.05	.02	.01
☐ 676 Danny Tartabull	.10	.05	.01
☐ 677 Joe Carter HL	.15	.07	.02
☐ 678 Cecil Espy	.05	.02	.01
☐ 679 Randy Velarde	.05	.02	.01
☐ 680 Bruce Ruffin	.05	.02	.01
☐ 681 Ted Wood	.05	.02	.01
☐ 682 Dan Plesac	.05	.02	.01
☐ 683 Eric Bullock	.05	.02	.01
☐ 684 Junior Ortiz	.05	.02	.01
☐ 685 Dave Hollins	.05	.02	.01
☐ 686 Dennis Martinez	.10	.05	.01
☐ 687 Larry Andersen	.05	.02	.01
☐ 688 Doug Simons	.05	.02	.01
☐ 689 Tim Spehr	.05	.02	.01
☐ 690 Calvin Jones	.05	.02	.01
☐ 691 Mark Guthrie	.05	.02	.01
☐ 692 Alfredo Griffin	.05	.02	.01
☐ 693 Joe Carter	.15	.07	.02
☐ 694 Terry Mathews	.05	.02	.01
☐ 695 Pascual Perez	.05	.02	.01
☐ 696 Gene Nelson	.05	.02	.01
☐ 697 Gerald Williams	.05	.02	.01

☐ 698 Chris Cron	.05	.02	.01
☐ 699 Steve Buechele	.05	.02	.01
☐ 700 Paul McClellan	.05	.02	.01
☐ 701 Jim Lindeman	.05	.02	.01
☐ 702 Francisco Oliveras	.05	.02	.01
☐ 703 Rob Maurer	.05	.02	.01
☐ 704 Pat Hentgen	.15	.07	.02
☐ 705 Jaime Navarro	.05	.02	.01
☐ 706 Mike Magnante	.05	.02	.01
☐ 707 Nolan Ryan	.75	.35	.09
☐ 708 Bobby Thigpen	.05	.02	.01
☐ 709 John Cerutti	.05	.02	.01
☐ 710 Steve Wilson	.05	.02	.01
☐ 711 Hensley Meulens	.05	.02	.01
☐ 712 Rheal Cormier	.05	.02	.01
☐ 713 Scott Bradley	.05	.02	.01
☐ 714 Mitch Webster	.05	.02	.01
☐ 715 Roger Mason	.05	.02	.01
☐ 716 Checklist 636-716	.05	.02	.01
☐ 717 Jeff Fassero	.05	.02	.01
☐ 718 Cal Eldred	.05	.02	.01
☐ 719 Sid Fernandez	.10	.05	.01
☐ 720 Bob Zupcic	.05	.02	.01
☐ 721 Jose Offerman	.05	.02	.01
☐ 722 Cliff Brantley	.05	.02	.01
☐ 723 Ron Darling	.05	.02	.01
☐ 724 Dave Stieb	.05	.02	.01
☐ 725 Hector Villanueva	.05	.02	.01
☐ 726 Mike Hartley	.05	.02	.01
☐ 727 Arthur Rhodes	.05	.02	.01
☐ 728 Randy Bush	.05	.02	.01
☐ 729 Steve Sax	.05	.02	.01
☐ 730 Dave Otto	.05	.02	.01
☐ 731 John Wehner	.05	.02	.01
☐ 732 Dave Martinez	.05	.02	.01
☐ 733 Ruben Amaro	.05	.02	.01
☐ 734 Billy Ripken	.05	.02	.01
☐ 735 Steve Farr	.05	.02	.01
☐ 736 Shawn Abner	.05	.02	.01
☐ 737 Gil Heredia	.05	.02	.01
☐ 738 Ron Jones	.05	.02	.01
☐ 739 Tony Castillo	.05	.02	.01
☐ 740 Sammy Sosa	.15	.07	.02
☐ 741 Julio Franco	.10	.05	.01
☐ 742 Tim Naehring	.05	.02	.01
☐ 743 Steve Wapnick	.05	.02	.01
☐ 744 Craig Wilson	.05	.02	.01
☐ 745 Darrin Chapin	.05	.02	.01
☐ 746 Chris George	.05	.02	.01
☐ 747 Mike Simms	.05	.02	.01
☐ 748 Rosario Rodriguez	.05	.02	.01
☐ 749 Skeeter Barnes	.05	.02	.01
☐ 750 Roger McDowell	.05	.02	.01
☐ 751 Dann Howitt	.05	.02	.01
☐ 752 Paul Sorrento	.05	.02	.01
☐ 753 Braulio Castillo	.05	.02	.01
☐ 754 Yorkis Perez	.05	.02	.01
☐ 755 Willie Fraser	.05	.02	.01
☐ 756 Jeremy Hernandez	.05	.02	.01
☐ 757 Curt Schilling	.05	.02	.01
☐ 758 Steve Lyons	.05	.02	.01
☐ 759 Dave Anderson	.05	.02	.01
☐ 760 Willie Banks	.05	.02	.01
☐ 761 Mark Leonard	.05	.02	.01
☐ 762 Jack Armstrong	.05	.02	.01
(Listed on Indians, but shown on Reds)			
☐ 763 Scott Servais	.05	.02	.01
☐ 764 Ray Stephens	.05	.02	.01
☐ 765 Junior Noboa	.05	.02	.01
☐ 766 Jim Olander	.05	.02	.01

☐ 767 Joe Magrane	.05	.02	.01
☐ 768 Lance Blankenship	.05	.02	.01
☐ 769 Mike Humphreys	.05	.02	.01
☐ 770 Jarvis Brown	.05	.02	.01
☐ 771 Damon Berryhill	.05	.02	.01
☐ 772 Alejandro Pena	.05	.02	.01
☐ 773 Jose Mesa	.05	.02	.01
☐ 774 Gary Cooper	.05	.02	.01
☐ 775 Carney Lansford	.10	.05	.01
☐ 776 Mike Bielecki	.05	.02	.01
(Shown on Cubs, but listed on Braves)			
☐ 777 Charlie O'Brien	.05	.02	.01
☐ 778 Carlos Hernandez	.05	.02	.01
☐ 779 Howard Farmer	.05	.02	.01
☐ 780 Mike Stanton	.05	.02	.01
☐ 781 Reggie Harris	.05	.02	.01
☐ 782 Xavier Hernandez	.05	.02	.01
☐ 783 Bryan Hickerson	4.00	.02	.01
☐ 784 Checklist 717-784 and BC1-BC8	.05	.02	.01

1992 Donruss Diamond Kings

These standard-size (2 1/2" by 3 1/2") cards were randomly inserted in 1992 Donruss I foil packs (cards 1-13 and the checklist only) and in 1992 Donruss II foil packs (cards 14-26). The fronts feature player portraits by noted sports artist Dick Perez. The words "Donruss Diamond Kings" are superimposed at the card top in a gold-trimmed blue and black banner, with the player's name in a similarly designed black stripe at the card bottom. On a white background with a dark blue border, the backs present career summary. The cards are numbered on the back with a DK prefix.

	MINT	NRMT	EXC
COMPLETE SET (27)	20.00	9.00	2.50
COMPLETE SERIES 1 (14)	16.00	7.25	2.00
COMPLETE SERIES 2 (13)	4.00	1.80	.50
COMMON CARD (DK1-DK27)	.50	.23	.06
☐ DK1 Paul Molitor	1.00	.45	.12
☐ DK2 Will Clark	1.25	.55	.16
☐ DK3 Joe Carter	1.00	.45	.12
☐ DK4 Julio Franco	.75	.35	.09
☐ DK5 Cal Ripken	8.00	3.60	1.00

☐ DK6 Dave Justice	1.25	.55	.16
☐ DK7 George Bell	.75	.35	.09
☐ DK8 Frank Thomas	8.00	3.60	1.00
☐ DK9 Wade Boggs	1.00	.45	.12
☐ DK10 Scott Sanderson	.50	.23	.06
☐ DK11 Jeff Bagwell	4.00	1.80	.50
☐ DK12 John Kruk	.75	.35	.09
☐ DK13 Felix Jose	.50	.23	.06
☐ DK14 Harold Baines	.75	.35	.09
☐ DK15 Dwight Gooden	.75	.35	.09
☐ DK16 Brian McRae	.75	.35	.09
☐ DK17 Jay Bell	.75	.35	.09
☐ DK18 Brett Butler	.75	.35	.09
☐ DK19 Hal Morris	.75	.35	.09
☐ DK20 Mark Langston	.75	.35	.09
☐ DK21 Scott Erickson	.75	.35	.09
☐ DK22 Randy Johnson	1.50	.70	.19
☐ DK23 Greg Swindell	.50	.23	.06
☐ DK24 Dennis Martinez	.75	.35	.09
☐ DK25 Tony Phillips	.50	.23	.06
☐ DK26 Fred McGriff	1.25	.55	.16
☐ DK27 Checklist 1-26 DP	.50	.23	.06
(Dick Perez)			

☐ 18 Frank Thomas	150.00	70.00	19.00
☐ L2 Rickey Henderson	70.00	32.00	8.75
(Legend Series)			
☐ S2 Cal Ripken	400.00	180.00	50.00
(Signature Series)			

1992 Donruss Rookies

After six years of issuing "The Rookies" as a 56-card boxed set, Donruss expanded it to a 132-card standard-size set available only as a foil pack product. An additional 20 Phenom cards were randomly inserted in the packs (numbered 1-12 in 12-card foil packs and numbered 13-20 in 30-card jumbo packs). The card design is the same as the 1992 Donruss regular issue except that the two-tone blue color bars have been replaced by green, as in the previous six Donruss Rookies sets. The cards are arranged in alphabetical order and numbered on the back. Rookie Cards in this set include Billy Ashley, Pedro Astacio, Chad Curtis, Brent Gates, Al Martin, David Nied, Manny Ramirez, and Tim Wakefield.

1992 Donruss Elite

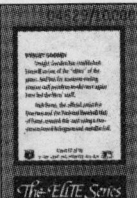

These cards were random inserts in 1992 Donruss foil packs. The numbering on the Elite cards is essentially a continuation of the series started the year before. The Signature Series Cal Ripken card was inserted in 1992 Donruss foil packs. Only 5,000 Ripken Signature Series cards were printed. The Rickey Henderson Legends Series card was inserted in 1992 Donruss foil packs; only 7,500 Henderson Legends cards were printed. All of these special limited cards are standard size, 2 1/2" by 3 1/2".

	MINT	NRMT	EXC
COMPLETE SET (12)	900.00	400.00	110.00
COMMON CARD (9-18)	20.00	9.00	2.50
☐ 9 Wade Boggs	30.00	13.50	3.70
☐ 10 Joe Carter	30.00	13.50	3.70
☐ 11 Will Clark	40.00	18.00	5.00
☐ 12 Dwight Gooden	20.00	9.00	2.50
☐ 13 Ken Griffey Jr.	150.00	70.00	19.00
☐ 14 Tony Gwynn	50.00	22.00	6.25
☐ 15 Howard Johnson	20.00	9.00	2.50
☐ 16 Terry Pendleton	20.00	9.00	2.50
☐ 17 Kirby Puckett	50.00	22.00	6.25

	MINT	NRMT	EXC
COMPLETE SET (132)	6.00	2.70	.75
COMMON CARD (1-132)	.05	.02	.01
☐ 1 Kyle Abbott	.05	.02	.01
☐ 2 Troy Afenir	.05	.02	.01
☐ 3 Rich Amaral	.05	.02	.01
☐ 4 Ruben Amaro	.05	.02	.01
☐ 5 Billy Ashley	.25	.11	.03
☐ 6 Pedro Astacio	.10	.05	.01
☐ 7 Jim Austin	.05	.02	.01
☐ 8 Robert Ayrault	.05	.02	.01
☐ 9 Kevin Baez	.05	.02	.01
☐ 10 Esteban Beltre	.05	.02	.01
☐ 11 Brian Bohanon	.05	.02	.01
☐ 12 Kent Bottenfield	.05	.02	.01
☐ 13 Jeff Branson	.05	.02	.01
☐ 14 Brad Brink	.05	.02	.01
☐ 15 John Briscoe	.05	.02	.01
☐ 16 Doug Brocail	.05	.02	.01
☐ 17 Rico Brogna	.05	.02	.01
☐ 18 J.T. Bruett	.05	.02	.01
☐ 19 Jacob Brumfield	.05	.02	.01
☐ 20 Jim Bullinger	.05	.02	.01

☐ 21 Kevin Campbell	.05	.02	.01
☐ 22 Pedro Castellano	.05	.02	.01
☐ 23 Mike Christopher	.05	.02	.01
☐ 24 Archi Cianfrocco	.05	.02	.01
☐ 25 Mark Clark	.15	.07	.02
☐ 26 Craig Colbert	.05	.02	.01
☐ 27 Victor Cole	.05	.02	.01
☐ 28 Steve Cooke	.05	.02	.01
☐ 29 Tim Costo	.05	.02	.01
☐ 30 Chad Curtis	.20	.09	.03
☐ 31 Doug Davis	.05	.02	.01
☐ 32 Gary DiSarcina	.05	.02	.01
☐ 33 John Doherty	.05	.02	.01
☐ 34 Mike Draper	.05	.02	.01
☐ 35 Monty Fariss	.05	.02	.01
☐ 36 Bien Figueroa	.05	.02	.01
☐ 37 John Flaherty	.05	.02	.01
☐ 38 Tim Fortugno	.05	.02	.01
☐ 39 Eric Fox	.05	.02	.01
☐ 40 Jeff Frye	.05	.02	.01
☐ 41 Ramon Garcia	.05	.02	.01
☐ 42 Brent Gates	.10	.05	.01
☐ 43 Tom Goodwin	.05	.02	.01
☐ 44 Buddy Groom	.05	.02	.01
☐ 45 Jeff Grotewold	.05	.02	.01
☐ 46 Juan Guerrero	.05	.02	.01
☐ 47 Johnny Guzman	.05	.02	.01
☐ 48 Shawn Hare	.05	.02	.01
☐ 49 Ryan Hawblitzel	.05	.02	.01
☐ 50 Bert Heffernan	.05	.02	.01
☐ 51 Butch Henry	.05	.02	.01
☐ 52 Cesar Hernandez	.05	.02	.01
☐ 53 Vince Horsman	.05	.02	.01
☐ 54 Steve Hosey	.05	.02	.01
☐ 55 Pat Howell	.05	.02	.01
☐ 56 Peter Hoy	.05	.02	.01
☐ 57 Jonathan Hurst	.05	.02	.01
☐ 58 Mark Hutton	.05	.02	.01
☐ 59 Shawn Jeter	.05	.02	.01
☐ 60 Joel Johnston	.05	.02	.01
☐ 61 Jeff Kent	.15	.07	.02
☐ 62 Kurt Knudsen	.05	.02	.01
☐ 63 Kevin Koslofski	.05	.02	.01
☐ 64 Danny Leon	.05	.02	.01
☐ 65 Jesse Levis	.05	.02	.01
☐ 66 Tom Marsh	.05	.02	.01
☐ 67 Ed Martel	.05	.02	.01
☐ 68 Al Martin	.05	.02	.01
☐ 69 Pedro Martinez	.25	.11	.03
☐ 70 Derrick May	.10	.05	.01
☐ 71 Matt Maysey	.05	.02	.01
☐ 72 Russ McGinnis	.05	.02	.01
☐ 73 Tim McIntosh	.05	.02	.01
☐ 74 Jim McNamara	.05	.02	.01
☐ 75 Jeff McNeely	.05	.02	.01
☐ 76 Rusty Meacham	.05	.02	.01
☐ 77 Tony Menendez	.05	.02	.01
☐ 78 Henry Mercedes	.05	.02	.01
☐ 79 Paul Miller	.05	.02	.01
☐ 80 Joe Millette	.05	.02	.01
☐ 81 Blas Minor	.05	.02	.01
☐ 82 Dennis Moeller	.05	.02	.01
☐ 83 Raul Mondesi	1.00	.45	.12
☐ 84 Rob Natal	.05	.02	.01
☐ 85 Troy Neel	.05	.02	.01
☐ 86 David Nied	.15	.07	.02
☐ 87 Jerry Nielson	.05	.02	.01
☐ 88 Donovan Osborne	.05	.02	.01
☐ 89 John Patterson	.05	.02	.01
☐ 90 Roger Pavlik	.10	.05	.01
☐ 91 Dan Peltier	.05	.02	.01
☐ 92 Jim Pena	.05	.02	.01
☐ 93 William Pennyfeather	.05	.02	.01
☐ 94 Mike Perez	.05	.02	.01
☐ 95 Hipolito Pichardo	.05	.02	.01
☐ 96 Greg Pirkl	.05	.02	.01
☐ 97 Harvey Pulliam	.05	.02	.01
☐ 98 Manny Ramirez	3.00	1.35	.35
☐ 99 Pat Rapp	.05	.02	.01
☐ 100 Jeff Reboulet	.05	.02	.01
☐ 101 Darren Reed	.05	.02	.01
☐ 102 Shane Reynolds	.25	.11	.03
☐ 103 Bill Risley	.05	.02	.01
☐ 104 Ben Rivera	.05	.02	.01
☐ 105 Henry Rodriguez	.05	.02	.01
☐ 106 Rico Rossy	.05	.02	.01
☐ 107 Johnny Ruffin	.05	.02	.01
☐ 108 Steve Scarsone	.05	.02	.01
☐ 109 Tim Scott	.05	.02	.01
☐ 110 Steve Shifflett	.05	.02	.01
☐ 111 Dave Silvestri	.05	.02	.01
☐ 112 Matt Stairs	.05	.02	.01
☐ 113 William Suero	.05	.02	.01
☐ 114 Jeff Tackett	.05	.02	.01
☐ 115 Eddie Taubensee	.05	.02	.01
☐ 116 Rick Trlicek	.05	.02	.01
☐ 117 Scooter Tucker	.05	.02	.01
☐ 118 Shane Turner	.05	.02	.01
☐ 119 Julio Valera	.05	.02	.01
☐ 120 Paul Wagner	.05	.02	.01
☐ 121 Tim Wakefield	.50	.23	.06
☐ 122 Mike Walker	.05	.02	.01
☐ 123 Bruce Walton	.05	.02	.01
☐ 124 Lenny Webster	.05	.02	.01
☐ 125 Bob Wickman	.05	.02	.01
☐ 126 Mike Williams	.05	.02	.01
☐ 127 Kerry Woodson	.05	.02	.01
☐ 128 Eric Young	.20	.09	.03
☐ 129 Kevin Young	.05	.02	.01
☐ 130 Pete Young	.05	.02	.01
☐ 131 Checklist 1-66	.05	.02	.01
☐ 132 Checklist 67-132	.05	.02	.01

1992 Donruss Rookies Phenoms

This 20-card set features baseball's most dynamic young prospects. The first 12 Phenom cards (1-12) were randomly inserted into 1992 Donruss The Rookies 12-card foil packs. The last eight Phenom cards (13-20) were inserted one per 30-card jumbo packs. The standard-size cards display nonaction color photos that are accented by gold-foil border stripes on a predominantly black card face. The set title "Phenoms" appears in gold foil lettering above the picture, while the player's name is given in the bottom border. In a horizontal format, the backs present biography, career highlights, and recent career performance statistics in a white and gray box enclosed by black and gold borders. The cards are arranged alphabetically and numbered on the back with a "BC" prefix.

	MINT	NRMT	EXC
COMPLETE SET (20)	35.00	16.00	4.40
COMPLETE FOIL SET (12)	25.00	11.00	3.10
COMPLETE JUMBO SET (8)	10.00	4.50	1.25
COMMON CARD (BC1-BC12)	.50	.23	.06
COMMON CARD (BC13-BC20)	.50	.23	.06
☐ BC1 Moises Alou	1.00	.45	.12
☐ BC2 Bret Boone	1.50	.70	.19
☐ BC3 Jeff Conine	2.00	.90	.25
☐ BC4 Dave Fleming	.50	.23	.06
☐ BC5 Tyler Green	.50	.23	.06
☐ BC6 Eric Karros	2.00	.90	.25
☐ BC7 Pat Listach	.50	.23	.06
☐ BC8 Kenny Lofton	8.00	3.60	1.00
☐ BC9 Mike Piazza	20.00	9.00	2.50
☐ BC10 Tim Salmon	6.00	2.70	.75
☐ BC11 Andy Stankiewicz	.50	.23	.06
☐ BC12 Dan Walters	.50	.23	.06
☐ BC13 Ramon Caraballo	.50	.23	.06
☐ BC14 Brian Jordan	.75	.35	.09
☐ BC15 Ryan Klesko	7.00	3.10	.85
☐ BC16 Sam Militello	.50	.23	.06
☐ BC17 Frank Seminara	.50	.23	.06
☐ BC18 Salomon Torres	.50	.23	.06
☐ BC19 John Valentin	3.00	1.35	.35
☐ BC20 Wil Cordero	1.25	.55	.16

1993 Donruss

The 1993 Donruss set was issued in two series, each with 396 standard-size cards. Several card subsets were randomly inserted in various Donruss products: Diamond Kings (featuring the artwork of Dick Perez and gold-foil stamping) in foil packs (1-15 in series I and 16-31 in series II); Elite series

in all packs (18 in all, nine in each series); Spirit of the Game (reportedly packed approximately two per box) in regular foil and jumbo packs (20 in total with ten in each series); Long Ball Leaders in 26-card magazine distributor packs (1-9 in series I and 10-18 in series II); and MVP cards in 23-card jumbo packs (26 in total with 13 in each series). Will Clark Signature Series (2,500 in each series) and Robin Yount Legend Series (10,000) cards were randomly inserted throughout the packs. Finally a Rated Rookies subset spotlights 20 top prospects; these Rated Rookies are sprinkled thoughout the set and are designated by RR in the checklist below. The fronts feature glossy color action photos bordered in white. At the bottom of the picture, the team logo appears in a team color-coded diamond with the player's name in a color-coded bar extending to the right. The backs have a second color player photo with biography and recent major league statistics filling up the rest of the card. The cards are numbered in a team color-coded home plate icon at the upper right corner. Rookie Cards in this set include Rene Arocha and J.T. Snow.

	MINT	NRMT	EXC
COMPLETE SET (792)	30.00	13.50	3.70
COMPLETE SERIES 1 (396)	15.00	6.75	1.85
COMPLETE SERIES 2 (396)	15.00	6.75	1.85
COMMON CARD (1-396)	.05	.02	.01
COMMON CARD (397-792)	.05	.02	.01
☐ 1 Craig Lefferts	.05	.02	.01
☐ 2 Kent Mercker	.10	.05	.01
☐ 3 Phil Plantier	.05	.02	.01
☐ 4 Alex Arias	.05	.02	.01
☐ 5 Julio Valera	.05	.02	.01
☐ 6 Dan Wilson	.05	.02	.01
☐ 7 Frank Thomas	2.00	.90	.25
☐ 8 Eric Anthony	.05	.02	.01
☐ 9 Derek Lilliquist	.05	.02	.01
☐ 10 Rafael Bournigal	.05	.02	.01
☐ 11 Manny Alexander RR	.05	.02	.01
☐ 12 Bret Barberie	.05	.02	.01
☐ 13 Mickey Tettleton	.10	.05	.01
☐ 14 Anthony Young	.05	.02	.01
☐ 15 Tim Spehr	.05	.02	.01
☐ 16 Bob Ayrault	.05	.02	.01
☐ 17 Bill Wegman	.05	.02	.01
☐ 18 Jay Bell	.10	.05	.01
☐ 19 Rick Aguilera	.10	.05	.01
☐ 20 Todd Zeile	.10	.05	.01
☐ 21 Steve Farr	.05	.02	.01
☐ 22 Andy Benes	.10	.05	.01
☐ 23 Lance Blankenship	.05	.02	.01
☐ 24 Ted Wood	.05	.02	.01
☐ 25 Omar Vizquel	.10	.05	.01
☐ 26 Steve Avery	.15	.07	.02
☐ 27 Brian Bohanon	.05	.02	.01
☐ 28 Rick Wilkins	.05	.02	.01
☐ 29 Devon White	.10	.05	.01
☐ 30 Bobby Ayala	.05	.02	.01
☐ 31 Leo Gomez	.05	.02	.01
☐ 32 Mike Simms	.05	.02	.01
☐ 33 Ellis Burks	.10	.05	.01
☐ 34 Steve Wilson	.05	.02	.01
☐ 35 Jim Abbott	.15	.07	.02

□	36	Tim Wallach	.05	.02	.01
□	37	Wilson Alvarez	.15	.07	.02
□	38	Daryl Boston	.05	.02	.01
□	39	Sandy Alomar Jr.	.10	.05	.01
□	40	Mitch Williams	.10	.05	.01
□	41	Rico Brogna	.15	.07	.02
□	42	Gary Varsho	.05	.02	.01
□	43	Kevin Appier	.10	.05	.01
□	44	Eric Wedge RR	.05	.02	.01
□	45	Dante Bichette	.25	.11	.03
□	46	Jose Oquendo	.05	.02	.01
□	47	Mike Trombley	.05	.02	.01
□	48	Dan Walters	.05	.02	.01
□	49	Gerald Williams	.05	.02	.01
□	50	Bud Black	.05	.02	.01
□	51	Bobby Witt	.05	.02	.01
□	52	Mark Davis	.05	.02	.01
□	53	Shawn Barton	.05	.02	.01
□	54	Paul Assenmacher	.05	.02	.01
□	55	Kevin Reimer	.05	.02	.01
□	56	Billy Ashley RR	.15	.07	.02
□	57	Eddie Zosky	.05	.02	.01
□	58	Chris Sabo	.05	.02	.01
□	59	Billy Ripken	.05	.02	.01
□	60	Scooter Tucker	.05	.02	.01
□	61	Tim Wakefield RR	.15	.07	.02
□	62	Mitch Webster	.05	.02	.01
□	63	Jack Clark	.10	.05	.01
□	64	Mark Gardner	.05	.02	.01
□	65	Lee Stevens	.05	.02	.01
□	66	Todd Hundley	.15	.07	.02
□	67	Bobby Thigpen	.05	.02	.01
□	68	Dave Hollins	.05	.02	.01
□	69	Jack Armstrong	.05	.02	.01
□	70	Alex Cole	.05	.02	.01
□	71	Mark Carreon	.05	.02	.01
□	72	Todd Worrell	.05	.02	.01
□	73	Steve Shifflett	.05	.02	.01
□	74	Jerald Clark	.05	.02	.01
□	75	Paul Molitor	.15	.07	.02
□	76	Larry Carter	.05	.02	.01
□	77	Rich Rowland RR	.05	.02	.01
□	78	Damon Berryhill	.05	.02	.01
□	79	Willie Banks	.05	.02	.01
□	80	Hector Villanueva	.05	.02	.01
□	81	Mike Gallego	.05	.02	.01
□	82	Tim Belcher	.05	.02	.01
□	83	Mike Bordick	.05	.02	.01
□	84	Craig Biggio	.15	.07	.02
□	85	Lance Parrish	.10	.05	.01
□	86	Brett Butler	.10	.05	.01
□	87	Mike Timlin	.05	.02	.01
□	88	Brian Barnes	.05	.02	.01
□	89	Brady Anderson	.10	.05	.01
□	90	D.J. Dozier	.05	.02	.01
□	91	Frank Viola	.10	.05	.01
□	92	Darren Daulton	.15	.07	.02
□	93	Chad Curtis	.10	.05	.01
□	94	Zane Smith	.05	.02	.01
□	95	George Bell	.10	.05	.01
□	96	Rex Hudler	.05	.02	.01
□	97	Mark Whiten	.05	.02	.01
□	98	Tim Teufel	.05	.02	.01
□	99	Kevin Ritz	.05	.02	.01
□	100	Jeff Brantley	.05	.02	.01
□	101	Jeff Conine	.15	.07	.02
□	102	Vinny Castilla	.15	.07	.02
□	103	Greg Vaughn	.05	.02	.01
□	104	Steve Buechele	.05	.02	.01
□	105	Darren Reed	.05	.02	.01
□	106	Bip Roberts	.05	.02	.01
□	107	John Habyan	.05	.02	.01
□	108	Scott Servais	.05	.02	.01
□	109	Walt Weiss	.05	.02	.01
□	110	J.T. Snow RR	.60	.25	.07
□	111	Jay Buhner	.15	.07	.02
□	112	Darryl Strawberry	.10	.05	.01
□	113	Roger Pavlik	.05	.02	.01
□	114	Chris Nabholz	.05	.02	.01
□	115	Pat Borders	.05	.02	.01
□	116	Pat Howell	.05	.02	.01
□	117	Gregg Olson	.05	.02	.01
□	118	Curt Schilling	.05	.02	.01
□	119	Roger Clemens	.30	.14	.04
□	120	Victor Cole	.05	.02	.01
□	121	Gary DiSarcina	.05	.02	.01
□	122	Checklist 1-80	.05	.02	.01
		(Gary Carter and			
		Kirt Manwaring)			
□	123	Steve Sax	.05	.02	.01
□	124	Chuck Carr	.05	.02	.01
□	125	Mark Lewis	.05	.02	.01
□	126	Tony Gwynn	.60	.25	.07
□	127	Travis Fryman	.15	.07	.02
□	128	Dave Burba	.05	.02	.01
□	129	Wally Joyner	.10	.05	.01
□	130	John Smoltz	.10	.05	.01
□	131	Cal Eldred	.05	.02	.01
□	132	Checklist 81-159	.10	.05	.01
		(Roberto Alomar and			
		Devon White)			
□	133	Arthur Rhodes	.10	.05	.01
□	134	Jeff Blauser	.10	.05	.01
□	135	Scott Cooper	.05	.02	.01
□	136	Doug Strange	.05	.02	.01
□	137	Luis Sojo	.05	.02	.01
□	138	Jeff Branson	.05	.02	.01
□	139	Alex Fernandez	.15	.07	.02
□	140	Ken Caminiti	.10	.05	.01
□	141	Charles Nagy	.10	.05	.01
□	142	Tom Candiotti	.05	.02	.01
□	143	Willie Greene RR	.10	.05	.01
□	144	John Vander Wal	.05	.02	.01
□	145	Kurt Knudsen	.05	.02	.01
□	146	John Franco	.10	.05	.01
□	147	Eddie Pierce	.05	.02	.01
□	148	Kim Batiste	.05	.02	.01
□	149	Darren Holmes	.05	.02	.01
□	150	Steve Cooke	.05	.02	.01
□	151	Terry Jorgensen	.05	.02	.01
□	152	Mark Clark	.05	.02	.01
□	153	Randy Velarde	.05	.02	.01
□	154	Greg W. Harris	.05	.02	.01
□	155	Kevin Campbell	.05	.02	.01
□	156	John Burkett	.05	.02	.01
□	157	Kevin Mitchell	.10	.05	.01
□	158	Deion Sanders	.40	.18	.05
□	159	Jose Canseco	.30	.14	.04
□	160	Jeff Hartsock	.05	.02	.01
□	161	Tom Quinlan	.05	.02	.01
□	162	Tim Pugh	.05	.02	.01
□	163	Glenn Davis	.05	.02	.01
□	164	Shane Reynolds	.05	.02	.01
□	165	Jody Reed	.05	.02	.01
□	166	Mike Sharperson	.05	.02	.01
□	167	Scott Lewis	.05	.02	.01
□	168	Dennis Martinez	.10	.05	.01
□	169	Scott Radinsky	.05	.02	.01
□	170	Dave Gallagher	.05	.02	.01
□	171	Jim Thome	.75	.35	.09
□	172	Terry Mulholland	.05	.02	.01
□	173	Milt Cuyler	.05	.02	.01

174	Bob Patterson	.05	.02	.01
175	Jeff Montgomery	.10	.05	.01
176	Tim Salmon RR	.60	.25	.07
177	Franklin Stubbs	.05	.02	.01
178	Donovan Osborne	.05	.02	.01
179	Jeff Reboulet	.05	.02	.01
180	Jeremy Hernandez	.05	.02	.01
181	Charlie Hayes	.10	.05	.01
182	Matt Williams	.30	.14	.04
183	Mike Raczka	.05	.02	.01
184	Francisco Cabrera	.05	.02	.01
185	Rich DeLucia	.05	.02	.01
186	Sammy Sosa	.15	.07	.02
187	Ivan Rodriguez	.15	.07	.02
188	Bret Boone RR	.15	.07	.02
189	Juan Guzman	.10	.05	.01
190	Tom Browning	.05	.02	.01
191	Randy Milligan	.05	.02	.01
192	Steve Finley	.10	.05	.01
193	John Patterson RR	.05	.02	.01
194	Kip Gross	.05	.02	.01
195	Tony Fossas	.05	.02	.01
196	Ivan Calderon	.05	.02	.01
197	Junior Felix	.05	.02	.01
198	Pete Schourek	.15	.07	.02
199	Craig Grebeck	.05	.02	.01
200	Juan Bell	.05	.02	.01
201	Glenallen Hill	.05	.02	.01
202	Danny Jackson	.05	.02	.01
203	John Kiely	.05	.02	.01
204	Bob Tewksbury	.05	.02	.01
205	Kevin Koslofski	.05	.02	.01
206	Craig Shipley	.05	.02	.01
207	John Jaha	.10	.05	.01
208	Royce Clayton	.10	.05	.01
209	Mike Piazza RR	1.50	.70	.19
210	Ron Gant	.15	.07	.02
211	Scott Erickson	.10	.05	.01
212	Doug Dascenzo	.05	.02	.01
213	Andy Stankiewicz	.05	.02	.01
214	Geronimo Berroa	.05	.02	.01
215	Dennis Eckersley	.15	.07	.02
216	Al Osuna	.05	.02	.01
217	Tino Martinez	.15	.07	.02
218	Henry Rodriguez	.05	.02	.01
219	Ed Sprague	.10	.05	.01
220	Ken Hill	.10	.05	.01
221	Chito Martinez	.05	.02	.01
222	Bret Saberhagen	.10	.05	.01
223	Mike Greenwell	.10	.05	.01
224	Mickey Morandini	.05	.02	.01
225	Chuck Finley	.10	.05	.01
226	Denny Neagle	.05	.02	.01
227	Kirk McCaskill	.05	.02	.01
228	Rheal Cormier	.05	.02	.01
229	Paul Sorrento	.05	.02	.01
230	Darrin Jackson	.05	.02	.01
231	Rob Deer	.05	.02	.01
232	Bill Swift	.10	.05	.01
233	Kevin McReynolds	.05	.02	.01
234	Terry Pendleton	.10	.05	.01
235	Dave Nilsson	.10	.05	.01
236	Chuck McElroy	.05	.02	.01
237	Derek Parks	.05	.02	.01
238	Norm Charlton	.05	.02	.01
239	Matt Nokes	.05	.02	.01
240	Juan Guerrero	.05	.02	.01
241	Jeff Parrett	.05	.02	.01
242	Ryan Thompson RR	.10	.05	.01
243	Dave Fleming	.05	.02	.01
244	Dave Hansen	.05	.02	.01
245	Monty Fariss	.05	.02	.01
246	Archi Cianfrocco	.05	.02	.01
247	Pat Hentgen	.10	.05	.01
248	Bill Pecota	.05	.02	.01
249	Ben McDonald	.05	.02	.01
250	Cliff Brantley	.05	.02	.01
251	John Valentin	.15	.07	.02
252	Jeff King	.05	.02	.01
253	Reggie Williams	.05	.02	.01
254	Checklist 160-238 (Damon Berryhill and Alex Arias)	.05	.02	.01
255	Ozzie Guillen	.05	.02	.01
256	Mike Perez	.05	.02	.01
257	Thomas Howard	.05	.02	.01
258	Kurt Stillwell	.05	.02	.01
259	Mike Henneman	.05	.02	.01
260	Steve Decker	.05	.02	.01
261	Brent Mayne	.05	.02	.01
262	Otis Nixon	.05	.02	.01
263	Mark Kiefer	.05	.02	.01
264	Checklist 239-317 (Don Mattingly and Mike Bordick)	.15	.07	.02
265	Richie Lewis	.05	.02	.01
266	Pat Gomez	.05	.02	.01
267	Scott Taylor	.05	.02	.01
268	Shawon Dunston	.05	.02	.01
269	Greg Myers	.05	.02	.01
270	Tim Costo	.05	.02	.01
271	Greg Hibbard	.05	.02	.01
272	Pete Harnisch	.05	.02	.01
273	Dave Mlicki	.05	.02	.01
274	Orel Hershiser	.10	.05	.01
275	Sean Berry RR	.05	.02	.01
276	Doug Simons	.05	.02	.01
277	John Doherty	.05	.02	.01
278	Eddie Murray	.30	.14	.04
279	Chris Haney	.05	.02	.01
280	Stan Javier	.05	.02	.01
281	Jaime Navarro	.05	.02	.01
282	Orlando Merced	.10	.05	.01
283	Kent Hrbek	.10	.05	.01
284	Bernard Gilkey	.10	.05	.01
285	Russ Springer	.05	.02	.01
286	Mike Maddux	.05	.02	.01
287	Eric Fox	.05	.02	.01
288	Mark Leonard	.05	.02	.01
289	Tim Leary	.05	.02	.01
290	Brian Hunter	.05	.02	.01
291	Donald Harris	.05	.02	.01
292	Bob Scanlan	.05	.02	.01
293	Turner Ward	.05	.02	.01
294	Hal Morris	.10	.05	.01
295	Jimmy Poole	.05	.02	.01
296	Doug Jones	.05	.02	.01
297	Tony Pena	.05	.02	.01
298	Ramon Martinez	.10	.05	.01
299	Tim Fortugno	.05	.02	.01
300	Marquis Grissom	.15	.07	.02
301	Lance Johnson	.05	.02	.01
302	Jeff Kent	.15	.07	.02
303	Reggie Jefferson	.05	.02	.01
304	Wes Chamberlain	.05	.02	.01
305	Shawn Hare	.05	.02	.01
306	Mike LaValliere	.05	.02	.01
307	Gregg Jefferies	.15	.07	.02
308	Troy Neel RR	.05	.02	.01
309	Pat Listach	.05	.02	.01
310	Geronimo Pena	.05	.02	.01
311	Pedro Munoz	.10	.05	.01

312	Guillermo Velasquez	.05	.02	.01
313	Roberto Kelly	.10	.05	.01
314	Mike Jackson	.05	.02	.01
315	Rickey Henderson	.15	.07	.02
316	Mark Lemke	.10	.05	.01
317	Erik Hanson	.10	.05	.01
318	Derrick May	.10	.05	.01
319	Geno Petralli	.05	.02	.01
320	Melvin Nieves RR	.15	.07	.02
321	Doug Linton	.05	.02	.01
322	Rob Dibble	.05	.02	.01
323	Chris Hoiles	.10	.05	.01
324	Jimmy Jones	.05	.02	.01
325	Dave Staton RR	.05	.02	.01
326	Pedro Martinez	.15	.07	.02
327	Paul Quantrill	.05	.02	.01
328	Greg Colbrunn	.15	.07	.02
329	Hilly Hathaway	.05	.02	.01
330	Jeff Innis	.05	.02	.01
331	Ron Karkovice	.05	.02	.01
332	Keith Shepherd	.05	.02	.01
333	Alan Embree	.05	.02	.01
334	Paul Wagner	.05	.02	.01
335	Dave Haas	.05	.02	.01
336	Ozzie Canseco	.05	.02	.01
337	Bill Sampen	.05	.02	.01
338	Rich Rodriguez	.05	.02	.01
339	Dean Palmer	.10	.05	.01
340	Greg Litton	.05	.02	.01
341	Jim Tatum RR	.05	.02	.01
342	Todd Haney	.05	.02	.01
343	Larry Casian	.05	.02	.01
344	Ryne Sandberg	.50	.23	.06
345	Sterling Hitchcock	.20	.09	.03
346	Chris Hammond	.05	.02	.01
347	Vince Horsman	.05	.02	.01
348	Butch Henry	.05	.02	.01
349	Dann Howitt	.05	.02	.01
350	Roger McDowell	.05	.02	.01
351	Jack Morris	.15	.07	.02
352	Bill Krueger	.05	.02	.01
353	Cris Colon	.05	.02	.01
354	Joe Vitko	.05	.02	.01
355	Willie McGee	.10	.05	.01
356	Jay Baller	.05	.02	.01
357	Pat Mahomes	.05	.02	.01
358	Roger Mason	.05	.02	.01
359	Jerry Nielsen	.05	.02	.01
360	Tom Pagnozzi	.05	.02	.01
361	Kevin Baez	.05	.02	.01
362	Tim Scott	.05	.02	.01
363	Domingo Martinez	.05	.02	.01
364	Kirt Manwaring	.05	.02	.01
365	Rafael Palmeiro	.15	.07	.02
366	Ray Lankford	.15	.07	.02
367	Tim McIntosh	.05	.02	.01
368	Jessie Hollins	.05	.02	.01
369	Scott Leius	.05	.02	.01
370	Bill Doran	.05	.02	.01
371	Sam Militello	.05	.02	.01
372	Ryan Bowen	.05	.02	.01
373	Dave Henderson	.05	.02	.01
374	Dan Smith RR	.05	.02	.01
375	Steve Reed RR	.10	.05	.01
376	Jose Offerman	.05	.02	.01
377	Kevin Brown	.05	.02	.01
378	Darrin Fletcher	.05	.02	.01
379	Duane Ward	.05	.02	.01
380	Wayne Kirby RR	.05	.02	.01
381	Steve Scarsone	.05	.02	.01
382	Mariano Duncan	.05	.02	.01
383	Ken Ryan	.05	.02	.01
384	Lloyd McClendon	.05	.02	.01
385	Brian Holman	.05	.02	.01
386	Braulio Castillo	.05	.02	.01
387	Danny Leon	.05	.02	.01
388	Omar Olivares	.05	.02	.01
389	Kevin Wickander	.05	.02	.01
390	Fred McGriff	.25	.11	.03
391	Phil Clark	.05	.02	.01
392	Darren Lewis	.05	.02	.01
393	Phil Hiatt	.05	.02	.01
394	Mike Morgan	.05	.02	.01
395	Shane Mack	.05	.02	.01
396	Checklist 318-396. (Dennis Eckersley and Art Kusnyer CO)	.05	.02	.01
397	David Segui	.05	.02	.01
398	Rafael Belliard	.05	.02	.01
399	Tim Naehring	.15	.07	.02
400	Frank Castillo	.05	.02	.01
401	Joe Grahe	.05	.02	.01
402	Reggie Sanders	.15	.07	.02
403	Roberto Hernandez	.10	.05	.01
404	Luis Gonzalez	.10	.05	.01
405	Carlos Baerga	.40	.18	.05
406	Carlos Hernandez	.05	.02	.01
407	Pedro Astacio RR	.05	.02	.01
408	Mel Rojas	.10	.05	.01
409	Scott Livingstone	.05	.02	.01
410	Chico Walker	.05	.02	.01
411	Brian McRae	.15	.07	.02
412	Ben Rivera	.05	.02	.01
413	Ricky Bones	.05	.02	.01
414	Andy Van Slyke	.10	.05	.01
415	Chuck Knoblauch	.15	.07	.02
416	Luis Alicea	.05	.02	.01
417	Bob Wickman	.05	.02	.01
418	Doug Brocail	.05	.02	.01
419	Scott Brosius	.05	.02	.01
420	Rod Beck	.15	.07	.02
421	Edgar Martinez	.15	.07	.02
422	Ryan Klesko	1.00	.45	.12
423	Nolan Ryan	2.00	.90	.25
424	Rey Sanchez	.05	.02	.01
425	Roberto Alomar	.40	.18	.05
426	Barry Larkin	.25	.11	.03
427	Mike Mussina	.30	.14	.04
428	Jeff Bagwell	.75	.35	.09
429	Mo Vaughn	.30	.14	.04
430	Eric Karros	.15	.07	.02
431	John Orton	.05	.02	.01
432	Wil Cordero	.15	.07	.02
433	Jack McDowell	.15	.07	.02
434	Howard Johnson	.05	.02	.01
435	Albert Belle	.75	.35	.09
436	John Kruk	.15	.07	.02
437	Skeeter Barnes	.05	.02	.01
438	Don Slaught	.05	.02	.01
439	Rusty Meacham	.05	.02	.01
440	Tim Laker RR	.05	.02	.01
441	Robin Yount	.25	.11	.03
442	Brian Jordan	.15	.07	.02
443	Kevin Tapani	.05	.02	.01
444	Gary Sheffield	.15	.07	.02
445	Rich Monteleone	.05	.02	.01
446	Will Clark	.25	.11	.03
447	Jerry Browne	.05	.02	.01
448	Jeff Treadway	.05	.02	.01
449	Mike Schooler	.05	.02	.01
450	Mike Harkey	.05	.02	.01
451	Julio Franco	.10	.05	.01

☐ 452 Kevin Young RR	.05	.02	.01
☐ 453 Kelly Gruber	.05	.02	.01
☐ 454 Jose Rijo	.10	.05	.01
☐ 455 Mike Devereaux	.10	.05	.01
☐ 456 Andujar Cedeno	.05	.02	.01
☐ 457 Damion Easley RR	.10	.05	.01
☐ 458 Kevin Gross	.05	.02	.01
☐ 459 Matt Young	.05	.02	.01
☐ 460 Matt Stairs	.05	.02	.01
☐ 461 Luis Polonia	.05	.02	.01
☐ 462 Dwight Gooden	.10	.05	.01
☐ 463 Warren Newson	.05	.02	.01
☐ 464 Jose DeLeon	.05	.02	.01
☐ 465 Jose Mesa	.05	.02	.01
☐ 466 Danny Cox	.05	.02	.01
☐ 467 Dan Gladden	.05	.02	.01
☐ 468 Gerald Perry	.05	.02	.01
☐ 469 Mike Boddicker	.05	.02	.01
☐ 470 Jeff Gardner	.05	.02	.01
☐ 471 Doug Henry	.05	.02	.01
☐ 472 Mike Benjamin	.05	.02	.01
☐ 473 Dan Peltier RR	.05	.02	.01
☐ 474 Mike Stanton	.05	.02	.01
☐ 475 John Smiley	.05	.02	.01
☐ 476 Dwight Smith	.05	.02	.01
☐ 477 Jim Leyritz	.05	.02	.01
☐ 478 Dwayne Henry	.05	.02	.01
☐ 479 Mark McGwire	.15	.07	.02
☐ 480 Pete Incaviglia	.05	.02	.01
☐ 481 Dave Cochrane	.05	.02	.01
☐ 482 Eric Davis	.05	.02	.01
☐ 483 John Olerud	.10	.05	.01
☐ 484 Kent Bottenfield	.05	.02	.01
☐ 485 Mark McLemore	.05	.02	.01
☐ 486 Dave Magadan	.05	.02	.01
☐ 487 John Marzano	.05	.02	.01
☐ 488 Ruben Amaro	.05	.02	.01
☐ 489 Rob Ducey	.05	.02	.01
☐ 490 Stan Belinda	.05	.02	.01
☐ 491 Dan Pasqua	.05	.02	.01
☐ 492 Joe Magrane	.05	.02	.01
☐ 493 Brook Jacoby	.05	.02	.01
☐ 494 Gene Harris	.05	.02	.01
☐ 495 Mark Leiter	.05	.02	.01
☐ 496 Bryan Hickerson	.05	.02	.01
☐ 497 Tom Gordon	.05	.02	.01
☐ 498 Pete Smith	.05	.02	.01
☐ 499 Chris Bosio	.05	.02	.01
☐ 500 Shawn Boskie	.05	.02	.01
☐ 501 Dave West	.05	.02	.01
☐ 502 Milt Hill	.05	.02	.01
☐ 503 Pat Kelly	.05	.02	.01
☐ 504 Joe Boever	.05	.02	.01
☐ 505 Terry Steinbach	.10	.05	.01
☐ 506 Butch Huskey RR	.15	.07	.02
☐ 507 David Valle	.05	.02	.01
☐ 508 Mike Scioscia	.05	.02	.01
☐ 509 Kenny Rogers	.10	.05	.01
☐ 510 Moises Alou	.15	.07	.02
☐ 511 David Wells	.05	.02	.01
☐ 512 Mackey Sasser	.05	.02	.01
☐ 513 Todd Frohwirth	.05	.02	.01
☐ 514 Ricky Jordan	.05	.02	.01
☐ 515 Mike Gardiner	.05	.02	.01
☐ 516 Gary Redus	.05	.02	.01
☐ 517 Gary Gaetti	.05	.02	.01
☐ 518 Checklist	.05	.02	.01
☐ 519 Carlton Fisk	.15	.07	.02
☐ 520 Ozzie Smith	.40	.18	.05
☐ 521 Rod Nichols	.05	.02	.01
☐ 522 Benito Santiago	.05	.02	.01

☐ 523 Bill Gullickson	.05	.02	.01
☐ 524 Robby Thompson	.05	.02	.01
☐ 525 Mike Macfarlane	.05	.02	.01
☐ 526 Sid Bream	.05	.02	.01
☐ 527 Darryl Hamilton	.05	.02	.01
☐ 528 Checklist	.05	.02	.01
☐ 529 Jeff Tackett	.05	.02	.01
☐ 530 Greg Olson	.05	.02	.01
☐ 531 Bob Zupcic	.05	.02	.01
☐ 532 Mark Grace	.15	.07	.02
☐ 533 Steve Frey	.05	.02	.01
☐ 534 Dave Martinez	.05	.02	.01
☐ 535 Robin Ventura	.15	.07	.02
☐ 536 Casey Candaele	.05	.02	.01
☐ 537 Kenny Lofton	.60	.25	.07
☐ 538 Jay Howell	.05	.02	.01
☐ 539 Fernando Ramsey RR	.05	.02	.01
☐ 540 Larry Walker	.25	.11	.03
☐ 541 Cecil Fielder	.15	.07	.02
☐ 542 Lee Guetterman	.05	.02	.01
☐ 543 Keith Miller	.05	.02	.01
☐ 544 Len Dykstra	.15	.07	.02
☐ 545 B.J. Surhoff	.10	.05	.01
☐ 546 Bob Walk	.05	.02	.01
☐ 547 Brian Harper	.05	.02	.01
☐ 548 Lee Smith	.15	.07	.02
☐ 549 Danny Tartabull	.10	.05	.01
☐ 550 Frank Seminara	.05	.02	.01
☐ 551 Henry Mercedes	.05	.02	.01
☐ 552 Dave Righetti	.05	.02	.01
☐ 553 Ken Griffey Jr.	2.00	.90	.25
☐ 554 Tom Glavine	.15	.07	.02
☐ 555 Juan Gonzalez	.40	.18	.05
☐ 556 Jim Bullinger	.05	.02	.01
☐ 557 Derek Bell	.15	.07	.02
☐ 558 Cesar Hernandez	.05	.02	.01
☐ 559 Cal Ripken	2.00	.90	.25
☐ 560 Eddie Taubensee	.05	.02	.01
☐ 561 John Flaherty	.05	.02	.01
☐ 562 Todd Benzinger	.05	.02	.01
☐ 563 Hubie Brooks	.05	.02	.01
☐ 564 Delino DeShields	.10	.05	.01
☐ 565 Tim Raines	.15	.07	.02
☐ 566 Sid Fernandez	.05	.02	.01
☐ 567 Steve Olin	.05	.02	.01
☐ 568 Tommy Greene	.05	.02	.01
☐ 569 Buddy Groom	.05	.02	.01
☐ 570 Randy Tomlin	.05	.02	.01
☐ 571 Hipolito Pichardo	.05	.02	.01
☐ 572 Rene Arocha RR	.10	.05	.01
☐ 573 Mike Fetters	.05	.02	.01
☐ 574 Felix Jose	.05	.02	.01
☐ 575 Gene Larkin	.05	.02	.01
☐ 576 Bruce Hurst	.05	.02	.01
☐ 577 Bernie Williams	.10	.05	.01
☐ 578 Trevor Wilson	.05	.02	.01
☐ 579 Bob Welch	.05	.02	.01
☐ 580 David Justice	.25	.11	.03
☐ 581 Randy Johnson	.40	.18	.05
☐ 582 Jose Vizcaino	.05	.02	.01
☐ 583 Jeff Huson	.05	.02	.01
☐ 584 Rob Maurer RR	.05	.02	.01
☐ 585 Todd Stottlemyre	.05	.02	.01
☐ 586 Joe Oliver	.05	.02	.01
☐ 587 Bob Milacki	.05	.02	.01
☐ 588 Rob Murphy	.05	.02	.01
☐ 589 Greg Pirkl RR	.05	.02	.01
☐ 590 Lenny Harris	.05	.02	.01
☐ 591 Luis Rivera	.05	.02	.01
☐ 592 John Wetteland	.10	.05	.01
☐ 593 Mark Langston	.15	.07	.02

☐ 594	Bobby Bonilla	.15	.07	.02
☐ 595	Esteban Beltre	.05	.02	.01
☐ 596	Mike Hartley	.05	.02	.01
☐ 597	Felix Fermin	.05	.02	.01
☐ 598	Carlos Garcia	.10	.05	.01
☐ 599	Frank Tanana	.05	.02	.01
☐ 600	Pedro Guerrero	.05	.02	.01
☐ 601	Terry Shumpert	.05	.02	.01
☐ 602	Wally Whitehurst	.05	.02	.01
☐ 603	Kevin Seitzer	.05	.02	.01
☐ 604	Chris James	.05	.02	.01
☐ 605	Greg Gohr RR	.05	.02	.01
☐ 606	Mark Wohlers	.05	.02	.01
☐ 607	Kirby Puckett	.60	.25	.07
☐ 608	Greg Maddux	2.00	.90	.25
☐ 609	Don Mattingly	1.00	.45	.12
☐ 610	Greg Cadaret	.05	.02	.01
☐ 611	Dave Stewart	.10	.05	.01
☐ 612	Mark Portugal	.05	.02	.01
☐ 613	Pete O'Brien	.05	.02	.01
☐ 614	Bobby Ojeda	.05	.02	.01
☐ 615	Joe Carter	.15	.07	.02
☐ 616	Pete Young	.05	.02	.01
☐ 617	Sam Horn	.05	.02	.01
☐ 618	Vince Coleman	.05	.02	.01
☐ 619	Wade Boggs	.15	.07	.02
☐ 620	Todd Pratt	.05	.02	.01
☐ 621	Ron Tingley	.05	.02	.01
☐ 622	Doug Drabek	.15	.07	.02
☐ 623	Scott Hemond	.05	.02	.01
☐ 624	Tim Jones	.05	.02	.01
☐ 625	Dennis Cook	.05	.02	.01
☐ 626	Jose Melendez	.05	.02	.01
☐ 627	Mike Munoz	.05	.02	.01
☐ 628	Jim Pena	.05	.02	.01
☐ 629	Gary Thurman	.05	.02	.01
☐ 630	Charlie Leibrandt	.05	.02	.01
☐ 631	Scott Fletcher	.05	.02	.01
☐ 632	Andre Dawson	.15	.07	.02
☐ 633	Greg Gagne	.05	.02	.01
☐ 634	Greg Swindell	.05	.02	.01
☐ 635	Kevin Maas	.05	.02	.01
☐ 636	Xavier Hernandez	.05	.02	.01
☐ 637	Ruben Sierra	.15	.07	.02
☐ 638	Dmitri Young RR	.10	.05	.01
☐ 639	Harold Reynolds	.05	.02	.01
☐ 640	Tom Goodwin	.05	.02	.01
☐ 641	Todd Burns	.05	.02	.01
☐ 642	Jeff Fassero	.05	.02	.01
☐ 643	Dave Winfield	.15	.07	.02
☐ 644	Willie Randolph	.10	.05	.01
☐ 645	Luis Mercedes	.05	.02	.01
☐ 646	Dale Murphy	.15	.07	.02
☐ 647	Danny Darwin	.05	.02	.01
☐ 648	Dennis Moeller	.05	.02	.01
☐ 649	Chuck Crim	.05	.02	.01
☐ 650	Checklist	.05	.02	.01
☐ 651	Shawn Abner	.05	.02	.01
☐ 652	Tracy Woodson	.05	.02	.01
☐ 653	Scott Scudder	.05	.02	.01
☐ 654	Tom Lampkin	.05	.02	.01
☐ 655	Alan Trammell	.15	.07	.02
☐ 656	Cory Snyder	.05	.02	.01
☐ 657	Chris Gwynn	.05	.02	.01
☐ 658	Lonnie Smith	.05	.02	.01
☐ 659	Jim Austin	.05	.02	.01
☐ 660	Checklist	.05	.02	.01
☐ 661	Tim Hulett	.05	.02	.01
☐ 662	Marvin Freeman	.05	.02	.01
☐ 663	Greg A. Harris	.05	.02	.01
☐ 664	Heathcliff Slocumb	.05	.02	.01
☐ 665	Mike Butcher	.05	.02	.01
☐ 666	Steve Foster	.05	.02	.01
☐ 667	Donn Pall	.05	.02	.01
☐ 668	Darryl Kile	.05	.02	.01
☐ 669	Jesse Levis	.05	.02	.01
☐ 670	Jim Gott	.05	.02	.01
☐ 671	Mark Hutton RR	.05	.02	.01
☐ 672	Brian Drahman	.05	.02	.01
☐ 673	Chad Kreuter	.05	.02	.01
☐ 674	Tony Fernandez	.05	.02	.01
☐ 675	Jose Lind	.05	.02	.01
☐ 676	Kyle Abbott	.05	.02	.01
☐ 677	Dan Plesac	.05	.02	.01
☐ 678	Barry Bonds	.50	.23	.06
☐ 679	Chili Davis	.10	.05	.01
☐ 680	Stan Royer	.05	.02	.01
☐ 681	Scott Kamieniecki	.05	.02	.01
☐ 682	Carlos Martinez	.05	.02	.01
☐ 683	Mike Moore	.05	.02	.01
☐ 684	Candy Maldonado	.05	.02	.01
☐ 685	Jeff Nelson	.05	.02	.01
☐ 686	Lou Whitaker	.15	.07	.02
☐ 687	Jose Guzman	.05	.02	.01
☐ 688	Manuel Lee	.05	.02	.01
☐ 689	Bob MacDonald	.05	.02	.01
☐ 690	Scott Bankhead	.05	.02	.01
☐ 691	Alan Mills	.05	.02	.01
☐ 692	Brian Williams	.05	.02	.01
☐ 693	Tom Brunansky	.05	.02	.01
☐ 694	Lenny Webster	.05	.02	.01
☐ 695	Greg Briley	.05	.02	.01
☐ 696	Paul O'Neill	.10	.05	.01
☐ 697	Joey Cora	.05	.02	.01
☐ 698	Charlie O'Brien	.05	.02	.01
☐ 699	Junior Ortiz	.05	.02	.01
☐ 700	Ron Darling	.05	.02	.01
☐ 701	Tony Phillips	.05	.02	.01
☐ 702	William Pennyfeather	.05	.02	.01
☐ 703	Mark Gubicza	.05	.02	.01
☐ 704	Steve Hosey RR	.05	.02	.01
☐ 705	Henry Cotto	.05	.02	.01
☐ 706	David Hulse	.05	.02	.01
☐ 707	Mike Pagliarulo	.05	.02	.01
☐ 708	Dave Stieb	.05	.02	.01
☐ 709	Melido Perez	.05	.02	.01
☐ 710	Jimmy Key	.10	.05	.01
☐ 711	Jeff Russell	.05	.02	.01
☐ 712	David Cone	.15	.07	.02
☐ 713	Russ Swan	.05	.02	.01
☐ 714	Mark Guthrie	.05	.02	.01
☐ 715	Checklist	.05	.02	.01
☐ 716	Al Martin RR	.10	.05	.01
☐ 717	Randy Knorr	.05	.02	.01
☐ 718	Mike Stanley	.10	.05	.01
☐ 719	Rick Sutcliffe	.10	.05	.01
☐ 720	Terry Leach	.05	.02	.01
☐ 721	Chipper Jones RR	2.00	.90	.25
☐ 722	Jim Eisenreich	.05	.02	.01
☐ 723	Tom Henke	.10	.05	.01
☐ 724	Jeff Frye	.05	.02	.01
☐ 725	Harold Baines	.10	.05	.01
☐ 726	Scott Sanderson	.05	.02	.01
☐ 727	Tom Foley	.05	.02	.01
☐ 728	Bryan Harvey	.10	.05	.01
☐ 729	Tom Edens	.05	.02	.01
☐ 730	Eric Young	.10	.05	.01
☐ 731	Dave Weathers	.05	.02	.01
☐ 732	Spike Owen	.05	.02	.01
☐ 733	Scott Aldred	.05	.02	.01
☐ 734	Cris Carpenter	.05	.02	.01
☐ 735	Dion James	.05	.02	.01

☐ 736	Joe Girardi	.05	.02	.01
☐ 737	Nigel Wilson RR	.10	.05	.01
☐ 738	Scott Chiamparino	.05	.02	.01
☐ 739	Jeff Reardon	.10	.05	.01
☐ 740	Willie Blair	.05	.02	.01
☐ 741	Jim Corsi	.05	.02	.01
☐ 742	Ken Patterson	.05	.02	.01
☐ 743	Andy Ashby	.05	.02	.01
☐ 744	Rob Natal	.05	.02	.01
☐ 745	Kevin Bass	.05	.02	.01
☐ 746	Freddie Benavides	.05	.02	.01
☐ 747	Chris Donnels	.05	.02	.01
☐ 748	Kerry Woodson	.05	.02	.01
☐ 749	Calvin Jones	.05	.02	.01
☐ 750	Gary Scott	.05	.02	.01
☐ 751	Joe Orsulak	.05	.02	.01
☐ 752	Armando Reynoso	.05	.02	.01
☐ 753	Monty Fariss	.05	.02	.01
☐ 754	Billy Hatcher	.05	.02	.01
☐ 755	Denis Boucher	.05	.02	.01
☐ 756	Walt Weiss	.10	.05	.01
☐ 757	Mike Fitzgerald	.05	.02	.01
☐ 758	Rudy Seanez	.05	.02	.01
☐ 759	Bret Barberie	.05	.02	.01
☐ 760	Mo Sanford	.05	.02	.01
☐ 761	Pedro Castellano	.05	.02	.01
☐ 762	Chuck Carr	.05	.02	.01
☐ 763	Steve Howe	.05	.02	.01
☐ 764	Andres Galarraga	.15	.07	.02
☐ 765	Jeff Conine	.15	.07	.02
☐ 766	Ted Power	.05	.02	.01
☐ 767	Butch Henry	.05	.02	.01
☐ 768	Steve Decker	.05	.02	.01
☐ 769	Storm Davis	.05	.02	.01
☐ 770	Vinny Castilla	.15	.07	.02
☐ 771	Junior Felix	.05	.02	.01
☐ 772	Walt Terrell	.05	.02	.01
☐ 773	Brad Ausmus	.05	.02	.01
☐ 774	Jamie McAndrew	.05	.02	.01
☐ 775	Milt Thompson	.05	.02	.01
☐ 776	Charlie Hayes	.10	.05	.01
☐ 777	Jack Armstrong	.05	.02	.01
☐ 778	Dennis Rasmussen	.05	.02	.01
☐ 779	Darren Holmes	.05	.02	.01
☐ 780	Alex Arias	.05	.02	.01
☐ 781	Randy Bush	.05	.02	.01
☐ 782	Javier Lopez RR	.60	.25	.07
☐ 783	Dante Bichette	.25	.11	.03
☐ 784	John Johnstone	.05	.02	.01
☐ 785	Rene Gonzales	.05	.02	.01
☐ 786	Alex Cole	.05	.02	.01
☐ 787	Jeromy Burnitz RR	.10	.05	.01
☐ 788	Michael Huff	.05	.02	.01
☐ 789	Anthony Telford	.05	.02	.01
☐ 790	Jerald Clark	.05	.02	.01
☐ 791	Joel Johnston	.05	.02	.01
☐ 792	David Nied RR	.10	.05	.01

1993 Donruss Diamond Kings

These standard-size (2 1/2" by 3 1/2") cards were randomly inserted in 1993 Donruss packs. The cards are gold-foil stamped and feature on the fronts player portraits by noted sports artist Dick Perez.

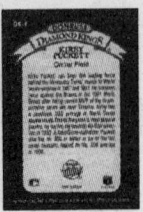

Inside green borders, the backs present career summaries. The first 15 cards were available in the first series of the 1993 Donruss and cards 16-31 were inserted with the second series. Diamond King numbers 27-28 honor the first draft picks of the new Florida Marlins and Colorado Rockies franchises. The cards are numbered on the back with a "DK" prefix. Collectors 16 years old and younger could enter Donruss' Diamond King contest by writing an essay of 75 words or less explaining who their favorite Diamond King player was and why. Winners were awarded one of 30 framed watercolors at the National Convention, held in Chicago, July 22-25, 1993.

	MINT	NRMT	EXC
COMPLETE SET (31)	30.00	13.50	3.70
COMPLETE SERIES 1 (15)	20.00	9.00	2.50
COMPLETE SERIES 2 (16)	10.00	4.50	1.25
COMMON CARD (DK1-DK15)	.50	.23	.06
COMMON CARD (DK16-DK31)	.50	.23	.06

☐ DK1	Ken Griffey Jr.	12.00	5.50	1.50
☐ DK2	Ryne Sandberg	3.00	1.35	.35
☐ DK3	Roger Clemens	2.00	.90	.25
☐ DK4	Kirby Puckett	4.00	1.80	.50
☐ DK5	Bill Swift	.50	.23	.06
☐ DK6	Larry Walker	1.50	.70	.19
☐ DK7	Juan Gonzalez	2.50	1.10	.30
☐ DK8	Wally Joyner	.50	.23	.06
☐ DK9	Andy Van Slyke	.50	.23	.06
☐ DK10	Robin Ventura	1.00	.45	.12
☐ DK11	Bip Roberts	.50	.23	.06
☐ DK12	Roberto Kelly	.50	.23	.06
☐ DK13	Carlos Baerga	2.50	1.10	.30
☐ DK14	Orel Hershiser	1.00	.45	.12
☐ DK15	Cecil Fielder	1.00	.45	.12
☐ DK16	Robin Yount	1.50	.70	.19
☐ DK17	Darren Daulton	.50	.23	.06
☐ DK18	Mark McGwire	1.00	.45	.12
☐ DK19	Tom Glavine	1.25	.55	.16
☐ DK20	Roberto Alomar	2.50	1.10	.30
☐ DK21	Gary Sheffield	1.00	.45	.12
☐ DK22	Bob Tewksbury	.50	.23	.06
☐ DK23	Brady Anderson	.50	.23	.06
☐ DK24	Craig Biggio	1.00	.45	.12
☐ DK25	Eddie Murray	2.00	.90	.25
☐ DK26	Luis Polonia	.50	.23	.06
☐ DK27	Nigel Wilson	.50	.23	.06
☐ DK28	David Nied	.50	.23	.06
☐ DK29	Pat Listach ROY	.50	.23	.06
☐ DK30	Eric Karros ROY	.50	.23	.06
☐ DK31	Checklist 1-31	.50	.23	.06

1993 Donruss Elite

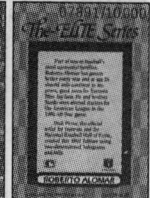

Cards 19-27 were random inserts in 1993
Donruss series I foil packs while cards 28-
36 were inserted in series II packs. The
numbering on the 1993 Elite cards follows
consecutively after that of the 1992 Elite
series cards, and each of the 10,000 Elite
cards is serially numbered. The Signature
Series Will Clark card was randomly inserted in 1993 Donruss foil packs; he personally autographed 5,000 cards. Featuring a
Dick Perez portrait, the ten thousand
Legends Series cards honor Robin Yount
for his 3,000th hit achievement. All these
special cards measure the standard size (2
1/2" by 3 1/2") and are numbered on the
back. The front design of the Elite cards
features a cutout color player photo superimposed on a neon-colored panel framed
by a gray inner border and a variegated silver metallic outer border. The player's
name appears in a neon-colored bar
toward the bottom of the card. On a gray
panel framed by a navy blue inner border
and a two-toned blue outer border, the
backs present player profile. The backs of
the Elite cards also carry the serial number
("X of 10,000) as well as the card number.

	MINT	NRMT	EXC
COMPLETE SET (20)	500.00	220.00	60.00
COMMON CARD (19-27)	10.00	4.50	1.25
COMMON CARD (28-36)	10.00	4.50	1.25
☐ 19 Fred McGriff	20.00	9.00	2.50
☐ 20 Ryne Sandberg	50.00	22.00	6.25
☐ 21 Eddie Murray	20.00	9.00	2.50
☐ 22 Paul Molitor	15.00	6.75	1.85
☐ 23 Barry Larkin	20.00	9.00	2.50
☐ 24 Don Mattingly	80.00	36.00	10.00
☐ 25 Dennis Eckersley	10.00	4.50	1.25
☐ 26 Roberto Alomar	30.00	13.50	3.70
☐ 27 Edgar Martinez	15.00	6.75	1.85
☐ 28 Gary Sheffield	10.00	4.50	1.25
☐ 29 Darren Daulton	10.00	4.50	1.25
☐ 30 Larry Walker	20.00	9.00	2.50
☐ 31 Barry Bonds	40.00	18.00	5.00
☐ 32 Andy Van Slyke	10.00	4.50	1.25
☐ 33 Mark McGwire	10.00	4.50	1.25
☐ 34 Cecil Fielder	10.00	4.50	1.25
☐ 35 Dave Winfield	10.00	4.50	1.25
☐ 36 Juan Gonzalez	40.00	18.00	5.00
☐ L3 Robin Yount	30.00	13.50	3.70

(Legend Series)			
☐ S3 Will Clark AU	150.00	70.00	19.00
(Signature Series)			

1993 Donruss Long Ball Leaders

Randomly inserted in 26-card magazine
distributor packs (1-9 in series I and 10-18
in series II), these standard-size (2 1/2" by
3 1/2") cards feature some of MLB's outstanding sluggers. The fronts feature full-
bleed color action player photos with a red
and bright yellow stripe design across the
bottom that carries the player's name and
team. The Donruss Long Ball Leaders icon
rests on the stripe at the lower left. The
player's longest home run is printed in gold
foil at the upper left. The backs carry color
photos of the ballpark in which the home
run occurred and some facts about the
player and his team. A red and yellow
stripe, similar to the front, contains the
words "1993 Edition." The cards are numbered on the back with an "LL" prefix.

	MINT	NRMT	EXC
COMPLETE SET (18)	80.00	36.00	10.00
COMPLETE SERIES 1 (9)	40.00	18.00	5.00
COMPLETE SERIES 2 (9)	40.00	18.00	5.00
COMMON CARD (LL1-LL9)	1.50	.70	.19
COMMON CARD (LL10-LL18)	1.50	.70	.19
☐ LL1 Rob Deer	1.50	.70	.19
☐ LL2 Fred McGriff	3.00	1.35	.35
☐ LL3 Albert Belle	10.00	4.50	1.25
☐ LL4 Mark McGwire	2.00	.90	.25
☐ LL5 David Justice	3.00	1.35	.35
☐ LL6 Jose Canseco	4.00	1.80	.50
☐ LL7 Kent Hrbek	1.50	.70	.19
☐ LL8 Roberto Alomar	5.00	2.20	.60
☐ LL9 Ken Griffey Jr	25.00	11.00	3.10
☐ LL10 Frank Thomas	25.00	11.00	3.10
☐ LL11 Darryl Strawberry	1.50	.70	.19
☐ LL12 Felix Jose	1.50	.70	.19
☐ LL13 Cecil Fielder	2.00	.90	.25
☐ LL14 Juan Gonzalez	5.00	2.20	.60
☐ LL15 Ryne Sandberg	6.00	2.70	.75
☐ LL16 Gary Sheffield	2.00	.90	.25
☐ LL17 Jeff Bagwell	10.00	4.50	1.25
☐ LL18 Larry Walker	3.00	1.35	.35

1993 Donruss MVPs

1993 Donruss Spirit of the Game

Thirteen MVP cards were issued in each series, and they were nserted one per 23-card jumbo packs. The cards measure the standard size. The fronts feature full-bleed color action player photos with a red, white, and blue ribbon design across the bottom that contains the player's name and team. The Donruss MVP icon is gold-foil stamped over the ribbon. The backs carry action player shots above a ribbon design similar to the front, and below the ribbon a pink granite panel contains player information and 1992 Spotlight stats. The cards are numbered on the back with an "MVP" prefix.

A new subset in 1993, these standard-size (2 1/2" by 3 1/2") cards were randomly inserted in 1993 Donruss packs and packed approximately two per box. Cards 1-10 were first-series inserts, and cards 11-20 were second-series inserts. The fronts feature borderless glossy color action player photos. The set title, "Spirit of the Game," is stamped in gold foil script across the top or bottom of the picture. The backs sport a second borderless color player photo; this photo concludes the action portrayed in the front photo. The caption to the second picture is printed in yellow block lettering. The cards are numbered on the back with an "SG" prefix.

	MINT	NRMT	EXC
COMPLETE SET (26)	30.00	13.50	3.70
COMPLETE SERIES 1 (13)	10.00	4.50	1.25
COMPLETE SERIES 2 (13)	20.00	9.00	2.50
COMMON CARD (1-13)	.30	.14	.04
COMMON CARD (14-26)	.30	.14	.04

		MINT	NRMT	EXC
☐ 1	Luis Polonia	.30	.14	.04
☐ 2	Frank Thomas	8.00	3.60	1.00
☐ 3	George Brett	3.00	1.35	.35
☐ 4	Paul Molitor	.50	.23	.06
☐ 5	Don Mattingly	4.00	1.80	.50
☐ 6	Roberto Alomar	1.50	.70	.19
☐ 7	Terry Pendleton	.30	.14	.04
☐ 8	Eric Karros	.50	.23	.06
☐ 9	Larry Walker	1.00	.45	.12
☐ 10	Eddie Murray	1.00	.45	.12
☐ 11	Darren Daulton	.50	.23	.06
☐ 12	Ray Lankford	.50	.23	.06
☐ 13	Will Clark	1.00	.45	.12
☐ 14	Cal Ripken	8.00	3.60	1.00
☐ 15	Roger Clemens	1.25	.55	.16
☐ 16	Carlos Baerga	1.50	.70	.19
☐ 17	Cecil Fielder	.50	.23	.06
☐ 18	Kirby Puckett	2.50	1.10	.30
☐ 19	Mark McGwire	.50	.23	.06
☐ 20	Ken Griffey Jr.	8.00	3.60	1.00
☐ 21	Juan Gonzalez	1.50	.70	.19
☐ 22	Ryne Sandberg	2.00	.90	.25
☐ 23	Bip Roberts	.30	.14	.04
☐ 24	Jeff Bagwell	3.00	1.35	.35
☐ 25	Barry Bonds	2.00	.90	.25
☐ 26	Gary Sheffield	.50	.23	.06

1993 Donruss Spirit of the Game

	MINT	NRMT	EXC
COMPLETE SET (20)	20.00	9.00	2.50
COMPLETE SERIES 1 (10)	8.00	3.60	1.00
COMPLETE SERIES 2 (10)	12.00	5.50	1.50
COMMON CARD (SG1-SG10)	.50	.23	.06
COMMON CARD (SG11-SG20)	.50	.23	.06

		MINT	NRMT	EXC
☐ SG1	Mike Bordick Turning Two	.50	.23	.06
☐ SG2	Dave Justice Play at the Plate	1.25	.55	.16
☐ SG3	Roberto Alomar In There	2.00	.90	.25
☐ SG4	Dennis Eckersley Pumped	1.00	.45	.12
☐ SG5	Juan Gonzalez and Jose Canseco Dynamic Duo	2.50	1.10	.30
☐ SG6	George Bell and Frank Thomas ... Gone	2.50	1.10	.30
☐ SG7	Wade Boggs and Luis Polonia Safe or Out	1.00	.45	.12
☐ SG8	Will Clark The Thrill	1.25	.55	.16
☐ SG9	Bip Roberts Safe at Home	.50	.23	.06
☐ SG10	Cecil Fielder Rob Deer Mickey Tettleton Thirty 3	1.00	.45	.12
☐ SG11	Kenny Lofton Bag Bandit	3.00	1.35	.35

		MINT	NRMT	EXC
☐ SG12	Gary Sheffield	1.00	.45	.12
	Fred McGriff			
	Back to Back			
☐ SG13	Greg Gagne	1.25	.55	.16
	Barry Larkin			
☐ SG14	Ryne Sandberg	2.50	1.10	.30
	The Ball Stops Here			
☐ SG15	Carlos Baerga	1.00	.45	.12
	Gary Gaetti			
	Over the Top			
☐ SG16	Danny Tartabull	.50	.23	.06
	At the Wall			
☐ SG17	Brady Anderson	.50	.23	.06
	Head First			
☐ SG18	Frank Thomas	10.00	4.50	1.25
	Big Hurt			
☐ SG19	Kevin Gross	.50	.23	.06
	No Hitter			
☐ SG20	Robin Yount	1.25	.55	.16
	3,000 Hits			

1994 Donruss

The 1994 Donruss set was issued in two separate series of 330 standard-size cards for a total of 660. The fronts feature borderless color player action photos on front. The player's name and position appear in gold foil within a team color-coded stripe near the bottom. The team logo appears within a black rectangle framed by a team color near the bottom. The set name and year, stamped in gold foil, also appear in this rectangle. Most of the backs are horizontal, and feature another borderless color player action photo. A black rectangle framed by a team color appears on one side and carries the player's name, team, uniform number, and biography. The player's stats appear within ghosted stripes near the bottom. Rookie Cards include Curtis Pride and Julian Tavarez.

	MINT	NRMT	EXC
COMPLETE SET (660)	50.00	22.00	6.25
COMPLETE SERIES 1 (330)	25.00	11.00	3.10
COMPLETE SERIES 2 (330)	25.00	11.00	3.10
COMMON CARD (1-330)	.10	.05	.01
COMMON CARD (331-660)	.10	.05	.01

		MINT	NRMT	EXC
☐ 1	Nolan Ryan	3.00	1.35	.35
☐ 2	Mike Piazza	1.25	.55	.16
☐ 3	Moises Alou	.30	.14	.04
☐ 4	Ken Griffey Jr.	3.00	1.35	.35
☐ 5	Gary Sheffield	.30	.14	.04
☐ 6	Roberto Alomar	.60	.25	.07
☐ 7	John Kruk	.20	.09	.03
☐ 8	Gregg Olson	.10	.05	.01
☐ 9	Gregg Jefferies	.30	.14	.04
☐ 10	Tony Gwynn	1.00	.45	.12
☐ 11	Chad Curtis	.20	.09	.03
☐ 12	Craig Biggio	.20	.09	.03
☐ 13	John Burkett	.10	.05	.01
☐ 14	Carlos Baerga	.60	.25	.07
☐ 15	Robin Yount	.40	.18	.05
☐ 16	Dennis Eckersley	.30	.14	.04
☐ 17	Dwight Gooden	.10	.05	.01
☐ 18	Ryne Sandberg	.75	.35	.09
☐ 19	Rickey Henderson	.30	.14	.04
☐ 20	Jack McDowell	.30	.14	.04
☐ 21	Jay Bell	.20	.09	.03
☐ 22	Kevin Brown	.10	.05	.01
☐ 23	Robin Ventura	.20	.09	.03
☐ 24	Paul Molitor	.30	.14	.04
☐ 25	David Justice	.40	.18	.05
☐ 26	Rafael Palmeiro	.30	.14	.04
☐ 27	Cecil Fielder	.30	.14	.04
☐ 28	Chuck Knoblauch	.30	.14	.04
☐ 29	Dave Hollins	.20	.09	.03
☐ 30	Jimmy Key	.20	.09	.03
☐ 31	Mark Langston	.20	.09	.03
☐ 32	Darryl Kile	.20	.09	.03
☐ 33	Ruben Sierra	.30	.14	.04
☐ 34	Ron Gant	.20	.09	.03
☐ 35	Ozzie Smith	.60	.25	.07
☐ 36	Wade Boggs	.30	.14	.04
☐ 37	Marquis Grissom	.30	.14	.04
☐ 38	Will Clark	.40	.18	.05
☐ 39	Kenny Lofton	1.00	.45	.12
☐ 40	Cal Ripken	3.00	1.35	.35
☐ 41	Steve Avery	.30	.14	.04
☐ 42	Mo Vaughn	.50	.23	.06
☐ 43	Brian McRae	.20	.09	.03
☐ 44	Mickey Tettleton	.20	.09	.03
☐ 45	Barry Larkin	.40	.18	.05
☐ 46	Charlie Hayes	.20	.09	.03
☐ 47	Kevin Appier	.20	.09	.03
☐ 48	Robby Thompson	.10	.05	.01
☐ 49	Juan Gonzalez	.75	.35	.09
☐ 50	Paul O'Neill	.20	.09	.03
☐ 51	Marcos Armas	.10	.05	.01
☐ 52	Mike Butcher	.10	.05	.01
☐ 53	Ken Caminiti	.20	.09	.03
☐ 54	Pat Borders	.10	.05	.01
☐ 55	Pedro Munoz	.10	.05	.01
☐ 56	Tim Belcher	.10	.05	.01
☐ 57	Paul Assenmacher	.10	.05	.01
☐ 58	Damon Berryhill	.10	.05	.01
☐ 59	Ricky Bones	.10	.05	.01
☐ 60	Rene Arocha	.20	.09	.03
☐ 61	Shawn Boskie	.10	.05	.01
☐ 62	Pedro Astacio	.20	.09	.03
☐ 63	Frank Bolick	.10	.05	.01
☐ 64	Bud Black	.10	.05	.01
☐ 65	Sandy Alomar Jr.	.20	.09	.03
☐ 66	Rich Amaral	.10	.05	.01
☐ 67	Luis Aquino	.10	.05	.01
☐ 68	Kevin Baez	.10	.05	.01
☐ 69	Mike Devereaux	.20	.09	.03
☐ 70	Andy Ashby	.10	.05	.01
☐ 71	Larry Andersen	.10	.05	.01
☐ 72	Steve Cooke	.10	.05	.01
☐ 73	Mario Diaz	.10	.05	.01

☐ 74	Rob Deer	.10	.05	.01
☐ 75	Bobby Ayala	.10	.05	.01
☐ 76	Freddie Benavides	.10	.05	.01
☐ 77	Stan Belinda	.10	.05	.01
☐ 78	John Doherty	.10	.05	.01
☐ 79	Willie Banks	.10	.05	.01
☐ 80	Spike Owen	.10	.05	.01
☐ 81	Mike Bordick	.10	.05	.01
☐ 82	Chili Davis	.20	.09	.03
☐ 83	Luis Gonzalez	.10	.05	.01
☐ 84	Ed Sprague	.10	.05	.01
☐ 85	Jeff Reboulet	.10	.05	.01
☐ 86	Jason Bere	.30	.14	.04
☐ 87	Mark Hutton	.10	.05	.01
☐ 88	Jeff Blauser	.20	.09	.03
☐ 89	Cal Eldred	.20	.09	.03
☐ 90	Bernard Gilkey	.10	.05	.01
☐ 91	Frank Castillo	.10	.05	.01
☐ 92	Jim Gott	.10	.05	.01
☐ 93	Greg Colbrunn	.10	.05	.01
☐ 94	Jeff Brantley	.10	.05	.01
☐ 95	Jeremy Hernandez	.10	.05	.01
☐ 96	Norm Charlton	.10	.05	.01
☐ 97	Alex Arias	.10	.05	.01
☐ 98	John Franco	.10	.05	.01
☐ 99	Chris Hoiles	.20	.09	.03
☐ 100	Brad Ausmus	.10	.05	.01
☐ 101	Wes Chamberlain	.10	.05	.01
☐ 102	Mark Dewey	.10	.05	.01
☐ 103	Benji Gil	.20	.09	.03
☐ 104	John Dopson	.10	.05	.01
☐ 105	John Smiley	.10	.05	.01
☐ 106	David Nied	.20	.09	.03
☐ 107	George Brett	1.25	.55	.16
☐ 108	Kirk Gibson	.20	.09	.03
☐ 109	Larry Casian	.10	.05	.01
☐ 110	Checklist 1-82	.10	.05	.01
	Ryne Sandberg			
☐ 111	Brent Gates	.20	.09	.03
☐ 112	Damion Easley	.10	.05	.01
☐ 113	Pete Harnisch	.10	.05	.01
☐ 114	Danny Cox	.10	.05	.01
☐ 115	Kevin Tapani	.10	.05	.01
☐ 116	Roberto Hernandez	.10	.05	.01
☐ 117	Domingo Jean	.10	.05	.01
☐ 118	Sid Bream	.10	.05	.01
☐ 119	Doug Henry	.10	.05	.01
☐ 120	Omar Olivares	.10	.05	.01
☐ 121	Mike Harkey	.10	.05	.01
☐ 122	Carlos Hernandez	.10	.05	.01
☐ 123	Jeff Fassero	.10	.05	.01
☐ 124	Dave Burba	.10	.05	.01
☐ 125	Wayne Kirby	.10	.05	.01
☐ 126	John Cummings	.10	.05	.01
☐ 127	Bret Barberie	.10	.05	.01
☐ 128	Todd Hundley	.20	.09	.03
☐ 129	Tim Hulett	.10	.05	.01
☐ 130	Phil Clark	.10	.05	.01
☐ 131	Danny Jackson	.10	.05	.01
☐ 132	Tom Foley	.10	.05	.01
☐ 133	Donald Harris	.10	.05	.01
☐ 134	Scott Fletcher	.10	.05	.01
☐ 135	Johnny Ruffin	.10	.05	.01
☐ 136	Jerald Clark	.10	.05	.01
☐ 137	Billy Brewer	.10	.05	.01
☐ 138	Dan Gladden	.10	.05	.01
☐ 139	Eddie Guardado	.10	.05	.01
☐ 140	Checklist 83-164	.10	.05	.01
	Cal Ripken			
☐ 141	Scott Hemond	.10	.05	.01
☐ 142	Steve Frey	.10	.05	.01
☐ 143	Xavier Hernandez	.10	.05	.01
☐ 144	Mark Eichhorn	.10	.05	.01
☐ 145	Ellis Burks	.20	.09	.03
☐ 146	Jim Leyritz	.10	.05	.01
☐ 147	Mark Lemke	.10	.05	.01
☐ 148	Pat Listach	.10	.05	.01
☐ 149	Donovan Osborne	.10	.05	.01
☐ 150	Glenallen Hill	.10	.05	.01
☐ 151	Orel Hershiser	.20	.09	.03
☐ 152	Darrin Fletcher	.10	.05	.01
☐ 153	Royce Clayton	.20	.09	.03
☐ 154	Derek Lilliquist	.10	.05	.01
☐ 155	Mike Felder	.10	.05	.01
☐ 156	Jeff Conine	.30	.14	.04
☐ 157	Ryan Thompson	.20	.09	.03
☐ 158	Ben McDonald	.20	.09	.03
☐ 159	Ricky Gutierrez	.10	.05	.01
☐ 160	Terry Mulholland	.10	.05	.01
☐ 161	Carlos Garcia	.10	.05	.01
☐ 162	Tom Henke	.10	.05	.01
☐ 163	Mike Greenwell	.20	.09	.03
☐ 164	Thomas Howard	.10	.05	.01
☐ 165	Joe Girardi	.10	.05	.01
☐ 166	Hubie Brooks	.10	.05	.01
☐ 167	Greg Gohr	.10	.05	.01
☐ 168	Chip Hale	.10	.05	.01
☐ 169	Rick Honeycutt	.10	.05	.01
☐ 170	Hilly Hathaway	.10	.05	.01
☐ 171	Todd Jones	.10	.05	.01
☐ 172	Tony Fernandez	.10	.05	.01
☐ 173	Bo Jackson	.30	.14	.04
☐ 174	Bobby Munoz	.10	.05	.01
☐ 175	Greg McMichael	.20	.09	.03
☐ 176	Graeme Lloyd	.10	.05	.01
☐ 177	Tom Pagnozzi	.10	.05	.01
☐ 178	Derrick May	.10	.05	.01
☐ 179	Pedro Martinez	.30	.14	.04
☐ 180	Ken Hill	.20	.09	.03
☐ 181	Bryan Hickerson	.10	.05	.01
☐ 182	Jose Mesa	.10	.05	.01
☐ 183	Dave Fleming	.10	.05	.01
☐ 184	Henry Cotto	.10	.05	.01
☐ 185	Jeff Kent	.20	.09	.03
☐ 186	Mark McLemore	.10	.05	.01
☐ 187	Trevor Hoffman	.10	.05	.01
☐ 188	Todd Pratt	.10	.05	.01
☐ 189	Blas Minor	.10	.05	.01
☐ 190	Charlie Leibrandt	.10	.05	.01
☐ 191	Tony Pena	.10	.05	.01
☐ 192	Larry Luebbers	.10	.05	.01
☐ 193	Greg W. Harris	.10	.05	.01
☐ 194	David Cone	.30	.14	.04
☐ 195	Bill Gullickson	.10	.05	.01
☐ 196	Brian Harper	.10	.05	.01
☐ 197	Steve Karsay	.10	.05	.01
☐ 198	Greg Myers	.10	.05	.01
☐ 199	Mark Portugal	.10	.05	.01
☐ 200	Pat Hentgen	.20	.09	.03
☐ 201	Mike LaValliere	.10	.05	.01
☐ 202	Mike Stanley	.10	.05	.01
☐ 203	Kent Mercker	.10	.05	.01
☐ 204	Dave Nilsson	.10	.05	.01
☐ 205	Erik Pappas	.10	.05	.01
☐ 206	Mike Morgan	.10	.05	.01
☐ 207	Roger McDowell	.10	.05	.01
☐ 208	Mike Lansing	.20	.09	.03
☐ 209	Kirt Manwaring	.10	.05	.01
☐ 210	Randy Milligan	.10	.05	.01
☐ 211	Erik Hanson	.10	.05	.01
☐ 212	Orestes Destrade	.10	.05	.01
☐ 213	Mike Maddux	.10	.05	.01

☐ 214 Alan Mills	.10	.05	.01
☐ 215 Tim Mauser	.10	.05	.01
☐ 216 Ben Rivera	.10	.05	.01
☐ 217 Don Slaught	.10	.05	.01
☐ 218 Bob Patterson	.10	.05	.01
☐ 219 Carlos Quintana	.10	.05	.01
☐ 220 Checklist 165-247	.10	.05	.01
Tim Raines			
☐ 221 Hal Morris	.20	.09	.03
☐ 222 Darren Holmes	.10	.05	.01
☐ 223 Chris Gwynn	.10	.05	.01
☐ 224 Chad Kreuter	.10	.05	.01
☐ 225 Mike Hartley	.10	.05	.01
☐ 226 Scott Lydy	.10	.05	.01
☐ 227 Eduardo Perez	.10	.05	.01
☐ 228 Greg Swindell	.10	.05	.01
☐ 229 Al Leiter	.10	.05	.01
☐ 230 Scott Radinsky	.10	.05	.01
☐ 231 Bob Wickman	.10	.05	.01
☐ 232 Otis Nixon	.10	.05	.01
☐ 233 Kevin Reimer	.10	.05	.01
☐ 234 Geronimo Pena	.10	.05	.01
☐ 235 Kevin Roberson	.10	.05	.01
☐ 236 Jody Reed	.10	.05	.01
☐ 237 Kirk Rueter	.10	.05	.01
☐ 238 Willie McGee	.10	.05	.01
☐ 239 Charles Nagy	.20	.09	.03
☐ 240 Tim Leary	.10	.05	.01
☐ 241 Carl Everett	.20	.09	.03
☐ 242 Charlie O'Brien	.10	.05	.01
☐ 243 Mike Pagliarulo	.10	.05	.01
☐ 244 Kerry Taylor	.10	.05	.01
☐ 245 Kevin Stocker	.20	.09	.03
☐ 246 Joel Johnston	.10	.05	.01
☐ 247 Geno Petralli	.10	.05	.01
☐ 248 Jeff Russell	.10	.05	.01
☐ 249 Joe Oliver	.10	.05	.01
☐ 250 Roberto Mejia	.20	.09	.03
☐ 251 Chris Haney	.10	.05	.01
☐ 252 Bill Krueger	.10	.05	.01
☐ 253 Shane Mack	.20	.09	.03
☐ 254 Terry Steinbach	.20	.09	.03
☐ 255 Luis Polonia	.10	.05	.01
☐ 256 Eddie Taubensee	.10	.05	.01
☐ 257 Dave Stewart	.20	.09	.03
☐ 258 Tim Raines	.30	.14	.04
☐ 259 Bernie Williams	.20	.09	.03
☐ 260 John Smoltz	.20	.09	.03
☐ 261 Kevin Seitzer	.10	.05	.01
☐ 262 Bob Tewksbury	.10	.05	.01
☐ 263 Bob Scanlan	.10	.05	.01
☐ 264 Henry Rodriguez	.10	.05	.01
☐ 265 Tim Scott	.10	.05	.01
☐ 266 Scott Sanderson	.10	.05	.01
☐ 267 Eric Plunk	.10	.05	.01
☐ 268 Edgar Martinez	.20	.09	.03
☐ 269 Charlie Hough	.10	.05	.01
☐ 270 Joe Orsulak	.10	.05	.01
☐ 271 Harold Reynolds	.10	.05	.01
☐ 272 Tim Teufel	.10	.05	.01
☐ 273 Bobby Thigpen	.10	.05	.01
☐ 274 Randy Tomlin	.10	.05	.01
☐ 275 Gary Redus	.10	.05	.01
☐ 276 Ken Ryan	.10	.05	.01
☐ 277 Tim Pugh	.10	.05	.01
☐ 278 J. Owens	.10	.05	.01
☐ 279 Phil Hiatt	.20	.09	.03
☐ 280 Alan Trammell	.30	.14	.04
☐ 281 Dave McCarty	.10	.05	.01
☐ 282 Bob Welch	.10	.05	.01
☐ 283 J.T. Snow	.20	.09	.03
☐ 284 Brian Williams	.10	.05	.01
☐ 285 Devon White	.20	.09	.03
☐ 286 Steve Sax	.10	.05	.01
☐ 287 Tony Tarasco	.30	.14	.04
☐ 288 Bill Spiers	.10	.05	.01
☐ 289 Allen Watson	.10	.05	.01
☐ 290 Checklist 248-330	.10	.05	.01
Rickey Henderson			
☐ 291 Jose Vizcaino	.10	.05	.01
☐ 292 Darryl Strawberry	.20	.09	.03
☐ 293 John Wetteland	.10	.05	.01
☐ 294 Bill Swift	.10	.05	.01
☐ 295 Jeff Treadway	.10	.05	.01
☐ 296 Tino Martinez	.20	.09	.03
☐ 297 Richie Lewis	.10	.05	.01
☐ 298 Bret Saberhagen	.20	.09	.03
☐ 299 Arthur Rhodes	.10	.05	.01
☐ 300 Guillermo Velasquez	.10	.05	.01
☐ 301 Milt Thompson	.10	.05	.01
☐ 302 Doug Strange	.10	.05	.01
☐ 303 Aaron Sele	.30	.14	.04
☐ 304 Bip Roberts	.10	.05	.01
☐ 305 Bruce Ruffin	.10	.05	.01
☐ 306 Jose Lind	.10	.05	.01
☐ 307 David Wells	.10	.05	.01
☐ 308 Bobby Witt	.10	.05	.01
☐ 309 Mark Wohlers	.10	.05	.01
☐ 310 B.J. Surhoff	.20	.09	.03
☐ 311 Mark Whiten	.10	.05	.01
☐ 312 Turk Wendell	.10	.05	.01
☐ 313 Raul Mondesi	1.00	.45	.12
☐ 314 Brian Turang	.10	.05	.01
☐ 315 Chris Hammond	.10	.05	.01
☐ 316 Tim Bogar	.10	.05	.01
☐ 317 Brad Pennington	.10	.05	.01
☐ 318 Tim Worrell	.10	.05	.01
☐ 319 Mitch Williams	.10	.05	.01
☐ 320 Rondell White	.30	.14	.04
☐ 321 Frank Viola	.10	.05	.01
☐ 322 Manny Ramirez	1.50	.70	.19
☐ 323 Gary Wayne	.10	.05	.01
☐ 324 Mike Macfarlane	.10	.05	.01
☐ 325 Russ Springer	.10	.05	.01
☐ 326 Tim Wallach	.10	.05	.01
☐ 327 Salomon Torres	.20	.09	.03
☐ 328 Omar Vizquel	.10	.05	.01
☐ 329 Andy Tomberlin	.10	.05	.01
☐ 330 Chris Sabo	.10	.05	.01
☐ 331 Mike Mussina	.40	.18	.05
☐ 332 Andy Benes	.20	.09	.03
☐ 333 Darren Daulton	.30	.14	.04
☐ 334 Orlando Merced	.20	.09	.03
☐ 335 Mark McGwire	.30	.14	.04
☐ 336 Dave Winfield	.30	.14	.04
☐ 337 Sammy Sosa	.30	.14	.04
☐ 338 Eric Karros	.20	.09	.03
☐ 339 Greg Vaughn	.20	.09	.03
☐ 340 Don Mattingly	1.50	.70	.19
☐ 341 Frank Thomas	3.00	1.35	.35
☐ 342 Fred McGriff	.40	.18	.05
☐ 343 Kirby Puckett	1.00	.45	.12
☐ 344 Roberto Kelly	.20	.09	.03
☐ 345 Wally Joyner	.20	.09	.03
☐ 346 Andres Galarraga	.30	.14	.04
☐ 347 Bobby Bonilla	.30	.14	.04
☐ 348 Benito Santiago	.10	.05	.01
☐ 349 Barry Bonds	.75	.35	.09
☐ 350 Delino DeShields	.20	.09	.03
☐ 351 Albert Belle	1.25	.55	.16
☐ 352 Randy Johnson	.60	.25	.07
☐ 353 Tim Salmon	.60	.25	.07

☐ 354 John Olerud	.30	.14	.04
☐ 355 Dean Palmer	.20	.09	.03
☐ 356 Roger Clemens	.50	.23	.06
☐ 357 Jim Abbott	.30	.14	.04
☐ 358 Mark Grace	.30	.14	.04
☐ 359 Ozzie Guillen	.10	.05	.01
☐ 360 Lou Whitaker	.30	.14	.04
☐ 361 Jose Rijo	.20	.09	.03
☐ 362 Jeff Montgomery	.20	.09	.03
☐ 363 Chuck Finley	.10	.05	.01
☐ 364 Tom Glavine	.30	.14	.04
☐ 365 Jeff Bagwell	1.00	.45	.12
☐ 366 Joe Carter	.30	.14	.04
☐ 367 Ray Lankford	.30	.14	.04
☐ 368 Ramon Martinez	.20	.09	.03
☐ 369 Jay Buhner	.20	.09	.03
☐ 370 Matt Williams	.50	.23	.06
☐ 371 Larry Walker	.40	.18	.05
☐ 372 Jose Canseco	.50	.23	.06
☐ 373 Lenny Dykstra	.30	.14	.04
☐ 374 Bryan Harvey	.10	.05	.01
☐ 375 Andy Van Slyke	.30	.14	.04
☐ 376 Ivan Rodriguez	.30	.14	.04
☐ 377 Kevin Mitchell	.20	.09	.03
☐ 378 Travis Fryman	.30	.14	.04
☐ 379 Duane Ward	.20	.09	.03
☐ 380 Greg Maddux	3.00	1.35	.35
☐ 381 Scott Servais	.10	.05	.01
☐ 382 Greg Olson	.10	.05	.01
☐ 383 Rey Sanchez	.10	.05	.01
☐ 384 Tom Kramer	.10	.05	.01
☐ 385 David Valle	.10	.05	.01
☐ 386 Eddie Murray	.40	.18	.05
☐ 387 Kevin Higgins	.10	.05	.01
☐ 388 Dan Wilson	.10	.05	.01
☐ 389 Todd Frohwith	.10	.05	.01
☐ 390 Gerald Williams	.20	.09	.03
☐ 391 Hipolito Pichardo	.10	.05	.01
☐ 392 Pat Meares	.10	.05	.01
☐ 393 Luis Lopez	.10	.05	.01
☐ 394 Ricky Jordan	.10	.05	.01
☐ 395 Bob Walk	.10	.05	.01
☐ 396 Sid Fernandez	.10	.05	.01
☐ 397 Todd Worrell	.10	.05	.01
☐ 398 Darryl Hamilton	.10	.05	.01
☐ 399 Randy Myers	.10	.05	.01
☐ 400 Rod Brewer	.10	.05	.01
☐ 401 Lance Blankenship	.10	.05	.01
☐ 402 Steve Finley	.10	.05	.01
☐ 403 Phil Leftwich	.10	.05	.01
☐ 404 Juan Guzman	.20	.09	.03
☐ 405 Anthony Young	.10	.05	.01
☐ 406 Jeff Gardner	.10	.05	.01
☐ 407 Ryan Bowen	.10	.05	.01
☐ 408 Fernando Valenzuela	.10	.05	.01
☐ 409 David West	.10	.05	.01
☐ 410 Kenny Rogers	.20	.09	.03
☐ 411 Bob Zupcic	.10	.05	.01
☐ 412 Eric Young	.20	.09	.03
☐ 413 Bret Boone	.30	.14	.04
☐ 414 Danny Tartabull	.20	.09	.03
☐ 415 Bob MacDonald	.10	.05	.01
☐ 416 Ron Karkovice	.10	.05	.01
☐ 417 Scott Cooper	.20	.09	.03
☐ 418 Dante Bichette	.40	.18	.05
☐ 419 Tripp Cromer	.20	.09	.03
☐ 420 Billy Ashley	.30	.14	.04
☐ 421 Roger Smithberg	.10	.05	.01
☐ 422 Dennis Martinez	.20	.09	.03
☐ 423 Mike Blowers	.20	.09	.03
☐ 424 Darren Lewis	.10	.05	.01

☐ 425 Junior Ortiz	.10	.05	.01
☐ 426 Butch Huskey	.20	.09	.03
☐ 427 Jimmy Poole	.10	.05	.01
☐ 428 Walt Weiss	.10	.05	.01
☐ 429 Scott Bankhead	.10	.05	.01
☐ 430 Deion Sanders	.60	.25	.07
☐ 431 Scott Bullett	.10	.05	.01
☐ 432 Jeff Huson	.10	.05	.01
☐ 433 Tyler Green	.20	.09	.03
☐ 434 Billy Hatcher	.10	.05	.01
☐ 435 Bob Hamelin	.10	.05	.01
☐ 436 Reggie Sanders	.20	.09	.03
☐ 437 Scott Erickson	.10	.05	.01
☐ 438 Steve Reed	.10	.05	.01
☐ 439 Randy Velarde	.10	.05	.01
☐ 440 Checklist 331-412	.10	.05	.01
(Tony Gwynn)			
☐ 441 Terry Leach	.10	.05	.01
☐ 442 Danny Bautista	.20	.09	.03
☐ 443 Kent Hrbek	.10	.05	.01
☐ 444 Rick Wilkins	.10	.05	.01
☐ 445 Tony Phillips	.10	.05	.01
☐ 446 Dion James	.10	.05	.01
☐ 447 Joey Cora	.10	.05	.01
☐ 448 Andre Dawson	.30	.14	.04
☐ 449 Pedro Castellano	.10	.05	.01
☐ 450 Tom Gordon	.10	.05	.01
☐ 451 Rob Dibble	.10	.05	.01
☐ 452 Ron Darling	.10	.05	.01
☐ 453 Chipper Jones	1.50	.70	.19
☐ 454 Joe Grahe	.10	.05	.01
☐ 455 Domingo Cedeno	.20	.09	.03
☐ 456 Tom Edens	.10	.05	.01
☐ 457 Mitch Webster	.10	.05	.01
☐ 458 Jose Bautista	.10	.05	.01
☐ 459 Troy O'Leary	.20	.09	.03
☐ 460 Todd Zeile	.20	.09	.03
☐ 461 Sean Berry	.10	.05	.01
☐ 462 Brad Holman	.10	.05	.01
☐ 463 Dave Martinez	.10	.05	.01
☐ 464 Mark Lewis	.10	.05	.01
☐ 465 Paul Carey	.10	.05	.01
☐ 466 Jack Armstrong	.10	.05	.01
☐ 467 David Telgheder	.10	.05	.01
☐ 468 Gene Harris	.10	.05	.01
☐ 469 Danny Darwin	.10	.05	.01
☐ 470 Kim Batiste	.10	.05	.01
☐ 471 Tim Wakefield	.20	.09	.03
☐ 472 Craig Lefferts	.10	.05	.01
☐ 473 Jacob Brumfield	.10	.05	.01
☐ 474 Lance Painter	.10	.05	.01
☐ 475 Milt Cuyler	.10	.05	.01
☐ 476 Melido Perez	.10	.05	.01
☐ 477 Derek Parks	.10	.05	.01
☐ 478 Gary DiSarcina	.10	.05	.01
☐ 479 Steve Bedrosian	.10	.05	.01
☐ 480 Eric Anthony	.10	.05	.01
☐ 481 Julio Franco	.20	.09	.03
☐ 482 Tommy Greene	.10	.05	.01
☐ 483 Pat Kelly	.10	.05	.01
☐ 484 Nate Minchey	.10	.05	.01
☐ 485 William Pennyfeather	.10	.05	.01
☐ 486 Harold Baines	.20	.09	.03
☐ 487 Howard Johnson	.10	.05	.01
☐ 488 Angel Miranda	.10	.05	.01
☐ 489 Scott Sanders	.20	.09	.03
☐ 490 Shawon Dunston	.10	.05	.01
☐ 491 Mel Rojas	.10	.05	.01
☐ 492 Jeff Nelson	.10	.05	.01
☐ 493 Archi Cianfrocco	.10	.05	.01
☐ 494 Al Martin	.10	.05	.01

☐ 495 Mike Gallego	.10	.05	.01
☐ 496 Mike Henneman	.10	.05	.01
☐ 497 Armando Reynoso	.10	.05	.01
☐ 498 Mickey Morandini	.10	.05	.01
☐ 499 Rick Renteria	.10	.05	.01
☐ 500 Rick Sutcliffe	.10	.05	.01
☐ 501 Bobby Jones	.30	.14	.04
☐ 502 Gary Gaetti	.10	.05	.01
☐ 503 Rick Aguilera	.20	.09	.03
☐ 504 Todd Stottlemyre	.10	.05	.01
☐ 505 Mike Mohler	.10	.05	.01
☐ 506 Mike Stanton	.10	.05	.01
☐ 507 Jose Guzman	.10	.05	.01
☐ 508 Kevin Rogers	.10	.05	.01
☐ 509 Chuck Carr	.10	.05	.01
☐ 510 Chris Jones	.10	.05	.01
☐ 511 Brent Mayne	.10	.05	.01
☐ 512 Greg Harris	.10	.05	.01
☐ 513 Dave Henderson	.10	.05	.01
☐ 514 Eric Hillman	.10	.05	.01
☐ 515 Dan Peltier	.10	.05	.01
☐ 516 Craig Shipley	.10	.05	.01
☐ 517 John Valentin	.30	.14	.04
☐ 518 Wilson Alvarez	.30	.14	.04
☐ 519 Andujar Cedeno	.10	.05	.01
☐ 520 Troy Neel	.10	.05	.01
☐ 521 Tom Candiotti	.10	.05	.01
☐ 522 Matt Mieske	.10	.05	.01
☐ 523 Jim Thome	.60	.25	.07
☐ 524 Lou Frazier	.10	.05	.01
☐ 525 Mike Jackson	.10	.05	.01
☐ 526 Pedro Martinez	.30	.14	.04
☐ 527 Roger Pavlik	.20	.09	.03
☐ 528 Kent Bottenfield	.10	.05	.01
☐ 529 Felix Jose	.10	.05	.01
☐ 530 Mark Guthrie	.10	.05	.01
☐ 531 Steve Farr	.10	.05	.01
☐ 532 Craig Paquette	.10	.05	.01
☐ 533 Doug Jones	.10	.05	.01
☐ 534 Luis Allcea	.10	.05	.01
☐ 535 Cory Snyder	.10	.05	.01
☐ 536 Paul Sorrento	.10	.05	.01
☐ 537 Nigel Wilson	.10	.05	.01
☐ 538 Jeff King	.10	.05	.01
☐ 539 Willie Greene	.10	.05	.01
☐ 540 Kirk McCaskill	.10	.05	.01
☐ 541 Al Osuna	.10	.05	.01
☐ 542 Greg Hibbard	.10	.05	.01
☐ 543 Brett Butler	.20	.09	.03
☐ 544 Jose Valentin	.10	.05	.01
☐ 545 Wil Cordero	.20	.09	.03
☐ 546 Chris Bosio	.10	.05	.01
☐ 547 Jamie Moyer	.10	.05	.01
☐ 548 Jim Eisenreich	.10	.05	.01
☐ 549 Vinny Castilla	.20	.09	.03
☐ 550 Checklist 413-494	.10	.05	.01
(Dave Winfield)			
☐ 551 John Roper	.10	.05	.01
☐ 552 Lance Johnson	.10	.05	.01
☐ 553 Scott Kamieniecki	.10	.05	.01
☐ 554 Mike Moore	.10	.05	.01
☐ 555 Steve Buechele	.10	.05	.01
☐ 556 Terry Pendleton	.30	.14	.04
☐ 557 Todd Van Poppel	.20	.09	.03
☐ 558 Rob Butler	.10	.05	.01
☐ 559 Zane Smith	.10	.05	.01
☐ 560 David Hulse	.10	.05	.01
☐ 561 Tim Costo	.10	.05	.01
☐ 562 John Habyan	.10	.05	.01
☐ 563 Terry Jorgensen	.10	.05	.01
☐ 564 Matt Nokes	.10	.05	.01

☐ 565 Kevin McReynolds	.10	.05	.01
☐ 566 Phil Plantier	.20	.09	.03
☐ 567 Chris Turner	.10	.05	.01
☐ 568 Carlos Delgado	.30	.14	.04
☐ 569 John Jaha	.10	.05	.01
☐ 570 Dwight Smith	.10	.05	.01
☐ 571 John Vander Wal	.10	.05	.01
☐ 572 Trevor Wilson	.10	.05	.01
☐ 573 Felix Fermin	.10	.05	.01
☐ 574 Marc Newfield	.20	.09	.03
☐ 575 Jeromy Burnitz	.10	.05	.01
☐ 576 Leo Gomez	.10	.05	.01
☐ 577 Curt Schilling	.10	.05	.01
☐ 578 Kevin Young	.10	.05	.01
☐ 579 Jerry Spradlin	.10	.05	.01
☐ 580 Curt Leskanic	.10	.05	.01
☐ 581 Carl Willis	.10	.05	.01
☐ 582 Alex Fernandez	.30	.14	.04
☐ 583 Mark Holzemer	.10	.05	.01
☐ 584 Domingo Martinez	.10	.05	.01
☐ 585 Pete Smith	.10	.05	.01
☐ 586 Brian Jordan	.20	.09	.03
☐ 587 Kevin Gross	.10	.05	.01
☐ 588 J.R. Phillips	.20	.09	.03
☐ 589 Chris Nabholz	.10	.05	.01
☐ 590 Bill Wertz	.10	.05	.01
☐ 591 Derek Bell	.20	.09	.03
☐ 592 Brady Anderson	.20	.09	.03
☐ 593 Matt Turner	.10	.05	.01
☐ 594 Pete Incaviglia	.10	.05	.01
☐ 595 Greg Gagne	.10	.05	.01
☐ 596 John Flaherty	.10	.05	.01
☐ 597 Scott Livingstone	.10	.05	.01
☐ 598 Rod Bolton	.10	.05	.01
☐ 599 Mike Perez	.10	.05	.01
☐ 600 Checklist 495-577	.10	.05	.01
(Roger Clemens)			
☐ 601 Tony Castillo	.10	.05	.01
☐ 602 Henry Mercedes	.10	.05	.01
☐ 603 Mike Fetters	.10	.05	.01
☐ 604 Rod Beck	.20	.09	.03
☐ 605 Damon Buford	.10	.05	.01
☐ 606 Matt Whiteside	.10	.05	.01
☐ 607 Shawn Green	.40	.18	.05
☐ 608 Midre Cummings	.20	.09	.03
☐ 609 Jeff McNeely	.10	.05	.01
☐ 610 Danny Sheaffer	.10	.05	.01
☐ 611 Paul Wagner	.10	.05	.01
☐ 612 Torey Lovullo	.10	.05	.01
☐ 613 Javier Lopez	.50	.23	.06
☐ 614 Mariano Duncan	.10	.05	.01
☐ 615 Doug Brocail	.10	.05	.01
☐ 616 Dave Hansen	.10	.05	.01
☐ 617 Ryan Klesko	.75	.35	.09
☐ 618 Eric Davis	.10	.05	.01
☐ 619 Scott Ruffcorn	.20	.09	.03
☐ 620 Mike Trombley	.10	.05	.01
☐ 621 Jaime Navarro	.10	.05	.01
☐ 622 Rheal Cormier	.10	.05	.01
☐ 623 Jose Offerman	.20	.09	.03
☐ 624 David Segui	.10	.05	.01
☐ 625 Robb Nen	.10	.05	.01
☐ 626 Dave Gallagher	.10	.05	.01
☐ 627 Julian Tavarez	.60	.25	.07
☐ 628 Chris Gomez	.20	.09	.03
☐ 629 Jeffrey Hammonds	.30	.14	.04
☐ 630 Scott Brosius	.10	.05	.01
☐ 631 Willie Blair	.10	.05	.01
☐ 632 Doug Drabek	.30	.14	.04
☐ 633 Bill Wegman	.10	.05	.01
☐ 634 Jeff McKnight	.10	.05	.01

☐ 635	Rich Rodriguez	.10	.05	.01
☐ 636	Steve Trachsel	.20	.09	.03
☐ 637	Buddy Groom	.10	.05	.01
☐ 638	Sterling Hitchcock	.20	.09	.03
☐ 639	Chuck McElroy	.10	.05	.01
☐ 640	Rene Gonzales	.10	.05	.01
☐ 641	Dan Plesac	.10	.05	.01
☐ 642	Jeff Branson	.10	.05	.01
☐ 643	Darrell Whitmore	.10	.05	.01
☐ 644	Paul Quantrill	.10	.05	.01
☐ 645	Rich Rowland	.10	.05	.01
☐ 646	Curtis Pride	.10	.05	.01
☐ 647	Erik Plantenberg	.10	.05	.01
☐ 648	Albie Lopez	.20	.09	.03
☐ 649	Rich Batchelor	.10	.05	.01
☐ 650	Lee Smith	.30	.14	.04
☐ 651	Cliff Floyd	.30	.14	.04
☐ 652	Pete Schourek	.20	.09	.03
☐ 653	Reggie Jefferson	.10	.05	.01
☐ 654	Bill Haselman	.10	.05	.01
☐ 655	Steve Hosey	.10	.05	.01
☐ 656	Mark Clark	.10	.05	.01
☐ 657	Mark Davis	.10	.05	.01
☐ 658	Dave Magadan	.10	.05	.01
☐ 659	Candy Maldonado	.10	.05	.01
☐ 660	Checklist 578-660	.10	.05	.01
	(Mark Langston)			

1994 Donruss
Anniversary '84

Randomly inserted in hobby foil packs at a rate of one in 12, this ten-card standard-size set reproduces selected cards from the 1984 Donruss baseball set. The cards feature white bordered color player photos on their fronts. The player's name appears in yellow lettering within a colored stripe at the bottom. The player's gold-foil team name is shown within wavy gold-foil lines near the bottom of the photo. The horizontal and white-bordered back carries the player's name and biography within a green-colored stripe across the top. A white area below contains the player's stats and, within a green panel further below, his career highlights. The cards are numbered on the back at the bottom right as "X of 10," and also carry the numbers from the original 1984 set at the upper left.

	MINT	NRMT	EXC
COMPLETE SET (10)	50.00	22.00	6.25
COMMON CARD (1-10)	2.00	.90	.25
☐ 1 Joe Carter	2.00	.90	.25
☐ 2 Robin Yount	2.50	1.10	.30
☐ 3 George Brett	6.00	2.70	.75
☐ 4 Rickey Henderson	2.00	.90	.25
☐ 5 Nolan Ryan	15.00	6.75	1.85
☐ 6 Cal Ripken	20.00	9.00	2.50
☐ 7 Wade Boggs UER	2.00	.90	.25
1983 runs 10, should be 100			
☐ 8 Don Mattingly	10.00	4.50	1.25
☐ 9 Ryne Sandberg	5.00	2.20	.60
☐ 10 Tony Gwynn	5.00	2.20	.60

1994 Donruss
Diamond Kings

 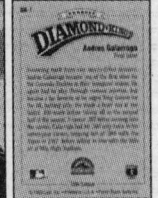

This 30-card set was split in two series. Cards 1-14 and 29 were randomly inserted in first series packs, while cards 15-28 and 30 were inserted in second series packs. With each series, the insertion rate was one in nine. The cards measure the standard size. Jumbo versions of these cards were inserted one per retail box and command up to twice the values below. The fronts feature full-bleed player portraits by noted sports artist Dick Perez. Red and silver holographic foil lettering across the top provides the set title. The player's name is printed in gold script lettering across the bottom. On a yellow background the backs provide a career summary in red print with a narrow red border. The cards are numbered on the back with the prefix DK.

	MINT	NRMT	EXC
COMPLETE SET (30)	55.00	25.00	7.00
COMPLETE SERIES 1 (15)	25.00	11.00	3.10
COMPLETE SERIES 2 (15)	30.00	13.50	3.70
COMMON CARD (1-30)	.40	.18	.05
☐ 1 Barry Bonds	2.50	1.10	.30
☐ 2 Mo Vaughn	1.50	.70	.19
☐ 3 Steve Avery	.75	.35	.09
☐ 4 Tim Salmon	2.00	.90	.25
☐ 5 Rick Wilkins	.40	.18	.05
☐ 6 Brian Harper	.40	.18	.05
☐ 7 Andres Galarraga	.75	.35	.09

		MINT	NRMT	EXC
☐ 8	Albert Belle	4.00	1.80	.50
☐ 9	John Kruk	.40	.18	.05
☐ 10	Ivan Rodriguez	.75	.35	.09
☐ 11	Tony Gwynn	3.00	1.35	.35
☐ 12	Brian McRae	.75	.35	.09
☐ 13	Bobby Bonilla	.75	.35	.09
☐ 14	Ken Griffey Jr.	10.00	4.50	1.25
☐ 15	Mike Piazza	4.00	1.80	.50
☐ 16	Don Mattingly	5.00	2.20	.60
☐ 17	Barry Larkin	1.00	.45	.12
☐ 18	Ruben Sierra	.75	.35	.09
☐ 19	Orlando Merced	.40	.18	.05
☐ 20	Greg Vaughn	.40	.18	.05
☐ 21	Gregg Jefferies	.75	.35	.09
☐ 22	Cecil Fielder	.75	.35	.09
☐ 23	Moises Alou	.75	.35	.09
☐ 24	John Olerud	.75	.35	.09
☐ 25	Gary Sheffield	.75	.35	.09
☐ 26	Mike Mussina	1.50	.70	.19
☐ 27	Jeff Bagwell	3.00	1.35	.35
☐ 28	Frank Thomas	10.00	4.50	1.25
☐ 29	Dave Winfield	.75	.35	.09
☐ 30	Checklist	.40	.18	.05

		MINT	NRMT	EXC
☐ A1	Cecil Fielder	1.00	.45	.12
☐ A2	Barry Bonds	2.50	1.10	.30
☐ A3	Fred McGriff	1.25	.55	.16
☐ A4	Matt Williams	1.50	.70	.19
☐ A5	Joe Carter	1.00	.45	.12
☐ A6	Juan Gonzalez	2.50	1.10	.30
☐ A7	Jose Canseco	1.50	.70	.19
☐ A8	Ron Gant	1.00	.45	.12
☐ A9	Ken Griffey Jr.	10.00	4.50	1.25
☐ A10	Mark McGwire	1.00	.45	.12
☐ B1	Tony Gwynn	3.00	1.35	.35
☐ B2	Frank Thomas	10.00	4.50	1.25
☐ B3	Paul Molitor	1.00	.45	.12
☐ B4	Edgar Martinez	1.00	.45	.12
☐ B5	Kirby Puckett	3.00	1.35	.35
☐ B6	Ken Griffey Jr.	10.00	4.50	1.25
☐ B7	Barry Bonds	2.50	1.10	.30
☐ B8	Willie McGee	.50	.23	.06
☐ B9	Lenny Dykstra	.50	.23	.06
☐ B10	John Kruk	.50	.23	.06

1994 Donruss Dominators

This 20-card, standard-size set was randomly inserted in all packs at a rate of one in 12. The 10 series 1 cards feature the top home run hitters of the '90s, while the 10 series 2 cards depict the decade's batting average leaders. The fronts displayed full-bleed color action shots with the set title printed along the bottom in gold and black lettering. The player's name appears within an oval gold bar. The horizontal backs carry a second player photo on approximately two-thirds of the card back. The remaining section contains the relevant statistics printed from the 1990s in a box. The player's ranking in the 1990s is also listed. Jumbo Dominators (3 1/2" by 5") were issued one per hobby box and are valued up to twice the prices below.

	MINT	NRMT	EXC
COMPLETE SET (20)	55.00	25.00	7.00
COMPLETE SER.1 SET (10)	25.00	11.00	3.10
COMPLETE SER.2 SET (10)	30.00	13.50	3.70
COMMON SER.1 CARD (A1-A10)	1.00	.45	.12
COMMON SER.2 CARD (B1-B10)	.50	.23	.06

1994 Donruss Elite

This 12-card set was issued in two series of six. Using a continued numbering system from previous years, cards 37-42 were randomly inserted in first series foil packs with cards 43-48 a second series offering. The cards measure the standard size. Only 10,000 of each card were produced. The color player photo inside a diamond design on the front rests on a marbleized panel framed by a red-and-white inner border and a silver foil outer border. Silver foil stripes radiate away from the edges of the picture. The player's name appears across the bottom of the front. The back design is similar, but with a color head shot in a small diamond and a player profile, both resting on a marbleized panel. The bottom carries the card number, the serial number, and the production run figure.

	MINT	NRMT	EXC
COMPLETE SET (12)	300.00	135.00	38.00
COMPLETE SERIES 1 (6)	150.00	70.00	19.00
COMPLETE SERIES 2 (6)	150.00	70.00	19.00
COMMON CARD (37-42)	10.00	4.50	1.25
COMMON CARD (43-48)	10.00	4.50	1.25
☐ 37 Frank Thomas	60.00	27.00	7.50
☐ 38 Tony Gwynn	20.00	9.00	2.50
☐ 39 Tim Salmon	12.00	5.50	1.50

		MINT	NRMT	EXC
☐ 40	Albert Belle	25.00	11.00	3.10
☐ 41	John Kruk	10.00	4.50	1.25
☐ 42	Juan Gonzalez	15.00	6.75	1.85
☐ 43	John Olerud	10.00	4.50	1.25
☐ 44	Barry Bonds	15.00	6.75	1.85
☐ 45	Ken Griffey Jr.	60.00	27.00	7.50
☐ 46	Mike Piazza	25.00	11.00	3.10
☐ 47	Jack McDowell	10.00	4.50	1.25
☐ 48	Andres Galarraga	10.00	4.50	1.25

1994 Donruss Long Ball Leaders

Inserted in second series hobby foil packs at a rate of one in 12, this 10-card set features some of top home run hitters and the distance of their longest home run of 1993. The card fronts have a color photo with a black right-hand border. Within the border is the Long Ball Leaders logo in silver foil. Also in silver foil at bottom, is the player's last name and the distance of the clout. Card backs contain a photo of the park with which the home run occurred as well as information such as the date, the pitcher and other particulars.

		MINT	NRMT	EXC
COMPLETE SET (10)		50.00	22.00	6.25
COMMON CARD (1-10)		1.00	.45	.12
☐ 1	Cecil Fielder	1.50	.70	.19
☐ 2	Dean Palmer	1.00	.45	.12
☐ 3	Andres Galarraga	1.00	.45	.12
☐ 4	Bo Jackson	1.50	.70	.19
☐ 5	Ken Griffey Jr.	15.00	6.75	1.85
☐ 6	David Justice	2.00	.90	.25
☐ 7	Mike Piazza	6.00	2.70	.75
☐ 8	Frank Thomas	15.00	6.75	1.85
☐ 9	Barry Bonds	4.00	1.80	.50
☐ 10	Juan Gonzalez	4.00	1.80	.50

1994 Donruss MVPs

Inserted at a rate of one per first and second series jumbo pack, this 28-card set was split into two series of 14; one player for each team. The first 14 are of National League players with the latter group being

American Leaguers. Full-bleed card fronts feature an action photo of the player with "MVP" in large red (American League) or blue (National) letters at the bottom. The player's name and, for Amercian League player cards only, team name are beneath the "MVP". A number of white stars stretches up the left border. The backs, which are horizontal, contain a photo, 1993 statistics, a short write-up and white stars within blue foil along the left border.

		MINT	NRMT	EXC
COMPLETE SET (28)		75.00	34.00	9.50
COMPLETE SERIES 1 (14)		15.00	6.75	1.85
COMPLETE SERIES 2 (14)		60.00	27.00	7.50
COMMON CARD (1-14)		.60	.25	.07
COMMON CARD (15-28)		.60	.25	.07
☐ 1	David Justice	2.00	.90	.25
☐ 2	Mark Grace	.75	.35	.09
☐ 3	Jose Rijo	.60	.25	.07
☐ 4	Andres Galarraga	.75	.35	.09
☐ 5	Bryan Harvey	.60	.25	.07
☐ 6	Jeff Bagwell	5.00	2.20	.60
☐ 7	Mike Piazza	6.00	2.70	.75
☐ 8	Moises Alou	.60	.25	.07
☐ 9	Bobby Bonilla	.75	.35	.09
☐ 10	Len Dykstra	.75	.35	.09
☐ 11	Jeff King	.60	.25	.07
☐ 12	Gregg Jefferies	.75	.35	.09
☐ 13	Tony Gwynn	5.00	2.20	.60
☐ 14	Barry Bonds	4.00	1.80	.50
☐ 15	Cal Ripken Jr.	16.00	7.25	2.00
☐ 16	Mo Vaughn	2.50	1.10	.30
☐ 17	Tim Salmon	3.00	1.35	.35
☐ 18	Frank Thomas	15.00	6.75	1.85
☐ 19	Albert Belle	6.00	2.70	.75
☐ 20	Cecil Fielder	.75	.35	.09
☐ 21	Wally Joyner	.60	.25	.07
☐ 22	Greg Vaughn	.60	.25	.07
☐ 23	Kirby Puckett	5.00	2.20	.60
☐ 24	Don Mattingly	8.00	3.60	1.00
☐ 25	Ruben Sierra	.75	.35	.09
☐ 26	Ken Griffey Jr.	15.00	6.75	1.85
☐ 27	Juan Gonzalez	4.00	1.80	.50
☐ 28	John Olerud	.60	.25	.07

1994 Donruss Spirit of the Game

Consisting of 10 cards, cards 1-5 were randomly inserted in first-series magazine

jumbo packs and cards 6-10 in second series magazine jumbo packs. Measuring the standard-size, the set features horizontal designs on its borderless fronts that have color action player photos superposed upon triple exposure sepia-toned action shots. The set's title appears in dark brown cursive lettering within a prismatic-foil stripe across the bottom. The horizontal back carries a color player close-up that is superposed upon red, white, and blue bunting. An outstanding achievement by the player appears in gold lettering at the upper right, and a ghosted panel immediately below carries black-lettered text providing details. The cards are numbered on the back. Jumbo sized Spirit of the Game cards, individually numbered out of 10,000, are issued one per magazine jumbo box and carry no additional premium.

	MINT	NRMT	EXC
COMPLETE SET (10)	70.00	32.00	8.75
COMPLETE SERIES 1 (5)	40.00	18.00	5.00
COMPLETE SERIES 2 (5)	30.00	13.50	3.70
COMMON CARD (1-10)	1.00	.45	.12
☐ 1 John Olerud	1.00	.45	.12
☐ 2 Barry Bonds	5.00	2.20	.60
☐ 3 Ken Griffey Jr.	20.00	9.00	2.50
☐ 4 Mike Piazza	8.00	3.60	1.00
☐ 5 Juan Gonzalez	5.00	2.20	.60
☐ 6 Frank Thomas	20.00	9.00	2.50
☐ 7 Tim Salmon	4.00	1.80	.50
☐ 8 David Justice	3.00	1.35	.35
☐ 9 Don Mattingly	10.00	4.50	1.25
☐ 10 Lenny Dykstra	1.00	.45	.12

1995 Donruss

The 1995 Donruss set consists of 550 cards. The first series had 330 cards while 220 cards comprised the second series. The fronts feature borderless color action player photos. A second, smaller color player photo in a homeplate shape with team color-coded borders appears in the lower left corner. The player's position in silver-foil is above this smaller photo, while his name is printed in a silver-foil bar under the photo. The borderless backs carry a color action player cutout superimposed

over the team logo, along with player biography and stats for the last five years. The cards are numbered on the back. There are no key Rookie Cards in this set.

	MINT	NRMT	EXC
COMPLETE SET (550)	40.00	18.00	5.00
COMPLETE SERIES 1 (330)	25.00	11.00	3.10
COMPLETE SERIES 2 (220)	15.00	6.75	1.85
COMMON CARD (1-330)	.10	.05	.01
COMMON CARD (331-550)	.10	.05	.01
SUPER PACKS CONTAIN COMPLETE INSERT SETS			
☐ 1 David Justice	.40	.18	.05
☐ 2 Rene Arocha	.10	.05	.01
☐ 3 Sandy Alomar Jr.	.20	.09	.03
☐ 4 Luis Lopez	.10	.05	.01
☐ 5 Mike Piazza	1.25	.55	.16
☐ 6 Bobby Jones	.20	.09	.03
☐ 7 Damion Easley	.10	.05	.01
☐ 8 Barry Bonds	.75	.35	.09
☐ 9 Mike Mussina	.40	.18	.05
☐ 10 Kevin Seitzer	.10	.05	.01
☐ 11 John Smiley	.10	.05	.01
☐ 12 Wm.VanLandingham	.20	.09	.03
☐ 13 Ron Darling	.10	.05	.01
☐ 14 Walt Weiss	.10	.05	.01
☐ 15 Mike Lansing	.10	.05	.01
☐ 16 Allen Watson	.20	.09	.03
☐ 17 Aaron Sele	.20	.09	.03
☐ 18 Randy Johnson	.60	.25	.07
☐ 19 Dean Palmer	.20	.09	.03
☐ 20 Jeff Bagwell	1.00	.45	.12
☐ 21 Curt Schilling	.10	.05	.01
☐ 22 Darrell Whitmore	.10	.05	.01
☐ 23 Steve Trachsel	.10	.05	.01
☐ 24 Dan Wilson	.20	.09	.03
☐ 25 Steve Finley	.20	.09	.03
☐ 26 Bret Boone	.30	.14	.04
☐ 27 Charles Johnson	.30	.14	.04
☐ 28 Mike Stanton	.10	.05	.01
☐ 29 Ismael Valdes	.10	.05	.01
☐ 30 Salomon Torres	.10	.05	.01
☐ 31 Eric Anthony	.10	.05	.01
☐ 32 Spike Owen	.10	.05	.01
☐ 33 Joey Cora	.10	.05	.01
☐ 34 Robert Eenhoorn	.10	.05	.01
☐ 35 Rick White	.10	.05	.01
☐ 36 Omar Vizquel	.20	.09	.03
☐ 37 Carlos Delgado	.20	.09	.03
☐ 38 Eddie Williams	.10	.05	.01
☐ 39 Shawon Dunston	.10	.05	.01
☐ 40 Darrin Fletcher	.10	.05	.01
☐ 41 Leo Gomez	.10	.05	.01
☐ 42 Juan Gonzalez	.75	.35	.09
☐ 43 Luis Alicea	.10	.05	.01

☐ 44	Ken Ryan	.10	.05	.01
☐ 45	Lou Whitaker	.30	.14	.04
☐ 46	Mike Blowers	.20	.09	.03
☐ 47	Willie Blair	.10	.05	.01
☐ 48	Todd Van Poppel	.10	.05	.01
☐ 49	Roberto Alomar	.60	.25	.07
☐ 50	Ozzie Smith	.60	.25	.07
☐ 51	Sterling Hitchcock	.20	.09	.03
☐ 52	Mo Vaughn	.50	.23	.06
☐ 53	Rick Aguilera	.20	.09	.03
☐ 54	Kent Mercker	.10	.05	.01
☐ 55	Don Mattingly	1.50	.70	.19
☐ 56	Bob Scanlan	.10	.05	.01
☐ 57	Wilson Alvarez	.20	.09	.03
☐ 58	Jose Mesa	.20	.09	.03
☐ 59	Scott Kamieniecki	.10	.05	.01
☐ 60	Todd Jones	.10	.05	.01
☐ 61	John Kruk	.30	.14	.04
☐ 62	Mike Stanley	.20	.09	.03
☐ 63	Tino Martinez	.30	.14	.04
☐ 64	Eddie Zambrano	.10	.05	.01
☐ 65	Todd Hundley	.20	.09	.03
☐ 66	Jamie Moyer	.10	.05	.01
☐ 67	Rich Amaral	.10	.05	.01
☐ 68	Jose Valentin	.10	.05	.01
☐ 69	Alex Gonzalez	.20	.09	.03
☐ 70	Kurt Abbott	.10	.05	.01
☐ 71	Delino DeShields	.20	.09	.03
☐ 72	Brian Anderson	.10	.05	.01
☐ 73	John Vander Wal	.10	.05	.01
☐ 74	Turner Ward	.10	.05	.01
☐ 75	Tim Raines	.30	.14	.04
☐ 76	Mark Acre	.10	.05	.01
☐ 77	Jose Offerman	.10	.05	.01
☐ 78	Jimmy Key	.20	.09	.03
☐ 79	Mark Whiten	.20	.09	.03
☐ 80	Mark Gubicza	.10	.05	.01
☐ 81	Darren Hall	.10	.05	.01
☐ 82	Travis Fryman	.30	.14	.04
☐ 83	Cal Ripken	3.00	1.35	.35
☐ 84	Geronimo Berroa	.10	.05	.01
☐ 85	Bret Barberie	.10	.05	.01
☐ 86	Andy Ashby	.10	.05	.01
☐ 87	Steve Avery	.30	.14	.04
☐ 88	Rich Becker	.20	.09	.03
☐ 89	John Valentin	.30	.14	.04
☐ 90	Glenallen Hill	.20	.09	.03
☐ 91	Carlos Garcia	.20	.09	.03
☐ 92	Dennis Martinez	.20	.09	.03
☐ 93	Pat Kelly	.10	.05	.01
☐ 94	Orlando Miller	.20	.09	.03
☐ 95	Felix Jose	.10	.05	.01
☐ 96	Mike Kingery	.10	.05	.01
☐ 97	Jeff Kent	.20	.09	.03
☐ 98	Pete Incaviglia	.10	.05	.01
☐ 99	Chad Curtis	.20	.09	.03
☐ 100	Thomas Howard	.10	.05	.01
☐ 101	Hector Carrasco	.10	.05	.01
☐ 102	Tom Pagnozzi	.10	.05	.01
☐ 103	Danny Tartabull	.20	.09	.03
☐ 104	Donnie Elliott	.10	.05	.01
☐ 105	Danny Jackson	.10	.05	.01
☐ 106	Steve Dunn	.10	.05	.01
☐ 107	Roger Salkeld	.10	.05	.01
☐ 108	Jeff King	.10	.05	.01
☐ 109	Cecil Fielder	.30	.14	.04
☐ 110	Checklist	.10	.05	.01
☐ 111	Denny Neagle	.10	.05	.01
☐ 112	Troy Neel	.10	.05	.01
☐ 113	Rod Beck	.20	.09	.03
☐ 114	Alex Rodriguez	.60	.25	.07
☐ 115	Joey Eischen	.10	.05	.01
☐ 116	Tom Candiotti	.10	.05	.01
☐ 117	Ray McDavid	.20	.09	.03
☐ 118	Vince Coleman	.10	.05	.01
☐ 119	Pete Harnisch	.10	.05	.01
☐ 120	David Nied	.20	.09	.03
☐ 121	Pat Rapp	.20	.09	.03
☐ 122	Sammy Sosa	.30	.14	.04
☐ 123	Steve Reed	.10	.05	.01
☐ 124	Jose Oliva	.20	.09	.03
☐ 125	Ricky Bottalico	.10	.05	.01
☐ 126	Jose DeLeon	.10	.05	.01
☐ 127	Pat Hentgen	.20	.09	.03
☐ 128	Will Clark	.40	.18	.05
☐ 129	Mark Dewey	.10	.05	.01
☐ 130	Greg Vaughn	.10	.05	.01
☐ 131	Darren Dreifort	.10	.05	.01
☐ 132	Ed Sprague	.10	.05	.01
☐ 133	Lee Smith	.30	.14	.04
☐ 134	Charles Nagy	.20	.09	.03
☐ 135	Phil Plantier	.10	.05	.01
☐ 136	Jason Jacome	.10	.05	.01
☐ 137	Jose Lima	.20	.09	.03
☐ 138	J.R. Phillips	.10	.05	.01
☐ 139	J.T. Snow	.30	.14	.04
☐ 140	Michael Huff	.10	.05	.01
☐ 141	Billy Brewer	.10	.05	.01
☐ 142	Jeromy Burnitz	.10	.05	.01
☐ 143	Ricky Bones	.10	.05	.01
☐ 144	Carlos Rodriguez	.10	.05	.01
☐ 145	Luis Gonzalez	.20	.09	.03
☐ 146	Mark Lemke	.20	.09	.03
☐ 147	Al Martin	.20	.09	.03
☐ 148	Mike Bordick	.10	.05	.01
☐ 149	Robb Nen	.20	.09	.03
☐ 150	Wil Cordero	.20	.09	.03
☐ 151	Edgar Martinez	.30	.14	.04
☐ 152	Gerald Williams	.10	.05	.01
☐ 153	Esteban Beltre	.10	.05	.01
☐ 154	Mike Moore	.10	.05	.01
☐ 155	Mark Langston	.30	.14	.04
☐ 156	Mark Clark	.10	.05	.01
☐ 157	Bobby Ayala	.10	.05	.01
☐ 158	Rick Wilkins	.10	.05	.01
☐ 159	Bobby Munoz	.10	.05	.01
☐ 160	B.Butler 2000 Hits CL	.10	.05	.01
☐ 161	Scott Erickson	.20	.09	.03
☐ 162	Paul Molitor	.30	.14	.04
☐ 163	Jon Lieber	.10	.05	.01
☐ 164	Jason Grimsley	.10	.05	.01
☐ 165	Norberto Martin	.10	.05	.01
☐ 166	Javier Lopez	.40	.18	.05
☐ 167	Brian McRae	.20	.09	.03
☐ 168	Gary Sheffield	.30	.14	.04
☐ 169	Marcus Moore	.10	.05	.01
☐ 170	John Hudek	.10	.05	.01
☐ 171	Kelly Stinnett	.10	.05	.01
☐ 172	Chris Gomez	.10	.05	.01
☐ 173	Rey Sanchez	.10	.05	.01
☐ 174	Juan Guzman	.20	.09	.03
☐ 175	Chan Ho Park	.20	.09	.03
☐ 176	Terry Shumpert	.10	.05	.01
☐ 177	Steve Ontiveros	.10	.05	.01
☐ 178	Brad Ausmus	.10	.05	.01
☐ 179	Tim Davis	.10	.05	.01
☐ 180	Billy Ashley	.20	.09	.03
☐ 181	Vinny Castilla	.30	.14	.04
☐ 182	Bill Spiers	.10	.05	.01
☐ 183	Randy Knorr	.10	.05	.01
☐ 184	Brian Hunter	.40	.18	.05
☐ 185	Pat Meares	.10	.05	.01

☐ 186 Steve Buechele	.10	.05	.01
☐ 187 Kirt Manwaring	.10	.05	.01
☐ 188 Tim Naehring	.20	.09	.03
☐ 189 Matt Mieske	.10	.05	.01
☐ 190 Josias Manzanillo	.10	.05	.01
☐ 191 Greg McMichael	.10	.05	.01
☐ 192 Chuck Carr	.10	.05	.01
☐ 193 Midre Cummings	.20	.09	.03
☐ 194 Darryl Strawberry	.20	.09	.03
☐ 195 Greg Gagne	.10	.05	.01
☐ 196 Steve Cooke	.10	.05	.01
☐ 197 Woody Williams	.10	.05	.01
☐ 198 Ron Karkovice	.10	.05	.01
☐ 199 Phil Leftwich	.10	.05	.01
☐ 200 Jim Thome	.50	.23	.06
☐ 201 Brady Anderson	.20	.09	.03
☐ 202 Pedro Martinez	.30	.14	.04
☐ 203 Steve Karsay	.10	.05	.01
☐ 204 Reggie Sanders	.30	.14	.04
☐ 205 Bill Risley	.10	.05	.01
☐ 206 Jay Bell	.20	.09	.03
☐ 207 Kevin Brown	.10	.05	.01
☐ 208 Tim Scott	.10	.05	.01
☐ 209 Lenny Dykstra	.30	.14	.04
☐ 210 Willie Greene	.20	.09	.03
☐ 211 Jim Eisenreich	.10	.05	.01
☐ 212 Cliff Floyd	.20	.09	.03
☐ 213 Otis Nixon	.10	.05	.01
☐ 214 Eduardo Perez	.10	.05	.01
☐ 215 Manuel Lee	.10	.05	.01
☐ 216 Armando Benitez	.10	.05	.01
☐ 217 Dave McCarty	.10	.05	.01
☐ 218 Scott Livingstone	.10	.05	.01
☐ 219 Chad Kreuter	.10	.05	.01
☐ 220 Don Mattingly CL	.75	.35	.09
☐ 221 Brian Jordan	.30	.14	.04
☐ 222 Matt Whiteside	.10	.05	.01
☐ 223 Jim Edmonds	.40	.18	.05
☐ 224 Tony Gwynn	1.00	.45	.12
☐ 225 Jose Lind	.10	.05	.01
☐ 226 Marvin Freeman	.10	.05	.01
☐ 227 Ken Hill	.20	.09	.03
☐ 228 David Hulse	.10	.05	.01
☐ 229 Joe Hesketh	.10	.05	.01
☐ 230 Roberto Petagine	.20	.09	.03
☐ 231 Jeffrey Hammonds	.20	.09	.03
☐ 232 John Jaha	.10	.05	.01
☐ 233 John Burkett	.10	.05	.01
☐ 234 Hal Morris	.20	.09	.03
☐ 235 Tony Castillo	.10	.05	.01
☐ 236 Ryan Bowen	.10	.05	.01
☐ 237 Wayne Kirby	.10	.05	.01
☐ 238 Brent Mayne	.10	.05	.01
☐ 239 Jim Bullinger	.10	.05	.01
☐ 240 Mike Lieberthal	.10	.05	.01
☐ 241 Barry Larkin	.40	.18	.05
☐ 242 David Segui	.10	.05	.01
☐ 243 Jose Bautista	.10	.05	.01
☐ 244 Hector Fajardo	.10	.05	.01
☐ 245 Orel Hershiser	.20	.09	.03
☐ 246 James Mouton	.10	.05	.01
☐ 247 Scott Leius	.10	.05	.01
☐ 248 Tom Glavine	.30	.14	.04
☐ 249 Danny Bautista	.10	.05	.01
☐ 250 Jose Mercedes	.10	.05	.01
☐ 251 Marquis Grissom	.30	.14	.04
☐ 252 Charlie Hayes	.20	.09	.03
☐ 253 Ryan Klesko	.60	.25	.07
☐ 254 Vicente Palacios	.10	.05	.01
☐ 255 Matias Carrillo	.10	.05	.01
☐ 256 Gary DiSarcina	.10	.05	.01
☐ 257 Kirk Gibson	.20	.09	.03
☐ 258 Garey Ingram	.10	.05	.01
☐ 259 Alex Fernandez	.20	.09	.03
☐ 260 John Mabry	.20	.09	.03
☐ 261 Chris Howard	.10	.05	.01
☐ 262 Miguel Jimenez	.10	.05	.01
☐ 263 Heath Slocumb	.10	.05	.01
☐ 264 Albert Belle	1.25	.55	.16
☐ 265 Dave Clark	.10	.05	.01
☐ 266 Joe Orsulak	.10	.05	.01
☐ 267 Joey Hamilton	.20	.09	.03
☐ 268 Mark Portugal	.10	.05	.01
☐ 269 Kevin Tapani	.10	.05	.01
☐ 270 Sid Fernandez	.10	.05	.01
☐ 271 Steve Dreyer	.10	.05	.01
☐ 272 Denny Hocking	.10	.05	.01
☐ 273 Troy O'Leary	.20	.09	.03
☐ 274 Milt Cuyler	.10	.05	.01
☐ 275 Frank Thomas	3.00	1.35	.35
☐ 276 Jorge Fabregas	.10	.05	.01
☐ 277 Mike Gallego	.10	.05	.01
☐ 278 Mickey Morandini	.10	.05	.01
☐ 279 Roberto Hernandez	.20	.09	.03
☐ 280 Henry Rodriguez	.10	.05	.01
☐ 281 Garret Anderson	.60	.25	.07
☐ 282 Bob Wickman	.10	.05	.01
☐ 283 Gar Finnvold	.10	.05	.01
☐ 284 Paul O'Neill	.20	.09	.03
☐ 285 Royce Clayton	.20	.09	.03
☐ 286 Chuck Knoblauch	.30	.14	.04
☐ 287 Johnny Ruffin	.10	.05	.01
☐ 288 Dave Nilsson	.20	.09	.03
☐ 289 David Cone	.30	.14	.04
☐ 290 Chuck McElroy	.10	.05	.01
☐ 291 Kevin Stocker	.20	.09	.03
☐ 292 Jose Rijo	.20	.09	.03
☐ 293 Sean Berry	.10	.05	.01
☐ 294 Ozzie Guillen	.10	.05	.01
☐ 295 Chris Hoiles	.20	.09	.03
☐ 296 Kevin Foster	.10	.05	.01
☐ 297 Jeff Frye	.10	.05	.01
☐ 298 Lance Johnson	.10	.05	.01
☐ 299 Mike Kelly	.20	.09	.03
☐ 300 Ellis Burks	.20	.09	.03
☐ 301 Roberto Kelly	.20	.09	.03
☐ 302 Dante Bichette	.40	.18	.05
☐ 303 Alvaro Espinoza	.10	.05	.01
☐ 304 Alex Cole	.10	.05	.01
☐ 305 Rickey Henderson	.30	.14	.04
☐ 306 Dave Weathers	.10	.05	.01
☐ 307 Shane Reynolds	.10	.05	.01
☐ 308 Bobby Bonilla	.30	.14	.04
☐ 309 Junior Felix	.10	.05	.01
☐ 310 Jeff Fassero	.20	.09	.03
☐ 311 Darren Lewis	.10	.05	.01
☐ 312 John Doherty	.10	.05	.01
☐ 313 Scott Servais	.10	.05	.01
☐ 314 Rick Helling	.10	.05	.01
☐ 315 Pedro Martinez	.30	.14	.04
☐ 316 Wes Chamberlain	.10	.05	.01
☐ 317 Bryan Eversgerd	.10	.05	.01
☐ 318 Trevor Hoffman	.20	.09	.03
☐ 319 John Patterson	.10	.05	.01
☐ 320 Matt Walbeck	.10	.05	.01
☐ 321 Jeff Montgomery	.20	.09	.03
☐ 322 Mel Rojas	.20	.09	.03
☐ 323 Eddie Taubensee	.10	.05	.01
☐ 324 Ray Lankford	.30	.14	.04
☐ 325 Jose Vizcaino	.10	.05	.01
☐ 326 Carlos Baerga	.60	.25	.07
☐ 327 Jack Voigt	.10	.05	.01

☐	328	Julio Franco	.20	.09	.03	☐	399	Mark McLemore	.10	.05	.01
☐	329	Brent Gates	.20	.09	.03	☐	400	Greg W.Harris	.10	.05	.01
☐	330	Kirby Puckett CL	.50	.23	.06	☐	401	Jim Leyritz	.10	.05	.01
☐	331	Greg Maddux	3.00	1.35	.35	☐	402	Doug Strange	.10	.05	.01
☐	332	Jason Bere	.20	.09	.03	☐	403	Tim Salmon	.50	.23	.06
☐	333	Bill Wegman	.10	.05	.01	☐	404	Terry Mulholland	.10	.05	.01
☐	334	Tuffy Rhodes	.10	.05	.01	☐	405	Robby Thompson	.10	.05	.01
☐	335	Kevin Young	.10	.05	.01	☐	406	Ruben Sierra	.30	.14	.04
☐	336	Andy Benes	.20	.09	.03	☐	407	Tony Phillips	.10	.05	.01
☐	337	Pedro Astacio	.10	.05	.01	☐	408	Moises Alou	.20	.09	.03
☐	338	Reggie Jefferson	.10	.05	.01	☐	409	Felix Fermin	.10	.05	.01
☐	339	Tim Belcher	.10	.05	.01	☐	410	Pat Listach	.10	.05	.01
☐	340	Ken Griffey Jr.	3.00	1.35	.35	☐	411	Kevin Bass	.10	.05	.01
☐	341	Mariano Duncan	.10	.05	.01	☐	412	Ben McDonald	.10	.05	.01
☐	342	Andres Galarraga	.30	.14	.04	☐	413	Scott Cooper	.10	.05	.01
☐	343	Rondell White	.30	.14	.04	☐	414	Jody Reed	.10	.05	.01
☐	344	Cory Bailey	.10	.05	.01	☐	415	Deion Sanders	.60	.25	.07
☐	345	Bryan Harvey	.20	.09	.03	☐	416	Ricky Gutierrez	.10	.05	.01
☐	346	John Franco	.20	.09	.03	☐	417	Gregg Jefferies	.30	.14	.04
☐	347	Greg Swindell	.10	.05	.01	☐	418	Jack McDowell	.30	.14	.04
☐	348	David West	.20	.09	.03	☐	419	Al Leiter	.10	.05	.01
☐	349	Fred McGriff	.40	.18	.05	☐	420	Tony Longmire	.10	.05	.01
☐	350	Jose Canseco	.50	.23	.06	☐	421	Paul Wagner	.10	.05	.01
☐	351	Orlando Merced	.20	.09	.03	☐	422	Geronimo Pena	.10	.05	.01
☐	352	Rheal Cormier	.10	.05	.01	☐	423	Ivan Rodriguez	.30	.14	.04
☐	353	Carlos Pulido	.10	.05	.01	☐	424	Kevin Gross	.10	.05	.01
☐	354	Terry Steinbach	.20	.09	.03	☐	425	Kirk McCaskill	.10	.05	.01
☐	355	Wade Boggs	.30	.14	.04	☐	426	Greg Myers	.10	.05	.01
☐	356	B.J. Surhoff	.20	.09	.03	☐	427	Roger Clemens	.50	.23	.06
☐	357	Rafael Palmeiro	.30	.14	.04	☐	428	Chris Hammond	.10	.05	.01
☐	358	Anthony Young	.10	.05	.01	☐	429	Randy Myers	.20	.09	.03
☐	359	Tom Brunansky	.10	.05	.01	☐	430	Roger Mason	.10	.05	.01
☐	360	Todd Stottlemyre	.10	.05	.01	☐	431	Bret Saberhagen	.20	.09	.03
☐	361	Chris Turner	.10	.05	.01	☐	432	Jeff Reboulet	.10	.05	.01
☐	362	Joe Boever	.10	.05	.01	☐	433	John Olerud	.20	.09	.03
☐	363	Jeff Blauser	.20	.09	.03	☐	434	Bill Gullickson	.10	.05	.01
☐	364	Derek Bell	.30	.14	.04	☐	435	Eddie Murray	.40	.18	.05
☐	365	Matt Williams	.50	.23	.06	☐	436	Pedro Munoz	.20	.09	.03
☐	366	Jeremy Hernandez	.10	.05	.01	☐	437	Charlie O'Brien	.10	.05	.01
☐	367	Joe Girardi	.10	.05	.01	☐	438	Jeff Nelson	.10	.05	.01
☐	368	Mike Devereaux	.10	.05	.01	☐	439	Mike Macfarlane	.10	.05	.01
☐	369	Jim Abbott	.30	.14	.04	☐	440	D.Mattingly 1000 RBI CL	.75	.35	.09
☐	370	Manny Ramirez	1.25	.55	.16	☐	441	Derrick May	.20	.09	.03
☐	371	Kenny Lofton	1.00	.45	.12	☐	442	John Roper	.10	.05	.01
☐	372	Mark Smith	.10	.05	.01	☐	443	Darryl Hamilton	.10	.05	.01
☐	373	Dave Fleming	.10	.05	.01	☐	444	Dan Miceli	.10	.05	.01
☐	374	Dave Stewart	.20	.09	.03	☐	445	Tony Eusebio	.10	.05	.01
☐	375	Roger Pavlik	.10	.05	.01	☐	446	Jerry Browne	.10	.05	.01
☐	376	Hipolito Pichardo	.10	.05	.01	☐	447	Wally Joyner	.20	.09	.03
☐	377	Bill Taylor	.10	.05	.01	☐	448	Brian Harper	.10	.05	.01
☐	378	Robin Ventura	.30	.14	.04	☐	449	Scott Fletcher	.10	.05	.01
☐	379	Bernard Gilkey	.20	.09	.03	☐	450	Bip Roberts	.10	.05	.01
☐	380	Kirby Puckett	1.00	.45	.12	☐	451	Pete Smith	.10	.05	.01
☐	381	Steve Howe	.10	.05	.01	☐	452	Chili Davis	.20	.09	.03
☐	382	Devon White	.20	.09	.03	☐	453	Dave Hollins	.10	.05	.01
☐	383	Roberto Mejia	.10	.05	.01	☐	454	Tony Pena	.10	.05	.01
☐	384	Darrin Jackson	.10	.05	.01	☐	455	Butch Henry	.10	.05	.01
☐	385	Mike Morgan	.10	.05	.01	☐	456	Craig Biggio	.30	.14	.04
☐	386	Rusty Meacham	.10	.05	.01	☐	457	Zane Smith	.10	.05	.01
☐	387	Bill Swift	.10	.05	.01	☐	458	Ryan Thompson	.20	.09	.03
☐	388	Lou Frazier	.10	.05	.01	☐	459	Mike Jackson	.10	.05	.01
☐	389	Andy Van Slyke	.20	.09	.03	☐	460	Mark McGwire	.30	.14	.04
☐	390	Brett Butler	.20	.09	.03	☐	461	John Smoltz	.20	.09	.03
☐	391	Bobby Witt	.10	.05	.01	☐	462	Steve Scarsone	.10	.05	.01
☐	392	Jeff Conine	.30	.14	.04	☐	463	Greg Colbrunn	.30	.14	.04
☐	393	Tim Hyers	.10	.05	.01	☐	464	Shawn Green	.30	.14	.04
☐	394	Terry Pendleton	.20	.09	.03	☐	465	David Wells	.10	.05	.01
☐	395	Ricky Jordan	.10	.05	.01	☐	466	Jose Hernandez	.10	.05	.01
☐	396	Eric Plunk	.10	.05	.01	☐	467	Chip Hale	.10	.05	.01
☐	397	Melido Perez	.10	.05	.01	☐	468	Tony Tarasco	.20	.09	.03
☐	398	Darryl Kile	.10	.05	.01	☐	469	Kevin Mitchell	.20	.09	.03

☐ 470	Billy Hatcher	.10	.05	.01
☐ 471	Jay Buhner	.30	.14	.04
☐ 472	Ken Caminiti	.20	.09	.03
☐ 473	Tom Henke	.20	.09	.03
☐ 474	Todd Worrell	.10	.05	.01
☐ 475	Mark Eichhorn	.10	.05	.01
☐ 476	Bruce Ruffin	.10	.05	.01
☐ 477	Chuck Finley	.20	.09	.03
☐ 478	Marc Newfield	.20	.09	.03
☐ 479	Paul Shuey	.10	.05	.01
☐ 480	Bob Tewksbury	.10	.05	.01
☐ 481	Ramon J.Martinez	.20	.09	.03
☐ 482	Melvin Nieves	.20	.09	.03
☐ 483	Todd Zeile	.20	.09	.03
☐ 484	Benito Santiago	.10	.05	.01
☐ 485	Stan Javier	.10	.05	.01
☐ 486	Kirk Rueter	.10	.05	.01
☐ 487	Andre Dawson	.30	.14	.04
☐ 488	Eric Karros	.30	.14	.04
☐ 489	Dave Magadan	.10	.05	.01
☐ 490	J.Carter 1000 RBI CL	.20	.09	.03
☐ 491	Randy Velarde	.10	.05	.01
☐ 492	Larry Walker	.40	.18	.05
☐ 493	Cris Carpenter	.10	.05	.01
☐ 494	Tom Gordon	.10	.05	.01
☐ 495	Dave Burba	.10	.05	.01
☐ 496	Darren Bragg	.10	.05	.01
☐ 497	Darren Daulton	.20	.09	.03
☐ 498	Don Slaught	.10	.05	.01
☐ 499	Pat Borders	.10	.05	.01
☐ 500	Lenny Harris	.10	.05	.01
☐ 501	Joe Ausanio	.10	.05	.01
☐ 502	Alan Trammell	.30	.14	.04
☐ 503	Mike Fetters	.10	.05	.01
☐ 504	Scott Ruffcorn	.10	.05	.01
☐ 505	Rich Rowland	.10	.05	.01
☐ 506	Juan Samuel	.10	.05	.01
☐ 507	Bo Jackson	.30	.14	.04
☐ 508	Jeff Branson	.10	.05	.01
☐ 509	Bernie Williams	.20	.09	.03
☐ 510	Paul Sorrento	.10	.05	.01
☐ 511	Dennis Eckersley	.30	.14	.04
☐ 512	Pat Mahomes	.10	.05	.01
☐ 513	Rusty Greer	.10	.05	.01
☐ 514	Luis Polonia	.10	.05	.01
☐ 515	Willie Banks	.10	.05	.01
☐ 516	John Wetteland	.20	.09	.03
☐ 517	Mike LaValliere	.10	.05	.01
☐ 518	Tommy Greene	.10	.05	.01
☐ 519	Mark Grace	.30	.14	.04
☐ 520	Bob Hamelin	.10	.05	.01
☐ 521	Scott Sanderson	.10	.05	.01
☐ 522	Joe Carter	.30	.14	.04
☐ 523	Jeff Brantley	.10	.05	.01
☐ 524	Andrew Lorraine	.20	.09	.03
☐ 525	Rico Brogna	.30	.14	.04
☐ 526	Shane Mack	.10	.05	.01
☐ 527	Mark Wohlers	.20	.09	.03
☐ 528	Scott Sanders	.10	.05	.01
☐ 529	Chris Bosio	.10	.05	.01
☐ 530	Andujar Cedeno	.10	.05	.01
☐ 531	Kenny Rogers	.10	.05	.01
☐ 532	Doug Drabek	.20	.09	.03
☐ 533	Curt Leskanic	.20	.09	.03
☐ 534	Craig Shipley	.10	.05	.01
☐ 535	Craig Grebeck	.10	.05	.01
☐ 536	Cal Eldred	.10	.05	.01
☐ 537	Mickey Tettleton	.20	.09	.03
☐ 538	Harold Baines	.20	.09	.03
☐ 539	Tim Wallach	.10	.05	.01
☐ 540	Damon Buford	.20	.09	.03

☐ 541	Lenny Webster	.10	.05	.01
☐ 542	Kevin Appier	.20	.09	.03
☐ 543	Raul Mondesi	.75	.35	.09
☐ 544	Eric Young	.20	.09	.03
☐ 545	Russ Davis	.20	.09	.03
☐ 546	Mike Benjamin	.10	.05	.01
☐ 547	Mike Greenwell	.20	.09	.03
☐ 548	Scott Brosius	.10	.05	.01
☐ 549	Brian Dorsett	.10	.05	.01
☐ 550	C.Davis 1000 RBI CL	.10	.05	.01

1995 Donruss
Press Proofs

Parallel to the basic Donruss set, the Press Proofs are distinguished by the player's name, team name and Donruss logo being done in gold foil on front. The words "Press Proof are also in gold at the top. The first 2,000 cards of the production run were stamped as such and inserted at a rate of one in every 20 packs.

	MINT	NRMT	EXC
COMPLETE SET (550)	2000.00	900.00	250.00
COMPLETE SERIES 1 (330)	1200.00	550.00	150.00
COMPLETE SERIES 2 (220)	800.00	350.00	100.00
COMMON CARD (1-330)	3.00	1.35	.35
COMMON CARD (331-550)	3.00	1.35	.35
SEMISTARS	6.00	2.70	.75
*VETERAN STARS: 20X to 35X BASIC CARDS			
*YOUNG STARS: 15X to 25X BASIC CARDS			

		MINT	NRMT	EXC
☐ 5	Mike Piazza	50.00	22.00	6.25
☐ 20	Jeff Bagwell	40.00	18.00	5.00
☐ 55	Don Mattingly	60.00	27.00	7.50
☐ 83	Cal Ripken	150.00	70.00	19.00
☐ 220	D.Mattingly 2000 Hits CL	30.00	13.50	3.70
☐ 224	Tony Gwynn	40.00	18.00	5.00
☐ 264	Albert Belle	50.00	22.00	6.25
☐ 275	Frank Thomas	125.00	55.00	15.50
☐ 330	K.Puckett 2000 Hits CL	20.00	9.00	2.50
☐ 331	Greg Maddux	125.00	55.00	15.50
☐ 340	Ken Griffey Jr.	125.00	55.00	15.50
☐ 370	Manny Ramirez	50.00	22.00	6.25
☐ 371	Kenny Lofton	40.00	18.00	5.00
☐ 380	Kirby Puckett	40.00	18.00	5.00
☐ 440	D.Mattingly 1000 RBI CL	30.00	13.50	3.70

1995 Donruss
All-Stars

This 18-card set was randomly inserted into retail packs. The first series has the nine 1994 American League starters while the second series honored the National League starters. The fronts feature the player's photo against a background of his league's all-star logo. The player and his team are identified on the bottom. His team is noted

in the upper left corner. All of this is on a borderless card with a gray background. The horizontal backs have a player photo, a quick blurb about his starting role in the game and his performance in the 1994 All-Star game. The cards are numbered in the upper right with either an "AL-X" or an "NL-X."

	MINT	NRMT	EXC
COMPLETE SET (18)	250.00	110.00	31.00
COMPLETE SERIES 1 (9)	175.00	80.00	22.00
COMPLETE SERIES 2 (9)	75.00	34.00	9.50
COMMON CARD (AL1-AL9)	2.50	1.10	.30
COMMON CARD (NL1-NL9)	2.50	1.10	.30

		MINT	NRMT	EXC
☐	AL1 Jimmy Key	2.50	1.10	.30
☐	AL2 Ivan Rodriguez	3.00	1.35	.35
☐	AL3 Frank Thomas	40.00	18.00	5.00
☐	AL4 Roberto Alomar	8.00	3.60	1.00
☐	AL5 Wade Boggs	3.00	1.35	.35
☐	AL6 Cal Ripken	50.00	22.00	6.25
☐	AL7 Joe Carter	3.00	1.35	.35
☐	AL8 Ken Griffey Jr.	40.00	18.00	5.00
☐	AL9 Kirby Puckett	12.00	5.50	1.50
☐	NL1 Greg Maddux	40.00	18.00	5.00
☐	NL2 Mike Piazza	18.00	8.00	2.20
☐	NL3 Gregg Jefferies	3.00	1.35	.35
☐	NL4 Mariano Duncan	2.50	1.10	.30
☐	NL5 Matt Williams	6.00	2.70	.75
☐	NL6 Ozzie Smith	8.00	3.60	1.00
☐	NL7 Barry Bonds	10.00	4.50	1.25
☐	NL8 Tony Gwynn	12.00	5.50	1.50
☐	NL9 David Justice	5.00	2.20	.60

1995 Donruss Bomb Squad

Randomly inserted one in every 24 retail packs and one in every 16 jumbo packs, this set features the top six home run hitters in the National and American League. These cards were only included in first series packs. Each of the six cards shows a different slugger on the either side of the card. Both the fronts and backs are horizontal and feature the player photo with a bomber as background. There are foil bombs to the left indicating how many homers the player hit in 1994. A doggie tag indicates the player's position and rank among home run leaders in his league.

	MINT	NRMT	EXC
COMPLETE SET (6)	25.00	11.00	3.10
COMMON CARD (1-6)	1.50	.70	.19

		MINT	NRMT	EXC
☐	1 Ken Griffey	8.00	3.60	1.00
	Matt Williams			
☐	2 Frank Thomas	10.00	4.50	1.25
	Jeff Bagwell			
☐	3 Albert Belle	5.00	2.20	.60
	Barry Bonds			
☐	4 Jose Canseco	2.50	1.10	.30
	Fred McGriff			
☐	5 Cecil Fielder	1.50	.70	.19
	Andres Galarraga			
☐	6 Joe Carter	1.50	.70	.19
	Kevin Mitchell			

1995 Donruss Diamond Kings

The 1995 Donruss Diamond King set consists of 29 standard-size cards that were randomly inserted in packs. The fronts feature water color player portraits by noted sports artist Dick Perez. The player's name and "Diamond Kings" are in gold foil. The backs have a dark blue border with a player photo and text. The cards are numbered on back with a DK prefix.

	MINT	NRMT	EXC
COMPLETE SET (29)	55.00	25.00	7.00
COMPLETE SERIES 1 (14)	25.00	11.00	3.10
COMPLETE SERIES 2 (15)	30.00	13.50	3.70
COMMON CARD (DK1-DK14)	1.00	.45	.12
COMMON CARD (DK15-DK29)	1.00	.45	.12

☐	DK1 Frank Thomas	12.00	5.50	1.50
☐	DK2 Jeff Bagwell	4.00	1.80	.50
☐	DK3 Chili Davis	1.25	.55	.16
☐	DK4 Dante Bichette	1.50	.70	.19
☐	DK5 Ruben Sierra	1.25	.55	.16
☐	DK6 Jeff Conine	1.25	.55	.16
☐	DK7 Paul O'Neill	1.25	.55	.16
☐	DK8 Bobby Bonilla	1.25	.55	.16
☐	DK9 Joe Carter	1.25	.55	.16
☐	DK10 Moises Alou	1.25	.55	.16
☐	DK11 Kenny Lofton	4.00	1.80	.50
☐	DK12 Matt Williams	2.00	.90	.25
☐	DK13 Kevin Seitzer	1.00	.45	.12
☐	DK14 Sammy Sosa	1.25	.55	.16
☐	DK15 Scott Cooper	1.00	.45	.12
☐	DK16 Raul Mondesi	3.00	1.35	.35
☐	DK17 Will Clark	1.50	.70	.19
☐	DK18 Lenny Dykstra	1.25	.55	.16
☐	DK19 Kirby Puckett	4.00	1.80	.50
☐	DK20 Hal Morris	1.00	.45	.12
☐	DK21 Travis Fryman	1.25	.55	.16
☐	DK22 Greg Maddux	12.00	5.50	1.50
☐	DK23 Rafael Palmeiro	1.25	.55	.16
☐	DK24 Tony Gwynn	4.00	1.80	.50
☐	DK25 David Cone	1.25	.55	.16
☐	DK26 Al Martin	1.00	.45	.12
☐	DK27 Ken Griffey Jr.	12.00	5.50	1.50
☐	DK28 Gregg Jefferies	1.25	.55	.16
☐	DK29 Checklist	1.00	.45	.12

	Greg Maddux			
☐ 2	Ivan Rodriguez	2.50	1.10	.30
	Mike Piazza			
	Darren Daulton			
☐ 3	Fred McGriff	10.00	4.50	1.25
	Frank Thomas			
	Jeff Bagwell			
☐ 4	Roberto Alomar	2.00	.90	.25
	Carlos Baerga			
	Craig Biggio			
☐ 5	Robin Ventura	1.00	.45	.12
	Travis Fryman			
	Matt Williams			
☐ 6	Cal Ripken	8.00	3.60	1.00
	Barry Larkin			
	Wil Cordero			
☐ 7	Albert Belle	3.00	1.35	.35
	Barry Bonds			
	Moises Alou			
☐ 8	Ken Griffey	10.00	4.50	1.25
	Kenny Lofton			
	Marquis Grissom			
☐ 9	Kirby Puckett	3.00	1.35	.35
	Paul O'Neill			
	Tony Gwynn			

1995 Donruss Elite

Randomly inserted one in every 210 packs, this set consists of 12 cards that are numbered (49-60) based on where the previous year's set left off. The fronts contain an action photo surrounded by a marble border. Silver holographic foil borders the card on all four sides. Limited to 10,000, the backs are individually numbered, contain a small photo and write-up.

	MINT	NRMT	EXC
COMPLETE SET (12)	380.00	170.00	47.50
COMPLETE SERIES 1 (6)	200.00	90.00	25.00
COMPLETE SERIES 2 (6)	180.00	80.00	22.00
COMMON CARD (49-54)	10.00	4.50	1.25
COMMON CARD (55-60)	12.00	5.50	1.50
☐ 49 Jeff Bagwell	25.00	11.00	3.10
☐ 50 Paul O'Neill	10.00	4.50	1.25
☐ 51 Greg Maddux	70.00	32.00	8.75
☐ 52 Mike Piazza	30.00	13.50	3.70
☐ 53 Matt Williams	15.00	6.75	1.85
☐ 54 Ken Griffey	75.00	34.00	9.50
☐ 55 Frank Thomas	75.00	34.00	9.50
☐ 56 Barry Bonds	20.00	9.00	2.50

1995 Donruss Dominators

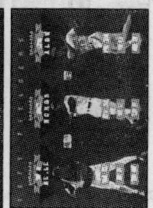

This nine-card set was randomly inserted in second series hobby packs. Each of these cards features three of the leading players at each position. The horizontal fronts have photos of all three players and identify only their last name. The words "remove protective film" cover a significant portion of the fronts as well. The backs have small action photos of the three players along with their 1994 stats. The cards are numbered in the upper right corner as "X" of 9.

	MINT	NRMT	EXC
COMPLETE SET (9)	30.00	13.50	3.70
COMMON CARD (1-9)	1.00	.45	.12
☐ 1 David Cone	8.00	3.60	1.00
	Mike Mussina			

		MINT	NRMT	EXC
☐ 57	Kirby Puckett	25.00	11.00	3.10
☐ 58	Fred McGriff	12.00	5.50	1.50
☐ 59	Jose Canseco	15.00	6.75	1.85
☐ 60	Albert Belle	30.00	13.50	3.70

1995 Donruss Long Ball Leaders

Inserted one in every 24 series one hobby packs, this set features eight top home run hitters. Metallic fronts have much ornamentation including a player photo, the length of the player's home run, the stadium and the date. Horizontal backs have a player photo and photo of the stadium with which the home run occurred. The back also includes all the particulars concerning the home run.

		MINT	NRMT	EXC
COMPLETE SET (8)		20.00	9.00	2.50
COMMON CARD (1-8)		1.25	.55	.16
☐ 1	Frank Thomas	8.00	3.60	1.00
☐ 2	Fred McGriff	1.25	.55	.16
☐ 3	Ken Griffey	8.00	3.60	1.00
☐ 4	Matt Williams	1.25	.55	.16
☐ 5	Mike Piazza	3.00	1.35	.35
☐ 6	Jose Canseco	1.25	.55	.16
☐ 7	Barry Bonds	2.00	.90	.25
☐ 8	Jeff Bagwell	2.50	1.10	.30

1995 Donruss Mound Marvels

This eight-card set was randomly inserted into second series magazine jumbo and retail packs. This set features eight of the leading major league starters. The horizontal fronts feature the player's photo on the left with the words "Donruss Mound Marvels" and the player's name on the right. The back features the player's photo within a circular inset along with all his 1994 stats. The cards are numbered in the left corner as "X" of eight.

		MINT	NRMT	EXC
COMPLETE SET (8)		25.00	11.00	3.10
COMMON CARD (1-8)		1.00	.45	.12
☐ 1	Greg Maddux	15.00	6.75	1.85
☐ 2	David Cone	1.50	.70	.19
☐ 3	Mike Mussina	2.50	1.10	.30
☐ 4	Bret Saberhagen	1.50	.70	.19
☐ 5	Jimmy Key	1.00	.45	.12
☐ 6	Doug Drabek	1.00	.45	.12
☐ 7	Randy Johnson	3.00	1.35	.35
☐ 8	Jason Bere	1.00	.45	.12

1996 Donruss

This 330-card first series was issued in 12-card packs. Suggested retail price of these packs was $1.79. The full-bleed fronts feature full-color action photos. The player's name is in white ink in the upper right. The Donruss logo, team name and team logo as well as uniform number and position are located in the bottom middle set against a silver foil background. The horizontal backs feature season and career stats, text, vital stats and another photo. The only Rookie Card in the first series is Angelo Encarnacion.

		MINT	NRMT	EXC
COMPLETE SERIES 1 (330)		25.00	11.00	3.10
COMMON CARD (1-330)		.10	.05	.01
☐ 1	Frank Thomas	3.00	1.35	.35
☐ 2	Jason Bates	.20	.09	.03
☐ 3	Steve Sparks	.10	.05	.01
☐ 4	Scott Servais	.10	.05	.01

☐ 5	Angelo Encarnacion	.25	.11	.03
☐ 6	Scott Sanders	.10	.05	.01
☐ 7	Billy Ashley	.10	.05	.01
☐ 8	Alex Rodriguez	.30	.14	.04
☐ 9	Sean Bergman	.10	.05	.01
☐ 10	Brad Radke	.10	.05	.01
☐ 11	Andy Van Slyke	.20	.09	.03
☐ 12	Joe Girardi	.10	.05	.01
☐ 13	Mark Grudzielanek	.10	.05	.01
☐ 14	Rick Aguilera	.20	.09	.03
☐ 15	Randy Veres	.10	.05	.01
☐ 16	Tim Bogar	.10	.05	.01
☐ 17	Dave Veres	.10	.05	.01
☐ 18	Kevin Stocker	.10	.05	.01
☐ 19	Marquis Grissom	.30	.14	.04
☐ 20	Will Clark	.40	.18	.05
☐ 21	Jay Bell	.20	.09	.03
☐ 22	Allen Battle	.10	.05	.01
☐ 23	Frank Rodriguez	.20	.09	.03
☐ 24	Terry Steinbach	.20	.09	.03
☐ 25	Gerald Williams	.10	.05	.01
☐ 26	Sid Roberson	.10	.05	.01
☐ 27	Greg Zaun	.10	.05	.01
☐ 28	Ozzie Timmons	.20	.09	.03
☐ 29	Vaughn Eshelman	.10	.05	.01
☐ 30	Ed Sprague	.10	.05	.01
☐ 31	Gary DiSarcina	.10	.05	.01
☐ 32	Joe Boever	.10	.05	.01
☐ 33	Steve Avery	.20	.09	.03
☐ 34	Brad Ausmus	.10	.05	.01
☐ 35	Kirt Manwaring	.10	.05	.01
☐ 36	Gary Sheffield	.30	.14	.04
☐ 37	Jason Bere	.20	.09	.03
☐ 38	Jeff Manto	.10	.05	.01
☐ 39	David Cone	.30	.14	.04
☐ 40	Manny Ramirez	1.25	.55	.16
☐ 41	Sandy Alomar Jr.	.20	.09	.03
☐ 42	Curtis Goodwin	.20	.09	.03
☐ 43	Tino Martinez	.30	.14	.04
☐ 44	Woody Williams	.10	.05	.01
☐ 45	Dean Palmer	.20	.09	.03
☐ 46	Hipolito Pichardo	.10	.05	.01
☐ 47	Jason Giambi	.20	.09	.03
☐ 48	Lance Johnson	.10	.05	.01
☐ 49	Bernard Gilkey	.20	.09	.03
☐ 50	Kirby Puckett	1.00	.45	.12
☐ 51	Tony Fernandez	.10	.05	.01
☐ 52	Alex Gonzalez	.20	.09	.03
☐ 53	Bret Saberhagen	.20	.09	.03
☐ 54	Lyle Mouton	.20	.09	.03
☐ 55	Brian McRae	.20	.09	.03
☐ 56	Mark Gubicza	.10	.05	.01
☐ 57	Sergio Valdez	.10	.05	.01
☐ 58	Darrin Fletcher	.10	.05	.01
☐ 59	Steve Parris	.10	.05	.01
☐ 60	Johnny Damon	.50	.23	.06
☐ 61	Rickey Henderson	.30	.14	.04
☐ 62	Darrell Whitmore	.10	.05	.01
☐ 63	Roberto Petagine	.20	.09	.03
☐ 64	Trenidad Hubbard	.10	.05	.01
☐ 65	Heathcliff Slocumb	.10	.05	.01
☐ 66	Steve Finley	.20	.09	.03
☐ 67	Mariano Rivera	.20	.09	.03
☐ 68	Brian Hunter	.10	.05	.01
☐ 69	Jamie Moyer	.10	.05	.01
☐ 70	Ellis Burks	.20	.09	.03
☐ 71	Pat Kelly	.10	.05	.01
☐ 72	Mickey Tettleton	.20	.09	.03
☐ 73	Garret Anderson	.30	.14	.04
☐ 74	Andy Pettitte	.30	.14	.04
☐ 75	Glenallen Hill	.10	.05	.01
☐ 76	Brent Gates	.10	.05	.01
☐ 77	Lou Whitaker	.30	.14	.04
☐ 78	David Segui	.10	.05	.01
☐ 79	Dan Wilson	.20	.09	.03
☐ 80	Pat Listach	.10	.05	.01
☐ 81	Jeff Bagwell	1.00	.45	.12
☐ 82	Ben McDonald	.10	.05	.01
☐ 83	John Valentin	.30	.14	.04
☐ 84	John Jaha	.20	.09	.03
☐ 85	Pete Schourek	.30	.14	.04
☐ 86	Bryce Florie	.10	.05	.01
☐ 87	Brian Jordan	.30	.14	.04
☐ 88	Ron Karkovice	.10	.05	.01
☐ 89	Al Leiter	.10	.05	.01
☐ 90	Tony Longmire	.10	.05	.01
☐ 91	Nelson Liriano	.10	.05	.01
☐ 92	David Bell	.20	.09	.03
☐ 93	Kevin Gross	.10	.05	.01
☐ 94	Tom Candiotti	.10	.05	.01
☐ 95	Dave Martinez	.10	.05	.01
☐ 96	Greg Myers	.10	.05	.01
☐ 97	Rheal Cormier	.10	.05	.01
☐ 98	Chris Hammond	.10	.05	.01
☐ 99	Randy Myers	.20	.09	.03
☐ 100	Bill Pulsipher	.30	.14	.04
☐ 101	Jason Isringhausen	.40	.18	.05
☐ 102	Dave Stevens	.10	.05	.01
☐ 103	Roberto Alomar	.60	.25	.07
☐ 104	Bob Higginson	.30	.14	.04
☐ 105	Eddie Murray	.40	.18	.05
☐ 106	Matt Walbeck	.10	.05	.01
☐ 107	Mark Wohlers	.20	.09	.03
☐ 108	Jeff Nelson	.10	.05	.01
☐ 109	Tom Goodwin	.10	.05	.01
☐ 110	Cal Ripken CL	1.50	.70	.19
☐ 111	Rey Sanchez	.10	.05	.01
☐ 112	Hector Carrasco	.10	.05	.01
☐ 113	B.J. Surhoff	.20	.09	.03
☐ 114	Dan Miceli	.10	.05	.01
☐ 115	Dean Hartgraves	.10	.05	.01
☐ 116	John Burkett	.10	.05	.01
☐ 117	Gary Gaetti	.20	.09	.03
☐ 118	Ricky Bones	.10	.05	.01
☐ 119	Mike Macfarlane	.10	.05	.01
☐ 120	Bip Roberts	.10	.05	.01
☐ 121	Dave Mlicki	.10	.05	.01
☐ 122	Chili Davis	.20	.09	.03
☐ 123	Mark Whiten	.20	.09	.03
☐ 124	Herbert Perry	.20	.09	.03
☐ 125	Butch Henry	.10	.05	.01
☐ 126	Derek Bell	.10	.05	.01
☐ 127	Al Martin	.20	.09	.03
☐ 128	John Franco	.20	.09	.03
☐ 129	W. VanLandingham	.20	.09	.03
☐ 130	Mike Bordick	.10	.05	.01
☐ 131	Mike Mordecai	.10	.05	.01
☐ 132	Robby Thompson	.10	.05	.01
☐ 133	Greg Colbrunn	.30	.14	.04
☐ 134	Domingo Cedeno	.10	.05	.01
☐ 135	Chad Curtis	.20	.09	.03
☐ 136	Jose Hernandez	.10	.05	.01
☐ 137	Scott Klingenbeck	.10	.05	.01
☐ 138	Ryan Klesko	.30	.14	.04
☐ 139	John Smiley	.10	.05	.01
☐ 140	Charlie Hayes	.20	.09	.03
☐ 141	Jay Buhner	.30	.14	.04
☐ 142	Doug Drabek	.20	.09	.03
☐ 143	Roger Pavlik	.10	.05	.01
☐ 144	Todd Worrell	.10	.05	.01
☐ 145	Cal Ripken	3.00	1.35	.35
☐ 146	Steve Reed	.10	.05	.01

☐ 147	Chuck Finley	.20	.09	.03
☐ 148	Mike Blowers	.20	.09	.03
☐ 149	Orel Hershiser	.20	.09	.03
☐ 150	Allen Watson	.20	.09	.03
☐ 151	Ramon Martinez	.10	.05	.01
☐ 152	Melvin Nieves	.10	.05	.01
☐ 153	Tripp Cromer	.10	.05	.01
☐ 154	Yorkis Perez	.10	.05	.01
☐ 155	Stan Javier	.10	.05	.01
☐ 156	Mel Rojas	.20	.09	.03
☐ 157	Aaron Sele	.20	.09	.03
☐ 158	Eric Karros	.30	.14	.04
☐ 159	Robb Nen	.20	.09	.03
☐ 160	Raul Mondesi	.60	.25	.07
☐ 161	John Wetteland	.20	.09	.03
☐ 162	Tim Scott	.10	.05	.01
☐ 163	Kenny Rogers	.10	.05	.01
☐ 164	Melvin Bunch	.10	.05	.01
☐ 165	Rod Beck	.20	.09	.03
☐ 166	Andy Benes	.20	.09	.03
☐ 167	Lenny Dykstra	.20	.09	.03
☐ 168	Orlando Merced	.20	.09	.03
☐ 169	Tomas Perez	.30	.14	.04
☐ 170	Xavier Hernandez	.10	.05	.01
☐ 171	Ruben Sierra	.20	.09	.03
☐ 172	Alan Trammell	.30	.14	.04
☐ 173	Mike Fetters	.10	.05	.01
☐ 174	Wilson Alvarez	.20	.09	.03
☐ 175	Erik Hanson	.20	.09	.03
☐ 176	Travis Fryman	.30	.14	.04
☐ 177	Jim Abbott	.30	.14	.04
☐ 178	Bret Boone	.20	.09	.03
☐ 179	Sterling Hitchcock	.20	.09	.03
☐ 180	Pat Mahomes	.10	.05	.01
☐ 181	Mark Acre	.10	.05	.01
☐ 182	Charles Nagy	.20	.09	.03
☐ 183	Rusty Greer	.10	.05	.01
☐ 184	Mike Stanley	.10	.05	.01
☐ 185	Jim Bullinger	.10	.05	.01
☐ 186	Shane Andrews	.10	.05	.01
☐ 187	Brian Keyser	.10	.05	.01
☐ 188	Tyler Green	.10	.05	.01
☐ 189	Mark Grace	.30	.14	.04
☐ 190	Bob Hamelin	.10	.05	.01
☐ 191	Luis Ortiz	.10	.05	.01
☐ 192	Joe Carter	.30	.14	.04
☐ 193	Eddie Taubensee	.10	.05	.01
☐ 194	Brian Anderson	.10	.05	.01
☐ 195	Edgardo Alfonzo	.20	.09	.03
☐ 196	Pedro Munoz	.20	.09	.03
☐ 197	David Justice	.40	.18	.05
☐ 198	Trevor Hoffman	.20	.09	.03
☐ 199	Bobby Ayala	.10	.05	.01
☐ 200	Tony Eusebio	.10	.05	.01
☐ 201	Jeff Russell	.10	.05	.01
☐ 202	Mike Hampton	.10	.05	.01
☐ 203	Walt Weiss	.20	.09	.03
☐ 204	Joey Hamilton	.20	.09	.03
☐ 205	Roberto Hernandez	.20	.09	.03
☐ 206	Greg Vaughn	.20	.09	.03
☐ 207	Felipe Lira	.10	.05	.01
☐ 208	Harold Baines	.20	.09	.03
☐ 209	Tim Wallach	.10	.05	.01
☐ 210	Manny Alexander	.10	.05	.01
☐ 211	Tim Laker	.10	.05	.01
☐ 212	Chris Haney	.10	.05	.01
☐ 213	Brian Maxcy	.10	.05	.01
☐ 214	Eric Young	.20	.09	.03
☐ 215	Darryl Strawberry	.20	.09	.03
☐ 216	Barry Bonds	.75	.35	.09
☐ 217	Tim Naehring	.20	.09	.03
☐ 218	Scott Brosius	.10	.05	.01
☐ 219	Reggie Sanders	.30	.14	.04
☐ 220	Eddie Murray CL	.20	.09	.03
☐ 221	Luis Alicea	.10	.05	.01
☐ 222	Albert Belle	1.25	.55	.16
☐ 223	Benji Gil	.10	.05	.01
☐ 224	Dante Bichette	.40	.18	.05
☐ 225	Bobby Bonilla	.30	.14	.04
☐ 226	Todd Stottlemyre	.10	.05	.01
☐ 227	Jim Edmonds	.30	.14	.04
☐ 228	Todd Jones	.10	.05	.01
☐ 229	Shawn Green	.30	.14	.04
☐ 230	Javier Lopez	.30	.14	.04
☐ 231	Ariel Prieto	.10	.05	.01
☐ 232	Tony Phillips	.10	.05	.01
☐ 233	James Mouton	.20	.09	.03
☐ 234	Jose Oquendo	.10	.05	.01
☐ 235	Royce Clayton	.10	.05	.01
☐ 236	Chuck Carr	.10	.05	.01
☐ 237	Doug Jones	.10	.05	.01
☐ 238	Mark McLemore	.10	.05	.01
☐ 239	Bill Swift	.10	.05	.01
☐ 240	Scott Leius	.10	.05	.01
☐ 241	Russ Davis	.20	.09	.03
☐ 242	Ray Durham	.30	.14	.04
☐ 243	Matt Mieske	.10	.05	.01
☐ 244	Brent Mayne	.10	.05	.01
☐ 245	Thomas Howard	.10	.05	.01
☐ 246	Troy O'Leary	.20	.09	.03
☐ 247	Jacob Brumfield	.10	.05	.01
☐ 248	Mickey Morandini	.10	.05	.01
☐ 249	Todd Hundley	.20	.09	.03
☐ 250	Chris Bosio	.10	.05	.01
☐ 251	Omar Vizquel	.20	.09	.03
☐ 252	Mike Lansing	.10	.05	.01
☐ 253	John Mabry	.20	.09	.03
☐ 254	Mike Perez	.10	.05	.01
☐ 255	Delino DeShields	.20	.09	.03
☐ 256	Wil Cordero	.20	.09	.03
☐ 257	Mike James	.10	.05	.01
☐ 258	Todd Van Poppel	.10	.05	.01
☐ 259	Joey Cora	.10	.05	.01
☐ 260	Andre Dawson	.30	.14	.04
☐ 261	Jerry DiPoto	.10	.05	.01
☐ 262	Rick Krivda	.10	.05	.01
☐ 263	Glenn Dishman	.20	.09	.03
☐ 264	Mike Mimbs	.10	.05	.01
☐ 265	John Ericks	.10	.05	.01
☐ 266	Jose Canseco	.50	.23	.06
☐ 267	Jeff Branson	.10	.05	.01
☐ 268	Curt Leskanic	.20	.09	.03
☐ 269	Jon Nunnally	.20	.09	.03
☐ 270	Scott Stahoviak	.10	.05	.01
☐ 271	Jeff Montgomery	.20	.09	.03
☐ 272	Hal Morris	.20	.09	.03
☐ 273	Esteban Loaiza	.10	.05	.01
☐ 274	Rico Brogna	.30	.14	.04
☐ 275	Dave Winfield	.30	.14	.04
☐ 276	J.R. Phillips	.10	.05	.01
☐ 277	Todd Zeile	.10	.05	.01
☐ 278	Tom Pagnozzi	.10	.05	.01
☐ 279	Mark Lemke	.20	.09	.03
☐ 280	Dave Magadan	.10	.05	.01
☐ 281	Greg McMichael	.10	.05	.01
☐ 282	Mike Morgan	.10	.05	.01
☐ 283	Moises Alou	.20	.09	.03
☐ 284	Dennis Martinez	.20	.09	.03
☐ 285	Jeff Kent	.20	.09	.03
☐ 286	Mark Johnson	.10	.05	.01
☐ 287	Darren Lewis	.10	.05	.01
☐ 288	Brad Clontz	.10	.05	.01

		MINT	NRMT	EXC
☐ 289	Chad Fonville	.20	.09	.03
☐ 290	Paul Sorrento	.10	.05	.01
☐ 291	Lee Smith	.30	.14	.04
☐ 292	Tom Glavine	.30	.14	.04
☐ 293	Antonio Osuna	.10	.05	.01
☐ 294	Kevin Foster	.10	.05	.01
☐ 295	Sandy Martinez	.20	.09	.03
☐ 296	Mark Leiter	.10	.05	.01
☐ 297	Julian Tavarez	.20	.09	.03
☐ 298	Mike Kelly	.10	.05	.01
☐ 299	Joe Oliver	.10	.05	.01
☐ 300	John Flaherty	.10	.05	.01
☐ 301	Don Mattingly	1.50	.70	.19
☐ 302	Pat Meares	.10	.05	.01
☐ 303	John Doherty	.10	.05	.01
☐ 304	Joe Vitiello	.20	.09	.03
☐ 305	Vinny Castilla	.30	.14	.04
☐ 306	Jeff Brantley	.10	.05	.01
☐ 307	Mike Greenwell	.20	.09	.03
☐ 308	Midre Cummings	.20	.09	.03
☐ 309	Curt Schilling	.10	.05	.01
☐ 310	Ken Caminiti	.10	.05	.01
☐ 311	Scott Erickson	.20	.09	.03
☐ 312	Carl Everett	.20	.09	.03
☐ 313	Charles Johnson	.30	.14	.04
☐ 314	Alex Diaz	.10	.05	.01
☐ 315	Jose Mesa	.20	.09	.03
☐ 316	Mark Carreon	.10	.05	.01
☐ 317	Carlos Perez	.30	.14	.04
☐ 318	Ismael Valdes	.10	.05	.01
☐ 319	Frank Castillo	.10	.05	.01
☐ 320	Tom Henke	.20	.09	.03
☐ 321	Spike Owen	.10	.05	.01
☐ 322	Joe Orsulak	.10	.05	.01
☐ 323	Paul Menhart	.10	.05	.01
☐ 324	Pedro Borbon	.10	.05	.01
☐ 325	Paul Molitor CL	.10	.05	.01
☐ 326	Jeff Cirillo	.10	.05	.01
☐ 327	Edwin Hurtado	.10	.05	.01
☐ 328	Orlando Miller	.20	.09	.03
☐ 329	Steve Ontiveros	.10	.05	.01
☐ 330	Kirby Puckett CL	.50	.23	.06

1996 Donruss Press Proofs

These cards are parallel to the regular Donruss issue. Even though they are not sequentially numbered, production on these cards were limited to 2,000 cards. Each card is noted as being a Press Proof in gold foil on the front and the cards are inserted one every 12 packs.

		MINT	NRMT	EXC
COMPLETE SERIES 1 (330)		1200.00	550.00	150.00
COMMON CARD (1-330)		2.00	.90	.25
SEMISTARS		5.00	2.20	.60
*VETERAN STARS: 15X TO 25X BASIC CARDS				
*YOUNG STARS: 9X TO 15X BASIC CARDS				
☐ 1	Frank Thomas	75.00	34.00	9.50
☐ 40	Manny Ramirez	30.00	13.50	3.70
☐ 50	Kirby Puckett	25.00	11.00	3.10
☐ 81	Jeff Bagwell	25.00	11.00	3.10

		MINT	NRMT	EXC
☐ 110	Cal Ripken CL	40.00	18.00	5.00
☐ 145	Cal Ripken	75.00	34.00	9.50
☐ 222	Albert Belle	25.00	11.00	3.10
☐ 301	Don Mattingly	30.00	13.50	3.70
☐ 330	Kirby Puckett CL	12.00	5.50	1.50

1996 Donruss Diamond Kings

These 30 cards were randomly inserted into packs and issued in two series of 14 and 16 cards. They were inserted at a ratio of approximately one every 60 packs. The cards are sequentially numbered in the back lower right as "X" of 10,000. The fronts feature player portraits by noted sports artist Dick Perez. These cards are gold-foil stamped and the portraits are surrounded by gold-foil borders. The backs feature text about the player as well as a player photo. The cards are numbered on the back with a "DK" prefix.

		MINT	NRMT	EXC
COMPLETE SERIES 1 (14)		150.00	70.00	19.00
COMMON CARD (1-14)		6.00	2.70	.75
☐ 1	Frank Thomas	50.00	22.00	6.25
☐ 2	Mo Vaughn	10.00	4.50	1.25
☐ 3	Manny Ramirez	20.00	9.00	2.50
☐ 4	Mark McGwire	6.00	2.70	.75
☐ 5	Juan Gonzalez	12.00	5.50	1.50
☐ 6	Roberto Alomar	12.00	5.50	1.50
☐ 7	Tim Salmon	10.00	4.50	1.25
☐ 8	Barry Bonds	15.00	6.75	1.85
☐ 9	Tony Gwynn	18.00	8.00	2.20
☐ 10	Reggie Sanders	8.00	3.60	1.00
☐ 11	Larry Walker	10.00	4.50	1.25
☐ 12	Pedro Martinez	6.00	2.70	.75
☐ 13	Jeff King	6.00	2.70	.75
☐ 14	Mark Grace	8.00	3.60	1.00

1996 Donruss Elite

Randomly inserted approximately one in every 140 packs, this 12-card set is continuously numbered (61-72) from the previous

year. The fronts contain an action photo surrounded by a silver photo. Limited to 10,000 and sequentially numbered, the backs contain a small photo and write up.

	MINT	NRMT	EXC
COMPLETE SERIES 1 (6)	175.00	80.00	22.00
COMMON CARD (61-66)	10.00	4.50	1.25
☐ 61 Cal Ripken	80.00	36.00	10.00
☐ 62 Hideo Nomo	35.00	16.00	4.40
☐ 63 Reggie Sanders	10.00	4.50	1.25
☐ 64 Mo Vaughn	15.00	6.75	1.85
☐ 65 Tim Salmon	15.00	6.75	1.85
☐ 66 Chipper Jones	40.00	18.00	5.00

1996 Donruss Hit List

This eight-card set was randomly inserted into packs. They were inserted at a ratio of approximately one in every 105 packs. The cards are sequentially numbered out of 10,000. The fronts feature full-color shots set against a silver-foil background that is complemented by a team color duotone and features a gold foil team logo and "Hit List" logo. The backs have a color action photo as well as having year-by-year and career hit and batting average stats.

	MINT	NRMT	EXC
COMPLETE SERIES 1 (8)	120.00	55.00	15.00
COMMON CARDS (1-8)	6.00	2.70	.75
☐ 1 Tony Gwynn	15.00	6.75	1.85
☐ 2 Ken Griffey Jr.	50.00	22.00	6.25

☐ 3 Will Clark	8.00	3.60	1.00
☐ 4 Mike Piazza	25.00	11.00	3.10
☐ 5 Carlos Baerga	12.00	5.50	1.50
☐ 6 Mo Vaughn	10.00	4.50	1.25
☐ 7 Mark Grace	6.00	2.70	.75
☐ 8 Kirby Puckett	15.00	6.75	1.85

1996 Donruss Power Alley

This ten-card set was randomly inserted into series one hobby packs. They were inserted at a rate of approximately one in every 92 packs. These cards are all sequentially numbered out of 5,000. The first 500 of these cards were issued in a diecut format. These cards feature a player photo set against a diamond design and team holographic background. The horizontal backs feature a player photo, some text and the player's 1995 power statistics.

	MINT	NRMT	EXC
COMPLETE SET (10)	300.00	135.00	38.00
COMMON CARD (1-10)	15.00	6.75	1.85
DIECUTS ARE FIRST 500 NUMBERS OF EACH CARD			
DIECUTS: 2.5X TO 4X BASIC CARDS			
☐ 1 Frank Thomas	80.00	36.00	10.00
☐ 2 Barry Bonds	25.00	11.00	3.10
☐ 3 Reggie Sanders	15.00	6.75	1.85
☐ 4 Albert Belle	40.00	18.00	5.00
☐ 5 Tim Salmon	20.00	9.00	2.50
☐ 6 Dante Bichette	18.00	8.00	2.20
☐ 7 Mo Vaughn	20.00	9.00	2.50
☐ 8 Jim Edmonds	15.00	6.75	1.85
☐ 9 Manny Ramirez	40.00	18.00	5.00
☐ 10 Ken Griffey Jr.	80.00	36.00	10.00

1996 Donruss Showdown

This eight-card set was randomly inserted in series one packs. These cards feature one top hitter and one top pitcher from each league. The cards are sequentially numbered out of 10,000. The horizontal fronts

feature gold foil stamping and have the words "Show Down" in the middle. The backs feature color player photos as well as some text about their accomplishments.

	MINT	NRMT	EXC
COMPLETE SET (8)	225.00	100.00	28.00
COMMON CARD (1-8)	8.00	3.60	1.00
☐ 1 Frank Thomas	50.00	22.00	6.25
Hideo Nomo			
☐ 2 Barry Bonds	20.00	9.00	2.50
Randy Johnson			
☐ 3 Greg Maddux	60.00	27.00	7.50
Ken Griffey Jr.			
☐ 4 Roger Clemens	20.00	9.00	2.50
Tony Gwynn			
☐ 5 Mike Piazza	25.00	11.00	3.10
Mike Mussina			
☐ 6 Cal Ripken	50.00	22.00	6.25
Pedro J.Martinez			
☐ 7 Tim Wakefield	8.00	3.60	1.00
Matt Williams			
☐ 8 Manny Ramirez	20.00	9.00	2.50
Carlos Perez			

1995 Emotion

This 200-card set was produced by Fleer/SkyBox. The first-year brand has double-thick card stock with borderless fronts. Card fronts and backs are either horizontal or vertical. On the front of each player card is a theme such as Class (Cal Ripken) and Confident (Barry Bonds). The backs have two player photos, '94 stats and career numbers. The checklist is arranged as such: Baltimore Orioles (1-8), Boston Red Sox (9-17), California Angels

(18-23), Chicago White Sox (24-30), Cleveland Indians (31-40), Detroit Tigers (41-47), Kansas City Royals (48-51), Milwaukee Brewers (52-55), Minnesota Twins (56-58), New York Yankees (59-68), Oakland Athletics (69-75), Seattle Mariners (76-82), Texas Rangers (83-89), Toronto Blue Jays (90-98). National League: Atlanta Braves (99-108), Chicago Cubs (109-114), Cincinnati Reds (115-121), Colorado Rockies (122-126), Florida Marlins (127-133), Houston Astros (134-140), Los Angeles Dodgers (141-147), Montreal Expos (148-156), New York Mets (157-162), Philadelphia Phillies (163-171), Pittsburgh Pirates (172-178), St. Louis Cardinals (179-183), San Diego Padres (184-190) and San Francisco Giants (191-197).

	MINT	NRMT	EXC
COMPLETE SET (200)	40.00	18.00	5.00
COMMON CARD (1-200)	.25	.11	.03
☐ 1 Brady Anderson	.30	.14	.04
☐ 2 Kevin Brown	.25	.11	.03
☐ 3 Curtis Goodwin	.40	.18	.05
☐ 4 Jeffrey Hammonds	.30	.14	.04
☐ 5 Ben McDonald	.25	.11	.03
☐ 6 Mike Mussina	.60	.25	.07
☐ 7 Rafael Palmeiro	.40	.18	.05
☐ 8 Cal Ripken Jr.	5.00	2.20	.60
☐ 9 Jose Canseco	.75	.35	.09
☐ 10 Roger Clemens	.75	.35	.09
☐ 11 Vaughn Eshelman	.25	.11	.03
☐ 12 Mike Greenwell	.30	.14	.04
☐ 13 Erik Hanson	.25	.11	.03
☐ 14 Tim Naehring	.25	.11	.03
☐ 15 Aaron Sele	.25	.11	.03
☐ 16 John Valentin	.40	.18	.05
☐ 17 Mo Vaughn	.75	.35	.09
☐ 18 Chili Davis	.30	.14	.04
☐ 19 Gary DiSarcina	.25	.11	.03
☐ 20 Chuck Finley	.25	.11	.03
☐ 21 Tim Salmon	.75	.35	.09
☐ 22 Lee Smith	.40	.18	.05
☐ 23 J.T. Snow	.40	.18	.05
☐ 24 Jim Abbott	.40	.18	.05
☐ 25 Jason Bere	.25	.11	.03
☐ 26 Ray Durham	.40	.18	.05
☐ 27 Ozzie Guillen	.25	.11	.03
☐ 28 Tim Raines	.40	.18	.05
☐ 29 Frank Thomas	5.00	2.20	.60
☐ 30 Robin Ventura	.40	.18	.05
☐ 31 Carlos Baerga	1.00	.45	.12
☐ 32 Albert Belle	2.00	.90	.25
☐ 33 Orel Hershiser	.30	.14	.04
☐ 34 Kenny Lofton	1.50	.70	.19
☐ 35 Dennis Martinez	.30	.14	.04
☐ 36 Eddie Murray	.60	.25	.07
☐ 37 Manny Ramirez	2.00	.90	.25
☐ 38 Julian Tavarez	.25	.11	.03
☐ 39 Jim Thome	.75	.35	.09
☐ 40 Dave Winfield	.40	.18	.05
☐ 41 Chad Curtis	.25	.11	.03
☐ 42 Cecil Fielder	.40	.18	.05
☐ 43 Travis Fryman	.40	.18	.05
☐ 44 Kirk Gibson	.40	.18	.05
☐ 45 Bob Higginson RC	.60	.25	.07
☐ 46 Alan Trammell	.40	.18	.05
☐ 47 Lou Whitaker	.40	.18	.05

☐ 48	Kevin Appier	.30	.14	.04
☐ 49	Gary Gaetti	.30	.14	.04
☐ 50	Jeff Montgomery	.30	.14	.04
☐ 51	Jon Nunnally	.40	.18	.05
☐ 52	Ricky Bones	.25	.11	.03
☐ 53	Cal Eldred	.25	.11	.03
☐ 54	Joe Oliver	.25	.11	.03
☐ 55	Kevin Seitzer	.25	.11	.03
☐ 56	Marty Cordova	.75	.35	.09
☐ 57	Chuck Knoblauch	.40	.18	.05
☐ 58	Kirby Puckett	1.50	.70	.19
☐ 59	Wade Boggs	.40	.18	.05
☐ 60	Derek Jeter	.75	.35	.09
☐ 61	Jimmy Key	.25	.11	.03
☐ 62	Don Mattingly	2.50	1.10	.30
☐ 63	Jack McDowell	.40	.18	.05
☐ 64	Paul O'Neill	.30	.14	.04
☐ 65	Andy Pettitte	.60	.25	.07
☐ 66	Ruben Rivera	3.00	1.35	.35
☐ 67	Mike Stanley	.25	.11	.03
☐ 68	John Wetteland	.30	.14	.04
☐ 69	Geronimo Berroa	.25	.11	.03
☐ 70	Dennis Eckersley	.40	.18	.05
☐ 71	Rickey Henderson	.40	.18	.05
☐ 72	Mark McGwire	.40	.18	.05
☐ 73	Steve Ontiveros	.25	.11	.03
☐ 74	Ruben Sierra	.40	.18	.05
☐ 75	Terry Steinbach	.30	.14	.04
☐ 76	Jay Buhner	.40	.18	.05
☐ 77	Ken Griffey Jr.	5.00	2.20	.60
☐ 78	Randy Johnson	1.00	.45	.12
☐ 79	Edgar Martinez	.40	.18	.05
☐ 80	Tino Martinez	.40	.18	.05
☐ 81	Marc Newfield	.30	.14	.04
☐ 82	Alex Rodriguez	1.00	.45	.12
☐ 83	Will Clark	.60	.25	.07
☐ 84	Benji Gil	.25	.11	.03
☐ 85	Juan Gonzalez	1.25	.55	.16
☐ 86	Rusty Greer	.25	.11	.03
☐ 87	Dean Palmer	.25	.11	.03
☐ 88	Ivan Rodriguez	.40	.18	.05
☐ 89	Kenny Rogers	.25	.11	.03
☐ 90	Roberto Alomar	1.00	.45	.12
☐ 91	Joe Carter	.40	.18	.05
☐ 92	David Cone	.40	.18	.05
☐ 93	Alex Gonzalez	.30	.14	.04
☐ 94	Shawn Green	.40	.18	.05
☐ 95	Pat Hentgen	.30	.14	.04
☐ 96	Paul Molitor	.40	.18	.05
☐ 97	John Olerud	.30	.14	.04
☐ 98	Devon White	.25	.11	.03
☐ 99	Steve Avery	.30	.14	.04
☐ 100	Tom Glavine	.40	.18	.05
☐ 101	Marquis Grissom	.40	.18	.05
☐ 102	Chipper Jones	2.00	.90	.25
☐ 103	David Justice	.60	.25	.07
☐ 104	Ryan Klesko	1.00	.45	.12
☐ 105	Javier Lopez	.60	.25	.07
☐ 106	Greg Maddux	5.00	2.20	.60
☐ 107	Fred McGriff	.60	.25	.07
☐ 108	John Smoltz	.30	.14	.04
☐ 109	Shawon Dunston	.25	.11	.03
☐ 110	Mark Grace	.40	.18	.05
☐ 111	Brian McRae	.30	.14	.04
☐ 112	Randy Myers	.30	.14	.04
☐ 113	Sammy Sosa	.40	.18	.05
☐ 114	Steve Trachsel	.25	.11	.03
☐ 115	Bret Boone	.30	.14	.04
☐ 116	Ron Gant	.40	.18	.05
☐ 117	Barry Larkin	.60	.25	.07
☐ 118	Deion Sanders	1.00	.45	.12
☐ 119	Reggie Sanders	.40	.18	.05
☐ 120	Pete Schourek	.40	.18	.05
☐ 121	John Smiley	.25	.11	.03
☐ 122	Jason Bates	.25	.11	.03
☐ 123	Dante Bichette	.60	.25	.07
☐ 124	Vinny Castilla	.40	.18	.05
☐ 125	Andres Galarraga	.40	.18	.05
☐ 126	Larry Walker	.60	.25	.07
☐ 127	Greg Colbrunn	.40	.18	.05
☐ 128	Jeff Conine	.40	.18	.05
☐ 129	Andre Dawson	.40	.18	.05
☐ 130	Chris Hammond	.25	.11	.03
☐ 131	Charles Johnson	.40	.18	.05
☐ 132	Gary Sheffield	.40	.18	.05
☐ 133	Quilvio Veras	.25	.11	.03
☐ 134	Jeff Bagwell	1.50	.70	.19
☐ 135	Derek Bell	.40	.18	.05
☐ 136	Craig Biggio	.40	.18	.05
☐ 137	Jim Dougherty	.25	.11	.03
☐ 138	John Hudek	.25	.11	.03
☐ 139	Orlando Miller	.25	.11	.03
☐ 140	Phil Plantier	.25	.11	.03
☐ 141	Eric Karros	.40	.18	.05
☐ 142	Ramon Martinez	.30	.14	.04
☐ 143	Raul Mondesi	1.25	.55	.16
☐ 144	Hideo Nomo	8.00	3.60	1.00
☐ 145	Mike Piazza	2.00	.90	.25
☐ 146	Ismael Valdes	.25	.11	.03
☐ 147	Todd Worrell	.25	.11	.03
☐ 148	Moises Alou	.30	.14	.04
☐ 149	Yamil Benitez	.60	.25	.07
☐ 150	Wil Cordero	.30	.14	.04
☐ 151	Jeff Fassero	.25	.11	.03
☐ 152	Cliff Floyd	.30	.14	.04
☐ 153	Pedro Martinez	.30	.14	.04
☐ 154	Carlos Perez	1.25	.55	.16
☐ 155	Tony Tarasco	.25	.11	.03
☐ 156	Rondell White	.40	.18	.05
☐ 157	Edgardo Alfonzo	.25	.11	.03
☐ 158	Bobby Bonilla	.40	.18	.05
☐ 159	Rico Brogna	.40	.18	.05
☐ 160	Bobby Jones	.25	.11	.03
☐ 161	Bill Pulsipher	.30	.14	.04
☐ 162	Bret Saberhagen	.25	.11	.03
☐ 163	Ricky Bottalico	.25	.11	.03
☐ 164	Darren Daulton	.30	.14	.04
☐ 165	Lenny Dykstra	.30	.14	.04
☐ 166	Charlie Hayes	.25	.11	.03
☐ 167	Dave Hollins	.25	.11	.03
☐ 168	Gregg Jefferies	.40	.18	.05
☐ 169	Michael Mimbs	.50	.23	.06
☐ 170	Curt Schilling	.25	.11	.03
☐ 171	Heathcliff Slocumb	.25	.11	.03
☐ 172	Jay Bell	.30	.14	.04
☐ 173	Micah Franklin	1.00	.45	.12
☐ 174	Mark Johnson	.25	.11	.03
☐ 175	Jeff King	.25	.11	.03
☐ 176	Al Martin	.30	.14	.04
☐ 177	Dan Miceli	.25	.11	.03
☐ 178	Denny Neagle	.25	.11	.03
☐ 179	Bernard Gilkey	.30	.14	.04
☐ 180	Ken Hill	.30	.14	.04
☐ 181	Brian Jordan	.40	.18	.05
☐ 182	Ray Lankford	.40	.18	.05
☐ 183	Ozzie Smith	1.00	.45	.12
☐ 184	Andy Benes	.30	.14	.04
☐ 185	Ken Caminiti	.25	.11	.03
☐ 186	Steve Finley	.25	.11	.03
☐ 187	Tony Gwynn	1.50	.70	.19
☐ 188	Joey Hamilton	.25	.11	.03
☐ 189	Melvin Nieves	.30	.14	.04

			MINT	NRMT	EXC
☐ 190	Scott Sanders		.25	.11	.03
☐ 191	Rod Beck		.25	.11	.03
☐ 192	Barry Bonds		1.25	.55	.16
☐ 193	Royce Clayton		.25	.11	.03
☐ 194	Glenallen Hill		.25	.11	.03
☐ 195	Darren Lewis		.25	.11	.03
☐ 196	Mark Portugal		.25	.11	.03
☐ 197	Matt Williams		.75	.35	.09
☐ 198	Checklist 1-82		.25	.11	.03
☐ 199	Checklist 83-162		.25	.11	.03
☐ 200	Checklist 163-200/Inserts	.25	.11	.03

1995 Emotion Masters

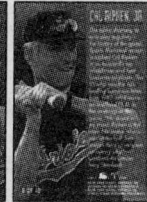

The theme of this 10-card set is the show-casing of players that come through in the clutch. Randomly inserted at a rate of one in eight packs, a player photo is superimposed over a larger photo that is ghosted in a color emblematic of that team. The player's name and the Emotion logo are at the bottom. The backs have a photo tot he left and text to the right. Both sides of the card are shaded in the color scheme of the player's team.

		MINT	NRMT	EXC
COMPLETE SET (10)		80.00	36.00	10.00
COMMON CARD (1-10)		3.00	1.35	.35
☐ 1	Barry Bonds	5.00	2.20	.60
☐ 2	Juan Gonzalez	5.00	2.20	.60
☐ 3	Ken Griffey Jr.	20.00	9.00	2.50
☐ 4	Tony Gwynn	6.00	2.70	.75
☐ 5	Kenny Lofton	6.00	2.70	.75
☐ 6	Greg Maddux	20.00	9.00	2.50
☐ 7	Raul Mondesi	5.00	2.20	.60
☐ 8	Cal Ripken	20.00	9.00	2.50
☐ 9	Frank Thomas	20.00	9.00	2.50
☐ 10	Matt Williams	3.00	1.35	.35

1995 Emotion N-Tense

Randomly inserted at a rate of one in 37 packs, this 12-card set features fronts that have a player photo surrounded by a

swirling color scheme and a large holographic "N" in the background. The backs feature a like color scheme with text and player photo.

		MINT	NRMT	EXC
COMPLETE SET (12)		225.00	100.00	28.00
COMMON CARD (1-12)		8.00	3.60	1.00
☐ 1	Jeff Bagwell	20.00	9.00	2.50
☐ 2	Albert Belle	25.00	11.00	3.10
☐ 3	Barry Bonds	15.00	6.75	1.85
☐ 4	Cecil Fielder	8.00	3.60	1.00
☐ 5	Ron Gant	8.00	3.60	1.00
☐ 6	Ken Griffey Jr.	65.00	29.00	8.00
☐ 7	Mark McGwire	8.00	3.60	1.00
☐ 8	Mike Piazza	25.00	11.00	3.10
☐ 9	Manny Ramirez	25.00	11.00	3.10
☐ 10	Frank Thomas	65.00	29.00	8.00
☐ 11	Mo Vaughn	12.00	5.50	1.50
☐ 12	Matt Williams	10.00	4.50	1.25

1995 Emotion Rookies

This 10-card set was inserted at a rate of one in five packs. Card fronts feature an action photo superimposed over background that is in a color consistent with that of the team's. The backs have a player photo and a write-up.

		MINT	NRMT	EXC
COMPLETE SET (10)		25.00	11.00	3.10
COMMON CARD (1-10)		1.00	.45	.12

		MINT	NRMT	EXC
☐	1 Edgardo Alfonzo	1.00	.45	.12
☐	2 Jason Bates	1.00	.45	.12
☐	3 Marty Cordova	2.50	1.10	.30
☐	4 Ray Durham	1.50	.70	.19
☐	5 Alex Gonzalez	1.00	.45	.12
☐	6 Shawn Green	1.50	.70	.19
☐	7 Charles Johnson	1.50	.70	.19
☐	8 Chipper Jones	8.00	3.60	1.00
☐	9 Hideo Nomo	12.00	5.50	1.50
☐	10 Alex Rodriguez	3.00	1.35	.35

1993 Finest

These 199 standard-size cards have metallic finishes on their fronts and feature color player action photos. The set's title appears at the top, and the player's name is shown at the bottom. The complete title of the set is Topps Baseball's Finest. The non-metallic, white-bordered horizontal back has a faded baseball action scene as a background and carries a color player action photo within a simulated metal frame on the left side. The player's name appears beneath the photo. The right side carries the set's title and the player's position, team, biography, and stats. The Mike Piazza card (199) was added to the set after the original 198 cards were released. The cards are numbered on the back. The key Rookie Card in this set is J.T. Snow.

		MINT	NRMT	EXC
COMPLETE SET (199)		250.00	110.00	31.00
COMMON CARD (1-199)		.75	.35	.09
☐	1 David Justice	4.00	1.80	.50
☐	2 Lou Whitaker	2.50	1.10	.30
☐	3 Bryan Harvey	.75	.35	.09
☐	4 Carlos Garcia	.75	.35	.09
☐	5 Sid Fernandez	.75	.35	.09
☐	6 Brett Butler	1.50	.70	.19
☐	7 Scott Cooper	.75	.35	.09
☐	8 B.J. Surhoff	1.50	.70	.19
☐	9 Steve Finley	.75	.35	.09
☐	10 Curt Schilling	.75	.35	.09
☐	11 Jeff Bagwell	12.00	5.50	1.50
☐	12 Alex Cole	.75	.35	.09
☐	13 John Olerud	1.50	.70	.19
☐	14 John Smiley	.75	.35	.09
☐	15 Bip Roberts	.75	.35	.09
☐	16 Albert Belle	12.00	5.50	1.50
☐	17 Duane Ward	.75	.35	.09
☐	18 Alan Trammell	2.50	1.10	.30
☐	19 Andy Benes	1.50	.70	.19
☐	20 Reggie Sanders	2.50	1.10	.30
☐	21 Todd Zeile	1.50	.70	.19
☐	22 Rick Aguilera	1.50	.70	.19
☐	23 Dave Hollins	.75	.35	.09
☐	24 Jose Rijo	.75	.35	.09
☐	25 Matt Williams	5.00	2.20	.60
☐	26 Sandy Alomar	1.50	.70	.19
☐	27 Alex Fernandez	1.50	.70	.19
☐	28 Ozzie Smith	6.00	2.70	.75
☐	29 Ramon Martinez	1.50	.70	.19
☐	30 Bernie Williams	1.50	.70	.19
☐	31 Gary Sheffield	2.50	1.10	.30
☐	32 Eric Karros	1.50	.70	.19
☐	33 Frank Viola	.75	.35	.09
☐	34 Kevin Young	.75	.35	.09
☐	35 Ken Hill	1.50	.70	.19
☐	36 Tony Fernandez	.75	.35	.09
☐	37 Tim Wakefield	2.50	1.10	.30
☐	38 John Kruk	2.50	1.10	.30
☐	39 Chris Sabo	.75	.35	.09
☐	40 Marquis Grissom	2.50	1.10	.30
☐	41 Glenn Davis	.75	.35	.09
☐	42 Jeff Montgomery	1.50	.70	.19
☐	43 Kenny Lofton	10.00	4.50	1.25
☐	44 John Burkett	.75	.35	.09
☐	45 Darryl Hamilton	.75	.35	.09
☐	46 Jim Abbott	2.50	1.10	.30
☐	47 Ivan Rodriguez	2.50	1.10	.30
☐	48 Eric Young	1.50	.70	.19
☐	49 Mitch Williams	.75	.35	.09
☐	50 Harold Reynolds	.75	.35	.09
☐	51 Brian Harper	.75	.35	.09
☐	52 Rafael Palmeiro	2.50	1.10	.30
☐	53 Bret Saberhagen	1.50	.70	.19
☐	54 Jeff Conine	2.50	1.10	.30
☐	55 Ivan Calderon	.75	.35	.09
☐	56 Juan Guzman	.75	.35	.09
☐	57 Carlos Baerga	6.00	2.70	.75
☐	58 Charles Nagy	1.50	.70	.19
☐	59 Wally Joyner	1.50	.70	.19
☐	60 Charlie Hayes	1.50	.70	.19
☐	61 Shane Mack	.75	.35	.09
☐	62 Pete Harnisch	.75	.35	.09
☐	63 George Brett	12.00	5.50	1.50
☐	64 Lance Johnson	.75	.35	.09
☐	65 Ben McDonald	.75	.35	.09
☐	66 Bobby Bonilla	2.50	1.10	.30
☐	67 Terry Steinbach	1.50	.70	.19
☐	68 Ron Gant	2.50	1.10	.30
☐	69 Doug Jones	.75	.35	.09
☐	70 Paul Molitor	2.50	1.10	.30
☐	71 Brady Anderson	1.50	.70	.19
☐	72 Chuck Finley	1.50	.70	.19
☐	73 Mark Grace	2.50	1.10	.30
☐	74 Mike Devereaux	.75	.35	.09
☐	75 Tony Phillips	.75	.35	.09
☐	76 Chuck Knoblauch	2.50	1.10	.30
☐	77 Tony Gwynn	10.00	4.50	1.25
☐	78 Kevin Appier	1.50	.70	.19
☐	79 Sammy Sosa	2.50	1.10	.30
☐	80 Mickey Tettleton	1.50	.70	.19
☐	81 Felix Jose	.75	.35	.09
☐	82 Mark Langston	1.50	.70	.19
☐	83 Gregg Jefferies	2.50	1.10	.30
☐	84 Andre Dawson AS	2.50	1.10	.30

☐ 85	Greg Maddux AS	30.00	13.50	3.70
☐ 86	Rickey Henderson AS	2.50	1.10	.30
☐ 87	Tom Glavine AS	2.50	1.10	.30
☐ 88	Roberto Alomar AS	6.00	2.70	.75
☐ 89	Darryl Strawberry AS	1.50	.70	.19
☐ 90	Wade Boggs AS	2.50	1.10	.30
☐ 91	Bo Jackson AS	2.50	1.10	.30
☐ 92	Mark McGwire AS	2.50	1.10	.30
☐ 93	Robin Ventura AS	2.50	1.10	.30
☐ 94	Joe Carter AS	2.50	1.10	.30
☐ 95	Lee Smith AS	2.50	1.10	.30
☐ 96	Cal Ripken AS	30.00	13.50	3.70
☐ 97	Larry Walker AS	4.00	1.80	.50
☐ 98	Don Mattingly AS	15.00	6.75	1.85
☐ 99	Jose Canseco AS	5.00	2.20	.60
☐ 100	Dennis Eckersley AS	2.50	1.10	.30
☐ 101	Terry Pendleton AS	1.50	.70	.19
☐ 102	Frank Thomas AS	30.00	13.50	3.70
☐ 103	Barry Bonds AS	8.00	3.60	1.00
☐ 104	Roger Clemens AS	5.00	2.20	.60
☐ 105	Ryne Sandberg AS	8.00	3.60	1.00
☐ 106	Fred McGriff AS	4.00	1.80	.50
☐ 107	Nolan Ryan AS	30.00	13.50	3.70
☐ 108	Will Clark AS	4.00	1.80	.50
☐ 109	Pat Listach AS	.75	.35	.09
☐ 110	Ken Griffey Jr. AS	30.00	13.50	3.70
☐ 111	Cecil Fielder AS	2.50	1.10	.30
☐ 112	Kirby Puckett AS	10.00	4.50	1.25
☐ 113	Dwight Gooden AS	1.50	.70	.19
☐ 114	Barry Larkin AS	4.00	1.80	.50
☐ 115	David Cone AS	2.50	1.10	.30
☐ 116	Juan Gonzalez AS	6.00	2.70	.75
☐ 117	Kent Hrbek	1.50	.70	.19
☐ 118	Tim Wallach	.75	.35	.09
☐ 119	Craig Biggio	2.50	1.10	.30
☐ 120	Roberto Kelly	1.50	.70	.19
☐ 121	Gregg Olson	.75	.35	.09
☐ 122	Eddie Murray UER	5.00	2.20	.60
	122 career strikeouts should be 1224			
☐ 123	Wil Cordero	1.50	.70	.19
☐ 124	Jay Buhner	2.50	1.10	.30
☐ 125	Carlton Fisk	2.50	1.10	.30
☐ 126	Eric Davis	.75	.35	.09
☐ 127	Doug Drabek	1.50	.70	.19
☐ 128	Ozzie Guillen	.75	.35	.09
☐ 129	John Wetteland	1.50	.70	.19
☐ 130	Andres Galarraga	2.50	1.10	.30
☐ 131	Ken Caminiti	1.50	.70	.19
☐ 132	Tom Candiotti	.75	.35	.09
☐ 133	Pat Borders	.75	.35	.09
☐ 134	Kevin Brown	.75	.35	.09
☐ 135	Travis Fryman	2.50	1.10	.30
☐ 136	Kevin Mitchell	1.50	.70	.19
☐ 137	Greg Swindell	.75	.35	.09
☐ 138	Benito Santiago	.75	.35	.09
☐ 139	Reggie Jefferson	.75	.35	.09
☐ 140	Chris Bosio	.75	.35	.09
☐ 141	Deion Sanders	6.00	2.70	.75
☐ 142	Scott Erickson	1.50	.70	.19
☐ 143	Howard Johnson	.75	.35	.09
☐ 144	Orestes Destrade	.75	.35	.09
☐ 145	Jose Guzman	.75	.35	.09
☐ 146	Chad Curtis	1.50	.70	.19
☐ 147	Cal Eldred	.75	.35	.09
☐ 148	Willie Greene	1.50	.70	.19
☐ 149	Tommy Greene	.75	.35	.09
☐ 150	Erik Hanson	1.50	.70	.19
☐ 151	Bob Welch	1.50	.70	.19
☐ 152	John Jaha	1.50	.70	.19
☐ 153	Harold Baines	1.50	.70	.19

☐ 154	Randy Johnson	6.00	2.70	.75
☐ 155	Al Martin	1.50	.70	.19
☐ 156	J.T. Snow	5.00	2.20	.60
☐ 157	Mike Mussina	4.00	1.80	.50
☐ 158	Ruben Sierra	2.50	1.10	.30
☐ 159	Dean Palmer	1.50	.70	.19
☐ 160	Steve Avery	2.50	1.10	.30
☐ 161	Julio Franco	1.50	.70	.19
☐ 162	Dave Winfield	2.50	1.10	.30
☐ 163	Tim Salmon	6.00	2.70	.75
☐ 164	Tom Henke	1.50	.70	.19
☐ 165	Mo Vaughn	5.00	2.20	.60
☐ 166	John Smoltz	1.50	.70	.19
☐ 167	Danny Tartabull	1.50	.70	.19
☐ 168	Delino DeShields	1.50	.70	.19
☐ 169	Charlie Hough	1.50	.70	.19
☐ 170	Paul O'Neill	1.50	.70	.19
☐ 171	Darren Daulton	2.50	1.10	.30
☐ 172	Jack McDowell	2.50	1.10	.30
☐ 173	Junior Felix	.75	.35	.09
☐ 174	Jimmy Key	1.50	.70	.19
☐ 175	George Bell	1.50	.70	.19
☐ 176	Mike Stanton	.75	.35	.09
☐ 177	Len Dykstra	2.50	1.10	.30
☐ 178	Norm Charlton	.75	.35	.09
☐ 179	Eric Anthony	.75	.35	.09
☐ 180	Rob Dibble	.75	.35	.09
☐ 181	Otis Nixon	.75	.35	.09
☐ 182	Randy Myers	1.50	.70	.19
☐ 183	Tim Raines	2.50	1.10	.30
☐ 184	Orel Hershiser	1.50	.70	.19
☐ 185	Andy Van Slyke	1.50	.70	.19
☐ 186	Mike Lansing	2.00	.90	.25
☐ 187	Ray Lankford	2.50	1.10	.30
☐ 188	Mike Morgan	.75	.35	.09
☐ 189	Moises Alou	2.50	1.10	.30
☐ 190	Edgar Martinez	2.50	1.10	.30
☐ 191	John Franco	1.50	.70	.19
☐ 192	Robin Yount	4.00	1.80	.50
☐ 193	Bob Tewksbury	.75	.35	.09
☐ 194	Jay Bell	1.50	.70	.19
☐ 195	Luis Gonzalez	1.50	.70	.19
☐ 196	Dave Fleming	.75	.35	.09
☐ 197	Mike Greenwell	1.50	.70	.19
☐ 198	David Nied	1.50	.70	.19
☐ 199	Mike Piazza	25.00	11.00	3.10

1993 Finest Refractors

Randomly inserted in packs, these 199 standard-size cards are identical to the reg-ular-issue 1993 Topps Finest except that their fronts have been laminated with a plastic diffraction grating that gives the card a colorful 3-D appearance. The horizontal backs, however, are the same. A color player action photo appears on the left side within gold or silver simulated picture frame. The player's name appears beneath. His position, team biography, and stats appear alongside on the right. All the back's design elements are superposed upon a ghosted and colorized baseball action photo.

	MINT	NRMT	EXC
COMPLETE SET (199)	22000.00	9900.00	2800.00
COMMON CARD (1-199)	30.00	13.50	3.70
SEMISTARS	50.00	22.00	6.25
STARS	100.00	45.00	12.50
ASTERISK CARDS PERCEIVED TO BE IN SHORT SUPPLY			

		MINT	NRMT	EXC
☐ 1	David Justice	200.00	90.00	25.00
☐ 3	Bryan Harvey*	200.00	90.00	25.00
☐ 10	Curt Schilling*	300.00	135.00	38.00
☐ 11	Jeff Bagwell	425.00	190.00	52.50
☐ 12	Alex Cole	175.00	80.00	22.00
☐ 16	Albert Belle	500.00	220.00	60.00
☐ 20	Reggie Sanders	125.00	55.00	15.50
☐ 25	Matt Williams	300.00	135.00	38.00
☐ 28	Ozzie Smith	175.00	80.00	22.00
☐ 32	Eric Karros	125.00	55.00	15.50
☐ 38	John Kruk	150.00	70.00	19.00
☐ 39	Chris Sabo*	150.00	70.00	19.00
☐ 40	Marquis Grissom*	400.00	180.00	50.00
☐ 41	Glenn Davis*	225.00	100.00	28.00
☐ 43	Kenny Lofton	350.00	160.00	45.00
☐ 54	Jeff Conine	125.00	55.00	15.50
☐ 57	Carlos Baerga	200.00	90.00	25.00
☐ 63	George Brett	600.00	275.00	75.00
☐ 70	Paul Molitor	400.00	180.00	50.00
☐ 76	Chuck Knoblauch	125.00	55.00	15.50
☐ 77	Tony Gwynn	425.00	190.00	52.50
☐ 79	Sammy Sosa*	450.00	200.00	55.00
☐ 80	Mickey Tettleton	125.00	55.00	15.50
☐ 81	Felix Jose*	150.00	70.00	19.00
☐ 84	Andre Dawson AS*	125.00	55.00	15.50
☐ 85	Greg Maddux AS	1500.00	700.00	190.00
☐ 87	Tom Glavine AS	150.00	70.00	19.00
☐ 88	Roberto Alomar AS	200.00	90.00	25.00
☐ 92	Mark McGwire AS	125.00	55.00	15.50
☐ 94	Joe Carter AS	125.00	55.00	15.50
☐ 96	Cal Ripken AS	2500.00	1100.00	300.00
☐ 97	Larry Walker AS	175.00	80.00	22.00
☐ 98	Don Mattingly AS	400.00	180.00	50.00
☐ 99	Jose Canseco AS	200.00	90.00	25.00
☐ 102	Frank Thomas AS	1250.00	550.00	160.00
☐ 103	Barry Bonds AS	275.00	125.00	34.00
☐ 104	Roger Clemens AS	200.00	90.00	25.00
☐ 105	Ryne Sandberg AS	300.00	135.00	38.00
☐ 106	Fred McGriff AS	150.00	70.00	19.00
☐ 107	Nolan Ryan AS	1250.00	550.00	160.00
☐ 108	Will Clark AS	150.00	70.00	19.00
☐ 110	Ken Griffey Jr. AS	1250.00	550.00	160.00
☐ 112	Kirby Puckett AS	300.00	135.00	38.00
☐ 114	Barry Larkin AS	150.00	70.00	19.00
☐ 116	Juan Gonzalez AS	700.00	325.00	90.00
☐ 122	Eddie Murray UER	275.00	125.00	34.00
	122 career strikeouts should be 1224			
☐ 124	Jay Buhner	150.00	70.00	19.00
☐ 134	Kevin Brown*	150.00	70.00	19.00
☐ 141	Deion Sanders	175.00	80.00	22.00
☐ 154	Randy Johnson	300.00	135.00	38.00
☐ 156	J.T. Snow	150.00	70.00	19.00
☐ 157	Mike Mussina	150.00	70.00	19.00
☐ 162	Dave Winfield	125.00	55.00	15.50
☐ 163	Tim Salmon	250.00	110.00	31.00
☐ 165	Mo Vaughn	225.00	100.00	28.00
☐ 173	Junior Felix*	250.00	110.00	31.00
☐ 189	Moises Alou*	150.00	70.00	19.00
☐ 190	Edgar Martinez	125.00	55.00	15.50
☐ 192	Robin Yount	175.00	80.00	22.00
☐ 193	Bob Tewksbury*	150.00	70.00	19.00
☐ 199	Mike Piazza	550.00	250.00	70.00

1994 Finest

The 1994 Topps Finest baseball set consists of two series of 220 cards each, for a total of 440 cards. Each series includes 40 special design Finest cards: 20 top 1993 rookies (1-20), 20 top 1994 rookies (421-440) and 40 top veterans (201-240). These glossy and metallic cards have a color photo on front with green and gold borders. A color photo on back is accompanied by statistics and a "Finest Moment" note. Rookie Cards include Brian Anderson and Chan Ho Park.

	MINT	NRMT	EXC
COMPLETE SET (440)	200.00	90.00	25.00
COMPLETE SERIES 1 (220)	100.00	45.00	12.50
COMPLETE SERIES 2 (220)	100.00	45.00	12.50
COMMON CARD (1-220)	.50	.23	.06
COMMON CARD (221-440)	.50	.23	.06
SOME SER.2 PACKS HAVE 1 OR 2 SER.1 CARDS			

		MINT	NRMT	EXC
☐ 1	Mike Piazza	5.00	2.20	.60
☐ 2	Kevin Stocker	.50	.23	.06
☐ 3	Greg McMichael	.50	.23	.06
☐ 4	Jeff Conine	1.00	.45	.12
☐ 5	Rene Arocha	.50	.23	.06
☐ 6	Aaron Sele	.75	.35	.09
☐ 7	Brent Gates	.50	.23	.06
☐ 8	Chuck Carr	.50	.23	.06
☐ 9	Kirk Rueter	.50	.23	.06
☐ 10	Mike Lansing	.75	.35	.09
☐ 11	Al Martin	.75	.35	.09
☐ 12	Jason Bere	.75	.35	.09
☐ 13	Troy Neel	.50	.23	.06
☐ 14	Armando Reynoso	.50	.23	.06
☐ 15	Jeromy Burnitz	.50	.23	.06
☐ 16	Rich Amaral	.50	.23	.06
☐ 17	David McCarty	.50	.23	.06
☐ 18	Tim Salmon	2.50	1.10	.30
☐ 19	Steve Cooke	.50	.23	.06
☐ 20	Wil Cordero	.75	.35	.09
☐ 21	Kevin Tapani	.50	.23	.06
☐ 22	Deion Sanders	2.50	1.10	.30
☐ 23	Jose Offerman	.50	.23	.06
☐ 24	Mark Langston	.75	.35	.09
☐ 25	Ken Hill	.75	.35	.09
☐ 26	Alex Fernandez	.75	.35	.09
☐ 27	Jeff Blauser	.50	.23	.06
☐ 28	Royce Clayton	.50	.23	.06
☐ 29	Brad Ausmus	.50	.23	.06
☐ 30	Ryan Bowen	.50	.23	.06
☐ 31	Steve Finley	.50	.23	.06

☐ 32	Charlie Hayes	.50	.23	.06
☐ 33	Jeff Kent	.75	.35	.09
☐ 34	Mike Henneman	.50	.23	.06
☐ 35	Andres Galarraga	1.00	.45	.12
☐ 36	Wayne Kirby	.50	.23	.06
☐ 37	Joe Oliver	.50	.23	.06
☐ 38	Terry Steinbach	.75	.35	.09
☐ 39	Ryan Thompson	.75	.35	.09
☐ 40	Luis Alicea	.50	.23	.06
☐ 41	Randy Velarde	.50	.23	.06
☐ 42	Bob Tewksbury	.50	.23	.06
☐ 43	Reggie Sanders	1.00	.45	.12
☐ 44	Brian Williams	.50	.23	.06
☐ 45	Joe Orsulak	.50	.23	.06
☐ 46	Jose Lind	.50	.23	.06
☐ 47	Dave Hollins	.50	.23	.06
☐ 48	Graeme Lloyd	.50	.23	.06
☐ 49	Jim Gott	.50	.23	.06
☐ 50	Andre Dawson	1.00	.45	.12
☐ 51	Steve Buechele	.50	.23	.06
☐ 52	David Cone	1.00	.45	.12
☐ 53	Ricky Gutierrez	.50	.23	.06
☐ 54	Lance Johnson	.50	.23	.06
☐ 55	Tino Martinez	1.00	.45	.12
☐ 56	Phil Hiatt	.50	.23	.06
☐ 57	Carlos Garcia	.75	.35	.09
☐ 58	Danny Darwin	.50	.23	.06
☐ 59	Dante Bichette	1.50	.70	.19
☐ 60	Scott Kamienicki	.50	.23	.06
☐ 61	Orlando Merced	.75	.35	.09
☐ 62	Brian McRae	.75	.35	.09
☐ 63	Pat Kelly	.50	.23	.06
☐ 64	Tom Henke	.75	.35	.09
☐ 65	Jeff King	.50	.23	.06
☐ 66	Mike Mussina	1.50	.70	.19
☐ 67	Tim Pugh	.50	.23	.06
☐ 68	Robby Thompson	.50	.23	.06
☐ 69	Paul O'Neill	.75	.35	.09
☐ 70	Hal Morris	.75	.35	.09
☐ 71	Ron Karkovice	.50	.23	.06
☐ 72	Joe Girardi	.50	.23	.06
☐ 73	Eduardo Perez	.50	.23	.06
☐ 74	Raul Mondesi	4.00	1.80	.50
☐ 75	Mike Gallego	.50	.23	.06
☐ 76	Mike Stanley	.50	.23	.06
☐ 77	Kevin Roberson	.50	.23	.06
☐ 78	Mark McGwire	1.00	.45	.12
☐ 79	Pat Listach	.50	.23	.06
☐ 80	Eric Davis	.50	.23	.06
☐ 81	Mike Bordick	.50	.23	.06
☐ 82	Doc Gooden	.75	.35	.09
☐ 83	Mike Moore	.50	.23	.06
☐ 84	Phil Plantier	.50	.23	.06
☐ 85	Darren Lewis	.50	.23	.06
☐ 86	Rick Wilkins	.50	.23	.06
☐ 87	Darryl Strawberry	.75	.35	.09
☐ 88	Rob Dibble	.50	.23	.06
☐ 89	Greg Vaughn	.50	.23	.06
☐ 90	Jeff Russell	.50	.23	.06
☐ 91	Mark Lewis	.50	.23	.06
☐ 92	Gregg Jefferies	1.00	.45	.12
☐ 93	Jose Guzman	.50	.23	.06
☐ 94	Kenny Rogers	.50	.23	.06
☐ 95	Mark Lemke	.50	.23	.06
☐ 96	Mike Morgan	.50	.23	.06
☐ 97	Andujar Cedeno	.50	.23	.06
☐ 98	Orel Hershiser	.75	.35	.09
☐ 99	Greg Swindell	.50	.23	.06
☐ 100	John Smoltz	.75	.35	.09
☐ 101	Pedro Martinez	.75	.35	.09
☐ 102	Jim Thome	2.50	1.10	.30
☐ 103	David Segui	.50	.23	.06
☐ 104	Charles Nagy	.75	.35	.09
☐ 105	Shane Mack	.50	.23	.06
☐ 106	John Jaha	.50	.23	.06
☐ 107	Tom Candiotti	.50	.23	.06
☐ 108	David Wells	.50	.23	.06
☐ 109	Bobby Jones	.75	.35	.09
☐ 110	Bob Hamelin	.50	.23	.06
☐ 111	Bernard Gilkey	.75	.35	.09
☐ 112	Chili Davis	.75	.35	.09
☐ 113	Todd Stottlemyre	.50	.23	.06
☐ 114	Derek Bell	.75	.35	.09
☐ 115	Mark McLemore	.50	.23	.06
☐ 116	Mark Whiten	.50	.23	.06
☐ 117	Mike Devereaux	.50	.23	.06
☐ 118	Terry Pendleton	.50	.23	.06
☐ 119	Pat Meares	.50	.23	.06
☐ 120	Pete Harnisch	.50	.23	.06
☐ 121	Moises Alou	.75	.35	.09
☐ 122	Jay Buhner	1.00	.45	.12
☐ 123	Wes Chamberlain	.50	.23	.06
☐ 124	Mike Perez	.50	.23	.06
☐ 125	Devon White	.50	.23	.06
☐ 126	Ivan Rodriguez	1.00	.45	.12
☐ 127	Don Slaught	.50	.23	.06
☐ 128	John Valentin	1.00	.45	.12
☐ 129	Jaime Navarro	.50	.23	.06
☐ 130	Dave Magadan	.50	.23	.06
☐ 131	Brady Anderson	.75	.35	.09
☐ 132	Juan Guzman	.50	.23	.06
☐ 133	John Wetteland	.75	.35	.09
☐ 134	Dave Stewart	.50	.23	.06
☐ 135	Scott Servais	.50	.23	.06
☐ 136	Ozzie Smith	2.50	1.10	.30
☐ 137	Darrin Fletcher	.50	.23	.06
☐ 138	Jose Mesa	.75	.35	.09
☐ 139	Wilson Alvarez	.75	.35	.09
☐ 140	Pete Incaviglia	.50	.23	.06
☐ 141	Chris Hoiles	.75	.35	.09
☐ 142	Darryl Hamilton	.50	.23	.06
☐ 143	Chuck Finley	.50	.23	.06
☐ 144	Archi Cianfrocco	.50	.23	.06
☐ 145	Bill Wegman	.50	.23	.06
☐ 146	Joey Cora	.50	.23	.06
☐ 147	Darrell Whitmore	.50	.23	.06
☐ 148	David Hulse	.50	.23	.06
☐ 149	Jim Abbott	.75	.35	.09
☐ 150	Curt Schilling	.50	.23	.06
☐ 151	Bill Swift	.50	.23	.06
☐ 152	Tommy Greene	.50	.23	.06
☐ 153	Roberto Mejia	.50	.23	.06
☐ 154	Edgar Martinez	1.00	.45	.12
☐ 155	Roger Pavlik	.50	.23	.06
☐ 156	Randy Tomlin	.50	.23	.06
☐ 157	J.T. Snow	.75	.35	.09
☐ 158	Bob Welch	.50	.23	.06
☐ 159	Alan Trammell	.75	.35	.09
☐ 160	Ed Sprague	.50	.23	.06
☐ 161	Ben McDonald	.75	.35	.09
☐ 162	Derrick May	.50	.23	.06
☐ 163	Roberto Kelly	.50	.23	.06
☐ 164	Bryan Harvey	.50	.23	.06
☐ 165	Ron Gant	.75	.35	.09
☐ 166	Scott Erickson	.75	.35	.09
☐ 167	Anthony Young	.50	.23	.06
☐ 168	Scott Cooper	.50	.23	.06
☐ 169	Rod Beck	.75	.35	.09
☐ 170	John Franco	.75	.35	.09
☐ 171	Gary DiSarcina	.50	.23	.06
☐ 172	Dave Fleming	.50	.23	.06
☐ 173	Wade Boggs	1.00	.45	.12

□	#	Name			
□	174	Kevin Appier	.75	.35	.09
□	175	Jose Bautista	.50	.23	.06
□	176	Wally Joyner	.50	.23	.06
□	177	Dean Palmer	.50	.23	.06
□	178	Tony Phillips	.50	.23	.06
□	179	John Smiley	.50	.23	.06
□	180	Charlie Hough	.50	.23	.06
□	181	Scott Fletcher	.50	.23	.06
□	182	Todd Van Poppel	.50	.23	.06
□	183	Mike Blowers	.75	.35	.09
□	184	Willie McGee	.50	.23	.06
□	185	Paul Sorrento	.50	.23	.06
□	186	Eric Young	.75	.35	.09
□	187	Bret Barberie	.50	.23	.06
□	188	Manuel Lee	.50	.23	.06
□	189	Jeff Branson	.50	.23	.06
□	190	Jim Deshaies	.50	.23	.06
□	191	Ken Caminiti	.75	.35	.09
□	192	Tim Raines	1.00	.45	.12
□	193	Joe Grahe	.50	.23	.06
□	194	Hipolito Pichardo	.50	.23	.06
□	195	Denny Neagle	.75	.35	.09
□	196	Jeff Gardner	.50	.23	.06
□	197	Mike Benjamin	.50	.23	.06
□	198	Milt Thompson	.50	.23	.06
□	199	Bruce Ruffin	.50	.23	.06
□	200	Chris Hammond UER	.50	.23	.06
		(Back of card has Mariners; should be Marlins)			
□	201	Tony Gwynn	4.00	1.80	.50
□	202	Robin Ventura	.75	.35	.09
□	203	Frank Thomas	12.00	5.50	1.50
□	204	Kirby Puckett	4.00	1.80	.50
□	205	Roberto Alomar	2.50	1.10	.30
□	206	Dennis Eckersley	1.00	.45	.12
□	207	Joe Carter	1.00	.45	.12
□	208	Albert Belle	5.00	2.20	.60
□	209	Greg Maddux	12.00	5.50	1.50
□	210	Ryne Sandberg	3.00	1.35	.35
□	211	Juan Gonzalez	2.50	1.10	.30
□	212	Jeff Bagwell	4.00	1.80	.50
□	213	Randy Johnson	2.50	1.10	.30
□	214	Matt Williams	2.00	.90	.25
□	215	Dave Winfield	1.00	.45	.12
□	216	Larry Walker	1.50	.70	.19
□	217	Roger Clemens	2.00	.90	.25
□	218	Kenny Lofton	4.00	1.80	.50
□	219	Cecil Fielder	1.00	.45	.12
□	220	Darren Daulton	.75	.35	.09
□	221	John Olerud	.75	.35	.09
□	222	Jose Canseco	2.00	.90	.25
□	223	Rickey Henderson	1.00	.45	.12
□	224	Fred McGriff	1.50	.70	.19
□	225	Gary Sheffield	1.00	.45	.12
□	226	Jack McDowell	.75	.35	.09
□	227	Rafael Palmeiro	1.00	.45	.12
□	228	Travis Fryman	1.00	.45	.12
□	229	Marquis Grissom	1.00	.45	.12
□	230	Barry Bonds	3.00	1.35	.35
□	231	Carlos Baerga	2.50	1.10	.30
□	232	Ken Griffey Jr.	12.00	5.50	1.50
□	233	David Justice	1.50	.70	.19
□	234	Bobby Bonilla	1.00	.45	.12
□	235	Cal Ripken	12.00	5.50	1.50
□	236	Sammy Sosa	1.00	.45	.12
□	237	Len Dykstra	.75	.35	.09
□	238	Will Clark	1.50	.70	.19
□	239	Paul Molitor	1.00	.45	.12
□	240	Barry Larkin	1.50	.70	.19
□	241	Bo Jackson	1.00	.45	.12
□	242	Mitch Williams	.50	.23	.06
□	243	Ron Darling	.50	.23	.06
□	244	Darryl Kile	.50	.23	.06
□	245	Geronimo Berroa	.50	.23	.06
□	246	Gregg Olson	.50	.23	.06
□	247	Brian Harper	.50	.23	.06
□	248	Rheal Cormier	.50	.23	.06
□	249	Rey Sanchez	.50	.23	.06
□	250	Jeff Fassero	.50	.23	.06
□	251	Sandy Alomar	.50	.23	.06
□	252	Chris Bosio	.50	.23	.06
□	253	Andy Stankiewicz	.50	.23	.06
□	254	Harold Baines	.75	.35	.09
□	255	Andy Ashby	.50	.23	.06
□	256	Tyler Green	.50	.23	.06
□	257	Kevin Brown	.50	.23	.06
□	258	Mo Vaughn	2.00	.90	.25
□	259	Mike Harkey	.50	.23	.06
□	260	Dave Henderson	.50	.23	.06
□	261	Kent Hrbek	.50	.23	.06
□	262	Darrin Jackson	.50	.23	.06
□	263	Bob Wickman	.50	.23	.06
□	264	Spike Owen	.50	.23	.06
□	265	Todd Jones	.50	.23	.06
□	266	Pat Borders	.50	.23	.06
□	267	Tom Glavine	1.00	.45	.12
□	268	Dave Nilsson	.50	.23	.06
□	269	Rich Batchelor	.50	.23	.06
□	270	Delino DeShields	.50	.23	.06
□	271	Felix Fermin	.50	.23	.06
□	272	Orestes Destrade	.50	.23	.06
□	273	Mickey Morandini	.50	.23	.06
□	274	Otis Nixon	.50	.23	.06
□	275	Ellis Burks	.50	.23	.06
□	276	Greg Gagne	.50	.23	.06
□	277	John Doherty	.50	.23	.06
□	278	Julio Franco	.75	.35	.09
□	279	Bernie Williams	.75	.35	.09
□	280	Rick Aguilera	.75	.35	.09
□	281	Mickey Tettleton	.75	.35	.09
□	282	David Nied	.75	.35	.09
□	283	Johnny Ruffin	.50	.23	.06
□	284	Dan Wilson	.75	.35	.09
□	285	Omar Vizquel	.75	.35	.09
□	286	Willie Banks	.50	.23	.06
□	287	Erik Pappas	.50	.23	.06
□	288	Cal Eldred	.50	.23	.06
□	289	Bobby Witt	.50	.23	.06
□	290	Luis Gonzalez	.75	.35	.09
□	291	Greg Pirkl	.50	.23	.06
□	292	Alex Cole	.50	.23	.06
□	293	Ricky Bones	.50	.23	.06
□	294	Denis Boucher	.50	.23	.06
□	295	John Burkett	.50	.23	.06
□	296	Steve Trachsel	.75	.35	.09
□	297	Ricky Jordan	.50	.23	.06
□	298	Mark Dewey	.50	.23	.06
□	299	Jimmy Key	.50	.23	.06
□	300	Mike Macfarlane	.50	.23	.06
□	301	Tim Belcher	.50	.23	.06
□	302	Carlos Reyes	.50	.23	.06
□	303	Greg A. Harris	.50	.23	.06
□	304	Brian Anderson	.75	.35	.09
□	305	Terry Mulholland	.50	.23	.06
□	306	Felix Jose	.50	.23	.06
□	307	Darren Holmes	.75	.35	.09
□	308	Jose Rijo	.50	.23	.06
□	309	Paul Wagner	.50	.23	.06
□	310	Bob Scanlan	.50	.23	.06
□	311	Mike Jackson	.50	.23	.06
□	312	Jose Vizcaino	.50	.23	.06
□	313	Rob Butler	.50	.23	.06

☐ 314 Kevin Seitzer	.50	.23	.06
☐ 315 Geronimo Pena	.50	.23	.06
☐ 316 Hector Carrasco	.50	.23	.06
☐ 317 Eddie Murray	1.50	.70	.19
☐ 318 Roger Salkeld	.50	.23	.06
☐ 319 Todd Hundley	.75	.35	.09
☐ 320 Danny Jackson	.50	.23	.06
☐ 321 Kevin Young	.50	.23	.06
☐ 322 Mike Greenwell	.50	.23	.06
☐ 323 Kevin Mitchell	.50	.23	.06
☐ 324 Chuck Knoblauch	1.00	.45	.12
☐ 325 Danny Tartabull	.75	.35	.09
☐ 326 Vince Coleman	.50	.23	.06
☐ 327 Marvin Freeman	.50	.23	.06
☐ 328 Andy Benes	.50	.23	.06
☐ 329 Mike Kelly	.50	.23	.06
☐ 330 Karl Rhodes	.50	.23	.06
☐ 331 Allen Watson	.50	.23	.06
☐ 332 Damion Easley	.50	.23	.06
☐ 333 Reggie Jefferson	.50	.23	.06
☐ 334 Kevin McReynolds	.50	.23	.06
☐ 335 Arthur Rhodes	.50	.23	.06
☐ 336 Brian Hunter	.50	.23	.06
☐ 337 Tom Browning	.50	.23	.06
☐ 338 Pedro Munoz	.75	.35	.09
☐ 339 Billy Ripken	.50	.23	.06
☐ 340 Gene Harris	.50	.23	.06
☐ 341 Fernando Vina	.50	.23	.06
☐ 342 Sean Berry	.50	.23	.06
☐ 343 Pedro Astacio	.50	.23	.06
☐ 344 B.J. Surhoff	.75	.35	.09
☐ 345 Doug Drabek	.50	.23	.06
☐ 346 Jody Reed	.50	.23	.06
☐ 347 Ray Lankford	.75	.35	.09
☐ 348 Steve Farr	.50	.23	.06
☐ 349 Eric Anthony	.50	.23	.06
☐ 350 Pete Smith	.50	.23	.06
☐ 351 Lee Smith	1.00	.45	.12
☐ 352 Mariano Duncan	.50	.23	.06
☐ 353 Doug Strange	.50	.23	.06
☐ 354 Tim Bogar	.50	.23	.06
☐ 355 Dave Weathers	.50	.23	.06
☐ 356 Eric Karros	1.00	.45	.12
☐ 357 Randy Myers	.75	.35	.09
☐ 358 Chad Curtis	.75	.35	.09
☐ 359 Steve Avery	.75	.35	.09
☐ 360 Brian Jordan	.75	.35	.09
☐ 361 Tim Wallach	.50	.23	.06
☐ 362 Pedro Martinez	.75	.35	.09
☐ 363 Bip Roberts	.50	.23	.06
☐ 364 Lou Whitaker	.75	.35	.09
☐ 365 Luis Polonia	.50	.23	.06
☐ 366 Benny Santiago	.50	.23	.06
☐ 367 Brett Butler	.75	.35	.09
☐ 368 Shawon Dunston	.50	.23	.06
☐ 369 Kelly Stinnett	.50	.23	.06
☐ 370 Chris Turner	.50	.23	.06
☐ 371 Ruben Sierra	.75	.35	.09
☐ 372 Greg A. Harris	.50	.23	.06
☐ 373 Xavier Hernandez	.50	.23	.06
☐ 374 Howard Johnson	.50	.23	.06
☐ 375 Duane Ward	.50	.23	.06
☐ 376 Roberto Hernandez	.50	.23	.06
☐ 377 Scott Leius	.50	.23	.06
☐ 378 Dave Valle	.50	.23	.06
☐ 379 Sid Fernandez	.50	.23	.06
☐ 380 Doug Jones	.50	.23	.06
☐ 381 Zane Smith	.50	.23	.06
☐ 382 Craig Biggio	1.00	.45	.12
☐ 383 Rick White	.50	.23	.06
☐ 384 Tom Pagnozzi	.50	.23	.06

☐ 385 Chris James	.50	.23	.06
☐ 386 Bret Boone	.75	.35	.09
☐ 387 Jeff Montgomery	.75	.35	.09
☐ 388 Chad Kreuter	.50	.23	.06
☐ 389 Greg Hibbard	.50	.23	.06
☐ 390 Mark Grace	1.00	.45	.12
☐ 391 Phil Leftwich	.50	.23	.06
☐ 392 Don Mattingly	6.00	2.70	.75
☐ 393 Ozzie Guillen	.50	.23	.06
☐ 394 Gary Gaetti	.50	.23	.06
☐ 395 Erik Hanson	.50	.23	.06
☐ 396 Scott Brosius	.50	.23	.06
☐ 397 Tom Gordon	.50	.23	.06
☐ 398 Bill Gullickson	.50	.23	.06
☐ 399 Matt Mieske	.50	.23	.06
☐ 400 Pat Hentgen	.75	.35	.09
☐ 401 Walt Weiss	.50	.23	.06
☐ 402 Greg Blosser	.50	.23	.06
☐ 403 Stan Javier	.50	.23	.06
☐ 404 Doug Henry	.50	.23	.06
☐ 405 Ramon Martinez	.75	.35	.09
☐ 406 Frank Viola	.50	.23	.06
☐ 407 Mike Hampton	.50	.23	.06
☐ 408 Andy Van Slyke	.75	.35	.09
☐ 409 Bobby Ayala	.50	.23	.06
☐ 410 Todd Zeile	.75	.35	.09
☐ 411 Jay Bell	.75	.35	.09
☐ 412 Denny Martinez	.75	.35	.09
☐ 413 Mark Portugal	.50	.23	.06
☐ 414 Bobby Munoz	.50	.23	.06
☐ 415 Kirt Manwaring	.50	.23	.06
☐ 416 John Kruk	.75	.35	.09
☐ 417 Trevor Hoffman	.75	.35	.09
☐ 418 Chris Sabo	.50	.23	.06
☐ 419 Bret Saberhagen	.75	.35	.09
☐ 420 Chris Nabholz	.50	.23	.06
☐ 421 James Mouton	.75	.35	.09
☐ 422 Tony Tarasco	.75	.35	.09
☐ 423 Carlos Delgado	.75	.35	.09
☐ 424 Rondell White	1.50	.70	.19
☐ 425 Javier Lopez	2.00	.90	.25
☐ 426 Chan Ho Park	1.25	.55	.16
☐ 427 Cliff Floyd	.75	.35	.09
☐ 428 Dave Staton	.50	.23	.06
☐ 429 J.R. Phillips	.75	.35	.09
☐ 430 Manny Ramirez	6.00	2.70	.75
☐ 431 Kurt Abbott	1.00	.45	.12
☐ 432 Melvin Nieves	.75	.35	.09
☐ 433 Alex Gonzalez	.75	.35	.09
☐ 434 Rick Helling	.50	.23	.06
☐ 435 Danny Bautista	.50	.23	.06
☐ 436 Matt Walbeck	.50	.23	.06
☐ 437 Ryan Klesko	3.00	1.35	.35
☐ 438 Steve Karsay	.50	.23	.06
☐ 439 Salomon Torres	.50	.23	.06
☐ 440 Scott Ruffcorn	.75	.35	.09

1994 Finest Refractors

The 1994 Topps Finest Refractors baseball set consists of two series of 220 cards each, for a total of 440 cards. These special cards were inserted at a rate of one in every nine packs. They are identical to the basic Finest card except for a more intense luster and 3-D appearance.

	MINT	NRMT	EXC
COMPLETE SET (440)	2800.00	1250.00	350.00
COMPLETE SERIES 1 (220)	1400.00	650.00	180.00
COMPLETE SERIES 2 (220)	1400.00	650.00	180.00
COMMON CARD (1-220)	3.00	1.35	.35
COMMON CARD (221-440)	3.00	1.35	.35
SEMISTARS	6.00	2.70	.75
STARS	10.00	4.50	1.25

*VETERAN STARS: 5X to 10X BASIC CARDS
*YOUNG STARS: 3X to 6X BASIC CARDS
*RCs: 2X to 4X BASIC CARDS

☐ 1 Mike Piazza FIN	50.00	22.00	6.25
☐ 74 Raul Mondesi FIN	40.00	18.00	5.00
☐ 201 Tony Gwynn FIN	40.00	18.00	5.00
☐ 203 Frank Thomas FIN	125.00	55.00	15.50
☐ 204 Kirby Puckett FIN	40.00	18.00	5.00
☐ 208 Albert Belle FIN	50.00	22.00	6.25
☐ 209 Greg Maddux FIN	125.00	55.00	15.50
☐ 212 Jeff Bagwell FIN	40.00	18.00	5.00
☐ 218 Kenny Lofton FIN	40.00	18.00	5.00
☐ 232 Ken Griffey Jr. FIN	125.00	55.00	15.50
☐ 235 Cal Ripken FIN	160.00	70.00	20.00
☐ 392 Don Mattingly FIN	60.00	27.00	7.50
☐ 430 Manny Ramirez FIN	60.00	27.00	7.50

1995 Finest

Consisting of 330 cards, this set was issued in series of 220 and 110. A protective film, designed to keep the card from scratching and to maintain original gloss, covers the front. With the Finest logo at the top, a silver baseball diamond design surrounded by green (field) form the background to an action photo. Horizontally designed backs have a photo to the right with statistical information to the left. A Finest Moment, or career highlight, is also included. Rookie Cards in this set include Hideo Nomo and Carlos Perez.

	MINT	NRMT	EXC
COMPLETE SET (330)	120.00	55.00	15.00
COMPLETE SERIES 1 (220)	80.00	36.00	10.00
COMPLETE SERIES 2 (110)	40.00	18.00	5.00
COMMON CARD (1-220)	.40	.18	.05
COMMON CARD (221-330)	.40	.18	.05

☐ 1 Raul Mondesi RT	2.50	1.10	.30
☐ 2 Kurt Abbott	.40	.18	.05
☐ 3 Chris Gomez	.40	.18	.05
☐ 4 Manny Ramirez RT	4.00	1.80	.50
☐ 5 Rondell White	.75	.35	.09
☐ 6 William VanLandingham	.40	.18	.05
☐ 7 Jon Lieber	.40	.18	.05
☐ 8 Ryan Klesko	2.00	.90	.25
☐ 9 John Hudek	.40	.18	.05
☐ 10 Joey Hamilton	.40	.18	.05
☐ 11 Bob Hamelin	.40	.18	.05
☐ 12 Brian Anderson	.40	.18	.05
☐ 13 Mike Lieberthal	.40	.18	.05
☐ 14 Rico Brogna	.75	.35	.09
☐ 15 Rusty Greer	.40	.18	.05
☐ 16 Carlos Delgado	.50	.23	.06
☐ 17 Jim Edmonds	1.25	.55	.16
☐ 18 Steve Trachsel	.40	.18	.05
☐ 19 Matt Walbeck	.40	.18	.05
☐ 20 Armando Benitez	.40	.18	.05
☐ 21 Steve Karsay	.40	.18	.05
☐ 22 Jose Oliva	.40	.18	.05
☐ 23 Cliff Floyd	.75	.35	.09
☐ 24 Kevin Foster	.40	.18	.05
☐ 25 Javier Lopez	1.25	.55	.16
☐ 26 Jose Valentin	.40	.18	.05
☐ 27 James Mouton	.40	.18	.05
☐ 28 Hector Carrasco	.40	.18	.05
☐ 29 Orlando Miller	.40	.18	.05
☐ 30 Garret Anderson	2.00	.90	.25
☐ 31 Marvin Freeman	.40	.18	.05
☐ 32 Brett Butler	.50	.23	.06
☐ 33 Roberto Kelly	.50	.23	.06
☐ 34 Rod Beck	.50	.23	.06
☐ 35 Jose Rijo	.50	.23	.06
☐ 36 Edgar Martinez	.75	.35	.09
☐ 37 Jim Thome	1.50	.70	.19
☐ 38 Rick Wilkins	.40	.18	.05
☐ 39 Wally Joyner	.50	.23	.06
☐ 40 Wil Cordero	.50	.23	.06
☐ 41 Tommy Greene	.40	.18	.05
☐ 42 Travis Fryman	.75	.35	.09
☐ 43 Don Slaught	.40	.18	.05
☐ 44 Brady Anderson	.50	.23	.06
☐ 45 Matt Williams	1.50	.70	.19
☐ 46 Rene Arocha	.40	.18	.05
☐ 47 Rickey Henderson	.75	.35	.09
☐ 48 Mike Mussina	1.25	.55	.16
☐ 49 Greg McMichael	.40	.18	.05
☐ 50 Jody Reed	.40	.18	.05
☐ 51 Tino Martinez	.75	.35	.09
☐ 52 Dave Clark	.40	.18	.05
☐ 53 John Valentin	.75	.35	.09
☐ 54 Bret Boone	.75	.35	.09
☐ 55 Walt Weiss	.50	.23	.06
☐ 56 Kenny Lofton	3.00	1.35	.35
☐ 57 Scott Leius	.40	.18	.05
☐ 58 Eric Karros	.75	.35	.09
☐ 59 John Olerud	.50	.23	.06
☐ 60 Chris Hoiles	.50	.23	.06
☐ 61 Sandy Alomar Jr.	.50	.23	.06
☐ 62 Tim Wallach	.40	.18	.05
☐ 63 Cal Eldred	.40	.18	.05
☐ 64 Tom Glavine	.75	.35	.09
☐ 65 Mark Grace	.75	.35	.09
☐ 66 Rey Sanchez	.40	.18	.05
☐ 67 Bobby Ayala	.40	.18	.05
☐ 68 Dante Bichette	1.25	.55	.16
☐ 69 Andres Galarraga	.75	.35	.09
☐ 70 Chuck Carr	.40	.18	.05
☐ 71 Bobby Witt	.40	.18	.05
☐ 72 Steve Avery	.50	.23	.06
☐ 73 Bobby Jones	.40	.18	.05
☐ 74 Delino DeShields	.50	.23	.06
☐ 75 Kevin Tapani	.40	.18	.05

☐ 76	Randy Johnson	2.00	.90	.25
☐ 77	David Nied	.40	.18	.05
☐ 78	Pat Hentgen	.50	.23	.06
☐ 79	Tim Salmon	1.50	.70	.19
☐ 80	Todd Zeile	.50	.23	.06
☐ 81	John Wetteland	.50	.23	.06
☐ 82	Albert Belle	4.00	1.80	.50
☐ 83	Ben McDonald	.40	.18	.05
☐ 84	Bobby Munoz	.40	.18	.05
☐ 85	Bip Roberts	.40	.18	.05
☐ 86	Mo Vaughn	1.50	.70	.19
☐ 87	Chuck Finley	.50	.23	.06
☐ 88	Chuck Knoblauch	.75	.35	.09
☐ 89	Frank Thomas	10.00	4.50	1.25
☐ 90	Danny Tartabull	.50	.23	.06
☐ 91	Dean Palmer	.50	.23	.06
☐ 92	Len Dykstra	.50	.23	.06
☐ 93	J.R. Phillips	.40	.18	.05
☐ 94	Tom Candiotti	.40	.18	.05
☐ 95	Marquis Grissom	.75	.35	.09
☐ 96	Barry Larkin	1.25	.55	.16
☐ 97	Bryan Harvey	.40	.18	.05
☐ 98	David Justice	1.25	.55	.16
☐ 99	David Cone	.75	.35	.09
☐ 100	Wade Boggs	.75	.35	.09
☐ 101	Jason Bere	.40	.18	.05
☐ 102	Hal Morris	.50	.23	.06
☐ 103	Fred McGriff	1.25	.55	.16
☐ 104	Bobby Bonilla	.75	.35	.09
☐ 105	Jay Buhner	.75	.35	.09
☐ 106	Allen Watson	.50	.23	.06
☐ 107	Mickey Tettleton	.40	.18	.05
☐ 108	Kevin Appier	.50	.23	.06
☐ 109	Ivan Rodriguez	.75	.35	.09
☐ 110	Carlos Garcia	.50	.23	.06
☐ 111	Andy Benes	.50	.23	.06
☐ 112	Eddie Murray	1.25	.55	.16
☐ 113	Mike Piazza	4.00	1.80	.50
☐ 114	Greg Vaughn	.40	.18	.05
☐ 115	Paul Molitor	.75	.35	.09
☐ 116	Terry Steinbach	.50	.23	.06
☐ 117	Jeff Bagwell	3.00	1.35	.35
☐ 118	Ken Griffey Jr.	10.00	4.50	1.25
☐ 119	Gary Sheffield	.75	.35	.09
☐ 120	Cal Ripken	10.00	4.50	1.25
☐ 121	Jeff Kent	.40	.18	.05
☐ 122	Jay Bell	.40	.18	.05
☐ 123	Will Clark	1.25	.55	.16
☐ 124	Cecil Fielder	.75	.35	.09
☐ 125	Alex Fernandez	.40	.18	.05
☐ 126	Don Mattingly	5.00	2.20	.60
☐ 127	Reggie Sanders	.75	.35	.09
☐ 128	Moises Alou	.50	.23	.06
☐ 129	Craig Biggio	.75	.35	.09
☐ 130	Eddie Williams	.40	.18	.05
☐ 131	John Franco	.50	.23	.06
☐ 132	John Kruk	.40	.18	.05
☐ 133	Jeff King	.40	.18	.05
☐ 134	Royce Clayton	.40	.18	.05
☐ 135	Doug Drabek	.50	.23	.06
☐ 136	Ray Lankford	.75	.35	.09
☐ 137	Roberto Alomar	2.00	.90	.25
☐ 138	Todd Hundley	.50	.23	.06
☐ 139	Alex Cole	.40	.18	.05
☐ 140	Shawon Dunston	.40	.18	.05
☐ 141	John Roper	.40	.18	.05
☐ 142	Mark Langston	.50	.23	.06
☐ 143	Tom Pagnozzi	.40	.18	.05
☐ 144	Wilson Alvarez	.50	.23	.06
☐ 145	Scott Cooper	.40	.18	.05
☐ 146	Kevin Mitchell	.50	.23	.06
☐ 147	Mark Whiten	.50	.23	.06
☐ 148	Jeff Conine	.75	.35	.09
☐ 149	Chili Davis	.50	.23	.06
☐ 150	Luis Gonzalez	.50	.23	.06
☐ 151	Juan Guzman	.50	.23	.06
☐ 152	Mike Greenwell	.50	.23	.06
☐ 153	Mike Henneman	.40	.18	.05
☐ 154	Rick Aguilera	.50	.23	.06
☐ 155	Dennis Eckersley	.75	.35	.09
☐ 156	Darrin Fletcher	.40	.18	.05
☐ 157	Darren Lewis	.40	.18	.05
☐ 158	Juan Gonzalez	2.50	1.10	.30
☐ 159	Dave Hollins	.40	.18	.05
☐ 160	Jimmy Key	.50	.23	.06
☐ 161	Roberto Hernandez	.50	.23	.06
☐ 162	Randy Myers	.50	.23	.06
☐ 163	Joe Carter	.75	.35	.09
☐ 164	Darren Daulton	.50	.23	.06
☐ 165	Mike Macfarlane	.40	.18	.05
☐ 166	Bret Saberhagen	.50	.23	.06
☐ 167	Kirby Puckett	3.00	1.35	.35
☐ 168	Lance Johnson	.40	.18	.05
☐ 169	Mark McGwire	.75	.35	.09
☐ 170	Jose Canseco	1.50	.70	.19
☐ 171	Mike Stanley	.40	.18	.05
☐ 172	Lee Smith	.75	.35	.09
☐ 173	Robin Ventura	.75	.35	.09
☐ 174	Greg Gagne	.40	.18	.05
☐ 175	Brian McRae	.40	.18	.05
☐ 176	Mike Bordick	.40	.18	.05
☐ 177	Rafael Palmeiro	.75	.35	.09
☐ 178	Kenny Rogers	.40	.18	.05
☐ 179	Chad Curtis	.50	.23	.06
☐ 180	Devon White	.50	.23	.06
☐ 181	Paul O'Neill	.50	.23	.06
☐ 182	Ken Caminiti	.50	.23	.06
☐ 183	Dave Nilsson	.50	.23	.06
☐ 184	Tim Naehring	.50	.23	.06
☐ 185	Roger Clemens	1.50	.70	.19
☐ 186	Otis Nixon	.40	.18	.05
☐ 187	Tim Raines	.75	.35	.09
☐ 188	Denny Martinez	.50	.23	.06
☐ 189	Pedro Martinez	.50	.23	.06
☐ 190	Jim Abbott	.75	.35	.09
☐ 191	Ryan Thompson	.40	.18	.05
☐ 192	Barry Bonds	2.50	1.10	.30
☐ 193	Joe Girardi	.40	.18	.05
☐ 194	Steve Finley	.50	.23	.06
☐ 195	John Jaha	.40	.18	.05
☐ 196	Tony Gwynn	3.00	1.35	.35
☐ 197	Sammy Sosa	.75	.35	.09
☐ 198	John Burkett	.40	.18	.05
☐ 199	Carlos Baerga	2.00	.90	.25
☐ 200	Ramon Martinez	.40	.18	.05
☐ 201	Aaron Sele	.40	.18	.05
☐ 202	Eduardo Perez	.40	.18	.05
☐ 203	Alan Trammell	.75	.35	.09
☐ 204	Orlando Merced	.40	.18	.05
☐ 205	Deion Sanders	2.00	.90	.25
☐ 206	Robb Nen	.40	.18	.05
☐ 207	Jack McDowell	.75	.35	.09
☐ 208	Ruben Sierra	.75	.35	.09
☐ 209	Bernie Williams	.50	.23	.06
☐ 210	Kevin Seitzer	.40	.18	.05
☐ 211	Charles Nagy	.40	.18	.05
☐ 212	Tony Phillips	.40	.18	.05
☐ 213	Greg Maddux	10.00	4.50	1.25
☐ 214	Jeff Montgomery	.50	.23	.06
☐ 215	Larry Walker	1.25	.55	.16
☐ 216	Andy Van Slyke	.40	.18	.05
☐ 217	Ozzie Smith	2.00	.90	.25

☐ 218	Geronimo Pena	.40	.18	.05
☐ 219	Gregg Jefferies	.75	.35	.09
☐ 220	Lou Whitaker	.75	.35	.09
☐ 221	Chipper Jones	4.00	1.80	.50
☐ 222	Benji Gil	.40	.18	.05
☐ 223	Tony Phillips	.40	.18	.05
☐ 224	Trevor Wilson	.40	.18	.05
☐ 225	Tony Tarasco	.50	.23	.06
☐ 226	Roberto Petagine	.50	.23	.06
☐ 227	Mike Macfarlane	.40	.18	.05
☐ 228	Hideo Nomo UER	12.00	5.50	1.50
	(In 3rd line agianst)			
☐ 229	Mark McLemore	.40	.18	.05
☐ 230	Ron Gant	.75	.35	.09
☐ 231	Andujar Cedeno	.40	.18	.05
☐ 232	Mike Mimbs	.75	.35	.09
☐ 233	Jim Abbott	.75	.35	.09
☐ 234	Ricky Bones	.40	.18	.05
☐ 235	Marty Cordova	1.50	.70	.19
☐ 236	Mark Johnson	.40	.18	.05
☐ 237	Marquis Grissom	.75	.35	.09
☐ 238	Tom Henke	.50	.23	.06
☐ 239	Terry Pendleton	.50	.23	.06
☐ 240	John Wetteland	.50	.23	.06
☐ 241	Lee Smith	.75	.35	.09
☐ 242	Jaime Navarro	.40	.18	.05
☐ 243	Luis Alicea	.40	.18	.05
☐ 244	Scott Cooper	.40	.18	.05
☐ 245	Gary Gaetti	.50	.23	.06
☐ 246	Edgardo Alfonzo UER	.40	.18	.05
	(Incomplete career BA)			
☐ 247	Brad Clontz	.40	.18	.05
☐ 248	Dave Mlicki	.40	.18	.05
☐ 249	Dave Winfield	.75	.35	.09
☐ 250	Mark Grudzielanek	.75	.35	.09
☐ 251	Alex Gonzalez	.50	.23	.06
☐ 252	Kevin Brown	.40	.18	.05
☐ 253	Esteban Loaiza	.40	.18	.05
☐ 254	Vaughn Eshelman	.40	.18	.05
☐ 255	Bill Swift	.40	.18	.05
☐ 256	Brian McRae	.40	.18	.05
☐ 257	Bobby Higginson	1.00	.45	.12
☐ 258	Jack McDowell	.75	.35	.09
☐ 259	Scott Stahoviak	.40	.18	.05
☐ 260	Jon Nunnally	.50	.23	.06
☐ 261	Charlie Hayes	.40	.18	.05
☐ 262	Jacob Brumfield	.40	.18	.05
☐ 263	Chad Curtis	.50	.23	.06
☐ 264	Heathcliff Slocumb	.40	.18	.05
☐ 265	Mark Whiten	.40	.18	.05
☐ 266	Mickey Tettleton	.50	.23	.06
☐ 267	Jose Mesa	.50	.23	.06
☐ 268	Doug Jones	.40	.18	.05
☐ 269	Trevor Hoffman	.50	.23	.06
☐ 270	Paul Sorrento	.40	.18	.05
☐ 271	Shane Andrews	.40	.18	.05
☐ 272	Brett Butler	.50	.23	.06
☐ 273	Curtis Goodwin	.50	.23	.06
☐ 274	Larry Walker	1.25	.55	.16
☐ 275	Phil Plantier	.40	.18	.05
☐ 276	Ken Hill	.50	.23	.06
☐ 277	Vinny Castilla UER	.75	.35	.09
	Rockies spelled Rockie			
☐ 278	Billy Ashley	.40	.18	.05
☐ 279	Derek Jeter	1.25	.55	.16
☐ 280	Bob Tewksbury	.40	.18	.05
☐ 281	Jose Offerman	.40	.18	.05
☐ 282	Glenallen Hill	.40	.18	.05
☐ 283	Tony Fernandez	.40	.18	.05
☐ 284	Mike Devereaux	.40	.18	.05
☐ 285	John Burkett	.40	.18	.05

☐ 286	Geronimo Berroa	.40	.18	.05
☐ 287	Quilvio Veras	.40	.18	.05
☐ 288	Jason Bates	.40	.18	.05
☐ 289	Lee Tinsley	.50	.23	.06
☐ 290	Derek Bell	.75	.35	.09
☐ 291	Jeff Fassero	.40	.18	.05
☐ 292	Ray Durham	.75	.35	.09
☐ 293	Chad Ogea	.40	.18	.05
☐ 294	Bill Pulsipher	.50	.23	.06
☐ 295	Phil Nevin	.40	.18	.05
☐ 296	Carlos Perez	2.00	.90	.25
☐ 297	Roberto Kelly	.50	.23	.06
☐ 298	Tim Wakefield	.50	.23	.06
☐ 299	Jeff Manto	.40	.18	.05
☐ 300	Brian Hunter	1.25	.55	.16
☐ 301	C.J. Nitkowski	.40	.18	.05
☐ 302	Dustin Hermanson	.40	.18	.05
☐ 303	John Mabry	.50	.23	.06
☐ 304	Orel Hershiser	.50	.23	.06
☐ 305	Ron Villone	.40	.18	.05
☐ 306	Sean Bergman	.40	.18	.05
☐ 307	Tom Goodwin	.40	.18	.05
☐ 308	Al Reyes	.40	.18	.05
☐ 309	Todd Stottlemyre	.40	.18	.05
☐ 310	Rich Becker	.40	.18	.05
☐ 311	Joey Cora	.40	.18	.05
☐ 312	Ed Sprague	.40	.18	.05
☐ 313	John Smoltz UER	.50	.23	.06
	(3rd line; from spelled as form)			
☐ 314	Frank Castillo	.40	.18	.05
☐ 315	Chris Hammond	.40	.18	.05
☐ 316	Ismael Valdes	.40	.18	.05
☐ 317	Pete Harnisch	.40	.18	.05
☐ 318	Bernard Gilkey	.50	.23	.06
☐ 319	John Kruk	.50	.23	.06
☐ 320	Marc Newfield	.50	.23	.06
☐ 321	Brian Johnson	.40	.18	.05
☐ 322	Mark Portugal	.40	.18	.05
☐ 323	David Hulse	.40	.18	.05
☐ 324	Luis Ortiz UER	.40	.18	.05
	(Below spelled beloe)			
☐ 325	Mike Benjamin	.40	.18	.05
☐ 326	Brian Jordan	.75	.35	.09
☐ 327	Shawn Green	.75	.35	.09
☐ 328	Joe Oliver	.40	.18	.05
☐ 329	Felipe Lira	.40	.18	.05
☐ 330	Andre Dawson	.75	.35	.09

1995 Finest
Refractors

This set is a parallel to the basic Finest set, including the use of protective coating, the difference can be found in the refractive sheen. The cards were inserted at a rate of one in 12 packs.

	MINT	NRMT	EXC
COMPLETE SET (330)	3800.00	1700.00	475.00
COMPLETE SERIES 1 (220)	2800.00	1250.00	350.00
COMPLETE SERIES 2 (110)	1000.00	450.00	125.00
COMMON CARD (1-220)	10.00	4.50	1.25
COMMON CARD (221-330)	10.00	4.50	1.25
STARS	25.00	11.00	3.10
*VETERAN STARS: 10X TO 18X BASIC CARDS			
*YOUNG STARS: 9X TO 15X BASIC CARDS			

□	1	Raul Mondesi	60.00	27.00	7.50
□	4	Manny Ramirez RT	125.00	55.00	15.50
□	8	Ryan Klesko	60.00	27.00	7.50
□	17	Jim Edmonds	30.00	13.50	3.70
□	25	Javier Lopez	30.00	13.50	3.70
□	30	Garret Anderson	50.00	22.00	6.25
□	37	Jim Thome	40.00	18.00	5.00
□	45	Matt Williams	40.00	18.00	5.00
□	48	Mike Mussina	30.00	13.50	3.70
□	56	Kenny Lofton	100.00	45.00	12.50
□	68	Dante Bichette	30.00	13.50	3.70
□	76	Randy Johnson	60.00	27.00	7.50
□	79	Tim Salmon	40.00	18.00	5.00
□	82	Albert Belle	125.00	55.00	15.50
□	86	Mo Vaughn	40.00	18.00	5.00
□	89	Frank Thomas	350.00	160.00	45.00
□	96	Barry Larkin	30.00	13.50	3.70
□	98	David Justice	30.00	13.50	3.70
□	103	Fred McGriff	30.00	13.50	3.70
□	112	Eddie Murray	30.00	13.50	3.70
□	113	Mike Piazza	125.00	55.00	15.50
□	117	Jeff Bagwell	100.00	45.00	12.50
□	118	Ken Griffey Jr.	350.00	160.00	45.00
□	120	Cal Ripken Jr.	350.00	160.00	45.00
□	123	Will Clark	30.00	13.50	3.70
□	126	Don Mattingly	125.00	55.00	15.50
□	137	Roberto Alomar	60.00	27.00	7.50
□	158	Juan Gonzalez	75.00	34.00	9.50
□	167	Kirby Puckett	100.00	45.00	12.50
□	170	Jose Canseco	50.00	22.00	6.25
□	185	Roger Clemens	40.00	18.00	5.00
□	192	Barry Bonds	75.00	34.00	9.50
□	196	Tony Gwynn	100.00	45.00	12.50
□	199	Carlos Baerga	60.00	27.00	7.50
□	205	Deion Sanders	60.00	27.00	7.50
□	213	Greg Maddux	350.00	160.00	45.00
□	215	Larry Walker	30.00	13.50	3.70
□	217	Ozzie Smith	60.00	27.00	7.50
□	221	Chipper Jones	125.00	55.00	15.50
□	228	Hideo Nomo	125.00	55.00	15.50
□	235	Marty Cordova	30.00	13.50	3.70
□	274	Larry Walker	30.00	13.50	3.70
□	279	Derek Jeter	30.00	13.50	3.70
□	300	Brian Hunter	30.00	13.50	3.70

1995 Finest Flame Throwers

Randomly inserted in packs, this nine-card set showcases strikeout leaders who bring on the heat. With a protective coating, a player photo is superimposed over a fiery orange background. The backs have a player photo with skills ratings such as velocity, etc.

		MINT	NRMT	EXC
COMPLETE SET (9)		110.00	50.00	14.00
COMMON CARD (1-9)		10.00	4.50	1.25

□	FT1	Jason Bere	10.00	4.50	1.25
□	FT2	Roger Clemens	25.00	11.00	3.10
□	FT3	Juan Guzman	10.00	4.50	1.25
□	FT4	John Hudek	10.00	4.50	1.25
□	FT5	Randy Johnson	30.00	13.50	3.70
□	FT6	Pedro Martinez	10.00	4.50	1.25
□	FT7	Jose Rijo	10.00	4.50	1.25
□	FT8	Bret Saberhagen	10.00	4.50	1.25
□	FT9	John Wetteland	10.00	4.50	1.25

1995 Finest Power Kings

Randomly inserted at a rate of one in 24 packs, Power Kings is an 18-card set highlighting top sluggers. With a protective coating, the fronts feature chromium technology that allows the player photo to be further enhanced as if to jump out from a blue lightning bolt background. Horizontal back contain two small photos and power production figures.

		MINT	NRMT	EXC
COMPLETE SET (18)		300.00	135.00	38.00
COMMON CARD (1-18)		5.00	2.20	.60

□	PK1	Bob Hamelin	5.00	2.20	.60
□	PK2	Raul Mondesi	15.00	6.75	1.85
□	PK3	Ryan Klesko	12.00	5.50	1.50
□	PK4	Carlos Delgado	5.00	2.20	.60
□	PK5	Manny Ramirez	25.00	11.00	3.10
□	PK6	Mike Piazza	25.00	11.00	3.10
□	PK7	Jeff Bagwell	20.00	9.00	2.50
□	PK8	Mo Vaughn	10.00	4.50	1.25
□	PK9	Frank Thomas	60.00	27.00	7.50
□	PK10	Ken Griffey Jr.	60.00	27.00	7.50
□	PK11	Albert Belle	25.00	11.00	3.10
□	PK12	Sammy Sosa	6.00	2.70	.75
□	PK13	Dante Bichette	8.00	3.60	1.00
□	PK14	Gary Sheffield	5.00	2.20	.60
□	PK15	Matt Williams	10.00	4.50	1.25

		MINT	NRMT	EXC
☐ PK16	Fred McGriff	8.00	3.60	1.00
☐ PK17	Barry Bonds	15.00	6.75	1.85
☐ PK18	Cecil Fielder	5.00	2.20	.60

1993 Flair

These 300 standard-size (2 1/2" by 3 1/2")
cards are made from heavy 24 point board
card stock, with an additional three points
of high-gloss laminate on each side, and
feature full-bleed color fronts that sport two
photos of each player, one superposed
upon the other. The Flair logo appears at
the top and the player's name rests at the
bottom, both stamped in gold foil. Another
borderless color player action photo graces
the back. Upon this slightly ghosted picture
appear the player's stats and, with a gold
foil start letter, career highlights. The player's team logo in the upper right rounds out
the back. The cards are numbered in gold
foil on the back, grouped alphabetically
within teams, and checklisted below alphabetically according to teams for National
League and American League as follows:
Atlanta Braves (1-12), Chicago Cubs (13-
23), Cincinnati Reds (24-34), Colorado
Rockies (35-44), Florida Marlins (45-55),
Houston Astros (56-67), Los Angeles
Dodgers (68-77), Montreal Expos (78-88),
New York Mets (89-96), Philadelphia
Phillies (97-108), Pittsburgh Pirates (109-
118), St. Louis Cardinals (119-130), San
Diego Padres (131-136), San Francisco
Giants (137-148), Baltimore Orioles (149-
159), Boston Red Sox (160-169), California
Angels (170-179), Chicago White Sox (180-
190), Cleveland Indians (191-199), Detroit
Tigers (200-211), Kansas City Royals (212-
222), Milwaukee Brewers (223-232),
Minnesota Twins (233-243), New York
Yankees (244-255), Oakland Athletics
(256-265), Seattle Mariners (266-276),
Texas Rangers (277-286), and Toronto
Blue Jays (287-297). The set closes with
checklists (298-300). Rookie Cards in this
set include Rene Arocha, David Hulse,
Mike Lansing, and J.T. Snow.

		MINT	NRMT	EXC
COMPLETE SET (300)		80.00	36.00	10.00
COMMON CARD (1-300)		.20	.09	.03

☐ 1	Steve Avery	.60	.25	.07
☐ 2	Jeff Blauser	.40	.18	.05
☐ 3	Ron Gant	.60	.25	.07
☐ 4	Tom Glavine	.60	.25	.07
☐ 5	David Justice	1.00	.45	.12
☐ 6	Mark Lemke	.40	.18	.05
☐ 7	Greg Maddux	8.00	3.60	1.00
☐ 8	Fred McGriff	1.00	.45	.12
☐ 9	Terry Pendleton	.40	.18	.05
☐ 10	Deion Sanders	1.50	.70	.19
☐ 11	John Smoltz	.40	.18	.05
☐ 12	Mike Stanton	.20	.09	.03
☐ 13	Steve Buechele	.20	.09	.03
☐ 14	Mark Grace	.60	.25	.07
☐ 15	Greg Hibbard	.20	.09	.03
☐ 16	Derrick May	.40	.18	.05
☐ 17	Chuck McElroy	.20	.09	.03
☐ 18	Mike Morgan	.20	.09	.03
☐ 19	Randy Myers	.40	.18	.05
☐ 20	Ryne Sandberg	2.00	.90	.25
☐ 21	Dwight Smith	.20	.09	.03
☐ 22	Sammy Sosa	.60	.25	.07
☐ 23	Jose Vizcaino	.20	.09	.03
☐ 24	Tim Belcher	.20	.09	.03
☐ 25	Rob Dibble	.20	.09	.03
☐ 26	Roberto Kelly	.40	.18	.05
☐ 27	Barry Larkin	1.00	.45	.12
☐ 28	Kevin Mitchell	.40	.18	.05
☐ 29	Hal Morris	.40	.18	.05
☐ 30	Joe Oliver	.20	.09	.03
☐ 31	Jose Rijo	.40	.18	.05
☐ 32	Bip Roberts	.20	.09	.03
☐ 33	Chris Sabo	.20	.09	.03
☐ 34	Reggie Sanders	.60	.25	.07
☐ 35	Dante Bichette	1.00	.45	.12
☐ 36	Willie Blair	.20	.09	.03
☐ 37	Jerald Clark	.20	.09	.03
☐ 38	Alex Cole	.20	.09	.03
☐ 39	Andres Galarraga	.60	.25	.07
☐ 40	Joe Girardi	.20	.09	.03
☐ 41	Charlie Hayes	.40	.18	.05
☐ 42	Chris Jones	.20	.09	.03
☐ 43	David Nied	.40	.18	.05
☐ 44	Eric Young	.40	.18	.05
☐ 45	Alex Arias	.20	.09	.03
☐ 46	Jack Armstrong	.20	.09	.03
☐ 47	Bret Barberie	.20	.09	.03
☐ 48	Chuck Carr	.20	.09	.03
☐ 49	Jeff Conine	.60	.25	.07
☐ 50	Orestes Destrade	.20	.09	.03
☐ 51	Chris Hammond	.20	.09	.03
☐ 52	Bryan Harvey	.40	.18	.05
☐ 53	Benito Santiago	.20	.09	.03
☐ 54	Gary Sheffield	.60	.25	.07
☐ 55	Walt Weiss	.40	.18	.05
☐ 56	Eric Anthony	.20	.09	.03
☐ 57	Jeff Bagwell	3.00	1.35	.35
☐ 58	Craig Biggio	.60	.25	.07
☐ 59	Ken Caminiti	.40	.18	.05
☐ 60	Andujar Cedeno	.20	.09	.03
☐ 61	Doug Drabek	.40	.18	.05
☐ 62	Steve Finley	.40	.18	.05
☐ 63	Luis Gonzalez	.40	.18	.05
☐ 64	Pete Harnisch	.20	.09	.03
☐ 65	Doug Jones	.20	.09	.03
☐ 66	Darryl Kile	.20	.09	.03
☐ 67	Greg Swindell	.20	.09	.03
☐ 68	Brett Butler	.40	.18	.05
☐ 69	Jim Gott	.20	.09	.03
☐ 70	Orel Hershiser	.40	.18	.05
☐ 71	Eric Karros	.40	.18	.05

☐	72	Pedro Martinez	.60	.25	.07
☐	73	Ramon Martinez	.40	.18	.05
☐	74	Roger McDowell	.20	.09	.03
☐	75	Mike Piazza	6.00	2.70	.75
☐	76	Jody Reed	.20	.09	.03
☐	77	Tim Wallach	.20	.09	.03
☐	78	Moises Alou	.20	.25	.07
☐	79	Greg Colbrunn	.20	.09	.03
☐	80	Wil Cordero	.40	.18	.05
☐	81	Delino DeShields	.40	.18	.05
☐	82	Jeff Fassero	.20	.09	.03
☐	83	Marquis Grissom	.60	.25	.07
☐	84	Ken Hill	.40	.18	.05
☐	85	Mike Lansing	.75	.35	.09
☐	86	Dennis Martinez	.40	.18	.05
☐	87	Larry Walker	1.00	.45	.12
☐	88	John Wetteland	.40	.18	.05
☐	89	Bobby Bonilla	.60	.25	.07
☐	90	Vince Coleman	.20	.09	.03
☐	91	Dwight Gooden	.40	.18	.05
☐	92	Todd Hundley	.60	.25	.07
☐	93	Howard Johnson	.20	.09	.03
☐	94	Eddie Murray	1.25	.55	.16
☐	95	Joe Orsulak	.20	.09	.03
☐	96	Bret Saberhagen	.40	.18	.05
☐	97	Darren Daulton	.60	.25	.07
☐	98	Mariano Duncan	.20	.09	.03
☐	99	Len Dykstra	.60	.25	.07
☐	100	Jim Eisenreich	.20	.09	.03
☐	101	Tommy Greene	.20	.09	.03
☐	102	Dave Hollins	.20	.09	.03
☐	103	Pete Incaviglia	.20	.09	.03
☐	104	Danny Jackson	.20	.09	.03
☐	105	John Kruk	.60	.25	.07
☐	106	Terry Mulholland	.20	.09	.03
☐	107	Curt Schilling	.40	.18	.05
☐	108	Mitch Williams	.40	.18	.05
☐	109	Stan Belinda	.20	.09	.03
☐	110	Jay Bell	.40	.18	.05
☐	111	Steve Cooke	.20	.09	.03
☐	112	Carlos Garcia	.40	.18	.05
☐	113	Jeff King	.20	.09	.03
☐	114	Al Martin	.40	.18	.05
☐	115	Orlando Merced	.40	.18	.05
☐	116	Don Slaught	.20	.09	.03
☐	117	Andy Van Slyke	.40	.18	.05
☐	118	Tim Wakefield	.60	.25	.07
☐	119	Rene Arocha	.40	.18	.05
☐	120	Bernard Gilkey	.40	.18	.05
☐	121	Gregg Jefferies	.60	.25	.07
☐	122	Ray Lankford	.60	.25	.07
☐	123	Donovan Osborne	.20	.09	.03
☐	124	Tom Pagnozzi	.20	.09	.03
☐	125	Erik Pappas	.20	.09	.03
☐	126	Geronimo Pena	.20	.09	.03
☐	127	Lee Smith	.60	.25	.07
☐	128	Ozzie Smith	1.50	.70	.19
☐	129	Bob Tewksbury	.20	.09	.03
☐	130	Mark Whiten	.40	.18	.05
☐	131	Derek Bell	.60	.25	.07
☐	132	Andy Benes	.40	.18	.05
☐	133	Tony Gwynn	2.50	1.10	.30
☐	134	Gene Harris	.20	.09	.03
☐	135	Trevor Hoffman	.40	.18	.05
☐	136	Phil Plantier	.20	.09	.03
☐	137	Rod Beck	.60	.25	.07
☐	138	Barry Bonds	2.00	.90	.25
☐	139	John Burkett	.20	.09	.03
☐	140	Will Clark	1.00	.45	.12
☐	141	Royce Clayton	.40	.18	.05
☐	142	Mike Jackson	.20	.09	.03
☐	143	Darren Lewis	.20	.09	.03
☐	144	Kirt Manwaring	.20	.09	.03
☐	145	Willie McGee	.20	.09	.03
☐	146	Bill Swift	.20	.09	.03
☐	147	Robby Thompson	.20	.09	.03
☐	148	Matt Williams	1.25	.55	.16
☐	149	Brady Anderson	.40	.18	.05
☐	150	Mike Devereaux	.40	.18	.05
☐	151	Chris Hoiles	.40	.18	.05
☐	152	Ben McDonald	.40	.18	.05
☐	153	Mark McLemore	.20	.09	.03
☐	154	Mike Mussina	1.25	.55	.16
☐	155	Gregg Olson	.20	.09	.03
☐	156	Harold Reynolds	.20	.09	.03
☐	157	Cal Ripken UER	8.00	3.60	1.00
		(Back refers to his games streak			
		going into 1992; should be 1993)			
		Also streak is spelled steak			
☐	158	Rick Sutcliffe	.40	.18	.05
☐	159	Fernando Valenzuela	.40	.18	.05
☐	160	Roger Clemens	1.25	.55	.16
☐	161	Scott Cooper	.20	.09	.03
☐	162	Andre Dawson	.60	.25	.07
☐	163	Scott Fletcher	.20	.09	.03
☐	164	Mike Greenwell	.40	.18	.05
☐	165	Greg A. Harris	.20	.09	.03
☐	166	Billy Hatcher	.20	.09	.03
☐	167	Jeff Russell	.20	.09	.03
☐	168	Mo Vaughn	1.25	.55	.16
☐	169	Frank Viola	.20	.09	.03
☐	170	Chad Curtis	.40	.18	.05
☐	171	Chili Davis	.40	.18	.05
☐	172	Gary DiScarcina	.20	.09	.03
☐	173	Damion Easley	.40	.18	.05
☐	174	Chuck Finley	.40	.18	.05
☐	175	Mark Langston	.60	.25	.07
☐	176	Luis Polonia	.20	.09	.03
☐	177	Tim Salmon	2.50	1.10	.30
☐	178	Scott Sanderson	.20	.09	.03
☐	179	J.T.Snow	2.00	.90	.25
☐	180	Wilson Alvarez	.60	.25	.07
☐	181	Ellis Burks	.40	.18	.05
☐	182	Joey Cora	.20	.09	.03
☐	183	Alex Fernandez	.60	.25	.07
☐	184	Ozzie Guillen	.20	.09	.03
☐	185	Roberto Hernandez	.40	.18	.05
☐	186	Bo Jackson	.60	.25	.07
☐	187	Lance Johnson	.20	.09	.03
☐	188	Jack McDowell	.60	.25	.07
☐	189	Frank Thomas	8.00	3.60	1.00
☐	190	Robin Ventura	.60	.25	.07
☐	191	Carlos Baerga	1.50	.70	.19
☐	192	Albert Belle	3.00	1.35	.35
☐	193	Wayne Kirby	.20	.09	.03
☐	194	Derek Lilliquist	.20	.09	.03
☐	195	Kenny Lofton	2.50	1.10	.30
☐	196	Carlos Martinez	.20	.09	.03
☐	197	Jose Mesa	.40	.18	.05
☐	198	Eric Plunk	.20	.09	.03
☐	199	Paul Sorrento	.20	.09	.03
☐	200	John Doherty	.20	.09	.03
☐	201	Cecil Fielder	.60	.25	.07
☐	202	Travis Fryman	.60	.25	.07
☐	203	Kirk Gibson	.40	.18	.05
☐	204	Mike Henneman	.20	.09	.03
☐	205	Chad Kreuter	.20	.09	.03
☐	206	Scott Livingstone	.20	.09	.03
☐	207	Tony Phillips	.20	.09	.03
☐	208	Mickey Tettleton	.40	.18	.05
☐	209	Alan Trammell	.60	.25	.07
☐	210	David Wells	.20	.09	.03

☐ 211	Lou Whitaker	.60	.25	.07
☐ 212	Kevin Appier	.40	.18	.05
☐ 213	George Brett	3.00	1.35	.35
☐ 214	David Cone	.60	.25	.07
☐ 215	Tom Gordon	.20	.09	.03
☐ 216	Phil Hiatt	.20	.09	.03
☐ 217	Felix Jose	.20	.09	.03
☐ 218	Wally Joyner	.40	.18	.05
☐ 219	Jose Lind	.20	.09	.03
☐ 220	Mike Macfarlane	.20	.09	.03
☐ 221	Brian McRae	.60	.25	.07
☐ 222	Jeff Montgomery	.40	.18	.05
☐ 223	Cal Eldred	.20	.09	.03
☐ 224	Darryl Hamilton	.20	.09	.03
☐ 225	John Jaha	.40	.18	.05
☐ 226	Pat Listach	.20	.09	.03
☐ 227	Graeme Lloyd	.20	.09	.03
☐ 228	Kevin Reimer	.20	.09	.03
☐ 229	Bill Spiers	.20	.09	.03
☐ 230	B.J.Surhoff	.40	.18	.05
☐ 231	Greg Vaughn	.20	.09	.03
☐ 232	Robin Yount	1.00	.45	.12
☐ 233	Rick Aguilera	.40	.18	.05
☐ 234	Jim Deshaies	.20	.09	.03
☐ 235	Brian Harper	.20	.09	.03
☐ 236	Kent Hrbek	.20	.09	.03
☐ 237	Chuck Knoblauch	.60	.25	.07
☐ 238	Shane Mack	.20	.09	.03
☐ 239	David McCarty	.20	.09	.03
☐ 240	Pedro Munoz	.40	.18	.05
☐ 241	Mike Pagliarulo	.20	.09	.03
☐ 242	Kirby Puckett	2.50	1.10	.30
☐ 243	Dave Winfield	.60	.25	.07
☐ 244	Jim Abbott	.60	.25	.07
☐ 245	Wade Boggs	.60	.25	.07
☐ 246	Pat Kelly	.20	.09	.03
☐ 247	Jimmy Key	.40	.18	.05
☐ 248	Jim Leyritz	.20	.09	.03
☐ 249	Don Mattingly	4.00	1.80	.50
☐ 250	Matt Nokes	.20	.09	.03
☐ 251	Paul O'Neill	.40	.18	.05
☐ 252	Mike Stanley	.40	.18	.05
☐ 253	Danny Tartabull	.40	.18	.05
☐ 254	Bob Wickman	.20	.09	.03
☐ 255	Bernie Williams	.40	.18	.05
☐ 256	Mike Bordick	.20	.09	.03
☐ 257	Dennis Eckersley	.60	.25	.07
☐ 258	Brent Gates	.40	.18	.05
☐ 259	Goose Gossage	.60	.25	.07
☐ 260	Rickey Henderson	.60	.25	.07
☐ 261	Mark McGwire	.60	.25	.07
☐ 262	Ruben Sierra	.60	.25	.07
☐ 263	Terry Steinbach	.40	.18	.05
☐ 264	Bob Welch	.40	.18	.05
☐ 265	Bobby Witt	.20	.09	.03
☐ 266	Rich Amaral	.20	.09	.03
☐ 267	Chris Bosio	.20	.09	.03
☐ 268	Jay Buhner	.60	.25	.07
☐ 269	Norm Charlton	.20	.09	.03
☐ 270	Ken Griffey Jr.	8.00	3.60	1.00
☐ 271	Erik Hanson	.40	.18	.05
☐ 272	Randy Johnson	1.50	.70	.19
☐ 273	Edgar Martinez	.60	.25	.07
☐ 274	Tino Martinez	.60	.25	.07
☐ 275	Dave Valle	.20	.09	.03
☐ 276	Omar Vizquel	.40	.18	.05
☐ 277	Kevin Brown	.20	.09	.03
☐ 278	Jose Canseco	1.25	.55	.16
☐ 279	Julio Franco	.40	.18	.05
☐ 280	Juan Gonzalez	1.50	.70	.19
☐ 281	Tom Henke	.40	.18	.05

☐ 282	David Hulse	.20	.09	.03
☐ 283	Rafael Palmeiro	.60	.25	.07
☐ 284	Dean Palmer	.40	.18	.05
☐ 285	Ivan Rodriguez	.60	.25	.07
☐ 286	Nolan Ryan	8.00	3.60	1.00
☐ 287	Roberto Alomar	1.50	.70	.19
☐ 288	Pat Borders	.20	.09	.03
☐ 289	Joe Carter	.60	.25	.07
☐ 290	Juan Guzman	.40	.18	.05
☐ 291	Pat Hentgen	.40	.18	.05
☐ 292	Paul Molitor	.60	.25	.07
☐ 293	John Olerud	.40	.18	.05
☐ 294	Ed Sprague	.20	.09	.03
☐ 295	Dave Stewart	.40	.18	.05
☐ 296	Duane Ward	.20	.09	.03
☐ 297	Devon White	.40	.18	.05
☐ 298	Checklist 1-100	.20	.09	.03
☐ 299	Checklist 101-200	.20	.09	.03
☐ 300	Checklist 201-300	.20	.09	.03

1993 Flair
Wave of the Future

This 20-card standard-size (2 1/2" by 3 1/2") limited edition subset is made of the same thick card stock as the regular-issue set and features full-bleed color player action photos on the fronts, with the Flair logo, player's name, and the "Wave of the Future" name and logo in gold foil, all superimposed upon an ocean breaker. The horizontal back carries the same wave photo, with a color player photo superposed on the right side. The Wave of the Future name and logo, along with the player's name and career highlights, appear in gold foil on the left side. The cards are numbered on the back in gold foil with the numbering following alphabetical order of players' names.

	MINT	NRMT	EXC
COMPLETE SET (20)	60.00	27.00	7.50
COMMON CARD (1-20)	1.00	.45	.12
☐ 1 Jason Bere	2.00	.90	.25
☐ 2 Jeromy Burnitz	1.00	.45	.12
☐ 3 Russ Davis	1.50	.70	.19
☐ 4 Jim Edmonds	8.00	3.60	1.00
☐ 5 Cliff Floyd	2.50	1.10	.30
☐ 6 Jeffrey Hammonds	2.00	.90	.25

		MINT	NRMT	EXC
☐ 7	Trevor Hoffman	1.00	.45	.12
☐ 8	Domingo Jean	1.00	.45	.12
☐ 9	David McCarty	1.00	.45	.12
☐ 10	Bobby Munoz	1.00	.45	.12
☐ 11	Brad Pennington	1.00	.45	.12
☐ 12	Mike Piazza	15.00	6.75	1.85
☐ 13	Manny Ramirez	15.00	6.75	1.85
☐ 14	John Roper	1.00	.45	.12
☐ 15	Tim Salmon	6.00	2.70	.75
☐ 16	Aaron Sele	2.00	.90	.25
☐ 17	Allen Watson	1.50	.70	.19
☐ 18	Rondell White	5.00	2.20	.60
☐ 19	Darrell Whitmore UER	1.00	.45	.12
	(Nigel Wilson back)			
☐ 20	Nigel Wilson UER	1.00	.45	.12
	(Darrell Whitmore back)			

1994 Flair

For the second consecutive year Fleer issued a Flair brand. The set consists of 450 full bleed cards in two series of 250 and 200. The card stock is thicker than the traditional standard card. Card fronts feature two photos with the player's name and team name at the bottom in gold foil. The first letter of the player's last name appears within a gold shield to add style to this premium brand product. The backs are horizontal with a player photo and statistics. The team logo and player's name are done in gold foil. The cards are grouped alphabetically by team within each league as follows: Baltimore Orioles (1-9/251-258), Boston Red Sox (10-18/259-266), California Angels (19-27/267-274), Chicago White Sox (28-36/275-281), Cleveland Indians (37-45/282-290), Detroit Tigers (46-53/291-296), Kansas City Royals (54-62/297-302), Milwaukee Brewers (63-71/303-310), Minnesota Twins (72-79/311-317), New York Yankees (80-88/318-326), Oakland Athletics (89-97/327-334), Seattle Mariners (98-106/335-342), Texas Rangers (107-114/343-347), Toronto Blue Jays (115-123/348-351), Atlanta Braves (124-133/352-359), Chicago Cubs (134-142/360-364), Cincinnati Reds (143-150/365-371), Colorado Rockies (151-159/372-377), Florida Marlins (160-167/378-384), Houston Astros (168-176/385-392), Los Angeles Dodgers (177-185/393-399), Montreal Expos (186-194/400-406), New York Mets

(195-203/407-410), Philadelphia Phillies (204-213/411-419), Pittsburgh Pirates (214-222/420-426), St. Louis Cardinals (223-230/427-432), San Diego Padres (231-237/433-441), and San Francisco Giants (238-247/442-448). Rookie Cards include Brian Anderson, John Hudek, Chan Ho Park, Alex Rodriguez and Will VanLandingham.

	MINT	NRMT	EXC
COMPLETE SET (450)	60.00	27.00	7.50
COMPLETE SERIES 1 (250)	35.00	16.00	4.40
COMPLETE SERIES 2 (200)	25.00	11.00	3.10
COMMON CARD (1-250)	.15	.07	.02
COMMON CARD (251-450)	.15	.07	.02

		MINT	NRMT	EXC
☐ 1	Harold Baines	.30	.14	.04
☐ 2	Jeffrey Hammonds	.40	.18	.05
☐ 3	Chris Hoiles	.30	.14	.04
☐ 4	Ben McDonald	.30	.14	.04
☐ 5	Mark McLemore	.15	.07	.02
☐ 6	Jamie Moyer	.15	.07	.02
☐ 7	Jim Poole	.15	.07	.02
☐ 8	Cal Ripken Jr.	5.00	2.20	.60
☐ 9	Chris Sabo	.15	.07	.02
☐ 10	Scott Bankhead	.15	.07	.02
☐ 11	Scott Cooper	.30	.14	.04
☐ 12	Danny Darwin	.15	.07	.02
☐ 13	Andre Dawson	.40	.18	.05
☐ 14	Billy Hatcher	.15	.07	.02
☐ 15	Aaron Sele	.30	.14	.04
☐ 16	John Valentin	.30	.14	.04
☐ 17	Dave Valle	.15	.07	.02
☐ 18	Mo Vaughn	.75	.35	.09
☐ 19	Brian Anderson	.40	.18	.05
☐ 20	Gary DiSarcina	.15	.07	.02
☐ 21	Jim Edmonds	.75	.35	.09
☐ 22	Chuck Finley	.15	.07	.02
☐ 23	Bo Jackson	.40	.18	.05
☐ 24	Mark Leiter	.15	.07	.02
☐ 25	Greg Myers	.15	.07	.02
☐ 26	Eduardo Perez	.15	.07	.02
☐ 27	Tim Salmon	1.00	.45	.12
☐ 28	Wilson Alvarez	.30	.14	.04
☐ 29	Jason Bere	.30	.14	.04
☐ 30	Alex Fernandez	.40	.18	.05
☐ 31	Ozzie Guillen	.15	.07	.02
☐ 32	Joe Hall	.15	.07	.02
☐ 33	Darrin Jackson	.15	.07	.02
☐ 34	Kirk McCaskill	.15	.07	.02
☐ 35	Tim Raines	.40	.18	.05
☐ 36	Frank Thomas	5.00	2.20	.60
☐ 37	Carlos Baerga	1.00	.45	.12
☐ 38	Albert Belle	2.00	.90	.25
☐ 39	Mark Clark	.15	.07	.02
☐ 40	Wayne Kirby	.15	.07	.02
☐ 41	Dennis Martinez	.30	.14	.04
☐ 42	Charles Nagy	.30	.14	.04
☐ 43	Manny Ramirez	2.00	.90	.25
☐ 44	Paul Sorrento	.15	.07	.02
☐ 45	Jim Thome	1.00	.45	.12
☐ 46	Eric Davis	.15	.07	.02
☐ 47	John Doherty	.15	.07	.02
☐ 48	Junior Felix	.15	.07	.02
☐ 49	Cecil Fielder	.40	.18	.05
☐ 50	Kirk Gibson	.30	.14	.04
☐ 51	Mike Moore	.15	.07	.02
☐ 52	Tony Phillips	.15	.07	.02
☐ 53	Alan Trammell	.40	.18	.05
☐ 54	Kevin Appier	.30	.14	.04

☐ 55 Stan Belinda	.15	.07	.02
☐ 56 Vince Coleman	.15	.07	.02
☐ 57 Greg Gagne	.15	.07	.02
☐ 58 Bob Hamelin	.15	.07	.02
☐ 59 Dave Henderson	.15	.07	.02
☐ 60 Wally Joyner	.30	.14	.04
☐ 61 Mike Macfarlane	.15	.07	.02
☐ 62 Jeff Montgomery	.30	.14	.04
☐ 63 Ricky Bones	.15	.07	.02
☐ 64 Jeff Bronkey	.15	.07	.02
☐ 65 Alex Diaz	.15	.07	.02
☐ 66 Cal Eldred	.30	.14	.04
☐ 67 Darryl Hamilton	.15	.07	.02
☐ 68 John Jaha	.15	.07	.02
☐ 69 Mark Kiefer	.15	.07	.02
☐ 70 Kevin Seitzer	.15	.07	.02
☐ 71 Turner Ward	.15	.07	.02
☐ 72 Rich Becker	.30	.14	.04
☐ 73 Scott Erickson	.15	.07	.02
☐ 74 Keith Garagozzo	.15	.07	.02
☐ 75 Kent Hrbek	.15	.07	.02
☐ 76 Scott Leius	.15	.07	.02
☐ 77 Kirby Puckett	1.50	.70	.19
☐ 78 Matt Walbeck	.15	.07	.02
☐ 79 Dave Winfield	.40	.18	.05
☐ 80 Mike Gallego	.15	.07	.02
☐ 81 Xavier Hernandez	.15	.07	.02
☐ 82 Jimmy Key	.30	.14	.04
☐ 83 Jim Leyritz	.15	.07	.02
☐ 84 Don Mattingly	2.50	1.10	.30
☐ 85 Matt Nokes	.15	.07	.02
☐ 86 Paul O'Neill	.30	.14	.04
☐ 87 Melido Perez	.15	.07	.02
☐ 88 Danny Tartabull	.30	.14	.04
☐ 89 Mike Bordick	.15	.07	.02
☐ 90 Ron Darling	.15	.07	.02
☐ 91 Dennis Eckersley	.40	.18	.05
☐ 92 Stan Javier	.15	.07	.02
☐ 93 Steve Karsay	.15	.07	.02
☐ 94 Mark McGwire	.40	.18	.05
☐ 95 Troy Neel	.15	.07	.02
☐ 96 Terry Steinbach	.30	.14	.04
☐ 97 Bill Taylor	.15	.07	.02
☐ 98 Eric Anthony	.15	.07	.02
☐ 99 Chris Bosio	.15	.07	.02
☐ 100 Tim Davis	.15	.07	.02
☐ 101 Felix Fermin	.15	.07	.02
☐ 102 Dave Fleming	.15	.07	.02
☐ 103 Ken Griffey Jr.	5.00	2.20	.60
☐ 104 Greg Hibbard	.15	.07	.02
☐ 105 Reggie Jefferson	.15	.07	.02
☐ 106 Tino Martinez	.30	.14	.04
☐ 107 Jack Armstrong	.15	.07	.02
☐ 108 Will Clark	.60	.25	.07
☐ 109 Juan Gonzalez	1.25	.55	.16
☐ 110 Rick Helling	.15	.07	.02
☐ 111 Tom Henke	.15	.07	.02
☐ 112 David Hulse	.15	.07	.02
☐ 113 Manuel Lee	.15	.07	.02
☐ 114 Doug Strange	.15	.07	.02
☐ 115 Roberto Alomar	1.00	.45	.12
☐ 116 Joe Carter	.40	.18	.05
☐ 117 Carlos Delgado	.40	.18	.05
☐ 118 Pat Hentgen	.30	.14	.04
☐ 119 Paul Molitor	.40	.18	.05
☐ 120 John Olerud	.40	.18	.05
☐ 121 Dave Stewart	.30	.14	.04
☐ 122 Todd Stottlemyre	.15	.07	.02
☐ 123 Mike Timlin	.15	.07	.02
☐ 124 Jeff Blauser	.30	.14	.04
☐ 125 Tom Glavine	.40	.18	.05

☐ 126 David Justice	.60	.25	.07
☐ 127 Mike Kelly	.30	.14	.04
☐ 128 Ryan Klesko	1.25	.55	.16
☐ 129 Javier Lopez	.75	.35	.09
☐ 130 Greg Maddux	5.00	2.20	.60
☐ 131 Fred McGriff	.60	.25	.07
☐ 132 Kent Mercker	.15	.07	.02
☐ 133 Mark Wohlers	.15	.07	.02
☐ 134 Willie Banks	.15	.07	.02
☐ 135 Steve Buechele	.15	.07	.02
☐ 136 Shawon Dunston	.15	.07	.02
☐ 137 Jose Guzman	.15	.07	.02
☐ 138 Glenallen Hill	.15	.07	.02
☐ 139 Randy Myers	.15	.07	.02
☐ 140 Karl Rhodes	.15	.07	.02
☐ 141 Ryne Sandberg	1.25	.55	.16
☐ 142 Steve Trachsel	.40	.18	.05
☐ 143 Bret Boone	.40	.18	.05
☐ 144 Tom Browning	.15	.07	.02
☐ 145 Hector Carrasco	.15	.07	.02
☐ 146 Barry Larkin	.60	.25	.07
☐ 147 Hal Morris	.30	.14	.04
☐ 148 Jose Rijo	.30	.14	.04
☐ 149 Reggie Sanders	.30	.14	.04
☐ 150 John Smiley	.15	.07	.02
☐ 151 Dante Bichette	.60	.25	.07
☐ 152 Ellis Burks	.30	.14	.04
☐ 153 Joe Girardi	.15	.07	.02
☐ 154 Mike Harkey	.15	.07	.02
☐ 155 Roberto Mejia	.15	.07	.02
☐ 156 Marcus Moore	.15	.07	.02
☐ 157 Armando Reynoso	.15	.07	.02
☐ 158 Bruce Ruffin	.15	.07	.02
☐ 159 Eric Young	.15	.07	.02
☐ 160 Kurt Abbott	.40	.18	.05
☐ 161 Jeff Conine	.40	.18	.05
☐ 162 Orestes Destrade	.15	.07	.02
☐ 163 Chris Hammond	.15	.07	.02
☐ 164 Bryan Harvey	.15	.07	.02
☐ 165 Dave Magadan	.15	.07	.02
☐ 166 Gary Sheffield	.40	.18	.05
☐ 167 David Weathers	.15	.07	.02
☐ 168 Andujar Cedeno	.15	.07	.02
☐ 169 Tom Edens	.15	.07	.02
☐ 170 Luis Gonzalez	.15	.07	.02
☐ 171 Pete Harnisch	.15	.07	.02
☐ 172 Todd Jones	.15	.07	.02
☐ 173 Darryl Kile	.30	.14	.04
☐ 174 James Mouton	.40	.18	.05
☐ 175 Scott Servais	.15	.07	.02
☐ 176 Mitch Williams	.15	.07	.02
☐ 177 Pedro Astacio	.30	.14	.04
☐ 178 Orel Hershiser	.30	.14	.04
☐ 179 Raul Mondesi	1.50	.70	.19
☐ 180 Jose Offerman	.15	.07	.02
☐ 181 Chan Ho Park	.50	.23	.06
☐ 182 Mike Piazza	2.00	.90	.25
☐ 183 Cory Snyder	.15	.07	.02
☐ 184 Tim Wallach	.15	.07	.02
☐ 185 Todd Worrell	.15	.07	.02
☐ 186 Sean Berry	.15	.07	.02
☐ 187 Wil Cordero	.40	.18	.05
☐ 188 Darrin Fletcher	.15	.07	.02
☐ 189 Cliff Floyd	.40	.18	.05
☐ 190 Marquis Grissom	.40	.18	.05
☐ 191 Rod Henderson	.30	.14	.04
☐ 192 Ken Hill	.30	.14	.04
☐ 193 Pedro Martinez	.40	.18	.05
☐ 194 Kirk Rueter	.15	.07	.02
☐ 195 Jeromy Burnitz	.15	.07	.02
☐ 196 John Franco	.15	.07	.02

☐ 197	Dwight Gooden	.15	.07	.02
☐ 198	Todd Hundley	.30	.14	.04
☐ 199	Bobby Jones	.40	.18	.05
☐ 200	Jeff Kent	.30	.14	.04
☐ 201	Mike Maddux	.15	.07	.02
☐ 202	Ryan Thompson	.30	.14	.04
☐ 203	Jose Vizcaino	.15	.07	.02
☐ 204	Darren Daulton	.40	.18	.05
☐ 205	Lenny Dykstra	.40	.18	.05
☐ 206	Jim Eisenreich	.15	.07	.02
☐ 207	Dave Hollins	.40	.18	.05
☐ 208	Danny Jackson	.15	.07	.02
☐ 209	Doug Jones	.15	.07	.02
☐ 210	Jeff Juden	.15	.07	.02
☐ 211	Ben Rivera	.15	.07	.02
☐ 212	Kevin Stocker	.30	.14	.04
☐ 213	Milt Thompson	.15	.07	.02
☐ 214	Jay Bell	.30	.14	.04
☐ 215	Steve Cooke	.15	.07	.02
☐ 216	Mark Dewey	.15	.07	.02
☐ 217	Al Martin	.15	.07	.02
☐ 218	Orlando Merced	.30	.14	.04
☐ 219	Don Slaught	.15	.07	.02
☐ 220	Zane Smith	.15	.07	.02
☐ 221	Rick White	.15	.07	.02
☐ 222	Kevin Young	.15	.07	.02
☐ 223	Rene Arocha	.15	.07	.02
☐ 224	Rheal Cormier	.15	.07	.02
☐ 225	Brian Jordan	.30	.14	.04
☐ 226	Ray Lankford	.40	.18	.05
☐ 227	Mike Perez	.15	.07	.02
☐ 228	Ozzie Smith	1.00	.45	.12
☐ 229	Mark Whiten	.30	.14	.04
☐ 230	Todd Zeile	.30	.14	.04
☐ 231	Derek Bell	.30	.14	.04
☐ 232	Archi Cianfrocco	.15	.07	.02
☐ 233	Ricky Gutierrez	.15	.07	.02
☐ 234	Trevor Hoffman	.15	.07	.02
☐ 235	Phil Plantier	.30	.14	.04
☐ 236	Dave Staton	.15	.07	.02
☐ 237	Wally Whitehurst	.15	.07	.02
☐ 238	Todd Benzinger	.15	.07	.02
☐ 239	Barry Bonds	1.25	.55	.16
☐ 240	John Burkett	.30	.14	.04
☐ 241	Royce Clayton	.30	.14	.04
☐ 242	Bryan Hickerson	.15	.07	.02
☐ 243	Mike Jackson	.15	.07	.02
☐ 244	Darren Lewis	.15	.07	.02
☐ 245	Kirt Manwaring	.15	.07	.02
☐ 246	Mark Portugal	.15	.07	.02
☐ 247	Salomon Torres	.30	.14	.04
☐ 248	Checklist	.15	.07	.02
☐ 249	Checklist	.15	.07	.02
☐ 250	Checklist	.15	.07	.02
☐ 251	Brady Anderson	.30	.14	.04
☐ 252	Mike Devereaux	.15	.07	.02
☐ 253	Sid Fernandez	.15	.07	.02
☐ 254	Leo Gomez	.15	.07	.02
☐ 255	Mike Mussina	.60	.25	.07
☐ 256	Mike Oquist	.15	.07	.02
☐ 257	Rafael Palmeiro	.40	.18	.05
☐ 258	Lee Smith	.30	.14	.04
☐ 259	Damon Berryhill	.15	.07	.02
☐ 260	Wes Chamberlain	.15	.07	.02
☐ 261	Roger Clemens	.75	.35	.09
☐ 262	Gar Finnvold	.15	.07	.02
☐ 263	Mike Greenwell	.30	.14	.04
☐ 264	Tim Naehring	.30	.14	.04
☐ 265	Otis Nixon	.15	.07	.02
☐ 266	Ken Ryan	.15	.07	.02
☐ 267	Chad Curtis	.30	.14	.04
☐ 268	Chili Davis	.30	.14	.04
☐ 269	Damion Easley	.15	.07	.02
☐ 270	Jorge Fabregas	.15	.07	.02
☐ 271	Mark Langston	.40	.18	.05
☐ 272	Phil Leftwich	.15	.07	.02
☐ 273	Harold Reynolds	.15	.07	.02
☐ 274	J.T. Snow	.30	.14	.04
☐ 275	Joey Cora	.15	.07	.02
☐ 276	Julio Franco	.30	.14	.04
☐ 277	Roberto Hernandez	.15	.07	.02
☐ 278	Lance Johnson	.15	.07	.02
☐ 279	Ron Karkovice	.15	.07	.02
☐ 280	Jack McDowell	.40	.18	.05
☐ 281	Robin Ventura	.30	.14	.04
☐ 282	Sandy Alomar Jr.	.30	.14	.04
☐ 283	Kenny Lofton	1.50	.70	.19
☐ 284	Jose Mesa	.15	.07	.02
☐ 285	Jack Morris	.40	.18	.05
☐ 286	Eddie Murray	.60	.25	.07
☐ 287	Chad Ogea	.30	.14	.04
☐ 288	Eric Plunk	.15	.07	.02
☐ 289	Paul Shuey	.15	.07	.02
☐ 290	Omar Vizquel	.15	.07	.02
☐ 291	Danny Bautista	.15	.07	.02
☐ 292	Travis Fryman	.40	.18	.05
☐ 293	Greg Gohr	.15	.07	.02
☐ 294	Chris Gomez	.40	.18	.05
☐ 295	Mickey Tettleton	.30	.14	.04
☐ 296	Lou Whitaker	.40	.18	.05
☐ 297	David Cone	.40	.18	.05
☐ 298	Gary Gaetti	.15	.07	.02
☐ 299	Tom Gordon	.15	.07	.02
☐ 300	Felix Jose	.15	.07	.02
☐ 301	Jose Lind	.15	.07	.02
☐ 302	Brian McRae	.30	.14	.04
☐ 303	Mike Fetters	.15	.07	.02
☐ 304	Brian Harper	.15	.07	.02
☐ 305	Pat Listach	.15	.07	.02
☐ 306	Matt Mieske	.15	.07	.02
☐ 307	Dave Nilsson	.15	.07	.02
☐ 308	Jody Reed	.15	.07	.02
☐ 309	Greg Vaughn	.30	.14	.04
☐ 310	Bill Wegman	.15	.07	.02
☐ 311	Rick Aguilera	.30	.14	.04
☐ 312	Alex Cole	.15	.07	.02
☐ 313	Denny Hocking	.15	.07	.02
☐ 314	Chuck Knoblauch	.40	.18	.05
☐ 315	Shane Mack	.30	.14	.04
☐ 316	Pat Meares	.15	.07	.02
☐ 317	Kevin Tapani	.15	.07	.02
☐ 318	Jim Abbott	.40	.18	.05
☐ 319	Wade Boggs	.40	.18	.05
☐ 320	Sterling Hitchcock	.30	.14	.04
☐ 321	Pat Kelly	.15	.07	.02
☐ 322	Terry Mulholland	.15	.07	.02
☐ 323	Luis Polonia	.15	.07	.02
☐ 324	Mike Stanley	.15	.07	.02
☐ 325	Bob Wickman	.15	.07	.02
☐ 326	Bernie Williams	.30	.14	.04
☐ 327	Mark Acre	.15	.07	.02
☐ 328	Geronimo Berroa	.15	.07	.02
☐ 329	Scott Brosius	.15	.07	.02
☐ 330	Brent Gates	.30	.14	.04
☐ 331	Rickey Henderson	.40	.18	.05
☐ 332	Carlos Reyes	.15	.07	.02
☐ 333	Ruben Sierra	.30	.14	.04
☐ 334	Bobby Witt	.15	.07	.02
☐ 335	Bobby Ayala	.15	.07	.02
☐ 336	Jay Buhner	.30	.14	.04
☐ 337	Randy Johnson	1.00	.45	.12
☐ 338	Edgar Martinez	.30	.14	.04

☐	339	Bill Risley	.15	.07	.02	☐	410	David Segui	.15	.07	.02

☐	339	Bill Risley	.15	.07	.02
☐	340	Alex Rodriguez	4.00	1.80	.50
☐	341	Roger Salkeld	.15	.07	.02
☐	342	Dan Wilson	.15	.07	.02
☐	343	Kevin Brown	.15	.07	.02
☐	344	Jose Canseco	.75	.35	.09
☐	345	Dean Palmer	.30	.14	.04
☐	346	Ivan Rodriguez	.40	.18	.05
☐	347	Kenny Rogers	.30	.14	.04
☐	348	Pat Borders	.15	.07	.02
☐	349	Juan Guzman	.30	.14	.04
☐	350	Ed Sprague	.15	.07	.02
☐	351	Devon White	.15	.07	.02
☐	352	Steve Avery	.40	.18	.05
☐	353	Roberto Kelly	.15	.07	.02
☐	354	Mark Lemke	.15	.07	.02
☐	355	Greg McMichael	.15	.07	.02
☐	356	Terry Pendleton	.15	.07	.02
☐	357	John Smoltz	.30	.14	.04
☐	358	Mike Stanton	.15	.07	.02
☐	359	Tony Tarasco	.40	.18	.05
☐	360	Mark Grace	.40	.18	.05
☐	361	Derrick May	.15	.07	.02
☐	362	Rey Sanchez	.15	.07	.02
☐	363	Sammy Sosa	.40	.18	.05
☐	364	Rick Wilkins	.15	.07	.02
☐	365	Jeff Brantley	.15	.07	.02
☐	366	Tony Fernandez	.15	.07	.02
☐	367	Chuck McElroy	.15	.07	.02
☐	368	Kevin Mitchell	.30	.14	.04
☐	369	John Roper	.15	.07	.02
☐	370	Johnny Ruffin	.15	.07	.02
☐	371	Deion Sanders	1.00	.45	.12
☐	372	Marvin Freeman	.15	.07	.02
☐	373	Andres Galarraga	.40	.18	.05
☐	374	Charlie Hayes	.30	.14	.04
☐	375	Nelson Liriano	.15	.07	.02
☐	376	David Nied	.30	.14	.04
☐	377	Walt Weiss	.15	.07	.02
☐	378	Bret Barberie	.15	.07	.02
☐	379	Jerry Browne	.15	.07	.02
☐	380	Chuck Carr	.15	.07	.02
☐	381	Greg Colbrunn	.30	.14	.04
☐	382	Charlie Hough	.30	.14	.04
☐	383	Kurt Miller	.15	.07	.02
☐	384	Benito Santiago	.15	.07	.02
☐	385	Jeff Bagwell	1.50	.70	.19
☐	386	Craig Biggio	.30	.14	.04
☐	387	Ken Caminiti	.30	.14	.04
☐	388	Doug Drabek	.40	.18	.05
☐	389	Steve Finley	.30	.14	.04
☐	390	John Hudek	.30	.14	.04
☐	391	Orlando Miller	.30	.14	.04
☐	392	Shane Reynolds	.15	.07	.02
☐	393	Brett Butler	.30	.14	.04
☐	394	Tom Candiotti	.15	.07	.02
☐	395	Delino DeShields	.30	.14	.04
☐	396	Kevin Gross	.15	.07	.02
☐	397	Eric Karros	.30	.14	.04
☐	398	Ramon Martinez	.30	.14	.04
☐	399	Henry Rodriguez	.15	.07	.02
☐	400	Moises Alou	.40	.18	.05
☐	401	Jeff Fassero	.15	.07	.02
☐	402	Mike Lansing	.30	.14	.04
☐	403	Mel Rojas	.15	.07	.02
☐	404	Larry Walker	.60	.25	.07
☐	405	John Wetteland	.15	.07	.02
☐	406	Gabe White	.15	.07	.02
☐	407	Bobby Bonilla	.40	.18	.05
☐	408	Josias Manzanillo	.15	.07	.02
☐	409	Bret Saberhagen	.30	.14	.04

☐	410	David Segui	.15	.07	.02
☐	411	Mariano Duncan	.15	.07	.02
☐	412	Tommy Greene	.15	.07	.02
☐	413	Billy Hatcher	.15	.07	.02
☐	414	Ricky Jordan	.15	.07	.02
☐	415	John Kruk	.30	.14	.04
☐	416	Bobby Munoz	.15	.07	.02
☐	417	Curt Schilling	.15	.07	.02
☐	418	Fernando Valenzuela	.15	.07	.02
☐	419	David West	.15	.07	.02
☐	420	Carlos Garcia	.15	.07	.02
☐	421	Brian Hunter	.15	.07	.02
☐	422	Jeff King	.15	.07	.02
☐	423	Jon Lieber	.15	.07	.02
☐	424	Ravelo Manzanillo	.15	.07	.02
☐	425	Denny Neagle	.30	.14	.04
☐	426	Andy Van Slyke	.40	.18	.05
☐	427	Bryan Eversgerd	.15	.07	.02
☐	428	Bernard Gilkey	.30	.14	.04
☐	429	Gregg Jefferies	.40	.18	.05
☐	430	Tom Pagnozzi	.15	.07	.02
☐	431	Bob Tewksbury	.15	.07	.02
☐	432	Allen Watson	.15	.07	.02
☐	433	Andy Ashby	.15	.07	.02
☐	434	Andy Benes	.30	.14	.04
☐	435	Donnie Elliott	.15	.07	.02
☐	436	Tony Gwynn	1.50	.70	.19
☐	437	Joey Hamilton	.40	.18	.05
☐	438	Tim Hyers	.15	.07	.02
☐	439	Luis Lopez	.15	.07	.02
☐	440	Bip Roberts	.15	.07	.02
☐	441	Scott Sanders	.15	.07	.02
☐	442	Rod Beck	.30	.14	.04
☐	443	Dave Burba	.15	.07	.02
☐	444	Darryl Strawberry	.30	.14	.04
☐	445	Bill Swift	.15	.07	.02
☐	446	Robby Thompson	.15	.07	.02
☐	447	Bill VanLandingham	.50	.23	.06
☐	448	Matt Williams	.75	.35	.09
☐	449	Checklist	.15	.07	.02
☐	450	Checklist	.15	.07	.02

1994 Flair
Hot Gloves

Randomly inserted in second series packs at a rate of one in 24, this set highlights 10 of the game's top players that also have outstanding defensive ability. The cards feature a special die-cut "glove" design with the player appearing within the glove. The back has a short write-up and a photo.

		MINT	NRMT	EXC
	COMPLETE SET (10)	400.00	180.00	50.00
	COMMON CARD (1-10)	15.00	6.75	1.85
☐ 1	Barry Bonds	25.00	11.00	3.10
☐ 2	Will Clark	15.00	6.75	1.85
☐ 3	Ken Griffey Jr.	125.00	55.00	15.50
☐ 4	Kenny Lofton	40.00	18.00	5.00
☐ 5	Greg Maddux	125.00	55.00	15.50
☐ 6	Don Mattingly	50.00	22.00	6.25
☐ 7	Kirby Puckett	35.00	16.00	4.40
☐ 8	Cal Ripken Jr.	140.00	65.00	17.50
☐ 9	Tim Salmon	25.00	11.00	3.10
☐ 10	Matt Williams	25.00	11.00	3.10

1994 Flair
Hot Numbers

This 10-card set was randomly inserted in first series packs at a rate of one in 24. Metallic fronts feature a player photo with various numbers or statistics serving as background. The player's uniform number is part of the Hot Numbers logo at bottom left or right. The player's name is also at the bottom. The backs have a small photo centered in the middle surrounded by text highlighting achievements.

		MINT	NRMT	EXC
	COMPLETE SET (10)	140.00	65.00	17.50
	COMMON CARD (1-10)	4.00	1.80	.50
☐ 1	Roberto Alomar	8.00	3.60	1.00
☐ 2	Carlos Baerga	8.00	3.60	1.00
☐ 3	Will Clark	5.00	2.20	.60
☐ 4	Fred McGriff	5.00	2.20	.60
☐ 5	Paul Molitor	4.00	1.80	.50
☐ 6	John Olerud	4.00	1.80	.50
☐ 7	Mike Piazza	15.00	6.75	1.85
☐ 8	Cal Ripken Jr.	50.00	22.00	6.25
☐ 9	Ryne Sandberg	10.00	4.50	1.25
☐ 10	Frank Thomas	40.00	18.00	5.00

1994 Flair
Infield Power

Randomly inserted in second series packs at a rate of one in five, this 10-card standard-size set spotlights major league

infielders who are power hitters. Card fronts feature a horizontal format with two photos of the player. The backs contain a short write-up with emphasis on power numbers. The back also has a small photo.

		MINT	NRMT	EXC
	COMPLETE SET (10)	40.00	18.00	5.00
	COMMON CARD (1-10)	.75	.35	.09
☐ 1	Jeff Bagwell	4.00	1.80	.50
☐ 2	Will Clark	1.50	.70	.19
☐ 3	Darren Daulton	.75	.35	.09
☐ 4	Don Mattingly	6.00	2.70	.75
☐ 5	Fred McGriff	1.50	.70	.19
☐ 6	Rafael Palmeiro	.75	.35	.09
☐ 7	Mike Piazza	5.00	2.20	.60
☐ 8	Cal Ripken Jr.	12.00	5.50	1.50
☐ 9	Frank Thomas	12.00	5.50	1.50
☐ 10	Matt Williams	2.00	.90	.25

1994 Flair
Outfield Power

This 10-card set was randomly inserted in both first and second series packs at a rate of one in five. Two photos on the front feature the player fielding and hitting. The player's name and Outfield Power serve as a dividing point between the photos. The back contains a small photo and text.

		MINT	NRMT	EXC
	COMPLETE SET (10)	30.00	13.50	3.70
	COMMON CARD (1-10)	.75	.35	.09

		MINT	NRMT	EXC
☐ 1	Albert Belle	5.00	2.20	.60
☐ 2	Barry Bonds	3.00	1.35	.35
☐ 3	Joe Carter	.75	.35	.09
☐ 4	Lenny Dykstra	.75	.35	.09
☐ 5	Juan Gonzalez	3.00	1.35	.35
☐ 6	Ken Griffey Jr.	12.00	5.50	1.50
☐ 7	David Justice	1.50	.70	.19
☐ 8	Kirby Puckett	4.00	1.80	.50
☐ 9	Tim Salmon	2.50	1.10	.30
☐ 10	Dave Winfield	.75	.35	.09

☐ B9	Tony Tarasco	1.00	.45	.12
☐ B10	William VanLandingham	1.25	.55	.16

1995 Flair

This set was issued in two series of 216 cards for a total of 432. Horizontally designed fronts have a 100 percent etched foil surface containing two player photos. The backs feature a full-bleed photo with yearly statistics superimposed. The checklist is arranged alphabetically by league according to series as follows: Baltimore Orioles (1-9/217-225), Boston Red Sox (10-15/226-232), California Angels (16-22/233-239), Chicago White Sox (23-28/240-248), Cleveland Indians (29-36/249-254), Detroit Tigers (37-42/255-261), Kansas City Royals (43-49/262-268), Milwaukee Brewers (50-56/269-276), Minnesota Twins (57-62/277-282), New York Yankees (63-69/283-290), Oakland Athletics (70-77/291-298), Seattle Mariners (78-85/299-304), Texas Rangers (86-93/305-312), Toronto Blue Jays (94-101/313-319), Atlanta Braves (102-110/320-329), Chicago Cubs (111-118/330-336), Cincinnati Reds (119-126/337-341), Colorado Rockies (127-135/342-348), Florida Marlins (136-142/349-356), Houston Astros (143-149/357-364), Los Angeles Dodgers (150-159/365-371), Montreal Expos (160-168/372-379), New York Mets (169-175/380-387), Philadelphia Phillies (176-183/388-396), Pittsburgh Pirates (184-190/397-405), St. Louis Cardinals (191-197/406-413), San Diego Padres (198-205/414-423) and San Francisco Giants (206-213/424-429).

1994 Flair
Wave of the Future

This 20-card standard-size set takes a look at potential big league stars. The cards were randomly inserted in packs at a rate of one in five -- the first 10 in series 1, the second 10 in series 2. The fronts and backs have the player superimposed over a wavy colored background. The front has the Wave of the Future logo and a paragraph or two about the player along with a photo on the back.

	MINT	NRMT	EXC
COMPLETE SET (20)	50.00	22.00	6.25
COMPLETE SER.1 SET (10)	20.00	9.00	2.50
COMPLETE SER.2 SET (10)	30.00	13.50	3.70
COMMON SER.1 CARD (A1-A10)	.75	.35	.09
COMMON SER.2 CARD (B1-B10)	.75	.35	.09

		MINT	NRMT	EXC
☐ A1	Kurt Abbott	1.00	.45	.12
☐ A2	Carlos Delgado	2.00	.90	.25
☐ A3	Steve Karsay	.75	.35	.09
☐ A4	Ryan Klesko	5.00	2.20	.60
☐ A5	Javier Lopez	3.00	1.35	.35
☐ A6	Raul Mondesi	6.00	2.70	.75
☐ A7	James Mouton	1.00	.45	.12
☐ A8	Chan Ho Park	1.50	.70	.19
☐ A9	Dave Staton	.75	.35	.09
☐ A10	Rick White	.75	.35	.09
☐ B1	Mark Acre	.75	.35	.09
☐ B2	Chris Gomez	.75	.35	.09
☐ B3	Joey Hamilton	2.00	.90	.25
☐ B4	John Hudek	.75	.35	.09
☐ B5	Jon Lieber	.75	.35	.09
☐ B6	Matt Mieske	.75	.35	.09
☐ B7	Orlando Miller	1.00	.45	.12
☐ B8	Alex Rodriguez	8.00	3.60	1.00

	MINT	NRMT	EXC
COMPLETE SET (432)	90.00	40.00	11.00
COMPLETE SERIES 1 (216)	50.00	22.00	6.25
COMPLETE SERIES (216)	40.00	18.00	5.00
COMMON CARD (1-216)	.25	.11	.03
COMMON CARD (217-429)	.25	.11	.03

		MINT	NRMT	EXC
☐ 1	Brady Anderson	.30	.14	.04
☐ 2	Harold Baines	.30	.14	.04
☐ 3	Leo Gomez	.25	.11	.03
☐ 4	Alan Mills	.25	.11	.03
☐ 5	Jamie Moyer	.25	.11	.03
☐ 6	Mike Mussina	.60	.25	.07

☐ 7	Mike Oquist	.25	.11	.03
☐ 8	Arthur Rhodes	.25	.11	.03
☐ 9	Cal Ripken Jr.	5.00	2.20	.60
☐ 10	Roger Clemens	.75	.35	.09
☐ 11	Scott Cooper	.25	.11	.03
☐ 12	Mike Greenwell	.30	.14	.04
☐ 13	Aaron Sele	.30	.14	.04
☐ 14	John Valentin	.40	.18	.05
☐ 15	Mo Vaughn	.75	.35	.09
☐ 16	Chad Curtis	.30	.14	.04
☐ 17	Gary DiSarcina	.25	.11	.03
☐ 18	Chuck Finley	.30	.14	.04
☐ 19	Andrew Lorraine	.30	.14	.04
☐ 20	Spike Owen	.25	.11	.03
☐ 21	Tim Salmon	.75	.35	.09
☐ 22	J.T. Snow	.40	.18	.05
☐ 23	Wilson Alvarez	.30	.14	.04
☐ 24	Jason Bere	.30	.14	.04
☐ 25	Ozzie Guillen	.25	.11	.03
☐ 26	Mike LaValliere	.25	.11	.03
☐ 27	Frank Thomas	5.00	2.20	.60
☐ 28	Robin Ventura	.40	.18	.05
☐ 29	Carlos Baerga	1.00	.45	.12
☐ 30	Albert Belle	2.00	.90	.25
☐ 31	Jason Grimsley	.25	.11	.03
☐ 32	Dennis Martinez	.30	.14	.04
☐ 33	Eddie Murray	.60	.25	.07
☐ 34	Charles Nagy	.30	.14	.04
☐ 35	Manny Ramirez	2.00	.90	.25
☐ 36	Paul Sorrento	.25	.11	.03
☐ 37	John Doherty	.25	.11	.03
☐ 38	Cecil Fielder	.40	.18	.05
☐ 39	Travis Fryman	.40	.18	.05
☐ 40	Chris Gomez	.25	.11	.03
☐ 41	Tony Phillips	.25	.11	.03
☐ 42	Lou Whitaker	.40	.18	.05
☐ 43	David Cone	.40	.18	.05
☐ 44	Gary Gaetti	.30	.14	.04
☐ 45	Mark Gubicza	.25	.11	.03
☐ 46	Bob Hamelin	.25	.11	.03
☐ 47	Wally Joyner	.30	.14	.04
☐ 48	Rusty Meacham	.25	.11	.03
☐ 49	Jeff Montgomery	.30	.14	.04
☐ 50	Ricky Bones	.25	.11	.03
☐ 51	Cal Eldred	.25	.11	.03
☐ 52	Pat Listach	.25	.11	.03
☐ 53	Matt Mieske	.25	.11	.03
☐ 54	Dave Nilsson	.30	.14	.04
☐ 55	Greg Vaughn	.25	.11	.03
☐ 56	Bill Wegman	.25	.11	.03
☐ 57	Chuck Knoblauch	.40	.18	.05
☐ 58	Scott Leius	.25	.11	.03
☐ 59	Pat Mahomes	.25	.11	.03
☐ 60	Pat Meares	.25	.11	.03
☐ 61	Pedro Munoz	.30	.14	.04
☐ 62	Kirby Puckett	1.50	.70	.19
☐ 63	Wade Boggs	.40	.18	.05
☐ 64	Jimmy Key	.30	.14	.04
☐ 65	Jim Leyritz	.25	.11	.03
☐ 66	Don Mattingly	2.50	1.10	.30
☐ 67	Paul O'Neill	.30	.14	.04
☐ 68	Melido Perez	.25	.11	.03
☐ 69	Danny Tartabull	.30	.14	.04
☐ 70	John Briscoe	.25	.11	.03
☐ 71	Scott Brosius	.25	.11	.03
☐ 72	Ron Darling	.25	.11	.03
☐ 73	Brent Gates	.30	.14	.04
☐ 74	Rickey Henderson	.40	.18	.05
☐ 75	Stan Javier	.25	.11	.03
☐ 76	Mark McGwire	.40	.18	.05
☐ 77	Todd Van Poppel	.25	.11	.03
☐ 78	Bobby Ayala	.25	.11	.03
☐ 79	Mike Blowers	.30	.14	.04
☐ 80	Jay Buhner	.40	.18	.05
☐ 81	Ken Griffey Jr.	5.00	2.20	.60
☐ 82	Randy Johnson	1.00	.45	.12
☐ 83	Tino Martinez	.40	.18	.05
☐ 84	Jeff Nelson	.25	.11	.03
☐ 85	Alex Rodriguez	1.00	.45	.12
☐ 86	Will Clark	.60	.25	.07
☐ 87	Jeff Frye	.25	.11	.03
☐ 88	Juan Gonzalez	1.25	.55	.16
☐ 89	Rusty Greer	.25	.11	.03
☐ 90	Darren Oliver	.25	.11	.03
☐ 91	Dean Palmer	.30	.14	.04
☐ 92	Ivan Rodriguez	.40	.18	.05
☐ 93	Matt Whiteside	.25	.11	.03
☐ 94	Roberto Alomar	1.00	.45	.12
☐ 95	Joe Carter	.40	.18	.05
☐ 96	Tony Castillo	.25	.11	.03
☐ 97	Juan Guzman	.25	.11	.03
☐ 98	Pat Hentgen	.30	.14	.04
☐ 99	Mike Huff	.25	.11	.03
☐ 100	John Olerud	.30	.14	.04
☐ 101	Woody Williams	.25	.11	.03
☐ 102	Roberto Kelly	.30	.14	.04
☐ 103	Ryan Klesko	1.00	.45	.12
☐ 104	Javier Lopez	.60	.25	.07
☐ 105	Greg Maddux	5.00	2.20	.60
☐ 106	Fred McGriff	.60	.25	.07
☐ 107	Jose Oliva	.25	.11	.03
☐ 108	John Smoltz	.30	.14	.04
☐ 109	Tony Tarasco	.30	.14	.04
☐ 110	Mark Wohlers	.30	.14	.04
☐ 111	Jim Bullinger	.25	.11	.03
☐ 112	Shawon Dunston	.25	.11	.03
☐ 113	Derrick May	.30	.14	.04
☐ 114	Randy Myers	.30	.14	.04
☐ 115	Karl Rhodes	.25	.11	.03
☐ 116	Rey Sanchez	.25	.11	.03
☐ 117	Steve Trachsel	.25	.11	.03
☐ 118	Eddie Zambrano	.25	.11	.03
☐ 119	Bret Boone	.40	.18	.05
☐ 120	Brian Dorsett	.25	.11	.03
☐ 121	Hal Morris	.30	.14	.04
☐ 122	Jose Rijo	.30	.14	.04
☐ 123	John Roper	.25	.11	.03
☐ 124	Reggie Sanders	.40	.18	.05
☐ 125	Pete Schourek	.40	.18	.05
☐ 126	John Smiley	.25	.11	.03
☐ 127	Ellis Burks	.30	.14	.04
☐ 128	Vinny Castilla	.40	.18	.05
☐ 129	Marvin Freeman	.25	.11	.03
☐ 130	Andres Galarraga	.40	.18	.05
☐ 131	Mike Munoz	.25	.11	.03
☐ 132	David Nied	.25	.11	.03
☐ 133	Bruce Ruffin	.25	.11	.03
☐ 134	Walt Weiss	.30	.14	.04
☐ 135	Eric Young	.30	.14	.04
☐ 136	Greg Colbrunn	.40	.18	.05
☐ 137	Jeff Conine	.40	.18	.05
☐ 138	Jeremy Hernandez	.25	.11	.03
☐ 139	Charles Johnson	.40	.18	.05
☐ 140	Robb Nen	.25	.11	.03
☐ 141	Gary Sheffield	.40	.18	.05
☐ 142	Dave Weathers	.25	.11	.03
☐ 143	Jeff Bagwell	1.50	.70	.19
☐ 144	Craig Biggio	.40	.18	.05
☐ 145	Tony Eusebio	.25	.11	.03
☐ 146	Luis Gonzalez	.30	.14	.04
☐ 147	John Hudek	.25	.11	.03
☐ 148	Darryl Kile	.25	.11	.03

☐ 149	Dave Veres	.25	.11	.03
☐ 150	Billy Ashley	.30	.14	.04
☐ 151	Pedro Astacio	.25	.11	.03
☐ 152	Rafael Bournigal	.25	.11	.03
☐ 153	Delino DeShields	.30	.14	.04
☐ 154	Raul Mondesi	1.25	.55	.16
☐ 155	Mike Piazza	2.00	.90	.25
☐ 156	Rudy Seanez	.25	.11	.03
☐ 157	Ismael Valdes	.25	.11	.03
☐ 158	Tim Wallach	.25	.11	.03
☐ 159	Todd Worrell	.25	.11	.03
☐ 160	Moises Alou	.30	.14	.04
☐ 161	Cliff Floyd	.40	.18	.05
☐ 162	Gil Heredia	.25	.11	.03
☐ 163	Mike Lansing	.25	.11	.03
☐ 164	Pedro Martinez	.30	.14	.04
☐ 165	Kirk Rueter	.25	.11	.03
☐ 166	Tim Scott	.25	.11	.03
☐ 167	Jeff Shaw	.25	.11	.03
☐ 168	Rondell White	.40	.18	.05
☐ 169	Bobby Bonilla	.40	.18	.05
☐ 170	Rico Brogna	.40	.18	.05
☐ 171	Todd Hundley	.30	.14	.04
☐ 172	Jeff Kent	.25	.11	.03
☐ 173	Jim Lindeman	.25	.11	.03
☐ 174	Joe Orsulak	.25	.11	.03
☐ 175	Bret Saberhagen	.30	.14	.04
☐ 176	Toby Borland	.25	.11	.03
☐ 177	Darren Daulton	.30	.14	.04
☐ 178	Lenny Dykstra	.30	.14	.04
☐ 179	Jim Eisenreich	.25	.11	.03
☐ 180	Tommy Greene	.25	.11	.03
☐ 181	Tony Longmire	.25	.11	.03
☐ 182	Bobby Munoz	.25	.11	.03
☐ 183	Kevin Stocker	.25	.11	.03
☐ 184	Jay Bell	.25	.11	.03
☐ 185	Steve Cooke	.25	.11	.03
☐ 186	Ravelo Manzanillo	.25	.11	.03
☐ 187	Al Martin	.30	.14	.04
☐ 188	Denny Neagle	.25	.11	.03
☐ 189	Don Slaught	.25	.11	.03
☐ 190	Paul Wagner	.25	.11	.03
☐ 191	Rene Arocha	.25	.11	.03
☐ 192	Bernard Gilkey	.30	.14	.04
☐ 193	Jose Oquendo	.25	.11	.03
☐ 194	Tom Pagnozzi	.25	.11	.03
☐ 195	Ozzie Smith	1.00	.45	.12
☐ 196	Allen Watson	.30	.14	.04
☐ 197	Mark Whiten	.30	.14	.04
☐ 198	Andy Ashby	.25	.11	.03
☐ 199	Donnie Elliott	.25	.11	.03
☐ 200	Bryce Florie	.25	.11	.03
☐ 201	Tony Gwynn	1.50	.70	.19
☐ 202	Trevor Hoffman	.30	.14	.04
☐ 203	Brian Johnson	.25	.11	.03
☐ 204	Tim Mauser	.25	.11	.03
☐ 205	Bip Roberts	.25	.11	.03
☐ 206	Rod Beck	.30	.14	.04
☐ 207	Barry Bonds	1.25	.55	.16
☐ 208	Royce Clayton	.30	.14	.04
☐ 209	Darren Lewis	.25	.11	.03
☐ 210	Mark Portugal	.25	.11	.03
☐ 211	Kevin Rogers	.25	.11	.03
☐ 212	Wm. VanLandingham	.30	.14	.04
☐ 213	Matt Williams	.75	.35	.09
☐ 214	Checklist	.25	.11	.03
☐ 215	Checklist	.25	.11	.03
☐ 216	Checklist	.25	.11	.03
☐ 217	Bret Barberie	.25	.11	.03
☐ 218	Armando Benitez	.25	.11	.03
☐ 219	Kevin Brown	.25	.11	.03
☐ 220	Sid Fernandez	.25	.11	.03
☐ 221	Chris Hoiles	.30	.14	.04
☐ 222	Doug Jones	.25	.11	.03
☐ 223	Ben McDonald	.25	.11	.03
☐ 224	Rafael Palmeiro	.40	.18	.05
☐ 225	Andy Van Slyke	.30	.14	.04
☐ 226	Jose Canseco	.75	.35	.09
☐ 227	Vaughn Eshelman	.25	.11	.03
☐ 228	Mike Macfarlane	.25	.11	.03
☐ 229	Tim Naehring	.30	.14	.04
☐ 230	Frank Rodriguez	.30	.14	.04
☐ 231	Lee Tinsley	.30	.14	.04
☐ 232	Mark Whiten	.30	.14	.04
☐ 233	Garret Anderson	1.00	.45	.12
☐ 234	Chili Davis	.30	.14	.04
☐ 235	Jim Edmonds	.60	.25	.07
☐ 236	Mark Langston	.30	.14	.04
☐ 237	Troy Percival	.30	.14	.04
☐ 238	Tony Phillips	.25	.11	.03
☐ 239	Lee Smith	.40	.18	.05
☐ 240	Jim Abbott	.40	.18	.05
☐ 241	James Baldwin	.25	.11	.03
☐ 242	Mike Devereaux	.25	.11	.03
☐ 243	Ray Durham	.40	.18	.05
☐ 244	Alex Fernandez	.30	.14	.04
☐ 245	Roberto Hernandez	.30	.14	.04
☐ 246	Lance Johnson	.25	.11	.03
☐ 247	Ron Karkovice	.25	.11	.03
☐ 248	Tim Raines	.40	.18	.05
☐ 249	Sandy Alomar Jr.	.30	.14	.04
☐ 250	Orel Hershiser	.30	.14	.04
☐ 251	Julian Tavarez	.30	.14	.04
☐ 252	Jim Thome	.75	.35	.09
☐ 253	Omar Vizquel	.30	.14	.04
☐ 254	Dave Winfield	.40	.18	.05
☐ 255	Chad Curtis	.25	.11	.03
☐ 256	Kirk Gibson	.30	.14	.04
☐ 257	Mike Henneman	.25	.11	.03
☐ 258	Bob Higginson	.60	.25	.07
☐ 259	Felipe Lira	.25	.11	.03
☐ 260	Rudy Pemberton	.25	.11	.03
☐ 261	Alan Trammell	.40	.18	.05
☐ 262	Kevin Appier	.30	.14	.04
☐ 263	Pat Borders	.25	.11	.03
☐ 264	Tom Gordon	.25	.11	.03
☐ 265	Jose Lind	.25	.11	.03
☐ 266	Jon Nunnally	.30	.14	.04
☐ 267	Dilson Torres	.25	.11	.03
☐ 268	Michael Tucker	.30	.14	.04
☐ 269	Jeff Cirillo	.30	.14	.04
☐ 270	Darryl Hamilton	.25	.11	.03
☐ 271	David Hulse	.25	.11	.03
☐ 272	Mark Kiefer	.25	.11	.03
☐ 273	Graeme Lloyd	.25	.11	.03
☐ 274	Joe Oliver	.25	.11	.03
☐ 275	Al Reyes	.25	.11	.03
☐ 276	Kevin Seitzer	.25	.11	.03
☐ 277	Rick Aguilera	.30	.14	.04
☐ 278	Marty Cordova	.75	.35	.09
☐ 279	Scott Erickson			
☐ 280	LaTroy Hawkins	.25	.11	.03
☐ 281	Brad Radke	.60	.25	.07
☐ 282	Kevin Tapani	.25	.11	.03
☐ 283	Tony Fernandez	.25	.11	.03
☐ 284	Sterling Hitchcock	.25	.11	.03
☐ 285	Pat Kelly	.25	.11	.03
☐ 286	Jack McDowell	.30	.14	.04
☐ 287	Andy Pettitte	.60	.25	.07
☐ 288	Mike Stanley	.30	.14	.04
☐ 289	John Wetteland	.30	.14	.04
☐ 290	Bernie Williams	.30	.14	.04

☐ 291	Mark Acre	.25	.11	.03
☐ 292	Geronimo Berroa	.25	.11	.03
☐ 293	Dennis Eckersley	.40	.18	.05
☐ 294	Steve Ontiveros	.25	.11	.03
☐ 295	Ruben Sierra	.40	.18	.05
☐ 296	Terry Steinbach	.30	.14	.04
☐ 297	Dave Stewart	.30	.14	.04
☐ 298	Todd Stottlemyre	.25	.11	.03
☐ 299	Darren Bragg	.25	.11	.03
☐ 300	Joey Cora	.25	.11	.03
☐ 301	Edgar Martinez	.40	.18	.05
☐ 302	Bill Risley	.25	.11	.03
☐ 303	Ron Villone	.25	.11	.03
☐ 304	Dan Wilson	.30	.14	.04
☐ 305	Benji Gil	.25	.11	.03
☐ 306	Wilson Heredia	.25	.11	.03
☐ 307	Mark McLemore	.25	.11	.03
☐ 308	Otis Nixon	.25	.11	.03
☐ 309	Kenny Rogers	.25	.11	.03
☐ 310	Jeff Russell	.25	.11	.03
☐ 311	Mickey Tettleton	.30	.14	.04
☐ 312	Bob Tewksbury	.25	.11	.03
☐ 313	David Cone	.40	.18	.05
☐ 314	Carlos Delgado	.30	.14	.04
☐ 315	Alex Gonzalez	.30	.14	.04
☐ 316	Shawn Green	.40	.18	.05
☐ 317	Paul Molitor	.40	.18	.05
☐ 318	Ed Sprague	.25	.11	.03
☐ 319	Devon White	.30	.14	.04
☐ 320	Steve Avery	.30	.14	.04
☐ 321	Jeff Blauser	.30	.14	.04
☐ 322	Brad Clontz	.25	.11	.03
☐ 323	Tom Glavine	.40	.18	.05
☐ 324	Marquis Grissom	.40	.18	.05
☐ 325	Chipper Jones	2.00	.90	.25
☐ 326	David Justice	.60	.25	.07
☐ 327	Mark Lemke	.30	.14	.04
☐ 328	Kent Mercker	.25	.11	.03
☐ 329	Jason Schmidt	.30	.14	.04
☐ 330	Steve Buechele	.25	.11	.03
☐ 331	Kevin Foster	.25	.11	.03
☐ 332	Mark Grace	.40	.18	.05
☐ 333	Brian McRae	.30	.14	.04
☐ 334	Sammy Sosa	.40	.18	.05
☐ 335	Ozzie Timmons	.25	.11	.03
☐ 336	Rick Wilkins	.25	.11	.03
☐ 337	Hector Carrasco	.25	.11	.03
☐ 338	Ron Gant	.40	.18	.05
☐ 339	Barry Larkin	.60	.25	.07
☐ 340	Deion Sanders	1.00	.45	.12
☐ 341	Benito Santiago	.25	.11	.03
☐ 342	Roger Bailey	.25	.11	.03
☐ 343	Jason Bates	.25	.11	.03
☐ 344	Dante Bichette	.60	.25	.07
☐ 345	Joe Girardi	.25	.11	.03
☐ 346	Bill Swift	.25	.11	.03
☐ 347	Mark Thompson	.25	.11	.03
☐ 348	Larry Walker	.60	.25	.07
☐ 349	Kurt Abbott	.25	.11	.03
☐ 350	John Burkett	.25	.11	.03
☐ 351	Chuck Carr	.25	.11	.03
☐ 352	Andre Dawson	.40	.18	.05
☐ 353	Chris Hammond	.25	.11	.03
☐ 354	Charles Johnson	.40	.18	.05
☐ 355	Terry Pendleton	.30	.14	.04
☐ 356	Quilvio Veras	.25	.11	.03
☐ 357	Derek Bell	.40	.18	.05
☐ 358	Jim Dougherty	.25	.11	.03
☐ 359	Doug Drabek	.30	.14	.04
☐ 360	Todd Jones	.25	.11	.03
☐ 361	Orlando Miller	.30	.14	.04
☐ 362	James Mouton	.30	.14	.04
☐ 363	Phil Plantier	.25	.11	.03
☐ 364	Shane Reynolds	.25	.11	.03
☐ 365	Todd Hollandsworth	.25	.11	.03
☐ 366	Eric Karros	.30	.14	.04
☐ 367	Ramon Martinez	.30	.14	.04
☐ 368	Hideo Nomo	8.00	3.60	1.00
☐ 369	Jose Offerman	.25	.11	.03
☐ 370	Antonio Osuna	.25	.11	.03
☐ 371	Todd Williams	.25	.11	.03
☐ 372	Shane Andrews	.25	.11	.03
☐ 373	Wil Cordero	.30	.14	.04
☐ 374	Jeff Fassero	.30	.14	.04
☐ 375	Darrin Fletcher	.25	.11	.03
☐ 376	Mark Grudzielanek	.30	.14	.04
☐ 377	Carlos Perez	1.25	.55	.16
☐ 378	Mel Rojas	.30	.14	.04
☐ 379	Tony Tarasco	.30	.14	.04
☐ 380	Edgardo Alfonzo	.25	.11	.03
☐ 381	Brett Butler	.30	.14	.04
☐ 382	Carl Everett	.30	.14	.04
☐ 383	John Franco	.30	.14	.04
☐ 384	Pete Harnisch	.25	.11	.03
☐ 385	Bobby Jones	.30	.14	.04
☐ 386	Dave Mlicki	.25	.11	.03
☐ 387	Jose Vizcaino	.25	.11	.03
☐ 388	Ricky Bottalico	.25	.11	.03
☐ 389	Tyler Green	.25	.11	.03
☐ 390	Charlie Hayes	.25	.11	.03
☐ 391	Dave Hollins	.25	.11	.03
☐ 392	Gregg Jefferies	.40	.18	.05
☐ 393	Michael Mimbs	.40	.18	.05
☐ 394	Mickey Morandini	.25	.11	.03
☐ 395	Curt Schilling	.25	.11	.03
☐ 396	Heathcliff Slocumb	.25	.11	.03
☐ 397	Jason Christiansen	.25	.11	.03
☐ 398	Midre Cummings	.30	.14	.04
☐ 399	Carlos Garcia	.30	.14	.04
☐ 400	Mark Johnson	.25	.11	.03
☐ 401	Jeff King	.25	.11	.03
☐ 402	Jon Lieber	.25	.11	.03
☐ 403	Esteban Loaiza	.25	.11	.03
☐ 404	Orlando Merced	.30	.14	.04
☐ 405	Gary Wilson	.25	.11	.03
☐ 406	Scott Cooper	.25	.11	.03
☐ 407	Tom Henke	.30	.14	.04
☐ 408	Ken Hill	.30	.14	.04
☐ 409	Danny Jackson	.25	.11	.03
☐ 410	Brian Jordan	.40	.18	.05
☐ 411	Ray Lankford	.40	.18	.05
☐ 412	John Mabry	.30	.14	.04
☐ 413	Todd Zeile	.30	.14	.04
☐ 414	Andy Benes	.30	.14	.04
☐ 415	Andres Berumen	.25	.11	.03
☐ 416	Ken Caminiti	.30	.14	.04
☐ 417	Andujar Cedeno	.25	.11	.03
☐ 418	Steve Finley	.30	.14	.04
☐ 419	Joey Hamilton	.30	.14	.04
☐ 420	Dustin Hermanson	.25	.11	.03
☐ 421	Melvin Nieves	.30	.14	.04
☐ 422	Roberto Petagine	.30	.14	.04
☐ 423	Eddie Williams	.25	.11	.03
☐ 424	Glenallen Hill	.30	.14	.04
☐ 425	Kirt Manwaring	.25	.11	.03
☐ 426	Terry Mulholland	.25	.11	.03
☐ 427	J.R. Phillips	.25	.11	.03
☐ 428	Joe Rosselli	.25	.11	.03
☐ 429	Robby Thompson	.25	.11	.03
☐ 430	Checklist	.25	.11	.03
☐ 431	Checklist	.25	.11	.03
☐ 432	Checklist	.25	.11	.03

1995 Flair
Hot Gloves

This 12-card set features players that are known for their defensive prowess. Randomly inserted in series two packs at a rate of one in 25, a player photo is superimposed over an embossed design of a bronze glove.The backs have a photo and write-up with a glove as background.

		MINT	NRMT	EXC
	COMPLETE SET (12)	275.00	125.00	34.00
	COMMON CARD (1-12)	8.00	3.60	1.00
☐ 1	Roberto Alomar	18.00	8.00	2.20
☐ 2	Barry Bonds	20.00	9.00	2.50
☐ 3	Ken Griffey Jr.	90.00	40.00	11.00
☐ 4	Marquis Grissom	12.00	5.50	1.50
☐ 5	Barry Larkin	15.00	6.75	1.85
☐ 6	Darren Lewis	8.00	3.60	1.00
☐ 7	Kenny Lofton	30.00	13.50	3.70
☐ 8	Don Mattingly	40.00	18.00	5.00
☐ 9	Cal Ripken	100.00	45.00	12.50
☐ 10	Ivan Rodriguez	12.00	5.50	1.50
☐ 11	Devon White	8.00	3.60	1.00
☐ 12	Matt Williams	18.00	8.00	2.20

1995 Flair
Hot Numbers

Randomly inserted in packs at a rate of one in nine, this 10-card set showcases top players. A player photo on front is superimposed over a gold background that contains player stats from 1994. Horizontal backs have a ghosted player photo to the right with highlights on the left.

		MINT	NRMT	EXC
	COMPLETE SET (10)	70.00	32.00	8.75
	COMMON CARD (1-10)	2.50	1.10	.30
☐ 1	Jeff Bagwell	5.00	2.20	.60
☐ 2	Albert Belle	6.00	2.70	.75
☐ 3	Barry Bonds	4.00	1.80	.50
☐ 4	Ken Griffey Jr.	15.00	6.75	1.85
☐ 5	Kenny Lofton	5.00	2.20	.60
☐ 6	Greg Maddux	15.00	6.75	1.85
☐ 7	Mike Piazza	6.00	2.70	.75
☐ 8	Cal Ripken	15.00	6.75	1.85
☐ 9	Frank Thomas	15.00	6.75	1.85
☐ 10	Matt Williams	2.50	1.10	.30

1995 Flair
Infield Power

Randomly inserted in second series packs at a rate of one in five, this 10-card set features sluggers that man the outfield. A player photo on front is surrounded by multiple color schemes with a horizontal back offering a player photo and highlights.

		MINT	NRMT	EXC
	COMPLETE SET (10)	18.00	8.00	2.20
	COMMON CARD (1-10)	.75	.35	.09
☐ 1	Jeff Bagwell	2.50	1.10	.30
☐ 2	Darren Daulton	.75	.35	.09
☐ 3	Cecil Fielder	.75	.35	.09
☐ 4	Andres Galarraga	.75	.35	.09
☐ 5	Fred McGriff	1.00	.45	.12
☐ 6	Rafael Palmeiro	.75	.35	.09
☐ 7	Mike Piazza	3.00	1.35	.35
☐ 8	Frank Thomas	8.00	3.60	1.00
☐ 9	Mo Vaughn	1.25	.55	.16
☐ 10	Matt Williams	1.25	.55	.16

1995 Flair
Outfield Power

Randomly inserted in first series packs at a rate of one in six, this 10-card set features

sluggers that patrol the outfield. A player photo on front is surrounded by multiple color schemes with a horizontal back offering a player photo and highlights.

	MINT	NRMT	EXC
COMPLETE SET (10)	18.00	8.00	2.20
COMMON CARD (1-10)	.75	.35	.09
☐ 1 Albert Belle	3.00	1.35	.35
☐ 2 Dante Bichette	1.00	.45	.12
☐ 3 Barry Bonds	2.00	.90	.25
☐ 4 Jose Canseco	1.25	.55	.16
☐ 5 Joe Carter	.75	.35	.09
☐ 6 Juan Gonzalez	2.00	.90	.25
☐ 7 Ken Griffey Jr.	8.00	3.60	1.00
☐ 8 Kirby Puckett	2.50	1.10	.30
☐ 9 Gary Sheffield	.75	.35	.09
☐ 10 Ruben Sierra	.75	.35	.09

1995 Flair
Today's Spotlight

This 12-card die-cut set was randomly inserted in first series packs at a rate of one in 25 packs. The upper portion of the player photo on front has the spotlight effect as the remainder of the photo is darkened. Horizontal backs have a circular player photo to the right with text off to the left.

	MINT	NRMT	EXC
COMPLETE SET (12)	180.00	80.00	22.00
COMMON CARD (1-12)	6.00	2.70	.75
☐ 1 Jeff Bagwell	20.00	9.00	2.50
☐ 2 Jason Bere	6.00	2.70	.75

☐ 3 Cliff Floyd	6.00	2.70	.75
☐ 4 Chuck Knoblauch	6.00	2.70	.75
☐ 5 Kenny Lofton	20.00	9.00	2.50
☐ 6 Javier Lopez	8.00	3.60	1.00
☐ 7 Raul Mondesi	15.00	6.75	1.85
☐ 8 Mike Mussina	8.00	3.60	1.00
☐ 9 Mike Piazza	25.00	11.00	3.10
☐ 10 Manny Ramirez	25.00	11.00	3.10
☐ 11 Tim Salmon	10.00	4.50	1.25
☐ 12 Frank Thomas	60.00	27.00	7.50

1995 Flair
Wave of the Future

Spotlighting 10 of the game's hottest young stars, cards were randomly inseretd in second series packs at a rate of one in eight. An action photo is superimposed over primarily a solid background save for the player's name, team and same name which appear several times. The backs are horizontal with a photo and write-up.

	MINT	NRMT	EXC
COMPLETE SET (10)	25.00	11.00	3.10
COMMON CARD (1-10)	1.25	.55	.16
☐ 1 Jason Bates	1.25	.55	.16
☐ 2 Armando Benitez	1.25	.55	.16
☐ 3 Marty Cordova	2.50	1.10	.30
☐ 4 Ray Durham	1.50	.70	.19
☐ 5 Vaughn Eshelman	1.25	.55	.16
☐ 6 Carl Everett	1.25	.55	.16
☐ 7 Shawn Green	1.50	.70	.19
☐ 8 Dustin Hermanson	1.50	.70	.19
☐ 9 Chipper Jones	8.00	3.60	1.00
☐ 10 Hideo Nomo	12.00	5.50	1.50

1981 Fleer

The cards in this 660-card set measure 2 1/2" by 3 1/2". This issue of cards marks Fleer's first entry into the current player baseball card market since 1963. Players from the same team are conveniently grouped together by number in the set. The teams are ordered (by 1980 standings) as

follows: Philadelphia (1-27), Kansas City
(28-50), Houston (51-78), New York
Yankees (79-109), Los Angeles (110-141),
Montreal (142-168), Baltimore (169-195),
Cincinnati (196-220), Boston (221-241),
Atlanta (242-267), California (268-290),
Chicago Cubs (291-315), New York Mets
(316-338), Chicago White Sox (339-350
and 352-359), Pittsburgh (360-386),
Cleveland (387-408), Toronto (409-431),
San Francisco (432-458), Detroit (459-483),
San Diego (484-506), Milwaukee (507-527),
St. Louis (528-550), Minnesota (551-571),
Oakland (351 and 572-594), Seattle (595-
616), and Texas (617-637). Cards 638-660
feature specials and checklists. The cards
of pitchers in this set erroneously show a
heading (on the card backs) of "Batting
Record" over their career pitching statistics.
There were three distinct printings: the two
following the primary run were designed to
correct numerous errors. The variations
caused by these multiple printings are
noted in the checklist below (P1, P2, or P3).
The C. Nettles variation was corrected
before the end of the first printing and thus
is not included in the complete set consid-
eration. The key Rookie Cards in this set
are Danny Ainge, Harold Baines, Kirk
Gibson, Jeff Reardon, and Fernando
Valenzuela, whose first name was erroneously spelled Fernand on the card front.

	NRMT-MT	EXC	G-VG
COMPLETE SET (660)	40.00	18.00	5.00
COMMON CARD (1-660)	.10	.05	.01

☐	1 Pete Rose UER (270 hits in '63, should be 170)	2.50	1.10	.30
☐	2 Larry Bowa	.20	.09	.03
☐	3 Manny Trillo	.10	.05	.01
☐	4 Bob Boone	.20	.09	.03
☐	5 Mike Schmidt (See also 640A)	2.00	.90	.25
☐	6A Steve Carlton P1 Golden Arm (Back "1066 Cardinals"; Number on back 6)	1.50	.70	.19
☐	6B Steve Carlton P2 Pitcher of Year (Back "1066 Cardinals")	1.50	.70	.19
☐	6C Steve Carlton P3 ("1966 Cardinals")	2.00	.90	.25
☐	7 Tug McGraw (See 657A)	.20	.09	.03
☐	8 Larry Christenson	.10	.05	.01
☐	9 Bake McBride	.10	.05	.01
☐	10 Greg Luzinski	.20	.09	.03
☐	11 Ron Reed	.10	.05	.01
☐	12 Dickie Noles	.10	.05	.01
☐	13 Keith Moreland	.20	.09	.03
☐	14 Bob Walk	.30	.14	.04
☐	15 Lonnie Smith	.10	.05	.01
☐	16 Dick Ruthven	.10	.05	.01
☐	17 Sparky Lyle	.20	.09	.03
☐	18 Greg Gross	.10	.05	.01
☐	19 Garry Maddox	.10	.05	.01
☐	20 Nino Espinosa	.10	.05	.01
☐	21 George Vukovich	.10	.05	.01
☐	22 John Vukovich	.10	.05	.01
☐	23 Ramon Aviles	.10	.05	.01
☐	24A Kevin Saucier P1 (Name on back "Ken")	.10	.05	.01
☐	24B Kevin Saucier P2 (Name on back "Ken")	.10	.05	.01
☐	24C Kevin Saucier P3 (Name on back "Kevin")	.20	.09	.03
☐	25 Randy Lerch	.10	.05	.01
☐	26 Del Unser	.10	.05	.01
☐	27 Tim McCarver	.30	.14	.04
☐	28 George Brett (See also 655A)	4.00	1.80	.50
☐	29 Willie Wilson (See also 653A)	.10	.05	.01
☐	30 Paul Splittorff	.10	.05	.01
☐	31 Dan Quisenberry	.30	.14	.04
☐	32A Amos Otis P1 (Batting Pose; "Outfield"; 32 on back)	.20	.09	.03
☐	32B Amos Otis P2 "Series Starter" (483 on back)	.20	.09	.03
☐	33 Steve Busby	.10	.05	.01
☐	34 U.L. Washington	.10	.05	.01
☐	35 Dave Chalk	.10	.05	.01
☐	36 Darrell Porter	.10	.05	.01
☐	37 Marty Pattin	.10	.05	.01
☐	38 Larry Gura	.10	.05	.01
☐	39 Renie Martin	.10	.05	.01
☐	40 Rich Gale	.10	.05	.01
☐	41A Hal McRae P1 ("Royals" on front in black letters)	.40	.18	.05
☐	41B Hal McRae P2 ("Royals" on front in blue letters)	.20	.09	.03
☐	42 Dennis Leonard	.10	.05	.01
☐	43 Willie Aikens	.10	.05	.01
☐	44 Frank White	.20	.09	.03
☐	45 Clint Hurdle	.10	.05	.01
☐	46 John Wathan	.10	.05	.01
☐	47 Pete LaCock	.10	.05	.01
☐	48 Rance Mulliniks	.10	.05	.01
☐	49 Jeff Twitty	.10	.05	.01
☐	50 Jamie Quirk	.10	.05	.01
☐	51 Art Howe	.20	.09	.03
☐	52 Ken Forsch	.10	.05	.01
☐	53 Vern Ruhle	.10	.05	.01
☐	54 Joe Niekro	.20	.09	.03
☐	55 Frank LaCorte	.10	.05	.01
☐	56 J.R. Richard	.20	.09	.03
☐	57 Nolan Ryan	6.00	2.70	.75
☐	58 Enos Cabell	.10	.05	.01
☐	59 Cesar Cedeno	.20	.09	.03
☐	60 Jose Cruz	.20	.09	.03

☐ 61	Bill Virdon MG	.10	.05	.01
☐ 62	Terry Puhl	.10	.05	.01
☐ 63	Joaquin Andujar	.20	.09	.03
☐ 64	Alan Ashby	.10	.05	.01
☐ 65	Joe Sambito	.10	.05	.01
☐ 66	Denny Walling	.10	.05	.01
☐ 67	Jeff Leonard	.20	.09	.03
☐ 68	Luis Pujols	.10	.05	.01
☐ 69	Bruce Bochy	.10	.05	.01
☐ 70	Rafael Landestoy	.10	.05	.01
☐ 71	Dave Smith	.10	.05	.01
☐ 72	Danny Heep	.10	.05	.01
☐ 73	Julio Gonzalez	.10	.05	.01
☐ 74	Craig Reynolds	.10	.05	.01
☐ 75	Gary Woods	.10	.05	.01
☐ 76	Dave Bergman	.10	.05	.01
☐ 77	Randy Niemann	.10	.05	.01
☐ 78	Joe Morgan	.75	.35	.09
☐ 79	Reggie Jackson	2.00	.90	.25
	(See also 650A)			
☐ 80	Bucky Dent	.20	.09	.03
☐ 81	Tommy John	.30	.14	.04
☐ 82	Luis Tiant	.20	.09	.03
☐ 83	Rick Cerone	.10	.05	.01
☐ 84	Dick Howser MG	.20	.09	.03
☐ 85	Lou Piniella	.20	.09	.03
☐ 86	Ron Davis	.10	.05	.01
☐ 87A	Craig Nettles P1	10.00	4.50	1.25
	ERR (Name on back misspelled "Craig")			
☐ 87B	Graig Nettles P2 COR	.25	.11	.03
	("Graig")			
☐ 88	Ron Guidry	.20	.09	.03
☐ 89	Rich Gossage	.30	.14	.04
☐ 90	Rudy May	.10	.05	.01
☐ 91	Gaylord Perry	.40	.18	.05
☐ 92	Eric Soderholm	.10	.05	.01
☐ 93	Bob Watson	.20	.09	.03
☐ 94	Bobby Murcer	.20	.09	.03
☐ 95	Bobby Brown	.10	.05	.01
☐ 96	Jim Spencer	.10	.05	.01
☐ 97	Tom Underwood	.10	.05	.01
☐ 98	Oscar Gamble	.10	.05	.01
☐ 99	Johnny Oates	.10	.05	.01
☐ 100	Fred Stanley	.10	.05	.01
☐ 101	Ruppert Jones	.10	.05	.01
☐ 102	Dennis Werth	.10	.05	.01
☐ 103	Joe Lefebvre	.10	.05	.01
☐ 104	Brian Doyle	.10	.05	.01
☐ 105	Aurelio Rodriguez	.10	.05	.01
☐ 106	Doug Bird	.10	.05	.01
☐ 107	Mike Griffin	.10	.05	.01
☐ 108	Tim Lollar	.10	.05	.01
☐ 109	Willie Randolph	.20	.09	.03
☐ 110	Steve Garvey	.40	.18	.05
☐ 111	Reggie Smith	.20	.09	.03
☐ 112	Don Sutton	.40	.18	.05
☐ 113	Burt Hooton	.10	.05	.01
☐ 114A	Dave Lopes P1	.40	.18	.05
	(Small hand on back)			
☐ 114B	Dave Lopes P2	.20	.09	.03
	(No hand)			
☐ 115	Dusty Baker	.30	.14	.04
☐ 116	Tom Lasorda MG	.20	.09	.03
☐ 117	Bill Russell	.20	.09	.03
☐ 118	Jerry Reuss UER	.20	.09	.03
	("Home:" omitted)			
☐ 119	Terry Forster	.10	.05	.01
☐ 120A	Bob Welch P1	.20	.09	.03
	(Name on back is "Bob")			
☐ 120B	Bob Welch P2	.30	.14	.04
	(Name on back is "Robert")			
☐ 121	Don Stanhouse	.10	.05	.01
☐ 122	Rick Monday	.20	.09	.03
☐ 123	Derrel Thomas	.10	.05	.01
☐ 124	Joe Ferguson	.10	.05	.01
☐ 125	Rick Sutcliffe	.30	.14	.04
☐ 126A	Ron Cey P1	.40	.18	.05
	(Small hand on back)			
☐ 126B	Ron Cey P2	.20	.09	.03
	(No hand)			
☐ 127	Dave Goltz	.10	.05	.01
☐ 128	Jay Johnstone	.20	.09	.03
☐ 129	Steve Yeager	.10	.05	.01
☐ 130	Gary Weiss	.10	.05	.01
☐ 131	Mike Scioscia	.50	.23	.06
☐ 132	Vic Davalillo	.10	.05	.01
☐ 133	Doug Rau	.10	.05	.01
☐ 134	Pepe Frias	.10	.05	.01
☐ 135	Mickey Hatcher	.10	.05	.01
☐ 136	Steve Howe	.20	.09	.03
☐ 137	Robert Castillo	.10	.05	.01
☐ 138	Gary Thomasson	.10	.05	.01
☐ 139	Rudy Law	.10	.05	.01
☐ 140	Fernando Valenzuela	2.00	.90	.25
	UER (Misspelled Fernand on card)			
☐ 141	Manny Mota	.20	.09	.03
☐ 142	Gary Carter	.75	.35	.09
☐ 143	Steve Rogers	.10	.05	.01
☐ 144	Warren Cromartie	.10	.05	.01
☐ 145	Andre Dawson	1.50	.70	.19
☐ 146	Larry Parrish	.10	.05	.01
☐ 147	Rowland Office	.10	.05	.01
☐ 148	Ellis Valentine	.10	.05	.01
☐ 149	Dick Williams MG	.10	.05	.01
☐ 150	Bill Gullickson	.30	.14	.04
☐ 151	Elias Sosa	.10	.05	.01
☐ 152	John Tamargo	.10	.05	.01
☐ 153	Chris Speier	.10	.05	.01
☐ 154	Ron LeFlore	.20	.09	.03
☐ 155	Rodney Scott	.10	.05	.01
☐ 156	Stan Bahnsen	.10	.05	.01
☐ 157	Bill Lee	.10	.05	.01
☐ 158	Fred Norman	.10	.05	.01
☐ 159	Woodie Fryman	.10	.05	.01
☐ 160	David Palmer	.10	.05	.01
☐ 161	Jerry White	.10	.05	.01
☐ 162	Roberto Ramos	.10	.05	.01
☐ 163	John D'Acquisto	.10	.05	.01
☐ 164	Tommy Hutton	.10	.05	.01
☐ 165	Charlie Lea	.10	.05	.01
☐ 166	Scott Sanderson	.20	.09	.03
☐ 167	Ken Macha	.10	.05	.01
☐ 168	Tony Bernazard	.10	.05	.01
☐ 169	Jim Palmer	.75	.35	.09
☐ 170	Steve Stone	.20	.09	.03
☐ 171	Mike Flanagan	.20	.09	.03
☐ 172	Al Bumbry	.20	.09	.03
☐ 173	Doug DeCinces	.20	.09	.03
☐ 174	Scott McGregor	.10	.05	.01
☐ 175	Mark Belanger	.20	.09	.03
☐ 176	Tim Stoddard	.10	.05	.01
☐ 177A	Rick Dempsey P1	.40	.18	.05
	(Small hand on front)			
☐ 177B	Rick Dempsey P2	.20	.09	.03
	(No hand)			
☐ 178	Earl Weaver MG	.20	.09	.03
☐ 179	Tippy Martinez	.20	.09	.03
☐ 180	Dennis Martinez	.20	.09	.03

□ 181 Sammy Stewart	.10	.05	.01
□ 182 Rich Dauer	.10	.05	.01
□ 183 Lee May	.20	.09	.03
□ 184 Eddie Murray	4.00	1.80	.50
□ 185 Benny Ayala	.10	.05	.01
□ 186 John Lowenstein	.10	.05	.01
□ 187 Gary Roenicke	.10	.05	.01
□ 188 Ken Singleton	.20	.09	.03
□ 189 Dan Graham	.10	.05	.01
□ 190 Terry Crowley	.10	.05	.01
□ 191 Kiko Garcia	.10	.05	.01
□ 192 Dave Ford	.10	.05	.01
□ 193 Mark Corey	.10	.05	.01
□ 194 Lenn Sakata	.10	.05	.01
□ 195 Doug DeCinces	.20	.09	.03
□ 196 Johnny Bench	1.25	.55	.16
□ 197 Dave Concepcion	.20	.09	.03
□ 198 Ray Knight	.20	.09	.03
□ 199 Ken Griffey	.10	.05	.01
□ 200 Tom Seaver	1.25	.55	.16
□ 201 Dave Collins	.10	.05	.01
□ 202A George Foster P1	.20	.09	.03
Slugger			
(Number on back 216)			
□ 202B George Foster P2	.20	.09	.03
Slugger			
(Number on back 202)			
□ 203 Junior Kennedy	.10	.05	.01
□ 204 Frank Pastore	.10	.05	.01
□ 205 Dan Driessen	.10	.05	.01
□ 206 Hector Cruz	.10	.05	.01
□ 207 Paul Moskau	.10	.05	.01
□ 208 Charlie Leibrandt	.30	.14	.04
□ 209 Harry Spilman	.10	.05	.01
□ 210 Joe Price	.10	.05	.01
□ 211 Tom Hume	.10	.05	.01
□ 212 Joe Nolan	.10	.05	.01
□ 213 Doug Bair	.10	.05	.01
□ 214 Mario Soto	.10	.05	.01
□ 215A Bill Bonham P1	.40	.18	.05
(Small hand on back)			
□ 215B Bill Bonham P2	.10	.05	.01
(No hand)			
□ 216 George Foster	.20	.09	.03
(See 202)			
□ 217 Paul Householder	.10	.05	.01
□ 218 Ron Oester	.10	.05	.01
□ 219 Sam Mejias	.10	.05	.01
□ 220 Sheldon Burnside	.10	.05	.01
□ 221 Carl Yastrzemski	1.00	.45	.12
□ 222 Jim Rice	.40	.18	.05
□ 223 Fred Lynn	.20	.09	.03
□ 224 Carlton Fisk	1.25	.55	.16
□ 225 Rick Burleson	.10	.05	.01
□ 226 Dennis Eckersley	.75	.35	.09
□ 227 Butch Hobson	.20	.09	.03
□ 228 Tom Burgmeier	.10	.05	.01
□ 229 Garry Hancock	.10	.05	.01
□ 230 Don Zimmer MG	.10	.05	.01
□ 231 Steve Renko	.10	.05	.01
□ 232 Dwight Evans	.30	.14	.04
□ 233 Mike Torrez	.10	.05	.01
□ 234 Bob Stanley	.10	.05	.01
□ 235 Jim Dwyer	.10	.05	.01
□ 236 Dave Stapleton	.10	.05	.01
□ 237 Glenn Hoffman	.10	.05	.01
□ 238 Jerry Remy	.10	.05	.01
□ 239 Dick Drago	.10	.05	.01
□ 240 Bill Campbell	.10	.05	.01
□ 241 Tony Perez	.40	.18	.05
□ 242 Phil Niekro	.40	.18	.05
□ 243 Dale Murphy	.75	.35	.09
□ 244 Bob Horner	.20	.09	.03
□ 245 Jeff Burroughs	.10	.05	.01
□ 246 Rick Camp	.10	.05	.01
□ 247 Bobby Cox MG	.10	.05	.01
□ 248 Bruce Benedict	.10	.05	.01
□ 249 Gene Garber	.10	.05	.01
□ 250 Jerry Royster	.10	.05	.01
□ 251A Gary Matthews P1	.40	.18	.05
(Small hand on back)			
□ 251B Gary Matthews P2	.20	.09	.03
(No hand)			
□ 252 Chris Chambliss	.20	.09	.03
□ 253 Luis Gomez	.10	.05	.01
□ 254 Bill Nahorodny	.10	.05	.01
□ 255 Doyle Alexander	.10	.05	.01
□ 256 Brian Asselstine	.10	.05	.01
□ 257 Biff Pocoroba	.10	.05	.01
□ 258 Mike Lum	.10	.05	.01
□ 259 Charlie Spikes	.10	.05	.01
□ 260 Glenn Hubbard	.10	.05	.01
□ 261 Tommy Boggs	.10	.05	.01
□ 262 Al Hrabosky	.10	.05	.01
□ 263 Rick Matula	.10	.05	.01
□ 264 Preston Hanna	.10	.05	.01
□ 265 Larry Bradford	.10	.05	.01
□ 266 Rafael Ramirez	.20	.09	.03
□ 267 Larry McWilliams	.10	.05	.01
□ 268 Rod Carew	.75	.35	.09
□ 269 Bobby Grich	.20	.09	.03
□ 270 Carney Lansford	.20	.09	.03
□ 271 Don Baylor	.30	.14	.04
□ 272 Joe Rudi	.20	.09	.03
□ 273 Dan Ford	.10	.05	.01
□ 274 Jim Fregosi MG	.10	.05	.01
□ 275 Dave Frost	.10	.05	.01
□ 276 Frank Tanana	.20	.09	.03
□ 277 Dickie Thon	.20	.09	.03
□ 278 Jason Thompson	.20	.09	.03
□ 279 Rick Miller	.10	.05	.01
□ 280 Bert Campaneris	.20	.09	.03
□ 281 Tom Donohue	.10	.05	.01
□ 282 Brian Downing	.20	.09	.03
□ 283 Fred Patek	.10	.05	.01
□ 284 Bruce Kison	.10	.05	.01
□ 285 Dave LaRoche	.10	.05	.01
□ 286 Don Aase	.10	.05	.01
□ 287 Jim Barr	.10	.05	.01
□ 288 Alfredo Martinez	.10	.05	.01
□ 289 Larry Harlow	.10	.05	.01
□ 290 Andy Hassler	.10	.05	.01
□ 291 Dave Kingman	.20	.09	.03
□ 292 Bill Buckner	.20	.09	.03
□ 293 Rick Reuschel	.20	.09	.03
□ 294 Bruce Sutter	.20	.09	.03
□ 295 Jerry Martin	.10	.05	.01
□ 296 Scot Thompson	.10	.05	.01
□ 297 Ivan DeJesus	.10	.05	.01
□ 298 Steve Dillard	.10	.05	.01
□ 299 Dick Tidrow	.10	.05	.01
□ 300 Randy Martz	.10	.05	.01
□ 301 Lenny Randle	.10	.05	.01
□ 302 Lynn McGlothen	.10	.05	.01
□ 303 Cliff Johnson	.10	.05	.01
□ 304 Tim Blackwell	.10	.05	.01
□ 305 Dennis Lamp	.10	.05	.01
□ 306 Bill Caudill	.10	.05	.01
□ 307 Carlos Lezcano	.10	.05	.01
□ 308 Jim Tracy	.10	.05	.01
□ 309 Doug Capilla UER	.10	.05	.01
(Cubs on front but			

Braves on back)

☐ 310	Willie Hernandez	.20	.09	.03
☐ 311	Mike Vail	.10	.05	.01
☐ 312	Mike Krukow	.10	.05	.01
☐ 313	Barry Foote	.10	.05	.01
☐ 314	Larry Biittner	.10	.05	.01
☐ 315	Mike Tyson	.10	.05	.01
☐ 316	Lee Mazzilli	.10	.05	.01
☐ 317	John Stearns	.10	.05	.01
☐ 318	Alex Trevino	.10	.05	.01
☐ 319	Craig Swan	.10	.05	.01
☐ 320	Frank Taveras	.10	.05	.01
☐ 321	Steve Henderson	.10	.05	.01
☐ 322	Neil Allen	.10	.05	.01
☐ 323	Mark Bomback	.10	.05	.01
☐ 324	Mike Jorgensen	.10	.05	.01
☐ 325	Joe Torre MG	.20	.09	.03
☐ 326	Elliott Maddox	.10	.05	.01
☐ 327	Pete Falcone	.10	.05	.01
☐ 328	Ray Burris	.10	.05	.01
☐ 329	Claudell Washington	.10	.05	.01
☐ 330	Doug Flynn	.10	.05	.01
☐ 331	Joel Youngblood	.10	.05	.01
☐ 332	Bill Almon	.10	.05	.01
☐ 333	Tom Hausman	.10	.05	.01
☐ 334	Pat Zachry	.10	.05	.01
☐ 335	Jeff Reardon	1.00	.45	.12
☐ 336	Wally Backman	.20	.09	.03
☐ 337	Dan Norman	.10	.05	.01
☐ 338	Jerry Morales	.10	.05	.01
☐ 339	Ed Farmer	.10	.05	.01
☐ 340	Bob Molinaro	.10	.05	.01
☐ 341	Todd Cruz	.10	.05	.01
☐ 342A	Britt Burns P1	.40	.18	.05
	(Small hand on front)			
☐ 342B	Britt Burns P2	.20	.09	.03
	(No hand)			
☐ 343	Kevin Bell	.10	.05	.01
☐ 344	Tony LaRussa MG	.20	.09	.03
☐ 345	Steve Trout	.10	.05	.01
☐ 346	Harold Baines	3.00	1.35	.35
☐ 347	Richard Wortham	.10	.05	.01
☐ 348	Wayne Nordhagen	.10	.05	.01
☐ 349	Mike Squires	.10	.05	.01
☐ 350	Lamar Johnson	.10	.05	.01
☐ 351	Rickey Henderson	3.00	1.35	.35
	(Most Stolen Bases AL)			
☐ 352	Francisco Barrios	.10	.05	.01
☐ 353	Thad Bosley	.10	.05	.01
☐ 354	Chet Lemon	.10	.05	.01
☐ 355	Bruce Kimm	.10	.05	.01
☐ 356	Richard Dotson	.20	.09	.03
☐ 357	Jim Morrison	.10	.05	.01
☐ 358	Mike Proly	.10	.05	.01
☐ 359	Greg Pryor	.10	.05	.01
☐ 360	Dave Parker	.30	.14	.04
☐ 361	Omar Moreno	.10	.05	.01
☐ 362A	Kent Tekulve P1	.20	.09	.03
	(Back "1071 Waterbury" and "1078 Pirates")			
☐ 362B	Kent Tekulve P2	.20	.09	.03
	("1971 Waterbury" and "1978 Pirates")			
☐ 363	Willie Stargell	.75	.35	.09
☐ 364	Phil Garner	.20	.09	.03
☐ 365	Ed Ott	.10	.05	.01
☐ 366	Don Robinson	.10	.05	.01
☐ 367	Chuck Tanner MG	.10	.05	.01
☐ 368	Jim Rooker	.10	.05	.01
☐ 369	Dale Berra	.10	.05	.01
☐ 370	Jim Bibby	.10	.05	.01
☐ 371	Steve Nicosia	.10	.05	.01
☐ 372	Mike Easler	.10	.05	.01
☐ 373	Bill Robinson	.20	.09	.03
☐ 374	Lee Lacy	.10	.05	.01
☐ 375	John Candelaria	.20	.09	.03
☐ 376	Manny Sanguillen	.20	.09	.03
☐ 377	Rick Rhoden	.10	.05	.01
☐ 378	Grant Jackson	.10	.05	.01
☐ 379	Tim Foli	.10	.05	.01
☐ 380	Rod Scurry	.10	.05	.01
☐ 381	Bill Madlock	.20	.09	.03
☐ 382A	Kurt Bevacqua P1 ERR	.20	.09	.03
	(P on cap backwards)			
☐ 382B	Kurt Bevacqua P2 COR	.10	.05	.01
☐ 383	Bert Blyleven	.30	.14	.04
☐ 384	Eddie Solomon	.10	.05	.01
☐ 385	Enrique Romo	.10	.05	.01
☐ 386	John Milner	.10	.05	.01
☐ 387	Mike Hargrove	.20	.09	.03
☐ 388	Jorge Orta	.10	.05	.01
☐ 389	Toby Harrah	.20	.09	.03
☐ 390	Tom Veryzer	.10	.05	.01
☐ 391	Miguel Dilone	.10	.05	.01
☐ 392	Dan Spillner	.10	.05	.01
☐ 393	Jack Brohamer	.10	.05	.01
☐ 394	Wayne Garland	.10	.05	.01
☐ 395	Sid Monge	.10	.05	.01
☐ 396	Rick Waits	.10	.05	.01
☐ 397	Joe Charboneau	.20	.09	.03
☐ 398	Gary Alexander	.10	.05	.01
☐ 399	Jerry Dybzinski	.10	.05	.01
☐ 400	Mike Stanton	.10	.05	.01
☐ 401	Mike Paxton	.10	.05	.01
☐ 402	Gary Gray	.10	.05	.01
☐ 403	Rick Manning	.10	.05	.01
☐ 404	Bo Diaz	.10	.05	.01
☐ 405	Ron Hassey	.10	.05	.01
☐ 406	Ross Grimsley	.10	.05	.01
☐ 407	Victor Cruz	.10	.05	.01
☐ 408	Len Barker	.10	.05	.01
☐ 409	Bob Bailor	.10	.05	.01
☐ 410	Otto Velez	.10	.05	.01
☐ 411	Ernie Whitt	.10	.05	.01
☐ 412	Jim Clancy	.10	.05	.01
☐ 413	Barry Bonnell	.10	.05	.01
☐ 414	Dave Stieb	.20	.09	.03
☐ 415	Damaso Garcia	.20	.09	.03
☐ 416	John Mayberry	.10	.05	.01
☐ 417	Roy Howell	.10	.05	.01
☐ 418	Danny Ainge	3.00	1.35	.35
☐ 419A	Jesse Jefferson P1	.10	.05	.01
	(Back says Pirates)			
☐ 419B	Jesse Jefferson P2	.10	.05	.01
	(Back says Pirates)			
☐ 419C	Jesse Jefferson P3	.20	.09	.03
	(Back says Blue Jays)			
☐ 420	Joey McLaughlin	.10	.05	.01
☐ 421	Lloyd Moseby	.20	.09	.03
☐ 422	Alvis Woods	.10	.05	.01
☐ 423	Garth Iorg	.10	.05	.01
☐ 424	Doug Ault	.10	.05	.01
☐ 425	Ken Schrom	.10	.05	.01
☐ 426	Mike Willis	.10	.05	.01
☐ 427	Steve Braun	.10	.05	.01
☐ 428	Bob Davis	.10	.05	.01
☐ 429	Jerry Garvin	.10	.05	.01
☐ 430	Alfredo Griffin	.10	.05	.01
☐ 431	Bob Mattick MG	.10	.05	.01
☐ 432	Vida Blue	.20	.09	.03

☐ 433 Jack Clark	.20	.09	.03	☐ 493A Tim Flannery P1 .... .20	.09	.03
☐ 434 Willie McCovey	.75	.35	.09	(Batting right)		
☐ 435 Mike Ivie	.10	.05	.01	☐ 493B Tim Flannery P2 .... .10	.05	.01
☐ 436A Darrel Evans P1 ERR.	.30	.14	.04	(Batting left)		

☐ 433 Jack Clark .20 .09 .03
☐ 434 Willie McCovey .75 .35 .09
☐ 435 Mike Ivie .10 .05 .01
☐ 436A Darrel Evans P1 ERR. .30 .14 .04
(Name on front
"Darrel")
☐ 436B Darrell Evans P2 COR .30 .14 .04
(Name on front
"Darrell")
☐ 437 Terry Whitfield .10 .05 .01
☐ 438 Rennie Stennett .10 .05 .01
☐ 439 John Montefusco .10 .05 .01
☐ 440 Jim Wohlford .10 .05 .01
☐ 441 Bill North .10 .05 .01
☐ 442 Milt May .10 .05 .01
☐ 443 Max Venable .10 .05 .01
☐ 444 Ed Whitson .10 .05 .01
☐ 445 Al Holland .10 .05 .01
☐ 446 Randy Moffitt .10 .05 .01
☐ 447 Bob Knepper .10 .05 .01
☐ 448 Gary Lavelle .10 .05 .01
☐ 449 Greg Minton .10 .05 .01
☐ 450 Johnnie LeMaster .10 .05 .01
☐ 451 Larry Herndon .10 .05 .01
☐ 452 Rich Murray .10 .05 .01
☐ 453 Joe Pettini .10 .05 .01
☐ 454 Allen Ripley .10 .05 .01
☐ 455 Dennis Littlejohn .10 .05 .01
☐ 456 Tom Griffin .10 .05 .01
☐ 457 Alan Hargesheimer .10 .05 .01
☐ 458 Joe Strain .10 .05 .01
☐ 459 Steve Kemp .10 .05 .01
☐ 460 Sparky Anderson MG .20 .09 .03
☐ 461 Alan Trammell 1.50 .70 .19
☐ 462 Mark Fidrych .20 .09 .03
☐ 463 Lou Whitaker 1.00 .45 .12
☐ 464 Dave Rozema .10 .05 .01
☐ 465 Milt Wilcox .10 .05 .01
☐ 466 Champ Summers .10 .05 .01
☐ 467 Lance Parrish .30 .14 .04
☐ 468 Dan Petry .20 .09 .03
☐ 469 Pat Underwood .10 .05 .01
☐ 470 Rick Peters .10 .05 .01
☐ 471 Al Cowens .10 .05 .01
☐ 472 John Wockenfuss .10 .05 .01
☐ 473 Tom Brookens .10 .05 .01
☐ 474 Richie Hebner .10 .05 .01
☐ 475 Jack Morris .40 .18 .05
☐ 476 Jim Lentine .10 .05 .01
☐ 477 Bruce Robbins .10 .05 .01
☐ 478 Mark Wagner .10 .05 .01
☐ 479 Tim Corcoran .10 .05 .01
☐ 480A Stan Papi P1 .20 .09 .03
(Front as Pitcher)
☐ 480B Stan Papi P2 .10 .05 .01
(Front as Shortstop)
☐ 481 Kirk Gibson 3.00 1.35 .35
☐ 482 Dan Schatzeder .10 .05 .01
☐ 483A Amos Otis P1 .20 .09 .03
(See card 32)
☐ 483B Amos Otis P2 .20 .09 .03
(See card 32)
☐ 484 Dave Winfield 2.00 .90 .25
☐ 485 Rollie Fingers .40 .18 .05
☐ 486 Gene Richards .10 .05 .01
☐ 487 Randy Jones .10 .05 .01
☐ 488 Ozzie Smith 3.50 1.55 .45
☐ 489 Gene Tenace .10 .05 .01
☐ 490 Bill Fahey .10 .05 .01
☐ 491 John Curtis .10 .05 .01
☐ 492 Dave Cash .10 .05 .01

☐ 493A Tim Flannery P1 .20 .09 .03
(Batting right)
☐ 493B Tim Flannery P2 .10 .05 .01
(Batting left)
☐ 494 Jerry Mumphrey .10 .05 .01
☐ 495 Bob Shirley .10 .05 .01
☐ 496 Steve Mura .10 .05 .01
☐ 497 Eric Rasmussen .10 .05 .01
☐ 498 Broderick Perkins .10 .05 .01
☐ 499 Barry Evans .10 .05 .01
☐ 500 Chuck Baker .10 .05 .01
☐ 501 Luis Salazar .10 .05 .01
☐ 502 Gary Lucas .10 .05 .01
☐ 503 Mike Armstrong .10 .05 .01
☐ 504 Jerry Turner .10 .05 .01
☐ 505 Dennis Kinney .10 .05 .01
☐ 506 Willie Montanez UER .... .10 .05 .01
(Misspelled Willy
on card front)
☐ 507 Gorman Thomas .20 .09 .03
☐ 508 Ben Oglivie .20 .09 .03
☐ 509 Larry Hisle .10 .05 .01
☐ 510 Sal Bando .20 .09 .03
☐ 511 Robin Yount 2.00 .90 .25
☐ 512 Mike Caldwell .10 .05 .01
☐ 513 Sixto Lezcano .10 .05 .01
☐ 514A Bill Travers P1 ERR .... .20 .09 .03
("Jerry Augustine"
with Augustine back)
☐ 514B Bill Travers P2 COR .... .10 .05 .01
☐ 515 Paul Molitor 1.50 .70 .19
☐ 516 Moose Haas .10 .05 .01
☐ 517 Bill Castro .10 .05 .01
☐ 518 Jim Slaton .10 .05 .01
☐ 519 Lary Sorensen .10 .05 .01
☐ 520 Bob McClure .10 .05 .01
☐ 521 Charlie Moore .10 .05 .01
☐ 522 Jim Gantner .20 .09 .03
☐ 523 Reggie Cleveland .10 .05 .01
☐ 524 Don Money .10 .05 .01
☐ 525 Bill Travers .10 .05 .01
☐ 526 Buck Martinez .10 .05 .01
☐ 527 Dick Davis .10 .05 .01
☐ 528 Ted Simmons .20 .09 .03
☐ 529 Garry Templeton .20 .09 .03
☐ 530 Ken Reitz .10 .05 .01
☐ 531 Tony Scott .10 .05 .01
☐ 532 Ken Oberkfell .10 .05 .01
☐ 533 Bob Sykes .10 .05 .01
☐ 534 Keith Smith .10 .05 .01
☐ 535 John Littlefield .10 .05 .01
☐ 536 Jim Kaat .20 .09 .03
☐ 537 Bob Forsch .10 .05 .01
☐ 538 Mike Phillips .10 .05 .01
☐ 539 Terry Landrum .10 .05 .01
☐ 540 Leon Durham .20 .09 .03
☐ 541 Terry Kennedy .10 .05 .01
☐ 542 George Hendrick .20 .09 .03
☐ 543 Dane Iorg .10 .05 .01
☐ 544 Mark Littell .10 .05 .01
☐ 545 Keith Hernandez .30 .14 .04
☐ 546 Silvio Martinez .10 .05 .01
☐ 547A Don Hood P1 ERR .... .20 .09 .03
("Pete Vuckovich"
with Vuckovich back)
☐ 547B Don Hood P2 COR ...... .10 .05 .01
☐ 548 Bobby Bonds .20 .09 .03
☐ 549 Mike Ramsey .10 .05 .01
☐ 550 Tom Herr .20 .09 .03
☐ 551 Roy Smalley .10 .05 .01
☐ 552 Jerry Koosman .20 .09 .03

☐ 553	Ken Landreaux	.10	.05	.01
☐ 554	John Castino	.10	.05	.01
☐ 555	Doug Corbett	.10	.05	.01
☐ 556	Bombo Rivera	.10	.05	.01
☐ 557	Ron Jackson	.10	.05	.01
☐ 558	Butch Wynegar	.10	.05	.01
☐ 559	Hosken Powell	.10	.05	.01
☐ 560	Pete Redfern	.10	.05	.01
☐ 561	Roger Erickson	.10	.05	.01
☐ 562	Glenn Adams	.10	.05	.01
☐ 563	Rick Sofield	.10	.05	.01
☐ 564	Geoff Zahn	.10	.05	.01
☐ 565	Pete Mackanin	.10	.05	.01
☐ 566	Mike Cubbage	.10	.05	.01
☐ 567	Darrell Jackson	.10	.05	.01
☐ 568	Dave Edwards	.10	.05	.01
☐ 569	Rob Wilfong	.10	.05	.01
☐ 570	Sal Butera	.10	.05	.01
☐ 571	Jose Morales	.10	.05	.01
☐ 572	Rick Langford	.10	.05	.01
☐ 573	Mike Norris	.10	.05	.01
☐ 574	Rickey Henderson	5.00	2.20	.60
☐ 575	Tony Armas	.20	.09	.03
☐ 576	Dave Revering	.10	.05	.01
☐ 577	Jeff Newman	.10	.05	.01
☐ 578	Bob Lacey	.10	.05	.01
☐ 579	Brian Kingman	.10	.05	.01
☐ 580	Mitchell Page	.10	.05	.01
☐ 581	Billy Martin MG	.30	.14	.04
☐ 582	Rob Picciolo	.10	.05	.01
☐ 583	Mike Heath	.10	.05	.01
☐ 584	Mickey Klutts	.10	.05	.01
☐ 585	Orlando Gonzalez	.10	.05	.01
☐ 586	Mike Davis	.10	.05	.01
☐ 587	Wayne Gross	.10	.05	.01
☐ 588	Matt Keough	.10	.05	.01
☐ 589	Steve McCatty	.10	.05	.01
☐ 590	Dwayne Murphy	.10	.05	.01
☐ 591	Mario Guerrero	.10	.05	.01
☐ 592	Dave McKay	.10	.05	.01
☐ 593	Jim Essian	.10	.05	.01
☐ 594	Dave Heaverlo	.10	.05	.01
☐ 595	Maury Wills MG	.20	.09	.03
☐ 596	Juan Beniquez	.10	.05	.01
☐ 597	Rodney Craig	.10	.05	.01
☐ 598	Jim Anderson	.10	.05	.01
☐ 599	Floyd Bannister	.10	.05	.01
☐ 600	Bruce Bochte	.10	.05	.01
☐ 601	Julio Cruz	.10	.05	.01
☐ 602	Ted Cox	.10	.05	.01
☐ 603	Dan Meyer	.10	.05	.01
☐ 604	Larry Cox	.10	.05	.01
☐ 605	Bill Stein	.10	.05	.01
☐ 606	Steve Garvey	.40	.18	.05
	(Most Hits NL)			
☐ 607	Dave Roberts	.10	.05	.01
☐ 608	Leon Roberts	.10	.05	.01
☐ 609	Reggie Walton	.10	.05	.01
☐ 610	Dave Edler	.10	.05	.01
☐ 611	Larry Milbourne	.10	.05	.01
☐ 612	Kim Allen	.10	.05	.01
☐ 613	Mario Mendoza	.10	.05	.01
☐ 614	Tom Paciorek	.20	.09	.03
☐ 615	Glenn Abbott	.10	.05	.01
☐ 616	Joe Simpson	.10	.05	.01
☐ 617	Mickey Rivers	.20	.09	.03
☐ 618	Jim Kern	.10	.05	.01
☐ 619	Jim Sundberg	.20	.09	.03
☐ 620	Richie Zisk	.10	.05	.01
☐ 621	Jon Matlack	.10	.05	.01
☐ 622	Ferguson Jenkins	.40	.18	.05

☐ 623	Pat Corrales MG	.10	.05	.01
☐ 624	Ed Figueroa	.10	.05	.01
☐ 625	Buddy Bell	.20	.09	.03
☐ 626	Al Oliver	.20	.09	.03
☐ 627	Doc Medich	.10	.05	.01
☐ 628	Bump Wills	.10	.05	.01
☐ 629	Rusty Staub	.20	.09	.03
☐ 630	Pat Putnam	.10	.05	.01
☐ 631	John Grubb	.10	.05	.01
☐ 632	Danny Darwin	.20	.09	.03
☐ 633	Ken Clay	.10	.05	.01
☐ 634	Jim Norris	.10	.05	.01
☐ 635	John Butcher	.10	.05	.01
☐ 636	Dave Roberts	.10	.05	.01
☐ 637	Billy Sample	.10	.05	.01
☐ 638	Carl Yastrzemski	1.00	.45	.12
☐ 639	Cecil Cooper	.20	.09	.03
☐ 640A	Mike Schmidt P1	2.00	.90	.25
	(Portrait;			
	"Third Base";			
	number on back 5)			
☐ 640B	Mike Schmidt P2	2.00	.90	.25
	("1980 Home Run King";			
	640 on back)			
☐ 641A	CL: Phils/Royals P1	.20	.09	.03
	41 is Hal McRae			
☐ 641B	CL: Phils/Royals P2	.20	.09	.03
	(41 is Hal McRae,			
	Double Threat)			
☐ 642	CL: Astros/Yankees	.20	.09	.03
☐ 643	CL: Expos/Dodgers	.20	.09	.03
☐ 644A	CL: Reds/Orioles P1	.20	.09	.03
	(202 is George Foster;			
	Joe Nolan pitcher;			
	should be catcher)			
☐ 644B	CL: Reds/Orioles P2	.20	.09	.03
	(202 is Foster Slugger;			
	Joe Nolan pitcher,			
	should be catcher)			
☐ 645A	Pete Rose	2.50	1.10	.30
	Larry Bowa			
	Mike Schmidt			
	Triple Threat P1			
	(No number on back)			
☐ 645B	Pete Rose	2.00	.90	.25
	Larry Bowa			
	Mike Schmidt			
	Triple Threat P2			
	(Back numbered 645)			
☐ 646	CL: Braves/Red Sox	.20	.09	.03
☐ 647	CL: Cubs/Angels	.20	.09	.03
☐ 648	CL: Mets/White Sox	.20	.09	.03
☐ 649	CL: Indians/Pirates	.20	.09	.03
☐ 650A	Reggie Jackson	2.00	.90	.25
	Mr. Baseball P1			
	(Number on back 79)			
☐ 650B	Reggie Jackson	2.00	.90	.25
	Mr. Baseball P2			
	(Number on back 650)			
☐ 651	CL: Giants/Blue Jays	.20	.09	.03
☐ 652A	CL: Tigers/Padres P1	.20	.09	.03
	(483 is listed)			
☐ 652B	CL: Tigers/Padres P2	.20	.09	.03
	(483 is deleted)			
☐ 653A	Willie Wilson P1	.20	.09	.03
	Most Hits Most Runs			
	(Number on back 29)			
☐ 653B	Willie Wilson P2	.20	.09	.03
	Most Hits Most Runs			
	(Number on back 653)			
☐ 654A	CL:Brewers/Cards P1	.20	.09	.03

		NRMT-MT	EXC	G-VG
	(514 Jerry Augustine; 547 Pete Vuckovich)			
☐ 654B	CL:Brewers/Cards P2. (514 Billy Travers; 547 Don Hood)	.20	.09	.03
☐ 655A	George Brett P1 .390 Average (Number on back 28)	4.00	1.80	.50
☐ 655B	George Brett P2 .390 Average (Number on back 655)	4.00	1.80	.50
☐ 656	CL: Twins/Oakland A's.	.20	.09	.03
☐ 657A	Tug McGraw P1 Game Saver (Number on back 7)	.20	.09	.03
☐ 657B	Tug McGraw P2 Game Saver (Number on back 657)	.20	.09	.03
☐ 658	CL: Rangers/Mariners..	.20	.09	.03
☐ 659A	Checklist P1 of Special Cards (Last lines on front, Wilson Most Hits)	.20	.09	.03
☐ 659B	Checklist P2 of Special Cards (Last lines on front, Otis Series Starter)	.20	.09	.03
☐ 660A	Steve Carlton P1 Golden Arm (Number on back 660; Back "1066 Cardinals")	1.50	.70	.19
☐ 660B	Steve Carlton P2 Golden Arm ("1966 Cardinals")	2.00	.90	.25

1982 Fleer

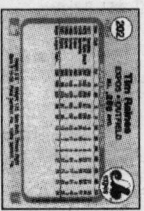

The cards in this 660-card set measure 2 1/2" by 3 1/2". The 1982 Fleer set is again ordered by teams; in fact, the players within each team are listed in alphabetical order. The teams are ordered (by 1981 standings) as follows: Los Angeles (1-29), New York Yankees (30-56), Cincinnati (57-84), Oakland (85-109), St. Louis (110-132), Milwaukee (133-156), Baltimore (157-182), Montreal (183-211), Houston (212-237), Philadelphia (238-262), Detroit (263-286), Boston (287-312), Texas (313-334), Chicago White Sox (335-358), Cleveland (359-382), San Francisco (383-403), Kansas City (404-427), Atlanta (428-449), California (450-474), Pittsburgh (475-501),

Seattle (502-519), New York Mets (520-544), Minnesota (545-565), San Diego (566-585), Chicago Cubs (586-607), and Toronto (608-627). Cards numbered 628 through 646 are special cards highlighting some of the stars and leaders of the 1981 season. The last 14 cards in the set (647-660) are checklist cards. The backs feature player statistics and a full-color team logo in the upper right-hand corner of each card. The complete set price below does not include any of the more valuable variation cards listed. Rookie Cards in this set include George Bell, Cal Ripken Jr., Steve Sax, Lee Smith, and Dave Stewart.

		NRMT-MT	EXC	G-VG
COMPLETE SET (660)		70.00	32.00	8.75
COMMON CARD (1-660)		.10	.05	.01
☐ 1	Dusty Baker	.30	.14	.04
☐ 2	Robert Castillo	.10	.05	.01
☐ 3	Ron Cey	.20	.09	.03
☐ 4	Terry Forster	.10	.05	.01
☐ 5	Steve Garvey	.40	.18	.05
☐ 6	Dave Goltz	.10	.05	.01
☐ 7	Pedro Guerrero	.20	.09	.03
☐ 8	Burt Hooton	.10	.05	.01
☐ 9	Steve Howe	.10	.05	.01
☐ 10	Jay Johnstone	.20	.09	.03
☐ 11	Ken Landreaux	.10	.05	.01
☐ 12	Dave Lopes	.20	.09	.03
☐ 13	Mike A. Marshall	.20	.09	.03
☐ 14	Bobby Mitchell	.10	.05	.01
☐ 15	Rick Monday	.10	.05	.01
☐ 16	Tom Niedenfuer	.10	.05	.01
☐ 17	Ted Power	.10	.05	.01
☐ 18	Jerry Reuss UER	.10	.05	.01
	("Home:" omitted)			
☐ 19	Ron Roenicke	.10	.05	.01
☐ 20	Bill Russell	.20	.09	.03
☐ 21	Steve Sax	.50	.23	.06
☐ 22	Mike Scioscia	.20	.09	.03
☐ 23	Reggie Smith	.20	.09	.03
☐ 24	Dave Stewart	1.50	.70	.19
☐ 25	Rick Sutcliffe	.20	.09	.03
☐ 26	Derrel Thomas	.10	.05	.01
☐ 27	Fernando Valenzuela	.30	.14	.04
☐ 28	Bob Welch	.20	.09	.03
☐ 29	Steve Yeager	.10	.05	.01
☐ 30	Bobby Brown	.10	.05	.01
☐ 31	Rick Cerone	.10	.05	.01
☐ 32	Ron Davis	.10	.05	.01
☐ 33	Bucky Dent	.20	.09	.03
☐ 34	Barry Foote	.10	.05	.01
☐ 35	George Frazier	.10	.05	.01
☐ 36	Oscar Gamble	.10	.05	.01
☐ 37	Rich Gossage	.30	.14	.04
☐ 38	Ron Guidry	.20	.09	.03
☐ 39	Reggie Jackson	1.00	.45	.12
☐ 40	Tommy John	.30	.14	.04
☐ 41	Rudy May	.10	.05	.01
☐ 42	Larry Milbourne	.10	.05	.01
☐ 43	Jerry Mumphrey	.10	.05	.01
☐ 44	Bobby Murcer	.20	.09	.03
☐ 45	Gene Nelson	.10	.05	.01
☐ 46	Graig Nettles	.20	.09	.03
☐ 47	Johnny Oates	.10	.05	.01
☐ 48	Lou Piniella	.20	.09	.03
☐ 49	Willie Randolph	.20	.09	.03
☐ 50	Rick Reuschel	.20	.09	.03

□	51	Dave Revering	.10	.05	.01
□	52	Dave Righetti	.40	.18	.05
□	53	Aurelio Rodriguez	.10	.05	.01
□	54	Bob Watson	.20	.09	.03
□	55	Dennis Werth	.10	.05	.01
□	56	Dave Winfield	1.50	.70	.19
□	57	Johnny Bench	.75	.35	.09
□	58	Bruce Berenyi	.10	.05	.01
□	59	Larry Biittner	.10	.05	.01
□	60	Scott Brown	.10	.05	.01
□	61	Dave Collins	.10	.05	.01
□	62	Geoff Combe	.10	.05	.01
□	63	Dave Concepcion	.20	.09	.03
□	64	Dan Driessen	.10	.05	.01
□	65	Joe Edelen	.10	.05	.01
□	66	George Foster	.20	.09	.03
□	67	Ken Griffey	.10	.05	.01
□	68	Paul Householder	.10	.05	.01
□	69	Tom Hume	.10	.05	.01
□	70	Junior Kennedy	.10	.05	.01
□	71	Ray Knight	.20	.09	.03
□	72	Mike LaCoss	.10	.05	.01
□	73	Rafael Landestoy	.10	.05	.01
□	74	Charlie Leibrandt	.10	.05	.01
□	75	Sam Mejias	.10	.05	.01
□	76	Paul Moskau	.10	.05	.01
□	77	Joe Nolan	.10	.05	.01
□	78	Mike O'Berry	.10	.05	.01
□	79	Ron Oester	.10	.05	.01
□	80	Frank Pastore	.10	.05	.01
□	81	Joe Price	.10	.05	.01
□	82	Tom Seaver	.75	.35	.09
□	83	Mario Soto	.10	.05	.01
□	84	Mike Vail	.10	.05	.01
□	85	Tony Armas	.10	.05	.01
□	86	Shooty Babitt	.10	.05	.01
□	87	Dave Beard	.10	.05	.01
□	88	Rick Bosetti	.10	.05	.01
□	89	Keith Drumwright	.10	.05	.01
□	90	Wayne Gross	.10	.05	.01
□	91	Mike Heath	.10	.05	.01
□	92	Rickey Henderson	3.00	1.35	.35
□	93	Cliff Johnson	.10	.05	.01
□	94	Jeff Jones	.10	.05	.01
□	95	Matt Keough	.10	.05	.01
□	96	Brian Kingman	.10	.05	.01
□	97	Mickey Klutts	.10	.05	.01
□	98	Rick Langford	.10	.05	.01
□	99	Steve McCatty	.10	.05	.01
□	100	Dave McKay	.10	.05	.01
□	101	Dwayne Murphy	.10	.05	.01
□	102	Jeff Newman	.10	.05	.01
□	103	Mike Norris	.10	.05	.01
□	104	Bob Owchinko	.10	.05	.01
□	105	Mitchell Page	.10	.05	.01
□	106	Rob Picciolo	.10	.05	.01
□	107	Jim Spencer	.10	.05	.01
□	108	Fred Stanley	.10	.05	.01
□	109	Tom Underwood	.10	.05	.01
□	110	Joaquin Andujar	.20	.09	.03
□	111	Steve Braun	.10	.05	.01
□	112	Bob Forsch	.10	.05	.01
□	113	George Hendrick	.20	.09	.03
□	114	Keith Hernandez	.30	.14	.04
□	115	Tom Herr	.20	.09	.03
□	116	Dane Iorg	.10	.05	.01
□	117	Jim Kaat	.20	.09	.03
□	118	Tito Landrum	.10	.05	.01
□	119	Sixto Lezcano	.10	.05	.01
□	120	Mark Littell	.10	.05	.01
□	121	John Martin	.10	.05	.01
□	122	Silvio Martinez	.10	.05	.01
□	123	Ken Oberkfell	.10	.05	.01
□	124	Darrell Porter	.10	.05	.01
□	125	Mike Ramsey	.10	.05	.01
□	126	Orlando Sanchez	.10	.05	.01
□	127	Bob Shirley	.10	.05	.01
□	128	Lary Sorensen	.10	.05	.01
□	129	Bruce Sutter	.20	.09	.03
□	130	Bob Sykes	.10	.05	.01
□	131	Garry Templeton	.20	.09	.03
□	132	Gene Tenace	.10	.05	.01
□	133	Jerry Augustine	.10	.05	.01
□	134	Sal Bando	.20	.09	.03
□	135	Mark Brouhard	.10	.05	.01
□	136	Mike Caldwell	.10	.05	.01
□	137	Reggie Cleveland	.10	.05	.01
□	138	Cecil Cooper	.20	.09	.03
□	139	Jamie Easterly	.10	.05	.01
□	140	Marshall Edwards	.10	.05	.01
□	141	Rollie Fingers	.40	.18	.05
□	142	Jim Gantner	.20	.09	.03
□	143	Moose Haas	.10	.05	.01
□	144	Larry Hisle	.10	.05	.01
□	145	Roy Howell	.10	.05	.01
□	146	Rickey Keeton	.10	.05	.01
□	147	Randy Lerch	.10	.05	.01
□	148	Paul Molitor	1.00	.45	.12
□	149	Don Money	.10	.05	.01
□	150	Charlie Moore	.10	.05	.01
□	151	Ben Oglivie	.20	.09	.03
□	152	Ted Simmons	.20	.09	.03
□	153	Jim Slaton	.10	.05	.01
□	154	Gorman Thomas	.20	.09	.03
□	155	Robin Yount	1.50	.70	.19
□	156	Pete Vuckovich	.20	.09	.03
		(Should precede Yount in the team order)			
□	157	Benny Ayala	.10	.05	.01
□	158	Mark Belanger	.20	.09	.03
□	159	Al Bumbry	.20	.09	.03
□	160	Terry Crowley	.10	.05	.01
□	161	Rich Dauer	.10	.05	.01
□	162	Doug DeCinces	.20	.09	.03
□	163	Rick Dempsey	.20	.09	.03
□	164	Jim Dwyer	.10	.05	.01
□	165	Mike Flanagan	.20	.09	.03
□	166	Dave Ford	.10	.05	.01
□	167	Dan Graham	.10	.05	.01
□	168	Wayne Krenchicki	.10	.05	.01
□	169	John Lowenstein	.10	.05	.01
□	170	Dennis Martinez	.20	.09	.03
□	171	Tippy Martinez	.10	.05	.01
□	172	Scott McGregor	.10	.05	.01
□	173	Jose Morales	.10	.05	.01
□	174	Eddie Murray	2.00	.90	.25
□	175	Jim Palmer	.60	.25	.07
□	176	Cal Ripken	55.00	25.00	7.00
		(Fleer Ripken cards from 1982 through 1993 erroneously have 22 games played in 1981; not 23.)			
□	177	Gary Roenicke	.10	.05	.01
□	178	Lenn Sakata	.10	.05	.01
□	179	Ken Singleton	.20	.09	.03
□	180	Sammy Stewart	.10	.05	.01
□	181	Tim Stoddard	.10	.05	.01
□	182	Steve Stone	.20	.09	.03
□	183	Stan Bahnsen	.10	.05	.01
□	184	Ray Burris	.10	.05	.01
□	185	Gary Carter	.50	.23	.06
□	186	Warren Cromartie	.10	.05	.01
□	187	Andre Dawson	1.00	.45	.12

☐	188	Terry Francona	.10	.05	.01	☐	257	Dick Ruthven	.10	.05	.01

☐ 188 Terry Francona	.10	.05	.01
☐ 189 Woodie Fryman	.10	.05	.01
☐ 190 Bill Gullickson	.20	.09	.03
☐ 191 Grant Jackson	.10	.05	.01
☐ 192 Wallace Johnson	.10	.05	.01
☐ 193 Charlie Lea	.10	.05	.01
☐ 194 Bill Lee	.10	.05	.01
☐ 195 Jerry Manuel	.10	.05	.01
☐ 196 Brad Mills	.10	.05	.01
☐ 197 John Milner	.10	.05	.01
☐ 198 Rowland Office	.10	.05	.01
☐ 199 David Palmer	.10	.05	.01
☐ 200 Larry Parrish	.10	.05	.01
☐ 201 Mike Phillips	.10	.05	.01
☐ 202 Tim Raines	2.00	.90	.25
☐ 203 Bobby Ramos	.10	.05	.01
☐ 204 Jeff Reardon	.40	.18	.05
☐ 205 Steve Rogers	.10	.05	.01
☐ 206 Scott Sanderson	.20	.09	.03
☐ 207 Rodney Scott UER	.30	.14	.04
(Photo actually			
Tim Raines)			
☐ 208 Elias Sosa	.10	.05	.01
☐ 209 Chris Speier	.10	.05	.01
☐ 210 Tim Wallach	.75	.35	.09
☐ 211 Jerry White	.10	.05	.01
☐ 212 Alan Ashby	.10	.05	.01
☐ 213 Cesar Cedeno	.20	.09	.03
☐ 214 Jose Cruz	.20	.09	.03
☐ 215 Kiko Garcia	.10	.05	.01
☐ 216 Phil Garner	.20	.09	.03
☐ 217 Danny Heep	.10	.05	.01
☐ 218 Art Howe	.10	.05	.01
☐ 219 Bob Knepper	.10	.05	.01
☐ 220 Frank LaCorte	.10	.05	.01
☐ 221 Joe Niekro	.20	.09	.03
☐ 222 Joe Pittman	.10	.05	.01
☐ 223 Terry Puhl	.10	.05	.01
☐ 224 Luis Pujols	.10	.05	.01
☐ 225 Craig Reynolds	.10	.05	.01
☐ 226 J.R. Richard	.20	.09	.03
☐ 227 Dave Roberts	.10	.05	.01
☐ 228 Vern Ruhle	.10	.05	.01
☐ 229 Nolan Ryan	6.00	2.70	.75
☐ 230 Joe Sambito	.10	.05	.01
☐ 231 Tony Scott	.10	.05	.01
☐ 232 Dave Smith	.10	.05	.01
☐ 233 Harry Spilman	.10	.05	.01
☐ 234 Don Sutton	.40	.18	.05
☐ 235 Dickie Thon	.10	.05	.01
☐ 236 Denny Walling	.10	.05	.01
☐ 237 Gary Woods	.10	.05	.01
☐ 238 Luis Aguayo	.10	.05	.01
☐ 239 Ramon Aviles	.10	.05	.01
☐ 240 Bob Boone	.20	.09	.03
☐ 241 Larry Bowa	.20	.09	.03
☐ 242 Warren Brusstar	.10	.05	.01
☐ 243 Steve Carlton	.75	.35	.09
☐ 244 Larry Christenson	.10	.05	.01
☐ 245 Dick Davis	.10	.05	.01
☐ 246 Greg Gross	.10	.05	.01
☐ 247 Sparky Lyle	.20	.09	.03
☐ 248 Garry Maddox	.10	.05	.01
☐ 249 Gary Matthews	.20	.09	.03
☐ 250 Bake McBride	.10	.05	.01
☐ 251 Tug McGraw	.20	.09	.03
☐ 252 Keith Moreland	.10	.05	.01
☐ 253 Dickie Noles	.10	.05	.01
☐ 254 Mike Proly	.10	.05	.01
☐ 255 Ron Reed	.10	.05	.01
☐ 256 Pete Rose	1.50	.70	.19
☐ 257 Dick Ruthven	.10	.05	.01
☐ 258 Mike Schmidt	2.00	.90	.25
☐ 259 Lonnie Smith	.20	.09	.03
☐ 260 Manny Trillo	.10	.05	.01
☐ 261 Del Unser	.10	.05	.01
☐ 262 George Vukovich	.10	.05	.01
☐ 263 Tom Brookens	.10	.05	.01
☐ 264 George Cappuzzello	.10	.05	.01
☐ 265 Marty Castillo	.10	.05	.01
☐ 266 Al Cowens	.10	.05	.01
☐ 267 Kirk Gibson	.75	.35	.09
☐ 268 Richie Hebner	.10	.05	.01
☐ 269 Ron Jackson	.10	.05	.01
☐ 270 Lynn Jones	.10	.05	.01
☐ 271 Steve Kemp	.10	.05	.01
☐ 272 Rick Leach	.10	.05	.01
☐ 273 Aurelio Lopez	.10	.05	.01
☐ 274 Jack Morris	.40	.18	.05
☐ 275 Kevin Saucier	.10	.05	.01
☐ 276 Lance Parrish	.30	.14	.04
☐ 277 Rick Peters	.10	.05	.01
☐ 278 Dan Petry	.10	.05	.01
☐ 279 Dave Rozema	.10	.05	.01
☐ 280 Stan Papi	.10	.05	.01
☐ 281 Dan Schatzeder	.10	.05	.01
☐ 282 Champ Summers	.10	.05	.01
☐ 283 Alan Trammell	1.00	.45	.12
☐ 284 Lou Whitaker	.50	.23	.06
☐ 285 Milt Wilcox	.10	.05	.01
☐ 286 John Wockenfuss	.10	.05	.01
☐ 287 Gary Allenson	.10	.05	.01
☐ 288 Tom Burgmeier	.10	.05	.01
☐ 289 Bill Campbell	.10	.05	.01
☐ 290 Mark Clear	.10	.05	.01
☐ 291 Steve Crawford	.10	.05	.01
☐ 292 Dennis Eckersley	.60	.25	.07
☐ 293 Dwight Evans	.30	.14	.04
☐ 294 Rich Gedman	.10	.05	.01
☐ 295 Garry Hancock	.10	.05	.01
☐ 296 Glenn Hoffman	.10	.05	.01
☐ 297 Bruce Hurst	.10	.05	.01
☐ 298 Carney Lansford	.20	.09	.03
☐ 299 Rick Miller	.10	.05	.01
☐ 300 Reid Nichols	.10	.05	.01
☐ 301 Bob Ojeda	.30	.14	.04
☐ 302 Tony Perez	.40	.18	.05
☐ 303 Chuck Rainey	.10	.05	.01
☐ 304 Jerry Remy	.10	.05	.01
☐ 305 Jim Rice	.30	.14	.04
☐ 306 Joe Rudi	.10	.05	.01
☐ 307 Bob Stanley	.10	.05	.01
☐ 308 Dave Stapleton	.10	.05	.01
☐ 309 Frank Tanana	.20	.09	.03
☐ 310 Mike Torrez	.10	.05	.01
☐ 311 John Tudor	.20	.09	.03
☐ 312 Carl Yastrzemski	.75	.35	.09
☐ 313 Buddy Bell	.20	.09	.03
☐ 314 Steve Comer	.10	.05	.01
☐ 315 Danny Darwin	.10	.05	.01
☐ 316 John Ellis	.10	.05	.01
☐ 317 John Grubb	.10	.05	.01
☐ 318 Rick Honeycutt	.10	.05	.01
☐ 319 Charlie Hough	.20	.09	.03
☐ 320 Ferguson Jenkins	.40	.18	.05
☐ 321 John Henry Johnson	.10	.05	.01
☐ 322 Jim Kern	.10	.05	.01
☐ 323 Jon Matlack	.10	.05	.01
☐ 324 Doc Medich	.10	.05	.01
☐ 325 Mario Mendoza	.10	.05	.01
☐ 326 Al Oliver	.20	.09	.03
☐ 327 Pat Putnam	.10	.05	.01

☐ 328	Mickey Rivers	.10	.05	.01
☐ 329	Leon Roberts	.10	.05	.01
☐ 330	Billy Sample	.10	.05	.01
☐ 331	Bill Stein	.10	.05	.01
☐ 332	Jim Sundberg	.20	.09	.03
☐ 333	Mark Wagner	.10	.05	.01
☐ 334	Bump Wills	.10	.05	.01
☐ 335	Bill Almon	.10	.05	.01
☐ 336	Harold Baines	.75	.35	.09
☐ 337	Ross Baumgarten	.10	.05	.01
☐ 338	Tony Bernazard	.10	.05	.01
☐ 339	Britt Burns	.10	.05	.01
☐ 340	Richard Dotson	.10	.05	.01
☐ 341	Jim Essian	.10	.05	.01
☐ 342	Ed Farmer	.10	.05	.01
☐ 343	Carlton Fisk	.75	.35	.09
☐ 344	Kevin Hickey	.10	.05	.01
☐ 345	LaMarr Hoyt	.10	.05	.01
☐ 346	Lamar Johnson	.10	.05	.01
☐ 347	Jerry Koosman	.20	.09	.03
☐ 348	Rusty Kuntz	.10	.05	.01
☐ 349	Dennis Lamp	.10	.05	.01
☐ 350	Ron LeFlore	.20	.09	.03
☐ 351	Chet Lemon	.10	.05	.01
☐ 352	Greg Luzinski	.20	.09	.03
☐ 353	Bob Molinaro	.10	.05	.01
☐ 354	Jim Morrison	.10	.05	.01
☐ 355	Wayne Nordhagen	.10	.05	.01
☐ 356	Greg Pryor	.10	.05	.01
☐ 357	Mike Squires	.10	.05	.01
☐ 358	Steve Trout	.10	.05	.01
☐ 359	Alan Bannister	.10	.05	.01
☐ 360	Len Barker	.10	.05	.01
☐ 361	Bert Blyleven	.30	.14	.04
☐ 362	Joe Charboneau	.10	.05	.01
☐ 363	John Denny	.10	.05	.01
☐ 364	Bo Diaz	.10	.05	.01
☐ 365	Miguel Dilone	.10	.05	.01
☐ 366	Jerry Dybzinski	.10	.05	.01
☐ 367	Wayne Garland	.10	.05	.01
☐ 368	Mike Hargrove	.20	.09	.03
☐ 369	Toby Harrah	.20	.09	.03
☐ 370	Ron Hassey	.10	.05	.01
☐ 371	Von Hayes	.20	.09	.03
☐ 372	Pat Kelly	.10	.05	.01
☐ 373	Duane Kuiper	.10	.05	.01
☐ 374	Rick Manning	.10	.05	.01
☐ 375	Sid Monge	.10	.05	.01
☐ 376	Jorge Orta	.10	.05	.01
☐ 377	Dave Rosello	.10	.05	.01
☐ 378	Dan Spillner	.10	.05	.01
☐ 379	Mike Stanton	.10	.05	.01
☐ 380	Andre Thornton	.20	.09	.03
☐ 381	Tom Veryzer	.10	.05	.01
☐ 382	Rick Waits	.10	.05	.01
☐ 383	Doyle Alexander	.10	.05	.01
☐ 384	Vida Blue	.20	.09	.03
☐ 385	Fred Breining	.10	.05	.01
☐ 386	Enos Cabell	.10	.05	.01
☐ 387	Jack Clark	.20	.09	.03
☐ 388	Darrell Evans	.20	.09	.03
☐ 389	Tom Griffin	.10	.05	.01
☐ 390	Larry Herndon	.10	.05	.01
☐ 391	Al Holland	.10	.05	.01
☐ 392	Gary Lavelle	.10	.05	.01
☐ 393	Johnnie LeMaster	.10	.05	.01
☐ 394	Jerry Martin	.10	.05	.01
☐ 395	Milt May	.10	.05	.01
☐ 396	Greg Minton	.10	.05	.01
☐ 397	Joe Morgan	.60	.25	.07
☐ 398	Joe Pettini	.10	.05	.01
☐ 399	Allen Ripley	.10	.05	.01
☐ 400	Billy Smith	.10	.05	.01
☐ 401	Rennie Stennett	.10	.05	.01
☐ 402	Ed Whitson	.10	.05	.01
☐ 403	Jim Wohlford	.10	.05	.01
☐ 404	Willie Aikens	.10	.05	.01
☐ 405	George Brett	3.50	1.55	.45
☐ 406	Ken Brett	.10	.05	.01
☐ 407	Dave Chalk	.10	.05	.01
☐ 408	Rich Gale	.10	.05	.01
☐ 409	Cesar Geronimo	.10	.05	.01
☐ 410	Larry Gura	.10	.05	.01
☐ 411	Clint Hurdle	.10	.05	.01
☐ 412	Mike Jones	.10	.05	.01
☐ 413	Dennis Leonard	.10	.05	.01
☐ 414	Renie Martin	.10	.05	.01
☐ 415	Lee May	.20	.09	.03
☐ 416	Hal McRae	.30	.14	.04
☐ 417	Darryl Motley	.10	.05	.01
☐ 418	Rance Mulliniks	.10	.05	.01
☐ 419	Amos Otis	.20	.09	.03
☐ 420	Ken Phelps	.10	.05	.01
☐ 421	Jamie Quirk	.10	.05	.01
☐ 422	Dan Quisenberry	.20	.09	.03
☐ 423	Paul Splittorff	.10	.05	.01
☐ 424	U.L. Washington	.10	.05	.01
☐ 425	John Wathan	.10	.05	.01
☐ 426	Frank White	.20	.09	.03
☐ 427	Willie Wilson	.20	.09	.03
☐ 428	Brian Asselstine	.10	.05	.01
☐ 429	Bruce Benedict	.10	.05	.01
☐ 430	Tommy Boggs	.10	.05	.01
☐ 431	Larry Bradford	.10	.05	.01
☐ 432	Rick Camp	.10	.05	.01
☐ 433	Chris Chambliss	.20	.09	.03
☐ 434	Gene Garber	.10	.05	.01
☐ 435	Preston Hanna	.10	.05	.01
☐ 436	Bob Horner	.20	.09	.03
☐ 437	Glenn Hubbard	.10	.05	.01
☐ 438A	Al Hrabosky ERR (Height 5'1", All on reverse)	20.00	9.00	2.50
☐ 438B	Al Hrabosky ERR (Height 5'1")	.40	.18	.05
☐ 438C	Al Hrabosky (Height 5'10")	.20	.09	.03
☐ 439	Rufino Linares	.10	.05	.01
☐ 440	Rick Mahler	.10	.05	.01
☐ 441	Ed Miller	.10	.05	.01
☐ 442	John Montefusco	.10	.05	.01
☐ 443	Dale Murphy	.60	.25	.07
☐ 444	Phil Niekro	.40	.18	.05
☐ 445	Gaylord Perry	.40	.18	.05
☐ 446	Biff Pocoroba	.10	.05	.01
☐ 447	Rafael Ramirez	.10	.05	.01
☐ 448	Jerry Royster	.10	.05	.01
☐ 449	Claudell Washington	.10	.05	.01
☐ 450	Don Aase	.10	.05	.01
☐ 451	Don Baylor	.30	.14	.04
☐ 452	Juan Beniquez	.10	.05	.01
☐ 453	Rick Burleson	.10	.05	.01
☐ 454	Bert Campaneris	.20	.09	.03
☐ 455	Rod Carew	.75	.35	.09
☐ 456	Bob Clark	.10	.05	.01
☐ 457	Brian Downing	.20	.09	.03
☐ 458	Dan Ford	.10	.05	.01
☐ 459	Ken Forsch	.10	.05	.01
☐ 460A	Dave Frost (5 mm space before ERA)	.10	.05	.01
☐ 460B	Dave Frost (1 mm space)	.10	.05	.01

☐ 461	Bobby Grich	.20	.09	.03	☐ 532	Mike G. Marshall	.10	.05	.01
☐ 462	Larry Harlow	.10	.05	.01	☐ 533	Lee Mazzilli	.10	.05	.01
☐ 463	John Harris	.10	.05	.01	☐ 534	Dyar Miller	.10	.05	.01
☐ 464	Andy Hassler	.10	.05	.01	☐ 535	Mike Scott	.20	.09	.03
☐ 465	Butch Hobson	.20	.09	.03	☐ 536	Rusty Staub	.20	.09	.03
☐ 466	Jesse Jefferson	.10	.05	.01	☐ 537	John Stearns	.10	.05	.01
☐ 467	Bruce Kison	.10	.05	.01	☐ 538	Craig Swan	.10	.05	.01
☐ 468	Fred Lynn	.20	.09	.03	☐ 539	Frank Taveras	.10	.05	.01
☐ 469	Angel Moreno	.10	.05	.01	☐ 540	Alex Trevino	.10	.05	.01
☐ 470	Ed Ott	.10	.05	.01	☐ 541	Ellis Valentine	.10	.05	.01
☐ 471	Fred Patek	.10	.05	.01	☐ 542	Mookie Wilson	.20	.09	.03
☐ 472	Steve Renko	.10	.05	.01	☐ 543	Joel Youngblood	.10	.05	.01
☐ 473	Mike Witt	.10	.05	.01	☐ 544	Pat Zachry	.10	.05	.01
☐ 474	Geoff Zahn	.10	.05	.01	☐ 545	Glenn Adams	.10	.05	.01
☐ 475	Gary Alexander	.10	.05	.01	☐ 546	Fernando Arroyo	.10	.05	.01
☐ 476	Dale Berra	.10	.05	.01	☐ 547	John Verhoeven	.10	.05	.01
☐ 477	Kurt Bevacqua	.10	.05	.01	☐ 548	Sal Butera	.10	.05	.01
☐ 478	Jim Bibby	.10	.05	.01	☐ 549	John Castino	.10	.05	.01
☐ 479	John Candelaria	.10	.05	.01	☐ 550	Don Cooper	.10	.05	.01
☐ 480	Victor Cruz	.10	.05	.01	☐ 551	Doug Corbett	.10	.05	.01
☐ 481	Mike Easler	.10	.05	.01	☐ 552	Dave Engle	.10	.05	.01
☐ 482	Tim Foli	.10	.05	.01	☐ 553	Roger Erickson	.10	.05	.01
☐ 483	Lee Lacy	.10	.05	.01	☐ 554	Danny Goodwin	.10	.05	.01
☐ 484	Vance Law	.10	.05	.01	☐ 555A	Darrell Jackson	.40	.18	.05
☐ 485	Bill Madlock	.20	.09	.03		(Black cap)			
☐ 486	Willie Montanez	.10	.05	.01	☐ 555B	Darrell Jackson	.20	.09	.03
☐ 487	Omar Moreno	.10	.05	.01		(Red cap with T)			
☐ 488	Steve Nicosia	.10	.05	.01	☐ 555C	Darrell Jackson	3.00	1.35	.35
☐ 489	Dave Parker	.30	.14	.04		(Red cap, no emblem)			
☐ 490	Tony Pena	.20	.09	.03	☐ 556	Pete Mackanin	.10	.05	.01
☐ 491	Pascual Perez	.10	.05	.01	☐ 557	Jack O'Connor	.10	.05	.01
☐ 492	Johnny Ray	.10	.05	.01	☐ 558	Hosken Powell	.10	.05	.01
☐ 493	Rick Rhoden	.10	.05	.01	☐ 559	Pete Redfern	.10	.05	.01
☐ 494	Bill Robinson	.20	.09	.03	☐ 560	Roy Smalley	.10	.05	.01
☐ 495	Don Robinson	.10	.05	.01	☐ 561	Chuck Baker UER	.10	.05	.01
☐ 496	Enrique Romo	.10	.05	.01		(Shortstop on front)			
☐ 497	Rod Scurry	.10	.05	.01	☐ 562	Gary Ward	.10	.05	.01
☐ 498	Eddie Solomon	.10	.05	.01	☐ 563	Rob Wilfong	.10	.05	.01
☐ 499	Willie Stargell	.50	.23	.06	☐ 564	Al Williams	.10	.05	.01
☐ 500	Kent Tekulve	.20	.09	.03	☐ 565	Butch Wynegar	.10	.05	.01
☐ 501	Jason Thompson	.10	.05	.01	☐ 566	Randy Bass	.30	.14	.04
☐ 502	Glenn Abbott	.10	.05	.01	☐ 567	Juan Bonilla	.10	.05	.01
☐ 503	Jim Anderson	.10	.05	.01	☐ 568	Danny Boone	.10	.05	.01
☐ 504	Floyd Bannister	.10	.05	.01	☐ 569	John Curtis	.10	.05	.01
☐ 505	Bruce Bochte	.10	.05	.01	☐ 570	Juan Eichelberger	.10	.05	.01
☐ 506	Jeff Burroughs	.10	.05	.01	☐ 571	Barry Evans	.10	.05	.01
☐ 507	Bryan Clark	.10	.05	.01	☐ 572	Tim Flannery	.10	.05	.01
☐ 508	Ken Clay	.10	.05	.01	☐ 573	Ruppert Jones	.10	.05	.01
☐ 509	Julio Cruz	.10	.05	.01	☐ 574	Terry Kennedy	.10	.05	.01
☐ 510	Dick Drago	.10	.05	.01	☐ 575	Joe Lefebvre	.10	.05	.01
☐ 511	Gary Gray	.10	.05	.01	☐ 576A	John Littlefield ERR	200.00	90.00	25.00
☐ 512	Dan Meyer	.10	.05	.01		(Left handed; reverse negative)			
☐ 513	Jerry Narron	.10	.05	.01					
☐ 514	Tom Paciorek	.20	.09	.03	☐ 576B	John Littlefield COR	.20	.09	.03
☐ 515	Casey Parsons	.10	.05	.01		(Right handed)			
☐ 516	Lenny Randle	.10	.05	.01	☐ 577	Gary Lucas	.10	.05	.01
☐ 517	Shane Rawley	.10	.05	.01	☐ 578	Steve Mura	.10	.05	.01
☐ 518	Joe Simpson	.10	.05	.01	☐ 579	Broderick Perkins	.10	.05	.01
☐ 519	Richie Zisk	.10	.05	.01	☐ 580	Gene Richards	.10	.05	.01
☐ 520	Neil Allen	.10	.05	.01	☐ 581	Luis Salazar	.10	.05	.01
☐ 521	Bob Bailor	.10	.05	.01	☐ 582	Ozzie Smith	3.00	1.35	.35
☐ 522	Hubie Brooks	.20	.09	.03	☐ 583	John Urrea	.10	.05	.01
☐ 523	Mike Cubbage	.10	.05	.01	☐ 584	Chris Welsh	.10	.05	.01
☐ 524	Pete Falcone	.10	.05	.01	☐ 585	Rick Wise	.10	.05	.01
☐ 525	Doug Flynn	.10	.05	.01	☐ 586	Doug Bird	.10	.05	.01
☐ 526	Tom Hausman	.10	.05	.01	☐ 587	Tim Blackwell	.10	.05	.01
☐ 527	Ron Hodges	.10	.05	.01	☐ 588	Bobby Bonds	.20	.09	.03
☐ 528	Randy Jones	.10	.05	.01	☐ 589	Bill Buckner	.20	.09	.03
☐ 529	Mike Jorgensen	.10	.05	.01	☐ 590	Bill Caudill	.10	.05	.01
☐ 530	Dave Kingman	.20	.09	.03	☐ 591	Hector Cruz	.10	.05	.01
☐ 531	Ed Lynch	.10	.05	.01	☐ 592	Jody Davis	.10	.05	.01

☐ 593	Ivan DeJesus	.10	.05	.01
☐ 594	Steve Dillard	.10	.05	.01
☐ 595	Leon Durham	.10	.05	.01
☐ 596	Rawly Eastwick	.10	.05	.01
☐ 597	Steve Henderson	.10	.05	.01
☐ 598	Mike Krukow	.10	.05	.01
☐ 599	Mike Lum	.10	.05	.01
☐ 600	Randy Martz	.10	.05	.01
☐ 601	Jerry Morales	.10	.05	.01
☐ 602	Ken Reitz	.10	.05	.01
☐ 603A	Lee Smith ERR	6.00	2.70	.75
	(Cubs logo reversed)			
☐ 603B	Lee Smith COR	6.00	2.70	.75
☐ 604	Dick Tidrow	.10	.05	.01
☐ 605	Jim Tracy	.10	.05	.01
☐ 606	Mike Tyson	.10	.05	.01
☐ 607	Ty Waller	.10	.05	.01
☐ 608	Danny Ainge	1.00	.45	.12
☐ 609	Jorge Bell	.75	.35	.09
☐ 610	Mark Bomback	.10	.05	.01
☐ 611	Barry Bonnell	.10	.05	.01
☐ 612	Jim Clancy	.10	.05	.01
☐ 613	Damaso Garcia	.10	.05	.01
☐ 614	Jerry Garvin	.10	.05	.01
☐ 615	Alfredo Griffin	.10	.05	.01
☐ 616	Garth Iorg	.10	.05	.01
☐ 617	Luis Leal	.10	.05	.01
☐ 618	Ken Macha	.10	.05	.01
☐ 619	John Mayberry	.10	.05	.01
☐ 620	Joey McLaughlin	.10	.05	.01
☐ 621	Lloyd Moseby	.10	.05	.01
☐ 622	Dave Stieb	.20	.09	.03
☐ 623	Jackson Todd	.10	.05	.01
☐ 624	Willie Upshaw	.10	.05	.01
☐ 625	Otto Velez	.10	.05	.01
☐ 626	Ernie Whitt	.10	.05	.01
☐ 627	Alvis Woods	.10	.05	.01
☐ 628	All Star Game	.20	.09	.03
	Cleveland, Ohio			
☐ 629	All Star Infielders	.20	.09	.03
	Frank White and			
	Bucky Dent			
☐ 630	Big Red Machine	.20	.09	.03
	Dan Driessen			
	Dave Concepcion			
	George Foster			
☐ 631	Bruce Sutter	.20	.09	.03
	Top NL Relief Pitcher			
☐ 632	"Steve and Carlton"	.75	.35	.09
	Steve Carlton and			
	Carlton Fisk			
☐ 633	Carl Yastrzemski	.60	.25	.07
	3000th Game			
☐ 634	Dynamic Duo	.75	.35	.09
	Johnny Bench and			
	Tom Seaver			
☐ 635	West Meets East	.20	.09	.03
	Fernando Valenzuela			
	and Gary Carter			
☐ 636A	Fernando Valenzuela:	.30	.14	.04
	NL SO King ("he" NL)			
☐ 636B	Fernando Valenzuela:	.30	.14	.04
	NL SO King ("the" NL)			
☐ 637	Mike Schmidt	1.00	.45	.12
	Home Run King			
☐ 638	NL All Stars	.30	.14	.04
	Gary Carter and			
	Dave Parker			
☐ 639	Perfect Game UER	.20	.09	.03
	Len Barker and			
	Bo Diaz			
	(Catcher actually			
	Ron Hassey)			
☐ 640	Pete and Re-Pete	1.00	.45	.12
	Pete Rose and Son			
☐ 641	Phillies Finest	.75	.35	.09
	Lonnie Smith			
	Mike Schmidt			
	Steve Carlton			
☐ 642	Red Sox Reunion	.20	.09	.03
	Fred Lynn and			
	Dwight Evans			
☐ 643	Rickey Henderson	1.00	.45	.12
	Most Hits and Runs			
☐ 644	Rollie Fingers	.40	.18	.05
	Most Saves AL			
☐ 645	Tom Seaver	.75	.35	.09
	Most 1981 Wins			
☐ 646A	Yankee Powerhouse	2.00	.90	.25
	Reggie Jackson and			
	Dave Winfield			
	(Comma on back			
	after outfielder)			
☐ 646B	Yankee Powerhouse	2.00	.90	.25
	Reggie Jackson and			
	Dave Winfield			
	(No comma)			
☐ 647	CL: Yankees/Dodgers	.20	.09	.03
☐ 648	CL: A's/Reds	.20	.09	.03
☐ 649	CL: Cards/Brewers	.20	.09	.03
☐ 650	CL: Expos/Orioles	.20	.09	.03
☐ 651	CL: Astros/Phillies	.20	.09	.03
☐ 652	CL: Tigers/Red Sox	.20	.09	.03
☐ 653	CL: Rangers/White Sox	.20	.09	.03
☐ 654	CL: Giants/Indians	.20	.09	.03
☐ 655	CL: Royals/Braves	.20	.09	.03
☐ 656	CL: Angels/Pirates	.20	.09	.03
☐ 657	CL: Mariners/Mets	.20	.09	.03
☐ 658	CL: Padres/Twins	.20	.09	.03
☐ 659	CL: Blue Jays/Cubs	.20	.09	.03
☐ 660	Specials Checklist	.20	.09	.03

1983 Fleer

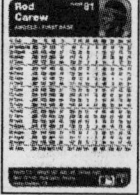

The cards in this 660-card set measure 2 1/2" by 3 1/2". In 1983, for the third straight year, Fleer has produced a baseball series numbering 660 cards. Of these, 1-628 are player cards, 629-646 are special cards, and 647-660 are checklist cards. The player cards are again ordered alphabetically within team. The team order relates back to each team's on-field performance during the previous year, i.e., World Champion

Cardinals (1-25), AL Champion Brewers (26-51), Baltimore (52-75), California (76-103), Kansas City (104-128), Atlanta (129-152), Philadelphia (153-176), Boston (177-200), Los Angeles (201-227), Chicago White Sox (228-251), San Francisco (252-276), Montreal (277-301), Pittsburgh (302-326), Detroit (327-351), San Diego (352-375), New York Yankees (376-399), Cleveland (400-423), Toronto (424-444), Houston (445-469), Seattle (470-489), Chicago Cubs (490-512), Oakland (513-535), New York Mets (536-561), Texas (562-583), Cincinnati (584-606), and Minnesota (607-628). The front of each card has a colorful team logo at bottom left and the player's name and position at lower right. The reverses are done in shades of brown on white. The cards are numbered on the back next to a small black and white photo of the player. The key Rookie Cards in this set are Wade Boggs, Tony Gwynn, Howard Johnson, Willie McGee, Ryne Sandberg, and Frank Viola.

	NRMT-MT	EXC	G-VG
COMPLETE SET (660)	90.00	40.00	11.00
COMMON CARD (1-660)	.10	.05	.01

		NRMT-MT	EXC	G-VG
☐ 1	Joaquin Andujar	.20	.09	.03
☐ 2	Doug Bair	.10	.05	.01
☐ 3	Steve Braun	.10	.05	.01
☐ 4	Glenn Brummer	.10	.05	.01
☐ 5	Bob Forsch	.10	.05	.01
☐ 6	David Green	.10	.05	.01
☐ 7	George Hendrick	.20	.09	.03
☐ 8	Keith Hernandez	.30	.14	.04
☐ 9	Tom Herr	.20	.09	.03
☐ 10	Dane Iorg	.10	.05	.01
☐ 11	Jim Kaat	.20	.09	.03
☐ 12	Jeff Lahti	.10	.05	.01
☐ 13	Tito Landrum	.10	.05	.01
☐ 14	Dave LaPoint	.10	.05	.01
☐ 15	Willie McGee	.75	.35	.09
☐ 16	Steve Mura	.10	.05	.01
☐ 17	Ken Oberkfell	.10	.05	.01
☐ 18	Darrell Porter	.10	.05	.01
☐ 19	Mike Ramsey	.10	.05	.01
☐ 20	Gene Roof	.10	.05	.01
☐ 21	Lonnie Smith	.20	.09	.03
☐ 22	Ozzie Smith	2.00	.90	.25
☐ 23	John Stuper	.10	.05	.01
☐ 24	Bruce Sutter	.20	.09	.03
☐ 25	Gene Tenace	.10	.05	.01
☐ 26	Jerry Augustine	.10	.05	.01
☐ 27	Dwight Bernard	.10	.05	.01
☐ 28	Mark Brouhard	.10	.05	.01
☐ 29	Mike Caldwell	.10	.05	.01
☐ 30	Cecil Cooper	.20	.09	.03
☐ 31	Jamie Easterly	.10	.05	.01
☐ 32	Marshall Edwards	.10	.05	.01
☐ 33	Rollie Fingers	.30	.14	.04
☐ 34	Jim Gantner	.20	.09	.03
☐ 35	Moose Haas	.10	.05	.01
☐ 36	Roy Howell	.10	.05	.01
☐ 37	Pete Ladd	.10	.05	.01
☐ 38	Bob McClure	.10	.05	.01
☐ 39	Doc Medich	.10	.05	.01
☐ 40	Paul Molitor	.75	.35	.09
☐ 41	Don Money	.10	.05	.01
☐ 42	Charlie Moore	.10	.05	.01
☐ 43	Ben Oglivie	.10	.05	.01
☐ 44	Ed Romero	.10	.05	.01
☐ 45	Ted Simmons	.20	.09	.03
☐ 46	Jim Slaton	.10	.05	.01
☐ 47	Don Sutton	.30	.14	.04
☐ 48	Gorman Thomas	.10	.05	.01
☐ 49	Pete Vuckovich	.10	.05	.01
☐ 50	Ned Yost	.10	.05	.01
☐ 51	Robin Yount	1.50	.70	.19
☐ 52	Benny Ayala	.10	.05	.01
☐ 53	Bob Bonner	.10	.05	.01
☐ 54	Al Bumbry	.20	.09	.03
☐ 55	Terry Crowley	.10	.05	.01
☐ 56	Storm Davis	.10	.05	.01
☐ 57	Rich Dauer	.10	.05	.01
☐ 58	Rick Dempsey UER	.20	.09	.03
	(Posing batting lefty)			
☐ 59	Jim Dwyer	.10	.05	.01
☐ 60	Mike Flanagan	.20	.09	.03
☐ 61	Dan Ford	.10	.05	.01
☐ 62	Glenn Gulliver	.10	.05	.01
☐ 63	John Lowenstein	.10	.05	.01
☐ 64	Dennis Martinez	.20	.09	.03
☐ 65	Tippy Martinez	.10	.05	.01
☐ 66	Scott McGregor	.10	.05	.01
☐ 67	Eddie Murray	2.00	.90	.25
☐ 68	Joe Nolan	.10	.05	.01
☐ 69	Jim Palmer	.60	.25	.07
☐ 70	Cal Ripken Jr.	16.00	7.25	2.00
☐ 71	Gary Roenicke	.10	.05	.01
☐ 72	Lenn Sakata	.10	.05	.01
☐ 73	Ken Singleton	.20	.09	.03
☐ 74	Sammy Stewart	.10	.05	.01
☐ 75	Tim Stoddard	.10	.05	.01
☐ 76	Don Aase	.10	.05	.01
☐ 77	Don Baylor	.30	.14	.04
☐ 78	Juan Beniquez	.10	.05	.01
☐ 79	Bob Boone	.20	.09	.03
☐ 80	Rick Burleson	.10	.05	.01
☐ 81	Rod Carew	.60	.25	.07
☐ 82	Bobby Clark	.10	.05	.01
☐ 83	Doug Corbett	.10	.05	.01
☐ 84	John Curtis	.10	.05	.01
☐ 85	Doug DeCinces	.20	.09	.03
☐ 86	Brian Downing	.20	.09	.03
☐ 87	Joe Ferguson	.10	.05	.01
☐ 88	Tim Foli	.10	.05	.01
☐ 89	Ken Forsch	.10	.05	.01
☐ 90	Dave Goltz	.10	.05	.01
☐ 91	Bobby Grich	.20	.09	.03
☐ 92	Andy Hassler	.10	.05	.01
☐ 93	Reggie Jackson	1.25	.55	.16
☐ 94	Ron Jackson	.10	.05	.01
☐ 95	Tommy John	.30	.14	.04
☐ 96	Bruce Kison	.10	.05	.01
☐ 97	Fred Lynn	.20	.09	.03
☐ 98	Ed Ott	.10	.05	.01
☐ 99	Steve Renko	.10	.05	.01
☐ 100	Luis Sanchez	.10	.05	.01
☐ 101	Rob Wilfong	.10	.05	.01
☐ 102	Mike Witt	.10	.05	.01
☐ 103	Geoff Zahn	.10	.05	.01
☐ 104	Willie Aikens	.10	.05	.01
☐ 105	Mike Armstrong	.10	.05	.01
☐ 106	Vida Blue	.20	.09	.03
☐ 107	Bud Black	.30	.14	.04
☐ 108	George Brett	3.00	1.35	.35
☐ 109	Bill Castro	.10	.05	.01
☐ 110	Onix Concepcion	.10	.05	.01
☐ 111	Dave Frost	.10	.05	.01
☐ 112	Cesar Geronimo	.10	.05	.01

☐ 113	Larry Gura	.10	.05	.01
☐ 114	Steve Hammond	.10	.05	.01
☐ 115	Don Hood	.10	.05	.01
☐ 116	Dennis Leonard	.10	.05	.01
☐ 117	Jerry Martin	.10	.05	.01
☐ 118	Lee May	.20	.09	.03
☐ 119	Hal McRae	.30	.14	.04
☐ 120	Amos Otis	.20	.09	.03
☐ 121	Greg Pryor	.10	.05	.01
☐ 122	Dan Quisenberry	.20	.09	.03
☐ 123	Don Slaught	.50	.23	.06
☐ 124	Paul Splittorff	.10	.05	.01
☐ 125	U.L. Washington	.10	.05	.01
☐ 126	John Wathan	.10	.05	.01
☐ 127	Frank White	.20	.09	.03
☐ 128	Willie Wilson	.20	.09	.03
☐ 129	Steve Bedrosian UER (Height 6'33")	.20	.09	.03
☐ 130	Bruce Benedict	.10	.05	.01
☐ 131	Tommy Boggs	.10	.05	.01
☐ 132	Brett Butler	.50	.23	.06
☐ 133	Rick Camp	.10	.05	.01
☐ 134	Chris Chambliss	.20	.09	.03
☐ 135	Ken Dayley	.10	.05	.01
☐ 136	Gene Garber	.10	.05	.01
☐ 137	Terry Harper	.10	.05	.01
☐ 138	Bob Horner	.20	.09	.03
☐ 139	Glenn Hubbard	.10	.05	.01
☐ 140	Rufino Linares	.10	.05	.01
☐ 141	Rick Mahler	.10	.05	.01
☐ 142	Dale Murphy	.50	.23	.06
☐ 143	Phil Niekro	.30	.14	.04
☐ 144	Pascual Perez	.10	.05	.01
☐ 145	Biff Pocoroba	.10	.05	.01
☐ 146	Rafael Ramirez	.10	.05	.01
☐ 147	Jerry Royster	.10	.05	.01
☐ 148	Ken Smith	.10	.05	.01
☐ 149	Bob Walk	.10	.05	.01
☐ 150	Claudell Washington	.10	.05	.01
☐ 151	Bob Watson	.20	.09	.03
☐ 152	Larry Whisenton	.10	.05	.01
☐ 153	Porfirio Altamirano	.10	.05	.01
☐ 154	Marty Bystrom	.10	.05	.01
☐ 155	Steve Carlton	.75	.35	.09
☐ 156	Larry Christenson	.10	.05	.01
☐ 157	Ivan DeJesus	.10	.05	.01
☐ 158	John Denny	.10	.05	.01
☐ 159	Bob Dernier	.10	.05	.01
☐ 160	Bo Diaz	.10	.05	.01
☐ 161	Ed Farmer	.10	.05	.01
☐ 162	Greg Gross	.10	.05	.01
☐ 163	Mike Krukow	.10	.05	.01
☐ 164	Garry Maddox	.10	.05	.01
☐ 165	Gary Matthews	.20	.09	.03
☐ 166	Tug McGraw	.20	.09	.03
☐ 167	Bob Molinaro	.10	.05	.01
☐ 168	Sid Monge	.10	.05	.01
☐ 169	Ron Reed	.10	.05	.01
☐ 170	Bill Robinson	.20	.09	.03
☐ 171	Pete Rose	1.50	.70	.19
☐ 172	Dick Ruthven	.10	.05	.01
☐ 173	Mike Schmidt	1.50	.70	.19
☐ 174	Manny Trillo	.10	.05	.01
☐ 175	Ozzie Virgil	.10	.05	.01
☐ 176	George Vukovich	.10	.05	.01
☐ 177	Gary Allenson	.10	.05	.01
☐ 178	Luis Aponte	.10	.05	.01
☐ 179	Wade Boggs	15.00	6.75	1.85
☐ 180	Tom Burgmeier	.10	.05	.01
☐ 181	Mark Clear	.10	.05	.01
☐ 182	Dennis Eckersley	.50	.23	.06
☐ 183	Dwight Evans	.20	.09	.03
☐ 184	Rich Gedman	.10	.05	.01
☐ 185	Glenn Hoffman	.10	.05	.01
☐ 186	Bruce Hurst	.20	.09	.03
☐ 187	Carney Lansford	.20	.09	.03
☐ 188	Rick Miller	.10	.05	.01
☐ 189	Reid Nichols	.10	.05	.01
☐ 190	Bob Ojeda	.20	.09	.03
☐ 191	Tony Perez	.30	.14	.04
☐ 192	Chuck Rainey	.10	.05	.01
☐ 193	Jerry Remy	.10	.05	.01
☐ 194	Jim Rice	.30	.14	.04
☐ 195	Bob Stanley	.10	.05	.01
☐ 196	Dave Stapleton	.10	.05	.01
☐ 197	Mike Torrez	.10	.05	.01
☐ 198	John Tudor	.20	.09	.03
☐ 199	Julio Valdez	.10	.05	.01
☐ 200	Carl Yastrzemski	.75	.35	.09
☐ 201	Dusty Baker	.30	.14	.04
☐ 202	Joe Beckwith	.10	.05	.01
☐ 203	Greg Brock	.10	.05	.01
☐ 204	Ron Cey	.20	.09	.03
☐ 205	Terry Forster	.10	.05	.01
☐ 206	Steve Garvey	.30	.14	.04
☐ 207	Pedro Guerrero	.20	.09	.03
☐ 208	Burt Hooton	.10	.05	.01
☐ 209	Steve Howe	.10	.05	.01
☐ 210	Ken Landreaux	.10	.05	.01
☐ 211	Mike Marshall	.10	.05	.01
☐ 212	Candy Maldonado	.20	.09	.03
☐ 213	Rick Monday	.10	.05	.01
☐ 214	Tom Niedenfuer	.10	.05	.01
☐ 215	Jorge Orta	.10	.05	.01
☐ 216	Jerry Reuss UER ("Home:" omitted)	.10	.05	.01
☐ 217	Ron Roenicke	.10	.05	.01
☐ 218	Vicente Romo	.10	.05	.01
☐ 219	Bill Russell	.20	.09	.03
☐ 220	Steve Sax	.20	.09	.03
☐ 221	Mike Scioscia	.20	.09	.03
☐ 222	Dave Stewart	.30	.14	.04
☐ 223	Derrel Thomas	.10	.05	.01
☐ 224	Fernando Valenzuela	.20	.09	.03
☐ 225	Bob Welch	.20	.09	.03
☐ 226	Ricky Wright	.10	.05	.01
☐ 227	Steve Yeager	.10	.05	.01
☐ 228	Bill Almon	.10	.05	.01
☐ 229	Harold Baines	.30	.14	.04
☐ 230	Salome Barojas	.10	.05	.01
☐ 231	Tony Bernazard	.10	.05	.01
☐ 232	Britt Burns	.10	.05	.01
☐ 233	Richard Dotson	.10	.05	.01
☐ 234	Ernesto Escarrega	.10	.05	.01
☐ 235	Carlton Fisk	.75	.35	.09
☐ 236	Jerry Hairston	.10	.05	.01
☐ 237	Kevin Hickey	.10	.05	.01
☐ 238	LaMarr Hoyt	.20	.09	.03
☐ 239	Steve Kemp	.10	.05	.01
☐ 240	Jim Kern	.10	.05	.01
☐ 241	Ron Kittle	.20	.09	.03
☐ 242	Jerry Koosman	.20	.09	.03
☐ 243	Dennis Lamp	.10	.05	.01
☐ 244	Rudy Law	.10	.05	.01
☐ 245	Vance Law	.10	.05	.01
☐ 246	Ron LeFlore	.20	.09	.03
☐ 247	Greg Luzinski	.20	.09	.03
☐ 248	Tom Paciorek	.20	.09	.03
☐ 249	Aurelio Rodriguez	.10	.05	.01
☐ 250	Mike Squires	.10	.05	.01
☐ 251	Steve Trout	.10	.05	.01
☐ 252	Jim Barr	.10	.05	.01

☐ 253	Dave Bergman	.10	.05	.01
☐ 254	Fred Breining	.10	.05	.01
☐ 255	Bob Brenly	.10	.05	.01
☐ 256	Jack Clark	.20	.09	.03
☐ 257	Chili Davis	.75	.35	.09
☐ 258	Darrell Evans	.20	.09	.03
☐ 259	Alan Fowlkes	.10	.05	.01
☐ 260	Rich Gale	.10	.05	.01
☐ 261	Atlee Hammaker	.10	.05	.01
☐ 262	Al Holland	.10	.05	.01
☐ 263	Duane Kuiper	.10	.05	.01
☐ 264	Bill Laskey	.10	.05	.01
☐ 265	Gary Lavelle	.10	.05	.01
☐ 266	Johnnie LeMaster	.10	.05	.01
☐ 267	Renie Martin	.10	.05	.01
☐ 268	Milt May	.10	.05	.01
☐ 269	Greg Minton	.10	.05	.01
☐ 270	Joe Morgan	.50	.23	.06
☐ 271	Tom O'Malley	.10	.05	.01
☐ 272	Reggie Smith	.20	.09	.03
☐ 273	Guy Sularz	.10	.05	.01
☐ 274	Champ Summers	.10	.05	.01
☐ 275	Max Venable	.10	.05	.01
☐ 276	Jim Wohlford	.10	.05	.01
☐ 277	Ray Burris	.10	.05	.01
☐ 278	Gary Carter	.30	.14	.04
☐ 279	Warren Cromartie	.10	.05	.01
☐ 280	Andre Dawson	.75	.35	.09
☐ 281	Terry Francona	.10	.05	.01
☐ 282	Doug Flynn	.10	.05	.01
☐ 283	Woodie Fryman	.10	.05	.01
☐ 284	Bill Gullickson	.20	.09	.03
☐ 285	Wallace Johnson	.10	.05	.01
☐ 286	Charlie Lea	.10	.05	.01
☐ 287	Randy Lerch	.10	.05	.01
☐ 288	Brad Mills	.10	.05	.01
☐ 289	Dan Norman	.10	.05	.01
☐ 290	Al Oliver	.20	.09	.03
☐ 291	David Palmer	.10	.05	.01
☐ 292	Tim Raines	.60	.25	.07
☐ 293	Jeff Reardon	.30	.14	.04
☐ 294	Steve Rogers	.10	.05	.01
☐ 295	Scott Sanderson	.10	.05	.01
☐ 296	Dan Schatzeder	.10	.05	.01
☐ 297	Bryn Smith	.10	.05	.01
☐ 298	Chris Speier	.10	.05	.01
☐ 299	Tim Wallach	.30	.14	.04
☐ 300	Jerry White	.10	.05	.01
☐ 301	Joel Youngblood	.10	.05	.01
☐ 302	Ross Baumgarten	.10	.05	.01
☐ 303	Dale Berra	.10	.05	.01
☐ 304	John Candelaria	.10	.05	.01
☐ 305	Dick Davis	.10	.05	.01
☐ 306	Mike Easler	.10	.05	.01
☐ 307	Richie Hebner	.10	.05	.01
☐ 308	Lee Lacy	.10	.05	.01
☐ 309	Bill Madlock	.20	.09	.03
☐ 310	Larry McWilliams	.10	.05	.01
☐ 311	John Milner	.10	.05	.01
☐ 312	Omar Moreno	.10	.05	.01
☐ 313	Jim Morrison	.10	.05	.01
☐ 314	Steve Nicosia	.10	.05	.01
☐ 315	Dave Parker	.30	.14	.04
☐ 316	Tony Pena	.20	.09	.03
☐ 317	Johnny Ray	.10	.05	.01
☐ 318	Rick Rhoden	.10	.05	.01
☐ 319	Don Robinson	.10	.05	.01
☐ 320	Enrique Romo	.10	.05	.01
☐ 321	Manny Sarmiento	.10	.05	.01
☐ 322	Rod Scurry	.10	.05	.01
☐ 323	Jimmy Smith	.10	.05	.01

☐ 324	Willie Stargell	.30	.14	.04
☐ 325	Jason Thompson	.10	.05	.01
☐ 326	Kent Tekulve	.20	.09	.03
☐ 327A	Tom Brookens	.10	.05	.01
	(Short .375" brown box shaded in on card back)			
☐ 327B	Tom Brookens	.10	.05	.01
	(Longer 1.25" brown box shaded in on card back)			
☐ 328	Enos Cabell	.10	.05	.01
☐ 329	Kirk Gibson	.60	.25	.07
☐ 330	Larry Herndon	.10	.05	.01
☐ 331	Mike Ivie	.10	.05	.01
☐ 332	Howard Johnson	.75	.35	.09
☐ 333	Lynn Jones	.10	.05	.01
☐ 334	Rick Leach	.10	.05	.01
☐ 335	Chet Lemon	.10	.05	.01
☐ 336	Jack Morris	.30	.14	.04
☐ 337	Lance Parrish	.20	.09	.03
☐ 338	Larry Pashnick	.10	.05	.01
☐ 339	Dan Petry	.10	.05	.01
☐ 340	Dave Rozema	.10	.05	.01
☐ 341	Dave Rucker	.10	.05	.01
☐ 342	Elias Sosa	.10	.05	.01
☐ 343	Dave Tobik	.10	.05	.01
☐ 344	Alan Trammell	.75	.35	.09
☐ 345	Jerry Turner	.10	.05	.01
☐ 346	Jerry Ujdur	.10	.05	.01
☐ 347	Pat Underwood	.10	.05	.01
☐ 348	Lou Whitaker	.50	.23	.06
☐ 349	Milt Wilcox	.10	.05	.01
☐ 350	Glenn Wilson	.20	.09	.03
☐ 351	John Wockenfuss	.10	.05	.01
☐ 352	Kurt Bevacqua	.10	.05	.01
☐ 353	Juan Bonilla	.10	.05	.01
☐ 354	Floyd Chiffer	.10	.05	.01
☐ 355	Luis DeLeon	.10	.05	.01
☐ 356	Dave Dravecky	.60	.25	.07
☐ 357	Dave Edwards	.10	.05	.01
☐ 358	Juan Eichelberger	.10	.05	.01
☐ 359	Tim Flannery	.10	.05	.01
☐ 360	Tony Gwynn	20.00	9.00	2.50
☐ 361	Ruppert Jones	.10	.05	.01
☐ 362	Terry Kennedy	.10	.05	.01
☐ 363	Joe Lefebvre	.10	.05	.01
☐ 364	Sixto Lezcano	.10	.05	.01
☐ 365	Tim Lollar	.10	.05	.01
☐ 366	Gary Lucas	.10	.05	.01
☐ 367	John Montefusco	.10	.05	.01
☐ 368	Broderick Perkins	.10	.05	.01
☐ 369	Joe Pittman	.10	.05	.01
☐ 370	Gene Richards	.10	.05	.01
☐ 371	Luis Salazar	.10	.05	.01
☐ 372	Eric Show	.20	.09	.03
☐ 373	Garry Templeton	.10	.05	.01
☐ 374	Chris Welsh	.10	.05	.01
☐ 375	Alan Wiggins	.10	.05	.01
☐ 376	Rick Cerone	.10	.05	.01
☐ 377	Dave Collins	.10	.05	.01
☐ 378	Roger Erickson	.10	.05	.01
☐ 379	George Frazier	.10	.05	.01
☐ 380	Oscar Gamble	.10	.05	.01
☐ 381	Rich Gossage	.30	.14	.04
☐ 382	Ken Griffey	.20	.09	.03
☐ 383	Ron Guidry	.20	.09	.03
☐ 384	Dave LaRoche	.10	.05	.01
☐ 385	Rudy May	.10	.05	.01
☐ 386	John Mayberry	.10	.05	.01
☐ 387	Lee Mazzilli	.10	.05	.01
☐ 388	Mike Morgan	.10	.05	.01
☐ 389	Jerry Mumphrey	.10	.05	.01

☐ 390 Bobby Murcer	.20	.09	.03
☐ 391 Graig Nettles	.20	.09	.03
☐ 392 Lou Piniella	.20	.09	.03
☐ 393 Willie Randolph	.20	.09	.03
☐ 394 Shane Rawley	.10	.05	.01
☐ 395 Dave Righetti	.20	.09	.03
☐ 396 Andre Robertson	.10	.05	.01
☐ 397 Roy Smalley	.10	.05	.01
☐ 398 Dave Winfield	1.50	.70	.19
☐ 399 Butch Wynegar	.10	.05	.01
☐ 400 Chris Bando	.10	.05	.01
☐ 401 Alan Bannister	.10	.05	.01
☐ 402 Len Barker	.10	.05	.01
☐ 403 Tom Brennan	.10	.05	.01
☐ 404 Carmelo Castillo	.10	.05	.01
☐ 405 Miguel Dilone	.10	.05	.01
☐ 406 Jerry Dybzinski	.10	.05	.01
☐ 407 Mike Fischlin	.10	.05	.01
☐ 408 Ed Glynn UER	.10	.05	.01
(Photo actually			
Bud Anderson)			
☐ 409 Mike Hargrove	.20	.09	.03
☐ 410 Toby Harrah	.10	.05	.01
☐ 411 Ron Hassey	.10	.05	.01
☐ 412 Von Hayes	.20	.09	.03
☐ 413 Rick Manning	.10	.05	.01
☐ 414 Bake McBride	.10	.05	.01
☐ 415 Larry Milbourne	.10	.05	.01
☐ 416 Bill Nahorodny	.10	.05	.01
☐ 417 Jack Perconte	.10	.05	.01
☐ 418 Lary Sorensen	.10	.05	.01
☐ 419 Dan Spillner	.10	.05	.01
☐ 420 Rick Sutcliffe	.20	.09	.03
☐ 421 Andre Thornton	.10	.05	.01
☐ 422 Rick Waits	.10	.05	.01
☐ 423 Eddie Whitson	.10	.05	.01
☐ 424 Jesse Barfield	.20	.09	.03
☐ 425 Barry Bonnell	.10	.05	.01
☐ 426 Jim Clancy	.10	.05	.01
☐ 427 Damaso García	.10	.05	.01
☐ 428 Jerry Garvin	.10	.05	.01
☐ 429 Alfredo Griffin	.10	.05	.01
☐ 430 Garth Iorg	.10	.05	.01
☐ 431 Roy Lee Jackson	.10	.05	.01
☐ 432 Luis Leal	.10	.05	.01
☐ 433 Buck Martinez	.10	.05	.01
☐ 434 Joey McLaughlin	.10	.05	.01
☐ 435 Lloyd Moseby	.10	.05	.01
☐ 436 Rance Mulliniks	.10	.05	.01
☐ 437 Dale Murray	.10	.05	.01
☐ 438 Wayne Nordhagen	.10	.05	.01
☐ 439 Geno Petralli	.20	.09	.03
☐ 440 Hosken Powell	.10	.05	.01
☐ 441 Dave Stieb	.20	.09	.03
☐ 442 Willie Upshaw	.10	.05	.01
☐ 443 Ernie Whitt	.10	.05	.01
☐ 444 Alvis Woods	.10	.05	.01
☐ 445 Alan Ashby	.10	.05	.01
☐ 446 Jose Cruz	.20	.09	.03
☐ 447 Kiko Garcia	.10	.05	.01
☐ 448 Phil Garner	.20	.09	.03
☐ 449 Danny Heep	.10	.05	.01
☐ 450 Art Howe	.10	.05	.01
☐ 451 Bob Knepper	.10	.05	.01
☐ 452 Alan Knicely	.10	.05	.01
☐ 453 Ray Knight	.20	.09	.03
☐ 454 Frank LaCorte	.10	.05	.01
☐ 455 Mike LaCoss	.10	.05	.01
☐ 456 Randy Moffitt	.10	.05	.01
☐ 457 Joe Niekro	.20	.09	.03
☐ 458 Terry Puhl	.10	.05	.01
☐ 459 Luis Pujols	.10	.05	.01
☐ 460 Craig Reynolds	.10	.05	.01
☐ 461 Bert Roberge	.10	.05	.01
☐ 462 Vern Ruhle	.10	.05	.01
☐ 463 Nolan Ryan	5.00	2.20	.60
☐ 464 Joe Sambito	.10	.05	.01
☐ 465 Tony Scott	.10	.05	.01
☐ 466 Dave Smith	.10	.05	.01
☐ 467 Harry Spilman	.10	.05	.01
☐ 468 Dickie Thon	.10	.05	.01
☐ 469 Denny Walling	.10	.05	.01
☐ 470 Larry Andersen	.10	.05	.01
☐ 471 Floyd Bannister	.10	.05	.01
☐ 472 Jim Beattie	.10	.05	.01
☐ 473 Bruce Bochte	.10	.05	.01
☐ 474 Manny Castillo	.10	.05	.01
☐ 475 Bill Caudill	.10	.05	.01
☐ 476 Bryan Clark	.10	.05	.01
☐ 477 Al Cowens	.10	.05	.01
☐ 478 Julio Cruz	.10	.05	.01
☐ 479 Todd Cruz	.10	.05	.01
☐ 480 Gary Gray	.10	.05	.01
☐ 481 Dave Henderson	.20	.09	.03
☐ 482 Mike Moore	.20	.09	.03
☐ 483 Gaylord Perry	.30	.14	.04
☐ 484 Dave Revering	.10	.05	.01
☐ 485 Joe Simpson	.10	.05	.01
☐ 486 Mike Stanton	.10	.05	.01
☐ 487 Rick Sweet	.10	.05	.01
☐ 488 Ed VandeBerg	.10	.05	.01
☐ 489 Richie Zisk	.10	.05	.01
☐ 490 Doug Bird	.10	.05	.01
☐ 491 Larry Bowa	.20	.09	.03
☐ 492 Bill Buckner	.20	.09	.03
☐ 493 Bill Campbell	.10	.05	.01
☐ 494 Jody Davis	.10	.05	.01
☐ 495 Leon Durham	.10	.05	.01
☐ 496 Steve Henderson	.10	.05	.01
☐ 497 Willie Hernandez	.20	.09	.03
☐ 498 Ferguson Jenkins	.30	.14	.04
☐ 499 Jay Johnstone	.20	.09	.03
☐ 500 Junior Kennedy	.10	.05	.01
☐ 501 Randy Martz	.10	.05	.01
☐ 502 Jerry Morales	.10	.05	.01
☐ 503 Keith Moreland	.10	.05	.01
☐ 504 Dickie Noles	.10	.05	.01
☐ 505 Mike Proly	.10	.05	.01
☐ 506 Allen Ripley	.10	.05	.01
☐ 507 Ryne Sandberg UER	20.00	9.00	2.50
(Should say High School			
in Spokane, Washington)			
☐ 508 Lee Smith	2.00	.90	.25
☐ 509 Pat Tabler	.10	.05	.01
☐ 510 Dick Tidrow	.10	.05	.01
☐ 511 Bump Wills	.10	.05	.01
☐ 512 Gary Woods	.10	.05	.01
☐ 513 Tony Armas	.10	.05	.01
☐ 514 Dave Beard	.10	.05	.01
☐ 515 Jeff Burroughs	.10	.05	.01
☐ 516 John D'Acquisto	.10	.05	.01
☐ 517 Wayne Gross	.10	.05	.01
☐ 518 Mike Heath	.10	.05	.01
☐ 519 Rickey Henderson UER	2.00	.90	.25
(Brock record listed			
as 120 steals)			
☐ 520 Cliff Johnson	.10	.05	.01
☐ 521 Matt Keough	.10	.05	.01
☐ 522 Brian Kingman	.10	.05	.01
☐ 523 Rick Langford	.10	.05	.01
☐ 524 Dave Lopes	.20	.09	.03
☐ 525 Steve McCatty	.10	.05	.01

☐ 526	Dave McKay	.10	.05	.01
☐ 527	Dan Meyer	.10	.05	.01
☐ 528	Dwayne Murphy	.10	.05	.01
☐ 529	Jeff Newman	.10	.05	.01
☐ 530	Mike Norris	.10	.05	.01
☐ 531	Bob Owchinko	.10	.05	.01
☐ 532	Joe Rudi	.10	.05	.01
☐ 533	Jimmy Sexton	.10	.05	.01
☐ 534	Fred Stanley	.10	.05	.01
☐ 535	Tom Underwood	.10	.05	.01
☐ 536	Neil Allen	.10	.05	.01
☐ 537	Wally Backman	.10	.05	.01
☐ 538	Bob Bailor	.10	.05	.01
☐ 539	Hubie Brooks	.20	.09	.03
☐ 540	Carlos Diaz	.10	.05	.01
☐ 541	Pete Falcone	.10	.05	.01
☐ 542	George Foster	.20	.09	.03
☐ 543	Ron Gardenhire	.10	.05	.01
☐ 544	Brian Giles	.10	.05	.01
☐ 545	Ron Hodges	.10	.05	.01
☐ 546	Randy Jones	.10	.05	.01
☐ 547	Mike Jorgensen	.10	.05	.01
☐ 548	Dave Kingman	.20	.09	.03
☐ 549	Ed Lynch	.10	.05	.01
☐ 550	Jesse Orosco	.10	.05	.01
☐ 551	Rick Ownbey	.10	.05	.01
☐ 552	Charlie Puleo	.10	.05	.01
☐ 553	Gary Rajsich	.10	.05	.01
☐ 554	Mike Scott	.20	.09	.03
☐ 555	Rusty Staub	.20	.09	.03
☐ 556	John Stearns	.10	.05	.01
☐ 557	Craig Swan	.10	.05	.01
☐ 558	Ellis Valentine	.10	.05	.01
☐ 559	Tom Veryzer	.10	.05	.01
☐ 560	Mookie Wilson	.20	.09	.03
☐ 561	Pat Zachry	.10	.05	.01
☐ 562	Buddy Bell	.20	.09	.03
☐ 563	John Butcher	.10	.05	.01
☐ 564	Steve Comer	.10	.05	.01
☐ 565	Danny Darwin	.10	.05	.01
☐ 566	Bucky Dent	.20	.09	.03
☐ 567	John Grubb	.10	.05	.01
☐ 568	Rick Honeycutt	.10	.05	.01
☐ 569	Dave Hostetler	.10	.05	.01
☐ 570	Charlie Hough	.20	.09	.03
☐ 571	Lamar Johnson	.10	.05	.01
☐ 572	Jon Matlack	.10	.05	.01
☐ 573	Paul Mirabella	.10	.05	.01
☐ 574	Larry Parrish	.10	.05	.01
☐ 575	Mike Richardt	.10	.05	.01
☐ 576	Mickey Rivers	.10	.05	.01
☐ 577	Billy Sample	.10	.05	.01
☐ 578	Dave Schmidt	.10	.05	.01
☐ 579	Bill Stein	.10	.05	.01
☐ 580	Jim Sundberg	.20	.09	.03
☐ 581	Frank Tanana	.20	.09	.03
☐ 582	Mark Wagner	.10	.05	.01
☐ 583	George Wright	.10	.05	.01
☐ 584	Johnny Bench	.75	.35	.09
☐ 585	Bruce Berenyi	.10	.05	.01
☐ 586	Larry Biittner	.10	.05	.01
☐ 587	Cesar Cedeno	.20	.09	.03
☐ 588	Dave Concepcion	.20	.09	.03
☐ 589	Dan Driessen	.10	.05	.01
☐ 590	Greg Harris	.10	.05	.01
☐ 591	Ben Hayes	.10	.05	.01
☐ 592	Paul Householder	.10	.05	.01
☐ 593	Tom Hume	.10	.05	.01
☐ 594	Wayne Krenchicki	.10	.05	.01
☐ 595	Rafael Landestoy	.10	.05	.01
☐ 596	Charlie Leibrandt	.20	.09	.03
☐ 597	Eddie Milner	.10	.05	.01
☐ 598	Ron Oester	.10	.05	.01
☐ 599	Frank Pastore	.10	.05	.01
☐ 600	Joe Price	.10	.05	.01
☐ 601	Tom Seaver	.75	.35	.09
☐ 602	Bob Shirley	.10	.05	.01
☐ 603	Mario Soto	.10	.05	.01
☐ 604	Alex Trevino	.10	.05	.01
☐ 605	Mike Vail	.10	.05	.01
☐ 606	Duane Walker	.10	.05	.01
☐ 607	Tom Brunansky	.20	.09	.03
☐ 608	Bobby Castillo	.10	.05	.01
☐ 609	John Castino	.10	.05	.01
☐ 610	Ron Davis	.10	.05	.01
☐ 611	Lenny Faedo	.10	.05	.01
☐ 612	Terry Felton	.10	.05	.01
☐ 613	Gary Gaetti	.75	.35	.09
☐ 614	Mickey Hatcher	.10	.05	.01
☐ 615	Brad Havens	.10	.05	.01
☐ 616	Kent Hrbek	.30	.14	.04
☐ 617	Randy Johnson	.10	.05	.01
☐ 618	Tim Laudner	.10	.05	.01
☐ 619	Jeff Little	.10	.05	.01
☐ 620	Bobby Mitchell	.10	.05	.01
☐ 621	Jack O'Connor	.10	.05	.01
☐ 622	John Pacella	.10	.05	.01
☐ 623	Pete Redfern	.10	.05	.01
☐ 624	Jesus Vega	.10	.05	.01
☐ 625	Frank Viola	.60	.25	.07
☐ 626	Ron Washington	.10	.05	.01
☐ 627	Gary Ward	.10	.05	.01
☐ 628	Al Williams	.10	.05	.01
☐ 629	Red Sox All-Stars	.60	.25	.07
	Carl Yastrzemski			
	Dennis Eckersley			
	Mark Clear			
☐ 630	"300 Career Wins"	.20	.09	.03
	Gaylord Perry and			
	Terry Bulling 5/6/82			
☐ 631	Pride of Venezuela	.20	.09	.03
	Dave Concepcion and			
	Manny Trillo			
☐ 632	All-Star Infielders	.30	.14	.04
	Robin Yount and			
	Buddy Bell			
☐ 633	Mr.Vet and Mr.Rookie	.75	.35	.09
	Dave Winfield and			
	Kent Hrbek			
☐ 634	Fountain of Youth	.60	.25	.07
	Willie Stargell and			
	Pete Rose			
☐ 635	Big Chiefs	.20	.09	.03
	Toby Harrah and			
	Andre Thornton			
☐ 636	Smith Brothers	.75	.35	.09
	Ozzie Smith			
	Lonnie Smith			
☐ 637	Base Stealers' Threat	.20	.09	.03
	Bo Diaz and			
	Gary Carter			
☐ 638	All-Star Catchers	.30	.14	.04
	Carlton Fisk and			
	Gary Carter			
☐ 639	The Silver Shoe	1.00	.45	.12
	Rickey Henderson			
☐ 640	Home Run Threats	.30	.14	.04
	Ben Oglivie and			
	Reggie Jackson			
☐ 641	Two Teams Same Day	.10	.05	.01
	Joel Youngblood			
	August 4, 1982			

☐ 642	Last Perfect Game .... Ron Hassey and Len Barker	.20	.09	.03
☐ 643	Black and Blue .... Vida Blue	.20	.09	.03
☐ 644	Black and Blue .... Bud Black	.20	.09	.03
☐ 645	Speed and Power.......... Reggie Jackson	.50	.23	.06
☐ 646	Speed and Power.......... Rickey Henderson	1.00	.45	.12
☐ 647	CL: Cards/Brewers	.20	.09	.03
☐ 648	CL: Orioles/Angels	.20	.09	.03
☐ 649	CL: Royals/Braves	.20	.09	.03
☐ 650	CL: Phillies/Red Sox	.20	.09	.03
☐ 651	CL: Dodgers/White Sox	.20	.09	.03
☐ 652	CL: Giants/Expos	.20	.09	.03
☐ 653	CL: Pirates/Tigers	.20	.09	.03
☐ 654	CL: Padres/Yankees	.20	.09	.03
☐ 655	CL: Indians/Blue Jays ...	.20	.09	.03
☐ 656	CL: Astros/Mariners	.20	.09	.03
☐ 657	CL: Cubs/A's	.20	.09	.03
☐ 658	CL: Mets/Rangers	.20	.09	.03
☐ 659	CL: Reds/Twins	.20	.09	.03
☐ 660	CL: Specials/Teams	.20	.09	.03

1984 Fleer

The cards in this 660-card set measure 2 1/2" by 3 1/2". The 1984 Fleer card set featured fronts with full-color team logos along with the player's name and position and the Fleer identification. The set features many imaginative photos, several multi-player cards, and many more action shots than the 1983 card set. The backs are quite similar to the 1983 backs except that blue rather than brown ink is used. The player cards are alphabetized within team and the teams are ordered by their 1983 season finish and won-lost record, e.g., Baltimore (1-23), Philadelphia (24-49), Chicago White Sox (50-73), Detroit (74-95), Los Angeles (96-118), New York Yankees (119-144), Toronto (145-169), Atlanta (170-193), Milwaukee (194-219), Houston (220-244), Pittsburgh (245-269), Montreal (270-293), San Diego (294-317), St. Louis (318-340), Kansas City (341-364), San Francisco (365-387), Boston (388-412), Texas (413-435), Oakland (436-461), Cincinnati (462-485), Chicago (486-507), California (508-532), Cleveland (533-555), Minnesota (556-

579), New York Mets (580-603), and Seattle (604-625). Specials (626-646) and checklist cards (647-660) make up the end of the set. The key Rookie Cards in this set are Tony Fernandez, Don Mattingly, Kevin McReynolds, Juan Samuel, Darryl Strawberry, and Andy Van Slyke.

	NRMT-MT	EXC	G-VG
COMPLETE SET (660)	90.00	40.00	11.00
COMMON CARD (1-660)	.15	.07	.02

☐ 1	Mike Boddicker	.30	.14	.04
☐ 2	Al Bumbry	.30	.14	.04
☐ 3	Todd Cruz	.15	.07	.02
☐ 4	Rich Dauer	.15	.07	.02
☐ 5	Storm Davis	.15	.07	.02
☐ 6	Rick Dempsey	.15	.07	.02
☐ 7	Jim Dwyer	.15	.07	.02
☐ 8	Mike Flanagan	.15	.07	.02
☐ 9	Dan Ford	.15	.07	.02
☐ 10	John Lowenstein	.15	.07	.02
☐ 11	Dennis Martinez	.30	.14	.04
☐ 12	Tippy Martinez	.15	.07	.02
☐ 13	Scott McGregor	.15	.07	.02
☐ 14	Eddie Murray	5.00	2.20	.60
☐ 15	Joe Nolan	.15	.07	.02
☐ 16	Jim Palmer	2.00	.90	.25
☐ 17	Cal Ripken	20.00	9.00	2.50
☐ 18	Gary Roenicke	.15	.07	.02
☐ 19	Lenn Sakata	.15	.07	.02
☐ 20	John Shelby	.15	.07	.02
☐ 21	Ken Singleton	.30	.14	.04
☐ 22	Sammy Stewart	.15	.07	.02
☐ 23	Tim Stoddard	.15	.07	.02
☐ 24	Marty Bystrom	.15	.07	.02
☐ 25	Steve Carlton	2.00	.90	.25
☐ 26	Ivan DeJesus	.15	.07	.02
☐ 27	John Denny	.15	.07	.02
☐ 28	Bob Dernier	.15	.07	.02
☐ 29	Bo Diaz	.15	.07	.02
☐ 30	Kiko Garcia	.15	.07	.02
☐ 31	Greg Gross	.15	.07	.02
☐ 32	Kevin Gross	.30	.14	.04
☐ 33	Von Hayes	.15	.07	.02
☐ 34	Willie Hernandez	.30	.14	.04
☐ 35	Al Holland	.15	.07	.02
☐ 36	Charles Hudson	.15	.07	.02
☐ 37	Joe Lefebvre	.15	.07	.02
☐ 38	Sixto Lezcano	.15	.07	.02
☐ 39	Garry Maddox	.15	.07	.02
☐ 40	Gary Matthews	.30	.14	.04
☐ 41	Len Matuszek	.15	.07	.02
☐ 42	Tug McGraw	.30	.14	.04
☐ 43	Joe Morgan	1.00	.45	.12
☐ 44	Tony Perez	.50	.23	.06
☐ 45	Ron Reed	.15	.07	.02
☐ 46	Pete Rose	3.00	1.35	.35
☐ 47	Juan Samuel	.50	.23	.06
☐ 48	Mike Schmidt	5.00	2.20	.60
☐ 49	Ozzie Virgil	.15	.07	.02
☐ 50	Juan Agosto	.15	.07	.02
☐ 51	Harold Baines	.50	.23	.06
☐ 52	Floyd Bannister	.15	.07	.02
☐ 53	Salome Barojas	.15	.07	.02
☐ 54	Britt Burns	.15	.07	.02
☐ 55	Julio Cruz	.15	.07	.02
☐ 56	Richard Dotson	.15	.07	.02
☐ 57	Jerry Dybzinski	.15	.07	.02
☐ 58	Carlton Fisk	2.00	.90	.25
☐ 59	Scott Fletcher	.15	.07	.02

☐ 60 Jerry Hairston	.15	.07	.02
☐ 61 Kevin Hickey	.15	.07	.02
☐ 62 Marc Hill	.15	.07	.02
☐ 63 LaMarr Hoyt	.15	.07	.02
☐ 64 Ron Kittle	.15	.07	.02
☐ 65 Jerry Koosman	.30	.14	.04
☐ 66 Dennis Lamp	.15	.07	.02
☐ 67 Rudy Law	.15	.07	.02
☐ 68 Vance Law	.15	.07	.02
☐ 69 Greg Luzinski	.30	.14	.04
☐ 70 Tom Paciorek	.30	.14	.04
☐ 71 Mike Squires	.15	.07	.02
☐ 72 Dick Tidrow	.15	.07	.02
☐ 73 Greg Walker	.15	.07	.02
☐ 74 Glenn Abbott	.15	.07	.02
☐ 75 Howard Bailey	.15	.07	.02
☐ 76 Doug Bair	.15	.07	.02
☐ 77 Juan Berenguer	.15	.07	.02
☐ 78 Tom Brookens	.30	.14	.04
☐ 79 Enos Cabell	.15	.07	.02
☐ 80 Kirk Gibson	1.00	.45	.12
☐ 81 John Grubb	.15	.07	.02
☐ 82 Larry Herndon	.30	.14	.04
☐ 83 Wayne Krenchicki	.15	.07	.02
☐ 84 Rick Leach	.15	.07	.02
☐ 85 Chet Lemon	.30	.14	.04
☐ 86 Aurelio Lopez	.30	.14	.04
☐ 87 Jack Morris	.50	.23	.06
☐ 88 Lance Parrish	.30	.14	.04
☐ 89 Dan Petry	.30	.14	.04
☐ 90 Dave Rozema	.15	.07	.02
☐ 91 Alan Trammell	1.50	.70	.19
☐ 92 Lou Whitaker	1.00	.45	.12
☐ 93 Milt Wilcox	.15	.07	.02
☐ 94 Glenn Wilson	.30	.14	.04
☐ 95 John Wockenfuss	.15	.07	.02
☐ 96 Dusty Baker	.50	.23	.06
☐ 97 Joe Beckwith	.15	.07	.02
☐ 98 Greg Brock	.15	.07	.02
☐ 99 Jack Fimple	.15	.07	.02
☐ 100 Pedro Guerrero	.30	.14	.04
☐ 101 Rick Honeycutt	.15	.07	.02
☐ 102 Burt Hooton	.15	.07	.02
☐ 103 Steve Howe	.15	.07	.02
☐ 104 Ken Landreaux	.15	.07	.02
☐ 105 Mike Marshall	.15	.07	.02
☐ 106 Rick Monday	.15	.07	.02
☐ 107 Jose Morales	.15	.07	.02
☐ 108 Tom Niedenfuer	.15	.07	.02
☐ 109 Alejandro Pena	.30	.14	.04
☐ 110 Jerry Reuss UER ("Home:" omitted)	.15	.07	.02
☐ 111 Bill Russell	.30	.14	.04
☐ 112 Steve Sax	.30	.14	.04
☐ 113 Mike Scioscia	.15	.07	.02
☐ 114 Derrel Thomas	.15	.07	.02
☐ 115 Fernando Valenzuela	.30	.14	.04
☐ 116 Bob Welch	.30	.14	.04
☐ 117 Steve Yeager	.15	.07	.02
☐ 118 Pat Zachry	.15	.07	.02
☐ 119 Don Baylor	.50	.23	.06
☐ 120 Bert Campaneris	.30	.14	.04
☐ 121 Rick Cerone	.15	.07	.02
☐ 122 Ray Fontenot	.15	.07	.02
☐ 123 George Frazier	.15	.07	.02
☐ 124 Oscar Gamble	.15	.07	.02
☐ 125 Rich Gossage	.50	.23	.06
☐ 126 Ken Griffey	.30	.14	.04
☐ 127 Ron Guidry	.30	.14	.04
☐ 128 Jay Howell	.30	.14	.04
☐ 129 Steve Kemp	.15	.07	.02
☐ 130 Matt Keough	.15	.07	.02
☐ 131 Don Mattingly	25.00	11.00	3.10
☐ 132 John Montefusco	.15	.07	.02
☐ 133 Omar Moreno	.15	.07	.02
☐ 134 Dale Murray	.15	.07	.02
☐ 135 Graig Nettles	.30	.14	.04
☐ 136 Lou Piniella	.30	.14	.04
☐ 137 Willie Randolph	.30	.14	.04
☐ 138 Shane Rawley	.15	.07	.02
☐ 139 Dave Righetti	.30	.14	.04
☐ 140 Andre Robertson	.15	.07	.02
☐ 141 Bob Shirley	.15	.07	.02
☐ 142 Roy Smalley	.15	.07	.02
☐ 143 Dave Winfield	3.00	1.35	.35
☐ 144 Butch Wynegar	.15	.07	.02
☐ 145 Jim Acker	.15	.07	.02
☐ 146 Doyle Alexander	.15	.07	.02
☐ 147 Jesse Barfield	.30	.14	.04
☐ 148 Jorge Bell	.30	.14	.04
☐ 149 Barry Bonnell	.15	.07	.02
☐ 150 Jim Clancy	.15	.07	.02
☐ 151 Dave Collins	.15	.07	.02
☐ 152 Tony Fernandez	1.50	.70	.19
☐ 153 Damaso Garcia	.15	.07	.02
☐ 154 Dave Geisel	.15	.07	.02
☐ 155 Jim Gott	.15	.07	.02
☐ 156 Alfredo Griffin	.15	.07	.02
☐ 157 Garth Iorg	.15	.07	.02
☐ 158 Roy Lee Jackson	.15	.07	.02
☐ 159 Cliff Johnson	.15	.07	.02
☐ 160 Luis Leal	.15	.07	.02
☐ 161 Buck Martinez	.15	.07	.02
☐ 162 Joey McLaughlin	.15	.07	.02
☐ 163 Randy Moffitt	.15	.07	.02
☐ 164 Lloyd Moseby	.15	.07	.02
☐ 165 Rance Mulliniks	.15	.07	.02
☐ 166 Jorge Orta	.15	.07	.02
☐ 167 Dave Stieb	.30	.14	.04
☐ 168 Willie Upshaw	.15	.07	.02
☐ 169 Ernie Whitt	.15	.07	.02
☐ 170 Len Barker	.15	.07	.02
☐ 171 Steve Bedrosian	.30	.14	.04
☐ 172 Bruce Benedict	.15	.07	.02
☐ 173 Brett Butler	.50	.23	.06
☐ 174 Rick Camp	.15	.07	.02
☐ 175 Chris Chambliss	.30	.14	.04
☐ 176 Ken Dayley	.15	.07	.02
☐ 177 Pete Falcone	.15	.07	.02
☐ 178 Terry Forster	.15	.07	.02
☐ 179 Gene Garber	.15	.07	.02
☐ 180 Terry Harper	.15	.07	.02
☐ 181 Bob Horner	.30	.14	.04
☐ 182 Glenn Hubbard	.15	.07	.02
☐ 183 Randy Johnson	.15	.07	.02
☐ 184 Craig McMurtry	.15	.07	.02
☐ 185 Donnie Moore	.15	.07	.02
☐ 186 Dale Murphy	1.00	.45	.12
☐ 187 Phil Niekro	.50	.23	.06
☐ 188 Pascual Perez	.15	.07	.02
☐ 189 Biff Pocoroba	.15	.07	.02
☐ 190 Rafael Ramirez	.15	.07	.02
☐ 191 Jerry Royster	.15	.07	.02
☐ 192 Claudell Washington	.15	.07	.02
☐ 193 Bob Watson	.30	.14	.04
☐ 194 Jerry Augustine	.15	.07	.02
☐ 195 Mark Brouhard	.15	.07	.02
☐ 196 Mike Caldwell	.15	.07	.02
☐ 197 Tom Candiotti	.75	.35	.09
☐ 198 Cecil Cooper	.30	.14	.04
☐ 199 Rollie Fingers	.50	.23	.06
☐ 200 Jim Gantner	.30	.14	.04

☐ 201	Bob L. Gibson	.15	.07	.02
☐ 202	Moose Haas	.15	.07	.02
☐ 203	Roy Howell	.15	.07	.02
☐ 204	Pete Ladd	.15	.07	.02
☐ 205	Rick Manning	.15	.07	.02
☐ 206	Bob McClure	.15	.07	.02
☐ 207	Paul Molitor UER	2.50	1.10	.30
	('83 stats should say			
	.270 BA and 608 AB)			
☐ 208	Don Money	.15	.07	.02
☐ 209	Charlie Moore	.15	.07	.02
☐ 210	Ben Oglivie	.15	.07	.02
☐ 211	Chuck Porter	.15	.07	.02
☐ 212	Ed Romero	.15	.07	.02
☐ 213	Ted Simmons	.30	.14	.04
☐ 214	Jim Slaton	.15	.07	.02
☐ 215	Don Sutton	.50	.23	.06
☐ 216	Tom Tellmann	.15	.07	.02
☐ 217	Pete Vuckovich	.15	.07	.02
☐ 218	Ned Yost	.15	.07	.02
☐ 219	Robin Yount	3.00	1.35	.35
☐ 220	Alan Ashby	.15	.07	.02
☐ 221	Kevin Bass	.15	.07	.02
☐ 222	Jose Cruz	.30	.14	.04
☐ 223	Bill Dawley	.15	.07	.02
☐ 224	Frank DiPino	.15	.07	.02
☐ 225	Bill Doran	.30	.14	.04
☐ 226	Phil Garner	.30	.14	.04
☐ 227	Art Howe	.15	.07	.02
☐ 228	Bob Knepper	.15	.07	.02
☐ 229	Ray Knight	.30	.14	.04
☐ 230	Frank LaCorte	.15	.07	.02
☐ 231	Mike LaCoss	.15	.07	.02
☐ 232	Mike Madden	.15	.07	.02
☐ 233	Jerry Mumphrey	.15	.07	.02
☐ 234	Joe Niekro	.30	.14	.04
☐ 235	Terry Puhl	.15	.07	.02
☐ 236	Luis Pujols	.15	.07	.02
☐ 237	Craig Reynolds	.15	.07	.02
☐ 238	Vern Ruhle	.15	.07	.02
☐ 239	Nolan Ryan	18.00	8.00	2.20
☐ 240	Mike Scott	.30	.14	.04
☐ 241	Tony Scott	.15	.07	.02
☐ 242	Dave Smith	.15	.07	.02
☐ 243	Dickie Thon	.15	.07	.02
☐ 244	Denny Walling	.15	.07	.02
☐ 245	Dale Berra	.15	.07	.02
☐ 246	Jim Bibby	.15	.07	.02
☐ 247	John Candelaria	.15	.07	.02
☐ 248	Jose DeLeon	.30	.14	.04
☐ 249	Mike Easler	.15	.07	.02
☐ 250	Cecilio Guante	.15	.07	.02
☐ 251	Richie Hebner	.15	.07	.02
☐ 252	Lee Lacy	.15	.07	.02
☐ 253	Bill Madlock	.30	.14	.04
☐ 254	Milt May	.15	.07	.02
☐ 255	Lee Mazzilli	.15	.07	.02
☐ 256	Larry McWilliams	.15	.07	.02
☐ 257	Jim Morrison	.15	.07	.02
☐ 258	Dave Parker	.50	.23	.06
☐ 259	Tony Pena	.30	.14	.04
☐ 260	Johnny Ray	.15	.07	.02
☐ 261	Rick Rhoden	.15	.07	.02
☐ 262	Don Robinson	.15	.07	.02
☐ 263	Manny Sarmiento	.15	.07	.02
☐ 264	Rod Scurry	.15	.07	.02
☐ 265	Kent Tekulve	.30	.14	.04
☐ 266	Gene Tenace	.15	.07	.02
☐ 267	Jason Thompson	.15	.07	.02
☐ 268	Lee Tunnell	.15	.07	.02
☐ 269	Marvell Wynne	.15	.07	.02
☐ 270	Ray Burris	.15	.07	.02
☐ 271	Gary Carter	.50	.23	.06
☐ 272	Warren Cromartie	.15	.07	.02
☐ 273	Andre Dawson	2.50	1.10	.30
☐ 274	Doug Flynn	.15	.07	.02
☐ 275	Terry Francona	.15	.07	.02
☐ 276	Bill Gullickson	.30	.14	.04
☐ 277	Bob James	.15	.07	.02
☐ 278	Charlie Lea	.15	.07	.02
☐ 279	Bryan Little	.15	.07	.02
☐ 280	Al Oliver	.30	.14	.04
☐ 281	Tim Raines	1.25	.55	.16
☐ 282	Bobby Ramos	.15	.07	.02
☐ 283	Jeff Reardon	.50	.23	.06
☐ 284	Steve Rogers	.15	.07	.02
☐ 285	Scott Sanderson	.15	.07	.02
☐ 286	Dan Schatzeder	.15	.07	.02
☐ 287	Bryn Smith	.15	.07	.02
☐ 288	Chris Speier	.15	.07	.02
☐ 289	Manny Trillo	.15	.07	.02
☐ 290	Mike Vail	.15	.07	.02
☐ 291	Tim Wallach	.30	.14	.04
☐ 292	Chris Welsh	.15	.07	.02
☐ 293	Jim Wohlford	.15	.07	.02
☐ 294	Kurt Bevacqua	.15	.07	.02
☐ 295	Juan Bonilla	.15	.07	.02
☐ 296	Bobby Brown	.15	.07	.02
☐ 297	Luis DeLeon	.15	.07	.02
☐ 298	Dave Dravecky	.30	.14	.02
☐ 299	Tim Flannery	.15	.07	.02
☐ 300	Steve Garvey	.50	.23	.06
☐ 301	Tony Gwynn	10.00	4.50	1.25
☐ 302	Andy Hawkins	.15	.07	.02
☐ 303	Ruppert Jones	.15	.07	.02
☐ 304	Terry Kennedy	.15	.07	.02
☐ 305	Tim Lollar	.15	.07	.02
☐ 306	Gary Lucas	.15	.07	.02
☐ 307	Kevin McReynolds	.50	.23	.06
☐ 308	Sid Monge	.15	.07	.02
☐ 309	Mario Ramirez	.15	.07	.02
☐ 310	Gene Richards	.15	.07	.02
☐ 311	Luis Salazar	.15	.07	.02
☐ 312	Eric Show	.15	.07	.02
☐ 313	Elias Sosa	.15	.07	.02
☐ 314	Garry Templeton	.15	.07	.02
☐ 315	Mark Thurmond	.15	.07	.02
☐ 316	Ed Whitson	.15	.07	.02
☐ 317	Alan Wiggins	.15	.07	.02
☐ 318	Neil Allen	.15	.07	.02
☐ 319	Joaquin Andujar	.15	.07	.02
☐ 320	Steve Braun	.15	.07	.02
☐ 321	Glenn Brummer	.15	.07	.02
☐ 322	Bob Forsch	.15	.07	.02
☐ 323	David Green	.15	.07	.02
☐ 324	George Hendrick	.15	.07	.02
☐ 325	Tom Herr	.30	.14	.04
☐ 326	Dane Iorg	.15	.07	.02
☐ 327	Jeff Lahti	.15	.07	.02
☐ 328	Dave LaPoint	.15	.07	.02
☐ 329	Willie McGee	.30	.14	.04
☐ 330	Ken Oberkfell	.15	.07	.02
☐ 331	Darrell Porter	.15	.07	.02
☐ 332	Jamie Quirk	.15	.07	.02
☐ 333	Mike Ramsey	.15	.07	.02
☐ 334	Floyd Rayford	.15	.07	.02
☐ 335	Lonnie Smith	.30	.14	.04
☐ 336	Ozzie Smith	4.00	1.80	.50
☐ 337	John Stuper	.15	.07	.02
☐ 338	Bruce Sutter	.30	.14	.04
☐ 339	Andy Van Slyke UER	2.00	.90	.25
	(Batting and throwing			

both wrong on card back)

☐ 340	Dave Von Ohlen	.15	.07	.02
☐ 341	Willie Aikens	.15	.07	.02
☐ 342	Mike Armstrong	.15	.07	.02
☐ 343	Bud Black	.15	.07	.02
☐ 344	George Brett	8.00	3.60	1.00
☐ 345	Onix Concepcion	.15	.07	.02
☐ 346	Keith Creel	.15	.07	.02
☐ 347	Larry Gura	.15	.07	.02
☐ 348	Don Hood	.15	.07	.02
☐ 349	Dennis Leonard	.15	.07	.02
☐ 350	Hal McRae	.50	.23	.06
☐ 351	Amos Otis	.30	.14	.04
☐ 352	Gaylord Perry	.50	.23	.06
☐ 353	Greg Pryor	.15	.07	.02
☐ 354	Dan Quisenberry	.30	.14	.04
☐ 355	Steve Renko	.15	.07	.02
☐ 356	Leon Roberts	.15	.07	.02
☐ 357	Pat Sheridan	.15	.07	.02
☐ 358	Joe Simpson	.15	.07	.02
☐ 359	Don Slaught	.30	.14	.04
☐ 360	Paul Splittorff	.15	.07	.02
☐ 361	U.L. Washington	.15	.07	.02
☐ 362	John Wathan	.15	.07	.02
☐ 363	Frank White	.30	.14	.04
☐ 364	Willie Wilson	.30	.14	.04
☐ 365	Jim Barr	.15	.07	.02
☐ 366	Dave Bergman	.15	.07	.02
☐ 367	Fred Breining	.15	.07	.02
☐ 368	Bob Brenly	.15	.07	.02
☐ 369	Jack Clark	.30	.14	.04
☐ 370	Chili Davis	.50	.23	.06
☐ 371	Mark Davis	.15	.07	.02
☐ 372	Darrell Evans	.30	.14	.04
☐ 373	Atlee Hammaker	.15	.07	.02
☐ 374	Mike Krukow	.15	.07	.02
☐ 375	Duane Kuiper	.15	.07	.02
☐ 376	Bill Laskey	.15	.07	.02
☐ 377	Gary Lavelle	.15	.07	.02
☐ 378	Johnnie LeMaster	.15	.07	.02
☐ 379	Jeff Leonard	.15	.07	.02
☐ 380	Randy Lerch	.15	.07	.02
☐ 381	Renie Martin	.15	.07	.02
☐ 382	Andy McGaffigan	.15	.07	.02
☐ 383	Greg Minton	.15	.07	.02
☐ 384	Tom O'Malley	.15	.07	.02
☐ 385	Max Venable	.15	.07	.02
☐ 386	Brad Wellman	.15	.07	.02
☐ 387	Joel Youngblood	.15	.07	.02
☐ 388	Gary Allenson	.15	.07	.02
☐ 389	Luis Aponte	.15	.07	.02
☐ 390	Tony Armas	.15	.07	.02
☐ 391	Doug Bird	.15	.07	.02
☐ 392	Wade Boggs	4.00	1.80	.50
☐ 393	Dennis Boyd	.30	.14	.04
☐ 394	Mike Brown UER P	.15	.07	.02

(shown with record
of 31-104)

☐ 395	Mark Clear	.15	.07	.02
☐ 396	Dennis Eckersley	1.25	.55	.16
☐ 397	Dwight Evans	.30	.14	.04
☐ 398	Rich Gedman	.15	.07	.02
☐ 399	Glenn Hoffman	.15	.07	.02
☐ 400	Bruce Hurst	.30	.14	.04
☐ 401	John Henry Johnson	.15	.07	.02
☐ 402	Ed Jurak	.15	.07	.02
☐ 403	Rick Miller	.15	.07	.02
☐ 404	Jeff Newman	.15	.07	.02
☐ 405	Reid Nichols	.15	.07	.02
☐ 406	Bob Ojeda	.30	.14	.04
☐ 407	Jerry Remy	.15	.07	.02

☐ 408	Jim Rice	.50	.23	.06
☐ 409	Bob Stanley	.15	.07	.02
☐ 410	Dave Stapleton	.15	.07	.02
☐ 411	John Tudor	.30	.14	.04
☐ 412	Carl Yastrzemski	1.50	.70	.19
☐ 413	Buddy Bell	.30	.14	.04
☐ 414	Larry Biittner	.15	.07	.02
☐ 415	John Butcher	.15	.07	.02
☐ 416	Danny Darwin	.15	.07	.02
☐ 417	Bucky Dent	.30	.14	.04
☐ 418	Dave Hostetler	.15	.07	.02
☐ 419	Charlie Hough	.30	.14	.04
☐ 420	Bobby Johnson	.15	.07	.02
☐ 421	Odell Jones	.15	.07	.02
☐ 422	Jon Matlack	.15	.07	.02
☐ 423	Pete O'Brien	.30	.14	.04
☐ 424	Larry Parrish	.15	.07	.02
☐ 425	Mickey Rivers	.15	.07	.02
☐ 426	Billy Sample	.15	.07	.02
☐ 427	Dave Schmidt	.15	.07	.02
☐ 428	Mike Smithson	.15	.07	.02
☐ 429	Bill Stein	.15	.07	.02
☐ 430	Dave Stewart	.50	.23	.06
☐ 431	Jim Sundberg	.30	.14	.04
☐ 432	Frank Tanana	.30	.14	.04
☐ 433	Dave Tobik	.15	.07	.02
☐ 434	Wayne Tolleson	.15	.07	.02
☐ 435	George Wright	.15	.07	.02
☐ 436	Bill Almon	.15	.07	.02
☐ 437	Keith Atherton	.15	.07	.02
☐ 438	Dave Beard	.15	.07	.02
☐ 439	Tom Burgmeier	.15	.07	.02
☐ 440	Jeff Burroughs	.15	.07	.02
☐ 441	Chris Codiroli	.15	.07	.02
☐ 442	Tim Conroy	.15	.07	.02
☐ 443	Mike Davis	.15	.07	.02
☐ 444	Wayne Gross	.15	.07	.02
☐ 445	Garry Hancock	.15	.07	.02
☐ 446	Mike Heath	.15	.07	.02
☐ 447	Rickey Henderson	3.00	1.35	.35
☐ 448	Donnie Hill	.15	.07	.02
☐ 449	Bob Kearney	.15	.07	.02
☐ 450	Bill Krueger	.15	.07	.02
☐ 451	Rick Langford	.15	.07	.02
☐ 452	Carney Lansford	.30	.14	.04
☐ 453	Dave Lopes	.30	.14	.04
☐ 454	Steve McCatty	.15	.07	.02
☐ 455	Dan Meyer	.15	.07	.02
☐ 456	Dwayne Murphy	.15	.07	.02
☐ 457	Mike Norris	.15	.07	.02
☐ 458	Ricky Peters	.15	.07	.02
☐ 459	Tony Phillips	2.00	.90	.25
☐ 460	Tom Underwood	.15	.07	.02
☐ 461	Mike Warren	.15	.07	.02
☐ 462	Johnny Bench	1.50	.70	.19
☐ 463	Bruce Berenyi	.15	.07	.02
☐ 464	Dann Bilardello	.15	.07	.02
☐ 465	Cesar Cedeno	.30	.14	.04
☐ 466	Dave Concepcion	.30	.14	.04
☐ 467	Dan Driessen	.15	.07	.02
☐ 468	Nick Esasky	.15	.07	.02
☐ 469	Rich Gale	.15	.07	.02
☐ 470	Ben Hayes	.15	.07	.02
☐ 471	Paul Householder	.15	.07	.02
☐ 472	Tom Hume	.15	.07	.02
☐ 473	Alan Knicely	.15	.07	.02
☐ 474	Eddie Milner	.15	.07	.02
☐ 475	Ron Oester	.15	.07	.02
☐ 476	Kelly Paris	.15	.07	.02
☐ 477	Frank Pastore	.15	.07	.02
☐ 478	Ted Power	.15	.07	.02

□	#	Name			
□	479	Joe Price	.15	.07	.02
□	480	Charlie Puleo	.15	.07	.02
□	481	Gary Redus	.30	.14	.04
□	482	Bill Scherrer	.15	.07	.02
□	483	Mario Soto	.15	.07	.02
□	484	Alex Trevino	.15	.07	.02
□	485	Duane Walker	.15	.07	.02
□	486	Larry Bowa	.30	.14	.04
□	487	Warren Brusstar	.15	.07	.02
□	488	Bill Buckner	.30	.14	.04
□	489	Bill Campbell	.15	.07	.02
□	490	Ron Cey	.30	.14	.04
□	491	Jody Davis	.15	.07	.02
□	492	Leon Durham	.15	.07	.02
□	493	Mel Hall	.30	.14	.04
□	494	Ferguson Jenkins	.50	.23	.06
□	495	Jay Johnstone	.30	.14	.04
□	496	Craig Lefferts	.15	.07	.02
□	497	Carmelo Martinez	.15	.07	.02
□	498	Jerry Morales	.15	.07	.02
□	499	Keith Moreland	.15	.07	.02
□	500	Dickie Noles	.15	.07	.02
□	501	Mike Proly	.15	.07	.02
□	502	Chuck Rainey	.15	.07	.02
□	503	Dick Ruthven	.15	.07	.02
□	504	Ryne Sandberg	10.00	4.50	1.25
□	505	Lee Smith	1.50	.70	.19
□	506	Steve Trout	.15	.07	.02
□	507	Gary Woods	.15	.07	.02
□	508	Juan Beniquez	.15	.07	.02
□	509	Bob Boone	.30	.14	.04
□	510	Rick Burleson	.15	.07	.02
□	511	Rod Carew	1.25	.55	.16
□	512	Bobby Clark	.15	.07	.02
□	513	John Curtis	.15	.07	.02
□	514	Doug DeCinces	.15	.07	.02
□	515	Brian Downing	.30	.14	.04
□	516	Tim Foli	.15	.07	.02
□	517	Ken Forsch	.15	.07	.02
□	518	Bobby Grich	.30	.14	.04
□	519	Andy Hassler	.15	.07	.02
□	520	Reggie Jackson	2.50	1.10	.30
□	521	Ron Jackson	.15	.07	.02
□	522	Tommy John	.50	.23	.06
□	523	Bruce Kison	.15	.07	.02
□	524	Steve Lubratich	.15	.07	.02
□	525	Fred Lynn	.30	.14	.04
□	526	Gary Pettis	.15	.07	.02
□	527	Luis Sanchez	.15	.07	.02
□	528	Daryl Sconiers	.15	.07	.02
□	529	Ellis Valentine	.15	.07	.02
□	530	Rob Wilfong	.15	.07	.02
□	531	Mike Witt	.15	.07	.02
□	532	Geoff Zahn	.15	.07	.02
□	533	Bud Anderson	.15	.07	.02
□	534	Chris Bando	.15	.07	.02
□	535	Alan Bannister	.15	.07	.02
□	536	Bert Blyleven	.50	.23	.06
□	537	Tom Brennan	.15	.07	.02
□	538	Jamie Easterly	.15	.07	.02
□	539	Juan Eichelberger	.15	.07	.02
□	540	Jim Essian	.15	.07	.02
□	541	Mike Fischlin	.15	.07	.02
□	542	Julio Franco	.75	.35	.09
□	543	Mike Hargrove	.30	.14	.04
□	544	Toby Harrah	.15	.07	.02
□	545	Ron Hassey	.15	.07	.02
□	546	Neal Heaton	.30	.14	.04
□	547	Bake McBride	.15	.07	.02
□	548	Broderick Perkins	.15	.07	.02
□	549	Lary Sorensen	.15	.07	.02
□	550	Dan Spillner	.15	.07	.02
□	551	Rick Sutcliffe	.30	.14	.04
□	552	Pat Tabler	.15	.07	.02
□	553	Gorman Thomas	.15	.07	.02
□	554	Andre Thornton	.15	.07	.02
□	555	George Vukovich	.15	.07	.02
□	556	Darrell Brown	.15	.07	.02
□	557	Tom Brunansky	.30	.14	.04
□	558	Randy Bush	.15	.07	.02
□	559	Bobby Castillo	.15	.07	.02
□	560	John Castino	.15	.07	.02
□	561	Ron Davis	.15	.07	.02
□	562	Dave Engle	.15	.07	.02
□	563	Lenny Faedo	.15	.07	.02
□	564	Pete Filson	.15	.07	.02
□	565	Gary Gaetti	.30	.14	.04
□	566	Mickey Hatcher	.15	.07	.02
□	567	Kent Hrbek	.50	.23	.06
□	568	Rusty Kuntz	.15	.07	.02
□	569	Tim Laudner	.15	.07	.02
□	570	Rick Lysander	.15	.07	.02
□	571	Bobby Mitchell	.15	.07	.02
□	572	Ken Schrom	.15	.07	.02
□	573	Ray Smith	.15	.07	.02
□	574	Tim Teufel	.15	.07	.02
□	575	Frank Viola	.30	.14	.04
□	576	Gary Ward	.15	.07	.02
□	577	Ron Washington	.15	.07	.02
□	578	Len Whitehouse	.15	.07	.02
□	579	Al Williams	.15	.07	.02
□	580	Bob Bailor	.15	.07	.02
□	581	Mark Bradley	.15	.07	.02
□	582	Hubie Brooks	.30	.14	.04
□	583	Carlos Diaz	.15	.07	.02
□	584	George Foster	.30	.14	.04
□	585	Brian Giles	.15	.07	.02
□	586	Danny Heep	.15	.07	.02
□	587	Keith Hernandez	.50	.23	.06
□	588	Ron Hodges	.15	.07	.02
□	589	Scott Holman	.15	.07	.02
□	590	Dave Kingman	.30	.14	.04
□	591	Ed Lynch	.15	.07	.02
□	592	Jose Oquendo	.30	.14	.04
□	593	Jesse Orosco	.15	.07	.02
□	594	Junior Ortiz	.15	.07	.02
□	595	Tom Seaver	2.00	.90	.25
□	596	Doug Sisk	.15	.07	.02
□	597	Rusty Staub	.30	.14	.04
□	598	John Stearns	.15	.07	.02
□	599	Darryl Strawberry	4.00	1.80	.50
□	600	Craig Swan	.15	.07	.02
□	601	Walt Terrell	.15	.07	.02
□	602	Mike Torrez	.15	.07	.02
□	603	Mookie Wilson	.30	.14	.04
□	604	Jamie Allen	.15	.07	.02
□	605	Jim Beattie	.15	.07	.02
□	606	Tony Bernazard	.15	.07	.02
□	607	Manny Castillo	.15	.07	.02
□	608	Bill Caudill	.15	.07	.02
□	609	Bryan Clark	.15	.07	.02
□	610	Al Cowens	.15	.07	.02
□	611	Dave Henderson	.30	.14	.04
□	612	Steve Henderson	.15	.07	.02
□	613	Orlando Mercado	.15	.07	.02
□	614	Mike Moore	.30	.14	.04
□	615	Ricky Nelson UER (Jamie Nelson's stats on back)	.15	.07	.02
□	616	Spike Owen	.30	.14	.04
□	617	Pat Putnam	.15	.07	.02
□	618	Ron Roenicke	.15	.07	.02

☐ 619	Mike Stanton	.15	.07	.02
☐ 620	Bob Stoddard	.15	.07	.02
☐ 621	Rick Sweet	.15	.07	.02
☐ 622	Roy Thomas	.15	.07	.02
☐ 623	Ed VandeBerg	.15	.07	.02
☐ 624	Matt Young	.15	.07	.02
☐ 625	Richie Zisk	.15	.07	.02
☐ 626	Fred Lynn 1982 AS Game RB	.30	.14	.04
☐ 627	Manny Trillo 1983 AS Game RB	.30	.14	.04
☐ 628	Steve Garvey NL Iron Man	.50	.23	.06
☐ 629	Rod Carew AL Batting Runner-Up	.50	.23	.06
☐ 630	Wade Boggs AL Batting Champion	1.50	.70	.19
☐ 631	Tim Raines: Letting Go of the Raines	.50	.23	.06
☐ 632	Al Oliver Double Trouble	.30	.14	.04
☐ 633	Steve Sax AS Second Base	.30	.14	.04
☐ 634	Dickie Thon AS Shortstop	.30	.14	.04
☐ 635	Ace Firemen Dan Quisenberry and Tippy Martinez	.30	.14	.04
☐ 636	Reds Reunited Joe Morgan Pete Rose Tony Perez	1.00	.45	.12
☐ 637	Backstop Stars Lance Parrish Bob Boone	.30	.14	.04
☐ 638	George Brett and Gaylord Perry Pine Tar 7/24/83	2.00	.90	.25
☐ 639	1983 No Hitters Dave Righetti Mike Warren Bob Forsch	.30	.14	.04
☐ 640	Johnny Bench and Carl Yastrzemski Retiring Superstars	2.00	.90	.25
☐ 641	Gaylord Perry Going Out In Style	.50	.23	.06
☐ 642	Steve Carlton 300 Club and Strikeout Record	1.00	.45	.12
☐ 643	Joe Altobelli and Paul Owens World Series Managers	.30	.14	.04
☐ 644	Rick Dempsey World Series MVP	.30	.14	.04
☐ 645	Mike Boddicker WS Rookie Winner	.30	.14	.04
☐ 646	Scott McGregor WS Clincher	.30	.14	.04
☐ 647	CL: Orioles/Royals Joe Altobelli MG	.30	.14	.04
☐ 648	CL: Phillies/Giants Paul Owens MG	.30	.14	.04
☐ 649	CL: White Sox/Red Sox Tony LaRussa MG	.30	.14	.04
☐ 650	CL: Tigers/Rangers Sparky Anderson MG	.30	.14	.04
☐ 651	CL: Dodgers/A's Tommy Lasorda MG	.30	.14	.04
☐ 652	CL: Yankees/Reds Billy Martin MG	.30	.14	.04
☐ 653	CL: Blue Jays/Cubs Bobby Cox MG	.30	.14	.04
☐ 654	CL: Braves/Angels Joe Torre MG	.30	.14	.04
☐ 655	CL: Brewers/Indians Rene Lachemann MG	.30	.14	.04
☐ 656	CL: Astros/Twins Bob Lillis MG	.30	.14	.04
☐ 657	CL: Pirates/Mets Chuck Tanner MG	.30	.14	.04
☐ 658	CL: Expos/Mariners Bill Virdon MG	.30	.14	.04
☐ 659	CL: Padres/Mariners Dick Williams MG	.30	.14	.04
☐ 660	CL: Cardinals/Teams Whitey Herzog MG	.30	.14	.04

1984 Fleer Update

 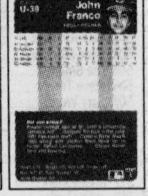

The cards in this 132-card set measure 2 1/2" by 3 1/2". For the first time, the Fleer Gum Company issued a traded, extended, or update set. The purpose of the set was the same as the traded sets issued by Topps over the past four years, i.e., to portray players with their proper team for the current year and to portray rookies who were not in their regular issue. Like the Topps Traded sets of the past four years, the Fleer Update sets were distributed through hobby dealers only. The set was quite popular with collectors, and, apparently, the print run was relatively short, as the set was quickly in short supply and exhibited a rapid and dramatic price increase. The cards are numbered on the back with a U prefix; the order corresponds to the alphabetical order of the subjects' names. The (extended) Rookie Cards in this set are Roger Clemens, Ron Darling, Alvin Davis, John Franco, Dwight Gooden, Jimmy Key, Mark Langston, Kirby Puckett, Jose Rijo, and Bret Saberhagen. Collectors are urged to be careful if purchasing single cards of Clemens, Darling, Gooden, Puckett, Rose, or Saberhagen as these specific cards have been illegally reprinted. These fakes are blurry when compared to the real cards.

	NRMT-MT	EXC	G-VG
COMPLETE FACT.SET (132)	600.00	275.00	75.00
COMMON CARD (1-132)	.50	.23	.06

☐	1	Willie Aikens	.50	.23	.06
☐	2	Luis Aponte	.50	.23	.06
☐	3	Mark Bailey	.50	.23	.06
☐	4	Bob Bailor	.50	.23	.06
☐	5	Dusty Baker	1.00	.45	.12
☐	6	Steve Balboni	.50	.23	.06
☐	7	Alan Bannister	.50	.23	.06
☐	8	Marty Barrett	.75	.35	.09
☐	9	Dave Beard	.50	.23	.06
☐	10	Joe Beckwith	.50	.23	.06
☐	11	Dave Bergman	.50	.23	.06
☐	12	Tony Bernazard	.50	.23	.06
☐	13	Bruce Bochte	.50	.23	.06
☐	14	Barry Bonnell	.50	.23	.06
☐	15	Phil Bradley	.75	.35	.09
☐	16	Fred Breining	.50	.23	.06
☐	17	Mike C. Brown	.50	.23	.06
☐	18	Bill Buckner	.75	.35	.09
☐	19	Ray Burris	.50	.23	.06
☐	20	John Butcher	.50	.23	.06
☐	21	Brett Butler	2.00	.90	.25
☐	22	Enos Cabell	.50	.23	.06
☐	23	Bill Campbell	.50	.23	.06
☐	24	Bill Caudill	.50	.23	.06
☐	25	Bobby Clark	.50	.23	.06
☐	26	Bryan Clark	.50	.23	.06
☐	27	Roger Clemens	200.00	90.00	25.00
☐	28	Jaime Cocanower	.50	.23	.06
☐	29	Ron Darling	1.00	.45	.12
☐	30	Alvin Davis	.75	.35	.09
☐	31	Bob Dernier	.50	.23	.06
☐	32	Carlos Diaz	.50	.23	.06
☐	33	Mike Easler	.50	.23	.06
☐	34	Dennis Eckersley	10.00	4.50	1.25
☐	35	Jim Essian	.50	.23	.06
☐	36	Darrell Evans	.75	.35	.09
☐	37	Mike Fitzgerald	.50	.23	.06
☐	38	Tim Foli	.50	.23	.06
☐	39	John Franco	6.00	2.70	.75
☐	40	George Frazier	.50	.23	.06
☐	41	Rich Gale	.50	.23	.06
☐	42	Barbaro Garbey	.50	.23	.06
☐	43	Dwight Gooden	10.00	4.50	1.25
☐	44	Rich Gossage	1.00	.45	.12
☐	45	Wayne Gross	.50	.23	.06
☐	46	Mark Gubicza	1.00	.45	.12
☐	47	Jackie Gutierrez	.50	.23	.06
☐	48	Toby Harrah	.50	.23	.06
☐	49	Ron Hassey	.50	.23	.06
☐	50	Richie Hebner	.50	.23	.06
☐	51	Willie Hernandez	.75	.35	.09
☐	52	Ed Hodge	.50	.23	.06
☐	53	Ricky Horton	.50	.23	.06
☐	54	Art Howe	.50	.23	.06
☐	55	Dane Iorg	.50	.23	.06
☐	56	Brook Jacoby	.75	.35	.09
☐	57	Dion James	.75	.35	.09
☐	58	Mike Jeffcoat	.50	.23	.06
☐	59	Ruppert Jones	.50	.23	.06
☐	60	Bob Kearney	.50	.23	.06
☐	61	Jimmy Key	12.00	5.50	1.50
☐	62	Dave Kingman	.75	.35	.09
☐	63	Brad Komminsk	.50	.23	.06
☐	64	Jerry Koosman	.75	.35	.09
☐	65	Wayne Krenchicki	.50	.23	.06
☐	66	Rusty Kuntz	.50	.23	.06
☐	67	Frank LaCorte	.50	.23	.06
☐	68	Dennis Lamp	.50	.23	.06
☐	69	Tito Landrum	.50	.23	.06
☐	70	Mark Langston	20.00	9.00	2.50
☐	71	Rick Leach	.50	.23	.06
☐	72	Craig Lefferts	.75	.35	.09
☐	73	Gary Lucas	.50	.23	.06
☐	74	Jerry Martin	.50	.23	.06
☐	75	Carmelo Martinez	.50	.23	.06
☐	76	Mike Mason	.50	.23	.06
☐	77	Gary Matthews	.75	.35	.09
☐	78	Andy McGaffigan	.50	.23	.06
☐	79	Joey McLaughlin	.50	.23	.06
☐	80	Joe Morgan	5.00	2.20	.60
☐	81	Darryl Motley	.50	.23	.06
☐	82	Graig Nettles	1.00	.45	.12
☐	83	Phil Niekro	2.00	.90	.25
☐	84	Ken Oberkfell	.50	.23	.06
☐	85	Al Oliver	.75	.35	.09
☐	86	Jorge Orta	.50	.23	.06
☐	87	Amos Otis	.75	.35	.09
☐	88	Bob Owchinko	.50	.23	.06
☐	89	Dave Parker	1.00	.45	.12
☐	90	Jack Perconte	.50	.23	.06
☐	91	Tony Perez	2.50	1.10	.30
☐	92	Gerald Perry	.75	.35	.09
☐	93	Kirby Puckett	300.00	135.00	38.00
☐	94	Shane Rawley	.50	.23	.06
☐	95	Floyd Rayford	.50	.23	.06
☐	96	Ron Reed	.50	.23	.06
☐	97	R.J. Reynolds	.50	.23	.06
☐	98	Gene Richards	.50	.23	.06
☐	99	Jose Rijo	15.00	6.75	1.85
☐	100	Jeff D. Robinson	.50	.23	.06
☐	101	Ron Romanick	.50	.23	.06
☐	102	Pete Rose	30.00	13.50	3.70
☐	103	Bret Saberhagen	30.00	13.50	3.70
☐	104	Scott Sanderson	.50	.23	.06
☐	105	Dick Schofield	.75	.35	.09
☐	106	Tom Seaver	12.00	5.50	1.50
☐	107	Jim Slaton	.50	.23	.06
☐	108	Mike Smithson	.50	.23	.06
☐	109	Lary Sorensen	.50	.23	.06
☐	110	Tim Stoddard	.50	.23	.06
☐	111	Jeff Stone	.50	.23	.06
☐	112	Champ Summers	.50	.23	.06
☐	113	Jim Sundberg	.75	.35	.09
☐	114	Rick Sutcliffe	1.00	.45	.12
☐	115	Craig Swan	.50	.23	.06
☐	116	Derrel Thomas	.50	.23	.06
☐	117	Gorman Thomas	.50	.23	.06
☐	118	Alex Trevino	.50	.23	.06
☐	119	Manny Trillo	.50	.23	.06
☐	120	John Tudor	.75	.35	.09
☐	121	Tom Underwood	.50	.23	.06
☐	122	Mike Vail	.50	.23	.06
☐	123	Tom Waddell	.50	.23	.06
☐	124	Gary Ward	.50	.23	.06
☐	125	Terry Whitfield	.50	.23	.06
☐	126	Curtis Wilkerson	.50	.23	.06
☐	127	Frank Williams	.50	.23	.06
☐	128	Glenn Wilson	.50	.23	.06
☐	129	John Wockenfuss	.50	.23	.06
☐	130	Ned Yost	.50	.23	.06
☐	131	Mike Young	.50	.23	.06
☐	132	Checklist 1-132	.50	.23	.06

1985 Fleer

*The cards in this 660-card set measure 2
1/2" by 3 1/2". The 1985 Fleer set features
fronts that contain the team logo along with*

 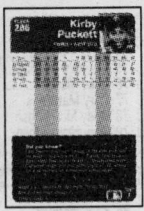

the player's name and position. The borders enclosing the photo are color-coded to correspond to the player's team. In each case, the color is one of the standard colors of that team, e.g., orange for Baltimore, red for St. Louis, etc. The backs feature the same name, number, and statistics format that Fleer has been using over the past few years. The cards are ordered alphabetically within team. The teams are ordered based on their respective performance during the prior year, e.g., World Champion Detroit Tigers (1-25), NL Champion San Diego (26-48), Chicago Cubs (49-71), New York Mets (72-95), Toronto (96-119), New York Yankees (120-147), Boston (148-169), Baltimore (170-195), Kansas City (196-218), St. Louis (219-243), Philadelphia (244-269), Minnesota (270-292), California (293-317), Atlanta (318-342), Houston (343-365), Los Angeles (366-391), Montreal (392-413), Oakland (414-436), Cleveland (437-460), Pittsburgh (461-481), Seattle (482-505), Chicago White Sox (506-530), Cincinnati (531-554), Texas (555-575), Milwaukee (576-601), and San Francisco (602-625). Subsets include Specials (626-643) and Major League Prospects (644-653). The black and white photo on the reverse is included for the third straight year. This set is noted for containing the Rookie Cards of Roger Clemens, Eric Davis, Shawon Dunston, Dwight Gooden, Orel Hershiser, Jimmy Key, Mark Langston, Terry Pendleton, Kirby Puckett, Jose Rijo, Bret Saberhagen, and Danny Tartabull.

	NRMT-MT	EXC	G-VG
COMPLETE SET (660)	120.00	55.00	15.00
COMMON CARD (1-660)	.10	.05	.01

☐ 1	Doug Bair	.10	.05	.01
☐ 2	Juan Berenguer	.10	.05	.01
☐ 3	Dave Bergman	.10	.05	.01
☐ 4	Tom Brookens	.10	.05	.01
☐ 5	Marty Castillo	.10	.05	.01
☐ 6	Darrell Evans	.20	.09	.03
☐ 7	Barbaro Garbey	.10	.05	.01
☐ 8	Kirk Gibson	.30	.14	.04
☐ 9	John Grubb	.10	.05	.01
☐ 10	Willie Hernandez	.10	.05	.01
☐ 11	Larry Herndon	.10	.05	.01
☐ 12	Howard Johnson	.20	.09	.03
☐ 13	Ruppert Jones	.10	.05	.01
☐ 14	Rusty Kuntz	.10	.05	.01
☐ 15	Chet Lemon	.10	.05	.01
☐ 16	Aurelio Lopez	.10	.05	.01
☐ 17	Sid Monge	.10	.05	.01
☐ 18	Jack Morris	.40	.18	.05
☐ 19	Lance Parrish	.20	.09	.03
☐ 20	Dan Petry	.10	.05	.01
☐ 21	Dave Rozema	.10	.05	.01
☐ 22	Bill Scherrer	.10	.05	.01
☐ 23	Alan Trammell	.75	.35	.09
☐ 24	Lou Whitaker	.60	.25	.07
☐ 25	Milt Wilcox	.10	.05	.01
☐ 26	Kurt Bevacqua	.10	.05	.01
☐ 27	Greg Booker	.10	.05	.01
☐ 28	Bobby Brown	.10	.05	.01
☐ 29	Luis DeLeon	.10	.05	.01
☐ 30	Dave Dravecky	.20	.09	.03
☐ 31	Tim Flannery	.10	.05	.01
☐ 32	Steve Garvey	.30	.14	.04
☐ 33	Rich Gossage	.30	.14	.04
☐ 34	Tony Gwynn	6.00	2.70	.75
☐ 35	Greg Harris	.10	.05	.01
☐ 36	Andy Hawkins	.10	.05	.01
☐ 37	Terry Kennedy	.10	.05	.01
☐ 38	Craig Lefferts	.20	.09	.03
☐ 39	Tim Lollar	.10	.05	.01
☐ 40	Carmelo Martinez	.10	.05	.01
☐ 41	Kevin McReynolds	.20	.09	.03
☐ 42	Graig Nettles	.20	.09	.03
☐ 43	Luis Salazar	.10	.05	.01
☐ 44	Eric Show	.10	.05	.01
☐ 45	Garry Templeton	.10	.05	.01
☐ 46	Mark Thurmond	.10	.05	.01
☐ 47	Ed Whitson	.10	.05	.01
☐ 48	Alan Wiggins	.10	.05	.01
☐ 49	Rich Bordi	.10	.05	.01
☐ 50	Larry Bowa	.20	.09	.03
☐ 51	Warren Brusstar	.10	.05	.01
☐ 52	Ron Cey	.20	.09	.03
☐ 53	Henry Cotto	.10	.05	.01
☐ 54	Jody Davis	.10	.05	.01
☐ 55	Bob Dernier	.10	.05	.01
☐ 56	Leon Durham	.10	.05	.01
☐ 57	Dennis Eckersley	.40	.18	.05
☐ 58	George Frazier	.10	.05	.01
☐ 59	Richie Hebner	.10	.05	.01
☐ 60	Dave Lopes	.20	.09	.03
☐ 61	Gary Matthews	.10	.05	.01
☐ 62	Keith Moreland	.10	.05	.01
☐ 63	Rick Reuschel	.20	.09	.03
☐ 64	Dick Ruthven	.10	.05	.01
☐ 65	Ryne Sandberg	6.00	2.70	.75
☐ 66	Scott Sanderson	.10	.05	.01
☐ 67	Lee Smith	1.00	.45	.12
☐ 68	Tim Stoddard	.10	.05	.01
☐ 69	Rick Sutcliffe	.20	.09	.03
☐ 70	Steve Trout	.10	.05	.01
☐ 71	Gary Woods	.10	.05	.01
☐ 72	Wally Backman	.10	.05	.01
☐ 73	Bruce Berenyi	.10	.05	.01
☐ 74	Hubie Brooks UER (Kelvin Chapman's stats on card back)	.20	.09	.03
☐ 75	Kelvin Chapman	.10	.05	.01
☐ 76	Ron Darling	.20	.09	.03
☐ 77	Sid Fernandez	.30	.14	.04
☐ 78	Mike Fitzgerald	.10	.05	.01
☐ 79	George Foster	.20	.09	.03
☐ 80	Brent Gaff	.10	.05	.01
☐ 81	Ron Gardenhire	.10	.05	.01
☐ 82	Dwight Gooden	1.00	.45	.12
☐ 83	Tom Gorman	.10	.05	.01

☐ 84	Danny Heep	.10	.05	.01
☐ 85	Keith Hernandez	.30	.14	.04
☐ 86	Ray Knight	.20	.09	.03
☐ 87	Ed Lynch	.10	.05	.01
☐ 88	Jose Oquendo	.10	.05	.01
☐ 89	Jesse Orosco	.10	.05	.01
☐ 90	Rafael Santana	.10	.05	.01
☐ 91	Doug Sisk	.10	.05	.01
☐ 92	Rusty Staub	.20	.09	.03
☐ 93	Darryl Strawberry	.75	.35	.09
☐ 94	Walt Terrell	.10	.05	.01
☐ 95	Mookie Wilson	.20	.09	.03
☐ 96	Jim Acker	.10	.05	.01
☐ 97	Willie Aikens	.10	.05	.01
☐ 98	Doyle Alexander	.10	.05	.01
☐ 99	Jesse Barfield	.10	.05	.01
☐ 100	George Bell	.20	.09	.03
☐ 101	Jim Clancy	.10	.05	.01
☐ 102	Dave Collins	.10	.05	.01
☐ 103	Tony Fernandez	.20	.09	.03
☐ 104	Damaso Garcia	.10	.05	.01
☐ 105	Jim Gott	.10	.05	.01
☐ 106	Alfredo Griffin	.10	.05	.01
☐ 107	Garth Iorg	.10	.05	.01
☐ 108	Roy Lee Jackson	.10	.05	.01
☐ 109	Cliff Johnson	.10	.05	.01
☐ 110	Jimmy Key	1.50	.70	.19
☐ 111	Dennis Lamp	.10	.05	.01
☐ 112	Rick Leach	.10	.05	.01
☐ 113	Luis Leal	.10	.05	.01
☐ 114	Buck Martinez	.10	.05	.01
☐ 115	Lloyd Moseby	.10	.05	.01
☐ 116	Rance Mulliniks	.10	.05	.01
☐ 117	Dave Stieb	.20	.09	.03
☐ 118	Willie Upshaw	.10	.05	.01
☐ 119	Ernie Whitt	.10	.05	.01
☐ 120	Mike Armstrong	.10	.05	.01
☐ 121	Don Baylor	.30	.14	.04
☐ 122	Marty Bystrom	.10	.05	.01
☐ 123	Rick Cerone	.10	.05	.01
☐ 124	Joe Cowley	.10	.05	.01
☐ 125	Brian Dayett	.10	.05	.01
☐ 126	Tim Foli	.10	.05	.01
☐ 127	Ray Fontenot	.10	.05	.01
☐ 128	Ken Griffey	.20	.09	.03
☐ 129	Ron Guidry	.20	.09	.03
☐ 130	Toby Harrah	.10	.05	.01
☐ 131	Jay Howell	.20	.09	.03
☐ 132	Steve Kemp	.10	.05	.01
☐ 133	Don Mattingly	8.00	3.60	1.00
☐ 134	Bobby Meacham	.10	.05	.01
☐ 135	John Montefusco	.10	.05	.01
☐ 136	Omar Moreno	.10	.05	.01
☐ 137	Dale Murray	.10	.05	.01
☐ 138	Phil Niekro	.30	.14	.04
☐ 139	Mike Pagliarulo	.10	.05	.01
☐ 140	Willie Randolph	.20	.09	.03
☐ 141	Dennis Rasmussen	.10	.05	.01
☐ 142	Dave Righetti	.20	.09	.03
☐ 143	Jose Rijo	2.00	.90	.25
☐ 144	Andre Robertson	.10	.05	.01
☐ 145	Bob Shirley	.10	.05	.01
☐ 146	Dave Winfield	1.50	.70	.19
☐ 147	Butch Wynegar	.10	.05	.01
☐ 148	Gary Allenson	.10	.05	.01
☐ 149	Tony Armas	.10	.05	.01
☐ 150	Marty Barrett	.10	.05	.01
☐ 151	Wade Boggs	2.50	1.10	.30
☐ 152	Dennis Boyd	.10	.05	.01
☐ 153	Bill Buckner	.20	.09	.03
☐ 154	Mark Clear	.10	.05	.01
☐ 155	Roger Clemens	20.00	9.00	2.50
☐ 156	Steve Crawford	.10	.05	.01
☐ 157	Mike Easler	.10	.05	.01
☐ 158	Dwight Evans	.20	.09	.03
☐ 159	Rich Gedman	.10	.05	.01
☐ 160	Jackie Gutierrez (Wade Boggs shown on deck)	.20	.09	.03
☐ 161	Bruce Hurst	.20	.09	.03
☐ 162	John Henry Johnson	.10	.05	.01
☐ 163	Rick Miller	.10	.05	.01
☐ 164	Reid Nichols	.10	.05	.01
☐ 165	Al Nipper	.10	.05	.01
☐ 166	Bob Ojeda	.20	.09	.03
☐ 167	Jerry Remy	.10	.05	.01
☐ 168	Jim Rice	.30	.14	.04
☐ 169	Bob Stanley	.10	.05	.01
☐ 170	Mike Boddicker	.10	.05	.01
☐ 171	Al Bumbry	.20	.09	.03
☐ 172	Todd Cruz	.10	.05	.01
☐ 173	Rich Dauer	.10	.05	.01
☐ 174	Storm Davis	.10	.05	.01
☐ 175	Rick Dempsey	.10	.05	.01
☐ 176	Jim Dwyer	.10	.05	.01
☐ 177	Mike Flanagan	.10	.05	.01
☐ 178	Dan Ford	.10	.05	.01
☐ 179	Wayne Gross	.10	.05	.01
☐ 180	John Lowenstein	.10	.05	.01
☐ 181	Dennis Martinez	.20	.09	.03
☐ 182	Tippy Martinez	.10	.05	.01
☐ 183	Scott McGregor	.10	.05	.01
☐ 184	Eddie Murray	2.50	1.10	.30
☐ 185	Joe Nolan	.10	.05	.01
☐ 186	Floyd Rayford	.10	.05	.01
☐ 187	Cal Ripken	8.00	3.60	1.00
☐ 188	Gary Roenicke	.10	.05	.01
☐ 189	Lenn Sakata	.10	.05	.01
☐ 190	John Shelby	.10	.05	.01
☐ 191	Ken Singleton	.20	.09	.03
☐ 192	Sammy Stewart	.10	.05	.01
☐ 193	Bill Swaggerty	.10	.05	.01
☐ 194	Tom Underwood	.10	.05	.01
☐ 195	Mike Young	.10	.05	.01
☐ 196	Steve Balboni	.10	.05	.01
☐ 197	Joe Beckwith	.10	.05	.01
☐ 198	Bud Black	.10	.05	.01
☐ 199	George Brett	4.00	1.80	.50
☐ 200	Onix Concepcion	.10	.05	.01
☐ 201	Mark Gubicza	.30	.14	.04
☐ 202	Larry Gura	.10	.05	.01
☐ 203	Mark Huismann	.10	.05	.01
☐ 204	Dane Iorg	.10	.05	.01
☐ 205	Danny Jackson	.20	.09	.03
☐ 206	Charlie Leibrandt	.10	.05	.01
☐ 207	Hal McRae	.30	.14	.04
☐ 208	Darryl Motley	.10	.05	.01
☐ 209	Jorge Orta	.10	.05	.01
☐ 210	Greg Pryor	.10	.05	.01
☐ 211	Dan Quisenberry	.20	.09	.03
☐ 212	Bret Saberhagen	4.00	1.80	.50
☐ 213	Pat Sheridan	.10	.05	.01
☐ 214	Don Slaught	.20	.09	.03
☐ 215	U.L. Washington	.10	.05	.01
☐ 216	John Wathan	.10	.05	.01
☐ 217	Frank White	.20	.09	.03
☐ 218	Willie Wilson	.20	.09	.03
☐ 219	Neil Allen	.10	.05	.01
☐ 220	Joaquin Andujar	.10	.05	.01
☐ 221	Steve Braun	.10	.05	.01
☐ 222	Danny Cox	.10	.05	.01
☐ 223	Bob Forsch	.10	.05	.01

☐ 224	David Green	.10	.05	.01
☐ 225	George Hendrick	.10	.05	.01
☐ 226	Tom Herr	.20	.09	.03
☐ 227	Ricky Horton	.10	.05	.01
☐ 228	Art Howe	.10	.05	.01
☐ 229	Mike Jorgensen	.10	.05	.01
☐ 230	Kurt Kepshire	.10	.05	.01
☐ 231	Jeff Lahti	.10	.05	.01
☐ 232	Tito Landrum	.10	.05	.01
☐ 233	Dave LaPoint	.10	.05	.01
☐ 234	Willie McGee	.20	.09	.03
☐ 235	Tom Nieto	.10	.05	.01
☐ 236	Terry Pendleton	2.00	.90	.25
☐ 237	Darrell Porter	.10	.05	.01
☐ 238	Dave Rucker	.10	.05	.01
☐ 239	Lonnie Smith	.10	.05	.01
☐ 240	Ozzie Smith	2.50	1.10	.30
☐ 241	Bruce Sutter	.20	.09	.03
☐ 242	Andy Van Slyke UER (Bats Right, Throws Left)	.50	.23	.06
☐ 243	Dave Von Ohlen	.10	.05	.01
☐ 244	Larry Andersen	.10	.05	.01
☐ 245	Bill Campbell	.10	.05	.01
☐ 246	Steve Carlton	.75	.35	.09
☐ 247	Tim Corcoran	.10	.05	.01
☐ 248	Ivan DeJesus	.10	.05	.01
☐ 249	John Denny	.10	.05	.01
☐ 250	Bo Diaz	.10	.05	.01
☐ 251	Greg Gross	.10	.05	.01
☐ 252	Kevin Gross	.10	.05	.01
☐ 253	Von Hayes	.10	.05	.01
☐ 254	Al Holland	.10	.05	.01
☐ 255	Charles Hudson	.10	.05	.01
☐ 256	Jerry Koosman	.20	.09	.03
☐ 257	Joe Lefebvre	.10	.05	.01
☐ 258	Sixto Lezcano	.10	.05	.01
☐ 259	Garry Maddox	.10	.05	.01
☐ 260	Len Matuszek	.10	.05	.01
☐ 261	Tug McGraw	.20	.09	.03
☐ 262	Al Oliver	.20	.09	.03
☐ 263	Shane Rawley	.10	.05	.01
☐ 264	Juan Samuel	.10	.05	.01
☐ 265	Mike Schmidt	3.00	1.35	.35
☐ 266	Jeff Stone	.10	.05	.01
☐ 267	Ozzie Virgil	.10	.05	.01
☐ 268	Glenn Wilson	.10	.05	.01
☐ 269	John Wockenfuss	.10	.05	.01
☐ 270	Darrell Brown	.10	.05	.01
☐ 271	Tom Brunansky	.10	.05	.01
☐ 272	Randy Bush	.10	.05	.01
☐ 273	John Butcher	.10	.05	.01
☐ 274	Bobby Castillo	.10	.05	.01
☐ 275	Ron Davis	.10	.05	.01
☐ 276	Dave Engle	.10	.05	.01
☐ 277	Pete Filson	.10	.05	.01
☐ 278	Gary Gaetti	.20	.09	.03
☐ 279	Mickey Hatcher	.10	.05	.01
☐ 280	Ed Hodge	.10	.05	.01
☐ 281	Kent Hrbek	.20	.09	.03
☐ 282	Houston Jimenez	.10	.05	.01
☐ 283	Tim Laudner	.10	.05	.01
☐ 284	Rick Lysander	.10	.05	.01
☐ 285	Dave Meier	.10	.05	.01
☐ 286	Kirby Puckett	30.00	13.50	3.70
☐ 287	Pat Putnam	.10	.05	.01
☐ 288	Ken Schrom	.10	.05	.01
☐ 289	Mike Smithson	.10	.05	.01
☐ 290	Tim Teufel	.10	.05	.01
☐ 291	Frank Viola	.20	.09	.03
☐ 292	Ron Washington	.10	.05	.01
☐ 293	Don Aase	.10	.05	.01
☐ 294	Juan Beniquez	.10	.05	.01
☐ 295	Bob Boone	.20	.09	.03
☐ 296	Mike C. Brown	.10	.05	.01
☐ 297	Rod Carew	.60	.25	.07
☐ 298	Doug Corbett	.10	.05	.01
☐ 299	Doug DeCinces	.10	.05	.01
☐ 300	Brian Downing	.20	.09	.03
☐ 301	Ken Forsch	.10	.05	.01
☐ 302	Bobby Grich	.20	.09	.03
☐ 303	Reggie Jackson	1.50	.70	.19
☐ 304	Tommy John	.30	.14	.04
☐ 305	Curt Kaufman	.10	.05	.01
☐ 306	Bruce Kison	.10	.05	.01
☐ 307	Fred Lynn	.20	.09	.03
☐ 308	Gary Pettis	.10	.05	.01
☐ 309	Ron Romanick	.10	.05	.01
☐ 310	Luis Sanchez	.10	.05	.01
☐ 311	Dick Schofield	.10	.05	.01
☐ 312	Daryl Sconiers	.10	.05	.01
☐ 313	Jim Slaton	.10	.05	.01
☐ 314	Derrel Thomas	.10	.05	.01
☐ 315	Rob Wilfong	.10	.05	.01
☐ 316	Mike Witt	.10	.05	.01
☐ 317	Geoff Zahn	.10	.05	.01
☐ 318	Len Barker	.10	.05	.01
☐ 319	Steve Bedrosian	.10	.05	.01
☐ 320	Bruce Benedict	.10	.05	.01
☐ 321	Rick Camp	.10	.05	.01
☐ 322	Chris Chambliss	.20	.09	.03
☐ 323	Jeff Dedmon	.10	.05	.01
☐ 324	Terry Forster	.10	.05	.01
☐ 325	Gene Garber	.10	.05	.01
☐ 326	Albert Hall	.10	.05	.01
☐ 327	Terry Harper	.10	.05	.01
☐ 328	Bob Horner	.10	.05	.01
☐ 329	Glenn Hubbard	.10	.05	.01
☐ 330	Randy Johnson	.10	.05	.01
☐ 331	Brad Komminsk	.10	.05	.01
☐ 332	Rick Mahler	.10	.05	.01
☐ 333	Craig McMurtry	.10	.05	.01
☐ 334	Donnie Moore	.10	.05	.01
☐ 335	Dale Murphy	.40	.18	.05
☐ 336	Ken Oberkfell	.10	.05	.01
☐ 337	Pascual Perez	.10	.05	.01
☐ 338	Gerald Perry	.10	.05	.01
☐ 339	Rafael Ramirez	.10	.05	.01
☐ 340	Jerry Royster	.10	.05	.01
☐ 341	Alex Trevino	.10	.05	.01
☐ 342	Claudell Washington	.10	.05	.01
☐ 343	Alan Ashby	.10	.05	.01
☐ 344	Mark Bailey	.10	.05	.01
☐ 345	Kevin Bass	.10	.05	.01
☐ 346	Enos Cabell	.10	.05	.01
☐ 347	Jose Cruz	.20	.09	.03
☐ 348	Bill Dawley	.10	.05	.01
☐ 349	Frank DiPino	.10	.05	.01
☐ 350	Bill Doran	.10	.05	.01
☐ 351	Phil Garner	.20	.09	.03
☐ 352	Bob Knepper	.10	.05	.01
☐ 353	Mike LaCoss	.10	.05	.01
☐ 354	Jerry Mumphrey	.10	.05	.01
☐ 355	Joe Niekro	.20	.09	.03
☐ 356	Terry Puhl	.10	.05	.01
☐ 357	Craig Reynolds	.10	.05	.01
☐ 358	Vern Ruhle	.10	.05	.01
☐ 359	Nolan Ryan	10.00	4.50	1.25
☐ 360	Joe Sambito	.10	.05	.01
☐ 361	Mike Scott	.20	.09	.03
☐ 362	Dave Smith	.10	.05	.01
☐ 363	Julio Solano	.10	.05	.01

☐ 364	Dickie Thon	.10	.05	.01	☐ 434	Lary Sorensen	.10	.05	.01

#	Player				#	Player			
364	Dickie Thon	.10	.05	.01	434	Lary Sorensen	.10	.05	.01
365	Denny Walling	.10	.05	.01	435	Mike Warren	.10	.05	.01
366	Dave Anderson	.10	.05	.01	436	Curt Young	.10	.05	.01
367	Bob Bailor	.10	.05	.01	437	Luis Aponte	.10	.05	.01
368	Greg Brock	.10	.05	.01	438	Chris Bando	.10	.05	.01
369	Carlos Diaz	.10	.05	.01	439	Tony Bernazard	.10	.05	.01
370	Pedro Guerrero	.20	.09	.03	440	Bert Blyleven	.30	.14	.04
371	Orel Hershiser	4.00	1.80	.50	441	Brett Butler	.30	.14	.04
372	Rick Honeycutt	.10	.05	.01	442	Ernie Camacho	.10	.05	.01
373	Burt Hooton	.10	.05	.01	443	Joe Carter	6.00	2.70	.75
374	Ken Howell	.10	.05	.01	444	Carmelo Castillo	.10	.05	.01
375	Ken Landreaux	.10	.05	.01	445	Jamie Easterly	.10	.05	.01
376	Candy Maldonado	.10	.05	.01	446	Steve Farr	.20	.09	.03
377	Mike Marshall	.10	.05	.01	447	Mike Fischlin	.10	.05	.01
378	Tom Niedenfuer	.10	.05	.01	448	Julio Franco	.30	.14	.04
379	Alejandro Pena	.10	.05	.01	449	Mel Hall	.10	.05	.01
380	Jerry Reuss UER	.10	.05	.01	450	Mike Hargrove	.20	.09	.03
	("Home." omitted)				451	Neal Heaton	.10	.05	.01
381	R.J. Reynolds	.10	.05	.01	452	Brook Jacoby	.10	.05	.01
382	German Rivera	.10	.05	.01	453	Mike Jeffcoat	.10	.05	.01
383	Bill Russell	.20	.09	.03	454	Don Schulze	.10	.05	.01
384	Steve Sax	.20	.09	.03	455	Roy Smith	.10	.05	.01
385	Mike Scioscia	.10	.05	.01	456	Pat Tabler	.10	.05	.01
386	Franklin Stubbs	.10	.05	.01	457	Andre Thornton	.10	.05	.01
387	Fernando Valenzuela	.20	.09	.03	458	George Vukovich	.10	.05	.01
388	Bob Welch	.20	.09	.03	459	Tom Waddell	.10	.05	.01
389	Terry Whitfield	.10	.05	.01	460	Jerry Willard	.10	.05	.01
390	Steve Yeager	.10	.05	.01	461	Dale Berra	.10	.05	.01
391	Pat Zachry	.10	.05	.01	462	John Candelaria	.10	.05	.01
392	Fred Breining	.10	.05	.01	463	Jose DeLeon	.10	.05	.01
393	Gary Carter	.30	.14	.04	464	Doug Frobel	.10	.05	.01
394	Andre Dawson	1.50	.70	.19	465	Cecilio Guante	.10	.05	.01
395	Miguel Dilone	.10	.05	.01	466	Brian Harper	.20	.09	.03
396	Dan Driessen	.10	.05	.01	467	Lee Lacy	.10	.05	.01
397	Doug Flynn	.10	.05	.01	468	Bill Madlock	.20	.09	.03
398	Terry Francona	.10	.05	.01	469	Lee Mazzilli	.10	.05	.01
399	Bill Gullickson	.20	.09	.03	470	Larry McWilliams	.10	.05	.01
400	Bob James	.10	.05	.01	471	Jim Morrison	.10	.05	.01
401	Charlie Lea	.10	.05	.01	472	Tony Pena	.10	.05	.01
402	Bryan Little	.10	.05	.01	473	Johnny Ray	.10	.05	.01
403	Gary Lucas	.10	.05	.01	474	Rick Rhoden	.10	.05	.01
404	David Palmer	.10	.05	.01	475	Don Robinson	.10	.05	.01
405	Tim Raines	.40	.18	.05	476	Rod Scurry	.10	.05	.01
406	Mike Ramsey	.10	.05	.01	477	Kent Tekulve	.10	.05	.01
407	Jeff Reardon	.30	.14	.04	478	Jason Thompson	.10	.05	.01
408	Steve Rogers	.10	.05	.01	479	John Tudor	.20	.09	.03
409	Dan Schatzeder	.10	.05	.01	480	Lee Tunnell	.10	.05	.01
410	Bryn Smith	.10	.05	.01	481	Marvell Wynne	.10	.05	.01
411	Mike Stenhouse	.10	.05	.01	482	Salome Barojas	.10	.05	.01
412	Tim Wallach	.20	.09	.03	483	Dave Beard	.10	.05	.01
413	Jim Wohlford	.10	.05	.01	484	Jim Beattie	.10	.05	.01
414	Bill Almon	.10	.05	.01	485	Barry Bonnell	.10	.05	.01
415	Keith Atherton	.10	.05	.01	486	Phil Bradley	.20	.09	.03
416	Bruce Bochte	.10	.05	.01	487	Al Cowens	.10	.05	.01
417	Tom Burgmeier	.10	.05	.01	488	Alvin Davis	.20	.09	.03
418	Ray Burris	.10	.05	.01	489	Dave Henderson	.20	.09	.03
419	Bill Caudill	.10	.05	.01	490	Steve Henderson	.10	.05	.01
420	Chris Codiroli	.10	.05	.01	491	Bob Kearney	.10	.05	.01
421	Tim Conroy	.10	.05	.01	492	Mark Langston	3.00	1.35	.35
422	Dave Kingman	.10	.05	.01	493	Larry Milbourne	.10	.05	.01
423	Jim Essian	.10	.05	.01	494	Paul Mirabella	.10	.05	.01
424	Mike Heath	.10	.05	.01	495	Mike Moore	.20	.09	.03
425	Rickey Henderson	1.50	.70	.19	496	Edwin Nunez	.10	.05	.01
426	Donnie Hill	.10	.05	.01	497	Spike Owen	.10	.05	.01
427	Dave Kingman	.20	.09	.03	498	Jack Perconte	.10	.05	.01
428	Bill Krueger	.10	.05	.01	499	Ken Phelps	.10	.05	.01
429	Carney Lansford	.20	.09	.03	500	Jim Presley	.10	.05	.01
430	Steve McCatty	.10	.05	.01	501	Mike Stanton	.10	.05	.01
431	Joe Morgan	.50	.23	.06	502	Bob Stoddard	.10	.05	.01
432	Dwayne Murphy	.10	.05	.01	503	Gorman Thomas	.10	.05	.01
433	Tony Phillips	.30	.14	.04	504	Ed VandeBerg	.10	.05	.01

☐ 505	Matt Young	.10	.05	.01
☐ 506	Juan Agosto	.10	.05	.01
☐ 507	Harold Baines	.30	.14	.04
☐ 508	Floyd Bannister	.10	.05	.01
☐ 509	Britt Burns	.10	.05	.01
☐ 510	Julio Cruz	.10	.05	.01
☐ 511	Richard Dotson	.10	.05	.01
☐ 512	Jerry Dybzinski	.10	.05	.01
☐ 513	Carlton Fisk	.75	.35	.09
☐ 514	Scott Fletcher	.10	.05	.01
☐ 515	Jerry Hairston	.10	.05	.01
☐ 516	Marc Hill	.10	.05	.01
☐ 517	LaMarr Hoyt	.10	.05	.01
☐ 518	Ron Kittle	.10	.05	.01
☐ 519	Rudy Law	.10	.05	.01
☐ 520	Vance Law	.10	.05	.01
☐ 521	Greg Luzinski	.20	.09	.03
☐ 522	Gene Nelson	.10	.05	.01
☐ 523	Tom Paciorek	.20	.09	.03
☐ 524	Ron Reed	.10	.05	.01
☐ 525	Bert Roberge	.10	.05	.01
☐ 526	Tom Seaver	.75	.35	.09
☐ 527	Roy Smalley	.10	.05	.01
☐ 528	Dan Spillner	.10	.05	.01
☐ 529	Mike Squires	.10	.05	.01
☐ 530	Greg Walker	.10	.05	.01
☐ 531	Cesar Cedeno	.20	.09	.03
☐ 532	Dave Concepcion	.20	.09	.03
☐ 533	Eric Davis	1.00	.45	.12
☐ 534	Nick Esasky	.10	.05	.01
☐ 535	Tom Foley	.10	.05	.01
☐ 536	John Franco UER	1.25	.55	.16
	(Koufax misspelled			
	as Kofax on back)			
☐ 537	Brad Gulden	.10	.05	.01
☐ 538	Tom Hume	.10	.05	.01
☐ 539	Wayne Krenchicki	.10	.05	.01
☐ 540	Andy McGaffigan	.10	.05	.01
☐ 541	Eddie Milner	.10	.05	.01
☐ 542	Ron Oester	.10	.05	.01
☐ 543	Bob Owchinko	.10	.05	.01
☐ 544	Dave Parker	.30	.14	.04
☐ 545	Frank Pastore	.10	.05	.01
☐ 546	Tony Perez	.30	.14	.04
☐ 547	Ted Power	.10	.05	.01
☐ 548	Joe Price	.10	.05	.01
☐ 549	Gary Redus	.10	.05	.01
☐ 550	Pete Rose	2.00	.90	.25
☐ 551	Jeff Russell	.20	.09	.03
☐ 552	Mario Soto	.10	.05	.01
☐ 553	Jay Tibbs	.10	.05	.01
☐ 554	Duane Walker	.10	.05	.01
☐ 555	Alan Bannister	.10	.05	.01
☐ 556	Buddy Bell	.20	.09	.03
☐ 557	Danny Darwin	.10	.05	.01
☐ 558	Charlie Hough	.20	.09	.03
☐ 559	Bobby Jones	.10	.05	.01
☐ 560	Odell Jones	.10	.05	.01
☐ 561	Jeff Kunkel	.10	.05	.01
☐ 562	Mike Mason	.10	.05	.01
☐ 563	Pete O'Brien	.20	.09	.03
☐ 564	Larry Parrish	.10	.05	.01
☐ 565	Mickey Rivers	.10	.05	.01
☐ 566	Billy Sample	.10	.05	.01
☐ 567	Dave Schmidt	.10	.05	.01
☐ 568	Donnie Scott	.10	.05	.01
☐ 569	Dave Stewart	.30	.14	.04
☐ 570	Frank Tanana	.20	.09	.03
☐ 571	Wayne Tolleson	.10	.05	.01
☐ 572	Gary Ward	.10	.05	.01
☐ 573	Curtis Wilkerson	.10	.05	.01
☐ 574	George Wright	.10	.05	.01
☐ 575	Ned Yost	.10	.05	.01
☐ 576	Mark Brouhard	.10	.05	.01
☐ 577	Mike Caldwell	.10	.05	.01
☐ 578	Bobby Clark	.10	.05	.01
☐ 579	Jaime Cocanower	.10	.05	.01
☐ 580	Cecil Cooper	.20	.09	.03
☐ 581	Rollie Fingers	.30	.14	.04
☐ 582	Jim Gantner	.10	.05	.01
☐ 583	Moose Haas	.10	.05	.01
☐ 584	Dion James	.10	.05	.01
☐ 585	Pete Ladd	.10	.05	.01
☐ 586	Rick Manning	.10	.05	.01
☐ 587	Bob McClure	.10	.05	.01
☐ 588	Paul Molitor	1.50	.70	.19
☐ 589	Charlie Moore	.10	.05	.01
☐ 590	Ben Oglivie	.10	.05	.01
☐ 591	Chuck Porter	.10	.05	.01
☐ 592	Randy Ready	.10	.05	.01
☐ 593	Ed Romero	.10	.05	.01
☐ 594	Bill Schroeder	.10	.05	.01
☐ 595	Ray Searage	.10	.05	.01
☐ 596	Ted Simmons	.20	.09	.03
☐ 597	Jim Sundberg	.20	.09	.03
☐ 598	Don Sutton	.30	.14	.04
☐ 599	Tom Tellmann	.10	.05	.01
☐ 600	Rick Waits	.10	.05	.01
☐ 601	Robin Yount	2.00	.90	.25
☐ 602	Dusty Baker	.30	.14	.04
☐ 603	Bob Brenly	.10	.05	.01
☐ 604	Jack Clark	.20	.09	.03
☐ 605	Chili Davis	.20	.09	.03
☐ 606	Mark Davis	.10	.05	.01
☐ 607	Dan Gladden	.20	.09	.03
☐ 608	Atlee Hammaker	.10	.05	.01
☐ 609	Mike Krukow	.10	.05	.01
☐ 610	Duane Kuiper	.10	.05	.01
☐ 611	Bob Lacey	.10	.05	.01
☐ 612	Bill Laskey	.10	.05	.01
☐ 613	Gary Lavelle	.10	.05	.01
☐ 614	Johnnie LeMaster	.10	.05	.01
☐ 615	Jeff Leonard	.10	.05	.01
☐ 616	Randy Lerch	.10	.05	.01
☐ 617	Greg Minton	.10	.05	.01
☐ 618	Steve Nicosia	.10	.05	.01
☐ 619	Gene Richards	.10	.05	.01
☐ 620	Jeff D. Robinson	.10	.05	.01
☐ 621	Scot Thompson	.10	.05	.01
☐ 622	Manny Trillo	.10	.05	.01
☐ 623	Brad Wellman	.10	.05	.01
☐ 624	Frank Williams	.10	.05	.01
☐ 625	Joel Youngblood	.10	.05	.01
☐ 626	Cal Ripken IA	5.00	2.20	.60
☐ 627	Mike Schmidt IA	1.50	.70	.19
☐ 628	Giving The Signs	.20	.09	.03
	Sparky Anderson			
☐ 629	AL Pitcher's Nightmare	1.50	.70	.19
	Dave Winfield			
	Rickey Henderson			
☐ 630	NL Pitcher's Nightmare	1.50	.70	.19
	Mike Schmidt			
	Ryne Sandberg			
☐ 631	NL All-Stars	.60	.25	.07
	Darryl Strawberry			
	Gary Carter			
	Steve Garvey			
	Ozzie Smith			
☐ 632	A-S Winning Battery	.30	.14	.04
	Gary Carter			
	Charlie Lea			
☐ 633	NL Pennant Clinchers	.30	.14	.04

Steve Garvey
Rich Gossage

		NRMT-MT	EXC	G-VG
☐ 634	NL Rookie Phenoms.....	.20	.09	.03

Dwight Gooden
Juan Samuel

☐ 635	Toronto's Big Guns.....	.20	.09	.03

Willie Upshaw

☐ 636	Toronto's Big Guns.....	.20	.09	.03

Lloyd Moseby

☐ 637	HOLLAND: Al Holland ..	.10	.05	.01
☐ 638	TUNNELL: Lee Tunnell.	.10	.05	.01
☐ 639	500th Homer..............	1.00	.45	.12

Reggie Jackson

☐ 640	4000th Hit.................	1.25	.55	.16

Pete Rose

☐ 641	Father and Son...........	5.00	2.20	.60

Cal Ripken Jr.
Cal Ripken Sr.

☐ 642	Cubs: Division Champs .20		.09	.03
☐ 643	Two Perfect Games......	.20	.09	.03

and One No-Hitter:
Mike Witt
David Palmer
Jack Morris

☐ 644	Willie Lozado and........	.10	.05	.01

Vic Mata

☐ 645	Kelly Gruber and	.20	.09	.03

Randy O'Neal

☐ 646	Jose Roman and	.10	.05	.01

Joel Skinner

☐ 647	Steve Kiefer and	1.50	.70	.19

Danny Tartabull

☐ 648	Rob Deer and..............	.20	.09	.03

Alejandro Sanchez

☐ 649	Billy Hatcher and........	1.25	.55	.16

Shawon Dunston

☐ 650	Ron Robinson and	.10	.05	.01

Mike Bielecki

☐ 651	Zane Smith and............	.20	.09	.03

Paul Zuvella

☐ 652	Joe Hesketh and	.20	.09	.03

Glenn Davis

☐ 653	John Russell and	.10	.05	.01

Steve Jeltz

☐ 654	CL: Tigers/Padres	.20	.09	.03

and Cubs/Mets

☐ 655	CL: Blue Jays/Yankees.	.20	.09	.03

and Red Sox/Orioles

☐ 656	CL: Royals/Cardinals...	.20	.09	.03

and Phillies/Twins

☐ 657	CL: Angels/Braves.......	.20	.09	.03

and Astros/Dodgers

☐ 658	CL: Expos/A's	.20	.09	.03

and Indians/Pirates

☐ 659	CL: Mariners/White Sox .20		.09	.03

and Reds/Rangers

☐ 660	CL: Brewers/Giants	.20	.09	.03

and Special Cards

1985 Fleer Update

This 132-card set was issued late in the collecting year and features new players and players on new teams compared to the 1985 Fleer regular issue cards. Cards measure 2 1/2" by 3 1/2" and were distributed together as a complete set in a special box. The cards are numbered with a U prefix

and are ordered alphabetically by the player's name. This set features the Extended Rookie Cards of Tom Browning, Ivan Calderon, Vince Coleman, Darren Daulton, Mariano Duncan, Ozzie Guillen, Teddy Higuera, and Mickey Tettleton.

		NRMT-MT	EXC	G-VG
	COMPLETE FACT.SET (132) ..	20.00	9.00	2.50
	COMMON CARD (1-132)	.15	.07	.02
☐ 1	Don Aase	.15	.07	.02
☐ 2	Bill Almon	.15	.07	.02
☐ 3	Dusty Baker	.30	.14	.04
☐ 4	Dale Berra	.15	.07	.02
☐ 5	Karl Best	.15	.07	.02
☐ 6	Tim Birtsas	.15	.07	.02
☐ 7	Vida Blue	.20	.09	.03
☐ 8	Rich Bordi	.15	.07	.02
☐ 9	Daryl Boston	.15	.07	.02
☐ 10	Hubie Brooks	.20	.09	.03
☐ 11	Chris Brown	.15	.07	.02
☐ 12	Tom Browning	.20	.09	.03
☐ 13	Al Bumbry	.15	.07	.02
☐ 14	Tim Burke	.15	.07	.02
☐ 15	Ray Burris	.15	.07	.02
☐ 16	Jeff Burroughs	.15	.07	.02
☐ 17	Ivan Calderon	.15	.07	.02
☐ 18	Jeff Calhoun	.15	.07	.02
☐ 19	Bill Campbell	.15	.07	.02
☐ 20	Don Carman	.15	.07	.02
☐ 21	Gary Carter	.30	.14	.04
☐ 22	Bobby Castillo	.15	.07	.02
☐ 23	Bill Caudill	.15	.07	.02
☐ 24	Rick Cerone	.15	.07	.02
☐ 25	Jack Clark	.20	.09	.03
☐ 26	Pat Clements	.15	.07	.02
☐ 27	Stewart Cliburn	.15	.07	.02
☐ 28	Vince Coleman	1.50	.70	.19
☐ 29	Dave Collins	.15	.07	.02
☐ 30	Fritz Connally	.15	.07	.02
☐ 31	Henry Cotto	.15	.07	.02
☐ 32	Danny Darwin	.15	.07	.02
☐ 33	Darren Daulton	10.00	4.50	1.25
☐ 34	Jerry Davis	.15	.07	.02
☐ 35	Brian Dayett	.15	.07	.02
☐ 36	Ken Dixon	.15	.07	.02
☐ 37	Tommy Dunbar	.15	.07	.02
☐ 38	Mariano Duncan	1.00	.45	.12
☐ 39	Bob Fallon	.15	.07	.02
☐ 40	Brian Fisher	.15	.07	.02
☐ 41	Mike Fitzgerald	.15	.07	.02
☐ 42	Ray Fontenot	.15	.07	.02
☐ 43	Greg Gagne	.20	.09	.03
☐ 44	Oscar Gamble	.15	.07	.02
☐ 45	Jim Gott	.15	.07	.02

☐ 46	David Green	.15	.07	.02
☐ 47	Alfredo Griffin	.15	.07	.02
☐ 48	Ozzie Guillen	2.00	.90	.25
☐ 49	Toby Harrah	.15	.07	.02
☐ 50	Ron Hassey	.15	.07	.02
☐ 51	Rickey Henderson	2.50	1.10	.30
☐ 52	Steve Henderson	.15	.07	.02
☐ 53	George Hendrick	.15	.07	.02
☐ 54	Teddy Higuera	.15	.07	.02
☐ 55	Al Holland	.15	.07	.02
☐ 56	Burt Hooton	.15	.07	.02
☐ 57	Jay Howell	.15	.07	.02
☐ 58	LaMarr Hoyt	.15	.07	.02
☐ 59	Tim Hulett	.15	.07	.02
☐ 60	Bob James	.15	.07	.02
☐ 61	Cliff Johnson	.15	.07	.02
☐ 62	Howard Johnson	.20	.09	.03
☐ 63	Ruppert Jones	.15	.07	.02
☐ 64	Steve Kemp	.15	.07	.02
☐ 65	Bruce Kison	.15	.07	.02
☐ 66	Mike LaCoss	.15	.07	.02
☐ 67	Lee Lacy	.15	.07	.02
☐ 68	Dave LaPoint	.15	.07	.02
☐ 69	Gary Lavelle	.15	.07	.02
☐ 70	Vance Law	.15	.07	.02
☐ 71	Manny Lee	.15	.07	.02
☐ 72	Sixto Lezcano	.15	.07	.02
☐ 73	Tim Lollar	.15	.07	.02
☐ 74	Urbano Lugo	.15	.07	.02
☐ 75	Fred Lynn	.20	.09	.03
☐ 76	Steve Lyons	.15	.07	.02
☐ 77	Mickey Mahler	.15	.07	.02
☐ 78	Ron Mathis	.15	.07	.02
☐ 79	Len Matuszek	.15	.07	.02
☐ 80	Oddibe McDowell UER	.15	.07	.02
	(Part of bio actually Roger's)			
☐ 81	Roger McDowell UER	.20	.09	.03
	(Part of bio actually Oddibe's)			
☐ 82	Donnie Moore	.15	.07	.02
☐ 83	Ron Musselman	.15	.07	.02
☐ 84	Al Oliver	.20	.09	.03
☐ 85	Joe Orsulak	.20	.09	.03
☐ 86	Dan Pasqua	.15	.07	.02
☐ 87	Chris Pittaro	.15	.07	.02
☐ 88	Rick Reuschel	.20	.09	.03
☐ 89	Earnie Riles	.15	.07	.02
☐ 90	Jerry Royster	.15	.07	.02
☐ 91	Dave Rozema	.15	.07	.02
☐ 92	Dave Rucker	.15	.07	.02
☐ 93	Vern Ruhle	.15	.07	.02
☐ 94	Mark Salas	.15	.07	.02
☐ 95	Luis Salazar	.15	.07	.02
☐ 96	Joe Sambito	.15	.07	.02
☐ 97	Billy Sample	.15	.07	.02
☐ 98	Alejandro Sanchez	.15	.07	.02
☐ 99	Calvin Schiraldi	.15	.07	.02
☐ 100	Rick Schu	.15	.07	.02
☐ 101	Larry Sheets	.15	.07	.02
☐ 102	Ron Shephard	.15	.07	.02
☐ 103	Nelson Simmons	.15	.07	.02
☐ 104	Don Slaught	.15	.07	.02
☐ 105	Roy Smalley	.15	.07	.02
☐ 106	Lonnie Smith	.15	.07	.02
☐ 107	Nate Snell	.15	.07	.02
☐ 108	Lary Sorensen	.15	.07	.02
☐ 109	Chris Speier	.15	.07	.02
☐ 110	Mike Stenhouse	.15	.07	.02
☐ 111	Tim Stoddard	.15	.07	.02
☐ 112	John Stuper	.15	.07	.02
☐ 113	Jim Sundberg	.20	.09	.03
☐ 114	Bruce Sutter	.30	.14	.04
☐ 115	Don Sutton	.30	.14	.04
☐ 116	Bruce Tanner	.15	.07	.02
☐ 117	Kent Tekulve	.15	.07	.02
☐ 118	Walt Terrell	.15	.07	.02
☐ 119	Mickey Tettleton	4.00	1.80	.50
☐ 120	Rich Thompson	.15	.07	.02
☐ 121	Louis Thornton	.15	.07	.02
☐ 122	Alex Trevino	.15	.07	.02
☐ 123	John Tudor	.15	.07	.02
☐ 124	Jose Uribe	.15	.07	.02
☐ 125	Dave Valle	.15	.07	.02
☐ 126	Dave Von Ohlen	.15	.07	.02
☐ 127	Curt Wardle	.15	.07	.02
☐ 128	U.L. Washington	.15	.07	.02
☐ 129	Ed Whitson	.15	.07	.02
☐ 130	Herm Winningham	.15	.07	.02
☐ 131	Rich Yett	.15	.07	.02
☐ 132	Checklist U1-U132	.15	.07	.02

1986 Fleer

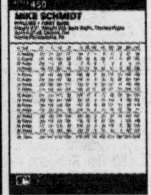

The cards in this 660-card set measure 2 1/2" by 3 1/2". The 1986 Fleer set features fronts that contain the team logo along with the player's name and position. The player cards are alphabetized within team and the teams are ordered by their 1985 season finish and won-lost record, e.g., Kansas City (1-25), St. Louis (26-49), Toronto (50-73), New York Mets (74-97), New York Yankees (98-122), Los Angeles (123-147), California (148-171), Cincinnati (172-196), Chicago White Sox (197-220), Detroit (221-243), Montreal (244-267), Baltimore (268-291), Houston (292-314), San Diego (315-338), Boston (339-360), Chicago Cubs (361-385), Minnesota (386-409), Oakland (410-432), Philadelphia (433-457), Seattle (458-481), Milwaukee (482-506), Atlanta (507-532), San Francisco (533-555), Texas (556-578), Cleveland (579-601), and Pittsburgh (602-625). Subsets include Specials (626-643) and Major League Prospects (644-653). The border enclosing the photo is dark blue. The backs feature the same name, number, and statistics format that Fleer has been using over the past few years. The Dennis and Tippy Martinez cards were apparently switched in the set numbering, as their adjacent numbers (279 and 280) were reversed on the Orioles checklist card.

The set includes the Rookie Cards of Rick Aguilera, Jose Canseco, Vince Coleman, Darren Daulton, Len Dykstra, Cecil Fielder, Paul O'Neill, Benito Santiago, and Mickey Tettleton.

	MINT	NRMT	EXC
COMPLETE SET (660)	70.00	32.00	8.75
COMPLETE FACT.SET (660)	80.00	36.00	10.00
COMMON CARD (1-660)	.10	.05	.01

☐ 1	Steve Balboni	.20	.09	.03
☐ 2	Joe Beckwith	.10	.05	.01
☐ 3	Buddy Biancalana	.10	.05	.01
☐ 4	Bud Black	.10	.05	.01
☐ 5	George Brett	2.50	1.10	.30
☐ 6	Onix Concepcion	.10	.05	.01
☐ 7	Steve Farr	.20	.09	.03
☐ 8	Mark Gubicza	.20	.09	.03
☐ 9	Dane Iorg	.10	.05	.01
☐ 10	Danny Jackson	.20	.09	.03
☐ 11	Lynn Jones	.10	.05	.01
☐ 12	Mike Jones	.10	.05	.01
☐ 13	Charlie Leibrandt	.10	.05	.01
☐ 14	Hal McRae	.30	.14	.04
☐ 15	Omar Moreno	.10	.05	.01
☐ 16	Darryl Motley	.10	.05	.01
☐ 17	Jorge Orta	.10	.05	.01
☐ 18	Dan Quisenberry	.20	.09	.03
☐ 19	Bret Saberhagen	.50	.23	.06
☐ 20	Pat Sheridan	.10	.05	.01
☐ 21	Lonnie Smith	.10	.05	.01
☐ 22	Jim Sundberg	.10	.05	.01
☐ 23	John Wathan	.10	.05	.01
☐ 24	Frank White	.20	.09	.03
☐ 25	Willie Wilson	.10	.05	.01
☐ 26	Joaquin Andujar	.10	.05	.01
☐ 27	Steve Braun	.10	.05	.01
☐ 28	Bill Campbell	.10	.05	.01
☐ 29	Cesar Cedeno	.20	.09	.03
☐ 30	Jack Clark	.20	.09	.03
☐ 31	Vince Coleman	.60	.25	.07
☐ 32	Danny Cox	.10	.05	.01
☐ 33	Ken Dayley	.10	.05	.01
☐ 34	Ivan DeJesus	.10	.05	.01
☐ 35	Bob Forsch	.10	.05	.01
☐ 36	Brian Harper	.20	.09	.03
☐ 37	Tom Herr	.10	.05	.01
☐ 38	Ricky Horton	.10	.05	.01
☐ 39	Kurt Kepshire	.10	.05	.01
☐ 40	Jeff Lahti	.10	.05	.01
☐ 41	Tito Landrum	.10	.05	.01
☐ 42	Willie McGee	.20	.09	.03
☐ 43	Tom Nieto	.10	.05	.01
☐ 44	Terry Pendleton	.30	.14	.04
☐ 45	Darrell Porter	.10	.05	.01
☐ 46	Ozzie Smith	1.25	.55	.16
☐ 47	John Tudor	.20	.09	.03
☐ 48	Andy Van Slyke	.20	.09	.03
☐ 49	Todd Worrell	.20	.09	.03
☐ 50	Jim Acker	.10	.05	.01
☐ 51	Doyle Alexander	.10	.05	.01
☐ 52	Jesse Barfield	.10	.05	.01
☐ 53	George Bell	.20	.09	.03
☐ 54	Jeff Burroughs	.10	.05	.01
☐ 55	Bill Caudill	.10	.05	.01
☐ 56	Jim Clancy	.10	.05	.01
☐ 57	Tony Fernandez	.20	.09	.03
☐ 58	Tom Filer	.10	.05	.01
☐ 59	Damaso Garcia	.10	.05	.01
☐ 60	Tom Henke	.20	.09	.03
☐ 61	Garth Iorg	.10	.05	.01
☐ 62	Cliff Johnson	.10	.05	.01
☐ 63	Jimmy Key	.30	.14	.04
☐ 64	Dennis Lamp	.10	.05	.01
☐ 65	Gary Lavelle	.10	.05	.01
☐ 66	Buck Martinez	.10	.05	.01
☐ 67	Lloyd Moseby	.10	.05	.01
☐ 68	Rance Mulliniks	.10	.05	.01
☐ 69	Al Oliver	.20	.09	.03
☐ 70	Dave Stieb	.20	.09	.03
☐ 71	Louis Thornton	.10	.05	.01
☐ 72	Willie Upshaw	.10	.05	.01
☐ 73	Ernie Whitt	.10	.05	.01
☐ 74	Rick Aguilera	1.00	.45	.12
☐ 75	Wally Backman	.10	.05	.01
☐ 76	Gary Carter	.30	.14	.04
☐ 77	Ron Darling	.20	.09	.03
☐ 78	Len Dykstra	2.00	.90	.25
☐ 79	Sid Fernandez	.20	.09	.03
☐ 80	George Foster	.20	.09	.03
☐ 81	Dwight Gooden	.30	.14	.04
☐ 82	Tom Gorman	.10	.05	.01
☐ 83	Danny Heep	.10	.05	.01
☐ 84	Keith Hernandez	.30	.14	.04
☐ 85	Howard Johnson	.20	.09	.03
☐ 86	Ray Knight	.20	.09	.03
☐ 87	Terry Leach	.10	.05	.01
☐ 88	Ed Lynch	.10	.05	.01
☐ 89	Roger McDowell	.20	.09	.03
☐ 90	Jesse Orosco	.10	.05	.01
☐ 91	Tom Paciorek	.20	.09	.03
☐ 92	Ronn Reynolds	.10	.05	.01
☐ 93	Rafael Santana	.10	.05	.01
☐ 94	Doug Sisk	.10	.05	.01
☐ 95	Rusty Staub	.20	.09	.03
☐ 96	Darryl Strawberry	.30	.14	.04
☐ 97	Mookie Wilson	.20	.09	.03
☐ 98	Neil Allen	.10	.05	.01
☐ 99	Don Baylor	.30	.14	.04
☐ 100	Dale Berra	.10	.05	.01
☐ 101	Rich Bordi	.10	.05	.01
☐ 102	Marty Bystrom	.10	.05	.01
☐ 103	Joe Cowley	.10	.05	.01
☐ 104	Brian Fisher	.10	.05	.01
☐ 105	Ken Griffey	.20	.09	.03
☐ 106	Ron Guidry	.20	.09	.03
☐ 107	Ron Hassey	.10	.05	.01
☐ 108	Rickey Henderson UER (SB Record of 120, sic)	.75	.35	.09
☐ 109	Don Mattingly	3.00	1.35	.35
☐ 110	Bobby Meacham	.10	.05	.01
☐ 111	John Montefusco	.10	.05	.01
☐ 112	Phil Niekro	.30	.14	.04
☐ 113	Mike Pagliarulo	.10	.05	.01
☐ 114	Dan Pasqua	.10	.05	.01
☐ 115	Willie Randolph	.20	.09	.03
☐ 116	Dave Righetti	.20	.09	.03
☐ 117	Andre Robertson	.10	.05	.01
☐ 118	Billy Sample	.10	.05	.01
☐ 119	Bob Shirley	.10	.05	.01
☐ 120	Ed Whitson	.10	.05	.01
☐ 121	Dave Winfield	.75	.35	.09
☐ 122	Butch Wynegar	.10	.05	.01
☐ 123	Dave Anderson	.10	.05	.01
☐ 124	Bob Bailor	.10	.05	.01
☐ 125	Greg Brock	.10	.05	.01
☐ 126	Enos Cabell	.10	.05	.01
☐ 127	Bobby Castillo	.10	.05	.01
☐ 128	Carlos Diaz	.10	.05	.01
☐ 129	Mariano Duncan	.30	.14	.04
☐ 130	Pedro Guerrero	.20	.09	.03

□	#	Name			
□	131	Orel Hershiser	.60	.25	.07
□	132	Rick Honeycutt	.10	.05	.01
□	133	Ken Howell	.10	.05	.01
□	134	Ken Landreaux	.10	.05	.01
□	135	Bill Madlock	.20	.09	.03
□	136	Candy Maldonado	.10	.05	.01
□	137	Mike Marshall	.10	.05	.01
□	138	Len Matuszek	.10	.05	.01
□	139	Tom Niedenfuer	.10	.05	.01
□	140	Alejandro Pena	.10	.05	.01
□	141	Jerry Reuss	.10	.05	.01
□	142	Bill Russell	.20	.09	.03
□	143	Steve Sax	.20	.09	.03
□	144	Mike Scioscia	.10	.05	.01
□	145	Fernando Valenzuela	.20	.09	.03
□	146	Bob Welch	.20	.09	.03
□	147	Terry Whitfield	.10	.05	.01
□	148	Juan Beniquez	.10	.05	.01
□	149	Bob Boone	.20	.09	.03
□	150	John Candelaria	.10	.05	.01
□	151	Rod Carew	.50	.23	.06
□	152	Stewart Cliburn	.10	.05	.01
□	153	Doug DeCinces	.10	.05	.01
□	154	Brian Downing	.20	.09	.03
□	155	Ken Forsch	.10	.05	.01
□	156	Craig Gerber	.10	.05	.01
□	157	Bobby Grich	.20	.09	.03
□	158	George Hendrick	.10	.05	.01
□	159	Al Holland	.10	.05	.01
□	160	Reggie Jackson	.75	.35	.09
□	161	Ruppert Jones	.10	.05	.01
□	162	Urbano Lugo	.10	.05	.01
□	163	Kirk McCaskill	.20	.09	.03
□	164	Donnie Moore	.10	.05	.01
□	165	Gary Pettis	.10	.05	.01
□	166	Ron Romanick	.10	.05	.01
□	167	Dick Schofield	.10	.05	.01
□	168	Daryl Sconiers	.10	.05	.01
□	169	Jim Slaton	.10	.05	.01
□	170	Don Sutton	.30	.14	.04
□	171	Mike Witt	.10	.05	.01
□	172	Buddy Bell	.20	.09	.03
□	173	Tom Browning	.20	.09	.03
□	174	Dave Concepcion	.20	.09	.03
□	175	Eric Davis	.30	.14	.04
□	176	Bo Diaz	.10	.05	.01
□	177	Nick Esasky	.10	.05	.01
□	178	John Franco	.20	.09	.03
□	179	Tom Hume	.10	.05	.01
□	180	Wayne Krenchicki	.10	.05	.01
□	181	Andy McGaffigan	.10	.05	.01
□	182	Eddie Milner	.10	.05	.01
□	183	Ron Oester	.10	.05	.01
□	184	Dave Parker	.30	.14	.04
□	185	Frank Pastore	.10	.05	.01
□	186	Tony Perez	.30	.14	.04
□	187	Ted Power	.10	.05	.01
□	188	Joe Price	.10	.05	.01
□	189	Gary Redus	.10	.05	.01
□	190	Ron Robinson	.10	.05	.01
□	191	Pete Rose	1.00	.45	.12
□	192	Mario Soto	.10	.05	.01
□	193	John Stuper	.10	.05	.01
□	194	Jay Tibbs	.10	.05	.01
□	195	Dave Van Gorder	.10	.05	.01
□	196	Max Venable	.10	.05	.01
□	197	Juan Agosto	.10	.05	.01
□	198	Harold Baines	.20	.09	.03
□	199	Floyd Bannister	.10	.05	.01
□	200	Britt Burns	.10	.05	.01
□	201	Julio Cruz	.10	.05	.01
□	202	Joel Davis	.10	.05	.01
□	203	Richard Dotson	.10	.05	.01
□	204	Carlton Fisk	.50	.23	.06
□	205	Scott Fletcher	.10	.05	.01
□	206	Ozzie Guillen	.75	.35	.09
□	207	Jerry Hairston	.10	.05	.01
□	208	Tim Hulett	.10	.05	.01
□	209	Bob James	.10	.05	.01
□	210	Ron Kittle	.10	.05	.01
□	211	Rudy Law	.10	.05	.01
□	212	Bryan Little	.10	.05	.01
□	213	Gene Nelson	.10	.05	.01
□	214	Reid Nichols	.10	.05	.01
□	215	Luis Salazar	.10	.05	.01
□	216	Tom Seaver	.50	.23	.06
□	217	Dan Spillner	.10	.05	.01
□	218	Bruce Tanner	.10	.05	.01
□	219	Greg Walker	.10	.05	.01
□	220	Dave Wehrmeister	.10	.05	.01
□	221	Juan Berenguer	.10	.05	.01
□	222	Dave Bergman	.10	.05	.01
□	223	Tom Brookens	.10	.05	.01
□	224	Darrell Evans	.20	.09	.03
□	225	Barbaro Garbey	.10	.05	.01
□	226	Kirk Gibson	.30	.14	.04
□	227	John Grubb	.10	.05	.01
□	228	Willie Hernandez	.10	.05	.01
□	229	Larry Herndon	.10	.05	.01
□	230	Chet Lemon	.10	.05	.01
□	231	Aurelio Lopez	.10	.05	.01
□	232	Jack Morris	.30	.14	.04
□	233	Randy O'Neal	.10	.05	.01
□	234	Lance Parrish	.20	.09	.03
□	235	Dan Petry	.10	.05	.01
□	236	Alejandro Sanchez	.10	.05	.01
□	237	Bill Scherrer	.10	.05	.01
□	238	Nelson Simmons	.10	.05	.01
□	239	Frank Tanana	.20	.09	.03
□	240	Walt Terrell	.10	.05	.01
□	241	Alan Trammell	.30	.14	.04
□	242	Lou Whitaker	.30	.14	.04
□	243	Milt Wilcox	.10	.05	.01
□	244	Hubie Brooks	.10	.05	.01
□	245	Tim Burke	.10	.05	.01
□	246	Andre Dawson	.50	.23	.06
□	247	Mike Fitzgerald	.10	.05	.01
□	248	Terry Francona	.10	.05	.01
□	249	Bill Gullickson	.20	.09	.03
□	250	Joe Hesketh	.10	.05	.01
□	251	Bill Laskey	.10	.05	.01
□	252	Vance Law	.10	.05	.01
□	253	Charlie Lea	.10	.05	.01
□	254	Gary Lucas	.10	.05	.01
□	255	David Palmer	.10	.05	.01
□	256	Tim Raines	.30	.14	.04
□	257	Jeff Reardon	.30	.14	.04
□	258	Bert Roberge	.10	.05	.01
□	259	Dan Schatzeder	.10	.05	.01
□	260	Bryn Smith	.10	.05	.01
□	261	Randy St.Claire	.10	.05	.01
□	262	Scot Thompson	.10	.05	.01
□	263	Tim Wallach	.20	.09	.03
□	264	U.L. Washington	.10	.05	.01
□	265	Mitch Webster	.10	.05	.01
□	266	Herm Winningham	.10	.05	.01
□	267	Floyd Youmans	.10	.05	.01
□	268	Don Aase	.10	.05	.01
□	269	Mike Boddicker	.10	.05	.01
□	270	Rich Dauer	.10	.05	.01
□	271	Storm Davis	.10	.05	.01
□	272	Rick Dempsey	.10	.05	.01

☐ 273	Ken Dixon	.10	.05	.01
☐ 274	Jim Dwyer	.10	.05	.01
☐ 275	Mike Flanagan	.10	.05	.01
☐ 276	Wayne Gross	.10	.05	.01
☐ 277	Lee Lacy	.10	.05	.01
☐ 278	Fred Lynn	.20	.09	.03
☐ 279	Tippy Martinez	.10	.05	.01
☐ 280	Dennis Martinez	.20	.09	.03
☐ 281	Scott McGregor	.10	.05	.01
☐ 282	Eddie Murray	1.00	.45	.12
☐ 283	Floyd Rayford	.10	.05	.01
☐ 284	Cal Ripken	5.00	2.20	.60
☐ 285	Gary Roenicke	.10	.05	.01
☐ 286	Larry Sheets	.10	.05	.01
☐ 287	John Shelby	.10	.05	.01
☐ 288	Nate Snell	.10	.05	.01
☐ 289	Sammy Stewart	.10	.05	.01
☐ 290	Alan Wiggins	.10	.05	.01
☐ 291	Mike Young	.10	.05	.01
☐ 292	Alan Ashby	.10	.05	.01
☐ 293	Mark Bailey	.10	.05	.01
☐ 294	Kevin Bass	.10	.05	.01
☐ 295	Jeff Calhoun	.10	.05	.01
☐ 296	Jose Cruz	.10	.05	.01
☐ 297	Glenn Davis	.10	.05	.01
☐ 298	Bill Dawley	.10	.05	.01
☐ 299	Frank DiPino	.10	.05	.01
☐ 300	Bill Doran	.10	.05	.01
☐ 301	Phil Garner	.20	.09	.03
☐ 302	Jeff Heathcock	.10	.05	.01
☐ 303	Charlie Kerfeld	.10	.05	.01
☐ 304	Bob Knepper	.10	.05	.01
☐ 305	Ron Mathis	.10	.05	.01
☐ 306	Jerry Mumphrey	.10	.05	.01
☐ 307	Jim Pankovits	.10	.05	.01
☐ 308	Terry Puhl	.10	.05	.01
☐ 309	Craig Reynolds	.10	.05	.01
☐ 310	Nolan Ryan	5.00	2.20	.60
☐ 311	Mike Scott	.10	.05	.01
☐ 312	Dave Smith	.10	.05	.01
☐ 313	Dickie Thon	.10	.05	.01
☐ 314	Denny Walling	.10	.05	.01
☐ 315	Kurt Bevacqua	.10	.05	.01
☐ 316	Al Bumbry	.10	.05	.01
☐ 317	Jerry Davis	.10	.05	.01
☐ 318	Luis DeLeon	.10	.05	.01
☐ 319	Dave Dravecky	.20	.09	.03
☐ 320	Tim Flannery	.10	.05	.01
☐ 321	Steve Garvey	.30	.14	.04
☐ 322	Rich Gossage	.30	.14	.04
☐ 323	Tony Gwynn	2.50	1.10	.30
☐ 324	Andy Hawkins	.10	.05	.01
☐ 325	LaMarr Hoyt	.10	.05	.01
☐ 326	Roy Lee Jackson	.10	.05	.01
☐ 327	Terry Kennedy	.10	.05	.01
☐ 328	Craig Lefferts	.10	.05	.01
☐ 329	Carmelo Martinez	.10	.05	.01
☐ 330	Lance McCullers	.10	.05	.01
☐ 331	Kevin McReynolds	.20	.09	.03
☐ 332	Graig Nettles	.20	.09	.03
☐ 333	Jerry Royster	.10	.05	.01
☐ 334	Eric Show	.10	.05	.01
☐ 335	Tim Stoddard	.10	.05	.01
☐ 336	Garry Templeton	.10	.05	.01
☐ 337	Mark Thurmond	.10	.05	.01
☐ 338	Ed Wojna	.10	.05	.01
☐ 339	Tony Armas	.10	.05	.01
☐ 340	Marty Barrett	.10	.05	.01
☐ 341	Wade Boggs	1.00	.45	.12
☐ 342	Dennis Boyd	.10	.05	.01
☐ 343	Bill Buckner	.20	.09	.03
☐ 344	Mark Clear	.10	.05	.01
☐ 345	Roger Clemens	2.50	1.10	.30
☐ 346	Steve Crawford	.10	.05	.01
☐ 347	Mike Easler	.10	.05	.01
☐ 348	Dwight Evans	.20	.09	.03
☐ 349	Rich Gedman	.10	.05	.01
☐ 350	Jackie Gutierrez	.10	.05	.01
☐ 351	Glenn Hoffman	.10	.05	.01
☐ 352	Bruce Hurst	.20	.09	.03
☐ 353	Bruce Kison	.10	.05	.01
☐ 354	Tim Lollar	.10	.05	.01
☐ 355	Steve Lyons	.10	.05	.01
☐ 356	Al Nipper	.10	.05	.01
☐ 357	Bob Ojeda	.20	.09	.03
☐ 358	Jim Rice	.30	.14	.04
☐ 359	Bob Stanley	.10	.05	.01
☐ 360	Mike Trujillo	.10	.05	.01
☐ 361	Thad Bosley	.10	.05	.01
☐ 362	Warren Brusstar	.10	.05	.01
☐ 363	Ron Cey	.20	.09	.03
☐ 364	Jody Davis	.10	.05	.01
☐ 365	Bob Dernier	.10	.05	.01
☐ 366	Shawon Dunston	.20	.09	.03
☐ 367	Leon Durham	.10	.05	.01
☐ 368	Dennis Eckersley	.30	.14	.04
☐ 369	Ray Fontenot	.10	.05	.01
☐ 370	George Frazier	.10	.05	.01
☐ 371	Billy Hatcher	.20	.09	.03
☐ 372	Dave Lopes	.20	.09	.03
☐ 373	Gary Matthews	.10	.05	.01
☐ 374	Ron Meridith	.10	.05	.01
☐ 375	Keith Moreland	.10	.05	.01
☐ 376	Reggie Patterson	.10	.05	.01
☐ 377	Dick Ruthven	.10	.05	.01
☐ 378	Ryne Sandberg	2.50	1.10	.30
☐ 379	Scott Sanderson	.10	.05	.01
☐ 380	Lee Smith	.30	.14	.04
☐ 381	Lary Sorensen	.10	.05	.01
☐ 382	Chris Speier	.10	.05	.01
☐ 383	Rick Sutcliffe	.20	.09	.03
☐ 384	Steve Trout	.10	.05	.01
☐ 385	Gary Woods	.10	.05	.01
☐ 386	Bert Blyleven	.30	.14	.04
☐ 387	Tom Brunansky	.10	.05	.01
☐ 388	Randy Bush	.10	.05	.01
☐ 389	John Butcher	.10	.05	.01
☐ 390	Ron Davis	.10	.05	.01
☐ 391	Dave Engle	.10	.05	.01
☐ 392	Frank Eufemia	.10	.05	.01
☐ 393	Pete Filson	.10	.05	.01
☐ 394	Gary Gaetti	.10	.05	.01
☐ 395	Greg Gagne	.20	.09	.03
☐ 396	Mickey Hatcher	.10	.05	.01
☐ 397	Kent Hrbek	.30	.14	.04
☐ 398	Tim Laudner	.10	.05	.01
☐ 399	Rick Lysander	.10	.05	.01
☐ 400	Dave Meier	.10	.05	.01
☐ 401	Kirby Puckett UER	5.00	2.20	.60
	(Card has him in NL, should be AL)			
☐ 402	Mark Salas	.10	.05	.01
☐ 403	Ken Schrom	.10	.05	.01
☐ 404	Roy Smalley	.10	.05	.01
☐ 405	Mike Smithson	.10	.05	.01
☐ 406	Mike Stenhouse	.10	.05	.01
☐ 407	Tim Teufel	.10	.05	.01
☐ 408	Frank Viola	.20	.09	.03
☐ 409	Ron Washington	.10	.05	.01
☐ 410	Keith Atherton	.10	.05	.01
☐ 411	Dusty Baker	.30	.14	.04
☐ 412	Tim Birtsas	.10	.05	.01

☐ 413	Bruce Bochte	.10	.05	.01	☐ 484	Cecil Cooper	.20	.09	.03
☐ 414	Chris Codiroli	.10	.05	.01	☐ 485	Danny Darwin	.10	.05	.01
☐ 415	Dave Collins	.10	.05	.01	☐ 486	Rollie Fingers	.30	.14	.04
☐ 416	Mike Davis	.10	.05	.01	☐ 487	Jim Gantner	.10	.05	.01
☐ 417	Alfredo Griffin	.10	.05	.01	☐ 488	Bob L. Gibson	.10	.05	.01
☐ 418	Mike Heath	.10	.05	.01	☐ 489	Moose Haas	.10	.05	.01
☐ 419	Steve Henderson	.10	.05	.01	☐ 490	Teddy Higuera	.10	.05	.01
☐ 420	Donnie Hill	.10	.05	.01	☐ 491	Paul Householder	.10	.05	.01
☐ 421	Jay Howell	.10	.05	.01	☐ 492	Pete Ladd	.10	.05	.01
☐ 422	Tommy John	.30	.14	.04	☐ 493	Rick Manning	.10	.05	.01
☐ 423	Dave Kingman	.20	.09	.03	☐ 494	Bob McClure	.10	.05	.01
☐ 424	Bill Krueger	.10	.05	.01	☐ 495	Paul Molitor	.50	.23	.06
☐ 425	Rick Langford	.10	.05	.01	☐ 496	Charlie Moore	.10	.05	.01
☐ 426	Carney Lansford	.20	.09	.03	☐ 497	Ben Oglivie	.10	.05	.01
☐ 427	Steve McCatty	.10	.05	.01	☐ 498	Randy Ready	.10	.05	.01
☐ 428	Dwayne Murphy	.10	.05	.01	☐ 499	Earnie Riles	.10	.05	.01
☐ 429	Steve Ontiveros	.50	.23	.06	☐ 500	Ed Romero	.10	.05	.01
☐ 430	Tony Phillips	.30	.14	.04	☐ 501	Bill Schroeder	.10	.05	.01
☐ 431	Jose Rijo	.50	.23	.06	☐ 502	Ray Searage	.10	.05	.01
☐ 432	Mickey Tettleton	2.00	.90	.25	☐ 503	Ted Simmons	.20	.09	.03
☐ 433	Luis Aguayo	.10	.05	.01	☐ 504	Pete Vuckovich	.10	.05	.01
☐ 434	Larry Andersen	.10	.05	.01	☐ 505	Rick Waits	.10	.05	.01
☐ 435	Steve Carlton	.50	.23	.06	☐ 506	Robin Yount	1.00	.45	.12
☐ 436	Don Carman	.10	.05	.01	☐ 507	Len Barker	.10	.05	.01
☐ 437	Tim Corcoran	.10	.05	.01	☐ 508	Steve Bedrosian	.10	.05	.01
☐ 438	Darren Daulton	3.00	1.35	.35	☐ 509	Bruce Benedict	.10	.05	.01
☐ 439	John Denny	.10	.05	.01	☐ 510	Rick Camp	.10	.05	.01
☐ 440	Tom Foley	.10	.05	.01	☐ 511	Rick Cerone	.10	.05	.01
☐ 441	Greg Gross	.10	.05	.01	☐ 512	Chris Chambliss	.20	.09	.03
☐ 442	Kevin Gross	.10	.05	.01	☐ 513	Jeff Dedmon	.10	.05	.01
☐ 443	Von Hayes	.10	.05	.01	☐ 514	Terry Forster	.10	.05	.01
☐ 444	Charles Hudson	.10	.05	.01	☐ 515	Gene Garber	.10	.05	.01
☐ 445	Garry Maddox	.10	.05	.01	☐ 516	Terry Harper	.10	.05	.01
☐ 446	Shane Rawley	.10	.05	.01	☐ 517	Bob Horner	.10	.05	.01
☐ 447	Dave Rucker	.10	.05	.01	☐ 518	Glenn Hubbard	.10	.05	.01
☐ 448	John Russell	.10	.05	.01	☐ 519	Joe Johnson	.10	.05	.01
☐ 449	Juan Samuel	.10	.05	.01	☐ 520	Brad Komminsk	.10	.05	.01
☐ 450	Mike Schmidt	1.00	.45	.12	☐ 521	Rick Mahler	.10	.05	.01
☐ 451	Rick Schu	.10	.05	.01	☐ 522	Dale Murphy	.30	.14	.04
☐ 452	Dave Shipanoff	.10	.05	.01	☐ 523	Ken Oberkfell	.10	.05	.01
☐ 453	Dave Stewart	.30	.14	.04	☐ 524	Pascual Perez	.10	.05	.01
☐ 454	Jeff Stone	.10	.05	.01	☐ 525	Gerald Perry	.10	.05	.01
☐ 455	Kent Tekulve	.10	.05	.01	☐ 526	Rafael Ramirez	.10	.05	.01
☐ 456	Ozzie Virgil	.10	.05	.01	☐ 527	Steve Shields	.10	.05	.01
☐ 457	Glenn Wilson	.10	.05	.01	☐ 528	Zane Smith	.10	.05	.01
☐ 458	Jim Beattie	.10	.05	.01	☐ 529	Bruce Sutter	.20	.09	.03
☐ 459	Karl Best	.10	.05	.01	☐ 530	Milt Thompson	.20	.09	.03
☐ 460	Barry Bonnell	.10	.05	.01	☐ 531	Claudell Washington	.10	.05	.01
☐ 461	Phil Bradley	.10	.05	.01	☐ 532	Paul Zuvella	.10	.05	.01
☐ 462	Ivan Calderon	.20	.09	.03	☐ 533	Vida Blue	.20	.09	.03
☐ 463	Al Cowens	.10	.05	.01	☐ 534	Bob Brenly	.10	.05	.01
☐ 464	Alvin Davis	.10	.05	.01	☐ 535	Chris Brown	.10	.05	.01
☐ 465	Dave Henderson	.10	.05	.01	☐ 536	Chili Davis	.30	.14	.04
☐ 466	Bob Kearney	.10	.05	.01	☐ 537	Mark Davis	.10	.05	.01
☐ 467	Mark Langston	.30	.14	.04	☐ 538	Rob Deer	.20	.09	.03
☐ 468	Bob Long	.10	.05	.01	☐ 539	Dan Driessen	.10	.05	.01
☐ 469	Mike Moore	.10	.05	.01	☐ 540	Scott Garrelts	.10	.05	.01
☐ 470	Edwin Nunez	.10	.05	.01	☐ 541	Dan Gladden	.10	.05	.01
☐ 471	Spike Owen	.10	.05	.01	☐ 542	Jim Gott	.10	.05	.01
☐ 472	Jack Perconte	.10	.05	.01	☐ 543	David Green	.10	.05	.01
☐ 473	Jim Presley	.10	.05	.01	☐ 544	Atlee Hammaker	.10	.05	.01
☐ 474	Donnie Scott	.10	.05	.01	☐ 545	Mike Jeffcoat	.10	.05	.01
☐ 475	Bill Swift	.20	.09	.03	☐ 546	Mike Krukow	.10	.05	.01
☐ 476	Danny Tartabull	.30	.14	.04	☐ 547	Dave LaPoint	.10	.05	.01
☐ 477	Gorman Thomas	.10	.05	.01	☐ 548	Jeff Leonard	.10	.05	.01
☐ 478	Roy Thomas	.10	.05	.01	☐ 549	Greg Minton	.10	.05	.01
☐ 479	Ed VandeBerg	.10	.05	.01	☐ 550	Alex Trevino	.10	.05	.01
☐ 480	Frank Wills	.10	.05	.01	☐ 551	Manny Trillo	.10	.05	.01
☐ 481	Matt Young	.10	.05	.01	☐ 552	Jose Uribe	.10	.05	.01
☐ 482	Ray Burris	.10	.05	.01	☐ 553	Brad Wellman	.10	.05	.01
☐ 483	Jaime Cocanower	.10	.05	.01	☐ 554	Frank Williams	.10	.05	.01

☐	555	Joel Youngblood	.10	.05	.01	☐	626	Dwight Gooden IA	.20	.09	.03

555	Joel Youngblood	.10	.05	.01
556	Alan Bannister	.10	.05	.01
557	Glenn Brummer	.10	.05	.01
558	Steve Buechele	.20	.09	.03
559	Jose Guzman	.10	.05	.01
560	Toby Harrah	.10	.05	.01
561	Greg Harris	.10	.05	.01
562	Dwayne Henry	.10	.05	.01
563	Burt Hooton	.10	.05	.01
564	Charlie Hough	.20	.09	.03
565	Mike Mason	.10	.05	.01
566	Oddibe McDowell	.10	.05	.01
567	Dickie Noles	.10	.05	.01
568	Pete O'Brien	.10	.05	.01
569	Larry Parrish	.10	.05	.01
570	Dave Rozema	.10	.05	.01
571	Dave Schmidt	.10	.05	.01
572	Don Slaught	.10	.05	.01
573	Wayne Tolleson	.10	.05	.01
574	Duane Walker	.10	.05	.01
575	Gary Ward	.10	.05	.01
576	Chris Welsh	.10	.05	.01
577	Curtis Wilkerson	.10	.05	.01
578	George Wright	.10	.05	.01
579	Chris Bando	.10	.05	.01
580	Tony Bernazard	.10	.05	.01
581	Brett Butler	.30	.14	.04
582	Ernie Camacho	.10	.05	.01
583	Joe Carter	2.50	1.10	.30
584	Carmen Castillo	.10	.05	.01
585	Jamie Easterly	.10	.05	.01
586	Julio Franco	.30	.14	.04
587	Mel Hall	.10	.05	.01
588	Mike Hargrove	.20	.09	.03
589	Neal Heaton	.10	.05	.01
590	Brook Jacoby	.10	.05	.01
591	Otis Nixon	.75	.35	.09
592	Jerry Reed	.10	.05	.01
593	Vern Ruhle	.10	.05	.01
594	Pat Tabler	.10	.05	.01
595	Rich Thompson	.10	.05	.01
596	Andre Thornton	.10	.05	.01
597	Dave Von Ohlen	.10	.05	.01
598	George Vukovich	.10	.05	.01
599	Tom Waddell	.10	.05	.01
600	Curt Wardle	.10	.05	.01
601	Jerry Willard	.10	.05	.01
602	Bill Almon	.10	.05	.01
603	Mike Bielecki	.10	.05	.01
604	Sid Bream	.20	.09	.03
605	Mike C. Brown	.10	.05	.01
606	Pat Clements	.10	.05	.01
607	Jose DeLeon	.10	.05	.01
608	Denny Gonzalez	.10	.05	.01
609	Cecilio Guante	.10	.05	.01
610	Steve Kemp	.10	.05	.01
611	Sammy Khalifa	.10	.05	.01
612	Lee Mazzilli	.10	.05	.01
613	Larry McWilliams	.10	.05	.01
614	Jim Morrison	.10	.05	.01
615	Joe Orsulak	.20	.09	.03
616	Tony Pena	.10	.05	.01
617	Johnny Ray	.10	.05	.01
618	Rick Reuschel	.10	.05	.01
619	R.J. Reynolds	.10	.05	.01
620	Rick Rhoden	.10	.05	.01
621	Don Robinson	.10	.05	.01
622	Jason Thompson	.10	.05	.01
623	Lee Tunnell	.10	.05	.01
624	Jim Winn	.10	.05	.01
625	Marvell Wynne	.10	.05	.01
626	Dwight Gooden IA	.20	.09	.03
627	Don Mattingly IA	1.25	.55	.16
628	4192 (Pete Rose)	.60	.25	.07
629	3000 Career Hits Rod Carew	.30	.14	.04
630	300 Career Wins Tom Seaver Phil Niekro	.30	.14	.04
631	Ouch (Don Baylor)	.20	.09	.03
632	Instant Offense Darryl Strawberry Tim Raines	.30	.14	.04
633	Shortstops Supreme Cal Ripken Alan Trammell	2.00	.90	.25
634	Boggs and "Hero" Wade Boggs George Brett	1.25	.55	.16
635	Braves Dynamic Duo Bob Horner Dale Murphy	.20	.09	.03
636	Cardinal Ignitors Willie McGee Vince Coleman	.20	.09	.03
637	Terror on Basepaths Vince Coleman	.20	.09	.03
638	Charlie Hustle / Dr.K Pete Rose Dwight Gooden	.40	.18	.05
639	1984 and 1985 AL Batting Champs Wade Boggs Don Mattingly	1.00	.45	.12
640	NL West Sluggers Dale Murphy Steve Garvey Dave Parker	.20	.09	.03
641	Staff Aces Fernando Valenzuela Dwight Gooden	.20	.09	.03
642	Blue Jay Stoppers Jimmy Key Dave Stieb	.30	.14	.04
643	AL All-Star Backstops Carlton Fisk Rich Gedman	.20	.09	.03
644	Gene Walter and Benito Santiago	.75	.35	.09
645	Mike Woodard and Colin Ward	.10	.05	.01
646	Kal Daniels and Paul O'Neill	2.00	.90	.25
647	Andres Galarraga and Fred Toliver	4.00	1.80	.50
648	Bob Kipper and Curt Ford	.10	.05	.01
649	Jose Canseco and Eric Plunk	15.00	6.75	1.85
650	Mark McLemore and Gus Polidor	.50	.23	.06
651	Rob Woodward and Mickey Brantley	.10	.05	.01
652	Billy Joe Robidoux and Mark Funderburk	.10	.05	.01
653	Cecil Fielder and Cory Snyder	6.00	2.70	.75
654	CL: Royals/Cardinals Blue Jays/Mets	.20	.09	.03
655	CL: Yankees/Dodgers Angels/Reds UER (168 Darly Sconiers)	.20	.09	.03

		MINT	NRMT	EXC
☐ 656	CL: White Sox/Tigers ... Expos/Orioles (279 Dennis, 280 Tippy)	.20	.09	.03
☐ 657	CL: Astros/Padres .... Red Sox/Cubs	.20	.09	.03
☐ 658	CL: Twins/A's............. Phillies/Mariners	.20	.09	.03
☐ 659	CL: Brewers/Braves ..... Giants/Rangers	.20	.09	.03
☐ 660	CL: Indians/Pirates....... Special Cards	.20	.09	.03

1986 Fleer Update

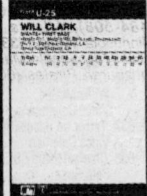

This 132-card set was distributed by Fleer to dealers as a complete set in a custom box. In addition to the complete set of 132 cards, the box also contains 25 Team Logo Stickers. The card fronts look very similar to the 1986 Fleer regular issue. The cards are numbered (with a U prefix) alphabetically according to player's last name. Cards measure the standard size, 2 1/2" by 3 1/2". The (extended) Rookie Cards in this set include Barry Bonds, Bobby Bonilla, Will Clark, Doug Drabek, Wally Joyner, John Kruk, Kevin Mitchell, and Ruben Sierra.

	MINT	NRMT	EXC
COMPLETE FACT.SET (132) ..	15.00	6.75	1.85
COMMON CARD (1-132)	.07	.03	.01

		MINT	NRMT	EXC
☐ 1	Mike Aldrete................	.07	.03	.01
☐ 2	Andy Allanson.............	.07	.03	.01
☐ 3	Neil Allen....................	.07	.03	.01
☐ 4	Joaquin Andujar.........	.07	.03	.01
☐ 5	Paul Assenmacher......	.07	.03	.01
☐ 6	Scott Bailes................	.07	.03	.01
☐ 7	Jay Baller....................	.07	.03	.01
☐ 8	Scott Bankhead..........	.07	.03	.01
☐ 9	Bill Bathe...................	.07	.03	.01
☐ 10	Don Baylor..................	.15	.07	.02
☐ 11	Billy Beane.................	.07	.03	.01
☐ 12	Steve Bedrosian..........	.07	.03	.01
☐ 13	Juan Beniquez............	.07	.03	.01
☐ 14	Barry Bonds................	5.00	2.20	.60
☐ 15	Bobby Bonilla UER ..... (Wrong birthday)	1.50	.70	.19
☐ 16	Rich Bordi..................	.07	.03	.01
☐ 17	Bill Campbell..............	.07	.03	.01
☐ 18	Tom Candiotti..............	.10	.05	.01
☐ 19	John Cangelosi............	.07	.03	.01
☐ 20	Jose Canseco UER.......	3.00	1.35	.35

(Headings on back for a pitcher)

		MINT	NRMT	EXC
☐ 21	Chuck Cary..................	.07	.03	.01
☐ 22	Juan Castillo...............	.07	.03	.01
☐ 23	Rick Cerone................	.07	.03	.01
☐ 24	John Cerutti................	.07	.03	.01
☐ 25	Will Clark	3.00	1.35	.35
☐ 26	Mark Clear..................	.07	.03	.01
☐ 27	Darnell Coles..............	.07	.03	.01
☐ 28	Dave Collins................	.07	.03	.01
☐ 29	Tim Conroy.................	.07	.03	.01
☐ 30	Ed Correa...................	.07	.03	.01
☐ 31	Joe Cowley.................	.07	.03	.01
☐ 32	Bill Dawley.................	.07	.03	.01
☐ 33	Rob Deer....................	.10	.05	.01
☐ 34	John Denny.................	.07	.03	.01
☐ 35	Jim Deshaies..............	.07	.03	.01
☐ 36	Doug Drabek................	.75	.35	.09
☐ 37	Mike Easler................	.07	.03	.01
☐ 38	Mark Eichhorn............	.07	.03	.01
☐ 39	Dave Engle.................	.07	.03	.01
☐ 40	Mike Fischlin..............	.07	.03	.01
☐ 41	Scott Fletcher.............	.07	.03	.01
☐ 42	Terry Forster..............	.07	.03	.01
☐ 43	Terry Francona............	.07	.03	.01
☐ 44	Andres Galarraga	2.00	.90	.25
☐ 45	Lee Guetterman	.07	.03	.01
☐ 46	Bill Gullickson............	.10	.05	.01
☐ 47	Jackie Gutierrez..........	.07	.03	.01
☐ 48	Moose Haas................	.07	.03	.01
☐ 49	Billy Hatcher...............	.07	.03	.01
☐ 50	Mike Heath.................	.07	.03	.01
☐ 51	Guy Hoffman...............	.07	.03	.01
☐ 52	Tom Hume...................	.07	.03	.01
☐ 53	Pete Incaviglia............	.15	.07	.02
☐ 54	Dane Iorg...................	.07	.03	.01
☐ 55	Chris James...............	.07	.03	.01
☐ 56	Stan Javier.................	.10	.05	.01
☐ 57	Tommy John................	.15	.07	.02
☐ 58	Tracy Jones................	.07	.03	.01
☐ 59	Wally Joyner...............	.75	.35	.09
☐ 60	Wayne Krenchicki........	.07	.03	.01
☐ 61	John Kruk...................	.75	.35	.09
☐ 62	Mike LaCoss...............	.07	.03	.01
☐ 63	Pete Ladd...................	.07	.03	.01
☐ 64	Dave LaPoint..............	.07	.03	.01
☐ 65	Mike LaValliere...........	.07	.03	.01
☐ 66	Rudy Law...................	.07	.03	.01
☐ 67	Dennis Leonard...........	.07	.03	.01
☐ 68	Steve Lombardozzi......	.07	.03	.01
☐ 69	Aurelio Lopez..............	.07	.03	.01
☐ 70	Mickey Mahler............	.07	.03	.01
☐ 71	Candy Maldonado........	.07	.03	.01
☐ 72	Roger Mason...............	.07	.03	.01
☐ 73	Greg Mathews.............	.07	.03	.01
☐ 74	Andy McGaffigan.........	.07	.03	.01
☐ 75	Joel McKeon...............	.07	.03	.01
☐ 76	Kevin Mitchell	.40	.18	.05
☐ 77	Bill Mooneyham..........	.07	.03	.01
☐ 78	Omar Moreno..............	.07	.03	.01
☐ 79	Jerry Mumphrey..........	.07	.03	.01
☐ 80	Al Newman.................	.07	.03	.01
☐ 81	Phil Niekro.................	.15	.07	.02
☐ 82	Randy Niemann...........	.07	.03	.01
☐ 83	Juan Nieves................	.07	.03	.01
☐ 84	Bob Ojeda..................	.10	.05	.01
☐ 85	Rick Ownbey...............	.07	.03	.01
☐ 86	Tom Paciorek..............	.10	.05	.01
☐ 87	David Palmer..............	.07	.03	.01
☐ 88	Jeff Parrett.................	.07	.03	.01
☐ 89	Pat Perry...................	.07	.03	.01

			MINT	NRMT	EXC
☐ 90	Dan Plesac	.07	.03	.01
☐ 91	Darrell Porter	.07	.03	.01
☐ 92	Luis Quinones	.07	.03	.01
☐ 93	Rey Quinones UER	.07	.03	.01
	(Misspelled Quinonez)			
☐ 94	Gary Redus	.07	.03	.01
☐ 95	Jeff Reed	.07	.03	.01
☐ 96	Bip Roberts	.50	.23	.06
☐ 97	Billy Joe Robidoux	.07	.03	.01
☐ 98	Gary Roenicke	.07	.03	.01
☐ 99	Ron Roenicke	.07	.03	.01
☐ 100	Angel Salazar	.07	.03	.01
☐ 101	Joe Sambito	.07	.03	.01
☐ 102	Billy Sample	.07	.03	.01
☐ 103	Dave Schmidt	.07	.03	.01
☐ 104	Ken Schrom	.07	.03	.01
☐ 105	Ruben Sierra	2.00	.90	.25
☐ 106	Ted Simmons	.10	.05	.01
☐ 107	Sammy Stewart	.07	.03	.01
☐ 108	Kurt Stillwell	.07	.03	.01
☐ 109	Dale Sveum	.07	.03	.01
☐ 110	Tim Teufel	.07	.03	.01
☐ 111	Bob Tewksbury	.10	.05	.01
☐ 112	Andres Thomas	.07	.03	.01
☐ 113	Jason Thompson	.07	.03	.01
☐ 114	Milt Thompson	.07	.03	.01
☐ 115	Robby Thompson	.15	.07	.02
☐ 116	Jay Tibbs	.07	.03	.01
☐ 117	Fred Toliver	.07	.03	.01
☐ 118	Wayne Tolleson	.07	.03	.01
☐ 119	Alex Trevino	.07	.03	.01
☐ 120	Manny Trillo	.07	.03	.01
☐ 121	Ed VandeBerg	.07	.03	.01
☐ 122	Ozzie Virgil	.07	.03	.01
☐ 123	Tony Walker	.07	.03	.01
☐ 124	Gene Walter	.07	.03	.01
☐ 125	Duane Ward	.10	.05	.01
☐ 126	Jerry Willard	.07	.03	.01
☐ 127	Mitch Williams	.10	.05	.01
☐ 128	Reggie Williams	.07	.03	.01
☐ 129	Bobby Witt	.10	.05	.01
☐ 130	Marvell Wynne	.07	.03	.01
☐ 131	Steve Yeager	.07	.03	.01
☐ 132	Checklist 1-132	.07	.03	.01

1987 Fleer

This 660-card set features a distinctive blue border, which fades to white on the card fronts. The backs are printed in blue, red, and pink on white card stock. The bottom of the card back shows an innovative graph of the player's ability, e.g., "He's got the stuff" for pitchers and "How he's hitting 'em," for hitters. Cards are numbered on the back and are again the standard 2 1/2" by 3 1/2". Cards are again organized numerically by teams, i.e., World Champion Mets (1-25), Boston Red Sox (26-48), Houston Astros (49-72), California Angels (73-95), New York Yankees (96-120), Texas Rangers (121-143), Detroit Tigers (144-168), Philadelphia Phillies (169-192), Cincinnati Reds (193-218), Toronto Blue Jays (219-240), Cleveland Indians (241-263), San Francisco Giants (264-288), St. Louis Cardinals (289-312), Montreal Expos (313-337), Milwaukee Brewers (338-361), Kansas City Royals (362-384), Oakland A's (385-410), San Diego Padres (411-435), Los Angeles Dodgers (436-460), Baltimore Orioles (461-483), Chicago White Sox (484-508), Atlanta Braves (509-532), Minnesota Twins (533-554), Chicago Cubs (555-578), Seattle Mariners (579-600), and Pittsburgh Pirates (601-624). The last 36 cards in the set consist of Specials (625-643), Rookie Pairs (644-653), and checklists (654-660). The key Rookie Cards in this set are Barry Bonds, Bobby Bonilla, Will Clark, Doug Drabek, Chuck Finley, Bo Jackson, Wally Joyner, John Kruk, Barry Larkin, Dave Magadan, Kevin Mitchell, Kevin Seitzer, Ruben Sierra, Greg Swindell, and Devon White. Fleer also produced a "limited" edition version of this set with glossy coating and packaged in a "tin." However, this glossy set was apparently not limited enough (estimated between 75,000 and 100,000 1987 tin sets produced by Fleer), since the values of the "tin" glossy cards are now the same as the values of the regular set cards.

	MINT	NRMT	EXC
COMPLETE SET (660)	50.00	22.00	6.25
COMPLETE FACT.SET (672)	50.00	22.00	6.25
COMPLETE WORLD SERIES (12)	2.00	.90	.25
COMMON CARD (1-660)	.08	.04	.01

			MINT	NRMT	EXC
☐ 1	Rick Aguilera	.30	.14	.04
☐ 2	Richard Anderson	.08	.04	.01
☐ 3	Wally Backman	.08	.04	.01
☐ 4	Gary Carter	.30	.14	.04
☐ 5	Ron Darling	.15	.07	.02
☐ 6	Len Dykstra	.30	.14	.04
☐ 7	Kevin Elster	.08	.04	.01
☐ 8	Sid Fernandez	.15	.07	.02
☐ 9	Dwight Gooden	.30	.14	.04
☐ 10	Ed Hearn	.08	.04	.01
☐ 11	Danny Heep	.08	.04	.01
☐ 12	Keith Hernandez	.15	.07	.02
☐ 13	Howard Johnson	.15	.07	.02
☐ 14	Ray Knight	.15	.07	.02
☐ 15	Lee Mazzilli	.08	.04	.01
☐ 16	Roger McDowell	.08	.04	.01
☐ 17	Kevin Mitchell	.50	.23	.06
☐ 18	Randy Niemann	.08	.04	.01
☐ 19	Bob Ojeda	.08	.04	.01
☐ 20	Jesse Orosco	.08	.04	.01
☐ 21	Rafael Santana	.08	.04	.01
☐ 22	Doug Sisk	.08	.04	.01
☐ 23	Darryl Strawberry	.30	.14	.04
☐ 24	Tim Teufel	.08	.04	.01
☐ 25	Mookie Wilson	.15	.07	.02

☐ 26	Tony Armas	.08	.04	.01
☐ 27	Marty Barrett	.08	.04	.01
☐ 28	Don Baylor	.30	.14	.04
☐ 29	Wade Boggs	.75	.35	.09
☐ 30	Oil Can Boyd	.08	.04	.01
☐ 31	Bill Buckner	.15	.07	.02
☐ 32	Roger Clemens	1.00	.45	.12
☐ 33	Steve Crawford	.08	.04	.01
☐ 34	Dwight Evans	.15	.07	.02
☐ 35	Rich Gedman	.08	.04	.01
☐ 36	Dave Henderson	.15	.07	.02
☐ 37	Bruce Hurst	.08	.04	.01
☐ 38	Tim Lollar	.08	.04	.01
☐ 39	Al Nipper	.08	.04	.01
☐ 40	Spike Owen	.08	.04	.01
☐ 41	Jim Rice	.30	.14	.04
☐ 42	Ed Romero	.08	.04	.01
☐ 43	Joe Sambito	.08	.04	.01
☐ 44	Calvin Schiraldi	.08	.04	.01
☐ 45	Tom Seaver	.50	.23	.06
☐ 46	Jeff Sellers	.08	.04	.01
☐ 47	Bob Stanley	.08	.04	.01
☐ 48	Sammy Stewart	.08	.04	.01
☐ 49	Larry Andersen	.08	.04	.01
☐ 50	Alan Ashby	.08	.04	.01
☐ 51	Kevin Bass	.08	.04	.01
☐ 52	Jeff Calhoun	.08	.04	.01
☐ 53	Jose Cruz	.08	.04	.01
☐ 54	Danny Darwin	.08	.04	.01
☐ 55	Glenn Davis	.08	.04	.01
☐ 56	Jim Deshaies	.08	.04	.01
☐ 57	Bill Doran	.08	.04	.01
☐ 58	Phil Garner	.15	.07	.02
☐ 59	Billy Hatcher	.08	.04	.01
☐ 60	Charlie Kerfeld	.08	.04	.01
☐ 61	Bob Knepper	.08	.04	.01
☐ 62	Dave Lopes	.15	.07	.02
☐ 63	Aurelio Lopez	.08	.04	.01
☐ 64	Jim Pankovits	.08	.04	.01
☐ 65	Terry Puhl	.08	.04	.01
☐ 66	Craig Reynolds	.08	.04	.01
☐ 67	Nolan Ryan	3.00	1.35	.35
☐ 68	Mike Scott	.08	.04	.01
☐ 69	Dave Smith	.08	.04	.01
☐ 70	Dickie Thon	.08	.04	.01
☐ 71	Tony Walker	.08	.04	.01
☐ 72	Denny Walling	.08	.04	.01
☐ 73	Bob Boone	.15	.07	.02
☐ 74	Rick Burleson	.08	.04	.01
☐ 75	John Candelaria	.08	.04	.01
☐ 76	Doug Corbett	.08	.04	.01
☐ 77	Doug DeCinces	.08	.04	.01
☐ 78	Brian Downing	.08	.04	.01
☐ 79	Chuck Finley	.50	.23	.06
☐ 80	Terry Forster	.08	.04	.01
☐ 81	Bob Grich	.15	.07	.02
☐ 82	George Hendrick	.08	.04	.01
☐ 83	Jack Howell	.08	.04	.01
☐ 84	Reggie Jackson	.60	.25	.07
☐ 85	Ruppert Jones	.08	.04	.01
☐ 86	Wally Joyner	1.00	.45	.12
☐ 87	Gary Lucas	.08	.04	.01
☐ 88	Kirk McCaskill	.08	.04	.01
☐ 89	Donnie Moore	.08	.04	.01
☐ 90	Gary Pettis	.08	.04	.01
☐ 91	Vern Ruhle	.08	.04	.01
☐ 92	Dick Schofield	.08	.04	.01
☐ 93	Don Sutton	.30	.14	.04
☐ 94	Rob Wilfong	.08	.04	.01
☐ 95	Mike Witt	.08	.04	.01
☐ 96	Doug Drabek	.75	.35	.09
☐ 97	Mike Easler	.08	.04	.01
☐ 98	Mike Fischlin	.08	.04	.01
☐ 99	Brian Fisher	.08	.04	.01
☐ 100	Ron Guidry	.15	.07	.02
☐ 101	Rickey Henderson	.50	.23	.06
☐ 102	Tommy John	.30	.14	.04
☐ 103	Ron Kittle	.08	.04	.01
☐ 104	Don Mattingly	2.00	.90	.25
☐ 105	Bobby Meacham	.08	.04	.01
☐ 106	Joe Niekro	.15	.07	.02
☐ 107	Mike Pagliarulo	.08	.04	.01
☐ 108	Dan Pasqua	.08	.04	.01
☐ 109	Willie Randolph	.15	.07	.02
☐ 110	Dennis Rasmussen	.08	.04	.01
☐ 111	Dave Righetti	.15	.07	.02
☐ 112	Gary Roenicke	.08	.04	.01
☐ 113	Rod Scurry	.08	.04	.01
☐ 114	Bob Shirley	.08	.04	.01
☐ 115	Joel Skinner	.08	.04	.01
☐ 116	Tim Stoddard	.08	.04	.01
☐ 117	Bob Tewksbury	.15	.07	.02
☐ 118	Wayne Tolleson	.08	.04	.01
☐ 119	Claudell Washington	.08	.04	.01
☐ 120	Dave Winfield	.40	.18	.05
☐ 121	Steve Buechele	.08	.04	.01
☐ 122	Ed Correa	.08	.04	.01
☐ 123	Scott Fletcher	.08	.04	.01
☐ 124	Jose Guzman	.08	.04	.01
☐ 125	Toby Harrah	.08	.04	.01
☐ 126	Greg Harris	.08	.04	.01
☐ 127	Charlie Hough	.15	.07	.02
☐ 128	Pete Incaviglia	.30	.14	.04
☐ 129	Mike Mason	.08	.04	.01
☐ 130	Oddibe McDowell	.08	.04	.01
☐ 131	Dale Mohorcic	.08	.04	.01
☐ 132	Pete O'Brien	.08	.04	.01
☐ 133	Tom Paciorek	.15	.07	.02
☐ 134	Larry Parrish	.08	.04	.01
☐ 135	Geno Petralli	.08	.04	.01
☐ 136	Darrell Porter	.08	.04	.01
☐ 137	Jeff Russell	.08	.04	.01
☐ 138	Ruben Sierra	4.00	1.80	.50
☐ 139	Don Slaught	.08	.04	.01
☐ 140	Gary Ward	.08	.04	.01
☐ 141	Curtis Wilkerson	.08	.04	.01
☐ 142	Mitch Williams	.15	.07	.02
☐ 143	Bobby Witt UER	.15	.07	.02
	(Tulsa misspelled as Tusla; ERA should be 6.43, not .643)			
☐ 144	Dave Bergman	.08	.04	.01
☐ 145	Tom Brookens	.08	.04	.01
☐ 146	Bill Campbell	.08	.04	.01
☐ 147	Chuck Cary	.08	.04	.01
☐ 148	Darnell Coles	.08	.04	.01
☐ 149	Dave Collins	.08	.04	.01
☐ 150	Darrell Evans	.15	.07	.02
☐ 151	Kirk Gibson	.30	.14	.04
☐ 152	John Grubb	.08	.04	.01
☐ 153	Willie Hernandez	.08	.04	.01
☐ 154	Larry Herndon	.08	.04	.01
☐ 155	Eric King	.08	.04	.01
☐ 156	Chet Lemon	.08	.04	.01
☐ 157	Dwight Lowry	.08	.04	.01
☐ 158	Jack Morris	.30	.14	.04
☐ 159	Randy O'Neal	.08	.04	.01
☐ 160	Lance Parrish	.15	.07	.02
☐ 161	Dan Petry	.08	.04	.01
☐ 162	Pat Sheridan	.08	.04	.01
☐ 163	Jim Slaton	.08	.04	.01
☐ 164	Frank Tanana	.08	.04	.01

☐ 165 Walt Terrell	.08	.04	.01
☐ 166 Mark Thurmond	.08	.04	.01
☐ 167 Alan Trammell	.30	.14	.04
☐ 168 Lou Whitaker	.30	.14	.04
☐ 169 Luis Aguayo	.08	.04	.01
☐ 170 Steve Bedrosian	.08	.04	.01
☐ 171 Don Carman	.08	.04	.01
☐ 172 Darren Daulton	.30	.14	.04
☐ 173 Greg Gross	.08	.04	.01
☐ 174 Kevin Gross	.08	.04	.01
☐ 175 Von Hayes	.08	.04	.01
☐ 176 Charles Hudson	.08	.04	.01
☐ 177 Tom Hume	.08	.04	.01
☐ 178 Steve Jeltz	.08	.04	.01
☐ 179 Mike Maddux	.08	.04	.01
☐ 180 Shane Rawley	.08	.04	.01
☐ 181 Gary Redus	.08	.04	.01
☐ 182 Ron Roenicke	.08	.04	.01
☐ 183 Bruce Ruffin	.15	.07	.02
☐ 184 John Russell	.08	.04	.01
☐ 185 Juan Samuel	.08	.04	.01
☐ 186 Dan Schatzeder	.08	.04	.01
☐ 187 Mike Schmidt	.75	.35	.09
☐ 188 Rick Schu	.08	.04	.01
☐ 189 Jeff Stone	.08	.04	.01
☐ 190 Kent Tekulve	.08	.04	.01
☐ 191 Milt Thompson	.08	.04	.01
☐ 192 Glenn Wilson	.08	.04	.01
☐ 193 Buddy Bell	.15	.07	.02
☐ 194 Tom Browning	.08	.04	.01
☐ 195 Sal Butera	.08	.04	.01
☐ 196 Dave Concepcion	.15	.07	.02
☐ 197 Kal Daniels	.08	.04	.01
☐ 198 Eric Davis	.30	.14	.04
☐ 199 John Denny	.08	.04	.01
☐ 200 Bo Diaz	.08	.04	.01
☐ 201 Nick Esasky	.08	.04	.01
☐ 202 John Franco	.15	.07	.02
☐ 203 Bill Gullickson	.08	.04	.01
☐ 204 Barry Larkin	6.00	2.70	.75
☐ 205 Eddie Milner	.08	.04	.01
☐ 206 Rob Murphy	.08	.04	.01
☐ 207 Ron Oester	.08	.04	.01
☐ 208 Dave Parker	.30	.14	.04
☐ 209 Tony Perez	.30	.14	.04
☐ 210 Ted Power	.08	.04	.01
☐ 211 Joe Price	.08	.04	.01
☐ 212 Ron Robinson	.08	.04	.01
☐ 213 Pete Rose	.75	.35	.09
☐ 214 Mario Soto	.08	.04	.01
☐ 215 Kurt Stillwell	.08	.04	.01
☐ 216 Max Venable	.08	.04	.01
☐ 217 Chris Welsh	.08	.04	.01
☐ 218 Carl Willis	.08	.04	.01
☐ 219 Jesse Barfield	.08	.04	.01
☐ 220 George Bell	.15	.07	.02
☐ 221 Bill Caudill	.08	.04	.01
☐ 222 John Cerutti	.08	.04	.01
☐ 223 Jim Clancy	.08	.04	.01
☐ 224 Mark Eichhorn	.08	.04	.01
☐ 225 Tony Fernandez	.15	.07	.02
☐ 226 Damaso Garcia	.08	.04	.01
☐ 227 Kelly Gruber ERR (Wrong birth year)	.08	.04	.01
☐ 228 Tom Henke	.15	.07	.02
☐ 229 Garth Iorg	.08	.04	.01
☐ 230 Joe Johnson	.08	.04	.01
☐ 231 Cliff Johnson	.08	.04	.01
☐ 232 Jimmy Key	.30	.14	.04
☐ 233 Dennis Lamp	.08	.04	.01
☐ 234 Rick Leach	.08	.04	.01
☐ 235 Buck Martinez	.08	.04	.01
☐ 236 Lloyd Moseby	.08	.04	.01
☐ 237 Rance Mulliniks	.08	.04	.01
☐ 238 Dave Stieb	.15	.07	.02
☐ 239 Willie Upshaw	.08	.04	.01
☐ 240 Ernie Whitt	.08	.04	.01
☐ 241 Andy Allanson	.08	.04	.01
☐ 242 Scott Bailes	.08	.04	.01
☐ 243 Chris Bando	.08	.04	.01
☐ 244 Tony Bernazard	.08	.04	.01
☐ 245 John Butcher	.08	.04	.01
☐ 246 Brett Butler	.30	.14	.04
☐ 247 Ernie Camacho	.08	.04	.01
☐ 248 Tom Candiotti	.15	.07	.02
☐ 249 Joe Carter	1.00	.45	.12
☐ 250 Carmen Castillo	.08	.04	.01
☐ 251 Julio Franco	.30	.14	.04
☐ 252 Mel Hall	.08	.04	.01
☐ 253 Brook Jacoby	.08	.04	.01
☐ 254 Phil Niekro	.30	.14	.04
☐ 255 Otis Nixon	.08	.04	.01
☐ 256 Dickie Noles	.08	.04	.01
☐ 257 Bryan Oelkers	.08	.04	.01
☐ 258 Ken Schrom	.08	.04	.01
☐ 259 Don Schulze	.08	.04	.01
☐ 260 Cory Snyder	.08	.04	.01
☐ 261 Pat Tabler	.08	.04	.01
☐ 262 Andre Thornton	.08	.04	.01
☐ 263 Rich Yett	.08	.04	.01
☐ 264 Mike Aldrete	.08	.04	.01
☐ 265 Juan Berenguer	.08	.04	.01
☐ 266 Vida Blue	.15	.07	.02
☐ 267 Bob Brenly	.08	.04	.01
☐ 268 Chris Brown	.08	.04	.01
☐ 269 Will Clark	6.00	2.70	.75
☐ 270 Chili Davis	.30	.14	.04
☐ 271 Mark Davis	.08	.04	.01
☐ 272 Kelly Downs	.08	.04	.01
☐ 273 Scott Garrelts	.08	.04	.01
☐ 274 Dan Gladden	.08	.04	.01
☐ 275 Mike Krukow	.08	.04	.01
☐ 276 Randy Kutcher	.08	.04	.01
☐ 277 Mike LaCoss	.08	.04	.01
☐ 278 Jeff Leonard	.08	.04	.01
☐ 279 Candy Maldonado	.08	.04	.01
☐ 280 Roger Mason	.08	.04	.01
☐ 281 Bob Melvin	.08	.04	.01
☐ 282 Greg Minton	.08	.04	.01
☐ 283 Jeff D. Robinson	.08	.04	.01
☐ 284 Harry Spilman	.08	.04	.01
☐ 285 Robby Thompson	.30	.14	.04
☐ 286 Jose Uribe	.08	.04	.01
☐ 287 Frank Williams	.08	.04	.01
☐ 288 Joel Youngblood	.08	.04	.01
☐ 289 Jack Clark	.15	.07	.02
☐ 290 Vince Coleman	.15	.07	.02
☐ 291 Tim Conroy	.08	.04	.01
☐ 292 Danny Cox	.08	.04	.01
☐ 293 Ken Dayley	.08	.04	.01
☐ 294 Curt Ford	.08	.04	.01
☐ 295 Bob Forsch	.08	.04	.01
☐ 296 Tom Herr	.08	.04	.01
☐ 297 Ricky Horton	.08	.04	.01
☐ 298 Clint Hurdle	.08	.04	.01
☐ 299 Jeff Lahti	.08	.04	.01
☐ 300 Steve Lake	.08	.04	.01
☐ 301 Tito Landrum	.08	.04	.01
☐ 302 Mike LaValliere	.08	.04	.01
☐ 303 Greg Mathews	.08	.04	.01
☐ 304 Willie McGee	.15	.07	.02
☐ 305 Jose Oquendo	.08	.04	.01

☐ 306	Terry Pendleton	.30	.14	.04
☐ 307	Pat Perry	.08	.04	.01
☐ 308	Ozzie Smith	1.00	.45	.12
☐ 309	Ray Soff	.08	.04	.01
☐ 310	John Tudor	.08	.04	.01
☐ 311	Andy Van Slyke UER	.15	.07	.02
	(Bats R, Throws L)			
☐ 312	Todd Worrell	.15	.07	.02
☐ 313	Dann Bilardello	.08	.04	.01
☐ 314	Hubie Brooks	.08	.04	.01
☐ 315	Tim Burke	.08	.04	.01
☐ 316	Andre Dawson	.30	.14	.04
☐ 317	Mike Fitzgerald	.08	.04	.01
☐ 318	Tom Foley	.08	.04	.01
☐ 319	Andres Galarraga	.75	.35	.09
☐ 320	Joe Hesketh	.08	.04	.01
☐ 321	Wallace Johnson	.08	.04	.01
☐ 322	Wayne Krenchicki	.08	.04	.01
☐ 323	Vance Law	.08	.04	.01
☐ 324	Dennis Martinez	.15	.07	.02
☐ 325	Bob McClure	.08	.04	.01
☐ 326	Andy McGaffigan	.08	.04	.01
☐ 327	Al Newman	.08	.04	.01
☐ 328	Tim Raines	.30	.14	.04
☐ 329	Jeff Reardon	.30	.14	.04
☐ 330	Luis Rivera	.08	.04	.01
☐ 331	Bob Sebra	.08	.04	.01
☐ 332	Bryn Smith	.08	.04	.01
☐ 333	Jay Tibbs	.08	.04	.01
☐ 334	Tim Wallach	.15	.07	.02
☐ 335	Mitch Webster	.08	.04	.01
☐ 336	Jim Wohlford	.08	.04	.01
☐ 337	Floyd Youmans	.08	.04	.01
☐ 338	Chris Bando	.40	.18	.05
☐ 339	Glenn Braggs	.08	.04	.01
☐ 340	Rick Cerone	.08	.04	.01
☐ 341	Mark Clear	.08	.04	.01
☐ 342	Bryan Clutterbuck	.08	.04	.01
☐ 343	Cecil Cooper	.15	.07	.02
☐ 344	Rob Deer	.08	.04	.01
☐ 345	Jim Gantner	.08	.04	.01
☐ 346	Ted Higuera	.08	.04	.01
☐ 347	John Henry Johnson	.08	.04	.01
☐ 348	Tim Leary	.08	.04	.01
☐ 349	Rick Manning	.08	.04	.01
☐ 350	Paul Molitor	.50	.23	.06
☐ 351	Charlie Moore	.08	.04	.01
☐ 352	Juan Nieves	.08	.04	.01
☐ 353	Ben Oglivie	.08	.04	.01
☐ 354	Dan Plesac	.08	.04	.01
☐ 355	Ernest Riles	.08	.04	.01
☐ 356	Billy Joe Robidoux	.08	.04	.01
☐ 357	Bill Schroeder	.08	.04	.01
☐ 358	Dale Sveum	.08	.04	.01
☐ 359	Gorman Thomas	.08	.04	.01
☐ 360	Bill Wegman	.08	.04	.01
☐ 361	Robin Yount	.60	.25	.07
☐ 362	Steve Balboni	.08	.04	.01
☐ 363	Scott Bankhead	.08	.04	.01
☐ 364	Buddy Biancalana	.08	.04	.01
☐ 365	Bud Black	.08	.04	.01
☐ 366	George Brett	2.00	.90	.25
☐ 367	Steve Farr	.08	.04	.01
☐ 368	Mark Gubicza	.08	.04	.01
☐ 369	Bo Jackson	3.00	1.35	.35
☐ 370	Danny Jackson	.15	.07	.02
☐ 371	Mike Kingery	.50	.23	.06
☐ 372	Rudy Law	.08	.04	.01
☐ 373	Charlie Leibrandt	.08	.04	.01
☐ 374	Dennis Leonard	.08	.04	.01
☐ 375	Hal McRae	.15	.07	.02
☐ 376	Jorge Orta	.08	.04	.01
☐ 377	Jamie Quirk	.08	.04	.01
☐ 378	Dan Quisenberry	.15	.07	.02
☐ 379	Bret Saberhagen	.30	.14	.04
☐ 380	Angel Salazar	.08	.04	.01
☐ 381	Lonnie Smith	.08	.04	.01
☐ 382	Jim Sundberg	.08	.04	.01
☐ 383	Frank White	.15	.07	.02
☐ 384	Willie Wilson	.08	.04	.01
☐ 385	Joaquin Andujar	.08	.04	.01
☐ 386	Doug Bair	.08	.04	.01
☐ 387	Dusty Baker	.30	.14	.04
☐ 388	Bruce Bochte	.08	.04	.01
☐ 389	Jose Canseco	3.00	1.35	.35
☐ 390	Chris Codiroli	.08	.04	.01
☐ 391	Mike Davis	.08	.04	.01
☐ 392	Alfredo Griffin	.08	.04	.01
☐ 393	Moose Haas	.08	.04	.01
☐ 394	Donnie Hill	.08	.04	.01
☐ 395	Jay Howell	.08	.04	.01
☐ 396	Dave Kingman	.15	.07	.02
☐ 397	Carney Lansford	.15	.07	.02
☐ 398	Dave Leiper	.08	.04	.01
☐ 399	Bill Mooneyham	.08	.04	.01
☐ 400	Dwayne Murphy	.08	.04	.01
☐ 401	Steve Ontiveros	.08	.04	.01
☐ 402	Tony Phillips	.30	.14	.04
☐ 403	Eric Plunk	.08	.04	.01
☐ 404	Jose Rijo	.30	.14	.04
☐ 405	Terry Steinbach	.50	.23	.06
☐ 406	Dave Stewart	.30	.14	.04
☐ 407	Mickey Tettleton	.15	.07	.02
☐ 408	Dave Von Ohlen	.08	.04	.01
☐ 409	Jerry Willard	.08	.04	.01
☐ 410	Curt Young	.08	.04	.01
☐ 411	Bruce Bochy	.08	.04	.01
☐ 412	Dave Dravecky	.15	.07	.02
☐ 413	Tim Flannery	.08	.04	.01
☐ 414	Steve Garvey	.30	.14	.04
☐ 415	Rich Gossage	.30	.14	.04
☐ 416	Tony Gwynn	2.00	.90	.25
☐ 417	Andy Hawkins	.08	.04	.01
☐ 418	LaMarr Hoyt	.08	.04	.01
☐ 419	Terry Kennedy	.08	.04	.01
☐ 420	John Kruk	1.00	.45	.12
☐ 421	Dave LaPoint	.08	.04	.01
☐ 422	Craig Lefferts	.08	.04	.01
☐ 423	Carmelo Martinez	.08	.04	.01
☐ 424	Lance McCullers	.08	.04	.01
☐ 425	Kevin McReynolds	.15	.07	.02
☐ 426	Graig Nettles	.15	.07	.02
☐ 427	Bip Roberts	.75	.35	.09
☐ 428	Jerry Royster	.08	.04	.01
☐ 429	Benito Santiago	.15	.07	.02
☐ 430	Eric Show	.08	.04	.01
☐ 431	Bob Stoddard	.08	.04	.01
☐ 432	Garry Templeton	.08	.04	.01
☐ 433	Gene Walter	.08	.04	.01
☐ 434	Ed Whitson	.08	.04	.01
☐ 435	Marvell Wynne	.08	.04	.01
☐ 436	Dave Anderson	.08	.04	.01
☐ 437	Greg Brock	.08	.04	.01
☐ 438	Enos Cabell	.08	.04	.01
☐ 439	Mariano Duncan	.08	.04	.01
☐ 440	Pedro Guerrero	.15	.07	.02
☐ 441	Orel Hershiser	.30	.14	.04
☐ 442	Rick Honeycutt	.08	.04	.01
☐ 443	Ken Howell	.08	.04	.01
☐ 444	Ken Landreaux	.08	.04	.01
☐ 445	Bill Madlock	.15	.07	.02
☐ 446	Mike Marshall	.08	.04	.01

☐ 447	Len Matuszek	.08	.04	.01
☐ 448	Tom Niedenfuer	.08	.04	.01
☐ 449	Alejandro Pena	.08	.04	.01
☐ 450	Dennis Powell	.08	.04	.01
☐ 451	Jerry Reuss	.08	.04	.01
☐ 452	Bill Russell	.15	.07	.02
☐ 453	Steve Sax	.08	.04	.01
☐ 454	Mike Scioscia	.08	.04	.01
☐ 455	Franklin Stubbs	.08	.04	.01
☐ 456	Alex Trevino	.08	.04	.01
☐ 457	Fernando Valenzuela	.08	.04	.01
☐ 458	Ed VandeBerg	.08	.04	.01
☐ 459	Bob Welch	.15	.07	.02
☐ 460	Reggie Williams	.08	.04	.01
☐ 461	Don Aase	.08	.04	.01
☐ 462	Juan Beniquez	.08	.04	.01
☐ 463	Mike Boddicker	.08	.04	.01
☐ 464	Juan Bonilla	.08	.04	.01
☐ 465	Rich Bordi	.08	.04	.01
☐ 466	Storm Davis	.08	.04	.01
☐ 467	Rick Dempsey	.08	.04	.01
☐ 468	Ken Dixon	.08	.04	.01
☐ 469	Jim Dwyer	.08	.04	.01
☐ 470	Mike Flanagan	.08	.04	.01
☐ 471	Jackie Gutierrez	.08	.04	.01
☐ 472	Brad Havens	.08	.04	.01
☐ 473	Lee Lacy	.08	.04	.01
☐ 474	Fred Lynn	.15	.07	.02
☐ 475	Scott McGregor	.08	.04	.01
☐ 476	Eddie Murray	.75	.35	.09
☐ 477	Tom O'Malley	.08	.04	.01
☐ 478	Cal Ripken Jr.	4.00	1.80	.50
☐ 479	Larry Sheets	.08	.04	.01
☐ 480	John Shelby	.08	.04	.01
☐ 481	Nate Snell	.08	.04	.01
☐ 482	Jim Traber	.08	.04	.01
☐ 483	Mike Young	.08	.04	.01
☐ 484	Neil Allen	.08	.04	.01
☐ 485	Harold Baines	.30	.14	.04
☐ 486	Floyd Bannister	.08	.04	.01
☐ 487	Daryl Boston	.08	.04	.01
☐ 488	Ivan Calderon	.08	.04	.01
☐ 489	John Cangelosi	.08	.04	.01
☐ 490	Steve Carlton	.50	.23	.06
☐ 491	Joe Cowley	.08	.04	.01
☐ 492	Julio Cruz	.08	.04	.01
☐ 493	Bill Dawley	.08	.04	.01
☐ 494	Jose DeLeon	.08	.04	.01
☐ 495	Richard Dotson	.08	.04	.01
☐ 496	Carlton Fisk	.50	.23	.06
☐ 497	Ozzie Guillen	.15	.07	.02
☐ 498	Jerry Hairston	.08	.04	.01
☐ 499	Ron Hassey	.08	.04	.01
☐ 500	Tim Hulett	.08	.04	.01
☐ 501	Bob James	.08	.04	.01
☐ 502	Steve Lyons	.08	.04	.01
☐ 503	Joel McKeon	.08	.04	.01
☐ 504	Gene Nelson	.08	.04	.01
☐ 505	Dave Schmidt	.08	.04	.01
☐ 506	Ray Searage	.08	.04	.01
☐ 507	Bobby Thigpen	.08	.04	.01
☐ 508	Greg Walker	.08	.04	.01
☐ 509	Jim Acker	.08	.04	.01
☐ 510	Doyle Alexander	.08	.04	.01
☐ 511	Paul Assenmacher	.08	.04	.01
☐ 512	Bruce Benedict	.08	.04	.01
☐ 513	Chris Chambliss	.15	.07	.02
☐ 514	Jeff Dedmon	.08	.04	.01
☐ 515	Gene Garber	.08	.04	.01
☐ 516	Ken Griffey	.15	.07	.02
☐ 517	Terry Harper	.08	.04	.01
☐ 518	Bob Horner	.08	.04	.01
☐ 519	Glenn Hubbard	.08	.04	.01
☐ 520	Rick Mahler	.08	.04	.01
☐ 521	Omar Moreno	.08	.04	.01
☐ 522	Dale Murphy	.30	.14	.04
☐ 523	Ken Oberkfell	.08	.04	.01
☐ 524	Ed Olwine	.08	.04	.01
☐ 525	David Palmer	.08	.04	.01
☐ 526	Rafael Ramirez	.08	.04	.01
☐ 527	Billy Sample	.08	.04	.01
☐ 528	Ted Simmons	.15	.07	.02
☐ 529	Zane Smith	.08	.04	.01
☐ 530	Bruce Sutter	.15	.07	.02
☐ 531	Andres Thomas	.08	.04	.01
☐ 532	Ozzie Virgil	.08	.04	.01
☐ 533	Allan Anderson	.08	.04	.01
☐ 534	Keith Atherton	.08	.04	.01
☐ 535	Billy Beane	.08	.04	.01
☐ 536	Bert Blyleven	.30	.14	.04
☐ 537	Tom Brunansky	.08	.04	.01
☐ 538	Randy Bush	.08	.04	.01
☐ 539	George Frazier	.08	.04	.01
☐ 540	Gary Gaetti	.08	.04	.01
☐ 541	Greg Gagne	.15	.07	.02
☐ 542	Mickey Hatcher	.08	.04	.01
☐ 543	Neal Heaton	.08	.04	.01
☐ 544	Kent Hrbek	.30	.14	.04
☐ 545	Roy Lee Jackson	.08	.04	.01
☐ 546	Tim Laudner	.08	.04	.01
☐ 547	Steve Lombardozzi	.08	.04	.01
☐ 548	Mark Portugal	.50	.23	.06
☐ 549	Kirby Puckett	3.00	1.35	.35
☐ 550	Jeff Reed	.08	.04	.01
☐ 551	Mark Salas	.08	.04	.01
☐ 552	Roy Smalley	.08	.04	.01
☐ 553	Mike Smithson	.08	.04	.01
☐ 554	Frank Viola	.15	.07	.02
☐ 555	Thad Bosley	.08	.04	.01
☐ 556	Ron Cey	.15	.07	.02
☐ 557	Jody Davis	.08	.04	.01
☐ 558	Ron Davis	.08	.04	.01
☐ 559	Bob Dernier	.08	.04	.01
☐ 560	Frank DiPino	.08	.04	.01
☐ 561	Shawon Dunston UER	.15	.07	.02
	(Wrong birth year listed on card back)			
☐ 562	Leon Durham	.08	.04	.01
☐ 563	Dennis Eckersley	.30	.14	.04
☐ 564	Terry Francona	.08	.04	.01
☐ 565	Dave Gumpert	.08	.04	.01
☐ 566	Guy Hoffman	.08	.04	.01
☐ 567	Ed Lynch	.08	.04	.01
☐ 568	Gary Matthews	.08	.04	.01
☐ 569	Keith Moreland	.08	.04	.01
☐ 570	Jamie Moyer	.15	.07	.02
☐ 571	Jerry Mumphrey	.08	.04	.01
☐ 572	Ryne Sandberg	2.00	.90	.25
☐ 573	Scott Sanderson	.08	.04	.01
☐ 574	Lee Smith	.30	.14	.04
☐ 575	Chris Speier	.08	.04	.01
☐ 576	Rick Sutcliffe	.15	.07	.02
☐ 577	Manny Trillo	.08	.04	.01
☐ 578	Steve Trout	.08	.04	.01
☐ 579	Karl Best	.08	.04	.01
☐ 580	Scott Bradley	.08	.04	.01
☐ 581	Phil Bradley	.08	.04	.01
☐ 582	Mickey Brantley	.08	.04	.01
☐ 583	Mike G. Brown P	.08	.04	.01
☐ 584	Alvin Davis	.08	.04	.01
☐ 585	Lee Guetterman	.08	.04	.01
☐ 586	Mark Huismann	.08	.04	.01

□				
587	Bob Kearney	.08	.04	.01
588	Pete Ladd	.08	.04	.01
589	Mark Langston	.30	.14	.04
590	Mike Moore	.08	.04	.01
591	Mike Morgan	.08	.04	.01
592	John Moses	.08	.04	.01
593	Ken Phelps	.08	.04	.01
594	Jim Presley	.08	.04	.01
595	Rey Quinones UER (Quinonez on front)	.08	.04	.01
596	Harold Reynolds	.08	.04	.01
597	Billy Swift	.15	.07	.02
598	Danny Tartabull	.15	.07	.02
599	Steve Yeager	.08	.04	.01
600	Matt Young	.08	.04	.01
601	Bill Almon	.08	.04	.01
602	Rafael Belliard	.08	.04	.01
603	Mike Bielecki	.08	.04	.01
604	Barry Bonds	20.00	9.00	2.50
605	Bobby Bonilla	2.50	1.10	.30
606	Sid Bream	.08	.04	.01
607	Mike C. Brown	.08	.04	.01
608	Pat Clements	.08	.04	.01
609	Mike Diaz	.08	.04	.01
610	Cecilio Guante	.08	.04	.01
611	Barry Jones	.08	.04	.01
612	Bob Kipper	.08	.04	.01
613	Larry McWilliams	.08	.04	.01
614	Jim Morrison	.08	.04	.01
615	Joe Orsulak	.08	.04	.01
616	Junior Ortiz	.08	.04	.01
617	Tony Pena	.08	.04	.01
618	Johnny Ray	.08	.04	.01
619	Rick Reuschel	.08	.04	.01
620	R.J. Reynolds	.08	.04	.01
621	Rick Rhoden	.08	.04	.01
622	Don Robinson	.08	.04	.01
623	Bob Walk	.08	.04	.01
624	Jim Winn	.08	.04	.01
625	Youthful Power Pete Incaviglia Jose Canseco	.50	.23	.06
626	300 Game Winners Don Sutton Phil Niekro	.15	.07	.02
627	AL Firemen Dave Righetti Don Aase	.08	.04	.01
628	Rookie All-Stars Wally Joyner Jose Canseco	.50	.23	.06
629	Magic Mets Gary Carter Sid Fernandez Dwight Gooden Keith Hernandez Darryl Strawberry	.15	.07	.02
630	NL Best Righties Mike Scott Mike Krukow	.08	.04	.01
631	Sensational Southpaws Fernando Valenzuela John Franco	.08	.04	.01
632	Count'Em Bob Horner	.08	.04	.01
633	AL Pitcher's Nightmare Jose Canseco Jim Rice Kirby Puckett	1.00	.45	.12
634	All-Star Battery Gary Carter	.30	.14	.04

□				
	Roger Clemens			
635	4000 Strikeouts Steve Carlton	.30	.14	.04
636	Big Bats at First Glenn Davis Eddie Murray	.40	.18	.05
637	On Base Wade Boggs Keith Hernandez	.30	.14	.04
638	Sluggers Left Side Don Mattingly Darryl Strawberry	.50	.23	.06
639	Former MVP's Dave Parker Ryne Sandberg	.15	.07	.02
640	Dr. K and Super K Dwight Gooden Roger Clemens	.40	.18	.05
641	AL West Stoppers Mike Witt Charlie Hough	.08	.04	.01
642	Doubles and Triples Juan Samuel Tim Raines	.15	.07	.02
643	Outfielders with Punch Harold Baines Jesse Barfield	.15	.07	.02
644	Dave Clark and Greg Swindell	.50	.23	.06
645	Ron Karkovice and Russ Morman	.15	.07	.02
646	Devon White and Willie Fraser	1.50	.70	.19
647	Mike Stanley and Jerry Browne	.60	.25	.07
648	Dave Magadan and Phil Lombardi	.15	.07	.02
649	Jose Gonzalez and Ralph Bryant	.08	.04	.01
650	Jimmy Jones and Randy Asadoor	.08	.04	.01
651	Tracy Jones and Marvin Freeman	.15	.07	.02
652	John Stefero and Kevin Seitzer	.40	.18	.05
653	Rob Nelson and Steve Fireovid	.08	.04	.01
654	CL: Mets/Red Sox Astros/Angels	.15	.07	.02
655	CL: Yankees/Rangers Tigers/Phillies	.15	.07	.02
656	CL: Reds/Blue Jays Indians/Giants ERR (230/231 wrong)	.15	.07	.02
657	CL: Cardinals/Expos Brewers/Royals	.15	.07	.02
658	CL: A's/Padres Dodgers/Orioles	.15	.07	.02
659	CL: White Sox/Braves Twins/Cubs	.15	.07	.02
660	CL: Mariners/Pirates Special Cards ER (580/581 wrong)	.15	.07	.02

1987 Fleer Update

This 132-card set was distributed by Fleer to dealers as a complete set in a custom

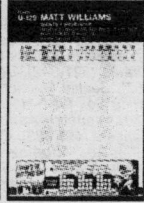

box. In addition to the complete set of 132
cards, the box also contains 25 Team Logo
stickers. The card fronts look very similar to
the 1987 Fleer regular issue. The cards are
numbered (with a U prefix) alphabetically
according to player's last name. Cards
measure the standard size, 2 1/2" by 3 1/2".
Fleer misalphabetized Jim Winn in their set
numbering by putting him ahead of the next
four players listed. The key (extended)
Rookie Cards in this set are Ellis Burks,
Mike Greenwell, Greg Maddux, Fred
McGriff, Mark McGwire and Matt Williams.
Fleer also produced a "limited" edition version of this set with glossy coating and
packaged in a "tin." However, this glossy tin
set was apparently not limited enough (estimated between 75,000 and 100,000 1987
Update tin sets produced by Fleer), since
the values of the "tin" glossy cards are now
the same as the values of the cards in the
regular set.

	MINT	NRMT	EXC
COMPLETE FACT.SET (132) ..	15.00	6.75	1.85
COMMON CARD (1-132)	.05	.02	.01

		MINT	NRMT	EXC
☐ 1	Scott Bankhead	.05	.02	.01
☐ 2	Eric Bell	.05	.02	.01
☐ 3	Juan Beniquez	.05	.02	.01
☐ 4	Juan Berenguer	.05	.02	.01
☐ 5	Mike Birkbeck	.05	.02	.01
☐ 6	Randy Bockus	.05	.02	.01
☐ 7	Rod Booker	.05	.02	.01
☐ 8	Thad Bosley	.05	.02	.01
☐ 9	Greg Brock	.05	.02	.01
☐ 10	Bob Brower	.05	.02	.01
☐ 11	Chris Brown	.05	.02	.01
☐ 12	Jerry Browne	.05	.02	.01
☐ 13	Ralph Bryant	.05	.02	.01
☐ 14	DeWayne Buice	.05	.02	.01
☐ 15	Ellis Burks	.50	.23	.06
☐ 16	Casey Candaele	.05	.02	.01
☐ 17	Steve Carlton	.15	.07	.02
☐ 18	Juan Castillo	.05	.02	.01
☐ 19	Chuck Crim	.05	.02	.01
☐ 20	Mark Davidson	.05	.02	.01
☐ 21	Mark Davis	.05	.02	.01
☐ 22	Storm Davis	.05	.02	.01
☐ 23	Bill Dawley	.05	.02	.01
☐ 24	Andre Dawson	.15	.07	.02
☐ 25	Brian Dayett	.05	.02	.01
☐ 26	Rick Dempsey	.05	.02	.01
☐ 27	Ken Dowell	.05	.02	.01
☐ 28	Dave Dravecky	.10	.05	.01
☐ 29	Mike Dunne	.05	.02	.01
☐ 30	Dennis Eckersley	.15	.07	.02
☐ 31	Cecil Fielder	1.00	.45	.12
☐ 32	Brian Fisher	.05	.02	.01
☐ 33	Willie Fraser	.05	.02	.01
☐ 34	Ken Gerhart	.05	.02	.01
☐ 35	Jim Gott	.05	.02	.01
☐ 36	Dan Gladden	.05	.02	.01
☐ 37	Mike Greenwell	.40	.18	.05
☐ 38	Cecilio Guante	.05	.02	.01
☐ 39	Albert Hall	.05	.02	.01
☐ 40	Atlee Hammaker	.05	.02	.01
☐ 41	Mickey Hatcher	.05	.02	.01
☐ 42	Mike Heath	.05	.02	.01
☐ 43	Neal Heaton	.05	.02	.01
☐ 44	Mike Henneman	.25	.11	.03
☐ 45	Guy Hoffman	.05	.02	.01
☐ 46	Charles Hudson	.05	.02	.01
☐ 47	Chuck Jackson	.05	.02	.01
☐ 48	Mike Jackson	.10	.05	.01
☐ 49	Reggie Jackson	.50	.23	.06
☐ 50	Chris James	.05	.02	.01
☐ 51	Dion James	.05	.02	.01
☐ 52	Stan Javier	.05	.02	.01
☐ 53	Stan Jefferson	.05	.02	.01
☐ 54	Jimmy Jones	.05	.02	.01
☐ 55	Tracy Jones	.05	.02	.01
☐ 56	Terry Kennedy	.05	.02	.01
☐ 57	Mike Kingery	.15	.07	.02
☐ 58	Ray Knight	.10	.05	.01
☐ 59	Gene Larkin	.10	.05	.01
☐ 60	Mike LaValliere	.05	.02	.01
☐ 61	Jack Lazorko	.05	.02	.01
☐ 62	Terry Leach	.05	.02	.01
☐ 63	Rick Leach	.05	.02	.01
☐ 64	Craig Lefferts	.05	.02	.01
☐ 65	Jim Lindeman	.05	.02	.01
☐ 66	Bill Long	.05	.02	.01
☐ 67	Mike Loynd	.05	.02	.01
☐ 68	Greg Maddux	10.00	4.50	1.25
☐ 69	Bill Madlock	.10	.05	.01
☐ 70	Dave Magadan	.10	.05	.01
☐ 71	Joe Magrane	.05	.02	.01
☐ 72	Fred Manrique	.05	.02	.01
☐ 73	Mike Mason	.05	.02	.01
☐ 74	Lloyd McClendon	.05	.02	.01
☐ 75	Fred McGriff	2.00	.90	.25
☐ 76	Mark McGwire	1.50	.70	.19
☐ 77	Mark McLemore	.05	.02	.01
☐ 78	Kevin McReynolds	.10	.05	.01
☐ 79	Dave Meads	.05	.02	.01
☐ 80	Greg Minton	.05	.02	.01
☐ 81	John Mitchell	.05	.02	.01
☐ 82	Kevin Mitchell	.15	.07	.02
☐ 83	John Morris	.05	.02	.01
☐ 84	Jeff Musselman	.05	.02	.01
☐ 85	Randy Myers	.40	.18	.05
☐ 86	Gene Nelson	.05	.02	.01
☐ 87	Joe Niekro	.10	.05	.01
☐ 88	Tom Nieto	.05	.02	.01
☐ 89	Reid Nichols	.05	.02	.01
☐ 90	Matt Nokes	.10	.05	.01
☐ 91	Dickie Noles	.05	.02	.01
☐ 92	Edwin Nunez	.05	.02	.01
☐ 93	Jose Nunez	.05	.02	.01
☐ 94	Paul O'Neill	.50	.23	.06
☐ 95	Jim Paciorek	.05	.02	.01
☐ 96	Lance Parrish	.10	.05	.01
☐ 97	Bill Pecota	.05	.02	.01
☐ 98	Tony Pena	.05	.02	.01
☐ 99	Luis Polonia	.30	.14	.04
☐ 100	Randy Ready	.05	.02	.01

			MINT	NRMT	EXC
☐ 101	Jeff Reardon	.15	.07	.02
☐ 102	Gary Redus	.05	.02	.01
☐ 103	Rick Rhoden	.05	.02	.01
☐ 104	Wally Ritchie	.05	.02	.01
☐ 105	Jeff M. Robinson UER	.05	.02	.01
	(Wrong Jeff's stats on back)			
☐ 106	Mark Salas	.05	.02	.01
☐ 107	Dave Schmidt	.05	.02	.01
☐ 108	Kevin Seitzer UER	.10	.05	.01
	(Wrong birth year)			
☐ 109	John Shelby	.05	.02	.01
☐ 110	John Smiley	.25	.11	.03
☐ 111	Lary Sorensen	.05	.02	.01
☐ 112	Chris Speier	.05	.02	.01
☐ 113	Randy St.Claire	.05	.02	.01
☐ 114	Jim Sundberg	.05	.02	.01
☐ 115	B.J. Surhoff	.30	.14	.04
☐ 116	Greg Swindell	.15	.07	.02
☐ 117	Danny Tartabull	.10	.05	.01
☐ 118	Dorn Taylor	.05	.02	.01
☐ 119	Lee Tunnell	.05	.02	.01
☐ 120	Ed VandeBerg	.05	.02	.01
☐ 121	Andy Van Slyke	.10	.05	.01
☐ 122	Gary Ward	.05	.02	.01
☐ 123	Devon White	.60	.25	.07
☐ 124	Alan Wiggins	.05	.02	.01
☐ 125	Bill Wilkinson	.05	.02	.01
☐ 126	Jim Winn	.05	.02	.01
☐ 127	Frank Williams	.05	.02	.01
☐ 128	Ken Williams	.05	.02	.01
☐ 129	Matt Williams	4.00	1.80	.50
☐ 130	Herm Willingham	.05	.02	.01
☐ 131	Matt Young	.05	.02	.01
☐ 132	Checklist 1-132	.05	.02	.01

1988 Fleer

This 660-card standard-size set features a distinctive white background with red and blue diagonal stripes across the center. The backs are printed in gray and red on white card stock. The bottom of the card back shows an innovative breakdown of the player's demonstrated ability with respect to day, night, home, and road games. Cards are again organized numerically by teams, i.e., World Champion Twins (1-25), N.L. Champion St. Louis Cardinals (26-50), Detroit Tigers (51-75), San Francisco Giants (76-101), Toronto Blue Jays (102-126), New York Mets (127-154), Milwaukee Brewers (155-178), Montreal Expos (179-

201), New York Yankees (202-226), Cincinnati Reds (227-250), Kansas City Royals (251-274), Oakland A's (275-296), Philadelphia Phillies (297-320), Pittsburgh Pirates (321-342), Boston Red Sox (343-367), Seattle Mariners (368-390), Chicago White Sox (391-413), Chicago Cubs (414-436), Houston Astros (437-460), Texas Rangers (461-483), California Angels (484-507), Los Angeles Dodgers (508-530), Atlanta Braves (531-552), Baltimore Orioles (553-575), San Diego Padres (576-599), and Cleveland Indians (600-621). The last 39 cards in the set consist of Specials (622-640), Rookie Pairs (641-653), and checklists (654-660). Cards 90 and 91 are incorrectly numbered on the checklist card number 654. Rookie Cards in this set include Jay Bell, Jeff Blauser, John Burkett, Ellis Burks, Ken Caminiti, Mike Devereaux, Ron Gant, Tom Glavine, Mark Grace, Gregg Jefferies, Roberto Kelly, Edgar Martinez, Jack McDowell, Jeff Montgomery, and Matt Williams. A subset of "Stadium Cards" was randomly inserted throughout the packs. These cards pictured all 26 stadiums used by Major League Baseball and presented facts about these ballparks. Fleer also produced a "limited" edition version of this set with glossy coating and packaged in a "tin." However, this tin set was apparently not limited enough (estimated between 40,000 and 60,000 1988 tin sets produced by Fleer), since the values of the "tin" glossy cards are now only double the values of the respective cards in the regular set.

	MINT	NRMT	EXC
COMPLETE SET (660)	20.00	9.00	2.50
COMPLETE RETAIL SET (660)	20.00	9.00	2.50
COMPLETE HOBBY SET (672)	25.00	11.00	3.10
COMPLETE WORLD SERIES (12)	2.00	.90	.25
COMMON CARD (1-660)	.06	.03	.01

			MINT	NRMT	EXC
☐ 1	Keith Atherton	.06	.03	.01
☐ 2	Don Baylor	.15	.07	.02
☐ 3	Juan Berenguer	.06	.03	.01
☐ 4	Bert Blyleven	.15	.07	.02
☐ 5	Tom Brunansky	.06	.03	.01
☐ 6	Randy Bush	.06	.03	.01
☐ 7	Steve Carlton	.15	.07	.02
☐ 8	Mark Davidson	.06	.03	.01
☐ 9	George Frazier	.06	.03	.01
☐ 10	Gary Gaetti	.06	.03	.01
☐ 11	Greg Gagne	.06	.03	.01
☐ 12	Dan Gladden	.06	.03	.01
☐ 13	Kent Hrbek	.15	.07	.02
☐ 14	Gene Larkin	.06	.03	.01
☐ 15	Tim Laudner	.06	.03	.01
☐ 16	Steve Lombardozzi	.06	.03	.01
☐ 17	Al Newman	.06	.03	.01
☐ 18	Joe Niekro	.10	.05	.01
☐ 19	Kirby Puckett	.75	.35	.09
☐ 20	Jeff Reardon	.15	.07	.02
☐ 21A	Dan Schatzeder ERR	.06	.03	.01
	(Misspelled Schatzader on card front)			
☐ 21B	Dan Schatzeder COR	.06	.03	.01
☐ 22	Roy Smalley	.06	.03	.01
☐ 23	Mike Smithson	.06	.03	.01
☐ 24	Les Straker	.06	.03	.01

□	25	Frank Viola	.10	.05	.01
□	26	Jack Clark	.10	.05	.01
□	27	Vince Coleman	.10	.05	.01
□	28	Danny Cox	.06	.03	.01
□	29	Bill Dawley	.06	.03	.01
□	30	Ken Dayley	.06	.03	.01
□	31	Doug DeCinces	.06	.03	.01
□	32	Curt Ford	.06	.03	.01
□	33	Bob Forsch	.06	.03	.01
□	34	David Green	.06	.03	.01
□	35	Tom Herr	.06	.03	.01
□	36	Ricky Horton	.06	.03	.01
□	37	Lance Johnson	.30	.14	.04
□	38	Steve Lake	.06	.03	.01
□	39	Jim Lindeman	.06	.03	.01
□	40	Joe Magrane	.06	.03	.01
□	41	Greg Mathews	.06	.03	.01
□	42	Willie McGee	.10	.05	.01
□	43	John Morris	.06	.03	.01
□	44	Jose Oquendo	.06	.03	.01
□	45	Tony Pena	.06	.03	.01
□	46	Terry Pendleton	.15	.07	.02
□	47	Ozzie Smith	.40	.18	.05
□	48	John Tudor	.06	.03	.01
□	49	Lee Tunnell	.06	.03	.01
□	50	Todd Worrell	.06	.03	.01
□	51	Doyle Alexander	.06	.03	.01
□	52	Dave Bergman	.06	.03	.01
□	53	Tom Brookens	.06	.03	.01
□	54	Darrell Evans	.10	.05	.01
□	55	Kirk Gibson	.15	.07	.02
□	56	Mike Heath	.06	.03	.01
□	57	Mike Henneman	.25	.11	.03
□	58	Willie Hernandez	.06	.03	.01
□	59	Larry Herndon	.06	.03	.01
□	60	Eric King	.06	.03	.01
□	61	Chet Lemon	.06	.03	.01
□	62	Scott Lusader	.06	.03	.01
□	63	Bill Madlock	.10	.05	.01
□	64	Jack Morris	.15	.07	.02
□	65	Jim Morrison	.06	.03	.01
□	66	Matt Nokes	.06	.03	.01
□	67	Dan Petry	.06	.03	.01
□	68A	Jeff M. Robinson ERR	.06	.03	.01
		(Stats for Jeff D. Robinson on card back, Born 12-13-60)			
□	68B	Jeff M. Robinson COR	.06	.03	.01
		(Born 12-14-61)			
□	69	Pat Sheridan	.06	.03	.01
□	70	Nate Snell	.06	.03	.01
□	71	Frank Tanana	.06	.03	.01
□	72	Walt Terrell	.06	.03	.01
□	73	Mark Thurmond	.06	.03	.01
□	74	Alan Trammell	.15	.07	.02
□	75	Lou Whitaker	.15	.07	.02
□	76	Mike Aldrete	.06	.03	.01
□	77	Bob Brenly	.06	.03	.01
□	78	Will Clark	.75	.35	.09
□	79	Chili Davis	.15	.07	.02
□	80	Kelly Downs	.06	.03	.01
□	81	Dave Dravecky	.10	.05	.01
□	82	Scott Garrelts	.06	.03	.01
□	83	Atlee Hammaker	.06	.03	.01
□	84	Dave Henderson	.10	.05	.01
□	85	Mike Krukow	.06	.03	.01
□	86	Mike LaCoss	.06	.03	.01
□	87	Craig Lefferts	.06	.03	.01
□	88	Jeff Leonard	.06	.03	.01
□	89	Candy Maldonado	.06	.03	.01
□	90	Eddie Milner	.06	.03	.01

□	91	Bob Melvin	.06	.03	.01
□	92	Kevin Mitchell	.10	.05	.01
□	93	Jon Perlman	.06	.03	.01
□	94	Rick Reuschel	.06	.03	.01
□	95	Don Robinson	.06	.03	.01
□	96	Chris Speier	.06	.03	.01
□	97	Harry Spilman	.06	.03	.01
□	98	Robby Thompson	.10	.05	.01
□	99	Jose Uribe	.06	.03	.01
□	100	Mark Wasinger	.06	.03	.01
□	101	Matt Williams	4.00	1.80	.50
□	102	Jesse Barfield	.06	.03	.01
□	103	George Bell	.06	.03	.01
□	104	Juan Beniquez	.06	.03	.01
□	105	John Cerutti	.06	.03	.01
□	106	Jim Clancy	.06	.03	.01
□	107	Rob Ducey	.06	.03	.01
□	108	Mark Eichhorn	.06	.03	.01
□	109	Tony Fernandez	.10	.05	.01
□	110	Cecil Fielder	.15	.07	.02
□	111	Kelly Gruber	.06	.03	.01
□	112	Tom Henke	.10	.05	.01
□	113A	Garth Iorg ERR	.06	.03	.01
		(Misspelled Iorg on card front)			
□	113B	Garth Iorg COR	.06	.03	.01
□	114	Jimmy Key	.15	.07	.02
□	115	Rick Leach	.06	.03	.01
□	116	Manny Lee	.06	.03	.01
□	117	Nelson Liriano	.06	.03	.01
□	118	Fred McGriff	1.50	.70	.19
□	119	Lloyd Moseby	.06	.03	.01
□	120	Rance Mulliniks	.06	.03	.01
□	121	Jeff Musselman	.06	.03	.01
□	122	Jose Nunez	.06	.03	.01
□	123	Dave Stieb	.10	.05	.01
□	124	Willie Upshaw	.06	.03	.01
□	125	Duane Ward	.10	.05	.01
□	126	Ernie Whitt	.06	.03	.01
□	127	Rick Aguilera	.15	.07	.02
□	128	Wally Backman	.06	.03	.01
□	129	Mark Carreon	.10	.05	.01
□	130	Gary Carter	.15	.07	.02
□	131	David Cone	1.00	.45	.12
□	132	Ron Darling	.10	.05	.01
□	133	Len Dykstra	.15	.07	.02
□	134	Sid Fernandez	.10	.05	.01
□	135	Dwight Gooden	.15	.07	.02
□	136	Keith Hernandez	.10	.05	.01
□	137	Gregg Jefferies	1.50	.70	.19
□	138	Howard Johnson	.10	.05	.01
□	139	Terry Leach	.06	.03	.01
□	140	Barry Lyons	.06	.03	.01
□	141	Dave Magadan	.10	.05	.01
□	142	Roger McDowell	.06	.03	.01
□	143	Kevin McReynolds	.10	.05	.01
□	144	Keith A. Miller	.06	.03	.01
□	145	John Mitchell	.06	.03	.01
□	146	Randy Myers	.15	.07	.02
□	147	Bob Ojeda	.06	.03	.01
□	148	Jesse Orosco	.06	.03	.01
□	149	Rafael Santana	.06	.03	.01
□	150	Doug Sisk	.06	.03	.01
□	151	Darryl Strawberry	.15	.07	.02
□	152	Tim Teufel	.06	.03	.01
□	153	Gene Walter	.06	.03	.01
□	154	Mookie Wilson	.10	.05	.01
□	155	Jay Aldrich	.06	.03	.01
□	156	Chris Bosio	.10	.05	.01
□	157	Glenn Braggs	.06	.03	.01
□	158	Greg Brock	.06	.03	.01

☐	159	Juan Castillo	.06	.03	.01
☐	160	Mark Clear	.06	.03	.01
☐	161	Cecil Cooper	.10	.05	.01
☐	162	Chuck Crim	.06	.03	.01
☐	163	Rob Deer	.06	.03	.01
☐	164	Mike Felder	.06	.03	.01
☐	165	Jim Gantner	.06	.03	.01
☐	166	Ted Higuera	.06	.03	.01
☐	167	Steve Kiefer	.06	.03	.01
☐	168	Rick Manning	.06	.03	.01
☐	169	Paul Molitor	.15	.07	.02
☐	170	Juan Nieves	.06	.03	.01
☐	171	Dan Plesac	.06	.03	.01
☐	172	Earnest Riles	.06	.03	.01
☐	173	Bill Schroeder	.06	.03	.01
☐	174	Steve Stanicek	.06	.03	.01
☐	175	B.J. Surhoff	.10	.05	.01
☐	176	Dale Sveum	.06	.03	.01
☐	177	Bill Wegman	.06	.03	.01
☐	178	Robin Yount	.30	.14	.04
☐	179	Hubie Brooks	.06	.03	.01
☐	180	Tim Burke	.06	.03	.01
☐	181	Casey Candaele	.06	.03	.01
☐	182	Mike Fitzgerald	.06	.03	.01
☐	183	Tom Foley	.06	.03	.01
☐	184	Andres Galarraga	.15	.07	.02
☐	185	Neal Heaton	.06	.03	.01
☐	186	Wallace Johnson	.06	.03	.01
☐	187	Vance Law	.06	.03	.01
☐	188	Dennis Martinez	.10	.05	.01
☐	189	Bob McClure	.06	.03	.01
☐	190	Andy McGaffigan	.06	.03	.01
☐	191	Reid Nichols	.06	.03	.01
☐	192	Pascual Perez	.06	.03	.01
☐	193	Tim Raines	.15	.07	.02
☐	194	Jeff Reed	.06	.03	.01
☐	195	Bob Sebra	.06	.03	.01
☐	196	Bryn Smith	.06	.03	.01
☐	197	Randy St.Claire	.06	.03	.01
☐	198	Tim Wallach	.10	.05	.01
☐	199	Mitch Webster	.06	.03	.01
☐	200	Herm Winningham	.06	.03	.01
☐	201	Floyd Youmans	.06	.03	.01
☐	202	Brad Arnsberg	.06	.03	.01
☐	203	Rick Cerone	.06	.03	.01
☐	204	Pat Clements	.06	.03	.01
☐	205	Henry Cotto	.06	.03	.01
☐	206	Mike Easler	.06	.03	.01
☐	207	Ron Guidry	.10	.05	.01
☐	208	Bill Gullickson	.06	.03	.01
☐	209	Rickey Henderson	.15	.07	.02
☐	210	Charles Hudson	.06	.03	.01
☐	211	Tommy John	.15	.07	.02
☐	212	Roberto Kelly	.40	.18	.05
☐	213	Ron Kittle	.06	.03	.01
☐	214	Don Mattingly	.75	.35	.09
☐	215	Bobby Meacham	.06	.03	.01
☐	216	Mike Pagliarulo	.06	.03	.01
☐	217	Dan Pasqua	.06	.03	.01
☐	218	Willie Randolph	.10	.05	.01
☐	219	Rick Rhoden	.06	.03	.01
☐	220	Dave Righetti	.06	.03	.01
☐	221	Jerry Royster	.06	.03	.01
☐	222	Tim Stoddard	.06	.03	.01
☐	223	Wayne Tolleson	.06	.03	.01
☐	224	Gary Ward	.06	.03	.01
☐	225	Claudell Washington	.06	.03	.01
☐	226	Dave Winfield	.15	.07	.02
☐	227	Buddy Bell	.10	.05	.01
☐	228	Tom Browning	.06	.03	.01
☐	229	Dave Concepcion	.10	.05	.01
☐	230	Kal Daniels	.06	.03	.01
☐	231	Eric Davis	.10	.05	.01
☐	232	Bo Diaz	.06	.03	.01
☐	233	Nick Esasky	.06	.03	.01
		(Has a dollar sign before '87 SB totals)			
☐	234	John Franco	.10	.05	.01
☐	235	Guy Hoffman	.06	.03	.01
☐	236	Tom Hume	.06	.03	.01
☐	237	Tracy Jones	.06	.03	.01
☐	238	Bill Landrum	.06	.03	.01
☐	239	Barry Larkin	.75	.35	.09
☐	240	Terry McGriff	.06	.03	.01
☐	241	Rob Murphy	.06	.03	.01
☐	242	Ron Oester	.06	.03	.01
☐	243	Dave Parker	.15	.07	.02
☐	244	Pat Perry	.06	.03	.01
☐	245	Ted Power	.06	.03	.01
☐	246	Dennis Rasmussen	.06	.03	.01
☐	247	Ron Robinson	.06	.03	.01
☐	248	Kurt Stillwell	.06	.03	.01
☐	249	Jeff Treadway	.06	.03	.01
☐	250	Frank Williams	.06	.03	.01
☐	251	Steve Balboni	.06	.03	.01
☐	252	Bud Black	.06	.03	.01
☐	253	Thad Bosley	.06	.03	.01
☐	254	George Brett	.75	.35	.09
☐	255	John Davis	.06	.03	.01
☐	256	Steve Farr	.06	.03	.01
☐	257	Gene Garber	.06	.03	.01
☐	258	Jerry Don Gleaton	.06	.03	.01
☐	259	Mark Gubicza	.06	.03	.01
☐	260	Bo Jackson	.50	.23	.06
☐	261	Danny Jackson	.06	.03	.01
☐	262	Ross Jones	.06	.03	.01
☐	263	Charlie Leibrandt	.06	.03	.01
☐	264	Bill Pecota	.06	.03	.01
☐	265	Melido Perez	.10	.05	.01
☐	266	Jamie Quirk	.06	.03	.01
☐	267	Dan Quisenberry	.10	.05	.01
☐	268	Bret Saberhagen	.15	.07	.02
☐	269	Angel Salazar	.06	.03	.01
☐	270	Kevin Seitzer UER	.10	.05	.01
		(Wrong birth year)			
☐	271	Danny Tartabull	.10	.05	.01
☐	272	Gary Thurman	.06	.03	.01
☐	273	Frank White	.10	.05	.01
☐	274	Willie Wilson	.06	.03	.01
☐	275	Tony Bernazard	.06	.03	.01
☐	276	Jose Canseco	1.00	.45	.12
☐	277	Mike Davis	.06	.03	.01
☐	278	Storm Davis	.06	.03	.01
☐	279	Dennis Eckersley	.15	.07	.02
☐	280	Alfredo Griffin	.06	.03	.01
☐	281	Rick Honeycutt	.06	.03	.01
☐	282	Jay Howell	.06	.03	.01
☐	283	Reggie Jackson	.50	.23	.06
☐	284	Dennis Lamp	.06	.03	.01
☐	285	Carney Lansford	.10	.05	.01
☐	286	Mark McGwire	.75	.35	.09
☐	287	Dwayne Murphy	.06	.03	.01
☐	288	Gene Nelson	.06	.03	.01
☐	289	Steve Ontiveros	.06	.03	.01
☐	290	Tony Phillips	.15	.07	.02
☐	291	Eric Plunk	.06	.03	.01
☐	292	Luis Polonia	.40	.18	.05
☐	293	Rick Rodriguez	.06	.03	.01
☐	294	Terry Steinbach	.10	.05	.01
☐	295	Dave Stewart	.15	.07	.02
☐	296	Curt Young	.06	.03	.01
☐	297	Luis Aguayo	.06	.03	.01

☐	298	Steve Bedrosian	.06	.03	.01			
☐	299	Jeff Calhoun	.06	.03	.01			
☐	300	Don Carman	.06	.03	.01			
☐	301	Todd Frohwirth	.06	.03	.01			
☐	302	Greg Gross	.06	.03	.01			
☐	303	Kevin Gross	.06	.03	.01			
☐	304	Von Hayes	.06	.03	.01			
☐	305	Keith Hughes	.06	.03	.01			
☐	306	Mike Jackson	.10	.05	.01			
☐	307	Chris James	.06	.03	.01			
☐	308	Steve Jeltz	.06	.03	.01			
☐	309	Mike Maddux	.06	.03	.01			
☐	310	Lance Parrish	.10	.05	.01			
☐	311	Shane Rawley	.06	.03	.01			
☐	312	Wally Ritchie	.06	.03	.01			
☐	313	Bruce Ruffin	.06	.03	.01			
☐	314	Juan Samuel	.06	.03	.01			
☐	315	Mike Schmidt	.35	.16	.04			
☐	316	Rick Schu	.06	.03	.01			
☐	317	Jeff Stone	.06	.03	.01			
☐	318	Kent Tekulve	.06	.03	.01			
☐	319	Milt Thompson	.06	.03	.01			
☐	320	Glenn Wilson	.06	.03	.01			
☐	321	Rafael Belliard	.06	.03	.01			
☐	322	Barry Bonds	1.25	.55	.16			
☐	323	Bobby Bonilla UER	.15	.07	.02			
		(Wrong birth year)						
☐	324	Sid Bream	.06	.03	.01			
☐	325	John Cangelosi	.06	.03	.01			
☐	326	Mike Diaz	.06	.03	.01			
☐	327	Doug Drabek	.15	.07	.02			
☐	328	Mike Dunne	.06	.03	.01			
☐	329	Brian Fisher	.06	.03	.01			
☐	330	Brett Gideon	.06	.03	.01			
☐	331	Terry Harper	.06	.03	.01			
☐	332	Bob Kipper	.06	.03	.01			
☐	333	Mike LaValliere	.06	.03	.01			
☐	334	Jose Lind	.06	.03	.01			
☐	335	Junior Ortiz	.06	.03	.01			
☐	336	Vicente Palacios	.06	.03	.01			
☐	337	Bob Patterson	.06	.03	.01			
☐	338	Al Pedrique	.06	.03	.01			
☐	339	R.J. Reynolds	.06	.03	.01			
☐	340	John Smiley	.30	.14	.04			
☐	341	Andy Van Slyke UER	.10	.05	.01			
		(Wrong batting and throwing listed)						
☐	342	Bob Walk	.06	.03	.01			
☐	343	Marty Barrett	.06	.03	.01			
☐	344	Todd Benzinger	.06	.03	.01			
☐	345	Wade Boggs	.15	.07	.02			
☐	346	Tom Bolton	.06	.03	.01			
☐	347	Oil Can Boyd	.06	.03	.01			
☐	348	Ellis Burks	.40	.18	.05			
☐	349	Roger Clemens	.30	.14	.04			
☐	350	Steve Crawford	.06	.03	.01			
☐	351	Dwight Evans	.10	.05	.01			
☐	352	Wes Gardner	.06	.03	.01			
☐	353	Rich Gedman	.06	.03	.01			
☐	354	Mike Greenwell	.15	.07	.02			
☐	355	Sam Horn	.06	.03	.01			
☐	356	Bruce Hurst	.06	.03	.01			
☐	357	John Marzano	.06	.03	.01			
☐	358	Al Nipper	.06	.03	.01			
☐	359	Spike Owen	.06	.03	.01			
☐	360	Jody Reed	.10	.05	.01			
☐	361	Jim Rice	.15	.07	.02			
☐	362	Ed Romero	.06	.03	.01			
☐	363	Kevin Romine	.06	.03	.01			
☐	364	Joe Sambito	.06	.03	.01			
☐	365	Calvin Schiraldi	.06	.03	.01			
☐	366	Jeff Sellers	.06	.03	.01			
☐	367	Bob Stanley	.06	.03	.01			
☐	368	Scott Bankhead	.06	.03	.01			
☐	369	Phil Bradley	.06	.03	.01			
☐	370	Scott Bradley	.06	.03	.01			
☐	371	Mickey Brantley	.06	.03	.01			
☐	372	Mike Campbell	.06	.03	.01			
☐	373	Alvin Davis	.06	.03	.01			
☐	374	Lee Guetterman	.06	.03	.01			
☐	375	Dave Hengel	.06	.03	.01			
☐	376	Mike Kingery	.06	.03	.01			
☐	377	Mark Langston	.15	.07	.02			
☐	378	Edgar Martinez	2.00	.90	.25			
☐	379	Mike Moore	.06	.03	.01			
☐	380	Mike Morgan	.06	.03	.01			
☐	381	John Moses	.06	.03	.01			
☐	382	Donell Nixon	.06	.03	.01			
☐	383	Edwin Nunez	.06	.03	.01			
☐	384	Ken Phelps	.06	.03	.01			
☐	385	Jim Presley	.06	.03	.01			
☐	386	Rey Quinones	.06	.03	.01			
☐	387	Jerry Reed	.06	.03	.01			
☐	388	Harold Reynolds	.06	.03	.01			
☐	389	Dave Valle	.06	.03	.01			
☐	390	Bill Wilkinson	.06	.03	.01			
☐	391	Harold Baines	.15	.07	.02			
☐	392	Floyd Bannister	.06	.03	.01			
☐	393	Daryl Boston	.06	.03	.01			
☐	394	Ivan Calderon	.06	.03	.01			
☐	395	Jose DeLeon	.06	.03	.01			
☐	396	Richard Dotson	.06	.03	.01			
☐	397	Carlton Fisk	.15	.07	.02			
☐	398	Ozzie Guillen	.10	.05	.01			
☐	399	Ron Hassey	.06	.03	.01			
☐	400	Donnie Hill	.06	.03	.01			
☐	401	Bob James	.06	.03	.01			
☐	402	Dave LaPoint	.06	.03	.01			
☐	403	Bill Lindsey	.06	.03	.01			
☐	404	Bill Long	.06	.03	.01			
☐	405	Steve Lyons	.06	.03	.01			
☐	406	Fred Manrique	.06	.03	.01			
☐	407	Jack McDowell	1.25	.55	.16			
☐	408	Gary Redus	.06	.03	.01			
☐	409	Ray Searage	.06	.03	.01			
☐	410	Bobby Thigpen	.06	.03	.01			
☐	411	Greg Walker	.06	.03	.01			
☐	412	Ken Williams	.06	.03	.01			
☐	413	Jim Winn	.06	.03	.01			
☐	414	Jody Davis	.06	.03	.01			
☐	415	Andre Dawson	.15	.07	.02			
☐	416	Brian Dayett	.06	.03	.01			
☐	417	Bob Dernier	.06	.03	.01			
☐	418	Frank DiPino	.06	.03	.01			
☐	419	Shawon Dunston	.10	.05	.01			
☐	420	Leon Durham	.06	.03	.01			
☐	421	Les Lancaster	.06	.03	.01			
☐	422	Ed Lynch	.06	.03	.01			
☐	423	Greg Maddux	4.00	1.80	.50			
☐	424	Dave Martinez	.06	.03	.01			
☐	425A	Keith Moreland ERR	1.50	.70	.19			
		(Photo actually Jody Davis)						
☐	425B	Keith Moreland COR	.06	.03	.01			
		(Bat on shoulder)						
☐	426	Jamie Moyer	.06	.03	.01			
☐	427	Jerry Mumphrey	.06	.03	.01			
☐	428	Paul Noce	.06	.03	.01			
☐	429	Rafael Palmeiro	1.25	.55	.16			
☐	430	Wade Rowdon	.06	.03	.01			
☐	431	Ryne Sandberg	.60	.25	.07			
☐	432	Scott Sanderson	.06	.03	.01			

☐ 433 Lee Smith	.15	.07	.02
☐ 434 Jim Sundberg	.06	.03	.01
☐ 435 Rick Sutcliffe	.10	.05	.01
☐ 436 Manny Trillo	.06	.03	.01
☐ 437 Juan Agosto	.06	.03	.01
☐ 438 Larry Andersen	.06	.03	.01
☐ 439 Alan Ashby	.06	.03	.01
☐ 440 Kevin Bass	.06	.03	.01
☐ 441 Ken Caminiti	1.00	.45	.12
☐ 442 Rocky Childress	.06	.03	.01
☐ 443 Jose Cruz	.06	.03	.01
☐ 444 Danny Darwin	.06	.03	.01
☐ 445 Glenn Davis	.06	.03	.01
☐ 446 Jim Deshaies	.06	.03	.01
☐ 447 Bill Doran	.06	.03	.01
☐ 448 Ty Gainey	.06	.03	.01
☐ 449 Billy Hatcher	.06	.03	.01
☐ 450 Jeff Heathcock	.06	.03	.01
☐ 451 Bob Knepper	.06	.03	.01
☐ 452 Rob Mallicoat	.06	.03	.01
☐ 453 Dave Meads	.06	.03	.01
☐ 454 Craig Reynolds	.06	.03	.01
☐ 455 Nolan Ryan	1.50	.70	.19
☐ 456 Mike Scott	.06	.03	.01
☐ 457 Dave Smith	.06	.03	.01
☐ 458 Denny Walling	.06	.03	.01
☐ 459 Robbie Wine	.06	.03	.01
☐ 460 Gerald Young	.06	.03	.01
☐ 461 Bob Brower	.06	.03	.01
☐ 462A Jerry Browne ERR	1.50	.70	.19
(Photo actually			
Bob Brower,			
white player)			
☐ 462B Jerry Browne COR	.06	.03	.01
(Black player)			
☐ 463 Steve Buechele	.06	.03	.01
☐ 464 Edwin Correa	.06	.03	.01
☐ 465 Cecil Espy	.06	.03	.01
☐ 466 Scott Fletcher	.06	.03	.01
☐ 467 Jose Guzman	.06	.03	.01
☐ 468 Greg Harris	.06	.03	.01
☐ 469 Charlie Hough	.10	.05	.01
☐ 470 Pete Incaviglia	.10	.05	.01
☐ 471 Paul Kilgus	.06	.03	.01
☐ 472 Mike Loynd	.06	.03	.01
☐ 473 Oddibe McDowell	.06	.03	.01
☐ 474 Dale Mohorcic	.06	.03	.01
☐ 475 Pete O'Brien	.06	.03	.01
☐ 476 Larry Parrish	.06	.03	.01
☐ 477 Geno Petralli	.06	.03	.01
☐ 478 Jeff Russell	.06	.03	.01
☐ 479 Ruben Sierra	.50	.23	.06
☐ 480 Mike Stanley	.10	.05	.01
☐ 481 Curtis Wilkerson	.06	.03	.01
☐ 482 Mitch Williams	.10	.05	.01
☐ 483 Bobby Witt	.10	.05	.01
☐ 484 Tony Armas	.06	.03	.01
☐ 485 Bob Boone	.10	.05	.01
☐ 486 Bill Buckner	.10	.05	.01
☐ 487 DeWayne Buice	.06	.03	.01
☐ 488 Brian Downing	.06	.03	.01
☐ 489 Chuck Finley	.10	.05	.01
☐ 490 Willie Fraser UER	.06	.03	.01
(Wrong bio stats,			
for George Hendrick)			
☐ 491 Jack Howell	.06	.03	.01
☐ 492 Ruppert Jones	.06	.03	.01
☐ 493 Wally Joyner	.10	.05	.01
☐ 494 Jack Lazorko	.06	.03	.01
☐ 495 Gary Lucas	.06	.03	.01
☐ 496 Kirk McCaskill	.06	.03	.01
☐ 497 Mark McLemore	.06	.03	.01
☐ 498 Darrell Miller	.06	.03	.01
☐ 499 Greg Minton	.06	.03	.01
☐ 500 Donnie Moore	.06	.03	.01
☐ 501 Gus Polidor	.06	.03	.01
☐ 502 Johnny Ray	.06	.03	.01
☐ 503 Mark Ryal	.06	.03	.01
☐ 504 Dick Schofield	.06	.03	.01
☐ 505 Don Sutton	.15	.07	.02
☐ 506 Devon White	.15	.07	.02
☐ 507 Mike Witt	.06	.03	.01
☐ 508 Dave Anderson	.06	.03	.01
☐ 509 Tim Belcher	.06	.03	.01
☐ 510 Ralph Bryant	.06	.03	.01
☐ 511 Tim Crews	.10	.05	.01
☐ 512 Mike Devereaux	.40	.18	.05
☐ 513 Mariano Duncan	.06	.03	.01
☐ 514 Pedro Guerrero	.10	.05	.01
☐ 515 Jeff Hamilton	.06	.03	.01
☐ 516 Mickey Hatcher	.06	.03	.01
☐ 517 Brad Havens	.06	.03	.01
☐ 518 Orel Hershiser	.15	.07	.02
☐ 519 Shawn Hillegas	.06	.03	.01
☐ 520 Ken Howell	.06	.03	.01
☐ 521 Tim Leary	.06	.03	.01
☐ 522 Mike Marshall	.06	.03	.01
☐ 523 Steve Sax	.06	.03	.01
☐ 524 Mike Scioscia	.06	.03	.01
☐ 525 Mike Sharperson	.06	.03	.01
☐ 526 John Shelby	.06	.03	.01
☐ 527 Franklin Stubbs	.06	.03	.01
☐ 528 Fernando Valenzuela	.06	.03	.01
☐ 529 Bob Welch	.10	.05	.01
☐ 530 Matt Young	.06	.03	.01
☐ 531 Jim Acker	.06	.03	.01
☐ 532 Paul Assenmacher	.06	.03	.01
☐ 533 Jeff Blauser	.30	.14	.04
☐ 534 Joe Boever	.06	.03	.01
☐ 535 Martin Clary	.06	.03	.01
☐ 536 Kevin Coffman	.06	.03	.01
☐ 537 Jeff Dedmon	.06	.03	.01
☐ 538 Ron Gant	2.00	.90	.25
☐ 539 Tom Glavine	2.50	1.10	.30
☐ 540 Ken Griffey	.10	.05	.01
☐ 541 Albert Hall	.06	.03	.01
☐ 542 Glenn Hubbard	.06	.03	.01
☐ 543 Dion James	.06	.03	.01
☐ 544 Dale Murphy	.15	.07	.02
☐ 545 Ken Oberkfell	.06	.03	.01
☐ 546 David Palmer	.06	.03	.01
☐ 547 Gerald Perry	.06	.03	.01
☐ 548 Charlie Puleo	.06	.03	.01
☐ 549 Ted Simmons	.10	.05	.01
☐ 550 Zane Smith	.06	.03	.01
☐ 551 Andres Thomas	.06	.03	.01
☐ 552 Ozzie Virgil	.06	.03	.01
☐ 553 Don Aase	.06	.03	.01
☐ 554 Jeff Ballard	.06	.03	.01
☐ 555 Eric Bell	.06	.03	.01
☐ 556 Mike Boddicker	.06	.03	.01
☐ 557 Ken Dixon	.06	.03	.01
☐ 558 Jim Dwyer	.06	.03	.01
☐ 559 Ken Gerhart	.06	.03	.01
☐ 560 Rene Gonzales	.06	.03	.01
☐ 561 Mike Griffin	.06	.03	.01
☐ 562 John Habyan UER	.06	.03	.01
(Misspelled Hayban on			
both sides of card)			
☐ 563 Terry Kennedy	.06	.03	.01
☐ 564 Ray Knight	.10	.05	.01
☐ 565 Lee Lacy	.06	.03	.01

☐ 566	Fred Lynn	.10	.05	.01
☐ 567	Eddie Murray	.35	.16	.04
☐ 568	Tom Niedenfuer	.06	.03	.01
☐ 569	Bill Ripken	.06	.03	.01
☐ 570	Cal Ripken	1.50	.70	.19
☐ 571	Dave Schmidt	.06	.03	.01
☐ 572	Larry Sheets	.06	.03	.01
☐ 573	Pete Stanicek	.06	.03	.01
☐ 574	Mark Williamson	.06	.03	.01
☐ 575	Mike Young	.06	.03	.01
☐ 576	Shawn Abner	.06	.03	.01
☐ 577	Greg Booker	.06	.03	.01
☐ 578	Chris Brown	.06	.03	.01
☐ 579	Keith Comstock	.06	.03	.01
☐ 580	Joey Cora	.20	.09	.03
☐ 581	Mark Davis	.06	.03	.01
☐ 582	Tim Flannery	.10	.05	.01
	(With surfboard)			
☐ 583	Goose Gossage	.15	.07	.02
☐ 584	Mark Grant	.06	.03	.01
☐ 585	Tony Gwynn	.60	.25	.07
☐ 586	Andy Hawkins	.06	.03	.01
☐ 587	Stan Jefferson	.06	.03	.01
☐ 588	Jimmy Jones	.06	.03	.01
☐ 589	John Kruk	.15	.07	.02
☐ 590	Shane Mack	.10	.05	.01
☐ 591	Carmelo Martinez	.06	.03	.01
☐ 592	Lance McCullers UER	.06	.03	.01
	(6'11" tall)			
☐ 593	Eric Nolte	.06	.03	.01
☐ 594	Randy Ready	.06	.03	.01
☐ 595	Luis Salazar	.06	.03	.01
☐ 596	Benito Santiago	.10	.05	.01
☐ 597	Eric Show	.06	.03	.01
☐ 598	Garry Templeton	.06	.03	.01
☐ 599	Ed Whitson	.06	.03	.01
☐ 600	Scott Bailes	.06	.03	.01
☐ 601	Chris Bando	.06	.03	.01
☐ 602	Jay Bell	.50	.23	.06
☐ 603	Brett Butler	.10	.05	.01
☐ 604	Tom Candiotti	.06	.03	.01
☐ 605	Joe Carter	.50	.23	.06
☐ 606	Carmen Castillo	.06	.03	.01
☐ 607	Brian Dorsett	.06	.03	.01
☐ 608	John Farrell	.06	.03	.01
☐ 609	Julio Franco	.10	.05	.01
☐ 610	Mel Hall	.06	.03	.01
☐ 611	Tommy Hinzo	.06	.03	.01
☐ 612	Brook Jacoby	.06	.03	.01
☐ 613	Doug Jones	.10	.05	.01
☐ 614	Ken Schrom	.06	.03	.01
☐ 615	Cory Snyder	.06	.03	.01
☐ 616	Sammy Stewart	.06	.03	.01
☐ 617	Greg Swindell	.10	.05	.01
☐ 618	Pat Tabler	.06	.03	.01
☐ 619	Ed VandeBerg	.06	.03	.01
☐ 620	Eddie Williams	.10	.05	.01
☐ 621	Rich Yett	.06	.03	.01
☐ 622	Slugging Sophomores	.10	.05	.01
	Wally Joyner			
	Cory Snyder			
☐ 623	Dominican Dynamite	.06	.03	.01
	George Bell			
	Pedro Guerrero			
☐ 624	Oakland's Power Team	.60	.25	.07
	Mark McGwire			
	Jose Canseco			
☐ 625	Classic Relief	.06	.03	.01
	Dave Righetti			
	Dan Plesac			
☐ 626	All Star Righties	.10	.05	.01

	Bret Saberhagen			
	Mike Witt			
	Jack Morris			
☐ 627	Game Closers	.06	.03	.01
	John Franco			
	Steve Bedrosian			
☐ 628	Masters/Double Play	.40	.18	.05
	Ozzie Smith			
	Ryne Sandberg			
☐ 629	Rookie Record Setter	.25	.11	.03
	Mark McGwire			
☐ 630	Changing the Guard	.15	.07	.02
	Mike Greenwell			
	Ellis Burks			
	Todd Benzinger			
☐ 631	NL Batting Champs	.15	.07	.02
	Tony Gwynn			
	Tim Raines			
☐ 632	Pitching Magic	.10	.05	.01
	Mike Scott			
	Orel Hershiser			
☐ 633	Big Bats at First	.20	.09	.03
	Pat Tabler			
	Mark McGwire			
☐ 634	Hitting King/Thief	.15	.07	.02
	Tony Gwynn			
	Vince Coleman			
☐ 635	Slugging Shortstops	.50	.23	.06
	Tony Fernandez			
	Cal Ripken			
	Alan Trammell			
☐ 636	Tried/True Sluggers	.15	.07	.02
	Mike Schmidt			
	Gary Carter			
☐ 637	Crunch Time	.10	.05	.01
	Darryl Strawberry			
	Eric Davis			
☐ 638	AL All-Stars	.15	.07	.02
	Matt Nokes			
	Kirby Puckett			
☐ 639	NL All-Stars	.10	.05	.01
	Keith Hernandez			
	Dale Murphy			
☐ 640	The O's Brothers	.75	.35	.09
	Billy Ripken			
	Cal Ripken			
☐ 641	Mark Grace and	1.50	.70	.19
	Darrin Jackson			
☐ 642	Damon Berryhill and	.40	.18	.05
	Jeff Montgomery			
☐ 643	Felix Fermin and	.08	.04	.01
	Jesse Reid			
☐ 644	Greg Myers and	.08	.04	.01
	Greg Tabor			
☐ 645	Joey Meyer and	.08	.04	.01
	Jim Eppard			
☐ 646	Adam Peterson and	.10	.05	.01
	Randy Velarde			
☐ 647	Pete Smith and	.10	.05	.01
	Chris Gwynn			
☐ 648	Tom Newell and	.08	.04	.01
	Greg Jelks			
☐ 649	Mario Diaz and	.08	.04	.01
	Clay Parker			
☐ 650	Jack Savage and	.08	.04	.01
	Todd Simmons			
☐ 651	John Burkett and	.50	.23	.06
	Kirt Manwaring			
☐ 652	Dave Otto and	.10	.05	.01
	Walt Weiss			
☐ 653	Jeff King and	.50	.23	.06

Randell Byers

		MINT	NRMT	EXC
☐ 654	CL: Twins/Cards........... (90 Bob Melvin, 91 Eddie Milner) Tigers/Giants UER	.10	.05	.01
☐ 655	CL: Blue Jays/Mets ...... Brewers/Expos UER (Mets listed before Blue Jays on card)	.10	.05	.01
☐ 656	CL: Yankees/Reds .... Royals/A's	.10	.05	.01
☐ 657	CL: Phillies/Pirates........ Red Sox/Mariners	.10	.05	.01
☐ 658	CL: White Sox/Cubs ..... Astros/Rangers	.10	.05	.01
☐ 659	CL: Angels/Dodgers ..... Braves/Orioles	.10	.05	.01
☐ 660	CL: Padres/Indians........ Rookies/Specials	.10	.05	.01

1988 Fleer Update

 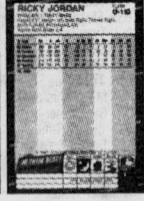

This 132-card set was distributed by Fleer to dealers as a complete set in a custom box. In addition to the complete set of 132 cards, the box also contains 25 Team Logo stickers. The card fronts look very similar to the 1988 Fleer regular issue. The cards are numbered (with a U prefix) alphabetically according to player's last name. Cards measure the standard size, 2 1/2" by 3 1/2". This was the first Fleer Update set to adopt the Fleer "alphabetical within team" numbering system. The key (extended) Rookie Cards in this set are Roberto Alomar, Craig Biggio, Bryan Harvey, Chris Sabo, and John Smoltz. Fleer also produced a "limited" edition version of this set with glossy coating and packaged in a "tin." However, this tin was apparently not limited enough (estimated between 40,000 and 60,000 1988 Update tin sets produced by Fleer), since the values of the "tin" glossy cards are now only double the values of the respective cards in the regular set.

	MINT	NRMT	EXC
COMPLETE FACT.SET (132) ..	10.00	4.50	1.25
COMMON CARD (1-132)	.05	.02	.01
☐ 1 Jose Bautista	.05	.02	.01
☐ 2 Joe Orsulak	.05	.02	.01
☐ 3 Doug Sisk	.05	.02	.01
☐ 4 Craig Worthington	.05	.02	.01
☐ 5 Mike Boddicker	.05	.02	.01
☐ 6 Rick Cerone	.05	.02	.01
☐ 7 Larry Parrish	.05	.02	.01
☐ 8 Lee Smith	.15	.07	.02
☐ 9 Mike Smithson	.05	.02	.01
☐ 10 John Trautwein	.05	.02	.01
☐ 11 Sherman Corbett	.05	.02	.01
☐ 12 Chili Davis	.15	.07	.02
☐ 13 Jim Eppard	.05	.02	.01
☐ 14 Bryan Harvey	.10	.05	.01
☐ 15 John Davis	.05	.02	.01
☐ 16 Dave Gallagher	.05	.02	.01
☐ 17 Ricky Horton	.05	.02	.01
☐ 18 Dan Pasqua	.05	.02	.01
☐ 19 Melido Perez	.10	.05	.01
☐ 20 Jose Segura	.05	.02	.01
☐ 21 Andy Allanson	.05	.02	.01
☐ 22 Jon Perlman	.05	.02	.01
☐ 23 Domingo Ramos	.05	.02	.01
☐ 24 Rick Rodriguez	.05	.02	.01
☐ 25 Willie Upshaw	.05	.02	.01
☐ 26 Paul Gibson	.05	.02	.01
☐ 27 Don Heinkel	.05	.02	.01
☐ 28 Ray Knight	.10	.05	.01
☐ 29 Gary Pettis	.05	.02	.01
☐ 30 Luis Salazar	.05	.02	.01
☐ 31 Mike Macfarlane	.30	.14	.04
☐ 32 Jeff Montgomery	.40	.18	.05
☐ 33 Ted Power	.05	.02	.01
☐ 34 Israel Sanchez	.05	.02	.01
☐ 35 Kurt Stillwell	.05	.02	.01
☐ 36 Pat Tabler	.05	.02	.01
☐ 37 Don August	.05	.02	.01
☐ 38 Darryl Hamilton	.10	.05	.01
☐ 39 Jeff Leonard	.05	.02	.01
☐ 40 Joey Meyer	.05	.02	.01
☐ 41 Allan Anderson	.05	.02	.01
☐ 42 Brian Harper	.10	.05	.01
☐ 43 Tom Herr	.05	.02	.01
☐ 44 Charlie Lea	.05	.02	.01
☐ 45 John Moses .... (Listed as Hohn on checklist card)	.05	.02	.01
☐ 46 John Candelaria	.05	.02	.01
☐ 47 Jack Clark	.10	.05	.01
☐ 48 Richard Dotson	.05	.02	.01
☐ 49 Al Leiter	.10	.05	.01
☐ 50 Rafael Santana	.05	.02	.01
☐ 51 Don Slaught	.05	.02	.01
☐ 52 Todd Burns	.05	.02	.01
☐ 53 Dave Henderson	.05	.02	.01
☐ 54 Doug Jennings	.05	.02	.01
☐ 55 Dave Parker	.15	.07	.02
☐ 56 Walt Weiss	.15	.07	.02
☐ 57 Bob Welch	.10	.05	.01
☐ 58 Henry Cotto	.05	.02	.01
☐ 59 Mario Diaz UER .... (Listed as Marion on card front)	.05	.02	.01
☐ 60 Mike Jackson	.05	.02	.01
☐ 61 Bill Swift	.10	.05	.01
☐ 62 Jose Cecena	.05	.02	.01
☐ 63 Ray Hayward	.05	.02	.01
☐ 64 Jim Steels UER .... (Listed as Jim Steele on card back)	.05	.02	.01
☐ 65 Pat Borders	.05	.02	.01
☐ 66 Sil Campusano	.05	.02	.01
☐ 67 Mike Flanagan	.05	.02	.01

☐ 68	Todd Stottlemyre	.50	.23	.06
☐ 69	David Wells	.40	.18	.05
☐ 70	Jose Alvarez	.05	.02	.01
☐ 71	Paul Runge	.05	.02	.01
☐ 72	Cesar Jimenez	.05	.02	.01
	(Card was intended			
	for German Jiminez,			
	it's his photo)			
☐ 73	Pete Smith	.05	.02	.01
☐ 74	John Smoltz	1.50	.70	.19
☐ 75	Damon Berryhill	.05	.02	.01
☐ 76	Goose Gossage	.15	.07	.02
☐ 77	Mark Grace	1.50	.70	.19
☐ 78	Darrin Jackson	.05	.02	.01
☐ 79	Vance Law	.05	.02	.01
☐ 80	Jeff Pico	.05	.02	.01
☐ 81	Gary Varsho	.05	.02	.01
☐ 82	Tim Birtsas	.05	.02	.01
☐ 83	Rob Dibble	.10	.05	.01
☐ 84	Danny Jackson	.05	.02	.01
☐ 85	Paul O'Neill	.15	.07	.02
☐ 86	Jose Rijo	.10	.05	.01
☐ 87	Chris Sabo	.10	.05	.01
☐ 88	John Fishel	.05	.02	.01
☐ 89	Craig Biggio	2.00	.90	.25
☐ 90	Terry Puhl	.05	.02	.01
☐ 91	Rafael Ramirez	.05	.02	.01
☐ 92	Louie Meadows	.05	.02	.01
☐ 93	Kirk Gibson	.15	.07	.02
☐ 94	Alfredo Griffin	.05	.02	.01
☐ 95	Jay Howell	.05	.02	.01
☐ 96	Jesse Orosco	.05	.02	.01
☐ 97	Alejandro Pena	.05	.02	.01
☐ 98	Tracy Woodson	.05	.02	.01
☐ 99	John Dopson	.05	.02	.01
☐ 100	Brian Holman	.05	.02	.01
☐ 101	Rex Hudler	.05	.02	.01
☐ 102	Jeff Parrett	.05	.02	.01
☐ 103	Nelson Santovenia	.05	.02	.01
☐ 104	Kevin Elster	.05	.02	.01
☐ 105	Jeff Innis	.05	.02	.01
☐ 106	Mackey Sasser	.05	.02	.01
☐ 107	Phil Bradley	.05	.02	.01
☐ 108	Danny Clay	.05	.02	.01
☐ 109	Greg A.Harris	.05	.02	.01
☐ 110	Ricky Jordan	.05	.02	.01
☐ 111	David Palmer	.05	.02	.01
☐ 112	Jim Gott	.05	.02	.01
☐ 113	Tommy Gregg UER	.05	.02	.01
	(Photo actually			
	Randy Milligan)			
☐ 114	Barry Jones	.05	.02	.01
☐ 115	Randy Milligan	.05	.02	.01
☐ 116	Luis Alicea	.05	.02	.01
☐ 117	Tom Brunansky	.05	.02	.01
☐ 118	John Costello	.05	.02	.01
☐ 119	Jose DeLeon	.05	.02	.01
☐ 120	Bob Horner	.05	.02	.01
☐ 121	Scott Terry	.05	.02	.01
☐ 122	Roberto Alomar	5.00	2.20	.60
☐ 123	Dave Leiper	.05	.02	.01
☐ 124	Keith Moreland	.05	.02	.01
☐ 125	Mark Parent	.05	.02	.01
☐ 126	Dennis Rasmussen	.05	.02	.01
☐ 127	Randy Bockus	.05	.02	.01
☐ 128	Brett Butler	.15	.07	.02
☐ 129	Donell Nixon	.05	.02	.01
☐ 130	Earnest Riles	.05	.02	.01
☐ 131	Roger Samuels	.05	.02	.01
☐ 132	Checklist U1-U132	.05	.02	.01

1989 Fleer

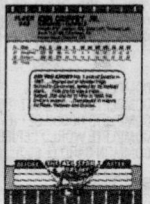

This 660-card set features a distinctive gray border background with white and yellow trim. The backs are printed in gray, black, and yellow on white card stock. The bottom of the card back shows an innovative breakdown of the player's demonstrated ability with respect to his performance before and after the All-Star break. Cards are numbered on the back and are again the standard 2 1/2" by 3 1/2". Cards are again organized numerically by teams and alphabetically within teams: Oakland A's (1-26), New York Mets (27-52), Los Angeles Dodgers (53-77), Boston Red Sox (78-101), Minnesota Twins (102-127), Detroit Tigers (128-151), Cincinnati Reds (152-175), Milwaukee Brewers (176-200), Pittsburgh Pirates (201-224), Toronto Blue Jays (225-248), New York Yankees (249-274), Kansas City Royals (275-298), San Diego Padres (299-322), San Francisco Giants. (323-347), Houston Astros (348-370), Montreal Expos (371-395), Cleveland Indians (396-417), Chicago Cubs (418-442), St. Louis Cardinals (443-466), California Angels (467-490), Chicago White Sox (491-513), Texas Rangers (514-537), Seattle Mariners (538-561), Philadelphia Phillies (562-584), Atlanta Braves (585-605), and Baltimore Orioles (606-627). However, pairs 148/149, 153/154, 272/273, 283/284, and 367/368 were apparently misalphabetized by Fleer. The last 33 cards in the set consist of Specials (628-639), Rookie Pairs (640-653), and checklists (654-660). Fleer arranged the teams according to regular season team record. Approximately half of the California Angels players have white rather than yellow halos. Certain Oakland A's player cards have red instead of green lines for front photo borders. Checklist cards are available either with or without positions listed for each player. Rookie Cards in this set include Sandy Alomar Jr., Brady Anderson, Dante Bichette, Craig Biggio, Ken Griffey Jr., Charlie Hayes, Ken Hill, Randy Johnson, Felix Jose, Ramon Martinez, Hal Morris, Gary Sheffield, and John Smoltz. Fleer also produced the last of their three-year run of "limited" edition glossy, tin sets. This tin set was limited, but only compared to the previous year, as collector and dealer interest in

the tin sets was apparently waning. It has been estimated that approximately 30,000 1989 tin sets were produced by Fleer; as a result, the price of the "tin" glossy cards now ranges from three to five times the price of the regular set cards.

	MINT	NRMT	EXC
COMPLETE SET (660)	12.00	5.50	1.50
COMPLETE RETAIL SET (660)	12.00	5.50	1.50
COMPLETE HOBBY SET (672)	14.00	6.25	1.75
COMPLETE WORLD SERIES (12)	2.00	.90	.25
COMMON CARD (1-660)	.05	.02	.01

☐ 1 Don Baylor	.15	.07	.02
☐ 2 Lance Blankenship	.05	.02	.01
☐ 3 Todd Burns UER	.05	.02	.01
(Wrong birthdate; before/after All-Star stats missing)			
☐ 4 Greg Cadaret UER	.05	.02	.01
(All-Star Break stats show 3 losses, should be 2)			
☐ 5 Jose Canseco	.30	.14	.04
☐ 6 Storm Davis	.05	.02	.01
☐ 7 Dennis Eckersley	.15	.07	.02
☐ 8 Mike Gallego	.05	.02	.01
☐ 9 Ron Hassey	.05	.02	.01
☐ 10 Dave Henderson	.05	.02	.01
☐ 11 Rick Honeycutt	.05	.02	.01
☐ 12 Glenn Hubbard	.05	.02	.01
☐ 13 Stan Javier	.05	.02	.01
☐ 14 Doug Jennings	.05	.02	.01
☐ 15 Felix Jose	.10	.05	.01
☐ 16 Carney Lansford	.10	.05	.01
☐ 17 Mark McGwire	.15	.07	.02
☐ 18 Gene Nelson	.05	.02	.01
☐ 19 Dave Parker	.15	.07	.02
☐ 20 Eric Plunk	.05	.02	.01
☐ 21 Luis Polonia	.10	.05	.01
☐ 22 Terry Steinbach	.10	.05	.01
☐ 23 Dave Stewart	.15	.07	.02
☐ 24 Walt Weiss	.05	.02	.01
☐ 25 Bob Welch	.10	.05	.01
☐ 26 Curt Young	.05	.02	.01
☐ 27 Rick Aguilera	.15	.07	.02
☐ 28 Wally Backman	.05	.02	.01
☐ 29 Mark Carreon UER	.05	.02	.01
(After All-Star Break batting 7.14)			
☐ 30 Gary Carter	.15	.07	.02
☐ 31 David Cone	.15	.07	.02
☐ 32 Ron Darling	.10	.05	.01
☐ 33 Len Dykstra	.15	.07	.02
☐ 34 Kevin Elster	.05	.02	.01
☐ 35 Sid Fernandez	.10	.05	.01
☐ 36 Dwight Gooden	.10	.05	.01
☐ 37 Keith Hernandez	.10	.05	.01
☐ 38 Gregg Jefferies	.20	.09	.03
☐ 39 Howard Johnson	.10	.05	.01
☐ 40 Terry Leach	.05	.02	.01
☐ 41 Dave Magadan UER	.05	.02	.01
(Bio says 15 doubles, should be 13)			
☐ 42 Bob McClure	.05	.02	.01
☐ 43 Roger McDowell UER	.05	.02	.01
(Led Mets with 58, should be 62)			
☐ 44 Kevin McReynolds	.05	.02	.01
☐ 45 Keith A. Miller	.05	.02	.01
☐ 46 Randy Myers	.15	.07	.02
☐ 47 Bob Ojeda	.05	.02	.01
☐ 48 Mackey Sasser	.05	.02	.01
☐ 49 Darryl Strawberry	.15	.07	.02
☐ 50 Tim Teufel	.05	.02	.01
☐ 51 Dave West	.10	.05	.01
☐ 52 Mookie Wilson	.10	.05	.01
☐ 53 Dave Anderson	.05	.02	.01
☐ 54 Tim Belcher	.05	.02	.01
☐ 55 Mike Davis	.05	.02	.01
☐ 56 Mike Devereaux	.10	.05	.01
☐ 57 Kirk Gibson	.10	.05	.01
☐ 58 Alfredo Griffin	.05	.02	.01
☐ 59 Chris Gwynn	.05	.02	.01
☐ 60 Jeff Hamilton	.05	.02	.01
☐ 61A Danny Heep	.10	.05	.01
(Home: Lake Hills)			
☐ 61B Danny Heep	.05	.02	.01
(Home: San Antonio)			
☐ 62 Orel Hershiser	.15	.07	.02
☐ 63 Brian Holton	.05	.02	.01
☐ 64 Jay Howell	.05	.02	.01
☐ 65 Tim Leary	.05	.02	.01
☐ 66 Mike Marshall	.05	.02	.01
☐ 67 Ramon Martinez	.30	.14	.04
☐ 68 Jesse Orosco	.05	.02	.01
☐ 69 Alejandro Pena	.05	.02	.01
☐ 70 Steve Sax	.05	.02	.01
☐ 71 Mike Scioscia	.05	.02	.01
☐ 72 Mike Sharperson	.05	.02	.01
☐ 73 John Shelby	.05	.02	.01
☐ 74 Franklin Stubbs	.05	.02	.01
☐ 75 John Tudor	.05	.02	.01
☐ 76 Fernando Valenzuela	.05	.02	.01
☐ 77 Tracy Woodson	.05	.02	.01
☐ 78 Marty Barrett	.05	.02	.01
☐ 79 Todd Benzinger	.05	.02	.01
☐ 80 Mike Boddicker UER	.05	.02	.01
(Rochester in '76, should be '78)			
☐ 81 Wade Boggs	.15	.07	.02
☐ 82 Oil Can Boyd	.05	.02	.01
☐ 83 Ellis Burks	.15	.07	.02
☐ 84 Rick Cerone	.05	.02	.01
☐ 85 Roger Clemens	.20	.09	.03
☐ 86 Steve Curry	.05	.02	.01
☐ 87 Dwight Evans	.10	.05	.01
☐ 88 Wes Gardner	.05	.02	.01
☐ 89 Rich Gedman	.05	.02	.01
☐ 90 Mike Greenwell	.10	.05	.01
☐ 91 Bruce Hurst	.05	.02	.01
☐ 92 Dennis Lamp	.05	.02	.01
☐ 93 Spike Owen	.05	.02	.01
☐ 94 Larry Parrish UER	.05	.02	.01
(Before All-Star Break batting 1.90)			
☐ 95 Carlos Quintana	.05	.02	.01
☐ 96 Jody Reed	.05	.02	.01
☐ 97 Jim Rice	.15	.07	.02
☐ 98A Kevin Romine ERR	.10	.05	.01
(Photo actually Randy Kutcher batting)			
☐ 98B Kevin Romine COR	.05	.02	.01
(Arms folded)			
☐ 99 Lee Smith	.15	.07	.02
☐ 100 Mike Smithson	.05	.02	.01
☐ 101 Bob Stanley	.05	.02	.01
☐ 102 Allan Anderson	.05	.02	.01
☐ 103 Keith Atherton	.05	.02	.01
☐ 104 Juan Berenguer	.05	.02	.01
☐ 105 Bert Blyleven	.15	.07	.02

☐ 106 Eric Bullock UER (Bats/Throws Right, should be Left)	.05	.02	.01
☐ 107 Randy Bush	.05	.02	.01
☐ 108 John Christensen	.05	.02	.01
☐ 109 Mark Davidson	.05	.02	.01
☐ 110 Gary Gaetti	.05	.02	.01
☐ 111 Greg Gagne	.05	.02	.01
☐ 112 Dan Gladden	.05	.02	.01
☐ 113 German Gonzalez	.05	.02	.01
☐ 114 Brian Harper	.10	.05	.01
☐ 115 Tom Herr	.05	.02	.01
☐ 116 Kent Hrbek	.10	.05	.01
☐ 117 Gene Larkin	.05	.02	.01
☐ 118 Tim Laudner	.05	.02	.01
☐ 119 Charlie Lea	.05	.02	.01
☐ 120 Steve Lombardozzi	.05	.02	.01
☐ 121A John Moses (Home: Tempe)	.10	.05	.01
☐ 121B John Moses (Home: Phoenix)	.05	.02	.01
☐ 122 Al Newman	.05	.02	.01
☐ 123 Mark Portugal	.10	.05	.01
☐ 124 Kirby Puckett	.40	.18	.05
☐ 125 Jeff Reardon	.15	.07	.02
☐ 126 Fred Toliver	.05	.02	.01
☐ 127 Frank Viola	.10	.05	.01
☐ 128 Doyle Alexander	.05	.02	.01
☐ 129 Dave Bergman	.05	.02	.01
☐ 130A Tom Brookens ERR (Mike Heath back)	.75	.35	.09
☐ 130B Tom Brookens COR	.05	.02	.01
☐ 131 Paul Gibson	.05	.02	.01
☐ 132A Mike Heath ERR (Tom Brookens back)	.75	.35	.09
☐ 132B Mike Heath COR	.05	.02	.01
☐ 133 Don Heinkel	.05	.02	.01
☐ 134 Mike Henneman	.10	.05	.01
☐ 135 Guillermo Hernandez	.05	.02	.01
☐ 136 Eric King	.05	.02	.01
☐ 137 Chet Lemon	.05	.02	.01
☐ 138 Fred Lynn UER ('74, '75 stats missing)	.10	.05	.01
☐ 139 Jack Morris	.15	.07	.02
☐ 140 Matt Nokes	.05	.02	.01
☐ 141 Gary Pettis	.05	.02	.01
☐ 142 Ted Power	.05	.02	.01
☐ 143 Jeff M. Robinson	.05	.02	.01
☐ 144 Luis Salazar	.05	.02	.01
☐ 145 Steve Searcy	.05	.02	.01
☐ 146 Pat Sheridan	.05	.02	.01
☐ 147 Frank Tanana	.05	.02	.01
☐ 148 Alan Trammell	.15	.07	.02
☐ 149 Walt Terrell	.05	.02	.01
☐ 150 Jim Walewander	.05	.02	.01
☐ 151 Lou Whitaker	.15	.07	.02
☐ 152 Tim Birtsas	.05	.02	.01
☐ 153 Tom Browning	.05	.02	.01
☐ 154 Keith Brown	.05	.02	.01
☐ 155 Norm Charlton	.10	.05	.01
☐ 156 Dave Concepcion	.10	.05	.01
☐ 157 Kal Daniels	.05	.02	.01
☐ 158 Eric Davis	.10	.05	.01
☐ 159 Bo Diaz	.05	.02	.01
☐ 160 Rob Dibble	.10	.05	.01
☐ 161 Nick Esasky	.05	.02	.01
☐ 162 John Franco	.10	.05	.01
☐ 163 Danny Jackson	.05	.02	.01
☐ 164 Barry Larkin	.20	.09	.03
☐ 165 Rob Murphy	.05	.02	.01

☐ 166 Paul O'Neill	.15	.07	.02
☐ 167 Jeff Reed	.05	.02	.01
☐ 168 Jose Rijo	.15	.07	.02
☐ 169 Ron Robinson	.05	.02	.01
☐ 170 Chris Sabo	.10	.05	.01
☐ 171 Candy Sierra	.05	.02	.01
☐ 172 Van Snider	.05	.02	.01
☐ 173A Jeff Treadway (Target registration mark above head on front in light blue)	5.00	2.20	.60
☐ 173B Jeff Treadway (No target on front)	.05	.02	.01
☐ 174 Frank Williams (After All-Star Break stats are jumbled!)	.05	.02	.01
☐ 175 Herm Winningham	.05	.02	.01
☐ 176 Jim Adduci	.05	.02	.01
☐ 177 Don August	.05	.02	.01
☐ 178 Mike Birkbeck	.05	.02	.01
☐ 179 Chris Bosio	.05	.02	.01
☐ 180 Glenn Braggs	.05	.02	.01
☐ 181 Greg Brock	.05	.02	.01
☐ 182 Mark Clear	.05	.02	.01
☐ 183 Chuck Crim	.05	.02	.01
☐ 184 Rob Deer	.05	.02	.01
☐ 185 Tom Filer	.05	.02	.01
☐ 186 Jim Gantner	.05	.02	.01
☐ 187 Darryl Hamilton	.10	.05	.01
☐ 188 Ted Higuera	.05	.02	.01
☐ 189 Odell Jones	.05	.02	.01
☐ 190 Jeffrey Leonard	.05	.02	.01
☐ 191 Joey Meyer	.05	.02	.01
☐ 192 Paul Mirabella	.05	.02	.01
☐ 193 Paul Molitor	.15	.07	.02
☐ 194 Charlie O'Brien	.05	.02	.01
☐ 195 Dan Plesac	.05	.02	.01
☐ 196 Gary Sheffield	.60	.25	.07
☐ 197 B.J. Surhoff	.05	.02	.01
☐ 198 Dale Sveum	.05	.02	.01
☐ 199 Bill Wegman	.05	.02	.01
☐ 200 Robin Yount	.20	.09	.03
☐ 201 Rafael Belliard	.05	.02	.01
☐ 202 Barry Bonds	.40	.18	.05
☐ 203 Bobby Bonilla	.15	.07	.02
☐ 204 Sid Bream	.05	.02	.01
☐ 205 Benny Distefano	.05	.02	.01
☐ 206 Doug Drabek	.15	.07	.02
☐ 207 Mike Dunne	.05	.02	.01
☐ 208 Felix Fermin	.05	.02	.01
☐ 209 Brian Fisher	.05	.02	.01
☐ 210 Jim Gott	.05	.02	.01
☐ 211 Bob Kipper	.05	.02	.01
☐ 212 Dave LaPoint	.05	.02	.01
☐ 213 Mike LaValliere	.05	.02	.01
☐ 214 Jose Lind	.05	.02	.01
☐ 215 Junior Ortiz	.05	.02	.01
☐ 216 Vicente Palacios	.05	.02	.01
☐ 217 Tom Prince	.05	.02	.01
☐ 218 Gary Redus	.05	.02	.01
☐ 219 R.J. Reynolds	.05	.02	.01
☐ 220 Jeff D. Robinson	.05	.02	.01
☐ 221 John Smiley	.05	.02	.01
☐ 222 Andy Van Slyke	.10	.05	.01
☐ 223 Bob Walk	.05	.02	.01
☐ 224 Glenn Wilson	.05	.02	.01
☐ 225 Jesse Barfield	.05	.02	.01
☐ 226 George Bell	.15	.07	.02
☐ 227 Pat Borders	.10	.05	.01
☐ 228 John Cerutti	.05	.02	.01

☐ 229	Jim Clancy	.05	.02	.01
☐ 230	Mark Eichhorn	.05	.02	.01
☐ 231	Tony Fernandez	.10	.05	.01
☐ 232	Cecil Fielder	.15	.07	.02
☐ 233	Mike Flanagan	.05	.02	.01
☐ 234	Kelly Gruber	.05	.02	.01
☐ 235	Tom Henke	.10	.05	.01
☐ 236	Jimmy Key	.15	.07	.02
☐ 237	Rick Leach	.05	.02	.01
☐ 238	Manny Lee UER	.05	.02	.01
	(Bio says regular			
	shortstop, sic,			
	Tony Fernandez)			
☐ 239	Nelson Liriano	.05	.02	.01
☐ 240	Fred McGriff	.25	.11	.03
☐ 241	Lloyd Moseby	.05	.02	.01
☐ 242	Rance Mulliniks	.05	.02	.01
☐ 243	Jeff Musselman	.05	.02	.01
☐ 244	Dave Stieb	.10	.05	.01
☐ 245	Todd Stottlemyre	.10	.05	.01
☐ 246	Duane Ward	.10	.05	.01
☐ 247	David Wells	.10	.05	.01
☐ 248	Ernie Whitt UER	.05	.02	.01
	(HR total 21,			
	should be 121)			
☐ 249	Luis Aguayo	.05	.02	.01
☐ 250A	Neil Allen	.75	.35	.09
	(Home: Sarasota, FL)			
☐ 250B	Neil Allen	.05	.02	.01
	(Home: Syosset, NY)			
☐ 251	John Candelaria	.05	.02	.01
☐ 252	Jack Clark	.10	.05	.01
☐ 253	Richard Dotson	.05	.02	.01
☐ 254	Rickey Henderson	.15	.07	.02
☐ 255	Tommy John	.15	.07	.02
☐ 256	Roberto Kelly	.10	.05	.01
☐ 257	Al Leiter	.05	.02	.01
☐ 258	Don Mattingly	.40	.18	.05
☐ 259	Dale Mohorcic	.05	.02	.01
☐ 260	Hal Morris	.15	.07	.02
☐ 261	Scott Nielsen	.05	.02	.01
☐ 262	Mike Pagliarulo UER	.05	.02	.01
	(Wrong birthdate)			
☐ 263	Hipolito Pena	.05	.02	.01
☐ 264	Ken Phelps	.05	.02	.01
☐ 265	Willie Randolph	.10	.05	.01
☐ 266	Rick Rhoden	.05	.02	.01
☐ 267	Dave Righetti	.05	.02	.01
☐ 268	Rafael Santana	.05	.02	.01
☐ 269	Steve Shields	.05	.02	.01
☐ 270	Joel Skinner	.05	.02	.01
☐ 271	Don Slaught	.05	.02	.01
☐ 272	Claudell Washington	.05	.02	.01
☐ 273	Gary Ward	.05	.02	.01
☐ 274	Dave Winfield	.15	.07	.02
☐ 275	Luis Aquino	.05	.02	.01
☐ 276	Floyd Bannister	.05	.02	.01
☐ 277	George Brett	.40	.18	.05
☐ 278	Bill Buckner	.10	.05	.01
☐ 279	Nick Capra	.05	.02	.01
☐ 280	Jose DeJesus	.05	.02	.01
☐ 281	Steve Farr	.05	.02	.01
☐ 282	Jerry Don Gleaton	.05	.02	.01
☐ 283	Mark Gubicza	.05	.02	.01
☐ 284	Tom Gordon UER	.15	.07	.02
	(16.2 innings in '88,			
	should be 15.2)			
☐ 285	Bo Jackson	.15	.07	.02
☐ 286	Charlie Leibrandt	.05	.02	.01
☐ 287	Mike Macfarlane	.10	.05	.01
☐ 288	Jeff Montgomery	.10	.05	.01
☐ 289	Bill Pecota UER	.05	.02	.01
	(Photo actually			
	Brad Wellman)			
☐ 290	Jamie Quirk	.05	.02	.01
☐ 291	Bret Saberhagen	.15	.07	.02
☐ 292	Kevin Seitzer	.05	.02	.01
☐ 293	Kurt Stillwell	.05	.02	.01
☐ 294	Pat Tabler	.05	.02	.01
☐ 295	Danny Tartabull	.10	.05	.01
☐ 296	Gary Thurman	.05	.02	.01
☐ 297	Frank White	.10	.05	.01
☐ 298	Willie Wilson	.05	.02	.01
☐ 299	Roberto Alomar	.50	.23	.06
☐ 300	Sandy Alomar Jr. UER	.20	.09	.03
	(Wrong birthdate, says			
	6/16/66, should say			
	6/18/66)			
☐ 301	Chris Brown	.05	.02	.01
☐ 302	Mike Brumley UER	.05	.02	.01
	(133 hits in '88,			
	should be 134)			
☐ 303	Mark Davis	.05	.02	.01
☐ 304	Mark Grant	.05	.02	.01
☐ 305	Tony Gwynn	.30	.14	.04
☐ 306	Greg W. Harris	.05	.02	.01
☐ 307	Andy Hawkins	.05	.02	.01
☐ 308	Jimmy Jones	.05	.02	.01
☐ 309	John Kruk	.15	.07	.02
☐ 310	Dave Leiper	.05	.02	.01
☐ 311	Carmelo Martinez	.05	.02	.01
☐ 312	Lance McCullers	.05	.02	.01
☐ 313	Keith Moreland	.05	.02	.01
☐ 314	Dennis Rasmussen	.05	.02	.01
☐ 315	Randy Ready UER	.05	.02	.01
	(1214 games in '88,			
	should be 114)			
☐ 316	Benito Santiago	.10	.05	.01
☐ 317	Eric Show	.05	.02	.01
☐ 318	Todd Simmons	.05	.02	.01
☐ 319	Garry Templeton	.05	.02	.01
☐ 320	Dickie Thon	.05	.02	.01
☐ 321	Ed Whitson	.05	.02	.01
☐ 322	Marvell Wynne	.05	.02	.01
☐ 323	Mike Aldrete	.05	.02	.01
☐ 324	Brett Butler	.15	.07	.02
☐ 325	Will Clark UER	.20	.09	.03
	(Three consecutive			
	100 RBI seasons)			
☐ 326	Kelly Downs UER	.05	.02	.01
	('88 stats missing)			
☐ 327	Dave Dravecky	.10	.05	.01
☐ 328	Scott Garrelts	.05	.02	.01
☐ 329	Atlee Hammaker	.05	.02	.01
☐ 330	Charlie Hayes	.20	.09	.03
☐ 331	Mike Krukow	.05	.02	.01
☐ 332	Craig Lefferts	.05	.02	.01
☐ 333	Candy Maldonado	.05	.02	.01
☐ 334	Kirt Manwaring UER	.05	.02	.01
	(Bats Rights)			
☐ 335	Bob Melvin	.05	.02	.01
☐ 336	Kevin Mitchell	.10	.05	.01
☐ 337	Donell Nixon	.05	.02	.01
☐ 338	Tony Perezchica	.05	.02	.01
☐ 339	Joe Price	.05	.02	.01
☐ 340	Rick Reuschel	.05	.02	.01
☐ 341	Earnest Riles	.05	.02	.01
☐ 342	Don Robinson	.05	.02	.01
☐ 343	Chris Speier	.05	.02	.01
☐ 344	Robby Thompson UER	.10	.05	.01
	(West Plam Beach)			
☐ 345	Jose Uribe	.05	.02	.01

☐ 346	Matt Williams	.50	.23	.06
☐ 347	Trevor Wilson	.05	.02	.01
☐ 348	Juan Agosto	.05	.02	.01
☐ 349	Larry Andersen	.05	.02	.01
☐ 350A	Alan Ashby ERR	2.00	.90	.25
	(Throws Rig)			
☐ 350B	Alan Ashby COR	.05	.02	.01
☐ 351	Kevin Bass	.05	.02	.01
☐ 352	Buddy Bell	.10	.05	.01
☐ 353	Craig Biggio	.60	.25	.07
☐ 354	Danny Darwin	.05	.02	.01
☐ 355	Glenn Davis	.05	.02	.01
☐ 356	Jim Deshaies	.05	.02	.01
☐ 357	Bill Doran	.05	.02	.01
☐ 358	John Fishel	.05	.02	.01
☐ 359	Billy Hatcher	.05	.02	.01
☐ 360	Bob Knepper	.05	.02	.01
☐ 361	Louie Meadows UER	.05	.02	.01
	(Bio says 10 EBH's			
	and 6 SB's in '88,			
	should be 3 and 4)			
☐ 362	Dave Meads	.05	.02	.01
☐ 363	Jim Pankovits	.05	.02	.01
☐ 364	Terry Puhl	.05	.02	.01
☐ 365	Rafael Ramirez	.05	.02	.01
☐ 366	Craig Reynolds	.05	.02	.01
☐ 367	Mike Scott	.05	.02	.01
	(Card number listed			
	as 368 on Astros CL)			
☐ 368	Nolan Ryan	.75	.35	.09
	(Card number listed			
	as 367 on Astros CL)			
☐ 369	Dave Smith	.05	.02	.01
☐ 370	Gerald Young	.05	.02	.01
☐ 371	Hubie Brooks	.05	.02	.01
☐ 372	Tim Burke	.05	.02	.01
☐ 373	John Dopson	.05	.02	.01
☐ 374	Mike R. Fitzgerald	.05	.02	.01
☐ 375	Tom Foley	.05	.02	.01
☐ 376	Andres Galarraga UER	.15	.07	.02
	(Home: Caracus)			
☐ 377	Neal Heaton	.05	.02	.01
☐ 378	Joe Hesketh	.05	.02	.01
☐ 379	Brian Holman	.05	.02	.01
☐ 380	Rex Hudler	.05	.02	.01
☐ 381	Randy Johnson UER	1.00	.45	.12
	(Innings for '85 and			
	'86 shown as 27 and			
	120, should be 27.1			
	and 119.2)			
☐ 382	Wallace Johnson	.05	.02	.01
☐ 383	Tracy Jones	.05	.02	.01
☐ 384	Dave Martinez	.05	.02	.01
☐ 385	Dennis Martinez	.10	.05	.01
☐ 386	Andy McGaffigan	.05	.02	.01
☐ 387	Otis Nixon	.10	.05	.01
☐ 388	Johnny Paredes	.05	.02	.01
☐ 389	Jeff Parrett	.05	.02	.01
☐ 390	Pascual Perez	.05	.02	.01
☐ 391	Tim Raines	.15	.07	.02
☐ 392	Luis Rivera	.05	.02	.01
☐ 393	Nelson Santovenia	.05	.02	.01
☐ 394	Bryn Smith	.05	.02	.01
☐ 395	Tim Wallach	.05	.02	.01
☐ 396	Andy Allanson UER	.05	.02	.01
	(1214 hits in '88,			
	should be 114)			
☐ 397	Rod Allen	.05	.02	.01
☐ 398	Scott Bailes	.05	.02	.01
☐ 399	Tom Candiotti	.05	.02	.01
☐ 400	Joe Carter	.20	.09	.03

☐ 401	Carmen Castillo UER	.05	.02	.01
	(After All-Star Break			
	batting 2.50)			
☐ 402	Dave Clark UER	.05	.02	.01
	(Card front shows			
	position as Rookie;			
	after All-Star Break			
	batting 3.14)			
☐ 403	John Farrell UER	.05	.02	.01
	(Typo in runs			
	allowed in '88)			
☐ 404	Julio Franco	.10	.05	.01
☐ 405	Don Gordon	.05	.02	.01
☐ 406	Mel Hall	.05	.02	.01
☐ 407	Brad Havens	.05	.02	.01
☐ 408	Brook Jacoby	.05	.02	.01
☐ 409	Doug Jones	.10	.05	.01
☐ 410	Jeff Kaiser	.05	.02	.01
☐ 411	Luis Medina	.05	.02	.01
☐ 412	Cory Snyder	.05	.02	.01
☐ 413	Greg Swindell	.10	.05	.01
☐ 414	Ron Tingley UER	.05	.02	.01
	(Hit HR in first ML			
	at-bat, should be			
	first AL at-bat)			
☐ 415	Willie Upshaw	.05	.02	.01
☐ 416	Ron Washington	.05	.02	.01
☐ 417	Rich Yett	.05	.02	.01
☐ 418	Damon Berryhill	.05	.02	.01
☐ 419	Mike Bielecki	.05	.02	.01
☐ 420	Doug Dascenzo	.05	.02	.01
☐ 421	Jody Davis UER	.05	.02	.01
	(Braves stats for			
	'88 missing)			
☐ 422	Andre Dawson	.15	.07	.02
☐ 423	Frank DiPino	.05	.02	.01
☐ 424	Shawon Dunston	.10	.05	.01
☐ 425	Rich Gossage	.15	.07	.02
☐ 426	Mark Grace UER	.15	.07	.02
	(Minor League stats			
	for '88 missing)			
☐ 427	Mike Harkey	.05	.02	.01
☐ 428	Darrin Jackson	.10	.05	.01
☐ 429	Les Lancaster	.05	.02	.01
☐ 430	Vance Law	.05	.02	.01
☐ 431	Greg Maddux	.75	.35	.09
☐ 432	Jamie Moyer	.05	.02	.01
☐ 433	Al Nipper	.05	.02	.01
☐ 434	Rafael Palmeiro UER	.25	.11	.03
	(170 hits in '88,			
	should be 178)			
☐ 435	Pat Perry	.05	.02	.01
☐ 436	Jeff Pico	.05	.02	.01
☐ 437	Ryne Sandberg	.30	.14	.04
☐ 438	Calvin Schiraldi	.05	.02	.01
☐ 439	Rick Sutcliffe	.10	.05	.01
☐ 440A	Manny Trillo ERR	2.00	.90	.25
	(Throws Rig)			
☐ 440B	Manny Trillo COR	.05	.02	.01
☐ 441	Gary Varsho UER	.05	.02	.01
	(Wrong birthdate;			
	.303 should be .302;			
	11/28 should be 9/19)			
☐ 442	Mitch Webster	.05	.02	.01
☐ 443	Luis Alicea	.05	.02	.01
☐ 444	Tom Brunansky	.05	.02	.01
☐ 445	Vince Coleman UER	.10	.05	.01
	(Third straight with			
	83, should be fourth			
	straight with 81)			
☐ 446	John Costello UER	.05	.02	.01

(Home California,
should be New York)
- 447 Danny Cox ... .05 .02 .01
- 448 Ken Dayley ... .05 .02 .01
- 449 Jose DeLeon ... .05 .02 .01
- 450 Curt Ford ... .05 .02 .01
- 451 Pedro Guerrero ... .10 .05 .01
- 452 Bob Horner ... .05 .02 .01
- 453 Tim Jones ... .05 .02 .01
- 454 Steve Lake ... .05 .02 .01
- 455 Joe Magrane UER ... .05 .02 .01
(Des Moines, IO)
- 456 Greg Mathews ... .05 .02 .01
- 457 Willie McGee ... .10 .05 .01
- 458 Larry McWilliams ... .05 .02 .01
- 459 Jose Oquendo ... .05 .02 .01
- 460 Tony Pena ... .05 .02 .01
- 461 Terry Pendleton ... .15 .07 .02
- 462 Steve Peters UER ... .05 .02 .01
(Lives in Harrah,
not Harah)
- 463 Ozzie Smith ... .30 .14 .04
- 464 Scott Terry ... .05 .02 .01
- 465 Denny Walling ... .05 .02 .01
- 466 Todd Worrell ... .05 .02 .01
- 467 Tony Armas UER ... .05 .02 .01
(Before All-Star Break
batting 2.39)
- 468 Dante Bichette ... .75 .35 .09
- 469 Bob Boone ... .10 .05 .01
- 470 Terry Clark ... .05 .02 .01
- 471 Stew Cliburn ... .05 .02 .01
- 472 Mike Cook UER ... .05 .02 .01
(TM near Angels logo
missing from front)
- 473 Sherman Corbett ... .05 .02 .01
- 474 Chili Davis ... .15 .07 .02
- 475 Brian Downing ... .05 .02 .01
- 476 Jim Eppard ... .05 .02 .01
- 477 Chuck Finley ... .10 .05 .01
- 478 Willie Fraser ... .05 .02 .01
- 479 Bryan Harvey UER ... .10 .05 .01
(ML record shows 0-0,
should be 7-5)
- 480 Jack Howell ... .05 .02 .01
- 481 Wally Joyner UER ... .10 .05 .01
(Yorba Linda, GA)
- 482 Jack Lazorko ... .05 .02 .01
- 483 Kirk McCaskill ... .05 .02 .01
- 484 Mark McLemore ... .05 .02 .01
- 485 Greg Minton ... .05 .02 .01
- 486 Dan Petry ... .05 .02 .01
- 487 Johnny Ray ... .05 .02 .01
- 488 Dick Schofield ... .05 .02 .01
- 489 Devon White ... .15 .07 .02
- 490 Mike Witt ... .05 .02 .01
- 491 Harold Baines ... .15 .07 .02
- 492 Daryl Boston ... .05 .02 .01
- 493 Ivan Calderon UER ... .05 .02 .01
('80 stats shifted)
- 494 Mike Diaz ... .05 .02 .01
- 495 Carlton Fisk ... .15 .07 .02
- 496 Dave Gallagher ... .05 .02 .01
- 497 Ozzie Guillen ... .10 .05 .01
- 498 Shawn Hillegas ... .05 .02 .01
- 499 Lance Johnson ... .10 .05 .01
- 500 Barry Jones ... .05 .02 .01
- 501 Bill Long ... .05 .02 .01
- 502 Steve Lyons ... .05 .02 .01
- 503 Fred Manrique ... .05 .02 .01
- 504 Jack McDowell ... .15 .07 .02
- 505 Donn Pall ... .05 .02 .01
- 506 Kelly Paris ... .05 .02 .01
- 507 Dan Pasqua ... .05 .02 .01
- 508 Ken Patterson ... .05 .02 .01
- 509 Melido Perez ... .05 .02 .01
- 510 Jerry Reuss ... .05 .02 .01
- 511 Mark Salas ... .05 .02 .01
- 512 Bobby Thigpen UER ... .05 .02 .01
('86 ERA 4.69,
should be 4.68)
- 513 Mike Woodard ... .05 .02 .01
- 514 Bob Brower ... .05 .02 .01
- 515 Steve Buechele ... .05 .02 .01
- 516 Jose Cecena ... .05 .02 .01
- 517 Cecil Espy ... .05 .02 .01
- 518 Scott Fletcher ... .05 .02 .01
- 519 Cecilio Guante ... .05 .02 .01
('87 Yankee stats
are off-centered)
- 520 Jose Guzman ... .05 .02 .01
- 521 Ray Hayward ... .05 .02 .01
- 522 Charlie Hough ... .10 .05 .01
- 523 Pete Incaviglia ... .10 .05 .01
- 524 Mike Jeffcoat ... .05 .02 .01
- 525 Paul Kilgus ... .05 .02 .01
- 526 Chad Kreuter ... .05 .02 .01
- 527 Jeff Kunkel ... .05 .02 .01
- 528 Oddibe McDowell ... .05 .02 .01
- 529 Pete O'Brien ... .05 .02 .01
- 530 Geno Petralli ... .05 .02 .01
- 531 Jeff Russell ... .05 .02 .01
- 532 Ruben Sierra ... .15 .07 .02
- 533 Mike Stanley ... .10 .05 .01
- 534A Ed VandeBerg ERR ... 2.00 .90 .25
(Throws Lef)
- 534B Ed VandeBerg COR ... .05 .02 .01
- 535 Curtis Wilkerson ERR ... .05 .02 .01
(Pitcher headings
at bottom)
- 536 Mitch Williams ... .10 .05 .01
- 537 Bobby Witt UER ... .10 .05 .01
('85 ERA .643,
should be 6.43)
- 538 Steve Balboni ... .05 .02 .01
- 539 Scott Bankhead ... .05 .02 .01
- 540 Scott Bradley ... .05 .02 .01
- 541 Mickey Brantley ... .05 .02 .01
- 542 Jay Buhner ... .15 .07 .02
- 543 Mike Campbell ... .05 .02 .01
- 544 Darnell Coles ... .05 .02 .01
- 545 Henry Cotto ... .05 .02 .01
- 546 Alvin Davis ... .05 .02 .01
- 547 Mario Diaz ... .05 .02 .01
- 548 Ken Griffey Jr. ... 5.00 2.20 .60
- 549 Erik Hanson ... .25 .11 .03
- 550 Mike Jackson UER ... .05 .02 .01
(Lifetime ERA 3.345,
should be 3.45)
- 551 Mark Langston ... .15 .07 .02
- 552 Edgar Martinez ... .20 .09 .03
- 553 Bill McGuire ... .05 .02 .01
- 554 Mike Moore ... .05 .02 .01
- 555 Jim Presley ... .05 .02 .01
- 556 Rey Quinones ... .05 .02 .01
- 557 Jerry Reed ... .05 .02 .01
- 558 Harold Reynolds ... .05 .02 .01
- 559 Mike Schooler ... .05 .02 .01
- 560 Bill Swift ... .10 .05 .01
- 561 Dave Valle ... .05 .02 .01
- 562 Steve Bedrosian ... .05 .02 .01
- 563 Phil Bradley ... .05 .02 .01

☐ 564	Don Carman	.05	.02	.01
☐ 565	Bob Dernier	.05	.02	.01
☐ 566	Marvin Freeman	.05	.02	.01
☐ 567	Todd Frohwirth	.05	.02	.01
☐ 568	Greg Gross	.05	.02	.01
☐ 569	Kevin Gross	.05	.02	.01
☐ 570	Greg A. Harris	.05	.02	.01
☐ 571	Von Hayes	.05	.02	.01
☐ 572	Chris James	.05	.02	.01
☐ 573	Steve Jeltz	.05	.02	.01
☐ 574	Ron Jones UER	.05	.02	.01
	(Led IL in '88 with 85, should be 75)			
☐ 575	Ricky Jordan	.05	.02	.01
☐ 576	Mike Maddux	.05	.02	.01
☐ 577	David Palmer	.05	.02	.01
☐ 578	Lance Parrish	.10	.05	.01
☐ 579	Shane Rawley	.05	.02	.01
☐ 580	Bruce Ruffin	.05	.02	.01
☐ 581	Juan Samuel	.05	.02	.01
☐ 582	Mike Schmidt	.25	.11	.03
☐ 583	Kent Tekulve	.05	.02	.01
☐ 584	Milt Thompson UER	.05	.02	.01
	(19 hits in '88, should be 109)			
☐ 585	Jose Alvarez	.05	.02	.01
☐ 586	Paul Assenmacher	.05	.02	.01
☐ 587	Bruce Benedict	.05	.02	.01
☐ 588	Jeff Blauser	.15	.07	.02
☐ 589	Terry Blocker	.05	.02	.01
☐ 590	Ron Gant	.25	.11	.03
☐ 591	Tom Glavine	.40	.18	.05
☐ 592	Tommy Gregg	.05	.02	.01
☐ 593	Albert Hall	.05	.02	.01
☐ 594	Dion James	.05	.02	.01
☐ 595	Rick Mahler	.05	.02	.01
☐ 596	Dale Murphy	.15	.07	.02
☐ 597	Gerald Perry	.05	.02	.01
☐ 598	Charlie Puleo	.05	.02	.01
☐ 599	Ted Simmons	.10	.05	.01
☐ 600	Pete Smith	.05	.02	.01
☐ 601	Zane Smith	.05	.02	.01
☐ 602	John Smoltz	.40	.18	.05
☐ 603	Bruce Sutter	.10	.05	.01
☐ 604	Andres Thomas	.05	.02	.01
☐ 605	Ozzie Virgil	.05	.02	.01
☐ 606	Brady Anderson	.40	.18	.05
☐ 607	Jeff Ballard	.05	.02	.01
☐ 608	Jose Bautista	.05	.02	.01
☐ 609	Ken Gerhart	.05	.02	.01
☐ 610	Terry Kennedy	.05	.02	.01
☐ 611	Eddie Murray	.20	.09	.03
☐ 612	Carl Nichols UER	.05	.02	.01
	(Before All-Star Break batting 1.88)			
☐ 613	Tom Niedenfuer	.05	.02	.01
☐ 614	Joe Orsulak	.05	.02	.01
☐ 615	Oswald Peraza UER	.05	.02	.01
	(Shown as Oswaldo)			
☐ 616A	Bill Ripken ERR	5.00	2.20	.60
	(Rick Face written on knob of bat)			
☐ 616B	Bill Ripken	40.00	18.00	5.00
	(Bat knob whited out)			
☐ 616C	Bill Ripken	5.00	2.20	.60
	(Words on bat knob scribbled out)			
☐ 616D	Bill Ripken DP	.10	.05	.01
	(Black box covering bat knob)			

☐ 617	Cal Ripken	.75	.35	.09
☐ 618	Dave Schmidt	.05	.02	.01
☐ 619	Rick Schu	.05	.02	.01
☐ 620	Larry Sheets	.05	.02	.01
☐ 621	Doug Sisk	.05	.02	.01
☐ 622	Pete Stanicek	.05	.02	.01
☐ 623	Mickey Tettleton	.10	.05	.01
☐ 624	Jay Tibbs	.05	.02	.01
☐ 625	Jim Traber	.05	.02	.01
☐ 626	Mark Williamson	.05	.02	.01
☐ 627	Craig Worthington	.05	.02	.01
☐ 628	Speed/Power	.15	.07	.02
	Jose Canseco			
☐ 629	Pitcher Perfect	.05	.02	.01
	Tom Browning			
☐ 630	Like Father/Like Sons	.30	.14	.04
	Roberto Alomar			
	Sandy Alomar Jr.			
	(Names on card listed in wrong order) UER			
☐ 631	NL All Stars UER	.25	.11	.03
	Will Clark			
	Rafael Palmeiro			
	(Gallaraga, sic; Clark 3 consecutive 100 RBI seasons; third with 102 RBI's)			
☐ 632	Homeruns - Coast	.10	.05	.01
	to Coast UER			
	Darryl Strawberry			
	Will Clark (Homeruns should be two words)			
☐ 633	Hot Corners - Hot	.10	.05	.01
	Hitters UER			
	Wade Boggs			
	Carney Lansford			
	(Boggs hit .366 in '86, should be '88)			
☐ 634	Triple A's	.10	.05	.01
	Jose Canseco			
	Terry Steinbach			
	Mark McGwire			
☐ 635	Dual Heat	.05	.02	.01
	Mark Davis			
	Dwight Gooden			
☐ 636	NL Pitching Power UER	.10	.05	.01
	Danny Jackson			
	David Cone			
	(Hersheiser, sic)			
☐ 637	Cannon Arms UER	.10	.05	.01
	Chris Sabo			
	Bobby Bonilla			
	(Bobby Bonds, sic)			
☐ 638	Double Trouble UER	.10	.05	.01
	Andres Galarraga			
	(Misspelled Gallaraga on card back)			
	Gerald Perry			
☐ 639	Power Center	.15	.07	.02
	Kirby Puckett			
	Eric Davis			
☐ 640	Steve Wilson and	.05	.02	.01
	Cameron Drew			
☐ 641	Kevin Brown and	.15	.07	.02
	Kevin Reimer			
☐ 642	Brad Pounders and	.05	.02	.01
	Jerald Clark			
☐ 643	Mike Capel and	.05	.02	.01
	Drew Hall			
☐ 644	Joe Girardi and	.10	.05	.01
	Rolando Roomes			

☐ 645	Lenny Harris and Marty Brown	.05	.02	.01
☐ 646	Luis DeLosSantos and Jim Campbell	.05	.02	.01
☐ 647	Randy Kramer and Miguel Garcia	.05	.02	.01
☐ 648	Torey Lovullo and Robert Palacios	.05	.02	.01
☐ 649	Jim Corsi and Bob Milacki	.05	.02	.01
☐ 650	Grady Hall and Mike Rochford	.05	.02	.01
☐ 651	Terry Taylor and Vance Lovelace	.05	.02	.01
☐ 652	Ken Hill and Dennis Cook	.50	.23	.06
☐ 653	Scott Service and Shane Turner	.05	.02	.01
☐ 654	CL: Oakland/Mets Dodgers/Red Sox (10 Hendersor; 68 Jess Orosco)	.05	.02	.01
☐ 655A	CL: Twins/Tigers ERR Reds/Brewers (179 Boslo and Twins/Tigers positions listed)	.05	.02	.01
☐ 655B	CL: Twins/Tigers COR Reds/Brewers (179 Boslo but Twins/Tigers positions not listed)	.05	.02	.01
☐ 656	CL: Pirates/Blue Jays Yankees/Royals (225 Jess Barfield)	.05	.02	.01
☐ 657	CL: Padres/Giants Astros/Expos (367/368 wrong)	.05	.02	.01
☐ 658	CL: Indians/Cubs Cardinals/Angels (449 Deleon)	.05	.02	.01
☐ 659	CL: White Sox/Rangers Mariners/Phillies	.05	.02	.01
☐ 660	CL: Braves/Orioles Specials/Checklists (632 hyphenated differently and 650 Hall; 595 Rich Mahler; 619 Rich Schu)	.05	.02	.01

1989 Fleer Update

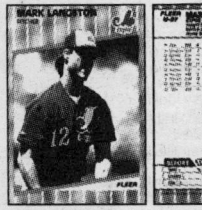 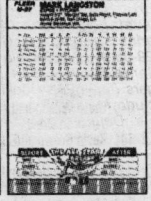

The 1989 Fleer Update set contains 132 standard-size cards. The fronts are gray with white pinstripes. The vertically oriented backs show lifetime stats and performance "Before and After the All-Star Break". The set numbering is in team order with players within teams ordered alphabetically. The set does includes special cards for Nolan Ryan's 5,000th strikeout and Mike Schmidt's retirement. Rookie Cards include Kevin Appier, Joey (Albert) Belle, Deion Sanders, Greg Vaughn. Robin Ventura and Todd Zeile. Fleer did NOT produce a limited (tin) edition version of this set with glossy coating.

	MINT	NRMT	EXC
COMPLETE FACT.SET (132)	6.00	2.70	.75
COMMON CARD (1-132)	.05	.02	.01

☐ 1	Phil Bradley	.05	.02	.01
☐ 2	Mike Devereaux	.10	.05	.01
☐ 3	Steve Finley	.20	.09	.03
☐ 4	Kevin Hickey	.05	.02	.01
☐ 5	Brian Holton	.05	.02	.01
☐ 6	Bob Milacki	.05	.02	.01
☐ 7	Randy Milligan	.05	.02	.01
☐ 8	John Dopson	.05	.02	.01
☐ 9	Nick Esasky	.05	.02	.01
☐ 10	Rob Murphy	.05	.02	.01
☐ 11	Jim Abbott	.25	.11	.03
☐ 12	Bert Blyleven	.15	.07	.02
☐ 13	Jeff Manto	.10	.05	.01
☐ 14	Bob McClure	.05	.02	.01
☐ 15	Lance Parrish	.10	.05	.01
☐ 16	Lee Stevens	.05	.02	.01
☐ 17	Claudell Washington	.05	.02	.01
☐ 18	Mark Davis	.05	.02	.01
☐ 19	Eric King	.05	.02	.01
☐ 20	Ron Kittle	.05	.02	.01
☐ 21	Matt Merullo	.05	.02	.01
☐ 22	Steve Rosenberg	.05	.02	.01
☐ 23	Robin Ventura	.50	.23	.06
☐ 24	Keith Atherton	.05	.02	.01
☐ 25	Joey Belle	3.00	1.35	.35
☐ 26	Jerry Browne	.05	.02	.01
☐ 27	Felix Fermin	.05	.02	.01
☐ 28	Brad Komminsk	.05	.02	.01
☐ 29	Pete O'Brien	.05	.02	.01
☐ 30	Mike Brumley	.05	.02	.01
☐ 31	Tracy Jones	.05	.02	.01
☐ 32	Mike Schwabe	.05	.02	.01
☐ 33	Gary Ward	.05	.02	.01
☐ 34	Frank Williams	.05	.02	.01
☐ 35	Kevin Appier	.50	.23	.06
☐ 36	Bob Boone	.10	.05	.01
☐ 37	Luis DeLosSantos	.05	.02	.01
☐ 38	Jim Eisenreich	.05	.02	.01
☐ 39	Jaime Navarro	.25	.11	.03
☐ 40	Bill Spiers	.05	.02	.01
☐ 41	Greg Vaughn	.30	.14	.04
☐ 42	Randy Veres	.05	.02	.01
☐ 43	Wally Backman	.05	.02	.01
☐ 44	Shane Rawley	.05	.02	.01
☐ 45	Steve Balboni	.05	.02	.01
☐ 46	Jesse Barfield	.05	.02	.01
☐ 47	Alvaro Espinoza	.05	.02	.01
☐ 48	Bob Geren	.05	.02	.01
☐ 49	Mel Hall	.05	.02	.01
☐ 50	Andy Hawkins	.05	.02	.01
☐ 51	Hensley Meulens	.05	.02	.01
☐ 52	Steve Sax	.05	.02	.01
☐ 53	Deion Sanders	1.50	.70	.19

☐ 54	Rickey Henderson	.15	.07	.02
☐ 55	Mike Moore	.05	.02	.01
☐ 56	Tony Phillips	.15	.07	.02
☐ 57	Greg Briley	.05	.02	.01
☐ 58	Gene Harris	.05	.02	.01
☐ 59	Randy Johnson	1.00	.45	.12
☐ 60	Jeffrey Leonard	.05	.02	.01
☐ 61	Dennis Powell	.05	.02	.01
☐ 62	Omar Vizquel	.25	.11	.03
☐ 63	Kevin Brown	.10	.05	.01
☐ 64	Julio Franco	.10	.05	.01
☐ 65	Jamie Moyer	.05	.02	.01
☐ 66	Rafael Palmeiro	.25	.11	.03
☐ 67	Nolan Ryan	1.50	.70	.19
☐ 68	Francisco Cabrera	.10	.05	.01
☐ 69	Junior Felix	.05	.02	.01
☐ 70	Al Leiter	.05	.02	.01
☐ 71	Alex Sanchez	.05	.02	.01
☐ 72	Geronimo Berroa	.10	.05	.01
☐ 73	Derek Lilliquist	.05	.02	.01
☐ 74	Lonnie Smith	.05	.02	.01
☐ 75	Jeff Treadway	.05	.02	.01
☐ 76	Paul Kilgus	.05	.02	.01
☐ 77	Lloyd McClendon	.05	.02	.01
☐ 78	Scott Sanderson	.05	.02	.01
☐ 79	Dwight Smith	.05	.02	.01
☐ 80	Jerome Walton	.05	.02	.01
☐ 81	Mitch Williams	.10	.05	.01
☐ 82	Steve Wilson	.05	.02	.01
☐ 83	Todd Benzinger	.05	.02	.01
☐ 84	Ken Griffey Sr.	.10	.05	.01
☐ 85	Rick Mahler	.05	.02	.01
☐ 86	Rolando Roomes	.05	.02	.01
☐ 87	Scott Scudder	.05	.02	.01
☐ 88	Jim Clancy	.05	.02	.01
☐ 89	Rick Rhoden	.05	.02	.01
☐ 90	Dan Schatzeder	.05	.02	.01
☐ 91	Mike Morgan	.05	.02	.01
☐ 92	Eddie Murray	.20	.09	.03
☐ 93	Willie Randolph	.10	.05	.01
☐ 94	Ray Searage	.05	.02	.01
☐ 95	Mike Aldrete	.05	.02	.01
☐ 96	Kevin Gross	.05	.02	.01
☐ 97	Mark Langston	.15	.07	.02
☐ 98	Spike Owen	.05	.02	.01
☐ 99	Zane Smith	.05	.02	.01
☐ 100	Don Aase	.05	.02	.01
☐ 101	Barry Lyons	.05	.02	.01
☐ 102	Juan Samuel	.05	.02	.01
☐ 103	Wally Whitehurst	.05	.02	.01
☐ 104	Dennis Cook	.05	.02	.01
☐ 105	Len Dykstra	.15	.07	.02
☐ 106	Charlie Hayes	.15	.07	.02
☐ 107	Tommy Herr	.05	.02	.01
☐ 108	Ken Howell	.05	.02	.01
☐ 109	John Kruk	.15	.07	.02
☐ 110	Roger McDowell	.05	.02	.01
☐ 111	Terry Mulholland	.10	.05	.01
☐ 112	Jeff Parrett	.05	.02	.01
☐ 113	Neal Heaton	.05	.02	.01
☐ 114	Jeff King	.10	.05	.01
☐ 115	Randy Kramer	.05	.02	.01
☐ 116	Bill Landrum	.05	.02	.01
☐ 117	Cris Carpenter	.05	.02	.01
☐ 118	Frank DiPino	.05	.02	.01
☐ 119	Ken Hill	.50	.23	.06
☐ 120	Dan Quisenberry	.10	.05	.01
☐ 121	Milt Thompson	.05	.02	.01
☐ 122	Todd Zeile	.40	.18	.05
☐ 123	Jack Clark	.10	.05	.01
☐ 124	Bruce Hurst	.05	.02	.01

☐ 125	Mark Parent	.05	.02	.01
☐ 126	Bip Roberts	.10	.05	.01
☐ 127	Jeff Brantley UER	.05	.02	.01
	(Photo actually			
	Joe Kmak)			
☐ 128	Terry Kennedy	.05	.02	.01
☐ 129	Mike LaCoss	.05	.02	.01
☐ 130	Greg Litton	.05	.02	.01
☐ 131	Mike Schmidt	.50	.23	.06
☐ 132	Checklist 1-132	.05	.02	.01

1990 Fleer

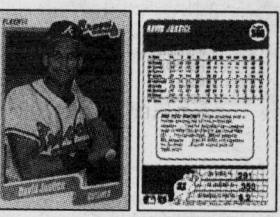

The 1990 Fleer set contains 660 standard-size (2 1/2" by 3 1/2") cards. The outer front borders are white; the inner, ribbon-like borders are different depending on the team. The vertically oriented backs are white, red, pink, and navy. The set is again ordered numerically by teams, followed by combination cards, rookie prospect pairs, and checklists. Fleer arranged the teams according to regular season team record. The complete team ordering is as follows: Oakland A's (1-24), Chicago Cubs (25-49), San Francisco Giants (50-75), Toronto Blue Jays (76-99), Kansas City Royals (100-124), California Angels (125-148), San Diego Padres (149-171), Baltimore Orioles (172-195), New York Mets (196-219), Houston Astros (220-241), St. Louis Cardinals (242-265), Boston Red Sox (266-289), Texas Rangers (290-315), Milwaukee Brewers (316-340), Montreal Expos (341-364), Minnesota Twins (365-388), Los Angeles Dodgers (389-411), Cincinnati Reds (412-435), New York Yankees (436-458), Pittsburgh Pirates (459-482), Cleveland Indians (483-504), Seattle Mariners (505-528), Chicago White Sox (529-551), Philadelphia Phillies (552-573), Atlanta Braves (574-598), and Detroit Tigers (599-620). Rookie Cards in this set include Moises Alou, Eric Anthony, Alex Cole, Delino DeShields, Juan Gonzalez, Tommy Greene, Marquis Grissom, Dave Justice, Derrick May, Ben McDonald, Sammy Sosa, and Larry Walker. The following five cards have minor printing differences, 6, 162, 260, 469, and 550; these differences are so minor that collectors have deemed them not significant enough to effect a price differential. Fleer also pro-

duced a separate set for Canada. The Canadian set only differs from the regular set in that it shows copyright "FLEER LTD./LTEE PTD. IN CANADA" on the card backs. Although these Canadian cards were undoubtedly produced in much lesser quantities compared to the U.S. issue, the fact that the versions are so similar has kept the demand (and the price differential) for the Canadian cards down.

	MINT	NRMT	EXC
COMPLETE SET (660)	8.00	3.60	1.00
COMPLETE RETAIL SET (660)	8.00	3.60	1.00
COMPLETE HOBBY SET (672)	10.00	4.50	1.25
COMPLETE WORLD SERIES (12)	1.00	.45	.12
COMMON CARD (1-660)	.05	.02	.01

☐ 1	Lance Blankenship	.05	.02	.01
☐ 2	Todd Burns	.05	.02	.01
☐ 3	Jose Canseco	.20	.09	.03
☐ 4	Jim Corsi	.05	.02	.01
☐ 5	Storm Davis	.05	.02	.01
☐ 6	Dennis Eckersley	.15	.07	.02
☐ 7	Mike Gallego	.05	.02	.01
☐ 8	Ron Hassey	.05	.02	.01
☐ 9	Dave Henderson	.05	.02	.01
☐ 10	Rickey Henderson	.15	.07	.02
☐ 11	Rick Honeycutt	.05	.02	.01
☐ 12	Stan Javier	.05	.02	.01
☐ 13	Felix Jose	.05	.02	.01
☐ 14	Carney Lansford	.10	.05	.01
☐ 15	Mark McGwire UER	.15	.07	.02
	(1989 runs listed as 4, should be 74)			
☐ 16	Mike Moore	.05	.02	.01
☐ 17	Gene Nelson	.05	.02	.01
☐ 18	Dave Parker	.10	.05	.01
☐ 19	Tony Phillips	.15	.07	.02
☐ 20	Terry Steinbach	.10	.05	.01
☐ 21	Dave Stewart	.15	.07	.02
☐ 22	Walt Weiss	.05	.02	.01
☐ 23	Bob Welch	.05	.02	.01
☐ 24	Curt Young	.05	.02	.01
☐ 25	Paul Assenmacher	.05	.02	.01
☐ 26	Damon Berryhill	.05	.02	.01
☐ 27	Mike Bielecki	.05	.02	.01
☐ 28	Kevin Blankenship	.05	.02	.01
☐ 29	Andre Dawson	.15	.07	.02
☐ 30	Shawon Dunston	.05	.02	.01
☐ 31	Joe Girardi	.05	.02	.01
☐ 32	Mark Grace	.15	.07	.02
☐ 33	Mike Harkey	.05	.02	.01
☐ 34	Paul Kilgus	.05	.02	.01
☐ 35	Les Lancaster	.05	.02	.01
☐ 36	Vance Law	.05	.02	.01
☐ 37	Greg Maddux	.60	.25	.07
☐ 38	Lloyd McClendon	.05	.02	.01
☐ 39	Jeff Pico	.05	.02	.01
☐ 40	Ryne Sandberg	.30	.14	.04
☐ 41	Scott Sanderson	.05	.02	.01
☐ 42	Dwight Smith	.05	.02	.01
☐ 43	Rick Sutcliffe	.10	.05	.01
☐ 44	Jerome Walton	.05	.02	.01
☐ 45	Mitch Webster	.05	.02	.01
☐ 46	Curt Wilkerson	.05	.02	.01
☐ 47	Dean Wilkins	.05	.02	.01
☐ 48	Mitch Williams	.10	.05	.01
☐ 49	Steve Wilson	.05	.02	.01
☐ 50	Steve Bedrosian	.05	.02	.01
☐ 51	Mike Benjamin	.05	.02	.01
☐ 52	Jeff Brantley	.05	.02	.01
☐ 53	Brett Butler	.15	.07	.02
☐ 54	Will Clark UER	.20	.09	.03
	("Did You Know" says first in runs, should say tied for first)			
☐ 55	Kelly Downs	.05	.02	.01
☐ 56	Scott Garrelts	.05	.02	.01
☐ 57	Atlee Hammaker	.05	.02	.01
☐ 58	Terry Kennedy	.05	.02	.01
☐ 59	Mike LaCoss	.05	.02	.01
☐ 60	Craig Lefferts	.05	.02	.01
☐ 61	Greg Litton	.05	.02	.01
☐ 62	Candy Maldonado	.05	.02	.01
☐ 63	Kirt Manwaring UER	.05	.02	.01
	(No '88 Phoenix stats as noted in box)			
☐ 64	Randy McCament	.05	.02	.01
☐ 65	Kevin Mitchell	.10	.05	.01
☐ 66	Donell Nixon	.05	.02	.01
☐ 67	Ken Oberkfell	.05	.02	.01
☐ 68	Rick Reuschel	.05	.02	.01
☐ 69	Ernest Riles	.05	.02	.01
☐ 70	Don Robinson	.05	.02	.01
☐ 71	Pat Sheridan	.05	.02	.01
☐ 72	Chris Speier	.05	.02	.01
☐ 73	Robby Thompson	.10	.05	.01
☐ 74	Jose Uribe	.05	.02	.01
☐ 75	Matt Williams	.30	.14	.04
☐ 76	George Bell	.10	.05	.01
☐ 77	Pat Borders	.05	.02	.01
☐ 78	John Cerutti	.05	.02	.01
☐ 79	Junior Felix	.05	.02	.01
☐ 80	Tony Fernandez	.10	.05	.01
☐ 81	Mike Flanagan	.05	.02	.01
☐ 82	Mauro Gozzo	.05	.02	.01
☐ 83	Kelly Gruber	.05	.02	.01
☐ 84	Tom Henke	.10	.05	.01
☐ 85	Jimmy Key	.10	.05	.01
☐ 86	Manny Lee	.05	.02	.01
☐ 87	Nelson Liriano UER	.05	.02	.01
	(Should say "led the IL" instead of "led the TL")			
☐ 88	Lee Mazzilli	.05	.02	.01
☐ 89	Fred McGriff	.20	.09	.03
☐ 90	Lloyd Moseby	.05	.02	.01
☐ 91	Rance Mulliniks	.05	.02	.01
☐ 92	Alex Sanchez	.05	.02	.01
☐ 93	Dave Stieb	.10	.05	.01
☐ 94	Todd Stottlemyre	.10	.05	.01
☐ 95	Duane Ward UER	.05	.02	.01
	(Double line of '87 Syracuse stats)			
☐ 96	David Wells	.05	.02	.01
☐ 97	Ernie Whitt	.05	.02	.01
☐ 98	Frank Wills	.05	.02	.01
☐ 99	Mookie Wilson	.05	.02	.01
☐ 100	Kevin Appier	.25	.11	.03
☐ 101	Luis Aquino	.05	.02	.01
☐ 102	Bob Boone	.10	.05	.01
☐ 103	George Brett	.40	.18	.05
☐ 104	Jose DeJesus	.05	.02	.01
☐ 105	Luis De Los Santos	.05	.02	.01
☐ 106	Jim Eisenreich	.05	.02	.01
☐ 107	Steve Farr	.05	.02	.01
☐ 108	Tom Gordon	.10	.05	.01
☐ 109	Mark Gubicza	.05	.02	.01
☐ 110	Bo Jackson	.15	.07	.02
☐ 111	Terry Leach	.05	.02	.01
☐ 112	Charlie Leibrandt	.05	.02	.01

☐ 113	Rick Luecken	.05	.02	.01
☐ 114	Mike Macfarlane	.05	.02	.01
☐ 115	Jeff Montgomery	.10	.05	.01
☐ 116	Bret Saberhagen	.15	.07	.02
☐ 117	Kevin Seitzer	.05	.02	.01
☐ 118	Kurt Stillwell	.05	.02	.01
☐ 119	Pat Tabler	.05	.02	.01
☐ 120	Danny Tartabull	.10	.05	.01
☐ 121	Gary Thurman	.05	.02	.01
☐ 122	Frank White	.10	.05	.01
☐ 123	Willie Wilson	.05	.02	.01
☐ 124	Matt Winters	.05	.02	.01
☐ 125	Jim Abbott	.15	.07	.02
☐ 126	Tony Armas	.05	.02	.01
☐ 127	Dante Bichette	.30	.14	.04
☐ 128	Bert Blyleven	.15	.07	.02
☐ 129	Chili Davis	.15	.07	.02
☐ 130	Brian Downing	.05	.02	.01
☐ 131	Mike Fetters	.05	.02	.01
☐ 132	Chuck Finley	.10	.05	.01
☐ 133	Willie Fraser	.05	.02	.01
☐ 134	Bryan Harvey	.10	.05	.01
☐ 135	Jack Howell	.05	.02	.01
☐ 136	Wally Joyner	.15	.07	.02
☐ 137	Jeff Manto	.05	.02	.01
☐ 138	Kirk McCaskill	.05	.02	.01
☐ 139	Bob McClure	.05	.02	.01
☐ 140	Greg Minton	.05	.02	.01
☐ 141	Lance Parrish	.10	.05	.01
☐ 142	Dan Petry	.05	.02	.01
☐ 143	Johnny Ray	.05	.02	.01
☐ 144	Dick Schofield	.05	.02	.01
☐ 145	Lee Stevens	.05	.02	.01
☐ 146	Claudell Washington	.05	.02	.01
☐ 147	Devon White	.10	.05	.01
☐ 148	Mike Witt	.05	.02	.01
☐ 149	Roberto Alomar	.30	.14	.04
☐ 150	Sandy Alomar Jr.	.10	.05	.01
☐ 151	Andy Benes	.10	.05	.01
☐ 152	Jack Clark	.10	.05	.01
☐ 153	Pat Clements	.05	.02	.01
☐ 154	Joey Cora	.10	.05	.01
☐ 155	Mark Davis	.05	.02	.01
☐ 156	Mark Grant	.05	.02	.01
☐ 157	Tony Gwynn	.30	.14	.04
☐ 158	Greg W. Harris	.05	.02	.01
☐ 159	Bruce Hurst	.05	.02	.01
☐ 160	Darrin Jackson	.05	.02	.01
☐ 161	Chris James	.05	.02	.01
☐ 162	Carmelo Martinez	.05	.02	.01
☐ 163	Mike Pagliarulo	.05	.02	.01
☐ 164	Mark Parent	.05	.02	.01
☐ 165	Dennis Rasmussen	.05	.02	.01
☐ 166	Bip Roberts	.10	.05	.01
☐ 167	Benito Santiago	.10	.05	.01
☐ 168	Calvin Schiraldi	.05	.02	.01
☐ 169	Eric Show	.05	.02	.01
☐ 170	Garry Templeton	.05	.02	.01
☐ 171	Ed Whitson	.05	.02	.01
☐ 172	Brady Anderson	.10	.05	.01
☐ 173	Jeff Ballard	.05	.02	.01
☐ 174	Phil Bradley	.05	.02	.01
☐ 175	Mike Devereaux	.10	.05	.01
☐ 176	Steve Finley	.10	.05	.01
☐ 177	Pete Harnisch	.10	.05	.01
☐ 178	Kevin Hickey	.05	.02	.01
☐ 179	Brian Holton	.05	.02	.01
☐ 180	Ben McDonald	.15	.07	.02
☐ 181	Bob Melvin	.05	.02	.01
☐ 182	Bob Milacki	.05	.02	.01
☐ 183	Randy Milligan UER	.05	.02	.01
	(Double line of '87 stats)			
☐ 184	Gregg Olson	.05	.02	.01
☐ 185	Joe Orsulak	.05	.02	.01
☐ 186	Bill Ripken	.05	.02	.01
☐ 187	Cal Ripken	.75	.35	.09
☐ 188	Dave Schmidt	.05	.02	.01
☐ 189	Larry Sheets	.05	.02	.01
☐ 190	Mickey Tettleton	.10	.05	.01
☐ 191	Mark Thurmond	.05	.02	.01
☐ 192	Jay Tibbs	.05	.02	.01
☐ 193	Jim Traber	.05	.02	.01
☐ 194	Mark Williamson	.05	.02	.01
☐ 195	Craig Worthington	.05	.02	.01
☐ 196	Don Aase	.05	.02	.01
☐ 197	Blaine Beatty	.05	.02	.01
☐ 198	Mark Carreon	.05	.02	.01
☐ 199	Gary Carter	.15	.07	.02
☐ 200	David Cone	.15	.07	.02
☐ 201	Ron Darling	.05	.02	.01
☐ 202	Kevin Elster	.05	.02	.01
☐ 203	Sid Fernandez	.10	.05	.01
☐ 204	Dwight Gooden	.05	.02	.01
☐ 205	Keith Hernandez	.10	.05	.01
☐ 206	Jeff Innis	.05	.02	.01
☐ 207	Gregg Jefferies	.25	.11	.03
☐ 208	Howard Johnson	.10	.05	.01
☐ 209	Barry Lyons UER	.05	.02	.01
	(Double line of '87 stats)			
☐ 210	Dave Magadan	.05	.02	.01
☐ 211	Kevin McReynolds	.05	.02	.01
☐ 212	Jeff Musselman	.05	.02	.01
☐ 213	Randy Myers	.15	.07	.02
☐ 214	Bob Ojeda	.05	.02	.01
☐ 215	Juan Samuel	.05	.02	.01
☐ 216	Mackey Sasser	.05	.02	.01
☐ 217	Darryl Strawberry	.10	.05	.01
☐ 218	Tim Teufel	.05	.02	.01
☐ 219	Frank Viola	.10	.05	.01
☐ 220	Juan Agosto	.05	.02	.01
☐ 221	Larry Andersen	.05	.02	.01
☐ 222	Eric Anthony	.05	.02	.01
☐ 223	Kevin Bass	.05	.02	.01
☐ 224	Craig Biggio	.15	.07	.02
☐ 225	Ken Caminiti	.15	.07	.02
☐ 226	Jim Clancy	.05	.02	.01
☐ 227	Danny Darwin	.05	.02	.01
☐ 228	Glenn Davis	.05	.02	.01
☐ 229	Jim Deshaies	.05	.02	.01
☐ 230	Bill Doran	.05	.02	.01
☐ 231	Bob Forsch	.05	.02	.01
☐ 232	Brian Meyer	.05	.02	.01
☐ 233	Terry Puhl	.05	.02	.01
☐ 234	Rafael Ramirez	.05	.02	.01
☐ 235	Rick Rhoden	.05	.02	.01
☐ 236	Dan Schatzeder	.05	.02	.01
☐ 237	Mike Scott	.05	.02	.01
☐ 238	Dave Smith	.05	.02	.01
☐ 239	Alex Trevino	.05	.02	.01
☐ 240	Glenn Wilson	.05	.02	.01
☐ 241	Gerald Young	.05	.02	.01
☐ 242	Tom Brunansky	.05	.02	.01
☐ 243	Cris Carpenter	.05	.02	.01
☐ 244	Alex Cole	.05	.02	.01
☐ 245	Vince Coleman	.10	.05	.01
☐ 246	John Costello	.05	.02	.01
☐ 247	Ken Dayley	.05	.02	.01
☐ 248	Jose DeLeon	.05	.02	.01
☐ 249	Frank DiPino	.05	.02	.01
☐ 250	Pedro Guerrero	.10	.05	.01

☐ 251	Ken Hill	.15	.07	.02
☐ 252	Joe Magrane	.05	.02	.01
☐ 253	Willie McGee UER	.10	.05	.01

(No decimal point
before 353)

☐ 254	John Morris	.05	.02	.01
☐ 255	Jose Oquendo	.05	.02	.01
☐ 256	Tony Pena	.05	.02	.01
☐ 257	Terry Pendleton	.15	.07	.02
☐ 258	Ted Power	.05	.02	.01
☐ 259	Dan Quisenberry	.05	.02	.01
☐ 260	Ozzie Smith	.20	.09	.03
☐ 261	Scott Terry	.05	.02	.01
☐ 262	Milt Thompson	.05	.02	.01
☐ 263	Denny Walling	.05	.02	.01
☐ 264	Todd Worrell	.05	.02	.01
☐ 265	Todd Zeile	.10	.05	.01
☐ 266	Marty Barrett	.05	.02	.01
☐ 267	Mike Boddicker	.05	.02	.01
☐ 268	Wade Boggs	.15	.07	.02
☐ 269	Ellis Burks	.10	.05	.01
☐ 270	Rick Cerone	.05	.02	.01
☐ 271	Roger Clemens	.15	.07	.02
☐ 272	John Dopson	.05	.02	.01
☐ 273	Nick Esasky	.05	.02	.01
☐ 274	Dwight Evans	.10	.05	.01
☐ 275	Wes Gardner	.05	.02	.01
☐ 276	Rich Gedman	.05	.02	.01
☐ 277	Mike Greenwell	.15	.07	.02
☐ 278	Danny Heep	.05	.02	.01
☐ 279	Eric Hetzel	.05	.02	.01
☐ 280	Dennis Lamp	.05	.02	.01
☐ 281	Rob Murphy UER	.05	.02	.01

('89 stats say Reds,
should say Red Sox)

☐ 282	Joe Price	.05	.02	.01
☐ 283	Carlos Quintana	.05	.02	.01
☐ 284	Jody Reed	.05	.02	.01
☐ 285	Luis Rivera	.05	.02	.01
☐ 286	Kevin Romine	.05	.02	.01
☐ 287	Lee Smith	.15	.07	.02
☐ 288	Mike Smithson	.05	.02	.01
☐ 289	Bob Stanley	.05	.02	.01
☐ 290	Harold Baines	.15	.07	.02
☐ 291	Kevin Brown	.10	.05	.01
☐ 292	Steve Buechele	.05	.02	.01
☐ 293	Scott Coolbaugh	.05	.02	.01
☐ 294	Jack Daugherty	.05	.02	.01
☐ 295	Cecil Espy	.05	.02	.01
☐ 296	Julio Franco	.10	.05	.01
☐ 297	Juan Gonzalez	1.25	.55	.16
☐ 298	Cecilio Guante	.05	.02	.01
☐ 299	Drew Hall	.05	.02	.01
☐ 300	Charlie Hough	.10	.05	.01
☐ 301	Pete Incaviglia	.05	.02	.01
☐ 302	Mike Jeffcoat	.05	.02	.01
☐ 303	Chad Kreuter	.05	.02	.01
☐ 304	Jeff Kunkel	.05	.02	.01
☐ 305	Rick Leach	.05	.02	.01
☐ 306	Fred Manrique	.05	.02	.01
☐ 307	Jamie Moyer	.05	.02	.01
☐ 308	Rafael Palmeiro	.15	.07	.02
☐ 309	Geno Petralli	.05	.02	.01
☐ 310	Kevin Reimer	.05	.02	.01
☐ 311	Kenny Rogers	.05	.02	.01
☐ 312	Jeff Russell	.05	.02	.01
☐ 313	Nolan Ryan	.75	.35	.09
☐ 314	Ruben Sierra	.15	.07	.02
☐ 315	Bobby Witt	.05	.02	.01
☐ 316	Chris Bosio	.05	.02	.01
☐ 317	Glenn Braggs UER	.05	.02	.01

(Stats say 111 K's,
but bio says 117 K's)

☐ 318	Greg Brock	.05	.02	.01
☐ 319	Chuck Crim	.05	.02	.01
☐ 320	Rob Deer	.05	.02	.01
☐ 321	Mike Felder	.05	.02	.01
☐ 322	Tom Filer	.05	.02	.01
☐ 323	Tony Fossas	.05	.02	.01
☐ 324	Jim Gantner	.05	.02	.01
☐ 325	Darryl Hamilton	.10	.05	.01
☐ 326	Teddy Higuera	.05	.02	.01
☐ 327	Mark Knudson	.05	.02	.01
☐ 328	Bill Krueger UER	.05	.02	.01

('86 stats missing)

☐ 329	Tim McIntosh	.05	.02	.01
☐ 330	Paul Molitor	.15	.07	.02
☐ 331	Jaime Navarro	.05	.02	.01
☐ 332	Charlie O'Brien	.05	.02	.01
☐ 333	Jeff Peterek	.05	.02	.01
☐ 334	Dan Plesac	.05	.02	.01
☐ 335	Jerry Reuss	.05	.02	.01
☐ 336	Gary Sheffield UER	.20	.09	.03

(Bio says played for
3 teams in '87, but
stats say in '88)

☐ 337	Bill Spiers	.05	.02	.01
☐ 338	B.J. Surhoff	.05	.02	.01
☐ 339	Greg Vaughn	.10	.05	.01
☐ 340	Robin Yount	.20	.09	.03
☐ 341	Hubie Brooks	.05	.02	.01
☐ 342	Tim Burke	.05	.02	.01
☐ 343	Mike Fitzgerald	.05	.02	.01
☐ 344	Tom Foley	.05	.02	.01
☐ 345	Andres Galarraga	.15	.07	.02
☐ 346	Damaso Garcia	.05	.02	.01
☐ 347	Marquis Grissom	.60	.25	.07
☐ 348	Kevin Gross	.05	.02	.01
☐ 349	Joe Hesketh	.05	.02	.01
☐ 350	Jeff Huson	.05	.02	.01
☐ 351	Wallace Johnson	.05	.02	.01
☐ 352	Mark Langston	.15	.07	.02
☐ 353A	Dave Martinez	2.00	.90	.25

(Yellow on front)

☐ 353B	Dave Martinez	.05	.02	.01

(Red on front)

☐ 354	Dennis Martinez UER	.10	.05	.01

('87 ERA is 616,
should be 6.16)

☐ 355	Andy McGaffigan	.05	.02	.01
☐ 356	Otis Nixon	.05	.02	.01
☐ 357	Spike Owen	.05	.02	.01
☐ 358	Pascual Perez	.05	.02	.01
☐ 359	Tim Raines	.15	.07	.02
☐ 360	Nelson Santovenia	.05	.02	.01
☐ 361	Bryn Smith	.05	.02	.01
☐ 362	Zane Smith	.05	.02	.01
☐ 363	Larry Walker	.75	.35	.09
☐ 364	Tim Wallach	.05	.02	.01
☐ 365	Rick Aguilera	.05	.02	.01
☐ 366	Allan Anderson	.05	.02	.01
☐ 367	Wally Backman	.05	.02	.01
☐ 368	Doug Baker	.05	.02	.01
☐ 369	Juan Berenguer	.05	.02	.01
☐ 370	Randy Bush	.05	.02	.01
☐ 371	Carmen Castillo	.05	.02	.01
☐ 372	Mike Dyer	.05	.02	.01
☐ 373	Gary Gaetti	.05	.02	.01
☐ 374	Greg Gagne	.05	.02	.01
☐ 375	Dan Gladden	.05	.02	.01
☐ 376	German Gonzalez UER	.05	.02	.01

(Bio says 31 saves in

	'88, but stats say 30)		
☐ 377	Brian Harper	.05	.02	.01
☐ 378	Kent Hrbek	.10	.05	.01
☐ 379	Gene Larkin	.05	.02	.01
☐ 380	Tim Laudner UER	.05	.02	.01
	(No decimal point before '85 BA of 238)		
☐ 381	John Moses	.05	.02	.01
☐ 382	Al Newman	.05	.02	.01
☐ 383	Kirby Puckett	.30	.14	.04
☐ 384	Shane Rawley	.05	.02	.01
☐ 385	Jeff Reardon	.15	.07	.02
☐ 386	Roy Smith	.05	.02	.01
☐ 387	Gary Wayne	.05	.02	.01
☐ 388	Dave West	.05	.02	.01
☐ 389	Tim Belcher	.05	.02	.01
☐ 390	Tim Crews UER	.10	.05	.01
	(Stats say 163 IP for '83, but bio says .136)		
☐ 391	Mike Davis	.05	.02	.01
☐ 392	Rick Dempsey	.05	.02	.01
☐ 393	Kirk Gibson	.15	.07	.02
☐ 394	Jose Gonzalez	.05	.02	.01
☐ 395	Alfredo Griffin	.05	.02	.01
☐ 396	Jeff Hamilton	.05	.02	.01
☐ 397	Lenny Harris	.05	.02	.01
☐ 398	Mickey Hatcher	.05	.02	.01
☐ 399	Orel Hershiser	.15	.07	.02
☐ 400	Jay Howell	.05	.02	.01
☐ 401	Mike Marshall	.05	.02	.01
☐ 402	Ramon Martinez	.15	.07	.02
☐ 403	Mike Morgan	.05	.02	.01
☐ 404	Eddie Murray	.25	.11	.03
☐ 405	Alejandro Pena	.05	.02	.01
☐ 406	Willie Randolph	.10	.05	.01
☐ 407	Mike Scioscia	.05	.02	.01
☐ 408	Ray Searage	.05	.02	.01
☐ 409	Fernando Valenzuela	.05	.02	.01
☐ 410	Jose Vizcaino	.05	.02	.01
☐ 411	John Wetteland	.10	.05	.01
☐ 412	Jack Armstrong	.05	.02	.01
☐ 413	Todd Benzinger UER	.05	.02	.01
	(Bio says .323 at Pawtucket, but stats say .321)		
☐ 414	Tim Birtsas	.05	.02	.01
☐ 415	Tom Browning	.05	.02	.01
☐ 416	Norm Charlton	.10	.05	.01
☐ 417	Eric Davis	.10	.05	.01
☐ 418	Rob Dibble	.10	.05	.01
☐ 419	John Franco	.15	.07	.02
☐ 420	Ken Griffey Sr.	.10	.05	.01
☐ 421	Chris Hammond	.10	.05	.01
	(No 1989 used for "Did Not Play" stat, actually did play for Nashville in 1989)		
☐ 422	Danny Jackson	.05	.02	.01
☐ 423	Barry Larkin	.20	.09	.03
☐ 424	Tim Leary	.05	.02	.01
☐ 425	Rick Mahler	.05	.02	.01
☐ 426	Joe Oliver	.05	.02	.01
☐ 427	Paul O'Neill	.15	.07	.02
☐ 428	Luis Quinones UER	.05	.02	.01
	('86-'88 stats are omitted from card but included in totals)		
☐ 429	Jeff Reed	.05	.02	.01
☐ 430	Jose Rijo	.10	.05	.01
☐ 431	Ron Robinson	.05	.02	.01
☐ 432	Rolando Roomes	.05	.02	.01
☐ 433	Chris Sabo	.05	.02	.01
☐ 434	Scott Scudder	.05	.02	.01
☐ 435	Herm Winningham	.05	.02	.01
☐ 436	Steve Balboni	.05	.02	.01
☐ 437	Jesse Barfield	.05	.02	.01
☐ 438	Mike Blowers	.20	.09	.03
☐ 439	Tom Brookens	.05	.02	.01
☐ 440	Greg Cadaret	.05	.02	.01
☐ 441	Alvaro Espinoza UER	.05	.02	.01
	(Career games say 218, should be 219)		
☐ 442	Bob Geren	.05	.02	.01
☐ 443	Lee Guetterman	.05	.02	.01
☐ 444	Mel Hall	.05	.02	.01
☐ 445	Andy Hawkins	.05	.02	.01
☐ 446	Roberto Kelly	.10	.05	.01
☐ 447	Don Mattingly	.40	.18	.05
☐ 448	Lance McCullers	.05	.02	.01
☐ 449	Hensley Meulens	.05	.02	.01
☐ 450	Dale Mohorcic	.05	.02	.01
☐ 451	Clay Parker	.05	.02	.01
☐ 452	Eric Plunk	.05	.02	.01
☐ 453	Dave Righetti	.05	.02	.01
☐ 454	Deion Sanders	.50	.23	.06
☐ 455	Steve Sax	.05	.02	.01
☐ 456	Don Slaught	.05	.02	.01
☐ 457	Walt Terrell	.05	.02	.01
☐ 458	Dave Winfield	.15	.07	.02
☐ 459	Jay Bell	.10	.05	.01
☐ 460	Rafael Belliard	.05	.02	.01
☐ 461	Barry Bonds	.30	.14	.04
☐ 462	Bobby Bonilla	.15	.07	.02
☐ 463	Sid Bream	.05	.02	.01
☐ 464	Benny Distefano	.05	.02	.01
☐ 465	Doug Drabek	.10	.05	.01
☐ 466	Jim Gott	.05	.02	.01
☐ 467	Billy Hatcher UER	.05	.02	.01
	(.1 hits for Cubs in 1984)		
☐ 468	Neal Heaton	.05	.02	.01
☐ 469	Jeff King	.10	.05	.01
☐ 470	Bob Kipper	.05	.02	.01
☐ 471	Randy Kramer	.05	.02	.01
☐ 472	Bill Landrum	.05	.02	.01
☐ 473	Mike LaValliere	.05	.02	.01
☐ 474	Jose Lind	.05	.02	.01
☐ 475	Junior Ortiz	.05	.02	.01
☐ 476	Gary Redus	.05	.02	.01
☐ 477	Rick Reed	.05	.02	.01
☐ 478	R.J. Reynolds	.05	.02	.01
☐ 479	Jeff D. Robinson	.05	.02	.01
☐ 480	John Smiley	.05	.02	.01
☐ 481	Andy Van Slyke	.10	.05	.01
☐ 482	Bob Walk	.05	.02	.01
☐ 483	Andy Allanson	.05	.02	.01
☐ 484	Scott Bailes	.05	.02	.01
☐ 485	Joey Belle UER	1.00	.45	.12
	(Has Jay Bell "Did You Know")		
☐ 486	Bud Black	.05	.02	.01
☐ 487	Jerry Browne	.05	.02	.01
☐ 488	Tom Candiotti	.05	.02	.01
☐ 489	Joe Carter	.15	.07	.02
☐ 490	Dave Clark	.05	.02	.01
	(No '84 stats)		
☐ 491	John Farrell	.05	.02	.01
☐ 492	Felix Fermin	.05	.02	.01
☐ 493	Brook Jacoby	.05	.02	.01
☐ 494	Dion James	.05	.02	.01
☐ 495	Doug Jones	.05	.02	.01
☐ 496	Brad Komminsk	.05	.02	.01

497 Rod Nichols	.05	.02	.01
498 Pete O'Brien	.05	.02	.01
499 Steve Olin	.10	.05	.01
500 Jesse Orosco	.05	.02	.01
501 Joel Skinner	.05	.02	.01
502 Cory Snyder	.05	.02	.01
503 Greg Swindell	.10	.05	.01
504 Rich Yett	.05	.02	.01
505 Scott Bankhead	.05	.02	.01
506 Scott Bradley	.05	.02	.01
507 Greg Briley UER	.05	.02	.01
(28 SB's in bio, but 27 in stats)			
508 Jay Buhner	.15	.07	.02
509 Darnell Coles	.05	.02	.01
510 Keith Comstock	.05	.02	.01
511 Henry Cotto	.05	.02	.01
512 Alvin Davis	.05	.02	.01
513 Ken Griffey Jr.	2.00	.90	.25
514 Erik Hanson	.10	.05	.01
515 Gene Harris	.05	.02	.01
516 Brian Holman	.05	.02	.01
517 Mike Jackson	.05	.02	.01
518 Randy Johnson	.40	.18	.05
519 Jeffrey Leonard	.05	.02	.01
520 Edgar Martinez	.15	.07	.02
521 Dennis Powell	.05	.02	.01
522 Jim Presley	.05	.02	.01
523 Jerry Reed	.05	.02	.01
524 Harold Reynolds	.05	.02	.01
525 Mike Schooler	.05	.02	.01
526 Bill Swift	.05	.02	.01
527 Dave Valle	.05	.02	.01
528 Omar Vizquel	.10	.05	.01
529 Ivan Calderon	.05	.02	.01
530 Carlton Fisk UER	.15	.07	.02
(Bellow Falls, should be Bellows Falls)			
531 Scott Fletcher	.05	.02	.01
532 Dave Gallagher	.05	.02	.01
533 Ozzie Guillen	.10	.05	.01
534 Greg Hibbard	.05	.02	.01
535 Shawn Hillegas	.05	.02	.01
536 Lance Johnson	.10	.05	.01
537 Eric King	.05	.02	.01
538 Ron Kittle	.05	.02	.01
539 Steve Lyons	.05	.02	.01
540 Carlos Martinez	.05	.02	.01
541 Tom McCarthy	.05	.02	.01
542 Matt Merullo	.05	.02	.01
(Had 5 ML runs scored entering '90, not 6)			
543 Donn Pall UER	.05	.02	.01
(Stats say pro career began in '85, bio says '88)			
544 Dan Pasqua	.05	.02	.01
545 Ken Patterson	.05	.02	.01
546 Melido Perez	.05	.02	.01
547 Steve Rosenberg	.05	.02	.01
548 Sammy Sosa	.75	.35	.09
549 Bobby Thigpen	.05	.02	.01
550 Robin Ventura	.25	.11	.03
551 Greg Walker	.05	.02	.01
552 Don Carman	.05	.02	.01
553 Pat Combs	.05	.02	.01
(6 walks for Phillies in '89 in stats, brief bio says 4)			
554 Dennis Cook	.05	.02	.01
555 Darren Daulton	.15	.07	.02
556 Len Dykstra	.15	.07	.02
557 Curt Ford	.05	.02	.01
558 Charlie Hayes	.10	.05	.01
559 Von Hayes	.05	.02	.01
560 Tommy Herr	.05	.02	.01
561 Ken Howell	.05	.02	.01
562 Steve Jeltz	.05	.02	.01
563 Ron Jones	.05	.02	.01
564 Ricky Jordan UER	.05	.02	.01
(Duplicate line of statistics on back)			
565 John Kruk	.15	.07	.02
566 Steve Lake	.05	.02	.01
567 Roger McDowell	.05	.02	.01
568 Terry Mulholland UER	.10	.05	.01
("Did You Know" refers to Dave Magadan)			
569 Dwayne Murphy	.05	.02	.01
570 Jeff Parrett	.05	.02	.01
571 Randy Ready	.05	.02	.01
572 Bruce Ruffin	.05	.02	.01
573 Dickie Thon	.05	.02	.01
574 Jose Alvarez UER	.05	.02	.01
('78 and '79 stats are reversed)			
575 Geronimo Berroa	.10	.05	.01
576 Jeff Blauser	.10	.05	.01
577 Joe Boever	.05	.02	.01
578 Marty Clary UER	.05	.02	.01
(No comma between city and state)			
579 Jody Davis	.05	.02	.01
580 Mark Eichhorn	.05	.02	.01
581 Darrell Evans	.10	.05	.01
582 Ron Gant	.15	.07	.02
583 Tom Glavine	.25	.11	.03
584 Tommy Greene	.15	.07	.02
585 Tommy Gregg	.05	.02	.01
586 Dave Justice UER	.75	.35	.09
(Actually had 16 2B in Sumter in '86)			
587 Mark Lemke	.10	.05	.01
588 Derek Lilliquist	.05	.02	.01
589 Oddibe McDowell	.05	.02	.01
590 Kent Mercker ERA	.20	.09	.03
(Bio says 2.75 ERA, stats say 2.68 ERA)			
591 Dale Murphy	.15	.07	.02
592 Gerald Perry	.05	.02	.01
593 Lonnie Smith	.05	.02	.01
594 Pete Smith	.05	.02	.01
595 John Smoltz	.15	.07	.02
596 Mike Stanton UER	.05	.02	.01
(No comma between city and state)			
597 Andres Thomas	.05	.02	.01
598 Jeff Treadway	.05	.02	.01
599 Doyle Alexander	.05	.02	.01
600 Dave Bergman	.05	.02	.01
601 Brian DuBois	.05	.02	.01
602 Paul Gibson	.05	.02	.01
603 Mike Heath	.05	.02	.01
604 Mike Henneman	.05	.02	.01
605 Guillermo Hernandez	.05	.02	.01
606 Shawn Holman	.05	.02	.01
607 Tracy Jones	.05	.02	.01
608 Chet Lemon	.05	.02	.01
609 Fred Lynn	.10	.05	.01
610 Jack Morris	.15	.07	.02
611 Matt Nokes	.05	.02	.01
612 Gary Pettis	.05	.02	.01

☐ 613 Kevin Ritz	.05	.02	.01
☐ 614 Jeff M. Robinson	.05	.02	.01
('88 stats are not in line)			
☐ 615 Steve Searcy	.05	.02	.01
☐ 616 Frank Tanana	.05	.02	.01
☐ 617 Alan Trammell	.15	.07	.02
☐ 618 Gary Ward	.05	.02	.01
☐ 619 Lou Whitaker	.15	.07	.02
☐ 620 Frank Williams	.05	.02	.01
☐ 621A George Brett '80 ERR (Had 10 .390 hitting seasons)	1.50	.70	.19
☐ 621B George Brett '80 COR	.20	.09	.03
☐ 622 Fern. Valenzuela '81	.05	.02	.01
☐ 623 Dale Murphy '82	.05	.02	.01
☐ 624A Cal Ripken '83 ERR (Misspelled Ripkin on card back)	5.00	2.20	.60
☐ 624B Cal Ripken '83 COR	.40	.18	.05
☐ 625 Ryne Sandberg '84	.15	.07	.02
☐ 626 Don Mattingly '85	.20	.09	.03
☐ 627 Roger Clemens '86	.15	.07	.02
☐ 628 George Bell '87	.05	.02	.01
☐ 629 Jose Canseco '88 UER (Reggie won MVP in '83, should say '73)	.15	.07	.02
☐ 630A Will Clark '89 ERR (32 total bases on card back)	1.00	.45	.12
☐ 630B Will Clark '89 COR (321 total bases; technically still an error, listing only 24 runs)	.15	.07	.02
☐ 631 Game Savers Mark Davis Mitch Williams	.05	.02	.01
☐ 632 Boston Igniters Wade Boggs Mike Greenwell	.15	.07	.02
☐ 633 Starter and Stopper Mark Gubicza Jeff Russell	.05	.02	.01
☐ 634 League's Best Shortstops Tony Fernandez Cal Ripken	.25	.11	.03
☐ 635 Human Dynamos Kirby Puckett Bo Jackson	.15	.07	.02
☐ 636 300 Strikeout Club Nolan Ryan Mike Scott	.25	.11	.03
☐ 637 The Dynamic Duo Will Clark Kevin Mitchell	.10	.05	.01
☐ 638 AL All-Stars Don Mattingly Mark McGwire	.25	.11	.03
☐ 639 NL East Rivals Howard Johnson Ryne Sandberg	.15	.07	.02
☐ 640 Rudy Seanez Colin Charland	.05	.02	.01
☐ 641 George Canale Kevin Maas UER (Canale listed as INF on front, 1B on back)	.05	.02	.01
☐ 642 Kelly Mann	.05	.02	.01

and Dave Hansen			
☐ 643 Greg Smith and Stu Tate	.05	.02	.01
☐ 644 Tom Drees and Dann Howitt	.05	.02	.01
☐ 645 Mike Roesler and Derrick May	.15	.07	.02
☐ 646 Scott Hemond and Mark Gardner	.05	.02	.01
☐ 647 John Orton and Scott Leius	.05	.02	.01
☐ 648 Rich Monteleone and Dana Williams	.05	.02	.01
☐ 649 Mike Huff and Steve Frey	.05	.02	.01
☐ 650 Chuck McElroy and Moises Alou	.25	.11	.03
☐ 651 Bobby Rose and Mike Hartley	.05	.02	.01
☐ 652 Matt Kinzer and Wayne Edwards	.05	.02	.01
☐ 653 Delino DeShields and Jason Grimsley	.15	.07	.02
☐ 654 CL: A's/Cubs Giants/Blue Jays	.05	.02	.01
☐ 655 CL: Royals/Angels Padres/Orioles	.05	.02	.01
☐ 656 CL: Mets/Astros Cards/Red Sox	.05	.02	.01
☐ 657 CL: Rangers/Brewers Expos/Twins	.05	.02	.01
☐ 658 CL: Dodgers/Reds Yankees/Pirates	.05	.02	.01
☐ 659 CL: Indians/Mariners White Sox/Phillies	.05	.02	.01
☐ 660A CL: Braves/Tigers Specials/Checklists (Checklist-660 in smaller print on card front)	.05	.02	.01
☐ 660B CL: Braves/Tigers Specials/Checklists (Checklist-660 in normal print on card front)	.05	.02	.01

1990 Fleer Update

The 1990 Fleer Update set contains 132 standard-size (2 1/2" by 3 1/2") cards. This set marked the seventh consecutive year Fleer issued an end of season Update set. The set was issued exclusively as a boxed set through hobby dealers. The set is checklisted alphabetically by team for each

league and then alphabetically within each team. The fronts are styled the same as the 1990 Fleer regular issue set. The backs are numbered with the prefix "U" for Update. Rookie Cards in this set include Carlos Baerga, Chuck Carr, Alex Fernandez, Travis Fryman, Chris Hoiles, Dave Hollins, Jose Offerman, John Olerud, Frank Thomas, and Mark Whiten.

	MINT	NRMT	EXC
COMPLETE FACT.SET (132)	6.00	2.70	.75
COMMON CARD (1-132)	.05	.02	.01

☐ 1	Steve Avery	.20	.09	.03
☐ 2	Francisco Cabrera	.05	.02	.01
☐ 3	Nick Esasky	.05	.02	.01
☐ 4	Jim Kremers	.05	.02	.01
☐ 5	Greg Olson	.05	.02	.01
☐ 6	Jim Presley	.05	.02	.01
☐ 7	Shawn Boskie	.05	.02	.01
☐ 8	Joe Kraemer	.05	.02	.01
☐ 9	Luis Salazar	.05	.02	.01
☐ 10	Hector Villanueva	.05	.02	.01
☐ 11	Glenn Braggs	.05	.02	.01
☐ 12	Mariano Duncan	.05	.02	.01
☐ 13	Billy Hatcher	.05	.02	.01
☐ 14	Tim Layana	.05	.02	.01
☐ 15	Hal Morris	.10	.05	.01
☐ 16	Javier Ortiz	.05	.02	.01
☐ 17	Dave Rohde	.05	.02	.01
☐ 18	Eric Yelding	.05	.02	.01
☐ 19	Hubie Brooks	.05	.02	.01
☐ 20	Kal Daniels	.05	.02	.01
☐ 21	Dave Hansen	.05	.02	.01
☐ 22	Mike Hartley	.05	.02	.01
☐ 23	Stan Javier	.05	.02	.01
☐ 24	Jose Offerman	.10	.05	.01
☐ 25	Juan Samuel	.05	.02	.01
☐ 26	Dennis Boyd	.05	.02	.01
☐ 27	Delino DeShields	.10	.05	.01
☐ 28	Steve Frey	.05	.02	.01
☐ 29	Mark Gardner	.05	.02	.01
☐ 30	Chris Nabholz	.05	.02	.01
☐ 31	Bill Sampen	.05	.02	.01
☐ 32	Dave Schmidt	.05	.02	.01
☐ 33	Daryl Boston	.05	.02	.01
☐ 34	Chuck Carr	.10	.05	.01
☐ 35	John Franco	.15	.07	.02
☐ 36	Todd Hundley	.10	.05	.01
☐ 37	Julio Machado	.05	.02	.01
☐ 38	Alejandro Pena	.05	.02	.01
☐ 39	Darren Reed	.05	.02	.01
☐ 40	Kelvin Torve	.05	.02	.01
☐ 41	Darrel Akerfelds	.05	.02	.01
☐ 42	Jose DeJesus	.05	.02	.01
☐ 43	Dave Hollins UER	.15	.07	.02
	(Misspelled Dane on card back)			
☐ 44	Carmelo Martinez	.05	.02	.01
☐ 45	Brad Moore	.05	.02	.01
☐ 46	Dale Murphy	.15	.07	.02
☐ 47	Wally Backman	.05	.02	.01
☐ 48	Stan Belinda	.05	.02	.01
☐ 49	Bob Patterson	.05	.02	.01
☐ 50	Ted Power	.05	.02	.01
☐ 51	Don Slaught	.05	.02	.01
☐ 52	Geronimo Pena	.05	.02	.01
☐ 53	Lee Smith	.15	.07	.02
☐ 54	John Tudor	.05	.02	.01
☐ 55	Joe Carter	.15	.07	.02
☐ 56	Thomas Howard	.05	.02	.01
☐ 57	Craig Lefferts	.05	.02	.01
☐ 58	Rafael Valdez	.05	.02	.01
☐ 59	Dave Anderson	.05	.02	.01
☐ 60	Kevin Bass	.05	.02	.01
☐ 61	John Burkett	.10	.05	.01
☐ 62	Gary Carter	.15	.07	.02
☐ 63	Rick Parker	.05	.02	.01
☐ 64	Trevor Wilson	.05	.02	.01
☐ 65	Chris Hoiles	.15	.07	.02
☐ 66	Tim Hulett	.05	.02	.01
☐ 67	Dave Johnson	.05	.02	.01
☐ 68	Curt Schilling	.10	.05	.01
☐ 69	David Segui	.05	.02	.01
☐ 70	Tom Brunansky	.05	.02	.01
☐ 71	Greg A. Harris	.05	.02	.01
☐ 72	Dana Kiecker	.05	.02	.01
☐ 73	Tim Naehring	.30	.14	.04
☐ 74	Tony Pena	.05	.02	.01
☐ 75	Jeff Reardon	.15	.07	.02
☐ 76	Jerry Reed	.05	.02	.01
☐ 77	Mark Eichhorn	.05	.02	.01
☐ 78	Mark Langston	.15	.07	.02
☐ 79	John Orton	.05	.02	.01
☐ 80	Luis Polonia	.10	.05	.01
☐ 81	Dave Winfield	.15	.07	.02
☐ 82	Cliff Young	.05	.02	.01
☐ 83	Wayne Edwards	.05	.02	.01
☐ 84	Alex Fernandez	.40	.18	.05
☐ 85	Craig Grebeck	.05	.02	.01
☐ 86	Scott Radinsky	.05	.02	.01
☐ 87	Frank Thomas	4.00	1.80	.50
☐ 88	Beau Allred	.05	.02	.01
☐ 89	Sandy Alomar Jr.	.10	.05	.01
☐ 90	Carlos Baerga	1.50	.70	.19
☐ 91	Kevin Bearse	.05	.02	.01
☐ 92	Chris James	.05	.02	.01
☐ 93	Candy Maldonado	.05	.02	.01
☐ 94	Jeff Manto	.05	.02	.01
☐ 95	Cecil Fielder	.15	.07	.02
☐ 96	Travis Fryman	.50	.23	.06
☐ 97	Lloyd Moseby	.05	.02	.01
☐ 98	Edwin Nunez	.05	.02	.01
☐ 99	Tony Phillips	.15	.07	.02
☐ 100	Larry Sheets	.05	.02	.01
☐ 101	Mark Davis	.05	.02	.01
☐ 102	Storm Davis	.05	.02	.01
☐ 103	Gerald Perry	.05	.02	.01
☐ 104	Terry Shumpert	.05	.02	.01
☐ 105	Edgar Diaz	.05	.02	.01
☐ 106	Dave Parker	.15	.07	.02
☐ 107	Tim Drummond	.05	.02	.01
☐ 108	Junior Ortiz	.05	.02	.01
☐ 109	Park Pittman	.05	.02	.01
☐ 110	Kevin Tapani	.15	.07	.02
☐ 111	Oscar Azocar	.05	.02	.01
☐ 112	Jim Leyritz	.10	.05	.01
☐ 113	Kevin Maas	.05	.02	.01
☐ 114	Alan Mills	.05	.02	.01
☐ 115	Matt Nokes	.05	.02	.01
☐ 116	Pascual Perez	.05	.02	.01
☐ 117	Ozzie Canseco	.05	.02	.01
☐ 118	Scott Sanderson	.05	.02	.01
☐ 119	Tino Martinez	.20	.09	.03
☐ 120	Jeff Schaefer	.05	.02	.01
☐ 121	Matt Young	.05	.02	.01
☐ 122	Brian Bohanon	.05	.02	.01
☐ 123	Jeff Huson	.05	.02	.01
☐ 124	Ramon Manon	.05	.02	.01
☐ 125	Gary Mielke UER	.05	.02	.01
	(Shown as Blue			

	Jay on front)		
☐ 126	Willie Blair..................	.05	.02	.01
☐ 127	Glenalien Hill..............	.05	.02	.01
☐ 128	John Olerud UER	.20	.09	.03
	(Listed as throwing right, should be left)		
☐ 129	Luis Sojo...................	.05	.02	.01
☐ 130	Mark Whiten	.15	.07	.02
☐ 131	Nolan Ryan	.75	.35	.09
☐ 132	Checklist U1-U132.......	.05	.02	.01

1991 Fleer

The 1991 Fleer set consists of 720 cards which measure the now standard size of 2 1/2" by 3 1/2". This set marks Fleer's eleventh consecutive year of issuing sets of current players. This set does not have what has been a Fleer tradition in recent years, the two-player rookie cards and there are less two-player special cards than in prior years. Apparently this was an attempt by Fleer to increase the number of single player cards in the set. The design features solid yellow borders with the information in black indicating name, position, and team. The backs feature beautiful full-color photos along with the career statistics and a biography for those players where there is room. The set is again ordered numerically by teams, followed by combination cards, rookie prospect pairs, and checklists. Again Fleer incorrectly anticipated the outcome of the 1990 Playoffs according to the team ordering. The A's, listed first, did not win the World Series and their opponents (and Series winners) were the Reds, not the Pirates. Fleer later reported that they merely arranged the teams according to regular season team record due to the early printing date. The complete team ordering is as follows: Oakland A's (1-28), Pittsburgh Pirates (29-54), Cincinnati Reds (55-82), Boston Red Sox (83-113), Chicago White Sox (114-139), New York Mets (140-166), Toronto Blue Jays (167-192), Los Angeles Dodgers (193-223), Montreal Expos (224-251), San Francisco Giants (252-277), Texas Rangers (278-304), California Angels (305-330), Detroit Tigers (331-357), Cleveland Indians (358-385), Philadelphia Phillies (386-412), Chicago Cubs (413-441), Seattle Mariners

(442-465), Baltimore Orioles (466-496), Houston Astros (497-522) San Diego Padres (523-548), Kansas City Royals (549-575), Milwaukee Brewers (576-601), Minnesota Twins (602-627), St. Louis Cardinals (628-654), New York Yankees (655-680), and Atlanta Braves (681-708). A number of the cards in the set can be found with photos cropped (very slightly) differently as Fleer used two separate printers in their attempt to maximize production. Rookie Cards in this set include Wes Chamberlain, Jeff Conine, Carlos Garcia, Luis Gonzalez, Brian McRae, Pedro Munoz, Phil Plantier, and Randy Tomlin.

	MINT	NRMT	EXC
COMPLETE SET (720)	8.00	3.60	1.00
COMPLETE RETAIL SET (732)	10.00	4.50	1.25
COMPLETE HOBBY SET (732)	10.00	4.50	1.25
COMPLETE WORLD SERIES (8)	2.00	.90	.25
COMMON CARD (1-720)	.05	.02	.01

☐ 1	Troy Afenir	.05	.02	.01
☐ 2	Harold Baines	.15	.07	.02
☐ 3	Lance Blankenship	.05	.02	.01
☐ 4	Todd Burns	.05	.02	.01
☐ 5	Jose Canseco	.20	.09	.03
☐ 6	Dennis Eckersley	.15	.07	.02
☐ 7	Mike Gallego	.05	.02	.01
☐ 8	Ron Hassey	.05	.02	.01
☐ 9	Dave Henderson	.05	.02	.01
☐ 10	Rickey Henderson	.15	.07	.02
☐ 11	Rick Honeycutt	.05	.02	.01
☐ 12	Doug Jennings	.05	.02	.01
☐ 13	Joe Klink	.05	.02	.01
☐ 14	Carney Lansford	.10	.05	.01
☐ 15	Darren Lewis	.10	.05	.01
☐ 16	Willie McGee UER	.10	.05	.01
	(Height 6'11")			
☐ 17	Mark McGwire UER	.15	.07	.02
	(183 extra base hits in 1987)			
☐ 18	Mike Moore	.05	.02	.01
☐ 19	Gene Nelson	.05	.02	.01
☐ 20	Dave Otto	.05	.02	.01
☐ 21	Jamie Quirk	.05	.02	.01
☐ 22	Willie Randolph	.10	.05	.01
☐ 23	Scott Sanderson	.05	.02	.01
☐ 24	Terry Steinbach	.10	.05	.01
☐ 25	Dave Stewart	.15	.07	.02
☐ 26	Walt Weiss	.05	.02	.01
☐ 27	Bob Welch	.05	.02	.01
☐ 28	Curt Young	.05	.02	.01
☐ 29	Wally Backman	.05	.02	.01
☐ 30	Stan Belinda UER	.05	.02	.01
	(Born in Huntington, should be State College)			
☐ 31	Jay Bell	.10	.05	.01
☐ 32	Rafael Belliard	.05	.02	.01
☐ 33	Barry Bonds	.30	.14	.04
☐ 34	Bobby Bonilla	.10	.05	.01
☐ 35	Sid Bream	.05	.02	.01
☐ 36	Doug Drabek	.10	.05	.01
☐ 37	Carlos Garcia	.15	.07	.02
☐ 38	Neal Heaton	.05	.02	.01
☐ 39	Jeff King	.05	.02	.01
☐ 40	Bob Kipper	.05	.02	.01
☐ 41	Bill Landrum	.05	.02	.01
☐ 42	Mike LaValliere	.05	.02	.01
☐ 43	Jose Lind	.05	.02	.01

☐ 44	Carmelo Martinez	.05	.02	.01
☐ 45	Bob Patterson	.05	.02	.01
☐ 46	Ted Power	.05	.02	.01
☐ 47	Gary Redus	.05	.02	.01
☐ 48	R.J. Reynolds	.05	.02	.01
☐ 49	Don Slaught	.05	.02	.01
☐ 50	John Smiley	.05	.02	.01
☐ 51	Zane Smith	.05	.02	.01
☐ 52	Randy Tomlin	.05	.02	.01
☐ 53	Andy Van Slyke	.10	.05	.01
☐ 54	Bob Walk	.05	.02	.01
☐ 55	Jack Armstrong	.05	.02	.01
☐ 56	Todd Benzinger	.05	.02	.01
☐ 57	Glenn Braggs	.05	.02	.01
☐ 58	Keith Brown	.05	.02	.01
☐ 59	Tom Browning	.05	.02	.01
☐ 60	Norm Charlton	.05	.02	.01
☐ 61	Eric Davis	.10	.05	.01
☐ 62	Rob Dibble	.10	.05	.01
☐ 63	Bill Doran	.05	.02	.01
☐ 64	Mariano Duncan	.05	.02	.01
☐ 65	Chris Hammond	.05	.02	.01
☐ 66	Billy Hatcher	.05	.02	.01
☐ 67	Danny Jackson	.05	.02	.01
☐ 68	Barry Larkin	.15	.07	.02
☐ 69	Tim Layana	.05	.02	.01
	(Black line over made in first text line)			
☐ 70	Terry Lee	.05	.02	.01
☐ 71	Rick Mahler	.05	.02	.01
☐ 72	Hal Morris	.10	.05	.01
☐ 73	Randy Myers	.15	.07	.02
☐ 74	Ron Oester	.05	.02	.01
☐ 75	Joe Oliver	.05	.02	.01
☐ 76	Paul O'Neill	.15	.07	.02
☐ 77	Luis Quinones	.05	.02	.01
☐ 78	Jeff Reed	.05	.02	.01
☐ 79	Jose Rijo	.10	.05	.01
☐ 80	Chris Sabo	.05	.02	.01
☐ 81	Scott Scudder	.05	.02	.01
☐ 82	Herm Winningham	.05	.02	.01
☐ 83	Larry Andersen	.05	.02	.01
☐ 84	Marty Barrett	.05	.02	.01
☐ 85	Mike Boddicker	.05	.02	.01
☐ 86	Wade Boggs	.15	.07	.02
☐ 87	Tom Bolton	.05	.02	.01
☐ 88	Tom Brunansky	.05	.02	.01
☐ 89	Ellis Burks	.10	.05	.01
☐ 90	Roger Clemens	.15	.07	.02
☐ 91	Scott Cooper	.10	.05	.01
☐ 92	John Dopson	.05	.02	.01
☐ 93	Dwight Evans	.10	.05	.01
☐ 94	Wes Gardner	.05	.02	.01
☐ 95	Jeff Gray	.05	.02	.01
☐ 96	Mike Greenwell	.15	.07	.02
☐ 97	Greg A. Harris	.05	.02	.01
☐ 98	Daryl Irvine	.05	.02	.01
☐ 99	Dana Kiecker	.05	.02	.01
☐ 100	Randy Kutcher	.05	.02	.01
☐ 101	Dennis Lamp	.05	.02	.01
☐ 102	Mike Marshall	.05	.02	.01
☐ 103	John Marzano	.05	.02	.01
☐ 104	Rob Murphy	.05	.02	.01
☐ 105	Tim Naehring	.05	.02	.01
☐ 106	Tony Pena	.05	.02	.01
☐ 107	Phil Plantier	.15	.07	.02
☐ 108	Carlos Quintana	.05	.02	.01
☐ 109	Jeff Reardon	.15	.07	.02
☐ 110	Jerry Reed	.05	.02	.01
☐ 111	Jody Reed	.05	.02	.01
☐ 112	Luis Rivera UER	.05	.02	.01

	(Born 1/3/84)			
☐ 113	Kevin Romine	.05	.02	.01
☐ 114	Phil Bradley	.05	.02	.01
☐ 115	Ivan Calderon	.05	.02	.01
☐ 116	Wayne Edwards	.05	.02	.01
☐ 117	Alex Fernandez	.10	.05	.01
☐ 118	Carlton Fisk	.15	.07	.02
☐ 119	Scott Fletcher	.05	.02	.01
☐ 120	Craig Grebeck	.05	.02	.01
☐ 121	Ozzie Guillen	.10	.05	.01
☐ 122	Greg Hibbard	.05	.02	.01
☐ 123	Lance Johnson UER	.05	.02	.01
	(Born Cincinnati, should be Lincoln Heights)			
☐ 124	Barry Jones	.05	.02	.01
☐ 125	Ron Karkovice	.05	.02	.01
☐ 126	Eric King	.05	.02	.01
☐ 127	Steve Lyons	.05	.02	.01
☐ 128	Carlos Martinez	.05	.02	.01
☐ 129	Jack McDowell UER	.15	.07	.02
	(Stanford misspelled as Standford on back)			
☐ 130	Donn Pall	.05	.02	.01
	(No dots over any i's in text)			
☐ 131	Dan Pasqua	.05	.02	.01
☐ 132	Ken Patterson	.05	.02	.01
☐ 133	Melido Perez	.05	.02	.01
☐ 134	Adam Peterson	.05	.02	.01
☐ 135	Scott Radinsky	.05	.02	.01
☐ 136	Sammy Sosa	.25	.11	.03
☐ 137	Bobby Thigpen	.05	.02	.01
☐ 138	Frank Thomas	2.00	.90	.25
☐ 139	Robin Ventura	.15	.07	.02
☐ 140	Daryl Boston	.05	.02	.01
☐ 141	Chuck Carr	.05	.02	.01
☐ 142	Mark Carreon	.05	.02	.01
☐ 143	David Cone	.15	.07	.02
☐ 144	Ron Darling	.05	.02	.01
☐ 145	Kevin Elster	.05	.02	.01
☐ 146	Sid Fernandez	.10	.05	.01
☐ 147	John Franco	.15	.07	.02
☐ 148	Dwight Gooden	.05	.02	.01
☐ 149	Tom Herr	.05	.02	.01
☐ 150	Todd Hundley	.10	.05	.01
☐ 151	Gregg Jefferies	.15	.07	.02
☐ 152	Howard Johnson	.05	.02	.01
☐ 153	Dave Magadan	.05	.02	.01
☐ 154	Kevin McReynolds	.05	.02	.01
☐ 155	Keith Miller UER	.05	.02	.01
	(Text says Rochester in '87, stats say Tidewater, mixed up with other Keith Miller)			
☐ 156	Bob Ojeda	.05	.02	.01
☐ 157	Tom O'Malley	.05	.02	.01
☐ 158	Alejandro Pena	.05	.02	.01
☐ 159	Darren Reed	.05	.02	.01
☐ 160	Mackey Sasser	.05	.02	.01
☐ 161	Darryl Strawberry	.10	.05	.01
☐ 162	Tim Teufel	.05	.02	.01
☐ 163	Kelvin Torve	.05	.02	.01
☐ 164	Julio Valera	.05	.02	.01
☐ 165	Frank Viola	.10	.05	.01
☐ 166	Wally Whitehurst	.05	.02	.01
☐ 167	Jim Acker	.05	.02	.01
☐ 168	Derek Bell	.15	.07	.02
☐ 169	George Bell	.05	.02	.01
☐ 170	Willie Blair	.05	.02	.01
☐ 171	Pat Borders	.05	.02	.01
☐ 172	John Cerutti	.05	.02	.01

☐ 173 Junior Felix	.05	.02	.01
☐ 174 Tony Fernandez	.05	.02	.01
☐ 175 Kelly Gruber UER	.05	.02	.01

(Born in Houston, should be Bellaire)

☐ 176 Tom Henke	.10	.05	.01
☐ 177 Glenallen Hill	.05	.02	.01
☐ 178 Jimmy Key	.10	.05	.01
☐ 179 Manny Lee	.05	.02	.01
☐ 180 Fred McGriff	.15	.07	.02
☐ 181 Rance Mulliniks	.05	.02	.01
☐ 182 Greg Myers	.05	.02	.01
☐ 183 John Olerud UER	.10	.05	.01

(Listed as throwing right, should be left)

☐ 184 Luis Sojo	.05	.02	.01
☐ 185 Dave Stieb	.05	.02	.01
☐ 186 Todd Stottlemyre	.05	.02	.01
☐ 187 Duane Ward	.05	.02	.01
☐ 188 David Wells	.05	.02	.01
☐ 189 Mark Whiten	.10	.05	.01
☐ 190 Ken Williams	.05	.02	.01
☐ 191 Frank Wills	.05	.02	.01
☐ 192 Mookie Wilson	.05	.02	.01
☐ 193 Don Aase	.05	.02	.01
☐ 194 Tim Belcher UER	.05	.02	.01

(Born Sparta, Ohio, should say Mt. Gilead)

☐ 195 Hubie Brooks	.05	.02	.01
☐ 196 Dennis Cook	.05	.02	.01
☐ 197 Tim Crews	.05	.02	.01
☐ 198 Kal Daniels	.05	.02	.01
☐ 199 Kirk Gibson	.15	.07	.02
☐ 200 Jim Gott	.05	.02	.01
☐ 201 Alfredo Griffin	.05	.02	.01
☐ 202 Chris Gwynn	.05	.02	.01
☐ 203 Dave Hansen	.05	.02	.01
☐ 204 Lenny Harris	.05	.02	.01
☐ 205 Mike Hartley	.05	.02	.01
☐ 206 Mickey Hatcher	.05	.02	.01
☐ 207 Carlos Hernandez	.05	.02	.01
☐ 208 Orel Hershiser	.15	.07	.02
☐ 209 Jay Howell UER	.05	.02	.01

(No 1982 Yankee stats)

☐ 210 Mike Huff	.05	.02	.01
☐ 211 Stan Javier	.05	.02	.01
☐ 212 Ramon Martinez	.15	.07	.02
☐ 213 Mike Morgan	.05	.02	.01
☐ 214 Eddie Murray	.20	.09	.03
☐ 215 Jim Neidlinger	.05	.02	.01
☐ 216 Jose Offerman	.10	.05	.01
☐ 217 Jim Poole	.05	.02	.01
☐ 218 Juan Samuel	.05	.02	.01
☐ 219 Mike Scioscia	.05	.02	.01
☐ 220 Ray Searage	.05	.02	.01
☐ 221 Mike Sharperson	.05	.02	.01
☐ 222 Fernando Valenzuela	.05	.02	.01
☐ 223 Jose Vizcaino	.05	.02	.01
☐ 224 Mike Aldrete	.05	.02	.01
☐ 225 Scott Anderson	.05	.02	.01
☐ 226 Dennis Boyd	.05	.02	.01
☐ 227 Tim Burke	.05	.02	.01
☐ 228 Delino DeShields	.10	.05	.01
☐ 229 Mike Fitzgerald	.05	.02	.01
☐ 230 Tom Foley	.05	.02	.01
☐ 231 Steve Frey	.05	.02	.01
☐ 232 Andres Galarraga	.15	.07	.02
☐ 233 Mark Gardner	.05	.02	.01
☐ 234 Marquis Grissom	.20	.09	.03
☐ 235 Kevin Gross	.05	.02	.01

(No date given for first Expos win)

☐ 236 Drew Hall	.05	.02	.01
☐ 237 Dave Martinez	.05	.02	.01
☐ 238 Dennis Martinez	.10	.05	.01
☐ 239 Dale Mohorcic	.05	.02	.01
☐ 240 Chris Nabholz	.05	.02	.01
☐ 241 Otis Nixon	.05	.02	.01
☐ 242 Junior Noboa	.05	.02	.01
☐ 243 Spike Owen	.05	.02	.01
☐ 244 Tim Raines	.10	.05	.01
☐ 245 Mel Rojas UER	.05	.02	.01

(Stats show 3.60 ERA, bio says 3.19 ERA)

☐ 246 Scott Ruskin	.05	.02	.01
☐ 247 Bill Sampen	.05	.02	.01
☐ 248 Nelson Santovenia	.05	.02	.01
☐ 249 Dave Schmidt	.05	.02	.01
☐ 250 Larry Walker	.25	.11	.03
☐ 251 Tim Wallach	.05	.02	.01
☐ 252 Dave Anderson	.05	.02	.01
☐ 253 Kevin Bass	.05	.02	.01
☐ 254 Steve Bedrosian	.05	.02	.01
☐ 255 Jeff Brantley	.05	.02	.01
☐ 256 John Burkett	.10	.05	.01
☐ 257 Brett Butler	.15	.07	.02
☐ 258 Gary Carter	.15	.07	.02
☐ 259 Will Clark	.15	.07	.02
☐ 260 Steve Decker	.05	.02	.01
☐ 261 Kelly Downs	.05	.02	.01
☐ 262 Scott Garrelts	.05	.02	.01
☐ 263 Terry Kennedy	.05	.02	.01
☐ 264 Mike LaCoss	.05	.02	.01
☐ 265 Mark Leonard	.05	.02	.01
☐ 266 Greg Litton	.05	.02	.01
☐ 267 Kevin Mitchell	.10	.05	.01
☐ 268 Randy O'Neal	.05	.02	.01
☐ 269 Rick Parker	.05	.02	.01
☐ 270 Rick Reuschel	.05	.02	.01
☐ 271 Ernest Riles	.05	.02	.01
☐ 272 Don Robinson	.05	.02	.01
☐ 273 Robby Thompson	.05	.02	.01
☐ 274 Mark Thurmond	.05	.02	.01
☐ 275 Jose Uribe	.05	.02	.01
☐ 276 Matt Williams	.20	.09	.03
☐ 277 Trevor Wilson	.05	.02	.01
☐ 278 Gerald Alexander	.05	.02	.01
☐ 279 Brad Arnsberg	.05	.02	.01
☐ 280 Kevin Belcher	.05	.02	.01
☐ 281 Joe Bitker	.05	.02	.01
☐ 282 Kevin Brown	.10	.05	.01
☐ 283 Steve Buechele	.05	.02	.01
☐ 284 Jack Daugherty	.05	.02	.01
☐ 285 Julio Franco	.10	.05	.01
☐ 286 Juan Gonzalez	.50	.23	.06
☐ 287 Bill Haselman	.05	.02	.01
☐ 288 Charlie Hough	.10	.05	.01
☐ 289 Jeff Huson	.05	.02	.01
☐ 290 Pete Incaviglia	.05	.02	.01
☐ 291 Mike Jeffcoat	.05	.02	.01
☐ 292 Jeff Kunkel	.05	.02	.01
☐ 293 Gary Mielke	.05	.02	.01
☐ 294 Jamie Moyer	.05	.02	.01
☐ 295 Rafael Palmeiro	.15	.07	.02
☐ 296 Geno Petralli	.05	.02	.01
☐ 297 Gary Pettis	.05	.02	.01
☐ 298 Kevin Reimer	.05	.02	.01
☐ 299 Kenny Rogers	.05	.02	.01
☐ 300 Jeff Russell	.05	.02	.01
☐ 301 John Russell	.05	.02	.01
☐ 302 Nolan Ryan	.75	.35	.09
☐ 303 Ruben Sierra	.10	.05	.01

☐ 304	Bobby Witt	.05	.02	.01
☐ 305	Jim Abbott UER	.15	.07	.02

(Text on back states he won
Sullivan Award (outstanding amateur
athlete) in 1989;should be '88)

☐ 306	Kent Anderson	.05	.02	.01
☐ 307	Dante Bichette	.20	.09	.03
☐ 308	Bert Blyleven	.15	.07	.02
☐ 309	Chili Davis	.15	.07	.02
☐ 310	Brian Downing	.05	.02	.01
☐ 311	Mark Eichhorn	.05	.02	.01
☐ 312	Mike Fetters	.05	.02	.01
☐ 313	Chuck Finley	.10	.05	.01
☐ 314	Willie Fraser	.05	.02	.01
☐ 315	Bryan Harvey	.05	.02	.01
☐ 316	Donnie Hill	.05	.02	.01
☐ 317	Wally Joyner	.15	.07	.02
☐ 318	Mark Langston	.15	.07	.02
☐ 319	Kirk McCaskill	.05	.02	.01
☐ 320	John Orton	.05	.02	.01
☐ 321	Lance Parrish	.10	.05	.01
☐ 322	Luis Polonia UER	.05	.02	.01

(1984 Madfison,
should be Madison)

☐ 323	Johnny Ray	.05	.02	.01
☐ 324	Bobby Rose	.05	.02	.01
☐ 325	Dick Schofield	.05	.02	.01
☐ 326	Rick Schu	.05	.02	.01
☐ 327	Lee Stevens	.05	.02	.01
☐ 328	Devon White	.10	.05	.01
☐ 329	Dave Winfield	.15	.07	.02
☐ 330	Cliff Young	.05	.02	.01
☐ 331	Dave Bergman	.05	.02	.01
☐ 332	Phil Clark	.05	.02	.01
☐ 333	Darnell Coles	.05	.02	.01
☐ 334	Milt Cuyler	.05	.02	.01
☐ 335	Cecil Fielder	.15	.07	.02
☐ 336	Travis Fryman	.20	.09	.03
☐ 337	Paul Gibson	.05	.02	.01
☐ 338	Jerry Don Gleaton	.05	.02	.01
☐ 339	Mike Heath	.05	.02	.01
☐ 340	Mike Henneman	.05	.02	.01
☐ 341	Chet Lemon	.05	.02	.01
☐ 342	Lance McCullers	.05	.02	.01
☐ 343	Jack Morris	.15	.07	.02
☐ 344	Lloyd Moseby	.05	.02	.01
☐ 345	Edwin Nunez	.05	.02	.01
☐ 346	Clay Parker	.05	.02	.01
☐ 347	Dan Petry	.05	.02	.01
☐ 348	Tony Phillips	.15	.07	.02
☐ 349	Jeff M. Robinson	.05	.02	.01
☐ 350	Mark Salas	.05	.02	.01
☐ 351	Mike Schwabe	.05	.02	.01
☐ 352	Larry Sheets	.05	.02	.01
☐ 353	John Shelby	.05	.02	.01
☐ 354	Frank Tanana	.05	.02	.01
☐ 355	Alan Trammell	.15	.07	.02
☐ 356	Gary Ward	.05	.02	.01
☐ 357	Lou Whitaker	.10	.05	.01
☐ 358	Beau Allred	.05	.02	.01
☐ 359	Sandy Alomar Jr.	.10	.05	.01
☐ 360	Carlos Baerga	.40	.18	.05
☐ 361	Kevin Bearse	.05	.02	.01
☐ 362	Tom Brookens	.05	.02	.01
☐ 363	Jerry Browne UER	.05	.02	.01

(No dot over i in
first line text)

☐ 364	Tom Candiotti	.05	.02	.01
☐ 365	Alex Cole	.05	.02	.01
☐ 366	John Farrell UER	.05	.02	.01

(Born in Neptune,
should be Monmouth)

☐ 367	Felix Fermin	.05	.02	.01
☐ 368	Keith Hernandez	.10	.05	.01
☐ 369	Brook Jacoby	.05	.02	.01
☐ 370	Chris James	.05	.02	.01
☐ 371	Dion James	.05	.02	.01
☐ 372	Doug Jones	.05	.02	.01
☐ 373	Candy Maldonado	.05	.02	.01
☐ 374	Steve Olin	.05	.02	.01
☐ 375	Jesse Orosco	.05	.02	.01
☐ 376	Rudy Seanez	.05	.02	.01
☐ 377	Joel Skinner	.05	.02	.01
☐ 378	Cory Snyder	.05	.02	.01
☐ 379	Greg Swindell	.05	.02	.01
☐ 380	Sergio Valdez	.05	.02	.01
☐ 381	Mike Walker	.05	.02	.01
☐ 382	Colby Ward	.05	.02	.01
☐ 383	Turner Ward	.05	.02	.01
☐ 384	Mitch Webster	.05	.02	.01
☐ 385	Kevin Wickander	.05	.02	.01
☐ 386	Darrel Akerfelds	.05	.02	.01
☐ 387	Joe Boever	.05	.02	.01
☐ 388	Rod Booker	.05	.02	.01
☐ 389	Sil Campusano	.05	.02	.01
☐ 390	Don Carman	.05	.02	.01
☐ 391	Wes Chamberlain	.05	.02	.01
☐ 392	Pat Combs	.05	.02	.01
☐ 393	Darren Daulton	.15	.07	.02
☐ 394	Jose DeJesus	.05	.02	.01
☐ 395A	Len Dykstra	.15	.07	.02

Name spelled Lenny on back

☐ 395B	Len Dykstra	.10	.05	.01

Name spelled Len on back

☐ 396	Jason Grimsley	.05	.02	.01
☐ 397	Charlie Hayes	.10	.05	.01
☐ 398	Von Hayes	.05	.02	.01
☐ 399	David Hollins UER	.05	.02	.01

(Atl-bats, should
say at-bats)

☐ 400	Ken Howell	.05	.02	.01
☐ 401	Ricky Jordan	.05	.02	.01
☐ 402	John Kruk	.15	.07	.02
☐ 403	Steve Lake	.05	.02	.01
☐ 404	Chuck Malone	.05	.02	.01
☐ 405	Roger McDowell UER	.05	.02	.01

(Says Phillies is
saves, should say in)

☐ 406	Chuck McElroy	.05	.02	.01
☐ 407	Mickey Morandini	.05	.02	.01
☐ 408	Terry Mulholland	.05	.02	.01
☐ 409	Dale Murphy	.15	.07	.02
☐ 410A	Randy Ready ERR	.05	.02	.01

(No Brewers stats
listed for 1983)

☐ 410B	Randy Ready COR	.05	.02	.01
☐ 411	Bruce Ruffin	.05	.02	.01
☐ 412	Dickie Thon	.05	.02	.01
☐ 413	Paul Assenmacher	.05	.02	.01
☐ 414	Damon Berryhill	.05	.02	.01
☐ 415	Mike Bielecki	.05	.02	.01
☐ 416	Shawn Boskie	.05	.02	.01
☐ 417	Dave Clark	.05	.02	.01
☐ 418	Doug Dascenzo	.05	.02	.01
☐ 419A	Andre Dawson ERR	.15	.07	.02

(No stats for 1976)

☐ 419B	Andre Dawson COR	.15	.07	.02
☐ 420	Shawon Dunston	.05	.02	.01
☐ 421	Joe Girardi	.05	.02	.01
☐ 422	Mark Grace	.15	.07	.02
☐ 423	Mike Harkey	.05	.02	.01
☐ 424	Les Lancaster	.05	.02	.01

□ 425	Bill Long	.05	.02	.01
□ 426	Greg Maddux	.60	.25	.07
□ 427	Derrick May	.10	.05	.01
□ 428	Jeff Pico	.05	.02	.01
□ 429	Domingo Ramos	.05	.02	.01
□ 430	Luis Salazar	.05	.02	.01
□ 431	Ryne Sandberg	.30	.14	.04
□ 432	Dwight Smith	.05	.02	.01
□ 433	Greg Smith	.05	.02	.01
□ 434	Rick Sutcliffe	.10	.05	.01
□ 435	Gary Varsho	.05	.02	.01
□ 436	Hector Villanueva	.05	.02	.01
□ 437	Jerome Walton	.05	.02	.01
□ 438	Curtis Wilkerson	.05	.02	.01
□ 439	Mitch Williams	.10	.05	.01
□ 440	Steve Wilson	.05	.02	.01
□ 441	Marvell Wynne	.05	.02	.01
□ 442	Scott Bankhead	.05	.02	.01
□ 443	Scott Bradley	.05	.02	.01
□ 444	Greg Briley	.05	.02	.01
□ 445	Mike Brumley UER (Text 40 SB's in 1988, stats say 41)	.05	.02	.01
□ 446	Jay Buhner	.15	.07	.02
□ 447	Dave Burba	.05	.02	.01
□ 448	Henry Cotto	.05	.02	.01
□ 449	Alvin Davis	.05	.02	.01
□ 450A	Ken Griffey Jr. (Bat .300)	1.50	.70	.19
□ 450B	Ken Griffey Jr. (Bat around .300)	1.50	.70	.19
□ 451	Erik Hanson	.05	.02	.01
□ 452	Gene Harris UER (63 career runs, should be 73)	.05	.02	.01
□ 453	Brian Holman	.05	.02	.01
□ 454	Mike Jackson	.05	.02	.01
□ 455	Randy Johnson	.25	.11	.03
□ 456	Jeffrey Leonard	.05	.02	.01
□ 457	Edgar Martinez	.15	.07	.02
□ 458	Tino Martinez	.15	.07	.02
□ 459	Pete O'Brien UER (1987 BA .266, should be .286)	.05	.02	.01
□ 460	Harold Reynolds	.05	.02	.01
□ 461	Mike Schooler	.05	.02	.01
□ 462	Bill Swift	.05	.02	.01
□ 463	David Valle	.05	.02	.01
□ 464	Omar Vizquel	.05	.02	.01
□ 465	Matt Young	.05	.02	.01
□ 466	Brady Anderson	.10	.05	.01
□ 467	Jeff Ballard UER (Missing top of right parenthesis after Saberhagen in last text line)	.05	.02	.01
□ 468	Juan Bell	.05	.02	.01
□ 469A	Mike Devereaux (First line of text ends with six)	.10	.05	.01
□ 469B	Mike Devereaux (First line of text ends with runs)	.10	.05	.01
□ 470	Steve Finley	.05	.02	.01
□ 471	Dave Gallagher	.05	.02	.01
□ 472	Leo Gomez	.05	.02	.01
□ 473	Rene Gonzales	.05	.02	.01
□ 474	Pete Harnisch	.10	.05	.01
□ 475	Kevin Hickey	.05	.02	.01
□ 476	Chris Hoiles	.10	.05	.01
□ 477	Sam Horn	.05	.02	.01

□ 478	Tim Hulett (Photo shows National Leaguer sliding into second base)	.05	.02	.01
□ 479	Dave Johnson	.05	.02	.01
□ 480	Ron Kittle UER (Edmonton misspelled as Edmundton)	.05	.02	.01
□ 481	Ben McDonald	.10	.05	.01
□ 482	Bob Melvin	.05	.02	.01
□ 483	Bob Milacki	.05	.02	.01
□ 484	Randy Milligan	.05	.02	.01
□ 485	John Mitchell	.05	.02	.01
□ 486	Gregg Olson	.05	.02	.01
□ 487	Joe Orsulak	.05	.02	.01
□ 488	Joe Price	.05	.02	.01
□ 489	Bill Ripken	.05	.02	.01
□ 490	Cal Ripken	.75	.35	.09
□ 491	Curt Schilling	.05	.02	.01
□ 492	David Segui	.05	.02	.01
□ 493	Anthony Telford	.05	.02	.01
□ 494	Mickey Tettleton	.10	.05	.01
□ 495	Mark Williamson	.05	.02	.01
□ 496	Craig Worthington	.05	.02	.01
□ 497	Juan Agosto	.05	.02	.01
□ 498	Eric Anthony	.05	.02	.01
□ 499	Craig Biggio	.15	.07	.02
□ 500	Ken Caminiti UER (Born 4/4, should be 4/21)	.15	.07	.02
□ 501	Casey Candaele	.05	.02	.01
□ 502	Andujar Cedeno	.05	.02	.01
□ 503	Danny Darwin	.05	.02	.01
□ 504	Mark Davidson	.05	.02	.01
□ 505	Glenn Davis	.05	.02	.01
□ 506	Jim Deshaies	.05	.02	.01
□ 507	Luis Gonzalez	.15	.07	.02
□ 508	Bill Gullickson	.05	.02	.01
□ 509	Xavier Hernandez	.05	.02	.01
□ 510	Brian Meyer	.05	.02	.01
□ 511	Ken Oberkfell	.05	.02	.01
□ 512	Mark Portugal	.05	.02	.01
□ 513	Rafael Ramirez	.05	.02	.01
□ 514	Karl Rhodes	.05	.02	.01
□ 515	Mike Scott	.05	.02	.01
□ 516	Mike Simms	.05	.02	.01
□ 517	Dave Smith	.05	.02	.01
□ 518	Franklin Stubbs	.05	.02	.01
□ 519	Glenn Wilson	.05	.02	.01
□ 520	Eric Yelding UER (Text has 63 steals, stats have 64, which is correct)	.05	.02	.01
□ 521	Gerald Young	.05	.02	.01
□ 522	Shawn Abner	.05	.02	.01
□ 523	Roberto Alomar	.25	.11	.03
□ 524	Andy Benes	.10	.05	.01
□ 525	Joe Carter	.15	.07	.02
□ 526	Jack Clark	.10	.05	.01
□ 527	Joey Cora	.05	.02	.01
□ 528	Paul Faries	.05	.02	.01
□ 529	Tony Gwynn	.30	.14	.04
□ 530	Atlee Hammaker	.05	.02	.01
□ 531	Greg W. Harris	.05	.02	.01
□ 532	Thomas Howard	.05	.02	.01
□ 533	Bruce Hurst	.05	.02	.01
□ 534	Craig Lefferts	.05	.02	.01
□ 535	Derek Lilliquist	.05	.02	.01
□ 536	Fred Lynn	.10	.05	.01
□ 537	Mike Pagliarulo	.05	.02	.01
□ 538	Mark Parent	.05	.02	.01

☐ 539	Dennis Rasmussen	.05	.02	.01
☐ 540	Bip Roberts	.10	.05	.01
☐ 541	Richard Rodriguez	.05	.02	.01
☐ 542	Benito Santiago	.05	.02	.01
☐ 543	Calvin Schiraldi	.05	.02	.01
☐ 544	Eric Show	.05	.02	.01
☐ 545	Phil Stephenson	.05	.02	.01
☐ 546	Garry Templeton UER	.05	.02	.01
	(Born 3/24/57, should be 3/24/56)			
☐ 547	Ed Whitson	.05	.02	.01
☐ 548	Eddie Williams	.05	.02	.01
☐ 549	Kevin Appier	.10	.05	.01
☐ 550	Luis Aquino	.05	.02	.01
☐ 551	Bob Boone	.10	.05	.01
☐ 552	George Brett	.40	.18	.05
☐ 553	Jeff Conine	.60	.25	.07
☐ 554	Steve Crawford	.05	.02	.01
☐ 555	Mark Davis	.05	.02	.01
☐ 556	Storm Davis	.05	.02	.01
☐ 557	Jim Eisenreich	.05	.02	.01
☐ 558	Steve Farr	.05	.02	.01
☐ 559	Tom Gordon	.10	.05	.01
☐ 560	Mark Gubicza	.05	.02	.01
☐ 561	Bo Jackson	.10	.05	.01
☐ 562	Mike Macfarlane	.05	.02	.01
☐ 563	Brian McRae	.30	.14	.04
☐ 564	Jeff Montgomery	.10	.05	.01
☐ 565	Bill Pecota	.05	.02	.01
☐ 566	Gerald Perry	.05	.02	.01
☐ 567	Bret Saberhagen	.15	.07	.02
☐ 568	Jeff Schulz	.05	.02	.01
☐ 569	Kevin Seitzer	.05	.02	.01
☐ 570	Terry Shumpert	.05	.02	.01
☐ 571	Kurt Stillwell	.05	.02	.01
☐ 572	Danny Tartabull	.10	.05	.01
☐ 573	Gary Thurman	.05	.02	.01
☐ 574	Frank White	.10	.05	.01
☐ 575	Willie Wilson	.05	.02	.01
☐ 576	Chris Bosio	.05	.02	.01
☐ 577	Greg Brock	.05	.02	.01
☐ 578	George Canale	.05	.02	.01
☐ 579	Chuck Crim	.05	.02	.01
☐ 580	Rob Deer	.05	.02	.01
☐ 581	Edgar Diaz	.05	.02	.01
☐ 582	Tom Edens	.05	.02	.01
☐ 583	Mike Felder	.05	.02	.01
☐ 584	Jim Gantner	.05	.02	.01
☐ 585	Darryl Hamilton	.10	.05	.01
☐ 586	Ted Higuera	.05	.02	.01
☐ 587	Mark Knudson	.05	.02	.01
☐ 588	Bill Krueger	.05	.02	.01
☐ 589	Tim McIntosh	.05	.02	.01
☐ 590	Paul Mirabella	.05	.02	.01
☐ 591	Paul Molitor	.15	.07	.02
☐ 592	Jaime Navarro	.05	.02	.01
☐ 593	Dave Parker	.10	.05	.01
☐ 594	Dan Plesac	.05	.02	.01
☐ 595	Ron Robinson	.05	.02	.01
☐ 596	Gary Sheffield	.15	.07	.02
☐ 597	Bill Spiers	.05	.02	.01
☐ 598	B.J. Surhoff	.05	.02	.01
☐ 599	Greg Vaughn	.10	.05	.01
☐ 600	Randy Veres	.05	.02	.01
☐ 601	Robin Yount	.15	.07	.02
☐ 602	Rick Aguilera	.10	.05	.01
☐ 603	Allan Anderson	.05	.02	.01
☐ 604	Juan Berenguer	.05	.02	.01
☐ 605	Randy Bush	.05	.02	.01
☐ 606	Carmen Castillo	.05	.02	.01
☐ 607	Tim Drummond	.05	.02	.01
☐ 608	Scott Erickson	.05	.02	.01
☐ 609	Gary Gaetti	.05	.02	.01
☐ 610	Greg Gagne	.05	.02	.01
☐ 611	Dan Gladden	.05	.02	.01
☐ 612	Mark Guthrie	.05	.02	.01
☐ 613	Brian Harper	.05	.02	.01
☐ 614	Kent Hrbek	.10	.05	.01
☐ 615	Gene Larkin	.05	.02	.01
☐ 616	Terry Leach	.05	.02	.01
☐ 617	Nelson Liriano	.05	.02	.01
☐ 618	Shane Mack	.05	.02	.01
☐ 619	John Moses	.05	.02	.01
☐ 620	Pedro Munoz	.10	.05	.01
☐ 621	Al Newman	.05	.02	.01
☐ 622	Junior Ortiz	.05	.02	.01
☐ 623	Kirby Puckett	.30	.14	.04
☐ 624	Roy Smith	.05	.02	.01
☐ 625	Kevin Tapani	.10	.05	.01
☐ 626	Gary Wayne	.05	.02	.01
☐ 627	David West	.05	.02	.01
☐ 628	Cris Carpenter	.05	.02	.01
☐ 629	Vince Coleman	.05	.02	.01
☐ 630	Ken Dayley	.05	.02	.01
☐ 631	Jose DeLeon	.05	.02	.01
☐ 632	Frank DiPino	.05	.02	.01
☐ 633	Bernard Gilkey	.10	.05	.01
☐ 634	Pedro Guerrero	.10	.05	.01
☐ 635	Ken Hill	.15	.07	.02
☐ 636	Felix Jose	.05	.02	.01
☐ 637	Ray Lankford	.10	.05	.01
☐ 638	Joe Magrane	.05	.02	.01
☐ 639	Tom Niedenfuer	.05	.02	.01
☐ 640	Jose Oquendo	.05	.02	.01
☐ 641	Tom Pagnozzi	.05	.02	.01
☐ 642	Terry Pendleton	.15	.07	.02
☐ 643	Mike Perez	.05	.02	.01
☐ 644	Bryn Smith	.05	.02	.01
☐ 645	Lee Smith	.15	.07	.02
☐ 646	Ozzie Smith	.20	.09	.03
☐ 647	Scott Terry	.05	.02	.01
☐ 648	Bob Tewksbury	.05	.02	.01
☐ 649	Milt Thompson	.05	.02	.01
☐ 650	John Tudor	.05	.02	.01
☐ 651	Denny Walling	.05	.02	.01
☐ 652	Craig Wilson	.05	.02	.01
☐ 653	Todd Worrell	.05	.02	.01
☐ 654	Todd Zeile	.10	.05	.01
☐ 655	Oscar Azocar	.05	.02	.01
☐ 656	Steve Balboni UER	.05	.02	.01
	(Born 1/5/57, should be 1/16)			
☐ 657	Jesse Barfield	.05	.02	.01
☐ 658	Greg Cadaret	.05	.02	.01
☐ 659	Chuck Cary	.05	.02	.01
☐ 660	Rick Cerone	.05	.02	.01
☐ 661	Dave Eiland	.05	.02	.01
☐ 662	Alvaro Espinoza	.05	.02	.01
☐ 663	Bob Geren	.05	.02	.01
☐ 664	Lee Guetterman	.05	.02	.01
☐ 665	Mel Hall	.05	.02	.01
☐ 666	Andy Hawkins	.05	.02	.01
☐ 667	Jimmy Jones	.05	.02	.01
☐ 668	Roberto Kelly	.10	.05	.01
☐ 669	Dave LaPoint UER	.05	.02	.01
	(No '81 Brewers stats, totals also are wrong)			
☐ 670	Tim Leary	.05	.02	.01
☐ 671	Jim Leyritz	.05	.02	.01
☐ 672	Kevin Maas	.05	.02	.01
☐ 673	Don Mattingly	.40	.18	.05
☐ 674	Matt Nokes	.05	.02	.01

☐	675	Pascual Perez	.05	.02	.01
☐	676	Eric Plunk	.05	.02	.01
☐	677	Dave Righetti	.05	.02	.01
☐	678	Jeff D. Robinson	.05	.02	.01
☐	679	Steve Sax	.05	.02	.01
☐	680	Mike Witt	.05	.02	.01
☐	681	Steve Avery UER (Born in New Jersey, should say Michigan)	.15	.07	.02
☐	682	Mike Bell	.05	.02	.01
☐	683	Jeff Blauser	.10	.05	.01
☐	684	Francisco Cabrera UER (Born 10/16, should say 10/10)	.05	.02	.01
☐	685	Tony Castillo	.05	.02	.01
☐	686	Marty Clary UER (Shown pitching righty, but bio has left)	.05	.02	.01
☐	687	Nick Esasky	.05	.02	.01
☐	688	Ron Gant	.15	.07	.02
☐	689	Tom Glavine	.20	.09	.03
☐	690	Mark Grant	.05	.02	.01
☐	691	Tommy Gregg	.05	.02	.01
☐	692	Dwayne Henry	.05	.02	.01
☐	693	Dave Justice	.20	.09	.03
☐	694	Jimmy Kremers	.05	.02	.01
☐	695	Charlie Leibrandt	.05	.02	.01
☐	696	Mark Lemke	.05	.02	.01
☐	697	Oddibe McDowell	.05	.02	.01
☐	698	Greg Olson	.05	.02	.01
☐	699	Jeff Parrett	.05	.02	.01
☐	700	Jim Presley	.05	.02	.01
☐	701	Victor Rosario	.05	.02	.01
☐	702	Lonnie Smith	.05	.02	.01
☐	703	Pete Smith	.05	.02	.01
☐	704	John Smoltz	.15	.07	.02
☐	705	Mike Stanton	.05	.02	.01
☐	706	Andres Thomas	.05	.02	.01
☐	707	Jeff Treadway	.05	.02	.01
☐	708	Jim Vatcher	.05	.02	.01
☐	709	Home Run Kings Ryne Sandberg Cecil Fielder	.15	.07	.02
☐	710	2nd Generation Stars Barry Bonds Ken Griffey Jr.	.50	.23	.06
☐	711	NLCS Team Leaders Bobby Bonilla Barry Larkin	.15	.07	.02
☐	712	Top Game Savers Bobby Thigpen John Franco	.05	.02	.01
☐	713	Chicago's 100 Club Andre Dawson Ryne Sandberg UER (Ryno misspelled Rhino)	.10	.05	.01
☐	714	CL:A's/Pirates Reds/Red Sox	.05	.02	.01
☐	715	CL:White Sox/Mets Blue Jays/Dodgers	.05	.02	.01
☐	716	CL:Expos/Giants Rangers/Angels	.05	.02	.01
☐	717	CL:Tigers/Indians Phillies/Cubs	.05	.02	.01
☐	718	CL:Mariners/Orioles Astros/Padres	.05	.02	.01
☐	719	CL:Royals/Brewers Twins/Cardinals	.05	.02	.01
☐	720	CL:Yankees/Braves Superstars/Specials	.05	.02	.01

1991 Fleer Update

The 1991 Fleer Update set contains 132 standard-size cards. The glossy color action photos on the fronts are placed on a yellow card face and accentuated by black lines above and below. The backs have a head shot (circular format), biography, and complete Major League statistics. The cards are checklisted below alphabetically within and according to teams for each league as follows: Baltimore Orioles (1-3), Boston Red Sox (4-7), California Angels (8-10), Chicago White Sox (11-15), Cleveland Indians (16-21), Detroit Tigers (22-24), Kansas City Royals (25-28), Milwaukee Brewers (29-35), Minnesota Twins (36-41), New York Yankees (42-49), Oakland Athletics (50-51), Seattle Mariners (52-57), Texas Rangers (58-62), Toronto Blue Jays (63-69), Atlanta Braves (70-76), Chicago Cubs (77-83), Cincinnati Reds (84-86), Houston Astros (87-90), Los Angeles Dodgers (91-96), Montreal Expos (97-99), New York Mets (100-104), Philadelphia Phillies (105-110), Pittsburgh Pirates (111-115), St. Louis Cardinals (116-119), San Diego Padres (120-127), and San Francisco Giants (128-131). The key Rookie Cards in this set are Jeff Bagwell and Ivan Rodriguez. Cards are numbered with a "U" prefix.

		MINT	NRMT	EXC
COMPLETE FACT.SET (132)		4.00	1.80	.50
COMMON CARD (1-132)		.05	.02	.01
☐	1 Glenn Davis	.05	.02	.01
☐	2 Dwight Evans	.10	.05	.01
☐	3 Jose Mesa	.05	.02	.01
☐	4 Jack Clark	.10	.05	.01
☐	5 Danny Darwin	.05	.02	.01
☐	6 Steve Lyons	.05	.02	.01
☐	7 Mo Vaughn	.50	.23	.06
☐	8 Floyd Bannister	.05	.02	.01
☐	9 Gary Gaetti	.05	.02	.01
☐	10 Dave Parker	.10	.05	.01
☐	11 Joey Cora	.05	.02	.01
☐	12 Charlie Hough	.10	.05	.01
☐	13 Matt Merullo	.05	.02	.01
☐	14 Warren Newson	.05	.02	.01
☐	15 Tim Raines	.15	.07	.02
☐	16 Albert Belle	.50	.23	.06
☐	17 Glenallen Hill	.05	.02	.01

☐ 18	Shawn Hillegas	.05	.02	.01
☐ 19	Mark Lewis	.05	.02	.01
☐ 20	Charles Nagy	.10	.05	.01
☐ 21	Mark Whiten	.15	.07	.02
☐ 22	John Cerutti	.05	.02	.01
☐ 23	Rob Deer	.05	.02	.01
☐ 24	Mickey Tettleton	.10	.05	.01
☐ 25	Warren Cromartie	.05	.02	.01
☐ 26	Kirk Gibson	.15	.07	.02
☐ 27	David Howard	.05	.02	.01
☐ 28	Brent Mayne	.05	.02	.01
☐ 29	Dante Bichette	.20	.09	.03
☐ 30	Mark Lee	.05	.02	.01
☐ 31	Julio Machado	.05	.02	.01
☐ 32	Edwin Nunez	.05	.02	.01
☐ 33	Willie Randolph	.10	.05	.01
☐ 34	Franklin Stubbs	.05	.02	.01
☐ 35	Bill Wegman	.05	.02	.01
☐ 36	Chili Davis	.15	.07	.02
☐ 37	Chuck Knoblauch	.25	.11	.03
☐ 38	Scott Leius	.05	.02	.01
☐ 39	Jack Morris	.15	.07	.02
☐ 40	Mike Pagliarulo	.05	.02	.01
☐ 41	Lenny Webster	.05	.02	.01
☐ 42	John Habyan	.05	.02	.01
☐ 43	Steve Howe	.05	.02	.01
☐ 44	Jeff Johnson	.05	.02	.01
☐ 45	Scott Kamieniecki	.05	.02	.01
☐ 46	Pat Kelly	.10	.05	.01
☐ 47	Hensley Meulens	.05	.02	.01
☐ 48	Wade Taylor	.05	.02	.01
☐ 49	Bernie Williams	.15	.07	.02
☐ 50	Kirk Dressendorfer	.05	.02	.01
☐ 51	Ernest Riles	.05	.02	.01
☐ 52	Rich DeLucia	.05	.02	.01
☐ 53	Tracy Jones	.05	.02	.01
☐ 54	Bill Krueger	.05	.02	.01
☐ 55	Alonzo Powell	.05	.02	.01
☐ 56	Jeff Schaefer	.05	.02	.01
☐ 57	Russ Swan	.05	.02	.01
☐ 58	John Barfield	.05	.02	.01
☐ 59	Rich Gossage	.15	.07	.02
☐ 60	Jose Guzman	.05	.02	.01
☐ 61	Dean Palmer	.10	.05	.01
☐ 62	Ivan Rodriguez	.50	.23	.06
☐ 63	Roberto Alomar	.25	.11	.03
☐ 64	Tom Candiotti	.05	.02	.01
☐ 65	Joe Carter	.15	.07	.02
☐ 66	Ed Sprague	.05	.02	.01
☐ 67	Pat Tabler	.05	.02	.01
☐ 68	Mike Timlin	.05	.02	.01
☐ 69	Devon White	.10	.05	.01
☐ 70	Rafael Belliard	.05	.02	.01
☐ 71	Juan Berenguer	.05	.02	.01
☐ 72	Sid Bream	.05	.02	.01
☐ 73	Marvin Freeman	.05	.02	.01
☐ 74	Kent Mercker	.05	.02	.01
☐ 75	Otis Nixon	.05	.02	.01
☐ 76	Terry Pendleton	.15	.07	.02
☐ 77	George Bell	.05	.02	.01
☐ 78	Danny Jackson	.05	.02	.01
☐ 79	Chuck McElroy	.05	.02	.01
☐ 80	Gary Scott	.05	.02	.01
☐ 81	Heathcliff Slocumb	.15	.07	.02
☐ 82	Dave Smith	.05	.02	.01
☐ 83	Rick Wilkins	.05	.02	.01
☐ 84	Freddie Benavides	.05	.02	.01
☐ 85	Ted Power	.05	.02	.01
☐ 86	Mo Sanford	.05	.02	.01
☐ 87	Jeff Bagwell	2.00	.90	.25
☐ 88	Steve Finley	.05	.02	.01

☐ 89	Pete Harnisch	.10	.05	.01
☐ 90	Darryl Kile	.05	.02	.01
☐ 91	Brett Butler	.15	.07	.02
☐ 92	John Candelaria	.05	.02	.01
☐ 93	Gary Carter	.15	.07	.02
☐ 94	Kevin Gross	.05	.02	.01
☐ 95	Bob Ojeda	.05	.02	.01
☐ 96	Darryl Strawberry	.05	.02	.01
☐ 97	Ivan Calderon	.05	.02	.01
☐ 98	Ron Hassey	.05	.02	.01
☐ 99	Gilberto Reyes	.05	.02	.01
☐ 100	Hubie Brooks	.05	.02	.01
☐ 101	Rick Cerone	.05	.02	.01
☐ 102	Vince Coleman	.05	.02	.01
☐ 103	Jeff Innis	.05	.02	.01
☐ 104	Pete Schourek	.40	.18	.05
☐ 105	Andy Ashby	.05	.02	.01
☐ 106	Wally Backman	.05	.02	.01
☐ 107	Darrin Fletcher	.05	.02	.01
☐ 108	Tommy Greene	.05	.02	.01
☐ 109	John Morris	.05	.02	.01
☐ 110	Mitch Williams	.10	.05	.01
☐ 111	Lloyd McClendon	.05	.02	.01
☐ 112	Orlando Merced	.15	.07	.02
☐ 113	Vicente Palacios	.05	.02	.01
☐ 114	Gary Varsho	.05	.02	.01
☐ 115	John Wehner	.05	.02	.01
☐ 116	Rex Hudler	.05	.02	.01
☐ 117	Tim Jones	.05	.02	.01
☐ 118	Geronimo Pena	.05	.02	.01
☐ 119	Gerald Perry	.05	.02	.01
☐ 120	Larry Andersen	.05	.02	.01
☐ 121	Jerald Clark	.05	.02	.01
☐ 122	Scott Coolbaugh	.05	.02	.01
☐ 123	Tony Fernandez	.05	.02	.01
☐ 124	Darrin Jackson	.05	.02	.01
☐ 125	Fred McGriff	.15	.07	.02
☐ 126	Jose Mota	.05	.02	.01
☐ 127	Tim Teufel	.05	.02	.01
☐ 128	Bud Black	.05	.02	.01
☐ 129	Mike Felder	.05	.02	.01
☐ 130	Willie McGee	.10	.05	.01
☐ 131	Dave Righetti	.05	.02	.01
☐ 132	Checklist U1-U132	.05	.02	.01

1992 Fleer

The 1992 Fleer set contains 720 standard-size cards. The card fronts shade from metallic pale green to white as one moves down the face. The team logo and player's name appear to the right of the picture, running the length of the card. The top portion

of the backs has a different color player photo and biography, while the bottom portion includes statistics and player profile. The cards are checklisted below alphabetically within and according to teams for each league as follows: Baltimore Orioles (1-31), Boston Red Sox (32-49), California Angels (50-73), Chicago White Sox (74-101), Cleveland Indians (102-126), Detroit Tigers (127-149), Kansas City Royals (150-172), Milwaukee Brewers (173-194), Minnesota Twins (195-220), New York Yankees (221-247), Oakland Athletics (248-272), Seattle Mariners (273-296), Texas Rangers (297-321), Toronto Blue Jays (322-348), Atlanta Braves (349-374), Chicago Cubs (375-397), Cincinnati Reds (398-423), Houston Astros (424-446), Los Angeles Dodgers (447-471), Montreal Expos (472-494), New York Mets (495-520), Philadelphia Phillies (521-547), Pittsburgh Pirates (548-573), St. Louis Cardinals (574-596), San Diego Padres (597-624), and San Francisco Giants (625-651). Topical subsets feature Major League Prospects (652-680), Record Setters (681-687), League Leaders (688-697), Super Star Specials (698-707) and Pro Visions (708-713). Rookie Cards in the set include Rod Beck.

	MINT	NRMT	EXC
COMPLETE SET (720)	15.00	6.75	1.85
COMPLETE HOBBY SET (732)	25.00	11.00	3.10
COMPLETE RETAIL SET (732)	25.00	11.00	3.10
COMMON CARD (1-720)	.05	.02	.01

☐ 1	Brady Anderson	.10	.05	.01
☐ 2	Jose Bautista	.05	.02	.01
☐ 3	Juan Bell	.05	.02	.01
☐ 4	Glenn Davis	.05	.02	.01
☐ 5	Mike Devereaux	.10	.05	.01
☐ 6	Dwight Evans	.10	.05	.01
☐ 7	Mike Flanagan	.05	.02	.01
☐ 8	Leo Gomez	.05	.02	.01
☐ 9	Chris Hoiles	.10	.05	.01
☐ 10	Sam Horn	.05	.02	.01
☐ 11	Tim Hulett	.05	.02	.01
☐ 12	Dave Johnson	.05	.02	.01
☐ 13	Chito Martinez	.05	.02	.01
☐ 14	Ben McDonald	.10	.05	.01
☐ 15	Bob Melvin	.05	.02	.01
☐ 16	Luis Mercedes	.05	.02	.01
☐ 17	Jose Mesa	.05	.02	.01
☐ 18	Bob Milacki	.05	.02	.01
☐ 19	Randy Milligan	.05	.02	.01
☐ 20	Mike Mussina UER (Card back refers to him as Jeff)	.25	.11	.03
☐ 21	Gregg Olson	.05	.02	.01
☐ 22	Joe Orsulak	.05	.02	.01
☐ 23	Jim Poole	.05	.02	.01
☐ 24	Arthur Rhodes	.05	.02	.01
☐ 25	Billy Ripken	.05	.02	.01
☐ 26	Cal Ripken	1.00	.45	.12
☐ 27	David Segui	.05	.02	.01
☐ 28	Roy Smith	.05	.02	.01
☐ 29	Anthony Telford	.05	.02	.01
☐ 30	Mark Williamson	.05	.02	.01
☐ 31	Craig Worthington	.05	.02	.01
☐ 32	Wade Boggs	.15	.07	.02
☐ 33	Tom Bolton	.05	.02	.01
☐ 34	Tom Brunansky	.05	.02	.01
☐ 35	Ellis Burks	.10	.05	.01
☐ 36	Jack Clark	.10	.05	.01
☐ 37	Roger Clemens	.20	.09	.03
☐ 38	Danny Darwin	.05	.02	.01
☐ 39	Mike Greenwell	.15	.07	.02
☐ 40	Joe Hesketh	.05	.02	.01
☐ 41	Daryl Irvine	.05	.02	.01
☐ 42	Dennis Lamp	.05	.02	.01
☐ 43	Tony Pena	.05	.02	.01
☐ 44	Phil Plantier	.10	.05	.01
☐ 45	Carlos Quintana	.05	.02	.01
☐ 46	Jeff Reardon	.10	.05	.01
☐ 47	Jody Reed	.05	.02	.01
☐ 48	Luis Rivera	.05	.02	.01
☐ 49	Mo Vaughn	.40	.18	.05
☐ 50	Jim Abbott	.15	.07	.02
☐ 51	Kyle Abbott	.05	.02	.01
☐ 52	Ruben Amaro Jr.	.05	.02	.01
☐ 53	Scott Bailes	.05	.02	.01
☐ 54	Chris Beasley	.05	.02	.01
☐ 55	Mark Eichhorn	.05	.02	.01
☐ 56	Mike Fetters	.05	.02	.01
☐ 57	Chuck Finley	.05	.02	.01
☐ 58	Gary Gaetti	.05	.02	.01
☐ 59	Dave Gallagher	.05	.02	.01
☐ 60	Donnie Hill	.05	.02	.01
☐ 61	Bryan Harvey UER (Lee Smith led the Majors with 47 saves)	.10	.05	.01
☐ 62	Wally Joyner	.15	.07	.02
☐ 63	Mark Langston	.15	.07	.02
☐ 64	Kirk McCaskill	.05	.02	.01
☐ 65	John Orton	.05	.02	.01
☐ 66	Lance Parrish	.10	.05	.01
☐ 67	Luis Polonia	.05	.02	.01
☐ 68	Bobby Rose	.05	.02	.01
☐ 69	Dick Schofield	.05	.02	.01
☐ 70	Luis Sojo	.05	.02	.01
☐ 71	Lee Stevens	.05	.02	.01
☐ 72	Dave Winfield	.15	.07	.02
☐ 73	Cliff Young	.05	.02	.01
☐ 74	Wilson Alvarez	.10	.05	.01
☐ 75	Esteban Beltre	.05	.02	.01
☐ 76	Joey Cora	.05	.02	.01
☐ 77	Brian Drahman	.05	.02	.01
☐ 78	Alex Fernandez	.15	.07	.02
☐ 79	Carlton Fisk	.15	.07	.02
☐ 80	Scott Fletcher	.05	.02	.01
☐ 81	Craig Grebeck	.05	.02	.01
☐ 82	Ozzie Guillen	.10	.05	.01
☐ 83	Greg Hibbard	.05	.02	.01
☐ 84	Charlie Hough	.10	.05	.01
☐ 85	Mike Huff	.05	.02	.01
☐ 86	Bo Jackson	.15	.07	.02
☐ 87	Lance Johnson	.05	.02	.01
☐ 88	Ron Karkovice	.05	.02	.01
☐ 89	Jack McDowell	.15	.07	.02
☐ 90	Matt Merullo	.05	.02	.01
☐ 91	Warren Newson	.05	.02	.01
☐ 92	Donn Pall UER (Called Dunn on card back)	.05	.02	.01
☐ 93	Dan Pasqua	.05	.02	.01
☐ 94	Ken Patterson	.05	.02	.01
☐ 95	Melido Perez	.05	.02	.01
☐ 96	Scott Radinsky	.05	.02	.01
☐ 97	Tim Raines	.10	.05	.01
☐ 98	Sammy Sosa	.15	.07	.02
☐ 99	Bobby Thigpen	.05	.02	.01
☐ 100	Frank Thomas	1.50	.70	.19

☐	101	Robin Ventura	.15	.07	.02	☐	170	Kurt Stillwell	.05	.02	.01
☐	102	Mike Aldrete	.05	.02	.01	☐	171	Danny Tartabull	.10	.05	.01
☐	103	Sandy Alomar Jr.	.10	.05	.01	☐	172	Gary Thurman	.05	.02	.01
☐	104	Carlos Baerga	.30	.14	.04	☐	173	Dante Bichette	.20	.09	.03
☐	105	Albert Belle	.50	.23	.06	☐	174	Kevin D. Brown	.05	.02	.01
☐	106	Willie Blair	.05	.02	.01	☐	175	Chuck Crim	.05	.02	.01
☐	107	Jerry Browne	.05	.02	.01	☐	176	Jim Gantner	.05	.02	.01
☐	108	Alex Cole	.05	.02	.01	☐	177	Darryl Hamilton	.10	.05	.01
☐	109	Felix Fermin	.05	.02	.01	☐	178	Ted Higuera	.05	.02	.01
☐	110	Glenallen Hill	.05	.02	.01	☐	179	Darren Holmes	.05	.02	.01
☐	111	Shawn Hillegas	.05	.02	.01	☐	180	Mark Lee	.05	.02	.01
☐	112	Chris James	.05	.02	.01	☐	181	Julio Machado	.05	.02	.01
☐	113	Reggie Jefferson	.05	.02	.01	☐	182	Paul Molitor	.15	.07	.02
☐	114	Doug Jones	.05	.02	.01	☐	183	Jaime Navarro	.05	.02	.01
☐	115	Eric King	.05	.02	.01	☐	184	Edwin Nunez	.05	.02	.01
☐	116	Mark Lewis	.05	.02	.01	☐	185	Dan Plesac	.05	.02	.01
☐	117	Carlos Martinez	.05	.02	.01	☐	186	Willie Randolph	.10	.05	.01
☐	118	Charles Nagy UER	.10	.05	.01	☐	187	Ron Robinson	.05	.02	.01
		(Throws right, but				☐	188	Gary Sheffield	.15	.07	.02
		card says left)				☐	189	Bill Spiers	.05	.02	.01
☐	119	Rod Nichols	.05	.02	.01	☐	190	B.J. Surhoff	.05	.02	.01
☐	120	Steve Olin	.05	.02	.01	☐	191	Dale Sveum	.05	.02	.01
☐	121	Jesse Orosco	.05	.02	.01	☐	192	Greg Vaughn	.10	.05	.01
☐	122	Rudy Seanez	.05	.02	.01	☐	193	Bill Wegman	.05	.02	.01
☐	123	Joel Skinner	.05	.02	.01	☐	194	Robin Yount	.15	.07	.02
☐	124	Greg Swindell	.05	.02	.01	☐	195	Rick Aguilera	.10	.05	.01
☐	125	Jim Thome	.75	.35	.09	☐	196	Allan Anderson	.05	.02	.01
☐	126	Mark Whiten	.10	.05	.01	☐	197	Steve Bedrosian	.05	.02	.01
☐	127	Scott Aldred	.05	.02	.01	☐	198	Randy Bush	.05	.02	.01
☐	128	Andy Allanson	.05	.02	.01	☐	199	Larry Casian	.05	.02	.01
☐	129	John Cerutti	.05	.02	.01	☐	200	Chili Davis	.15	.07	.02
☐	130	Milt Cuyler	.05	.02	.01	☐	201	Scott Erickson	.05	.02	.01
☐	131	Mike Dalton	.05	.02	.01	☐	202	Greg Gagne	.05	.02	.01
☐	132	Rob Deer	.05	.02	.01	☐	203	Dan Gladden	.05	.02	.01
☐	133	Cecil Fielder	.10	.05	.01	☐	204	Brian Harper	.05	.02	.01
☐	134	Travis Fryman	.15	.07	.02	☐	205	Kent Hrbek	.10	.05	.01
☐	135	Dan Gakeler	.05	.02	.01	☐	206	Chuck Knoblauch UER	.15	.07	.02
☐	136	Paul Gibson	.05	.02	.01			(Career hit total			
☐	137	Bill Gullickson	.05	.02	.01			of 59 is wrong)			
☐	138	Mike Henneman	.05	.02	.01	☐	207	Gene Larkin	.05	.02	.01
☐	139	Pete Incaviglia	.05	.02	.01	☐	208	Terry Leach	.05	.02	.01
☐	140	Mark Leiter	.05	.02	.01	☐	209	Scott Leius	.05	.02	.01
☐	141	Scott Livingstone	.05	.02	.01	☐	210	Shane Mack	.05	.02	.01
☐	142	Lloyd Moseby	.05	.02	.01	☐	211	Jack Morris	.15	.07	.02
☐	143	Tony Phillips	.05	.02	.01	☐	212	Pedro Munoz	.10	.05	.01
☐	144	Mark Salas	.05	.02	.01	☐	213	Denny Neagle	.05	.02	.01
☐	145	Frank Tanana	.05	.02	.01	☐	214	Al Newman	.05	.02	.01
☐	146	Walt Terrell	.05	.02	.01	☐	215	Junior Ortiz	.05	.02	.01
☐	147	Mickey Tettleton	.10	.05	.01	☐	216	Mike Pagliarulo	.05	.02	.01
☐	148	Alan Trammell	.15	.07	.02	☐	217	Kirby Puckett	.30	.14	.04
☐	149	Lou Whitaker	.15	.07	.02	☐	218	Paul Sorrento	.10	.05	.01
☐	150	Kevin Appier	.10	.05	.01	☐	219	Kevin Tapani	.05	.02	.01
☐	151	Luis Aquino	.05	.02	.01	☐	220	Lenny Webster	.05	.02	.01
☐	152	Todd Benzinger	.05	.02	.01	☐	221	Jesse Barfield	.05	.02	.01
☐	153	Mike Boddicker	.05	.02	.01	☐	222	Greg Cadaret	.05	.02	.01
☐	154	George Brett	.40	.18	.05	☐	223	Dave Eiland	.05	.02	.01
☐	155	Storm Davis	.05	.02	.01	☐	224	Alvaro Espinoza	.05	.02	.01
☐	156	Jim Eisenreich	.05	.02	.01	☐	225	Steve Farr	.05	.02	.01
☐	157	Kirk Gibson	.15	.07	.02	☐	226	Bob Geren	.05	.02	.01
☐	158	Tom Gordon	.10	.05	.01	☐	227	Lee Guetterman	.05	.02	.01
☐	159	Mark Gubicza	.05	.02	.01	☐	228	John Habyan	.05	.02	.01
☐	160	David Howard	.05	.02	.01	☐	229	Mel Hall	.05	.02	.01
☐	161	Mike Macfarlane	.05	.02	.01	☐	230	Steve Howe	.05	.02	.01
☐	162	Brent Mayne	.05	.02	.01	☐	231	Mike Humphreys	.05	.02	.01
☐	163	Brian McRae	.15	.07	.02	☐	232	Scott Kamieniecki	.05	.02	.01
☐	164	Jeff Montgomery	.10	.05	.01	☐	233	Pat Kelly	.05	.02	.01
☐	165	Bill Pecota	.05	.02	.01	☐	234	Roberto Kelly	.10	.05	.01
☐	166	Harvey Pulliam	.05	.02	.01	☐	235	Tim Leary	.05	.02	.01
☐	167	Bret Saberhagen	.15	.07	.02	☐	236	Kevin Maas	.05	.02	.01
☐	168	Kevin Seitzer	.05	.02	.01	☐	237	Don Mattingly	.50	.23	.06
☐	169	Terry Shumpert	.05	.02	.01	☐	238	Hensley Meulens	.05	.02	.01

☐ 239	Matt Nokes	.05	.02	.01
☐ 240	Pascual Perez	.05	.02	.01
☐ 241	Eric Plunk	.05	.02	.01
☐ 242	John Ramos	.05	.02	.01
☐ 243	Scott Sanderson	.05	.02	.01
☐ 244	Steve Sax	.05	.02	.01
☐ 245	Wade Taylor	.05	.02	.01
☐ 246	Randy Velarde	.05	.02	.01
☐ 247	Bernie Williams	.15	.07	.02
☐ 248	Troy Afenir	.05	.02	.01
☐ 249	Harold Baines	.15	.07	.02
☐ 250	Lance Blankenship	.05	.02	.01
☐ 251	Mike Bordick	.05	.02	.01
☐ 252	Jose Canseco	.15	.07	.02
☐ 253	Steve Chitren	.05	.02	.01
☐ 254	Ron Darling	.05	.02	.01
☐ 255	Dennis Eckersley	.15	.07	.02
☐ 256	Mike Gallego	.05	.02	.01
☐ 257	Dave Henderson	.05	.02	.01
☐ 258	Rickey Henderson UER	.15	.07	.02
	(Wearing 24 on front			
	and 22 on back)			
☐ 259	Rick Honeycutt	.05	.02	.01
☐ 260	Brook Jacoby	.05	.02	.01
☐ 261	Carney Lansford	.10	.05	.01
☐ 262	Mark McGwire	.15	.07	.02
☐ 263	Mike Moore	.05	.02	.01
☐ 264	Gene Nelson	.05	.02	.01
☐ 265	Jamie Quirk	.05	.02	.01
☐ 266	Joe Slusarski	.05	.02	.01
☐ 267	Terry Steinbach	.10	.05	.01
☐ 268	Dave Stewart	.15	.07	.02
☐ 269	Todd Van Poppel	.10	.05	.01
☐ 270	Walt Weiss	.05	.02	.01
☐ 271	Bob Welch	.05	.02	.01
☐ 272	Curt Young	.05	.02	.01
☐ 273	Scott Bradley	.05	.02	.01
☐ 274	Greg Briley	.05	.02	.01
☐ 275	Jay Buhner	.15	.07	.02
☐ 276	Henry Cotto	.05	.02	.01
☐ 277	Alvin Davis	.05	.02	.01
☐ 278	Rich DeLucia	.05	.02	.01
☐ 279	Ken Griffey Jr.	1.50	.70	.19
☐ 280	Erik Hanson	.05	.02	.01
☐ 281	Brian Holman	.05	.02	.01
☐ 282	Mike Jackson	.05	.02	.01
☐ 283	Randy Johnson	.25	.11	.03
☐ 284	Tracy Jones	.05	.02	.01
☐ 285	Bill Krueger	.05	.02	.01
☐ 286	Edgar Martinez	.15	.07	.02
☐ 287	Tino Martinez	.15	.07	.02
☐ 288	Rob Murphy	.05	.02	.01
☐ 289	Pete O'Brien	.05	.02	.01
☐ 290	Alonzo Powell	.05	.02	.01
☐ 291	Harold Reynolds	.05	.02	.01
☐ 292	Mike Schooler	.05	.02	.01
☐ 293	Russ Swan	.05	.02	.01
☐ 294	Bill Swift	.05	.02	.01
☐ 295	Dave Valle	.05	.02	.01
☐ 296	Omar Vizquel	.05	.02	.01
☐ 297	Gerald Alexander	.05	.02	.01
☐ 298	Brad Arnsberg	.05	.02	.01
☐ 299	Kevin Brown	.10	.05	.01
☐ 300	Jack Daugherty	.05	.02	.01
☐ 301	Mario Diaz	.05	.02	.01
☐ 302	Brian Downing	.05	.02	.01
☐ 303	Julio Franco	.10	.05	.01
☐ 304	Juan Gonzalez	.40	.18	.05
☐ 305	Rich Gossage	.10	.05	.01
☐ 306	Jose Guzman	.05	.02	.01
☐ 307	Jose Hernandez	.05	.02	.01
☐ 308	Jeff Huson	.05	.02	.01
☐ 309	Mike Jeffcoat	.05	.02	.01
☐ 310	Terry Mathews	.05	.02	.01
☐ 311	Rafael Palmeiro	.15	.07	.02
☐ 312	Dean Palmer	.10	.05	.01
☐ 313	Geno Petralli	.05	.02	.01
☐ 314	Gary Pettis	.05	.02	.01
☐ 315	Kevin Reimer	.05	.02	.01
☐ 316	Ivan Rodriguez	.15	.07	.02
☐ 317	Kenny Rogers	.05	.02	.01
☐ 318	Wayne Rosenthal	.05	.02	.01
☐ 319	Jeff Russell	.05	.02	.01
☐ 320	Nolan Ryan	.75	.35	.09
☐ 321	Ruben Sierra	.10	.05	.01
☐ 322	Jim Acker	.05	.02	.01
☐ 323	Roberto Alomar	.20	.09	.03
☐ 324	Derek Bell	.10	.05	.01
☐ 325	Pat Borders	.05	.02	.01
☐ 326	Tom Candiotti	.05	.02	.01
☐ 327	Joe Carter	.15	.07	.02
☐ 328	Rob Ducey	.05	.02	.01
☐ 329	Kelly Gruber	.05	.02	.01
☐ 330	Juan Guzman	.10	.05	.01
☐ 331	Tom Henke	.10	.05	.01
☐ 332	Jimmy Key	.10	.05	.01
☐ 333	Manny Lee	.05	.02	.01
☐ 334	Al Leiter	.05	.02	.01
☐ 335	Bob MacDonald	.05	.02	.01
☐ 336	Candy Maldonado	.05	.02	.01
☐ 337	Rance Mulliniks	.05	.02	.01
☐ 338	Greg Myers	.05	.02	.01
☐ 339	John Olerud UER	.10	.05	.01
	(1991 BA has .256,			
	but text says .258)			
☐ 340	Ed Sprague	.10	.05	.01
☐ 341	Dave Stieb	.05	.02	.01
☐ 342	Todd Stottlemyre	.05	.02	.01
☐ 343	Mike Timlin	.05	.02	.01
☐ 344	Duane Ward	.05	.02	.01
☐ 345	David Wells	.10	.05	.01
☐ 346	Devon White	.10	.05	.01
☐ 347	Mookie Wilson	.05	.02	.01
☐ 348	Eddie Zosky	.05	.02	.01
☐ 349	Steve Avery	.15	.07	.02
☐ 350	Mike Bell	.05	.02	.01
☐ 351	Rafael Belliard	.05	.02	.01
☐ 352	Juan Berenguer	.05	.02	.01
☐ 353	Jeff Blauser	.10	.05	.01
☐ 354	Sid Bream	.05	.02	.01
☐ 355	Francisco Cabrera	.05	.02	.01
☐ 356	Marvin Freeman	.05	.02	.01
☐ 357	Ron Gant	.15	.07	.02
☐ 358	Tom Glavine	.15	.07	.02
☐ 359	Brian Hunter	.05	.02	.01
☐ 360	Dave Justice	.15	.07	.02
☐ 361	Charlie Leibrandt	.05	.02	.01
☐ 362	Mark Lemke	.05	.02	.01
☐ 363	Kent Mercker	.05	.02	.01
☐ 364	Keith Mitchell	.05	.02	.01
☐ 365	Greg Olson	.05	.02	.01
☐ 366	Terry Pendleton	.15	.07	.02
☐ 367	Armando Reynoso	.05	.02	.01
☐ 368	Deion Sanders	.20	.09	.03
☐ 369	Lonnie Smith	.05	.02	.01
☐ 370	Pete Smith	.05	.02	.01
☐ 371	John Smoltz	.15	.07	.02
☐ 372	Mike Stanton	.05	.02	.01
☐ 373	Jeff Treadway	.05	.02	.01
☐ 374	Mark Wohlers	.10	.05	.01
☐ 375	Paul Assenmacher	.05	.02	.01
☐ 376	George Bell	.05	.02	.01

☐ 377	Shawn Boskie	.05	.02	.01
☐ 378	Frank Castillo	.05	.02	.01
☐ 379	Andre Dawson	.15	.07	.02
☐ 380	Shawon Dunston	.05	.02	.01
☐ 381	Mark Grace	.15	.07	.02
☐ 382	Mike Harkey	.05	.02	.01
☐ 383	Danny Jackson	.05	.02	.01
☐ 384	Les Lancaster	.05	.02	.01
☐ 385	Ced Landrum	.05	.02	.01
☐ 386	Greg Maddux	.75	.35	.09
☐ 387	Derrick May	.10	.05	.01
☐ 388	Chuck McElroy	.05	.02	.01
☐ 389	Ryne Sandberg	.25	.11	.03
☐ 390	Heathcliff Slocumb	.10	.05	.01
☐ 391	Dave Smith	.05	.02	.01
☐ 392	Dwight Smith	.05	.02	.01
☐ 393	Rick Sutcliffe	.10	.05	.01
☐ 394	Hector Villanueva	.05	.02	.01
☐ 395	Chico Walker	.05	.02	.01
☐ 396	Jerome Walton	.05	.02	.01
☐ 397	Rick Wilkins	.05	.02	.01
☐ 398	Jack Armstrong	.05	.02	.01
☐ 399	Freddie Benavides	.05	.02	.01
☐ 400	Glenn Braggs	.05	.02	.01
☐ 401	Tom Browning	.05	.02	.01
☐ 402	Norm Charlton	.05	.02	.01
☐ 403	Eric Davis	.10	.05	.01
☐ 404	Rob Dibble	.05	.02	.01
☐ 405	Bill Doran	.05	.02	.01
☐ 406	Mariano Duncan	.05	.02	.01
☐ 407	Kip Gross	.05	.02	.01
☐ 408	Chris Hammond	.05	.02	.01
☐ 409	Billy Hatcher	.05	.02	.01
☐ 410	Chris Jones	.05	.02	.01
☐ 411	Barry Larkin	.15	.07	.02
☐ 412	Hal Morris	.10	.05	.01
☐ 413	Randy Myers	.15	.07	.02
☐ 414	Joe Oliver	.05	.02	.01
☐ 415	Paul O'Neill	.15	.07	.02
☐ 416	Ted Power	.05	.02	.01
☐ 417	Luis Quinones	.05	.02	.01
☐ 418	Jeff Reed	.05	.02	.01
☐ 419	Jose Rijo	.10	.05	.01
☐ 420	Chris Sabo	.05	.02	.01
☐ 421	Reggie Sanders	.20	.09	.03
☐ 422	Scott Scudder	.05	.02	.01
☐ 423	Glenn Sutko	.05	.02	.01
☐ 424	Eric Anthony	.05	.02	.01
☐ 425	Jeff Bagwell	.50	.23	.06
☐ 426	Craig Biggio	.15	.07	.02
☐ 427	Ken Caminiti	.15	.07	.02
☐ 428	Casey Candaele	.05	.02	.01
☐ 429	Mike Capel	.05	.02	.01
☐ 430	Andujar Cedeno	.05	.02	.01
☐ 431	Jim Corsi	.05	.02	.01
☐ 432	Mark Davidson	.05	.02	.01
☐ 433	Steve Finley	.10	.05	.01
☐ 434	Luis Gonzalez	.10	.05	.01
☐ 435	Pete Harnisch	.05	.02	.01
☐ 436	Dwayne Henry	.05	.02	.01
☐ 437	Xavier Hernandez	.05	.02	.01
☐ 438	Jimmy Jones	.05	.02	.01
☐ 439	Darryl Kile	.05	.02	.01
☐ 440	Rob Mallicoat	.05	.02	.01
☐ 441	Andy Mota	.05	.02	.01
☐ 442	Al Osuna	.05	.02	.01
☐ 443	Mark Portugal	.05	.02	.01
☐ 444	Scott Servais	.05	.02	.01
☐ 445	Mike Simms	.05	.02	.01
☐ 446	Gerald Young	.05	.02	.01
☐ 447	Tim Belcher	.05	.02	.01
☐ 448	Brett Butler	.15	.07	.02
☐ 449	John Candelaria	.05	.02	.01
☐ 450	Gary Carter	.15	.07	.02
☐ 451	Dennis Cook	.05	.02	.01
☐ 452	Tim Crews	.05	.02	.01
☐ 453	Kal Daniels	.05	.02	.01
☐ 454	Jim Gott	.05	.02	.01
☐ 455	Alfredo Griffin	.05	.02	.01
☐ 456	Kevin Gross	.05	.02	.01
☐ 457	Chris Gwynn	.05	.02	.01
☐ 458	Lenny Harris	.05	.02	.01
☐ 459	Orel Hershiser	.15	.07	.02
☐ 460	Jay Howell	.05	.02	.01
☐ 461	Stan Javier	.05	.02	.01
☐ 462	Eric Karros	.20	.09	.03
☐ 463	Ramon Martinez UER	.15	.07	.02
	(Card says bats right, should be left)			
☐ 464	Roger McDowell UER	.05	.02	.01
	(Wins add up to 54, totals have 51)			
☐ 465	Mike Morgan	.05	.02	.01
☐ 466	Eddie Murray	.15	.07	.02
☐ 467	Jose Offerman	.05	.02	.01
☐ 468	Bob Ojeda	.05	.02	.01
☐ 469	Juan Samuel	.05	.02	.01
☐ 470	Mike Scioscia	.05	.02	.01
☐ 471	Darryl Strawberry	.10	.05	.01
☐ 472	Bret Barberie	.05	.02	.01
☐ 473	Brian Barnes	.05	.02	.01
☐ 474	Eric Bullock	.05	.02	.01
☐ 475	Ivan Calderon	.05	.02	.01
☐ 476	Delino DeShields	.10	.05	.01
☐ 477	Jeff Fassero	.05	.02	.01
☐ 478	Mike Fitzgerald	.05	.02	.01
☐ 479	Steve Frey	.05	.02	.01
☐ 480	Andres Galarraga	.15	.07	.02
☐ 481	Mark Gardner	.05	.02	.01
☐ 482	Marquis Grissom	.15	.07	.02
☐ 483	Chris Haney	.05	.02	.01
☐ 484	Barry Jones	.05	.02	.01
☐ 485	Dave Martinez	.05	.02	.01
☐ 486	Dennis Martinez	.10	.05	.01
☐ 487	Chris Nabholz	.05	.02	.01
☐ 488	Spike Owen	.05	.02	.01
☐ 489	Gilberto Reyes	.05	.02	.01
☐ 490	Mel Rojas	.10	.05	.01
☐ 491	Scott Ruskin	.05	.02	.01
☐ 492	Bill Sampen	.05	.02	.01
☐ 493	Larry Walker	.15	.07	.02
☐ 494	Tim Wallach	.05	.02	.01
☐ 495	Daryl Boston	.05	.02	.01
☐ 496	Hubie Brooks	.05	.02	.01
☐ 497	Tim Burke	.05	.02	.01
☐ 498	Mark Carreon	.05	.02	.01
☐ 499	Tony Castillo	.05	.02	.01
☐ 500	Vince Coleman	.05	.02	.01
☐ 501	David Cone	.15	.07	.02
☐ 502	Kevin Elster	.05	.02	.01
☐ 503	Sid Fernandez	.10	.05	.01
☐ 504	John Franco	.15	.07	.02
☐ 505	Dwight Gooden	.05	.02	.01
☐ 506	Todd Hundley	.05	.02	.01
☐ 507	Jeff Innis	.05	.02	.01
☐ 508	Gregg Jefferies	.15	.07	.02
☐ 509	Howard Johnson	.05	.02	.01
☐ 510	Dave Magadan	.05	.02	.01
☐ 511	Terry McDaniel	.05	.02	.01
☐ 512	Kevin McReynolds	.05	.02	.01
☐ 513	Keith Miller	.05	.02	.01
☐ 514	Charlie O'Brien	.05	.02	.01

☐ 515	Mackey Sasser	.05	.02	.01
☐ 516	Pete Schourek	.10	.05	.01
☐ 517	Julio Valera	.05	.02	.01
☐ 518	Frank Viola	.05	.02	.01
☐ 519	Wally Whitehurst	.05	.02	.01
☐ 520	Anthony Young	.05	.02	.01
☐ 521	Andy Ashby	.05	.02	.01
☐ 522	Kim Batiste	.05	.02	.01
☐ 523	Joe Boever	.05	.02	.01
☐ 524	Wes Chamberlain	.05	.02	.01
☐ 525	Pat Combs	.05	.02	.01
☐ 526	Danny Cox	.05	.02	.01
☐ 527	Darren Daulton	.15	.07	.02
☐ 528	Jose DeJesus	.05	.02	.01
☐ 529	Len Dykstra	.15	.07	.02
☐ 530	Darrin Fletcher	.05	.02	.01
☐ 531	Tommy Greene	.05	.02	.01
☐ 532	Jason Grimsley	.05	.02	.01
☐ 533	Charlie Hayes	.10	.05	.01
☐ 534	Von Hayes	.05	.02	.01
☐ 535	Dave Hollins	.05	.02	.01
☐ 536	Ricky Jordan	.05	.02	.01
☐ 537	John Kruk	.15	.07	.02
☐ 538	Jim Lindeman	.05	.02	.01
☐ 539	Mickey Morandini	.05	.02	.01
☐ 540	Terry Mulholland	.05	.02	.01
☐ 541	Dale Murphy	.15	.07	.02
☐ 542	Randy Ready	.05	.02	.01
☐ 543	Wally Ritchie UER	.05	.02	.01
	(Letters in data are cut off on card)			
☐ 544	Bruce Ruffin	.05	.02	.01
☐ 545	Steve Searcy	.05	.02	.01
☐ 546	Dickie Thon	.05	.02	.01
☐ 547	Mitch Williams	.10	.05	.01
☐ 548	Stan Belinda	.05	.02	.01
☐ 549	Jay Bell	.10	.05	.01
☐ 550	Barry Bonds	.25	.11	.03
☐ 551	Bobby Bonilla	.10	.05	.01
☐ 552	Steve Buechele	.05	.02	.01
☐ 553	Doug Drabek	.10	.05	.01
☐ 554	Neal Heaton	.05	.02	.01
☐ 555	Jeff King	.10	.05	.01
☐ 556	Bob Kipper	.05	.02	.01
☐ 557	Bill Landrum	.05	.02	.01
☐ 558	Mike LaValliere	.05	.02	.01
☐ 559	Jose Lind	.05	.02	.01
☐ 560	Lloyd McClendon	.05	.02	.01
☐ 561	Orlando Merced	.05	.02	.01
☐ 562	Bob Patterson	.05	.02	.01
☐ 563	Joe Redfield	.05	.02	.01
☐ 564	Gary Redus	.05	.02	.01
☐ 565	Rosario Rodriguez	.05	.02	.01
☐ 566	Don Slaught	.05	.02	.01
☐ 567	John Smiley	.05	.02	.01
☐ 568	Zane Smith	.05	.02	.01
☐ 569	Randy Tomlin	.05	.02	.01
☐ 570	Andy Van Slyke	.10	.05	.01
☐ 571	Gary Varsho	.05	.02	.01
☐ 572	Bob Walk	.05	.02	.01
☐ 573	John Wehner UER	.05	.02	.01
	(Actually played for Carolina in 1991, not Cards)			
☐ 574	Juan Agosto	.05	.02	.01
☐ 575	Cris Carpenter	.05	.02	.01
☐ 576	Jose DeLeon	.05	.02	.01
☐ 577	Rich Gedman	.05	.02	.01
☐ 578	Bernard Gilkey	.10	.05	.01
☐ 579	Pedro Guerrero	.05	.02	.01
☐ 580	Ken Hill	.15	.07	.02
☐ 581	Rex Hudler	.05	.02	.01
☐ 582	Felix Jose	.05	.02	.01
☐ 583	Ray Lankford	.15	.07	.02
☐ 584	Omar Olivares	.05	.02	.01
☐ 585	Jose Oquendo	.05	.02	.01
☐ 586	Tom Pagnozzi	.05	.02	.01
☐ 587	Geronimo Pena	.05	.02	.01
☐ 588	Mike Perez	.05	.02	.01
☐ 589	Gerald Perry	.05	.02	.01
☐ 590	Bryn Smith	.05	.02	.01
☐ 591	Lee Smith	.15	.07	.02
☐ 592	Ozzie Smith	.20	.09	.03
☐ 593	Scott Terry	.05	.02	.01
☐ 594	Bob Tewksbury	.05	.02	.01
☐ 595	Milt Thompson	.05	.02	.01
☐ 596	Todd Zeile	.10	.05	.01
☐ 597	Larry Andersen	.05	.02	.01
☐ 598	Oscar Azocar	.05	.02	.01
☐ 599	Andy Benes	.10	.05	.01
☐ 600	Ricky Bones	.05	.02	.01
☐ 601	Jerald Clark	.05	.02	.01
☐ 602	Pat Clements	.05	.02	.01
☐ 603	Paul Faries	.05	.02	.01
☐ 604	Tony Fernandez	.05	.02	.01
☐ 605	Tony Gwynn	.30	.14	.04
☐ 606	Greg W. Harris	.05	.02	.01
☐ 607	Thomas Howard	.05	.02	.01
☐ 608	Bruce Hurst	.05	.02	.01
☐ 609	Darrin Jackson	.05	.02	.01
☐ 610	Tom Lampkin	.05	.02	.01
☐ 611	Craig Lefferts	.05	.02	.01
☐ 612	Jim Lewis	.05	.02	.01
☐ 613	Mike Maddux	.05	.02	.01
☐ 614	Fred McGriff	.15	.07	.02
☐ 615	Jose Melendez	.05	.02	.01
☐ 616	Jose Mota	.05	.02	.01
☐ 617	Dennis Rasmussen	.05	.02	.01
☐ 618	Bip Roberts	.05	.02	.01
☐ 619	Rich Rodriguez	.05	.02	.01
☐ 620	Benito Santiago	.05	.02	.01
☐ 621	Craig Shipley	.05	.02	.01
☐ 622	Tim Teufel	.05	.02	.01
☐ 623	Kevin Ward	.05	.02	.01
☐ 624	Ed Whitson	.05	.02	.01
☐ 625	Dave Anderson	.05	.02	.01
☐ 626	Kevin Bass	.05	.02	.01
☐ 627	Rod Beck	.25	.11	.03
☐ 628	Bud Black	.05	.02	.01
☐ 629	Jeff Brantley	.05	.02	.01
☐ 630	John Burkett	.10	.05	.01
☐ 631	Will Clark	.15	.07	.02
☐ 632	Royce Clayton	.10	.05	.01
☐ 633	Steve Decker	.05	.02	.01
☐ 634	Kelly Downs	.05	.02	.01
☐ 635	Mike Felder	.05	.02	.01
☐ 636	Scott Garrelts	.05	.02	.01
☐ 637	Eric Gunderson	.05	.02	.01
☐ 638	Bryan Hickerson	.05	.02	.01
☐ 639	Darren Lewis	.10	.05	.01
☐ 640	Greg Litton	.05	.02	.01
☐ 641	Kirt Manwaring	.05	.02	.01
☐ 642	Paul McClellan	.05	.02	.01
☐ 643	Willie McGee	.10	.05	.01
☐ 644	Kevin Mitchell	.10	.05	.01
☐ 645	Francisco Oliveras	.05	.02	.01
☐ 646	Mike Remlinger	.05	.02	.01
☐ 647	Dave Righetti	.05	.02	.01
☐ 648	Robby Thompson	.10	.05	.01
☐ 649	Jose Uribe	.05	.02	.01
☐ 650	Matt Williams	.20	.09	.03
☐ 651	Trevor Wilson	.05	.02	.01

☐ 652	Tom Goodwin MLP UER (Timed in 3.5, should be be timed)	.10	.05	.01
☐ 653	Terry Bross MLP	.05	.02	.01
☐ 654	Mike Christopher MLP	.05	.02	.01
☐ 655	Kenny Lofton MLP	1.00	.45	.12
☐ 656	Chris Cron MLP	.05	.02	.01
☐ 657	Willie Banks MLP	.05	.02	.01
☐ 658	Pat Rice MLP	.05	.02	.01
☐ 659A	Rob Maurer MLP ERR (Name misspelled as Mauer on card front)	.75	.35	.09
☐ 659B	Rob Maurer MLP COR	.05	.02	.01
☐ 660	Don Harris MLP	.05	.02	.01
☐ 661	Henry Rodriguez MLP	.05	.02	.01
☐ 662	Cliff Brantley MLP	.05	.02	.01
☐ 663	Mike Linskey MLP UER (220 pounds in data, 200 in text)	.05	.02	.01
☐ 664	Gary DiSarcina MLP	.05	.02	.01
☐ 665	Gil Heredia MLP	.05	.02	.01
☐ 666	Vinny Castilla RC	.50	.23	.06
☐ 667	Paul Abbott MLP	.05	.02	.01
☐ 668	Monty Fariss MLP UER (Called Paul on back)	.05	.02	.01
☐ 669	Jarvis Brown MLP	.05	.02	.01
☐ 670	Wayne Kirby MLP	.10	.05	.01
☐ 671	Scott Brosius MLP	.05	.02	.01
☐ 672	Bob Hamelin MLP	.10	.05	.01
☐ 673	Joel Johnston MLP	.05	.02	.01
☐ 674	Tim Spehr MLP	.05	.02	.01
☐ 675A	Jeff Gardner MLP ERR (P on front, should be SS)	.75	.35	.09
☐ 675B	Jeff Gardner MLP COR	.25	.11	.03
☐ 676	Rico Rossy MLP	.05	.02	.01
☐ 677	Roberto Hernandez MLP	.10	.05	.01
☐ 678	Ted Wood MLP	.05	.02	.01
☐ 679	Cal Eldred MLP	.05	.02	.01
☐ 680	Sean Berry MLP	.10	.05	.01
☐ 681	Rickey Henderson RS	.15	.07	.02
☐ 682	Nolan Ryan RS	.40	.18	.05
☐ 683	Dennis Martinez RS	.05	.02	.01
☐ 684	Wilson Alvarez RS	.10	.05	.01
☐ 685	Joe Carter RS	.15	.07	.02
☐ 686	Dave Winfield RS	.15	.07	.02
☐ 687	David Cone RS	.10	.05	.01
☐ 688	Jose Canseco LL UER (Text on back has 42 stolen bases in '88; should be 40)	.15	.07	.02
☐ 689	Howard Johnson LL	.05	.02	.01
☐ 690	Julio Franco LL	.05	.02	.01
☐ 691	Terry Pendleton LL	.10	.05	.01
☐ 692	Cecil Fielder LL	.10	.05	.01
☐ 693	Scott Erickson LL	.05	.02	.01
☐ 694	Tom Glavine LL	.10	.05	.01
☐ 695	Dennis Martinez LL	.05	.02	.01
☐ 696	Bryan Harvey LL	.05	.02	.01
☐ 697	Lee Smith LL	.10	.05	.01
☐ 698	Super Siblings Roberto Alomar Sandy Alomar Jr.	.10	.05	.01
☐ 699	The Indispensables Bobby Bonilla Will Clark	.10	.05	.01
☐ 700	Teamwork Mark Wohlers Kent Mercker Alejandro Pena	.05	.02	.01
☐ 701	Tiger Tandems Stacy Jones	.50	.23	.06

	Bo Jackson Gregg Olson Frank Thomas			
☐ 702	The Ignitors Paul Molitor Brett Butler	.15	.07	.02
☐ 703	Indispensables II Cal Ripken Joe Carter	.50	.23	.06
☐ 704	Power Packs Barry Larkin Kirby Puckett	.15	.07	.02
☐ 705	Today and Tomorrow Mo Vaughn Cecil Fielder	.20	.09	.03
☐ 706	Teenage Sensations Ramon Martinez Ozzie Guillen	.10	.05	.01
☐ 707	Designated Hitters Harold Baines Wade Boggs	.15	.07	.02
☐ 708	Robin Yount PV	.10	.05	.01
☐ 709	Ken Griffey Jr. PV UER (Missing quotations on back; BA has .322, but was actually .327)	.75	.35	.09
☐ 710	Nolan Ryan PV	.40	.18	.05
☐ 711	Cal Ripken PV	.50	.23	.06
☐ 712	Frank Thomas PV	.75	.35	.09
☐ 713	Dave Justice PV	.15	.07	.02
☐ 714	Checklist 1-101	.05	.02	.01
☐ 715	Checklist 102-194	.05	.02	.01
☐ 716	Checklist 195-296	.05	.02	.01
☐ 717	Checklist 297-397	.05	.02	.01
☐ 718	Checklist 398-494	.05	.02	.01
☐ 719	Checklist 495-596	.05	.02	.01
☐ 720A	Checklist 597-720 ERR (659 Rob Mauer)	.05	.02	.01
☐ 720B	Checklist 597-720 COR (659 Rob Maurer)	.05	.02	.01

1992 Fleer All-Stars

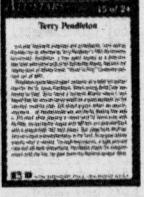

The 24-card All-Stars series was randomly inserted in 1992 Fleer wax packs (fin-sealed single packs). The cards measure the standard size (2 1/2" by 3 1/2"). The glossy color photos on the fronts are bordered in black and accented above and below with gold stripes and lettering. A diamond with a color head shot of the player is superimposed at the lower right corner of the picture. The player's name and the words "Fleer '92 All-Stars" appear above and below the picture respectively in gold foil lettering. On a white background with black borders, the back has career highlights with the words "Fleer '92 All-Stars" appearing at the top in yellow lettering. The cards are numbered on the back.

	MINT	NRMT	EXC
COMPLETE SET (24)	35.00	16.00	4.40
COMMON CARD (1-24)	.50	.23	.06
☐ 1 Felix Jose	.50	.23	.06
☐ 2 Tony Gwynn	2.00	.90	.25
☐ 3 Barry Bonds	2.00	.90	.25
☐ 4 Bobby Bonilla	.75	.35	.09
☐ 5 Mike LaValliere	.50	.23	.06
☐ 6 Tom Glavine	1.00	.45	.12
☐ 7 Ramon Martinez	.75	.35	.09
☐ 8 Lee Smith	.75	.35	.09
☐ 9 Mickey Tettleton	.50	.23	.06
☐ 10 Scott Erickson	.75	.35	.09
☐ 11 Frank Thomas	10.00	4.50	1.25
☐ 12 Danny Tartabull	.75	.35	.09
☐ 13 Will Clark	1.00	.45	.12
☐ 14 Ryne Sandberg	1.50	.70	.19
☐ 15 Terry Pendleton	.75	.35	.09
☐ 16 Barry Larkin	1.00	.45	.12
☐ 17 Rafael Palmeiro	1.25	.55	.16
☐ 18 Julio Franco	.75	.35	.09
☐ 19 Robin Ventura	.75	.35	.09
☐ 20 Cal Ripken UER	8.00	3.60	1.00
(Candidte; total bases misspelled as based)			
☐ 21 Joe Carter	1.25	.55	.16
☐ 22 Kirby Puckett	2.00	.90	.25
☐ 23 Ken Griffey Jr.	10.00	4.50	1.25
☐ 24 Jose Canseco	1.25	.55	.16

1992 Fleer Rookie Sensations

The 20-card Fleer Rookie Sensations series was randomly inserted in 1992 Fleer 35-card cello packs. The cards measure the standard size (2 1/2" by 3 1/2"). The glossy color photos on the fronts have a white border on a royal blue card face. The words "Rookie Sensations" appear above the picture in gold foil lettering, while the player's name appears on a gold foil plaque

beneath the picture. On a light blue background with royal blue borders, the backs have career summary. The cards are numbered on the back. Through a mail-in offer for ten Fleer baseball card wrappers and 1.00 for postage and handling, Fleer offered an uncut 8 1/2" by 11" numbered promo sheet picturing ten of the 20-card set on each side in a reduced-size front-only format. The offer indicated an expiration date of July 31, 1992, or whenever the production quantity of 250,000 sheets was exhausted.

	MINT	NRMT	EXC
COMPLETE SET (20)	60.00	27.00	7.50
COMMON CARD (1-20)	1.00	.45	.12
☐ 1 Frank Thomas	30.00	13.50	3.70
☐ 2 Todd Van Poppel	1.50	.70	.19
☐ 3 Orlando Merced	1.50	.70	.19
☐ 4 Jeff Bagwell	12.00	5.50	1.50
☐ 5 Jeff Fassero	1.50	.70	.19
☐ 6 Darren Lewis	1.50	.70	.19
☐ 7 Milt Cuyler	1.00	.45	.12
☐ 8 Mike Timlin	1.00	.45	.12
☐ 9 Brian McRae	2.00	.90	.25
☐ 10 Chuck Knoblauch	3.00	1.35	.35
☐ 11 Rich DeLucia	1.00	.45	.12
☐ 12 Ivan Rodriguez	2.50	1.10	.30
☐ 13 Juan Guzman	1.50	.70	.19
☐ 14 Steve Chitren	1.00	.45	.12
☐ 15 Mark Wohlers	2.50	1.10	.30
☐ 16 Wes Chamberlain	1.00	.45	.12
☐ 17 Ray Lankford	3.00	1.35	.35
☐ 18 Chito Martinez	1.00	.45	.12
☐ 19 Phil Plantier	1.50	.70	.19
☐ 20 Scott Leius UER	1.00	.45	.12
(Misspelled Lieus on card front)			

1992 Fleer Team Leaders

The 20-card Fleer Team Leaders series was randomly inserted in 1992 Fleer 42-card rack packs. The cards measure the standard size (2 1/2" by 3 1/2"). The glossy color photos on the fronts are bordered in white and green. Two gold foil stripes below the picture intersect a diamond-shaped "Team Leaders" emblem. On a pale green background with green borders, the backs have career summary. The cards are numbered on the back.

	MINT	NRMT	EXC
COMPLETE SET (20)	50.00	22.00	6.25
COMMON CARD (1-20)	1.00	.45	.12
☐ 1 Don Mattingly	8.00	3.60	1.00
☐ 2 Howard Johnson	1.00	.45	.12
☐ 3 Chris Sabo UER	1.00	.45	.12
(Where he it, should			
be Where he hit)			
☐ 4 Carlton Fisk	1.50	.70	.19
☐ 5 Kirby Puckett	5.00	2.20	.60
☐ 6 Cecil Fielder	1.50	.70	.19
☐ 7 Tony Gwynn	5.00	2.20	.60
☐ 8 Will Clark	2.50	1.10	.30
☐ 9 Bobby Bonilla	1.50	.70	.19
☐ 10 Len Dykstra	1.50	.70	.19
☐ 11 Tom Glavine	2.00	.90	.25
☐ 12 Rafael Palmeiro	2.00	.90	.25
☐ 13 Wade Boggs	1.50	.70	.19
☐ 14 Joe Carter	2.00	.90	.25
☐ 15 Ken Griffey Jr	20.00	9.00	2.50
☐ 16 Darryl Strawberry	1.50	.70	.19
☐ 17 Cal Ripken	16.00	7.25	2.00
☐ 18 Danny Tartabull	1.50	.70	.19
☐ 19 Jose Canseco	2.50	1.10	.30
☐ 20 Andre Dawson	1.50	.70	.19

1992 Fleer Update

The 1992 Fleer Update set contains 132 standard-size cards. Factory sets included a four-card, black-bordered "92 Headliners" insert set for a total of 136 cards. The basic card fronts have color action player photos with a metallic blue-green border that fades to white as one moves down the card face. The team logo, player's name, and his position appear in the wider right border. The top half of the backs has a close-up photo, while the bottom half carry biography and complete career statistics. The cards are checklisted below alphabetically within and according to teams for each league as follows: Baltimore Orioles (1-3), Boston Red Sox (4-6), California Angels (7-11), Chicago White Sox (12-14), Cleveland Indians (15-18), Detroit Tigers (19-25), Kansas City Royals (26-32), Milwaukee

Brewers (33-38), Minnesota Twins (39-41), New York Yankees (42-46), Oakland Athletics (47-53), Seattle Mariners (54-58), Texas Rangers (59-62), Toronto Blue Jays (63-67), Atlanta Braves (68-71), Chicago Cubs (72-77), Cincinnati Reds (78-84), Houston Astros (85-88), Los Angeles Dodgers (89-94), Montreal Expos (95-100), New York Mets (101-107), Philadelphia Phillies (108-112), Pittsburgh Pirates (113-117), St. Louis Cardinals (118-121), San Diego Padres (122-126), and San Francisco Giants (127-132). The cards are numbered on the back with a "U" prefix. Rookie Cards in this set include Chad Curtis, Damion Easley, John Jaha, Jeff Kent, Pat Listach, Pat Mahomes, Al Martin, Troy Neel, David Nied, Mike Piazza, Tim Wakefield, and Eric Young.

	MINT	NRMT	EXC
COMPLETE FACT.SET (136)	150.00	70.00	19.00
COMPLETE SET (132)	125.00	55.00	15.50
COMMON CARD (1-132)	.25	.11	.03
☐ 1 Todd Frohwirth	.25	.11	.03
☐ 2 Alan Mills	.25	.11	.03
☐ 3 Rick Sutcliffe	.40	.18	.05
☐ 4 John Valentin	6.00	2.70	.75
☐ 5 Frank Viola	.25	.11	.03
☐ 6 Bob Zupcic	.25	.11	.03
☐ 7 Mike Butcher	.25	.11	.03
☐ 8 Chad Curtis	4.00	1.80	.50
☐ 9 Damion Easley	1.50	.70	.19
☐ 10 Tim Salmon	20.00	9.00	2.50
☐ 11 Julio Valera	.25	.11	.03
☐ 12 George Bell	.25	.11	.03
☐ 13 Roberto Hernandez	.40	.18	.05
☐ 14 Shawn Jeter	.25	.11	.03
☐ 15 Thomas Howard	.25	.11	.03
☐ 16 Jesse Levis	.25	.11	.03
☐ 17 Kenny Lofton	35.00	16.00	4.40
☐ 18 Paul Sorrento	.40	.18	.05
☐ 19 Rico Brogna	3.00	1.35	.35
☐ 20 John Doherty	.25	.11	.03
☐ 21 Dan Gladden	.25	.11	.03
☐ 22 Buddy Groom	.25	.11	.03
☐ 23 Shawn Hare	.25	.11	.03
☐ 24 John Kiely	.25	.11	.03
☐ 25 Kurt Knudsen	.25	.11	.03
☐ 26 Gregg Jefferies	.60	.25	.07
☐ 27 Wally Joyner	.60	.25	.07
☐ 28 Kevin Koslofski	.25	.11	.03
☐ 29 Kevin McReynolds	.25	.11	.03
☐ 30 Rusty Meacham	.25	.11	.03
☐ 31 Keith Miller	.25	.11	.03
☐ 32 Hipolito Pichardo	.25	.11	.03
☐ 33 James Austin	.25	.11	.03
☐ 34 Scott Fletcher	.25	.11	.03
☐ 35 John Jaha	1.50	.70	.19
☐ 36 Pat Listach	.40	.18	.05
☐ 37 Dave Nilsson	2.00	.90	.25
☐ 38 Kevin Seitzer	.25	.11	.03
☐ 39 Tom Edens	.25	.11	.03
☐ 40 Pat Mahomes	.25	.11	.03
☐ 41 John Smiley	.25	.11	.03
☐ 42 Charlie Hayes	.40	.18	.05
☐ 43 Sam Militello	.25	.11	.03
☐ 44 Andy Stankiewicz	.25	.11	.03
☐ 45 Danny Tartabull	.40	.18	.05
☐ 46 Bob Wickman	.25	.11	.03

☐ 47	Jerry Browne	.25	.11	.03
☐ 48	Kevin Campbell	.25	.11	.03
☐ 49	Vince Horsman	.25	.11	.03
☐ 50	Troy Neel	.25	.11	.03
☐ 51	Ruben Sierra	.75	.35	.09
☐ 52	Bruce Walton	.25	.11	.03
☐ 53	Willie Wilson	.25	.11	.03
☐ 54	Bret Boone	5.00	2.20	.60
☐ 55	Dave Fleming	.25	.11	.03
☐ 56	Kevin Mitchell	.60	.25	.07
☐ 57	Jeff Nelson	.25	.11	.03
☐ 58	Shane Turner	.25	.11	.03
☐ 59	Jose Canseco	3.00	1.35	.35
☐ 60	Jeff Frye	.25	.11	.03
☐ 61	Danny Leon	.25	.11	.03
☐ 62	Roger Pavlik	.40	.18	.05
☐ 63	David Cone	.60	.25	.07
☐ 64	Pat Hentgen	2.00	.90	.25
☐ 65	Randy Knorr	.25	.11	.03
☐ 66	Jack Morris	.40	.18	.05
☐ 67	Dave Winfield	1.50	.70	.19
☐ 68	David Nied	1.00	.45	.12
☐ 69	Otis Nixon	.25	.11	.03
☐ 70	Alejandro Pena	.25	.11	.03
☐ 71	Jeff Reardon	.40	.18	.05
☐ 72	Alex Arias	.40	.18	.05
☐ 73	Jim Bullinger	.25	.11	.03
☐ 74	Mike Morgan	.25	.11	.03
☐ 75	Rey Sanchez	.25	.11	.03
☐ 76	Bob Scanlan	.25	.11	.03
☐ 77	Sammy Sosa	3.00	1.35	.35
☐ 78	Scott Bankhead	.25	.11	.03
☐ 79	Tim Belcher	.25	.11	.03
☐ 80	Steve Foster	.25	.11	.03
☐ 81	Willie Greene	.25	.11	.03
☐ 82	Bip Roberts	.40	.18	.05
☐ 83	Scott Ruskin	.25	.11	.03
☐ 84	Greg Swindell	.25	.11	.03
☐ 85	Juan Guerrero	.25	.11	.03
☐ 86	Butch Henry	.25	.11	.03
☐ 87	Doug Jones	.25	.11	.03
☐ 88	Brian Williams	.25	.11	.03
☐ 89	Tom Candiotti	.25	.11	.03
☐ 90	Eric Davis	.40	.18	.05
☐ 91	Carlos Hernandez	.25	.11	.03
☐ 92	Mike Piazza	75.00	34.00	9.50
☐ 93	Mike Sharperson	.25	.11	.03
☐ 94	Eric Young	1.50	.70	.19
☐ 95	Moises Alou	3.00	1.35	.35
☐ 96	Greg Colbrunn	1.00	.45	.12
☐ 97	Wil Cordero	4.00	1.80	.50
☐ 98	Ken Hill	1.50	.70	.19
☐ 99	John Vander Wal	.25	.11	.03
☐ 100	John Wetteland	1.00	.45	.12
☐ 101	Bobby Bonilla	.75	.35	.09
☐ 102	Eric Hillman	.25	.11	.03
☐ 103	Pat Howell	.25	.11	.03
☐ 104	Jeff Kent	3.00	1.35	.35
☐ 105	Dick Schofield	.25	.11	.03
☐ 106	Ryan Thompson	1.50	.70	.19
☐ 107	Chico Walker	.25	.11	.03
☐ 108	Juan Bell	.25	.11	.03
☐ 109	Mariano Duncan	.25	.11	.03
☐ 110	Jeff Grotewold	.25	.11	.03
☐ 111	Ben Rivera	.25	.11	.03
☐ 112	Curt Schilling	.25	.11	.03
☐ 113	Victor Cole	.25	.11	.03
☐ 114	Albert Martin	.60	.25	.07
☐ 115	Roger Mason	.25	.11	.03
☐ 116	Blas Minor	.25	.11	.03
☐ 117	Tim Wakefield	5.00	2.20	.60

☐ 118	Mark Clark	1.00	.45	.12
☐ 119	Rheal Cormier	.25	.11	.03
☐ 120	Donovan Osborne	.25	.11	.03
☐ 121	Todd Worrell	.25	.11	.03
☐ 122	Jeremy Hernandez	.25	.11	.03
☐ 123	Randy Myers	.60	.25	.07
☐ 124	Frank Seminara	.25	.11	.03
☐ 125	Gary Sheffield	1.50	.70	.19
☐ 126	Dan Walters	.25	.11	.03
☐ 127	Steve Hosey	.25	.11	.03
☐ 128	Mike Jackson	.25	.11	.03
☐ 129	Jim Pena	.25	.11	.03
☐ 130	Cory Snyder	.25	.11	.03
☐ 131	Bill Swift	.25	.11	.03
☐ 132	Checklist U1-U132	.25	.11	.03

1993 Fleer

The 1993 Fleer baseball set contains two series of 360 standard-size cards. Randomly inserted in the first series wax packs were a three-card Golden Moments subset, a 12-card NL All-Stars subset, an 18-card Major League Prospects subset, and three Pro-Visions cards. The fronts show glossy color action player photos bordered in silver. A team color-coded stripe edges the left side of the picture and carries the player's name and team name. On a background that shades from white to silver, the horizontally oriented backs have the player's last name in team-color coded block lettering, a cut out color player photo, and a box displaying biographical and statistical information. The cards are checklisted below alphabetically within and according to teams for each league as follows: Atlanta Braves (1-16), Chicago Cubs (17-28), Cincinnati Reds (29-44), Houston Astros (45-56), Los Angeles Dodgers (57-69), Montreal Expos (70-83), New York Mets (84-96), Philadelphia Phillies (97-109), Pittsburgh Pirates (110-123), St. Louis Cardinals (124-136), San Diego Padres (137-149), San Francisco Giants (150-162), Baltimore Orioles (163-175), Boston Red Sox (176-186), California Angels (187-198), Chicago White Sox (199-211), Cleveland Indians (212-223), Detroit Tigers (224-234), Kansas City Royals (235-246), Milwaukee Brewers (247-260), Minnesota Twins (261-275), New York Yankees (276-289), Oakland Athletics (290-303), Seattle

Mariners (304-316), Texas Rangers (317-329), and Toronto Blue Jays (330-343). Topical subsets featured include League Leaders (344-348), NL Round Trippers (349-353), and Super Star Specials (354-357). The set concludes with checklists (358-360). The second series consists of 360 cards and includes cards of players from the expansion teams, the Florida Marlins and the Colorado Rockies. Three Golden Moments cards, three Pro-Vision cards, 18 Major League Prospects cards, and 12 American League All-Stars cards were inserted in series II wax packs. The rack packs included ten Team Leader cards while the jumbo packs offered ten Rookie Sensations. The 12-card Tom Glavine "Career Highlights" set continued to be randomly inserted in all series II cards; though some cards were autographed, series I wax variations were not repeated in series II. The cards are numbered on the back, grouped alphabetically within teams, and checklisted below alphabetically according to teams for each league as follows: Atlanta Braves (361-372), Chicago Cubs (373-385), Cincinnati Reds (386-400), Colorado Rockies (401-416), Florida Marlins (417-431), Houston Astros (432-442), Los Angeles Dodgers (443-456), Montreal Expos (457-465), New York Mets (466-482), Philadelphia Phillies (483-498), Pittsburgh Pirates (499-506), St. Louis Cardinals (507-517), San Diego Padres (518-525), San Francisco Giants (526-540), Baltimore Orioles (541-553), Boston Red Sox (554-567), California Angels (568-578), Chicago White Sox (579-589), Cleveland Indians (590-602), Detroit Tigers (603-614), Kansas City Royals (615-627), Milwaukee Brewers (628-636), Minnesota Twins (637-646), New York Yankees (647-658), Oakland Athletics (659-669), Seattle Mariners (670-681), Texas Rangers (682-690), and Toronto Blue Jays (691-703). The set closes with the following topical subsets: League Leaders (704-708), AL Round Trippers (709-713), Super Star Specials (714-717), and checklists (718-720).

	MINT	NRMT	EXC
COMPLETE SET (720)	45.00	20.00	5.50
COMPLETE SERIES 1 (360)	22.50	10.00	2.80
COMPLETE SERIES 2 (360)	22.50	10.00	2.80
COMMON CARD (1-360)	.05	.02	.01
COMMON CARD (361-720)	.05	.02	.01

☐ 1	Steve Avery	.15	.07	.02
☐ 2	Sid Bream	.05	.02	.01
☐ 3	Ron Gant	.15	.07	.02
☐ 4	Tom Glavine	.15	.07	.02
☐ 5	Brian Hunter	.05	.02	.01
☐ 6	Ryan Klesko	1.00	.45	.12
☐ 7	Charlie Leibrandt	.05	.02	.01
☐ 8	Kent Mercker	.05	.02	.01
☐ 9	David Nied	.10	.05	.01
☐ 10	Otis Nixon	.05	.02	.01
☐ 11	Greg Olson	.05	.02	.01
☐ 12	Terry Pendleton	.10	.05	.01
☐ 13	Deion Sanders	.40	.18	.05
☐ 14	John Smoltz	.10	.05	.01
☐ 15	Mike Stanton	.05	.02	.01
☐ 16	Mark Wohlers	.05	.02	.01
☐ 17	Paul Assenmacher	.05	.02	.01
☐ 18	Steve Buechele	.05	.02	.01
☐ 19	Shawon Dunston	.05	.02	.01
☐ 20	Mark Grace	.15	.07	.02
☐ 21	Derrick May	.10	.05	.01
☐ 22	Chuck McElroy	.05	.02	.01
☐ 23	Mike Morgan	.05	.02	.01
☐ 24	Rey Sanchez	.05	.02	.01
☐ 25	Ryne Sandberg	.50	.23	.06
☐ 26	Bob Scanlan	.05	.02	.01
☐ 27	Sammy Sosa	.15	.07	.02
☐ 28	Rick Wilkins	.05	.02	.01
☐ 29	Bobby Ayala	.10	.05	.01
☐ 30	Tim Belcher	.05	.02	.01
☐ 31	Jeff Branson	.05	.02	.01
☐ 32	Norm Charlton	.05	.02	.01
☐ 33	Steve Foster	.05	.02	.01
☐ 34	Willie Greene	.10	.05	.01
☐ 35	Chris Hammond	.05	.02	.01
☐ 36	Milt Hill	.05	.02	.01
☐ 37	Hal Morris	.10	.05	.01
☐ 38	Joe Oliver	.05	.02	.01
☐ 39	Paul O'Neill	.10	.05	.01
☐ 40	Tim Pugh	.05	.02	.01
☐ 41	Jose Rijo	.10	.05	.01
☐ 42	Bip Roberts	.05	.02	.01
☐ 43	Chris Sabo	.05	.02	.01
☐ 44	Reggie Sanders	.15	.07	.02
☐ 45	Eric Anthony	.05	.02	.01
☐ 46	Jeff Bagwell	.75	.35	.09
☐ 47	Craig Biggio	.15	.07	.02
☐ 48	Joe Boever	.05	.02	.01
☐ 49	Casey Candaele	.05	.02	.01
☐ 50	Steve Finley	.10	.05	.01
☐ 51	Luis Gonzalez	.10	.05	.01
☐ 52	Pete Harnisch	.05	.02	.01
☐ 53	Xavier Hernandez	.05	.02	.01
☐ 54	Doug Jones	.05	.02	.01
☐ 55	Eddie Taubensee	.05	.02	.01
☐ 56	Brian Williams	.05	.02	.01
☐ 57	Pedro Astacio	.05	.02	.01
☐ 58	Todd Benzinger	.05	.02	.01
☐ 59	Brett Butler	.10	.05	.01
☐ 60	Tom Candiotti	.05	.02	.01
☐ 61	Lenny Harris	.05	.02	.01
☐ 62	Carlos Hernandez	.05	.02	.01
☐ 63	Orel Hershiser	.10	.05	.01
☐ 64	Eric Karros	.10	.05	.01
☐ 65	Ramon Martinez	.10	.05	.01
☐ 66	Jose Offerman	.05	.02	.01
☐ 67	Mike Scioscia	.05	.02	.01
☐ 68	Mike Sharperson	.05	.02	.01
☐ 69	Eric Young	.10	.05	.01
☐ 70	Moises Alou	.15	.07	.02
☐ 71	Ivan Calderon	.05	.02	.01
☐ 72	Archi Cianfrocco	.05	.02	.01
☐ 73	Wil Cordero	.10	.05	.01
☐ 74	Delino DeShields	.10	.05	.01
☐ 75	Mark Gardner	.05	.02	.01
☐ 76	Ken Hill	.10	.05	.01
☐ 77	Tim Laker	.05	.02	.01
☐ 78	Chris Nabholz	.05	.02	.01
☐ 79	Mel Rojas	.05	.02	.01
☐ 80	John Vander Wal UER	.05	.02	.01
	(Misspelled Vander Wall in letters on back)			
☐ 81	Larry Walker	.25	.11	.03
☐ 82	Tim Wallach	.05	.02	.01

☐ 83 John Wetteland .... .10	.05	.01
☐ 84 Bobby Bonilla .... .15	.07	.02
☐ 85 Daryl Boston .... .05	.02	.01
☐ 86 Sid Fernandez .... .05	.02	.01
☐ 87 Eric Hillman .... .05	.02	.01
☐ 88 Todd Hundley .... .15	.07	.02
☐ 89 Howard Johnson .... .05	.02	.01
☐ 90 Jeff Kent .... .15	.07	.02
☐ 91 Eddie Murray .... .30	.14	.04
☐ 92 Bill Pecota .... .05	.02	.01
☐ 93 Bret Saberhagen .... .10	.05	.01
☐ 94 Dick Schofield .... .05	.02	.01
☐ 95 Pete Schourek .... .15	.07	.02
☐ 96 Anthony Young .... .05	.02	.01
☐ 97 Ruben Amaro Jr .... .05	.02	.01
☐ 98 Juan Bell .... .05	.02	.01
☐ 99 Wes Chamberlain .... .05	.02	.01
☐ 100 Darren Daulton .... .15	.07	.02
☐ 101 Mariano Duncan .... .05	.02	.01
☐ 102 Mike Hartley .... .05	.02	.01
☐ 103 Ricky Jordan .... .05	.02	.01
☐ 104 John Kruk .... .15	.07	.02
☐ 105 Mickey Morandini .... .05	.02	.01
☐ 106 Terry Mulholland .... .05	.02	.01
☐ 107 Ben Rivera .... .05	.02	.01
☐ 108 Curt Schilling .... .05	.02	.01
☐ 109 Keith Shepherd .... .05	.02	.01
☐ 110 Stan Belinda .... .05	.02	.01
☐ 111 Jay Bell .... .10	.05	.01
☐ 112 Barry Bonds .... .50	.23	.06
☐ 113 Jeff King .... .05	.02	.01
☐ 114 Mike LaValliere .... .05	.02	.01
☐ 115 Jose Lind .... .05	.02	.01
☐ 116 Roger Mason .... .05	.02	.01
☐ 117 Orlando Merced .... .10	.05	.01
☐ 118 Bob Patterson .... .05	.02	.01
☐ 119 Don Slaught .... .05	.02	.01
☐ 120 Zane Smith .... .05	.02	.01
☐ 121 Randy Tomlin .... .05	.02	.01
☐ 122 Andy Van Slyke .... .10	.05	.01
☐ 123 Tim Wakefield .... .15	.07	.02
☐ 124 Rheal Cormier .... .05	.02	.01
☐ 125 Bernard Gilkey .... .10	.05	.01
☐ 126 Felix Jose .... .05	.02	.01
☐ 127 Ray Lankford .... .15	.07	.02
☐ 128 Bob McClure .... .05	.02	.01
☐ 129 Donovan Osborne .... .05	.02	.01
☐ 130 Tom Pagnozzi .... .05	.02	.01
☐ 131 Geronimo Pena .... .05	.02	.01
☐ 132 Mike Perez .... .05	.02	.01
☐ 133 Lee Smith .... .15	.07	.02
☐ 134 Bob Tewksbury .... .05	.02	.01
☐ 135 Todd Worrell .... .05	.02	.01
☐ 136 Todd Zeile .... .10	.05	.01
☐ 137 Jerald Clark .... .05	.02	.01
☐ 138 Tony Gwynn .... .60	.25	.07
☐ 139 Greg W. Harris .... .05	.02	.01
☐ 140 Jeremy Hernandez .... .05	.02	.01
☐ 141 Darrin Jackson .... .05	.02	.01
☐ 142 Mike Maddux .... .05	.02	.01
☐ 143 Fred McGriff .... .25	.11	.03
☐ 144 Jose Melendez .... .05	.02	.01
☐ 145 Rich Rodriguez .... .05	.02	.01
☐ 146 Frank Seminara .... .05	.02	.01
☐ 147 Gary Sheffield .... .15	.07	.02
☐ 148 Kurt Stillwell .... .05	.02	.01
☐ 149 Dan Walters .... .05	.02	.01
☐ 150 Rod Beck .... .15	.07	.02
☐ 151 Bud Black .... .05	.02	.01
☐ 152 Jeff Brantley .... .05	.02	.01
☐ 153 John Burkett .... .05	.02	.01
☐ 154 Will Clark .... .25	.11	.03
☐ 155 Royce Clayton .... .10	.05	.01
☐ 156 Mike Jackson .... .05	.02	.01
☐ 157 Darren Lewis .... .05	.02	.01
☐ 158 Kirt Manwaring .... .05	.02	.01
☐ 159 Willie McGee .... .10	.05	.01
☐ 160 Cory Snyder .... .05	.02	.01
☐ 161 Bill Swift .... .05	.02	.01
☐ 162 Trevor Wilson .... .05	.02	.01
☐ 163 Brady Anderson .... .10	.05	.01
☐ 164 Glenn Davis .... .05	.02	.01
☐ 165 Mike Devereaux .... .10	.05	.01
☐ 166 Todd Frohwirth .... .05	.02	.01
☐ 167 Leo Gomez .... .05	.02	.01
☐ 168 Chris Hoiles .... .10	.05	.01
☐ 169 Ben McDonald .... .05	.02	.01
☐ 170 Randy Milligan .... .05	.02	.01
☐ 171 Alan Mills .... .05	.02	.01
☐ 172 Mike Mussina .... .30	.14	.04
☐ 173 Gregg Olson .... .05	.02	.01
☐ 174 Arthur Rhodes .... .10	.05	.01
☐ 175 David Segui .... .05	.02	.01
☐ 176 Ellis Burks .... .10	.05	.01
☐ 177 Roger Clemens .... .30	.14	.04
☐ 178 Scott Cooper .... .05	.02	.01
☐ 179 Danny Darwin .... .05	.02	.01
☐ 180 Tony Fossas .... .05	.02	.01
☐ 181 Paul Quantrill .... .05	.02	.01
☐ 182 Jody Reed .... .05	.02	.01
☐ 183 John Valentin .... .15	.07	.02
☐ 184 Mo Vaughn .... .30	.14	.04
☐ 185 Frank Viola .... .10	.05	.01
☐ 186 Bob Zupcic .... .05	.02	.01
☐ 187 Jim Abbott .... .15	.07	.02
☐ 188 Gary DiSarcina .... .10	.05	.01
☐ 189 Damion Easley .... .10	.05	.01
☐ 190 Junior Felix .... .05	.02	.01
☐ 191 Chuck Finley .... .05	.02	.01
☐ 192 Joe Grahe .... .05	.02	.01
☐ 193 Bryan Harvey .... .10	.05	.01
☐ 194 Mark Langston .... .15	.07	.02
☐ 195 John Orton .... .05	.02	.01
☐ 196 Luis Polonia .... .05	.02	.01
☐ 197 Tim Salmon .... .60	.25	.07
☐ 198 Luis Sojo .... .05	.02	.01
☐ 199 Wilson Alvarez .... .15	.07	.02
☐ 200 George Bell .... .10	.05	.01
☐ 201 Alex Fernandez .... .15	.07	.02
☐ 202 Craig Grebeck .... .05	.02	.01
☐ 203 Ozzie Guillen .... .05	.02	.01
☐ 204 Lance Johnson .... .05	.02	.01
☐ 205 Ron Karkovice .... .05	.02	.01
☐ 206 Kirk McCaskill .... .05	.02	.01
☐ 207 Jack McDowell .... .15	.07	.02
☐ 208 Scott Radinsky .... .05	.02	.01
☐ 209 Tim Raines .... .15	.07	.02
☐ 210 Frank Thomas 2.00	.90	.25
☐ 211 Robin Ventura .... .15	.07	.02
☐ 212 Sandy Alomar Jr .... .10	.05	.01
☐ 213 Carlos Baerga .... .40	.18	.05
☐ 214 Dennis Cook .... .05	.02	.01
☐ 215 Thomas Howard .... .05	.02	.01
☐ 216 Mark Lewis .... .05	.02	.01
☐ 217 Derek Lilliquist .... .05	.02	.01
☐ 218 Kenny Lofton .... .60	.25	.07
☐ 219 Charles Nagy .... .10	.05	.01
☐ 220 Steve Olin .... .05	.02	.01
☐ 221 Paul Sorrento .... .05	.02	.01
☐ 222 Jim Thome .... .75	.35	.09
☐ 223 Mark Whiten .... .10	.05	.01
☐ 224 Milt Cuyler .... .05	.02	.01

☐ 225 Rob Deer	.05	.02	.01
☐ 226 John Doherty	.05	.02	.01
☐ 227 Cecil Fielder	.15	.07	.02
☐ 228 Travis Fryman	.15	.07	.02
☐ 229 Mike Henneman	.05	.02	.01
☐ 230 John Kiely UER	.05	.02	.01
(Card has batting stats of Pat Kelly)			
☐ 231 Kurt Knudsen	.05	.02	.01
☐ 232 Scott Livingstone	.05	.02	.01
☐ 233 Tony Phillips	.05	.02	.01
☐ 234 Mickey Tettleton	.10	.05	.01
☐ 235 Kevin Appier	.10	.05	.01
☐ 236 George Brett	.75	.35	.09
☐ 237 Tom Gordon	.05	.02	.01
☐ 238 Gregg Jefferies	.15	.07	.02
☐ 239 Wally Joyner	.10	.05	.01
☐ 240 Kevin Koslofski	.05	.02	.01
☐ 241 Mike Macfarlane	.05	.02	.01
☐ 242 Brian McRae	.15	.07	.02
☐ 243 Rusty Meacham	.05	.02	.01
☐ 244 Keith Miller	.05	.02	.01
☐ 245 Jeff Montgomery	.10	.05	.01
☐ 246 Hipolito Pichardo	.05	.02	.01
☐ 247 Ricky Bones	.05	.02	.01
☐ 248 Cal Eldred	.05	.02	.01
☐ 249 Mike Fetters	.05	.02	.01
☐ 250 Darryl Hamilton	.05	.02	.01
☐ 251 Doug Henry	.05	.02	.01
☐ 252 John Jaha	.10	.05	.01
☐ 253 Pat Listach	.05	.02	.01
☐ 254 Paul Molitor	.15	.07	.02
☐ 255 Jaime Navarro	.05	.02	.01
☐ 256 Kevin Seitzer	.05	.02	.01
☐ 257 B.J. Surhoff	.10	.05	.01
☐ 258 Greg Vaughn	.05	.02	.01
☐ 259 Bill Wegman	.05	.02	.01
☐ 260 Robin Yount	.25	.11	.03
☐ 261 Rick Aguilera	.10	.05	.01
☐ 262 Chili Davis	.10	.05	.01
☐ 263 Scott Erickson	.10	.05	.01
☐ 264 Greg Gagne	.05	.02	.01
☐ 265 Mark Guthrie	.05	.02	.01
☐ 266 Brian Harper	.05	.02	.01
☐ 267 Kent Hrbek	.10	.05	.01
☐ 268 Terry Jorgensen	.05	.02	.01
☐ 269 Gene Larkin	.05	.02	.01
☐ 270 Scott Leius	.05	.02	.01
☐ 271 Pat Mahomes	.05	.02	.01
☐ 272 Pedro Munoz	.10	.05	.01
☐ 273 Kirby Puckett	.60	.25	.07
☐ 274 Kevin Tapani	.05	.02	.01
☐ 275 Carl Willis	.05	.02	.01
☐ 276 Steve Farr	.05	.02	.01
☐ 277 John Habyan	.05	.02	.01
☐ 278 Mel Hall	.05	.02	.01
☐ 279 Charlie Hayes	.10	.05	.01
☐ 280 Pat Kelly	.05	.02	.01
☐ 281 Don Mattingly	1.00	.45	.12
☐ 282 Sam Militello	.05	.02	.01
☐ 283 Matt Nokes	.05	.02	.01
☐ 284 Melido Perez	.05	.02	.01
☐ 285 Andy Stankiewicz	.05	.02	.01
☐ 286 Danny Tartabull	.10	.05	.01
☐ 287 Randy Velarde	.05	.02	.01
☐ 288 Bob Wickman	.05	.02	.01
☐ 289 Bernie Williams	.10	.05	.01
☐ 290 Lance Blankenship	.05	.02	.01
☐ 291 Mike Bordick	.10	.05	.01
☐ 292 Jerry Browne	.05	.02	.01
☐ 293 Dennis Eckersley	.15	.07	.02
☐ 294 Rickey Henderson	.15	.07	.02
☐ 295 Vince Horsman	.05	.02	.01
☐ 296 Mark McGwire	.15	.07	.02
☐ 297 Jeff Parrett	.05	.02	.01
☐ 298 Ruben Sierra	.15	.07	.02
☐ 299 Terry Steinbach	.10	.05	.01
☐ 300 Walt Weiss	.10	.05	.01
☐ 301 Bob Welch	.10	.05	.01
☐ 302 Willie Wilson	.05	.02	.01
☐ 303 Bobby Witt	.05	.02	.01
☐ 304 Bret Boone	.15	.07	.02
☐ 305 Jay Buhner	.15	.07	.02
☐ 306 Dave Fleming	.05	.02	.01
☐ 307 Ken Griffey Jr	2.00	.90	.25
☐ 308 Erik Hanson	.05	.02	.01
☐ 309 Edgar Martinez	.15	.07	.02
☐ 310 Tino Martinez	.15	.07	.02
☐ 311 Jeff Nelson	.05	.02	.01
☐ 312 Dennis Powell	.05	.02	.01
☐ 313 Mike Schooler	.05	.02	.01
☐ 314 Russ Swan	.05	.02	.01
☐ 315 Dave Valle	.05	.02	.01
☐ 316 Omar Vizquel	.10	.05	.01
☐ 317 Kevin Brown	.05	.02	.01
☐ 318 Todd Burns	.05	.02	.01
☐ 319 Jose Canseco	.30	.14	.04
☐ 320 Julio Franco	.10	.05	.01
☐ 321 Jeff Frye	.05	.02	.01
☐ 322 Juan Gonzalez	.40	.18	.05
☐ 323 Jose Guzman	.05	.02	.01
☐ 324 Jeff Huson	.05	.02	.01
☐ 325 Dean Palmer	.10	.05	.01
☐ 326 Kevin Reimer	.05	.02	.01
☐ 327 Ivan Rodriguez	.15	.07	.02
☐ 328 Kenny Rogers	.05	.02	.01
☐ 329 Dan Smith	.05	.02	.01
☐ 330 Roberto Alomar	.40	.18	.05
☐ 331 Derek Bell	.15	.07	.02
☐ 332 Pat Borders	.05	.02	.01
☐ 333 Joe Carter	.15	.07	.02
☐ 334 Kelly Gruber	.05	.02	.01
☐ 335 Tom Henke	.10	.05	.01
☐ 336 Jimmy Key	.10	.05	.01
☐ 337 Manuel Lee	.05	.02	.01
☐ 338 Candy Maldonado	.05	.02	.01
☐ 339 John Olerud	.10	.05	.01
☐ 340 Todd Stottlemyre	.05	.02	.01
☐ 341 Duane Ward	.05	.02	.01
☐ 342 Devon White	.10	.05	.01
☐ 343 Dave Winfield	.15	.07	.02
☐ 344 Edgar Martinez LL	.10	.05	.01
☐ 345 Cecil Fielder LL	.10	.05	.01
☐ 346 Kenny Lofton LL	.30	.14	.04
☐ 347 Jack Morris LL	.10	.05	.01
☐ 348 Roger Clemens LL	.15	.07	.02
☐ 349 Fred McGriff RT	.10	.05	.01
☐ 350 Barry Bonds RT	.25	.11	.03
☐ 351 Gary Sheffield RT	.10	.05	.01
☐ 352 Darren Daulton RT	.10	.05	.01
☐ 353 Dave Hollins RT	.05	.02	.01
☐ 354 Brothers in Blue	.05	.02	.01
Pedro Martinez			
Ramon Martinez			
☐ 355 Power Packs	.15	.07	.02
Ivan Rodriguez			
Kirby Puckett			
☐ 356 Triple Threats	.10	.05	.01
Ryne Sandberg			
Gary Sheffield			
☐ 357 Infield Trifecta	.10	.05	.01
Roberto Alomar			

Chuck Knoblauch
Carlos Baerga

☐	358	Checklist 1-120	.05	.02	.01
☐	359	Checklist 121-240	.05	.02	.01
☐	360	Checklist 241-360	.05	.02	.01
☐	361	Rafael Belliard	.05	.02	.01
☐	362	Damon Berryhill	.05	.02	.01
☐	363	Mike Bielecki	.05	.02	.01
☐	364	Jeff Blauser	.10	.05	.01
☐	365	Francisco Cabrera	.05	.02	.01
☐	366	Marvin Freeman	.05	.02	.01
☐	367	David Justice	.25	.11	.03
☐	368	Mark Lemke	.10	.05	.01
☐	369	Alejandro Pena	.05	.02	.01
☐	370	Jeff Reardon	.10	.05	.01
☐	371	Lonnie Smith	.05	.02	.01
☐	372	Pete Smith	.05	.02	.01
☐	373	Shawn Boskie	.05	.02	.01
☐	374	Jim Bullinger	.05	.02	.01
☐	375	Frank Castillo	.05	.02	.01
☐	376	Doug Dascenzo	.05	.02	.01
☐	377	Andre Dawson	.15	.07	.02
☐	378	Mike Harkey	.05	.02	.01
☐	379	Greg Hibbard	.05	.02	.01
☐	380	Greg Maddux	2.00	.90	.25
☐	381	Ken Patterson	.05	.02	.01
☐	382	Jeff D. Robinson	.05	.02	.01
☐	383	Luis Salazar	.05	.02	.01
☐	384	Dwight Smith	.05	.02	.01
☐	385	Jose Vizcaino	.05	.02	.01
☐	386	Scott Bankhead	.05	.02	.01
☐	387	Tom Browning	.05	.02	.01
☐	388	Darnell Coles	.05	.02	.01
☐	389	Rob Dibble	.05	.02	.01
☐	390	Bill Doran	.05	.02	.01
☐	391	Dwayne Henry	.05	.02	.01
☐	392	Cesar Hernandez	.05	.02	.01
☐	393	Roberto Kelly	.10	.05	.01
☐	394	Barry Larkin	.25	.11	.03
☐	395	Dave Martinez	.05	.02	.01
☐	396	Kevin Mitchell	.10	.05	.01
☐	397	Jeff Reed	.05	.02	.01
☐	398	Scott Ruskin	.05	.02	.01
☐	399	Greg Swindell	.05	.02	.01
☐	400	Dan Wilson	.10	.05	.01
☐	401	Andy Ashby	.05	.02	.01
☐	402	Freddie Benavides	.05	.02	.01
☐	403	Dante Bichette	.25	.11	.03
☐	404	Willie Blair	.05	.02	.01
☐	405	Denis Boucher	.05	.02	.01
☐	406	Vinny Castilla	.15	.07	.02
☐	407	Braulio Castillo	.05	.02	.01
☐	408	Alex Cole	.05	.02	.01
☐	409	Andres Galarraga	.15	.07	.02
☐	410	Joe Girardi	.05	.02	.01
☐	411	Butch Henry	.05	.02	.01
☐	412	Darren Holmes	.10	.05	.01
☐	413	Calvin Jones	.05	.02	.01
☐	414	Steve Reed	.05	.02	.01
☐	415	Kevin Ritz	.05	.02	.01
☐	416	Jim Tatum	.05	.02	.01
☐	417	Jack Armstrong	.05	.02	.01
☐	418	Bret Barberie	.05	.02	.01
☐	419	Ryan Bowen	.05	.02	.01
☐	420	Cris Carpenter	.05	.02	.01
☐	421	Chuck Carr	.05	.02	.01
☐	422	Scott Chiamparino	.05	.02	.01
☐	423	Jeff Conine	.15	.07	.02
☐	424	Jim Corsi	.05	.02	.01
☐	425	Steve Decker	.05	.02	.01
☐	426	Chris Donnels	.05	.02	.01
☐	427	Monty Fariss	.05	.02	.01
☐	428	Bob Natal	.05	.02	.01
☐	429	Pat Rapp	.10	.05	.01
☐	430	Dave Weathers	.05	.02	.01
☐	431	Nigel Wilson	.10	.05	.01
☐	432	Ken Caminiti	.10	.05	.01
☐	433	Andujar Cedeno	.05	.02	.01
☐	434	Tom Edens	.05	.02	.01
☐	435	Juan Guerrero	.05	.02	.01
☐	436	Pete Incaviglia	.05	.02	.01
☐	437	Jimmy Jones	.05	.02	.01
☐	438	Darryl Kile	.05	.02	.01
☐	439	Rob Murphy	.05	.02	.01
☐	440	Al Osuna	.05	.02	.01
☐	441	Mark Portugal	.05	.02	.01
☐	442	Scott Servais	.05	.02	.01
☐	443	John Candelaria	.05	.02	.01
☐	444	Tim Crews	.05	.02	.01
☐	445	Eric Davis	.05	.02	.01
☐	446	Tom Goodwin	.05	.02	.01
☐	447	Jim Gott	.05	.02	.01
☐	448	Kevin Gross	.05	.02	.01
☐	449	Dave Hansen	.05	.02	.01
☐	450	Jay Howell	.05	.02	.01
☐	451	Roger McDowell	.05	.02	.01
☐	452	Bob Ojeda	.05	.02	.01
☐	453	Henry Rodriguez	.05	.02	.01
☐	454	Darryl Strawberry	.10	.05	.01
☐	455	Mitch Webster	.05	.02	.01
☐	456	Steve Wilson	.05	.02	.01
☐	457	Brian Barnes	.05	.02	.01
☐	458	Sean Berry	.05	.02	.01
☐	459	Jeff Fassero	.10	.05	.01
☐	460	Darrin Fletcher	.05	.02	.01
☐	461	Marquis Grissom	.15	.07	.02
☐	462	Dennis Martinez	.10	.05	.01
☐	463	Spike Owen	.05	.02	.01
☐	464	Matt Stairs	.05	.02	.01
☐	465	Sergio Valdez	.05	.02	.01
☐	466	Kevin Bass	.05	.02	.01
☐	467	Vince Coleman	.05	.02	.01
☐	468	Mark Dewey	.05	.02	.01
☐	469	Kevin Elster	.05	.02	.01
☐	470	Tony Fernandez	.05	.02	.01
☐	471	John Franco	.10	.05	.01
☐	472	Dave Gallagher	.05	.02	.01
☐	473	Paul Gibson	.05	.02	.01
☐	474	Dwight Gooden	.10	.05	.01
☐	475	Lee Guetterman	.05	.02	.01
☐	476	Jeff Innis	.05	.02	.01
☐	477	Dave Magadan	.05	.02	.01
☐	478	Charlie O'Brien	.05	.02	.01
☐	479	Willie Randolph	.10	.05	.01
☐	480	Mackey Sasser	.05	.02	.01
☐	481	Ryan Thompson	.15	.07	.02
☐	482	Chico Walker	.05	.02	.01
☐	483	Kyle Abbott	.05	.02	.01
☐	484	Bob Ayrault	.05	.02	.01
☐	485	Kim Batiste	.05	.02	.01
☐	486	Cliff Brantley	.05	.02	.01
☐	487	Jose DeLeon	.05	.02	.01
☐	488	Len Dykstra	.15	.07	.02
☐	489	Tommy Greene	.05	.02	.01
☐	490	Jeff Grotewold	.05	.02	.01
☐	491	Dave Hollins	.05	.02	.01
☐	492	Danny Jackson	.05	.02	.01
☐	493	Stan Javier	.05	.02	.01
☐	494	Tom Marsh	.05	.02	.01
☐	495	Greg Mathews	.05	.02	.01
☐	496	Dale Murphy	.15	.07	.02
☐	497	Todd Pratt	.05	.02	.01

☐	498	Mitch Williams	.10	.05	.01			
☐	499	Danny Cox	.05	.02	.01			
☐	500	Doug Drabek	.10	.05	.01			
☐	501	Carlos Garcia	.10	.05	.01			
☐	502	Lloyd McClendon	.05	.02	.01			
☐	503	Denny Neagle	.05	.02	.01			
☐	504	Gary Redus	.05	.02	.01			
☐	505	Bob Walk	.05	.02	.01			
☐	506	John Wehner	.05	.02	.01			
☐	507	Luis Alicea	.05	.02	.01			
☐	508	Mark Clark	.10	.05	.01			
☐	509	Pedro Guerrero	.05	.02	.01			
☐	510	Rex Hudler	.05	.02	.01			
☐	511	Brian Jordan	.15	.07	.02			
☐	512	Omar Olivares	.05	.02	.01			
☐	513	Jose Oquendo	.05	.02	.01			
☐	514	Gerald Perry	.05	.02	.01			
☐	515	Bryn Smith	.05	.02	.01			
☐	516	Craig Wilson	.05	.02	.01			
☐	517	Tracy Woodson	.05	.02	.01			
☐	518	Larry Andersen	.05	.02	.01			
☐	519	Andy Benes	.10	.05	.01			
☐	520	Jim Deshaies	.05	.02	.01			
☐	521	Bruce Hurst	.05	.02	.01			
☐	522	Randy Myers	.10	.05	.01			
☐	523	Benito Santiago	.05	.02	.01			
☐	524	Tim Scott	.05	.02	.01			
☐	525	Tim Teufel	.05	.02	.01			
☐	526	Mike Benjamin	.05	.02	.01			
☐	527	Dave Burba	.05	.02	.01			
☐	528	Craig Colbert	.05	.02	.01			
☐	529	Mike Felder	.05	.02	.01			
☐	530	Bryan Hickerson	.05	.02	.01			
☐	531	Chris James	.05	.02	.01			
☐	532	Mark Leonard	.05	.02	.01			
☐	533	Greg Litton	.05	.02	.01			
☐	534	Francisco Oliveras	.05	.02	.01			
☐	535	John Patterson	.05	.02	.01			
☐	536	Jim Pena	.05	.02	.01			
☐	537	Dave Righetti	.05	.02	.01			
☐	538	Robby Thompson	.05	.02	.01			
☐	539	Jose Uribe	.05	.02	.01			
☐	540	Matt Williams	.30	.14	.04			
☐	541	Storm Davis	.05	.02	.01			
☐	542	Sam Horn	.05	.02	.01			
☐	543	Tim Hulett	.05	.02	.01			
☐	544	Craig Lefferts	.05	.02	.01			
☐	545	Chito Martinez	.05	.02	.01			
☐	546	Mark McLemore	.05	.02	.01			
☐	547	Luis Mercedes	.05	.02	.01			
☐	548	Bob Milacki	.05	.02	.01			
☐	549	Joe Orsulak	.05	.02	.01			
☐	550	Billy Ripken	.05	.02	.01			
☐	551	Cal Ripken Jr.	2.00	.90	.25			
☐	552	Rick Sutcliffe	.10	.05	.01			
☐	553	Jeff Tackett	.05	.02	.01			
☐	554	Wade Boggs	.15	.07	.02			
☐	555	Tom Brunansky	.05	.02	.01			
☐	556	Jack Clark	.05	.02	.01			
☐	557	John Dopson	.05	.02	.01			
☐	558	Mike Gardiner	.05	.02	.01			
☐	559	Mike Greenwell	.10	.05	.01			
☐	560	Greg A. Harris	.05	.02	.01			
☐	561	Billy Hatcher	.05	.02	.01			
☐	562	Joe Hesketh	.05	.02	.01			
☐	563	Tony Pena	.05	.02	.01			
☐	564	Phil Plantier	.05	.02	.01			
☐	565	Luis Rivera	.05	.02	.01			
☐	566	Herm Winningham	.05	.02	.01			
☐	567	Matt Young	.05	.02	.01			
☐	568	Bert Blyleven	.15	.07	.02			
☐	569	Mike Butcher	.05	.02	.01			
☐	570	Chuck Crim	.05	.02	.01			
☐	571	Chad Curtis	.10	.05	.01			
☐	572	Tim Fortugno	.05	.02	.01			
☐	573	Steve Frey	.05	.02	.01			
☐	574	Gary Gaetti	.10	.05	.01			
☐	575	Scott Lewis	.05	.02	.01			
☐	576	Lee Stevens	.05	.02	.01			
☐	577	Ron Tingley	.05	.02	.01			
☐	578	Julio Valera	.05	.02	.01			
☐	579	Shawn Abner	.05	.02	.01			
☐	580	Joey Cora	.05	.02	.01			
☐	581	Chris Cron	.05	.02	.01			
☐	582	Carlton Fisk	.15	.07	.02			
☐	583	Roberto Hernandez	.10	.05	.01			
☐	584	Charlie Hough	.10	.05	.01			
☐	585	Terry Leach	.05	.02	.01			
☐	586	Donn Pall	.05	.02	.01			
☐	587	Dan Pasqua	.05	.02	.01			
☐	588	Steve Sax	.05	.02	.01			
☐	589	Bobby Thigpen	.05	.02	.01			
☐	590	Albert Belle	.75	.35	.09			
☐	591	Felix Fermin	.05	.02	.01			
☐	592	Glenallen Hill	.10	.05	.01			
☐	593	Brook Jacoby	.05	.02	.01			
☐	594	Reggie Jefferson	.05	.02	.01			
☐	595	Carlos Martinez	.05	.02	.01			
☐	596	Jose Mesa	.10	.05	.01			
☐	597	Rod Nichols	.05	.02	.01			
☐	598	Junior Ortiz	.05	.02	.01			
☐	599	Eric Plunk	.05	.02	.01			
☐	600	Ted Power	.05	.02	.01			
☐	601	Scott Scudder	.05	.02	.01			
☐	602	Kevin Wickander	.05	.02	.01			
☐	603	Skeeter Barnes	.05	.02	.01			
☐	604	Mark Carreon	.05	.02	.01			
☐	605	Dan Gladden	.05	.02	.01			
☐	606	Bill Gullickson	.05	.02	.01			
☐	607	Chad Kreuter	.05	.02	.01			
☐	608	Mark Leiter	.05	.02	.01			
☐	609	Mike Munoz	.05	.02	.01			
☐	610	Rich Rowland	.05	.02	.01			
☐	611	Frank Tanana	.05	.02	.01			
☐	612	Walt Terrell	.05	.02	.01			
☐	613	Alan Trammell	.15	.07	.02			
☐	614	Lou Whitaker	.15	.07	.02			
☐	615	Luis Aquino	.05	.02	.01			
☐	616	Mike Boddicker	.05	.02	.01			
☐	617	Jim Eisenreich	.05	.02	.01			
☐	618	Mark Gubicza	.05	.02	.01			
☐	619	David Howard	.05	.02	.01			
☐	620	Mike Magnante	.05	.02	.01			
☐	621	Brent Mayne	.05	.02	.01			
☐	622	Kevin McReynolds	.05	.02	.01			
☐	623	Ed Pierce	.05	.02	.01			
☐	624	Bill Sampen	.05	.02	.01			
☐	625	Steve Shifflett	.05	.02	.01			
☐	626	Gary Thurman	.05	.02	.01			
☐	627	Curtis Wilkerson	.05	.02	.01			
☐	628	Chris Bosio	.05	.02	.01			
☐	629	Scott Fletcher	.05	.02	.01			
☐	630	Jim Gantner	.05	.02	.01			
☐	631	Dave Nilsson	.10	.05	.01			
☐	632	Jesse Orosco	.05	.02	.01			
☐	633	Dan Plesac	.05	.02	.01			
☐	634	Ron Robinson	.05	.02	.01			
☐	635	Bill Spiers	.05	.02	.01			
☐	636	Franklin Stubbs	.05	.02	.01			
☐	637	Willie Banks	.05	.02	.01			
☐	638	Randy Bush	.05	.02	.01			
☐	639	Chuck Knoblauch	.15	.07	.02			

			MINT	NRMT	EXC
☐ 640	Shane Mack	.05	.02	.01	
☐ 641	Mike Pagliarulo	.05	.02	.01	
☐ 642	Jeff Reboulet	.05	.02	.01	
☐ 643	John Smiley	.05	.02	.01	
☐ 644	Mike Trombley	.05	.02	.01	
☐ 645	Gary Wayne	.05	.02	.01	
☐ 646	Lenny Webster	.05	.02	.01	
☐ 647	Tim Burke	.05	.02	.01	
☐ 648	Mike Gallego	.05	.02	.01	
☐ 649	Dion James	.05	.02	.01	
☐ 650	Jeff Johnson	.05	.02	.01	
☐ 651	Scott Kamieniecki	.05	.02	.01	
☐ 652	Kevin Maas	.05	.02	.01	
☐ 653	Rich Monteleone	.05	.02	.01	
☐ 654	Jerry Nielsen	.05	.02	.01	
☐ 655	Scott Sanderson	.05	.02	.01	
☐ 656	Mike Stanley	.10	.05	.01	
☐ 657	Gerald Williams	.05	.02	.01	
☐ 658	Curt Young	.05	.02	.01	
☐ 659	Harold Baines	.10	.05	.01	
☐ 660	Kevin Campbell	.05	.02	.01	
☐ 661	Ron Darling	.05	.02	.01	
☐ 662	Kelly Downs	.05	.02	.01	
☐ 663	Eric Fox	.05	.02	.01	
☐ 664	Dave Henderson	.05	.02	.01	
☐ 665	Rick Honeycutt	.05	.02	.01	
☐ 666	Mike Moore	.05	.02	.01	
☐ 667	Jamie Quirk	.05	.02	.01	
☐ 668	Jeff Russell	.05	.02	.01	
☐ 669	Dave Stewart	.10	.05	.01	
☐ 670	Greg Briley	.05	.02	.01	
☐ 671	Dave Cochrane	.05	.02	.01	
☐ 672	Henry Cotto	.05	.02	.01	
☐ 673	Rich DeLucia	.05	.02	.01	
☐ 674	Brian Fisher	.05	.02	.01	
☐ 675	Mark Grant	.05	.02	.01	
☐ 676	Randy Johnson	.40	.18	.05	
☐ 677	Tim Leary	.05	.02	.01	
☐ 678	Pete O'Brien	.05	.02	.01	
☐ 679	Lance Parrish	.10	.05	.01	
☐ 680	Harold Reynolds	.05	.02	.01	
☐ 681	Shane Turner	.05	.02	.01	
☐ 682	Jack Daugherty	.05	.02	.01	
☐ 683	David Hulse	.05	.02	.01	
☐ 684	Terry Mathews	.05	.02	.01	
☐ 685	Al Newman	.05	.02	.01	
☐ 686	Edwin Nunez	.05	.02	.01	
☐ 687	Rafael Palmeiro	.15	.07	.02	
☐ 688	Roger Pavlik	.05	.02	.01	
☐ 689	Geno Petralli	.05	.02	.01	
☐ 690	Nolan Ryan	2.00	.90	.25	
☐ 691	David Cone	.15	.07	.02	
☐ 692	Alfredo Griffin	.05	.02	.01	
☐ 693	Juan Guzman	.10	.05	.01	
☐ 694	Pat Hentgen	.10	.05	.01	
☐ 695	Randy Knorr	.05	.02	.01	
☐ 696	Bob MacDonald	.05	.02	.01	
☐ 697	Jack Morris	.15	.07	.02	
☐ 698	Ed Sprague	.05	.02	.01	
☐ 699	Dave Stieb	.05	.02	.01	
☐ 700	Pat Tabler	.05	.02	.01	
☐ 701	Mike Timlin	.05	.02	.01	
☐ 702	David Wells	.05	.02	.01	
☐ 703	Eddie Zosky	.05	.02	.01	
☐ 704	Gary Sheffield LL	.10	.05	.01	
☐ 705	Darren Daulton LL	.10	.05	.01	
☐ 706	Marquis Grissom LL	.10	.05	.01	
☐ 707	Greg Maddux LL	1.00	.45	.12	
☐ 708	Bill Swift LL	.05	.02	.01	
☐ 709	Juan Gonzalez RT	.15	.07	.02	
☐ 710	Mark McGwire RT	.10	.05	.01	

			MINT	NRMT	EXC
☐ 711	Cecil Fielder RT	.10	.05	.01
☐ 712	Albert Belle RT	.40	.18	.05
☐ 713	Joe Carter RT	.10	.05	.01
☐ 714	Cecil Fielder SS Frank Thomas Power Brokers	.50	.23	.06
☐ 715	Larry Walker SS Darren Daulton Unsung Heroes	.10	.05	.01
☐ 716	Edgar Martinez SS Robin Ventura Hot Corner Hammers	.10	.05	.01
☐ 717	Roger Clemens SS Dennis Eckersley Start to Finish	.10	.05	.01
☐ 718	Checklist 361-480	.05	.02	.01
☐ 719	Checklist 481-600	.05	.02	.01
☐ 720	Checklist 601-720	.05	.02	.01

1993 Fleer All-Stars

 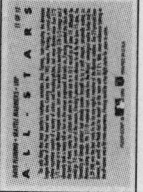

This 24-card standard-size (2 1/2" by 3 1/2") set was randomly inserted in wax packs, 12 American League players in series 1 and 12 National League players in series 2. The horizontal fronts feature a color close-up photo cut out and super-posed upon a black-and-white action scene framed by white borders. The player's name and the word "All-Stars" are printed in gold foil lettering across the bottom of the picture. On a pastel yellow panel, each horizontal back carries a career summary. The cards are numbered on the back "No. X of 12."

		MINT	NRMT	EXC
COMPLETE SET (24)		35.00	16.00	4.40
COMPLETE SER.1 (12)		25.00	11.00	3.10
COMPLETE SER.2 (12)		10.00	4.50	1.25
COMMON CARD (AL1-AL12)		.50	.23	.06
COMMON CARD (NL1-NL12)		.50	.23	.06
☐ AL1	Frank Thomas	12.00	5.50	1.50
☐ AL2	Roberto Alomar	2.50	1.10	.30
☐ AL3	Edgar Martinez	1.00	.45	.12
☐ AL4	Pat Listach	.50	.23	.06
☐ AL5	Cecil Fielder	1.00	.45	.12
☐ AL6	Juan Gonzalez	2.50	1.10	.30
☐ AL7	Ken Griffey Jr.	12.00	5.50	1.50
☐ AL8	Joe Carter	1.00	.45	.12
☐ AL9	Kirby Puckett	4.00	1.80	.50
☐ AL10	Brian Harper	.50	.23	.06

		MINT	NRMT	EXC
☐ AL11	Dave Fleming	.50	.23	.06
☐ AL12	Jack McDowell	1.00	.45	.12
☐ NL1	Fred McGriff	1.50	.70	.19
☐ NL2	Delino DeShields	1.00	.45	.12
☐ NL3	Gary Sheffield	1.00	.45	.12
☐ NL4	Barry Larkin	1.50	.70	.19
☐ NL5	Felix Jose	.50	.23	.06
☐ NL6	Larry Walker	1.00	.45	.12
☐ NL7	Barry Bonds	3.00	1.35	.35
☐ NL8	Andy Van Slyke	1.00	.45	.12
☐ NL9	Darren Daulton	1.00	.45	.12
☐ NL10	Greg Maddux	12.00	5.50	1.50
☐ NL11	Tom Glavine	1.25	.55	.16
☐ NL12	Lee Smith	1.00	.45	.12

1993 Fleer Final Edition

The cards are numbered on the back (with an "F" prefix), grouped alphabetically within teams, and checklisted below alphabetically according to teams for the National League and American League as follows: Atlanta Braves (1-5), Chicago Cubs (6-13), Cincinnati Reds (14-20), Colorado Rockies (21-47), Florida Marlins (48-75), Houston Astros (76-80), Los Angeles Dodgers (81-87), Montreal Expos (88- 97), New York Mets (98-107), Philadelphia Phillies (108-112), Pittsburgh Pirates (113-122), St. Louis Cardinals (123-133), San Diego Padres (134-148), San Francisco Giants (149-155), Baltimore Orioles (156-168), Boston Red Sox (169- 178), California Angels (179-191), Chicago White Sox (192-198), Cleveland Indians (199-208), Detroit Tigers (209-214), Kansas City Royals (215-221), Milwaukee Brewers (222-232), Minnesota Twins (233-241), New York Yankees (242-252), Oakland Athletics (253-262), Seattle Mariners (263-276), Texas Rangers (277-285), and Toronto Blue Jays (286-297). The set closes with checklist cards (298-300). Rookie Cards in this set include Rene Arocha, Russ Davis, Scott Lydy, J.T. Snow, Tony Tarasco, and Darrell Whitmore.

	MINT	NRMT	EXC
COMPLETE FACT.SET (310)	10.00	4.50	1.25
COMPLETE SET (300)	6.00	2.70	.75
COMMON CARD (1-300)	.05	.02	.01

☐ 1	Steve Bedrosian	.05	.02	.01
☐ 2	Jay Howell	.05	.02	.01
☐ 3	Greg Maddux	2.00	.90	.25
☐ 4	Greg McMichael	.10	.05	.01
☐ 5	Tony Tarasco	.25	.11	.03
☐ 6	Jose Bautista	.05	.02	.01
☐ 7	Jose Guzman	.05	.02	.01
☐ 8	Greg Hibbard	.05	.02	.01
☐ 9	Candy Maldonado	.05	.02	.01
☐ 10	Randy Myers	.10	.05	.01
☐ 11	Matt Walbeck	.10	.05	.01
☐ 12	Turk Wendell	.10	.05	.01
☐ 13	Willie Wilson	.05	.02	.01
☐ 14	Greg Cadaret	.05	.02	.01
☐ 15	Roberto Kelly	.10	.05	.01
☐ 16	Randy Milligan	.05	.02	.01
☐ 17	Kevin Mitchell	.10	.05	.01
☐ 18	Jeff Reardon	.10	.05	.01
☐ 19	John Roper	.10	.05	.01
☐ 20	John Smiley	.05	.02	.01
☐ 21	Andy Ashby	.05	.02	.01
☐ 22	Dante Bichette	.25	.11	.03
☐ 23	Willie Blair	.05	.02	.01
☐ 24	Pedro Castellano	.05	.02	.01
☐ 25	Vinny Castilla	.15	.07	.02
☐ 26	Jerald Clark	.05	.02	.01
☐ 27	Alex Cole	.05	.02	.01
☐ 28	Scott Fredrickson	.05	.02	.01
☐ 29	Jay Gainer	.05	.02	.01
☐ 30	Andres Galarraga	.15	.07	.02
☐ 31	Joe Girardi	.05	.02	.01
☐ 32	Ryan Hawblitzel	.05	.02	.01
☐ 33	Charlie Hayes	.10	.05	.01
☐ 34	Darren Holmes	.05	.02	.01
☐ 35	Chris Jones	.05	.02	.01
☐ 36	David Nied	.10	.05	.01
☐ 37	J.Owens	.10	.05	.01
☐ 38	Lance Painter	.05	.02	.01
☐ 39	Jeff Parrett	.05	.02	.01
☐ 40	Steve Reed	.05	.02	.01
☐ 41	Armando Reynoso	.05	.02	.01
☐ 42	Bruce Ruffin	.05	.02	.01
☐ 43	Danny Sheaffer	.05	.02	.01
☐ 44	Keith Shepherd	.05	.02	.01
☐ 45	Jim Tatum	.05	.02	.01
☐ 46	Gary Wayne	.05	.02	.01
☐ 47	Eric Young	.10	.05	.01
☐ 48	Luis Aquino	.05	.02	.01
☐ 49	Alex Arias	.05	.02	.01
☐ 50	Jack Armstrong	.05	.02	.01
☐ 51	Bret Barberie	.05	.02	.01
☐ 52	Geronimo Berroa	.05	.02	.01
☐ 53	Ryan Bowen	.05	.02	.01
☐ 54	Greg Briley	.05	.02	.01
☐ 55	Cris Carpenter	.05	.02	.01
☐ 56	Chuck Carr	.05	.02	.01
☐ 57	Jeff Conine	.15	.07	.02
☐ 58	Jim Corsi	.05	.02	.01
☐ 59	Orestes Destrade	.05	.02	.01
☐ 60	Junior Felix	.05	.02	.01
☐ 61	Chris Hammond	.05	.02	.01
☐ 62	Bryan Harvey	.10	.05	.01
☐ 63	Charlie Hough	.10	.05	.01
☐ 64	Joe Klink	.05	.02	.01
☐ 65	Richie Lewis UER	.05	.02	.01
	(Refers to place of birth and residence as Illinois instead of Indiana)			
☐ 66	Mitch Lyden	.05	.02	.01
☐ 67	Bob Natal	.05	.02	.01
☐ 68	Scott Pose	.05	.02	.01
☐ 69	Rich Renteria	.05	.02	.01

☐ 70	Benito Santiago	.05	.02	.01	☐ 141	Gene Harris	.05	.02	.01
☐ 71	Gary Sheffield	.15	.07	.02	☐ 142	Kevin Higgins	.05	.02	.01
☐ 72	Matt Turner	.05	.02	.01	☐ 143	Trevor Hoffman	.10	.05	.01
☐ 73	Walt Weiss	.10	.05	.01	☐ 144	Phil Plantier	.10	.05	.01
☐ 74	Darrell Whitmore	.05	.02	.01	☐ 145	Kerry Taylor	.05	.02	.01
☐ 75	Nigel Wilson	.10	.05	.01	☐ 146	Guillermo Velasquez	.05	.02	.01
☐ 76	Kevin Bass	.05	.02	.01	☐ 147	Wally Whitehurst	.05	.02	.01
☐ 77	Doug Drabek	.10	.05	.01	☐ 148	Tim Worrell	.05	.02	.01
☐ 78	Tom Edens	.05	.02	.01	☐ 149	Todd Benzinger	.05	.02	.01
☐ 79	Chris James	.05	.02	.01	☐ 150	Barry Bonds	.50	.23	.06
☐ 80	Greg Swindell	.05	.02	.01	☐ 151	Greg Brummett	.05	.02	.01
☐ 81	Omar Daal	.10	.05	.01	☐ 152	Mark Carreon	.05	.02	.01
☐ 82	Raul Mondesi	1.25	.55	.16	☐ 153	Dave Martinez	.05	.02	.01
☐ 83	Jody Reed	.05	.02	.01	☐ 154	Jeff Reed	.05	.02	.01
☐ 84	Cory Snyder	.05	.02	.01	☐ 155	Kevin Rogers	.05	.02	.01
☐ 85	Rick Trlicek	.05	.02	.01	☐ 156	Harold Baines	.10	.05	.01
☐ 86	Tim Wallach	.05	.02	.01	☐ 157	Damon Buford	.05	.02	.01
☐ 87	Todd Worrell	.05	.02	.01	☐ 158	Paul Carey	.05	.02	.01
☐ 88	Tavo Alvarez	.05	.02	.01	☐ 159	Jeffrey Hammonds	.10	.05	.01
☐ 89	Frank Bolick	.05	.02	.01	☐ 160	Jamie Moyer	.05	.02	.01
☐ 90	Kent Bottenfield	.05	.02	.01	☐ 161	Sherman Obando	.10	.05	.01
☐ 91	Greg Colbrunn	.15	.07	.02	☐ 162	John O'Donoghue	.05	.02	.01
☐ 92	Cliff Floyd	.15	.07	.02	☐ 163	Brad Pennington	.05	.02	.01
☐ 93	Lou Frazier	.05	.02	.01	☐ 164	Jim Poole	.05	.02	.01
☐ 94	Mike Gardiner	.05	.02	.01	☐ 165	Harold Reynolds	.05	.02	.01
☐ 95	Mike Lansing	.15	.07	.02	☐ 166	Fernando Valenzuela	.10	.05	.01
☐ 96	Bill Risley	.05	.02	.01	☐ 167	Jack Voigt	.05	.02	.01
☐ 97	Jeff Shaw	.05	.02	.01	☐ 168	Mark Williamson	.05	.02	.01
☐ 98	Kevin Baez	.05	.02	.01	☐ 169	Scott Bankhead	.05	.02	.01
☐ 99	Tim Bogar	.05	.02	.01	☐ 170	Greg Blosser	.05	.02	.01
☐ 100	Jeromy Burnitz	.05	.02	.01	☐ 171	Jim Byrd	.05	.02	.01
☐ 101	Mike Draper	.05	.02	.01	☐ 172	Ivan Calderson	.05	.02	.01
☐ 102	Darrin Jackson	.05	.02	.01	☐ 173	Andre Dawson	.15	.07	.02
☐ 103	Mike Maddux	.05	.02	.01	☐ 174	Scott Fletcher	.05	.02	.01
☐ 104	Joe Orsulak	.05	.02	.01	☐ 175	Jose Melendez	.05	.02	.01
☐ 105	Doug Saunders	.05	.02	.01	☐ 176	Carlos Quintana	.05	.02	.01
☐ 106	Frank Tanana	.05	.02	.01	☐ 177	Jeff Russell	.05	.02	.01
☐ 107	Dave Telgheder	.05	.02	.01	☐ 178	Aaron Sele	.10	.05	.01
☐ 108	Larry Andersen	.05	.02	.01	☐ 179	Rod Correia	.05	.02	.01
☐ 109	Jim Eisenreich	.05	.02	.01	☐ 180	Chili Davis	.10	.05	.01
☐ 110	Pete Incaviglia	.05	.02	.01	☐ 181	Jim Edmonds	1.25	.55	.16
☐ 111	Danny Jackson	.05	.02	.01	☐ 182	Rene Gonzales	.05	.02	.01
☐ 112	David West	.05	.02	.01	☐ 183	Hilly Hathaway	.05	.02	.01
☐ 113	Al Martin	.10	.05	.01	☐ 184	Torey Lovullo	.05	.02	.01
☐ 114	Blas Minor	.05	.02	.01	☐ 185	Greg Myers	.05	.02	.01
☐ 115	Dennis Moeller	.05	.02	.01	☐ 186	Gene Nelson	.05	.02	.01
☐ 116	William Pennyfeather	.05	.02	.01	☐ 187	Troy Percival	.05	.02	.01
☐ 117	Rich Robertson	.05	.02	.01	☐ 188	Scott Sanderson	.05	.02	.01
☐ 118	Ben Shelton	.05	.02	.01	☐ 189	Darryl Scott	.05	.02	.01
☐ 119	Lonnie Smith	.05	.02	.01	☐ 190	J.T. Snow	.60	.25	.07
☐ 120	Freddie Toliver	.05	.02	.01	☐ 191	Russ Springer	.05	.02	.01
☐ 121	Paul Wagner	.05	.02	.01	☐ 192	Jason Bere	.10	.05	.01
☐ 122	Kevin Young	.05	.02	.01	☐ 193	Rodney Bolton	.05	.02	.01
☐ 123	Rene Arocha	.10	.05	.01	☐ 194	Ellis Burks	.10	.05	.01
☐ 124	Gregg Jefferies	.15	.07	.02	☐ 195	Bo Jackson	.15	.07	.02
☐ 125	Paul Kilgus	.05	.02	.01	☐ 196	Mike LaValliere	.05	.02	.01
☐ 126	Les Lancaster	.05	.02	.01	☐ 197	Scott Ruffcorn	.10	.05	.01
☐ 127	Joe Magrane	.05	.02	.01	☐ 198	Jeff Schwartz	.05	.02	.01
☐ 128	Rob Murphy	.05	.02	.01	☐ 199	Jerry DiPoto	.05	.02	.01
☐ 129	Erik Pappas	.05	.02	.01	☐ 200	Alvaro Espinoza	.05	.02	.01
☐ 130	Stan Royer	.05	.02	.01	☐ 201	Wayne Kirby	.05	.02	.01
☐ 131	Ozzie Smith	.40	.18	.05	☐ 202	Tom Kramer	.05	.02	.01
☐ 132	Tom Urbani	.05	.02	.01	☐ 203	Jesse Levis	.05	.02	.01
☐ 133	Mark Whiten	.10	.05	.01	☐ 204	Manny Ramirez	1.50	.70	.19
☐ 134	Derek Bell	.15	.07	.02	☐ 205	Jeff Treadway	.05	.02	.01
☐ 135	Doug Brocail	.05	.02	.01	☐ 206	Bill Wertz	.05	.02	.01
☐ 136	Phil Clark	.05	.02	.01	☐ 207	Cliff Young	.05	.02	.01
☐ 137	Mark Ettles	.05	.02	.01	☐ 208	Matt Young	.05	.02	.01
☐ 138	Jeff Gardner	.05	.02	.01	☐ 209	Kirk Gibson	.10	.05	.01
☐ 139	Pat Gomez	.05	.02	.01	☐ 210	Greg Gohr	.05	.02	.01
☐ 140	Ricky Gutierrez	.05	.02	.01	☐ 211	Bill Krueger	.05	.02	.01

		MINT	NRMT	EXC
☐ 212	Bob MacDonald	.05	.02	.01
☐ 213	Mike Moore	.05	.02	.01
☐ 214	David Wells	.05	.02	.01
☐ 215	Billy Brewer	.05	.02	.01
☐ 216	David Cone	.15	.07	.02
☐ 217	Greg Gagne	.05	.02	.01
☐ 218	Mark Gardner	.05	.02	.01
☐ 219	Chris Haney	.05	.02	.01
☐ 220	Phil Hiatt	.05	.02	.01
☐ 221	Jose Lind	.05	.02	.01
☐ 222	Juan Bell	.05	.02	.01
☐ 223	Tom Brunansky	.05	.02	.01
☐ 224	Mike Ignasiak	.05	.02	.01
☐ 225	Joe Kmak	.05	.02	.01
☐ 226	Tom Lampkin	.05	.02	.01
☐ 227	Graeme Lloyd	.05	.02	.01
☐ 228	Carlos Maldonado	.05	.02	.01
☐ 229	Matt Mieske	.10	.05	.01
☐ 230	Angel Miranda	.05	.02	.01
☐ 231	Troy O'Leary	.40	.18	.05
☐ 232	Kevin Reimer	.05	.02	.01
☐ 233	Larry Casian	.05	.02	.01
☐ 234	Jim Deshaies	.05	.02	.01
☐ 235	Eddie Guardado	.05	.02	.01
☐ 236	Chip Hale	.05	.02	.01
☐ 237	Mike Maksudian	.05	.02	.01
☐ 238	David McCarty	.10	.05	.01
☐ 239	Pat Meares	.10	.05	.01
☐ 240	George Tsamis	.05	.02	.01
☐ 241	Dave Winfield	.15	.07	.02
☐ 242	Jim Abbott	.15	.07	.02
☐ 243	Wade Boggs	.15	.07	.02
☐ 244	Andy Cook	.05	.02	.01
☐ 245	Russ Davis	.20	.09	.03
☐ 246	Mike Humphreys	.05	.02	.01
☐ 247	Jimmy Key	.10	.05	.01
☐ 248	Jim Leyritz	.05	.02	.01
☐ 249	Bobby Munoz	.05	.02	.01
☐ 250	Paul O'Neill	.10	.05	.01
☐ 251	Spike Owen	.05	.02	.01
☐ 252	Dave Silvestri	.05	.02	.01
☐ 253	Marcos Armas	.05	.02	.01
☐ 254	Brent Gates	.10	.05	.01
☐ 255	Goose Gossage	.15	.07	.02
☐ 256	Scott Lydy	.05	.02	.01
☐ 257	Henry Mercedes	.05	.02	.01
☐ 258	Mike Mohler	.05	.02	.01
☐ 259	Troy Neel	.05	.02	.01
☐ 260	Edwin Nunez	.05	.02	.01
☐ 261	Craig Paquette	.05	.02	.01
☐ 262	Kevin Seitzer	.05	.02	.01
☐ 263	Rich Amaral	.05	.02	.01
☐ 264	Mike Blowers	.05	.02	.01
☐ 265	Chris Bosio	.05	.02	.01
☐ 266	Norm Charlton	.05	.02	.01
☐ 267	Jim Converse	.10	.05	.01
☐ 268	John Cummings	.10	.05	.01
☐ 269	Mike Felder	.05	.02	.01
☐ 270	Mike Hampton	.05	.02	.01
☐ 271	Bill Haselman	.05	.02	.01
☐ 272	Dwayne Henry	.05	.02	.01
☐ 273	Greg Litton	.05	.02	.01
☐ 274	Mackey Sasser	.05	.02	.01
☐ 275	Lee Tinsley	.10	.05	.01
☐ 276	David Wainhouse	.05	.02	.01
☐ 277	Jeff Bronkey	.05	.02	.01
☐ 278	Benji Gil	.10	.05	.01
☐ 279	Tom Henke	.10	.05	.01
☐ 280	Charlie Leibrandt	.05	.02	.01
☐ 281	Robb Nen	.05	.02	.01
☐ 282	Bill Ripken	.05	.02	.01

		MINT	NRMT	EXC
☐ 283	Jon Shave	.05	.02	.01
☐ 284	Doug Strange	.05	.02	.01
☐ 285	Matt Whiteside	.05	.02	.01
☐ 286	Scott Brow	.05	.02	.01
☐ 287	Willie Canate	.05	.02	.01
☐ 288	Tony Castillo	.05	.02	.01
☐ 289	Domingo Cedeno	.05	.02	.01
☐ 290	Darnell Coles	.05	.02	.01
☐ 291	Danny Cox	.05	.02	.01
☐ 292	Mark Eichhorn	.05	.02	.01
☐ 293	Tony Fernandez	.05	.02	.01
☐ 294	Al Leiter	.05	.02	.01
☐ 295	Paul Molitor	.15	.07	.02
☐ 296	Dave Stewart	.10	.05	.01
☐ 297	Woody Williams	.05	.02	.01
☐ 298	Checklist F1-F100	.05	.02	.01
☐ 299	Checklist F101-F200	.05	.02	.01
☐ 300	Checklist F201-F300	.05	.02	.01

1993 Fleer
Golden Moments

This six-card standard-size (2 1/2" by 3 1/2") set was randomly inserted in 1993 Fleer wax packs, three each in series 1 and 2. The fronts feature glossy color action photos framed by thin aqua and white lines and a black outer border. A gold foil baseball icon appears at each corner of the picture, and the player's name and the set title "Golden Moments" appears in a gold foil bar toward the bottom of the picture. The black-bordered backs have a similar design to that on the fronts, only with a small color head shot and a summary of the player's outstanding achievement on a white panel. The cards are unnumbered and checklisted below in alphabetical order.

		MINT	NRMT	EXC
COMPLETE SET (6)		16.00	7.25	2.00
COMPLETE SER.1 (3)		6.00	2.70	.75
COMPLETE SER.2 (3)		10.00	4.50	1.25
COMMON SERIES 1 (A1-A3)		.50	.23	.06
COMMON SERIES 2 (B1-B3)		.50	.23	.06
☐ A1	George Brett 3,000 Hits	5.00	2.20	.60
☐ A2	Mickey Morandini Unassisted Triple Play	.50	.23	.06
☐ A3	Dave Winfield	1.00	.45	.12

		MINT	NRMT	EXC
☐	Oldest Player with 100 RBI Season			
☐ B1	Dennis Eckersley Consecutive Saves Record	1.00	.45	.12
☐ B2	Bip Roberts Ties NL Consecutive Hits Record	.50	.23	.06
☐ B3	Frank Thomas and Juan Gonzalez 100 Plus RBI Seasons, First Two Years	9.00	4.00	1.10

		MINT	NRMT	EXC
☐ A13	Mike Piazza	18.00	8.00	2.20
☐ A14	Jesse Levis	.50	.23	.06
☐ A15	Rico Brogna	1.50	.70	.19
☐ A16	Alex Arias	.50	.23	.06
☐ A17	Rod Brewer	.50	.23	.06
☐ A18	Troy Neel	.50	.23	.06
☐ B1	Scooter Tucker	.50	.23	.06
☐ B2	Kerry Woodson	.50	.23	.06
☐ B3	Greg Colbrunn	.75	.35	.09
☐ B4	Pedro Martinez	2.00	.90	.25
☐ B5	Dave Silvestri	.50	.23	.06
☐ B6	Kent Bottenfield	.50	.23	.06
☐ B7	Rafael Bournigal	.50	.23	.06
☐ B8	J.T. Bruett	.50	.23	.06
☐ B9	Dave Mlicki	.50	.23	.06
☐ B10	Paul Wagner	.50	.23	.06
☐ B11	Mike Williams	.50	.23	.06
☐ B12	Henry Mercedes	.50	.23	.06
☐ B13	Scott Taylor	.50	.23	.06
☐ B14	Dennis Moeller	.50	.23	.06
☐ B15	Javier Lopez	6.00	2.70	.75
☐ B16	Steve Cooke	.50	.23	.06
☐ B17	Pete Young	.50	.23	.06
☐ B18	Ken Ryan	.50	.23	.06

1993 Fleer Major League Prospects

This 36-card set was randomly inserted in wax packs, 18 each in series 1 and 2. These standard-size (2 1/2" by 3 1/2") cards feature black-bordered color player action photos on their fronts. The player's name appears in gold foil at the top, and the set's name and logo appear in gold foil and black at the bottom. The black-bordered horizontal back carries a color player head shot in the upper left. The player's name, biography, and career highlights are displayed on a white background alongside and below. The cards are numbered on the back. The key card in this set is Mike Piazza.

	MINT	NRMT	EXC
COMPLETE SET (36)	30.00	13.50	3.70
COMPLETE SERIES 1 (18)	20.00	9.00	2.50
COMPLETE SERIES 2 (18)	10.00	4.50	1.25
COMMON SERIES 1 (A1-A18)	.50	.23	.06
COMMON SERIES 2 (B1-B18)	.50	.23	.06

		MINT	NRMT	EXC
☐ A1	Melvin Nieves	1.25	.55	.16
☐ A2	Sterling Hitchcock	.50	.23	.06
☐ A3	Tim Costo	.50	.23	.06
☐ A4	Manny Alexander	.50	.23	.06
☐ A5	Alan Embree	.50	.23	.06
☐ A6	Kevin Young	.50	.23	.06
☐ A7	J.T. Snow	5.00	2.20	.60
☐ A8	Russ Springer	.50	.23	.06
☐ A9	Billy Ashley	2.00	.90	.25
☐ A10	Kevin Rogers	.50	.23	.06
☐ A11	Steve Hosey	.50	.23	.06
☐ A12	Eric Wedge	.50	.23	.06

1993 Fleer Pro-Visions

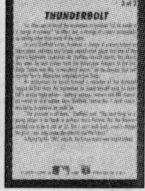

THUNDERBOLT

This six-card set was randomly inserted in wax packs, three each in series 1 and 2. These standard-size cards feature black-bordered fanciful color artwork of the players in action. The player's name appears in gold foil within the bottom black margin of each. The back carries player career highlights within a black-bordered white panel.

	MINT	NRMT	EXC
COMPLETE SET (6)	6.00	2.70	.75
COMPLETE SERIES 1 (3)	4.00	1.80	.50
COMPLETE SERIES 2 (3)	2.00	.90	.25
COMMON SERIES 1 (A1-A3)	1.00	.45	.12
COMMON SERIES 2 (B1-B3)	.75	.35	.09

		MINT	NRMT	EXC
☐ A1	Roberto Alomar	2.50	1.10	.30
☐ A2	Dennis Eckersley	1.00	.45	.12
☐ A3	Gary Sheffield	1.00	.45	.12
☐ B1	Andy Van Slyke	.75	.35	.09
☐ B2	Tom Glavine	1.25	.55	.16
☐ B3	Cecil Fielder	1.00	.45	.12

1993 Fleer
Rookie Sensations

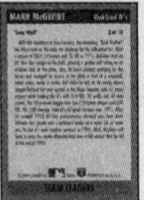

This 20-card set was randomly inserted in cello packs, 10 each in series 1 and 2. These standard-size (2 1/2" by 3 1/2") cards feature on their blue-bordered fronts cutout color player photos, each superposed upon a silver-colored background. The set's title and the player's name appear in gold foil in an upper corner. The back has the same blue-bordered and silver-colored background design. A color player head shot appears in the upper left and the player's career highlights follow alongside and below. The cards are numbered on the back "X of 10."

racks included 10 American League players, while series 2 racks included 10 National League players. Each of the tan-bordered standard-size (2 1/2" by 3 1/2") cards comprising this set feature a posed color player photo on its front with a smaller cutout color action photo superposed in a lower corner. The player's name and the set's title appear vertically in gold foil along the left side within team color-coded bars. The tan-bordered backs carry the player's name and team at the top within a team color-coded bar, and the set's title at the bottom within another team color-coded bar. Between these, the player's career highlights appear on a white background. The cards are numbered on the back.

	MINT	NRMT	EXC
COMPLETE SET (20)	30.00	13.50	3.70
COMPLETE SERIES 1 (10)	20.00	9.00	2.50
COMPLETE SERIES 2 (10)	10.00	4.50	1.25
COMMON CARD (RSA1-RSA10)	1.00	.45	.12
COMMON CARD (RSB1-RSB10)	1.00	.45	.12
☐ RSA1 Kenny Lofton	15.00	6.75	1.85
☐ RSA2 Cal Eldred	1.00	.45	.12
☐ RSA3 Pat Listach	1.00	.45	.12
☐ RSA4 Roberto Hernandez	1.50	.70	.19
☐ RSA5 Dave Fleming	1.00	.45	.12
☐ RSA6 Eric Karros	4.00	1.80	.50
☐ RSA7 Reggie Sanders	4.00	1.80	.50
☐ RSA8 Derrick May	1.00	.45	.12
☐ RSA9 Mike Perez	1.00	.45	.12
☐ RSA10 Donovan Osborne	1.00	.45	.12
☐ RSB1 Moises Alou	2.00	.90	.25
☐ RSB2 Pedro Astacio	1.00	.45	.12
☐ RSB3 Jim Austin	1.00	.45	.12
☐ RSB4 Chad Curtis	1.50	.70	.19
☐ RSB5 Gary DiSarcina	1.00	.45	.12
☐ RSB6 Scott Livingstone	1.00	.45	.12
☐ RSB7 Sam Militello	1.00	.45	.12
☐ RSB8 Arthur Rhodes	1.00	.45	.12
☐ RSB9 Tim Wakefield	1.50	.70	.19
☐ RSB10 Bob Zupcic	1.00	.45	.12

1993 Fleer
Team Leaders

One Team Leader or Tom Glavine was inserted into each Fleer rack pack. Series 1

	MINT	NRMT	EXC
COMPLETE SET (20)	75.00	34.00	9.50
COMPLETE SERIES 1 (10)	50.00	22.00	6.25
COMPLETE SERIES 2 (10)	25.00	11.00	3.10
COMMON CARD (AL1-AL10)	1.00	.45	.12
COMMON CARD (NL1-NL10)	2.00	.90	.25
☐ AL1 Kirby Puckett	6.00	2.70	.75
☐ AL2 Mark McGwire	2.00	.90	.25
☐ AL3 Pat Listach	1.00	.45	.12
☐ AL4 Roger Clemens	3.00	1.35	.35
☐ AL5 Frank Thomas	20.00	9.00	2.50
☐ AL6 Carlos Baerga	4.00	1.80	.50
☐ AL7 Brady Anderson	1.00	.45	.12
☐ AL8 Juan Gonzalez	4.00	1.80	.50
☐ AL9 Roberto Alomar	4.00	1.80	.50
☐ AL10 Ken Griffey Jr.	20.00	9.00	2.50
☐ NL1 Will Clark	2.50	1.10	.30
☐ NL2 Terry Pendleton	2.00	.90	.25
☐ NL3 Ray Lankford	2.00	.90	.25
☐ NL4 Eric Karros	2.50	1.10	.30
☐ NL5 Gary Sheffield	2.00	.90	.25
☐ NL6 Ryne Sandberg	5.00	2.20	.60
☐ NL7 Marquis Grissom	2.00	.90	.25
☐ NL8 John Kruk	2.00	.90	.25
☐ NL9 Jeff Bagwell	8.00	3.60	1.00
☐ NL10 Andy Van Slyke	2.00	.90	.25

1994 Fleer

The 1994 Fleer baseball set consists of 720 standard-size cards. The white-bordered fronts feature color player action photos. In one corner, the player's name and position appear in a gold foil lettered arc; his team

logo appears within. The backs are also white-bordered and feature a color player photo, some action, others posed. One side of the picture is ghosted and color-screened, and carries the player's name, biography, and career highlights. The bottom of the photo is also color-screened and ghosted, and carries the player's statistics. The cards are numbered on the back, grouped alphabetically within teams, and checklisted below alphabetically according to teams for each league as follows: Baltimore Orioles (1-24), Boston Red Sox (25-47), California Angels (48-72), Chicago White Sox (73-97), Cleveland Indians (98-123), Detroit Tigers (124-146), Kansas City Royals (147-172), Milwaukee Brewers (173-197), Minnesota Twins (198-223), New York Yankees (224-251), Oakland Athletics (252-277), Seattle Mariners (278-301), Texas Rangers (302-323), Toronto Blue Jays (324-349), Atlanta Braves (350-378), Chicago Cubs (379-403), Cincinnati Reds (404-431), Colorado Rockies (432-457), Florida Marlins (458-481), Houston Astros (482-503), Los Angeles Dodgers (504-530), Montreal Expos (531-556), New York Mets (557-580), Philadelphia Phillies (581-604), Pittsburgh Pirates (605-626), St. Louis Cardinals (627-651), San Diego Padres (652-679), and San Francisco Giants (680-705). The set closes with a Superstar Specials (706-713) subset.

	MINT	NRMT	EXC
COMPLETE SET (720)	50.00	22.00	6.25
COMMON CARD (1-720)	.10	.05	.01
ONE INSERT PER PACK			

☐ 1	Brady Anderson	.20	.09	.03
☐ 2	Harold Baines	.20	.09	.03
☐ 3	Mike Devereaux	.20	.09	.03
☐ 4	Todd Frohwirth	.10	.05	.01
☐ 5	Jeffrey Hammonds	.30	.14	.04
☐ 6	Chris Hoiles	.20	.09	.03
☐ 7	Tim Hulett	.10	.05	.01
☐ 8	Ben McDonald	.20	.09	.03
☐ 9	Mark McLemore	.10	.05	.01
☐ 10	Alan Mills	.10	.05	.01
☐ 11	Jamie Moyer	.10	.05	.01
☐ 12	Mike Mussina	.40	.18	.05
☐ 13	Gregg Olson	.10	.05	.01
☐ 14	Mike Pagliarulo	.10	.05	.01
☐ 15	Brad Pennington	.10	.05	.01
☐ 16	Jim Poole	.10	.05	.01
☐ 17	Harold Reynolds	.10	.05	.01
☐ 18	Arthur Rhodes	.10	.05	.01
☐ 19	Cal Ripken Jr.	3.00	1.35	.35
☐ 20	David Segui	.10	.05	.01
☐ 21	Rick Sutcliffe	.20	.09	.03
☐ 22	Fernando Valenzuela	.10	.05	.01
☐ 23	Jack Voigt	.10	.05	.01
☐ 24	Mark Williamson	.10	.05	.01
☐ 25	Scott Bankhead	.10	.05	.01
☐ 26	Roger Clemens	.50	.23	.06
☐ 27	Scott Cooper	.20	.09	.03
☐ 28	Danny Darwin	.10	.05	.01
☐ 29	Andre Dawson	.30	.14	.04
☐ 30	Rob Deer	.10	.05	.01
☐ 31	John Dopson	.10	.05	.01
☐ 32	Scott Fletcher	.10	.05	.01
☐ 33	Mike Greenwell	.20	.09	.03
☐ 34	Greg A. Harris	.10	.05	.01
☐ 35	Billy Hatcher	.10	.05	.01
☐ 36	Bob Melvin	.10	.05	.01
☐ 37	Tony Pena	.10	.05	.01
☐ 38	Paul Quantrill	.10	.05	.01
☐ 39	Carlos Quintana	.10	.05	.01
☐ 40	Ernest Riles	.10	.05	.01
☐ 41	Jeff Russell	.10	.05	.01
☐ 42	Ken Ryan	.10	.05	.01
☐ 43	Aaron Sele	.20	.09	.03
☐ 44	John Valentin	.20	.09	.03
☐ 45	Mo Vaughn	.50	.23	.06
☐ 46	Frank Viola	.10	.05	.01
☐ 47	Bob Zupcic	.10	.05	.01
☐ 48	Mike Butcher	.10	.05	.01
☐ 49	Rod Correia	.10	.05	.01
☐ 50	Chad Curtis	.20	.09	.03
☐ 51	Chili Davis	.20	.09	.03
☐ 52	Gary DiSarcina	.10	.05	.01
☐ 53	Damion Easley	.10	.05	.01
☐ 54	Jim Edmonds	.50	.23	.06
☐ 55	Chuck Finley	.10	.05	.01
☐ 56	Steve Frey	.10	.05	.01
☐ 57	Rene Gonzales	.10	.05	.01
☐ 58	Joe Grahe	.10	.05	.01
☐ 59	Hilly Hathaway	.10	.05	.01
☐ 60	Stan Javier	.10	.05	.01
☐ 61	Mark Langston	.30	.14	.04
☐ 62	Phil Leftwich	.10	.05	.01
☐ 63	Torey Lovullo	.10	.05	.01
☐ 64	Joe Magrane	.10	.05	.01
☐ 65	Greg Myers	.10	.05	.01
☐ 66	Ken Patterson	.10	.05	.01
☐ 67	Eduardo Perez	.10	.05	.01
☐ 68	Luis Polonia	.10	.05	.01
☐ 69	Tim Salmon	.60	.25	.07
☐ 70	J.T. Snow	.20	.09	.03
☐ 71	Ron Tingley	.10	.05	.01
☐ 72	Julio Valera	.10	.05	.01
☐ 73	Wilson Alvarez	.20	.09	.03
☐ 74	Tim Belcher	.10	.05	.01
☐ 75	George Bell	.20	.09	.03
☐ 76	Jason Bere	.20	.09	.03
☐ 77	Rod Bolton	.10	.05	.01
☐ 78	Ellis Burks	.20	.09	.03
☐ 79	Joey Cora	.10	.05	.01
☐ 80	Alex Fernandez	.30	.14	.04
☐ 81	Craig Grebeck	.10	.05	.01
☐ 82	Ozzie Guillen	.10	.05	.01
☐ 83	Roberto Hernandez	.10	.05	.01
☐ 84	Bo Jackson	.30	.14	.04
☐ 85	Lance Johnson	.10	.05	.01
☐ 86	Ron Karkovice	.10	.05	.01
☐ 87	Mike LaValliere	.10	.05	.01
☐ 88	Kirk McCaskill	.10	.05	.01

□	#	Player			
□	89	Jack McDowell	.30	.14	.04
□	90	Warren Newson	.10	.05	.01
□	91	Dan Pasqua	.10	.05	.01
□	92	Scott Radinsky	.10	.05	.01
□	93	Tim Raines	.30	.14	.04
□	94	Steve Sax	.10	.05	.01
□	95	Jeff Schwarz	.10	.05	.01
□	96	Frank Thomas	3.00	1.35	.35
□	97	Robin Ventura	.20	.09	.03
□	98	Sandy Alomar Jr.	.20	.09	.03
□	99	Carlos Baerga	.60	.25	.07
□	100	Albert Belle	1.25	.55	.16
□	101	Mark Clark	.10	.05	.01
□	102	Jerry DiPoto	.10	.05	.01
□	103	Alvaro Espinoza	.10	.05	.01
□	104	Felix Fermin	.10	.05	.01
□	105	Jeremy Hernandez	.10	.05	.01
□	106	Reggie Jefferson	.10	.05	.01
□	107	Wayne Kirby	.10	.05	.01
□	108	Tom Kramer	.10	.05	.01
□	109	Mark Lewis	.10	.05	.01
□	110	Derek Lilliquist	.10	.05	.01
□	111	Kenny Lofton	1.00	.45	.12
□	112	Candy Maldonado	.10	.05	.01
□	113	Jose Mesa	.10	.05	.01
□	114	Jeff Mutis	.10	.05	.01
□	115	Charles Nagy	.20	.09	.03
□	116	Bob Ojeda	.10	.05	.01
□	117	Junior Ortiz	.10	.05	.01
□	118	Eric Plunk	.10	.05	.01
□	119	Manny Ramirez	1.50	.70	.19
□	120	Paul Sorrento	.10	.05	.01
□	121	Jim Thome	.60	.25	.07
□	122	Jeff Treadway	.10	.05	.01
□	123	Bill Wertz	.10	.05	.01
□	124	Skeeter Barnes	.10	.05	.01
□	125	Milt Cuyler	.10	.05	.01
□	126	Eric Davis	.10	.05	.01
□	127	John Doherty	.10	.05	.01
□	128	Cecil Fielder	.30	.14	.04
□	129	Travis Fryman	.30	.14	.04
□	130	Kirk Gibson	.20	.09	.03
□	131	Dan Gladden	.10	.05	.01
□	132	Greg Gohr	.10	.05	.01
□	133	Chris Gomez	.30	.14	.04
□	134	Bill Gullickson	.10	.05	.01
□	135	Mike Henneman	.10	.05	.01
□	136	Kurt Knudsen	.10	.05	.01
□	137	Chad Kreuter	.10	.05	.01
□	138	Bill Krueger	.10	.05	.01
□	139	Scott Livingstone	.10	.05	.01
□	140	Bob MacDonald	.10	.05	.01
□	141	Mike Moore	.10	.05	.01
□	142	Tony Phillips	.10	.05	.01
□	143	Mickey Tettleton	.20	.09	.03
□	144	Alan Trammell	.30	.14	.04
□	145	David Wells	.10	.05	.01
□	146	Lou Whitaker	.30	.14	.04
□	147	Kevin Appier	.20	.09	.03
□	148	Stan Belinda	.10	.05	.01
□	149	George Brett	1.25	.55	.16
□	150	Billy Brewer	.10	.05	.01
□	151	Hubie Brooks	.10	.05	.01
□	152	David Cone	.30	.14	.04
□	153	Gary Gaetti	.10	.05	.01
□	154	Greg Gagne	.10	.05	.01
□	155	Tom Gordon	.10	.05	.01
□	156	Mark Gubicza	.10	.05	.01
□	157	Chris Gwynn	.10	.05	.01
□	158	John Habyan	.10	.05	.01
□	159	Chris Haney	.10	.05	.01
□	160	Phil Hiatt	.20	.09	.03
□	161	Felix Jose	.10	.05	.01
□	162	Wally Joyner	.20	.09	.03
□	163	Jose Lind	.10	.05	.01
□	164	Mike Macfarlane	.10	.05	.01
□	165	Mike Magnante	.10	.05	.01
□	166	Brent Mayne	.10	.05	.01
□	167	Brian McRae	.20	.09	.03
□	168	Kevin McReynolds	.10	.05	.01
□	169	Keith Miller	.10	.05	.01
□	170	Jeff Montgomery	.20	.09	.03
□	171	Hipolito Pichardo	.10	.05	.01
□	172	Rico Rossy	.10	.05	.01
□	173	Juan Bell	.10	.05	.01
□	174	Ricky Bones	.10	.05	.01
□	175	Cal Eldred	.20	.09	.03
□	176	Mike Fetters	.10	.05	.01
□	177	Darryl Hamilton	.10	.05	.01
□	178	Doug Henry	.10	.05	.01
□	179	Mike Ignasiak	.10	.05	.01
□	180	John Jaha	.10	.05	.01
□	181	Pat Listach	.10	.05	.01
□	182	Graeme Lloyd	.10	.05	.01
□	183	Matt Mieske	.10	.05	.01
□	184	Angel Miranda	.10	.05	.01
□	185	Jaime Navarro	.10	.05	.01
□	186	Dave Nilsson	.10	.05	.01
□	187	Troy O'Leary	.20	.09	.03
□	188	Jesse Orosco	.10	.05	.01
□	189	Kevin Reimer	.10	.05	.01
□	190	Kevin Seitzer	.10	.05	.01
□	191	Bill Spiers	.10	.05	.01
□	192	B.J. Surhoff	.10	.05	.01
□	193	Dickie Thon	.10	.05	.01
□	194	Jose Valentin	.20	.05	.01
□	195	Greg Vaughn	.20	.09	.03
□	196	Bill Wegman	.10	.05	.01
□	197	Robin Yount	.40	.18	.05
□	198	Rick Aguilera	.20	.09	.03
□	199	Willie Banks	.10	.05	.01
□	200	Bernardo Brito	.10	.05	.01
□	201	Larry Casian	.10	.05	.01
□	202	Scott Erickson	.10	.05	.01
□	203	Eddie Guardado	.10	.05	.01
□	204	Mark Guthrie	.10	.05	.01
□	205	Chip Hale	.10	.05	.01
□	206	Brian Harper	.10	.05	.01
□	207	Mike Hartley	.10	.05	.01
□	208	Kent Hrbek	.10	.05	.01
□	209	Terry Jorgensen	.10	.05	.01
□	210	Chuck Knoblauch	.30	.14	.04
□	211	Gene Larkin	.10	.05	.01
□	212	Shane Mack	.20	.09	.03
□	213	David McCarty	.10	.05	.01
□	214	Pat Meares	.10	.05	.01
□	215	Pedro Munoz	.10	.05	.01
□	216	Derek Parks	.10	.05	.01
□	217	Kirby Puckett	1.00	.45	.12
□	218	Jeff Reboulet	.10	.05	.01
□	219	Kevin Tapani	.10	.05	.01
□	220	Mike Trombley	.10	.05	.01
□	221	George Tsamis	.10	.05	.01
□	222	Carl Willis	.10	.05	.01
□	223	Dave Winfield	.30	.14	.04
□	224	Jim Abbott	.30	.14	.04
□	225	Paul Assenmacher	.10	.05	.01
□	226	Wade Boggs	.30	.14	.04
□	227	Russ Davis	.20	.09	.03
□	228	Steve Farr	.10	.05	.01
□	229	Mike Gallego	.10	.05	.01
□	230	Paul Gibson	.10	.05	.01

☐ 231	Steve Howe	.10	.05	.01
☐ 232	Dion James	.10	.05	.01
☐ 233	Domingo Jean	.10	.05	.01
☐ 234	Scott Kamieniecki	.10	.05	.01
☐ 235	Pat Kelly	.10	.05	.01
☐ 236	Jimmy Key	.20	.09	.03
☐ 237	Jim Leyritz	.10	.05	.01
☐ 238	Kevin Maas	.10	.05	.01
☐ 239	Don Mattingly	1.50	.70	.19
☐ 240	Rich Monteleone	.10	.05	.01
☐ 241	Bobby Munoz	.10	.05	.01
☐ 242	Matt Nokes	.10	.05	.01
☐ 243	Paul O'Neill	.20	.09	.03
☐ 244	Spike Owen	.10	.05	.01
☐ 245	Melido Perez	.10	.05	.01
☐ 246	Lee Smith	.30	.14	.04
☐ 247	Mike Stanley	.10	.05	.01
☐ 248	Danny Tartabull	.20	.09	.03
☐ 249	Randy Velarde	.10	.05	.01
☐ 250	Bob Wickman	.10	.05	.01
☐ 251	Bernie Williams	.20	.09	.03
☐ 252	Mike Aldrete	.10	.05	.01
☐ 253	Marcos Armas	.10	.05	.01
☐ 254	Lance Blankenship	.10	.05	.01
☐ 255	Mike Bordick	.10	.05	.01
☐ 256	Scott Brosius	.10	.05	.01
☐ 257	Jerry Browne	.10	.05	.01
☐ 258	Ron Darling	.10	.05	.01
☐ 259	Kelly Downs	.10	.05	.01
☐ 260	Dennis Eckersley	.30	.14	.04
☐ 261	Brent Gates	.20	.09	.03
☐ 262	Goose Gossage	.20	.09	.03
☐ 263	Scott Hemond	.10	.05	.01
☐ 264	Dave Henderson	.10	.05	.01
☐ 265	Rick Honeycutt	.10	.05	.01
☐ 266	Vince Horsman	.10	.05	.01
☐ 267	Scott Lydy	.10	.05	.01
☐ 268	Mark McGwire	.30	.14	.04
☐ 269	Mike Mohler	.10	.05	.01
☐ 270	Troy Neel	.10	.05	.01
☐ 271	Edwin Nunez	.10	.05	.01
☐ 272	Craig Paquette	.10	.05	.01
☐ 273	Ruben Sierra	.30	.14	.04
☐ 274	Terry Steinbach	.20	.09	.03
☐ 275	Todd Van Poppel	.20	.09	.03
☐ 276	Bob Welch	.10	.05	.01
☐ 277	Bobby Witt	.10	.05	.01
☐ 278	Rich Amaral	.10	.05	.01
☐ 279	Mike Blowers	.20	.09	.03
☐ 280	Bret Boone UER	.30	.14	.04
	(Name spelled Brett on front)			
☐ 281	Chris Bosio	.10	.05	.01
☐ 282	Jay Buhner	.20	.09	.03
☐ 283	Norm Charlton	.10	.05	.01
☐ 284	Mike Felder	.10	.05	.01
☐ 285	Dave Fleming	.10	.05	.01
☐ 286	Ken Griffey, Jr.	3.00	1.35	.35
☐ 287	Erik Hanson	.10	.05	.01
☐ 288	Bill Haselman	.10	.05	.01
☐ 289	Brad Holman	.10	.05	.01
☐ 290	Randy Johnson	.60	.25	.07
☐ 291	Tim Leary	.10	.05	.01
☐ 292	Greg Litton	.10	.05	.01
☐ 293	Dave Magadan	.10	.05	.01
☐ 294	Edgar Martinez	.20	.09	.03
☐ 295	Tino Martinez	.20	.09	.03
☐ 296	Jeff Nelson	.10	.05	.01
☐ 297	Erik Plantenberg	.10	.05	.01
☐ 298	Mackey Sasser	.10	.05	.01
☐ 299	Brian Turang	.10	.05	.01
☐ 300	Dave Valle	.10	.05	.01
☐ 301	Omar Vizquel	.10	.05	.01
☐ 302	Brian Bohanon	.10	.05	.01
☐ 303	Kevin Brown	.10	.05	.01
☐ 304	Jose Canseco UER	.50	.23	.06
	(Back mentions 1991 as his 40/40 MVP season; should be '88)			
☐ 305	Mario Diaz	.10	.05	.01
☐ 306	Julio Franco	.20	.09	.03
☐ 307	Juan Gonzalez	.75	.35	.09
☐ 308	Tom Henke	.10	.05	.01
☐ 309	David Hulse	.10	.05	.01
☐ 310	Manuel Lee	.10	.05	.01
☐ 311	Craig Lefferts	.10	.05	.01
☐ 312	Charlie Leibrandt	.10	.05	.01
☐ 313	Rafael Palmeiro	.30	.14	.04
☐ 314	Dean Palmer	.20	.09	.03
☐ 315	Roger Pavlik	.10	.05	.01
☐ 316	Dan Peltier	.10	.05	.01
☐ 317	Gene Petralli	.10	.05	.01
☐ 318	Gary Redus	.10	.05	.01
☐ 319	Ivan Rodriguez	.30	.14	.04
☐ 320	Kenny Rogers	.10	.05	.01
☐ 321	Nolan Ryan	3.00	1.35	.35
☐ 322	Doug Strange	.10	.05	.01
☐ 323	Matt Whiteside	.10	.05	.01
☐ 324	Roberto Alomar	.60	.25	.07
☐ 325	Pat Borders	.10	.05	.01
☐ 326	Joe Carter	.30	.14	.04
☐ 327	Tony Castillo	.10	.05	.01
☐ 328	Darnell Coles	.10	.05	.01
☐ 329	Danny Cox	.10	.05	.01
☐ 330	Mark Eichhorn	.10	.05	.01
☐ 331	Tony Fernandez	.10	.05	.01
☐ 332	Alfredo Griffin	.10	.05	.01
☐ 333	Juan Guzman	.20	.09	.03
☐ 334	Rickey Henderson	.30	.14	.04
☐ 335	Pat Hentgen	.20	.09	.03
☐ 336	Randy Knorr	.10	.05	.01
☐ 337	Al Leiter	.10	.05	.01
☐ 338	Paul Molitor	.30	.14	.04
☐ 339	Jack Morris	.30	.14	.04
☐ 340	John Olerud	.30	.14	.04
☐ 341	Dick Schofield	.10	.05	.01
☐ 342	Ed Sprague	.10	.05	.01
☐ 343	Dave Stewart	.20	.09	.03
☐ 344	Todd Stottlemyre	.10	.05	.01
☐ 345	Mike Timlin	.10	.05	.01
☐ 346	Duane Ward	.20	.09	.03
☐ 347	Turner Ward	.10	.05	.01
☐ 348	Devon White	.20	.09	.03
☐ 349	Woody Williams	.10	.05	.01
☐ 350	Steve Avery	.30	.14	.04
☐ 351	Steve Bedrosian	.10	.05	.01
☐ 352	Rafael Belliard	.10	.05	.01
☐ 353	Damon Berryhill	.10	.05	.01
☐ 354	Jeff Blauser	.20	.09	.03
☐ 355	Sid Bream	.10	.05	.01
☐ 356	Francisco Cabrera	.10	.05	.01
☐ 357	Marvin Freeman	.10	.05	.01
☐ 358	Ron Gant	.20	.09	.03
☐ 359	Tom Glavine	.30	.14	.04
☐ 360	Jay Howell	.10	.05	.01
☐ 361	David Justice	.40	.18	.05
☐ 362	Ryan Klesko	.75	.35	.09
☐ 363	Mark Lemke	.10	.05	.01
☐ 364	Javier Lopez	.50	.23	.06
☐ 365	Greg Maddux	3.00	1.35	.35
☐ 366	Fred McGriff	.40	.18	.05
☐ 367	Greg McMichael	.10	.05	.01
☐ 368	Kent Mercker	.10	.05	.01
☐ 369	Otis Nixon	.10	.05	.01

☐ 370 Greg Olson	.10	.05	.01
☐ 371 Bill Pecota	.10	.05	.01
☐ 372 Terry Pendleton	.30	.14	.04
☐ 373 Deion Sanders	.60	.25	.07
☐ 374 Pete Smith	.10	.05	.01
☐ 375 John Smoltz	.20	.09	.03
☐ 376 Mike Stanton	.10	.05	.01
☐ 377 Tony Tarasco	.30	.14	.04
☐ 378 Mark Wohlers	.10	.05	.01
☐ 379 Jose Bautista	.10	.05	.01
☐ 380 Shawn Boskie	.10	.05	.01
☐ 381 Steve Buechele	.10	.05	.01
☐ 382 Frank Castillo	.10	.05	.01
☐ 383 Mark Grace	.30	.14	.04
☐ 384 Jose Guzman	.10	.05	.01
☐ 385 Mike Harkey	.10	.05	.01
☐ 386 Greg Hibbard	.10	.05	.01
☐ 387 Glenallen Hill	.10	.05	.01
☐ 388 Steve Lake	.10	.05	.01
☐ 389 Derrick May	.10	.05	.01
☐ 390 Chuck McElroy	.10	.05	.01
☐ 391 Mike Morgan	.10	.05	.01
☐ 392 Randy Myers	.10	.05	.01
☐ 393 Dan Plesac	.10	.05	.01
☐ 394 Kevin Roberson	.10	.05	.01
☐ 395 Rey Sanchez	.10	.05	.01
☐ 396 Ryne Sandberg	.75	.35	.09
☐ 397 Bob Scanlan	.10	.05	.01
☐ 398 Dwight Smith	.10	.05	.01
☐ 399 Sammy Sosa	.30	.14	.04
☐ 400 Jose Vizcaino	.10	.05	.01
☐ 401 Rick Wilkins	.10	.05	.01
☐ 402 Willie Wilson	.10	.05	.01
☐ 403 Eric Yelding	.10	.05	.01
☐ 404 Bobby Ayala	.10	.05	.01
☐ 405 Jeff Branson	.10	.05	.01
☐ 406 Tom Browning	.10	.05	.01
☐ 407 Jacob Brumfield	.10	.05	.01
☐ 408 Tim Costo	.10	.05	.01
☐ 409 Rob Dibble	.10	.05	.01
☐ 410 Willie Greene	.10	.05	.01
☐ 411 Thomas Howard	.10	.05	.01
☐ 412 Roberto Kelly	.20	.09	.03
☐ 413 Bill Landrum	.10	.05	.01
☐ 414 Barry Larkin	.40	.18	.05
☐ 415 Larry Luebbers	.10	.05	.01
☐ 416 Kevin Mitchell	.20	.09	.03
☐ 417 Hal Morris	.20	.09	.03
☐ 418 Joe Oliver	.10	.05	.01
☐ 419 Tim Pugh	.10	.05	.01
☐ 420 Jeff Reardon	.20	.09	.03
☐ 421 Jose Rijo	.20	.09	.03
☐ 422 Bip Roberts	.10	.05	.01
☐ 423 John Roper	.20	.09	.03
☐ 424 Johnny Ruffin	.10	.05	.01
☐ 425 Chris Sabo	.10	.05	.01
☐ 426 Juan Samuel	.10	.05	.01
☐ 427 Reggie Sanders	.20	.09	.03
☐ 428 Scott Service	.10	.05	.01
☐ 429 John Smiley	.10	.05	.01
☐ 430 Jerry Spradlin	.10	.05	.01
☐ 431 Kevin Wickander	.10	.05	.01
☐ 432 Freddie Benavides	.10	.05	.01
☐ 433 Dante Bichette	.40	.18	.05
☐ 434 Willie Blair	.10	.05	.01
☐ 435 Daryl Boston	.10	.05	.01
☐ 436 Kent Bottenfield	.10	.05	.01
☐ 437 Vinny Castilla	.10	.05	.01
☐ 438 Jerald Clark	.10	.05	.01
☐ 439 Alex Cole	.10	.05	.01
☐ 440 Andres Galarraga	.30	.14	.04
☐ 441 Joe Girardi	.10	.05	.01
☐ 442 Greg W. Harris	.10	.05	.01
☐ 443 Charlie Hayes	.20	.09	.03
☐ 444 Darren Holmes	.10	.05	.01
☐ 445 Chris Jones	.10	.05	.01
☐ 446 Roberto Mejia	.10	.05	.01
☐ 447 David Nied	.20	.09	.03
☐ 448 J. Owens	.10	.05	.01
☐ 449 Jeff Parrett	.10	.05	.01
☐ 450 Steve Reed	.10	.05	.01
☐ 451 Armando Reynoso	.10	.05	.01
☐ 452 Bruce Ruffin	.10	.05	.01
☐ 453 Mo Sanford	.10	.05	.01
☐ 454 Danny Sheaffer	.10	.05	.01
☐ 455 Jim Tatum	.10	.05	.01
☐ 456 Gary Wayne	.10	.05	.01
☐ 457 Eric Young	.10	.05	.01
☐ 458 Luis Aquino	.10	.05	.01
☐ 459 Alex Arias	.10	.05	.01
☐ 460 Jack Armstrong	.10	.05	.01
☐ 461 Bret Barberie	.10	.05	.01
☐ 462 Ryan Bowen	.10	.05	.01
☐ 463 Chuck Carr	.10	.05	.01
☐ 464 Jeff Conine	.30	.14	.04
☐ 465 Henry Cotto	.10	.05	.01
☐ 466 Orestes Destrade	.10	.05	.01
☐ 467 Chris Hammond	.10	.05	.01
☐ 468 Bryan Harvey	.10	.05	.01
☐ 469 Charlie Hough	.10	.05	.01
☐ 470 Joe Klink	.10	.05	.01
☐ 471 Richie Lewis	.10	.05	.01
☐ 472 Bob Natal	.10	.05	.01
☐ 473 Pat Rapp	.10	.05	.01
☐ 474 Rich Renteria	.10	.05	.01
☐ 475 Rich Rodriguez	.10	.05	.01
☐ 476 Benito Santiago	.10	.05	.01
☐ 477 Gary Sheffield	.30	.14	.04
☐ 478 Matt Turner	.10	.05	.01
☐ 479 David Weathers	.10	.05	.01
☐ 480 Walt Weiss	.10	.05	.01
☐ 481 Darrell Whitmore	.20	.09	.03
☐ 482 Eric Anthony	.10	.05	.01
☐ 483 Jeff Bagwell	1.00	.45	.12
☐ 484 Kevin Bass	.10	.05	.01
☐ 485 Craig Biggio	.20	.09	.03
☐ 486 Ken Caminiti	.20	.09	.03
☐ 487 Andujar Cedeno	.10	.05	.01
☐ 488 Chris Donnels	.10	.05	.01
☐ 489 Doug Drabek	.30	.14	.04
☐ 490 Steve Finley	.10	.05	.01
☐ 491 Luis Gonzalez	.10	.05	.01
☐ 492 Pete Harnisch	.10	.05	.01
☐ 493 Xavier Hernandez	.10	.05	.01
☐ 494 Doug Jones	.10	.05	.01
☐ 495 Todd Jones	.10	.05	.01
☐ 496 Darryl Kile	.20	.09	.03
☐ 497 Al Osuna	.10	.05	.01
☐ 498 Mark Portugal	.10	.05	.01
☐ 499 Scott Servais	.10	.05	.01
☐ 500 Greg Swindell	.10	.05	.01
☐ 501 Eddie Taubensee	.10	.05	.01
☐ 502 Jose Uribe	.10	.05	.01
☐ 503 Brian Williams	.10	.05	.01
☐ 504 Billy Wagner	.30	.14	.04
☐ 505 Pedro Astacio	.20	.09	.03
☐ 506 Brett Butler	.20	.09	.03
☐ 507 Tom Candiotti	.10	.05	.01
☐ 508 Omar Daal	.10	.05	.01
☐ 509 Jim Gott	.10	.05	.01
☐ 510 Kevin Gross	.10	.05	.01
☐ 511 Dave Hansen	.10	.05	.01

□	512	Carlos Hernandez	.10	.05	.01
□	513	Orel Hershiser	.10	.05	.01
□	514	Eric Karros	.20	.09	.03
□	515	Pedro Martinez	.30	.14	.04
□	516	Ramon Martinez	.20	.09	.03
□	517	Roger McDowell	.10	.05	.01
□	518	Raul Mondesi	1.00	.45	.12
□	519	Jose Offerman	.10	.05	.01
□	520	Mike Piazza	1.25	.55	.16
□	521	Jody Reed	.10	.05	.01
□	522	Henry Rodriguez	.10	.05	.01
□	523	Mike Sharperson	.10	.05	.01
□	524	Cory Snyder	.10	.05	.01
□	525	Darryl Strawberry	.20	.09	.03
□	526	Rick Trlicek	.10	.05	.01
□	527	Tim Wallach	.10	.05	.01
□	528	Mitch Webster	.10	.05	.01
□	529	Steve Wilson	.10	.05	.01
□	530	Todd Worrell	.10	.05	.01
□	531	Moises Alou	.30	.14	.04
□	532	Brian Barnes	.10	.05	.01
□	533	Sean Berry	.10	.05	.01
□	534	Greg Colbrunn	.10	.05	.01
□	535	Delino DeShields	.20	.09	.03
□	536	Jeff Fassero	.10	.05	.01
□	537	Darrin Fletcher	.10	.05	.01
□	538	Cliff Floyd	.30	.14	.04
□	539	Lou Frazier	.10	.05	.01
□	540	Marquis Grissom	.30	.14	.04
□	541	Butch Henry	.10	.05	.01
□	542	Ken Hill	.20	.09	.03
□	543	Mike Lansing	.20	.09	.03
□	544	Brian Looney	.10	.05	.01
□	545	Dennis Martinez	.20	.09	.03
□	546	Chris Nabholz	.10	.05	.01
□	547	Randy Ready	.10	.05	.01
□	548	Mel Rojas	.10	.05	.01
□	549	Kirk Rueter	.10	.05	.01
□	550	Tim Scott	.10	.05	.01
□	551	Jeff Shaw	.10	.05	.01
□	552	Tim Spehr	.10	.05	.01
□	553	John VanderWal	.10	.05	.01
□	554	Larry Walker	.40	.18	.05
□	555	John Wetteland	.10	.05	.01
□	556	Rondell White	.30	.14	.04
□	557	Tim Bogar	.10	.05	.01
□	558	Bobby Bonilla	.30	.14	.04
□	559	Jeromy Burnitz	.10	.05	.01
□	560	Sid Fernandez	.10	.05	.01
□	561	John Franco	.10	.05	.01
□	562	Dave Gallagher	.10	.05	.01
□	563	Dwight Gooden	.10	.05	.01
□	564	Eric Hillman	.10	.05	.01
□	565	Todd Hundley	.20	.09	.03
□	566	Jeff Innis	.10	.05	.01
□	567	Darrin Jackson	.10	.05	.01
□	568	Howard Johnson	.10	.05	.01
□	569	Bobby Jones	.30	.14	.04
□	570	Jeff Kent	.20	.09	.03
□	571	Mike Maddux	.10	.05	.01
□	572	Jeff McKnight	.10	.05	.01
□	573	Eddie Murray	.40	.18	.05
□	574	Charlie O'Brien	.10	.05	.01
□	575	Joe Orsulak	.10	.05	.01
□	576	Bret Saberhagen	.20	.09	.03
□	577	Pete Schourek	.20	.09	.03
□	578	Dave Telgheder	.10	.05	.01
□	579	Ryan Thompson	.20	.09	.03
□	580	Anthony Young	.10	.05	.01
□	581	Ruben Amaro	.10	.05	.01
□	582	Larry Andersen	.10	.05	.01
□	583	Kim Batiste	.10	.05	.01
□	584	Wes Chamberlain	.10	.05	.01
□	585	Darren Daulton	.30	.14	.04
□	586	Mariano Duncan	.10	.05	.01
□	587	Lenny Dykstra	.30	.14	.04
□	588	Jim Eisenreich	.10	.05	.01
□	589	Tommy Greene	.10	.05	.01
□	590	Dave Hollins	.20	.09	.03
□	591	Pete Incaviglia	.10	.05	.01
□	592	Danny Jackson	.10	.05	.01
□	593	Ricky Jordan	.10	.05	.01
□	594	John Kruk	.20	.09	.03
□	595	Roger Mason	.10	.05	.01
□	596	Mickey Morandini	.10	.05	.01
□	597	Terry Mulholland	.10	.05	.01
□	598	Todd Pratt	.10	.05	.01
□	599	Ben Rivera	.10	.05	.01
□	600	Curt Schilling	.10	.05	.01
□	601	Kevin Stocker	.20	.09	.03
□	602	Milt Thompson	.10	.05	.01
□	603	David West	.10	.05	.01
□	604	Mitch Williams	.10	.05	.01
□	605	Jay Bell	.20	.09	.03
□	606	Dave Clark	.10	.05	.01
□	607	Steve Cooke	.10	.05	.01
□	608	Tom Foley	.10	.05	.01
□	609	Carlos Garcia	.10	.05	.01
□	610	Joel Johnston	.10	.05	.01
□	611	Jeff King	.10	.05	.01
□	612	Al Martin	.10	.05	.01
□	613	Lloyd McClendon	.10	.05	.01
□	614	Orlando Merced	.20	.09	.03
□	615	Blas Minor	.10	.05	.01
□	616	Denny Neagle	.20	.09	.03
□	617	Mark Petkovsek	.10	.05	.01
□	618	Tom Prince	.10	.05	.01
□	619	Don Slaught	.10	.05	.01
□	620	Zane Smith	.10	.05	.01
□	621	Randy Tomlin	.10	.05	.01
□	622	Andy Van Slyke	.30	.14	.04
□	623	Paul Wagner	.10	.05	.01
□	624	Tim Wakefield	.20	.09	.03
□	625	Bob Walk	.10	.05	.01
□	626	Kevin Young	.10	.05	.01
□	627	Luis Alicea	.10	.05	.01
□	628	Rene Arocha	.20	.09	.03
□	629	Rod Brewer	.10	.05	.01
□	630	Rheal Cormier	.10	.05	.01
□	631	Bernard Gilkey	.20	.09	.03
□	632	Lee Guetterman	.10	.05	.01
□	633	Gregg Jefferies	.30	.14	.04
□	634	Brian Jordan	.20	.09	.03
□	635	Les Lancaster	.10	.05	.01
□	636	Ray Lankford	.30	.14	.04
□	637	Rob Murphy	.10	.05	.01
□	638	Omar Olivares	.10	.05	.01
□	639	Jose Oquendo	.10	.05	.01
□	640	Donovan Osborne	.10	.05	.01
□	641	Tom Pagnozzi	.10	.05	.01
□	642	Erik Pappas	.10	.05	.01
□	643	Geronimo Pena	.10	.05	.01
□	644	Mike Perez	.10	.05	.01
□	645	Gerald Perry	.10	.05	.01
□	646	Ozzie Smith	.60	.25	.07
□	647	Bob Tewksbury	.10	.05	.01
□	648	Allen Watson	.10	.05	.01
□	649	Mark Whiten	.20	.09	.03
□	650	Tracy Woodson	.10	.05	.01
□	651	Todd Zeile	.20	.09	.03
□	652	Andy Ashby	.10	.05	.01
□	653	Brad Ausmus	.10	.05	.01

☐ 654	Billy Bean	.10	.05	.01
☐ 655	Derek Bell	.20	.09	.03
☐ 656	Andy Benes	.20	.09	.03
☐ 657	Doug Brocail	.10	.05	.01
☐ 658	Jarvis Brown	.10	.05	.01
☐ 659	Archi Cianfrocco	.10	.05	.01
☐ 660	Phil Clark	.10	.05	.01
☐ 661	Mark Davis	.10	.05	.01
☐ 662	Jeff Gardner	.10	.05	.01
☐ 663	Pat Gomez	.10	.05	.01
☐ 664	Ricky Gutierrez	.10	.05	.01
☐ 665	Tony Gwynn	1.00	.45	.12
☐ 666	Gene Harris	.10	.05	.01
☐ 667	Kevin Higgins	.10	.05	.01
☐ 668	Trevor Hoffman	.10	.05	.01
☐ 669	Pedro Martinez	.10	.05	.01
☐ 670	Tim Mauser	.10	.05	.01
☐ 671	Melvin Nieves	.30	.14	.04
☐ 672	Phil Plantier	.20	.09	.03
☐ 673	Frank Seminara	.10	.05	.01
☐ 674	Craig Shipley	.10	.05	.01
☐ 675	Kerry Taylor	.10	.05	.01
☐ 676	Tim Teufel	.10	.05	.01
☐ 677	Guillermo Velasquez	.10	.05	.01
☐ 678	Wally Whitehurst	.10	.05	.01
☐ 679	Tim Worrell	.10	.05	.01
☐ 680	Rod Beck	.20	.09	.03
☐ 681	Mike Benjamin	.10	.05	.01
☐ 682	Todd Benzinger	.10	.05	.01
☐ 683	Bud Black	.10	.05	.01
☐ 684	Barry Bonds	.75	.35	.09
☐ 685	Jeff Brantley	.10	.05	.01
☐ 686	Dave Burba	.10	.05	.01
☐ 687	John Burkett	.20	.09	.03
☐ 688	Mark Carreon	.10	.05	.01
☐ 689	Will Clark	.40	.18	.05
☐ 690	Royce Clayton	.20	.09	.03
☐ 691	Bryan Hickerson	.10	.05	.01
☐ 692	Mike Jackson	.10	.05	.01
☐ 693	Darren Lewis	.10	.05	.01
☐ 694	Kirt Manwaring	.10	.05	.01
☐ 695	Dave Martinez	.10	.05	.01
☐ 696	Willie McGee	.10	.05	.01
☐ 697	John Patterson	.10	.05	.01
☐ 698	Jeff Reed	.10	.05	.01
☐ 699	Kevin Rogers	.10	.05	.01
☐ 700	Scott Sanderson	.10	.05	.01
☐ 701	Steve Scarsone	.10	.05	.01
☐ 702	Billy Swift	.10	.05	.01
☐ 703	Robby Thompson	.10	.05	.01
☐ 704	Matt Williams	.50	.23	.06
☐ 705	Trevor Wilson	.10	.05	.01
☐ 706	Brave New World	.10	.05	.01
	Fred McGriff			
	Ron Gant			
	David Justice			
☐ 707	1-2 Punch	.10	.05	.01
	John Olerud			
	Paul Molitor			
☐ 708	American Heat	.10	.05	.01
	Mike Mussina			
	Jack McDowell			
☐ 709	Together Again	.10	.05	.01
	Lou Whitaker			
	Alan Trammell			
☐ 710	Lone Star Lumber	.30	.14	.04
	Rafael Palmeiro			
	Juan Gonzalez			
☐ 711	Batmen	.30	.14	.04
	Brett Butler			
	Tony Gwyn			

☐ 712	Twin Peaks	.30	.14	.04
	Kirby Puckett			
	Chuck Knoblauch			
☐ 713	Back to Back	.50	.23	.06
	Mike Piazza			
	Eric Karros			
☐ 714	Checklist 1	.10	.05	.01
☐ 715	Checklist 2	.10	.05	.01
☐ 716	Checklist 3	.10	.05	.01
☐ 717	Checklist 4	.10	.05	.01
☐ 718	Checklist 5	.10	.05	.01
☐ 719	Checklist 6	.10	.05	.01
☐ 720	Checklist 7	.10	.05	.01

1994 Fleer All-Stars

Fleer issued this 50-card set in 1994, to commemorate the All-Stars of the 1993 season. The cards were exclusively available in the Fleer wax packs at a rate of one in two. The set features 25 American League (1-25) and 25 National League (26-50) All-Stars. The cards measure standard size. The full-bleed fronts feature color action player cut-out photos with an American flag background. The player's name is stamped in gold foil along the bottom edge adjacent to a 1993 All-Stars Game logo. The borderless backs carry a similar flag background with a player head shot near the bottom. The player's name and career highlights round out the back.

	MINT	NRMT	EXC
COMPLETE SET (50)	25.00	11.00	3.10
COMMON CARD (1-50)	.25	.11	.03

☐ 1	Roberto Alomar	.75	.35	.09
☐ 2	Carlos Baerga	.75	.35	.09
☐ 3	Albert Belle	1.50	.70	.19
☐ 4	Wade Boggs	.40	.18	.05
☐ 5	Joe Carter	.40	.18	.05
☐ 6	Scott Cooper	.25	.11	.03
☐ 7	Cecil Fielder	.40	.18	.05
☐ 8	Travis Fryman	.40	.18	.05
☐ 9	Juan Gonzalez	1.00	.45	.12
☐ 10	Ken Griffey Jr	4.00	1.80	.50
☐ 11	Pat Hentgen	.25	.11	.03
☐ 12	Randy Johnson	.75	.35	.09
☐ 13	Jimmy Key	.25	.11	.03
☐ 14	Mark Langston	.25	.11	.03
☐ 15	Jack McDowell	.25	.11	.03

☐	16 Paul Molitor	.40	.18	.05
☐	17 Jeff Montgomery	.25	.11	.03
☐	18 Mike Mussina	.50	.23	.06
☐	19 John Olerud	.40	.18	.05
☐	20 Kirby Puckett	1.25	.55	.16
☐	21 Cal Ripken	5.00	2.20	.60
☐	22 Ivan Rodriguez	.40	.18	.05
☐	23 Frank Thomas	4.00	1.80	.50
☐	24 Greg Vaughn	.25	.11	.03
☐	25 Duane Ward	.25	.11	.03
☐	26 Steve Avery	.40	.18	.05
☐	27 Rod Beck	.25	.11	.03
☐	28 Jay Bell	.25	.11	.03
☐	29 Andy Benes	.25	.11	.03
☐	30 Jeff Blauser	.25	.11	.03
☐	31 Barry Bonds	1.00	.45	.12
☐	32 Bobby Bonilla	.40	.18	.05
☐	33 John Burkett	.25	.11	.03
☐	34 Darren Daulton	.40	.18	.05
☐	35 Andres Galarraga	.40	.18	.05
☐	36 Tom Glavine	.40	.18	.05
☐	37 Mark Grace	.40	.18	.05
☐	38 Marquis Grissom	.40	.18	.05
☐	39 Tony Gwynn	1.25	.55	.16
☐	40 Bryan Harvey	.25	.11	.03
☐	41 Dave Hollins	.25	.11	.03
☐	42 David Justice	.50	.23	.06
☐	43 Darryl Kile	.25	.11	.03
☐	44 John Kruk	.25	.11	.03
☐	45 Barry Larkin	.50	.23	.06
☐	46 Terry Mulholland	.25	.11	.03
☐	47 Mike Piazza	1.50	.70	.19
☐	48 Ryne Sandberg	1.00	.45	.12
☐	49 Gary Sheffield	.40	.18	.05
☐	50 John Smoltz	.25	.11	.03

1994 Fleer Award Winners

Randomly inserted in foil packs at a rate of one in 37, this six-card standard-size set spotlights six outstanding players who received awards. Inside beige borders, the horizontal fronts feature three views of the same color player photo. The words "Fleer Award Winners" and the player's name are printed in gold toward the bottom. The backs have a similar design to the fronts, only with one color player cutout and a season summary.

	MINT	NRMT	EXC
COMPLETE SET (6)	12.00	5.50	1.50
COMMON CARD (1-6)	.50	.23	.06

☐ 1 Frank Thomas 5.00	2.20	.60	
AL Most Valuable Player			
☐ 2 Barry Bonds 1.25	.55	.16	
NL Most Valuable Player			
☐ 3 Jack McDowell .50	.23	.06	
AL Pitcher of the Year			
☐ 4 Greg Maddux 5.00	2.20	.60	
NL Pitcher of the Year			
☐ 5 Tim Salmon 1.00	.45	.12	
AL Rookie of the Year			
☐ 6 Mike Piazza 2.00	.90	.25	
NL Rookie of the Year			

1994 Fleer League Leaders

Randomly inserted in all pack types at a rate of one in 17, this 28-card standard-size set features six statistical leaders each for the American (1-6) and the National (7-12) Leagues. Inside a beige border, the fronts feature a color action player cutout superimposed on a black-and-white player photo. The player's name and the set title are gold foil stamped in the bottom border, while the player's achievement is printed vertically along the right edge of the picture. The horizontal backs have a color close-up shot on the left portion and a player summary on the right.

	MINT	NRMT	EXC
COMPLETE SET (12)	8.00	3.60	1.00
COMMON CARD (1-12)	.25	.11	.03

☐ 1 John Olerud .50	.23	.06	
AL Batting Crown			
☐ 2 Albert Belle 2.00	.90	.25	
AL RBI Leader			
☐ 3 Rafael Palmeiro .50	.23	.06	
AL Runs Scored Leader			
☐ 4 Kenny Lofton 1.50	.70	.19	
AL Stolen Base Leader			
☐ 5 Jack McDowell .50	.23	.06	
AL Winningest Pitcher			
☐ 6 Kevin Appier .50	.23	.06	
AL ERA Leader			

		MINT	NRMT	EXC
☐ 7	Andres Galarraga	.50	.23	.06
	NL Batting Crown			
☐ 8	Barry Bonds	1.25	.55	.16
	NL RBI Leader			
☐ 9	Lenny Dykstra	.50	.23	.06
	NL Runs Scored Leader			
☐ 10	Chuck Carr	.25	.11	.03
	NL Stolen Base Leader			
☐ 11	Tom Glavine	.50	.23	.06
	NL Winningest Pitcher			
☐ 12	Greg Maddux	5.00	2.20	.60
	NL ERA Leader			

		MINT	NRMT	EXC
☐ 16	Butch Huskey	.50	.23	.06
☐ 17	Miguel Jimenez	.50	.23	.06
☐ 18	Chipper Jones	8.00	3.60	1.00
☐ 19	Steve Karsay	.50	.23	.06
☐ 20	Mike Kelly	.50	.23	.06
☐ 21	Mike Lieberthal	.25	.11	.03
☐ 22	Albie Lopez	.50	.23	.06
☐ 23	Jeff McNeely	.25	.11	.03
☐ 24	Dan Miceli	.25	.11	.03
☐ 25	Nate Minchey	.25	.11	.03
☐ 26	Marc Newfield	.50	.23	.06
☐ 27	Darren Oliver	.25	.11	.03
☐ 28	Luis Ortiz	.50	.23	.06
☐ 29	Curtis Pride	.50	.23	.06
☐ 30	Roger Salked	.25	.11	.03
☐ 31	Scott Sanders	.50	.23	.06
☐ 32	Dave Staton	.25	.11	.03
☐ 33	Salomon Torres	.50	.23	.06
☐ 34	Steve Trachsel	.50	.23	.06
☐ 35	Chris Turner	.25	.11	.03

1994 Fleer Major League Prospects

Randomly inserted in all pack types at a rate of one in six, this 35-card standard-size set showcases some of the outstanding young players in Major League Baseball. Inside beige borders, the fronts display color action photos superimposed over ghosted versions of the team logos. The set title and the player's name are gold foil stamped across the bottom of the card. On a beige background with thin blue pin-stripes, the backs show a color player cutout and, on a powder blue panel, a player profile. The cards are numbered on the back "X of 35."

	MINT	NRMT	EXC
COMPLETE SET (35)	20.00	9.00	2.50
COMMON CARD (1-35)	.25	.11	.03
☐ 1 Kurt Abbott	.75	.35	.09
☐ 2 Brian Anderson	.50	.23	.06
☐ 3 Rich Aude	.50	.23	.06
☐ 4 Cory Bailey	.25	.11	.03
☐ 5 Danny Bautista	.25	.11	.03
☐ 6 Marty Cordova	3.00	1.35	.35
☐ 7 Tripp Cromer	.25	.11	.03
☐ 8 Midre Cummings	.50	.23	.06
☐ 9 Carlos Delgado	2.00	.90	.25
☐ 10 Steve Dreyer	.25	.11	.03
☐ 11 Steve Dunn	.25	.11	.03
☐ 12 Jeff Granger	.50	.23	.06
☐ 13 Tyrone Hill	.50	.23	.06
☐ 14 Denny Hocking	.50	.23	.06
☐ 15 John Hope	.25	.11	.03

1994 Fleer Pro-Visions

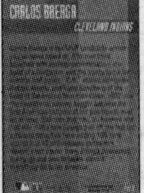

Randomly inserted in all pack types at a rate of one in 12, this nine-card standard-size set features on its fronts colorful artistic player caricatures with surrealistic backgrounds drawn by illustrator Wayne Still. The player's name is gold foil stamped at the lower right corner. When all nine cards are placed in order in a collector sheet, the backgrounds fit together to form a composite. The backs shade from one bright color to another and present career summaries. The cards are numbered on the back "X of 9."

	MINT	NRMT	EXC
COMPLETE SET (9)	5.00	2.20	.60
COMMON CARD (1-9)	.25	.11	.03
☐ 1 Darren Daulton	.25	.11	.03
☐ 2 John Olerud	.25	.11	.03
☐ 3 Matt Williams	.60	.25	.07
☐ 4 Carlos Baerga	.75	.35	.09
☐ 5 Ozzie Smith	.75	.35	.09
☐ 6 Juan Gonzalez	1.00	.45	.12
☐ 7 Jack McDowell	.25	.11	.03
☐ 8 Mike Piazza	1.50	.70	.19
☐ 9 Tony Gwynn	1.25	.55	.16

1994 Fleer
Rookie Sensations

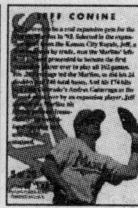

Randomly inserted in jumbo packs at a rate of one in four, this 20-card standard-size set features outstanding rookies. The fronts are "double exposed," with a player action cutout superimposed over a second photo. The team logo also appears in the team color-coded background. The set title is gold foil stamped toward the top, and the player's name is gold foil stamped on a team color-coded ribbon toward the bottom. On a white background featuring a ghosted version of the team logo, the backs have a player cutout photo and a season summary. The cards are numbered on the back "X of 20."

		MINT	NRMT	EXC
	COMPLETE SET (20)	18.00	8.00	2.20
	COMMON CARD (1-20)	.75	.35	.09
☐	1 Rene Arocha	.75	.35	.09
☐	2 Jason Bere	1.50	.70	.19
☐	3 Jeromy Burnitz	.75	.35	.09
☐	4 Chuck Carr	.75	.35	.09
☐	5 Jeff Conine	2.00	.90	.25
☐	6 Steve Cooke	.75	.35	.09
☐	7 Cliff Floyd	1.50	.70	.19
☐	8 Jeffrey Hammonds	1.50	.70	.19
☐	9 Wayne Kirby	.75	.35	.09
☐	10 Mike Lansing	.75	.35	.09
☐	11 Al Martin	1.50	.70	.19
☐	12 Greg McMichael	.75	.35	.09
☐	13 Troy Neel	.75	.35	.09
☐	14 Mike Piazza	8.00	3.60	1.00
☐	15 Armando Reynoso	.75	.35	.09
☐	16 Kirk Rueter	.75	.35	.09
☐	17 Tim Salmon	4.00	1.80	.50
☐	18 Aaron Sele	1.50	.70	.19
☐	19 J.T. Snow	1.50	.70	.19
☐	20 Kevin Stocker	.75	.35	.09

1994 Fleer
Smoke 'n Heat

Randomly inserted in wax packs at a rate of one in 36, this 12-card standard-size set showcases the best pitchers in the game.

On the fronts, color action player cutouts are superimposed on a red-and-gold fiery background that has a metallic sheen to it. The set title "Smoke 'n Heat" is printed in large block lettering. On a reddish marbleized background, the backs have another player cutout and season summary. mary. The cards are numbered on the back "X of 12."

		MINT	NRMT	EXC
	COMPLETE SET (12)	80.00	36.00	10.00
	COMMON CARD (1-12)	2.00	.90	.25
☐	1 Roger Clemens	6.00	2.70	.75
☐	2 David Cone	3.00	1.35	.35
☐	3 Juan Guzman	2.00	.90	.25
☐	4 Pete Harnisch	2.00	.90	.25
☐	5 Randy Johnson	6.00	2.70	.75
☐	6 Mark Langston	2.00	.90	.25
☐	7 Greg Maddux	30.00	13.50	3.70
☐	8 Mike Mussina	5.00	2.20	.60
☐	9 Jose Rijo	2.00	.90	.25
☐	10 Nolan Ryan	30.00	13.50	3.70
☐	11 Curt Schilling	2.00	.90	.25
☐	12 John Smoltz	3.00	1.35	.35

1994 Fleer
Team Leaders

Randomly inserted in all pack types, this 28-card standard-size set features Fleer's selected top player from each of the 28 major league teams. The fronts feature an action player cutout superposed on a larger close-up photo with a team color-coded background, all inside beige borders. The set title, player's name, team name, and position are printed in gold foil across the bottom. On a white background with a ghosted version of the team logo, the horizontal backs carry a second color player cutout and a summary of the player's performance. The card numbering is arranged alphabetically by city according to the American (1-14) and the National (15-28) Leagues.

		MINT	NRMT	EXC
	COMPLETE SET (28)	25.00	11.00	3.10
	COMMON CARD (1-28)	.25	.11	.03

		MINT	NRMT	EXC
☐ 1	Cal Ripken	5.00	2.20	.60
☐ 2	Mo Vaughn	.75	.35	.09
☐ 3	Tim Salmon	1.00	.45	.12
☐ 4	Frank Thomas	5.00	2.20	.60
☐ 5	Carlos Baerga	1.00	.45	.12
☐ 6	Cecil Fielder	.50	.23	.06
☐ 7	Brian McRae	.25	.11	.03
☐ 8	Greg Vaughn	.25	.11	.03
☐ 9	Kirby Puckett	1.50	.70	.19
☐ 10	Don Mattingly	2.50	1.10	.30
☐ 11	Mark McGwire	.50	.23	.06
☐ 12	Ken Griffey Jr.	5.00	2.20	.60
☐ 13	Juan Gonzalez	1.25	.55	.16
☐ 14	Paul Molitor	.50	.23	.06
☐ 15	David Justice	.60	.25	.07
☐ 16	Ryne Sandberg	1.25	.55	.16
☐ 17	Barry Larkin	.60	.25	.07
☐ 18	Andres Galarraga	.50	.23	.06
☐ 19	Gary Sheffield	.50	.23	.06
☐ 20	Jeff Bagwell	1.50	.70	.19
☐ 21	Mike Piazza	2.00	.90	.25
☐ 22	Marquis Grissom	.50	.23	.06
☐ 23	Bobby Bonilla	.50	.23	.06
☐ 24	Lenny Dykstra	.50	.23	.06
☐ 25	Jay Bell	.25	.11	.03
☐ 26	Gregg Jefferies	.50	.23	.06
☐ 27	Tony Gwynn	1.50	.70	.19
☐ 28	Will Clark	.60	.25	.07

1994 Fleer Update

This 200-card standard-size set highlights traded players in their new uniforms and promising young rookies. A ten card Diamond Tribute set was included in each factory set for a total of 210 cards. The cards are numbered on the back, grouped alphabetically by team in league as follows: Baltimore Orioles (1-8), Boston Red Sox (9-14), California Angels (15-22), Chicago White Sox (23-30), Cleveland Indians (31-38), Detroit Tigers (39-46), Kansas City Royals (47-51), Milwaukee Brewers (52-58), Minnesota Twins (59-66), New York Yankees (67-71), Oakland Athletics (72-78), Seattle Mariners (79-88), Texas Rangers (89-95), Toronto Blue Jays (96-100), Atlanta Braves (101-105), Chicago Cubs (106-113), Cincinnati Reds (114-121), Colorado Rockies (122-131), Florida Marlins (132-139), Houston Astros (140-147), Los Angeles Dodgers (148-151), Montreal Expos (152-155), New York Mets

(156-163), Philadelphia Phillies (164-171), Pittsburgh Pirates (172-177), St. Louis Cardinals (178-183), San Diego Padres (184-191), and San Francisco Giants (192-198). Rookie Cards include Brian Anderson, John Hudek, Chan Ho Park, Alex Rodriguez and Will VanLandingham.

		MINT	NRMT	EXC
	COMPLETE FACT.SET (210)	15.00	6.75	1.85
	COMPLETE SET (200)	10.00	4.50	1.25
	COMMON CARD (U1-U200)	.10	.05	.01
☐ U1	Mark Eichhorn	.10	.05	.01
☐ U2	Sid Fernandez	.10	.05	.01
☐ U3	Leo Gomez	.10	.05	.01
☐ U4	Mike Oquist	.10	.05	.01
☐ U5	Rafael Palmeiro	.40	.18	.05
☐ U6	Chris Sabo	.10	.05	.01
☐ U7	Dwight Smith	.10	.05	.01
☐ U8	Lee Smith	.40	.18	.05
☐ U9	Damon Berryhill	.10	.05	.01
☐ U10	Wes Chamberlain	.10	.05	.01
☐ U11	Gar Finnvold	.10	.05	.01
☐ U12	Chris Howard	.10	.05	.01
☐ U13	Tim Naehring	.25	.11	.03
☐ U14	Otis Nixon	.10	.05	.01
☐ U15	Brian Anderson	.40	.18	.05
☐ U16	Jorge Fabregas	.10	.05	.01
☐ U17	Rex Hudler	.10	.05	.01
☐ U18	Bo Jackson	.40	.18	.05
☐ U19	Mark Leiter	.10	.05	.01
☐ U20	Spike Owen	.10	.05	.01
☐ U21	Harold Reynolds	.10	.05	.01
☐ U22	Chris Turner	.10	.05	.01
☐ U23	Dennis Cook	.10	.05	.01
☐ U24	Jose DeLeon	.10	.05	.01
☐ U25	Julio Franco	.25	.11	.03
☐ U26	Joe Hall	.10	.05	.01
☐ U27	Darrin Jackson	.10	.05	.01
☐ U28	Dane Johnson	.10	.05	.01
☐ U29	Norberto Martin	.10	.05	.01
☐ U30	Scott Sanderson	.10	.05	.01
☐ U31	Jason Grimsley	.10	.05	.01
☐ U32	Dennis Martinez	.25	.11	.03
☐ U33	Jack Morris	.25	.11	.03
☐ U34	Eddie Murray	.75	.35	.09
☐ U35	Chad Ogea	.25	.11	.03
☐ U36	Tony Pena	.10	.05	.01
☐ U37	Paul Shuey	.25	.11	.03
☐ U38	Omar Vizquel	.10	.05	.01
☐ U39	Danny Bautista	.25	.11	.03
☐ U40	Tim Belcher	.10	.05	.01
☐ U41	Joe Boever	.10	.05	.01
☐ U42	Storm Davis	.10	.05	.01
☐ U43	Junior Felix	.10	.05	.01
☐ U44	Mike Gardiner	.10	.05	.01
☐ U45	Buddy Groom	.10	.05	.01
☐ U46	Juan Samuel	.10	.05	.01
☐ U47	Vince Coleman	.10	.05	.01
☐ U48	Bob Hamelin	.10	.05	.01
☐ U49	Dave Henderson	.10	.05	.01
☐ U50	Rusty Meacham	.10	.05	.01
☐ U51	Terry Shumpert	.10	.05	.01
☐ U52	Jeff Bronkey	.10	.05	.01
☐ U53	Alex Diaz	.10	.05	.01
☐ U54	Brian Harper	.10	.05	.01
☐ U55	Jose Mercedes	.10	.05	.01
☐ U56	Jody Reed	.10	.05	.01
☐ U57	Bob Scanlan	.10	.05	.01
☐ U58	Turner Ward	.10	.05	.01

☐ U59 Rich Becker	.25	.11	.03
☐ U60 Alex Cole	.10	.05	.01
☐ U61 Denny Hocking	.10	.05	.01
☐ U62 Scott Leius	.10	.05	.01
☐ U63 Pat Mahomes	.10	.05	.01
☐ U64 Carlos Pulido	.10	.05	.01
☐ U65 Dave Stevens	.10	.05	.01
☐ U66 Matt Walbeck	.10	.05	.01
☐ U67 Xavier Hernandez	.10	.05	.01
☐ U68 Sterling Hitchcock	.25	.11	.03
☐ U69 Terry Mulholland	.10	.05	.01
☐ U70 Luis Polonia	.10	.05	.01
☐ U71 Gerald Williams	.10	.05	.01
☐ U72 Mark Acre	.10	.05	.01
☐ U73 Geronimo Berroa	.10	.05	.01
☐ U74 Rickey Henderson	.40	.18	.05
☐ U75 Stan Javier	.10	.05	.01
☐ U76 Steve Karsay	.10	.05	.01
☐ U77 Carlos Reyes	.10	.05	.01
☐ U78 Bill Taylor	.10	.05	.01
☐ U79 Eric Anthony	.10	.05	.01
☐ U80 Bobby Ayala	.10	.05	.01
☐ U81 Tim Davis	.10	.05	.01
☐ U82 Felix Fermin	.10	.05	.01
☐ U83 Reggie Jefferson	.10	.05	.01
☐ U84 Keith Mitchell	.10	.05	.01
☐ U85 Bill Risley	.10	.05	.01
☐ U86 Alex Rodriguez	4.00	1.80	.50
☐ U87 Roger Salkeld	.10	.05	.01
☐ U88 Dan Wilson	.10	.05	.01
☐ U89 Cris Carpenter	.10	.05	.01
☐ U90 Will Clark	.75	.35	.09
☐ U91 Jeff Frye	.10	.05	.01
☐ U92 Rick Helling	.10	.05	.01
☐ U93 Chris James	.10	.05	.01
☐ U94 Oddibe McDowell	.10	.05	.01
☐ U95 Billy Ripken	.10	.05	.01
☐ U96 Carlos Delgado	.40	.18	.05
☐ U97 Alex Gonzalez	.40	.18	.05
☐ U98 Shawn Green	1.00	.45	.12
☐ U99 Darren Hall	.10	.05	.01
☐ U100 Mike Huff	.10	.05	.01
☐ U101 Mike Kelly	.25	.11	.03
☐ U102 Roberto Kelly	.10	.05	.01
☐ U103 Charlie O'Brien	.10	.05	.01
☐ U104 Jose Oliva	.25	.11	.03
☐ U105 Gregg Olson	.10	.05	.01
☐ U106 Willie Banks	.10	.05	.01
☐ U107 Jim Bullinger	.10	.05	.01
☐ U108 Chuck Crim	.10	.05	.01
☐ U109 Shawon Dunston	.10	.05	.01
☐ U110 Karl Rhodes	.10	.05	.01
☐ U111 Steve Trachsel	.40	.18	.05
☐ U112 Anthony Young	.10	.05	.01
☐ U113 Eddie Zambrano	.10	.05	.01
☐ U114 Bret Boone	.40	.18	.05
☐ U115 Jeff Brantley	.10	.05	.01
☐ U116 Hector Carrasco	.10	.05	.01
☐ U117 Tony Fernandez	.10	.05	.01
☐ U118 Tim Fortugno	.10	.05	.01
☐ U119 Erik Hanson	.10	.05	.01
☐ U120 Chuck McElroy	.10	.05	.01
☐ U121 Deion Sanders	1.25	.55	.16
☐ U122 Ellis Burks	.25	.11	.03
☐ U123 Marvin Freeman	.10	.05	.01
☐ U124 Mike Harkey	.10	.05	.01
☐ U125 Howard Johnson	.10	.05	.01
☐ U126 Mike Kingery	.10	.05	.01
☐ U127 Nelson Liriano	.10	.05	.01
☐ U128 Marcus Moore	.10	.05	.01
☐ U129 Mike Munoz	.10	.05	.01
☐ U130 Kevin Ritz	.10	.05	.01
☐ U131 Walt Weiss	.10	.05	.01
☐ U132 Kurt Abbott	.40	.18	.05
☐ U133 Jerry Browne	.10	.05	.01
☐ U134 Greg Colbrunn	.25	.11	.03
☐ U135 Jeremy Hernandez	.10	.05	.01
☐ U136 Dave Magadan	.10	.05	.01
☐ U137 Kurt Miller	.10	.05	.01
☐ U138 Robb Nen	.10	.05	.01
☐ U139 Jesus Tavarez	.25	.11	.03
☐ U140 Sid Bream	.10	.05	.01
☐ U141 Tom Edens	.10	.05	.01
☐ U142 Tony Eusebio	.10	.05	.01
☐ U143 John Hudek	.25	.11	.03
☐ U144 Brian L. Hunter	1.50	.70	.19
☐ U145 Orlando Miller	.25	.11	.03
☐ U146 James Mouton	.25	.11	.03
☐ U147 Shane Reynolds	.10	.05	.01
☐ U148 Rafael Bournigal	.10	.05	.01
☐ U149 Delino DeShields	.25	.11	.03
☐ U150 Garey Ingram	.10	.05	.01
☐ U151 Chan Ho Park	.50	.23	.06
☐ U152 Wil Cordero	.25	.11	.03
☐ U153 Pedro Martinez	.40	.18	.05
☐ U154 Randy Milligan	.10	.05	.01
☐ U155 Lenny Webster	.10	.05	.01
☐ U156 Rico Brogna	.25	.11	.03
☐ U157 Josias Manzanillo	.10	.05	.01
☐ U158 Kevin McReynolds	.10	.05	.01
☐ U159 Mike Remlinger	.10	.05	.01
☐ U160 David Segui	.10	.05	.01
☐ U161 Pete Smith	.10	.05	.01
☐ U162 Kelly Stinnett	.10	.05	.01
☐ U163 Jose Vizcaino	.10	.05	.01
☐ U164 Billy Hatcher	.10	.05	.01
☐ U165 Doug Jones	.10	.05	.01
☐ U166 Mike Lieberthal	.10	.05	.01
☐ U167 Tony Longmire	.10	.05	.01
☐ U168 Bobby Munoz	.10	.05	.01
☐ U169 Paul Quantrill	.10	.05	.01
☐ U170 Heathcliff Slocumb	.10	.05	.01
☐ U171 Fernando Valenzuela	.10	.05	.01
☐ U172 Mark Dewey	.10	.05	.01
☐ U173 Brian R. Hunter	.10	.05	.01
☐ U174 Jon Lieber	.10	.05	.01
☐ U175 Ravelo Manzanillo	.10	.05	.01
☐ U176 Dan Miceli	.10	.05	.01
☐ U177 Rick White	.10	.05	.01
☐ U178 Bryan Eversgerd	.10	.05	.01
☐ U179 John Habyan	.10	.05	.01
☐ U180 Terry McGriff	.10	.05	.01
☐ U181 Vicente Palacios	.10	.05	.01
☐ U182 Rich Rodriguez	.10	.05	.01
☐ U183 Rick Sutcliffe	.25	.11	.03
☐ U184 Donnie Elliott	.10	.05	.01
☐ U185 Joey Hamilton	.50	.23	.06
☐ U186 Tim Hyers	.10	.05	.01
☐ U187 Luis Lopez	.10	.05	.01
☐ U188 Ray McDavid	.25	.11	.03
☐ U189 Bip Roberts	.10	.05	.01
☐ U190 Scott Sanders	.25	.11	.03
☐ U191 Eddie Williams	.10	.05	.01
☐ U192 Steve Frey	.10	.05	.01
☐ U193 Pat Gomez	.10	.05	.01
☐ U194 Rich Monteleone	.10	.05	.01
☐ U195 Mark Portugal	.10	.05	.01
☐ U196 Darryl Strawberry	.25	.11	.03
☐ U197 Salomon Torres	.25	.11	.03
☐ U198 W.VanLandingham	.50	.23	.06
☐ U199 Checklist	.10	.05	.01
☐ U200 Checklist	.10	.05	.01

1995 Fleer

The 1995 Fleer set consists of 600 standard-size cards issued as one series. Full-bleed fronts have two player photos and, atypical of baseball cards fronts, biographical information such as height, weight, etc. The backgrounds are multi-colored. The backs are horizontal and contain year-by-year statistics along with a photo. There was a different design for each of baseball's six divisions. The checklist is arranged alphabetically by teams within each league as follows: Baltimore Orioles (1-22), Boston Red Sox (23-43), Detroit Tigers (44-64), New York Yankees (65-86), Toronto Blue Jays (87-108), Chicago White Sox (109-129), Cleveland Indians (130-151), Kansas City Royals (152-173), Milwaukee Brewers (174-195), Minnesota Twins (196-217), California Angels (218-237), Oakland Athletics (238-257), Seattle Mariners (258-279), Texas Rangers (280-298), Atlanta Braves (299-322), Florida Marlins (323-343), Montreal Expos (344-364), New York Mets (365-385), Philadelphia Phillies (386-407), Chicago Cubs (408-428), Cincinnati Reds (429-450), Houston Astros (451-471), Pittsburgh Pirates (472-492), St. Louis Cardinals (493-513), Colorado Rockies (514-531), Los Angeles Dodgers (532-552), San Diego Padres (553-571), and San Francisco Giants (572-593).

	MINT	NRMT	EXC
COMPLETE SET (600)	50.00	22.00	6.25
COMMON CARD (1-600)	.10	.05	.01
ONE INSERT PER PACK			
HOT PACKS CONTAIN INSERTS ONLY			

☐	1 Brady Anderson	.20	.09	.03
☐	2 Harold Baines	.20	.09	.03
☐	3 Damon Buford	.10	.05	.01
☐	4 Mike Devereaux	.20	.09	.03
☐	5 Mark Eichhorn	.10	.05	.01
☐	6 Sid Fernandez	.10	.05	.01
☐	7 Leo Gomez	.10	.05	.01
☐	8 Jeffrey Hammonds	.30	.14	.04
☐	9 Chris Hoiles	.20	.09	.03
☐	10 Rick Krivda	.10	.05	.01
☐	11 Ben McDonald	.10	.05	.01
☐	12 Mark McLemore	.10	.05	.01
☐	13 Alan Mills	.10	.05	.01
☐	14 Jamie Moyer	.10	.05	.01
☐	15 Mike Mussina	.40	.18	.05
☐	16 Mike Oquist	.10	.05	.01
☐	17 Rafael Palmeiro	.30	.14	.04
☐	18 Arthur Rhodes	.10	.05	.01
☐	19 Cal Ripken Jr.	3.00	1.35	.35
☐	20 Chris Sabo	.10	.05	.01
☐	21 Lee Smith	.30	.14	.04
☐	22 Jack Voigt	.10	.05	.01
☐	23 Damon Berryhill	.10	.05	.01
☐	24 Tom Brunansky	.10	.05	.01
☐	25 Wes Chamberlain	.10	.05	.01
☐	26 Roger Clemens	.50	.23	.06
☐	27 Scott Cooper	.10	.05	.01
☐	28 Andre Dawson	.30	.14	.04
☐	29 Gar Finnvold	.10	.05	.01
☐	30 Tony Fossas	.10	.05	.01
☐	31 Mike Greenwell	.20	.09	.03
☐	32 Joe Hesketh	.10	.05	.01
☐	33 Chris Howard	.10	.05	.01
☐	34 Chris Nabholz	.10	.05	.01
☐	35 Tim Naehring	.20	.09	.03
☐	36 Otis Nixon	.10	.05	.01
☐	37 Carlos Rodriguez	.10	.05	.01
☐	38 Rich Rowland	.10	.05	.01
☐	39 Ken Ryan	.10	.05	.01
☐	40 Aaron Sele	.20	.09	.03
☐	41 John Valentin	.30	.14	.04
☐	42 Mo Vaughn	.50	.23	.06
☐	43 Frank Viola	.20	.09	.03
☐	44 Danny Bautista	.10	.05	.01
☐	45 Joe Boever	.10	.05	.01
☐	46 Milt Cuyler	.10	.05	.01
☐	47 Storm Davis	.10	.05	.01
☐	48 John Doherty	.10	.05	.01
☐	49 Junior Felix	.10	.05	.01
☐	50 Cecil Fielder	.30	.14	.04
☐	51 Travis Fryman	.30	.14	.04
☐	52 Mike Gardiner	.10	.05	.01
☐	53 Kirk Gibson	.20	.09	.03
☐	54 Chris Gomez	.20	.09	.03
☐	55 Buddy Groom	.10	.05	.01
☐	56 Mike Henneman	.10	.05	.01
☐	57 Chad Kreuter	.10	.05	.01
☐	58 Mike Moore	.10	.05	.01
☐	59 Tony Phillips	.10	.05	.01
☐	60 Juan Samuel	.10	.05	.01
☐	61 Mickey Tettleton	.20	.09	.03
☐	62 Alan Trammell	.30	.14	.04
☐	63 David Wells	.10	.05	.01
☐	64 Lou Whitaker	.30	.14	.04
☐	65 Jim Abbott	.30	.14	.04
☐	66 Joe Ausanio	.10	.05	.01
☐	67 Wade Boggs	.30	.14	.04
☐	68 Mike Gallego	.10	.05	.01
☐	69 Xavier Hernandez	.10	.05	.01
☐	70 Sterling Hitchcock	.10	.05	.01
☐	71 Steve Howe	.10	.05	.01
☐	72 Scott Kamieniecki	.10	.05	.01
☐	73 Pat Kelly	.10	.05	.01
☐	74 Jimmy Key	.20	.09	.03
☐	75 Jim Leyritz	.10	.05	.01
☐	76 Don Mattingly UER	1.50	.70	.19
	Photo is a reversed negative			
☐	77 Terry Mulholland	.10	.05	.01
☐	78 Paul O'Neill	.20	.09	.03
☐	79 Melido Perez	.10	.05	.01
☐	80 Luis Polonia	.10	.05	.01
☐	81 Mike Stanley	.20	.09	.03
☐	82 Danny Tartabull	.20	.09	.03
☐	83 Randy Velarde	.10	.05	.01
☐	84 Bob Wickman	.10	.05	.01

☐ 85	Bernie Williams	.20	.09	.03	☐ 156	Gary Gaetti	.20	.09	.03
☐ 86	Gerald Williams	.10	.05	.01	☐ 157	Greg Gagne	.10	.05	.01
☐ 87	Roberto Alomar	.60	.25	.07	☐ 158	Tom Gordon	.10	.05	.01
☐ 88	Pat Borders	.10	.05	.01	☐ 159	Mark Gubicza	.10	.05	.01
☐ 89	Joe Carter	.30	.14	.04	☐ 160	Bob Hamelin	.10	.05	.01
☐ 90	Tony Castillo	.10	.05	.01	☐ 161	Dave Henderson	.10	.05	.01
☐ 91	Brad Cornett	.10	.05	.01	☐ 162	Felix Jose	.10	.05	.01
☐ 92	Carlos Delgado	.20	.09	.03	☐ 163	Wally Joyner	.20	.09	.03
☐ 93	Alex Gonzalez	.20	.09	.03	☐ 164	Jose Lind	.10	.05	.01
☐ 94	Shawn Green	.30	.14	.04	☐ 165	Mike Macfarlane	.10	.05	.01
☐ 95	Juan Guzman	.20	.09	.03	☐ 166	Mike Magnante	.10	.05	.01
☐ 96	Darren Hall	.10	.05	.01	☐ 167	Brent Mayne	.10	.05	.01
☐ 97	Pat Hentgen	.20	.09	.03	☐ 168	Brian McRae	.20	.09	.03
☐ 98	Mike Huff	.10	.05	.01	☐ 169	Rusty Meacham	.10	.05	.01
☐ 99	Randy Knorr	.10	.05	.01	☐ 170	Jeff Montgomery	.20	.09	.03
☐ 100	Al Leiter	.10	.05	.01	☐ 171	Hipolito Pichardo	.10	.05	.01
☐ 101	Paul Molitor	.30	.14	.04	☐ 172	Terry Shumpert	.10	.05	.01
☐ 102	John Olerud	.20	.09	.03	☐ 173	Michael Tucker	.20	.09	.03
☐ 103	Dick Schofield	.10	.05	.01	☐ 174	Ricky Bones	.10	.05	.01
☐ 104	Ed Sprague	.10	.05	.01	☐ 175	Jeff Cirillo	.20	.09	.03
☐ 105	Dave Stewart	.20	.09	.03	☐ 176	Alex Diaz	.10	.05	.01
☐ 106	Todd Stottlemyre	.10	.05	.01	☐ 177	Cal Eldred	.10	.05	.01
☐ 107	Devon White	.20	.09	.03	☐ 178	Mike Fetters	.10	.05	.01
☐ 108	Woody Williams	.10	.05	.01	☐ 179	Darryl Hamilton	.10	.05	.01
☐ 109	Wilson Alvarez	.20	.09	.03	☐ 180	Brian Harper	.10	.05	.01
☐ 110	Paul Assenmacher	.10	.05	.01	☐ 181	John Jaha	.20	.09	.03
☐ 111	Jason Bere	.20	.09	.03	☐ 182	Pat Listach	.10	.05	.01
☐ 112	Dennis Cook	.10	.05	.01	☐ 183	Graeme Lloyd	.10	.05	.01
☐ 113	Joey Cora	.10	.05	.01	☐ 184	Jose Mercedes	.10	.05	.01
☐ 114	Jose DeLeon	.10	.05	.01	☐ 185	Matt Mieske	.20	.09	.03
☐ 115	Alex Fernandez	.20	.09	.03	☐ 186	Dave Nilsson	.20	.09	.03
☐ 116	Julio Franco	.20	.09	.03	☐ 187	Jody Reed	.10	.05	.01
☐ 117	Craig Grebeck	.10	.05	.01	☐ 188	Bob Scanlan	.10	.05	.01
☐ 118	Ozzie Guillen	.10	.05	.01	☐ 189	Kevin Seitzer	.10	.05	.01
☐ 119	Roberto Hernandez	.20	.09	.03	☐ 190	Bill Spiers	.10	.05	.01
☐ 120	Darrin Jackson	.10	.05	.01	☐ 191	B.J. Surhoff	.20	.09	.03
☐ 121	Lance Johnson	.10	.05	.01	☐ 192	Jose Valentin	.10	.05	.01
☐ 122	Ron Karkovice	.10	.05	.01	☐ 193	Greg Vaughn	.10	.05	.01
☐ 123	Mike LaValliere	.10	.05	.01	☐ 194	Turner Ward	.10	.05	.01
☐ 124	Norberto Martin	.10	.05	.01	☐ 195	Bill Wegman	.10	.05	.01
☐ 125	Kirk McCaskill	.10	.05	.01	☐ 196	Rick Aguilera	.20	.09	.03
☐ 126	Jack McDowell	.30	.14	.04	☐ 197	Rich Becker	.10	.05	.01
☐ 127	Tim Raines	.20	.09	.03	☐ 198	Alex Cole	.10	.05	.01
☐ 128	Frank Thomas	3.00	1.35	.35	☐ 199	Marty Cordova	.50	.23	.06
☐ 129	Robin Ventura	.30	.14	.04	☐ 200	Steve Dunn	.10	.05	.01
☐ 130	Sandy Alomar Jr.	.20	.09	.03	☐ 201	Scott Erickson	.20	.09	.03
☐ 131	Carlos Baerga	.60	.25	.07	☐ 202	Mark Guthrie	.10	.05	.01
☐ 132	Albert Belle	1.25	.55	.16	☐ 203	Chip Hale	.10	.05	.01
☐ 133	Mark Clark	.10	.05	.01	☐ 204	LaTroy Hawkins	.10	.05	.01
☐ 134	Alvaro Espinoza	.10	.05	.01	☐ 205	Denny Hocking	.10	.05	.01
☐ 135	Jason Grimsley	.10	.05	.01	☐ 206	Chuck Knoblauch	.30	.14	.04
☐ 136	Wayne Kirby	.10	.05	.01	☐ 207	Scott Leius	.10	.05	.01
☐ 137	Kenny Lofton	1.00	.45	.12	☐ 208	Shane Mack	.10	.05	.01
☐ 138	Albie Lopez	.10	.05	.01	☐ 209	Pat Mahomes	.10	.05	.01
☐ 139	Dennis Martinez	.20	.09	.03	☐ 210	Pat Meares	.10	.05	.01
☐ 140	Jose Mesa	.20	.09	.03	☐ 211	Pedro Munoz	.20	.09	.03
☐ 141	Eddie Murray	.40	.18	.05	☐ 212	Kirby Puckett	1.00	.45	.12
☐ 142	Charles Nagy	.20	.09	.03	☐ 213	Jeff Reboulet	.10	.05	.01
☐ 143	Tony Pena	.10	.05	.01	☐ 214	Dave Stevens	.10	.05	.01
☐ 144	Eric Plunk	.10	.05	.01	☐ 215	Kevin Tapani	.10	.05	.01
☐ 145	Manny Ramirez	1.25	.55	.16	☐ 216	Matt Walbeck	.10	.05	.01
☐ 146	Jeff Russell	.10	.05	.01	☐ 217	Carl Willis	.10	.05	.01
☐ 147	Paul Shuey	.10	.05	.01	☐ 218	Brian Anderson	.10	.05	.01
☐ 148	Paul Sorrento	.10	.05	.01	☐ 219	Chad Curtis	.20	.09	.03
☐ 149	Jim Thome	.50	.23	.06	☐ 220	Chili Davis	.20	.09	.03
☐ 150	Omar Vizquel	.20	.09	.03	☐ 221	Gary DiSarcina	.10	.05	.01
☐ 151	Dave Winfield	.30	.14	.04	☐ 222	Damion Easley	.10	.05	.01
☐ 152	Kevin Appier	.20	.09	.03	☐ 223	Jim Edmonds	.40	.18	.05
☐ 153	Billy Brewer	.10	.05	.01	☐ 224	Chuck Finley	.20	.09	.03
☐ 154	Vince Coleman	.10	.05	.01	☐ 225	Joe Grahe	.10	.05	.01
☐ 155	David Cone	.30	.14	.04	☐ 226	Rex Hudler	.10	.05	.01

☐ 227	Bo Jackson	.30	.14	.04	☐ 298	Matt Whiteside	.10	.05	.01
☐ 228	Mark Langston	.20	.09	.03	☐ 299	Steve Avery	.30	.14	.04
☐ 229	Phil Leftwich	.10	.05	.01	☐ 300	Steve Bedrosian	.10	.05	.01
☐ 230	Mark Leiter	.10	.05	.01	☐ 301	Rafael Belliard	.10	.05	.01
☐ 231	Spike Owen	.10	.05	.01	☐ 302	Jeff Blauser	.20	.09	.03
☐ 232	Bob Patterson	.10	.05	.01	☐ 303	Dave Gallagher	.10	.05	.01
☐ 233	Troy Percival	.20	.09	.03	☐ 304	Tom Glavine	.30	.14	.04
☐ 234	Eduardo Perez	.10	.05	.01	☐ 305	David Justice	.40	.18	.05
☐ 235	Tim Salmon	.50	.23	.06	☐ 306	Mike Kelly	.10	.05	.01
☐ 236	J.T. Snow	.30	.14	.04	☐ 307	Roberto Kelly	.20	.09	.03
☐ 237	Chris Turner	.10	.05	.01	☐ 308	Ryan Klesko	.60	.25	.07
☐ 238	Mark Acre	.10	.05	.01	☐ 309	Mark Lemke	.20	.09	.03
☐ 239	Geronimo Berroa	.10	.05	.01	☐ 310	Javier Lopez	.40	.18	.05
☐ 240	Mike Bordick	.10	.05	.01	☐ 311	Greg Maddux	3.00	1.35	.35
☐ 241	John Briscoe	.10	.05	.01	☐ 312	Fred McGriff	.40	.18	.05
☐ 242	Scott Brosius	.10	.05	.01	☐ 313	Greg McMichael	.10	.05	.01
☐ 243	Ron Darling	.10	.05	.01	☐ 314	Kent Mercker	.10	.05	.01
☐ 244	Dennis Eckersley	.30	.14	.04	☐ 315	Charlie O'Brien	.10	.05	.01
☐ 245	Brent Gates	.20	.09	.03	☐ 316	Jose Oliva	.20	.09	.03
☐ 246	Rickey Henderson	.30	.14	.04	☐ 317	Terry Pendleton	.10	.05	.01
☐ 247	Stan Javier	.10	.05	.01	☐ 318	John Smoltz	.30	.14	.04
☐ 248	Steve Karsay	.10	.05	.01	☐ 319	Mike Stanton	.10	.05	.01
☐ 249	Mark McGwire	.30	.14	.04	☐ 320	Tony Tarasco	.20	.09	.03
☐ 250	Troy Neel	.10	.05	.01	☐ 321	Terrell Wade	.10	.05	.01
☐ 251	Steve Ontiveros	.10	.05	.01	☐ 322	Mark Wohlers	.20	.09	.03
☐ 252	Carlos Reyes	.10	.05	.01	☐ 323	Kurt Abbott	.10	.05	.01
☐ 253	Ruben Sierra	.30	.14	.04	☐ 324	Luis Aquino	.10	.05	.01
☐ 254	Terry Steinbach	.20	.09	.03	☐ 325	Bret Barberie	.10	.05	.01
☐ 255	Bill Taylor	.10	.05	.01	☐ 326	Ryan Bowen	.10	.05	.01
☐ 256	Todd Van Poppel	.20	.09	.03	☐ 327	Jerry Browne	.10	.05	.01
☐ 257	Bobby Witt	.10	.05	.01	☐ 328	Chuck Carr	.10	.05	.01
☐ 258	Rich Amaral	.10	.05	.01	☐ 329	Matias Carrillo	.10	.05	.01
☐ 259	Eric Anthony	.10	.05	.01	☐ 330	Greg Colbrunn	.30	.14	.04
☐ 260	Bobby Ayala	.10	.05	.01	☐ 331	Jeff Conine	.30	.14	.04
☐ 261	Mike Blowers	.20	.09	.03	☐ 332	Mark Gardner	.10	.05	.01
☐ 262	Chris Bosio	.10	.05	.01	☐ 333	Chris Hammond	.10	.05	.01
☐ 263	Jay Buhner	.30	.14	.04	☐ 334	Bryan Harvey	.10	.05	.01
☐ 264	John Cummings	.10	.05	.01	☐ 335	Richie Lewis	.10	.05	.01
☐ 265	Tim Davis	.10	.05	.01	☐ 336	Dave Magadan	.10	.05	.01
☐ 266	Felix Fermin	.10	.05	.01	☐ 337	Terry Mathews	.10	.05	.01
☐ 267	Dave Fleming	.10	.05	.01	☐ 338	Robb Nen	.20	.09	.03
☐ 268	Goose Gossage	.20	.09	.03	☐ 339	Yorkis Perez	.10	.05	.01
☐ 269	Ken Griffey Jr.	3.00	1.35	.35	☐ 340	Pat Rapp	.20	.09	.03
☐ 270	Reggie Jefferson	.10	.05	.01	☐ 341	Benito Santiago	.10	.05	.01
☐ 271	Randy Johnson	.60	.25	.07	☐ 342	Gary Sheffield	.30	.14	.04
☐ 272	Edgar Martinez	.30	.14	.04	☐ 343	Dave Weathers	.10	.05	.01
☐ 273	Tino Martinez	.30	.14	.04	☐ 344	Moises Alou	.20	.09	.03
☐ 274	Greg Pirkl	.10	.05	.01	☐ 345	Sean Berry	.10	.05	.01
☐ 275	Bill Risley	.10	.05	.01	☐ 346	Wil Cordero	.20	.09	.03
☐ 276	Roger Salkeld	.10	.05	.01	☐ 347	Joey Eischen	.10	.05	.01
☐ 277	Luis Sojo	.10	.05	.01	☐ 348	Jeff Fassero	.20	.09	.03
☐ 278	Mac Suzuki	.20	.09	.03	☐ 349	Darrin Fletcher	.10	.05	.01
☐ 279	Dan Wilson	.20	.09	.03	☐ 350	Cliff Floyd	.30	.14	.04
☐ 280	Kevin Brown	.10	.05	.01	☐ 351	Marquis Grissom	.30	.14	.04
☐ 281	Jose Canseco	.50	.23	.06	☐ 352	Butch Henry	.10	.05	.01
☐ 282	Cris Carpenter	.10	.05	.01	☐ 353	Gil Heredia	.10	.05	.01
☐ 283	Will Clark	.40	.18	.05	☐ 354	Ken Hill	.20	.09	.03
☐ 284	Jeff Frye	.10	.05	.01	☐ 355	Mike Lansing	.10	.05	.01
☐ 285	Juan Gonzalez	.75	.35	.09	☐ 356	Pedro Martinez	.20	.09	.03
☐ 286	Rick Helling	.10	.05	.01	☐ 357	Mel Rojas	.10	.05	.01
☐ 287	Tom Henke	.20	.09	.03	☐ 358	Kirk Rueter	.10	.05	.01
☐ 288	David Hulse	.10	.05	.01	☐ 359	Tim Scott	.10	.05	.01
☐ 289	Chris James	.10	.05	.01	☐ 360	Jeff Shaw	.10	.05	.01
☐ 290	Manuel Lee	.10	.05	.01	☐ 361	Larry Walker	.40	.18	.05
☐ 291	Oddibe McDowell	.10	.05	.01	☐ 362	Lenny Webster	.10	.05	.01
☐ 292	Dean Palmer	.10	.05	.01	☐ 363	John Wetteland	.20	.09	.03
☐ 293	Roger Pavlik	.10	.05	.01	☐ 364	Rondell White	.30	.14	.04
☐ 294	Bill Ripken	.10	.05	.01	☐ 365	Bobby Bonilla	.20	.09	.03
☐ 295	Ivan Rodriguez	.30	.14	.04	☐ 366	Rico Brogna	.30	.14	.04
☐ 296	Kenny Rogers	.10	.05	.01	☐ 367	Jeromy Burnitz	.10	.05	.01
☐ 297	Doug Strange	.10	.05	.01	☐ 368	John Franco	.20	.09	.03

☐ 369	Dwight Gooden	.20	.09	.03
☐ 370	Todd Hundley	.20	.09	.03
☐ 371	Jason Jacome	.10	.05	.01
☐ 372	Bobby Jones	.20	.09	.03
☐ 373	Jeff Kent	.20	.09	.03
☐ 374	Jim Lindeman	.10	.05	.01
☐ 375	Josias Manzanillo	.10	.05	.01
☐ 376	Roger Mason	.10	.05	.01
☐ 377	Kevin McReynolds	.10	.05	.01
☐ 378	Joe Orsulak	.10	.05	.01
☐ 379	Bill Pulsipher	.30	.14	.04
☐ 380	Bret Saberhagen	.20	.09	.03
☐ 381	David Segui	.10	.05	.01
☐ 382	Pete Smith	.10	.05	.01
☐ 383	Kelly Stinnett	.10	.05	.01
☐ 384	Ryan Thompson	.10	.05	.01
☐ 385	Jose Vizcaino	.10	.05	.01
☐ 386	Toby Borland	.10	.05	.01
☐ 387	Ricky Bottalico	.10	.05	.01
☐ 388	Darren Daulton	.30	.14	.04
☐ 389	Mariano Duncan	.10	.05	.01
☐ 390	Lenny Dykstra	.30	.14	.04
☐ 391	Jim Eisenreich	.10	.05	.01
☐ 392	Tommy Greene	.10	.05	.01
☐ 393	Dave Hollins	.10	.05	.01
☐ 394	Pete Incaviglia	.10	.05	.01
☐ 395	Danny Jackson	.10	.05	.01
☐ 396	Doug Jones	.10	.05	.01
☐ 397	Ricky Jordan	.10	.05	.01
☐ 398	John Kruk	.20	.09	.03
☐ 399	Mike Lieberthal	.10	.05	.01
☐ 400	Tony Longmire	.10	.05	.01
☐ 401	Mickey Morandini	.10	.05	.01
☐ 402	Bobby Munoz	.10	.05	.01
☐ 403	Curt Schilling	.10	.05	.01
☐ 404	Heathcliff Slocumb	.10	.05	.01
☐ 405	Kevin Stocker	.20	.09	.03
☐ 406	Fernando Valenzuela	.20	.09	.03
☐ 407	David West	.10	.05	.01
☐ 408	Willie Banks	.10	.05	.01
☐ 409	Jose Bautista	.10	.05	.01
☐ 410	Steve Buechele	.10	.05	.01
☐ 411	Jim Bullinger	.10	.05	.01
☐ 412	Chuck Crim	.10	.05	.01
☐ 413	Shawon Dunston	.10	.05	.01
☐ 414	Kevin Foster	.10	.05	.01
☐ 415	Mark Grace	.30	.14	.04
☐ 416	Jose Hernandez	.10	.05	.01
☐ 417	Glenallen Hill	.20	.09	.03
☐ 418	Brooks Kieschnick	.60	.25	.07
☐ 419	Derrick May	.20	.09	.03
☐ 420	Randy Myers	.20	.09	.03
☐ 421	Dan Plesac	.10	.05	.01
☐ 422	Karl Rhodes	.10	.05	.01
☐ 423	Rey Sanchez	.10	.05	.01
☐ 424	Sammy Sosa	.30	.14	.04
☐ 425	Steve Trachsel	.20	.09	.03
☐ 426	Rick Wilkins	.10	.05	.01
☐ 427	Anthony Young	.10	.05	.01
☐ 428	Eddie Zambrano	.10	.05	.01
☐ 429	Bret Boone	.30	.14	.04
☐ 430	Jeff Branson	.10	.05	.01
☐ 431	Jeff Brantley	.10	.05	.01
☐ 432	Hector Carrasco	.10	.05	.01
☐ 433	Brian Dorsett	.10	.05	.01
☐ 434	Tony Fernandez	.10	.05	.01
☐ 435	Tim Fortugno	.10	.05	.01
☐ 436	Erik Hanson	.20	.09	.03
☐ 437	Thomas Howard	.10	.05	.01
☐ 438	Kevin Jarvis	.10	.05	.01
☐ 439	Barry Larkin	.40	.18	.05
☐ 440	Chuck McElroy	.10	.05	.01
☐ 441	Kevin Mitchell	.20	.09	.03
☐ 442	Hal Morris	.20	.09	.03
☐ 443	Jose Rijo	.20	.09	.03
☐ 444	John Roper	.10	.05	.01
☐ 445	Johnny Ruffin	.10	.05	.01
☐ 446	Deion Sanders	.60	.25	.07
☐ 447	Reggie Sanders	.30	.14	.04
☐ 448	Pete Schourek	.30	.14	.04
☐ 449	John Smiley	.10	.05	.01
☐ 450	Eddie Taubensee	.10	.05	.01
☐ 451	Jeff Bagwell	1.00	.45	.12
☐ 452	Kevin Bass	.10	.05	.01
☐ 453	Craig Biggio	.30	.14	.04
☐ 454	Ken Caminiti	.20	.09	.03
☐ 455	Andujar Cedeno	.10	.05	.01
☐ 456	Doug Drabek	.20	.09	.03
☐ 457	Tony Eusebio	.10	.05	.01
☐ 458	Mike Felder	.10	.05	.01
☐ 459	Steve Finley	.20	.09	.03
☐ 460	Luis Gonzalez	.20	.09	.03
☐ 461	Mike Hampton	.10	.05	.01
☐ 462	Pete Harnisch	.10	.05	.01
☐ 463	John Hudek	.10	.05	.01
☐ 464	Todd Jones	.10	.05	.01
☐ 465	Darryl Kile	.10	.05	.01
☐ 466	James Mouton	.20	.09	.03
☐ 467	Shane Reynolds	.10	.05	.01
☐ 468	Scott Servais	.10	.05	.01
☐ 469	Greg Swindell	.10	.05	.01
☐ 470	Dave Veres	.10	.05	.01
☐ 471	Brian Williams	.10	.05	.01
☐ 472	Jay Bell	.20	.09	.03
☐ 473	Jacob Brumfield	.10	.05	.01
☐ 474	Dave Clark	.10	.05	.01
☐ 475	Steve Cooke	.10	.05	.01
☐ 476	Midre Cummings	.20	.09	.03
☐ 477	Mark Dewey	.10	.05	.01
☐ 478	Tom Foley	.10	.05	.01
☐ 479	Carlos Garcia	.20	.09	.03
☐ 480	Jeff King	.10	.05	.01
☐ 481	Jon Lieber	.10	.05	.01
☐ 482	Ravelo Manzanillo	.10	.05	.01
☐ 483	Al Martin	.20	.09	.03
☐ 484	Orlando Merced	.10	.05	.01
☐ 485	Danny Miceli	.10	.05	.01
☐ 486	Denny Neagle	.10	.05	.01
☐ 487	Lance Parrish	.20	.09	.03
☐ 488	Don Slaught	.10	.05	.01
☐ 489	Zane Smith	.10	.05	.01
☐ 490	Andy Van Slyke	.20	.09	.03
☐ 491	Paul Wagner	.10	.05	.01
☐ 492	Rick White	.10	.05	.01
☐ 493	Luis Alicea	.10	.05	.01
☐ 494	Rene Arocha	.10	.05	.01
☐ 495	Rheal Cormier	.10	.05	.01
☐ 496	Bryan Eversgerd	.10	.05	.01
☐ 497	Bernard Gilkey	.20	.09	.03
☐ 498	John Habyan	.10	.05	.01
☐ 499	Gregg Jefferies	.30	.14	.04
☐ 500	Brian Jordan	.30	.14	.04
☐ 501	Ray Lankford	.30	.14	.04
☐ 502	John Mabry	.20	.09	.03
☐ 503	Terry McGriff	.10	.05	.01
☐ 504	Tom Pagnozzi	.10	.05	.01
☐ 505	Vicente Palacios	.10	.05	.01
☐ 506	Geronimo Pena	.10	.05	.01
☐ 507	Gerald Perry	.10	.05	.01
☐ 508	Rich Rodriguez	.10	.05	.01
☐ 509	Ozzie Smith	.60	.25	.07
☐ 510	Bob Tewksbury	.10	.05	.01

☐ 511	Allen Watson	.20	.09	.03
☐ 512	Mark Whiten	.20	.09	.03
☐ 513	Todd Zeile	.20	.09	.03
☐ 514	Dante Bichette	.40	.18	.05
☐ 515	Willie Blair	.10	.05	.01
☐ 516	Ellis Burks	.20	.09	.03
☐ 517	Marvin Freeman	.10	.05	.01
☐ 518	Andres Galarraga	.30	.14	.04
☐ 519	Joe Girardi	.10	.05	.01
☐ 520	Greg W. Harris	.10	.05	.01
☐ 521	Charlie Hayes	.20	.09	.03
☐ 522	Mike Kingery	.10	.05	.01
☐ 523	Nelson Liriano	.10	.05	.01
☐ 524	Mike Munoz	.10	.05	.01
☐ 525	David Nied	.20	.09	.03
☐ 526	Steve Reed	.10	.05	.01
☐ 527	Kevin Ritz	.10	.05	.01
☐ 528	Bruce Ruffin	.10	.05	.01
☐ 529	John Vander Wal	.10	.05	.01
☐ 530	Walt Weiss	.20	.09	.03
☐ 531	Eric Young	.20	.09	.03
☐ 532	Billy Ashley	.30	.14	.04
☐ 533	Pedro Astacio	.10	.05	.01
☐ 534	Rafael Bournigal	.10	.05	.01
☐ 535	Brett Butler	.20	.09	.03
☐ 536	Tom Candiotti	.10	.05	.01
☐ 537	Omar Daal	.10	.05	.01
☐ 538	Delino DeShields	.20	.09	.03
☐ 539	Darren Dreifort	.10	.05	.01
☐ 540	Kevin Gross	.10	.05	.01
☐ 541	Orel Hershiser	.20	.09	.03
☐ 542	Garey Ingram	.10	.05	.01
☐ 543	Eric Karros	.30	.14	.04
☐ 544	Ramon Martinez	.20	.09	.03
☐ 545	Raul Mondesi	.75	.35	.09
☐ 546	Chan Ho Park	.20	.09	.03
☐ 547	Mike Piazza	1.25	.55	.16
☐ 548	Henry Rodriguez	.10	.05	.01
☐ 549	Rudy Seanez	.10	.05	.01
☐ 550	Ismael Valdes	.10	.05	.01
☐ 551	Tim Wallach	.10	.05	.01
☐ 552	Todd Worrell	.10	.05	.01
☐ 553	Andy Ashby	.10	.05	.01
☐ 554	Brad Ausmus	.10	.05	.01
☐ 555	Derek Bell	.30	.14	.04
☐ 556	Andy Benes	.20	.09	.03
☐ 557	Phil Clark	.10	.05	.01
☐ 558	Donnie Elliott	.10	.05	.01
☐ 559	Ricky Gutierrez	.10	.05	.01
☐ 560	Tony Gwynn	1.00	.45	.12
☐ 561	Joey Hamilton	.30	.14	.04
☐ 562	Trevor Hoffman	.20	.09	.03
☐ 563	Luis Lopez	.10	.05	.01
☐ 564	Pedro A. Martinez	.10	.05	.01
☐ 565	Tim Mauser	.10	.05	.01
☐ 566	Phil Plantier	.10	.05	.01
☐ 567	Bip Roberts	.10	.05	.01
☐ 568	Scott Sanders	.10	.05	.01
☐ 569	Craig Shipley	.10	.05	.01
☐ 570	Jeff Tabaka	.10	.05	.01
☐ 571	Eddie Williams	.10	.05	.01
☐ 572	Rod Beck	.30	.14	.04
☐ 573	Mike Benjamin	.10	.05	.01
☐ 574	Barry Bonds	.75	.35	.09
☐ 575	Dave Burba	.10	.05	.01
☐ 576	John Burkett	.10	.05	.01
☐ 577	Mark Carreon	.10	.05	.01
☐ 578	Royce Clayton	.20	.09	.03
☐ 579	Steve Frey	.10	.05	.01
☐ 580	Bryan Hickerson	.10	.05	.01
☐ 581	Mike Jackson	.10	.05	.01

☐ 582	Darren Lewis	.10	.05	.01
☐ 583	Kirt Manwaring	.10	.05	.01
☐ 584	Rich Monteleone	.10	.05	.01
☐ 585	John Patterson	.10	.05	.01
☐ 586	J.R. Phillips	.10	.05	.01
☐ 587	Mark Portugal	.10	.05	.01
☐ 588	Joe Rosselli	.10	.05	.01
☐ 589	Darryl Strawberry	.20	.09	.03
☐ 590	Bill Swift	.10	.05	.01
☐ 591	Robby Thompson	.10	.05	.01
☐ 592	William VanLandingham	.20	.09	.03
☐ 593	Matt Williams	.50	.23	.06
☐ 594	Checklist	.10	.05	.01
☐ 595	Checklist	.10	.05	.01
☐ 596	Checklist	.10	.05	.01
☐ 597	Checklist	.10	.05	.01
☐ 598	Checklist	.10	.05	.01
☐ 599	Checklist	.10	.05	.01
☐ 600	Checklist	.10	.05	.01

1995 Fleer
Award Winners

Randomly inserted in all pack types at a rate of one in 24, this six card set highlights the major award winners of 1994. Card fronts feature action photos that are full-bleed on the right border and have gold border on the left. Within the gold border are the player's name and Fleer Award Winner. The backs contain a photo with text that references 1994 accomplishments.

	MINT	NRMT	EXC
COMPLETE SET (6)	10.00	4.50	1.25
COMMON CARD (1-6)	.50	.23	.06
☐ 1 Frank Thomas AL MVP	5.00	2.20	.60
☐ 2 Jeff Bagwell NL MVP	1.50	.70	.19
☐ 3 David Cone AL Pitcher of the Year	.50	.23	.06
☐ 4 Greg Maddux NL Pitcher of the Year	5.00	2.20	.60
☐ 5 Bob Hamelin AL ROY	.50	.23	.06
☐ 6 Raul Mondesi NL ROY	1.25	.55	.16

1995 Fleer
League Leaders

Randomly inserted in all pack types at a rate of one in 12, this 10-card set features 1994 American and National League leaders in various categories. The horizontal cards have player photos on front and back. The back also has a brief write-up concerning the accomplishment.

	MINT	NRMT	EXC
COMPLETE SET (10)	10.00	4.50	1.25
COMMON CARD (1-10)	.50	.23	.06
☐ 1 Paul O'Neill	.50	.23	.06
AL Batting Leader			
☐ 2 Ken Griffey Jr.	5.00	2.20	.60
AL Home Run Leader			
☐ 3 Kirby Puckett	1.50	.70	.19
AL RBI Leader			
☐ 4 Jimmy Key	.50	.23	.06
AL Winningest Pitcher			
☐ 5 Randy Johnson	1.00	.45	.12
AL Strikeout Leader			
☐ 6 Tony Gwynn	1.50	.70	.19
NL Batting Leader			
☐ 7 Matt Williams	.75	.35	.09
NL Home Run Leader			
☐ 8 Jeff Bagwell	1.50	.70	.19
NL RBI Leader			
☐ 9 Greg Maddux	2.50	1.10	.30
Ken Hill			
NL Winningest Pitchers			
☐ 10 Andy Benes	.50	.23	.06
NL Strikeout Leader			

1995 Fleer
Lumber Company

Randomly inserted in retail packs at a rate of one in 24, this set highlights 10 of the game's top sluggers. Full-bleed card fronts feature an action photo with the Lumber Company logo, which includes the player's name, toward the bottom of the photo. Card backs have a player photo and woodgrain background with a write-up that highlights individual achievements.

	MINT	NRMT	EXC
COMPLETE SET (10)	40.00	18.00	5.00
COMMON CARD (1-10)	1.00	.45	.12
☐ 1 Jeff Bagwell	5.00	2.20	.60
☐ 2 Albert Belle	6.00	2.70	.75
☐ 3 Barry Bonds	4.00	1.80	.50
☐ 4 Jose Canseco	2.50	1.10	.30
☐ 5 Joe Carter	1.50	.70	.19
☐ 6 Ken Griffey Jr.	15.00	6.75	1.85
☐ 7 Fred McGriff	2.00	.90	.25
☐ 8 Kevin Mitchell	1.00	.45	.12
☐ 9 Frank Thomas	15.00	6.75	1.85
☐ 10 Matt Williams	2.50	1.10	.30

1995 Fleer Major
League Prospects

Randomly inserted in all pack types at a rate of one in six, this 10-card set spotlights major league hopefuls. Card fronts feature a player photo with the words "Major League Prospects" serving as part of the background. The player's name and team appear in silver foil at the bottom. The backs have a photo and a write-up on his minor league career.

	MINT	NRMT	EXC
COMPLETE SET (10)	10.00	4.50	1.25
COMMON CARD (1-10)	.50	.23	.06
☐ 1 Garret Anderson	3.00	1.35	.35
☐ 2 James Baldwin	.75	.35	.09
☐ 3 Alan Benes	1.00	.45	.12
☐ 4 Armando Benitez	.50	.23	.06

		MINT	NRMT	EXC
☐ 5	Ray Durham	1.00	.45	.12
☐ 6	Brian L. Hunter	1.50	.70	.19
☐ 7	Derek Jeter	1.50	.70	.19
☐ 8	Charles Johnson	1.25	.55	.16
☐ 9	Orlando Miller	.75	.35	.09
☐ 10	Alex Rodriguez	2.50	1.10	.30

1995 Fleer
Rookie Sensations

Randomly inserted in 18-card packs, this 20-card set features top rookies from the 1994 season. The fronts have full-bleed color photos with the team and player's name in gold foil along the right edge. The backs also have full-bleed color photos along with player information.

		MINT	NRMT	EXC
COMPLETE SET (20)		50.00	22.00	6.25
COMMON CARD (1-20)		1.00	.45	.12
☐ 1	Kurt Abbott	2.00	.90	.25
☐ 2	Rico Brogna	2.00	.90	.25
☐ 3	Hector Carrasco	1.00	.45	.12
☐ 4	Kevin Foster	1.00	.45	.12
☐ 5	Chris Gomez	1.50	.70	.19
☐ 6	Darren Hall	1.00	.45	.12
☐ 7	Bob Hamelin	1.00	.45	.12
☐ 8	Joey Hamilton	1.50	.70	.19
☐ 9	John Hudek	1.00	.45	.12
☐ 10	Ryan Klesko	8.00	3.60	1.00
☐ 11	Javier Lopez	6.00	2.70	.75
☐ 12	Matt Mieske	1.00	.45	.12
☐ 13	Raul Mondesi	10.00	4.50	1.25
☐ 14	Manny Ramirez	20.00	9.00	2.50
☐ 15	Shane Reynolds	1.50	.70	.19
☐ 16	Bill Risley	1.00	.45	.12
☐ 17	Johnny Ruffin	1.00	.45	.12
☐ 18	Steve Trachsel	1.50	.70	.19
☐ 19	William VanLandingham	1.50	.70	.19
☐ 20	Rondell White	5.00	2.20	.60

1995 Fleer
Team Leaders

Randomly inserted in 12-card hobby packs at a rate of one in 24, this 28-card set features top players from each team. Each

team is represented with card the has the team's leading hitter on one side with the leading pitcher on the other side. The team logo, "Team Leaders" and the player's name are gold foil stamped on front and back.

		MINT	NRMT	EXC
COMPLETE SET (28)		240.00	110.00	30.00
COMMON PAIR (1-28)		3.00	1.35	.35
☐ 1	Cal Ripken Jr. / Mike Mussina	45.00	20.00	5.50
☐ 2	Mo Vaughn / Roger Clemens	15.00	6.75	1.85
☐ 3	Tim Salmon / Chuck Finley	6.00	2.70	.75
☐ 4	Frank Thomas / Jack McDowell	40.00	18.00	5.00
☐ 5	Albert Belle / Dennis Martinez	18.00	8.00	2.20
☐ 6	Cecil Fielder / Mike Moore	3.00	1.35	.35
☐ 7	Bob Hamelin / David Cone	3.00	1.35	.35
☐ 8	Greg Vaughn / Ricky Bones	3.00	1.35	.35
☐ 9	Kirby Puckett / Rick Aguilara	12.00	5.50	1.50
☐ 10	Don Mattingly / Jimmy Key	20.00	9.00	2.50
☐ 11	Ruben Sierra / Dennis Eckersley	3.00	1.35	.35
☐ 12	Ken Griffey Jr. / Randy Johnson	50.00	22.00	6.25
☐ 13	Jose Canseco / Kenny Rogers	6.00	2.70	.75
☐ 14	Joe Carter / Pat Hentgen	3.00	1.35	.35
☐ 15	David Justice / Greg Maddux	45.00	20.00	5.50
☐ 16	Sammy Sosa / Steve Trachsel	4.00	1.80	.50
☐ 17	Kevin Mitchell / Jose Rijo	3.00	1.35	.35
☐ 18	Dante Bichette / Bruce Ruffin	5.00	2.20	.60
☐ 19	Jeff Conine / Robb Nen	3.00	1.35	.35
☐ 20	Jeff Bagwell / Doug Drabek	12.00	5.50	1.50
☐ 21	Mike Piazza / Ramon Martinez	18.00	8.00	2.20
☐ 22	Moises Alou / Ken Hill	3.00	1.35	.35

☐ 23	Bobby Bonilla	3.00	1.35	.35
	Bret Saberhagen			
☐ 24	Darren Daulton	3.00	1.35	.35
	Danny Jackson			
☐ 25	Jay Bell	3.00	1.35	.35
	Zane Smith			
☐ 26	Gregg Jefferies	3.00	1.35	.35
	Bob Tewksbury			
☐ 27	Tony Gwynn	12.00	5.50	1.50
	Andy Benes			
☐ 28	Matt Williams	6.00	2.70	.75
	Rod Beck			

1995 Fleer Update

This 200-card set features many players who were either rookies in 1995 or played for new teams. These cards were issued in either 12-card packs with a suggested retail price of $1.49 or 18-card packs that had a suggested retail price of $2.29. Each Fleer Update pack included one card from several insert sets produced with this product. Hot packs featuring only these insert cards were included one every 72 packs. The full-bleed fronts have two player photos and, atypical of baseball card fronts, biographical information such as height, weight, etc. The backgrounds are multi-colored. The backs are horizontal and contain yearly statistics along with a photo. The backs are numbered with the prefix "U". The checklist is arranged alphabetically by team within each league's divisions: Baltimore Orioles (1-7), Boston Red Sox (8-16), Detroit Tigers (17-24), New York Yankees (25-28), Toronto Blue Jays (29-31), Chicago White Sox (32-38), Cleveland Indians (39-43), Kansas City Royals (44-50), Milwaukee Brewers (51-57), Minnesota Twins (58-63), California Angels (64-69), Oakland Athletics (70-73), Seattle Mariners (74-79), Texas Rangers (80-88), Atlanta Braves (89-93), Florida Marlins (94-102), Montreal Expos (103-109), New York Mets (110-117), Philadelphia Phillies (118-124), Chicago Cubs (125-130), Cincinnati Reds (131-137), Houston Astros (138-144), Pittsburgh Pirates (145-152), St. Louis Cardinals (153-163), Colorado Rockies (164-171), Los Angeles Dodgers (172-179), San Diego Padres (180-191) and San Francisco Giants (192-197). Rookie Cards in this set include Hideo Nomo and Carlos Perez.

		MINT	NRMT	EXC
	COMPLETE SET (200)	20.00	9.00	2.50
	COMMON CARD (1-200)	.05	.02	.01
☐ 1	Manny Alexander	.05	.02	.01
☐ 2	Bret Barberie	.05	.02	.01
☐ 3	Armando Benitez	.05	.02	.01
☐ 4	Kevin Brown	.05	.02	.01
☐ 5	Doug Jones	.05	.02	.01
☐ 6	Sherman Obando	.05	.02	.01
☐ 7	Andy Van Slyke	.05	.02	.01
☐ 8	Stan Belinda	.05	.02	.01
☐ 9	Jose Canseco	.30	.14	.04
☐ 10	Vaughn Eshelman	.05	.02	.01
☐ 11	Mike Macfarlane	.05	.02	.01
☐ 12	Troy O'Leary	.10	.05	.01
☐ 13	Steve Rodriguez	.05	.02	.01
☐ 14	Lee Tinsley	.10	.05	.01
☐ 15	Tim Vanegmond	.05	.02	.01
☐ 16	Mark Whiten	.05	.02	.01
☐ 17	Sean Bergman	.05	.02	.01
☐ 18	Chad Curtis	.10	.05	.01
☐ 19	John Flaherty	.05	.02	.01
☐ 20	Bob Higginson	.20	.09	.03
☐ 21	Felipe Lira	.05	.02	.01
☐ 22	Shannon Penn	.05	.02	.01
☐ 23	Todd Steverson	.05	.02	.01
☐ 24	Sean Whiteside	.05	.02	.01
☐ 25	Tony Fernandez	.05	.02	.01
☐ 26	Jack McDowell	.15	.07	.02
☐ 27	Andy Pettitte	.25	.11	.03
☐ 28	John Wetteland	.10	.05	.01
☐ 29	David Cone	.15	.07	.02
☐ 30	Mike Timlin	.05	.02	.01
☐ 31	Duane Ward	.05	.02	.01
☐ 32	Jim Abbott	.10	.05	.01
☐ 33	James Baldwin	.10	.05	.01
☐ 34	Mike Devereaux	.05	.02	.01
☐ 35	Ray Durham	.15	.07	.02
☐ 36	Tim Fortugno	.05	.02	.01
☐ 37	Scott Ruffcorn	.05	.02	.01
☐ 38	Chris Sabo	.05	.02	.01
☐ 39	Paul Assenmacher	.05	.02	.01
☐ 40	Bud Black	.05	.02	.01
☐ 41	Orel Hershiser	.10	.05	.01
☐ 42	Julian Tavarez	.10	.05	.01
☐ 43	Dave Winfield	.15	.07	.02
☐ 44	Pat Borders	.05	.02	.01
☐ 45	Melvin Bunch	.10	.05	.01
☐ 46	Tom Goodwin	.05	.02	.01
☐ 47	Jon Nunnally	.10	.05	.01
☐ 48	Joe Randa	.05	.02	.01
☐ 49	Dilson Torres	.05	.02	.01
☐ 50	Joe Vitiello	.10	.05	.01
☐ 51	David Hulse	.05	.02	.01
☐ 52	Scott Karl	.05	.02	.01
☐ 53	Mark Kiefer	.05	.02	.01
☐ 54	Derrick May	.05	.02	.01
☐ 55	Joe Oliver	.05	.02	.01
☐ 56	Al Reyes	.05	.02	.01
☐ 57	Steve Sparks	.15	.07	.02
☐ 58	Jerald Clark	.05	.02	.01
☐ 59	Eddie Guardado	.05	.02	.01
☐ 60	Kevin Maas	.05	.02	.01
☐ 61	David McCarty	.05	.02	.01
☐ 62	Brad Radke	.25	.11	.03
☐ 63	Scott Stahoviak	.05	.02	.01
☐ 64	Garret Anderson	.40	.18	.05
☐ 65	Shawn Boskie	.05	.02	.01
☐ 66	Mike James	.05	.02	.01
☐ 67	Tony Phillips	.05	.02	.01

□					□				
68	Lee Smith	.15	.07	.02	139	Doug Brocail	.05	.02	.01
69	Mitch Williams	.05	.02	.01	140	Ricky Gutierrez	.05	.02	.01
70	Jim Corsi	.05	.02	.01	141	Pedro Martinez	.05	.02	.01
71	Mark Harkey	.05	.02	.01	142	Orlando Miller	.05	.02	.01
72	Dave Stewart	.10	.05	.01	143	Phil Plantier	.05	.02	.01
73	Todd Stottlemyre	.05	.02	.01	144	Craig Shipley	.05	.02	.01
74	Joey Cora	.05	.02	.01	145	Rich Aude	.05	.02	.01
75	Chad Kreuter	.05	.02	.01	146	Jason Christiansen	.05	.02	.01
76	Jeff Nelson	.05	.02	.01	147	Freddy Garcia	.15	.07	.02
77	Alex Rodriguez	.40	.18	.05	148	Jim Gott	.05	.02	.01
78	Ron Villone	.05	.02	.01	149	Mark Johnson	.05	.02	.01
79	Bob Wells	.05	.02	.01	150	Esteban Loaiza	.05	.02	.01
80	Jose Alberro	.05	.02	.01	151	Dan Plesac	.05	.02	.01
81	Terry Burrows	.05	.02	.01	152	Gary Wilson	.05	.02	.01
82	Kevin Gross	.05	.02	.01	153	Allen Battle	.05	.02	.01
83	Wilson Heredia	.05	.02	.01	154	Terry Bradshaw	.05	.02	.01
84	Mark McLemore	.05	.02	.01	155	Scott Cooper	.05	.02	.01
85	Otis Nixon	.05	.02	.01	156	Tripp Cromer	.05	.02	.01
86	Jeff Russell	.05	.02	.01	157	John Frascatore	.05	.02	.01
87	Mickey Tettleton	.10	.05	.01	158	John Habyan	.05	.02	.01
88	Bob Tewksbury	.05	.02	.01	159	Tom Henke	.10	.05	.01
89	Pedro Borbon	.05	.02	.01	160	Ken Hill	.10	.05	.01
90	Marquis Grissom	.15	.07	.02	161	Danny Jackson	.05	.02	.01
91	Chipper Jones	.75	.35	.09	162	Donovan Osborne	.05	.02	.01
92	Mike Mordecai	.05	.02	.01	163	Tom Urbani	.05	.02	.01
93	Jason Schmidt	.10	.05	.01	164	Roger Bailey	.05	.02	.01
94	John Burkett	.05	.02	.01	165	Jorge Brito	.05	.02	.01
95	Andre Dawson	.15	.07	.02	166	Vinny Castilla	.15	.07	.02
96	Matt Dunbar	.05	.02	.01	167	Darren Holmes	.10	.05	.01
97	Charles Johnson	.15	.07	.02	168	Roberto Mejia	.05	.02	.01
98	Terry Pendleton	.10	.05	.01	169	Bill Swift	.05	.02	.01
99	Rich Scheid	.05	.02	.01	170	Mark Thompson	.05	.02	.01
100	Quilvio Veras	.05	.02	.01	171	Larry Walker	.25	.11	.03
101	Bobby Witt	.05	.02	.01	172	Greg Hansell	.05	.02	.01
102	Eddie Zosky	.05	.02	.01	173	Dave Hansen	.05	.02	.01
103	Shane Andrews	.05	.02	.01	174	Carlos Hernandez	.05	.02	.01
104	Reid Cornelius	.05	.02	.01	175	Hideo Nomo	4.00	1.80	.50
105	Chad Fonville	.30	.14	.04	176	Jose Offerman	.05	.02	.01
106	Mark Grudzielanek	.20	.09	.03	177	Antonio Osuna	.05	.02	.01
107	Roberto Kelly	.10	.05	.01	178	Reggie Williams	.05	.02	.01
108	Carlos Perez	.50	.23	.06	179	Todd Williams	.05	.02	.01
109	Tony Tarasco	.10	.05	.01	180	Andres Berumen	.05	.02	.01
110	Brett Butler	.10	.05	.01	181	Ken Caminiti	.10	.05	.01
111	Carl Everett	.10	.05	.01	182	Andujar Cedeno	.05	.02	.01
112	Pete Harnisch	.05	.02	.01	183	Steve Finley	.10	.05	.01
113	Doug Henry	.05	.02	.01	184	Bryce Florie	.05	.02	.01
114	Kevin Lomon	.05	.02	.01	185	Dustin Hermanson	.10	.05	.01
115	Blas Minor	.05	.02	.01	186	Ray Holbert	.05	.02	.01
116	Dave Mlicki	.05	.02	.01	187	Melvin Nieves	.10	.05	.01
117	Ricky Otero	.05	.02	.01	188	Roberto Petagine	.10	.05	.01
118	Norm Charlton	.05	.02	.01	189	Jody Reed	.05	.02	.01
119	Tyler Green	.05	.02	.01	190	Fernando Valenzuela	.10	.05	.01
120	Gene Harris	.05	.02	.01	191	Brian Williams	.05	.02	.01
121	Charlie Hayes	.05	.02	.01	192	Mark Dewey	.05	.02	.01
122	Gregg Jefferies	.15	.07	.02	193	Glenallen Hill	.10	.05	.01
123	Michael Mimbs	.20	.09	.03	194	Chris Hook	.05	.02	.01
124	Paul Quantrill	.05	.02	.01	195	Terry Mulholland	.05	.02	.01
125	Frank Castillo	.05	.02	.01	196	Steve Scarsone	.05	.02	.01
126	Brian McRae	.10	.05	.01	197	Trevor Wilson	.05	.02	.01
127	Jaime Navarro	.05	.02	.01	198	Checklist	.05	.02	.01
128	Mike Perez	.05	.02	.01	199	Checklist	.05	.02	.01
129	Tanyon Sturtze	.05	.02	.01	200	Checklist	.05	.02	.01
130	Ozzie Timmons	.10	.05	.01					
131	John Courtright	.05	.02	.01					
132	Ron Gant	.15	.07	.02					
133	Xavier Hernandez	.05	.02	.01					
134	Brian Hunter	.05	.02	.01					
135	Benito Santiago	.05	.02	.01					
136	Pete Smith	.05	.02	.01					
137	Scott Sullivan	.05	.02	.01					
138	Derek Bell	.15	.07	.02					

1995 Fleer Update
Rookie Update

Inserted one in every four packs, this 10-card standard-size set features some of

tures a glove. All of this information as well as the "Fleer 95" logo is in gold print. All of this is on a card with a special "leather like" coating. The back features a photo as well as fielding information. The cards are numbered in the lower left as "X" of 10 and are sequenced in alphabetical order.

	MINT	NRMT	EXC
COMPLETE SET (10)	30.00	13.50	3.70
COMMON CARD (1-10)	.75	.35	.09
☐ 1 Roberto Alomar	2.50	1.10	.30
☐ 2 Barry Bonds	3.00	1.35	.35
☐ 3 Ken Griffey Jr	12.00	5.50	1.50
☐ 4 Marquis Grissom	1.50	.70	.19
☐ 5 Darren Lewis	.75	.35	.09
☐ 6 Kenny Lofton	4.00	1.80	.50
☐ 7 Don Mattingly	6.00	2.70	.75
☐ 8 Cal Ripken	12.00	5.50	1.50
☐ 9 Ivan Rodriguez	1.50	.70	.19
☐ 10 Matt Williams	2.00	.90	.25

1995s best rookies. The horizontal fronts feature the words "Rookie Update" in large letters at the top, and the "Fleer 95" logo as well as the player's name at the bottom. The rest of the card has the player's photo. To the left, the back has background information as well as a photo on the right. The cards are numbered as "X" of 10. Chipper Jones and Hideo Nomo are among the players included in this set. The set is sequenced in alphabetical order.

	MINT	NRMT	EXC
COMPLETE SET (10)	15.00	6.75	1.85
COMMON CARD (1-10)	.30	.14	.04
☐ 1 Shane Andrews	.30	.14	.04
☐ 2 Ray Durham	.75	.35	.09
☐ 3 Shawn Green	1.00	.45	.12
☐ 4 Charles Johnson	1.00	.45	.12
☐ 5 Chipper Jones	5.00	2.20	.60
☐ 6 Esteban Loaiza	.30	.14	.04
☐ 7 Hideo Nomo	7.00	3.10	.85
☐ 8 Jon Nunnally	.75	.35	.09
☐ 9 Alex Rodriguez	2.00	.90	.25
☐ 10 Julian Tavarez	.30	.14	.04

1995 Fleer Update Soaring Stars

This nine-card set was inserted one every 36 packs. The fronts feature the player's photo set against a prismatic background of baseballs. The player's name, the "Soaring Stars" logo as well as a star are all printed in gold foil at the bottom. The back has a player photo, his name as well as some career information. The cards are numbered in the upper right "X" of 9 and are sequenced in alphabetical order.

1995 Fleer Update Smooth Leather

Inserted one every five packs, this 10-card set features many leading defensive wizards. The card fronts feature a player photo. Underneath the player photo, is his name along with the words "smooth leather" on the bottom. The right corner fea-

	MINT	NRMT	EXC
COMPLETE SET (9)	60.00	27.00	7.50
COMMON CARD (1-9)	2.50	1.10	.30
☐ 1 Moises Alou	2.50	1.10	.30
☐ 2 Jason Bere	2.50	1.10	.30
☐ 3 Jeff Conine	4.00	1.80	.50
☐ 4 Cliff Floyd	2.50	1.10	.30
☐ 5 Pat Hentgen	2.50	1.10	.30
☐ 6 Kenny Lofton	15.00	6.75	1.85
☐ 7 Raul Mondesi	12.00	5.50	1.50
☐ 8 Mike Piazza	20.00	9.00	2.50
☐ 9 Tim Salmon	8.00	3.60	1.00

1990 Leaf

 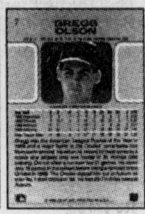

GREGG OLSON

The 1990 Leaf set was another major, premium set introduced by Donruss in 1990. This set, which was produced on high quality paper stock, was issued in two separate series of 264 cards each. The second series was issued approximately six weeks after the release of the first series. The cards are in the standard size of 2 1/2" by 3 1/2" and have full-color photos on both the front and the back of the cards. The first card of the set includes a brief history of the Leaf company and the checklists feature player photos in a style very reminiscent to the Topps checklists of the late 1960s. The card style is very similar to Upper Deck, but the Leaf sets were only distributed through hobby channels and were not available in factory sets. Rookie Cards in the set include Eric Anthony, Carlos Baerga, Delino DeShields, Bernard Gilkey, Marquis Grissom, Chris Hoiles, David Justice, Kevin Maas, Ben McDonald, Jose Offerman, John Olerud, Sammy Sosa, Kevin Tapani, Frank Thomas, Larry Walker, and Mark Whiten. Each pack contained 15 cards and one three-piece puzzle card of a 63-piece Yogi Berra "Donruss Hall of Fame Diamond King" puzzle.

	MINT	NRMT	EXC
COMPLETE SET (528)	225.00	100.00	28.00
COMPLETE SERIES 1 (264)	100.00	45.00	12.50
COMPLETE SERIES 2 (264)	125.00	55.00	15.50
COMMON CARD (1-264)	.25	.11	.03
COMMON CARD (265-528)	.25	.11	.03
COVER CARD (NNO)	.30	.14	.04
BEWARE THOMAS COUNTERFEIT			

☐	1	Introductory Card	.25	.11	.03
☐	2	Mike Henneman	.25	.11	.03
☐	3	Steve Bedrosian	.25	.11	.03
☐	4	Mike Scott	.25	.11	.03
☐	5	Allan Anderson	.25	.11	.03
☐	6	Rick Sutcliffe	.40	.18	.05
☐	7	Gregg Olson	.25	.11	.03
☐	8	Kevin Elster	.25	.11	.03
☐	9	Pete O'Brien	.25	.11	.03
☐	10	Carlton Fisk	.60	.25	.07
☐	11	Joe Magrane	.25	.11	.03
☐	12	Roger Clemens	1.50	.70	.19
☐	13	Tom Glavine	2.50	1.10	.30
☐	14	Tom Gordon	.40	.18	.05
☐	15	Todd Benzinger	.25	.11	.03
☐	16	Hubie Brooks	.25	.11	.03
☐	17	Roberto Kelly	.60	.25	.07
☐	18	Barry Larkin	1.25	.55	.16
☐	19	Mike Boddicker	.25	.11	.03
☐	20	Roger McDowell	.25	.11	.03
☐	21	Nolan Ryan	7.00	3.10	.85
☐	22	John Farrell	.25	.11	.03
☐	23	Bruce Hurst	.25	.11	.03
☐	24	Wally Joyner	.60	.25	.07
☐	25	Greg Maddux	20.00	9.00	2.50
☐	26	Chris Bosio	.25	.11	.03
☐	27	John Cerutti	.25	.11	.03
☐	28	Tim Burke	.25	.11	.03
☐	29	Dennis Eckersley	.60	.25	.07
☐	30	Glenn Davis	.25	.11	.03
☐	31	Jim Abbott	1.00	.45	.12
☐	32	Mike LaValliere	.25	.11	.03
☐	33	Andres Thomas	.25	.11	.03
☐	34	Lou Whitaker	.60	.25	.07
☐	35	Alvin Davis	.25	.11	.03
☐	36	Melido Perez	.25	.11	.03
☐	37	Craig Biggio	1.50	.70	.19
☐	38	Rick Aguilera	.40	.18	.05
☐	39	Pete Harnisch	.40	.18	.05
☐	40	David Cone	1.50	.70	.19
☐	41	Scott Garrelts	.25	.11	.03
☐	42	Jay Howell	.25	.11	.03
☐	43	Eric King	.25	.11	.03
☐	44	Pedro Guerrero	.40	.18	.05
☐	45	Mike Bielecki	.25	.11	.03
☐	46	Bob Boone	.40	.18	.05
☐	47	Kevin Brown	.40	.18	.05
☐	48	Jerry Browne	.25	.11	.03
☐	49	Mike Scioscia	.25	.11	.03
☐	50	Chuck Cary	.25	.11	.03
☐	51	Wade Boggs	1.25	.55	.16
☐	52	Von Hayes	.25	.11	.03
☐	53	Tony Fernandez	.40	.18	.05
☐	54	Dennis Martinez	.40	.18	.05
☐	55	Tom Candiotti	.25	.11	.03
☐	56	Andy Benes	.40	.18	.05
☐	57	Rob Dibble	.40	.18	.05
☐	58	Chuck Crim	.25	.11	.03
☐	59	John Smoltz	1.00	.45	.12
☐	60	Mike Heath	.25	.11	.03
☐	61	Kevin Gross	.25	.11	.03
☐	62	Mark McGwire	2.00	.90	.25
☐	63	Bert Blyleven	.60	.25	.07
☐	64	Bob Walk	.25	.11	.03
☐	65	Mickey Tettleton	.40	.18	.05
☐	66	Sid Fernandez	.40	.18	.05
☐	67	Terry Kennedy	.25	.11	.03
☐	68	Fernando Valenzuela	.25	.11	.03
☐	69	Don Mattingly	4.00	1.80	.50
☐	70	Paul O'Neill	.60	.25	.07
☐	71	Robin Yount	1.50	.70	.19
☐	72	Bret Saberhagen	.40	.18	.05
☐	73	Geno Petralli	.25	.11	.03
☐	74	Brook Jacoby	.25	.11	.03
☐	75	Roberto Alomar	3.00	1.35	.35
☐	76	Devon White	.40	.18	.05
☐	77	Jose Lind	.25	.11	.03
☐	78	Pat Combs	.25	.11	.03
☐	79	Dave Stieb	.40	.18	.05
☐	80	Tim Wallach	.25	.11	.03
☐	81	Dave Stewart	.60	.25	.07
☐	82	Eric Anthony	.25	.11	.03
☐	83	Randy Bush	.25	.11	.03
☐	84	Checklist 1-88	.40	.18	.05
		(Rickey Henderson)			

85	Jaime Navarro	.25	.11	.03
86	Tommy Gregg	.25	.11	.03
87	Frank Tanana	.25	.11	.03
88	Omar Vizquel	.75	.35	.09
89	Ivan Calderon	.25	.11	.03
90	Vince Coleman	.40	.18	.05
91	Barry Bonds	2.50	1.10	.30
92	Randy Milligan	.25	.11	.03
93	Frank Viola	.40	.18	.05
94	Matt Williams	5.00	2.20	.60
95	Alfredo Griffin	.25	.11	.03
96	Steve Sax	.25	.11	.03
97	Gary Gaetti	.25	.11	.03
98	Ryne Sandberg	3.00	1.35	.35
99	Danny Tartabull	.25	.11	.03
100	Rafael Palmeiro	2.00	.90	.25
101	Jesse Orosco	.25	.11	.03
102	Garry Templeton	.25	.11	.03
103	Frank DiPino	.25	.11	.03
104	Tony Pena	.25	.11	.03
105	Dickie Thon	.25	.11	.03
106	Kelly Gruber	.25	.11	.03
107	Marquis Grissom	7.00	3.10	.85
108	Jose Canseco	2.00	.90	.25
109	Mike Blowers	1.25	.55	.16
110	Tom Browning	.25	.11	.03
111	Greg Vaughn	.40	.18	.05
112	Oddibe McDowell	.25	.11	.03
113	Gary Ward	.25	.11	.03
114	Jay Buhner	1.50	.70	.19
115	Eric Show	.25	.11	.03
116	Bryan Harvey	.40	.18	.05
117	Andy Van Slyke	.40	.18	.05
118	Jeff Ballard	.25	.11	.03
119	Barry Lyons	.25	.11	.03
120	Kevin Mitchell	.40	.18	.05
121	Mike Gallego	.25	.11	.03
122	Dave Smith	.25	.11	.03
123	Kirby Puckett	3.00	1.35	.35
124	Jerome Walton	.25	.11	.03
125	Bo Jackson	1.00	.45	.12
126	Harold Baines	.60	.25	.07
127	Scott Bankhead	.25	.11	.03
128	Ozzie Guillen	.40	.18	.05
129	Jose Oquendo UER	.25	.11	.03
	(League misspelled as Legue)			
130	John Dopson	.25	.11	.03
131	Charlie Hayes	.40	.18	.05
132	Fred McGriff	1.25	.55	.16
133	Chet Lemon	.25	.11	.03
134	Gary Carter	.60	.25	.07
135	Rafael Ramirez	.25	.11	.03
136	Shane Mack	.25	.11	.03
137	Mark Grace UER	1.00	.45	.12
	(Card back has OB:L, should be B:L)			
138	Phil Bradley	.25	.11	.03
139	Dwight Gooden	.25	.11	.03
140	Harold Reynolds	.25	.11	.03
141	Scott Fletcher	.25	.11	.03
142	Ozzie Smith	1.50	.70	.19
143	Mike Greenwell	.60	.25	.07
144	Pete Smith	.25	.11	.03
145	Mark Gubicza	.25	.11	.03
146	Chris Sabo	.25	.11	.03
147	Ramon Martinez	1.00	.45	.12
148	Tim Leary	.25	.11	.03
149	Randy Myers	.60	.25	.07
150	Jody Reed	.25	.11	.03
151	Bruce Ruffin	.25	.11	.03
152	Jeff Russell	.25	.11	.03
153	Doug Jones	.25	.11	.03
154	Tony Gwynn	3.00	1.35	.35
155	Mark Langston	.60	.25	.07
156	Mitch Williams	.40	.18	.05
157	Gary Sheffield	2.50	1.10	.30
158	Tom Henke	.40	.18	.05
159	Oil Can Boyd	.25	.11	.03
160	Rickey Henderson	1.00	.45	.12
161	Bill Doran	.25	.11	.03
162	Chuck Finley	.40	.18	.05
163	Jeff King	.40	.18	.05
164	Nick Esasky	.25	.11	.03
165	Cecil Fielder	1.00	.45	.12
166	Dave Valle	.25	.11	.03
167	Robin Ventura	2.50	1.10	.30
168	Jim Deshaies	.25	.11	.03
169	Juan Berenguer	.25	.11	.03
170	Craig Worthington	.25	.11	.03
171	Gregg Jefferies	1.50	.70	.19
172	Will Clark	1.25	.55	.16
173	Kirk Gibson	.60	.25	.07
174	Checklist 89-176	.60	.25	.07
	(Carlton Fisk)			
175	Bobby Thigpen	.25	.11	.03
176	John Tudor	.25	.11	.03
177	Andre Dawson	.60	.25	.07
178	George Brett	4.00	1.80	.50
179	Steve Buechele	.25	.11	.03
180	Joey Belle	18.00	8.00	2.20
181	Eddie Murray	1.50	.70	.19
182	Bob Geren	.25	.11	.03
183	Rob Murphy	.25	.11	.03
184	Tom Herr	.25	.11	.03
185	George Bell	.25	.11	.03
186	Spike Owen	.25	.11	.03
187	Cory Snyder	.25	.11	.03
188	Fred Lynn	.40	.18	.05
189	Eric Davis	.40	.18	.05
190	Dave Parker	.40	.18	.05
191	Jeff Blauser	.40	.18	.05
192	Matt Nokes	.25	.11	.03
193	Delino DeShields	1.25	.55	.16
194	Scott Sanderson	.25	.11	.03
195	Lance Parrish	.40	.18	.05
196	Bobby Bonilla	.60	.25	.07
197	Cal Ripken UER	8.00	3.60	1.00
	(Reistertown, should be Reisterstown)			
198	Kevin McReynolds	.25	.11	.03
199	Robby Thompson	.40	.18	.05
200	Tim Belcher	.25	.11	.03
201	Jesse Barfield	.25	.11	.03
202	Mariano Duncan	.25	.11	.03
203	Bill Spiers	.25	.11	.03
204	Frank White	.40	.18	.05
205	Julio Franco	.40	.18	.05
206	Greg Swindell	.40	.18	.05
207	Benito Santiago	.40	.18	.05
208	Johnny Ray	.25	.11	.03
209	Gary Redus	.25	.11	.03
210	Jeff Parrett	.25	.11	.03
211	Jimmy Key	.40	.18	.05
212	Tim Raines	.40	.18	.05
213	Carney Lansford	.40	.18	.05
214	Gerald Young	.25	.11	.03
215	Gene Larkin	.25	.11	.03
216	Dan Plesac	.25	.11	.03
217	Lonnie Smith	.25	.11	.03
218	Alan Trammell	.60	.25	.07
219	Jeffrey Leonard	.25	.11	.03

☐ 220	Sammy Sosa	8.00	3.60	1.00
☐ 221	Todd Zeile	1.00	.45	.12
☐ 222	Bill Landrum	.25	.11	.03
☐ 223	Mike Devereaux	.40	.18	.05
☐ 224	Mike Marshall	.25	.11	.03
☐ 225	Jose Uribe	.25	.11	.03
☐ 226	Juan Samuel	.25	.11	.03
☐ 227	Mel Hall	.25	.11	.03
☐ 228	Kent Hrbek	.40	.18	.05
☐ 229	Shawon Dunston	.25	.11	.03
☐ 230	Kevin Seitzer	.25	.11	.03
☐ 231	Pete Incaviglia	.25	.11	.03
☐ 232	Sandy Alomar Jr.	.40	.18	.05
☐ 233	Bip Roberts	.40	.18	.05
☐ 234	Scott Terry	.25	.11	.03
☐ 235	Dwight Evans	.40	.18	.05
☐ 236	Ricky Jordan	.25	.11	.03
☐ 237	John Olerud	2.00	.90	.25
☐ 238	Zane Smith	.25	.11	.03
☐ 239	Walt Weiss	.25	.11	.03
☐ 240	Alvaro Espinoza	.25	.11	.03
☐ 241	Billy Hatcher	.25	.11	.03
☐ 242	Paul Molitor	1.00	.45	.12
☐ 243	Dale Murphy	.60	.25	.07
☐ 244	Dave Bergman	.25	.11	.03
☐ 245	Ken Griffey Jr.	25.00	11.00	3.10
☐ 246	Ed Whitson	.25	.11	.03
☐ 247	Kirk McCaskill	.25	.11	.03
☐ 248	Jay Bell	.40	.18	.05
☐ 249	Ben McDonald	1.50	.70	.19
☐ 250	Darryl Strawberry	.40	.18	.05
☐ 251	Brett Butler	.60	.25	.07
☐ 252	Terry Steinbach	.40	.18	.05
☐ 253	Ken Caminiti	.60	.25	.07
☐ 254	Dan Gladden	.25	.11	.03
☐ 255	Dwight Smith	.25	.11	.03
☐ 256	Kurt Stillwell	.25	.11	.03
☐ 257	Ruben Sierra	.60	.25	.07
☐ 258	Mike Schooler	.25	.11	.03
☐ 259	Lance Johnson	.40	.18	.05
☐ 260	Terry Pendleton	.25	.11	.03
☐ 261	Ellis Burks	.60	.25	.07
☐ 262	Len Dykstra	.60	.25	.07
☐ 263	Mookie Wilson	.25	.11	.03
☐ 264	Checklist 177-264	.50	.23	.06
	(Nolan Ryan) UER			
	(No TM after Ranger			
	logo)			
☐ 265	No Hit King	4.00	1.80	.50
	(Nolan Ryan)			
☐ 266	Brian DuBois	.25	.11	.03
☐ 267	Don Robinson	.25	.11	.03
☐ 268	Glenn Wilson	.25	.11	.03
☐ 269	Kevin Tapani	1.00	.45	.12
☐ 270	Marvell Wynne	.25	.11	.03
☐ 271	Billy Ripken	.25	.11	.03
☐ 272	Howard Johnson	.40	.18	.05
☐ 273	Brian Holman	.25	.11	.03
☐ 274	Dan Pasqua	.25	.11	.03
☐ 275	Ken Dayley	.25	.11	.03
☐ 276	Jeff Reardon	.60	.25	.07
☐ 277	Jim Presley	.25	.11	.03
☐ 278	Jim Eisenreich	.25	.11	.03
☐ 279	Danny Jackson	.25	.11	.03
☐ 280	Orel Hershiser	.60	.25	.07
☐ 281	Andy Hawkins	.25	.11	.03
☐ 282	Jose Rijo	.40	.18	.05
☐ 283	Luis Rivera	.25	.11	.03
☐ 284	John Kruk	.60	.25	.07
☐ 285	Jeff Huson	.25	.11	.03
☐ 286	Joel Skinner	.25	.11	.03
☐ 287	Jack Clark	.40	.18	.05
☐ 288	Chili Davis	.60	.25	.07
☐ 289	Joe Girardi	.25	.11	.03
☐ 290	B.J. Surhoff	.40	.18	.05
☐ 291	Luis Sojo	.25	.11	.03
☐ 292	Tom Foley	.25	.11	.03
☐ 293	Mike Moore	.25	.11	.03
☐ 294	Ken Oberkfell	.25	.11	.03
☐ 295	Luis Polonia	.40	.18	.05
☐ 296	Doug Drabek	.40	.18	.05
☐ 297	Dave Justice	8.00	3.60	1.00
☐ 298	Paul Gibson	.25	.11	.03
☐ 299	Edgar Martinez	2.00	.90	.25
☐ 300	Frank Thomas UER	85.00	38.00	10.50
	(No B in front			
	of birthdate)			
☐ 301	Eric Yelding	.25	.11	.03
☐ 302	Greg Gagne	.25	.11	.03
☐ 303	Brad Komminsk	.25	.11	.03
☐ 304	Ron Darling	.25	.11	.03
☐ 305	Kevin Bass	.25	.11	.03
☐ 306	Jeff Hamilton	.25	.11	.03
☐ 307	Ron Karkovice	.25	.11	.03
☐ 308	Milt Thompson UER	.25	.11	.03
	(Ray Lankford pictured			
	on card back)			
☐ 309	Mike Harkey	.25	.11	.03
☐ 310	Mel Stottlemyre Jr.	.25	.11	.03
☐ 311	Kenny Rogers	1.00	.45	.12
☐ 312	Mitch Webster	.25	.11	.03
☐ 313	Kal Daniels	.25	.11	.03
☐ 314	Matt Nokes	.25	.11	.03
☐ 315	Dennis Lamp	.25	.11	.03
☐ 316	Ken Howell	.25	.11	.03
☐ 317	Glenallen Hill	.25	.11	.03
☐ 318	Dave Martinez	.25	.11	.03
☐ 319	Chris James	.25	.11	.03
☐ 320	Mike Pagliarulo	.25	.11	.03
☐ 321	Hal Morris	.40	.18	.05
☐ 322	Rob Deer	.25	.11	.03
☐ 323	Greg Olson	.25	.11	.03
☐ 324	Tony Phillips	.60	.25	.07
☐ 325	Larry Walker	8.00	3.60	1.00
☐ 326	Ron Hassey	.25	.11	.03
☐ 327	Jack Howell	.25	.11	.03
☐ 328	John Smiley	.25	.11	.03
☐ 329	Steve Finley	.40	.18	.05
☐ 330	Dave Magadan	.25	.11	.03
☐ 331	Greg Litton	.25	.11	.03
☐ 332	Mickey Hatcher	.25	.11	.03
☐ 333	Lee Guetterman	.25	.11	.03
☐ 334	Norm Charlton	.25	.11	.03
☐ 335	Edgar Diaz	.25	.11	.03
☐ 336	Willie Wilson	.25	.11	.03
☐ 337	Bobby Witt	.40	.18	.05
☐ 338	Candy Maldonado	.25	.11	.03
☐ 339	Craig Lefferts	.25	.11	.03
☐ 340	Dante Bichette	4.00	1.80	.50
☐ 341	Wally Backman	.25	.11	.03
☐ 342	Dennis Cook	.25	.11	.03
☐ 343	Pat Borders	.25	.11	.03
☐ 344	Wallace Johnson	.25	.11	.03
☐ 345	Willie Randolph	.40	.18	.05
☐ 346	Danny Darwin	.25	.11	.03
☐ 347	Al Newman	.25	.11	.03
☐ 348	Mark Knudson	.25	.11	.03
☐ 349	Joe Boever	.25	.11	.03
☐ 350	Larry Sheets	.25	.11	.03
☐ 351	Mike Jackson	.25	.11	.03
☐ 352	Wayne Edwards	.25	.11	.03
☐ 353	Bernard Gilkey	1.50	.70	.19

□	354	Don Slaught	.25	.11	.03
□	355	Joe Orsulak	.25	.11	.03
□	356	John Franco	.60	.25	.07
□	357	Jeff Brantley	.25	.11	.03
□	358	Mike Morgan	.25	.11	.03
□	359	Deion Sanders	7.00	3.10	.85
□	360	Terry Leach	.25	.11	.03
□	361	Les Lancaster	.25	.11	.03
□	362	Storm Davis	.25	.11	.03
□	363	Scott Coolbaugh	.25	.11	.03
□	364	Checklist 265-352	.60	.25	.07
		(Ozzie Smith)			
□	365	Cecilio Guante	.25	.11	.03
□	366	Joey Cora	.40	.18	.05
□	367	Willie McGee	.40	.18	.05
□	368	Jerry Reed	.25	.11	.03
□	369	Darren Daulton	.60	.25	.07
□	370	Manny Lee	.25	.11	.03
□	371	Mark Gardner	.25	.11	.03
□	372	Rick Honeycutt	.25	.11	.03
□	373	Steve Balboni	.25	.11	.03
□	374	Jack Armstrong	.25	.11	.03
□	375	Charlie O'Brien	.25	.11	.03
□	376	Ron Gant	2.00	.90	.25
□	377	Lloyd Moseby	.25	.11	.03
□	378	Gene Harris	.25	.11	.03
□	379	Joe Carter	1.00	.45	.12
□	380	Scott Bailes	.25	.11	.03
□	381	R.J. Reynolds	.25	.11	.03
□	382	Bob Melvin	.25	.11	.03
□	383	Tim Teufel	.25	.11	.03
□	384	John Burkett	.40	.18	.05
□	385	Felix Jose	.25	.11	.03
□	386	Larry Andersen	.25	.11	.03
□	387	David West	.25	.11	.03
□	388	Luis Salazar	.25	.11	.03
□	389	Mike Macfarlane	.40	.18	.05
□	390	Charlie Hough	.40	.18	.05
□	391	Greg Briley	.25	.11	.03
□	392	Donn Pall	.25	.11	.03
□	393	Bryn Smith	.25	.11	.03
□	394	Carlos Quintana	.25	.11	.03
□	395	Steve Lake	.25	.11	.03
□	396	Mark Whiten	.75	.35	.09
□	397	Edwin Nunez	.25	.11	.03
□	398	Rick Parker	.25	.11	.03
□	399	Mark Portugal	.25	.11	.03
□	400	Roy Smith	.25	.11	.03
□	401	Hector Villanueva	.25	.11	.03
□	402	Bob Milacki	.25	.11	.03
□	403	Alejandro Pena	.25	.11	.03
□	404	Scott Bradley	.25	.11	.03
□	405	Ron Kittle	.25	.11	.03
□	406	Bob Tewksbury	.25	.11	.03
□	407	Wes Gardner	.25	.11	.03
□	408	Ernie Whitt	.25	.11	.03
□	409	Terry Shumpert	.25	.11	.03
□	410	Tim Layana	.25	.11	.03
□	411	Chris Gwynn	.25	.11	.03
□	412	Jeff D. Robinson	.25	.11	.03
□	413	Scott Scudder	.25	.11	.03
□	414	Kevin Romine	.25	.11	.03
□	415	Jose DeJesus	.25	.11	.03
□	416	Mike Jeffcoat	.25	.11	.03
□	417	Rudy Seanez	.25	.11	.03
□	418	Mike Dunne	.25	.11	.03
□	419	Dick Schofield	.25	.11	.03
□	420	Steve Wilson	.25	.11	.03
□	421	Bill Krueger	.25	.11	.03
□	422	Junior Felix	.25	.11	.03
□	423	Drew Hall	.25	.11	.03
□	424	Curt Young	.25	.11	.03
□	425	Franklin Stubbs	.25	.11	.03
□	426	Dave Winfield	1.00	.45	.12
□	427	Rick Reed	.25	.11	.03
□	428	Charlie Leibrandt	.25	.11	.03
□	429	Jeff M. Robinson	.25	.11	.03
□	430	Erik Hanson	.40	.18	.05
□	431	Barry Jones	.25	.11	.03
□	432	Alex Trevino	.25	.11	.03
□	433	John Moses	.25	.11	.03
□	434	Dave Johnson	.25	.11	.03
□	435	Mackey Sasser	.25	.11	.03
□	436	Rick Leach	.25	.11	.03
□	437	Lenny Harris	.25	.11	.03
□	438	Carlos Martinez	.25	.11	.03
□	439	Rex Hudler	.25	.11	.03
□	440	Domingo Ramos	.25	.11	.03
□	441	Gerald Perry	.25	.11	.03
□	442	Jeff Russell	.25	.11	.03
□	443	Carlos Baerga	15.00	6.75	1.85
□	444	Checklist 353-440	.60	.25	.07
		(Will Clark)			
□	445	Stan Javier	.25	.11	.03
□	446	Kevin Maas	.25	.11	.03
□	447	Tom Brunansky	.25	.11	.03
□	448	Carmelo Martinez	.25	.11	.03
□	449	Willie Blair	.25	.11	.03
□	450	Andres Galarraga	1.00	.45	.12
□	451	Bud Black	.25	.11	.03
□	452	Greg W. Harris	.25	.11	.03
□	453	Joe Oliver	.25	.11	.03
□	454	Greg Brock	.25	.11	.03
□	455	Jeff Treadway	.25	.11	.03
□	456	Lance McCullers	.25	.11	.03
□	457	Dave Schmidt	.25	.11	.03
□	458	Todd Burns	.25	.11	.03
□	459	Max Venable	.25	.11	.03
□	460	Neal Heaton	.25	.11	.03
□	461	Mark Williamson	.25	.11	.03
□	462	Keith Miller	.25	.11	.03
□	463	Mike LaCoss	.25	.11	.03
□	464	Jose Offerman	.40	.18	.05
□	465	Jim Leyritz	.25	.11	.03
□	466	Glenn Braggs	.25	.11	.03
□	467	Ron Robinson	.25	.11	.03
□	468	Mark Davis	.25	.11	.03
□	469	Gary Pettis	.25	.11	.03
□	470	Keith Hernandez	.40	.18	.05
□	471	Dennis Rasmussen	.25	.11	.03
□	472	Mark Eichhorn	.25	.11	.03
□	473	Ted Power	.25	.11	.03
□	474	Terry Mulholland	.40	.18	.05
□	475	Todd Stottlemyre	.40	.18	.05
□	476	Jerry Goff	.25	.11	.03
□	477	Gene Nelson	.25	.11	.03
□	478	Rich Gedman	.25	.11	.03
□	479	Brian Harper	.25	.11	.03
□	480	Mike Felder	.25	.11	.03
□	481	Steve Avery	2.00	.90	.25
□	482	Jack Morris	.60	.25	.07
□	483	Randy Johnson	5.00	2.20	.60
□	484	Scott Radinsky	.25	.11	.03
□	485	Jose DeLeon	.25	.11	.03
□	486	Stan Belinda	.25	.11	.03
□	487	Brian Holton	.25	.11	.03
□	488	Mark Carreon	.25	.11	.03
□	489	Trevor Wilson	.25	.11	.03
□	490	Mike Sharperson	.25	.11	.03
□	491	Alan Mills	.25	.11	.03
□	492	John Candelaria	.25	.11	.03
□	493	Paul Assenmacher	.25	.11	.03

☐ 494	Steve Crawford	.25	.11	.03
☐ 495	Brad Arnsberg	.25	.11	.03
☐ 496	Sergio Valdez	.25	.11	.03
☐ 497	Mark Parent	.25	.11	.03
☐ 498	Tom Pagnozzi	.40	.18	.05
☐ 499	Greg A. Harris	.25	.11	.03
☐ 500	Randy Ready	.25	.11	.03
☐ 501	Duane Ward	.25	.11	.03
☐ 502	Nelson Santovenia	.25	.11	.03
☐ 503	Joe Klink	.25	.11	.03
☐ 504	Eric Plunk	.25	.11	.03
☐ 505	Jeff Reed	.25	.11	.03
☐ 506	Ted Higuera	.25	.11	.03
☐ 507	Joe Hesketh	.25	.11	.03
☐ 508	Dan Petry	.25	.11	.03
☐ 509	Matt Young	.25	.11	.03
☐ 510	Jerald Clark	.25	.11	.03
☐ 511	John Orton	.25	.11	.03
☐ 512	Scott Ruskin	.25	.11	.03
☐ 513	Chris Hoiles	1.50	.70	.19
☐ 514	Daryl Boston	.25	.11	.03
☐ 515	Francisco Oliveras	.25	.11	.03
☐ 516	Ozzie Canseco	.25	.11	.03
☐ 517	Xavier Hernandez	.25	.11	.03
☐ 518	Fred Manrique	.25	.11	.03
☐ 519	Shawn Boskie	.25	.11	.03
☐ 520	Jeff Montgomery	.40	.18	.05
☐ 521	Jack Daugherty	.25	.11	.03
☐ 522	Keith Comstock	.25	.11	.03
☐ 523	Greg Hibbard	.25	.11	.03
☐ 524	Lee Smith	.60	.25	.07
☐ 525	Dana Kiecker	.25	.11	.03
☐ 526	Darrel Akerfelds	.25	.11	.03
☐ 527	Greg Myers	.25	.11	.03
☐ 528	Checklist 441-528	.40	.18	.05
	(Ryne Sandberg)			

1991 Leaf

This 528-card standard size 2 1/2" by 3 1/2" set marks the second year Donruss has produced a two-series premium set using the Leaf name. This set features a photo of the player which is surrounded by black and white borders. The whole card is framed in gray borders. The Leaf logo is in the upper right corner of the card. The back of the card features a gray, red and black back with white lettering on the black background and black lettering on the gray and red backgrounds. The backs of the cards also features biographical and statistical information along with a write-up when

room is provided. The set was issued using the Donruss dealer distribution network with very little Leaf product being released in other fashions. The cards are numbered on the back. Rookie Cards in the set include Wes Chamberlain, Brian McRae, Orlando Merced, Denny Neagle, and Randy Tomlin.

	MINT	NRMT	EXC
COMPLETE SET (528)	20.00	9.00	2.50
COMPLETE SERIES 1 (264)	10.00	4.50	1.25
COMPLETE SERIES 2 (264)	10.00	4.50	1.25
COMMON CARD (1-264)	.05	.02	.01
COMMON CARD (265-528)	.05	.02	.01
COVER CARD (NNO)	.05	.02	.01

☐ 1	The Leaf Card	.05	.02	.01
☐ 2	Kurt Stillwell	.05	.02	.01
☐ 3	Bobby Witt	.05	.02	.01
☐ 4	Tony Phillips	.15	.07	.02
☐ 5	Scott Garrelts	.05	.02	.01
☐ 6	Greg Swindell	.05	.02	.01
☐ 7	Billy Ripken	.05	.02	.01
☐ 8	Dave Martinez	.05	.02	.01
☐ 9	Kelly Gruber	.05	.02	.01
☐ 10	Juan Samuel	.05	.02	.01
☐ 11	Brian Holman	.05	.02	.01
☐ 12	Craig Biggio	.15	.07	.02
☐ 13	Lonnie Smith	.05	.02	.01
☐ 14	Ron Robinson	.05	.02	.01
☐ 15	Mike LaValliere	.05	.02	.01
☐ 16	Mark Davis	.05	.02	.01
☐ 17	Jack Daugherty	.05	.02	.01
☐ 18	Mike Henneman	.05	.02	.01
☐ 19	Mike Greenwell	.15	.07	.02
☐ 20	Dave Magadan	.05	.02	.01
☐ 21	Mark Williamson	.05	.02	.01
☐ 22	Marquis Grissom	.30	.14	.04
☐ 23	Pat Borders	.05	.02	.01
☐ 24	Mike Scioscia	.05	.02	.01
☐ 25	Shawon Dunston	.05	.02	.01
☐ 26	Randy Bush	.05	.02	.01
☐ 27	John Smoltz	.15	.07	.02
☐ 28	Chuck Crim	.05	.02	.01
☐ 29	Don Slaught	.05	.02	.01
☐ 30	Mike Macfarlane	.05	.02	.01
☐ 31	Wally Joyner	.15	.07	.02
☐ 32	Pat Combs	.05	.02	.01
☐ 33	Tony Pena	.05	.02	.01
☐ 34	Howard Johnson	.05	.02	.01
☐ 35	Leo Gomez	.05	.02	.01
☐ 36	Spike Owen	.05	.02	.01
☐ 37	Eric Davis	.10	.05	.01
☐ 38	Roberto Kelly	.10	.05	.01
☐ 39	Jerome Walton	.05	.02	.01
☐ 40	Shane Mack	.05	.02	.01
☐ 41	Kent Mercker	.05	.02	.01
☐ 42	B.J. Surhoff	.05	.02	.01
☐ 43	Jerry Browne	.05	.02	.01
☐ 44	Lee Smith	.15	.07	.02
☐ 45	Chuck Finley	.10	.05	.01
☐ 46	Terry Mulholland	.05	.02	.01
☐ 47	Tom Bolton	.05	.02	.01
☐ 48	Tom Herr	.05	.02	.01
☐ 49	Jim Deshaies	.05	.02	.01
☐ 50	Walt Weiss	.05	.02	.01
☐ 51	Hal Morris	.10	.05	.01
☐ 52	Lee Guetterman	.05	.02	.01
☐ 53	Paul Assenmacher	.05	.02	.01
☐ 54	Brian Harper	.05	.02	.01
☐ 55	Paul Gibson	.05	.02	.01

☐ 56	John Burkett	.10	.05	.01
☐ 57	Doug Jones	.05	.02	.01
☐ 58	Jose Oquendo	.05	.02	.01
☐ 59	Dick Schofield	.05	.02	.01
☐ 60	Dickie Thon	.05	.02	.01
☐ 61	Ramon Martinez	.15	.07	.02
☐ 62	Jay Buhner	.15	.07	.02
☐ 63	Mark Portugal	.05	.02	.01
☐ 64	Bob Welch	.05	.02	.01
☐ 65	Chris Sabo	.05	.02	.01
☐ 66	Chuck Cary	.05	.02	.01
☐ 67	Mark Langston	.15	.07	.02
☐ 68	Joe Boever	.05	.02	.01
☐ 69	Jody Reed	.05	.02	.01
☐ 70	Alejandro Pena	.05	.02	.01
☐ 71	Jeff King	.05	.02	.01
☐ 72	Tom Pagnozzi	.05	.02	.01
☐ 73	Joe Oliver	.05	.02	.01
☐ 74	Mike Witt	.05	.02	.01
☐ 75	Hector Villanueva	.05	.02	.01
☐ 76	Dan Gladden	.05	.02	.01
☐ 77	Dave Justice	.40	.18	.05
☐ 78	Mike Gallego	.05	.02	.01
☐ 79	Tom Candiotti	.05	.02	.01
☐ 80	Ozzie Smith	.30	.14	.04
☐ 81	Luis Polonia	.05	.02	.01
☐ 82	Randy Ready	.05	.02	.01
☐ 83	Greg A. Harris	.05	.02	.01
☐ 84	Checklist 1-92	.05	.02	.01
	Dave Justice			
☐ 85	Kevin Mitchell	.10	.05	.01
☐ 86	Mark McLemore	.05	.02	.01
☐ 87	Terry Steinbach	.10	.05	.01
☐ 88	Tom Browning	.05	.02	.01
☐ 89	Matt Nokes	.05	.02	.01
☐ 90	Mike Harkey	.05	.02	.01
☐ 91	Omar Vizquel	.05	.02	.01
☐ 92	Dave Bergman	.05	.02	.01
☐ 93	Matt Williams	.50	.23	.06
☐ 94	Steve Olin	.05	.02	.01
☐ 95	Craig Wilson	.05	.02	.01
☐ 96	Dave Stieb	.05	.02	.01
☐ 97	Ruben Sierra	.10	.05	.01
☐ 98	Jay Howell	.05	.02	.01
☐ 99	Scott Bradley	.05	.02	.01
☐ 100	Eric Yelding	.05	.02	.01
☐ 101	Rickey Henderson	.15	.07	.02
☐ 102	Jeff Reed	.05	.02	.01
☐ 103	Jimmy Key	.10	.05	.01
☐ 104	Terry Shumpert	.05	.02	.01
☐ 105	Kenny Rogers	.10	.05	.01
☐ 106	Cecil Fielder	.10	.05	.01
☐ 107	Robby Thompson	.05	.02	.01
☐ 108	Alex Cole	.05	.02	.01
☐ 109	Randy Milligan	.05	.02	.01
☐ 110	Andres Galarraga	.15	.07	.02
☐ 111	Bill Spiers	.05	.02	.01
☐ 112	Kal Daniels	.05	.02	.01
☐ 113	Henry Cotto	.05	.02	.01
☐ 114	Casey Candaele	.05	.02	.01
☐ 115	Jeff Blauser	.10	.05	.01
☐ 116	Robin Yount	.30	.14	.04
☐ 117	Ben McDonald	.10	.05	.01
☐ 118	Bret Saberhagen	.15	.07	.02
☐ 119	Juan Gonzalez	1.25	.55	.16
☐ 120	Lou Whitaker	.10	.05	.01
☐ 121	Ellis Burks	.10	.05	.01
☐ 122	Charlie O'Brien	.05	.02	.01
☐ 123	John Smiley	.05	.02	.01
☐ 124	Tim Burke	.05	.02	.01
☐ 125	John Olerud	.10	.05	.01

☐ 126	Eddie Murray	.40	.18	.05
☐ 127	Greg Maddux	1.25	.55	.16
☐ 128	Kevin Tapani	.10	.05	.01
☐ 129	Ron Gant	.15	.07	.02
☐ 130	Jay Bell	.10	.05	.01
☐ 131	Chris Hoiles	.10	.05	.01
☐ 132	Tom Gordon	.10	.05	.01
☐ 133	Kevin Seitzer	.05	.02	.01
☐ 134	Jeff Huson	.05	.02	.01
☐ 135	Jerry Don Gleaton	.05	.02	.01
☐ 136	Jeff Brantley UER	.05	.02	.01
	(Photo actually Rick			
	Leach on back)			
☐ 137	Felix Fermin	.05	.02	.01
☐ 138	Mike Devereaux	.10	.05	.01
☐ 139	Delino DeShields	.10	.05	.01
☐ 140	David Wells	.05	.02	.01
☐ 141	Tim Crews	.05	.02	.01
☐ 142	Erik Hanson	.05	.02	.01
☐ 143	Mark Davidson	.05	.02	.01
☐ 144	Tommy Gregg	.05	.02	.01
☐ 145	Jim Gantner	.05	.02	.01
☐ 146	Jose Lind	.05	.02	.01
☐ 147	Danny Tartabull	.10	.05	.01
☐ 148	Geno Petralli	.05	.02	.01
☐ 149	Travis Fryman	.40	.18	.05
☐ 150	Tim Naehring	.10	.05	.01
☐ 151	Kevin McReynolds	.05	.02	.01
☐ 152	Joe Orsulak	.05	.02	.01
☐ 153	Steve Frey	.05	.02	.01
☐ 154	Duane Ward	.05	.02	.01
☐ 155	Stan Javier	.05	.02	.01
☐ 156	Damon Berryhill	.05	.02	.01
☐ 157	Gene Larkin	.05	.02	.01
☐ 158	Greg Olson	.05	.02	.01
☐ 159	Mark Knudson	.05	.02	.01
☐ 160	Carmelo Martinez	.05	.02	.01
☐ 161	Storm Davis	.05	.02	.01
☐ 162	Jim Abbott	.15	.07	.02
☐ 163	Len Dykstra	.15	.07	.02
☐ 164	Tom Brunansky	.05	.02	.01
☐ 165	Dwight Gooden	.15	.07	.02
☐ 166	Jose Mesa	.05	.02	.01
☐ 167	Oil Can Boyd	.05	.02	.01
☐ 168	Barry Larkin	.30	.14	.04
☐ 169	Scott Sanderson	.05	.02	.01
☐ 170	Mark Grace	.15	.07	.02
☐ 171	Mark Guthrie	.05	.02	.01
☐ 172	Tom Glavine	.30	.14	.04
☐ 173	Gary Sheffield	.15	.07	.02
☐ 174	Checklist 93-184	.10	.05	.01
	Roger Clemens			
☐ 175	Chris James	.05	.02	.01
☐ 176	Milt Thompson	.05	.02	.01
☐ 177	Donnie Hill	.05	.02	.01
☐ 178	Wes Chamberlain	.05	.02	.01
☐ 179	John Marzano	.05	.02	.01
☐ 180	Frank Viola	.10	.05	.01
☐ 181	Eric Anthony	.05	.02	.01
☐ 182	Jose Canseco	.30	.14	.04
☐ 183	Scott Scudder	.05	.02	.01
☐ 184	Dave Eiland	.05	.02	.01
☐ 185	Luis Salazar	.05	.02	.01
☐ 186	Pedro Munoz	.10	.05	.01
☐ 187	Steve Searcy	.05	.02	.01
☐ 188	Don Robinson	.05	.02	.01
☐ 189	Sandy Alomar Jr.	.10	.05	.01
☐ 190	Jose DeLeon	.05	.02	.01
☐ 191	John Orton	.05	.02	.01
☐ 192	Darren Daulton	.15	.07	.02
☐ 193	Mike Morgan	.05	.02	.01

☐ 194	Greg Briley	.05	.02	.01
☐ 195	Karl Rhodes	.05	.02	.01
☐ 196	Harold Baines	.15	.07	.02
☐ 197	Bill Doran	.05	.02	.01
☐ 198	Alvaro Espinoza	.05	.02	.01
☐ 199	Kirk McCaskill	.05	.02	.01
☐ 200	Jose DeJesus	.05	.02	.01
☐ 201	Jack Clark	.10	.05	.01
☐ 202	Daryl Boston	.05	.02	.01
☐ 203	Randy Tomlin	.05	.02	.01
☐ 204	Pedro Guerrero	.10	.05	.01
☐ 205	Billy Hatcher	.05	.02	.01
☐ 206	Tim Leary	.05	.02	.01
☐ 207	Ryne Sandberg	.60	.25	.07
☐ 208	Kirby Puckett	.60	.25	.07
☐ 209	Charlie Leibrandt	.05	.02	.01
☐ 210	Rick Honeycutt	.05	.02	.01
☐ 211	Joel Skinner	.05	.02	.01
☐ 212	Rex Hudler	.05	.02	.01
☐ 213	Bryan Harvey	.05	.02	.01
☐ 214	Charlie Hayes	.10	.05	.01
☐ 215	Matt Young	.05	.02	.01
☐ 216	Terry Kennedy	.05	.02	.01
☐ 217	Carl Nichols	.05	.02	.01
☐ 218	Mike Moore	.05	.02	.01
☐ 219	Paul O'Neill	.15	.07	.02
☐ 220	Steve Sax	.05	.02	.01
☐ 221	Shawn Boskie	.05	.02	.01
☐ 222	Rich DeLucia	.05	.02	.01
☐ 223	Lloyd Moseby	.05	.02	.01
☐ 224	Mike Kingery	.05	.02	.01
☐ 225	Carlos Baerga	.75	.35	.09
☐ 226	Bryn Smith	.05	.02	.01
☐ 227	Todd Stottlemyre	.05	.02	.01
☐ 228	Julio Franco	.10	.05	.01
☐ 229	Jim Gott	.05	.02	.01
☐ 230	Mike Schooler	.05	.02	.01
☐ 231	Steve Finley	.05	.02	.01
☐ 232	Dave Henderson	.05	.02	.01
☐ 233	Luis Quinones	.05	.02	.01
☐ 234	Mark Whiten	.10	.05	.01
☐ 235	Brian McRae	.60	.25	.07
☐ 236	Rich Gossage	.10	.05	.01
☐ 237	Rob Deer	.05	.02	.01
☐ 238	Will Clark	.30	.14	.04
☐ 239	Albert Belle	1.00	.45	.12
☐ 240	Bob Melvin	.05	.02	.01
☐ 241	Larry Walker	.40	.18	.05
☐ 242	Dante Bichette	.30	.14	.04
☐ 243	Orel Hershiser	.15	.07	.02
☐ 244	Pete O'Brien	.05	.02	.01
☐ 245	Pete Harnisch	.10	.05	.01
☐ 246	Jeff Treadway	.05	.02	.01
☐ 247	Julio Machado	.05	.02	.01
☐ 248	Dave Johnson	.05	.02	.01
☐ 249	Kirk Gibson	.15	.07	.02
☐ 250	Kevin Brown	.10	.05	.01
☐ 251	Milt Cuyler	.05	.02	.01
☐ 252	Jeff Reardon	.15	.07	.02
☐ 253	David Cone	.15	.07	.02
☐ 254	Gary Redus	.05	.02	.01
☐ 255	Junior Noboa	.05	.02	.01
☐ 256	Greg Myers	.05	.02	.01
☐ 257	Dennis Cook	.05	.02	.01
☐ 258	Joe Girardi	.05	.02	.01
☐ 259	Allan Anderson	.05	.02	.01
☐ 260	Paul Marak	.05	.02	.01
☐ 261	Barry Bonds	.50	.23	.06
☐ 262	Juan Bell	.05	.02	.01
☐ 263	Russ Morman	.05	.02	.01
☐ 264	Checklist 185-264	.05	.02	.01
	and BC1-BC12			
	George Brett			
☐ 265	Jerald Clark	.05	.02	.01
☐ 266	Dwight Evans	.10	.05	.01
☐ 267	Roberto Alomar	.50	.23	.06
☐ 268	Danny Jackson	.05	.02	.01
☐ 269	Brian Downing	.05	.02	.01
☐ 270	John Cerutti	.05	.02	.01
☐ 271	Robin Ventura			
☐ 272	Gerald Perry	.05	.02	.01
☐ 273	Wade Boggs	.15	.07	.02
☐ 274	Dennis Martinez	.10	.05	.01
☐ 275	Andy Benes	.10	.05	.01
☐ 276	Tony Fossas	.05	.02	.01
☐ 277	Franklin Stubbs	.05	.02	.01
☐ 278	John Kruk	.15	.07	.02
☐ 279	Kevin Gross	.05	.02	.01
☐ 280	Von Hayes	.05	.02	.01
☐ 281	Frank Thomas	4.00	1.80	.50
☐ 282	Rob Dibble	.10	.05	.01
☐ 283	Mel Hall	.05	.02	.01
☐ 284	Rick Mahler	.05	.02	.01
☐ 285	Dennis Eckersley	.15	.07	.02
☐ 286	Bernard Gilkey	.10	.05	.01
☐ 287	Dan Plesac	.05	.02	.01
☐ 288	Jason Grimsley	.05	.02	.01
☐ 289	Mark Lewis	.05	.02	.01
☐ 290	Tony Gwynn	.60	.25	.07
☐ 291	Jeff Russell	.05	.02	.01
☐ 292	Curt Schilling	.05	.02	.01
☐ 293	Pascual Perez	.05	.02	.01
☐ 294	Jack Morris	.15	.07	.02
☐ 295	Hubie Brooks	.05	.02	.01
☐ 296	Alex Fernandez	.15	.07	.02
☐ 297	Harold Reynolds	.05	.02	.01
☐ 298	Craig Worthington	.05	.02	.01
☐ 299	Willie Wilson	.05	.02	.01
☐ 300	Mike Maddux	.05	.02	.01
☐ 301	Dave Righetti	.05	.02	.01
☐ 302	Paul Molitor	.15	.07	.02
☐ 303	Gary Gaetti	.05	.02	.01
☐ 304	Terry Pendleton	.15	.07	.02
☐ 305	Kevin Elster	.05	.02	.01
☐ 306	Scott Fletcher	.05	.02	.01
☐ 307	Jeff Robinson	.05	.02	.01
☐ 308	Jesse Barfield	.05	.02	.01
☐ 309	Mike LaCoss	.05	.02	.01
☐ 310	Andy Van Slyke	.10	.05	.01
☐ 311	Glenallen Hill	.05	.02	.01
☐ 312	Bud Black	.05	.02	.01
☐ 313	Kent Hrbek	.10	.05	.01
☐ 314	Tim Teufel	.05	.02	.01
☐ 315	Tony Fernandez	.05	.02	.01
☐ 316	Beau Allred	.05	.02	.01
☐ 317	Curtis Wilkerson	.05	.02	.01
☐ 318	Bill Sampen	.05	.02	.01
☐ 319	Randy Johnson	.50	.23	.06
☐ 320	Mike Heath	.05	.02	.01
☐ 321	Sammy Sosa	.40	.18	.05
☐ 322	Mickey Tettleton	.10	.05	.01
☐ 323	Jose Vizcaino	.05	.02	.01
☐ 324	John Candelaria	.05	.02	.01
☐ 325	Dave Howard	.05	.02	.01
☐ 326	Jose Rijo	.10	.05	.01
☐ 327	Todd Zeile	.10	.05	.01
☐ 328	Gene Nelson	.05	.02	.01
☐ 329	Dwayne Henry	.05	.02	.01
☐ 330	Mike Boddicker	.05	.02	.01
☐ 331	Ozzie Guillen	.10	.05	.01
☐ 332	Sam Horn	.05	.02	.01
☐ 333	Wally Whitehurst	.05	.02	.01

☐ 334 Dave Parker	.10	.05	.01
☐ 335 George Brett	.75	.35	.09
☐ 336 Bobby Thigpen	.05	.02	.01
☐ 337 Ed Whitson	.05	.02	.01
☐ 338 Ivan Calderon	.05	.02	.01
☐ 339 Mike Pagliarulo	.05	.02	.01
☐ 340 Jack McDowell	.15	.07	.02
☐ 341 Dana Kiecker	.05	.02	.01
☐ 342 Fred McGriff	.30	.14	.04
☐ 343 Mark Lee	.05	.02	.01
☐ 344 Alfredo Griffin	.05	.02	.01
☐ 345 Scott Bankhead	.05	.02	.01
☐ 346 Darrin Jackson	.05	.02	.01
☐ 347 Rafael Palmeiro	.15	.07	.02
☐ 348 Steve Farr	.05	.02	.01
☐ 349 Hensley Meulens	.05	.02	.01
☐ 350 Danny Cox	.05	.02	.01
☐ 351 Alan Trammell	.15	.07	.02
☐ 352 Edwin Nunez	.05	.02	.01
☐ 353 Joe Carter	.15	.07	.02
☐ 354 Eric Show	.05	.02	.01
☐ 355 Vance Law	.05	.02	.01
☐ 356 Jeff Gray	.05	.02	.01
☐ 357 Bobby Bonilla	.10	.05	.01
☐ 358 Ernest Riles	.05	.02	.01
☐ 359 Ron Hassey	.05	.02	.01
☐ 360 Willie McGee	.10	.05	.01
☐ 361 Mackey Sasser	.05	.02	.01
☐ 362 Glenn Braggs	.05	.02	.01
☐ 363 Mario Diaz	.05	.02	.01
☐ 364 Checklist 355-356	.10	.05	.01
Barry Bonds			
☐ 365 Kevin Bass	.05	.02	.01
☐ 366 Pete Incaviglia	.05	.02	.01
☐ 367 Luis Sojo UER	.05	.02	.01
(1989 stats inter-			
spersed with 1990's)			
☐ 368 Lance Parrish	.10	.05	.01
☐ 369 Mark Leonard	.05	.02	.01
☐ 370 Heathcliff Slocumb	.30	.14	.04
☐ 371 Jimmy Jones	.05	.02	.01
☐ 372 Ken Griffey Jr.	3.00	1.35	.35
☐ 373 Chris Hammond	.05	.02	.01
☐ 374 Chili Davis	.15	.07	.02
☐ 375 Joey Cora	.05	.02	.01
☐ 376 Ken Hill	.15	.07	.02
☐ 377 Darryl Strawberry	.10	.05	.01
☐ 378 Ron Darling	.05	.02	.01
☐ 379 Sid Bream	.05	.02	.01
☐ 380 Bill Swift	.05	.02	.01
☐ 381 Shawn Abner	.05	.02	.01
☐ 382 Eric King	.05	.02	.01
☐ 383 Mickey Morandini	.05	.02	.01
☐ 384 Carlton Fisk	.15	.07	.02
☐ 385 Steve Lake	.05	.02	.01
☐ 386 Mike Jeffcoat	.05	.02	.01
☐ 387 Darren Holmes	.05	.02	.01
☐ 388 Tim Wallach	.05	.02	.01
☐ 389 George Bell	.05	.02	.01
☐ 390 Craig Lefferts	.05	.02	.01
☐ 391 Ernie Whitt	.05	.02	.01
☐ 392 Felix Jose	.05	.02	.01
☐ 393 Kevin Maas	.05	.02	.01
☐ 394 Devon White	.10	.05	.01
☐ 395 Otis Nixon	.05	.02	.01
☐ 396 Chuck Knoblauch	.50	.23	.06
☐ 397 Scott Coolbaugh	.05	.02	.01
☐ 398 Glenn Davis	.05	.02	.01
☐ 399 Manny Lee	.05	.02	.01
☐ 400 Andre Dawson	.15	.07	.02
☐ 401 Scott Chiamparino	.05	.02	.01
☐ 402 Bill Gullickson	.05	.02	.01
☐ 403 Lance Johnson	.05	.02	.01
☐ 404 Juan Agosto	.05	.02	.01
☐ 405 Danny Darwin	.05	.02	.01
☐ 406 Barry Jones	.05	.02	.01
☐ 407 Larry Andersen	.05	.02	.01
☐ 408 Luis Rivera	.05	.02	.01
☐ 409 Jaime Navarro	.05	.02	.01
☐ 410 Roger McDowell	.05	.02	.01
☐ 411 Brett Butler	.15	.07	.02
☐ 412 Dale Murphy	.15	.07	.02
☐ 413 Tim Raines UER	.10	.05	.01
(Listed as hitting .500			
in 1980, should be .050)			
☐ 414 Norm Charlton	.05	.02	.01
☐ 415 Greg Cadaret	.05	.02	.01
☐ 416 Chris Nabholz	.05	.02	.01
☐ 417 Dave Stewart	.15	.07	.02
☐ 418 Rich Gedman	.05	.02	.01
☐ 419 Willie Randolph	.10	.05	.01
☐ 420 Mitch Williams	.10	.05	.01
☐ 421 Brook Jacoby	.05	.02	.01
☐ 422 Greg W. Harris	.05	.02	.01
☐ 423 Nolan Ryan	1.50	.70	.19
☐ 424 Dave Rohde	.05	.02	.01
☐ 425 Don Mattingly	1.00	.45	.12
☐ 426 Greg Gagne	.05	.02	.01
☐ 427 Vince Coleman	.05	.02	.01
☐ 428 Dan Pasqua	.05	.02	.01
☐ 429 Alvin Davis	.05	.02	.01
☐ 430 Cal Ripken	2.00	.90	.25
☐ 431 Jamie Quirk	.05	.02	.01
☐ 432 Benito Santiago	.05	.02	.01
☐ 433 Jose Uribe	.05	.02	.01
☐ 434 Candy Maldonado	.05	.02	.01
☐ 435 Junior Felix	.05	.02	.01
☐ 436 Deion Sanders	.50	.23	.06
☐ 437 John Franco	.15	.07	.02
☐ 438 Greg Hibbard	.05	.02	.01
☐ 439 Floyd Bannister	.05	.02	.01
☐ 440 Steve Howe	.05	.02	.01
☐ 441 Steve Decker	.05	.02	.01
☐ 442 Vicente Palacios	.05	.02	.01
☐ 443 Pat Tabler	.05	.02	.01
☐ 444 Checklist 357-448	.05	.02	.01
Darryl Strawberry			
☐ 445 Mike Felder	.05	.02	.01
☐ 446 Al Newman	.05	.02	.01
☐ 447 Chris Donnels	.05	.02	.01
☐ 448 Rich Rodriguez	.05	.02	.01
☐ 449 Turner Ward	.05	.02	.01
☐ 450 Bob Walk	.05	.02	.01
☐ 451 Gilberto Reyes	.05	.02	.01
☐ 452 Mike Jackson	.05	.02	.01
☐ 453 Rafael Belliard	.05	.02	.01
☐ 454 Wayne Edwards	.05	.02	.01
☐ 455 Andy Allanson	.05	.02	.01
☐ 456 Dave Smith	.05	.02	.01
☐ 457 Gary Carter	.15	.07	.02
☐ 458 Warren Cromartie	.05	.02	.01
☐ 459 Jack Armstrong	.05	.02	.01
☐ 460 Bob Tewksbury	.05	.02	.01
☐ 461 Joe Klink	.05	.02	.01
☐ 462 Xavier Hernandez	.05	.02	.01
☐ 463 Scott Radinsky	.05	.02	.01
☐ 464 Jeff Robinson	.05	.02	.01
☐ 465 Gregg Jefferies	.15	.07	.02
☐ 466 Denny Neagle	.30	.14	.04
☐ 467 Carmelo Martinez	.05	.02	.01
☐ 468 Donn Pall	.05	.02	.01
☐ 469 Bruce Hurst	.05	.02	.01

☐ 470	Eric Bullock	.05	.02	.01
☐ 471	Rick Aguilera	.10	.05	.01
☐ 472	Charlie Hough	.10	.05	.01
☐ 473	Carlos Quintana	.05	.02	.01
☐ 474	Marty Barrett	.05	.02	.01
☐ 475	Kevin D. Brown	.05	.02	.01
☐ 476	Bobby Ojeda	.05	.02	.01
☐ 477	Edgar Martinez	.15	.07	.02
☐ 478	Bip Roberts	.10	.05	.01
☐ 479	Mike Flanagan	.05	.02	.01
☐ 480	John Habyan	.05	.02	.01
☐ 481	Larry Casian	.05	.02	.01
☐ 482	Wally Backman	.05	.02	.01
☐ 483	Doug Dascenzo	.05	.02	.01
☐ 484	Rick Dempsey	.05	.02	.01
☐ 485	Ed Sprague	.05	.02	.01
☐ 486	Steve Chitren	.05	.02	.01
☐ 487	Mark McGwire	.15	.07	.02
☐ 488	Roger Clemens	.30	.14	.04
☐ 489	Orlando Merced	.30	.14	.04
☐ 490	Rene Gonzales	.05	.02	.01
☐ 491	Mike Stanton	.05	.02	.01
☐ 492	Al Osuna	.05	.02	.01
☐ 493	Rick Cerone	.05	.02	.01
☐ 494	Mariano Duncan	.05	.02	.01
☐ 495	Zane Smith	.05	.02	.01
☐ 496	John Morris	.05	.02	.01
☐ 497	Frank Tanana	.05	.02	.01
☐ 498	Junior Ortiz	.05	.02	.01
☐ 499	Dave Winfield	.15	.07	.02
☐ 500	Gary Varsho	.05	.02	.01
☐ 501	Chico Walker	.05	.02	.01
☐ 502	Ken Caminiti	.15	.07	.02
☐ 503	Ken Griffey Sr.	.10	.05	.01
☐ 504	Randy Myers	.15	.07	.02
☐ 505	Steve Bedrosian	.05	.02	.01
☐ 506	Cory Snyder	.05	.02	.01
☐ 507	Cris Carpenter	.05	.02	.01
☐ 508	Tim Belcher	.05	.02	.01
☐ 509	Jeff Hamilton	.05	.02	.01
☐ 510	Steve Avery	.15	.07	.02
☐ 511	Dave Valle	.05	.02	.01
☐ 512	Tom Lampkin	.05	.02	.01
☐ 513	Shawn Hillegas	.05	.02	.01
☐ 514	Reggie Jefferson	.10	.05	.01
☐ 515	Ron Karkovice	.05	.02	.01
☐ 516	Doug Drabek	.05	.02	.01
☐ 517	Tom Henke	.10	.05	.01
☐ 518	Chris Bosio	.05	.02	.01
☐ 519	Gregg Olson	.05	.02	.01
☐ 520	Bob Scanlan	.05	.02	.01
☐ 521	Alonzo Powell	.05	.02	.01
☐ 522	Jeff Ballard	.05	.02	.01
☐ 523	Ray Lankford	.40	.18	.05
☐ 524	Tommy Greene	.10	.05	.01
☐ 525	Mike Timlin	.05	.02	.01
☐ 526	Juan Berenguer	.05	.02	.01
☐ 527	Scott Erickson	.05	.02	.01
☐ 528	Checklist 449-528	.05	.02	.01
	and BC13-BC26			
	Sandy Alomar Jr.			

1991 Leaf Gold Rookies

This 26-card standard size (2 1/2" by 3 1/2") set was issued by Leaf as an adjunct

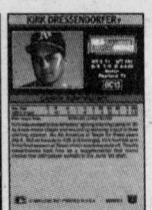

(inserted in packs) to their 1991 Leaf regular issue. The set features some of the most popular prospects active in baseball. This set marks the first time Leaf Inc. and/or Donruss had produced a card utilizing any of the first 24 young players. The first twelve cards were issued as random inserts in with the first series of 1991 Leaf foil packs. The rest were issued as random inserts in with the second series. The card numbers have a BC prefix. The earliest Leaf Gold Rookie cards issued with the first series can sometimes be found with erroneous regular numbered backs 265 through 276 instead of the correct BC1 through BC12. These numbered variations are very tough to find and are valued at ten times the values listed below.

	MINT	NRMT	EXC
COMPLETE SET (26)	20.00	9.00	2.50
COMMON CARD (BC1-BC12)	.50	.23	.06
COMMON CARD (BC13-BC26)	.50	.23	.06

☐ BC1	Scott Leius	.50	.23	.06
☐ BC2	Luis Gonzalez	1.00	.45	.12
☐ BC3	Wil Cordero	1.25	.55	.16
☐ BC4	Gary Scott	.50	.23	.06
☐ BC5	Willie Banks	.50	.23	.06
☐ BC6	Arthur Rhodes	1.00	.45	.12
☐ BC7	Mo Vaughn	5.00	2.20	.60
☐ BC8	Henry Rodriguez	.50	.23	.06
☐ BC9	Todd Van Poppel	1.00	.45	.12
☐ BC10	Reggie Sanders	1.50	.70	.19
☐ BC11	Rico Brogna	1.25	.55	.16
☐ BC12	Mike Mussina	3.00	1.35	.35
☐ BC13	Kirk Dressendorfer	.50	.23	.06
☐ BC14	Jeff Bagwell	6.00	2.70	.75
☐ BC15	Pete Schourek	1.25	.55	.16
☐ BC16	Wade Taylor	.50	.23	.06
☐ BC17	Pat Kelly	1.00	.45	.12
☐ BC18	Tim Costo	.50	.23	.06
☐ BC19	Roger Salkeld	.50	.23	.06
☐ BC20	Andujar Cedeno	1.00	.45	.12
☐ BC21	Ryan Klesko UER	5.00	2.20	.60
	(1990 Sumter BA .289; should be .368)			
☐ BC22	Mike Huff	.50	.23	.06
☐ BC23	Anthony Young	1.00	.45	.12
☐ BC24	Eddie Zosky	.50	.23	.06
☐ BC25	Nolan Ryan DP UER	1.50	.70	.19
	No Hitter 7 (Word other repeated in 7th line)			
☐ BC26	Rickey Henderson DP	1.00	.45	.12
	Record Steal			

1992 Leaf

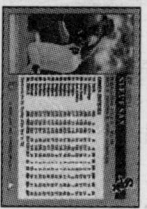

The 1992 Leaf set consists of 528 cards, issued in two series each with 264 cards measuring the standard size (2 1/2" by 3 1/2"). The fronts feature color action player photos on a silver card face. The player's name appears in a black bar edged at the bottom by a thin red stripe. The team logo overlaps the bar at the right corner. The horizontally oriented backs have color action player photos on left portion of the card. The right portion carries the player's name and team logo in a black bar as well as career statistics and career highlights in a white box. The card backs have a silver background. The cards are numbered on the back. Leaf also produced a Gold Foil Version of the complete set (series I and II), featuring gold metallic ink and gold foil highlights instead of the traditional silver. One of these "black gold inserts" was included in each 15-card foil pack. Twelve "Gold Leaf Rookie" bonus cards, numbered BC1-BC12, were randomly inserted in first series foil packs and twelve, numbered BC13-24, were randomly inserted in second series foil packs. Rookie Cards in the set include Archi Cianfrocco, Chris Gardner, Brian Jordan, Jeff Kent, and Pat Listach.

	MINT	NRMT	EXC
COMPLETE SET (528)	16.00	7.25	2.00
COMPLETE SERIES 1 (264)	8.00	3.60	1.00
COMPLETE SERIES 2 (264)	8.00	3.60	1.00
COMMON CARD (1-264)	.05	.02	.01
COMMON CARD (265-528)	.05	.02	.01
COMP. BLACK GOLD SET (528)	90.00	40.00	11.00
COMMON BLACK GOLD (1-528)	.10	.05	.01
BLACK GOLD SEMISTARS	.20	.09	.03
*BLACK GOLD VETERAN STARS: 3X TO 6X BASIC CARDS			
*BLACK GOLD YOUNG STARS: 2X TO 4X BASIC CARDS			

☐	1 Jim Abbott	.15	.07	.02
☐	2 Cal Eldred	.05	.02	.01
☐	3 Bud Black	.05	.02	.01
☐	4 Dave Howard	.05	.02	.01
☐	5 Luis Sojo	.05	.02	.01
☐	6 Gary Scott	.05	.02	.01
☐	7 Joe Oliver	.05	.02	.01
☐	8 Chris Gardner	.05	.02	.01
☐	9 Sandy Alomar Jr.	.10	.05	.01
☐	10 Greg W. Harris	.05	.02	.01
☐	11 Doug Drabek	.10	.05	.01
☐	12 Darryl Hamilton	.10	.05	.01
☐	13 Mike Mussina	.40	.18	.05
☐	14 Kevin Tapani	.05	.02	.01
☐	15 Ron Gant	.15	.07	.02
☐	16 Mark McGwire	.20	.09	.03
☐	17 Robin Ventura	.15	.07	.02
☐	18 Pedro Guerrero	.05	.02	.01
☐	19 Roger Clemens	.25	.11	.03
☐	20 Steve Farr	.05	.02	.01
☐	21 Frank Tanana	.05	.02	.01
☐	22 Joe Hesketh	.05	.02	.01
☐	23 Erik Hanson	.05	.02	.01
☐	24 Greg Cadaret	.05	.02	.01
☐	25 Rex Hudler	.05	.02	.01
☐	26 Mark Grace	.20	.09	.03
☐	27 Kelly Gruber	.05	.02	.01
☐	28 Jeff Bagwell	.75	.35	.09
☐	29 Darryl Strawberry	.10	.05	.01
☐	30 Dave Smith	.05	.02	.01
☐	31 Kevin Appier	.10	.05	.01
☐	32 Steve Chitren	.05	.02	.01
☐	33 Kevin Gross	.05	.02	.01
☐	34 Rick Aguilera	.10	.05	.01
☐	35 Juan Guzman	.10	.05	.01
☐	36 Joe Orsulak	.05	.02	.01
☐	37 Tim Raines	.20	.09	.03
☐	38 Harold Reynolds	.05	.02	.01
☐	39 Charlie Hough	.10	.05	.01
☐	40 Tony Phillips	.15	.07	.02
☐	41 Nolan Ryan	1.25	.55	.16
☐	42 Vince Coleman	.05	.02	.01
☐	43 Andy Van Slyke	.10	.05	.01
☐	44 Tim Burke	.05	.02	.01
☐	45 Luis Polonia	.05	.02	.01
☐	46 Tom Browning	.05	.02	.01
☐	47 Willie McGee	.10	.05	.01
☐	48 Gary DiSarcina	.05	.02	.01
☐	49 Mark Lewis	.05	.02	.01
☐	50 Phil Plantier	.10	.05	.01
☐	51 Doug Dascenzo	.05	.02	.01
☐	52 Cal Ripken	1.50	.70	.19
☐	53 Pedro Munoz	.10	.05	.01
☐	54 Carlos Hernandez	.05	.02	.01
☐	55 Jerald Clark	.05	.02	.01
☐	56 Jeff Brantley	.05	.02	.01
☐	57 Don Mattingly	.75	.35	.09
☐	58 Roger McDowell	.05	.02	.01
☐	59 Steve Avery	.15	.07	.02
☐	60 John Olerud	.10	.05	.01
☐	61 Bill Gullickson	.05	.02	.01
☐	62 Juan Gonzalez	.60	.25	.07
☐	63 Felix Jose	.05	.02	.01
☐	64 Robin Yount	.25	.11	.03
☐	65 Greg Briley	.05	.02	.01
☐	66 Steve Finley	.10	.05	.01
☐	67 Checklist 1-88	.20	.09	.03
	Frank Thomas			
☐	68 Tom Gordon	.10	.05	.01
☐	69 Rob Dibble	.05	.02	.01
☐	70 Glenallen Hill	.05	.02	.01
☐	71 Calvin Jones	.05	.02	.01
☐	72 Joe Girardi	.05	.02	.01
☐	73 Barry Larkin	.25	.11	.03
☐	74 Andy Benes	.10	.05	.01
☐	75 Milt Cuyler	.05	.02	.01
☐	76 Kevin Bass	.05	.02	.01
☐	77 Pete Harnisch	.10	.05	.01
☐	78 Wilson Alvarez	.15	.07	.02
☐	79 Mike Devereaux	.10	.05	.01
☐	80 Doug Henry	.05	.02	.01

☐ 81	Orel Hershiser	.15	.07	.02
☐ 82	Shane Mack	.05	.02	.01
☐ 83	Mike Macfarlane	.05	.02	.01
☐ 84	Thomas Howard	.05	.02	.01
☐ 85	Alex Fernandez	.15	.07	.02
☐ 86	Reggie Jefferson	.05	.02	.01
☐ 87	Leo Gomez	.05	.02	.01
☐ 88	Mel Hall	.05	.02	.01
☐ 89	Mike Greenwell	.15	.07	.02
☐ 90	Jeff Russell	.05	.02	.01
☐ 91	Steve Buechele	.05	.02	.01
☐ 92	David Cone	.15	.07	.02
☐ 93	Kevin Reimer	.05	.02	.01
☐ 94	Mark Lemke	.05	.02	.01
☐ 95	Bob Tewksbury	.05	.02	.01
☐ 96	Zane Smith	.05	.02	.01
☐ 97	Mark Eichhorn	.05	.02	.01
☐ 98	Kirby Puckett	.50	.23	.06
☐ 99	Paul O'Neill	.15	.07	.02
☐ 100	Dennis Eckersley	.15	.07	.02
☐ 101	Duane Ward	.05	.02	.01
☐ 102	Matt Nokes	.05	.02	.01
☐ 103	Mo Vaughn	.50	.23	.06
☐ 104	Pat Kelly	.05	.02	.01
☐ 105	Ron Karkovice	.05	.02	.01
☐ 106	Bill Spiers	.05	.02	.01
☐ 107	Gary Gaetti	.05	.02	.01
☐ 108	Mackey Sasser	.05	.02	.01
☐ 109	Robby Thompson	.05	.02	.01
☐ 110	Marvin Freeman	.05	.02	.01
☐ 111	Jimmy Key	.10	.05	.01
☐ 112	Dwight Gooden	.05	.02	.01
☐ 113	Charlie Leibrandt	.05	.02	.01
☐ 114	Devon White	.10	.05	.01
☐ 115	Charles Nagy	.10	.05	.01
☐ 116	Rickey Henderson	.20	.09	.03
☐ 117	Paul Assenmacher	.05	.02	.01
☐ 118	Junior Felix	.05	.02	.01
☐ 119	Julio Franco	.10	.05	.01
☐ 120	Norm Charlton	.05	.02	.01
☐ 121	Scott Servais	.05	.02	.01
☐ 122	Gerald Perry	.05	.02	.01
☐ 123	Brian McRae	.15	.07	.02
☐ 124	Don Slaught	.05	.02	.01
☐ 125	Juan Samuel	.05	.02	.01
☐ 126	Harold Baines	.15	.07	.02
☐ 127	Scott Livingstone	.05	.02	.01
☐ 128	Jay Buhner	.20	.09	.03
☐ 129	Darrin Jackson	.05	.02	.01
☐ 130	Luis Mercedes	.05	.02	.01
☐ 131	Brian Harper	.05	.02	.01
☐ 132	Howard Johnson	.05	.02	.01
☐ 133	Checklist 89-176	.15	.07	.02
	Nolan Ryan			
☐ 134	Dante Bichette	.25	.11	.03
☐ 135	Dave Righetti	.05	.02	.01
☐ 136	Jeff Montgomery	.10	.05	.01
☐ 137	Joe Grahe	.05	.02	.01
☐ 138	Delino DeShields	.15	.07	.02
☐ 139	Jose Rijo	.10	.05	.01
☐ 140	Ken Caminiti	.15	.07	.02
☐ 141	Steve Olin	.05	.02	.01
☐ 142	Kurt Stillwell	.05	.02	.01
☐ 143	Jay Bell	.10	.05	.01
☐ 144	Jaime Navarro	.05	.02	.01
☐ 145	Ben McDonald	.10	.05	.01
☐ 146	Greg Gagne	.05	.02	.01
☐ 147	Jeff Blauser	.10	.05	.01
☐ 148	Carney Lansford	.10	.05	.01
☐ 149	Ozzie Guillen	.10	.05	.01
☐ 150	Milt Thompson	.05	.02	.01
☐ 151	Jeff Reardon	.10	.05	.01
☐ 152	Scott Sanderson	.05	.02	.01
☐ 153	Cecil Fielder	.20	.09	.03
☐ 154	Greg A. Harris	.05	.02	.01
☐ 155	Rich DeLucia	.05	.02	.01
☐ 156	Roberto Kelly	.10	.05	.01
☐ 157	Bryn Smith	.05	.02	.01
☐ 158	Chuck McElroy	.05	.02	.01
☐ 159	Tom Henke	.10	.05	.01
☐ 160	Luis Gonzalez	.10	.05	.01
☐ 161	Steve Wilson	.05	.02	.01
☐ 162	Shawn Boskie	.05	.02	.01
☐ 163	Mark Davis	.05	.02	.01
☐ 164	Mike Moore	.05	.02	.01
☐ 165	Mike Scioscia	.05	.02	.01
☐ 166	Scott Erickson	.05	.02	.01
☐ 167	Todd Stottlemyre	.05	.02	.01
☐ 168	Alvin Davis	.05	.02	.01
☐ 169	Greg Hibbard	.05	.02	.01
☐ 170	David Valle	.05	.02	.01
☐ 171	Dave Winfield	.20	.09	.03
☐ 172	Alan Trammell	.15	.07	.02
☐ 173	Kenny Rogers	.10	.05	.01
☐ 174	John Franco	.15	.07	.02
☐ 175	Jose Lind	.05	.02	.01
☐ 176	Pete Schourek	.10	.05	.01
☐ 177	Von Hayes	.05	.02	.01
☐ 178	Chris Hammond	.05	.02	.01
☐ 179	John Burkett	.10	.05	.01
☐ 180	Dickie Thon	.05	.02	.01
☐ 181	Joel Skinner	.05	.02	.01
☐ 182	Scott Cooper	.10	.05	.01
☐ 183	Andre Dawson	.15	.07	.02
☐ 184	Billy Ripken	.05	.02	.01
☐ 185	Kevin Mitchell	.10	.05	.01
☐ 186	Brett Butler	.15	.07	.02
☐ 187	Tony Fernandez	.05	.02	.01
☐ 188	Cory Snyder	.05	.02	.01
☐ 189	John Habyan	.05	.02	.01
☐ 190	Dennis Martinez	.10	.05	.01
☐ 191	John Smoltz	.15	.07	.02
☐ 192	Greg Myers	.05	.02	.01
☐ 193	Rob Deer	.05	.02	.01
☐ 194	Ivan Rodriguez	.15	.07	.02
☐ 195	Ray Lankford	.15	.07	.02
☐ 196	Bill Wegman	.05	.02	.01
☐ 197	Edgar Martinez	.20	.09	.03
☐ 198	Darryl Kile	.05	.02	.01
☐ 199	Checklist 177-264	.15	.07	.02
	Cal Ripken			
☐ 200	Brent Mayne	.05	.02	.01
☐ 201	Larry Walker	.20	.09	.03
☐ 202	Carlos Baerga	.40	.18	.05
☐ 203	Russ Swan	.05	.02	.01
☐ 204	Mike Morgan	.05	.02	.01
☐ 205	Hal Morris	.10	.05	.01
☐ 206	Tony Gwynn	.50	.23	.06
☐ 207	Mark Leiter	.05	.02	.01
☐ 208	Kirt Manwaring	.05	.02	.01
☐ 209	Al Osuna	.05	.02	.01
☐ 210	Bobby Thigpen	.05	.02	.01
☐ 211	Chris Hoiles	.10	.05	.01
☐ 212	B.J. Surhoff	.05	.02	.01
☐ 213	Lenny Harris	.05	.02	.01
☐ 214	Scott Leius	.05	.02	.01
☐ 215	Gregg Jefferies	.15	.07	.02
☐ 216	Bruce Hurst	.05	.02	.01
☐ 217	Steve Sax	.05	.02	.01
☐ 218	Dave Otto	.05	.02	.01
☐ 219	Sam Horn	.05	.02	.01
☐ 220	Charlie Hayes	.10	.05	.01

☐ 221 Frank Viola	.05	.02	.01
☐ 222 Jose Guzman	.10	.05	.01
☐ 223 Gary Redus	.05	.02	.01
☐ 224 Dave Gallagher	.05	.02	.01
☐ 225 Dean Palmer	.10	.05	.01
☐ 226 Greg Olson	.05	.02	.01
☐ 227 Jose DeLeon	.05	.02	.01
☐ 228 Mike LaValliere	.05	.02	.01
☐ 229 Mark Langston	.15	.07	.02
☐ 230 Chuck Knoblauch	.20	.09	.03
☐ 231 Bill Doran	.05	.02	.01
☐ 232 Dave Henderson	.05	.02	.01
☐ 233 Roberto Alomar	.30	.14	.04
☐ 234 Scott Fletcher	.05	.02	.01
☐ 235 Tim Naehring	.05	.02	.01
☐ 236 Mike Gallego	.05	.02	.01
☐ 237 Lance Johnson	.05	.02	.01
☐ 238 Paul Molitor	.20	.09	.03
☐ 239 Dan Gladden	.05	.02	.01
☐ 240 Willie Randolph	.10	.05	.01
☐ 241 Will Clark	.25	.11	.03
☐ 242 Sid Bream	.05	.02	.01
☐ 243 Derek Bell	.10	.05	.01
☐ 244 Bill Pecota	.05	.02	.01
☐ 245 Terry Pendleton	.15	.07	.02
☐ 246 Randy Ready	.05	.02	.01
☐ 247 Jack Armstrong	.05	.02	.01
☐ 248 Todd Van Poppel	.10	.05	.01
☐ 249 Shawon Dunston	.05	.02	.01
☐ 250 Bobby Rose	.05	.02	.01
☐ 251 Jeff Huson	.05	.02	.01
☐ 252 Bip Roberts	.10	.05	.01
☐ 253 Doug Jones	.05	.02	.01
☐ 254 Lee Smith	.15	.07	.02
☐ 255 George Brett	.60	.25	.07
☐ 256 Randy Tomlin	.05	.02	.01
☐ 257 Todd Benzinger	.05	.02	.01
☐ 258 Dave Stewart	.15	.07	.02
☐ 259 Mark Carreon	.05	.02	.01
☐ 260 Pete O'Brien	.05	.02	.01
☐ 261 Tim Teufel	.05	.02	.01
☐ 262 Bob Milacki	.05	.02	.01
☐ 263 Mark Guthrie	.05	.02	.01
☐ 264 Darrin Fletcher	.05	.02	.01
☐ 265 Omar Vizquel	.05	.02	.01
☐ 266 Chris Bosio	.05	.02	.01
☐ 267 Jose Canseco	.25	.11	.03
☐ 268 Mike Boddicker	.05	.02	.01
☐ 269 Lance Parrish	.10	.05	.01
☐ 270 Jose Vizcaino	.05	.02	.01
☐ 271 Chris Sabo	.05	.02	.01
☐ 272 Royce Clayton	.10	.05	.01
☐ 273 Marquis Grissom	.15	.07	.02
☐ 274 Fred McGriff	.25	.11	.03
☐ 275 Barry Bonds	.40	.18	.05
☐ 276 Greg Vaughn	.10	.05	.01
☐ 277 Gregg Olson	.05	.02	.01
☐ 278 Dave Hollins	.05	.02	.01
☐ 279 Tom Glavine	.15	.07	.02
☐ 280 Bryan Hickerson UER	.05	.02	.01
Name spelled Brian on front			
☐ 281 Scott Radinsky	.05	.02	.01
☐ 282 Omar Olivares	.05	.02	.01
☐ 283 Ivan Calderon	.05	.02	.01
☐ 284 Kevin Maas	.05	.02	.01
☐ 285 Mickey Tettleton	.10	.05	.01
☐ 286 Wade Boggs	.20	.09	.03
☐ 287 Stan Belinda	.05	.02	.01
☐ 288 Bret Barberie	.05	.02	.01
☐ 289 Jose Oquendo	.05	.02	.01
☐ 290 Frank Castillo	.05	.02	.01

☐ 291 Dave Stieb	.05	.02	.01
☐ 292 Tommy Greene	.05	.02	.01
☐ 293 Eric Karros	.30	.14	.04
☐ 294 Greg Maddux	1.25	.55	.16
☐ 295 Jim Eisenreich	.05	.02	.01
☐ 296 Rafael Palmeiro	.20	.09	.03
☐ 297 Ramon Martinez	.15	.07	.02
☐ 298 Tim Wallach	.05	.02	.01
☐ 299 Jim Thome	1.25	.55	.16
☐ 300 Chito Martinez	.05	.02	.01
☐ 301 Mitch Williams	.10	.05	.01
☐ 302 Randy Johnson	.40	.18	.05
☐ 303 Carlton Fisk	.15	.07	.02
☐ 304 Travis Fryman	.15	.07	.02
☐ 305 Bobby Witt	.05	.02	.01
☐ 306 Dave Magadan	.05	.02	.01
☐ 307 Alex Cole	.05	.02	.01
☐ 308 Bobby Bonilla	.20	.09	.03
☐ 309 Bryan Harvey	.05	.02	.01
☐ 310 Rafael Belliard	.05	.02	.01
☐ 311 Mariano Duncan	.05	.02	.01
☐ 312 Chuck Crim	.05	.02	.01
☐ 313 John Kruk	.15	.07	.02
☐ 314 Ellis Burks	.10	.05	.01
☐ 315 Craig Biggio	.15	.07	.02
☐ 316 Glenn Davis	.05	.02	.01
☐ 317 Ryne Sandberg	.40	.18	.05
☐ 318 Mike Sharperson	.05	.02	.01
☐ 319 Rich Rodriguez	.05	.02	.01
☐ 320 Lee Guetterman	.05	.02	.01
☐ 321 Benito Santiago	.05	.02	.01
☐ 322 Jose Offerman	.05	.02	.01
☐ 323 Tony Pena	.05	.02	.01
☐ 324 Pat Borders	.05	.02	.01
☐ 325 Mike Henneman	.05	.02	.01
☐ 326 Kevin Brown	.10	.05	.01
☐ 327 Chris Nabholz	.05	.02	.01
☐ 328 Franklin Stubbs	.05	.02	.01
☐ 329 Tino Martinez	.15	.07	.02
☐ 330 Mickey Morandini	.05	.02	.01
☐ 331 Checklist 265-352	.15	.07	.02
Ryne Sandberg			
☐ 332 Mark Gubicza	.05	.02	.01
☐ 333 Bill Landrum	.05	.02	.01
☐ 334 Mark Whiten	.10	.05	.01
☐ 335 Darren Daulton	.15	.07	.02
☐ 336 Rick Wilkins	.05	.02	.01
☐ 337 Brian Jordan	.30	.14	.04
☐ 338 Kevin Ward	.05	.02	.01
☐ 339 Ruben Amaro	.05	.02	.01
☐ 340 Trevor Wilson	.05	.02	.01
☐ 341 Andujar Cedeno	.05	.02	.01
☐ 342 Michael Huff	.05	.02	.01
☐ 343 Brady Anderson	.10	.05	.01
☐ 344 Craig Grebeck	.05	.02	.01
☐ 345 Bobby Ojeda	.05	.02	.01
☐ 346 Mike Pagliarulo	.05	.02	.01
☐ 347 Terry Shumpert	.05	.02	.01
☐ 348 Dann Bilardello	.05	.02	.01
☐ 349 Frank Thomas	2.50	1.10	.30
☐ 350 Albert Belle	.60	.25	.07
☐ 351 Jose Mesa	.05	.02	.01
☐ 352 Rich Monteleone	.05	.02	.01
☐ 353 Bob Walk	.05	.02	.01
☐ 354 Monty Fariss	.05	.02	.01
☐ 355 Luis Rivera	.05	.02	.01
☐ 356 Anthony Young	.05	.02	.01
☐ 357 Geno Petralli	.05	.02	.01
☐ 358 Otis Nixon	.05	.02	.01
☐ 359 Tom Pagnozzi	.05	.02	.01
☐ 360 Reggie Sanders	.30	.14	.04

☐ 361	Lee Stevens	.05	.02	.01	☐ 429	Scott Scudder	.05	.02	.01
☐ 362	Kent Hrbek	.10	.05	.01	☐ 430	Eric Davis	.10	.05	.01
☐ 363	Orlando Merced	.05	.02	.01	☐ 431	Joe Slusarski	.05	.02	.01
☐ 364	Mike Bordick	.05	.02	.01	☐ 432	Todd Zeile	.10	.05	.01
☐ 365	Dion James UER	.05	.02	.01	☐ 433	Dwayne Henry	.05	.02	.01
	(Blue Jays logo				☐ 434	Cliff Brantley	.05	.02	.01
	on card back)				☐ 435	Butch Henry	.10	.05	.01
☐ 366	Jack Clark	.10	.05	.01	☐ 436	Todd Worrell	.05	.02	.01
☐ 367	Mike Stanley	.10	.05	.01	☐ 437	Bob Scanlan	.05	.02	.01
☐ 368	Randy Velarde	.05	.02	.01	☐ 438	Wally Joyner	.10	.05	.01
☐ 369	Dan Pasqua	.05	.02	.01	☐ 439	John Flaherty	.10	.05	.01
☐ 370	Pat Listach	.10	.05	.01	☐ 440	Brian Downing	.05	.02	.01
☐ 371	Mike Fitzgerald	.05	.02	.01	☐ 441	Darren Lewis	.10	.05	.01
☐ 372	Tom Foley	.05	.02	.01	☐ 442	Gary Carter	.15	.07	.02
☐ 373	Matt Williams	.30	.14	.04	☐ 443	Wally Ritchie	.05	.02	.01
☐ 374	Brian Hunter	.05	.02	.01	☐ 444	Chris Jones	.05	.02	.01
☐ 375	Joe Carter	.20	.09	.03	☐ 445	Jeff Kent	.25	.11	.03
☐ 376	Bret Saberhagen	.15	.07	.02	☐ 446	Gary Sheffield	.15	.07	.02
☐ 377	Mike Stanton	.05	.02	.01	☐ 447	Ron Darling	.05	.02	.01
☐ 378	Hubie Brooks	.05	.02	.01	☐ 448	Deion Sanders	.30	.14	.04
☐ 379	Eric Bell	.05	.02	.01	☐ 449	Andres Galarraga	.20	.09	.03
☐ 380	Walt Weiss	.05	.02	.01	☐ 450	Chuck Finley	.05	.02	.01
☐ 381	Danny Jackson	.05	.02	.01	☐ 451	Derek Lilliquist	.05	.02	.01
☐ 382	Manuel Lee	.05	.02	.01	☐ 452	Carl Willis	.05	.02	.01
☐ 383	Ruben Sierra	.20	.09	.03	☐ 453	Wes Chamberlain	.05	.02	.01
☐ 384	Greg Swindell	.05	.02	.01	☐ 454	Roger Mason	.05	.02	.01
☐ 385	Ryan Bowen	.05	.02	.01	☐ 455	Spike Owen	.05	.02	.01
☐ 386	Kevin Ritz	.05	.02	.01	☐ 456	Thomas Howard	.05	.02	.01
☐ 387	Curtis Wilkerson	.05	.02	.01	☐ 457	Dave Martinez	.05	.02	.01
☐ 388	Gary Varsho	.05	.02	.01	☐ 458	Pete Incaviglia	.05	.02	.01
☐ 389	Dave Hansen	.05	.02	.01	☐ 459	Keith A. Miller	.05	.02	.01
☐ 390	Bob Welch	.05	.02	.01	☐ 460	Mike Fetters	.05	.02	.01
☐ 391	Lou Whitaker	.15	.07	.02	☐ 461	Paul Gibson	.05	.02	.01
☐ 392	Ken Griffey Jr.	2.50	1.10	.30	☐ 462	George Bell	.05	.02	.01
☐ 393	Mike Maddux	.05	.02	.01	☐ 463	Checklist 441-528	.10	.05	.01
☐ 394	Arthur Rhodes	.05	.02	.01		Bobby Bonilla			
☐ 395	Chili Davis	.15	.07	.02	☐ 464	Terry Mulholland	.05	.02	.01
☐ 396	Eddie Murray	.25	.11	.03	☐ 465	Storm Davis	.05	.02	.01
☐ 397	Checklist 353-440	.10	.05	.01	☐ 466	Gary Pettis	.05	.02	.01
	Robin Yount				☐ 467	Randy Bush	.05	.02	.01
☐ 398	Dave Cochrane	.05	.02	.01	☐ 468	Ken Hill	.15	.07	.02
☐ 399	Kevin Seitzer	.05	.02	.01	☐ 469	Rheal Cormier	.05	.02	.01
☐ 400	Ozzie Smith	.30	.14	.04	☐ 470	Andy Stankiewicz	.05	.02	.01
☐ 401	Paul Sorrento	.05	.02	.01	☐ 471	Dave Burba	.05	.02	.01
☐ 402	Les Lancaster	.05	.02	.01	☐ 472	Henry Cotto	.05	.02	.01
☐ 403	Junior Noboa	.05	.02	.01	☐ 473	Dale Sveum	.05	.02	.01
☐ 404	David Justice	.25	.11	.03	☐ 474	Rich Gossage	.10	.05	.01
☐ 405	Andy Ashby	.05	.02	.01	☐ 475	William Suero	.05	.02	.01
☐ 406	Danny Tartabull	.10	.05	.01	☐ 476	Doug Strange	.05	.02	.01
☐ 407	Bill Swift	.05	.02	.01	☐ 477	Bill Krueger	.05	.02	.01
☐ 408	Craig Lefferts	.05	.02	.01	☐ 478	John Wetteland	.10	.05	.01
☐ 409	Tom Candiotti	.05	.02	.01	☐ 479	Melido Perez	.05	.02	.01
☐ 410	Lance Blankenship	.05	.02	.01	☐ 480	Lonnie Smith	.05	.02	.01
☐ 411	Jeff Tackett	.05	.02	.01	☐ 481	Mike Jackson	.05	.02	.01
☐ 412	Sammy Sosa	.25	.11	.03	☐ 482	Mike Gardiner	.05	.02	.01
☐ 413	Jody Reed	.05	.02	.01	☐ 483	David Wells	.10	.05	.01
☐ 414	Bruce Ruffin	.05	.02	.01	☐ 484	Barry Jones	.05	.02	.01
☐ 415	Gene Larkin	.05	.02	.01	☐ 485	Scott Bankhead	.05	.02	.01
☐ 416	John Vander Wal	.05	.02	.01	☐ 486	Terry Leach	.05	.02	.01
☐ 417	Tim Belcher	.05	.02	.01	☐ 487	Vince Horsman	.05	.02	.01
☐ 418	Steve Frey	.05	.02	.01	☐ 488	Dave Eiland	.05	.02	.01
☐ 419	Dick Schofield	.05	.02	.01	☐ 489	Alejandro Pena	.05	.02	.01
☐ 420	Jeff King	.10	.05	.01	☐ 490	Julio Valera	.05	.02	.01
☐ 421	Kim Batiste	.05	.02	.01	☐ 491	Joe Boever	.05	.02	.01
☐ 422	Jack McDowell	.15	.07	.02	☐ 492	Paul Miller	.05	.02	.01
☐ 423	Damon Berryhill	.05	.02	.01	☐ 493	Archi Cianfrocco	.05	.02	.01
☐ 424	Gary Wayne	.05	.02	.01	☐ 494	Dave Fleming	.05	.02	.01
☐ 425	Jack Morris	.15	.07	.02	☐ 495	Kyle Abbott	.05	.02	.01
☐ 426	Moises Alou	.15	.07	.02	☐ 496	Chad Kreuter	.05	.02	.01
☐ 427	Mark McLemore	.05	.02	.01	☐ 497	Chris James	.05	.02	.01
☐ 428	Juan Guerrero	.05	.02	.01	☐ 498	Donnie Hill	.05	.02	.01

			MINT	NRMT	EXC
☐ 499	Jacob Brumfield	.05	.02	.01	
☐ 500	Ricky Bones	.05	.02	.01	
☐ 501	Terry Steinbach	.10	.05	.01	
☐ 502	Bernard Gilkey	.10	.05	.01	
☐ 503	Dennis Cook	.05	.02	.01	
☐ 504	Len Dykstra	.15	.07	.02	
☐ 505	Mike Bielecki	.05	.02	.01	
☐ 506	Bob Kipper	.05	.02	.01	
☐ 507	Jose Melendez	.05	.02	.01	
☐ 508	Rick Sutcliffe	.10	.05	.01	
☐ 509	Ken Patterson	.05	.02	.01	
☐ 510	Andy Allanson	.05	.02	.01	
☐ 511	Al Newman	.05	.02	.01	
☐ 512	Mark Gardner	.05	.02	.01	
☐ 513	Jeff Schaefer	.05	.02	.01	
☐ 514	Jim McNamara	.05	.02	.01	
☐ 515	Peter Hoy	.05	.02	.01	
☐ 516	Curt Schilling	.05	.02	.01	
☐ 517	Kirk McCaskill	.05	.02	.01	
☐ 518	Chris Gwynn	.05	.02	.01	
☐ 519	Sid Fernandez	.10	.05	.01	
☐ 520	Jeff Parrett	.05	.02	.01	
☐ 521	Scott Ruskin	.05	.02	.01	
☐ 522	Kevin McReynolds	.05	.02	.01	
☐ 523	Rick Cerone	.05	.02	.01	
☐ 524	Jesse Orosco	.05	.02	.01	
☐ 525	Troy Afenir	.05	.02	.01	
☐ 526	John Smiley	.05	.02	.01	
☐ 527	Dale Murphy	.15	.07	.02	
☐ 528	Leaf Set Card	.05	.02	.01	

		MINT	NRMT	EXC
COMPLETE SET (24)		20.00	9.00	2.50
COMPLETE SERIES 1 (12)		8.00	3.60	1.00
COMPLETE SERIES 2 (12)		12.00	5.50	1.50
COMMON CARD (BC1-BC12)		.25	.11	.03
COMMON CARD (BC13-BC24)		.25	.11	.03
☐ BC1	Chad Curtis	1.50	.70	.19
☐ BC2	Brent Gates	.50	.23	.06
☐ BC3	Pedro Martinez	1.50	.70	.19
☐ BC4	Kenny Lofton	6.00	2.70	.75
☐ BC5	Turk Wendell	.25	.11	.03
☐ BC6	Mark Hutton	.25	.11	.03
☐ BC7	Todd Hundley	.50	.23	.06
☐ BC8	Matt Stairs	.25	.11	.03
☐ BC9	Eddie Taubensee	.50	.23	.06
☐ BC10	David Nied	.75	.35	.09
☐ BC11	Salomon Torres	.25	.11	.03
☐ BC12	Bret Boone	1.25	.55	.16
☐ BC13	Johnny Ruffin	.25	.11	.03
☐ BC14	Ed Martel	.25	.11	.03
☐ BC15	Rick Trlicek	.25	.11	.03
☐ BC16	Raul Mondesi	10.00	4.50	1.25
☐ BC17	Pat Mahomes	.25	.11	.03
☐ BC18	Dan Wilson	.50	.23	.06
☐ BC19	Donovan Osborne	.25	.11	.03
☐ BC20	Dave Silvestri	.25	.11	.03
☐ BC21	Gary DiSarcina	.25	.11	.03
☐ BC22	Denny Neagle	1.00	.45	.12
☐ BC23	Steve Hosey	.25	.11	.03
☐ BC24	John Doherty	.25	.11	.03

1992 Leaf Gold Rookies

This 24-card standard-size (2 1/2" by 3 1/2") set honors 1992's most promising newcomers. The first 12 cards were randomly inserted in Leaf series I foil packs, while the second 12 cards were featured only in series II packs. The card numbers show a BC prefix. The fronts display full-bleed color action photos highlighted by gold foil border stripes. A gold foil diamond appears at the corners of the picture frame, and the player's name appears in a black bar that extends between the bottom two diamonds. On a gold background, the horizontally oriented backs feature a second color player photo, biography, and, on a white panel, career statistics and career summary. The cards are numbered on the back.

1993 Leaf

The 1993 Leaf baseball set consists of three series of 220, 220, and 110 cards, respectively. Three insert subsets, Gold Leaf Rookies, Heading for the Hall, and Frank Thomas, were randomly packed in the 14-card foil packs. Two other insert sets, Gold Leaf All Stars and Fasttrack, were randomly packed only in jumbo and magazine distributor packs respectively. Players from five MLB teams were found only in second series packs to show them in their new uniforms (Colorado Rockies, Florida Marlins, Cincinnati Reds, California Angels, and Seattle Mariners). All the cards measure the standard size (2 1/2" by 3 1/2"). The fronts feature color action photos that are full-bleed except at the bottom where a diagonal black stripe (gold-foil stamped with the player's name) separates

the picture from a team color-coded slate triangle. The Leaf seal embossed with gold foil is superimposed at the lower right corner. The backs have the same design as the fronts, only the player action shot is cutout and superimposed on a cityscape background. A holographic team logo appears in the upper left corner, while biography and statistics are printed diagonally across the bottom of the photo. The cards are numbered on the back. Rookie Cards in this set include Marcos Armas, Greg McMichael, J. Owens, Kevin Roberson, J.T. Snow, and Tony Tarasco.

	MINT	NRMT	EXC
COMPLETE SET (550)	40.00	18.00	5.00
COMPLETE SERIES 1 (220)	18.00	8.00	2.20
COMPLETE SERIES 2 (220)	18.00	8.00	2.20
COMPLETE UPDATE (110)	5.00	2.20	.60
COMMON CARD (1-220)	.10	.05	.01
COMMON CARD (221-440)	.10	.05	.01
COMMON CARD (441-550)	.10	.05	.01

		MINT	NRMT	EXC
☐	1 Ben McDonald	.10	.05	.01
☐	2 Sid Fernandez	.10	.05	.01
☐	3 Juan Guzman	.20	.09	.03
☐	4 Curt Schilling	.10	.05	.01
☐	5 Ivan Rodriguez	.30	.14	.04
☐	6 Don Slaught	.10	.05	.01
☐	7 Terry Steinbach	.20	.09	.03
☐	8 Todd Zeile	.20	.09	.03
☐	9 Andy Stankiewicz	.10	.05	.01
☐	10 Tim Teufel	.10	.05	.01
☐	11 Marvin Freeman	.10	.05	.01
☐	12 Jim Austin	.10	.05	.01
☐	13 Bob Scanlan	.10	.05	.01
☐	14 Rusty Meacham	.10	.05	.01
☐	15 Casey Candaele	.10	.05	.01
☐	16 Travis Fryman	.30	.14	.04
☐	17 Jose Offerman	.10	.05	.01
☐	18 Albert Belle	1.25	.55	.16
☐	19 John Vander Wal	.10	.05	.01
☐	20 Dan Pasqua	.10	.05	.01
☐	21 Frank Viola	.20	.09	.03
☐	22 Terry Mulholland	.10	.05	.01
☐	23 Gregg Olson	.10	.05	.01
☐	24 Randy Tomlin	.10	.05	.01
☐	25 Todd Stottlemyre	.10	.05	.01
☐	26 Jose Oquendo	.10	.05	.01
☐	27 Julio Franco	.20	.09	.03
☐	28 Tony Gwynn	1.00	.45	.12
☐	29 Ruben Sierra	.30	.14	.04
☐	30 Robby Thompson	.10	.05	.01
☐	31 Jim Bullinger	.10	.05	.01
☐	32 Rick Aguilera	.20	.09	.03
☐	33 Scott Servais	.10	.05	.01
☐	34 Cal Eldred	.10	.05	.01
☐	35 Mike Piazza	2.50	1.10	.30
☐	36 Brent Mayne	.10	.05	.01
☐	37 Wil Cordero	.20	.09	.03
☐	38 Milt Cuyler	.10	.05	.01
☐	39 Howard Johnson	.10	.05	.01
☐	40 Kenny Lofton	1.00	.45	.12
☐	41 Alex Fernandez	.30	.14	.04
☐	42 Denny Neagle	.10	.05	.01
☐	43 Tony Pena	.10	.05	.01
☐	44 Bob Tewksbury	.10	.05	.01
☐	45 Glenn Davis	.10	.05	.01
☐	46 Fred McGriff	.40	.18	.05
☐	47 John Olerud	.20	.09	.03
☐	48 Steve Hosey	.10	.05	.01
☐	49 Rafael Palmeiro	.30	.14	.04
☐	50 David Justice	.40	.18	.05
☐	51 Pete Harnisch	.10	.05	.01
☐	52 Sam Militello	.10	.05	.01
☐	53 Orel Hershiser	.20	.09	.03
☐	54 Pat Mahomes	.10	.05	.01
☐	55 Greg Colbrunn	.30	.14	.04
☐	56 Greg Vaughn	.10	.05	.01
☐	57 Vince Coleman	.10	.05	.01
☐	58 Brian McRae	.30	.14	.04
☐	59 Len Dykstra	.30	.14	.04
☐	60 Dan Gladden	.10	.05	.01
☐	61 Ted Power	.10	.05	.01
☐	62 Donovan Osborne	.10	.05	.01
☐	63 Ron Karkovice	.10	.05	.01
☐	64 Frank Seminara	.10	.05	.01
☐	65 Bob Zupcic	.10	.05	.01
☐	66 Kirt Manwaring	.10	.05	.01
☐	67 Mike Devereaux	.20	.09	.03
☐	68 Mark Lemke	.10	.05	.01
☐	69 Devon White	.20	.09	.03
☐	70 Sammy Sosa	.30	.14	.04
☐	71 Pedro Astacio	.10	.05	.01
☐	72 Dennis Eckersley	.30	.14	.04
☐	73 Chris Nabholz	.10	.05	.01
☐	74 Melido Perez	.10	.05	.01
☐	75 Todd Hundley	.30	.14	.04
☐	76 Kent Hrbek	.20	.09	.03
☐	77 Mickey Morandini	.10	.05	.01
☐	78 Tim McIntosh	.10	.05	.01
☐	79 Andy Van Slyke	.30	.14	.04
☐	80 Kevin McReynolds	.10	.05	.01
☐	81 Mike Henneman	.10	.05	.01
☐	82 Greg W. Harris	.10	.05	.01
☐	83 Sandy Alomar Jr.	.20	.09	.03
☐	84 Mike Jackson	.10	.05	.01
☐	85 Ozzie Guillen	.10	.05	.01
☐	86 Jeff Blauser	.20	.09	.03
☐	87 John Valentin	.30	.14	.04
☐	88 Rey Sanchez	.10	.05	.01
☐	89 Rick Sutcliffe	.20	.09	.03
☐	90 Luis Gonzalez	.20	.09	.03
☐	91 Jeff Fassero	.20	.09	.03
☐	92 Kenny Rogers	.10	.05	.01
☐	93 Bret Saberhagen	.20	.09	.03
☐	94 Bob Welch	.20	.09	.03
☐	95 Darren Daulton	.30	.14	.04
☐	96 Mike Gallego	.10	.05	.01
☐	97 Orlando Merced	.20	.09	.03
☐	98 Chuck Knoblauch	.30	.14	.04
☐	99 Bernard Gilkey	.20	.09	.03
☐	100 Billy Ashley	.20	.09	.03
☐	101 Kevin Appier	.20	.09	.03
☐	102 Jeff Brantley	.10	.05	.01
☐	103 Bill Gullickson	.10	.05	.01
☐	104 John Smoltz	.20	.09	.03
☐	105 Paul Sorrento	.10	.05	.01
☐	106 Steve Buechele	.10	.05	.01
☐	107 Steve Sax	.10	.05	.01
☐	108 Andujar Cedeno	.10	.05	.01
☐	109 Billy Hatcher	.10	.05	.01
☐	110 Checklist	.10	.05	.01
☐	111 Alan Mills	.10	.05	.01
☐	112 John Franco	.20	.09	.03
☐	113 Jack Morris	.30	.14	.04
☐	114 Mitch Williams	.20	.09	.03
☐	115 Nolan Ryan	2.50	1.10	.30
☐	116 Jay Bell	.20	.09	.03
☐	117 Mike Bordick	.10	.05	.01
☐	118 Geronimo Pena	.10	.05	.01

☐	119	Danny Tartabull	.20	.09	.03				
☐	120	Checklist	.10	.05	.01				
☐	121	Steve Avery	.30	.14	.04				
☐	122	Ricky Bones	.10	.05	.01				
☐	123	Mike Morgan	.10	.05	.01				
☐	124	Jeff Montgomery	.20	.09	.03				
☐	125	Jeff Bagwell	1.25	.55	.16				
☐	126	Tony Phillips	.10	.05	.01				
☐	127	Lenny Harris	.10	.05	.01				
☐	128	Glenallen Hill	.10	.05	.01				
☐	129	Marquis Grissom	.30	.14	.04				
☐	130	Gerald Williams UER	.10	.05	.01				
		(Bernie Williams picture and stats)							
☐	131	Greg A. Harris	.10	.05	.01				
☐	132	Tommy Greene	.10	.05	.01				
☐	133	Chris Hoiles	.20	.09	.03				
☐	134	Bob Walk	.10	.05	.01				
☐	135	Duane Ward	.10	.05	.01				
☐	136	Tom Pagnozzi	.10	.05	.01				
☐	137	Jeff Huson	.10	.05	.01				
☐	138	Kurt Stillwell	.10	.05	.01				
☐	139	Dave Henderson	.10	.05	.01				
☐	140	Darrin Jackson	.10	.05	.01				
☐	141	Frank Castillo	.10	.05	.01				
☐	142	Scott Erickson	.10	.05	.01				
☐	143	Darryl Kile	.10	.05	.01				
☐	144	Bill Wegman	.10	.05	.01				
☐	145	Steve Wilson	.10	.05	.01				
☐	146	George Brett	1.25	.55	.16				
☐	147	Moises Alou	.30	.14	.04				
☐	148	Lou Whitaker	.30	.14	.04				
☐	149	Chico Walker	.10	.05	.01				
☐	150	Jerry Browne	.10	.05	.01				
☐	151	Kirk McCaskill	.10	.05	.01				
☐	152	Zane Smith	.10	.05	.01				
☐	153	Matt Young	.10	.05	.01				
☐	154	Lee Smith	.30	.14	.04				
☐	155	Leo Gomez	.10	.05	.01				
☐	156	Dan Walters	.10	.05	.01				
☐	157	Pat Borders	.10	.05	.01				
☐	158	Matt Williams	.50	.23	.06				
☐	159	Dean Palmer	.20	.09	.03				
☐	160	John Patterson	.10	.05	.01				
☐	161	Doug Jones	.10	.05	.01				
☐	162	John Habyan	.10	.05	.01				
☐	163	Pedro Martinez	.30	.14	.04				
☐	164	Carl Willis	.10	.05	.01				
☐	165	Darrin Fletcher	.10	.05	.01				
☐	166	B.J. Surhoff	.20	.09	.03				
☐	167	Eddie Murray	.50	.23	.06				
☐	168	Keith Miller	.10	.05	.01				
☐	169	Ricky Jordan	.10	.05	.01				
☐	170	Juan Gonzalez	.60	.25	.07				
☐	171	Charles Nagy	.20	.09	.03				
☐	172	Mark Clark	.20	.09	.03				
☐	173	Bobby Thigpen	.10	.05	.01				
☐	174	Tim Scott	.10	.05	.01				
☐	175	Scott Cooper	.10	.05	.01				
☐	176	Royce Clayton	.20	.09	.03				
☐	177	Brady Anderson	.20	.09	.03				
☐	178	Sid Bream	.10	.05	.01				
☐	179	Derek Bell	.30	.14	.04				
☐	180	Otis Nixon	.10	.05	.01				
☐	181	Kevin Gross	.10	.05	.01				
☐	182	Ron Darling	.10	.05	.01				
☐	183	John Wetteland	.20	.09	.03				
☐	184	Mike Stanley	.20	.09	.03				
☐	185	Jeff Kent	.30	.14	.04				
☐	186	Brian Harper	.10	.05	.01				
☐	187	Mariano Duncan	.10	.05	.01				
☐	188	Robin Yount	.40	.18	.05				
☐	189	Al Martin	.20	.09	.03				
☐	190	Eddie Zosky	.10	.05	.01				
☐	191	Mike Munoz	.10	.05	.01				
☐	192	Andy Benes	.20	.09	.03				
☐	193	Dennis Cook	.10	.05	.01				
☐	194	Bill Swift	.10	.05	.01				
☐	195	Frank Thomas	3.00	1.35	.35				
☐	196	Damon Berryhill	.10	.05	.01				
☐	197	Mike Greenwell	.20	.09	.03				
☐	198	Mark Grace	.30	.14	.04				
☐	199	Darryl Hamilton	.10	.05	.01				
☐	200	Derrick May	.20	.09	.03				
☐	201	Ken Hill	.20	.09	.03				
☐	202	Kevin Brown	.10	.05	.01				
☐	203	Dwight Gooden	.20	.09	.03				
☐	204	Bobby Witt	.10	.05	.01				
☐	205	Juan Bell	.10	.05	.01				
☐	206	Kevin Maas	.10	.05	.01				
☐	207	Jeff King	.10	.05	.01				
☐	208	Scott Leius	.10	.05	.01				
☐	209	Rheal Cormier	.10	.05	.01				
☐	210	Darryl Strawberry	.20	.09	.03				
☐	211	Tom Gordon	.10	.05	.01				
☐	212	Bud Black	.10	.05	.01				
☐	213	Mickey Tettleton	.20	.09	.03				
☐	214	Pete Smith	.10	.05	.01				
☐	215	Felix Fermin	.10	.05	.01				
☐	216	Rick Wilkins	.10	.05	.01				
☐	217	George Bell	.20	.09	.03				
☐	218	Eric Anthony	.10	.05	.01				
☐	219	Pedro Munoz	.20	.09	.03				
☐	220	Checklist	.10	.05	.01				
☐	221	Lance Blankenship	.10	.05	.01				
☐	222	Deion Sanders	.60	.25	.07				
☐	223	Craig Biggio	.30	.14	.04				
☐	224	Ryne Sandberg	.75	.35	.09				
☐	225	Ron Gant	.30	.14	.04				
☐	226	Tom Brunansky	.10	.05	.01				
☐	227	Chad Curtis	.20	.09	.03				
☐	228	Joe Carter	.30	.14	.04				
☐	229	Brian Jordan	.30	.14	.04				
☐	230	Brett Butler	.20	.09	.03				
☐	231	Frank Bolick	.10	.05	.01				
☐	232	Rod Beck	.30	.14	.04				
☐	233	Carlos Baerga	.60	.25	.07				
☐	234	Eric Karros	.30	.14	.04				
☐	235	Jack Armstrong	.10	.05	.01				
☐	236	Bobby Bonilla	.30	.14	.04				
☐	237	Don Mattingly	1.50	.70	.19				
☐	238	Jeff Gardner	.10	.05	.01				
☐	239	Dave Hollins	.20	.09	.03				
☐	240	Steve Cooke	.10	.05	.01				
☐	241	Jose Canseco	.50	.23	.06				
☐	242	Ivan Calderon	.10	.05	.01				
☐	243	Tim Belcher	.10	.05	.01				
☐	244	Freddie Benavides	.10	.05	.01				
☐	245	Roberto Alomar	.60	.25	.07				
☐	246	Rob Deer	.10	.05	.01				
☐	247	Will Clark	.40	.18	.05				
☐	248	Mike Felder	.10	.05	.01				
☐	249	Harold Baines	.20	.09	.03				
☐	250	David Cone	.30	.14	.04				
☐	251	Mark Guthrie	.10	.05	.01				
☐	252	Ellis Burks	.20	.09	.03				
☐	253	Jim Abbott	.30	.14	.04				
☐	254	Chili Davis	.20	.09	.03				
☐	255	Chris Bosio	.10	.05	.01				
☐	256	Bret Barberie	.10	.05	.01				
☐	257	Hal Morris	.20	.09	.03				
☐	258	Dante Bichette	.40	.18	.05				

□	No.	Player			
□	259	Storm Davis	.10	.05	.01
□	260	Gary DiSarcina	.10	.05	.01
□	261	Ken Caminiti	.20	.09	.03
□	262	Paul Molitor	.30	.14	.04
□	263	Joe Oliver	.10	.05	.01
□	264	Pat Listach	.10	.05	.01
□	265	Gregg Jefferies	.30	.14	.04
□	266	Jose Guzman	.10	.05	.01
□	267	Eric Davis	.10	.05	.01
□	268	Delino DeShields	.20	.09	.03
□	269	Barry Bonds	.75	.35	.09
□	270	Mike Bielecki	.10	.05	.01
□	271	Jay Buhner	.30	.14	.04
□	272	Scott Pose	.10	.05	.01
□	273	Tony Fernandez	.10	.05	.01
□	274	Chito Martinez	.10	.05	.01
□	275	Phil Plantier	.10	.05	.01
□	276	Pete Incaviglia	.10	.05	.01
□	277	Carlos Garcia	.20	.09	.03
□	278	Tom Henke	.20	.09	.03
□	279	Roger Clemens	.50	.23	.06
□	280	Rob Dibble	.10	.05	.01
□	281	Daryl Boston	.10	.05	.01
□	282	Greg Gagne	.10	.05	.01
□	283	Cecil Fielder	.30	.14	.04
□	284	Carlton Fisk	.30	.14	.04
□	285	Wade Boggs	.30	.14	.04
□	286	Damion Easley	.20	.09	.03
□	287	Norm Charlton	.10	.05	.01
□	288	Jeff Conine	.30	.14	.04
□	289	Roberto Kelly	.20	.09	.03
□	290	Jerald Clark	.10	.05	.01
□	291	Rickey Henderson	.30	.14	.04
□	292	Chuck Finley	.20	.09	.03
□	293	Doug Drabek	.20	.09	.03
□	294	Dave Stewart	.20	.09	.03
□	295	Tom Glavine	.30	.14	.04
□	296	Jaime Navarro	.10	.05	.01
□	297	Ray Lankford	.30	.14	.04
□	298	Greg Hibbard	.10	.05	.01
□	299	Jody Reed	.10	.05	.01
□	300	Dennis Martinez	.20	.09	.03
□	301	Dave Martinez	.10	.05	.01
□	302	Reggie Jefferson	.10	.05	.01
□	303	John Cummings	.20	.09	.03
□	304	Orestes Destrade	.10	.05	.01
□	305	Mike Maddux	.10	.05	.01
□	306	David Segui	.10	.05	.01
□	307	Gary Sheffield	.30	.14	.04
□	308	Danny Jackson	.10	.05	.01
□	309	Craig Lefferts	.10	.05	.01
□	310	Andre Dawson	.30	.14	.04
□	311	Barry Larkin	.40	.18	.05
□	312	Alex Cole	.10	.05	.01
□	313	Mark Gardner	.10	.05	.01
□	314	Kirk Gibson	.20	.09	.03
□	315	Shane Mack	.10	.05	.01
□	316	Bo Jackson	.30	.14	.04
□	317	Jimmy Key	.20	.09	.03
□	318	Greg Myers	.10	.05	.01
□	319	Ken Griffey Jr.	3.00	1.35	.35
□	320	Monty Fariss	.10	.05	.01
□	321	Kevin Mitchell	.20	.09	.03
□	322	Andres Galarraga	.30	.14	.04
□	323	Mark McGwire	.30	.14	.04
□	324	Mark Langston	.30	.14	.04
□	325	Steve Finley	.20	.09	.03
□	326	Greg Maddux	3.00	1.35	.35
□	327	Dave Nilsson	.20	.09	.03
□	328	Ozzie Smith	.60	.25	.07
□	329	Candy Maldonado	.10	.05	.01
□	330	Checklist	.10	.05	.01
□	331	Tim Pugh	.10	.05	.01
□	332	Joe Girardi	.10	.05	.01
□	333	Junior Felix	.10	.05	.01
□	334	Greg Swindell	.10	.05	.01
□	335	Ramon Martinez	.20	.09	.03
□	336	Sean Berry	.10	.05	.01
□	337	Joe Orsulak	.10	.05	.01
□	338	Wes Chamberlain	.10	.05	.01
□	339	Stan Belinda	.10	.05	.01
□	340	Checklist UER	.10	.05	.01
		(306 Luis Mercedes)			
□	341	Bruce Hurst	.10	.05	.01
□	342	John Burkett	.10	.05	.01
□	343	Mike Mussina	.50	.23	.06
□	344	Scott Fletcher	.10	.05	.01
□	345	Rene Gonzales	.10	.05	.01
□	346	Roberto Hernandez	.20	.09	.03
□	347	Carlos Martinez	.10	.05	.01
□	348	Bill Krueger	.10	.05	.01
□	349	Felix Jose	.10	.05	.01
□	350	John Jaha	.20	.09	.03
□	351	Willie Banks	.10	.05	.01
□	352	Matt Nokes	.10	.05	.01
□	353	Kevin Seitzer	.10	.05	.01
□	354	Erik Hanson	.20	.09	.03
□	355	David Hulse	.10	.05	.01
□	356	Domingo Martinez	.10	.05	.01
□	357	Greg Olson	.10	.05	.01
□	358	Randy Myers	.20	.09	.03
□	359	Tom Browning	.10	.05	.01
□	360	Charlie Hayes	.20	.09	.03
□	361	Bryan Harvey	.20	.09	.03
□	362	Eddie Taubensee	.10	.05	.01
□	363	Tim Wallach	.10	.05	.01
□	364	Mel Rojas	.20	.09	.03
□	365	Frank Tanana	.10	.05	.01
□	366	John Kruk	.30	.14	.04
□	367	Tim Laker	.10	.05	.01
□	368	Rich Rodriguez	.10	.05	.01
□	369	Darren Lewis	.10	.05	.01
□	370	Harold Reynolds	.10	.05	.01
□	371	Jose Melendez	.10	.05	.01
□	372	Joe Grahe	.10	.05	.01
□	373	Lance Johnson	.10	.05	.01
□	374	Jose Mesa	.20	.09	.03
□	375	Scott Livingstone	.10	.05	.01
□	376	Wally Joyner	.20	.09	.03
□	377	Kevin Reimer	.10	.05	.01
□	378	Kirby Puckett	1.00	.45	.12
□	379	Paul O'Neill	.20	.09	.03
□	380	Randy Johnson	.60	.25	.07
□	381	Manuel Lee	.10	.05	.01
□	382	Dick Schofield	.10	.05	.01
□	383	Darren Holmes	.20	.09	.03
□	384	Charlie Hough	.20	.09	.03
□	385	John Orton	.10	.05	.01
□	386	Edgar Martinez	.30	.14	.04
□	387	Terry Pendleton	.20	.09	.03
□	388	Dan Plesac	.10	.05	.01
□	389	Jeff Reardon	.20	.09	.03
□	390	David Nied	.20	.09	.03
□	391	Dave Magadan	.10	.05	.01
□	392	Larry Walker	.40	.18	.05
□	393	Ben Rivera	.10	.05	.01
□	394	Lonnie Smith	.10	.05	.01
□	395	Craig Shipley	.10	.05	.01
□	396	Willie McGee	.20	.09	.03
□	397	Arthur Rhodes	.20	.09	.03
□	398	Mike Stanton	.10	.05	.01
□	399	Luis Polonia	.10	.05	.01

☐ 400	Jack McDowell	.30	.14	.04	☐ 471	Guillermo Velasquez	.10	.05	.01
☐ 401	Mike Moore	.10	.05	.01	☐ 472	Fernando Valenzuela	.20	.09	.03
☐ 402	Jose Lind	.10	.05	.01	☐ 473	Raul Mondesi	2.00	.90	.25
☐ 403	Bill Spiers	.10	.05	.01	☐ 474	Mike Pagliarulo	.10	.05	.01
☐ 404	Kevin Tapani	.10	.05	.01	☐ 475	Chris Hammond	.10	.05	.01
☐ 405	Spike Owen	.10	.05	.01	☐ 476	Torey Lovullo	.10	.05	.01
☐ 406	Tino Martinez	.30	.14	.04	☐ 477	Trevor Wilson	.10	.05	.01
☐ 407	Charlie Leibrandt	.10	.05	.01	☐ 478	Marcos Armas	.10	.05	.01
☐ 408	Ed Sprague	.10	.05	.01	☐ 479	Dave Gallagher	.10	.05	.01
☐ 409	Bryn Smith	.10	.05	.01	☐ 480	Jeff Treadway	.10	.05	.01
☐ 410	Benito Santiago	.10	.05	.01	☐ 481	Jeff Branson	.10	.05	.01
☐ 411	Jose Rijo	.20	.09	.03	☐ 482	Dickie Thon	.10	.05	.01
☐ 412	Pete O'Brien	.10	.05	.01	☐ 483	Eduardo Perez	.20	.09	.03
☐ 413	Willie Wilson	.10	.05	.01	☐ 484	David Wells	.10	.05	.01
☐ 414	Bip Roberts	.10	.05	.01	☐ 485	Brian Williams	.10	.05	.01
☐ 415	Eric Young	.20	.09	.03	☐ 486	Domingo Cedeno	.10	.05	.01
☐ 416	Walt Weiss	.20	.09	.03	☐ 487	Tom Candiotti	.10	.05	.01
☐ 417	Milt Thompson	.10	.05	.01	☐ 488	Steve Frey	.10	.05	.01
☐ 418	Chris Sabo	.10	.05	.01	☐ 489	Greg McMichael	.20	.09	.03
☐ 419	Scott Sanderson	.10	.05	.01	☐ 490	Marc Newfield	.20	.09	.03
☐ 420	Tim Raines	.30	.14	.04	☐ 491	Larry Andersen	.10	.05	.01
☐ 421	Alan Trammell	.30	.14	.04	☐ 492	Damon Buford	.10	.05	.01
☐ 422	Mike Macfarlane	.10	.05	.01	☐ 493	Ricky Gutierrez	.10	.05	.01
☐ 423	Dave Winfield	.30	.14	.04	☐ 494	Jeff Russell	.10	.05	.01
☐ 424	Bob Wickman	.10	.05	.01	☐ 495	Vinny Castilla	.10	.05	.01
☐ 425	David Valle	.10	.05	.01	☐ 496	Wilson Alvarez	.30	.14	.04
☐ 426	Gary Redus	.10	.05	.01	☐ 497	Scott Bullett	.10	.05	.01
☐ 427	Turner Ward	.10	.05	.01	☐ 498	Larry Casian	.10	.05	.01
☐ 428	Reggie Sanders	.30	.14	.04	☐ 499	Jose Vizcaino	.10	.05	.01
☐ 429	Todd Worrell	.10	.05	.01	☐ 500	J.T. Snow	1.00	.45	.12
☐ 430	Julio Valera	.10	.05	.01	☐ 501	Bryan Hickerson	.10	.05	.01
☐ 431	Cal Ripken Jr.	3.00	1.35	.35	☐ 502	Jeremy Hernandez	.10	.05	.01
☐ 432	Mo Vaughn	.50	.23	.06	☐ 503	Jeromy Burnitz	.20	.09	.03
☐ 433	John Smiley	.10	.05	.01	☐ 504	Steve Farr	.10	.05	.01
☐ 434	Omar Vizquel	.20	.09	.03	☐ 505	J. Owens	.20	.09	.03
☐ 435	Billy Ripken	.10	.05	.01	☐ 506	Craig Paquette	.10	.05	.01
☐ 436	Cory Snyder	.10	.05	.01	☐ 507	Jim Eisenreich	.10	.05	.01
☐ 437	Carlos Quintana	.10	.05	.01	☐ 508	Matt Whiteside	.10	.05	.01
☐ 438	Omar Olivares	.10	.05	.01	☐ 509	Luis Aquino	.10	.05	.01
☐ 439	Robin Ventura	.30	.14	.04	☐ 510	Mike LaValliere	.10	.05	.01
☐ 440	Checklist	.10	.05	.01	☐ 511	Jim Gott	.10	.05	.01
☐ 441	Kevin Higgins	.10	.05	.01	☐ 512	Mark McLemore	.10	.05	.01
☐ 442	Carlos Hernandez	.10	.05	.01	☐ 513	Randy Milligan	.10	.05	.01
☐ 443	Dan Peltier	.10	.05	.01	☐ 514	Gary Gaetti	.20	.09	.03
☐ 444	Derek Lilliquist	.10	.05	.01	☐ 515	Lou Frazier	.10	.05	.01
☐ 445	Tim Salmon	1.00	.45	.12	☐ 516	Rich Amaral	.10	.05	.01
☐ 446	Sherman Obando	.20	.09	.03	☐ 517	Gene Harris	.10	.05	.01
☐ 447	Pat Kelly	.10	.05	.01	☐ 518	Aaron Sele	.30	.14	.04
☐ 448	Todd Van Poppel	.20	.09	.03	☐ 519	Mark Wohlers	.10	.05	.01
☐ 449	Mark Whiten	.20	.09	.03	☐ 520	Scott Kamieniecki	.10	.05	.01
☐ 450	Checklist	.10	.05	.01	☐ 521	Kent Mercker	.10	.05	.01
☐ 451	Pat Meares	.20	.09	.03	☐ 522	Jim Deshaies	.10	.05	.01
☐ 452	Tony Tarasco	.40	.18	.05	☐ 523	Kevin Stocker	.20	.09	.03
☐ 453	Chris Gwynn	.10	.05	.01	☐ 524	Jason Bere	.30	.14	.04
☐ 454	Armando Reynoso	.10	.05	.01	☐ 525	Tim Bogar	.10	.05	.01
☐ 455	Danny Darwin	.10	.05	.01	☐ 526	Brad Pennington	.10	.05	.01
☐ 456	Willie Greene	.20	.09	.03	☐ 527	Curt Leskanic	.10	.05	.01
☐ 457	Mike Blowers	.20	.09	.03	☐ 528	Wayne Kirby	.10	.05	.01
☐ 458	Kevin Roberson	.10	.05	.01	☐ 529	Tim Costo	.10	.05	.01
☐ 459	Graeme Lloyd	.10	.05	.01	☐ 530	Doug Henry	.10	.05	.01
☐ 460	David West	.10	.05	.01	☐ 531	Trevor Hoffman	.20	.09	.03
☐ 461	Joey Cora	.10	.05	.01	☐ 532	Kelly Gruber	.10	.05	.01
☐ 462	Alex Arias	.10	.05	.01	☐ 533	Mike Harkey	.10	.05	.01
☐ 463	Chad Kreuter	.10	.05	.01	☐ 534	John Doherty	.10	.05	.01
☐ 464	Mike Lansing	.20	.09	.03	☐ 535	Erik Pappas	.10	.05	.01
☐ 465	Mike Timlin	.10	.05	.01	☐ 536	Brent Gates	.20	.09	.03
☐ 466	Paul Wagner	.10	.05	.01	☐ 537	Roger McDowell	.10	.05	.01
☐ 467	Mark Portugal	.10	.05	.01	☐ 538	Chris Haney	.10	.05	.01
☐ 468	Jim Leyritz	.10	.05	.01	☐ 539	Blas Minor	.10	.05	.01
☐ 469	Ryan Klesko	1.50	.70	.19	☐ 540	Pat Hentgen	.20	.09	.03
☐ 470	Mario Diaz	.10	.05	.01	☐ 541	Chuck Carr	.10	.05	.01

		MINT	NRMT	EXC
☐	542 Doug Strange	.10	.05	.01
☐	543 Xavier Hernandez	.10	.05	.01
☐	544 Paul Quantrill	.10	.05	.01
☐	545 Anthony Young	.10	.05	.01
☐	546 Bret Boone	.30	.14	.04
☐	547 Dwight Smith	.10	.05	.01
☐	548 Bobby Munoz	.10	.05	.01
☐	549 Russ Springer	.10	.05	.01
☐	550 Roger Pavlik	.10	.05	.01
☐	DW Dave Winfield 3000 Hits	1.00	.45	.12
☐	FT Frank Thomas AU/3500 (Certified autograph)	250.00	110.00	31.00

☐	9 Juan Guzman	2.00	.90	.25
☐	10 Pat Listach	2.00	.90	.25
☐	11 Carlos Baerga	8.00	3.60	1.00
☐	12 Felix Jose	2.00	.90	.25
☐	13 Steve Avery	3.00	1.35	.35
☐	14 Robin Ventura	3.00	1.35	.35
☐	15 Ivan Rodriguez	3.00	1.35	.35
☐	16 Cal Eldred	2.00	.90	.25
☐	17 Jeff Bagwell	15.00	6.75	1.85
☐	18 David Justice	5.00	2.20	.60
☐	19 Travis Fryman	3.00	1.35	.35
☐	20 Marquis Grissom	3.00	1.35	.35

1993 Leaf Fasttrack

These 20 standard-size (2 1/2" by 3 1/2") cards were randomly inserted into 1993 Leaf retail packs; the first ten were series I inserts, the second ten were series II inserts. The fronts feature color player action photos that are borderless, except in the lower right corner, where an oblique white stripe carries the motion-streaked set title. Beneath this is a black stripe that contains the player's name and team name and, further below, a black marbleized design. The gold-foil-embossed Leaf seal appears in an upper corner. The similarly designed backs carry a second color player action photo. The player's name, position, biography, and career highlights appear above and parallel to the oblique corner design. The player's prismatic-foil-embossed team name appears in an upper corner. The cards are numbered on the back.

	MINT	NRMT	EXC
COMPLETE SET (20)	100.00	45.00	12.50
COMPLETE SERIES 1 (10)	60.00	27.00	7.50
COMPLETE SERIES 2 (10)	40.00	18.00	5.00
COMMON CARD (1-10)	2.00	.90	.25
COMMON CARD (11-20)	2.00	.90	.25

☐	1 Frank Thomas	40.00	18.00	5.00
☐	2 Tim Wakefield	2.00	.90	.25
☐	3 Kenny Lofton	12.00	5.50	1.50
☐	4 Mike Mussina	6.00	2.70	.75
☐	5 Juan Gonzalez	8.00	3.60	1.00
☐	6 Chuck Knoblauch	3.00	1.35	.35
☐	7 Eric Karros	5.00	2.20	.60
☐	8 Ray Lankford	3.00	1.35	.35

1993 Leaf Gold All-Stars

These standard-size cards were inserted one per 1993 Leaf jumbo packs; the first ten were series I inserts, the second ten were series II inserts. One side of each card features a color player action photo of a National League All-Star that is borderless, except in the lower right corner, where oblique red, white, and blue stripes carry the set's title, with the word "Stars" printed in gold foil. Beneath this is a black marbleized design that contains the player's name in white lettering, and his position, which is printed in gold foil. The gold-foil-embossed Leaf seal appears in an upper corner. The design of the other side is almost identical and carries a color player action photo of an American League All-Star. The AL side carries the year and copyright symbol, and the Major League Baseball and MLBPA logos. The NL side carries the card's number. An additional 10-card update set was randomly inserted in 1993 Leaf Update packs.

	MINT	NRMT	EXC
COMPLETE REG.SET (20)	40.00	18.00	5.00
COMPLETE UPDATE SET (10)	12.00	5.50	1.50
COMMON REG.CARD (R1-R20)	.50	.23	.06
COMMON UPDATE CARD (U1-U10)	.50	.23	.06

☐	R1 Ivan Rodriguez Darren Daulton	.75	.35	.09
☐	R2 Don Mattingly Fred McGriff	3.00	1.35	.35
☐	R3 Cecil Fielder	3.00	1.35	.35

☐		Jeff Bagwell		
☐	R4	Carlos Baerga	3.00	1.35	.35
		Ryne Sandberg		
☐	R5	Chuck Knoblauch	.75	.35	.09
		Delino DeShields		
☐	R6	Robin Ventura	.50	.23	.06
		Terry Pendleton		
☐	R7	Ken Griffey Jr.	5.00	2.20	.60
		Andy Van Slyke		
☐	R8	Joe Carter	1.50	.70	.19
		Dave Justice		
☐	R9	Jose Canseco	3.00	1.35	.35
		Tony Gwynn		
☐	R10	Dennis Eckersley	.50	.23	.06
		Rob Dibble		
☐	R11	Mark McGwire	1.50	.70	.19
		Will Clark		
☐	R12	Frank Thomas	5.00	2.20	.60
		Mark Grace		
☐	R13	Roberto Alomar	1.50	.70	.19
		Craig Biggio		
☐	R14	Cal Ripken	6.00	2.70	.75
		Barry Larkin		
☐	R15	Edgar Martinez	.75	.35	.09
		Gary Sheffield		
☐	R16	Juan Gonzalez	2.50	1.10	.30
		Barry Bonds		
☐	R17	Kirby Puckett	2.50	1.10	.30
		Marquis Grissom		
☐	R18	Jim Abbott	.75	.35	.09
		Tom Glavine		
☐	R19	Nolan Ryan	12.00	5.50	1.50
		Greg Maddux		
☐	R20	Roger Clemens	1.50	.70	.19
		Doug Drabek		
☐	U1	Mark Langston	.50	.23	.06
		Terry Mulholland		
☐	U2	Ivan Rodriguez	.75	.35	.09
		Darren Daulton		
☐	U3	John Olerud	.50	.23	.06
		John Kruk		
☐	U4	Roberto Alomar	2.00	.90	.25
		Ryne Sandberg		
☐	U5	Wade Boggs	.75	.35	.09
		Gary Sheffield		
☐	U6	Cal Ripken	6.00	2.70	.75
		Barry Larkin		
☐	U7	Kirby Puckett	3.00	1.35	.35
		Bobby Bonds		
☐	U8	Ken Griffey Jr.	5.00	2.20	.60
		Marquis Grissom		
☐	U9	Joe Carter	1.00	.45	.12
		David Justice		
☐	U10	Paul Molitor	.75	.35	.09
		Mark Grace		

1993 Leaf
Gold Rookies

These cards of promising newcomers were randomly inserted into 1993 Leaf packs; the first ten in series I, the last ten in series II, and five in the Update product. The front of each standard-size (2 1/2" by 3 1/2") card features a borderless color player action shot. The player's name appears in white

cursive lettering within a wide gray lithic stripe near the bottom, which is set off by gold-foil lines and carries the set's title in simulated bas-relief. The gold foil-embossed Leaf seal appears in an upper corner. The back carries another borderless color player action photo, which is cut out and projected upon a picture of the player's ballpark. His prismatic foil-embossed team logo appears in an upper corner. His name and biography, along with his 1992 minor league stats within a gray lithic stripe, appear near the bottom. The cards are numbered on the back.

		MINT	NRMT	EXC
COMPLETE REG.SET (20)		50.00	22.00	6.25
COMPLETE UPDATE SET (5)		16.00	7.25	2.00
COMMON REG.CARD (R1-R20)		1.00	.45	.12
COMMON UPDATE CARD (U1-U5)		.75	.35	.09

			MINT	NRMT	EXC
☐	R1	Kevin Young	1.00	.45	.12
☐	R2	Wil Cordero	2.50	1.10	.30
☐	R3	Mark Kiefer	1.00	.45	.12
☐	R4	Gerald Williams	1.00	.45	.12
☐	R5	Brandon Wilson	1.00	.45	.12
☐	R6	Greg Gohr	1.00	.45	.12
☐	R7	Ryan Thompson	1.00	.45	.12
☐	R8	Tim Wakefield	1.50	.70	.19
☐	R9	Troy Neel	1.00	.45	.12
☐	R10	Tim Salmon	10.00	4.50	1.25
☐	R11	Kevin Rogers	1.00	.45	.12
☐	R12	Rod Bolton	1.00	.45	.12
☐	R13	Ken Ryan	1.00	.45	.12
☐	R14	Phil Hiatt	1.00	.45	.12
☐	R15	Rene Arocha	1.00	.45	.12
☐	R16	Nigel Wilson	1.00	.45	.12
☐	R17	J.T. Snow	8.00	3.60	1.00
☐	R18	Benji Gil	1.50	.70	.19
☐	R19	Chipper Jones	30.00	13.50	3.70
☐	R20	Darrell Sherman	1.00	.45	.12
☐	U1	Allen Watson	1.50	.70	.19
☐	U2	Jeffrey Hammonds	2.00	.90	.25
☐	U3	Dave McCarty	.75	.35	.09
☐	U4	Mike Piazza	15.00	6.75	1.85
☐	U5	Roberto Mejia	.75	.35	.09

1993 Leaf
Heading for the Hall

Randomly inserted into all 1993 Leaf packs, this ten-card standard-size (2 1/2" by 3

1/2") set features potential Hall of Famers. Cards 1-5 were series I inserts and cards 6-10 were series II inserts. The fronts feature borderless color player action shots, with the player's name appearing within a lithic banner near the bottom, below the set's logo. The gold foil-embossed Leaf seal appears in an upper corner. The horizontal backs carry a cutout color player action photo superposed upon an exterior view of the Hall of Fame building and a blowup of a road map of the Cooperstown area. A Hall of Fame-style plaque appears on the right, which bears the player's name, likeness, and achievements that merit his induction into the Hall. The cards are numbered on the back.

of 440. The fronts feature color action player photos, with team color-coded designs on the bottom. The player's name and the Leaf logo are foil stamped, the team name appears under the player's name. The backs carry a photo of the player's home stadium in the background with a silhouetted photo of the player in the foreground. Additionally, a headshot appears in a ticket stub-like design with biographical information, while player statistics appear on the bottom. Cards featuring players from the Texas Rangers, Cleveland Indians, Milwaukee Brewers and Houston Astros were held out of the first series in order to have up-to-date photography in each team's new uniforms. A limited number of players from the San Francisco Giants are featured in the first series because of minor modifications to the team's uniforms. Randomly inserted in hobby packs at a rate of one in 36 was a stamped version of Frank Thomas' 1990 Leaf rookie card.

	MINT	NRMT	EXC
COMPLETE SET (440)	30.00	13.50	3.70
COMPLETE SERIES 1 (220)	14.00	6.25	1.75
COMPLETE SERIES 2 (220)	16.00	7.25	2.00
COMMON CARD (1-220)	.10	.05	.01
COMMON CARD (221-440)	.10	.05	.01
SUPER PACKS CONTAIN COMPLETE INSERT SETS			

	MINT	NRMT	EXC
COMPLETE SET (10)	30.00	13.50	3.70
COMPLETE SERIES 1 (5)	20.00	9.00	2.50
COMPLETE SERIES 2 (5)	10.00	4.50	1.25
COMMON CARD (1-10)	1.50	.70	.19
☐ 1 Nolan Ryan	12.00	5.50	1.50
☐ 2 Tony Gwynn	4.00	1.80	.50
☐ 3 Robin Yount	1.50	.70	.19
☐ 4 Eddie Murray	2.00	.90	.25
☐ 5 Cal Ripken	15.00	6.75	1.85
☐ 6 Roger Clemens	2.00	.90	.25
☐ 7 George Brett	5.00	2.20	.60
☐ 8 Ryne Sandberg	3.00	1.35	.35
☐ 9 Kirby Puckett	4.00	1.80	.50
☐ 10 Ozzie Smith	3.00	1.35	.35

1994 Leaf

The 1994 Leaf baseball set consists of two series of 220 standard-size cards for a total

	MINT	NRMT	EXC
☐ 1 Cal Ripken Jr.	3.00	1.35	.35
☐ 2 Tony Tarasco	.30	.14	.04
☐ 3 Joe Girardi	.10	.05	.01
☐ 4 Bernie Williams	.20	.09	.03
☐ 5 Chad Kreuter	.10	.05	.01
☐ 6 Troy Neel	.10	.05	.01
☐ 7 Tom Pagnozzi	.10	.05	.01
☐ 8 Kirk Rueter	.10	.05	.01
☐ 9 Chris Bosio	.10	.05	.01
☐ 10 Dwight Gooden	.10	.05	.01
☐ 11 Mariano Duncan	.10	.05	.01
☐ 12 Jay Bell	.20	.09	.03
☐ 13 Lance Johnson	.10	.05	.01
☐ 14 Richie Lewis	.10	.05	.01
☐ 15 Dave Martinez	.10	.05	.01
☐ 16 Orel Hershiser	.20	.09	.03
☐ 17 Rob Butler	.10	.05	.01
☐ 18 Glenallen Hill	.10	.05	.01
☐ 19 Chad Curtis	.20	.09	.03
☐ 20 Mike Stanton	.10	.05	.01
☐ 21 Tim Wallach	.10	.05	.01
☐ 22 Milt Thompson	.10	.05	.01
☐ 23 Kevin Young	.10	.05	.01
☐ 24 John Smiley	.10	.05	.01
☐ 25 Jeff Montgomery	.20	.09	.03
☐ 26 Robin Ventura	.20	.09	.03
☐ 27 Scott Lydy	.10	.05	.01
☐ 28 Todd Stottlemyre	.10	.05	.01
☐ 29 Mark Whiten	.20	.09	.03
☐ 30 Robby Thompson	.10	.05	.01
☐ 31 Bobby Bonilla	.30	.14	.04
☐ 32 Andy Ashby	.10	.05	.01
☐ 33 Greg Myers	.10	.05	.01
☐ 34 Billy Hatcher	.10	.05	.01
☐ 35 Brad Holman	.10	.05	.01
☐ 36 Mark McLemore	.10	.05	.01
☐ 37 Scott Sanders	.20	.09	.03
☐ 38 Jim Abbott	.30	.14	.04
☐ 39 David Wells	.10	.05	.01

☐ 40	Roberto Kelly	.10	.05	.01
☐ 41	Jeff Conine	.30	.14	.04
☐ 42	Sean Berry	.10	.05	.01
☐ 43	Mark Grace	.30	.14	.04
☐ 44	Eric Young	.20	.09	.03
☐ 45	Rick Aguilera	.20	.09	.03
☐ 46	Chipper Jones	1.50	.70	.19
☐ 47	Mel Rojas	.10	.05	.01
☐ 48	Ryan Thompson	.20	.09	.03
☐ 49	Al Martin	.10	.05	.01
☐ 50	Cecil Fielder	.30	.14	.04
☐ 51	Pat Kelly	.10	.05	.01
☐ 52	Kevin Tapani	.10	.05	.01
☐ 53	Tim Costo	.10	.05	.01
☐ 54	Dave Hollins	.20	.09	.03
☐ 55	Kirt Manwaring	.10	.05	.01
☐ 56	Gregg Jefferies	.30	.14	.04
☐ 57	Ron Darling	.10	.05	.01
☐ 58	Bill Haselman	.10	.05	.01
☐ 59	Phil Plantier	.20	.09	.03
☐ 60	Frank Viola	.10	.05	.01
☐ 61	Todd Zeile	.20	.09	.03
☐ 62	Bret Barberie	.10	.05	.01
☐ 63	Roberto Mejia	.20	.09	.03
☐ 64	Chuck Knoblauch	.30	.14	.04
☐ 65	Jose Lind	.10	.05	.01
☐ 66	Brady Anderson	.20	.09	.03
☐ 67	Ruben Sierra	.30	.14	.04
☐ 68	Jose Vizcaino	.10	.05	.01
☐ 69	Joe Grahe	.10	.05	.01
☐ 70	Kevin Appier	.20	.09	.03
☐ 71	Wilson Alvarez	.30	.14	.04
☐ 72	Tom Candiotti	.10	.05	.01
☐ 73	John Burkett	.20	.09	.03
☐ 74	Anthony Young	.10	.05	.01
☐ 75	Scott Cooper	.20	.09	.03
☐ 76	Nigel Wilson	.20	.09	.03
☐ 77	John Valentin	.30	.14	.04
☐ 78	Dave McCarty	.10	.05	.01
☐ 79	Archi Cianfrocco	.10	.05	.01
☐ 80	Lou Whitaker	.30	.14	.04
☐ 81	Dante Bichette	.40	.18	.05
☐ 82	Mark Dewey	.10	.05	.01
☐ 83	Danny Jackson	.10	.05	.01
☐ 84	Harold Baines	.20	.09	.03
☐ 85	Todd Benzinger	.10	.05	.01
☐ 86	Damion Easley	.10	.05	.01
☐ 87	Danny Cox	.10	.05	.01
☐ 88	Jose Bautista	.10	.05	.01
☐ 89	Mike Lansing	.20	.09	.03
☐ 90	Phil Hiatt	.10	.05	.01
☐ 91	Tim Pugh	.10	.05	.01
☐ 92	Tino Martinez	.20	.09	.03
☐ 93	Raul Mondesi	1.00	.45	.12
☐ 94	Greg Maddux	3.00	1.35	.35
☐ 95	Al Leiter	.10	.05	.01
☐ 96	Benito Santiago	.10	.05	.01
☐ 97	Lenny Dykstra	.30	.14	.04
☐ 98	Sammy Sosa	.30	.14	.04
☐ 99	Tim Bogar	.10	.05	.01
☐ 100	Checklist	.10	.05	.01
☐ 101	Deion Sanders	.60	.25	.07
☐ 102	Bobby Witt	.10	.05	.01
☐ 103	Wil Cordero	.30	.14	.04
☐ 104	Rich Amaral	.10	.05	.01
☐ 105	Mike Mussina	.40	.18	.05
☐ 106	Reggie Sanders	.20	.09	.03
☐ 107	Ozzie Guillen	.10	.05	.01
☐ 108	Paul O'Neill	.20	.09	.03
☐ 109	Tim Salmon	.60	.25	.07
☐ 110	Rheal Cormier	.10	.05	.01
☐ 111	Billy Ashley	.30	.14	.04
☐ 112	Jeff Kent	.20	.09	.03
☐ 113	Derek Bell	.20	.09	.03
☐ 114	Danny Darwin	.10	.05	.01
☐ 115	Chip Hale	.10	.05	.01
☐ 116	Tim Raines	.30	.14	.04
☐ 117	Ed Sprague	.10	.05	.01
☐ 118	Darrin Fletcher	.10	.05	.01
☐ 119	Darren Holmes	.10	.05	.01
☐ 120	Alan Trammell	.30	.14	.04
☐ 121	Don Mattingly	1.50	.70	.19
☐ 122	Greg Gagne	.10	.05	.01
☐ 123	Jose Offerman	.10	.05	.01
☐ 124	Joe Orsulak	.10	.05	.01
☐ 125	Jack McDowell	.30	.14	.04
☐ 126	Barry Larkin	.40	.18	.05
☐ 127	Ben McDonald	.20	.09	.03
☐ 128	Mike Bordick	.10	.05	.01
☐ 129	Devon White	.10	.05	.01
☐ 130	Mike Perez	.10	.05	.01
☐ 131	Jay Buhner	.20	.09	.03
☐ 132	Phil Leftwich	.10	.05	.01
☐ 133	Tommy Greene	.10	.05	.01
☐ 134	Charlie Hayes	.20	.09	.03
☐ 135	Don Slaught	.10	.05	.01
☐ 136	Mike Gallego	.10	.05	.01
☐ 137	Dave Winfield	.30	.14	.04
☐ 138	Steve Avery	.30	.14	.04
☐ 139	Derrick May	.10	.05	.01
☐ 140	Bryan Harvey	.10	.05	.01
☐ 141	Wally Joyner	.20	.09	.03
☐ 142	Andre Dawson	.30	.14	.04
☐ 143	Andy Benes	.20	.09	.03
☐ 144	John Franco	.10	.05	.01
☐ 145	Jeff King	.10	.05	.01
☐ 146	Joe Oliver	.10	.05	.01
☐ 147	Bill Gullickson	.10	.05	.01
☐ 148	Armando Reynoso	.10	.05	.01
☐ 149	Dave Fleming	.10	.05	.01
☐ 150	Checklist	.10	.05	.01
☐ 151	Todd Van Poppel	.20	.09	.03
☐ 152	Bernard Gilkey	.20	.09	.03
☐ 153	Kevin Gross	.10	.05	.01
☐ 154	Mike Devereaux	.20	.09	.03
☐ 155	Tim Wakefield	.20	.09	.03
☐ 156	Andres Galarraga	.30	.14	.04
☐ 157	Pat Meares	.10	.05	.01
☐ 158	Jim Leyritz	.10	.05	.01
☐ 159	Mike Macfarlane	.10	.05	.01
☐ 160	Tony Phillips	.10	.05	.01
☐ 161	Brent Gates	.20	.09	.03
☐ 162	Mark Langston	.30	.14	.04
☐ 163	Allen Watson	.10	.05	.01
☐ 164	Randy Johnson	.60	.25	.07
☐ 165	Doug Brocail	.10	.05	.01
☐ 166	Rob Dibble	.10	.05	.01
☐ 167	Roberto Hernandez	.10	.05	.01
☐ 168	Felix Jose	.10	.05	.01
☐ 169	Steve Cooke	.10	.05	.01
☐ 170	Darren Daulton	.30	.14	.04
☐ 171	Eric Karros	.20	.09	.03
☐ 172	Geronimo Pena	.10	.05	.01
☐ 173	Gary DiSarcina	.10	.05	.01
☐ 174	Marquis Grissom	.30	.14	.04
☐ 175	Joey Cora	.10	.05	.01
☐ 176	Jim Eisenreich	.10	.05	.01
☐ 177	Brad Pennington	.10	.05	.01
☐ 178	Terry Steinbach	.20	.09	.03
☐ 179	Pat Borders	.10	.05	.01
☐ 180	Steve Buechele	.10	.05	.01
☐ 181	Jeff Fassero	.10	.05	.01

☐ 182	Mike Greenwell	.20	.09	.03			
☐ 183	Mike Henneman	.10	.05	.01			
☐ 184	Ron Karkovice	.10	.05	.01			
☐ 185	Pat Hentgen	.20	.09	.03			
☐ 186	Jose Guzman	.10	.05	.01			
☐ 187	Brett Butler	.20	.09	.03			
☐ 188	Charlie Hough	.20	.09	.03			
☐ 189	Terry Pendleton	.10	.05	.01			
☐ 190	Melido Perez	.10	.05	.01			
☐ 191	Orestes Destrade	.10	.05	.01			
☐ 192	Mike Morgan	.10	.05	.01			
☐ 193	Joe Carter	.30	.14	.04			
☐ 194	Jeff Blauser	.20	.09	.03			
☐ 195	Chris Hoiles	.20	.09	.03			
☐ 196	Ricky Gutierrez	.10	.05	.01			
☐ 197	Mike Moore	.10	.05	.01			
☐ 198	Carl Willis	.10	.05	.01			
☐ 199	Aaron Sele	.30	.14	.04			
☐ 200	Checklist	.10	.05	.01			
☐ 201	Tim Naehring	.20	.09	.03			
☐ 202	Scott Livingstone	.10	.05	.01			
☐ 203	Luis Alicea	.10	.05	.01			
☐ 204	Torey Lovullo	.10	.05	.01			
☐ 205	Jim Gott	.10	.05	.01			
☐ 206	Bob Wickman	.10	.05	.01			
☐ 207	Greg McMichael	.10	.05	.01			
☐ 208	Scott Brosius	.10	.05	.01			
☐ 209	Chris Gwynn	.10	.05	.01			
☐ 210	Steve Sax	.10	.05	.01			
☐ 211	Dick Schofield	.10	.05	.01			
☐ 212	Robb Nen	.10	.05	.01			
☐ 213	Ben Rivera	.10	.05	.01			
☐ 214	Vinny Castilla	.20	.09	.03			
☐ 215	Jamie Moyer	.10	.05	.01			
☐ 216	Wally Whitehurst	.10	.05	.01			
☐ 217	Frank Castillo	.10	.05	.01			
☐ 218	Mike Blowers	.10	.05	.01			
☐ 219	Tim Scott	.10	.05	.01			
☐ 220	Paul Wagner	.10	.05	.01			
☐ 221	Jeff Bagwell	1.00	.45	.12			
☐ 222	Ricky Bones	.10	.05	.01			
☐ 223	Sandy Alomar Jr.	.20	.09	.03			
☐ 224	Rod Beck	.20	.09	.03			
☐ 225	Roberto Alomar	.60	.25	.07			
☐ 226	Jack Armstrong	.10	.05	.01			
☐ 227	Scott Erickson	.10	.05	.01			
☐ 228	Rene Arocha	.20	.09	.03			
☐ 229	Eric Anthony	.10	.05	.01			
☐ 230	Jeromy Burnitz	.20	.09	.03			
☐ 231	Kevin Brown	.10	.05	.01			
☐ 232	Tim Belcher	.10	.05	.01			
☐ 233	Bret Boone	.30	.14	.04			
☐ 234	Dennis Eckersley	.30	.14	.04			
☐ 235	Tom Glavine	.30	.14	.04			
☐ 236	Craig Biggio	.30	.14	.04			
☐ 237	Pedro Astacio	.20	.09	.03			
☐ 238	Ryan Bowen	.10	.05	.01			
☐ 239	Brad Ausmus	.10	.05	.01			
☐ 240	Vince Coleman	.10	.05	.01			
☐ 241	Jason Bere	.30	.14	.04			
☐ 242	Ellis Burks	.20	.09	.03			
☐ 243	Wes Chamberlain	.10	.05	.01			
☐ 244	Ken Caminiti	.20	.09	.03			
☐ 245	Willie Banks	.10	.05	.01			
☐ 246	Sid Fernandez	.10	.05	.01			
☐ 247	Carlos Baerga	.60	.25	.07			
☐ 248	Carlos Garcia	.10	.05	.01			
☐ 249	Jose Canseco	.50	.23	.06			
☐ 250	Alex Diaz	.10	.05	.01			
☐ 251	Albert Belle	1.25	.55	.16			
☐ 252	Moises Alou	.30	.14	.04			

☐ 253	Bobby Ayala	.10	.05	.01
☐ 254	Tony Gwynn	1.00	.45	.12
☐ 255	Roger Clemens	.50	.23	.06
☐ 256	Eric Davis	.10	.05	.01
☐ 257	Wade Boggs	.30	.14	.04
☐ 258	Chili Davis	.20	.09	.03
☐ 259	Rickey Henderson	.30	.14	.04
☐ 260	Andujar Cedeno	.10	.05	.01
☐ 261	Cris Carpenter	.10	.05	.01
☐ 262	Juan Guzman	.20	.09	.03
☐ 263	David Justice	.40	.18	.05
☐ 264	Barry Bonds	.75	.35	.09
☐ 265	Pete Incaviglia	.10	.05	.01
☐ 266	Tony Fernandez	.10	.05	.01
☐ 267	Cal Eldred	.20	.09	.03
☐ 268	Alex Fernandez	.30	.14	.04
☐ 269	Kent Hrbek	.20	.09	.03
☐ 270	Steve Farr	.10	.05	.01
☐ 271	Doug Drabek	.30	.14	.04
☐ 272	Brian Jordan	.20	.09	.03
☐ 273	Xavier Hernandez	.10	.05	.01
☐ 274	David Cone	.30	.14	.04
☐ 275	Brian Hunter	.10	.05	.01
☐ 276	Mike Harkey	.10	.05	.01
☐ 277	Delino DeShields	.20	.09	.03
☐ 278	David Hulse	.10	.05	.01
☐ 279	Mickey Tettleton	.20	.09	.03
☐ 280	Kevin McReynolds	.10	.05	.01
☐ 281	Darryl Hamilton	.10	.05	.01
☐ 282	Ken Hill	.20	.09	.03
☐ 283	Wayne Kirby	.10	.05	.01
☐ 284	Chris Hammond	.10	.05	.01
☐ 285	Mo Vaughn	.50	.23	.06
☐ 286	Ryan Klesko	.75	.35	.09
☐ 287	Rick Wilkins	.10	.05	.01
☐ 288	Bill Swift	.10	.05	.01
☐ 289	Rafael Palmeiro	.30	.14	.04
☐ 290	Brian Harper	.10	.05	.01
☐ 291	Chris Turner	.10	.05	.01
☐ 292	Luis Gonzalez	.10	.05	.01
☐ 293	Kenny Rogers	.20	.09	.03
☐ 294	Kirby Puckett	1.00	.45	.12
☐ 295	Mike Stanley	.10	.05	.01
☐ 296	Carlos Reyes	.10	.05	.01
☐ 297	Charles Nagy	.10	.05	.01
☐ 298	Reggie Jefferson	.10	.05	.01
☐ 299	Bip Roberts	.10	.05	.01
☐ 300	Darrin Jackson	.10	.05	.01
☐ 301	Mike Jackson	.10	.05	.01
☐ 302	Dave Nilsson	.10	.05	.01
☐ 303	Ramon Martinez	.20	.09	.03
☐ 304	Bobby Jones	.30	.14	.04
☐ 305	Johnny Ruffin	.10	.05	.01
☐ 306	Brian McRae	.20	.09	.03
☐ 307	Bo Jackson	.30	.14	.04
☐ 308	Dave Stewart	.20	.09	.03
☐ 309	John Smoltz	.20	.09	.03
☐ 310	Dennis Martinez	.20	.09	.03
☐ 311	Dean Palmer	.20	.09	.03
☐ 312	David Nied	.20	.09	.03
☐ 313	Eddie Murray	.40	.18	.05
☐ 314	Darryl Kile	.20	.09	.03
☐ 315	Rick Sutcliffe	.20	.09	.03
☐ 316	Shawon Dunston	.10	.05	.01
☐ 317	John Jaha	.10	.05	.01
☐ 318	Salomon Torres	.20	.09	.03
☐ 319	Gary Sheffield	.30	.14	.04
☐ 320	Curt Schilling	.10	.05	.01
☐ 321	Greg Vaughn	.20	.09	.03
☐ 322	Jay Howell	.10	.05	.01
☐ 323	Todd Hundley	.20	.09	.03

☐ 324 Chris Sabo	.10	.05	.01
☐ 325 Stan Javier	.10	.05	.01
☐ 326 Willie Greene	.20	.09	.03
☐ 327 Hipolito Pichardo	.10	.05	.01
☐ 328 Doug Strange	.10	.05	.01
☐ 329 Dan Wilson	.10	.05	.01
☐ 330 Checklist	.10	.05	.01
☐ 331 Omar Vizquel	.10	.05	.01
☐ 332 Scott Servais	.10	.05	.01
☐ 333 Bob Tewksbury	.10	.05	.01
☐ 334 Matt Williams	.50	.23	.06
☐ 335 Tom Foley	.10	.05	.01
☐ 336 Jeff Russell	.10	.05	.01
☐ 337 Scott Leius	.10	.05	.01
☐ 338 Ivan Rodriguez	.30	.14	.04
☐ 339 Kevin Seitzer	.10	.05	.01
☐ 340 Jose Rijo	.20	.09	.03
☐ 341 Eduardo Perez	.10	.05	.01
☐ 342 Kirk Gibson	.20	.09	.03
☐ 343 Randy Milligan	.10	.05	.01
☐ 344 Edgar Martinez	.20	.09	.03
☐ 345 Fred McGriff	.40	.18	.05
☐ 346 Kurt Abbott	.25	.11	.03
☐ 347 John Kruk	.20	.09	.03
☐ 348 Mike Felder	.10	.05	.01
☐ 349 Dave Staton	.10	.05	.01
☐ 350 Kenny Lofton	1.00	.45	.12
☐ 351 Graeme Lloyd	.10	.05	.01
☐ 352 David Segui	.10	.05	.01
☐ 353 Danny Tartabull	.20	.09	.03
☐ 354 Bob Welch	.10	.05	.01
☐ 355 Duane Ward	.10	.05	.01
☐ 356 Karl Rhodes	.10	.05	.01
☐ 357 Lee Smith	.30	.14	.04
☐ 358 Chris James	.10	.05	.01
☐ 359 Walt Weiss	.10	.05	.01
☐ 360 Pedro Munoz	.10	.05	.01
☐ 361 Paul Sorrento	.10	.05	.01
☐ 362 Todd Worrell	.10	.05	.01
☐ 363 Bob Hamelin	.10	.05	.01
☐ 364 Julio Franco	.20	.09	.03
☐ 365 Roberto Petagine	.20	.09	.03
☐ 366 Willie McGee	.10	.05	.01
☐ 367 Pedro Martinez	.30	.14	.04
☐ 368 Ken Griffey Jr.	3.00	1.35	.35
☐ 369 B.J. Surhoff	.10	.05	.01
☐ 370 Kevin Mitchell	.20	.09	.03
☐ 371 John Doherty	.10	.05	.01
☐ 372 Manuel Lee	.10	.05	.01
☐ 373 Terry Mulholland	.10	.05	.01
☐ 374 Zane Smith	.10	.05	.01
☐ 375 Otis Nixon	.10	.05	.01
☐ 376 Jody Reed	.10	.05	.01
☐ 377 Doug Jones	.10	.05	.01
☐ 378 John Olerud	.30	.14	.04
☐ 379 Greg Swindell	.10	.05	.01
☐ 380 Checklist	.10	.05	.01
☐ 381 Royce Clayton	.20	.09	.03
☐ 382 Jim Thome	.60	.25	.07
☐ 383 Steve Finley	.10	.05	.01
☐ 384 Ray Lankford	.30	.14	.04
☐ 385 Henry Rodriguez	.10	.05	.01
☐ 386 Dave Magadan	.10	.05	.01
☐ 387 Gary Redus	.10	.05	.01
☐ 388 Orlando Merced	.20	.09	.03
☐ 389 Tom Gordon	.10	.05	.01
☐ 390 Luis Polonia	.10	.05	.01
☐ 391 Mark McGwire	.30	.14	.04
☐ 392 Mark Lemke	.10	.05	.01
☐ 393 Doug Henry	.10	.05	.01
☐ 394 Chuck Finley	.10	.05	.01
☐ 395 Paul Molitor	.30	.14	.04
☐ 396 Randy Myers	.10	.05	.01
☐ 397 Larry Walker	.40	.18	.05
☐ 398 Pete Harnisch	.10	.05	.01
☐ 399 Darren Lewis	.10	.05	.01
☐ 400 Frank Thomas	3.00	1.35	.35
☐ 401 Jack Morris	.20	.09	.03
☐ 402 Greg Hibbard	.10	.05	.01
☐ 403 Jeffrey Hammonds	.30	.14	.04
☐ 404 Will Clark	.40	.18	.05
☐ 405 Travis Fryman	.30	.14	.04
☐ 406 Scott Sanderson	.10	.05	.01
☐ 407 Gene Harris	.10	.05	.01
☐ 408 Chuck Carr	.10	.05	.01
☐ 409 Ozzie Smith	.60	.25	.07
☐ 410 Kent Mercker	.10	.05	.01
☐ 411 Andy Van Slyke	.30	.14	.04
☐ 412 Jimmy Key	.20	.09	.03
☐ 413 Pat Mahomes	.10	.05	.01
☐ 414 John Wetteland	.10	.05	.01
☐ 415 Todd Jones	.10	.05	.01
☐ 416 Greg Harris	.10	.05	.01
☐ 417 Kevin Stocker	.20	.09	.03
☐ 418 Juan Gonzalez	.75	.35	.09
☐ 419 Pete Smith	.10	.05	.01
☐ 420 Pat Listach	.10	.05	.01
☐ 421 Trevor Hoffman	.10	.05	.01
☐ 422 Scott Fletcher	.10	.05	.01
☐ 423 Mark Lewis	.10	.05	.01
☐ 424 Mickey Morandini	.10	.05	.01
☐ 425 Ryne Sandberg	.75	.35	.09
☐ 426 Erik Hanson	.10	.05	.01
☐ 427 Gary Gaetti	.10	.05	.01
☐ 428 Harold Reynolds	.10	.05	.01
☐ 429 Mark Portugal	.10	.05	.01
☐ 430 David Valle	.10	.05	.01
☐ 431 Mitch Williams	.10	.05	.01
☐ 432 Howard Johnson	.10	.05	.01
☐ 433 Hal Morris	.20	.09	.03
☐ 434 Tom Henke	.10	.05	.01
☐ 435 Shane Mack	.20	.09	.03
☐ 436 Mike Piazza	1.25	.55	.16
☐ 437 Bret Saberhagen	.20	.09	.03
☐ 438 Jose Mesa	.10	.05	.01
☐ 439 Jaime Navarro	.10	.05	.01
☐ 440 Checklist	.10	.05	.01
☐ A300 Frank Thomas	4.00	1.80	.50
Leaf 5th Anniversary			

1994 Leaf Clean-Up Crew

Inserted in magazine jumbo packs at a rate of one in 12, this 12-card set was issued in two series of six. Full-bleed fronts contain an action photo with the Clean-Up Crew logo at bottom right and the player's name in a colored band toward bottom left. The backs contain a photo and 1993 statistics when batting fourth. The home plate area serves as background.

	MINT	NRMT	EXC
COMPLETE SET (12)	60.00	27.00	7.50
COMPLETE SERIES 1 (6)	10.00	4.50	1.25
COMPLETE SERIES 2 (6)	50.00	22.00	6.25

	MINT	NRMT	EXC
COMMON CARD (1-6)	3.00	1.35	.35
COMMON CARD (7-12)	3.00	1.35	.35

		MINT	NRMT	EXC
☐ 1	Larry Walker	6.00	2.70	.75
☐ 2	Andres Galarraga	5.00	2.20	.60
☐ 3	Dave Hollins	3.00	1.35	.35
☐ 4	Bobby Bonilla	3.00	1.35	.35
☐ 5	Cecil Fielder	5.00	2.20	.60
☐ 6	Danny Tartabull	3.00	1.35	.35
☐ 7	Juan Gonzalez	12.00	5.50	1.50
☐ 8	Joe Carter	5.00	2.20	.60
☐ 9	Fred McGriff	6.00	2.70	.75
☐ 10	Matt Williams	8.00	3.60	1.00
☐ 11	Albert Belle	20.00	9.00	2.50
☐ 12	Harold Baines	3.00	1.35	.35

1994 Leaf Gamers

A close-up photo of the player highlights this 12-card set that was issued in two series of six. They were randomly inserted in jumbo packs at a rate of one in eight. The player's name appears at the top of the photo with the Leaf Gamers hologram logo at the bottom. The backs feature a variety of color photos including a frame by frame series resembling a film strip. There is also a small write-up.

	MINT	NRMT	EXC
COMPLETE SET (12)	200.00	90.00	25.00
COMPLETE SERIES 1 (6)	90.00	40.00	11.00
COMPLETE SERIES 2 (6)	110.00	50.00	14.00
COMMON CARD (1-6)	5.00	2.20	.60
COMMON CARD (7-12)	5.00	2.20	.60

		MINT	NRMT	EXC
☐ 1	Ken Griffey Jr.	60.00	27.00	7.50
☐ 2	Lenny Dykstra	5.00	2.20	.60

		MINT	NRMT	EXC
☐ 3	Juan Gonzalez	15.00	6.75	1.85
☐ 4	Don Mattingly	30.00	13.50	3.70
☐ 5	David Justice	8.00	3.60	1.00
☐ 6	Mark Grace	5.00	2.20	.60
☐ 7	Frank Thomas	60.00	27.00	7.50
☐ 8	Barry Bonds	15.00	6.75	1.85
☐ 9	Kirby Puckett	20.00	9.00	2.50
☐ 10	Will Clark	8.00	3.60	1.00
☐ 11	John Kruk	5.00	2.20	.60
☐ 12	Mike Piazza	25.00	11.00	3.10

1994 Leaf Gold Rookies

This set, which was randomly inserted in all packs at a rate of one in 18, features ten of the hottest young stars in the majors. A color player cutout is layed over a dark brownish background that contains "94 Gold Leaf Rookie". The player's name and team appear at the bottom in silver. Horizontal backs include career highlights and two photos.

	MINT	NRMT	EXC
COMPLETE SET (20)	25.00	11.00	3.10
COMPLETE SERIES 1 (10)	15.00	6.75	1.85
COMPLETE SERIES 2 (10)	10.00	4.50	1.25
COMMON CARD (1-10)	.50	.23	.06
COMMON CARD (11-20)	.50	.23	.06

		MINT	NRMT	EXC
☐ 1	Javier Lopez	2.50	1.10	.30
☐ 2	Rondell White	2.00	.90	.25
☐ 3	Butch Huskey	1.00	.45	.12
☐ 4	Midre Cummings	1.00	.45	.12
☐ 5	Scott Ruffcorn	1.00	.45	.12
☐ 6	Manny Ramirez	8.00	3.60	1.00
☐ 7	Danny Bautista	.50	.23	.06
☐ 8	Russ Davis	.50	.23	.06
☐ 9	Steve Karsay	.50	.23	.06
☐ 10	Carlos Delgado	1.50	.70	.19
☐ 11	Bob Hamelin	1.00	.45	.12
☐ 12	Marcus Moore	.50	.23	.06
☐ 13	Miguel Jimenez	.50	.23	.06
☐ 14	Matt Walbeck	.50	.23	.06
☐ 15	James Mouton	1.00	.45	.12
☐ 16	Rich Becker	1.00	.45	.12
☐ 17	Brian Anderson	1.00	.45	.12
☐ 18	Cliff Floyd	1.00	.45	.12
☐ 19	Steve Trachsel	1.00	.45	.12
☐ 20	Hector Carrasco	.50	.23	.06

1994 Leaf Gold Stars

Randomly inserted in all packs at a rate of one in 90, the 15 cards in this set are individually numbered and limited to 10,000 per player. The cards were issued in two series with eight cards in series one and seven in series two. The fronts are bordered by gold and have a green marble appearance with the player appearing within a diamond (outlined in gold) in the card's upper half. The player's name, gold facsimile autograph and team name appear below the photo. The backs are similar to the fronts except for 1993 highlights and the individual numbering. They are numbered "X/10,000".

	MINT	NRMT	EXC
COMPLETE SET (15)	250.00	110.00	31.00
COMPLETE SERIES 1 (8)....	150.00	70.00	19.00
COMPLETE SERIES 2 (7)....	100.00	45.00	12.50
COMMON CARD (1-8)	8.00	3.60	1.00
COMMON CARD (9-15)	8.00	3.60	1.00
☐ 1 Roberto Alomar	12.00	5.50	1.50
☐ 2 Barry Bonds.................	15.00	6.75	1.85
☐ 3 David Justice	10.00	4.50	1.25
☐ 4 Ken Griffey Jr.............	60.00	27.00	7.50
☐ 5 Lenny Dykstra.............	8.00	3.60	1.00
☐ 6 Don Mattingly.............	30.00	13.50	3.70
☐ 7 Andres Galarraga	8.00	3.60	1.00
☐ 8 Greg Maddux.............	60.00	27.00	7.50
☐ 9 Carlos Baerga............	12.00	5.50	1.50
☐ 10 Paul Molitor.............	8.00	3.60	1.00
☐ 11 Frank Thomas...........	60.00	27.00	7.50
☐ 12 John Olerud.............	8.00	3.60	1.00
☐ 13 Juan Gonzalez.........	15.00	6.75	1.85
☐ 14 Fred McGriff.............	10.00	4.50	1.25
☐ 15 Jack McDowell..........	8.00	3.60	1.00

1994 Leaf MVP Contenders

This 30-card set contains 15 players from each league who were projected to be 1994 MVP hopefuls. These unnumbered

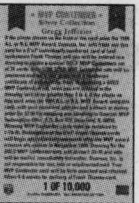

cards were randomly inserted in all second series packs at a rate of one in 36. If the player appearing on the card was named his league's MVP (Frank Thomas American League and Jeff Bagwell National League), the card could be redeemed for a 5" x 7" Frank Thomas card individually numbered out of 20,000. Also, the collector was entered in a drawing to win one of 5,000 special Gold MVP Contenders sets. The fronts contain a color player photo with a black and white National or American League logo serving as a background. The backs contain all the rules and read "1 of 10,000". The expiration for redeeming Thomas and Bagwell cards was early February 1995.

	MINT	NRMT	EXC
COMPLETE SILVER SET (30)	200.00	90.00	25.00
COMMON AL PLAYER (A1-A15)	2.00	.90	.25
COMMON NL PLAYER (N1-N15)	2.00	.90	.25
GOLD VERSIONS: SAME VALUE			
☐ A1 Carlos Baerga	7.00	3.10	.85
☐ A2 Albert Belle	14.00	6.25	1.75
☐ A3 Jose Canseco	6.00	2.70	.75
☐ A4 Joe Carter	3.00	1.35	.35
☐ A5 Will Clark	5.00	2.20	.60
☐ A6 Cecil Fielder	2.00	.90	.25
☐ A7 Juan Gonzalez...........	8.00	3.60	1.00
☐ A8 Ken Griffey Jr............	35.00	16.00	4.40
☐ A9 Paul Molitor..............	3.00	1.35	.35
☐ A10 Rafael Palmeiro........	3.00	1.35	.35
☐ A11 Kirby Puckett...........	10.00	4.50	1.25
☐ A12 Cal Ripken Jr...........	35.00	16.00	4.40
☐ A14 Mo Vaughn..............	6.00	2.70	.75
☐ A15 AL Bonus Card..........	2.00	.90	.25
☐ N1 Jeff Bagwell..............	12.00	5.50	1.50
☐ N2 Dante Bichette..........	5.00	2.20	.60
☐ N3 Barry Bonds.............	8.00	3.60	1.00
☐ N4 Darren Daulton..........	2.00	.90	.25
☐ N5 Andres Galarraga......	3.00	1.35	.35
☐ N6 Gregg Jefferies.........	3.00	1.35	.35
☐ N7 David Justice............	5.00	2.20	.60
☐ N8 Ray Lankford............	3.00	1.35	.35
☐ N9 Barry Larkin.............	5.00	2.20	.60
☐ N10 Fred McGriff............	5.00	2.20	.60
☐ N11 Mike Piazza............	14.00	6.25	1.75
☐ N12 Deion Sanders.........	7.00	3.10	.85
☐ N13 Gary Sheffield.........	3.00	1.35	.35
☐ N14 Matt Williams..........	6.00	2.70	.75
☐ N15 NL Bonus Card	2.00	.90	.25
☐ J400 Frank Thomas Jumbo	20.00	9.00	2.50
☐ A13 Frank Thomas..........	35.00	16.00	4.40

1994 Leaf
Power Brokers

appearance of the slide's reverse image, carries comments about the player from Frank Thomas.

	MINT	NRMT	EXC
COMPLETE SET (10)	70.00	32.00	8.75
COMPLETE SERIES 1 (5)	35.00	16.00	4.40
COMPLETE SERIES 2 (5)	35.00	16.00	4.40
COMMON CARD (1-5)	1.50	.70	.19
COMMON CARD (6-10)	2.50	1.10	.30
☐ 1 Frank Thomas	20.00	9.00	2.50
☐ 2 Mike Piazza	8.00	3.60	1.00
☐ 3 Darren Daulton	1.50	.70	.19
☐ 4 Ryne Sandberg	5.00	2.20	.60
☐ 5 Roberto Alomar	4.00	1.80	.50
☐ 6 Barry Bonds	5.00	2.20	.60
☐ 7 Juan Gonzalez	5.00	2.20	.60
☐ 8 Tim Salmon	4.00	1.80	.50
☐ 9 Ken Griffey Jr.	20.00	9.00	2.50
☐ 10 David Justice	2.50	1.10	.30

Inserted in second series retail and hobby foil packs at a rate of one in 12, this 10-card set spotlights top sluggers. Both fronts and backs are horizontal. The fronts have a small player cutout with a black background and "Power Brokers" dominating the card. Fireworks appear within "Power". The backs contain various pie charts that document the player's home run tendencies as far as home vs. away etc. There is also a small photo.

	MINT	NRMT	EXC
COMPLETE SET (10)	20.00	9.00	2.50
COMMON CARD (1-10)	.75	.35	.09
☐ 1 Frank Thomas	8.00	3.60	1.00
☐ 2 David Justice	1.00	.45	.12
☐ 3 Barry Bonds	2.00	.90	.25
☐ 4 Juan Gonzalez	2.00	.90	.25
☐ 5 Ken Griffey Jr.	8.00	3.60	1.00
☐ 6 Mike Piazza	3.00	1.35	.35
☐ 7 Cecil Fielder	.75	.35	.09
☐ 8 Fred McGriff	1.00	.45	.12
☐ 9 Joe Carter	.75	.35	.09
☐ 10 Albert Belle	3.00	1.35	.35

1994 Leaf Statistical
Standouts

1994 Leaf
Slideshow

Randomly inserted in first and second series packs at a rate of one in 54, these ten standard-size cards simulate mounted photographic slides, but the images of the players are actually printed on acetate. The color transparencies can be seen best when they are held up to the light. The front of each transparency is framed by a simulated white slide holder, which at its bottom bears the player's name and the game from which the photo was shot. The insert set's title is shown in blue and merges with the blue-edged bottom. The remaining edges are black. The back, in addition to the

Inserted in retail and hobby foil packs at a rate of one in 12, this 10-card set features players that had significant statistical achievements in 1993. For example: Cal Ripken's home run record for a shortstop. Card fronts contain a player photo that stands out from a background that is the colors of that player's team. The back contains a photo and statistical information.

	MINT	NRMT	EXC
COMPLETE SET (10)	20.00	9.00	2.50
COMMON CARD (1-10)	.50	.23	.06

		MINT	NRMT	EXC
☐ 1	Frank Thomas	5.00	2.20	.60
☐ 2	Barry Bonds	1.25	.55	.16
☐ 3	Juan Gonzalez	1.25	.55	.16
☐ 4	Mike Piazza	2.00	.90	.25
☐ 5	Greg Maddux	5.00	2.20	.60
☐ 6	Ken Griffey Jr.	5.00	2.20	.60
☐ 7	Joe Carter	.50	.23	.06
☐ 8	Dave Winfield	.50	.23	.06
☐ 9	Tony Gwynn	1.50	.70	.19
☐ 10	Cal Ripken	5.00	2.20	.60

1994 Leaf Limited

This 160-card standard-size set was issued exclusively to hobby dealers. The fronts display silver holographic Spectra Tech foiling and a silhouetted player action photo over full silver foil. The backs contain silver holographic Spectra Tech foil, two photos, and a quote about the player by well-known baseball personalities. The cards are numbered on the back, grouped alphabetically within teams, and checklisted below alphabetically according to teams for each league as follows: Baltimore Orioles (1-6), Boston Red Sox (7-12), California Angels (13-18), Chicago White Sox (19-25), Cleveland Indians (26-30), Detroit Tigers (31-35), Kansas City Royals (36-41), Milwaukee Brewers (42-47), Minnesota Twins (48-52), New York Yankees (53-58), Oakland Athletics (59-63), Seattle Mariners (64-69), Texas Rangers (70-74), Toronto Blue Jays (75-80), Atlanta Braves (81-88), Chicago Cubs (89-93), Cincinnati Reds (94-99), Colorado Rockies (100-104), Florida Marlins (105-109), Houston Astros (110-115), Los Angeles Dodgers (116-122), Montreal Expos (123-128), New York Mets (129-133), Philadelphia Phillies (134-138), Pittsburgh Pirates (139-143), St. Louis Cardinals (144-149), San Diego Padres (150-154), and San Francisco Giants (155-160). The only Rookie Card is Brian Anderson.

		MINT	NRMT	EXC
COMPLETE SET (160)		80.00	36.00	10.00
COMMON CARD (1-160)		.40	.18	.05
☐ 1	Jeffrey Hammonds	1.00	.45	.12
☐ 2	Ben McDonald	.75	.35	.09

		MINT	NRMT	EXC
☐ 3	Mike Mussina	1.25	.55	.16
☐ 4	Rafael Palmeiro	1.00	.45	.12
☐ 5	Cal Ripken Jr.	10.00	4.50	1.25
☐ 6	Lee Smith	1.00	.45	.12
☐ 7	Roger Clemens	1.50	.70	.19
☐ 8	Scott Cooper	.75	.35	.09
☐ 9	Andre Dawson	1.00	.45	.12
☐ 10	Mike Greenwell	.75	.35	.09
☐ 11	Aaron Sele	1.00	.45	.12
☐ 12	Mo Vaughn	1.50	.70	.19
☐ 13	Brian Anderson	1.00	.45	.12
☐ 14	Chad Curtis	.75	.35	.09
☐ 15	Chili Davis	.75	.35	.09
☐ 16	Gary DiSarcina	.40	.18	.05
☐ 17	Mark Langston	1.00	.45	.12
☐ 18	Tim Salmon	2.00	.90	.25
☐ 19	Wilson Alvarez	1.00	.45	.12
☐ 20	Jason Bere	1.00	.45	.12
☐ 21	Julio Franco	.75	.35	.09
☐ 22	Jack McDowell	1.00	.45	.12
☐ 23	Tim Raines	1.00	.45	.12
☐ 24	Frank Thomas	10.00	4.50	1.25
☐ 25	Robin Ventura	.75	.35	.09
☐ 26	Carlos Baerga	2.00	.90	.25
☐ 27	Albert Belle	4.00	1.80	.50
☐ 28	Kenny Lofton	3.00	1.35	.35
☐ 29	Eddie Murray	1.25	.55	.16
☐ 30	Manny Ramirez	5.00	2.20	.60
☐ 31	Cecil Fielder	1.00	.45	.12
☐ 32	Travis Fryman	1.00	.45	.12
☐ 33	Mickey Tettleton	.75	.35	.09
☐ 34	Alan Trammell	1.00	.45	.12
☐ 35	Lou Whitaker	1.00	.45	.12
☐ 36	David Cone	1.00	.45	.12
☐ 37	Gary Gaetti	.75	.35	.09
☐ 38	Greg Gagne	.40	.18	.05
☐ 39	Bob Hamelin	.75	.35	.09
☐ 40	Wally Joyner	.75	.35	.09
☐ 41	Brian McRae	.75	.35	.09
☐ 42	Ricky Bones	.40	.18	.05
☐ 43	Brian Harper	.40	.18	.05
☐ 44	John Jaha	.75	.35	.09
☐ 45	Pat Listach	.40	.18	.05
☐ 46	Dave Nilsson	.40	.18	.05
☐ 47	Greg Vaughn	.75	.35	.09
☐ 48	Kent Hrbek	.75	.35	.09
☐ 49	Chuck Knoblauch	1.00	.45	.12
☐ 50	Shane Mack	.75	.35	.09
☐ 51	Kirby Puckett	3.00	1.35	.35
☐ 52	Dave Winfield	1.00	.45	.12
☐ 53	Jim Abbott	1.00	.45	.12
☐ 54	Wade Boggs	1.00	.45	.12
☐ 55	Jimmy Key	.75	.35	.09
☐ 56	Don Mattingly	5.00	2.20	.60
☐ 57	Paul O'Neill	.75	.35	.09
☐ 58	Danny Tartabull	.75	.35	.09
☐ 59	Dennis Eckersley	1.00	.45	.12
☐ 60	Rickey Henderson	1.00	.45	.12
☐ 61	Mark McGwire	1.00	.45	.12
☐ 62	Troy Neel	.40	.18	.05
☐ 63	Ruben Sierra	1.00	.45	.12
☐ 64	Eric Anthony	.40	.18	.05
☐ 65	Jay Buhner	1.00	.45	.12
☐ 66	Ken Griffey Jr	10.00	4.50	1.25
☐ 67	Randy Johnson	2.00	.90	.25
☐ 68	Edgar Martinez	1.00	.45	.12
☐ 69	Tino Martinez	1.00	.45	.12
☐ 70	Jose Canseco	1.50	.70	.19
☐ 71	Will Clark	1.25	.55	.16
☐ 72	Juan Gonzalez	2.50	1.10	.30
☐ 73	Dean Palmer	.75	.35	.09

☐ 74	Ivan Rodriguez	1.00	.45	.12
☐ 75	Roberto Alomar	2.00	.90	.25
☐ 76	Joe Carter	1.00	.45	.12
☐ 77	Carlos Delgado	1.00	.45	.12
☐ 78	Paul Molitor	1.00	.45	.12
☐ 79	John Olerud	1.00	.45	.12
☐ 80	Devon White	.75	.35	.09
☐ 81	Steve Avery	1.00	.45	.12
☐ 82	Tom Glavine	1.00	.45	.12
☐ 83	David Justice	1.25	.55	.16
☐ 84	Roberto Kelly	.75	.35	.09
☐ 85	Ryan Klesko	2.50	1.10	.30
☐ 86	Javier Lopez	1.50	.70	.19
☐ 87	Greg Maddux	10.00	4.50	1.25
☐ 88	Fred McGriff	1.25	.55	.16
☐ 89	Shawon Dunston	.40	.18	.05
☐ 90	Mark Grace	1.00	.45	.12
☐ 91	Derrick May	.40	.18	.05
☐ 92	Sammy Sosa	1.00	.45	.12
☐ 93	Rick Wilkins	.40	.18	.05
☐ 94	Bret Boone	1.00	.45	.12
☐ 95	Barry Larkin	1.25	.55	.16
☐ 96	Kevin Mitchell	.75	.35	.09
☐ 97	Hal Morris	.75	.35	.09
☐ 98	Deion Sanders	2.00	.90	.25
☐ 99	Reggie Sanders	.75	.35	.09
☐ 100	Dante Bichette	1.25	.55	.16
☐ 101	Ellis Burks	.75	.35	.09
☐ 102	Andres Galarraga	1.00	.45	.12
☐ 103	Joe Girardi	.40	.18	.05
☐ 104	Charlie Hayes	.75	.35	.09
☐ 105	Chuck Carr	.40	.18	.05
☐ 106	Jeff Conine	1.00	.45	.12
☐ 107	Bryan Harvey	.40	.18	.05
☐ 108	Benito Santiago	.40	.18	.05
☐ 109	Gary Sheffield	1.00	.45	.12
☐ 110	Jeff Bagwell	3.00	1.35	.35
☐ 111	Craig Biggio	.75	.35	.09
☐ 112	Ken Caminiti	.75	.35	.09
☐ 113	Andujar Cedeno	.40	.18	.05
☐ 114	Doug Drabek	1.00	.45	.12
☐ 115	Luis Gonzalez	.40	.18	.05
☐ 116	Brett Butler	.75	.35	.09
☐ 117	Delino DeShields	.75	.35	.09
☐ 118	Eric Karros	.75	.35	.09
☐ 119	Raul Mondesi	3.00	1.35	.35
☐ 120	Mike Piazza	4.00	1.80	.50
☐ 121	Henry Rodriguez	.40	.18	.05
☐ 122	Tim Wallach	.40	.18	.05
☐ 123	Moises Alou	1.00	.45	.12
☐ 124	Cliff Floyd	1.00	.45	.12
☐ 125	Marquis Grissom	1.00	.45	.12
☐ 126	Ken Hill	.75	.35	.09
☐ 127	Larry Walker	1.25	.55	.16
☐ 128	John Wetteland	.75	.35	.09
☐ 129	Bobby Bonilla	1.00	.45	.12
☐ 130	John Franco	.75	.35	.09
☐ 131	Jeff Kent	.75	.35	.09
☐ 132	Bret Saberhagen	.75	.35	.09
☐ 133	Ryan Thompson	.75	.35	.09
☐ 134	Darren Daulton	1.00	.45	.12
☐ 135	Mariano Duncan	.40	.18	.05
☐ 136	Lenny Dykstra	1.00	.45	.12
☐ 137	Danny Jackson	.40	.18	.05
☐ 138	John Kruk	.75	.35	.09
☐ 139	Jay Bell	.75	.35	.09
☐ 140	Jeff King	.40	.18	.05
☐ 141	Al Martin	.40	.18	.05
☐ 142	Orlando Merced	.75	.35	.09
☐ 143	Andy Van Slyke	.75	.35	.09
☐ 144	Bernard Gilkey	.75	.35	.09

☐ 145	Gregg Jefferies	1.00	.45	.12
☐ 146	Ray Lankford	1.00	.45	.12
☐ 147	Ozzie Smith	2.00	.90	.25
☐ 148	Mark Whiten	.75	.35	.09
☐ 149	Todd Zeile	.75	.35	.09
☐ 150	Derek Bell	.75	.35	.09
☐ 151	Andy Benes	.75	.35	.09
☐ 152	Tony Gwynn	3.00	1.35	.35
☐ 153	Phil Plantier	.75	.35	.09
☐ 154	Bip Roberts	.40	.18	.05
☐ 155	Rod Beck	.75	.35	.09
☐ 156	Barry Bonds	2.00	.90	.25
☐ 157	John Burkett	.75	.35	.09
☐ 158	Royce Clayton	.75	.35	.09
☐ 159	Bill Swift	.40	.18	.05
☐ 160	Matt Williams	1.50	.70	.19

1994 Leaf Limited Gold All-Stars

Randomly inserted in packs at a rate of one in eight, this 18-card standard-size set features the starting players at each position in both the National and American leagues for the 1994 All-Star Game. They are identical in design to the basic Limited product except for being gold and individually numbered out of 10,000.

	MINT	NRMT	EXC
COMPLETE SET (18)	300.00	135.00	38.00
COMMON CARD (1-18)	6.00	2.70	.75

☐ 1	Frank Thomas	50.00	22.00	6.25
☐ 2	Gregg Jefferies	8.00	3.60	1.00
☐ 3	Roberto Alomar	10.00	4.50	1.25
☐ 4	Mariano Duncan	6.00	2.70	.75
☐ 5	Wade Boggs	8.00	3.60	1.00
☐ 6	Matt Williams	8.00	3.60	1.00
☐ 7	Cal Ripken Jr.	60.00	27.00	7.50
☐ 8	Ozzie Smith	10.00	4.50	1.25
☐ 9	Kirby Puckett	15.00	6.75	1.85
☐ 10	Barry Bonds	12.00	5.50	1.50
☐ 11	Ken Griffey Jr.	50.00	22.00	6.25
☐ 12	Tony Gwynn	15.00	6.75	1.85
☐ 13	Joe Carter	8.00	3.60	1.00
☐ 14	David Justice	8.00	3.60	1.00
☐ 15	Ivan Rodriguez	8.00	3.60	1.00
☐ 16	Mike Piazza	20.00	9.00	2.50
☐ 17	Jimmy Key	6.00	2.70	.75
☐ 18	Greg Maddux	50.00	22.00	6.25

1994 Leaf Limited Rookies

This 80-card standard-size set was issued exclusively to hobby dealers. The set showcases top rookies and prospects of 1994. The fronts display silver holographic Spectra Tech foiling and a silhouetted player action photo over full silver foil. The word "Rookies" appears in black letters above the Leaf Limited logo at top. The backs contain silver holographic Spectra Tech foil, two photos, and a quote about the player by well-known baseball personalities. Rookie Cards in this set include Kurt Abbott, Rusty Greer, Bill VanLandingham and Ismael Valdes.

	MINT	NRMT	EXC
COMPLETE SET (80)	35.00	16.00	4.40
COMMON CARD (1-80)	.40	.18	.05

		MINT	NRMT	EXC
☐ 1	Charles Johnson	1.25	.55	.16
☐ 2	Rico Brogna	.60	.25	.07
☐ 3	Melvin Nieves	.60	.25	.07
☐ 4	Rich Becker	.60	.25	.07
☐ 5	Russ Davis	.60	.25	.07
☐ 6	Matt Mieske	.40	.18	.05
☐ 7	Paul Shuey	.40	.18	.05
☐ 8	Hector Carrasco	.40	.18	.05
☐ 9	J.R. Phillips	.60	.25	.07
☐ 10	Scott Ruffcorn	.60	.25	.07
☐ 11	Kurt Abbott	1.25	.55	.16
☐ 12	Danny Bautista	.40	.18	.05
☐ 13	Rick White	.40	.18	.05
☐ 14	Steve Dunn	.40	.18	.05
☐ 15	Joe Ausanio	.40	.18	.05
☐ 16	Salomon Torres	.60	.25	.07
☐ 17	Ricky Bottalico	.40	.18	.05
☐ 18	Johnny Ruffin	.40	.18	.05
☐ 19	Kevin Foster	.40	.18	.05
☐ 20	W.VanLandingham	1.25	.55	.16
☐ 21	Troy O'Leary	.60	.25	.07
☐ 22	Mark Acre	.40	.18	.05
☐ 23	Norberto Martin	.40	.18	.05
☐ 24	Jason Jacome	1.00	.45	.12
☐ 25	Steve Trachsel	.60	.25	.07
☐ 26	Denny Hocking	.60	.25	.07
☐ 27	Mike Lieberthal	.40	.18	.05
☐ 28	Gerald Williams	.40	.18	.05
☐ 29	John Mabry	.60	.25	.07
☐ 30	Greg Blosser	.40	.18	.05
☐ 31	Carl Everett	.60	.25	.07
☐ 32	Steve Karsay	.60	.25	.07
☐ 33	Jose Valentin	.40	.18	.05
☐ 34	Jon Lieber	.40	.18	.05
☐ 35	Chris Gomez	.60	.25	.07
☐ 36	Jesus Tavarez	.60	.25	.07
☐ 37	Tony Longmire	.40	.18	.05
☐ 38	Luis Lopez	.40	.18	.05
☐ 39	Matt Walbeck	.40	.18	.05
☐ 40	Rikkert Faneyte	.40	.18	.05
☐ 41	Shane Reynolds	.40	.18	.05
☐ 42	Joey Hamilton	1.00	.45	.12
☐ 43	Ismael Valdes	2.50	1.10	.30
☐ 44	Danny Miceli	.40	.18	.05
☐ 45	Darren Bragg	.60	.25	.07
☐ 46	Alex Gonzalez	.60	.25	.07
☐ 47	Rick Helling	.40	.18	.05
☐ 48	Jose Oliva	.60	.25	.07
☐ 49	Jim Edmonds	2.00	.90	.25
☐ 50	Miguel Jimenez	.40	.18	.05
☐ 51	Tony Eusebio	.40	.18	.05
☐ 52	Shawn Green	2.00	.90	.25
☐ 53	Billy Ashley	.60	.25	.07
☐ 54	Rondell White	1.25	.55	.16
☐ 55	Cory Bailey	.40	.18	.05
☐ 56	Tim Davis	.40	.18	.05
☐ 57	John Hudek	.60	.25	.07
☐ 58	Darren Hall	.40	.18	.05
☐ 59	Darren Dreifort	.60	.25	.07
☐ 60	Mike Kelly	.60	.25	.07
☐ 61	Marcus Moore	.40	.18	.05
☐ 62	Garret Anderson	4.00	1.80	.50
☐ 63	Brian L.Hunter	2.50	1.10	.30
☐ 64	Mark Smith	.60	.25	.07
☐ 65	Garey Ingram	.40	.18	.05
☐ 66	Rusty Greer	1.25	.55	.16
☐ 67	Marc Newfield	.60	.25	.07
☐ 68	Gar Finnvold	.40	.18	.05
☐ 69	Paul Spoljaric	.40	.18	.05
☐ 70	Ray McDavid	.60	.25	.07
☐ 71	Orlando Miller	.60	.25	.07
☐ 72	Jorge Fabregas	.40	.18	.05
☐ 73	Ray Holbert	.40	.18	.05
☐ 74	Armando Benitez	.40	.18	.05
☐ 75	Ernie Young	.60	.25	.07
☐ 76	James Mouton	.40	.18	.05
☐ 77	Robert Perez	.40	.18	.05
☐ 78	Chan Ho Park	1.00	.45	.12
☐ 79	Roger Salkeld	.40	.18	.05
☐ 80	Tony Tarasco	.60	.25	.07

1994 Leaf Limited Rookies Phenoms

This 10-card set was randomly inserted in Leaf Limited Rookies packs at a rate of approximately of one in eight. Limited to 5,000, the set showcases top 1994 rookies. The fronts are designed much like the Limited Rookies except the card is comprised of gold foil instead of silver. Gold backs are also virtually identical to the Limited Rookies in terms of content and layout. The cards are individually numbered on back out of 5,000.

	MINT	NRMT	EXC
COMPLETE SET (10)	225.00	100.00	28.00
COMMON CARD (1-10)	8.00	3.60	1.00

		MINT	NRMT	EXC
☐ 1	Raul Mondesi	35.00	16.00	4.40
☐ 2	Bob Hamelin	8.00	3.60	1.00
☐ 3	Midre Cummings	8.00	3.60	1.00
☐ 4	Carlos Delgado	12.00	5.50	1.50
☐ 5	Cliff Floyd	10.00	4.50	1.25
☐ 6	Jeffrey Hammonds	8.00	3.60	1.00
☐ 7	Ryan Klesko	30.00	13.50	3.70
☐ 8	Javier Lopez	20.00	9.00	2.50
☐ 9	Manny Ramirez	60.00	27.00	7.50
☐ 10	Alex Rodriguez	50.00	22.00	6.25

1995 Leaf

The 1995 Leaf set was issued in two series of 200 cards for a total of 400. Full-bleed fronts contain diamond-shaped player hologram in the upper left. The team name is done in silver foil up the left side. Peculiar backs contain two photos, the card number within a stamp or seal like emblem in the upper right and '94 and career stats graph toward bottom left. There are no key Rookie Cards in this set.

	MINT	NRMT	EXC
COMPLETE SET (400)	40.00	18.00	5.00
COMPLETE SERIES 1 (200)	15.00	6.75	1.85
COMPLETE SERIES 2 (200)	25.00	11.00	3.10
COMMON CARD (1-200)	.10	.05	.01
COMMON CARD (201-400)	.10	.05	.01

		MINT	NRMT	EXC
☐ 1	Frank Thomas	3.00	1.35	.35
☐ 2	Carlos Garcia	.20	.09	.03
☐ 3	Todd Hundley	.20	.09	.03
☐ 4	Damion Easley	.10	.05	.01
☐ 5	Roberto Mejia	.10	.05	.01
☐ 6	John Mabry	.20	.09	.03
☐ 7	Aaron Sele	.20	.09	.03
☐ 8	Kenny Lofton	1.00	.45	.12
☐ 9	John Doherty	.10	.05	.01
☐ 10	Joe Carter	.30	.14	.04
☐ 11	Mike Lansing	.10	.05	.01
☐ 12	John Valentin	.30	.14	.04
☐ 13	Ismael Valdes	.10	.05	.01
☐ 14	Dave McCarty	.10	.05	.01
☐ 15	Melvin Nieves	.20	.09	.03
☐ 16	Bobby Jones	.20	.09	.03
☐ 17	Trevor Hoffman	.20	.09	.03
☐ 18	John Smoltz	.20	.09	.03
☐ 19	Leo Gomez	.10	.05	.01
☐ 20	Roger Pavlik	.10	.05	.01
☐ 21	Dean Palmer	.20	.09	.03
☐ 22	Rickey Henderson	.30	.14	.04
☐ 23	Eddie Taubensee	.10	.05	.01
☐ 24	Damon Buford	.10	.05	.01
☐ 25	Mark Wohlers	.20	.09	.03
☐ 26	Jim Edmonds	.40	.18	.05
☐ 27	Wilson Alvarez	.20	.09	.03
☐ 28	Matt Williams	.50	.23	.06
☐ 29	Jeff Montgomery	.20	.09	.03
☐ 30	Shawon Dunston	.10	.05	.01
☐ 31	Tom Pagnozzi	.10	.05	.01
☐ 32	Jose Lind	.10	.05	.01
☐ 33	Royce Clayton	.10	.05	.01
☐ 34	Cal Eldred	.10	.05	.01
☐ 35	Chris Gomez	.10	.05	.01
☐ 36	Henry Rodriguez	.10	.05	.01
☐ 37	Dave Fleming	.10	.05	.01
☐ 38	Jon Lieber	.10	.05	.01
☐ 39	Scott Servais	.10	.05	.01
☐ 40	Wade Boggs	.30	.14	.04
☐ 41	John Olerud	.20	.09	.03
☐ 42	Eddie Williams	.10	.05	.01
☐ 43	Paul Sorrento	.10	.05	.01
☐ 44	Ron Karkovice	.10	.05	.01
☐ 45	Kevin Foster	.10	.05	.01
☐ 46	Miguel Jimenez	.10	.05	.01
☐ 47	Reggie Sanders	.30	.14	.04
☐ 48	Rondell White	.30	.14	.04
☐ 49	Scott Leius	.10	.05	.01
☐ 50	Jose Valentin	.10	.05	.01
☐ 51	Wm. VanLandingham	.20	.09	.03
☐ 52	Denny Hocking	.10	.05	.01
☐ 53	Jeff Fassero	.20	.09	.03
☐ 54	Chris Hoiles	.20	.09	.03
☐ 55	Walt Weiss	.20	.09	.03
☐ 56	Geronimo Berroa	.10	.05	.01
☐ 57	Rich Rowland	.10	.05	.01
☐ 58	Dave Weathers	.10	.05	.01
☐ 59	Sterling Hitchcock	.10	.05	.01
☐ 60	Raul Mondesi	.75	.35	.09
☐ 61	Rusty Greer	.10	.05	.01
☐ 62	David Justice	.40	.18	.05
☐ 63	Cecil Fielder	.30	.14	.04
☐ 64	Brian Jordan	.30	.14	.04
☐ 65	Mike Lieberthal	.10	.05	.01
☐ 66	Rick Aguilera	.20	.09	.03
☐ 67	Chuck Finley	.20	.09	.03
☐ 68	Andy Ashby	.10	.05	.01
☐ 69	Alex Fernandez	.20	.09	.03
☐ 70	Ed Sprague	.10	.05	.01
☐ 71	Steve Buechele	.10	.05	.01
☐ 72	Willie Greene	.10	.05	.01
☐ 73	Dave Nilsson	.20	.09	.03
☐ 74	Bret Saberhagen	.20	.09	.03

☐ 75	Jimmy Key	.20	.09	.03	☐ 146	Felix Fermin	.10	.05	.01
☐ 76	Darren Lewis	.10	.05	.01	☐ 147	Jeff Frye	.10	.05	.01
☐ 77	Steve Cooke	.10	.05	.01	☐ 148	Terry Steinbach	.20	.09	.03
☐ 78	Kirk Gibson	.20	.09	.03	☐ 149	Jim Eisenreich	.10	.05	.01
☐ 79	Ray Lankford	.30	.14	.04	☐ 150	Brad Ausmus	.10	.05	.01
☐ 80	Paul O'Neill	.20	.09	.03	☐ 151	Randy Myers	.20	.09	.03
☐ 81	Mike Bordick	.10	.05	.01	☐ 152	Rick White	.10	.05	.01
☐ 82	Wes Chamberlain	.10	.05	.01	☐ 153	Mark Portugal	.10	.05	.01
☐ 83	Rico Brogna	.30	.14	.04	☐ 154	Delino DeShields	.20	.09	.03
☐ 84	Kevin Appier	.20	.09	.03	☐ 155	Scott Cooper	.10	.05	.01
☐ 85	Juan Guzman	.10	.05	.01	☐ 156	Pat Hentgen	.20	.09	.03
☐ 86	Kevin Seitzer	.10	.05	.01	☐ 157	Mark Gubicza	.10	.05	.01
☐ 87	Mickey Morandini	.10	.05	.01	☐ 158	Carlos Baerga	.60	.25	.07
☐ 88	Pedro Martinez	.10	.05	.01	☐ 159	Joe Girardi	.10	.05	.01
☐ 89	Matt Mieske	.10	.05	.01	☐ 160	Rey Sanchez	.10	.05	.01
☐ 90	Tino Martinez	.30	.14	.04	☐ 161	Todd Jones	.10	.05	.01
☐ 91	Paul Shuey	.10	.05	.01	☐ 162	Luis Polonia	.10	.05	.01
☐ 92	Bip Roberts	.10	.05	.01	☐ 163	Steve Trachsel	.10	.05	.01
☐ 93	Chili Davis	.10	.05	.01	☐ 164	Roberto Hernandez	.20	.09	.03
☐ 94	Deion Sanders	.60	.25	.07	☐ 165	John Patterson	.10	.05	.01
☐ 95	Darrell Whitmore	.10	.05	.01	☐ 166	Rene Arocha	.10	.05	.01
☐ 96	Joe Orsulak	.10	.05	.01	☐ 167	Will Clark	.40	.18	.05
☐ 97	Bret Boone	.30	.14	.04	☐ 168	Jim Leyritz	.10	.05	.01
☐ 98	Kent Mercker	.10	.05	.01	☐ 169	Todd Van Poppel	.10	.05	.01
☐ 99	Scott Livingstone	.10	.05	.01	☐ 170	Robb Nen	.20	.09	.03
☐ 100	Brady Anderson	.20	.09	.03	☐ 171	Midre Cummings	.20	.09	.03
☐ 101	James Mouton	.20	.09	.03	☐ 172	Jay Buhner	.30	.14	.04
☐ 102	Jose Rijo	.10	.05	.01	☐ 173	Kevin Tapani	.10	.05	.01
☐ 103	Bobby Munoz	.10	.05	.01	☐ 174	Mark Lemke	.20	.09	.03
☐ 104	Ramon Martinez	.20	.09	.03	☐ 175	Marcus Moore	.10	.05	.01
☐ 105	Bernie Williams	.20	.09	.03	☐ 176	Wayne Kirby	.10	.05	.01
☐ 106	Troy Neel	.10	.05	.01	☐ 177	Rich Amaral	.10	.05	.01
☐ 107	Ivan Rodriguez	.30	.14	.04	☐ 178	Lou Whitaker	.30	.14	.04
☐ 108	Salomon Torres	.10	.05	.01	☐ 179	Jay Bell	.20	.09	.03
☐ 109	Johnny Ruffin	.10	.05	.01	☐ 180	Rick Wilkins	.10	.05	.01
☐ 110	Darryl Kile	.10	.05	.01	☐ 181	Paul Molitor	.30	.14	.04
☐ 111	Bobby Ayala	.10	.05	.01	☐ 182	Gary Sheffield	.30	.14	.04
☐ 112	Ron Darling	.10	.05	.01	☐ 183	Kirby Puckett	1.00	.45	.12
☐ 113	Jose Lima	.10	.05	.01	☐ 184	Cliff Floyd	.30	.14	.04
☐ 114	Joey Hamilton	.10	.05	.01	☐ 185	Darren Oliver	.10	.05	.01
☐ 115	Greg Maddux	3.00	1.35	.35	☐ 186	Tim Naehring	.10	.05	.01
☐ 116	Greg Colbrunn	.30	.14	.04	☐ 187	John Hudek	.10	.05	.01
☐ 117	Ozzie Guillen	.10	.05	.01	☐ 188	Eric Young	.20	.09	.03
☐ 118	Brian Anderson	.10	.05	.01	☐ 189	Roger Salkeld	.10	.05	.01
☐ 119	Jeff Bagwell	1.00	.45	.12	☐ 190	Kirt Manwaring	.10	.05	.01
☐ 120	Pat Listach	.10	.05	.01	☐ 191	Kurt Abbott	.10	.05	.01
☐ 121	Sandy Alomar Jr.	.10	.05	.01	☐ 192	David Nied	.10	.05	.01
☐ 122	Jose Vizcaino	.10	.05	.01	☐ 193	Todd Zeile	.20	.09	.03
☐ 123	Rick Helling	.10	.05	.01	☐ 194	Wally Joyner	.20	.09	.03
☐ 124	Allen Watson	.20	.09	.03	☐ 195	Dennis Martinez	.20	.09	.03
☐ 125	Pedro Munoz	.20	.09	.03	☐ 196	Billy Ashley	.20	.09	.03
☐ 126	Craig Biggio	.30	.14	.04	☐ 197	Ben McDonald	.10	.05	.01
☐ 127	Kevin Stocker	.10	.05	.01	☐ 198	Bob Hamelin	.10	.05	.01
☐ 128	Wil Cordero	.20	.09	.03	☐ 199	Chris Turner	.10	.05	.01
☐ 129	Rafael Palmeiro	.30	.14	.04	☐ 200	Lance Johnson	.10	.05	.01
☐ 130	Gar Finnvold	.10	.05	.01	☐ 201	Willie Banks	.10	.05	.01
☐ 131	Darren Hall	.10	.05	.01	☐ 202	Juan Gonzalez	.75	.35	.09
☐ 132	Heath Slocumb	.10	.05	.01	☐ 203	Scott Sanders	.10	.05	.01
☐ 133	Darrin Fletcher	.10	.05	.01	☐ 204	Scott Brosius	.10	.05	.01
☐ 134	Cal Ripken	3.00	1.35	.35	☐ 205	Curt Schilling	.10	.05	.01
☐ 135	Dante Bichette	.40	.18	.05	☐ 206	Alex Gonzalez	.20	.09	.03
☐ 136	Don Slaught	.10	.05	.01	☐ 207	Travis Fryman	.30	.14	.04
☐ 137	Pedro Astacio	.10	.05	.01	☐ 208	Tim Raines	.30	.14	.04
☐ 138	Ryan Thompson	.10	.05	.01	☐ 209	Steve Avery	.20	.09	.03
☐ 139	Greg Gohr	.10	.05	.01	☐ 210	Hal Morris	.20	.09	.03
☐ 140	Javier Lopez	.40	.18	.05	☐ 211	Ken Griffey Jr.	3.00	1.35	.35
☐ 141	Lenny Dykstra	.20	.09	.03	☐ 212	Ozzie Smith	.60	.25	.07
☐ 142	Pat Rapp	.20	.09	.03	☐ 213	Chuck Carr	.10	.05	.01
☐ 143	Mark Kiefer	.10	.05	.01	☐ 214	Ryan Klesko	.60	.25	.07
☐ 144	Greg Gagne	.10	.05	.01	☐ 215	Robin Ventura	.30	.14	.04
☐ 145	Eduardo Perez	.10	.05	.01	☐ 216	Luis Gonzalez	.20	.09	.03

☐ 217	Ken Ryan	.10	.05	.01
☐ 218	Mike Piazza	1.25	.55	.16
☐ 219	Matt Walbeck	.10	.05	.01
☐ 220	Jeff Kent	.20	.09	.03
☐ 221	Orlando Miller	.20	.09	.03
☐ 222	Kenny Rogers	.10	.05	.01
☐ 223	J.T. Snow	.30	.14	.04
☐ 224	Alan Trammell	.30	.14	.04
☐ 225	John Franco	.20	.09	.03
☐ 226	Gerald Williams	.10	.05	.01
☐ 227	Andy Benes	.20	.09	.03
☐ 228	Dan Wilson	.20	.09	.03
☐ 229	Dave Hollins	.10	.05	.01
☐ 230	Vinny Castilla	.30	.14	.04
☐ 231	Devon White	.20	.09	.03
☐ 232	Fred McGriff	.40	.18	.05
☐ 233	Quilvio Veras	.10	.05	.01
☐ 234	Tom Candiotti	.10	.05	.01
☐ 235	Jason Bere	.10	.05	.01
☐ 236	Mark Langston	.20	.09	.03
☐ 237	Mel Rojas	.20	.09	.03
☐ 238	Chuck Knoblauch	.30	.14	.04
☐ 239	Bernard Gilkey	.20	.09	.03
☐ 240	Mark McGwire	.30	.14	.04
☐ 241	Kirk Rueter	.10	.05	.01
☐ 242	Pat Kelly	.10	.05	.01
☐ 243	Ruben Sierra	.30	.14	.04
☐ 244	Randy Johnson	.60	.25	.07
☐ 245	Shane Reynolds	.20	.09	.03
☐ 246	Danny Tartabull	.20	.09	.03
☐ 247	Darryl Hamilton	.10	.05	.01
☐ 248	Danny Bautista	.10	.05	.01
☐ 249	Tom Gordon	.10	.05	.01
☐ 250	Tom Glavine	.30	.14	.04
☐ 251	Orlando Merced	.20	.09	.03
☐ 252	Eric Karros	.30	.14	.04
☐ 253	Benji Gil	.10	.05	.01
☐ 254	Sean Bergman	.10	.05	.01
☐ 255	Roger Clemens	.50	.23	.06
☐ 256	Roberto Alomar	.60	.25	.07
☐ 257	Benito Santiago	.10	.05	.01
☐ 258	Robby Thompson	.10	.05	.01
☐ 259	Marvin Freeman	.10	.05	.01
☐ 260	Jose Offerman	.10	.05	.01
☐ 261	Greg Vaughn	.10	.05	.01
☐ 262	David Segui	.10	.05	.01
☐ 263	Geronimo Pena	.10	.05	.01
☐ 264	Tim Salmon	.50	.23	.06
☐ 265	Eddie Murray	.40	.18	.05
☐ 266	Mariano Duncan	.10	.05	.01
☐ 267	Hideo Nomo	6.00	2.70	.75
☐ 268	Derek Bell	.30	.14	.04
☐ 269	Mo Vaughn	.50	.23	.06
☐ 270	Jeff King	.10	.05	.01
☐ 271	Edgar Martinez	.30	.14	.04
☐ 272	Sammy Sosa	.30	.14	.04
☐ 273	Scott Ruffcorn	.10	.05	.01
☐ 274	Darren Daulton	.20	.09	.03
☐ 275	John Jaha	.20	.09	.03
☐ 276	Andres Galarraga	.30	.14	.04
☐ 277	Mark Grace	.30	.14	.04
☐ 278	Mike Moore	.10	.05	.01
☐ 279	Barry Bonds	.75	.35	.09
☐ 280	Manny Ramirez	1.25	.55	.16
☐ 281	Ellis Burks	.10	.05	.01
☐ 282	Greg Swindell	.10	.05	.01
☐ 283	Barry Larkin	.40	.18	.05
☐ 284	Albert Belle	1.25	.55	.16
☐ 285	Shawn Green	.30	.14	.04
☐ 286	John Roper	.10	.05	.01
☐ 287	Scott Erickson	.20	.09	.03
☐ 288	Moises Alou	.20	.09	.03
☐ 289	Mike Blowers	.20	.09	.03
☐ 290	Brent Gates	.20	.09	.03
☐ 291	Sean Berry	.10	.05	.01
☐ 292	Mike Stanley	.20	.09	.03
☐ 293	Jeff Conine	.30	.14	.04
☐ 294	Tim Wallach	.10	.05	.01
☐ 295	Bobby Bonilla	.30	.14	.04
☐ 296	Bruce Ruffin	.10	.05	.01
☐ 297	Chad Curtis	.20	.09	.03
☐ 298	Mike Greenwell	.10	.05	.01
☐ 299	Tony Gwynn	1.00	.45	.12
☐ 300	Russ Davis	.10	.05	.01
☐ 301	Danny Jackson	.10	.05	.01
☐ 302	Pete Harnisch	.10	.05	.01
☐ 303	Don Mattingly	1.50	.70	.19
☐ 304	Rheal Cormier	.10	.05	.01
☐ 305	Larry Walker	.40	.18	.05
☐ 306	Hector Carrasco	.10	.05	.01
☐ 307	Jason Jacome	.10	.05	.01
☐ 308	Phil Plantier	.10	.05	.01
☐ 309	Harold Baines	.20	.09	.03
☐ 310	Mitch Williams	.10	.05	.01
☐ 311	Charles Nagy	.10	.05	.01
☐ 312	Ken Caminiti	.20	.09	.03
☐ 313	Alex Rodriguez	.60	.25	.07
☐ 314	Chris Sabo	.10	.05	.01
☐ 315	Gary Gaetti	.20	.09	.03
☐ 316	Andre Dawson	.30	.14	.04
☐ 317	Mark Clark	.10	.05	.01
☐ 318	Vince Coleman	.10	.05	.01
☐ 319	Brad Clontz	.10	.05	.01
☐ 320	Steve Finley	.20	.09	.03
☐ 321	Doug Drabek	.20	.09	.03
☐ 322	Mark McLemore	.10	.05	.01
☐ 323	Stan Javier	.10	.05	.01
☐ 324	Ron Gant	.30	.14	.04
☐ 325	Charlie Hayes	.10	.05	.01
☐ 326	Carlos Delgado	.20	.09	.03
☐ 327	Ricky Bottalico	.10	.05	.01
☐ 328	Rod Beck	.20	.09	.03
☐ 329	Mark Acre	.10	.05	.01
☐ 330	Chris Bosio	.10	.05	.01
☐ 331	Tony Phillips	.10	.05	.01
☐ 332	Garret Anderson	.60	.25	.07
☐ 333	Pat Meares	.10	.05	.01
☐ 334	Todd Worrell	.10	.05	.01
☐ 335	Marquis Grissom	.30	.14	.04
☐ 336	Brent Mayne	.10	.05	.01
☐ 337	Lee Tinsley	.20	.09	.03
☐ 338	Terry Pendleton	.20	.09	.03
☐ 339	David Cone	.30	.14	.04
☐ 340	Tony Fernandez	.10	.05	.01
☐ 341	Jim Bullinger	.10	.05	.01
☐ 342	Armando Benitez	.10	.05	.01
☐ 343	John Smiley	.10	.05	.01
☐ 344	Dan Miceli	.10	.05	.01
☐ 345	Charles Johnson	.30	.14	.04
☐ 346	Lee Smith	.30	.14	.04
☐ 347	Brian McRae	.20	.09	.03
☐ 348	Jim Thome	.50	.23	.06
☐ 349	Jose Oliva	.10	.05	.01
☐ 350	Terry Mulholland	.10	.05	.01
☐ 351	Tom Henke	.20	.09	.03
☐ 352	Dennis Eckersley	.30	.14	.04
☐ 353	Sid Fernandez	.10	.05	.01
☐ 354	Paul Wagner	.10	.05	.01
☐ 355	John Dettmer	.10	.05	.01
☐ 356	John Wetteland	.30	.14	.04
☐ 357	John Burkett	.10	.05	.01
☐ 358	Marty Cordova	.50	.23	.06

		MINT	NRMT	EXC
☐ 359	Norm Charlton	.10	.05	.01
☐ 360	Mike Devereaux	.10	.05	.01
☐ 361	Alex Cole	.10	.05	.01
☐ 362	Brett Butler	.20	.09	.03
☐ 363	Mickey Tettleton	.20	.09	.03
☐ 364	Al Martin	.20	.09	.03
☐ 365	Tony Tarasco	.20	.09	.03
☐ 366	Pat Mahomes	.10	.05	.01
☐ 367	Gary DiSarcina	.10	.05	.01
☐ 368	Bill Swift	.10	.05	.01
☐ 369	Chipper Jones	1.25	.55	.16
☐ 370	Orel Hershiser	.20	.09	.03
☐ 371	Kevin Gross	.10	.05	.01
☐ 372	Dave Winfield	.30	.14	.04
☐ 373	Andujar Cedeno	.10	.05	.01
☐ 374	Jim Abbott	.20	.09	.03
☐ 375	Glenallen Hill	.20	.09	.03
☐ 376	Otis Nixon	.10	.05	.01
☐ 377	Roberto Kelly	.20	.09	.03
☐ 378	Chris Hammond	.10	.05	.01
☐ 379	Mike Macfarlane	.10	.05	.01
☐ 380	J.R. Phillips	.10	.05	.01
☐ 381	Luis Alicea	.10	.05	.01
☐ 382	Bret Barberie	.10	.05	.01
☐ 383	Tom Goodwin	.10	.05	.01
☐ 384	Mark Whiten	.10	.05	.01
☐ 385	Jeffrey Hammonds	.20	.09	.03
☐ 386	Omar Vizquel	.10	.05	.01
☐ 387	Mike Mussina	.40	.18	.05
☐ 388	Ricky Bones	.10	.05	.01
☐ 389	Steve Ontiveros	.10	.05	.01
☐ 390	Jeff Blauser	.10	.05	.01
☐ 391	Jose Canseco	.50	.23	.06
☐ 392	Bob Tewksbury	.10	.05	.01
☐ 393	Jacob Brumfield	.10	.05	.01
☐ 394	Doug Jones	.10	.05	.01
☐ 395	Ken Hill	.20	.09	.03
☐ 396	Pat Borders	.10	.05	.01
☐ 397	Carl Everett	.20	.09	.03
☐ 398	Gregg Jefferies	.30	.14	.04
☐ 399	Jack McDowell	.30	.14	.04
☐ 400	Denny Neagle	.10	.05	.01

1995 Leaf 300 Club

Randomly inserted in first and second series mini and retail packs on a three per box basis, this set depicts all 18 players who had a career average of .300 or better entering the 1995 campaign. A large ghosted 300 serves as background to a player photo. Gold foil is at the bottom in either corner including career average in the right corner. Full-bleed backs list the 18 players and their averages to that point.

	MINT	NRMT	EXC
COMPLETE SET (18)	135.00	60.00	17.00
COMPLETE SERIES 1 (9)	55.00	25.00	7.00
COMPLETE SERIES 2 (9)	80.00	36.00	10.00
COMMON CARD (1-9)	3.00	1.35	.35
COMMON CARD (10-18)	3.00	1.35	.35
☐ 1 Frank Thomas	35.00	16.00	4.40
☐ 2 Paul Molitor	3.00	1.35	.35
☐ 3 Mike Piazza	15.00	6.75	1.85
☐ 4 Moises Alou	3.00	1.35	.35
☐ 5 Mike Greenwell	3.00	1.35	.35
☐ 6 Will Clark	5.00	2.20	.60
☐ 7 Hal Morris	3.00	1.35	.35
☐ 8 Edgar Martinez	4.00	1.80	.50
☐ 9 Carlos Baerga	7.00	3.10	.85
☐ 10 Ken Griffey Jr.	35.00	16.00	4.40
☐ 11 Wade Boggs	3.00	1.35	.35
☐ 12 Jeff Bagwell	12.00	5.50	1.50
☐ 13 Tony Gwynn	12.00	5.50	1.50
☐ 14 John Kruk	3.00	1.35	.35
☐ 15 Don Mattingly	18.00	8.00	2.20
☐ 16 Mark Grace	3.00	1.35	.35
☐ 17 Kirby Puckett	12.00	5.50	1.50
☐ 18 Kenny Lofton	12.00	5.50	1.50

1995 Leaf Cornerstones

Cards from this six-card set were randomly inserted in first series packs. Horizontally designed, leading first and thrid basemen from the same team are featured. The fronts have silver foil borders and team names with the team logo serving as background to the photos. The backs have a photo of either player with offensive and defensive stats.

	MINT	NRMT	EXC
COMPLETE SET (6)	15.00	6.75	1.85
COMMON CARD (1-6)	1.00	.45	.12
☐ 1 Frank Thomas Robin Ventura	8.00	3.60	1.00
☐ 2 Cecil Fielder Travis Fryman	1.00	.45	.12
☐ 3 Don Mattingly Wade Boggs	4.00	1.80	.50
☐ 4 Jeff Bagwell	2.50	1.10	.30

	Ken Caminiti			
☐ 5	Will Clark	1.00	.45	.12
	Dean Palmer			
☐ 6	J.R.Phillips	1.50	.70	.19
	Matt Williams			

1995 Leaf
Gold Stars

Randomly inserted in first and second series packs at a rate of one in 110, this 14-card set (eight first series, six second series) showcases some of the game's superstars. Individually numbered on back out of 10,000, the cards feature fronts that have a player photo superimposed metallic, refractive background. A die-cut star is in the lower left corner. The backs have a small player photo and brief write-up in addition to the numbering.

	MINT	NRMT	EXC
COMPLETE SET (14)	350.00	160.00	45.00
COMPLETE SERIES 1 (8)	200.00	90.00	25.00
COMPLETE SERIES 2 (6)	150.00	70.00	19.00
COMMON CARD (1-8)	8.00	3.60	1.00
COMMON CARD (9-14)	10.00	4.50	1.25
☐ 1 Jeff Bagwell	20.00	9.00	2.50
☐ 2 Albert Belle	25.00	11.00	3.10
☐ 3 Tony Gwynn	20.00	9.00	2.50
☐ 4 Ken Griffey Jr.	60.00	27.00	7.50
☐ 5 Barry Bonds	15.00	6.75	1.85
☐ 6 Don Mattingly	30.00	13.50	3.70
☐ 7 Raul Mondesi	15.00	6.75	1.85
☐ 8 Joe Carter	8.00	3.60	1.00
☐ 9 Greg Maddux	60.00	27.00	7.50
☐ 10 Frank Thomas	60.00	27.00	7.50
☐ 11 Mike Piazza	25.00	11.00	3.10
☐ 12 Jose Canseco	10.00	4.50	1.25
☐ 13 Kirby Puckett	20.00	9.00	2.50
☐ 14 Matt Williams	10.00	4.50	1.25

1995 Leaf
Heading for the Hall

This eight-card standard-size set was randomly inserted into series two hobby packs.

The cards are cut in the shape of a Hall of Fame plaque and are designed as if this were the actual information on the player's plaque in Cooperstown. The backs feature a black and white photo along with career statistics. The cards are individually numbered out of 5,000 as well.

	MINT	NRMT	EXC
COMPLETE SET (8)	500.00	220.00	60.00
COMMON CARD (1-8)	15.00	6.75	1.85
☐ 1 Frank Thomas	120.00	55.00	15.00
☐ 2 Ken Griffey Jr.	120.00	55.00	15.00
☐ 3 Jeff Bagwell	40.00	18.00	5.00
☐ 4 Barry Bonds	25.00	11.00	3.10
☐ 5 Kirby Puckett	40.00	18.00	5.00
☐ 6 Cal Ripken	140.00	65.00	17.50
☐ 7 Tony Gwynn	40.00	18.00	5.00
☐ 8 Paul Molitor	15.00	6.75	1.85

1995 Leaf
Slideshow

This 16-card set was issued eight per series and randomly inserted at a rate of per box. The eight cards in the first series are numbered 1A-8A and repeated with different photos in tyhe second series as 1B-8B. Both version carry the same value. The left-hand side of the card front is semi-circular featuring three player translucent "slides".

	MINT	NRMT	EXC
COMPLETE SET (16)	90.00	40.00	11.00
COMPLETE SERIES 1 (8)	45.00	20.00	5.50

	MINT	NRMT	EXC
COMPLETE SERIES 2 (8)........	45.00	20.00	5.50
COMMON CARD (1-8)	2.00	.90	.25
☐ 1 Raul Mondesi.................	4.00	1.80	.50
☐ 2 Frank Thomas..................	15.00	6.75	1.85
☐ 3 Fred McGriff.....................	2.00	.90	.25
☐ 4 Cal Ripken.......................	15.00	6.75	1.85
☐ 5 Jeff Bagwell.....................	5.00	2.20	.60
☐ 6 Will Clark.........................	2.00	.90	.25
☐ 7 Matt Williams...................	2.50	1.10	.30
☐ 8 Ken Griffey Jr..................	15.00	6.75	1.85

1995 Leaf Statistical Standouts

 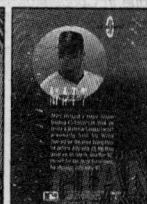

Randomly inserted in first series hobby packs at a rate of one in 70, this set features nine players who stood out from the rest statistically. The fronts contain a player photo between embossed seams or stitches of a baseball. The backs have a small circular player photo with 1994 highlights.

	MINT	NRMT	EXC
COMPLETE SET (9)	600.00	275.00	75.00
COMMON CARD (1-9)	20.00	9.00	2.50
☐ 1 Joe Carter	20.00	9.00	2.50
☐ 2 Ken Griffey Jr.................	140.00	65.00	17.50
☐ 3 Don Mattingly.................	60.00	27.00	7.50
☐ 4 Fred McGriff....................	25.00	11.00	3.10
☐ 5 Paul Molitor	20.00	9.00	2.50
☐ 6 Kirby Puckett..................	45.00	20.00	5.50
☐ 7 Cal Ripken......................	160.00	70.00	20.00
☐ 8 Frank Thomas.................	140.00	65.00	17.50
☐ 9 Matt Williams.................	30.00	13.50	3.70

1995 Leaf Limited

This 192 standard-size card set was issued in two series. Each series contained 96 cards. These cards were issued in six-box cases with 20 packs per box and five cards per pack. Dealer initial cost was $60 per box. Forty-five thousand boxes of each series was produced. The fronts feature a player photo shot against a silver holographic foil background. The player is identified on the top with his team name on the

right. The "Leaf Limited" logo is on the bottom of the card. The horizontal backs contain two player photos along with career stats broken down on a monthly basis. The cards are numbered in the upper right corner. Rookie Cards in this set include Bob Higginson, Ariel Prieto and Carlos Perez.

	MINT	NRMT	EXC
COMPLETE SET (192)	80.00	36.00	10.00
COMPLETE SERIES 1 (96)....	40.00	18.00	5.00
COMPLETE SERIES 2 (96)....	40.00	18.00	5.00
COMMON CARD (1-192)	.30	.14	.04
☐ 1 Frank Thomas.................	8.00	3.60	1.00
☐ 2 Geronimo Berroa	.30	.14	.04
☐ 3 Tony Phillips	.30	.14	.04
☐ 4 Roberto Alomar	1.50	.70	.19
☐ 5 Steve Avery	.30	.14	.04
☐ 6 Darryl Hamilton.............	.30	.14	.04
☐ 7 Scott Cooper	.30	.14	.04
☐ 8 Mark Grace	.60	.25	.07
☐ 9 Billy Ashley	.30	.14	.04
☐ 10 Wil Cordero..................	.30	.14	.04
☐ 11 Barry Bonds.................	2.00	.90	.25
☐ 12 Kenny Lofton...............	2.50	1.10	.30
☐ 13 Jay Buhner	.60	.25	.07
☐ 14 Alex Rodriguez............	1.50	.70	.19
☐ 15 Bobby Bonilla	.60	.25	.07
☐ 16 Brady Anderson	.30	.14	.04
☐ 17 Ken Caminiti.................	.30	.14	.04
☐ 18 Charlie Hayes	.30	.14	.04
☐ 19 Jay Bell	.30	.14	.04
☐ 20 Will Clark	1.00	.45	.12
☐ 21 Jose Canseco	1.25	.55	.16
☐ 22 Bret Boone	.60	.25	.07
☐ 23 Dante Bichette..............	1.00	.45	.12
☐ 24 Kevin Appier	.30	.14	.04
☐ 25 Chad Curtis	.30	.14	.04
☐ 26 Marty Cordova	1.25	.55	.16
☐ 27 Jason Bere	.30	.14	.04
☐ 28 Jimmy Key	.30	.14	.04
☐ 29 Rickey Henderson	.60	.25	.07
☐ 30 Tim Salmon	1.25	.55	.16
☐ 31 Joe Carter	.60	.25	.07
☐ 32 Tom Glavine.................	.60	.25	.07
☐ 33 Pat Listach	.30	.14	.04
☐ 34 Brian Jordan	.60	.25	.07
☐ 35 Brian McRae	.30	.14	.04
☐ 36 Eric Karros	.60	.25	.07
☐ 37 Pedro Martinez	.30	.14	.04
☐ 38 Royce Clayton	.30	.14	.04
☐ 39 Eddie Murray	1.00	.45	.12
☐ 40 Randy Johnson.............	1.50	.70	.19
☐ 41 Jeff Conine...................	.60	.25	.07

☐ 42	Brett Butler	.30	.14	.04
☐ 43	Jeffrey Hammonds	.30	.14	.04
☐ 44	Andujar Cedeno	.30	.14	.04
☐ 45	Dave Hollins	.30	.14	.04
☐ 46	Jeff King	.30	.14	.04
☐ 47	Benji Gil	.30	.14	.04
☐ 48	Roger Clemens	1.25	.55	.16
☐ 49	Barry Larkin	1.00	.45	.12
☐ 50	Joe Girardi	.30	.14	.04
☐ 51	Bob Hamelin	.30	.14	.04
☐ 52	Travis Fryman	.60	.25	.07
☐ 53	Chuck Knoblauch	.60	.25	.07
☐ 54	Ray Durham	.60	.25	.07
☐ 55	Don Mattingly	4.00	1.80	.50
☐ 56	Ruben Sierra	.60	.25	.07
☐ 57	J.T. Snow	.60	.25	.07
☐ 58	Derek Bell	.60	.25	.07
☐ 59	David Cone	.60	.25	.07
☐ 60	Marquis Grissom	.60	.25	.07
☐ 61	Kevin Seitzer	.30	.14	.04
☐ 62	Ozzie Smith	1.50	.70	.19
☐ 63	Rick Wilkins	.30	.14	.04
☐ 64	Hideo Nomo	10.00	4.50	1.25
☐ 65	Tony Tarasco	.30	.14	.04
☐ 66	Manny Ramirez	3.00	1.35	.35
☐ 67	Charles Johnson	.60	.25	.07
☐ 68	Craig Biggio	.60	.25	.07
☐ 69	Bobby Jones	.30	.14	.04
☐ 70	Mike Mussina	1.00	.45	.12
☐ 71	Alex Gonzalez	.30	.14	.04
☐ 72	Gregg Jefferies	.60	.25	.07
☐ 73	Rusty Greer	.30	.14	.04
☐ 74	Mike Greenwell	.30	.14	.04
☐ 75	Hal Morris	.30	.14	.04
☐ 76	Paul O'Neill	.30	.14	.04
☐ 77	Luis Gonzalez	.30	.14	.04
☐ 78	Chipper Jones	4.00	1.80	.50
☐ 79	Mike Piazza	3.00	1.35	.35
☐ 80	Rondell White	.60	.25	.07
☐ 81	Glenallen Hill	.30	.14	.04
☐ 82	Shawn Green	.60	.25	.07
☐ 83	Bernie Williams	.30	.14	.04
☐ 84	Jim Thome	1.25	.55	.16
☐ 85	Terry Pendleton	.30	.14	.04
☐ 86	Rafael Palmeiro	.60	.25	.07
☐ 87	Tony Gwynn	2.50	1.10	.30
☐ 88	Mickey Tettleton	.30	.14	.04
☐ 89	John Valentin	.60	.25	.07
☐ 90	Deion Sanders	1.50	.70	.19
☐ 91	Larry Walker	1.00	.45	.12
☐ 92	Michael Tucker	.30	.14	.04
☐ 93	Alan Trammell	.60	.25	.07
☐ 94	Tim Raines	.60	.25	.07
☐ 95	David Justice	1.00	.45	.12
☐ 96	Tino Martinez	.60	.25	.07
☐ 97	Cal Ripken, Jr.	8.00	3.60	1.00
☐ 98	Deion Sanders	1.50	.70	.19
☐ 99	Darren Daulton	.30	.14	.04
☐ 100	Paul Molitor	.60	.25	.07
☐ 101	Randy Myers	.30	.14	.04
☐ 102	Wally Joyner	.30	.14	.04
☐ 103	Carlos Perez	1.50	.70	.19
☐ 104	Brian Hunter	1.00	.45	.12
☐ 105	Wade Boggs	.60	.25	.07
☐ 106	Bob Higginson	1.00	.45	.12
☐ 107	Jeff Kent	.30	.14	.04
☐ 108	Jose Offerman	.30	.14	.04
☐ 109	Dennis Eckersley	.60	.25	.07
☐ 110	Dave Nilsson	.30	.14	.04
☐ 111	Chuck Finley	.30	.14	.04
☐ 112	Devon White	.30	.14	.04
☐ 113	Bip Roberts	.30	.14	.04
☐ 114	Ramon Martinez	.30	.14	.04
☐ 115	Greg Maddux	8.00	3.60	1.00
☐ 116	Curtis Goodwin	.30	.14	.04
☐ 117	John Jaha	.30	.14	.04
☐ 118	Ken Griffey, Jr.	8.00	3.60	1.00
☐ 119	Geronimo Pena	.30	.14	.04
☐ 120	Shawon Dunston	.30	.14	.04
☐ 121	Ariel Prieto	1.25	.55	.16
☐ 122	Kirby Puckett	2.50	1.10	.30
☐ 123	Carlos Baerga	1.50	.70	.19
☐ 124	Todd Hundley	.30	.14	.04
☐ 125	Tim Naehring	.30	.14	.04
☐ 126	Gary Sheffield	.60	.25	.07
☐ 127	Dean Palmer	.30	.14	.04
☐ 128	Rondell White	.60	.25	.07
☐ 129	Greg Gagne	.30	.14	.04
☐ 130	Jose Rijo	.30	.14	.04
☐ 131	Ivan Rodriguez	.60	.25	.07
☐ 132	Jeff Bagwell	2.50	1.10	.30
☐ 133	Greg Vaughn	.30	.14	.04
☐ 134	Chili Davis	.30	.14	.04
☐ 135	Al Martin	.30	.14	.04
☐ 136	Kenny Rogers	.30	.14	.04
☐ 137	Aaron Sele	.30	.14	.04
☐ 138	Raul Mondesi	1.50	.70	.19
☐ 139	Cecil Fielder	.60	.25	.07
☐ 140	Tim Wallach	.30	.14	.04
☐ 141	Andres Galarraga	.60	.25	.07
☐ 142	Lou Whitaker	.60	.25	.07
☐ 143	Jack McDowell	.60	.25	.07
☐ 144	Matt Williams	1.25	.55	.16
☐ 145	Ryan Klesko	1.50	.70	.19
☐ 146	Carlos Garcia	.30	.14	.04
☐ 147	Albert Belle	3.00	1.35	.35
☐ 148	Ryan Thompson	.30	.14	.04
☐ 149	Roberto Kelly	.30	.14	.04
☐ 150	Edgar Martinez	.60	.25	.07
☐ 151	Robby Thompson	.30	.14	.04
☐ 152	Mo Vaughn	1.25	.55	.16
☐ 153	Todd Zeile	.30	.14	.04
☐ 154	Harold Baines	.30	.14	.04
☐ 155	Phil Plantier	.30	.14	.04
☐ 156	Mike Stanley	.30	.14	.04
☐ 157	Ed Sprague	.30	.14	.04
☐ 158	Moises Alou	.30	.14	.04
☐ 159	Quilvio Veras	.30	.14	.04
☐ 160	Reggie Sanders	.60	.25	.07
☐ 161	Delino DeShields	.30	.14	.04
☐ 162	Rico Brogna	.60	.25	.07
☐ 163	Greg Colbrunn	.60	.25	.07
☐ 164	Steve Finley	.30	.14	.04
☐ 165	Orlando Merced	.30	.14	.04
☐ 166	Mark McGwire	.60	.25	.07
☐ 167	Garret Anderson	1.50	.70	.19
☐ 168	Paul Sorrento	.30	.14	.04
☐ 169	Mark Langston	.30	.14	.04
☐ 170	Danny Tartabull	.30	.14	.04
☐ 171	Vinny Castilla	.60	.25	.07
☐ 172	Javier Lopez	1.00	.45	.12
☐ 173	Bret Saberhagen	.30	.14	.04
☐ 174	Eddie Williams	.30	.14	.04
☐ 175	Scott Leius	.30	.14	.04
☐ 176	Juan Gonzalez	2.00	.90	.25
☐ 177	Gary Gaetti	.30	.14	.04
☐ 178	Jim Edmonds	1.00	.45	.12
☐ 179	John Olerud	.30	.14	.04
☐ 180	Lenny Dykstra	.30	.14	.04
☐ 181	Ray Lankford	.60	.25	.07
☐ 182	Ron Gant	.60	.25	.07
☐ 183	Doug Drabek	.30	.14	.04

		MINT	NRMT	EXC
☐	184 Fred McGriff	1.00	.45	.12
☐	185 Andy Benes	.30	.14	.04
☐	186 Kurt Abbott	.30	.14	.04
☐	187 Bernard Gilkey	.30	.14	.04
☐	188 Sammy Sosa	.60	.25	.07
☐	189 Lee Smith	.60	.25	.07
☐	190 Dennis Martinez	.30	.14	.04
☐	191 Ozzie Guillen	.30	.14	.04
☐	192 Robin Ventura	.60	.25	.07

1995 Leaf Limited Lumberjacks

These eight standard-size cards were randomly inserted into second series packs. The cards are individually numbered out of 5,000. The fronts of the cards feature a player photo surrounded by his name, the word "Lumberjacks" and "Handcrafted" in an semi-circular pattern. The team logo is in the background. The UV-coated horizontal backs feature a player photo against a forest background on the right along with some information on the left side. The player's career statistics are directly above the individual numbering (out of 5,000) of the card. The cards are numbered in the upper right corner.

	MINT	NRMT	EXC
COMPLETE SET (16)	700.00	325.00	90.00
COMPLETE SERIES 1 (8)	325.00	145.00	40.00
COMPLETE SERIES 2 (8)	375.00	170.00	47.50
COMMON CARD (1-16)	15.00	6.75	1.85

		MINT	NRMT	EXC
☐	1 Albert Belle	50.00	22.00	6.25
☐	2 Barry Bonds	25.00	11.00	3.10
☐	3 Juan Gonzalez	25.00	11.00	3.10
☐	4 Ken Griffey Jr.	120.00	55.00	15.00
☐	5 Fred McGriff	20.00	9.00	2.50
☐	6 Mike Piazza	50.00	22.00	6.25
☐	7 Kirby Puckett	35.00	16.00	4.40
☐	8 Mo Vaughn	25.00	11.00	3.10
☐	9 Frank Thomas	120.00	55.00	15.00
☐	10 Jeff Bagwell	35.00	16.00	4.40
☐	11 Matt Williams	25.00	11.00	3.10
☐	12 Jose Canseco	25.00	11.00	3.10
☐	13 Raul Mondesi	25.00	11.00	3.10
☐	14 Manny Ramirez	50.00	22.00	6.25
☐	15 Cecil Fielder	15.00	6.75	1.85
☐	16 Cal Ripken, Jr.	140.00	65.00	17.50

1992 Pinnacle

The 1992 Score Pinnacle baseball set consists of two series each with 310 cards measuring the standard size (2 1/2" by 3 1/2"). Series I count goods pack had 16 cards per pack, while the cello pack featured 27 cards. Two 12-card bonus subsets, displaying the artwork of Chris Greco, were randomly inserted in series I and II count good packs. The fronts feature glossy color player photos, on a black background accented by thin white borders. On a black background, the horizontally oriented backs carry a close-up portrait, statistics (1991 and career), and an in-depth player profile. An anti-counterfeit device appears in the bottom border of each card back. Special subsets featured include '92 Rookie Prospects (52, 55, 168, 247-261, 263-280), Idols (281-286), Sidelines (287-294), Draft Picks (295-304), Shades (305-310), Idols (584-591), Sidelines (592-596), Shades (601-605), Grips (606-612), and Technicians (614-620). The cards are numbered on the back. Rookie Cards in the set include Chad Curtis, Cliff Floyd, Benji Gil, Tyler Green, Bobby Jones, Pat Listach, Manny Ramirez, Scott Ruffcorn, Al Shirley, Allen Watson, and Bob Zupcic.

	MINT	NRMT	EXC
COMPLETE SET (620)	40.00	18.00	5.00
COMPLETE SERIES 1 (310)	25.00	11.00	3.10
COMPLETE SERIES 2 (310)	15.00	6.75	1.85
COMMON CARD (1-310)	.10	.05	.01
COMMON CARD (311-620)	.10	.05	.01

		MINT	NRMT	EXC
☐	1 Frank Thomas	3.00	1.35	.35
☐	2 Benito Santiago	.10	.05	.01
☐	3 Carlos Baerga	.60	.25	.07
☐	4 Cecil Fielder	.25	.11	.03
☐	5 Barry Larkin	.30	.14	.04
☐	6 Ozzie Smith	.40	.18	.05
☐	7 Willie McGee	.15	.07	.02
☐	8 Paul Molitor	.25	.11	.03
☐	9 Andy Van Slyke	.15	.07	.02
☐	10 Ryne Sandberg	.50	.23	.06
☐	11 Kevin Seitzer	.10	.05	.01
☐	12 Len Dykstra	.25	.11	.03
☐	13 Edgar Martinez	.25	.11	.03
☐	14 Ruben Sierra	.25	.11	.03
☐	15 Howard Johnson	.10	.05	.01
☐	16 Dave Henderson	.10	.05	.01

□	No.	Player			
□	17	Devon White	.15	.07	.02
□	18	Terry Pendleton	.25	.11	.03
□	19	Steve Finley	.15	.07	.02
□	20	Kirby Puckett	.60	.25	.07
□	21	Orel Hershiser	.25	.11	.03
□	22	Hal Morris	.15	.07	.02
□	23	Don Mattingly	1.00	.45	.12
□	24	Delino DeShields	.15	.07	.02
□	25	Dennis Eckersley	.25	.11	.03
□	26	Ellis Burks	.15	.07	.02
□	27	Jay Buhner	.25	.11	.03
□	28	Matt Williams	.40	.18	.05
□	29	Lou Whitaker	.25	.11	.03
□	30	Alex Fernandez	.25	.11	.03
□	31	Albert Belle	1.00	.45	.12
□	32	Todd Zeile	.15	.07	.02
□	33	Tony Pena	.10	.05	.01
□	34	Jay Bell	.15	.07	.02
□	35	Rafael Palmeiro	.25	.11	.03
□	36	Wes Chamberlain	.10	.05	.01
□	37	George Bell	.10	.05	.01
□	38	Robin Yount	.30	.14	.04
□	39	Vince Coleman	.10	.05	.01
□	40	Bruce Hurst	.10	.05	.01
□	41	Harold Baines	.25	.11	.03
□	42	Chuck Finley	.10	.05	.01
□	43	Ken Caminiti	.25	.11	.03
□	44	Ben McDonald	.15	.07	.02
□	45	Roberto Alomar	.40	.18	.05
□	46	Chili Davis	.25	.11	.03
□	47	Bill Doran	.10	.05	.01
□	48	Jerald Clark	.10	.05	.01
□	49	Jose Lind	.10	.05	.01
□	50	Nolan Ryan	1.50	.70	.19
□	51	Phil Plantier	.15	.07	.02
□	52	Gary DiSarcina	.10	.05	.01
□	53	Kevin Bass	.10	.05	.01
□	54	Pat Kelly	.10	.05	.01
□	55	Mark Wohlers	.15	.07	.02
□	56	Walt Weiss	.10	.05	.01
□	57	Lenny Harris	.10	.05	.01
□	58	Ivan Calderon	.10	.05	.01
□	59	Harold Reynolds	.10	.05	.01
□	60	George Brett	.75	.35	.09
□	61	Gregg Olson	.10	.05	.01
□	62	Orlando Merced	.10	.05	.01
□	63	Steve Decker	.10	.05	.01
□	64	John Franco	.25	.11	.03
□	65	Greg Maddux	1.50	.70	.19
□	66	Alex Cole	.10	.05	.01
□	67	Dave Hollins	.10	.05	.01
□	68	Kent Hrbek	.15	.07	.02
□	69	Tom Pagnozzi	.10	.05	.01
□	70	Jeff Bagwell	1.00	.45	.12
□	71	Jim Gantner	.10	.05	.01
□	72	Matt Nokes	.10	.05	.01
□	73	Brian Harper	.10	.05	.01
□	74	Andy Benes	.15	.07	.02
□	75	Tom Glavine	.25	.11	.03
□	76	Terry Steinbach	.15	.07	.02
□	77	Dennis Martinez	.15	.07	.02
□	78	John Olerud	.15	.07	.02
□	79	Ozzie Guillen	.15	.07	.02
□	80	Darryl Strawberry	.15	.07	.02
□	81	Gary Gaetti	.10	.05	.01
□	82	Dave Righetti	.10	.05	.01
□	83	Chris Hoiles	.15	.07	.02
□	84	Andujar Cedeno	.10	.05	.01
□	85	Jack Clark	.15	.07	.02
□	86	David Howard	.10	.05	.01
□	87	Bill Gullickson	.10	.05	.01
□	88	Bernard Gilkey	.15	.07	.02
□	89	Kevin Elster	.10	.05	.01
□	90	Kevin Maas	.10	.05	.01
□	91	Mark Lewis	.10	.05	.01
□	92	Greg Vaughn	.15	.07	.02
□	93	Bret Barberie	.10	.05	.01
□	94	Dave Smith	.10	.05	.01
□	95	Roger Clemens	.30	.14	.04
□	96	Doug Drabek	.15	.07	.02
□	97	Omar Vizquel	.10	.05	.01
□	98	Jose Guzman	.10	.05	.01
□	99	Juan Samuel	.10	.05	.01
□	100	Dave Justice	.30	.14	.04
□	101	Tom Browning	.10	.05	.01
□	102	Mark Gubicza	.10	.05	.01
□	103	Mickey Morandini	.10	.05	.01
□	104	Ed Whitson	.10	.05	.01
□	105	Lance Parrish	.15	.07	.02
□	106	Scott Erickson	.10	.05	.01
□	107	Jack McDowell	.25	.11	.03
□	108	Dave Stieb	.10	.05	.01
□	109	Mike Moore	.10	.05	.01
□	110	Travis Fryman	.25	.11	.03
□	111	Dwight Gooden	.10	.05	.01
□	112	Fred McGriff	.30	.14	.04
□	113	Alan Trammell	.25	.11	.03
□	114	Roberto Kelly	.15	.07	.02
□	115	Andre Dawson	.25	.11	.03
□	116	Bill Landrum	.10	.05	.01
□	117	Brian McRae	.25	.11	.03
□	118	B.J. Surhoff	.10	.05	.01
□	119	Chuck Knoblauch	.30	.14	.04
□	120	Steve Olin	.10	.05	.01
□	121	Robin Ventura	.25	.11	.03
□	122	Will Clark	.30	.14	.04
□	123	Tino Martinez	.25	.11	.03
□	124	Dale Murphy	.25	.11	.03
□	125	Pete O'Brien	.10	.05	.01
□	126	Ray Lankford	.25	.11	.03
□	127	Juan Gonzalez	.75	.35	.09
□	128	Ron Gant	.25	.11	.03
□	129	Marquis Grissom	.25	.11	.03
□	130	Jose Canseco	.30	.14	.04
□	131	Mike Greenwell	.25	.11	.03
□	132	Mark Langston	.25	.11	.03
□	133	Brett Butler	.25	.11	.03
□	134	Kelly Gruber	.10	.05	.01
□	135	Chris Sabo	.10	.05	.01
□	136	Mark Grace	.25	.11	.03
□	137	Tony Fernandez	.10	.05	.01
□	138	Glenn Davis	.10	.05	.01
□	139	Pedro Munoz	.15	.07	.02
□	140	Craig Biggio	.25	.11	.03
□	141	Pete Schourek	.15	.07	.02
□	142	Mike Boddicker	.10	.05	.01
□	143	Robby Thompson	.15	.07	.02
□	144	Mel Hall	.10	.05	.01
□	145	Bryan Harvey	.10	.05	.01
□	146	Mike LaValliere	.10	.05	.01
□	147	John Kruk	.25	.11	.03
□	148	Joe Carter	.25	.11	.03
□	149	Greg Olson	.10	.05	.01
□	150	Julio Franco	.15	.07	.02
□	151	Darryl Hamilton	.15	.07	.02
□	152	Felix Fermin	.10	.05	.01
□	153	Jose Offerman	.15	.07	.02
□	154	Paul O'Neill	.25	.11	.03
□	155	Tommy Greene	.10	.05	.01
□	156	Ivan Rodriguez	.25	.11	.03
□	157	Dave Stewart	.25	.11	.03
□	158	Jeff Reardon	.15	.07	.02

☐ 159	Felix Jose	.10	.05	.01
☐ 160	Doug Dascenzo	.10	.05	.01
☐ 161	Tim Wallach	.10	.05	.01
☐ 162	Dan Plesac	.10	.05	.01
☐ 163	Luis Gonzalez	.15	.07	.02
☐ 164	Mike Henneman	.10	.05	.01
☐ 165	Mike Devereaux	.15	.07	.02
☐ 166	Luis Polonia	.10	.05	.01
☐ 167	Mike Sharperson	.10	.05	.01
☐ 168	Chris Donnels	.10	.05	.01
☐ 169	Greg W. Harris	.10	.05	.01
☐ 170	Deion Sanders	.40	.18	.05
☐ 171	Mike Schooler	.10	.05	.01
☐ 172	Jose DeJesus	.10	.05	.01
☐ 173	Jeff Montgomery	.15	.07	.02
☐ 174	Milt Cuyler	.10	.05	.01
☐ 175	Wade Boggs	.25	.11	.03
☐ 176	Kevin Tapani	.10	.05	.01
☐ 177	Bill Spiers	.10	.05	.01
☐ 178	Tim Raines	.25	.11	.03
☐ 179	Randy Milligan	.10	.05	.01
☐ 180	Rob Dibble	.10	.05	.01
☐ 181	Kirt Manwaring	.10	.05	.01
☐ 182	Pascual Perez	.10	.05	.01
☐ 183	Juan Guzman	.15	.07	.02
☐ 184	John Smiley	.10	.05	.01
☐ 185	David Segui	.10	.05	.01
☐ 186	Omar Olivares	.10	.05	.01
☐ 187	Joe Slusarski	.10	.05	.01
☐ 188	Erik Hanson	.10	.05	.01
☐ 189	Mark Portugal	.10	.05	.01
☐ 190	Walt Terrell	.10	.05	.01
☐ 191	John Smoltz	.25	.11	.03
☐ 192	Wilson Alvarez	.15	.07	.02
☐ 193	Jimmy Key	.15	.07	.02
☐ 194	Larry Walker	.30	.14	.04
☐ 195	Lee Smith	.25	.11	.03
☐ 196	Pete Harnisch	.15	.07	.02
☐ 197	Mike Harkey	.10	.05	.01
☐ 198	Frank Tanana	.10	.05	.01
☐ 199	Terry Mulholland	.10	.05	.01
☐ 200	Cal Ripken	2.00	.90	.25
☐ 201	Dave Magadan	.10	.05	.01
☐ 202	Bud Black	.10	.05	.01
☐ 203	Terry Shumpert	.10	.05	.01
☐ 204	Mike Mussina	.50	.23	.06
☐ 205	Mo Vaughn	.75	.35	.09
☐ 206	Steve Farr	.10	.05	.01
☐ 207	Darrin Jackson	.10	.05	.01
☐ 208	Jerry Browne	.10	.05	.01
☐ 209	Jeff Russell	.10	.05	.01
☐ 210	Mike Scioscia	.10	.05	.01
☐ 211	Rick Aguilera	.15	.07	.02
☐ 212	Jaime Navarro	.10	.05	.01
☐ 213	Randy Tomlin	.10	.05	.01
☐ 214	Bobby Thigpen	.10	.05	.01
☐ 215	Mark Gardner	.10	.05	.01
☐ 216	Norm Charlton	.10	.05	.01
☐ 217	Mark McGwire	.15	.07	.02
☐ 218	Skeeter Barnes	.10	.05	.01
☐ 219	Bob Tewksbury	.10	.05	.01
☐ 220	Junior Felix	.10	.05	.01
☐ 221	Sam Horn	.10	.05	.01
☐ 222	Jody Reed	.10	.05	.01
☐ 223	Luis Sojo	.10	.05	.01
☐ 224	Jerome Walton	.10	.05	.01
☐ 225	Darryl Kile	.10	.05	.01
☐ 226	Mickey Tettleton	.15	.07	.02
☐ 227	Dan Pasqua	.10	.05	.01
☐ 228	Jim Gott	.10	.05	.01
☐ 229	Bernie Williams	.25	.11	.03
☐ 230	Shane Mack	.10	.05	.01
☐ 231	Steve Avery	.25	.11	.03
☐ 232	Dave Valle	.10	.05	.01
☐ 233	Mark Leonard	.10	.05	.01
☐ 234	Spike Owen	.10	.05	.01
☐ 235	Gary Sheffield	.25	.11	.03
☐ 236	Steve Chitren	.10	.05	.01
☐ 237	Zane Smith	.10	.05	.01
☐ 238	Tom Gordon	.15	.07	.02
☐ 239	Jose Oquendo	.10	.05	.01
☐ 240	Todd Stottlemyre	.10	.05	.01
☐ 241	Darren Daulton	.25	.11	.03
☐ 242	Tim Naehring	.15	.07	.02
☐ 243	Tony Phillips	.25	.11	.03
☐ 244	Shawon Dunston	.10	.05	.01
☐ 245	Manuel Lee	.10	.05	.01
☐ 246	Mike Pagliarulo	.10	.05	.01
☐ 247	Jim Thome	1.50	.70	.19
☐ 248	Luis Mercedes	.10	.05	.01
☐ 249	Cal Eldred	.10	.05	.01
☐ 250	Derek Bell	.15	.07	.02
☐ 251	Arthur Rhodes	.10	.05	.01
☐ 252	Scott Cooper	.15	.07	.02
☐ 253	Roberto Hernandez	.15	.07	.02
☐ 254	Mo Sanford	.10	.05	.01
☐ 255	Scott Servais	.10	.05	.01
☐ 256	Eric Karros	.50	.23	.06
☐ 257	Andy Mota	.10	.05	.01
☐ 258	Keith Mitchell	.10	.05	.01
☐ 259	Joel Johnston	.10	.05	.01
☐ 260	John Wehner	.10	.05	.01
☐ 261	Gino Minutelli	.10	.05	.01
☐ 262	Greg Gagne	.10	.05	.01
☐ 263	Stan Royer	.10	.05	.01
☐ 264	Carlos Garcia	.15	.07	.02
☐ 265	Andy Ashby	.10	.05	.01
☐ 266	Kim Batiste	.10	.05	.01
☐ 267	Julio Valera	.10	.05	.01
☐ 268	Royce Clayton	.15	.07	.02
☐ 269	Gary Scott	.10	.05	.01
☐ 270	Kirk Dressendorfer	.10	.05	.01
☐ 271	Sean Berry	.15	.07	.02
☐ 272	Lance Dickson	.10	.05	.01
☐ 273	Rob Maurer	.10	.05	.01
☐ 274	Scott Brosius	.10	.05	.01
☐ 275	Dave Fleming	.10	.05	.01
☐ 276	Lenny Webster	.10	.05	.01
☐ 277	Mike Humphreys	.10	.05	.01
☐ 278	Freddie Benavides	.10	.05	.01
☐ 279	Harvey Pulliam	.10	.05	.01
☐ 280	Jeff Carter	.10	.05	.01
☐ 281	Jim Abbott I	.50	.23	.06
	Nolan Ryan			
☐ 282	Wade Boggs I	.40	.18	.05
	George Brett			
☐ 283	Ken Griffey Jr. I	.75	.35	.09
	Rickey Henderson			
☐ 284	Wally Joyner I	.15	.07	.02
	Dale Murphy			
☐ 285	Chuck Knoblauch I	.25	.11	.03
	Ozzie Smith			
☐ 286	Robin Ventura I	.50	.23	.06
	Lou Gehrig			
☐ 287	Robin Yount SIDE	.15	.07	.02
☐ 288	Bob Tewksbury SIDE	.10	.05	.01
☐ 289	Kirby Puckett SIDE	.30	.14	.04
☐ 290	Kenny Lofton SIDE	1.25	.55	.16
☐ 291	Jack McDowell SIDE	.15	.07	.02
☐ 292	John Burkett SIDE	.15	.07	.02
☐ 293	Dwight Smith SIDE	.10	.05	.01
☐ 294	Nolan Ryan SIDE	.75	.35	.09

☐ 295	Manny Ramirez DP 6.00	2.70	.75
☐ 296	Cliff Floyd DP UER .... .75	.35	.09
	(Throws right, not left as		
	indicated on back)		
☐ 297	Al Shirley DP................ .20	.09	.03
☐ 298	Brian Barber DP............ .20	.09	.03
☐ 299	Jon Farrell DP............... .10	.05	.01
☐ 300	Scott Ruffcorn DP......... .15	.07	.02
☐ 301	Tyrone Hill DP.............. .15	.07	.02
☐ 302	Benji Gil DP................. .50	.23	.06
☐ 303	Tyler Green DP............. .15	.07	.02
☐ 304	Allen Watson DP .... .20	.09	.03
☐ 305	Jay Buhner SH .... .25	.11	.03
☐ 306	Roberto Alomar SH........ .20	.09	.03
☐ 307	Chuck Knoblauch SH.... .15	.07	.02
☐ 308	Darryl Strawberry SH.... .15	.07	.02
☐ 309	Danny Tartabull SH....... .10	.05	.01
☐ 310	Bobby Bonilla SH.......... .15	.07	.02
☐ 311	Mike Felder.................. .10	.05	.01
☐ 312	Storm Davis.................. .10	.05	.01
☐ 313	Tim Teufel.................... .10	.05	.01
☐ 314	Tom Brunansky............. .10	.05	.01
☐ 315	Rex Hudler................... .10	.05	.01
☐ 316	Dave Otto .... .10	.05	.01
☐ 317	Jeff King..................... .15	.07	.02
☐ 318	Dan Gladden .... .10	.05	.01
☐ 319	Bill Pecota .... .10	.05	.01
☐ 320	Franklin Stubbs............ .10	.05	.01
☐ 321	Gary Carter.................. .25	.11	.03
☐ 322	Melido Perez................ .10	.05	.01
☐ 323	Eric Davis.................... .10	.05	.01
☐ 324	Greg Myers................... .10	.05	.01
☐ 325	Pete Incaviglia............. .10	.05	.01
☐ 326	Von Hayes .... .10	.05	.01
☐ 327	Greg Swindell............... .10	.05	.01
☐ 328	Steve Sax .... .10	.05	.01
☐ 329	Chuck McElroy.............. .10	.05	.01
☐ 330	Gregg Jefferies .... .25	.11	.03
☐ 331	Joe Oliver.................... .10	.05	.01
☐ 332	Paul Faries.................. .10	.05	.01
☐ 333	David West................... .10	.05	.01
☐ 334	Craig Grebeck............... .10	.05	.01
☐ 335	Chris Hammond............. .10	.05	.01
☐ 336	Billy Ripken .... .10	.05	.01
☐ 337	Scott Sanderson............ .10	.05	.01
☐ 338	Dick Schofield .... .10	.05	.01
☐ 339	Bob Milacki................. .10	.05	.01
☐ 340	Kevin Reimer................ .10	.05	.01
☐ 341	Jose DeLeon .... .10	.05	.01
☐ 342	Henry Cotto.................. .10	.05	.01
☐ 343	Daryl Boston .... .10	.05	.01
☐ 344	Kevin Gross.................. .10	.05	.01
☐ 345	Milt Thompson.............. .10	.05	.01
☐ 346	Luis Rivera................... .10	.05	.01
☐ 347	Al Osuna...................... .10	.05	.01
☐ 348	Rob Deer...................... .10	.05	.01
☐ 349	Tim Leary..................... .10	.05	.01
☐ 350	Mike Stanton................ .10	.05	.01
☐ 351	Dean Palmer................. .15	.07	.02
☐ 352	Trevor Wilson .... .10	.05	.01
☐ 353	Mark Eichhorn............... .10	.05	.01
☐ 354	Scott Aldred .... .10	.05	.01
☐ 355	Mark Whiten .... .15	.07	.02
☐ 356	Leo Gomez.................... .10	.05	.01
☐ 357	Rafael Belliard.............. .10	.05	.01
☐ 358	Carlos Quintana .... .10	.05	.01
☐ 359	Mark Davis................... .10	.05	.01
☐ 360	Chris Nabholz .... .10	.05	.01
☐ 361	Carlton Fisk................. .25	.11	.03
☐ 362	Joe Orsulak.................. .10	.05	.01
☐ 363	Eric Anthony .... .10	.05	.01
☐ 364	Greg Hibbard .... .10	.05	.01
☐ 365	Scott Leius................... .10	.05	.01
☐ 366	Hensley Meulens........... .10	.05	.01
☐ 367	Chris Bosio.................. .10	.05	.01
☐ 368	Brian Downing .... .10	.05	.01
☐ 369	Sammy Sosa.................. .30	.14	.04
☐ 370	Stan Belinda................ .10	.05	.01
☐ 371	Joe Grahe.................... .10	.05	.01
☐ 372	Luis Salazar................. .10	.05	.01
☐ 373	Lance Johnson .... .10	.05	.01
☐ 374	Kal Daniels.................. .10	.05	.01
☐ 375	Dave Winfield............... .15	.07	.02
☐ 376	Brook Jacoby .... .10	.05	.01
☐ 377	Mariano Duncan .... .10	.05	.01
☐ 378	Ron Darling.................. .10	.05	.01
☐ 379	Randy Johnson.............. .50	.23	.06
☐ 380	Chito Martinez.............. .10	.05	.01
☐ 381	Andres Galarraga........... .25	.11	.03
☐ 382	Willie Randolph............ .15	.07	.02
☐ 383	Charles Nagy................ .15	.07	.02
☐ 384	Tim Belcher................. .10	.05	.01
☐ 385	Duane Ward .... .10	.05	.01
☐ 386	Vicente Palacios........... .10	.05	.01
☐ 387	Mike Gallego .... .10	.05	.01
☐ 388	Rich DeLucia................ .10	.05	.01
☐ 389	Scott Radinsky.............. .10	.05	.01
☐ 390	Damon Berryhill............ .10	.05	.01
☐ 391	Kirk McCaskill.............. .10	.05	.01
☐ 392	Pedro Guerrero.............. .10	.05	.01
☐ 393	Kevin Mitchell .... .15	.07	.02
☐ 394	Dickie Thon .... .10	.05	.01
☐ 395	Bobby Bonilla............... .25	.11	.03
☐ 396	Bill Wegman................. .10	.05	.01
☐ 397	Dave Martinez............... .10	.05	.01
☐ 398	Rick Sutcliffe............... .15	.07	.02
☐ 399	Larry Andersen.............. .10	.05	.01
☐ 400	Tony Gwynn................... .60	.25	.07
☐ 401	Rickey Henderson.......... .25	.11	.03
☐ 402	Greg Cadaret................ .10	.05	.01
☐ 403	Keith Miller .... .10	.05	.01
☐ 404	Bip Roberts.................. .15	.07	.02
☐ 405	Kevin Brown .... .15	.07	.02
☐ 406	Mitch Williams.............. .15	.07	.02
☐ 407	Frank Viola .... .10	.05	.01
☐ 408	Darren Lewis................ .15	.07	.02
☐ 409	Bob Welch .... .10	.05	.01
☐ 410	Bob Walk .... .10	.05	.01
☐ 411	Todd Frohwirth.............. .10	.05	.01
☐ 412	Brian Hunter .... .10	.05	.01
☐ 413	Ron Karkovice............... .10	.05	.01
☐ 414	Mike Morgan................. .10	.05	.01
☐ 415	Joe Hesketh................. .10	.05	.01
☐ 416	Don Slaught.................. .10	.05	.01
☐ 417	Tom Henke .... .15	.07	.02
☐ 418	Kurt Stillwell............... .10	.05	.01
☐ 419	Hector Villanueva.......... .10	.05	.01
☐ 420	Glenallen Hill.............. .10	.05	.01
☐ 421	Pat Borders.................. .10	.05	.01
☐ 422	Charlie Hough............... .15	.07	.02
☐ 423	Charlie Leibrandt.......... .10	.05	.01
☐ 424	Eddie Murray................ .30	.14	.04
☐ 425	Jesse Barfield .... .10	.05	.01
☐ 426	Mark Lemke.................. .10	.05	.01
☐ 427	Kevin McReynolds.......... .10	.05	.01
☐ 428	Gilberto Reyes .... .10	.05	.01
☐ 429	Ramon Martinez .... .25	.11	.03
☐ 430	Steve Buechele............. .10	.05	.01
☐ 431	David Wells.................. .15	.07	.02
☐ 432	Kyle Abbott.................. .10	.05	.01
☐ 433	John Habyan................. .10	.05	.01
☐ 434	Kevin Appier................. .15	.07	.02

□	435	Gene Larkin	.10	.05	.01
□	436	Sandy Alomar Jr.	.15	.07	.02
□	437	Mike Jackson	.10	.05	.01
□	438	Todd Benzinger	.10	.05	.01
□	439	Teddy Higuera	.10	.05	.01
□	440	Reggie Sanders	.40	.18	.05
□	441	Mark Carreon	.10	.05	.01
□	442	Bret Saberhagen	.25	.11	.03
□	443	Gene Nelson	.10	.05	.01
□	444	Jay Howell	.10	.05	.01
□	445	Roger McDowell	.10	.05	.01
□	446	Sid Bream	.10	.05	.01
□	447	Mackey Sasser	.10	.05	.01
□	448	Bill Swift	.10	.05	.01
□	449	Hubie Brooks	.10	.05	.01
□	450	David Cone	.25	.11	.03
□	451	Bobby Witt	.10	.05	.01
□	452	Brady Anderson	.15	.07	.02
□	453	Lee Stevens	.10	.05	.01
□	454	Luis Aquino	.10	.05	.01
□	455	Carney Lansford	.15	.07	.02
□	456	Carlos Hernandez	.10	.05	.01
□	457	Danny Jackson	.10	.05	.01
□	458	Gerald Young	.10	.05	.01
□	459	Tom Candiotti	.10	.05	.01
□	460	Billy Hatcher	.10	.05	.01
□	461	John Wetteland	.10	.05	.01
□	462	Mike Bordick	.10	.05	.01
□	463	Don Robinson	.10	.05	.01
□	464	Jeff Johnson	.10	.05	.01
□	465	Lonnie Smith	.10	.05	.01
□	466	Paul Assenmacher	.10	.05	.01
□	467	Alvin Davis	.10	.05	.01
□	468	Jim Eisenreich	.10	.05	.01
□	469	Brent Mayne	.10	.05	.01
□	470	Jeff Brantley	.10	.05	.01
□	471	Tim Burke	.10	.05	.01
□	472	Pat Mahomes	.10	.05	.01
□	473	Ryan Bowen	.10	.05	.01
□	474	Bryn Smith	.10	.05	.01
□	475	Mike Flanagan	.10	.05	.01
□	476	Reggie Jefferson	.10	.05	.01
□	477	Jeff Blauser	.15	.07	.02
□	478	Craig Lefferts	.10	.05	.01
□	479	Todd Worrell	.10	.05	.01
□	480	Scott Scudder	.10	.05	.01
□	481	Kirk Gibson	.25	.11	.03
□	482	Kenny Rogers	.10	.05	.01
□	483	Jack Morris	.25	.11	.03
□	484	Russ Swan	.10	.05	.01
□	485	Mike Huff	.10	.05	.01
□	486	Ken Hill	.25	.11	.03
□	487	Geronimo Pena	.10	.05	.01
□	488	Charlie O'Brien	.10	.05	.01
□	489	Mike Maddux	.10	.05	.01
□	490	Scott Livingstone	.10	.05	.01
□	491	Carl Willis	.10	.05	.01
□	492	Kelly Downs	.10	.05	.01
□	493	Dennis Cook	.10	.05	.01
□	494	Joe Magrane	.10	.05	.01
□	495	Bob Kipper	.10	.05	.01
□	496	Jose Mesa	.10	.05	.01
□	497	Charlie Hayes	.15	.07	.02
□	498	Joe Girardi	.10	.05	.01
□	499	Doug Jones	.10	.05	.01
□	500	Barry Bonds	.50	.23	.06
□	501	Bill Krueger	.10	.05	.01
□	502	Glenn Braggs	.10	.05	.01
□	503	Eric King	.10	.05	.01
□	504	Frank Castillo	.10	.05	.01
□	505	Mike Gardiner	.10	.05	.01
□	506	Cory Snyder	.10	.05	.01
□	507	Steve Howe	.10	.05	.01
□	508	Jose Rijo	.15	.07	.02
□	509	Sid Fernandez	.15	.07	.02
□	510	Archi Cianfrocco	.10	.05	.01
□	511	Mark Guthrie	.10	.05	.01
□	512	Bob Ojeda	.10	.05	.01
□	513	John Doherty	.10	.05	.01
□	514	Dante Bichette	.30	.14	.04
□	515	Juan Berenguer	.10	.05	.01
□	516	Jeff M. Robinson	.10	.05	.01
□	517	Mike Macfarlane	.10	.05	.01
□	518	Matt Young	.10	.05	.01
□	519	Otis Nixon	.10	.05	.01
□	520	Brian Holman	.10	.05	.01
□	521	Chris Haney	.10	.05	.01
□	522	Jeff Kent	.30	.14	.04
□	523	Chad Curtis	.40	.18	.05
□	524	Vince Horsman	.10	.05	.01
□	525	Rod Nichols	.10	.05	.01
□	526	Peter Hoy	.10	.05	.01
□	527	Shawn Boskie	.10	.05	.01
□	528	Alejandro Pena	.10	.05	.01
□	529	Dave Burba	.10	.05	.01
□	530	Ricky Jordan	.10	.05	.01
□	531	Dave Silvestri	.10	.05	.01
□	532	John Patterson UER	.10	.05	.01
		(Listed as being born in 1960; should be 1967)			
□	533	Jeff Branson	.10	.05	.01
□	534	Derrick May	.15	.07	.02
□	535	Esteban Beltre	.10	.05	.01
□	536	Jose Melendez	.10	.05	.01
□	537	Wally Joyner	.25	.11	.03
□	538	Eddie Taubensee	.10	.05	.01
□	539	Jim Abbott	.25	.11	.03
□	540	Brian Williams	.10	.05	.01
□	541	Donovan Osborne	.10	.05	.01
□	542	Patrick Lennon	.10	.05	.01
□	543	Mike Groppuso	.10	.05	.01
□	544	Jarvis Brown	.10	.05	.01
□	545	Shawn Livsey	.10	.05	.01
□	546	Jeff Ware	.10	.05	.01
□	547	Danny Tartabull	.15	.07	.02
□	548	Bobby Jones	.60	.25	.07
□	549	Ken Griffey Jr.	3.00	1.35	.35
□	550	Rey Sanchez	.10	.05	.01
□	551	Pedro Astacio	.15	.07	.02
□	552	Juan Guerrero	.10	.05	.01
□	553	Jacob Brumfield	.10	.05	.01
□	554	Ben Rivera	.10	.05	.01
□	555	Brian Jordan	.50	.23	.06
□	556	Denny Neagle	.10	.05	.01
□	557	Cliff Brantley	.10	.05	.01
□	558	Anthony Young	.10	.05	.01
□	559	John Vander Wal	.10	.05	.01
□	560	Monty Fariss	.10	.05	.01
□	561	Russ Springer	.10	.05	.01
□	562	Pat Listach	.15	.07	.02
□	563	Pat Hentgen	.25	.11	.03
□	564	Andy Stankiewicz	.10	.05	.01
□	565	Mike Perez	.10	.05	.01
□	566	Mike Bielecki	.10	.05	.01
□	567	Butch Henry	.15	.07	.02
□	568	Dave Nilsson	.10	.05	.01
□	569	Scott Hatteberg	.10	.05	.01
□	570	Ruben Amaro Jr.	.10	.05	.01
□	571	Todd Hundley	.10	.05	.01
□	572	Moises Alou	.25	.11	.03
□	573	Hector Fajardo	.10	.05	.01
□	574	Todd Van Poppel	.15	.07	.02

☐ 575	Willie Banks	.10	.05	.01
☐ 576	Bob Zupcic	.10	.05	.01
☐ 577	J.J. Johnson	.20	.09	.03
☐ 578	John Burkett	.15	.07	.02
☐ 579	Trever Miller	.10	.05	.01
☐ 580	Scott Bankhead	.10	.05	.01
☐ 581	Rich Amaral	.10	.05	.01
☐ 582	Kenny Lofton	2.50	1.10	.30
☐ 583	Matt Stairs	.10	.05	.01
☐ 584	Don Mattingly	.40	.18	.05
	Rod Carew IDOLS			
☐ 585	Steve Avery	.15	.07	.02
	Jack Morris IDOLS			
☐ 586	Roberto Alomar	.20	.09	.03
	Sandy Alomar SR. IDOLS			
☐ 587	Scott Sanderson	.10	.05	.01
	Catfish Hunter IDOLS			
☐ 588	Dave Justice	.20	.09	.03
	Willie Stargell IDOLS			
☐ 589	Rex Hudler	.25	.11	.03
	Roger Staubach IDOLS			
☐ 590	David Cone	.25	.11	.03
	Jackie Gleason IDOLS			
☐ 591	Tony Gwynn	.20	.09	.03
	Willie Davis IDOLS			
☐ 592	Orel Hershiser SIDE	.15	.07	.02
☐ 593	John Wetteland SIDE	.10	.05	.01
☐ 594	Tom Glavine SIDE	.15	.07	.02
☐ 595	Randy Johnson SIDE	.25	.11	.03
☐ 596	Jim Gott SIDE	.10	.05	.01
☐ 597	Donald Harris	.10	.05	.01
☐ 598	Shawn Hare	.10	.05	.01
☐ 599	Chris Gardner	.10	.05	.01
☐ 600	Rusty Meacham	.10	.05	.01
☐ 601	Benito Santiago	.10	.05	.01
☐ 602	Eric Davis SHADE	.10	.05	.01
☐ 603	Jose Lind SHADE	.10	.05	.01
☐ 604	Dave Justice SHADE	.20	.09	.03
☐ 605	Tim Raines SHADE	.25	.11	.03
☐ 606	Randy Tomlin GRIP	.10	.05	.01
☐ 607	Jack McDowell GRIP	.15	.07	.02
☐ 608	Greg Maddux GRIP	.60	.25	.07
☐ 609	Charles Nagy GRIP	.15	.07	.02
☐ 610	Tom Candiotti GRIP	.10	.05	.01
☐ 611	David Cone GRIP	.15	.07	.02
☐ 612	Steve Avery GRIP	.15	.07	.02
☐ 613	Rod Beck GRIP	.50	.23	.06
☐ 614	Rickey Henderson TECH	.25	.11	.03
☐ 615	Benito Santiago TECH	.10	.05	.01
☐ 616	Ruben Sierra TECH	.15	.07	.02
☐ 617	Ryne Sandberg TECH	.25	.11	.03
☐ 618	Nolan Ryan TECH	.75	.35	.09
☐ 619	Brett Butler TECH	.15	.07	.02
☐ 620	Dave Justice TECH	.20	.09	.03

1992 Pinnacle Rookie Idols

This 18-card insert set is a spin-off on the Idols subset featured in the regular series. The set features full-bleed color photos of 18 rookies along with their pick of sports figures or other individuals who had the greatest impact on their careers. The standard-size (2 1/2" by 3 1/2") cards were randomly inserted in Series II wax packs. Both sides of the cards are horizontally oriented.

The fronts carry a close-up photo of the rookie superimposed on an action game shot of his idol. On a background that shades from white to light blue, the backs feature text comparing the two players flanked by a color photo of each player. The cards are numbered on the back.

		MINT	NRMT	EXC
COMPLETE SET (18)		140.00	65.00	17.50
COMMON PAIR (1-18)		3.00	1.35	.35
☐ 1	Reggie Sanders and Eric Davis	8.00	3.60	1.00
☐ 2	Hector Fajardo and Jim Abbott	3.00	1.35	.35
☐ 3	Gary Cooper and George Brett	15.00	6.75	1.85
☐ 4	Mark Wohlers and Roger Clemens	10.00	4.50	1.25
☐ 5	Luis Mercedes and Julio Franco	3.00	1.35	.35
☐ 6	Willie Banks and Doc Gooden	3.00	1.35	.35
☐ 7	Kenny Lofton and Rickey Henderson	30.00	13.50	3.70
☐ 8	Keith Mitchell and Dave Henderson	3.00	1.35	.35
☐ 9	Kim Batiste and Barry Larkin	6.00	2.70	.75
☐ 10	Todd Hundley and Thurman Munson	4.00	1.80	.50
☐ 11	Eddie Zosky and Cal Ripken	30.00	13.50	3.70
☐ 12	Todd Van Poppel and Nolan Ryan	25.00	11.00	3.10
☐ 13	Jim Thome and Ryne Sandberg	25.00	11.00	3.10
☐ 14	Dave Fleming and Bobby Murcer	3.00	1.35	.35
☐ 15	Royce Clayton and Ozzie Smith	8.00	3.60	1.00
☐ 16	Donald Harris and Darryl Strawberry	3.00	1.35	.35
☐ 17	Chad Curtis and Alan Trammell	5.00	2.20	.60
☐ 18	Derek Bell and Dave Winfield	8.00	3.60	1.00

1992 Pinnacle Team 2000

This 80-card standard-size (2 1/2" by 3 1/2") set focuses on young players who will

be still be stars in the year 2000. Cards 1-40 were inserted in Series 1 jumbo packs while cards 41-80 were featured in Series 2 jumbo packs. The fronts features action color player photos. The cards are bordered by a 1/2" black stripe that runs along the left edge and bottom forming a right angle. The two ends of the black stripe are sloped. The words "Team 2000" and the player's name appear in gold foil in the stripe. The team logo is displayed in the lower left corner. The horizontally oriented backs show a close-up color player photo and a career summary on a black background. The cards are numbered on the back.

	MINT	NRMT	EXC
COMPLETE SET (80)	30.00	13.50	3.70
COMPLETE SERIES 1 (40)	20.00	9.00	2.50
COMPLETE SERIES 2 (40)	10.00	4.50	1.25
COMMON CARD (1-40)	.15	.07	.02
COMMON CARD (41-80)	.15	.07	.02

☐ 1	Mike Mussina	.75	.35	.09
☐ 2	Phil Plantier	.15	.07	.02
☐ 3	Frank Thomas	5.00	2.20	.60
☐ 4	Travis Fryman	.25	.11	.03
☐ 5	Kevin Appier	.25	.11	.03
☐ 6	Chuck Knoblauch	.40	.18	.05
☐ 7	Pat Kelly	.15	.07	.02
☐ 8	Ivan Rodriguez	.30	.14	.04
☐ 9	Dave Justice	.40	.18	.05
☐ 10	Jeff Bagwell	1.50	.70	.19
☐ 11	Marquis Grissom	.25	.11	.03
☐ 12	Andy Benes	.15	.07	.02
☐ 13	Gregg Olson	.15	.07	.02
☐ 14	Kevin Morton	.15	.07	.02
☐ 15	Tim Naehring	.25	.11	.03
☐ 16	Dave Hollins	.15	.07	.02
☐ 17	Sandy Alomar Jr.	.25	.11	.03
☐ 18	Albert Belle	1.50	.70	.19
☐ 19	Charles Nagy	.15	.07	.02
☐ 20	Brian McRae	.25	.11	.03
☐ 21	Larry Walker	.40	.18	.05
☐ 22	Delino DeShields	.25	.11	.03
☐ 23	Jeff Johnson	.15	.07	.02
☐ 24	Bernie Williams	.25	.11	.03
☐ 25	Jose Offerman	.15	.07	.02
☐ 26	Juan Gonzalez	1.25	.55	.16
☐ 27A	Juan Guzman (Pinnacle logo at top)	.25	.11	.03
☐ 27B	Juan Guzman (Pinnacle logo at bottom)	.25	.11	.03
☐ 28	Eric Anthony	.15	.07	.02
☐ 29	Brian Hunter	.15	.07	.02
☐ 30	John Smoltz	.25	.11	.03
☐ 31	Deion Sanders	.60	.25	.07
☐ 32	Greg Maddux	3.00	1.35	.35
☐ 33	Andujar Cedeno	.15	.07	.02
☐ 34	Royce Clayton	.25	.11	.03
☐ 35	Kenny Lofton	2.50	1.10	.30
☐ 36	Cal Eldred	.15	.07	.02
☐ 37	Jim Thome	2.50	1.10	.30
☐ 38	Gary DiSarcina	.15	.07	.02
☐ 39	Brian Jordan	.60	.25	.07
☐ 40	Chad Curtis	.50	.23	.06
☐ 41	Ben McDonald	.25	.11	.03
☐ 42	Jim Abbott	.25	.11	.03
☐ 43	Robin Ventura	.25	.11	.03
☐ 44	Milt Cuyler	.15	.07	.02
☐ 45	Gregg Jefferies	.25	.11	.03
☐ 46	Scott Radinsky	.15	.07	.02
☐ 47	Ken Griffey Jr.	5.00	2.20	.60
☐ 48	Roberto Alomar	.60	.25	.07
☐ 49	Ramon Martinez	.25	.11	.03
☐ 50	Bret Barberie	.15	.07	.02
☐ 51	Ray Lankford	.25	.11	.03
☐ 52	Leo Gomez	.15	.07	.02
☐ 53	Tommy Greene	.15	.07	.02
☐ 54	Mo Vaughn	1.25	.55	.16
☐ 55	Sammy Sosa	.30	.14	.04
☐ 56	Carlos Baerga	1.00	.45	.12
☐ 57	Mark Lewis	.15	.07	.02
☐ 58	Tom Gordon	.25	.11	.03
☐ 59	Gary Sheffield	.25	.11	.03
☐ 60	Scott Erickson	.25	.11	.03
☐ 61	Pedro Munoz	.25	.11	.03
☐ 62	Tino Martinez	.25	.11	.03
☐ 63	Darren Lewis	.15	.07	.02
☐ 64	Dean Palmer	.15	.07	.02
☐ 65	John Olerud	.25	.11	.03
☐ 66	Steve Avery	.30	.14	.04
☐ 67	Pete Harnisch	.15	.07	.02
☐ 68	Luis Gonzalez	.25	.11	.03
☐ 69	Kim Batiste	.15	.07	.02
☐ 70	Reggie Sanders	.75	.35	.09
☐ 71	Luis Mercedes	.15	.07	.02
☐ 72	Todd Van Poppel	.15	.07	.02
☐ 73	Gary Scott	.15	.07	.02
☐ 74	Monty Fariss	.15	.07	.02
☐ 75	Kyle Abbott	.15	.07	.02
☐ 76	Eric Karros	.75	.35	.09
☐ 77	Mo Sanford	.15	.07	.02
☐ 78	Todd Hundley	.25	.11	.03
☐ 79	Reggie Jefferson	.15	.07	.02
☐ 80	Pat Mahomes	.15	.07	.02

1992 Pinnacle Team Pinnacle

This 12-card, double-sided subset features the National League and American League All-Star team as selected by Pinnacle. The standard-size (2 1/2" by 3 1/2") were randomly inserted in Series I wax packs. There is one card per position, including two cards for pitchers and two cards for relief pitchers for a total set of twelve. The cards feature illustrations by sports artist Chris Greco of the National League All-Star on one side and the American League All-Star on the

other. The words "Team Pinnacle" are printed vertically down the left side of the card in red for American League on one side and blue for National League on the other. The player's name appears in a gold stripe at the bottom. There is no text. The cards are numbered in the black bottom stripe on the side featuring the National League All-Star.

	MINT	NRMT	EXC
COMPLETE SET (12)	100.00	45.00	12.50
COMMON PAIR (1-12)	5.00	2.20	.60
☐ 1 Roger Clemens and Ramon Martinez	8.00	3.60	1.00
☐ 2 Jim Abbott and Steve Avery	6.00	2.70	.75
☐ 3 Ivan Rodriguez and Benito Santiago	6.00	2.70	.75
☐ 4 Frank Thomas and Will Clark	35.00	16.00	4.40
☐ 5 Roberto Alomar and Ryne Sandberg	20.00	9.00	2.50
☐ 6 Robin Ventura and Matt Williams	10.00	4.50	1.25
☐ 7 Cal Ripken and Barry Larkin	35.00	16.00	4.40
☐ 8 Danny Tartabull and Barry Bonds	10.00	4.50	1.25
☐ 9 Ken Griffey Jr. and Brett Butler	25.00	11.00	3.10
☐ 10 Ruben Sierra and Dave Justice	8.00	3.60	1.00
☐ 11 Dennis Eckersley and Rob Dibble	5.00	2.20	.60
☐ 12 Scott Radinsky and John Franco	5.00	2.20	.60

1993 Pinnacle

The 1993 Score Pinnacle baseball set contains 620 standard-size cards issued in two series. A ten-card Team Pinnacle subset was randomly inserted in Series I packs, and a ten-card Rookie Team Pinnacle subset was randomly inserted in Series II, as was the ten-card Tribute subset. The fronts feature color action player photos bordered in white and set on a black card face. The player's name appears below the photo, the player's team is above. The horizontal backs are black and carry a color close-up in the center and reversed out text including biographical information, career highlights, and statistics. The set includes the following topical subsets: Rookies (238-288, 575-620), Now and Then (289-296, 470-476), Idols (297-303, 477-483), Hometown Heroes (304-310, 484-490), and Draft Picks (455-469). Rookie Cards in this set include Rene Arocha, Derek Jeter, Jason Kendall, J.T. Snow, and Todd Steverson.

	MINT	NRMT	EXC
COMPLETE SET (620)	50.00	22.00	6.25
COMPLETE SERIES 1 (310)	25.00	11.00	3.10
COMPLETE SERIES 2 (310)	25.00	11.00	3.10
COMMON CARD (1-310)	.10	.05	.01
COMMON CARD (311-620)	.10	.05	.01
☐ 1 Gary Sheffield	.30	.14	.04
☐ 2 Cal Eldred	.10	.05	.01
☐ 3 Larry Walker	.40	.18	.05
☐ 4 Deion Sanders	.60	.25	.07
☐ 5 Dave Fleming	.10	.05	.01
☐ 6 Carlos Baerga	.60	.25	.07
☐ 7 Bernie Williams	.20	.09	.03
☐ 8 John Kruk	.30	.14	.04
☐ 9 Jimmy Key	.20	.09	.03
☐ 10 Jeff Bagwell	1.25	.55	.16
☐ 11 Jim Abbott	.30	.14	.04
☐ 12 Terry Steinbach	.20	.09	.03
☐ 13 Bob Tewksbury	.10	.05	.01
☐ 14 Eric Karros	.30	.14	.04
☐ 15 Ryne Sandberg	.75	.35	.09
☐ 16 Will Clark	.40	.18	.05
☐ 17 Edgar Martinez	.30	.14	.04
☐ 18 Eddie Murray	.50	.23	.06
☐ 19 Andy Van Slyke	.20	.09	.03
☐ 20 Cal Ripken Jr.	3.00	1.35	.35
☐ 21 Ivan Rodriguez	.30	.14	.04
☐ 22 Barry Larkin	.40	.18	.05
☐ 23 Don Mattingly	1.50	.70	.19
☐ 24 Gregg Jefferies	.30	.14	.04
☐ 25 Roger Clemens	.50	.23	.06
☐ 26 Cecil Fielder	.30	.14	.04
☐ 27 Kent Hrbek	.20	.09	.03
☐ 28 Robin Ventura	.30	.14	.04
☐ 29 Rickey Henderson	.30	.14	.04
☐ 30 Roberto Alomar	.60	.25	.07
☐ 31 Luis Polonia	.10	.05	.01
☐ 32 Andujar Cedeno	.10	.05	.01
☐ 33 Pat Listach	.10	.05	.01
☐ 34 Mark Grace	.30	.14	.04
☐ 35 Otis Nixon	.10	.05	.01
☐ 36 Felix Jose	.10	.05	.01

☐ 37	Mike Sharperson	.10	.05	.01
☐ 38	Dennis Martinez	.20	.09	.03
☐ 39	Willie McGee	.20	.09	.03
☐ 40	Kenny Lofton	1.00	.45	.12
☐ 41	Randy Johnson	.60	.25	.07
☐ 42	Andy Benes	.20	.09	.03
☐ 43	Bobby Bonilla	.30	.14	.04
☐ 44	Mike Mussina	.50	.23	.06
☐ 45	Len Dykstra	.30	.14	.04
☐ 46	Ellis Burks	.20	.09	.03
☐ 47	Chris Sabo	.10	.05	.01
☐ 48	Jay Bell	.20	.09	.03
☐ 49	Jose Canseco	.50	.23	.06
☐ 50	Craig Biggio	.30	.14	.04
☐ 51	Wally Joyner	.20	.09	.03
☐ 52	Mickey Tettleton	.20	.09	.03
☐ 53	Tim Raines	.30	.14	.04
☐ 54	Brian Harper	.10	.05	.01
☐ 55	Rene Gonzales	.10	.05	.01
☐ 56	Mark Langston	.30	.14	.04
☐ 57	Jack Morris	.30	.14	.04
☐ 58	Mark McGwire	.30	.14	.04
☐ 59	Ken Caminiti	.20	.09	.03
☐ 60	Terry Pendleton	.20	.09	.03
☐ 61	Dave Nilsson	.20	.09	.03
☐ 62	Tom Pagnozzi	.10	.05	.01
☐ 63	Mike Morgan	.10	.05	.01
☐ 64	Darryl Strawberry	.20	.09	.03
☐ 65	Charles Nagy	.20	.09	.03
☐ 66	Ken Hill	.20	.09	.03
☐ 67	Matt Williams	.50	.23	.06
☐ 68	Jay Buhner	.30	.14	.04
☐ 69	Vince Coleman	.10	.05	.01
☐ 70	Brady Anderson	.20	.09	.03
☐ 71	Fred McGriff	.40	.18	.05
☐ 72	Ben McDonald	.10	.05	.01
☐ 73	Terry Mulholland	.10	.05	.01
☐ 74	Randy Tomlin	.10	.05	.01
☐ 75	Nolan Ryan	2.50	1.10	.30
☐ 76	Frank Viola UER	.20	.09	.03
	(Card incorrectly states			
	he has a surgically			
	repaired elbow)			
☐ 77	Jose Rijo	.20	.09	.03
☐ 78	Shane Mack	.10	.05	.01
☐ 79	Travis Fryman	.30	.14	.04
☐ 80	Jack McDowell	.30	.14	.04
☐ 81	Mark Gubicza	.10	.05	.01
☐ 82	Matt Nokes	.10	.05	.01
☐ 83	Bert Blyleven	.30	.14	.04
☐ 84	Eric Anthony	.10	.05	.01
☐ 85	Mike Bordick	.10	.05	.01
☐ 86	John Olerud	.20	.09	.03
☐ 87	B.J. Surhoff	.20	.09	.03
☐ 88	Bernard Gilkey	.20	.09	.03
☐ 89	Shawon Dunston	.10	.05	.01
☐ 90	Tom Glavine	.30	.14	.04
☐ 91	Brett Butler	.20	.09	.03
☐ 92	Moises Alou	.30	.14	.04
☐ 93	Albert Belle	1.25	.55	.16
☐ 94	Darren Lewis	.10	.05	.01
☐ 95	Omar Vizquel	.20	.09	.03
☐ 96	Dwight Gooden	.20	.09	.03
☐ 97	Gregg Olson	.10	.05	.01
☐ 98	Tony Gwynn	1.00	.45	.12
☐ 99	Darren Daulton	.30	.14	.04
☐ 100	Dennis Eckersley	.30	.14	.04
☐ 101	Rob Dibble	.10	.05	.01
☐ 102	Mike Greenwell	.20	.09	.03
☐ 103	Jose Lind	.10	.05	.01
☐ 104	Julio Franco	.20	.09	.03
☐ 105	Tom Gordon	.10	.05	.01
☐ 106	Scott Livingstone	.10	.05	.01
☐ 107	Chuck Knoblauch	.30	.14	.04
☐ 108	Frank Thomas	3.00	1.35	.35
☐ 109	Melido Perez	.10	.05	.01
☐ 110	Ken Griffey Jr.	3.00	1.35	.35
☐ 111	Harold Baines	.20	.09	.03
☐ 112	Gary Gaetti	.20	.09	.03
☐ 113	Pete Harnisch	.10	.05	.01
☐ 114	David Wells	.10	.05	.01
☐ 115	Charlie Leibrandt	.10	.05	.01
☐ 116	Ray Lankford	.30	.14	.04
☐ 117	Kevin Seitzer	.10	.05	.01
☐ 118	Robin Yount	.40	.18	.05
☐ 119	Lenny Harris	.10	.05	.01
☐ 120	Chris James	.10	.05	.01
☐ 121	Delino DeShields	.20	.09	.03
☐ 122	Kirt Manwaring	.10	.05	.01
☐ 123	Glenallen Hill	.20	.09	.03
☐ 124	Hensley Meulens	.10	.05	.01
☐ 125	Darrin Jackson	.10	.05	.01
☐ 126	Todd Hundley	.30	.14	.04
☐ 127	Dave Hollins	.10	.05	.01
☐ 128	Sam Horn	.10	.05	.01
☐ 129	Roberto Hernandez	.20	.09	.03
☐ 130	Vicente Palacios	.10	.05	.01
☐ 131	George Brett	1.25	.55	.16
☐ 132	Dave Martinez	.10	.05	.01
☐ 133	Kevin Appier	.20	.09	.03
☐ 134	Pat Kelly	.10	.05	.01
☐ 135	Pedro Munoz	.20	.09	.03
☐ 136	Mark Carreon	.10	.05	.01
☐ 137	Lance Johnson	.10	.05	.01
☐ 138	Devon White	.20	.09	.03
☐ 139	Julio Valera	.10	.05	.01
☐ 140	Eddie Taubensee	.10	.05	.01
☐ 141	Willie Wilson	.10	.05	.01
☐ 142	Stan Belinda	.10	.05	.01
☐ 143	John Smoltz	.20	.09	.03
☐ 144	Darryl Hamilton	.10	.05	.01
☐ 145	Sammy Sosa	.30	.14	.04
☐ 146	Carlos Hernandez	.10	.05	.01
☐ 147	Tom Candiotti	.10	.05	.01
☐ 148	Mike Felder	.10	.05	.01
☐ 149	Rusty Meacham	.10	.05	.01
☐ 150	Ivan Calderon	.10	.05	.01
☐ 151	Pete O'Brien	.10	.05	.01
☐ 152	Erik Hanson	.20	.09	.03
☐ 153	Billy Ripken	.10	.05	.01
☐ 154	Kurt Stillwell	.10	.05	.01
☐ 155	Jeff Kent	.30	.14	.04
☐ 156	Mickey Morandini	.10	.05	.01
☐ 157	Randy Milligan	.10	.05	.01
☐ 158	Reggie Sanders	.30	.14	.04
☐ 159	Luis Rivera	.10	.05	.01
☐ 160	Orlando Merced	.20	.09	.03
☐ 161	Dean Palmer	.20	.09	.03
☐ 162	Mike Perez	.10	.05	.01
☐ 163	Scott Erickson	.20	.09	.03
☐ 164	Kevin McReynolds	.10	.05	.01
☐ 165	Kevin Maas	.10	.05	.01
☐ 166	Ozzie Guillen	.10	.05	.01
☐ 167	Rob Deer	.10	.05	.01
☐ 168	Danny Tartabull	.20	.09	.03
☐ 169	Lee Stevens	.10	.05	.01
☐ 170	Dave Henderson	.10	.05	.01
☐ 171	Derek Bell	.30	.14	.04
☐ 172	Steve Finley	.10	.05	.01
☐ 173	Greg Olson	.10	.05	.01
☐ 174	Geronimo Pena	.10	.05	.01
☐ 175	Paul Quantrill	.10	.05	.01

☐ 176	Steve Buechele	.10	.05	.01
☐ 177	Kevin Gross	.10	.05	.01
☐ 178	Tim Wallach	.10	.05	.01
☐ 179	Dave Valle	.10	.05	.01
☐ 180	Dave Silvestri	.10	.05	.01
☐ 181	Bud Black	.10	.05	.01
☐ 182	Henry Rodriguez	.10	.05	.01
☐ 183	Tim Teufel	.10	.05	.01
☐ 184	Mark McLemore	.10	.05	.01
☐ 185	Bret Saberhagen	.20	.09	.03
☐ 186	Chris Hoiles	.20	.09	.03
☐ 187	Ricky Jordan	.10	.05	.01
☐ 188	Don Slaught	.10	.05	.01
☐ 189	Mo Vaughn	.50	.23	.06
☐ 190	Joe Oliver	.10	.05	.01
☐ 191	Juan Gonzalez	.60	.25	.07
☐ 192	Scott Leius	.10	.05	.01
☐ 193	Milt Cuyler	.10	.05	.01
☐ 194	Chris Haney	.10	.05	.01
☐ 195	Ron Karkovice	.10	.05	.01
☐ 196	Steve Farr	.10	.05	.01
☐ 197	John Orton	.10	.05	.01
☐ 198	Kelly Gruber	.10	.05	.01
☐ 199	Ron Darling	.10	.05	.01
☐ 200	Ruben Sierra	.30	.14	.04
☐ 201	Chuck Finley	.10	.05	.01
☐ 202	Mike Moore	.10	.05	.01
☐ 203	Pat Borders	.10	.05	.01
☐ 204	Sid Bream	.10	.05	.01
☐ 205	Todd Zeile	.20	.09	.03
☐ 206	Rick Wilkins	.10	.05	.01
☐ 207	Jim Gantner	.10	.05	.01
☐ 208	Frank Castillo	.10	.05	.01
☐ 209	Dave Hansen	.10	.05	.01
☐ 210	Trevor Wilson	.10	.05	.01
☐ 211	Sandy Alomar Jr.	.20	.09	.03
☐ 212	Sean Berry	.10	.05	.01
☐ 213	Tino Martinez	.30	.14	.04
☐ 214	Chito Martinez	.10	.05	.01
☐ 215	Dan Walters	.10	.05	.01
☐ 216	John Franco	.20	.09	.03
☐ 217	Glenn Davis	.10	.05	.01
☐ 218	Mariano Duncan	.10	.05	.01
☐ 219	Mike LaValliere	.10	.05	.01
☐ 220	Rafael Palmeiro	.30	.14	.04
☐ 221	Jack Clark	.10	.05	.01
☐ 222	Hal Morris	.20	.09	.03
☐ 223	Ed Sprague	.10	.05	.01
☐ 224	John Valentin	.30	.14	.04
☐ 225	Sam Militello	.10	.05	.01
☐ 226	Bob Wickman	.10	.05	.01
☐ 227	Damion Easley	.20	.09	.03
☐ 228	John Jaha	.20	.09	.03
☐ 229	Bob Ayrault	.10	.05	.01
☐ 230	Mo Sanford	.10	.05	.01
☐ 231	Walt Weiss	.20	.09	.03
☐ 232	Dante Bichette	.40	.18	.05
☐ 233	Steve Decker	.10	.05	.01
☐ 234	Jerald Clark	.10	.05	.01
☐ 235	Bryan Harvey	.20	.09	.03
☐ 236	Joe Girardi	.10	.05	.01
☐ 237	Dave Magadan	.10	.05	.01
☐ 238	David Nied	.20	.09	.03
☐ 239	Eric Wedge	.10	.05	.01
☐ 240	Rico Brogna	.20	.09	.03
☐ 241	J.T.Bruett	.10	.05	.01
☐ 242	Jonathan Hurst	.10	.05	.01
☐ 243	Bret Boone	.30	.14	.04
☐ 244	Manny Alexander	.10	.05	.01
☐ 245	Scooter Tucker	.10	.05	.01
☐ 246	Troy Neel	.10	.05	.01
☐ 247	Eddie Zosky	.10	.05	.01
☐ 248	Melvin Nieves	.30	.14	.04
☐ 249	Ryan Thompson	.20	.09	.03
☐ 250	Shawn Barton	.10	.05	.01
☐ 251	Ryan Klesko	1.50	.70	.19
☐ 252	Mike Piazza	2.50	1.10	.30
☐ 253	Steve Hosey	.10	.05	.01
☐ 254	Shane Reynolds	.20	.09	.03
☐ 255	Dan Wilson	.20	.09	.03
☐ 256	Tom Marsh	.10	.05	.01
☐ 257	Barry Manuel	.10	.05	.01
☐ 258	Paul Miller	.10	.05	.01
☐ 259	Pedro Martinez	.30	.14	.04
☐ 260	Steve Cooke	.10	.05	.01
☐ 261	Johnny Guzman	.10	.05	.01
☐ 262	Mike Butcher	.10	.05	.01
☐ 263	Bien Figueroa	.10	.05	.01
☐ 264	Rich Rowland	.10	.05	.01
☐ 265	Shawn Jeter	.10	.05	.01
☐ 266	Gerald Williams	.10	.05	.01
☐ 267	Derek Parks	.10	.05	.01
☐ 268	Henry Mercedes	.10	.05	.01
☐ 269	David Hulse	.10	.05	.01
☐ 270	Tim Pugh	.10	.05	.01
☐ 271	William Suero	.10	.05	.01
☐ 272	Ozzie Canseco	.10	.05	.01
☐ 273	Fernando Ramsey	.10	.05	.01
☐ 274	Bernardo Brito	.10	.05	.01
☐ 275	Dave Mlicki	.10	.05	.01
☐ 276	Tim Salmon	1.00	.45	.12
☐ 277	Mike Raczka	.10	.05	.01
☐ 278	Ken Ryan	.10	.05	.01
☐ 279	Rafael Bournigal	.10	.05	.01
☐ 280	Wil Cordero	.30	.14	.04
☐ 281	Billy Ashley	.30	.14	.04
☐ 282	Paul Wagner	.10	.05	.01
☐ 283	Blas Minor	.10	.05	.01
☐ 284	Rick Trlicek	.10	.05	.01
☐ 285	Willie Greene	.20	.09	.03
☐ 286	Ted Wood	.10	.05	.01
☐ 287	Phil Clark	.10	.05	.01
☐ 288	Jesse Levis	.10	.05	.01
☐ 289	Tony Gwynn NT	.50	.23	.06
☐ 290	Nolan Ryan NT	1.50	.70	.19
☐ 291	Dennis Martinez NT	.10	.05	.01
☐ 292	Eddie Murray NT	.20	.09	.03
☐ 293	Robin Yount NT	.20	.09	.03
☐ 294	George Brett NT	.60	.25	.07
☐ 295	Dave Winfield NT	.20	.09	.03
☐ 296	Bert Blyleven NT	.10	.05	.01
☐ 297	Jeff Bagwell Carl Yastrzemski	.40	.18	.05
☐ 298	John Smoltz Jack Morris	.20	.09	.03
☐ 299	Larry Walker Mike Bossy	.25	.11	.03
☐ 300	Gary Sheffield Barry Larkin	.20	.09	.03
☐ 301	Ivan Rodriguez Carlton Fisk	.20	.09	.03
☐ 302	Delino DeShields Malcolm X	.20	.09	.03
☐ 303	Tim Salmon Dwight Evans	.25	.11	.03
☐ 304	Bernard Gilkey HH	.10	.05	.01
☐ 305	Cal Ripken Jr. HH	1.50	.70	.19
☐ 306	Barry Larkin HH	.20	.09	.03
☐ 307	Kent Hrbek HH	.10	.05	.01
☐ 308	Rickey Henderson HH	.20	.09	.03
☐ 309	Darryl Strawberry HH	.20	.09	.03
☐ 310	John Franco HH	.10	.05	.01

□				
□ 311	Todd Stottlemyre	.10	.05	.01
□ 312	Luis Gonzalez	.20	.09	.03
□ 313	Tommy Greene	.10	.05	.01
□ 314	Randy Velarde	.10	.05	.01
□ 315	Steve Avery	.30	.14	.04
□ 316	Jose Oquendo	.10	.05	.01
□ 317	Rey Sanchez	.10	.05	.01
□ 318	Greg Vaughn	.10	.05	.01
□ 319	Orel Hershiser	.20	.09	.03
□ 320	Paul Sorrento	.10	.05	.01
□ 321	Royce Clayton	.20	.09	.03
□ 322	John Vander Wal	.10	.05	.01
□ 323	Henry Cotto	.10	.05	.01
□ 324	Pete Schourek	.30	.14	.04
□ 325	David Segui	.10	.05	.01
□ 326	Arthur Rhodes	.20	.09	.03
□ 327	Bruce Hurst	.10	.05	.01
□ 328	Wes Chamberlain	.10	.05	.01
□ 329	Ozzie Smith	.60	.25	.07
□ 330	Scott Cooper	.10	.05	.01
□ 331	Felix Fermin	.10	.05	.01
□ 332	Mike Macfarlane	.10	.05	.01
□ 333	Dan Gladden	.10	.05	.01
□ 334	Kevin Tapani	.10	.05	.01
□ 335	Steve Sax	.10	.05	.01
□ 336	Jeff Montgomery	.20	.09	.03
□ 337	Gary DiSarcina	.10	.05	.01
□ 338	Lance Blankenship	.10	.05	.01
□ 339	Brian Williams	.10	.05	.01
□ 340	Duane Ward	.10	.05	.01
□ 341	Chuck McElroy	.10	.05	.01
□ 342	Joe Magrane	.10	.05	.01
□ 343	Jaime Navarro	.10	.05	.01
□ 344	Dave Justice	.40	.18	.05
□ 345	Jose Offerman	.10	.05	.01
□ 346	Marquis Grissom	.30	.14	.04
□ 347	Bill Swift	.10	.05	.01
□ 348	Jim Thome	1.25	.55	.16
□ 349	Archi Cianfrocco	.10	.05	.01
□ 350	Anthony Young	.10	.05	.01
□ 351	Leo Gomez	.10	.05	.01
□ 352	Bill Gullickson	.10	.05	.01
□ 353	Alan Trammell	.30	.14	.04
□ 354	Dan Pasqua	.10	.05	.01
□ 355	Jeff King	.10	.05	.01
□ 356	Kevin Brown	.10	.05	.01
□ 357	Tim Belcher	.10	.05	.01
□ 358	Bip Roberts	.10	.05	.01
□ 359	Brent Mayne	.10	.05	.01
□ 360	Rheal Cormier	.10	.05	.01
□ 361	Mark Guthrie	.10	.05	.01
□ 362	Craig Grebeck	.10	.05	.01
□ 363	Andy Stankiewicz	.10	.05	.01
□ 364	Juan Guzman	.20	.09	.03
□ 365	Bobby Witt	.10	.05	.01
□ 366	Mark Portugal	.10	.05	.01
□ 367	Brian McRae	.30	.14	.04
□ 368	Mark Lemke	.10	.05	.01
□ 369	Bill Wegman	.10	.05	.01
□ 370	Donovan Osborne	.10	.05	.01
□ 371	Derrick May	.20	.09	.03
□ 372	Carl Willis	.10	.05	.01
□ 373	Chris Nabholz	.10	.05	.01
□ 374	Mark Lewis	.10	.05	.01
□ 375	John Burkett	.10	.05	.01
□ 376	Luis Mercedes	.10	.05	.01
□ 377	Ramon Martinez	.20	.09	.03
□ 378	Kyle Abbott	.10	.05	.01
□ 379	Mark Wohlers	.10	.05	.01
□ 380	Bob Walk	.10	.05	.01
□ 381	Kenny Rogers	.10	.05	.01
□ 382	Tim Naehring	.10	.05	.01
□ 383	Alex Fernandez	.30	.14	.04
□ 384	Keith Miller	.10	.05	.01
□ 385	Mike Henneman	.10	.05	.01
□ 386	Rick Aguilera	.20	.09	.03
□ 387	George Bell	.20	.09	.03
□ 388	Mike Gallego	.10	.05	.01
□ 389	Howard Johnson	.10	.05	.01
□ 390	Kim Batiste	.10	.05	.01
□ 391	Jerry Browne	.10	.05	.01
□ 392	Damon Berryhill	.10	.05	.01
□ 393	Ricky Bones	.10	.05	.01
□ 394	Omar Olivares	.10	.05	.01
□ 395	Mike Harkey	.10	.05	.01
□ 396	Pedro Astacio	.10	.05	.01
□ 397	John Wetteland	.20	.09	.03
□ 398	Rod Beck	.30	.14	.04
□ 399	Thomas Howard	.10	.05	.01
□ 400	Mike Devereaux	.20	.09	.03
□ 401	Tim Wakefield	.30	.14	.04
□ 402	Curt Schilling	.10	.05	.01
□ 403	Zane Smith	.10	.05	.01
□ 404	Bob Zupcic	.10	.05	.01
□ 405	Tom Browning	.10	.05	.01
□ 406	Tony Phillips	.10	.05	.01
□ 407	John Doherty	.10	.05	.01
□ 408	Pat Mahomes	.10	.05	.01
□ 409	John Habyan	.10	.05	.01
□ 410	Steve Olin	.10	.05	.01
□ 411	Chad Curtis	.20	.09	.03
□ 412	Joe Grahe	.10	.05	.01
□ 413	John Patterson	.10	.05	.01
□ 414	Brian Hunter	.10	.05	.01
□ 415	Doug Henry	.10	.05	.01
□ 416	Lee Smith	.30	.14	.04
□ 417	Bob Scanlan	.10	.05	.01
□ 418	Kent Mercker	.10	.05	.01
□ 419	Mel Rojas	.20	.09	.03
□ 420	Mark Whiten	.20	.09	.03
□ 421	Carlton Fisk	.30	.14	.04
□ 422	Candy Maldonado	.10	.05	.01
□ 423	Doug Drabek	.20	.09	.03
□ 424	Wade Boggs	.30	.14	.04
□ 425	Mark Davis	.10	.05	.01
□ 426	Kirby Puckett	1.00	.45	.12
□ 427	Joe Carter	.30	.14	.04
□ 428	Paul Molitor	.30	.14	.04
□ 429	Eric Davis	.10	.05	.01
□ 430	Darryl Kile	.10	.05	.01
□ 431	Jeff Parrett	.10	.05	.01
□ 432	Jeff Blauser	.20	.09	.03
□ 433	Dan Plesac	.10	.05	.01
□ 434	Andres Galarraga	.30	.14	.04
□ 435	Jim Gott	.10	.05	.01
□ 436	Jose Mesa	.20	.09	.03
□ 437	Ben Rivera	.10	.05	.01
□ 438	Dave Winfield	.30	.14	.04
□ 439	Norm Charlton	.10	.05	.01
□ 440	Chris Bosio	.10	.05	.01
□ 441	Wilson Alvarez	.30	.14	.04
□ 442	Dave Stewart	.20	.09	.03
□ 443	Doug Jones	.10	.05	.01
□ 444	Jeff Russell	.10	.05	.01
□ 445	Ron Gant	.30	.14	.04
□ 446	Paul O'Neill	.20	.09	.03
□ 447	Charlie Hayes	.20	.09	.03
□ 448	Joe Hesketh	.10	.05	.01
□ 449	Chris Hammond	.10	.05	.01
□ 450	Hipolito Pichardo	.10	.05	.01
□ 451	Scott Radinsky	.10	.05	.01
□ 452	Bobby Thigpen	.10	.05	.01

☐ 453 Xavier Hernandez	.10	.05	.01
☐ 454 Lonnie Smith	.10	.05	.01
☐ 455 Jamie Arnold DP	.20	.09	.03
☐ 456 B.J. Wallace DP	.20	.09	.03
☐ 457 Derek Jeter DP	2.50	1.10	.30
☐ 458 Jason Kendall DP	1.00	.45	.12
☐ 459 Rick Helling DP	.10	.05	.01
☐ 460 Derek Wallace DP	.10	.05	.01
☐ 461 Sean Lowe DP	.20	.09	.03
☐ 462 Shannon Stewart DP	.40	.18	.05
☐ 463 Benji Grigsby DP	.10	.05	.01
☐ 464 Todd Steverson DP	.20	.09	.03
☐ 465 Dan Serafini DP	.50	.23	.06
☐ 466 Michael Tucker DP	.30	.14	.04
☐ 467 Chris Roberts DP	.20	.09	.03
☐ 468 Pete Janicki DP	.10	.05	.01
☐ 469 Jeff Schmidt DP	.10	.05	.01
☐ 470 Don Mattingly NT	.75	.35	.09
☐ 471 Cal Ripken Jr. NT	1.50	.70	.19
☐ 472 Jack Morris NT	.20	.09	.03
☐ 473 Terry Pendleton NT	.10	.05	.01
☐ 474 Dennis Eckersley NT	.20	.09	.03
☐ 475 Carlton Fisk NT	.20	.09	.03
☐ 476 Wade Boggs NT	.20	.09	.03
☐ 477 Len Dykstra	.20	.09	.03
Ken Stabler			
☐ 478 Danny Tartabull	.20	.09	.03
Jose Tartabull			
☐ 479 Jeff Conine	.20	.09	.03
Dale Murphy			
☐ 480 Gregg Jefferies	.20	.09	.03
Ron Cey			
☐ 481 Paul Molitor	.20	.09	.03
Harmon Killebrew			
☐ 482 John Valentin	.10	.05	.01
Dave Concepcion			
☐ 483 Alex Arias	.10	.05	.01
Dave Winfield			
☐ 484 Barry Bonds HH	.40	.18	.05
☐ 485 Doug Drabek HH	.10	.05	.01
☐ 486 Dave Winfield HH	.20	.09	.03
☐ 487 Brett Butler HH	.10	.05	.01
☐ 488 Harold Baines HH	.10	.05	.01
☐ 489 David Cone HH	.10	.05	.01
☐ 490 Willie McGee HH	.10	.05	.01
☐ 491 Robby Thompson	.10	.05	.01
☐ 492 Pete Incaviglia	.10	.05	.01
☐ 493 Manuel Lee	.10	.05	.01
☐ 494 Rafael Belliard	.10	.05	.01
☐ 495 Scott Fletcher	.10	.05	.01
☐ 496 Jeff Frye	.10	.05	.01
☐ 497 Andre Dawson	.30	.14	.04
☐ 498 Mike Scioscia	.10	.05	.01
☐ 499 Spike Owen	.10	.05	.01
☐ 500 Sid Fernandez	.10	.05	.01
☐ 501 Joe Orsulak	.10	.05	.01
☐ 502 Benito Santiago	.10	.05	.01
☐ 503 Dale Murphy	.30	.14	.04
☐ 504 Barry Bonds	.75	.35	.09
☐ 505 Jose Guzman	.10	.05	.01
☐ 506 Tony Pena	.10	.05	.01
☐ 507 Greg Swindell	.10	.05	.01
☐ 508 Mike Pagliarulo	.10	.05	.01
☐ 509 Lou Whitaker	.30	.14	.04
☐ 510 Greg Gagne	.10	.05	.01
☐ 511 Butch Henry	.10	.05	.01
☐ 512 Jeff Brantley	.10	.05	.01
☐ 513 Jack Armstrong	.10	.05	.01
☐ 514 Danny Jackson	.10	.05	.01
☐ 515 Junior Felix	.10	.05	.01
☐ 516 Milt Thompson	.10	.05	.01
☐ 517 Greg Maddux	3.00	1.35	.35
☐ 518 Eric Young	.20	.09	.03
☐ 519 Jody Reed	.10	.05	.01
☐ 520 Roberto Kelly	.20	.09	.03
☐ 521 Darren Holmes	.20	.09	.03
☐ 522 Craig Lefferts	.10	.05	.01
☐ 523 Charlie Hough	.20	.09	.03
☐ 524 Bo Jackson	.30	.14	.04
☐ 525 Bill Spiers	.10	.05	.01
☐ 526 Orestes Destrade	.10	.05	.01
☐ 527 Greg Hibbard	.10	.05	.01
☐ 528 Roger McDowell	.10	.05	.01
☐ 529 Cory Snyder	.10	.05	.01
☐ 530 Harold Reynolds	.10	.05	.01
☐ 531 Kevin Reimer	.10	.05	.01
☐ 532 Rick Sutcliffe	.20	.09	.03
☐ 533 Tony Fernandez	.10	.05	.01
☐ 534 Tom Brunansky	.10	.05	.01
☐ 535 Jeff Reardon	.20	.09	.03
☐ 536 Chili Davis	.20	.09	.03
☐ 537 Bob Ojeda	.10	.05	.01
☐ 538 Greg Colbrunn	.30	.14	.04
☐ 539 Phil Plantier	.10	.05	.01
☐ 540 Brian Jordan	.30	.14	.04
☐ 541 Pete Smith	.10	.05	.01
☐ 542 Frank Tanana	.10	.05	.01
☐ 543 John Smiley	.10	.05	.01
☐ 544 David Cone	.30	.14	.04
☐ 545 Daryl Boston	.10	.05	.01
☐ 546 Tom Henke	.20	.09	.03
☐ 547 Bill Krueger	.10	.05	.01
☐ 548 Freddie Benavides	.10	.05	.01
☐ 549 Randy Myers	.20	.09	.03
☐ 550 Reggie Jefferson	.10	.05	.01
☐ 551 Kevin Mitchell	.20	.09	.03
☐ 552 Dave Stieb	.10	.05	.01
☐ 553 Bret Barberie	.10	.05	.01
☐ 554 Tim Crews	.10	.05	.01
☐ 555 Doug Dascenzo	.10	.05	.01
☐ 556 Alex Cole	.10	.05	.01
☐ 557 Jeff Innis	.10	.05	.01
☐ 558 Carlos Garcia	.20	.09	.03
☐ 559 Steve Howe	.10	.05	.01
☐ 560 Kirk McCaskill	.10	.05	.01
☐ 561 Frank Seminara	.10	.05	.01
☐ 562 Cris Carpenter	.10	.05	.01
☐ 563 Mike Stanley	.20	.09	.03
☐ 564 Carlos Quintana	.10	.05	.01
☐ 565 Mitch Williams	.20	.09	.03
☐ 566 Juan Bell	.10	.05	.01
☐ 567 Eric Fox	.10	.05	.01
☐ 568 Al Leiter	.10	.05	.01
☐ 569 Mike Stanton	.10	.05	.01
☐ 570 Scott Kamieniecki	.10	.05	.01
☐ 571 Ryan Bowen	.10	.05	.01
☐ 572 Andy Ashby	.10	.05	.01
☐ 573 Bob Welch	.20	.09	.03
☐ 574 Scott Sanderson	.10	.05	.01
☐ 575 Joe Kmak	.10	.05	.01
☐ 576 Scott Pose	.10	.05	.01
☐ 577 Ricky Gutierrez	.10	.05	.01
☐ 578 Mike Trombley	.10	.05	.01
☐ 579 Sterling Hitchcock	.25	.11	.03
☐ 580 Rodney Bolton	.10	.05	.01
☐ 581 Tyler Green	.10	.05	.01
☐ 582 Tim Costo	.10	.05	.01
☐ 583 Tim Laker	.10	.05	.01
☐ 584 Steve Reed	.10	.05	.01
☐ 585 Tom Kramer	.10	.05	.01
☐ 586 Robb Nen	.10	.05	.01
☐ 587 Jim Tatum	.10	.05	.01

			MINT	NRMT	EXC
☐	588	Frank Bolick	.10	.05	.01
☐	589	Kevin Young	.10	.05	.01
☐	590	Matt Whiteside	.10	.05	.01
☐	591	Cesar Hernandez	.10	.05	.01
☐	592	Mike Mohler	.10	.05	.01
☐	593	Alan Embree	.10	.05	.01
☐	594	Terry Jorgensen	.10	.05	.01
☐	595	John Cummings	.20	.09	.03
☐	596	Domingo Martinez	.10	.05	.01
☐	597	Benji Gil	.20	.09	.03
☐	598	Todd Pratt	.10	.05	.01
☐	599	Rene Arocha	.20	.09	.03
☐	600	Dennis Moeller	.10	.05	.01
☐	601	Jeff Conine	.30	.14	.04
☐	602	Trevor Hoffman	.20	.09	.03
☐	603	Daniel Smith	.10	.05	.01
☐	604	Lee Tinsley	.10	.05	.01
☐	605	Dan Peltier	.10	.05	.01
☐	606	Billy Brewer	.10	.05	.01
☐	607	Matt Walbeck	.20	.09	.03
☐	608	Richie Lewis	.10	.05	.01
☐	609	J.T. Snow	1.00	.45	.12
☐	610	Pat Gomez	.10	.05	.01
☐	611	Phil Hiatt	.10	.05	.01
☐	612	Alex Arias	.10	.05	.01
☐	613	Kevin Rogers	.10	.05	.01
☐	614	Al Martin	.20	.09	.03
☐	615	Greg Gohr	.10	.05	.01
☐	616	Graeme Lloyd	.10	.05	.01
☐	617	Kent Bottenfield	.10	.05	.01
☐	618	Chuck Carr	.10	.05	.01
☐	619	Darrell Sherman	.10	.05	.01
☐	620	Mike Lansing	.20	.09	.03

ing within a colored stripe beneath the picture, blue for the American League, red for the National League. The set's title appears in gold foil above each painting. The cards are numbered on the front and back. According to Score, the chances of finding a Rookie Team Pinnacle card are not less than one in 90 packs.

		MINT	NRMT	EXC
COMPLETE SET (10)		135.00	60.00	17.00
COMMON PAIR (1-10)		5.00	2.20	.60
☐ 1	Pedro Martinez Mike Trombley	8.00	3.60	1.00
☐ 2	Kevin Rogers Sterling Hitchcock	5.00	2.20	.60
☐ 3	Mike Piazza Jesse Levis	60.00	27.00	7.50
☐ 4	Ryan Klesko J.T. Snow	40.00	18.00	5.00
☐ 5	John Patterson Bret Boone	8.00	3.60	1.00
☐ 6	Kevin Young Domingo Martinez	5.00	2.20	.60
☐ 7	Wil Cordero Manny Alexander	8.00	3.60	1.00
☐ 8	Steve Hosey Tim Salmon	25.00	11.00	3.10
☐ 9	Ryan Thompson Gerald Williams	5.00	2.20	.60
☐ 10	Melvin Nieves David Hulse	5.00	2.20	.60

1993 Pinnacle Rookie Team Pinnacle

These ten standard-size (2 1/2" by 3 1/2") cards were randomly inserted in Series II foil packs and each features an American League rookie on one side and a National League rookie on the other. Both sides feature black-bordered color player paintings that resemble grainy photographs and are trimmed by a thin white line. Each double-sided card displays paintings by artist Christopher Greco. The player's name, position, and league appear in white letter-

1993 Pinnacle Slugfest

These 30 standard-size (2 1/2" by 3 1/2") cards salute baseball's top hitters and were randomly inserted in series II 27-card superpacks. The fronts feature color player action shots that are borderless, except at the bottom, where a black stripe carries the player's name in white lettering. The set's title appears below in black lettering within a gold foil stripe. The horizontal back carries a posed color player photo on its right side. On the left side appears the player's name, the set's title, and the player's career highlights and team logo. The cards are numbered on the back.

	MINT	NRMT	EXC
COMPLETE SET (30)	60.00	27.00	7.50
COMMON CARD (1-30)	.75	.35	.09

		MINT	NRMT	EXC
☐ 1	Juan Gonzalez	3.00	1.35	.35
☐ 2	Mark McGwire	1.50	.70	.19
☐ 3	Cecil Fielder	1.50	.70	.19
☐ 4	Joe Carter	1.50	.70	.19
☐ 5	Fred McGriff	2.00	.90	.25
☐ 6	Barry Bonds	4.00	1.80	.50
☐ 7	Gary Sheffield	1.50	.70	.19
☐ 8	Dave Hollins	.75	.35	.09
☐ 9	Frank Thomas	15.00	6.75	1.85
☐ 10	Danny Tartabull	.75	.35	.09
☐ 11	Albert Belle	6.00	2.70	.75
☐ 12	Ruben Sierra	1.50	.70	.19
☐ 13	Larry Walker	2.00	.90	.25
☐ 14	Jeff Bagwell	6.00	2.70	.75
☐ 15	David Justice	2.00	.90	.25
☐ 16	Kirby Puckett	5.00	2.20	.60
☐ 17	John Kruk	.75	.35	.09
☐ 18	Howard Johnson	.75	.35	.09
☐ 19	Darryl Strawberry	.75	.35	.09
☐ 20	Will Clark	2.00	.90	.25
☐ 21	Kevin Mitchell	.75	.35	.09
☐ 22	Mickey Tettleton	.75	.35	.09
☐ 23	Don Mattingly	6.00	2.70	.75
☐ 24	Jose Canseco	2.50	1.10	.30
☐ 25	George Bell	.75	.35	.09
☐ 26	Andre Dawson	1.50	.70	.19
☐ 27	Ryne Sandberg	4.00	1.80	.50
☐ 28	Ken Griffey Jr.	15.00	6.75	1.85
☐ 29	Carlos Baerga	3.00	1.35	.35
☐ 30	Travis Fryman	1.50	.70	.19

the left, the player's name in gold foil, followed by his team name, position, and career highlights. The set's vertical title reappears in gold foil near the left edge. The cards are numbered on the back.

		MINT	NRMT	EXC
COMPLETE SET (30)		40.00	18.00	5.00
COMMON CARD (1-30)		.75	.35	.09

		MINT	NRMT	EXC
☐ 1	Wil Cordero	.75	.35	.09
☐ 2	Cal Eldred	.75	.35	.09
☐ 3	Mike Mussina	2.50	1.10	.30
☐ 4	Chuck Knoblauch	2.00	.90	.25
☐ 5	Melvin Nieves	.75	.35	.09
☐ 6	Tim Wakefield	.75	.35	.09
☐ 7	Carlos Baerga	3.00	1.35	.35
☐ 8	Bret Boone	1.50	.70	.19
☐ 9	Jeff Bagwell	6.00	2.70	.75
☐ 10	Travis Fryman	1.50	.70	.19
☐ 11	Royce Clayton	.75	.35	.09
☐ 12	Delino DeShields	.75	.35	.09
☐ 13	Juan Gonzalez	3.00	1.35	.35
☐ 14	Pedro Martinez	.75	.35	.09
☐ 15	Bernie Williams	.75	.35	.09
☐ 16	Billy Ashley	.75	.35	.09
☐ 17	Marquis Grissom	1.50	.70	.19
☐ 18	Kenny Lofton	5.00	2.20	.60
☐ 19	Ray Lankford	1.50	.70	.19
☐ 20	Tim Salmon	3.00	1.35	.35
☐ 21	Steve Hosey	.75	.35	.09
☐ 22	Charles Nagy	.75	.35	.09
☐ 23	Dave Fleming	.75	.35	.09
☐ 24	Reggie Sanders	2.00	.90	.25
☐ 25	Sam Militello	.75	.35	.09
☐ 26	Eric Karros	2.00	.90	.25
☐ 27	Ryan Klesko	5.00	2.20	.60
☐ 28	Dean Palmer	.75	.35	.09
☐ 29	Ivan Rodriguez	1.50	.70	.19
☐ 30	Sterling Hitchcock	.75	.35	.09

1993 Pinnacle Team 2001

This 30-card standard-size (2 1/2" by 3 1/2") set salutes players expected to be stars in the year 2001. The cards were inserted one per pack in first series 27-card superpacks and feature color player action shots on their fronts. These photos are borderless at the top and right, and black-bordered on the bottom and left. The player's name appears in gold-foil in the bottom margin, and his gold-foil-encircled team logo rests in the bottom left. The set's title appears vertically in gold foil in the left margin. The horizontal back carries a posed color player photo in its right half, and on

1993 Pinnacle Team Pinnacle

This ten-card Team Pinnacle subset was randomly inserted in first series foil packs. According to Score, the chances of finding one are not less than one in 24 packs. Each double-sided card displays paintings by artist Christopher Greco. One side features the best player at his position in the American League, while the opposite has his National League counterpart. A special bonus Team Pinnacle card (11) was available to collectors only through a mail-in offer for ten 1993 Pinnacle baseball wrappers plus 1.50 for shipping and handling. Moreover, hobby dealers who ordered Pinnacle received two bonus cards and an advertisement display promoting the offer.

	MINT	NRMT	EXC
COMPLETE SET (10)	90.00	40.00	11.00
COMMON PAIR (1-10/B11)	3.00	1.35	.35
☐ 1 Greg Maddux Mike Mussina	30.00	13.50	3.70
☐ 2 Tom Glavine John Smiley	5.00	2.20	.60
☐ 3 Darren Daulton Ivan Rodriguez	5.00	2.20	.60
☐ 4 Fred McGriff Frank Thomas	30.00	13.50	3.70
☐ 5 Delino DeShields Carlos Baerga	10.00	4.50	1.25
☐ 6 Gary Sheffield Edgar Martinez	5.00	2.20	.60
☐ 7 Ozzie Smith Pat Listach	8.00	3.60	1.00
☐ 8 Barry Bonds Juan Gonzalez	15.00	6.75	1.85
☐ 9 Andy Van Slyke Kirby Puckett	10.00	4.50	1.25
☐ 10 Larry Walker Joe Carter	8.00	3.60	1.00
☐ B11 Rob Dibble Rick Aguilera	3.00	1.35	.35

1994 Pinnacle

The 540-card 1994 Pinnacle set was issued in two series of 270. The fronts feature full-bleed color action player photos. In one of the upper corners, the new Pinnacle logo appears with the brand name immediately below in small white lettering. Toward the bottom, the player's last name in gold foil on a black bar overlays a two-color emblem carrying his first name and his team name. On most of the backs, a ghosted version of the front picture forms the background for a player cutout, biography, and statistics. The series closes with a Rookie Prospects subset (224-261) and a Draft Picks subset (262-270). The cards are

numbered on the back. Rookie Cards include Brian Anderson, Brooks Kieschnick, Derrek Lee, Trot Nixon and Kirk Presley.

	MINT	NRMT	EXC
COMPLETE SET (540)	30.00	13.50	3.70
COMPLETE SERIES 1 (270)	15.00	6.75	1.85
COMPLETE SERIES 2 (270)	15.00	6.75	1.85
COMMON CARD (1-270)	.10	.05	.01
COMMON CARD (271-540)	.10	.05	.01
☐ 1 Frank Thomas	3.00	1.35	.35
☐ 2 Carlos Baerga	.60	.25	.07
☐ 3 Sammy Sosa	.30	.14	.04
☐ 4 Tony Gwynn	1.00	.45	.12
☐ 5 John Olerud	.30	.14	.04
☐ 6 Ryne Sandberg	.75	.35	.09
☐ 7 Moises Alou	.30	.14	.04
☐ 8 Steve Avery	.30	.14	.04
☐ 9 Tim Salmon	.60	.25	.07
☐ 10 Cecil Fielder	.30	.14	.04
☐ 11 Greg Maddux	3.00	1.35	.35
☐ 12 Barry Larkin	.40	.18	.05
☐ 13 Mike Devereaux	.20	.09	.03
☐ 14 Charlie Hayes	.20	.09	.03
☐ 15 Albert Belle	1.25	.55	.16
☐ 16 Andy Van Slyke	.30	.14	.04
☐ 17 Mo Vaughn	.50	.23	.06
☐ 18 Brian McRae	.20	.09	.03
☐ 19 Cal Eldred	.20	.09	.03
☐ 20 Craig Biggio	.20	.09	.03
☐ 21 Kirby Puckett	1.00	.45	.12
☐ 22 Derek Bell	.20	.09	.03
☐ 23 Don Mattingly	1.50	.70	.19
☐ 24 John Burkett	.20	.09	.03
☐ 25 Roger Clemens	.50	.23	.06
☐ 26 Barry Bonds	.75	.35	.09
☐ 27 Paul Molitor	.30	.14	.04
☐ 28 Mike Piazza	1.25	.55	.16
☐ 29 Robin Ventura	.20	.09	.03
☐ 30 Jeff Conine	.30	.14	.04
☐ 31 Wade Boggs	.30	.14	.04
☐ 32 Dennis Eckersley	.30	.14	.04
☐ 33 Bobby Bonilla	.30	.14	.04
☐ 34 Lenny Dykstra	.30	.14	.04
☐ 35 Manny Alexander	.10	.05	.01
☐ 36 Ray Lankford	.30	.14	.04
☐ 37 Greg Vaughn	.20	.09	.03
☐ 38 Chuck Finley	.10	.05	.01
☐ 39 Todd Benzinger	.10	.05	.01
☐ 40 Dave Justice	.40	.18	.05
☐ 41 Rob Dibble	.10	.05	.01
☐ 42 Tom Henke	.10	.05	.01
☐ 43 David Nied	.20	.09	.03
☐ 44 Sandy Alomar Jr.	.20	.09	.03
☐ 45 Pete Harnisch	.10	.05	.01
☐ 46 Jeff Russell	.10	.05	.01
☐ 47 Terry Mulholland	.20	.09	.03
☐ 48 Kevin Appier	.20	.09	.03
☐ 49 Randy Tomlin	.10	.05	.01
☐ 50 Cal Ripken Jr.	3.00	1.35	.35
☐ 51 Andy Benes	.20	.09	.03
☐ 52 Jimmy Key	.20	.09	.03
☐ 53 Kirt Manwaring	.10	.05	.01
☐ 54 Kevin Tapani	.10	.05	.01
☐ 55 Jose Guzman	.10	.05	.01
☐ 56 Todd Stottlemyre	.10	.05	.01
☐ 57 Jack McDowell	.30	.14	.04
☐ 58 Orel Hershiser	.20	.09	.03
☐ 59 Chris Hammond	.10	.05	.01
☐ 60 Chris Nabholz	.10	.05	.01

☐ 61	Ruben Sierra	.30	.14	.04	☐ 132	Wayne Kirby	.10	.05	.01
☐ 62	Dwight Gooden	.10	.05	.01	☐ 133	Eric Young	.20	.09	.03
☐ 63	John Kruk	.20	.09	.03	☐ 134	Scott Servais	.10	.05	.01
☐ 64	Omar Vizquel	.10	.05	.01	☐ 135	Scott Radinsky	.10	.05	.01
☐ 65	Tim Naehring	.20	.09	.03	☐ 136	Bret Barberie	.10	.05	.01
☐ 66	Dwight Smith	.10	.05	.01	☐ 137	John Roper	.10	.05	.01
☐ 67	Mickey Tettleton	.20	.09	.03	☐ 138	Ricky Gutierrez	.10	.05	.01
☐ 68	J.T. Snow	.20	.09	.03	☐ 139	Bernie Williams	.20	.09	.03
☐ 69	Greg McMichael	.20	.09	.03	☐ 140	Bud Black	.10	.05	.01
☐ 70	Kevin Mitchell	.20	.09	.03	☐ 141	Jose Vizcaino	.10	.05	.01
☐ 71	Kevin Brown	.10	.05	.01	☐ 142	Gerald Williams	.20	.09	.03
☐ 72	Scott Cooper	.20	.09	.03	☐ 143	Duane Ward	.20	.09	.03
☐ 73	Jim Thome	.60	.25	.07	☐ 144	Danny Jackson	.10	.05	.01
☐ 74	Joe Girardi	.10	.05	.01	☐ 145	Allen Watson	.10	.05	.01
☐ 75	Eric Anthony	.10	.05	.01	☐ 146	Scott Fletcher	.10	.05	.01
☐ 76	Orlando Merced	.20	.09	.03	☐ 147	Delino DeShields	.20	.09	.03
☐ 77	Felix Jose	.10	.05	.01	☐ 148	Shane Mack	.20	.09	.03
☐ 78	Tommy Greene	.10	.05	.01	☐ 149	Jim Eisenreich	.10	.05	.01
☐ 79	Bernard Gilkey	.20	.09	.03	☐ 150	Troy Neel	.20	.09	.03
☐ 80	Phil Plantier	.20	.09	.03	☐ 151	Jay Bell	.20	.09	.03
☐ 81	Danny Tartabull	.20	.09	.03	☐ 152	B.J. Surhoff	.10	.05	.01
☐ 82	Trevor Wilson	.10	.05	.01	☐ 153	Mark Whiten	.20	.09	.03
☐ 83	Chuck Knoblauch	.30	.14	.04	☐ 154	Mike Henneman	.10	.05	.01
☐ 84	Rick Wilkins	.10	.05	.01	☐ 155	Todd Hundley	.20	.09	.03
☐ 85	Devon White	.20	.09	.03	☐ 156	Greg Myers	.10	.05	.01
☐ 86	Lance Johnson	.10	.05	.01	☐ 157	Ryan Klesko	.75	.35	.09
☐ 87	Eric Karros	.20	.09	.03	☐ 158	Dave Fleming	.10	.05	.01
☐ 88	Gary Sheffield	.30	.14	.04	☐ 159	Mickey Morandini	.10	.05	.01
☐ 89	Wil Cordero	.30	.14	.04	☐ 160	Blas Minor	.10	.05	.01
☐ 90	Ron Darling	.10	.05	.01	☐ 161	Reggie Jefferson	.10	.05	.01
☐ 91	Darren Daulton	.30	.14	.04	☐ 162	David Hulse	.10	.05	.01
☐ 92	Joe Orsulak	.10	.05	.01	☐ 163	Greg Swindell	.10	.05	.01
☐ 93	Steve Cooke	.10	.05	.01	☐ 164	Roberto Hernandez	.10	.05	.01
☐ 94	Darryl Hamilton	.10	.05	.01	☐ 165	Brady Anderson	.20	.09	.03
☐ 95	Aaron Sele	.30	.14	.04	☐ 166	Jack Armstrong	.10	.05	.01
☐ 96	John Doherty	.10	.05	.01	☐ 167	Phil Clark	.10	.05	.01
☐ 97	Gary DiSarcina	.10	.05	.01	☐ 168	Melido Perez	.10	.05	.01
☐ 98	Jeff Blauser	.20	.09	.03	☐ 169	Darren Lewis	.10	.05	.01
☐ 99	John Smiley	.10	.05	.01	☐ 170	Sam Horn	.10	.05	.01
☐ 100	Ken Griffey Jr.	3.00	1.35	.35	☐ 171	Mike Harkey	.10	.05	.01
☐ 101	Dean Palmer	.20	.09	.03	☐ 172	Juan Guzman	.20	.09	.03
☐ 102	Felix Fermin	.10	.05	.01	☐ 173	Bob Natal	.10	.05	.01
☐ 103	Jerald Clark	.10	.05	.01	☐ 174	Deion Sanders	.60	.25	.07
☐ 104	Doug Drabek	.30	.14	.04	☐ 175	Carlos Quintana	.10	.05	.01
☐ 105	Curt Schilling	.10	.05	.01	☐ 176	Mel Rojas	.10	.05	.01
☐ 106	Jeff Montgomery	.20	.09	.03	☐ 177	Willie Banks	.10	.05	.01
☐ 107	Rene Arocha	.20	.05	.01	☐ 178	Ben Rivera	.10	.05	.01
☐ 108	Carlos Garcia	.10	.05	.01	☐ 179	Kenny Lofton	1.00	.45	.12
☐ 109	Wally Whitehurst	.10	.05	.01	☐ 180	Leo Gomez	.10	.05	.01
☐ 110	Jim Abbott	.30	.14	.04	☐ 181	Roberto Mejia	.10	.05	.01
☐ 111	Royce Clayton	.20	.09	.03	☐ 182	Mike Perez	.10	.05	.01
☐ 112	Chris Hoiles	.20	.09	.03	☐ 183	Travis Fryman	.30	.14	.04
☐ 113	Mike Morgan	.10	.05	.01	☐ 184	Ben McDonald	.20	.09	.03
☐ 114	Joe Magrane	.10	.05	.01	☐ 185	Steve Frey	.10	.05	.01
☐ 115	Tom Candiotti	.10	.05	.01	☐ 186	Kevin Young	.10	.05	.01
☐ 116	Ron Karkovice	.10	.05	.01	☐ 187	Dave Magadan	.10	.05	.01
☐ 117	Ryan Bowen	.10	.05	.01	☐ 188	Bobby Munoz	.20	.09	.03
☐ 118	Rod Beck	.20	.09	.03	☐ 189	Pat Rapp	.10	.05	.01
☐ 119	John Wetteland	.10	.05	.01	☐ 190	Jose Offerman	.20	.09	.03
☐ 120	Terry Steinbach	.20	.09	.03	☐ 191	Vinny Castilla	.20	.09	.03
☐ 121	Dave Hollins	.20	.09	.03	☐ 192	Ivan Calderon	.10	.05	.01
☐ 122	Jeff Kent	.20	.09	.03	☐ 193	Ken Caminiti	.20	.09	.03
☐ 123	Ricky Bones	.10	.05	.01	☐ 194	Benji Gil	.20	.09	.03
☐ 124	Brian Jordan	.20	.09	.03	☐ 195	Chuck Carr	.10	.05	.01
☐ 125	Chad Kreuter	.10	.05	.01	☐ 196	Derrick May	.10	.05	.01
☐ 126	John Valentin	.30	.14	.04	☐ 197	Pat Kelly	.10	.05	.01
☐ 127	Hilly Hathaway	.10	.05	.01	☐ 198	Jeff Brantley	.10	.05	.01
☐ 128	Wilson Alvarez	.30	.14	.04	☐ 199	Jose Lind	.10	.05	.01
☐ 129	Tino Martinez	.20	.09	.03	☐ 200	Steve Buechele	.10	.05	.01
☐ 130	Rodney Bolton	.10	.05	.01	☐ 201	Wes Chamberlain	.10	.05	.01
☐ 131	David Segui	.10	.05	.01	☐ 202	Eduardo Perez	.10	.05	.01

□	#	Player			
□	203	Bret Saberhagen	.20	.09	.03
□	204	Gregg Jefferies	.30	.14	.04
□	205	Darrin Fletcher	.10	.05	.01
□	206	Kent Hrbek	.10	.05	.01
□	207	Kim Batiste	.10	.05	.01
□	208	Jeff King	.10	.05	.01
□	209	Donovan Osborne	.10	.05	.01
□	210	Dave Nilsson	.10	.05	.01
□	211	Al Martin	.10	.05	.01
□	212	Mike Moore	.10	.05	.01
□	213	Sterling Hitchcock	.20	.09	.03
□	214	Geronimo Pena	.10	.05	.01
□	215	Kevin Higgins	.10	.05	.01
□	216	Norm Charlton	.10	.05	.01
□	217	Don Slaught	.10	.05	.01
□	218	Mitch Williams	.10	.05	.01
□	219	Derek Lilliquist	.10	.05	.01
□	220	Armando Reynoso	.10	.05	.01
□	221	Kenny Rogers	.20	.09	.03
□	222	Doug Jones	.10	.05	.01
□	223	Luis Aquino	.10	.05	.01
□	224	Mike Oquist	.20	.09	.03
□	225	Darryl Scott	.10	.05	.01
□	226	Kurt Abbott	.25	.11	.03
□	227	Andy Tomberlin	.10	.05	.01
□	228	Norberto Martin	.20	.09	.03
□	229	Pedro Castellano	.10	.05	.01
□	230	Curtis Pride	.20	.09	.03
□	231	Jeff McNeely	.10	.05	.01
□	232	Scott Lydy	.10	.05	.01
□	233	Darren Oliver	.10	.05	.01
□	234	Danny Bautista	.20	.09	.03
□	235	Butch Huskey	.10	.05	.01
□	236	Chipper Jones	1.50	.70	.19
□	237	Eddie Zambrano	.10	.05	.01
□	238	Domingo Jean	.10	.05	.01
□	239	Javier Lopez	.50	.23	.06
□	240	Nigel Wilson	.20	.09	.03
□	241	Drew Denson	.10	.05	.01
□	242	Raul Mondesi	1.00	.45	.12
□	243	Luis Ortiz	.10	.05	.01
□	244	Manny Ramirez	1.50	.70	.19
□	245	Greg Blosser	.10	.05	.01
□	246	Rondell White	.30	.14	.04
□	247	Steve Karsay	.20	.09	.03
□	248	Scott Stahoviak	.10	.05	.01
□	249	Jose Valentin	.20	.09	.03
□	250	Marc Newfield	.30	.14	.04
□	251	Keith Kessinger	.10	.05	.01
□	252	Carl Everett	.20	.09	.03
□	253	John O'Donoghue	.10	.05	.01
□	254	Turk Wendell	.10	.05	.01
□	255	Scott Ruffcorn	.20	.09	.03
□	256	Tony Tarasco	.30	.14	.04
□	257	Andy Cook	.20	.09	.03
□	258	Matt Mieske	.10	.05	.01
□	259	Luis Lopez	.10	.05	.01
□	260	Ramon Caraballo	.20	.09	.03
□	261	Salomon Torres	.20	.09	.03
□	262	Brooks Kieschnick	2.50	1.10	.30
□	263	Daron Kirkreit	.20	.09	.03
□	264	Bill Wagner	.60	.25	.07
□	265	Matt Drews	.75	.35	.09
□	266	Scott Christman	.20	.09	.03
□	267	Torii Hunter	.25	.11	.03
□	268	Jamey Wright	.30	.14	.04
□	269	Jeff Granger	.20	.09	.03
□	270	Trot Nixon	.75	.35	.09
□	271	Randy Myers	.10	.05	.01
□	272	Trevor Hoffman	.10	.05	.01
□	273	Bob Wickman	.10	.05	.01
□	274	Willie McGee	.10	.05	.01
□	275	Hipolito Pichardo	.10	.05	.01
□	276	Bobby Witt	.10	.05	.01
□	277	Gregg Olson	.10	.05	.01
□	278	Randy Johnson	.60	.25	.07
□	279	Robb Nen	.10	.05	.01
□	280	Paul O'Neill	.20	.09	.03
□	281	Lou Whitaker	.30	.14	.04
□	282	Chad Curtis	.20	.09	.03
□	283	Doug Henry	.10	.05	.01
□	284	Tom Glavine	.30	.14	.04
□	285	Mike Greenwell	.20	.09	.03
□	286	Roberto Kelly	.10	.05	.01
□	287	Roberto Alomar	.60	.25	.07
□	288	Charlie Hough	.20	.09	.03
□	289	Alex Fernandez	.30	.14	.04
□	290	Jeff Bagwell	1.00	.45	.12
□	291	Wally Joyner	.20	.09	.03
□	292	Andujar Cedeno	.10	.05	.01
□	293	Rick Aguilera	.20	.09	.03
□	294	Darryl Strawberry	.20	.09	.03
□	295	Mike Mussina	.40	.18	.05
□	296	Jeff Gardner	.10	.05	.01
□	297	Chris Gwynn	.10	.05	.01
□	298	Matt Williams	.50	.23	.06
□	299	Brent Gates	.20	.09	.03
□	300	Mark McGwire	.30	.14	.04
□	301	Jim Deshaies	.10	.05	.01
□	302	Edgar Martinez	.20	.09	.03
□	303	Danny Darwin	.10	.05	.01
□	304	Pat Meares	.10	.05	.01
□	305	Benito Santiago	.10	.05	.01
□	306	Jose Canseco	.50	.23	.06
□	307	Jim Gott	.10	.05	.01
□	308	Paul Sorrento	.10	.05	.01
□	309	Scott Kamienicki	.10	.05	.01
□	310	Larry Walker	.40	.18	.05
□	311	Mark Langston	.30	.14	.04
□	312	John Jaha	.10	.05	.01
□	313	Stan Javier	.10	.05	.01
□	314	Hal Morris	.20	.09	.03
□	315	Robby Thompson	.10	.05	.01
□	316	Pat Hentgen	.20	.09	.03
□	317	Tom Gordon	.10	.05	.01
□	318	Joey Cora	.10	.05	.01
□	319	Luis Alicea	.10	.05	.01
□	320	Andre Dawson	.30	.14	.04
□	321	Darryl Kile	.20	.09	.03
□	322	Jose Rijo	.20	.09	.03
□	323	Luis Gonzalez	.10	.05	.01
□	324	Billy Ashley	.30	.14	.04
□	325	David Cone	.30	.14	.04
□	326	Bill Swift	.10	.05	.01
□	327	Phil Hiatt	.10	.05	.01
□	328	Craig Paquette	.10	.05	.01
□	329	Bob Welch	.10	.05	.01
□	330	Tony Phillips	.10	.05	.01
□	331	Archi Cianfrocco	.10	.05	.01
□	332	Dave Winfield	.30	.14	.04
□	333	David McCarty	.10	.05	.01
□	334	Al Leiter	.10	.05	.01
□	335	Tom Browning	.10	.05	.01
□	336	Mark Grace	.30	.14	.04
□	337	Jose Mesa	.20	.09	.03
□	338	Mike Stanley	.10	.05	.01
□	339	Roger McDowell	.10	.05	.01
□	340	Damion Easley	.10	.05	.01
□	341	Angel Miranda	.10	.05	.01
□	342	John Smoltz	.20	.09	.03
□	343	Jay Buhner	.30	.14	.04
□	344	Bryan Harvey	.10	.05	.01

☐ 345 Joe Carter	.30	.14	.04	
☐ 346 Dante Bichette	.40	.18	.05	
☐ 347 Jason Bere	.30	.14	.04	
☐ 348 Frank Viola	.10	.05	.01	
☐ 349 Ivan Rodriguez	.30	.14	.04	
☐ 350 Juan Gonzalez	.75	.35	.09	
☐ 351 Steve Finley	.10	.05	.01	
☐ 352 Mike Felder	.10	.05	.01	
☐ 353 Ramon Martinez	.20	.09	.03	
☐ 354 Greg Gagne	.10	.05	.01	
☐ 355 Ken Hill	.20	.09	.03	
☐ 356 Pedro Munoz	.10	.05	.01	
☐ 357 Todd Van Poppel	.20	.09	.03	
☐ 358 Marquis Grissom	.30	.14	.04	
☐ 359 Milt Cuyler	.10	.05	.01	
☐ 360 Reggie Sanders	.30	.14	.04	
☐ 361 Scott Erickson	.10	.05	.01	
☐ 362 Billy Hatcher	.10	.05	.01	
☐ 363 Gene Harris	.10	.05	.01	
☐ 364 Rene Gonzales	.10	.05	.01	
☐ 365 Kevin Rogers	.10	.05	.01	
☐ 366 Eric Plunk	.10	.05	.01	
☐ 367 Todd Zeile	.10	.05	.01	
☐ 368 John Franco	.10	.05	.01	
☐ 369 Brett Butler	.20	.09	.03	
☐ 370 Bill Spiers	.10	.05	.01	
☐ 371 Terry Pendleton	.10	.05	.01	
☐ 372 Chris Bosio	.10	.05	.01	
☐ 373 Orestes Destrade	.10	.05	.01	
☐ 374 Dave Stewart	.20	.09	.03	
☐ 375 Darren Holmes	.10	.05	.01	
☐ 376 Doug Strange	.10	.05	.01	
☐ 377 Brian Turang	.10	.05	.01	
☐ 378 Carl Wills	.10	.05	.01	
☐ 379 Mark McLemore	.10	.05	.01	
☐ 380 Bobby Jones	.30	.14	.04	
☐ 381 Scott Sanders	.10	.05	.01	
☐ 382 Kirk Rueter	.10	.05	.01	
☐ 383 Randy Velarde	.10	.05	.01	
☐ 384 Fred McGriff	.40	.18	.05	
☐ 385 Charles Nagy	.20	.09	.03	
☐ 386 Rich Amaral	.10	.05	.01	
☐ 387 Geronimo Berroa	.10	.05	.01	
☐ 388 Eric Davis	.10	.05	.01	
☐ 389 Ozzie Smith	.60	.25	.07	
☐ 390 Alex Arias	.10	.05	.01	
☐ 391 Brad Ausmus	.10	.05	.01	
☐ 392 Cliff Floyd	.30	.14	.04	
☐ 393 Roger Salkeld	.10	.05	.01	
☐ 394 Jim Edmonds	.50	.23	.06	
☐ 395 Jeromy Burnitz	.10	.05	.01	
☐ 396 Dave Staton	.10	.05	.01	
☐ 397 Rob Butler	.10	.05	.01	
☐ 398 Marcos Armas	.10	.05	.01	
☐ 399 Darrell Whitmore	.10	.05	.01	
☐ 400 Ryan Thompson	.20	.09	.03	
☐ 401 Ross Powell	.10	.05	.01	
☐ 402 Joe Oliver	.10	.05	.01	
☐ 403 Paul Carey	.10	.05	.01	
☐ 404 Bob Hamelin	.20	.09	.03	
☐ 405 Chris Turner	.10	.05	.01	
☐ 406 Nate Minchey	.10	.05	.01	
☐ 407 Lonnie Maclin	.10	.05	.01	
☐ 408 Harold Baines	.20	.09	.03	
☐ 409 Brian Williams	.10	.05	.01	
☐ 410 Johnny Ruffin	.10	.05	.01	
☐ 411 Julian Tavarez	.60	.25	.07	
☐ 412 Mark Hutton	.10	.05	.01	
☐ 413 Carlos Delgado	.30	.14	.04	
☐ 414 Chris Gomez	.30	.14	.04	
☐ 415 Mike Hampton	.10	.05	.01	
☐ 416 Alex Diaz	.10	.05	.01	
☐ 417 Jeffrey Hammonds	.30	.14	.04	
☐ 418 Jayhawk Owens	.10	.05	.01	
☐ 419 J.R. Phillips	.20	.09	.03	
☐ 420 Cory Bailey	.10	.05	.01	
☐ 421 Denny Hocking	.10	.05	.01	
☐ 422 Jon Shave	.10	.05	.01	
☐ 423 Damon Buford	.10	.05	.01	
☐ 424 Troy O'Leary	.20	.09	.03	
☐ 425 Tripp Cromer	.10	.05	.01	
☐ 426 Albie Lopez	.20	.09	.03	
☐ 427 Tony Fernandez	.10	.05	.01	
☐ 428 Ozzie Guillen	.10	.05	.01	
☐ 429 Alan Trammell	.30	.14	.04	
☐ 430 John Wasdin	.60	.25	.07	
☐ 431 Marc Valdes	.20	.09	.03	
☐ 432 Brian Anderson	.30	.14	.04	
☐ 433 Matt Brunson	.25	.11	.03	
☐ 434 Wayne Gomes	.40	.18	.05	
☐ 435 Jay Powell	.30	.14	.04	
☐ 436 Kirk Presley	.30	.14	.04	
☐ 437 Jon Ratliff	.20	.09	.03	
☐ 438 Derrek Lee	1.25	.55	.16	
☐ 439 Tom Pagnozzi	.10	.05	.01	
☐ 440 Kent Mercker	.10	.05	.01	
☐ 441 Phil Leftwich	.10	.05	.01	
☐ 442 Jamie Moyer	.10	.05	.01	
☐ 443 John Flaherty	.10	.05	.01	
☐ 444 Mark Wohlers	.10	.05	.01	
☐ 445 Jose Bautista	.10	.05	.01	
☐ 446 Andres Galarraga	.30	.14	.04	
☐ 447 Mark Lemke	.10	.05	.01	
☐ 448 Tim Wakefield	.20	.09	.03	
☐ 449 Pat Listach	.10	.05	.01	
☐ 450 Rickey Henderson	.30	.14	.04	
☐ 451 Mike Gallego	.10	.05	.01	
☐ 452 Bob Tewksbury	.10	.05	.01	
☐ 453 Kirk Gibson	.20	.09	.03	
☐ 454 Pedro Astacio	.20	.09	.03	
☐ 455 Mike Lansing	.20	.09	.03	
☐ 456 Sean Berry	.10	.05	.01	
☐ 457 Bob Walk	.10	.05	.01	
☐ 458 Chili Davis	.20	.09	.03	
☐ 459 Ed Sprague	.10	.05	.01	
☐ 460 Kevin Stocker	.20	.09	.03	
☐ 461 Mike Stanton	.10	.05	.01	
☐ 462 Tim Raines	.30	.14	.04	
☐ 463 Mike Bordick	.10	.05	.01	
☐ 464 David Wells	.10	.05	.01	
☐ 465 Tim Laker	.10	.05	.01	
☐ 466 Cory Snyder	.10	.05	.01	
☐ 467 Alex Cole	.10	.05	.01	
☐ 468 Pete Incaviglia	.10	.05	.01	
☐ 469 Roger Pavlik	.10	.05	.01	
☐ 470 Greg W. Harris	.10	.05	.01	
☐ 471 Xavier Hernandez	.10	.05	.01	
☐ 472 Erik Hanson	.10	.05	.01	
☐ 473 Jesse Orosco	.10	.05	.01	
☐ 474 Greg Colbrunn	.20	.09	.03	
☐ 475 Harold Reynolds	.10	.05	.01	
☐ 476 Greg A. Harris	.10	.05	.01	
☐ 477 Pat Borders	.10	.05	.01	
☐ 478 Melvin Nieves	.30	.14	.04	
☐ 479 Mariano Duncan	.10	.05	.01	
☐ 480 Greg Hibbard	.10	.05	.01	
☐ 481 Tim Pugh	.10	.05	.01	
☐ 482 Bobby Ayala	.10	.05	.01	
☐ 483 Sid Fernandez	.10	.05	.01	
☐ 484 Tim Wallach	.10	.05	.01	
☐ 485 Randy Milligan	.10	.05	.01	
☐ 486 Walt Weiss	.10	.05	.01	

			MINT	NRMT	EXC
☐ 487	Matt Walbeck	.10	.05	.01	
☐ 488	Mike Macfarlane	.10	.05	.01	
☐ 489	Jerry Browne	.10	.05	.01	
☐ 490	Chris Sabo	.10	.05	.01	
☐ 491	Tim Belcher	.10	.05	.01	
☐ 492	Spike Owen	.10	.05	.01	
☐ 493	Rafael Palmeiro	.30	.14	.04	
☐ 494	Brian Harper	.10	.05	.01	
☐ 495	Eddie Murray	.40	.18	.05	
☐ 496	Ellis Burks	.20	.09	.03	
☐ 497	Karl Rhodes	.10	.05	.01	
☐ 498	Otis Nixon	.10	.05	.01	
☐ 499	Lee Smith	.30	.14	.04	
☐ 500	Bip Roberts	.10	.05	.01	
☐ 501	Pedro Martinez	.30	.14	.04	
☐ 502	Brian Hunter	.10	.05	.01	
☐ 503	Tyler Green	.20	.09	.03	
☐ 504	Bruce Hurst	.10	.05	.01	
☐ 505	Alex Gonzalez	.30	.14	.04	
☐ 506	Mark Portugal	.10	.05	.01	
☐ 507	Bob Ojeda	.10	.05	.01	
☐ 508	Dave Henderson	.10	.05	.01	
☐ 509	Bo Jackson	.30	.14	.04	
☐ 510	Bret Boone	.30	.14	.04	
☐ 511	Mark Eichhorn	.10	.05	.01	
☐ 512	Luis Polonia	.10	.05	.01	
☐ 513	Will Clark	.40	.18	.05	
☐ 514	Dave Valle	.10	.05	.01	
☐ 515	Dan Wilson	.10	.05	.01	
☐ 516	Dennis Martinez	.20	.09	.03	
☐ 517	Jim Leyritz	.10	.05	.01	
☐ 518	Howard Johnson	.10	.05	.01	
☐ 519	Jody Reed	.10	.05	.01	
☐ 520	Julio Franco	.20	.09	.03	
☐ 521	Jeff Reardon	.20	.09	.03	
☐ 522	Willie Greene	.20	.09	.03	
☐ 523	Shawon Dunston	.10	.05	.01	
☐ 524	Keith Mitchell	.10	.05	.01	
☐ 525	Rick Helling	.10	.05	.01	
☐ 526	Mark Kiefer	.10	.05	.01	
☐ 527	Chan Ho Park	.30	.14	.04	
☐ 528	Tony Longmire	.10	.05	.01	
☐ 529	Rich Becker	.20	.09	.03	
☐ 530	Tim Hyers	.10	.05	.01	
☐ 531	Darrin Jackson	.10	.05	.01	
☐ 532	Jack Morris	.20	.09	.03	
☐ 533	Rick White	.10	.05	.01	
☐ 534	Mike Kelly	.20	.09	.03	
☐ 535	James Mouton	.20	.09	.03	
☐ 536	Steve Trachsel	.30	.14	.04	
☐ 537	Tony Eusebio	.10	.05	.01	
☐ 538	Kelly Stinnett	.10	.05	.01	
☐ 539	Paul Spoljaric	.10	.05	.01	
☐ 540	Darren Dreifort	.20	.09	.03	
☐ SR1	C.Delgado Super Rk.	10.00	4.50	1.25	

1994 Pinnacle
Artist's Proofs

Randomly inserted at a rate of one in 26 hobby and retail packs, this 540-card set parallels that of the basic Pinnacle issue. Each card is embossed with a gold-foil-stamped "Artist's Proof" logo just above the player name. The Pinnacle logo is also done in gold foil. Just 1,000 of each card were printed.

	MINT	NRMT	EXC
COMPLETE SET (540)	3500.00	1600.00	450.00
COMPLETE SERIES 1 (270)	2250.00	1000.00	275.00
COMPLETE SERIES 2 (270)	1250.00	550.00	160.00
COMMON CARD (1-270)	3.00	1.35	.35
COMMON CARD (271-540)	3.00	1.35	.35
SEMISTARS	6.00	2.70	.75
STARS	10.00	4.50	1.25
*VETERAN STARS:25X to 40X BASIC CARDS			
*YOUNG STARS: 18X to 30X BASIC CARDS			
*RCs:12X to 20X BASIC CARDS			

			MINT	NRMT	EXC
☐ 1	Frank Thomas	125.00	55.00	15.50	
☐ 4	Tony Gwynn	40.00	18.00	5.00	
☐ 11	Greg Maddux	125.00	55.00	15.50	
☐ 15	Albert Belle	50.00	22.00	6.25	
☐ 21	Kirby Puckett	40.00	18.00	5.00	
☐ 23	Don Mattingly	60.00	27.00	7.50	
☐ 28	Mike Piazza	50.00	22.00	6.25	
☐ 50	Cal Ripken	140.00	65.00	17.50	
☐ 100	Ken Griffey Jr.	125.00	55.00	15.50	
☐ 179	Kenny Lofton	40.00	18.00	5.00	
☐ 236	Chipper Jones	75.00	34.00	9.50	
☐ 242	Raul Mondesi	40.00	18.00	5.00	
☐ 244	Manny Ramirez	60.00	27.00	7.50	
☐ 262	Brooks Kieschnick	50.00	22.00	6.25	
☐ 290	Jeff Bagwell	40.00	18.00	5.00	

1994 Pinnacle
Museum Collection

This 540-card set is a parallel dufex to that of the basic Pinnacle issue. They were randomly inserted at a rate of one in four hobby and retail packs. A Museum Collection logo replaces the anti-counterfeit device. Only 6,500 of each card were printed.

	MINT	NRMT	EXC
COMPLETE SET (540)	900.00	400.00	110.00
COMPLETE SERIES 1 (270)	550.00	250.00	70.00
COMPLETE SERIES 2 (270)	350.00	160.00	45.00
COMMON CARD (1-270)	1.00	.45	.12
COMMON CARD (271-540)	1.00	.45	.12
TRADE (279/313/328/382/387)	3.00	1.35	.35
EXPIRED TRADE CARDS	.50	.23	.06
SEMISTARS	2.50	1.10	.30
STARS	4.00	1.80	.50
*VETERAN STARS: 7X to 14X BASIC CARDS			
*YOUNG STARS: 5X to 10X BASIC CARDS			
*RCs: 3X to 6X BASIC CARDS			

			MINT	NRMT	EXC
☐ 1	Frank Thomas	40.00	18.00	5.00	
☐ 4	Tony Gwynn	12.00	5.50	1.50	
☐ 11	Greg Maddux	40.00	18.00	5.00	
☐ 15	Albert Belle	16.00	7.25	2.00	
☐ 21	Kirby Puckett	12.00	5.50	1.50	
☐ 23	Don Mattingly	20.00	9.00	2.50	
☐ 28	Mike Piazza	16.00	7.25	2.00	
☐ 50	Cal Ripken	45.00	20.00	5.50	
☐ 100	Ken Griffey Jr.	40.00	18.00	5.00	
☐ 179	Kenny Lofton	12.00	5.50	1.50	
☐ 236	Chipper Jones	25.00	11.00	3.10	
☐ 242	Raul Mondesi	12.00	5.50	1.50	
☐ 244	Manny Ramirez	20.00	9.00	2.50	
☐ 262	Brooks Kieschnick	16.00	7.25	2.00	
☐ 290	Jeff Bagwell	12.00	5.50	1.50	

1994 Pinnacle Rookie Team Pinnacle

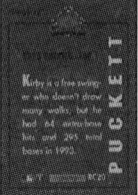

gold foil. The Run Creators logo is at bottom center. A solid colored back contains the team logo as background to statistical highlights including runs created.

These nine double-front cards of the "Rookie Team Pinnacle" set feature a top AL and a top NL rookie prospect by position. The insertion rate for these is one per 48 packs. These special portrait cards were painted by artists Christopher Greco and Ron DeFelice. The front features the National League player and card number. Both sides contain a gold Rookie Team Pinnacle logo.

	MINT	NRMT	EXC
COMPLETE SET (9)	125.00	55.00	15.50
COMMON PAIR (1-9)............	5.00	2.20	.60
☐ 1 Carlos Delgado	15.00	6.75	1.85
Javier Lopez			
☐ 2 Bob Hamelin	10.00	4.50	1.25
J.R. Phillips			
☐ 3 Jon Shave	5.00	2.20	.60
Keith Kessinger			
☐ 4 Luis Ortiz	10.00	4.50	1.25
Butch Huskey			
☐ 5 Kurt Abbott	35.00	16.00	4.40
Chipper Jones			
☐ 6 Manny Ramirez.............	40.00	18.00	5.00
Rondell White			
☐ 7 Jeffrey Hammonds	10.00	4.50	1.25
Cliff Floyd			
☐ 8 Marc Newfield...............	10.00	4.50	1.25
Nigel Wilson			
☐ 9 Mark Hutton..................	5.00	2.20	.60
Salomon Torres			

1994 Pinnacle Run Creators

Randomly inserted at an approximate rate of one in four jumbo packs, this 22-card standard-size set spotlights top run producers. The player stands out from a solid background on front. His last name and the Pinnacle logo run up the right border in

	MINT	NRMT	EXC
COMPLETE SET (44)	160.00	70.00	20.00
COMPLETE SERIES 1 (22)....	90.00	40.00	11.00
COMPLETE SERIES 2 (22).....	70.00	32.00	8.75
COMMON CARD (RC1-RC22)..	1.00	.45	.12
COMMON CARD (RC23-RC44)	1.00	.45	.12
☐ RC1 John Olerud	1.50	.70	.19
☐ RC2 Frank Thomas	20.00	9.00	2.50
☐ RC3 Ken Griffey Jr.	20.00	9.00	2.50
☐ RC4 Paul Molitor	1.50	.70	.19
☐ RC5 Rafael Palmeiro	1.50	.70	.19
☐ RC6 Roberto Alomar..........	4.00	1.80	.50
☐ RC7 Juan Gonzalez...........	5.00	2.20	.60
☐ RC8 Albert Belle................	8.00	3.60	1.00
☐ RC9 Travis Fryman	1.50	.70	.19
☐ RC10 Rickey Henderson	1.50	.70	.19
☐ RC11 Tony Phillips	1.00	.45	.12
☐ RC12 Mo Vaughn...............	3.00	1.35	.35
☐ RC13 Tim Salmon	4.00	1.80	.50
☐ RC14 Kenny Lofton............	6.00	2.70	.75
☐ RC15 Carlos Baerga	4.00	1.80	.50
☐ RC16 Greg Vaughn............	1.00	.45	.12
☐ RC17 Jay Buhner	2.00	.90	.25
☐ RC18 Chris Hoiles..............	1.00	.45	.12
☐ RC19 Mickey Tettleton......	1.00	.45	.12
☐ RC20 Kirby Puckett............	6.00	2.70	.75
☐ RC21 Danny Tartabull........	1.00	.45	.12
☐ RC22 Devon White..............	1.00	.45	.12
☐ RC23 Barry Bonds	5.00	2.20	.60
☐ RC24 Lenny Dykstra	1.50	.70	.19
☐ RC25 John Kruk.................	1.00	.45	.12
☐ RC26 Fred McGriff.............	2.50	1.10	.30
☐ RC27 Gregg Jefferies.........	1.50	.70	.19
☐ RC28 Mike Piazza..............	8.00	3.60	1.00
☐ RC29 Jeff Blauser..............	1.00	.45	.12
☐ RC30 Andres Galarraga......	1.50	.70	.19
☐ RC31 Darren Daulton..........	1.50	.70	.19
☐ RC32 Dave Justice.............	2.50	1.10	.30
☐ RC33 Craig Biggio	1.50	.70	.19
☐ RC34 Mark Grace...............	1.50	.70	.19
☐ RC35 Tony Gwynn..............	6.00	2.70	.75
☐ RC36 Jeff Bagwell..............	6.00	2.70	.75
☐ RC37 Jay Bell....................	1.00	.45	.12
☐ RC38 Marquis Grissom......	1.50	.70	.19
☐ RC39 Matt Williams............	3.00	1.35	.35
☐ RC40 Charlie Hayes...........	1.00	.45	.12
☐ RC41 Dante Bichette..........	2.50	1.10	.30
☐ RC42 Bernard Gilkey..........	1.50	.70	.19
☐ RC43 Brett Butler...............	1.00	.45	.12
☐ RC44 Rick Wilkins	1.00	.45	.12

1994 Pinnacle Team Pinnacle

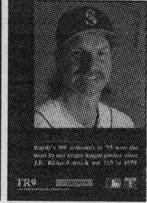

to describe the player. The backs are primarily black with a close-up photo of the player. The cards are numbered with a TR prefix.

Identical in design to the Rookie Team Pinnacle set, these double-front cards feature top players from each of the nine positions. Randomly inserted in second series hobby and retail packs at a rate of one in 48, these special portrait cards were painted by artists Christopher Greco and Ron DeFelice. The front features the National League player and card number. Both sides contain a gold Team Pinnacle logo.

	MINT	NRMT	EXC
COMPLETE SET (9)	200.00	90.00	25.00
COMMON PAIR (1-9)	10.00	4.50	1.25
1 Jeff Bagwell / Frank Thomas	75.00	34.00	9.50
2 Carlos Baerga / Robby Thompson	12.00	5.50	1.50
3 Matt Williams / Dean Palmer	10.00	4.50	1.25
4 Cal Ripken Jr. / Jay Bell	50.00	22.00	6.25
5 Ivan Rodriguez / Mike Piazza	18.00	8.00	2.20
6 Lenny Dykstra / Ken Griffey Jr.	40.00	18.00	5.00
7 Juan Gonzalez / Barry Bonds	20.00	9.00	2.50
8 Tim Salmon / Dave Justice	15.00	6.75	1.85
9 Greg Maddux / Jack McDowell	40.00	18.00	5.00

1994 Pinnacle Tribute

Randomly inserted in hobby packs at a rate of one in 18, this 18-card set was issued in two series of nine. Showcasing some of the top superstar veterans, the fronts have a color player photo with "Tribute" up the left border in a black stripe. The player's name appears at the bottom with a notation given

	MINT	NRMT	EXC
COMPLETE SET (18)	100.00	45.00	12.50
COMPLETE SERIES 1 (9)	40.00	18.00	5.00
COMPLETE SERIES 2 (9)	60.00	27.00	7.50
COMMON CARD (TR1-TR9)	1.00	.45	.12
COMMON CARD (TR10-TR18)	1.00	.45	.12
TR1 Paul Molitor	1.50	.70	.19
TR2 Jim Abbott	1.00	.45	.12
TR3 Dave Winfield	1.50	.70	.19
TR4 Bo Jackson	1.50	.70	.19
TR5 David Justice	2.50	1.10	.30
TR6 Len Dykstra	1.50	.70	.19
TR7 Mike Piazza	8.00	3.60	1.00
TR8 Barry Bonds	5.00	2.20	.60
TR9 Randy Johnson	4.00	1.80	.50
TR10 Ozzie Smith	4.00	1.80	.50
TR11 Mark Whiten	1.00	.45	.12
TR12 Greg Maddux	20.00	9.00	2.50
TR13 Cal Ripken Jr.	25.00	11.00	3.10
TR14 Frank Thomas	20.00	9.00	2.50
TR15 Juan Gonzalez	5.00	2.20	.60
TR16 Roberto Alomar	4.00	1.80	.50
TR17 Ken Griffey Jr.	20.00	9.00	2.50
TR18 Lee Smith	1.50	.70	.19

1995 Pinnacle

This 450-card set was issued in two series of 225 cards. They were released in 12-card packs, 24 packs to a box and 18 boxes in a case. The full-bleed fronts feature action photos. The player's last name is printed in black ink against a gold foil background. The horizontal backs feature a

portrait, an action shot and brief text about the player's career. Seasonal and career stats are on the bottom. Rookie Cards in this set include Scott Elarton and Antone Williamson.

	MINT	NRMT	EXC
COMPLETE SET (450)	40.00	18.00	5.00
COMPLETE SERIES 1 (225)	20.00	9.00	2.50
COMPLETE SERIES 2 (225)	20.00	9.00	2.50
COMMON CARD (1-225)	.10	.05	.01
COMMON CARD (226-450)	.10	.05	.01

☐ 1	Jeff Bagwell	1.00	.45	.12
☐ 2	Roger Clemens	.50	.23	.06
☐ 3	Mark Whiten	.10	.05	.01
☐ 4	Shawon Dunston	.10	.05	.01
☐ 5	Bobby Bonilla	.30	.14	.04
☐ 6	Kevin Tapani	.10	.05	.01
☐ 7	Eric Karros	.30	.14	.04
☐ 8	Cliff Floyd	.30	.14	.04
☐ 9	Pat Kelly	.10	.05	.01
☐ 10	Jeffrey Hammonds	.20	.09	.03
☐ 11	Jeff Conine	.10	.05	.01
☐ 12	Fred McGriff	.40	.18	.05
☐ 13	Chris Bosio	.10	.05	.01
☐ 14	Mike Mussina	.40	.18	.05
☐ 15	Danny Bautista	.10	.05	.01
☐ 16	Mickey Morandini	.10	.05	.01
☐ 17	Chuck Finley	.20	.09	.03
☐ 18	Jim Thome	.50	.23	.06
☐ 19	Luis Ortiz	.10	.05	.01
☐ 20	Walt Weiss	.20	.09	.03
☐ 21	Don Mattingly	1.50	.70	.19
☐ 22	Bob Hamelin	.10	.05	.01
☐ 23	Melido Perez	.10	.05	.01
☐ 24	Keith Mitchell	.10	.05	.01
☐ 25	John Smoltz	.20	.09	.03
☐ 26	Hector Carrasco	.10	.05	.01
☐ 27	Pat Hentgen	.20	.09	.03
☐ 28	Derrick May	.20	.09	.03
☐ 29	Mike Kingery	.10	.05	.01
☐ 30	Chuck Carr	.10	.05	.01
☐ 31	Billy Ashley	.20	.09	.03
☐ 32	Todd Hundley	.30	.14	.04
☐ 33	Luis Gonzalez	.20	.09	.03
☐ 34	Marquis Grissom	.30	.14	.04
☐ 35	Jeff King	.10	.05	.01
☐ 36	Eddie Williams	.10	.05	.01
☐ 37	Tom Pagnozzi	.10	.05	.01
☐ 38	Chris Hoiles	.10	.05	.01
☐ 39	Sandy Alomar Jr.	.10	.05	.01
☐ 40	Mike Greenwell	.20	.09	.03
☐ 41	Lance Johnson	.10	.05	.01
☐ 42	Junior Felix	.10	.05	.01
☐ 43	Felix Jose	.10	.05	.01
☐ 44	Scott Leius	.10	.05	.01
☐ 45	Ruben Sierra	.30	.14	.04
☐ 46	Kevin Seitzer	.10	.05	.01
☐ 47	Wade Boggs	.30	.14	.04
☐ 48	Reggie Jefferson	.10	.05	.01
☐ 49	Jose Canseco	.50	.23	.06
☐ 50	David Justice	.40	.18	.05
☐ 51	John Smiley	.10	.05	.01
☐ 52	Joe Carter	.30	.14	.04
☐ 53	Rick Wilkins	.10	.05	.01
☐ 54	Ellis Burks	.10	.05	.01
☐ 55	Dave Weathers	.10	.05	.01
☐ 56	Pedro Astacio	.10	.05	.01
☐ 57	Ryan Thompson	.10	.05	.01
☐ 58	James Mouton	.20	.09	.03
☐ 59	Mel Rojas	.20	.09	.03
☐ 60	Orlando Merced	.10	.05	.01
☐ 61	Matt Williams	.50	.23	.06
☐ 62	Bernard Gilkey	.20	.09	.03
☐ 63	J.R. Phillips	.10	.05	.01
☐ 64	Lee Smith	.30	.14	.04
☐ 65	Jim Edmonds	.40	.18	.05
☐ 66	Darrin Jackson	.10	.05	.01
☐ 67	Scott Cooper	.10	.05	.01
☐ 68	Ron Karkovice	.10	.05	.01
☐ 69	Chris Gomez	.10	.05	.01
☐ 70	Kevin Appier	.20	.09	.03
☐ 71	Bobby Jones	.20	.09	.03
☐ 72	Doug Drabek	.20	.09	.03
☐ 73	Matt Mieske	.10	.05	.01
☐ 74	Sterling Hitchcock	.10	.05	.01
☐ 75	John Valentin	.30	.14	.04
☐ 76	Reggie Sanders	.30	.14	.04
☐ 77	Wally Joyner	.20	.09	.03
☐ 78	Turk Wendell	.10	.05	.01
☐ 79	Charlie Hayes	.10	.05	.01
☐ 80	Bret Barberie	.10	.05	.01
☐ 81	Troy Neel	.10	.05	.01
☐ 82	Ken Caminiti	.20	.09	.03
☐ 83	Milt Thompson	.10	.05	.01
☐ 84	Paul Sorrento	.10	.05	.01
☐ 85	Trevor Hoffman	.20	.09	.03
☐ 86	Jay Bell	.20	.09	.03
☐ 87	Mark Portugal	.10	.05	.01
☐ 88	Sid Fernandez	.10	.05	.01
☐ 89	Charles Nagy	.20	.09	.03
☐ 90	Jeff Montgomery	.20	.09	.03
☐ 91	Chuck Knoblauch	.30	.14	.04
☐ 92	Jeff Frye	.10	.05	.01
☐ 93	Tony Gwynn	1.00	.45	.12
☐ 94	John Olerud	.20	.09	.03
☐ 95	David Nied	.10	.05	.01
☐ 96	Chris Hammond	.10	.05	.01
☐ 97	Edgar Martinez	.30	.14	.04
☐ 98	Kevin Stocker	.10	.05	.01
☐ 99	Jeff Fassero	.20	.09	.03
☐ 100	Curt Schilling	.10	.05	.01
☐ 101	Dave Clark	.10	.05	.01
☐ 102	Delino DeShields	.20	.09	.03
☐ 103	Leo Gomez	.10	.05	.01
☐ 104	Dave Hollins	.20	.09	.03
☐ 105	Tim Naehring	.20	.09	.03
☐ 106	Otis Nixon	.10	.05	.01
☐ 107	Ozzie Guillen	.10	.05	.01
☐ 108	Jose Lind	.10	.05	.01
☐ 109	Stan Javier	.10	.05	.01
☐ 110	Greg Vaughn	.10	.05	.01
☐ 111	Chipper Jones	1.25	.55	.16
☐ 112	Ed Sprague	.10	.05	.01
☐ 113	Mike Macfarlane	.10	.05	.01
☐ 114	Steve Finley	.20	.09	.03
☐ 115	Ken Hill	.20	.09	.03
☐ 116	Carlos Garcia	.20	.09	.03
☐ 117	Lou Whitaker	.30	.14	.04
☐ 118	Todd Zeile	.20	.09	.03
☐ 119	Gary Sheffield	.30	.14	.04
☐ 120	Ben McDonald	.10	.05	.01
☐ 121	Pete Harnisch	.10	.05	.01
☐ 122	Ivan Rodriguez	.30	.14	.04
☐ 123	Wilson Alvarez	.20	.09	.03
☐ 124	Travis Fryman	.30	.14	.04
☐ 125	Pedro Munoz	.20	.09	.03
☐ 126	Mark Lemke	.20	.09	.03
☐ 127	Jose Valentin	.10	.05	.01
☐ 128	Ken Griffey Jr.	3.00	1.35	.35
☐ 129	Omar Vizquel	.20	.09	.03

☐ 130	Milt Cuyler	.10	.05	.01
☐ 131	Steve Trachsel	.10	.05	.01
☐ 132	Alex Rodriguez	.60	.25	.07
☐ 133	Garret Anderson	.60	.25	.07
☐ 134	Armando Benitez	.10	.05	.01
☐ 135	Shawn Green	.30	.14	.04
☐ 136	Jorge Fabregas	.10	.05	.01
☐ 137	Orlando Miller	.20	.09	.03
☐ 138	Rikkert Faneyte	.10	.05	.01
☐ 139	Ismael Valdes	.10	.05	.01
☐ 140	Jose Oliva	.10	.05	.01
☐ 141	Aaron Small	.10	.05	.01
☐ 142	Tim Davis	.10	.05	.01
☐ 143	Ricky Bottalico	.10	.05	.01
☐ 144	Mike Matheny	.10	.05	.01
☐ 145	Roberto Petagine	.20	.09	.03
☐ 146	Fausto Cruz	.10	.05	.01
☐ 147	Bryce Florie	.10	.05	.01
☐ 148	Jose Lima	.10	.05	.01
☐ 149	John Hudek	.10	.05	.01
☐ 150	Duane Singleton	.20	.09	.03
☐ 151	John Mabry	.20	.09	.03
☐ 152	Robert Eenhoorn	.10	.05	.01
☐ 153	Jon Lieber	.10	.05	.01
☐ 154	Garey Ingram	.10	.05	.01
☐ 155	Paul Shuey	.10	.05	.01
☐ 156	Mike Lieberthal	.10	.05	.01
☐ 157	Steve Dunn	.10	.05	.01
☐ 158	Charles Johnson	.30	.14	.04
☐ 159	Ernie Young	.10	.05	.01
☐ 160	Jose Martinez	.10	.05	.01
☐ 161	Kurt Miller	.10	.05	.01
☐ 162	Joey Eischen	.10	.05	.01
☐ 163	Dave Stevens	.10	.05	.01
☐ 164	Brian L.Hunter	.40	.18	.05
☐ 165	Jeff Cirillo	.20	.09	.03
☐ 166	Mark Smith	.10	.05	.01
☐ 167	McKay Christensen	.25	.11	.03
☐ 168	C.J. Nitkowski	.10	.05	.01
☐ 169	Antone Williamson	.75	.35	.09
☐ 170	Paul Konerko	.20	.09	.03
☐ 171	Scott Elarton	.50	.23	.06
☐ 172	Jacob Shumate	.20	.09	.03
☐ 173	Terrence Long	.20	.09	.03
☐ 174	Mark Johnson	.30	.14	.04
☐ 175	Ben Grieve	.75	.35	.09
☐ 176	Jayson Peterson	.30	.14	.04
☐ 177	Checklist	.10	.05	.01
☐ 178	Checklist	.10	.05	.01
☐ 179	Checklist	.10	.05	.01
☐ 180	Checklist	.10	.05	.01
☐ 181	Brian Anderson	.10	.05	.01
☐ 182	Steve Buechele	.10	.05	.01
☐ 183	Mark Clark	.10	.05	.01
☐ 184	Cecil Fielder	.30	.14	.04
☐ 185	Steve Avery	.20	.09	.03
☐ 186	Devon White	.20	.09	.03
☐ 187	Craig Shipley	.10	.05	.01
☐ 188	Brady Anderson	.20	.09	.03
☐ 189	Kenny Lofton	1.00	.45	.12
☐ 190	Alex Cole	.10	.05	.01
☐ 191	Brent Gates	.20	.09	.03
☐ 192	Dean Palmer	.10	.05	.01
☐ 193	Alex Gonzalez	.20	.09	.03
☐ 194	Steve Cooke	.10	.05	.01
☐ 195	Ray Lankford	.30	.14	.04
☐ 196	Mark McGwire	.30	.14	.04
☐ 197	Marc Newfield	.20	.09	.03
☐ 198	Pat Rapp	.20	.09	.03
☐ 199	Darren Lewis	.10	.05	.01
☐ 200	Carlos Baerga	.60	.25	.07
☐ 201	Rickey Henderson	.30	.14	.04
☐ 202	Kurt Abbott	.20	.09	.03
☐ 203	Kirt Manwaring	.10	.05	.01
☐ 204	Cal Ripken	3.00	1.35	.35
☐ 205	Darren Daulton	.20	.09	.03
☐ 206	Greg Colbrunn	.30	.14	.04
☐ 207	Darryl Hamilton	.10	.05	.01
☐ 208	Bo Jackson	.30	.14	.04
☐ 209	Tony Phillips	.10	.05	.01
☐ 210	Geronimo Berroa	.10	.05	.01
☐ 211	Rich Becker	.10	.05	.01
☐ 212	Tony Tarasco	.20	.09	.03
☐ 213	Karl Rhodes	.10	.05	.01
☐ 214	Phil Plantier	.10	.05	.01
☐ 215	J.T. Snow	.30	.14	.04
☐ 216	Mo Vaughn	.50	.23	.06
☐ 217	Greg Gagne	.10	.05	.01
☐ 218	Ricky Bones	.10	.05	.01
☐ 219	Mike Bordick	.10	.05	.01
☐ 220	Chad Curtis	.20	.09	.03
☐ 221	Royce Clayton	.20	.09	.03
☐ 222	Roberto Alomar	.60	.25	.07
☐ 223	Jose Rijo	.10	.05	.01
☐ 224	Ryan Klesko	.60	.25	.07
☐ 225	Mark Langston	.20	.09	.03
☐ 226	Frank Thomas	3.00	1.35	.35
☐ 227	Juan Gonzalez	.75	.35	.09
☐ 228	Ron Gant	.30	.14	.04
☐ 229	Javier Lopez	.40	.18	.05
☐ 230	Sammy Sosa	.30	.14	.04
☐ 231	Kevin Brown	.10	.05	.01
☐ 232	Gary DiSarcina	.10	.05	.01
☐ 233	Albert Belle	1.25	.55	.16
☐ 234	Jay Buhner	.30	.14	.04
☐ 235	Pedro J.Martinez	.20	.09	.03
☐ 236	Bob Tewksbury	.10	.05	.01
☐ 237	Mike Piazza	1.25	.55	.16
☐ 238	Darryl Kile	.10	.05	.01
☐ 239	Bryan Harvey	.20	.09	.03
☐ 240	Andres Galarraga	.30	.14	.04
☐ 241	Jeff Blauser	.20	.09	.03
☐ 242	Jeff Kent	.20	.09	.03
☐ 243	Bobby Munoz	.10	.05	.01
☐ 244	Greg Maddux	3.00	1.35	.35
☐ 245	Paul O'Neill	.20	.09	.03
☐ 246	Lenny Dykstra	.20	.09	.03
☐ 247	Todd Van Poppel	.10	.05	.01
☐ 248	Bernie Williams	.20	.09	.03
☐ 249	Glenallen Hill	.10	.05	.01
☐ 250	Duane Ward	.10	.05	.01
☐ 251	Dennis Eckersley	.30	.14	.04
☐ 252	Pat Mahomes	.10	.05	.01
☐ 253	Rusty Greer	.10	.05	.01
☐ 254	Roberto Kelly	.20	.09	.03
☐ 255	Randy Myers	.20	.09	.03
☐ 256	Scott Ruffcorn	.10	.05	.01
☐ 257	Robin Ventura	.30	.14	.04
☐ 258	Eduardo Perez	.10	.05	.01
☐ 259	Aaron Sele	.10	.05	.01
☐ 260	Paul Molitor	.30	.14	.04
☐ 261	Juan Guzman	.10	.05	.01
☐ 262	Darren Oliver	.10	.05	.01
☐ 263	Mike Stanley	.20	.09	.03
☐ 264	Tom Glavine	.30	.14	.04
☐ 265	Rico Brogna	.30	.14	.04
☐ 266	Craig Biggio	.30	.14	.04
☐ 267	Darrell Whitmore	.10	.05	.01
☐ 268	Jimmy Key	.20	.09	.03
☐ 269	Will Clark	.40	.18	.05
☐ 270	David Cone	.30	.14	.04
☐ 271	Brian Jordan	.30	.14	.04

☐ 272	Barry Bonds	.75	.35	.09
☐ 273	Danny Tartabull	.20	.09	.03
☐ 274	Ramon J.Martinez	.10	.05	.01
☐ 275	Al Martin	.20	.09	.03
☐ 276	Fred McGriff SM	.20	.09	.03
☐ 277	Carlos Delgado SM	.10	.05	.01
☐ 278	Juan Gonzalez SM	.30	.14	.04
☐ 279	Shawn Green SM	.20	.09	.03
☐ 280	Carlos Baerga SM	.30	.14	.04
☐ 281	Cliff Floyd SM	.10	.05	.01
☐ 282	Ozzie Smith SM	.30	.14	.04
☐ 283	Alex Rodriguez SM	.30	.14	.04
☐ 284	Kenny Lofton SM	.50	.23	.06
☐ 285	Dave Justice SM	.20	.09	.03
☐ 286	Tim Salmon SM	.30	.14	.04
☐ 287	Manny Ramirez SM	.60	.25	.07
☐ 288	Will Clark SM	.20	.09	.03
☐ 289	Garret Anderson SM	.30	.14	.04
☐ 290	Billy Ashley SM	.10	.05	.01
☐ 291	Tony Gwynn SM	.40	.18	.05
☐ 292	Raul Mondesi SM	.40	.18	.05
☐ 293	Rafael Palmeiro SM	.10	.05	.01
☐ 294	Matt Williams SM	.30	.14	.04
☐ 295	Don Mattingly SM	.75	.35	.09
☐ 296	Kirby Puckett SM	.50	.23	.06
☐ 297	Paul Molitor SM	.20	.09	.03
☐ 298	Albert Belle SM	.60	.25	.07
☐ 299	Barry Bonds SM	.40	.18	.05
☐ 300	Mike Piazza SM	.60	.25	.07
☐ 301	Jeff Bagwell SM	.50	.23	.06
☐ 302	Frank Thomas SM	1.50	.70	.19
☐ 303	Chipper Jones SM	.60	.25	.07
☐ 304	Ken Griffey Jr. SM	1.50	.70	.19
☐ 305	Cal Ripken Jr. SM	1.50	.70	.19
☐ 306	Eric Anthony	.10	.05	.01
☐ 307	Todd Benzinger	.10	.05	.01
☐ 308	Jacob Brumfield	.10	.05	.01
☐ 309	Wes Chamberlain	.10	.05	.01
☐ 310	Tino Martinez	.30	.14	.04
☐ 311	Roberto Mejia	.10	.05	.01
☐ 312	Jose Offerman	.10	.05	.01
☐ 313	David Segui	.10	.05	.01
☐ 314	Eric Young	.10	.05	.01
☐ 315	Rey Sanchez	.10	.05	.01
☐ 316	Raul Mondesi	.75	.35	.09
☐ 317	Bret Boone	.30	.14	.04
☐ 318	Andre Dawson	.30	.14	.04
☐ 319	Brian McRae	.20	.09	.03
☐ 320	Dave Nilsson	.20	.09	.03
☐ 321	Moises Alou	.20	.09	.03
☐ 322	Don Slaught	.10	.05	.01
☐ 323	Dave McCarty	.10	.05	.01
☐ 324	Mike Huff	.10	.05	.01
☐ 325	Rick Aguilera	.20	.09	.03
☐ 326	Rod Beck	.20	.09	.03
☐ 327	Kenny Rogers	.10	.05	.01
☐ 328	Andy Benes	.20	.09	.03
☐ 329	Allen Watson	.20	.09	.03
☐ 330	Randy Johnson	.60	.25	.07
☐ 331	Willie Greene	.10	.05	.01
☐ 332	Hal Morris	.20	.09	.03
☐ 333	Ozzie Smith	.60	.25	.07
☐ 334	Jason Bere	.20	.09	.03
☐ 335	Scott Erickson	.20	.09	.03
☐ 336	Dante Bichette	.40	.18	.05
☐ 337	Willie Banks	.10	.05	.01
☐ 338	Eric Davis	.10	.05	.01
☐ 339	Rondell White	.30	.14	.04
☐ 340	Kirby Puckett	1.00	.45	.12
☐ 341	Deion Sanders	.60	.25	.07
☐ 342	Eddie Murray	.40	.18	.05
☐ 343	Mike Harkey	.10	.05	.01
☐ 344	Joey Hamilton	.20	.09	.03
☐ 345	Roger Salkeld	.10	.05	.01
☐ 346	Wil Cordero	.20	.09	.03
☐ 347	John Wetteland	.20	.09	.03
☐ 348	Geronimo Pena	.10	.05	.01
☐ 349	Kirk Gibson	.20	.09	.03
☐ 350	Manny Ramirez	1.25	.55	.16
☐ 351	Wm.VanLandingham	.20	.09	.03
☐ 352	B.J. Surhoff	.20	.09	.03
☐ 353	Ken Ryan	.10	.05	.01
☐ 354	Terry Steinbach	.20	.09	.03
☐ 355	Bret Saberhagen	.20	.09	.03
☐ 356	John Jaha	.20	.09	.03
☐ 357	Joe Girardi	.10	.05	.01
☐ 358	Steve Karsay	.10	.05	.01
☐ 359	Alex Fernandez	.20	.09	.03
☐ 360	Salomon Torres	.10	.05	.01
☐ 361	John Burkett	.10	.05	.01
☐ 362	Derek Bell	.30	.14	.04
☐ 363	Tom Henke	.20	.09	.03
☐ 364	Gregg Jefferies	.30	.14	.04
☐ 365	Jack McDowell	.30	.14	.04
☐ 366	Andujar Cedeno	.10	.05	.01
☐ 367	Dave Winfield	.30	.14	.04
☐ 368	Carl Everett	.20	.09	.03
☐ 369	Danny Jackson	.10	.05	.01
☐ 370	Jeromy Burnitz	.10	.05	.01
☐ 371	Mark Grace	.30	.14	.04
☐ 372	Larry Walker	.40	.18	.05
☐ 373	Bill Swift	.10	.05	.01
☐ 374	Dennis Martinez	.20	.09	.03
☐ 375	Mickey Tettleton	.20	.09	.03
☐ 376	Mel Nieves	.20	.09	.03
☐ 377	Cal Eldred	.10	.05	.01
☐ 378	Orel Hershiser	.20	.09	.03
☐ 379	David Wells	.10	.05	.01
☐ 380	Gary Gaetti	.20	.09	.03
☐ 381	Jeromy Burnitz	.10	.05	.01
☐ 382	Barry Larkin	.40	.18	.05
☐ 383	Jason Jacome	.10	.05	.01
☐ 384	Tim Wallach	.10	.05	.01
☐ 385	Robby Thompson	.10	.05	.01
☐ 386	Frank Viola	.20	.09	.03
☐ 387	Dave Stewart	.20	.09	.03
☐ 388	Bip Roberts	.10	.05	.01
☐ 389	Ron Darling	.10	.05	.01
☐ 390	Carlos Delgado	.20	.09	.03
☐ 391	Tim Salmon	.50	.23	.06
☐ 392	Alan Trammell	.30	.14	.04
☐ 393	Kevin Foster	.10	.05	.01
☐ 394	Jim Abbott	.30	.14	.04
☐ 395	John Kruk	.20	.09	.03
☐ 396	Andy Van Slyke	.20	.09	.03
☐ 397	Dave Magadan	.10	.05	.01
☐ 398	Rafael Palmeiro	.30	.14	.04
☐ 399	Mike Devereaux	.10	.05	.01
☐ 400	Benito Santiago	.20	.09	.03
☐ 401	Brett Butler	.20	.09	.03
☐ 402	John Franco	.20	.09	.03
☐ 403	Matt Walbeck	.10	.05	.01
☐ 404	Terry Pendleton	.20	.09	.03
☐ 405	Chris Sabo	.10	.05	.01
☐ 406	Andrew Lorraine	.20	.09	.03
☐ 407	Dan Wilson	.20	.09	.03
☐ 408	Mike Lansing	.10	.05	.01
☐ 409	Ray McDavid	.20	.09	.03
☐ 410	Shane Andrews	.10	.05	.01
☐ 411	Tom Gordon	.10	.05	.01
☐ 412	Chad Ogea	.20	.09	.03
☐ 413	James Baldwin	.20	.09	.03

		MINT	NRMT	EXC
☐ 414	Russ Davis	.20	.09	.03
☐ 415	Ray Holbert	.10	.05	.01
☐ 416	Ray Durham	.30	.14	.04
☐ 417	Matt Nokes	.10	.05	.01
☐ 418	Rodney Henderson	.10	.05	.01
☐ 419	Gabe White	.10	.05	.01
☐ 420	Todd Hollandsworth	.10	.05	.01
☐ 421	Midre Cummings	.20	.09	.03
☐ 422	Harold Baines	.20	.09	.03
☐ 423	Troy Percival	.20	.09	.03
☐ 424	Joe Vitiello	.20	.09	.03
☐ 425	Andy Ashby	.10	.05	.01
☐ 426	Michael Tucker	.20	.09	.03
☐ 427	Mark Gubicza	.10	.05	.01
☐ 428	Jim Bullinger	.10	.05	.01
☐ 429	Jose Malave	.10	.05	.01
☐ 430	Pete Schourek	.30	.14	.04
☐ 431	Bobby Ayala	.10	.05	.01
☐ 432	Marvin Freeman	.10	.05	.01
☐ 433	Pat Listach	.10	.05	.01
☐ 434	Eddie Taubensee	.10	.05	.01
☐ 435	Steve Howe	.10	.05	.01
☐ 436	Kent Mercker	.10	.05	.01
☐ 437	Hector Fajardo	.10	.05	.01
☐ 438	Scott Kamieniecki	.10	.05	.01
☐ 439	Robb Nen	.20	.09	.03
☐ 440	Mike Kelly	.10	.05	.01
☐ 441	Tom Candiotti	.10	.05	.01
☐ 442	Albie Lopez	.10	.05	.01
☐ 443	Jeff Granger	.10	.05	.01
☐ 444	Rich Aude	.10	.05	.01
☐ 445	Luis Polonia	.10	.05	.01
☐ 446	Frank Thomas Checklist	1.50	.70	.19
☐ 447	Ken Griffey Jr. Checklist	1.50	.70	.19
☐ 448	Mike Piazza Checklist	.60	.25	.07
☐ 449	Jeff Bagwell Checklist	.50	.23	.06
☐ 450	Checklist	2.00	.90	.25
	Jeff Bagwell			
	Frank Thomas			
	Ken Griffey Jr.			
	Mike Piazza			

1995 Pinnacle Artist's Proofs

Inserted one per 36 packs, this is a parallel set to the regular Pinnacle issue. The words "Artist Proof" are clearly labeled in silver. The name on the bottom is also set against a silvery background.

		MINT	NRMT	EXC
COMPLETE SET (450)		2000.00	900.00	250.00
COMPLETE SERIES 1 (225)		1000.00	450.00	125.00
COMPLETE SERIES 2 (225)		1000.00	450.00	125.00
COMMON CARD (1-225)		3.00	1.35	.35
COMMON CARD (226-450)		3.00	1.35	.35
SEMISTARS		6.00	2.70	.75

*VETERAN STARS: 30X to 45X BASIC CARDS
*YOUNG STARS: 20X to 35X BASIC CARDS
*RCs: 10X to 20X BASIC CARDS

☐ 1	Jeff Bagwell	40.00	18.00	5.00
☐ 21	Don Mattingly	60.00	27.00	7.50
☐ 93	Tony Gwynn	40.00	18.00	5.00
☐ 111	Chipper Jones	50.00	22.00	6.25

☐ 128	Ken Griffey Jr.	125.00	55.00	15.50
☐ 189	Kenny Lofton	40.00	18.00	5.00
☐ 204	Cal Ripken	140.00	65.00	17.50
☐ 226	Frank Thomas	125.00	55.00	15.50
☐ 233	Albert Belle	50.00	22.00	6.25
☐ 237	Mike Piazza	50.00	22.00	6.25
☐ 244	Greg Maddux	125.00	55.00	15.50
☐ 284	Kenny Lofton SM	20.00	9.00	2.50
☐ 302	Frank Thomas SM	60.00	27.00	7.50
☐ 303	Chipper Jones SM	25.00	11.00	3.10
☐ 304	Ken Griffey Jr. SM	60.00	27.00	7.50
☐ 305	Cal Ripken SM	70.00	32.00	8.75
☐ 340	Kirby Puckett	40.00	18.00	5.00
☐ 350	Manny Ramirez	50.00	22.00	6.25
☐ 446	Frank Thomas CL	60.00	27.00	7.50
☐ 447	Ken Griffey CL	60.00	27.00	7.50
☐ 450	Jeff Bagwell CL	110.00	50.00	14.00
	Frank Thomas			
	Ken Griffey Jr.			
	Mike Piazza			

1995 Pinnacle Museum Collection

Inserted one in four packs, this is a parallel to the regular Pinnacle issue. These cards use the Dufex technology and are clearly labeled on the back as Museum Collection Cards.

	MINT	NRMT	EXC
COMPLETE SET (450)	800.00	350.00	100.00
COMPLETE SERIES 1 (225)	400.00	180.00	50.00
COMPLETE SERIES 2 (225)	400.00	180.00	50.00
COMMON CARD (1-225)	1.50	.70	.19
COMMON CARD (226-450)	1.50	.70	.19
SEMISTARS	3.00	1.35	.35
TRADE (410/413/416/-	3.00	1.35	.35
420/423/426/444)			

*VETERAN STARS: 10X to 18X BASIC CARDS
*YOUNG STARS: 8X to 14X BASIC CARDS
*RCs: 4X to 8X BASIC CARDS
TRADE CARDS EXPIRED 12/31/95

☐ 1	Jeff Bagwell	15.00	6.75	1.85
☐ 21	Don Mattingly	25.00	11.00	3.10
☐ 93	Tony Gwynn	15.00	6.75	1.85
☐ 111	Chipper Jones	20.00	9.00	2.50
☐ 128	Ken Griffey Jr.	50.00	22.00	6.25
☐ 189	Kenny Lofton	15.00	6.75	1.85
☐ 204	Cal Ripken	55.00	25.00	7.00
☐ 226	Frank Thomas	50.00	22.00	6.25
☐ 233	Albert Belle	20.00	9.00	2.50
☐ 237	Mike Piazza	20.00	9.00	2.50
☐ 244	Greg Maddux	50.00	22.00	6.25
☐ 284	Kenny Lofton SM	8.00	3.60	1.00
☐ 302	Frank Thomas SM	25.00	11.00	3.10
☐ 303	Chipper Jones SM	10.00	4.50	1.25
☐ 304	Ken Griffey Jr. SM	25.00	11.00	3.10
☐ 305	Cal Ripken SM	30.00	13.50	3.70
☐ 340	Kirby Puckett	15.00	6.75	1.85
☐ 350	Manny Ramirez	20.00	9.00	2.50
☐ 446	Frank Thomas CL	25.00	11.00	3.10
☐ 447	Ken Griffey Jr. CL	25.00	11.00	3.10
☐ 450	Jeff Bagwell CL	45.00	20.00	5.50
	Frank Thomas			

Ken Griffey Jr.
Mike Piazza

1995 Pinnacle ETA

This six-card set was randomly inserted approximately one in every 24 first series hobby packs. This set features players who were among the leading prospects for major league stardom. The fronts feature a player photo as well as a quick information bit. The player's name is located on the top. The busy full-bleed backs feature a player photo and some quick comments. On the bottom is the player's name and the card is numbered with an "ETA" prefix in the upper left corner.

	MINT	NRMT	EXC
COMPLETE SET (6)	30.00	13.50	3.70
COMMON CARD (1-6)	2.50	1.10	.30
☐ 1 Ben Grieve	10.00	4.50	1.25
☐ 2 Alex Ochoa	4.00	1.80	.50
☐ 3 Joe Vitiello	2.50	1.10	.30
☐ 4 Johnny Damon	15.00	6.75	1.85
☐ 5 Trey Beamon	4.00	1.80	.50
☐ 6 Brooks Kieschnick	10.00	4.50	1.25

1995 Pinnacle Gate Attractions

This 18-card set was inserted approximately one every 12 second series jumbo packs. The fronts feature two photos, with the words "Gate Attraction" at the bottom left. The player is identified on the top. The horizontal full-bleed backs have the player's name on the left, a player photo in the middle and some career information in the lower right. The cards are numbered with a "GA" prefix in the upper right corner.

	MINT	NRMT	EXC
COMPLETE SET (18)	180.00	80.00	22.00
COMMON PLAYER (GA1-GA18)	3.00	1.35	.35
☐ GA1 Ken Griffey Jr.	30.00	13.50	3.70
☐ GA2 Frank Thomas	30.00	13.50	3.70
☐ GA3 Cal Ripken	40.00	18.00	5.00
☐ GA4 Jeff Bagwell	10.00	4.50	1.25
☐ GA5 Mike Piazza	12.00	5.50	1.50
☐ GA6 Barry Bonds	8.00	3.60	1.00
☐ GA7 Kirby Puckett	10.00	4.50	1.25
☐ GA8 Albert Belle	12.00	5.50	1.50
☐ GA9 Tony Gwynn	10.00	4.50	1.25
☐ GA10 Raul Mondesi	8.00	3.60	1.00
☐ GA11 Will Clark	4.00	1.80	.50
☐ GA12 Don Mattingly	20.00	9.00	2.50
☐ GA13 Roger Clemens	5.00	2.20	.60
☐ GA14 Paul Molitor	3.00	1.35	.35
☐ GA15 Matt Williams	5.00	2.20	.60
☐ GA16 Greg Maddux	30.00	13.50	3.70
☐ GA17 Kenny Lofton	10.00	4.50	1.25
☐ GA18 Cliff Floyd	3.00	1.35	.35

1995 Pinnacle New Blood

This nine-card set was inserted approximately one in every 90 second series hobby and retail packs. This set features nine players who were leading prospects entering the 1995 season. The Dufex enhanced fronts feature two player photos. One photo is a color shot while the other one is a black and white background photo. The words "New Blood" and player's name are on the bottom. The full-bleed backs feature two more photos. Player information is set against these photos. The card is numbered with an "NB" prefix in the upper left corner.

	MINT	NRMT	EXC
COMPLETE SET (9)	150.00	70.00	19.00
COMMON CARD (NB1-NB9)	5.00	2.20	.60

		MINT	NRMT	EXC
☐	NB1 Alex Rodriguez........	25.00	11.00	3.10
☐	NB2 Shawn Green........	12.00	5.50	1.50
☐	NB3 Brian Hunter........	15.00	6.75	1.85
☐	NB4 Garret Anderson......	30.00	13.50	3.70
☐	NB5 Charles Johnson......	12.00	5.50	1.50
☐	NB6 Chipper Jones........	60.00	27.00	7.50
☐	NB7 Carlos Delgado......	12.00	5.50	1.50
☐	NB8 Billy Ashley............	6.00	2.70	.75
☐	NB9 J.R. Phillips UER	5.00	2.20	.60

Dodgers logo on back
Phillips plays for the Giants

1995 Pinnacle Performers

These 18 cards were randomly inserted approximately one in every 12 first series jumbo packs. The full-bleed fronts feature a player photo against a shiny background. The player's name is in white lettering in the upper right corner. The backs have two photos: one a color portrait with the other one being a shaded black and white. There is also some text pertaining to that player. The cards are numbered in the upper right corner with a "PP" prefix.

	MINT	NRMT	EXC
COMPLETE SERIES 1 (18) .	125.00	55.00	15.50
COMMON CARD (1-18)	2.50	1.10	.30

		MINT	NRMT	EXC
☐	PP1 Frank Thomas	30.00	13.50	3.70
☐	PP2 Albert Belle	12.00	5.50	1.50
☐	PP3 Barry Bonds	8.00	3.60	1.00
☐	PP4 Juan Gonzalez	8.00	3.60	1.00
☐	PP5 Andres Galarraga	4.00	1.80	.50
☐	PP6 Raul Mondesi	8.00	3.60	1.00
☐	PP7 Paul Molitor	4.00	1.80	.50
☐	PP8 Tim Salmon	5.00	2.20	.60
☐	PP9 Mike Piazza	12.00	5.50	1.50
☐	PP10 Gregg Jefferies	4.00	1.80	.50
☐	PP11 Will Clark	4.00	1.80	.50
☐	PP12 Greg Maddux	30.00	13.50	3.70
☐	PP13 Manny Ramirez	12.00	5.50	1.50
☐	PP14 Kirby Puckett	10.00	4.50	1.25
☐	PP15 Shawn Green	4.00	1.80	.50
☐	PP16 Rafael Palmeiro	4.00	1.80	.50
☐	PP17 Paul O'Neill	4.00	1.80	.50
☐	PP18 Jason Bere	2.50	1.10	.30

1995 Pinnacle Pin Redemption

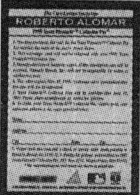

This 18-card set was randomly inserted in all second series packs. Printed odds indicate that these cards were inserted approximately one every in 48 hobby and retail packs and one in every 36 jumbo packs. The horizontal full-bleed fronts feature an action photo, a team logo and another small player photo. The backs explain the rules for ordering the "Team Pinnacle" Collector Pin. The offer expired on November 15, 1995.

	MINT	NRMT	EXC
COMPLETE SET (18)	140.00	65.00	17.50
COMMON CARD (1-18)	2.00	.90	.25

		MINT	NRMT	EXC
☐	1 Greg Maddux..............	25.00	11.00	3.10
☐	2 Mike Mussina..............	3.00	1.35	.35
☐	3 Mike Piazza................	10.00	4.50	1.25
☐	4 Carlos Delgado............	2.00	.90	.25
☐	5 Jeff Bagwell................	8.00	3.60	1.00
☐	6 Frank Thomas..............	25.00	11.00	3.10
☐	7 Craig Biggio................	4.00	1.80	.50
☐	8 Roberto Alomar............	5.00	2.20	.60
☐	9 Ozzie Smith................	5.00	2.20	.60
☐	10 Cal Ripken Jr.	25.00	11.00	3.10
☐	11 Matt Williams............	4.00	1.80	.50
☐	12 Travis Fryman............	4.00	1.80	.50
☐	13 Barry Bonds..............	6.00	2.70	.75
☐	14 Ken Griffey Jr.............	25.00	11.00	3.10
☐	15 Dave Justice..............	3.00	1.35	.35
☐	16 Albert Belle..............	10.00	4.50	1.25
☐	17 Tony Gwynn..............	8.00	3.60	1.00
☐	18 Kirby Puckett..............	8.00	3.60	1.00

1995 Pinnacle Red Hot/White Hot

This 25-card set was randomly inserted into second series packs. The Red Hots were inserted in both hobby and retail packs while the White Hots were only in hobby packs. The fronts feature a player photo on the right, with his name, an inset portrait and either the words "Red Hot or White Hot" on the left. The upper right corner has either an "r" or a "w" in a circle. The back

ground is either white or red depending on the card. The backs have the words "Red Hot" or "White Hot" in the background with a player photo and some information set against it. The cards are numbered in the upper right corner with either a "WH" or a "RH" prefix.

	MINT	NRMT	EXC
COMPLETE SET (25)	125.00	55.00	15.50
COMMON CARD (1-25)	2.00	.90	.25
COMP.WHITE HOT SET (25)	700.00	325.00	90.00
COM.WH.HOT (WH1-WH25)	16.00	7.25	2.00
WHITE HOT: 4X VALUE			

		MINT	NRMT	EXC
☐	1 Cal Ripken Jr.	20.00	9.00	2.50
☐	2 Ken Griffey Jr.	20.00	9.00	2.50
☐	3 Frank Thomas	20.00	9.00	2.50
☐	4 Jeff Bagwell	6.00	2.70	.75
☐	5 Mike Piazza	8.00	3.60	1.00
☐	6 Barry Bonds	5.00	2.20	.60
☐	7 Albert Belle	8.00	3.60	1.00
☐	8 Tony Gwynn	6.00	2.70	.75
☐	9 Kirby Puckett	6.00	2.70	.75
☐	10 Don Mattingly	10.00	4.50	1.25
☐	11 Matt Williams	4.00	1.80	.50
☐	12 Greg Maddux	20.00	9.00	2.50
☐	13 Raul Mondesi	5.00	2.20	.60
☐	14 Paul Molitor	3.00	1.35	.35
☐	15 Manny Ramirez	8.00	3.60	1.00
☐	16 Joe Carter	3.00	1.35	.35
☐	17 Will Clark	3.00	1.35	.35
☐	18 Roger Clemens	4.00	1.80	.50
☐	19 Tim Salmon	4.00	1.80	.50
☐	20 Dave Justice	3.00	1.35	.35
☐	21 Kenny Lofton	6.00	2.70	.75
☐	22 Deion Sanders	4.00	1.80	.50
☐	23 Roberto Alomar	4.00	1.80	.50
☐	24 Cliff Floyd	2.00	.90	.25
☐	25 Carlos Baerga	4.00	1.80	.50

1995 Pinnacle Team Pinnacle

Randomly inserted in series one hobby and retail packs at a rate of one in 90, this nine-card set showcases the game's top players in an etched-foil design. A player photo is superimposed over the player's team logo. The Team Pinnacle logo, player's name and position are printed in silver foil on a black strip at the bottom left of the card. Cards are numbered with the prefix "TP".

	MINT	NRMT	EXC
COMPLETE SET (9)	275.00	125.00	34.00
COMMON CARD (1-9)	10.00	4.50	1.25
KEY SIDE DUFEX: 1.25X VALUE			

		MINT	NRMT	EXC
☐	TP1 Mike Mussina	50.00	22.00	6.25
	Greg Maddux			
☐	TP2 Carlos Delgado	25.00	11.00	3.10
	Mike Piazza			
☐	TP3 Frank Thomas	75.00	34.00	9.50
	Jeff Bagwell			
☐	TP4 Roberto Alomar	12.00	5.50	1.50
	Craig Biggio			
☐	TP5 Cal Ripken	70.00	32.00	8.75
	Ozzie Smith			
☐	TP6 Travis Fryman	10.00	4.50	1.25
	Matt Williams			
☐	TP7 Ken Griffey Jr.	60.00	27.00	7.50
	Barry Bonds			
☐	TP8 Albert Belle	25.00	11.00	3.10
	David Justice			
☐	TP9 Kirby Puckett	25.00	11.00	3.10
	Tony Gwynn			

1995 Pinnacle Upstarts

Top young players are featured in this 30-card set. The cards were randomly inserted in series one hobby and retail packs at a rate of one in eight. Multi-colored foil fronts feature the player in a action cutout set against a star background. The player's name is wrapped around the "Upstarts" logo which is printed on the lower left of the front. The player's team logo is printed at *the top right of the front. Backs are full-bleed color action photos of the player and are numbered at the top right with the prefix "US". A gold polygonal box encloses the player's name and '94 stats along with the team logo. The Pinnacle and '95 Upstarts logo are printed on the top left of the back.*

	MINT	NRMT	EXC
COMPLETE SET (30)	75.00	34.00	9.50
COMMON CARD (US1-US30)	.75	.35	.09

		MINT	NRMT	EXC
☐	US1 Frank Thomas	20.00	9.00	2.50
☐	US2 Roberto Alomar	4.00	1.80	.50
☐	US3 Mike Piazza	8.00	3.60	1.00
☐	US4 Javier Lopez	3.00	1.35	.35
☐	US5 Albert Belle	8.00	3.60	1.00
☐	US6 Carlos Delgado	1.50	.70	.19
☐	US7 Brent Gates	.75	.35	.09
☐	US8 Tim Salmon	3.00	1.35	.35
☐	US9 Raul Mondesi	5.00	2.20	.60
☐	US10 Juan Gonzalez	5.00	2.20	.60
☐	US11 Manny Ramirez	8.00	3.60	1.00
☐	US12 Sammy Sosa	2.50	1.10	.30
☐	US13 Jeff Kent	.75	.35	.09
☐	US14 Melvin Nieves	.75	.35	.09
☐	US15 Rondell White	1.50	.70	.19
☐	US16 Shawn Green	1.50	.70	.19
☐	US17 Bernie Williams	.75	.35	.09
☐	US18 Aaron Sele	.75	.35	.09
☐	US19 Jason Bere	1.50	.70	.19
☐	US20 Joey Hamilton	1.50	.70	.19
☐	US21 Mike Kelly	.75	.35	.09
☐	US22 Wil Cordero	.75	.35	.09
☐	US23 Moises Alou	.75	.35	.09
☐	US24 Roberto Kelly	.75	.35	.09
☐	US25 Deion Sanders	4.00	1.80	.50
☐	US26 Steve Karsay	.75	.35	.09
☐	US27 Bret Boone	1.50	.70	.19
☐	US28 Willie Greene	.75	.35	.09
☐	US29 Billy Ashley	.75	.35	.09
☐	US30 Brian Anderson	.75	.35	.09

1988 Score

This 660-card set was distributed by Major League Marketing. Cards measure 2 1/2" by 3 1/2" and feature six distinctive border colors on the front. Highlights (652-660) and Rookie Prospects (623-647) are included in the set. Reggie Jackson's career is honored with a five-card subset on cards 500-504. Card number 501, showing

Reggie as a member of the Baltimore Orioles, is one of the few opportunities collectors have to visually remember (on a regular card) Reggie's one-year stay with the Orioles. The set is distinguished by the fact that each card back shows a full-color picture of the player. Rookie Cards in this set include Jeff Blauser, Ellis Burks, Mike Devereaux, Ron Gant, Tom Glavine, Gregg Jefferies, Roberto Kelly, Jeff Montgomery, and Matt Williams. The company also produced a very limited "glossy" set, that is valued at ten times the value of the regular (non-glossy) set. Although exact production quantities of this glossy set are not known, it has been speculated, but not confirmed, that 5,000 glossy sets were produced. It is generally accepted that the number of Score glossy sets produced in 1988 was much smaller (estimated only 10 percent to 15 percent as many) than the number of Topps Tiffany or Fleer Tin sets. These Score glossy sets, when bought or sold individually, are valued approximately five to ten times the values listed below.

	MINT	NRMT	EXC
COMPLETE SET (660)	12.00	5.50	1.50
COMPLETE FACT.SET (660)	12.00	5.50	1.50
COMMON CARD (1-660)	.05	.02	.01

		MINT	NRMT	EXC
☐	1 Don Mattingly	.40	.18	.05
☐	2 Wade Boggs	.15	.07	.02
☐	3 Tim Raines	.15	.07	.02
☐	4 Andre Dawson	.15	.07	.02
☐	5 Mark McGwire	.50	.23	.06
☐	6 Kevin Seitzer	.10	.05	.01
☐	7 Wally Joyner	.10	.05	.01
☐	8 Jesse Barfield	.05	.02	.01
☐	9 Pedro Guerrero	.05	.02	.01
☐	10 Eric Davis	.10	.05	.01
☐	11 George Brett	.40	.18	.05
☐	12 Ozzie Smith	.30	.14	.04
☐	13 Rickey Henderson	.15	.07	.02
☐	14 Jim Rice	.15	.07	.02
☐	15 Matt Nokes	.05	.02	.01
☐	16 Mike Schmidt	.25	.11	.03
☐	17 Dave Parker	.15	.07	.02
☐	18 Eddie Murray	.25	.11	.03
☐	19 Andres Galarraga	.15	.07	.02
☐	20 Tony Fernandez	.10	.05	.01
☐	21 Kevin McReynolds	.10	.05	.01
☐	22 B.J. Surhoff	.10	.05	.01
☐	23 Pat Tabler	.05	.02	.01
☐	24 Kirby Puckett	.40	.18	.05
☐	25 Benny Santiago	.10	.05	.01
☐	26 Ryne Sandberg	.30	.14	.04
☐	27 Kelly Downs (Will Clark in background, out of focus)	.05	.02	.01
☐	28 Jose Cruz	.05	.02	.01
☐	29 Pete O'Brien	.05	.02	.01
☐	30 Mark Langston	.15	.07	.02
☐	31 Lee Smith	.15	.07	.02
☐	32 Juan Samuel	.05	.02	.01
☐	33 Kevin Bass	.05	.02	.01
☐	34 R.J. Reynolds	.05	.02	.01
☐	35 Steve Sax	.10	.05	.01
☐	36 John Kruk	.15	.07	.02
☐	37 Alan Trammell	.15	.07	.02
☐	38 Chris Bosio	.10	.05	.01

☐ 39	Brook Jacoby	.05	.02	.01
☐ 40	Willie McGee UER	.10	.05	.01
	(Excited misspelled as excitd)			
☐ 41	Dave Magadan	.10	.05	.01
☐ 42	Fred Lynn	.10	.05	.01
☐ 43	Kent Hrbek	.15	.07	.02
☐ 44	Brian Downing	.05	.02	.01
☐ 45	Jose Canseco	.50	.23	.06
☐ 46	Jim Presley	.05	.02	.01
☐ 47	Mike Stanley	.10	.05	.01
☐ 48	Tony Pena	.05	.02	.01
☐ 49	David Cone	.35	.16	.04
☐ 50	Rick Sutcliffe	.10	.05	.01
☐ 51	Doug Drabek	.15	.07	.02
☐ 52	Bill Doran	.05	.02	.01
☐ 53	Mike Scioscia	.05	.02	.01
☐ 54	Candy Maldonado	.05	.02	.01
☐ 55	Dave Winfield	.15	.07	.02
☐ 56	Lou Whitaker	.15	.07	.02
☐ 57	Tom Henke	.10	.05	.01
☐ 58	Ken Gerhart	.05	.02	.01
☐ 59	Glenn Braggs	.05	.02	.01
☐ 60	Julio Franco	.10	.05	.01
☐ 61	Charlie Leibrandt	.05	.02	.01
☐ 62	Gary Gaetti	.05	.02	.01
☐ 63	Bob Boone	.10	.05	.01
☐ 64	Luis Polonia	.20	.09	.03
☐ 65	Dwight Evans	.10	.05	.01
☐ 66	Phil Bradley	.05	.02	.01
☐ 67	Mike Boddicker	.05	.02	.01
☐ 68	Vince Coleman	.10	.05	.01
☐ 69	Howard Johnson	.10	.05	.01
☐ 70	Tim Wallach	.10	.05	.01
☐ 71	Keith Moreland	.05	.02	.01
☐ 72	Barry Larkin	.30	.14	.04
☐ 73	Alan Ashby	.05	.02	.01
☐ 74	Rick Rhoden	.05	.02	.01
☐ 75	Darrell Evans	.10	.05	.01
☐ 76	Dave Stieb	.10	.05	.01
☐ 77	Dan Plesac	.05	.02	.01
☐ 78	Will Clark UER	.30	.14	.04
	(Born 3/17/64, should be 3/13/64)			
☐ 79	Frank White	.10	.05	.01
☐ 80	Joe Carter	.20	.09	.03
☐ 81	Mike Witt	.05	.02	.01
☐ 82	Terry Steinbach	.10	.05	.01
☐ 83	Alvin Davis	.05	.02	.01
☐ 84	Tommy Herr	.10	.05	.01
	(Will Clark shown sliding into second)			
☐ 85	Vance Law	.05	.02	.01
☐ 86	Kal Daniels	.05	.02	.01
☐ 87	Rick Honeycutt UER	.05	.02	.01
	(Wrong years for stats on back)			
☐ 88	Alfredo Griffin	.05	.02	.01
☐ 89	Bret Saberhagen	.15	.07	.02
☐ 90	Bert Blyleven	.15	.07	.02
☐ 91	Jeff Reardon	.15	.07	.02
☐ 92	Cory Snyder	.05	.02	.01
☐ 93A	Greg Walker ERR	2.00	.90	.25
	(93 of 66)			
☐ 93B	Greg Walker COR	.05	.02	.01
	(93 of 660)			
☐ 94	Joe Magrane	.05	.02	.01
☐ 95	Rob Deer	.05	.02	.01
☐ 96	Ray Knight	.10	.05	.01
☐ 97	Casey Candaele	.05	.02	.01
☐ 98	John Cerutti	.05	.02	.01
☐ 99	Buddy Bell	.10	.05	.01
☐ 100	Jack Clark	.10	.05	.01
☐ 101	Eric Bell	.05	.02	.01
☐ 102	Willie Wilson	.05	.02	.01
☐ 103	Dave Schmidt	.05	.02	.01
☐ 104	Dennis Eckersley UER	.15	.07	.02
	(Complete games stats are wrong)			
☐ 105	Don Sutton	.15	.07	.02
☐ 106	Danny Tartabull	.10	.05	.01
☐ 107	Fred McGriff	.40	.18	.05
☐ 108	Les Straker	.05	.02	.01
☐ 109	Lloyd Moseby	.05	.02	.01
☐ 110	Roger Clemens	.25	.11	.03
☐ 111	Glenn Hubbard	.05	.02	.01
☐ 112	Ken Williams	.05	.02	.01
☐ 113	Ruben Sierra	.25	.11	.03
☐ 114	Stan Jefferson	.05	.02	.01
☐ 115	Milt Thompson	.05	.02	.01
☐ 116	Bobby Bonilla	.15	.07	.02
☐ 117	Wayne Tolleson	.05	.02	.01
☐ 118	Matt Williams	1.50	.70	.19
☐ 119	Chet Lemon	.05	.02	.01
☐ 120	Dale Sveum	.05	.02	.01
☐ 121	Dennis Boyd	.05	.02	.01
☐ 122	Brett Butler	.15	.07	.02
☐ 123	Terry Kennedy	.05	.02	.01
☐ 124	Jack Howell	.05	.02	.01
☐ 125	Curt Young	.05	.02	.01
☐ 126A	Dave Valle ERR	.05	.02	.01
	(Misspelled Dale on card front)			
☐ 126B	Dave Valle COR	.05	.02	.01
☐ 127	Curt Wilkerson	.05	.02	.01
☐ 128	Tim Teufel	.05	.02	.01
☐ 129	Ozzie Virgil	.05	.02	.01
☐ 130	Brian Fisher	.05	.02	.01
☐ 131	Lance Parrish	.10	.05	.01
☐ 132	Tom Browning	.05	.02	.01
☐ 133A	Larry Andersen ERR	.05	.02	.01
	(Misspelled Anderson on card front)			
☐ 133B	Larry Andersen COR	.05	.02	.01
☐ 134A	Bob Brenly ERR	.05	.02	.01
	(Misspelled Brenley on card front)			
☐ 134B	Bob Brenly COR	.05	.02	.01
☐ 135	Mike Marshall	.05	.02	.01
☐ 136	Gerald Perry	.05	.02	.01
☐ 137	Bobby Meacham	.05	.02	.01
☐ 138	Larry Herndon	.05	.02	.01
☐ 139	Fred Manrique	.05	.02	.01
☐ 140	Charlie Hough	.10	.05	.01
☐ 141	Ron Darling	.10	.05	.01
☐ 142	Herm Winningham	.05	.02	.01
☐ 143	Mike Diaz	.05	.02	.01
☐ 144	Mike Jackson	.10	.05	.01
☐ 145	Denny Walling	.05	.02	.01
☐ 146	Robby Thompson	.10	.05	.01
☐ 147	Franklin Stubbs	.05	.02	.01
☐ 148	Albert Hall	.05	.02	.01
☐ 149	Bobby Witt	.10	.05	.01
☐ 150	Lance McCullers	.05	.02	.01
☐ 151	Scott Bradley	.05	.02	.01
☐ 152	Mark McLemore	.05	.02	.01
☐ 153	Tim Laudner	.05	.02	.01
☐ 154	Greg Swindell	.10	.05	.01
☐ 155	Marty Barrett	.05	.02	.01
☐ 156	Mike Heath	.05	.02	.01
☐ 157	Gary Ward	.05	.02	.01
☐ 158A	Lee Mazzilli ERR	.05	.02	.01

	(Misspelled Mazilli on card front)		
☐ 158B	Lee Mazzilli COR	.05	.02	.01
☐ 159	Tom Foley	.05	.02	.01
☐ 160	Robin Yount	.20	.09	.03
☐ 161	Steve Bedrosian	.05	.02	.01
☐ 162	Bob Walk	.05	.02	.01
☐ 163	Nick Esasky	.05	.02	.01
☐ 164	Ken Caminiti	.50	.23	.06
☐ 165	Jose Uribe	.05	.02	.01
☐ 166	Dave Anderson	.05	.02	.01
☐ 167	Ed Whitson	.05	.02	.01
☐ 168	Ernie Whitt	.05	.02	.01
☐ 169	Cecil Cooper	.10	.05	.01
☐ 170	Mike Pagliarulo	.05	.02	.01
☐ 171	Pat Sheridan	.05	.02	.01
☐ 172	Chris Bando	.05	.02	.01
☐ 173	Lee Lacy	.05	.02	.01
☐ 174	Steve Lombardozzi	.05	.02	.01
☐ 175	Mike Greenwell	.15	.07	.02
☐ 176	Greg Minton	.05	.02	.01
☐ 177	Moose Haas	.05	.02	.01
☐ 178	Mike Kingery	.05	.02	.01
☐ 179	Greg A. Harris	.05	.02	.01
☐ 180	Bo Jackson	.25	.11	.03
☐ 181	Carmelo Martinez	.05	.02	.01
☐ 182	Alex Trevino	.05	.02	.01
☐ 183	Ron Oester	.05	.02	.01
☐ 184	Danny Darwin	.05	.02	.01
☐ 185	Mike Krukow	.05	.02	.01
☐ 186	Rafael Palmeiro	.40	.18	.05
☐ 187	Tim Burke	.05	.02	.01
☐ 188	Roger McDowell	.05	.02	.01
☐ 189	Garry Templeton	.05	.02	.01
☐ 190	Terry Pendleton	.15	.07	.02
☐ 191	Larry Parrish	.05	.02	.01
☐ 192	Rey Quinones	.05	.02	.01
☐ 193	Joaquin Andujar	.05	.02	.01
☐ 194	Tom Brunansky	.05	.02	.01
☐ 195	Donnie Moore	.05	.02	.01
☐ 196	Dan Pasqua	.05	.02	.01
☐ 197	Jim Gantner	.05	.02	.01
☐ 198	Mark Eichhorn	.05	.02	.01
☐ 199	John Grubb	.05	.02	.01
☐ 200	Bill Ripken	.05	.02	.01
☐ 201	Sam Horn	.05	.02	.01
☐ 202	Todd Worrell	.05	.02	.01
☐ 203	Terry Leach	.05	.02	.01
☐ 204	Garth Iorg	.05	.02	.01
☐ 205	Brian Dayett	.05	.02	.01
☐ 206	Bo Diaz	.05	.02	.01
☐ 207	Craig Reynolds	.05	.02	.01
☐ 208	Brian Holton	.05	.02	.01
☐ 209	Marvell Wynne UER	.05	.02	.01
	(Misspelled Marvelle on card front)			
☐ 210	Dave Concepcion	.10	.05	.01
☐ 211	Mike Davis	.05	.02	.01
☐ 212	Devon White	.15	.07	.02
☐ 213	Mickey Brantley	.05	.02	.01
☐ 214	Greg Gagne	.05	.02	.01
☐ 215	Oddibe McDowell	.05	.02	.01
☐ 216	Jimmy Key	.15	.07	.02
☐ 217	Dave Bergman	.05	.02	.01
☐ 218	Calvin Schiraldi	.05	.02	.01
☐ 219	Larry Sheets	.05	.02	.01
☐ 220	Mike Easler	.05	.02	.01
☐ 221	Kurt Stillwell	.05	.02	.01
☐ 222	Chuck Jackson	.05	.02	.01
☐ 223	Dave Martinez	.05	.02	.01
☐ 224	Tim Leary	.05	.02	.01
☐ 225	Steve Garvey	.15	.07	.02
☐ 226	Greg Mathews	.05	.02	.01
☐ 227	Doug Sisk	.05	.02	.01
☐ 228	Dave Henderson	.05	.02	.01
	(Wearing Red Sox uniform; Red Sox logo on back)			
☐ 229	Jimmy Dwyer	.05	.02	.01
☐ 230	Larry Owen	.05	.02	.01
☐ 231	Andre Thornton	.05	.02	.01
☐ 232	Mark Salas	.05	.02	.01
☐ 233	Tom Brookens	.05	.02	.01
☐ 234	Greg Brock	.05	.02	.01
☐ 235	Rance Mulliniks	.05	.02	.01
☐ 236	Bob Brower	.05	.02	.01
☐ 237	Joe Niekro	.10	.05	.01
☐ 238	Scott Bankhead	.05	.02	.01
☐ 239	Doug DeCinces	.05	.02	.01
☐ 240	Tommy John	.15	.07	.02
☐ 241	Rich Gedman	.05	.02	.01
☐ 242	Ted Power	.05	.02	.01
☐ 243	Dave Meads	.05	.02	.01
☐ 244	Jim Sundberg	.05	.02	.01
☐ 245	Ken Oberkfell	.05	.02	.01
☐ 246	Jimmy Jones	.05	.02	.01
☐ 247	Ken Landreaux	.05	.02	.01
☐ 248	Jose Oquendo	.05	.02	.01
☐ 249	John Mitchell	.05	.02	.01
☐ 250	Don Baylor	.15	.07	.02
☐ 251	Scott Fletcher	.05	.02	.01
☐ 252	Al Newman	.05	.02	.01
☐ 253	Carney Lansford	.10	.05	.01
☐ 254	Johnny Ray	.05	.02	.01
☐ 255	Gary Pettis	.05	.02	.01
☐ 256	Ken Phelps	.05	.02	.01
☐ 257	Rick Leach	.05	.02	.01
☐ 258	Tim Stoddard	.05	.02	.01
☐ 259	Ed Romero	.05	.02	.01
☐ 260	Sid Bream	.05	.02	.01
☐ 261A	Tom Niedenfuer ERR	.05	.02	.01
	(Misspelled Neidenfuer on card front)			
☐ 261B	Tom Niedenfuer COR	.05	.02	.01
☐ 262	Rick Dempsey	.05	.02	.01
☐ 263	Lonnie Smith	.05	.02	.01
☐ 264	Bob Forsch	.05	.02	.01
☐ 265	Barry Bonds	.60	.25	.07
☐ 266	Willie Randolph	.10	.05	.01
☐ 267	Mike Ramsey	.05	.02	.01
☐ 268	Don Slaught	.05	.02	.01
☐ 269	Mickey Tettleton	.10	.05	.01
☐ 270	Jerry Reuss	.05	.02	.01
☐ 271	Marc Sullivan	.05	.02	.01
☐ 272	Jim Morrison	.05	.02	.01
☐ 273	Steve Balboni	.05	.02	.01
☐ 274	Dick Schofield	.05	.02	.01
☐ 275	John Tudor	.05	.02	.01
☐ 276	Gene Larkin	.05	.02	.01
☐ 277	Harold Reynolds	.05	.02	.01
☐ 278	Jerry Browne	.05	.02	.01
☐ 279	Willie Upshaw	.05	.02	.01
☐ 280	Ted Higuera	.05	.02	.01
☐ 281	Terry McGriff	.05	.02	.01
☐ 282	Terry Puhl	.05	.02	.01
☐ 283	Mark Wasinger	.05	.02	.01
☐ 284	Luis Salazar	.05	.02	.01
☐ 285	Ted Simmons	.10	.05	.01
☐ 286	John Shelby	.05	.02	.01
☐ 287	John Smiley	.20	.09	.03
☐ 288	Curt Ford	.05	.02	.01
☐ 289	Steve Crawford	.05	.02	.01
☐ 290	Dan Quisenberry	.10	.05	.01

☐ 291 Alan Wiggins	.05	.02	.01	☐ 359 Floyd Rayford	.05	.02	.01
☐ 292 Randy Bush	.05	.02	.01	☐ 360 Darryl Strawberry	.15	.07	.02
☐ 293 John Candelaria	.05	.02	.01	☐ 361 Sal Butera	.05	.02	.01
☐ 294 Tony Phillips	.15	.07	.02	☐ 362 Domingo Ramos	.05	.02	.01
☐ 295 Mike Morgan	.05	.02	.01	☐ 363 Chris Brown	.05	.02	.01
☐ 296 Bill Wegman	.05	.02	.01	☐ 364 Jose Gonzalez	.05	.02	.01
☐ 297A Terry Francona ERR...	.05	.02	.01	☐ 365 Dave Smith	.05	.02	.01
(Misspelled Franconia				☐ 366 Andy McGaffigan	.05	.02	.01
on card front)				☐ 367 Stan Javier	.05	.02	.01
☐ 297B Terry Francona COR ..	.05	.02	.01	☐ 368 Henry Cotto	.05	.02	.01
☐ 298 Mickey Hatcher	.05	.02	.01	☐ 369 Mike Birkbeck	.05	.02	.01
☐ 299 Andres Thomas	.05	.02	.01	☐ 370 Len Dykstra	.15	.07	.02
☐ 300 Bob Stanley	.05	.02	.01	☐ 371 Dave Collins	.05	.02	.01
☐ 301 Al Pedrique	.05	.02	.01	☐ 372 Spike Owen	.05	.02	.01
☐ 302 Jim Lindeman	.05	.02	.01	☐ 373 Geno Petralli	.05	.02	.01
☐ 303 Wally Backman	.05	.02	.01	☐ 374 Ron Karkovice	.05	.02	.01
☐ 304 Paul O'Neill	.15	.07	.02	☐ 375 Shane Rawley	.05	.02	.01
☐ 305 Hubie Brooks	.05	.02	.01	☐ 376 DeWayne Buice	.05	.02	.01
☐ 306 Steve Buechele	.05	.02	.01	☐ 377 Bill Pecota	.05	.02	.01
☐ 307 Bobby Thigpen	.05	.02	.01	☐ 378 Leon Durham	.05	.02	.01
☐ 308 George Hendrick	.05	.02	.01	☐ 379 Ed Olwine	.05	.02	.01
☐ 309 John Moses	.05	.02	.01	☐ 380 Bruce Hurst	.05	.02	.01
☐ 310 Ron Guidry	.10	.05	.01	☐ 381 Bob McClure	.05	.02	.01
☐ 311 Bill Schroeder	.05	.02	.01	☐ 382 Mark Thurmond	.05	.02	.01
☐ 312 Jose Nunez	.05	.02	.01	☐ 383 Buddy Biancalana	.05	.02	.01
☐ 313 Bud Black	.05	.02	.01	☐ 384 Tim Conroy	.05	.02	.01
☐ 314 Joe Sambito	.05	.02	.01	☐ 385 Tony Gwynn	.30	.14	.04
☐ 315 Scott McGregor	.05	.02	.01	☐ 386 Greg Gross	.05	.02	.01
☐ 316 Rafael Santana	.05	.02	.01	☐ 387 Barry Lyons	.05	.02	.01
☐ 317 Frank Williams	.05	.02	.01	☐ 388 Mike Felder	.05	.02	.01
☐ 318 Mike Fitzgerald	.05	.02	.01	☐ 389 Pat Clements	.05	.02	.01
☐ 319 Rick Mahler	.05	.02	.01	☐ 390 Ken Griffey	.10	.05	.01
☐ 320 Jim Gott	.05	.02	.01	☐ 391 Mark Davis	.05	.02	.01
☐ 321 Mariano Duncan	.05	.02	.01	☐ 392 Jose Rijo	.15	.07	.02
☐ 322 Jose Guzman	.05	.02	.01	☐ 393 Mike Young	.05	.02	.01
☐ 323 Lee Guetterman	.05	.02	.01	☐ 394 Willie Fraser	.05	.02	.01
☐ 324 Dan Gladden	.05	.02	.01	☐ 395 Dion James	.05	.02	.01
☐ 325 Gary Carter	.15	.07	.02	☐ 396 Steve Shields	.05	.02	.01
☐ 326 Tracy Jones	.05	.02	.01	☐ 397 Randy St.Claire	.05	.02	.01
☐ 327 Floyd Youmans	.05	.02	.01	☐ 398 Danny Jackson	.05	.02	.01
☐ 328 Bill Dawley	.05	.02	.01	☐ 399 Cecil Fielder	.15	.07	.02
☐ 329 Paul Noce	.05	.02	.01	☐ 400 Keith Hernandez	.10	.05	.01
☐ 330 Angel Salazar	.05	.02	.01	☐ 401 Don Carman	.05	.02	.01
☐ 331 Goose Gossage	.15	.07	.02	☐ 402 Chuck Crim	.05	.02	.01
☐ 332 George Frazier	.05	.02	.01	☐ 403 Rob Woodward	.05	.02	.01
☐ 333 Ruppert Jones	.05	.02	.01	☐ 404 Junior Ortiz	.05	.02	.01
☐ 334 Billy Joe Robidoux	.05	.02	.01	☐ 405 Glenn Wilson	.05	.02	.01
☐ 335 Mike Scott	.05	.02	.01	☐ 406 Ken Howell	.05	.02	.01
☐ 336 Randy Myers	.10	.05	.01	☐ 407 Jeff Kunkel	.05	.02	.01
☐ 337 Bob Sebra	.05	.02	.01	☐ 408 Jeff Reed	.05	.02	.01
☐ 338 Eric Show	.05	.02	.01	☐ 409 Chris James	.05	.02	.01
☐ 339 Mitch Williams	.10	.05	.01	☐ 410 Zane Smith	.05	.02	.01
☐ 340 Paul Molitor	.15	.07	.02	☐ 411 Ken Dixon	.05	.02	.01
☐ 341 Gus Polidor	.05	.02	.01	☐ 412 Ricky Horton	.05	.02	.01
☐ 342 Steve Trout	.05	.02	.01	☐ 413 Frank DiPino	.05	.02	.01
☐ 343 Jerry Don Gleaton	.05	.02	.01	☐ 414 Shane Mack	.10	.05	.01
☐ 344 Bob Knepper	.05	.02	.01	☐ 415 Danny Cox	.05	.02	.01
☐ 345 Mitch Webster	.05	.02	.01	☐ 416 Andy Van Slyke	.10	.05	.01
☐ 346 John Morris	.05	.02	.01	☐ 417 Danny Heep	.05	.02	.01
☐ 347 Andy Hawkins	.05	.02	.01	☐ 418 John Cangelosi	.05	.02	.01
☐ 348 Dave Leiper	.05	.02	.01	☐ 419A John Christensen ERR	.05	.02	.01
☐ 349 Ernest Riles	.05	.02	.01	(Christiansen			
☐ 350 Dwight Gooden	.10	.05	.01	on card front)			
☐ 351 Dave Righetti	.05	.02	.01	☐ 419B John Christensen COR	.05	.02	.01
☐ 352 Pat Dodson	.05	.02	.01	☐ 420 Joey Cora	.15	.07	.02
☐ 353 John Habyan	.05	.02	.01	☐ 421 Mike LaValliere	.05	.02	.01
☐ 354 Jim Deshaies	.05	.02	.01	☐ 422 Kelly Gruber	.05	.02	.01
☐ 355 Butch Wynegar	.05	.02	.01	☐ 423 Bruce Benedict	.05	.02	.01
☐ 356 Bryn Smith	.05	.02	.01	☐ 424 Len Matuszek	.05	.02	.01
☐ 357 Matt Young	.05	.02	.01	☐ 425 Kent Tekulve	.05	.02	.01
☐ 358 Tom Pagnozzi	.10	.05	.01	☐ 426 Rafael Ramirez	.05	.02	.01

☐ 427	Mike Flanagan	.05	.02	.01
☐ 428	Mike Gallego	.05	.02	.01
☐ 429	Juan Castillo	.05	.02	.01
☐ 430	Neal Heaton	.05	.02	.01
☐ 431	Phil Garner	.10	.05	.01
☐ 432	Mike Dunne	.05	.02	.01
☐ 433	Wallace Johnson	.05	.02	.01
☐ 434	Jack O'Connor	.05	.02	.01
☐ 435	Steve Jeltz	.05	.02	.01
☐ 436	Donell Nixon	.05	.02	.01
☐ 437	Jack Lazorko	.05	.02	.01
☐ 438	Keith Comstock	.05	.02	.01
☐ 439	Jeff D. Robinson	.05	.02	.01
☐ 440	Graig Nettles	.10	.05	.01
☐ 441	Mel Hall	.05	.02	.01
☐ 442	Gerald Young	.05	.02	.01
☐ 443	Gary Redus	.05	.02	.01
☐ 444	Charlie Moore	.05	.02	.01
☐ 445	Bill Madlock	.10	.05	.01
☐ 446	Mark Clear	.05	.02	.01
☐ 447	Greg Booker	.05	.02	.01
☐ 448	Rick Schu	.05	.02	.01
☐ 449	Ron Kittle	.05	.02	.01
☐ 450	Dale Murphy	.15	.07	.02
☐ 451	Bob Dernier	.05	.02	.01
☐ 452	Dale Mohorcic	.05	.02	.01
☐ 453	Rafael Belliard	.05	.02	.01
☐ 454	Charlie Puleo	.05	.02	.01
☐ 455	Dwayne Murphy	.05	.02	.01
☐ 456	Jim Eisenreich	.10	.05	.01
☐ 457	David Palmer	.05	.02	.01
☐ 458	Dave Stewart	.15	.07	.02
☐ 459	Pascual Perez	.05	.02	.01
☐ 460	Glenn Davis	.05	.02	.01
☐ 461	Dan Petry	.05	.02	.01
☐ 462	Jim Winn	.05	.02	.01
☐ 463	Darrell Miller	.05	.02	.01
☐ 464	Mike Moore	.05	.02	.01
☐ 465	Mike LaCoss	.05	.02	.01
☐ 466	Steve Farr	.05	.02	.01
☐ 467	Jerry Mumphrey	.05	.02	.01
☐ 468	Kevin Gross	.05	.02	.01
☐ 469	Bruce Bochy	.05	.02	.01
☐ 470	Orel Hershiser	.15	.07	.02
☐ 471	Eric King	.05	.02	.01
☐ 472	Ellis Burks	.15	.07	.02
☐ 473	Darren Daulton	.15	.07	.02
☐ 474	Mookie Wilson	.10	.05	.01
☐ 475	Frank Viola	.10	.05	.01
☐ 476	Ron Robinson	.05	.02	.01
☐ 477	Bob Melvin	.05	.02	.01
☐ 478	Jeff Musselman	.05	.02	.01
☐ 479	Charlie Kerfeld	.05	.02	.01
☐ 480	Richard Dotson	.05	.02	.01
☐ 481	Kevin Mitchell	.15	.07	.02
☐ 482	Gary Roenicke	.05	.02	.01
☐ 483	Tim Flannery	.05	.02	.01
☐ 484	Rich Yett	.05	.02	.01
☐ 485	Pete Incaviglia	.10	.05	.01
☐ 486	Rick Cerone	.05	.02	.01
☐ 487	Tony Armas	.05	.02	.01
☐ 488	Jerry Reed	.05	.02	.01
☐ 489	Dave Lopes	.10	.05	.01
☐ 490	Frank Tanana	.05	.02	.01
☐ 491	Mike Loynd	.05	.02	.01
☐ 492	Bruce Ruffin	.05	.02	.01
☐ 493	Chris Speier	.05	.02	.01
☐ 494	Tom Hume	.05	.02	.01
☐ 495	Jesse Orosco	.05	.02	.01
☐ 496	Robbie Wine UER	.05	.02	.01
	(Misspelled Robby			
	on card front)			
☐ 497	Jeff Montgomery	.20	.09	.03
☐ 498	Jeff Dedmon	.05	.02	.01
☐ 499	Luis Aguayo	.05	.02	.01
☐ 500	Reggie Jackson	.15	.07	.02
	(Oakland A's)			
☐ 501	Reggie Jackson	.15	.07	.02
	(Baltimore Orioles)			
☐ 502	Reggie Jackson	.15	.07	.02
	(New York Yankees)			
☐ 503	Reggie Jackson	.15	.07	.02
	(California Angels)			
☐ 504	Reggie Jackson	.15	.07	.02
	(Oakland A's)			
☐ 505	Billy Hatcher	.05	.02	.01
☐ 506	Ed Lynch	.05	.02	.01
☐ 507	Willie Hernandez	.05	.02	.01
☐ 508	Jose DeLeon	.05	.02	.01
☐ 509	Joel Youngblood	.05	.02	.01
☐ 510	Bob Welch	.10	.05	.01
☐ 511	Steve Ontiveros	.05	.02	.01
☐ 512	Randy Ready	.05	.02	.01
☐ 513	Juan Nieves	.05	.02	.01
☐ 514	Jeff Russell	.05	.02	.01
☐ 515	Von Hayes	.05	.02	.01
☐ 516	Mark Gubicza	.05	.02	.01
☐ 517	Ken Dayley	.05	.02	.01
☐ 518	Don Aase	.05	.02	.01
☐ 519	Rick Reuschel	.05	.02	.01
☐ 520	Mike Henneman	.15	.07	.02
☐ 521	Rick Aguilera	.15	.07	.02
☐ 522	Jay Howell	.05	.02	.01
☐ 523	Ed Correa	.05	.02	.01
☐ 524	Manny Trillo	.05	.02	.01
☐ 525	Kirk Gibson	.15	.07	.02
☐ 526	Wally Ritchie	.05	.02	.01
☐ 527	Al Nipper	.05	.02	.01
☐ 528	Atlee Hammaker	.05	.02	.01
☐ 529	Shawon Dunston	.10	.05	.01
☐ 530	Jim Clancy	.05	.02	.01
☐ 531	Tom Paciorek	.10	.05	.01
☐ 532	Joel Skinner	.05	.02	.01
☐ 533	Scott Garrelts	.05	.02	.01
☐ 534	Tom O'Malley	.05	.02	.01
☐ 535	John Franco	.10	.05	.01
☐ 536	Paul Kilgus	.05	.02	.01
☐ 537	Darrell Porter	.05	.02	.01
☐ 538	Walt Terrell	.05	.02	.01
☐ 539	Bill Long	.05	.02	.01
☐ 540	George Bell	.05	.02	.01
☐ 541	Jeff Sellers	.05	.02	.01
☐ 542	Joe Boever	.05	.02	.01
☐ 543	Steve Howe	.05	.02	.01
☐ 544	Scott Sanderson	.05	.02	.01
☐ 545	Jack Morris	.15	.07	.02
☐ 546	Todd Benzinger	.05	.02	.01
☐ 547	Steve Henderson	.05	.02	.01
☐ 548	Eddie Milner	.05	.02	.01
☐ 549	Jeff M. Robinson	.05	.02	.01
☐ 550	Cal Ripken	.75	.35	.09
☐ 551	Jody Davis	.05	.02	.01
☐ 552	Kirk McCaskill	.05	.02	.01
☐ 553	Craig Lefferts	.05	.02	.01
☐ 554	Darnell Coles	.05	.02	.01
☐ 555	Phil Niekro	.15	.07	.02
☐ 556	Mike Aldrete	.05	.02	.01
☐ 557	Pat Perry	.05	.02	.01
☐ 558	Juan Agosto	.05	.02	.01
☐ 559	Rob Murphy	.05	.02	.01
☐ 560	Dennis Rasmussen	.05	.02	.01
☐ 561	Manny Lee	.05	.02	.01

☐ 562	Jeff Blauser	.15	.07	.02
☐ 563	Bob Ojeda	.05	.02	.01
☐ 564	Dave Dravecky	.10	.05	.01
☐ 565	Gene Garber	.05	.02	.01
☐ 566	Ron Roenicke	.05	.02	.01
☐ 567	Tommy Hinzo	.05	.02	.01
☐ 568	Eric Nolte	.05	.02	.01
☐ 569	Ed Hearn	.05	.02	.01
☐ 570	Mark Davidson	.05	.02	.01
☐ 571	Jim Walewander	.05	.02	.01
☐ 572	Donnie Hill UER	.05	.02	.01
	(84 Stolen Base total listed as 7)			
☐ 573	Jamie Moyer	.05	.02	.01
☐ 574	Ken Schrom	.05	.02	.01
☐ 575	Nolan Ryan	.75	.35	.09
☐ 576	Jim Acker	.05	.02	.01
☐ 577	Jamie Quirk	.05	.02	.01
☐ 578	Jay Aldrich	.05	.02	.01
☐ 579	Claudell Washington	.05	.02	.01
☐ 580	Jeff Leonard	.05	.02	.01
☐ 581	Carmen Castillo	.05	.02	.01
☐ 582	Daryl Boston	.05	.02	.01
☐ 583	Jeff DeWillis	.05	.02	.01
☐ 584	John Marzano	.05	.02	.01
☐ 585	Bill Gullickson	.05	.02	.01
☐ 586	Andy Allanson	.05	.02	.01
☐ 587	Lee Tunnell UER	.05	.02	.01
	(1987 stat line reads .4.84 ERA)			
☐ 588	Gene Nelson	.05	.02	.01
☐ 589	Dave LaPoint	.05	.02	.01
☐ 590	Harold Baines	.15	.07	.02
☐ 591	Bill Buckner	.10	.05	.01
☐ 592	Carlton Fisk	.15	.07	.02
☐ 593	Rick Manning	.05	.02	.01
☐ 594	Doug Jones	.10	.05	.01
☐ 595	Tom Candiotti	.05	.02	.01
☐ 596	Steve Lake	.05	.02	.01
☐ 597	Jose Lind	.05	.02	.01
☐ 598	Ross Jones	.05	.02	.01
☐ 599	Gary Matthews	.05	.02	.01
☐ 600	Fernando Valenzuela	.05	.02	.01
☐ 601	Dennis Martinez	.10	.05	.01
☐ 602	Les Lancaster	.05	.02	.01
☐ 603	Ozzie Guillen	.10	.05	.01
☐ 604	Tony Bernazard	.05	.02	.01
☐ 605	Chili Davis	.15	.07	.02
☐ 606	Roy Smalley	.05	.02	.01
☐ 607	Ivan Calderon	.05	.02	.01
☐ 608	Jay Tibbs	.05	.02	.01
☐ 609	Guy Hoffman	.05	.02	.01
☐ 610	Doyle Alexander	.05	.02	.01
☐ 611	Mike Bielecki	.05	.02	.01
☐ 612	Shawn Hillegas	.05	.02	.01
☐ 613	Keith Atherton	.05	.02	.01
☐ 614	Eric Plunk	.05	.02	.01
☐ 615	Sid Fernandez	.10	.05	.01
☐ 616	Dennis Lamp	.05	.02	.01
☐ 617	Dave Engle	.05	.02	.01
☐ 618	Harry Spilman	.05	.02	.01
☐ 619	Don Robinson	.05	.02	.01
☐ 620	John Farrell	.05	.02	.01
☐ 621	Nelson Liriano	.05	.02	.01
☐ 622	Floyd Bannister	.05	.02	.01
☐ 623	Randy Milligan	.05	.02	.01
☐ 624	Kevin Elster	.05	.02	.01
☐ 625	Jody Reed	.10	.05	.01
☐ 626	Shawn Abner	.05	.02	.01
☐ 627	Kirt Manwaring	.10	.05	.01
☐ 628	Pete Stanicek	.05	.02	.01

☐ 629	Rob Ducey	.05	.02	.01
☐ 630	Steve Kiefer	.05	.02	.01
☐ 631	Gary Thurman	.05	.02	.01
☐ 632	Darrel Akerfelds	.05	.02	.01
☐ 633	Dave Clark	.05	.02	.01
☐ 634	Roberto Kelly	.20	.09	.03
☐ 635	Keith Hughes	.05	.02	.01
☐ 636	John Davis	.05	.02	.01
☐ 637	Mike Devereaux	.20	.09	.03
☐ 638	Tom Glavine	1.25	.55	.16
☐ 639	Keith A. Miller	.05	.02	.01
☐ 640	Chris Gwynn UER	.10	.05	.01
	(Wrong batting and throwing on back)			
☐ 641	Tim Crews	.10	.05	.01
☐ 642	Mackey Sasser	.05	.02	.01
☐ 643	Vicente Palacios	.05	.02	.01
☐ 644	Kevin Romine	.05	.02	.01
☐ 645	Gregg Jefferies	.75	.35	.09
☐ 646	Jeff Treadway	.05	.02	.01
☐ 647	Ron Gant	1.00	.45	.12
☐ 648	Mark McGwire and	.15	.07	.02
	Matt Nokes (Rookie Sluggers)			
☐ 649	Eric Davis and	.10	.05	.01
	Tim Raines (Speed and Power)			
☐ 650	Don Mattingly and	.20	.09	.03
	Jack Clark			
☐ 651	Tony Fernandez,	.30	.14	.04
	Alan Trammell, and Cal Ripken			
☐ 652	Vince Coleman HL	.10	.05	.01
	100 Stolen Bases			
☐ 653	Kirby Puckett HL	.20	.09	.03
	10 Hits in a Row			
☐ 654	Benito Santiago HL	.05	.02	.01
	Hitting Streak			
☐ 655	Juan Nieves HL	.05	.02	.01
	No Hitter			
☐ 656	Steve Bedrosian HL	.05	.02	.01
	Saves Record			
☐ 657	Mike Schmidt HL	.15	.07	.02
	500 Homers			
☐ 658	Don Mattingly HL	.25	.11	.03
	Home Run Streak			
☐ 659	Mark McGwire HL	.15	.07	.02
	Rookie HR Record			
☐ 660	Paul Molitor HL	.15	.07	.02
	Hitting Streak			

1988 Score Rookie/Traded

This 110-card set featured traded players (1-65) and rookies (66-110) for the 1988 season. The cards are distinguishable from the regular Score set by the orange borders and by the fact that the numbering on the back has a T suffix. The cards are standard size, 2 1/2" by 3 1/2", and were distributed by Score as a collated set in a special collector box along with some trivia cards. Score also produced a limited "glossy" Rookie and Traded set, that is valued at three times the value of the regular (non-glossy) set. It should be noted that the set

itself (non-glossy) is now considered somewhat scarce. Apparently Score's first attempt at a Rookie/Traded set was produced very conservatively, resulting in a set which is now recognized as being much tougher to find than the other Rookie/Traded sets from the other major companies of that year. The key (extended) Rookie Cards in this set are Roberto Alomar, Brady Anderson, Craig Biggio, Pat Borders, Jay Buhner, Orestes Destrade, Rob Dibble, Mark Grace, Darryl Hamilton, Bryan Harvey, Mike Macfarlane, Jack McDowell, Melido Perez, Chris Sabo, Todd Stottlemyre, and Walt Weiss.

	MINT	NRMT	EXC
COMPLETE FACT.SET (110)	50.00	22.00	6.25
COMMON CARD (1T-110T)	.15	.07	.02
☐ 1T Jack Clark	.30	.14	.04
☐ 2T Danny Jackson	.15	.07	.02
☐ 3T Brett Butler	.50	.23	.06
☐ 4T Kurt Stillwell	.15	.07	.02
☐ 5T Tom Brunansky	.15	.07	.02
☐ 6T Dennis Lamp	.15	.07	.02
☐ 7T Jose DeLeon	.15	.07	.02
☐ 8T Tom Herr	.15	.07	.02
☐ 9T Keith Moreland	.15	.07	.02
☐ 10T Kirk Gibson	.50	.23	.06
☐ 11T Bud Black	.15	.07	.02
☐ 12T Rafael Ramirez	.15	.07	.02
☐ 13T Luis Salazar	.15	.07	.02
☐ 14T Goose Gossage	.50	.23	.06
☐ 15T Bob Welch	.30	.14	.04
☐ 16T Vance Law	.15	.07	.02
☐ 17T Ray Knight	.30	.14	.04
☐ 18T Dan Quisenberry	.30	.14	.04
☐ 19T Don Slaught	.15	.07	.02
☐ 20T Lee Smith	.50	.23	.06
☐ 21T Rick Cerone	.15	.07	.02
☐ 22T Pat Tabler	.15	.07	.02
☐ 23T Larry McWilliams	.15	.07	.02
☐ 24T Ricky Horton	.15	.07	.02
☐ 25T Graig Nettles	.30	.14	.04
☐ 26T Dan Petry	.15	.07	.02
☐ 27T Jose Rijo	.50	.23	.06
☐ 28T Chili Davis	.50	.23	.06
☐ 29T Dickie Thon	.15	.07	.02
☐ 30T Mackey Sasser	.15	.07	.02
☐ 31T Mickey Tettleton	.30	.14	.04
☐ 32T Rick Dempsey	.15	.07	.02
☐ 33T Ron Hassey	.15	.07	.02
☐ 34T Phil Bradley	.15	.07	.02
☐ 35T Jay Howell	.15	.07	.02
☐ 36T Bill Buckner	.30	.14	.04
☐ 37T Alfredo Griffin	.15	.07	.02
☐ 38T Gary Pettis	.15	.07	.02
☐ 39T Calvin Schiraldi	.15	.07	.02
☐ 40T John Candelaria	.15	.07	.02
☐ 41T Joe Orsulak	.15	.07	.02
☐ 42T Willie Upshaw	.15	.07	.02
☐ 43T Herm Winningham	.15	.07	.02
☐ 44T Ron Kittle	.15	.07	.02
☐ 45T Bob Dernier	.15	.07	.02
☐ 46T Steve Balboni	.15	.07	.02
☐ 47T Steve Shields	.15	.07	.02
☐ 48T Henry Cotto	.15	.07	.02
☐ 49T Dave Henderson	.15	.07	.02
☐ 50T Dave Parker	.50	.23	.06
☐ 51T Mike Young	.15	.07	.02
☐ 52T Mark Salas	.15	.07	.02
☐ 53T Mike Davis	.15	.07	.02
☐ 54T Rafael Santana	.15	.07	.02
☐ 55T Don Baylor	.50	.23	.06
☐ 56T Dan Pasqua	.15	.07	.02
☐ 57T Ernest Riles	.15	.07	.02
☐ 58T Glenn Hubbard	.15	.07	.02
☐ 59T Mike Smithson	.15	.07	.02
☐ 60T Richard Dotson	.15	.07	.02
☐ 61T Jerry Reuss	.15	.07	.02
☐ 62T Mike Jackson	.15	.07	.02
☐ 63T Floyd Bannister	.15	.07	.02
☐ 64T Jesse Orosco	.15	.07	.02
☐ 65T Larry Parrish	.15	.07	.02
☐ 66T Jeff Bittiger	.15	.07	.02
☐ 67T Ray Hayward	.15	.07	.02
☐ 68T Ricky Jordan	.15	.07	.02
☐ 69T Tommy Gregg	.15	.07	.02
☐ 70T Brady Anderson	2.00	.90	.25
☐ 71T Jeff Montgomery	1.50	.70	.19
☐ 72T Darryl Hamilton	.30	.14	.04
☐ 73T Cecil Espy	.15	.07	.02
☐ 74T Greg Briley	.15	.07	.02
☐ 75T Joey Meyer	.15	.07	.02
☐ 76T Mike Macfarlane	1.00	.45	.12
☐ 77T Oswald Peraza	.15	.07	.02
☐ 78T Jack Armstrong	.15	.07	.02
☐ 79T Don Heinkel	.15	.07	.02
☐ 80T Mark Grace	8.00	3.60	1.00
☐ 81T Steve Curry	.15	.07	.02
☐ 82T Damon Berryhill	.15	.07	.02
☐ 83T Steve Ellsworth	.15	.07	.02
☐ 84T Pete Smith	.15	.07	.02
☐ 85T Jack McDowell	6.00	2.70	.75
☐ 86T Rob Dibble	.30	.14	.04
☐ 87T Bryan Harvey UER	.50	.23	.06
(Games Pitched 47, Innings 5)			
☐ 88T John Dopson	.15	.07	.02
☐ 89T Dave Gallagher	.15	.07	.02
☐ 90T Todd Stottlemyre	1.50	.70	.19
☐ 91T Mike Schooler	.15	.07	.02
☐ 92T Don Gordon	.15	.07	.02
☐ 93T Sil Campusano	.15	.07	.02
☐ 94T Jeff Pico	.15	.07	.02
☐ 95T Jay Buhner	8.00	3.60	1.00
☐ 96T Nelson Santovenia	.15	.07	.02
☐ 97T Al Leiter	.30	.14	.04
☐ 98T Luis Alicea	.15	.07	.02
☐ 99T Pat Borders	.30	.14	.04
☐ 100T Chris Sabo	.30	.14	.04
☐ 101T Tim Belcher	.15	.07	.02
☐ 102T Walt Weiss	.30	.14	.04
☐ 103T Craig Biggio	8.00	3.60	1.00
☐ 104T Don August	.15	.07	.02
☐ 105T Roberto Alomar	30.00	13.50	3.70

		MINT	NRMT	EXC
☐ 106T	Todd Burns	.15	.07	.02
☐ 107T	John Costello	.15	.07	.02
☐ 108T	Melido Perez	.30	.14	.04
☐ 109T	Darrin Jackson	.30	.14	.04
☐ 110T	Orestes Destrade	.15	.07	.02

1989 Score

This 660-card set was distributed by Major League Marketing. Cards measure 2 1/2" by 3 1/2" and feature six distinctive inner border (inside a white outer border) colors on the front. Highlights (652-660) and Rookie Prospects (621-651) are included in the set. The set is distinguished by the fact that each card back shows a full-color picture (portrait) of the player. Score "missed" many of the mid-season and later trades; there are numerous examples of inconsistency with regard to the treatment of these players. Study as examples of this inconsistency of handling of late trades, cards numbered 49, 71, 77, 83, 106, 126, 139, 145, 173, 177, 242, 348, 384, 420, 439, 488, 494, and 525. Rookie Cards in this set include Sandy Alomar Jr., Brady Anderson, Craig Biggio, Charlie Hayes, Randy Johnson, Felix Jose, Ramon Martinez, Gary Sheffield, and John Smoltz.

		MINT	NRMT	EXC
	COMPLETE SET (660)	10.00	4.50	1.25
	COMPLETE FACT.SET (660)	10.00	4.50	1.25
	COMMON CARD (1-660)	.05	.02	.01
☐ 1	Jose Canseco	.30	.14	.04
☐ 2	Andre Dawson	.15	.07	.02
☐ 3	Mark McGwire	.15	.07	.02
☐ 4	Benito Santiago	.10	.05	.01
☐ 5	Rick Reuschel	.05	.02	.01
☐ 6	Fred McGriff	.25	.11	.03
☐ 7	Kal Daniels	.05	.02	.01
☐ 8	Gary Gaetti	.05	.02	.01
☐ 9	Ellis Burks	.15	.07	.02
☐ 10	Darryl Strawberry	.15	.07	.02
☐ 11	Julio Franco	.10	.05	.01
☐ 12	Lloyd Moseby	.05	.02	.01
☐ 13	Jeff Pico	.05	.02	.01
☐ 14	Johnny Ray	.05	.02	.01
☐ 15	Cal Ripken	.75	.35	.09
☐ 16	Dick Schofield	.05	.02	.01
☐ 17	Mel Hall	.05	.02	.01
☐ 18	Bill Ripken	.05	.02	.01
☐ 19	Brook Jacoby	.05	.02	.01
☐ 20	Kirby Puckett	.40	.18	.05
☐ 21	Bill Doran	.05	.02	.01
☐ 22	Pete O'Brien	.05	.02	.01
☐ 23	Matt Nokes	.05	.02	.01
☐ 24	Brian Fisher	.05	.02	.01
☐ 25	Jack Clark	.10	.05	.01
☐ 26	Gary Pettis	.05	.02	.01
☐ 27	Dave Valle	.05	.02	.01
☐ 28	Willie Wilson	.05	.02	.01
☐ 29	Curt Young	.05	.02	.01
☐ 30	Dale Murphy	.15	.07	.02
☐ 31	Barry Larkin	.20	.09	.03
☐ 32	Dave Stewart	.15	.07	.02
☐ 33	Mike LaValliere	.05	.02	.01
☐ 34	Glenn Hubbard	.05	.02	.01
☐ 35	Ryne Sandberg	.30	.14	.04
☐ 36	Tony Pena	.05	.02	.01
☐ 37	Greg Walker	.05	.02	.01
☐ 38	Von Hayes	.05	.02	.01
☐ 39	Kevin Mitchell	.10	.05	.01
☐ 40	Tim Raines	.15	.07	.02
☐ 41	Keith Hernandez	.10	.05	.01
☐ 42	Keith Moreland	.05	.02	.01
☐ 43	Ruben Sierra	.15	.07	.02
☐ 44	Chet Lemon	.05	.02	.01
☐ 45	Willie Randolph	.10	.05	.01
☐ 46	Andy Allanson	.05	.02	.01
☐ 47	Candy Maldonado	.05	.02	.01
☐ 48	Sid Bream	.05	.02	.01
☐ 49	Denny Walling	.05	.02	.01
☐ 50	Dave Winfield	.15	.07	.02
☐ 51	Alvin Davis	.05	.02	.01
☐ 52	Cory Snyder	.05	.02	.01
☐ 53	Hubie Brooks	.05	.02	.01
☐ 54	Chili Davis	.15	.07	.02
☐ 55	Kevin Seitzer	.05	.02	.01
☐ 56	Jose Uribe	.05	.02	.01
☐ 57	Tony Fernandez	.10	.05	.01
☐ 58	Tim Teufel	.05	.02	.01
☐ 59	Oddibe McDowell	.05	.02	.01
☐ 60	Les Lancaster	.05	.02	.01
☐ 61	Billy Hatcher	.05	.02	.01
☐ 62	Dan Gladden	.05	.02	.01
☐ 63	Marty Barrett	.05	.02	.01
☐ 64	Nick Esasky	.05	.02	.01
☐ 65	Wally Joyner	.10	.05	.01
☐ 66	Mike Greenwell	.10	.05	.01
☐ 67	Ken Williams	.05	.02	.01
☐ 68	Bob Horner	.05	.02	.01
☐ 69	Steve Sax	.05	.02	.01
☐ 70	Rickey Henderson	.15	.07	.02
☐ 71	Mitch Webster	.05	.02	.01
☐ 72	Rob Deer	.05	.02	.01
☐ 73	Jim Presley	.05	.02	.01
☐ 74	Albert Hall	.05	.02	.01
☐ 75A	George Brett ERR (At age 33)	.75	.35	.09
☐ 75B	George Brett COR (At age 35)	.40	.18	.05
☐ 76	Brian Downing	.05	.02	.01
☐ 77	Dave Martinez	.05	.02	.01
☐ 78	Scott Fletcher	.05	.02	.01
☐ 79	Phil Bradley	.05	.02	.01
☐ 80	Ozzie Smith	.30	.14	.04
☐ 81	Larry Sheets	.05	.02	.01
☐ 82	Mike Aldrete	.05	.02	.01
☐ 83	Darnell Coles	.05	.02	.01
☐ 84	Len Dykstra	.15	.07	.02
☐ 85	Jim Rice	.15	.07	.02

☐ 86	Jeff Treadway	.05	.02	.01
☐ 87	Jose Lind	.05	.02	.01
☐ 88	Willie McGee	.10	.05	.01
☐ 89	Mickey Brantley	.05	.02	.01
☐ 90	Tony Gwynn	.30	.14	.04
☐ 91	R.J. Reynolds	.05	.02	.01
☐ 92	Milt Thompson	.05	.02	.01
☐ 93	Kevin McReynolds	.05	.02	.01
☐ 94	Eddie Murray UER	.20	.09	.03
	('86 batting .205, should be .305)			
☐ 95	Lance Parrish	.10	.05	.01
☐ 96	Ron Kittle	.05	.02	.01
☐ 97	Gerald Young	.05	.02	.01
☐ 98	Ernie Whitt	.05	.02	.01
☐ 99	Jeff Reed	.05	.02	.01
☐ 100	Don Mattingly	.40	.18	.05
☐ 101	Gerald Perry	.05	.02	.01
☐ 102	Vance Law	.05	.02	.01
☐ 103	John Shelby	.05	.02	.01
☐ 104	Chris Sabo	.10	.05	.01
☐ 105	Danny Tartabull	.10	.05	.01
☐ 106	Glenn Wilson	.05	.02	.01
☐ 107	Mark Davidson	.05	.02	.01
☐ 108	Dave Parker	.15	.07	.02
☐ 109	Eric Davis	.10	.05	.01
☐ 110	Alan Trammell	.15	.07	.02
☐ 111	Ozzie Virgil	.05	.02	.01
☐ 112	Frank Tanana	.05	.02	.01
☐ 113	Rafael Ramirez	.05	.02	.01
☐ 114	Dennis Martinez	.10	.05	.01
☐ 115	Jose DeLeon	.05	.02	.01
☐ 116	Bob Ojeda	.05	.02	.01
☐ 117	Doug Drabek	.15	.07	.02
☐ 118	Andy Hawkins	.05	.02	.01
☐ 119	Greg Maddux	.75	.35	.09
☐ 120	Cecil Fielder UER	.15	.07	.02
	(Photo on back reversed)			
☐ 121	Mike Scioscia	.05	.02	.01
☐ 122	Dan Petry	.05	.02	.01
☐ 123	Terry Kennedy	.05	.02	.01
☐ 124	Kelly Downs	.05	.02	.01
☐ 125	Greg Gross UER	.05	.02	.01
	(Gregg on back)			
☐ 126	Fred Lynn	.10	.05	.01
☐ 127	Barry Bonds	.40	.18	.05
☐ 128	Harold Baines	.15	.07	.02
☐ 129	Doyle Alexander	.05	.02	.01
☐ 130	Kevin Elster	.05	.02	.01
☐ 131	Mike Heath	.05	.02	.01
☐ 132	Teddy Higuera	.05	.02	.01
☐ 133	Charlie Leibrandt	.05	.02	.01
☐ 134	Tim Laudner	.05	.02	.01
☐ 135A	Ray Knight ERR	.15	.07	.02
	(Reverse negative)			
☐ 135B	Ray Knight COR	.05	.02	.01
☐ 136	Howard Johnson	.10	.05	.01
☐ 137	Terry Pendleton	.15	.07	.02
☐ 138	Andy McGaffigan	.05	.02	.01
☐ 139	Ken Oberkfell	.05	.02	.01
☐ 140	Butch Wynegar	.05	.02	.01
☐ 141	Rob Murphy	.05	.02	.01
☐ 142	Rich Renteria	.05	.02	.01
☐ 143	Jose Guzman	.05	.02	.01
☐ 144	Andres Galarraga	.15	.07	.02
☐ 145	Ricky Horton	.05	.02	.01
☐ 146	Frank DiPino	.05	.02	.01
☐ 147	Glenn Braggs	.05	.02	.01
☐ 148	John Kruk	.15	.07	.02
☐ 149	Mike Schmidt	.25	.11	.03
☐ 150	Lee Smith	.15	.07	.02
☐ 151	Robin Yount	.20	.09	.03
☐ 152	Mark Eichhorn	.05	.02	.01
☐ 153	DeWayne Buice	.05	.02	.01
☐ 154	B.J. Surhoff	.10	.05	.01
☐ 155	Vince Coleman	.10	.05	.01
☐ 156	Tony Phillips	.15	.07	.02
☐ 157	Willie Fraser	.05	.02	.01
☐ 158	Lance McCullers	.05	.02	.01
☐ 159	Greg Gagne	.05	.02	.01
☐ 160	Jesse Barfield	.05	.02	.01
☐ 161	Mark Langston	.15	.07	.02
☐ 162	Kurt Stillwell	.05	.02	.01
☐ 163	Dion James	.05	.02	.01
☐ 164	Glenn Davis	.05	.02	.01
☐ 165	Walt Weiss	.05	.02	.01
☐ 166	Dave Concepcion	.10	.05	.01
☐ 167	Alfredo Griffin	.05	.02	.01
☐ 168	Don Heinkel	.05	.02	.01
☐ 169	Luis Rivera	.05	.02	.01
☐ 170	Shane Rawley	.05	.02	.01
☐ 171	Darrell Evans	.05	.02	.01
☐ 172	Robby Thompson	.10	.05	.01
☐ 173	Jody Davis	.05	.02	.01
☐ 174	Andy Van Slyke	.10	.05	.01
☐ 175	Wade Boggs UER	.15	.07	.02
	(Bio says .364, should be .356)			
☐ 176	Garry Templeton	.05	.02	.01
	('85 stats off-centered)			
☐ 177	Gary Redus	.05	.02	.01
☐ 178	Craig Lefferts	.05	.02	.01
☐ 179	Carney Lansford	.10	.05	.01
☐ 180	Ron Darling	.10	.05	.01
☐ 181	Kirk McCaskill	.05	.02	.01
☐ 182	Tony Armas	.05	.02	.01
☐ 183	Steve Farr	.05	.02	.01
☐ 184	Tom Brunansky	.05	.02	.01
☐ 185	Bryan Harvey UER	.10	.05	.01
	('87 games 47, should be 3)			
☐ 186	Mike Marshall	.05	.02	.01
☐ 187	Bo Diaz	.05	.02	.01
☐ 188	Willie Upshaw	.05	.02	.01
☐ 189	Mike Pagliarulo	.05	.02	.01
☐ 190	Mike Krukow	.05	.02	.01
☐ 191	Tommy Herr	.05	.02	.01
☐ 192	Jim Pankovits	.05	.02	.01
☐ 193	Dwight Evans	.10	.05	.01
☐ 194	Kelly Gruber	.05	.02	.01
☐ 195	Bobby Bonilla	.15	.07	.02
☐ 196	Wallace Johnson	.05	.02	.01
☐ 197	Dave Stieb	.10	.05	.01
☐ 198	Pat Borders	.10	.05	.01
☐ 199	Rafael Palmeiro	.25	.11	.03
☐ 200	Dwight Gooden	.10	.05	.01
☐ 201	Pete Incaviglia	.10	.05	.01
☐ 202	Chris James	.05	.02	.01
☐ 203	Marvell Wynne	.05	.02	.01
☐ 204	Pat Sheridan	.05	.02	.01
☐ 205	Don Baylor	.15	.07	.02
☐ 206	Paul O'Neill	.15	.07	.02
☐ 207	Pete Smith	.05	.02	.01
☐ 208	Mark McLemore	.05	.02	.01
☐ 209	Henry Cotto	.05	.02	.01
☐ 210	Kirk Gibson	.15	.07	.02
☐ 211	Claudell Washington	.05	.02	.01
☐ 212	Randy Bush	.05	.02	.01
☐ 213	Joe Carter	.20	.09	.03
☐ 214	Bill Buckner	.10	.05	.01

☐ 215	Bert Blyleven UER (Wrong birth year)	.15	.07	.02
☐ 216	Brett Butler	.15	.07	.02
☐ 217	Lee Mazzilli	.05	.02	.01
☐ 218	Spike Owen	.05	.02	.01
☐ 219	Bill Swift	.10	.05	.01
☐ 220	Tim Wallach	.05	.02	.01
☐ 221	David Cone	.15	.07	.02
☐ 222	Don Carman	.05	.02	.01
☐ 223	Rich Gossage	.15	.07	.02
☐ 224	Bob Walk	.05	.02	.01
☐ 225	Dave Righetti	.05	.02	.01
☐ 226	Kevin Bass	.05	.02	.01
☐ 227	Kevin Gross	.05	.02	.01
☐ 228	Tim Burke	.05	.02	.01
☐ 229	Rick Mahler	.05	.02	.01
☐ 230	Lou Whitaker UER (252 games in '85, should be 152)	.15	.07	.02
☐ 231	Luis Alicea	.05	.02	.01
☐ 232	Roberto Alomar	.50	.23	.06
☐ 233	Bob Boone	.10	.05	.01
☐ 234	Dickie Thon	.05	.02	.01
☐ 235	Shawon Dunston	.10	.05	.01
☐ 236	Pete Stanicek	.05	.02	.01
☐ 237	Craig Biggio (Inconsistent design, portrait on front)	.60	.25	.07
☐ 238	Dennis Boyd	.05	.02	.01
☐ 239	Tom Candiotti	.05	.02	.01
☐ 240	Gary Carter	.15	.07	.02
☐ 241	Mike Stanley	.10	.05	.01
☐ 242	Ken Phelps	.05	.02	.01
☐ 243	Chris Bosio	.05	.02	.01
☐ 244	Les Straker	.05	.02	.01
☐ 245	Dave Smith	.05	.02	.01
☐ 246	John Candelaria	.05	.02	.01
☐ 247	Joe Orsulak	.05	.02	.01
☐ 248	Storm Davis	.05	.02	.01
☐ 249	Floyd Bannister UER (ML Batting Record)	.05	.02	.01
☐ 250	Jack Morris	.15	.07	.02
☐ 251	Bret Saberhagen	.15	.07	.02
☐ 252	Tom Niedenfuer	.05	.02	.01
☐ 253	Neal Heaton	.05	.02	.01
☐ 254	Eric Show	.05	.02	.01
☐ 255	Juan Samuel	.05	.02	.01
☐ 256	Dale Sveum	.05	.02	.01
☐ 257	Jim Gott	.05	.02	.01
☐ 258	Scott Garrelts	.05	.02	.01
☐ 259	Larry McWilliams	.05	.02	.01
☐ 260	Steve Bedrosian	.05	.02	.01
☐ 261	Jack Howell	.05	.02	.01
☐ 262	Jay Tibbs	.05	.02	.01
☐ 263	Jamie Moyer	.05	.02	.01
☐ 264	Doug Sisk	.05	.02	.01
☐ 265	Todd Worrell	.05	.02	.01
☐ 266	John Farrell	.05	.02	.01
☐ 267	Dave Collins	.05	.02	.01
☐ 268	Sid Fernandez	.10	.05	.01
☐ 269	Tom Brookens	.05	.02	.01
☐ 270	Shane Mack	.10	.05	.01
☐ 271	Paul Kilgus	.05	.02	.01
☐ 272	Chuck Crim	.05	.02	.01
☐ 273	Bob Knepper	.05	.02	.01
☐ 274	Mike Moore	.05	.02	.01
☐ 275	Guillermo Hernandez	.05	.02	.01
☐ 276	Dennis Eckersley	.15	.07	.02
☐ 277	Graig Nettles	.10	.05	.01
☐ 278	Rich Dotson	.05	.02	.01
☐ 279	Larry Herndon	.05	.02	.01
☐ 280	Gene Larkin	.05	.02	.01
☐ 281	Roger McDowell	.05	.02	.01
☐ 282	Greg Swindell	.10	.05	.01
☐ 283	Juan Agosto	.05	.02	.01
☐ 284	Jeff M. Robinson	.05	.02	.01
☐ 285	Mike Dunne	.05	.02	.01
☐ 286	Greg Mathews	.05	.02	.01
☐ 287	Kent Tekulve	.05	.02	.01
☐ 288	Jerry Mumphrey	.05	.02	.01
☐ 289	Jack McDowell	.15	.07	.02
☐ 290	Frank Viola	.10	.05	.01
☐ 291	Mark Gubicza	.05	.02	.01
☐ 292	Dave Schmidt	.05	.02	.01
☐ 293	Mike Henneman	.10	.05	.01
☐ 294	Jimmy Jones	.05	.02	.01
☐ 295	Charlie Hough	.10	.05	.01
☐ 296	Rafael Santana	.05	.02	.01
☐ 297	Chris Speier	.05	.02	.01
☐ 298	Mike Witt	.05	.02	.01
☐ 299	Pascual Perez	.05	.02	.01
☐ 300	Nolan Ryan	.75	.35	.09
☐ 301	Mitch Williams	.10	.05	.01
☐ 302	Mookie Wilson	.10	.05	.01
☐ 303	Mackey Sasser	.05	.02	.01
☐ 304	John Cerutti	.05	.02	.01
☐ 305	Jeff Reardon	.15	.07	.02
☐ 306	Randy Myers UER (6 hits in '87, should be 61)	.15	.07	.02
☐ 307	Greg Brock	.05	.02	.01
☐ 308	Bob Welch	.10	.05	.01
☐ 309	Jeff D. Robinson	.05	.02	.01
☐ 310	Harold Reynolds	.05	.02	.01
☐ 311	Jim Walewander	.05	.02	.01
☐ 312	Dave Magadan	.05	.02	.01
☐ 313	Jim Gantner	.05	.02	.01
☐ 314	Walt Terrell	.05	.02	.01
☐ 315	Wally Backman	.05	.02	.01
☐ 316	Luis Salazar	.05	.02	.01
☐ 317	Rick Rhoden	.05	.02	.01
☐ 318	Tom Henke	.10	.05	.01
☐ 319	Mike Macfarlane	.10	.05	.01
☐ 320	Dan Plesac	.05	.02	.01
☐ 321	Calvin Schiraldi	.05	.02	.01
☐ 322	Stan Javier	.05	.02	.01
☐ 323	Devon White	.15	.07	.02
☐ 324	Scott Bradley	.05	.02	.01
☐ 325	Bruce Hurst	.05	.02	.01
☐ 326	Manny Lee	.05	.02	.01
☐ 327	Rick Aguilera	.15	.07	.02
☐ 328	Bruce Ruffin	.05	.02	.01
☐ 329	Ed Whitson	.05	.02	.01
☐ 330	Bo Jackson	.15	.07	.02
☐ 331	Ivan Calderon	.05	.02	.01
☐ 332	Mickey Hatcher	.05	.02	.01
☐ 333	Barry Jones	.05	.02	.01
☐ 334	Ron Hassey	.05	.02	.01
☐ 335	Bill Wegman	.05	.02	.01
☐ 336	Damon Berryhill	.05	.02	.01
☐ 337	Steve Ontiveros	.05	.02	.01
☐ 338	Dan Pasqua	.05	.02	.01
☐ 339	Bill Pecota	.05	.02	.01
☐ 340	Greg Cadaret	.05	.02	.01
☐ 341	Scott Bankhead	.05	.02	.01
☐ 342	Ron Guidry	.10	.05	.01
☐ 343	Danny Heep	.05	.02	.01
☐ 344	Bob Brower	.05	.02	.01
☐ 345	Rich Gedman	.05	.02	.01
☐ 346	Nelson Santovenia	.05	.02	.01
☐ 347	George Bell	.05	.02	.01
☐ 348	Ted Power	.05	.02	.01

☐ 349 Mark Grant	.05	.02	.01
☐ 350A Roger Clemens ERR	2.00	.90	.25
(778 career wins)			
☐ 350B Roger Clemens COR	.20	.09	.03
(78 career wins)			
☐ 351 Bill Long	.05	.02	.01
☐ 352 Jay Bell	.15	.07	.02
☐ 353 Steve Balboni	.05	.02	.01
☐ 354 Bob Kipper	.05	.02	.01
☐ 355 Steve Jeltz	.05	.02	.01
☐ 356 Jesse Orosco	.05	.02	.01
☐ 357 Bob Dernier	.05	.02	.01
☐ 358 Mickey Tettleton	.10	.05	.01
☐ 359 Duane Ward	.10	.05	.01
☐ 360 Darrin Jackson	.05	.02	.01
☐ 361 Rey Quinones	.05	.02	.01
☐ 362 Mark Grace	.15	.07	.02
☐ 363 Steve Lake	.05	.02	.01
☐ 364 Pat Perry	.05	.02	.01
☐ 365 Terry Steinbach	.10	.05	.01
☐ 366 Alan Ashby	.05	.02	.01
☐ 367 Jeff Montgomery	.10	.05	.01
☐ 368 Steve Buechele	.05	.02	.01
☐ 369 Chris Brown	.05	.02	.01
☐ 370 Orel Hershiser	.15	.07	.02
☐ 371 Todd Benzinger	.05	.02	.01
☐ 372 Ron Gant	.20	.09	.03
☐ 373 Paul Assenmacher	.05	.02	.01
☐ 374 Joey Meyer	.05	.02	.01
☐ 375 Neil Allen	.05	.02	.01
☐ 376 Mike Davis	.05	.02	.01
☐ 377 Jeff Parrett	.05	.02	.01
☐ 378 Jay Howell	.05	.02	.01
☐ 379 Rafael Belliard	.05	.02	.01
☐ 380 Luis Polonia UER	.10	.05	.01
(2 triples in '87,			
should be 10)			
☐ 381 Keith Atherton	.05	.02	.01
☐ 382 Kent Hrbek	.10	.05	.01
☐ 383 Bob Stanley	.05	.02	.01
☐ 384 Dave LaPoint	.05	.02	.01
☐ 385 Rance Mulliniks	.05	.02	.01
☐ 386 Melido Perez	.05	.02	.01
☐ 387 Doug Jones	.10	.05	.01
☐ 388 Steve Lyons	.05	.02	.01
☐ 389 Alejandro Pena	.05	.02	.01
☐ 390 Frank White	.10	.05	.01
☐ 391 Pat Tabler	.05	.02	.01
☐ 392 Eric Plunk	.05	.02	.01
☐ 393 Mike Maddux	.05	.02	.01
☐ 394 Allan Anderson	.05	.02	.01
☐ 395 Bob Brenly	.05	.02	.01
☐ 396 Rick Cerone	.05	.02	.01
☐ 397 Scott Terry	.05	.02	.01
☐ 398 Mike Jackson	.05	.02	.01
☐ 399 Bobby Thigpen UER	.05	.02	.01
(Bio says 37 saves in			
'88, should be 34)			
☐ 400 Don Sutton	.15	.07	.02
☐ 401 Cecil Espy	.05	.02	.01
☐ 402 Junior Ortiz	.05	.02	.01
☐ 403 Mike Smithson	.05	.02	.01
☐ 404 Bud Black	.05	.02	.01
☐ 405 Tom Foley	.05	.02	.01
☐ 406 Andres Thomas	.05	.02	.01
☐ 407 Rick Sutcliffe	.10	.05	.01
☐ 408 Brian Harper	.10	.05	.01
☐ 409 John Smiley	.05	.02	.01
☐ 410 Juan Nieves	.05	.02	.01
☐ 411 Shawn Abner	.05	.02	.01
☐ 412 Wes Gardner	.05	.02	.01

☐ 413 Darren Daulton	.15	.07	.02
☐ 414 Juan Berenguer	.05	.02	.01
☐ 415 Charles Hudson	.05	.02	.01
☐ 416 Rick Honeycutt	.05	.02	.01
☐ 417 Greg Booker	.05	.02	.01
☐ 418 Tim Belcher	.05	.02	.01
☐ 419 Don August	.05	.02	.01
☐ 420 Dale Mohorcic	.05	.02	.01
☐ 421 Steve Lombardozzi	.05	.02	.01
☐ 422 Atlee Hammaker	.05	.02	.01
☐ 423 Jerry Don Gleaton	.05	.02	.01
☐ 424 Scott Bailes	.05	.02	.01
☐ 425 Bruce Sutter	.10	.05	.01
☐ 426 Randy Ready	.05	.02	.01
☐ 427 Jerry Reed	.05	.02	.01
☐ 428 Bryn Smith	.05	.02	.01
☐ 429 Tim Leary	.05	.02	.01
☐ 430 Mark Clear	.05	.02	.01
☐ 431 Terry Leach	.05	.02	.01
☐ 432 John Moses	.05	.02	.01
☐ 433 Ozzie Guillen	.10	.05	.01
☐ 434 Gene Nelson	.05	.02	.01
☐ 435 Gary Ward	.05	.02	.01
☐ 436 Luis Aguayo	.05	.02	.01
☐ 437 Fernando Valenzuela	.05	.02	.01
☐ 438 Jeff Russell UER	.05	.02	.01
(Saves total does			
not add up correctly)			
☐ 439 Cecilio Guante	.05	.02	.01
☐ 440 Don Robinson	.05	.02	.01
☐ 441 Rick Anderson	.05	.02	.01
☐ 442 Tom Glavine	.40	.18	.05
☐ 443 Daryl Boston	.05	.02	.01
☐ 444 Joe Price	.05	.02	.01
☐ 445 Stewart Cliburn	.05	.02	.01
☐ 446 Manny Trillo	.05	.02	.01
☐ 447 Joel Skinner	.05	.02	.01
☐ 448 Charlie Puleo	.05	.02	.01
☐ 449 Carlton Fisk	.15	.07	.02
☐ 450 Will Clark	.20	.09	.03
☐ 451 Otis Nixon	.05	.02	.01
☐ 452 Rick Schu	.05	.02	.01
☐ 453 Todd Stottlemyre UER	.10	.05	.01
(ML Batting Record)			
☐ 454 Tim Birtsas	.05	.02	.01
☐ 455 Dave Gallagher	.05	.02	.01
☐ 456 Barry Lyons	.05	.02	.01
☐ 457 Fred Manrique	.05	.02	.01
☐ 458 Ernest Riles	.05	.02	.01
☐ 459 Doug Jennings	.05	.02	.01
☐ 460 Joe Magrane	.05	.02	.01
☐ 461 Jamie Quirk	.05	.02	.01
☐ 462 Jack Armstrong	.05	.02	.01
☐ 463 Bobby Witt	.10	.05	.01
☐ 464 Keith A. Miller	.05	.02	.01
☐ 465 Todd Burns	.05	.02	.01
☐ 466 John Dopson	.05	.02	.01
☐ 467 Rich Yett	.05	.02	.01
☐ 468 Craig Reynolds	.05	.02	.01
☐ 469 Dave Bergman	.05	.02	.01
☐ 470 Rex Hudler	.05	.02	.01
☐ 471 Eric King	.05	.02	.01
☐ 472 Joaquin Andujar	.05	.02	.01
☐ 473 Sil Campusano	.05	.02	.01
☐ 474 Terry Mulholland	.10	.05	.01
☐ 475 Mike Flanagan	.05	.02	.01
☐ 476 Greg A. Harris	.05	.02	.01
☐ 477 Tommy John	.15	.07	.02
☐ 478 Dave Anderson	.05	.02	.01
☐ 479 Fred Toliver	.05	.02	.01
☐ 480 Jimmy Key	.15	.07	.02

☐ 481 Donell Nixon	.05	.02	.01
☐ 482 Mark Portugal	.10	.05	.01
☐ 483 Tom Pagnozzi	.05	.02	.01
☐ 484 Jeff Kunkel	.05	.02	.01
☐ 485 Frank Williams	.05	.02	.01
☐ 486 Jody Reed	.05	.02	.01
☐ 487 Roberto Kelly	.10	.05	.01
☐ 488 Shawn Hillegas UER	.05	.02	.01
(165 innings in '87, should be 165.2)			
☐ 489 Jerry Reuss	.05	.02	.01
☐ 490 Mark Davis	.05	.02	.01
☐ 491 Jeff Sellers	.05	.02	.01
☐ 492 Zane Smith	.05	.02	.01
☐ 493 Al Newman	.05	.02	.01
☐ 494 Mike Young	.05	.02	.01
☐ 495 Larry Parrish	.05	.02	.01
☐ 496 Herm Winningham	.05	.02	.01
☐ 497 Carmen Castillo	.05	.02	.01
☐ 498 Joe Hesketh	.05	.02	.01
☐ 499 Darrell Miller	.05	.02	.01
☐ 500 Mike LaCoss	.05	.02	.01
☐ 501 Charlie Lea	.05	.02	.01
☐ 502 Bruce Benedict	.05	.02	.01
☐ 503 Chuck Finley	.10	.05	.01
☐ 504 Brad Wellman	.05	.02	.01
☐ 505 Tim Crews	.05	.02	.01
☐ 506 Ken Gerhart	.05	.02	.01
☐ 507A Brian Holton ERR	.05	.02	.01
(Born 1/25/65 Denver, should be 11/29/59 in McKeesport)			
☐ 507B Brian Holton COR	2.00	.90	.25
☐ 508 Dennis Lamp	.05	.02	.01
☐ 509 Bobby Meacham UER	.05	.02	.01
('84 games 099)			
☐ 510 Tracy Jones	.05	.02	.01
☐ 511 Mike R. Fitzgerald	.05	.02	.01
☐ 512 Jeff Bittiger	.05	.02	.01
☐ 513 Tim Flannery	.05	.02	.01
☐ 514 Ray Hayward	.05	.02	.01
☐ 515 Dave Leiper	.05	.02	.01
☐ 516 Rod Scurry	.05	.02	.01
☐ 517 Carmelo Martinez	.05	.02	.01
☐ 518 Curtis Wilkerson	.05	.02	.01
☐ 519 Stan Jefferson	.05	.02	.01
☐ 520 Dan Quisenberry	.10	.05	.01
☐ 521 Lloyd McClendon	.05	.02	.01
☐ 522 Steve Trout	.05	.02	.01
☐ 523 Larry Andersen	.05	.02	.01
☐ 524 Don Aase	.05	.02	.01
☐ 525 Bob Forsch	.05	.02	.01
☐ 526 Geno Petralli	.05	.02	.01
☐ 527 Angel Salazar	.05	.02	.01
☐ 528 Mike Schooler	.05	.02	.01
☐ 529 Jose Oquendo	.05	.02	.01
☐ 530 Jay Buhner UER	.15	.07	.02
(Wearing 43 on front, listed as 34 on back)			
☐ 531 Tom Bolton	.05	.02	.01
☐ 532 Al Nipper	.05	.02	.01
☐ 533 Dave Henderson	.05	.02	.01
☐ 534 John Costello	.05	.02	.01
☐ 535 Donnie Moore	.05	.02	.01
☐ 536 Mike Laga	.05	.02	.01
☐ 537 Mike Gallego	.05	.02	.01
☐ 538 Jim Clancy	.05	.02	.01
☐ 539 Joel Youngblood	.05	.02	.01
☐ 540 Rick Leach	.05	.02	.01
☐ 541 Kevin Romine	.05	.02	.01
☐ 542 Mark Salas	.05	.02	.01
☐ 543 Greg Minton	.05	.02	.01
☐ 544 Dave Palmer	.05	.02	.01
☐ 545 Dwayne Murphy UER	.05	.02	.01
(Game-sinning)			
☐ 546 Jim Deshaies	.05	.02	.01
☐ 547 Don Gordon	.05	.02	.01
☐ 548 Ricky Jordan	.05	.02	.01
☐ 549 Mike Boddicker	.05	.02	.01
☐ 550 Mike Scott	.05	.02	.01
☐ 551 Jeff Ballard	.05	.02	.01
☐ 552A Jose Rijo ERR	.15	.07	.02
(Uniform listed as 27 on back)			
☐ 552B Jose Rijo COR	.15	.07	.02
(Uniform listed as 24 on back)			
☐ 553 Danny Darwin	.05	.02	.01
☐ 554 Tom Browning	.05	.02	.01
☐ 555 Danny Jackson	.05	.02	.01
☐ 556 Rick Dempsey	.05	.02	.01
☐ 557 Jeffrey Leonard	.05	.02	.01
☐ 558 Jeff Musselman	.05	.02	.01
☐ 559 Ron Robinson	.05	.02	.01
☐ 560 John Tudor	.05	.02	.01
☐ 561 Don Slaught UER	.05	.02	.01
(237 games in 1987)			
☐ 562 Dennis Rasmussen	.05	.02	.01
☐ 563 Brady Anderson	.40	.18	.05
☐ 564 Pedro Guerrero	.10	.05	.01
☐ 565 Paul Molitor	.15	.07	.02
☐ 566 Terry Clark	.05	.02	.01
☐ 567 Terry Puhl	.05	.02	.01
☐ 568 Mike Campbell	.05	.02	.01
☐ 569 Paul Mirabella	.05	.02	.01
☐ 570 Jeff Hamilton	.05	.02	.01
☐ 571 Oswald Peraza	.05	.02	.01
☐ 572 Bob McClure	.05	.02	.01
☐ 573 Jose Bautista	.05	.02	.01
☐ 574 Alex Trevino	.05	.02	.01
☐ 575 John Franco	.10	.05	.01
☐ 576 Mark Parent	.05	.02	.01
☐ 577 Nelson Liriano	.05	.02	.01
☐ 578 Steve Shields	.05	.02	.01
☐ 579 Odell Jones	.05	.02	.01
☐ 580 Al Leiter	.05	.02	.01
☐ 581 Dave Stapleton	.05	.02	.01
☐ 582 World Series '88	.10	.05	.01
Orel Hershiser			
Jose Canseco			
Kirk Gibson			
Dave Stewart			
☐ 583 Donnie Hill	.05	.02	.01
☐ 584 Chuck Jackson	.05	.02	.01
☐ 585 Rene Gonzales	.05	.02	.01
☐ 586 Tracy Woodson	.05	.02	.01
☐ 587 Jim Adduci	.05	.02	.01
☐ 588 Mario Soto	.05	.02	.01
☐ 589 Jeff Blauser	.15	.07	.02
☐ 590 Jim Traber	.05	.02	.01
☐ 591 Jon Perlman	.05	.02	.01
☐ 592 Mark Williamson	.05	.02	.01
☐ 593 Dave Meads	.05	.02	.01
☐ 594 Jim Eisenreich	.05	.02	.01
☐ 595A Paul Gibson P1	1.00	.45	.12
☐ 595B Paul Gibson P2	.05	.02	.01
(Airbrushed leg on player in background)			
☐ 596 Mike Birkbeck	.05	.02	.01
☐ 597 Terry Francona	.05	.02	.01
☐ 598 Paul Zuvella	.05	.02	.01
☐ 599 Franklin Stubbs	.05	.02	.01

☐ 600	Gregg Jefferies	.20	.09	.03
☐ 601	John Cangelosi	.05	.02	.01
☐ 602	Mike Sharperson	.05	.02	.01
☐ 603	Mike Diaz	.05	.02	.01
☐ 604	Gary Varsho	.05	.02	.01
☐ 605	Terry Blocker	.05	.02	.01
☐ 606	Charlie O'Brien	.05	.02	.01
☐ 607	Jim Eppard	.05	.02	.01
☐ 608	John Davis	.05	.02	.01
☐ 609	Ken Griffey Sr.	.10	.05	.01
☐ 610	Buddy Bell	.10	.05	.01
☐ 611	Ted Simmons UER	.10	.05	.01
	('78 stats Cardinal)			
☐ 612	Matt Williams	.50	.23	.06
☐ 613	Danny Cox	.05	.02	.01
☐ 614	Al Pedrique	.05	.02	.01
☐ 615	Ron Oester	.05	.02	.01
☐ 616	John Smoltz	.40	.18	.05
☐ 617	Bob Melvin	.05	.02	.01
☐ 618	Rob Dibble	.10	.05	.01
☐ 619	Kirt Manwaring	.05	.02	.01
☐ 620	Felix Fermin	.05	.02	.01
☐ 621	Doug Dascenzo	.05	.02	.01
☐ 622	Bill Brennan	.05	.02	.01
☐ 623	Carlos Quintana	.05	.02	.01
☐ 624	Mike Harkey UER	.05	.02	.01
	(13 and 31 walks in '88, should be 35 and 33)			
☐ 625	Gary Sheffield	.60	.25	.07
☐ 626	Tom Prince	.05	.02	.01
☐ 627	Steve Searcy	.05	.02	.01
☐ 628	Charlie Hayes	.20	.09	.03
	(Listed as outfielder)			
☐ 629	Felix Jose UER	.10	.05	.01
	(Modesto misspelled as Modesta)			
☐ 630	Sandy Alomar Jr.	.20	.09	.03
	(Inconsistent design, portrait on front)			
☐ 631	Derek Lilliquist	.05	.02	.01
☐ 632	Geronimo Berroa	.10	.05	.01
☐ 633	Luis Medina	.05	.02	.01
☐ 634	Tom Gordon UER	.15	.07	.02
	(Height 6'0")			
☐ 635	Ramon Martinez	.30	.14	.04
☐ 636	Craig Worthington	.05	.02	.01
☐ 637	Edgar Martinez	.25	.11	.03
☐ 638	Chad Kreuter	.05	.02	.01
☐ 639	Ron Jones	.05	.02	.01
☐ 640	Van Snider	.05	.02	.01
☐ 641	Lance Blankenship	.05	.02	.01
☐ 642	Dwight Smith UER	.05	.02	.01
	(10 HR's in '87, should be 18)			
☐ 643	Cameron Drew	.05	.02	.01
☐ 644	Jerald Clark	.05	.02	.01
☐ 645	Randy Johnson	1.00	.45	.12
☐ 646	Norm Charlton	.10	.05	.01
☐ 647	Todd Frohwirth UER	.05	.02	.01
	(Southpaw on back)			
☐ 648	Luis De Los Santos	.05	.02	.01
☐ 649	Tim Jones	.05	.02	.01
☐ 650	Dave West UER	.10	.05	.01
	(ML hits 3, should be 6)			
☐ 651	Bob Milacki	.05	.02	.01
☐ 652	Wrigley Field HL	.10	.05	.01
	(Let There Be Lights)			
☐ 653	Orel Hershiser HL	.10	.05	.01
	(The Streak)			

☐ 654A	Wade Boggs HL ERR	1.50	.70	.19
	(Wade Whacks 'Em) ("seaason" on back)			
☐ 654B	Wade Boggs HL COR.	.15	.07	.02
	(Wade Whacks 'Em)			
☐ 655	Jose Canseco HL	.15	.07	.02
	(One of a Kind)			
☐ 656	Doug Jones HL	.05	.02	.01
	(Doug Sets Saves)			
☐ 657	Rickey Henderson HL	.15	.07	.02
	(Rickey Rocks 'Em)			
☐ 658	Tom Browning HL	.05	.02	.01
	(Tom Perfect Pitches)			
☐ 659	Mike Greenwell HL	.10	.05	.01
	(Greenwell Gamers)			
☐ 660	Boston Red Sox HL	.05	.02	.01
	(Joe Morgan MG, Sox Sock 'Em)			

1989 Score Rookie/Traded

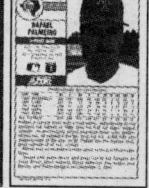

The 1989 Score Rookie and Traded set contains 110 standard-size (2 1/2" by 3 1/2") cards. The fronts have coral green borders with pink diamonds at the bottom. The vertically oriented backs have color facial shots, career stats, and biographical information. Cards 1-80 feature traded players; cards 81-110 feature 1989 rookies. The set was distributed in a blue box with 10 Magic Motion trivia cards. Rookie Cards in this set include Jim Abbott, Joey (Albert) Belle, Junior Felix, Ken Griffey Jr., Ken Hill, Gregg Olson, Jerome Walton, and John Wetteland.

	MINT	NRMT	EXC
COMPLETE FACT.SET (110)	8.00	3.60	1.00
COMMON CARD (1T-110T)	.05	.02	.01
☐ 1T Rafael Palmeiro	.25	.11	.03
☐ 2T Nolan Ryan	1.50	.70	.19
☐ 3T Jack Clark	.10	.05	.01
☐ 4T Dave LaPoint	.05	.02	.01
☐ 5T Mike Moore	.05	.02	.01
☐ 6T Pete O'Brien	.05	.02	.01
☐ 7T Jeffrey Leonard	.05	.02	.01
☐ 8T Rob Murphy	.05	.02	.01

☐ 9T Tom Herr	.05	.02	.01
☐ 10T Claudell Washington	.05	.02	.01
☐ 11T Mike Pagliarulo	.05	.02	.01
☐ 12T Steve Lake	.05	.02	.01
☐ 13T Spike Owen	.05	.02	.01
☐ 14T Andy Hawkins	.05	.02	.01
☐ 15T Todd Benzinger	.05	.02	.01
☐ 16T Mookie Wilson	.10	.05	.01
☐ 17T Bert Blyleven	.15	.07	.02
☐ 18T Jeff Treadway	.05	.02	.01
☐ 19T Bruce Hurst	.05	.02	.01
☐ 20T Steve Sax	.05	.02	.01
☐ 21T Juan Samuel	.05	.02	.01
☐ 22T Jesse Barfield	.05	.02	.01
☐ 23T Carmen Castillo	.05	.02	.01
☐ 24T Terry Leach	.05	.02	.01
☐ 25T Mark Langston	.15	.07	.02
☐ 26T Eric King	.05	.02	.01
☐ 27T Steve Balboni	.05	.02	.01
☐ 28T Len Dykstra	.15	.07	.02
☐ 29T Keith Moreland	.05	.02	.01
☐ 30T Terry Kennedy	.05	.02	.01
☐ 31T Eddie Murray	.20	.09	.03
☐ 32T Mitch Williams	.10	.05	.01
☐ 33T Jeff Parrett	.05	.02	.01
☐ 34T Wally Backman	.05	.02	.01
☐ 35T Julio Franco	.10	.05	.01
☐ 36T Lance Parrish	.10	.05	.01
☐ 37T Nick Esasky	.05	.02	.01
☐ 38T Luis Polonia	.10	.05	.01
☐ 39T Kevin Gross	.05	.02	.01
☐ 40T John Dopson	.05	.02	.01
☐ 41T Willie Randolph	.10	.05	.01
☐ 42T Jim Clancy	.05	.02	.01
☐ 43T Tracy Jones	.05	.02	.01
☐ 44T Phil Bradley	.05	.02	.01
☐ 45T Milt Thompson	.05	.02	.01
☐ 46T Chris James	.05	.02	.01
☐ 47T Scott Fletcher	.05	.02	.01
☐ 48T Kal Daniels	.05	.02	.01
☐ 49T Steve Bedrosian	.05	.02	.01
☐ 50T Rickey Henderson	.15	.07	.02
☐ 51T Dion James	.05	.02	.01
☐ 52T Tim Leary	.05	.02	.01
☐ 53T Roger McDowell	.05	.02	.01
☐ 54T Mel Hall	.05	.02	.01
☐ 55T Dickie Thon	.05	.02	.01
☐ 56T Zane Smith	.05	.02	.01
☐ 57T Danny Heep	.05	.02	.01
☐ 58T Bob McClure	.05	.02	.01
☐ 59T Brian Holton	.05	.02	.01
☐ 60T Randy Ready	.05	.02	.01
☐ 61T Bob Melvin	.05	.02	.01
☐ 62T Harold Baines	.15	.07	.02
☐ 63T Lance McCullers	.05	.02	.01
☐ 64T Jody Davis	.05	.02	.01
☐ 65T Darrell Evans	.10	.05	.01
☐ 66T Joel Youngblood	.05	.02	.01
☐ 67T Frank Viola	.10	.05	.01
☐ 68T Mike Aldrete	.05	.02	.01
☐ 69T Greg Cadaret	.05	.02	.01
☐ 70T John Kruk	.15	.07	.02
☐ 71T Pat Sheridan	.05	.02	.01
☐ 72T Oddibe McDowell	.05	.02	.01
☐ 73T Tom Brookens	.05	.02	.01
☐ 74T Bob Boone	.10	.05	.01
☐ 75T Walt Terrell	.05	.02	.01
☐ 76T Joel Skinner	.05	.02	.01
☐ 77T Randy Johnson	1.00	.45	.12
☐ 78T Felix Fermin	.05	.02	.01
☐ 79T Rick Mahler	.05	.02	.01

☐ 80T Richard Dotson	.05	.02	.01
☐ 81T Cris Carpenter	.05	.02	.01
☐ 82T Bill Spiers	.05	.02	.01
☐ 83T Junior Felix	.05	.02	.01
☐ 84T Joe Girardi	.10	.05	.01
☐ 85T Jerome Walton	.05	.02	.01
☐ 86T Greg Litton	.05	.02	.01
☐ 87T Greg W.Harris	.05	.02	.01
☐ 88T Jim Abbott	.25	.11	.03
☐ 89T Kevin Brown	.10	.05	.01
☐ 90T John Wetteland	.50	.23	.06
☐ 91T Gary Wayne	.05	.02	.01
☐ 92T Rich Monteleone	.05	.02	.01
☐ 93T Bob Geren	.05	.02	.01
☐ 94T Clay Parker	.05	.02	.01
☐ 95T Steve Finley	.20	.09	.03
☐ 96T Gregg Olson	.15	.07	.02
☐ 97T Ken Patterson	.05	.02	.01
☐ 98T Ken Hill	.50	.23	.06
☐ 99T Scott Scudder	.05	.02	.01
☐ 100T Ken Griffey Jr.	5.00	2.20	.60
☐ 101T Jeff Brantley	.05	.02	.01
☐ 102T Donn Pall	.05	.02	.01
☐ 103T Carlos Martinez	.05	.02	.01
☐ 104T Joe Oliver	.15	.07	.02
☐ 105T Omar Vizquel	.25	.11	.03
☐ 106T Joey Belle	3.00	1.35	.35
☐ 107T Kenny Rogers	.30	.14	.04
☐ 108T Mark Carreon	.05	.02	.01
☐ 109T Rolando Roomes	.05	.02	.01
☐ 110T Pete Harnisch	.10	.05	.01

1990 Score

The 1990 Score set contains 704 standard-size (2 1/2" by 3 1/2") cards. The front borders are red, blue, green or white. The vertically oriented backs are white with borders that match the fronts, and feature color mugshots. Cards numbered 661-682 contain the first round draft picks subset noted as DC for "draft choice" in the checklist below. Cards numbered 683-695 contain the "Dream Team" subset noted by DT in the checklist below. Rookie Cards in this set include Scott Cooper, Delino DeShields, Cal Eldred, Juan Gonzalez, Tommy Greene, Marquis Grissom, Dave Justice, Chuck Knoblauch, Kevin Maas, Ben McDonald, John Olerud, Dean Palmer, Sammy Sosa, Frank Thomas, Mo Vaughn, and Larry Walker. A ten-card set of Dream

Team Rookies was inserted into each hobby factory set, but was not included in retail factory sets. These cards carry a B prefix on the card number and include a player at each position plus a commemorative card honoring the late Baseball Commissioner A. Bartlett Giamatti.

	MINT	NRMT	EXC
COMPLETE SET (704)	12.00	5.50	1.50
COMPLETE RETAIL SET (704)	12.00	5.50	1.50
COMPLETE HOBBY SET (714)	18.00	8.00	2.20
COMMON CARD (1-704)	.05	.02	.01

☐	1 Don Mattingly	.40	.18	.05
☐	2 Cal Ripken	.75	.35	.09
☐	3 Dwight Evans	.10	.05	.01
☐	4 Barry Bonds	.30	.14	.04
☐	5 Kevin McReynolds	.05	.02	.01
☐	6 Ozzie Guillen	.10	.05	.01
☐	7 Terry Kennedy	.05	.02	.01
☐	8 Bryan Harvey	.10	.05	.01
☐	9 Alan Trammell	.15	.07	.02
☐	10 Cory Snyder	.05	.02	.01
☐	11 Jody Reed	.05	.02	.01
☐	12 Roberto Alomar	.30	.14	.04
☐	13 Pedro Guerrero	.10	.05	.01
☐	14 Gary Redus	.05	.02	.01
☐	15 Marty Barrett	.05	.02	.01
☐	16 Ricky Jordan	.05	.02	.01
☐	17 Joe Magrane	.05	.02	.01
☐	18 Sid Fernandez	.10	.05	.01
☐	19 Richard Dotson	.05	.02	.01
☐	20 Jack Clark	.10	.05	.01
☐	21 Bob Walk	.05	.02	.01
☐	22 Ron Karkovice	.05	.02	.01
☐	23 Lenny Harris	.05	.02	.01
☐	24 Phil Bradley	.05	.02	.01
☐	25 Andres Galarraga	.15	.07	.02
☐	26 Brian Downing	.05	.02	.01
☐	27 Dave Martinez	.05	.02	.01
☐	28 Eric King	.05	.02	.01
☐	29 Barry Lyons	.05	.02	.01
☐	30 Dave Schmidt	.05	.02	.01
☐	31 Mike Boddicker	.05	.02	.01
☐	32 Tom Foley	.05	.02	.01
☐	33 Brady Anderson	.10	.05	.01
☐	34 Jim Presley	.05	.02	.01
☐	35 Lance Parrish	.10	.05	.01
☐	36 Von Hayes	.05	.02	.01
☐	37 Lee Smith	.15	.07	.02
☐	38 Herm Winningham	.05	.02	.01
☐	39 Alejandro Pena	.05	.02	.01
☐	40 Mike Scott	.05	.02	.01
☐	41 Joe Orsulak	.05	.02	.01
☐	42 Rafael Ramirez	.05	.02	.01
☐	43 Gerald Young	.05	.02	.01
☐	44 Dick Schofield	.05	.02	.01
☐	45 Dave Smith	.05	.02	.01
☐	46 Dave Magadan	.05	.02	.01
☐	47 Dennis Martinez	.10	.05	.01
☐	48 Greg Minton	.05	.02	.01
☐	49 Milt Thompson	.05	.02	.01
☐	50 Orel Hershiser	.15	.07	.02
☐	51 Bip Roberts	.10	.05	.01
☐	52 Jerry Browne	.05	.02	.01
☐	53 Bob Ojeda	.05	.02	.01
☐	54 Fernando Valenzuela	.05	.02	.01
☐	55 Matt Nokes	.05	.02	.01
☐	56 Brook Jacoby	.05	.02	.01
☐	57 Frank Tanana	.05	.02	.01
☐	58 Scott Fletcher	.05	.02	.01
☐	59 Ron Oester	.05	.02	.01
☐	60 Bob Boone	.10	.05	.01
☐	61 Dan Gladden	.05	.02	.01
☐	62 Darnell Coles	.05	.02	.01
☐	63 Gregg Olson	.05	.02	.01
☐	64 Todd Burns	.05	.02	.01
☐	65 Todd Benzinger	.05	.02	.01
☐	66 Dale Murphy	.15	.07	.02
☐	67 Mike Flanagan	.05	.02	.01
☐	68 Jose Oquendo	.05	.02	.01
☐	69 Cecil Espy	.05	.02	.01
☐	70 Chris Sabo	.05	.02	.01
☐	71 Shane Rawley	.05	.02	.01
☐	72 Tom Brunansky	.05	.02	.01
☐	73 Vance Law	.05	.02	.01
☐	74 B.J. Surhoff	.05	.02	.01
☐	75 Lou Whitaker	.15	.07	.02
☐	76 Ken Caminiti UER	.15	.07	.02
	(Euclid, Ohio should be Hanford, California)			
☐	77 Nelson Liriano	.05	.02	.01
☐	78 Tommy Gregg	.05	.02	.01
☐	79 Don Slaught	.05	.02	.01
☐	80 Eddie Murray	.25	.11	.03
☐	81 Joe Boever	.05	.02	.01
☐	82 Charlie Leibrandt	.05	.02	.01
☐	83 Jose Lind	.05	.02	.01
☐	84 Tony Phillips	.15	.07	.02
☐	85 Mitch Webster	.05	.02	.01
☐	86 Dan Plesac	.05	.02	.01
☐	87 Rick Mahler	.05	.02	.01
☐	88 Steve Lyons	.05	.02	.01
☐	89 Tony Fernandez	.10	.05	.01
☐	90 Ryne Sandberg	.30	.14	.04
☐	91 Nick Esasky	.05	.02	.01
☐	92 Luis Salazar	.05	.02	.01
☐	93 Pete Incaviglia	.05	.02	.01
☐	94 Ivan Calderon	.05	.02	.01
☐	95 Jeff Treadway	.05	.02	.01
☐	96 Kurt Stillwell	.05	.02	.01
☐	97 Gary Sheffield	.20	.09	.03
☐	98 Jeffrey Leonard	.05	.02	.01
☐	99 Andres Thomas	.05	.02	.01
☐	100 Roberto Kelly	.10	.05	.01
☐	101 Alvaro Espinoza	.05	.02	.01
☐	102 Greg Gagne	.05	.02	.01
☐	103 John Farrell	.05	.02	.01
☐	104 Willie Wilson	.05	.02	.01
☐	105 Glenn Braggs	.05	.02	.01
☐	106 Chet Lemon	.05	.02	.01
☐	107A Jamie Moyer ERR	.05	.02	.01
	(Scintilating)			
☐	107B Jamie Moyer COR	.05	.02	.01
	(Scintilating)			
☐	108 Chuck Crim	.05	.02	.01
☐	109 Dave Valle	.05	.02	.01
☐	110 Walt Weiss	.05	.02	.01
☐	111 Larry Sheets	.05	.02	.01
☐	112 Don Robinson	.05	.02	.01
☐	113 Danny Heep	.05	.02	.01
☐	114 Carmelo Martinez	.05	.02	.01
☐	115 Dave Gallagher	.05	.02	.01
☐	116 Mike LaValliere	.05	.02	.01
☐	117 Bob McClure	.05	.02	.01
☐	118 Rene Gonzales	.05	.02	.01
☐	119 Mark Parent	.05	.02	.01
☐	120 Wally Joyner	.15	.07	.02
☐	121 Mark Gubicza	.05	.02	.01
☐	122 Tony Pena	.05	.02	.01
☐	123 Carmen Castillo	.05	.02	.01

☐ 124	Howard Johnson	.10	.05	.01		
☐ 125	Steve Sax	.05	.02	.01		
☐ 126	Tim Belcher	.05	.02	.01		
☐ 127	Tim Burke	.05	.02	.01		
☐ 128	Al Newman	.05	.02	.01		
☐ 129	Dennis Rasmussen	.05	.02	.01		
☐ 130	Doug Jones	.05	.02	.01		
☐ 131	Fred Lynn	.10	.05	.01		
☐ 132	Jeff Hamilton	.05	.02	.01		
☐ 133	German Gonzalez	.05	.02	.01		
☐ 134	John Morris	.05	.02	.01		
☐ 135	Dave Parker	.10	.05	.01		
☐ 136	Gary Pettis	.05	.02	.01		
☐ 137	Dennis Boyd	.05	.02	.01		
☐ 138	Candy Maldonado	.05	.02	.01		
☐ 139	Rick Cerone	.05	.02	.01		
☐ 140	George Brett	.40	.18	.05		
☐ 141	Dave Clark	.05	.02	.01		
☐ 142	Dickie Thon	.05	.02	.01		
☐ 143	Junior Ortiz	.05	.02	.01		
☐ 144	Don August	.05	.02	.01		
☐ 145	Gary Gaetti	.05	.02	.01		
☐ 146	Kirt Manwaring	.05	.02	.01		
☐ 147	Jeff Reed	.05	.02	.01		
☐ 148	Jose Alvarez	.05	.02	.01		
☐ 149	Mike Schooler	.05	.02	.01		
☐ 150	Mark Grace	.15	.07	.02		
☐ 151	Geronimo Berroa	.10	.05	.01		
☐ 152	Barry Jones	.05	.02	.01		
☐ 153	Geno Petralli	.05	.02	.01		
☐ 154	Jim Deshaies	.05	.02	.01		
☐ 155	Barry Larkin	.20	.09	.03		
☐ 156	Alfredo Griffin	.05	.02	.01		
☐ 157	Tom Henke	.10	.05	.01		
☐ 158	Mike Jeffcoat	.05	.02	.01		
☐ 159	Bob Welch	.05	.02	.01		
☐ 160	Julio Franco	.10	.05	.01		
☐ 161	Henry Cotto	.05	.02	.01		
☐ 162	Terry Steinbach	.10	.05	.01		
☐ 163	Damon Berryhill	.05	.02	.01		
☐ 164	Tim Crews	.10	.05	.01		
☐ 165	Tom Browning	.05	.02	.01		
☐ 166	Fred Manrique	.05	.02	.01		
☐ 167	Harold Reynolds	.05	.02	.01		
☐ 168A	Ron Hassey ERR (27 on back)	.05	.02	.01		
☐ 168B	Ron Hassey COR (24 on back)	.50	.23	.06		
☐ 169	Shawon Dunston	.05	.02	.01		
☐ 170	Bobby Bonilla	.15	.07	.02		
☐ 171	Tommy Herr	.05	.02	.01		
☐ 172	Mike Heath	.05	.02	.01		
☐ 173	Rich Gedman	.05	.02	.01		
☐ 174	Bill Ripken	.05	.02	.01		
☐ 175	Pete O'Brien	.05	.02	.01		
☐ 176A	Lloyd McClendon ERR (Uniform number on back listed as 1)	.50	.23	.06		
☐ 176B	Lloyd McClendon COR (Uniform number on back listed as 10)	.05	.02	.01		
☐ 177	Brian Holton	.05	.02	.01		
☐ 178	Jeff Blauser	.10	.05	.01		
☐ 179	Jim Eisenreich	.05	.02	.01		
☐ 180	Bert Blyleven	.15	.07	.02		
☐ 181	Rob Murphy	.05	.02	.01		
☐ 182	Bill Doran	.05	.02	.01		
☐ 183	Curt Ford	.05	.02	.01		
☐ 184	Mike Henneman	.05	.02	.01		
☐ 185	Eric Davis	.10	.05	.01		
☐ 186	Lance McCullers	.05	.02	.01		
☐ 187	Steve Davis	.05	.02	.01		
☐ 188	Bill Wegman	.05	.02	.01		
☐ 189	Brian Harper	.05	.02	.01		
☐ 190	Mike Moore	.05	.02	.01		
☐ 191	Dale Mohorcic	.05	.02	.01		
☐ 192	Tim Wallach	.05	.02	.01		
☐ 193	Keith Hernandez	.10	.05	.01		
☐ 194	Dave Righetti	.05	.02	.01		
☐ 195A	Bret Saberhagen ERR (Joke)	.10	.05	.01		
☐ 195B	Bret Saberhagen COR (Joker)	.10	.05	.01		
☐ 196	Paul Kilgus	.05	.02	.01		
☐ 197	Bud Black	.05	.02	.01		
☐ 198	Juan Samuel	.05	.02	.01		
☐ 199	Kevin Seitzer	.05	.02	.01		
☐ 200	Darryl Strawberry	.10	.05	.01		
☐ 201	Dave Stieb	.10	.05	.01		
☐ 202	Charlie Hough	.10	.05	.01		
☐ 203	Jack Morris	.15	.07	.02		
☐ 204	Rance Mulliniks	.05	.02	.01		
☐ 205	Alvin Davis	.05	.02	.01		
☐ 206	Jack Howell	.05	.02	.01		
☐ 207	Ken Patterson	.05	.02	.01		
☐ 208	Terry Pendleton	.15	.07	.02		
☐ 209	Craig Lefferts	.05	.02	.01		
☐ 210	Kevin Brown UER (First mention of '89 Rangers should be '88)	.10	.05	.01		
☐ 211	Dan Petry	.05	.02	.01		
☐ 212	Dave Leiper	.05	.02	.01		
☐ 213	Daryl Boston	.05	.02	.01		
☐ 214	Kevin Hickey	.05	.02	.01		
☐ 215	Mike Krukow	.05	.02	.01		
☐ 216	Terry Francona	.05	.02	.01		
☐ 217	Kirk McCaskill	.05	.02	.01		
☐ 218	Scott Bailes	.05	.02	.01		
☐ 219	Bob Forsch	.05	.02	.01		
☐ 220A	Mike Aldrete ERR (25 on back)	.05	.02	.01		
☐ 220B	Mike Aldrete COR (24 on back)	.05	.02	.01		
☐ 221	Steve Buechele	.05	.02	.01		
☐ 222	Jesse Barfield	.05	.02	.01		
☐ 223	Juan Berenguer	.05	.02	.01		
☐ 224	Andy McGaffigan	.05	.02	.01		
☐ 225	Pete Smith	.05	.02	.01		
☐ 226	Mike Witt	.05	.02	.01		
☐ 227	Jay Howell	.05	.02	.01		
☐ 228	Scott Bradley	.05	.02	.01		
☐ 229	Jerome Walton	.05	.02	.01		
☐ 230	Greg Swindell	.10	.05	.01		
☐ 231	Atlee Hammaker	.05	.02	.01		
☐ 232A	Mike Devereaux ERR (RF on front)	.10	.05	.01		
☐ 232B	Mike Devereaux COR (CF on front)	.50	.23	.06		
☐ 233	Ken Hill	.15	.07	.02		
☐ 234	Craig Worthington	.05	.02	.01		
☐ 235	Scott Terry	.05	.02	.01		
☐ 236	Brett Butler	.15	.07	.02		
☐ 237	Doyle Alexander	.05	.02	.01		
☐ 238	Dave Anderson	.05	.02	.01		
☐ 239	Bob Milacki	.05	.02	.01		
☐ 240	Dwight Smith	.05	.02	.01		
☐ 241	Otis Nixon	.05	.02	.01		
☐ 242	Pat Tabler	.05	.02	.01		
☐ 243	Derek Lilliquist	.05	.02	.01		
☐ 244	Danny Tartabull	.10	.05	.01		
☐ 245	Wade Boggs	.15	.07	.02		
☐ 246	Scott Garrelts	.05	.02	.01		

(Should say Relief
Pitcher on front)

☐ 247	Spike Owen	.05	.02	.01
☐ 248	Norm Charlton	.10	.05	.01
☐ 249	Gerald Perry	.05	.02	.01
☐ 250	Nolan Ryan	.75	.35	.09
☐ 251	Kevin Gross	.05	.02	.01
☐ 252	Randy Milligan	.05	.02	.01
☐ 253	Mike LaCoss	.05	.02	.01
☐ 254	Dave Bergman	.05	.02	.01
☐ 255	Tony Gwynn	.30	.14	.04
☐ 256	Felix Fermin	.05	.02	.01
☐ 257	Greg W. Harris	.05	.02	.01
☐ 258	Junior Felix	.05	.02	.01
☐ 259	Mark Davis	.05	.02	.01
☐ 260	Vince Coleman	.10	.05	.01
☐ 261	Paul Gibson	.05	.02	.01
☐ 262	Mitch Williams	.10	.05	.01
☐ 263	Jeff Russell	.05	.02	.01
☐ 264	Omar Vizquel	.05	.02	.01
☐ 265	Andre Dawson	.15	.07	.02
☐ 266	Storm Davis	.05	.02	.01
☐ 267	Guillermo Hernandez	.05	.02	.01
☐ 268	Mike Felder	.05	.02	.01
☐ 269	Tom Candiotti	.05	.02	.01
☐ 270	Bruce Hurst	.05	.02	.01
☐ 271	Fred McGriff	.20	.09	.03
☐ 272	Glenn Davis	.05	.02	.01
☐ 273	John Franco	.15	.07	.02
☐ 274	Rich Yett	.05	.02	.01
☐ 275	Craig Biggio	.15	.07	.02
☐ 276	Gene Larkin	.05	.02	.01
☐ 277	Rob Dibble	.10	.05	.01
☐ 278	Randy Bush	.05	.02	.01
☐ 279	Kevin Bass	.05	.02	.01
☐ 280A	Bo Jackson ERR	.15	.07	.02
	(Watham)			
☐ 280B	Bo Jackson COR	.15	.07	.02
	(Wathan)			
☐ 281	Wally Backman	.05	.02	.01
☐ 282	Larry Andersen	.05	.02	.01
☐ 283	Chris Bosio	.05	.02	.01
☐ 284	Juan Agosto	.05	.02	.01
☐ 285	Ozzie Smith	.20	.09	.03
☐ 286	George Bell	.05	.02	.01
☐ 287	Rex Hudler	.05	.02	.01
☐ 288	Pat Borders	.05	.02	.01
☐ 289	Danny Jackson	.05	.02	.01
☐ 290	Carlton Fisk	.15	.07	.02
☐ 291	Tracy Jones	.05	.02	.01
☐ 292	Allan Anderson	.05	.02	.01
☐ 293	Johnny Ray	.05	.02	.01
☐ 294	Lee Guetterman	.05	.02	.01
☐ 295	Paul O'Neill	.15	.07	.02
☐ 296	Carney Lansford	.10	.05	.01
☐ 297	Tom Brookens	.05	.02	.01
☐ 298	Claudell Washington	.05	.02	.01
☐ 299	Hubie Brooks	.05	.02	.01
☐ 300	Will Clark	.20	.09	.03
☐ 301	Kenny Rogers	.05	.02	.01
☐ 302	Darrell Evans	.10	.05	.01
☐ 303	Greg Briley	.05	.02	.01
☐ 304	Donn Pall	.05	.02	.01
☐ 305	Teddy Higuera	.05	.02	.01
☐ 306	Dan Pasqua	.05	.02	.01
☐ 307	Dave Winfield	.15	.07	.02
☐ 308	Dennis Powell	.05	.02	.01
☐ 309	Jose DeLeon	.05	.02	.01
☐ 310	Roger Clemens UER	.15	.07	.02
	(Dominate, should			
	say dominant)			
☐ 311	Melido Perez	.05	.02	.01
☐ 312	Devon White	.10	.05	.01
☐ 313	Dwight Gooden	.05	.02	.01
☐ 314	Carlos Martinez	.05	.02	.01
☐ 315	Dennis Eckersley	.15	.07	.02
☐ 316	Clay Parker UER	.05	.02	.01
	(Height 6'11")			
☐ 317	Rick Honeycutt	.05	.02	.01
☐ 318	Tim Laudner	.05	.02	.01
☐ 319	Joe Carter	.15	.07	.02
☐ 320	Robin Yount	.20	.09	.03
☐ 321	Felix Jose	.05	.02	.01
☐ 322	Mickey Tettleton	.10	.05	.01
☐ 323	Mike Gallego	.05	.02	.01
☐ 324	Edgar Martinez	.15	.07	.02
☐ 325	Dave Henderson	.05	.02	.01
☐ 326	Chili Davis	.15	.07	.02
☐ 327	Steve Balboni	.05	.02	.01
☐ 328	Jody Davis	.05	.02	.01
☐ 329	Shawn Hillegas	.05	.02	.01
☐ 330	Jim Abbott	.15	.07	.02
☐ 331	John Dopson	.05	.02	.01
☐ 332	Mark Williamson	.05	.02	.01
☐ 333	Jeff D. Robinson	.05	.02	.01
☐ 334	John Smiley	.05	.02	.01
☐ 335	Bobby Thigpen	.05	.02	.01
☐ 336	Garry Templeton	.05	.02	.01
☐ 337	Marvell Wynne	.05	.02	.01
☐ 338A	Ken Griffey Sr. ERR	.05	.02	.01
	(Uniform number on			
	back listed as 25)			
☐ 338B	Ken Griffey Sr. COR	.50	.23	.06
	(Uniform number on			
	back listed as 30)			
☐ 339	Steve Finley	.10	.05	.01
☐ 340	Ellis Burks	.10	.05	.01
☐ 341	Frank Williams	.05	.02	.01
☐ 342	Mike Morgan	.05	.02	.01
☐ 343	Kevin Mitchell	.10	.05	.01
☐ 344	Joel Youngblood	.05	.02	.01
☐ 345	Mike Greenwell	.15	.07	.02
☐ 346	Glenn Wilson	.05	.02	.01
☐ 347	John Costello	.05	.02	.01
☐ 348	Wes Gardner	.05	.02	.01
☐ 349	Jeff Ballard	.05	.02	.01
☐ 350	Mark Thurmond UER	.05	.02	.01
	(ERA is 192,			
	should be 1.92)			
☐ 351	Randy Myers	.15	.07	.02
☐ 352	Shawn Abner	.05	.02	.01
☐ 353	Jesse Orosco	.05	.02	.01
☐ 354	Greg Walker	.05	.02	.01
☐ 355	Pete Harnisch	.10	.05	.01
☐ 356	Steve Farr	.05	.02	.01
☐ 357	Dave LaPoint	.05	.02	.01
☐ 358	Willie Fraser	.05	.02	.01
☐ 359	Mickey Hatcher	.05	.02	.01
☐ 360	Rickey Henderson	.15	.07	.02
☐ 361	Mike Fitzgerald	.05	.02	.01
☐ 362	Bill Schroeder	.05	.02	.01
☐ 363	Mark Carreon	.05	.02	.01
☐ 364	Ron Jones	.05	.02	.01
☐ 365	Jeff Montgomery	.10	.05	.01
☐ 366	Bill Krueger	.05	.02	.01
☐ 367	John Cangelosi	.05	.02	.01
☐ 368	Jose Gonzalez	.05	.02	.01
☐ 369	Greg Hibbard	.05	.02	.01
☐ 370	John Smoltz	.15	.07	.02
☐ 371	Jeff Brantley	.05	.02	.01
☐ 372	Frank White	.10	.05	.01
☐ 373	Ed Whitson	.05	.02	.01

☐ 374 Willie McGee	.10	.05	.01
☐ 375 Jose Canseco	.20	.09	.03
☐ 376 Randy Ready	.05	.02	.01
☐ 377 Don Aase	.05	.02	.01
☐ 378 Tony Armas	.05	.02	.01
☐ 379 Steve Bedrosian	.05	.02	.01
☐ 380 Chuck Finley	.10	.05	.01
☐ 381 Kent Hrbek	.10	.05	.01
☐ 382 Jim Gantner	.05	.02	.01
☐ 383 Mel Hall	.05	.02	.01
☐ 384 Mike Marshall	.05	.02	.01
☐ 385 Mark McGwire	.15	.07	.02
☐ 386 Wayne Tolleson	.05	.02	.01
☐ 387 Brian Holman	.05	.02	.01
☐ 388 John Wetteland	.10	.05	.01
☐ 389 Darren Daulton	.15	.07	.02
☐ 390 Rob Deer	.05	.02	.01
☐ 391 John Moses	.05	.02	.01
☐ 392 Todd Worrell	.05	.02	.01
☐ 393 Chuck Cary	.05	.02	.01
☐ 394 Stan Javier	.05	.02	.01
☐ 395 Willie Randolph	.10	.05	.01
☐ 396 Bill Buckner	.10	.05	.01
☐ 397 Robby Thompson	.10	.05	.01
☐ 398 Mike Scioscia	.05	.02	.01
☐ 399 Lonnie Smith	.05	.02	.01
☐ 400 Kirby Puckett	.30	.14	.04
☐ 401 Mark Langston	.15	.07	.02
☐ 402 Danny Darwin	.05	.02	.01
☐ 403 Greg Maddux	.60	.25	.07
☐ 404 Lloyd Moseby	.05	.02	.01
☐ 405 Rafael Palmeiro	.15	.07	.02
☐ 406 Chad Kreuter	.05	.02	.01
☐ 407 Jimmy Key	.10	.05	.01
☐ 408 Tim Birtsas	.05	.02	.01
☐ 409 Tim Raines	.15	.07	.02
☐ 410 Dave Stewart	.15	.07	.02
☐ 411 Eric Yelding	.05	.02	.01
☐ 412 Kent Anderson	.05	.02	.01
☐ 413 Les Lancaster	.05	.02	.01
☐ 414 Rick Dempsey	.05	.02	.01
☐ 415 Randy Johnson	.40	.18	.05
☐ 416 Gary Carter	.15	.07	.02
☐ 417 Rolando Roomes	.05	.02	.01
☐ 418 Dan Schatzeder	.05	.02	.01
☐ 419 Bryn Smith	.05	.02	.01
☐ 420 Ruben Sierra	.15	.07	.02
☐ 421 Steve Jeltz	.05	.02	.01
☐ 422 Ken Oberkfell	.05	.02	.01
☐ 423 Sid Bream	.05	.02	.01
☐ 424 Jim Clancy	.05	.02	.01
☐ 425 Kelly Gruber	.05	.02	.01
☐ 426 Rick Leach	.05	.02	.01
☐ 427 Len Dykstra	.15	.07	.02
☐ 428 Jeff Pico	.05	.02	.01
☐ 429 John Cerutti	.05	.02	.01
☐ 430 David Cone	.15	.07	.02
☐ 431 Jeff Kunkel	.05	.02	.01
☐ 432 Luis Aquino	.05	.02	.01
☐ 433 Ernie Whitt	.05	.02	.01
☐ 434 Bo Diaz	.05	.02	.01
☐ 435 Steve Lake	.05	.02	.01
☐ 436 Pat Perry	.05	.02	.01
☐ 437 Mike Davis	.05	.02	.01
☐ 438 Cecilio Guante	.05	.02	.01
☐ 439 Duane Ward	.05	.02	.01
☐ 440 Andy Van Slyke	.10	.05	.01
☐ 441 Gene Nelson	.05	.02	.01
☐ 442 Luis Polonia	.10	.05	.01
☐ 443 Kevin Elster	.05	.02	.01
☐ 444 Keith Moreland	.05	.02	.01

☐ 445 Roger McDowell	.05	.02	.01
☐ 446 Ron Darling	.05	.02	.01
☐ 447 Ernest Riles	.05	.02	.01
☐ 448 Mookie Wilson	.05	.02	.01
☐ 449A Billy Spiers ERR	.05	.02	.01
(No birth year)			
☐ 449B Billy Spiers COR	.05	.02	.01
(Born in 1966)			
☐ 450 Rick Sutcliffe	.10	.05	.01
☐ 451 Nelson Santovenia	.05	.02	.01
☐ 452 Andy Allanson	.05	.02	.01
☐ 453 Bob Melvin	.05	.02	.01
☐ 454 Benito Santiago	.10	.05	.01
☐ 455 Jose Uribe	.05	.02	.01
☐ 456 Bill Landrum	.05	.02	.01
☐ 457 Bobby Witt	.05	.02	.01
☐ 458 Kevin Romine	.05	.02	.01
☐ 459 Lee Mazzilli	.05	.02	.01
☐ 460 Paul Molitor	.15	.07	.02
☐ 461 Ramon Martinez	.15	.07	.02
☐ 462 Frank DiPino	.05	.02	.01
☐ 463 Walt Terrell	.05	.02	.01
☐ 464 Bob Geren	.05	.02	.01
☐ 465 Rick Reuschel	.05	.02	.01
☐ 466 Mark Grant	.05	.02	.01
☐ 467 John Kruk	.15	.07	.02
☐ 468 Gregg Jefferies	.10	.05	.01
☐ 469 R.J. Reynolds	.05	.02	.01
☐ 470 Harold Baines	.15	.07	.02
☐ 471 Dennis Lamp	.05	.02	.01
☐ 472 Tom Gordon	.10	.05	.01
☐ 473 Terry Puhl	.05	.02	.01
☐ 474 Curt Wilkerson	.05	.02	.01
☐ 475 Dan Quisenberry	.05	.02	.01
☐ 476 Oddibe McDowell	.05	.02	.01
☐ 477 Zane Smith UER	.05	.02	.01
(Career ERA .393)			
☐ 478 Franklin Stubbs	.05	.02	.01
☐ 479 Wallace Johnson	.05	.02	.01
☐ 480 Jay Tibbs	.05	.02	.01
☐ 481 Tom Glavine	.25	.11	.03
☐ 482 Manny Lee	.05	.02	.01
☐ 483 Joe Hesketh UER	.05	.02	.01
(Says Rookiess on back,			
should say Rookies)			
☐ 484 Mike Bielecki	.05	.02	.01
☐ 485 Greg Brock	.05	.02	.01
☐ 486 Pascual Perez	.05	.02	.01
☐ 487 Kirk Gibson	.15	.07	.02
☐ 488 Scott Sanderson	.05	.02	.01
☐ 489 Domingo Ramos	.05	.02	.01
☐ 490 Kal Daniels	.05	.02	.01
☐ 491A David Wells ERR	.50	.23	.06
(Reverse negative			
photo on card back)			
☐ 491B David Wells COR	.05	.02	.01
☐ 492 Jerry Reed	.05	.02	.01
☐ 493 Eric Show	.05	.02	.01
☐ 494 Mike Pagliarulo	.05	.02	.01
☐ 495 Ron Robinson	.05	.02	.01
☐ 496 Brad Komminsk	.05	.02	.01
☐ 497 Greg Litton	.05	.02	.01
☐ 498 Chris James	.05	.02	.01
☐ 499 Luis Quinones	.05	.02	.01
☐ 500 Frank Viola	.10	.05	.01
☐ 501 Tim Teufel UER	.05	.02	.01
(Twins '85, the s is			
lower case, should			
be upper case)			
☐ 502 Terry Leach	.05	.02	.01
☐ 503 Matt Williams UER	.30	.14	.04

(Wearing 10 on front, listed as 9 on back)
- [ ] 504 Tim Leary .05 .02 .01
- [ ] 505 Doug Drabek .10 .05 .01
- [ ] 506 Mariano Duncan .05 .02 .01
- [ ] 507 Charlie Hayes .10 .05 .01
- [ ] 508 Joey Belle 1.00 .45 .12
- [ ] 509 Pat Sheridan .05 .02 .01
- [ ] 510 Mackey Sasser .05 .02 .01
- [ ] 511 Jose Rijo .10 .05 .01
- [ ] 512 Mike Smithson .05 .02 .01
- [ ] 513 Gary Ward .05 .02 .01
- [ ] 514 Dion James .05 .02 .01
- [ ] 515 Jim Gott .05 .02 .01
- [ ] 516 Drew Hall .05 .02 .01
- [ ] 517 Doug Bair .05 .02 .01
- [ ] 518 Scott Scudder .05 .02 .01
- [ ] 519 Rick Aguilera .10 .05 .01
- [ ] 520 Rafael Belliard .05 .02 .01
- [ ] 521 Jay Buhner .15 .07 .02
- [ ] 522 Jeff Reardon .15 .07 .02
- [ ] 523 Steve Rosenberg .05 .02 .01
- [ ] 524 Randy Velarde .05 .02 .01
- [ ] 525 Jeff Musselman .05 .02 .01
- [ ] 526 Bill Long .05 .02 .01
- [ ] 527 Gary Wayne .05 .02 .01
- [ ] 528 Dave Johnson (P) .05 .02 .01
- [ ] 529 Ron Kittle .05 .02 .01
- [ ] 530 Erik Hanson UER .10 .05 .01
(5th line on back says seson, should say season)
- [ ] 531 Steve Wilson .05 .02 .01
- [ ] 532 Joey Meyer .05 .02 .01
- [ ] 533 Curt Young .05 .02 .01
- [ ] 534 Kelly Downs .05 .02 .01
- [ ] 535 Joe Girardi .05 .02 .01
- [ ] 536 Lance Blankenship .05 .02 .01
- [ ] 537 Greg Mathews .05 .02 .01
- [ ] 538 Donell Nixon .05 .02 .01
- [ ] 539 Mark Knudson .05 .02 .01
- [ ] 540 Jeff Wetherby .05 .02 .01
- [ ] 541 Darrin Jackson .05 .02 .01
- [ ] 542 Terry Mulholland .10 .05 .01
- [ ] 543 Eric Hetzel .05 .02 .01
- [ ] 544 Rick Reed .05 .02 .01
- [ ] 545 Dennis Cook .05 .02 .01
- [ ] 546 Mike Jackson .05 .02 .01
- [ ] 547 Brian Fisher .05 .02 .01
- [ ] 548 Gene Harris .05 .02 .01
- [ ] 549 Jeff King .10 .05 .01
- [ ] 550 Dave Dravecky .10 .05 .01
- [ ] 551 Randy Kutcher .05 .02 .01
- [ ] 552 Mark Portugal .05 .02 .01
- [ ] 553 Jim Corsi .05 .02 .01
- [ ] 554 Todd Stottlemyre .10 .05 .01
- [ ] 555 Scott Bankhead .05 .02 .01
- [ ] 556 Ken Dayley .05 .02 .01
- [ ] 557 Rick Wrona .05 .02 .01
- [ ] 558 Sammy Sosa .75 .35 .09
- [ ] 559 Keith Miller .05 .02 .01
- [ ] 560 Ken Griffey Jr. 2.00 .90 .25
- [ ] 561A Ryne Sandberg HL ERR 8.00 3.60 1.00
(Position on front listed as 3B)
- [ ] 561B Ryne Sandberg HL COR .15 .07 .02
- [ ] 562 Billy Hatcher .05 .02 .01
- [ ] 563 Jay Bell .10 .05 .01
- [ ] 564 Jack Daugherty .05 .02 .01
- [ ] 565 Rich Monteleone .05 .02 .01
- [ ] 566 Bo Jackson AS-MVP .15 .07 .02

- [ ] 567 Tony Fossas .05 .02 .01
- [ ] 568 Roy Smith .05 .02 .01
- [ ] 569 Jaime Navarro .05 .02 .01
- [ ] 570 Lance Johnson .10 .05 .01
- [ ] 571 Mike Dyer .05 .02 .01
- [ ] 572 Kevin Ritz .05 .02 .01
- [ ] 573 Dave West .05 .02 .01
- [ ] 574 Gary Mielke .05 .02 .01
- [ ] 575 Scott Lusader .05 .02 .01
- [ ] 576 Joe Oliver .05 .02 .01
- [ ] 577 Sandy Alomar Jr. .10 .05 .01
- [ ] 578 Andy Benes UER .10 .05 .01
(Extra comma between day and year)
- [ ] 579 Tim Jones .05 .02 .01
- [ ] 580 Randy McCament .05 .02 .01
- [ ] 581 Curt Schilling .10 .05 .01
- [ ] 582 John Orton .05 .02 .01
- [ ] 583A Milt Cuyler ERR .15 .07 .02
(998 games)
- [ ] 583B Milt Cuyler COR .05 .02 .01
(98 games; the extra 9 was ghosted out and may still be visible)
- [ ] 584 Eric Anthony .05 .02 .01
- [ ] 585 Greg Vaughn .10 .05 .01
- [ ] 586 Deion Sanders .50 .23 .06
- [ ] 587 Jose DeJesus .05 .02 .01
- [ ] 588 Chip Hale .05 .02 .01
- [ ] 589 John Olerud .20 .09 .03
- [ ] 590 Steve Olin .10 .05 .01
- [ ] 591 Marquis Grissom .60 .25 .07
- [ ] 592 Moises Alou .25 .11 .03
- [ ] 593 Mark Lemke .10 .05 .01
- [ ] 594 Dean Palmer .20 .09 .03
- [ ] 595 Robin Ventura .25 .11 .03
- [ ] 596 Tino Martinez .20 .09 .03
- [ ] 597 Mike Huff .05 .02 .01
- [ ] 598 Scott Hemond .05 .02 .01
- [ ] 599 Wally Whitehurst .05 .02 .01
- [ ] 600 Todd Zeile .10 .05 .01
- [ ] 601 Glenallen Hill .05 .02 .01
- [ ] 602 Hal Morris .10 .05 .01
- [ ] 603 Juan Bell .05 .02 .01
- [ ] 604 Bobby Rose .05 .02 .01
- [ ] 605 Matt Merullo .05 .02 .01
- [ ] 606 Kevin Maas .05 .02 .01
- [ ] 607 Randy Nosek .05 .02 .01
- [ ] 608A Billy Bates .05 .02 .01
(Text mentions 12 triples in tenth line)
- [ ] 608B Billy Bates .05 .02 .01
(Text has no mention of triples)
- [ ] 609 Mike Stanton .05 .02 .01
- [ ] 610 Mauro Gozzo .05 .02 .01
- [ ] 611 Charles Nagy .25 .11 .03
- [ ] 612 Scott Coolbaugh .05 .02 .01
- [ ] 613 Jose Vizcaino .05 .02 .01
- [ ] 614 Greg Smith .05 .02 .01
- [ ] 615 Jeff Huson .05 .02 .01
- [ ] 616 Mickey Weston .05 .02 .01
- [ ] 617 John Pawlowski .05 .02 .01
- [ ] 618A Joe Skalski ERR .05 .02 .01
(27 on back)
- [ ] 618B Joe Skalski COR .50 .23 .06
(67 on back)
- [ ] 619 Bernie Williams .30 .14 .04
- [ ] 620 Shawn Holman .05 .02 .01
- [ ] 621 Gary Eave .05 .02 .01
- [ ] 622 Darrin Fletcher UER .10 .05 .01

(Elmherst, should
be Elmhurst)
☐ 623	Pat Combs	.05	.02	.01
☐ 624	Mike Blowers	.20	.09	.03
☐ 625	Kevin Appier	.25	.11	.03
☐ 626	Pat Austin	.05	.02	.01
☐ 627	Kelly Mann	.05	.02	.01
☐ 628	Matt Kinzer	.10	.05	.01
☐ 629	Chris Hammond	.10	.05	.01
☐ 630	Dean Wilkins	.05	.02	.01
☐ 631	Larry Walker UER	.75	.35	.09

(Uniform number 55 on
front and 33 on back;
Home is Maple Ridge,
not Maple River)

☐ 632	Blaine Beatty	.05	.02	.01
☐ 633A	Tommy Barrett ERR	.05	.02	.01

(29 on back)

☐ 633B	Tommy Barrett COR	.50	.23	.06

(14 on back)

☐ 634	Stan Belinda	.05	.02	.01
☐ 635	Mike (Tex) Smith	.05	.02	.01
☐ 636	Hensley Meulens	.05	.02	.01
☐ 637	Juan Gonzalez UER	1.25	.55	.16

(Sarasots on back,
should be Sarasota)

☐ 638	Lenny Webster	.05	.02	.01
☐ 639	Mark Gardner	.05	.02	.01
☐ 640	Tommy Greene	.15	.07	.02
☐ 641	Mike Hartley	.05	.02	.01
☐ 642	Phil Stephenson	.05	.02	.01
☐ 643	Kevin Mmahat	.05	.02	.01
☐ 644	Ed Whited	.05	.02	.01
☐ 645	Delino DeShields	.15	.07	.02
☐ 646	Kevin Blankenship	.05	.02	.01
☐ 647	Paul Sorrento	.20	.09	.03
☐ 648	Mike Roesler	.05	.02	.01
☐ 649	Jason Grimsley	.05	.02	.01
☐ 650	Dave Justice	.75	.35	.09
☐ 651	Scott Cooper	.15	.07	.02
☐ 652	Dave Eiland	.05	.02	.01
☐ 653	Mike Munoz	.05	.02	.01
☐ 654	Jeff Fischer	.05	.02	.01
☐ 655	Terry Jorgensen	.05	.02	.01
☐ 656	George Canale	.05	.02	.01
☐ 657	Brian DuBois UER	.05	.02	.01

(Misspelled Dubois
on card)

☐ 658	Carlos Quintana	.05	.02	.01
☐ 659	Luis de los Santos	.05	.02	.01
☐ 660	Jerald Clark	.05	.02	.01
☐ 661	Donald Harris DC	.05	.02	.01
☐ 662	Paul Coleman DC	.05	.02	.01
☐ 663	Frank Thomas DC	4.00	1.80	.50
☐ 664	Brent Mayne DC	.05	.02	.01
☐ 665	Eddie Zosky DC	.05	.02	.01
☐ 666	Steve Hosey DC	.05	.02	.01
☐ 667	Scott Bryant DC	.05	.02	.01
☐ 668	Tom Goodwin DC	.15	.07	.02
☐ 669	Cal Eldred DC	.10	.05	.01
☐ 670	Earl Cunningham DC	.05	.02	.01
☐ 671	Alan Zinter DC	.05	.02	.01
☐ 672	Chuck Knoblauch DC	.50	.23	.06
☐ 673	Kyle Abbott DC	.05	.02	.01
☐ 674	Roger Salkeld DC	.05	.02	.01
☐ 675	Maurice Vaughn DC	1.25	.55	.16
☐ 676	Keith(Kiki) Jones DC	.05	.02	.01
☐ 677	Tyler Houston DC	.05	.02	.01
☐ 678	Jeff Jackson DC	.05	.02	.01
☐ 679	Greg Gohr DC	.05	.02	.01
☐ 680	Ben McDonald DC	.15	.07	.02

☐ 681	Greg Blosser DC	.05	.02	.01
☐ 682	Willie Green DC UER	.05	.02	.01

(Name misspelled on
card, should be Greene)

☐ 683	Wade Boggs DT UER	.15	.07	.02

(Text says 215 hits in
'89, should be 205)

☐ 684	Will Clark DT	.15	.07	.02
☐ 685	Tony Gwynn DT UER	.15	.07	.02

(Text reads battling
instead of batting)

☐ 686	Rickey Henderson DT	.15	.07	.02
☐ 687	Bo Jackson DT	.15	.07	.02
☐ 688	Mark Langston DT	.10	.05	.01
☐ 689	Barry Larkin DT	.15	.07	.02
☐ 690	Kirby Puckett DT	.20	.09	.03
☐ 691	Ryne Sandberg DT	.20	.09	.03
☐ 692	Mike Scott DT	.05	.02	.01
☐ 693A	Terry Steinbach DT	.05	.02	.01

ERR (cathers)

☐ 693B	Terry Steinbach DT	.05	.02	.01

COR (catchers)

☐ 694	Bobby Thigpen DT	.05	.02	.01
☐ 695	Mitch Williams DT	.05	.02	.01
☐ 696	Nolan Ryan HL	.40	.18	.05
☐ 697	Bo Jackson FB/BB	1.00	.45	.12
☐ 698	Rickey Henderson	.15	.07	.02

ALCS-MVP

☐ 699	Will Clark	.20	.09	.03

NLCS-MVP

☐ 700	WS Games 1/2	.10	.05	.01

(Dave Stewart and
Mike Moore)

☐ 701	Lights Out:	.15	.07	.02

Candlestick
5:04pm (10/17/89)

☐ 702	WS Game 3	.15	.07	.02

Bashers Blast Giants
(Carney Lansford,
Ricky Henderson,
Jose Canseco,
Dave Henderson)

☐ 703	WS Game 4/Wrap-up	.05	.02	.01

A's Sweep Battle of
of the Bay
(A's Celebrate)

☐ 704	Wade Boggs HL	.15	.07	.02

Wade Raps 200

1990 Score
Rookie/Traded

*The 1990 Score Rookie and Traded set
marks the third consecutive year Score has*

issued an end of the year set to mark trades and give rookies early cards. The set consists of 110 standard-size cards. The first 66 cards are traded players while the last 44 cards are rookie cards. Included in the set are multi-sport athletes Eric Lindros (hockey) and D.J. Dozier (football). Rookie Cards in the set include Carlos Baerga, Derek Bell, Dave Hollins, and Ray Lankford.

	MINT	NRMT	EXC
COMPLETE FACT.SET (110)	10.00	4.50	1.25
COMMON CARD (1T-110T)	.05	.02	.01

☐ 1T	Dave Winfield	.15	.07	.02
☐ 2T	Kevin Bass	.05	.02	.01
☐ 3T	Nick Esasky	.05	.02	.01
☐ 4T	Mitch Webster	.05	.02	.01
☐ 5T	Pascual Perez	.05	.02	.01
☐ 6T	Gary Pettis	.05	.02	.01
☐ 7T	Tony Pena	.05	.02	.01
☐ 8T	Candy Maldonado	.05	.02	.01
☐ 9T	Cecil Fielder	.15	.07	.02
☐ 10T	Carmelo Martinez	.05	.02	.01
☐ 11T	Mark Langston	.10	.05	.01
☐ 12T	Dave Parker	.15	.07	.02
☐ 13T	Don Slaught	.05	.02	.01
☐ 14T	Tony Phillips	.15	.07	.02
☐ 15T	John Franco	.15	.07	.02
☐ 16T	Randy Myers	.15	.07	.02
☐ 17T	Jeff Reardon	.15	.07	.02
☐ 18T	Sandy Alomar Jr.	.10	.05	.01
☐ 19T	Joe Carter	.15	.07	.02
☐ 20T	Fred Lynn	.10	.05	.01
☐ 21T	Storm Davis	.05	.02	.01
☐ 22T	Craig Lefferts	.05	.02	.01
☐ 23T	Pete O'Brien	.05	.02	.01
☐ 24T	Dennis Boyd	.05	.02	.01
☐ 25T	Lloyd Moseby	.05	.02	.01
☐ 26T	Mark Davis	.05	.02	.01
☐ 27T	Tim Leary	.05	.02	.01
☐ 28T	Gerald Perry	.05	.02	.01
☐ 29T	Don Aase	.05	.02	.01
☐ 30T	Ernie Whitt	.05	.02	.01
☐ 31T	Dale Murphy	.15	.07	.02
☐ 32T	Alejandro Pena	.05	.02	.01
☐ 33T	Juan Samuel	.05	.02	.01
☐ 34T	Hubie Brooks	.05	.02	.01
☐ 35T	Gary Carter	.15	.07	.02
☐ 36T	Jim Presley	.05	.02	.01
☐ 37T	Wally Backman	.05	.02	.01
☐ 38T	Matt Nokes	.05	.02	.01
☐ 39T	Dan Petry	.05	.02	.01
☐ 40T	Franklin Stubbs	.05	.02	.01
☐ 41T	Jeff Huson	.05	.02	.01
☐ 42T	Billy Hatcher	.05	.02	.01
☐ 43T	Terry Leach	.05	.02	.01
☐ 44T	Phil Bradley	.05	.02	.01
☐ 45T	Claudell Washington	.05	.02	.01
☐ 46T	Luis Polonia	.10	.05	.01
☐ 47T	Daryl Boston	.05	.02	.01
☐ 48T	Lee Smith	.15	.07	.02
☐ 49T	Tom Brunansky	.05	.02	.01
☐ 50T	Mike Witt	.05	.02	.01
☐ 51T	Willie Randolph	.10	.05	.01
☐ 52T	Stan Javier	.05	.02	.01
☐ 53T	Brad Komminsk	.05	.02	.01
☐ 54T	John Candelaria	.05	.02	.01
☐ 55T	Bryn Smith	.05	.02	.01
☐ 56T	Glenn Braggs	.05	.02	.01
☐ 57T	Keith Hernandez	.10	.05	.01
☐ 58T	Ken Oberkfell	.05	.02	.01
☐ 59T	Steve Jeltz	.05	.02	.01
☐ 60T	Chris James	.05	.02	.01
☐ 61T	Scott Sanderson	.05	.02	.01
☐ 62T	Bill Long	.05	.02	.01
☐ 63T	Rick Cerone	.05	.02	.01
☐ 64T	Scott Bailes	.05	.02	.01
☐ 65T	Larry Sheets	.05	.02	.01
☐ 66T	Junior Ortiz	.05	.02	.01
☐ 67T	Francisco Cabrera	.05	.02	.01
☐ 68T	Gary DiSarcina	.15	.07	.02
☐ 69T	Greg Olson	.05	.02	.01
☐ 70T	Beau Allred	.05	.02	.01
☐ 71T	Oscar Azocar	.05	.02	.01
☐ 72T	Kent Mercker	.20	.09	.03
☐ 73T	John Burkett	.05	.02	.01
☐ 74T	Carlos Baerga	1.50	.70	.19
☐ 75T	Dave Hollins	.15	.07	.02
☐ 76T	Todd Hundley	.10	.05	.01
☐ 77T	Rick Parker	.05	.02	.01
☐ 78T	Steve Cummings	.05	.02	.01
☐ 79T	Bill Sampen	.05	.02	.01
☐ 80T	Jerry Kutzler	.05	.02	.01
☐ 81T	Derek Bell	.50	.23	.06
☐ 82T	Kevin Tapani	.15	.07	.02
☐ 83T	Jim Leyritz	.10	.05	.01
☐ 84T	Ray Lankford	.50	.23	.06
☐ 85T	Wayne Edwards	.05	.02	.01
☐ 86T	Frank Thomas	4.00	1.80	.50
☐ 87T	Tim Naehring	.30	.14	.04
☐ 88T	Willie Blair	.05	.02	.01
☐ 89T	Alan Mills	.05	.02	.01
☐ 90T	Scott Radinsky	.05	.02	.01
☐ 91T	Howard Farmer	.05	.02	.01
☐ 92T	Julio Machado	.05	.02	.01
☐ 93T	Rafael Valdez	.05	.02	.01
☐ 94T	Shawn Boskie	.05	.02	.01
☐ 95T	David Segui	.05	.02	.01
☐ 96T	Chris Hoiles	.15	.07	.02
☐ 97T	D.J. Dozier	.05	.02	.01
☐ 98T	Hector Villanueva	.05	.02	.01
☐ 99T	Eric Gunderson	.05	.02	.01
☐ 100T	Eric Lindros	3.00	1.35	.35
☐ 101T	Dave Otto	.05	.02	.01
☐ 102T	Dana Kiecker	.05	.02	.01
☐ 103T	Tim Drummond	.05	.02	.01
☐ 104T	Mickey Pina	.05	.02	.01
☐ 105T	Craig Grebeck	.05	.02	.01
☐ 106T	Bernard Gilkey	.25	.11	.03
☐ 107T	Tim Layana	.05	.02	.01
☐ 108T	Scott Chiamparino	.05	.02	.01
☐ 109T	Steve Avery	.20	.09	.03
☐ 110T	Terry Shumpert	.05	.02	.01

1991 Score

The 1991 Score set contains 893 cards. The cards feature a solid color border framing the full-color photo of the cards. The cards measure the standard card size of 2 1/2" by 3 1/2" and also feature Score trademark full-color photos on the back. The backs also include a brief biography on each player. This set marks the fourth consecutive year that Score has issued a major set but the first time Score issued the set in two series. Score also reused their

successful Dream Team concept by using non-baseball photos of Today's stars. Series one contains 441 cards and ends with the Annie Leibowitz photo of Jose Canseco used in American Express ads. This first series also includes 49 Rookie Prospects (331-379), 12 First Round Draft Picks (380-393), and five each of the Master Blaster (402-406), K-Man (407-411), and Rifleman (412-416) subsets. The All-Star sets in the first series are all American Leaguers (which are all caricatures). Rookie Cards in the set include Jeromy Burnitz, Wes Chamberlain, Chipper Jones, Steve Karsay, Brian McRae, Mike Mussina, Marc Newfield, Phil Plantier, Todd Van Poppel, and Rondell White. There are a number of pitchers whose card backs show Innings Pitched totals which do not equal the added year-by-year total; the following card numbers were affected, 4, 24, 29, 30, 51, 81, 109, 111, 118, 141, 150, 156, 177, 204, 218, 232, 235, 255, 287, 289, 311, and 328. The second series was issued approximately three months after the release of series one and included many of the special cards Score is noted for, e.g., the continuation of the Dream Team set begun in Series One, All-Star Cartoons featuring National Leaguers, a continuation of the 1990 first round draft picks, and 61 rookie prospects. An American Flag card (737) was issued to honor the American soldiers involved in Desert Storm.

	MINT	NRMT	EXC
COMPLETE SET (893)	12.00	5.50	1.50
COMPLETE FACT.SET (900)	20.00	9.00	2.50
COMMON CARD (1-893)	.05	.02	.01

☐ 1	Jose Canseco	.20	.09	.03
☐ 2	Ken Griffey Jr.	1.50	.70	.19
☐ 3	Ryne Sandberg	.30	.14	.04
☐ 4	Nolan Ryan	.75	.35	.09
☐ 5	Bo Jackson	.15	.07	.02
☐ 6	Bret Saberhagen UER	.15	.07	.02
	(In bio, missed misspelled as mised)			
☐ 7	Will Clark	.15	.07	.02
☐ 8	Ellis Burks	.10	.05	.01
☐ 9	Joe Carter	.15	.07	.02
☐ 10	Rickey Henderson	.15	.07	.02
☐ 11	Ozzie Guillen	.10	.05	.01
☐ 12	Wade Boggs	.15	.07	.02
☐ 13	Jerome Walton	.05	.02	.01
☐ 14	John Franco	.15	.07	.02
☐ 15	Ricky Jordan UER	.05	.02	.01
	(League misspelled as legue)			
☐ 16	Wally Backman	.05	.02	.01
☐ 17	Rob Dibble	.10	.05	.01
☐ 18	Glenn Braggs	.05	.02	.01
☐ 19	Cory Snyder	.05	.02	.01
☐ 20	Kal Daniels	.05	.02	.01
☐ 21	Mark Langston	.15	.07	.02
☐ 22	Kevin Gross	.05	.02	.01
☐ 23	Don Mattingly UER	.40	.18	.05
	(First line, ' is missing from Yankee)			
☐ 24	Dave Righetti	.05	.02	.01
☐ 25	Roberto Alomar	.25	.11	.03
☐ 26	Robby Thompson	.05	.02	.01
☐ 27	Jack McDowell	.15	.07	.02
☐ 28	Bip Roberts UER	.10	.05	.01
	(Bio reads playd)			
☐ 29	Jay Howell	.05	.02	.01
☐ 30	Dave Stieb UER	.05	.02	.01
	(17 wins in bio, 18 in stats)			
☐ 31	Johnny Ray	.05	.02	.01
☐ 32	Steve Sax	.05	.02	.01
☐ 33	Terry Mulholland	.05	.02	.01
☐ 34	Lee Guetterman	.05	.02	.01
☐ 35	Tim Raines	.15	.07	.02
☐ 36	Scott Fletcher	.05	.02	.01
☐ 37	Lance Parrish	.10	.05	.01
☐ 38	Tony Phillips UER	.15	.07	.02
	(Born 4/15, should be 4/25)			
☐ 39	Todd Stottlemyre	.05	.02	.01
☐ 40	Alan Trammell	.15	.07	.02
☐ 41	Todd Burns	.05	.02	.01
☐ 42	Mookie Wilson	.05	.02	.01
☐ 43	Chris Bosio	.05	.02	.01
☐ 44	Jeffrey Leonard	.05	.02	.01
☐ 45	Doug Jones	.05	.02	.01
☐ 46	Mike Scott UER	.05	.02	.01
	(In first line, dominate should read dominating)			
☐ 47	Andy Hawkins	.05	.02	.01
☐ 48	Harold Reynolds	.05	.02	.01
☐ 49	Paul Molitor	.15	.07	.02
☐ 50	John Farrell	.05	.02	.01
☐ 51	Danny Darwin	.05	.02	.01
☐ 52	Jeff Blauser	.10	.05	.01
☐ 53	John Tudor UER	.05	.02	.01
	(41 wins in '81)			
☐ 54	Milt Thompson	.05	.02	.01
☐ 55	Dave Justice	.20	.09	.03
☐ 56	Greg Olson	.05	.02	.01
☐ 57	Willie Blair	.05	.02	.01
☐ 58	Rick Parker	.05	.02	.01
☐ 59	Shawn Boskie	.05	.02	.01
☐ 60	Kevin Tapani	.05	.02	.01
☐ 61	Dave Hollins	.05	.02	.01
☐ 62	Scott Radinsky	.05	.02	.01
☐ 63	Francisco Cabrera	.05	.02	.01
☐ 64	Tim Layana	.05	.02	.01
☐ 65	Jim Leyritz	.05	.02	.01
☐ 66	Wayne Edwards	.05	.02	.01
☐ 67	Lee Stevens	.05	.02	.01
☐ 68	Bill Sampen UER	.05	.02	.01
	(Fourth line, long is spelled along)			
☐ 69	Craig Grebeck UER	.05	.02	.01
	(Born in Cerritos,			

□	#	Player			
□	70	John Burkett	.10	.05	.01
□	71	Hector Villanueva	.05	.02	.01
□	72	Oscar Azocar	.05	.02	.01
□	73	Alan Mills	.05	.02	.01
□	74	Carlos Baerga	.40	.18	.05
□	75	Charles Nagy	.10	.05	.01
□	76	Tim Drummond	.05	.02	.01
□	77	Dana Kiecker	.05	.02	.01
□	78	Tom Edens	.05	.02	.01
□	79	Kent Mercker	.05	.02	.01
□	80	Steve Avery	.15	.07	.02
□	81	Lee Smith	.15	.07	.02
□	82	Dave Martinez	.05	.02	.01
□	83	Dave Winfield	.15	.07	.02
□	84	Bill Spiers	.05	.02	.01
□	85	Dan Pasqua	.05	.02	.01
□	86	Randy Milligan	.05	.02	.01
□	87	Tracy Jones	.05	.02	.01
□	88	Greg Myers	.05	.02	.01
□	89	Keith Hernandez	.10	.05	.01
□	90	Todd Benzinger	.05	.02	.01
□	91	Mike Jackson	.05	.02	.01
□	92	Mike Stanley	.10	.05	.01
□	93	Candy Maldonado	.05	.02	.01
□	94	John Kruk UER	.15	.07	.02
		(No decimal point before 1990 BA)			
□	95	Cal Ripken UER	.75	.35	.09
		(Genius spelled genuis)			
□	96	Willie Fraser	.05	.02	.01
□	97	Mike Felder	.05	.02	.01
□	98	Bill Landrum	.05	.02	.01
□	99	Chuck Crim	.05	.02	.01
□	100	Chuck Finley	.10	.05	.01
□	101	Kirt Manwaring	.05	.02	.01
□	102	Jaime Navarro	.05	.02	.01
□	103	Dickie Thon	.05	.02	.01
□	104	Brian Downing	.05	.02	.01
□	105	Jim Abbott	.15	.07	.02
□	106	Tom Brookens	.05	.02	.01
□	107	Darryl Hamilton UER	.10	.05	.01
		(Bio info is for Jeff Hamilton)			
□	108	Bryan Harvey	.05	.02	.01
□	109	Greg A. Harris UER	.05	.02	.01
		(Shown pitching lefty, bio says righty)			
□	110	Greg Swindell	.05	.02	.01
□	111	Juan Berenguer	.05	.02	.01
□	112	Mike Heath	.05	.02	.01
□	113	Scott Bradley	.05	.02	.01
□	114	Jack Morris	.15	.07	.02
□	115	Barry Jones	.05	.02	.01
□	116	Kevin Romine	.05	.02	.01
□	117	Garry Templeton	.05	.02	.01
□	118	Scott Sanderson	.05	.02	.01
□	119	Roberto Kelly	.10	.05	.01
□	120	George Brett	.40	.18	.05
□	121	Oddibe McDowell	.05	.02	.01
□	122	Jim Acker	.05	.02	.01
□	123	Bill Swift UER	.05	.02	.01
		(Born 12/27/61, should be 10/27)			
□	124	Eric King	.05	.02	.01
□	125	Jay Buhner	.15	.07	.02
□	126	Matt Young	.05	.02	.01
□	127	Alvaro Espinoza	.05	.02	.01
□	128	Greg Hibbard	.05	.02	.01
□	129	Jeff M. Robinson	.05	.02	.01
□	130	Mike Greenwell	.15	.07	.02
□	131	Dion James	.05	.02	.01
□	132	Donn Pall UER	.05	.02	.01
		(1988 ERA in stats 0.00)			
□	133	Lloyd Moseby	.05	.02	.01
□	134	Randy Velarde	.05	.02	.01
□	135	Allan Anderson	.05	.02	.01
□	136	Mark Davis	.05	.02	.01
□	137	Eric Davis	.10	.05	.01
□	138	Phil Stephenson	.05	.02	.01
□	139	Felix Fermin	.05	.02	.01
□	140	Pedro Guerrero	.10	.05	.01
□	141	Charlie Hough	.10	.05	.01
□	142	Mike Henneman	.05	.02	.01
□	143	Jeff Montgomery	.10	.05	.01
□	144	Lenny Harris	.05	.02	.01
□	145	Bruce Hurst	.05	.02	.01
□	146	Eric Anthony	.05	.02	.01
□	147	Paul Assenmacher	.05	.02	.01
□	148	Jesse Barfield	.05	.02	.01
□	149	Carlos Quintana	.05	.02	.01
□	150	Dave Stewart	.15	.07	.02
□	151	Roy Smith	.05	.02	.01
□	152	Paul Gibson	.05	.02	.01
□	153	Mickey Hatcher	.05	.02	.01
□	154	Jim Eisenreich	.05	.02	.01
□	155	Kenny Rogers	.10	.05	.01
□	156	Dave Schmidt	.05	.02	.01
□	157	Lance Johnson	.05	.02	.01
□	158	Dave West	.05	.02	.01
□	159	Steve Balboni	.05	.02	.01
□	160	Jeff Brantley	.05	.02	.01
□	161	Craig Biggio	.15	.07	.02
□	162	Brook Jacoby	.05	.02	.01
□	163	Dan Gladden	.05	.02	.01
□	164	Jeff Reardon UER	.10	.05	.01
		(Total IP shown as 943.2, should be 943.1)			
□	165	Mark Carreon	.05	.02	.01
□	166	Mel Hall	.05	.02	.01
□	167	Gary Mielke	.05	.02	.01
□	168	Cecil Fielder	.15	.07	.02
□	169	Darrin Jackson	.05	.02	.01
□	170	Rick Aguilera	.10	.05	.01
□	171	Walt Weiss	.05	.02	.01
□	172	Steve Farr	.05	.02	.01
□	173	Jody Reed	.05	.02	.01
□	174	Mike Jeffcoat	.05	.02	.01
□	175	Mark Grace	.15	.07	.02
□	176	Larry Sheets	.05	.02	.01
□	177	Bill Gullickson	.05	.02	.01
□	178	Chris Gwynn	.05	.02	.01
□	179	Melido Perez	.05	.02	.01
□	180	Sid Fernandez UER	.10	.05	.01
		(779 runs in 1990)			
□	181	Tim Burke	.05	.02	.01
□	182	Gary Pettis	.05	.02	.01
□	183	Rob Murphy	.05	.02	.01
□	184	Craig Lefferts	.05	.02	.01
□	185	Howard Johnson	.05	.02	.01
□	186	Ken Caminiti	.15	.07	.02
□	187	Tim Belcher	.05	.02	.01
□	188	Greg Cadaret	.05	.02	.01
□	189	Matt Williams	.20	.09	.03
□	190	Dave Magadan	.05	.02	.01
□	191	Geno Petralli	.05	.02	.01
□	192	Jeff D. Robinson	.05	.02	.01
□	193	Jim Deshaies	.05	.02	.01
□	194	Willie Randolph	.10	.05	.01
□	195	George Bell	.05	.02	.01
□	196	Hubie Brooks	.05	.02	.01
□	197	Tom Gordon	.10	.05	.01

☐ 198 Mike Fitzgerald	.05	.02	.01
☐ 199 Mike Pagliarulo	.05	.02	.01
☐ 200 Kirby Puckett	.30	.14	.04
☐ 201 Shawon Dunston	.05	.02	.01
☐ 202 Dennis Boyd	.05	.02	.01
☐ 203 Junior Felix UER	.05	.02	.01
(Text has him in NL)			
☐ 204 Alejandro Pena	.05	.02	.01
☐ 205 Pete Smith	.05	.02	.01
☐ 206 Tom Glavine UER	.20	.09	.03
(Lefty spelled leftie)			
☐ 207 Luis Salazar	.05	.02	.01
☐ 208 John Smoltz	.15	.07	.02
☐ 209 Doug Dascenzo	.05	.02	.01
☐ 210 Tim Wallach	.05	.02	.01
☐ 211 Greg Gagne	.05	.02	.01
☐ 212 Mark Gubicza	.05	.02	.01
☐ 213 Mark Parent	.05	.02	.01
☐ 214 Ken Oberkfell	.05	.02	.01
☐ 215 Gary Carter	.15	.07	.02
☐ 216 Rafael Palmeiro	.15	.07	.02
☐ 217 Tom Niedenfuer	.05	.02	.01
☐ 218 Dave LaPoint	.05	.02	.01
☐ 219 Jeff Treadway	.05	.02	.01
☐ 220 Mitch Williams UER	.10	.05	.01
('89 ERA shown as 2.76, should be 2.64)			
☐ 221 Jose DeLeon	.05	.02	.01
☐ 222 Mike LaValliere	.05	.02	.01
☐ 223 Darrel Akerfelds	.05	.02	.01
☐ 224A Kent Anderson ERR	.05	.02	.01
(First line, flachy should read flashy)			
☐ 224B Kent Anderson COR	.05	.02	.01
(Corrected in factory sets)			
☐ 225 Dwight Evans	.10	.05	.01
☐ 226 Gary Redus	.05	.02	.01
☐ 227 Paul O'Neill	.15	.07	.02
☐ 228 Marty Barrett	.05	.02	.01
☐ 229 Tom Browning	.05	.02	.01
☐ 230 Terry Pendleton	.15	.07	.02
☐ 231 Jack Armstrong	.05	.02	.01
☐ 232 Mike Boddicker	.05	.02	.01
☐ 233 Neal Heaton	.05	.02	.01
☐ 234 Marquis Grissom	.20	.09	.03
☐ 235 Bert Blyleven	.15	.07	.02
☐ 236 Curt Young	.05	.02	.01
☐ 237 Don Carman	.05	.02	.01
☐ 238 Charlie Hayes	.10	.05	.01
☐ 239 Mark Knudson	.05	.02	.01
☐ 240 Todd Zeile	.10	.05	.01
☐ 241 Larry Walker UER	.25	.11	.03
(Maple River, should be Maple Ridge)			
☐ 242 Jerald Clark	.05	.02	.01
☐ 243 Jeff Ballard	.05	.02	.01
☐ 244 Jeff King	.05	.02	.01
☐ 245 Tom Brunansky	.05	.02	.01
☐ 246 Darren Daulton	.15	.07	.02
☐ 247 Scott Terry	.05	.02	.01
☐ 248 Rob Deer	.05	.02	.01
☐ 249 Brady Anderson UER	.10	.05	.01
(1990 Hagerstown 1 hit, should say 13 hits)			
☐ 250 Len Dykstra	.15	.07	.02
☐ 251 Greg W. Harris	.05	.02	.01
☐ 252 Mike Hartley	.05	.02	.01
☐ 253 Joey Cora	.05	.02	.01
☐ 254 Ivan Calderon	.05	.02	.01
☐ 255 Ted Power	.05	.02	.01
☐ 256 Sammy Sosa	.25	.11	.03
☐ 257 Steve Buechele	.05	.02	.01
☐ 258 Mike Devereaux UER	.10	.05	.01
(No comma between city and state)			
☐ 259 Brad Komminsk UER	.05	.02	.01
(Last text line, Ba should be BA)			
☐ 260 Teddy Higuera	.05	.02	.01
☐ 261 Shawn Abner	.05	.02	.01
☐ 262 Dave Valle	.05	.02	.01
☐ 263 Jeff Huson	.05	.02	.01
☐ 264 Edgar Martinez	.15	.07	.02
☐ 265 Carlton Fisk	.15	.07	.02
☐ 266 Steve Finley	.10	.05	.01
☐ 267 John Wetteland	.10	.05	.01
☐ 268 Kevin Appier	.10	.05	.01
☐ 269 Steve Lyons	.05	.02	.01
☐ 270 Mickey Tettleton	.10	.05	.01
☐ 271 Luis Rivera	.05	.02	.01
☐ 272 Steve Jeltz	.05	.02	.01
☐ 273 R.J. Reynolds	.05	.02	.01
☐ 274 Carlos Martinez	.05	.02	.01
☐ 275 Dan Plesac	.05	.02	.01
☐ 276 Mike Morgan UER	.05	.02	.01
(Total IP shown as 1149.1, should be 1149)			
☐ 277 Jeff Russell	.05	.02	.01
☐ 278 Pete Incaviglia	.05	.02	.01
☐ 279 Kevin Seitzer UER	.05	.02	.01
(Bio has 200 hits twice and .300 four times, should be once and three times)			
☐ 280 Bobby Thigpen	.05	.02	.01
☐ 281 Stan Javier UER	.05	.02	.01
(Born 1/9, should say 9/1)			
☐ 282 Henry Cotto	.05	.02	.01
☐ 283 Gary Wayne	.05	.02	.01
☐ 284 Shane Mack	.05	.02	.01
☐ 285 Brian Holman	.05	.02	.01
☐ 286 Gerald Perry	.05	.02	.01
☐ 287 Steve Crawford	.05	.02	.01
☐ 288 Nelson Liriano	.05	.02	.01
☐ 289 Don Aase	.05	.02	.01
☐ 290 Randy Johnson	.25	.11	.03
☐ 291 Harold Baines	.15	.07	.02
☐ 292 Kent Hrbek	.10	.05	.01
☐ 293A Les Lancaster ERR	.05	.02	.01
(No comma between Dallas and Texas)			
☐ 293B Les Lancaster COR	.05	.02	.01
(Corrected in factory sets)			
☐ 294 Jeff Musselman	.05	.02	.01
☐ 295 Kurt Stillwell	.05	.02	.01
☐ 296 Stan Belinda	.05	.02	.01
☐ 297 Lou Whitaker	.10	.05	.01
☐ 298 Glenn Wilson	.05	.02	.01
☐ 299 Omar Vizquel UER	.05	.02	.01
(Born 5/15, should be 4/24, there is a decimal before GP total for '90)			
☐ 300 Ramon Martinez	.15	.07	.02
☐ 301 Dwight Smith	.05	.02	.01
☐ 302 Tim Crews	.05	.02	.01
☐ 303 Lance Blankenship	.05	.02	.01
☐ 304 Sid Bream	.05	.02	.01
☐ 305 Rafael Ramirez	.05	.02	.01
☐ 306 Steve Wilson	.05	.02	.01

#				
☐ 307	Mackey Sasser	.05	.02	.01
☐ 308	Franklin Stubbs	.05	.02	.01
☐ 309	Jack Daugherty UER (Born 6/3/60, should say July)	.05	.02	.01
☐ 310	Eddie Murray	.20	.09	.03
☐ 311	Bob Welch	.05	.02	.01
☐ 312	Brian Harper	.05	.02	.01
☐ 313	Lance McCullers	.05	.02	.01
☐ 314	Dave Smith	.05	.02	.01
☐ 315	Bobby Bonilla	.15	.07	.02
☐ 316	Jerry Don Gleaton	.05	.02	.01
☐ 317	Greg Maddux	.60	.25	.07
☐ 318	Keith Miller	.05	.02	.01
☐ 319	Mark Portugal	.05	.02	.01
☐ 320	Robin Ventura	.15	.07	.02
☐ 321	Bob Ojeda	.05	.02	.01
☐ 322	Mike Harkey	.05	.02	.01
☐ 323	Jay Bell	.10	.05	.01
☐ 324	Mark McGwire	.15	.07	.02
☐ 325	Gary Gaetti	.05	.02	.01
☐ 326	Jeff Pico	.05	.02	.01
☐ 327	Kevin McReynolds	.05	.02	.01
☐ 328	Frank Tanana	.05	.02	.01
☐ 329	Eric Yelding UER (Listed as 6'3", should be 5'11")	.05	.02	.01
☐ 330	Barry Bonds	.30	.14	.04
☐ 331	Brian McRae UER (No comma between city and state)	.30	.14	.04
☐ 332	Pedro Munoz	.10	.05	.01
☐ 333	Daryl Irvine	.05	.02	.01
☐ 334	Chris Hoiles	.10	.05	.01
☐ 335	Thomas Howard	.05	.02	.01
☐ 336	Jeff Schulz	.05	.02	.01
☐ 337	Jeff Manto	.05	.02	.01
☐ 338	Beau Allred	.05	.02	.01
☐ 339	Mike Bordick	.10	.05	.01
☐ 340	Todd Hundley	.10	.05	.01
☐ 341	Jim Vatcher UER (Height 6'9", should be 5'9")	.05	.02	.01
☐ 342	Luis Sojo	.05	.02	.01
☐ 343	Jose Offerman UER (Born 1969, should say 1968)	.10	.05	.01
☐ 344	Pete Coachman	.05	.02	.01
☐ 345	Mike Benjamin	.05	.02	.01
☐ 346	Ozzie Canseco	.05	.02	.01
☐ 347	Tim McIntosh	.05	.02	.01
☐ 348	Phil Plantier	.15	.07	.02
☐ 349	Terry Shumpert	.05	.02	.01
☐ 350	Darren Lewis	.10	.05	.01
☐ 351	David Walsh	.05	.02	.01
☐ 352A	Scott Chiamparino ERR (Bats left, should be right)	.05	.02	.01
☐ 352B	Scott Chiamparino COR (corrected in factory sets)	.05	.02	.01
☐ 353	Julio Valera UER (Progressed mis-spelled as progessed)	.05	.02	.01
☐ 354	Anthony Telford	.05	.02	.01
☐ 355	Kevin Wickander	.05	.02	.01
☐ 356	Tim Naehring	.05	.02	.01
☐ 357	Jim Poole	.05	.02	.01
☐ 358	Mark Whiten UER (Shown hitting lefty, bio says righty)	.10	.05	.01
☐ 359	Terry Wells	.05	.02	.01
☐ 360	Rafael Valdez	.05	.02	.01
☐ 361	Mel Stottlemyre Jr.	.05	.02	.01
☐ 362	David Segui	.05	.02	.01
☐ 363	Paul Abbott	.05	.02	.01
☐ 364	Steve Howard	.05	.02	.01
☐ 365	Karl Rhodes	.05	.02	.01
☐ 366	Rafael Novoa	.05	.02	.01
☐ 367	Joe Grahe	.05	.02	.01
☐ 368	Darren Reed	.05	.02	.01
☐ 369	Jeff McKnight	.05	.02	.01
☐ 370	Scott Leius	.05	.02	.01
☐ 371	Mark Dewey	.05	.02	.01
☐ 372	Mark Lee UER (Shown hitting lefty, bio says righty, born in Dakota, should say North Dakota)	.05	.02	.01
☐ 373	Rosario Rodriguez (Shown hitting lefty, bio says righty) UER	.05	.02	.01
☐ 374	Chuck McElroy	.05	.02	.01
☐ 375	Mike Bell	.05	.02	.01
☐ 376	Mickey Morandini	.05	.02	.01
☐ 377	Bill Haselman	.05	.02	.01
☐ 378	Dave Pavlas	.05	.02	.01
☐ 379	Derrick May	.10	.05	.01
☐ 380	Jeromy Burnitz FDP	.05	.02	.01
☐ 381	Donald Peters FDP	.05	.02	.01
☐ 382	Alex Fernandez FDP	.10	.05	.01
☐ 383	Mike Mussina FDP	1.00	.45	.12
☐ 384	Dan Smith FDP	.05	.02	.01
☐ 385	Lance Dickson FDP	.05	.02	.01
☐ 386	Carl Everett FDP	.25	.11	.03
☐ 387	Thomas Nevers FDP	.05	.02	.01
☐ 388	Adam Hyzdu FDP	.05	.02	.01
☐ 389	Todd Van Poppel FDP	.05	.02	.01
☐ 390	Rondell White FDP	1.00	.45	.12
☐ 391	Marc Newfield FDP	.20	.09	.03
☐ 392	Julio Franco AS	.05	.02	.01
☐ 393	Wade Boggs AS	.10	.05	.01
☐ 394	Ozzie Guillen AS	.05	.02	.01
☐ 395	Cecil Fielder AS	.10	.05	.01
☐ 396	Ken Griffey Jr. AS	.75	.35	.09
☐ 397	Rickey Henderson AS	.15	.07	.02
☐ 398	Jose Canseco AS	.15	.07	.02
☐ 399	Roger Clemens AS	.15	.07	.02
☐ 400	Sandy Alomar Jr. AS	.10	.05	.01
☐ 401	Bobby Thigpen AS	.05	.02	.01
☐ 402	Bobby Bonilla MB	.10	.05	.01
☐ 403	Eric Davis MB	.05	.02	.01
☐ 404	Fred McGriff MB	.10	.05	.01
☐ 405	Glenn Davis MB	.05	.02	.01
☐ 406	Kevin Mitchell MB	.05	.02	.01
☐ 407	Rob Dibble KM	.05	.02	.01
☐ 408	Ramon Martinez KM	.05	.02	.01
☐ 409	David Cone KM	.15	.07	.02
☐ 410	Bobby Witt KM	.05	.02	.01
☐ 411	Mark Langston KM	.10	.05	.01
☐ 412	Bo Jackson RIF	.15	.07	.02
☐ 413	Shawon Dunston RIF UER (In the baseball, should say in baseball)	.05	.02	.01
☐ 414	Jesse Barfield RIF	.05	.02	.01
☐ 415	Ken Caminiti RIF	.10	.05	.01
☐ 416	Benito Santiago RIF	.05	.02	.01
☐ 417	Nolan Ryan HL	.40	.18	.05
☐ 418	Bobby Thigpen HL UER (Back refers to Hal McRae Jr., should say Brian McRae)	.05	.02	.01

☐ 419	Ramon Martinez HL	.05	.02	.01
☐ 420	Bo Jackson HL	.15	.07	.02
☐ 421	Carlton Fisk HL	.10	.05	.01
☐ 422	Jimmy Key	.10	.05	.01
☐ 423	Junior Noboa	.05	.02	.01
☐ 424	Al Newman	.05	.02	.01
☐ 425	Pat Borders	.05	.02	.01
☐ 426	Von Hayes	.05	.02	.01
☐ 427	Tim Teufel	.05	.02	.01
☐ 428	Eric Plunk UER	.05	.02	.01
	(Text says Eric's had, no apostrophe needed)			
☐ 429	John Moses	.05	.02	.01
☐ 430	Mike Witt	.05	.02	.01
☐ 431	Otis Nixon	.05	.02	.01
☐ 432	Tony Fernandez	.05	.02	.01
☐ 433	Rance Mulliniks	.05	.02	.01
☐ 434	Dan Petry	.05	.02	.01
☐ 435	Bob Geren	.05	.02	.01
☐ 436	Steve Frey	.05	.02	.01
☐ 437	Jamie Moyer	.05	.02	.01
☐ 438	Junior Ortiz	.05	.02	.01
☐ 439	Tom O'Malley	.05	.02	.01
☐ 440	Pat Combs	.05	.02	.01
☐ 441	Jose Canseco DT	.50	.23	.06
☐ 442	Alfredo Griffin	.05	.02	.01
☐ 443	Andres Galarraga	.15	.07	.02
☐ 444	Bryn Smith	.05	.02	.01
☐ 445	Andre Dawson	.15	.07	.02
☐ 446	Juan Samuel	.05	.02	.01
☐ 447	Mike Aldrete	.05	.02	.01
☐ 448	Ron Gant	.15	.07	.02
☐ 449	Fernando Valenzuela	.05	.02	.01
☐ 450	Vince Coleman UER	.05	.02	.01
	(Should say topped majors in steals four times, not three times)			
☐ 451	Kevin Mitchell	.10	.05	.01
☐ 452	Spike Owen	.05	.02	.01
☐ 453	Mike Bielecki	.05	.02	.01
☐ 454	Dennis Martinez	.10	.05	.01
☐ 455	Brett Butler	.15	.07	.02
☐ 456	Ron Darling	.05	.02	.01
☐ 457	Dennis Rasmussen	.05	.02	.01
☐ 458	Ken Howell	.05	.02	.01
☐ 459	Steve Bedrosian	.05	.02	.01
☐ 460	Frank Viola	.05	.02	.01
☐ 461	Jose Lind	.05	.02	.01
☐ 462	Chris Sabo	.05	.02	.01
☐ 463	Dante Bichette	.20	.09	.03
☐ 464	Rick Mahler	.05	.02	.01
☐ 465	John Smiley	.05	.02	.01
☐ 466	Devon White	.10	.05	.01
☐ 467	John Orton	.05	.02	.01
☐ 468	Mike Stanton	.05	.02	.01
☐ 469	Billy Hatcher	.05	.02	.01
☐ 470	Wally Joyner	.15	.07	.02
☐ 471	Gene Larkin	.05	.02	.01
☐ 472	Doug Drabek	.10	.05	.01
☐ 473	Gary Sheffield	.15	.07	.02
☐ 474	David Wells	.05	.02	.01
☐ 475	Andy Van Slyke	.10	.05	.01
☐ 476	Mike Gallego	.05	.02	.01
☐ 477	B.J. Surhoff	.05	.02	.01
☐ 478	Gene Nelson	.05	.02	.01
☐ 479	Mariano Duncan	.05	.02	.01
☐ 480	Fred McGriff	.15	.07	.02
☐ 481	Jerry Browne	.05	.02	.01
☐ 482	Alvin Davis	.05	.02	.01
☐ 483	Bill Wegman	.05	.02	.01
☐ 484	Dave Parker	.10	.05	.01
☐ 485	Dennis Eckersley	.15	.07	.02
☐ 486	Erik Hanson UER	.05	.02	.01
	(Basketball misspelled as baseketball)			
☐ 487	Bill Ripken	.05	.02	.01
☐ 488	Tom Candiotti	.05	.02	.01
☐ 489	Mike Schooler	.05	.02	.01
☐ 490	Gregg Olson	.05	.02	.01
☐ 491	Chris James	.05	.02	.01
☐ 492	Pete Harnisch	.10	.05	.01
☐ 493	Julio Franco	.10	.05	.01
☐ 494	Greg Briley	.05	.02	.01
☐ 495	Ruben Sierra	.15	.07	.02
☐ 496	Steve Olin	.05	.02	.01
☐ 497	Mike Fetters	.05	.02	.01
☐ 498	Mark Williamson	.05	.02	.01
☐ 499	Bob Tewksbury	.05	.02	.01
☐ 500	Tony Gwynn	.30	.14	.04
☐ 501	Randy Myers	.15	.07	.02
☐ 502	Keith Comstock	.05	.02	.01
☐ 503	Craig Worthington UER	.05	.02	.01
	(DeCinces misspelled DiCinces on back)			
☐ 504	Mark Eichhorn UER	.05	.02	.01
	(Stats incomplete, doesn't have '89 Braves stint)			
☐ 505	Barry Larkin	.15	.07	.02
☐ 506	Dave Johnson	.05	.02	.01
☐ 507	Bobby Witt	.05	.02	.01
☐ 508	Joe Orsulak	.05	.02	.01
☐ 509	Pete O'Brien	.05	.02	.01
☐ 510	Brad Arnsberg	.05	.02	.01
☐ 511	Storm Davis	.05	.02	.01
☐ 512	Bob Milacki	.05	.02	.01
☐ 513	Bill Pecota	.05	.02	.01
☐ 514	Glenallen Hill	.05	.02	.01
☐ 515	Danny Tartabull	.10	.05	.01
☐ 516	Mike Moore	.05	.02	.01
☐ 517	Ron Robinson UER	.05	.02	.01
	(577 K's in 1990)			
☐ 518	Mark Gardner	.05	.02	.01
☐ 519	Rick Wrona	.05	.02	.01
☐ 520	Mike Scioscia	.05	.02	.01
☐ 521	Frank Wills	.05	.02	.01
☐ 522	Greg Brock	.05	.02	.01
☐ 523	Jack Clark	.10	.05	.01
☐ 524	Bruce Ruffin	.05	.02	.01
☐ 525	Robin Yount	.15	.07	.02
☐ 526	Tom Foley	.05	.02	.01
☐ 527	Pat Perry	.05	.02	.01
☐ 528	Greg Vaughn	.10	.05	.01
☐ 529	Wally Whitehurst	.05	.02	.01
☐ 530	Norm Charlton	.05	.02	.01
☐ 531	Marvell Wynne	.05	.02	.01
☐ 532	Jim Gantner	.05	.02	.01
☐ 533	Greg Litton	.05	.02	.01
☐ 534	Manny Lee	.05	.02	.01
☐ 535	Scott Bailes	.05	.02	.01
☐ 536	Charlie Leibrandt	.05	.02	.01
☐ 537	Roger McDowell	.05	.02	.01
☐ 538	Andy Benes	.10	.05	.01
☐ 539	Rick Honeycutt	.05	.02	.01
☐ 540	Dwight Gooden	.05	.02	.01
☐ 541	Scott Garrelts	.05	.02	.01
☐ 542	Dave Clark	.05	.02	.01
☐ 543	Lonnie Smith	.05	.02	.01
☐ 544	Rick Reuschel	.05	.02	.01
☐ 545	Delino DeShields UER	.10	.05	.01
	(Rockford misspelled as Rock Ford in '88)			

☐ 546	Mike Sharperson	.05	.02	.01
☐ 547	Mike Kingery	.05	.02	.01
☐ 548	Terry Kennedy	.05	.02	.01
☐ 549	David Cone	.15	.07	.02
☐ 550	Orel Hershiser	.15	.07	.01
☐ 551	Matt Nokes	.05	.02	.01
☐ 552	Eddie Williams	.05	.02	.01
☐ 553	Frank DiPino	.05	.02	.01
☐ 554	Fred Lynn	.10	.05	.01
☐ 555	Alex Cole	.05	.02	.01
☐ 556	Terry Leach	.05	.02	.01
☐ 557	Chet Lemon	.05	.02	.01
☐ 558	Paul Mirabella	.05	.02	.01
☐ 559	Bill Long	.05	.02	.01
☐ 560	Phil Bradley	.05	.02	.01
☐ 561	Duane Ward	.05	.02	.01
☐ 562	Dave Bergman	.05	.02	.01
☐ 563	Eric Show	.05	.02	.01
☐ 564	Xavier Hernandez	.05	.02	.01
☐ 565	Jeff Parrett	.05	.02	.01
☐ 566	Chuck Cary	.05	.02	.01
☐ 567	Ken Hill	.15	.07	.02
☐ 568	Bob Welch Hand	.05	.02	.01
	(Complement should be compliment) UER			
☐ 569	John Mitchell	.05	.02	.01
☐ 570	Travis Fryman	.20	.09	.03
☐ 571	Derek Lilliquist	.05	.02	.01
☐ 572	Steve Lake	.05	.02	.01
☐ 573	John Barfield	.05	.02	.01
☐ 574	Randy Bush	.05	.02	.01
☐ 575	Joe Magrane	.05	.02	.01
☐ 576	Eddie Diaz	.05	.02	.01
☐ 577	Casey Candaele	.05	.02	.01
☐ 578	Jesse Orosco	.05	.02	.01
☐ 579	Tom Henke	.10	.05	.01
☐ 580	Rick Cerone UER	.05	.02	.01
	(Actually his third go-round with Yankees)			
☐ 581	Drew Hall	.05	.02	.01
☐ 582	Tony Castillo	.05	.02	.01
☐ 583	Jimmy Jones	.05	.02	.01
☐ 584	Rick Reed	.05	.02	.01
☐ 585	Joe Girardi	.05	.02	.01
☐ 586	Jeff Gray	.05	.02	.01
☐ 587	Luis Polonia	.05	.02	.01
☐ 588	Joe Klink	.05	.02	.01
☐ 589	Rex Hudler	.05	.02	.01
☐ 590	Kirk McCaskill	.05	.02	.01
☐ 591	Juan Agosto	.05	.02	.01
☐ 592	Wes Gardner	.05	.02	.01
☐ 593	Rich Rodriguez	.05	.02	.01
☐ 594	Mitch Webster	.05	.02	.01
☐ 595	Kelly Gruber	.05	.02	.01
☐ 596	Dale Mohorcic	.05	.02	.01
☐ 597	Willie McGee	.10	.05	.01
☐ 598	Bill Krueger	.05	.02	.01
☐ 599	Bob Walk UER	.05	.02	.01
	(Cards says he's 33, but actually he's 34)			
☐ 600	Kevin Maas	.05	.02	.01
☐ 601	Danny Jackson	.05	.02	.01
☐ 602	Craig McMurtry UER	.05	.02	.01
	(Anonymously misspelled anonimously)			
☐ 603	Curtis Wilkerson	.05	.02	.01
☐ 604	Adam Peterson	.05	.02	.01
☐ 605	Sam Horn	.05	.02	.01
☐ 606	Tommy Gregg	.05	.02	.01
☐ 607	Ken Dayley	.05	.02	.01
☐ 608	Carmelo Castillo	.05	.02	.01
☐ 609	John Shelby	.05	.02	.01
☐ 610	Don Slaught	.05	.02	.01
☐ 611	Calvin Schiraldi	.05	.02	.01
☐ 612	Dennis Lamp	.05	.02	.01
☐ 613	Andres Thomas	.05	.02	.01
☐ 614	Jose Gonzalez	.05	.02	.01
☐ 615	Randy Ready	.05	.02	.01
☐ 616	Kevin Bass	.05	.02	.01
☐ 617	Mike Marshall	.05	.02	.01
☐ 618	Daryl Boston	.05	.02	.01
☐ 619	Andy McGaffigan	.05	.02	.01
☐ 620	Joe Oliver	.05	.02	.01
☐ 621	Jim Gott	.05	.02	.01
☐ 622	Jose Oquendo	.05	.02	.01
☐ 623	Jose DeJesus	.05	.02	.01
☐ 624	Mike Brumley	.05	.02	.01
☐ 625	John Olerud	.10	.05	.01
☐ 626	Ernest Riles	.05	.02	.01
☐ 627	Gene Harris	.05	.02	.01
☐ 628	Jose Uribe	.05	.02	.01
☐ 629	Darnell Coles	.05	.02	.01
☐ 630	Carney Lansford	.10	.05	.01
☐ 631	Tim Leary	.05	.02	.01
☐ 632	Tim Hulett	.05	.02	.01
☐ 633	Kevin Elster	.05	.02	.01
☐ 634	Tony Fossas	.05	.02	.01
☐ 635	Francisco Oliveras	.05	.02	.01
☐ 636	Bob Patterson	.05	.02	.01
☐ 637	Gary Ward	.05	.02	.01
☐ 638	Rene Gonzales	.05	.02	.01
☐ 639	Don Robinson	.05	.02	.01
☐ 640	Darryl Strawberry	.10	.05	.01
☐ 641	Dave Anderson	.05	.02	.01
☐ 642	Scott Scudder	.05	.02	.01
☐ 643	Reggie Harris UER	.05	.02	.01
	(Hepatitis misspelled as hepititis)			
☐ 644	Dave Henderson	.05	.02	.01
☐ 645	Ben McDonald	.10	.05	.01
☐ 646	Bob Kipper	.05	.02	.01
☐ 647	Hal Morris UER	.10	.05	.01
	(It's should be its)			
☐ 648	Tim Birtsas	.05	.02	.01
☐ 649	Steve Searcy	.05	.02	.01
☐ 650	Dale Murphy	.15	.07	.02
☐ 651	Ron Oester	.05	.02	.01
☐ 652	Mike LaCoss	.05	.02	.01
☐ 653	Ron Jones	.05	.02	.01
☐ 654	Kelly Downs	.05	.02	.01
☐ 655	Roger Clemens	.15	.07	.02
☐ 656	Herm Winningham	.05	.02	.01
☐ 657	Trevor Wilson	.05	.02	.01
☐ 658	Jose Rijo	.10	.05	.01
☐ 659	Dann Bilardello UER	.05	.02	.01
	(Bio has 13 games, 1 hit, and 32 AB, stats show 19, 2, and 37)			
☐ 660	Gregg Jefferies	.15	.07	.02
☐ 661	Doug Drabek AS UER	.05	.02	.01
	(Through is misspelled though)			
☐ 662	Randy Myers AS	.10	.05	.01
☐ 663	Benny Santiago AS	.10	.05	.01
☐ 664	Will Clark AS	.15	.07	.02
☐ 665	Ryne Sandberg AS	.15	.07	.02
☐ 666	Barry Larkin AS UER	.10	.05	.01
	(Line 13, coolly misspelled cooly)			
☐ 667	Matt Williams AS	.15	.07	.02
☐ 668	Barry Bonds AS	.15	.07	.02
☐ 669	Eric Davis AS	.05	.02	.01

☐ 670 Bobby Bonilla AS	.10	.05	.01
☐ 671 Chipper Jones FDP	3.00	1.35	.35
☐ 672 Eric Christopherson FDP	.05	.02	.01
☐ 673 Robbie Beckett FDP	.05	.02	.01
☐ 674 Shane Andrews FDP	.10	.05	.01
☐ 675 Steve Karsay FDP	.10	.05	.01
☐ 676 Aaron Holbert FDP	.05	.02	.01
☐ 677 Donovan Osborne FDP	.05	.02	.01
☐ 678 Todd Ritchie FDP	.05	.02	.01
☐ 679 Ron Walden FDP	.05	.02	.01
☐ 680 Tim Costo FDP	.05	.02	.01
☐ 681 Dan Wilson FDP	.05	.02	.01
☐ 682 Kurt Miller FDP	.05	.02	.01
☐ 683 Mike Lieberthal FDP	.10	.05	.01
☐ 684 Roger Clemens KM	.15	.07	.02
☐ 685 Doc Gooden KM	.05	.02	.01
☐ 686 Nolan Ryan KM	.40	.18	.05
☐ 687 Frank Viola KM	.05	.02	.01
☐ 688 Erik Hanson KM	.05	.02	.01
☐ 689 Matt Williams MB	.15	.07	.02
☐ 690 Jose Canseco MB UER (Mammoth misspelled as monmouth)	.15	.07	.02
☐ 691 Darryl Strawberry MB	.05	.02	.01
☐ 692 Bo Jackson MB	.15	.07	.02
☐ 693 Cecil Fielder MB	.10	.05	.01
☐ 694 Sandy Alomar Jr. RF	.05	.02	.01
☐ 695 Cory Snyder RF	.05	.02	.01
☐ 696 Eric Davis RF	.05	.02	.01
☐ 697 Ken Griffey Jr. RF	.75	.35	.09
☐ 698 Andy Van Slyke RF UER (Line 2, outfielders does not need)	.10	.05	.01
☐ 699 Langston/Witt NH Mark Langston Mike Witt	.10	.05	.01
☐ 700 Randy Johnson NH	.15	.07	.02
☐ 701 Nolan Ryan NH	.40	.18	.05
☐ 702 Dave Stewart NH	.10	.05	.01
☐ 703 Fernando Valenzuela NH	.05	.02	.01
☐ 704 Andy Hawkins NH	.05	.02	.01
☐ 705 Melido Perez NH	.05	.02	.01
☐ 706 Terry Mulholland NH	.05	.02	.01
☐ 707 Dave Stieb NH	.05	.02	.01
☐ 708 Brian Barnes	.05	.02	.01
☐ 709 Bernard Gilkey	.10	.05	.01
☐ 710 Steve Decker	.05	.02	.01
☐ 711 Paul Faries	.05	.02	.01
☐ 712 Paul Marak	.05	.02	.01
☐ 713 Wes Chamberlain	.05	.02	.01
☐ 714 Kevin Belcher	.05	.02	.01
☐ 715 Dan Boone UER (IP adds up to 101, but card has 101.2)	.05	.02	.01
☐ 716 Steve Adkins	.05	.02	.01
☐ 717 Geronimo Pena	.05	.02	.01
☐ 718 Howard Farmer	.05	.02	.01
☐ 719 Mark Leonard	.05	.02	.01
☐ 720 Tom Lampkin	.05	.02	.01
☐ 721 Mike Gardiner	.05	.02	.01
☐ 722 Jeff Conine	.60	.25	.07
☐ 723 Efrain Valdez	.05	.02	.01
☐ 724 Chuck Malone	.05	.02	.01
☐ 725 Leo Gomez	.05	.02	.01
☐ 726 Paul McClellan	.05	.02	.01
☐ 727 Mark Leiter	.05	.02	.01
☐ 728 Rich DeLucia UER (Line 2, all told is written alltold)	.05	.02	.01
☐ 729 Mel Rojas	.05	.02	.01
☐ 730 Hector Wagner	.05	.02	.01
☐ 731 Ray Lankford	.10	.05	.01
☐ 732 Turner Ward	.05	.02	.01
☐ 733 Gerald Alexander	.05	.02	.01
☐ 734 Scott Anderson	.05	.02	.01
☐ 735 Tony Perezchica	.05	.02	.01
☐ 736 Jimmy Kremers	.05	.02	.01
☐ 737 American Flag (Pray for Peace)	.15	.07	.02
☐ 738 Mike York	.05	.02	.01
☐ 739 Mike Rochford	.05	.02	.01
☐ 740 Scott Aldred	.05	.02	.01
☐ 741 Rico Brogna	.10	.05	.01
☐ 742 Dave Burba	.05	.02	.01
☐ 743 Ray Stephens	.05	.02	.01
☐ 744 Eric Gunderson	.05	.02	.01
☐ 745 Troy Afenir	.05	.02	.01
☐ 746 Jeff Shaw	.05	.02	.01
☐ 747 Orlando Merced	.15	.07	.02
☐ 748 Omar Olivares UER (Line 9, league is misspelled legaue)	.05	.02	.01
☐ 749 Jerry Kutzler	.05	.02	.01
☐ 750 Mo Vaughn UER (44 SB's in 1990)	.50	.23	.06
☐ 751 Matt Stark	.05	.02	.01
☐ 752 Randy Hennis	.05	.02	.01
☐ 753 Andujar Cedeno	.05	.02	.01
☐ 754 Kelvin Torve	.05	.02	.01
☐ 755 Joe Kraemer	.05	.02	.01
☐ 756 Phil Clark	.05	.02	.01
☐ 757 Ed Vosberg	.05	.02	.01
☐ 758 Mike Perez	.05	.02	.01
☐ 759 Scott Lewis	.05	.02	.01
☐ 760 Steve Chitren	.05	.02	.01
☐ 761 Ray Young	.05	.02	.01
☐ 762 Andres Santana	.05	.02	.01
☐ 763 Rodney McCray	.05	.02	.01
☐ 764 Sean Berry UER (Name misspelled Barry on card front)	.10	.05	.01
☐ 765 Brent Mayne	.05	.02	.01
☐ 766 Mike Simms	.05	.02	.01
☐ 767 Glenn Sutko	.05	.02	.01
☐ 768 Gary DiSarcina	.05	.02	.01
☐ 769 George Brett HL	.20	.09	.03
☐ 770 Cecil Fielder HL	.10	.05	.01
☐ 771 Jim Presley	.05	.02	.01
☐ 772 John Dopson	.05	.02	.01
☐ 773 Bo Jackson Breaker	.15	.07	.02
☐ 774 Brent Knackert UER (Born in 1954, shown throwing righty, but bio says lefty)	.05	.02	.01
☐ 775 Bill Doran UER (Reds in NL East)	.05	.02	.01
☐ 776 Dick Schofield	.05	.02	.01
☐ 777 Nelson Santovenia	.05	.02	.01
☐ 778 Mark Guthrie	.05	.02	.01
☐ 779 Mark Lemke	.05	.02	.01
☐ 780 Terry Steinbach	.10	.05	.01
☐ 781 Tom Bolton	.05	.02	.01
☐ 782 Randy Tomlin	.05	.02	.01
☐ 783 Jeff Kunkel	.05	.02	.01
☐ 784 Felix Jose	.05	.02	.01
☐ 785 Rick Sutcliffe	.10	.05	.01
☐ 786 John Cerutti	.05	.02	.01
☐ 787 Jose Vizcaino UER (Offerman, not Opperman)	.05	.02	.01
☐ 788 Curt Schilling	.05	.02	.01
☐ 789 Ed Whitson	.05	.02	.01

☐ 790 Tony Pena	.05	.02	.01
☐ 791 John Candelaria	.05	.02	.01
☐ 792 Carmelo Martinez	.05	.02	.01
☐ 793 Sandy Alomar Jr. UER	.10	.05	.01
(Indian's should			
say Indians')			
☐ 794 Jim Neidlinger	.05	.02	.01
☐ 795 Barry Larkin WS	.10	.05	.01
and Chris Sabo			
☐ 796 Paul Sorrento	.10	.05	.01
☐ 797 Tom Pagnozzi	.05	.02	.01
☐ 798 Tino Martinez	.15	.07	.02
☐ 799 Scott Ruskin UER	.05	.02	.01
(Text says first three			
seasons but lists			
averages for four)			
☐ 800 Kirk Gibson	.15	.07	.02
☐ 801 Walt Terrell	.05	.02	.01
☐ 802 John Russell	.05	.02	.01
☐ 803 Chili Davis	.15	.07	.02
☐ 804 Chris Nabholz	.05	.02	.01
☐ 805 Juan Gonzalez	.50	.23	.06
☐ 806 Ron Hassey	.05	.02	.01
☐ 807 Todd Worrell	.05	.02	.01
☐ 808 Tommy Greene	.10	.05	.01
☐ 809 Joel Skinner UER	.05	.02	.01
(Joel, not Bob, was			
drafted in 1979)			
☐ 810 Benito Santiago	.05	.02	.01
☐ 811 Pat Tabler UER	.05	.02	.01
(Line 3, always			
misspelled alway)			
☐ 812 Scott Erickson UER	.05	.02	.01
(Record spelled rcord)			
☐ 813 Moises Alou	.15	.07	.02
☐ 814 Dale Sveum	.05	.02	.01
☐ 815 Ryne Sandberg MANYR	.15	.07	.02
☐ 816 Rick Dempsey	.05	.02	.01
☐ 817 Scott Bankhead	.05	.02	.01
☐ 818 Jason Grimsley	.05	.02	.01
☐ 819 Doug Jennings	.05	.02	.01
☐ 820 Tom Herr	.05	.02	.01
☐ 821 Rob Ducey	.05	.02	.01
☐ 822 Luis Quinones	.05	.02	.01
☐ 823 Greg Minton	.05	.02	.01
☐ 824 Mark Grant	.05	.02	.01
☐ 825 Ozzie Smith UER	.20	.09	.03
(Shortstop misspelled			
shortsop)			
☐ 826 Dave Eiland	.05	.02	.01
☐ 827 Danny Heep	.05	.02	.01
☐ 828 Hensley Meulens	.05	.02	.01
☐ 829 Charlie O'Brien	.05	.02	.01
☐ 830 Glenn Davis	.05	.02	.01
☐ 831 John Marzano UER	.05	.02	.01
(International mis-			
spelled Internaional)			
☐ 832 Steve Ontiveros	.05	.02	.01
☐ 833 Ron Karkovice	.05	.02	.01
☐ 834 Jerry Goff	.05	.02	.01
☐ 835 Ken Griffey Sr.	.10	.05	.01
☐ 836 Kevin Reimer	.05	.02	.01
☐ 837 Randy Kutcher UER	.05	.02	.01
(Infectious mis-			
spelled infectous)			
☐ 838 Mike Blowers	.05	.02	.01
☐ 839 Mike Macfarlane	.05	.02	.01
☐ 840 Frank Thomas UER	2.00	.90	.25
(1989 Sarasota stats,			
15 games but 188 AB)			
☐ 841 The Griffeys	.75	.35	.09
Ken Griffey Jr.			
Ken Griffey Sr.			
☐ 842 Jack Howell	.05	.02	.01
☐ 843 Goose Gozzo	.05	.02	.01
☐ 844 Gerald Young	.05	.02	.01
☐ 845 Zane Smith	.05	.02	.01
☐ 846 Kevin Brown	.10	.05	.01
☐ 847 Sil Campusano	.05	.02	.01
☐ 848 Larry Andersen	.05	.02	.01
☐ 849 Cal Ripken FRAN	.40	.18	.05
☐ 850 Roger Clemens FRAN	.15	.07	.02
☐ 851 Sandy Alomar Jr. FRAN	.10	.05	.01
☐ 852 Alan Trammell FRAN	.10	.05	.01
☐ 853 George Brett FRAN	.20	.09	.03
☐ 854 Robin Yount FRAN	.15	.07	.02
☐ 855 Kirby Puckett FRAN	.20	.09	.03
☐ 856 Don Mattingly FRAN	.20	.09	.03
☐ 857 Rickey Henderson FRAN	.15	.07	.02
☐ 858 Ken Griffey Jr. FRAN	.75	.35	.09
☐ 859 Ruben Sierra FRAN	.15	.07	.02
☐ 860 John Olerud FRAN	.10	.05	.01
☐ 861 Dave Justice FRAN	.10	.05	.01
☐ 862 Ryne Sandberg FRAN	.20	.09	.03
☐ 863 Eric Davis FRAN	.05	.02	.01
☐ 864 Darryl Strawberry FRAN	.05	.02	.01
☐ 865 Tim Wallach FRAN	.05	.02	.01
☐ 866 Doc Gooden FRAN	.05	.02	.01
☐ 867 Len Dykstra FRAN	.10	.05	.01
☐ 868 Barry Bonds FRAN	.15	.07	.02
☐ 869 Todd Zeile FRAN	.05	.02	.01
(Powerful misspelled			
as poweful)			
☐ 870 Benito Santiago FRAN	.10	.05	.01
☐ 871 Will Clark FRAN	.15	.07	.02
☐ 872 Craig Biggio FRAN	.10	.05	.01
☐ 873 Wally Joyner FRAN	.10	.05	.01
☐ 874 Frank Thomas FRAN	1.00	.45	.12
☐ 875 Rickey Henderson MVP	.15	.07	.02
☐ 876 Barry Bonds MVP	.15	.07	.02
☐ 877 Bob Welch CY	.05	.02	.01
☐ 878 Doug Drabek CY	.10	.05	.01
☐ 879 Sandy Alomar Jr ROY	.05	.02	.01
☐ 880 Dave Justice ROY	.10	.05	.01
☐ 881 Damon Berryhill	.05	.02	.01
☐ 882 Frank Viola DT	.05	.02	.01
☐ 883 Dave Stewart DT	.10	.05	.01
☐ 884 Doug Jones DT	.05	.02	.01
☐ 885 Randy Myers DT	.10	.05	.01
☐ 886 Will Clark DT	.20	.09	.03
☐ 887 Roberto Alomar DT	.30	.14	.04
☐ 888 Barry Larkin DT	.20	.09	.03
☐ 889 Wade Boggs DT	.10	.05	.01
☐ 890 Rickey Henderson DT	.15	.07	.02
☐ 891 Kirby Puckett DT	.30	.14	.04
☐ 892 Ken Griffey Jr DT	1.50	.70	.19
☐ 893 Benny Santiago DT	.10	.05	.01

1991 Score
Rookie/Traded

The 1991 Score Rookie and Traded set contains 110 standard-size (2 1/2" by 3 1/2") player cards and 10 "World Series II" magic motion trivia cards. The front design features glossy color action photos, with

white and purple borders on a mauve card face. The player's name, team, and position are given above the pictures. In a horizontal format, the left portion of the back has a color head shot and biography, while the right portion has statistics and player profile on a pale yellow background. The cards are numbered on the back. Cards 1T-80T feature traded players, while cards 81T-110T focus on rookies. The only noteworthy Rookie Cards in the set are Jeff Bagwell, Luis Gonzalez, Ivan Rodriguez, and Rick Wilkins.

	MINT	NRMT	EXC
COMPLETE FACT.SET (110)	4.00	1.80	.50
COMMON CARD (1T-110T)	.05	.02	.01

		MINT	NRMT	EXC
☐	1T Bo Jackson	.20	.09	.03
☐	2T Mike Flanagan	.05	.02	.01
☐	3T Pete Incaviglia	.05	.02	.01
☐	4T Jack Clark	.10	.05	.01
☐	5T Hubie Brooks	.05	.02	.01
☐	6T Ivan Calderon	.05	.02	.01
☐	7T Glenn Davis	.05	.02	.01
☐	8T Wally Backman	.05	.02	.01
☐	9T Dave Smith	.05	.02	.01
☐	10T Tim Raines	.15	.07	.02
☐	11T Joe Carter	.15	.07	.02
☐	12T Sid Bream	.05	.02	.01
☐	13T George Bell	.05	.02	.01
☐	14T Steve Bedrosian	.05	.02	.01
☐	15T Willie Wilson	.05	.02	.01
☐	16T Darryl Strawberry	.05	.02	.01
☐	17T Danny Jackson	.05	.02	.01
☐	18T Kirk Gibson	.15	.07	.02
☐	19T Willie McGee	.10	.05	.01
☐	20T Junior Felix	.05	.02	.01
☐	21T Steve Farr	.05	.02	.01
☐	22T Pat Tabler	.05	.02	.01
☐	23T Brett Butler	.15	.07	.02
☐	24T Danny Darwin	.05	.02	.01
☐	25T Mickey Tettleton	.10	.05	.01
☐	26T Gary Carter	.15	.07	.02
☐	27T Mitch Williams	.10	.05	.01
☐	28T Candy Maldonado	.05	.02	.01
☐	29T Otis Nixon	.05	.02	.01
☐	30T Brian Downing	.05	.02	.01
☐	31T Tom Candiotti	.05	.02	.01
☐	32T John Candelaria	.05	.02	.01
☐	33T Rob Murphy	.05	.02	.01
☐	34T Deion Sanders	.25	.11	.03
☐	35T Willie Randolph	.10	.05	.01
☐	36T Pete Harnisch	.05	.02	.01
☐	37T Dante Bichette	.20	.09	.03
☐	38T Garry Templeton	.05	.02	.01
☐	39T Gary Gaetti	.05	.02	.01
☐	40T John Cerutti	.05	.02	.01
☐	41T Rick Cerone	.05	.02	.01
☐	42T Mike Pagliarulo	.05	.02	.01
☐	43T Ron Hassey	.05	.02	.01
☐	44T Roberto Alomar	.25	.11	.03
☐	45T Mike Boddicker	.05	.02	.01
☐	46T Bud Black	.05	.02	.01
☐	47T Rob Deer	.05	.02	.01
☐	48T Devon White	.10	.05	.01
☐	49T Luis Sojo	.05	.02	.01
☐	50T Terry Pendleton	.15	.07	.02
☐	51T Kevin Gross	.05	.02	.01
☐	52T Mike Huff	.05	.02	.01
☐	53T Dave Righetti	.05	.02	.01
☐	54T Matt Young	.05	.02	.01
☐	55T Earnest Riles	.05	.02	.01
☐	56T Bill Gullickson	.05	.02	.01
☐	57T Vince Coleman	.05	.02	.01
☐	58T Fred McGriff	.15	.07	.02
☐	59T Franklin Stubbs	.05	.02	.01
☐	60T Eric King	.05	.02	.01
☐	61T Cory Snyder	.05	.02	.01
☐	62T Dwight Evans	.10	.05	.01
☐	63T Gerald Perry	.05	.02	.01
☐	64T Eric Show	.05	.02	.01
☐	65T Shawn Hillegas	.05	.02	.01
☐	66T Tony Fernandez	.05	.02	.01
☐	67T Tim Teufel	.05	.02	.01
☐	68T Mitch Webster	.05	.02	.01
☐	69T Mike Heath	.05	.02	.01
☐	70T Chili Davis	.15	.07	.02
☐	71T Larry Andersen	.05	.02	.01
☐	72T Gary Varsho	.05	.02	.01
☐	73T Juan Berenguer	.05	.02	.01
☐	74T Jack Morris	.15	.07	.02
☐	75T Barry Jones	.05	.02	.01
☐	76T Rafael Belliard	.05	.02	.01
☐	77T Steve Buechele	.05	.02	.01
☐	78T Scott Sanderson	.05	.02	.01
☐	79T Bob Ojeda	.05	.02	.01
☐	80T Curt Schilling	.10	.05	.01
☐	81T Brian Drahman	.05	.02	.01
☐	82T Ivan Rodriguez	.50	.23	.06
☐	83T David Howard	.05	.02	.01
☐	84T Heathcliff Slocumb	.15	.07	.02
☐	85T Mike Timlin	.05	.02	.01
☐	86T Darryl Kile	.05	.02	.01
☐	87T Pete Schourek	.40	.18	.05
☐	88T Bruce Walton	.05	.02	.01
☐	89T Al Osuna	.05	.02	.01
☐	90T Gary Scott	.05	.02	.01
☐	91T Doug Simons	.05	.02	.01
☐	92T Chris Jones	.05	.02	.01
☐	93T Chuck Knoblauch	.25	.11	.03
☐	94T Dana Allison	.05	.02	.01
☐	95T Erik Pappas	.05	.02	.01
☐	96T Jeff Bagwell	2.00	.90	.25
☐	97T Kirk Dressendorfer	.05	.02	.01
☐	98T Freddie Benavides	.05	.02	.01
☐	99T Luis Gonzalez	.15	.07	.02
☐	100T Wade Taylor	.05	.02	.01
☐	101T Ed Sprague	.05	.02	.01
☐	102T Bob Scanlan	.05	.02	.01
☐	103T Rick Wilkins	.05	.02	.01
☐	104T Chris Donnels	.05	.02	.01
☐	105T Joe Slusarski	.05	.02	.01
☐	106T Mark Lewis	.05	.02	.01
☐	107T Pat Kelly	.10	.05	.01
☐	108T John Briscoe	.05	.02	.01
☐	109T Luis Lopez	.05	.02	.01
☐	110T Jeff Johnson	.05	.02	.01

1992 Score

The 1992 Score set marked the second year that Score released their set in two different series. The first series contains 442 cards measuring the standard size (2 1/2" by 3 1/2"). The second series contains 451 more cards sequentially numbered. The glossy color action photos on the fronts are bordered above and below by stripes of the same color, and a thicker, different color stripe runs the length of the card to one side of the picture. The backs have a color close-up shot in the upper right corner, with biography, complete career statistics, and player profile printed on a yellow background. Hall of Famer Joe DiMaggio is remembered in a five-card subset. He autographed 2,500 cards; 2,495 of these were randomly inserted in Series I packs, while the other five were given away through a mail-in sweepstakes. Another 150,000 unsigned DiMaggio cards were inserted in Series I Count Goods packs only. Score later extended its DiMaggio promotion to Series I blister packs; one hundred signed and twelve thousand unsigned cards were randomly inserted in these packs. Also a special "World Series II" trivia card was inserted into each pack. These cards highlight crucial games and heroes from past Octobers. Topical subsets included in the set focus on Rookie Prospects (395-424), No-Hit Club (425-428), Highlights (429-430), AL All-Stars (431-440); with color montages displaying Chris Greco's player caricatures; Dream Team (441-442), Rookie Prospects (736-772), NL All-Stars (773-782), Highlights (783, 795-797), No-Hit Club (784-787), Draft Picks (799-810), Memorabilia (878-882), and Dream Team (883-893). All of the Rookie Prospects (736-772) can be found with or without the Rookie Prospect stripe. The cards are numbered on the back. Rookie Cards in the set include Cliff Floyd, Brent Gates, Benji Gil, Tyler Green, Manny Ramirez, Scott Ruffcorn, Aaron Sele, Allen Watson, and Bob Zupcic. Chuck Knoblauch, 1991 American League Rookie of the Year, autographed 3,000 of his own 1990 Score Draft Pick cards (card number 672) in gold ink, 2,989 were randomly inserted in Series 2 poly packs, while the other 11 were given away in a sweepstakes. The backs of these Knoblauch

autograph cards have special holograms to differentiate them.

	MINT	NRMT	EXC
COMPLETE SET (893)	16.00	7.25	2.00
COMPLETE FACT.SET (910)	20.00	9.00	2.50
COMPLETE SERIES 1 (442)	8.00	3.60	1.00
COMPLETE SERIES 2 (451)	8.00	3.60	1.00
COMMON CARD (1-442)	.05	.02	.01
COMMON CARD (443-893)	.05	.02	.01
☐ 1 Ken Griffey Jr.	1.50	.70	.19
☐ 2 Nolan Ryan	.75	.35	.09
☐ 3 Will Clark	.15	.07	.02
☐ 4 Dave Justice	.15	.07	.02
☐ 5 Dave Henderson	.05	.02	.01
☐ 6 Bret Saberhagen	.15	.07	.02
☐ 7 Fred McGriff	.15	.07	.02
☐ 8 Erik Hanson	.05	.02	.01
☐ 9 Darryl Strawberry	.10	.05	.01
☐ 10 Dwight Gooden	.05	.02	.01
☐ 11 Juan Gonzalez	.40	.18	.05
☐ 12 Mark Langston	.15	.07	.02
☐ 13 Lonnie Smith	.05	.02	.01
☐ 14 Jeff Montgomery	.10	.05	.01
☐ 15 Roberto Alomar	.20	.09	.03
☐ 16 Delino DeShields	.10	.05	.01
☐ 17 Steve Bedrosian	.05	.02	.01
☐ 18 Terry Pendleton	.15	.07	.02
☐ 19 Mark Carreon	.05	.02	.01
☐ 20 Mark McGwire	.15	.07	.02
☐ 21 Roger Clemens	.20	.09	.03
☐ 22 Chuck Crim	.05	.02	.01
☐ 23 Don Mattingly	.50	.23	.06
☐ 24 Dickie Thon	.05	.02	.01
☐ 25 Ron Gant	.15	.07	.02
☐ 26 Milt Cuyler	.05	.02	.01
☐ 27 Mike Macfarlane	.05	.02	.01
☐ 28 Dan Gladden	.05	.02	.01
☐ 29 Melido Perez	.05	.02	.01
☐ 30 Willie Randolph	.10	.05	.01
☐ 31 Albert Belle	.50	.23	.06
☐ 32 Dave Winfield	.15	.07	.02
☐ 33 Jimmy Jones	.05	.02	.01
☐ 34 Kevin Gross	.05	.02	.01
☐ 35 Andres Galarraga	.15	.07	.02
☐ 36 Mike Devereaux	.10	.05	.01
☐ 37 Chris Bosio	.05	.02	.01
☐ 38 Mike LaValliere	.05	.02	.01
☐ 39 Gary Gaetti	.05	.02	.01
☐ 40 Felix Jose	.05	.02	.01
☐ 41 Alvaro Espinoza	.05	.02	.01
☐ 42 Rick Aguilera	.10	.05	.01
☐ 43 Mike Gallego	.05	.02	.01
☐ 44 Eric Gunderson	.10	.05	.01
☐ 45 George Bell	.05	.02	.01
☐ 46 Tom Brunansky	.05	.02	.01
☐ 47 Steve Farr	.05	.02	.01
☐ 48 Duane Ward	.05	.02	.01
☐ 49 David Wells	.10	.05	.01
☐ 50 Cecil Fielder	.15	.07	.02
☐ 51 Walt Weiss	.05	.02	.01
☐ 52 Todd Zeile	.10	.05	.01
☐ 53 Doug Jones	.05	.02	.01
☐ 54 Bob Walk	.05	.02	.01
☐ 55 Rafael Palmeiro	.15	.07	.02
☐ 56 Rob Deer	.05	.02	.01
☐ 57 Paul O'Neill	.15	.07	.02
☐ 58 Jeff Reardon	.10	.05	.01
☐ 59 Randy Ready	.05	.02	.01
☐ 60 Scott Erickson	.05	.02	.01

☐ 61	Paul Molitor	.15	.07	.02
☐ 62	Jack McDowell	.15	.07	.02
☐ 63	Jim Acker	.05	.02	.01
☐ 64	Jay Buhner	.15	.07	.02
☐ 65	Travis Fryman	.15	.07	.02
☐ 66	Marquis Grissom	.15	.07	.02
☐ 67	Mike Harkey	.05	.02	.01
☐ 68	Luis Polonia	.05	.02	.01
☐ 69	Ken Caminiti	.15	.07	.02
☐ 70	Chris Sabo	.05	.02	.01
☐ 71	Gregg Olson	.05	.02	.01
☐ 72	Carlton Fisk	.15	.07	.02
☐ 73	Juan Samuel	.05	.02	.01
☐ 74	Todd Stottlemyre	.05	.02	.01
☐ 75	Andre Dawson	.15	.07	.02
☐ 76	Alvin Davis	.05	.02	.01
☐ 77	Bill Doran	.05	.02	.01
☐ 78	B.J. Surhoff	.05	.02	.01
☐ 79	Kirk McCaskill	.05	.02	.01
☐ 80	Dale Murphy	.15	.07	.02
☐ 81	Jose DeLeon	.05	.02	.01
☐ 82	Alex Fernandez	.15	.07	.02
☐ 83	Ivan Calderon	.05	.02	.01
☐ 84	Brent Mayne	.05	.02	.01
☐ 85	Jody Reed	.05	.02	.01
☐ 86	Randy Tomlin	.05	.02	.01
☐ 87	Randy Milligan	.05	.02	.01
☐ 88	Pascual Perez	.05	.02	.01
☐ 89	Hensley Meulens	.05	.02	.01
☐ 90	Joe Carter	.15	.07	.02
☐ 91	Mike Moore	.05	.02	.01
☐ 92	Ozzie Guillen	.10	.05	.01
☐ 93	Shawn Hillegas	.05	.02	.01
☐ 94	Chili Davis	.15	.07	.02
☐ 95	Vince Coleman	.05	.02	.01
☐ 96	Jimmy Key	.10	.05	.01
☐ 97	Billy Ripken	.05	.02	.01
☐ 98	Dave Smith	.05	.02	.01
☐ 99	Tom Bolton	.05	.02	.01
☐ 100	Barry Larkin	.15	.07	.02
☐ 101	Kenny Rogers	.05	.02	.01
☐ 102	Mike Boddicker	.05	.02	.01
☐ 103	Kevin Elster	.05	.02	.01
☐ 104	Ken Hill	.15	.07	.02
☐ 105	Charlie Leibrandt	.05	.02	.01
☐ 106	Pat Combs	.05	.02	.01
☐ 107	Hubie Brooks	.05	.02	.01
☐ 108	Julio Franco	.10	.05	.01
☐ 109	Vicente Palacios	.05	.02	.01
☐ 110	Kal Daniels	.05	.02	.01
☐ 111	Bruce Hurst	.05	.02	.01
☐ 112	Willie McGee	.10	.05	.01
☐ 113	Ted Power	.05	.02	.01
☐ 114	Milt Thompson	.05	.02	.01
☐ 115	Doug Drabek	.10	.05	.01
☐ 116	Rafael Belliard	.05	.02	.01
☐ 117	Scott Garrelts	.05	.02	.01
☐ 118	Terry Mulholland	.05	.02	.01
☐ 119	Jay Howell	.05	.02	.01
☐ 120	Danny Jackson	.05	.02	.01
☐ 121	Scott Ruskin	.05	.02	.01
☐ 122	Robin Ventura	.15	.07	.02
☐ 123	Bip Roberts	.05	.02	.01
☐ 124	Jeff Russell	.05	.02	.01
☐ 125	Hal Morris	.10	.05	.01
☐ 126	Teddy Higuera	.05	.02	.01
☐ 127	Luis Sojo	.05	.02	.01
☐ 128	Carlos Baerga	.30	.14	.04
☐ 129	Jeff Ballard	.05	.02	.01
☐ 130	Tom Gordon	.05	.02	.01
☐ 131	Sid Bream	.05	.02	.01
☐ 132	Rance Mulliniks	.05	.02	.01
☐ 133	Andy Benes	.10	.05	.01
☐ 134	Mickey Tettleton	.10	.05	.01
☐ 135	Rich DeLucia	.05	.02	.01
☐ 136	Tom Pagnozzi	.05	.02	.01
☐ 137	Harold Baines	.15	.07	.02
☐ 138	Danny Darwin	.05	.02	.01
☐ 139	Kevin Bass	.05	.02	.01
☐ 140	Chris Nabholz	.05	.02	.01
☐ 141	Pete O'Brien	.05	.02	.01
☐ 142	Jeff Treadway	.05	.02	.01
☐ 143	Mickey Morandini	.05	.02	.01
☐ 144	Eric King	.05	.02	.01
☐ 145	Danny Tartabull	.10	.05	.01
☐ 146	Lance Johnson	.05	.02	.01
☐ 147	Casey Candaele	.05	.02	.01
☐ 148	Felix Fermin	.05	.02	.01
☐ 149	Rich Rodriguez	.05	.02	.01
☐ 150	Dwight Evans	.10	.05	.01
☐ 151	Joe Klink	.05	.02	.01
☐ 152	Kevin Reimer	.05	.02	.01
☐ 153	Orlando Merced	.05	.02	.01
☐ 154	Mel Hall	.05	.02	.01
☐ 155	Randy Myers	.15	.07	.02
☐ 156	Greg A. Harris	.05	.02	.01
☐ 157	Jeff Brantley	.05	.02	.01
☐ 158	Jim Eisenreich	.05	.02	.01
☐ 159	Luis Rivera	.05	.02	.01
☐ 160	Cris Carpenter	.05	.02	.01
☐ 161	Bruce Ruffin	.05	.02	.01
☐ 162	Omar Vizquel	.05	.02	.01
☐ 163	Gerald Alexander	.05	.02	.01
☐ 164	Mark Guthrie	.05	.02	.01
☐ 165	Scott Lewis	.05	.02	.01
☐ 166	Bill Sampen	.05	.02	.01
☐ 167	Dave Anderson	.05	.02	.01
☐ 168	Kevin McReynolds	.05	.02	.01
☐ 169	Jose Vizcaino	.05	.02	.01
☐ 170	Bob Geren	.05	.02	.01
☐ 171	Mike Morgan	.05	.02	.01
☐ 172	Jim Gott	.05	.02	.01
☐ 173	Mike Pagliarulo	.05	.02	.01
☐ 174	Mike Jeffcoat	.05	.02	.01
☐ 175	Craig Lefferts	.05	.02	.01
☐ 176	Steve Finley	.10	.05	.01
☐ 177	Wally Backman	.05	.02	.01
☐ 178	Kent Mercker	.05	.02	.01
☐ 179	John Cerutti	.05	.02	.01
☐ 180	Jay Bell	.10	.05	.01
☐ 181	Dale Sveum	.05	.02	.01
☐ 182	Greg Gagne	.05	.02	.01
☐ 183	Donnie Hill	.05	.02	.01
☐ 184	Rex Hudler	.05	.02	.01
☐ 185	Pat Kelly	.05	.02	.01
☐ 186	Jeff D. Robinson	.05	.02	.01
☐ 187	Jeff Gray	.05	.02	.01
☐ 188	Jerry Willard	.05	.02	.01
☐ 189	Carlos Quintana	.05	.02	.01
☐ 190	Dennis Eckersley	.10	.05	.01
☐ 191	Kelly Downs	.05	.02	.01
☐ 192	Gregg Jefferies	.15	.07	.02
☐ 193	Darrin Fletcher	.05	.02	.01
☐ 194	Mike Jackson	.05	.02	.01
☐ 195	Eddie Murray	.15	.07	.02
☐ 196	Bill Landrum	.05	.02	.01
☐ 197	Eric Yelding	.05	.02	.01
☐ 198	Devon White	.10	.05	.01
☐ 199	Larry Walker	.15	.07	.02
☐ 200	Ryne Sandberg	.25	.11	.03
☐ 201	Dave Magadan	.05	.02	.01
☐ 202	Steve Chitren	.05	.02	.01

☐ 203 Scott Fletcher	.05	.02	.01
☐ 204 Dwayne Henry	.05	.02	.01
☐ 205 Scott Coolbaugh	.05	.02	.01
☐ 206 Tracy Jones	.05	.02	.01
☐ 207 Von Hayes	.05	.02	.01
☐ 208 Bob Melvin	.05	.02	.01
☐ 209 Scott Scudder	.05	.02	.01
☐ 210 Luis Gonzalez	.10	.05	.01
☐ 211 Scott Sanderson	.05	.02	.01
☐ 212 Chris Donnels	.05	.02	.01
☐ 213 Heathcliff Slocumb	.10	.05	.01
☐ 214 Mike Timlin	.05	.02	.01
☐ 215 Brian Harper	.05	.02	.01
☐ 216 Juan Berenguer UER	.05	.02	.01
(Decimal point missing in IP total)			
☐ 217 Mike Henneman	.05	.02	.01
☐ 218 Bill Spiers	.05	.02	.01
☐ 219 Scott Terry	.05	.02	.01
☐ 220 Frank Viola	.05	.02	.01
☐ 221 Mark Eichhorn	.05	.02	.01
☐ 222 Ernest Riles	.05	.02	.01
☐ 223 Ray Lankford	.15	.07	.02
☐ 224 Pete Harnisch	.05	.02	.01
☐ 225 Bobby Bonilla	.15	.07	.02
☐ 226 Mike Scioscia	.05	.02	.01
☐ 227 Joel Skinner	.05	.02	.01
☐ 228 Brian Holman	.05	.02	.01
☐ 229 Gilberto Reyes	.05	.02	.01
☐ 230 Matt Williams	.20	.09	.03
☐ 231 Jaime Navarro	.05	.02	.01
☐ 232 Jose Rijo	.10	.05	.01
☐ 233 Atlee Hammaker	.05	.02	.01
☐ 234 Tim Teufel	.05	.02	.01
☐ 235 John Kruk	.15	.07	.02
☐ 236 Kurt Stillwell	.05	.02	.01
☐ 237 Dan Pasqua	.05	.02	.01
☐ 238 Tim Crews	.05	.02	.01
☐ 239 Dave Gallagher	.05	.02	.01
☐ 240 Leo Gomez	.05	.02	.01
☐ 241 Steve Avery	.15	.07	.02
☐ 242 Bill Gullickson	.05	.02	.01
☐ 243 Mark Portugal	.05	.02	.01
☐ 244 Lee Guetterman	.05	.02	.01
☐ 245 Benito Santiago	.05	.02	.01
☐ 246 Jim Gantner	.05	.02	.01
☐ 247 Robby Thompson	.05	.02	.01
☐ 248 Terry Shumpert	.05	.02	.01
☐ 249 Mike Bell	.05	.02	.01
☐ 250 Harold Reynolds	.05	.02	.01
☐ 251 Mike Felder	.05	.02	.01
☐ 252 Bill Pecota	.05	.02	.01
☐ 253 Bill Krueger	.05	.02	.01
☐ 254 Alfredo Griffin	.05	.02	.01
☐ 255 Lou Whitaker	.15	.07	.02
☐ 256 Roy Smith	.05	.02	.01
☐ 257 Jerald Clark	.05	.02	.01
☐ 258 Sammy Sosa	.15	.07	.02
☐ 259 Tim Naehring	.05	.02	.01
☐ 260 Dave Righetti	.05	.02	.01
☐ 261 Paul Gibson	.05	.02	.01
☐ 262 Chris James	.05	.02	.01
☐ 263 Larry Andersen	.05	.02	.01
☐ 264 Storm Davis	.05	.02	.01
☐ 265 Jose Lind	.05	.02	.01
☐ 266 Greg Hibbard	.05	.02	.01
☐ 267 Norm Charlton	.05	.02	.01
☐ 268 Paul Kilgus	.05	.02	.01
☐ 269 Greg Maddux	.75	.35	.09
☐ 270 Ellis Burks	.10	.05	.01
☐ 271 Frank Tanana	.05	.02	.01
☐ 272 Gene Larkin	.05	.02	.01
☐ 273 Ron Hassey	.05	.02	.01
☐ 274 Jeff M. Robinson	.05	.02	.01
☐ 275 Steve Howe	.05	.02	.01
☐ 276 Daryl Boston	.05	.02	.01
☐ 277 Mark Lee	.05	.02	.01
☐ 278 Jose Segura	.05	.02	.01
☐ 279 Lance Blankenship	.05	.02	.01
☐ 280 Don Slaught	.05	.02	.01
☐ 281 Russ Swan	.05	.02	.01
☐ 282 Bob Tewksbury	.05	.02	.01
☐ 283 Geno Petralli	.05	.02	.01
☐ 284 Shane Mack	.05	.02	.01
☐ 285 Bob Scanlan	.05	.02	.01
☐ 286 Tim Leary	.05	.02	.01
☐ 287 John Smoltz	.15	.07	.02
☐ 288 Pat Borders	.05	.02	.01
☐ 289 Mark Davidson	.05	.02	.01
☐ 290 Sam Horn	.05	.02	.01
☐ 291 Lenny Harris	.05	.02	.01
☐ 292 Franklin Stubbs	.05	.02	.01
☐ 293 Thomas Howard	.05	.02	.01
☐ 294 Steve Lyons	.05	.02	.01
☐ 295 Francisco Oliveras	.05	.02	.01
☐ 296 Terry Leach	.05	.02	.01
☐ 297 Barry Jones	.05	.02	.01
☐ 298 Lance Parrish	.10	.05	.01
☐ 299 Wally Whitehurst	.05	.02	.01
☐ 300 Bob Welch	.05	.02	.01
☐ 301 Charlie Hayes	.10	.05	.01
☐ 302 Charlie Hough	.10	.05	.01
☐ 303 Gary Redus	.05	.02	.01
☐ 304 Scott Bradley	.05	.02	.01
☐ 305 Jose Oquendo	.05	.02	.01
☐ 306 Pete Incaviglia	.05	.02	.01
☐ 307 Marvin Freeman	.05	.02	.01
☐ 308 Gary Pettis	.05	.02	.01
☐ 309 Joe Slusarski	.05	.02	.01
☐ 310 Kevin Seitzer	.05	.02	.01
☐ 311 Jeff Reed	.05	.02	.01
☐ 312 Pat Tabler	.05	.02	.01
☐ 313 Mike Maddux	.05	.02	.01
☐ 314 Bob Milacki	.05	.02	.01
☐ 315 Eric Anthony	.05	.02	.01
☐ 316 Dante Bichette	.20	.09	.03
☐ 317 Steve Decker	.05	.02	.01
☐ 318 Jack Clark	.10	.05	.01
☐ 319 Doug Dascenzo	.05	.02	.01
☐ 320 Scott Leius	.05	.02	.01
☐ 321 Jim Lindeman	.05	.02	.01
☐ 322 Bryan Harvey	.05	.02	.01
☐ 323 Spike Owen	.05	.02	.01
☐ 324 Roberto Kelly	.10	.05	.01
☐ 325 Stan Belinda	.05	.02	.01
☐ 326 Joey Cora	.05	.02	.01
☐ 327 Jeff Innis	.05	.02	.01
☐ 328 Willie Wilson	.05	.02	.01
☐ 329 Juan Agosto	.05	.02	.01
☐ 330 Charles Nagy	.10	.05	.01
☐ 331 Scott Bailes	.05	.02	.01
☐ 332 Pete Schourek	.10	.05	.01
☐ 333 Mike Flanagan	.05	.02	.01
☐ 334 Omar Olivares	.05	.02	.01
☐ 335 Dennis Lamp	.05	.02	.01
☐ 336 Tommy Greene	.05	.02	.01
☐ 337 Randy Velarde	.05	.02	.01
☐ 338 Tom Lampkin	.05	.02	.01
☐ 339 John Russell	.05	.02	.01
☐ 340 Bob Kipper	.05	.02	.01
☐ 341 Todd Burns	.05	.02	.01
☐ 342 Ron Jones	.05	.02	.01

☐ 343	Dave Valle	.05	.02	.01
☐ 344	Mike Heath	.05	.02	.01
☐ 345	John Olerud	.15	.07	.02
☐ 346	Gerald Young	.05	.02	.01
☐ 347	Ken Patterson	.05	.02	.01
☐ 348	Les Lancaster	.05	.02	.01
☐ 349	Steve Crawford	.05	.02	.01
☐ 350	John Candelaria	.05	.02	.01
☐ 351	Mike Aldrete	.05	.02	.01
☐ 352	Mariano Duncan	.05	.02	.01
☐ 353	Julio Machado	.05	.02	.01
☐ 354	Ken Williams	.05	.02	.01
☐ 355	Walt Terrell	.05	.02	.01
☐ 356	Mitch Williams	.10	.05	.01
☐ 357	Al Newman	.05	.02	.01
☐ 358	Bud Black	.05	.02	.01
☐ 359	Joe Hesketh	.05	.02	.01
☐ 360	Paul Assenmacher	.05	.02	.01
☐ 361	Bo Jackson	.15	.07	.02
☐ 362	Jeff Blauser	.10	.05	.01
☐ 363	Mike Brumley	.05	.02	.01
☐ 364	Jim Deshaies	.05	.02	.01
☐ 365	Brady Anderson	.10	.05	.01
☐ 366	Chuck McElroy	.05	.02	.01
☐ 367	Matt Merullo	.05	.02	.01
☐ 368	Tim Belcher	.05	.02	.01
☐ 369	Luis Aquino	.05	.02	.01
☐ 370	Joe Oliver	.05	.02	.01
☐ 371	Greg Swindell	.05	.02	.01
☐ 372	Lee Stevens	.05	.02	.01
☐ 373	Mark Knudson	.05	.02	.01
☐ 374	Bill Wegman	.05	.02	.01
☐ 375	Jerry Don Gleaton	.05	.02	.01
☐ 376	Pedro Guerrero	.05	.02	.01
☐ 377	Randy Bush	.05	.02	.01
☐ 378	Greg W. Harris	.05	.02	.01
☐ 379	Eric Plunk	.05	.02	.01
☐ 380	Jose DeJesus	.05	.02	.01
☐ 381	Bobby Witt	.05	.02	.01
☐ 382	Curtis Wilkerson	.05	.02	.01
☐ 383	Gene Nelson	.05	.02	.01
☐ 384	Wes Chamberlain	.05	.02	.01
☐ 385	Tom Henke	.10	.05	.01
☐ 386	Mark Lemke	.05	.02	.01
☐ 387	Greg Briley	.05	.02	.01
☐ 388	Rafael Ramirez	.05	.02	.01
☐ 389	Tony Fossas	.05	.02	.01
☐ 390	Henry Cotto	.05	.02	.01
☐ 391	Tim Hulett	.05	.02	.01
☐ 392	Dean Palmer	.10	.05	.01
☐ 393	Glenn Braggs	.05	.02	.01
☐ 394	Mark Salas	.05	.02	.01
☐ 395	Rusty Meacham	.05	.02	.01
☐ 396	Andy Ashby	.05	.02	.01
☐ 397	Jose Melendez	.05	.02	.01
☐ 398	Warren Newson	.05	.02	.01
☐ 399	Frank Castillo	.05	.02	.01
☐ 400	Chito Martinez	.05	.02	.01
☐ 401	Bernie Williams	.15	.07	.02
☐ 402	Derek Bell	.10	.05	.01
☐ 403	Javier Ortiz	.05	.02	.01
☐ 404	Tim Sherrill	.05	.02	.01
☐ 405	Rob MacDonald	.05	.02	.01
☐ 406	Phil Plantier	.10	.05	.01
☐ 407	Troy Afenir	.05	.02	.01
☐ 408	Gino Minutelli	.05	.02	.01
☐ 409	Reggie Jefferson	.05	.02	.01
☐ 410	Mike Remlinger	.05	.02	.01
☐ 411	Carlos Rodriguez	.05	.02	.01
☐ 412	Joe Redfield	.05	.02	.01
☐ 413	Alonzo Powell	.05	.02	.01

☐ 414	Scott Livingstone UER (Travis Fryman, not Woody, should be referenced on back)	.05	.02	.01
☐ 415	Scott Kamieniecki	.05	.02	.01
☐ 416	Tim Spehr	.05	.02	.01
☐ 417	Brian Hunter	.05	.02	.01
☐ 418	Ced Landrum	.05	.02	.01
☐ 419	Bret Barberie	.05	.02	.01
☐ 420	Kevin Morton	.05	.02	.01
☐ 421	Doug Henry	.05	.02	.01
☐ 422	Doug Piatt	.05	.02	.01
☐ 423	Pat Rice	.05	.02	.01
☐ 424	Juan Guzman	.10	.05	.01
☐ 425	Nolan Ryan NH	.40	.18	.05
☐ 426	Tommy Greene NH	.05	.02	.01
☐ 427	Bob Milacki and Mike Flanagan NH (Mark Williamson and Gregg Olson)	.05	.02	.01
☐ 428	Wilson Alvarez NH	.10	.05	.01
☐ 429	Otis Nixon HL	.05	.02	.01
☐ 430	Rickey Henderson HL	.15	.07	.02
☐ 431	Cecil Fielder AS	.10	.05	.01
☐ 432	Julio Franco AS	.05	.02	.01
☐ 433	Cal Ripken AS	.50	.23	.06
☐ 434	Wade Boggs AS	.15	.07	.02
☐ 435	Joe Carter AS	.15	.07	.02
☐ 436	Ken Griffey Jr. AS	.75	.35	.09
☐ 437	Ruben Sierra AS	.10	.05	.01
☐ 438	Scott Erickson AS	.05	.02	.01
☐ 439	Tom Henke AS	.05	.02	.01
☐ 440	Terry Steinbach AS	.05	.02	.01
☐ 441	Rickey Henderson DT	.15	.07	.02
☐ 442	Ryne Sandberg DT	.25	.11	.03
☐ 443	Otis Nixon	.05	.02	.01
☐ 444	Scott Radinsky	.05	.02	.01
☐ 445	Mark Grace	.15	.07	.02
☐ 446	Tony Pena	.05	.02	.01
☐ 447	Billy Hatcher	.05	.02	.01
☐ 448	Glenallen Hill	.05	.02	.01
☐ 449	Chris Gwynn	.05	.02	.01
☐ 450	Tom Glavine	.15	.07	.02
☐ 451	John Habyan	.05	.02	.01
☐ 452	Al Osuna	.05	.02	.01
☐ 453	Tony Phillips	.15	.07	.02
☐ 454	Greg Cadaret	.05	.02	.01
☐ 455	Rob Dibble	.05	.02	.01
☐ 456	Rick Honeycutt	.05	.02	.01
☐ 457	Jerome Walton	.05	.02	.01
☐ 458	Mookie Wilson	.05	.02	.01
☐ 459	Mark Gubicza	.05	.02	.01
☐ 460	Craig Biggio	.15	.07	.02
☐ 461	Dave Cochrane	.05	.02	.01
☐ 462	Keith Miller	.05	.02	.01
☐ 463	Alex Cole	.05	.02	.01
☐ 464	Pete Smith	.05	.02	.01
☐ 465	Brett Butler	.15	.07	.02
☐ 466	Jeff Huson	.05	.02	.01
☐ 467	Steve Lake	.05	.02	.01
☐ 468	Lloyd Moseby	.05	.02	.01
☐ 469	Tim McIntosh	.05	.02	.01
☐ 470	Dennis Martinez	.10	.05	.01
☐ 471	Greg Myers	.05	.02	.01
☐ 472	Mackey Sasser	.05	.02	.01
☐ 473	Junior Ortiz	.05	.02	.01
☐ 474	Greg Olson	.05	.02	.01
☐ 475	Steve Sax	.05	.02	.01
☐ 476	Ricky Jordan	.05	.02	.01
☐ 477	Max Venable	.05	.02	.01
☐ 478	Brian McRae	.15	.07	.02

☐ 479	Doug Simons	.05	.02	.01
☐ 480	Rickey Henderson	.15	.07	.02
☐ 481	Gary Varsho	.05	.02	.01
☐ 482	Carl Willis	.05	.02	.01
☐ 483	Rick Wilkins	.05	.02	.01
☐ 484	Donn Pall	.05	.02	.01
☐ 485	Edgar Martinez	.15	.07	.02
☐ 486	Tom Foley	.05	.02	.01
☐ 487	Mark Williamson	.05	.02	.01
☐ 488	Jack Armstrong	.05	.02	.01
☐ 489	Gary Carter	.15	.07	.02
☐ 490	Ruben Sierra	.15	.07	.02
☐ 491	Gerald Perry	.05	.02	.01
☐ 492	Rob Murphy	.05	.02	.01
☐ 493	Zane Smith	.05	.02	.01
☐ 494	Darryl Kile	.05	.02	.01
☐ 495	Kelly Gruber	.05	.02	.01
☐ 496	Jerry Browne	.05	.02	.01
☐ 497	Darryl Hamilton	.10	.05	.01
☐ 498	Mike Stanton	.05	.02	.01
☐ 499	Mark Leonard	.05	.02	.01
☐ 500	Jose Canseco	.15	.07	.02
☐ 501	Dave Martinez	.05	.02	.01
☐ 502	Jose Guzman	.05	.02	.01
☐ 503	Terry Kennedy	.05	.02	.01
☐ 504	Ed Sprague	.10	.05	.01
☐ 505	Frank Thomas UER (His Gulf Coast League stats are wrong)	1.50	.70	.19
☐ 506	Darren Daulton	.15	.07	.02
☐ 507	Kevin Tapani	.05	.02	.01
☐ 508	Luis Salazar	.05	.02	.01
☐ 509	Paul Faries	.05	.02	.01
☐ 510	Sandy Alomar Jr.	.10	.05	.01
☐ 511	Jeff King	.05	.02	.01
☐ 512	Gary Thurman	.05	.02	.01
☐ 513	Chris Hammond	.05	.02	.01
☐ 514	Pedro Munoz	.10	.05	.01
☐ 515	Alan Trammell	.15	.07	.02
☐ 516	Geronimo Pena	.05	.02	.01
☐ 517	Rodney McCray UER (Stole 6 bases in 1990, not 5; career totals are correct at 7)	.05	.02	.01
☐ 518	Manny Lee	.05	.02	.01
☐ 519	Junior Felix	.05	.02	.01
☐ 520	Kirk Gibson	.15	.07	.02
☐ 521	Darrin Jackson	.05	.02	.01
☐ 522	John Burkett	.10	.05	.01
☐ 523	Jeff Johnson	.05	.02	.01
☐ 524	Jim Corsi	.05	.02	.01
☐ 525	Robin Yount	.15	.07	.02
☐ 526	Jamie Quirk	.05	.02	.01
☐ 527	Bob Ojeda	.05	.02	.01
☐ 528	Mark Lewis	.05	.02	.01
☐ 529	Bryn Smith	.05	.02	.01
☐ 530	Kent Hrbek	.10	.05	.01
☐ 531	Dennis Boyd	.05	.02	.01
☐ 532	Ron Karkovice	.05	.02	.01
☐ 533	Don August	.05	.02	.01
☐ 534	Todd Frohwirth	.05	.02	.01
☐ 535	Wally Joyner	.10	.05	.01
☐ 536	Dennis Rasmussen	.05	.02	.01
☐ 537	Andy Allanson	.05	.02	.01
☐ 538	Goose Gossage	.10	.05	.01
☐ 539	John Marzano	.05	.02	.01
☐ 540	Cal Ripken	1.00	.45	.12
☐ 541	Bill Swift UER (Brewers logo on front)	.05	.02	.01
☐ 542	Kevin Appier	.10	.05	.01
☐ 543	Dave Bergman	.05	.02	.01
☐ 544	Bernard Gilkey	.10	.05	.01
☐ 545	Mike Greenwell	.15	.07	.02
☐ 546	Jose Uribe	.05	.02	.01
☐ 547	Jesse Orosco	.05	.02	.01
☐ 548	Bob Patterson	.05	.02	.01
☐ 549	Mike Stanley	.10	.05	.01
☐ 550	Howard Johnson	.05	.02	.01
☐ 551	Joe Orsulak	.05	.02	.01
☐ 552	Dick Schofield	.05	.02	.01
☐ 553	Dave Hollins	.05	.02	.01
☐ 554	David Segui	.05	.02	.01
☐ 555	Barry Bonds	.25	.11	.03
☐ 556	Mo Vaughn	.40	.18	.05
☐ 557	Craig Wilson	.05	.02	.01
☐ 558	Bobby Rose	.05	.02	.01
☐ 559	Rod Nichols	.05	.02	.01
☐ 560	Len Dykstra	.15	.07	.02
☐ 561	Craig Grebeck	.05	.02	.01
☐ 562	Darren Lewis	.10	.05	.01
☐ 563	Todd Benzinger	.05	.02	.01
☐ 564	Ed Whitson	.05	.02	.01
☐ 565	Jesse Barfield	.05	.02	.01
☐ 566	Lloyd McClendon	.05	.02	.01
☐ 567	Dan Plesac	.05	.02	.01
☐ 568	Danny Cox	.05	.02	.01
☐ 569	Skeeter Barnes	.05	.02	.01
☐ 570	Bobby Thigpen	.05	.02	.01
☐ 571	Deion Sanders	.20	.09	.03
☐ 572	Chuck Knoblauch	.15	.07	.02
☐ 573	Matt Nokes	.05	.02	.01
☐ 574	Herm Winningham	.05	.02	.01
☐ 575	Tom Candiotti	.05	.02	.01
☐ 576	Jeff Bagwell	.50	.23	.06
☐ 577	Brook Jacoby	.05	.02	.01
☐ 578	Chico Walker	.05	.02	.01
☐ 579	Brian Downing	.05	.02	.01
☐ 580	Dave Stewart	.15	.07	.02
☐ 581	Francisco Cabrera	.05	.02	.01
☐ 582	Rene Gonzales	.05	.02	.01
☐ 583	Stan Javier	.05	.02	.01
☐ 584	Randy Johnson	.25	.11	.03
☐ 585	Chuck Finley	.05	.02	.01
☐ 586	Mark Gardner	.05	.02	.01
☐ 587	Mark Whiten	.10	.05	.01
☐ 588	Garry Templeton	.05	.02	.01
☐ 589	Gary Sheffield	.15	.07	.02
☐ 590	Ozzie Smith	.20	.09	.03
☐ 591	Candy Maldonado	.05	.02	.01
☐ 592	Mike Sharperson	.05	.02	.01
☐ 593	Carlos Martinez	.05	.02	.01
☐ 594	Scott Bankhead	.05	.02	.01
☐ 595	Tim Wallach	.05	.02	.01
☐ 596	Tino Martinez	.15	.07	.02
☐ 597	Roger McDowell	.05	.02	.01
☐ 598	Cory Snyder	.05	.02	.01
☐ 599	Andujar Cedeno	.05	.02	.01
☐ 600	Kirby Puckett	.30	.14	.04
☐ 601	Rick Parker	.05	.02	.01
☐ 602	Todd Hundley	.05	.02	.01
☐ 603	Greg Litton	.05	.02	.01
☐ 604	Dave Johnson	.05	.02	.01
☐ 605	John Franco	.15	.07	.02
☐ 606	Mike Fetters	.05	.02	.01
☐ 607	Luis Alicea	.05	.02	.01
☐ 608	Trevor Wilson	.05	.02	.01
☐ 609	Rob Ducey	.05	.02	.01
☐ 610	Ramon Martinez	.15	.07	.02
☐ 611	Dave Burba	.05	.02	.01
☐ 612	Dwight Smith	.05	.02	.01
☐ 613	Kevin Maas	.05	.02	.01
☐ 614	John Costello	.05	.02	.01

☐ 615	Glenn Davis	.05	.02	.01			
☐ 616	Shawn Abner	.05	.02	.01			
☐ 617	Scott Hemond	.05	.02	.01			
☐ 618	Tom Prince	.05	.02	.01			
☐ 619	Wally Ritchie	.05	.02	.01			
☐ 620	Jim Abbott	.15	.07	.02			
☐ 621	Charlie O'Brien	.05	.02	.01			
☐ 622	Jack Daugherty	.05	.02	.01			
☐ 623	Tommy Gregg	.05	.02	.01			
☐ 624	Jeff Shaw	.05	.02	.01			
☐ 625	Tony Gwynn	.30	.14	.04			
☐ 626	Mark Leiter	.05	.02	.01			
☐ 627	Jim Clancy	.05	.02	.01			
☐ 628	Tim Layana	.05	.02	.01			
☐ 629	Jeff Schaefer	.05	.02	.01			
☐ 630	Lee Smith	.15	.07	.02			
☐ 631	Wade Taylor	.05	.02	.01			
☐ 632	Mike Simms	.05	.02	.01			
☐ 633	Terry Steinbach	.10	.05	.01			
☐ 634	Shawon Dunston	.05	.02	.01			
☐ 635	Tim Raines	.15	.07	.02			
☐ 636	Kirt Manwaring	.05	.02	.01			
☐ 637	Warren Cromartie	.05	.02	.01			
☐ 638	Luis Quinones	.05	.02	.01			
☐ 639	Greg Vaughn	.10	.05	.01			
☐ 640	Kevin Mitchell	.10	.05	.01			
☐ 641	Chris Hoiles	.10	.05	.01			
☐ 642	Tom Browning	.05	.02	.01			
☐ 643	Mitch Webster	.05	.02	.01			
☐ 644	Steve Olin	.05	.02	.01			
☐ 645	Tony Fernandez	.05	.02	.01			
☐ 646	Juan Bell	.05	.02	.01			
☐ 647	Joe Boever	.05	.02	.01			
☐ 648	Carney Lansford	.10	.05	.01			
☐ 649	Mike Benjamin	.05	.02	.01			
☐ 650	George Brett	.40	.18	.05			
☐ 651	Tim Burke	.05	.02	.01			
☐ 652	Jack Morris	.15	.07	.02			
☐ 653	Orel Hershiser	.15	.07	.02			
☐ 654	Mike Schooler	.05	.02	.01			
☐ 655	Andy Van Slyke	.10	.05	.01			
☐ 656	Dave Stieb	.05	.02	.01			
☐ 657	Dave Clark	.05	.02	.01			
☐ 658	Ben McDonald	.10	.05	.01			
☐ 659	John Smiley	.05	.02	.01			
☐ 660	Wade Boggs	.15	.07	.02			
☐ 661	Eric Bullock	.05	.02	.01			
☐ 662	Eric Show	.05	.02	.01			
☐ 663	Lenny Webster	.05	.02	.01			
☐ 664	Mike Huff	.05	.02	.01			
☐ 665	Rick Sutcliffe	.10	.05	.01			
☐ 666	Jeff Manto	.05	.02	.01			
☐ 667	Mike Fitzgerald	.05	.02	.01			
☐ 668	Matt Young	.05	.02	.01			
☐ 669	Dave West	.05	.02	.01			
☐ 670	Mike Hartley	.05	.02	.01			
☐ 671	Curt Schilling	.05	.02	.01			
☐ 672	Brian Bohanon	.05	.02	.01			
☐ 673	Cecil Espy	.05	.02	.01			
☐ 674	Joe Grahe	.05	.02	.01			
☐ 675	Sid Fernandez	.10	.05	.01			
☐ 676	Edwin Nunez	.05	.02	.01			
☐ 677	Hector Villanueva	.05	.02	.01			
☐ 678	Sean Berry	.10	.05	.01			
☐ 679	Dave Eiland	.05	.02	.01			
☐ 680	Dave Cone	.15	.07	.02			
☐ 681	Mike Bordick	.05	.02	.01			
☐ 682	Tony Castillo	.05	.02	.01			
☐ 683	John Barfield	.05	.02	.01			
☐ 684	Jeff Hamilton	.05	.02	.01			
☐ 685	Ken Dayley	.05	.02	.01			
☐ 686	Carmelo Martinez	.05	.02	.01
☐ 687	Mike Capel	.05	.02	.01
☐ 688	Scott Chiamparino	.05	.02	.01
☐ 689	Rich Gedman	.05	.02	.01
☐ 690	Rich Monteleone	.05	.02	.01
☐ 691	Alejandro Pena	.05	.02	.01
☐ 692	Oscar Azocar	.05	.02	.01
☐ 693	Jim Poole	.05	.02	.01
☐ 694	Mike Gardiner	.05	.02	.01
☐ 695	Steve Buechele	.05	.02	.01
☐ 696	Rudy Seanez	.05	.02	.01
☐ 697	Paul Abbott	.05	.02	.01
☐ 698	Steve Searcy	.05	.02	.01
☐ 699	Jose Offerman	.05	.02	.01
☐ 700	Ivan Rodriguez	.15	.07	.02
☐ 701	Joe Girardi	.05	.02	.01
☐ 702	Tony Perezchica	.05	.02	.01
☐ 703	Paul McClellan	.05	.02	.01
☐ 704	David Howard	.05	.02	.01
☐ 705	Dan Petry	.05	.02	.01
☐ 706	Jack Howell	.05	.02	.01
☐ 707	Jose Mesa	.05	.02	.01
☐ 708	Randy St. Claire	.05	.02	.01
☐ 709	Kevin Brown	.10	.05	.01
☐ 710	Ron Darling	.05	.02	.01
☐ 711	Jason Grimsley	.05	.02	.01
☐ 712	John Orton	.05	.02	.01
☐ 713	Shawn Boskie	.05	.02	.01
☐ 714	Pat Clements	.05	.02	.01
☐ 715	Brian Barnes	.05	.02	.01
☐ 716	Luis Lopez	.05	.02	.01
☐ 717	Bob McClure	.05	.02	.01
☐ 718	Mark Davis	.05	.02	.01
☐ 719	Dann Bilardello	.05	.02	.01
☐ 720	Tom Edens	.05	.02	.01
☐ 721	Willie Fraser	.05	.02	.01
☐ 722	Curt Young	.05	.02	.01
☐ 723	Neal Heaton	.05	.02	.01
☐ 724	Craig Worthington	.05	.02	.01
☐ 725	Mel Rojas	.05	.02	.01
☐ 726	Daryl Irvine	.05	.02	.01
☐ 727	Roger Mason	.05	.02	.01
☐ 728	Kirk Dressendorfer	.05	.02	.01
☐ 729	Scott Aldred	.05	.02	.01
☐ 730	Willie Blair	.05	.02	.01
☐ 731	Allan Anderson	.05	.02	.01
☐ 732	Dana Kiecker	.05	.02	.01
☐ 733	Jose Gonzalez	.05	.02	.01
☐ 734	Brian Drahman	.05	.02	.01
☐ 735	Brad Komminsk	.05	.02	.01
☐ 736	Arthur Rhodes	.05	.02	.01
☐ 737	Terry Mathews	.05	.02	.01
☐ 738	Jeff Fassero	.05	.02	.01
☐ 739	Mike Magnante	.05	.02	.01
☐ 740	Kip Gross	.05	.02	.01
☐ 741	Jim Hunter	.05	.02	.01
☐ 742	Jose Mota	.05	.02	.01
☐ 743	Joe Bitker	.05	.02	.01
☐ 744	Tim Mauser	.05	.02	.01
☐ 745	Ramon Garcia	.05	.02	.01
☐ 746	Rod Beck	.25	.11	.03
☐ 747	Jim Austin	.05	.02	.01
☐ 748	Keith Mitchell	.05	.02	.01
☐ 749	Wayne Rosenthal	.05	.02	.01
☐ 750	Bryan Hickerson	.05	.02	.01
☐ 751	Bruce Egloff	.05	.02	.01
☐ 752	John Wehner	.05	.02	.01
☐ 753	Darren Holmes	.05	.02	.01
☐ 754	Dave Hansen	.05	.02	.01
☐ 755	Mike Mussina	.25	.11	.03
☐ 756	Anthony Young	.05	.02	.01

☐ 757 Ron Tingley	.05	.02	.01
☐ 758 Ricky Bones	.05	.02	.01
☐ 759 Mark Wohlers	.10	.05	.01
☐ 760 Wilson Alvarez	.15	.07	.02
☐ 761 Harvey Pulliam	.05	.02	.01
☐ 762 Ryan Bowen	.05	.02	.01
☐ 763 Terry Bross	.05	.02	.01
☐ 764 Joel Johnston	.05	.02	.01
☐ 765 Terry McDaniel	.05	.02	.01
☐ 766 Esteban Beltre	.05	.02	.01
☐ 767 Rob Maurer	.05	.02	.01
☐ 768 Ted Wood	.05	.02	.01
☐ 769 Mo Sanford	.05	.02	.01
☐ 770 Jeff Carter	.05	.02	.01
☐ 771 Gil Heredia	.05	.02	.01
☐ 772 Monty Fariss	.05	.02	.01
☐ 773 Will Clark AS	.10	.05	.01
☐ 774 Ryne Sandberg AS	.15	.07	.02
☐ 775 Barry Larkin AS	.15	.07	.02
☐ 776 Howard Johnson AS	.05	.02	.01
☐ 777 Barry Bonds AS	.15	.07	.02
☐ 778 Brett Butler AS	.05	.02	.01
☐ 779 Tony Gwynn AS	.15	.07	.02
☐ 780 Ramon Martinez AS	.10	.05	.01
☐ 781 Lee Smith AS	.10	.05	.01
☐ 782 Mike Scioscia AS	.05	.02	.01
☐ 783 Dennis Martinez HL UER	.05	.02	.01
(Card has both 13th			
and 15th perfect game			
in Major League history)			
☐ 784 Dennis Martinez NH	.05	.02	.01
☐ 785 Mark Gardner NH	.05	.02	.01
☐ 786 Bret Saberhagen NH	.10	.05	.01
☐ 787 Kent Mercker NH	.05	.02	.01
Mark Wohlers			
Alejandro Pena			
☐ 788 Cal Ripken MVP	.50	.23	.06
☐ 789 Terry Pendleton MVP	.10	.05	.01
☐ 790 Roger Clemens CY	.15	.07	.02
☐ 791 Tom Glavine CY	.10	.05	.01
☐ 792 Chuck Knoblauch ROY	.10	.05	.01
☐ 793 Jeff Bagwell ROY	.25	.11	.03
☐ 794 Cal Ripken MANYR	.50	.23	.06
☐ 795 David Cone HL	.10	.05	.01
☐ 796 Kirby Puckett HL	.15	.07	.02
☐ 797 Steve Avery HL	.10	.05	.01
☐ 798 Jack Morris HL	.10	.05	.01
☐ 799 Allen Watson DC	.15	.07	.02
☐ 800 Manny Ramirez DC	3.00	1.35	.35
☐ 801 Cliff Floyd DC	.40	.18	.05
☐ 802 Al Shirley DC	.15	.07	.02
☐ 803 Brian Barber DC	.15	.07	.02
☐ 804 Jon Farrell DC	.05	.02	.01
☐ 805 Brent Gates DC	.10	.05	.01
☐ 806 Scott Ruffcorn DC	.05	.02	.01
☐ 807 Tyrone Hill DC	.05	.02	.01
☐ 808 Benji Gil DC	.25	.11	.03
☐ 809 Aaron Sele DC	.30	.14	.04
☐ 810 Tyler Green DC	.10	.05	.01
☐ 811 Chris Jones	.05	.02	.01
☐ 812 Steve Wilson	.05	.02	.01
☐ 813 Freddie Benavides	.05	.02	.01
☐ 814 Don Wakamatsu	.05	.02	.01
☐ 815 Mike Humphreys	.05	.02	.01
☐ 816 Scott Servais	.05	.02	.01
☐ 817 Rico Rossy	.05	.02	.01
☐ 818 John Ramos	.05	.02	.01
☐ 819 Rob Mallicoat	.05	.02	.01
☐ 820 Milt Hill	.05	.02	.01
☐ 821 Carlos Garcia	.10	.05	.01
☐ 822 Stan Royer	.05	.02	.01
☐ 823 Jeff Plympton	.05	.02	.01
☐ 824 Braulio Castillo	.05	.02	.01
☐ 825 David Haas	.05	.02	.01
☐ 826 Luis Mercedes	.05	.02	.01
☐ 827 Eric Karros	.20	.09	.03
☐ 828 Shawn Hare	.05	.02	.01
☐ 829 Reggie Sanders	.20	.09	.03
☐ 830 Tom Goodwin	.05	.02	.01
☐ 831 Dan Gakeler	.05	.02	.01
☐ 832 Stacy Jones	.05	.02	.01
☐ 833 Kim Batiste	.05	.02	.01
☐ 834 Cal Eldred	.05	.02	.01
☐ 835 Chris George	.05	.02	.01
☐ 836 Wayne Housie	.05	.02	.01
☐ 837 Mike Ignasiak	.05	.02	.01
☐ 838 Josias Manzanillo	.05	.02	.01
☐ 839 Jim Olander	.05	.02	.01
☐ 840 Gary Cooper	.05	.02	.01
☐ 841 Royce Clayton	.10	.05	.01
☐ 842 Hector Fajardo	.05	.02	.01
☐ 843 Blaine Beatty	.05	.02	.01
☐ 844 Jorge Pedre	.05	.02	.01
☐ 845 Kenny Lofton	1.00	.45	.12
☐ 846 Scott Brosius	.05	.02	.01
☐ 847 Chris Cron	.05	.02	.01
☐ 848 Denis Boucher	.05	.02	.01
☐ 849 Kyle Abbott	.05	.02	.01
☐ 850 Robert Zupcic	.05	.02	.01
☐ 851 Rheal Cormier	.05	.02	.01
☐ 852 Jim Lewis	.05	.02	.01
☐ 853 Anthony Telford	.05	.02	.01
☐ 854 Cliff Brantley	.05	.02	.01
☐ 855 Kevin Campbell	.05	.02	.01
☐ 856 Craig Shipley	.05	.02	.01
☐ 857 Chuck Carr	.05	.02	.01
☐ 858 Tony Eusebio	.05	.02	.01
☐ 859 Jim Thome	.75	.35	.09
☐ 860 Vinny Castilla RC	.50	.23	.06
☐ 861 Dann Howitt	.05	.02	.01
☐ 862 Kevin Ward	.05	.02	.01
☐ 863 Steve Wapnick	.05	.02	.01
☐ 864 Rod Brewer	.05	.02	.01
☐ 865 Todd Van Poppel	.15	.07	.02
☐ 866 Jose Hernandez	.05	.02	.01
☐ 867 Amalio Carreno	.05	.02	.01
☐ 868 Calvin Jones	.05	.02	.01
☐ 869 Jeff Gardner	.05	.02	.01
☐ 870 Jarvis Brown	.05	.02	.01
☐ 871 Eddie Taubensee	.05	.02	.01
☐ 872 Andy Mota	.05	.02	.01
☐ 873 Chris Haney	.05	.02	.01
☐ 874 Roberto Hernandez	.10	.05	.01
☐ 875 Laddie Renfroe	.05	.02	.01
☐ 876 Scott Cooper	.10	.05	.01
☐ 877 Armando Reynoso	.05	.02	.01
☐ 878 Ty Cobb MEMO	.25	.11	.03
☐ 879 Babe Ruth MEMO	.30	.14	.04
☐ 880 Honus Wagner MEMO	.15	.07	.02
☐ 881 Lou Gehrig MEMO	.25	.11	.03
☐ 882 Satchel Paige MEMO	.15	.07	.02
☐ 883 Will Clark DT	.20	.09	.03
☐ 884 Cal Ripken DT	2.00	.90	.25
☐ 885 Wade Boggs DT	.15	.07	.02
☐ 886 Kirby Puckett DT	.30	.14	.04
☐ 887 Tony Gwynn DT	.30	.14	.04
☐ 888 Craig Biggio DT	.10	.05	.01
☐ 889 Scott Erickson DT	.05	.02	.01
☐ 890 Tom Glavine DT	.10	.05	.01
☐ 891 Rob Dibble DT	.05	.02	.01
☐ 892 Mitch Williams DT	.05	.02	.01
☐ 893 Frank Thomas DT	1.50	.70	.19

☐ X672 Chuck Knoblauch AU 60.00 27.00   7.50
   (1990 Score card,
   autographed with
   special hologram on back)

1992 Score Impact Players

The 1992 Score Impact Players insert set was issued in two series each with 45 cards with the respective series of the 1992 regular issue Score cards. Five cards from the 45-card first (second) series were randomly inserted in each 1992 Score I (II) jumbo pack. The cards measure the standard size (2 1/2" by 3 1/2") and the fronts feature full-bleed color action player photos. The pictures are enhanced by a wide vertical stripe running near the left edge containing the words "90's Impact Player" and a narrower stripe at the bottom printed with the player's name. The stripes are team color-coded and intersect at the team logo in the lower left corner. The backs display close-up color player photos. The picture borders and background colors reflect the team's colors. A white box below the photo contains biographical and statistical information as well as a career summary. The cards are numbered on the back.

	MINT	NRMT	EXC
COMPLETE SET (90)	20.00	9.00	2.50
COMPLETE SERIES 1 (45)	14.00	6.25	1.75
COMPLETE SERIES 2 (45)	6.00	2.70	.75
COMMON CARD (1-45)	.10	.05	.01
COMMON CARD (46-90)	.10	.05	.01

☐	1 Chuck Knoblauch	.40	.18	.05
☐	2 Jeff Bagwell	1.25	.55	.16
☐	3 Juan Guzman	.10	.05	.01
☐	4 Milt Cuyler	.10	.05	.01
☐	5 Ivan Rodriguez	.30	.14	.04
☐	6 Rich DeLucia	.10	.05	.01
☐	7 Orlando Merced	.20	.09	.03
☐	8 Ray Lankford	.30	.14	.04
☐	9 Brian Hunter	.10	.05	.01
☐	10 Roberto Alomar	.50	.23	.06
☐	11 Wes Chamberlain	.10	.05	.01
☐	12 Steve Avery	.30	.14	.04
☐	13 Scott Erickson	.20	.09	.03
☐	14 Jim Abbott	.30	.14	.04
☐	15 Mark Whiten	.10	.05	.01
☐	16 Leo Gomez	.10	.05	.01
☐	17 Doug Henry	.10	.05	.01
☐	18 Brent Mayne	.10	.05	.01
☐	19 Charles Nagy	.20	.09	.03
☐	20 Phil Plantier	.10	.05	.01
☐	21 Mo Vaughn	1.00	.45	.12
☐	22 Craig Biggio	.30	.14	.04
☐	23 Derek Bell	.20	.09	.03
☐	24 Royce Clayton	.20	.09	.03
☐	25 Gary Cooper	.10	.05	.01
☐	26 Scott Cooper	.10	.05	.01
☐	27 Juan Gonzalez	1.00	.45	.12
☐	28 Ken Griffey Jr.	4.00	1.80	.50
☐	29 Larry Walker	.40	.18	.05
☐	30 John Smoltz	.30	.14	.04
☐	31 Todd Hundley	.20	.09	.03
☐	32 Kenny Lofton	2.50	1.10	.30
☐	33 Andy Mota	.10	.05	.01
☐	34 Todd Zeile	.20	.09	.03
☐	35 Arthur Rhodes	.10	.05	.01
☐	36 Jim Thome	2.00	.90	.25
☐	37 Todd Van Poppel	.10	.05	.01
☐	38 Mark Wohlers	.10	.05	.01
☐	39 Anthony Young	.10	.05	.01
☐	40 Sandy Alomar Jr.	.10	.05	.01
☐	41 John Olerud	.20	.09	.03
☐	42 Robin Ventura	.30	.14	.04
☐	43 Frank Thomas	4.00	1.80	.50
☐	44 Dave Justice	.40	.18	.05
☐	45 Hal Morris	.20	.09	.03
☐	46 Ruben Sierra	.30	.14	.04
☐	47 Travis Fryman	.30	.14	.04
☐	48 Mike Mussina	.75	.35	.09
☐	49 Tom Glavine	.30	.14	.04
☐	50 Barry Larkin	.40	.18	.05
☐	51 Will Clark UER	.40	.18	.05
	Career Totals spelled To als			
☐	52 Jose Canseco	.40	.18	.05
☐	53 Bo Jackson	.30	.14	.04
☐	54 Dwight Gooden	.10	.05	.01
☐	55 Barry Bonds	.75	.35	.09
☐	56 Fred McGriff	.40	.18	.05
☐	57 Roger Clemens	.40	.18	.05
☐	58 Benito Santiago	.10	.05	.01
☐	59 Darryl Strawberry	.20	.09	.03
☐	60 Cecil Fielder	.30	.14	.04
☐	61 John Franco	.10	.05	.01
☐	62 Matt Williams	.60	.25	.07
☐	63 Marquis Grissom	.30	.14	.04
☐	64 Danny Tartabull	.20	.09	.03
☐	65 Ron Gant	.30	.14	.04
☐	66 Paul O'Neill	.30	.14	.04
☐	67 Devon White	.20	.09	.03
☐	68 Rafael Palmeiro	.30	.14	.04
☐	69 Tom Gordon	.10	.05	.01
☐	70 Shawon Dunston	.10	.05	.01
☐	71 Rob Dibble	.10	.05	.01
☐	72 Eddie Zosky	.10	.05	.01
☐	73 Jack McDowell	.30	.14	.04
☐	74 Len Dykstra	.30	.14	.04
☐	75 Ramon Martinez	.30	.14	.04
☐	76 Reggie Sanders	.40	.18	.05
☐	77 Greg Maddux	2.00	.90	.25
☐	78 Ellis Burks	.20	.09	.03
☐	79 John Smiley	.10	.05	.01
☐	80 Roberto Kelly	.10	.05	.01
☐	81 Ben McDonald	.10	.05	.01
☐	82 Mark Lewis	.10	.05	.01
☐	83 Jose Rijo	.20	.09	.03

			MINT	NRMT	EXC
☐	84	Ozzie Guillen	.10	.05	.01
☐	85	Lance Dickson	.10	.05	.01
☐	86	Kim Batiste	.10	.05	.01
☐	87	Gregg Olson	.10	.05	.01
☐	88	Andy Benes	.10	.05	.01
☐	89	Cal Eldred	.10	.05	.01
☐	90	David Cone	.30	.14	.04

1992 Score Rookie/Traded

The 1992 Score Rookie and Traded set contains 110 standard-size cards featuring traded veterans and rookies. The fronts display color action player photos edged on one side by an orange stripe that fades to white as one moves down the card face. The player's name appears in a purple bar above the picture, while his position is printed in a purple bar below the picture. The backs carry a color close-up photo, biography, and on a yellow panel, batting or pitching statistics and career summary. The cards are numbered on the back with the "T" suffix. The set is arranged numerically such that cards 1T-79T are traded players and cards 80T-110T feature rookies. Rookie Cards in this set include Chad Curtis, Brian Jordan, and Jeff Kent.

		MINT	NRMT	EXC
COMPLETE FACT.SET (110)		25.00	11.00	3.10
COMMON CARD (1T-110T)		.10	.05	.01

			MINT	NRMT	EXC
☐	1T	Gary Sheffield	.30	.14	.04
☐	2T	Kevin Seitzer	.10	.05	.01
☐	3T	Danny Tartabull	.20	.09	.03
☐	4T	Steve Sax	.10	.05	.01
☐	5T	Bobby Bonilla	.30	.14	.04
☐	6T	Frank Viola	.20	.09	.03
☐	7T	Dave Winfield	.60	.25	.07
☐	8T	Rick Sutcliffe	.20	.09	.03
☐	9T	Jose Canseco	1.00	.45	.12
☐	10T	Greg Swindell	.10	.05	.01
☐	11T	Eddie Murray	.60	.25	.07
☐	12T	Randy Myers	.30	.14	.04
☐	13T	Wally Joyner	.20	.09	.03
☐	14T	Kenny Lofton	8.00	3.60	1.00
☐	15T	Jack Morris	.30	.14	.04
☐	16T	Charlie Hayes	.20	.09	.03
☐	17T	Pete Incaviglia	.10	.05	.01
☐	18T	Kevin Mitchell	.20	.09	.03
☐	19T	Kurt Stillwell	.10	.05	.01
☐	20T	Bret Saberhagen	.30	.14	.04
☐	21T	Steve Buechele	.10	.05	.01
☐	22T	John Smiley	.10	.05	.01
☐	23T	Sammy Sosa	.75	.35	.09
☐	24T	George Bell	.20	.09	.03
☐	25T	Curt Schilling	.10	.05	.01
☐	26T	Dick Schofield	.10	.05	.01
☐	27T	David Cone	.30	.14	.04
☐	28T	Dan Gladden	.10	.05	.01
☐	29T	Kirk McCaskill	.10	.05	.01
☐	30T	Mike Gallego	.10	.05	.01
☐	31T	Kevin McReynolds	.10	.05	.01
☐	32T	Bill Swift	.20	.09	.03
☐	33T	Dave Martinez	.10	.05	.01
☐	34T	Storm Davis	.10	.05	.01
☐	35T	Willie Randolph	.20	.09	.03
☐	36T	Melido Perez	.10	.05	.01
☐	37T	Mark Carreon	.10	.05	.01
☐	38T	Doug Jones	.10	.05	.01
☐	39T	Gregg Jefferies	.30	.14	.04
☐	40T	Mike Jackson	.10	.05	.01
☐	41T	Dickie Thon	.10	.05	.01
☐	42T	Eric King	.10	.05	.01
☐	43T	Herm Winningham	.10	.05	.01
☐	44T	Derek Lilliquist	.10	.05	.01
☐	45T	Dave Anderson	.10	.05	.01
☐	46T	Jeff Reardon	.20	.09	.03
☐	47T	Scott Bankhead	.10	.05	.01
☐	48T	Cory Snyder	.10	.05	.01
☐	49T	Al Newman	.10	.05	.01
☐	50T	Keith Miller	.10	.05	.01
☐	51T	Dave Burba	.10	.05	.01
☐	52T	Bill Pecota	.10	.05	.01
☐	53T	Chuck Crim	.10	.05	.01
☐	54T	Mariano Duncan	.10	.05	.01
☐	55T	Dave Gallagher	.10	.05	.01
☐	56T	Chris Gwynn	.10	.05	.01
☐	57T	Scott Ruskin	.10	.05	.01
☐	58T	Jack Armstrong	.10	.05	.01
☐	59T	Gary Carter	.30	.14	.04
☐	60T	Andres Galarraga	.30	.14	.04
☐	61T	Ken Hill	.20	.09	.03
☐	62T	Eric Davis	.10	.05	.01
☐	63T	Ruben Sierra	.30	.14	.04
☐	64T	Darrin Fletcher	.10	.05	.01
☐	65T	Tim Belcher	.10	.05	.01
☐	66T	Mike Morgan	.10	.05	.01
☐	67T	Scott Scudder	.10	.05	.01
☐	68T	Tom Candiotti	.10	.05	.01
☐	69T	Hubie Brooks	.10	.05	.01
☐	70T	Kal Daniels	.10	.05	.01
☐	71T	Bruce Ruffin	.10	.05	.01
☐	72T	Billy Hatcher	.10	.05	.01
☐	73T	Bob Melvin	.10	.05	.01
☐	74T	Lee Guetterman	.10	.05	.01
☐	75T	Rene Gonzales	.10	.05	.01
☐	76T	Kevin Bass	.10	.05	.01
☐	77T	Tom Bolton	.10	.05	.01
☐	78T	John Wetteland	.30	.14	.04
☐	79T	Bip Roberts	.10	.05	.01
☐	80T	Pat Listach	.20	.09	.03
☐	81T	John Doherty	.10	.05	.01
☐	82T	Sam Militello	.10	.05	.01
☐	83T	Brian Jordan	1.00	.45	.12
☐	84T	Jeff Kent	1.00	.45	.12
☐	85T	Dave Fleming	.20	.09	.03
☐	86T	Jeff Tackett	.10	.05	.01
☐	87T	Chad Curtis	1.00	.45	.12
☐	88T	Eric Fox	.10	.05	.01

☐ 89T	Denny Neagle	.50	.23	.06
☐ 90T	Donovan Osborne	.10	.05	.01
☐ 91T	Carlos Hernandez	.10	.05	.01
☐ 92T	Tim Wakefield	1.50	.70	.19
☐ 93T	Tim Salmon	6.00	2.70	.75
☐ 94T	Dave Nilsson	.50	.23	.06
☐ 95T	Mike Perez	.10	.05	.01
☐ 96T	Pat Hentgen	.30	.14	.04
☐ 97T	Frank Seminara	.20	.09	.03
☐ 98T	Ruben Amaro Jr.	.10	.05	.01
☐ 99T	Archi Cianfrocco	.10	.05	.01
☐ 100T	Andy Stankiewicz	.10	.05	.01
☐ 101T	Jim Bullinger	.10	.05	.01
☐ 102T	Pat Mahomes	.10	.05	.01
☐ 103T	Hipolito Pichardo	.10	.05	.01
☐ 104T	Bret Boone	1.50	.70	.19
☐ 105T	John Vander Wal	.20	.09	.03
☐ 106T	Vince Horsman	.20	.09	.03
☐ 107T	James Austin	.10	.05	.01
☐ 108T	Brian Williams	.10	.05	.01
☐ 109T	Dan Walters	.20	.09	.03
☐ 110T	Wil Cordero	1.25	.55	.16

1993 Score

The 1993 Score baseball set consists of 660 standard-size cards. The fronts feature color action player photos surrounded by white borders. The player's name appears in the bottom white border, while the team name and position appear in a team color-coded stripe that edges the left side of the picture. The backs carry a close-up color photo, biography, and team logo on the top portion; full career statistics and player profile appear on the bottom portion on a pastel color panel. Topical subsets featured are Rookie (221-222, 224-255, 257-260, 262-312, 314-316, 318-322, 324-330, 458, 561, 565, 569, 573, 586), Award Winners (481-486), Draft Picks (487-501), All-Star Caricature (502-512 [AL], 522-531 [NL]), Highlight (513-519), World Series Highlight (520-521), and Dream Team (532-542). The cards are numbered on the back. Rookie Cards in this set include Derek Jeter, Jason Kendall and J.T. Snow.

	MINT	NRMT	EXC
COMPLETE SET (660)	40.00	18.00	5.00
COMMON CARD (1-660)	.05	.02	.01

☐ 1	Ken Griffey Jr.	2.00	.90	.25
☐ 2	Gary Sheffield	.15	.07	.02
☐ 3	Frank Thomas	2.00	.90	.25
☐ 4	Ryne Sandberg	.50	.23	.06
☐ 5	Larry Walker	.25	.11	.03
☐ 6	Cal Ripken Jr.	2.00	.90	.25
☐ 7	Roger Clemens	.30	.14	.04
☐ 8	Bobby Bonilla	.15	.07	.02
☐ 9	Carlos Baerga	.40	.18	.05
☐ 10	Darren Daulton	.15	.07	.02
☐ 11	Travis Fryman	.15	.07	.02
☐ 12	Andy Van Slyke	.10	.05	.01
☐ 13	Jose Canseco	.30	.14	.04
☐ 14	Roberto Alomar	.40	.18	.05
☐ 15	Tom Glavine	.15	.07	.02
☐ 16	Barry Larkin	.25	.11	.03
☐ 17	Gregg Jefferies	.15	.07	.02
☐ 18	Craig Biggio	.15	.07	.02
☐ 19	Shane Mack	.05	.02	.01
☐ 20	Brett Butler	.10	.05	.01
☐ 21	Dennis Eckersley	.15	.07	.02
☐ 22	Will Clark	.25	.11	.03
☐ 23	Don Mattingly	1.00	.45	.12
☐ 24	Tony Gwynn	.60	.25	.07
☐ 25	Ivan Rodriguez	.15	.07	.02
☐ 26	Shawon Dunston	.05	.02	.01
☐ 27	Mike Mussina	.30	.14	.04
☐ 28	Marquis Grissom	.15	.07	.02
☐ 29	Charles Nagy	.10	.05	.01
☐ 30	Len Dykstra	.15	.07	.02
☐ 31	Cecil Fielder	.15	.07	.02
☐ 32	Jay Bell	.10	.05	.01
☐ 33	B.J. Surhoff	.10	.05	.01
☐ 34	Bob Tewksbury	.05	.02	.01
☐ 35	Danny Tartabull	.10	.05	.01
☐ 36	Terry Pendleton	.10	.05	.01
☐ 37	Jack Morris	.15	.07	.02
☐ 38	Hal Morris	.10	.05	.01
☐ 39	Luis Polonia	.05	.02	.01
☐ 40	Ken Caminiti	.10	.05	.01
☐ 41	Robin Ventura	.15	.07	.02
☐ 42	Darryl Strawberry	.10	.05	.01
☐ 43	Wally Joyner	.10	.05	.01
☐ 44	Fred McGriff	.25	.11	.03
☐ 45	Kevin Tapani	.05	.02	.01
☐ 46	Matt Williams	.30	.14	.04
☐ 47	Robin Yount	.25	.11	.03
☐ 48	Ken Hill	.10	.05	.01
☐ 49	Edgar Martinez	.15	.07	.02
☐ 50	Mark Grace	.15	.07	.02
☐ 51	Juan Gonzalez	.40	.18	.05
☐ 52	Curt Schilling	.05	.02	.01
☐ 53	Dwight Gooden	.05	.02	.01
☐ 54	Chris Hoiles	.10	.05	.01
☐ 55	Frank Viola	.10	.05	.01
☐ 56	Ray Lankford	.15	.07	.02
☐ 57	George Brett	.75	.35	.09
☐ 58	Kenny Lofton	.60	.25	.07
☐ 59	Nolan Ryan	2.00	.90	.25
☐ 60	Mickey Tettleton	.10	.05	.01
☐ 61	John Smoltz	.10	.05	.01
☐ 62	Howard Johnson	.05	.02	.01
☐ 63	Eric Karros	.10	.05	.01
☐ 64	Rick Aguilera	.10	.05	.01
☐ 65	Steve Finley	.10	.05	.01
☐ 66	Mark Langston	.15	.07	.02
☐ 67	Bill Swift	.05	.02	.01
☐ 68	John Olerud	.15	.07	.02
☐ 69	Kevin McReynolds	.05	.02	.01
☐ 70	Jack McDowell	.15	.07	.02
☐ 71	Rickey Henderson	.15	.07	.02

☐	72	Brian Harper	.05	.02	.01			
☐	73	Mike Morgan	.05	.02	.01			
☐	74	Rafael Palmeiro	.15	.07	.02			
☐	75	Dennis Martinez	.10	.05	.01			
☐	76	Tino Martinez	.15	.07	.02			
☐	77	Eddie Murray	.30	.14	.04			
☐	78	Ellis Burks	.10	.05	.01			
☐	79	John Kruk	.15	.07	.02			
☐	81	Gregg Olson	.05	.02	.01			
☐	81	Bernard Gilkey	.10	.05	.01			
☐	82	Milt Cuyler	.05	.02	.01			
☐	83	Mike LaValliere	.05	.02	.01			
☐	84	Albert Belle	.75	.35	.09			
☐	85	Bip Roberts	.05	.02	.01			
☐	86	Melido Perez	.05	.02	.01			
☐	87	Otis Nixon	.05	.02	.01			
☐	88	Bill Spiers	.05	.02	.01			
☐	89	Jeff Bagwell	.75	.35	.09			
☐	90	Orel Hershiser	.10	.05	.01			
☐	91	Andy Benes	.10	.05	.01			
☐	92	Devon White	.10	.05	.01			
☐	93	Willie McGee	.10	.05	.01			
☐	94	Ozzie Guillen	.05	.02	.01			
☐	95	Ivan Calderon	.05	.02	.01			
☐	96	Keith Miller	.05	.02	.01			
☐	97	Steve Buechele	.05	.02	.01			
☐	98	Kent Hrbek	.10	.05	.01			
☐	99	Dave Hollins	.05	.02	.01			
☐	100	Mike Bordick	.05	.02	.01			
☐	101	Randy Tomlin	.05	.02	.01			
☐	102	Omar Vizquel	.10	.05	.01			
☐	103	Lee Smith	.15	.07	.02			
☐	104	Leo Gomez	.05	.02	.01			
☐	105	Jose Rijo	.10	.05	.01			
☐	106	Mark Whiten	.10	.05	.01			
☐	107	Dave Justice	.25	.11	.03			
☐	108	Eddie Taubensee	.05	.02	.01			
☐	109	Lance Johnson	.05	.02	.01			
☐	110	Felix Jose	.05	.02	.01			
☐	111	Mike Harkey	.05	.02	.01			
☐	112	Randy Milligan	.05	.02	.01			
☐	113	Anthony Young	.05	.02	.01			
☐	114	Rico Brogna	.10	.05	.01			
☐	115	Bret Saberhagen	.10	.05	.01			
☐	116	Sandy Alomar	.10	.05	.01			
☐	117	Terry Mulholland	.05	.02	.01			
☐	118	Darryl Hamilton	.05	.02	.01			
☐	119	Todd Zeile	.10	.05	.01			
☐	120	Bernie Williams	.10	.05	.01			
☐	121	Zane Smith	.05	.02	.01			
☐	122	Derek Bell	.15	.07	.02			
☐	123	Deion Sanders	.40	.18	.05			
☐	124	Luis Sojo	.05	.02	.01			
☐	125	Joe Oliver	.05	.02	.01			
☐	126	Craig Grebeck	.05	.02	.01			
☐	127	Andujar Cedeno	.05	.02	.01			
☐	128	Brian McRae	.15	.07	.02			
☐	129	Jose Offerman	.05	.02	.01			
☐	130	Pedro Munoz	.10	.05	.01			
☐	131	Bud Black	.05	.02	.01			
☐	132	Mo Vaughn	.30	.14	.04			
☐	133	Bruce Hurst	.05	.02	.01			
☐	134	Dave Henderson	.05	.02	.01			
☐	135	Tom Pagnozzi	.05	.02	.01			
☐	136	Erik Hanson	.10	.05	.01			
☐	137	Orlando Merced	.10	.05	.01			
☐	138	Dean Palmer	.10	.05	.01			
☐	139	John Franco	.10	.05	.01			
☐	140	Brady Anderson	.10	.05	.01			
☐	141	Ricky Jordan	.05	.02	.01			
☐	142	Jeff Blauser	.10	.05	.01			
☐	143	Sammy Sosa	.15	.07	.02			
☐	144	Bob Walk	.05	.02	.01			
☐	145	Delino DeShields	.10	.05	.01			
☐	146	Kevin Brown	.05	.02	.01			
☐	147	Mark Lemke	.10	.05	.01			
☐	148	Chuck Knoblauch	.15	.07	.02			
☐	149	Chris Sabo	.05	.02	.01			
☐	150	Bobby Witt	.05	.02	.01			
☐	151	Luis Gonzalez	.10	.05	.01			
☐	152	Ron Karkovice	.05	.02	.01			
☐	153	Jeff Brantley	.05	.02	.01			
☐	154	Kevin Appier	.10	.05	.01			
☐	155	Darrin Jackson	.05	.02	.01			
☐	156	Kelly Gruber	.05	.02	.01			
☐	157	Royce Clayton	.10	.05	.01			
☐	158	Chuck Finley	.10	.05	.01			
☐	159	Jeff King	.05	.02	.01			
☐	160	Greg Vaughn	.05	.02	.01			
☐	161	Geronimo Pena	.05	.02	.01			
☐	162	Steve Farr	.05	.02	.01			
☐	163	Jose Oquendo	.05	.02	.01			
☐	164	Mark Lewis	.05	.02	.01			
☐	165	John Wetteland	.10	.05	.01			
☐	166	Mike Henneman	.05	.02	.01			
☐	167	Todd Hundley	.15	.07	.02			
☐	168	Wes Chamberlain	.05	.02	.01			
☐	169	Steve Avery	.15	.07	.02			
☐	170	Mike Devereaux	.10	.05	.01			
☐	171	Reggie Sanders	.15	.07	.02			
☐	172	Jay Buhner	.15	.07	.02			
☐	173	Eric Anthony	.05	.02	.01			
☐	174	John Burkett	.05	.02	.01			
☐	175	Tom Candiotti	.05	.02	.01			
☐	176	Phil Plantier	.05	.02	.01			
☐	177	Doug Henry	.05	.02	.01			
☐	178	Scott Leius	.05	.02	.01			
☐	179	Kirt Manwaring	.05	.02	.01			
☐	180	Jeff Parrett	.05	.02	.01			
☐	181	Don Slaught	.05	.02	.01			
☐	182	Scott Radinsky	.05	.02	.01			
☐	183	Luis Alicea	.05	.02	.01			
☐	184	Tom Gordon	.05	.02	.01			
☐	185	Rick Wilkins	.05	.02	.01			
☐	186	Todd Stottlemyre	.05	.02	.01			
☐	187	Moises Alou	.15	.07	.02			
☐	188	Joe Grahe	.05	.02	.01			
☐	189	Jeff Kent	.15	.07	.02			
☐	190	Bill Wegman	.05	.02	.01			
☐	191	Kim Batiste	.05	.02	.01			
☐	192	Matt Nokes	.05	.02	.01			
☐	193	Mark Wohlers	.05	.02	.01			
☐	194	Paul Sorrento	.05	.02	.01			
☐	195	Chris Hammond	.05	.02	.01			
☐	196	Scott Livingstone	.05	.02	.01			
☐	197	Doug Jones	.05	.02	.01			
☐	198	Scott Cooper	.05	.02	.01			
☐	199	Ramon Martinez	.10	.05	.01			
☐	200	Dave Valle	.05	.02	.01			
☐	201	Mariano Duncan	.05	.02	.01			
☐	202	Ben McDonald	.05	.02	.01			
☐	203	Darren Lewis	.05	.02	.01			
☐	204	Kenny Rogers	.05	.02	.01			
☐	205	Manuel Lee	.05	.02	.01			
☐	206	Scott Erickson	.10	.05	.01			
☐	207	Dan Gladden	.05	.02	.01			
☐	208	Bob Welch	.10	.05	.01			
☐	209	Greg Olson	.05	.02	.01			
☐	210	Dan Pasqua	.05	.02	.01			
☐	211	Tim Wallach	.05	.02	.01			
☐	212	Jeff Montgomery	.10	.05	.01			
☐	213	Derrick May	.10	.05	.01			

□	#	Player			
□	214	Ed Sprague	.05	.02	.01
□	215	David Haas	.05	.02	.01
□	216	Darrin Fletcher	.05	.02	.01
□	217	Brian Jordan	.15	.07	.02
□	218	Jaime Navarro	.05	.02	.01
□	219	Randy Velarde	.05	.02	.01
□	220	Ron Gant	.15	.07	.02
□	221	Paul Quantrill	.05	.02	.01
□	222	Damion Easley	.10	.05	.01
□	223	Charlie Hough	.10	.05	.01
□	224	Brad Brink	.05	.02	.01
□	225	Barry Manuel	.05	.02	.01
□	226	Kevin Koslofski	.05	.02	.01
□	227	Ryan Thompson	.10	.05	.01
□	228	Mike Munoz	.05	.02	.01
□	229	Dan Wilson	.10	.05	.01
□	230	Peter Hoy	.05	.02	.01
□	231	Pedro Astacio	.05	.02	.01
□	232	Matt Stairs	.05	.02	.01
□	233	Jeff Reboulet	.05	.02	.01
□	234	Manny Alexander	.05	.02	.01
□	235	Willie Banks	.05	.02	.01
□	236	John Jaha	.10	.05	.01
□	237	Scooter Tucker	.05	.02	.01
□	238	Russ Springer	.05	.02	.01
□	239	Paul Miller	.05	.02	.01
□	240	Dan Peltier	.05	.02	.01
□	241	Ozzie Canseco	.05	.02	.01
□	242	Ben Rivera	.05	.02	.01
□	243	John Valentin	.15	.07	.02
□	244	Henry Rodriguez	.05	.02	.01
□	245	Derek Parks	.05	.02	.01
□	246	Carlos Garcia	.10	.05	.01
□	247	Tim Pugh	.05	.02	.01
□	248	Melvin Nieves	.15	.07	.02
□	249	Rich Amaral	.05	.02	.01
□	250	Willie Greene	.10	.05	.01
□	251	Tim Scott	.05	.02	.01
□	252	Dave Silvestri	.05	.02	.01
□	253	Rob Mallicoat	.05	.02	.01
□	254	Donald Harris	.05	.02	.01
□	255	Craig Colbert	.05	.02	.01
□	256	Jose Guzman	.05	.02	.01
□	257	Domingo Martinez	.05	.02	.01
□	258	William Suero	.05	.02	.01
□	259	Juan Guerrero	.05	.02	.01
□	260	J.T. Snow	.60	.25	.07
□	261	Tony Pena	.05	.02	.01
□	262	Tim Fortugno	.05	.02	.01
□	263	Tom Marsh	.05	.02	.01
□	264	Kurt Knudsen	.05	.02	.01
□	265	Tim Costo	.05	.02	.01
□	266	Steve Shifflett	.05	.02	.01
□	267	Billy Ashley	.15	.07	.02
□	268	Jerry Nielsen	.05	.02	.01
□	269	Pete Young	.05	.02	.01
□	270	Johnny Guzman	.05	.02	.01
□	271	Greg Colbrunn	.15	.07	.02
□	272	Jeff Nelson	.05	.02	.01
□	273	Kevin Young	.05	.02	.01
□	274	Jeff Frye	.05	.02	.01
□	275	J.T. Bruett	.05	.02	.01
□	276	Todd Pratt	.05	.02	.01
□	277	Mike Butcher	.05	.02	.01
□	278	John Flaherty	.05	.02	.01
□	279	John Patterson	.05	.02	.01
□	280	Eric Hillman	.05	.02	.01
□	281	Bien Figueroa	.05	.02	.01
□	282	Shane Reynolds	.10	.05	.01
□	283	Rich Rowland	.05	.02	.01
□	284	Steve Foster	.05	.02	.01
□	285	Dave Mlicki	.05	.02	.01
□	286	Mike Piazza	1.50	.70	.19
□	287	Mike Trombley	.05	.02	.01
□	288	Jim Pena	.05	.02	.01
□	289	Bob Ayrault	.05	.02	.01
□	290	Henry Mercedes	.05	.02	.01
□	291	Bob Wickman	.05	.02	.01
□	292	Jacob Brumfield	.05	.02	.01
□	293	David Hulse	.05	.02	.01
□	294	Ryan Klesko	1.00	.45	.12
□	295	Doug Linton	.05	.02	.01
□	296	Steve Cooke	.05	.02	.01
□	297	Eddie Zosky	.05	.02	.01
□	298	Gerald Williams	.05	.02	.01
□	299	Jonathan Hurst	.05	.02	.01
□	300	Larry Carter	.05	.02	.01
□	301	William Pennyfeather	.05	.02	.01
□	302	Cesar Hernandez	.05	.02	.01
□	303	Steve Hosey	.05	.02	.01
□	304	Blas Minor	.05	.02	.01
□	305	Jeff Grotewald	.05	.02	.01
□	306	Bernardo Brito	.05	.02	.01
□	307	Rafael Bournigal	.05	.02	.01
□	308	Jeff Branson	.05	.02	.01
□	309	Tom Quinlan	.05	.02	.01
□	310	Pat Gomez	.05	.02	.01
□	311	Sterling Hitchcock	.20	.09	.03
□	312	Kent Bottenfield	.05	.02	.01
□	313	Alan Trammell	.15	.07	.02
□	314	Cris Colon	.05	.02	.01
□	315	Paul Wagner	.05	.02	.01
□	316	Matt Maysey	.05	.02	.01
□	317	Mike Stanton	.05	.02	.01
□	318	Rick Trlicek	.05	.02	.01
□	319	Kevin Rogers	.05	.02	.01
□	320	Mark Clark	.10	.05	.01
□	321	Pedro Martinez	.15	.07	.02
□	322	Al Martin	.10	.05	.01
□	323	Mike Macfarlane	.05	.02	.01
□	324	Rey Sanchez	.10	.05	.01
□	325	Roger Pavlik	.05	.02	.01
□	326	Troy Neel	.05	.02	.01
□	327	Kerry Woodson	.05	.02	.01
□	328	Wayne Kirby	.05	.02	.01
□	329	Ken Ryan	.05	.02	.01
□	330	Jesse Levis	.05	.02	.01
□	331	James Austin	.05	.02	.01
□	332	Dan Walters	.05	.02	.01
□	333	Brian Williams	.05	.02	.01
□	334	Wil Cordero	.15	.07	.02
□	335	Bret Boone	.15	.07	.02
□	336	Hipolito Pichardo	.05	.02	.01
□	337	Pat Mahomes	.05	.02	.01
□	338	Andy Stankiewicz	.05	.02	.01
□	339	Jim Bullinger	.05	.02	.01
□	340	Archi Cianfrocco	.05	.02	.01
□	341	Ruben Amaro Jr.	.05	.02	.01
□	342	Frank Seminara	.05	.02	.01
□	343	Pat Hentgen	.10	.05	.01
□	344	Dave Nilsson	.10	.05	.01
□	345	Mike Perez	.05	.02	.01
□	346	Tim Salmon	.60	.25	.07
□	347	Tim Wakefield	.15	.07	.02
□	348	Carlos Hernandez	.05	.02	.01
□	349	Donovan Osborne	.05	.02	.01
□	350	Denny Neagle	.05	.02	.01
□	351	Sam Militello	.05	.02	.01
□	352	Eric Fox	.05	.02	.01
□	353	John Doherty	.05	.02	.01
□	354	Chad Curtis	.10	.05	.01
□	355	Jeff Tackett	.05	.02	.01

☐ 356	Dave Fleming	.05	.02	.01
☐ 357	Pat Listach	.05	.02	.01
☐ 358	Kevin Wickander	.05	.02	.01
☐ 359	John Vander Wal	.05	.02	.01
☐ 360	Arthur Rhodes	.10	.05	.01
☐ 361	Bob Scanlan	.05	.02	.01
☐ 362	Bob Zupcic	.05	.02	.01
☐ 363	Mel Rojas	.10	.05	.01
☐ 364	Jim Thome	.75	.35	.09
☐ 365	Bill Pecota	.05	.02	.01
☐ 366	Mark Carreon	.05	.02	.01
☐ 367	Mitch Williams	.10	.05	.01
☐ 368	Cal Eldred	.05	.02	.01
☐ 369	Stan Belinda	.05	.02	.01
☐ 370	Pat Kelly	.05	.02	.01
☐ 371	Rheal Cormier	.05	.02	.01
☐ 372	Juan Guzman	.10	.05	.01
☐ 373	Damon Berryhill	.05	.02	.01
☐ 374	Gary DiSarcina	.05	.02	.01
☐ 375	Norm Charlton	.05	.02	.01
☐ 376	Roberto Hernandez	.10	.05	.01
☐ 377	Scott Kamieniecki	.05	.02	.01
☐ 378	Rusty Meacham	.05	.02	.01
☐ 379	Kurt Stillwell	.05	.02	.01
☐ 380	Lloyd McClendon	.05	.02	.01
☐ 381	Mark Leonard	.05	.02	.01
☐ 382	Jerry Browne	.05	.02	.01
☐ 383	Glenn Davis	.05	.02	.01
☐ 384	Randy Johnson	.40	.18	.05
☐ 385	Mike Greenwell	.10	.05	.01
☐ 386	Scott Chiamparino	.05	.02	.01
☐ 387	George Bell	.10	.05	.01
☐ 388	Steve Olin	.05	.02	.01
☐ 389	Chuck McElroy	.05	.02	.01
☐ 390	Mark Gardner	.05	.02	.01
☐ 391	Rod Beck	.15	.07	.02
☐ 392	Dennis Rasmussen	.05	.02	.01
☐ 393	Charlie Leibrandt	.05	.02	.01
☐ 394	Julio Franco	.10	.05	.01
☐ 395	Pete Harnisch	.05	.02	.01
☐ 396	Sid Bream	.05	.02	.01
☐ 397	Milt Thompson	.05	.02	.01
☐ 398	Glenallen Hill	.05	.02	.01
☐ 399	Chico Walker	.05	.02	.01
☐ 400	Alex Cole	.05	.02	.01
☑ 401	Trevor Wilson	.05	.02	.01
☐ 402	Jeff Conine	.15	.07	.02
☐ 403	Kyle Abbott	.05	.02	.01
☐ 404	Tom Browning	.05	.02	.01
☐ 405	Jerald Clark	.05	.02	.01
☐ 406	Vince Horsman	.05	.02	.01
☐ 407	Kevin Mitchell	.10	.05	.01
☐ 408	Pete Smith	.05	.02	.01
☐ 409	Jeff Innis	.05	.02	.01
☐ 410	Mike Timlin	.05	.02	.01
☐ 411	Charlie Hayes	.10	.05	.01
☐ 412	Alex Fernandez	.15	.07	.02
☐ 413	Jeff Russell	.05	.02	.01
☐ 414	Jody Reed	.05	.02	.01
☐ 415	Mickey Morandini	.05	.02	.01
☐ 416	Darnell Coles	.05	.02	.01
☐ 417	Xavier Hernandez	.05	.02	.01
☐ 418	Steve Sax	.05	.02	.01
☐ 419	Joe Girardi	.05	.02	.01
☐ 420	Mike Fetters	.05	.02	.01
☐ 421	Danny Jackson	.05	.02	.01
☐ 422	Jim Gott	.05	.02	.01
☐ 423	Tim Belcher	.05	.02	.01
☐ 424	Jose Mesa	.10	.05	.01
☐ 425	Junior Felix	.05	.02	.01
☐ 426	Thomas Howard	.05	.02	.01
☐ 427	Julio Valera	.05	.02	.01
☐ 428	Dante Bichette	.25	.11	.03
☐ 429	Mike Sharperson	.05	.02	.01
☐ 430	Darryl Kile	.05	.02	.01
☐ 431	Lonnie Smith	.05	.02	.01
☐ 432	Monty Fariss	.05	.02	.01
☐ 433	Reggie Jefferson	.05	.02	.01
☐ 434	Bob McClure	.05	.02	.01
☐ 435	Craig Lefferts	.05	.02	.01
☐ 436	Duane Ward	.05	.02	.01
☐ 437	Shawn Abner	.05	.02	.01
☐ 438	Roberto Kelly	.10	.05	.01
☐ 439	Paul O'Neill	.10	.05	.01
☐ 440	Alan Mills	.05	.02	.01
☐ 441	Roger Mason	.05	.02	.01
☐ 442	Gary Pettis	.05	.02	.01
☐ 443	Steve Lake	.05	.02	.01
☐ 444	Gene Larkin	.05	.02	.01
☐ 445	Larry Andersen	.05	.02	.01
☐ 446	Doug Dascenzo	.05	.02	.01
☐ 447	Daryl Boston	.05	.02	.01
☐ 448	John Candelaria	.05	.02	.01
☐ 449	Storm Davis	.05	.02	.01
☐ 450	Tom Edens	.05	.02	.01
☐ 451	Mike Maddux	.05	.02	.01
☐ 452	Tim Naehring	.10	.05	.01
☐ 453	John Orton	.05	.02	.01
☐ 454	Joey Cora	.05	.02	.01
☐ 455	Chuck Crim	.05	.02	.01
☐ 456	Dan Plesac	.05	.02	.01
☐ 457	Mike Bielecki	.05	.02	.01
☐ 458	Terry Jorgensen	.05	.02	.01
☐ 459	John Habyan	.05	.02	.01
☐ 460	Pete O'Brien	.05	.02	.01
☐ 461	Jeff Treadway	.05	.02	.01
☐ 462	Frank Castillo	.05	.02	.01
☐ 463	Jimmy Jones	.05	.02	.01
☐ 464	Tommy Greene	.05	.02	.01
☐ 465	Tracy Woodson	.05	.02	.01
☐ 466	Rich Rodriguez	.05	.02	.01
☐ 467	Joe Hesketh	.05	.02	.01
☐ 468	Greg Myers	.05	.02	.01
☐ 469	Kirk McCaskill	.05	.02	.01
☐ 470	Ricky Bones	.05	.02	.01
☐ 471	Lenny Webster	.05	.02	.01
☐ 472	Francisco Cabrera	.05	.02	.01
☐ 473	Turner Ward	.05	.02	.01
☐ 474	Dwayne Henry	.05	.02	.01
☐ 475	Al Osuna	.05	.02	.01
☐ 476	Craig Wilson	.05	.02	.01
☐ 477	Chris Nabholz	.05	.02	.01
☐ 478	Rafael Belliard	.05	.02	.01
☐ 479	Terry Leach	.05	.02	.01
☐ 480	Tim Teufel	.05	.02	.01
☐ 481	Dennis Eckersley AW	.10	.05	.01
☐ 482	Barry Bonds AW	.25	.11	.03
☐ 483	Dennis Eckersley AW	.10	.05	.01
☐ 484	Greg Maddux AW	1.00	.45	.12
☐ 485	Pat Listach AW	.05	.02	.01
☐ 486	Eric Karros AW	.10	.05	.01
☐ 487	Jamie Arnold DP	.15	.07	.02
☐ 488	B.J. Wallace DP	.05	.02	.01
☐ 489	Derek Jeter DP	1.50	.70	.19
☐ 490	Jason Kendall DP	.60	.25	.07
☐ 491	Rick Helling DP	.10	.05	.01
☐ 492	Derek Wallace DP	.05	.02	.01
☐ 493	Sean Lowe DP	.15	.07	.02
☐ 494	Shannon Stewart DP	.25	.11	.03
☐ 495	Benji Grigsby DP	.10	.05	.01
☐ 496	Todd Steverson DP	.10	.05	.01
☐ 497	Dan Serafini DP	.30	.14	.04

☐ 498 Michael Tucker DP	.15	.07	.02
☐ 499 Chris Roberts DP	.10	.05	.01
☐ 500 Pete Janicki DP	.05	.02	.01
☐ 501 Jeff Schmidt DP	.05	.02	.01
☐ 502 Edgar Martinez AS	.10	.05	.01
☐ 503 Omar Vizquel AS	.05	.02	.01
☐ 504 Ken Griffey Jr. AS	1.00	.45	.12
☐ 505 Kirby Puckett AS	.30	.14	.04
☐ 506 Joe Carter AS	.10	.05	.01
☐ 507 Ivan Rodriguez AS	.10	.05	.01
☐ 508 Jack Morris AS	.10	.05	.01
☐ 509 Dennis Eckersley AS	.10	.05	.01
☐ 510 Frank Thomas AS	1.00	.45	.12
☐ 511 Roberto Alomar AS	.10	.05	.01
☐ 512 Mickey Morandini AS	.05	.02	.01
☐ 513 Dennis Eckersley HL	.10	.05	.01
☐ 514 Jeff Reardon HL	.10	.05	.01
☐ 515 Danny Tartabull HL	.10	.05	.01
☐ 516 Bip Roberts HL	.05	.02	.01
☐ 517 George Brett HL	.40	.18	.05
☐ 518 Robin Yount HL	.10	.05	.01
☐ 519 Kevin Gross HL	.05	.02	.01
☐ 520 Ed Sprague WS	.05	.02	.01
☐ 521 Dave Winfield WS	.10	.05	.01
☐ 522 Ozzie Smith AS	.10	.05	.01
☐ 523 Barry Bonds AS	.25	.11	.03
☐ 524 Andy Van Slyke AS	.05	.02	.01
☐ 525 Tony Gwynn AS	.30	.14	.04
☐ 526 Darren Daulton AS	.10	.05	.01
☐ 527 Greg Maddux AS	1.00	.45	.12
☐ 528 Fred McGriff AS	.10	.05	.01
☐ 529 Lee Smith AS	.10	.05	.01
☐ 530 Ryne Sandberg AS	.25	.11	.03
☐ 531 Gary Sheffield AS	.10	.05	.01
☐ 532 Ozzie Smith DT	.10	.05	.01
☐ 533 Kirby Puckett DT	.30	.14	.04
☐ 534 Gary Sheffield DT	.10	.05	.01
☐ 535 Andy Van Slyke DT	.05	.02	.01
☐ 536 Ken Griffey Jr. DT	1.00	.45	.12
☐ 537 Ivan Rodriguez DT	.10	.05	.01
☐ 538 Charles Nagy DT	.05	.02	.01
☐ 539 Tom Glavine DT	.10	.05	.01
☐ 540 Dennis Eckersley DT	.10	.05	.01
☐ 541 Frank Thomas DT	1.00	.45	.12
☐ 542 Roberto Alomar DT	.10	.05	.01
☐ 543 Sean Berry	.05	.02	.01
☐ 544 Mike Schooler	.05	.02	.01
☐ 545 Chuck Carr	.05	.02	.01
☐ 546 Lenny Harris	.05	.02	.01
☐ 547 Gary Scott	.05	.02	.01
☐ 548 Derek Lilliquist	.05	.02	.01
☐ 549 Brian Hunter	.05	.02	.01
☐ 550 Kirby Puckett MOY	.30	.14	.04
☐ 551 Jim Eisenreich	.05	.02	.01
☐ 552 Andre Dawson	.15	.07	.02
☐ 553 David Nied	.10	.05	.01
☐ 554 Spike Owen	.05	.02	.01
☐ 555 Greg Gagne	.05	.02	.01
☐ 556 Sid Fernandez	.05	.02	.01
☐ 557 Mark McGwire	.15	.07	.02
☐ 558 Bryan Harvey	.10	.05	.01
☐ 559 Harold Reynolds	.05	.02	.01
☐ 560 Barry Bonds	.50	.23	.06
☐ 561 Eric Wedge	.05	.02	.01
☐ 562 Ozzie Smith	.40	.18	.05
☐ 563 Rick Sutcliffe	.10	.05	.01
☐ 564 Jeff Reardon	.10	.05	.01
☐ 565 Alex Arias	.05	.02	.01
☐ 566 Greg Swindell	.05	.02	.01
☐ 567 Brook Jacoby	.05	.02	.01
☐ 568 Pete Incaviglia	.05	.02	.01
☐ 569 Butch Henry	.05	.02	.01
☐ 570 Eric Davis	.05	.02	.01
☐ 571 Kevin Seitzer	.05	.02	.01
☐ 572 Tony Fernandez	.05	.02	.01
☐ 573 Steve Reed	.05	.02	.01
☐ 574 Cory Snyder	.05	.02	.01
☐ 575 Joe Carter	.15	.07	.02
☐ 576 Greg Maddux	2.00	.90	.25
☐ 577 Bert Blyleven UER	.15	.07	.02
(Should say 3701 career strikeouts)			
☐ 578 Kevin Bass	.05	.02	.01
☐ 579 Carlton Fisk	.15	.07	.02
☐ 580 Doug Drabek	.15	.07	.02
☐ 581 Mark Gubicza	.05	.02	.01
☐ 582 Bobby Thigpen	.05	.02	.01
☐ 583 Chili Davis	.10	.05	.01
☐ 584 Scott Bankhead	.05	.02	.01
☐ 585 Harold Baines	.10	.05	.01
☐ 586 Eric Young	.10	.05	.01
☐ 587 Lance Parrish	.10	.05	.01
☐ 588 Juan Bell	.05	.02	.01
☐ 589 Bob Ojeda	.05	.02	.01
☐ 590 Joe Orsulak	.05	.02	.01
☐ 591 Benito Santiago	.05	.02	.01
☐ 592 Wade Boggs	.15	.07	.02
☐ 593 Robby Thompson	.05	.02	.01
☐ 594 Eric Plunk	.05	.02	.01
☐ 595 Hensley Meulens	.05	.02	.01
☐ 596 Lou Whitaker	.15	.07	.02
☐ 597 Dale Murphy	.15	.07	.02
☐ 598 Paul Molitor	.15	.07	.02
☐ 599 Greg W. Harris	.05	.02	.01
☐ 600 Darren Holmes	.10	.05	.01
☐ 601 Dave Martinez	.05	.02	.01
☐ 602 Tom Henke	.10	.05	.01
☐ 603 Mike Benjamin	.05	.02	.01
☐ 604 Rene Gonzales	.05	.02	.01
☐ 605 Roger McDowell	.05	.02	.01
☐ 606 Kirby Puckett	.60	.25	.07
☐ 607 Randy Myers	.10	.05	.01
☐ 608 Ruben Sierra	.15	.07	.02
☐ 609 Wilson Alvarez	.15	.07	.02
☐ 610 David Segui	.05	.02	.01
☐ 611 Juan Samuel	.05	.02	.01
☐ 612 Tom Brunansky	.05	.02	.01
☐ 613 Willie Randolph	.10	.05	.01
☐ 614 Tony Phillips	.05	.02	.01
☐ 615 Candy Maldonado	.05	.02	.01
☐ 616 Chris Bosio	.05	.02	.01
☐ 617 Bret Barberie	.05	.02	.01
☐ 618 Scott Sanderson	.05	.02	.01
☐ 619 Ron Darling	.05	.02	.01
☐ 620 Dave Winfield	.15	.07	.02
☐ 621 Mike Felder	.05	.02	.01
☐ 622 Greg Hibbard	.05	.02	.01
☐ 623 Mike Scioscia	.05	.02	.01
☐ 624 John Smiley	.05	.02	.01
☐ 625 Alejandro Pena	.05	.02	.01
☐ 626 Terry Steinbach	.10	.05	.01
☐ 627 Freddie Benavides	.05	.02	.01
☐ 628 Kevin Reimer	.05	.02	.01
☐ 629 Braulio Castillo	.05	.02	.01
☐ 630 Dave Stieb	.05	.02	.01
☐ 631 Dave Magadan	.05	.02	.01
☐ 632 Scott Fletcher	.05	.02	.01
☐ 633 Cris Carpenter	.05	.02	.01
☐ 634 Kevin Maas	.05	.02	.01
☐ 635 Todd Worrell	.05	.02	.01
☐ 636 Rob Deer	.05	.02	.01
☐ 637 Dwight Smith	.05	.02	.01

☐	638	Chito Martinez	.05	.02	.01
☐	639	Jimmy Key	.10	.05	.01
☐	640	Greg A. Harris	.05	.02	.01
☐	641	Mike Moore	.05	.02	.01
☐	642	Pat Borders	.05	.02	.01
☐	643	Bill Gullickson	.05	.02	.01
☐	644	Gary Gaetti	.10	.05	.01
☐	645	David Howard	.05	.02	.01
☐	646	Jim Abbott	.15	.07	.02
☐	647	Willie Wilson	.05	.02	.01
☐	648	David Wells	.05	.02	.01
☐	649	Andres Galarraga	.15	.07	.02
☐	650	Vince Coleman	.05	.02	.01
☐	651	Rob Dibble	.05	.02	.01
☐	652	Frank Tanana	.05	.02	.01
☐	653	Steve Decker	.05	.02	.01
☐	654	David Cone	.15	.07	.02
☐	655	Jack Armstrong	.05	.02	.01
☐	656	Dave Stewart	.10	.05	.01
☐	657	Billy Hatcher	.05	.02	.01
☐	658	Tim Raines	.15	.07	.02
☐	659	Walt Weiss	.10	.05	.01
☐	660	Jose Lind	.05	.02	.01

☐	3	Pedro Martinez	3.00	1.35	.35
☐	4	Luis Mercedes	.50	.23	.06
☐	5	Mike Piazza	25.00	11.00	3.10
☐	6	Troy Neel	.50	.23	.06
☐	7	Melvin Nieves	1.00	.45	.12
☐	8	Ryan Klesko	12.00	5.50	1.50
☐	9	Ryan Thompson	.50	.23	.06
☐	10	Kevin Young	.50	.23	.06
☐	11	Gerald Williams	.50	.23	.06
☐	12	Willie Greene	1.00	.45	.12
☐	13	John Patterson	.50	.23	.06
☐	14	Carlos Garcia	1.00	.45	.12
☐	15	Ed Zosky	.50	.23	.06
☐	16	Sean Berry	.50	.23	.06
☐	17	Rico Brogna	2.50	1.10	.30
☐	18	Larry Carter	.50	.23	.06
☐	19	Bobby Ayala	1.00	.45	.12
☐	20	Alan Embree	.50	.23	.06
☐	21	Donald Harris	.50	.23	.06
☐	22	Sterling Hitchcock	.50	.23	.06
☐	23	David Nied	.50	.23	.06
☐	24	Henry Mercedes	.50	.23	.06
☐	25	Ozzie Canseco	.50	.23	.06
☐	26	David Hulse	.50	.23	.06
☐	27	Al Martin	.50	.23	.06
☐	28	Dan Wilson	1.00	.45	.12
☐	29	Paul Miller	.50	.23	.06
☐	30	Rich Rowland	.50	.23	.06

1993 Score Boys of Summer

Randomly inserted in 1993 Score 35-card super packs only, this standard-size (2 1/2" by 3 1/2") set features 30 rookies expected to be the best in their class. The fronts are borderless with a color action player photo superimposed over an illustration of the sun. The player's name appears in cursive lettering within a greenish stripe across the bottom. The back carries a posed color player photo in the upper left that is also superimposed over an illustration of the sun. The player's name, profile, and team logo appear within the greenish area beneath the photo. According to Score, the odds of finding one of these cards are at least one in every four super packs. The cards are numbered on the back.

	MINT	NRMT	EXC
COMPLETE SET (30)	60.00	27.00	7.50
COMMON CARD (1-30)	.50	.23	.06
☐ 1 Billy Ashley	3.00	1.35	.35
☐ 2 Tim Salmon	10.00	4.50	1.25

1993 Score Franchise

This 28-card set honors the top player on each of the 28 teams. These cards were randomly inserted in 16-card count goods packs. According to Score, the chances of finding one of these cards is not less than one in 24 packs. The full-bleed, color action photos on the fronts have the background darkened so that the player stands out. His name appears in white lettering within a team color-coded bar near the bottom, which conjoins with the set logo in the lower left. The back features a borderless color posed player photo. His name and team appear within a darkened rectangle near the bottom, within which is a white rectangle that carries a player profile. The cards are numbered on the back.

	MINT	NRMT	EXC
COMPLETE SET (28)	130.00	57.50	16.00
COMMON CARD (1-28)	1.50	.70	.19
☐ 1 Cal Ripken	40.00	18.00	5.00
☐ 2 Roger Clemens	5.00	2.20	.60
☐ 3 Mark Langston	1.50	.70	.19
☐ 4 Frank Thomas	35.00	16.00	4.40
☐ 5 Carlos Baerga	7.00	3.10	.85
☐ 6 Cecil Fielder	2.50	1.10	.30
☐ 7 Gregg Jefferies	2.50	1.10	.30
☐ 8 Robin Yount	4.00	1.80	.50
☐ 9 Kirby Puckett	12.00	5.50	1.50
☐ 10 Don Mattingly	18.00	8.00	2.20
☐ 11 Dennis Eckersley	2.50	1.10	.30
☐ 12 Ken Griffey Jr.	35.00	16.00	4.40
☐ 13 Juan Gonzalez	7.00	3.10	.85
☐ 14 Roberto Alomar	7.00	3.10	.85
☐ 15 Terry Pendleton	1.50	.70	.19
☐ 16 Ryne Sandberg	9.00	4.00	1.10
☐ 17 Barry Larkin	4.00	1.80	.50
☐ 18 Jeff Bagwell	15.00	6.75	1.85
☐ 19 Brett Butler	1.50	.70	.19
☐ 20 Larry Walker	4.00	1.80	.50
☐ 21 Bobby Bonilla	2.50	1.10	.30
☐ 22 Darren Daulton	1.50	.70	.19
☐ 23 Andy Van Slyke	1.50	.70	.19
☐ 24 Ray Lankford	1.50	.70	.19
☐ 25 Gary Sheffield	2.50	1.10	.30
☐ 26 Will Clark	4.00	1.80	.50
☐ 27 Bryan Harvey	1.50	.70	.19
☐ 28 David Nied	2.50	1.10	.30

1994 Score

The 1994 Score set of 660 cards was issued in two series of 330. The cards are standard size. The navy blue bordered fronts feature color action photos with the player's name and team name appearing on two team color-coded stripes across the bottom. The horizontal back features a narrow-cropped color player close-up shot on the left side. On a team color-coded stripe at the top are the player's name and position, and below are the team logo, biography, player profile, and career statistics. Among the subsets are American League stadiums (317-330) and National League stadiums (647-660). The cards are numbered on the back. Rookie Cards include

Brian Anderson, Brooks Kieschnick, Derrek Lee, Trot Nixon and Kirk Presley.

	MINT	NRMT	EXC
COMPLETE SET (660)	30.00	13.50	3.70
COMPLETE SERIES 1 (330)	15.00	6.75	1.85
COMPLETE SERIES 2 (330)	15.00	6.75	1.85
COMMON CARD (1-330)	.05	.02	.01
COMMON CARD (331-660)	.05	.02	.01
COMP. GOLD RUSH SET (660)	180.00	80.00	22.00
GOLD RUSH COMMON (1-660)	.25	.11	.03
GOLD RUSH SEMISTAR	.50	.23	.06
*GOLD RUSH VETERAN STARS: 4X TO 7X BASIC CARDS			
*GOLD RUSH YOUNG STARS 2.5X TO 5X BASIC CARDS			
*GOLD RUSH ROOKIE CARDS: 2X TO 4X BASIC CARDS			
☐ 1 Barry Bonds	.50	.23	.06
☐ 2 John Olerud	.15	.07	.02
☐ 3 Ken Griffey Jr.	2.00	.90	.25
☐ 4 Jeff Bagwell	.60	.25	.07
☐ 5 John Burkett	.10	.05	.01
☐ 6 Jack McDowell	.15	.07	.02
☐ 7 Albert Belle	.75	.35	.09
☐ 8 Andres Galarraga	.15	.07	.02
☐ 9 Mike Mussina	.25	.11	.03
☐ 10 Will Clark	.25	.11	.03
☐ 11 Travis Fryman	.15	.07	.02
☐ 12 Tony Gwynn	.60	.25	.07
☐ 13 Robin Yount	.25	.11	.03
☐ 14 Dave Magadan	.05	.02	.01
☐ 15 Paul O'Neill	.10	.05	.01
☐ 16 Ray Lankford	.15	.07	.02
☐ 17 Damion Easley	.05	.02	.01
☐ 18 Andy Van Slyke	.10	.05	.01
☐ 19 Brian McRae	.10	.05	.01
☐ 20 Ryne Sandberg	.50	.23	.06
☐ 21 Kirby Puckett	.60	.25	.07
☐ 22 Dwight Gooden	.05	.02	.01
☐ 23 Don Mattingly	1.00	.45	.12
☐ 24 Kevin Mitchell	.10	.05	.01
☐ 25 Roger Clemens	.30	.14	.04
☐ 26 Eric Karros	.10	.05	.01
☐ 27 Juan Gonzalez	.50	.23	.06
☐ 28 John Kruk	.10	.05	.01
☐ 29 Gregg Jefferies	.15	.07	.02
☐ 30 Tom Glavine	.15	.07	.02
☐ 31 Ivan Rodriguez	.15	.07	.02
☐ 32 Jay Bell	.10	.05	.01
☐ 33 Randy Johnson	.40	.18	.05
☐ 34 Darren Daulton	.15	.07	.02
☐ 35 Rickey Henderson	.15	.07	.02
☐ 36 Eddie Murray	.25	.11	.03
☐ 37 Brian Harper	.05	.02	.01
☐ 38 Delino DeShields	.10	.05	.01
☐ 39 Jose Lind	.05	.02	.01
☐ 40 Benito Santiago	.05	.02	.01
☐ 41 Frank Thomas	2.00	.90	.25
☐ 42 Mark Grace	.15	.07	.02
☐ 43 Roberto Alomar	.40	.18	.05
☐ 44 Andy Benes	.10	.05	.01
☐ 45 Luis Polonia	.05	.02	.01
☐ 46 Brett Butler	.10	.05	.01
☐ 47 Terry Steinbach	.10	.05	.01
☐ 48 Craig Biggio	.10	.05	.01
☐ 49 Greg Vaughn	.10	.05	.01
☐ 50 Charlie Hayes	.10	.05	.01
☐ 51 Mickey Tettleton	.10	.05	.01
☐ 52 Jose Rijo	.10	.05	.01
☐ 53 Carlos Baerga	.40	.18	.05
☐ 54 Jeff Blauser	.10	.05	.01

☐ 55	Leo Gomez	.05	.02	.01
☐ 56	Bob Tewksbury	.05	.02	.01
☐ 57	Mo Vaughn	.30	.14	.04
☐ 58	Orlando Merced	.10	.05	.01
☐ 59	Tino Martinez	.10	.05	.01
☐ 60	Lenny Dykstra	.15	.07	.02
☐ 61	Jose Canseco	.30	.14	.04
☐ 62	Tony Fernandez	.05	.02	.01
☐ 63	Donovan Osborne	.05	.02	.01
☐ 64	Ken Hill	.10	.05	.01
☐ 65	Kent Hrbek	.05	.02	.01
☐ 66	Bryan Harvey	.05	.02	.01
☐ 67	Wally Joyner	.10	.05	.01
☐ 68	Derrick May	.05	.02	.01
☐ 69	Lance Johnson	.05	.02	.01
☐ 70	Willie McGee	.05	.02	.01
☐ 71	Mark Langston	.15	.07	.02
☐ 72	Terry Pendleton	.10	.05	.01
☐ 73	Joe Carter	.30	.14	.04
☐ 74	Barry Larkin	.25	.11	.03
☐ 75	Jimmy Key	.10	.05	.01
☐ 76	Joe Girardi	.05	.02	.01
☐ 77	B.J. Surhoff	.05	.02	.01
☐ 78	Pete Harnisch	.05	.02	.01
☐ 79	Lou Whitaker UER	.15	.07	.02
	(Milt Cuyler			
	pictured on front)			
☐ 80	Cory Snyder	.05	.02	.01
☐ 81	Kenny Lofton	.60	.25	.07
☐ 82	Fred McGriff	.25	.11	.03
☐ 83	Mike Greenwell	.10	.05	.01
☐ 84	Mike Perez	.05	.02	.01
☐ 85	Cal Ripken	2.00	.90	.25
☐ 86	Don Slaught	.05	.02	.01
☐ 87	Omar Vizquel	.05	.02	.01
☐ 88	Curt Schilling	.05	.02	.01
☐ 89	Chuck Knoblauch	.15	.07	.02
☐ 90	Moises Alou	.15	.07	.02
☐ 91	Greg Gagne	.05	.02	.01
☐ 92	Bret Saberhagen	.10	.05	.01
☐ 93	Ozzie Guillen	.05	.02	.01
☐ 94	Matt Williams	.30	.14	.04
☐ 95	Chad Curtis	.10	.05	.01
☐ 96	Mike Harkey	.05	.02	.01
☐ 97	Devon White	.10	.05	.01
☐ 98	Walt Weiss	.05	.02	.01
☐ 99	Kevin Brown	.05	.02	.01
☐ 100	Gary Sheffield	.15	.07	.02
☐ 101	Wade Boggs	.15	.07	.02
☐ 102	Orel Hershiser	.10	.05	.01
☐ 103	Tony Phillips	.05	.02	.01
☐ 104	Andujar Cedeno	.05	.02	.01
☐ 105	Bill Spiers	.05	.02	.01
☐ 106	Otis Nixon	.05	.02	.01
☐ 107	Felix Fermin	.05	.02	.01
☐ 108	Bip Roberts	.05	.02	.01
☐ 109	Dennis Eckersley	.15	.07	.02
☐ 110	Dante Bichette	.25	.11	.03
☐ 111	Ben McDonald	.10	.05	.01
☐ 112	Jim Poole	.05	.02	.01
☐ 113	John Dopson	.05	.02	.01
☐ 114	Rob Dibble	.05	.02	.01
☐ 115	Jeff Treadway	.05	.02	.01
☐ 116	Ricky Jordan	.05	.02	.01
☐ 117	Mike Henneman	.05	.02	.01
☐ 118	Willie Blair	.05	.02	.01
☐ 119	Doug Henry	.05	.02	.01
☐ 120	Gerald Perry	.05	.02	.01
☐ 121	Greg Myers	.05	.02	.01
☐ 122	John Franco	.05	.02	.01
☐ 123	Roger Mason	.05	.02	.01
☐ 124	Chris Hammond	.05	.02	.01
☐ 125	Hubie Brooks	.05	.02	.01
☐ 126	Kent Mercker	.05	.02	.01
☐ 127	Jim Abbott	.15	.07	.02
☐ 128	Kevin Bass	.05	.02	.01
☐ 129	Rick Aguilera	.10	.05	.01
☐ 130	Mitch Webster	.05	.02	.01
☐ 131	Eric Plunk	.05	.02	.01
☐ 132	Mark Carreon	.05	.02	.01
☐ 133	Dave Stewart	.10	.05	.01
☐ 134	Willie Wilson	.05	.02	.01
☐ 135	Dave Fleming	.05	.02	.01
☐ 136	Jeff Tackett	.05	.02	.01
☐ 137	Geno Petralli	.05	.02	.01
☐ 138	Gene Harris	.05	.02	.01
☐ 139	Scott Bankhead	.05	.02	.01
☐ 140	Trevor Wilson	.05	.02	.01
☐ 141	Alvaro Espinoza	.05	.02	.01
☐ 142	Ryan Bowen	.05	.02	.01
☐ 143	Mike Moore	.05	.02	.01
☐ 144	Bill Pecota	.05	.02	.01
☐ 145	Jaime Navarro	.05	.02	.01
☐ 146	Jack Daugherty	.05	.02	.01
☐ 147	Bob Wickman	.05	.02	.01
☐ 148	Chris Jones	.05	.02	.01
☐ 149	Todd Stottlemyre	.05	.02	.01
☐ 150	Brian Williams	.05	.02	.01
☐ 151	Chuck Finley	.05	.02	.01
☐ 152	Lenny Harris	.05	.02	.01
☐ 153	Alex Fernandez	.15	.07	.02
☐ 154	Candy Maldonado	.05	.02	.01
☐ 155	Jeff Montgomery	.10	.05	.01
☐ 156	David West	.05	.02	.01
☐ 157	Mark Williamson	.05	.02	.01
☐ 158	Milt Thompson	.05	.02	.01
☐ 159	Ron Darling	.05	.02	.01
☐ 160	Stan Belinda	.05	.02	.01
☐ 161	Henry Cotto	.05	.02	.01
☐ 162	Mel Rojas	.05	.02	.01
☐ 163	Doug Strange	.05	.02	.01
☐ 164	Rene Arocha	.10	.05	.01
☐ 165	Tim Hulett	.05	.02	.01
☐ 166	Steve Avery	.15	.07	.02
☐ 167	Jim Thome	.40	.18	.05
☐ 168	Tom Browning	.05	.02	.01
☐ 169	Mario Diaz	.05	.02	.01
☐ 170	Steve Reed	.05	.02	.01
☐ 171	Scott Livingstone	.05	.02	.01
☐ 172	Chris Donnels	.05	.02	.01
☐ 173	John Jaha	.05	.02	.01
☐ 174	Carlos Hernandez	.05	.02	.01
☐ 175	Dion James	.05	.02	.01
☐ 176	Bud Black	.05	.02	.01
☐ 177	Tony Castillo	.05	.02	.01
☐ 178	Jose Guzman	.05	.02	.01
☐ 179	Torey Lovullo	.05	.02	.01
☐ 180	John Vander Wal	.05	.02	.01
☐ 181	Mike LaValliere	.05	.02	.01
☐ 182	Sid Fernandez	.05	.02	.01
☐ 183	Brent Mayne	.05	.02	.01
☐ 184	Terry Mulholland	.05	.02	.01
☐ 185	Willie Banks	.05	.02	.01
☐ 186	Steve Cooke	.05	.02	.01
☐ 187	Brent Gates	.10	.05	.01
☐ 188	Erik Pappas	.05	.02	.01
☐ 189	Bill Haselman	.05	.02	.01
☐ 190	Fernando Valenzuela	.05	.02	.01
☐ 191	Gary Redus	.05	.02	.01
☐ 192	Danny Darwin	.05	.02	.01
☐ 193	Mark Portugal	.05	.02	.01
☐ 194	Derek Lilliquist	.05	.02	.01

#	Player			
☐ 195	Charlie O'Brien	.05	.02	.01
☐ 196	Matt Nokes	.05	.02	.01
☐ 197	Danny Sheaffer	.05	.02	.01
☐ 198	Bill Gullickson	.05	.02	.01
☐ 199	Alex Arias	.05	.02	.01
☐ 200	Mike Fetters	.05	.02	.01
☐ 201	Brian Jordan	.10	.05	.01
☐ 202	Joe Grahe	.05	.02	.01
☐ 203	Tom Candiotti	.05	.02	.01
☐ 204	Jeremy Hernández	.05	.02	.01
☐ 205	Mike Stanton	.05	.02	.01
☐ 206	David Howard	.05	.02	.01
☐ 207	Darren Holmes	.05	.02	.01
☐ 208	Rick Honeycutt	.05	.02	.01
☐ 209	Danny Jackson	.05	.02	.01
☐ 210	Rich Amaral	.05	.02	.01
☐ 211	Blas Minor	.05	.02	.01
☐ 212	Kenny Rogers	.10	.05	.01
☐ 213	Jim Leyritz	.05	.02	.01
☐ 214	Mike Morgan	.05	.02	.01
☐ 215	Dan Gladden	.05	.02	.01
☐ 216	Randy Velarde	.05	.02	.01
☐ 217	Mitch Williams	.05	.02	.01
☐ 218	Hipolito Pichardo	.05	.02	.01
☐ 219	Dave Burba	.05	.02	.01
☐ 220	Wilson Alvarez	.15	.07	.02
☐ 221	Bob Zupcic	.05	.02	.01
☐ 222	Francisco Cabrera	.05	.02	.01
☐ 223	Julio Valera	.05	.02	.01
☐ 224	Paul Assenmacher	.05	.02	.01
☐ 225	Jeff Branson	.05	.02	.01
☐ 226	Todd Frohwirth	.05	.02	.01
☐ 227	Armando Reynoso	.05	.02	.01
☐ 228	Rich Rowland	.05	.02	.01
☐ 229	Freddie Benavides	.05	.02	.01
☐ 230	Wayne Kirby	.05	.02	.01
☐ 231	Darryl Kile	.10	.05	.01
☐ 232	Skeeter Barnes	.05	.02	.01
☐ 233	Ramon Martinez	.10	.05	.01
☐ 234	Tom Gordon	.05	.02	.01
☐ 235	Dave Gallagher	.05	.02	.01
☐ 236	Ricky Bones	.05	.02	.01
☐ 237	Larry Andersen	.05	.02	.01
☐ 238	Pat Meares	.05	.02	.01
☐ 239	Zane Smith	.05	.02	.01
☐ 240	Tim Leary	.05	.02	.01
☐ 241	Phil Clark	.05	.02	.01
☐ 242	Danny Cox	.05	.02	.01
☐ 243	Mike Jackson	.05	.02	.01
☐ 244	Mike Gallego	.05	.02	.01
☐ 245	Lee Smith	.15	.07	.02
☐ 246	Todd Jones	.05	.02	.01
☐ 247	Steve Bedrosian	.05	.02	.01
☐ 248	Troy Neel	.05	.02	.01
☐ 249	Jose Bautista	.05	.02	.01
☐ 250	Steve Frey	.05	.02	.01
☐ 251	Jeff Reardon	.10	.05	.01
☐ 252	Stan Javier	.05	.02	.01
☐ 253	Mo Sanford	.05	.02	.01
☐ 254	Steve Sax	.05	.02	.01
☐ 255	Luis Aquino	.05	.02	.01
☐ 256	Domingo Jean	.05	.02	.01
☐ 257	Scott Servais	.05	.02	.01
☐ 258	Brad Pennington	.05	.02	.01
☐ 259	Dave Hansen	.05	.02	.01
☐ 260	Goose Gossage	.10	.05	.01
☐ 261	Jeff Fassero	.05	.02	.01
☐ 262	Junior Ortiz	.05	.02	.01
☐ 263	Anthony Young	.05	.02	.01
☐ 264	Chris Bosio	.05	.02	.01
☐ 265	Ruben Amaro Jr.	.05	.02	.01
☐ 266	Mark Eichhorn	.05	.02	.01
☐ 267	Dave Clark	.05	.02	.01
☐ 268	Gary Thurman	.05	.02	.01
☐ 269	Les Lancaster	.05	.02	.01
☐ 270	Jamie Moyer	.05	.02	.01
☐ 271	Ricky Gutierrez	.05	.02	.01
☐ 272	Greg A.Harris	.05	.02	.01
☐ 273	Mike Benjamin	.05	.02	.01
☐ 274	Gene Nelson	.05	.02	.01
☐ 275	Damon Berryhill	.05	.02	.01
☐ 276	Scott Radinsky	.05	.02	.01
☐ 277	Mike Aldrete	.05	.02	.01
☐ 278	Jerry DiPoto	.05	.02	.01
☐ 279	Chris Haney	.05	.02	.01
☐ 280	Richie Lewis	.05	.02	.01
☐ 281	Jarvis Brown	.05	.02	.01
☐ 282	Juan Bell	.05	.02	.01
☐ 283	Joe Klink	.05	.02	.01
☐ 284	Graeme Lloyd	.05	.02	.01
☐ 285	Casey Candaele	.05	.02	.01
☐ 286	Bob MacDonald	.05	.02	.01
☐ 287	Mike Sharperson	.05	.02	.01
☐ 288	Gene Larkin	.05	.02	.01
☐ 289	Brian Barnes	.05	.02	.01
☐ 290	David McCarty	.05	.02	.01
☐ 291	Jeff Innis	.05	.02	.01
☐ 292	Bob Patterson	.05	.02	.01
☐ 293	Ben Rivera	.05	.02	.01
☐ 294	John Habyan	.05	.02	.01
☐ 295	Rich Rodriguez	.05	.02	.01
☐ 296	Edwin Nunez	.05	.02	.01
☐ 297	Rod Brewer	.05	.02	.01
☐ 298	Mike Timlin	.05	.02	.01
☐ 299	Jesse Orosco	.05	.02	.01
☐ 300	Gary Gaetti	.05	.02	.01
☐ 301	Todd Benzinger	.05	.02	.01
☐ 302	Jeff Nelson	.05	.02	.01
☐ 303	Rafael Belliard	.05	.02	.01
☐ 304	Matt Whiteside	.05	.02	.01
☐ 305	Vinny Castilla	.10	.05	.01
☐ 306	Matt Turner	.05	.02	.01
☐ 307	Eduardo Perez	.05	.02	.01
☐ 308	Joel Johnston	.05	.02	.01
☐ 309	Chris Gomez	.15	.07	.02
☐ 310	Pat Rapp	.05	.02	.01
☐ 311	Jim Tatum	.05	.02	.01
☐ 312	Kirk Rueter	.05	.02	.01
☐ 313	John Flaherty	.05	.02	.01
☐ 314	Tom Kramer	.05	.02	.01
☐ 315	Mark Whiten	.05	.02	.01
☐ 316	Chris Bosio	.05	.02	.01
☐ 317	Baltimore Orioles CL	.10	.05	.01
☐ 318	Boston Red Sox CL UER (Viola listed as 316; should be 331)	.10	.05	.01
☐ 319	California Angels CL	.10	.05	.01
☐ 320	Chicago White Sox CL	.10	.05	.01
☐ 321	Cleveland Indians CL	.10	.05	.01
☐ 322	Detroit Tigers CL	.10	.05	.01
☐ 323	Kansas City Royals CL	.10	.05	.01
☐ 324	Milwaukee Brewers CL	.10	.05	.01
☐ 325	Minnesota Twins CL	.10	.05	.01
☐ 326	New York Yankees CL	.10	.05	.01
☐ 327	Oakland Athletics CL	.10	.05	.01
☐ 328	Seattle Mariners CL	.10	.05	.01
☐ 329	Texas Rangers CL	.10	.05	.01
☐ 330	Toronto Blue Jays CL	.10	.05	.01
☐ 331	Frank Viola	.05	.02	.01
☐ 332	Ron Gant	.10	.05	.01
☐ 333	Charles Nagy	.10	.05	.01
☐ 334	Roberto Kelly	.05	.02	.01

□	#	Player			
□	335	Brady Anderson	.10	.05	.01
□	336	Alex Cole	.05	.02	.01
□	337	Alan Trammell	.15	.07	.02
□	338	Derek Bell	.10	.05	.01
□	339	Bernie Williams	.10	.05	.01
□	340	Jose Offerman	.05	.02	.01
□	341	Bill Wegman	.05	.02	.01
□	342	Ken Caminiti	.10	.05	.01
□	343	Pat Borders	.05	.02	.01
□	344	Kirt Manwaring	.05	.02	.01
□	345	Chili Davis	.10	.05	.01
□	346	Steve Buechele	.05	.02	.01
□	347	Robin Ventura	.10	.05	.01
□	348	Teddy Higuera	.05	.02	.01
□	349	Jerry Browne	.05	.02	.01
□	350	Scott Kamieniecki	.05	.02	.01
□	351	Kevin Tapani	.05	.02	.01
□	352	Marquis Grissom	.15	.07	.02
□	353	Jay Buhner	.15	.07	.02
□	354	Dave Hollins	.15	.07	.02
□	355	Dan Wilson	.05	.02	.01
□	356	Bob Walk	.05	.02	.01
□	357	Chris Hoiles	.10	.05	.01
□	358	Todd Zeile	.10	.05	.01
□	359	Kevin Appier	.10	.05	.01
□	360	Chris Sabo	.05	.02	.01
□	361	David Segui	.05	.02	.01
□	362	Jerald Clark	.05	.02	.01
□	363	Tony Pena	.05	.02	.01
□	364	Steve Finley	.05	.02	.01
□	365	Roger Pavlik	.05	.02	.01
□	366	John Smoltz	.10	.05	.01
□	367	Scott Fletcher	.05	.02	.01
□	368	Jody Reed	.05	.02	.01
□	369	David Wells	.05	.02	.01
□	370	Jose Vizcaino	.05	.02	.01
□	371	Pat Listach	.05	.02	.01
□	372	Orestes Destrade	.05	.02	.01
□	373	Danny Tartabull	.10	.05	.01
□	374	Greg W. Harris	.05	.02	.01
□	375	Juan Guzman	.10	.05	.01
□	376	Larry Walker	.25	.11	.03
□	377	Gary DiSarcina	.05	.02	.01
□	378	Bobby Bonilla	.15	.07	.02
□	379	Tim Raines	.15	.07	.02
□	380	Tommy Greene	.05	.02	.01
□	381	Chris Gwynn	.05	.02	.01
□	382	Jeff King	.05	.02	.01
□	383	Shane Mack	.10	.05	.01
□	384	Ozzie Smith	.40	.18	.05
□	385	Eddie Zambrano	.05	.02	.01
□	386	Mike Devereaux	.10	.05	.01
□	387	Erik Hanson	.05	.02	.01
□	388	Scott Cooper	.10	.05	.01
□	389	Dean Palmer	.10	.05	.01
□	390	John Wetteland	.05	.02	.01
□	391	Reggie Jefferson	.05	.02	.01
□	392	Mark Lemke	.05	.02	.01
□	393	Cecil Fielder	.15	.07	.02
□	394	Reggie Sanders	.15	.07	.02
□	395	Darryl Hamilton	.05	.02	.01
□	396	Daryl Boston	.05	.02	.01
□	397	Pat Kelly	.05	.02	.01
□	398	Joe Orsulak	.05	.02	.01
□	399	Ed Sprague	.05	.02	.01
□	400	Eric Anthony	.05	.02	.01
□	401	Scott Sanderson	.05	.02	.01
□	402	Jim Gott	.05	.02	.01
□	403	Ron Karkovice	.05	.02	.01
□	404	Phil Plantier	.10	.05	.01
□	405	David Cone	.15	.07	.02
□	406	Robby Thompson	.05	.02	.01
□	407	Dave Winfield	.15	.07	.02
□	408	Dwight Smith	.05	.02	.01
□	409	Ruben Sierra	.15	.07	.02
□	410	Jack Armstrong	.05	.02	.01
□	411	Mike Felder	.05	.02	.01
□	412	Wil Cordero	.15	.07	.02
□	413	Julio Franco	.10	.05	.01
□	414	Howard Johnson	.05	.02	.01
□	415	Mark McLemore	.05	.02	.01
□	416	Pete Incaviglia	.05	.02	.01
□	417	John Valentin	.10	.05	.01
□	418	Tim Wakefield	.05	.02	.01
□	419	Jose Mesa	.05	.02	.01
□	420	Bernard Gilkey	.10	.05	.01
□	421	Kirk Gibson	.10	.05	.01
□	422	Dave Justice	.25	.11	.03
□	423	Tom Brunansky	.05	.02	.01
□	424	John Smiley	.05	.02	.01
□	425	Kevin Maas	.05	.02	.01
□	426	Doug Drabek	.15	.07	.02
□	427	Paul Molitor	.15	.07	.02
□	428	Darryl Strawberry	.10	.05	.01
□	429	Tim Naehring	.05	.02	.01
□	430	Bill Swift	.05	.02	.01
□	431	Ellis Burks	.10	.05	.01
□	432	Greg Hibbard	.05	.02	.01
□	433	Felix Jose	.05	.02	.01
□	434	Bret Barberie	.05	.02	.01
□	435	Pedro Munoz	.05	.02	.01
□	436	Darrin Fletcher	.05	.02	.01
□	437	Bobby Witt	.05	.02	.01
□	438	Wes Chamberlain	.05	.02	.01
□	439	Mackey Sasser	.05	.02	.01
□	440	Mark Whiten	.10	.05	.01
□	441	Harold Reynolds	.05	.02	.01
□	442	Greg Olson	.05	.02	.01
□	443	Billy Hatcher	.05	.02	.01
□	444	Joe Oliver	.05	.02	.01
□	445	Sandy Alomar Jr.	.10	.05	.01
□	446	Tim Wallach	.05	.02	.01
□	447	Karl Rhodes	.05	.02	.01
□	448	Royce Clayton	.10	.05	.01
□	449	Cal Eldred	.10	.05	.01
□	450	Rick Wilkins	.05	.02	.01
□	451	Mike Stanley	.05	.02	.01
□	452	Charlie Hough	.10	.05	.01
□	453	Jack Morris	.15	.07	.02
□	454	Jon Ratliff	.15	.07	.02
□	455	Rene Gonzales	.05	.02	.01
□	456	Eddie Taubensee	.05	.02	.01
□	457	Roberto Hernandez	.05	.02	.01
□	458	Todd Hundley	.05	.02	.01
□	459	Mike Macfarlane	.05	.02	.01
□	460	Mickey Morandini	.05	.02	.01
□	461	Scott Erickson	.05	.02	.01
□	462	Lonnie Smith	.05	.02	.01
□	463	Dave Henderson	.05	.02	.01
□	464	Ryan Klesko	.50	.23	.06
□	465	Edgar Martinez	.05	.02	.01
□	466	Tom Pagnozzi	.05	.02	.01
□	467	Charlie Leibrandt	.05	.02	.01
□	468	Brian Anderson	.15	.07	.02
□	469	Harold Baines	.10	.05	.01
□	470	Tim Belcher	.05	.02	.01
□	471	Andre Dawson	.15	.07	.02
□	472	Eric Young	.10	.05	.01
□	473	Paul Sorrento	.05	.02	.01
□	474	Luis Gonzalez	.05	.02	.01
□	475	Rob Deer	.05	.02	.01
□	476	Mike Piazza	.75	.35	.09

☐ 477 Kevin Reimer	.05	.02	.01	☐ 546 Al Martin	.05	.02	.01
☐ 478 Jeff Gardner	.05	.02	.01	☐ 547 Bob Welch	.05	.02	.01
☐ 479 Melido Perez	.05	.02	.01	☐ 548 Scott Christmas	.10	.05	.01
☐ 480 Darren Lewis	.05	.02	.01	☐ 549 Norm Charlton	.05	.02	.01
☐ 481 Duane Ward	.05	.02	.01	☐ 550 Mark McGwire	.15	.07	.02
☐ 482 Rey Sanchez	.05	.02	.01	☐ 551 Greg McMichael	.05	.02	.01
☐ 483 Mark Lewis	.05	.02	.01	☐ 552 Tim Costo	.05	.02	.01
☐ 484 Jeff Conine	.15	.07	.02	☐ 553 Rodney Bolton	.05	.02	.01
☐ 485 Joey Cora	.05	.02	.01	☐ 554 Pedro Martinez	.15	.07	.02
☐ 486 Trot Nixon	.50	.23	.06	☐ 555 Marc Valdes	.10	.05	.01
☐ 487 Kevin McReynolds	.05	.02	.01	☐ 556 Darrell Whitmore	.05	.02	.01
☐ 488 Mike Lansing	.10	.05	.01	☐ 557 Tim Bogar	.05	.02	.01
☐ 489 Mike Pagliarulo	.05	.02	.01	☐ 558 Steve Karsay	.10	.05	.01
☐ 490 Mariano Duncan	.05	.02	.01	☐ 559 Danny Bautista	.10	.05	.01
☐ 491 Mike Bordick	.05	.02	.01	☐ 560 Jeffrey Hammonds	.15	.07	.02
☐ 492 Kevin Young	.05	.02	.01	☐ 561 Aaron Sele	.15	.07	.02
☐ 493 Dave Valle	.05	.02	.01	☐ 562 Russ Springer	.05	.02	.01
☐ 494 Wayne Gomes	.25	.11	.03	☐ 563 Jason Bere	.15	.07	.02
☐ 495 Rafael Palmeiro	.15	.07	.02	☐ 564 Billy Brewer	.05	.02	.01
☐ 496 Deion Sanders	.40	.18	.05	☐ 565 Sterling Hitchcock	.10	.05	.01
☐ 497 Rick Sutcliffe	.10	.05	.01	☐ 566 Bobby Munoz	.05	.02	.01
☐ 498 Randy Milligan	.05	.02	.01	☐ 567 Craig Paquette	.05	.02	.01
☐ 499 Carlos Quintana	.05	.02	.01	☐ 568 Bret Boone	.15	.07	.02
☐ 500 Chris Turner	.05	.02	.01	☐ 569 Dan Peltier	.05	.02	.01
☐ 501 Thomas Howard	.05	.02	.01	☐ 570 Jeromy Burnitz	.10	.05	.01
☐ 502 Greg Swindell	.05	.02	.01	☐ 571 John Wasdin	.40	.18	.05
☐ 503 Chad Kreuter	.05	.02	.01	☐ 572 Chipper Jones	1.00	.45	.12
☐ 504 Eric Davis	.05	.02	.01	☐ 573 Jamey Wright	.20	.09	.03
☐ 505 Dickie Thon	.05	.02	.01	☐ 574 Jeff Granger	.10	.05	.01
☐ 506 Matt Drews	.50	.23	.06	☐ 575 Jay Powell	.20	.09	.03
☐ 507 Spike Owen	.05	.02	.01	☐ 576 Ryan Thompson	.10	.05	.01
☐ 508 Rod Beck	.10	.05	.01	☐ 577 Lou Frazier	.05	.02	.01
☐ 509 Pat Hentgen	.10	.05	.01	☐ 578 Paul Wagner	.05	.02	.01
☐ 510 Sammy Sosa	.15	.07	.02	☐ 579 Brad Ausmus	.05	.02	.01
☐ 511 J.T. Snow	.10	.05	.01	☐ 580 Jack Voigt	.05	.02	.01
☐ 512 Chuck Carr	.05	.02	.01	☐ 581 Kevin Rogers	.05	.02	.01
☐ 513 Bo Jackson	.15	.07	.02	☐ 582 Damon Buford	.05	.02	.01
☐ 514 Dennis Martinez	.10	.05	.01	☐ 583 Paul Quantrill	.05	.02	.01
☐ 515 Phil Hiatt	.05	.02	.01	☐ 584 Marc Newfield	.15	.07	.02
☐ 516 Jeff Kent	.10	.05	.01	☐ 585 Derrek Lee	.75	.35	.09
☐ 517 Brooks Kieschnick	1.50	.70	.19	☐ 586 Shane Reynolds	.05	.02	.01
☐ 518 Kirk Presley	.20	.09	.03	☐ 587 Cliff Floyd	.15	.07	.02
☐ 519 Kevin Seitzer	.05	.02	.01	☐ 588 Jeff Schwarz	.05	.02	.01
☐ 520 Carlos Garcia	.05	.02	.01	☐ 589 Ross Powell	.05	.02	.01
☐ 521 Mike Blowers	.10	.05	.01	☐ 590 Gerald Williams	.05	.02	.01
☐ 522 Luis Alicea	.05	.02	.01	☐ 591 Mike Trombley	.05	.02	.01
☐ 523 David Hulse	.05	.02	.01	☐ 592 Ken Ryan	.05	.02	.01
☐ 524 Greg Maddux UER	2.00	.90	.25	☐ 593 John O'Donoghue	.05	.02	.01
(career strikeout totals listed as 113; should be 1134)				☐ 594 Rod Correia	.05	.02	.01
				☐ 595 Darrell Sherman	.05	.02	.01
☐ 525 Gregg Olson	.05	.02	.01	☐ 596 Steve Scarsone	.05	.02	.01
☐ 526 Hal Morris	.10	.05	.01	☐ 597 Sherman Obando	.05	.02	.01
☐ 527 Daron Kirkreit	.10	.05	.01	☐ 598 Kurt Abbott	.15	.07	.02
☐ 528 David Nied	.15	.07	.02	☐ 599 Dave Telgheder	.05	.02	.01
☐ 529 Jeff Russell	.05	.02	.01	☐ 600 Rick Trlicek	.05	.02	.01
☐ 530 Kevin Gross	.05	.02	.01	☐ 601 Carl Everett	.10	.05	.01
☐ 531 John Doherty	.05	.02	.01	☐ 602 Luis Ortiz	.05	.02	.01
☐ 532 Matt Brunson	.15	.07	.02	☐ 603 Larry Luebbers	.05	.02	.01
☐ 533 Dave Nilsson	.05	.02	.01	☐ 604 Kevin Roberson	.05	.02	.01
☐ 534 Randy Myers	.05	.02	.01	☐ 605 Butch Huskey	.10	.05	.01
☐ 535 Steve Farr	.05	.02	.01	☐ 606 Benji Gil	.10	.05	.01
☐ 536 Billy Wagner	.40	.18	.05	☐ 607 Todd Van Poppel	.10	.05	.01
☐ 537 Darnell Coles	.05	.02	.01	☐ 608 Mark Hutton	.05	.02	.01
☐ 538 Frank Tanana	.05	.02	.01	☐ 609 Chip Hale	.05	.02	.01
☐ 539 Tim Salmon	.40	.18	.05	☐ 610 Matt Maysey	.05	.02	.01
☐ 540 Kim Batiste	.05	.02	.01	☐ 611 Scott Ruffcorn	.15	.07	.02
☐ 541 George Bell	.05	.02	.01	☐ 612 Hilly Hathaway	.05	.02	.01
☐ 542 Tom Henke	.05	.02	.01	☐ 613 Allen Watson	.05	.02	.01
☐ 543 Sam Horn	.05	.02	.01	☐ 614 Carlos Delgado	.15	.07	.02
☐ 544 Doug Jones	.05	.02	.01	☐ 615 Roberto Mejia	.10	.05	.01
☐ 545 Scott Leius	.05	.02	.01	☐ 616 Turk Wendell	.05	.02	.01

☐ 617	Tony Tarasco	.15	.07	.02
☐ 618	Raul Mondesi	.60	.25	.07
☐ 619	Kevin Stocker	.10	.05	.01
☐ 620	Javier Lopez	.30	.14	.04
☐ 621	Keith Kessinger	.05	.02	.01
☐ 622	Bob Hamelin	.10	.05	.01
☐ 623	John Roper	.10	.05	.01
☐ 624	Lenny Dykstra WS	.05	.02	.01
☐ 625	Joe Carter WS	.15	.07	.02
☐ 626	Jim Abbott HL	.05	.02	.01
☐ 627	Lee Smith HL	.05	.02	.01
☐ 628	Ken Griffey Jr. HL	1.00	.45	.12
☐ 629	Dave Winfield HL	.15	.07	.02
☐ 630	Darryl Kile HL	.05	.02	.01
☐ 631	Frank Thomas AL MVP	1.00	.45	.12
☐ 632	Barry Bonds NL MVP	.25	.11	.03
☐ 633	Jack McDowell AL CY	.05	.02	.01
☐ 634	Greg Maddux NL CY	1.00	.45	.12
☐ 635	Tim Salmon AL ROY	.15	.07	.02
☐ 636	Mike Piazza NL ROY	.40	.18	.05
☐ 637	Brian Turang	.05	.02	.01
☐ 638	Rondell White	.15	.07	.02
☐ 639	Nigel Wilson	.05	.02	.01
☐ 640	Torii Hunter	.15	.07	.02
☐ 641	Salomon Torres	.10	.05	.01
☐ 642	Kevin Higgins	.05	.02	.01
☐ 643	Eric Wedge	.05	.02	.01
☐ 644	Roger Salkeld	.05	.02	.01
☐ 645	Manny Ramirez	1.00	.45	.12
☐ 646	Jeff McNeely	.05	.02	.01
☐ 647	Checklist	.10	.05	.01
	Atlanta Braves			
☐ 648	Checklist	.10	.05	.01
	Chicago Cubs			
☐ 649	Checklist	.10	.05	.01
	Cincinnati Reds			
☐ 650	Checklist	.10	.05	.01
	Colorado Rockies			
☐ 651	Checklist	.10	.05	.01
	Florida Marlins			
☐ 652	Checklist	.10	.05	.01
	Houston Astros			
☐ 653	Checklist	.10	.05	.01
	Los Angeles Dodgers			
☐ 654	Checklist	.10	.05	.01
	Montreal Expos			
☐ 655	Checklist	.10	.05	.01
	New York Mets			
☐ 656	Checklist	.10	.05	.01
	Philadelphia Phillies			
☐ 657	Checklist	.10	.05	.01
	Pittsburgh Pirates			
☐ 658	Checklist	.10	.05	.01
	St. Louis Cardinals			
☐ 659	Checklist	.10	.05	.01
	San Diego Padres			
☐ 660	Checklist	.10	.05	.01
	San Francisco Giants			

1994 Score
Boys of Summer

Randomly inserted in super packs at a rate of one in four, this 60-card set features top young stars and hopefuls. The set was issued in two series of 30 cards. The fronts

have a color player photo that is outlined by what resembles static electricity. The backgrounds are blurred and the player's name and Boys of Summer logo appear up the right-hand side. An orange back contains a player photo and text.

	MINT	NRMT	EXC
COMPLETE SET (60)	120.00	55.00	15.00
COMPLETE SERIES 1 (30)	60.00	27.00	7.50
COMPLETE SERIES 2 (30)	60.00	27.00	7.50
COMMON CARD (1-30)	1.50	.70	.19
COMMON CARD (31-60)	1.50	.70	.19

☐ 1	Jeff Conine	4.00	1.80	.50
☐ 2	Aaron Sele	3.00	1.35	.35
☐ 3	Kevin Stocker	2.00	.90	.25
☐ 4	Pat Meares	1.50	.70	.19
☐ 5	Jeromy Burnitz	1.50	.70	.19
☐ 6	Mike Piazza	18.00	8.00	2.20
☐ 7	Allen Watson	2.00	.90	.25
☐ 8	Jeffrey Hammonds	3.00	1.35	.35
☐ 9	Kevin Roberson	1.50	.70	.19
☐ 10	Hilly Hathaway	1.50	.70	.19
☐ 11	Kirk Rueter	1.50	.70	.19
☐ 12	Eduardo Perez	1.50	.70	.19
☐ 13	Ricky Gutierrez	1.50	.70	.19
☐ 14	Domingo Jean	1.50	.70	.19
☐ 15	David Nied	2.00	.90	.25
☐ 16	Wayne Kirby	1.50	.70	.19
☐ 17	Mike Lansing	2.00	.90	.25
☐ 18	Jason Bere	3.00	1.35	.35
☐ 19	Brent Gates	2.00	.90	.25
☐ 20	Javier Lopez	6.00	2.70	.75
☐ 21	Greg McMichael	1.50	.70	.19
☐ 22	David Hulse	1.50	.70	.19
☐ 23	Roberto Mejia	1.50	.70	.19
☐ 24	Tim Salmon	8.00	3.60	1.00
☐ 25	Rene Arocha	1.50	.70	.19
☐ 26	Bret Boone	3.00	1.35	.35
☐ 27	David McCarty	1.50	.70	.19
☐ 28	Todd Van Poppel	2.00	.90	.25
☐ 29	Lance Painter	1.50	.70	.19
☐ 30	Erik Pappas	1.50	.70	.19
☐ 31	Chuck Carr	1.50	.70	.19
☐ 32	Mark Hutton	1.50	.70	.19
☐ 33	Jeff McNeely	1.50	.70	.19
☐ 34	Willie Greene	2.00	.90	.25
☐ 35	Nigel Wilson	2.00	.90	.25
☐ 36	Rondell White	5.00	2.20	.60
☐ 37	Brian Turang	1.50	.70	.19
☐ 38	Manny Ramirez	20.00	9.00	2.50
☐ 39	Salomon Torres	2.00	.90	.25
☐ 40	Melvin Nieves	3.00	1.35	.35
☐ 41	Ryan Klesko	10.00	4.50	1.25
☐ 42	Keith Kessinger	1.50	.70	.19
☐ 43	Brad Ausmus	1.50	.70	.19

		MINT	NRMT	EXC
☐ 44	Bob Hamelin	2.00	.90	.25
☐ 45	Carlos Delgado	4.00	1.80	.50
☐ 46	Marc Newfield	3.00	1.35	.35
☐ 47	Raul Mondesi	12.00	5.50	1.50
☐ 48	Tim Costo	1.50	.70	.19
☐ 49	Pedro Martinez	3.00	1.35	.35
☐ 50	Steve Karsay	3.00	1.35	.35
☐ 51	Danny Bautista	1.50	.70	.19
☐ 52	Butch Huskey	2.00	.90	.25
☐ 53	Kurt Abbott	3.00	1.35	.35
☐ 54	Darrell Sherman	1.50	.70	.19
☐ 55	Damon Buford	2.00	.90	.25
☐ 56	Ross Powell	1.50	.70	.19
☐ 57	Darrell Whitmore	1.50	.70	.19
☐ 58	Chipper Jones	20.00	9.00	2.50
☐ 59	Jeff Granger	2.00	.90	.25
☐ 60	Cliff Floyd	3.00	1.35	.35

1994 Score Cycle

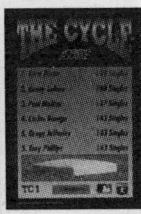

This 20-card set was randomly inserted in second series foil and jumbo packs at a rate of one in 90. The set is arranged according to players with the most singles (1-5), doubles (6-10), triples (11-15) and home runs (16-20). The front contains an oval player photo with "The Cycle" at top and the players name at the bottom. Also at the bottom, is the number of of that particular base hit the player accumulated in 1993. A small baseball diamond appears beneath the oval photo. The back lists the top five of the given base hit category. A dark blue border surrounds both sides. The cards are number with a TC prefix.

		MINT	NRMT	EXC
COMPLETE SET (20)		250.00	110.00	31.00
COMMON CARD (TC1-TC20)		3.00	1.35	.35
☐ TC1	Brett Butler	3.00	1.35	.35
☐ TC2	Kenny Lofton	20.00	9.00	2.50
☐ TC3	Paul Molitor	5.00	2.20	.60
☐ TC4	Carlos Baerga	12.00	5.50	1.50
☐ TC5	Gregg Jefferies	5.00	2.20	.60
	Tony Phillips			
☐ TC6	John Olerud	5.00	2.20	.60
☐ TC7	Charlie Hayes	3.00	1.35	.35
☐ TC8	Lenny Dykstra	5.00	2.20	.60
☐ TC9	Dante Bichette	8.00	3.60	1.00
☐ TC10	Devon White	5.00	2.20	.60
☐ TC11	Lance Johnson	3.00	1.35	.35
☐ TC12	Joey Cora	3.00	1.35	.35
	Steve Finley			
☐ TC13	Tony Fernandez	3.00	1.35	.35
☐ TC14	David Hulse	3.00	1.35	.35
	Brett Butler			
☐ TC15	Jay Bell	3.00	1.35	.35
	Brian McRae			
	Mickey Morandini			
☐ TC16	Juan Gonzalez	15.00	6.75	1.85
	Barry Bonds			
☐ TC17	Ken Griffey Jr.	60.00	27.00	7.50
☐ TC18	Frank Thomas	60.00	27.00	7.50
☐ TC19	Dave Justice	8.00	3.60	1.00
☐ TC20	Matt Williams	25.00	11.00	3.10
	Albert Belle			

1994 Score Dream Team

Randomly inserted in first series foil and jumbo packs at a rate of one in 72, this ten-card set feature's baseball's Dream Team as selected by Pinnacle Brands. Banded by forest green stripes above and below, the player photos on the fronts feature ten of baseball's best players sporting historical team uniforms from the 1930's. The set title and player's name appear in gold foil lettering on black bars above and below the picture. The backs carry a color head shot and brief player profile.

		MINT	NRMT	EXC
COMPLETE SET (10)		90.00	40.00	11.00
COMMON CARD (1-10)		3.00	1.35	.35
☐ 1	Mike Mussina	8.00	3.60	1.00
☐ 2	Tom Glavine	6.00	2.70	.75
☐ 3	John Kruk	25.00	11.00	3.10
☐ 4	Carlos Baerga	12.00	5.50	1.50
☐ 5	Barry Larkin	6.00	2.70	.75
☐ 6	Matt Williams	10.00	4.50	1.25
☐ 7	Barry Bonds	15.00	6.75	1.85
☐ 8	Andy Van Slyke	3.00	1.35	.35
☐ 9	Larry Walker	8.00	3.60	1.00
☐ 10	Mike Stanley	3.00	1.35	.35

1994 Score Gold Stars

Randomly inserted at a rate of one in every 18 hobby packs, this 60-card set features

National and American stars. Split into two series of 30 cards, the first series (1-30) comprises of National League players and the second series (31-60) American Leaguers. The fronts feature a color action player photo cut out and superimposed on a foil background. At the bottom, a navy blue triangle carries the set title and the player's name appears in a white bar. The backs have a color close-up shot and a player profile.

	MINT	NRMT	EXC
COMPLETE SET (60)	350.00	160.00	45.00
COMPLETE NL SERIES (30)	150.00	70.00	19.00
COMPLETE AL SERIES (30)	200.00	90.00	25.00
COMMON CARD (1-30)	2.00	.90	.25
COMMON CARD (31-60)	2.00	.90	.25

		MINT	NRMT	EXC
☐ 1	Barry Bonds	10.00	4.50	1.25
☐ 2	Orlando Merced	2.00	.90	.25
☐ 3	Mark Grace	3.00	1.35	.35
☐ 4	Darren Daulton	4.00	1.80	.50
☐ 5	Jeff Blauser	2.00	.90	.25
☐ 6	Deion Sanders	8.00	3.60	1.00
☐ 7	John Kruk	3.00	1.35	.35
☐ 8	Jeff Bagwell	12.00	5.50	1.50
☐ 9	Gregg Jefferies	4.00	1.80	.50
☐ 10	Matt Williams	6.00	2.70	.75
☐ 11	Andres Galarraga	4.00	1.80	.50
☐ 12	Jay Bell	2.00	.90	.25
☐ 13	Mike Piazza	15.00	6.75	1.85
☐ 14	Ron Gant	3.00	1.35	.35
☐ 15	Barry Larkin	5.00	2.20	.60
☐ 16	Tom Glavine	5.00	2.20	.60
☐ 17	Lenny Dykstra	4.00	1.80	.50
☐ 18	Fred McGriff	5.00	2.20	.60
☐ 19	Andy Van Slyke	3.00	1.35	.35
☐ 20	Gary Sheffield	4.00	1.80	.50
☐ 21	John Burkett	2.00	.90	.25
☐ 22	Dante Bichette	5.00	2.20	.60
☐ 23	Tony Gwynn	12.00	5.50	1.50
☐ 24	Dave Justice	5.00	2.20	.60
☐ 25	Marquis Grissom	4.00	1.80	.50
☐ 26	Bobby Bonilla	3.00	1.35	.35
☐ 27	Larry Walker	5.00	2.20	.60
☐ 28	Brett Butler	2.00	.90	.25
☐ 29	Robby Thompson	2.00	.90	.25
☐ 30	Jeff Conine	4.00	1.80	.50
☐ 31	Joe Carter	4.00	1.80	.50
☐ 32	Ken Griffey Jr.	40.00	18.00	5.00
☐ 33	Juan Gonzalez	10.00	4.50	1.25
☐ 34	Rickey Henderson	4.00	1.80	.50
☐ 35	Bo Jackson	4.00	1.80	.50
☐ 36	Cal Ripken	40.00	18.00	5.00
☐ 37	John Olerud	4.00	1.80	.50
☐ 38	Carlos Baerga	8.00	3.60	1.00
☐ 39	Jack McDowell	4.00	1.80	.50
☐ 40	Cecil Fielder	4.00	1.80	.50
☐ 41	Kenny Lofton	12.00	5.50	1.50
☐ 42	Roberto Alomar	8.00	3.60	1.00
☐ 43	Randy Johnson	8.00	3.60	1.00
☐ 44	Tim Salmon	8.00	3.60	1.00
☐ 45	Frank Thomas	40.00	18.00	5.00
☐ 46	Albert Belle	15.00	6.75	1.85
☐ 47	Greg Vaughn	2.00	.90	.25
☐ 48	Travis Fryman	4.00	1.80	.50
☐ 49	Don Mattingly	20.00	9.00	2.50
☐ 50	Wade Boggs	4.00	1.80	.50
☐ 51	Mo Vaughn	6.00	2.70	.75
☐ 52	Kirby Puckett	12.00	5.50	1.50
☐ 53	Devon White	3.00	1.35	.35
☐ 54	Tony Phillips	2.00	.90	.25
☐ 55	Brian Harper	2.00	.90	.25
☐ 56	Chad Curtis	2.00	.90	.25
☐ 57	Paul Molitor	4.00	1.80	.50
☐ 58	Ivan Rodriguez	3.00	1.35	.35
☐ 59	Rafael Palmeiro	4.00	1.80	.50
☐ 60	Brian McRae	3.00	1.35	.35

1994 Score Rookie/Traded

The 1994 Score Rookie and Traded set consists of 165 standard-size cards featuring rookie standouts, traded players, and new young prospects. Each foil pack contained one Gold Rush card. The cards are numbered on the back with an "RT" prefix. A special unnumbered September Call-Up Redemption card could be exchanged for an Alex Rodriguez card. The expiration date was January 31, 1995. Odds of finding a redemption card are approximately one in 240 retail and hobby packs. Rookie Cards include John Hudek and Chan Ho Park.

	MINT	NRMT	EXC
COMPLETE SET (165)	10.00	4.50	1.25
COMMON CARD (RT1-RT165)	.05	.02	.01
COMP. GOLD RUSH SET (165)	50.00	22.00	6.25
GOLD RUSH COMMON (1-165)	.25	.11	.03
GOLD RUSH SEMISTARS	.50	.23	.06
*GOLD RUSH VETERAN STARS: 4X TO 7X BASIC CARDS			
*GOLD RUSH YOUNG STARS: 2.5X TO 5X BASIC CARDS			
*GOLD RUSH ROOKIE CARDS: 2X TO 4X BASIC CARDS			

#	Player			
☐ RT1	Will Clark	.25	.11	.03
☐ RT2	Lee Smith	.15	.07	.02
☐ RT3	Bo Jackson	.15	.07	.02
☐ RT4	Ellis Burks	.10	.05	.01
☐ RT5	Eddie Murray	.25	.11	.03
☐ RT6	Delino DeShields	.10	.05	.01
☐ RT7	Erik Hanson	.05	.02	.01
☐ RT8	Rafael Palmeiro	.15	.07	.02
☐ RT9	Luis Polonia	.05	.02	.01
☐ RT10	Omar Vizquel	.05	.02	.01
☐ RT11	Kurt Abbott	.10	.05	.01
☐ RT12	Vince Coleman	.05	.02	.01
☐ RT13	Rickey Henderson	.15	.07	.02
☐ RT14	Terry Mulholland	.05	.02	.01
☐ RT15	Greg Hibbard	.05	.02	.01
☐ RT16	Walt Weiss	.05	.02	.01
☐ RT17	Chris Sabo	.05	.02	.01
☐ RT18	Dave Henderson	.05	.02	.01
☐ RT19	Rick Sutcliffe	.10	.05	.01
☐ RT20	Harold Reynolds	.05	.02	.01
☐ RT21	Jack Morris	.10	.05	.01
☐ RT22	Dan Wilson	.05	.02	.01
☐ RT23	Dave Magadan	.05	.02	.01
☐ RT24	Dennis Martinez	.10	.05	.01
☐ RT25	Wes Chamberlain	.05	.02	.01
☐ RT26	Otis Nixon	.05	.02	.01
☐ RT27	Eric Anthony	.05	.02	.01
☐ RT28	Randy Milligan	.05	.02	.01
☐ RT29	Julio Franco	.10	.05	.01
☐ RT30	Kevin McReynolds	.05	.02	.01
☐ RT31	Anthony Young	.05	.02	.01
☐ RT32	Brian Harper	.05	.02	.01
☐ RT33	Gene Harris	.05	.02	.01
☐ RT34	Eddie Taubensee	.05	.02	.01
☐ RT35	David Segui	.05	.02	.01
☐ RT36	Stan Javier	.05	.02	.01
☐ RT37	Felix Fermin	.05	.02	.01
☐ RT38	Darrin Jackson	.05	.02	.01
☐ RT39	Tony Fernandez	.05	.02	.01
☐ RT40	Jose Vizcaino	.05	.02	.01
☐ RT41	Willie Banks	.05	.02	.01
☐ RT42	Brian Hunter	.05	.02	.01
☐ RT43	Reggie Jefferson	.05	.02	.01
☐ RT44	Junior Felix	.05	.02	.01
☐ RT45	Jack Armstrong	.05	.02	.01
☐ RT46	Bip Roberts	.05	.02	.01
☐ RT47	Jerry Browne	.05	.02	.01
☐ RT48	Marvin Freeman	.05	.02	.01
☐ RT49	Jody Reed	.05	.02	.01
☐ RT50	Alex Cole	.05	.02	.01
☐ RT51	Sid Fernandez	.05	.02	.01
☐ RT52	Pete Smith	.05	.02	.01
☐ RT53	Xavier Hernandez	.05	.02	.01
☐ RT54	Scott Sanderson	.05	.02	.01
☐ RT55	Turner Ward	.05	.02	.01
☐ RT56	Rex Hudler	.05	.02	.01
☐ RT57	Deion Sanders	.40	.18	.05
☐ RT58	Sid Bream	.05	.02	.01
☐ RT59	Tony Pena	.05	.02	.01
☐ RT60	Bret Boone	.15	.07	.02
☐ RT61	Bobby Ayala	.05	.02	.01
☐ RT62	Pedro Martinez	.15	.07	.02
☐ RT63	Howard Johnson	.05	.02	.01
☐ RT64	Mark Portugal	.05	.02	.01
☐ RT65	Roberto Kelly	.05	.02	.01
☐ RT66	Spike Owen	.05	.02	.01
☐ RT67	Jeff Treadway	.05	.02	.01
☐ RT68	Mike Harkey	.05	.02	.01
☐ RT69	Doug Jones	.05	.02	.01
☐ RT70	Steve Farr	.05	.02	.01
☐ RT71	Billy Taylor	.05	.02	.01
☐ RT72	Manny Ramirez	1.00	.45	.12
☐ RT73	Bob Hamelin	.10	.05	.01
☐ RT74	Steve Karsay	.10	.05	.01
☐ RT75	Ryan Klesko	.50	.23	.06
☐ RT76	Cliff Floyd	.15	.07	.02
☐ RT77	Jeffrey Hammonds	.15	.07	.02
☐ RT78	Javier Lopez	.30	.14	.04
☐ RT79	Roger Salkeld	.05	.02	.01
☐ RT80	Hector Carrasco	.05	.02	.01
☐ RT81	Gerald Williams	.05	.02	.01
☐ RT82	Raul Mondesi	.60	.25	.07
☐ RT83	Sterling Hitchcock	.10	.05	.01
☐ RT84	Danny Bautista	.10	.05	.01
☐ RT85	Chris Turner	.05	.02	.01
☐ RT86	Shane Reynolds	.05	.02	.01
☐ RT87	Rondell White	.15	.07	.02
☐ RT88	Salomon Torres	.10	.05	.01
☐ RT89	Turk Wendell	.05	.02	.01
☐ RT90	Tony Tarasco	.15	.07	.02
☐ RT91	Shawn Green	.30	.14	.04
☐ RT92	Greg Colbrunn	.10	.05	.01
☐ RT93	Eddie Zambrano	.05	.02	.01
☐ RT94	Rich Becker	.10	.05	.01
☐ RT95	Chris Gomez	.10	.05	.01
☐ RT96	John Patterson	.05	.02	.01
☐ RT97	Derek Parks	.05	.02	.01
☐ RT98	Rich Rowland	.05	.02	.01
☐ RT99	James Mouton	.10	.05	.01
☐ RT100	Tim Hyers	.05	.02	.01
☐ RT101	Jose Valentin	.05	.02	.01
☐ RT102	Carlos Delgado	.15	.07	.02
☐ RT103	Robert Eenhoorn	.05	.02	.01
☐ RT104	John Hudek	.10	.05	.01
☐ RT105	Domingo Cedeno	.05	.02	.01
☐ RT106	Denny Hocking	.05	.02	.01
☐ RT107	Greg Pirkl	.05	.02	.01
☐ RT108	Mark Smith	.05	.02	.01
☐ RT109	Paul Shuey	.05	.02	.01
☐ RT110	Jorge Fabregas	.05	.02	.01
☐ RT111	Rikkert Faneyte	.05	.02	.01
☐ RT112	Rob Butler	.05	.02	.01
☐ RT113	Darren Oliver	.05	.02	.01
☐ RT114	Troy O'Leary	.10	.05	.01
☐ RT115	Scott Brow	.05	.02	.01
☐ RT116	Tony Eusebio	.05	.02	.01
☐ RT117	Carlos Reyes	.05	.02	.01
☐ RT118	J.R. Phillips	.10	.05	.01
☐ RT119	Alex Diaz	.05	.02	.01
☐ RT120	Charles Johnson	.15	.07	.02
☐ RT121	Nate Minchey	.05	.02	.01
☐ RT122	Scott Sanders	.05	.02	.01
☐ RT123	Daryl Boston	.05	.02	.01
☐ RT124	Joey Hamilton	.15	.07	.02
☐ RT125	Brian Anderson	.15	.07	.02
☐ RT126	Dan Miceli	.05	.02	.01
☐ RT127	Tom Brunansky	.05	.02	.01
☐ RT128	Dave Staton	.05	.02	.01
☐ RT129	Mike Oquist	.05	.02	.01
☐ RT130	John Mabry	.15	.07	.02
☐ RT131	Norberto Martin	.05	.02	.01
☐ RT132	Hector Fajardo	.05	.02	.01
☐ RT133	Mark Hutton	.05	.02	.01
☐ RT134	Fernando Vina	.05	.02	.01
☐ RT135	Lee Tinsley	.05	.02	.01
☐ RT136	Chan Ho Park	.20	.09	.03
☐ RT137	Paul Spoljaric	.05	.02	.01
☐ RT138	Matias Carillo	.05	.02	.01
☐ RT139	Mark Kiefer	.05	.02	.01
☐ RT140	Stan Royer	.05	.02	.01
☐ RT141	Bryan Eversgerd	.05	.02	.01
☐ RT142	Brian L.Hunter	.50	.23	.06

☐ RT143	Joe Hall	.05	.02 .01
☐ RT144	Johnny Ruffin	.05	.02 .01
☐ RT145	Alex Gonzalez	.15	.07 .02
☐ RT146	Keith Lockhart	.05	.02 .01
☐ RT147	Tom Marsh	.05	.02 .01
☐ RT148	Tony Longmire	.05	.02 .01
☐ RT149	Keith Mitchell	.05	.02 .01
☐ RT150	Melvin Nieves	.15	.07 .02
☐ RT151	Kelly Stinnett	.05	.02 .01
☐ RT152	Miguel Jimenez	.05	.02 .01
☐ RT153	Jeff Juden	.05	.02 .01
☐ RT154	Matt Walbeck	.05	.02 .01
☐ RT155	Marc Newfield	.15	.07 .02
☐ RT156	Matt Mieske	.05	.02 .01
☐ RT157	Marcus Moore	.05	.02 .01
☐ RT158	Jose Lima	.30	.14 .04
☐ RT159	Mike Kelly	.10	.05 .01
☐ RT160	Jim Edmonds	.30	.14 .04
☐ RT161	Steve Trachsel	.15	.07 .02
☐ RT162	Greg Blosser	.05	.02 .01
☐ RT163	Marc Acre	.05	.02 .01
☐ RT164	AL Checklist	.05	.02 .01
☐ RT165	NL Checklist	.05	.02 .01
☐ NNO	Sept. Call-Up Redemp.	15.00	6.75 1.85

1994 Score R/T Changing Places

Randomly inserted in both retail and hobby packs at a rate of one in 36 Rookie/Traded packs, this 10-card standard-size set focuses on ten veteran superstar players who were traded prior to or during the 1994 season. Cards fronts feature a color photo with a slanted design. The backs have a short write-up and a distorted photo.

		MINT	NRMT	EXC
COMPLETE SET (10)		35.00	16.00	4.40
COMMON CARD (CP1-CP10)		2.50	1.10	.30
☐ CP1	Will Clark	8.00	3.60	1.00
☐ CP2	Rafael Palmeiro	6.00	2.70	.75
☐ CP3	Roberto Kelly	2.50	1.10	.30
☐ CP4	Bo Jackson	4.00	1.80	.50
☐ CP5	Otis Nixon	2.50	1.10	.30
☐ CP6	Rickey Henderson	4.00	1.80	.50
☐ CP7	Ellis Burks	2.50	1.10	.30
☐ CP8	Lee Smith	4.00	1.80	.50
☐ CP9	Delino DeShields	2.50	1.10	.30
☐ CP10	Deion Sanders	12.00	5.50	1.50

1994 Score R/T Super Rookies

Randomly inserted in hobby packs at a rate of one in 36, this 18-card standard-size set focuses on top rookies of 1994. Odds of finding one of these cards is approximately one in 36 hobby packs. Designed much like the Gold Rush, the cards have an all-foil design. The fronts have a player photo and the backs have a photo that serves as background to the Super Rookies logo and text.

		MINT	NRMT	EXC
COMPLETE SET (18)		100.00	45.00	12.50
COMMON CARD (SU1-SU18)		2.50	1.10	.30
☐ SU1	Carlos Delgado	5.00	2.20	.60
☐ SU2	Manny Ramirez	25.00	11.00	3.10
☐ SU3	Ryan Klesko	12.00	5.50	1.50
☐ SU4	Raul Mondesi	15.00	6.75	1.85
☐ SU5	Bob Hamelin	2.50	1.10	.30
☐ SU6	Steve Karsay	2.50	1.10	.30
☐ SU7	Jeffrey Hammonds	4.00	1.80	.50
☐ SU8	Cliff Floyd	4.00	1.80	.50
☐ SU9	Kurt Abbott	2.50	1.10	.30
☐ SU10	Marc Newfield	2.50	1.10	.30
☐ SU11	Javier Lopez	8.00	3.60	1.00
☐ SU12	Rich Becker	2.50	1.10	.30
☐ SU13	Greg Pirkl	2.50	1.10	.30
☐ SU14	Rondell White	6.00	2.70	.75
☐ SU15	James Mouton	2.50	1.10	.30
☐ SU16	Tony Tarasco	2.50	1.10	.30
☐ SU17	Brian Anderson	2.50	1.10	.30
☐ SU18	Jim Edmonds	10.00	4.50	1.25

1995 Score

The 1995 Score set consists of 605 standard-size cards. The horizontal and vertical fronts feature color action player shots with irregular dark green and sand brown borders. The player's name, position and the team logo appear in a blue bar under the photo. The horizontal backs have the same design as the fronts. They carry another

small color headshot on the left, with the player's name, short biography, career highlights and statistics on the right. Hobby packs featured a special signed Ryan Klesko (RG1) card. Retail packs also had a Klesko card (SG1) but these were not signed. There are no key Rookie Cards in this set

	MINT	NRMT	EXC
COMPLETE SERIES 1 (330)...	20.00	9.00	2.50
COMPLETE SET (605)	10.00	4.50	1.25
COMPLETE SERIES 2 (275) .	10.00	4.50	1.25
COMPLETE TRADE SET (11) .	1.50	.70	.19
COMMON CARD (1-330)	.05	.02	.01
COMMON CARD (331-605)	.05	.02	.01
COMP. GOLD RUSH SET (605)	220.00	100.00	28.00
GOLD RUSH COMMON (1-605).	.30	.14	.04
GOLD RUSH SEMISTARS..........	.50	.23	.06
*GOLD RUSH VETERAN STARS: 4X TO 8X BASIC CARDS
*GOLD RUSH YOUNG STARS: 3X TO 6X BASIC CARDS

☐ 1 Ken Griffey Jr.............	2.00	.90	.25
☐ 2 Roberto Alomar	.40	.18	.05
☐ 3 Cal Ripken..................	2.00	.90	.25
☐ 4 Jose Canseco...............	.30	.14	.04
☐ 5 Matt Williams..............	.30	.14	.04
☐ 6 Esteban Beltre..............	.05	.02	.01
☐ 7 Domingo Cedeno	.05	.02	.01
☐ 8 John Valentin..............	.15	.07	.02
☐ 9 Glenallen Hill..............	.10	.05	.01
☐ 10 Rafael Belliard.............	.05	.02	.01
☐ 11 Randy Myers...............	.05	.02	.01
☐ 12 Mo Vaughn................	.30	.14	.04
☐ 13 Hector Carrasco...........	.05	.02	.01
☐ 14 Chili Davis................	.10	.05	.01
☐ 15 Dante Bichette.............	.25	.11	.03
☐ 16 Darrin Jackson.............	.05	.02	.01
☐ 17 Mike Piazza	.75	.35	.09
☐ 18 Junior Felix..............	.05	.02	.01
☐ 19 Moises Alou..............	.10	.05	.01
☐ 20 Mark Gubicza..............	.05	.02	.01
☐ 21 Bret Saberhagen..........	.10	.05	.01
☐ 22 Lenny Dykstra.............	.15	.07	.02
☐ 23 Steve Howe...............	.05	.02	.01
☐ 24 Mark Dewey..............	.05	.02	.01
☐ 25 Brian Harper..............	.05	.02	.01
☐ 26 Ozzie Smith...............	.40	.18	.05
☐ 27 Scott Erickson.............	.10	.05	.01
☐ 28 Tony Gwynn..............	.60	.25	.07
☐ 29 Bob Welch...............	.10	.05	.01
☐ 30 Barry Bonds..............	.50	.23	.06
☐ 31 Leo Gomez................	.05	.02	.01
☐ 32 Greg Maddux.............	2.00	.90	.25
☐ 33 Mike Greenwell.............	.10	.05	.01

☐ 34 Sammy Sosa...............	.15	.07	.02
☐ 35 Darnell Coles..............	.05	.02	.01
☐ 36 Tommy Greene............	.05	.02	.01
☐ 37 Will Clark.................	.25	.11	.03
☐ 38 Steve Ontiveros............	.05	.02	.01
☐ 39 Stan Javier...............	.05	.02	.01
☐ 40 Bip Roberts...............	.05	.02	.01
☐ 41 Paul O'Neill...............	.10	.05	.01
☐ 42 Bill Haselman.............	.05	.02	.01
☐ 43 Shane Mack..............	.05	.02	.01
☐ 44 Orlando Merced............	.10	.05	.01
☐ 45 Kevin Seitzer	.05	.02	.01
☐ 46 Trevor Hoffman............	.10	.05	.01
☐ 47 Greg Gagne...............	.05	.02	.01
☐ 48 Jeff Kent.................	.10	.05	.01
☐ 49 Tony Phillips..............	.05	.02	.01
☐ 50 Ken Hill	.10	.05	.01
☐ 51 Carlos Baerga.............	.40	.18	.05
☐ 52 Henry Rodriguez...........	.05	.02	.01
☐ 53 Scott Sanderson..........	.05	.02	.01
☐ 54 Jeff Conine...............	.15	.07	.02
☐ 55 Chris Turner..............	.05	.02	.01
☐ 56 Ken Caminiti..............	.10	.05	.01
☐ 57 Harold Baines.............	.10	.05	.01
☐ 58 Charlie Hayes.............	.10	.05	.01
☐ 59 Roberto Kelly.............	.10	.05	.01
☐ 60 John Olerud	.10	.05	.01
☐ 61 Tim Davis................	.05	.02	.01
☐ 62 Rich Rowland.............	.05	.02	.01
☐ 63 Rey Sanchez	.05	.02	.01
☐ 64 Junior Ortiz...............	.05	.02	.01
☐ 65 Ricky Gutierrez...........	.05	.02	.01
☐ 66 Rex Hudler...............	.05	.02	.01
☐ 67 Johnny Ruffin.............	.05	.02	.01
☐ 68 Jay Buhner...............	.15	.07	.02
☐ 69 Tom Pagnozzi.............	.05	.02	.01
☐ 70 Julio Franco...............	.10	.05	.01
☐ 71 Eric Young................	.10	.05	.01
☐ 72 Mike Bordick..............	.05	.02	.01
☐ 73 Don Slaught..............	.05	.02	.01
☐ 74 Goose Gossage...........	.15	.07	.02
☐ 75 Lonnie Smith..............	.05	.02	.01
☐ 76 Jimmy Key................	.10	.05	.01
☐ 77 Dave Hollins..............	.05	.02	.01
☐ 78 Mickey Tettleton	.10	.05	.01
☐ 79 Luis Gonzalez.............	.10	.05	.01
☐ 80 Dave Winfield.............	.15	.07	.02
☐ 81 Ryan Thompson...........	.10	.05	.01
☐ 82 Felix Jose................	.05	.02	.01
☐ 83 Rusty Meacham...........	.05	.02	.01
☐ 84 Darryl Hamilton...........	.05	.02	.01
☐ 85 John Wetteland...........	.10	.05	.01
☐ 86 Tom Brunansky...........	.05	.02	.01
☐ 87 Mark Lemke..............	.10	.05	.01
☐ 88 Spike Owen...............	.05	.02	.01
☐ 89 Shawon Dunston.........	.05	.02	.01
☐ 90 Wilson Alvarez...........	.05	.02	.01
☐ 91 Lee Smith................	.15	.07	.02
☐ 92 Scott Kamieniecki.........	.05	.02	.01
☐ 93 Jacob Brumfield..........	.05	.02	.01
☐ 94 Kirk Gibson...............	.10	.05	.01
☐ 95 Joe Girardi...............	.05	.02	.01
☐ 96 Mike Macfarlane	.05	.02	.01
☐ 97 Greg Colbrunn............	.15	.07	.02
☐ 98 Ricky Bones..............	.05	.02	.01
☐ 99 Delino DeShields..........	.10	.05	.01
☐ 100 Pat Meares..............	.05	.02	.01
☐ 101 Jeff Fassero.............	.10	.05	.01
☐ 102 Jim Leyritz..............	.05	.02	.01
☐ 103 Gary Redus..............	.05	.02	.01
☐ 104 Terry Steinbach..........	.10	.05	.01

#	Player			
☐ 105	Kevin McReynolds	.05	.02	.01
☐ 106	Felix Fermin	.05	.02	.01
☐ 107	Danny Jackson	.05	.02	.01
☐ 108	Chris James	.05	.02	.01
☐ 109	Jeff King	.05	.02	.01
☐ 110	Pat Hentgen	.10	.05	.01
☐ 111	Gerald Perry	.05	.02	.01
☐ 112	Tim Raines	.15	.07	.02
☐ 113	Eddie Williams	.05	.02	.01
☐ 114	Jamie Moyer	.05	.02	.01
☐ 115	Bud Black	.05	.02	.01
☐ 116	Chris Gomez	.10	.05	.01
☐ 117	Luis Lopez	.05	.02	.01
☐ 118	Roger Clemens	.30	.14	.04
☐ 119	Javier Lopez	.25	.11	.03
☐ 120	Dave Nilsson	.10	.05	.01
☐ 121	Karl Rhodes	.05	.02	.01
☐ 122	Rick Aguilera	.10	.05	.01
☐ 123	Tony Fernandez	.05	.02	.01
☐ 124	Bernie Williams	.10	.05	.01
☐ 125	James Mouton	.10	.05	.01
☐ 126	Mark Langston	.10	.05	.01
☐ 127	Mike Lansing	.05	.02	.01
☐ 128	Tino Martinez	.15	.07	.02
☐ 129	Joe Orsulak	.05	.02	.01
☐ 130	David Hulse	.05	.02	.01
☐ 131	Pete Incaviglia	.05	.02	.01
☐ 132	Mark Clark	.05	.02	.01
☐ 133	Tony Eusebio	.05	.02	.01
☐ 134	Chuck Finley	.10	.05	.01
☐ 135	Lou Frazier	.05	.02	.01
☐ 136	Craig Grebeck	.05	.02	.01
☐ 137	Kelly Stinnett	.05	.02	.01
☐ 138	Paul Shuey	.05	.02	.01
☐ 139	David Nied	.10	.05	.01
☐ 140	Billy Brewer	.05	.02	.01
☐ 141	Dave Weathers	.05	.02	.01
☐ 142	Scott Leius	.05	.02	.01
☐ 143	Brian Jordan	.15	.07	.02
☐ 144	Melido Perez	.05	.02	.01
☐ 145	Tony Tarasco	.10	.05	.01
☐ 146	Dan Wilson	.10	.05	.01
☐ 147	Rondell White	.15	.07	.02
☐ 148	Mike Henneman	.05	.02	.01
☐ 149	Brian Johnson	.05	.02	.01
☐ 150	Tom Henke	.10	.05	.01
☐ 151	John Patterson	.05	.02	.01
☐ 152	Bobby Witt	.05	.02	.01
☐ 153	Eddie Taubensee	.05	.02	.01
☐ 154	Pat Borders	.05	.02	.01
☐ 155	Ramon Martinez	.10	.05	.01
☐ 156	Mike Kingery	.05	.02	.01
☐ 157	Zane Smith	.05	.02	.01
☐ 158	Benito Santiago	.05	.02	.01
☐ 159	Matias Carrillo	.05	.02	.01
☐ 160	Scott Brosius	.05	.02	.01
☐ 161	Dave Clark	.05	.02	.01
☐ 162	Mark McLemore	.05	.02	.01
☐ 163	Curt Schilling	.05	.02	.01
☐ 164	J.T. Snow	.15	.07	.02
☐ 165	Rod Beck	.10	.05	.01
☐ 166	Scott Fletcher	.05	.02	.01
☐ 167	Bob Tewksbury	.05	.02	.01
☐ 168	Mike LaValliere	.05	.02	.01
☐ 169	Dave Hansen	.05	.02	.01
☐ 170	Pedro Martinez	.15	.07	.02
☐ 171	Kirk Rueter	.05	.02	.01
☐ 172	Jose Lind	.05	.02	.01
☐ 173	Luis Alicea	.05	.02	.01
☐ 174	Mike Moore	.05	.02	.01
☐ 175	Andy Ashby	.05	.02	.01
☐ 176	Jody Reed	.05	.02	.01
☐ 177	Darryl Kile	.05	.02	.01
☐ 178	Carl Willis	.05	.02	.01
☐ 179	Jeromy Burnitz	.05	.02	.01
☐ 180	Mike Gallego	.05	.02	.01
☐ 181	Bill VanLandingham	.10	.05	.01
☐ 182	Sid Fernandez	.05	.02	.01
☐ 183	Kim Batiste	.05	.02	.01
☐ 184	Greg Myers	.05	.02	.01
☐ 185	Steve Avery	.15	.07	.02
☐ 186	Steve Farr	.05	.02	.01
☐ 187	Robb Nen	.10	.05	.01
☐ 188	Dan Pasqua	.05	.02	.01
☐ 189	Bruce Ruffin	.05	.02	.01
☐ 190	Jose Valentin	.05	.02	.01
☐ 191	Willie Banks	.05	.02	.01
☐ 192	Mike Aldrete	.05	.02	.01
☐ 193	Randy Milligan	.05	.02	.01
☐ 194	Steve Karsay	.05	.02	.01
☐ 195	Mike Stanley	.10	.05	.01
☐ 196	Jose Mesa	.05	.02	.01
☐ 197	Tom Browning	.05	.02	.01
☐ 198	John Vander Wal	.05	.02	.01
☐ 199	Kevin Brown	.05	.02	.01
☐ 200	Mike Oquist	.05	.02	.01
☐ 201	Greg Swindell	.05	.02	.01
☐ 202	Eddie Zambrano	.05	.02	.01
☐ 203	Joe Boever	.05	.02	.01
☐ 204	Gary Varsho	.05	.02	.01
☐ 205	Chris Gwynn	.05	.02	.01
☐ 206	David Howard	.05	.02	.01
☐ 207	Jerome Walton	.05	.02	.01
☐ 208	Danny Darwin	.05	.02	.01
☐ 209	Darryl Strawberry	.10	.05	.01
☐ 210	Todd Van Poppel	.10	.05	.01
☐ 211	Scott Livingstone	.05	.02	.01
☐ 212	Dave Fleming	.05	.02	.01
☐ 213	Todd Worrell	.05	.02	.01
☐ 214	Carlos Delgado	.10	.05	.01
☐ 215	Bill Pecota	.05	.02	.01
☐ 216	Jim Lindeman	.05	.02	.01
☐ 217	Rick White	.05	.02	.01
☐ 218	Jose Oquendo	.05	.02	.01
☐ 219	Tony Castillo	.05	.02	.01
☐ 220	Fernando Vina	.05	.02	.01
☐ 221	Jeff Bagwell	.60	.25	.07
☐ 222	Randy Johnson	.40	.18	.05
☐ 223	Albert Belle	.75	.35	.09
☐ 224	Chuck Carr	.05	.02	.01
☐ 225	Mark Leiter	.05	.02	.01
☐ 226	Hal Morris	.10	.05	.01
☐ 227	Robin Ventura	.15	.07	.02
☐ 228	Mike Munoz	.05	.02	.01
☐ 229	Jim Thome	.30	.14	.04
☐ 230	Mario Diaz	.05	.02	.01
☐ 231	John Doherty	.05	.02	.01
☐ 232	Bobby Jones	.10	.05	.01
☐ 233	Raul Mondesi	.50	.23	.06
☐ 234	Ricky Jordan	.05	.02	.01
☐ 235	John Jaha	.10	.05	.01
☐ 236	Carlos Garcia	.10	.05	.01
☐ 237	Kirby Puckett	.60	.25	.07
☐ 238	Orel Hershiser	.10	.05	.01
☐ 239	Don Mattingly	1.00	.45	.12
☐ 240	Sid Bream	.05	.02	.01
☐ 241	Brent Gates	.10	.05	.01
☐ 242	Tony Longmire	.05	.02	.01
☐ 243	Robby Thompson	.05	.02	.01
☐ 244	Rick Sutcliffe	.10	.05	.01
☐ 245	Dean Palmer	.10	.05	.01
☐ 246	Marquis Grissom	.15	.07	.02

☐ 247 Paul Molitor	.15	.07	.02
☐ 248 Mark Carreon	.05	.02	.01
☐ 249 Jack Voigt	.05	.02	.01
☐ 250 Greg McMichael	.05	.02	.01
☐ 251 Damon Berryhill	.05	.02	.01
☐ 252 Brian Dorsett	.05	.02	.01
☐ 253 Jim Edmonds	.25	.11	.03
☐ 254 Barry Larkin	.25	.11	.03
☐ 255 Jack McDowell	.15	.07	.02
☐ 256 Wally Joyner	.10	.05	.01
☐ 257 Eddie Murray	.25	.11	.03
☐ 258 Lenny Webster	.05	.02	.01
☐ 259 Milt Cuyler	.05	.02	.01
☐ 260 Todd Benzinger	.05	.02	.01
☐ 261 Vince Coleman	.05	.02	.01
☐ 262 Todd Stottlemyre	.05	.02	.01
☐ 263 Turner Ward	.05	.02	.01
☐ 264 Ray Lankford	.15	.07	.02
☐ 265 Matt Walbeck	.05	.02	.01
☐ 266 Deion Sanders	.40	.18	.05
☐ 267 Gerald Williams	.05	.02	.01
☐ 268 Jim Gott	.05	.02	.01
☐ 269 Jeff Frye	.05	.02	.01
☐ 270 Jose Rijo	.10	.05	.01
☐ 271 Dave Justice	.25	.11	.03
☐ 272 Ismael Valdes	.05	.02	.01
☐ 273 Ben McDonald	.05	.02	.01
☐ 274 Darren Lewis	.05	.02	.01
☐ 275 Graeme Lloyd	.05	.02	.01
☐ 276 Luis Ortiz	.05	.02	.01
☐ 277 Julian Tavarez	.10	.05	.01
☐ 278 Mark Dalesandro	.05	.02	.01
☐ 279 Brett Merriman	.05	.02	.01
☐ 280 Ricky Bottalico	.05	.02	.01
☐ 281 Robert Eenhoorn	.05	.02	.01
☐ 282 Rikkert Faneyte	.05	.02	.01
☐ 283 Mike Kelly	.10	.05	.01
☐ 284 Mark Smith	.05	.02	.01
☐ 285 Turk Wendell	.05	.02	.01
☐ 286 Greg Blosser	.05	.02	.01
☐ 287 Garey Ingram	.05	.02	.01
☐ 288 Jorge Fabregas	.05	.02	.01
☐ 289 Blaise Ilsley	.05	.02	.01
☐ 290 Joe Hall	.05	.02	.01
☐ 291 Orlando Miller	.10	.05	.01
☐ 292 Jose Lima	.05	.02	.01
☐ 293 Greg O'Halloran	.05	.02	.01
☐ 294 Mark Kiefer	.05	.02	.01
☐ 295 Jose Oliva	.10	.05	.01
☐ 296 Rich Becker	.10	.05	.01
☐ 297 Brian L. Hunter	.25	.11	.03
☐ 298 Dave Silvestri	.05	.02	.01
☐ 299 Armando Benitez	.05	.02	.01
☐ 300 Darren Dreifort	.05	.02	.01
☐ 301 John Mabry	.10	.05	.01
☐ 302 Greg Pirkl	.05	.02	.01
☐ 303 J.R. Phillips	.05	.02	.01
☐ 304 Shawn Green	.15	.07	.02
☐ 305 Roberto Petagine	.10	.05	.01
☐ 306 Keith Lockhart	.05	.02	.01
☐ 307 Jonathan Hurst	.05	.02	.01
☐ 308 Paul Spoljaric	.05	.02	.01
☐ 309 Mike Lieberthal	.05	.02	.01
☐ 310 Garret Anderson	.40	.18	.05
☐ 311 John Johnstone	.05	.02	.01
☐ 312 Alex Rodriguez	.40	.18	.05
☐ 313 Kent Mercker HL	.05	.02	.01
☐ 314 John Valentin HL	.10	.05	.01
☐ 315 Kenny Rogers HL	.05	.02	.01
☐ 316 Fred McGriff HL	.30	.14	.04
☐ 317 Team Checklists	.05	.02	.01
☐ 318 Team Checklists	.05	.02	.01
☐ 319 Team Checklists	.05	.02	.01
☐ 320 Team Checklists	.05	.02	.01
☐ 321 Team Checklists	.05	.02	.01
☐ 322 Team Checklists	.05	.02	.01
☐ 323 Team Checklists	.05	.02	.01
☐ 324 Team Checklists	.05	.02	.01
☐ 325 Team Checklists	.05	.02	.01
☐ 326 Team Checklists	.05	.02	.01
☐ 327 Team Checklists	.05	.02	.01
☐ 328 Team Checklists	.05	.02	.01
☐ 329 Team Checklists	.05	.02	.01
☐ 330 Team Checklists	.05	.02	.01
☐ 331 Pedro Munoz	.10	.05	.01
☐ 332 Ryan Klesko	.40	.18	.05
☐ 333 Andre Dawson	.15	.07	.02
☐ 333T Andre Dawson Marlins	.15	.07	.02
☐ 334 Derrick May	.10	.05	.01
☐ 335 Aaron Sele	.10	.05	.01
☐ 336 Kevin Mitchell	.10	.05	.01
☐ 337 Steve Trachsel	.05	.02	.01
☐ 338 Andres Galarraga	.15	.07	.02
☐ 339 Terry Pendleton	.10	.05	.01
☐ 339T Terry Pendleton Marlins	.10	.05	.01
☐ 340 Gary Sheffield	.15	.07	.02
☐ 341 Travis Fryman	.15	.07	.02
☐ 342 Bo Jackson	.15	.07	.02
☐ 343 Gary Gaetti	.10	.05	.01
☐ 344 Brett Butler	.10	.05	.01
☐ 344T Brett Butler Mets	.10	.05	.01
☐ 345 B.J. Surhoff	.10	.05	.01
☐ 346 Larry Walker	.25	.11	.03
☐ 346T Larry Walker Rockies	.50	.23	.06
☐ 347 Kevin Tapani	.05	.02	.01
☐ 348 Rick Wilkins	.05	.02	.01
☐ 349 Wade Boggs	.15	.07	.02
☐ 350 Mariano Duncan	.05	.02	.01
☐ 351 Ruben Sierra	.15	.07	.02
☐ 352 Andy Van Slyke	.10	.05	.01
☐ 352T Andy Van Slyke Orioles	.05	.02	.01
☐ 353 Reggie Jefferson	.05	.02	.01
☐ 354 Gregg Jefferies	.15	.07	.02
☐ 355 Tim Naehring	.05	.02	.01
☐ 356 John Roper	.05	.02	.01
☐ 357 Joe Carter	.15	.07	.02
☐ 358 Kurt Abbott	.05	.02	.01
☐ 359 Lenny Harris	.05	.02	.01
☐ 360 Lance Johnson	.05	.02	.01
☐ 361 Brian Anderson	.05	.02	.01
☐ 362 Jim Eisenreich	.05	.02	.01
☐ 363 Jerry Browne	.05	.02	.01
☐ 364 Mark Grace	.15	.07	.02
☐ 365 Devon White	.10	.05	.01
☐ 366 Reggie Sanders	.15	.07	.02
☐ 367 Ivan Rodriguez	.15	.07	.02
☐ 368 Kirt Manwaring	.05	.02	.01
☐ 369 Pat Kelly	.05	.02	.01
☐ 370 Ellis Burks	.10	.05	.01
☐ 371 Charles Nagy	.10	.05	.01
☐ 372 Kevin Bass	.05	.02	.01
☐ 373 Lou Whitaker	.15	.07	.02
☐ 374 Rene Arocha	.05	.02	.01
☐ 375 Derek Parks	.05	.02	.01
☐ 376 Mark Whiten	.10	.05	.01
☐ 377 Mark McGwire	.15	.07	.02
☐ 378 Doug Drabek	.10	.05	.01
☐ 379 Greg Vaughn	.05	.02	.01
☐ 380 Al Martin	.10	.05	.01
☐ 381 Ron Darling	.05	.02	.01
☐ 382 Tim Wallach	.05	.02	.01
☐ 383 Alan Trammell	.15	.07	.02

#	Player			
☐ 384	Randy Velarde	.05	.02	.01
☐ 385	Chris Sabo	.05	.02	.01
☐ 386	Wil Cordero	.10	.05	.01
☐ 387	Darrin Fletcher	.05	.02	.01
☐ 388	David Segui	.05	.02	.01
☐ 389	Steve Buechele	.05	.02	.01
☐ 390	Dave Gallagher	.05	.02	.01
☐ 391	Thomas Howard	.05	.02	.01
☐ 392	Chad Curtis	.10	.05	.01
☐ 392T	Chad Curtis Tigers	.10	.05	.01
☐ 393	Cal Eldred	.05	.02	.01
☐ 394	Jason Bere	.10	.05	.01
☐ 395	Bret Barberie	.05	.02	.01
☐ 396	Paul Sorrento	.05	.02	.01
☐ 397	Steve Finley	.10	.05	.01
☐ 398	Cecil Fielder	.10	.05	.01
☐ 399	Eric Karros	.15	.07	.02
☐ 400	Jeff Montgomery	.10	.05	.01
☐ 401	Cliff Floyd	.15	.07	.02
☐ 402	Matt Mieske	.05	.02	.01
☐ 403	Brian Hunter	.05	.02	.01
☐ 404	Alex Cole	.05	.02	.01
☐ 405	Kevin Stocker	.05	.02	.01
☐ 406	Eric Davis	.10	.05	.01
☐ 407	Marvin Freeman	.05	.02	.01
☐ 408	Dennis Eckersley	.15	.07	.02
☐ 409	Todd Zeile	.10	.05	.01
☐ 410	Keith Mitchell	.05	.02	.01
☐ 411	Andy Benes	.10	.05	.01
☐ 412	Juan Bell	.05	.02	.01
☐ 413	Royce Clayton	.05	.02	.01
☐ 414	Ed Sprague	.05	.02	.01
☐ 415	Mike Mussina	.25	.11	.03
☐ 416	Todd Hundley	.10	.05	.01
☐ 417	Pat Listach	.05	.02	.01
☐ 418	Joe Oliver	.05	.02	.01
☐ 419	Rafael Palmeiro	.15	.07	.02
☐ 420	Tim Salmon	.30	.14	.04
☐ 421	Brady Anderson	.05	.02	.01
☐ 422	Kenny Lofton	.60	.25	.07
☐ 423	Craig Biggio	.15	.07	.02
☐ 424	Bobby Bonilla	.15	.07	.02
☐ 425	Kenny Rogers	.05	.02	.01
☐ 426	Derek Bell	.15	.07	.02
☐ 427	Scott Cooper	.05	.02	.01
☐ 427T	Scott Cooper Cardinals	.05	.02	.01
☐ 428	Ozzie Guillen	.05	.02	.01
☐ 429	Omar Vizquel	.10	.05	.01
☐ 430	Phil Plantier	.05	.02	.01
☐ 431	Chuck Knoblauch	.15	.07	.02
☐ 432	Darren Daulton	.05	.02	.01
☐ 433	Bob Hamelin	.05	.02	.01
☐ 434	Tom Glavine	.15	.07	.02
☐ 435	Walt Weiss	.10	.05	.01
☐ 436	Jose Vizcaino	.05	.02	.01
☐ 437	Ken Griffey Jr.	2.00	.90	.25
☐ 438	Jay Bell	.10	.05	.01
☐ 439	Juan Gonzalez	.50	.23	.06
☐ 440	Jeff Blauser	.10	.05	.01
☐ 441	Rickey Henderson	.15	.07	.02
☐ 442	Bobby Ayala	.05	.02	.01
☐ 443	David Cone	.15	.07	.02
☐ 443T	David Cone Blue Jays	.15	.07	.02
☐ 444	Pedro J. Martinez	.10	.05	.01
☐ 445	Manny Ramirez	.75	.35	.09
☐ 446	Mark Portugal	.05	.02	.01
☐ 447	Damion Easley	.05	.02	.01
☐ 448	Gary DiSarcina	.05	.02	.01
☐ 449	Roberto Hernandez	.10	.05	.01
☐ 450	Jeffrey Hammonds	.10	.05	.01
☐ 451	Jeff Treadway	.05	.02	.01
☐ 452	Jim Abbott	.15	.07	.02
☐ 452T	Jim Abbott White Sox	.15	.07	.02
☐ 453	Carlos Rodriguez	.05	.02	.01
☐ 454	Joey Cora	.05	.02	.01
☐ 455	Bret Boone	.15	.07	.02
☐ 456	Danny Tartabull	.05	.02	.01
☐ 457	John Franco	.10	.05	.01
☐ 458	Roger Salkeld	.05	.02	.01
☐ 459	Fred McGriff	.25	.11	.03
☐ 460	Pedro Astacio	.05	.02	.01
☐ 461	Jon Lieber	.05	.02	.01
☐ 462	Luis Polonia	.05	.02	.01
☐ 463	Geronimo Pena	.05	.02	.01
☐ 464	Tom Gordon	.05	.02	.01
☐ 465	Brad Ausmus	.05	.02	.01
☐ 466	Willie McGee	.05	.02	.01
☐ 467	Doug Jones	.05	.02	.01
☐ 468	John Smoltz	.10	.05	.01
☐ 469	Troy Neel	.05	.02	.01
☐ 470	Luis Sojo	.05	.02	.01
☐ 471	John Smiley	.05	.02	.01
☐ 472	Rafael Bournigal	.05	.02	.01
☐ 473	Bill Taylor	.05	.02	.01
☐ 474	Juan Guzman	.10	.05	.01
☐ 475	Dave Magadan	.05	.02	.01
☐ 476	Mike Devereaux	.05	.02	.01
☐ 477	Andujar Cedeno	.05	.02	.01
☐ 478	Edgar Martinez	.15	.07	.02
☐ 479	Milt Thompson	.05	.02	.01
☐ 480	Ailen Watson	.10	.05	.01
☐ 481	Ron Karkovice	.05	.02	.01
☐ 482	Joey Hamilton	.10	.05	.01
☐ 483	Vinny Castilla	.15	.07	.02
☐ 484	Tim Belcher	.05	.02	.01
☐ 485	Bernard Gilkey	.10	.05	.01
☐ 486	Scott Servais	.05	.02	.01
☐ 487	Cory Snyder	.05	.02	.01
☐ 488	Mel Rojas	.10	.05	.01
☐ 489	Carlos Reyes	.05	.02	.01
☐ 490	Chip Hale	.05	.02	.01
☐ 491	Bill Swift	.05	.02	.01
☐ 492	Pat Rapp	.10	.05	.01
☐ 493	Brian McRae	.05	.02	.01
☐ 493T	Brian McRae Cubs	.10	.05	.01
☐ 494	Mickey Morandini	.05	.02	.01
☐ 495	Tony Pena	.05	.02	.01
☐ 496	Danny Bautista	.05	.02	.01
☐ 497	Armando Reynoso	.05	.02	.01
☐ 498	Ken Ryan	.05	.02	.01
☐ 499	Billy Ripken	.05	.02	.01
☐ 500	Pat Mahomes	.05	.02	.01
☐ 501	Mark Acre	.05	.02	.01
☐ 502	Geronimo Berroa	.05	.02	.01
☐ 503	Norberto Martin	.05	.02	.01
☐ 504	Chad Kreuter	.05	.02	.01
☐ 505	Howard Johnson	.05	.02	.01
☐ 506	Eric Anthony	.05	.02	.01
☐ 507	Mark Wohlers	.10	.05	.01
☐ 508	Scott Sanders	.05	.02	.01
☐ 509	Pete Harnisch	.05	.02	.01
☐ 510	Wes Chamberlain	.05	.02	.01
☐ 511	Tom Candiotti	.05	.02	.01
☐ 512	Albie Lopez	.05	.02	.01
☐ 513	Denny Neagle	.05	.02	.01
☐ 514	Sean Berry	.05	.02	.01
☐ 515	Billy Hatcher	.05	.02	.01
☐ 516	Todd Jones	.05	.02	.01
☐ 517	Wayne Kirby	.05	.02	.01
☐ 518	Butch Henry	.05	.02	.01
☐ 519	Sandy Alomar Jr.	.10	.05	.01
☐ 520	Kevin Appier	.10	.05	.01

☐ 521	Roberto Mejia	.05	.02	.01
☐ 522	Steve Cooke	.05	.02	.01
☐ 523	Terry Shumpert	.05	.02	.01
☐ 524	Mike Jackson	.05	.02	.01
☐ 525	Kent Mercker	.05	.02	.01
☐ 526	David Wells	.05	.02	.01
☐ 527	Juan Samuel	.05	.02	.01
☐ 528	Salomon Torres	.05	.02	.01
☐ 529	Duane Ward	.05	.02	.01
☐ 530	Rob Dibble	.05	.02	.01
☐ 530T	Rob Dibble White Sox	.05	.02	.01
☐ 531	Mike Blowers	.10	.05	.01
☐ 532	Mark Eichhorn	.05	.02	.01
☐ 533	Alex Diaz	.05	.02	.01
☐ 534	Dan Miceli	.05	.02	.01
☐ 535	Jeff Branson	.05	.02	.01
☐ 536	Dave Stevens	.05	.02	.01
☐ 537	Charlie O'Brien	.05	.02	.01
☐ 538	Shane Reynolds	.05	.02	.01
☐ 539	Rich Amaral	.05	.02	.01
☐ 540	Rusty Greer	.05	.02	.01
☐ 541	Alex Arias	.05	.02	.01
☐ 542	Eric Plunk	.05	.02	.01
☐ 543	John Hudek	.05	.02	.01
☐ 544	Kirk McCaskill	.05	.02	.01
☐ 545	Jeff Reboulet	.05	.02	.01
☐ 546	Sterling Hitchcock	.05	.02	.01
☐ 547	Warren Newson	.05	.02	.01
☐ 548	Bryan Harvey	.05	.02	.01
☐ 549	Mike Huff	.05	.02	.01
☐ 550	Lance Parrish	.10	.05	.01
☐ 551	Ken Griffey Jr. HIT	1.00	.45	.12
☐ 552	Matt Williams HIT	.15	.07	.02
☐ 553	Roberto Alomar HIT UER	.15	.07	.02
	(Card says he's a NL All-Star He plays in the AL)			
☐ 554	Jeff Bagwell HIT	.30	.14	.04
☐ 555	Dave Justice HIT	.10	.05	.01
☐ 556	Cal Ripken Jr. HIT	1.00	.45	.12
☐ 557	Albert Belle HIT	.40	.18	.05
☐ 558	Mike Piazza HIT	.40	.18	.05
☐ 559	Kirby Puckett HIT	.30	.14	.04
☐ 560	Wade Boggs HIT	.10	.05	.01
☐ 561	Tony Gwynn HIT	.30	.14	.04
☐ 562	Barry Bonds HIT	.25	.11	.03
☐ 563	Mo Vaughn HIT	.15	.07	.02
☐ 564	Don Mattingly HIT	.50	.23	.06
☐ 565	Carlos Baerga HIT	.15	.07	.02
☐ 566	Paul Molitor HIT	.10	.05	.01
☐ 567	Raul Mondesi HIT	.25	.11	.03
☐ 568	Manny Ramirez HIT	.40	.18	.05
☐ 569	Alex Rodriguez HIT	.15	.07	.02
☐ 570	Will Clark HIT	.10	.05	.01
☐ 571	Frank Thomas HIT	1.00	.45	.12
☐ 572	Moises Alou HIT	.05	.02	.01
☐ 573	Jeff Conine HIT	.05	.02	.01
☐ 574	Joe Ausanio	.05	.02	.01
☐ 575	Charles Johnson	.15	.07	.02
☐ 576	Ernie Young	.05	.02	.01
☐ 577	Jeff Granger	.05	.02	.01
☐ 578	Robert Perez	.05	.02	.01
☐ 579	Melvin Nieves	.10	.05	.01
☐ 580	Gar Finnvold	.05	.02	.01
☐ 581	Duane Singleton	.05	.02	.01
☐ 582	Chan Ho Park	.10	.05	.01
☐ 583	Fausto Cruz	.05	.02	.01
☐ 584	Dave Staton	.05	.02	.01
☐ 585	Denny Hocking	.05	.02	.01
☐ 586	Nate Minchey	.05	.02	.01
☐ 587	Marc Newfield	.10	.05	.01
☐ 588	Jayhawk Owens	.05	.02	.01

☐ 589	Darren Bragg	.05	.02	.01
☐ 590	Kevin King	.05	.02	.01
☐ 591	Kurt Miller	.05	.02	.01
☐ 592	Aaron Small	.05	.02	.01
☐ 593	Troy O'Leary	.10	.05	.01
☐ 594	Phil Stidham	.05	.02	.01
☐ 595	Steve Dunn	.05	.02	.01
☐ 596	Cory Bailey	.05	.02	.01
☐ 597	Alex Gonzalez	.10	.05	.01
☐ 598	Jim Bowie	.05	.02	.01
☐ 599	Jeff Cirillo	.10	.05	.01
☐ 600	Mark Hutton	.05	.02	.01
☐ 601	Russ Davis	.10	.05	.01
☐ 602	Checklist	.05	.02	.01
☐ 603	Checklist	.05	.02	.01
☐ 604	Checklist	.05	.02	.01
☐ 605	Checklist	.05	.02	.01
☐ RG1	R.Klesko Rook.Greatness	20.00	9.00	2.50
☐ SG1	Ryan Klesko AU/6100	40.00	18.00	5.00
☐ NNO	Trade Hall of Gold	1.00	.45	.12

1995 Score Airmail

This 18-card set was randomly inserted in series two jumbo packs at a rate of one in eight. The fronts have a color photo of the player in a home run swing with the sky in the background. Broken red and blue inner borders frame the player. A gold stamp with the words "Air Mail" is prominent in upper left. The backs have a color photo with player information including how many home runs per at-bats he averaged. A sunset serves as background.

		MINT	NRMT	EXC
COMPLETE SET (18)		100.00	45.00	12.50
COMMON CARD (1-18)		3.00	1.35	.35
☐ AM1	Bob Hamelin	3.00	1.35	.35
☐ AM2	John Mabry	5.00	2.20	.60
☐ AM3	Marc Newfield	3.00	1.35	.35
☐ AM4	Jose Oliva	3.00	1.35	.35
☐ AM5	Charles Johnson	6.00	2.70	.75
☐ AM6	Russ Davis	3.00	1.35	.35
☐ AM7	Ernie Young	3.00	1.35	.35
☐ AM8	Billy Ashley	3.00	1.35	.35
☐ AM9	Ryan Klesko	15.00	6.75	1.85
☐ AM10	J.R. Phillips	3.00	1.35	.35
☐ AM11	Cliff Floyd	5.00	2.20	.60
☐ AM12	Carlos Delgado	6.00	2.70	.75
☐ AM13	Melvin Nieves	3.00	1.35	.35

☐ AM14	Raul Mondesi	20.00	9.00	2.50
☐ AM15	Manny Ramirez	30.00	13.50	3.70
☐ AM16	Mike Kelly	3.00	1.35	.35
☐ AM17	Alex Rodriguez	12.00	5.50	1.50
☐ AM18	Rusty Greer	3.00	1.35	.35

1995 Score Double Gold Champs

This 12-card set was randomly inserted in second series hobby packs at a rate of one in 36. Horizontally-designed fronts have a color action photo with the words "Double Gold Champs" in gold-foil at the bottom above the player's name. The backs have a color photo and a list of the player's accomplishments.

	MINT	NRMT	EXC
COMPLETE SET (12)	120.00	55.00	15.00
COMMON CARD (1-12)	4.00	1.80	.50
☐ GC1 Frank Thomas	25.00	11.00	3.10
☐ GC2 Ken Griffey Jr.	25.00	11.00	3.10
☐ GC3 Barry Bonds	6.00	2.70	.75
☐ GC4 Tony Gwynn	8.00	3.60	1.00
☐ GC5 Don Mattingly	12.00	5.50	1.50
☐ GC6 Greg Maddux	25.00	11.00	3.10
☐ GC7 Roger Clemens	4.00	1.80	.50
☐ GC8 Kenny Lofton	8.00	3.60	1.00
☐ GC9 Jeff Bagwell	8.00	3.60	1.00
☐ GC10 Matt Williams	4.00	1.80	.50
☐ GC11 Kirby Puckett	8.00	3.60	1.00
☐ GC12 Cal Ripken.............	25.00	11.00	3.10

1995 Score Draft Picks

Randomly inserted in first series hobby packs at a rate of one in 36, this 18-card set takes a look at top picks selected in June of 1994. Horizontal fronts have two player photos on a white background. Vertical backs have a player photo and 1994 season's highlights. The cards are numbered with a DP prefix.

	MINT	NRMT	EXC
COMPLETE SET (18)	75.00	34.00	9.50
COMMON CARD (DP1-DP18) ..	3.00	1.35	.35
☐ DP1 McKay Christensen ...	3.00	1.35	.35
☐ DP2 Brett Wagner.............	4.00	1.80	.50
☐ DP3 Paul Wilson	10.00	4.50	1.25
☐ DP4 C.J. Nitkowski.........	3.00	1.35	.35
☐ DP5 Josh Booty................	6.00	2.70	.75
☐ DP6 Antone Williamson....	8.00	3.60	1.00
☐ DP7 Paul Konerko.............	6.00	2.70	.75
☐ DP8 Scott Elarton.............	6.00	2.70	.75
☐ DP9 Jacob Shumate	3.00	1.35	.35
☐ DP10 Terrance Long	4.00	1.80	.50
☐ DP11 Mark Johnson	3.00	1.35	.35
☐ DP12 Ben Grieve.............	12.00	5.50	1.50
☐ DP13 Doug Million.............	4.00	1.80	.50
☐ DP14 Jayson Peterson.......	3.00	1.35	.35
☐ DP15 Dustin Hermanson ..	4.00	1.80	.50
☐ DP16 Matt Smith.............	3.00	1.35	.35
☐ DP17 Kevin Witt................	4.00	1.80	.50
☐ DP18 Brian Buchanan.......	3.00	1.35	.35

1995 Score Dream Team

Randomly inserted in first series hobby and retail packs at a rate of one in 72 packs, this 12-card hologram set showcases top performers from the 1994 season. The holographic fronts have two player images. The horizontal backs are not holographic. They are multi-colored with a small player close-up and a brief write-up. The cards are numbered with a DG prefix.

	MINT	NRMT	EXC
COMPLETE SET (12)	150.00	70.00	19.00
COMMON CARD (DG1-DG12) .	3.00	1.35	.35

		MINT	NRMT	EXC
☐	DG1 Frank Thomas.............	40.00	18.00	5.00
☐	DG2 Roberto Alomar...........	8.00	3.60	1.00
☐	DG3 Cal Ripken.................	40.00	18.00	5.00
☐	DG4 Matt Williams.............	6.00	2.70	.75
☐	DG5 Mike Piazza...............	15.00	6.75	1.85
☐	DG6 Albert Belle................	15.00	6.75	1.85
☐	DG7 Ken Griffey Jr.............	40.00	18.00	5.00
☐	DG8 Tony Gwynn...............	12.00	5.50	1.50
☐	DG9 Paul Molitor...............	4.00	1.80	.50
☐	DG10 Jimmy Key...............	3.00	1.35	.35
☐	DG11 Greg Maddux...........	40.00	18.00	5.00
☐	DG12 Lee Smith................	3.00	1.35	.35

1995 Score Hall of Gold

Randomly inserted in packs at a rate one in six, this 110-card set is a collection of top stars and young hopefuls. Metallic fronts are presented in shades of silver and gold that overlay a player photo. The Hall of Gold logo appears in the upper right-hand corner. Black backs contain a brief write-up and a player photo. The cards are numbered with an HG prefix. Five cards of players who switched team were issued later in the year. These five cards are not considered part of the complete set.

	MINT	NRMT	EXC
COMPLETE SET (110)	100.00	45.00	12.50
COMPLETE SERIES 1 (55)..	60.00	27.00	7.50
COMPLETE SERIES 2 (55)..	40.00	18.00	5.00
COMPLETE TRADE SET (5) ...	4.00	1.80	.50
COMMON CARD (HG1-HG55) ...	.75	.35	.09
COMMON CARD (HG56-HG110)	.75	.35	.09

		MINT	NRMT	EXC
☐	HG1 Ken Griffey Jr...........	12.00	5.50	1.50
☐	HG2 Matt Williams............	2.00	.90	.25
☐	HG3 Roberto Alomar........	2.50	1.10	.30
☐	HG4 Jeff Bagwell.............	4.00	1.80	.50
☐	HG5 Dave Justice............	1.50	.70	.19
☐	HG6 Cal Ripken................	12.00	5.50	1.50
☐	HG7 Randy Johnson.........	2.50	1.10	.30
☐	HG8 Barry Larkin.............	1.50	.70	.19
☐	HG9 Albert Belle..............	5.00	2.20	.60
☐	HG10 Mike Piazza.............	5.00	2.20	.60
☐	HG11 Kirby Puckett............	4.00	1.80	.50
☐	HG12 Moises Alou.............	.75	.35	.09
☐	HG13 Jose Canseco............	2.00	.90	.25
☐	HG14 Tony Gwynn..............	4.00	1.80	.50
☐	HG15 Roger Clemens.........	2.00	.90	.25
☐	HG16 Barry Bonds.............	3.00	1.35	.35
☐	HG17 Mo Vaughn...............	2.00	.90	.25
☐	HG18 Greg Maddux............	12.00	5.50	1.50
☐	HG19 Dante Bichette..........	1.50	.70	.19
☐	HG20 Will Clark.................	1.50	.70	.19
☐	HG21 Lenny Dykstra...........	1.00	.45	.12
☐	HG22 Don Mattingly...........	6.00	2.70	.75
☐	HG23 Carlos Baerga...........	2.50	1.10	.30
☐	HG24 Ozzie Smith..............	2.50	1.10	.30
☐	HG25 Paul Molitor.............	1.00	.45	.12
☐	HG26 Paul O'Neill..............	1.00	.45	.12
☐	HG27 Deion Sanders...........	2.50	1.10	.30
☐	HG28 Jeff Conine...............	1.00	.45	.12
☐	HG29 John Olerud..............	.75	.35	.09
☐	HG30 Jose Rijo.................	.75	.35	.09
☐	HG31 Sammy Sosa.............	1.00	.45	.12
☐	HG32 Robin Ventura...........	1.00	.45	.12
☐	HG33 Raul Mondesi............	3.00	1.35	.35
☐	HG34 Eddie Murray............	1.50	.70	.19
☐	HG35 Marquis Grissom........	1.00	.45	.12
☐	HG36 Darryl Strawberry......	.75	.35	.09
☐	HG37 Dave Nilsson............	.75	.35	.09
☐	HG38 Manny Ramirez........	5.00	2.20	.60
☐	HG39 Delino DeShields.......	.75	.35	.09
☐	HG40 Lee Smith................	1.00	.45	.12
☐	HG41 Alex Rodriguez..........	2.50	1.10	.30
☐	HG42 Julio Franco.............	.75	.35	.09
☐	HG43 Bret Saberhagen........	.75	.35	.09
☐	HG44 Ken Hill..................	.75	.35	.09
☐	HG45 Roberto Kelly...........	.75	.35	.09
☐	HG46 Hal Morris................	.75	.35	.09
☐	HG47 Jimmy Key...............	.75	.35	.09
☐	HG48 Terry Steinbach.........	.75	.35	.09
☐	HG49 Mickey Tettleton........	.75	.35	.09
☐	HG50 Tony Phillips............	.75	.35	.09
☐	HG51 Carlos Garcia	.75	.35	.09
☐	HG52 Jim Edmonds............	1.50	.70	.19
☐	HG53 Rod Beck.................	.75	.35	.09
☐	HG54 Shane Mack..............	.75	.35	.09
☐	HG55 Ken Caminiti.............	.75	.35	.09
☐	HG56 Frank Thomas...........	12.00	5.50	1.50
☐	HG57 Kenny Lofton............	4.00	1.80	.50
☐	HG58 Juan Gonzalez..........	3.00	1.35	.35
☐	HG59 Jason Bere...............	.75	.35	.09
☐	HG60 Joe Carter...............	1.00	.45	.12
☐	HG61 Gary Sheffield..........	1.00	.45	.12
☐	HG62 Andres Galarraga ...	1.00	.45	.12
☐	HG63 Ellis Burks...............	.75	.35	.09
☐	HG64 Bobby Bonilla	1.00	.45	.12
☐	HG65 Tom Glavine	1.00	.45	.12
☐	HG66 John Smoltz............	.75	.35	.09
☐	HG67 Fred McGriff............	1.50	.70	.19
☐	HG68 Craig Biggio............	1.00	.45	.12
☐	HG69 Reggie Sanders........	1.00	.45	.12
☐	HG70 Kevin Mitchell	.75	.35	.09
☐	HG71 Larry Walker	1.50	.70	.19
☐	HG71T Larry Walker Rockies	2.00	.90	.25
☐	HG72 Carlos Delgado	.75	.35	.09
☐	HG73 Alex Gonzalez	.75	.35	.09
☐	HG74 Ivan Rodriguez	1.00	.45	.12
☐	HG75 Ryan Klesko	2.50	1.10	.30
☐	HG76 John Kruk	.75	.35	.09
☐	HG76T John Kruk White Sox	.75	.35	.09
☐	HG77 Brian McRae	.75	.35	.09
☐	HG77T Brian McRae Cubs ..	.75	.35	.09

☐ HG78 Tim Salmon	2.00	.90	.25
☐ HG79 Travis Fryman	1.00	.45	.12
☐ HG80 Chuck Knoblauch ..	1.00	.45	.12
☐ HG81 Jay Bell	.75	.35	.09
☐ HG82 Cecil Fielder	1.00	.45	.12
☐ HG83 Cliff Floyd	.75	.35	.09
☐ HG84 Ruben Sierra	.75	.35	.09
☐ HG85 Mike Mussina	1.50	.70	.19
☐ HG86 Mark Grace	1.00	.45	.12
☐ HG87 Dennis Eckersley ..	1.00	.45	.12
☐ HG88 Dennis Martinez	.75	.35	.09
☐ HG89 Rafael Palmeiro	1.00	.45	.12
☐ HG90 Ben McDonald	.75	.35	.09
☐ HG91 Dave Hollins	.75	.35	.09
☐ HG92 Steve Avery	.75	.35	.09
☐ HG93 David Cone	1.00	.45	.12
☐ HG93T David Cone Blue Jays	1.00	.45	.12
☐ HG94 Darren Daulton	.75	.35	.09
☐ HG95 Bret Boone	.75	.35	.09
☐ HG96 Wade Boggs	1.00	.45	.12
☐ HG97 Doug Drabek	.75	.35	.09
☐ HG98 Andy Benes	.75	.35	.09
☐ HG99 Jim Thome	2.00	.90	.25
☐ HG100 Chili Davis	.75	.35	.09
☐ HG101 Jeffrey Hammonds	.75	.35	.09
☐ HG102 Rickey Henderson	1.00	.45	.12
☐ HG103 Brett Butler	.75	.35	.09
☐ HG104 Tim Wallach	.75	.35	.09
☐ HG105 Wil Cordero	.75	.35	.09
☐ HG106 Mark Whiten	.75	.35	.09
☐ HG107 Bob Hamelin	.75	.35	.09
☐ HG108 Rondell White	.75	.35	.09
☐ HG109 Devon White	.75	.35	.09
☐ HG110 Tony Tarasco	.75	.35	.09
☐ HG110T Tony Tarasco Expos	.75	.35	.09
☐ NNO Trade Hall of Gold	2.00	.90	.25

1995 Score Rookie Dream Team

This 12-card set was randomly inserted in second series retail and hobby packs at a rate of one in 12. The fronts contain a color photo with a metallic background. The "Rookie Dream Team" title occupy two of the borders. The player's name is at the bottom in gold-foil. The backs are horizontally designed, have a head shot and player information with the sky serving as a background.

	MINT	NRMT	EXC
COMPLETE SET (12)	70.00	32.00	8.75
COMMON CARD (1-12)	3.00	1.35	.35
RDT PREFIX ON CARD NUMBERS....			
☐ RDT1 J.R. Phillips	3.00	1.35	.35
☐ RDT2 Alex Gonzalez	4.00	1.80	.50
☐ RDT3 Alex Rodriguez	12.00	5.50	1.50
☐ RDT4 Jose Oliva	3.00	1.35	.35
☐ RDT5 Charles Johnson	6.00	2.70	.75
☐ RDT6 Shawn Green	8.00	3.60	1.00
☐ RDT7 Brian Hunter	10.00	4.50	1.25
☐ RDT8 Garret Anderson	15.00	6.75	1.85
☐ RDT9 Julian Tavarez	4.00	1.80	.50
☐ RDT10 Jose Lima	4.00	1.80	.50
☐ RDT11 Armando Benitez	3.00	1.35	.35
☐ RDT12 Ricky Bottalico	3.00	1.35	.35

1995 Score Rules

Randomly inserted in first series jumbo packs, this 30-card standard-size set features top big league players. Card fronts offer a player photo to the left. At right, the player's name is spelled vertically within a green vapor trail left by a baseball that is at the top. A horizontally designed back features three images of the player and a brief write-up. The cards are numbered with an "SR" prefix.

	MINT	NRMT	EXC
COMPLETE SET (30)	200.00	90.00	25.00
COMMON CARD (SR1-SR30) ..	2.00	.90	.25
☐ SR1 Ken Griffey Jr.	40.00	18.00	5.00
☐ SR2 Frank Thomas	40.00	18.00	5.00
☐ SR3 Mike Piazza	15.00	6.75	1.85
☐ SR4 Jeff Bagwell	12.00	5.50	1.50
☐ SR5 Alex Rodriguez	8.00	3.60	1.00
☐ SR6 Albert Belle	15.00	6.75	1.85
☐ SR7 Matt Williams	6.00	2.70	.75
☐ SR8 Roberto Alomar	8.00	3.60	1.00
☐ SR9 Barry Bonds	10.00	4.50	1.25
☐ SR10 Raul Mondesi	10.00	4.50	1.25
☐ SR11 Jose Canseco	6.00	2.70	.75
☐ SR12 Kirby Puckett	12.00	5.50	1.50
☐ SR13 Fred McGriff	5.00	2.20	.60
☐ SR14 Kenny Lofton	12.00	5.50	1.50
☐ SR15 Greg Maddux	40.00	18.00	5.00
☐ SR16 Juan Gonzalez	10.00	4.50	1.25
☐ SR17 Cliff Floyd	2.00	.90	.25
☐ SR18 Cal Ripken Jr.	40.00	18.00	5.00

		MINT	NRMT	EXC
☐ SR19	Will Clark	5.00	2.20	.60
☐ SR20	Tim Salmon	6.00	2.70	.75
☐ SR21	Paul O'Neill	2.00	.90	.25
☐ SR22	Jason Bere	2.00	.90	.25
☐ SR23	Tony Gwynn	12.00	5.50	1.50
☐ SR24	Manny Ramirez	15.00	6.75	1.85
☐ SR25	Don Mattingly	20.00	9.00	2.50
☐ SR26	Dave Justice	5.00	2.20	.60
☐ SR27	Javier Lopez	5.00	2.20	.60
☐ SR28	Ryan Klesko	8.00	3.60	1.00
☐ SR29	Carlos Delgado	2.00	.90	.25
☐ SR30	Mike Mussina	5.00	2.20	.60

1996 Score

This first series issue consists of 275 cards. These cards were issued in packs of 15 that retailed for 99 cents per pack. A Cal Ripken tribute card was issued at a rate of 1 every 300 packs. The fronts feature an action photo surrounded by white borders. The "Score 96" logo is in the upper left, while the player is identified on the bottom. The backs have season and career stats as well as a player photo and some text.

		MINT	NRMT	EXC
	COMPLETE SERIES 1 (275)	10.00	4.50	1.25
	COMMON CARD (1-275)	.05	.02	.01
☐ 1	Will Clark	.25	.11	.03
☐ 2	Rich Becker	.05	.02	.01
☐ 3	Ryan Klesko	.15	.07	.02
☐ 4	Jim Edmonds	.15	.07	.02
☐ 5	Barry Larkin	.25	.11	.03
☐ 6	Jim Thome	.15	.07	.02
☐ 7	Raul Mondesi	.40	.18	.05
☐ 8	Don Mattingly	1.00	.45	.12
☐ 9	Jeff Conine	.15	.07	.02
☐ 10	Rickey Henderson	.15	.07	.02
☐ 11	Chad Curtis	.10	.05	.01
☐ 12	Darren Daulton	.10	.05	.01
☐ 13	Larry Walker	.25	.11	.03
☐ 14	Carlos Garcia	.05	.02	.01
☐ 15	Carlos Baerga	.40	.18	.05
☐ 16	Tony Gwynn	.60	.25	.07
☐ 17	Jon Nunnally	.10	.05	.01
☐ 18	Deion Sanders	.40	.18	.05
☐ 19	Mark Grace	.15	.07	.02
☐ 20	Alex Rodriguez	.15	.07	.02
☐ 21	Frank Thomas	2.00	.90	.25
☐ 22	Brian Jordan	.15	.07	.02
☐ 23	J.T. Snow	.15	.07	.02
☐ 24	Shawn Green	.15	.07	.02
☐ 25	Tim Wakefield	.10	.05	.01
☐ 26	Curtis Goodwin	.10	.05	.01
☐ 27	John Smoltz	.10	.05	.01
☐ 28	Devon White	.10	.05	.01
☐ 29	Brian L.Hunter	.15	.07	.02
☐ 30	Rusty Greer	.05	.02	.01
☐ 31	Rafael Palmeiro	.15	.07	.02
☐ 32	Bernard Gilkey	.10	.05	.01
☐ 33	John Valentin	.15	.07	.02
☐ 34	Randy Johnson	.40	.18	.05
☐ 35	Garret Anderson			
☐ 36	Rikkert Faneyte	.05	.02	.01
☐ 37	Ray Durham	.15	.07	.02
☐ 38	Bip Roberts	.05	.02	.01
☐ 39	Jaime Navarro	.05	.02	.01
☐ 40	Mark Johnson	.05	.02	.01
☐ 41	Darren Lewis	.05	.02	.01
☐ 42	Tyler Green	.05	.02	.01
☐ 43	Bill Pulsipher	.15	.07	.02
☐ 44	Jason Giambi	.10	.05	.01
☐ 45	Kevin Ritz	.05	.02	.01
☐ 46	Jack McDowell	.15	.07	.02
☐ 47	Felipe Lira	.05	.02	.01
☐ 48	Rico Brogna	.15	.07	.02
☐ 49	Terry Pendleton	.10	.05	.01
☐ 50	Rondell White	.15	.07	.02
☐ 51	Andre Dawson	.15	.07	.02
☐ 52	Kirby Puckett	.60	.25	.07
☐ 53	Wally Joyner	.10	.05	.01
☐ 54	B.J. Surhoff	.10	.05	.01
☐ 55	Randy Velarde	.05	.02	.01
☐ 56	Greg Vaughn	.05	.02	.01
☐ 57	Roberto Alomar	.40	.18	.05
☐ 58	David Justice	.25	.11	.03
☐ 59	Kevin Seitzer	.05	.02	.01
☐ 60	Cal Ripken	2.00	.90	.25
☐ 61	Ozzie Smith	.40	.18	.05
☐ 62	Mo Vaughn	.30	.14	.04
☐ 63	Ricky Bones	.05	.02	.01
☐ 64	Gary DiSarcina	.05	.02	.01
☐ 65	Matt Williams	.30	.14	.04
☐ 66	Wilson Alvarez	.10	.05	.01
☐ 67	Lenny Dykstra	.10	.05	.01
☐ 68	Brian McRae	.10	.05	.01
☐ 69	Todd Stottlemyre	.05	.02	.01
☐ 70	Bret Boone	.10	.05	.01
☐ 71	Sterling Hitchcock	.10	.05	.01
☐ 72	Albert Belle	.75	.35	.09
☐ 73	Todd Hundley	.10	.05	.01
☐ 74	Vinny Castilla	.15	.07	.02
☐ 75	Moises Alou	.10	.05	.01
☐ 76	Cecil Fielder	.15	.07	.02
☐ 77	Brad Radke	.05	.02	.01
☐ 78	Quilvio Veras	.10	.05	.01
☐ 79	Eddie Murray	.25	.11	.03
☐ 80	James Mouton	.10	.05	.01
☐ 81	Pat Listach	.05	.02	.01
☐ 82	Mark Gubicza	.05	.02	.01
☐ 83	Dave Winfield	.15	.07	.02
☐ 84	Fred McGriff	.25	.11	.03
☐ 85	Darryl Hamilton	.05	.02	.01
☐ 86	Jeffrey Hammonds	.05	.02	.01
☐ 87	Pedro Munoz	.10	.05	.01
☐ 88	Craig Biggio	.15	.07	.02
☐ 89	Cliff Floyd	.15	.07	.02
☐ 90	Tim Naehring	.10	.05	.01
☐ 91	Brett Butler	.10	.05	.01
☐ 92	Kevin Foster	.05	.02	.01
☐ 93	Pat Kelly	.05	.02	.01
☐ 94	John Smiley	.05	.02	.01

☐ 95	Terry Steinbach	.10	.05	.01
☐ 96	Orel Hershiser	.10	.05	.01
☐ 97	Darrin Fletcher	.05	.02	.01
☐ 98	Walt Weiss	.10	.05	.01
☐ 99	John Wetteland	.10	.05	.01
☐ 100	Alan Trammell	.15	.07	.02
☐ 101	Steve Avery	.10	.05	.01
☐ 102	Tony Eusebio	.05	.02	.01
☐ 103	Sandy Alomar Jr.	.05	.02	.01
☐ 104	Joe Girardi	.05	.02	.01
☐ 105	Rick Aguilera	.10	.05	.01
☐ 106	Tony Tarasco	.10	.05	.01
☐ 107	Chris Hammond	.05	.02	.01
☐ 108	Mike Macfarlane	.10	.05	.01
☐ 109	Doug Drabek	.10	.05	.01
☐ 110	Derek Bell	.10	.05	.01
☐ 111	Ed Sprague	.05	.02	.01
☐ 112	Todd Hollandsworth	.05	.02	.01
☐ 113	Otis Nixon	.05	.02	.01
☐ 114	Keith Lockhart	.05	.02	.01
☐ 115	Donovan Osborne	.05	.02	.01
☐ 116	Dave Magadan	.05	.02	.01
☐ 117	Edgar Martinez	.15	.07	.02
☐ 118	Chuck Carr	.05	.02	.01
☐ 119	J.R. Phillips	.05	.02	.01
☐ 120	Sean Bergman	.05	.02	.01
☐ 121	Andujar Cedeno	.05	.02	.01
☐ 122	Eric Young	.10	.05	.01
☐ 123	Al Martin	.10	.05	.01
☐ 124	Mark Lemke	.10	.05	.01
☐ 125	Jim Eisenreich	.05	.02	.01
☐ 126	Benito Santiago	.05	.02	.01
☐ 127	Ariel Prieto	.10	.05	.01
☐ 128	Jim Bullinger	.05	.02	.01
☐ 129	Russ Davis	.10	.05	.01
☐ 130	Jim Abbott	.15	.07	.02
☐ 131	Jason Isringhausen	.25	.11	.03
☐ 132	Carlos Perez	.15	.07	.02
☐ 133	David Segui	.05	.02	.01
☐ 134	Troy O'Leary	.10	.05	.01
☐ 135	Pat Meares	.05	.02	.01
☐ 136	Chris Hoiles	.10	.05	.01
☐ 137	Ismael Valdes	.05	.02	.01
☐ 138	Jose Oliva	.05	.02	.01
☐ 139	Carlos Delgado	.10	.05	.01
☐ 140	Tom Goodwin	.05	.02	.01
☐ 141	Bob Tewksbury	.05	.02	.01
☐ 142	Chris Gomez	.05	.02	.01
☐ 143	Jose Oquendo	.05	.02	.01
☐ 144	Mark Lewis	.05	.02	.01
☐ 145	Salomon Torres	.05	.02	.01
☐ 146	Luis Gonzalez	.10	.05	.01
☐ 147	Mark Carreon	.05	.02	.01
☐ 148	Lance Johnson	.05	.02	.01
☐ 149	Melvin Nieves	.05	.02	.01
☐ 150	Lee Smith	.15	.07	.02
☐ 151	Jacob Brumfield	.05	.02	.01
☐ 152	Armando Benitez	.05	.02	.01
☐ 153	Curt Schilling	.05	.02	.01
☐ 154	Javier Lopez	.15	.07	.02
☐ 155	Frank Rodriguez	.10	.05	.01
☐ 156	Alex Gonzalez	.10	.05	.01
☐ 157	Todd Worrell	.05	.02	.01
☐ 158	Benji Gil	.05	.02	.01
☐ 159	Greg Gagne	.05	.02	.01
☐ 160	Tom Henke	.10	.05	.01
☐ 161	Randy Myers	.10	.05	.01
☐ 162	Joey Cora	.05	.02	.01
☐ 163	Scott Ruffcorn	.05	.02	.01
☐ 164	W. VanLandingham	.10	.05	.01
☐ 165	Tony Phillips	.05	.02	.01
☐ 166	Eddie Williams	.05	.02	.01
☐ 167	Bobby Bonilla	.15	.07	.02
☐ 168	Denny Neagle	.05	.02	.01
☐ 169	Troy Percival	.10	.05	.01
☐ 170	Billy Ashley	.05	.02	.01
☐ 171	Andy Van Slyke	.10	.05	.01
☐ 172	Jose Offerman	.05	.02	.01
☐ 173	Mark Parent	.05	.02	.01
☐ 174	Edgardo Alfonzo	.10	.05	.01
☐ 175	Trevor Hoffman	.10	.05	.01
☐ 176	David Cone	.15	.07	.02
☐ 177	Dan Wilson	.10	.05	.01
☐ 178	Steve Ontiveros	.05	.02	.01
☐ 179	Dean Palmer	.10	.05	.01
☐ 180	Mike Kelly	.05	.02	.01
☐ 181	Jim Leyritz	.05	.02	.01
☐ 182	Ron Karkovice	.05	.02	.01
☐ 183	Kevin Brown	.05	.02	.01
☐ 184	Jose Valentin	.05	.02	.01
☐ 185	Jorge Fabregas	.05	.02	.01
☐ 186	Jose Mesa	.10	.05	.01
☐ 187	Brent Mayne	.05	.02	.01
☐ 188	Carl Everett	.10	.05	.01
☐ 189	Paul Sorrento	.05	.02	.01
☐ 190	Pete Schourek	.15	.07	.02
☐ 191	Scott Kamieniecki	.05	.02	.01
☐ 192	Roberto Hernandez	.10	.05	.01
☐ 193	Randy Johnson RR	.15	.07	.02
☐ 194	Greg Maddux RR	1.00	.45	.12
☐ 195	Hideo Nomo RR	.40	.18	.05
☐ 196	David Cone RR	.05	.02	.01
☐ 197	Mike Mussina RR	.05	.02	.01
☐ 198	Andy Benes RR	.05	.02	.01
☐ 199	Kevin Appier RR	.05	.02	.01
☐ 200	John Smoltz RR	.05	.02	.01
☐ 201	John Wetteland RR	.05	.02	.01
☐ 202	Mark Wohlers RR	.05	.02	.01
☐ 203	Stan Belinda	.05	.02	.01
☐ 204	Brian Anderson	.05	.02	.01
☐ 205	Mike Devereaux	.05	.02	.01
☐ 206	Mark Wohlers	.10	.05	.01
☐ 207	Omar Vizquel	.10	.05	.01
☐ 208	Jose Rijo	.05	.02	.01
☐ 209	Willie Blair	.05	.02	.01
☐ 210	Jamie Moyer	.05	.02	.01
☐ 211	Craig Shipley	.05	.02	.01
☐ 212	Shane Reynolds	.10	.05	.01
☐ 213	Chad Fonville	.10	.05	.01
☐ 214	Jose Vizcaino	.05	.02	.01
☐ 215	Sid Fernandez	.05	.02	.01
☐ 216	Andy Ashby	.05	.02	.01
☐ 217	Frank Castillo	.05	.02	.01
☐ 218	Kevin Tapani	.05	.02	.01
☐ 219	Kent Mercker	.05	.02	.01
☐ 220	Karim Garcia	.25	.11	.03
☐ 221	Antonio Osuna	.05	.02	.01
☐ 222	Tim Unroe	.05	.02	.01
☐ 223	Johnny Damon	.30	.14	.04
☐ 224	LaTroy Hawkins	.05	.02	.01
☐ 225	Mariano Rivera	.10	.05	.01
☐ 226	Jose Alberro	.05	.02	.01
☐ 227	Angel Martinez	.10	.05	.01
☐ 228	Jason Schmidt	.15	.07	.02
☐ 229	Tony Clark	.10	.05	.01
☐ 230	Kevin Jordan	.05	.02	.01
☐ 231	Mark Thompson	.05	.02	.01
☐ 232	Jim Dougherty	.05	.02	.01
☐ 233	Roger Cedeno	.15	.07	.02
☐ 234	Ugueth Urbina	.10	.05	.01
☐ 235	Ricky Otero	.05	.02	.01
☐ 236	Mark Smith	.05	.02	.01

☐ 237	Brian Barber	.05	.02	.01
☐ 238	Kevin Flora	.05	.02	.01
☐ 239	Joe Rosselli	.05	.02	.01
☐ 240	Derek Jeter	.15	.07	.02
☐ 241	Michael Tucker	.10	.05	.01
☐ 242	Ben Blomdahl	.05	.02	.01
☐ 243	Joe Vitiello	.05	.02	.01
☐ 244	Todd Steverson	.05	.02	.01
☐ 245	James Baldwin	.10	.05	.01
☐ 246	Alan Embree	.05	.02	.01
☐ 247	Shannon Penn	.05	.02	.01
☐ 248	Chris Stynes	.10	.05	.01
☐ 249	Oscar Munoz	.05	.02	.01
☐ 250	Jose Herrera	.05	.02	.01
☐ 251	Scott Sullivan	.05	.02	.01
☐ 252	Reggie Williams	.05	.02	.01
☐ 253	Mark Grudzielanek	.05	.02	.01
☐ 254	Steve Rodriguez	.05	.02	.01
☐ 255	Terry Bradshaw	.05	.02	.01
☐ 256	F.P. Santangelo	.05	.02	.01
☐ 257	Lyle Mouton	.10	.05	.01
☐ 258	George Williams	.05	.02	.01
☐ 259	Larry Thomas	.05	.02	.01
☐ 260	Rudy Pemberton	.05	.02	.01
☐ 261	Jim Pittsley	.15	.07	.02
☐ 262	Les Norman	.05	.02	.01
☐ 263	Ruben Rivera	.30	.14	.04
☐ 264	Cesar Devarez	.05	.02	.01
☐ 265	Greg Zaun	.05	.02	.01
☐ 266	Dustin Hermanson	.10	.05	.01
☐ 267	John Frascatore	.05	.02	.01
☐ 268	Joe Randa	.05	.02	.01
☐ 269	Jeff Bagwell CL	.30	.14	.04
☐ 270	Mike Piazza CL	.40	.18	.05
☐ 271	Dante Bichette CL	.10	.05	.01
☐ 272	Frank Thomas CL	1.00	.45	.12
☐ 273	Ken Griffey, Jr. CL	1.00	.45	.12
☐ 274	Cal Ripken CL	1.00	.45	.12
☐ 275	Greg Maddux CL	.75	.35	.09
	Albert Belle			
☐ NNO	Cal Ripken 2131	50.00	22.00	6.25

		MINT	NRMT	EXC
COMPLETE SET (20)		150.00	70.00	19.00
COMMON CARD (1-20)		3.00	1.35	.35
☐ 1	Cal Ripken	30.00	13.50	3.70
☐ 2	Ken Griffey Jr.	30.00	13.50	3.70
☐ 3	Frank Thomas	30.00	13.50	3.70
☐ 4	Jeff Bagwell	10.00	4.50	1.25
☐ 5	Mike Piazza	12.00	5.50	1.50
☐ 6	Barry Bonds	8.00	3.60	1.00
☐ 7	Matt Williams	5.00	2.20	.60
☐ 8	Raul Mondesi	6.00	2.70	.75
☐ 9	Tony Gwynn	10.00	4.50	1.25
☐ 10	Albert Belle	12.00	5.50	1.50
☐ 11	Manny Ramirez	12.00	5.50	1.50
☐ 12	Carlos Baerga	6.00	2.70	.75
☐ 13	Mo Vaughn	5.00	2.20	.60
☐ 14	Derek Bell	3.00	1.35	.35
☐ 15	Larry Walker	4.00	1.80	.50
☐ 16	Kenny Lofton	10.00	4.50	1.25
☐ 17	Edgar Martinez	3.00	1.35	.35
☐ 18	Reggie Sanders	3.00	1.35	.35
☐ 19	Eddie Murray	4.00	1.80	.50
☐ 20	Chipper Jones	12.00	5.50	1.50

1996 Score Dream Team

This nine-card set was randomly inserted in approximately one in 72 packs. This set features a leading player at each position. The fronts feature a player photo set against a holographic foil background. The words "1995 Dream Team" as well as his name and team are printed on the bottom of the card. The horizontal backs feature a player photo and some text. The cards are numbered in the upper right as "X" of nine.

		MINT	NRMT	EXC
COMPLETE SET (9)		125.00	55.00	15.50
COMMON CARD (1-9)		5.00	2.20	.60
☐ 1	Cal Ripken	30.00	13.50	3.70
☐ 2	Frank Thomas	30.00	13.50	3.70
☐ 3	Carlos Baerga	6.00	2.70	.75
☐ 4	Matt Williams	5.00	2.20	.60
☐ 5	Mike Piazza	12.00	5.50	1.50
☐ 6	Barry Bonds	8.00	3.60	1.00
☐ 7	Ken Griffey Jr.	30.00	13.50	3.70
☐ 8	Manny Ramirez	12.00	5.50	1.50
☐ 9	Greg Maddux	30.00	13.50	3.70

1996 Score Big Bats

This 20-card set was randomly inserted in retail packs at a rate of approximately one in 31. The fronts feature a player photo set against a gold-foil background. The words "Big Bats" as well as the player's name is printed in white at the bottom. The backs feature a photo against a multi-colored background. The cards are numbered "X" of 20 in the upper left corner.

1996 Score Dugout Collection

This set is a mini-parallel to the regular issue. In the first series, only 110 of the 275 cards were issued as Dugout Collection cards. These cards were inserted approximately one in every three packs. These cards have all-foil printing that gives these cards a shiny copper cast. The words "Dugout Collection" are printed in the back.

	MINT	NRMT	EXC
COMPLETE SERIES 1 (110)..	50.00	22.00	6.25
COMMON CARD (1-110)	.40	.18	.05
SEMISTARS..............................	.60	.25	.07
☐ 1 Will Clark	1.00	.45	.12
☐ 5 Barry Larkin	1.00	.45	.12
☐ 7 Raul Mondesi...............	1.50	.70	.19
☐ 8 Don Mattingly	4.00	1.80	.50
☐ 13 Larry Walker	1.00	.45	.12
☐ 14 Carlos Baerga............	1.50	.70	.19
☐ 15 Tony Gwynn	2.50	1.10	.30
☐ 17 Deion Sanders	1.50	.70	.19
☐ 20 Frank Thomas............	8.00	3.60	1.00
☐ 33 Randy Johnson...........	1.50	.70	.19
☐ 45 Kirby Puckett.............	2.50	1.10	.30
☐ 50 Roberto Alomar...........	1.50	.70	.19
☐ 51 David Justice	1.00	.45	.12
☐ 52 Cal Ripken.................	8.00	3.60	1.00
☐ 53 Ozzie Smith	1.50	.70	.19
☐ 54 Mo Vaughn	1.25	.55	.16
☐ 56 Matt Williams.............	1.25	.55	.16
☐ 59 Albert Belle	3.00	1.35	.35
☐ 65 Eddie Murray	1.00	.45	.12
☐ 67 Fred McGriff..............	1.00	.45	.12
☐ 82 Jason Isringhausen.....	1.00	.45	.12
☐ 102 Karim Garcia............	1.00	.45	.12
☐ 103 Johnny Damon..........	1.25	.55	.16
☐ 109 Ruben Rivera............	1.25	.55	.16

1996 Score Dugout Collection Artist's Proofs

This set is a parallel to the Dugout Collection set. These cards are different from the regular Dugout Collection as they have the words Artist Proof printed on the front. These cards are inserted approximately one in every 36 packs.

	MINT	NRMT	EXC
COMPLETE SERIES 1 (110).	350.00	160.00	45.00
COMMON CARD (1-110)	2.00	.90	.25
SEMISTARS..............................	4.00	1.80	.50
*VETERAN STARS: 4X to 7X BASIC CARDS			
*YOUNG STARS: 2.5X to 5X BASIC CARDS			
☐ 8 Don Mattingly	30.00	13.50	3.70
☐ 15 Tony Gwynn	20.00	9.00	2.50

☐ 20 Frank Thomas............	60.00	27.00	7.50
☐ 45 Kirby Puckett.............	20.00	9.00	2.50
☐ 52 Cal Ripken.................	60.00	27.00	7.50
☐ 59 Albert Belle	25.00	11.00	3.10

1996 Score Numbers Game

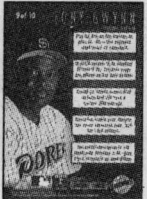

This 30-card set was inserted approximately one in every 15 packs. The fronts feature two player photos. The player's name is spelled vertically on the right while the words "Numbers Game" are printed against a gold-foil background. The backs contain five quick information bytes that feature that player's accomplishments. The cards are numbered as "X" of 30 in the upper left corner.

	MINT	NRMT	EXC
COMPLETE SET (30)	55.00	25.00	7.00
COMMON CARD (1-30)	.75	.35	.09
☐ 1 Cal Ripken....................	10.00	4.50	1.25
☐ 2 Frank Thomas	10.00	4.50	1.25
☐ 3 Ken Griffey Jr.	10.00	4.50	1.25
☐ 4 Mike Piazza	4.00	1.80	.50
☐ 5 Barry Bonds	2.50	1.10	.30
☐ 6 Greg Maddux	10.00	4.50	1.25
☐ 7 Jeff Bagwell	3.00	1.35	.35
☐ 8 Derek Bell	.75	.35	.09
☐ 9 Tony Gwynn	3.00	1.35	.35
☐ 10 Hideo Nomo	4.00	1.80	.50
☐ 11 Raul Mondesi.............	2.00	.90	.25
☐ 12 Manny Ramirez...........	4.00	1.80	.50
☐ 13 Albert Belle	4.00	1.80	.50
☐ 14 Matt Williams.............	1.50	.70	.19
☐ 15 Jim Edmonds	.75	.35	.09
☐ 16 Edgar Martinez...........	.75	.35	.09
☐ 17 Mo Vaughn	1.50	.70	.19
☐ 18 Reggie Sanders..........	.75	.35	.09
☐ 19 Chipper Jones	5.00	2.20	.60
☐ 20 Larry Walker	1.25	.55	.16
☐ 21 Juan Gonzalez...........	2.50	1.10	.30
☐ 22 Kenny Lofton	3.00	1.35	.35
☐ 23 Don Mattingly	5.00	2.20	.60
☐ 24 Ivan Rodriguez...........	.75	.35	.09
☐ 25 Randy Johnson...........	2.00	.90	.25
☐ 26 Derek Jeter	.75	.35	.09
☐ 27 J.T. Snow	.75	.35	.09
☐ 28 Will Clark	1.25	.55	.16

		MINT	NRMT	EXC
☐ 29	Rafael Palmeiro	.75	.35	.09
☐ 30	Alex Rodriguez	.75	.35	.09

☐ 19	Jim Thome	2.00	.90	.25
	Dean Palmer			
☐ 20	Chuck Knoblauch	2.00	.90	.25
	Craig Biggio			

1996 Score Reflextions

This 20-card set was randomly inserted approximately one in every 31 hobby packs. Two players per card are featured, a veteran player and a younger star playing the same position. These cards feature a mirror effect on the front.

		MINT	NRMT	EXC
COMPLETE SET (20)		135.00	60.00	17.00
COMMON CARD (1-20)		2.00	.90	.25
☐ 1	Cal Ripken	35.00	16.00	4.40
	Chipper Jones			
☐ 2	Ken Griffey Jr.	20.00	9.00	2.50
	Alex Rodriguez			
☐ 3	Frank Thomas	25.00	11.00	3.10
	Mo Vaughn			
☐ 4	K. Lofton/Brian L.Hunter	8.00	3.60	1.00
☐ 5	Don Mattingly/J.T.Snow	10.00	4.50	1.25
☐ 6	Manny Ramirez	10.00	4.50	1.25
	Raul Mondesi			
☐ 7	Tony Gwynn	8.00	3.60	1.00
	Garret Anderson			
☐ 8	Roberto Alomar	5.00	2.20	.60
	Carlos Baerga			
☐ 9	Andre Dawson	3.00	1.35	.35
	Larry Walker			
☐ 10	Barry Larkin	3.00	1.35	.35
	Derek Jeter			
☐ 11	Barry Bonds	5.00	2.20	.60
	Reggie Sanders			
☐ 12	Mike Piazza	15.00	6.75	1.85
	Albert Belle			
☐ 13	Wade Boggs	2.00	.90	.25
	Edgar Martinez			
☐ 14	David Cone	2.00	.90	.25
	John Smoltz			
☐ 15	Will Clark	8.00	3.60	1.00
	Jeff Bagwell			
☐ 16	Mark McGwire	2.00	.90	.25
	Cecil Fielder			
☐ 17	Greg Maddux	20.00	9.00	2.50
	Mike Mussina			
☐ 18	Randy Johnson	12.00	5.50	1.50
	Hideo Nomo			

1993 Select

Seeking a niche in the premium, mid-price market, Score produced a new 405-card baseball set. The set includes regular players, rookies, and draft picks, and was sold in 15-card packs and 28-card super packs. Themed Chase Cards (24 in all) were randomly inserted into the 15-card packs. The cards measure the standard size (2 1/2" by 3 1/2"). The front photos, composed either horizontally or vertically, are ultra-violet coated while the two-toned green borders received a matte finish. The player's name appears in mustard-colored lettering in the bottom border. The backs carry a second color photo as well as 1992 statistics, career totals, and an in-depth player profile, all on a two-toned green background. The cards are numbered on the back. The set includes Draft Pick (291, 297, 303, 310, 352-360) and Rookie (271-290, 292-296, 298-302, 304-309, 311-351, 383, 385, 391, 394, 400-405) subsets. Rookie Cards in this set include Derek Jeter, Jason Kendall and J.T. Snow.

		MINT	NRMT	EXC
COMPLETE SET (405)		30.00	13.50	3.70
COMMON CARD (1-405)		.10	.05	.01
☐ 1	Barry Bonds	.75	.35	.09
☐ 2	Ken Griffey Jr	3.00	1.35	.35
☐ 3	Will Clark	.40	.18	.05
☐ 4	Kirby Puckett	1.00	.45	.12
☐ 5	Tony Gwynn	1.00	.45	.12
☐ 6	Frank Thomas	3.00	1.35	.35
☐ 7	Tom Glavine	.30	.14	.04
☐ 8	Roberto Alomar	.60	.25	.07
☐ 9	Andre Dawson	.30	.14	.04
☐ 10	Ron Darling	.10	.05	.01
☐ 11	Bobby Bonilla	.30	.14	.04
☐ 12	Danny Tartabull	.20	.09	.03
☐ 13	Darren Daulton	.30	.14	.04
☐ 14	Roger Clemens	.50	.23	.06
☐ 15	Ozzie Smith	.60	.25	.07
☐ 16	Mark McGwire	.30	.14	.04

☐ 17	Terry Pendleton	.20	.09	.03
☐ 18	Cal Ripken	3.00	1.35	.35
☐ 19	Fred McGriff	.40	.18	.05
☐ 20	Cecil Fielder	.30	.14	.04
☐ 21	Darryl Strawberry	.20	.09	.03
☐ 22	Robin Yount	.40	.18	.05
☐ 23	Barry Larkin	.40	.18	.05
☐ 24	Don Mattingly	1.50	.70	.19
☐ 25	Craig Biggio	.30	.14	.04
☐ 26	Sandy Alomar Jr.	.20	.09	.03
☐ 27	Larry Walker	.40	.18	.05
☐ 28	Junior Felix	.10	.05	.01
☐ 29	Eddie Murray	.50	.23	.06
☐ 30	Robin Ventura	.30	.14	.04
☐ 31	Greg Maddux	3.00	1.35	.35
☐ 32	Dave Winfield	.30	.14	.04
☐ 33	John Kruk	.30	.14	.04
☐ 34	Wally Joyner	.20	.09	.03
☐ 35	Andy Van Slyke	.20	.09	.03
☐ 36	Chuck Knoblauch	.30	.14	.04
☐ 37	Tom Pagnozzi	.10	.05	.01
☐ 38	Dennis Eckersley	.30	.14	.04
☐ 39	Dave Justice	.40	.18	.05
☐ 40	Juan Gonzalez	.60	.25	.07
☐ 41	Gary Sheffield	.30	.14	.04
☐ 42	Paul Molitor	.30	.14	.04
☐ 43	Delino DeShields	.20	.09	.03
☐ 44	Travis Fryman	.30	.14	.04
☐ 45	Hal Morris	.20	.09	.03
☐ 46	Greg Olson	.10	.05	.01
☐ 47	Ken Caminiti	.20	.09	.03
☐ 48	Wade Boggs	.30	.14	.04
☐ 49	Orel Hershiser	.20	.09	.03
☐ 50	Albert Belle	1.25	.55	.16
☐ 51	Bill Swift	.10	.05	.01
☐ 52	Mark Langston	.30	.14	.04
☐ 53	Joe Girardi	.10	.05	.01
☐ 54	Keith Miller	.10	.05	.01
☐ 55	Gary Carter	.30	.14	.04
☐ 56	Brady Anderson	.20	.09	.03
☐ 57	Dwight Gooden	.20	.09	.03
☐ 58	Julio Franco	.20	.09	.03
☐ 59	Lenny Dykstra	.30	.14	.04
☐ 60	Mickey Tettleton	.20	.09	.03
☐ 61	Randy Tomlin	.10	.05	.01
☐ 62	B.J. Surhoff	.20	.09	.03
☐ 63	Todd Zeile	.20	.09	.03
☐ 64	Roberto Kelly	.20	.09	.03
☐ 65	Rob Dibble	.10	.05	.01
☐ 66	Leo Gomez	.10	.05	.01
☐ 67	Doug Jones	.10	.05	.01
☐ 68	Ellis Burks	.20	.09	.03
☐ 69	Mike Scioscia	.10	.05	.01
☐ 70	Charles Nagy	.20	.09	.03
☐ 71	Cory Snyder	.10	.05	.01
☐ 72	Devon White	.20	.09	.03
☐ 73	Mark Grace	.30	.14	.04
☐ 74	Luis Polonia	.10	.05	.01
☐ 75	John Smiley 2X	.20	.09	.03
☐ 76	Carlton Fisk	.30	.14	.04
☐ 77	Luis Sojo	.10	.05	.01
☐ 78	George Brett	1.25	.55	.16
☐ 79	Mitch Williams	.20	.09	.03
☐ 80	Kent Hrbek	.20	.09	.03
☐ 81	Jay Bell	.20	.09	.03
☐ 82	Edgar Martinez	.30	.14	.04
☐ 83	Lee Smith	.30	.14	.04
☐ 84	Deion Sanders	.60	.25	.07
☐ 85	Bill Gullickson	.10	.05	.01
☐ 86	Paul O'Neill	.20	.09	.03
☐ 87	Kevin Seitzer	.10	.05	.01
☐ 88	Steve Finley	.20	.09	.03
☐ 89	Mel Hall	.10	.05	.01
☐ 90	Nolan Ryan	2.50	1.10	.30
☐ 91	Eric Davis	.10	.05	.01
☐ 92	Mike Mussina	.50	.23	.06
☐ 93	Tony Fernandez	.10	.05	.01
☐ 94	Frank Viola	.20	.09	.03
☐ 95	Matt Williams	.50	.23	.06
☐ 96	Joe Carter	.30	.14	.04
☐ 97	Ryne Sandberg	.75	.35	.09
☐ 98	Jim Abbott	.30	.14	.04
☐ 99	Marquis Grissom	.30	.14	.04
☐ 100	George Bell	.20	.09	.03
☐ 101	Howard Johnson	.10	.05	.01
☐ 102	Kevin Appier	.20	.09	.03
☐ 103	Dale Murphy	.30	.14	.04
☐ 104	Shane Mack	.10	.05	.01
☐ 105	Jose Lind	.10	.05	.01
☐ 106	Rickey Henderson	.30	.14	.04
☐ 107	Bob Tewksbury	.10	.05	.01
☐ 108	Kevin Mitchell	.20	.09	.03
☐ 109	Steve Avery	.30	.14	.04
☐ 110	Candy Maldonado	.10	.05	.01
☐ 111	Bip Roberts	.20	.09	.03
☐ 112	Lou Whitaker	.30	.14	.04
☐ 113	Jeff Bagwell	1.25	.55	.16
☐ 114	Dante Bichette	.40	.18	.05
☐ 115	Brett Butler	.20	.09	.03
☐ 116	Melido Perez	.10	.05	.01
☐ 117	Andy Benes	.20	.09	.03
☐ 118	Randy Johnson	.60	.25	.07
☐ 119	Willie McGee	.20	.09	.03
☐ 120	Jody Reed	.10	.05	.01
☐ 121	Shawon Dunston	.10	.05	.01
☐ 122	Carlos Baerga	.60	.25	.07
☐ 123	Bret Saberhagen	.20	.09	.03
☐ 124	John Olerud	.20	.09	.03
☐ 125	Ivan Calderon	.10	.05	.01
☐ 126	Bryan Harvey	.20	.09	.03
☐ 127	Terry Mulholland	.10	.05	.01
☐ 128	Ozzie Guillen	.10	.05	.01
☐ 129	Steve Buechele	.10	.05	.01
☐ 130	Kevin Tapani	.10	.05	.01
☐ 131	Felix Jose	.10	.05	.01
☐ 132	Terry Steinbach	.20	.09	.03
☐ 133	Ron Gant	.30	.14	.04
☐ 134	Harold Reynolds	.10	.05	.01
☐ 135	Chris Sabo	.10	.05	.01
☐ 136	Ivan Rodriguez	.30	.14	.04
☐ 137	Eric Anthony	.10	.05	.01
☐ 138	Mike Henneman	.10	.05	.01
☐ 139	Robby Thompson	.10	.05	.01
☐ 140	Scott Fletcher	.10	.05	.01
☐ 141	Bruce Hurst	.10	.05	.01
☐ 142	Kevin Maas	.10	.05	.01
☐ 143	Tom Candiotti	.10	.05	.01
☐ 144	Chris Hoiles	.20	.09	.03
☐ 145	Mike Morgan	.10	.05	.01
☐ 146	Mark Whiten	.20	.09	.03
☐ 147	Dennis Martinez	.20	.09	.03
☐ 148	Tony Pena	.10	.05	.01
☐ 149	Dave Magadan	.10	.05	.01
☐ 150	Mark Lewis	.10	.05	.01
☐ 151	Mariano Duncan	.10	.05	.01
☐ 152	Gregg Jefferies	.30	.14	.04
☐ 153	Doug Drabek	.30	.14	.04
☐ 154	Brian Harper	.10	.05	.01
☐ 155	Ray Lankford	.30	.14	.04
☐ 156	Carney Lansford	.20	.09	.03
☐ 157	Mike Sharperson	.10	.05	.01
☐ 158	Jack Morris	.30	.14	.04

☐ 159	Otis Nixon	.10	.05	.01
☐ 160	Steve Sax	.10	.05	.01
☐ 161	Mark Lemke	.20	.09	.03
☐ 162	Rafael Palmeiro	.30	.14	.04
☐ 163	Jose Rijo	.20	.09	.03
☐ 164	Omar Vizquel	.20	.09	.03
☐ 165	Sammy Sosa	.30	.14	.04
☐ 166	Milt Cuyler	.10	.05	.01
☐ 167	John Franco	.20	.09	.03
☐ 168	Darryl Hamilton	.10	.05	.01
☐ 169	Ken Hill	.20	.09	.03
☐ 170	Mike Devereaux	.20	.09	.03
☐ 171	Don Slaught	.10	.05	.01
☐ 172	Steve Farr	.10	.05	.01
☐ 173	Bernard Gilkey	.20	.09	.03
☐ 174	Mike Fetters	.10	.05	.01
☐ 175	Vince Coleman	.10	.05	.01
☐ 176	Kevin McReynolds	.10	.05	.01
☐ 177	John Smoltz	.20	.09	.03
☐ 178	Greg Gagne	.10	.05	.01
☐ 179	Greg Swindell	.10	.05	.01
☐ 180	Juan Guzman	.20	.09	.03
☐ 181	Kal Daniels	.10	.05	.01
☐ 182	Rick Sutcliffe	.20	.09	.03
☐ 183	Orlando Merced	.20	.09	.03
☐ 184	Bill Wegman	.10	.05	.01
☐ 185	Mark Gardner	.10	.05	.01
☐ 186	Rob Deer	.10	.05	.01
☐ 187	Dave Hollins	.10	.05	.01
☐ 188	Jack Clark	.20	.09	.03
☐ 189	Brian Hunter	.10	.05	.01
☐ 190	Tim Wallach	.10	.05	.01
☐ 191	Tim Belcher	.10	.05	.01
☐ 192	Walt Weiss	.20	.09	.03
☐ 193	Kurt Stillwell	.10	.05	.01
☐ 194	Charlie Hayes	.20	.09	.03
☐ 195	Willie Randolph	.20	.09	.03
☐ 196	Jack McDowell	.30	.14	.04
☐ 197	Jose Offerman	.10	.05	.01
☐ 198	Chuck Finley	.10	.05	.01
☐ 199	Darrin Jackson	.10	.05	.01
☐ 200	Kelly Gruber	.10	.05	.01
☐ 201	John Wetteland	.20	.09	.03
☐ 202	Jay Buhner	.30	.14	.04
☐ 203	Mike LaValliere	.10	.05	.01
☐ 204	Kevin Brown	.10	.05	.01
☐ 205	Luis Gonzalez	.20	.09	.03
☐ 206	Rick Aguilera	.20	.09	.03
☐ 207	Norm Charlton	.10	.05	.01
☐ 208	Mike Bordick	.20	.09	.03
☐ 209	Charlie Leibrandt	.10	.05	.01
☐ 210	Tom Brunansky	.10	.05	.01
☐ 211	Tom Henke	.20	.09	.03
☐ 212	Randy Milligan	.10	.05	.01
☐ 213	Ramon Martinez	.20	.09	.03
☐ 214	Mo Vaughn	.50	.23	.06
☐ 215	Randy Myers	.20	.09	.03
☐ 216	Greg Hibbard	.10	.05	.01
☐ 217	Wes Chamberlain	.10	.05	.01
☐ 218	Tony Phillips	.10	.05	.01
☐ 219	Pete Harnisch	.10	.05	.01
☐ 220	Mike Gallego	.10	.05	.01
☐ 221	Bud Black	.10	.05	.01
☐ 222	Greg Vaughn	.10	.05	.01
☐ 223	Milt Thompson	.10	.05	.01
☐ 224	Ben McDonald	.10	.05	.01
☐ 225	Billy Hatcher	.10	.05	.01
☐ 226	Paul Sorrento	.10	.05	.01
☐ 227	Mark Gubicza	.10	.05	.01
☐ 228	Mike Greenwell	.20	.09	.03
☐ 229	Curt Schilling	.10	.05	.01
☐ 230	Alan Trammell	.30	.14	.04
☐ 231	Zane Smith	.10	.05	.01
☐ 232	Bobby Thigpen	.10	.05	.01
☐ 233	Greg Olson	.10	.05	.01
☐ 234	Joe Orsulak	.10	.05	.01
☐ 235	Joe Oliver	.10	.05	.01
☐ 236	Tim Raines	.30	.14	.04
☐ 237	Juan Samuel	.10	.05	.01
☐ 238	Chili Davis	.20	.09	.03
☐ 239	Spike Owen	.10	.05	.01
☐ 240	Dave Stewart	.20	.09	.03
☐ 241	Jim Eisenreich	.10	.05	.01
☐ 242	Phil Plantier	.10	.05	.01
☐ 243	Sid Fernandez	.10	.05	.01
☐ 244	Dan Gladden	.10	.05	.01
☐ 245	Mickey Morandini	.10	.05	.01
☐ 246	Tino Martinez	.30	.14	.04
☐ 247	Kirt Manwaring	.10	.05	.01
☐ 248	Dean Palmer	.20	.09	.03
☐ 249	Tom Browning	.10	.05	.01
☐ 250	Brian McRae	.30	.14	.04
☐ 251	Scott Leius	.10	.05	.01
☐ 252	Bert Blyleven	.30	.14	.04
☐ 253	Scott Erickson	.20	.09	.03
☐ 254	Bob Welch	.20	.09	.03
☐ 255	Pat Kelly	.10	.05	.01
☐ 256	Felix Fermin	.10	.05	.01
☐ 257	Harold Baines	.20	.09	.03
☐ 258	Duane Ward	.10	.05	.01
☐ 259	Bill Spiers	.10	.05	.01
☐ 260	Jaime Navarro	.10	.05	.01
☐ 261	Scott Sanderson	.10	.05	.01
☐ 262	Gary Gaetti	.20	.09	.03
☐ 263	Bob Ojeda	.10	.05	.01
☐ 264	Jeff Montgomery	.20	.09	.03
☐ 265	Scott Bankhead	.10	.05	.01
☐ 266	Lance Johnson	.10	.05	.01
☐ 267	Rafael Belliard	.10	.05	.01
☐ 268	Kevin Reimer	.10	.05	.01
☐ 269	Benito Santiago	.10	.05	.01
☐ 270	Mike Moore	.10	.05	.01
☐ 271	Dave Fleming	.10	.05	.01
☐ 272	Moises Alou	.30	.14	.04
☐ 273	Pat Listach	.10	.05	.01
☐ 274	Reggie Sanders	.30	.14	.04
☐ 275	Kenny Lofton	1.00	.45	.12
☐ 276	Donovan Osborne	.10	.05	.01
☐ 277	Rusty Meacham	.10	.05	.01
☐ 278	Eric Karros	.30	.14	.04
☐ 279	Andy Stankiewicz	.10	.05	.01
☐ 280	Brian Jordan	.30	.14	.04
☐ 281	Gary DiSarcina	.10	.05	.01
☐ 282	Mark Wohlers	.30	.14	.04
☐ 283	Dave Nilsson	.20	.09	.03
☐ 284	Anthony Young	.10	.05	.01
☐ 285	Jim Bullinger	.10	.05	.01
☐ 286	Derek Bell	.30	.14	.04
☐ 287	Brian Williams	.10	.05	.01
☐ 288	Julio Valera	.10	.05	.01
☐ 289	Dan Walters	.10	.05	.01
☐ 290	Chad Curtis	.20	.09	.03
☐ 291	Michael Tucker DP	.30	.14	.04
☐ 292	Bob Zupcic	.10	.05	.01
☐ 293	Todd Hundley	.10	.05	.01
☐ 294	Jeff Tackett	.10	.05	.01
☐ 295	Greg Colbrunn	.30	.14	.04
☐ 296	Cal Eldred	.20	.09	.03
☐ 297	Chris Roberts DP	.20	.09	.03
☐ 298	John Doherty	.10	.05	.01
☐ 299	Denny Neagle	.10	.05	.01
☐ 300	Arthur Rhodes	.20	.09	.03

☐ 301	Mark Clark	.20	.09	.03
☐ 302	Scott Cooper	.10	.05	.01
☐ 303	Jamie Arnold DP	.20	.09	.03
☐ 304	Jim Thome	1.25	.55	.16
☐ 305	Frank Seminara	.10	.05	.01
☐ 306	Kurt Knudsen	.10	.05	.01
☐ 307	Tim Wakefield	.30	.14	.04
☐ 308	John Jaha	.20	.09	.03
☐ 309	Pat Hentgen	.20	.09	.03
☐ 310	B.J. Wallace DP	.10	.05	.01
☐ 311	Roberto Hernandez	.10	.05	.01
☐ 312	Hipolito Pichardo	.10	.05	.01
☐ 313	Eric Fox	.10	.05	.01
☐ 314	Willie Banks	.10	.05	.01
☐ 315	Sam Militello	.10	.05	.01
☐ 316	Vince Horsman	.10	.05	.01
☐ 317	Carlos Hernandez	.10	.05	.01
☐ 318	Jeff Kent	.30	.14	.04
☐ 319	Mike Perez	.10	.05	.01
☐ 320	Scott Livingstone	.10	.05	.01
☐ 321	Jeff Conine	.30	.14	.04
☐ 322	James Austin	.10	.05	.01
☐ 323	John Vander Wal	.10	.05	.01
☐ 324	Pat Mahomes	.10	.05	.01
☐ 325	Pedro Astacio	.10	.05	.01
☐ 326	Bret Boone UER	.30	.14	.04
	(Misspelled Brett)			
☐ 327	Matt Stairs	.10	.05	.01
☐ 328	Damion Easley	.20	.09	.03
☐ 329	Ben Rivera	.10	.05	.01
☐ 330	Reggie Jefferson	.10	.05	.01
☐ 331	Luis Mercedes	.10	.05	.01
☐ 332	Kyle Abbott	.10	.05	.01
☐ 333	Eddie Taubensee	.10	.05	.01
☐ 334	Tim McIntosh	.10	.05	.01
☐ 335	Phil Clark	.10	.05	.01
☐ 336	Wil Cordero	.30	.14	.04
☐ 337	Russ Springer	.10	.05	.01
☐ 338	Craig Colbert	.10	.05	.01
☐ 339	Tim Salmon	1.00	.45	.12
☐ 340	Braulio Castillo	.10	.05	.01
☐ 341	Donald Harris	.10	.05	.01
☐ 342	Eric Young	.20	.09	.03
☐ 343	Bob Wickman	.10	.05	.01
☐ 344	John Valentin	.30	.14	.04
☐ 345	Dan Wilson	.20	.09	.03
☐ 346	Steve Hosey	.10	.05	.01
☐ 347	Mike Piazza	2.50	1.10	.30
☐ 348	Willie Greene	.20	.09	.03
☐ 349	Tom Goodwin	.10	.05	.01
☐ 350	Eric Hillman	.10	.05	.01
☐ 351	Steve Reed	.10	.05	.01
☐ 352	Dan Serafini DP	.50	.23	.06
☐ 353	Todd Steverson DP	.20	.09	.03
☐ 354	Benji Grigsby DP	.10	.05	.01
☐ 355	Shannon Stewart DP	.40	.18	.05
☐ 356	Sean Lowe DP	.10	.05	.01
☐ 357	Derek Wallace DP	.10	.05	.01
☐ 358	Rick Helling DP	.10	.05	.01
☐ 359	Jason Kendall DP	1.00	.45	.12
☐ 360	Derek Jeter DP	2.50	1.10	.30
☐ 361	David Cone	.30	.14	.04
☐ 362	Jeff Reardon	.20	.09	.03
☐ 363	Bobby Witt	.10	.05	.01
☐ 364	Jose Canseco	.50	.23	.06
☐ 365	Jeff Russell	.10	.05	.01
☐ 366	Ruben Sierra	.30	.14	.04
☐ 367	Alan Mills	.10	.05	.01
☐ 368	Matt Nokes	.10	.05	.01
☐ 369	Pat Borders	.10	.05	.01
☐ 370	Pedro Munoz	.20	.09	.03

☐ 371	Danny Jackson	.10	.05	.01
☐ 372	Geronimo Pena	.10	.05	.01
☐ 373	Craig Lefferts	.10	.05	.01
☐ 374	Joe Grahe	.10	.05	.01
☐ 375	Roger McDowell	.10	.05	.01
☐ 376	Jimmy Key	.20	.09	.03
☐ 377	Steve Olin	.10	.05	.01
☐ 378	Glenn Davis	.10	.05	.01
☐ 379	Rene Gonzales	.10	.05	.01
☐ 380	Manuel Lee	.10	.05	.01
☐ 381	Ron Karkovice	.10	.05	.01
☐ 382	Sid Bream	.10	.05	.01
☐ 383	Gerald Williams	.10	.05	.01
☐ 384	Lenny Harris	.10	.05	.01
☐ 385	J.T. Snow	1.00	.45	.12
☐ 386	Dave Stieb	.10	.05	.01
☐ 387	Kirk McCaskill	.10	.05	.01
☐ 388	Lance Parrish	.20	.09	.03
☐ 389	Craig Grebeck	.10	.05	.01
☐ 390	Rick Wilkins	.10	.05	.01
☐ 391	Manny Alexander	.10	.05	.01
☐ 392	Mike Schooler	.10	.05	.01
☐ 393	Bernie Williams	.20	.09	.03
☐ 394	Kevin Koslofski	.10	.05	.01
☐ 395	Willie Wilson	.10	.05	.01
☐ 396	Jeff Parrett	.10	.05	.01
☐ 397	Mike Harkey	.10	.05	.01
☐ 398	Frank Tanana	.10	.05	.01
☐ 399	Doug Henry	.10	.05	.01
☐ 400	Royce Clayton	.20	.09	.03
☐ 401	Eric Wedge	.10	.05	.01
☐ 402	Derrick May	.20	.09	.03
☐ 403	Carlos Garcia	.20	.09	.03
☐ 404	Henry Rodriguez	.20	.09	.03
☐ 405	Ryan Klesko	1.50	.70	.19

1993 Select Aces

This 24-card set of the top starting pitchers in both leagues was randomly inserted in 1993 Score Select 28-card super packs. According to Score, the chances of finding an Ace card are not less than one in eight packs. The fronts display an action player pose cut out and superimposed on a metallic variegated red and silver diamond design. The diamond itself rests on a background consisting of silver metallic streaks that emanate from the center of the card. In imitation of playing card design, the fronts have a large "A" for Ace in upper left and lower right corners. The player's name in the upper right corner rounds out the card

face. On a red background, the horizontal backs have a white "Ace" playing card with a color head shot emanating from a diamond, team logo, and player profile. The cards are numbered on the back.

	MINT	NRMT	EXC
COMPLETE SET (24)	90.00	40.00	11.00
COMMON CARD (1-24)	2.50	1.10	.30
☐ 1 Roger Clemens	8.00	3.60	1.00
☐ 2 Tom Glavine	8.00	3.60	1.00
☐ 3 Jack McDowell	4.00	1.80	.50
☐ 4 Greg Maddux	50.00	22.00	6.25
☐ 5 Jack Morris	4.00	1.80	.50
☐ 6 Dennis Martinez	4.00	1.80	.50
☐ 7 Kevin Brown	2.50	1.10	.30
☐ 8 Dwight Gooden	4.00	1.80	.50
☐ 9 Kevin Appier	4.00	1.80	.50
☐ 10 Mike Morgan	2.50	1.10	.30
☐ 11 Juan Guzman	4.00	1.80	.50
☐ 12 Charles Nagy	4.00	1.80	.50
☐ 13 John Smiley	2.50	1.10	.30
☐ 14 Ken Hill	4.00	1.80	.50
☐ 15 Bob Tewksbury	2.50	1.10	.30
☐ 16 Doug Drabek	4.00	1.80	.50
☐ 17 John Smoltz	4.00	1.80	.50
☐ 18 Greg Swindell	2.50	1.10	.30
☐ 19 Bruce Hurst	2.50	1.10	.30
☐ 20 Mike Mussina	8.00	3.60	1.00
☐ 21 Cal Eldred	2.50	1.10	.30
☐ 22 Melido Perez	2.50	1.10	.30
☐ 23 Dave Fleming	2.50	1.10	.30
☐ 24 Kevin Tapani	2.50	1.10	.30

1993 Select
Chase Rookies

This 21-card set showcases rookies. The cards were randomly inserted in hobby packs only with at least two cards per box of 36 15-card packs. The fronts exhibit Score's "dufex" printing process, in which a color photo is printed on a metallic base creating an unusual, three-dimensional look. The pictures are tilted slightly to the left and edged on the left and bottom by red metallic borders. On a two-toned red background, the backs present a color headshot in a triangular design and player profile. The cards are numbered on the back at the bottom center.

	MINT	NRMT	EXC
COMPLETE SET (21)	150.00	70.00	19.00
COMMON CARD (1-21)	2.50	1.10	.30
☐ 1 Pat Listach	2.50	1.10	.30
☐ 2 Moises Alou	6.00	2.70	.75
☐ 3 Reggie Sanders	15.00	6.75	1.85
☐ 4 Kenny Lofton	50.00	22.00	6.25
☐ 5 Eric Karros	15.00	6.75	1.85
☐ 6 Brian Williams	2.50	1.10	.30
☐ 7 Donovan Osborne	2.50	1.10	.30
☐ 8 Sam Militello	2.50	1.10	.30
☐ 9 Chad Curtis	4.00	1.80	.50
☐ 10 Bob Zupcic	2.50	1.10	.30
☐ 11 Tim Salmon	30.00	13.50	3.70
☐ 12 Jeff Conine	15.00	6.75	1.85
☐ 13 Pedro Astacio	2.50	1.10	.30
☐ 14 Arthur Rhodes	2.50	1.10	.30
☐ 15 Cal Eldred	2.50	1.10	.30
☐ 16 Tim Wakefield	4.00	1.80	.50
☐ 17 Andy Stankiewicz	2.50	1.10	.30
☐ 18 Wil Cordero	8.00	3.60	1.00
☐ 19 Todd Hundley	4.00	1.80	.50
☐ 20 Dave Fleming	2.50	1.10	.30
☐ 21 Bret Boone	8.00	3.60	1.00

1993 Select
Chase Stars

This 24-card set showcases the top players in Major League Baseball. The cards were randomly inserted in retail packs only with at least two cards per box of 36 15-card packs. The fronts exhibit Score's "dufex" printing process, in which a color photo is printed on a metallic base creating an unusual, three-dimensional look. The pictures are tilted slightly to the left and edged on the left and bottom by green metallic borders. On a two-toned green background, the backs present a color headshot in a triangular design and player profile. The cards are numbered on the back at the bottom center.

	MINT	NRMT	EXC
COMPLETE SET (24)	170.00	75.00	21.00
COMMON CARD (1-24)	2.50	1.10	.30
☐ 1 Fred McGriff	6.00	2.70	.75
☐ 2 Ryne Sandberg	12.00	5.50	1.50

		MINT	NRMT	EXC
☐ 3	Ozzie Smith	10.00	4.50	1.25
☐ 4	Gary Sheffield	4.00	1.80	.50
☐ 5	Darren Daulton	4.00	1.80	.50
☐ 6	Andy Van Slyke	2.50	1.10	.30
☐ 7	Barry Bonds	12.00	5.50	1.50
☐ 8	Tony Gwynn	15.00	6.75	1.85
☐ 9	Greg Maddux	40.00	18.00	5.00
☐ 10	Tom Glavine	6.00	2.70	.75
☐ 11	John Franco	2.50	1.10	.30
☐ 12	Lee Smith	4.00	1.80	.50
☐ 13	Cecil Fielder	4.00	1.80	.50
☐ 14	Roberto Alomar	10.00	4.50	1.25
☐ 15	Cal Ripken	60.00	27.00	7.50
☐ 16	Edgar Martinez	5.00	2.20	.60
☐ 17	Ivan Rodriguez	4.00	1.80	.50
☐ 18	Kirby Puckett	15.00	6.75	1.85
☐ 19	Ken Griffey Jr	50.00	22.00	6.25
☐ 20	Joe Carter	4.00	1.80	.50
☐ 21	Roger Clemens	8.00	3.60	1.00
☐ 22	Dave Fleming	2.50	1.10	.30
☐ 23	Paul Molitor	4.00	1.80	.50
☐ 24	Dennis Eckersley	4.00	1.80	.50

1993 Select Triple Crown

Honoring Triple Crown winners, this 3-card set was randomly inserted in hobby packs only with at least two cards per box of 36 15-cards packs. The fronts exhibit Score's "dufex" printing process, in which a color photo is printed on a metallic base creating an unusual, three-dimensional look. The color player photos on the fronts have a forest green metallic border. The player's name and the year he won the Triple Crown appear above the picture, while the words "Triple Crown" are written in script beneath it. On a forest green background, the backs carry a black and white close-up photo of the player wearing a crown and a summary of the player's award winning performance. The cards are numbered on the back "X of 3" at the lower right corner.

		MINT	NRMT	EXC
COMPLETE SET (3)		110.00	50.00	14.00
COMMON CARD (1-3)		20.00	9.00	2.50
☐ 1	Mickey Mantle	80.00	36.00	10.00
☐ 2	Carl Yastrzemski	20.00	9.00	2.50
☐ 3	Frank Robinson	20.00	9.00	2.50

1993 Select Rookie/Traded

These 150 standard-size cards feature rookies and traded veteran players. The production run comprised 1,950 individually numbered cases. A ten-card All-Star Rookies subset, a two-card Rookie of the Year subset, and a Nolan Ryan Tribute card were randomly inserted in the foil packs. The chances of finding a Nolan Ryan card was listed at not less than one per 288 packs. The two-card set of ROY's featuring American League Rookie of the Year, Tim Salmon and National League Rookie of the Year, Mike Piazza was reportedly randomly inserted at a rate of not less than one in 576 foil packs of 1993 Select Rookie and Traded. The set has horizontal and vertical fronts that carry glossy color player photos, some action, others posed. These photos are borderless on their top and right sides, and have oblique blue-and-black borders set off by gold-foil lines on their bottom and left sides. The player's name is stamped in gold foil and rests in the lower right. The blue-and-black back carries another obliquely bordered color player photo in the upper right. His career highlights appear in white lettering alongside on the left, and his stats and team logo appear below. The cards are numbered on the back with a "T" suffix. Rookie Cards inclue Chris Gomez and Kirk Reuter.

		MINT	NRMT	EXC
COMPLETE SET (150)		20.00	9.00	2.50
COMMON CARD (1T-150T)		.10	.05	.01
☐ 1T	Rickey Henderson	.30	.14	.04
☐ 2T	Rob Deer	.10	.05	.01
☐ 3T	Tim Belcher	.10	.05	.01
☐ 4T	Gary Sheffield	.30	.14	.04
☐ 5T	Fred McGriff	1.00	.45	.12
☐ 6T	Matt Whiten	.20	.09	.03
☐ 7T	Jeff Russell	.10	.05	.01
☐ 8T	Harold Baines	.20	.09	.03
☐ 9T	Dave Winfield	.30	.14	.04
☐ 10T	Ellis Burks	.20	.09	.03
☐ 11T	Andre Dawson	.30	.14	.04

☐ 12T Gregg Jefferies	.30	.14	.04	☐ 83T Brad Ausmus	.20	.09	.03
☐ 13T Jimmy Key	.20	.09	.03	☐ 84T Kevin Stocker	.20	.09	.03
☐ 14T Harold Reynolds	.10	.05	.01	☐ 85T Jeromy Burnitz	.10	.05	.01
☐ 15T Tom Henke	.20	.09	.03	☐ 86T Aaron Sele	.30	.14	.04
☐ 16T Paul Molitor	.30	.14	.04	☐ 87T Roberto Mejia	.20	.09	.03
☐ 17T Wade Boggs	.30	.14	.04	☐ 88T Kirk Rueter	.20	.09	.03
☐ 18T David Cone	.30	.14	.04	☐ 89T Kevin Roberson	.10	.05	.01
☐ 19T Tony Fernandez	.10	.05	.01	☐ 90T Allen Watson	.20	.09	.03
☐ 20T Roberto Kelly	.20	.09	.03	☐ 91T Charlie Leibrandt	.10	.05	.01
☐ 21T Paul O'Neill	.20	.09	.03	☐ 92T Eric Davis	.10	.05	.01
☐ 22T Jose Lind	.10	.05	.01	☐ 93T Jody Reed	.10	.05	.01
☐ 23T Barry Bonds	1.50	.70	.19	☐ 94T Danny Jackson	.10	.05	.01
☐ 24T Dave Stewart	.20	.09	.03	☐ 95T Gary Gaetti	.20	.09	.03
☐ 25T Randy Myers	.20	.09	.03	☐ 96T Norm Charlton	.20	.09	.03
☐ 26T Benito Santiago	.10	.05	.01	☐ 97T Doug Drabek	.20	.09	.03
☐ 27T Tim Wallach	.10	.05	.01	☐ 98T Scott Fletcher	.10	.05	.01
☐ 28T Greg Gagne	.10	.05	.01	☐ 99T Greg Swindell	.10	.05	.01
☐ 29T Kevin Mitchell	.20	.09	.03	☐ 100T John Smiley	.10	.05	.01
☐ 30T Jim Abbott	.30	.14	.04	☐ 101T Kevin Reimer	.10	.05	.01
☐ 31T Lee Smith	.30	.14	.04	☐ 102T Andres Galarraga	.30	.14	.04
☐ 32T Bobby Munoz	.10	.05	.01	☐ 103T Greg Hibbard	.10	.05	.01
☐ 33T Mo Sanford	.10	.05	.01	☐ 104T Chris Hammond	.10	.05	.01
☐ 34T John Roper	.20	.09	.03	☐ 105T Darnell Coles	.10	.05	.01
☐ 35T David Hulse	.10	.05	.01	☐ 106T Mike Felder	.10	.05	.01
☐ 36T Pedro Martinez	.30	.14	.04	☐ 107T Jose Guzman	.10	.05	.01
☐ 37T Chuck Carr	.10	.05	.01	☐ 108T Chris Bosio	.10	.05	.01
☐ 38T Armando Reynoso	.10	.05	.01	☐ 109T Spike Owen	.10	.05	.01
☐ 39T Ryan Thompson	.20	.09	.03	☐ 110T Felix Jose	.10	.05	.01
☐ 40T Carlos Garcia	.20	.09	.03	☐ 111T Cory Snyder	.10	.05	.01
☐ 41T Matt Whiteside	.10	.05	.01	☐ 112T Craig Lefferts	.10	.05	.01
☐ 42T Benji Gil	.20	.09	.03	☐ 113T David Wells	.10	.05	.01
☐ 43T Rodney Bolton	.10	.05	.01	☐ 114T Pete Incaviglia	.10	.05	.01
☐ 44T J.T. Snow	1.00	.45	.12	☐ 115T Mike Pagliarulo	.10	.05	.01
☐ 45T David McCarty	.10	.05	.01	☐ 116T Dave Magadan	.10	.05	.01
☐ 46T Paul Quantrill	.10	.05	.01	☐ 117T Charlie Hough	.20	.09	.03
☐ 47T Al Martin	.20	.09	.03	☐ 118T Ivan Calderon	.10	.05	.01
☐ 48T Lance Painter	.10	.05	.01	☐ 119T Manuel Lee	.10	.05	.01
☐ 49T Lou Frazier	.10	.05	.01	☐ 120T Bob Patterson	.10	.05	.01
☐ 50T Eduardo Perez	.20	.09	.03	☐ 121T Bob Ojeda	.10	.05	.01
☐ 51T Kevin Young	.10	.05	.01	☐ 122T Scott Bankhead	.10	.05	.01
☐ 52T Mike Trombley	.10	.05	.01	☐ 123T Greg Maddux	6.00	2.70	.75
☐ 53T Sterling Hitchcock	.50	.23	.06	☐ 124T Chili Davis	.20	.09	.03
☐ 54T Tim Bogar	.10	.05	.01	☐ 125T Milt Thompson	.10	.05	.01
☐ 55T Hilly Hathaway	.10	.05	.01	☐ 126T Dave Martinez	.10	.05	.01
☐ 56T Wayne Kirby	.10	.05	.01	☐ 127T Frank Tanana	.10	.05	.01
☐ 57T Craig Paquette	.10	.05	.01	☐ 128T Phil Plantier	.10	.05	.01
☐ 58T Bret Boone	.30	.14	.04	☐ 129T Juan Samuel	.10	.05	.01
☐ 59T Greg McMichael	.20	.09	.03	☐ 130T Eric Young	.20	.09	.03
☐ 60T Mike Lansing	.50	.23	.06	☐ 131T Joe Orsulak	.10	.05	.01
☐ 61T Brent Gates	.20	.09	.03	☐ 132T Derek Bell	.30	.14	.04
☐ 62T Rene Arocha	.20	.09	.03	☐ 133T Darrin Jackson	.10	.05	.01
☐ 63T Ricky Gutierrez	.10	.05	.01	☐ 134T Tom Brunansky	.10	.05	.01
☐ 64T Kevin Rogers	.10	.05	.01	☐ 135T Jeff Reardon	.20	.09	.03
☐ 65T Ken Ryan	.10	.05	.01	☐ 136T Kevin Higgins	.10	.05	.01
☐ 66T Phil Hiatt	.10	.05	.01	☐ 137T Joel Johnston	.10	.05	.01
☐ 67T Pat Meares	.20	.09	.03	☐ 138T Rick Trlicek	.10	.05	.01
☐ 68T Troy Neel	.10	.05	.01	☐ 139T Richie Lewis	.10	.05	.01
☐ 69T Steve Cooke	.10	.05	.01	☐ 140T Jeff Gardner	.10	.05	.01
☐ 70T Sherman Obando	.20	.09	.03	☐ 141T Jack Voigt	.10	.05	.01
☐ 71T Blas Minor	.10	.05	.01	☐ 142T Rod Correia	.10	.05	.01
☐ 72T Angel Miranda	.10	.05	.01	☐ 143T Billy Brewer	.10	.05	.01
☐ 73T Tom Kramer	.10	.05	.01	☐ 144T Terry Jorgensen	.10	.05	.01
☐ 74T Chip Hale	.10	.05	.01	☐ 145T Rich Amaral	.10	.05	.01
☐ 75T Brad Pennington	.10	.05	.01	☐ 146T Sean Berry	.10	.05	.01
☐ 76T Graeme Lloyd	.10	.05	.01	☐ 147T Dan Peltier	.10	.05	.01
☐ 77T Darrell Whitmore	.10	.05	.01	☐ 148T Paul Wagner	.10	.05	.01
☐ 78T David Neid	.20	.09	.03	☐ 149T Damon Buford	.10	.05	.01
☐ 79T Todd Van Poppel	.20	.09	.03	☐ 150T Wil Cordero	.20	.09	.03
☐ 80T Chris Gomez	.50	.23	.06	☐ NR1 Nolan Ryan Tribute	120.00	55.00	15.00
☐ 81T Jason Bere	.30	.14	.04	☐ ROY1 Tim Salmon AL ROY	30.00	13.50	3.70
☐ 82T Jeffrey Hammonds	.30	.14	.04	☐ ROY2 Mike Piazza NL ROY	75.00	34.00	9.50

1993 Select R/T
All-Star Rookies

This ten-card set was randomly inserted in foil packs of 1993 Select Rookie and Traded. The insertion rate was reportedly not less than one in 36 packs. The cards measure the standard size (2 1/2" by 3 1/2") and feature on their fronts color player action shots that have a grainy metallic appearance. These photos are borderless, except at the top, where the silver-colored player's name is displayed upon red and blue metallic stripes. The set's title appears within a metallic silver-colored stripe near the bottom, which has a star-and-baseball icon emblazoned over its center. This combination of the set's title, stripe, and star-and-baseball icon reappears at the top of the non-metallic back, but in a red, white, and blue design. The player's name, position, and team logo are shown on the red-colored right half of the card. His career highlights appear in white lettering on the blue-colored left half. The cards are numbered on the back.

	MINT	NRMT	EXC
COMPLETE SET (10)	150.00	70.00	19.00
COMMON CARD (1-10)	5.00	2.20	.60

		MINT	NRMT	EXC
☐	1 Jeff Conine	15.00	6.75	1.85
☐	2 Brent Gates	7.00	3.10	.85
☐	3 Mike Lansing	7.00	3.10	.85
☐	4 Kevin Stocker	7.00	3.10	.85
☐	5 Mike Piazza	75.00	34.00	9.50
☐	6 Jeffrey Hammonds	10.00	4.50	1.25
☐	7 David Hulse	5.00	2.20	.60
☐	8 Tim Salmon	30.00	13.50	3.70
☐	9 Rene Arocha	5.00	2.20	.60
☐	10 Greg McMichael	5.00	2.20	.60

1994 Select

Measuring the standard size, the 1994 Select set consists of 420 cards that were issued in two series of 210. The horizontal fronts feature a color player action photo

and a duo-tone player shot. The backs are vertical and contain a photo, 1993 and career statistics and highlights. Special Dave Winfield and Cal Ripken cards were insertd in first series packs. A Paul Molitor MVP card and a Carlos Delgado Rookie of the Year card were inserted in second series packs. The insertion rate for ech card was one in 360 packs. Rookie Cards include Brian Anderson, John Hudek and Chan Ho Park.

	MINT	NRMT	EXC
COMPLETE SET (420)	30.00	13.50	3.70
COMPLETE SERIES 1 (210)	18.00	8.00	2.20
COMPLETE SERIES 2 (210)	12.00	5.50	1.50
COMMON CARD (1-210)	.10	.05	.01
COMMON CARD (211-420)	.10	.05	.01

		MINT	NRMT	EXC
☐	1 Ken Griffey Jr.	3.00	1.35	.35
☐	2 Greg Maddux	3.00	1.35	.35
☐	3 Paul Molitor	.30	.14	.04
☐	4 Mike Piazza	1.25	.55	.16
☐	5 Jay Bell	.10	.05	.01
☐	6 Frank Thomas	3.00	1.35	.35
☐	7 Barry Larkin	.40	.18	.05
☐	8 Paul O'Neill	.20	.09	.03
☐	9 Darren Daulton	.30	.14	.04
☐	10 Mike Greenwell	.10	.05	.01
☐	11 Chuck Carr	.10	.05	.01
☐	12 Joe Carter	.30	.14	.04
☐	13 Lance Johnson	.10	.05	.01
☐	14 Jeff Blauser	.10	.05	.01
☐	15 Chris Hoiles	.20	.09	.03
☐	16 Rick Wilkins	.10	.05	.01
☐	17 Kirby Puckett	1.00	.45	.12
☐	18 Larry Walker	.40	.18	.05
☐	19 Randy Johnson	.60	.25	.07
☐	20 Bernard Gilkey	.20	.09	.03
☐	21 Devon White	.10	.05	.01
☐	22 Randy Myers	.10	.05	.01
☐	23 Don Mattingly	1.50	.70	.19
☐	24 John Kruk	.20	.09	.03
☐	25 Ozzie Guillen	.10	.05	.01
☐	26 Jeff Conine	.30	.14	.04
☐	27 Mike Macfarlane	.10	.05	.01
☐	28 Dave Hollins	.30	.14	.04
☐	29 Chuck Knoblauch	.30	.14	.04
☐	30 Ozzie Smith	.60	.25	.07
☐	31 Harold Baines	.20	.09	.03
☐	32 Ryne Sandberg	.75	.35	.09
☐	33 Ron Karkovice	.10	.05	.01
☐	34 Terry Pendleton	.10	.05	.01
☐	35 Wally Joyner	.20	.09	.03
☐	36 Mike Mussina	.40	.18	.05
☐	37 Felix Jose	.10	.05	.01
☐	38 Derrick May	.10	.05	.01

☐	39	Scott Cooper	.20	.09	.03			
☐	40	Jose Rijo	.20	.09	.03			
☐	41	Robin Ventura	.20	.09	.03			
☐	42	Charlie Hayes	.20	.09	.03			
☐	43	Jimmy Key	.20	.09	.03			
☐	44	Eric Karros	.20	.09	.03			
☐	45	Ruben Sierra	.30	.14	.04			
☐	46	Ryan Thompson	.20	.09	.03			
☐	47	Brian McRae	.20	.09	.03			
☐	48	Pat Hentgen	.20	.09	.03			
☐	49	John Valentin	.30	.14	.04			
☐	50	Al Martin	.10	.05	.01			
☐	51	Jose Lind	.10	.05	.01			
☐	52	Kevin Stocker	.20	.09	.03			
☐	53	Mike Gallego	.10	.05	.01			
☐	54	Dwight Gooden	.10	.05	.01			
☐	55	Brady Anderson	.20	.09	.03			
☐	56	Jeff King	.10	.05	.01			
☐	57	Mark McGwire	.30	.14	.04			
☐	58	Sammy Sosa	.30	.14	.04			
☐	59	Ryan Bowen	.10	.05	.01			
☐	60	Mark Lemke	.10	.05	.01			
☐	61	Roger Clemens	.50	.23	.06			
☐	62	Brian Jordan	.20	.09	.03			
☐	63	Andres Galarraga	.30	.14	.04			
☐	64	Kevin Appier	.20	.09	.03			
☐	65	Don Slaught	.10	.05	.01			
☐	66	Mike Blowers	.20	.09	.03			
☐	67	Wes Chamberlain	.10	.05	.01			
☐	68	Troy Neel	.10	.05	.01			
☐	69	John Wetteland	.10	.05	.01			
☐	70	Joe Girardi	.10	.05	.01			
☐	71	Reggie Sanders	.30	.14	.04			
☐	72	Edgar Martinez	.20	.09	.03			
☐	73	Todd Hundley	.20	.09	.03			
☐	74	Pat Borders	.10	.05	.01			
☐	75	Roberto Mejia	.10	.05	.01			
☐	76	David Cone	.30	.14	.04			
☐	77	Tony Gwynn	1.00	.45	.12			
☐	78	Jim Abbott	.30	.14	.04			
☐	79	Jay Buhner	.30	.14	.04			
☐	80	Mark McLemore	.10	.05	.01			
☐	81	Wil Cordero	.30	.14	.04			
☐	82	Pedro Astacio	.20	.09	.03			
☐	83	Bob Tewksbury	.10	.05	.01			
☐	84	Dave Winfield	.30	.14	.04			
☐	85	Jeff Kent	.20	.09	.03			
☐	86	Todd Van Poppel	.20	.09	.03			
☐	87	Steve Avery	.30	.14	.04			
☐	88	Mike Lansing	.20	.09	.03			
☐	89	Lenny Dykstra	.30	.14	.04			
☐	90	Jose Guzman	.10	.05	.01			
☐	91	Brian R. Hunter	.10	.05	.01			
☐	92	Tim Raines	.30	.14	.04			
☐	93	Andre Dawson	.30	.14	.04			
☐	94	Joe Orsulak	.10	.05	.01			
☐	95	Ricky Jordan	.10	.05	.01			
☐	96	Billy Hatcher	.10	.05	.01			
☐	97	Jack McDowell	.30	.14	.04			
☐	98	Tom Pagnozzi	.10	.05	.01			
☐	99	Darryl Strawberry	.20	.09	.03			
☐	100	Mike Stanley	.10	.05	.01			
☐	101	Bret Saberhagen	.20	.09	.03			
☐	102	Willie Greene	.20	.09	.03			
☐	103	Bryan Harvey	.10	.05	.01			
☐	104	Tim Bogar	.10	.05	.01			
☐	105	Jack Voigt	.10	.05	.01			
☐	106	Brad Ausmus	.10	.05	.01			
☐	107	Ramon Martinez	.20	.09	.03			
☐	108	Mike Perez	.10	.05	.01			
☐	109	Jeff Montgomery	.20	.09	.03			
☐	110	Danny Darwin	.10	.05	.01			
☐	111	Wilson Alvarez	.30	.14	.04			
☐	112	Kevin Mitchell	.20	.09	.03			
☐	113	David Nied	.20	.09	.03			
☐	114	Rich Amaral	.10	.05	.01			
☐	115	Stan Javier	.10	.05	.01			
☐	116	Mo Vaughn	.50	.23	.06			
☐	117	Ben McDonald	.20	.09	.03			
☐	118	Tom Gordon	.10	.05	.01			
☐	119	Carlos Garcia	.10	.05	.01			
☐	120	Phil Plantier	.20	.09	.03			
☐	121	Mike Morgan	.10	.05	.01			
☐	122	Pat Meares	.10	.05	.01			
☐	123	Kevin Young	.10	.05	.01			
☐	124	Jeff Fassero	.10	.05	.01			
☐	125	Gene Harris	.10	.05	.01			
☐	126	Bob Welch	.10	.05	.01			
☐	127	Walt Weiss	.10	.05	.01			
☐	128	Bobby Witt	.10	.05	.01			
☐	129	Andy Van Slyke	.30	.14	.04			
☐	130	Steve Cooke	.10	.05	.01			
☐	131	Mike Devereaux	.20	.09	.03			
☐	132	Joey Cora	.10	.05	.01			
☐	133	Bret Barberie	.10	.05	.01			
☐	134	Orel Hershiser	.20	.09	.03			
☐	135	Ed Sprague	.10	.05	.01			
☐	136	Shawon Dunston	.10	.05	.01			
☐	137	Alex Arias	.10	.05	.01			
☐	138	Archi Cianfrocco	.10	.05	.01			
☐	139	Tim Wallach	.10	.05	.01			
☐	140	Bernie Williams	.20	.09	.03			
☐	141	Karl Rhodes	.10	.05	.01			
☐	142	Pat Kelly	.10	.05	.01			
☐	143	Dave Magadan	.10	.05	.01			
☐	144	Kevin Tapani	.10	.05	.01			
☐	145	Eric Young	.20	.09	.03			
☐	146	Derek Bell	.20	.09	.03			
☐	147	Dante Bichette	.40	.18	.05			
☐	148	Geronimo Pena	.10	.05	.01			
☐	149	Joe Oliver	.10	.05	.01			
☐	150	Orestes Destrade	.10	.05	.01			
☐	151	Tim Naehring	.20	.09	.03			
☐	152	Ray Lankford	.30	.14	.04			
☐	153	Phil Clark	.10	.05	.01			
☐	154	David McCarty	.10	.05	.01			
☐	155	Tommy Greene	.10	.05	.01			
☐	156	Wade Boggs	.20	.09	.03			
☐	157	Kevin Gross	.10	.05	.01			
☐	158	Hal Morris	.20	.09	.03			
☐	159	Moises Alou	.30	.14	.04			
☐	160	Rick Aguilera	.20	.09	.03			
☐	161	Curt Schilling	.10	.05	.01			
☐	162	Chip Hale	.10	.05	.01			
☐	163	Tino Martinez	.20	.09	.03			
☐	164	Mark Whiten	.10	.05	.01			
☐	165	Dave Stewart	.20	.09	.03			
☐	166	Steve Buechele	.10	.05	.01			
☐	167	Bobby Jones	.30	.14	.04			
☐	168	Darrin Fletcher	.10	.05	.01			
☐	169	John Smiley	.10	.05	.01			
☐	170	Cory Snyder	.10	.05	.01			
☐	171	Scott Erickson	.10	.05	.01			
☐	172	Kirk Rueter	.10	.05	.01			
☐	173	Dave Fleming	.10	.05	.01			
☐	174	John Smoltz	.20	.09	.03			
☐	175	Ricky Gutierrez	.10	.05	.01			
☐	176	Mike Bordick	.10	.05	.01			
☐	177	Chan Ho Park	.30	.14	.04			
☐	178	Alex Gonzalez	.30	.14	.04			
☐	179	Steve Karsay	.10	.05	.01			
☐	180	Jeffrey Hammonds	.30	.14	.04			

□	181	Manny Ramirez	1.50	.70	.19
□	182	Salomon Torres	.20	.09	.03
□	183	Raul Mondesi	1.00	.45	.12
□	184	James Mouton	.20	.09	.03
□	185	Cliff Floyd	.30	.14	.04
□	186	Danny Bautista	.20	.09	.03
□	187	Kurt Abbott	.25	.11	.03
□	188	Javier Lopez	.50	.23	.06
□	189	John Patterson	.10	.05	.01
□	190	Greg Blosser	.10	.05	.01
□	191	Bob Hamelin	.20	.09	.03
□	192	Tony Eusebio	.10	.05	.01
□	193	Carlos Delgado	.30	.14	.04
□	194	Chris Gomez	.30	.14	.04
□	195	Kelly Stinnett	.10	.05	.01
□	196	Shane Reynolds	.10	.05	.01
□	197	Ryan Klesko	.75	.35	.09
□	198	Jim Edmonds UER	.50	.23	.06
		Player throwing right on front			
		Edmonds is a lefty			
□	199	James Hurst	.10	.05	.01
□	200	Dave Staton	.10	.05	.01
□	201	Rondell White	.30	.14	.04
□	202	Keith Mitchell	.10	.05	.01
□	203	Darren Oliver	.10	.05	.01
□	204	Mike Matheny	.10	.05	.01
□	205	Chris Turner	.10	.05	.01
□	206	Matt Mieske	.10	.05	.01
□	207	NL Team Checklist	.10	.05	.01
□	208	NL Team Checklist	.10	.05	.01
□	209	AL Team Checklist	.10	.05	.01
□	210	AL Team Checklist	.10	.05	.01
□	211	Barry Bonds	.75	.35	.09
□	212	Juan Gonzalez	.75	.35	.09
□	213	Jim Eisenreich	.10	.05	.01
□	214	Ivan Rodriguez	.30	.14	.04
□	215	Tony Phillips	.10	.05	.01
□	216	John Jaha	.10	.05	.01
□	217	Lee Smith	.30	.14	.04
□	218	Bip Roberts	.10	.05	.01
□	219	Dave Hansen	.10	.05	.01
□	220	Pat Listach	.10	.05	.01
□	221	Willie McGee	.10	.05	.01
□	222	Damion Easley	.10	.05	.01
□	223	Dean Palmer	.20	.09	.03
□	224	Mike Moore	.10	.05	.01
□	225	Brian Harper	.10	.05	.01
□	226	Gary DiSarcina	.10	.05	.01
□	227	Delino DeShields	.20	.09	.03
□	228	Otis Nixon	.10	.05	.01
□	229	Roberto Alomar	.60	.25	.07
□	230	Mark Grace	.30	.14	.04
□	231	Kenny Lofton	1.00	.45	.12
□	232	Gregg Jefferies	.30	.14	.04
□	233	Cecil Fielder	.30	.14	.04
□	234	Jeff Bagwell	1.00	.45	.12
□	235	Albert Belle	1.25	.55	.16
□	236	Dave Justice	.40	.18	.05
□	237	Tom Henke	.10	.05	.01
□	238	Bobby Bonilla	.30	.14	.04
□	239	John Olerud	.30	.14	.04
□	240	Robby Thompson	.10	.05	.01
□	241	Dave Valle	.10	.05	.01
□	242	Marquis Grissom	.30	.14	.04
□	243	Greg Swindell	.10	.05	.01
□	244	Todd Zeile	.20	.09	.03
□	245	Dennis Eckersley	.30	.14	.04
□	246	Jose Offerman	.10	.05	.01
□	247	Greg McMichael	.10	.05	.01
□	248	Tim Belcher	.10	.05	.01
□	249	Cal Ripken Jr.	3.00	1.35	.35

□	250	Tom Glavine	.30	.14	.04
□	251	Luis Polonia	.10	.05	.01
□	252	Bill Swift	.10	.05	.01
□	253	Juan Guzman	.20	.09	.03
□	254	Rickey Henderson	.30	.14	.04
□	255	Terry Mulholland	.10	.05	.01
□	256	Gary Sheffield	.30	.14	.04
□	257	Terry Steinbach	.20	.09	.03
□	258	Brett Butler	.20	.09	.03
□	259	Jason Bere	.30	.14	.04
□	260	Doug Strange	.10	.05	.01
□	261	Kent Hrbek	.10	.05	.01
□	262	Graeme Lloyd	.10	.05	.01
□	263	Lou Frazier	.10	.05	.01
□	264	Charles Nagy	.20	.09	.03
□	265	Bret Boone	.30	.14	.04
□	266	Kirk Gibson	.20	.09	.03
□	267	Kevin Brown	.10	.05	.01
□	268	Fred McGriff	.40	.18	.05
□	269	Matt Williams	.50	.23	.06
□	270	Greg Gagne	.10	.05	.01
□	271	Mariano Duncan	.10	.05	.01
□	272	Jeff Russell	.10	.05	.01
□	273	Eric Davis	.10	.05	.01
□	274	Shane Mack	.20	.09	.03
□	275	Jose Vizcaino	.10	.05	.01
□	276	Jose Canseco	.50	.23	.06
□	277	Roberto Hernandez	.10	.05	.01
□	278	Royce Clayton	.20	.09	.03
□	279	Carlos Baerga	.60	.25	.07
□	280	Pete Incaviglia	.10	.05	.01
□	281	Brent Gates	.20	.09	.03
□	282	Jeromy Burnitz	.10	.05	.01
□	283	Chili Davis	.20	.09	.03
□	284	Pete Harnisch	.10	.05	.01
□	285	Alan Trammell	.30	.14	.04
□	286	Eric Anthony	.10	.05	.01
□	287	Ellis Burks	.20	.09	.03
□	288	Julio Franco	.20	.09	.03
□	289	Jack Morris	.30	.14	.04
□	290	Erik Hanson	.10	.05	.01
□	291	Chuck Finley	.10	.05	.01
□	292	Reggie Jefferson	.10	.05	.01
□	293	Kevin McReynolds	.10	.05	.01
□	294	Greg Hibbard	.10	.05	.01
□	295	Travis Fryman	.30	.14	.04
□	296	Craig Biggio	.20	.09	.03
□	297	Kenny Rogers	.20	.09	.03
□	298	Dave Henderson	.10	.05	.01
□	299	Jim Thome	.60	.25	.07
□	300	Rene Arocha	.20	.09	.03
□	301	Pedro Munoz	.10	.05	.01
□	302	David Hulse	.10	.05	.01
□	303	Greg Vaughn	.20	.09	.03
□	304	Darren Lewis	.10	.05	.01
□	305	Deion Sanders	.60	.25	.07
□	306	Danny Tartabull	.20	.09	.03
□	307	Darryl Hamilton	.10	.05	.01
□	308	Andujar Cedeno	.10	.05	.01
□	309	Tim Salmon	.60	.25	.07
□	310	Tony Fernandez	.10	.05	.01
□	311	Alex Fernandez	.30	.14	.04
□	312	Roberto Kelly	.10	.05	.01
□	313	Harold Reynolds	.10	.05	.01
□	314	Chris Sabo	.10	.05	.01
□	315	Howard Johnson	.10	.05	.01
□	316	Mark Portugal	.10	.05	.01
□	317	Rafael Palmeiro	.30	.14	.04
□	318	Pete Smith	.10	.05	.01
□	319	Will Clark	.40	.18	.05
□	320	Henry Rodriguez	.10	.05	.01

☐ 321	Omar Vizquel	.10	.05	.01
☐ 322	David Segui	.10	.05	.01
☐ 323	Lou Whitaker	.30	.14	.04
☐ 324	Felix Fermin	.10	.05	.01
☐ 325	Spike Owen	.10	.05	.01
☐ 326	Darryl Kile	.20	.09	.03
☐ 327	Chad Kreuter	.10	.05	.01
☐ 328	Rod Beck	.20	.09	.03
☐ 329	Eddie Murray	.40	.18	.05
☐ 330	B.J. Surhoff	.10	.05	.01
☐ 331	Mickey Tettleton	.20	.09	.03
☐ 332	Pedro Martinez	.30	.14	.04
☐ 333	Roger Pavlik	.10	.05	.01
☐ 334	Eddie Taubensee	.10	.05	.01
☐ 335	John Doherty	.10	.05	.01
☐ 336	Jody Reed	.10	.05	.01
☐ 337	Aaron Sele	.30	.14	.04
☐ 338	Leo Gomez	.10	.05	.01
☐ 339	Dave Nilsson	.10	.05	.01
☐ 340	Rob Dibble	.10	.05	.01
☐ 341	John Burkett	.20	.09	.03
☐ 342	Wayne Kirby	.10	.05	.01
☐ 343	Dan Wilson	.10	.05	.01
☐ 344	Armando Reynoso	.10	.05	.01
☐ 345	Chad Curtis	.20	.09	.03
☐ 346	Dennis Martinez	.20	.09	.03
☐ 347	Cal Eldred	.20	.09	.03
☐ 348	Luis Gonzalez	.10	.05	.01
☐ 349	Doug Drabek	.30	.14	.04
☐ 350	Jim Leyritz	.10	.05	.01
☐ 351	Mark Langston	.30	.14	.04
☐ 352	Darrin Jackson	.10	.05	.01
☐ 353	Sid Fernandez	.10	.05	.01
☐ 354	Benito Santiago	.10	.05	.01
☐ 355	Kevin Seitzer	.10	.05	.01
☐ 356	Bo Jackson	.30	.14	.04
☐ 357	David Wells	.10	.05	.01
☐ 358	Paul Sorrento	.10	.05	.01
☐ 359	Ken Caminiti	.20	.09	.03
☐ 360	Eduardo Perez	.10	.05	.01
☐ 361	Orlando Merced	.20	.09	.03
☐ 362	Steve Finley	.10	.05	.01
☐ 363	Andy Benes	.20	.09	.03
☐ 364	Manuel Lee	.10	.05	.01
☐ 365	Todd Benzinger	.10	.05	.01
☐ 366	Sandy Alomar Jr.	.20	.09	.03
☐ 367	Rex Hudler	.10	.05	.01
☐ 368	Mike Henneman	.10	.05	.01
☐ 369	Vince Coleman	.10	.05	.01
☐ 370	Kirt Manwaring	.10	.05	.01
☐ 371	Ken Hill	.20	.09	.03
☐ 372	Glenallen Hill	.10	.05	.01
☐ 373	Sean Berry	.10	.05	.01
☐ 374	Geronimo Berroa	.10	.05	.01
☐ 375	Duane Ward	.10	.05	.01
☐ 376	Allen Watson	.10	.05	.01
☐ 377	Marc Newfield	.30	.14	.04
☐ 378	Dan Miceli	.10	.05	.01
☐ 379	Denny Hocking	.10	.05	.01
☐ 380	Mark Kiefer	.10	.05	.01
☐ 381	Tony Tarasco	.30	.14	.04
☐ 382	Tony Longmire	.10	.05	.01
☐ 383	Brian Anderson	.30	.14	.04
☐ 384	Fernando Vina	.10	.05	.01
☐ 385	Hector Carrasco	.10	.05	.01
☐ 386	Mike Kelly	.20	.09	.03
☐ 387	Greg Colbrunn	.20	.09	.03
☐ 388	Roger Salkeld	.10	.05	.01
☐ 389	Steve Trachsel	.30	.14	.04
☐ 390	Rich Becker	.20	.09	.03
☐ 391	Billy Taylor	.10	.05	.01

☐ 392	Rich Rowland	.10	.05	.01
☐ 393	Carl Everett	.20	.09	.03
☐ 394	Johnny Ruffin	.10	.05	.01
☐ 395	Keith Lockhart	.10	.05	.01
☐ 396	J.R. Phillips	.20	.09	.03
☐ 397	Sterling Hitchcock	.20	.09	.03
☐ 398	Jorge Fabregas	.10	.05	.01
☐ 399	Jeff Granger	.20	.09	.03
☐ 400	Eddie Zambrano	.10	.05	.01
☐ 401	Rikkert Faneyte	.10	.05	.01
☐ 402	Gerald Williams	.10	.05	.01
☐ 403	Joey Hamilton	.30	.14	.04
☐ 404	Joe Hall	.10	.05	.01
☐ 405	John Hudek	.30	.14	.04
☐ 406	Roberto Petagine	.20	.09	.03
☐ 407	Charles Johnson	.30	.14	.04
☐ 408	Mark Smith	.10	.05	.01
☐ 409	Jeff Juden	.10	.05	.01
☐ 410	Carlos Pulido	.10	.05	.01
☐ 411	Paul Shuey	.10	.05	.01
☐ 412	Rob Butler	.10	.05	.01
☐ 413	Mark Acre	.10	.05	.01
☐ 414	Greg Pirkl	.10	.05	.01
☐ 415	Melvin Nieves	.30	.14	.04
☐ 416	Tim Hyers	.10	.05	.01
☐ 417	NL Checklist	.10	.05	.01
☐ 418	NL Checklist	.10	.05	.01
☐ 419	AL Checklist	.10	.05	.01
☐ 420	AL Checklist	.10	.05	.01
☐ RY1	Carlos Delgado	10.00	4.50	1.25
☐ SS1	Cal Ripken Jr.	100.00	45.00	12.50
	Salute			
☐ SS2	Dave Winfield	10.00	4.50	1.25
	Salute			
☐ MVP1	Paul Molitor	10.00	4.50	1.25

1994 Select
Crown Contenders

This ten-card set showcases top contenders for various awards such as batting champion, Cy Young Award winner and Most Valuable Player. The cards were inserted in packs at a rate of one in 24 and measure the standard size. The horizontal fronts feature color action player shots on a holographic gold foil background. The backs carry a color player close-up photo and highlights. The cards are numbered on the back with a CC prefix..

	MINT	NRMT	EXC
COMPLETE SET (10)	100.00	45.00	12.50
COMMON CARD (CC1-CC10)	3.00	1.35	.35
☐ CC1 Lenny Dykstra	3.00	1.35	.35
☐ CC2 Greg Maddux	25.00	11.00	3.10
☐ CC3 Roger Clemens	4.00	1.80	.50
☐ CC4 Randy Johnson	5.00	2.20	.60
☐ CC5 Frank Thomas	25.00	11.00	3.10
☐ CC6 Barry Bonds	6.00	2.70	.75
☐ CC7 Juan Gonzalez	6.00	2.70	.75
☐ CC8 John Olerud	3.00	1.35	.35
☐ CC9 Mike Piazza	10.00	4.50	1.25
☐ CC10 Ken Griffey Jr.	25.00	11.00	3.10

1994 Select Rookie Surge

This 18-card set standard-size showcased potential top rookies for 1994. The set was divided into two series of nine cards. The cards were randomly inserted in packs at a rate of one in 48. The fronts exhibit Score's "dufex" printing process, in which a color photo is printed on a metallic base creating an unusual, three-dimensional look. On a multi-colored background, the horizontal backs present a color player headshot. The cards are numbered on the back with an RS prefix.

	MINT	NRMT	EXC
COMPLETE SET (18)	225.00	100.00	28.00
COMPLETE SERIES 1 (9)	100.00	45.00	12.50
COMPLETE SERIES 2 (9)	125.00	55.00	15.50
COMMON CARD (RS1-RS9)	4.00	1.80	.50
COMMON CARD (RS10-RS18)	4.00	1.80	.50
☐ RS1 Cliff Floyd	10.00	4.50	1.25
☐ RS2 Bob Hamelin	4.00	1.80	.50
☐ RS3 Ryan Klesko	30.00	13.50	3.70
☐ RS4 Carlos Delgado	12.00	5.50	1.50
☐ RS5 Jeffrey Hammonds	6.00	2.70	.75
☐ RS6 Rondell White	15.00	6.75	1.85
☐ RS7 Salomon Torres	4.00	1.80	.50
☐ RS8 Steve Karsay	4.00	1.80	.50
☐ RS9 Javier Lopez	20.00	9.00	2.50
☐ RS10 Manny Ramirez	60.00	27.00	7.50
☐ RS11 Tony Tarasco	6.00	2.70	.75
☐ RS12 Kurt Abbott	4.00	1.80	.50
☐ RS13 Chan Ho Park	10.00	4.50	1.25

☐ RS14 Rich Becker	4.00	1.80	.50
☐ RS15 James Mouton	4.00	1.80	.50
☐ RS16 Alex Gonzalez	6.00	2.70	.75
☐ RS17 Raul Mondesi	35.00	16.00	4.40
☐ RS18 Steve Trachsel	4.00	1.80	.50

1994 Select Skills

This 10-card standard-size set takes an up close look at the leagues top statistical leaders. The cards were randomly inserted in second series packs at a rate of approximately one in 24. A foil front has a holographic appearance that allows the player to stand out. The bottom of the front notes the player as being the best at something. For example, the front of Barry Bonds' card notes, "Select's Best Run Producer". The back has a small photo with text. The cards are numbered with an "SK" prefix.

	MINT	NRMT	EXC
COMPLETE SET (10)	65.00	29.00	8.00
COMMON CARD (SK1-SK10)	3.00	1.35	.35
☐ SK1 Randy Johnson	10.00	4.50	1.25
☐ SK2 Barry Larkin	6.00	2.70	.75
☐ SK3 Lenny Dykstra	3.00	1.35	.35
☐ SK4 Kenny Lofton	15.00	6.75	1.85
☐ SK5 Juan Gonzalez	12.00	5.50	1.50
☐ SK6 Barry Bonds	12.00	5.50	1.50
☐ SK7 Marquis Grissom	5.00	2.20	.60
☐ SK8 Ivan Rodriguez	5.00	2.20	.60
☐ SK9 Larry Walker	6.00	2.70	.75
☐ SK10 Travis Fryman	5.00	2.20	.60

1995 Select

This 250-card set was issued in 12-card packs with 24 packs per box and 24 boxes per case. There was an announced production run of 4,950 cases. These horizontal cards feature an action photo over most of the card with the player's profile and name on the right side. The "Select 95" logo is in the upper left corner. The vertical backs have a black and white photo on the top. The middle of the card is dedicated to a brief biography as well as seasonal and

career stats. A specific important stat is included at the bottom of the card. A special card of Hideo Nomo (#251) was issued to hobby dealers who had bought cases of the Select product.

	MINT	NRMT	EXC
COMPLETE SET (250)	15.00	6.75	1.85
COMMON CARD (1-250)	.05	.02	.01

☐ 1	Cal Ripken Jr.	2.00	.90	.25
☐ 2	Robin Ventura	.15	.07	.02
☐ 3	Al Martin	.10	.05	.01
☐ 4	Jeff Frye	.05	.02	.01
☐ 5	Darryl Strawberry	.10	.05	.01
☐ 6	Chan Ho Park	.10	.05	.01
☐ 7	Steve Avery	.10	.05	.01
☐ 8	Bret Boone	.15	.07	.02
☐ 9	Danny Tartabull	.10	.05	.01
☐ 10	Dante Bichette	.25	.11	.03
☐ 11	Rondell White	.15	.07	.02
☐ 12	Dave McCarty	.05	.02	.01
☐ 13	Bernard Gilkey	.10	.05	.01
☐ 14	Mark McGwire	.15	.07	.02
☐ 15	Ruben Sierra	.15	.07	.02
☐ 16	Wade Boggs	.15	.07	.02
☐ 17	Mike Piazza	.75	.35	.09
☐ 18	Jeffrey Hammonds	.10	.05	.01
☐ 19	Mike Mussina	.25	.11	.03
☐ 20	Darryl Kile	.05	.02	.01
☐ 21	Greg Maddux	2.00	.90	.25
☐ 22	Frank Thomas	2.00	.90	.25
☐ 23	Kevin Appier	.10	.05	.01
☐ 24	Jay Bell	.10	.05	.01
☐ 25	Kirk Gibson	.10	.05	.01
☐ 26	Pat Hentgen	.10	.05	.01
☐ 27	Joey Hamilton	.10	.05	.01
☐ 28	Bernie Williams	.10	.05	.01
☐ 29	Aaron Sele	.05	.02	.01
☐ 30	Delino DeShields	.10	.05	.01
☐ 31	Danny Bautista	.05	.02	.01
☐ 32	Jim Thome	.30	.14	.04
☐ 33	Rikkert Faneyte	.05	.02	.01
☐ 34	Roberto Alomar	.40	.18	.05
☐ 35	Paul Molitor	.15	.07	.02
☐ 36	Allen Watson	.10	.05	.01
☐ 37	Jeff Bagwell	.60	.25	.07
☐ 38	Jay Buhner	.15	.07	.02
☐ 39	Marquis Grissom	.15	.07	.02
☐ 40	Jim Edmonds	.25	.11	.03
☐ 41	Ryan Klesko	.40	.18	.05
☐ 42	Fred McGriff	.25	.11	.03
☐ 43	Tony Tarasco	.05	.02	.01
☐ 44	Darren Daulton	.10	.05	.01
☐ 45	Marc Newfield	.05	.02	.01
☐ 46	Barry Bonds	.50	.23	.06
☐ 47	Bobby Bonilla	.15	.07	.02
☐ 48	Greg Pirkl	.05	.02	.01
☐ 49	Steve Karsay	.05	.02	.01
☐ 50	Bob Hamelin	.05	.02	.01
☐ 51	Javier Lopez	.25	.11	.03
☐ 52	Barry Larkin	.25	.11	.03
☐ 53	Kevin Young	.05	.02	.01
☐ 54	Sterling Hitchcock	.05	.02	.01
☐ 55	Tom Glavine	.15	.07	.02
☐ 56	Carlos Delgado	.05	.02	.01
☐ 57	Darren Oliver	.05	.02	.01
☐ 58	Cliff Floyd	.10	.05	.01
☐ 59	Tim Salmon	.30	.14	.04
☐ 60	Albert Belle	.75	.35	.09
☐ 61	Salomon Torres	.05	.02	.01
☐ 62	Gary Sheffield	.15	.07	.02
☐ 63	Ivan Rodriguez	.15	.07	.02
☐ 64	Charles Nagy	.10	.05	.01
☐ 65	Eduardo Perez	.05	.02	.01
☐ 66	Terry Steinbach	.10	.05	.01
☐ 67	Dave Justice	.25	.11	.03
☐ 68	Jason Bere	.05	.02	.01
☐ 69	Dave Nilsson	.10	.05	.01
☐ 70	Brian Anderson	.05	.02	.01
☐ 71	Billy Ashley	.05	.02	.01
☐ 72	Roger Clemens	.30	.14	.04
☐ 73	Jimmy Key	.10	.05	.01
☐ 74	Wally Joyner	.10	.05	.01
☐ 75	Andy Benes	.10	.05	.01
☐ 76	Ray Lankford	.15	.07	.02
☐ 77	Jeff Kent	.10	.05	.01
☐ 78	Moises Alou	.10	.05	.01
☐ 79	Kirby Puckett	.60	.25	.07
☐ 80	Joe Carter	.15	.07	.02
☐ 81	Manny Ramirez	.75	.35	.09
☐ 82	J.R. Phillips	.05	.02	.01
☐ 83	Matt Mieske	.05	.02	.01
☐ 84	John Olerud	.10	.05	.01
☐ 85	Andres Galarraga	.15	.07	.02
☐ 86	Juan Gonzalez	.50	.23	.06
☐ 87	Pedro Martinez	.05	.02	.01
☐ 88	Dean Palmer	.05	.02	.01
☐ 89	Ken Griffey Jr.	2.00	.90	.25
☐ 90	Brian Jordan	.15	.07	.02
☐ 91	Hal Morris	.05	.02	.01
☐ 92	Lenny Dykstra	.10	.05	.01
☐ 93	Wil Cordero	.05	.02	.01
☐ 94	Tony Gwynn	.60	.25	.07
☐ 95	Alex Gonzalez	.05	.02	.01
☐ 96	Cecil Fielder	.15	.07	.02
☐ 97	Mo Vaughn	.30	.14	.04
☐ 98	John Valentin	.15	.07	.02
☐ 99	Will Clark	.25	.11	.03
☐ 100	Geronimo Pena	.05	.02	.01
☐ 101	Don Mattingly	1.00	.45	.12
☐ 102	Charles Johnson	.10	.05	.01
☐ 103	Raul Mondesi	.50	.23	.06
☐ 104	Reggie Sanders	.15	.07	.02
☐ 105	Royce Clayton	.05	.02	.01
☐ 106	Reggie Jefferson	.05	.02	.01
☐ 107	Craig Biggio	.15	.07	.02
☐ 108	Jack McDowell	.15	.07	.02
☐ 109	James Mouton	.10	.05	.01
☐ 110	Mike Greenwell	.05	.02	.01
☐ 111	David Cone	.15	.07	.02
☐ 112	Matt Williams	.30	.14	.04
☐ 113	Garret Anderson	.40	.18	.05
☐ 114	Carlos Garcia	.05	.02	.01
☐ 115	Alex Fernandez	.05	.02	.01
☐ 116	Deion Sanders	.40	.18	.05

☐ 117 Chili Davis	.10	.05	.01
☐ 118 Mike Kelly	.05	.02	.01
☐ 119 Jeff Conine	.15	.07	.02
☐ 120 Kenny Lofton	.60	.25	.07
☐ 121 Rafael Palmeiro	.15	.07	.02
☐ 122 Chuck Knoblauch	.15	.07	.02
☐ 123 Ozzie Smith	.40	.18	.05
☐ 124 Carlos Baerga	.40	.18	.05
☐ 125 Brett Butler	.10	.05	.01
☐ 126 Sammy Sosa	.15	.07	.02
☐ 127 Ellis Burks	.10	.05	.01
☐ 128 Bret Saberhagen	.10	.05	.01
☐ 129 Doug Drabek	.10	.05	.01
☐ 130 Dennis Martinez	.10	.05	.01
☐ 131 Paul O'Neill	.10	.05	.01
☐ 132 Travis Fryman	.15	.07	.02
☐ 133 Brent Gates	.10	.05	.01
☐ 134 Rickey Henderson	.15	.07	.02
☐ 135 Randy Johnson	.40	.18	.05
☐ 136 Mark Langston	.10	.05	.01
☐ 137 Greg Colbrunn	.15	.07	.02
☐ 138 Jose Rijo	.05	.02	.01
☐ 139 Bryan Harvey	.05	.02	.01
☐ 140 Dennis Eckersley	.15	.07	.02
☐ 141 Ron Gant	.15	.07	.02
☐ 142 Carl Everett	.10	.05	.01
☐ 143 Jeff Granger	.05	.02	.01
☐ 144 Ben McDonald	.05	.02	.01
☐ 145 Kurt Abbott	.05	.02	.01
☐ 146 Jim Abbott	.15	.07	.02
☐ 147 Jason Jacome	.05	.02	.01
☐ 148 Rico Brogna	.15	.07	.02
☐ 149 Cal Eldred	.05	.02	.01
☐ 150 Rich Becker	.05	.02	.01
☐ 151 Pete Harnisch	.05	.02	.01
☐ 152 Roberto Petagine	.05	.02	.01
☐ 153 Jacob Brumfield	.05	.02	.01
☐ 154 Todd Hundley	.10	.05	.01
☐ 155 Roger Cedeno	.15	.07	.02
☐ 156 Harold Baines	.10	.05	.01
☐ 157 Steve Dunn	.05	.02	.01
☐ 158 Tim Belk	.05	.02	.01
☐ 159 Marty Cordova	.30	.14	.04
☐ 160 Russ Davis	.10	.05	.01
☐ 161 Jose Malave	.05	.02	.01
☐ 162 Brian Hunter	.25	.11	.03
☐ 163 Andy Pettitte	.25	.11	.03
☐ 164 Brooks Kieschnick	.40	.18	.05
☐ 165 Midre Cummings	.10	.05	.01
☐ 166 Frank Rodriguez	.10	.05	.01
☐ 167 Chad Mottola	.10	.05	.01
☐ 168 Brian Barber	.05	.02	.01
☐ 169 Tim Unroe	.25	.11	.03
☐ 170 Shane Andrews	.05	.02	.01
☐ 171 Kevin Flora	.05	.02	.01
☐ 172 Ray Durham	.15	.07	.02
☐ 173 Chipper Jones	.75	.35	.09
☐ 174 Butch Huskey	.10	.05	.01
☐ 175 Ray McDavid	.10	.05	.01
☐ 176 Jeff Cirillo	.10	.05	.01
☐ 177 Terry Pendleton	.05	.02	.01
☐ 178 Scott Ruffcorn	.05	.02	.01
☐ 179 Ray Holbert	.05	.02	.01
☐ 180 Joe Randa	.05	.02	.01
☐ 181 Jose Oliva	.05	.02	.01
☐ 182 Andy Van Slyke	.05	.02	.01
☐ 183 Albie Lopez	.05	.02	.01
☐ 184 Chad Curtis	.10	.05	.01
☐ 185 Ozzie Guillen	.05	.02	.01
☐ 186 Chad Ogea	.10	.05	.01
☐ 187 Dan Wilson	.10	.05	.01
☐ 188 Tony Fernandez	.05	.02	.01
☐ 189 John Smoltz	.10	.05	.01
☐ 190 Willie Greene	.05	.02	.01
☐ 191 Darren Lewis	.05	.02	.01
☐ 192 Orlando Miller	.10	.05	.01
☐ 193 Kurt Miller	.05	.02	.01
☐ 194 Andrew Lorraine	.05	.02	.01
☐ 195 Ernie Young	.05	.02	.01
☐ 196 Jimmy Haynes	.15	.07	.02
☐ 197 Raul Casanova	.50	.23	.06
☐ 198 Joe Vitiello	.10	.05	.01
☐ 199 Brad Woodall	.05	.02	.01
☐ 200 Juan Acevedo	.05	.02	.01
☐ 201 Michael Tucker	.10	.05	.01
☐ 202 Shawn Green	.15	.07	.02
☐ 203 Alex Rodriguez	.40	.18	.05
☐ 204 Julian Tavarez	.10	.05	.01
☐ 205 Jose Lima	.05	.02	.01
☐ 206 Wilson Alvarez	.10	.05	.01
☐ 207 Rich Aude	.05	.02	.01
☐ 208 Armando Benitez	.05	.02	.01
☐ 209 Dwayne Hosey	.05	.02	.01
☐ 210 Gabe White	.05	.02	.01
☐ 211 Joey Eischen	.05	.02	.01
☐ 212 Bill Pulsipher	.10	.05	.01
☐ 213 Robby Thompson	.05	.02	.01
☐ 214 Toby Borland	.05	.02	.01
☐ 215 Rusty Greer	.05	.02	.01
☐ 216 Fausto Cruz	.05	.02	.01
☐ 217 Luis Ortiz	.05	.02	.01
☐ 218 Duane Singleton	.05	.02	.01
☐ 219 Troy Percival	.10	.05	.01
☐ 220 Gregg Jefferies	.15	.07	.02
☐ 221 Mark Grace	.15	.07	.02
☐ 222 Mickey Tettleton	.10	.05	.01
☐ 223 Phil Plantier	.05	.02	.01
☐ 224 Larry Walker	.25	.11	.03
☐ 225 Ken Caminiti	.05	.02	.01
☐ 226 Dave Winfield	.15	.07	.02
☐ 227 Brady Anderson	.05	.02	.01
☐ 228 Kevin Brown	.05	.02	.01
☐ 229 Andujar Cedeno	.05	.02	.01
☐ 230 Roberto Kelly	.10	.05	.01
☐ 231 Jose Canseco	.30	.14	.04
☐ 232 Scott Ruffcorn ST	.05	.02	.01
☐ 233 Billy Ashley ST	.05	.02	.01
☐ 234 J.R. Phillips ST	.05	.02	.01
☐ 235 Chipper Jones ST	.40	.18	.05
☐ 236 Charles Johnson ST	.10	.05	.01
☐ 237 Midre Cummings ST	.10	.05	.01
☐ 238 Brian L. Hunter ST	.10	.05	.01
☐ 239 Garret Anderson ST	.15	.07	.02
☐ 240 Shawn Green ST	.10	.05	.01
☐ 241 Alex Rodriguez ST	.15	.07	.02
☐ 242 Frank Thomas CL	1.00	.45	.12
☐ 243 Ken Griffey Jr. CL	1.00	.45	.12
☐ 244 Albert Belle CL	.40	.18	.05
☐ 245 Cal Ripken Jr. CL	1.00	.45	.12
☐ 246 Barry Bonds CL	.25	.11	.03
☐ 247 Raul Mondesi CL	.25	.11	.03
☐ 248 Mike Piazza CL	.40	.18	.05
☐ 249 Jeff Bagwell CL	.30	.14	.04
☐ 250 Jeff Bagwell	1.50	.70	.19
Ken Griffey Jr.			
Frank Thomas			
Mike Piazza CL			
☐ 251S Hideo Nomo	4.00	1.80	.50

1995 Select Artist's Proofs

This 250-card set is parallel to the regular Select set. These cards were inserted at a rate of one per 24 packs. The only difference between these cards and the regular issue cards are the words "Artist's Proof" printed in the lower left corner.

	MINT	NRMT	EXC
COMPLETE SET (250)	6000.00	2700.00	750.00
COMMON CARD (1-250)	10.00	4.50	1.25
SEMISTARS	20.00	9.00	2.50
STARS	30.00	13.50	3.70

*VETERAN STARS: 50X TO 75X BASIC CARDS
*YOUNG STARS: 30X TO 50X BASIC CARDS
*RCs: 20X TO 40X BASIC CARDS

		MINT	NRMT	EXC
☐	1 Cal Ripken	400.00	180.00	50.00
☐	10 Dante Bichette	40.00	18.00	5.00
☐	17 Mike Piazza	150.00	70.00	19.00
☐	19 Mike Mussina	40.00	18.00	5.00
☐	21 Greg Maddux	325.00	145.00	40.00
☐	22 Frank Thomas	325.00	145.00	40.00
☐	32 Jim Thome	50.00	22.00	6.25
☐	34 Roberto Alomar	75.00	34.00	9.50
☐	37 Jeff Bagwell	125.00	55.00	15.50
☐	40 Jim Edmonds	40.00	18.00	5.00
☐	41 Ryan Klesko	60.00	27.00	7.50
☐	42 Fred McGriff	40.00	18.00	5.00
☐	46 Barry Bonds	90.00	40.00	11.00
☐	51 Javier Lopez	40.00	18.00	5.00
☐	52 Barry Larkin	40.00	18.00	5.00
☐	59 Tim Salmon	50.00	22.00	6.25
☐	60 Albert Belle	150.00	70.00	19.00
☐	67 Dave Justice	40.00	18.00	5.00
☐	72 Roger Clemens	50.00	22.00	6.25
☐	79 Kirby Puckett	125.00	55.00	15.50
☐	81 Manny Ramirez	150.00	70.00	19.00
☐	86 Juan Gonzalez	90.00	40.00	11.00
☐	89 Ken Griffey Jr.	325.00	145.00	40.00
☐	94 Tony Gwynn	125.00	55.00	15.50
☐	97 Mo Vaughn	50.00	22.00	6.25
☐	99 Will Clark	40.00	18.00	5.00
☐	101 Don Mattingly	160.00	70.00	20.00
☐	103 Raul Mondesi	75.00	34.00	9.50
☐	112 Matt Williams	50.00	22.00	6.25
☐	113 Garret Anderson	60.00	27.00	7.50
☐	116 Deion Sanders	75.00	34.00	9.50
☐	120 Kenny Lofton	125.00	55.00	15.50
☐	123 Ozzie Smith	75.00	34.00	9.50
☐	124 Carlos Baerga	75.00	34.00	9.50
☐	135 Randy Johnson	75.00	34.00	9.50
☐	159 Marty Cordova	40.00	18.00	5.00
☐	162 Brian Hunter	40.00	18.00	5.00
☐	163 Andy Pettitte	40.00	18.00	5.00
☐	164 Brooks Kieschnick	60.00	27.00	7.50
☐	173 Chipper Jones	160.00	70.00	20.00
☐	197 Raul Casanova	40.00	18.00	5.00
☐	203 Alex Rodriguez	60.00	27.00	7.50
☐	224 Larry Walker	40.00	18.00	5.00
☐	231 Jose Canseco	60.00	27.00	7.50
☐	235 Chipper Jones ST	80.00	36.00	10.00
☐	242 Frank Thomas CL	150.00	70.00	19.00
☐	243 Ken Griffey Jr. CL	150.00	70.00	19.00
☐	244 Albert Belle CL	60.00	27.00	7.50
☐	245 Cal Ripken CL	180.00	80.00	22.00
☐	246 Barry Bonds CL	40.00	18.00	5.00
☐	247 Raul Mondesi CL	35.00	16.00	4.40
☐	248 Mike Piazza CL	60.00	27.00	7.50
☐	249 Jeff Bagwell CL	50.00	22.00	6.25
☐	250 Bag/Thom/Grif/Piaz CL	275.00	125.00	34.00
☐	251S Hideo Nomo	125.00	55.00	15.50

1995 Select Big Sticks

Randomly inserted in packs, these 12 cards feature leading hitters. The fronts picture the player's photo against a metallic background. The words "Big Sticks 95" as well as the player's name is on the bottom. The player's team is noted in the middle of the background. The backs contain a player photo, personal information as well as some notes about his career. The cards are numbered in the upper right corner with a "BS" prefix.

		MINT	NRMT	EXC
	COMPLETE SET (12)	225.00	100.00	28.00
	COMMON CARD (1-12)	5.00	2.20	.60
☐	BS1 Frank Thomas	50.00	22.00	6.25
☐	BS2 Ken Griffey Jr.	50.00	22.00	6.25
☐	BS3 Cal Ripken Jr.	50.00	22.00	6.25
☐	BS4 Mike Piazza	20.00	9.00	2.50
☐	BS5 Don Mattingly	25.00	11.00	3.10
☐	BS6 Will Clark	6.00	2.70	.75
☐	BS7 Tony Gwynn	15.00	6.75	1.85
☐	BS8 Jeff Bagwell	15.00	6.75	1.85
☐	BS9 Barry Bonds	12.00	5.50	1.50
☐	BS10 Paul Molitor	5.00	2.20	.60
☐	BS11 Matt Williams	8.00	3.60	1.00
☐	BS12 Albert Belle	20.00	9.00	2.50

1995 Select Can't Miss

These 12 cards featuring promising young players were inserted one per 24 packs.

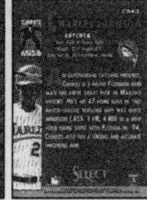

The player is pictured against a wavy red background. His last name is identified on the bottom left with the "Can't Miss" logo directly above the name. In the middle of the "Can't Miss" logo is a drawing of an umpire signaling safe. The backs have a blue background and include an inset photo, some professional information and biographical data. The cards are numbered with a "CM" prefix in the upper right corner.

	MINT	NRMT	EXC
COMPLETE SET (12)	90.00	40.00	11.00
COMMON CARD (1-12)	2.50	1.10	.30
☐ CM1 Cliff Floyd	3.00	1.35	.35
☐ CM2 Ryan Klesko	10.00	4.50	1.25
☐ CM3 Charles Johnson	4.00	1.80	.50
☐ CM4 Raul Mondesi	12.00	5.50	1.50
☐ CM5 Manny Ramirez	20.00	9.00	2.50
☐ CM6 Billy Ashley	2.50	1.10	.30
☐ CM7 Alex Gonzalez	2.50	1.10	.30
☐ CM8 Carlos Delgado	4.00	1.80	.50
☐ CM9 Garret Anderson	10.00	4.50	1.25
☐ CM10 Alex Rodriguez	8.00	3.60	1.00
☐ CM11 Chipper Jones	25.00	11.00	3.10
☐ CM12 Shawn Green	5.00	2.20	.60

1995 Select
Sure Shots

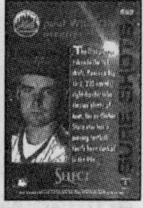

These 10 cards were randomly inserted into packs. This set features some of the top 1994 draft picks. The fronts feature the player's photo against a gold metallic background. The phrase "Sure Shots" is printed on gold ink against a blue background on the left. The player is identified in white ink

on the bottom. The backs contain some information about the player as well as an inset photo. All of this information is set against a blue background with a white light effect. The cards are numbered with an "SS" prefix in the upper right corner.

	MINT	NRMT	EXC
COMPLETE SET (10)	140.00	65.00	17.50
COMMON CARD (1-10)	10.00	4.50	1.25
☐ SS1 Ben Grieve	30.00	13.50	3.70
☐ SS2 Kevin Witt	12.00	5.50	1.50
☐ SS3 Mark Farris	10.00	4.50	1.25
☐ SS4 Paul Konerko	15.00	6.75	1.85
☐ SS5 Dustin Hermanson	12.00	5.50	1.50
☐ SS6 Ramon Castro	10.00	4.50	1.25
☐ SS7 McKay Christensen	10.00	4.50	1.25
☐ SS8 Brian Buchanan	10.00	4.50	1.25
☐ SS9 Paul Wilson	25.00	11.00	3.10
☐ SS10 Terrence Long	12.00	5.50	1.50

1995 Select
Certified

This 135-card set was issued through hobby outlets only. This set was issued in six-card packs. There are also tribute cards to Eddie Murray and Cal Ripken in this set. The cards are made with 24 point stock and are all metallic and double laminated. The fronts feature a player photo, his name in the lower right and the "Select '95 Certified" logo in the upper right. The horizontal backs feature a team by team seasonal summary and a player photo. The cards are numbered in the upper right corner. Rookie Cards in this set include Hideo Nomo and Carlos Perez.

	MINT	NRMT	EXC
COMPLETE SET (135)	50.00	22.00	6.25
COMMON CARD (1-135)	.25	.11	.03
COMP. CHECKLIST SET (7)	4.00	1.80	.50
☐ 1 Barry Bonds	1.25	.55	.16
☐ 2 Reggie Sanders	.50	.23	.06
☐ 3 Terry Steinbach	.25	.11	.03
☐ 4 Eduardo Perez	.25	.11	.03
☐ 5 Frank Thomas	5.00	2.20	.60
☐ 6 Wil Cordero	.25	.11	.03
☐ 7 John Olerud	.25	.11	.03

☐ 8 Deion Sanders	1.00	.45	.12
☐ 9 Mike Mussina	.60	.25	.07
☐ 10 Mo Vaughn	.75	.35	.09
☐ 11 Will Clark	.60	.25	.07
☐ 12 Chili Davis	.25	.11	.03
☐ 13 Jimmy Key	.25	.11	.03
☐ 14 Eddie Murray	.60	.25	.07
☐ 15 Bernard Gilkey	.25	.11	.03
☐ 16 David Cone	.50	.23	.06
☐ 17 Tim Salmon	.75	.35	.09
☐ 19 Steve Ontiveros	.25	.11	.03
☐ 20 Andres Galarraga	.50	.23	.06
☐ 21 Don Mattingly	2.50	1.10	.30
☐ 22 Kevin Appier	.25	.11	.03
☐ 23 Paul Molitor	.50	.23	.06
☐ 24 Edgar Martinez	.50	.23	.06
☐ 25 Andy Benes	.25	.11	.03
☐ 26 Rafael Palmeiro	.50	.23	.06
☐ 27 Barry Larkin	.60	.25	.07
☐ 28 Gary Sheffield	.50	.23	.06
☐ 29 Wally Joyner	.25	.11	.03
☐ 30 Wade Boggs	.50	.23	.06
☐ 31 Rico Brogna	.50	.23	.06
☐ 32 Eddie Murray 3000th Hit	.60	.25	.07
☐ 33 Kirby Puckett	1.50	.70	.19
☐ 34 Bobby Bonilla	.50	.23	.06
☐ 35 Hal Morris	.25	.11	.03
☐ 36 Moises Alou	.25	.11	.03
☐ 37 Javier Lopez	.60	.25	.07
☐ 38 Chuck Knoblauch	.50	.23	.06
☐ 39 Mike Piazza	2.00	.90	.25
☐ 40 Travis Fryman	.50	.23	.06
☐ 41 Rickey Henderson	.50	.23	.06
☐ 42 Jim Thome	.60	.25	.07
☐ 43 Carlos Baerga	1.00	.45	.12
☐ 44 Dean Palmer	.25	.11	.03
☐ 45 Kirk Gibson	.50	.23	.06
☐ 46 Bret Saberhagen	.25	.11	.03
☐ 47 Cecil Fielder	.50	.23	.06
☐ 48 Manny Ramirez	2.00	.90	.25
☐ 49 Derek Bell	.25	.11	.03
☐ 50 Mark McGwire	.50	.23	.06
☐ 51 Jim Edmonds	.60	.25	.07
☐ 52 Robin Ventura			
☐ 53 Ryan Klesko	1.00	.45	.12
☐ 54 Jeff Bagwell	1.50	.70	.19
☐ 55 Ozzie Smith	1.00	.45	.12
☐ 56 Albert Belle	2.00	.90	.25
☐ 57 Darren Daulton	.50	.23	.06
☐ 58 Jeff Conine	.50	.23	.06
☐ 59 Greg Maddux	5.00	2.20	.60
☐ 60 Lenny Dykstra	.50	.23	.06
☐ 61 Randy Johnson	1.00	.45	.12
☐ 62 Fred McGriff	.60	.25	.07
☐ 63 Ray Lankford	.50	.23	.06
☐ 64 David Justice	.60	.25	.07
☐ 65 Paul O'Neill	.25	.11	.03
☐ 66 Tony Gwynn	1.50	.70	.19
☐ 67 Matt Williams	.75	.35	.09
☐ 68 Dante Bichette	.60	.25	.07
☐ 69 Craig Biggio	.50	.23	.06
☐ 70 Ken Griffey Jr.	5.00	2.20	.60
☐ 71 J.T. Snow	.50	.23	.06
☐ 72 Cal Ripken	5.00	2.20	.60
☐ 73 Jay Bell	.25	.11	.03
☐ 74 Joe Carter	.50	.23	.06
☐ 75 Roberto Alomar	1.00	.45	.12
☐ 76 Benji Gil	.25	.11	.03
☐ 77 Ivan Rodriguez	.50	.23	.06
☐ 78 Raul Mondesi	1.25	.55	.16
☐ 79 Cliff Floyd	.25	.11	.03

☐ 80 Karros/Piazza/Mondesi	1.00	.45	.12
☐ 81 Royce Clayton	.25	.11	.03
☐ 82 Billy Ashley	.25	.11	.03
☐ 83 Joey Hamilton	.25	.11	.03
☐ 84 Sammy Sosa	.50	.23	.06
☐ 85 Jason Bere	.25	.11	.03
☐ 86 Dennis Martinez	.50	.23	.06
☐ 87 Greg Vaughn	.25	.11	.03
☐ 88 Roger Clemens	.75	.35	.09
☐ 89 Larry Walker	.60	.25	.07
☐ 90 Mark Grace	.50	.23	.06
☐ 91 Kenny Lofton	1.50	.70	.19
☐ 92 Carlos Perez	1.25	.55	.16
☐ 93 Roger Cedeno	.25	.11	.03
☐ 94 Scott Ruffcorn	.25	.11	.03
☐ 95 Jim Pittsley	.25	.11	.03
☐ 96 Andy Pettitte	.60	.25	.07
☐ 97 James Baldwin	.25	.11	.03
☐ 98 Hideo Nomo	8.00	3.60	1.00
☐ 99 Ismael Valdes	.25	.11	.03
☐ 100 Armando Benitez	.25	.11	.03
☐ 101 Jose Malave	.25	.11	.03
☐ 102 Bob Higginson	.75	.35	.09
☐ 103 LaTroy Hawkins	.25	.11	.03
☐ 104 Russ Davis	.25	.11	.03
☐ 105 Shawn Green	.50	.23	.06
☐ 106 Joe Vitiello	.25	.11	.03
☐ 107 Chipper Jones	2.00	.90	.25
☐ 108 Shane Andrews	.25	.11	.03
☐ 109 Jose Oliva	.25	.11	.03
☐ 110 Ray Durham	.50	.23	.06
☐ 111 Jon Nunnally	.25	.11	.03
☐ 112 Alex Gonzalez	.25	.11	.03
☐ 113 Vaughn Eshelman	.25	.11	.03
☐ 114 Marty Cordova	.75	.35	.09
☐ 115 Mark Grudzielanek	.50	.23	.06
☐ 116 Brian L.Hunter	.60	.25	.07
☐ 117 Charles Johnson	.50	.23	.06
☐ 118 Alex Rodriguez	1.00	.45	.12
☐ 119 David Bell	.25	.11	.03
☐ 120 Todd Hollandsworth	.25	.11	.03
☐ 121 Joe Randa	.25	.11	.03
☐ 122 Derek Jeter	.60	.25	.07
☐ 123 Frank Rodriguez	.25	.11	.03
☐ 124 Curtis Goodwin	.25	.11	.03
☐ 125 Bill Pulsipher	.50	.23	.06
☐ 126 John Mabry	.25	.11	.03
☐ 127 Julian Tavarez	.25	.11	.03
☐ 128 Edgardo Alfonzo	.25	.11	.03
☐ 129 Orlando Miller	.25	.11	.03
☐ 130 Juan Acevedo	.25	.11	.03
☐ 131 Jeff Cirillo	.50	.23	.06
☐ 132 Roberto Petagine	.25	.11	.03
☐ 133 Antonio Osuna	.25	.11	.03
☐ 134 Michael Tucker	.25	.11	.03
☐ 135 Garret Anderson	1.00	.45	.12
☐ 2131 Cal Ripken TRIB	5.00	2.20	.60

1995 Select Certified Mirror Gold

This 135-card set is a parallel to the regular issue. Pinnacle used their all-holographic foil technology on the fronts. The backs are identical to the regular issue but the words "Mirror Gold" are in the middle. These cards were inserted approximately one every five packs.

	MINT	NRMT	EXC
COMPLETE SET (135)	800.00	350.00	100.00
COMMON CARD (1-135)	2.50	1.10	.30
SEMISTARS	5.00	2.20	.60

*VETERAN STARS: 7.5X to 15X BASIC CARDS
*YOUNG STARS: 6X to 12X BASIC CARDS
*RCs: 3X to 6X BASIC CARDS

		MINT	NRMT	EXC
☐ 5	Frank Thomas	75.00	34.00	9.50
☐ 21	Don Mattingly	35.00	16.00	4.40
☐ 39	Mike Piazza	30.00	13.50	3.70
☐ 48	Manny Ramirez	30.00	13.50	3.70
☐ 56	Albert Belle	30.00	13.50	3.70
☐ 59	Greg Maddux	75.00	34.00	9.50
☐ 70	Ken Griffey Jr	75.00	34.00	9.50
☐ 72	Cal Ripken	75.00	34.00	9.50
☐ 98	Hideo Nomo	50.00	22.00	6.25
☐ 107	Chipper Jones	35.00	16.00	4.40
☐ 2131	Cal Ripken TRIB	75.00	34.00	9.50

1995 Select Certified Future

Ray Durham

This ten-card set was inserted approximately one in every 19 packs. Ten leading 1995 rookie players are included in this set. These cards were produced using Pinnacle's Dufex technology. The fronts feature a player photo with his name on the bottom. The words "Certified Future" are spelled vertically on the right. The horizontal backs feature some textual information and a player photo.

		MINT	NRMT	EXC
COMPLETE SET (10)		100.00	45.00	12.50
COMMON CARD (1-10)		6.00	2.70	.75
☐ 1	Chipper Jones	25.00	11.00	3.10
☐ 2	Curtis Goodwin	6.00	2.70	.75
☐ 3	Hideo Nomo	20.00	9.00	2.50
☐ 4	Shawn Green	8.00	3.60	1.00
☐ 5	Ray Durham	6.00	2.70	.75
☐ 6	Todd Hollandsworth	6.00	2.70	.75
☐ 7	Brian L.Hunter	10.00	4.50	1.25
☐ 8	Carlos Delgado	8.00	3.60	1.00
☐ 9	Michael Tucker	8.00	3.60	1.00
☐ 10	Alex Rodriguez	12.00	5.50	1.50

1995 Select Certified Gold Team

This 12-card was inserted approximately one in every 41 packs. This set features some of the leading players in baseball. These cards feature double-sided all-gold-foil Dufex technology.

		MINT	NRMT	EXC
COMPLETE SET (12)		375.00	170.00	47.50
COMMON CARD (1-12)		10.00	4.50	1.25
☐ 1	Ken Griffey Jr	80.00	36.00	10.00
☐ 2	Frank Thomas	80.00	36.00	10.00
☐ 3	Cal Ripken	80.00	36.00	10.00
☐ 4	Jeff Bagwell	25.00	11.00	3.10
☐ 5	Mike Piazza	30.00	13.50	3.70
☐ 6	Barry Bonds	18.00	8.00	2.20
☐ 7	Matt Williams	12.00	5.50	1.50
☐ 8	Don Mattingly	40.00	18.00	5.00
☐ 9	Will Clark	10.00	4.50	1.25
☐ 10	Tony Gwynn	25.00	11.00	3.10
☐ 11	Kirby Puckett	25.00	11.00	3.10
☐ 12	Jose Canseco	12.00	5.50	1.50

1995 Select Certified Potential Unlimited

These 20 were randomly inserted into packs. Two varieties of each card were produced. Cards numbered out of 1,975 were randomly inserted into packs while cards numbered out of 903 were randomly inserted on top of boxes. These cards feature Pinnacle's all-foil Dufex printing technology. The fronts feature a player photo in the middle. The words "Potential Unlimited" appear in the upper left and the player's name in the bottom left. The horizontal

back has a player photo and some text set against a background of a baseball. The cards are numbered 1 of either 1,975 or 903 at bottom right. The cards are also numbered as part of the set as "X" of 20 in the upper right. According to Pinnacle, across the production run these cards were inserted one every 29 packs. Prices below reflect cards numbered out of 1975.

	MINT	NRMT	EXC
COMP. 1975 NUM. SET (20)	300.00	135.00	38.00
COMMON 1975 CARD (1-20) ..	8.00	3.60	1.00
COMP. 903 NUM. SET (20) ..	450.00	200.00	55.00
COMMON 903 CARD (1-20) ..	12.00	5.50	1.50
903 NUMBERED CARDS: .75X TO 1.5X			

		MINT	NRMT	EXC
☐	1 Cliff Floyd	12.00	5.50	1.50
☐	2 Manny Ramirez	50.00	22.00	6.25
☐	3 Raul Mondesi	30.00	13.50	3.70
☐	4 Scott Ruffcorn	8.00	3.60	1.00
☐	5 Billy Ashley	8.00	3.60	1.00
☐	6 Alex Gonzalez	10.00	4.50	1.25
☐	7 Midre Cummings	10.00	4.50	1.25
☐	8 Charles Johnson	15.00	6.75	1.85
☐	9 Garret Anderson	25.00	11.00	3.10
☐	10 Hideo Nomo	40.00	18.00	5.00
☐	11 Chipper Jones	60.00	27.00	7.50
☐	12 Curtis Goodwin	12.00	5.50	1.50
☐	13 Frank Rodriguez	8.00	3.60	1.00
☐	14 Shawn Green	15.00	6.75	1.85
☐	15 Ray Durham	12.00	5.50	1.50
☐	16 Todd Hollandsworth ..	12.00	5.50	1.50
☐	17 Brian L.Hunter	20.00	9.00	2.50
☐	18 Carlos Delgado	15.00	6.75	1.85
☐	19 Michael Tucker	15.00	6.75	1.85
☐	20 Alex Rodriguez	20.00	9.00	2.50

1993 SP

This 290-card standard-size (2 1/2" by 3 1/2") set features fronts with action color player photos. The player's name and position appear within a team-colored stripe at the bottom edge that shades from dark to light, left to right. A team color-checkered stripe is in the upper left and the team name in a gold-lettered arc appears at the top with a gold underline that extends down the right side. The copper foil-stamped SP logo appears at the bottom right. The back displays an action shot of the player in the top half with a team color-checkered stripe

in the upper right. The bottom half carries the player's biography, statistics, and career highlights. Special subsets include All Star players (1-18) and Foil Prospects (271-290). Cards 19-270 are in alphabetical order by team nickname. The cards are numbered on the back. The six foil rookies are the key Rookie Cards in the set: Roger Cedeno, Johnny Damon, Russ Davis, Derek Jeter, Chad Mottola, and Todd Steverson. Other Rookie Cards in the set are Ray McDavid and Roberto Mejia.

	MINT	NRMT	EXC
COMPLETE SET (290)	75.00	34.00	9.50
COMMON CARD (1-290)	.15	.07	.02
FOIL PROSPECTS (271-290)	.50	.23	.06

		MINT	NRMT	EXC
☐	1 Roberto Alomar AS	1.50	.70	.19
☐	2 Wade Boggs AS	.50	.23	.06
☐	3 Joe Carter AS	.50	.23	.06
☐	4 Ken Griffey Jr. AS	8.00	3.60	1.00
☐	5 Mark Langston AS	.30	.14	.04
☐	6 John Olerud AS	.30	.14	.04
☐	7 Kirby Puckett AS	2.50	1.10	.30
☐	8 Cal Ripken Jr. AS	8.00	3.60	1.00
☐	9 Ivan Rodriguez AS	.50	.23	.06
☐	10 Barry Bonds AS	2.00	.90	.25
☐	11 Darren Daulton AS	.50	.23	.06
☐	12 Marquis Grissom AS	.50	.23	.06
☐	13 David Justice AS	1.00	.45	.12
☐	14 John Kruk AS	.30	.14	.04
☐	15 Barry Larkin AS	1.00	.45	.12
☐	16 Terry Mulholland AS	.15	.07	.02
☐	17 Ryne Sandberg AS	2.00	.90	.25
☐	18 Gary Sheffield AS	.50	.23	.06
☐	19 Chad Curtis	.30	.14	.04
☐	20 Chili Davis	.30	.14	.04
☐	21 Gary DiSarcina	.15	.07	.02
☐	22 Damion Easley	.30	.14	.04
☐	23 Chuck Finley	.30	.14	.04
☐	24 Luis Polonia	.15	.07	.02
☐	25 Tim Salmon	2.50	1.10	.30
☐	26 J.T. Snow	2.00	.90	.25
☐	27 Russ Springer	.15	.07	.02
☐	28 Jeff Bagwell	3.00	1.35	.35
☐	29 Craig Biggio	.50	.23	.06
☐	30 Ken Caminiti	.30	.14	.04
☐	31 Andujar Cedeno	.15	.07	.02
☐	32 Doug Drabek	.30	.14	.04
☐	33 Steve Finley	.30	.14	.04
☐	34 Luis Gonzalez	.30	.14	.04
☐	35 Pete Harnisch	.15	.07	.02
☐	36 Darryl Kile	.15	.07	.02
☐	37 Mike Bordick	.15	.07	.02
☐	38 Dennis Eckersley	.50	.23	.06
☐	39 Brent Gates	.50	.23	.06
☐	40 Rickey Henderson	.50	.23	.06
☐	41 Mark McGwire	.50	.23	.06
☐	42 Craig Paquette	.15	.07	.02
☐	43 Ruben Sierra	.50	.23	.06
☐	44 Terry Steinbach	.30	.14	.04
☐	45 Todd Van Poppel	.30	.14	.04
☐	46 Pat Borders	.15	.07	.02
☐	47 Tony Fernandez	.15	.07	.02
☐	48 Juan Guzman	.30	.14	.04
☐	49 Pat Hentgen	.30	.14	.04
☐	50 Paul Molitor	.50	.23	.06
☐	51 Jack Morris	.50	.23	.06
☐	52 Ed Sprague	.15	.07	.02
☐	53 Duane Ward	.15	.07	.02

☐ 54	Devon White	.30	.14	.04	☐ 125	Charles Nagy	.30	.14	.04
☐ 55	Steve Avery	.50	.23	.06	☐ 126	Paul Sorrento	.15	.07	.02
☐ 56	Jeff Blauser	.30	.14	.04	☐ 127	Rich Amaral	.15	.07	.02
☐ 57	Ron Gant	.50	.23	.06	☐ 128	Jay Buhner	.50	.23	.06
☐ 58	Tom Glavine	.50	.23	.06	☐ 129	Norm Charlton	.15	.07	.02
☐ 59	Greg Maddux	8.00	3.60	1.00	☐ 130	Dave Fleming	.15	.07	.02
☐ 60	Fred McGriff	1.00	.45	.12	☐ 131	Erik Hanson	.30	.14	.04
☐ 61	Terry Pendleton	.30	.14	.04	☐ 132	Randy Johnson	1.50	.70	.19
☐ 62	Deion Sanders	1.50	.70	.19	☐ 133	Edgar Martinez	.50	.23	.06
☐ 63	John Smoltz	.30	.14	.04	☐ 134	Tino Martinez	.50	.23	.06
☐ 64	Cal Eldred	.15	.07	.02	☐ 135	Omar Vizquel	.30	.14	.04
☐ 65	Darryl Hamilton	.15	.07	.02	☐ 136	Bret Barberie	.15	.07	.02
☐ 66	John Jaha	.30	.14	.04	☐ 137	Chuck Carr	.15	.07	.02
☐ 67	Pat Listach	.15	.07	.02	☐ 138	Jeff Conine	.50	.23	.06
☐ 68	Jaime Navarro	.15	.07	.02	☐ 139	Orestes Destrade	.15	.07	.02
☐ 69	Kevin Reimer	.15	.07	.02	☐ 140	Chris Hammond	.15	.07	.02
☐ 70	B.J. Surhoff	.30	.14	.04	☐ 141	Bryan Harvey	.30	.14	.04
☐ 71	Greg Vaughn	.15	.07	.02	☐ 142	Benito Santiago	.15	.07	.02
☐ 72	Robin Yount	1.00	.45	.12	☐ 143	Walt Weiss	.30	.14	.04
☐ 73	Rene Arocha	.30	.14	.04	☐ 144	Darrell Whitmore	.15	.07	.02
☐ 74	Bernard Gilkey	.30	.14	.04	☐ 145	Tim Bogar	.15	.07	.02
☐ 75	Gregg Jefferies	.50	.23	.06	☐ 146	Bobby Bonilla	.50	.23	.06
☐ 76	Ray Lankford	.50	.23	.06	☐ 147	Jeromy Burnitz	.15	.07	.02
☐ 77	Tom Pagnozzi	.15	.07	.02	☐ 148	Vince Coleman	.15	.07	.02
☐ 78	Lee Smith	.50	.23	.06	☐ 149	Dwight Gooden	.30	.14	.04
☐ 79	Ozzie Smith	1.50	.70	.19	☐ 150	Todd Hundley	.30	.14	.04
☐ 80	Bob Tewksbury	.15	.07	.02	☐ 151	Howard Johnson	.15	.07	.02
☐ 81	Mark Whiten	.30	.14	.04	☐ 152	Eddie Murray	1.25	.55	.16
☐ 82	Steve Buechele	.15	.07	.02	☐ 153	Bret Saberhagen	.30	.14	.04
☐ 83	Mark Grace	.50	.23	.06	☐ 154	Brady Anderson	.30	.14	.04
☐ 84	Jose Guzman	.15	.07	.02	☐ 155	Mike Devereaux	.30	.14	.04
☐ 85	Derrick May	.30	.14	.04	☐ 156	Jeffrey Hammonds	.50	.23	.06
☐ 86	Mike Morgan	.15	.07	.02	☐ 157	Chris Hoiles	.30	.14	.04
☐ 87	Randy Myers	.30	.14	.04	☐ 158	Ben McDonald	.15	.07	.02
☐ 88	Kevin Roberson	.15	.07	.02	☐ 159	Mark McLemore	.15	.07	.02
☐ 89	Sammy Sosa	.50	.23	.06	☐ 160	Mike Mussina	1.25	.55	.16
☐ 90	Rick Wilkins	.15	.07	.02	☐ 161	Gregg Olson	.15	.07	.02
☐ 91	Brett Butler	.30	.14	.04	☐ 162	David Segui	.15	.07	.02
☐ 92	Eric Davis	.15	.07	.02	☐ 163	Derek Bell	.50	.23	.06
☐ 93	Orel Hershiser	.30	.14	.04	☐ 164	Andy Benes	.30	.14	.04
☐ 94	Eric Karros	.50	.23	.06	☐ 165	Archi Cianfrocco	.15	.07	.02
☐ 95	Ramon Martinez	.30	.14	.04	☐ 166	Ricky Gutierrez	.15	.07	.02
☐ 96	Raul Mondesi	5.00	2.20	.60	☐ 167	Tony Gwynn	2.50	1.10	.30
☐ 97	Jose Offerman	.15	.07	.02	☐ 168	Gene Harris	.15	.07	.02
☐ 98	Mike Piazza	6.00	2.70	.75	☐ 169	Trevor Hoffman	.30	.14	.04
☐ 99	Darryl Strawberry	.30	.14	.04	☐ 170	Ray McDavid	.50	.23	.06
☐ 100	Moises Alou	.50	.23	.06	☐ 171	Phil Plantier	.15	.07	.02
☐ 101	Wil Cordero	.30	.14	.04	☐ 172	Mariano Duncan	.15	.07	.02
☐ 102	Delino DeShields	.30	.14	.04	☐ 173	Len Dykstra	.50	.23	.06
☐ 103	Darrin Fletcher	.15	.07	.02	☐ 174	Tommy Greene	.15	.07	.02
☐ 104	Ken Hill	.30	.14	.04	☐ 175	Dave Hollins	.15	.07	.02
☐ 105	Mike Lansing	.75	.35	.09	☐ 176	Pete Incaviglia	.15	.07	.02
☐ 106	Dennis Martinez	.30	.14	.04	☐ 177	Mickey Morandini	.15	.07	.02
☐ 107	Larry Walker	1.00	.45	.12	☐ 178	Curt Schilling	.15	.07	.02
☐ 108	John Wetteland	.30	.14	.04	☐ 179	Kevin Stocker	.30	.14	.04
☐ 109	Rod Beck	.50	.23	.06	☐ 180	Mitch Williams	.30	.14	.04
☐ 110	John Burkett	.15	.07	.02	☐ 181	Stan Belinda	.15	.07	.02
☐ 111	Will Clark	1.00	.45	.12	☐ 182	Jay Bell	.30	.14	.04
☐ 112	Royce Clayton	.30	.14	.04	☐ 183	Steve Cooke	.15	.07	.02
☐ 113	Darren Lewis	.15	.07	.02	☐ 184	Carlos Garcia	.30	.14	.04
☐ 114	Willie McGee	.30	.14	.04	☐ 185	Jeff King	.15	.07	.02
☐ 115	Bill Swift	.15	.07	.02	☐ 186	Orlando Merced	.30	.14	.04
☐ 116	Robby Thompson	.15	.07	.02	☐ 187	Don Slaught	.15	.07	.02
☐ 117	Matt Williams	1.25	.55	.16	☐ 188	Andy Van Slyke	.30	.14	.04
☐ 118	Sandy Alomar Jr.	.30	.14	.04	☐ 189	Kevin Young	.15	.07	.02
☐ 119	Carlos Baerga	1.50	.70	.19	☐ 190	Kevin Brown	.15	.07	.02
☐ 120	Albert Belle	3.00	1.35	.35	☐ 191	Jose Canseco	1.25	.55	.16
☐ 121	Reggie Jefferson	.15	.07	.02	☐ 192	Julio Franco	.30	.14	.04
☐ 122	Wayne Kirby	.15	.07	.02	☐ 193	Benji Gil	.30	.14	.04
☐ 123	Kenny Lofton	2.50	1.10	.30	☐ 194	Juan Gonzalez	1.50	.70	.19
☐ 124	Carlos Martinez	.15	.07	.02	☐ 195	Tom Henke	.30	.14	.04

		MINT	NRMT	EXC
☐ 196	Rafael Palmeiro	.50	.23	.06
☐ 197	Dean Palmer	.30	.14	.04
☐ 198	Nolan Ryan	8.00	3.60	1.00
☐ 199	Roger Clemens	1.25	.55	.16
☐ 200	Scott Cooper	.15	.07	.02
☐ 201	Andre Dawson	.50	.23	.06
☐ 202	Mike Greenwell	.30	.14	.04
☐ 203	Carlos Quintana	.15	.07	.02
☐ 204	Jeff Russell	.15	.07	.02
☐ 205	Aaron Sele	.30	.14	.04
☐ 206	Mo Vaughn	1.25	.55	.16
☐ 207	Frank Viola	.30	.14	.04
☐ 208	Rob Dibble	.15	.07	.02
☐ 209	Roberto Kelly	.30	.14	.04
☐ 210	Kevin Mitchell	.30	.14	.04
☐ 211	Hal Morris	.30	.14	.04
☐ 212	Joe Oliver	.15	.07	.02
☐ 213	Jose Rijo	.30	.14	.04
☐ 214	Bip Roberts	.15	.07	.02
☐ 215	Chris Sabo	.15	.07	.02
☐ 216	Reggie Sanders	.50	.23	.06
☐ 217	Dante Bichette	1.00	.45	.12
☐ 218	Jerald Clark	.15	.07	.02
☐ 219	Alex Cole	.15	.07	.02
☐ 220	Andres Galarraga	.50	.23	.06
☐ 221	Joe Girardi	.15	.07	.02
☐ 222	Charlie Hayes	.30	.14	.04
☐ 223	Roberto Mejia	.15	.07	.02
☐ 224	Armando Reynoso	.15	.07	.02
☐ 225	Eric Young	.30	.14	.04
☐ 226	Kevin Appier	.30	.14	.04
☐ 227	George Brett	3.00	1.35	.35
☐ 228	David Cone	.50	.23	.06
☐ 229	Phil Hiatt	.30	.14	.04
☐ 230	Felix Jose	.15	.07	.02
☐ 231	Wally Joyner	.30	.14	.04
☐ 232	Mike Macfarlane	.15	.07	.02
☐ 233	Brian McRae	.50	.23	.06
☐ 234	Jeff Montgomery	.30	.14	.04
☐ 235	Rob Deer	.15	.07	.02
☐ 236	Cecil Fielder	.50	.23	.06
☐ 237	Travis Fryman	.50	.23	.06
☐ 238	Mike Henneman	.15	.07	.02
☐ 239	Tony Phillips	.15	.07	.02
☐ 240	Mickey Tettleton	.30	.14	.04
☐ 241	Alan Trammell	.50	.23	.06
☐ 242	David Wells	.15	.07	.02
☐ 243	Lou Whitaker	.50	.23	.06
☐ 244	Rick Aguilera	.30	.14	.04
☐ 245	Scott Erickson	.30	.14	.04
☐ 246	Brian Harper	.15	.07	.02
☐ 247	Kent Hrbek	.30	.14	.04
☐ 248	Chuck Knoblauch	.50	.23	.06
☐ 249	Shane Mack	.15	.07	.02
☐ 250	David McCarty	.15	.07	.02
☐ 251	Pedro Munoz	.30	.14	.04
☐ 252	Dave Winfield	.50	.23	.06
☐ 253	Alex Fernandez	.50	.23	.06
☐ 254	Ozzie Guillen	.15	.07	.02
☐ 255	Bo Jackson	.50	.23	.06
☐ 256	Lance Johnson	.15	.07	.02
☐ 257	Ron Karkovice	.15	.07	.02
☐ 258	Jack McDowell	.50	.23	.06
☐ 259	Tim Raines	.50	.23	.06
☐ 260	Frank Thomas	8.00	3.60	1.00
☐ 261	Robin Ventura	.50	.23	.06
☐ 262	Jim Abbott	.50	.23	.06
☐ 263	Steve Farr	.15	.07	.02
☐ 264	Jimmy Key	.30	.14	.04
☐ 265	Don Mattingly	4.00	1.80	.50
☐ 266	Paul O'Neill	.30	.14	.04
☐ 267	Mike Stanley	.30	.14	.04
☐ 268	Danny Tartabull	.30	.14	.04
☐ 269	Bob Wickman	.15	.07	.02
☐ 270	Bernie Williams	.30	.14	.04
☐ 271	Jason Bere FOIL	1.25	.55	.16
☐ 272	Roger Cedeno FOIL	5.00	2.20	.60
☐ 273	Johnny Damon FOIL	12.00	5.50	1.50
☐ 274	Russ Davis FOIL	1.00	.45	.12
☐ 275	Carlos Delgado FOIL	2.50	1.10	.30
☐ 276	Carl Everett FOIL	1.00	.45	.12
☐ 277	Cliff Floyd FOIL	1.50	.70	.19
☐ 278	Alex Gonzalez FOIL	1.25	.55	.16
☐ 279	Derek Jeter FOIL	8.00	3.60	1.00
☐ 280	Chipper Jones FOIL	12.00	5.50	1.50
☐ 281	Javier Lopez FOIL	4.00	1.80	.50
☐ 282	Chad Mottola FOIL	1.00	.45	.12
☐ 283	Marc Newfield FOIL	.50	.23	.06
☐ 284	Eduardo Perez FOIL	.50	.23	.06
☐ 285	Manny Ramirez FOIL	10.00	4.50	1.25
☐ 286	Todd Steverson FOIL	.50	.23	.06
☐ 287	Michael Tucker FOIL	1.25	.55	.16
☐ 288	Allen Watson FOIL	.50	.23	.06
☐ 289	Rondell White FOIL	3.00	1.35	.35
☐ 290	Dmitri Young FOIL	.50	.23	.06

1993 SP
Platinum Power

Cards from this 20-card set were randomly inserted in packs. The standard-size (2 1/2" by 3 1/2") cards feature power hitters from the American and National Leagues. The color action cut-out shot is superimposed on a royal blue background that contains lettering for Upper Deck Platinum Power and about the player. The top edge of the front is cut out in an arc with a copper foil stripe containing the player's name. The copper foil-stamped Platinum Power logo appears in the lower right. The back displays a color action player photo over the same royal blue background as depicted on the front. On a white background below the player photo is a career summary. The cards are numbered on the back with a "PP" prefix alphabetically by player's name.

	MINT	NRMT	EXC
COMPLETE SET (20)	250.00	110.00	31.00
COMMON CARD (PP1-PP20)	5.00	2.20	.60

		MINT	NRMT	EXC
☐	PP1 Albert Belle	30.00	13.50	3.70
☐	PP2 Barry Bonds	15.00	6.75	1.85
☐	PP3 Joe Carter	6.00	2.70	.75
☐	PP4 Will Clark	8.00	3.60	1.00
☐	PP5 Darren Daulton	6.00	2.70	.75
☐	PP6 Cecil Fielder	6.00	2.70	.75
☐	PP7 Ron Gant	6.00	2.70	.75
☐	PP8 Juan Gonzalez	12.00	5.50	1.50
☐	PP9 Ken Griffey Jr.	60.00	27.00	7.50
☐	PP10 Dave Hollins	5.00	2.20	.60
☐	PP11 David Justice	8.00	3.60	1.00
☐	PP12 Fred McGriff	8.00	3.60	1.00
☐	PP13 Mark McGwire	6.00	2.70	.75
☐	PP14 Dean Palmer	5.00	2.20	.60
☐	PP15 Mike Piazza	35.00	16.00	4.40
☐	PP16 Tim Salmon	12.00	5.50	1.50
☐	PP17 Ryne Sandberg	18.00	8.00	2.20
☐	PP18 Gary Sheffield	6.00	2.70	.75
☐	PP19 Frank Thomas	60.00	27.00	7.50
☐	PP20 Matt Williams	12.00	5.50	1.50

		MINT	NRMT	EXC
☐	WR3 Ken Griffey Jr.	30.00	13.50	3.70
☐	WR4 Mike Piazza	12.00	5.50	1.50
☐	WR5 Tim Salmon	6.00	2.70	.75

1994 SP

This 200-card set primarily contains the game's top players and prospects. The first 20 cards in the set are Foil Prospects which are brighter and more metallic than the rest of the set. In either case, card fronts have a metallic finish with color player photos and a gold right-hand border. The backs contain a color player photo, 1993, career and best season statistics. The left side has a black border. The Upper Deck hologram on back is gold. Rookie Cards include Brooks Kieschnick, Chan Ho Park, Alex Rodriguez and Glenn Williams.

1994 SP Previews

These 15 cards were distributed regionally as inserts in second series Upper Deck hobby packs. They were inserted at a rate of one in 35. The manner of distribution was five cards per Central, East and West region. The cards are nearly identical to the basic SP issue. Card fronts differ in that the region is at bottom right where the team name is located on the SP cards.

	MINT	NRMT	EXC
COMPLETE SET (15)	190.00	85.00	24.00
COMPLETE CENTRAL (5)	85.00	38.00	10.50
COMPLETE EAST (5)	40.00	18.00	5.00
COMPLETE WEST (5)	65.00	29.00	8.00
COMMON CARD	2.00	.90	.25

		MINT	NRMT	EXC
☐	CR1 Jeff Bagwell	10.00	4.50	1.25
☐	CR2 Michael Jordan	30.00	13.50	3.70
☐	CR3 Kirby Puckett	10.00	4.50	1.25
☐	CR4 Manny Ramirez	15.00	6.75	1.85
☐	CR5 Frank Thomas	30.00	13.50	3.70
☐	ER1 Roberto Alomar	5.00	2.20	.60
☐	ER2 Cliff Floyd	2.00	.90	.25
☐	ER3 Javier Lopez	4.00	1.80	.50
☐	ER4 Don Mattingly	12.00	5.50	1.50
☐	ER5 Cal Ripken	25.00	11.00	3.10
☐	WR1 Barry Bonds	8.00	3.60	1.00
☐	WR2 Juan Gonzalez	8.00	3.60	1.00

	MINT	NRMT	EXC
COMPLETE SET (200)	40.00	18.00	5.00
COMMON CARD (1-200)	.15	.07	.02
COMP. DIECUTS SET (200)	150.00	70.00	19.00
DIECUT COMMON (1-200)	.25	.11	.03
DIECUT SEMISTARS	.50	.23	.06

*DIECUT VETERAN STARS: 1.5X TO 3X BASIC CARDS
*DIECUT YOUNG STARS: 1.25X TO 2.5X BASIC CARDS
*DIECUT RC'S: 1X TO 2X BASIC CARDS

		MINT	NRMT	EXC
☐	1 Mike Bell FOIL	.50	.23	.06
☐	2 D.J. Boston FOIL	.30	.14	.04
☐	3 Johnny Damon FOIL	3.00	1.35	.35
☐	4 Brad Fullmer FOIL	.60	.25	.07
☐	5 Joey Hamilton FOIL	.75	.35	.09
☐	6 Todd Hollandsworth FOIL	.75	.35	.09
☐	7 Brian L. Hunter FOIL	2.00	.90	.25
☐	8 LaTroy Hawkins FOIL	.75	.35	.09
☐	9 Brooks Kieschnick FOIL	4.00	1.80	.50
☐	10 Derrek Lee FOIL	2.50	1.10	.30
☐	11 Trot Nixon FOIL	2.00	.90	.25
☐	12 Alex Ochoa FOIL	.40	.18	.05
☐	13 Chan Ho Park FOIL	.50	.23	.06
☐	14 Kirk Presley FOIL	.75	.35	.09
☐	15 Alex Rodriguez FOIL	5.00	2.20	.60
☐	16 Jose Silva FOIL	1.00	.45	.12
☐	17 Terrell Wade FOIL	1.00	.45	.12
☐	18 Billy Wagner FOIL	1.50	.70	.19
☐	19 Glenn Williams FOIL	1.25	.55	.16
☐	20 Preston Wilson FOIL	.40	.18	.05
☐	21 Brian Anderson	.40	.18	.05
☐	22 Chad Curtis	.15	.07	.02

□	#	Player			
□	23	Chili Davis	.30	.14	.04
□	24	Bo Jackson	.40	.18	.05
□	25	Mark Langston	.40	.18	.05
□	26	Tim Salmon	1.00	.45	.12
□	27	Jeff Bagwell	1.50	.70	.19
□	28	Craig Biggio	.30	.14	.04
□	29	Ken Caminiti	.30	.14	.04
□	30	Doug Drabek	.40	.18	.05
□	31	John Hudek	.40	.18	.05
□	32	Greg Swindell	.15	.07	.02
□	33	Brent Gates	.40	.18	.05
□	34	Rickey Henderson	.40	.18	.05
□	35	Steve Karsay	.15	.07	.02
□	36	Mark McGwire	.40	.18	.05
□	37	Ruben Sierra	.40	.18	.05
□	38	Terry Steinbach	.30	.14	.04
□	39	Roberto Alomar	1.00	.45	.12
□	40	Joe Carter	.40	.18	.05
□	41	Carlos Delgado	.40	.18	.05
□	42	Alex Gonzalez	.40	.18	.05
□	43	Juan Guzman	.30	.14	.04
□	44	Paul Molitor	.40	.18	.05
□	45	John Olerud	.40	.18	.05
□	46	Devon White	.15	.07	.02
□	47	Steve Avery	.40	.18	.05
□	48	Jeff Blauser	.30	.14	.04
□	49	Tom Glavine	.40	.18	.05
□	50	David Justice	.60	.25	.07
□	51	Roberto Kelly	.15	.07	.02
□	52	Ryan Klesko	1.25	.55	.16
□	53	Javier Lopez	.75	.35	.09
□	54	Greg Maddux	5.00	2.20	.60
□	55	Fred McGriff	.60	.25	.07
□	56	Ricky Bones	.15	.07	.02
□	57	Cal Eldred	.30	.14	.04
□	58	Brian Harper	.15	.07	.02
□	59	Pat Listach	.15	.07	.02
□	60	B.J. Surhoff	.15	.07	.02
□	61	Greg Vaughn	.30	.14	.04
□	62	Bernard Gilkey	.30	.14	.04
□	63	Gregg Jefferies	.40	.18	.05
□	64	Ray Lankford	.40	.18	.05
□	65	Ozzie Smith	1.00	.45	.12
□	66	Bob Tewksbury	.15	.07	.02
□	67	Mark Whiten	.30	.14	.04
□	68	Todd Zeile	.30	.14	.04
□	69	Mark Grace	.40	.18	.05
□	70	Randy Myers	.15	.07	.02
□	71	Ryne Sandberg	1.25	.55	.16
□	72	Sammy Sosa	.40	.18	.05
□	73	Steve Trachsel	.40	.18	.05
□	74	Rick Wilkins	.15	.07	.02
□	75	Brett Butler	.30	.14	.04
□	76	Delino DeShields	.30	.14	.04
□	77	Orel Hershiser	.30	.14	.04
□	78	Eric Karros	.30	.14	.04
□	79	Raul Mondesi	1.50	.70	.19
□	80	Mike Piazza	2.00	.90	.25
□	81	Tim Wallach	.15	.07	.02
□	82	Moises Alou	.40	.18	.05
□	83	Cliff Floyd	.40	.18	.05
□	84	Marquis Grissom	.40	.18	.05
□	85	Pedro J. Martinez	.40	.18	.05
□	86	Larry Walker	.60	.25	.07
□	87	John Wetteland	.15	.07	.02
□	88	Rondell White	.40	.18	.05
□	89	Rod Beck	.30	.14	.04
□	90	Barry Bonds	1.25	.55	.16
□	91	John Burkett	.30	.14	.04
□	92	Royce Clayton	.30	.14	.04
□	93	Billy Swift	.15	.07	.02
□	94	Robby Thompson	.15	.07	.02
□	95	Matt Williams	.75	.35	.09
□	96	Carlos Baerga	1.00	.45	.12
□	97	Albert Belle	2.00	.90	.25
□	98	Kenny Lofton	1.50	.70	.19
□	99	Dennis Martinez	.30	.14	.04
□	100	Eddie Murray	.60	.25	.07
□	101	Manny Ramirez	2.50	1.10	.30
□	102	Eric Anthony	.15	.07	.02
□	103	Chris Bosio	.15	.07	.02
□	104	Jay Buhner	.40	.18	.05
□	105	Ken Griffey Jr.	5.00	2.20	.60
□	106	Randy Johnson	1.00	.45	.12
□	107	Edgar Martinez	.30	.14	.04
□	108	Chuck Carr	.15	.07	.02
□	109	Jeff Conine	.40	.18	.05
□	110	Carl Everett	.30	.14	.04
□	111	Chris Hammond	.15	.07	.02
□	112	Bryan Harvey	.15	.07	.02
□	113	Charles Johnson	.40	.18	.05
□	114	Gary Sheffield	.40	.18	.05
□	115	Bobby Bonilla	.40	.18	.05
□	116	Dwight Gooden	.15	.07	.02
□	117	Todd Hundley	.30	.14	.04
□	118	Bobby Jones	.40	.18	.05
□	119	Jeff Kent	.30	.14	.04
□	120	Bret Saberhagen	.30	.14	.04
□	121	Jeffrey Hammonds	.40	.18	.05
□	122	Chris Hoiles	.30	.14	.04
□	123	Ben McDonald	.30	.14	.04
□	124	Mike Mussina	.60	.25	.07
□	125	Rafael Palmeiro	.40	.18	.05
□	126	Cal Ripken Jr.	5.00	2.20	.60
□	127	Lee Smith	.40	.18	.05
□	128	Derek Bell	.30	.14	.04
□	129	Andy Benes	.30	.14	.04
□	130	Tony Gwynn	1.50	.70	.19
□	131	Trevor Hoffman	.15	.07	.02
□	132	Phil Plantier	.30	.14	.04
□	133	Bip Roberts	.15	.07	.02
□	134	Darren Daulton	.40	.18	.05
□	135	Lenny Dykstra	.40	.18	.05
□	136	Dave Hollins	.40	.18	.05
□	137	Danny Jackson	.15	.07	.02
□	138	John Kruk	.30	.14	.04
□	139	Kevin Stocker	.30	.14	.04
□	140	Jay Bell	.30	.14	.04
□	141	Carlos Garcia	.15	.07	.02
□	142	Jeff King	.15	.07	.02
□	143	Orlando Merced	.30	.14	.04
□	144	Andy Van Slyke	.40	.18	.05
□	145	Rick White	.15	.07	.02
□	146	Jose Canseco	.75	.35	.09
□	147	Will Clark	.60	.25	.07
□	148	Juan Gonzalez	1.25	.55	.16
□	149	Rick Helling	.15	.07	.02
□	150	Dean Palmer	.30	.14	.04
□	151	Ivan Rodriguez	.40	.18	.05
□	152	Roger Clemens	.75	.35	.09
□	153	Scott Cooper	.30	.14	.04
□	154	Andre Dawson	.40	.18	.05
□	155	Mike Greenwell	.30	.14	.04
□	156	Aaron Sele	.40	.18	.05
□	157	Mo Vaughn	.75	.35	.09
□	158	Bret Boone	.40	.18	.05
□	159	Barry Larkin	.60	.25	.07
□	160	Kevin Mitchell	.30	.14	.04
□	161	Jose Rijo	.30	.14	.04
□	162	Deion Sanders	1.00	.45	.12
□	163	Reggie Sanders	.30	.14	.04
□	164	Dante Bichette	.60	.25	.07

		MINT	NRMT	EXC
☐ 165	Ellis Burks	.30	.14	.04
☐ 166	Andres Galarraga	.40	.18	.05
☐ 167	Charlie Hayes	.30	.14	.04
☐ 168	David Nied	.40	.18	.05
☐ 169	Walt Weiss	.15	.07	.02
☐ 170	Kevin Appier	.30	.14	.04
☐ 171	David Cone	.40	.18	.05
☐ 172	Jeff Granger	.30	.14	.04
☐ 173	Felix Jose	.15	.07	.02
☐ 174	Wally Joyner	.30	.14	.04
☐ 175	Brian McRae	.30	.14	.04
☐ 176	Cecil Fielder	.40	.18	.05
☐ 177	Travis Fryman	.40	.18	.05
☐ 178	Mike Henneman	.15	.07	.02
☐ 179	Tony Phillips	.15	.07	.02
☐ 180	Mickey Tettleton	.30	.14	.04
☐ 181	Alan Trammell	.40	.18	.05
☐ 182	Rick Aguilera	.30	.14	.04
☐ 183	Rich Becker	.30	.14	.04
☐ 184	Scott Erickson	.15	.07	.02
☐ 185	Chuck Knoblauch	.40	.18	.05
☐ 186	Kirby Puckett	1.50	.70	.19
☐ 187	Dave Winfield	.40	.18	.05
☐ 188	Wilson Alvarez	.40	.18	.05
☐ 189	Jason Bere	.40	.18	.05
☐ 190	Alex Fernandez	.40	.18	.05
☐ 191	Julio Franco	.30	.14	.04
☐ 192	Jack McDowell	.40	.18	.05
☐ 193	Frank Thomas	5.00	2.20	.60
☐ 194	Robin Ventura	.30	.14	.04
☐ 195	Jim Abbott	.40	.18	.05
☐ 196	Wade Boggs	.40	.18	.05
☐ 197	Jimmy Key	.30	.14	.04
☐ 198	Don Mattingly	2.50	1.10	.30
☐ 199	Paul O'Neill	.30	.14	.04
☐ 200	Danny Tartabull	.30	.14	.04

		MINT	NRMT	EXC
☐ 1	Roberto Alomar	6.00	2.70	.75
☐ 2	Kevin Appier	2.50	1.10	.30
☐ 3	Jeff Bagwell	10.00	4.50	1.25
☐ 4	Barry Bonds	5.00	2.20	.60
☐ 5	Roger Clemens	5.00	2.20	.60
☐ 6	Carlos Delgado	2.50	1.10	.30
☐ 7	Cecil Fielder	2.50	1.10	.30
☐ 8	Cliff Floyd	2.50	1.10	.30
☐ 9	Travis Fryman	2.50	1.10	.30
☐ 10	Andres Galarraga	2.50	1.10	.30
☐ 11	Juan Gonzalez	6.00	2.70	.75
☐ 12	Ken Griffey Jr.	30.00	13.50	3.70
☐ 13	Tony Gwynn	10.00	4.50	1.25
☐ 14	Jeffrey Hammonds	2.50	1.10	.30
☐ 15	Bo Jackson	2.50	1.10	.30
☐ 16	Michael Jordan	35.00	16.00	4.40
☐ 17	David Justice	4.00	1.80	.50
☐ 18	Steve Karsay	2.00	.90	.25
☐ 19	Jeff Kent	2.00	.90	.25
☐ 20	Brooks Kieschnick	8.00	3.60	1.00
☐ 21	Ryan Klesko	6.00	2.70	.75
☐ 22	John Kruk	2.00	.90	.25
☐ 23	Barry Larkin	4.00	1.80	.50
☐ 24	Pat Listach	2.00	.90	.25
☐ 25	Don Mattingly	15.00	6.75	1.85
☐ 26	Mark McGwire	2.50	1.10	.30
☐ 27	Raul Mondesi	10.00	4.50	1.25
☐ 28	Trot Nixon	4.00	1.80	.50
☐ 29	Mike Piazza	12.00	5.50	1.50
☐ 30	Kirby Puckett	10.00	4.50	1.25
☐ 31	Manny Ramirez	12.00	5.50	1.50
☐ 32	Cal Ripken	35.00	16.00	4.40
☐ 33	Alex Rodriguez	10.00	4.50	1.25
☐ 34	Tim Salmon	6.00	2.70	.75
☐ 35	Gary Sheffield	2.50	1.10	.30
☐ 36	Ozzie Smith	6.00	2.70	.75
☐ 37	Sammy Sosa	3.00	1.35	.35
☐ 38	Andy Van Slyke	2.00	.90	.25

1994 SP
Holoview Blue

Randomly inserted in SP foil packs at a rate of one in five, this 38-card set contains top stars and prospects. Card fronts have a color player photo with a black and blue border to the right with which the player's name appears. A player hologram that runs the width of the card is at the bottom. The backs are primarily blue with a player photo and text.

	MINT	NRMT	EXC
COMPLETE SET (38)	150.00	70.00	19.00
COMMON CARD (1-38)	2.00	.90	.25

1994 SP
Holoview Red

Parallel to the Holoview Blue set, this 38-card issue was also randomly inserted in SP packs. They are much more difficult to pull than the Blue version with an insertion rate of one in 75. Card fronts have a color player photo with a black and red border to the right with which the player's name appears. A player hologram that runs the width of the card is at the bottom. The backs are primarily red with a player photo and text.

	MINT	NRMT	EXC
COMPLETE SET (38)	2800.00	1250.00	350.00
COMMON CARD (1-38)	16.00	7.25	2.00
☐ 1 Roberto Alomar	80.00	36.00	10.00
☐ 2 Kevin Appier	30.00	13.50	3.70
☐ 3 Jeff Bagwell	120.00	55.00	15.00
☐ 4 Barry Bonds	60.00	27.00	7.50
☐ 5 Roger Clemens	60.00	27.00	7.50
☐ 6 Carlos Delgado	40.00	18.00	5.00
☐ 7 Cecil Fielder	30.00	13.50	3.70

☐ 8	Cliff Floyd	30.00	13.50	3.70
☐ 9	Travis Fryman	30.00	13.50	3.70
☐ 10	Andres Galarraga	30.00	13.50	3.70
☐ 11	Juan Gonzalez	80.00	36.00	10.00
☐ 12	Ken Griffey Jr.	350.00	160.00	45.00
☐ 13	Tony Gwynn	120.00	55.00	15.00
☐ 14	Jeffrey Hammonds	30.00	13.50	3.70
☐ 15	Bo Jackson	30.00	13.50	3.70
☐ 16	Michael Jordan	400.00	180.00	50.00
☐ 17	David Justice	50.00	22.00	6.25
☐ 18	Steve Karsay	16.00	7.25	2.00
☐ 19	Jeff Kent	16.00	7.25	2.00
☐ 20	Brooks Kieschnick	90.00	40.00	11.00
☐ 21	Ryan Klesko	80.00	36.00	10.00
☐ 22	John Kruk	16.00	7.25	2.00
☐ 23	Barry Larkin	50.00	22.00	6.25
☐ 24	Pat Listach	16.00	7.25	2.00
☐ 25	Don Mattingly	150.00	70.00	19.00
☐ 26	Mark McGwire	40.00	18.00	5.00
☐ 27	Raul Mondesi	100.00	45.00	12.50
☐ 28	Trot Nixon	50.00	22.00	6.25
☐ 29	Mike Piazza	160.00	70.00	20.00
☐ 30	Kirby Puckett	120.00	55.00	15.00
☐ 31	manny Ramirez	160.00	70.00	20.00
☐ 32	Cal Ripken	400.00	180.00	50.00
☐ 33	Alex Rodriguez	100.00	45.00	12.50
☐ 34	Tim Salmon	80.00	36.00	10.00
☐ 35	Gary Sheffield	30.00	13.50	3.70
☐ 36	Ozzie Smith	80.00	36.00	10.00
☐ 37	Sammy Sosa	60.00	27.00	7.50
☐ 38	Andy Van Slyke	16.00	7.25	2.00

1995 SP

This set consists of 207 cards being sold in eight-card, hobby-only packs with a suggested retail price of $3.99. The fronts have full-bleed photos and a large chevron on the left. The chevron consists of red and gold foil for American League players and blue and gold for National Leaguers. The backs have a photo with player information and statistics at the bottom. The backs also have a gold hologram to prevent counterfeiting. Subsets featured are Salute (1-4) and Premier Prospects (5-24).

	MINT	NRMT	EXC
COMPLETE SET (207)	40.00	18.00	5.00
COMMON CARD (1-207)	.15	.07	.02

COMPLETE SILVER SET (207)	150.00	70.00	19.00
SILVER COMMONS (1-207)	.25	.11	.03
SILVER SEMISTARS	.50	.23	.06

*SILVER VETERAN STARS: 1.5X TO 3X BASIC CARDS
*SILVER YOUNG STARS: 1.25X TO 2.5X BASIC CARDS
*SILVER RC'S: 1X TO 2X BASIC CARDS

☐ 1	Cal Ripken Salute	4.00	1.80	.50
☐ 2	Nolan Ryan Salute	2.50	1.10	.30
☐ 3	George Brett Salute	1.00	.45	.12
☐ 4	Mike Schmidt Salute	.60	.25	.07
☐ 5	Dustin Hermanson FOIL	.15	.07	.02
☐ 6	Antonio Osuna FOIL	.15	.07	.02
☐ 7	Mark Grudzielanek FOIL	.25	.11	.03
☐ 8	Ray Durham FOIL	.40	.18	.05
☐ 9	Ugueth Urbina FOIL	.30	.14	.04
☐ 10	Ruben Rivera FOIL	2.50	1.10	.30
☐ 11	Curtis Goodwin FOIL	.30	.14	.04
☐ 12	Jimmy Hurst FOIL	.30	.14	.04
☐ 13	Jose Malave FOIL	.15	.07	.02
☐ 14	Hideo Nomo FOIL	8.00	3.60	1.00
☐ 15	Juan Acevedo FOIL	.15	.07	.02
☐ 16	Tony Clark FOIL	.15	.07	.02
☐ 17	Jim Pittsley FOIL	.15	.07	.02
☐ 18	Freddy Garcia FOIL	.30	.14	.04
☐ 19	Carlos Perez FOIL	1.00	.45	.12
☐ 20	Raul Casanova FOIL	1.00	.45	.12
☐ 21	Quilvio Veras FOIL	.15	.07	.02
☐ 22	Edgardo Alfonzo FOIL	.15	.07	.02
☐ 23	Marty Cordova FOIL	.60	.25	.07
☐ 24	C.J. Nitkowski FOIL	.15	.07	.02
☐ 25	Wade Boggs CL	.15	.07	.02
☐ 26	Dave Winfield CL	.15	.07	.02
☐ 27	Eddie Murray CL	.50	.23	.06
☐ 28	David Justice	.50	.23	.06
☐ 29	Marquis Grissom	.40	.18	.05
☐ 30	Fred McGriff	.50	.23	.06
☐ 31	Greg Maddux	4.00	1.80	.50
☐ 32	Tom Glavine	.40	.18	.05
☐ 33	Steve Avery	.30	.14	.04
☐ 34	Chipper Jones	1.50	.70	.19
☐ 35	Sammy Sosa	.40	.18	.05
☐ 36	Jaime Navarro	.15	.07	.02
☐ 37	Randy Myers	.30	.14	.04
☐ 38	Mark Grace	.40	.18	.05
☐ 39	Todd Zeile	.30	.14	.04
☐ 40	Brian McRae	.30	.14	.04
☐ 41	Reggie Sanders	.40	.18	.05
☐ 42	Ron Gant	.40	.18	.05
☐ 43	Deion Sanders	.75	.35	.09
☐ 44	Bret Boone	.30	.14	.04
☐ 45	Barry Larkin	.50	.23	.06
☐ 46	Jose Rijo	.15	.07	.02
☐ 47	Jason Bates	.15	.07	.02
☐ 48	Andres Galarraga	.40	.18	.05
☐ 49	Bill Swift	.15	.07	.02
☐ 50	Larry Walker	.50	.23	.06
☐ 51	Vinny Castilla	.40	.18	.05
☐ 52	Dante Bichette	.50	.23	.06
☐ 53	Jeff Conine	.40	.18	.05
☐ 54	John Burkett	.15	.07	.02
☐ 55	Gary Sheffield	.40	.18	.05
☐ 56	Andre Dawson	.40	.18	.05
☐ 57	Terry Pendleton	.30	.14	.04
☐ 58	Charles Johnson	.40	.18	.05
☐ 59	Brian L. Hunter	.50	.23	.06
☐ 60	Jeff Bagwell	1.25	.55	.16
☐ 61	Craig Biggio	.40	.18	.05
☐ 62	Phil Nevin	.15	.07	.02
☐ 63	Doug Drabek	.30	.14	.04
☐ 64	Derek Bell	.15	.07	.02

☐ 65	Raul Mondesi	1.00	.45	.12
☐ 66	Eric Karros	.40	.18	.05
☐ 67	Roger Cedeno	.40	.18	.05
☐ 68	Delino DeShields	.15	.07	.02
☐ 69	Ramon Martinez	.15	.07	.02
☐ 70	Mike Piazza	1.50	.70	.19
☐ 71	Billy Ashley	.15	.07	.02
☐ 72	Jeff Fassero	.15	.07	.02
☐ 73	Shane Andrews	.15	.07	.02
☐ 74	Wil Cordero	.15	.07	.02
☐ 75	Tony Tarasco	.15	.07	.02
☐ 76	Rondell White	.40	.18	.05
☐ 77	Pedro J. Martinez	.30	.14	.04
☐ 78	Moises Alou	.15	.07	.02
☐ 79	Rico Brogna	.40	.18	.05
☐ 80	Bobby Bonilla	.40	.18	.05
☐ 81	Jeff Kent	.30	.14	.04
☐ 82	Brett Butler	.30	.14	.04
☐ 83	Bobby Jones	.15	.07	.02
☐ 84	Bill Pulsipher	.30	.14	.04
☐ 85	Bret Saberhagen	.30	.14	.04
☐ 86	Gregg Jefferies	.40	.18	.05
☐ 87	Lenny Dykstra	.30	.14	.04
☐ 88	Dave Hollins	.15	.07	.02
☐ 89	Charlie Hayes	.15	.07	.02
☐ 90	Darren Daulton	.30	.14	.04
☐ 91	Curt Schilling	.15	.07	.02
☐ 92	Heathcliff Slocumb	.15	.07	.02
☐ 93	Carlos Garcia	.15	.07	.02
☐ 94	Denny Neagle	.15	.07	.02
☐ 95	Jay Bell	.15	.07	.02
☐ 96	Orlando Merced	.15	.07	.02
☐ 97	Dave Clark	.15	.07	.02
☐ 98	Bernard Gilkey	.15	.07	.02
☐ 99	Scott Cooper	.15	.07	.02
☐ 100	Ozzie Smith	.75	.35	.09
☐ 101	Tom Henke	.30	.14	.04
☐ 102	Ken Hill	.30	.14	.04
☐ 103	Brian Jordan	.40	.18	.05
☐ 104	Ray Lankford	.40	.18	.05
☐ 105	Tony Gwynn	1.25	.55	.16
☐ 106	Andy Benes	.30	.14	.04
☐ 107	Ken Caminiti	.15	.07	.02
☐ 108	Steve Finley	.15	.07	.02
☐ 109	Joey Hamilton	.30	.14	.04
☐ 110	Bip Roberts	.15	.07	.02
☐ 111	Eddie Williams	.15	.07	.02
☐ 112	Rod Beck	.15	.07	.02
☐ 113	Matt Williams	.60	.25	.07
☐ 114	Glenallen Hill	.15	.07	.02
☐ 115	Barry Bonds	1.00	.45	.12
☐ 116	Robby Thompson	.15	.07	.02
☐ 117	Mark Portugal	.15	.07	.02
☐ 118	Brady Anderson	.15	.07	.02
☐ 119	Mike Mussina	.50	.23	.06
☐ 120	Rafael Palmeiro	.40	.18	.05
☐ 121	Chris Hoiles	.15	.07	.02
☐ 122	Harold Baines	.30	.14	.04
☐ 123	Jeffrey Hammonds	.30	.14	.04
☐ 124	Tim Naehring	.15	.07	.02
☐ 125	Mo Vaughn	.60	.25	.07
☐ 126	Mike Macfarlane	.15	.07	.02
☐ 127	Roger Clemens	.60	.25	.07
☐ 128	John Valentin	.40	.18	.05
☐ 129	Aaron Sele	.15	.07	.02
☐ 130	Jose Canseco	.60	.25	.07
☐ 131	J.T. Snow	.40	.18	.05
☐ 132	Mark Langston	.15	.07	.02
☐ 133	Chili Davis	.30	.14	.04
☐ 134	Chuck Finley	.15	.07	.02
☐ 135	Tim Salmon	.60	.25	.07
☐ 136	Tony Phillips	.15	.07	.02
☐ 137	Jason Bere	.15	.07	.02
☐ 138	Robin Ventura	.40	.18	.05
☐ 139	Tim Raines	.40	.18	.05
☐ 140A	Frank Thomas ERR..	8.00	3.60	1.00
☐ 140B	Frank Thomas COR..	4.00	1.80	.50
☐ 141	Alex Fernandez	.30	.14	.04
☐ 142	Jim Abbott	.40	.18	.05
☐ 143	Wilson Alvarez	.15	.07	.02
☐ 144	Carlos Baerga	.75	.35	.09
☐ 145	Albert Belle	1.50	.70	.19
☐ 146	Jim Thome	.60	.25	.07
☐ 147	Dennis Martinez	.30	.14	.04
☐ 148	Eddie Murray	.50	.23	.06
☐ 149	Dave Winfield	.40	.18	.05
☐ 150	Kenny Lofton	1.25	.55	.16
☐ 151	Manny Ramirez	1.50	.70	.19
☐ 152	Chad Curtis	.30	.14	.04
☐ 153	Lou Whitaker	.40	.18	.05
☐ 154	Alan Trammell	.40	.18	.05
☐ 155	Cecil Fielder	.40	.18	.05
☐ 156	Kirk Gibson	.30	.14	.04
☐ 157	Michael Tucker	.30	.14	.04
☐ 158	Jon Nunnally	.30	.14	.04
☐ 159	Wally Joyner	.30	.14	.04
☐ 160	Kevin Appier	.30	.14	.04
☐ 161	Jeff Montgomery	.30	.14	.04
☐ 162	Greg Gagne	.15	.07	.02
☐ 163	Ricky Bones	.15	.07	.02
☐ 164	Cal Eldred	.15	.07	.02
☐ 165	Greg Vaughn	.15	.07	.02
☐ 166	Kevin Seitzer	.15	.07	.02
☐ 167	Jose Valentin	.15	.07	.02
☐ 168	Joe Oliver	.15	.07	.02
☐ 169	Rick Aguilera	.30	.14	.04
☐ 170	Kirby Puckett	1.25	.55	.16
☐ 171	Scott Stahoviak	.15	.07	.02
☐ 172	Kevin Tapani	.15	.07	.02
☐ 173	Chuck Knoblauch	.40	.18	.05
☐ 174	Rich Becker	.15	.07	.02*
☐ 175	Don Mattingly	2.00	.90	.25
☐ 176	Jack McDowell	.40	.18	.05
☐ 177	Jimmy Key	.30	.14	.04
☐ 178	Paul O'Neill	.30	.14	.04
☐ 179	Jim Wetteland	.30	.14	.04
☐ 180	Wade Boggs	.40	.18	.05
☐ 181	Derek Jeter	.50	.23	.06
☐ 182	Rickey Henderson	.40	.18	.05
☐ 183	Terry Steinbach	.30	.14	.04
☐ 184	Ruben Sierra	.40	.18	.05
☐ 185	Mark McGwire	.40	.18	.05
☐ 186	Todd Stottlemyre	.15	.07	.02
☐ 187	Dennis Eckersley	.40	.18	.05
☐ 188	Alex Rodriguez	.75	.35	.09
☐ 189	Randy Johnson	.75	.35	.09
☐ 190	Ken Griffey Jr	4.00	1.80	.50
☐ 191	Tino Martinez UER	.30	.14	.04
	Mike Blowers pictured on back			
☐ 192	Jay Buhner	.40	.18	.05
☐ 193	Edgar Martinez	.40	.18	.05
☐ 194	Mickey Tettleton	.30	.14	.04
☐ 195	Juan Gonzalez	1.00	.45	.12
☐ 196	Benji Gil	.15	.07	.02
☐ 197	Dean Palmer	.15	.07	.02
☐ 198	Ivan Rodriguez	.40	.18	.05
☐ 199	Kenny Rogers	.15	.07	.02
☐ 200	Will Clark	.50	.23	.06
☐ 201	Roberto Alomar	.75	.35	.09
☐ 202	David Cone	.40	.18	.05
☐ 203	Paul Molitor	.40	.18	.05
☐ 204	Shawn Green	.40	.18	.05

☐ 205 Joe Carter	.40	.18	.05
☐ 206 Alex Gonzalez	.15	.07	.02
☐ 207 Pat Hentgen	.30	.14	.04

1995 SP Platinum Power

This 20-card set was randomly inserted in packs at a rate of one in five. This die-cut set is comprised of the top home run hitters in baseball. The fronts have an action photo with a bronze background and rays of light coming out of the "SP" emblem at bottom right. The backs have a player photo in a box at the middle of the card with player statistics at the bottom.

	MINT	NRMT	EXC
COMPLETE SET (20)	40.00	18.00	5.00
COMMON CARD (PP1-PP20)	.75	.35	.09

☐ PP1	Jeff Bagwell	2.50	1.10	.30
☐ PP2	Barry Bonds	2.00	.90	.25
☐ PP3	Ron Gant	.75	.35	.09
☐ PP4	Fred McGriff	1.00	.45	.12
☐ PP5	Raul Mondesi	2.00	.90	.25
☐ PP6	Mike Piazza	3.00	1.35	.35
☐ PP7	Larry Walker	1.00	.45	.12
☐ PP8	Matt Williams	1.25	.55	.16
☐ PP9	Albert Belle	3.00	1.35	.35
☐ PP10	Cecil Fielder	.75	.35	.09
☐ PP11	Juan Gonzalez	2.00	.90	.25
☐ PP12	Ken Griffey Jr.	8.00	3.60	1.00
☐ PP13	Mark McGwire	.75	.35	.09
☐ PP14	Eddie Murray	1.00	.45	.12
☐ PP15	Manny Ramirez	3.00	1.35	.35
☐ PP16	Cal Ripken	8.00	3.60	1.00
☐ PP17	Tim Salmon	1.25	.55	.16
☐ PP18	Frank Thomas	8.00	3.60	1.00
☐ PP19	Jim Thome	1.25	.55	.16
☐ PP20	Mo Vaughn	1.25	.55	.16

1995 SP Special FX

This 48-card set was randomly inserted in packs at a rate of one in 75. The set is comprised of the top names in baseball. The fronts have an action photo on a sky-

colored foil background. There is also a hologram of the player's face that allows you to see a 50-degree, 3-D image. The backs have a photo with player information and statistics. The cards are numbered on the back "X/48."

	MINT	NRMT	EXC
COMPLETE SET (48)	2000.00	900.00	250.00
COMMON CARD (1-48)	15.00	6.75	1.85

☐ 1	Jose Canseco	40.00	18.00	5.00
☐ 2	Roger Clemens	40.00	18.00	5.00
☐ 3	Mo Vaughn	40.00	18.00	5.00
☐ 4	Tim Salmon	40.00	18.00	5.00
☐ 5	Chuck Finley	15.00	6.75	1.85
☐ 6	Robin Ventura	20.00	9.00	2.50
☐ 7	Jason Bere	15.00	6.75	1.85
☐ 8	Carlos Baerga	50.00	22.00	6.25
☐ 9	Albert Belle	100.00	45.00	12.50
☐ 10	Kenny Lofton	75.00	34.00	9.50
☐ 11	Manny Ramirez	100.00	45.00	12.50
☐ 12	Jeff Montgomery	15.00	6.75	1.85
☐ 13	Kirby Puckett	75.00	34.00	9.50
☐ 14	Wade Boggs	20.00	9.00	2.50
☐ 15	Don Mattingly	100.00	45.00	12.50
☐ 16	Cal Ripken	250.00	110.00	31.00
☐ 17	Ruben Sierra	15.00	6.75	1.85
☐ 18	Ken Griffey Jr.	250.00	110.00	31.00
☐ 19	Randy Johnson	50.00	22.00	6.25
☐ 20	Alex Rodriguez	40.00	18.00	5.00
☐ 21	Will Clark	30.00	13.50	3.70
☐ 22	Juan Gonzalez	60.00	27.00	7.50
☐ 23	Roberto Alomar	50.00	22.00	6.25
☐ 24	Joe Carter	20.00	9.00	2.50
☐ 25	Alex Gonzalez	15.00	6.75	1.85
☐ 26	Paul Molitor	20.00	9.00	2.50
☐ 27	Ryan Klesko	50.00	22.00	6.25
☐ 28	Fred McGriff	30.00	13.50	3.70
☐ 29	Greg Maddux	250.00	110.00	31.00
☐ 30	Sammy Sosa	25.00	11.00	3.10
☐ 31	Bret Boone	15.00	6.75	1.85
☐ 32	Barry Larkin	30.00	13.50	3.70
☐ 33	Reggie Sanders	20.00	9.00	2.50
☐ 34	Dante Bichette	30.00	13.50	3.70
☐ 35	Andres Galarraga	20.00	9.00	2.50
☐ 36	Charles Johnson	20.00	9.00	2.50
☐ 37	Gary Sheffield	20.00	9.00	2.50
☐ 38	Jeff Bagwell	75.00	34.00	9.50
☐ 39	Craig Biggio	25.00	11.00	3.10
☐ 40	Eric Karros	20.00	9.00	2.50
☐ 41	Billy Ashley	15.00	6.75	1.85
☐ 42	Raul Mondesi	60.00	27.00	7.50
☐ 43	Mike Piazza	100.00	45.00	12.50
☐ 44	Rondell White	20.00	9.00	2.50
☐ 45	Bret Saberhagen	20.00	9.00	2.50

		MINT	NRMT	EXC
☐ 46	Tony Gwynn	75.00	34.00	9.50
☐ 47	Melvin Nieves	15.00	6.75	1.85
☐ 48	Matt Williams	40.00	18.00	5.00

1995 SP Championship

This set contains 200 cards that were sold in six-card retail packs for a suggested price of $2.99. The fronts have a full-bleed action photo with the words "SP Championship Series" in gold-foil in the bottom left-hand corner. In the bottom right-hand corner is the team's name in blue (National League) and red (American League) foil. The backs have a small head shot and player information. Statistics and team name are also on the back in blue or red just like on the front. Subsets featured are: Diamonds in the Rough (1-20), October Legends (100-114) and Major League Profiles.

	MINT	NRMT	EXC
COMPLETE SET (200)	40.00	18.00	5.00
COMMON CARD (1-200)	.15	.07	.02
COMPLETE DIECUT SET (200)	150.00	70.00	19.00
DIECUT COMMON CARDS (1-200)	.25	.11	.03
DIECUT SEMISTARS	.50	.23	.06

*DIECUT VETERAN STARS: 1.5X TO 3X BASIC CARDS
*DIECUT YOUNG STARS: 1.25X TO 2.5X BASIC CARDS
*DIECUT ROOKIE STARS: 1X TO 2X BASIC CARDS

☐ 1	Hideo Nomo	8.00	3.60	1.00
☐ 2	Roger Cedeno	.30	.14	.04
☐ 3	Curtis Goodwin	.30	.14	.04
☐ 4	Jon Nunnally	.30	.14	.04
☐ 5	Bill Pulsipher	.30	.14	.04
☐ 6	Garret Anderson	.75	.35	.09
☐ 7	Dustin Hermanson	.15	.07	.02
☐ 8	Marty Cordova	.60	.25	.07
☐ 9	Ruben Rivera	2.50	1.10	.30
☐ 10	Ariel Prieto	.40	.18	.05
☐ 11	Edgardo Alfonzo	.30	.14	.04
☐ 12	Ray Durham	.30	.14	.04
☐ 13	Quilvio Veras	.30	.14	.04
☐ 14	Ugueth Urbina	.30	.14	.04
☐ 15	Carlos Perez	1.00	.45	.12
☐ 16	Glenn Dishman	.30	.14	.04
☐ 17	Jeff Suppan	.30	.14	.04
☐ 18	Jason Bates	.30	.14	.04
☐ 19	Jason Isringhausen	2.00	.90	.25
☐ 20	Derek Jeter	.50	.23	.06
☐ 21	Fred McGriff MLP	.15	.07	.02
☐ 22	Marquis Grissom	.30	.14	.04
☐ 23	Fred McGriff	.50	.23	.06
☐ 24	Tom Glavine	.30	.14	.04
☐ 25	Greg Maddux	4.00	1.80	.50
☐ 26	Chipper Jones	1.50	.70	.19
☐ 27	Sammy Sosa MLP	.15	.07	.02
☐ 28	Randy Myers	.15	.07	.02
☐ 29	Mark Grace	.30	.14	.04
☐ 30	Sammy Sosa	.30	.14	.04
☐ 31	Todd Zeile	.15	.07	.02
☐ 32	Brian McRae	.15	.07	.02
☐ 33	Ron Gant MLP	.15	.07	.02
☐ 34	Reggie Sanders	.30	.14	.04
☐ 35	Ron Gant	.30	.14	.04
☐ 36	Barry Larkin	.50	.23	.06
☐ 37	Bret Boone	.15	.07	.02
☐ 38	John Smiley	.15	.07	.02
☐ 39	Larry Walker MLP	.30	.14	.04
☐ 40	Andres Galarraga	.30	.14	.04
☐ 41	Bill Swift	.15	.07	.02
☐ 42	Larry Walker	.50	.23	.06
☐ 43	Vinny Castilla	.30	.14	.04
☐ 44	Dante Bichette	.50	.23	.06
☐ 45	Jeff Conine MLP	.15	.07	.02
☐ 46	Charles Johnson	.30	.14	.04
☐ 47	Gary Sheffield	.30	.14	.04
☐ 48	Andre Dawson	.30	.14	.04
☐ 49	Jeff Conine	.30	.14	.04
☐ 50	Jeff Bagwell MLP	.60	.25	.07
☐ 51	Phil Nevin	.15	.07	.02
☐ 52	Craig Biggio	.30	.14	.04
☐ 53	Brian L. Hunter	.50	.23	.06
☐ 54	Doug Drabek	.15	.07	.02
☐ 55	Jeff Bagwell	1.25	.55	.16
☐ 56	Derek Bell	.15	.07	.02
☐ 57	Mike Piazza MLP	.75	.35	.09
☐ 58	Raul Mondesi	1.00	.45	.12
☐ 59	Eric Karros	.30	.14	.04
☐ 60	Mike Piazza	1.50	.70	.19
☐ 61	Ramon Martinez	.15	.07	.02
☐ 62	Billy Ashley	.15	.07	.02
☐ 63	Rondell White MLP	.30	.14	.04
☐ 64	Jeff Fassero	.15	.07	.02
☐ 65	Moises Alou	.15	.07	.02
☐ 66	Tony Tarasco	.15	.07	.02
☐ 67	Rondell White	.30	.14	.04
☐ 68	Pedro J. Martinez	.15	.07	.02
☐ 69	Bobby Jones MLP	.15	.07	.02
☐ 70	Bobby Bonilla	.30	.14	.04
☐ 71	Bobby Jones	.15	.07	.02
☐ 72	Bret Saberhagen	.15	.07	.02
☐ 73	Darren Daulton MLP	.15	.07	.02
☐ 74	Darren Daulton	.30	.14	.04
☐ 75	Gregg Jefferies	.30	.14	.04
☐ 76	Tyler Green	.15	.07	.02
☐ 77	Heathcliff Slocumb	.15	.07	.02
☐ 78	Lenny Dykstra	.30	.14	.04
☐ 79	Jay Bell MLP	.15	.07	.02
☐ 80	Denny Neagle	.15	.07	.02
☐ 81	Orlando Merced	.15	.07	.02
☐ 82	Jay Bell	.15	.07	.02
☐ 83	Ozzie Smith MLP	.40	.18	.05
☐ 84	Ken Hill	.15	.07	.02
☐ 85	Ozzie Smith	.75	.35	.09
☐ 86	Bernard Gilkey	.15	.07	.02
☐ 87	Ray Lankford	.30	.14	.04
☐ 88	Tony Gwynn MLP	.60	.25	.07
☐ 89	Ken Caminiti	.15	.07	.02

□				
□	90 Tony Gwynn	1.25	.55	.16
□	91 Joey Hamilton	.15	.07	.02
□	92 Bip Roberts	.15	.07	.02
□	93 Deion Sanders MLP	.40	.18	.05
□	94 Glenallen Hill	.15	.07	.02
□	95 Matt Williams	.60	.25	.07
□	96 Barry Bonds	1.00	.45	.12
□	97 Rod Beck	.15	.07	.02
□	98 Eddie Murray CL	.30	.14	.04
□	99 Cal Ripken Jr. CL	2.00	.90	.25
□	100 Roberto Alomar	.40	.18	.05
□	101 George Brett OL	1.00	.45	.12
□	102 Joe Carter OL	.15	.07	.02
□	103 Will Clark OL	.30	.14	.04
□	104 Dennis Eckersley OL	.15	.07	.02
□	105 Whitey Ford OL	.50	.23	.06
□	106 Steve Garvey OL	.30	.14	.04
□	107 Kirk Gibson OL	.15	.07	.02
□	108 Orel Hershiser OL	.15	.07	.02
□	109 Reggie Jackson OL	.50	.23	.06
□	110 Paul Molitor OL	.15	.07	.02
□	111 Kirby Puckett OL	.60	.25	.07
□	112 Mike Schmidt OL	.60	.25	.07
□	113 Dave Stewart OL	.15	.07	.02
□	114 Alan Trammell OL	.15	.07	.02
□	115 Cal Ripken Jr. MLP	2.00	.90	.25
□	116 Brady Anderson	.15	.07	.02
□	117 Mike Mussina	.50	.23	.06
□	118 Rafael Palmeiro	.30	.14	.04
□	119 Chris Hoiles	.15	.07	.02
□	120 Cal Ripken	4.00	1.80	.50
□	121 Mo Vaughn MLP	.30	.14	.04
□	122 Roger Clemens	.60	.25	.07
□	123 Tim Naehring	.15	.07	.02
□	124 John Valentin	.30	.14	.04
□	125 Mo Vaughn	.60	.25	.07
□	126 Tim Wakefield	.15	.07	.02
□	127 Jose Canseco	.60	.25	.07
□	128 Rick Aguilera	.15	.07	.02
□	129 Chili Davis MLP	.15	.07	.02
□	130 Lee Smith	.30	.14	.04
□	131 Jim Edmonds	.50	.23	.06
□	132 Chuck Finley	.15	.07	.02
□	133 Chili Davis	.15	.07	.02
□	134 J.T. Snow	.30	.14	.04
□	135 Tim Salmon	.60	.25	.07
□	136 Frank Thomas MLP	2.00	.90	.25
□	137 Jason Bere	.15	.07	.02
□	138 Robin Ventura	.30	.14	.04
□	139 Tim Raines	.30	.14	.04
□	140 Frank Thomas	4.00	1.80	.50
□	141 Alex Fernandez	.15	.07	.02
□	142 Eddie Murray MLP	.30	.14	.04
□	143 Carlos Baerga	.75	.35	.09
□	144 Eddie Murray	.50	.23	.06
□	145 Albert Belle	1.50	.70	.19
□	146 Jim Thome	.60	.25	.07
□	147 Dennis Martinez	.15	.07	.02
□	148 Dave Winfield	.30	.14	.04
□	149 Kenny Lofton	1.25	.55	.16
□	150 Manny Ramirez	1.50	.70	.19
□	151 Cecil Fielder MLP	.30	.14	.04
□	152 Lou Whitaker	.30	.14	.04
□	153 Alan Trammell	.30	.14	.04
□	154 Kirk Gibson	.15	.07	.02
□	155 Cecil Fielder	.30	.14	.04
□	156 Bobby Higginson	.40	.18	.05
□	157 Kevin Appier MLP	.15	.07	.02
□	158 Wally Joyner	.15	.07	.02
□	159 Jeff Montgomery	.15	.07	.02
□	160 Kevin Appier	.15	.07	.02

□				
□	161 Gary Gaetti	.15	.07	.02
□	162 Greg Gagne	.15	.07	.02
□	163 Ricky Bones MLP	.15	.07	.02
□	164 Greg Vaughn	.15	.07	.02
□	165 Kevin Seitzer	.15	.07	.02
□	166 Ricky Bones	.15	.07	.02
□	167 Kirby Puckett MLP	.60	.25	.07
□	168 Pedro Munoz	.15	.07	.02
□	169 Chuck Knoblauch	.30	.14	.04
□	170 Kirby Puckett	1.25	.55	.16
□	171 Don Mattingly MLP	1.00	.45	.12
□	172 Wade Boggs	.30	.14	.04
□	173 Paul O'Neill	.15	.07	.02
□	174 John Wetteland	.15	.07	.02
□	175 Don Mattingly	2.00	.90	.25
□	176 Jack McDowell	.15	.07	.02
□	177 Mark McGwire MLP	.15	.07	.02
□	178 Rickey Henderson	.30	.14	.04
□	179 Terry Steinbach	.15	.07	.02
□	180 Ruben Sierra	.15	.07	.02
□	181 Mark McGwire	.30	.14	.04
□	182 Dennis Eckersley	.30	.14	.04
□	183 Ken Griffey Jr. MLP	2.00	.90	.25
□	184 Alex Rodriguez	.75	.35	.09
□	185 Ken Griffey Jr.	4.00	1.80	.50
□	186 Randy Johnson	.75	.35	.09
□	187 Jay Buhner	.30	.14	.04
□	188 Edgar Martinez	.30	.14	.04
□	189 Will Clark MLP	.30	.14	.04
□	190 Juan Gonzalez	1.00	.45	.12
□	191 Benji Gil	.15	.07	.02
□	192 Ivan Rodriguez	.30	.14	.04
□	193 Kenny Rogers	.15	.07	.02
□	194 Will Clark	.50	.23	.06
□	195 Paul Molitor MLP	.15	.07	.02
□	196 Roberto Alomar	.75	.35	.09
□	197 David Cone	.30	.14	.04
□	198 Paul Molitor	.30	.14	.04
□	199 Shawn Green	.30	.14	.04
□	200 Joe Carter	.30	.14	.04
□	CR1 Cal Ripken, Jr. Tribute	65.00	29.00	8.00
□	CR1DC Cal Ripken 2131 DC	200.00	90.00	25.00

1995 SP Championship Classic Performances

This 10-card set was randomly inserted in packs at a rate of one in 15. The set con-

sists of 10 of the most memorable highlights since the 1969 Miracle Mets. The
fronts have a series action photo highlighted with the words "Classic Performances"
at the top in gold-foil enclosed by red. The
backs have a color head shot with information and statistics from the series. Diecut
versions were inserted at a rate of 72 packs
and are valued at three to six times the
prices below.

	MINT	NRMT	EXC
COMPLETE SET (10)	45.00	20.00	5.50
COMMON CARD (CP1-CP10)	2.00	.90	.25
*DIE CUT: 3X TO 6X BASIC CARDS..			

☐ CP1	Reggie Jackson	3.00	1.35	.35
☐ CP2	Nolan Ryan	20.00	9.00	2.50
☐ CP3	Kirk Gibson	2.00	.90	.25
☐ CP4	Joe Carter	2.50	1.10	.30
☐ CP5	George Brett	8.00	3.60	1.00
☐ CP6	Roberto Alomar	4.00	1.80	.50
☐ CP7	Ozzie Smith	4.00	1.80	.50
☐ CP8	Kirby Puckett	7.00	3.10	.85
☐ CP9	Bret Saberhagen	2.00	.90	.25
☐ CP10	Steve Garvey	2.00	.90	.25

1995 SP Championship Fall Classic

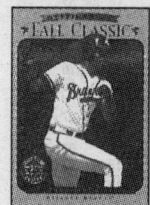

This nine-card set was randomly inserted in
packs at a rate of one in 40. The set is
comprised of players who had never been
to the World Series prior to the 1995 Fall
Classic. The fronts have a color-action
photo with the game background in foil.
There is a grain-colored border with the
word "Destination" at the top in bronze-foil
and "Fall Classic" underneath in black. The
backs have a small, color picture inside a
black box with player information underneath. Diecut versions were inserted at a
rate of one in 72 packs and are valued at
1.5X to 3X the prices below.

	MINT	NRMT	EXC
COMPLETE SET (9)	175.00	80.00	22.00
COMMON CARD (1-9)	8.00	3.60	1.00
*DIECUTS: 1.25X TO 2.5X BASIC CARDS			

☐ 1	Ken Griffey Jr.	40.00	18.00	5.00
☐ 2	Frank Thomas	40.00	18.00	5.00
☐ 3	Albert Belle	15.00	6.75	1.85
☐ 4	Mike Piazza	15.00	6.75	1.85
☐ 5	Don Mattingly	20.00	9.00	2.50
☐ 6	Hideo Nomo	25.00	11.00	3.10
☐ 7	Greg Maddux	40.00	18.00	5.00
☐ 8	Fred McGriff	8.00	3.60	1.00
☐ 9	Barry Bonds	10.00	4.50	1.25

1991 Stadium Club

This 600-card standard size set marked
Topps first entry into the mass market with
a premium quality set. The set features borderless full-color action photos on the front
with the name of the player and the Topps
Stadium club logo on the bottom of the
card, while the back of the card has the
basic biographical information as well as
making use of the Fastball BARS system
and an inset photo of the player's Topps
rookie card. The set was issued in two
series of 300 cards each. Series II cards were
also available at McDonald's restaurants in
the Northeast at three cards per pack.
Rookie Cards include Jeff Bagwell, Jeff
Conine, Luis Gonzalez, Brian McRae,
Pedro Munoz, and Phil Plantier.

	MINT	NRMT	EXC
COMPLETE SET (600)	120.00	55.00	15.00
COMPLETE SERIES 1 (300)	80.00	36.00	10.00
COMPLETE SERIES 2 (300)	40.00	18.00	5.00
COMMON CARD (1-300)	.15	.07	.02
COMMON CARD (301-600)	.15	.07	.02

☐ 1	Dave Stewart TUX	.50	.23	.06
☐ 2	Wally Joyner	.50	.23	.06
☐ 3	Shawon Dunston	.15	.07	.02
☐ 4	Darren Daulton	.50	.23	.06
☐ 5	Will Clark	1.00	.45	.12
☐ 6	Sammy Sosa	1.50	.70	.19
☐ 7	Dan Plesac	.15	.07	.02
☐ 8	Marquis Grissom	1.25	.55	.16
☐ 9	Erik Hanson	.15	.07	.02
☐ 10	Geno Petralli	.15	.07	.02
☐ 11	Jose Rijo	.30	.14	.04
☐ 12	Carlos Quintana	.15	.07	.02
☐ 13	Junior Ortiz	.15	.07	.02
☐ 14	Bob Walk	.15	.07	.02

☐ 15 Mike Macfarlane	.15	.07	.02
☐ 16 Eric Yelding	.15	.07	.02
☐ 17 Bryn Smith	.15	.07	.02
☐ 18 Bip Roberts	.30	.14	.04
☐ 19 Mike Scioscia	.15	.07	.02
☐ 20 Mark Williamson	.15	.07	.02
☐ 21 Don Mattingly	3.00	1.35	.35
☐ 22 John Franco	.50	.23	.06
☐ 23 Chet Lemon	.15	.07	.02
☐ 24 Tom Henke	.30	.14	.04
☐ 25 Jerry Browne	.15	.07	.02
☐ 26 Dave Justice	1.50	.70	.19
☐ 27 Mark Langston	.50	.23	.06
☐ 28 Damon Berryhill	.15	.07	.02
☐ 29 Kevin Bass	.15	.07	.02
☐ 30 Scott Fletcher	.15	.07	.02
☐ 31 Moises Alou	1.25	.55	.16
☐ 32 Dave Valle	.15	.07	.02
☐ 33 Jody Reed	.15	.07	.02
☐ 34 Dave West	.15	.07	.02
☐ 35 Kevin McReynolds	.15	.07	.02
☐ 36 Pat Combs	.15	.07	.02
☐ 37 Eric Davis	.30	.14	.04
☐ 38 Bret Saberhagen	.50	.23	.06
☐ 39 Stan Javier	.15	.07	.02
☐ 40 Chuck Cary	.15	.07	.02
☐ 41 Tony Phillips	.50	.23	.06
☐ 42 Lee Smith	.50	.23	.06
☐ 43 Tim Teufel	.15	.07	.02
☐ 44 Lance Dickson	.15	.07	.02
☐ 45 Greg Litton	.15	.07	.02
☐ 46 Teddy Higuera	.15	.07	.02
☐ 47 Edgar Martinez	1.00	.45	.12
☐ 48 Steve Avery	.75	.35	.09
☐ 49 Walt Weiss	.15	.07	.02
☐ 50 David Segui	.15	.07	.02
☐ 51 Andy Benes	.30	.14	.04
☐ 52 Karl Rhodes	.15	.07	.02
☐ 53 Neal Heaton	.15	.07	.02
☐ 54 Danny Gladden	.15	.07	.02
☐ 55 Luis Rivera	.15	.07	.02
☐ 56 Kevin Brown	.15	.07	.02
☐ 57 Frank Thomas	15.00	6.75	1.85
☐ 58 Terry Mulholland	.15	.07	.02
☐ 59 Dick Schofield	.15	.07	.02
☐ 60 Ron Darling	.15	.07	.02
☐ 61 Sandy Alomar Jr.	.30	.14	.04
☐ 62 Dave Stieb	.15	.07	.02
☐ 63 Alan Trammell	.50	.23	.06
☐ 64 Matt Nokes	.15	.07	.02
☐ 65 Lenny Harris	.15	.07	.02
☐ 66 Milt Thompson	.15	.07	.02
☐ 67 Storm Davis	.15	.07	.02
☐ 68 Joe Oliver	.15	.07	.02
☐ 69 Andres Galarraga	.50	.23	.06
☐ 70 Ozzie Guillen	.50	.23	.06
☐ 71 Ken Howell	.15	.07	.02
☐ 72 Garry Templeton	.15	.07	.02
☐ 73 Derrick May	.30	.14	.04
☐ 74 Xavier Hernandez	.15	.07	.02
☐ 75 Dave Parker	.30	.14	.04
☐ 76 Rick Aguilera	.30	.14	.04
☐ 77 Robby Thompson	.30	.14	.04
☐ 78 Pete Incaviglia	.15	.07	.02
☐ 79 Bob Welch	.15	.07	.02
☐ 80 Randy Milligan	.15	.07	.02
☐ 81 Chuck Finley	.30	.14	.04
☐ 82 Alvin Davis	.15	.07	.02
☐ 83 Tim Naehring	1.00	.45	.12
☐ 84 Jay Bell	.30	.14	.04
☐ 85 Joe Magrane	.15	.07	.02
☐ 86 Howard Johnson	.15	.07	.02
☐ 87 Jack McDowell	.50	.23	.06
☐ 88 Kevin Seitzer	.15	.07	.02
☐ 89 Bruce Ruffin	.15	.07	.02
☐ 90 Fernando Valenzuela	.15	.07	.02
☐ 91 Terry Kennedy	.15	.07	.02
☐ 92 Barry Larkin	1.00	.45	.12
☐ 93 Larry Walker	1.50	.70	.19
☐ 94 Luis Salazar	.15	.07	.02
☐ 95 Gary Sheffield	1.25	.55	.16
☐ 96 Bobby Witt	.15	.07	.02
☐ 97 Lonnie Smith	.15	.07	.02
☐ 98 Bryan Harvey	.15	.07	.02
☐ 99 Mookie Wilson	.15	.07	.02
☐ 100 Dwight Gooden	.15	.07	.02
☐ 101 Lou Whitaker	.30	.14	.04
☐ 102 Ron Karkovice	.15	.07	.02
☐ 103 Jesse Barfield	.15	.07	.02
☐ 104 Jose DeJesus	.15	.07	.02
☐ 105 Benito Santiago	.30	.14	.04
☐ 106 Brian Holman	.15	.07	.02
☐ 107 Rafael Ramirez	.15	.07	.02
☐ 108 Ellis Burks	.30	.14	.04
☐ 109 Mike Bielecki	.15	.07	.02
☐ 110 Kirby Puckett	2.00	.90	.25
☐ 111 Terry Shumpert	.15	.07	.02
☐ 112 Chuck Crim	.15	.07	.02
☐ 113 Todd Benzinger	.15	.07	.02
☐ 114 Brian Barnes	.15	.07	.02
☐ 115 Carlos Baerga	3.00	1.35	.35
☐ 116 Kal Daniels	.15	.07	.02
☐ 117 Dave Johnson	.15	.07	.02
☐ 118 Andy Van Slyke	.30	.14	.04
☐ 119 John Burkett	.30	.14	.04
☐ 120 Rickey Henderson	.60	.25	.07
☐ 121 Tim Jones	.15	.07	.02
☐ 122 Daryl Irvine	.15	.07	.02
☐ 123 Ruben Sierra	.50	.23	.06
☐ 124 Jim Abbott	.50	.23	.06
☐ 125 Daryl Boston	.15	.07	.02
☐ 126 Greg Maddux	6.00	2.70	.75
☐ 127 Von Hayes	.15	.07	.02
☐ 128 Mike Fitzgerald	.15	.07	.02
☐ 129 Wayne Edwards	.15	.07	.02
☐ 130 Greg Briley	.15	.07	.02
☐ 131 Rob Dibble	.15	.07	.02
☐ 132 Gene Larkin	.15	.07	.02
☐ 133 David Wells	.15	.07	.02
☐ 134 Steve Balboni	.15	.07	.02
☐ 135 Greg Vaughn	.30	.14	.04
☐ 136 Mark Davis	.15	.07	.02
☐ 137 Dave Rhode	.15	.07	.02
☐ 138 Eric Show	.15	.07	.02
☐ 139 Bobby Bonilla	.50	.23	.06
☐ 140 Dana Kiecker	.15	.07	.02
☐ 141 Gary Pettis	.15	.07	.02
☐ 142 Dennis Boyd	.15	.07	.02
☐ 143 Mike Benjamin	.15	.07	.02
☐ 144 Luis Polonia	.30	.14	.04
☐ 145 Doug Jones	.15	.07	.02
☐ 146 Al Newman	.15	.07	.02
☐ 147 Alex Fernandez	1.50	.70	.19
☐ 148 Bill Doran	.15	.07	.02
☐ 149 Kevin Elster	.15	.07	.02
☐ 150 Len Dykstra	.50	.23	.06
☐ 151 Mike Gallego	.15	.07	.02
☐ 152 Tim Belcher	.15	.07	.02
☐ 153 Jay Buhner	.75	.35	.09
☐ 154 Ozzie Smith UER	1.25	.55	.16
(Rookie card is 1979,			
but card back says '78)			

☐ 155 Jose Canseco	1.00	.45	.12
☐ 156 Gregg Olson	.15	.07	.02
☐ 157 Charlie O'Brien	.15	.07	.02
☐ 158 Frank Tanana	.15	.07	.02
☐ 159 George Brett	2.50	1.10	.30
☐ 160 Jeff Huson	.15	.07	.02
☐ 161 Kevin Tapani	.15	.07	.02
☐ 162 Jerome Walton	.15	.07	.02
☐ 163 Charlie Hayes	.30	.14	.04
☐ 164 Chris Bosio	.15	.07	.02
☐ 165 Chris Sabo	.15	.07	.02
☐ 166 Lance Parrish	.30	.14	.04
☐ 167 Don Robinson	.15	.07	.02
☐ 168 Manny Lee	.15	.07	.02
☐ 169 Dennis Rasmussen	.15	.07	.02
☐ 170 Wade Boggs	.75	.35	.09
☐ 171 Bob Geren	.15	.07	.02
☐ 172 Mackey Sasser	.15	.07	.02
☐ 173 Julio Franco	.30	.14	.04
☐ 174 Otis Nixon	.15	.07	.02
☐ 175 Bert Blyleven	.50	.23	.06
☐ 176 Craig Biggio	.60	.25	.07
☐ 177 Eddie Murray	.60	.25	.07
☐ 178 Randy Tomlin	.15	.07	.02
☐ 179 Tino Martinez	1.00	.45	.12
☐ 180 Carlton Fisk	.50	.23	.06
☐ 181 Dwight Smith	.15	.07	.02
☐ 182 Scott Garrelts	.15	.07	.02
☐ 183 Jim Gantner	.15	.07	.02
☐ 184 Dickie Thon	.15	.07	.02
☐ 185 John Farrell	.15	.07	.02
☐ 186 Cecil Fielder	.75	.35	.09
☐ 187 Glenn Braggs	.15	.07	.02
☐ 188 Allan Anderson	.15	.07	.02
☐ 189 Kurt Stillwell	.15	.07	.02
☐ 190 Jose Oquendo	.15	.07	.02
☐ 191 Joe Orsulak	.15	.07	.02
☐ 192 Ricky Jordan	.15	.07	.02
☐ 193 Kelly Downs	.15	.07	.02
☐ 194 Delino DeShields	.30	.14	.04
☐ 195 Omar Vizquel	.15	.07	.02
☐ 196 Mark Carreon	.15	.07	.02
☐ 197 Mike Harkey	.15	.07	.02
☐ 198 Jack Howell	.15	.07	.02
☐ 199 Lance Johnson	.30	.14	.04
☐ 200 Nolan Ryan TUX	8.00	3.60	1.00
☐ 201 John Marzano	.15	.07	.02
☐ 202 Doug Drabek	.30	.14	.04
☐ 203 Mark Lemke	.15	.07	.02
☐ 204 Steve Sax	.15	.07	.02
☐ 205 Greg Harris	.15	.07	.02
☐ 206 B.J. Surhoff	.15	.07	.02
☐ 207 Todd Burns	.15	.07	.02
☐ 208 Jose Gonzalez	.15	.07	.02
☐ 209 Mike Scott	.15	.07	.02
☐ 210 Dave Magadan	.15	.07	.02
☐ 211 Dante Bichette	1.50	.70	.19
☐ 212 Trevor Wilson	.15	.07	.02
☐ 213 Hector Villanueva	.15	.07	.02
☐ 214 Dan Pasqua	.15	.07	.02
☐ 215 Greg Colbrunn	.75	.35	.09
☐ 216 Mike Jeffcoat	.15	.07	.02
☐ 217 Harold Reynolds	.15	.07	.02
☐ 218 Paul O'Neill	.50	.23	.06
☐ 219 Mark Guthrie	.15	.07	.02
☐ 220 Barry Bonds	2.00	.90	.25
☐ 221 Jimmy Key	.30	.14	.04
☐ 222 Billy Ripken	.15	.07	.02
☐ 223 Tom Pagnozzi	.15	.07	.02
☐ 224 Bo Jackson	.50	.23	.06
☐ 225 Sid Fernandez	.30	.14	.04
☐ 226 Mike Marshall	.15	.07	.02
☐ 227 John Kruk	.50	.23	.06
☐ 228 Mike Fetters	.15	.07	.02
☐ 229 Eric Anthony	.15	.07	.02
☐ 230 Ryne Sandberg	2.00	.90	.25
☐ 231 Carney Lansford	.30	.14	.04
☐ 232 Melido Perez	.15	.07	.02
☐ 233 Jose Lind	.15	.07	.02
☐ 234 Darryl Hamilton	.30	.14	.04
☐ 235 Tom Browning	.15	.07	.02
☐ 236 Spike Owen	.15	.07	.02
☐ 237 Juan Gonzalez	5.00	2.20	.60
☐ 238 Felix Fermin	.15	.07	.02
☐ 239 Keith Miller	.15	.07	.02
☐ 240 Mark Gubicza	.15	.07	.02
☐ 241 Kent Anderson	.15	.07	.02
☐ 242 Alvaro Espinoza	.15	.07	.02
☐ 243 Dale Murphy	.15	.07	.02
☐ 244 Orel Hershiser	.50	.23	.06
☐ 245 Paul Molitor	.75	.35	.09
☐ 246 Eddie Whitson	.15	.07	.02
☐ 247 Joe Girardi	.15	.07	.02
☐ 248 Kent Hrbek	.30	.14	.04
☐ 249 Bill Sampen	.15	.07	.02
☐ 250 Kevin Mitchell	.30	.14	.04
☐ 251 Mariano Duncan	.15	.07	.02
☐ 252 Scott Bradley	.15	.07	.02
☐ 253 Mike Greenwell	.50	.23	.06
☐ 254 Tom Gordon	.30	.14	.04
☐ 255 Todd Zeile	.30	.14	.04
☐ 256 Bobby Thigpen	.15	.07	.02
☐ 257 Gregg Jefferies	.50	.23	.06
☐ 258 Kenny Rogers	.15	.07	.02
☐ 259 Shane Mack	.15	.07	.02
☐ 260 Zane Smith	.15	.07	.02
☐ 261 Mitch Williams	.30	.14	.04
☐ 262 Jim Deshaies	.15	.07	.02
☐ 263 Dave Winfield	.50	.23	.06
☐ 264 Ben McDonald	.30	.14	.04
☐ 265 Randy Ready	.15	.07	.02
☐ 266 Pat Borders	.15	.07	.02
☐ 267 Jose Uribe	.15	.07	.02
☐ 268 Derek Lilliquist	.15	.07	.02
☐ 269 Greg Brock	.15	.07	.02
☐ 270 Ken Griffey Jr.	15.00	6.75	1.85
☐ 271 Jeff Gray	.15	.07	.02
☐ 272 Danny Tartabull	.30	.14	.04
☐ 273 Denny Martinez	.30	.14	.04
☐ 274 Robin Ventura	1.00	.45	.12
☐ 275 Randy Myers	.50	.23	.06
☐ 276 Jack Daugherty	.15	.07	.02
☐ 277 Greg Gagne	.15	.07	.02
☐ 278 Jay Howell	.15	.07	.02
☐ 279 Mike LaValliere	.15	.07	.02
☐ 280 Rex Hudler	.15	.07	.02
☐ 281 Mike Simms	.15	.07	.02
☐ 282 Kevin Maas	.15	.07	.02
☐ 283 Jeff Ballard	.15	.07	.02
☐ 284 Dave Henderson	.15	.07	.02
☐ 285 Pete O'Brien	.15	.07	.02
☐ 286 Brook Jacoby	.15	.07	.02
☐ 287 Mike Henneman	.15	.07	.02
☐ 288 Greg Olson	.15	.07	.02
☐ 289 Greg Myers	.15	.07	.02
☐ 290 Mark Grace	.60	.25	.07
☐ 291 Shawn Abner	.15	.07	.02
☐ 292 Frank Viola	.15	.07	.02
☐ 293 Lee Stevens	.15	.07	.02
☐ 294 Jason Grimsley	.15	.07	.02
☐ 295 Matt Williams	2.00	.90	.25
☐ 296 Ron Robinson	.15	.07	.02

☐ 297 Tom Brunansky	.15	.07	.02
☐ 298 Checklist 1-100	.15	.07	.02
☐ 299 Checklist 101-200	.15	.07	.02
☐ 300 Checklist 201-300	.15	.07	.02
☐ 301 Darryl Strawberry	.30	.14	.04
☐ 302 Bud Black	.15	.07	.02
☐ 303 Harold Baines	.50	.23	.06
☐ 304 Roberto Alomar	1.50	.70	.19
☐ 305 Norm Charlton	.15	.07	.02
☐ 306 Gary Thurman	.15	.07	.02
☐ 307 Mike Felder	.15	.07	.02
☐ 308 Tony Gwynn	2.00	.90	.25
☐ 309 Roger Clemens	1.25	.55	.16
☐ 310 Andre Dawson	.50	.23	.06
☐ 311 Scott Radinsky	.15	.07	.02
☐ 312 Bob Melvin	.15	.07	.02
☐ 313 Kirk McCaskill	.15	.07	.02
☐ 314 Pedro Guerrero	.30	.14	.04
☐ 315 Walt Terrell	.15	.07	.02
☐ 316 Sam Horn	.15	.07	.02
☐ 317 Wes Chamberlain UER	.15	.07	.02
(Card listed as 1989			
Debut card, should be 1990)			
☐ 318 Pedro Munoz	.30	.14	.04
☐ 319 Roberto Kelly	.30	.14	.04
☐ 320 Mark Portugal	.15	.07	.02
☐ 321 Tim McIntosh	.15	.07	.02
☐ 322 Jesse Orosco	.15	.07	.02
☐ 323 Gary Green	.15	.07	.02
☐ 324 Greg Harris	.15	.07	.02
☐ 325 Hubie Brooks	.15	.07	.02
☐ 326 Chris Nabholz	.15	.07	.02
☐ 327 Terry Pendleton	.15	.07	.02
☐ 328 Eric King	.15	.07	.02
☐ 329 Chili Davis	.50	.23	.06
☐ 330 Anthony Telford	.15	.07	.02
☐ 331 Kelly Gruber	.15	.07	.02
☐ 332 Dennis Eckersley	.50	.23	.06
☐ 333 Mel Hall	.15	.07	.02
☐ 334 Bob Kipper	.15	.07	.02
☐ 335 Willie McGee	.30	.14	.04
☐ 336 Steve Olin	.15	.07	.02
☐ 337 Steve Buechele	.15	.07	.02
☐ 338 Scott Leius	.15	.07	.02
☐ 339 Hal Morris	.30	.14	.04
☐ 340 Jose Offerman	.30	.14	.04
☐ 341 Kent Mercker	.75	.35	.09
☐ 342 Ken Griffey Sr.	.30	.14	.04
☐ 343 Pete Harnisch	.30	.14	.04
☐ 344 Kirk Gibson	.50	.23	.06
☐ 345 Dave Smith	.15	.07	.02
☐ 346 Dave Martinez	.15	.07	.02
☐ 347 Atlee Hammaker	.15	.07	.02
☐ 348 Brian Downing	.15	.07	.02
☐ 349 Todd Hundley	.30	.14	.04
☐ 350 Candy Maldonado	.15	.07	.02
☐ 351 Dwight Evans	.30	.14	.04
☐ 352 Steve Searcy	.15	.07	.02
☐ 353 Gary Gaetti	.15	.07	.02
☐ 354 Jeff Reardon	.30	.14	.04
☐ 355 Travis Fryman	2.00	.90	.25
☐ 356 Dave Righetti	.15	.07	.02
☐ 357 Fred McGriff	1.00	.45	.12
☐ 358 Don Slaught	.15	.07	.02
☐ 359 Gene Nelson	.15	.07	.02
☐ 360 Billy Spiers	.15	.07	.02
☐ 361 Lee Guetterman	.15	.07	.02
☐ 362 Darren Lewis	.30	.14	.04
☐ 363 Duane Ward	.15	.07	.02
☐ 364 Lloyd Moseby	.15	.07	.02
☐ 365 John Smoltz	.50	.23	.06
☐ 366 Felix Jose	.15	.07	.02
☐ 367 David Cone	.75	.35	.09
☐ 368 Wally Backman	.15	.07	.02
☐ 369 Jeff Montgomery	.30	.14	.04
☐ 370 Rich Garces	.15	.07	.02
☐ 371 Billy Hatcher	.15	.07	.02
☐ 372 Bill Swift	.15	.07	.02
☐ 373 Jim Eisenreich	.15	.07	.02
☐ 374 Rob Ducey	.15	.07	.02
☐ 375 Tim Crews	.15	.07	.02
☐ 376 Steve Finley	.15	.07	.02
☐ 377 Jeff Blauser	.30	.14	.04
☐ 378 Willie Wilson	.15	.07	.02
☐ 379 Gerald Perry	.15	.07	.02
☐ 380 Jose Mesa	.15	.07	.02
☐ 381 Pat Kelly	.30	.14	.04
☐ 382 Matt Merullo	.15	.07	.02
☐ 383 Ivan Calderon	.15	.07	.02
☐ 384 Scott Chiamparino	.15	.07	.02
☐ 385 Lloyd McClendon	.15	.07	.02
☐ 386 Dave Bergman	.15	.07	.02
☐ 387 Ed Sprague	.15	.07	.02
☐ 388 Jeff Bagwell	6.00	2.70	.75
☐ 389 Brett Butler	.50	.23	.06
☐ 390 Larry Andersen	.15	.07	.02
☐ 391 Glenn Davis	.15	.07	.02
☐ 392 Alex Cole UER	.15	.07	.02
(Front photo actually			
Otis Nixon)			
☐ 393 Mike Heath	.15	.07	.02
☐ 394 Danny Darwin	.15	.07	.02
☐ 395 Steve Lake	.15	.07	.02
☐ 396 Tim Layana	.15	.07	.02
☐ 397 Terry Leach	.15	.07	.02
☐ 398 Bill Wegman	.15	.07	.02
☐ 399 Mark McGwire	1.00	.45	.12
☐ 400 Mike Boddicker	.15	.07	.02
☐ 401 Steve Howe	.15	.07	.02
☐ 402 Bernard Gilkey	.30	.14	.04
☐ 403 Thomas Howard	.15	.07	.02
☐ 404 Rafael Belliard	.15	.07	.02
☐ 405 Tom Candiotti	.15	.07	.02
☐ 406 Rene Gonzales	.15	.07	.02
☐ 407 Chuck McElroy	.15	.07	.02
☐ 408 Paul Sorrento	1.00	.45	.12
☐ 409 Randy Johnson	2.00	.90	.25
☐ 410 Brady Anderson	.30	.14	.04
☐ 411 Dennis Cook	.15	.07	.02
☐ 412 Mickey Tettleton	.30	.14	.04
☐ 413 Mike Stanton	.15	.07	.02
☐ 414 Ken Oberkfell	.15	.07	.02
☐ 415 Rick Honeycutt	.15	.07	.02
☐ 416 Nelson Santovenia	.15	.07	.02
☐ 417 Bob Tewksbury	.15	.07	.02
☐ 418 Brent Mayne	.15	.07	.02
☐ 419 Steve Farr	.15	.07	.02
☐ 420 Phil Stephenson	.15	.07	.02
☐ 421 Jeff Russell	.15	.07	.02
☐ 422 Chris James	.15	.07	.02
☐ 423 Tim Leary	.15	.07	.02
☐ 424 Gary Carter	.50	.23	.06
☐ 425 Glenallen Hill	.15	.07	.02
☐ 426 Matt Young UER	.15	.07	.02
(Card mentions 83T/Tr			
as RC, but 84T shown)			
☐ 427 Sid Bream	.15	.07	.02
☐ 428 Greg Swindell	.15	.07	.02
☐ 429 Scott Aldred	.15	.07	.02
☐ 430 Cal Ripken	6.00	2.70	.75
☐ 431 Bill Landrum	.15	.07	.02
☐ 432 Earnest Riles	.15	.07	.02

☐ 433 Danny Jackson	.15	.07	.02
☐ 434 Casey Candaele	.15	.07	.02
☐ 435 Ken Hill	.75	.35	.09
☐ 436 Jaime Navarro	.15	.07	.02
☐ 437 Lance Blankenship	.15	.07	.02
☐ 438 Randy Velarde	.15	.07	.02
☐ 439 Frank DiPino	.15	.07	.02
☐ 440 Carl Nichols	.15	.07	.02
☐ 441 Jeff M. Robinson	.15	.07	.02
☐ 442 Deion Sanders	2.00	.90	.25
☐ 443 Vicente Palacios	.15	.07	.02
☐ 444 Devon White	.30	.14	.04
☐ 445 John Cerutti	.15	.07	.02
☐ 446 Tracy Jones	.15	.07	.02
☐ 447 Jack Morris	.50	.23	.06
☐ 448 Mitch Webster	.15	.07	.02
☐ 449 Bob Ojeda	.15	.07	.02
☐ 450 Oscar Azocar	.15	.07	.02
☐ 451 Luis Aquino	.15	.07	.02
☐ 452 Mark Whiten	.30	.14	.04
☐ 453 Stan Belinda	.15	.07	.02
☐ 454 Ron Gant	1.00	.45	.12
☐ 455 Jose DeLeon	.15	.07	.02
☐ 456 Mark Salas UER	.15	.07	.02
(Back has 85T photo, but calls it 86T)			
☐ 457 Junior Felix	.15	.07	.02
☐ 458 Wally Whitehurst	.15	.07	.02
☐ 459 Phil Plantier	.75	.35	.09
☐ 460 Juan Berenguer	.15	.07	.02
☐ 461 Franklin Stubbs	.15	.07	.02
☐ 462 Joe Boever	.15	.07	.02
☐ 463 Tim Wallach	.15	.07	.02
☐ 464 Mike Moore	.15	.07	.02
☐ 465 Albert Belle	5.00	2.20	.60
☐ 466 Mike Witt	.15	.07	.02
☐ 467 Craig Worthington	.15	.07	.02
☐ 468 Jerald Clark	.15	.07	.02
☐ 469 Scott Terry	.15	.07	.02
☐ 470 Milt Cuyler	.15	.07	.02
☐ 471 John Smiley	.15	.07	.02
☐ 472 Charles Nagy	.30	.14	.04
☐ 473 Alan Mills	.15	.07	.02
☐ 474 John Russell	.15	.07	.02
☐ 475 Bruce Hurst	.15	.07	.02
☐ 476 Andujar Cedeno	.30	.14	.04
☐ 477 Dave Eiland	.15	.07	.02
☐ 478 Brian McRae	1.25	.55	.16
☐ 479 Mike LaCoss	.15	.07	.02
☐ 480 Chris Gwynn	.15	.07	.02
☐ 481 Jamie Moyer	.15	.07	.02
☐ 482 John Olerud	.30	.14	.04
☐ 483 Efrain Valdez	.15	.07	.02
☐ 484 Sil Campusano	.15	.07	.02
☐ 485 Pascual Perez	.15	.07	.02
☐ 486 Gary Redus	.15	.07	.02
☐ 487 Andy Hawkins	.15	.07	.02
☐ 488 Cory Snyder	.15	.07	.02
☐ 489 Chris Hoiles	.30	.14	.04
☐ 490 Ron Hassey	.15	.07	.02
☐ 491 Gary Wayne	.15	.07	.02
☐ 492 Mark Lewis	.15	.07	.02
☐ 493 Scott Coolbaugh	.15	.07	.02
☐ 494 Gerald Young	.15	.07	.02
☐ 495 Juan Samuel	.15	.07	.02
☐ 496 Willie Fraser	.15	.07	.02
☐ 497 Jeff Treadway	.15	.07	.02
☐ 498 Vince Coleman	.15	.07	.02
☐ 499 Cris Carpenter	.15	.07	.02
☐ 500 Jack Clark	.30	.14	.04
☐ 501 Kevin Appier	1.25	.55	.16
☐ 502 Rafael Palmeiro	1.00	.45	.12
☐ 503 Hensley Meulens	.15	.07	.02
☐ 504 George Bell	.15	.07	.02
☐ 505 Tony Pena	.15	.07	.02
☐ 506 Roger McDowell	.15	.07	.02
☐ 507 Luis Sojo	.15	.07	.02
☐ 508 Mike Schooler	.15	.07	.02
☐ 509 Robin Yount	1.00	.45	.12
☐ 510 Jack Armstrong	.15	.07	.02
☐ 511 Rick Cerone	.15	.07	.02
☐ 512 Curt Wilkerson	.15	.07	.02
☐ 513 Joe Carter	1.00	.45	.12
☐ 514 Tim Burke	.15	.07	.02
☐ 515 Tony Fernandez	.15	.07	.02
☐ 516 Ramon Martinez	.50	.23	.06
☐ 517 Tim Hulett	.15	.07	.02
☐ 518 Terry Steinbach	.30	.14	.04
☐ 519 Pete Smith	.15	.07	.02
☐ 520 Ken Caminiti	.50	.23	.06
☐ 521 Shawn Boskie	.15	.07	.02
☐ 522 Mike Pagliarulo	.15	.07	.02
☐ 523 Tim Raines	.50	.23	.06
☐ 524 Alfredo Griffin	.15	.07	.02
☐ 525 Henry Cotto	.15	.07	.02
☐ 526 Mike Stanley	.30	.14	.04
☐ 527 Charlie Leibrandt	.15	.07	.02
☐ 528 Jeff King	.30	.14	.04
☐ 529 Eric Plunk	.15	.07	.02
☐ 530 Tom Lampkin	.15	.07	.02
☐ 531 Steve Bedrosian	.15	.07	.02
☐ 532 Tom Herr	.15	.07	.02
☐ 533 Craig Lefferts	.15	.07	.02
☐ 534 Jeff Reed	.15	.07	.02
☐ 535 Mickey Morandini	.15	.07	.02
☐ 536 Greg Cadaret	.15	.07	.02
☐ 537 Ray Lankford	2.00	.90	.25
☐ 538 John Candelaria	.15	.07	.02
☐ 539 Rob Deer	.15	.07	.02
☐ 540 Brad Arnsberg	.15	.07	.02
☐ 541 Mike Sharperson	.15	.07	.02
☐ 542 Jeff D. Robinson	.15	.07	.02
☐ 543 Mo Vaughn	5.00	2.20	.60
☐ 544 Jeff Parrett	.15	.07	.02
☐ 545 Willie Randolph	.30	.14	.04
☐ 546 Herm Winningham	.15	.07	.02
☐ 547 Jeff Innis	.15	.07	.02
☐ 548 Chuck Knoblauch	2.00	.90	.25
☐ 549 Tommy Greene UER	.30	.14	.04
(Born in North Carolina, not South Carolina)			
☐ 550 Jeff Hamilton	.15	.07	.02
☐ 551 Barry Jones	.15	.07	.02
☐ 552 Ken Dayley	.15	.07	.02
☐ 553 Rick Dempsey	.15	.07	.02
☐ 554 Greg Smith	.15	.07	.02
☐ 555 Mike Devereaux	.30	.14	.04
☐ 556 Keith Comstock	.15	.07	.02
☐ 557 Paul Faries	.15	.07	.02
☐ 558 Tom Glavine	1.00	.45	.12
☐ 559 Craig Grebeck	.15	.07	.02
☐ 560 Scott Erickson	.15	.07	.02
☐ 561 Joel Skinner	.15	.07	.02
☐ 562 Mike Morgan	.15	.07	.02
☐ 563 Dave Gallagher	.15	.07	.02
☐ 564 Todd Stottlemyre	.15	.07	.02
☐ 565 Rich Rodriguez	.15	.07	.02
☐ 566 Craig Wilson	.15	.07	.02
☐ 567 Jeff Brantley	.15	.07	.02
☐ 568 Scott Kamieniecki	.15	.07	.02
☐ 569 Steve Decker	.15	.07	.02
☐ 570 Juan Agosto	.15	.07	.02

☐ 571	Tommy Gregg	.15	.07	.02
☐ 572	Kevin Wickander	.15	.07	.02
☐ 573	Jamie Quirk UER	.15	.07	.02
	(Rookie card is 1976, but card back is 1990)			
☐ 574	Jerry Don Gleaton	.15	.07	.02
☐ 575	Chris Hammond	.15	.07	.02
☐ 576	Luis Gonzalez	.75	.35	.09
☐ 577	Russ Swan	.15	.07	.02
☐ 578	Jeff Conine	2.50	1.10	.30
☐ 579	Charlie Hough	.30	.14	.04
☐ 580	Jeff Kunkel	.15	.07	.02
☐ 581	Darrel Akerfelds	.15	.07	.02
☐ 582	Jeff Manto	.15	.07	.02
☐ 583	Alejandro Pena	.15	.07	.02
☐ 584	Mark Davidson	.15	.07	.02
☐ 585	Bob MacDonald	.15	.07	.02
☐ 586	Paul Assenmacher	.15	.07	.02
☐ 587	Dan Wilson	.15	.07	.02
☐ 588	Tom Bolton	.15	.07	.02
☐ 589	Brian Harper	.15	.07	.02
☐ 590	John Habyan	.15	.07	.02
☐ 591	John Orton	.15	.07	.02
☐ 592	Mark Gardner	.15	.07	.02
☐ 593	Turner Ward	.15	.07	.02
☐ 594	Bob Patterson	.15	.07	.02
☐ 595	Ed Nunez	.15	.07	.02
☐ 596	Gary Scott UER	.15	.07	.02
	(Major League Batting Record should be Minor League)			
☐ 597	Scott Bankhead	.15	.07	.02
☐ 598	Checklist 301-400	.15	.07	.02
☐ 599	Checklist 401-500	.15	.07	.02
☐ 600	Checklist 501-600	.15	.07	.02

1992 Stadium Club

The 1992 Topps Stadium Club baseball card set consists of 900 standard-size cards issued in three series of 300 cards each. The glossy color player photos on the fronts are full-bleed. The "Topps Stadium Club" logo is superimposed at the bottom of the card face, with the player's name appearing immediately below the logo. Some cards in the set have the Stadium Club logo printed upside down. The backs display a mini reprint of the player's rookie card and "BARS" (Baseball Analysis and Reporting System) statistics. A card-like application form for membership in Topps Stadium Club was inserted in each wax pack. Card numbers 591-600 in the second series form a "Members Choice" subset. Card numbers 601-610 in the third series form a "Members Choice" subset. Rookie Cards include Pat Listach and Bill Pulsipher.

	MINT	NRMT	EXC
COMPLETE SET (900)	60.00	27.00	7.50
COMPLETE SERIES 1 (300)	20.00	9.00	2.50
COMPLETE SERIES 2 (300)	20.00	9.00	2.50
COMPLETE SERIES 3 (300)	20.00	9.00	2.50
COMMON CARD (1-300)	.10	.05	.01
COMMON CARD (301-600)	.10	.05	.01
COMMON CARD (601-900)	.10	.05	.01

☐ 1	Cal Ripken UER	2.00	.90	.25
	(Misspelled Ripkin on card back)			
☐ 2	Eric Yelding	.10	.05	.01
☐ 3	Geno Petralli	.10	.05	.01
☐ 4	Wally Backman	.10	.05	.01
☐ 5	Milt Cuyler	.10	.05	.01
☐ 6	Kevin Bass	.10	.05	.01
☐ 7	Dante Bichette	.30	.14	.04
☐ 8	Ray Lankford	.25	.11	.03
☐ 9	Mel Hall	.10	.05	.01
☐ 10	Joe Carter	.25	.11	.03
☐ 11	Juan Samuel	.10	.05	.01
☐ 12	Jeff Montgomery	.15	.07	.02
☐ 13	Glenn Braggs	.10	.05	.01
☐ 14	Henry Cotto	.10	.05	.01
☐ 15	Deion Sanders	.40	.18	.05
☐ 16	Dick Schofield	.10	.05	.01
☐ 17	David Cone	.25	.11	.03
☐ 18	Chili Davis	.25	.11	.03
☐ 19	Tom Foley	.10	.05	.01
☐ 20	Ozzie Guillen	.15	.07	.02
☐ 21	Luis Salazar	.10	.05	.01
☐ 22	Terry Steinbach	.15	.07	.02
☐ 23	Chris James	.10	.05	.01
☐ 24	Jeff King	.15	.07	.02
☐ 25	Carlos Quintana	.10	.05	.01
☐ 26	Mike Maddux	.10	.05	.01
☐ 27	Tommy Greene	.10	.05	.01
☐ 28	Jeff Russell	.10	.05	.01
☐ 29	Steve Finley	.15	.07	.02
☐ 30	Mike Flanagan	.10	.05	.01
☐ 31	Darren Lewis	.15	.07	.02
☐ 32	Mark Lee	.10	.05	.01
☐ 33	Willie Fraser	.10	.05	.01
☐ 34	Mike Henneman	.10	.05	.01
☐ 35	Kevin Maas	.10	.05	.01
☐ 36	Dave Hansen	.10	.05	.01
☐ 37	Erik Hanson	.10	.05	.01
☐ 38	Bill Doran	.10	.05	.01
☐ 39	Mike Boddicker	.10	.05	.01
☐ 40	Vince Coleman	.10	.05	.01
☐ 41	Devon White	.15	.07	.02
☐ 42	Mark Gardner	.10	.05	.01
☐ 43	Scott Lewis	.10	.05	.01
☐ 44	Juan Berenguer	.10	.05	.01
☐ 45	Carney Lansford	.15	.07	.02
☐ 46	Curt Wilkerson	.10	.05	.01
☐ 47	Shane Mack	.10	.05	.01
☐ 48	Bip Roberts	.15	.07	.02
☐ 49	Greg A. Harris	.10	.05	.01
☐ 50	Ryne Sandberg	.50	.23	.06
☐ 51	Mark Whiten	.15	.07	.02
☐ 52	Jack McDowell	.25	.11	.03
☐ 53	Jimmy Jones	.10	.05	.01

☐ 54	Steve Lake	.10	.05	.01
☐ 55	Bud Black	.10	.05	.01
☐ 56	Dave Valle	.10	.05	.01
☐ 57	Kevin Reimer	.10	.05	.01
☐ 58	Rich Gedman UER	.10	.05	.01
	(Wrong BARS chart used)			
☐ 59	Travis Fryman	.25	.11	.03
☐ 60	Steve Avery	.25	.11	.03
☐ 61	Francisco de la Rosa	.10	.05	.01
☐ 62	Scott Hemond	.10	.05	.01
☐ 63	Hal Morris	.15	.07	.02
☐ 64	Hensley Meulens	.10	.05	.01
☐ 65	Frank Castillo	.10	.05	.01
☐ 66	Gene Larkin	.10	.05	.01
☐ 67	Jose DeLeon	.10	.05	.01
☐ 68	Al Osuna	.10	.05	.01
☐ 69	Dave Cochrane	.10	.05	.01
☐ 70	Robin Ventura	.25	.11	.03
☐ 71	John Cerutti	.10	.05	.01
☐ 72	Kevin Gross	.10	.05	.01
☐ 73	Ivan Calderon	.10	.05	.01
☐ 74	Mike Macfarlane	.10	.05	.01
☐ 75	Stan Belinda	.10	.05	.01
☐ 76	Shawn Hillegas	.10	.05	.01
☐ 77	Pat Borders	.10	.05	.01
☐ 78	Jim Vatcher	.10	.05	.01
☐ 79	Bobby Rose	.10	.05	.01
☐ 80	Roger Clemens	.30	.14	.04
☐ 81	Craig Worthington	.10	.05	.01
☐ 82	Jeff Treadway	.10	.05	.01
☐ 83	Jamie Quirk	.10	.05	.01
☐ 84	Randy Bush	.10	.05	.01
☐ 85	Anthony Young	.10	.05	.01
☐ 86	Trevor Wilson	.10	.05	.01
☐ 87	Jaime Navarro	.10	.05	.01
☐ 88	Les Lancaster	.10	.05	.01
☐ 89	Pat Kelly	.10	.05	.01
☐ 90	Alvin Davis	.10	.05	.01
☐ 91	Larry Andersen	.10	.05	.01
☐ 92	Rob Deer	.10	.05	.01
☐ 93	Mike Sharperson	.10	.05	.01
☐ 94	Lance Parrish	.15	.07	.02
☐ 95	Cecil Espy	.10	.05	.01
☐ 96	Tim Spehr	.10	.05	.01
☐ 97	Dave Stieb	.10	.05	.01
☐ 98	Terry Mulholland	.10	.05	.01
☐ 99	Dennis Boyd	.10	.05	.01
☐ 100	Barry Larkin	.30	.14	.04
☐ 101	Ryan Bowen	.10	.05	.01
☐ 102	Felix Fermin	.10	.05	.01
☐ 103	Luis Alicea	.10	.05	.01
☐ 104	Tim Hulett	.10	.05	.01
☐ 105	Rafael Belliard	.10	.05	.01
☐ 106	Mike Gallego	.10	.05	.01
☐ 107	Dave Righetti	.10	.05	.01
☐ 108	Jeff Schaefer	.10	.05	.01
☐ 109	Ricky Bones	.15	.07	.02
☐ 110	Scott Erickson	.10	.05	.01
☐ 111	Matt Nokes	.10	.05	.01
☐ 112	Bob Scanlan	.10	.05	.01
☐ 113	Tom Candiotti	.10	.05	.01
☐ 114	Sean Berry	.15	.07	.02
☐ 115	Kevin Morton	.10	.05	.01
☐ 116	Scott Fletcher	.10	.05	.01
☐ 117	B.J. Surhoff	.10	.05	.01
☐ 118	Dave Magadan UER	.10	.05	.01
	(Born Tampa, not Tamps)			
☐ 119	Bill Gullickson	.10	.05	.01
☐ 120	Marquis Grissom	.25	.11	.03
☐ 121	Lenny Harris	.10	.05	.01
☐ 122	Wally Joyner	.15	.07	.02
☐ 123	Kevin Brown	.15	.07	.02
☐ 124	Braulio Castillo	.10	.05	.01
☐ 125	Eric King	.10	.05	.01
☐ 126	Mark Portugal	.10	.05	.01
☐ 127	Calvin Jones	.10	.05	.01
☐ 128	Mike Heath	.10	.05	.01
☐ 129	Todd Van Poppel	.15	.07	.02
☐ 130	Benny Santiago	.15	.07	.02
☐ 131	Gary Thurman	.10	.05	.01
☐ 132	Joe Girardi	.10	.05	.01
☐ 133	Dave Eiland	.10	.05	.01
☐ 134	Orlando Merced	.15	.07	.02
☐ 135	Joe Orsulak	.10	.05	.01
☐ 136	John Burkett	.15	.07	.02
☐ 137	Ken Dayley	.10	.05	.01
☐ 138	Ken Hill	.25	.11	.03
☐ 139	Walt Terrell	.10	.05	.01
☐ 140	Mike Scioscia	.10	.05	.01
☐ 141	Junior Felix	.10	.05	.01
☐ 142	Ken Caminiti	.25	.11	.03
☐ 143	Carlos Baerga	.60	.25	.07
☐ 144	Tony Fossas	.10	.05	.01
☐ 145	Craig Grebeck	.10	.05	.01
☐ 146	Scott Bradley	.10	.05	.01
☐ 147	Kent Mercker	.10	.05	.01
☐ 148	Derrick May	.15	.07	.02
☐ 149	Jerald Clark	.10	.05	.01
☐ 150	George Brett	.75	.35	.09
☐ 151	Luis Quinones	.10	.05	.01
☐ 152	Mike Pagliarulo	.10	.05	.01
☐ 153	Jose Guzman	.10	.05	.01
☐ 154	Charlie O'Brien	.10	.05	.01
☐ 155	Darren Holmes	.10	.05	.01
☐ 156	Joe Boever	.10	.05	.01
☐ 157	Rich Monteleone	.10	.05	.01
☐ 158	Reggie Harris	.10	.05	.01
☐ 159	Roberto Alomar	.40	.18	.05
☐ 160	Robby Thompson	.15	.07	.02
☐ 161	Chris Hoiles	.15	.07	.02
☐ 162	Tom Pagnozzi	.10	.05	.01
☐ 163	Omar Vizquel	.10	.05	.01
☐ 164	John Candelaria	.10	.05	.01
☐ 165	Terry Shumpert	.10	.05	.01
☐ 166	Andy Mota	.10	.05	.01
☐ 167	Scott Bailes	.10	.05	.01
☐ 168	Jeff Blauser	.15	.07	.02
☐ 169	Steve Olin	.10	.05	.01
☐ 170	Doug Drabek	.15	.07	.02
☐ 171	Dave Bergman	.10	.05	.01
☐ 172	Eddie Whitson	.10	.05	.01
☐ 173	Gilberto Reyes	.10	.05	.01
☐ 174	Mark Grace	.25	.11	.03
☐ 175	Paul O'Neill	.25	.11	.03
☐ 176	Greg Cadaret	.10	.05	.01
☐ 177	Mark Williamson	.10	.05	.01
☐ 178	Casey Candaele	.10	.05	.01
☐ 179	Candy Maldonado	.10	.05	.01
☐ 180	Lee Smith	.25	.11	.03
☐ 181	Harold Reynolds	.10	.05	.01
☐ 182	David Justice	.30	.14	.04
☐ 183	Lenny Webster	.10	.05	.01
☐ 184	Donn Pall	.10	.05	.01
☐ 185	Gerald Alexander	.10	.05	.01
☐ 186	Jack Clark	.15	.07	.02
☐ 187	Stan Javier	.10	.05	.01
☐ 188	Ricky Jordan	.10	.05	.01
☐ 189	Franklin Stubbs	.10	.05	.01
☐ 190	Dennis Eckersley	.25	.11	.03
☐ 191	Danny Tartabull	.15	.07	.02
☐ 192	Pete O'Brien	.10	.05	.01
☐ 193	Mark Lewis	.10	.05	.01

☐ 194	Mike Felder	.10	.05	.01
☐ 195	Mickey Tettleton	.15	.07	.02
☐ 196	Dwight Smith	.10	.05	.01
☐ 197	Shawn Abner	.10	.05	.01
☐ 198	Jim Leyritz UER	.10	.05	.01
	(Career totals less			
	than 1991 totals)			
☐ 199	Mike Devereaux	.15	.07	.02
☐ 200	Craig Biggio	.25	.11	.03
☐ 201	Kevin Elster	.10	.05	.01
☐ 202	Rance Mulliniks	.10	.05	.01
☐ 203	Tony Fernandez	.10	.05	.01
☐ 204	Allan Anderson	.10	.05	.01
☐ 205	Herm Winningham	.10	.05	.01
☐ 206	Tim Jones	.10	.05	.01
☐ 207	Ramon Martinez	.25	.11	.03
☐ 208	Teddy Higuera	.10	.05	.01
☐ 209	John Kruk	.25	.11	.03
☐ 210	Jim Abbott	.25	.11	.03
☐ 211	Dean Palmer	.15	.07	.02
☐ 212	Mark Davis	.10	.05	.01
☐ 213	Jay Buhner	.25	.11	.03
☐ 214	Jesse Barfield	.10	.05	.01
☐ 215	Kevin Mitchell	.15	.07	.02
☐ 216	Mike LaValliere	.10	.05	.01
☐ 217	Mark Wohlers	.15	.07	.02
☐ 218	Dave Henderson	.10	.05	.01
☐ 219	Dave Smith	.10	.05	.01
☐ 220	Albert Belle	1.00	.45	.12
☐ 221	Spike Owen	.10	.05	.01
☐ 222	Jeff Gray	.10	.05	.01
☐ 223	Paul Gibson	.10	.05	.01
☐ 224	Bobby Thigpen	.10	.05	.01
☐ 225	Mike Mussina	.50	.23	.06
☐ 226	Darrin Jackson	.10	.05	.01
☐ 227	Luis Gonzalez	.15	.07	.02
☐ 228	Greg Briley	.10	.05	.01
☐ 229	Brent Mayne	.10	.05	.01
☐ 230	Paul Molitor	.25	.11	.03
☐ 231	Al Leiter	.10	.05	.01
☐ 232	Andy Van Slyke	.15	.07	.02
☐ 233	Ron Tingley	.10	.05	.01
☐ 234	Bernard Gilkey	.15	.07	.02
☐ 235	Kent Hrbek	.15	.07	.02
☐ 236	Eric Karros	.50	.23	.06
☐ 237	Randy Velarde	.10	.05	.01
☐ 238	Andy Allanson	.10	.05	.01
☐ 239	Willie McGee	.15	.07	.02
☐ 240	Juan Gonzalez	.75	.35	.09
☐ 241	Karl Rhodes	.10	.05	.01
☐ 242	Luis Mercedes	.10	.05	.01
☐ 243	Billy Swift	.15	.07	.02
☐ 244	Tommy Gregg	.10	.05	.01
☐ 245	David Howard	.10	.05	.01
☐ 246	Dave Hollins	.10	.05	.01
☐ 247	Kip Gross	.10	.05	.01
☐ 248	Walt Weiss	.10	.05	.01
☐ 249	Mackey Sasser	.10	.05	.01
☐ 250	Cecil Fielder	.25	.11	.03
☐ 251	Jerry Browne	.10	.05	.01
☐ 252	Doug Dascenzo	.10	.05	.01
☐ 253	Darryl Hamilton	.15	.07	.02
☐ 254	Dann Bilardello	.10	.05	.01
☐ 255	Luis Rivera	.10	.05	.01
☐ 256	Larry Walker	.30	.14	.04
☐ 257	Ron Karkovice	.10	.05	.01
☐ 258	Bob Tewksbury	.10	.05	.01
☐ 259	Jimmy Key	.15	.07	.02
☐ 260	Bernie Williams	.25	.11	.03
☐ 261	Gary Wayne	.10	.05	.01
☐ 262	Mike Simms UER	.10	.05	.01

	(Reversed negative)			
☐ 263	John Orton	.10	.05	.01
☐ 264	Marvin Freeman	.10	.05	.01
☐ 265	Mike Jeffcoat	.10	.05	.01
☐ 266	Roger Mason	.10	.05	.01
☐ 267	Edgar Martinez	.25	.11	.03
☐ 268	Henry Rodriguez	.15	.07	.02
☐ 269	Sam Horn	.10	.05	.01
☐ 270	Brian McRae	.25	.11	.03
☐ 271	Kirt Manwaring	.10	.05	.01
☐ 272	Mike Bordick	.10	.05	.01
☐ 273	Chris Sabo	.10	.05	.01
☐ 274	Jim Olander	.10	.05	.01
☐ 275	Greg W. Harris	.10	.05	.01
☐ 276	Dan Gakeler	.10	.05	.01
☐ 277	Bill Sampen	.10	.05	.01
☐ 278	Joel Skinner	.10	.05	.01
☐ 279	Curt Schilling	.10	.05	.01
☐ 280	Dale Murphy	.25	.11	.03
☐ 281	Lee Stevens	.10	.05	.01
☐ 282	Lonnie Smith	.10	.05	.01
☐ 283	Manuel Lee	.10	.05	.01
☐ 284	Shawn Boskie	.10	.05	.01
☐ 285	Kevin Seitzer	.10	.05	.01
☐ 286	Stan Royer	.10	.05	.01
☐ 287	John Dopson	.10	.05	.01
☐ 288	Scott Bullett	.10	.05	.01
☐ 289	Ken Patterson	.10	.05	.01
☐ 290	Todd Hundley	.10	.05	.01
☐ 291	Tim Leary	.10	.05	.01
☐ 292	Brett Butler	.25	.11	.03
☐ 293	Gregg Olson	.10	.05	.01
☐ 294	Jeff Brantley	.10	.05	.01
☐ 295	Brian Holman	.10	.05	.01
☐ 296	Brian Harper	.10	.05	.01
☐ 297	Brian Bohanon	.10	.05	.01
☐ 298	Checklist 1-100	.10	.05	.01
☐ 299	Checklist 101-200	.10	.05	.01
☐ 300	Checklist 201-300	.10	.05	.01
☐ 301	Frank Thomas	3.00	1.35	.35
☐ 302	Lloyd McClendon	.10	.05	.01
☐ 303	Brady Anderson	.15	.07	.02
☐ 304	Julio Valera	.10	.05	.01
☐ 305	Mike Aldrete	.10	.05	.01
☐ 306	Joe Oliver	.10	.05	.01
☐ 307	Todd Stottlemyre	.10	.05	.01
☐ 308	Rey Sanchez	.10	.05	.01
☐ 309	Gary Sheffield UER	.25	.11	.03
	(Listed as 5'1",			
	should be 5'11")			
☐ 310	Andujar Cedeno	.10	.05	.01
☐ 311	Kenny Rogers	.15	.07	.02
☐ 312	Bruce Hurst	.10	.05	.01
☐ 313	Mike Schooler	.10	.05	.01
☐ 314	Mike Benjamin	.10	.05	.01
☐ 315	Chuck Finley	.10	.05	.01
☐ 316	Mark Lemke	.10	.05	.01
☐ 317	Scott Livingstone	.10	.05	.01
☐ 318	Chris Nabholz	.10	.05	.01
☐ 319	Mike Humphreys	.10	.05	.01
☐ 320	Pedro Guerrero	.10	.05	.01
☐ 321	Willie Banks	.10	.05	.01
☐ 322	Tom Goodwin	.10	.05	.01
☐ 323	Hector Wagner	.10	.05	.01
☐ 324	Wally Ritchie	.10	.05	.01
☐ 325	Mo Vaughn	.75	.35	.09
☐ 326	Joe Klink	.10	.05	.01
☐ 327	Cal Eldred	.10	.05	.01
☐ 328	Daryl Boston	.10	.05	.01
☐ 329	Mike Huff	.10	.05	.01
☐ 330	Jeff Bagwell	1.00	.45	.12

331	Bob Milacki	.10	.05	.01
332	Tom Prince	.10	.05	.01
333	Pat Tabler	.10	.05	.01
334	Ced Landrum	.10	.05	.01
335	Reggie Jefferson	.10	.05	.01
336	Mo Sanford	.10	.05	.01
337	Kevin Ritz	.10	.05	.01
338	Gerald Perry	.10	.05	.01
339	Jeff Hamilton	.10	.05	.01
340	Tim Wallach	.10	.05	.01
341	Jeff Huson	.10	.05	.01
342	Jose Melendez	.10	.05	.01
343	Willie Wilson	.10	.05	.01
344	Mike Stanton	.10	.05	.01
345	Joel Johnston	.10	.05	.01
346	Lee Guetterman	.10	.05	.01
347	Francisco Oliveras	.10	.05	.01
348	Dave Burba	.10	.05	.01
349	Tim Crews	.10	.05	.01
350	Scott Leius	.10	.05	.01
351	Danny Cox	.10	.05	.01
352	Wayne Housie	.10	.05	.01
353	Chris Donnels	.10	.05	.01
354	Chris George	.10	.05	.01
355	Gerald Young	.10	.05	.01
356	Roberto Hernandez	.15	.07	.02
357	Neal Heaton	.10	.05	.01
358	Todd Frohwirth	.10	.05	.01
359	Jose Vizcaino	.10	.05	.01
360	Jim Thome	1.50	.70	.19
361	Craig Wilson	.10	.05	.01
362	Dave Haas	.10	.05	.01
363	Billy Hatcher	.10	.05	.01
364	John Barfield	.10	.05	.01
365	Luis Aquino	.10	.05	.01
366	Charlie Leibrandt	.10	.05	.01
367	Howard Farmer	.10	.05	.01
368	Bryn Smith	.10	.05	.01
369	Mickey Morandini	.10	.05	.01
370	Jose Canseco	.30	.14	.04
	(See also 597)			
371	Jose Uribe	.10	.05	.01
372	Bob MacDonald	.10	.05	.01
373	Luis Sojo	.10	.05	.01
374	Craig Shipley	.10	.05	.01
375	Scott Bankhead	.10	.05	.01
376	Greg Gagne	.10	.05	.01
377	Scott Cooper	.15	.07	.02
378	Jose Offerman	.10	.05	.01
379	Billy Spiers	.10	.05	.01
380	John Smiley	.10	.05	.01
381	Jeff Carter	.10	.05	.01
382	Heathcliff Slocumb	.15	.07	.02
383	Jeff Tackett	.10	.05	.01
384	John Kiely	.10	.05	.01
385	John Vander Wal	.10	.05	.01
386	Omar Olivares	.10	.05	.01
387	Ruben Sierra	.25	.11	.03
388	Tom Gordon	.15	.07	.02
389	Charles Nagy	.15	.07	.02
390	Dave Stewart	.25	.11	.03
391	Pete Harnisch	.10	.05	.01
392	Tim Burke	.10	.05	.01
393	Roberto Kelly	.15	.07	.02
394	Freddie Benavides	.10	.05	.01
395	Tom Glavine	.25	.11	.03
396	Wes Chamberlain	.10	.05	.01
397	Eric Gunderson	.10	.05	.01
398	Dave West	.10	.05	.01
399	Ellis Burks	.15	.07	.02
400	Ken Griffey Jr.	3.00	1.35	.35
401	Thomas Howard	.10	.05	.01
402	Juan Guzman	.15	.07	.02
403	Mitch Webster	.10	.05	.01
404	Matt Merullo	.10	.05	.01
405	Steve Buechele	.10	.05	.01
406	Danny Jackson	.10	.05	.01
407	Felix Jose	.10	.05	.01
408	Doug Piatt	.10	.05	.01
409	Jim Eisenreich	.10	.05	.01
410	Bryan Harvey	.10	.05	.01
411	Jim Austin	.10	.05	.01
412	Jim Poole	.10	.05	.01
413	Glenallen Hill	.10	.05	.01
414	Gene Nelson	.10	.05	.01
415	Ivan Rodriguez	.30	.14	.04
416	Frank Tanana	.10	.05	.01
417	Steve Decker	.10	.05	.01
418	Jason Grimsley	.10	.05	.01
419	Tim Layana	.10	.05	.01
420	Don Mattingly	1.00	.45	.12
421	Jerome Walton	.10	.05	.01
422	Rob Ducey	.10	.05	.01
423	Andy Benes	.15	.07	.02
424	John Marzano	.10	.05	.01
425	Gene Harris	.10	.05	.01
426	Tim Raines	.25	.11	.03
427	Bret Barberie	.10	.05	.01
428	Harvey Pulliam	.10	.05	.01
429	Cris Carpenter	.10	.05	.01
430	Howard Johnson	.10	.05	.01
431	Orel Hershiser	.25	.11	.03
432	Brian Hunter	.10	.05	.01
433	Kevin Tapani	.10	.05	.01
434	Rick Reed	.10	.05	.01
435	Ron Witmeyer	.10	.05	.01
436	Gary Gaetti	.10	.05	.01
437	Alex Cole	.10	.05	.01
438	Chito Martinez	.10	.05	.01
439	Greg Litton	.10	.05	.01
440	Julio Franco	.15	.07	.02
441	Mike Munoz	.10	.05	.01
442	Erik Pappas	.10	.05	.01
443	Pat Combs	.10	.05	.01
444	Lance Johnson	.10	.05	.01
445	Ed Sprague	.15	.07	.02
446	Mike Greenwell	.25	.11	.03
447	Milt Thompson	.10	.05	.01
448	Mike Magnante	.10	.05	.01
449	Chris Haney	.10	.05	.01
450	Robin Yount	.30	.14	.04
451	Rafael Ramirez	.10	.05	.01
452	Gino Minutelli	.10	.05	.01
453	Tom Lampkin	.10	.05	.01
454	Tony Perezchica	.10	.05	.01
455	Dwight Gooden	.10	.05	.01
456	Mark Guthrie	.10	.05	.01
457	Jay Howell	.10	.05	.01
458	Gary DiSarcina	.10	.05	.01
459	John Smoltz	.25	.11	.03
460	Will Clark	.30	.14	.04
461	Dave Otto	.10	.05	.01
462	Rob Maurer	.10	.05	.01
463	Dwight Evans	.15	.07	.02
464	Tom Brunansky	.10	.05	.01
465	Shawn Hare	.10	.05	.01
466	Geronimo Pena	.10	.05	.01
467	Alex Fernandez	.25	.11	.03
468	Greg Myers	.10	.05	.01
469	Jeff Fassero	.10	.05	.01
470	Len Dykstra	.25	.11	.03
471	Jeff Johnson	.10	.05	.01

□	472	Russ Swan	.10	.05	.01
□	473	Archie Corbin	.10	.05	.01
□	474	Chuck McElroy	.10	.05	.01
□	475	Mark McGwire	.25	.11	.03
□	476	Wally Whitehurst	.10	.05	.01
□	477	Tim McIntosh	.10	.05	.01
□	478	Sid Bream	.10	.05	.01
□	479	Jeff Juden	.15	.07	.02
□	480	Carlton Fisk	.25	.11	.03
□	481	Jeff Plympton	.10	.05	.01
□	482	Carlos Martinez	.10	.05	.01
□	483	Jim Gott	.10	.05	.01
□	484	Bob McClure	.10	.05	.01
□	485	Tim Teufel	.10	.05	.01
□	486	Vicente Palacios	.10	.05	.01
□	487	Jeff Reed	.10	.05	.01
□	488	Tony Phillips	.25	.11	.03
□	489	Mel Rojas	.15	.07	.02
□	490	Ben McDonald	.15	.07	.02
□	491	Andres Santana	.10	.05	.01
□	492	Chris Beasley	.10	.05	.01
□	493	Mike Timlin	.10	.05	.01
□	494	Brian Downing	.10	.05	.01
□	495	Kirk Gibson	.25	.11	.03
□	496	Scott Sanderson	.10	.05	.01
□	497	Nick Esasky	.10	.05	.01
□	498	Johnny Guzman	.10	.05	.01
□	499	Mitch Williams	.15	.07	.02
□	500	Kirby Puckett	.60	.25	.07
□	501	Mike Harkey	.10	.05	.01
□	502	Jim Gantner	.10	.05	.01
□	503	Bruce Egloff	.10	.05	.01
□	504	Josias Manzanillo	.10	.05	.01
□	505	Delino DeShields	.15	.07	.02
□	506	Rheal Cormier	.10	.05	.01
□	507	Jay Bell	.15	.07	.02
□	508	Rich Rowland	.10	.05	.01
□	509	Scott Servais	.10	.05	.01
□	510	Terry Pendleton	.25	.11	.03
□	511	Rich DeLucia	.10	.05	.01
□	512	Warren Newson	.10	.05	.01
□	513	Paul Faries	.10	.05	.01
□	514	Kal Daniels	.10	.05	.01
□	515	Jarvis Brown	.15	.07	.02
□	516	Rafael Palmeiro	.25	.11	.03
□	517	Kelly Downs	.10	.05	.01
□	518	Steve Chitren	.10	.05	.01
□	519	Moises Alou	.25	.11	.03
□	520	Wade Boggs	.25	.11	.03
□	521	Pete Schourek	.15	.07	.02
□	522	Scott Terry	.10	.05	.01
□	523	Kevin Appier	.15	.07	.02
□	524	Gary Redus	.10	.05	.01
□	525	George Bell	.10	.05	.01
□	526	Jeff Kaiser	.10	.05	.01
□	527	Alvaro Espinoza	.10	.05	.01
□	528	Luis Polonia	.10	.05	.01
□	529	Darren Daulton	.25	.11	.03
□	530	Norm Charlton	.10	.05	.01
□	531	John Olerud	.15	.07	.02
□	532	Dan Plesac	.10	.05	.01
□	533	Billy Ripken	.10	.05	.01
□	534	Rod Nichols	.10	.05	.01
□	535	Joey Cora	.10	.05	.01
□	536	Harold Baines	.25	.11	.03
□	537	Bob Ojeda	.10	.05	.01
□	538	Mark Leonard	.10	.05	.01
□	539	Danny Darwin	.10	.05	.01
□	540	Shawon Dunston	.10	.05	.01
□	541	Pedro Munoz	.15	.07	.02
□	542	Mark Gubicza	.10	.05	.01
□	543	Kevin Baez	.10	.05	.01
□	544	Todd Zeile	.15	.07	.02
□	545	Don Slaught	.10	.05	.01
□	546	Tony Eusebio	.10	.05	.01
□	547	Alonzo Powell	.10	.05	.01
□	548	Gary Pettis	.10	.05	.01
□	549	Brian Barnes	.10	.05	.01
□	550	Lou Whitaker	.25	.11	.03
□	551	Keith Mitchell	.10	.05	.01
□	552	Oscar Azocar	.10	.05	.01
□	553	Stu Cole	.10	.05	.01
□	554	Steve Wapnick	.10	.05	.01
□	555	Derek Bell	.15	.07	.02
□	556	Luis Lopez	.10	.05	.01
□	557	Anthony Telford	.10	.05	.01
□	558	Tim Mauser	.10	.05	.01
□	559	Glen Sutko	.10	.05	.01
□	560	Darryl Strawberry	.10	.05	.01
□	561	Tom Bolton	.10	.05	.01
□	562	Cliff Young	.10	.05	.01
□	563	Bruce Walton	.10	.05	.01
□	564	Chico Walker	.10	.05	.01
□	565	John Franco	.25	.11	.03
□	566	Paul McClellan	.10	.05	.01
□	567	Paul Abbott	.10	.05	.01
□	568	Gary Varsho	.10	.05	.01
□	569	Carlos Maldonado	.10	.05	.01
□	570	Kelly Gruber	.10	.05	.01
□	571	Jose Oquendo	.10	.05	.01
□	572	Steve Frey	.10	.05	.01
□	573	Tino Martinez	.25	.11	.03
□	574	Bill Haselman	.10	.05	.01
□	575	Eric Anthony	.10	.05	.01
□	576	John Habyan	.10	.05	.01
□	577	Jeff McNeeley	.10	.05	.01
□	578	Chris Bosio	.10	.05	.01
□	579	Joe Grahe	.10	.05	.01
□	580	Fred McGriff	.30	.14	.04
□	581	Rick Honeycutt	.10	.05	.01
□	582	Matt Williams	.40	.18	.05
□	583	Cliff Brantley	.15	.07	.02
□	584	Rob Dibble	.10	.05	.01
□	585	Skeeter Barnes	.10	.05	.01
□	586	Greg Hibbard	.10	.05	.01
□	587	Randy Milligan	.10	.05	.01
□	588	Checklist 301-400	.10	.05	.01
□	589	Checklist 401-500	.10	.05	.01
□	590	Checklist 501-600	.10	.05	.01
□	591	Frank Thomas MC	1.50	.70	.19
□	592	David Justice MC	.20	.09	.03
□	593	Roger Clemens MC	.25	.11	.03
□	594	Steve Avery MC	.25	.11	.03
□	595	Cal Ripken MC	1.00	.45	.12
□	596	Barry Larkin MC UER (Ranked in AL, should be NL)	.25	.11	.03
□	597	Jose Canseco MC UER (Mistakenly numbered 370 on card back)	.30	.14	.04
□	598	Will Clark MC	.30	.14	.04
□	599	Cecil Fielder MC	.25	.11	.03
□	600	Ryne Sandberg MC	.30	.14	.04
□	601	Chuck Knoblauch MC	.25	.11	.03
□	602	Dwight Gooden MC	.10	.05	.01
□	603	Ken Griffey Jr. MC	1.50	.70	.19
□	604	Barry Bonds MC	.25	.11	.03
□	605	Nolan Ryan MC	1.00	.45	.12
□	606	Jeff Bagwell MC	.50	.23	.06
□	607	Robin Yount MC	.25	.11	.03
□	608	Bobby Bonilla MC	.25	.11	.03
□	609	George Brett MC	.40	.18	.05

☐ 610 Howard Johnson MC ...	.10	.05	.01
☐ 611 Esteban Beltre	.10	.05	.01
☐ 612 Mike Christopher	.10	.05	.01
☐ 613 Troy Afenir	.10	.05	.01
☐ 614 Mariano Duncan	.10	.05	.01
☐ 615 Doug Henry	.10	.05	.01
☐ 616 Doug Jones	.10	.05	.01
☐ 617 Alvin Davis	.10	.05	.01
☐ 618 Craig Lefferts	.10	.05	.01
☐ 619 Kevin McReynolds	.10	.05	.01
☐ 620 Barry Bonds	.50	.23	.06
☐ 621 Turner Ward	.10	.05	.01
☐ 622 Joe Magrane	.10	.05	.01
☐ 623 Mark Parent	.10	.05	.01
☐ 624 Tom Browning	.10	.05	.01
☐ 625 John Smiley	.10	.05	.01
☐ 626 Steve Wilson	.10	.05	.01
☐ 627 Mike Gallego	.10	.05	.01
☐ 628 Sammy Sosa	.30	.14	.04
☐ 629 Rico Rossy	.10	.05	.01
☐ 630 Royce Clayton	.15	.07	.02
☐ 631 Clay Parker	.10	.05	.01
☐ 632 Pete Smith	.10	.05	.01
☐ 633 Jeff McKnight	.10	.05	.01
☐ 634 Jack Daugherty	.10	.05	.01
☐ 635 Steve Sax	.10	.05	.01
☐ 636 Joe Hesketh	.10	.05	.01
☐ 637 Vince Horsman	.15	.07	.02
☐ 638 Eric King	.10	.05	.01
☐ 639 Joe Boever	.10	.05	.01
☐ 640 Jack Morris	.15	.07	.02
☐ 641 Arthur Rhodes	.10	.05	.01
☐ 642 Bob Melvin	.10	.05	.01
☐ 643 Rick Wilkins	.10	.05	.01
☐ 644 Scott Scudder	.10	.05	.01
☐ 645 Bip Roberts	.10	.05	.01
☐ 646 Julio Valera	.10	.05	.01
☐ 647 Kevin Campbell	.10	.05	.01
☐ 648 Steve Searcy	.10	.05	.01
☐ 649 Scott Kamieniecki	.10	.05	.01
☐ 650 Kurt Stillwell	.10	.05	.01
☐ 651 Bob Welch	.10	.05	.01
☐ 652 Andres Galarraga	.25	.11	.03
☐ 653 Mike Jackson	.10	.05	.01
☐ 654 Bo Jackson	.25	.11	.03
☐ 655 Sid Fernandez	.15	.07	.02
☐ 656 Mike Bielecki	.10	.05	.01
☐ 657 Jeff Reardon	.15	.07	.02
☐ 658 Wayne Rosenthal	.10	.05	.01
☐ 659 Eric Bullock	.10	.05	.01
☐ 660 Eric Davis	.15	.07	.02
☐ 661 Randy Tomlin	.10	.05	.01
☐ 662 Tom Edens	.10	.05	.01
☐ 663 Rob Murphy	.10	.05	.01
☐ 664 Leo Gomez	.10	.05	.01
☐ 665 Greg Maddux	1.50	.70	.19
☐ 666 Greg Vaughn	.15	.07	.02
☐ 667 Wade Taylor	.10	.05	.01
☐ 668 Brad Arnsberg	.10	.05	.01
☐ 669 Mike Moore	.10	.05	.01
☐ 670 Mark Langston	.25	.11	.03
☐ 671 Barry Jones	.10	.05	.01
☐ 672 Bill Landrum	.10	.05	.01
☐ 673 Greg Swindell	.10	.05	.01
☐ 674 Wayne Edwards	.10	.05	.01
☐ 675 Greg Olson	.10	.05	.01
☐ 676 Bill Pulsipher	2.00	.90	.25
☐ 677 Bobby Witt	.10	.05	.01
☐ 678 Mark Carreon	.10	.05	.01
☐ 679 Patrick Lennon	.10	.05	.01
☐ 680 Ozzie Smith	.40	.18	.05
☐ 681 John Briscoe	.10	.05	.01
☐ 682 Matt Young	.10	.05	.01
☐ 683 Jeff Conine	.50	.23	.06
☐ 684 Phil Stephenson	.10	.05	.01
☐ 685 Ron Darling	.10	.05	.01
☐ 686 Bryan Hickerson	.10	.05	.01
☐ 687 Dale Sveum	.10	.05	.01
☐ 688 Kirk McCaskill	.10	.05	.01
☐ 689 Rich Amaral	.10	.05	.01
☐ 690 Danny Tartabull	.15	.07	.02
☐ 691 Donald Harris	.10	.05	.01
☐ 692 Doug Davis	.10	.05	.01
☐ 693 John Farrell	.10	.05	.01
☐ 694 Paul Gibson	.10	.05	.01
☐ 695 Kenny Lofton	2.50	1.10	.30
☐ 696 Mike Fetters	.10	.05	.01
☐ 697 Rosario Rodriguez	.10	.05	.01
☐ 698 Chris Jones	.10	.05	.01
☐ 699 Jeff Manto	.10	.05	.01
☐ 700 Rick Sutcliffe	.15	.07	.02
☐ 701 Scott Bankhead	.10	.05	.01
☐ 702 Donnie Hill	.10	.05	.01
☐ 703 Todd Worrell	.10	.05	.01
☐ 704 Rene Gonzales	.10	.05	.01
☐ 705 Rick Cerone	.10	.05	.01
☐ 706 Tony Pena	.10	.05	.01
☐ 707 Paul Sorrento	.10	.05	.01
☐ 708 Gary Scott	.10	.05	.01
☐ 709 Junior Noboa	.10	.05	.01
☐ 710 Wally Joyner	.25	.11	.03
☐ 711 Charlie Hayes	.15	.07	.02
☐ 712 Rich Rodriguez	.10	.05	.01
☐ 713 Rudy Seanez	.10	.05	.01
☐ 714 Jim Bullinger	.10	.05	.01
☐ 715 Jeff M. Robinson	.10	.05	.01
☐ 716 Jeff Branson	.10	.05	.01
☐ 717 Andy Ashby	.10	.05	.01
☐ 718 Dave Burba	.10	.05	.01
☐ 719 Rich Gossage	.15	.07	.02
☐ 720 Randy Johnson	.50	.23	.06
☐ 721 David Wells	.10	.05	.01
☐ 722 Paul Kilgus	.10	.05	.01
☐ 723 Dave Martinez	.10	.05	.01
☐ 724 Denny Neagle	.10	.05	.01
☐ 725 Andy Stankiewicz	.10	.05	.01
☐ 726 Rick Aguilera	.15	.07	.02
☐ 727 Junior Ortiz	.10	.05	.01
☐ 728 Storm Davis	.10	.05	.01
☐ 729 Don Robinson	.10	.05	.01
☐ 730 Ron Gant	.25	.11	.03
☐ 731 Paul Assenmacher	.10	.05	.01
☐ 732 Mike Gardiner	.10	.05	.01
☐ 733 Milt Hill	.10	.05	.01
☐ 734 Jeremy Hernandez	.10	.05	.01
☐ 735 Ken Hill	.25	.11	.03
☐ 736 Xavier Hernandez	.10	.05	.01
☐ 737 Gregg Jefferies	.25	.11	.03
☐ 738 Dick Schofield	.10	.05	.01
☐ 739 Ron Robinson	.10	.05	.01
☐ 740 Sandy Alomar	.15	.07	.02
☐ 741 Mike Stanley	.15	.07	.02
☐ 742 Butch Henry	.10	.05	.01
☐ 743 Floyd Bannister	.10	.05	.01
☐ 744 Brian Drahman	.10	.05	.01
☐ 745 Dave Winfield	.25	.11	.03
☐ 746 Bob Walk	.10	.05	.01
☐ 747 Chris James	.10	.05	.01
☐ 748 Don Prybylinski	.10	.05	.01
☐ 749 Dennis Rasmussen	.10	.05	.01
☐ 750 Rickey Henderson	.25	.11	.03
☐ 751 Chris Hammond	.10	.05	.01

☐ 752	Bob Kipper	.10	.05	.01
☐ 753	Dave Rohde	.10	.05	.01
☐ 754	Hubie Brooks	.10	.05	.01
☐ 755	Bret Saberhagen	.25	.11	.03
☐ 756	Jeff D. Robinson	.10	.05	.01
☐ 757	Pat Listach	.15	.07	.02
☐ 758	Bill Wegman	.10	.05	.01
☐ 759	John Wetteland	.10	.05	.01
☐ 760	Phil Plantier	.15	.07	.02
☐ 761	Wilson Alvarez	.25	.11	.03
☐ 762	Scott Aldred	.10	.05	.01
☐ 763	Armando Reynoso	.10	.05	.01
☐ 764	Todd Benzinger	.10	.05	.01
☐ 765	Kevin Mitchell	.15	.07	.02
☐ 766	Gary Sheffield	.25	.11	.03
☐ 767	Allan Anderson	.10	.05	.01
☐ 768	Rusty Meacham	.10	.05	.01
☐ 769	Rick Parker	.10	.05	.01
☐ 770	Nolan Ryan	2.00	.90	.25
☐ 771	Jeff Ballard	.10	.05	.01
☐ 772	Cory Snyder	.10	.05	.01
☐ 773	Denis Boucher	.10	.05	.01
☐ 774	Jose Gonzalez	.10	.05	.01
☐ 775	Juan Guerrero	.10	.05	.01
☐ 776	Ed Nunez	.10	.05	.01
☐ 777	Scott Ruskin	.10	.05	.01
☐ 778	Terry Leach	.10	.05	.01
☐ 779	Carl Willis	.10	.05	.01
☐ 780	Bobby Bonilla	.25	.11	.03
☐ 781	Duane Ward	.10	.05	.01
☐ 782	Joe Slusarski	.10	.05	.01
☐ 783	David Segui	.10	.05	.01
☐ 784	Kirk Gibson	.25	.11	.03
☐ 785	Frank Viola	.10	.05	.01
☐ 786	Keith Miller	.10	.05	.01
☐ 787	Mike Morgan	.10	.05	.01
☐ 788	Kim Batiste	.10	.05	.01
☐ 789	Sergio Valdez	.10	.05	.01
☐ 790	Eddie Taubensee	.10	.05	.01
☐ 791	Jack Armstrong	.10	.05	.01
☐ 792	Scott Fletcher	.10	.05	.01
☐ 793	Steve Farr	.10	.05	.01
☐ 794	Dan Pasqua	.10	.05	.01
☐ 795	Eddie Murray	.30	.14	.04
☐ 796	John Morris	.10	.05	.01
☐ 797	Francisco Cabrera	.10	.05	.01
☐ 798	Mike Perez	.10	.05	.01
☐ 799	Ted Wood	.10	.05	.01
☐ 800	Jose Rijo	.15	.07	.02
☐ 801	Danny Gladden	.10	.05	.01
☐ 802	Archi Cianfrocco	.10	.05	.01
☐ 803	Monty Fariss	.10	.05	.01
☐ 804	Roger McDowell	.10	.05	.01
☐ 805	Randy Myers	.25	.11	.03
☐ 806	Kirk Dressendorfer	.10	.05	.01
☐ 807	Zane Smith	.10	.05	.01
☐ 808	Glenn Davis	.10	.05	.01
☐ 809	Torey Lovullo	.10	.05	.01
☐ 810	Andre Dawson	.25	.11	.03
☐ 811	Bill Pecota	.10	.05	.01
☐ 812	Ted Power	.10	.05	.01
☐ 813	Willie Blair	.10	.05	.01
☐ 814	Dave Fleming	.10	.05	.01
☐ 815	Chris Gwynn	.10	.05	.01
☐ 816	Jody Reed	.10	.05	.01
☐ 817	Mark Dewey	.10	.05	.01
☐ 818	Kyle Abbott	.10	.05	.01
☐ 819	Tom Henke	.15	.07	.02
☐ 820	Kevin Seitzer	.10	.05	.01
☐ 821	Al Newman	.10	.05	.01
☐ 822	Tim Sherrill	.10	.05	.01
☐ 823	Chuck Crim	.10	.05	.01
☐ 824	Darren Reed	.10	.05	.01
☐ 825	Tony Gwynn	.60	.25	.07
☐ 826	Steve Foster	.10	.05	.01
☐ 827	Steve Howe	.10	.05	.01
☐ 828	Brook Jacoby	.10	.05	.01
☐ 829	Rodney McCray	.10	.05	.01
☐ 830	Chuck Knoblauch	.30	.14	.04
☐ 831	John Wehner	.10	.05	.01
☐ 832	Scott Garrelts	.10	.05	.01
☐ 833	Alejandro Pena	.10	.05	.01
☐ 834	Jeff Parrett UER	.10	.05	.01
	(Kentucy)			
☐ 835	Juan Bell	.10	.05	.01
☐ 836	Lance Dickson	.10	.05	.01
☐ 837	Darryl Kile	.10	.05	.01
☐ 838	Efrain Valdez	.10	.05	.01
☐ 839	Bob Zupcic	.10	.05	.01
☐ 840	George Bell	.10	.05	.01
☐ 841	Dave Gallagher	.10	.05	.01
☐ 842	Tim Belcher	.10	.05	.01
☐ 843	Jeff Shaw	.10	.05	.01
☐ 844	Mike Fitzgerald	.10	.05	.01
☐ 845	Gary Carter	.25	.11	.03
☐ 846	John Russell	.10	.05	.01
☐ 847	Eric Hillman	.10	.05	.01
☐ 848	Mike Witt	.10	.05	.01
☐ 849	Curt Wilkerson	.10	.05	.01
☐ 850	Alan Trammell	.25	.11	.03
☐ 851	Rex Hudler	.10	.05	.01
☐ 852	Mike Walkden	.10	.05	.01
☐ 853	Kevin Ward	.10	.05	.01
☐ 854	Tim Naehring	.10	.05	.01
☐ 855	Bill Swift	.10	.05	.01
☐ 856	Damon Berryhill	.10	.05	.01
☐ 857	Mark Eichhorn	.10	.05	.01
☐ 858	Hector Villanueva	.10	.05	.01
☐ 859	Jose Lind	.10	.05	.01
☐ 860	Denny Martinez	.15	.07	.02
☐ 861	Bill Krueger	.10	.05	.01
☐ 862	Mike Kingery	.10	.05	.01
☐ 863	Jeff Innis	.10	.05	.01
☐ 864	Derek Lilliquist	.10	.05	.01
☐ 865	Reggie Sanders	.40	.18	.05
☐ 866	Ramon Garcia	.10	.05	.01
☐ 867	Bruce Ruffin	.10	.05	.01
☐ 868	Dickie Thon	.10	.05	.01
☐ 869	Melido Perez	.10	.05	.01
☐ 870	Ruben Amaro	.10	.05	.01
☐ 871	Alan Mills	.10	.05	.01
☐ 872	Matt Sinatro	.10	.05	.01
☐ 873	Eddie Zosky	.10	.05	.01
☐ 874	Pete Incaviglia	.10	.05	.01
☐ 875	Tom Candiotti	.10	.05	.01
☐ 876	Bob Patterson	.10	.05	.01
☐ 877	Neal Heaton	.10	.05	.01
☐ 878	Terrel Hansen	.10	.05	.01
☐ 879	Dave Eiland	.10	.05	.01
☐ 880	Von Hayes	.10	.05	.01
☐ 881	Tim Scott	.10	.05	.01
☐ 882	Otis Nixon	.10	.05	.01
☐ 883	Herm Winningham	.10	.05	.01
☐ 884	Dion James	.10	.05	.01
☐ 885	Dave Wainhouse	.10	.05	.01
☐ 886	Frank DiPino	.10	.05	.01
☐ 887	Dennis Cook	.10	.05	.01
☐ 888	Jose Mesa	.10	.05	.01
☐ 889	Mark Leiter	.10	.05	.01
☐ 890	Willie Randolph	.15	.07	.02
☐ 891	Craig Colbert	.10	.05	.01
☐ 892	Dwayne Henry	.10	.05	.01

		MINT	NRMT	EXC
☐ 893	Jim Lindeman	.10	.05	.01
☐ 894	Charlie Hough	.15	.07	.02
☐ 895	Gil Heredia	.10	.05	.01
☐ 896	Scott Chiamparino	.10	.05	.01
☐ 897	Lance Blankenship	.10	.05	.01
☐ 898	Checklist 601-700	.10	.05	.01
☐ 899	Checklist 701-800	.10	.05	.01
☐ 900	Checklist 801-900	.10	.05	.01

1993 Stadium Club

The 1993 Stadium Club baseball set consists of 750 cards issued in three series of 300, 300, and 150 cards respectively. Randomly inserted throughout first series packs were a Stadium Club Master Photo winner card (redeemable for three master photos), a 1st Day Production card, and four special bonus cards featuring the newest members of the 3,000 Hit Club (Robin Yount and George Brett) and the Number One Expansion Draft Picks of the Florida Marlins and Colorado Rockies (Nigel Wilson and David Nied). Fewer than 2,000 of each card were imprinted with a special foil First Day Production logo. According to Topps, one of these insert cards were to be found in approximately one in every 24 packs. Also every hobby box contained a Stadium Club Master Photo. The cards measure the standard size (2 1/2" by 3 1/2"). The fronts display full-bleed glossy color player photos. A red stripe carrying the player's name and edged on the bottom by a gold stripe cuts across the bottom of the picture. A white baseball icon with gold motion streaks rounds out the front. Award Winner and League Leader cards are studded with gold foil stars. On a background consisting of an artistic drawing of a baseball player's arm extended with ball in glove, the backs carry a second color action photo, biographical information, 1992 Stats Player Profile, the player's ranking (either on his team and/or the AL or NL), statistics, and a miniature reproduction of his Topps rookie card. Each series closes with a Members Choice subset (291-300, 591-600, and 746-750. The cards are numbered on the back. Rookie Cards in this set include Roberto Mejia, J.T.

Snow, Tony Tarasco, and Darrell Whitmore. A 1993 Stadium Club "Members Only" set was also issued as a direct-mail offer to members of Topps Stadium Club. Also issued in three series, this set is identical to the regular 750-set, except that each card has in its upper corner a gold foil "Members Only" seal. With the third and final shipment, the collector received a certificate of authenticity registering the set serial number out of a production run of 12,000 sets.

	MINT	NRMT	EXC
COMPLETE SET (750)	60.00	27.00	7.50
COMPLETE SERIES 1 (300)	20.00	9.00	2.50
COMPLETE SERIES 2 (300)	25.00	11.00	3.10
COMPLETE SERIES 3 (150)	15.00	6.75	1.85
COMMON CARD (1-300)	.10	.05	.01
COMMON CARD (301-600)	.10	.05	.01
COMMON CARD (601-750)	.10	.05	.01

		MINT	NRMT	EXC
☐ 1	Pat Borders	.10	.05	.01
☐ 2	Greg Maddux	3.00	1.35	.35
☐ 3	Daryl Boston	.10	.05	.01
☐ 4	Bob Ayrault	.10	.05	.01
☐ 5	Tony Phillips IF	.10	.05	.01
☐ 6	Damion Easley	.20	.09	.03
☐ 7	Kip Gross	.10	.05	.01
☐ 8	Jim Thome	1.25	.55	.16
☐ 9	Tim Belcher	.10	.05	.01
☐ 10	Gary Wayne	.10	.05	.01
☐ 11	Sam Militello	.10	.05	.01
☐ 12	Mike Magnante	.10	.05	.01
☐ 13	Tim Wakefield	.30	.14	.04
☐ 14	Tim Hulett	.10	.05	.01
☐ 15	Rheal Cormier	.10	.05	.01
☐ 16	Juan Guerrero	.10	.05	.01
☐ 17	Rich Gossage	.30	.14	.04
☐ 18	Tim Laker	.10	.05	.01
☐ 19	Darrin Jackson	.10	.05	.01
☐ 20	Jack Clark	.10	.05	.01
☐ 21	Roberto Hernandez	.20	.09	.03
☐ 22	Dean Palmer	.20	.09	.03
☐ 23	Harold Reynolds	.10	.05	.01
☐ 24	Dan Plesac	.10	.05	.01
☐ 25	Brent Mayne	.10	.05	.01
☐ 26	Pat Hentgen	.20	.09	.03
☐ 27	Luis Sojo	.10	.05	.01
☐ 28	Ron Gant	.30	.14	.04
☐ 29	Paul Gibson	.10	.05	.01
☐ 30	Bip Roberts	.10	.05	.01
☐ 31	Mickey Tettleton	.20	.09	.03
☐ 32	Randy Velarde	.10	.05	.01
☐ 33	Brian McRae	.20	.09	.03
☐ 34	Wes Chamberlain	.10	.05	.01
☐ 35	Wayne Kirby	.10	.05	.01
☐ 36	Rey Sanchez	.10	.05	.01
☐ 37	Jesse Orosco	.10	.05	.01
☐ 38	Mike Stanton	.10	.05	.01
☐ 39	Royce Clayton	.20	.09	.03
☐ 40	Cal Ripken UER	3.00	1.35	.35
	(Place of birth Havre de Grave; should be Havre de Grace)			
☐ 41	John Dopson	.10	.05	.01
☐ 42	Gene Larkin	.10	.05	.01
☐ 43	Tim Raines	.30	.14	.04
☐ 44	Randy Myers	.20	.09	.03
☐ 45	Clay Parker	.10	.05	.01
☐ 46	Mike Scioscia	.10	.05	.01
☐ 47	Pete Incaviglia	.10	.05	.01
☐ 48	Todd Van Poppel	.20	.09	.03

☐ 49	Ray Lankford	.30	.14	.04
☐ 50	Eddie Murray	.50	.23	.06
☐ 51A	Barry Bonds ERR	.75	.35	.09
	(Missing four stars over name to indicate NL MVP)			
☐ 51B	Barry Bonds COR	.75	.35	.09
☐ 52	Gary Thurman	.10	.05	.01
☐ 53	Bob Wickman	.10	.05	.01
☐ 54	Joey Cora	.10	.05	.01
☐ 55	Kenny Rogers	.10	.05	.01
☐ 56	Mike Devereaux	.20	.09	.03
☐ 57	Kevin Seitzer	.10	.05	.01
☐ 58	Rafael Belliard	.10	.05	.01
☐ 59	David Wells	.10	.05	.01
☐ 60	Mark Clark	.10	.05	.01
☐ 61	Carlos Baerga	.60	.25	.07
☐ 62	Scott Brosius	.10	.05	.01
☐ 63	Jeff Grotewold	.10	.05	.01
☐ 64	Rick Wrona	.10	.05	.01
☐ 65	Kurt Knudsen	.10	.05	.01
☐ 66	Lloyd McClendon	.10	.05	.01
☐ 67	Omar Vizquel	.20	.09	.03
☐ 68	Jose Vizcaino	.10	.05	.01
☐ 69	Rob Ducey	.10	.05	.01
☐ 70	Casey Candaele	.10	.05	.01
☐ 71	Ramon Martinez	.20	.09	.03
☐ 72	Todd Hundley	.20	.09	.03
☐ 73	John Marzano	.10	.05	.01
☐ 74	Derek Parks	.10	.05	.01
☐ 75	Jack McDowell	.30	.14	.04
☐ 76	Tim Scott	.10	.05	.01
☐ 77	Mike Mussina	.50	.23	.06
☐ 78	Delino DeShields	.20	.09	.03
☐ 79	Chris Bosio	.10	.05	.01
☐ 80	Mike Bordick	.10	.05	.01
☐ 81	Rod Beck	.30	.14	.04
☐ 82	Ted Power	.10	.05	.01
☐ 83	John Kruk	.30	.14	.04
☐ 84	Steve Shifflett	.10	.05	.01
☐ 85	Danny Tartabull	.20	.09	.03
☐ 86	Mike Greenwell	.20	.09	.03
☐ 87	Jose Melendez	.10	.05	.01
☐ 88	Craig Wilson	.10	.05	.01
☐ 89	Melvin Nieves	.30	.14	.04
☐ 90	Ed Sprague	.10	.05	.01
☐ 91	Willie McGee	.20	.09	.03
☐ 92	Joe Orsulak	.10	.05	.01
☐ 93	Jeff King	.10	.05	.01
☐ 94	Dan Pasqua	.10	.05	.01
☐ 95	Brian Harper	.10	.05	.01
☐ 96	Joe Oliver	.10	.05	.01
☐ 97	Shane Turner	.10	.05	.01
☐ 98	Lenny Harris	.10	.05	.01
☐ 99	Jeff Parrett	.10	.05	.01
☐ 100	Luis Polonia	.10	.05	.01
☐ 101	Kent Bottenfield	.10	.05	.01
☐ 102	Albert Belle	1.25	.55	.16
☐ 103	Mike Maddux	.10	.05	.01
☐ 104	Randy Tomlin	.10	.05	.01
☐ 105	Andy Stankiewicz	.10	.05	.01
☐ 106	Rico Rossy	.10	.05	.01
☐ 107	Joe Hesketh	.10	.05	.01
☐ 108	Dennis Powell	.10	.05	.01
☐ 109	Derrick May	.20	.09	.03
☐ 110	Pete Harnisch	.10	.05	.01
☐ 111	Kent Mercker	.10	.05	.01
☐ 112	Scott Fletcher	.10	.05	.01
☐ 113	Rex Hudler	.10	.05	.01
☐ 114	Chico Walker	.10	.05	.01
☐ 115	Rafael Palmeiro	.30	.14	.04
☐ 116	Mark Leiter	.10	.05	.01
☐ 117	Pedro Munoz	.20	.09	.03
☐ 118	Jim Bullinger	.10	.05	.01
☐ 119	Ivan Calderon	.10	.05	.01
☐ 120	Mike Timlin	.10	.05	.01
☐ 121	Rene Gonzales	.10	.05	.01
☐ 122	Greg Vaughn	.10	.05	.01
☐ 123	Mike Flanagan	.10	.05	.01
☐ 124	Mike Hartley	.10	.05	.01
☐ 125	Jeff Montgomery	.20	.09	.03
☐ 126	Mike Gallego	.10	.05	.01
☐ 127	Don Slaught	.10	.05	.01
☐ 128	Charlie O'Brien	.10	.05	.01
☐ 129	Jose Offerman	.10	.05	.01
	(Can be found with home town missing on back)			
☐ 130	Mark Wohlers	.10	.05	.01
☐ 131	Eric Fox	.10	.05	.01
☐ 132	Doug Strange	.10	.05	.01
☐ 133	Jeff Frye	.10	.05	.01
☐ 134	Wade Boggs UER	.30	.14	.04
	(Redundantly lists lefty breakdown)			
☐ 135	Lou Whitaker	.30	.14	.04
☐ 136	Craig Grebeck	.10	.05	.01
☐ 137	Rich Rodriguez	.10	.05	.01
☐ 138	Jay Bell	.20	.09	.03
☐ 139	Felix Fermin	.10	.05	.01
☐ 140	Denny Martinez	.20	.09	.03
☐ 141	Eric Anthony	.10	.05	.01
☐ 142	Roberto Alomar	.60	.25	.07
☐ 143	Darren Lewis	.10	.05	.01
☐ 144	Mike Blowers	.10	.05	.01
☐ 145	Scott Bankhead	.10	.05	.01
☐ 146	Jeff Reboulet	.10	.05	.01
☐ 147	Frank Viola	.20	.09	.03
☐ 148	Bill Pecota	.10	.05	.01
☐ 149	Carlos Hernandez	.10	.05	.01
☐ 150	Bobby Witt	.10	.05	.01
☐ 151	Sid Bream	.10	.05	.01
☐ 152	Todd Zeile	.20	.09	.03
☐ 153	Dennis Cook	.10	.05	.01
☐ 154	Brian Bohanon	.10	.05	.01
☐ 155	Pat Kelly	.10	.05	.01
☐ 156	Milt Cuyler	.10	.05	.01
☐ 157	Juan Bell	.10	.05	.01
☐ 158	Randy Milligan	.10	.05	.01
☐ 159	Mark Gardner	.10	.05	.01
☐ 160	Pat Tabler	.10	.05	.01
☐ 161	Jeff Reardon	.20	.09	.03
☐ 162	Ken Patterson	.10	.05	.01
☐ 163	Bobby Bonilla	.30	.14	.04
☐ 164	Tony Pena	.10	.05	.01
☐ 165	Greg Swindell	.10	.05	.01
☐ 166	Kirk McCaskill	.10	.05	.01
☐ 167	Doug Drabek	.30	.14	.04
☐ 168	Franklin Stubbs	.10	.05	.01
☐ 169	Ron Tingley	.10	.05	.01
☐ 170	Willie Banks	.10	.05	.01
☐ 171	Sergio Valdez	.10	.05	.01
☐ 172	Mark Lemke	.10	.05	.01
☐ 173	Robin Yount	.40	.18	.05
☐ 174	Storm Davis	.10	.05	.01
☐ 175	Dan Walters	.10	.05	.01
☐ 176	Steve Farr	.10	.05	.01
☐ 177	Curt Wilkerson	.10	.05	.01
☐ 178	Luis Alicea	.10	.05	.01
☐ 179	Russ Swan	.10	.05	.01
☐ 180	Mitch Williams	.20	.09	.03
☐ 181	Wilson Alvarez	.30	.14	.04
☐ 182	Carl Willis	.10	.05	.01
☐ 183	Craig Biggio	.30	.14	.04

☐ 184	Sean Berry	.10	.05	.01
☐ 185	Trevor Wilson	.10	.05	.01
☐ 186	Jeff Tackett	.10	.05	.01
☐ 187	Ellis Burks	.20	.09	.03
☐ 188	Jeff Branson	.10	.05	.01
☐ 189	Matt Nokes	.10	.05	.01
☐ 190	John Smiley	.10	.05	.01
☐ 191	Danny Gladden	.10	.05	.01
☐ 192	Mike Boddicker	.10	.05	.01
☐ 193	Roger Pavlik	.10	.05	.01
☐ 194	Paul Sorrento	.10	.05	.01
☐ 195	Vince Coleman	.10	.05	.01
☐ 196	Gary DiSarcina	.10	.05	.01
☐ 197	Rafael Bournigal	.10	.05	.01
☐ 198	Mike Schooler	.10	.05	.01
☐ 199	Scott Ruskin	.10	.05	.01
☐ 200	Frank Thomas	3.00	1.35	.35
☐ 201	Kyle Abbott	.10	.05	.01
☐ 202	Mike Perez	.10	.05	.01
☐ 203	Andre Dawson	.30	.14	.04
☐ 204	Bill Swift	.20	.09	.03
☐ 205	Alejandro Pena	.10	.05	.01
☐ 206	Dave Winfield	.30	.14	.04
☐ 207	Andujar Cedeno	.10	.05	.01
☐ 208	Terry Steinbach	.20	.09	.03
☐ 209	Chris Hammond	.10	.05	.01
☐ 210	Todd Burns	.10	.05	.01
☐ 211	Hipolito Pichardo	.10	.05	.01
☐ 212	John Kiely	.10	.05	.01
☐ 213	Tim Teufel	.10	.05	.01
☐ 214	Lee Guetterman	.10	.05	.01
☐ 215	Geronimo Pena	.10	.05	.01
☐ 216	Brett Butler	.20	.09	.03
☐ 217	Bryan Hickerson	.10	.05	.01
☐ 218	Rick Trlicek	.10	.05	.01
☐ 219	Lee Stevens	.10	.05	.01
☐ 220	Roger Clemens	.50	.23	.06
☐ 221	Carlton Fisk	.30	.14	.04
☐ 222	Chili Davis	.20	.09	.03
☐ 223	Walt Terrell	.10	.05	.01
☐ 224	Jim Eisenreich	.10	.05	.01
☐ 225	Ricky Bones	.10	.05	.01
☐ 226	Henry Rodriguez	.10	.05	.01
☐ 227	Ken Hill	.20	.09	.03
☐ 228	Rick Wilkins	.10	.05	.01
☐ 229	Ricky Jordan	.10	.05	.01
☐ 230	Bernard Gilkey	.20	.09	.03
☐ 231	Tim Fortugno	.10	.05	.01
☐ 232	Geno Petralli	.10	.05	.01
☐ 233	Jose Rijo	.20	.09	.03
☐ 234	Jim Leyritz	.10	.05	.01
☐ 235	Kevin Campbell	.10	.05	.01
☐ 236	Al Osuna	.10	.05	.01
☐ 237	Pete Smith	.10	.05	.01
☐ 238	Pete Schourek	.20	.09	.03
☐ 239	Moises Alou	.30	.14	.04
☐ 240	Donn Pall	.10	.05	.01
☐ 241	Denny Neagle	.10	.05	.01
☐ 242	Dan Peltier	.10	.05	.01
☐ 243	Scott Scudder	.10	.05	.01
☐ 244	Juan Guzman	.20	.09	.03
☐ 245	Dave Burba	.10	.05	.01
☐ 246	Rick Sutcliffe	.20	.09	.03
☐ 247	Tony Fossas	.10	.05	.01
☐ 248	Mike Munoz	.10	.05	.01
☐ 249	Tim Salmon	1.00	.45	.12
☐ 250	Rob Murphy	.10	.05	.01
☐ 251	Roger McDowell	.10	.05	.01
☐ 252	Lance Parrish	.20	.09	.03
☐ 253	Cliff Brantley	.10	.05	.01
☐ 254	Scott Leius	.10	.05	.01
☐ 255	Carlos Martinez	.10	.05	.01
☐ 256	Vince Horsman	.10	.05	.01
☐ 257	Oscar Azocar	.10	.05	.01
☐ 258	Craig Shipley	.10	.05	.01
☐ 259	Ben McDonald	.10	.05	.01
☐ 260	Jeff Brantley	.10	.05	.01
☐ 261	Damon Berryhill	.10	.05	.01
☐ 262	Joe Grahe	.10	.05	.01
☐ 263	Dave Hansen	.10	.05	.01
☐ 264	Rich Amaral	.10	.05	.01
☐ 265	Tim Pugh	.10	.05	.01
☐ 266	Dion James	.10	.05	.01
☐ 267	Frank Tanana	.10	.05	.01
☐ 268	Stan Belinda	.10	.05	.01
☐ 269	Jeff Kent	.30	.14	.04
☐ 270	Bruce Ruffin	.10	.05	.01
☐ 271	Xavier Hernandez	.10	.05	.01
☐ 272	Darrin Fletcher	.10	.05	.01
☐ 273	Tino Martinez	.30	.14	.04
☐ 274	Benny Santiago	.10	.05	.01
☐ 275	Scott Radinsky	.10	.05	.01
☐ 276	Mariano Duncan	.10	.05	.01
☐ 277	Kenny Lofton	1.00	.45	.12
☐ 278	Dwight Smith	.10	.05	.01
☐ 279	Joe Carter	.30	.14	.04
☐ 280	Tim Jones	.10	.05	.01
☐ 281	Jeff Huson	.10	.05	.01
☐ 282	Phil Plantier	.10	.05	.01
☐ 283	Kirby Puckett	1.00	.45	.12
☐ 284	Johnny Guzman	.10	.05	.01
☐ 285	Mike Morgan	.10	.05	.01
☐ 286	Chris Sabo	.10	.05	.01
☐ 287	Matt Williams	.50	.23	.06
☐ 288	Checklist 1-100	.10	.05	.01
☐ 289	Checklist 101-200	.10	.05	.01
☐ 290	Checklist 201-300	.10	.05	.01
☐ 291	Dennis Eckersley MC	.30	.14	.04
☐ 292	Eric Karros MC	.30	.14	.04
☐ 293	Pat Listach MC	.10	.05	.01
☐ 294	Andy Van Slyke MC	.20	.09	.03
☐ 295	Robin Ventura MC	.30	.14	.04
☐ 296	Tom Glavine MC	.30	.14	.04
☐ 297	Juan Gonzalez MC UER (Misspelled Gonzales)	.30	.14	.04
☐ 298	Travis Fryman MC	.30	.14	.04
☐ 299	Larry Walker MC	.30	.14	.04
☐ 300	Gary Sheffield MC	.30	.14	.04
☐ 301	Chuck Finley	.20	.09	.03
☐ 302	Luis Gonzalez	.20	.09	.03
☐ 303	Darryl Hamilton	.10	.05	.01
☐ 304	Bien Figueroa	.10	.05	.01
☐ 305	Ron Darling	.10	.05	.01
☐ 306	Jonathan Hurst	.10	.05	.01
☐ 307	Mike Sharperson	.10	.05	.01
☐ 308	Mike Christopher	.10	.05	.01
☐ 309	Marvin Freeman	.10	.05	.01
☐ 310	Jay Buhner	.30	.14	.04
☐ 311	Butch Henry	.10	.05	.01
☐ 312	Greg W. Harris	.10	.05	.01
☐ 313	Darren Daulton	.30	.14	.04
☐ 314	Chuck Knoblauch	.30	.14	.04
☐ 315	Greg A. Harris	.10	.05	.01
☐ 316	John Franco	.20	.09	.03
☐ 317	John Wehner	.10	.05	.01
☐ 318	Donald Harris	.10	.05	.01
☐ 319	Benny Santiago	.10	.05	.01
☐ 320	Larry Walker	.40	.18	.05
☐ 321	Randy Knorr	.10	.05	.01
☐ 322	Ramon Martinez	.10	.05	.01
☐ 323	Mike Stanley	.10	.05	.01
☐ 324	Bill Wegman	.10	.05	.01

☐ 325	Tom Candiotti	.10	.05	.01	☐ 396	Kevin Brown	.10	.05	.01
☐ 326	Glenn Davis	.10	.05	.01	☐ 397	J.T. Bruett	.10	.05	.01
☐ 327	Chuck Crim	.10	.05	.01	☐ 398	Darryl Strawberry	.20	.09	.03
☐ 328	Scott Livingstone	.10	.05	.01	☐ 399	Tom Pagnozzi	.10	.05	.01
☐ 329	Eddie Taubensee	.10	.05	.01	☐ 400	Sandy Alomar Jr.	.10	.05	.01
☐ 330	George Bell	.20	.09	.03	☐ 401	Keith Miller	.10	.05	.01
☐ 331	Edgar Martinez	.30	.14	.04	☐ 402	Rich DeLucia	.10	.05	.01
☐ 332	Paul Assenmacher	.10	.05	.01	☐ 403	Shawn Abner	.10	.05	.01
☐ 333	Steve Hosey	.10	.05	.01	☐ 404	Howard Johnson	.10	.05	.01
☐ 334	Mo Vaughn	.50	.23	.06	☐ 405	Mike Benjamin	.10	.05	.01
☐ 335	Bret Saberhagen	.20	.09	.03	☐ 406	Roberto Mejia	.10	.05	.01
☐ 336	Mike Trombley	.10	.05	.01	☐ 407	Mike Butcher	.10	.05	.01
☐ 337	Mark Lewis	.10	.05	.01	☐ 408	Deion Sanders UER	.60	.25	.07
☐ 338	Terry Pendleton	.20	.09	.03		(Braves on front and Yankees on back)			
☐ 339	Dave Hollins	.10	.05	.01	☐ 409	Todd Stottlemyre	.10	.05	.01
☐ 340	Jeff Conine	.30	.14	.04	☐ 410	Scott Kamieniecki	.10	.05	.01
☐ 341	Bob Tewksbury	.10	.05	.01	☐ 411	Doug Jones	.10	.05	.01
☐ 342	Billy Ashley	.20	.09	.03	☐ 412	John Burkett	.10	.05	.01
☐ 343	Zane Smith	.10	.05	.01	☐ 413	Lance Blankenship	.10	.05	.01
☐ 344	John Wetteland	.10	.05	.01	☐ 414	Jeff Parrett	.10	.05	.01
☐ 345	Chris Hoiles	.20	.09	.03	☐ 415	Barry Larkin	.40	.18	.05
☐ 346	Frank Castillo	.10	.05	.01	☐ 416	Alan Trammell	.30	.14	.04
☐ 347	Bruce Hurst	.10	.05	.01	☐ 417	Mark Kiefer	.10	.05	.01
☐ 348	Kevin McReynolds	.10	.05	.01	☐ 418	Gregg Olson	.10	.05	.01
☐ 349	Dave Henderson	.10	.05	.01	☐ 419	Mark Grace	.30	.14	.04
☐ 350	Ryan Bowen	.10	.05	.01	☐ 420	Shane Mack	.10	.05	.01
☐ 351	Sid Fernandez	.10	.05	.01	☐ 421	Bob Walk	.10	.05	.01
☐ 352	Mark Whiten	.20	.09	.03	☐ 422	Curt Schilling	.10	.05	.01
☐ 353	Nolan Ryan	2.50	1.10	.30	☐ 423	Erik Hanson	.10	.05	.01
☐ 354	Rick Aguilera	.20	.09	.03	☐ 424	George Brett	1.25	.55	.16
☐ 355	Mark Langston	.30	.14	.04	☐ 425	Reggie Jefferson	.10	.05	.01
☐ 356	Jack Morris	.30	.14	.04	☐ 426	Mark Portugal	.10	.05	.01
☐ 357	Rob Deer	.10	.05	.01	☐ 427	Ron Karkovice	.10	.05	.01
☐ 358	Dave Fleming	.10	.05	.01	☐ 428	Matt Young	.10	.05	.01
☐ 359	Lance Johnson	.10	.05	.01	☐ 429	Troy Neel	.10	.05	.01
☐ 360	Joe Millette	.10	.05	.01	☐ 430	Hector Fajardo	.10	.05	.01
☐ 361	Wil Cordero	.20	.09	.03	☐ 431	Dave Righetti	.10	.05	.01
☐ 362	Chito Martinez	.10	.05	.01	☐ 432	Pat Listach	.10	.05	.01
☐ 363	Scott Servais	.10	.05	.01	☐ 433	Jeff Innis	.10	.05	.01
☐ 364	Bernie Williams	.20	.09	.03	☐ 434	Bob MacDonald	.10	.05	.01
☐ 365	Pedro Martinez	.30	.14	.04	☐ 435	Brian Jordan	.30	.14	.04
☐ 366	Ryne Sandberg	.75	.35	.09	☐ 436	Jeff Blauser	.20	.09	.03
☐ 367	Brad Ausmus	.10	.05	.01	☐ 437	Mike Myers	.10	.05	.01
☐ 368	Scott Cooper	.10	.05	.01	☐ 438	Frank Seminara	.10	.05	.01
☐ 369	Rob Dibble	.10	.05	.01	☐ 439	Rusty Meacham	.10	.05	.01
☐ 370	Walt Weiss	.10	.05	.01	☐ 440	Greg Briley	.10	.05	.01
☐ 371	Mark Davis	.10	.05	.01	☐ 441	Derek Lilliquist	.10	.05	.01
☐ 372	Orlando Merced	.20	.09	.03	☐ 442	John Vander Wal	.10	.05	.01
☐ 373	Mike Jackson	.10	.05	.01	☐ 443	Scott Erickson	.10	.05	.01
☐ 374	Kevin Appier	.20	.09	.03	☐ 444	Bob Scanlan	.10	.05	.01
☐ 375	Esteban Beltre	.10	.05	.01	☐ 445	Todd Frohwirth	.10	.05	.01
☐ 376	Joe Slusarski	.10	.05	.01	☐ 446	Tom Goodwin	.10	.05	.01
☐ 377	William Suero	.10	.05	.01	☐ 447	William Pennyfeather	.10	.05	.01
☐ 378	Pete O'Brien	.10	.05	.01	☐ 448	Travis Fryman	.30	.14	.04
☐ 379	Alan Embree	.10	.05	.01	☐ 449	Mickey Morandini	.10	.05	.01
☐ 380	Lenny Webster	.10	.05	.01	☐ 450	Greg Olson	.10	.05	.01
☐ 381	Eric Davis	.10	.05	.01	☐ 451	Trevor Hoffman	.20	.09	.03
☐ 382	Duane Ward	.10	.05	.01	☐ 452	Dave Magadan	.10	.05	.01
☐ 383	John Habyan	.10	.05	.01	☐ 453	Shawn Jeter	.10	.05	.01
☐ 384	Jeff Bagwell	1.25	.55	.16	☐ 454	Andres Galarraga	.30	.14	.04
☐ 385	Ruben Amaro	.10	.05	.01	☐ 455	Ted Wood	.10	.05	.01
☐ 386	Julio Valera	.10	.05	.01	☐ 456	Freddie Benavides	.10	.05	.01
☐ 387	Robin Ventura	.30	.14	.04	☐ 457	Junior Felix	.10	.05	.01
☐ 388	Archi Cianfrocco	.10	.05	.01	☐ 458	Alex Cole	.10	.05	.01
☐ 389	Skeeter Barnes	.10	.05	.01	☐ 459	John Orton	.10	.05	.01
☐ 390	Tim Costo	.10	.05	.01	☐ 460	Eddie Zosky	.10	.05	.01
☐ 391	Luis Mercedes	.10	.05	.01	☐ 461	Dennis Eckersley	.30	.14	.04
☐ 392	Jeremy Hernandez	.10	.05	.01	☐ 462	Lee Smith	.30	.14	.04
☐ 393	Shawon Dunston	.10	.05	.01	☐ 463	John Smoltz	.20	.09	.03
☐ 394	Andy Van Slyke	.20	.09	.03	☐ 464	Ken Caminiti	.20	.09	.03
☐ 395	Kevin Maas	.10	.05	.01	☐ 465	Melido Perez	.10	.05	.01

☐ 466 Tom Marsh	.10	.05	.01
☐ 467 Jeff Nelson	.10	.05	.01
☐ 468 Jesse Levis	.10	.05	.01
☐ 469 Chris Nabholz	.10	.05	.01
☐ 470 Mike Macfarlane	.10	.05	.01
☐ 471 Reggie Sanders	.30	.14	.04
☐ 472 Chuck McElroy	.10	.05	.01
☐ 473 Kevin Gross	.10	.05	.01
☐ 474 Matt Whiteside	.10	.05	.01
☐ 475 Cal Eldred	.10	.05	.01
☐ 476 Dave Gallagher	.10	.05	.01
☐ 477 Len Dykstra	.30	.14	.04
☐ 478 Mark McGwire	.30	.14	.04
☐ 479 David Segui	.10	.05	.01
☐ 480 Mike Henneman	.10	.05	.01
☐ 481 Bret Barberie	.10	.05	.01
☐ 482 Steve Sax	.10	.05	.01
☐ 483 Dave Valle	.10	.05	.01
☐ 484 Danny Darwin	.10	.05	.01
☐ 485 Devon White	.20	.09	.03
☐ 486 Eric Plunk	.10	.05	.01
☐ 487 Jim Gott	.10	.05	.01
☐ 488 Scooter Tucker	.10	.05	.01
☐ 489 Omar Olivares	.10	.05	.01
☐ 490 Greg Myers	.10	.05	.01
☐ 491 Brian Hunter	.10	.05	.01
☐ 492 Kevin Tapani	.10	.05	.01
☐ 493 Rich Monteleone	.10	.05	.01
☐ 494 Steve Buechele	.10	.05	.01
☐ 495 Bo Jackson	.30	.14	.04
☐ 496 Mike LaValliere	.10	.05	.01
☐ 497 Mark Leonard	.10	.05	.01
☐ 498 Daryl Boston	.10	.05	.01
☐ 499 Jose Canseco	.50	.23	.06
☐ 500 Brian Barnes	.10	.05	.01
☐ 501 Randy Johnson	.60	.25	.07
☐ 502 Tim McIntosh	.10	.05	.01
☐ 503 Cecil Fielder	.30	.14	.04
☐ 504 Derek Bell	.20	.09	.03
☐ 505 Kevin Koslofski	.10	.05	.01
☐ 506 Darren Holmes	.20	.09	.03
☐ 507 Brady Anderson	.20	.09	.03
☐ 508 John Valentin	.30	.14	.04
☐ 509 Jerry Browne	.10	.05	.01
☐ 510 Fred McGriff	.40	.18	.05
☐ 511 Pedro Astacio	.10	.05	.01
☐ 512 Gary Gaetti	.10	.05	.01
☐ 513 John Burke	.10	.05	.01
☐ 514 Dwight Gooden	.20	.09	.03
☐ 515 Thomas Howard	.10	.05	.01
☐ 516 Darrell Whitmore UER	.10	.05	.01
(11 games played in 1992; should			
be 121)			
☐ 517 Ozzie Guillen	.10	.05	.01
☐ 518 Darryl Kile	.10	.05	.01
☐ 519 Rich Rowland	.10	.05	.01
☐ 520 Carlos Delgado	.60	.25	.07
☐ 521 Doug Henry	.10	.05	.01
☐ 522 Greg Colbrunn	.30	.14	.04
☐ 523 Tom Gordon	.10	.05	.01
☐ 524 Ivan Rodriguez	.30	.14	.04
☐ 525 Kent Hrbek	.20	.09	.03
☐ 526 Eric Young	.20	.09	.03
☐ 527 Rod Brewer	.10	.05	.01
☐ 528 Eric Karros	.30	.14	.04
☐ 529 Marquis Grissom	.30	.14	.04
☐ 530 Rico Brogna	.30	.14	.04
☐ 531 Sammy Sosa	.30	.14	.04
☐ 532 Bret Boone	.30	.14	.04
☐ 533 Luis Rivera	.10	.05	.01
☐ 534 Hal Morris	.20	.09	.03
☐ 535 Monty Fariss	.10	.05	.01
☐ 536 Leo Gomez	.10	.05	.01
☐ 537 Wally Joyner	.20	.09	.03
☐ 538 Tony Gwynn	1.00	.45	.12
☐ 539 Mike Williams	.10	.05	.01
☐ 540 Juan Gonzalez	.60	.25	.07
☐ 541 Ryan Klesko	1.50	.70	.19
☐ 542 Ryan Thompson	.20	.09	.03
☐ 543 Chad Curtis	.20	.09	.03
☐ 544 Orel Hershiser	.20	.09	.03
☐ 545 Carlos Garcia	.20	.09	.03
☐ 546 Bob Welch	.20	.09	.03
☐ 547 Vinny Castilla	.30	.14	.04
☐ 548 Ozzie Smith	.60	.25	.07
☐ 549 Luis Salazar	.10	.05	.01
☐ 550 Mark Guthrie	.10	.05	.01
☐ 551 Charles Nagy	.20	.09	.03
☐ 552 Alex Fernandez	.30	.14	.04
☐ 553 Mel Rojas	.20	.09	.03
☐ 554 Orestes Destrade	.10	.05	.01
☐ 555 Mark Gubicza	.10	.05	.01
☐ 556 Steve Finley	.10	.05	.01
☐ 557 Don Mattingly	1.50	.70	.19
☐ 558 Rickey Henderson	.30	.14	.04
☐ 559 Tommy Greene	.10	.05	.01
☐ 560 Arthur Rhodes	.10	.05	.01
☐ 561 Alfredo Griffin	.10	.05	.01
☐ 562 Will Clark	.40	.18	.05
☐ 563 Bob Zupcic	.10	.05	.01
☐ 564 Chuck Carr	.10	.05	.01
☐ 565 Henry Cotto	.10	.05	.01
☐ 566 Billy Spiers	.10	.05	.01
☐ 567 Jack Armstrong	.10	.05	.01
☐ 568 Kurt Stillwell	.10	.05	.01
☐ 569 David McCarty	.10	.05	.01
☐ 570 Joe Vitiello	.20	.09	.03
☐ 571 Gerald Williams	.10	.05	.01
☐ 572 Dale Murphy	.30	.14	.04
☐ 573 Scott Aldred	.10	.05	.01
☐ 574 Bill Gullickson	.10	.05	.01
☐ 575 Bobby Thigpen	.10	.05	.01
☐ 576 Glenallen Hill	.20	.09	.03
☐ 577 Dwayne Henry	.10	.05	.01
☐ 578 Calvin Jones	.10	.05	.01
☐ 579 Al Martin	.20	.09	.03
☐ 580 Ruben Sierra	.30	.14	.04
☐ 581 Andy Benes	.20	.09	.03
☐ 582 Anthony Young	.10	.05	.01
☐ 583 Shawn Boskie	.10	.05	.01
☐ 584 Scott Pose	.10	.05	.01
☐ 585 Mike Piazza	2.50	1.10	.30
☐ 586 Donovan Osborne	.10	.05	.01
☐ 587 James Austin	.10	.05	.01
☐ 588 Checklist 301-400	.10	.05	.01
☐ 589 Checklist 401-500	.10	.05	.01
☐ 590 Checklist 501-600	.10	.05	.01
☐ 591 Ken Griffey Jr. MC	1.50	.70	.19
☐ 592 Ivan Rodriguez MC	.30	.14	.04
☐ 593 Carlos Baerga MC	.30	.14	.04
☐ 594 Fred McGriff MC	.30	.14	.04
☐ 595 Mark McGwire MC	.30	.14	.04
☐ 596 Roberto Alomar MC	.30	.14	.04
☐ 597 Kirby Puckett MC	.50	.23	.06
☐ 598 Marquis Grissom MC	.30	.14	.04
☐ 599 John Smoltz MC	.20	.09	.03
☐ 600 Ryne Sandberg MC	.40	.18	.05
☐ 601 Wade Boggs	.30	.14	.04
☐ 602 Jeff Reardon	.20	.09	.03
☐ 603 Billy Ripken	.10	.05	.01
☐ 604 Bryan Harvey	.20	.09	.03
☐ 605 Carlos Quintana	.10	.05	.01

□	#	Player			
□	606	Greg Hibbard	.10	.05	.01
□	607	Ellis Burks	.20	.09	.03
□	608	Greg Swindell	.10	.05	.01
□	609	Dave Winfield	.30	.14	.04
□	610	Charlie Hough	.20	.09	.03
□	611	Chili Davis	.20	.09	.03
□	612	Jody Reed	.10	.05	.01
□	613	Mark Williamson	.10	.05	.01
□	614	Phil Plantier	.10	.05	.01
□	615	Jim Abbott	.30	.14	.04
□	616	Dante Bichette	.40	.18	.05
□	617	Mark Eichhorn	.10	.05	.01
□	618	Gary Sheffield	.30	.14	.04
□	619	Richie Lewis	.10	.05	.01
□	620	Joe Girardi	.10	.05	.01
□	621	Jaime Navarro	.10	.05	.01
□	622	Willie Wilson	.10	.05	.01
□	623	Scott Fletcher	.10	.05	.01
□	624	Bud Black	.10	.05	.01
□	625	Tom Brunansky	.10	.05	.01
□	626	Steve Avery	.30	.14	.04
□	627	Paul Molitor	.30	.14	.04
□	628	Gregg Jefferies	.30	.14	.04
□	629	Dave Stewart	.20	.09	.03
□	630	Javier Lopez	1.00	.45	.12
□	631	Greg Gagne	.10	.05	.01
□	632	Roberto Kelly	.20	.09	.03
□	633	Mike Fetters	.10	.05	.01
□	634	Ozzie Canseco	.10	.05	.01
□	635	Jeff Russell	.10	.05	.01
□	636	Pete Incaviglia	.10	.05	.01
□	637	Tom Henke	.20	.09	.03
□	638	Chipper Jones	3.00	1.35	.35
□	639	Jimmy Key	.20	.09	.03
□	640	Dave Martinez	.10	.05	.01
□	641	Dave Stieb	.10	.05	.01
□	642	Milt Thompson	.10	.05	.01
□	643	Alan Mills	.10	.05	.01
□	644	Tony Fernandez	.10	.05	.01
□	645	Randy Bush	.10	.05	.01
□	646	Joe Magrane	.10	.05	.01
□	647	Ivan Calderon	.10	.05	.01
□	648	Jose Guzman	.10	.05	.01
□	649	John Olerud	.20	.09	.03
□	650	Tom Glavine	.30	.14	.04
□	651	Julio Franco	.20	.09	.03
□	652	Armando Reynoso	.10	.05	.01
□	653	Felix Jose	.10	.05	.01
□	654	Ben Rivera	.10	.05	.01
□	655	Andre Dawson	.30	.14	.04
□	656	Mike Harkey	.10	.05	.01
□	657	Kevin Seitzer	.10	.05	.01
□	658	Lonnie Smith	.10	.05	.01
□	659	Norm Charlton	.10	.05	.01
□	660	David Justice	.40	.18	.05
□	661	Fernando Valenzuela	.20	.09	.03
□	662	Dan Wilson	.20	.09	.03
□	663	Mark Gardner	.10	.05	.01
□	664	Doug Dascenzo	.10	.05	.01
□	665	Greg Maddux	3.00	1.35	.35
□	666	Harold Baines	.20	.09	.03
□	667	Randy Myers	.20	.09	.03
□	668	Harold Reynolds	.10	.05	.01
□	669	Candy Maldonado	.10	.05	.01
□	670	Al Leiter	.10	.05	.01
□	671	Jerald Clark	.10	.05	.01
□	672	Doug Drabek	.30	.14	.04
□	673	Kirk Gibson	.20	.09	.03
□	674	Steve Reed	.10	.05	.01
□	675	Mike Felder	.10	.05	.01
□	676	Ricky Gutierrez	.10	.05	.01
□	677	Spike Owen	.10	.05	.01
□	678	Otis Nixon	.10	.05	.01
□	679	Scott Sanderson	.10	.05	.01
□	680	Mark Carreon	.10	.05	.01
□	681	Troy Percival	.10	.05	.01
□	682	Kevin Stocker	.20	.09	.03
□	683	Jim Converse	.20	.09	.03
□	684	Barry Bonds	.75	.35	.09
□	685	Greg Gohr	.10	.05	.01
□	686	Tim Wallach	.10	.05	.01
□	687	Matt Mieske	.20	.09	.03
□	688	Robby Thompson	.10	.05	.01
□	689	Brien Taylor	.20	.09	.03
□	690	Kirt Manwaring	.10	.05	.01
□	691	Mike Lansing	.20	.09	.03
□	692	Steve Decker	.10	.05	.01
□	693	Mike Moore	.10	.05	.01
□	694	Kevin Mitchell	.20	.09	.03
□	695	Phil Hiatt	.10	.05	.01
□	696	Tony Tarasco	.40	.18	.05
□	697	Benji Gil	.20	.09	.03
□	698	Jeff Juden	.10	.05	.01
□	699	Kevin Reimer	.10	.05	.01
□	700	Andy Ashby	.10	.05	.01
□	701	John Jaha	.20	.09	.03
□	702	Tim Bogar	.10	.05	.01
□	703	David Cone	.30	.14	.04
□	704	Willie Greene	.20	.09	.03
□	705	David Hulse	.10	.05	.01
□	706	Cris Carpenter	.10	.05	.01
□	707	Ken Griffey Jr.	3.00	1.35	.35
□	708	Steve Bedrosian	.10	.05	.01
□	709	Dave Nilsson	.20	.09	.03
□	710	Paul Wagner	.10	.05	.01
□	711	B.J. Surhoff	.20	.09	.03
□	712	Rene Arocha	.20	.09	.03
□	713	Manuel Lee	.10	.05	.01
□	714	Brian Williams	.10	.05	.01
□	715	Sherman Obando	.20	.09	.03
□	716	Terry Mulholland	.10	.05	.01
□	717	Paul O'Neill	.20	.09	.03
□	718	David Nied	.20	.09	.03
□	719	J.T. Snow	1.00	.45	.12
□	720	Nigel Wilson	.20	.09	.03
□	721	Mike Bielecki	.10	.05	.01
□	722	Kevin Young	.10	.05	.01
□	723	Charlie Leibrandt	.10	.05	.01
□	724	Frank Bolick	.10	.05	.01
□	725	Jon Shave	.10	.05	.01
□	726	Steve Cooke	.10	.05	.01
□	727	Domingo Martinez	.10	.05	.01
□	728	Todd Worrell	.10	.05	.01
□	729	Jose Lind	.10	.05	.01
□	730	Jim Tatum	.10	.05	.01
□	731	Mike Hampton	.10	.05	.01
□	732	Mike Draper	.10	.05	.01
□	733	Henry Mercedes	.10	.05	.01
□	734	John Johnstone	.10	.05	.01
□	735	Mitch Webster	.10	.05	.01
□	736	Russ Springer	.10	.05	.01
□	737	Rob Natal	.10	.05	.01
□	738	Steve Howe	.10	.05	.01
□	739	Darrell Sherman	.10	.05	.01
□	740	Pat Mahomes	.10	.05	.01
□	741	Alex Arias	.10	.05	.01
□	742	Damon Buford	.10	.05	.01
□	743	Charlie Hayes	.20	.09	.03
□	744	Guillermo Velasquez	.10	.05	.01
□	745	Checklist 601-750 UER (650 Tom Glavine)	.10	.05	.01
□	746	Frank Thomas MC	1.50	.70	.19

☐	747	Barry Bonds MC	.40	.18	.05
☐	748	Roger Clemens MC	.30	.14	.04
☐	749	Joe Carter MC	.30	.14	.04
☐	750	Greg Maddux MC	1.50	.70	.19

1993 Stadium Club First Day Issue

Two thousand of each 1993 Stadium Club baseball card were produced on the first day and then randomly inserted in packs. These standard-size (2 1/2" by 3 1/2") cards are identical to the regular-issue 1993 Stadium Club cards, except for the embossed prismatic-foil "1st Day Production" logo stamped in an upper corner. The fronts feature unbordered color player action shots and carry the player's name in gold foil backed by a red stripe near the bottom. A baseball icon appears in the lower right with gold-foil motion-streaking. The back carries another color player action photo in the upper left. His name appears in white lettering upon a black stripe alongside on the right. Beneath are the player's team, biography, and 1992 stats. Further below are a picture of the player's first Topps card, his ranking, and career stats. All the back's design elements are superposed upon a ghosted and grainy photo of a player's gloved hand holding a baseball. The cards are numbered on the back.

	MINT	NRMT	EXC
COMPLETE SET (750)	3200.00	1450.00	400.00
COMPLETE SERIES 1 (300)	1200.00	550.00	150.00
COMPLETE SERIES 2 (300)	1200.00	550.00	150.00
COMPLETE SERIES 3 (150)	800.00	350.00	100.00
COMMON FDI (1-300)	2.50	1.10	.30
COMMON FDI (301-600)	2.50	1.10	.30
COMMON FDI (601-750)	2.50	1.10	.30
SEMISTARS	5.00	2.20	.60

BEWARE OF TRANSFERRED FDI LOGOS
*VETERAN STARS: 25X to 40X BASIC CARDS
*YOUNG STARS: 18X to 30X BASIC CARDS
*RCs: 10X to 20X BASIC CARDS

			MINT	NRMT	EXC
☐	2	Greg Maddux	120.00	55.00	15.00
☐	40	Cal Ripken	140.00	65.00	17.50
☐	102	Albert Belle	50.00	22.00	6.25
☐	200	Frank Thomas	120.00	55.00	15.00
☐	277	Kenny Lofton	40.00	18.00	5.00
☐	283	Kirby Puckett	40.00	18.00	5.00
☐	353	Nolan Ryan	120.00	55.00	15.00
☐	384	Jeff Bagwell	50.00	22.00	6.25
☐	424	George Brett	50.00	22.00	6.25
☐	538	Tony Gwynn	40.00	18.00	5.00
☐	557	Don Mattingly	60.00	27.00	7.50
☐	585	Mike Piazza	60.00	27.00	7.50
☐	591	Ken Griffey Jr. MC	60.00	27.00	7.50
☐	638	Chipper Jones	80.00	36.00	10.00
☐	665	Greg Maddux	120.00	55.00	15.00
☐	707	Ken Griffey Jr.	120.00	55.00	15.00
☐	746	Frank Thomas MC	60.00	27.00	7.50
☐	750	Greg Maddux MC	60.00	27.00	7.50

1994 Stadium Club

The 720 standard-size cards comprising this set were issued two series of 270 and a third series of 180. Card fronts feature borderless color player action photos. The player's last name appears in white lettering within a red-foil-stamped rectangle at the bottom. His first name appears alongside in black "typewritten" lettering within a division color-coded "tearaway." The red-foil-stamped Stadium Club logo appears in an upper corner. The back carries a color player action cutout superimposed upon a blue and black background. The player's name, team, biography, career highlights and statistics appear in lettering of several different colors and typefaces. There are a number of subsets including Home Run Club (258-268), Tale of Two Players (525/526), Division Leaders (527-532), Quick Starts (533-538), Career Contributors (541-543), Rookie Rocker (626-630), Rookie Rocket (631-634) and Fantastic Finishes (714-719). Rookie Cards include Brian Anderson, Chan Ho Park and Julian Tavarez.

	MINT	NRMT	EXC
COMPLETE SET (720)	55.00	25.00	7.00
COMPLETE SERIES 1 (270)	20.00	9.00	2.50
COMPLETE SERIES 2 (270)	20.00	9.00	2.50
COMPLETE SERIES 3 (180)	15.00	6.75	1.85
COMMON CARD (1-270)	.10	.05	.01
COMMON CARD (271-540)	.10	.05	.01
COMMON CARD (541-720)	.10	.05	.01
COMP. GOLD. RAINBOW (720)	170.00	75.00	21.00
GOLD. RAINBOW COM. CARDS (1-720)	.25	.11	.03
GOLD. RAINBOW SEMISTARS	.50	.23	.06

*GOLD. RAINBOW VETERAN STARS: 2X TO 4X BASIC CARDS
*GOLD. RAINBOW YOUNG STARS: 1.25X TO 2.5X BASIC CARDS
*GOLD. RAINBOW RC's: 1.25X TO 2.5X BASIC CARDS

☐	1	Robin Yount	.40	.18	.05
☐	2	Rick Wilkins	.10	.05	.01
☐	3	Steve Scarsone	.10	.05	.01
☐	4	Gary Sheffield	.30	.14	.04
☐	5	George Brett UER	1.25	.55	.16
		(birthdate listed as 1963; should be 1953)			
☐	6	Al Martin	.10	.05	.01
☐	7	Joe Oliver	.10	.05	.01
☐	8	Stan Belinda	.10	.05	.01
☐	9	Denny Hocking	.10	.05	.01
☐	10	Roberto Alomar	.60	.25	.07

☐ 11	Luis Polonia	.10	.05	.01
☐ 12	Scott Hemond	.10	.05	.01
☐ 13	Jody Reed	.10	.05	.01
☐ 14	Mel Rojas	.10	.05	.01
☐ 15	Junior Ortiz	.10	.05	.01
☐ 16	Harold Baines	.20	.09	.03
☐ 17	Brad Pennington	.10	.05	.01
☐ 18	Jay Bell	.10	.05	.01
☐ 19	Tom Henke	.10	.05	.01
☐ 20	Jeff Branson	.10	.05	.01
☐ 21	Roberto Mejia	.10	.05	.01
☐ 22	Pedro Munoz	.10	.05	.01
☐ 23	Matt Nokes	.10	.05	.01
☐ 24	Jack McDowell	.30	.14	.04
☐ 25	Cecil Fielder	.30	.14	.04
☐ 26	Tony Fossas	.10	.05	.01
☐ 27	Jim Eisenreich	.10	.05	.01
☐ 28	Anthony Young	.10	.05	.01
☐ 29	Chuck Carr	.10	.05	.01
☐ 30	Jeff Treadway	.10	.05	.01
☐ 31	Chris Nabholz	.10	.05	.01
☐ 32	Tom Candiotti	.10	.05	.01
☐ 33	Mike Maddux	.10	.05	.01
☐ 34	Nolan Ryan	3.00	1.35	.35
☐ 35	Luis Gonzalez	.10	.05	.01
☐ 36	Tim Salmon	.60	.25	.07
☐ 37	Mark Whiten	.20	.09	.03
☐ 38	Roger McDowell	.10	.05	.01
☐ 39	Royce Clayton	.20	.09	.03
☐ 40	Troy Neel	.10	.05	.01
☐ 41	Mike Harkey	.10	.05	.01
☐ 42	Darrin Fletcher	.10	.05	.01
☐ 43	Wayne Kirby	.10	.05	.01
☐ 44	Rich Amaral	.10	.05	.01
☐ 45	Robb Nen UER	.10	.05	.01
	(Nenn on back)			
☐ 46	Tim Teufel	.10	.05	.01
☐ 47	Steve Cooke	.10	.05	.01
☐ 48	Jeff McNeely	.10	.05	.01
☐ 49	Jeff Montgomery	.20	.09	.03
☐ 50	Skeeter Barnes	.10	.05	.01
☐ 51	Scott Stahoviak	.10	.05	.01
☐ 52	Pat Kelly	.10	.05	.01
☐ 53	Brady Anderson	.20	.09	.03
☐ 54	Mariano Duncan	.10	.05	.01
☐ 55	Brian Bohanon	.10	.05	.01
☐ 56	Jerry Spradlin	.10	.05	.01
☐ 57	Ron Karkovice	.10	.05	.01
☐ 58	Jeff Gardner	.10	.05	.01
☐ 59	Bobby Bonilla	.30	.14	.04
☐ 60	Tino Martinez	.20	.09	.03
☐ 61	Todd Benzinger	.10	.05	.01
☐ 62	Steve Trachsel	.30	.14	.04
☐ 63	Brian Jordan	.20	.09	.03
☐ 64	Steve Bedrosian	.10	.05	.01
☐ 65	Brent Gates	.20	.09	.03
☐ 66	Shawn Green	.40	.18	.05
☐ 67	Sean Berry	.10	.05	.01
☐ 68	Joe Klink	.10	.05	.01
☐ 69	Fernando Valenzuela	.10	.05	.01
☐ 70	Andy Tomberlin	.10	.05	.01
☐ 71	Tony Pena	.10	.05	.01
☐ 72	Eric Young	.10	.05	.01
☐ 73	Chris Gomez	.30	.14	.04
☐ 74	Paul O'Neill	.20	.09	.03
☐ 75	Ricky Gutierrez	.10	.05	.01
☐ 76	Brad Holman	.10	.05	.01
☐ 77	Lance Painter	.10	.05	.01
☐ 78	Mike Butcher	.10	.05	.01
☐ 79	Sid Bream	.10	.05	.01
☐ 80	Sammy Sosa	.30	.14	.04
☐ 81	Felix Fermin	.10	.05	.01
☐ 82	Todd Hundley	.20	.09	.03
☐ 83	Kevin Higgins	.10	.05	.01
☐ 84	Todd Pratt	.10	.05	.01
☐ 85	Ken Griffey Jr.	3.00	1.35	.35
☐ 86	John O'Donoghue	.10	.05	.01
☐ 87	Rick Renteria	.10	.05	.01
☐ 88	John Burkett	.20	.09	.03
☐ 89	Jose Vizcaino	.10	.05	.01
☐ 90	Kevin Seitzer	.10	.05	.01
☐ 91	Bobby Witt	.10	.05	.01
☐ 92	Chris Turner	.10	.05	.01
☐ 93	Omar Vizquel	.10	.05	.01
☐ 94	David Justice	.40	.18	.05
☐ 95	David Segui	.10	.05	.01
☐ 96	Dave Hollins	.20	.09	.03
☐ 97	Doug Strange	.10	.05	.01
☐ 98	Jerald Clark	.10	.05	.01
☐ 99	Mike Moore	.10	.05	.01
☐ 100	Joey Cora	.10	.05	.01
☐ 101	Scott Kamieniecki	.10	.05	.01
☐ 102	Andy Benes	.20	.09	.03
☐ 103	Chris Bosio	.10	.05	.01
☐ 104	Rey Sanchez	.10	.05	.01
☐ 105	John Jaha	.10	.05	.01
☐ 106	Otis Nixon	.10	.05	.01
☐ 107	Rickey Henderson	.30	.14	.04
☐ 108	Jeff Bagwell	1.00	.45	.12
☐ 109	Gregg Jefferies	.30	.14	.04
☐ 110	Blue Jays Trio	.30	.14	.04
	(Roberto Alomar/Paul Molitor/ John Olerud)			
☐ 111	Braves Trio	.30	.14	.04
	(Ron Gant/David Justice/ Fred McGriff)			
☐ 112	Rangers Trio	.30	.14	.04
	(Juan Gonzalez/Rafael Palmeiro/ Dean Palmer)			
☐ 113	Greg Swindell	.10	.05	.01
☐ 114	Bill Haselman	.10	.05	.01
☐ 115	Phil Plantier	.20	.09	.03
☐ 116	Ivan Rodriguez	.30	.14	.04
☐ 117	Kevin Tapani	.10	.05	.01
☐ 118	Mike LaValliere	.10	.05	.01
☐ 119	Tim Costo	.10	.05	.01
☐ 120	Mickey Morandini	.10	.05	.01
☐ 121	Brett Butler	.20	.09	.03
☐ 122	Tom Pagnozzi	.10	.05	.01
☐ 123	Ron Gant	.20	.09	.03
☐ 124	Damion Easley	.10	.05	.01
☐ 125	Dennis Eckersley	.30	.14	.04
☐ 126	Matt Mieske	.10	.05	.01
☐ 127	Cliff Floyd	.30	.14	.04
☐ 128	Julian Tavarez	.60	.25	.07
☐ 129	Arthur Rhodes	.10	.05	.01
☐ 130	Dave West	.10	.05	.01
☐ 131	Tim Naehring	.20	.09	.03
☐ 132	Freddie Benavides	.10	.05	.01
☐ 133	Paul Assenmacher	.10	.05	.01
☐ 134	David McCarty	.10	.05	.01
☐ 135	Jose Lind	.10	.05	.01
☐ 136	Reggie Sanders	.30	.14	.04
☐ 137	Don Slaught	.10	.05	.01
☐ 138	Andujar Cedeno	.10	.05	.01
☐ 139	Rob Deer	.10	.05	.01
☐ 140	Mike Piazza UER	1.25	.55	.16
	(listed as outfielder)			
☐ 141	Moises Alou	.20	.09	.03
☐ 142	Tom Foley	.10	.05	.01
☐ 143	Benito Santiago	.10	.05	.01
☐ 144	Sandy Alomar	.20	.09	.03

☐ 145	Carlos Hernandez	.10	.05	.01
☐ 146	Luis Alicea	.10	.05	.01
☐ 147	Tom Lampkin	.10	.05	.01
☐ 148	Ryan Klesko	.75	.35	.09
☐ 149	Juan Guzman	.20	.09	.03
☐ 150	Scott Servais	.10	.05	.01
☐ 151	Tony Gwynn	1.00	.45	.12
☐ 152	Tim Wakefield	.20	.09	.03
☐ 153	David Nied	.20	.09	.03
☐ 154	Chris Haney	.10	.05	.01
☐ 155	Danny Bautista	.20	.09	.03
☐ 156	Randy Velarde	.10	.05	.01
☐ 157	Darrin Jackson	.10	.05	.01
☐ 158	J.R. Phillips	.20	.09	.03
☐ 159	Greg Gagne	.10	.05	.01
☐ 160	Luis Aquino	.10	.05	.01
☐ 161	John Vander Wal	.10	.05	.01
☐ 162	Randy Myers	.10	.05	.01
☐ 163	Ted Power	.10	.05	.01
☐ 164	Scott Brosius	.10	.05	.01
☐ 165	Len Dykstra	.30	.14	.04
☐ 166	Jacob Brumfield	.10	.05	.01
☐ 167	Bo Jackson	.30	.14	.04
☐ 168	Eddie Taubensee	.10	.05	.01
☐ 169	Carlos Baerga	.60	.25	.07
☐ 170	Tim Bogar	.10	.05	.01
☐ 171	Jose Canseco	.50	.23	.06
☐ 172	Greg Blosser UER	.10	.05	.01
	(Gregg on front)			
☐ 173	Chili Davis	.20	.09	.03
☐ 174	Randy Knorr	.10	.05	.01
☐ 175	Mike Perez	.10	.05	.01
☐ 176	Henry Rodriguez	.10	.05	.01
☐ 177	Brian Turang	.10	.05	.01
☐ 178	Roger Pavlik	.10	.05	.01
☐ 179	Aaron Sele	.30	.14	.04
☐ 180	Fred McGriff	.30	.14	.04
	Gary Sheffield			
	Tale of 2 Players			
☐ 181	J.T. Snow	.20	.09	.03
	Tim Salmon			
	Tale of 2 Players			
☐ 182	Roberto Hernandez	.10	.05	.01
☐ 183	Jeff Reboulet	.10	.05	.01
☐ 184	John Doherty	.10	.05	.01
☐ 185	Danny Sheaffer	.10	.05	.01
☐ 186	Bip Roberts	.10	.05	.01
☐ 187	Denny Martinez	.20	.09	.03
☐ 188	Darryl Hamilton	.10	.05	.01
☐ 189	Eduardo Perez	.10	.05	.01
☐ 190	Pete Harnisch	.10	.05	.01
☐ 191	Rich Gossage	.20	.09	.03
☐ 192	Mickey Tettleton	.20	.09	.03
☐ 193	Lenny Webster	.10	.05	.01
☐ 194	Lance Johnson	.10	.05	.01
☐ 195	Don Mattingly	1.50	.70	.19
☐ 196	Gregg Olson	.10	.05	.01
☐ 197	Mark Gubicza	.10	.05	.01
☐ 198	Scott Fletcher	.10	.05	.01
☐ 199	Jon Shave	.10	.05	.01
☐ 200	Tim Mauser	.10	.05	.01
☐ 201	Jeromy Burnitz	.10	.05	.01
☐ 202	Rob Dibble	.10	.05	.01
☐ 203	Will Clark	.40	.18	.05
☐ 204	Steve Buechele	.10	.05	.01
☐ 205	Brian Williams	.10	.05	.01
☐ 206	Carlos Garcia	.10	.05	.01
☐ 207	Mark Clark	.10	.05	.01
☐ 208	Rafael Palmeiro	.30	.14	.04
☐ 209	Eric Davis	.10	.05	.01
☐ 210	Pat Meares	.10	.05	.01
☐ 211	Chuck Finley	.10	.05	.01
☐ 212	Jason Bere	.30	.14	.04
☐ 213	Gary DiSarcina	.10	.05	.01
☐ 214	Tony Fernandez	.10	.05	.01
☐ 215	B.J. Surhoff	.10	.05	.01
☐ 216	Lee Guetterman	.10	.05	.01
☐ 217	Tim Wallach	.10	.05	.01
☐ 218	Kirt Manwaring	.10	.05	.01
☐ 219	Albert Belle	1.25	.55	.16
☐ 220	Doc Gooden	.10	.05	.01
☐ 221	Archi Cianfrocco	.10	.05	.01
☐ 222	Terry Mulholland	.10	.05	.01
☐ 223	Hipolito Pichardo	.10	.05	.01
☐ 224	Kent Hrbek	.10	.05	.01
☐ 225	Craig Grebeck	.10	.05	.01
☐ 226	Todd Jones	.10	.05	.01
☐ 227	Mike Bordick	.10	.05	.01
☐ 228	John Olerud	.30	.14	.04
☐ 229	Jeff Blauser	.10	.05	.01
☐ 230	Alex Arias	.10	.05	.01
☐ 231	Bernard Gilkey	.20	.09	.03
☐ 232	Denny Neagle	.20	.09	.03
☐ 233	Pedro Borbon	.10	.05	.01
☐ 234	Dick Schofield	.10	.05	.01
☐ 235	Matias Carrillo	.10	.05	.01
☐ 236	Juan Bell	.10	.05	.01
☐ 237	Mike Hampton	.10	.05	.01
☐ 238	Barry Bonds	.75	.35	.09
☐ 239	Cris Carpenter	.10	.05	.01
☐ 240	Eric Karros	.20	.09	.03
☐ 241	Greg McMichael	.10	.05	.01
☐ 242	Pat Hentgen	.20	.09	.03
☐ 243	Tim Pugh	.10	.05	.01
☐ 244	Vinny Castilla	.20	.09	.03
☐ 245	Charlie Hough	.10	.05	.01
☐ 246	Bobby Munoz	.10	.05	.01
☐ 247	Kevin Baez	.10	.05	.01
☐ 248	Todd Frohwirth	.10	.05	.01
☐ 249	Charlie Hayes	.20	.09	.03
☐ 250	Mike Macfarlane	.10	.05	.01
☐ 251	Danny Darwin	.10	.05	.01
☐ 252	Ben Rivera	.10	.05	.01
☐ 253	Dave Henderson	.10	.05	.01
☐ 254	Steve Avery	.30	.14	.04
☐ 255	Tim Belcher	.10	.05	.01
☐ 256	Dan Plesac	.10	.05	.01
☐ 257	Jim Thome	.60	.25	.07
☐ 258	Albert Belle 35	.60	.25	.07
☐ 259	Barry Bonds 35	.40	.18	.05
☐ 260	Ron Gant 35	.20	.09	.03
☐ 261	Juan Gonzalez 35	.30	.14	.04
☐ 262	Ken Griffey Jr. 35	1.50	.70	.19
☐ 263	David Justice 35	.30	.14	.04
☐ 264	Fred McGriff 35	.30	.14	.04
☐ 265	Rafael Palmeiro 35	.30	.14	.04
☐ 266	Mike Piazza 35	.60	.25	.07
☐ 267	Frank Thomas 35	1.50	.70	.19
☐ 268	Matt Williams 35	.30	.14	.04
☐ 269	Checklist 1-135	.10	.05	.01
☐ 270	Checklist 136-270	.10	.05	.01
☐ 271	Mike Stanley	.10	.05	.01
☐ 272	Tony Tarasco	.30	.14	.04
☐ 273	Teddy Higuera	.10	.05	.01
☐ 274	Ryan Thompson	.20	.09	.03
☐ 275	Rick Aguilera	.20	.09	.03
☐ 276	Ramon Martinez	.20	.09	.03
☐ 277	Orlando Merced	.20	.09	.03
☐ 278	Guillermo Velasquez	.10	.05	.01
☐ 279	Mark Hutton	.10	.05	.01
☐ 280	Larry Walker	.40	.18	.05
☐ 281	Kevin Gross	.10	.05	.01

□	#	Name			
□	282	Jose Offerman	.10	.05	.01
□	283	Jim Leyritz	.10	.05	.01
□	284	Jamie Moyer	.10	.05	.01
□	285	Frank Thomas	3.00	1.35	.35
□	286	Derek Bell	.20	.09	.03
□	287	Derrick May	.10	.05	.01
□	288	Dave Winfield	.30	.14	.04
□	289	Curt Schilling	.10	.05	.01
□	290	Carlos Quintana	.10	.05	.01
□	291	Bob Natal	.10	.05	.01
□	292	David Cone	.30	.14	.04
□	293	Al Osuna	.10	.05	.01
□	294	Bob Hamelin	.20	.09	.03
□	295	Chad Curtis	.20	.09	.03
□	296	Danny Jackson	.10	.05	.01
□	297	Bob Welch	.10	.05	.01
□	298	Felix Jose	.10	.05	.01
□	299	Jay Buhner	.30	.14	.04
□	300	Joe Carter	.30	.14	.04
□	301	Kenny Lofton	1.00	.45	.12
□	302	Kirk Rueter	.10	.05	.01
□	303	Kim Batiste	.10	.05	.01
□	304	Mike Morgan	.10	.05	.01
□	305	Pat Borders	.10	.05	.01
□	306	Rene Arocha	.20	.09	.03
□	307	Ruben Sierra	.30	.14	.04
□	308	Steve Finley	.10	.05	.01
□	309	Travis Fryman	.30	.14	.04
□	310	Zane Smith	.10	.05	.01
□	311	Willie Wilson	.10	.05	.01
□	312	Trevor Hoffman	.10	.05	.01
□	313	Terry Pendleton	.10	.05	.01
□	314	Salomon Torres	.20	.09	.03
□	315	Robin Ventura	.20	.09	.03
□	316	Randy Tomlin	.10	.05	.01
□	317	Dave Stewart	.20	.09	.03
□	318	Mike Benjamin	.10	.05	.01
□	319	Matt Turner	.10	.05	.01
□	320	Manny Ramirez	1.50	.70	.19
□	321	Kevin Young	.10	.05	.01
□	322	Ken Caminiti	.20	.09	.03
□	323	Joe Girardi	.10	.05	.01
□	324	Jeff McKnight	.10	.05	.01
□	325	Gene Harris	.10	.05	.01
□	326	Devon White	.20	.09	.03
□	327	Darryl Kile	.20	.09	.03
□	328	Craig Paquette	.10	.05	.01
□	329	Cal Eldred	.20	.09	.03
□	330	Bill Swift	.10	.05	.01
□	331	Alan Trammell	.30	.14	.04
□	332	Armando Reynoso	.10	.05	.01
□	333	Brent Mayne	.10	.05	.01
□	334	Chris Donnels	.10	.05	.01
□	335	Darryl Strawberry	.20	.09	.03
□	336	Dean Palmer	.20	.09	.03
□	337	Frank Castillo	.10	.05	.01
□	338	Jeff King	.10	.05	.01
□	339	John Franco	.10	.05	.01
□	340	Kevin Appier	.20	.09	.03
□	341	Lance Blankenship	.10	.05	.01
□	342	Mark McLemore	.10	.05	.01
□	343	Pedro Astacio	.20	.09	.03
□	344	Rich Batchelor	.10	.05	.01
□	345	Ryan Bowen	.10	.05	.01
□	346	Terry Steinbach	.20	.09	.03
□	347	Troy O'Leary	.20	.09	.03
□	348	Willie Blair	.10	.05	.01
□	349	Wade Boggs	.30	.14	.04
□	350	Tim Raines	.30	.14	.04
□	351	Scott Livingstone	.10	.05	.01
□	352	Rod Correia	.10	.05	.01
□	353	Ray Lankford	.30	.14	.04
□	354	Pat Listach	.10	.05	.01
□	355	Milt Thompson	.10	.05	.01
□	356	Miguel Jimenez	.20	.09	.03
□	357	Marc Newfield	.30	.14	.04
□	358	Mark McGwire	.30	.14	.04
□	359	Kirby Puckett	1.00	.45	.12
□	360	Kent Mercker	.10	.05	.01
□	361	John Kruk	.20	.09	.03
□	362	Jeff Kent	.20	.09	.03
□	363	Hal Morris	.20	.09	.03
□	364	Edgar Martinez	.20	.09	.03
□	365	Dave Magadan	.10	.05	.01
□	366	Dante Bichette	.40	.18	.05
□	367	Chris Hammond	.10	.05	.01
□	368	Bret Saberhagen	.20	.09	.03
□	369	Billy Ripken	.10	.05	.01
□	370	Bill Gullickson	.10	.05	.01
□	371	Andre Dawson	.30	.14	.04
□	372	Roberto Kelly	.10	.05	.01
□	373	Cal Ripken	3.00	1.35	.35
□	374	Craig Biggio	.20	.09	.03
□	375	Dan Pasqua	.10	.05	.01
□	376	Dave Nilsson	.10	.05	.01
□	377	Duane Ward	.10	.05	.01
□	378	Greg Vaughn	.20	.09	.03
□	379	Jeff Fassero	.10	.05	.01
□	380	Jerry DiPoto	.10	.05	.01
□	381	John Patterson	.10	.05	.01
□	382	Kevin Brown	.10	.05	.01
□	383	Kevin Roberson	.10	.05	.01
□	384	Joe Orsulak	.10	.05	.01
□	385	Hilly Hathaway	.10	.05	.01
□	386	Mike Greenwell	.20	.09	.03
□	387	Orestes Destrade	.10	.05	.01
□	388	Mike Gallego	.10	.05	.01
□	389	Ozzie Guillen	.10	.05	.01
□	390	Raul Mondesi	1.00	.45	.12
□	391	Scott Lydy	.10	.05	.01
□	392	Tom Urbani	.10	.05	.01
□	393	Wil Cordero	.30	.14	.04
□	394	Tony Longmire	.10	.05	.01
□	395	Todd Zeile	.20	.09	.03
□	396	Scott Cooper	.20	.09	.03
□	397	Ryne Sandberg	.75	.35	.09
□	398	Ricky Bones	.10	.05	.01
□	399	Phil Clark	.10	.05	.01
□	400	Orel Hershiser	.20	.09	.03
□	401	Mike Henneman	.10	.05	.01
□	402	Mark Lemke	.10	.05	.01
□	403	Mark Grace	.30	.14	.04
□	404	Ken Ryan	.10	.05	.01
□	405	John Smoltz	.20	.09	.03
□	406	Jeff Conine	.30	.14	.04
□	407	Greg Harris	.10	.05	.01
□	408	Doug Drabek	.20	.09	.03
□	409	Dave Fleming	.10	.05	.01
□	410	Danny Tartabull	.20	.09	.03
□	411	Chad Kreuter	.10	.05	.01
□	412	Brad Ausmus	.10	.05	.01
□	413	Ben McDonald	.20	.09	.03
□	414	Barry Larkin	.40	.18	.05
□	415	Bret Barberie	.10	.05	.01
□	416	Chuck Knoblauch	.30	.14	.04
□	417	Ozzie Smith	.60	.25	.07
□	418	Ed Sprague	.10	.05	.01
□	419	Matt Williams	.50	.23	.06
□	420	Jeremy Hernandez	.10	.05	.01
□	421	Jose Bautista	.10	.05	.01
□	422	Kevin Mitchell	.20	.09	.03
□	423	Manuel Lee	.10	.05	.01

☐ 424	Mike Devereaux	.20	.09	.03
☐ 425	Omar Olivares	.10	.05	.01
☐ 426	Rafael Belliard	.10	.05	.01
☐ 427	Richie Lewis	.10	.05	.01
☐ 428	Ron Darling	.10	.05	.01
☐ 429	Shane Mack	.20	.09	.03
☐ 430	Tim Hulett	.10	.05	.01
☐ 431	Wally Joyner	.20	.09	.03
☐ 432	Wes Chamberlain	.10	.05	.01
☐ 433	Tom Browning	.10	.05	.01
☐ 434	Scott Radinsky	.10	.05	.01
☐ 435	Rondell White	.30	.14	.04
☐ 436	Rod Beck	.20	.09	.03
☐ 437	Rheal Cormier	.10	.05	.01
☐ 438	Randy Johnson	.60	.25	.07
☐ 439	Pete Schourek	.20	.09	.03
☐ 440	Mo Vaughn	.50	.23	.06
☐ 441	Mike Timlin	.10	.05	.01
☐ 442	Mark Langston	.30	.14	.04
☐ 443	Lou Whitaker	.30	.14	.04
☐ 444	Kevin Stocker	.20	.09	.03
☐ 445	Ken Hill	.20	.09	.03
☐ 446	John Wetteland	.10	.05	.01
☐ 447	J.T. Snow	.20	.09	.03
☐ 448	Erik Pappas	.10	.05	.01
☐ 449	David Hulse	.10	.05	.01
☐ 450	Darren Daulton	.30	.14	.04
☐ 451	Chris Hoiles	.20	.09	.03
☐ 452	Bryan Harvey	.10	.05	.01
☐ 453	Darren Lewis	.10	.05	.01
☐ 454	Andres Galarraga	.30	.14	.04
☐ 455	Joe Hesketh	.10	.05	.01
☐ 456	Jose Valentin	.10	.05	.01
☐ 457	Dan Peltier	.10	.05	.01
☐ 458	Joe Boever	.10	.05	.01
☐ 459	Kevin Rogers	.10	.05	.01
☐ 460	Craig Shipley	.10	.05	.01
☐ 461	Alvaro Espinoza	.10	.05	.01
☐ 462	Wilson Alvarez	.30	.14	.04
☐ 463	Cory Snyder	.10	.05	.01
☐ 464	Candy Maldonado	.10	.05	.01
☐ 465	Blas Minor	.10	.05	.01
☐ 466	Rod Bolton	.10	.05	.01
☐ 467	Kenny Rogers	.20	.09	.03
☐ 468	Greg Myers	.10	.05	.01
☐ 469	Jimmy Key	.20	.09	.03
☐ 470	Tony Castillo	.10	.05	.01
☐ 471	Mike Stanton	.10	.05	.01
☐ 472	Deion Sanders	.60	.25	.07
☐ 473	Tito Navarro	.10	.05	.01
☐ 474	Mike Gardiner	.10	.05	.01
☐ 475	Steve Reed	.10	.05	.01
☐ 476	John Roper	.10	.05	.01
☐ 477	Mike Trombley	.10	.05	.01
☐ 478	Charles Nagy	.20	.09	.03
☐ 479	Larry Casian	.10	.05	.01
☐ 480	Eric Hillman	.10	.05	.01
☐ 481	Bill Wertz	.10	.05	.01
☐ 482	Jeff Schwarz	.10	.05	.01
☐ 483	John Valentin	.20	.09	.03
☐ 484	Carl Willis	.10	.05	.01
☐ 485	Gary Gaetti	.10	.05	.01
☐ 486	Bill Pecota	.10	.05	.01
☐ 487	John Smiley	.10	.05	.01
☐ 488	Mike Mussina	.40	.18	.05
☐ 489	Mike Ignasiak	.10	.05	.01
☐ 490	Billy Brewer	.10	.05	.01
☐ 491	Jack Voigt	.10	.05	.01
☐ 492	Mike Munoz	.10	.05	.01
☐ 493	Lee Tinsley	.10	.05	.01
☐ 494	Bob Wickman	.10	.05	.01

☐ 495	Roger Salkeld	.10	.05	.01
☐ 496	Thomas Howard	.10	.05	.01
☐ 497	Mark Davis	.10	.05	.01
☐ 498	Dave Clark	.10	.05	.01
☐ 499	Turk Wendell	.10	.05	.01
☐ 500	Rafael Bournigal	.10	.05	.01
☐ 501	Chip Hale	.10	.05	.01
☐ 502	Matt Whiteside	.10	.05	.01
☐ 503	Brian Koelling	.10	.05	.01
☐ 504	Jeff Reed	.10	.05	.01
☐ 505	Paul Wagner	.10	.05	.01
☐ 506	Torey Lovullo	.10	.05	.01
☐ 507	Curtis Leskanic	.10	.05	.01
☐ 508	Derek Lilliquist	.10	.05	.01
☐ 509	Joe Magrane	.10	.05	.01
☐ 510	Mackey Sasser	.10	.05	.01
☐ 511	Lloyd McClendon	.10	.05	.01
☐ 512	Jayhawk Owens	.10	.05	.01
☐ 513	Woody Williams	.10	.05	.01
☐ 514	Gary Redus	.10	.05	.01
☐ 515	Tim Spehr	.10	.05	.01
☐ 516	Jim Abbott	.30	.14	.04
☐ 517	Lou Frazier	.10	.05	.01
☐ 518	Erik Plantenberg	.10	.05	.01
☐ 519	Tim Worrell	.10	.05	.01
☐ 520	Brian McRae	.20	.09	.03
☐ 521	Chan Ho Park	.30	.14	.04
☐ 522	Mark Wohlers	.10	.05	.01
☐ 523	Geronimo Pena	.10	.05	.01
☐ 524	Andy Ashby	.10	.05	.01
☐ 525	Tim Raines TA	.20	.09	.03
☐ 526	Paul Molitor TA	.20	.09	.03
☐ 527	Joe Carter DL	.30	.14	.04
☐ 528	Frank Thomas DL UER	1.50	.70	.19
	(listed as third in RBI in			
	1993; was actually second)			
☐ 529	Ken Griffey Jr. DL	1.50	.70	.19
☐ 530	David Justice DL	.20	.09	.03
☐ 531	Gregg Jefferies DL	.20	.09	.03
☐ 532	Barry Bonds DL	.40	.18	.05
☐ 533	John Kruk QS	.20	.09	.03
☐ 534	Roger Clemens QS	.20	.09	.03
☐ 535	Cecil Fielder QS	.20	.09	.03
☐ 536	Ruben Sierra QS	.20	.09	.03
☐ 537	Tony Gwynn QS	.50	.23	.06
☐ 538	Tom Glavine QS	.20	.09	.03
☐ 539	Checklist 271-405 UER	.10	.05	.01
	(number on back is 269)			
☐ 540	Checklist 406-540 UER	.10	.05	.01
	(numbered 270 on back)			
☐ 541	Ozzie Smith	.30	.14	.04
☐ 542	Eddie Murray	.40	.18	.05
☐ 543	Lee Smith	.30	.14	.04
☐ 544	Greg Maddux	3.00	1.35	.35
☐ 545	Denis Boucher	.10	.05	.01
☐ 546	Mark Gardner	.10	.05	.01
☐ 547	Bo Jackson	.30	.14	.04
☐ 548	Eric Anthony	.10	.05	.01
☐ 549	Delino DeShields	.20	.09	.03
☐ 550	Turner Ward	.10	.05	.01
☐ 551	Scott Sanderson	.10	.05	.01
☐ 552	Hector Carrasco	.10	.05	.01
☐ 553	Tony Phillips	.10	.05	.01
☐ 554	Melido Perez	.10	.05	.01
☐ 555	Mike Felder	.10	.05	.01
☐ 556	Jack Morris	.30	.14	.04
☐ 557	Rafael Palmeiro	.30	.14	.04
☐ 558	Shane Reynolds	.10	.05	.01
☐ 559	Pete Incaviglia	.10	.05	.01
☐ 560	Greg Harris	.10	.05	.01
☐ 561	Matt Walbeck	.10	.05	.01

☐ 562	Todd Van Poppel	.20	.09	.03
☐ 563	Todd Stottlemyre	.10	.05	.01
☐ 564	Ricky Bones	.10	.05	.01
☐ 565	Mike Jackson	.10	.05	.01
☐ 566	Kevin McReynolds	.10	.05	.01
☐ 567	Melvin Nieves	.30	.14	.04
☐ 568	Juan Gonzalez	.75	.35	.09
☐ 569	Frank Viola	.10	.05	.01
☐ 570	Vince Coleman	.10	.05	.01
☐ 571	Brian Anderson	.30	.14	.04
☐ 572	Omar Vizquel	.10	.05	.01
☐ 573	Bernie Williams	.20	.09	.03
☐ 574	Tom Glavine	.30	.14	.04
☐ 575	Mitch Williams	.10	.05	.01
☐ 576	Shawon Dunston	.10	.05	.01
☐ 577	Mike Lansing	.20	.09	.03
☐ 578	Greg Pirkl	.10	.05	.01
☐ 579	Sid Fernandez	.10	.05	.01
☐ 580	Doug Jones	.10	.05	.01
☐ 581	Walt Weiss	.10	.05	.01
☐ 582	Tim Belcher	.10	.05	.01
☐ 583	Alex Fernandez	.30	.14	.04
☐ 584	Alex Cole	.10	.05	.01
☐ 585	Greg Cadaret	.10	.05	.01
☐ 586	Bob Tewksbury	.10	.05	.01
☐ 587	Dave Hansen	.10	.05	.01
☐ 588	Kurt Abbott	.25	.11	.03
☐ 589	Rick White	.10	.05	.01
☐ 590	Kevin Bass	.10	.05	.01
☐ 591	Geronimo Berroa	.10	.05	.01
☐ 592	Jaime Navarro	.10	.05	.01
☐ 593	Steve Farr	.10	.05	.01
☐ 594	Jack Armstrong	.10	.05	.01
☐ 595	Steve Howe	.10	.05	.01
☐ 596	Jose Rijo	.20	.09	.03
☐ 597	Otis Nixon	.10	.05	.01
☐ 598	Robby Thompson	.10	.05	.01
☐ 599	Kelly Stinnett	.10	.05	.01
☐ 600	Carlos Delgado	.30	.14	.04
☐ 601	Brian Johnson	.10	.05	.01
☐ 602	Gregg Olson	.10	.05	.01
☐ 603	Jim Edmonds	.50	.23	.06
☐ 604	Mike Blowers	.20	.09	.03
☐ 605	Lee Smith	.30	.14	.04
☐ 606	Pat Rapp	.10	.05	.01
☐ 607	Mike Magnante	.10	.05	.01
☐ 608	Karl Rhodes	.10	.05	.01
☐ 609	Jeff Juden	.10	.05	.01
☐ 610	Rusty Meacham	.10	.05	.01
☐ 611	Pedro Martinez	.30	.14	.04
☐ 612	Todd Worrell	.10	.05	.01
☐ 613	Stan Javier	.10	.05	.01
☐ 614	Mike Hampton	.10	.05	.01
☐ 615	Jose Guzman	.10	.05	.01
☐ 616	Xavier Hernandez	.10	.05	.01
☐ 617	David Wells	.10	.05	.01
☐ 618	John Habyan	.10	.05	.01
☐ 619	Chris Nabholz	.10	.05	.01
☐ 620	Bobby Jones	.30	.14	.04
☐ 621	Chris James	.10	.05	.01
☐ 622	Ellis Burks	.20	.09	.03
☐ 623	Erik Hanson	.10	.05	.01
☐ 624	Pat Meares	.10	.05	.01
☐ 625	Harold Reynolds	.10	.05	.01
☐ 626	Bob Hamelin	.20	.09	.03
☐ 627	Manny Ramirez	.75	.35	.09
☐ 628	Ryan Klesko	.30	.14	.04
☐ 629	Carlos Delgado	.30	.14	.04
☐ 630	Javier Lopez	.30	.14	.04
☐ 631	Steve Karsay	.10	.05	.01
☐ 632	Rick Helling	.10	.05	.01
☐ 633	Steve Trachsel	.30	.14	.04
☐ 634	Hector Carrasco	.10	.05	.01
☐ 635	Andy Stankiewicz	.10	.05	.01
☐ 636	Paul Sorrento	.10	.05	.01
☐ 637	Scott Erickson	.10	.05	.01
☐ 638	Chipper Jones	1.50	.70	.19
☐ 639	Luis Polonia	.10	.05	.01
☐ 640	Howard Johnson	.10	.05	.01
☐ 641	John Dopson	.10	.05	.01
☐ 642	Jody Reed	.10	.05	.01
☐ 643	Lonnie Smith	.10	.05	.01
☐ 644	Mark Portugal	.10	.05	.01
☐ 645	Paul Molitor	.30	.14	.04
☐ 646	Paul Assenmacher	.10	.05	.01
☐ 647	Hubie Brooks	.10	.05	.01
☐ 648	Gary Wayne	.10	.05	.01
☐ 649	Sean Berry	.10	.05	.01
☐ 650	Roger Clemens	.50	.23	.06
☐ 651	Brian L. Hunter	.75	.35	.09
☐ 652	Wally Whitehurst	.10	.05	.01
☐ 653	Allen Watson	.10	.05	.01
☐ 654	Rickey Henderson	.30	.14	.04
☐ 655	Sid Bream	.10	.05	.01
☐ 656	Dan Wilson	.10	.05	.01
☐ 657	Ricky Jordan	.10	.05	.01
☐ 658	Sterling Hitchcock	.20	.09	.03
☐ 659	Darrin Jackson	.10	.05	.01
☐ 660	Junior Felix	.10	.05	.01
☐ 661	Tom Brunansky	.10	.05	.01
☐ 662	Jose Vizcaino	.10	.05	.01
☐ 663	Mark Leiter	.10	.05	.01
☐ 664	Gil Heredia	.10	.05	.01
☐ 665	Fred McGriff	.40	.18	.05
☐ 666	Will Clark	.40	.18	.05
☐ 667	Al Leiter	.10	.05	.01
☐ 668	James Mouton	.20	.09	.03
☐ 669	Billy Bean	.10	.05	.01
☐ 670	Scott Leius	.10	.05	.01
☐ 671	Bret Boone	.30	.14	.04
☐ 672	Darren Holmes	.10	.05	.01
☐ 673	Dave Weathers	.10	.05	.01
☐ 674	Eddie Murray	.40	.18	.05
☐ 675	Felix Fermin	.10	.05	.01
☐ 676	Chris Sabo	.10	.05	.01
☐ 677	Billy Spiers	.10	.05	.01
☐ 678	Aaron Sele	.30	.14	.04
☐ 679	Juan Samuel	.10	.05	.01
☐ 680	Julio Franco	.20	.09	.03
☐ 681	Heathcliff Slocumb	.10	.05	.01
☐ 682	Denny Martinez	.20	.09	.03
☐ 683	Jerry Browne	.10	.05	.01
☐ 684	Pedro Martinez	.30	.14	.04
☐ 685	Rex Hudler	.10	.05	.01
☐ 686	Willie McGee	.10	.05	.01
☐ 687	Andy Van Slyke	.30	.14	.04
☐ 688	Pat Mahomes	.10	.05	.01
☐ 689	Dave Henderson	.10	.05	.01
☐ 690	Tony Eusebio	.10	.05	.01
☐ 691	Rick Sutcliffe	.20	.09	.03
☐ 692	Willie Banks	.10	.05	.01
☐ 693	Alan Mills	.10	.05	.01
☐ 694	Jeff Treadway	.10	.05	.01
☐ 695	Alex Gonzalez	.30	.14	.04
☐ 696	David Segui	.10	.05	.01
☐ 697	Rick Helling	.10	.05	.01
☐ 698	Bip Roberts	.10	.05	.01
☐ 699	Jeff Cirillo	.20	.09	.03
☐ 700	Terry Mulholland	.10	.05	.01
☐ 701	Marvin Freeman	.10	.05	.01
☐ 702	Jason Bere	.30	.14	.04
☐ 703	Javier Lopez	.50	.23	.06

		MINT	NRMT	EXC
☐ 704	Greg Hibbard	.10	.05	.01
☐ 705	Tommy Greene	.10	.05	.01
☐ 706	Marquis Grissom	.30	.14	.04
☐ 707	Brian Harper	.10	.05	.01
☐ 708	Steve Karsay	.10	.05	.01
☐ 709	Jeff Brantley	.10	.05	.01
☐ 710	Jeff Russell	.10	.05	.01
☐ 711	Bryan Hickerson	.10	.05	.01
☐ 712	Jim Pittsley	.40	.18	.05
☐ 713	Bobby Ayala	.10	.05	.01
☐ 714	John Smoltz	.20	.09	.03
☐ 715	Jose Rijo	.20	.09	.03
☐ 716	Greg Maddux	1.50	.70	.19
☐ 717	Matt Williams	.30	.14	.04
☐ 718	Frank Thomas	1.50	.70	.19
☐ 719	Ryne Sandberg	.40	.18	.05
☐ 720	Checklist	.10	.05	.01

1994 Stadium Club Finest

This set contains 10 standard-size metallic cards of top players. They were randomly inserted one in 24 third series packs. The fronts feature a color player photo with a red and yellow background. Backs contain a color player photo with 1993 and career statistics. Jumbo versions measuring approximately five inches by seven inches were issued for retail repacks and are valued approximately 1.5X the regular versions.

		MINT	NRMT	EXC
COMPLETE SET (10)		35.00	16.00	4.40
COMMON CARD (1-10)		1.00	.45	.12
☐ 1	Jeff Bagwell	3.00	1.35	.35
☐ 2	Albert Belle	4.00	1.80	.50
☐ 3	Barry Bonds	2.50	1.10	.30
☐ 4	Juan Gonzalez	2.50	1.10	.30
☐ 5	Ken Griffey Jr.	10.00	4.50	1.25
☐ 6	Marquis Grissom	1.00	.45	.12
☐ 7	David Justice	1.50	.70	.19
☐ 8	Mike Piazza	4.00	1.80	.50
☐ 9	Tim Salmon	2.00	.90	.25
☐ 10	Frank Thomas	10.00	4.50	1.25

1994 Stadium Club First Day Issue

Randomly inserted in one of every 24 packs, these First Day Production cards are identical to the regular issues except for a special 1st Day foil stamp engraved on the front of each card. No more than 2,000 of each Stadium Club card was issued as First Day Issue.

	MINT	NRMT	EXC
COMPLETE SET (720)	2700.00	1200.00	350.00
COMPLETE SERIES 1 (270)	1200.00	550.00	150.00
COMPLETE SERIES 2 (270)	1000.00	450.00	125.00
COMPLETE SERIES 3 (180)	500.00	220.00	60.00
COMMON CARD (1-270)	2.00	.90	.25
COMMON CARD (271-540)	2.00	.90	.25
COMMON CARD (541-720)	2.00	.90	.25
SEMISTARS	4.00	1.80	.50

BEWARE OF TRANSFERRED FDI LOGOS
*VETERAN STARS: 30X to 50X BASIC CARDS
*YOUNG STARS: 20X to 40X BASIC CARDS
*RCs: 15X to 30X BASIC CARDS

☐ 5	George Brett	40.00	18.00	5.00
☐ 34	Nolan Ryan	100.00	45.00	12.50
☐ 85	Ken Griffey Jr.	100.00	45.00	12.50
☐ 108	Jeff Bagwell	30.00	13.50	3.70
☐ 140	Mike Piazza	40.00	18.00	5.00
☐ 151	Tony Gwynn	30.00	13.50	3.70
☐ 195	Don Mattingly	50.00	22.00	6.25
☐ 219	Albert Belle	40.00	18.00	5.00
☐ 262	Ken Griffey Jr. HR	50.00	22.00	6.25
☐ 267	FRank Thomas HR	50.00	22.00	6.25
☐ 285	Frank Thomas HR	100.00	45.00	12.50
☐ 301	Kenny Lofton	30.00	13.50	3.70
☐ 320	Manny Ramirez	50.00	22.00	6.25
☐ 359	Kirby Puckett	30.00	13.50	3.70
☐ 373	Cal Ripken	120.00	55.00	15.00
☐ 390	Raul Mondesi	30.00	13.50	3.70
☐ 528	Frank Thomas DL	50.00	22.00	6.25
☐ 529	Ken Griffey Jr. DL	50.00	22.00	6.25
☐ 544	Greg Maddux	100.00	45.00	12.50
☐ 627	Manny Ramirez RR	25.00	11.00	3.10
☐ 638	Chipper Jones	50.00	22.00	6.25
☐ 716	Greg Maddux FAN	50.00	22.00	6.25
☐ 718	Frank Thomas FAN	50.00	22.00	6.25

1994 Stadium Club Super Teams

Randomly inserted at a rate of one per 24 first series packs only, this 28-card standard-size features one card for each of the 28 MLB teams. Collectors holding team cards could redeem them for special prizes if those teams won a division title, a league championship, or the World Series. But, since the strike affected the 1994 season, Topps postponed the promotion until the 1995 season. The expiration was pushed back to January 31, 1996.

	MINT	NRMT	EXC
COMPLETE SET (28)	75.00	34.00	9.50
COMMON TEAM (1-28)	1.50	.70	.19

		MINT	NRMT	EXC
☐ 1	Atlanta Braves (Jeff Blauser Terry Pendleton)	25.00	11.00	3.10
☐ 2	Chicago Cubs (Sammy Sosa Derrick May)	1.50	.70	.19
☐ 3	Cincinnati Reds (Reggie Sanders Barry Larkin)	4.00	1.80	.50
☐ 4	Colorado Rockies (Vinny Castilla Eric Young)	1.50	.70	.19
☐ 5	Florida Marlins (Alex Arias)	1.50	.70	.19
☐ 6	Houston Astros (Eric Anthony Steve Finley)	1.50	.70	.19
☐ 7	Los Angeles Dodgers (Mike Piazza)	4.00	1.80	.50
☐ 8	Montreal Expos (Marquis Grissom)	1.50	.70	.19
☐ 9	New York Mets (Bobby Bonilla)	1.50	.70	.19
☐ 10	Philadelphia Phillies (Mickey Morandini)	1.50	.70	.19
☐ 11	Pittsburgh Pirates (Andy Van Slyke Jay Bell)	1.50	.70	.19
☐ 12	St. Louis Cardinals (Todd Zeile Gregg Jefferies)	1.50	.70	.19
☐ 13	San Diego Padres (Ricky Gutierrez)	1.50	.70	.19
☐ 14	San Francisco Giants (Matt Williams Kirt Manwaring)	2.00	.90	.25
☐ 15	Baltimore Orioles (Cal Ripken)	8.00	3.60	1.00
☐ 16	Boston Red Sox (Luis Rivera John Valentin)	4.00	1.80	.50
☐ 17	California Angels (Tim Salmon)	1.50	.70	.19
☐ 18	Chicago White Sox (Joey Cora)	1.50	.70	.19
☐ 19	Cleveland Indians (Kenny Lofton Carlos Baerga Albert Belle)	8.00	3.60	1.00
☐ 20	Detroit Tigers (Alan Trammell Tony Phillips)	1.50	.70	.19
☐ 21	Kansas City Royals (Jose Lind Curt Wilkerson)	1.50	.70	.19
☐ 22	Milwaukee Brewers (Julio Navarro John Jaha Cal Eldred)	1.50	.70	.19
☐ 23	Minnesota Twins (Kirby Puckett Kent Hrbek)	3.00	1.35	.35
☐ 24	New York Yankees (Don Mattingly Bernie Williams)	4.00	1.80	.50
☐ 25	Oakland Athletics (Mike Bordick Brent Gates)	1.50	.70	.19
☐ 26	Seattle Mariners (Jay Buhner Mike Blowers)	4.00	1.80	.50
☐ 27	Texas Rangers (Ivan Rodriguez Dean Palmer Jose Canseco Juan Gonzalez)	2.00	.90	.25
☐ 28	Toronto Blue Jays (John Olerud)	1.50	.70	.19

1995 Stadium Club

The 1995 Stadium Club baseball card collection was issued in three series of 270, 225 and 135 cards for a total of 630. The cards were distributed in 14-card packs at a suggested retail price of $2.50 and contained 24 packs per box. Cards feature players in full-bleed action photos with team logo and player's name in gold foil at the bottom of the card. Backs feature statistical bar graphs and action photos of players. Rookie Cards include Scott Elarton and Hideo Nomo.

		MINT	NRMT	EXC
COMPLETE SET (630)		55.00	25.00	7.00
COMPLETE SERIES 1 (270)		20.00	9.00	2.50
COMPLETE SERIES 2 (225)		20.00	9.00	2.50
COMPLETE SERIES 3 (135)		15.00	6.75	1.85
COMMON CARD (1-270)		.10	.05	.01
COMMON CARD (271-495)		.10	.05	.01
COMMON CARD (496-630)		.10	.05	.01
☐ 1	Cal Ripken	3.00	1.35	.35
☐ 2	Bo Jackson	.30	.14	.04
☐ 3	Bryan Harvey	.10	.05	.01
☐ 4	Curt Schilling	.10	.05	.01
☐ 5	Bruce Ruffin	.10	.05	.01
☐ 6	Travis Fryman	.30	.14	.04
☐ 7	Jim Abbott	.30	.14	.04
☐ 8	David McCarty	.10	.05	.01

☐ 9	Gary Gaetti	.20	.09	.03
☐ 10	Roger Clemens	.50	.23	.06
☐ 11	Carlos Garcia	.10	.05	.01
☐ 12	Lee Smith	.30	.14	.04
☐ 13	Bobby Ayala	.10	.05	.01
☐ 14	Charles Nagy	.20	.09	.03
☐ 15	Lou Frazier	.10	.05	.01
☐ 16	Rene Arocha	.10	.05	.01
☐ 17	Carlos Delgado	.20	.09	.03
☐ 18	Steve Finley	.10	.05	.01
☐ 19	Ryan Klesko	.60	.25	.07
☐ 20	Cal Eldred	.10	.05	.01
☐ 21	Rey Sanchez	.10	.05	.01
☐ 22	Ken Hill	.10	.05	.01
☐ 23	Benito Santiago	.10	.05	.01
☐ 24	Julian Tavarez	.20	.09	.03
☐ 25	Jose Vizcaino	.10	.05	.01
☐ 26	Andy Benes	.20	.09	.03
☐ 27	Mariano Duncan	.10	.05	.01
☐ 28	Checklist A	.10	.05	.01
☐ 29	Shawon Dunston	.10	.05	.01
☐ 30	Rafael Palmeiro	.30	.14	.04
☐ 31	Dean Palmer	.20	.09	.03
☐ 32	Andres Galarraga	.30	.14	.04
☐ 33	Joey Cora	.10	.05	.01
☐ 34	Mickey Tettleton	.20	.09	.03
☐ 35	Barry Larkin	.40	.18	.05
☐ 36	Carlos Baerga	.60	.25	.07
☐ 37	Orel Hershiser	.20	.09	.03
☐ 38	Jody Reed	.10	.05	.01
☐ 39	Paul Molitor	.30	.14	.04
☐ 40	Jim Edmonds	.40	.18	.05
☐ 41	Bob Tewksbury	.10	.05	.01
☐ 42	John Patterson	.10	.05	.01
☐ 43	Ray McDavid	.20	.09	.03
☐ 44	Zane Smith	.10	.05	.01
☐ 45	Bret Saberhagen SE	.10	.05	.01
☐ 46	Greg Maddux SE	1.50	.70	.19
☐ 47	Frank Thomas SE	1.50	.70	.19
☐ 48	Carlos Baerga SE	.30	.14	.04
☐ 49	Billy Spiers	.10	.05	.01
☐ 50	Stan Javier	.10	.05	.01
☐ 51	Rex Hudler	.10	.05	.01
☐ 52	Denny Hocking	.10	.05	.01
☐ 53	Todd Worrell	.10	.05	.01
☐ 54	Mark Clark	.10	.05	.01
☐ 55	Hipolito Pichardo	.10	.05	.01
☐ 56	Bob Wickman	.10	.05	.01
☐ 57	Raul Mondesi	.75	.35	.09
☐ 58	Steve Cooke	.10	.05	.01
☐ 59	Rod Beck	.10	.05	.01
☐ 60	Tim Davis	.10	.05	.01
☐ 61	Jeff Kent	.10	.05	.01
☐ 62	John Valentin	.30	.14	.04
☐ 63	Alex Arias	.10	.05	.01
☐ 64	Steve Reed	.10	.05	.01
☐ 65	Ozzie Smith	.60	.25	.07
☐ 66	Terry Pendleton	.10	.05	.01
☐ 67	Kenny Rogers	.10	.05	.01
☐ 68	Vince Coleman	.10	.05	.01
☐ 69	Tom Pagnozzi	.10	.05	.01
☐ 70	Roberto Alomar	.60	.25	.07
☐ 71	Darrin Jackson	.10	.05	.01
☐ 72	Dennis Eckersley	.30	.14	.04
☐ 73	Jay Buhner	.30	.14	.04
☐ 74	Darren Lewis	.10	.05	.01
☐ 75	Dave Weathers	.10	.05	.01
☐ 76	Matt Walbeck	.10	.05	.01
☐ 77	Brad Ausmus	.10	.05	.01
☐ 78	Danny Bautista	.10	.05	.01
☐ 79	Bob Hamelin	.10	.05	.01
☐ 80	Steve Trachsel	.10	.05	.01
☐ 81	Ken Ryan	.10	.05	.01
☐ 82	Chris Turner	.10	.05	.01
☐ 83	David Segui	.10	.05	.01
☐ 84	Ben McDonald	.10	.05	.01
☐ 85	Wade Boggs	.30	.14	.04
☐ 86	John VanderWal	.10	.05	.01
☐ 87	Sandy Alomar Jr.	.20	.09	.03
☐ 88	Ron Karkovice	.10	.05	.01
☐ 89	Doug Jones	.10	.05	.01
☐ 90	Gary Sheffield	.30	.14	.04
☐ 91	Ken Caminiti	.20	.09	.03
☐ 92	Chris Bosio	.10	.05	.01
☐ 93	Kevin Tapani	.10	.05	.01
☐ 94	Walt Weiss	.20	.09	.03
☐ 95	Erik Hanson	.10	.05	.01
☐ 96	Ruben Sierra	.10	.05	.01
☐ 97	Nomar Garciaparra	.30	.14	.04
☐ 98	Terrence Long	.20	.09	.03
☐ 99	Jacob Shumate	.20	.09	.03
☐ 100	Paul Wilson	.60	.25	.07
☐ 101	Kevin Witt	.20	.09	.03
☐ 102	Paul Konerko	.20	.09	.03
☐ 103	Ben Grieve	.75	.35	.09
☐ 104	Mark Johnson	.30	.14	.04
☐ 105	Cade Gaspar	.30	.14	.04
☐ 106	Mark Farris	.20	.09	.03
☐ 107	Dustin Hermanson	.20	.09	.03
☐ 108	Scott Elarton	.50	.23	.06
☐ 109	Doug Million RC	.20	.09	.03
☐ 110	Matt Smith	.20	.09	.03
☐ 111	Brian Buchanan	.25	.11	.03
☐ 112	Jayson Peterson	.30	.14	.04
☐ 113	Bret Wagner	.20	.09	.03
☐ 114	C.J. Nitkowski	.20	.09	.03
☐ 115	Ramon Castro	.40	.18	.05
☐ 116	Rafael Bournigal	.10	.05	.01
☐ 117	Jeff Fassero	.10	.05	.01
☐ 118	Bobby Bonilla	.30	.14	.04
☐ 119	Ricky Gutierrez	.10	.05	.01
☐ 120	Roger Pavlik	.10	.05	.01
☐ 121	Mike Greenwell	.20	.09	.03
☐ 122	Deion Sanders	.60	.25	.07
☐ 123	Charlie Hayes	.10	.05	.01
☐ 124	Paul O'Neill	.20	.09	.03
☐ 125	Jay Bell	.10	.05	.01
☐ 126	Royce Clayton	.10	.05	.01
☐ 127	Willie Banks	.10	.05	.01
☐ 128	Mark Wohlers	.20	.09	.03
☐ 129	Todd Jones	.10	.05	.01
☐ 130	Todd Stottlemyre	.10	.05	.01
☐ 131	Will Clark	.40	.18	.05
☐ 132	Wilson Alvarez	.20	.09	.03
☐ 133	Chili Davis	.20	.09	.03
☐ 134	Dave Burba	.10	.05	.01
☐ 135	Chris Hoiles	.20	.09	.03
☐ 136	Jeff Blauser	.10	.05	.01
☐ 137	Jeff Reboulet	.10	.05	.01
☐ 138	Bret Saberhagen	.20	.09	.03
☐ 139	Kirk Rueter	.10	.05	.01
☐ 140	Dave Nilsson	.10	.05	.01
☐ 141	Pat Borders	.10	.05	.01
☐ 142	Ron Darling	.10	.05	.01
☐ 143	Derek Bell	.30	.14	.04
☐ 144	Dave Hollins	.10	.05	.01
☐ 145	Juan Gonzalez	.75	.35	.09
☐ 146	Andre Dawson	.30	.14	.04
☐ 147	Jim Thome	.50	.23	.06
☐ 148	Larry Walker	.40	.18	.05
☐ 149	Mike Piazza	1.25	.55	.16
☐ 150	Mike Perez	.10	.05	.01

☐ 151	Steve Avery	.20	.09	.03
☐ 152	Dan Wilson	.20	.09	.03
☐ 153	Andy Van Slyke	.10	.05	.01
☐ 154	Junior Felix	.10	.05	.01
☐ 155	Jack McDowell	.30	.14	.04
☐ 156	Danny Tartabull	.20	.09	.03
☐ 157	Willie Blair	.10	.05	.01
☐ 158	Wm.VanLandingham	.10	.05	.01
☐ 159	Robb Nen	.20	.09	.03
☐ 160	Lee Tinsley	.20	.09	.03
☐ 161	Ismael Valdes	.10	.05	.01
☐ 162	Juan Guzman	.10	.05	.01
☐ 163	Scott Servais	.10	.05	.01
☐ 164	Cliff Floyd	.20	.09	.03
☐ 165	Allen Watson	.20	.09	.03
☐ 166	Eddie Taubensee	.10	.05	.01
☐ 167	Scott Hemond	.10	.05	.01
☐ 168	Jeff Tackett	.10	.05	.01
☐ 169	Chad Curtis	.20	.09	.03
☐ 170	Rico Brogna	.30	.14	.04
☐ 171	Luis Polonia	.10	.05	.01
☐ 172	Checklist B	.10	.05	.01
☐ 173	Lance Johnson	.10	.05	.01
☐ 174	Sammy Sosa	.30	.14	.04
☐ 175	Mike MacFarlane	.10	.05	.01
☐ 176	Darryl Hamilton	.10	.05	.01
☐ 177	Rick Aguilera	.10	.05	.01
☐ 178	Dave West	.10	.05	.01
☐ 179	Mike Gallego	.10	.05	.01
☐ 180	Marc Newfield	.20	.09	.03
☐ 181	Steve Buechele	.10	.05	.01
☐ 182	David Wells	.10	.05	.01
☐ 183	Tom Glavine	.30	.14	.04
☐ 184	Joe Girardi	.10	.05	.01
☐ 185	Craig Biggio	.30	.14	.04
☐ 186	Eddie Murray	.40	.18	.05
☐ 187	Kevin Gross	.10	.05	.01
☐ 188	Sid Fernandez	.10	.05	.01
☐ 189	John Franco	.20	.09	.03
☐ 190	Bernard Gilkey	.10	.05	.01
☐ 191	Matt Williams	.50	.23	.06
☐ 192	Darrin Fletcher	.10	.05	.01
☐ 193	Jeff Conine	.30	.14	.04
☐ 194	Ed Sprague	.10	.05	.01
☐ 195	Eduardo Perez	.10	.05	.01
☐ 196	Scott Livingstone	.10	.05	.01
☐ 197	Ivan Rodriguez	.30	.14	.04
☐ 198	Orlando Merced	.10	.05	.01
☐ 199	Ricky Bones	.10	.05	.01
☐ 200	Javier Lopez	.40	.18	.05
☐ 201	Miguel Jimenez	.10	.05	.01
☐ 202	Terry McGriff	.10	.05	.01
☐ 203	Mike Lieberthal	.10	.05	.01
☐ 204	David Cone	.30	.14	.04
☐ 205	Todd Hundley	.30	.14	.04
☐ 206	Ozzie Guillen	.10	.05	.01
☐ 207	Alex Cole	.10	.05	.01
☐ 208	Tony Phillips	.10	.05	.01
☐ 209	Jim Eisenreich	.10	.05	.01
☐ 210	Greg Vaughn BES	.10	.05	.01
☐ 211	Barry Larkin BES	.20	.09	.03
☐ 212	Don Mattingly BES	.75	.35	.09
☐ 213	Mark Grace BES	.20	.09	.03
☐ 214	Jose Canseco BES	.20	.09	.03
☐ 215	Joe Carter BES	.20	.09	.03
☐ 216	David Cone BES	.10	.05	.01
☐ 217	Sandy Alomar Jr. BES	.10	.05	.01
☐ 218	Al Martin BES	.10	.05	.01
☐ 219	Roberto Kelly BES	.10	.05	.01
☐ 220	Paul Sorrento	.10	.05	.01
☐ 221	Tony Fernandez	.10	.05	.01
☐ 222	Stan Belinda	.10	.05	.01
☐ 223	Mike Stanley	.20	.09	.03
☐ 224	Doug Drabek	.20	.09	.03
☐ 225	Todd Van Poppel	.10	.05	.01
☐ 226	Matt Mieske	.10	.05	.01
☐ 227	Tino Martinez	.30	.14	.04
☐ 228	Andy Ashby	.10	.05	.01
☐ 229	Midre Cummings	.20	.09	.03
☐ 230	Jeff Frye	.10	.05	.01
☐ 231	Hal Morris	.10	.05	.01
☐ 232	Jose Lind	.10	.05	.01
☐ 233	Shawn Green	.30	.14	.04
☐ 234	Rafael Belliard	.10	.05	.01
☐ 235	Randy Myers	.20	.09	.03
☐ 236	Frank Thomas CE	1.50	.70	.19
☐ 237	Darren Daulton CE	.10	.05	.01
☐ 238	Sammy Sosa CE	.20	.09	.03
☐ 239	Cal Ripken CE	1.50	.70	.19
☐ 240	Jeff Bagwell CE	.50	.23	.06
☐ 241	Ken Griffey Jr.	3.00	1.35	.35
☐ 242	Brett Butler	.20	.09	.03
☐ 243	Derrick May	.10	.05	.01
☐ 244	Pat Listach	.10	.05	.01
☐ 245	Mike Bordick	.10	.05	.01
☐ 246	Mark Langston	.10	.05	.01
☐ 247	Randy Velarde	.10	.05	.01
☐ 248	Julio Franco	.20	.09	.03
☐ 249	Chuck Knoblauch	.30	.14	.04
☐ 250	Bill Gullickson	.10	.05	.01
☐ 251	Dave Henderson	.10	.05	.01
☐ 252	Bret Boone	.30	.14	.04
☐ 253	Al Martin	.20	.09	.03
☐ 254	Armando Benitez	.10	.05	.01
☐ 255	Wil Cordero	.20	.09	.03
☐ 256	Al Leiter	.10	.05	.01
☐ 257	Luis Gonzalez	.20	.09	.03
☐ 258	Charlie O'Brien	.10	.05	.01
☐ 259	Tim Wallach	.10	.05	.01
☐ 260	Scott Sanders	.10	.05	.01
☐ 261	Tom Henke	.20	.09	.03
☐ 262	Otis Nixon	.10	.05	.01
☐ 263	Darren Daulton	.10	.05	.01
☐ 264	Manny Ramirez	1.25	.55	.16
☐ 265	Bret Barberie	.10	.05	.01
☐ 266	Mel Rojas	.20	.09	.03
☐ 267	John Burkett	.10	.05	.01
☐ 268	Brady Anderson	.20	.09	.03
☐ 269	John Roper	.10	.05	.01
☐ 270	Shane Reynolds	.10	.05	.01
☐ 271	Barry Bonds	.75	.35	.09
☐ 272	Alex Fernandez	.20	.09	.03
☐ 273	Brian McRae	.20	.09	.03
☐ 274	Todd Zeile	.20	.09	.03
☐ 275	Greg Swindell	.10	.05	.01
☐ 276	Johnny Ruffin	.10	.05	.01
☐ 277	Troy Neel	.10	.05	.01
☐ 278	Eric Karros	.30	.14	.04
☐ 279	John Hudek	.10	.05	.01
☐ 280	Thomas Howard	.10	.05	.01
☐ 281	Joe Carter	.30	.14	.04
☐ 282	Mike Devereaux	.10	.05	.01
☐ 283	Butch Henry	.10	.05	.01
☐ 284	Reggie Jefferson	.10	.05	.01
☐ 285	Mark Lemke	.20	.09	.03
☐ 286	Jeff Montgomery	.20	.09	.03
☐ 287	Ryan Thompson	.10	.05	.01
☐ 288	Paul Shuey	.10	.05	.01
☐ 289	Mark McGwire	.30	.14	.04
☐ 290	Bernie Williams	.20	.09	.03
☐ 291	Mickey Morandini	.10	.05	.01
☐ 292	Scott Leius	.10	.05	.01

☐ 293	David Hulse	.10	.05	.01	☐ 364	Pat Rapp	.20	.09	.03
☐ 294	Greg Gagne	.10	.05	.01	☐ 365	Bill Swift	.10	.05	.01
☐ 295	Moises Alou	.30	.14	.04	☐ 366	Checklist	.10	.05	.01
☐ 296	Geronimo Berroa	.10	.05	.01	☐ 367	Robin Ventura	.30	.14	.04
☐ 297	Eddie Zambrano	.10	.05	.01	☐ 368	Bobby Witt	.10	.05	.01
☐ 298	Alan Trammell	.30	.14	.04	☐ 369	Karl Rhodes	.10	.05	.01
☐ 299	Don Slaught	.10	.05	.01	☐ 370	Eddie Williams	.10	.05	.01
☐ 300	Jose Rijo	.20	.09	.03	☐ 371	John Jaha	.20	.09	.03
☐ 301	Joe Ausanio	.10	.05	.01	☐ 372	Steve Howe	.10	.05	.01
☐ 302	Tim Raines	.30	.14	.04	☐ 373	Leo Gomez	.10	.05	.01
☐ 303	Melido Perez	.10	.05	.01	☐ 374	Hector Fajardo	.10	.05	.01
☐ 304	Kent Mercker	.10	.05	.01	☐ 375	Jeff Bagwell	1.00	.45	.12
☐ 305	James Mouton	.20	.09	.03	☐ 376	Mark Acre	.10	.05	.01
☐ 306	Luis Lopez	.10	.05	.01	☐ 377	Wayne Kirby	.10	.05	.01
☐ 307	Mike Kingery	.10	.05	.01	☐ 378	Mark Portugal	.10	.05	.01
☐ 308	Willie Greene	.10	.05	.01	☐ 379	Jesus Tavarez	.10	.05	.01
☐ 309	Cecil Fielder	.30	.14	.04	☐ 380	Jim Lindeman	.10	.05	.01
☐ 310	Scott Kamieniecki	.10	.05	.01	☐ 381	Don Mattingly	1.50	.70	.19
☐ 311	Mike Greenwell BES	.10	.05	.01	☐ 382	Trevor Hoffman	.20	.09	.03
☐ 312	Bobby Bonilla BES	.20	.09	.03	☐ 383	Chris Gomez	.10	.05	.01
☐ 313	Andres Galarraga BES	.20	.09	.03	☐ 384	Garret Anderson	.60	.25	.07
☐ 314	Cal Ripken BES	1.50	.70	.19	☐ 385	Bobby Munoz	.10	.05	.01
☐ 315	Matt Williams BES	.20	.09	.03	☐ 386	Jon Lieber	.10	.05	.01
☐ 316	Tom Pagnozzi BES	.10	.05	.01	☐ 387	Rick Helling	.10	.05	.01
☐ 317	Len Dykstra BES	.10	.05	.01	☐ 388	Marvin Freeman	.10	.05	.01
☐ 318	Frank Thomas BES	1.50	.70	.19	☐ 389	Juan Castillo	.10	.05	.01
☐ 319	Kirby Puckett BES	.50	.23	.06	☐ 390	Jeff Cirillo	.20	.09	.03
☐ 320	Mike Piazza BES	.60	.25	.07	☐ 391	Sean Berry	.10	.05	.01
☐ 321	Jason Jacome	.10	.05	.01	☐ 392	Hector Carrasco	.10	.05	.01
☐ 322	Brian Hunter	.10	.05	.01	☐ 393	Mark Grace	.30	.14	.04
☐ 323	Brent Gates	.20	.09	.03	☐ 394	Pat Kelly	.10	.05	.01
☐ 324	Jim Converse	.10	.05	.01	☐ 395	Tim Naehring	.20	.09	.03
☐ 325	Damion Easley	.10	.05	.01	☐ 396	Greg Pirkl	.10	.05	.01
☐ 326	Dante Bichette	.40	.18	.05	☐ 397	John Smoltz	.20	.09	.03
☐ 327	Kurt Abbott	.10	.05	.01	☐ 398	Robby Thompson	.10	.05	.01
☐ 328	Scott Cooper	.10	.05	.01	☐ 399	Rick White	.10	.05	.01
☐ 329	Mike Henneman	.10	.05	.01	☐ 400	Frank Thomas	3.00	1.35	.35
☐ 330	Orlando Miller	.10	.05	.01	☐ 401	Jeff Conine CS	.10	.05	.01
☐ 331	John Kruk	.20	.09	.03	☐ 402	Jose Valentin CS	.10	.05	.01
☐ 332	Jose Oliva	.10	.05	.01	☐ 403	Carlos Baerga CS	.30	.14	.04
☐ 333	Reggie Sanders	.30	.14	.04	☐ 404	Rick Aguilera CS	.10	.05	.01
☐ 334	Omar Vizquel	.20	.09	.03	☐ 405	Wilson Alvarez CS	.10	.05	.01
☐ 335	Devon White	.20	.09	.03	☐ 406	Juan Gonzalez CS	.30	.14	.04
☐ 336	Mike Morgan	.10	.05	.01	☐ 407	Barry Larkin CS	.20	.09	.03
☐ 337	J.R. Phillips	.10	.05	.01	☐ 408	Ken Hill CS	.10	.05	.01
☐ 338	Gary DiSarcina	.10	.05	.01	☐ 409	Chuck Carr CS	.10	.05	.01
☐ 339	Joey Hamilton	.10	.05	.01	☐ 410	Tim Raines CS	.10	.05	.01
☐ 340	Randy Johnson	.60	.25	.07	☐ 411	Bryan Eversgerd	.10	.05	.01
☐ 341	Jim Leyritz	.10	.05	.01	☐ 412	Phil Plantier	.10	.05	.01
☐ 342	Bobby Jones	.10	.05	.01	☐ 413	Josias Manzanillo	.10	.05	.01
☐ 343	Jaime Navarro	.10	.05	.01	☐ 414	Roberto Kelly	.20	.09	.03
☐ 344	Bip Roberts	.10	.05	.01	☐ 415	Rickey Henderson	.30	.14	.04
☐ 345	Steve Karsay	.10	.05	.01	☐ 416	John Smiley	.10	.05	.01
☐ 346	Kevin Stocker	.10	.05	.01	☐ 417	Kevin Brown	.10	.05	.01
☐ 347	Jose Canseco	.50	.23	.06	☐ 418	Jimmy Key	.10	.05	.01
☐ 348	Bill Wegman	.10	.05	.01	☐ 419	Wally Joyner	.20	.09	.03
☐ 349	Rondell White	.30	.14	.04	☐ 420	Roberto Hernandez	.20	.09	.03
☐ 350	Mo Vaughn	.50	.23	.06	☐ 421	Felix Fermin	.10	.05	.01
☐ 351	Joe Orsulak	.10	.05	.01	☐ 422	Checklist	.10	.05	.01
☐ 352	Pat Meares	.10	.05	.01	☐ 423	Greg Vaughn	.10	.05	.01
☐ 353	Albie Lopez	.10	.05	.01	☐ 424	Ray Lankford	.30	.14	.04
☐ 354	Edgar Martinez	.30	.14	.04	☐ 425	Greg Maddux	3.00	1.35	.35
☐ 355	Brian Jordan	.30	.14	.04	☐ 426	Mike Mussina	.40	.18	.05
☐ 356	Tommy Greene	.10	.05	.01	☐ 427	Geronimo Pena	.10	.05	.01
☐ 357	Chuck Carr	.10	.05	.01	☐ 428	David Nied	.10	.05	.01
☐ 358	Pedro Astacio	.10	.05	.01	☐ 429	Scott Erickson	.20	.09	.03
☐ 359	Russ Davis	.20	.09	.03	☐ 430	Kevin Mitchell	.20	.09	.03
☐ 360	Chris Hammond	.10	.05	.01	☐ 431	Mike Lansing	.10	.05	.01
☐ 361	Gregg Jefferies	.30	.14	.04	☐ 432	Brian Anderson	.10	.05	.01
☐ 362	Shane Mack	.10	.05	.01	☐ 433	Jeff King	.10	.05	.01
☐ 363	Fred McGriff	.40	.18	.05	☐ 434	Ramon Martinez	.20	.09	.03

☐	435	Kevin Seitzer	.10	.05	.01	☐ 506 Jeff King EC	.10	.05	.01
☐	436	Salomon Torres	.10	.05	.01	☐ 507 Ray Lankford EC	.10	.05	.01
☐	437	Brian L.Hunter	.40	.18	.05	☐ 508 Tony Gwynn EC	.50	.23	.06
☐	438	Melvin Nieves	.20	.09	.03	☐ 509 Barry Bonds EC	.40	.18	.05
☐	439	Mike Kelly	.20	.09	.03	☐ 510 Cal Ripken EC	1.50	.70	.19
☐	440	Marquis Grissom	.30	.14	.04	☐ 511 Mo Vaughn EC	.30	.14	.04
☐	441	Chuck Finley	.20	.09	.03	☐ 512 Tim Salmon EC	.30	.14	.04
☐	442	Len Dykstra	.20	.09	.03	☐ 513 Frank Thomas EC	1.50	.70	.19
☐	443	Ellis Burks	.10	.05	.01	☐ 514 Albert Belle EC	.60	.25	.07
☐	444	Harold Baines	.20	.09	.03	☐ 515 Cecil Fielder EC	.10	.05	.01
☐	445	Kevin Appier	.10	.05	.01	☐ 516 Kevin Appier EC	.10	.05	.01
☐	446	David Justice	.40	.18	.05	☐ 517 Greg Vaughn EC	.10	.05	.01
☐	447	Darryl Kile	.10	.05	.01	☐ 518 Kirby Puckett EC	.50	.23	.06
☐	448	John Olerud	.20	.09	.03	☐ 519 Paul O'Neill EC	.10	.05	.01
☐	449	Greg McMichael	.10	.05	.01	☐ 520 Ruben Sierra EC	.10	.05	.01
☐	450	Kirby Puckett	1.00	.45	.12	☐ 521 Ken Griffey Jr. EC	1.50	.70	.19
☐	451	Jose Valentin	.10	.05	.01	☐ 522 Will Clark EC	.20	.09	.03
☐	452	Rick Wilkins	.10	.05	.01	☐ 523 Joe Carter EC	.10	.05	.01
☐	453	Arthur Rhodes	.10	.05	.01	☐ 524 Antonio Osuna	.10	.05	.01
☐	454	Pat Hentgen	.20	.09	.03	☐ 525 Glenallen Hill	.20	.09	.03
☐	455	Tom Gordon	.10	.05	.01	☐ 526 Alex Gonzalez	.20	.09	.03
☐	456	Tom Candiotti	.10	.05	.01	☐ 527 Dave Stewart	.20	.09	.03
☐	457	Jason Bere	.10	.05	.01	☐ 528 Ron Gant	.30	.14	.04
☐	458	Wes Chamberlain	.10	.05	.01	☐ 529 Jason Bates	.20	.09	.03
☐	459	Greg Colbrunn	.30	.14	.04	☐ 530 Mike Macfarlane	.10	.05	.01
☐	460	John Doherty	.10	.05	.01	☐ 531 Esteban Loaiza	.10	.05	.01
☐	461	Kevin Foster	.10	.05	.01	☐ 532 Joe Randa	.10	.05	.01
☐	462	Mark Whiten	.10	.05	.01	☐ 533 Dave Winfield	.30	.14	.04
☐	463	Terry Steinbach	.20	.09	.03	☐ 534 Danny Darwin	.10	.05	.01
☐	464	Aaron Sele	.10	.05	.01	☐ 535 Pete Harnisch	.10	.05	.01
☐	465	Kirt Manwaring	.10	.05	.01	☐ 536 Joey Cora	.10	.05	.01
☐	466	Darren Hall	.10	.05	.01	☐ 537 Jaime Navarro	.10	.05	.01
☐	467	Delino DeShields	.20	.09	.03	☐ 538 Marty Cordova	.50	.23	.06
☐	468	Andujar Cedeno	.10	.05	.01	☐ 539 Andujar Cedeno	.10	.05	.01
☐	469	Billy Ashley	.10	.05	.01	☐ 540 Mickey Tettleton	.20	.09	.03
☐	470	Kenny Lofton	1.00	.45	.12	☐ 541 Andy Van Slyke	.20	.09	.03
☐	471	Pedro Munoz	.20	.09	.03	☐ 542 Carlos Perez	.75	.35	.09
☐	472	John Wetteland	.20	.09	.03	☐ 543 Chipper Jones	1.25	.55	.16
☐	473	Tim Salmon	.50	.23	.06	☐ 544 Tony Fernandez	.10	.05	.01
☐	474	Denny Neagle	.10	.05	.01	☐ 545 Tom Henke	.20	.09	.03
☐	475	Tony Gwynn	1.00	.45	.12	☐ 546 Pat Borders	.10	.05	.01
☐	476	Vinny Castilla	.30	.14	.04	☐ 547 Chad Curtis	.20	.09	.03
☐	477	Steve Dreyer	.10	.05	.01	☐ 548 Ray Durham	.30	.14	.04
☐	478	Jeff Shaw	.10	.05	.01	☐ 549 Joe Oliver	.10	.05	.01
☐	479	Chad Ogea	.20	.09	.03	☐ 550 Jose Mesa	.20	.09	.03
☐	480	Scott Ruffcorn	.10	.05	.01	☐ 551 Steve Finley	.10	.05	.01
☐	481	Lou Whitaker	.30	.14	.04	☐ 552 Otis Nixon	.10	.05	.01
☐	482	J.T. Snow	.30	.14	.04	☐ 553 Jacob Brumfield	.10	.05	.01
☐	483	Rich Rowland	.10	.05	.01	☐ 554 Bill Swift	.10	.05	.01
☐	484	Denny Martinez	.20	.09	.03	☐ 555 Quilvio Veras	.10	.05	.01
☐	485	Pedro Martinez	.10	.05	.01	☐ 556 Hideo Nomo	6.00	2.70	.75
☐	486	Rusty Greer	.10	.05	.01	☐ 557 Joe Vitiello	.10	.05	.01
☐	487	Dave Fleming	.10	.05	.01	☐ 558 Mike Perez	.10	.05	.01
☐	488	John Dettmer	.10	.05	.01	☐ 559 Charlie Hayes	.20	.09	.03
☐	489	Albert Belle	1.25	.55	.16	☐ 560 Brad Radke	.30	.14	.04
☐	490	Ravelo Manzanillo	.10	.05	.01	☐ 561 Darren Bragg	.10	.05	.01
☐	491	Henry Rodriguez	.10	.05	.01	☐ 562 Orel Hershiser	.20	.09	.03
☐	492	Andrew Lorraine	.20	.09	.03	☐ 563 Edgardo Alfonzo	.20	.09	.03
☐	493	Dwayne Hosey	.10	.05	.01	☐ 564 Doug Jones	.10	.05	.01
☐	494	Mike Blowers	.20	.09	.03	☐ 565 Andy Pettitte	.40	.18	.05
☐	495	Turner Ward	.10	.05	.01	☐ 566 Benito Santiago	.10	.05	.01
☐	496	Fred McGriff EC	.20	.09	.03	☐ 567 John Burkett	.10	.05	.01
☐	497	Sammy Sosa EC	.10	.05	.01	☐ 568 Brad Clontz	.10	.05	.01
☐	498	Barry Larkin EC	.20	.09	.03	☐ 569 Jim Abbott	.30	.14	.04
☐	499	Andres Galarraga EC	.10	.05	.01	☐ 570 Joe Rosselli	.10	.05	.01
☐	500	Gary Sheffield EC	.10	.05	.01	☐ 571 Mark Grudzielanek	.20	.09	.03
☐	501	Jeff Bagwell EC	.50	.23	.06	☐ 572 Dustin Hermanson	.10	.05	.01
☐	502	Mike Piazza EC	.60	.25	.07	☐ 573 Benji Gil	.10	.05	.01
☐	503	Moises Alou EC	.10	.05	.01	☐ 574 Mark Whiten	.10	.05	.01
☐	504	Bobby Bonilla EC	.10	.05	.01	☐ 575 Mike Ignasiak	.10	.05	.01
☐	505	Darren Daulton EC	.10	.05	.01	☐ 576 Kevin Ritz	.10	.05	.01

☐ 577	Paul Quantrill	.10	.05	.01
☐ 578	Andre Dawson	.30	.14	.04
☐ 579	Jerald Clark	.10	.05	.01
☐ 580	Frank Rodriguez	.20	.09	.03
☐ 581	Mark Kiefer	.10	.05	.01
☐ 582	Trevor Wilson	.10	.05	.01
☐ 583	Gary Wilson	.10	.05	.01
☐ 584	Andy Stankiewicz	.10	.05	.01
☐ 585	Felipe Lira	.10	.05	.01
☐ 586	Mike Mimbs	.30	.14	.04
☐ 587	Jon Nunnally	.20	.09	.03
☐ 588	Tomas Perez	.25	.11	.03
☐ 589	Checklist	.10	.05	.01
☐ 590	Todd Hollandsworth	.10	.05	.01
☐ 591	Roberto Petagine	.10	.05	.01
☐ 592	Mariano Rivera	.20	.09	.03
☐ 593	Mark McLemore	.10	.05	.01
☐ 594	Bobby Witt	.10	.05	.01
☐ 595	Jose Offerman	.10	.05	.01
☐ 596	Jason Christiansen	.20	.09	.03
☐ 597	Jeff Manto	.10	.05	.01
☐ 598	Jim Dougherty	.10	.05	.01
☐ 599	Juan Acevedo	.10	.05	.01
☐ 600	Troy O'Leary	.20	.09	.03
☐ 601	Ron Villone	.10	.05	.01
☐ 602	Tripp Cromer	.10	.05	.01
☐ 603	Steve Scarsone	.10	.05	.01
☐ 604	Lance Parrish	.20	.09	.03
☐ 605	Ozzie Timmons	.20	.09	.03
☐ 606	Ray Holbert	.10	.05	.01
☐ 607	Tony Phillips	.10	.05	.01
☐ 608	Phil Plantier	.10	.05	.01
☐ 609	Shane Andrews	.10	.05	.01
☐ 610	Heathcliff Slocumb	.10	.05	.01
☐ 611	Bobby Higginson	.30	.14	.04
☐ 612	Bob Tewksbury	.10	.05	.01
☐ 613	Terry Pendleton	.20	.09	.03
☐ 614	Scott Cooper TA	.10	.05	.01
☐ 615	John Wetteland TA	.10	.05	.01
☐ 616	Ken Hill TA	.10	.05	.01
☐ 617	Marquis Grissom TA	.10	.05	.01
☐ 618	Larry Walker TA	.20	.09	.03
☐ 619	Derek Bell TA	.10	.05	.01
☐ 620	David Cone TA	.10	.05	.01
☐ 621	Ken Caminiti TA	.10	.05	.01
☐ 622	Jack McDowell TA	.10	.05	.01
☐ 623	Vaughn Eshelman TA	.10	.05	.01
☐ 624	Brian McRae TA	.10	.05	.01
☐ 625	Gregg Jefferies TA	.10	.05	.01
☐ 626	Kevin Brown TA	.10	.05	.01
☐ 627	Lee Smith TA	.10	.05	.01
☐ 628	Tony Tarasco TA	.10	.05	.01
☐ 629	Brett Butler TA	.10	.05	.01
☐ 630	Jose Canseco TA	.30	.14	.04

1995 Stadium Club First Day Issue

Parallel to the basic first series Stadium Club issue, these cards, for the most part were inserted in second series Topps packs. The double printed cards (indicated by DP in the checklist below) were issued in both series. There are nine such cards. They were also inserted at a rate of ten per Topps factory set.

	MINT	NRMT	EXC
COMPLETE SET (270)	275.00	125.00	34.00
COMMON CARD (1-270)	1.00	.45	.12
COMMON DP (29/39/79/96)	.50	.23	.06
COMMON DP (153/168/197)	.50	.23	.06
SEMISTARS	1.50	.70	.19

BEWARE OF TRANSFERRED FDI LOGOS
*VETERAN STARS: 12X TO 20X BASIC CARDS
*YOUNG STARS: 9X TO 15X BASIC CARDS
*RCs: 6X TO 12X BASIC CARDS

☐ 131	Will Clark DP	2.00	.90	.25
☐ 149	Mike Piazza DP	5.00	2.20	.60

1995 Stadium Club Clear Cut

Randomly inserted at a rate of one in 16 packs, this 28-card set features a full color action photo of the player against a clear acetate background with the player's name printed vertically. Backs highlight the season achievement of the player on a thin horizontal strip.

	MINT	NRMT	EXC
COMPLETE SET (28)	100.00	45.00	12.50
COMPLETE SET (14)	50.00	22.00	6.25
COMPLETE SERIES 2 (14)	50.00	22.00	6.25
COMMON CARD (1-14)	1.00	.45	.12
COMMON CARD (15-28)	1.00	.45	.12

☐ 1	Mike Piazza	10.00	4.50	1.25
☐ 2	Ruben Sierra	2.00	.90	.25
☐ 3	Tony Gwynn	8.00	3.60	1.00
☐ 4	Frank Thomas	25.00	11.00	3.10
☐ 5	Fred McGriff	3.00	1.35	.35
☐ 6	Rafael Palmeiro	2.00	.90	.25
☐ 7	Bobby Bonilla	2.00	.90	.25
☐ 8	Chili Davis	2.00	.90	.25
☐ 9	Hal Morris	1.00	.45	.12
☐ 10	Jose Canseco	4.00	1.80	.50
☐ 11	Jay Bell	1.00	.45	.12
☐ 12	Kirby Puckett	8.00	3.60	1.00
☐ 13	Gary Sheffield	2.00	.90	.25
☐ 14	Bob Hamelin	1.00	.45	.12
☐ 15	Jeff Bagwell	8.00	3.60	1.00
☐ 16	Albert Belle	10.00	4.50	1.25
☐ 17	Sammy Sosa	2.50	1.10	.30
☐ 18	Ken Griffey Jr.	25.00	11.00	3.10

		MINT	NRMT	EXC
☐ 19	Todd Zeile	1.00	.45	.12
☐ 20	Mo Vaughn	4.00	1.80	.50
☐ 21	Moises Alou	1.00	.45	.12
☐ 22	Paul O'Neill	2.00	.90	.25
☐ 23	Andres Galarraga	2.00	.90	.25
☐ 24	Greg Vaughn	1.00	.45	.12
☐ 25	Len Dykstra	2.00	.90	.25
☐ 26	Joe Carter	2.00	.90	.25
☐ 27	Barry Bonds	6.00	2.70	.75
☐ 28	Cecil Fielder	2.00	.90	.25

1995 Stadium Club Crystal Ball

This 15-card standard-size set was inserted into series three packs at a rate of one in 24. Fifteen leading 1995 rookies and prospects were featured in this set. The fronts feature a player photo in the middle with the words "Crystal Ball" on the top with the player's name on the bottom. The backs have season-by-season stats with a sentence about the player's accomplishments during that season. There is a player photo in the upper right set in a crystal ball. The player is identified on the top and the cards are numbered with a "CB" prefix in the upper left corner.

		MINT	NRMT	EXC
	COMPLETE SET (15)	90.00	40.00	11.00
	COMMON CARD (CB1-CB15)	3.00	1.35	.35
☐ CB1	Chipper Jones	30.00	13.50	3.70
☐ CB2	Dustin Hermanson	4.00	1.80	.50
☐ CB3	Ray Durham	5.00	2.20	.60
☐ CB4	Phil Nevin	3.00	1.35	.35
☐ CB5	Billy Ashley	4.00	1.80	.50
☐ CB6	Shawn Green	6.00	2.70	.75
☐ CB7	Jason Bates	3.00	1.35	.35
☐ CB8	Benji Gil	3.00	1.35	.35
☐ CB9	Marty Cordova	8.00	3.60	1.00
☐ CB10	Quilvio Veras	4.00	1.80	.50
☐ CB11	Mark Grudzielanek	3.00	1.35	.35
☐ CB12	Ruben Rivera	25.00	11.00	3.10
☐ CB13	Bill Pulsipher	6.00	2.70	.75
☐ CB14	Derek Jeter	8.00	3.60	1.00
☐ CB15	LaTroy Hawkins	3.00	1.35	.35

1995 Stadium Club Power Zone

This 12-card standard-size set was inserted into series three packs at a rate of one in 24. The fronts feature a player photo and his name on the right. The left side of the card has the bat powering through an explosion. The words "Power Zone" are on the bottom. The horizontal backs feature a close-up photo, some vital information as well as some seasonal highlights. The cards are numbered in the upper right corner with a "PZ" prefix. The set is sequenced in alphabetical order.

		MINT	NRMT	EXC
	COMPLETE SET (12)	90.00	40.00	11.00
	COMMON PLAYER (PZ1-PZ12)	3.00	1.35	.35
☐ PZ1	Jeff Bagwell	10.00	4.50	1.25
☐ PZ2	Albert Belle	12.00	5.50	1.50
☐ PZ3	Barry Bonds	8.00	3.60	1.00
☐ PZ4	Joe Carter	3.00	1.35	.35
☐ PZ5	Cecil Fielder	3.00	1.35	.35
☐ PZ6	Andres Galarraga	3.00	1.35	.35
☐ PZ7	Ken Griffey Jr	30.00	13.50	3.70
☐ PZ8	Paul Molitor	3.00	1.35	.35
☐ PZ9	Fred McGriff	4.00	1.80	.50
☐ PZ10	Rafael Palmeiro	3.00	1.35	.35
☐ PZ11	Frank Thomas	30.00	13.50	3.70
☐ PZ12	Matt Williams	5.00	2.20	.60

1995 Stadium Club Ring Leaders

Randomly inserted in packs, this set features players who have won various awards or titles. This set was also redeemable as a prize with winning regular phone cards. This set features Stadium Club's "Power Matrix Technology," which makes the cards shine and glow. The horizontal fronts feature a player photo, rings in both upper corners as well as other designs that make for a very busy front. The backs have information on how the player earned his rings, along with a player photo and some other pertinent information.

player photo against a multi-colored background. The background was enhanced using Stadium Club's "Power Matrix" Technology. The "Super Skills" logo is in the lower left corner. The backs have a full-bleed photo with a description of the player's special skill. The cards are numbered in the upper left as "X" of 9.

	MINT	NRMT	EXC
COMPLETE SET (40)	275.00	125.00	34.00
COMPLETE SERIES 1 (20)	125.00	55.00	15.50
COMPLETE SERIES 2 (20)	150.00	70.00	19.00
COMMON CARD (1-20)	1.50	.70	.19
COMMON CARD (21-40)	1.50	.70	.19

		MINT	NRMT	EXC
☐ 1	Jeff Bagwell	10.00	4.50	1.25
☐ 2	Mark McGwire	2.50	1.10	.30
☐ 3	Ozzie Smith	6.00	2.70	.75
☐ 4	Paul Molitor	2.50	1.10	.30
☐ 5	Darryl Strawberry	2.00	.90	.25
☐ 6	Eddie Murray	4.00	1.80	.50
☐ 7	Tony Gwynn	10.00	4.50	1.25
☐ 8	Jose Canseco	5.00	2.20	.60
☐ 9	Howard Johnson	2.00	.90	.25
☐ 10	Andre Dawson	2.50	1.10	.30
☐ 11	Matt Williams	5.00	2.20	.60
☐ 12	Tim Raines	2.50	1.10	.30
☐ 13	Fred McGriff	4.00	1.80	.50
☐ 14	Ken Griffey Jr.	30.00	13.50	3.70
☐ 15	Gary Sheffield	2.50	1.10	.30
☐ 16	Dennis Eckersley	2.50	1.10	.30
☐ 17	Kevin Mitchell	2.00	.90	.25
☐ 18	Will Clark	4.00	1.80	.50
☐ 19	Darren Daulton	1.50	.70	.19
☐ 20	Paul O'Neill	2.00	.90	.25
☐ 21	Julio Franco	1.50	.70	.19
☐ 22	Albert Belle	12.00	5.50	1.50
☐ 23	Juan Gonzalez	8.00	3.60	1.00
☐ 24	Kirby Puckett	10.00	4.50	1.25
☐ 25	Joe Carter	2.50	1.10	.30
☐ 26	Frank Thomas	30.00	13.50	3.70
☐ 27	Cal Ripken	30.00	13.50	3.70
☐ 28	John Olerud	1.50	.70	.19
☐ 29	Ruben Sierra	1.50	.70	.19
☐ 30	Barry Bonds	8.00	3.60	1.00
☐ 31	Cecil Fielder	2.50	1.10	.30
☐ 32	Roger Clemens	5.00	2.20	.60
☐ 33	Don Mattingly	15.00	6.75	1.85
☐ 34	Terry Pendleton	1.50	.70	.19
☐ 35	Rickey Henderson	2.50	1.10	.30
☐ 36	Dave Winfield	2.50	1.10	.30
☐ 37	Edgar Martinez	3.00	1.35	.35
☐ 38	Wade Boggs	2.50	1.10	.30
☐ 39	Willie McGee	1.50	.70	.19
☐ 40	Andres Galarraga	2.50	1.10	.30

	MINT	NRMT	EXC
COMPLETE SET (20)	80.00	36.00	10.00
COMPLETE SERIES 1 (9)	35.00	16.00	4.40
COMPLETE SERIES 2 (11)	45.00	20.00	5.50
COMMON CARD (1-9)	1.50	.70	.19
COMMON CARD (10-20)	1.50	.70	.19

		MINT	NRMT	EXC
☐ 1	Roberto Alomar	5.00	2.20	.60
☐ 2	Barry Bonds	6.00	2.70	.75
☐ 3	Jay Buhner	2.00	.90	.25
☐ 4	Chuck Carr	1.50	.70	.19
☐ 5	Don Mattingly	12.00	5.50	1.50
☐ 6	Raul Mondesi	6.00	2.70	.75
☐ 7	Tim Salmon	4.00	1.80	.50
☐ 8	Deion Sanders	5.00	2.20	.60
☐ 9	Devon White	1.50	.70	.19
☐ 10	Mark Whiten	1.50	.70	.19
☐ 11	Ken Griffey Jr.	25.00	11.00	3.10
☐ 12	Marquis Grissom	2.00	.90	.25
☐ 13	Paul O'Neill	2.00	.90	.25
☐ 14	Kenny Lofton	8.00	3.60	1.00
☐ 15	Larry Walker	3.00	1.35	.35
☐ 16	Scott Cooper	1.50	.70	.19
☐ 17	Barry Larkin	3.00	1.35	.35
☐ 18	Matt Williams	4.00	1.80	.50
☐ 19	John Wetteland	2.00	.90	.25
☐ 20	Randy Johnson	5.00	2.20	.60

1991 Studio

1995 Stadium Club Super Skills

This 20-card set was randomly inserted into hobby packs. The full-bleed front features a

The 1991 Studio set (issued by Donruss/Leaf) contains 264 cards and a

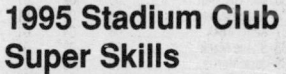

puzzle of recently inducted Hall of Famer Rod Carew. The Carew puzzle was issued on twenty-one 2 1/2" by 3 1/2" cards, with 3 puzzle pieces per card, for a total of 63 pieces. The player cards measure the standard-size (2 1/2" by 3 1/2"), and the fronts feature posed black and white head-and-shoulders player photos with mauve borders. The team logo, player's name, and position appear along the bottom of the card face. The backs are printed in black and white and have four categories of information: personal, career, hobbies and interests, and heroes. The cards are numbered on the back. The cards are checklisted below alphabetically within and according to teams for each league as follows: Baltimore Orioles (1-10), Boston Red Sox (11-20), California Angels (21-30), Chicago White Sox (31-40), Cleveland Indians (41-50), Detroit Tigers (51-60), Kansas City Royals (61-70), Milwaukee Brewers (71-80), Minnesota Twins (81-90), New York Yankees (91-100), Oakland Athletics (101-110), Seattle Mariners (111-120), Texas Rangers (121-130), Toronto Blue Jays (131-140), Atlanta Braves (141-150), Chicago Cubs (151-160), Cincinnati Reds (161-170), Houston Astros (171-180), Los Angeles Dodgers (181-190), Montreal Expos (191-200), New York Mets (201-210), Philadelphia Phillies (211-220), Pittsburgh Pirates (221-230), St. Louis Cardinals (231-240), San Diego Padres (241-250), and San Francisco Giants (251-260). Rookie Cards in the set include Jeff Bagwell, Wes Chamberlain, Jeff Conine, Brian McRae, Phil Plantier, and Todd Van Poppel. Among the other notable cards are Frank Thomas and Dave Justice.

		MINT	NRMT	EXC
	COMPLETE SET (264)	15.00	6.75	1.85
	COMMON CARD (1-263)	.05	.02	.01
	COVER CARD (NNO)	.05	.02	.01
☐ 1	Glenn Davis	.05	.02	.01
☐ 2	Dwight Evans	.08	.04	.01
☐ 3	Leo Gomez	.05	.02	.01
☐ 4	Chris Hoiles	.08	.04	.01
☐ 5	Sam Horn	.05	.02	.01
☐ 6	Ben McDonald	.10	.05	.01
☐ 7	Randy Milligan	.05	.02	.01
☐ 8	Gregg Olson	.05	.02	.01
☐ 9	Cal Ripken	2.00	.90	.25
☐ 10	David Segui	.05	.02	.01
☐ 11	Wade Boggs	.20	.09	.03
☐ 12	Ellis Burks	.08	.04	.01
☐ 13	Jack Clark	.08	.04	.01
☐ 14	Roger Clemens	.30	.14	.04
☐ 15	Mike Greenwell	.10	.05	.01
☐ 16	Tim Naehring	.05	.02	.01
☐ 17	Tony Pena	.05	.02	.01
☐ 18	Phil Plantier	.30	.14	.04
☐ 19	Jeff Reardon	.08	.04	.01
☐ 20	Mo Vaughn	1.25	.55	.16
☐ 21	Jimmy Reese CO	.25	.11	.03
☐ 22	Jim Abbott UER	.10	.05	.01
	(Born in 1967, not 1969)			
☐ 23	Bert Blyleven	.10	.05	.01
☐ 24	Chuck Finley	.08	.04	.01
☐ 25	Gary Gaetti	.05	.02	.01
☐ 26	Wally Joyner	.10	.05	.01
☐ 27	Mark Langston	.10	.05	.01
☐ 28	Kirk McCaskill	.05	.02	.01
☐ 29	Lance Parrish	.08	.04	.01
☐ 30	Dave Winfield	.20	.09	.03
☐ 31	Alex Fernandez	.08	.04	.01
☐ 32	Carlton Fisk	.10	.05	.01
☐ 33	Scott Fletcher	.05	.02	.01
☐ 34	Greg Hibbard	.05	.02	.01
☐ 35	Charlie Hough	.08	.04	.01
☐ 36	Jack McDowell	.20	.09	.03
☐ 37	Tim Raines	.20	.09	.03
☐ 38	Sammy Sosa	.40	.18	.05
☐ 39	Bobby Thigpen	.05	.02	.01
☐ 40	Frank Thomas	4.00	1.80	.50
☐ 41	Sandy Alomar Jr.	.08	.04	.01
☐ 42	John Farrell	.05	.02	.01
☐ 43	Glenallen Hill	.05	.02	.01
☐ 44	Brook Jacoby	.05	.02	.01
☐ 45	Chris James	.05	.02	.01
☐ 46	Doug Jones	.05	.02	.01
☐ 47	Eric King	.05	.02	.01
☐ 48	Mark Lewis	.05	.02	.01
☐ 49	Greg Swindell UER	.05	.02	.01
	(Photo actually Turner Ward)			
☐ 50	Mark Whiten	.08	.04	.01
☐ 51	Milt Cuyler	.05	.02	.01
☐ 52	Rob Deer	.05	.02	.01
☐ 53	Cecil Fielder	.20	.09	.03
☐ 54	Travis Fryman	.40	.18	.05
☐ 55	Bill Gullickson	.05	.02	.01
☐ 56	Lloyd Moseby	.05	.02	.01
☐ 57	Frank Tanana	.05	.02	.01
☐ 58	Mickey Tettleton	.08	.04	.01
☐ 59	Alan Trammell	.10	.05	.01
☐ 60	Lou Whitaker	.10	.05	.01
☐ 61	Mike Boddicker	.05	.02	.01
☐ 62	George Brett	.75	.35	.09
☐ 63	Jeff Conine	1.00	.45	.12
☐ 64	Warren Cromartie	.05	.02	.01
☐ 65	Storm Davis	.05	.02	.01
☐ 66	Kirk Gibson	.10	.05	.01
☐ 67	Mark Gubicza	.05	.02	.01
☐ 68	Brian McRae	.40	.18	.05
☐ 69	Bret Saberhagen	.10	.05	.01
☐ 70	Kurt Stillwell	.05	.02	.01
☐ 71	Tim McIntosh	.05	.02	.01
☐ 72	Candy Maldonado	.05	.02	.01
☐ 73	Paul Molitor	.20	.09	.03
☐ 74	Willie Randolph	.08	.04	.01
☐ 75	Ron Robinson	.05	.02	.01
☐ 76	Gary Sheffield	.10	.05	.01
☐ 77	Franklin Stubbs	.05	.02	.01
☐ 78	B.J. Surhoff	.05	.02	.01
☐ 79	Greg Vaughn	.08	.04	.01
☐ 80	Robin Yount	.30	.14	.04
☐ 81	Rick Aguilera	.08	.04	.01
☐ 82	Steve Bedrosian	.05	.02	.01
☐ 83	Scott Erickson	.05	.02	.01
☐ 84	Greg Gagne	.05	.02	.01
☐ 85	Dan Gladden	.05	.02	.01
☐ 86	Brian Harper	.05	.02	.01
☐ 87	Kent Hrbek	.08	.04	.01
☐ 88	Shane Mack	.05	.02	.01
☐ 89	Jack Morris	.10	.05	.01
☐ 90	Kirby Puckett	.60	.25	.07
☐ 91	Jesse Barfield	.05	.02	.01
☐ 92	Steve Farr	.05	.02	.01
☐ 93	Steve Howe	.05	.02	.01

☐ 94 Roberto Kelly	.08	.04	.01	☐ 161 Tom Browning	.05	.02	.01
☐ 95 Tim Leary	.05	.02	.01	☐ 162 Eric Davis	.08	.04	.01
☐ 96 Kevin Maas	.05	.02	.01	☐ 163 Rob Dibble	.08	.04	.01
☐ 97 Don Mattingly	1.00	.45	.12	☐ 164 Mariano Duncan	.05	.02	.01
☐ 98 Hensley Meulens	.05	.02	.01	☐ 165 Chris Hammond	.05	.02	.01
☐ 99 Scott Sanderson	.05	.02	.01	☐ 166 Billy Hatcher	.05	.02	.01
☐ 100 Steve Sax	.05	.02	.01	☐ 167 Barry Larkin	.30	.14	.04
☐ 101 Jose Canseco	.30	.14	.04	☐ 168 Hal Morris	.08	.04	.01
☐ 102 Dennis Eckersley	.10	.05	.01	☐ 169 Paul O'Neill	.10	.05	.01
☐ 103 Dave Henderson	.05	.02	.01	☐ 170 Chris Sabo	.05	.02	.01
☐ 104 Rickey Henderson	.20	.09	.03	☐ 171 Eric Anthony	.05	.02	.01
☐ 105 Rick Honeycutt	.05	.02	.01	☐ 172 Jeff Bagwell	3.00	1.35	.35
☐ 106 Mark McGwire	.20	.09	.03	☐ 173 Craig Biggio	.10	.05	.01
☐ 107 Dave Stewart UER	.10	.05	.01	☐ 174 Ken Caminiti	.10	.05	.01
(No-hitter against Toronto, not Texas)				☐ 175 Jim Deshaies	.05	.02	.01
				☐ 176 Steve Finley	.05	.02	.01
☐ 108 Eric Show	.05	.02	.01	☐ 177 Pete Harnisch	.08	.04	.01
☐ 109 Todd Van Poppel	.08	.04	.01	☐ 178 Darryl Kile	.05	.02	.01
☐ 110 Bob Welch	.05	.02	.01	☐ 179 Curt Schilling	.05	.02	.01
☐ 111 Alvin Davis	.05	.02	.01	☐ 180 Mike Scott	.05	.02	.01
☐ 112 Ken Griffey Jr.	3.00	1.35	.35	☐ 181 Brett Butler	.10	.05	.01
☐ 113 Ken Griffey Sr.	.08	.04	.01	☐ 182 Gary Carter	.10	.05	.01
☐ 114 Erik Hanson UER	.05	.02	.01	☐ 183 Orel Hershiser	.10	.05	.01
(Misspelled Eric)				☐ 184 Ramon Martinez	.10	.05	.01
☐ 115 Brian Holman	.05	.02	.01	☐ 185 Eddie Murray	.40	.18	.05
☐ 116 Randy Johnson	.50	.23	.06	☐ 186 Jose Offerman	.08	.04	.01
☐ 117 Edgar Martinez	.20	.09	.03	☐ 187 Bob Ojeda	.05	.02	.01
☐ 118 Tino Martinez	.10	.05	.01	☐ 188 Juan Samuel	.05	.02	.01
☐ 119 Harold Reynolds	.05	.02	.01	☐ 189 Mike Scioscia	.05	.02	.01
☐ 120 David Valle	.05	.02	.01	☐ 190 Darryl Strawberry	.08	.04	.01
☐ 121 Kevin Belcher	.05	.02	.01	☐ 191 Moises Alou	.10	.05	.01
☐ 122 Scott Chiamparino	.05	.02	.01	☐ 192 Brian Barnes	.05	.02	.01
☐ 123 Julio Franco	.08	.04	.01	☐ 193 Oil Can Boyd	.05	.02	.01
☐ 124 Juan Gonzalez	1.25	.55	.16	☐ 194 Ivan Calderon	.05	.02	.01
☐ 125 Rich Gossage	.10	.05	.01	☐ 195 Delino DeShields	.10	.05	.01
☐ 126 Jeff Kunkel	.05	.02	.01	☐ 196 Mike Fitzgerald	.05	.02	.01
☐ 127 Rafael Palmeiro	.20	.09	.03	☐ 197 Andres Galarraga	.20	.09	.03
☐ 128 Nolan Ryan	1.50	.70	.19	☐ 198 Marquis Grissom	.35	.16	.04
☐ 129 Ruben Sierra	.20	.09	.03	☐ 199 Bill Sampen	.05	.02	.01
☐ 130 Bobby Witt	.05	.02	.01	☐ 200 Tim Wallach	.05	.02	.01
☐ 131 Roberto Alomar	.50	.23	.06	☐ 201 Daryl Boston	.05	.02	.01
☐ 132 Tom Candiotti	.05	.02	.01	☐ 202 Vince Coleman	.05	.02	.01
☐ 133 Joe Carter	.20	.09	.03	☐ 203 John Franco	.10	.05	.01
☐ 134 Ken Dayley	.05	.02	.01	☐ 204 Dwight Gooden	.10	.05	.01
☐ 135 Kelly Gruber	.05	.02	.01	☐ 205 Tom Herr	.05	.02	.01
☐ 136 John Olerud	.08	.04	.01	☐ 206 Gregg Jefferies	.10	.05	.01
☐ 137 Dave Stieb	.05	.02	.01	☐ 207 Howard Johnson	.10	.05	.01
☐ 138 Turner Ward	.05	.02	.01	☐ 208 Dave Magadan UER	.05	.02	.01
☐ 139 Devon White	.08	.04	.01	(Born 1862, should be 1962)			
☐ 140 Mookie Wilson	.05	.02	.01				
☐ 141 Steve Avery	.10	.05	.01	☐ 209 Kevin McReynolds	.05	.02	.01
☐ 142 Sid Bream	.05	.02	.01	☐ 210 Frank Viola	.08	.04	.01
☐ 143 Nick Esasky UER	.05	.02	.01	☐ 211 Wes Chamberlain	.05	.02	.01
(Homers abbreviated RH)				☐ 212 Darren Daulton	.10	.05	.01
☐ 144 Ron Gant	.10	.05	.01	☐ 213 Len Dykstra	.05	.02	.01
☐ 145 Tom Glavine	.30	.14	.04	☐ 214 Charlie Hayes	.08	.04	.01
☐ 146 David Justice	.40	.18	.05	☐ 215 Ricky Jordan	.05	.02	.01
☐ 147 Kelly Mann	.05	.02	.01	☐ 216 Steve Lake	.05	.02	.01
☐ 148 Terry Pendleton	.10	.05	.01	(Pictured with parrot on his shoulder)			
☐ 149 John Smoltz	.10	.05	.01				
☐ 150 Jeff Treadway	.05	.02	.01	☐ 217 Roger McDowell	.05	.02	.01
☐ 151 George Bell	.10	.05	.01	☐ 218 Mickey Morandini	.05	.02	.01
☐ 152 Shawn Boskie	.05	.02	.01	☐ 219 Terry Mulholland	.05	.02	.01
☐ 153 Andre Dawson	.10	.05	.01	☐ 220 Dale Murphy	.10	.05	.01
☐ 154 Lance Dickson	.05	.02	.01	☐ 221 Jay Bell	.08	.04	.01
☐ 155 Shawon Dunston	.05	.02	.01	☐ 222 Barry Bonds	.60	.25	.07
☐ 156 Joe Girardi	.05	.02	.01	☐ 223 Bobby Bonilla	.20	.09	.03
☐ 157 Mark Grace	.20	.09	.03	☐ 224 Doug Drabek	.10	.05	.01
☐ 158 Ryne Sandberg	.60	.25	.07	☐ 225 Bill Landrum	.05	.02	.01
☐ 159 Gary Scott	.05	.02	.01	☐ 226 Mike LaValliere	.05	.02	.01
☐ 160 Dave Smith	.05	.02	.01	☐ 227 Jose Lind	.05	.02	.01

		MINT	NRMT	EXC
☐ 228	Don Slaught	.05	.02	.01
☐ 229	John Smiley	.05	.02	.01
☐ 230	Andy Van Slyke	.10	.05	.01
☐ 231	Bernard Gilkey	.08	.04	.01
☐ 232	Pedro Guerrero	.08	.04	.01
☐ 233	Rex Hudler	.05	.02	.01
☐ 234	Ray Lankford	.40	.18	.05
☐ 235	Joe Magrane	.05	.02	.01
☐ 236	Jose Oquendo	.05	.02	.01
☐ 237	Lee Smith	.10	.05	.01
☐ 238	Ozzie Smith	.30	.14	.04
☐ 239	Milt Thompson	.05	.02	.01
☐ 240	Todd Zeile	.08	.04	.01
☐ 241	Larry Andersen	.05	.02	.01
☐ 242	Andy Benes	.08	.04	.01
☐ 243	Paul Faries	.05	.02	.01
☐ 244	Tony Fernandez	.05	.02	.01
☐ 245	Tony Gwynn	.60	.25	.07
☐ 246	Atlee Hammaker	.05	.02	.01
☐ 247	Fred McGriff	.30	.14	.04
☐ 248	Bip Roberts	.08	.04	.01
☐ 249	Bentio Santiago	.05	.02	.01
☐ 250	Ed Whitson	.05	.02	.01
☐ 251	Dave Anderson	.05	.02	.01
☐ 252	Mike Benjamin	.05	.02	.01
☐ 253	John Burkett UER	.08	.04	.01
	(Front photo actually Trevor Wilson)			
☐ 254	Will Clark	.30	.14	.04
☐ 255	Scott Garrelts	.05	.02	.01
☐ 256	Willie McGee	.08	.04	.01
☐ 257	Kevin Mitchell	.08	.04	.01
☐ 258	Dave Righetti	.05	.02	.01
☐ 259	Matt Williams	.40	.18	.05
☐ 260	Black and Decker	.05	.02	.01
	Bud Black			
	Steve Decker			
☐ 261	Checklist Card 1-88	.05	.02	.01
	Sparky Anderson MG			
☐ 262	Checklist Card 89-176	.05	.02	.01
	Tom Lasorda MG			
☐ 263	Checklist Card 177-263	.05	.02	.01
	Tony LaRussa MG			
☐ NNO	Title Card	.05	.02	.01

1992 Studio

 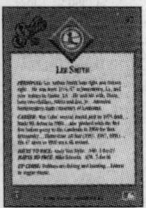

The 1992 Studio set consists of ten players from each of the 26 major league teams, three checklists, and an introduction card for a total of 264 cards. A Heritage series eight-card subset, featuring today's star players dressed in vintage uniforms, was randomly inserted in 12-card foil packs. Six additional Heritage cards were featured only in 28-card jumbo packs. The cards measure the standard size (2 1/2" by 3 1/2"). Inside champagne color metallic borders, the fronts carry a color close-up shot superimposed on a black and white action player photo. The backs focus on the personal side of each player by providing an up-close look, and unusual statistics show the batter or pitcher each player "Loves to Face" or "Hates to Face". The cards are numbered on the back. The key Rookie Cards in this set are Chad Curtis and Pat Mahomes.

		MINT	NRMT	EXC
COMPLETE SET (264)		15.00	6.75	1.85
COMMON CARD (1-264)		.05	.02	.01
☐ 1	Steve Avery	.20	.09	.03
☐ 2	Sid Bream	.05	.02	.01
☐ 3	Ron Gant	.20	.09	.03
☐ 4	Tom Glavine	.20	.09	.03
☐ 5	David Justice	.25	.11	.03
☐ 6	Mark Lemke	.05	.02	.01
☐ 7	Greg Olson	.05	.02	.01
☐ 8	Terry Pendleton	.20	.09	.03
☐ 9	Deion Sanders	.30	.14	.04
☐ 10	John Smoltz	.20	.09	.03
☐ 11	Doug Dascenzo	.05	.02	.01
☐ 12	Andre Dawson	.20	.09	.03
☐ 13	Joe Girardi	.05	.02	.01
☐ 14	Mark Grace	.20	.09	.03
☐ 15	Greg Maddux	1.25	.55	.16
☐ 16	Chuck McElroy	.05	.02	.01
☐ 17	Mike Morgan	.05	.02	.01
☐ 18	Ryne Sandberg	.40	.18	.05
☐ 19	Gary Scott	.05	.02	.01
☐ 20	Sammy Sosa	.25	.11	.03
☐ 21	Norm Charlton	.05	.02	.01
☐ 22	Rob Dibble	.05	.02	.01
☐ 23	Barry Larkin	.25	.11	.03
☐ 24	Hal Morris	.10	.05	.01
☐ 25	Paul O'Neill	.20	.09	.03
☐ 26	Jose Rijo	.10	.05	.01
☐ 27	Bip Roberts	.05	.02	.01
☐ 28	Chris Sabo	.05	.02	.01
☐ 29	Reggie Sanders	.30	.14	.04
☐ 30	Greg Swindell	.05	.02	.01
☐ 31	Jeff Bagwell	.75	.35	.09
☐ 32	Craig Biggio	.20	.09	.03
☐ 33	Ken Caminiti	.20	.09	.03
☐ 34	Andujar Cedeno	.05	.02	.01
☐ 35	Steve Finley	.10	.05	.01
☐ 36	Pete Harnisch	.05	.02	.01
☐ 37	Butch Henry	.10	.05	.01
☐ 38	Doug Jones	.05	.02	.01
☐ 39	Darryl Kile	.05	.02	.01
☐ 40	Eddie Taubensee	.05	.02	.01
☐ 41	Brett Butler	.20	.09	.03
☐ 42	Tom Candiotti	.05	.02	.01
☐ 43	Eric Davis	.10	.05	.01
☐ 44	Orel Hershiser	.20	.09	.03
☐ 45	Eric Karros	.30	.14	.04
☐ 46	Ramon Martinez	.20	.09	.03
☐ 47	Jose Offerman	.05	.02	.01
☐ 48	Mike Scioscia	.05	.02	.01
☐ 49	Mike Sharperson	.05	.02	.01
☐ 50	Darryl Strawberry	.10	.05	.01
☐ 51	Bret Barberie	.05	.02	.01

☐ 52	Ivan Calderon	.05	.02	.01
☐ 53	Gary Carter	.20	.09	.03
☐ 54	Delino DeShields	.20	.09	.03
☐ 55	Marquis Grissom	.20	.09	.03
☐ 56	Ken Hill	.20	.09	.03
☐ 57	Dennis Martinez	.10	.05	.01
☐ 58	Spike Owen	.05	.02	.01
☐ 59	Larry Walker	.20	.09	.03
☐ 60	Tim Wallach	.05	.02	.01
☐ 61	Bobby Bonilla	.20	.09	.03
☐ 62	Tim Burke	.05	.02	.01
☐ 63	Vince Coleman	.05	.02	.01
☐ 64	John Franco	.20	.09	.03
☐ 65	Dwight Gooden	.05	.02	.01
☐ 66	Todd Hundley	.05	.02	.01
☐ 67	Howard Johnson	.05	.02	.01
☐ 68	Eddie Murray UER	.25	.11	.03
	(He's not all-time switch homer leader, but he has most games with homers from both sides)			
☐ 69	Bret Saberhagen	.20	.09	.03
☐ 70	Anthony Young	.05	.02	.01
☐ 71	Kim Batiste	.05	.02	.01
☐ 72	Wes Chamberlain	.05	.02	.01
☐ 73	Darren Daulton	.20	.09	.03
☐ 74	Mariano Duncan	.05	.02	.01
☐ 75	Len Dykstra	.20	.09	.03
☐ 76	John Kruk	.20	.09	.03
☐ 77	Mickey Morandini	.05	.02	.01
☐ 78	Terry Mulholland	.05	.02	.01
☐ 79	Dale Murphy	.20	.09	.03
☐ 80	Mitch Williams	.10	.05	.01
☐ 81	Jay Bell	.10	.05	.01
☐ 82	Barry Bonds	.40	.18	.05
☐ 83	Steve Buechele	.05	.02	.01
☐ 84	Doug Drabek	.20	.09	.03
☐ 85	Mike LaValliere	.05	.02	.01
☐ 86	Jose Lind	.05	.02	.01
☐ 87	Denny Neagle	.05	.02	.01
☐ 88	Randy Tomlin	.05	.02	.01
☐ 89	Andy Van Slyke	.10	.05	.01
☐ 90	Gary Varsho	.05	.02	.01
☐ 91	Pedro Guerrero	.05	.02	.01
☐ 92	Rex Hudler	.05	.02	.01
☐ 93	Brian Jordan	.30	.14	.04
☐ 94	Felix Jose	.05	.02	.01
☐ 95	Donovan Osborne	.05	.02	.01
☐ 96	Tom Pagnozzi	.05	.02	.01
☐ 97	Lee Smith	.20	.09	.03
☐ 98	Ozzie Smith	.30	.14	.04
☐ 99	Todd Worrell	.05	.02	.01
☐ 100	Todd Zeile	.10	.05	.01
☐ 101	Andy Benes	.10	.05	.01
☐ 102	Jerald Clark	.05	.02	.01
☐ 103	Tony Fernandez	.05	.02	.01
☐ 104	Tony Gwynn	.50	.23	.06
☐ 105	Greg W. Harris	.05	.02	.01
☐ 106	Fred McGriff	.25	.11	.03
☐ 107	Benito Santiago	.05	.02	.01
☐ 108	Gary Sheffield	.20	.09	.03
☐ 109	Kurt Stillwell	.05	.02	.01
☐ 110	Tim Teufel	.05	.02	.01
☐ 111	Kevin Bass	.05	.02	.01
☐ 112	Jeff Brantley	.05	.02	.01
☐ 113	John Burkett	.10	.05	.01
☐ 114	Will Clark	.25	.11	.03
☐ 115	Royce Clayton	.10	.05	.01
☐ 116	Mike Jackson	.05	.02	.01
☐ 117	Darren Lewis	.10	.05	.01
☐ 118	Bill Swift	.05	.02	.01
☐ 119	Robby Thompson	.10	.05	.01
☐ 120	Matt Williams	.30	.14	.04
☐ 121	Brady Anderson	.10	.05	.01
☐ 122	Glenn Davis	.05	.02	.01
☐ 123	Mike Devereaux	.10	.05	.01
☐ 124	Chris Hoiles	.10	.05	.01
☐ 125	Sam Horn	.05	.02	.01
☐ 126	Ben McDonald	.10	.05	.01
☐ 127	Mike Mussina	.40	.18	.05
☐ 128	Gregg Olson	.05	.02	.01
☐ 129	Cal Ripken Jr.	1.50	.70	.19
☐ 130	Rick Sutcliffe	.10	.05	.01
☐ 131	Wade Boggs	.20	.09	.03
☐ 132	Roger Clemens	.25	.11	.03
☐ 133	Greg A. Harris	.05	.02	.01
☐ 134	Tim Naehring	.05	.02	.01
☐ 135	Tony Pena	.05	.02	.01
☐ 136	Phil Plantier	.20	.09	.03
☐ 137	Jeff Reardon	.10	.05	.01
☐ 138	Jody Reed	.05	.02	.01
☐ 139	Mo Vaughn	.50	.23	.06
☐ 140	Frank Viola	.05	.02	.01
☐ 141	Jim Abbott	.20	.09	.03
☐ 142	Hubie Brooks	.05	.02	.01
☐ 143	Chad Curtis	.25	.11	.03
☐ 144	Gary DiSarcina	.05	.02	.01
☐ 145	Chuck Finley	.05	.02	.01
☐ 146	Bryan Harvey	.05	.02	.01
☐ 147	Von Hayes	.05	.02	.01
☐ 148	Mark Langston	.20	.09	.03
☐ 149	Lance Parrish	.10	.05	.01
☐ 150	Lee Stevens	.05	.02	.01
☐ 151	George Bell	.05	.02	.01
☐ 152	Alex Fernandez	.20	.09	.03
☐ 153	Greg Hibbard	.05	.02	.01
☐ 154	Lance Johnson	.05	.02	.01
☐ 155	Kirk McCaskill	.05	.02	.01
☐ 156	Tim Raines	.20	.09	.03
☐ 157	Steve Sax	.05	.02	.01
☐ 158	Bobby Thigpen	.05	.02	.01
☐ 159	Frank Thomas	2.50	1.10	.30
☐ 160	Robin Ventura	.20	.09	.03
☐ 161	Sandy Alomar Jr.	.10	.05	.01
☐ 162	Jack Armstrong	.05	.02	.01
☐ 163	Carlos Baerga	.40	.18	.05
☐ 164	Albert Belle	.60	.25	.07
☐ 165	Alex Cole	.05	.02	.01
☐ 166	Glenallen Hill	.05	.02	.01
☐ 167	Mark Lewis	.05	.02	.01
☐ 168	Kenny Lofton	2.00	.90	.25
☐ 169	Paul Sorrento	.10	.05	.01
☐ 170	Mark Whiten	.10	.05	.01
☐ 171	Milt Cuyler	.05	.02	.01
☐ 172	Rob Deer	.05	.02	.01
☐ 173	Cecil Fielder	.20	.09	.03
☐ 174	Travis Fryman	.20	.09	.03
☐ 175	Mike Henneman	.05	.02	.01
☐ 176	Tony Phillips	.20	.09	.03
☐ 177	Frank Tanana	.05	.02	.01
☐ 178	Mickey Tettleton	.10	.05	.01
☐ 179	Alan Trammell	.20	.09	.03
☐ 180	Lou Whitaker	.20	.09	.03
☐ 181	George Brett	.60	.25	.07
☐ 182	Tom Gordon	.05	.02	.01
☐ 183	Mark Gubicza	.05	.02	.01
☐ 184	Gregg Jefferies	.20	.09	.03
☐ 185	Wally Joyner	.20	.09	.03
☐ 186	Brent Mayne	.05	.02	.01
☐ 187	Brian McRae	.20	.09	.03
☐ 188	Kevin McReynolds	.05	.02	.01
☐ 189	Keith Miller	.05	.02	.01

☐ 190	Jeff Montgomery	.10	.05	.01
☐ 191	Dante Bichette	.25	.11	.03
☐ 192	Ricky Bones	.05	.02	.01
☐ 193	Scott Fletcher	.05	.02	.01
☐ 194	Paul Molitor	.20	.09	.03
☐ 195	Jaime Navarro	.05	.02	.01
☐ 196	Franklin Stubbs	.05	.02	.01
☐ 197	B.J. Surhoff	.05	.02	.01
☐ 198	Greg Vaughn	.10	.05	.01
☐ 199	Bill Wegman	.05	.02	.01
☐ 200	Robin Yount	.25	.11	.03
☐ 201	Rick Aguilera	.10	.05	.01
☐ 202	Scott Erickson	.05	.02	.01
☐ 203	Greg Gagne	.05	.02	.01
☐ 204	Brian Harper	.05	.02	.01
☐ 205	Kent Hrbek	.10	.05	.01
☐ 206	Scott Leius	.05	.02	.01
☐ 207	Shane Mack	.05	.02	.01
☐ 208	Pat Mahomes	.05	.02	.01
☐ 209	Kirby Puckett	.50	.23	.06
☐ 210	John Smiley	.05	.02	.01
☐ 211	Mike Gallego	.05	.02	.01
☐ 212	Charlie Hayes	.10	.05	.01
☐ 213	Pat Kelly	.05	.02	.01
☐ 214	Roberto Kelly	.10	.05	.01
☐ 215	Kevin Maas	.05	.02	.01
☐ 216	Don Mattingly	.75	.35	.09
☐ 217	Matt Nokes	.05	.02	.01
☐ 218	Melido Perez	.05	.02	.01
☐ 219	Scott Sanderson	.05	.02	.01
☐ 220	Danny Tartabull	.10	.05	.01
☐ 221	Harold Baines	.20	.09	.03
☐ 222	Jose Canseco	.25	.11	.03
☐ 223	Dennis Eckersley	.20	.09	.03
☐ 224	Dave Henderson	.05	.02	.01
☐ 225	Carney Lansford	.10	.05	.01
☐ 226	Mark McGwire	.20	.09	.03
☐ 227	Mike Moore	.05	.02	.01
☐ 228	Randy Ready	.05	.02	.01
☐ 229	Terry Steinbach	.10	.05	.01
☐ 230	Dave Stewart	.20	.09	.03
☐ 231	Jay Buhner	.20	.09	.03
☐ 232	Ken Griffey Jr.	2.50	1.10	.30
☐ 233	Erik Hanson	.05	.02	.01
☐ 234	Randy Johnson	.40	.18	.05
☐ 235	Edgar Martinez	.20	.09	.03
☐ 236	Tino Martinez	.20	.09	.03
☐ 237	Kevin Mitchell	.10	.05	.01
☐ 238	Pete O'Brien	.05	.02	.01
☐ 239	Harold Reynolds	.05	.02	.01
☐ 240	David Valle	.05	.02	.01
☐ 241	Julio Franco	.10	.05	.01
☐ 242	Juan Gonzalez	.60	.25	.07
☐ 243	Jose Guzman	.05	.02	.01
☐ 244	Rafael Palmeiro	.20	.09	.03
☐ 245	Dean Palmer	.10	.05	.01
☐ 246	Ivan Rodriguez	.20	.09	.03
☐ 247	Jeff Russell	.05	.02	.01
☐ 248	Nolan Ryan	1.25	.55	.16
☐ 249	Ruben Sierra	.20	.09	.03
☐ 250	Dickie Thon	.05	.02	.01
☐ 251	Roberto Alomar	.30	.14	.04
☐ 252	Derek Bell	.10	.05	.01
☐ 253	Pat Borders	.05	.02	.01
☐ 254	Joe Carter	.20	.09	.03
☐ 255	Kelly Gruber	.05	.02	.01
☐ 256	Juan Guzman	.10	.05	.01
☐ 257	Jack Morris	.20	.09	.03
☐ 258	John Olerud	.10	.05	.01
☐ 259	Devon White	.10	.05	.01
☐ 260	Dave Winfield	.20	.09	.03

☐ 261	Checklist	.10	.05	.01
☐ 262	Checklist	.10	.05	.01
☐ 263	Checklist	.10	.05	.01
☐ 264	History Card	.05	.02	.01

1992 Studio Heritage

The 1992 Studio Heritage series subset presents today's star players dressed in vintage uniforms. Cards numbered 1-8 were randomly inserted in 12-card Studio foil packs while cards numbered 9-14 were inserted one per pack in 28-card Studio jumbo packs. The cards measure the standard size (2 1/2" by 3 1/2"). The fronts display sepia-toned portraits of the players dressed in vintage uniforms of their current teams. The pictures are bordered by dark turquoise and have bronze foil picture holders at each corner. The set title "Heritage Series" also appears in bronze foil lettering above the pictures. Within a bronze picture frame design on dark turquoise, the backs give a brief history of the team with special reference to the year of the vintage uniform. The cards are numbered on the back with a "BC" prefix.

	MINT	NRMT	EXC
COMPLETE SET (14)	25.00	11.00	3.10
COMPLETE FOIL SET (8)	15.00	6.75	1.85
COMPLETE JUMBO SET (6)	10.00	4.50	1.25
COMMON CARD (BC1-BC8)	.75	.35	.09
COMMON CARD (BC9-BC14)	.75	.35	.09
☐ BC1 Ryne Sandberg	2.50	1.10	.30
1908 Cubs			
☐ BC2 Carlton Fisk	1.25	.55	.16
1917 White Sox			
☐ BC3 Wade Boggs	1.25	.55	.16
1918 Red Sox			
☐ BC4 Jose Canseco	1.50	.70	.19
1929 Athletics			
☐ BC5 Don Mattingly	4.00	1.80	.50
1939 Yankees			
☐ BC6 Darryl Strawberry	.75	.35	.09
1944 Dodgers			
☐ BC7 Cal Ripken	8.00	3.60	1.00
1951 Browns			
☐ BC8 Will Clark	1.50	.70	.19

	1951 Giants	MINT	NRMT	EXC
☐ BC9	Andre Dawson	1.25	.55	.16
	1944 Cubs			
☐ BC10	Andy Van Slyke	.75	.35	.09
	1960 Pirates			
☐ BC11	Paul Molitor	1.25	.55	.16
	1969 Pilots			
☐ BC12	Jeff Bagwell	4.00	1.80	.50
	1962 Colt 45s			
☐ BC13	Darren Daulton	.75	.35	.09
	1945 Phillies			
☐ BC14	Kirby Puckett	2.50	1.10	.30
	1960 Senators			

1993 Studio

The 220 standard-size (2 1/2" by 3 1/2")
cards comprising this set feature borderless
fronts with posed color player photos that
are cut out and superposed upon a closeup
of an embroidered team logo. A facsimile
player autograph appears in prismatic gold
foil across the lower portion of the photo.
The borderless black backs carry another
posed color player photo shunted to the
right side, with the player's name, position,
team, biography, and personal profile
appearing in white lettering on the left side.
The cards are numbered on the back. The
key Rookie Card in this set is J.T. Snow.

	MINT	NRMT	EXC
COMPLETE SET (220)	20.00	9.00	2.50
COMMON CARD (1-220)	.10	.05	.01

		MINT	NRMT	EXC
☐ 1	Dennis Eckersley	.30	.14	.04
☐ 2	Chad Curtis	.20	.09	.03
☐ 3	Eric Anthony	.10	.05	.01
☐ 4	Roberto Alomar	.50	.23	.06
☐ 5	Steve Avery	.30	.14	.04
☐ 6	Cal Eldred	.10	.05	.01
☐ 7	Bernard Gilkey	.20	.09	.03
☐ 8	Steve Buechele	.10	.05	.01
☐ 9	Brett Butler	.20	.09	.03
☐ 10	Terry Mulholland	.10	.05	.01
☐ 11	Moises Alou	.30	.14	.04
☐ 12	Barry Bonds	.60	.25	.07
☐ 13	Sandy Alomar Jr.	.20	.09	.03
☐ 14	Chris Bosio	.10	.05	.01
☐ 15	Scott Sanderson	.10	.05	.01
☐ 16	Bobby Bonilla	.30	.14	.04
☐ 17	Brady Anderson	.20	.09	.03
☐ 18	Derek Bell	.30	.14	.04
☐ 19	Wes Chamberlain	.10	.05	.01
☐ 20	Jay Bell	.20	.09	.03
☐ 21	Kevin Brown	.10	.05	.01
☐ 22	Roger Clemens	.40	.18	.05
☐ 23	Roberto Kelly	.20	.09	.03
☐ 24	Dante Bichette	.30	.14	.04
☐ 25	George Brett	1.00	.45	.12
☐ 26	Rob Deer	.10	.05	.01
☐ 27	Brian Harper	.10	.05	.01
☐ 28	George Bell	.20	.09	.03
☐ 29	Jim Abbott	.30	.14	.04
☐ 30	Dave Henderson	.10	.05	.01
☐ 31	Wade Boggs	.30	.14	.04
☐ 32	Chili Davis	.20	.09	.03
☐ 33	Ellis Burks	.20	.09	.03
☐ 34	Jeff Bagwell	1.00	.45	.12
☐ 35	Kent Hrbek	.20	.09	.03
☐ 36	Pat Borders	.10	.05	.01
☐ 37	Cecil Fielder	.30	.14	.04
☐ 38	Sid Bream	.10	.05	.01
☐ 39	Greg Gagne	.10	.05	.01
☐ 40	Darryl Hamilton	.10	.05	.01
☐ 41	Jerald Clark	.10	.05	.01
☐ 42	Mark Grace	.30	.14	.04
☐ 43	Barry Larkin	.30	.14	.04
☐ 44	John Burkett	.10	.05	.01
☐ 45	Scott Cooper	.10	.05	.01
☐ 46	Mike Lansing	.20	.09	.03
☐ 47	Jose Canseco	.40	.18	.05
☐ 48	Will Clark	.30	.14	.04
☐ 49	Carlos Garcia	.20	.09	.03
☐ 50	Carlos Baerga	.50	.23	.06
☐ 51	Darren Daulton	.30	.14	.04
☐ 52	Jay Buhner	.30	.14	.04
☐ 53	Andy Benes	.20	.09	.03
☐ 54	Jeff Conine	.30	.14	.04
☐ 55	Mike Devereaux	.20	.09	.03
☐ 56	Vince Coleman	.10	.05	.01
☐ 57	Terry Steinbach	.20	.09	.03
☐ 58	J.T. Snow	.75	.35	.09
☐ 59	Greg Swindell	.10	.05	.01
☐ 60	Devon White	.20	.09	.03
☐ 61	John Smoltz	.20	.09	.03
☐ 62	Todd Zeile	.20	.09	.03
☐ 63	Rick Wilkins	.10	.05	.01
☐ 64	Tim Wallach	.10	.05	.01
☐ 65	John Wetteland	.20	.09	.03
☐ 66	Matt Williams	.40	.18	.05
☐ 67	Paul Sorrento	.10	.05	.01
☐ 68	David Valle	.10	.05	.01
☐ 69	Walt Weiss	.20	.09	.03
☐ 70	John Franco	.20	.09	.03
☐ 71	Nolan Ryan	2.50	1.10	.30
☐ 72	Frank Viola	.10	.05	.01
☐ 73	Chris Sabo	.20	.09	.03
☐ 74	David Nied	.20	.09	.03
☐ 75	Kevin McReynolds	.10	.05	.01
☐ 76	Lou Whitaker	.30	.14	.04
☐ 77	Dave Winfield	.30	.14	.04
☐ 78	Robin Ventura	.30	.14	.04
☐ 79	Spike Owen	.10	.05	.01
☐ 80	Cal Ripken Jr.	2.50	1.10	.30
☐ 81	Dan Walters	.10	.05	.01
☐ 82	Mitch Williams	.20	.09	.03
☐ 83	Tim Wakefield	.10	.05	.01
☐ 84	Rickey Henderson	.30	.14	.04
☐ 85	Gary DiSarcina	.10	.05	.01
☐ 86	Craig Biggio	.30	.14	.04
☐ 87	Joe Carter	.30	.14	.04
☐ 88	Ron Gant	.30	.14	.04
☐ 89	John Jaha	.20	.09	.03

☐ 90 Gregg Jefferies	.30	.14	.04
☐ 91 Jose Guzman	.10	.05	.01
☐ 92 Eric Karros	.30	.14	.04
☐ 93 Wil Cordero	.20	.09	.03
☐ 94 Royce Clayton	.20	.09	.03
☐ 95 Albert Belle	1.00	.45	.12
☐ 96 Ken Griffey Jr.	2.50	1.10	.30
☐ 97 Orestes Destrade	.10	.05	.01
☐ 98 Tony Fernandez	.10	.05	.01
☐ 99 Leo Gomez	.10	.05	.01
☐ 100 Tony Gwynn	.75	.35	.09
☐ 101 Len Dykstra	.30	.14	.04
☐ 102 Jeff King	.10	.05	.01
☐ 103 Julio Franco	.20	.09	.03
☐ 104 Andre Dawson	.30	.14	.04
☐ 105 Randy Milligan	.10	.05	.01
☐ 106 Alex Cole	.10	.05	.01
☐ 107 Phil Hiatt	.10	.05	.01
☐ 108 Travis Fryman	.30	.14	.04
☐ 109 Chuck Knoblauch	.30	.14	.04
☐ 110 Bo Jackson	.30	.14	.04
☐ 111 Pat Kelly	.10	.05	.01
☐ 112 Bret Saberhagen	.20	.09	.03
☐ 113 Ruben Sierra	.30	.14	.04
☐ 114 Tim Salmon	.75	.35	.09
☐ 115 Doug Jones	.10	.05	.01
☐ 116 Ed Sprague	.10	.05	.01
☐ 117 Terry Pendleton	.20	.09	.03
☐ 118 Robin Yount	.30	.14	.04
☐ 119 Mark Whiten	.20	.09	.03
☐ 120 Checklist 1-110	.10	.05	.01
☐ 121 Sammy Sosa	.30	.14	.04
☐ 122 Darryl Strawberry	.20	.09	.03
☐ 123 Larry Walker	.30	.14	.04
☐ 124 Robby Thompson	.10	.05	.01
☐ 125 Carlos Martinez	.10	.05	.01
☐ 126 Edgar Martinez	.30	.14	.04
☐ 127 Benito Santiago	.10	.05	.01
☐ 128 Howard Johnson	.10	.05	.01
☐ 129 Harold Reynolds	.10	.05	.01
☐ 130 Craig Shipley	.10	.05	.01
☐ 131 Curt Schilling	.10	.05	.01
☐ 132 Andy Van Slyke	.20	.09	.03
☐ 133 Ivan Rodriguez	.30	.14	.04
☐ 134 Mo Vaughn	.40	.18	.05
☐ 135 Bip Roberts	.10	.05	.01
☐ 136 Charlie Hayes	.20	.09	.03
☐ 137 Brian McRae	.30	.14	.04
☐ 138 Mickey Tettleton	.20	.09	.03
☐ 139 Frank Thomas	2.50	1.10	.30
☐ 140 Paul O'Neill	.20	.09	.03
☐ 141 Mark McGwire	.30	.14	.04
☐ 142 Damion Easley	.20	.09	.03
☐ 143 Ken Caminiti	.20	.09	.03
☐ 144 Juan Guzman	.20	.09	.03
☐ 145 Tom Glavine	.30	.14	.04
☐ 146 Pat Listach	.10	.05	.01
☐ 147 Lee Smith	.30	.14	.04
☐ 148 Derrick May	.20	.09	.03
☐ 149 Ramon Martinez	.20	.09	.03
☐ 150 Delino DeShields	.20	.09	.03
☐ 151 Kirt Manwaring	.10	.05	.01
☐ 152 Reggie Jefferson	.10	.05	.01
☐ 153 Randy Johnson	.50	.23	.06
☐ 154 Dave Magadan	.10	.05	.01
☐ 155 Dwight Gooden	.20	.09	.03
☐ 156 Chris Hoiles	.20	.09	.03
☐ 157 Fred McGriff	.30	.14	.04
☐ 158 Dave Hollins	.10	.05	.01
☐ 159 Al Martin	.20	.09	.03
☐ 160 Juan Gonzalez	.50	.23	.06

☐ 161 Mike Greenwell	.20	.09	.03
☐ 162 Kevin Mitchell	.20	.09	.03
☐ 163 Andres Galarraga	.30	.14	.04
☐ 164 Wally Joyner	.20	.09	.03
☐ 165 Kirk Gibson	.20	.09	.03
☐ 166 Pedro Munoz	.20	.09	.03
☐ 167 Ozzie Guillen	.10	.05	.01
☐ 168 Jimmy Key	.20	.09	.03
☐ 169 Kevin Seitzer	.10	.05	.01
☐ 170 Luis Polonia	.10	.05	.01
☐ 171 Luis Gonzalez	.20	.09	.03
☐ 172 Paul Molitor	.30	.14	.04
☐ 173 David Justice	.30	.14	.04
☐ 174 B.J. Surhoff	.20	.09	.03
☐ 175 Ray Lankford	.30	.14	.04
☐ 176 Ryne Sandberg	.60	.25	.07
☐ 177 Jody Reed	.10	.05	.01
☐ 178 Marquis Grissom	.30	.14	.04
☐ 179 Willie McGee	.20	.09	.03
☐ 180 Kenny Lofton	.75	.35	.09
☐ 181 Junior Felix	.10	.05	.01
☐ 182 Jose Offerman	.10	.05	.01
☐ 183 John Kruk	.30	.14	.04
☐ 184 Orlando Merced	.20	.09	.03
☐ 185 Rafael Palmeiro	.30	.14	.04
☐ 186 Billy Hatcher	.10	.05	.01
☐ 187 Joe Oliver	.10	.05	.01
☐ 188 Joe Girardi	.10	.05	.01
☐ 189 Jose Lind	.10	.05	.01
☐ 190 Harold Baines	.20	.09	.03
☐ 191 Mike Pagliarulo	.10	.05	.01
☐ 192 Lance Johnson	.10	.05	.01
☐ 193 Don Mattingly	1.25	.55	.16
☐ 194 Doug Drabek	.20	.09	.03
☐ 195 John Olerud	.20	.09	.03
☐ 196 Greg Maddux	2.50	1.10	.30
☐ 197 Greg Vaughn	.10	.05	.01
☐ 198 Tom Pagnozzi	.10	.05	.01
☐ 199 Willie Wilson	.10	.05	.01
☐ 200 Jack McDowell	.30	.14	.04
☐ 201 Mike Piazza	2.00	.90	.25
☐ 202 Mike Mussina	.40	.18	.05
☐ 203 Charles Nagy	.20	.09	.03
☐ 204 Tino Martinez	.30	.14	.04
☐ 205 Charlie Hough	.20	.09	.03
☐ 206 Todd Hundley	.20	.09	.03
☐ 207 Gary Sheffield	.30	.14	.04
☐ 208 Mickey Morandini	.10	.05	.01
☐ 209 Don Slaught	.10	.05	.01
☐ 210 Dean Palmer	.20	.09	.03
☐ 211 Jose Rijo	.20	.09	.03
☐ 212 Vinny Castilla	.30	.14	.04
☐ 213 Tony Phillips	.10	.05	.01
☐ 214 Kirby Puckett	.75	.35	.09
☐ 215 Tim Raines	.30	.14	.04
☐ 216 Otis Nixon	.10	.05	.01
☐ 217 Ozzie Smith	.50	.23	.06
☐ 218 Jose Vizcaino	.10	.05	.01
☐ 219 Randy Tomlin	.10	.05	.01
☐ 220 Checklist 111-220	.10	.05	.01

1993 Studio
Heritage

This 12-card set was randomly inserted in all 1993 Leaf Studio foil packs, measures

the standard size (2 1/2" by 3 1/2"), and features sepia-toned portraits of current players in vintage team uniforms. The pictures are bordered in turquoise blue and have bronze-foil simulated picture holders at each corner. The set title appears in white lettering above the picture, and the player's name is printed in white below. The horizontal and turquoise-blue-bordered back shades from beige to red from top to bottom, and carries a posed sepia-toned player picture on the right within an oval set off by red and black lines. His name appears in white lettering at the top within a black arc. A brief story of the team represented by the player's vintage uniform follows below. The cards are numbered on the back.

	MINT	NRMT	EXC
COMPLETE SET (12)	30.00	13.50	3.70
COMMON CARD (1-12)	.75	.35	.09
☐ 1 George Brett	6.00	2.70	.75
☐ 2 Juan Gonzalez	3.00	1.35	.35
☐ 3 Roger Clemens	2.50	1.10	.30
☐ 4 Mark McGwire	1.50	.70	.19
☐ 5 Mark Grace	1.50	.70	.19
☐ 6 Ozzie Smith	3.00	1.35	.35
☐ 7 Barry Larkin	2.00	.90	.25
☐ 8 Frank Thomas	15.00	6.75	1.85
☐ 9 Carlos Baerga	3.00	1.35	.35
☐ 10 Eric Karros	2.50	1.10	.30
☐ 11 J.T. Snow	2.50	1.10	.30
☐ 12 John Kruk	.75	.35	.09

1993 Studio Superstars on Canvas

This ten-card set was randomly inserted in 1993 Studio hobby and retail foil packs. The cards measure the standard size (2 1/2" by 3 1/2") and feature players in gray-bordered portraits that blend photography and artwork. The design of each front simulates a canvas painting of a player displayed on an artist's easel. The player's name appears in copper foil across the easel's base near the bottom. The set's title appears in white lettering beneath. The horizontal back carries a cutout color action

player photo on one side and the player's name and career highlights within a black rectangle on the other, all superposed upon an abstract team color-coded design.

	MINT	NRMT	EXC
COMPLETE SET (10)	35.00	16.00	4.40
COMMON CARD (1-10)	.75	.35	.09
☐ 1 Ken Griffey Jr.	15.00	6.75	1.85
☐ 2 Jose Canseco	2.50	1.10	.30
☐ 3 Mark McGwire	1.50	.70	.19
☐ 4 Mike Mussina	2.50	1.10	.30
☐ 5 Joe Carter	1.50	.70	.19
☐ 6 Frank Thomas	15.00	6.75	1.85
☐ 7 Darren Daulton	.75	.35	.09
☐ 8 Mark Grace	1.50	.70	.19
☐ 9 Andres Galarraga	1.50	.70	.19
☐ 10 Barry Bonds	4.00	1.80	.50

1994 Studio

The 1994 Studio set consists of 220 full-bleed, standard-size cards. Card fronts offer a player photo with his jersey hanging in a locker room setting in the background. Backs contain statistics and a small photo. The set is grouped by team as follows: Oakland Athletics (1-7), California Angels (8-15), Houston Astros (16-23), Toronto Blue Jays (24-32), Atlanta Braves (33-41), Milwaukee Brewers (42-49), St. Louis Cardinals (50-57), Chicago Cubs (58-65), Los Angeles Dodgers (66-73), Montreal Expos (74-81), San Francisco Giants (82-89), Cleveland Indians (90-97), Seattle Mariners (98-104), Florida Marlins (105-112), New York Mets (113-120), Baltimore Orioles (121-128), San Diego Padres (129-135), Philadelphia Phillies (136-143),

556 / 1994 Studio

Pittsburgh Pirates (144-150), Texas Rangers (151-158), Boston Red Sox (159-166), Cincinnati Reds (167-174), Colorado Rockies (175-181), Kansas City Royals (182-188), Detroit Tigers (189-195), Minnesota Twins (196-202), Chicago White Sox (203-210), and New York Yankees (211-218).

		MINT	NRMT	EXC
	COMPLETE SET (220)	15.00	6.75	1.85
	COMMON CARD (1-220)	.10	.05	.01
☐ 1	Dennis Eckersley	.30	.14	.04
☐ 2	Brent Gates	.30	.14	.04
☐ 3	Rickey Henderson	.30	.14	.04
☐ 4	Mark McGwire	.30	.14	.04
☐ 5	Troy Neel	.10	.05	.01
☐ 6	Ruben Sierra	.30	.14	.04
☐ 7	Terry Steinbach	.20	.09	.03
☐ 8	Chad Curtis	.20	.09	.03
☐ 9	Chili Davis	.20	.09	.03
☐ 10	Gary DiSarcina	.10	.05	.01
☐ 11	Damion Easley	.10	.05	.01
☐ 12	Bo Jackson	.30	.14	.04
☐ 13	Mark Langston	.30	.14	.04
☐ 14	Eduardo Perez	.10	.05	.01
☐ 15	Tim Salmon	.60	.25	.07
☐ 16	Jeff Bagwell	1.00	.45	.12
☐ 17	Craig Biggio	.20	.09	.03
☐ 18	Ken Caminiti	.20	.09	.03
☐ 19	Andujar Cedeno	.10	.05	.01
☐ 20	Doug Drabek	.30	.14	.04
☐ 21	Steve Finley	.10	.05	.01
☐ 22	Luis Gonzalez	.10	.05	.01
☐ 23	Darryl Kile	.20	.09	.03
☐ 24	Roberto Alomar	.60	.25	.07
☐ 25	Pat Borders	.10	.05	.01
☐ 26	Joe Carter	.30	.14	.04
☐ 27	Carlos Delgado	.30	.14	.04
☐ 28	Pat Hentgen	.20	.09	.03
☐ 29	Paul Molitor	.30	.14	.04
☐ 30	John Olerud	.30	.14	.04
☐ 31	Ed Sprague	.10	.05	.01
☐ 32	Devon White	.10	.05	.01
☐ 33	Steve Avery	.30	.14	.04
☐ 34	Tom Glavine	.30	.14	.04
☐ 35	David Justice	.40	.18	.05
☐ 36	Roberto Kelly	.10	.05	.01
☐ 37	Ryan Klesko	.75	.35	.09
☐ 38	Javier Lopez	.50	.23	.06
☐ 39	Greg Maddux	3.00	1.35	.35
☐ 40	Fred McGriff	.40	.18	.05
☐ 41	Terry Pendleton	.10	.05	.01
☐ 42	Ricky Bones	.10	.05	.01
☐ 43	Darryl Hamilton	.10	.05	.01
☐ 44	Brian Harper	.10	.05	.01
☐ 45	John Jaha	.10	.05	.01
☐ 46	Dave Nilsson	.10	.05	.01
☐ 47	Kevin Seitzer	.10	.05	.01
☐ 48	Greg Vaughn	.20	.09	.03
☐ 49	Turner Ward	.10	.05	.01
☐ 50	Bernard Gilkey	.20	.09	.03
☐ 51	Gregg Jefferies	.30	.14	.04
☐ 52	Ray Lankford	.30	.14	.04
☐ 53	Tom Pagnozzi	.10	.05	.01
☐ 54	Ozzie Smith	.60	.25	.07
☐ 55	Bob Tewksbury	.10	.05	.01
☐ 56	Mark Whiten	.20	.09	.03
☐ 57	Todd Zeile	.20	.09	.03
☐ 58	Steve Buechele	.10	.05	.01
☐ 59	Shawon Dunston	.10	.05	.01
☐ 60	Mark Grace	.30	.14	.04
☐ 61	Derrick May	.10	.05	.01
☐ 62	Karl Rhodes	.10	.05	.01
☐ 63	Ryne Sandberg	.75	.35	.09
☐ 64	Sammy Sosa	.30	.14	.04
☐ 65	Rick Wilkins	.10	.05	.01
☐ 66	Brett Butler	.20	.09	.03
☐ 67	Delino DeShields	.20	.09	.03
☐ 68	Orel Hershiser	.20	.09	.03
☐ 69	Eric Karros	.20	.09	.03
☐ 70	Raul Mondesi	1.00	.45	.12
☐ 71	Jose Offerman	.10	.05	.01
☐ 72	Mike Piazza	1.25	.55	.16
☐ 73	Tim Wallach	.10	.05	.01
☐ 74	Moises Alou	.30	.14	.04
☐ 75	Sean Berry	.10	.05	.01
☐ 76	Wil Cordero	.30	.14	.04
☐ 77	Cliff Floyd	.30	.14	.04
☐ 78	Marquis Grissom	.30	.14	.04
☐ 79	Ken Hill	.20	.09	.03
☐ 80	Larry Walker	.40	.18	.05
☐ 81	John Wetteland	.10	.05	.01
☐ 82	Rod Beck	.20	.09	.03
☐ 83	Barry Bonds	.75	.35	.09
☐ 84	Royce Clayton	.20	.09	.03
☐ 85	Darren Lewis	.10	.05	.01
☐ 86	Willie McGee	.10	.05	.01
☐ 87	Bill Swift	.10	.05	.01
☐ 88	Robby Thompson	.10	.05	.01
☐ 89	Matt Williams	.50	.23	.06
☐ 90	Sandy Alomar Jr.	.20	.09	.03
☐ 91	Carlos Baerga	.60	.25	.07
☐ 92	Albert Belle	1.25	.55	.16
☐ 93	Kenny Lofton	1.00	.45	.12
☐ 94	Eddie Murray	.40	.18	.05
☐ 95	Manny Ramirez	1.50	.70	.19
☐ 96	Paul Sorrento	.10	.05	.01
☐ 97	Jim Thome	.60	.25	.07
☐ 98	Rich Amaral	.10	.05	.01
☐ 99	Eric Anthony	.10	.05	.01
☐ 100	Jay Buhner	.20	.09	.03
☐ 101	Ken Griffey Jr.	3.00	1.35	.35
☐ 102	Randy Johnson	.60	.25	.07
☐ 103	Edgar Martinez	.20	.09	.03
☐ 104	Tino Martinez	.20	.09	.03
☐ 105	Kurt Abbott	.25	.11	.03
☐ 106	Bret Barberie	.10	.05	.01
☐ 107	Chuck Carr	.10	.05	.01
☐ 108	Jeff Conine	.30	.14	.04
☐ 109	Chris Hammond	.10	.05	.01
☐ 110	Bryan Harvey	.10	.05	.01
☐ 111	Benito Santiago	.10	.05	.01
☐ 112	Gary Sheffield	.30	.14	.04
☐ 113	Bobby Bonilla	.30	.14	.04
☐ 114	Dwight Gooden	.10	.05	.01
☐ 115	Todd Hundley	.20	.09	.03
☐ 116	Bobby Jones	.30	.14	.04
☐ 117	Jeff Kent	.20	.09	.03
☐ 118	Kevin McReynolds	.10	.05	.01
☐ 119	Bret Saberhagen	.20	.09	.03
☐ 120	Ryan Thompson	.20	.09	.03
☐ 121	Harold Baines	.20	.09	.03
☐ 122	Mike Devereaux	.20	.09	.03
☐ 123	Jeffrey Hammonds	.30	.14	.04
☐ 124	Ben McDonald	.20	.09	.03
☐ 125	Mike Mussina	.40	.18	.05
☐ 126	Rafael Palmeiro	.30	.14	.04
☐ 127	Cal Ripken Jr.	3.00	1.35	.35
☐ 128	Lee Smith	.30	.14	.04
☐ 129	Brad Ausmus	.10	.05	.01

☐ 130	Derek Bell	.20	.09	.03
☐ 131	Andy Benes	.20	.09	.03
☐ 132	Tony Gwynn	1.00	.45	.12
☐ 133	Trevor Hoffman	.10	.05	.01
☐ 134	Scott Livingstone	.10	.05	.01
☐ 135	Phil Plantier	.20	.09	.03
☐ 136	Darren Daulton	.30	.14	.04
☐ 137	Mariano Duncan	.10	.05	.01
☐ 138	Lenny Dykstra	.30	.14	.04
☐ 139	Dave Hollins	.30	.14	.04
☐ 140	Pete Incaviglia	.10	.05	.01
☐ 141	Danny Jackson	.10	.05	.01
☐ 142	John Kruk	.20	.09	.03
☐ 143	Kevin Stocker	.20	.09	.03
☐ 144	Jay Bell	.20	.09	.03
☐ 145	Carlos Garcia	.10	.05	.01
☐ 146	Jeff King	.10	.05	.01
☐ 147	Al Martin	.10	.05	.01
☐ 148	Orlando Merced	.20	.09	.03
☐ 149	Don Slaught	.10	.05	.01
☐ 150	Andy Van Slyke	.30	.14	.04
☐ 151	Kevin Brown	.10	.05	.01
☐ 152	Jose Canseco	.50	.23	.06
☐ 153	Will Clark	.40	.18	.05
☐ 154	Juan Gonzalez	.75	.35	.09
☐ 155	David Hulse	.10	.05	.01
☐ 156	Dean Palmer	.20	.09	.03
☐ 157	Ivan Rodriguez	.30	.14	.04
☐ 158	Kenny Rogers	.20	.09	.03
☐ 159	Roger Clemens	.50	.23	.06
☐ 160	Scott Cooper	.20	.09	.03
☐ 161	Andre Dawson	.30	.14	.04
☐ 162	Mike Greenwell	.20	.09	.03
☐ 163	Otis Nixon	.10	.05	.01
☐ 164	Aaron Sele	.30	.14	.04
☐ 165	John Valentin	.30	.14	.04
☐ 166	Mo Vaughn	.50	.23	.06
☐ 167	Bret Boone	.30	.14	.04
☐ 168	Barry Larkin	.40	.18	.05
☐ 169	Kevin Mitchell	.20	.09	.03
☐ 170	Hal Morris	.20	.09	.03
☐ 171	Jose Rijo	.20	.09	.03
☐ 172	Deion Sanders	.60	.25	.07
☐ 173	Reggie Sanders	.20	.09	.03
☐ 174	John Smiley	.10	.05	.01
☐ 175	Dante Bichette	.40	.18	.05
☐ 176	Ellis Burks	.20	.09	.03
☐ 177	Andres Galarraga	.30	.14	.04
☐ 178	Joe Girardi	.10	.05	.01
☐ 179	Charlie Hayes	.20	.09	.03
☐ 180	Roberto Mejia	.20	.09	.03
☐ 181	Walt Weiss	.10	.05	.01
☐ 182	David Cone	.30	.14	.04
☐ 183	Gary Gaetti	.10	.05	.01
☐ 184	Greg Gagne	.10	.05	.01
☐ 185	Felix Jose	.10	.05	.01
☐ 186	Wally Joyner	.20	.09	.03
☐ 187	Mike Macfarlane	.10	.05	.01
☐ 188	Brian McRae	.20	.09	.03
☐ 189	Eric Davis	.10	.05	.01
☐ 190	Cecil Fielder	.30	.14	.04
☐ 191	Travis Fryman	.30	.14	.04
☐ 192	Tony Phillips	.10	.05	.01
☐ 193	Mickey Tettleton	.20	.09	.03
☐ 194	Alan Trammell	.30	.14	.04
☐ 195	Lou Whitaker	.30	.14	.04
☐ 196	Kent Hrbek	.20	.09	.03
☐ 197	Chuck Knoblauch	.30	.14	.04
☐ 198	Shane Mack	.20	.09	.03
☐ 199	Pat Meares	.10	.05	.01
☐ 200	Kirby Puckett	1.00	.45	.12
☐ 201	Matt Walbeck	.10	.05	.01
☐ 202	Dave Winfield	.30	.14	.04
☐ 203	Wilson Alvarez	.30	.14	.04
☐ 204	Alex Fernandez	.30	.14	.04
☐ 205	Julio Franco	.20	.09	.03
☐ 206	Ozzie Guillen	.10	.05	.01
☐ 207	Jack McDowell	.30	.14	.04
☐ 208	Tim Raines	.30	.14	.04
☐ 209	Frank Thomas	3.00	1.35	.35
☐ 210	Robin Ventura	.20	.09	.03
☐ 211	Jim Abbott	.30	.14	.04
☐ 212	Wade Boggs	.30	.14	.04
☐ 213	Pat Kelly	.10	.05	.01
☐ 214	Jimmy Key	.20	.09	.03
☐ 215	Don Mattingly	1.50	.70	.19
☐ 216	Paul O'Neill	.20	.09	.03
☐ 217	Mike Stanley	.10	.05	.01
☐ 218	Danny Tartabull	.20	.09	.03
☐ 219	Checklist	.10	.05	.01
☐ 220	Checklist	.10	.05	.01

1994 Studio Editor's Choice

This eight-card set was randomly inserted in foil packs at a rate of one in 36. These standard-size cards are acetate and were designed much like a film strip with black borders. The fronts have various stop-action shots of the player and no back.

	MINT	NRMT	EXC
COMPLETE SET (8)	40.00	18.00	5.00
COMMON CARD (1-8)	1.50	.70	.19
☐ 1 Barry Bonds	4.00	1.80	.50
☐ 2 Frank Thomas	15.00	6.75	1.85
☐ 3 Ken Griffey Jr.	15.00	6.75	1.85
☐ 4 Andres Galarraga	1.50	.70	.19
☐ 5 Juan Gonzalez	4.00	1.80	.50
☐ 6 Tim Salmon	3.00	1.35	.35
☐ 7 Paul O'Neill	1.50	.70	.19
☐ 8 Mike Piazza	6.00	2.70	.75

1994 Studio Heritage

Each player in this eight-card insert set (randomly inserted in foil packs at a rate of

	MINT	NRMT	EXC
COMPLETE SILVER SET (10)	180.00	80.00	22.00
COMMON SILVER (1-10)	5.00	2.20	.60
*GOLD VERSIONS: 2X VALUES BELOW			

		MINT	NRMT	EXC
☐ 1	Tony Gwynn	12.00	5.50	1.50
☐ 2	Barry Bonds	10.00	4.50	1.25
☐ 3	Frank Thomas	40.00	18.00	5.00
☐ 4	Ken Griffey Jr.	40.00	18.00	5.00
☐ 5	Joe Carter	5.00	2.20	.60
☐ 6	Mike Piazza	16.00	7.25	2.00
☐ 7	Cal Ripken Jr.	40.00	18.00	5.00
☐ 8	Greg Maddux	40.00	18.00	5.00
☐ 9	Juan Gonzalez	10.00	4.50	1.25
☐ 10	Don Mattingly	20.00	9.00	2.50

one in nine) is modelling a vintage uniform of his team. The year of the uniform is noted in gold lettering at the top with a gold Heritage Collection logo at the bottom. A black and white photo of the stadium that the team used from the era of the depicted uniform serves as background. The back has a small photo a team highlight from that year.

	MINT	NRMT	EXC
COMPLETE SET (8)	20.00	9.00	2.50
COMMON CARD (1-8)	.50	.23	.06

		MINT	NRMT	EXC
☐ 1	Barry Bonds	2.00	.90	.25
☐ 2	Frank Thomas	8.00	3.60	1.00
☐ 3	Joe Carter	.75	.35	.09
☐ 4	Don Mattingly	4.00	1.80	.50
☐ 5	Ryne Sandberg	2.00	.90	.25
☐ 6	Javier Lopez	1.25	.55	.16
☐ 7	Gregg Jefferies	.50	.23	.06
☐ 8	Mike Mussina	1.25	.55	.16

1994 Studio Series Stars

This 10-card acetate set showcases top stars and was limited to 10,000 of each card. They were randomly inserted in foil packs at a rate of one in 60. The player cutout is surrounded by a small circle of stars with the player's name at the top. The team name, limited edition notation and the Series Stars logo are at the bottom. The back of the cutout contains a photo. Gold versions of this set were more difficult to obtain in packs (one in 120, 5,000 total) and are valued at twice the prices below.

1995 Studio

This 200-card horizontal set was issued by Donruss for the fifth consecutive year. Using a different design than past Studio issues, these cards were designed similarly to credit cards. The cards were issued in five-card packs with a suggested retail price of $1.49. The fronts have a player photo on the right with holographic team logo in the right corner. The rest of the card has the player identified in the upper left. Underneath that information are 1994 stats as well as various vital statistics. There is also the "Studio" logo in the upper left corner. The horizontal backs have an action photo on the left. The right has the player's signature along with a pertinent fact and his career statistics.

	MINT	NRMT	EXC
COMPLETE SET (200)	45.00	20.00	5.50
COMMON CARD (1-200)	.15	.07	.02

		MINT	NRMT	EXC
☐ 1	Frank Thomas	4.00	1.80	.50
☐ 2	Jeff Bagwell	1.25	.55	.16
☐ 3	Don Mattingly	2.00	.90	.25
☐ 4	Mike Piazza	1.50	.70	.19
☐ 5	Ken Griffey	4.00	1.80	.50
☐ 6	Greg Maddux	4.00	1.80	.50
☐ 7	Barry Bonds	1.00	.45	.12
☐ 8	Cal Ripken Jr.	4.00	1.80	.50
☐ 9	Jose Canseco	.60	.25	.07
☐ 10	Paul Molitor	.30	.14	.04
☐ 11	Kenny Lofton	1.25	.55	.16
☐ 12	Will Clark	.50	.23	.06
☐ 13	Tim Salmon	.60	.25	.07
☐ 14	Joe Carter	.30	.14	.04

☐ 15	Albert Belle	1.50	.70	.19	☐ 86	Jeff Montgomery	.15	.07	.02
☐ 16	Roger Clemens	.60	.25	.07	☐ 87	Mark Langston	.15	.07	.02
☐ 17	Roberto Alomar	.75	.35	.09	☐ 88	Reggie Sanders	.30	.14	.04
☐ 18	Alex Rodriguez	.75	.35	.09	☐ 89	Rusty Greer	.15	.07	.02
☐ 19	Raul Mondesi	1.00	.45	.12	☐ 90	Delino DeShields	.15	.07	.02
☐ 20	Deion Sanders	.75	.35	.09	☐ 91	Jason Bere	.15	.07	.02
☐ 21	Juan Gonzalez	1.00	.45	.12	☐ 92	Lee Smith	.30	.14	.04
☐ 22	Kirby Puckett	1.25	.55	.16	☐ 93	Devon White	.15	.07	.02
☐ 23	Fred McGriff	.50	.23	.06	☐ 94	John Wetteland	.15	.07	.02
☐ 24	Matt Williams	.60	.25	.07	☐ 95	Luis Gonzalez	.15	.07	.02
☐ 25	Tony Gwynn	1.25	.55	.16	☐ 96	Greg Vaughn	.15	.07	.02
☐ 26	Cliff Floyd	.30	.14	.04	☐ 97	Lance Johnson	.15	.07	.02
☐ 27	Travis Fryman	.30	.14	.04	☐ 98	Alan Trammell	.30	.14	.04
☐ 28	Shawn Green	.30	.14	.04	☐ 99	Bret Saberhagen	.15	.07	.02
☐ 29	Mike Mussina	.50	.23	.06	☐ 100	Jack McDowell	.30	.14	.04
☐ 30	Bob Hamelin	.15	.07	.02	☐ 101	Trevor Hoffman	.15	.07	.02
☐ 31	David Justice	.50	.23	.06	☐ 102	Dave Nilsson	.15	.07	.02
☐ 32	Manny Ramirez	1.50	.70	.19	☐ 103	Bryan Harvey	.15	.07	.02
☐ 33	David Cone	.30	.14	.04	☐ 104	Chuck Knoblauch	.30	.14	.04
☐ 34	Marquis Grissom	.30	.14	.04	☐ 105	Bobby Bonilla	.30	.14	.04
☐ 35	Moises Alou	.15	.07	.02	☐ 106	Hal Morris	.15	.07	.02
☐ 36	Carlos Baerga	.75	.35	.09	☐ 107	Mark Whiten	.15	.07	.02
☐ 37	Barry Larkin	.50	.23	.06	☐ 108	Phil Plantier	.15	.07	.02
☐ 38	Robin Ventura	.30	.14	.04	☐ 109	Ryan Klesko	.75	.35	.09
☐ 39	Mo Vaughn	.60	.25	.07	☐ 110	Greg Gagne	.15	.07	.02
☐ 40	Jeffrey Hammonds	.15	.07	.02	☐ 111	Ruben Sierra	.15	.07	.02
☐ 41	Ozzie Smith	.75	.35	.09	☐ 112	J.R. Phillips	.15	.07	.02
☐ 42	Andres Galarraga	.30	.14	.04	☐ 113	Terry Steinbach	.15	.07	.02
☐ 43	Carlos Delgado	.15	.07	.02	☐ 114	Jay Buhner	.30	.14	.04
☐ 44	Lenny Dykstra	.30	.14	.04	☐ 115	Ken Caminiti	.15	.07	.02
☐ 45	Cecil Fielder	.30	.14	.04	☐ 116	Gary DiSarcina	.15	.07	.02
☐ 46	Wade Boggs	.30	.14	.04	☐ 117	Ivan Rodriguez	.30	.14	.04
☐ 47	Gregg Jefferies	.30	.14	.04	☐ 118	Bip Roberts	.15	.07	.02
☐ 48	Randy Johnson	.75	.35	.09	☐ 119	Jay Bell	.15	.07	.02
☐ 49	Rafael Palmeiro	.30	.14	.04	☐ 120	Ken Hill	.15	.07	.02
☐ 50	Craig Biggio	.30	.14	.04	☐ 121	Mike Greenwell	.15	.07	.02
☐ 51	Steve Avery	.15	.07	.02	☐ 122	Rick Wilkins	.15	.07	.02
☐ 52	Ricky Bottalico	.15	.07	.02	☐ 123	Rickey Henderson	.30	.14	.04
☐ 53	Chris Gomez	.15	.07	.02	☐ 124	Dave Hollins	.15	.07	.02
☐ 54	Carlos Garcia	.15	.07	.02	☐ 125	Terry Pendleton	.15	.07	.02
☐ 55	Brian Anderson	.15	.07	.02	☐ 126	Rich Becker	.15	.07	.02
☐ 56	Wilson Alvarez	.15	.07	.02	☐ 127	Billy Ashley	.15	.07	.02
☐ 57	Roberto Kelly	.15	.07	.02	☐ 128	Derek Bell	.30	.14	.04
☐ 58	Larry Walker	.50	.23	.06	☐ 129	Dennis Eckersley	.30	.14	.04
☐ 59	Dean Palmer	.15	.07	.02	☐ 130	Andujar Cedeno	.15	.07	.02
☐ 60	Rick Aguilera	.15	.07	.02	☐ 131	John Jaha	.15	.07	.02
☐ 61	Javier Lopez	.50	.23	.06	☐ 132	Chuck Finley	.15	.07	.02
☐ 62	Shawon Dunston	.15	.07	.02	☐ 133	Steve Finley	.15	.07	.02
☐ 63	Wm. VanLandingham	.15	.07	.02	☐ 134	Danny Tartabull	.15	.07	.02
☐ 64	Jeff Kent	.15	.07	.02	☐ 135	Jeff Conine	.30	.14	.04
☐ 65	David McCarty	.15	.07	.02	☐ 136	Jon Lieber	.15	.07	.02
☐ 66	Armando Benitez	.15	.07	.02	☐ 137	Jim Abbott	.15	.07	.02
☐ 67	Brett Butler	.15	.07	.02	☐ 138	Steve Trachsel	.15	.07	.02
☐ 68	Bernard Gilkey	.15	.07	.02	☐ 139	Bret Boone	.15	.07	.02
☐ 69	Joey Hamilton	.15	.07	.02	☐ 140	Charles Johnson	.30	.14	.04
☐ 70	Chad Curtis	.15	.07	.02	☐ 141	Mark McGwire	.30	.14	.04
☐ 71	Dante Bichette	.50	.23	.06	☐ 142	Eddie Murray	.50	.23	.06
☐ 72	Chuck Carr	.15	.07	.02	☐ 143	Doug Drabek	.15	.07	.02
☐ 73	Pedro Martinez	.15	.07	.02	☐ 144	Steve Cooke	.15	.07	.02
☐ 74	Ramon Martinez	.15	.07	.02	☐ 145	Kevin Seitzer	.15	.07	.02
☐ 75	Rondell White	.30	.14	.04	☐ 146	Rod Beck	.15	.07	.02
☐ 76	Alex Fernandez	.15	.07	.02	☐ 147	Eric Karros	.30	.14	.04
☐ 77	Dennis Martinez	.15	.07	.02	☐ 148	Tim Raines	.30	.14	.04
☐ 78	Sammy Sosa	.30	.14	.04	☐ 149	Joe Girardi	.15	.07	.02
☐ 79	Bernie Williams	.15	.07	.02	☐ 150	Aaron Sele	.15	.07	.02
☐ 80	Lou Whitaker	.30	.14	.04	☐ 151	Robby Thompson	.15	.07	.02
☐ 81	Kurt Abbott	.15	.07	.02	☐ 152	Chan Ho Park	.30	.14	.04
☐ 82	Tino Martinez	.30	.14	.04	☐ 153	Ellis Burks	.15	.07	.02
☐ 83	Willie Greene	.15	.07	.02	☐ 154	Brian McRae	.15	.07	.02
☐ 84	Garret Anderson	.75	.35	.09	☐ 155	Jimmy Key	.15	.07	.02
☐ 85	Jose Rijo	.15	.07	.02	☐ 156	Rico Brogna	.30	.14	.04

			MINT	NRMT	EXC
☐	157	Ozzie Guillen	.15	.07	.02
☐	158	Chili Davis	.15	.07	.02
☐	159	Darren Daulton	.15	.07	.02
☐	160	Chipper Jones	1.50	.70	.19
☐	161	Walt Weiss	.15	.07	.02
☐	162	Paul O'Neill	.15	.07	.02
☐	163	Al Martin	.15	.07	.02
☐	164	John Valentin	.30	.14	.04
☐	165	Tim Wallach	.15	.07	.02
☐	166	Scott Erickson	.15	.07	.02
☐	167	Ryan Thompson	.15	.07	.02
☐	168	Todd Zeile	.15	.07	.02
☐	169	Scott Cooper	.15	.07	.02
☐	170	Matt Mieske	.15	.07	.02
☐	171	Allen Watson	.15	.07	.02
☐	172	Brian L.Hunter	.50	.23	.06
☐	173	Kevin Stocker	.15	.07	.02
☐	174	Cal Eldred	.15	.07	.02
☐	175	Tony Phillips	.15	.07	.02
☐	176	Ben McDonald	.15	.07	.02
☐	177	Mark Grace	.30	.14	.04
☐	178	Midre Cummings	.15	.07	.02
☐	179	Orlando Merced	.15	.07	.02
☐	180	Jeff King	.15	.07	.02
☐	181	Gary Sheffield	.30	.14	.04
☐	182	Tom Glavine	.30	.14	.04
☐	183	Edgar Martinez	.30	.14	.04
☐	184	Steve Karsay	.15	.07	.02
☐	185	Pat Listach	.15	.07	.02
☐	186	Wil Cordero	.15	.07	.02
☐	187	Brady Anderson	.15	.07	.02
☐	188	Bobby Jones	.15	.07	.02
☐	189	Andy Benes	.15	.07	.02
☐	190	Ray Lankford	.30	.14	.04
☐	191	John Doherty	.15	.07	.02
☐	192	Wally Joyner	.15	.07	.02
☐	193	Jim Thome	.60	.25	.07
☐	194	Royce Clayton	.15	.07	.02
☐	195	John Olerud	.15	.07	.02
☐	196	Steve Buechele	.15	.07	.02
☐	197	Harold Baines	.15	.07	.02
☐	198	Geronimo Berroa	.15	.07	.02
☐	199	Checklist	.15	.07	.02
☐	200	Checklist	.15	.07	.02

1995 Studio Gold Series

This 50-card set was inserted one per packs. This set parallels the first 50 cards of the regular studio set. The only differences between these cards and the regular issue are they were printed with a gold background and are numbered in the right corner as "X" of 50. Also the words "Studio Gold" are printed in the upper front left corner.

	MINT	NRMT	EXC
COMPLETE SET (50)	45.00	20.00	5.50
COMMON CARD (1-50)	.50	.23	.06
SEMISTARS	.75	.35	.09
*GOLD: 1.5X REGULAR CARDS			

1995 Studio Platinum Series

This 25-card set was randomly inserted into packs at a rate of one in 10 packs. This set parallels the first 25 cards of the regular issue. These cards are different from the regular issue in that they have a platinum background, the words "Studio Platinum" in the upper left corner and are numbered on the back as "X" of 25.

	MINT	NRMT	EXC
COMPLETE SET (25)	150.00	70.00	19.00
COMMON CARD (1-25)	2.00	.90	.25
SEMISTARS	3.00	1.35	.35
*PLATINUM: 6X REGULAR CARDS			

1995 Summit

This set contains 200 cards and was sold in seven-card retail packs for a suggested price of $1.99. This set is a premium product issued by Pinnacle Brands and produced on thicker paper than the regular set. The fronts have an action photo on a white background with the player's name and team emblem at the bottom in gold-foil. The backs have a player color photo on the left side with a baseball diamond on the right that gives the player's statistics month by month for the season. Subsets featured are Rookies (112-173), Bat Speed (174-188) and Special Delivery (189-193).

			MINT	NRMT	EXC
COMPLETE SET (200)			25.00	11.00	3.10
COMMON CARD (1-200)			.10	.05	.01
☐	1	Ken Griffey Jr.	3.00	1.35	.35
☐	2	Alex Fernandez	.10	.05	.01
☐	3	Fred McGriff	.40	.18	.05
☐	4	Ben McDonald	.10	.05	.01
☐	5	Rafael Palmeiro	.20	.09	.03
☐	6	Tony Gwynn	1.00	.45	.12
☐	7	Jim Thome	.50	.23	.06
☐	8	Ken Hill	.10	.05	.01
☐	9	Barry Bonds	.75	.35	.09
☐	10	Barry Larkin	.40	.18	.05

☐ 11	Albert Belle	1.25	.55	.16
☐ 12	Billy Ashley	.10	.05	.01
☐ 13	Matt Williams	.50	.23	.06
☐ 14	Andy Benes	.10	.05	.01
☐ 15	Midre Cummings	.10	.05	.01
☐ 16	J.R. Phillips	.10	.05	.01
☐ 17	Edgar Martinez	.30	.14	.04
☐ 18	Manny Ramirez	1.25	.55	.16
☐ 19	Jose Canseco	.50	.23	.06
☐ 20	Chili Davis	.20	.09	.03
☐ 21	Don Mattingly	1.50	.70	.19
☐ 22	Bernie Williams	.10	.05	.01
☐ 23	Tom Glavine	.30	.14	.04
☐ 24	Robin Ventura	.30	.14	.04
☐ 25	Jeff Conine	.30	.14	.04
☐ 26	Mark Grace	.30	.14	.04
☐ 27	Mark McGwire	.30	.14	.04
☐ 28	Carlos Delgado	.10	.05	.01
☐ 29	Greg Colbrunn	.30	.14	.04
☐ 30	Greg Maddux	3.00	1.35	.35
☐ 31	Craig Biggio	.30	.14	.04
☐ 32	Kirby Puckett	1.00	.45	.12
☐ 33	Derek Bell	.20	.09	.03
☐ 34	Lenny Dykstra	.20	.09	.03
☐ 35	Tim Salmon	.50	.23	.06
☐ 36	Deion Sanders	.60	.25	.07
☐ 37	Moises Alou	.10	.05	.01
☐ 38	Ray Lankford	.20	.09	.03
☐ 39	Willie Greene	.10	.05	.01
☐ 40	Ozzie Smith	.60	.25	.07
☐ 41	Roger Clemens	.50	.23	.06
☐ 42	Andres Galarraga	.30	.14	.04
☐ 43	Gary Sheffield	.30	.14	.04
☐ 44	Sammy Sosa	.30	.14	.04
☐ 45	Larry Walker	.40	.18	.05
☐ 46	Kevin Appier	.10	.05	.01
☐ 47	Raul Mondesi	.75	.35	.09
☐ 48	Kenny Lofton	1.00	.45	.12
☐ 49	Darryl Hamilton	.10	.05	.01
☐ 50	Roberto Alomar	.60	.25	.07
☐ 51	Hal Morris	.10	.05	.01
☐ 52	Cliff Floyd	.20	.09	.03
☐ 53	Brent Gates	.20	.09	.03
☐ 54	Rickey Henderson	.30	.14	.04
☐ 55	John Olerud	.10	.05	.01
☐ 56	Gregg Jefferies	.30	.14	.04
☐ 57	Cecil Fielder	.30	.14	.04
☐ 58	Paul Molitor	.30	.14	.04
☐ 59	Bret Boone	.20	.09	.03
☐ 60	Greg Vaughn	.10	.05	.01
☐ 61	Wally Joyner	.20	.09	.03
☐ 62	Jeffrey Hammonds	.10	.05	.01
☐ 63	James Mouton	.10	.05	.01
☐ 64	Omar Vizquel	.10	.05	.01
☐ 65	Wade Boggs	.30	.14	.04
☐ 66	Terry Steinbach	.20	.09	.03
☐ 67	Wil Cordero	.10	.05	.01
☐ 68	Joey Hamilton	.10	.05	.01
☐ 69	Rico Brogna	.20	.09	.03
☐ 70	Darren Daulton	.20	.09	.03
☐ 71	Chuck Knoblauch	.30	.14	.04
☐ 72	Bob Hamelin	.10	.05	.01
☐ 73	Carl Everett	.20	.09	.03
☐ 74	Joe Carter	.30	.14	.04
☐ 75	Dave Winfield	.30	.14	.04
☐ 76	Bobby Bonilla	.30	.14	.04
☐ 77	Paul O'Neill	.20	.09	.03
☐ 78	Javier Lopez	.40	.18	.05
☐ 79	Cal Ripken	3.00	1.35	.35
☐ 80	David Cone	.30	.14	.04
☐ 81	Bernard Gilkey	.10	.05	.01
☐ 82	Ivan Rodriguez	.30	.14	.04
☐ 83	Dean Palmer	.10	.05	.01
☐ 84	Jason Bere	.10	.05	.01
☐ 85	Will Clark	.40	.18	.05
☐ 86	Scott Cooper	.10	.05	.01
☐ 87	Royce Clayton	.10	.05	.01
☐ 88	Mike Piazza	1.25	.55	.16
☐ 89	Ryan Klesko	.60	.25	.07
☐ 90	Juan Gonzalez	.75	.35	.09
☐ 91	Travis Fryman	.30	.14	.04
☐ 92	Frank Thomas	3.00	1.35	.35
☐ 93	Eduardo Perez	.10	.05	.01
☐ 94	Mo Vaughn	.50	.23	.06
☐ 95	Jay Bell	.10	.05	.01
☐ 96	Jeff Bagwell	1.00	.45	.12
☐ 97	Randy Johnson	.60	.25	.07
☐ 98	Jimmy Key	.10	.05	.01
☐ 99	Dennis Eckersley	.30	.14	.04
☐ 100	Carlos Baerga	.60	.25	.07
☐ 101	Eddie Murray	.40	.18	.05
☐ 102	Mike Mussina	.40	.18	.05
☐ 103	Brian Anderson	.10	.05	.01
☐ 104	Jeff Cirillo	.10	.05	.01
☐ 105	Dante Bichette	.40	.18	.05
☐ 106	Bret Saberhagen	.20	.09	.03
☐ 107	Jeff Kent	.20	.09	.03
☐ 108	Ruben Sierra	.20	.09	.03
☐ 109	Kirk Gibson	.20	.09	.03
☐ 110	Steve Karsay	.10	.05	.01
☐ 111	David Justice	.40	.18	.05
☐ 112	Benji Gil	.10	.05	.01
☐ 113	Vaughn Eshelman	.10	.05	.01
☐ 114	Carlos Perez	.75	.35	.09
☐ 115	Chipper Jones	1.25	.55	.16
☐ 116	Shane Andrews	.10	.05	.01
☐ 117	Orlando Miller	.10	.05	.01
☐ 118	Scott Ruffcorn	.10	.05	.01
☐ 119	Jose Oliva	.10	.05	.01
☐ 120	Joe Vitiello	.10	.05	.01
☐ 121	Jon Nunnally	.20	.09	.03
☐ 122	Garret Anderson	.60	.25	.07
☐ 123	Curtis Goodwin	.20	.09	.03
☐ 124	Mark Grudzielanek	.20	.09	.03
☐ 125	Alex Gonzalez	.20	.09	.03
☐ 126	David Bell	.10	.05	.01
☐ 127	Dustin Hermanson	.10	.05	.01
☐ 128	Dave Nilsson	.10	.05	.01
☐ 129	Wilson Heredia	.10	.05	.01
☐ 130	Charles Johnson	.30	.14	.04
☐ 131	Frank Rodriguez	.10	.05	.01
☐ 132	Alex Ochoa	.20	.09	.03
☐ 133	Alex Rodriguez	.60	.25	.07
☐ 134	Bobby Higginson	.30	.14	.04
☐ 135	Edgardo Alfonzo	.20	.09	.03
☐ 136	Armando Benitez	.10	.05	.01
☐ 137	Rich Aude	.10	.05	.01
☐ 138	Tim Naehring	.10	.05	.01
☐ 139	Joe Randa	.10	.05	.01
☐ 140	Quilvio Veras	.10	.05	.01
☐ 141	Hideo Nomo	6.00	2.70	.75
☐ 142	Ray Holbert	.10	.05	.01
☐ 143	Michael Tucker	.20	.09	.03
☐ 144	Chad Mottola	.20	.09	.03
☐ 145	John Valentin	.20	.09	.03
☐ 146	James Baldwin	.10	.05	.01
☐ 147	Esteban Loaiza	.10	.05	.01
☐ 148	Marty Cordova	.50	.23	.06
☐ 149	Juan Acevedo	.10	.05	.01
☐ 150	Tim Unroe UER	.25	.11	.03
	Cardinals logo			
☐ 151	Brad Clontz UER	.10	.05	.01

	A's logo			
☐ 152	Steve Rodriguez UER...	.10	.05	.01
	Yankees logo			
☐ 153	Rudy Pemberton UER..	.10	.05	.01
	Dodgers logo			
☐ 154	Ozzie Timmons UER	.20	.09	.03
	Tigers logo			
☐ 155	Ricky Otero	.10	.05	.01
☐ 156	Allen Battle	.10	.05	.01
☐ 157	Joe Rosselli	.10	.05	.01
☐ 158	Roberto Petagine	.20	.09	.03
☐ 159	Todd Hollandsworth	.10	.05	.01
☐ 160	Shannon Penn UER	.10	.05	.01
	Cubs logo			
☐ 161	Antonio Osuna UER	.10	.05	.01
	Tigers logo			
☐ 162	Russ Davis UER	.20	.09	.03
	Red Sox logo			
☐ 163	Jason Giambi UER	.20	.09	.03
	Brewers logo			
☐ 164	Terry Bradshaw UER....	.10	.05	.01
	Brewers logo			
☐ 165	Ray Durham	.30	.14	.04
☐ 166	Todd Steverson	.10	.05	.01
☐ 167	Tim Belk	.10	.05	.01
☐ 168	Andy Pettitte	.40	.18	.05
☐ 169	Roger Cedeno	.30	.14	.04
☐ 170	Jose Parra	.20	.09	.03
☐ 171	Scott Sullivan	.10	.05	.01
☐ 172	LaTroy Hawkins	.10	.05	.01
☐ 173	Jeff McCurry	.10	.05	.01
☐ 174	Ken Griffey Jr. BS	1.50	.70	.19
☐ 175	Frank Thomas BS	1.50	.70	.19
☐ 176	Cal Ripken Jr. BS	1.50	.70	.19
☐ 177	Jeff Bagwell BS	.50	.23	.06
☐ 178	Mike Piazza BS	.60	.25	.07
☐ 179	Barry Bonds BS	.40	.18	.05
☐ 180	Matt Williams BS	.30	.14	.04
☐ 181	Don Mattingly BS	.75	.35	.09
☐ 182	Will Clark BS	.20	.09	.03
☐ 183	Tony Gwynn BS	.50	.23	.06
☐ 184	Kirby Puckett BS	.50	.23	.06
☐ 185	Jose Canseco BS	.20	.09	.03
☐ 186	Paul Molitor BS	.10	.05	.01
☐ 187	Albert Belle BS	.60	.25	.07
☐ 188	Joe Carter BS	.10	.05	.01
☐ 189	Greg Maddux SD	1.50	.70	.19
☐ 190	Roger Clemens SD	.20	.09	.03
☐ 191	David Cone SD	.10	.05	.01
☐ 192	Mike Mussina SD	.10	.05	.01
☐ 193	Randy Johnson SD	.30	.14	.04
☐ 194	Frank Thomas CL	1.50	.70	.19
☐ 195	Ken Griffey Jr. CL	1.50	.70	.19
☐ 196	Cal Ripken CL	1.50	.70	.19
☐ 197	Jeff Bagwell CL	.50	.23	.06
☐ 198	Mike Piazza CL	.60	.25	.07
☐ 199	Barry Bonds CL	.40	.18	.05
☐ 200	Mo Vaughn CL	.10	.05	.01
	Matt Williams			

1995 Summit Nth Degree

This set is a parallel of the 200 regular cards from the Collector's Choice set and

inserted one per four packs. The only difference between these cards and the regular set is that "Nth degree" has a prismatic foil background.

	MINT	NRMT	EXC
COMPLETE SET (200)	450.00	200.00	55.00
COMMON CARD (1-200)	1.50	.70	.19
SEMISTARS	2.50	1.10	.30

*VETERAN STARS: 5X TO 10X BASIC CARDS
*YOUNG STARS: 4X TO 8X BASIC CARDS
*RCs: 3X to 6X BASIC CARDS

		MINT	NRMT	EXC
☐ 1	Ken Griffey Jr.	50.00	22.00	6.25
☐ 6	Tony Gwynn	15.00	6.75	1.85
☐ 11	Albert Belle	20.00	9.00	2.50
☐ 18	Manny Ramirez	20.00	9.00	2.50
☐ 21	Don Mattingly	25.00	11.00	3.10
☐ 30	Greg Maddux	50.00	22.00	6.25
☐ 32	Kirby Puckett	15.00	6.75	1.85
☐ 48	Kenny Lofton	15.00	6.75	1.85
☐ 79	Cal Ripken	50.00	22.00	6.25
☐ 88	Mike Piazza	20.00	9.00	2.50
☐ 92	Frank Thomas	50.00	22.00	6.25
☐ 96	Jeff Bagwell	15.00	6.75	1.85
☐ 115	Chipper Jones	25.00	11.00	3.10
☐ 141	Hideo Nomo	40.00	18.00	5.00
☐ 174	Ken Griffey Jr. BS	25.00	11.00	3.10
☐ 175	Frank Thomas BS	25.00	11.00	3.10
☐ 176	Cal Ripken BS	25.00	11.00	3.10
☐ 189	Greg Maddux SPD	25.00	11.00	3.10
☐ 194	Frank Thomas CL	25.00	11.00	3.10
☐ 195	Ken Griffey Jr. CL	25.00	11.00	3.10
☐ 196	Cal Ripken CL	25.00	11.00	3.10

1995 Summit 21 Club

This nine-card set was randomly inserted in packs at a rate of one in 36. The set is comprised of young players with bright futures. Both sides of the card are done in foil with the front having a color photo with a gold background with "21 Club" in gray and red in the bottom right hand corner. The backs are laid out horizontally with a player head shot and information done in foil.

	MINT	NRMT	EXC
COMPLETE SET (9)	60.00	27.00	7.50
COMMON CARD (TC1-TC9)	6.00	2.70	.75

		MINT	NRMT	EXC
☐ TC1	Bob Abreu	8.00	3.60	1.00
☐ TC2	Pokey Reese	6.00	2.70	.75
☐ TC3	Edgardo Alfonzo	6.00	2.70	.75
☐ TC4	Jim Pittsley	6.00	2.70	.75
☐ TC5	Ruben Rivera	20.00	9.00	2.50
☐ TC6	Chan Ho Park	6.00	2.70	.75
☐ TC7	Julian Tavarez	8.00	3.60	1.00
☐ TC8	Ismael Valdes	8.00	3.60	1.00
☐ TC9	Dmitri Young	6.00	2.70	.75

1995 Summit
Big Bang

This 20-card set was randomly inserted in packs at a rate of one in 72. The set is comprised of the best home run hitters in the game. The set uses a process called "Spectrotech" which allows the card to be made of foil and have a holographic image. The fronts have an action photo with a game background which also shows the player. The backs have a player photo and information on his power exploits.

	MINT	NRMT	EXC
COMPLETE SET (20)	550.00	250.00	70.00
COMMON CARD (BB1-BB20)	12.00	5.50	1.50

		MINT	NRMT	EXC
☐ BB1	Ken Griffey Jr.	80.00	36.00	10.00
☐ BB2	Frank Thomas	80.00	36.00	10.00
☐ BB3	Cal Ripken	80.00	36.00	10.00
☐ BB4	Jeff Bagwell	30.00	13.50	3.70
☐ BB5	Mike Piazza	35.00	16.00	4.40
☐ BB6	Barry Bonds	20.00	9.00	2.50
☐ BB7	Matt Williams	18.00	8.00	2.20
☐ BB8	Don Mattingly	40.00	18.00	5.00
☐ BB9	Will Clark	15.00	6.75	1.85
☐ BB10	Tony Gwynn	30.00	13.50	3.70
☐ BB11	Kirby Puckett	30.00	13.50	3.70
☐ BB12	Jose Canseco	18.00	8.00	2.20
☐ BB13	Paul Molitor	12.00	5.50	1.50
☐ BB14	Albert Belle	35.00	16.00	4.40
☐ BB15	Joe Carter	12.00	5.50	1.50
☐ BB16	Rafael Palmeiro	12.00	5.50	1.50
☐ BB17	Fred McGriff	15.00	6.75	1.85
☐ BB18	David Justice	15.00	6.75	1.85
☐ BB19	Tim Salmon	18.00	8.00	2.20
☐ BB20	Mo Vaughn	18.00	8.00	2.20

1995 Summit
New Age

This 15-card set was randomly inserted in packs at a rate of one in 18. The set is comprised 15 of the best young players in baseball. The fronts are horizontally designed and have a color-action photo with a background of a baseball stadium with a red and gray background. The backs have a photo with player information and the words "New Age" at the bottom in red and white.

	MINT	NRMT	EXC
COMPLETE SET (15)	90.00	40.00	11.00
COMMON CARD (NA1-NA15)	2.50	1.10	.30

		MINT	NRMT	EXC
☐ NA1	Cliff Floyd	3.00	1.35	.35
☐ NA2	Manny Ramirez	25.00	11.00	3.10
☐ NA3	Raul Mondesi	15.00	6.75	1.85
☐ NA4	Alex Rodriguez	10.00	4.50	1.25
☐ NA5	Billy Ashley	2.50	1.10	.30
☐ NA6	Alex Gonzalez	2.50	1.10	.30
☐ NA7	Michael Tucker	2.50	1.10	.30
☐ NA8	Charles Johnson	4.00	1.80	.50
☐ NA9	Carlos Delgado	4.00	1.80	.50
☐ NA10	Benji Gil	2.50	1.10	.30
☐ NA11	Chipper Jones	30.00	13.50	3.70
☐ NA12	Todd Hollandsworth	2.50	1.10	.30
☐ NA13	Frankie Rodriguez	2.50	1.10	.30
☐ NA14	Shawn Green	4.00	1.80	.50
☐ NA15	Ray Durham	3.00	1.35	.35

1951 Topps
Blue Backs

The cards in this 52-card set measure approximately 2" by 2 5/8". The 1951 Topps series of blue-backed baseball cards could be used to play a baseball game by shuffling the cards and drawing them from a pile. These cards were marketed with a piece of caramel candy, which often melted or was squashed in such a way as to damage the card and wrapper (despite the fact that a paper shield was inserted between

		NRMT	VG-E	GOOD
☐ 47	Herman Wehmeier.....	30.00	13.50	3.70
☐ 48	Billy Cox....................	30.00	13.50	3.70
☐ 49	Hank Sauer...............	30.00	13.50	3.70
☐ 50	Johnny Mize	110.00	50.00	14.00
☐ 51	Eddie Waitkus............	30.00	13.50	3.70
☐ 52	Sam Chapman...........	40.00	13.50	5.00

1951 Topps Red Backs

candy and card). Blue Backs are more diffi-
cult to obtain than the similarly styled Red
Backs. The set is denoted on the cards as
"Set B" and the Red Back set is corre-
spondingly Set A. The only notable Rookie
Card in the set is Billy Pierce.

		NRMT	VG-E	GOOD
COMPLETE SET (52)		1800.00	800.00	220.00
COMMON CARD (1-52)		30.00	13.50	3.70

		NRMT	VG-E	GOOD
☐ 1	Eddie Yost...................	60.00	18.00	6.00
☐ 2	Hank Majeski.............	30.00	13.50	3.70
☐ 3	Richie Ashburn	225.00	100.00	28.00
☐ 4	Del Ennis....................	35.00	16.00	4.40
☐ 5	Johnny Pesky	35.00	16.00	4.40
☐ 6	Red Schoendienst.......	100.00	45.00	12.50
☐ 7	Gerry Staley	30.00	13.50	3.70
☐ 8	Dick Sisler.................	30.00	13.50	3.70
☐ 9	Johnny Sain................	50.00	22.00	6.25
☐ 10	Joe Page....................	30.00	13.50	3.70
☐ 11	Johnny Groth..............	30.00	13.50	3.70
☐ 12	Sam Jethroe	35.00	16.00	4.40
☐ 13	Mickey Vernon............	30.00	13.50	3.70
☐ 14	Red Munger................	30.00	13.50	3.70
☐ 15	Eddie Joost................	30.00	13.50	3.70
☐ 16	Murry Dickson............	30.00	13.50	3.70
☐ 17	Roy Smalley	30.00	13.50	3.70
☐ 18	Ned Garver.................	30.00	13.50	3.70
☐ 19	Phil Masi...................	30.00	13.50	3.70
☐ 20	Ralph Branca	50.00	22.00	6.25
☐ 21	Billy Johnson	30.00	13.50	3.70
☐ 22	Bob Kuzava................	30.00	13.50	3.70
☐ 23	Dizzy Trout.................	35.00	16.00	4.40
☐ 24	Sherman Lollar...........	35.00	16.00	4.40
☐ 25	Sam Mele	30.00	13.50	3.70
☐ 26	Chico Carrasquel........	35.00	16.00	4.40
☐ 27	Andy Pafko	35.00	16.00	4.40
☐ 28	Harry Brecheen...........	35.00	16.00	4.40
☐ 29	Granville Hamner	30.00	13.50	3.70
☐ 30	Enos Slaughter...........	100.00	45.00	12.50
☐ 31	Lou Brissie	30.00	13.50	3.70
☐ 32	Bob Elliott..................	35.00	16.00	4.40
☐ 33	Don Lenhardt.............	30.00	13.50	3.70
☐ 34	Earl Torgeson	30.00	13.50	3.70
☐ 35	Tommy Byrne	30.00	13.50	3.70
☐ 36	Cliff Fannin................	30.00	13.50	3.70
☐ 37	Bobby Doerr...............	90.00	40.00	11.00
☐ 38	Irv Noren...................	35.00	16.00	4.40
☐ 39	Ed Lopat....................	40.00	18.00	5.00
☐ 40	Vic Wertz...................	35.00	16.00	4.40
☐ 41	Johnny Schmitz...........	30.00	13.50	3.70
☐ 42	Bruce Edwards............	30.00	13.50	3.70
☐ 43	Willie Jones	30.00	13.50	3.70
☐ 44	Johnny Wyrostek..........	30.00	13.50	3.70
☐ 45	Billy Pierce	50.00	22.00	6.25
☐ 46	Gerry Priddy	30.00	13.50	3.70

The cards in this 52-card set measure
approximately 2" by 2 5/8". The 1951 Topps
Red Back set is identical in style to the Blue
Back set of the same year. The cards have
rounded corners and were designed to be
used as a baseball game. Zernial, number
36, is listed with either the White Sox or
Athletics, and Holmes, number 52, with
either the Braves or Hartford. The set is
denoted on the cards as "Set A" and the
Blue Back set is correspondingly Set B.
The only notable Rookie Card in the set is
Monte Irvin.

		NRMT	VG-E	GOOD
COMPLETE SET (54)		850.00	375.00	105.00
COMMON CARD (1-52)		10.00	4.50	1.25

		NRMT	VG-E	GOOD
☐ 1	Yogi Berra	125.00	45.00	12.50
☐ 2	Sid Gordon	10.00	4.50	1.25
☐ 3	Ferris Fain	12.00	5.50	1.50
☐ 4	Vern Stephens	12.00	5.50	1.50
☐ 5	Phil Rizzuto	55.00	25.00	7.00
☐ 6	Allie Reynolds	18.00	8.00	2.20
☐ 7	Howie Pollet	10.00	4.50	1.25
☐ 8	Early Wynn	25.00	11.00	3.10
☐ 9	Roy Sievers	12.00	5.50	1.50
☐ 10	Mel Parnell	12.00	5.50	1.50
☐ 11	Gene Hermanski	10.00	4.50	1.25
☐ 12	Jim Hegan.................	12.00	5.50	1.50
☐ 13	Dale Mitchell	12.00	5.50	1.50
☐ 14	Wayne Terwilliger	10.00	4.50	1.25
☐ 15	Ralph Kiner	35.00	16.00	4.40
☐ 16	Preacher Roe	12.00	5.50	1.50
☐ 17	Gus Bell	15.00	6.75	1.85
☐ 18	Jerry Coleman	12.00	5.50	1.50
☐ 19	Dick Kokos	10.00	4.50	1.25
☐ 20	Dom DiMaggio	18.00	8.00	2.20
☐ 21	Larry Jansen	12.00	5.50	1.50
☐ 22	Bob Feller	55.00	25.00	7.00
☐ 23	Ray Boone	15.00	6.75	1.85
☐ 24	Hank Bauer	18.00	8.00	2.20
☐ 25	Cliff Chambers	10.00	4.50	1.25

			NRMT	VG-E	GOOD
☐ 26	Luke Easter	12.00	5.50	1.50
☐ 27	Wally Westlake	10.00	4.50	1.25
☐ 28	Elmer Valo	10.00	4.50	1.25
☐ 29	Bob Kennedy	12.00	5.50	1.50
☐ 30	Warren Spahn	55.00	25.00	7.00
☐ 31	Gil Hodges	40.00	18.00	5.00
☐ 32	Henry Thompson	12.00	5.50	1.50
☐ 33	William Werle	10.00	4.50	1.25
☐ 34	Grady Hatton	10.00	4.50	1.25
☐ 35	Al Rosen	12.00	5.50	1.50
☐ 36A	Gus Zernial (Chicago)	40.00	18.00	5.00
☐ 36B	Gus Zernial (Philadelphia)	20.00	9.00	2.50
☐ 37	Wes Westrum	12.00	5.50	1.50
☐ 38	Duke Snider	80.00	36.00	10.00
☐ 39	Ted Kluszewski	20.00	9.00	2.50
☐ 40	Mike Garcia	12.00	5.50	1.50
☐ 41	Whitey Lockman	12.00	5.50	1.50
☐ 42	Ray Scarborough	10.00	4.50	1.25
☐ 43	Maurice McDermott	10.00	4.50	1.25
☐ 44	Sid Hudson	10.00	4.50	1.25
☐ 45	Andy Seminick	10.00	4.50	1.25
☐ 46	Billy Goodman	12.00	5.50	1.50
☐ 47	Tommy Glaviano	10.00	4.50	1.25
☐ 48	Eddie Stanky	12.00	5.50	1.50
☐ 49	Al Zarilla	10.00	4.50	1.25
☐ 50	Monte Irvin	40.00	18.00	5.00
☐ 51	Eddie Robinson	10.00	4.50	1.25
☐ 52A	Tommy Holmes (Boston)	40.00	10.00	4.00
☐ 52B	Tommy Holmes (Hartford)	25.00	6.25	2.50

1952 Topps

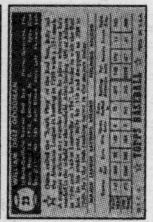

The cards in this 407-card set measure approximately 2 5/8" by 3 3/4". The 1952 Topps set is Topps' first truly major set. Card numbers 1 to 80 were issued with red or black backs, both of which are less plentiful than card numbers 81 to 250. In fact, the first series is considered the most difficult with respect to finding perfect condition cards. Card number 48 (Joe Page) and number 49 (Johnny Sain) can be found with each other's write-up on their back. Card numbers 251 to 310 are somewhat scarce and numbers 311 to 407 are quite scarce. Cards 281-300 were single printed compared to the other cards in the next to last series. Cards 311-313 were double printed

on the last high number printing sheet. The key card in the set is obviously Mickey Mantle, number 311, Mickey's first of many Topps cards. Although rarely seen, there exist salesman sample panels of three cards containing the fronts of regular cards with ad information on the back. Two such panels seen are Bob Mahoney/Robin Roberts/Sid Hudson and Wally Westlake/Dizzy Trout/Irv Noren. The key Rookie Cards in this set are Billy Martin, Eddie Mathews (the last card in the set), and Hoyt Wilhelm.

		NRMT	VG-E	GOOD
COMP. SET (407)		65000.00	29200.00	8100.00
COMMON CARD (1-80)		50.00	22.00	6.25
COMMON CARD (81-250)		30.00	13.50	3.70
COMMON CARD (251-310)		50.00	22.00	6.25
COMMON CARD (311-407)		250.00	110.00	31.00
*RED/BLACK BACKS 1-80 SAME VALUE				

			NRMT	VG-E	GOOD
☐ 1	Andy Pafko	1200.00	120.00	40.00
☐ 2	Pete Runnels	65.00	29.00	8.00
☐ 3	Hank Thompson	55.00	25.00	7.00
☐ 4	Don Lenhardt	50.00	22.00	6.25
☐ 5	Larry Jansen	55.00	25.00	7.00
☐ 6	Grady Hatton	50.00	22.00	6.25
☐ 7	Wayne Terwilliger	55.00	25.00	7.00
☐ 8	Fred Marsh	50.00	22.00	6.25
☐ 9	Robert Hogue	50.00	22.00	6.25
☐ 10	Al Rosen	60.00	27.00	7.50
☐ 11	Phil Rizzuto	200.00	90.00	25.00
☐ 12	Monty Basgall	50.00	22.00	6.25
☐ 13	Johnny Wyrostek	50.00	22.00	6.25
☐ 14	Bob Elliott	55.00	25.00	7.00
☐ 15	Johnny Pesky	55.00	25.00	7.00
☐ 16	Gene Hermanski	50.00	22.00	6.25
☐ 17	Jim Hegan	55.00	25.00	7.00
☐ 18	Merrill Combs	50.00	22.00	6.25
☐ 19	Johnny Bucha	50.00	22.00	6.25
☐ 20	Billy Loes	100.00	45.00	12.50
☐ 21	Ferris Fain	55.00	25.00	7.00
☐ 22	Dom DiMaggio	90.00	40.00	11.00
☐ 23	Billy Goodman	55.00	25.00	7.00
☐ 24	Luke Easter	55.00	25.00	7.00
☐ 25	Johnny Groth	50.00	22.00	6.25
☐ 26	Monte Irvin	90.00	40.00	11.00
☐ 27	Sam Jethroe	55.00	25.00	7.00
☐ 28	Jerry Priddy	50.00	22.00	6.25
☐ 29	Ted Kluszewski	90.00	40.00	11.00
☐ 30	Mel Parnell	55.00	25.00	7.00
☐ 31	Gus Zernial	80.00	36.00	10.00
☐ 32	Eddie Robinson	50.00	22.00	6.25
☐ 33	Warren Spahn	200.00	90.00	25.00
☐ 34	Elmer Valo	50.00	22.00	6.25
☐ 35	Hank Sauer	60.00	27.00	7.50
☐ 36	Gil Hodges	150.00	70.00	19.00
☐ 37	Duke Snider	275.00	125.00	34.00
☐ 38	Wally Westlake	50.00	22.00	6.25
☐ 39	Dizzy Trout	55.00	25.00	7.00
☐ 40	Irv Noren	55.00	25.00	7.00
☐ 41	Bob Wellman	50.00	22.00	6.25
☐ 42	Lou Kretlow	50.00	22.00	6.25
☐ 43	Ray Scarborough	50.00	22.00	6.25
☐ 44	Con Dempsey	50.00	22.00	6.25
☐ 45	Eddie Joost	50.00	22.00	6.25
☐ 46	Gordon Goldsberry	50.00	22.00	6.25
☐ 47	Willie Jones	50.00	22.00	6.25
☐ 48A	Joe Page COR	75.00	34.00	9.50
☐ 48B	Joe Page ERR	275.00	125.00	34.00

	(Bio for Sain)			
☐	49A Johnny Sain COR.....	75.00	34.00	9.50
☐	49B Johnny Sain ERR...	275.00	125.00	34.00
	(Bio for Page)			
☐	50 Marv Rickert	50.00	22.00	6.25
☐	51 Jim Russell	50.00	22.00	6.25
☐	52 Don Mueller	55.00	25.00	7.00
☐	53 Chris Van Cuyk	50.00	22.00	6.25
☐	54 Leo Kiely	50.00	22.00	6.25
☐	55 Ray Boone	55.00	25.00	7.00
☐	56 Tommy Glaviano	50.00	22.00	6.25
☐	57 Ed Lopat	90.00	40.00	11.00
☐	58 Bob Mahoney..............	50.00	22.00	6.25
☐	59 Robin Roberts............	140.00	65.00	17.50
☐	60 Sid Hudson	50.00	22.00	6.25
☐	61 Tookie Gilbert	50.00	22.00	6.25
☐	62 Chuck Stobbs	50.00	22.00	6.25
☐	63 Howie Pollet..............	50.00	22.00	6.25
☐	64 Roy Sievers	55.00	25.00	7.00
☐	65 Enos Slaughter	140.00	65.00	17.50
☐	66 Preacher Roe	90.00	40.00	11.00
☐	67 Allie Reynolds	90.00	40.00	11.00
☐	68 Cliff Chambers	50.00	22.00	6.25
☐	69 Virgil Stallcup	50.00	22.00	6.25
☐	70 Al Zarilla..................	50.00	22.00	6.25
☐	71 Tom Upton	50.00	22.00	6.25
☐	72 Karl Olson	50.00	22.00	6.25
☐	73 Bill Werle	50.00	22.00	6.25
☐	74 Andy Hansen..............	50.00	22.00	6.25
☐	75 Wes Westrum..............	55.00	25.00	7.00
☐	76 Eddie Stanky	55.00	25.00	7.00
☐	77 Bob Kennedy..............	55.00	25.00	7.00
☐	78 Ellis Kinder	50.00	22.00	6.25
☐	79 Gerry Staley	50.00	22.00	6.25
☐	80 Herman Wehmeier	50.00	22.00	6.25
☐	81 Vernon Law................	30.00	13.50	3.70
☐	82 Duane Pillette............	30.00	13.50	3.70
☐	83 Billy Johnson	30.00	13.50	3.70
☐	84 Vern Stephens	35.00	16.00	4.40
☐	85 Bob Kuzava	35.00	16.00	4.40
☐	86 Ted Gray	30.00	13.50	3.70
☐	87 Dale Coogan	30.00	13.50	3.70
☐	88 Bob Feller..................	200.00	90.00	25.00
☐	89 Johnny Lipon	30.00	13.50	3.70
☐	90 Mickey Grasso	30.00	13.50	3.70
☐	91 Red Schoendienst.......	75.00	34.00	9.50
☐	92 Dale Mitchell	35.00	16.00	4.40
☐	93 Al Sima	30.00	13.50	3.70
☐	94 Sam Mele	30.00	13.50	3.70
☐	95 Ken Holcombe	30.00	13.50	3.70
☐	96 Willard Marshall..........	30.00	13.50	3.70
☐	97 Earl Torgeson	30.00	13.50	3.70
☐	98 Billy Pierce	30.00	13.50	3.70
☐	99 Gene Woodling	40.00	18.00	5.00
☐	100 Del Rice	30.00	13.50	3.70
☐	101 Max Lanier	30.00	13.50	3.70
☐	102 Bill Kennedy..............	30.00	13.50	3.70
☐	103 Cliff Mapes..............	30.00	13.50	3.70
☐	104 Don Kolloway............	30.00	13.50	3.70
☐	105 Johnny Pramesa	30.00	13.50	3.70
☐	106 Mickey Vernon............	40.00	18.00	5.00
☐	107 Connie Ryan	30.00	13.50	3.70
☐	108 Jim Konstanty............	40.00	18.00	5.00
☐	109 Ted Wilks	30.00	13.50	3.70
☐	110 Dutch Leonard	30.00	13.50	3.70
☐	111 Peanuts Lowrey	30.00	13.50	3.70
☐	112 Hank Majeski	30.00	13.50	3.70
☐	113 Dick Sisler	35.00	16.00	4.40
☐	114 Willard Ramsdell..........	30.00	13.50	3.70
☐	115 Red Munger..............	30.00	13.50	3.70
☐	116 Carl Scheib	30.00	13.50	3.70
☐	117 Sherm Lollar............	35.00	16.00	4.40
☐	118 Ken Raffensberger ...	30.00	13.50	3.70
☐	119 Mickey McDermott ..	30.00	13.50	3.70
☐	120 Bob Chakales	30.00	13.50	3.70
☐	121 Gus Niarhos............	30.00	13.50	3.70
☐	122 Jackie Jensen	70.00	32.00	8.75
☐	123 Eddie Yost................	35.00	16.00	4.40
☐	124 Monte Kennedy	30.00	13.50	3.70
☐	125 Bill Rigney................	30.00	13.50	3.70
☐	126 Fred Hutchinson	35.00	16.00	4.40
☐	127 Paul Minner	30.00	13.50	3.70
☐	128 Don Bollweg..............	30.00	13.50	3.70
☐	129 Johnny Mize..............	90.00	40.00	11.00
☐	130 Sheldon Jones	30.00	13.50	3.70
☐	131 Morrie Martin............	30.00	13.50	3.70
☐	132 Clyde Kluttz..............	30.00	13.50	3.70
☐	133 Al Widmar................	30.00	13.50	3.70
☐	134 Joe Tipton................	30.00	13.50	3.70
☐	135 Dixie Howell	30.00	13.50	3.70
☐	136 Johnny Schmitz..........	30.00	13.50	3.70
☐	137 Roy McMillan............	35.00	16.00	4.40
☐	138 Bill MacDonald	30.00	13.50	3.70
☐	139 Ken Wood	30.00	13.50	3.70
☐	140 Johnny Antonelli	35.00	16.00	4.40
☐	141 Clint Hartung............	30.00	13.50	3.70
☐	142 Harry Perkowski.........	30.00	13.50	3.70
☐	143 Les Moss	30.00	13.50	3.70
☐	144 Ed Blake	30.00	13.50	3.70
☐	145 Joe Haynes	30.00	13.50	3.70
☐	146 Frank House..............	30.00	13.50	3.70
☐	147 Bob Young................	30.00	13.50	3.70
☐	148 Johnny Klippstein	30.00	13.50	3.70
☐	149 Dick Kryhoski............	30.00	13.50	3.70
☐	150 Ted Beard	30.00	13.50	3.70
☐	151 Wally Post................	35.00	16.00	4.40
☐	152 Al Evans	30.00	13.50	3.70
☐	153 Bob Rush	30.00	13.50	3.70
☐	154 Joe Muir	30.00	13.50	3.70
☐	155 Frank Overmire	30.00	13.50	3.70
☐	156 Frank Hiller	30.00	13.50	3.70
☐	157 Bob Usher................	30.00	13.50	3.70
☐	158 Eddie Waitkus	30.00	13.50	3.70
☐	159 Saul Rogovin............	30.00	13.50	3.70
☐	160 Owen Friend............	30.00	13.50	3.70
☐	161 Bud Byerly	30.00	13.50	3.70
☐	162 Del Crandall............	35.00	16.00	4.40
☐	163 Stan Rojek	30.00	13.50	3.70
☐	164 Walt Dubiel	30.00	13.50	3.70
☐	165 Eddie Kazak..............	30.00	13.50	3.70
☐	166 Paul LaPalme............	30.00	13.50	3.70
☐	167 Bill Howerton............	30.00	13.50	3.70
☐	168 Charlie Silvera..........	35.00	16.00	4.40
☐	169 Howie Judson............	30.00	13.50	3.70
☐	170 Gus Bell	35.00	16.00	4.40
☐	171 Ed Erautt................	30.00	13.50	3.70
☐	172 Eddie Miksis	30.00	13.50	3.70
☐	173 Roy Smalley	30.00	13.50	3.70
☐	174 Clarence Marshall	30.00	13.50	3.70
☐	175 Billy Martin	225.00	100.00	28.00
☐	176 Hank Edwards............	30.00	13.50	3.70
☐	177 Bill Wight................	30.00	13.50	3.70
☐	178 Cass Michaels............	30.00	13.50	3.70
☐	179 Frank Smith	30.00	13.50	3.70
☐	180 Charlie Maxwell..........	35.00	16.00	4.40
☐	181 Bob Swift	30.00	13.50	3.70
☐	182 Billy Hitchcock..........	30.00	13.50	3.70
☐	183 Erv Dusak	30.00	13.50	3.70
☐	184 Bob Ramazzotti..........	30.00	13.50	3.70
☐	185 Bill Nicholson............	35.00	16.00	4.40
☐	186 Walt Masterson..........	30.00	13.50	3.70
☐	187 Bob Miller	30.00	13.50	3.70

☐ 188	Clarence Podbielan ..	30.00	13.50	3.70
☐ 189	Pete Reiser	40.00	18.00	5.00
☐ 190	Don Johnson	30.00	13.50	3.70
☐ 191	Yogi Berra	350.00	160.00	45.00
☐ 192	Myron Ginsberg	30.00	13.50	3.70
☐ 193	Harry Simpson	35.00	16.00	4.40
☐ 194	Joe Hatton	30.00	13.50	3.70
☐ 195	Minnie Minoso	150.00	70.00	19.00
☐ 196	Solly Hemus	40.00	18.00	5.00
☐ 197	George Strickland	30.00	13.50	3.70
☐ 198	Phil Haugstad	30.00	13.50	3.70
☐ 199	George Zuverink	30.00	13.50	3.70
☐ 200	Ralph Houk	70.00	32.00	8.75
☐ 201	Alex Kellner	30.00	13.50	3.70
☐ 202	Joe Collins	40.00	18.00	5.00
☐ 203	Curt Simmons	40.00	18.00	5.00
☐ 204	Ron Northey	30.00	13.50	3.70
☐ 205	Clyde King	35.00	16.00	4.40
☐ 206	Joe Ostrowski	30.00	13.50	3.70
☐ 207	Mickey Harris	30.00	13.50	3.70
☐ 208	Marlin Stuart	30.00	13.50	3.70
☐ 209	Howie Fox	30.00	13.50	3.70
☐ 210	Dick Fowler	30.00	13.50	3.70
☐ 211	Ray Coleman	30.00	13.50	3.70
☐ 212	Ned Garver	30.00	13.50	3.70
☐ 213	Nippy Jones	30.00	13.50	3.70
☐ 214	Johnny Hopp	35.00	16.00	4.40
☐ 215	Hank Bauer	50.00	22.00	6.25
☐ 216	Richie Ashburn	150.00	70.00	19.00
☐ 217	Snuffy Stirnweiss	35.00	16.00	4.40
☐ 218	Clyde McCullough	30.00	13.50	3.70
☐ 219	Bobby Shantz	40.00	18.00	5.00
☐ 220	Joe Presko	30.00	13.50	3.70
☐ 221	Granny Hamner	30.00	13.50	3.70
☐ 222	Hoot Evers	30.00	13.50	3.70
☐ 223	Del Ennis	35.00	16.00	4.40
☐ 224	Bruce Edwards	30.00	13.50	3.70
☐ 225	Frank Baumholtz	30.00	13.50	3.70
☐ 226	Dave Philley	30.00	13.50	3.70
☐ 227	Joe Garagiola	80.00	36.00	10.00
☐ 228	Al Brazle	30.00	13.50	3.70
☐ 229	Gene Bearden UER.... (Misspelled Beardon)	30.00	13.50	3.70
☐ 230	Matt Batts	30.00	13.50	3.70
☐ 231	Sam Zoldak	30.00	13.50	3.70
☐ 232	Billy Cox	30.00	13.50	3.70
☐ 233	Bob Friend	50.00	22.00	6.25
☐ 234	Steve Souchock	30.00	13.50	3.70
☐ 235	Walt Dropo	30.00	13.50	3.70
☐ 236	Ed Fitzgerald	30.00	13.50	3.70
☐ 237	Jerry Coleman	40.00	18.00	5.00
☐ 238	Art Houtteman	30.00	13.50	3.70
☐ 239	Rocky Bridges	35.00	16.00	4.40
☐ 240	Jack Phillips	30.00	13.50	3.70
☐ 241	Tommy Byrne	30.00	13.50	3.70
☐ 242	Tom Poholsky	30.00	13.50	3.70
☐ 243	Larry Doby	65.00	29.00	8.00
☐ 244	Vic Wertz	35.00	16.00	4.40
☐ 245	Sherry Robertson	30.00	13.50	3.70
☐ 246	George Kell	70.00	32.00	8.75
☐ 247	Randy Gumpert	30.00	13.50	3.70
☐ 248	Frank Shea	30.00	13.50	3.70
☐ 249	Bobby Adams	30.00	13.50	3.70
☐ 250	Carl Erskine	80.00	36.00	10.00
☐ 251	Chico Carrasquel	50.00	22.00	6.25
☐ 252	Vern Bickford	50.00	22.00	6.25
☐ 253	Johnny Berardino	55.00	25.00	7.00
☐ 254	Joe Dobson	50.00	22.00	6.25
☐ 255	Clyde Vollmer	50.00	22.00	6.25
☐ 256	Pete Suder	50.00	22.00	6.25
☐ 257	Bobby Avila	55.00	25.00	7.00
☐ 258	Steve Gromek	50.00	22.00	6.25
☐ 259	Bob Addis	50.00	22.00	6.25
☐ 260	Pete Castiglione	50.00	22.00	6.25
☐ 261	Willie Mays	2700.00	1200.00	350.00
☐ 262	Virgil Trucks	55.00	25.00	7.00
☐ 263	Harry Brecheen	55.00	25.00	7.00
☐ 264	Roy Hartsfield	50.00	22.00	6.25
☐ 265	Chuck Diering	50.00	22.00	6.25
☐ 266	Murry Dickson	50.00	22.00	6.25
☐ 267	Sid Gordon	50.00	22.00	6.25
☐ 268	Bob Lemon	140.00	65.00	17.50
☐ 269	Willard Nixon	50.00	22.00	6.25
☐ 270	Lou Brissie	50.00	22.00	6.25
☐ 271	Jim Delsing	50.00	22.00	6.25
☐ 272	Mike Garcia	55.00	25.00	7.00
☐ 273	Erv Palica	50.00	22.00	6.25
☐ 274	Ralph Branca	100.00	45.00	12.50
☐ 275	Pat Mullin	50.00	22.00	6.25
☐ 276	Jim Wilson	50.00	22.00	6.25
☐ 277	Early Wynn	140.00	65.00	17.50
☐ 278	Allie Clark	50.00	22.00	6.25
☐ 279	Eddie Stewart	50.00	22.00	6.25
☐ 280	Cloyd Boyer	55.00	25.00	7.00
☐ 281	Tommy Brown SP	50.00	22.00	6.25
☐ 282	Birdie Tebbetts SP	55.00	25.00	7.00
☐ 283	Phil Masi SP	50.00	22.00	6.25
☐ 284	Hank Arft SP	50.00	22.00	6.25
☐ 285	Cliff Fannin SP	50.00	22.00	6.25
☐ 286	Joe DeMaestri SP	50.00	22.00	6.25
☐ 287	Steve Bilko SP	50.00	22.00	6.25
☐ 288	Chet Nichols SP	50.00	22.00	6.25
☐ 289	Tommy Holmes SP..	55.00	25.00	7.00
☐ 290	Joe Astroth SP	50.00	22.00	6.25
☐ 291	Gil Coan SP	50.00	22.00	6.25
☐ 292	Floyd Baker SP	50.00	22.00	6.25
☐ 293	Sibby Sisti SP	50.00	22.00	6.25
☐ 294	Walker Cooper SP	50.00	22.00	6.25
☐ 295	Phil Cavarretta SP..	55.00	25.00	7.00
☐ 296	Red Rolfe MG SP	55.00	25.00	7.00
☐ 297	Andy Seminick SP	50.00	22.00	6.25
☐ 298	Bob Ross SP	50.00	22.00	6.25
☐ 299	Ray Murray SP	50.00	22.00	6.25
☐ 300	Barney McCosky SP.	50.00	22.00	6.25
☐ 301	Bob Porterfield	50.00	22.00	6.25
☐ 302	Max Surkont	50.00	22.00	6.25
☐ 303	Harry Dorish	50.00	22.00	6.25
☐ 304	Sam Dente	50.00	22.00	6.25
☐ 305	Paul Richards MG	55.00	25.00	7.00
☐ 306	Lou Sleater	50.00	22.00	6.25
☐ 307	Frank Campos	50.00	22.00	6.25
☐ 308	Luis Aloma	50.00	22.00	6.25
☐ 309	Jim Busby	50.00	22.00	6.25
☐ 310	George Metkovich....	55.00	25.00	7.00
☐ 311	Mickey Mantle	25000.00	11200.00	3100.00
☐ 312	Jackie Robinson DP	1400.00	650.00	180.00
☐ 313	Bobby Thomson	300.00	135.00	38.00
☐ 314	Roy Campanella	2100.00	950.00	250.00
☐ 315	Leo Durocher MG ..	375.00	170.00	47.50
☐ 316	Dave Williams	275.00	125.00	34.00
☐ 317	Conrado Marrero ...	275.00	125.00	34.00
☐ 318	Harold Gregg	250.00	110.00	31.00
☐ 319	Al Walker	250.00	110.00	31.00
☐ 320	John Rutherford	275.00	125.00	34.00
☐ 321	Joe Black	300.00	135.00	38.00
☐ 322	Randy Jackson	250.00	110.00	31.00
☐ 323	Bubba Church	250.00	110.00	31.00
☐ 324	Warren Hacker	250.00	110.00	31.00
☐ 325	Bill Serena	250.00	110.00	31.00
☐ 326	George Shuba	300.00	135.00	38.00
☐ 327	Al Wilson	250.00	110.00	31.00
☐ 328	Bob Borkowski	250.00	110.00	31.00

☐ 329	Ike Delock	250.00	110.00	31.00
☐ 330	Turk Lown	250.00	110.00	31.00
☐ 331	Tom Morgan	250.00	110.00	31.00
☐ 332	Anthony Bartirome	250.00	110.00	31.00
☐ 333	Pee Wee Reese	1400.00	650.00	180.00
☐ 334	Wilmer Mizell	300.00	135.00	38.00
☐ 335	Ted Lepcio	250.00	110.00	31.00
☐ 336	Dave Koslo	250.00	110.00	31.00
☐ 337	Jim Hearn	250.00	110.00	31.00
☐ 338	Sal Yvars	250.00	110.00	31.00
☐ 339	Russ Meyer	250.00	110.00	31.00
☐ 340	Bob Hooper	250.00	110.00	31.00
☐ 341	Hal Jeffcoat	250.00	110.00	31.00
☐ 342	Clem Labine	300.00	135.00	38.00
☐ 343	Dick Gernert	250.00	110.00	31.00
☐ 344	Ewell Blackwell	300.00	135.00	38.00
☐ 345	Sammy White	250.00	110.00	31.00
☐ 346	George Spencer	250.00	110.00	31.00
☐ 347	Joe Adcock	300.00	135.00	38.00
☐ 348	Robert Kelly	250.00	110.00	31.00
☐ 349	Bob Cain	250.00	110.00	31.00
☐ 350	Cal Abrams	250.00	110.00	31.00
☐ 351	Alvin Dark	300.00	135.00	38.00
☐ 352	Karl Drews	250.00	110.00	31.00
☐ 353	Bobby Del Greco	250.00	110.00	31.00
☐ 354	Fred Hatfield	250.00	110.00	31.00
☐ 355	Bobby Morgan	250.00	110.00	31.00
☐ 356	Toby Atwell	250.00	110.00	31.00
☐ 357	Smoky Burgess	300.00	135.00	38.00
☐ 358	John Kucab	250.00	110.00	31.00
☐ 359	Dee Fondy	250.00	110.00	31.00
☐ 360	George Crowe	275.00	125.00	34.00
☐ 361	William Posedel CO	250.00	110.00	31.00
☐ 362	Ken Heintzelman	250.00	110.00	31.00
☐ 363	Dick Rozek	250.00	110.00	31.00
☐ 364	Clyde Sukeforth CO	250.00	110.00	31.00
☐ 365	Cookie Lavagetto CO	275.00	125.00	34.00
☐ 366	Dave Madison	250.00	110.00	31.00
☐ 367	Ben Thorpe	250.00	110.00	31.00
☐ 368	Ed Wright	250.00	110.00	31.00
☐ 369	Dick Groat	350.00	160.00	45.00
☐ 370	Billy Hoeft	275.00	125.00	34.00
☐ 371	Bobby Hofman	250.00	110.00	31.00
☐ 372	Gil McDougald	350.00	160.00	45.00
☐ 373	Jim Turner CO	300.00	135.00	38.00
☐ 374	John Benton	250.00	110.00	31.00
☐ 375	John Merson	250.00	110.00	31.00
☐ 376	Faye Throneberry	250.00	110.00	31.00
☐ 377	Chuck Dressen MG	250.00	110.00	31.00
☐ 378	Leroy Fusselman	250.00	110.00	31.00
☐ 379	Joe Rossi	250.00	110.00	31.00
☐ 380	Clem Koshorek	250.00	110.00	31.00
☐ 381	Milton Stock CO	250.00	110.00	31.00
☐ 382	Sam Jones	300.00	135.00	38.00
☐ 383	Del Wilber	250.00	110.00	31.00
☐ 384	Frank Crosetti CO	300.00	135.00	38.00
☐ 385	Herman Franks CO	250.00	110.00	31.00
☐ 386	John Yuhas	250.00	110.00	31.00
☐ 387	Billy Meyer MG	250.00	110.00	31.00
☐ 388	Bob Chipman	250.00	110.00	31.00
☐ 389	Ben Wade	250.00	110.00	31.00
☐ 390	Glenn Nelson	250.00	110.00	31.00
☐ 391	Ben Chapman UER CO (Photo actually Sam Chapman)	250.00	110.00	31.00
☐ 392	Hoyt Wilhelm	700.00	325.00	90.00
☐ 393	Ebba St.Claire	250.00	110.00	31.00
☐ 394	Billy Herman CO	300.00	135.00	38.00
☐ 395	Jake Pitler CO	250.00	110.00	31.00
☐ 396	Dick Williams	300.00	135.00	38.00
☐ 397	Forrest Main	250.00	110.00	31.00

☐ 398	Hal Rice	250.00	110.00	31.00
☐ 399	Jim Fridley	250.00	110.00	31.00
☐ 400	Bill Dickey CO	700.00	325.00	90.00
☐ 401	Bob Schultz	250.00	110.00	31.00
☐ 402	Earl Harrist	250.00	110.00	31.00
☐ 403	Bill Miller	250.00	110.00	31.00
☐ 404	Dick Brodowski	250.00	110.00	31.00
☐ 405	Eddie Pellagrini	250.00	110.00	31.00
☐ 406	Joe Nuxhall	300.00	135.00	38.00
☐ 407	Eddie Mathews	3200.00	800.00	325.00

1953 Topps

The cards in this 274-card set measure 2 5/8" by 3 3/4". Although the last card is numbered 280, there are only 274 cards in the set since numbers 253, 261, 267, 268, 271, and 275 were never issued. The 1953 Topps series contains line drawings of players in full color. The name and team panel at the card base is easily damaged, making it very difficult to complete a mint set. The high number series, 221 to 280, was produced in shorter supply late in the year and hence is more difficult to complete than the lower numbers. The key cards in the set are Mickey Mantle (82) and Willie Mays (244). The key Rookie Cards in this set are Roy Face, Jim Gilliam, and Johnny Podres, all from the last series. There are a number of double-printed cards (actually not double but 50 percent more of each of these numbers were printed compared to the other cards in the series) indicated by DP in the checklist below. There were five players (10 Smoky Burgess, 44 Ellis Kinder, 61 Early Wynn, 72 Fred Hutchinson, and 81 Joe Black) held out of the first run of 1-85 (but printed with numbers 86-165), who are each marked by SP in the checklist below. In addition, there are five numbers which were printed with the more plentiful series 166-220; these cards (94, 107, 131, 145, and 156) are also indicated by DP in the checklist below. There were some three-card advertising panels produced by Topps; the players include Johnny Mize/Clem Koshorek/Toby Atwell and Mickey Mantle/Johnny Wyrostek/Sal Yvars. When cut apart, these advertising cards are distinguished by the non-standard card back, i.e., part of an advertisement for the 1953 Topps set instead of the

typical statistics and biographical information about the player pictured.

	NRMT	VG-E	GOOD
COMPLETE SET (274)	13500.00	6100.00	1700.00
COMMON CARD (1-165)	25.00	11.00	3.10
COMMON CARD (166-220)	20.00	9.00	2.50
COMMON CARD (221-280)	90.00	40.00	11.00

		NRMT	VG-E	GOOD
☐	1 Jackie Robinson DP	450.00	125.00	45.00
☐	2 Luke Easter DP	18.00	8.00	2.20
☐	3 George Crowe	25.00	11.00	3.10
☐	4 Ben Wade	25.00	11.00	3.10
☐	5 Joe Dobson	25.00	11.00	3.10
☐	6 Sam Jones	30.00	13.50	3.70
☐	7 Bob Borkowski DP	15.00	6.75	1.85
☐	8 Clem Koshorek DP	15.00	6.75	1.85
☐	9 Joe Collins	35.00	16.00	4.40
☐	10 Smoky Burgess SP	60.00	27.00	7.50
☐	11 Sal Yvars	25.00	11.00	3.10
☐	12 Howie Judson DP	15.00	6.75	1.85
☐	13 Conrado Marrero DP	15.00	6.75	1.85
☐	14 Clem Labine DP	15.00	6.75	1.85
☐	15 Bobo Newsom DP	18.00	8.00	2.20
☐	16 Peanuts Lowrey DP	15.00	6.75	1.85
☐	17 Billy Hitchcock	25.00	11.00	3.10
☐	18 Ted Lepcio DP	15.00	6.75	1.85
☐	19 Mel Parnell DP	18.00	8.00	2.20
☐	20 Hank Thompson	30.00	13.50	3.70
☐	21 Billy Johnson	25.00	11.00	3.10
☐	22 Howie Fox	25.00	11.00	3.10
☐	23 Toby Atwell DP	15.00	6.75	1.85
☐	24 Ferris Fain	30.00	13.50	3.70
☐	25 Ray Boone	30.00	13.50	3.70
☐	26 Dale Mitchell DP	18.00	8.00	2.20
☐	27 Roy Campanella DP	200.00	90.00	25.00
☐	28 Eddie Pellagrini	25.00	11.00	3.10
☐	29 Hal Jeffcoat	25.00	11.00	3.10
☐	30 Willard Nixon	25.00	11.00	3.10
☐	31 Ewell Blackwell	50.00	22.00	6.25
☐	32 Clyde Vollmer	25.00	11.00	3.10
☐	33 Bob Kennedy DP	18.00	8.00	2.20
☐	34 George Shuba	30.00	13.50	3.70
☐	35 Irv Noren DP	18.00	8.00	2.20
☐	36 Johnny Groth DP	15.00	6.75	1.85
☐	37 Eddie Mathews DP	100.00	45.00	12.50
☐	38 Jim Hearn DP	15.00	6.75	1.85
☐	39 Eddie Miksis	25.00	11.00	3.10
☐	40 John Lipon	25.00	11.00	3.10
☐	41 Enos Slaughter	80.00	36.00	10.00
☐	42 Gus Zernial DP	15.00	6.75	1.85
☐	43 Gil McDougald	50.00	22.00	6.25
☐	44 Ellis Kinder SP	35.00	16.00	4.40
☐	45 Grady Hatton DP	15.00	6.75	1.85
☐	46 Johnny Klippstein DP	15.00	6.75	1.85
☐	47 Bubba Church DP	15.00	6.75	1.85
☐	48 Bob Del Greco DP	15.00	6.75	1.85
☐	49 Faye Throneberry DP	15.00	6.75	1.85
☐	50 Chuck Dressen MG DP	18.00	8.00	2.20
☐	51 Frank Campos DP	15.00	6.75	1.85
☐	52 Ted Gray DP	15.00	6.75	1.85
☐	53 Sherm Lollar DP	18.00	8.00	2.20
☐	54 Bob Feller DP	100.00	45.00	12.50
☐	55 Maurice McDermott DP	15.00	6.75	1.85
☐	56 Gerry Staley DP	15.00	6.75	1.85
☐	57 Carl Scheib	25.00	11.00	3.10
☐	58 George Metkovich	25.00	11.00	3.10
☐	59 Karl Drews DP	15.00	6.75	1.85
☐	60 Cloyd Boyer DP	15.00	6.75	1.85
☐	61 Early Wynn SP	100.00	45.00	12.50
☐	62 Monte Irvin DP	35.00	16.00	4.40
☐	63 Gus Niarhos DP	15.00	6.75	1.85
☐	64 Dave Philley	25.00	11.00	3.10
☐	65 Earl Harrist	25.00	11.00	3.10
☐	66 Minnie Minoso	50.00	22.00	6.25
☐	67 Roy Sievers DP	18.00	8.00	2.20
☐	68 Del Rice	25.00	11.00	3.10
☐	69 Dick Brodowski	25.00	11.00	3.10
☐	70 Ed Yuhas	25.00	11.00	3.10
☐	71 Tony Bartirome	25.00	11.00	3.10
☐	72 Fred Hutchinson MG SP	50.00	22.00	6.25
☐	73 Eddie Robinson	25.00	11.00	3.10
☐	74 Joe Rossi	25.00	11.00	3.10
☐	75 Mike Garcia	30.00	13.50	3.70
☐	76 Pee Wee Reese	175.00	80.00	22.00
☐	77 Johnny Mize DP	55.00	25.00	7.00
☐	78 Red Schoendienst	60.00	27.00	7.50
☐	79 Johnny Wyrostek	25.00	11.00	3.10
☐	80 Jim Hegan	30.00	13.50	3.70
☐	81 Joe Black SP	60.00	27.00	7.50
☐	82 Mickey Mantle	3200.00	1450.00	400.00
☐	83 Howie Pollet	25.00	11.00	3.10
☐	84 Bob Hooper DP	15.00	6.75	1.85
☐	85 Bobby Morgan DP	15.00	6.75	1.85
☐	86 Billy Martin	120.00	55.00	15.00
☐	87 Ed Lopat	45.00	20.00	5.50
☐	88 Willie Jones DP	15.00	6.75	1.85
☐	89 Chuck Stobbs DP	15.00	6.75	1.85
☐	90 Hank Edwards DP	15.00	6.75	1.85
☐	91 Ebba St.Claire DP	15.00	6.75	1.85
☐	92 Paul Minner DP	15.00	6.75	1.85
☐	93 Hal Rice DP	15.00	6.75	1.85
☐	94 Bill Kennedy DP	15.00	6.75	1.85
☐	95 Willard Marshall DP	15.00	6.75	1.85
☐	96 Virgil Trucks	30.00	13.50	3.70
☐	97 Don Kolloway DP	15.00	6.75	1.85
☐	98 Cal Abrams DP	15.00	6.75	1.85
☐	99 Dave Madison	25.00	11.00	3.10
☐	100 Bill Miller	25.00	11.00	3.10
☐	101 Ted Wilks	25.00	11.00	3.10
☐	102 Connie Ryan DP	15.00	6.75	1.85
☐	103 Joe Astroth DP	15.00	6.75	1.85
☐	104 Yogi Berra	200.00	90.00	25.00
☐	105 Joe Nuxhall DP	18.00	8.00	2.20
☐	106 Johnny Antonelli	25.00	11.00	3.10
☐	107 Danny O'Connell DP	15.00	6.75	1.85
☐	108 Bob Porterfield DP	15.00	6.75	1.85
☐	109 Alvin Dark	30.00	13.50	3.70
☐	110 Herman Wehmeier DP	15.00	6.75	1.85
☐	111 Hank Sauer DP	18.00	8.00	2.20
☐	112 Ned Garver DP	15.00	6.75	1.85
☐	113 Jerry Priddy	25.00	11.00	3.10
☐	114 Phil Rizzuto	150.00	70.00	19.00
☐	115 George Spencer	25.00	11.00	3.10
☐	116 Frank Smith DP	15.00	6.75	1.85
☐	117 Sid Gordon DP	15.00	6.75	1.85
☐	118 Gus Bell DP	18.00	8.00	2.20
☐	119 Johnny Sain SP	50.00	22.00	6.25
☐	120 Davey Williams	30.00	13.50	3.70
☐	121 Walt Dropo	30.00	13.50	3.70
☐	122 Elmer Valo	25.00	11.00	3.10
☐	123 Tommy Byrne DP	15.00	6.75	1.85
☐	124 Sibby Sisti DP	15.00	6.75	1.85
☐	125 Dick Williams DP	18.00	8.00	2.20
☐	126 Bill Connelly DP	15.00	6.75	1.85
☐	127 Clint Courtney DP	15.00	6.75	1.85
☐	128 Wilmer Mizell DP	18.00	8.00	2.20
	(Inconsistent design, logo on front with black birds)			
☐	129 Keith Thomas	25.00	11.00	3.10
☐	130 Turk Lown DP	15.00	6.75	1.85

☐ 131	Harry Byrd DP	15.00	6.75	1.85
☐ 132	Tom Morgan	25.00	11.00	3.10
☐ 133	Gil Coan	25.00	11.00	3.10
☐ 134	Rube Walker	30.00	13.50	3.70
☐ 135	Al Rosen DP	25.00	11.00	3.10
☐ 136	Ken Heintzelman DP	15.00	6.75	1.85
☐ 137	John Rutherford DP	15.00	6.75	1.85
☐ 138	George Kell	50.00	22.00	6.25
☐ 139	Sammy White	25.00	11.00	3.10
☐ 140	Tommy Glaviano	25.00	11.00	3.10
☐ 141	Allie Reynolds DP	25.00	11.00	3.10
☐ 142	Vic Wertz	30.00	13.50	3.70
☐ 143	Billy Pierce	30.00	13.50	3.70
☐ 144	Bob Schultz DP	15.00	6.75	1.85
☐ 145	Harry Dorish DP	15.00	6.75	1.85
☐ 146	Granny Hamner	25.00	11.00	3.10
☐ 147	Warren Spahn	150.00	70.00	19.00
☐ 148	Mickey Grasso	25.00	11.00	3.10
☐ 149	Dom DiMaggio DP	35.00	16.00	4.40
☐ 150	Harry Simpson DP	15.00	6.75	1.85
☐ 151	Hoyt Wilhelm	80.00	36.00	10.00
☐ 152	Bob Adams DP	15.00	6.75	1.85
☐ 153	Andy Seminick DP	15.00	6.75	1.85
☐ 154	Dick Groat	30.00	13.50	3.70
☐ 155	Dutch Leonard	25.00	11.00	3.10
☐ 156	Jim Rivera DP	18.00	8.00	2.20
☐ 157	Bob Addis DP	15.00	6.75	1.85
☐ 158	Johnny Logan	35.00	16.00	4.40
☐ 159	Wayne Terwilliger DP	15.00	6.75	1.85
☐ 160	Bob Young	25.00	11.00	3.10
☐ 161	Vern Bickford DP	15.00	6.75	1.85
☐ 162	Ted Kluszewski	50.00	22.00	6.25
☐ 163	Fred Hatfield DP	15.00	6.75	1.85
☐ 164	Frank Shea DP	15.00	6.75	1.85
☐ 165	Billy Hoeft	25.00	11.00	3.10
☐ 166	Billy Hunter	20.00	9.00	2.50
☐ 167	Art Schult	20.00	9.00	2.50
☐ 168	Willard Schmidt	20.00	9.00	2.50
☐ 169	Dizzy Trout	22.00	10.00	2.70
☐ 170	Bill Werle	20.00	9.00	2.50
☐ 171	Bill Glynn	20.00	9.00	2.50
☐ 172	Rip Repulski	20.00	9.00	2.50
☐ 173	Preston Ward	20.00	9.00	2.50
☐ 174	Billy Loes	25.00	11.00	3.10
☐ 175	Ron Kline	20.00	9.00	2.50
☐ 176	Don Hoak	25.00	11.00	3.10
☐ 177	Jim Dyck	20.00	9.00	2.50
☐ 178	Jim Waugh	20.00	9.00	2.50
☐ 179	Gene Hermanski	20.00	9.00	2.50
☐ 180	Virgil Stallcup	20.00	9.00	2.50
☐ 181	Al Zarilla	20.00	9.00	2.50
☐ 182	Bobby Hofman	20.00	9.00	2.50
☐ 183	Stu Miller	25.00	11.00	3.10
☐ 184	Hal Brown	20.00	9.00	2.50
☐ 185	Jim Pendleton	20.00	9.00	2.50
☐ 186	Charlie Bishop	20.00	9.00	2.50
☐ 187	Jim Fridley	20.00	9.00	2.50
☐ 188	Andy Carey	35.00	16.00	4.40
☐ 189	Ray Jablonski	20.00	9.00	2.50
☐ 190	Dixie Walker CO	22.00	10.00	2.70
☐ 191	Ralph Kiner	70.00	32.00	8.75
☐ 192	Wally Westlake	20.00	9.00	2.50
☐ 193	Mike Clark	20.00	9.00	2.50
☐ 194	Eddie Kazak	20.00	9.00	2.50
☐ 195	Ed McGhee	20.00	9.00	2.50
☐ 196	Bob Keegan	20.00	9.00	2.50
☐ 197	Del Crandall	22.00	10.00	2.70
☐ 198	Forrest Main	20.00	9.00	2.50
☐ 199	Marion Fricano	20.00	9.00	2.50
☐ 200	Gordon Goldsberry	20.00	9.00	2.50
☐ 201	Paul LaPalme	20.00	9.00	2.50
☐ 202	Carl Sawatski	20.00	9.00	2.50
☐ 203	Cliff Fannin	20.00	9.00	2.50
☐ 204	Dick Bokelman	20.00	9.00	2.50
☐ 205	Vern Benson	20.00	9.00	2.50
☐ 206	Ed Bailey	20.00	9.00	2.50
☐ 207	Whitey Ford	125.00	55.00	15.50
☐ 208	Jim Wilson	20.00	9.00	2.50
☐ 209	Jim Greengrass	20.00	9.00	2.50
☐ 210	Bob Cerv	30.00	13.50	3.70
☐ 211	J.W. Porter	20.00	9.00	2.50
☐ 212	Jack Dittmer	20.00	9.00	2.50
☐ 213	Ray Scarborough	20.00	9.00	2.50
☐ 214	Bill Bruton	25.00	11.00	3.10
☐ 215	Gene Conley	25.00	11.00	3.10
☐ 216	Jim Hughes	20.00	9.00	2.50
☐ 217	Murray Wall	20.00	9.00	2.50
☐ 218	Les Fusselman	20.00	9.00	2.50
☐ 219	Pete Runnels UER	22.00	10.00	2.70
	(Photo actually			
	Don Johnson)			
☐ 220	Satchel Paige UER	450.00	200.00	55.00
	(Misspelled Satchell			
	on card front)			
☐ 221	Bob Milliken	90.00	40.00	11.00
☐ 222	Vic Janowicz DP	55.00	25.00	7.00
☐ 223	Johnny O'Brien DP	55.00	25.00	7.00
☐ 224	Lou Sleater DP	50.00	22.00	6.25
☐ 225	Bobby Shantz	100.00	45.00	12.50
☐ 226	Ed Erautt	90.00	40.00	11.00
☐ 227	Morrie Martin	90.00	40.00	11.00
☐ 228	Hal Newhouser	150.00	70.00	19.00
☐ 229	Rocky Krsnich	90.00	40.00	11.00
☐ 230	Johnny Lindell DP	50.00	22.00	6.25
☐ 231	Solly Hemus DP	50.00	22.00	6.25
☐ 232	Dick Kokos	90.00	40.00	11.00
☐ 233	Al Aber	90.00	40.00	11.00
☐ 234	Ray Murray DP	50.00	22.00	6.25
☐ 235	John Hetki DP	50.00	22.00	6.25
☐ 236	Harry Perkowski DP	50.00	22.00	6.25
☐ 237	Bud Podbielan DP	50.00	22.00	6.25
☐ 238	Cal Hogue DP	50.00	22.00	6.25
☐ 239	Jim Delsing	90.00	40.00	11.00
☐ 240	Fred Marsh	90.00	40.00	11.00
☐ 241	Al Sima DP	50.00	22.00	6.25
☐ 242	Charlie Silvera	100.00	45.00	12.50
☐ 243	Carlos Bernier DP	50.00	22.00	6.25
☐ 244	Willie Mays	2800.00	1250.00	350.00
☐ 245	Bill Norman CO	90.00	40.00	11.00
☐ 246	Roy Face DP	80.00	36.00	10.00
☐ 247	Mike Sandlock DP	50.00	22.00	6.25
☐ 248	Gene Stephens DP	50.00	22.00	6.25
☐ 249	Eddie O'Brien	90.00	40.00	11.00
☐ 250	Bob Wilson	90.00	40.00	11.00
☐ 251	Sid Hudson	90.00	40.00	11.00
☐ 252	Hank Foiles	90.00	40.00	11.00
☐ 253	Does not exist			
☐ 254	Preacher Roe DP	80.00	36.00	10.00
☐ 255	Dixie Howell	90.00	40.00	11.00
☐ 256	Les Peden	90.00	40.00	11.00
☐ 257	Bob Boyd	90.00	40.00	11.00
☐ 258	Jim Gilliam	275.00	125.00	34.00
☐ 259	Roy McMillan DP	55.00	25.00	7.00
☐ 260	Sam Calderone	90.00	40.00	11.00
☐ 261	Does not exist			
☐ 262	Bob Oldis	90.00	40.00	11.00
☐ 263	Johnny Podres	275.00	125.00	34.00
☐ 264	Gene Woodling DP	50.00	22.00	6.25
☐ 265	Jackie Jensen	110.00	50.00	14.00
☐ 266	Bob Cain	90.00	40.00	11.00
☐ 267	Does not exist			
☐ 268	Does not exist			

		NRMT	VG-E	GOOD
☐ 269	Duane Pillette	90.00	40.00	11.00
☐ 270	Vern Stephens	100.00	45.00	12.50
☐ 271	Does not exist			
☐ 272	Bill Antonello	90.00	40.00	11.00
☐ 273	Harvey Haddix	120.00	55.00	15.00
☐ 274	John Riddle CO	90.00	40.00	11.00
☐ 275	Does not exist			
☐ 276	Ken Raffensberger	90.00	40.00	11.00
☐ 277	Don Lund	90.00	40.00	11.00
☐ 278	Willie Miranda	90.00	40.00	11.00
☐ 279	Joe Coleman DP	50.00	22.00	6.25
☐ 280	Milt Bolling	300.00	50.00	20.00

1954 Topps

The cards in this 250-card set measure approximately 2 5/8" by 3 3/4". Each of the cards in the 1954 Topps set contains a large "head" shot of the player in color plus a smaller full-length photo in black and white set against a color background. This series contains the Rookie Cards of Hank Aaron, Ernie Banks, and Al Kaline and two separate cards of Ted Williams (number 1 and number 250). Conspicuous by his absence is Mickey Mantle who apparently was the exclusive property of Bowman during 1954 (and 1955). The first two issues of Sports Illustrated magazine contained "card" inserts on regular paper stock. The first issue showed actual cards in the set in color, while the second issue showed some created cards of New York Yankees players in black and white, including Mickey Mantle.

	NRMT	VG-E	GOOD
COMPLETE SET (250)	7800.00	3500.00	1000.00
COMMON CARD (1-50)	15.00	6.75	1.85
COMMON CARD (51-75)	25.00	11.00	3.10
COMMON CARD (76-250)	15.00	6.75	1.85

		NRMT	VG-E	GOOD
☐ 1	Ted Williams	700.00	250.00	70.00
☐ 2	Gus Zernial	20.00	9.00	2.50
☐ 3	Monte Irvin	40.00	18.00	5.00
☐ 4	Hank Sauer	20.00	9.00	2.50
☐ 5	Ed Lopat	25.00	11.00	3.10
☐ 6	Pete Runnels	20.00	9.00	2.50
☐ 7	Ted Kluszewski	40.00	18.00	5.00
☐ 8	Bob Young	15.00	6.75	1.85
☐ 9	Harvey Haddix	20.00	9.00	2.50
☐ 10	Jackie Robinson	250.00	110.00	31.00

		NRMT	VG-E	GOOD
☐ 11	Paul Leslie Smith	15.00	6.75	1.85
☐ 12	Del Crandall	20.00	9.00	2.50
☐ 13	Billy Martin	50.00	22.00	6.25
☐ 14	Preacher Roe	25.00	11.00	3.10
☐ 15	Al Rosen	25.00	11.00	3.10
☐ 16	Vic Janowicz	25.00	11.00	3.10
☐ 17	Phil Rizzuto	75.00	34.00	9.50
☐ 18	Walt Dropo	20.00	9.00	2.50
☐ 19	Johnny Lipon	15.00	6.75	1.85
☐ 20	Warren Spahn	75.00	34.00	9.50
☐ 21	Bobby Shantz	20.00	9.00	2.50
☐ 22	Jim Greengrass	15.00	6.75	1.85
☐ 23	Luke Easter	20.00	9.00	2.50
☐ 24	Granny Hamner	15.00	6.75	1.85
☐ 25	Harvey Kuenn	40.00	18.00	5.00
☐ 26	Ray Jablonski	15.00	6.75	1.85
☐ 27	Ferris Fain	20.00	9.00	2.50
☐ 28	Paul Minner	15.00	6.75	1.85
☐ 29	Jim Hegan	20.00	9.00	2.50
☐ 30	Eddie Mathews	75.00	34.00	9.50
☐ 31	Johnny Klippstein	15.00	6.75	1.85
☐ 32	Duke Snider	125.00	55.00	15.50
☐ 33	Johnny Schmitz	15.00	6.75	1.85
☐ 34	Jim Rivera	15.00	6.75	1.85
☐ 35	Jim Gilliam	30.00	13.50	3.70
☐ 36	Hoyt Wilhelm	50.00	22.00	6.25
☐ 37	Whitey Ford	100.00	45.00	12.50
☐ 38	Eddie Stanky MG	20.00	9.00	2.50
☐ 39	Sherm Lollar	20.00	9.00	2.50
☐ 40	Mel Parnell	20.00	9.00	2.50
☐ 41	Willie Jones	15.00	6.75	1.85
☐ 42	Don Mueller	20.00	9.00	2.50
☐ 43	Dick Groat	25.00	11.00	3.10
☐ 44	Ned Garver	15.00	6.75	1.85
☐ 45	Richie Ashburn	70.00	32.00	8.75
☐ 46	Ken Raffensberger	15.00	6.75	1.85
☐ 47	Ellis Kinder	15.00	6.75	1.85
☐ 48	Billy Hunter	20.00	9.00	2.50
☐ 49	Ray Murray	15.00	6.75	1.85
☐ 50	Yogi Berra	150.00	70.00	19.00
☐ 51	Johnny Lindell	30.00	13.50	3.70
☐ 52	Vic Power	35.00	16.00	4.40
☐ 53	Jack Dittmer	25.00	11.00	3.10
☐ 54	Vern Stephens	30.00	13.50	3.70
☐ 55	Phil Cavarretta MG	30.00	13.50	3.70
☐ 56	Willie Miranda	25.00	11.00	3.10
☐ 57	Luis Aloma	25.00	11.00	3.10
☐ 58	Bob Wilson	25.00	11.00	3.10
☐ 59	Gene Conley	30.00	13.50	3.70
☐ 60	Frank Baumholtz	25.00	11.00	3.10
☐ 61	Bob Cain	25.00	11.00	3.10
☐ 62	Eddie Robinson	25.00	11.00	3.10
☐ 63	Johnny Pesky	25.00	11.00	3.10
☐ 64	Hank Thompson	30.00	13.50	3.70
☐ 65	Bob Swift CO	25.00	11.00	3.10
☐ 66	Ted Lepcio	25.00	11.00	3.10
☐ 67	Jim Willis	25.00	11.00	3.10
☐ 68	Sam Calderone	25.00	11.00	3.10
☐ 69	Bud Podbielan	25.00	11.00	3.10
☐ 70	Larry Doby	60.00	27.00	7.50
☐ 71	Frank Smith	25.00	11.00	3.10
☐ 72	Preston Ward	25.00	11.00	3.10
☐ 73	Wayne Terwilliger	25.00	11.00	3.10
☐ 74	Bill Taylor	25.00	11.00	3.10
☐ 75	Fred Haney MG	25.00	11.00	3.10
☐ 76	Bob Scheffing CO	15.00	6.75	1.85
☐ 77	Ray Boone	20.00	9.00	2.50
☐ 78	Ted Kazanski	15.00	6.75	1.85
☐ 79	Andy Pafko	20.00	9.00	2.50
☐ 80	Jackie Jensen	25.00	11.00	3.10
☐ 81	Dave Hoskins	15.00	6.75	1.85

☐ 82	Milt Bolling	15.00	6.75	1.85
☐ 83	Joe Collins	15.00	6.75	1.85
☐ 84	Dick Cole	15.00	6.75	1.85
☐ 85	Bob Turley	30.00	13.50	3.70
☐ 86	Billy Herman CO	25.00	11.00	3.10
☐ 87	Roy Face	20.00	9.00	2.50
☐ 88	Matt Batts	15.00	6.75	1.85
☐ 89	Howie Pollet	15.00	6.75	1.85
☐ 90	Willie Mays	500.00	220.00	60.00
☐ 91	Bob Oldis	15.00	6.75	1.85
☐ 92	Wally Westlake	15.00	6.75	1.85
☐ 93	Sid Hudson	15.00	6.75	1.85
☐ 94	Ernie Banks	800.00	350.00	100.00
☐ 95	Hal Rice	15.00	6.75	1.85
☐ 96	Charlie Silvera	20.00	9.00	2.50
☐ 97	Jerald Hal Lane	15.00	6.75	1.85
☐ 98	Joe Black	25.00	11.00	3.10
☐ 99	Bobby Hofman	15.00	6.75	1.85
☐ 100	Bob Keegan	15.00	6.75	1.85
☐ 101	Gene Woodling	25.00	11.00	3.10
☐ 102	Gil Hodges	70.00	32.00	8.75
☐ 103	Jim Lemon	15.00	6.75	1.85
☐ 104	Mike Sandlock	15.00	6.75	1.85
☐ 105	Andy Carey	15.00	6.75	1.85
☐ 106	Dick Kokos	15.00	6.75	1.85
☐ 107	Duane Pillette	15.00	6.75	1.85
☐ 108	Thornton Kipper	15.00	6.75	1.85
☐ 109	Bill Bruton	20.00	9.00	2.50
☐ 110	Harry Dorish	15.00	6.75	1.85
☐ 111	Jim Delsing	15.00	6.75	1.85
☐ 112	Bill Renna	15.00	6.75	1.85
☐ 113	Bob Boyd	15.00	6.75	1.85
☐ 114	Dean Stone	15.00	6.75	1.85
☐ 115	Rip Repulski	15.00	6.75	1.85
☐ 116	Steve Bilko	15.00	6.75	1.85
☐ 117	Solly Hemus	15.00	6.75	1.85
☐ 118	Carl Scheib	15.00	6.75	1.85
☐ 119	Johnny Antonelli	20.00	9.00	2.50
☐ 120	Roy McMillan	20.00	9.00	2.50
☐ 121	Clem Labine	15.00	6.75	1.85
☐ 122	Johnny Logan	20.00	9.00	2.50
☐ 123	Bobby Adams	15.00	6.75	1.85
☐ 124	Marion Fricano	15.00	6.75	1.85
☐ 125	Harry Perkowski	15.00	6.75	1.85
☐ 126	Ben Wade	15.00	6.75	1.85
☐ 127	Steve O'Neill MG	15.00	6.75	1.85
☐ 128	Hank Aaron	1500.00	700.00	190.00
☐ 129	Forrest Jacobs	15.00	6.75	1.85
☐ 130	Hank Bauer	25.00	11.00	3.10
☐ 131	Reno Bertoia	15.00	6.75	1.85
☐ 132	Tom Lasorda	125.00	55.00	15.50
☐ 133	Dave Baker CO	15.00	6.75	1.85
☐ 134	Cal Hogue	15.00	6.75	1.85
☐ 135	Joe Presko	15.00	6.75	1.85
☐ 136	Connie Ryan	15.00	6.75	1.85
☐ 137	Wally Moon	30.00	13.50	3.70
☐ 138	Bob Borkowski	15.00	6.75	1.85
☐ 139	The O'Briens	40.00	18.00	5.00
	Johnny O'Brien			
	Eddie O'Brien			
☐ 140	Tom Wright	15.00	6.75	1.85
☐ 141	Joey Jay	15.00	6.75	1.85
☐ 142	Tom Poholsky	15.00	6.75	1.85
☐ 143	Rollie Hemsley CO	15.00	6.75	1.85
☐ 144	Bill Werle	15.00	6.75	1.85
☐ 145	Elmer Valo	15.00	6.75	1.85
☐ 146	Don Johnson	15.00	6.75	1.85
☐ 147	Johnny Riddle CO	15.00	6.75	1.85
☐ 148	Bob Trice	15.00	6.75	1.85
☐ 149	Al Robertson	15.00	6.75	1.85
☐ 150	Dick Kryhoski	15.00	6.75	1.85
☐ 151	Alex Grammas	15.00	6.75	1.85
☐ 152	Michael Blyzka	15.00	6.75	1.85
☐ 153	Al Walker	15.00	6.75	1.85
☐ 154	Mike Fornieles	15.00	6.75	1.85
☐ 155	Bob Kennedy	20.00	9.00	2.50
☐ 156	Joe Coleman	15.00	6.75	1.85
☐ 157	Don Lenhardt	15.00	6.75	1.85
☐ 158	Peanuts Lowrey	15.00	6.75	1.85
☐ 159	Dave Philley	15.00	6.75	1.85
☐ 160	Ralph Kress CO	15.00	6.75	1.85
☐ 161	John Hetki	15.00	6.75	1.85
☐ 162	Herman Wehmeier	15.00	6.75	1.85
☐ 163	Frank House	15.00	6.75	1.85
☐ 164	Stu Miller	20.00	9.00	2.50
☐ 165	Jim Pendleton	15.00	6.75	1.85
☐ 166	Johnny Podres	30.00	13.50	3.70
☐ 167	Don Lund	15.00	6.75	1.85
☐ 168	Morrie Martin	15.00	6.75	1.85
☐ 169	Jim Hughes	15.00	6.75	1.85
☐ 170	James(Dusty) Rhodes	25.00	11.00	3.10
☐ 171	Leo Kiely	15.00	6.75	1.85
☐ 172	Harold Brown	15.00	6.75	1.85
☐ 173	Jack Harshman	15.00	6.75	1.85
☐ 174	Tom Qualters	15.00	6.75	1.85
☐ 175	Frank Leja	20.00	9.00	2.50
☐ 176	Robert Keely CO	15.00	6.75	1.85
☐ 177	Bob Milliken	15.00	6.75	1.85
☐ 178	Bill Glynn	15.00	6.75	1.85
☐ 179	Gair Allie	15.00	6.75	1.85
☐ 180	Wes Westrum	20.00	9.00	2.50
☐ 181	Mel Roach	15.00	6.75	1.85
☐ 182	Chuck Harmon	15.00	6.75	1.85
☐ 183	Earle Combs CO	25.00	11.00	3.10
☐ 184	Ed Bailey	15.00	6.75	1.85
☐ 185	Chuck Stobbs	15.00	6.75	1.85
☐ 186	Karl Olson	15.00	6.75	1.85
☐ 187	Heinie Manush CO	25.00	11.00	3.10
☐ 188	Dave Jolly	15.00	6.75	1.85
☐ 189	Bob Ross	15.00	6.75	1.85
☐ 190	Ray Herbert	15.00	6.75	1.85
☐ 191	John(Dick) Schofield	20.00	9.00	2.50
☐ 192	Ellis Deal CO	15.00	6.75	1.85
☐ 193	Johnny Hopp CO	20.00	9.00	2.50
☐ 194	Bill Sarni	15.00	6.75	1.85
☐ 195	Billy Consolo	15.00	6.75	1.85
☐ 196	Stan Jok	15.00	6.75	1.85
☐ 197	Lynwood Rowe CO	20.00	9.00	2.50
	("Schoolboy")			
☐ 198	Carl Sawatski	15.00	6.75	1.85
☐ 199	Glenn(Rocky) Nelson	15.00	6.75	1.85
☐ 200	Larry Jansen	20.00	9.00	2.50
☐ 201	Al Kaline	750.00	350.00	95.00
☐ 202	Bob Purkey	20.00	9.00	2.50
☐ 203	Harry Brecheen CO	20.00	9.00	2.50
☐ 204	Angel Scull	15.00	6.75	1.85
☐ 205	Johnny Sain	30.00	13.50	3.70
☐ 206	Ray Crone	15.00	6.75	1.85
☐ 207	Tom Oliver CO	15.00	6.75	1.85
☐ 208	Grady Hatton	15.00	6.75	1.85
☐ 209	Chuck Thompson	15.00	6.75	1.85
☐ 210	Bob Buhl	25.00	11.00	3.10
☐ 211	Don Hoak	15.00	6.75	1.85
☐ 212	Bob Micelotta	15.00	6.75	1.85
☐ 213	Johnny Fitzpatrick CO	15.00	6.75	1.85
☐ 214	Arnie Portocarrero	15.00	6.75	1.85
☐ 215	Ed McGhee	15.00	6.75	1.85
☐ 216	Al Sima	15.00	6.75	1.85
☐ 217	Paul Schreiber CO	15.00	6.75	1.85
☐ 218	Fred Marsh	15.00	6.75	1.85
☐ 219	Chuck Kress	15.00	6.75	1.85
☐ 220	Ruben Gomez	20.00	9.00	2.50

			NRMT	VG-E	GOOD
☐ 221	Dick Brodowski	15.00	6.75	1.85
☐ 222	Bill Wilson	15.00	6.75	1.85
☐ 223	Joe Haynes CO	15.00	6.75	1.85
☐ 224	Dick Weik	15.00	6.75	1.85
☐ 225	Don Liddle	15.00	6.75	1.85
☐ 226	Jehosie Heard	15.00	6.75	1.85
☐ 227	Colonel Mills CO	15.00	6.75	1.85
☐ 228	Gene Hermanski	15.00	6.75	1.85
☐ 229	Bob Talbot	15.00	6.75	1.85
☐ 230	Bob Kuzava	20.00	9.00	2.50
☐ 231	Roy Smalley	15.00	6.75	1.85
☐ 232	Lou Limmer	15.00	6.75	1.85
☐ 233	Augie Galan CO	15.00	6.75	1.85
☐ 234	Jerry Lynch	15.00	6.75	1.85
☐ 235	Vernon Law	20.00	9.00	2.50
☐ 236	Paul Penson	15.00	6.75	1.85
☐ 237	Mike Ryba CO	15.00	6.75	1.85
☐ 238	Al Aber	15.00	6.75	1.85
☐ 239	Bill Skowron	100.00	45.00	12.50
☐ 240	Sam Mele	20.00	9.00	2.50
☐ 241	Robert Miller	15.00	6.75	1.85
☐ 242	Curt Roberts	15.00	6.75	1.85
☐ 243	Ray Blades CO	15.00	6.75	1.85
☐ 244	Leroy Wheat	15.00	6.75	1.85
☐ 245	Roy Sievers	15.00	6.75	1.85
☐ 246	Howie Fox	15.00	6.75	1.85
☐ 247	Ed Mayo CO	15.00	6.75	1.85
☐ 248	Al Smith	20.00	9.00	2.50
☐ 249	Wilmer Mizell	20.00	9.00	2.50
☐ 250	Ted Williams	725.00	300.00	70.00

1955 Topps

The cards in this 206-card set measure approximately 2 5/8" by 3 3/4". Both the large "head" shot and the smaller full-length photos used on each card of the 1955 Topps set are in color. The card fronts are designed horizontally for the first time in Topps' history. The first card features Dusty Rhodes, hitting star for the Giants' 1954 World Series sweep over the Indians. A "high" series, 161 to 210, is more difficult to find than cards 1 to 160. Numbers 175, 186, 203, and 209 were never issued. To fill in for the four cards not issued in the high number series, Topps double printed four players, those appearing on cards 170, 172, 184, and 188. Although rarely seen, there exist salesman sample panels of three cards containing the fronts of regular cards with ad information for the 1955 Topps regular and the 1955 Topps

Doubleheaders on the back. One such ad panel depicts (from top to bottom) Danny Schell, Jake Thies, and Howie Pollet. The key Rookie Cards in this set are Ken Boyer, Roberto Clemente, Harmon Killebrew, and Sandy Koufax.

		NRMT	VG-E	GOOD
COMPLETE SET (206)		7500.00	3400.00	950.00
COMMON CARD (1-150)		14.00	6.25	1.75
COMMON CARD (151-160)		20.00	9.00	2.50
COMMON CARD (161-210)		30.00	13.50	3.70

			NRMT	VG-E	GOOD
☐ 1	Dusty Rhodes		45.00	9.00	3.00
☐ 2	Ted Williams		450.00	200.00	55.00
☐ 3	Art Fowler		18.00	8.00	2.20
☐ 4	Al Kaline		180.00	80.00	22.00
☐ 5	Jim Gilliam		20.00	9.00	2.50
☐ 6	Stan Hack MG		18.00	8.00	2.20
☐ 7	Jim Hegan		18.00	8.00	2.20
☐ 8	Harold Smith		14.00	6.25	1.75
☐ 9	Robert Miller		14.00	6.25	1.75
☐ 10	Bob Keegan		14.00	6.25	1.75
☐ 11	Ferris Fain		18.00	8.00	2.20
☐ 12	Vernon(Jake) Thies		14.00	6.25	1.75
☐ 13	Fred Marsh		14.00	6.25	1.75
☐ 14	Jim Finigan		14.00	6.25	1.75
☐ 15	Jim Pendleton		14.00	6.25	1.75
☐ 16	Roy Sievers		18.00	8.00	2.20
☐ 17	Bobby Hofman		14.00	6.25	1.75
☐ 18	Russ Kemmerer		14.00	6.25	1.75
☐ 19	Billy Herman CO		18.00	8.00	2.20
☐ 20	Andy Carey		18.00	8.00	2.20
☐ 21	Alex Grammas		14.00	6.25	1.75
☐ 22	Bill Skowron		20.00	9.00	2.50
☐ 23	Jack Parks		14.00	6.25	1.75
☐ 24	Hal Newhouser		20.00	9.00	2.50
☐ 25	Johnny Podres		20.00	9.00	2.50
☐ 26	Dick Groat		18.00	8.00	2.20
☐ 27	Billy Gardner		18.00	8.00	2.20
☐ 28	Ernie Banks		180.00	80.00	22.00
☐ 29	Herman Wehmeier		14.00	6.25	1.75
☐ 30	Vic Power		18.00	8.00	2.20
☐ 31	Warren Spahn		80.00	36.00	10.00
☐ 32	Warren McGhee		14.00	6.25	1.75
☐ 33	Tom Qualters		14.00	6.25	1.75
☐ 34	Wayne Terwilliger		14.00	6.25	1.75
☐ 35	Dave Jolly		14.00	6.25	1.75
☐ 36	Leo Kiely		14.00	6.25	1.75
☐ 37	Joe Cunningham		18.00	8.00	2.20
☐ 38	Bob Turley		18.00	8.00	2.20
☐ 39	Bill Glynn		14.00	6.25	1.75
☐ 40	Don Hoak		18.00	8.00	2.20
☐ 41	Chuck Stobbs		14.00	6.25	1.75
☐ 42	John(Windy) McCall		14.00	6.25	1.75
☐ 43	Harvey Haddix		18.00	8.00	2.20
☐ 44	Harold Valentine		14.00	6.25	1.75
☐ 45	Hank Sauer		18.00	8.00	2.20
☐ 46	Ted Kazanski		14.00	6.25	1.75
☐ 47	Hank Aaron UER		350.00	160.00	45.00
	(Birth incorrectly listed as 2/10)				
☐ 48	Bob Kennedy		18.00	8.00	2.20
☐ 49	J.W. Porter		14.00	6.25	1.75
☐ 50	Jackie Robinson		250.00	110.00	31.00
☐ 51	Jim Hughes		18.00	8.00	2.20
☐ 52	Bill Tremel		14.00	6.25	1.75
☐ 53	Bill Taylor		14.00	6.25	1.75
☐ 54	Lou Limmer		14.00	6.25	1.75
☐ 55	Rip Repulski		14.00	6.25	1.75
☐ 56	Ray Jablonski		14.00	6.25	1.75

☐ 57	Billy O'Dell	14.00	6.25	1.75
☐ 58	Jim Rivera	14.00	6.25	1.75
☐ 59	Gair Allie	14.00	6.25	1.75
☐ 60	Dean Stone	14.00	6.25	1.75
☐ 61	Forrest Jacobs	14.00	6.25	1.75
☐ 62	Thornton Kipper	14.00	6.25	1.75
☐ 63	Joe Collins	18.00	8.00	2.20
☐ 64	Gus Triandos	18.00	8.00	2.20
☐ 65	Ray Boone	18.00	8.00	2.20
☐ 66	Ron Jackson	14.00	6.25	1.75
☐ 67	Wally Moon	18.00	8.00	2.20
☐ 68	Jim Davis	14.00	6.25	1.75
☐ 69	Ed Bailey	18.00	8.00	2.20
☐ 70	Al Rosen	18.00	8.00	2.20
☐ 71	Ruben Gomez	14.00	6.25	1.75
☐ 72	Karl Olson	14.00	6.25	1.75
☐ 73	Jack Shepard	14.00	6.25	1.75
☐ 74	Bob Borkowski	14.00	6.25	1.75
☐ 75	Sandy Amoros	30.00	13.50	3.70
☐ 76	Howie Pollet	14.00	6.25	1.75
☐ 77	Arnie Portocarrero	14.00	6.25	1.75
☐ 78	Gordon Jones	14.00	6.25	1.75
☐ 79	Clyde(Danny) Schell	14.00	6.25	1.75
☐ 80	Bob Grim	18.00	8.00	2.20
☐ 81	Gene Conley	18.00	8.00	2.20
☐ 82	Chuck Harmon	14.00	6.25	1.75
☐ 83	Tom Brewer	14.00	6.25	1.75
☐ 84	Camilo Pascual	18.00	8.00	2.20
☐ 85	Don Mossi RC	20.00	9.00	2.50
☐ 86	Bill Wilson	14.00	6.25	1.75
☐ 87	Frank House	14.00	6.25	1.75
☐ 88	Bob Skinner	18.00	8.00	2.20
☐ 89	Joe Frazier	18.00	8.00	2.20
☐ 90	Karl Spooner	18.00	8.00	2.20
☐ 91	Milt Bolling	14.00	6.25	1.75
☐ 92	Don Zimmer	25.00	11.00	3.10
☐ 93	Steve Bilko	14.00	6.25	1.75
☐ 94	Reno Bertoia	14.00	6.25	1.75
☐ 95	Preston Ward	14.00	6.25	1.75
☐ 96	Chuck Bishop	14.00	6.25	1.75
☐ 97	Carlos Paula	14.00	6.25	1.75
☐ 98	John Riddle CO	14.00	6.25	1.75
☐ 99	Frank Leja	14.00	6.25	1.75
☐ 100	Monte Irvin	35.00	16.00	4.40
☐ 101	Johnny Gray	14.00	6.25	1.75
☐ 102	Wally Westlake	14.00	6.25	1.75
☐ 103	Chuck White	14.00	6.25	1.75
☐ 104	Jack Harshman	14.00	6.25	1.75
☐ 105	Chuck Diering	14.00	6.25	1.75
☐ 106	Frank Sullivan	14.00	6.25	1.75
☐ 107	Curt Roberts	14.00	6.25	1.75
☐ 108	Al Walker	18.00	8.00	2.20
☐ 109	Ed Lopat	18.00	8.00	2.20
☐ 110	Gus Zernial	18.00	8.00	2.20
☐ 111	Bob Milliken	18.00	8.00	2.20
☐ 112	Nelson King	14.00	6.25	1.75
☐ 113	Harry Brecheen CO	18.00	8.00	2.20
☐ 114	Louis Ortiz	14.00	6.25	1.75
☐ 115	Ellis Kinder	14.00	6.25	1.75
☐ 116	Tom Hurd	14.00	6.25	1.75
☐ 117	Mel Roach	14.00	6.25	1.75
☐ 118	Bob Purkey	14.00	6.25	1.75
☐ 119	Bob Lennon	14.00	6.25	1.75
☐ 120	Ted Kluszewski	35.00	16.00	4.40
☐ 121	Bill Renna	14.00	6.25	1.75
☐ 122	Carl Sawatski	14.00	6.25	1.75
☐ 123	Sandy Koufax	900.00	400.00	110.00
☐ 124	Harmon Killebrew	250.00	110.00	31.00
☐ 125	Ken Boyer	70.00	32.00	8.75
☐ 126	Dick Hall	14.00	6.25	1.75
☐ 127	Dale Long	18.00	8.00	2.20
☐ 128	Ted Lepcio	14.00	6.25	1.75
☐ 129	Elvin Tappe	14.00	6.25	1.75
☐ 130	Mayo Smith MG	14.00	6.25	1.75
☐ 131	Grady Hatton	14.00	6.25	1.75
☐ 132	Bob Trice	14.00	6.25	1.75
☐ 133	Dave Hoskins	14.00	6.25	1.75
☐ 134	Joey Jay	18.00	8.00	2.20
☐ 135	Johnny O'Brien	18.00	8.00	2.20
☐ 136	Veston(Bunky) Stewart	14.00	6.25	1.75
☐ 137	Harry Elliott	14.00	6.25	1.75
☐ 138	Ray Herbert	14.00	6.25	1.75
☐ 139	Steve Kraly	14.00	6.25	1.75
☐ 140	Mel Parnell	18.00	8.00	2.20
☐ 141	Tom Wright	14.00	6.25	1.75
☐ 142	Jerry Lynch	18.00	8.00	2.20
☐ 143	John(Dick) Schofield	18.00	8.00	2.20
☐ 144	John(Joe) Amalfitano	14.00	6.25	1.75
☐ 145	Elmer Valo	14.00	6.25	1.75
☐ 146	Dick Donovan	14.00	6.25	1.75
☐ 147	Hugh Pepper	14.00	6.25	1.75
☐ 148	Hector Brown	14.00	6.25	1.75
☐ 149	Ray Crone	14.00	6.25	1.75
☐ 150	Mike Higgins MG	14.00	6.25	1.75
☐ 151	Ralph Kress CO	20.00	9.00	2.50
☐ 152	Harry Agganis	60.00	27.00	7.50
☐ 153	Bud Podbielan	20.00	9.00	2.50
☐ 154	Willie Miranda	20.00	9.00	2.50
☐ 155	Eddie Mathews	90.00	40.00	11.00
☐ 156	Joe Black	35.00	16.00	4.40
☐ 157	Robert Miller	20.00	9.00	2.50
☐ 158	Tommy Carroll	20.00	9.00	2.50
☐ 159	Johnny Schmitz	20.00	9.00	2.50
☐ 160	Ray Narleski	20.00	9.00	2.50
☐ 161	Chuck Tanner	35.00	16.00	4.40
☐ 162	Joe Coleman	30.00	13.50	3.70
☐ 163	Faye Throneberry	30.00	13.50	3.70
☐ 164	Roberto Clemente	2200.00	1000.00	275.00
☐ 165	Don Johnson	30.00	13.50	3.70
☐ 166	Hank Bauer	35.00	16.00	4.40
☐ 167	Thomas Casagrande	30.00	13.50	3.70
☐ 168	Duane Pillette	30.00	13.50	3.70
☐ 169	Bob Oldis	30.00	13.50	3.70
☐ 170	Jim Pearce DP	15.00	6.75	1.85
☐ 171	Dick Brodowski	30.00	13.50	3.70
☐ 172	Frank Baumholtz DP	15.00	6.75	1.85
☐ 173	Bob Kline	30.00	13.50	3.70
☐ 174	Rudy Minarcin	30.00	13.50	3.70
☐ 175	Does not exist			
☐ 176	Norm Zauchin	30.00	13.50	3.70
☐ 177	Al Robertson	30.00	13.50	3.70
☐ 178	Bobby Adams	30.00	13.50	3.70
☐ 179	Jim Bolger	30.00	13.50	3.70
☐ 180	Clem Labine	35.00	16.00	4.40
☐ 181	Roy McMillan	35.00	16.00	4.40
☐ 182	Humberto Robinson	30.00	13.50	3.70
☐ 183	Anthony Jacobs	30.00	13.50	3.70
☐ 184	Harry Perkowski DP	15.00	6.75	1.85
☐ 185	Don Ferrarese	30.00	13.50	3.70
☐ 186	Does not exist			
☐ 187	Gil Hodges	120.00	55.00	15.00
☐ 188	Charlie Silvera DP	15.00	6.75	1.85
☐ 189	Phil Rizzuto	125.00	55.00	15.50
☐ 190	Gene Woodling	30.00	13.50	3.70
☐ 191	Eddie Stanky MG	30.00	13.50	3.70
☐ 192	Jim Delsing	30.00	13.50	3.70
☐ 193	Johnny Sain	35.00	16.00	4.40
☐ 194	Willie Mays	475.00	210.00	60.00
☐ 195	Ed Roebuck	30.00	13.50	3.70
☐ 196	Gale Wade	30.00	13.50	3.70
☐ 197	Al Smith	35.00	16.00	4.40
☐ 198	Yogi Berra	200.00	90.00	25.00

			NRMT	VG-E	GOOD
☐	199	Odbert Hamric	35.00	16.00	4.40
☐	200	Jackie Jensen	35.00	16.00	4.40
☐	201	Sherm Lollar	35.00	16.00	4.40
☐	202	Jim Owens	30.00	13.50	3.70
☐	203	Does not exist			
☐	204	Frank Smith	30.00	13.50	3.70
☐	205	Gene Freese	30.00	13.50	3.70
☐	206	Pete Daley	30.00	13.50	3.70
☐	207	Billy Consolo	30.00	13.50	3.70
☐	208	Ray Moore	30.00	13.50	3.70
☐	209	Does not exist			
☐	210	Duke Snider	450.00	135.00	45.00

1956 Topps

The cards in this 340-card set measure approximately 2 5/8" by 3 3/4". Following up with another horizontally oriented card in 1956, Topps improved the format by layering the color "head" shot onto an actual action sequence involving the player. Cards 1 to 180 come with either white or gray backs: in the 1 to 100 sequence, gray backs are less common (worth about 10 percent more) and in the 101 to 180 sequence, white backs are less common (worth 30 percent more). The team cards, used for the first time in a regular set by Topps, are found dated 1955, or undated, with the team name appearing on either side. The dated team cards in the first series were not printed on the gray stock. The two unnumbered checklist cards are highly prized (must be unmarked to qualify as excellent or mint). The complete set price below does not include the unnumbered checklist cards or any of the variations. The key Rookie Cards in this set are Walt Alston, Luis Aparicio, and Roger Craig. There are ten double-printed cards in the first series as evidenced by the discovery of an uncut sheet of 110 cards (10 by 11); these DP's are listed below.

	NRMT	VG-E	GOOD
COMPLETE SET (340)	7000.00	3200.00	900.00
COMMON CARD (1-100)	12.00	5.50	1.50
COMMON CARD (101-180)	13.00	5.75	1.60
COMMON CARD (181-260)	16.00	7.25	2.00
COMMON CARD (261-340)	13.00	5.75	1.60

			NRMT	VG-E	GOOD
☐	1	William Harridge	90.00	25.00	9.00
		(AL President)			
☐	2	Warren Giles	24.00	11.00	3.00
		(NL President)			
☐	3	Elmer Valo	12.00	5.50	1.50
☐	4	Carlos Paula	12.00	5.50	1.50
☐	5	Ted Williams	350.00	160.00	45.00
☐	6	Ray Boone	14.00	6.25	1.75
☐	7	Ron Negray	12.00	5.50	1.50
☐	8	Walter Alston MG	40.00	18.00	5.00
☐	9	Ruben Gomez DP	9.00	4.00	1.10
☐	10	Warren Spahn	70.00	32.00	8.75
☐	11A	Chicago Cubs	30.00	13.50	3.70
		(Centered)			
☐	11B	Cubs Team	75.00	34.00	9.50
		(Dated 1955)			
☐	11C	Cubs Team	30.00	13.50	3.70
		(Name at far left)			
☐	12	Andy Carey	14.00	6.25	1.75
☐	13	Roy Face	12.00	5.50	1.50
☐	14	Ken Boyer DP	14.00	6.25	1.75
☐	15	Ernie Banks DP	80.00	36.00	10.00
☐	16	Hector Lopez	14.00	6.25	1.75
☐	17	Gene Conley	14.00	6.25	1.75
☐	18	Dick Donovan	12.00	5.50	1.50
☐	19	Chuck Diering	12.00	5.50	1.50
☐	20	Al Kaline	90.00	40.00	11.00
☐	21	Joe Collins DP	10.00	4.50	1.25
☐	22	Jim Finigan	12.00	5.50	1.50
☐	23	Fred Marsh	12.00	5.50	1.50
☐	24	Dick Groat	14.00	6.25	1.75
☐	25	Ted Kluszewski	30.00	13.50	3.70
☐	26	Grady Hatton	12.00	5.50	1.50
☐	27	Nelson Burbrink	12.00	5.50	1.50
☐	28	Bobby Hofman	12.00	5.50	1.50
☐	29	Jack Harshman	12.00	5.50	1.50
☐	30	Jackie Robinson DP	150.00	70.00	19.00
☐	31	Hank Aaron UER	275.00	125.00	34.00
		(Small photo			
		actually Willie Mays)			
☐	32	Frank House	12.00	5.50	1.50
☐	33	Roberto Clemente	475.00	210.00	60.00
☐	34	Tom Brewer	12.00	5.50	1.50
☐	35	Al Rosen	14.00	6.25	1.75
☐	36	Rudy Minarcin	12.00	5.50	1.50
☐	37	Alex Grammas	12.00	5.50	1.50
☐	38	Bob Kennedy	14.00	6.25	1.75
☐	39	Don Mossi	14.00	6.25	1.75
☐	40	Bob Turley	14.00	6.25	1.75
☐	41	Hank Sauer	14.00	6.25	1.75
☐	42	Sandy Amoros	14.00	6.25	1.75
☐	43	Ray Moore	12.00	5.50	1.50
☐	44	Windy McCall	12.00	5.50	1.50
☐	45	Gus Zernial	14.00	6.25	1.75
☐	46	Gene Freese DP	9.00	4.00	1.10
☐	47	Art Fowler	12.00	5.50	1.50
☐	48	Jim Hegan	14.00	6.25	1.75
☐	49	Pedro Ramos	12.00	5.50	1.50
☐	50	Dusty Rhodes	14.00	6.25	1.75
☐	51	Ernie Oravetz	12.00	5.50	1.50
☐	52	Bob Grim	14.00	6.25	1.75
☐	53	Arnie Portocarrero	12.00	5.50	1.50
☐	54	Bob Keegan	12.00	5.50	1.50
☐	55	Wally Moon	14.00	6.25	1.75
☐	56	Dale Long	14.00	6.25	1.75
☐	57	Duke Maas	12.00	5.50	1.50
☐	58	Ed Roebuck	14.00	6.25	1.75
☐	59	Jose Santiago	12.00	5.50	1.50
☐	60	Mayo Smith MG DP	9.00	4.00	1.10
☐	61	Bill Skowron	14.00	6.25	1.75
☐	62	Hal Smith	12.00	5.50	1.50
☐	63	Roger Craig	20.00	9.00	2.50
☐	64	Luis Arroyo	12.00	5.50	1.50

□ 65 Johnny O'Brien	14.00	6.25	1.75
□ 66 Bob Speake	12.00	5.50	1.50
□ 67 Vic Power	14.00	6.25	1.75
□ 68 Chuck Stobbs	12.00	5.50	1.50
□ 69 Chuck Tanner	14.00	6.25	1.75
□ 70 Jim Rivera	12.00	5.50	1.50
□ 71 Frank Sullivan	12.00	5.50	1.50
□ 72A Phillies Team (Centered)	30.00	13.50	3.70
□ 72B Phillies Team (Dated 1955)	75.00	34.00	9.50
□ 72C Phillies Team (Name at far left)	30.00	13.50	3.70
□ 73 Wayne Terwilliger	12.00	5.50	1.50
□ 74 Jim King	12.00	5.50	1.50
□ 75 Roy Sievers DP	10.00	4.50	1.25
□ 76 Ray Crone	12.00	5.50	1.50
□ 77 Harvey Haddix	14.00	6.25	1.75
□ 78 Herman Wehmeier	12.00	5.50	1.50
□ 79 Sandy Koufax	350.00	160.00	45.00
□ 80 Gus Triandos DP	10.00	4.50	1.25
□ 81 Wally Westlake	12.00	5.50	1.50
□ 82 Bill Renna	12.00	5.50	1.50
□ 83 Karl Spooner	14.00	6.25	1.75
□ 84 Babe Birrer	12.00	5.50	1.50
□ 85A Cleveland Indians (Centered)	30.00	13.50	3.70
□ 85B Indians Team (Dated 1955)	75.00	34.00	9.50
□ 85C Indians Team (Name at far left)	30.00	13.50	3.70
□ 86 Ray Jablonski DP	9.00	4.00	1.10
□ 87 Dean Stone	12.00	5.50	1.50
□ 88 Johnny Kucks	12.00	5.50	1.50
□ 89 Norm Zauchin	12.00	5.50	1.50
□ 90A Cincinnati Redlegs Team (Centered)	30.00	13.50	3.70
□ 90B Reds Team (Dated 1955)	75.00	34.00	9.50
□ 90C Reds Team (Name at far left)	30.00	13.50	3.70
□ 91 Gail Harris	12.00	5.50	1.50
□ 92 Bob(Red) Wilson	12.00	5.50	1.50
□ 93 George Susce	12.00	5.50	1.50
□ 94 Ron Kline	12.00	5.50	1.50
□ 95A Milwaukee Braves Team (Centered)	42.00	19.00	5.25
□ 95B Braves Team (Dated 1955)	75.00	34.00	9.50
□ 95C Braves Team (Name at far left)	42.00	19.00	5.25
□ 96 Bill Tremel	12.00	5.50	1.50
□ 97 Jerry Lynch	14.00	6.25	1.75
□ 98 Camilo Pascual	14.00	6.25	1.75
□ 99 Don Zimmer	14.00	6.25	1.75
□ 100A Baltimore Orioles Team (centered)	35.00	16.00	4.40
□ 100B Orioles Team (Dated 1955)	75.00	34.00	9.50
□ 100C Orioles Team (Name at far left)	35.00	16.00	4.40
□ 101 Roy Campanella	150.00	70.00	19.00
□ 102 Jim Davis	13.00	5.75	1.60
□ 103 Willie Miranda	13.00	5.75	1.60
□ 104 Bob Lennon	13.00	5.75	1.60
□ 105 Al Smith	13.00	5.75	1.60
□ 106 Joe Astroth	13.00	5.75	1.60
□ 107 Eddie Mathews	50.00	22.00	6.25
□ 108 Laurin Pepper	13.00	5.75	1.60
□ 109 Enos Slaughter	35.00	16.00	4.40
□ 110 Yogi Berra	125.00	55.00	15.50
□ 111 Boston Red Sox Team Card	35.00	16.00	4.40
□ 112 Dee Fondy	13.00	5.75	1.60
□ 113 Phil Rizzuto	80.00	36.00	10.00
□ 114 Jim Owens	13.00	5.75	1.60
□ 115 Jackie Jensen	18.00	8.00	2.20
□ 116 Eddie O'Brien	13.00	5.75	1.60
□ 117 Virgil Trucks	16.00	7.25	2.00
□ 118 Nellie Fox	40.00	18.00	5.00
□ 119 Larry Jackson	13.00	5.75	1.60
□ 120 Richie Ashburn	50.00	22.00	6.25
□ 121 Pittsburgh Pirates Team Card	35.00	16.00	4.40
□ 122 Willard Nixon	13.00	5.75	1.60
□ 123 Roy McMillan	16.00	7.25	2.00
□ 124 Don Kaiser	13.00	5.75	1.60
□ 125 Minnie Minoso	25.00	11.00	3.10
□ 126 Jim Brady	13.00	5.75	1.60
□ 127 Willie Jones	16.00	7.25	2.00
□ 128 Eddie Yost	16.00	7.25	2.00
□ 129 Jake Martin	13.00	5.75	1.60
□ 130 Willie Mays	325.00	145.00	40.00
□ 131 Bob Roselli	13.00	5.75	1.60
□ 132 Bobby Avila	13.00	5.75	1.60
□ 133 Ray Narleski	13.00	5.75	1.60
□ 134 St. Louis Cardinals Team Card	35.00	16.00	4.40
□ 135 Mickey Mantle	1400.00	650.00	180.00
□ 136 Johnny Logan	16.00	7.25	2.00
□ 137 Al Silvera	13.00	5.75	1.60
□ 138 Johnny Antonelli	16.00	7.25	2.00
□ 139 Tommy Carroll	13.00	5.75	1.60
□ 140 Herb Score	60.00	27.00	7.50
□ 141 Joe Frazier	13.00	5.75	1.60
□ 142 Gene Baker	13.00	5.75	1.60
□ 143 Jim Piersall	18.00	8.00	2.20
□ 144 Leroy Powell	13.00	5.75	1.60
□ 145 Gil Hodges	50.00	22.00	6.25
□ 146 Washington Nationals Team Card	35.00	16.00	4.40
□ 147 Earl Torgeson	13.00	5.75	1.60
□ 148 Alvin Dark	16.00	7.25	2.00
□ 149 Dixie Howell	13.00	5.75	1.60
□ 150 Duke Snider	100.00	45.00	12.50
□ 151 Spook Jacobs	16.00	7.25	2.00
□ 152 Billy Hoeft	16.00	7.25	2.00
□ 153 Frank Thomas	16.00	7.25	2.00
□ 154 Dave Pope	13.00	5.75	1.60
□ 155 Harvey Kuenn	18.00	8.00	2.20
□ 156 Wes Westrum	16.00	7.25	2.00
□ 157 Dick Brodowski	13.00	5.75	1.60
□ 158 Wally Post	16.00	7.25	2.00
□ 159 Clint Courtney	13.00	5.75	1.60
□ 160 Billy Pierce	16.00	7.25	2.00
□ 161 Joe DeMaestri	13.00	5.75	1.60
□ 162 Dave(Gus) Bell	16.00	7.25	2.00
□ 163 Gene Woodling	16.00	7.25	2.00
□ 164 Harmon Killebrew	100.00	45.00	12.50
□ 165 Red Schoendienst	25.00	11.00	3.10
□ 166 Brooklyn Dodgers Team Card	200.00	90.00	25.00
□ 167 Harry Dorish	13.00	5.75	1.60
□ 168 Sammy White	13.00	5.75	1.60
□ 169 Bob Nelson	13.00	5.75	1.60
□ 170 Bill Virdon	16.00	7.25	2.00
□ 171 Jim Wilson	13.00	5.75	1.60
□ 172 Frank Torre	13.00	5.75	1.60
□ 173 Johnny Podres	18.00	8.00	2.20
□ 174 Glen Gorbous	13.00	5.75	1.60
□ 175 Del Crandall	16.00	7.25	2.00
□ 176 Alex Kellner	13.00	5.75	1.60

☐	177	Hank Bauer	18.00	8.00	2.20
☐	178	Joe Black	16.00	7.25	2.00
☐	179	Harry Chiti	13.00	5.75	1.60
☐	180	Robin Roberts	40.00	18.00	5.00
☐	181	Billy Martin	40.00	18.00	5.00
☐	182	Paul Minner	16.00	7.25	2.00
☐	183	Stan Lopata	16.00	7.25	2.00
☐	184	Don Bessent	16.00	7.25	2.00
☐	185	Bill Bruton	18.00	8.00	2.20
☐	186	Ron Jackson	16.00	7.25	2.00
☐	187	Early Wynn	40.00	18.00	5.00
☐	188	Chicago White Sox... Team Card	40.00	18.00	5.00
☐	189	Ned Garver	16.00	7.25	2.00
☐	190	Carl Furillo	25.00	11.00	3.10
☐	191	Frank Lary	20.00	9.00	2.50
☐	192	Smoky Burgess	18.00	8.00	2.20
☐	193	Wilmer Mizell	18.00	8.00	2.20
☐	194	Monte Irvin	35.00	16.00	4.40
☐	195	George Kell	35.00	16.00	4.40
☐	196	Tom Poholsky	16.00	7.25	2.00
☐	197	Granny Hamner	16.00	7.25	2.00
☐	198	Ed Fitzgerald	16.00	7.25	2.00
☐	199	Hank Thompson	18.00	8.00	2.20
☐	200	Bob Feller	100.00	45.00	12.50
☐	201	Rip Repulski	16.00	7.25	2.00
☐	202	Jim Hearn	16.00	7.25	2.00
☐	203	Bill Tuttle	16.00	7.25	2.00
☐	204	Art Swanson	16.00	7.25	2.00
☐	205	Whitey Lockman	18.00	8.00	2.20
☐	206	Erv Palica	16.00	7.25	2.00
☐	207	Jim Small	16.00	7.25	2.00
☐	208	Elston Howard	50.00	22.00	6.25
☐	209	Max Surkont	16.00	7.25	2.00
☐	210	Mike Garcia	20.00	9.00	2.50
☐	211	Murry Dickson	16.00	7.25	2.00
☐	212	Johnny Temple	16.00	7.25	2.00
☐	213	Detroit Tigers Team Card	55.00	25.00	7.00
☐	214	Bob Rush	16.00	7.25	2.00
☐	215	Tommy Byrne	16.00	7.25	2.00
☐	216	Jerry Schoonmaker..	16.00	7.25	2.00
☐	217	Billy Klaus	16.00	7.25	2.00
☐	218	Joe Nuxhall UER (Misspelled Nuxall)	18.00	8.00	2.20
☐	219	Lew Burdette	18.00	8.00	2.20
☐	220	Del Ennis	20.00	9.00	2.50
☐	221	Bob Friend	18.00	8.00	2.20
☐	222	Dave Philley	16.00	7.25	2.00
☐	223	Randy Jackson	16.00	7.25	2.00
☐	224	Bud Podbielan	16.00	7.25	2.00
☐	225	Gil McDougald	30.00	13.50	3.70
☐	226	New York Giants Team Card	75.00	34.00	9.50
☐	227	Russ Meyer	16.00	7.25	2.00
☐	228	Mickey Vernon	18.00	8.00	2.20
☐	229	Harry Brecheen CO ..	18.00	8.00	2.20
☐	230	Chico Carrasquel	16.00	7.25	2.00
☐	231	Bob Hale	16.00	7.25	2.00
☐	232	Toby Atwell	16.00	7.25	2.00
☐	233	Carl Erskine	30.00	13.50	3.70
☐	234	Pete Runnels	18.00	8.00	2.20
☐	235	Don Newcombe	50.00	22.00	6.25
☐	236	Kansas City Athletics Team Card	35.00	16.00	4.40
☐	237	Jose Valdivielso	16.00	7.25	2.00
☐	238	Walt Dropo	18.00	8.00	2.20
☐	239	Harry Simpson	16.00	7.25	2.00
☐	240	Whitey Ford	100.00	45.00	12.50
☐	241	Don Mueller UER (6" tall)	18.00	8.00	2.20
☐	242	Hershell Freeman	16.00	7.25	2.00
☐	243	Sherm Lollar	18.00	8.00	2.20
☐	244	Bob Buhl	18.00	8.00	2.20
☐	245	Billy Goodman	18.00	8.00	2.20
☐	246	Tom Gorman	16.00	7.25	2.00
☐	247	Bill Sarni	16.00	7.25	2.00
☐	248	Bob Porterfield	16.00	7.25	2.00
☐	249	Johnny Klippstein	16.00	7.25	2.00
☐	250	Larry Doby	30.00	13.50	3.70
☐	251	New York Yankees. Team Card UER (Don Larsen misspelled as Larson on front)	250.00	110.00	31.00
☐	252	Vern Law	18.00	8.00	2.20
☐	253	Irv Noren	16.00	7.25	2.00
☐	254	George Crowe	16.00	7.25	2.00
☐	255	Bob Lemon	30.00	13.50	3.70
☐	256	Tom Hurd	16.00	7.25	2.00
☐	257	Bobby Thomson	30.00	13.50	3.70
☐	258	Art Ditmar	16.00	7.25	2.00
☐	259	Sam Jones	18.00	8.00	2.20
☐	260	Pee Wee Reese	125.00	55.00	15.50
☐	261	Bobby Shantz	16.00	7.25	2.00
☐	262	Howie Pollet	13.00	5.75	1.60
☐	263	Bob Miller	13.00	5.75	1.60
☐	264	Ray Monzant	13.00	5.75	1.60
☐	265	Sandy Consuegra	13.00	5.75	1.60
☐	266	Don Ferrarese	13.00	5.75	1.60
☐	267	Bob Nieman	13.00	5.75	1.60
☐	268	Dale Mitchell	18.00	8.00	2.20
☐	269	Jack Meyer	13.00	5.75	1.60
☐	270	Billy Loes	16.00	7.25	2.00
☐	271	Foster Castleman	13.00	5.75	1.60
☐	272	Danny O'Connell	13.00	5.75	1.60
☐	273	Walker Cooper	13.00	5.75	1.60
☐	274	Frank Baumholtz	13.00	5.75	1.60
☐	275	Jim Greengrass	13.00	5.75	1.60
☐	276	George Zuverink	13.00	5.75	1.60
☐	277	Daryl Spencer	13.00	5.75	1.60
☐	278	Chet Nichols	13.00	5.75	1.60
☐	279	Johnny Groth	13.00	5.75	1.60
☐	280	Jim Gilliam	20.00	9.00	2.50
☐	281	Art Houtteman	13.00	5.75	1.60
☐	282	Warren Hacker	13.00	5.75	1.60
☐	283	Hal Smith	13.00	5.75	1.60
☐	284	Ike Delock	13.00	5.75	1.60
☐	285	Eddie Miksis	13.00	5.75	1.60
☐	286	Bill Wight	13.00	5.75	1.60
☐	287	Bobby Adams	13.00	5.75	1.60
☐	288	Bob Cerv	35.00	16.00	4.40
☐	289	Hal Jeffcoat	13.00	5.75	1.60
☐	290	Curt Simmons	16.00	7.25	2.00
☐	291	Frank Kellert	13.00	5.75	1.60
☐	292	Luis Aparicio	125.00	55.00	15.50
☐	293	Stu Miller	16.00	7.25	2.00
☐	294	Ernie Johnson	16.00	7.25	2.00
☐	295	Clem Labine	16.00	7.25	2.00
☐	296	Andy Seminick	13.00	5.75	1.60
☐	297	Bob Skinner	16.00	7.25	2.00
☐	298	Johnny Schmitz	13.00	5.75	1.60
☐	299	Charlie Neal	35.00	16.00	4.40
☐	300	Vic Wertz	18.00	8.00	2.20
☐	301	Marv Grissom	13.00	5.75	1.60
☐	302	Eddie Robinson	13.00	5.75	1.60
☐	303	Jim Dyck	13.00	5.75	1.60
☐	304	Frank Malzone	20.00	9.00	2.50
☐	305	Brooks Lawrence	13.00	5.75	1.60
☐	306	Curt Roberts	13.00	5.75	1.60
☐	307	Hoyt Wilhelm	35.00	16.00	4.40
☐	308	Chuck Harmon	13.00	5.75	1.60
☐	309	Don Blasingame	16.00	7.25	2.00

		NRMT	VG-E	GOOD
☐	310 Steve Gromek	13.00	5.75	1.60
☐	311 Hal Naragon	13.00	5.75	1.60
☐	312 Andy Pafko	16.00	7.25	2.00
☐	313 Gene Stephens	13.00	5.75	1.60
☐	314 Hobie Landrith	13.00	5.75	1.60
☐	315 Milt Bolling	13.00	5.75	1.60
☐	316 Jerry Coleman	16.00	7.25	2.00
☐	317 Al Aber	13.00	5.75	1.60
☐	318 Fred Hatfield	13.00	5.75	1.60
☐	319 Jack Crimian	13.00	5.75	1.60
☐	320 Joe Adcock	18.00	8.00	2.20
☐	321 Jim Konstanty	16.00	7.25	2.00
☐	322 Karl Olson	13.00	5.75	1.60
☐	323 Willard Schmidt	13.00	5.75	1.60
☐	324 Rocky Bridges	16.00	7.25	2.00
☐	325 Don Liddle	13.00	5.75	1.60
☐	326 Connie Johnson	13.00	5.75	1.60
☐	327 Bob Wiesler	13.00	5.75	1.60
☐	328 Preston Ward	13.00	5.75	1.60
☐	329 Lou Berberet	13.00	5.75	1.60
☐	330 Jim Busby	13.00	5.75	1.60
☐	331 Dick Hall	13.00	5.75	1.60
☐	332 Don Larsen	60.00	27.00	7.50
☐	333 Rube Walker	13.00	5.75	1.60
☐	334 Bob Miller	13.00	5.75	1.60
☐	335 Don Hoak	16.00	7.25	2.00
☐	336 Ellis Kinder	13.00	5.75	1.60
☐	337 Bobby Morgan	13.00	5.75	1.60
☐	338 Jim Delsing	13.00	5.75	1.60
☐	339 Rance Pless	13.00	5.75	1.60
☐	340 Mickey McDermott	50.00	10.00	3.00
☐	NNO Checklist 2/4 !	300.00	95.00	45.00
☐	NNO Checklist 1/3	300.00	95.00	45.00

1957 Topps

The cards in this 407-card set measure 2 1/2" by 3 1/2". In 1957, Topps returned to the vertical obverse, adopted what we now call the standard card size, and used a large, uncluttered color photo for the first time since 1952. Cards in the series 265 to 352 and the unnumbered checklist cards are scarcer than other cards in the set. However within this scarce series (265-352) there are 22 cards which were printed in double the quantity of the other cards in the series; these 22 double prints are indicated by DP in the checklist below. The first star combination cards, cards 400 and 407, are quite popular with collectors. They feature the big stars of the previous season's World Series teams, the Dodgers (Furillo,

Hodges, Campanella, and Snider) and Yankees (Berra and Mantle). The complete set price below does not include the unnumbered checklist cards. The key Rookie Cards in this set are Jim Bunning, Rocky Colavito, Don Drysdale, Whitey Herzog, Tony Kubek, Bobby Richardson, Brooks Robinson, and Frank Robinson.

		NRMT	VG-E	GOOD
COMPLETE SET (407)		7250.00	3300.00	900.00
COMMON CARD (1-88)		9.00	4.00	1.10
COMMON CARD (89-176)		8.00	3.60	1.00
COMMON CARD (177-264)		7.00	3.10	.85
COMMON CARD (265-352)		20.00	9.00	2.50
COMMON CARD (353-407)		8.00	3.60	1.00

☐ 1	Ted Williams	500.00	150.00	50.00
☐ 2	Yogi Berra	125.00	55.00	15.50
☐ 3	Dale Long	10.00	4.50	1.25
☐ 4	Johnny Logan	10.00	4.50	1.25
☐ 5	Sal Maglie	12.00	5.50	1.50
☐ 6	Hector Lopez	10.00	4.50	1.25
☐ 7	Luis Aparicio	40.00	18.00	5.00
☐ 8	Don Mossi	10.00	4.50	1.25
☐ 9	Johnny Temple	10.00	4.50	1.25
☐ 10	Willie Mays	225.00	100.00	28.00
☐ 11	George Zuverink	9.00	4.00	1.10
☐ 12	Dick Groat	10.00	4.50	1.25
☐ 13	Wally Burnette	9.00	4.00	1.10
☐ 14	Bob Nieman	9.00	4.00	1.10
☐ 15	Robin Roberts	35.00	16.00	4.40
☐ 16	Walt Moryn	9.00	4.00	1.10
☐ 17	Billy Gardner	9.00	4.00	1.10
☐ 18	Don Drysdale	180.00	80.00	22.00
☐ 19	Bob Wilson	9.00	4.00	1.10
☐ 20	Hank Aaron UER	225.00	100.00	28.00
	(Reverse negative photo on front)			
☐ 21	Frank Sullivan	9.00	4.00	1.10
☐ 22	Jerry Snyder UER	9.00	4.00	1.10
	(Photo actually Ed Fitzgerald)			
☐ 23	Sherm Lollar	10.00	4.50	1.25
☐ 24	Bill Mazeroski	75.00	34.00	9.50
☐ 25	Whitey Ford	65.00	29.00	8.00
☐ 26	Bob Boyd	9.00	4.00	1.10
☐ 27	Ted Kazanski	9.00	4.00	1.10
☐ 28	Gene Conley	10.00	4.50	1.25
☐ 29	Whitey Herzog	25.00	11.00	3.10
☐ 30	Pee Wee Reese	75.00	34.00	9.50
☐ 31	Ron Northey	9.00	4.00	1.10
☐ 32	Hershell Freeman	9.00	4.00	1.10
☐ 33	Jim Small	9.00	4.00	1.10
☐ 34	Tom Sturdivant	9.00	4.00	1.10
☐ 35	Frank Robinson	200.00	90.00	25.00
☐ 36	Bob Grim	9.00	4.00	1.10
☐ 37	Frank Torre	10.00	4.50	1.25
☐ 38	Nellie Fox	30.00	13.50	3.70
☐ 39	Al Worthington	9.00	4.00	1.10
☐ 40	Early Wynn	30.00	13.50	3.70
☐ 41	Hal W. Smith	9.00	4.00	1.10
☐ 42	Dee Fondy	9.00	4.00	1.10
☐ 43	Connie Johnson	9.00	4.00	1.10
☐ 44	Joe DeMaestri	9.00	4.00	1.10
☐ 45	Carl Furillo	20.00	9.00	2.50
☐ 46	Robert J. Miller	9.00	4.00	1.10
☐ 47	Don Blasingame	9.00	4.00	1.10
☐ 48	Bill Bruton	9.00	4.00	1.10
☐ 49	Daryl Spencer	9.00	4.00	1.10
☐ 50	Herb Score	20.00	9.00	2.50

☐ 51	Clint Courtney	9.00	4.00	1.10
☐ 52	Lee Walls	9.00	4.00	1.10
☐ 53	Clem Labine	9.00	4.00	1.10
☐ 54	Elmer Valo	9.00	4.00	1.10
☐ 55	Ernie Banks	120.00	55.00	15.00
☐ 56	Dave Sisler	9.00	4.00	1.10
☐ 57	Jim Lemon	10.00	4.50	1.25
☐ 58	Ruben Gomez	9.00	4.00	1.10
☐ 59	Dick Williams	10.00	4.50	1.25
☐ 60	Billy Hoeft	10.00	4.50	1.25
☐ 61	James(Dusty) Rhodes	10.00	4.50	1.25
☐ 62	Billy Martin	30.00	13.50	3.70
☐ 63	Ike Delock	9.00	4.00	1.10
☐ 64	Pete Runnels	10.00	4.50	1.25
☐ 65	Wally Moon	10.00	4.50	1.25
☐ 66	Brooks Lawrence	9.00	4.00	1.10
☐ 67	Chico Carrasquel	9.00	4.00	1.10
☐ 68	Ray Crone	9.00	4.00	1.10
☐ 69	Roy McMillan	10.00	4.50	1.25
☐ 70	Richie Ashburn	45.00	20.00	5.50
☐ 71	Murry Dickson	9.00	4.00	1.10
☐ 72	Bill Tuttle	9.00	4.00	1.10
☐ 73	George Crowe	9.00	4.00	1.10
☐ 74	Vito Valentinetti	9.00	4.00	1.10
☐ 75	Jim Piersall	12.00	5.50	1.50
☐ 76	Roberto Clemente	250.00	110.00	31.00
☐ 77	Paul Foytack	9.00	4.00	1.10
☐ 78	Vic Wertz	10.00	4.50	1.25
☐ 79	Lindy McDaniel	15.00	6.75	1.85
☐ 80	Gil Hodges	40.00	18.00	5.00
☐ 81	Herman Wehmeier	9.00	4.00	1.10
☐ 82	Elston Howard	20.00	9.00	2.50
☐ 83	Lou Skizas	9.00	4.00	1.10
☐ 84	Moe Drabowsky	10.00	4.50	1.25
☐ 85	Larry Doby	12.00	5.50	1.50
☐ 86	Bill Sarni	9.00	4.00	1.10
☐ 87	Tom Gorman	9.00	4.00	1.10
☐ 88	Harvey Kuenn	12.00	5.50	1.50
☐ 89	Roy Sievers	10.00	4.50	1.25
☐ 90	Warren Spahn	65.00	29.00	8.00
☐ 91	Mack Burk	8.00	3.60	1.00
☐ 92	Mickey Vernon	10.00	4.50	1.25
☐ 93	Hal Jeffcoat	8.00	3.60	1.00
☐ 94	Bobby Del Greco	8.00	3.60	1.00
☐ 95	Mickey Mantle	1100.00	500.00	140.00
☐ 96	Hank Aguirre	8.00	3.60	1.00
☐ 97	New York Yankees	80.00	36.00	10.00
	Team Card			
☐ 98	Alvin Dark	10.00	4.50	1.25
☐ 99	Bob Keegan	8.00	3.60	1.00
☐ 100	League Presidents	14.00	6.25	1.75
	Warren Giles			
	Will Harridge			
☐ 101	Chuck Stobbs	8.00	3.60	1.00
☐ 102	Ray Boone	10.00	4.50	1.25
☐ 103	Joe Nuxhall	10.00	4.50	1.25
☐ 104	Hank Foiles	8.00	3.60	1.00
☐ 105	Johnny Antonelli	10.00	4.50	1.25
☐ 106	Ray Moore	8.00	3.60	1.00
☐ 107	Jim Rivera	8.00	3.60	1.00
☐ 108	Tommy Byrne	8.00	3.60	1.00
☐ 109	Hank Thompson	10.00	4.50	1.25
☐ 110	Bill Virdon	8.00	3.60	1.00
☐ 111	Hal R. Smith	8.00	3.60	1.00
☐ 112	Tom Brewer	8.00	3.60	1.00
☐ 113	Wilmer Mizell	10.00	4.50	1.25
☐ 114	Milwaukee Braves	22.00	10.00	2.70
	Team Card			
☐ 115	Jim Gilliam	10.00	4.50	1.25
☐ 116	Mike Fornieles	8.00	3.60	1.00
☐ 117	Joe Adcock	10.00	4.50	1.25
☐ 118	Bob Porterfield	8.00	3.60	1.00
☐ 119	Stan Lopata	8.00	3.60	1.00
☐ 120	Bob Lemon	20.00	9.00	2.50
☐ 121	Clete Boyer	25.00	11.00	3.10
☐ 122	Ken Boyer	15.00	6.75	1.85
☐ 123	Steve Ridzik	8.00	3.60	1.00
☐ 124	Dave Philley	8.00	3.60	1.00
☐ 125	Al Kaline	85.00	38.00	10.50
☐ 126	Bob Wiesler	8.00	3.60	1.00
☐ 127	Bob Buhl	10.00	4.50	1.25
☐ 128	Ed Bailey	10.00	4.50	1.25
☐ 129	Saul Rogovin	8.00	3.60	1.00
☐ 130	Don Newcombe	15.00	6.75	1.85
☐ 131	Milt Bolling	8.00	3.60	1.00
☐ 132	Art Ditmar	10.00	4.50	1.25
☐ 133	Del Crandall	10.00	4.50	1.25
☐ 134	Don Kaiser	8.00	3.60	1.00
☐ 135	Bill Skowron	15.00	6.75	1.85
☐ 136	Jim Hegan	10.00	4.50	1.25
☐ 137	Bob Rush	8.00	3.60	1.00
☐ 138	Minnie Minoso	15.00	6.75	1.85
☐ 139	Lou Kretlow	8.00	3.60	1.00
☐ 140	Frank Thomas	10.00	4.50	1.25
☐ 141	Al Aber	8.00	3.60	1.00
☐ 142	Charley Thompson	8.00	3.60	1.00
☐ 143	Andy Pafko	10.00	4.50	1.25
☐ 144	Ray Narleski	8.00	3.60	1.00
☐ 145	Al Smith	8.00	3.60	1.00
☐ 146	Don Ferrarese	8.00	3.60	1.00
☐ 147	Al Walker	8.00	3.60	1.00
☐ 148	Don Mueller	10.00	4.50	1.25
☐ 149	Bob Kennedy	10.00	4.50	1.25
☐ 150	Bob Friend	10.00	4.50	1.25
☐ 151	Willie Miranda	8.00	3.60	1.00
☐ 152	Jack Harshman	8.00	3.60	1.00
☐ 153	Karl Olson	8.00	3.60	1.00
☐ 154	Red Schoendienst	20.00	9.00	2.50
☐ 155	Jim Brosnan	10.00	4.50	1.25
☐ 156	Gus Triandos	10.00	4.50	1.25
☐ 157	Wally Post	10.00	4.50	1.25
☐ 158	Curt Simmons	10.00	4.50	1.25
☐ 159	Solly Drake	8.00	3.60	1.00
☐ 160	Billy Pierce	8.00	3.60	1.00
☐ 161	Pittsburgh Pirates	18.00	8.00	2.20
	Team Card			
☐ 162	Jack Meyer	8.00	3.60	1.00
☐ 163	Sammy White	8.00	3.60	1.00
☐ 164	Tommy Carroll	8.00	3.60	1.00
☐ 165	Ted Kluszewski	50.00	22.00	6.25
☐ 166	Roy Face	10.00	4.50	1.25
☐ 167	Vic Power	10.00	4.50	1.25
☐ 168	Frank Lary	10.00	4.50	1.25
☐ 169	Herb Plews	8.00	3.60	1.00
☐ 170	Duke Snider	110.00	50.00	14.00
☐ 171	Boston Red Sox	18.00	8.00	2.20
	Team Card			
☐ 172	Gene Woodling	10.00	4.50	1.25
☐ 173	Roger Craig	15.00	6.75	1.85
☐ 174	Willie Jones	8.00	3.60	1.00
☐ 175	Don Larsen	25.00	11.00	3.10
☐ 176A	Gene Baker ERR	350.00	160.00	45.00
	(Misspelled Bakep			
	on card back)			
☐ 176B	Gene Baker COR	8.00	3.60	1.00
☐ 177	Eddie Yost	10.00	4.50	1.25
☐ 178	Don Bessent	7.00	3.10	.85
☐ 179	Ernie Oravetz	7.00	3.10	.85
☐ 180	Gus Bell	10.00	4.50	1.25
☐ 181	Dick Donovan	7.00	3.10	.85
☐ 182	Hobie Landrith	7.00	3.10	.85
☐ 183	Chicago Cubs	18.00	8.00	2.20

Team Card

☐ 184	Tito Francona	7.00	3.10	.85
☐ 185	Johnny Kucks	7.00	3.10	.85
☐ 186	Jim King	7.00	3.10	.85
☐ 187	Virgil Trucks	10.00	4.50	1.25
☐ 188	Felix Mantilla	7.00	3.10	.85
☐ 189	Willard Nixon	7.00	3.10	.85
☐ 190	Randy Jackson	7.00	3.10	.85
☐ 191	Joe Margoneri	7.00	3.10	.85
☐ 192	Jerry Coleman	10.00	4.50	1.25
☐ 193	Del Rice	7.00	3.10	.85
☐ 194	Hal Brown	7.00	3.10	.85
☐ 195	Bobby Avila	7.00	3.10	.85
☐ 196	Larry Jackson	10.00	4.50	1.25
☐ 197	Hank Sauer	10.00	4.50	1.25
☐ 198	Detroit Tigers	18.00	8.00	2.20

Team Card

☐ 199	Vern Law	10.00	4.50	1.25
☐ 200	Gil McDougald	15.00	6.75	1.85
☐ 201	Sandy Amoros	10.00	4.50	1.25
☐ 202	Dick Gernert	7.00	3.10	.85
☐ 203	Hoyt Wilhelm	20.00	9.00	2.50
☐ 204	Kansas City Athletics	18.00	8.00	2.20

Team Card

☐ 205	Charlie Maxwell	10.00	4.50	1.25
☐ 206	Willard Schmidt	7.00	3.10	.85
☐ 207	Gordon(Billy) Hunter	7.00	3.10	.85
☐ 208	Lou Burdette	7.00	3.10	.85
☐ 209	Bob Skinner	10.00	4.50	1.25
☐ 210	Roy Campanella	125.00	55.00	15.50
☐ 211	Camilo Pascual	10.00	4.50	1.25
☐ 212	Rocky Colavito	175.00	80.00	22.00
☐ 213	Les Moss	7.00	3.10	.85
☐ 214	Philadelphia Phillies	18.00	8.00	2.20

Team Card

☐ 215	Enos Slaughter	25.00	11.00	3.10
☐ 216	Marv Grissom	7.00	3.10	.85
☐ 217	Gene Stephens	7.00	3.10	.85
☐ 218	Ray Jablonski	7.00	3.10	.85
☐ 219	Tom Acker	7.00	3.10	.85
☐ 220	Jackie Jensen	10.00	4.50	1.25
☐ 221	Dixie Howell	7.00	3.10	.85
☐ 222	Alex Grammas	7.00	3.10	.85
☐ 223	Frank House	7.00	3.10	.85
☐ 224	Marv Blaylock	7.00	3.10	.85
☐ 225	Harry Simpson	7.00	3.10	.85
☐ 226	Preston Ward	7.00	3.10	.85
☐ 227	Gerry Staley	7.00	3.10	.85
☐ 228	Smoky Burgess UER	10.00	4.50	1.25

(Misspelled Smokey
on card back)

☐ 229	George Susce	7.00	3.10	.85
☐ 230	George Kell	20.00	9.00	2.50
☐ 231	Solly Hemus	7.00	3.10	.85
☐ 232	Whitey Lockman	10.00	4.50	1.25
☐ 233	Art Fowler	7.00	3.10	.85
☐ 234	Dick Cole	7.00	3.10	.85
☐ 235	Tom Poholsky	7.00	3.10	.85
☐ 236	Joe Ginsberg	7.00	3.10	.85
☐ 237	Foster Castleman	7.00	3.10	.85
☐ 238	Eddie Robinson	7.00	3.10	.85
☐ 239	Tom Morgan	7.00	3.10	.85
☐ 240	Hank Bauer	10.00	4.50	1.25
☐ 241	Joe Lonnett	7.00	3.10	.85
☐ 242	Charlie Neal	10.00	4.50	1.25
☐ 243	St. Louis Cardinals	18.00	8.00	2.20

Team Card

☐ 244	Billy Loes	10.00	4.50	1.25
☐ 245	Rip Repulski	7.00	3.10	.85
☐ 246	Jose Valdivielso	7.00	3.10	.85
☐ 247	Turk Lown	7.00	3.10	.85
☐ 248	Jim Finigan	7.00	3.10	.85
☐ 249	Dave Pope	7.00	3.10	.85
☐ 250	Eddie Mathews	35.00	16.00	4.40
☐ 251	Baltimore Orioles	18.00	8.00	2.20

Team Card

☐ 252	Carl Erskine	10.00	4.50	1.25
☐ 253	Gus Zernial	10.00	4.50	1.25
☐ 254	Ron Negray	7.00	3.10	.85
☐ 255	Charlie Silvera	10.00	4.50	1.25
☐ 256	Ron Kline	7.00	3.10	.85
☐ 257	Walt Dropo	7.00	3.10	.85
☐ 258	Steve Gromek	7.00	3.10	.85
☐ 259	Eddie O'Brien	7.00	3.10	.85
☐ 260	Del Ennis	10.00	4.50	1.25
☐ 261	Bob Chakales	7.00	3.10	.85
☐ 262	Bobby Thomson	10.00	4.50	1.25
☐ 263	George Strickland	7.00	3.10	.85
☐ 264	Bob Turley	10.00	4.50	1.25
☐ 265	Harvey Haddix DP	14.00	6.25	1.75
☐ 266	Ken Kuhn DP	14.00	6.25	1.75
☐ 267	Danny Kravitz	20.00	9.00	2.50
☐ 268	Jack Collum	20.00	9.00	2.50
☐ 269	Bob Cerv	20.00	9.00	2.50
☐ 270	Washington Senators	60.00	27.00	7.50

Team Card

☐ 271	Danny O'Connell DP	14.00	6.25	1.75
☐ 272	Bobby Shantz	25.00	11.00	3.10
☐ 273	Jim Davis	20.00	9.00	2.50
☐ 274	Don Hoak	20.00	9.00	2.50
☐ 275	Cleveland Indians	60.00	27.00	7.50

Team Card UER
(Text on back credits Tribe
with winning AL title in '28.
The Yankees won that year.)

☐ 276	Jim Pyburn	20.00	9.00	2.50
☐ 277	Johnny Podres DP	45.00	20.00	5.50
☐ 278	Fred Hatfield DP	14.00	6.25	1.75
☐ 279	Bob Thurman	20.00	9.00	2.50
☐ 280	Alex Kellner	20.00	9.00	2.50
☐ 281	Gail Harris	20.00	9.00	2.50
☐ 282	Jack Dittmer DP	14.00	6.25	1.75
☐ 283	Wes Covington DP	14.00	6.25	1.75
☐ 284	Don Zimmer	25.00	11.00	3.10
☐ 285	Ned Garver	20.00	9.00	2.50
☐ 286	Bobby Richardson	120.00	55.00	15.00
☐ 287	Sam Jones	20.00	9.00	2.50
☐ 288	Ted Lepcio	20.00	9.00	2.50
☐ 289	Jim Bolger DP	14.00	6.25	1.75
☐ 290	Andy Carey DP	14.00	6.25	1.75
☐ 291	Windy McCall	20.00	9.00	2.50
☐ 292	Billy Klaus	20.00	9.00	2.50
☐ 293	Ted Abernathy	20.00	9.00	2.50
☐ 294	Rocky Bridges DP	14.00	6.25	1.75
☐ 295	Joe Collins DP	14.00	6.25	1.75
☐ 296	Johnny Klippstein	20.00	9.00	2.50
☐ 297	Jack Crimian	20.00	9.00	2.50
☐ 298	Irv Noren DP	14.00	6.25	1.75
☐ 299	Chuck Harmon	20.00	9.00	2.50
☐ 300	Mike Garcia	20.00	9.00	2.50
☐ 301	Sammy Esposito DP	14.00	6.25	1.75
☐ 302	Sandy Koufax DP	250.00	110.00	31.00
☐ 303	Billy Goodman	20.00	9.00	2.50
☐ 304	Joe Cunningham	20.00	9.00	2.50
☐ 305	Chico Fernandez	20.00	9.00	2.50
☐ 306	Darrell Johnson DP	14.00	6.25	1.75
☐ 307	Jack D. Phillips DP	14.00	6.25	1.75
☐ 308	Dick Hall	20.00	9.00	2.50
☐ 309	Jim Busby DP	14.00	6.25	1.75
☐ 310	Max Surkont DP	14.00	6.25	1.75
☐ 311	Al Pilarcik DP	14.00	6.25	1.75
☐ 312	Tony Kubek DP	60.00	27.00	7.50

☐	313	Mel Parnell	20.00	9.00	2.50				
☐	314	Ed Bouchee DP	14.00	6.25	1.75				
☐	315	Lou Berberet DP	14.00	6.25	1.75				
☐	316	Billy O'Dell	20.00	9.00	2.50				
☐	317	New York Giants	70.00	32.00	8.75				
		Team Card							
☐	318	Mickey McDermott	20.00	9.00	2.50				
☐	319	Gino Cimoli	20.00	9.00	2.50				
☐	320	Neil Chrisley	20.00	9.00	2.50				
☐	321	John(Red) Murff	20.00	9.00	2.50				
☐	322	Cincinnati Reds	70.00	32.00	8.75				
		Team Card							
☐	323	Wes Westrum	20.00	9.00	2.50				
☐	324	Brooklyn Dodgers	125.00	55.00	15.50				
		Team Card							
☐	325	Frank Bolling	20.00	9.00	2.50				
☐	326	Pedro Ramos	20.00	9.00	2.50				
☐	327	Jim Pendleton	20.00	9.00	2.50				
☐	328	Brooks Robinson	375.00	170.00	47.50				
☐	329	Chicago White Sox	60.00	27.00	7.50				
		Team Card							
☐	330	Jim Wilson	20.00	9.00	2.50				
☐	331	Ray Katt	20.00	9.00	2.50				
☐	332	Bob Bowman	20.00	9.00	2.50				
☐	333	Ernie Johnson	20.00	9.00	2.50				
☐	334	Jerry Schoonmaker	20.00	9.00	2.50				
☐	335	Granny Hamner	20.00	9.00	2.50				
☐	336	Haywood Sullivan	20.00	9.00	2.50				
☐	337	Rene Valdes	20.00	9.00	2.50				
☐	338	Jim Bunning	125.00	55.00	15.50				
☐	339	Bob Speake	20.00	9.00	2.50				
☐	340	Bill Wight	20.00	9.00	2.50				
☐	341	Don Gross	20.00	9.00	2.50				
☐	342	Gene Mauch	20.00	9.00	2.50				
☐	343	Taylor Phillips	20.00	9.00	2.50				
☐	344	Paul LaPalme	20.00	9.00	2.50				
☐	345	Paul Smith	20.00	9.00	2.50				
☐	346	Dick Littlefield	20.00	9.00	2.50				
☐	347	Hal Naragon	20.00	9.00	2.50				
☐	348	Jim Hearn	20.00	9.00	2.50				
☐	349	Nellie King	20.00	9.00	2.50				
☐	350	Eddie Miksis	20.00	9.00	2.50				
☐	351	Dave Hillman	20.00	9.00	2.50				
☐	352	Ellis Kinder	20.00	9.00	2.50				
☐	353	Cal Neeman	8.00	3.60	1.00				
☐	354	W. (Rip) Coleman	8.00	3.60	1.00				
☐	355	Frank Malzone	10.00	4.50	1.25				
☐	356	Faye Throneberry	8.00	3.60	1.00				
☐	357	Earl Torgeson	8.00	3.60	1.00				
☐	358	Jerry Lynch	10.00	4.50	1.25				
☐	359	Tom Cheney	10.00	4.50	1.25				
☐	360	Johnny Groth	8.00	3.60	1.00				
☐	361	Curt Barclay	8.00	3.60	1.00				
☐	362	Roman Mejias	10.00	4.50	1.25				
☐	363	Eddie Kasko	8.00	3.60	1.00				
☐	364	Cal McLish	10.00	4.50	1.25				
☐	365	Ozzie Virgil	8.00	3.60	1.00				
☐	366	Ken Lehman	8.00	3.60	1.00				
☐	367	Ed Fitzgerald	8.00	3.60	1.00				
☐	368	Bob Purkey	8.00	3.60	1.00				
☐	369	Milt Graff	8.00	3.60	1.00				
☐	370	Warren Hacker	8.00	3.60	1.00				
☐	371	Bob Lennon	8.00	3.60	1.00				
☐	372	Norm Zauchin	8.00	3.60	1.00				
☐	373	Pete Whisenant	8.00	3.60	1.00				
☐	374	Don Cardwell	8.00	3.60	1.00				
☐	375	Jim Landis	10.00	4.50	1.25				
☐	376	Don Elston	8.00	3.60	1.00				
☐	377	Andre Rodgers	8.00	3.60	1.00				
☐	378	Elmer Singleton	8.00	3.60	1.00				
☐	379	Don Lee	8.00	3.60	1.00				

☐	380	Walker Cooper	8.00	3.60	1.00
☐	381	Dean Stone	8.00	3.60	1.00
☐	382	Jim Brideweser	8.00	3.60	1.00
☐	383	Juan Pizarro	8.00	3.60	1.00
☐	384	Bobby G. Smith	8.00	3.60	1.00
☐	385	Art Houtteman	8.00	3.60	1.00
☐	386	Lyle Luttrell	8.00	3.60	1.00
☐	387	Jack Sanford	12.00	5.50	1.50
☐	388	Pete Daley	8.00	3.60	1.00
☐	389	Dave Jolly	8.00	3.60	1.00
☐	390	Reno Bertoia	8.00	3.60	1.00
☐	391	Ralph Terry	12.00	5.50	1.50
☐	392	Chuck Tanner	12.00	5.50	1.50
☐	393	Raul Sanchez	8.00	3.60	1.00
☐	394	Luis Arroyo	10.00	4.50	1.25
☐	395	Bubba Phillips	8.00	3.60	1.00
☐	396	Casey Wise	8.00	3.60	1.00
☐	397	Roy Smalley	8.00	3.60	1.00
☐	398	Al Cicotte	10.00	4.50	1.25
☐	399	Billy Consolo	8.00	3.60	1.00
☐	400	Dodgers' Sluggers	250.00	110.00	31.00
		Carl Furillo			
		Gil Hodges			
		Roy Campanella			
		Duke Snider			
☐	401	Earl Battey	14.00	6.25	1.75
☐	402	Jim Pisoni	8.00	3.60	1.00
☐	403	Dick Hyde	8.00	3.60	1.00
☐	404	Harry Anderson	8.00	3.60	1.00
☐	405	Duke Maas	8.00	3.60	1.00
☐	406	Bob Hale	8.00	3.60	1.00
☐	407	Yankee Power Hitters	525.00	160.00	52.50
		Mickey Mantle			
		Yogi Berra			
☐	NNO1	Checklist 1/2	250.00	75.00	25.00
☐	NNO2	Checklist 2/3	400.00	100.00	40.00
☐	NNO3	Checklist 3/4	750.00	170.00	75.00
☐	NNO4	Checklist 4/5	900.00	200.00	90.00
☐	NNO5	Saturday, May 4th	60.00	27.00	7.50
		Boston Red Sox			
		vs. Cincinnati Redlegs			
		Cleveland Indians			
		vs. New York Giants			
☐	NNO6	Saturday, May 25th	60.00	27.00	7.50
☐	NNO7	Saturday, June 22nd	80.00	36.00	10.00
		Brooklyn Dodgers			
		vs. Chicago White Sox			
		St. Louis Cardinals			
		vs. New York Yankees			
☐	NNO8	Saturday, July 19th	90.00	40.00	11.00
		Milwaukee Braves			
		vs. New York Giants			
		Baltimore Orioles			
		vs. Kansas City Athletics			
☐	NNO9	Lucky Penny Charm	50.00	22.00	6.25
		and Key Chain			
		offer card			

1958 Topps

The cards in this 494-card set measure 2 1/2" by 3 1/2". Although the last card is numbered 495, number 145 was not issued, bringing the set total to 494 cards. The 1958 Topps set contains the first Sport Magazine All-Star Selection series (475-495) and expanded use of combination

cards. The team cards carried series checklists on back (Milwaukee, Detroit, Baltimore, and Cincinnati are also found with players listed alphabetically). Cards with the scarce yellow name (YL) or team (YT) lettering, as opposed to the common white lettering, are noted in the checklist. In the last series, cards of Stan Musial and Mickey Mantle were triple printed; the cards they replaced (443, 446, 450, and 462) on the printing sheet were hence printed in shorter supply than other cards in the last series and are marked with an SP in the list below. Technically the New York Giants team card (19) is an error as the Giants had already moved to San Francisco. The key Rookie Cards in this set are Orlando Cepeda, Curt Flood, Roger Maris, and Vada Pinson.

	NRMT	VG-E	GOOD
COMPLETE SET (494)	5000.00	2200.00	600.00
COMMON CARD (1-110)	12.00	5.50	1.50
COMMON CARD (111-198)	7.00	3.10	.85
COMMON CARD (199-352)	7.00	3.10	.85
COMMON CARD (353-440)	7.00	3.10	.85
COMMON AS (441-474)	7.00	3.10	.85
COMMON CARD (475-495)	7.00	3.10	.85

		NRMT	VG-E	GOOD
☐ 1	Ted Williams	425.00	150.00	42.50
☐ 2A	Bob Lemon	30.00	13.50	3.70
☐ 2B	Bob Lemon YT	60.00	27.00	7.50
☐ 3	Alex Kellner	12.00	5.50	1.50
☐ 4	Hank Foiles	12.00	5.50	1.50
☐ 5	Willie Mays	225.00	100.00	28.00
☐ 6	George Zuverink	12.00	5.50	1.50
☐ 7	Dale Long	14.00	6.25	1.75
☐ 8A	Eddie Kasko	12.00	5.50	1.50
☐ 8B	Eddie Kasko YL	45.00	20.00	5.50
☐ 9	Hank Bauer	14.00	6.25	1.75
☐ 10	Lou Burdette	14.00	6.25	1.75
☐ 11A	Jim Rivera	12.00	5.50	1.50
☐ 11B	Jim Rivera YT	45.00	20.00	5.50
☐ 12	George Crowe	12.00	5.50	1.50
☐ 13A	Billy Hoeft	12.00	5.50	1.50
☐ 13B	Billy Hoeft YL	45.00	20.00	5.50
☐ 14	Rip Repulski	12.00	5.50	1.50
☐ 15	Jim Lemon	14.00	6.25	1.75
☐ 16	Charlie Neal	14.00	6.25	1.75
☐ 17	Felix Mantilla	12.00	5.50	1.50
☐ 18	Frank Sullivan	12.00	5.50	1.50
☐ 19	New York Giants Team Card (Checklist on back)	35.00	16.00	4.40
☐ 20A	Gil McDougald	15.00	6.75	1.85
☐ 20B	Gil McDougald YL	60.00	27.00	7.50
☐ 21	Curt Barclay	12.00	5.50	1.50
☐ 22	Hal Naragon	12.00	5.50	1.50
☐ 23A	Bill Tuttle	12.00	5.50	1.50
☐ 23B	Bill Tuttle YL	45.00	20.00	5.50
☐ 24A	Hobie Landrith	12.00	5.50	1.50
☐ 24B	Hobie Landrith YL	45.00	20.00	5.50
☐ 25	Don Drysdale	75.00	34.00	9.50
☐ 26	Ron Jackson	12.00	5.50	1.50
☐ 27	Bud Freeman	12.00	5.50	1.50
☐ 28	Jim Busby	12.00	5.50	1.50
☐ 29	Ted Lepcio	12.00	5.50	1.50
☐ 30A	Hank Aaron	225.00	100.00	28.00
☐ 30B	Hank Aaron YL	450.00	200.00	55.00
☐ 31	Tex Clevenger	12.00	5.50	1.50
☐ 32A	J.W. Porter	12.00	5.50	1.50
☐ 32B	J.W. Porter YL	45.00	20.00	5.50
☐ 33A	Cal Neeman	12.00	5.50	1.50
☐ 33B	Cal Neeman YT	45.00	20.00	5.50
☐ 34	Bob Thurman	12.00	5.50	1.50
☐ 35A	Don Mossi	12.00	5.50	1.50
☐ 35B	Don Mossi YT	45.00	20.00	5.50
☐ 36	Ted Kazanski	12.00	5.50	1.50
☐ 37	Mike McCormick UER (Photo actually Ray Monzant)	15.00	6.75	1.95
☐ 38	Dick Gernert	12.00	5.50	1.50
☐ 39	Bob Martyn	12.00	5.50	1.50
☐ 40	George Kell	15.00	6.75	1.85
☐ 41	Dave Hillman	12.00	5.50	1.50
☐ 42	John Roseboro	24.00	11.00	3.00
☐ 43	Sal Maglie	14.00	6.25	1.75
☐ 44	Washington Senators Team Card (Checklist on back)	20.00	9.00	2.50
☐ 45	Dick Groat	14.00	6.25	1.75
☐ 46A	Lou Sleater	12.00	5.50	1.50
☐ 46B	Lou Sleater YL	45.00	20.00	5.50
☐ 47	Roger Maris	450.00	200.00	55.00
☐ 48	Chuck Harmon	12.00	5.50	1.50
☐ 49	Smoky Burgess	14.00	6.25	1.75
☐ 50A	Billy Pierce	14.00	6.25	1.75
☐ 50B	Billy Pierce YT	50.00	22.00	6.25
☐ 51	Del Rice	12.00	5.50	1.50
☐ 52A	Bob Clemente	225.00	100.00	28.00
☐ 52B	Bob Clemente YT	450.00	200.00	55.00
☐ 53A	Morrie Martin	12.00	5.50	1.50
☐ 53B	Morrie Martin YL	45.00	20.00	5.50
☐ 54	Norm Siebern	12.00	5.50	1.50
☐ 55	Chico Carrasquel	12.00	5.50	1.50
☐ 56	Bill Fischer	12.00	5.50	1.50
☐ 57A	Tim Thompson	12.00	5.50	1.50
☐ 57B	Tim Thompson YL	45.00	20.00	5.50
☐ 58A	Art Schult	12.00	5.50	1.50
☐ 58B	Art Schult YT	45.00	20.00	5.50
☐ 59	Dave Sisler	12.00	5.50	1.50
☐ 60A	Del Ennis	14.00	6.25	1.75
☐ 60B	Del Ennis YL	50.00	22.00	6.25
☐ 61A	Darrell Johnson	12.00	5.50	1.50
☐ 61B	Darrell Johnson YL	45.00	20.00	5.50
☐ 62	Joe DeMaestri	12.00	5.50	1.50
☐ 63	Joe Nuxhall	14.00	6.25	1.75
☐ 64	Joe Lonnett	12.00	5.50	1.50
☐ 65A	Von McDaniel	12.00	5.50	1.50
☐ 65B	Von McDaniel YL	45.00	20.00	5.50
☐ 66	Lee Walls	12.00	5.50	1.50
☐ 67	Joe Ginsberg	12.00	5.50	1.50
☐ 68	Daryl Spencer	12.00	5.50	1.50
☐ 69	Wally Burnette	12.00	5.50	1.50
☐ 70A	Al Kaline	90.00	40.00	11.00
☐ 70B	Al Kaline YL	180.00	80.00	22.00
☐ 71	Dodgers Team	50.00	22.00	6.25

(Checklist on back)

☐ 72	Bud Byerly	12.00	5.50	1.50
☐ 73	Pete Daley	12.00	5.50	1.50
☐ 74	Roy Face	14.00	6.25	1.75
☐ 75	Gus Bell	14.00	6.25	1.75
☐ 76A	Dick Farrell	12.00	5.50	1.50
☐ 76B	Dick Farrell YT	45.00	20.00	5.50
☐ 77A	Don Zimmer	14.00	6.25	1.75
☐ 77B	Don Zimmer YT	50.00	22.00	6.25
☐ 78A	Ernie Johnson	14.00	6.25	1.75
☐ 78B	Ernie Johnson YT	50.00	22.00	6.25
☐ 79A	Dick Williams	14.00	6.25	1.75
☐ 79B	Dick Williams YT	50.00	22.00	6.25
☐ 80	Dick Drott	12.00	5.50	1.50
☐ 81A	Steve Boros	12.00	5.50	1.50
☐ 81B	Steve Boros YT	45.00	20.00	5.50
☐ 82	Ron Kline	12.00	5.50	1.50
☐ 83	Bob Hazle	12.00	5.50	1.50
☐ 84	Billy O'Dell	12.00	5.50	1.50
☐ 85A	Luis Aparicio	30.00	13.50	3.70
☐ 85B	Luis Aparicio YT	70.00	32.00	8.75
☐ 86	Valmy Thomas	12.00	5.50	1.50
☐ 87	Johnny Kucks	12.00	5.50	1.50
☐ 88	Duke Snider	75.00	34.00	9.50
☐ 89	Billy Klaus	12.00	5.50	1.50
☐ 90	Robin Roberts	30.00	13.50	3.70
☐ 91	Chuck Tanner	14.00	6.25	1.75
☐ 92A	Clint Courtney	12.00	5.50	1.50
☐ 92B	Clint Courtney YL	45.00	20.00	5.50
☐ 93	Sandy Amoros	14.00	6.25	1.75
☐ 94	Bob Skinner	14.00	6.25	1.75
☐ 95	Frank Bolling	12.00	5.50	1.50
☐ 96	Joe Durham	12.00	5.50	1.50
☐ 97A	Larry Jackson	12.00	5.50	1.50
☐ 97B	Larry Jackson YL	45.00	20.00	5.50
☐ 98A	Billy Hunter	12.00	5.50	1.50
☐ 98B	Billy Hunter YL	45.00	20.00	5.50
☐ 99	Bobby Adams	12.00	5.50	1.50
☐ 100A	Early Wynn	25.00	11.00	3.10
☐ 100B	Early Wynn YT	60.00	27.00	7.50
☐ 101A	Bobby Richardson	24.00	11.00	3.00
☐ 101B	Bobby Richardson YL	55.00	25.00	7.00
☐ 102	George Strickland	12.00	5.50	1.50
☐ 103	Jerry Lynch	14.00	6.25	1.75
☐ 104	Jim Pendleton	12.00	5.50	1.50
☐ 105	Billy Gardner	12.00	5.50	1.50
☐ 106	Dick Schofield	14.00	6.25	1.75
☐ 107	Ossie Virgil	12.00	5.50	1.50
☐ 108A	Jim Landis	12.00	5.50	1.50
☐ 108B	Jim Landis YT	45.00	20.00	5.50
☐ 109	Herb Plews	12.00	5.50	1.50
☐ 110	Johnny Logan	14.00	6.25	1.75
☐ 111	Stu Miller	8.00	3.60	1.00
☐ 112	Gus Zernial	8.00	3.60	1.00
☐ 113	Jerry Walker	7.00	3.10	.85
☐ 114	Irv Noren	8.00	3.60	1.00
☐ 115	Jim Bunning	25.00	11.00	3.10
☐ 116	Dave Philley	7.00	3.10	.85
☐ 117	Frank Torre	8.00	3.60	1.00
☐ 118	Harvey Haddix	9.00	4.00	1.10
☐ 119	Harry Chiti	7.00	3.10	.85
☐ 120	Johnny Podres	10.00	4.50	1.25
☐ 121	Eddie Miksis	7.00	3.10	.85
☐ 122	Walt Moryn	7.00	3.10	.85
☐ 123	Dick Tomanek	7.00	3.10	.85
☐ 124	Bobby Usher	7.00	3.10	.85
☐ 125	Alvin Dark	9.00	4.00	1.10
☐ 126	Stan Palys	7.00	3.10	.85
☐ 127	Tom Sturdivant	8.00	3.60	1.00
☐ 128	Willie Kirkland	8.00	3.60	1.00
☐ 129	Jim Derrington	7.00	3.10	.85

☐ 130	Jackie Jensen	8.00	3.60	1.00
☐ 131	Bob Henrich	7.00	3.10	.85
☐ 132	Vern Law	9.00	4.00	1.10
☐ 133	Russ Nixon	7.00	3.10	.85
☐ 134	Philadelphia Phillies	15.00	6.75	1.85
	Team Card			
	(Checklist on back)			
☐ 135	Mike(Moe) Drabowsky	8.00	3.60	1.00
☐ 136	Jim Finigan	7.00	3.10	.85
☐ 137	Russ Kemmerer	7.00	3.10	.85
☐ 138	Earl Torgeson	7.00	3.10	.85
☐ 139	George Brunet	7.00	3.10	.85
☐ 140	Wes Covington	8.00	3.60	1.00
☐ 141	Ken Lehman	7.00	3.10	.85
☐ 142	Enos Slaughter	24.00	11.00	3.00
☐ 143	Billy Muffett	7.00	3.10	.85
☐ 144	Bobby Morgan	7.00	3.10	.85
☐ 145	Never issued			
☐ 146	Dick Gray	7.00	3.10	.85
☐ 147	Don McMahon	7.00	3.10	.85
☐ 148	Billy Consolo	7.00	3.10	.85
☐ 149	Tom Acker	7.00	3.10	.85
☐ 150	Mickey Mantle	750.00	350.00	95.00
☐ 151	Buddy Pritchard	7.00	3.10	.85
☐ 152	Johnny Antonelli	9.00	4.00	1.10
☐ 153	Les Moss	7.00	3.10	.85
☐ 154	Harry Byrd	7.00	3.10	.85
☐ 155	Hector Lopez	8.00	3.60	1.00
☐ 156	Dick Hyde	7.00	3.10	.85
☐ 157	Dee Fondy	7.00	3.10	.85
☐ 158	Cleveland Indians	15.00	6.75	1.85
	Team Card			
	(Checklist on back)			
☐ 159	Taylor Phillips	7.00	3.10	.85
☐ 160	Don Hoak	8.00	3.60	1.00
☐ 161	Don Larsen	14.00	6.25	1.75
☐ 162	Gil Hodges	25.00	11.00	3.10
☐ 163	Jim Wilson	7.00	3.10	.85
☐ 164	Bob Taylor	7.00	3.10	.85
☐ 165	Bob Nieman	7.00	3.10	.85
☐ 166	Danny O'Connell	7.00	3.10	.85
☐ 167	Frank Baumann	7.00	3.10	.85
☐ 168	Joe Cunningham	8.00	3.60	1.00
☐ 169	Ralph Terry	8.00	3.60	1.00
☐ 170	Vic Wertz	9.00	4.00	1.10
☐ 171	Harry Anderson	7.00	3.10	.85
☐ 172	Don Gross	7.00	3.10	.85
☐ 173	Eddie Yost	8.00	3.60	1.00
☐ 174	Athletics Team	15.00	6.75	1.85
	(Checklist on back)			
☐ 175	Marv Throneberry	16.00	7.25	2.00
☐ 176	Bob Buhl	8.00	3.60	1.00
☐ 177	Al Smith	7.00	3.10	.85
☐ 178	Ted Kluszewski	16.00	7.25	2.00
☐ 179	Willie Miranda	7.00	3.10	.85
☐ 180	Lindy McDaniel	8.00	3.60	1.00
☐ 181	Willie Jones	7.00	3.10	.85
☐ 182	Joe Caffie	7.00	3.10	.85
☐ 183	Dave Jolly	7.00	3.10	.85
☐ 184	Elvin Tappe	7.00	3.10	.85
☐ 185	Ray Boone	8.00	3.60	1.00
☐ 186	Jack Meyer	7.00	3.10	.85
☐ 187	Sandy Koufax	225.00	100.00	28.00
☐ 188	Milt Bolling UER	7.00	3.10	.85
	(Photo actually			
	Lou Berberet)			
☐ 189	George Susce	7.00	3.10	.85
☐ 190	Red Schoendienst	18.00	8.00	2.20
☐ 191	Art Ceccarelli	7.00	3.10	.85
☐ 192	Milt Graff	7.00	3.10	.85
☐ 193	Jerry Lumpe	7.00	3.10	.85

☐ 194 Roger Craig	8.00	3.60	1.00
☐ 195 Whitey Lockman	8.00	3.60	1.00
☐ 196 Mike Garcia	9.00	4.00	1.10
☐ 197 Haywood Sullivan	8.00	3.60	1.00
☐ 198 Bill Virdon	9.00	4.00	1.10
☐ 199 Don Blasingame	7.00	3.10	.85
☐ 200 Bob Keegan	7.00	3.10	.85
☐ 201 Jim Bolger	7.00	3.10	.85
☐ 202 Woody Held	7.00	3.10	.85
☐ 203 Al Walker	7.00	3.10	.85
☐ 204 Leo Kiely	7.00	3.10	.85
☐ 205 Johnny Temple	8.00	3.60	1.00
☐ 206 Bob Shaw	7.00	3.10	.85
☐ 207 Solly Hemus	7.00	3.10	.85
☐ 208 Cal McLish	7.00	3.10	.85
☐ 209 Bob Anderson	7.00	3.10	.85
☐ 210 Wally Moon	8.00	3.60	1.00
☐ 211 Pete Burnside	7.00	3.10	.85
☐ 212 Bubba Phillips	7.00	3.10	.85
☐ 213 Red Wilson	7.00	3.10	.85
☐ 214 Willard Schmidt	7.00	3.10	.85
☐ 215 Jim Gilliam	10.00	4.50	1.25
☐ 216 St. Louis Cardinals	15.00	6.75	1.85
Team Card			
(Checklist on back)			
☐ 217 Jack Harshman	7.00	3.10	.85
☐ 218 Dick Rand	7.00	3.10	.85
☐ 219 Camilo Pascual	8.00	3.60	1.00
☐ 220 Tom Brewer	7.00	3.10	.85
☐ 221 Jerry Kindall	7.00	3.10	.85
☐ 222 Bud Daley	7.00	3.10	.85
☐ 223 Andy Pafko	8.00	3.60	1.00
☐ 224 Bob Grim	8.00	3.60	1.00
☐ 225 Billy Goodman	8.00	3.60	1.00
☐ 226 Bob Smith	7.00	3.10	.85
☐ 227 Gene Stephens	7.00	3.10	.85
☐ 228 Duke Maas	7.00	3.10	.85
☐ 229 Frank Zupo	7.00	3.10	.85
☐ 230 Richie Ashburn	35.00	16.00	4.40
☐ 231 Lloyd Merritt	7.00	3.10	.85
☐ 232 Reno Bertoia	7.00	3.10	.85
☐ 233 Mickey Vernon	8.00	3.60	1.00
☐ 234 Carl Sawatski	7.00	3.10	.85
☐ 235 Tom Gorman	7.00	3.10	.85
☐ 236 Ed Fitzgerald	7.00	3.10	.85
☐ 237 Bill Wight	7.00	3.10	.85
☐ 238 Bill Mazeroski	24.00	11.00	3.00
☐ 239 Chuck Stobbs	7.00	3.10	.85
☐ 240 Bill Skowron	16.00	7.25	2.00
☐ 241 Dick Littlefield	7.00	3.10	.85
☐ 242 Johnny Klippstein	7.00	3.10	.85
☐ 243 Larry Raines	7.00	3.10	.85
☐ 244 Don Demeter	7.00	3.10	.85
☐ 245 Frank Lary	8.00	3.60	1.00
☐ 246 New York Yankees	80.00	36.00	10.00
Team Card			
(Checklist on back)			
☐ 247 Casey Wise	7.00	3.10	.85
☐ 248 Herman Wehmeier	7.00	3.10	.85
☐ 249 Ray Moore	7.00	3.10	.85
☐ 250 Roy Sievers	8.00	3.60	1.00
☐ 251 Warren Hacker	7.00	3.10	.85
☐ 252 Bob Trowbridge	7.00	3.10	.85
☐ 253 Don Mueller	8.00	3.60	1.00
☐ 254 Alex Grammas	7.00	3.10	.85
☐ 255 Bob Turley	8.00	3.60	1.00
☐ 256 Chicago White Sox	15.00	6.75	1.85
Team Card			
(Checklist on back)			
☐ 257 Hal Smith	7.00	3.10	.85
☐ 258 Carl Erskine	10.00	4.50	1.25
☐ 259 Al Pilarcik	7.00	3.10	.85
☐ 260 Frank Malzone	8.00	3.60	1.00
☐ 261 Turk Lown	7.00	3.10	.85
☐ 262 Johnny Groth	7.00	3.10	.85
☐ 263 Eddie Bressoud	8.00	3.60	1.00
☐ 264 Jack Sanford	8.00	3.60	1.00
☐ 265 Pete Runnels	8.00	3.60	1.00
☐ 266 Connie Johnson	7.00	3.10	.85
☐ 267 Sherm Lollar	8.00	3.60	1.00
☐ 268 Granny Hamner	7.00	3.10	.85
☐ 269 Paul Smith	7.00	3.10	.85
☐ 270 Warren Spahn	55.00	25.00	7.00
☐ 271 Billy Martin	18.00	8.00	2.20
☐ 272 Ray Crone	7.00	3.10	.85
☐ 273 Hal Smith	7.00	3.10	.85
☐ 274 Rocky Bridges	7.00	3.10	.85
☐ 275 Elston Howard	16.00	7.25	2.00
☐ 276 Bobby Avila	7.00	3.10	.85
☐ 277 Virgil Trucks	8.00	3.60	1.00
☐ 278 Mack Burk	7.00	3.10	.85
☐ 279 Bob Boyd	7.00	3.10	.85
☐ 280 Jim Piersall	9.00	4.00	1.10
☐ 281 Sammy Taylor	7.00	3.10	.85
☐ 282 Paul Foytack	7.00	3.10	.85
☐ 283 Ray Shearer	7.00	3.10	.85
☐ 284 Ray Katt	7.00	3.10	.85
☐ 285 Frank Robinson	100.00	45.00	12.50
☐ 286 Gino Cimoli	7.00	3.10	.85
☐ 287 Sam Jones	8.00	3.60	1.00
☐ 288 Harmon Killebrew	85.00	38.00	10.50
☐ 289 Series Hurling Rivals	7.00	3.10	.85
Lou Burdette			
Bobby Shantz			
☐ 290 Dick Donovan	7.00	3.10	.85
☐ 291 Don Landrum	7.00	3.10	.85
☐ 292 Ned Garver	7.00	3.10	.85
☐ 293 Gene Freese	7.00	3.10	.85
☐ 294 Hal Jeffcoat	7.00	3.10	.85
☐ 295 Minnie Minoso	10.00	4.50	1.25
☐ 296 Ryne Duren	16.00	7.25	2.00
☐ 297 Don Buddin	7.00	3.10	.85
☐ 298 Jim Hearn	7.00	3.10	.85
☐ 299 Harry Simpson	7.00	3.10	.85
☐ 300 League Presidents	10.00	4.50	1.25
Will Harridge			
Warren Giles			
☐ 301 Randy Jackson	7.00	3.10	.85
☐ 302 Mike Baxes	7.00	3.10	.85
☐ 303 Neil Chrisley	7.00	3.10	.85
☐ 304 Tigers' Big Bats	20.00	9.00	2.50
Harvey Kuenn			
Al Kaline			
☐ 305 Clem Labine	8.00	3.60	1.00
☐ 306 Whammy Douglas	7.00	3.10	.85
☐ 307 Brooks Robinson	100.00	45.00	12.50
☐ 308 Paul Giel	8.00	3.60	1.00
☐ 309 Gail Harris	7.00	3.10	.85
☐ 310 Ernie Banks	100.00	45.00	12.50
☐ 311 Bob Purkey	7.00	3.10	.85
☐ 312 Boston Red Sox	15.00	6.75	1.85
Team Card			
(Checklist on back)			
☐ 313 Bob Rush	7.00	3.10	.85
☐ 314 Dodgers' Boss and	25.00	11.00	3.10
Power: Duke Snider			
Walt Alston MG			
☐ 315 Bob Friend	9.00	4.00	1.10
☐ 316 Tito Francona	8.00	3.60	1.00
☐ 317 Albie Pearson	8.00	3.60	1.00
☐ 318 Frank House	7.00	3.10	.85
☐ 319 Lou Skizas	7.00	3.10	.85

☐ 320 Whitey Ford	50.00	22.00	6.25
☐ 321 Sluggers Supreme	70.00	32.00	8.75
Ted Kluszewski			
Ted Williams			
☐ 322 Harding Peterson	8.00	3.60	1.00
☐ 323 Elmer Valo	7.00	3.10	.85
☐ 324 Hoyt Wilhelm	18.00	8.00	2.20
☐ 325 Joe Adcock	9.00	4.00	1.10
☐ 326 Bob Miller	7.00	3.10	.85
☐ 327 Chicago Cubs	15.00	6.75	1.85
Team Card			
(Checklist on back)			
☐ 328 Ike Delock	7.00	3.10	.85
☐ 329 Bob Cerv	8.00	3.60	1.00
☐ 330 Ed Bailey	8.00	3.60	1.00
☐ 331 Pedro Ramos	7.00	3.10	.85
☐ 332 Jim King	7.00	3.10	.85
☐ 333 Andy Carey	8.00	3.60	1.00
☐ 334 Mound Aces	9.00	4.00	1.10
8. Bob Friend			
8. Billy Pierce			
☐ 335 Ruben Gomez	7.00	3.10	.85
☐ 336 Bert Hamric	7.00	3.10	.85
☐ 337 Hank Aguirre	7.00	3.10	.85
☐ 338 Walt Dropo	9.00	4.00	1.10
☐ 339 Fred Hatfield	7.00	3.10	.85
☐ 340 Don Newcombe	10.00	4.50	1.25
☐ 341 Pittsburgh Pirates	15.00	6.75	1.85
Team Card			
(Checklist on back)			
☐ 342 Jim Brosnan	8.00	3.60	1.00
☐ 343 Orlando Cepeda	90.00	40.00	11.00
☐ 344 Bob Porterfield	7.00	3.10	.85
☐ 345 Jim Hegan	8.00	3.60	1.00
☐ 346 Steve Bilko	7.00	3.10	.85
☐ 347 Don Rudolph	7.00	3.10	.85
☐ 348 Chico Fernandez	7.00	3.10	.85
☐ 349 Murry Dickson	7.00	3.10	.85
☐ 350 Ken Boyer	16.00	7.25	2.00
☐ 351 Braves Fence Busters	35.00	16.00	4.40
Del Crandall			
Eddie Mathews			
Hank Aaron			
Joe Adcock			
☐ 352 Herb Score	14.00	6.25	1.75
☐ 353 Stan Lopata	7.00	3.10	.85
☐ 354 Art Ditmar	8.00	3.60	1.00
☐ 355 Bill Bruton	8.00	3.60	1.00
☐ 356 Bob Malkmus	7.00	3.10	.85
☐ 357 Danny McDevitt	7.00	3.10	.85
☐ 358 Gene Baker	7.00	3.10	.85
☐ 359 Billy Loes	8.00	3.60	1.00
☐ 360 Roy McMillan	8.00	3.60	1.00
☐ 361 Mike Fornieles	7.00	3.10	.85
☐ 362 Ray Jablonski	7.00	3.10	.85
☐ 363 Don Elston	7.00	3.10	.85
☐ 364 Earl Battey	7.00	3.10	.85
☐ 365 Tom Morgan	7.00	3.10	.85
☐ 366 Gene Green	7.00	3.10	.85
☐ 367 Jack Urban	7.00	3.10	.85
☐ 368 Rocky Colavito	50.00	22.00	6.25
☐ 369 Ralph Lumenti	7.00	3.10	.85
☐ 370 Yogi Berra	85.00	38.00	10.50
☐ 371 Marty Keough	7.00	3.10	.85
☐ 372 Don Cardwell	7.00	3.10	.85
☐ 373 Joe Pignatano	7.00	3.10	.85
☐ 374 Brooks Lawrence	7.00	3.10	.85
☐ 375 Pee Wee Reese	55.00	25.00	7.00
☐ 376 Charley Rabe	7.00	3.10	.85
☐ 377A Milwaukee Braves	15.00	6.75	1.85
Team Card			
(Alphabetical)			
☐ 377B Milwaukee Team	100.00	45.00	12.50
numerical checklist			
☐ 378 Hank Sauer	9.00	4.00	1.10
☐ 379 Ray Herbert	7.00	3.10	.85
☐ 380 Charlie Maxwell	8.00	3.60	1.00
☐ 381 Hal Brown	7.00	3.10	.85
☐ 382 Al Cicotte	7.00	3.10	.85
☐ 383 Lou Berberet	7.00	3.10	.85
☐ 384 John Goryl	7.00	3.10	.85
☐ 385 Wilmer Mizell	8.00	3.60	1.00
☐ 386 Birdie's Sluggers	14.00	6.25	1.75
Ed Bailey			
Birdie Tebbetts MG			
Frank Robinson			
☐ 387 Wally Post	9.00	4.00	1.10
☐ 388 Billy Moran	7.00	3.10	.85
☐ 389 Bill Taylor	7.00	3.10	.85
☐ 390 Del Crandall	8.00	3.60	1.00
☐ 391 Dave Melton	7.00	3.10	.85
☐ 392 Bennie Daniels	7.00	3.10	.85
☐ 393 Tony Kubek	18.00	8.00	2.20
☐ 394 Jim Grant	7.00	3.10	.85
☐ 395 Willard Nixon	7.00	3.10	.85
☐ 396 Dutch Dotterer	7.00	3.10	.85
☐ 397A Detroit Tigers	15.00	6.75	1.85
Team Card			
(Alphabetical)			
☐ 397B Detroit Team	100.00	45.00	12.50
numerical checklist			
☐ 398 Gene Woodling	8.00	3.60	1.00
☐ 399 Marv Grissom	7.00	3.10	.85
☐ 400 Nellie Fox	16.00	7.25	2.00
☐ 401 Don Bessent	7.00	3.10	.85
☐ 402 Bobby Gene Smith	7.00	3.10	.85
☐ 403 Steve Korcheck	7.00	3.10	.85
☐ 404 Curt Simmons	8.00	3.60	1.00
☐ 405 Ken Aspromonte	7.00	3.10	.85
☐ 406 Vic Power	8.00	3.60	1.00
☐ 407 Carlton Willey	8.00	3.60	1.00
☐ 408A Baltimore Orioles	15.00	6.75	1.85
Team Card			
(Alphabetical)			
☐ 408B Baltimore Team	100.00	45.00	12.50
numerical checklist			
☐ 409 Frank Thomas	8.00	3.60	1.00
☐ 410 Murray Wall	7.00	3.10	.85
☐ 411 Tony Taylor	9.00	4.00	1.10
☐ 412 Gerry Staley	7.00	3.10	.85
☐ 413 Jim Davenport	7.00	3.10	.85
☐ 414 Sammy White	7.00	3.10	.85
☐ 415 Bob Bowman	7.00	3.10	.85
☐ 416 Foster Castleman	7.00	3.10	.85
☐ 417 Carl Furillo	10.00	4.50	1.25
☐ 418 World Series Batting	250.00	110.00	31.00
Foes: Mickey Mantle			
Hank Aaron			
☐ 419 Bobby Shantz	8.00	3.60	1.00
☐ 420 Vada Pinson	40.00	18.00	5.00
☐ 421 Dixie Howell	7.00	3.10	.85
☐ 422 Norm Zauchin	7.00	3.10	.85
☐ 423 Phil Clark	7.00	3.10	.85
☐ 424 Larry Doby	10.00	4.50	1.25
☐ 425 Sammy Esposito	7.00	3.10	.85
☐ 426 Johnny O'Brien	8.00	3.60	1.00
☐ 427 Al Worthington	7.00	3.10	.85
☐ 428A Cincinnati Reds	15.00	6.75	1.85
Team Card			
(Alphabetical)			
☐ 428B Cincinnati Team	100.00	45.00	12.50
numerical checklist			

☐	429	Gus Triandos	8.00	3.60	1.00
☐	430	Bobby Thomson	8.00	3.60	1.00
☐	431	Gene Conley	8.00	3.60	1.00
☐	432	John Powers	7.00	3.10	.85
☐	433A	Pancho Herrer ERR	650.00	300.00	80.00
☐	433B	Pancho Herrera COR	7.00	3.10	.85
☐	434	Harvey Kuenn	8.00	3.60	1.00
☐	435	Ed Roebuck	8.00	3.60	1.00
☐	436	Rival Fence Busters .	75.00	34.00	9.50
		Willie Mays			
		Duke Snider			
☐	437	Bob Speake	7.00	3.10	.85
☐	438	Whitey Herzog	8.00	3.60	1.00
☐	439	Ray Narleski	7.00	3.10	.85
☐	440	Eddie Mathews	35.00	16.00	4.40
☐	441	Jim Marshall	8.00	3.60	1.00
☐	442	Phil Paine	7.00	3.10	.85
☐	443	Billy Harrell SP	18.00	8.00	2.20
☐	444	Danny Kravitz	7.00	3.10	.85
☐	445	Bob Smith	7.00	3.10	.85
☐	446	Carroll Hardy SP	18.00	8.00	2.20
☐	447	Ray Monzant	7.00	3.10	.85
☐	448	Charlie Lau	8.00	3.60	1.00
☐	449	Gene Fodge	7.00	3.10	.85
☐	450	Preston Ward SP	18.00	8.00	2.20
☐	451	Joe Taylor	7.00	3.10	.85
☐	452	Roman Mejias	7.00	3.10	.85
☐	453	Tom Qualters	7.00	3.10	.85
☐	454	Harry Hanebrink	7.00	3.10	.85
☐	455	Hal Griggs	7.00	3.10	.85
☐	456	Dick Brown	7.00	3.10	.85
☐	457	Milt Pappas	8.00	3.60	1.00
☐	458	Julio Becquer	7.00	3.10	.85
☐	459	Ron Blackburn	7.00	3.10	.85
☐	460	Chuck Essegian	7.00	3.10	.85
☐	461	Ed Mayer	7.00	3.10	.85
☐	462	Gary Geiger SP	18.00	8.00	2.20
☐	463	Vito Valentinetti	7.00	3.10	.85
☐	464	Curt Flood	25.00	11.00	3.10
☐	465	Arnie Portocarrero	7.00	3.10	.85
☐	466	Pete Whisenant	7.00	3.10	.85
☐	467	Glen Hobbie	7.00	3.10	.85
☐	468	Bob Schmidt	7.00	3.10	.85
☐	469	Don Ferrarese	7.00	3.10	.85
☐	470	R.C. Stevens	7.00	3.10	.85
☐	471	Lenny Green	7.00	3.10	.85
☐	472	Joey Jay	8.00	3.60	1.00
☐	473	Bill Renna	7.00	3.10	.85
☐	474	Roman Semproch	7.00	3.10	.85
☐	475	Fred Haney AS MG and	20.00	9.00	2.50
		Casey Stengel AS MG			
		(Checklist back)			
☐	476	Stan Musial AS TP	45.00	20.00	5.50
☐	477	Bill Skowron AS	9.00	4.00	1.10
☐	478	Johnny Temple AS	7.00	3.10	.85
☐	479	Nellie Fox AS	10.00	4.50	1.25
☐	480	Eddie Mathews AS	16.00	7.25	2.00
☐	481	Frank Malzone AS	7.00	3.10	.85
☐	482	Ernie Banks AS	35.00	16.00	4.40
☐	483	Luis Aparicio AS	16.00	7.25	2.00
☐	484	Frank Robinson AS	25.00	11.00	3.10
☐	485	Ted Williams AS	120.00	55.00	15.00
☐	486	Willie Mays AS	50.00	22.00	6.25
☐	487	Mickey Mantle AS TP	175.00	80.00	22.00
☐	488	Hank Aaron AS	50.00	22.00	6.25
☐	489	Jackie Jensen AS	8.00	3.60	1.00
☐	490	Ed Bailey AS	7.00	3.10	.85
☐	491	Sherm Lollar AS	7.00	3.10	.85
☐	492	Bob Friend AS	7.00	3.10	.85
☐	493	Bob Turley AS	8.00	3.60	1.00
☐	494	Warren Spahn AS	24.00	11.00	3.00
☐	495	Herb Score AS	15.00	3.00	1.00
☐	xx	Contest Cards	40.00	18.00	5.00

1959 Topps

The cards in this 572-card set measure 2 1/2" by 3 1/2". The 1959 Topps set contains bust pictures of the players in a colored circle. Card numbers 551 to 572 are Sporting News All-Star Selections. High numbers 507 to 572 have the card number in a black background on the reverse rather than a green background as in the lower numbers. The high numbers are more difficult to obtain. Several cards in the 300s exist with or without an extra traded or option line on the back of the card. Cards 199 to 286 exist with either white or gray backs. Cards 461 to 470 contain "Highlights" while cards 116 to 146 give an alphabetically ordered listing of "Rookie Prospects." These Rookie Prospects (RP) were Topps' first organized inclusion of untested "Rookie" cards. Card 440 features Lew Burdette erroneously posing as a left-handed pitcher. There were some three-card advertising panels produced by Topps; the players included are from the first series. One advertising panel shows Don McMahon, Red Wilson and Bob Boyd on the front with Ted Kluszewski's card back on the back of the panel. Other panels are: Joe Pignatano, Sam Jones and Jack Urban also with Kluszewski's card back on back, Billy Hunter, Chuck Stobbs and Carl Sawatski on the front with the back of Nellie Fox's card on the back, Vito Valentinetti, Ken Lehman and Ed Bouchee on the front with Fox's card back on back and Mel Roach, Brooks Lawrence and Warren Spahn also with Fox on back. When separated, these advertising cards are distinguished by the non-standard card back, i.e., part of an advertisement for the 1959 Topps instead of the typical statistics and biographical information about the player pictured. The key Rookie Cards in this set are Felipe Alou, Sparky Anderson, Bob Gibson, and Bill White.

	NRMT	VG-E	GOOD
COMPLETE SET (572)	4500.00	2000.00	550.00
COMMON CARD (1-110)	6.00	2.70	.75
COMMON CARD (111-506)	4.00	1.80	.50

COMMON CARD (507-550)	16.00	7.25	2.00
COMMON AS (551-572)	16.00	7.25	2.00
☐ 1 Ford Frick COMM	55.00	15.00	4.90
☐ 2 Eddie Yost	7.00	3.10	.85
☐ 3 Don McMahon	7.00	3.10	.85
☐ 4 Albie Pearson	7.00	3.10	.85
☐ 5 Dick Donovan	7.00	3.10	.85
☐ 6 Alex Grammas	6.00	2.70	.75
☐ 7 Al Pilarcik	6.00	2.70	.75
☐ 8 Phillies Team	65.00	29.00	8.00
(Checklist on back)			
☐ 9 Paul Giel	7.00	3.10	.85
☐ 10 Mickey Mantle	600.00	275.00	75.00
☐ 11 Billy Hunter	7.00	3.10	.85
☐ 12 Vern Law	10.00	4.50	1.25
☐ 13 Dick Gernert	6.00	2.70	.75
☐ 14 Pete Whisenant	6.00	2.70	.75
☐ 15 Dick Drott	6.00	2.70	.75
☐ 16 Joe Pignatano	6.00	2.70	.75
☐ 17 Danny's Stars	7.00	3.10	.85
Frank Thomas			
Danny Murtaugh MG			
Ted Kluszewski			
☐ 18 Jack Urban	6.00	2.70	.75
☐ 19 Eddie Bressoud	6.00	2.70	.75
☐ 20 Duke Snider	50.00	22.00	6.25
☐ 21 Connie Johnson	6.00	2.70	.75
☐ 22 Al Smith	7.00	3.10	.85
☐ 23 Murry Dickson	7.00	3.10	.85
☐ 24 Red Wilson	6.00	2.70	.75
☐ 25 Don Hoak	7.00	3.10	.85
☐ 26 Chuck Stobbs	6.00	2.70	.75
☐ 27 Andy Pafko	7.00	3.10	.85
☐ 28 Al Worthington	6.00	2.70	.75
☐ 29 Jim Bolger	6.00	2.70	.75
☐ 30 Nellie Fox	20.00	9.00	2.50
☐ 31 Ken Lehman	6.00	2.70	.75
☐ 32 Don Buddin	6.00	2.70	.75
☐ 33 Ed Fitzgerald	6.00	2.70	.75
☐ 34 Pitchers Beware	20.00	9.00	2.50
Al Kaline			
Charley Maxwell			
☐ 35 Ted Kluszewski	16.00	7.25	2.00
☐ 36 Hank Aguirre	6.00	2.70	.75
☐ 37 Gene Green	6.00	2.70	.75
☐ 38 Morrie Martin	6.00	2.70	.75
☐ 39 Ed Bouchee	6.00	2.70	.75
☐ 40A Warren Spahn ERR	75.00	34.00	9.50
(Born 1931)			
☐ 40B Warren Spahn	100.00	45.00	12.50
(Born 1931, but three			
is partially obscured)			
☐ 40C Warren Spahn COR	55.00	25.00	7.00
(Born 1921)			
☐ 41 Bob Martyn	6.00	2.70	.75
☐ 42 Murray Wall	6.00	2.70	.75
☐ 43 Steve Bilko	6.00	2.70	.75
☐ 44 Vito Valentinetti	6.00	2.70	.75
☐ 45 Andy Carey	7.00	3.10	.85
☐ 46 Bill R. Henry	6.00	2.70	.75
☐ 47 Jim Finigan	6.00	2.70	.75
☐ 48 Orioles Team	24.00	11.00	3.00
(Checklist on back)			
☐ 49 Bill Hall	6.00	2.70	.75
☐ 50 Willie Mays	125.00	55.00	15.50
☐ 51 Rip Coleman	6.00	2.70	.75
☐ 52 Coot Veal	6.00	2.70	.75
☐ 53 Stan Williams	10.00	4.50	1.25
☐ 54 Mel Roach	6.00	2.70	.75
☐ 55 Tom Brewer	6.00	2.70	.75
☐ 56 Carl Sawatski	6.00	2.70	.75
☐ 57 Al Cicotte	6.00	2.70	.75
☐ 58 Eddie Miksis	6.00	2.70	.75
☐ 59 Irv Noren	7.00	3.10	.85
☐ 60 Bob Turley	7.00	3.10	.85
☐ 61 Dick Brown	6.00	2.70	.75
☐ 62 Tony Taylor	7.00	3.10	.85
☐ 63 Jim Hearn	6.00	2.70	.75
☐ 64 Joe DeMaestri	6.00	2.70	.75
☐ 65 Frank Torre	7.00	3.10	.85
☐ 66 Joe Ginsberg	6.00	2.70	.75
☐ 67 Brooks Lawrence	6.00	2.70	.75
☐ 68 Dick Schofield	7.00	3.10	.85
☐ 69 Giants Team	24.00	11.00	3.00
(Checklist on back)			
☐ 70 Harvey Kuenn	8.00	3.60	1.00
☐ 71 Don Bessent	6.00	2.70	.75
☐ 72 Bill Renna	6.00	2.70	.75
☐ 73 Ron Jackson	7.00	3.10	.85
☐ 74 Directing Power	7.00	3.10	.85
Jim Lemon			
Cookie Lavagetto MG			
Roy Sievers			
☐ 75 Sam Jones	7.00	3.10	.85
☐ 76 Bobby Richardson	20.00	9.00	2.50
☐ 77 John Goryl	6.00	2.70	.75
☐ 78 Pedro Ramos	6.00	2.70	.75
☐ 79 Harry Chiti	6.00	2.70	.75
☐ 80 Minnie Minoso	10.00	4.50	1.25
☐ 81 Hal Jeffcoat	6.00	2.70	.75
☐ 82 Bob Boyd	6.00	2.70	.75
☐ 83 Bob Smith	6.00	2.70	.75
☐ 84 Reno Bertoia	6.00	2.70	.75
☐ 85 Harry Anderson	6.00	2.70	.75
☐ 86 Bob Keegan	7.00	3.10	.85
☐ 87 Danny O'Connell	6.00	2.70	.75
☐ 88 Herb Score	10.00	4.50	1.25
☐ 89 Billy Gardner	6.00	2.70	.75
☐ 90 Bill Skowron	16.00	7.25	2.00
☐ 91 Herb Moford	6.00	2.70	.75
☐ 92 Dave Philley	6.00	2.70	.75
☐ 93 Julio Becquer	6.00	2.70	.75
☐ 94 White Sox Team	35.00	16.00	4.40
(Checklist on back)			
☐ 95 Carl Willey	6.00	2.70	.75
☐ 96 Lou Berberet	6.00	2.70	.75
☐ 97 Jerry Lynch	7.00	3.10	.85
☐ 98 Arnie Portocarrero	6.00	2.70	.75
☐ 99 Ted Kazanski	6.00	2.70	.75
☐ 100 Bob Cerv	7.00	3.10	.85
☐ 101 Alex Kellner	6.00	2.70	.75
☐ 102 Felipe Alou	30.00	13.50	3.70
☐ 103 Billy Goodman	7.00	3.10	.85
☐ 104 Del Rice	7.00	3.10	.85
☐ 105 Lee Walls	7.00	3.10	.85
☐ 106 Hal Woodeshick	6.00	2.70	.75
☐ 107 Norm Larker	7.00	3.10	.85
☐ 108 Zack Monroe	7.00	3.10	.85
☐ 109 Bob Schmidt	6.00	2.70	.75
☐ 110 George Witt	7.00	3.10	.85
☐ 111 Redlegs Team	15.00	6.75	1.85
(Checklist on back)			
☐ 112 Billy Consolo	4.00	1.80	.50
☐ 113 Taylor Phillips	4.00	1.80	.50
☐ 114 Earl Battey	7.00	3.10	.85
☐ 115 Mickey Vernon	7.00	3.10	.85
☐ 116 Bob Allison RP	10.00	4.50	1.25
☐ 117 John Blanchard RP	7.00	3.10	.85
☐ 118 John Buzhardt RP	5.00	2.20	.60
☐ 119 John Callison RP	12.00	5.50	1.50
☐ 120 Chuck Coles RP	5.00	2.20	.60

☐ 121	Bob Conley RP	5.00	2.20	.60
☐ 122	Bennie Daniels RP	5.00	2.20	.60
☐ 123	Don Dillard RP	5.00	2.20	.60
☐ 124	Dan Dobbek RP	5.00	2.20	.60
☐ 125	Ron Fairly RP	7.00	3.10	.85
☐ 126	Ed Haas RP	5.00	2.20	.60
☐ 127	Kent Hadley RP	5.00	2.20	.60
☐ 128	Bob Hartman RP	5.00	2.20	.60
☐ 129	Frank Herrera RP	5.00	2.20	.60
☐ 130	Lou Jackson RP	5.00	2.20	.60
☐ 131	Deron Johnson RP	7.00	3.10	.85
☐ 132	Don Lee RP	5.00	2.20	.60
☐ 133	Bob Lillis RP	5.00	2.20	.60
☐ 134	Jim McDaniel RP	5.00	2.20	.60
☐ 135	Gene Oliver RP	5.00	2.20	.60
☐ 136	Jim O'Toole RP	5.00	2.20	.60
☐ 137	Dick Ricketts RP	5.00	2.20	.60
☐ 138	John Romano RP	5.00	2.20	.60
☐ 139	Ed Sadowski RP	5.00	2.20	.60
☐ 140	Charlie Secrest RP	5.00	2.20	.60
☐ 141	Joe Shipley RP	5.00	2.20	.60
☐ 142	Dick Stigman RP	5.00	2.20	.60
☐ 143	Willie Tasby RP	5.00	2.20	.60
☐ 144	Jerry Walker RP	5.00	2.20	.60
☐ 145	Dom Zanni RP	5.00	2.20	.60
☐ 146	Jerry Zimmerman RP	5.00	2.20	.60
☐ 147	Cubs Clubbers	25.00	11.00	3.10
	Dale Long			
	Ernie Banks			
	Walt Moryn			
☐ 148	Mike McCormick	5.00	2.20	.60
☐ 149	Jim Bunning	16.00	7.25	2.00
☐ 150	Stan Musial	140.00	65.00	17.50
☐ 151	Bob Malkmus	4.00	1.80	.50
☐ 152	Johnny Klippstein	4.00	1.80	.50
☐ 153	Jim Marshall	4.00	1.80	.50
☐ 154	Ray Herbert	4.00	1.80	.50
☐ 155	Enos Slaughter	20.00	9.00	2.50
☐ 156	Ace Hurlers	10.00	4.50	1.25
	Billy Pierce			
	Robin Roberts			
☐ 157	Felix Mantilla	4.00	1.80	.50
☐ 158	Walt Dropo	4.00	1.80	.50
☐ 159	Bob Shaw	5.00	2.20	.60
☐ 160	Dick Groat	5.00	2.20	.60
☐ 161	Frank Baumann	4.00	1.80	.50
☐ 162	Bobby G. Smith	4.00	1.80	.50
☐ 163	Sandy Koufax	150.00	70.00	19.00
☐ 164	Johnny Groth	4.00	1.80	.50
☐ 165	Bill Bruton	4.00	1.80	.50
☐ 166	Destruction Crew	12.00	5.50	1.50
	Minnie Minoso			
	Rocky Colavito			
	(Misspelled Colovito			
	on card back)			
	Larry Doby			
☐ 167	Duke Maas	4.00	1.80	.50
☐ 168	Carroll Hardy	4.00	1.80	.50
☐ 169	Ted Abernathy	4.00	1.80	.50
☐ 170	Gene Woodling	5.00	2.20	.60
☐ 171	Willard Schmidt	4.00	1.80	.50
☐ 172	Athletics Team	15.00	6.75	1.85
	(Checklist on back)			
☐ 173	Bill Monbouquette	5.00	2.20	.60
☐ 174	Jim Pendleton	4.00	1.80	.50
☐ 175	Dick Farrell	5.00	2.20	.60
☐ 176	Preston Ward	4.00	1.80	.50
☐ 177	John Briggs	4.00	1.80	.50
☐ 178	Ruben Amaro	5.00	2.20	.60
☐ 179	Don Rudolph	4.00	1.80	.50
☐ 180	Yogi Berra	75.00	34.00	9.50
☐ 181	Bob Porterfield	4.00	1.80	.50
☐ 182	Milt Graff	4.00	1.80	.50
☐ 183	Stu Miller	5.00	2.20	.60
☐ 184	Harvey Haddix	5.00	2.20	.60
☐ 185	Jim Busby	4.00	1.80	.50
☐ 186	Mudcat Grant	5.00	2.20	.60
☐ 187	Bubba Phillips	5.00	2.20	.60
☐ 188	Juan Pizarro	4.00	1.80	.50
☐ 189	Neil Chrisley	4.00	1.80	.50
☐ 190	Bill Virdon	4.00	1.80	.50
☐ 191	Russ Kemmerer	4.00	1.80	.50
☐ 192	Charlie Beamon	4.00	1.80	.50
☐ 193	Sammy Taylor	4.00	1.80	.50
☐ 194	Jim Brosnan	5.00	2.20	.60
☐ 195	Rip Repulski	4.00	1.80	.50
☐ 196	Billy Moran	4.00	1.80	.50
☐ 197	Ray Semproch	4.00	1.80	.50
☐ 198	Jim Davenport	5.00	2.20	.60
☐ 199	Leo Kiely	4.00	1.80	.50
☐ 200	Warren Giles	8.00	3.60	1.00
	(NL President)			
☐ 201	Tom Acker	4.00	1.80	.50
☐ 202	Roger Maris	110.00	50.00	14.00
☐ 203	Ossie Virgil	4.00	1.80	.50
☐ 204	Casey Wise	4.00	1.80	.50
☐ 205	Don Larsen	7.00	3.10	.85
☐ 206	Carl Furillo	4.00	1.80	.50
☐ 207	George Strickland	4.00	1.80	.50
☐ 208	Willie Jones	4.00	1.80	.50
☐ 209	Lenny Green	4.00	1.80	.50
☐ 210	Ed Bailey	4.00	1.80	.50
☐ 211	Bob Blaylock	4.00	1.80	.50
☐ 212	Fence Busters	75.00	34.00	9.50
	Hank Aaron			
	Eddie Mathews			
☐ 213	Jim Rivera	5.00	2.20	.60
☐ 214	Marcelino Solis	4.00	1.80	.50
☐ 215	Jim Lemon	5.00	2.20	.60
☐ 216	Andre Rodgers	4.00	1.80	.50
☐ 217	Carl Erskine	5.00	2.20	.60
☐ 218	Roman Mejias	4.00	1.80	.50
☐ 219	George Zuverink	4.00	1.80	.50
☐ 220	Frank Malzone	5.00	2.20	.60
☐ 221	Bob Bowman	4.00	1.80	.50
☐ 222	Bobby Shantz	4.00	1.80	.50
☐ 223	Cardinals Team	15.00	6.75	1.85
	(Checklist on back)			
☐ 224	Claude Osteen	5.00	2.20	.60
☐ 225	Johnny Logan	5.00	2.20	.60
☐ 226	Art Ceccarelli	4.00	1.80	.50
☐ 227	Hal W. Smith	4.00	1.80	.50
☐ 228	Don Gross	4.00	1.80	.50
☐ 229	Vic Power	5.00	2.20	.60
☐ 230	Bill Fischer	4.00	1.80	.50
☐ 231	Ellis Burton	4.00	1.80	.50
☐ 232	Eddie Kasko	4.00	1.80	.50
☐ 233	Paul Foytack	4.00	1.80	.50
☐ 234	Chuck Tanner	5.00	2.20	.60
☐ 235	Valmy Thomas	4.00	1.80	.50
☐ 236	Ted Bowsfield	4.00	1.80	.50
☐ 237	Run Preventers	12.00	5.50	1.50
	Gil McDougald			
	Bob Turley			
	Bobby Richardson			
☐ 238	Gene Baker	4.00	1.80	.50
☐ 239	Bob Trowbridge	4.00	1.80	.50
☐ 240	Hank Bauer	5.00	2.20	.60
☐ 241	Billy Muffett	4.00	1.80	.50
☐ 242	Ron Samford	4.00	1.80	.50
☐ 243	Marv Grissom	4.00	1.80	.50
☐ 244	Ted Gray	4.00	1.80	.50

☐ 245	Ned Garver	4.00	1.80	.50
☐ 246	J.W. Porter	4.00	1.80	.50
☐ 247	Don Ferrarese	4.00	1.80	.50
☐ 248	Red Sox Team	15.00	6.75	1.85
	(Checklist on back)			
☐ 249	Bobby Adams	4.00	1.80	.50
☐ 250	Billy O'Dell	4.00	1.80	.50
☐ 251	Clete Boyer	5.00	2.20	.60
☐ 252	Ray Boone	5.00	2.20	.60
☐ 253	Seth Morehead	4.00	1.80	.50
☐ 254	Zeke Bella	4.00	1.80	.50
☐ 255	Del Ennis	5.00	2.20	.60
☐ 256	Jerry Davie	4.00	1.80	.50
☐ 257	Leon Wagner	5.00	2.20	.60
☐ 258	Fred Kipp	4.00	1.80	.50
☐ 259	Jim Pisoni	4.00	1.80	.50
☐ 260	Early Wynn UER	16.00	7.25	2.00
	(1957 Cleevland)			
☐ 261	Gene Stephens	4.00	1.80	.50
☐ 262	Hitters' Foes	16.00	7.25	2.00
	Johnny Podres			
	Clem Labine			
	Don Drysdale			
☐ 263	Bud Daley	4.00	1.80	.50
☐ 264	Chico Carrasquel	4.00	1.80	.50
☐ 265	Ron Kline	4.00	1.80	.50
☐ 266	Woody Held	4.00	1.80	.50
☐ 267	John Romonosky	4.00	1.80	.50
☐ 268	Tito Francona	5.00	2.20	.60
☐ 269	Jack Meyer	4.00	1.80	.50
☐ 270	Gil Hodges	25.00	11.00	3.10
☐ 271	Orlando Pena	4.00	1.80	.50
☐ 272	Jerry Lumpe	4.00	1.80	.50
☐ 273	Joey Jay	5.00	2.20	.60
☐ 274	Jerry Kindall	5.00	2.20	.60
☐ 275	Jack Sanford	5.00	2.20	.60
☐ 276	Pete Daley	4.00	1.80	.50
☐ 277	Turk Lown	5.00	2.20	.60
☐ 278	Chuck Essegian	4.00	1.80	.50
☐ 279	Ernie Johnson	5.00	2.20	.60
☐ 280	Frank Bolling	4.00	1.80	.50
☐ 281	Walt Craddock	4.00	1.80	.50
☐ 282	R.C. Stevens	4.00	1.80	.50
☐ 283	Russ Heman	4.00	1.80	.50
☐ 284	Steve Korcheck	4.00	1.80	.50
☐ 285	Joe Cunningham	5.00	2.20	.60
☐ 286	Dean Stone	4.00	1.80	.50
☐ 287	Don Zimmer	5.00	2.20	.60
☐ 288	Dutch Dotterer	4.00	1.80	.50
☐ 289	Johnny Kucks	4.00	1.80	.50
☐ 290	Wes Covington	5.00	2.20	.60
☐ 291	Pitching Partners	5.00	2.20	.60
	Pedro Ramos			
	Camilo Pascual			
☐ 292	Dick Williams	5.00	2.20	.60
☐ 293	Ray Moore	4.00	1.80	.50
☐ 294	Hank Foiles	4.00	1.80	.50
☐ 295	Billy Martin	14.00	6.25	1.75
☐ 296	Ernie Broglio	4.00	1.80	.50
☐ 297	Jackie Brandt	4.00	1.80	.50
☐ 298	Tex Clevenger	4.00	1.80	.50
☐ 299	Billy Klaus	4.00	1.80	.50
☐ 300	Richie Ashburn	25.00	11.00	3.10
☐ 301	Earl Averill	4.00	1.80	.50
☐ 302	Don Mossi	5.00	2.20	.60
☐ 303	Marty Keough	4.00	1.80	.50
☐ 304	Cubs Team	15.00	6.75	1.85
	(Checklist on back)			
☐ 305	Curt Raydon	4.00	1.80	.50
☐ 306	Jim Gilliam	5.00	2.20	.60
☐ 307	Curt Barclay	4.00	1.80	.50

☐ 308	Norm Siebern	4.00	1.80	.50
☐ 309	Sal Maglie	5.00	2.20	.60
☐ 310	Luis Aparicio	20.00	9.00	2.50
☐ 311	Norm Zauchin	4.00	1.80	.50
☐ 312	Don Newcombe	5.00	2.20	.60
☐ 313	Frank House	4.00	1.80	.50
☐ 314	Don Cardwell	4.00	1.80	.50
☐ 315	Joe Adcock	5.00	2.20	.60
☐ 316A	Ralph Lumenti UER	4.00	1.80	.50
	(Option)			
	(Photo actually			
	Camilo Pascual)			
☐ 316B	Ralph Lumenti UER	80.00	36.00	10.00
	(No option)			
	(Photo actually			
	Camilo Pascual)			
☐ 317	Hitting Kings	65.00	29.00	8.00
	Willie Mays			
	Richie Ashburn			
☐ 318	Rocky Bridges	4.00	1.80	.50
☐ 319	Dave Hillman	4.00	1.80	.50
☐ 320	Bob Skinner	5.00	2.20	.60
☐ 321A	Bob Giallombardo	4.00	1.80	.50
	(Option)			
☐ 321B	Bob Giallombardo	80.00	36.00	10.00
	(No option)			
☐ 322A	Harry Hanebrink	4.00	1.80	.50
	(Traded)			
☐ 322B	Harry Hanebrink	80.00	36.00	10.00
	(No trade)			
☐ 323	Frank Sullivan	4.00	1.80	.50
☐ 324	Don Demeter	4.00	1.80	.50
☐ 325	Ken Boyer	10.00	4.50	1.25
☐ 326	Marv Throneberry	5.00	2.20	.60
☐ 327	Gary Bell	4.00	1.80	.50
☐ 328	Lou Skizas	4.00	1.80	.50
☐ 329	Tigers Team	15.00	6.75	1.85
	(Checklist on back)			
☐ 330	Gus Triandos	5.00	2.20	.60
☐ 331	Steve Boros	4.00	1.80	.50
☐ 332	Ray Monzant	4.00	1.80	.50
☐ 333	Harry Simpson	4.00	1.80	.50
☐ 334	Glen Hobbie	4.00	1.80	.50
☐ 335	Johnny Temple	5.00	2.20	.60
☐ 336A	Billy Loes	5.00	2.20	.60
	(With traded line)			
☐ 336B	Billy Loes	80.00	36.00	10.00
	(No trade)			
☐ 337	George Crowe	4.00	1.80	.50
☐ 338	Sparky Anderson	90.00	40.00	11.00
☐ 339	Roy Face	4.00	1.80	.50
☐ 340	Roy Sievers	5.00	2.20	.60
☐ 341	Tom Qualters	4.00	1.80	.50
☐ 342	Ray Jablonski	4.00	1.80	.50
☐ 343	Billy Hoeft	4.00	1.80	.50
☐ 344	Russ Nixon	4.00	1.80	.50
☐ 345	Gil McDougald	8.00	3.60	1.00
☐ 346	Batter Bafflers	4.00	1.80	.50
	Dave Sisler			
	Tom Brewer			
☐ 347	Bob Buhl	5.00	2.20	.60
☐ 348	Ted Lepcio	4.00	1.80	.50
☐ 349	Hoyt Wilhelm	16.00	7.25	2.00
☐ 350	Ernie Banks	75.00	34.00	9.50
☐ 351	Earl Torgeson	4.00	1.80	.50
☐ 352	Robin Roberts	20.00	9.00	2.50
☐ 353	Curt Flood	5.00	2.20	.60
☐ 354	Pete Burnside	4.00	1.80	.50
☐ 355	Jim Piersall	5.00	2.20	.60
☐ 356	Bob Mabe	4.00	1.80	.50
☐ 357	Dick Stuart	5.00	2.20	.60

☐	358	Ralph Terry	5.00	2.20	.60
☐	359	Bill White	25.00	11.00	3.10
☐	360	Al Kaline	65.00	29.00	8.00
☐	361	Willard Nixon	4.00	1.80	.50
☐	362A	Dolan Nichols	4.00	1.80	.50
		(With option line)			
☐	362B	Dolan Nichols	80.00	36.00	10.00
		(No option)			
☐	363	Bobby Avila	4.00	1.80	.50
☐	364	Danny McDevitt	4.00	1.80	.50
☐	365	Gus Bell	5.00	2.20	.60
☐	366	Humberto Robinson	4.00	1.80	.50
☐	367	Cal Neeman	4.00	1.80	.50
☐	368	Don Mueller	5.00	2.20	.60
☐	369	Dick Tomanek	4.00	1.80	.50
☐	370	Pete Runnels	5.00	2.20	.60
☐	371	Dick Brodowski	4.00	1.80	.50
☐	372	Jim Hegan	5.00	2.20	.60
☐	373	Herb Plews	4.00	1.80	.50
☐	374	Art Ditmar	4.00	1.80	.50
☐	375	Bob Nieman	4.00	1.80	.50
☐	376	Hal Naragon	4.00	1.80	.50
☐	377	John Antonelli	5.00	2.20	.60
☐	378	Gail Harris	4.00	1.80	.50
☐	379	Bob Miller	4.00	1.80	.50
☐	380	Hank Aaron	125.00	55.00	15.50
☐	381	Mike Baxes	4.00	1.80	.50
☐	382	Curt Simmons	5.00	2.20	.60
☐	383	Words of Wisdom	12.00	5.50	1.50
		Don Larsen			
		Casey Stengel MG			
☐	384	Dave Sisler	4.00	1.80	.50
☐	385	Sherm Lollar	5.00	2.20	.60
☐	386	Jim Delsing	4.00	1.80	.50
☐	387	Don Drysdale	35.00	16.00	4.40
☐	388	Bob Will	4.00	1.80	.50
☐	389	Joe Nuxhall	5.00	2.20	.60
☐	390	Orlando Cepeda	16.00	7.25	2.00
☐	391	Milt Pappas	5.00	2.20	.60
☐	392	Whitey Herzog	5.00	2.20	.60
☐	393	Frank Lary	5.00	2.20	.60
☐	394	Randy Jackson	4.00	1.80	.50
☐	395	Elston Howard	10.00	4.50	1.25
☐	396	Bob Rush	4.00	1.80	.50
☐	397	Senators Team	15.00	6.75	1.85
		(Checklist on back)			
☐	398	Wally Post	5.00	2.20	.60
☐	399	Larry Jackson	4.00	1.80	.50
☐	400	Jackie Jensen	5.00	2.20	.60
☐	401	Ron Blackburn	4.00	1.80	.50
☐	402	Hector Lopez	5.00	2.20	.60
☐	403	Clem Labine	5.00	2.20	.60
☐	404	Hank Sauer	5.00	2.20	.60
☐	405	Roy McMillan	5.00	2.20	.60
☐	406	Solly Drake	4.00	1.80	.50
☐	407	Moe Drabowsky	5.00	2.20	.60
☐	408	Keystone Combo	18.00	8.00	2.20
		Nellie Fox			
		Luis Aparicio			
☐	409	Gus Zernial	5.00	2.20	.60
☐	410	Billy Pierce	5.00	2.20	.60
☐	411	Whitey Lockman	5.00	2.20	.60
☐	412	Stan Lopata	4.00	1.80	.50
☐	413	Camilo Pascual UER	5.00	2.20	.60
		(Listed as Camillo			
		on front and Pasqual			
		on back)			
☐	414	Dale Long	5.00	2.20	.60
☐	415	Bill Mazeroski	12.00	5.50	1.50
☐	416	Haywood Sullivan	5.00	2.20	.60
☐	417	Virgil Trucks	5.00	2.20	.60
☐	418	Gino Cimoli	4.00	1.80	.50
☐	419	Braves Team	15.00	6.75	1.85
		(Checklist on back)			
☐	420	Rocky Colavito	30.00	13.50	3.70
☐	421	Herman Wehmeier	4.00	1.80	.50
☐	422	Hobie Landrith	4.00	1.80	.50
☐	423	Bob Grim	5.00	2.20	.60
☐	424	Ken Aspromonte	4.00	1.80	.50
☐	425	Del Crandall	5.00	2.20	.60
☐	426	Gerry Staley	5.00	2.20	.60
☐	427	Charlie Neal	5.00	2.20	.60
☐	428	Buc Hill Aces	5.00	2.20	.60
		Ron Kline			
		Bob Friend			
		Vernon Law			
		Roy Face			
☐	429	Bobby Thomson	4.00	1.80	.50
☐	430	Whitey Ford	40.00	18.00	5.00
☐	431	Whammy Douglas	4.00	1.80	.50
☐	432	Smoky Burgess	5.00	2.20	.60
☐	433	Billy Harrell	4.00	1.80	.50
☐	434	Hal Griggs	4.00	1.80	.50
☐	435	Frank Robinson	50.00	22.00	6.25
☐	436	Granny Hamner	4.00	1.80	.50
☐	437	Ike Delock	4.00	1.80	.50
☐	438	Sammy Esposito	4.00	1.80	.50
☐	439	Brooks Robinson	50.00	22.00	6.25
☐	440	Lou Burdette	8.00	3.60	1.00
		(Posing as if			
		lefthanded)			
☐	441	John Roseboro	5.00	2.20	.60
☐	442	Ray Narleski	4.00	1.80	.50
☐	443	Daryl Spencer	4.00	1.80	.50
☐	444	Ron Hansen	5.00	2.20	.60
☐	445	Cal McLish	4.00	1.80	.50
☐	446	Rocky Nelson	4.00	1.80	.50
☐	447	Bob Anderson	4.00	1.80	.50
☐	448	Vada Pinson UER	10.00	4.50	1.25
		(Born: 8/8/38,			
		should be 8/11/38)			
☐	449	Tom Gorman	4.00	1.80	.50
☐	450	Eddie Mathews	30.00	13.50	3.70
☐	451	Jimmy Constable	4.00	1.80	.50
☐	452	Chico Fernandez	4.00	1.80	.50
☐	453	Les Moss	4.00	1.80	.50
☐	454	Phil Clark	4.00	1.80	.50
☐	455	Larry Doby	5.00	2.20	.60
☐	456	Jerry Casale	4.00	1.80	.50
☐	457	Dodgers Team	25.00	11.00	3.10
		(Checklist on back)			
☐	458	Gordon Jones	4.00	1.80	.50
☐	459	Bill Tuttle	4.00	1.80	.50
☐	460	Bob Friend	5.00	2.20	.60
☐	461	Mickey Mantle Hits Homer	125.00	55.00	15.50
☐	462	Rocky Colavito's Catch	12.00	5.50	1.50
☐	463	Al Kaline Batting Champ	18.00	8.00	2.20
☐	464	Willie Mays' Series Catch	35.00	16.00	4.40
☐	465	Roy Sievers Sets Mark	5.00	2.20	.60
☐	466	Billy Pierce All-Star	5.00	2.20	.60
☐	467	Hank Aaron Clubs Homer	30.00	13.50	3.70
☐	468	Duke Snider's Play	18.00	8.00	2.20
☐	469	Hustler Ernie Banks	18.00	8.00	2.20
☐	470	Stan Musial's 3000th Hit	20.00	9.00	2.50
☐	471	Tom Sturdivant	4.00	1.80	.50
☐	472	Gene Freese	4.00	1.80	.50

☐ 473	Mike Fornieles	4.00	1.80	.50
☐ 474	Moe Thacker	4.00	1.80	.50
☐ 475	Jack Harshman	4.00	1.80	.50
☐ 476	Indians Team (Checklist on back)	15.00	6.75	1.85
☐ 477	Barry Latman	4.00	1.80	.50
☐ 478	Bob Clemente	150.00	70.00	19.00
☐ 479	Lindy McDaniel	5.00	2.20	.60
☐ 480	Red Schoendienst	14.00	6.25	1.75
☐ 481	Charlie Maxwell	5.00	2.20	.60
☐ 482	Russ Meyer	4.00	1.80	.50
☐ 483	Clint Courtney	4.00	1.80	.50
☐ 484	Willie Kirkland	4.00	1.80	.50
☐ 485	Ryne Duren	7.00	3.10	.85
☐ 486	Sammy White	4.00	1.80	.50
☐ 487	Hal Brown	4.00	1.80	.50
☐ 488	Walt Moryn	4.00	1.80	.50
☐ 489	John Powers	4.00	1.80	.50
☐ 490	Frank Thomas	5.00	2.20	.60
☐ 491	Don Blasingame	4.00	1.80	.50
☐ 492	Gene Conley	5.00	2.20	.60
☐ 493	Jim Landis	5.00	2.20	.60
☐ 494	Don Pavletich	4.00	1.80	.50
☐ 495	Johnny Podres	5.00	2.20	.60
☐ 496	Wayne Terwilliger UER (Athlitics on front)	4.00	1.80	.50
☐ 497	Hal R. Smith	4.00	1.80	.50
☐ 498	Dick Hyde	4.00	1.80	.50
☐ 499	Johnny O'Brien	5.00	2.20	.60
☐ 500	Vic Wertz	5.00	2.20	.60
☐ 501	Bob Tiefenauer	4.00	1.80	.50
☐ 502	Alvin Dark	5.00	2.20	.60
☐ 503	Jim Owens	4.00	1.80	.50
☐ 504	Ossie Alvarez	4.00	1.80	.50
☐ 505	Tony Kubek	10.00	4.50	1.25
☐ 506	Bob Purkey	4.00	1.80	.50
☐ 507	Bob Hale	16.00	7.25	2.00
☐ 508	Art Fowler	16.00	7.25	2.00
☐ 509	Norm Cash	65.00	29.00	8.00
☐ 510	Yankees Team (Checklist on back)	120.00	55.00	15.00
☐ 511	George Susce	16.00	7.25	2.00
☐ 512	George Altman	16.00	7.25	2.00
☐ 513	Tommy Carroll	16.00	7.25	2.00
☐ 514	Bob Gibson	240.00	110.00	30.00
☐ 515	Harmon Killebrew	125.00	55.00	15.50
☐ 516	Mike Garcia	18.00	8.00	2.20
☐ 517	Joe Koppe	16.00	7.25	2.00
☐ 518	Mike Cueller UER (Sic, Cuellar)	30.00	13.50	3.70
☐ 519	Infield Power Pete Runnels Dick Gernert Frank Malzone	18.00	8.00	2.20
☐ 520	Don Elston	16.00	7.25	2.00
☐ 521	Gary Geiger	16.00	7.25	2.00
☐ 522	Gene Snyder	16.00	7.25	2.00
☐ 523	Harry Bright	16.00	7.25	2.00
☐ 524	Larry Osborne	16.00	7.25	2.00
☐ 525	Jim Coates	18.00	8.00	2.20
☐ 526	Bob Speake	16.00	7.25	2.00
☐ 527	Solly Hemus	16.00	7.25	2.00
☐ 528	Pirates Team (Checklist on back)	65.00	29.00	8.00
☐ 529	George Bamberger	20.00	9.00	2.50
☐ 530	Wally Moon	18.00	8.00	2.20
☐ 531	Ray Webster	16.00	7.25	2.00
☐ 532	Mark Freeman	16.00	7.25	2.00
☐ 533	Darrell Johnson	18.00	8.00	2.20
☐ 534	Faye Throneberry	16.00	7.25	2.00
☐ 535	Ruben Gomez	16.00	7.25	2.00

☐ 536	Danny Kravitz	16.00	7.25	2.00
☐ 537	Rudolph Arias	16.00	7.25	2.00
☐ 538	Chick King	16.00	7.25	2.00
☐ 539	Gary Blaylock	16.00	7.25	2.00
☐ 540	Willie Miranda	16.00	7.25	2.00
☐ 541	Bob Thurman	16.00	7.25	2.00
☐ 542	Jim Perry	30.00	13.50	3.70
☐ 543	Corsair Trio Bob Skinner Bill Virdon Roberto Clemente	140.00	65.00	17.50
☐ 544	Lee Tate	16.00	7.25	2.00
☐ 545	Tom Morgan	16.00	7.25	2.00
☐ 546	Al Schroll	16.00	7.25	2.00
☐ 547	Jim Baxes	16.00	7.25	2.00
☐ 548	Elmer Singleton	16.00	7.25	2.00
☐ 549	Howie Nunn	16.00	7.25	2.00
☐ 550	Roy Campanella (Symbol of Courage)	170.00	75.00	21.00
☐ 551	Fred Haney AS MG	16.00	7.25	2.00
☐ 552	Casey Stengel AS MG	35.00	16.00	4.40
☐ 553	Orlando Cepeda AS	25.00	11.00	3.10
☐ 554	Bill Skowron AS	25.00	11.00	3.10
☐ 555	Bill Mazeroski AS	25.00	11.00	3.10
☐ 556	Nellie Fox AS	25.00	11.00	3.10
☐ 557	Ken Boyer AS	25.00	11.00	3.10
☐ 558	Frank Malzone AS	16.00	7.25	2.00
☐ 559	Ernie Banks AS	65.00	29.00	8.00
☐ 560	Luis Aparicio AS	30.00	13.50	3.70
☐ 561	Hank Aaron AS	125.00	55.00	15.50
☐ 562	Al Kaline AS	65.00	29.00	8.00
☐ 563	Willie Mays AS	125.00	55.00	15.50
☐ 564	Mickey Mantle AS	325.00	145.00	40.00
☐ 565	Wes Covington AS	16.00	7.25	2.00
☐ 566	Roy Sievers AS	16.00	7.25	2.00
☐ 567	Del Crandall AS	16.00	7.25	2.00
☐ 568	Gus Triandos AS	16.00	7.25	2.00
☐ 569	Bob Friend AS	16.00	7.25	2.00
☐ 570	Bob Turley AS	16.00	7.25	2.00
☐ 571	Warren Spahn AS	40.00	18.00	5.00
☐ 572	Billy Pierce AS	25.00	8.00	2.50

1960 Topps

The cards in this 572-card set measure 2 1/2" by 3 1/2". The 1960 Topps set is the only Topps standard size issue to use a horizontally oriented front. World Series cards appeared for the first time (385 to 391), and there is a Rookie Prospect (RP) series (117-148), the most famous of which is Carl Yastrzemski, and a Sport Magazine All-Star Selection (AS) series (553-572).

There are 16 manager cards listed alpha-betically from 212 through 227. The 1959 Topps All-Rookie team is featured on cards 316-325. The coaching staff of each team was also afforded their own card in a 16-card subset (455-470). Cards 375 to 440 come with either gray or white backs, and the high series (507-572) were printed on a more limited basis than the rest of the set. The team cards have series checklists on the reverse. The key Rookie Cards in this set are Willie McCovey and Carl Yastrzemski.

	NRMT	VG-E	GOOD
COMPLETE SET (572)	3500.00	1600.00	450.00
COMMON CARD (1-440)	4.00	1.80	.50
COMMON CARD (441-506)	7.00	3.10	.85
COMMON CARD (507-552)	16.00	7.25	2.00
COMMON AS (553-572)	16.00	7.25	2.00

		NRMT	VG-E	GOOD
☐ 1	Early Wynn	30.00	7.50	3.00
☐ 2	Roman Mejias	4.00	1.80	.50
☐ 3	Joe Adcock	5.00	2.20	.60
☐ 4	Bob Purkey	4.00	1.80	.50
☐ 5	Wally Moon	5.00	2.20	.60
☐ 6	Lou Berberet	4.00	1.80	.50
☐ 7	Master and Mentor	20.00	9.00	2.50
	Willie Mays			
	Bill Rigney MG			
☐ 8	Bud Daley	4.00	1.80	.50
☐ 9	Faye Throneberry	4.00	1.80	.50
☐ 10	Ernie Banks	50.00	22.00	6.25
☐ 11	Norm Siebern	4.00	1.80	.50
☐ 12	Milt Pappas	5.00	2.20	.60
☐ 13	Wally Post	5.00	2.20	.60
☐ 14	Jim Grant	5.00	2.20	.60
☐ 15	Pete Runnels	5.00	2.20	.60
☐ 16	Ernie Broglio	5.00	2.20	.60
☐ 17	Johnny Callison	4.00	1.80	.50
☐ 18	Dodgers Team	35.00	16.00	4.40
	(Checklist on back)			
☐ 19	Felix Mantilla	4.00	1.80	.50
☐ 20	Roy Face	5.00	2.20	.60
☐ 21	Dutch Dotterer	4.00	1.80	.50
☐ 22	Rocky Bridges	4.00	1.80	.50
☐ 23	Eddie Fisher	4.00	1.80	.50
☐ 24	Dick Gray	4.00	1.80	.50
☐ 25	Roy Sievers	5.00	2.20	.60
☐ 26	Wayne Terwilliger	4.00	1.80	.50
☐ 27	Dick Drott	4.00	1.80	.50
☐ 28	Brooks Robinson	50.00	22.00	6.25
☐ 29	Clem Labine	5.00	2.20	.60
☐ 30	Tito Francona	4.00	1.80	.50
☐ 31	Sammy Esposito	4.00	1.80	.50
☐ 32	Sophomore Stalwarts	4.00	1.80	.50
	Jim O'Toole			
	Vada Pinson			
☐ 33	Tom Morgan	4.00	1.80	.50
☐ 34	Sparky Anderson	20.00	9.00	2.50
☐ 35	Whitey Ford	50.00	22.00	6.25
☐ 36	Russ Nixon	4.00	1.80	.50
☐ 37	Bill Bruton	4.00	1.80	.50
☐ 38	Jerry Casale	4.00	1.80	.50
☐ 39	Earl Averill	4.00	1.80	.50
☐ 40	Joe Cunningham	5.00	2.20	.60
☐ 41	Barry Latman	4.00	1.80	.50
☐ 42	Hobie Landrith	4.00	1.80	.50
☐ 43	Senators Team	10.00	4.50	1.25
	(Checklist on back)			
☐ 44	Bobby Locke	4.00	1.80	.50

		NRMT	VG-E	GOOD
☐ 45	Roy McMillan	5.00	2.20	.60
☐ 46	Jerry Fisher	4.00	1.80	.50
☐ 47	Don Zimmer	5.00	2.20	.60
☐ 48	Hal W. Smith	4.00	1.80	.50
☐ 49	Curt Raydon	4.00	1.80	.50
☐ 50	Al Kaline	50.00	22.00	6.25
☐ 51	Jim Coates	4.00	1.80	.50
☐ 52	Dave Philley	4.00	1.80	.50
☐ 53	Jackie Brandt	4.00	1.80	.50
☐ 54	Mike Fornieles	4.00	1.80	.50
☐ 55	Bill Mazeroski	10.00	4.50	1.25
☐ 56	Steve Korcheck	4.00	1.80	.50
☐ 57	Win Savers	4.00	1.80	.50
	Turk Lown			
	Gerry Staley			
☐ 58	Gino Cimoli	4.00	1.80	.50
☐ 59	Juan Pizarro	4.00	1.80	.50
☐ 60	Gus Triandos	5.00	2.20	.60
☐ 61	Eddie Kasko	4.00	1.80	.50
☐ 62	Roger Craig	4.00	1.80	.50
☐ 63	George Strickland	4.00	1.80	.50
☐ 64	Jack Meyer	4.00	1.80	.50
☐ 65	Elston Howard	6.00	2.70	.75
☐ 66	Bob Trowbridge	4.00	1.80	.50
☐ 67	Jose Pagan	4.00	1.80	.50
☐ 68	Dave Hillman	4.00	1.80	.50
☐ 69	Billy Goodman	5.00	2.20	.60
☐ 70	Lew Burdette	4.00	1.80	.50
☐ 71	Marty Keough	4.00	1.80	.50
☐ 72	Tigers Team	18.00	8.00	2.20
	(Checklist on back)			
☐ 73	Bob Gibson	45.00	20.00	5.50
☐ 74	Walt Moryn	4.00	1.80	.50
☐ 75	Vic Power	5.00	2.20	.60
☐ 76	Bill Fischer	4.00	1.80	.50
☐ 77	Hank Foiles	4.00	1.80	.50
☐ 78	Bob Grim	4.00	1.80	.50
☐ 79	Walt Dropo	4.00	1.80	.50
☐ 80	Johnny Antonelli	5.00	2.20	.60
☐ 81	Russ Snyder	4.00	1.80	.50
☐ 82	Ruben Gomez	4.00	1.80	.50
☐ 83	Tony Kubek	6.00	2.70	.75
☐ 84	Hal R. Smith	4.00	1.80	.50
☐ 85	Frank Lary	5.00	2.20	.60
☐ 86	Dick Gernert	4.00	1.80	.50
☐ 87	John Romonosky	4.00	1.80	.50
☐ 88	John Roseboro	5.00	2.20	.60
☐ 89	Hal Brown	4.00	1.80	.50
☐ 90	Bobby Avila	4.00	1.80	.50
☐ 91	Bennie Daniels	4.00	1.80	.50
☐ 92	Whitey Herzog	5.00	2.20	.60
☐ 93	Art Schult	4.00	1.80	.50
☐ 94	Leo Kiely	4.00	1.80	.50
☐ 95	Frank Thomas	5.00	2.20	.60
☐ 96	Ralph Terry	5.00	2.20	.60
☐ 97	Ted Lepcio	4.00	1.80	.50
☐ 98	Gordon Jones	4.00	1.80	.50
☐ 99	Lenny Green	4.00	1.80	.50
☐ 100	Nellie Fox	12.00	5.50	1.50
☐ 101	Bob Miller	4.00	1.80	.50
☐ 102	Kent Hadley	4.00	1.80	.50
☐ 103	Dick Farrell	5.00	2.20	.60
☐ 104	Dick Schofield	5.00	2.20	.60
☐ 105	Larry Sherry	8.00	3.60	1.00
☐ 106	Billy Gardner	4.00	1.80	.50
☐ 107	Carlton Willey	4.00	1.80	.50
☐ 108	Pete Daley	4.00	1.80	.50
☐ 109	Clete Boyer	5.00	2.20	.60
☐ 110	Cal McLish	4.00	1.80	.50
☐ 111	Vic Wertz	5.00	2.20	.60
☐ 112	Jack Harshman	4.00	1.80	.50

113	Bob Skinner	4.00	1.80	.50
114	Ken Aspromonte	4.00	1.80	.50
115	Fork and Knuckler	6.00	2.70	.75
	Roy Face			
	Hoyt Wilhelm			
116	Jim Rivera	4.00	1.80	.50
117	Tom Borland RP	4.00	1.80	.50
118	Bob Bruce RP	4.00	1.80	.50
119	Chico Cardenas RP	5.00	2.20	.60
120	Duke Carmel RP	4.00	1.80	.50
121	Camilo Carreon RP	4.00	1.80	.50
122	Don Dillard RP	4.00	1.80	.50
123	Dan Dobbek RP	4.00	1.80	.50
124	Jim Donohue RP	4.00	1.80	.50
125	Dick Ellsworth RP	5.00	2.20	.60
126	Chuck Estrada RP	4.00	1.80	.50
127	Ron Hansen RP	5.00	2.20	.60
128	Bill Harris RP	4.00	1.80	.50
129	Bob Hartman RP	4.00	1.80	.50
130	Frank Herrera RP	4.00	1.80	.50
131	Ed Hobaugh RP	4.00	1.80	.50
132	Frank Howard RP	20.00	9.00	2.50
133	Manuel Javier RP	5.00	2.20	.60
	(Sic, Julian)			
134	Deron Johnson RP	5.00	2.20	.60
135	Ken Johnson RP	4.00	1.80	.50
136	Jim Kaat RP	40.00	18.00	5.00
137	Lou Klimchock RP	4.00	1.80	.50
138	Art Mahaffey RP	5.00	2.20	.60
139	Carl Mathias RP	4.00	1.80	.50
140	Julio Navarro RP	4.00	1.80	.50
141	Jim Proctor RP	4.00	1.80	.50
142	Bill Short RP	4.00	1.80	.50
143	Al Spangler RP	4.00	1.80	.50
144	Al Stieglitz RP	4.00	1.80	.50
145	Jim Umbricht RP	4.00	1.80	.50
146	Ted Wieand RP	4.00	1.80	.50
147	Bob Will RP	4.00	1.80	.50
148	Carl Yastrzemski RP	140.00	65.00	17.50
149	Bob Nieman	4.00	1.80	.50
150	Billy Pierce	5.00	2.20	.60
151	Giants Team	10.00	2.00	1.00
	(Checklist on back)			
152	Gail Harris	4.00	1.80	.50
153	Bobby Thomson	5.00	2.20	.60
154	Jim Davenport	5.00	2.20	.60
155	Charlie Neal	5.00	2.20	.60
156	Art Ceccarelli	4.00	1.80	.50
157	Rocky Nelson	4.00	1.80	.50
158	Wes Covington	5.00	2.20	.60
159	Jim Piersall	4.00	1.80	.50
160	Rival All-Stars	100.00	45.00	12.50
	Mickey Mantle			
	Ken Boyer			
161	Ray Narleski	4.00	1.80	.50
162	Sammy Taylor	4.00	1.80	.50
163	Hector Lopez	5.00	2.20	.60
164	Reds Team	10.00	2.00	1.00
	(Checklist on back)			
165	Jack Sanford	5.00	2.20	.60
166	Chuck Essegian	4.00	1.80	.50
167	Valmy Thomas	4.00	1.80	.50
168	Alex Grammas	4.00	1.80	.50
169	Jake Striker	4.00	1.80	.50
170	Del Crandall	5.00	2.20	.60
171	Johnny Groth	4.00	1.80	.50
172	Willie Kirkland	4.00	1.80	.50
173	Billy Martin	10.00	4.50	1.25
174	Indians Team	10.00	2.00	1.00
	(Checklist on back)			
175	Pedro Ramos	4.00	1.80	.50
176	Vada Pinson	6.00	2.70	.75
177	Johnny Kucks	4.00	1.80	.50
178	Woody Held	4.00	1.80	.50
179	Rip Coleman	4.00	1.80	.50
180	Harry Simpson	4.00	1.80	.50
181	Billy Loes	5.00	2.20	.60
182	Glen Hobbie	4.00	1.80	.50
183	Eli Grba	4.00	1.80	.50
184	Gary Geiger	4.00	1.80	.50
185	Jim Owens	4.00	1.80	.50
186	Dave Sisler	4.00	1.80	.50
187	Jay Hook	4.00	1.80	.50
188	Dick Williams	5.00	2.20	.60
189	Don McMahon	4.00	1.80	.50
190	Gene Woodling	5.00	2.20	.60
191	Johnny Klippstein	4.00	1.80	.50
192	Danny O'Connell	4.00	1.80	.50
193	Dick Hyde	4.00	1.80	.50
194	Bobby Gene Smith	4.00	1.80	.50
195	Lindy McDaniel	5.00	2.20	.60
196	Andy Carey	5.00	2.20	.60
197	Ron Kline	4.00	1.80	.50
198	Jerry Lynch	5.00	2.20	.60
199	Dick Donovan	5.00	2.20	.60
200	Willie Mays	90.00	40.00	11.00
201	Larry Osborne	4.00	1.80	.50
202	Fred Kipp	4.00	1.80	.50
203	Sammy White	4.00	1.80	.50
204	Ryne Duren	5.00	2.20	.60
205	Johnny Logan	5.00	2.20	.60
206	Claude Osteen	5.00	2.20	.60
207	Bob Boyd	4.00	1.80	.50
208	White Sox Team	10.00	4.50	1.25
	(Checklist on back)			
209	Ron Blackburn	4.00	1.80	.50
210	Harmon Killebrew	25.00	11.00	3.10
211	Taylor Phillips	4.00	1.80	.50
212	Walt Alston MG	12.00	5.50	1.50
213	Chuck Dressen MG	5.00	2.20	.60
214	Jimmy Dykes MG	5.00	2.20	.60
215	Bob Elliott MG	5.00	2.20	.60
216	Joe Gordon MG	5.00	2.20	.60
217	Charlie Grimm MG	5.00	2.20	.60
218	Solly Hemus MG	4.00	1.80	.50
219	Fred Hutchinson MG	5.00	2.20	.60
220	Billy Jurges MG	4.00	1.80	.50
221	Cookie Lavagetto MG	4.00	1.80	.50
222	Al Lopez MG	5.00	2.20	.60
223	Danny Murtaugh MG	4.00	1.80	.50
224	Paul Richards MG	5.00	2.20	.60
225	Bill Rigney MG	4.00	1.80	.50
226	Eddie Sawyer MG	4.00	1.80	.50
227	Casey Stengel MG	16.00	7.25	2.00
228	Ernie Johnson	5.00	2.20	.60
229	Joe M. Morgan	4.00	1.80	.50
230	Mound Magicians	12.00	5.50	1.50
	Lou Burdette			
	Warren Spahn			
	Bob Buhl			
231	Hal Naragon	4.00	1.80	.50
232	Jim Busby	4.00	1.80	.50
233	Don Elston	4.00	1.80	.50
234	Don Demeter	4.00	1.80	.50
235	Gus Bell	5.00	2.20	.60
236	Dick Ricketts	4.00	1.80	.50
237	Elmer Valo	4.00	1.80	.50
238	Danny Kravitz	4.00	1.80	.50
239	Joe Shipley	4.00	1.80	.50
240	Luis Aparicio	14.00	6.25	1.75
241	Albie Pearson	5.00	2.20	.60
242	Cardinals Team	10.00	4.50	1.25

(Checklist on back)

☐ 243	Bubba Phillips	4.00	1.80	.50
☐ 244	Hal Griggs	4.00	1.80	.50
☐ 245	Eddie Yost	5.00	2.20	.60
☐ 246	Lee Maye	5.00	2.20	.60
☐ 247	Gil McDougald	5.00	2.20	.60
☐ 248	Del Rice	4.00	1.80	.50
☐ 249	Earl Wilson	5.00	2.20	.60
☐ 250	Stan Musial	100.00	45.00	12.50
☐ 251	Bob Malkmus	4.00	1.80	.50
☐ 252	Ray Herbert	4.00	1.80	.50
☐ 253	Eddie Bressoud	4.00	1.80	.50
☐ 254	Arnie Portocarrero	4.00	1.80	.50
☐ 255	Jim Gilliam	5.00	2.20	.60
☐ 256	Dick Brown	4.00	1.80	.50
☐ 257	Gordy Coleman	4.00	1.80	.50
☐ 258	Dick Groat	5.00	2.20	.60
☐ 259	George Altman	4.00	1.80	.50
☐ 260	Power Plus	12.00	5.50	1.50
	Rocky Colavito			
	Tito Francona			
☐ 261	Pete Burnside	4.00	1.80	.50
☐ 262	Hank Bauer	4.00	1.80	.50
☐ 263	Darrell Johnson	4.00	1.80	.50
☐ 264	Robin Roberts	14.00	6.25	1.75
☐ 265	Rip Repulski	4.00	1.80	.50
☐ 266	Joey Jay	5.00	2.20	.60
☐ 267	Jim Marshall	4.00	1.80	.50
☐ 268	Al Worthington	4.00	1.80	.50
☐ 269	Gene Green	4.00	1.80	.50
☐ 270	Bob Turley	5.00	1.80	.50
☐ 271	Julio Becquer	4.00	1.80	.50
☐ 272	Fred Green	4.00	1.80	.50
☐ 273	Neil Chrisley	4.00	1.80	.50
☐ 274	Tom Acker	4.00	1.80	.50
☐ 275	Curt Flood	5.00	2.20	.60
☐ 276	Ken McBride	4.00	1.80	.50
☐ 277	Harry Bright	4.00	1.80	.50
☐ 278	Stan Williams	5.00	2.20	.60
☐ 279	Chuck Tanner	5.00	2.20	.60
☐ 280	Frank Sullivan	4.00	1.80	.50
☐ 281	Ray Boone	5.00	2.20	.60
☐ 282	Joe Nuxhall	5.00	2.20	.60
☐ 283	John Blanchard	4.00	1.80	.50
☐ 284	Don Gross	4.00	1.80	.50
☐ 285	Harry Anderson	4.00	1.80	.50
☐ 286	Ray Semproch	4.00	1.80	.50
☐ 287	Felipe Alou	6.00	2.70	.75
☐ 288	Bob Mabe	4.00	1.80	.50
☐ 289	Willie Jones	4.00	1.80	.50
☐ 290	Jerry Lumpe	4.00	1.80	.50
☐ 291	Bob Keegan	4.00	1.80	.50
☐ 292	Dodger Backstops	5.00	2.20	.60
	Joe Pignatano			
	John Roseboro			
☐ 293	Gene Conley	5.00	2.20	.60
☐ 294	Tony Taylor	5.00	2.20	.60
☐ 295	Gil Hodges	18.00	8.00	2.20
☐ 296	Nelson Chittum	4.00	1.80	.50
☐ 297	Reno Bertoia	4.00	1.80	.50
☐ 298	George Witt	4.00	1.80	.50
☐ 299	Earl Torgeson	4.00	1.80	.50
☐ 300	Hank Aaron	90.00	40.00	11.00
☐ 301	Jerry Davie	4.00	1.80	.50
☐ 302	Phillies Team	10.00	4.50	1.25
	(Checklist on back)			
☐ 303	Billy O'Dell	4.00	1.80	.50
☐ 304	Joe Ginsberg	4.00	1.80	.50
☐ 305	Richie Ashburn	18.00	8.00	2.20
☐ 306	Frank Baumann	4.00	1.80	.50
☐ 307	Gene Oliver	4.00	1.80	.50

☐ 308	Dick Hall	4.00	1.80	.50
☐ 309	Bob Hale	4.00	1.80	.50
☐ 310	Frank Malzone	5.00	2.20	.60
☐ 311	Raul Sanchez	4.00	1.80	.50
☐ 312	Charley Lau	5.00	2.20	.60
☐ 313	Turk Lown	4.00	1.80	.50
☐ 314	Chico Fernandez	4.00	1.80	.50
☐ 315	Bobby Shantz	5.00	2.20	.60
☐ 316	Willie McCovey	115.00	52.50	14.50
☐ 317	Pumpsie Green	5.00	2.20	.60
☐ 318	Jim Baxes	5.00	2.20	.60
☐ 319	Joe Koppe	5.00	2.20	.60
☐ 320	Bob Allison	5.00	2.20	.60
☐ 321	Ron Fairly	5.00	2.20	.60
☐ 322	Willie Tasby	5.00	2.20	.60
☐ 323	John Romano	5.00	2.20	.60
☐ 324	Jim Perry	5.00	2.20	.60
☐ 325	Jim O'Toole	5.00	2.20	.60
☐ 326	Bob Clemente	150.00	70.00	19.00
☐ 327	Ray Sadecki	4.00	1.80	.50
☐ 328	Earl Battey	4.00	1.80	.50
☐ 329	Zack Monroe	4.00	1.80	.50
☐ 330	Harvey Kuenn	5.00	2.20	.60
☐ 331	Henry Mason	4.00	1.80	.50
☐ 332	Yankees Team	50.00	22.00	6.25
	(Checklist on back)			
☐ 333	Danny McDevitt	4.00	1.80	.50
☐ 334	Ted Abernathy	4.00	1.80	.50
☐ 335	Red Schoendienst	12.00	5.50	1.50
☐ 336	Ike Delock	4.00	1.80	.50
☐ 337	Cal Neeman	4.00	1.80	.50
☐ 338	Ray Monzant	4.00	1.80	.50
☐ 339	Harry Chiti	4.00	1.80	.50
☐ 340	Harvey Haddix	5.00	2.20	.60
☐ 341	Carroll Hardy	4.00	1.80	.50
☐ 342	Casey Wise	4.00	1.80	.50
☐ 343	Sandy Koufax	135.00	60.00	17.00
☐ 344	Clint Courtney	4.00	1.80	.50
☐ 345	Don Newcombe	5.00	2.20	.60
☐ 346	J.C. Martin UER	5.00	2.20	.60
	(Face actually			
	Gary Peters)			
☐ 347	Ed Bouchee	4.00	1.80	.50
☐ 348	Barry Shetrone	4.00	1.80	.50
☐ 349	Moe Drabowsky	5.00	2.20	.60
☐ 350	Mickey Mantle	500.00	220.00	60.00
☐ 351	Don Nottebart	4.00	1.80	.50
☐ 352	Cincy Clouters	8.00	3.60	1.00
	Gus Bell			
	Frank Robinson			
	Jerry Lynch			
☐ 353	Don Larsen	5.00	2.20	.60
☐ 354	Bob Lillis	4.00	1.80	.50
☐ 355	Bill White	6.00	2.70	.75
☐ 356	Joe Amalfitano	4.00	1.80	.50
☐ 357	Al Schroll	4.00	1.80	.50
☐ 358	Joe DeMaestri	4.00	1.80	.50
☐ 359	Buddy Gilbert	4.00	1.80	.50
☐ 360	Herb Score	5.00	2.20	.60
☐ 361	Bob Oldis	4.00	1.80	.50
☐ 362	Russ Kemmerer	4.00	1.80	.50
☐ 363	Gene Stephens	4.00	1.80	.50
☐ 364	Paul Foytack	4.00	1.80	.50
☐ 365	Minnie Minoso	6.00	2.70	.75
☐ 366	Dallas Green	8.00	3.60	1.00
☐ 367	Bill Tuttle	4.00	1.80	.50
☐ 368	Daryl Spencer	4.00	1.80	.50
☐ 369	Billy Hoeft	4.00	1.80	.50
☐ 370	Bill Skowron	6.00	2.70	.75
☐ 371	Bud Byerly	4.00	1.80	.50
☐ 372	Frank House	4.00	1.80	.50

☐	373 Don Hoak	5.00	2.20	.60
☐	374 Bob Buhl	5.00	2.20	.60
☐	375 Dale Long	5.00	2.20	.60
☐	376 John Briggs	4.00	1.80	.50
☐	377 Roger Maris	90.00	40.00	11.00
☐	378 Stu Miller	5.00	2.20	.60
☐	379 Red Wilson	4.00	1.80	.50
☐	380 Bob Shaw	4.00	1.80	.50
☐	381 Braves Team	10.00	2.00	1.00
	(Checklist on back)			
☐	382 Ted Bowsfield	4.00	1.80	.50
☐	383 Leon Wagner	4.00	1.80	.50
☐	384 Don Cardwell	4.00	1.80	.50
☐	385 World Series Game 1.	7.00	3.10	.85
	Charlie Neal			
	Steals Second			
☐	386 World Series Game 2.	7.00	3.10	.85
	Charlie Neal			
	Belts Second Homer			
☐	387 World Series Game 3.	7.00	3.10	.85
	Carl Furillo			
	Breaks Game			
☐	388 World Series Game 4	10.00	4.50	1.25
	Gil Hodges' Homer			
☐	389 World Series Game 5	12.00	5.50	1.50
	Luis Aparicio			
	Swipes Base			
	(Maury Wills			
	applies late tag)			
☐	390 World Series Game 6.	7.00	3.10	.85
	Scrambling After Ball			
☐	391 World Series Summary	7.00	3.10	.85
	The Champs Celebrate			
☐	392 Tex Clevenger	4.00	1.80	.50
☐	393 Smoky Burgess	5.00	2.20	.60
☐	394 Norm Larker	5.00	2.20	.60
☐	395 Hoyt Wilhelm	14.00	6.25	1.75
☐	396 Steve Bilko	4.00	1.80	.50
☐	397 Don Blasingame	4.00	1.80	.50
☐	398 Mike Cuellar	5.00	2.20	.60
☐	399 Young Hill Stars	5.00	2.20	.60
	Milt Pappas			
	Jack Fisher			
	Jerry Walker			
☐	400 Rocky Colavito	20.00	9.00	2.50
☐	401 Bob Duliba	4.00	1.80	.50
☐	402 Dick Stuart	5.00	2.20	.60
☐	403 Ed Sadowski	4.00	1.80	.50
☐	404 Bob Rush	4.00	1.80	.50
☐	405 Bobby Richardson	14.00	6.25	1.75
☐	406 Billy Klaus	4.00	1.80	.50
☐	407 Gary Peters UER	5.00	2.20	.60
	(Face actually			
	J.C. Martin)			
☐	408 Carl Furillo	5.00	2.20	.60
☐	409 Ron Samford	4.00	1.80	.50
☐	410 Sam Jones	5.00	2.20	.60
☐	411 Ed Bailey	4.00	1.80	.50
☐	412 Bob Anderson	4.00	1.80	.50
☐	413 Athletics Team	10.00	2.00	1.00
	(Checklist on back)			
☐	414 Don Williams	4.00	1.80	.50
☐	415 Bob Cerv	4.00	1.80	.50
☐	416 Humberto Robinson	4.00	1.80	.50
☐	417 Chuck Cottier	4.00	1.80	.50
☐	418 Don Mossi	5.00	2.20	.60
☐	419 George Crowe	4.00	1.80	.50
☐	420 Eddie Mathews	25.00	11.00	3.10
☐	421 Duke Maas	4.00	1.80	.50
☐	422 John Powers	4.00	1.80	.50
☐	423 Ed Fitzgerald	4.00	1.80	.50
☐	424 Pete Whisenant	4.00	1.80	.50
☐	425 Johnny Podres	5.00	2.20	.60
☐	426 Ron Jackson	4.00	1.80	.50
☐	427 Al Grunwald	4.00	1.80	.50
☐	428 Al Smith	4.00	1.80	.50
☐	429 AL Kings	8.00	3.60	1.00
	Nellie Fox			
	Harvey Kuenn			
☐	430 Art Ditmar	4.00	1.80	.50
☐	431 Andre Rodgers	4.00	1.80	.50
☐	432 Chuck Stobbs	4.00	1.80	.50
☐	433 Irv Noren	4.00	1.80	.50
☐	434 Brooks Lawrence	4.00	1.80	.50
☐	435 Gene Freese	4.00	1.80	.50
☐	436 Marv Throneberry	5.00	2.20	.60
☐	437 Bob Friend	5.00	2.20	.60
☐	438 Jim Coker	4.00	1.80	.50
☐	439 Tom Brewer	4.00	1.80	.50
☐	440 Jim Lemon	5.00	2.20	.60
☐	441 Gary Bell	7.00	3.10	.85
☐	442 Joe Pignatano	7.00	3.10	.85
☐	443 Charlie Maxwell	7.00	3.10	.85
☐	444 Jerry Kindall	7.00	3.10	.85
☐	445 Warren Spahn	45.00	20.00	5.50
☐	446 Ellis Burton	7.00	3.10	.85
☐	447 Ray Moore	7.00	3.10	.85
☐	448 Jim Gentile	20.00	9.00	2.50
☐	449 Jim Brosnan	7.00	3.10	.85
☐	450 Orlando Cepeda	18.00	8.00	2.20
☐	451 Curt Simmons	7.00	3.10	.85
☐	452 Ray Webster	7.00	3.10	.85
☐	453 Vern Law	8.00	3.60	1.00
☐	454 Hal Woodeshick	7.00	3.10	.85
☐	455 Baltimore Coaches	7.00	3.10	.85
	Eddie Robinson			
	Harry Brecheen			
	Luman Harris			
☐	456 Red Sox Coaches	8.00	3.60	1.00
	Rudy York			
	Billy Herman			
	Sal Maglie			
	Del Baker			
☐	457 Cubs Coaches	7.00	3.10	.85
	Charlie Root			
	Lou Klein			
	Elvin Tappe			
☐	458 White Sox Coaches	7.00	3.10	.85
	Johnny Cooney			
	Don Gutteridge			
	Tony Cuccinello			
	Ray Berres			
☐	459 Reds Coaches	7.00	3.10	.85
	Reggie Otero			
	Cot Deal			
	Wally Moses			
☐	460 Indians Coaches	8.00	3.60	1.00
	Mel Harder			
	Jo-Jo White			
	Bob Lemon			
	Ralph(Red) Kress			
☐	461 Tigers Coaches	8.00	3.60	1.00
	Tom Ferrick			
	Luke Appling			
	Billy Hitchcock			
☐	462 Athletics Coaches	7.00	3.10	.85
	Fred Fitzsimmons			
	Don Heffner			
	Walker Cooper			
☐	463 Dodgers Coaches	7.00	3.10	.85
	Bobby Bragan			
	Pete Reiser			

	Joe Becker			
	Greg Mulleavy			
□ 464	Braves Coaches	7.00	3.10	.85
	Bob Scheffing			
	Whitlow Wyatt			
	Andy Pafko			
	George Myatt			
□ 465	Yankees Coaches	12.00	5.50	1.50
	Bill Dickey			
	Ralph Houk			
	Frank Crosetti			
	Ed Lopat			
□ 466	Phillies Coaches	7.00	3.10	.85
	Ken Silvestri			
	Dick Carter			
	Andy Cohen			
□ 467	Pirates Coaches	7.00	3.10	.85
	Mickey Vernon			
	Frank Oceak			
	Sam Narron			
	Bill Burwell			
□ 468	Cardinals Coaches	7.00	3.10	.85
	Johnny Keane			
	Howie Pollet			
	Ray Katt			
	Harry Walker			
□ 469	Giants Coaches	7.00	3.10	.85
	Wes Westrum			
	Salty Parker			
	Bill Posedel			
□ 470	Senators Coaches	7.00	3.10	.85
	Bob Swift			
	Ellis Clary			
	Sam Mele			
□ 471	Ned Garver	7.00	3.10	.85
□ 472	Alvin Dark	7.00	3.10	.85
□ 473	Al Cicotte	7.00	3.10	.85
□ 474	Haywood Sullivan	7.00	3.10	.85
□ 475	Don Drysdale	35.00	16.00	4.40
□ 476	Lou Johnson	7.00	3.10	.85
□ 477	Don Ferrarese	7.00	3.10	.85
□ 478	Frank Torre	7.00	3.10	.85
□ 479	Georges Maranda	7.00	3.10	.85
□ 480	Yogi Berra	70.00	32.00	8.75
□ 481	Wes Stock	7.00	3.10	.85
□ 482	Frank Bolling	7.00	3.10	.85
□ 483	Camilo Pascual	7.00	3.10	.85
□ 484	Pirates Team	40.00	18.00	5.00
	(Checklist on back)			
□ 485	Ken Boyer	14.00	6.25	1.75
□ 486	Bobby Del Greco	7.00	3.10	.85
□ 487	Tom Sturdivant	7.00	3.10	.85
□ 488	Norm Cash	15.00	6.75	1.85
□ 489	Steve Ridzik	7.00	3.10	.85
□ 490	Frank Robinson	50.00	22.00	6.25
□ 491	Mel Roach	7.00	3.10	.85
□ 492	Larry Jackson	7.00	3.10	.85
□ 493	Duke Snider	50.00	22.00	6.25
□ 494	Orioles Team	20.00	9.00	2.50
	(Checklist on back)			
□ 495	Sherm Lollar	7.00	3.10	.85
□ 496	Bill Virdon	8.00	3.60	1.00
□ 497	John Tsitouris	7.00	3.10	.85
□ 498	Al Pilarcik	7.00	3.10	.85
□ 499	Johnny James	7.00	3.10	.85
□ 500	Johnny Temple	7.00	3.10	.85
□ 501	Bob Schmidt	7.00	3.10	.85
□ 502	Jim Bunning	15.00	6.75	1.85
□ 503	Don Lee	7.00	3.10	.85
□ 504	Seth Morehead	7.00	3.10	.85
□ 505	Ted Kluszewski	15.00	6.75	1.85
□ 506	Lee Walls	7.00	3.10	.85
□ 507	Dick Stigman	18.00	8.00	2.20
□ 508	Billy Consolo	16.00	7.25	2.00
□ 509	Tommy Davis	25.00	11.00	3.10
□ 510	Gerry Staley	16.00	7.25	2.00
□ 511	Ken Walters	16.00	7.25	2.00
□ 512	Joe Gibbon	16.00	7.25	2.00
□ 513	Chicago Cubs	30.00	13.50	3.70
	Team Card			
	(Checklist on back)			
□ 514	Steve Barber	18.00	8.00	2.20
□ 515	Stan Lopata	16.00	7.25	2.00
□ 516	Marty Kutyna	16.00	7.25	2.00
□ 517	Charlie James	16.00	7.25	2.00
□ 518	Tony Gonzalez	18.00	8.00	2.20
□ 519	Ed Roebuck	16.00	7.25	2.00
□ 520	Don Buddin	16.00	7.25	2.00
□ 521	Mike Lee	16.00	7.25	2.00
□ 522	Ken Hunt	16.00	7.25	2.00
□ 523	Clay Dalrymple	16.00	7.25	2.00
□ 524	Bill Henry	16.00	7.25	2.00
□ 525	Marv Breeding	16.00	7.25	2.00
□ 526	Paul Giel	16.00	7.25	2.00
□ 527	Jose Valdivielso	16.00	7.25	2.00
□ 528	Ben Johnson	16.00	7.25	2.00
□ 529	Norm Sherry	18.00	8.00	2.20
□ 530	Mike McCormick	18.00	8.00	2.20
□ 531	Sandy Amoros	18.00	8.00	2.20
□ 532	Mike Garcia	18.00	8.00	2.20
□ 533	Lu Clinton	16.00	7.25	2.00
□ 534	Ken MacKenzie	16.00	7.25	2.00
□ 535	Whitey Lockman	18.00	8.00	2.20
□ 536	Wynn Hawkins	16.00	7.25	2.00
□ 537	Boston Red Sox	30.00	13.50	3.70
	Team Card			
	(Checklist on back)			
□ 538	Frank Barnes	16.00	7.25	2.00
□ 539	Gene Baker	16.00	7.25	2.00
□ 540	Jerry Walker	16.00	7.25	2.00
□ 541	Tony Curry	16.00	7.25	2.00
□ 542	Ken Hamlin	16.00	7.25	2.00
□ 543	Elio Chacon	16.00	7.25	2.00
□ 544	Bill Monbouquette	16.00	7.25	2.00
□ 545	Carl Sawatski	16.00	7.25	2.00
□ 546	Hank Aguirre	16.00	7.25	2.00
□ 547	Bob Aspromonte	16.00	7.25	2.00
□ 548	Don Mincher	18.00	8.00	2.20
□ 549	John Buzhardt	16.00	7.25	2.00
□ 550	Jim Landis	16.00	7.25	2.00
□ 551	Ed Rakow	16.00	7.25	2.00
□ 552	Walt Bond	16.00	7.25	2.00
□ 553	Bill Skowron AS	16.00	7.25	2.00
□ 554	Willie McCovey AS	45.00	20.00	5.50
□ 555	Nellie Fox AS	20.00	9.00	2.50
□ 556	Charlie Neal AS	16.00	7.25	2.00
□ 557	Frank Malzone AS	16.00	7.25	2.00
□ 558	Eddie Mathews AS	30.00	13.50	3.70
□ 559	Luis Aparicio AS	25.00	11.00	3.10
□ 560	Ernie Banks AS	60.00	27.00	7.50
□ 561	Al Kaline AS	60.00	27.00	7.50
□ 562	Joe Cunningham AS	16.00	7.25	2.00
□ 563	Mickey Mantle AS	350.00	160.00	45.00
□ 564	Willie Mays AS	115.00	52.50	14.50
□ 565	Roger Maris AS	90.00	40.00	11.00
□ 566	Hank Aaron AS	125.00	55.00	15.50
□ 567	Sherm Lollar AS	16.00	7.25	2.00
□ 568	Del Crandall AS	16.00	7.25	2.00
□ 569	Camilo Pascual AS	16.00	7.25	2.00
□ 570	Don Drysdale AS	30.00	13.50	3.70
□ 571	Billy Pierce AS	16.00	7.25	2.00
□ 572	Johnny Antonelli AS	24.00	7.25	2.40

1961 Topps

The cards in this 587-card set measure 2 1/2" by 3 1/2". In 1961, Topps returned to the vertical obverse format. Introduced for the first time were "League Leaders" (41 to 50) and separate, numbered checklist cards. Two number 463s exist: the Braves team card carrying that number was meant to be number 426. There are three versions of the second series checklist card number 98; the variations are distinguished by the color of the "CHECKLIST" headline on the front of the card, the color of the printing of the card number on the bottom of the reverse, and the presence of the copyright notice running vertically on the card back. There are two groups of managers (131-139 and 219-226) as well as separate series of World Series cards (306-313), Baseball Thrills (401 to 410), previous MVP's (AL 471-478 and NL 479-486) and Sporting News All-Stars (566 to 589). The usual last series scarcity (523 to 589) exists. The set actually totals 587 cards since numbers 587 and 588 were never issued. The key Rookie Cards in this set are Juan Marichal, Ron Santo and Billy Williams.

	NRMT	VG-E	GOOD
COMPLETE SET (587)	5000.00	2200.00	600.00
COMMON CARD (1-370)	3.00	1.35	.35
COMMON CARD (371-446)	4.00	1.80	.50
COMMON CARD (447-522)	7.00	3.10	.85
COMMON CARD (523-565)	30.00	13.50	3.70
COMMON AS (566-589)	30.00	13.50	3.70

☐ 1	Dick Groat	30.00	6.00	3.00
☐ 2	Roger Maris	175.00	80.00	22.00
☐ 3	John Buzhardt	3.00	1.35	.35
☐ 4	Lenny Green	3.00	1.35	.35
☐ 5	John Romano	3.00	1.35	.35
☐ 6	Ed Roebuck	3.00	1.35	.35
☐ 7	White Sox Team	9.00	4.00	1.10
☐ 8	Dick Williams	5.00	2.20	.60
☐ 9	Bob Purkey	3.00	1.35	.35
☐ 10	Brooks Robinson	35.00	16.00	4.40
☐ 11	Curt Simmons	5.00	2.20	.60
☐ 12	Moe Thacker	3.00	1.35	.35
☐ 13	Chuck Cottier	3.00	1.35	.35
☐ 14	Don Mossi	5.00	2.20	.60
☐ 15	Willie Kirkland	3.00	1.35	.35
☐ 16	Billy Muffett	3.00	1.35	.35
☐ 17	Checklist 1	10.00	2.00	1.00
☐ 18	Jim Grant	5.00	2.20	.60
☐ 19	Clete Boyer	6.00	2.70	.75
☐ 20	Robin Roberts	14.00	6.25	1.75
☐ 21	Zorro Versalles UER	4.00	1.80	.50
	(First name should be Zoilo)			
☐ 22	Clem Labine	5.00	2.20	.60
☐ 23	Don Demeter	3.00	1.35	.35
☐ 24	Ken Johnson	3.00	1.35	.35
☐ 25	Reds' Heavy Artillery	8.00	3.60	1.00
	Vada Pinson			
	Gus Bell			
	Frank Robinson			
☐ 26	Wes Stock	3.00	1.35	.35
☐ 27	Jerry Kindall	3.00	1.35	.35
☐ 28	Hector Lopez	3.00	1.35	.35
☐ 29	Don Nottebart	3.00	1.35	.35
☐ 30	Nellie Fox	8.00	3.60	1.00
☐ 31	Bob Schmidt	3.00	1.35	.35
☐ 32	Ray Sadecki	3.00	1.35	.35
☐ 33	Gary Geiger	3.00	1.35	.35
☐ 34	Wynn Hawkins	3.00	1.35	.35
☐ 35	Ron Santo	60.00	27.00	7.50
☐ 36	Jack Kralick	3.00	1.35	.35
☐ 37	Charley Maxwell	5.00	2.20	.60
☐ 38	Bob Lillis	3.00	1.35	.35
☐ 39	Leo Posada	3.00	1.35	.35
☐ 40	Bob Turley	5.00	2.20	.60
☐ 41	NL Batting Leaders	20.00	9.00	2.50
	Dick Groat			
	Norm Larker			
	Willie Mays			
	Roberto Clemente			
☐ 42	AL Batting Leaders	7.00	3.10	.85
	Pete Runnels			
	Al Smith			
	Minnie Minoso			
	Bill Skowron			
☐ 43	NL Home Run Leaders	24.00	11.00	3.00
	Ernie Banks			
	Hank Aaron			
	Ed Mathews			
	Ken Boyer			
☐ 44	AL Home Run Leaders	80.00	36.00	10.00
	Mickey Mantle			
	Roger Maris			
	Jim Lemon			
	Rocky Colavito			
☐ 45	NL ERA Leaders	7.00	3.10	.85
	Mike McCormick			
	Ernie Broglio			
	Don Drysdale			
	Bob Friend			
	Stan Williams			
☐ 46	AL ERA Leaders	7.00	3.10	.85
	Frank Baumann			
	Jim Bunning			
	Art Ditmar			
	Hal Brown			
☐ 47	NL Pitching Leaders	7.00	3.10	.85
	Ernie Broglio			
	Warren Spahn			
	Vern Law			
	Lou Burdette			
☐ 48	AL Pitching Leaders	7.00	3.10	.85
	Chuck Estrada			
	Jim Perry UER			
	(Listed as an Oriole)			
	Bud Daley			
	Art Ditmar			

Frank Lary
Milt Pappas

☐ 49	NL Strikeout Leaders .	18.00	8.00	2.20
	Don Drysdale			
	Sandy Koufax			
	Sam Jones			
	Ernie Broglio			
☐ 50	AL Strikeout Leaders ...	7.00	3.10	.85
	Jim Bunning			
	Pedro Ramos			
	Early Wynn			
	Frank Lary			
☐ 51	Detroit Tigers	9.00	4.00	1.10
	Team Card			
☐ 52	George Crowe	3.00	1.35	.35
☐ 53	Russ Nixon	3.00	1.35	.35
☐ 54	Earl Francis	3.00	1.35	.35
☐ 55	Jim Davenport	5.00	2.20	.60
☐ 56	Russ Kemmerer	3.00	1.35	.35
☐ 57	Marv Throneberry	5.00	2.20	.60
☐ 58	Joe Schaffernoth	3.00	1.35	.35
☐ 59	Jim Woods	3.00	1.35	.35
☐ 60	Woody Held	3.00	1.35	.35
☐ 61	Ron Piche	3.00	1.35	.35
☐ 62	Al Pilarcik	3.00	1.35	.35
☐ 63	Jim Kaat	8.00	3.60	1.00
☐ 64	Alex Grammas	3.00	1.35	.35
☐ 65	Ted Kluszewski	7.00	3.10	.85
☐ 66	Bill Henry	3.00	1.35	.35
☐ 67	Ossie Virgil	3.00	1.35	.35
☐ 68	Deron Johnson	5.00	2.20	.60
☐ 69	Earl Wilson	5.00	2.20	.60
☐ 70	Bill Virdon	5.00	2.20	.60
☐ 71	Jerry Adair	3.00	1.35	.35
☐ 72	Stu Miller	5.00	2.20	.60
☐ 73	Al Spangler	3.00	1.35	.35
☐ 74	Joe Pignatano	3.00	1.35	.35
☐ 75	Lindy Shows Larry	5.00	2.20	.60
	Lindy McDaniel			
	Larry Jackson			
☐ 76	Harry Anderson	3.00	1.35	.35
☐ 77	Dick Stigman	3.00	1.35	.35
☐ 78	Lee Walls	3.00	1.35	.35
☐ 79	Joe Ginsberg	3.00	1.35	.35
☐ 80	Harmon Killebrew	20.00	9.00	2.50
☐ 81	Tracy Stallard	3.00	1.35	.35
☐ 82	Joe Christopher	3.00	1.35	.35
☐ 83	Bob Bruce	3.00	1.35	.35
☐ 84	Lee Maye	3.00	1.35	.35
☐ 85	Jerry Walker	3.00	1.35	.35
☐ 86	Los Angeles Dodgers	9.00	4.00	1.10
	Team Card			
☐ 87	Joe Amalfitano	3.00	1.35	.35
☐ 88	Richie Ashburn	15.00	6.75	1.85
☐ 89	Billy Martin	8.00	3.60	1.00
☐ 90	Gerry Staley	3.00	1.35	.35
☐ 91	Walt Moryn	3.00	1.35	.35
☐ 92	Hal Naragon	3.00	1.35	.35
☐ 93	Tony Gonzalez	3.00	1.35	.35
☐ 94	Johnny Kucks	3.00	1.35	.35
☐ 95	Norm Cash	7.00	3.10	.85
☐ 96	Billy O'Dell	3.00	1.35	.35
☐ 97	Jerry Lynch	5.00	2.20	.60
☐ 98A	Checklist 2	10.00	2.00	1.00
	(Red "Checklist",			
	98 black on white)			
☐ 98B	Checklist 2	10.00	2.00	1.00
	(Yellow "Checklist",			
	98 black on white)			
☐ 98C	Checklist 2	10.00	2.00	1.00
	(Yellow "Checklist",			
	98 white on black,			
	no copyright)			
☐ 99	Don Buddin UER	3.00	1.35	.35
	(66 HR's)			
☐ 100	Harvey Haddix	5.00	2.20	.60
☐ 101	Bubba Phillips	3.00	1.35	.35
☐ 102	Gene Stephens	3.00	1.35	.35
☐ 103	Ruben Amaro	3.00	1.35	.35
☐ 104	John Blanchard	5.00	2.20	.60
☐ 105	Carl Willey	3.00	1.35	.35
☐ 106	Whitey Herzog	5.00	2.20	.60
☐ 107	Seth Morehead	3.00	1.35	.35
☐ 108	Dan Dobbek	3.00	1.35	.35
☐ 109	Johnny Podres	5.00	2.20	.60
☐ 110	Vada Pinson	5.00	2.20	.60
☐ 111	Jack Meyer	3.00	1.35	.35
☐ 112	Chico Fernandez	3.00	1.35	.35
☐ 113	Mike Fornieles	3.00	1.35	.35
☐ 114	Hobie Landrith	3.00	1.35	.35
☐ 115	Johnny Antonelli	5.00	2.20	.60
☐ 116	Joe DeMaestri	3.00	1.35	.35
☐ 117	Dale Long	5.00	2.20	.60
☐ 118	Chris Cannizzaro	3.00	1.35	.35
☐ 119	A's Big Armor	5.00	2.20	.60
	Norm Siebern			
	Hank Bauer			
	Jerry Lumpe			
☐ 120	Eddie Mathews	25.00	11.00	3.10
☐ 121	Eli Grba	5.00	2.20	.60
☐ 122	Chicago Cubs	9.00	4.00	1.10
	Team Card			
☐ 123	Billy Gardner	3.00	1.35	.35
☐ 124	J.C. Martin	3.00	1.35	.35
☐ 125	Steve Barber	3.00	1.35	.35
☐ 126	Dick Stuart	5.00	2.20	.60
☐ 127	Ron Kline	3.00	1.35	.35
☐ 128	Rip Repulski	3.00	1.35	.35
☐ 129	Ed Hobaugh	3.00	1.35	.35
☐ 130	Norm Larker	3.00	1.35	.35
☐ 131	Paul Richards MG	5.00	2.20	.60
☐ 132	Al Lopez MG	5.00	2.20	.60
☐ 133	Ralph Houk MG	5.00	2.20	.60
☐ 134	Mickey Vernon MG	5.00	2.20	.60
☐ 135	Fred Hutchinson MG .	5.00	2.20	.60
☐ 136	Walt Alston MG	6.00	2.70	.75
☐ 137	Chuck Dressen MG	5.00	2.20	.60
☐ 138	Danny Murtaugh MG .	5.00	2.20	.60
☐ 139	Solly Hemus MG	5.00	2.20	.60
☐ 140	Gus Triandos	5.00	2.20	.60
☐ 141	Billy Williams	60.00	27.00	7.50
☐ 142	Luis Arroyo	5.00	2.20	.60
☐ 143	Russ Snyder	3.00	1.35	.35
☐ 144	Jim Coker	3.00	1.35	.35
☐ 145	Bob Buhl	5.00	2.20	.60
☐ 146	Marty Keough	3.00	1.35	.35
☐ 147	Ed Rakow	3.00	1.35	.35
☐ 148	Julian Javier	5.00	2.20	.60
☐ 149	Bob Oldis	3.00	1.35	.35
☐ 150	Willie Mays	100.00	45.00	12.50
☐ 151	Jim Donohue	3.00	1.35	.35
☐ 152	Earl Torgeson	3.00	1.35	.35
☐ 153	Don Lee	3.00	1.35	.35
☐ 154	Bobby Del Greco	3.00	1.35	.35
☐ 155	Johnny Temple	5.00	2.20	.60
☐ 156	Ken Hunt	5.00	2.20	.60
☐ 157	Cal McLish	3.00	1.35	.35
☐ 158	Pete Daley	3.00	1.35	.35
☐ 159	Orioles Team	9.00	4.00	1.10
☐ 160	Whitey Ford UER	40.00	18.00	5.00
	(Incorrectly listed			
	as 5'0" tall)			

☐ 161	Sherman Jones UER (Photo actually Eddie Fisher)	3.00	1.35	.35
☐ 162	Jay Hook	3.00	1.35	.35
☐ 163	Ed Sadowski	3.00	1.35	.35
☐ 164	Felix Mantilla	3.00	1.35	.35
☐ 165	Gino Cimoli	3.00	1.35	.35
☐ 166	Danny Kravitz	3.00	1.35	.35
☐ 167	San Francisco Giants Team Card	9.00	4.00	1.10
☐ 168	Tommy Davis	6.00	2.70	.75
☐ 169	Don Elston	3.00	1.35	.35
☐ 170	Al Smith	3.00	1.35	.35
☐ 171	Paul Foytack	3.00	1.35	.35
☐ 172	Don Dillard	3.00	1.35	.35
☐ 173	Beantown Bombers Frank Malzone Vic Wertz Jackie Jensen	5.00	2.20	.60
☐ 174	Ray Semproch	3.00	1.35	.35
☐ 175	Gene Freese	3.00	1.35	.35
☐ 176	Ken Aspromonte	3.00	1.35	.35
☐ 177	Don Larsen	5.00	2.20	.60
☐ 178	Bob Nieman	3.00	1.35	.35
☐ 179	Joe Koppe	3.00	1.35	.35
☐ 180	Bobby Richardson	12.00	5.50	1.50
☐ 181	Fred Green	3.00	1.35	.35
☐ 182	Dave Nicholson	3.00	1.35	.35
☐ 183	Andre Rodgers	3.00	1.35	.35
☐ 184	Steve Bilko	5.00	2.20	.60
☐ 185	Herb Score	5.00	2.20	.60
☐ 186	Elmer Valo	5.00	2.20	.60
☐ 187	Billy Klaus	3.00	1.35	.35
☐ 188	Jim Marshall	3.00	1.35	.35
☐ 189A	Checklist 3 (Copyright symbol almost adjacent to 263 Ken Hamlin)	10.00	2.00	1.00
☐ 189B	Checklist 3 (Copyright symbol adjacent to 264 Glen Hobbie)	10.00	2.00	1.00
☐ 190	Stan Williams	5.00	2.20	.60
☐ 191	Mike de la Hoz	3.00	1.35	.35
☐ 192	Dick Brown	3.00	1.35	.35
☐ 193	Gene Conley	5.00	2.20	.60
☐ 194	Gordy Coleman	5.00	2.20	.60
☐ 195	Jerry Casale	3.00	1.35	.35
☐ 196	Ed Bouchee	3.00	1.35	.35
☐ 197	Dick Hall	3.00	1.35	.35
☐ 198	Carl Sawatski	3.00	1.35	.35
☐ 199	Bob Boyd	3.00	1.35	.35
☐ 200	Warren Spahn	30.00	13.50	3.70
☐ 201	Pete Whisenant	3.00	1.35	.35
☐ 202	Al Neiger	3.00	1.35	.35
☐ 203	Eddie Bressoud	3.00	1.35	.35
☐ 204	Bob Skinner	5.00	2.20	.60
☐ 205	Billy Pierce	5.00	2.20	.60
☐ 206	Gene Green	3.00	1.35	.35
☐ 207	Dodger Southpaws Sandy Koufax Johnny Podres	25.00	11.00	3.10
☐ 208	Larry Osborne	3.00	1.35	.35
☐ 209	Ken McBride	3.00	1.35	.35
☐ 210	Pete Runnels	5.00	2.20	.60
☐ 211	Bob Gibson	40.00	18.00	5.00
☐ 212	Haywood Sullivan	5.00	2.20	.60
☐ 213	Bill Stafford	3.00	1.35	.35
☐ 214	Danny Murphy	3.00	1.35	.35
☐ 215	Gus Bell	5.00	2.20	.60
☐ 216	Ted Bowsfield	3.00	1.35	.35
☐ 217	Mel Roach	3.00	1.35	.35
☐ 218	Hal Brown	3.00	1.35	.35
☐ 219	Gene Mauch MG	5.00	2.20	.60
☐ 220	Alvin Dark MG	5.00	2.20	.60
☐ 221	Mike Higgins MG	3.00	1.35	.35
☐ 222	Jimmy Dykes MG	5.00	2.20	.60
☐ 223	Bob Scheffing MG	3.00	1.35	.35
☐ 224	Joe Gordon MG	5.00	2.20	.60
☐ 225	Bill Rigney MG	5.00	2.20	.60
☐ 226	Cookie Lavagetto MG	5.00	2.20	.60
☐ 227	Juan Pizarro	3.00	1.35	.35
☐ 228	New York Yankees Team Card	55.00	25.00	7.00
☐ 229	Rudy Hernandez	3.00	1.35	.35
☐ 230	Don Hoak	5.00	2.20	.60
☐ 231	Dick Drott	3.00	1.35	.35
☐ 232	Bill White	6.00	2.70	.75
☐ 233	Joey Jay	5.00	2.20	.60
☐ 234	Ted Lepcio	3.00	1.35	.35
☐ 235	Camilo Pascual	5.00	2.20	.60
☐ 236	Don Gile	3.00	1.35	.35
☐ 237	Billy Loes	5.00	2.20	.60
☐ 238	Jim Gilliam	5.00	2.20	.60
☐ 239	Dave Sisler	3.00	1.35	.35
☐ 240	Ron Hansen	3.00	1.35	.35
☐ 241	Al Cicotte	3.00	1.35	.35
☐ 242	Hal Smith	3.00	1.35	.35
☐ 243	Frank Lary	5.00	2.20	.60
☐ 244	Chico Cardenas	5.00	2.20	.60
☐ 245	Joe Adcock	5.00	2.20	.60
☐ 246	Bob Davis	3.00	1.35	.35
☐ 247	Billy Goodman	5.00	2.20	.60
☐ 248	Ed Keegan	3.00	1.35	.35
☐ 249	Cincinnati Reds Team Card	9.00	4.00	1.10
☐ 250	Buc Hill Aces Vern Law Roy Face	5.00	2.20	.60
☐ 251	Bill Bruton	3.00	1.35	.35
☐ 252	Bill Short	3.00	1.35	.35
☐ 253	Sammy Taylor	3.00	1.35	.35
☐ 254	Ted Sadowski	3.00	1.35	.35
☐ 255	Vic Power	5.00	2.20	.60
☐ 256	Billy Hoeft	3.00	1.35	.35
☐ 257	Carroll Hardy	3.00	1.35	.35
☐ 258	Jack Sanford	5.00	2.20	.60
☐ 259	John Schaive	3.00	1.35	.35
☐ 260	Don Drysdale	30.00	13.50	3.70
☐ 261	Charlie Lau	5.00	2.20	.60
☐ 262	Tony Curry	3.00	1.35	.35
☐ 263	Ken Hamlin	3.00	1.35	.35
☐ 264	Glen Hobbie	3.00	1.35	.35
☐ 265	Tony Kubek	8.00	3.60	1.00
☐ 266	Lindy McDaniel	5.00	2.20	.60
☐ 267	Norm Siebern	3.00	1.35	.35
☐ 268	Ike Delock	3.00	1.35	.35
☐ 269	Harry Chiti	3.00	1.35	.35
☐ 270	Bob Friend	5.00	2.20	.60
☐ 271	Jim Landis	3.00	1.35	.35
☐ 272	Tom Morgan	3.00	1.35	.35
☐ 273A	Checklist 4 (Copyright symbol adjacent to 336 Don Mincher)	15.00	3.00	1.50
☐ 273B	Checklist 4 (Copyright symbol adjacent to 339 Gene Baker)	10.00	2.00	1.00
☐ 274	Gary Bell	3.00	1.35	.35
☐ 275	Gene Woodling	5.00	2.20	.60
☐ 276	Ray Rippelmeyer	3.00	1.35	.35

☐ 277	Hank Foiles	3.00	1.35	.35
☐ 278	Don McMahon	3.00	1.35	.35
☐ 279	Jose Pagan	3.00	1.35	.35
☐ 280	Frank Howard	8.00	3.60	1.00
☐ 281	Frank Sullivan	3.00	1.35	.35
☐ 282	Faye Throneberry	3.00	1.35	.35
☐ 283	Bob Anderson	3.00	1.35	.35
☐ 284	Dick Gernert	3.00	1.35	.35
☐ 285	Sherm Lollar	5.00	2.20	.60
☐ 286	George Witt	3.00	1.35	.35
☐ 287	Carl Yastrzemski	60.00	27.00	7.50
☐ 288	Albie Pearson	5.00	2.20	.60
☐ 289	Ray Moore	3.00	1.35	.35
☐ 290	Stan Musial	100.00	45.00	12.50
☐ 291	Tex Clevenger	3.00	1.35	.35
☐ 292	Jim Baumer	3.00	1.35	.35
☐ 293	Tom Sturdivant	3.00	1.35	.35
☐ 294	Don Blasingame	3.00	1.35	.35
☐ 295	Milt Pappas	5.00	2.20	.60
☐ 296	Wes Covington	5.00	2.20	.60
☐ 297	Athletics Team	9.00	4.00	1.10
☐ 298	Jim Golden	3.00	1.35	.35
☐ 299	Clay Dalrymple	3.00	1.35	.35
☐ 300	Mickey Mantle	500.00	220.00	60.00
☐ 301	Chet Nichols	3.00	1.35	.35
☐ 302	Al Heist	3.00	1.35	.35
☐ 303	Gary Peters	5.00	2.20	.60
☐ 304	Rocky Nelson	3.00	1.35	.35
☐ 305	Mike McCormick	5.00	2.20	.60
☐ 306	World Series Game 1. Bill Virdon Saves Game	8.00	3.60	1.00
☐ 307	World Series Game 2 Mickey Mantle Two Homers	90.00	40.00	11.00
☐ 308	World Series Game 3 Bobby Richardson Is Hero	10.00	4.50	1.25
☐ 309	World Series Game 4. Gino Cimoli Safe	8.00	3.60	1.00
☐ 310	World Series Game 5. Roy Face Saves Day	8.00	3.60	1.00
☐ 311	World Series Game 6 Whitey Ford Second Shutout	16.00	7.25	2.00
☐ 312	World Series Game 7 Bill Mazeroski's Homer	20.00	9.00	2.50
☐ 313	World Series Summary Pirates Celebrate	16.00	7.25	2.00
☐ 314	Bob Miller	3.00	1.35	.35
☐ 315	Earl Battey	5.00	2.20	.60
☐ 316	Bobby Gene Smith	3.00	1.35	.35
☐ 317	Jim Brewer	3.00	1.35	.35
☐ 318	Danny O'Connell	3.00	1.35	.35
☐ 319	Valmy Thomas	3.00	1.35	.35
☐ 320	Lou Burdette	5.00	2.20	.60
☐ 321	Marv Breeding	3.00	1.35	.35
☐ 322	Bill Kunkel	5.00	2.20	.60
☐ 323	Sammy Esposito	3.00	1.35	.35
☐ 324	Hank Aguirre	3.00	1.35	.35
☐ 325	Wally Moon	5.00	2.20	.60
☐ 326	Dave Hillman	3.00	1.35	.35
☐ 327	Matty Alou	10.00	4.50	1.25
☐ 328	Jim O'Toole	5.00	2.20	.60
☐ 329	Julio Becquer	3.00	1.35	.35
☐ 330	Rocky Colavito	20.00	9.00	2.50
☐ 331	Ned Garver	3.00	1.35	.35
☐ 332	Dutch Dotterer UER (Photo actually Tommy Dotterer, Dutch's brother)	3.00	1.35	.35
☐ 333	Fritz Brickell	3.00	1.35	.35

☐ 334	Walt Bond	3.00	1.35	.35
☐ 335	Frank Bolling	3.00	1.35	.35
☐ 336	Don Mincher	5.00	2.20	.60
☐ 337	Al's Aces Early Wynn Al Lopez Herb Score	6.00	2.70	.75
☐ 338	Don Landrum	3.00	1.35	.35
☐ 339	Gene Baker	3.00	1.35	.35
☐ 340	Vic Wertz	5.00	2.20	.60
☐ 341	Jim Owens	3.00	1.35	.35
☐ 342	Clint Courtney	3.00	1.35	.35
☐ 343	Earl Robinson	3.00	1.35	.35
☐ 344	Sandy Koufax	100.00	45.00	12.50
☐ 345	Jim Piersall	5.00	2.20	.60
☐ 346	Howie Nunn	3.00	1.35	.35
☐ 347	St. Louis Cardinals Team Card	9.00	4.00	1.10
☐ 348	Steve Boros	3.00	1.35	.35
☐ 349	Danny McDevitt	3.00	1.35	.35 ☐
☐ 350	Ernie Banks	45.00	20.00	5.50 ☐
☐ 351	Jim King	3.00	1.35	.35
☐ 352	Bob Shaw	3.00	1.35	.35 ☐
☐ 353	Howie Bedell	3.00	1.35	.35
☐ 354	Billy Harrell	3.00	1.35	.35
☐ 355	Bob Allison	5.00	2.20	.60
☐ 356	Ryne Duren	3.00	1.35	.35
☐ 357	Daryl Spencer	3.00	1.35	.35
☐ 358	Earl Averill	5.00	2.20	.60
☐ 359	Dallas Green	3.00	1.35	.35
☐ 360	Frank Robinson	45.00	20.00	5.50
☐ 361A	Checklist 5 (No ad on back)	10.00	2.00	1.00
☐ 361B	Checklist 5 (Special Feature ad on back)	15.00	3.00	1.50
☐ 362	Frank Funk	3.00	1.35	.35
☐ 363	John Roseboro	5.00	2.20	.60
☐ 364	Moe Drabowsky	5.00	2.20	.60
☐ 365	Jerry Lumpe	3.00	1.35	.35
☐ 366	Eddie Fisher	3.00	1.35	.35
☐ 367	Jim Rivera	3.00	1.35	.35
☐ 368	Bennie Daniels	3.00	1.35	.35
☐ 369	Dave Philley	3.00	1.35	.35
☐ 370	Roy Face	5.00	2.20	.60
☐ 371	Bill Skowron SP	60.00	27.00	7.50
☐ 372	Bob Hendley	4.00	1.80	.50
☐ 373	Boston Red Sox Team Card	10.00	4.50	1.25
☐ 374	Paul Giel	4.00	1.80	.50
☐ 375	Ken Boyer	10.00	4.50	1.25
☐ 376	Mike Roarke	4.00	1.80	.50
☐ 377	Ruben Gomez	4.00	1.80	.50
☐ 378	Wally Post	6.00	2.70	.75
☐ 379	Bobby Shantz	4.00	1.80	.50
☐ 380	Minnie Minoso	7.00	3.10	.85
☐ 381	Dave Wickersham	4.00	1.80	.50
☐ 382	Frank Thomas	6.00	2.70	.75
☐ 383	Frisco First Liners Mike McCormick Jack Sanford Billy O'Dell	6.00	2.70	.75
☐ 384	Chuck Essegian	4.00	1.80	.50
☐ 385	Jim Perry	6.00	2.70	.75
☐ 386	Joe Hicks	4.00	1.80	.50
☐ 387	Duke Maas	4.00	1.80	.50
☐ 388	Bob Clemente	125.00	55.00	15.50
☐ 389	Ralph Terry	6.00	2.70	.75
☐ 390	Del Crandall	6.00	2.70	.75
☐ 391	Winston Brown	4.00	1.80	.50
☐ 392	Reno Bertoia	4.00	1.80	.50

☐ 393	Batter Bafflers	4.00	1.80	.50
	Don Cardwell			
	Glen Hobbie			
☐ 394	Ken Walters	4.00	1.80	.50
☐ 395	Chuck Estrada	6.00	2.70	.75
☐ 396	Bob Aspromonte	4.00	1.80	.50
☐ 397	Hal Woodeshick	4.00	1.80	.50
☐ 398	Hank Bauer	4.00	1.80	.50
☐ 399	Cliff Cook	4.00	1.80	.50
☐ 400	Vern Law	6.00	2.70	.75
☐ 401	Babe Ruth 60th Homer	50.00	22.00	6.25
☐ 402	Perfect Game	25.00	11.00	3.10
	(Don Larsen)			
☐ 403	26 Inning Tie	6.00	2.70	.75
☐ 404	Rogers Hornsby .424	10.00	4.50	1.25
	Average			
☐ 405	Lou Gehrig's Streak	80.00	36.00	10.00
☐ 406	Mickey Mantle 565	80.00	36.00	10.00
	Foot Homer			
☐ 407	Jack Chesbro Wins 41	6.00	2.70	.75
☐ 408	Christy Mathewson	20.00	9.00	2.50
	Fans 267			
☐ 409	Walter Johnson	12.00	5.50	1.50
	Shutouts			
☐ 410	Harvey Haddix 12	6.00	2.70	.75
	Perfect Innings			
☐ 411	Tony Taylor	6.00	2.70	.75
☐ 412	Larry Sherry	6.00	2.70	.75
☐ 413	Eddie Yost	6.00	2.70	.75
☐ 414	Dick Donovan	6.00	2.70	.75
☐ 415	Hank Aaron	100.00	45.00	12.50
☐ 416	Dick Howser	10.00	4.50	1.25
☐ 417	Juan Marichal's	125.00	55.00	15.50
☐ 418	Ed Bailey	6.00	2.70	.75
☐ 419	Tom Borland	4.00	1.80	.50
☐ 420	Ernie Broglio	6.00	2.70	.75
☐ 421	Ty Cline SP	18.00	8.00	2.20
☐ 422	Bud Daley	4.00	1.80	.50
☐ 423	Charlie Neal SP	18.00	8.00	2.20
☐ 424	Turk Lown	4.00	1.80	.50
☐ 425	Yogi Berra	70.00	32.00	8.75
☐ 426	Milwaukee Braves	12.00	5.50	1.50
	Team Card			
	(Back numbered 463)			
☐ 427	Dick Ellsworth	6.00	2.70	.75
☐ 428	Ray Barker SP	18.00	8.00	2.20
☐ 429	Al Kaline	45.00	20.00	5.50
☐ 430	Bill Mazeroski SP	60.00	27.00	7.50
☐ 431	Chuck Stobbs	4.00	1.80	.50
☐ 432	Coot Veal	6.00	2.70	.75
☐ 433	Art Mahaffey	4.00	1.80	.50
☐ 434	Tom Brewer	4.00	1.80	.50
☐ 435	Orlando Cepeda UER	14.00	6.25	1.75
	(San Francis on			
	card front)			
☐ 436	Jim Maloney	20.00	9.00	2.50
☐ 437A	Checklist 6	15.00	3.00	1.50
	440 Louis Aparicio			
☐ 437B	Checklist 6	15.00	3.00	1.50
	440 Luis Aparicio			
☐ 438	Curt Flood	6.00	2.70	.75
☐ 439	Phil Regan	6.00	2.70	.75
☐ 440	Luis Aparicio	16.00	7.25	2.00
☐ 441	Dick Bertell	4.00	1.80	.50
☐ 442	Gordon Jones	4.00	1.80	.50
☐ 443	Duke Snider	40.00	18.00	5.00
☐ 444	Joe Nuxhall	6.00	2.70	.75
☐ 445	Frank Malzone	6.00	2.70	.75
☐ 446	Bob Taylor	4.00	1.80	.50
☐ 447	Harry Bright	7.00	3.10	.85
☐ 448	Del Rice	7.00	3.10	.85

☐ 449	Bob Bolin	7.00	3.10	.85
☐ 450	Jim Lemon	7.00	3.10	.85
☐ 451	Power for Ernie	7.00	3.10	.85
	Daryl Spencer			
	Bill White			
	Ernie Broglio			
☐ 452	Bob Allen	7.00	3.10	.85
☐ 453	Dick Schofield	7.00	3.10	.85
☐ 454	Pumpsie Green	7.00	3.10	.85
☐ 455	Early Wynn	15.00	6.75	1.85
☐ 456	Hal Bevan	7.00	3.10	.85
☐ 457	Johnny James	7.00	3.10	.85
	(Listed as Angel,			
	but wearing Yankee			
	uniform and cap)			
☐ 458	Willie Tasby	7.00	3.10	.85
☐ 459	Terry Fox	7.00	3.10	.85
☐ 460	Gil Hodges	16.00	7.25	2.00
☐ 461	Smoky Burgess	10.00	4.50	1.25
☐ 462	Lou Klimchock	7.00	3.10	.85
☐ 463	Jack Fisher	7.00	3.10	.85
	(See also 426)			
☐ 464	Lee Thomas	8.00	3.60	1.00
	(Pictured with Yankee			
	cap but listed as			
	Los Angeles Angel)			
☐ 465	Roy McMillan	7.00	3.10	.85
☐ 466	Ron Moeller	7.00	3.10	.85
☐ 467	Cleveland Indians	12.00	5.50	1.50
	Team Card			
☐ 468	John Callison	10.00	4.50	1.25
☐ 469	Ralph Lumenti	7.00	3.10	.85
☐ 470	Roy Sievers	10.00	4.50	1.25
☐ 471	Phil Rizzuto MVP	18.00	8.00	2.20
☐ 472	Yogi Berra MVP	60.00	27.00	7.50
☐ 473	Bob Shantz MVP	7.00	3.10	.85
☐ 474	Al Rosen MVP	10.00	4.50	1.25
☐ 475	Mickey Mantle MVP	175.00	80.00	22.00
☐ 476	Jackie Jensen MVP	10.00	4.50	1.25
☐ 477	Nellie Fox MVP	12.00	5.50	1.50
☐ 478	Roger Maris MVP	45.00	20.00	5.50
☐ 479	Jim Konstanty MVP	7.00	3.10	.85
☐ 480	Roy Campanella MVP	35.00	16.00	4.40
☐ 481	Hank Sauer MVP	7.00	3.10	.85
☐ 482	Willie Mays MVP	50.00	22.00	6.25
☐ 483	Don Newcombe MVP	10.00	4.50	1.25
☐ 484	Hank Aaron MVP	50.00	22.00	6.25
☐ 485	Ernie Banks MVP	35.00	16.00	4.40
☐ 486	Dick Groat MVP	10.00	4.50	1.25
☐ 487	Gene Oliver	7.00	3.10	.85
☐ 488	Joe McClain	10.00	4.50	1.25
☐ 489	Walt Dropo	7.00	3.10	.85
☐ 490	Jim Bunning	15.00	6.75	1.85
☐ 491	Philadelphia Phillies	12.00	5.50	1.50
	Team Card			
☐ 492	Ron Fairly	10.00	4.50	1.25
☐ 493	Don Zimmer UER	10.00	4.50	1.25
	(Brooklyn A.L.)			
☐ 494	Tom Cheney	7.00	3.10	.85
☐ 495	Elston Howard	12.00	5.50	1.50
☐ 496	Ken MacKenzie	7.00	3.10	.85
☐ 497	Willie Jones	7.00	3.10	.85
☐ 498	Ray Herbert	7.00	3.10	.85
☐ 499	Chuck Schilling	7.00	3.10	.85
☐ 500	Harvey Kuenn	10.00	4.50	1.25
☐ 501	John DeMerit	7.00	3.10	.85
☐ 502	Clarence Coleman	10.00	4.50	1.25
☐ 503	Tito Francona	7.00	3.10	.85
☐ 504	Billy Consolo	7.00	3.10	.85
☐ 505	Red Schoendienst	14.00	6.25	1.75
☐ 506	Willie Davis	20.00	9.00	2.50

☐ 507	Pete Burnside	10.00	4.50	1.25
☐ 508	Rocky Bridges	10.00	4.50	1.25
☐ 509	Camilo Carreon	7.00	3.10	.85
☐ 510	Art Ditmar	7.00	3.10	.85
☐ 511	Joe M. Morgan	7.00	3.10	.85
☐ 512	Bob Will	7.00	3.10	.85
☐ 513	Jim Brosnan	10.00	4.50	1.25
☐ 514	Jake Wood	7.00	3.10	.85
☐ 515	Jackie Brandt	7.00	3.10	.85
☐ 516	Checklist 7	15.00	6.75	1.85
☐ 517	Willie McCovey	50.00	22.00	6.25
☐ 518	Andy Carey	10.00	4.50	1.25
☐ 519	Jim Pagliaroni	10.00	4.50	1.25
☐ 520	Joe Cunningham	10.00	4.50	1.25
☐ 521	Brother Battery	10.00	4.50	1.25
	Norm Sherry			
	Larry Sherry			
☐ 522	Dick Farrell UER	10.00	4.50	1.25
	(Phillies cap, but			
	listed on Dodgers)			
☐ 523	Joe Gibbon	30.00	13.50	3.70
☐ 524	Johnny Logan	30.00	13.50	3.70
☐ 525	Ron Perranoski	35.00	16.00	4.40
☐ 526	R.C. Stevens	30.00	13.50	3.70
☐ 527	Gene Leek	30.00	13.50	3.70
☐ 528	Pedro Ramos	30.00	13.50	3.70
☐ 529	Bob Roselli	30.00	13.50	3.70
☐ 530	Bob Malkmus	30.00	13.50	3.70
☐ 531	Jim Coates	30.00	13.50	3.70
☐ 532	Bob Hale	30.00	13.50	3.70
☐ 533	Jack Curtis	30.00	13.50	3.70
☐ 534	Eddie Kasko	30.00	13.50	3.70
☐ 535	Larry Jackson	30.00	13.50	3.70
☐ 536	Bill Tuttle	30.00	13.50	3.70
☐ 537	Bobby Locke	30.00	13.50	3.70
☐ 538	Chuck Hiller	30.00	13.50	3.70
☐ 539	Johnny Klippstein	30.00	13.50	3.70
☐ 540	Jackie Jensen	35.00	16.00	4.40
☐ 541	Roland Sheldon	35.00	16.00	4.40
☐ 542	Minnesota Twins	70.00	32.00	8.75
	Team Card			
☐ 543	Roger Craig	30.00	13.50	3.70
☐ 544	George Thomas	30.00	13.50	3.70
☐ 545	Hoyt Wilhelm	50.00	22.00	6.25
☐ 546	Marty Kutyna	30.00	13.50	3.70
☐ 547	Leon Wagner	30.00	13.50	3.70
☐ 548	Ted Wills	30.00	13.50	3.70
☐ 549	Hal R. Smith	30.00	13.50	3.70
☐ 550	Frank Baumann	30.00	13.50	3.70
☐ 551	George Altman	30.00	13.50	3.70
☐ 552	Jim Archer	30.00	13.50	3.70
☐ 553	Bill Fischer	30.00	13.50	3.70
☐ 554	Pittsburgh Pirates	70.00	32.00	8.75
	Team Card			
☐ 555	Sam Jones	30.00	13.50	3.70
☐ 556	Ken R. Hunt	30.00	13.50	3.70
☐ 557	Jose Valdivielso	30.00	13.50	3.70
☐ 558	Don Ferrarese	30.00	13.50	3.70
☐ 559	Jim Gentile	55.00	25.00	7.00
☐ 560	Barry Latman	30.00	13.50	3.70
☐ 561	Charley James	30.00	13.50	3.70
☐ 562	Bill Monbouquette	30.00	13.50	3.70
☐ 563	Bob Cerv	45.00	20.00	5.50
☐ 564	Don Cardwell	30.00	13.50	3.70
☐ 565	Felipe Alou	45.00	20.00	5.50
☐ 566	Paul Richards AS MG	30.00	13.50	3.70
☐ 567	Danny Murtaugh AS MG	30.00	13.50	3.70
☐ 568	Bill Skowron AS	35.00	16.00	4.40
☐ 569	Frank Herrera AS	30.00	13.50	3.70
☐ 570	Nellie Fox AS	35.00	16.00	4.40
☐ 571	Bill Mazeroski AS	35.00	16.00	4.40

☐ 572	Brooks Robinson AS	90.00	40.00	11.00
☐ 573	Ken Boyer AS	35.00	16.00	4.40
☐ 574	Luis Aparicio AS	45.00	20.00	5.50
☐ 575	Ernie Banks AS	90.00	40.00	11.00
☐ 576	Roger Maris AS	175.00	80.00	22.00
☐ 577	Hank Aaron AS	175.00	80.00	22.00
☐ 578	Mickey Mantle AS	450.00	200.00	55.00
☐ 579	Willie Mays AS	160.00	70.00	20.00
☐ 580	Al Kaline AS	90.00	40.00	11.00
☐ 581	Frank Robinson AS	90.00	40.00	11.00
☐ 582	Earl Battey AS	30.00	13.50	3.70
☐ 583	Del Crandall AS	30.00	13.50	3.70
☐ 584	Jim Perry AS	30.00	13.50	3.70
☐ 585	Bob Friend AS	30.00	13.50	3.70
☐ 586	Whitey Ford AS	90.00	40.00	11.00
☐ 587	Does not exist	30.00	13.50	3.70
☐ 588	Does not exist	30.00	13.50	3.70
☐ 589	Warren Spahn AS	100.00	30.00	10.00

1962 Topps

The cards in this 598-card set measure 2 1/2" by 3 1/2". The 1962 Topps set contains a mini-series spotlighting Babe Ruth (135-144). Other subsets in the set include League Leaders (51-60), World Series cards (232-237), In Action cards (311-319), NL All Stars (390-399), AL All Stars (466-475), and Rookie Prospects (591-598). The All-Star selections were again provided by Sport Magazine, as in 1958 and 1960. The second series had two distinct printings which are distinguishable by numerous color and pose variations. Those cards with a distinctive "green tint" are valued at a slight premium as they are basically the result of a flawed printing process occurring early in the second series run. Card number 139 exists as A: Babe Ruth Special card, B: Hal Reniff with arms over head, or C: Hal Reniff in the same pose as card number 159. In addition, two poses exist for players depicted on card numbers 129, 132, 134, 147, 174, 176, and 190. The high number series, 523 to 598, is somewhat more difficult to obtain than other cards in the set. Within the last series (523-598) there are 43 cards which were printed in lesser quantities; these are marked SP in the checklist below. In particular, the Rookie Parade subset (591-598) of this last series is even more difficult. This was the first year Topps produced multi-player Rookie Cards. The set price listed does not include the pose variations (see checklist

below for individual values). The key Rookie Cards in this set are Lou Brock, Tim McCarver, Gaylord Perry, and Bob Uecker.

		NRMT	VG-E	GOOD
	COMPLETE SET (598)	4600.00	2100.00	575.00
	COMMON CARD (1-370)	5.00	2.20	.60
	COMMON CARD (371-446)	6.00	2.70	.75
	COMMON CARD (447-522)	12.00	5.50	1.50
	COMMON CARD (523-590)	20.00	9.00	2.50
	COMMON ROOKIES (591-598)	45.00	20.00	5.50
☐ 1	Roger Maris	200.00	50.00	20.00
☐ 2	Jim Brosnan	5.00	2.20	.60
☐ 3	Pete Runnels	5.00	2.20	.60
☐ 4	John DeMerit	5.00	2.20	.60
☐ 5	Sandy Koufax UER	150.00	70.00	19.00
	(Struck ou 18)			
☐ 6	Marv Breeding	5.00	2.20	.60
☐ 7	Frank Thomas	5.00	2.20	.60
☐ 8	Ray Herbert	5.00	2.20	.60
☐ 9	Jim Davenport	5.00	2.20	.60
☐ 10	Bob Clemente	175.00	80.00	22.00
☐ 11	Tom Morgan	5.00	2.20	.60
☐ 12	Harry Craft MG	5.00	2.20	.60
☐ 13	Dick Howser	5.00	2.20	.60
☐ 14	Bill White	6.00	2.70	.75
☐ 15	Dick Donovan	5.00	2.20	.60
☐ 16	Darrell Johnson	5.00	2.20	.60
☐ 17	John Callison	5.00	2.20	.60
☐ 18	Managers' Dream	200.00	90.00	25.00
	Mickey Mantle			
	Willie Mays			
☐ 19	Ray Washburn	5.00	2.20	.60
☐ 20	Rocky Colavito	15.00	6.75	1.85
☐ 21	Jim Kaat	8.00	3.60	1.00
☐ 22A	Checklist 1 ERR	12.00	2.40	1.20
	(121-176 on back)			
☐ 22B	Checklist 1 COR	12.00	2.40	1.20
☐ 23	Norm Larker	5.00	2.20	.60
☐ 24	Tigers Team	8.00	3.60	1.00
☐ 25	Ernie Banks	45.00	20.00	5.50
☐ 26	Chris Cannizzaro	5.00	2.20	.60
☐ 27	Chuck Cottier	5.00	2.20	.60
☐ 28	Minnie Minoso	6.00	2.70	.75
☐ 29	Casey Stengel MG	20.00	9.00	2.50
☐ 30	Eddie Mathews	20.00	9.00	2.50
☐ 31	Tom Tresh	20.00	9.00	2.50
☐ 32	John Roseboro	5.00	2.20	.60
☐ 33	Don Larsen	8.00	2.20	.60
☐ 34	Johnny Temple	5.00	2.20	.60
☐ 35	Don Schwall	5.00	2.20	.60
☐ 36	Don Leppert	5.00	2.20	.60
☐ 37	Tribe Hill Trio	5.00	2.20	.60
	Barry Latman			
	Dick Stigman			
	Jim Perry			
☐ 38	Gene Stephens	5.00	2.20	.60
☐ 39	Joe Koppe	5.00	2.20	.60
☐ 40	Orlando Cepeda	14.00	6.25	1.75
☐ 41	Cliff Cook	5.00	2.20	.60
☐ 42	Jim King	5.00	2.20	.60
☐ 43	Los Angeles Dodgers	8.00	3.60	1.00
	Team Card			
☐ 44	Don Taussig	5.00	2.20	.60
☐ 45	Brooks Robinson	45.00	20.00	5.50
☐ 46	Jack Baldschun	5.00	2.20	.60
☐ 47	Bob Will	5.00	2.20	.60
☐ 48	Ralph Terry	5.00	2.20	.60
☐ 49	Hal Jones	5.00	2.20	.60
☐ 50	Stan Musial	100.00	45.00	12.50

		NRMT	VG-E	GOOD
☐ 51	AL Batting Leaders	8.00	3.60	1.00
	Norm Cash			
	Jim Piersall			
	Al Kaline			
	Elston Howard			
☐ 52	NL Batting Leaders	12.00	5.50	1.50
	Bob Clemente			
	Vada Pinson			
	Ken Boyer			
	Wally Moon			
☐ 53	AL Home Run Leaders	80.00	36.00	10.00
	Roger Maris			
	Mickey Mantle			
	Jim Gentile			
	Harmon Killebrew			
☐ 54	NL Home Run Leaders	12.00	5.50	1.50
	Orlando Cepeda			
	Willie Mays			
	Frank Robinson			
☐ 55	AL ERA Leaders	7.00	3.10	.85
	Dick Donovan			
	Bill Stafford			
	Don Mossi			
	Milt Pappas			
☐ 56	NL ERA Leaders	8.00	3.60	1.00
	Warren Spahn			
	Jim O'Toole			
	Curt Simmons			
	Mike McCormick			
☐ 57	AL Wins Leaders	8.00	3.60	1.00
	Whitey Ford			
	Frank Lary			
	Steve Barber			
	Jim Bunning			
☐ 58	NL Wins Leaders	8.00	3.60	1.00
	Warren Spahn			
	Joe Jay			
	Jim O'Toole			
☐ 59	AL Strikeout Leaders	8.00	3.60	1.00
	Camilo Pascual			
	Whitey Ford			
	Jim Bunning			
	Juan Pizzaro			
☐ 60	NL Strikeout Leaders	12.00	5.50	1.50
	Sandy Koufax			
	Stan Williams			
	Don Drysdale			
	Jim O'Toole			
☐ 61	Cardinals Team	8.00	3.60	1.00
☐ 62	Steve Boros	5.00	2.20	.60
☐ 63	Tony Cloninger	6.00	2.70	.75
☐ 64	Russ Snyder	5.00	2.20	.60
☐ 65	Bobby Richardson	12.00	5.50	1.50
☐ 66	Cuno Barragan	5.00	2.20	.60
☐ 67	Harvey Haddix	5.00	2.20	.60
☐ 68	Ken Hunt	5.00	2.20	.60
☐ 69	Phil Ortega	5.00	2.20	.60
☐ 70	Harmon Killebrew	25.00	11.00	3.10
☐ 71	Dick LeMay	5.00	2.20	.60
☐ 72	Bob's Pupils	5.00	2.20	.60
	Steve Boros			
	Bob Scheffing MG			
	Jake Wood			
☐ 73	Nellie Fox	10.00	4.50	1.25
☐ 74	Bob Lillis	5.00	2.20	.60
☐ 75	Milt Pappas	5.00	2.20	.60
☐ 76	Howie Bedell	5.00	2.20	.60
☐ 77	Tony Taylor	5.00	2.20	.60
☐ 78	Gene Green	5.00	2.20	.60
☐ 79	Ed Hobaugh	5.00	2.20	.60
☐ 80	Vada Pinson	7.00	3.10	.85

☐ 81 Jim Pagliaroni	5.00	2.20	.60
☐ 82 Deron Johnson	5.00	2.20	.60
☐ 83 Larry Jackson	5.00	2.20	.60
☐ 84 Lenny Green	5.00	2.20	.60
☐ 85 Gil Hodges	15.00	6.75	1.85
☐ 86 Donn Clendenon	6.00	2.70	.75
☐ 87 Mike Roarke	5.00	2.20	.60
☐ 88 Ralph Houk MG	5.00	2.20	.60
(Berra in background)			
☐ 89 Barney Schultz	5.00	2.20	.60
☐ 90 Jim Piersall	5.00	2.20	.60
☐ 91 J.C. Martin	5.00	2.20	.60
☐ 92 Sam Jones	5.00	2.20	.60
☐ 93 John Blanchard	5.00	2.20	.60
☐ 94 Jay Hook	5.00	2.20	.60
☐ 95 Don Hoak	5.00	2.20	.60
☐ 96 Eli Grba	5.00	2.20	.60
☐ 97 Tito Francona	5.00	2.20	.60
☐ 98 Checklist 2	12.00	2.40	1.20
☐ 99 John (Boog) Powell	30.00	13.50	3.70
☐ 100 Warren Spahn	30.00	13.50	3.70
☐ 101 Carroll Hardy	5.00	2.20	.60
☐ 102 Al Schroll	5.00	2.20	.60
☐ 103 Don Blasingame	5.00	2.20	.60
☐ 104 Ted Savage	5.00	2.20	.60
☐ 105 Don Mossi	5.00	2.20	.60
☐ 106 Carl Sawatski	5.00	2.20	.60
☐ 107 Mike McCormick	5.00	2.20	.60
☐ 108 Willie Davis	5.00	2.20	.60
☐ 109 Bob Shaw	5.00	2.20	.60
☐ 110 Bill Skowron	6.00	2.70	.75
☐ 111 Dallas Green	5.00	2.20	.60
☐ 112 Hank Foiles	5.00	2.20	.60
☐ 113 Chicago White Sox	7.00	3.10	.85
Team Card			
☐ 114 Howie Koplitz	5.00	2.20	.60
☐ 115 Bob Skinner	5.00	2.20	.60
☐ 116 Herb Score	5.00	2.20	.60
☐ 117 Gary Geiger	5.00	2.20	.60
☐ 118 Julian Javier	5.00	2.20	.60
☐ 119 Danny Murphy	5.00	2.20	.60
☐ 120 Bob Purkey	5.00	2.20	.60
☐ 121 Billy Hitchcock MG	5.00	2.20	.60
☐ 122 Norm Bass	5.00	2.20	.60
☐ 123 Mike de la Hoz	5.00	2.20	.60
☐ 124 Bill Pleis	5.00	2.20	.60
☐ 125 Gene Woodling	5.00	2.20	.60
☐ 126 Al Cicotte	5.00	2.20	.60
☐ 127 Pride of A's	5.00	2.20	.60
Norm Siebern			
Hank Bauer MG			
Jerry Lumpe			
☐ 128 Art Fowler	5.00	2.20	.60
☐ 129A Lee Walls	5.00	2.20	.60
(Facing right)			
☐ 129B Lee Walls	25.00	11.00	3.10
(Facing left)			
☐ 130 Frank Bolling	5.00	2.20	.60
☐ 131 Pete Richert	5.00	2.20	.60
☐ 132A Angels Team	8.00	3.60	1.00
(Without photo)			
☐ 132B Angels Team	25.00	11.00	3.10
(With photo)			
☐ 133 Felipe Alou	6.00	2.70	.75
☐ 134A Billy Hoeft	5.00	2.20	.60
(Facing right)			
☐ 134B Billy Hoeft	25.00	11.00	3.10
(Facing straight)			
☐ 135 Babe Ruth Special 1.	20.00	9.00	2.50
Babe as a Boy			
☐ 136 Babe Ruth Special 2.	20.00	9.00	2.50

Babe Joins Yanks			
☐ 137 Babe Ruth Special 3.	20.00	9.00	2.50
With Miller Huggins			
☐ 138 Babe Ruth Special 4.	20.00	9.00	2.50
Famous Slugger			
☐ 139A Babe Ruth Special 5	30.00	13.50	3.70
Babe Hits 60			
☐ 139B Hal Reniff PORT	12.00	5.50	1.50
☐ 139C Hal Reniff	65.00	29.00	8.00
(Pitching)			
☐ 140 Babe Ruth Special 6.	45.00	20.00	5.50
With Lou Gehrig			
☐ 141 Babe Ruth Special 7.	20.00	9.00	2.50
Twilight Years			
☐ 142 Babe Ruth Special 8.	20.00	9.00	2.50
Coaching Dodgers			
☐ 143 Babe Ruth Special 9.	20.00	9.00	2.50
Greatest Sports Hero			
☐ 144 Babe Ruth Special 10	20.00	9.00	2.50
Farewell Speech			
☐ 145 Barry Latman	5.00	2.20	.60
☐ 146 Don Demeter	5.00	2.20	.60
☐ 147A Bill Kunkel PORT	5.00	2.20	.60
☐ 147B Bill Kunkel	25.00	11.00	3.10
(Pitching pose)			
☐ 148 Wally Post	5.00	2.20	.60
☐ 149 Bob Duliba	5.00	2.20	.60
☐ 150 Al Kaline	45.00	20.00	5.50
☐ 151 Johnny Klippstein	5.00	2.20	.60
☐ 152 Mickey Vernon MG	5.00	2.20	.60
☐ 153 Pumpsie Green	5.00	2.20	.60
☐ 154 Lee Thomas	5.00	2.20	.60
☐ 155 Stu Miller	5.00	2.20	.60
☐ 156 Merritt Ranew	5.00	2.20	.60
☐ 157 Wes Covington	5.00	2.20	.60
☐ 158 Braves Team	8.00	3.60	1.00
☐ 159 Hal Reniff	6.00	2.70	.75
☐ 160 Dick Stuart	5.00	2.20	.60
☐ 161 Frank Baumann	5.00	2.20	.60
☐ 162 Sammy Drake	5.00	2.20	.60
☐ 163 Hot Corner Guard	5.00	2.20	.60
Billy Gardner			
Cletis Boyer			
☐ 164 Hal Naragon	5.00	2.20	.60
☐ 165 Jackie Brandt	5.00	2.20	.60
☐ 166 Don Lee	5.00	2.20	.60
☐ 167 Tim McCarver	30.00	13.50	3.70
☐ 168 Leo Posada	5.00	2.20	.60
☐ 169 Bob Cerv	5.00	2.20	.60
☐ 170 Ron Santo	15.00	6.75	1.85
☐ 171 Dave Sisler	5.00	2.20	.60
☐ 172 Fred Hutchinson MG	5.00	2.20	.60
☐ 173 Chico Fernandez	5.00	2.20	.60
☐ 174A Carl Willey	5.00	2.20	.60
(Capless)			
☐ 174B Carl Willey	25.00	11.00	3.10
(With cap)			
☐ 175 Frank Howard	6.00	2.70	.75
☐ 176A Eddie Yost PORT	5.00	2.20	.60
☐ 176B Eddie Yost BATTING	28.00	12.50	3.50
☐ 177 Bobby Shantz	5.00	2.20	.60
☐ 178 Camilo Carreon	5.00	2.20	.60
☐ 179 Tom Sturdivant	5.00	2.20	.60
☐ 180 Bob Allison	5.00	2.20	.60
☐ 181 Paul Brown	5.00	2.20	.60
☐ 182 Bob Nieman	5.00	2.20	.60
☐ 183 Roger Craig	5.00	2.20	.60
☐ 184 Haywood Sullivan	5.00	2.20	.60
☐ 185 Roland Sheldon	5.00	2.20	.60
☐ 186 Mack Jones	5.00	2.20	.60
☐ 187 Gene Conley	5.00	2.20	.60

☐ 188	Chuck Hiller	5.00	2.20	.60
☐ 189	Dick Hall	5.00	2.20	.60
☐ 190A	Wally Moon PORT	5.00	2.20	.60
☐ 190B	Wally Moon BATTING	28.00	12.50	3.50
☐ 191	Jim Brewer	5.00	2.20	.60
☐ 192A	Checklist 3 (Without comma)	12.00	2.40	1.20
☐ 192B	Checklist 3 (Comma after Checklist)	12.00	2.40	1.20
☐ 193	Eddie Kasko	5.00	2.20	.60
☐ 194	Dean Chance	6.00	2.70	.75
☐ 195	Joe Cunningham	5.00	2.20	.60
☐ 196	Terry Fox	5.00	2.20	.60
☐ 197	Daryl Spencer	5.00	2.20	.60
☐ 198	Johnny Keane MG	5.00	2.20	.60
☐ 199	Gaylord Perry	90.00	40.00	11.00
☐ 200	Mickey Mantle	550.00	250.00	70.00
☐ 201	Ike Delock	5.00	2.20	.60
☐ 202	Carl Warwick	5.00	2.20	.60
☐ 203	Jack Fisher	5.00	2.20	.60
☐ 204	Johnny Weekly	5.00	2.20	.60
☐ 205	Gene Freese	5.00	2.20	.60
☐ 206	Senators Team	8.00	3.60	1.00
☐ 207	Pete Burnside	5.00	2.20	.60
☐ 208	Billy Martin	10.00	4.50	1.25
☐ 209	Jim Fregosi	15.00	6.75	1.85
☐ 210	Roy Face	5.00	2.20	.60
☐ 211	Midway Masters Frank Bolling Roy McMillan	5.00	2.20	.60
☐ 212	Jim Owens	5.00	2.20	.60
☐ 213	Richie Ashburn	20.00	9.00	2.50
☐ 214	Dom Zanni	5.00	2.20	.60
☐ 215	Woody Held	5.00	2.20	.60
☐ 216	Ron Kline	5.00	2.20	.60
☐ 217	Walt Alston MG	6.00	2.70	.75
☐ 218	Joe Torre	30.00	13.50	3.70
☐ 219	Al Downing	6.00	2.70	.75
☐ 220	Roy Sievers	5.00	2.20	.60
☐ 221	Bill Short	5.00	2.20	.60
☐ 222	Jerry Zimmerman	5.00	2.20	.60
☐ 223	Alex Grammas	5.00	2.20	.60
☐ 224	Don Rudolph	5.00	2.20	.60
☐ 225	Frank Malzone	5.00	2.20	.60
☐ 226	San Francisco Giants Team Card	8.00	3.60	1.00
☐ 227	Bob Tiefenauer	5.00	2.20	.60
☐ 228	Dale Long	5.00	2.20	.60
☐ 229	Jesus McFarlane	5.00	2.20	.60
☐ 230	Camilo Pascual	5.00	2.20	.60
☐ 231	Ernie Bowman	5.00	2.20	.60
☐ 232	World Series Game 1. Yanks win opener	7.00	3.10	.85
☐ 233	World Series Game 2. Joey Jay ties it up	7.00	3.10	.85
☐ 234	World Series Game 3 Roger Maris wins in 9th	20.00	9.00	2.50
☐ 235	World Series Game 4 Whitey Ford sets new mark	10.00	4.50	1.25
☐ 236	World Series Game 5. Yanks crush Reds	7.00	3.10	.85
☐ 237	World Series Summary Yanks celebrate	7.00	3.10	.85
☐ 238	Norm Sherry	5.00	2.20	.60
☐ 239	Cecil Butler	5.00	2.20	.60
☐ 240	George Altman	5.00	2.20	.60
☐ 241	Johnny Kucks	5.00	2.20	.60
☐ 242	Mel McGaha MG	5.00	2.20	.60
☐ 243	Robin Roberts	16.00	7.25	2.00
☐ 244	Don Gile	5.00	2.20	.60
☐ 245	Ron Hansen	5.00	2.20	.60
☐ 246	Art Ditmar	5.00	2.20	.60
☐ 247	Joe Pignatano	5.00	2.20	.60
☐ 248	Bob Aspromonte	5.00	2.20	.60
☐ 249	Ed Keegan	5.00	2.20	.60
☐ 250	Norm Cash	10.00	4.50	1.25
☐ 251	New York Yankees Team Card	50.00	22.00	6.25
☐ 252	Earl Francis	5.00	2.20	.60
☐ 253	Harry Chiti MG	5.00	2.20	.60
☐ 254	Gordon Windhorn	5.00	2.20	.60
☐ 255	Juan Pizarro	5.00	2.20	.60
☐ 256	Elio Chacon	5.00	2.20	.60
☐ 257	Jack Spring	5.00	2.20	.60
☐ 258	Marty Keough	5.00	2.20	.60
☐ 259	Lou Klimchock	5.00	2.20	.60
☐ 260	Billy Pierce	5.00	2.20	.60
☐ 261	George Alusik	5.00	2.20	.60
☐ 262	Bob Schmidt	5.00	2.20	.60
☐ 263	The Right Pitch Bob Purkey Jim Turner CO Joe Jay	5.00	2.20	.60
☐ 264	Dick Ellsworth	5.00	2.20	.60
☐ 265	Joe Adcock	5.00	2.20	.60
☐ 266	John Anderson	5.00	2.20	.60
☐ 267	Dan Dobbek	5.00	2.20	.60
☐ 268	Ken McBride	5.00	2.20	.60
☐ 269	Bob Oldis	5.00	2.20	.60
☐ 270	Dick Groat	5.00	2.20	.60
☐ 271	Ray Rippelmeyer	5.00	2.20	.60
☐ 272	Earl Robinson	5.00	2.20	.60
☐ 273	Gary Bell	5.00	2.20	.60
☐ 274	Sammy Taylor	5.00	2.20	.60
☐ 275	Norm Siebern	5.00	2.20	.60
☐ 276	Hal Kolstad	5.00	2.20	.60
☐ 277	Checklist 4	12.00	2.40	1.20
☐ 278	Ken Johnson	5.00	2.20	.60
☐ 279	Hobie Landrith UER (Wrong birthdate)	5.00	2.20	.60
☐ 280	Johnny Podres	5.00	2.20	.60
☐ 281	Jake Gibbs	5.00	2.20	.60
☐ 282	Dave Hillman	5.00	2.20	.60
☐ 283	Charlie Smith	5.00	2.20	.60
☐ 284	Ruben Amaro	5.00	2.20	.60
☐ 285	Curt Simmons	5.00	2.20	.60
☐ 286	Al Lopez MG	6.00	2.70	.75
☐ 287	George Witt	5.00	2.20	.60
☐ 288	Billy Williams	30.00	13.50	3.70
☐ 289	Mike Krsnich	5.00	2.20	.60
☐ 290	Jim Gentile	5.00	2.20	.60
☐ 291	Hal Stowe	5.00	2.20	.60
☐ 292	Jerry Kindall	5.00	2.20	.60
☐ 293	Bob Miller	5.00	2.20	.60
☐ 294	Phillies Team	9.00	4.00	1.10
☐ 295	Vern Law	5.00	2.20	.60
☐ 296	Ken Hamlin	5.00	2.20	.60
☐ 297	Ron Perranoski	5.00	2.20	.60
☐ 298	Bill Tuttle	5.00	2.20	.60
☐ 299	Don Wert	5.00	2.20	.60
☐ 300	Willie Mays	150.00	70.00	19.00
☐ 301	Galen Cisco	5.00	2.20	.60
☐ 302	Johnny Edwards	5.00	2.20	.60
☐ 303	Frank Torre	5.00	2.20	.60
☐ 304	Dick Farrell	5.00	2.20	.60
☐ 305	Jerry Lumpe	5.00	2.20	.60
☐ 306	Redbird Rippers Lindy McDaniel Larry Jackson	5.00	2.20	.60

☐ 307	Jim Grant	5.00	2.20	.60
☐ 308	Neil Chrisley	5.00	2.20	.60
☐ 309	Moe Morhardt	5.00	2.20	.60
☐ 310	Whitey Ford	40.00	18.00	5.00
☐ 311	Tony Kubek IA	7.00	3.10	.85
☐ 312	Warren Spahn IA	14.00	6.25	1.75
☐ 313	Roger Maris IA	35.00	16.00	4.40
☐ 314	Rocky Colavito IA	12.00	5.50	1.50
☐ 315	Whitey Ford IA	15.00	6.75	1.85
☐ 316	Harmon Killebrew IA	15.00	6.75	1.85
☐ 317	Stan Musial IA	20.00	9.00	2.50
☐ 318	Mickey Mantle IA	125.00	55.00	15.50
☐ 319	Mike McCormick IA	5.00	2.20	.60
☐ 320	Hank Aaron	150.00	70.00	19.00
☐ 321	Lee Stange	5.00	2.20	.60
☐ 322	Alvin Dark MG	5.00	2.20	.60
☐ 323	Don Landrum	5.00	2.20	.60
☐ 324	Joe McClain	5.00	2.20	.60
☐ 325	Luis Aparicio	16.00	7.25	2.00
☐ 326	Tom Parsons	5.00	2.20	.60
☐ 327	Ozzie Virgil	5.00	2.20	.60
☐ 328	Ken Walters	5.00	2.20	.60
☐ 329	Bob Bolin	5.00	2.20	.60
☐ 330	John Romano	5.00	2.20	.60
☐ 331	Moe Drabowsky	5.00	2.20	.60
☐ 332	Don Buddin	5.00	2.20	.60
☐ 333	Frank Cipriani	5.00	2.20	.60
☐ 334	Boston Red Sox	9.00	4.00	1.10
	Team Card			
☐ 335	Bill Bruton	5.00	2.20	.60
☐ 336	Billy Muffett	5.00	2.20	.60
☐ 337	Jim Marshall	5.00	2.20	.60
☐ 338	Billy Gardner	5.00	2.20	.60
☐ 339	Jose Valdivielso	5.00	2.20	.60
☐ 340	Don Drysdale	35.00	16.00	4.40
☐ 341	Mike Hershberger	5.00	2.20	.60
☐ 342	Ed Rakow	5.00	2.20	.60
☐ 343	Albie Pearson	5.00	2.20	.60
☐ 344	Ed Bauta	5.00	2.20	.60
☐ 345	Chuck Schilling	5.00	2.20	.60
☐ 346	Jack Kralick	5.00	2.20	.60
☐ 347	Chuck Hinton	5.00	2.20	.60
☐ 348	Larry Burright	5.00	2.20	.60
☐ 349	Paul Foytack	5.00	2.20	.60
☐ 350	Frank Robinson	50.00	22.00	6.25
☐ 351	Braves' Backstops	7.00	3.10	.85
	Joe Torre			
	Del Crandall			
☐ 352	Frank Sullivan	5.00	2.20	.60
☐ 353	Bill Mazeroski	10.00	4.50	1.25
☐ 354	Roman Mejias	5.00	2.20	.60
☐ 355	Steve Barber	5.00	2.20	.60
☐ 356	Tom Haller	5.00	2.20	.60
☐ 357	Jerry Walker	5.00	2.20	.60
☐ 358	Tommy Davis	5.00	2.20	.60
☐ 359	Bobby Locke	5.00	2.20	.60
☐ 360	Yogi Berra	75.00	34.00	9.50
☐ 361	Bob Hendley	5.00	2.20	.60
☐ 362	Ty Cline	5.00	2.20	.60
☐ 363	Bob Roselli	5.00	2.20	.60
☐ 364	Ken Hunt	5.00	2.20	.60
☐ 365	Charlie Neal	5.00	2.20	.60
☐ 366	Phil Regan	5.00	2.20	.60
☐ 367	Checklist 5	12.00	2.40	1.20
☐ 368	Bob Tillman	5.00	2.20	.60
☐ 369	Ted Bowsfield	5.00	2.20	.60
☐ 370	Ken Boyer	6.00	2.70	.75
☐ 371	Earl Battey	6.00	2.70	.75
☐ 372	Jack Curtis	6.00	2.70	.75
☐ 373	Al Heist	6.00	2.70	.75
☐ 374	Gene Mauch MG	7.00	3.10	.85
☐ 375	Ron Fairly	7.00	3.10	.85
☐ 376	Bud Daley	6.00	2.70	.75
☐ 377	John Orsino	6.00	2.70	.75
☐ 378	Bennie Daniels	6.00	2.70	.75
☐ 379	Chuck Essegian	6.00	2.70	.75
☐ 380	Lou Burdette	6.00	2.70	.75
☐ 381	Chico Cardenas	7.00	3.10	.85
☐ 382	Dick Williams	7.00	3.10	.85
☐ 383	Ray Sadecki	6.00	2.70	.75
☐ 384	K.C. Athletics	12.00	5.50	1.50
	Team Card			
☐ 385	Early Wynn	18.00	8.00	2.20
☐ 386	Don Mincher	7.00	3.10	.85
☐ 387	Lou Brock	125.00	55.00	15.50
☐ 388	Ryne Duren	6.00	2.70	.75
☐ 389	Smoky Burgess	7.00	3.10	.85
☐ 390	Orlando Cepeda AS	10.00	4.50	1.25
☐ 391	Bill Mazeroski AS	10.00	4.50	1.25
☐ 392	Ken Boyer AS	6.00	2.70	.75
☐ 393	Roy McMillan AS	6.00	2.70	.75
☐ 394	Hank Aaron AS	50.00	22.00	6.25
☐ 395	Willie Mays AS	50.00	22.00	6.25
☐ 396	Frank Robinson AS	16.00	7.25	2.00
☐ 397	John Roseboro AS	6.00	2.70	.75
☐ 398	Don Drysdale AS	16.00	7.25	2.00
☐ 399	Warren Spahn AS	16.00	7.25	2.00
☐ 400	Elston Howard	10.00	4.50	1.25
☐ 401	AL/NL Homer Kings	50.00	22.00	6.25
	Roger Maris			
	Orlando Cepeda			
☐ 402	Gino Cimoli	6.00	2.70	.75
☐ 403	Chet Nichols	6.00	2.70	.75
☐ 404	Tim Harkness	6.00	2.70	.75
☐ 405	Jim Perry	6.00	2.70	.75
☐ 406	Bob Taylor	6.00	2.70	.75
☐ 407	Hank Aguirre	6.00	2.70	.75
☐ 408	Gus Bell	7.00	3.10	.85
☐ 409	Pittsburgh Pirates	12.00	5.50	1.50
	Team Card			
☐ 410	Al Smith	6.00	2.70	.75
☐ 411	Danny O'Connell	6.00	2.70	.75
☐ 412	Charlie James	6.00	2.70	.75
☐ 413	Matty Alou	7.00	3.10	.85
☐ 414	Joe Gaines	6.00	2.70	.75
☐ 415	Bill Virdon	7.00	3.10	.85
☐ 416	Bob Scheffing MG	6.00	2.70	.75
☐ 417	Joe Azcue	6.00	2.70	.75
☐ 418	Andy Carey	6.00	2.70	.75
☐ 419	Bob Bruce	7.00	3.10	.85
☐ 420	Gus Triandos	7.00	3.10	.85
☐ 421	Ken MacKenzie	7.00	3.10	.85
☐ 422	Steve Bilko	6.00	2.70	.75
☐ 423	Rival League	8.00	3.60	1.00
	Relief Aces:			
	Roy Face			
	Hoyt Wilhelm			
☐ 424	Al McBean	6.00	2.70	.75
☐ 425	Carl Yastrzemski	125.00	55.00	15.50
☐ 426	Bob Farley	6.00	2.70	.75
☐ 427	Jake Wood	6.00	2.70	.75
☐ 428	Joe Hicks	6.00	2.70	.75
☐ 429	Billy O'Dell	6.00	2.70	.75
☐ 430	Tony Kubek	10.00	4.50	1.25
☐ 431	Bob Rodgers	6.00	2.70	.75
☐ 432	Jim Pendleton	6.00	2.70	.75
☐ 433	Jim Archer	6.00	2.70	.75
☐ 434	Clay Dalrymple	6.00	2.70	.75
☐ 435	Larry Sherry	7.00	3.10	.85
☐ 436	Felix Mantilla	7.00	3.10	.85
☐ 437	Ray Moore	6.00	2.70	.75
☐ 438	Dick Brown	6.00	2.70	.75

☐	439	Jerry Buchek	6.00	2.70	.75	☐	499	Zoilo Versalles	13.00	5.75	1.60
☐	440	Joey Jay	6.00	2.70	.75	☐	500	Duke Snider	50.00	22.00	6.25
☐	441	Checklist 6	16.00	7.25	2.00	☐	501	Claude Osteen	13.00	5.75	1.60
☐	442	Wes Stock	6.00	2.70	.75	☐	502	Hector Lopez	13.00	5.75	1.60
☐	443	Del Crandall	7.00	3.10	.85	☐	503	Danny Murtaugh MG	13.00	5.75	1.60
☐	444	Ted Wills	6.00	2.70	.75	☐	504	Eddie Bressoud	12.00	5.50	1.50
☐	445	Vic Power	7.00	3.10	.85	☐	505	Juan Marichal	40.00	18.00	5.00
☐	446	Don Elston	6.00	2.70	.75	☐	506	Charlie Maxwell	13.00	5.75	1.60
☐	447	Willie Kirkland	12.00	5.50	1.50	☐	507	Ernie Broglio	13.00	5.75	1.60
☐	448	Joe Gibbon	12.00	5.50	1.50	☐	508	Gordy Coleman	13.00	5.75	1.60
☐	449	Jerry Adair	12.00	5.50	1.50	☐	509	Dave Giusti	13.00	5.75	1.60
☐	450	Jim O'Toole	13.00	5.75	1.60	☐	510	Jim Lemon	12.00	5.50	1.50
☐	451	Jose Tartabull	13.00	5.75	1.60	☐	511	Bubba Phillips	12.00	5.50	1.50
☐	452	Earl Averill Jr.	12.00	5.50	1.50	☐	512	Mike Fornieles	12.00	5.50	1.50
☐	453	Cal McLish	12.00	5.50	1.50	☐	513	Whitey Herzog	13.00	5.75	1.60
☐	454	Floyd Robinson	12.00	5.50	1.50	☐	514	Sherm Lollar	13.00	5.75	1.60
☐	455	Luis Arroyo	13.00	5.75	1.60	☐	515	Stan Williams	13.00	5.75	1.60
☐	456	Joe Amalfitano	13.00	5.75	1.60	☐	516	Checklist 7	16.00	3.20	1.60
☐	457	Lou Clinton	12.00	5.50	1.50	☐	517	Dave Wickersham	12.00	5.50	1.50
☐	458A	Bob Buhl	13.00	5.75	1.60	☐	518	Lee Maye	12.00	5.50	1.50
		(Braves emblem				☐	519	Bob Johnson	12.00	5.50	1.50
		on cap)				☐	520	Bob Friend	13.00	5.75	1.60
☐	458B	Bob Buhl	50.00	22.00	6.25	☐	521	Jacke Davis UER	12.00	5.50	1.50
		(No emblem on cap)						(Listed as OF on			
☐	459	Ed Bailey	12.00	5.50	1.50			front and P on back)			
☐	460	Jim Bunning	14.00	6.25	1.75	☐	522	Lindy McDaniel	13.00	5.75	1.60
☐	461	Ken Hubbs	32.00	14.50	4.00	☐	523	Russ Nixon SP	32.00	14.50	4.00
☐	462A	Willie Tasby	12.00	5.50	1.50	☐	524	Howie Nunn SP	32.00	14.50	4.00
		(Senators emblem				☐	525	George Thomas	20.00	9.00	2.50
		on cap)				☐	526	Hal Woodeshick SP	32.00	14.50	4.00
☐	462B	Willie Tasby	50.00	22.00	6.25	☐	527	Dick McAuliffe	25.00	11.00	3.10
		(No emblem on cap)				☐	528	Turk Lown	20.00	9.00	2.50
☐	463	Hank Bauer MG	13.00	5.75	1.60	☐	529	John Schaive SP	32.00	14.50	4.00
☐	464	Al Jackson	13.00	5.75	1.60	☐	530	Bob Gibson SP	150.00	70.00	19.00
☐	465	Reds Team	16.00	7.25	2.00	☐	531	Bobby G. Smith	20.00	9.00	2.50
☐	466	Norm Cash AS	13.00	5.75	1.60	☐	532	Dick Stigman	20.00	9.00	2.50
☐	467	Chuck Schilling AS	12.00	5.50	1.50	☐	533	Charley Lau SP	35.00	16.00	4.40
☐	468	Brooks Robinson AS	20.00	9.00	2.50	☐	534	Tony Gonzalez SP	32.00	14.50	4.00
☐	469	Luis Aparicio AS	16.00	7.25	2.00	☐	535	Ed Roebuck	20.00	9.00	2.50
☐	470	Al Kaline AS	20.00	9.00	2.50	☐	536	Dick Gernert	20.00	9.00	2.50
☐	471	Mickey Mantle AS	180.00	80.00	22.00	☐	537	Cleveland Indians	50.00	22.00	6.25
☐	472	Rocky Colavito AS	16.00	7.25	2.00			Team Card			
☐	473	Elston Howard AS	13.00	5.75	1.60	☐	538	Jack Sanford	20.00	9.00	2.50
☐	474	Frank Lary AS	12.00	5.50	1.50	☐	539	Billy Moran	20.00	9.00	2.50
☐	475	Whitey Ford AS	16.00	7.25	2.00	☐	540	Jim Landis SP	32.00	14.50	4.00
☐	476	Orioles Team	16.00	7.25	2.00	☐	541	Don Nottebart SP	32.00	14.50	4.00
☐	477	Andre Rodgers	12.00	5.50	1.50	☐	542	Dave Philley	20.00	9.00	2.50
☐	478	Don Zimmer	13.00	5.75	1.60	☐	543	Bob Allen SP	32.00	14.50	4.00
		(Shown with Mets cap,				☐	544	Willie McCovey SP	115.00	52.50	14.50
		but listed as with				☐	545	Hoyt Wilhelm SP	55.00	25.00	7.00
		Cincinnati)				☐	546	Moe Thacker SP	32.00	14.50	4.00
☐	479	Joel Horlen	12.00	5.50	1.50	☐	547	Don Ferrarese	20.00	9.00	2.50
☐	480	Harvey Kuenn	13.00	5.75	1.60	☐	548	Bobby Del Greco	20.00	9.00	2.50
☐	481	Vic Wertz	13.00	5.75	1.60	☐	549	Bill Rigney MG SP	32.00	14.50	4.00
☐	482	Sam Mele MG	12.00	5.50	1.50	☐	550	Art Mahaffey SP	32.00	14.50	4.00
☐	483	Don McMahon	12.00	5.50	1.50	☐	551	Harry Bright	20.00	9.00	2.50
☐	484	Dick Schofield	12.00	5.50	1.50	☐	552	Chicago Cubs SP	55.00	25.00	7.00
☐	485	Pedro Ramos	12.00	5.50	1.50			Team Card			
☐	486	Jim Gilliam	13.00	5.75	1.60	☐	553	Jim Coates	20.00	9.00	2.50
☐	487	Jerry Lynch	12.00	5.50	1.50	☐	554	Bubba Morton SP	32.00	14.50	4.00
☐	488	Hal Brown	12.00	5.50	1.50	☐	555	John Buzhardt SP	32.00	14.50	4.00
☐	489	Julio Gotay	12.00	5.50	1.50	☐	556	Al Spangler	20.00	9.00	2.50
☐	490	Clete Boyer	13.00	5.75	1.60	☐	557	Bob Anderson SP	32.00	14.50	4.00
☐	491	Leon Wagner	12.00	5.50	1.50	☐	558	John Goryl	20.00	9.00	2.50
☐	492	Hal W. Smith	13.00	5.75	1.60	☐	559	Mike Higgins MG	20.00	9.00	2.50
☐	493	Danny McDevitt	12.00	5.50	1.50	☐	560	Chuck Estrada SP	32.00	14.50	4.00
☐	494	Sammy White	12.00	5.50	1.50	☐	561	Gene Oliver SP	32.00	14.50	4.00
☐	495	Don Cardwell	12.00	5.50	1.50	☐	562	Bill Henry	20.00	9.00	2.50
☐	496	Wayne Causey	12.00	5.50	1.50	☐	563	Ken Aspromonte	20.00	9.00	2.50
☐	497	Ed Bouchee	13.00	5.75	1.60	☐	564	Bob Grim	20.00	9.00	2.50
☐	498	Jim Donohue	12.00	5.50	1.50	☐	565	Jose Pagan	20.00	9.00	2.50

			NRMT	VG-E	GOOD
☐	566	Marty Kutyna SP	32.00	14.50	4.00
☐	567	Tracy Stallard SP	32.00	14.50	4.00
☐	568	Jim Golden	20.00	9.00	2.50
☐	569	Ed Sadowski SP	32.00	14.50	4.00
☐	570	Bill Stafford SP	32.00	14.50	4.00
☐	571	Billy Klaus SP	32.00	14.50	4.00
☐	572	Bob G. Miller SP	35.00	16.00	4.40
☐	573	Johnny Logan	20.00	9.00	2.50
☐	574	Dean Stone	20.00	9.00	2.50
☐	575	Red Schoendienst SP	45.00	20.00	5.50
☐	576	Russ Kemmerer SP	32.00	14.50	4.00
☐	577	Dave Nicholson SP	32.00	14.50	4.00
☐	578	Jim Duffalo	20.00	9.00	2.50
☐	579	Jim Schaffer SP	32.00	14.50	4.00
☐	580	Bill Monbouquette	20.00	9.00	2.50
☐	581	Mel Roach	20.00	9.00	2.50
☐	582	Ron Piche	20.00	9.00	2.50
☐	583	Larry Osborne	20.00	9.00	2.50
☐	584	Minnesota Twins SP Team Card	55.00	25.00	7.00
☐	585	Glen Hobbie SP	32.00	14.50	4.00
☐	586	Sammy Esposito SP	32.00	14.50	4.00
☐	587	Frank Funk SP	32.00	14.50	4.00
☐	588	Birdie Tebbetts MG	20.00	9.00	2.50
☐	589	Bob Turley	20.00	9.00	2.50
☐	590	Curt Flood	25.00	11.00	3.10
☐	591	Rookie Pitchers SP	70.00	32.00	8.75
		Sam McDowell			
		Ron Taylor			
		Ron Nischwitz			
		Art Quirk			
		Dick Radatz			
☐	592	Rookie Pitchers SP	70.00	32.00	8.75
		Dan Pfister			
		Bo Belinsky			
		Dave Stenhouse			
		Jim Bouton			
		Joe Bonikowski			
☐	593	Rookie Pitchers SP	48.00	22.00	6.00
		Jack Lamabe			
		Craig Anderson			
		Jack Hamilton			
		Bob Moorhead			
		Bob Veale			
☐	594	Rookie Catchers SP	75.00	34.00	9.50
		Doc Edwards			
		Ken Retzer			
		Bob Uecker			
		Doug Camilli			
		Don Pavletich			
☐	595	Rookie Infielders SP	45.00	20.00	5.50
		Bob Sadowski			
		Felix Torres			
		Marlan Coughtry			
		Ed Charles			
☐	596	Rookie Infielders SP	70.00	32.00	8.75
		Bernie Allen			
		Joe Pepitone			
		Phil Linz			
		Rich Rollins			
☐	597	Rookie Infielders SP	45.00	20.00	5.50
		Jim McKnight			
		Rod Kanehl			
		Amado Samuel			
		Denis Menke			
☐	598	Rookie Outfielders SP	70.00	20.00	7.00
		Al Luplow			
		Manny Jimenez			
		Howie Goss			
		Jim Hickman			
		Ed Olivares			

1963 Topps

 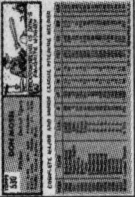

The cards in this 576-card set measure 2 1/2" by 3 1/2". The sharp color photographs of the 1963 set are a vivid contrast to the drab pictures of 1962. In addition to the "League Leaders" series (1-10) and World Series cards (142-148), the seventh and last series of cards (523-576) contains seven rookie cards (each depicting four players). There were some three-card advertising panels produced by Topps; the players included are from the first series; one panel shows Hoyt Wilhelm, Don Lock, and Bob Duliba on the front with a Stan Musial ad/endorsement on one of the backs. This set has gained special prominence in recent years since it contains the Rookie Card of Pete Rose (537). Other key Rookie Cards in this set are Bill Freehan, Tony Oliva, Willie Stargell, and Rusty Staub.

	NRMT	VG-E	GOOD
COMPLETE SET (576)	5000.00	2200.00	600.00
COMMON CARD (1-196)	4.00	1.80	.50
COMMON CARD (197-283)	5.00	2.20	.60
COMMON CARD (284-370)	5.00	2.20	.60
COMMON CARD (371-446)	5.00	2.20	.60
COMMON CARD (447-522)	20.00	9.00	2.50
COMMON CARD (523-576)	15.00	6.75	1.85

			NRMT	VG-E	GOOD
☐	1	NL Batting Leaders	40.00	8.00	4.00
		Tommy Davis			
		Frank Robinson			
		Stan Musial			
		Hank Aaron			
		Bill White			
☐	2	AL Batting Leaders	40.00	18.00	5.00
		Pete Runnels			
		Mickey Mantle			
		Floyd Robinson			
		Norm Siebern			
		Chuck Hinton			
☐	3	NL Home Run Leaders	30.00	13.50	3.70
		Willie Mays			
		Hank Aaron			
		Frank Robinson			
		Orlando Cepeda			
		Ernie Banks			
☐	4	AL Home Run Leaders	14.00	6.25	1.75
		Harmon Killebrew			
		Norm Cash			
		Rocky Colavito			
		Roger Maris			
		Jim Gentile			

	Leon Wagner			
☐ 5	NL ERA Leaders	20.00	9.00	2.50
	Sandy Koufax			
	Bob Shaw			
	Bob Purkey			
	Bob Gibson			
	Don Drysdale			
☐ 6	AL ERA Leaders	8.00	3.60	1.00
	Hank Aguirre			
	Robin Roberts			
	Whitey Ford			
	Eddie Fisher			
	Dean Chance			
☐ 7	NL Pitching Leaders	8.00	3.60	1.00
	Don Drysdale			
	Jack Sanford			
	Bob Purkey			
	Billy O'Dell			
	Art Mahaffey			
	Joe Jay			
☐ 8	AL Pitching Leaders	6.00	2.70	.75
	Ralph Terry			
	Dick Donovan			
	Ray Herbert			
	Jim Bunning			
	Camilo Pascual			
☐ 9	NL Strikeout Leaders	16.00	7.25	2.00
	Don Drysdale			
	Sandy Koufax			
	Bob Gibson			
	Billy O'Dell			
	Dick Farrell			
☐ 10	AL Strikeout Leaders	6.00	2.70	.75
	Camilo Pascual			
	Jim Bunning			
	Ralph Terry			
	Juan Pizarro			
	Jim Kaat			
☐ 11	Lee Walls	4.00	1.80	.50
☐ 12	Steve Barber	4.00	1.80	.50
☐ 13	Philadelphia Phillies Team Card	6.00	2.70	.75
☐ 14	Pedro Ramos	4.00	1.80	.50
☐ 15	Ken Hubbs UER (No position listed on front of card)	6.00	2.70	.75
☐ 16	Al Smith	4.00	1.80	.50
☐ 17	Ryne Duren	5.00	2.20	.60
☐ 18	Buc Blasters	40.00	18.00	5.00
	Smoky Burgess			
	Dick Stuart			
	Bob Clemente			
	Bob Skinner			
☐ 19	Pete Burnside	4.00	1.80	.50
☐ 20	Tony Kubek	5.00	2.20	.60
☐ 21	Marty Keough	4.00	1.80	.50
☐ 22	Curt Simmons	5.00	2.20	.60
☐ 23	Ed Lopat MG	5.00	2.20	.60
☐ 24	Bob Bruce	4.00	1.80	.50
☐ 25	Al Kaline	35.00	16.00	4.40
☐ 26	Ray Moore	4.00	1.80	.50
☐ 27	Choo Choo Coleman	4.00	1.80	.50
☐ 28	Mike Fornieles	4.00	1.80	.50
☐ 29A	1962 Rookie Stars	6.00	2.70	.75
	Sammy Ellis			
	Ray Culp			
	John Boozer			
	Jesse Gonder			
☐ 29B	1963 Rookie Stars	4.00	1.80	.50
	Sammy Ellis			
	Ray Culp			
	John Boozer			
	Jesse Gonder			
☐ 30	Harvey Kuenn	5.00	2.20	.60
☐ 31	Cal Koonce	4.00	1.80	.50
☐ 32	Tony Gonzalez	4.00	1.80	.50
☐ 33	Bo Belinsky	5.00	2.20	.60
☐ 34	Dick Schofield	4.00	1.80	.50
☐ 35	John Buzhardt	4.00	1.80	.50
☐ 36	Jerry Kindall	4.00	1.80	.50
☐ 37	Jerry Lynch	4.00	1.80	.50
☐ 38	Bud Daley	4.00	1.80	.50
☐ 39	Angels Team	6.00	2.70	.75
☐ 40	Vic Power	5.00	2.20	.60
☐ 41	Charley Lau	5.00	2.20	.60
☐ 42	Stan Williams (Listed as Yankee on card but LA cap)	5.00	2.20	.60
☐ 43	Veteran Masters	5.00	2.20	.60
	Casey Stengel MG			
	Gene Woodling			
☐ 44	Terry Fox	4.00	1.80	.50
☐ 45	Bob Aspromonte	4.00	1.80	.50
☐ 46	Tommie Aaron	5.00	2.20	.60
☐ 47	Don Lock	4.00	1.80	.50
☐ 48	Birdie Tebbetts MG	5.00	2.20	.60
☐ 49	Dal Maxvill	5.00	2.20	.60
☐ 50	Billy Pierce	5.00	2.20	.60
☐ 51	George Alusik	4.00	1.80	.50
☐ 52	Chuck Schilling	4.00	1.80	.50
☐ 53	Joe Moeller	4.00	1.80	.50
☐ 54A	1962 Rookie Stars	16.00	7.25	2.00
	Nelson Mathews			
	Harry Fanok			
	Jack Cullen			
	Dave DeBusschere			
☐ 54B	1963 Rookie Stars	7.00	3.10	.85
	Nelson Mathews			
	Harry Fanok			
	Jack Cullen			
	Dave DeBusschere			
☐ 55	Bill Virdon	5.00	2.20	.60
☐ 56	Dennis Bennett	4.00	1.80	.50
☐ 57	Billy Moran	4.00	1.80	.50
☐ 58	Bob Will	4.00	1.80	.50
☐ 59	Craig Anderson	4.00	1.80	.50
☐ 60	Elston Howard	5.00	2.20	.60
☐ 61	Ernie Bowman	4.00	1.80	.50
☐ 62	Bob Hendley	4.00	1.80	.50
☐ 63	Reds Team	6.00	2.70	.75
☐ 64	Dick McAuliffe	5.00	2.20	.60
☐ 65	Jackie Brandt	4.00	1.80	.50
☐ 66	Mike Joyce	4.00	1.80	.50
☐ 67	Ed Charles	4.00	1.80	.50
☐ 68	Friendly Foes	20.00	9.00	2.50
	Duke Snider			
	Gil Hodges			
☐ 69	Bud Zipfel	4.00	1.80	.50
☐ 70	Jim O'Toole	5.00	2.20	.60
☐ 71	Bobby Wine	5.00	2.20	.60
☐ 72	Johnny Romano	4.00	1.80	.50
☐ 73	Bobby Bragan MG	5.00	2.20	.60
☐ 74	Denny Lemaster	4.00	1.80	.50
☐ 75	Bob Allison	5.00	2.20	.60
☐ 76	Earl Wilson	5.00	2.20	.60
☐ 77	Al Spangler	4.00	1.80	.50
☐ 78	Marv Throneberry	4.00	1.80	.50
☐ 79	Checklist 1	10.00	2.00	1.00
☐ 80	Jim Gilliam	4.00	1.80	.50
☐ 81	Jim Schaffer	4.00	1.80	.50
☐ 82	Ed Rakow	4.00	1.80	.50
☐ 83	Charley James	4.00	1.80	.50

☐ 84 Ron Kline	4.00	1.80	.50
☐ 85 Tom Haller	5.00	2.20	.60
☐ 86 Charley Maxwell	5.00	2.20	.60
☐ 87 Bob Veale	5.00	2.20	.60
☐ 88 Ron Hansen	4.00	1.80	.50
☐ 89 Dick Stigman	4.00	1.80	.50
☐ 90 Gordy Coleman	5.00	2.20	.60
☐ 91 Dallas Green	5.00	2.20	.60
☐ 92 Hector Lopez	5.00	2.20	.60
☐ 93 Galen Cisco	4.00	1.80	.50
☐ 94 Bob Schmidt	4.00	1.80	.50
☐ 95 Larry Jackson	4.00	1.80	.50
☐ 96 Lou Clinton	4.00	1.80	.50
☐ 97 Bob Duliba	4.00	1.80	.50
☐ 98 George Thomas	4.00	1.80	.50
☐ 99 Jim Umbricht	4.00	1.80	.50
☐ 100 Joe Cunningham	5.00	2.20	.60
☐ 101 Joe Gibbon	4.00	1.80	.50
☐ 102A Checklist 2	12.00	2.40	1.20
(Red on yellow)			
☐ 102B Checklist 2	12.00	2.40	1.20
(White on red)			
☐ 103 Chuck Essegian	4.00	1.80	.50
☐ 104 Lew Krausse	4.00	1.80	.50
☐ 105 Ron Fairly	5.00	2.20	.60
☐ 106 Bobby Bolin	4.00	1.80	.50
☐ 107 Jim Hickman	5.00	2.20	.60
☐ 108 Hoyt Wilhelm	10.00	4.50	1.25
☐ 109 Lee Maye	4.00	1.80	.50
☐ 110 Rich Rollins	5.00	2.20	.60
☐ 111 Al Jackson	4.00	1.80	.50
☐ 112 Dick Brown	4.00	1.80	.50
☐ 113 Don Landrum UER	4.00	1.80	.50
(Photo actually			
Ron Santo)			
☐ 114 Dan Osinski	4.00	1.80	.50
☐ 115 Carl Yastrzemski	40.00	18.00	5.00
☐ 116 Jim Brosnan	5.00	2.20	.60
☐ 117 Jacke Davis	4.00	1.80	.50
☐ 118 Sherm Lollar	4.00	1.80	.50
☐ 119 Bob Lillis	4.00	1.80	.50
☐ 120 Roger Maris	55.00	25.00	7.00
☐ 121 Jim Hannan	4.00	1.80	.50
☐ 122 Julio Gotay	4.00	1.80	.50
☐ 123 Frank Howard	5.00	2.20	.60
☐ 124 Dick Howser	5.00	2.20	.60
☐ 125 Robin Roberts	14.00	6.25	1.75
☐ 126 Bob Uecker	14.00	6.25	1.75
☐ 127 Bill Tuttle	4.00	1.80	.50
☐ 128 Matty Alou	5.00	2.20	.60
☐ 129 Gary Bell	4.00	1.80	.50
☐ 130 Dick Groat	5.00	2.20	.60
☐ 131 Washington Senators	6.00	2.70	.75
Team Card			
☐ 132 Jack Hamilton	4.00	1.80	.50
☐ 133 Gene Freese	4.00	1.80	.50
☐ 134 Bob Scheffing MG	4.00	1.80	.50
☐ 135 Richie Ashburn	18.00	8.00	2.20
☐ 136 Ike Delock	4.00	1.80	.50
☐ 137 Mack Jones	4.00	1.80	.50
☐ 138 Pride of NL	70.00	32.00	8.75
Willie Mays			
Stan Musial			
☐ 139 Earl Averill	4.00	1.80	.50
☐ 140 Frank Lary	5.00	2.20	.60
☐ 141 Manny Mota	7.00	3.10	.85
☐ 142 World Series Game 1.	8.00	3.60	1.00
Whitey Ford wins			
series opener			
☐ 143 World Series Game 2.	6.00	2.70	.75
Jack Sanford flashes			
shutout magic			
☐ 144 World Series Game 3	12.00	5.50	1.50
Roger Maris sparks			
Yankee rally			
☐ 145 World Series Game 4.	6.00	2.70	.75
Chuck Hiller blasts			
grand slammer			
☐ 146 World Series Game 5.	6.00	2.70	.75
Tom Tresh's homer			
defeats Giants			
☐ 147 World Series Game 6.	6.00	-2.70	.75
Billy Pierce stars in			
3 hit victory			
☐ 148 World Series Game 7.	6.00	2.70	.75
Yanks celebrate			
as Ralph Terry wins			
☐ 149 Marv Breeding	4.00	1.80	.50
☐ 150 Johnny Podres	5.00	2.20	.60
☐ 151 Pirates Team	6.00	2.70	.75
☐ 152 Ron Nischwitz	4.00	1.80	.50
☐ 153 Hal Smith	4.00	1.80	.50
☐ 154 Walt Alston MG	5.00	2.20	.60
☐ 155 Bill Stafford	4.00	1.80	.50
☐ 156 Roy McMillan	5.00	2.20	.60
☐ 157 Diego Segui	5.00	2.20	.60
☐ 158 Rookie Stars	6.00	2.70	.75
Rogelio Alvares			
Dave Roberts			
Tommy Harper			
Bob Saverine			
☐ 159 Jim Pagliaroni	4.00	1.80	.50
☐ 160 Juan Pizarro	4.00	1.80	.50
☐ 161 Frank Torre	5.00	2.20	.60
☐ 162 Twins Team	6.00	2.70	.75
☐ 163 Don Larsen	5.00	2.20	.60
☐ 164 Bubba Morton	4.00	1.80	.50
☐ 165 Jim Kaat	6.00	2.70	.75
☐ 166 Johnny Keane MG	4.00	1.80	.50
☐ 167 Jim Fregosi	6.00	2.70	.75
☐ 168 Russ Nixon	4.00	1.80	.50
☐ 169 Rookie Stars	25.00	11.00	3.10
Dick Egan			
Julio Navarro			
Tommie Sisk			
Gaylord Perry			
☐ 170 Joe Adcock	4.00	1.80	.50
☐ 171 Steve Hamilton	4.00	1.80	.50
☐ 172 Gene Oliver	4.00	1.80	.50
☐ 173 Bombers' Best	135.00	60.00	17.00
Tom Tresh			
Mickey Mantle			
Bobby Richardson			
☐ 174 Larry Burright	4.00	1.80	.50
☐ 175 Bob Buhl	5.00	2.20	.60
☐ 176 Jim King	4.00	1.80	.50
☐ 177 Bubba Phillips	4.00	1.80	.50
☐ 178 Johnny Edwards	4.00	1.80	.50
☐ 179 Ron Piche	4.00	1.80	.50
☐ 180 Bill Skowron	5.00	2.20	.60
☐ 181 Sammy Esposito	4.00	1.80	.50
☐ 182 Albie Pearson	5.00	2.20	.60
☐ 183 Joe Pepitone	5.00	2.20	.60
☐ 184 Vern Law	5.00	2.20	.60
☐ 185 Chuck Hiller	4.00	1.80	.50
☐ 186 Jerry Zimmerman	4.00	1.80	.50
☐ 187 Willie Kirkland	4.00	1.80	.50
☐ 188 Eddie Bressoud	4.00	1.80	.50
☐ 189 Dave Giusti	5.00	2.20	.60
☐ 190 Minnie Minoso	5.00	2.20	.60
☐ 191 Checklist 3	12.00	2.40	1.20
☐ 192 Clay Dalrymple	4.00	1.80	.50

☐ 193	Andre Rodgers	4.00	1.80	.50
☐ 194	Joe Nuxhall	5.00	2.20	.60
☐ 195	Manny Jimenez	4.00	1.80	.50
☐ 196	Doug Camilli	4.00	1.80	.50
☐ 197	Roger Craig	5.00	2.20	.60
☐ 198	Lenny Green	5.00	2.20	.60
☐ 199	Joe Amalfitano	5.00	2.20	.60
☐ 200	Mickey Mantle	550.00	250.00	70.00
☐ 201	Cecil Butler	5.00	2.20	.60
☐ 202	Boston Red Sox	7.00	3.10	.85
	Team Card			
☐ 203	Chico Cardenas	5.00	2.20	.60
☐ 204	Don Nottebart	5.00	2.20	.60
☐ 205	Luis Aparicio	16.00	7.25	2.00
☐ 206	Ray Washburn	5.00	2.20	.60
☐ 207	Ken Hunt	5.00	2.20	.60
☐ 208	Rookie Stars	5.00	2.20	.60
	Ron Herbel			
	John Miller			
	Wally Wolf			
	Ron Taylor			
☐ 209	Hobie Landrith	5.00	2.20	.60
☐ 210	Sandy Koufax	160.00	70.00	20.00
☐ 211	Fred Whitfield	5.00	2.20	.60
☐ 212	Glen Hobbie	5.00	2.20	.60
☐ 213	Billy Hitchcock MG	5.00	2.20	.60
☐ 214	Orlando Pena	5.00	2.20	.60
☐ 215	Bob Skinner	5.00	2.20	.60
☐ 216	Gene Conley	5.00	2.20	.60
☐ 217	Joe Christopher	5.00	2.20	.60
☐ 218	Tiger Twirlers	5.00	2.20	.60
	Frank Lary			
	Don Mossi			
	Jim Bunning			
☐ 219	Chuck Cottier	5.00	2.20	.60
☐ 220	Camilo Pascual	5.00	2.20	.60
☐ 221	Cookie Rojas	6.00	2.70	.75
☐ 222	Cubs Team	7.00	3.10	.85
☐ 223	Eddie Fisher	5.00	2.20	.60
☐ 224	Mike Roarke	5.00	2.20	.60
☐ 225	Joey Jay	5.00	2.20	.60
☐ 226	Julian Javier	5.00	2.20	.60
☐ 227	Jim Grant	5.00	2.20	.60
☐ 228	Rookie Stars	45.00	20.00	5.50
	Max Alvis			
	Bob Bailey			
	Tony Oliva			
	(Listed as Pedro)			
	Ed Kranepool			
☐ 229	Willie Davis	5.00	2.20	.60
☐ 230	Pete Runnels	5.00	2.20	.60
☐ 231	Eli Grba UER	5.00	2.20	.60
	(Large photo is			
	Ryne Duren)			
☐ 232	Frank Malzone	5.00	2.20	.60
☐ 233	Casey Stengel MG	18.00	8.00	2.20
☐ 234	Dave Nicholson	5.00	2.20	.60
☐ 235	Billy O'Dell	5.00	2.20	.60
☐ 236	Bill Bryan	5.00	2.20	.60
☐ 237	Jim Coates	5.00	2.20	.60
☐ 238	Lou Johnson	5.00	2.20	.60
☐ 239	Harvey Haddix	5.00	2.20	.60
☐ 240	Rocky Colavito	16.00	7.25	2.00
☐ 241	Bob Smith	5.00	2.20	.60
☐ 242	Power Plus	55.00	25.00	7.00
	Ernie Banks			
	Hank Aaron			
☐ 243	Don Leppert	5.00	2.20	.60
☐ 244	John Tsitouris	5.00	2.20	.60
☐ 245	Gil Hodges	18.00	8.00	2.20
☐ 246	Lee Stange	5.00	2.20	.60
☐ 247	Yankees Team	35.00	16.00	4.40
☐ 248	Tito Francona	5.00	2.20	.60
☐ 249	Leo Burke	5.00	2.20	.60
☐ 250	Stan Musial	135.00	60.00	17.00
☐ 251	Jack Lamabe	5.00	2.20	.60
☐ 252	Ron Santo	10.00	4.50	1.25
☐ 253	Rookie Stars	5.00	2.20	.60
	Len Gabrielson			
	Pete Jernigan			
	John Wojcik			
	Deacon Jones			
☐ 254	Mike Hershberger	5.00	2.20	.60
☐ 255	Bob Shaw	5.00	2.20	.60
☐ 256	Jerry Lumpe	5.00	2.20	.60
☐ 257	Hank Aguirre	5.00	2.20	.60
☐ 258	Alvin Dark MG	5.00	2.20	.60
☐ 259	Johnny Logan	5.00	2.20	.60
☐ 260	Jim Gentile	5.00	2.20	.60
☐ 261	Bob Miller	5.00	2.20	.60
☐ 262	Ellis Burton	5.00	2.20	.60
☐ 263	Dave Stenhouse	5.00	2.20	.60
☐ 264	Phil Linz	5.00	2.20	.60
☐ 265	Vada Pinson	6.00	2.70	.75
☐ 266	Bob Allen	5.00	2.20	.60
☐ 267	Carl Sawatski	5.00	2.20	.60
☐ 268	Don Demeter	5.00	2.20	.60
☐ 269	Don Mincher	5.00	2.20	.60
☐ 270	Felipe Alou	6.00	2.70	.75
☐ 271	Dean Stone	5.00	2.20	.60
☐ 272	Danny Murphy	5.00	2.20	.60
☐ 273	Sammy Taylor	5.00	2.20	.60
☐ 274	Checklist 4	12.00	2.40	1.20
☐ 275	Eddie Mathews	18.00	8.00	2.20
☐ 276	Barry Shetrone	5.00	2.20	.60
☐ 277	Dick Farrell	5.00	2.20	.60
☐ 278	Chico Fernandez	5.00	2.20	.60
☐ 279	Wally Moon	5.00	2.20	.60
☐ 280	Bob Rodgers	5.00	2.20	.60
☐ 281	Tom Sturdivant	5.00	2.20	.60
☐ 282	Bobby Del Greco	5.00	2.20	.60
☐ 283	Roy Sievers	5.00	2.20	.60
☐ 284	Dave Sisler	5.00	2.20	.60
☐ 285	Dick Stuart	5.00	2.20	.60
☐ 286	Stu Miller	5.00	2.20	.60
☐ 287	Dick Bertell	5.00	2.20	.60
☐ 288	Chicago White Sox	10.00	4.50	1.25
	Team Card			
☐ 289	Hal Brown	5.00	2.20	.60
☐ 290	Bill White	6.00	2.70	.75
☐ 291	Don Rudolph	5.00	2.20	.60
☐ 292	Pumpsie Green	5.00	2.20	.60
☐ 293	Bill Pleis	5.00	2.20	.60
☐ 294	Bill Rigney MG	5.00	2.20	.60
☐ 295	Ed Roebuck	5.00	2.20	.60
☐ 296	Doc Edwards	5.00	2.20	.60
☐ 297	Jim Golden	5.00	2.20	.60
☐ 298	Don Dillard	5.00	2.20	.60
☐ 299	Rookie Stars	5.00	2.20	.60
	Dave Morehead			
	Bob Dustal			
	Tom Butters			
	Dan Schneider			
☐ 300	Willie Mays	135.00	60.00	17.00
☐ 301	Bill Fischer	5.00	2.20	.60
☐ 302	Whitey Herzog	6.00	2.70	.75
☐ 303	Earl Francis	5.00	2.20	.60
☐ 304	Harry Bright	5.00	2.20	.60
☐ 305	Don Hoak	5.00	2.20	.60
☐ 306	Star Receivers	6.00	2.70	.75
	Earl Battey			
	Elston Howard			

☐ 307	Chet Nichols	5.00	2.20	.60
☐ 308	Camilo Carreon	5.00	2.20	.60
☐ 309	Jim Brewer	5.00	2.20	.60
☐ 310	Tommy Davis	5.00	2.20	.60
☐ 311	Joe McClain	5.00	2.20	.60
☐ 312	Houston Colts	25.00	11.00	3.10
	Team Card			
☐ 313	Ernie Broglio	5.00	2.20	.60
☐ 314	John Goryl	5.00	2.20	.60
☐ 315	Ralph Terry	5.00	2.20	.60
☐ 316	Norm Sherry	5.00	2.20	.60
☐ 317	Sam McDowell	8.00	3.60	1.00
☐ 318	Gene Mauch MG	5.00	2.20	.60
☐ 319	Joe Gaines	5.00	2.20	.60
☐ 320	Warren Spahn	40.00	18.00	5.00
☐ 321	Gino Cimoli	5.00	2.20	.60
☐ 322	Bob Turley	5.00	2.20	.60
☐ 323	Bill Mazeroski	8.00	3.60	1.00
☐ 324	Rookie Stars	6.00	2.70	.75
	George Williams			
	Pete Ward			
	Phil Roof			
	Vic Davalillo			
☐ 325	Jack Sanford	5.00	2.20	.60
☐ 326	Hank Foiles	5.00	2.20	.60
☐ 327	Paul Foytack	5.00	2.20	.60
☐ 328	Dick Williams	5.00	2.20	.60
☐ 329	Lindy McDaniel	5.00	2.20	.60
☐ 330	Chuck Hinton	5.00	2.20	.60
☐ 331	Series Foes	5.00	2.20	.60
	Bill Stafford			
	Bill Pierce			
☐ 332	Joel Horlen	5.00	2.20	.60
☐ 333	Carl Warwick	5.00	2.20	.60
☐ 334	Wynn Hawkins	5.00	2.20	.60
☐ 335	Leon Wagner	5.00	2.20	.60
☐ 336	Ed Bauta	5.00	2.20	.60
☐ 337	Dodgers Team	20.00	9.00	2.50
☐ 338	Russ Kemmerer	5.00	2.20	.60
☐ 339	Ted Bowsfield	5.00	2.20	.60
☐ 340	Yogi Berra P/CO	70.00	32.00	8.75
☐ 341	Jack Baldschun	5.00	2.20	.60
☐ 342	Gene Woodling	5.00	2.20	.60
☐ 343	Johnny Pesky MG	5.00	2.20	.60
☐ 344	Don Schwall	5.00	2.20	.60
☐ 345	Brooks Robinson	55.00	25.00	7.00
☐ 346	Billy Hoeft	5.00	2.20	.60
☐ 347	Joe Torre	10.00	4.50	1.25
☐ 348	Vic Wertz	5.00	2.20	.60
☐ 349	Zoilo Versalles	5.00	2.20	.60
☐ 350	Bob Purkey	5.00	2.20	.60
☐ 351	Al Luplow	5.00	2.20	.60
☐ 352	Ken Johnson	5.00	2.20	.60
☐ 353	Billy Williams	30.00	13.50	3.70
☐ 354	Dom Zanni	5.00	2.20	.60
☐ 355	Dean Chance	5.00	2.20	.60
☐ 356	John Schaive	5.00	2.20	.60
☐ 357	George Altman	5.00	2.20	.60
☐ 358	Milt Pappas	5.00	2.20	.60
☐ 359	Haywood Sullivan	5.00	2.20	.60
☐ 360	Don Drysdale	40.00	18.00	5.00
☐ 361	Clete Boyer	7.00	3.10	.85
☐ 362	Checklist 5	12.00	2.40	1.20
☐ 363	Dick Radatz	5.00	2.20	.60
☐ 364	Howie Goss	5.00	2.20	.60
☐ 365	Jim Bunning	12.00	5.50	1.50
☐ 366	Tony Taylor	5.00	2.20	.60
☐ 367	Tony Cloninger	5.00	2.20	.60
☐ 368	Ed Bailey	5.00	2.20	.60
☐ 369	Jim Lemon	5.00	2.20	.60
☐ 370	Dick Donovan	5.00	2.20	.60
☐ 371	Rod Kanehl	5.00	2.20	.60
☐ 372	Don Lee	5.00	2.20	.60
☐ 373	Jim Campbell	5.00	2.20	.60
☐ 374	Claude Osteen	6.00	2.70	.75
☐ 375	Ken Boyer	8.00	3.60	1.00
☐ 376	John Wyatt	5.00	2.20	.60
☐ 377	Baltimore Orioles	10.00	4.50	1.25
	Team Card			
☐ 378	Bill Henry	5.00	2.20	.60
☐ 379	Bob Anderson	5.00	2.20	.60
☐ 380	Ernie Banks UER	80.00	36.00	10.00
	(Back has career Major			
	and Minor, but he			
	never played in Minors)			
☐ 381	Frank Baumann	5.00	2.20	.60
☐ 382	Ralph Houk MG	8.00	2.20	.60
☐ 383	Pete Richert	5.00	2.20	.60
☐ 384	Bob Tillman	5.00	2.20	.60
☐ 385	Art Mahaffey	5.00	2.20	.60
☐ 386	Rookie Stars	5.00	2.20	.60
	Ed Kirkpatrick			
	John Bateman			
	Larry Bearnarth			
	Garry Roggenburk			
☐ 387	Al McBean	5.00	2.20	.60
☐ 388	Jim Davenport	6.00	2.70	.75
☐ 389	Frank Sullivan	5.00	2.20	.60
☐ 390	Hank Aaron	135.00	60.00	17.00
☐ 391	Bill Dailey	5.00	2.20	.60
☐ 392	Tribe Thumpers	5.00	2.20	.60
	Johnny Romano			
	Tito Francona			
☐ 393	Ken MacKenzie	5.00	2.20	.60
☐ 394	Tim McCarver	14.00	6.25	1.75
☐ 395	Don McMahon	5.00	2.20	.60
☐ 396	Joe Koppe	5.00	2.20	.60
☐ 397	Kansas City Athletics	10.00	4.50	1.25
	Team Card			
☐ 398	Boog Powell	25.00	11.00	3.10
☐ 399	Dick Ellsworth	6.00	2.70	.75
☐ 400	Frank Robinson	55.00	25.00	7.00
☐ 401	Jim Bouton	14.00	6.25	1.75
☐ 402	Mickey Vernon MG	6.00	2.70	.75
☐ 403	Ron Perranoski	6.00	2.70	.75
☐ 404	Bob Oldis	5.00	2.20	.60
☐ 405	Floyd Robinson	5.00	2.20	.60
☐ 406	Howie Koplitz	5.00	2.20	.60
☐ 407	Rookie Stars	5.00	2.20	.60
	Frank Kostro			
	Chico Ruiz			
	Larry Elliot			
	Dick Simpson			
☐ 408	Billy Gardner	5.00	2.20	.60
☐ 409	Roy Face	6.00	2.70	.75
☐ 410	Earl Battey	5.00	2.20	.60
☐ 411	Jim Constable	5.00	2.20	.60
☐ 412	Dodger Big Three	40.00	18.00	5.00
	Johnny Podres			
	Don Drysdale			
	Sandy Koufax			
☐ 413	Jerry Walker	5.00	2.20	.60
☐ 414	Ty Cline	5.00	2.20	.60
☐ 415	Bob Gibson	55.00	25.00	7.00
☐ 416	Alex Grammas	5.00	2.20	.60
☐ 417	Giants Team	10.00	4.50	1.25
☐ 418	John Orsino	5.00	2.20	.60
☐ 419	Tracy Stallard	5.00	2.20	.60
☐ 420	Bobby Richardson	14.00	6.25	1.75
☐ 421	Tom Morgan	5.00	2.20	.60
☐ 422	Fred Hutchinson MG	6.00	2.70	.75
☐ 423	Ed Hobaugh	5.00	2.20	.60

☐ 424	Charlie Smith	5.00	2.20	.60
☐ 425	Smoky Burgess	6.00	2.70	.75
☐ 426	Barry Latman	5.00	2.20	.60
☐ 427	Bernie Allen	5.00	2.20	.60
☐ 428	Carl Boles	5.00	2.20	.60
☐ 429	Lou Burdette	5.00	2.20	.60
☐ 430	Norm Siebern	5.00	2.20	.60
☐ 431A	Checklist 6	12.00	2.40	1.20
	(White on red)			
☐ 431B	Checklist 6	20.00	4.00	2.00
	(Black on orange)			
☐ 432	Roman Mejias	5.00	2.20	.60
☐ 433	Denis Menke	5.00	2.20	.60
☐ 434	John Callison	6.00	2.70	.75
☐ 435	Woody Held	5.00	2.20	.60
☐ 436	Tim Harkness	5.00	2.20	.60
☐ 437	Bill Bruton	5.00	2.20	.60
☐ 438	Wes Stock	5.00	2.20	.60
☐ 439	Don Zimmer	5.00	2.20	.60
☐ 440	Juan Marichal	30.00	13.50	3.70
☐ 441	Lee Thomas	6.00	2.70	.75
☐ 442	J.C. Hartman	5.00	2.20	.60
☐ 443	Jim Piersall	6.00	2.70	.75
☐ 444	Jim Maloney	5.00	2.20	.60
☐ 445	Norm Cash	7.00	3.10	.85
☐ 446	Whitey Ford	40.00	18.00	5.00
☐ 447	Felix Mantilla	20.00	9.00	2.50
☐ 448	Jack Kralick	20.00	9.00	2.50
☐ 449	Jose Tartabull	20.00	9.00	2.50
☐ 450	Bob Friend	22.50	10.00	2.80
☐ 451	Indians Team	40.00	18.00	5.00
☐ 452	Barney Schultz	20.00	9.00	2.50
☐ 453	Jake Wood	20.00	9.00	2.50
☐ 454A	Art Fowler	20.00	9.00	2.50
	(Card number on			
	white background)			
☐ 454B	Art Fowler	30.00	13.50	3.70
	(Card number on			
	orange background)			
☐ 455	Ruben Amaro	20.00	9.00	2.50
☐ 456	Jim Coker	20.00	9.00	2.50
☐ 457	Tex Clevenger	20.00	9.00	2.50
☐ 458	Al Lopez MG	22.50	10.00	2.80
☐ 459	Dick LeMay	20.00	9.00	2.50
☐ 460	Del Crandall	22.50	10.00	2.80
☐ 461	Norm Bass	20.00	9.00	2.50
☐ 462	Wally Post	22.50	10.00	2.80
☐ 463	Joe Schaffernoth	20.00	9.00	2.50
☐ 464	Ken Aspromonte	20.00	9.00	2.50
☐ 465	Chuck Estrada	20.00	9.00	2.50
☐ 466	Rookie Stars SP	60.00	27.00	7.50
	Nate Oliver			
	Tony Martinez			
	Bill Freehan			
	Jerry Robinson			
☐ 467	Phil Ortega	20.00	9.00	2.50
☐ 468	Carroll Hardy	22.50	10.00	2.80
☐ 469	Jay Hook	20.00	9.00	2.50
☐ 470	Tom Tresh SP	60.00	27.00	7.50
☐ 471	Ken Retzer	20.00	9.00	2.50
☐ 472	Lou Brock	100.00	45.00	12.50
☐ 473	New York Mets	100.00	45.00	12.50
	Team Card			
☐ 474	Jack Fisher	20.00	9.00	2.50
☐ 475	Gus Triandos	22.50	10.00	2.80
☐ 476	Frank Funk	20.00	9.00	2.50
☐ 477	Donn Clendenon	22.50	10.00	2.80
☐ 478	Paul Brown	20.00	9.00	2.50
☐ 479	Ed Brinkman	20.00	9.00	2.50
☐ 480	Bill Monbouquette	20.00	9.00	2.50
☐ 481	Bob Taylor	20.00	9.00	2.50
☐ 482	Felix Torres	20.00	9.00	2.50
☐ 483	Jim Owens UER	20.00	9.00	2.50
	(Stat column for Wins			
	has an R instead)			
☐ 484	Dale Long SP	25.00	11.00	3.10
☐ 485	Jim Landis	20.00	9.00	2.50
☐ 486	Ray Sadecki	20.00	9.00	2.50
☐ 487	John Roseboro	22.50	10.00	2.80
☐ 488	Jerry Adair	20.00	9.00	2.50
☐ 489	Paul Toth	20.00	9.00	2.50
☐ 490	Willie McCovey	125.00	55.00	15.50
☐ 491	Harry Craft MG	20.00	9.00	2.50
☐ 492	Dave Wickersham	20.00	9.00	2.50
☐ 493	Walt Bond	20.00	9.00	2.50
☐ 494	Phil Regan	22.50	10.00	2.80
☐ 495	Frank Thomas SP	25.00	11.00	3.10
☐ 496	Rookie Stars	22.50	10.00	2.80
	Steve Dalkowski			
	Fred Newman			
	Jack Smith			
	Carl Bouldin			
☐ 497	Bennie Daniels	20.00	9.00	2.50
☐ 498	Eddie Kasko	20.00	9.00	2.50
☐ 499	J.C. Martin	20.00	9.00	2.50
☐ 500	Harmon Killebrew SP	150.00	70.00	19.00
☐ 501	Joe Azcue	20.00	9.00	2.50
☐ 502	Daryl Spencer	20.00	9.00	2.50
☐ 503	Braves Team	40.00	18.00	5.00
☐ 504	Bob Johnson	20.00	9.00	2.50
☐ 505	Curt Flood	22.50	10.00	2.80
☐ 506	Gene Green	20.00	9.00	2.50
☐ 507	Roland Sheldon	20.00	9.00	2.50
☐ 508	Ted Savage	20.00	9.00	2.50
☐ 509A	Checklist 7	30.00	10.00	3.00
	(Copyright centered)			
☐ 509B	Checklist 7	30.00	10.00	3.00
	(Copyright to right)			
☐ 510	Ken McBride	20.00	9.00	2.50
☐ 511	Charlie Neal	22.50	10.00	2.80
☐ 512	Cal McLish	20.00	9.00	2.50
☐ 513	Gary Geiger	20.00	9.00	2.50
☐ 514	Larry Osborne	20.00	9.00	2.50
☐ 515	Don Elston	20.00	9.00	2.50
☐ 516	Purnell Goldy	20.00	9.00	2.50
☐ 517	Hal Woodeshick	20.00	9.00	2.50
☐ 518	Don Blasingame	20.00	9.00	2.50
☐ 519	Claude Raymond	20.00	9.00	2.50
☐ 520	Orlando Cepeda	30.00	13.50	3.70
☐ 521	Dan Pfister	20.00	9.00	2.50
☐ 522	Rookie Stars	22.50	10.00	2.80
	Mel Nelson			
	Gary Peters			
	Jim Roland			
	Art Quirk			
☐ 523	Bill Kunkel	15.00	6.75	1.85
☐ 524	Cardinals Team	30.00	13.50	3.70
☐ 525	Nellie Fox	30.00	13.50	3.70
☐ 526	Dick Hall	15.00	6.75	1.85
☐ 527	Ed Sadowski	15.00	6.75	1.85
☐ 528	Carl Willey	15.00	6.75	1.85
☐ 529	Wes Covington	15.00	6.75	1.85
☐ 530	Don Mossi	15.00	6.75	1.85
☐ 531	Sam Mele MG	15.00	6.75	1.85
☐ 532	Steve Boros	15.00	6.75	1.85
☐ 533	Bobby Shantz	15.00	6.75	1.85
☐ 534	Ken Walters	15.00	6.75	1.85
☐ 535	Jim Perry	15.00	6.75	1.85
☐ 536	Norm Larker	15.00	6.75	1.85
☐ 537	Rookie Stars	1000.00	450.00	125.00
	Pedro Gonzalez			
	Ken McMullen			

			NRMT	VG-E	GOOD
	Al Weis				
	Pete Rose				
☐ 538	George Brunet	15.00	6.75	1.85	
☐ 539	Wayne Causey	15.00	6.75	1.85	
☐ 540	Bob Clemente	350.00	160.00	45.00	
☐ 541	Ron Moeller	15.00	6.75	1.85	
☐ 542	Lou Klimchock	15.00	6.75	1.85	
☐ 543	Russ Snyder	15.00	6.75	1.85	
☐ 544	Rookie Stars	45.00	20.00	5.50	
	Duke Carmel				
	Bill Haas				
	Rusty Staub				
	Dick Phillips				
☐ 545	Jose Pagan	15.00	6.75	1.85	
☐ 546	Hal Reniff	15.00	6.75	1.85	
☐ 547	Gus Bell	15.00	6.75	1.85	
☐ 548	Tom Satriano	15.00	6.75	1.85	
☐ 549	Rookie Stars	15.00	6.75	1.85	
	Marcelino Lopez				
	Pete Lovrich				
	Paul Ratliff				
	Elmo Plaskett				
☐ 550	Duke Snider	75.00	34.00	9.50	
☐ 551	Billy Klaus	15.00	6.75	1.85	
☐ 552	Detroit Tigers	45.00	20.00	5.50	
	Team Card				
☐ 553	Rookie Stars	125.00	55.00	15.50	
	Brock Davis				
	Jim Gosger				
	Willie Stargell				
	John Herrnstein				
☐ 554	Hank Fischer	15.00	6.75	1.85	
☐ 555	John Blanchard	15.00	6.75	1.85	
☐ 556	Al Worthington	15.00	6.75	1.85	
☐ 557	Cuno Barragan	15.00	6.75	1.85	
☐ 558	Rookie Stars	16.00	7.25	2.00	
	Bill Faul				
	Ron Hunt				
	Al Moran				
	Bob Lipski				
☐ 559	Danny Murtaugh MG	15.00	6.75	1.85	
☐ 560	Ray Herbert	15.00	6.75	1.85	
☐ 561	Mike De La Hoz	15.00	6.75	1.85	
☐ 562	Rookie Stars	25.00	11.00	3.10	
	Randy Cardinal				
	Dave McNally				
	Ken Rowe				
	Don Rowe				
☐ 563	Mike McCormick	15.00	6.75	1.85	
☐ 564	George Banks	15.00	6.75	1.85	
☐ 565	Larry Sherry	15.00	6.75	1.85	
☐ 566	Cliff Cook	15.00	6.75	1.85	
☐ 567	Jim Duffalo	15.00	6.75	1.85	
☐ 568	Bob Sadowski	15.00	6.75	1.85	
☐ 569	Luis Arroyo	15.00	6.75	1.85	
☐ 570	Frank Bolling	15.00	6.75	1.85	
☐ 571	Johnny Klippstein	15.00	6.75	1.85	
☐ 572	Jack Spring	15.00	6.75	1.85	
☐ 573	Coot Veal	15.00	6.75	1.85	
☐ 574	Hal Kolstad	15.00	6.75	1.85	
☐ 575	Don Cardwell	15.00	6.75	1.85	
☐ 576	Johnny Temple	18.00	6.75	1.85	

1964 Topps

The cards in this 587-card set measure 2 1/2" by 3 1/2". Players in the 1964 Topps baseball series were easy to sort by team

due to the giant block lettering found at the top of each card. The name and position of the player are found underneath the picture, and the card is numbered in a ball design on the orange-colored back. The usual last series scarcity holds for this set (523 to 587). Subsets within this set include League Leaders (1-12) and World Series cards (136-140). There were some three-card advertising panels produced by Topps; the players included are from the first series; one panel shows Walt Alston, Bill Henry, and Vada Pinson on the front with a Mickey Mantle card back on one of the backs. Another panel shows Carl Willey, White Sox Rookies, and Bob Friend on the front with a Mickey Mantle card back on one of the backs. The key Rookie Cards in this set are Richie Allen, Tommy John, Tony LaRussa, Lou Piniella, and Phil Niekro.

	NRMT	VG-E	GOOD
COMPLETE SET (587)	3000.00	1350.00	375.00
COMMON CARD (1-196)	3.00	1.35	.35
COMMON CARD (197-370)	4.00	1.80	.50
COMMON CARD (371-522)	7.00	3.10	.85
COMMON CARD (523-587)	16.00	7.25	2.00
☐ 1 NL ERA Leaders	30.00	9.00	3.00
Sandy Koufax			
Dick Ellsworth			
Bob Friend			
☐ 2 AL ERA Leaders	6.00	2.70	.75
Gary Peters			
Juan Pizarro			
Camilo Pascual			
☐ 3 NL Pitching Leaders	18.00	8.00	2.20
Sandy Koufax			
Juan Marichal			
Warren Spahn			
Jim Maloney			
☐ 4 AL Pitching Leaders	10.00	4.50	1.25
Whitey Ford			
Camilo Pascual			
Jim Bouton			
☐ 5 NL Strikeout Leaders	14.00	6.25	1.75
Sandy Koufax			
Jim Maloney			
Don Drysdale			
☐ 6 AL Strikeout Leaders	6.00	2.70	.75
Camilo Pascual			
Jim Bunning			
Dick Stigman			
☐ 7 NL Batting Leaders	18.00	8.00	2.20
Tommy Davis			

☐	Bob Clemente			
	Dick Groat			
	Hank Aaron			
☐ 8	AL Batting Leaders	12.00	5.50	1.50
	Carl Yastrzemski			
	Al Kaline			
	Rich Rollins			
☐ 9	NL Home Run Leaders	30.00	13.50	3.70
	Hank Aaron			
	Willie McCovey			
	Willie Mays			
	Orlando Cepeda			
☐ 10	AL Home Run Leaders	10.00	4.50	1.25
	Harmon Killebrew			
	Dick Stuart			
	Bob Allison			
☐ 11	NL RBI Leaders	12.00	5.50	1.50
	Hank Aaron			
	Ken Boyer			
	Bill White			
☐ 12	AL RBI Leaders	10.00	4.50	1.25
	Dick Stuart			
	Al Kaline			
	Harmon Killebrew			
☐ 13	Hoyt Wilhelm	8.00	3.60	1.00
☐ 14	Dodgers Rookies	3.00	1.35	.35
	Dick Nen			
	Nick Willhite			
☐ 15	Zoilo Versalles	4.00	1.80	.50
☐ 16	John Boozer	3.00	1.35	.35
☐ 17	Willie Kirkland	3.00	1.35	.35
☐ 18	Billy O'Dell	3.00	1.35	.35
☐ 19	Don Wert	3.00	1.35	.35
☐ 20	Bob Friend	4.00	1.80	.50
☐ 21	Yogi Berra MG	30.00	13.50	3.70
☐ 22	Jerry Adair	3.00	1.35	.35
☐ 23	Chris Zachary	3.00	1.35	.35
☐ 24	Carl Sawatski	3.00	1.35	.35
☐ 25	Bill Monbouquette	3.00	1.35	.35
☐ 26	Gino Cimoli	3.00	1.35	.35
☐ 27	New York Mets	8.00	3.60	1.00
	Team Card			
☐ 28	Claude Osteen	4.00	1.80	.50
☐ 29	Lou Brock	35.00	16.00	4.40
☐ 30	Ron Perranoski	4.00	1.80	.50
☐ 31	Dave Nicholson	3.00	1.35	.35
☐ 32	Dean Chance	4.00	1.80	.50
☐ 33	Reds Rookies	4.00	1.80	.50
	Sammy Ellis			
	Mel Queen			
☐ 34	Jim Perry	4.00	1.80	.50
☐ 35	Eddie Mathews	20.00	9.00	2.50
☐ 36	Hal Reniff	3.00	1.35	.35
☐ 37	Smoky Burgess	4.00	1.80	.50
☐ 38	Jim Wynn	7.00	3.10	.85
☐ 39	Hank Aguirre	3.00	1.35	.35
☐ 40	Dick Groat	4.00	1.80	.50
☐ 41	Friendly Foes	8.00	3.60	1.00
	Willie McCovey			
	Leon Wagner			
☐ 42	Moe Drabowsky	4.00	1.80	.50
☐ 43	Roy Sievers	4.00	1.80	.50
☐ 44	Duke Carmel	3.00	1.35	.35
☐ 45	Milt Pappas	4.00	1.80	.50
☐ 46	Ed Brinkman	3.00	1.35	.35
☐ 47	Giants Rookies	5.00	2.20	.60
	Jesus Alou			
	Ron Herbel			
☐ 48	Bob Perry	3.00	1.35	.35
☐ 49	Bill Henry	3.00	1.35	.35
☐ 50	Mickey Mantle	325.00	145.00	40.00
☐ 51	Pete Richert	3.00	1.35	.35
☐ 52	Chuck Hinton	3.00	1.35	.35
☐ 53	Denis Menke	3.00	1.35	.35
☐ 54	Sam Mele MG	3.00	1.35	.35
☐ 55	Ernie Banks	40.00	18.00	5.00
☐ 56	Hal Brown	3.00	1.35	.35
☐ 57	Tim Harkness	3.00	1.35	.35
☐ 58	Don Demeter	3.00	1.35	.35
☐ 59	Ernie Broglio	3.00	1.35	.35
☐ 60	Frank Malzone	4.00	1.80	.50
☐ 61	Angel Backstops	4.00	1.80	.50
	Bob Rodgers			
	Ed Sadowski			
☐ 62	Ted Savage	3.00	1.35	.35
☐ 63	John Orsino	3.00	1.35	.35
☐ 64	Ted Abernathy	3.00	1.35	.35
☐ 65	Felipe Alou	4.00	1.80	.50
☐ 66	Eddie Fisher	3.00	1.35	.35
☐ 67	Tigers Team	6.00	2.70	.75
☐ 68	Willie Davis	4.00	1.80	.50
☐ 69	Clete Boyer	3.00	1.35	.35
☐ 70	Joe Torre	5.00	2.20	.60
☐ 71	Jack Spring	3.00	1.35	.35
☐ 72	Chico Cardenas	4.00	1.80	.50
☐ 73	Jimmie Hall	4.00	1.80	.50
☐ 74	Pirates Rookies	3.00	1.35	.35
	Bob Priddy			
	Tom Butters			
☐ 75	Wayne Causey	3.00	1.35	.35
☐ 76	Checklist 1	10.00	2.00	1.00
☐ 77	Jerry Walker	3.00	1.35	.35
☐ 78	Merritt Ranew	3.00	1.35	.35
☐ 79	Bob Heffner	3.00	1.35	.35
☐ 80	Vada Pinson	4.00	1.80	.50
☐ 81	All-Star Vets	8.00	3.60	1.00
	Nellie Fox			
	Harmon Killebrew			
☐ 82	Jim Davenport	4.00	1.80	.50
☐ 83	Gus Triandos	4.00	1.80	.50
☐ 84	Carl Willey	3.00	1.35	.35
☐ 85	Pete Ward	3.00	1.35	.35
☐ 86	Al Downing	3.00	1.35	.35
☐ 87	St. Louis Cardinals	6.00	2.70	.75
	Team Card			
☐ 88	John Roseboro	4.00	1.80	.50
☐ 89	Boog Powell	6.00	2.70	.75
☐ 90	Earl Battey	3.00	1.35	.35
☐ 91	Bob Bailey	4.00	1.80	.50
☐ 92	Steve Ridzik	3.00	1.35	.35
☐ 93	Gary Geiger	3.00	1.35	.35
☐ 94	Braves Rookies	3.00	1.35	.35
	Jim Britton			
	Larry Maxie			
☐ 95	George Altman	3.00	1.35	.35
☐ 96	Bob Buhl	4.00	1.80	.50
☐ 97	Jim Fregosi	4.00	1.80	.50
☐ 98	Bill Bruton	3.00	1.35	.35
☐ 99	Al Stanek	3.00	1.35	.35
☐ 100	Elston Howard	4.00	1.80	.50
☐ 101	Walt Alston MG	4.00	1.80	.50
☐ 102	Checklist 2	10.00	2.00	1.00
☐ 103	Curt Flood	4.00	1.80	.50
☐ 104	Art Mahaffey	4.00	1.80	.50
☐ 105	Woody Held	3.00	1.35	.35
☐ 106	Joe Nuxhall	4.00	1.80	.50
☐ 107	White Sox Rookies	3.00	1.35	.35
	Bruce Howard			
	Frank Kreutzer			
☐ 108	John Wyatt	3.00	1.35	.35
☐ 109	Rusty Staub	5.00	2.20	.60
☐ 110	Albie Pearson	4.00	1.80	.50

☐ 111	Don Elston	3.00	1.35	.35
☐ 112	Bob Tillman	3.00	1.35	.35
☐ 113	Grover Powell	3.00	1.35	.35
☐ 114	Don Lock	3.00	1.35	.35
☐ 115	Frank Bolling	3.00	1.35	.35
☐ 116	Twins Rookies	12.00	5.50	1.50
	Jay Ward			
	Tony Oliva			
☐ 117	Earl Francis	3.00	1.35	.35
☐ 118	John Blanchard	4.00	1.80	.50
☐ 119	Gary Kolb	3.00	1.35	.35
☐ 120	Don Drysdale	20.00	9.00	2.50
☐ 121	Pete Runnels	4.00	1.80	.50
☐ 122	Don McMahon	3.00	1.35	.35
☐ 123	Jose Pagan	3.00	1.35	.35
☐ 124	Orlando Pena	3.00	1.35	.35
☐ 125	Pete Rose	150.00	70.00	19.00
☐ 126	Russ Snyder	3.00	1.35	.35
☐ 127	Angels Rookies	3.00	1.35	.35
	Aubrey Gatewood			
	Dick Simpson			
☐ 128	Mickey Lolich	20.00	9.00	2.50
☐ 129	Amado Samuel	3.00	1.35	.35
☐ 130	Gary Peters	4.00	1.80	.50
☐ 131	Steve Boros	3.00	1.35	.35
☐ 132	Braves Team	6.00	2.70	.75
☐ 133	Jim Grant	4.00	1.80	.50
☐ 134	Don Zimmer	4.00	1.80	.50
☐ 135	Johnny Callison	4.00	1.80	.50
☐ 136	World Series Game 1	16.00	7.25	2.00
	Sandy Koufax			
	strikes out 15			
☐ 137	World Series Game 2	6.00	2.70	.75
	Tommy Davis			
	sparks rally			
☐ 138	World Series Game 3	6.00	2.70	.75
	LA Three Straight			
	(Ron Fairly)			
☐ 139	World Series Game 4	6.00	2.70	.75
	Sealing Yanks doom			
	(Frank Howard)			
☐ 140	World Series Summary	6.00	2.70	.75
	Dodgers celebrate			
☐ 141	Danny Murtaugh MG	4.00	1.80	.50
☐ 142	John Bateman	3.00	1.35	.35
☐ 143	Bubba Phillips	3.00	1.35	.35
☐ 144	Al Worthington	3.00	1.35	.35
☐ 145	Norm Siebern	3.00	1.35	.35
☐ 146	Indians Rookies	30.00	13.50	3.70
	Tommy John			
	Bob Chance			
☐ 147	Ray Sadecki	3.00	1.35	.35
☐ 148	J.C. Martin	3.00	1.35	.35
☐ 149	Paul Foytack	3.00	1.35	.35
☐ 150	Willie Mays	100.00	45.00	12.50
☐ 151	Athletics Team	6.00	2.70	.75
☐ 152	Denny Lemaster	3.00	1.35	.35
☐ 153	Dick Williams	4.00	1.80	.50
☐ 154	Dick Tracewski	4.00	1.80	.50
☐ 155	Duke Snider	30.00	13.50	3.70
☐ 156	Bill Dailey	3.00	1.35	.35
☐ 157	Gene Mauch MG	4.00	1.80	.50
☐ 158	Ken Johnson	3.00	1.35	.35
☐ 159	Charlie Dees	3.00	1.35	.35
☐ 160	Ken Boyer	5.00	2.20	.60
☐ 161	Dave McNally	4.00	1.80	.50
☐ 162	Hitting Area	4.00	1.80	.50
	Dick Sisler CO			
	Vada Pinson			
☐ 163	Donn Clendenon	4.00	1.80	.50
☐ 164	Bud Daley	3.00	1.35	.35
☐ 165	Jerry Lumpe	3.00	1.35	.35
☐ 166	Marty Keough	3.00	1.35	.35
☐ 167	Senators Rookies	30.00	13.50	3.70
	Mike Brumley			
	Lou Piniella			
☐ 168	Al Weis	3.00	1.35	.35
☐ 169	Del Crandall	4.00	1.80	.50
☐ 170	Dick Radatz	4.00	1.80	.50
☐ 171	Ty Cline	3.00	1.35	.35
☐ 172	Indians Team	6.00	2.70	.75
☐ 173	Ryne Duren	4.00	1.80	.50
☐ 174	Doc Edwards	3.00	1.35	.35
☐ 175	Billy Williams	14.00	6.25	1.75
☐ 176	Tracy Stallard	3.00	1.35	.35
☐ 177	Harmon Killebrew	20.00	9.00	2.50
☐ 178	Hank Bauer MG	4.00	1.80	.50
☐ 179	Carl Warwick	3.00	1.35	.35
☐ 180	Tommy Davis	3.00	1.35	.35
☐ 181	Dave Wickersham	3.00	1.35	.35
☐ 182	Sox Sockers	14.00	6.25	1.75
	Carl Yastrzemski			
	Chuck Schilling			
☐ 183	Ron Taylor	3.00	1.35	.35
☐ 184	Al Luplow	3.00	1.35	.35
☐ 185	Jim O'Toole	4.00	1.80	.50
☐ 186	Roman Mejias	3.00	1.35	.35
☐ 187	Ed Roebuck	3.00	1.35	.35
☐ 188	Checklist 3	10.00	2.00	1.00
☐ 189	Bob Hendley	3.00	1.35	.35
☐ 190	Bobby Richardson	8.00	3.60	1.00
☐ 191	Clay Dalrymple	4.00	1.80	.50
☐ 192	Cubs Rookies	3.00	1.35	.35
	John Boccabella			
	Billy Cowan			
☐ 193	Jerry Lynch	3.00	1.35	.35
☐ 194	John Goryl	3.00	1.35	.35
☐ 195	Floyd Robinson	3.00	1.35	.35
☐ 196	Jim Gentile	3.00	1.35	.35
☐ 197	Frank Lary	5.00	2.20	.60
☐ 198	Len Gabrielson	4.00	1.80	.50
☐ 199	Joe Azcue	4.00	1.80	.50
☐ 200	Sandy Koufax	110.00	50.00	14.00
☐ 201	Orioles Rookies	5.00	2.20	.60
	Sam Bowens			
	Wally Bunker			
☐ 202	Galen Cisco	5.00	2.20	.60
☐ 203	John Kennedy	5.00	2.20	.60
☐ 204	Matty Alou	4.00	1.80	.50
☐ 205	Nellie Fox	8.00	3.60	1.00
☐ 206	Steve Hamilton	4.00	1.80	.50
☐ 207	Fred Hutchinson MG	5.00	2.20	.60
☐ 208	Wes Covington	5.00	2.20	.60
☐ 209	Bob Allen	4.00	1.80	.50
☐ 210	Carl Yastrzemski	40.00	18.00	5.00
☐ 211	Jim Coker	4.00	1.80	.50
☐ 212	Pete Lovrich	4.00	1.80	.50
☐ 213	Angels Team	7.00	3.10	.85
☐ 214	Ken McMullen	5.00	2.20	.60
☐ 215	Ray Herbert	4.00	1.80	.50
☐ 216	Mike de la Hoz	4.00	1.80	.50
☐ 217	Jim King	4.00	1.80	.50
☐ 218	Hank Fischer	4.00	1.80	.50
☐ 219	Young Aces	5.00	2.20	.60
	Al Downing			
	Jim Bouton			
☐ 220	Dick Ellsworth	5.00	2.20	.60
☐ 221	Bob Saverine	4.00	1.80	.50
☐ 222	Billy Pierce	5.00	2.20	.60
☐ 223	George Banks	4.00	1.80	.50
☐ 224	Tommie Sisk	4.00	1.80	.50
☐ 225	Roger Maris	60.00	27.00	7.50

☐ 226	Colts Rookies.............. 7.00	3.10	.85
	Jerry Grote		
	Larry Yellen		
☐ 227	Barry Latman 4.00	1.80	.50
☐ 228	Felix Mantilla.............. 4.00	1.80	.50
☐ 229	Charley Lau 5.00	2.20	.60
☐ 230	Brooks Robinson 40.00	18.00	5.00
☐ 231	Dick Calmus............... 4.00	1.80	.50
☐ 232	Al Lopez MG 5.00	2.20	.60
☐ 233	Hal Smith................... 4.00	1.80	.50
☐ 234	Gary Bell 4.00	1.80	.50
☐ 235	Ron Hunt 4.00	1.80	.50
☐ 236	Bill Faul 4.00	1.80	.50
☐ 237	Cubs Team................. 7.00	3.10	.85
☐ 238	Roy McMillan............. 5.00	2.20	.60
☐ 239	Herm Starrette 4.00	1.80	.50
☐ 240	Bill White 5.00	2.20	.60
☐ 241	Jim Owens................. 4.00	1.80	.50
☐ 242	Harvey Kuenn 5.00	2.20	.60
☐ 243	Phillies Rookies 30.00	13.50	3.70
	Richie Allen		
	John Herrnstein		
☐ 244	Tony LaRussa 30.00	13.50	3.70
☐ 245	Dick Stigman 4.00	1.80	.50
☐ 246	Manny Mota................ 4.00	1.80	.50
☐ 247	Dave DeBusschere....... 6.00	2.70	.75
☐ 248	Johnny Pesky MG........ 5.00	2.20	.60
☐ 249	Doug Camilli 4.00	1.80	.50
☐ 250	Al Kaline 40.00	18.00	5.00
☐ 251	Choo Choo Coleman 4.00	1.80	.50
☐ 252	Ken Aspromonte 4.00	1.80	.50
☐ 253	Wally Post 5.00	2.20	.60
☐ 254	Don Hoak 5.00	2.20	.60
☐ 255	Lee Thomas 5.00	2.20	.60
☐ 256	Johnny Weekly 4.00	1.80	.50
☐ 257	San Francisco Giants . 7.00	3.10	.85
	Team Card		
☐ 258	Garry Roggenburk 4.00	1.80	.50
☐ 259	Harry Bright 4.00	1.80	.50
☐ 260	Frank Robinson 40.00	18.00	5.00
☐ 261	Jim Hannan 4.00	1.80	.50
☐ 262	Cards Rookies............. 8.00	3.60	1.00
	Mike Shannon		
	Harry Fanok		
☐ 263	Chuck Estrada 4.00	1.80	.50
☐ 264	Jim Landis 4.00	1.80	.50
☐ 265	Jim Bunning 8.00	3.60	1.00
☐ 266	Gene Freese 4.00	1.80	.50
☐ 267	Wilbur Wood............... 8.00	3.60	1.00
☐ 268	Bill's Got It................. 5.00	2.20	.60
	Danny Murtaugh MG		
	Bill Virdon		
☐ 269	Ellis Burton 4.00	1.80	.50
☐ 270	Rich Rollins 5.00	2.20	.60
☐ 271	Bob Sadowski 4.00	1.80	.50
☐ 272	Jake Wood 4.00	1.80	.50
☐ 273	Mel Nelson 4.00	1.80	.50
☐ 274	Checklist 4 .... 10.00	2.00	1.00
☐ 275	John Tsitouris 4.00	1.80	.50
☐ 276	Jose Tartabull 5.00	2.20	.60
☐ 277	Ken Retzer 4.00	1.80	.50
☐ 278	Bobby Shantz 5.00	2.20	.60
☐ 279	Joe Koppe UER 4.00	1.80	.50
	(Glove on wrong hand)		
☐ 280	Juan Marichal 14.00	6.25	1.75
☐ 281	Yankees Rookies......... 5.00	2.20	.60
	Jake Gibbs		
	Tom Metcalf		
☐ 282	Bob Bruce 4.00	1.80	.50
☐ 283	Tom McCraw 4.00	1.80	.50
☐ 284	Dick Schofield............. 4.00	1.80	.50
☐ 285	Robin Roberts.......... 14.00	6.25	1.75
☐ 286	Don Landrum................ 4.00	1.80	.50
☐ 287	Red Sox Rookies 50.00	22.00	6.25
	Tony Conigliaro		
	Bill Spanswick		
☐ 288	Al Moran 4.00	1.80	.50
☐ 289	Frank Funk 4.00	1.80	.50
☐ 290	Bob Allison 5.00	2.20	.60
☐ 291	Phil Ortega 4.00	1.80	.50
☐ 292	Mike Roarke............... 4.00	1.80	.50
☐ 293	Phillies Team 7.00	3.10	.85
☐ 294	Ken L. Hunt............... 4.00	1.80	.50
☐ 295	Roger Craig 5.00	2.20	.60
☐ 296	Ed Kirkpatrick 4.00	1.80	.50
☐ 297	Ken MacKenzie 4.00	1.80	.50
☐ 298	Harry Craft MG........... 4.00	1.80	.50
☐ 299	Bill Stafford 4.00	1.80	.50
☐ 300	Hank Aaron 100.00	45.00	12.50
☐ 301	Larry Brown 4.00	1.80	.50
☐ 302	Dan Pfister 4.00	1.80	.50
☐ 303	Jim Campbell.............. 4.00	1.80	.50
☐ 304	Bob Johnson............... 4.00	1.80	.50
☐ 305	Jack Lamabe 4.00	1.80	.50
☐ 306	Giant Gunners 35.00	16.00	4.40
	Willie Mays		
	Orlando Cepeda		
☐ 307	Joe Gibbon 4.00	1.80	.50
☐ 308	Gene Stephens............ 4.00	1.80	.50
☐ 309	Paul Toth 4.00	1.80	.50
☐ 310	Jim Gilliam................. 4.00	1.80	.50
☐ 311	Tom Brown 5.00	2.20	.60
☐ 312	Tigers Rookies............ 4.00	1.80	.50
	Fritz Fisher		
	Fred Gladding		
☐ 313	Chuck Hiller 4.00	1.80	.50
☐ 314	Jerry Buchek............... 4.00	1.80	.50
☐ 315	Bo Belinsky 5.00	2.20	.60
☐ 316	Gene Oliver 4.00	1.80	.50
☐ 317	Al Smith 4.00	1.80	.50
☐ 318	Minnesota Twins 7.00	3.10	.85
	Team Card		
☐ 319	Paul Brown 4.00	1.80	.50
☐ 320	Rocky Colavito 14.00	6.25	1.75
☐ 321	Bob Lillis 4.00	1.80	.50
☐ 322	George Brunet............. 4.00	1.80	.50
☐ 323	John Buzhardt............. 4.00	1.80	.50
☐ 324	Casey Stengel MG..... 16.00	7.25	2.00
☐ 325	Hector Lopez 5.00	2.20	.60
☐ 326	Ron Brand.................. 4.00	1.80	.50
☐ 327	Don Blasingame........... 4.00	1.80	.50
☐ 328	Bob Shaw 4.00	1.80	.50
☐ 329	Russ Nixon 4.00	1.80	.50
☐ 330	Tommy Harper............. 5.00	2.20	.60
☐ 331	AL Bombers 160.00	70.00	20.00
	Roger Maris		
	Norm Cash		
	Mickey Mantle		
	Al Kaline		
☐ 332	Ray Washburn 4.00	1.80	.50
☐ 333	Billy Moran 4.00	1.80	.50
☐ 334	Lew Krausse 4.00	1.80	.50
☐ 335	Don Mossi 5.00	2.20	.60
☐ 336	Andre Rodgers............. 4.00	1.80	.50
☐ 337	Dodgers Rookies 8.00	3.60	1.00
	Al Ferrara		
	Jeff Torborg		
☐ 338	Jack Kralick................ 4.00	1.80	.50
☐ 339	Walt Bond 4.00	1.80	.50
☐ 340	Joe Cunningham 5.00	2.20	.60
☐ 341	Jim Roland 4.00	1.80	.50
☐ 342	Willie Stargell............ 30.00	13.50	3.70

343	Senators Team	7.00	3.10	.85
344	Phil Linz	5.00	2.20	.60
345	Frank Thomas	5.00	2.20	.60
346	Joey Jay	4.00	1.80	.50
347	Bobby Wine	5.00	2.20	.60
348	Ed Lopat MG	5.00	2.20	.60
349	Art Fowler	4.00	1.80	.50
350	Willie McCovey	20.00	9.00	2.50
351	Dan Schneider	4.00	1.80	.50
352	Eddie Bressoud	4.00	1.80	.50
353	Wally Moon	5.00	2.20	.60
354	Dave Giusti	4.00	1.80	.50
355	Vic Power	5.00	2.20	.60
356	Reds Rookies	5.00	2.20	.60
	Bill McCool			
	Chico Ruiz			
357	Charley James	4.00	1.80	.50
358	Ron Kline	4.00	1.80	.50
359	Jim Schaffer	4.00	1.80	.50
360	Joe Pepitone	7.00	3.10	.85
361	Jay Hook	4.00	1.80	.50
362	Checklist 5	10.00	2.00	1.00
363	Dick McAuliffe	5.00	2.20	.60
364	Joe Gaines	4.00	1.80	.50
365	Cal McLish	5.00	2.20	.60
366	Nelson Mathews	4.00	1.80	.50
367	Fred Whitfield	4.00	1.80	.50
368	White Sox Rookies	7.00	3.10	.85
	Fritz Ackley			
	Don Buford			
369	Jerry Zimmerman	4.00	1.80	.50
370	Hal Woodeshick	4.00	1.80	.50
371	Frank Howard	7.50	3.40	.95
372	Howie Koplitz	7.00	3.10	.85
373	Pirates Team	12.00	5.50	1.50
374	Bobby Bolin	7.00	3.10	.85
375	Ron Santo	10.00	4.50	1.25
376	Dave Morehead	7.00	3.10	.85
377	Bob Skinner	7.50	3.40	.95
378	Braves Rookies	7.50	3.40	.95
	Woody Woodward			
	Jack Smith			
379	Tony Gonzalez	7.50	3.40	.95
380	Whitey Ford	35.00	16.00	4.40
381	Bob Taylor	7.00	3.10	.85
382	Wes Stock	7.00	3.10	.85
383	Bill Rigney MG	7.00	3.10	.85
384	Ron Hansen	7.00	3.10	.85
385	Curt Simmons	7.50	3.40	.95
386	Lenny Green	7.00	3.10	.85
387	Terry Fox	7.00	3.10	.85
388	A's Rookies	7.50	3.40	.95
	John O'Donoghue			
	George Williams			
389	Jim Umbricht	7.50	3.40	.95
	(Card back mentions			
	his death)			
390	Orlando Cepeda	8.00	3.60	1.00
391	Sam McDowell	7.50	3.40	.95
392	Jim Pagliaroni	7.00	3.10	.85
393	Casey Teaches	10.00	4.50	1.25
	Casey Stengel MG			
	Ed Kranepool			
394	Bob Miller	7.00	3.10	.85
395	Tom Tresh	7.50	3.40	.95
396	Dennis Bennett	7.00	3.10	.85
397	Chuck Cottier	7.00	3.10	.85
398	Mets Rookies	7.00	3.10	.85
	Bill Haas			
	Dick Smith			
399	Jackie Brandt	7.00	3.10	.85
400	Warren Spahn	40.00	18.00	5.00
401	Charlie Maxwell	7.50	3.40	.95
402	Tom Sturdivant	7.00	3.10	.85
403	Reds Team	12.00	5.50	1.50
404	Tony Martinez	7.00	3.10	.85
405	Ken McBride	7.00	3.10	.85
406	Al Spangler	7.00	3.10	.85
407	Bill Freehan	8.00	3.60	1.00
408	Cubs Rookies	7.00	3.10	.85
	Jim Stewart			
	Fred Burdette			
409	Bill Fischer	7.00	3.10	.85
410	Dick Stuart	7.50	3.40	.95
411	Lee Walls	7.00	3.10	.85
412	Ray Culp	7.50	3.40	.95
413	Johnny Keane MG	7.00	3.10	.85
414	Jack Sanford	7.00	3.10	.85
415	Tony Kubek	8.00	3.60	1.00
416	Lee Maye	7.00	3.10	.85
417	Don Cardwell	7.00	3.10	.85
418	Orioles Rookies	7.50	3.40	.95
	Darold Knowles			
	Les Narum			
419	Ken Harrelson	14.00	6.25	1.75
420	Jim Maloney	7.50	3.40	.95
421	Camilo Carreon	7.00	3.10	.85
422	Jack Fisher	7.00	3.10	.85
423	Tops in NL	125.00	55.00	15.50
	Hank Aaron			
	Willie Mays			
424	Dick Bertell	7.00	3.10	.85
425	Norm Cash	8.00	3.60	1.00
426	Bob Rodgers	7.50	3.40	.95
427	Don Rudolph	7.00	3.10	.85
428	Red Sox Rookies	7.00	3.10	.85
	Archie Skeen			
	Pete Smith			
	(Back states Archie			
	has retired)			
429	Tim McCarver	10.00	4.50	1.25
430	Juan Pizarro	7.00	3.10	.85
431	George Alusik	7.00	3.10	.85
432	Ruben Amaro	7.50	3.40	.95
433	Yankees Team	30.00	13.50	3.70
434	Don Nottebart	7.00	3.10	.85
435	Vic Davalillo	7.50	3.40	.95
436	Charlie Neal	7.50	3.40	.95
437	Ed Bailey	7.00	3.10	.85
438	Checklist 6	16.00	3.20	1.60
439	Harvey Haddix	7.50	3.40	.95
440	Bob Clemente UER	225.00	100.00	28.00
	(1960 Pittsburfh)			
441	Bob Duliba	7.00	3.10	.85
442	Pumpsie Green	7.50	3.40	.95
443	Chuck Dressen MG	7.50	3.40	.95
444	Larry Jackson	7.00	3.10	.85
445	Bill Skowron	7.50	3.40	.95
446	Julian Javier	7.50	3.40	.95
447	Ted Bowsfield	7.00	3.10	.85
448	Cookie Rojas	7.50	3.40	.95
449	Deron Johnson	7.50	3.40	.95
450	Steve Barber	7.00	3.10	.85
451	Joe Amalfitano	7.00	3.10	.85
452	Giants Rookies	7.50	3.40	.95
	Gil Garrido			
	Jim Ray Hart			
453	Frank Baumann	7.00	3.10	.85
454	Tommie Aaron	7.50	3.40	.95
455	Bernie Allen	7.00	3.10	.85
456	Dodgers Rookies	8.00	3.60	1.00
	Wes Parker			

	John Werhas			
☐ 457	Jesse Gonder	7.00	3.10	.85
☐ 458	Ralph Terry	7.50	3.40	.95
☐ 459	Red Sox Rookies	7.00	3.10	.85
	Pete Charton			
	Dalton Jones			
☐ 460	Bob Gibson	40.00	18.00	5.00
☐ 461	George Thomas	7.00	3.10	.85
☐ 462	Birdie Tebbetts MG	7.50	3.40	.95
☐ 463	Don Leppert	7.00	3.10	.85
☐ 464	Dallas Green	7.50	3.40	.95
☐ 465	Mike Hershberger	7.00	3.10	.85
☐ 466	A's Rookies	7.50	3.40	.95
	Dick Green			
	Aurelio Monteagudo			
☐ 467	Bob Aspromonte	7.00	3.10	.85
☐ 468	Gaylord Perry	40.00	18.00	5.00
☐ 469	Cubs Rookies	7.50	3.40	.95
	Fred Norman			
	Sterling Slaughter			
☐ 470	Jim Bouton	8.00	3.60	1.00
☐ 471	Gates Brown	10.00	4.50	1.25
☐ 472	Vern Law	7.50	3.40	.95
☐ 473	Baltimore Orioles	12.00	5.50	1.50
	Team Card			
☐ 474	Larry Sherry	7.50	3.40	.95
☐ 475	Ed Charles	7.00	3.10	.85
☐ 476	Braves Rookies	14.00	6.25	1.75
	Rico Carty			
	Dick Kelley			
☐ 477	Mike Joyce	7.00	3.10	.85
☐ 478	Dick Howser	7.50	3.40	.95
☐ 479	Cardinals Rookies	7.00	3.10	.85
	Dave Bakenhaster			
	Johnny Lewis			
☐ 480	Bob Purkey	7.00	3.10	.85
☐ 481	Chuck Schilling	7.00	3.10	.85
☐ 482	Phillies Rookies	7.50	3.40	.95
	John Briggs			
	Danny Cater			
☐ 483	Fred Valentine	7.00	3.10	.85
☐ 484	Bill Pleis	7.00	3.10	.85
☐ 485	Tom Haller	7.50	3.40	.95
☐ 486	Bob Kennedy MG	7.50	3.40	.95
☐ 487	Mike McCormick	7.50	3.40	.95
☐ 488	Yankees Rookies	7.50	3.40	.95
	Pete Mikkelsen			
	Bob Meyer			
☐ 489	Julio Navarro	7.00	3.10	.85
☐ 490	Ron Fairly	7.50	3.40	.95
☐ 491	Ed Rakow	7.00	3.10	.85
☐ 492	Colts Rookies	7.00	3.10	.85
	Jim Beauchamp			
	Mike White			
☐ 493	Don Lee	7.00	3.10	.85
☐ 494	Al Jackson	7.00	3.10	.85
☐ 495	Bill Virdon	7.50	3.40	.95
☐ 496	White Sox Team	12.00	5.50	1.50
☐ 497	Jeoff Long	7.00	3.10	.85
☐ 498	Dave Stenhouse	7.00	3.10	.85
☐ 499	Indians Rookies	7.50	3.40	.95
	Chico Salmon			
	Gordon Seyfried			
☐ 500	Camilo Pascual	7.50	3.40	.95
☐ 501	Bob Veale	7.50	3.40	.95
☐ 502	Angels Rookies	7.00	3.10	.85
	Bobby Knoop			
	Bob Lee			
☐ 503	Earl Wilson	7.50	3.40	.95
☐ 504	Claude Raymond	7.50	3.40	.95
☐ 505	Stan Williams	7.50	3.40	.95
☐ 506	Bobby Bragan MG	7.00	3.10	.85
☐ 507	Johnny Edwards	7.00	3.10	.85
☐ 508	Diego Segui	7.00	3.10	.85
☐ 509	Pirates Rookies	7.50	3.40	.95
	Gene Alley			
	Orlando McFarlane			
☐ 510	Lindy McDaniel	7.50	3.40	.95
☐ 511	Lou Jackson	7.50	3.40	.95
☐ 512	Tigers Rookies	14.00	6.25	1.75
	Willie Horton			
	Joe Sparma			
☐ 513	Don Larsen	7.00	3.10	.85
☐ 514	Jim Hickman	7.50	3.40	.95
☐ 515	Johnny Romano	7.00	3.10	.85
☐ 516	Twins Rookies	7.00	3.10	.85
	Jerry Arrigo			
	Dwight Siebler			
☐ 517A	Checklist 7 ERR	25.00	5.00	2.50
	(Incorrect numbering sequence on back)			
☐ 517B	Checklist 7 COR	16.00	3.20	1.60
	(Correct numbering on back)			
☐ 518	Carl Bouldin	7.00	3.10	.85
☐ 519	Charlie Smith	7.00	3.10	.85
☐ 520	Jack Baldschun	7.50	3.40	.95
☐ 521	Tom Satriano	7.00	3.10	.85
☐ 522	Bob Tiefenauer	7.00	3.10	.85
☐ 523	Lou Burdette UER	16.00	7.25	2.00
	(Pitching lefty)			
☐ 524	Reds Rookies	16.00	7.25	2.00
	Jim Dickson			
	Bobby Klaus			
☐ 525	Al McBean	16.00	7.25	2.00
☐ 526	Lou Clinton	16.00	7.25	2.00
☐ 527	Larry Bearnarth	16.00	7.25	2.00
☐ 528	A's Rookies	16.00	7.25	2.00
	Dave Duncan			
	Tommie Reynolds			
☐ 529	Alvin Dark MG	16.00	7.25	2.00
☐ 530	Leon Wagner	16.00	7.25	2.00
☐ 531	Los Angeles Dodgers	24.00	11.00	3.00
	Team Card			
☐ 532	Twins Rookies	16.00	7.25	2.00
	Bud Bloomfield			
	(Bloomfield photo actually Jay Ward)			
	Joe Nossek			
☐ 533	Johnny Klippstein	16.00	7.25	2.00
☐ 534	Gus Bell	16.00	7.25	2.00
☐ 535	Phil Regan	16.00	7.25	2.00
☐ 536	Mets Rookies	16.00	7.25	2.00
	Larry Elliot			
	John Stephenson			
☐ 537	Dan Osinski	16.00	7.25	2.00
☐ 538	Minnie Minoso	16.00	7.25	2.00
☐ 539	Roy Face	16.00	7.25	2.00
☐ 540	Luis Aparicio	20.00	9.00	2.50
☐ 541	Braves Rookies	100.00	45.00	12.50
	Phil Roof			
	Phil Niekro			
☐ 542	Don Mincher	16.00	7.25	2.00
☐ 543	Bob Uecker	40.00	18.00	5.00
☐ 544	Colts Rookies	16.00	7.25	2.00
	Steve Hertz			
	Joe Hoerner			
☐ 545	Max Alvis	16.00	7.25	2.00
☐ 546	Joe Christopher	16.00	7.25	2.00
☐ 547	Gil Hodges MG	20.00	9.00	2.50
☐ 548	NL Rookies	16.00	7.25	2.00
	Wayne Schurr			

Paul Speckenbach
☐ 549	Joe Moeller	16.00	7.25	2.00
☐ 550	Ken Hubbs MEM	35.00	16.00	4.40
☐ 551	Billy Hoeft	16.00	7.25	2.00
☐ 552	Indians Rookies	16.00	7.25	2.00

Tom Kelley
Sonny Siebert
☐ 553	Jim Brewer	16.00	7.25	2.00
☐ 554	Hank Foiles	16.00	7.25	2.00
☐ 555	Lee Stange	16.00	7.25	2.00
☐ 556	Mets Rookies	16.00	7.25	2.00

Steve Dillon
Ron Locke
☐ 557	Leo Burke	16.00	7.25	2.00
☐ 558	Don Schwall	16.00	7.25	2.00
☐ 559	Dick Phillips	16.00	7.25	2.00
☐ 560	Dick Farrell	16.00	7.25	2.00
☐ 561	Phillies Rookies UER	20.00	9.00	2.50

Dave Bennett
(19 ... is 18)
Rick Wise
☐ 562	Pedro Ramos	16.00	7.25	2.00
☐ 563	Dal Maxvill	16.00	7.25	2.00
☐ 564	AL Rookies	16.00	7.25	2.00

Joe McCabe
Jerry McNertney
☐ 565	Stu Miller	16.00	7.25	2.00
☐ 566	Ed Kranepool	16.00	7.25	2.00
☐ 567	Jim Kaat	18.00	8.00	2.20
☐ 568	NL Rookies	16.00	7.25	2.00

Phil Gagliano
Cap Peterson
☐ 569	Fred Newman	16.00	7.25	2.00
☐ 570	Bill Mazeroski	18.00	8.00	2.20
☐ 571	Gene Conley	16.00	7.25	2.00
☐ 572	AL Rookies	16.00	7.25	2.00

Dave Gray
Dick Egan
☐ 573	Jim Duffalo	16.00	7.25	2.00
☐ 574	Manny Jimenez	16.00	7.25	2.00
☐ 575	Tony Cloninger	16.00	7.25	2.00
☐ 576	Mets Rookies	16.00	7.25	2.00

Jerry Hinsley
Bill Wakefield
☐ 577	Gordy Coleman	16.00	7.25	2.00
☐ 578	Glen Hobbie	16.00	7.25	2.00
☐ 579	Red Sox Team	24.00	11.00	3.00
☐ 580	Johnny Podres	16.00	7.25	2.00
☐ 581	Yankees Rookies	16.00	7.25	2.00

Pedro Gonzalez
Archie Moore
☐ 582	Rod Kanehl	16.00	7.25	2.00
☐ 583	Tito Francona	16.00	7.25	2.00
☐ 584	Joel Horlen	16.00	7.25	2.00
☐ 585	Tony Taylor	16.00	7.25	2.00
☐ 586	Jim Piersall	16.00	7.25	2.00
☐ 587	Bennie Daniels	18.00	7.25	2.00

1965 Topps

The cards in this 598-card set measure 2 1/2" by 3 1/2". The cards comprising the 1965 Topps set have team names located within a distinctive pennant design below the picture. The cards have blue borders on the reverse and were issued by series. Cards 523 to 598 are more difficult to obtain than all other series. Within this last

series there are 44 cards that were printed in lesser quantities than the other cards in that series; these shorter-printed cards are marked by SP in the checklist below. In addition, the sixth series (447-522) is more difficult to obtain than series one through five. Featured subsets within this set include League Leaders (1-12) and World Series cards (132-139). Key cards in this set include Steve Carlton's Rookie Card, Mickey Mantle, and Pete Rose. Other key Rookie Cards in this set are Jim Hunter, Joe Morgan, and Tony Perez.

	NRMT	VG-E	GOOD
COMPLETE SET (598)	3500.00	1600.00	450.00
COMMON CARD (1-196)	2.00	.90	.25
COMMON CARD (197-283)	2.50	1.10	.30
COMMON CARD (284-370)	4.00	1.80	.50
COMMON CARD (371-598)	7.00	3.10	.85

		NRMT	VG-E	GOOD
☐ 1	AL Batting Leaders	20.00	6.00	2.00

Tony Oliva
Elston Howard
Brooks Robinson
☐ 2	NL Batting Leaders	20.00	9.00	2.50

Bob Clemente
Hank Aaron
Rico Carty
☐ 3	AL Home Run Leaders	40.00	18.00	5.00

Harmon Killebrew
Mickey Mantle
Boog Powell
☐ 4	NL Home Run Leaders	14.00	6.25	1.75

Willie Mays
Billy Williams
Jim Ray Hart
Orlando Cepeda
Johnny Callison
☐ 5	AL RBI Leaders	40.00	18.00	5.00

Brooks Robinson
Harmon Killebrew
Mickey Mantle
Dick Stuart
☐ 6	NL RBI Leaders	8.00	3.60	1.00

Ken Boyer
Willie Mays
Ron Santo
☐ 7	AL ERA Leaders	4.00	1.80	.50

Dean Chance
Joel Horlen
☐ 8	NL ERA Leaders	20.00	9.00	2.50

Sandy Koufax
Don Drysdale
☐ 9	AL Pitching Leaders	4.00	1.80	.50

Dean Chance

	Gary Peters			
	Dave Wickersham			
	Juan Pizarro			
	Wally Bunker			
☐ 10	NL Pitching Leaders.....	4.00	1.80	.50
	Larry Jackson			
	Ray Sadecki			
	Juan Marichal			
☐ 11	AL Strikeout Leaders ...	4.00	1.80	.50
	Al Downing			
	Dean Chance			
	Camilo Pascual			
☐ 12	NL Strikeout Leaders ...	8.00	3.60	1.00
	Bob Veale			
	Don Drysdale			
	Bob Gibson			
☐ 13	Pedro Ramos	2.00	.90	.25
☐ 14	Len Gabrielson	2.00	.90	.25
☐ 15	Robin Roberts	12.00	5.50	1.50
☐ 16	Houston Rookies	70.00	32.00	8.75
	Joe Morgan			
	Sonny Jackson			
☐ 17	Johnny Romano	2.00	.90	.25
☐ 18	Bill McCool	2.00	.90	.25
☐ 19	Gates Brown	2.50	1.10	.30
☐ 20	Jim Bunning	5.00	2.20	.60
☐ 21	Don Blasingame	2.00	.90	.25
☐ 22	Charlie Smith	2.00	.90	.25
☐ 23	Bob Tiefenauer	2.00	.90	.25
☐ 24	Minnesota Twins...........	4.00	1.80	.50
	Team Card			
☐ 25	Al McBean...................	2.00	.90	.25
☐ 26	Bobby Knoop	2.00	.90	.25
☐ 27	Dick Bertell	2.00	.90	.25
☐ 28	Barney Schultz	2.00	.90	.25
☐ 29	Felix Mantilla	2.00	.90	.25
☐ 30	Jim Bouton	5.00	2.20	.60
☐ 31	Mike White..................	2.00	.90	.25
☐ 32	Herman Franks MG	2.00	.90	.25
☐ 33	Jackie Brandt...............	2.00	.90	.25
☐ 34	Cal Koonce.................	2.00	.90	.25
☐ 35	Ed Charles..................	2.00	.90	.25
☐ 36	Bobby Wine	2.00	.90	.25
☐ 37	Fred Gladding	2.00	.90	.25
☐ 38	Jim King	2.00	.90	.25
☐ 39	Gerry Arrigo	2.00	.90	.25
☐ 40	Frank Howard	2.50	1.10	.30
☐ 41	White Sox Rookies........	2.00	.90	.25
	Bruce Howard			
	Marv Staehle			
☐ 42	Earl Wilson	2.50	1.10	.30
☐ 43	Mike Shannon	2.50	1.10	.30
	(Name in red, other			
	Cardinals in yellow)			
☐ 44	Wade Blasingame	2.00	.90	.25
☐ 45	Roy McMillan...............	2.50	1.10	.30
☐ 46	Bob Lee......................	2.00	.90	.25
☐ 47	Tommy Harper.............	2.50	1.10	.30
☐ 48	Claude Raymond...........	2.50	1.10	.30
☐ 49	Orioles Rookies............	3.50	1.55	.45
	Curt Blefary			
	John Miller			
☐ 50	Juan Marichal	12.00	5.50	1.50
☐ 51	Bill Bryan	2.00	.90	.25
☐ 52	Ed Roebuck..................	2.00	.90	.25
☐ 53	Dick McAuliffe..............	2.50	1.10	.30
☐ 54	Joe Gibbon	2.00	.90	.25
☐ 55	Tony Conigliaro	15.00	6.75	1.85
☐ 56	Ron Kline	2.00	.90	.25
☐ 57	Cardinals Team.............	4.00	1.80	.50
☐ 58	Fred Talbot..................	2.00	.90	.25

☐ 59	Nate Oliver..................	2.00	.90	.25
☐ 60	Jim O'Toole	2.50	1.10	.30
☐ 61	Chris Cannizzaro	2.00	.90	.25
☐ 62	Jim Kaat UER...............	5.00	2.20	.60
	(Misspelled Katt)			
☐ 63	Ty Cline.....................	2.00	.90	.25
☐ 64	Lou Burdette................	2.50	1.10	.30
☐ 65	Tony Kubek	4.00	1.80	.50
☐ 66	Bill Rigney MG	2.00	.90	.25
☐ 67	Harvey Haddix	2.50	1.10	.30
☐ 68	Del Crandall................	2.50	1.10	.30
☐ 69	Bill Virdon	2.50	1.10	.30
☐ 70	Bill Skowron	2.50	1.10	.30
☐ 71	John O'Donoghue	2.00	.90	.25
☐ 72	Tony Gonzalez..............	2.00	.90	.25
☐ 73	Dennis Ribant..............	2.00	.90	.25
☐ 74	Red Sox Rookies	12.00	5.50	1.50
	Rico Petrocelli			
	Jerry Stephenson			
☐ 75	Deron Johnson	2.50	1.10	.30
☐ 76	Sam McDowell.............	2.50	1.10	.30
☐ 77	Doug Camilli	2.00	.90	.25
☐ 78	Dal Maxvill	2.00	.90	.25
☐ 79A	Checklist 1	10.00	2.00	1.00
	(61 Cannizzaro)			
☐ 79B	Checklist 1	10.00	2.00	1.00
	(61 C.Cannizzaro)			
☐ 80	Turk Farrell	2.00	.90	.25
☐ 81	Don Buford	2.50	1.10	.30
☐ 82	Braves Rookies	6.00	2.70	.75
	Santos Alomar			
	John Braun			
☐ 83	George Thomas	2.00	.90	.25
☐ 84	Ron Herbel.................	2.00	.90	.25
☐ 85	Willie Smith	2.00	.90	.25
☐ 86	Les Narum	2.00	.90	.25
☐ 87	Nelson Mathews	2.00	.90	.25
☐ 88	Jack Lamabe...............	2.00	.90	.25
☐ 89	Mike Hershberger	2.00	.90	.25
☐ 90	Rich Rollins	2.50	1.10	.30
☐ 91	Cubs Team..................	4.00	1.80	.50
☐ 92	Dick Howser	2.50	1.10	.30
☐ 93	Jack Fisher	2.00	.90	.25
☐ 94	Charlie Lau..................	2.50	1.10	.30
☐ 95	Bill Mazeroski	4.00	1.80	.50
☐ 96	Sonny Siebert	2.50	1.10	.30
☐ 97	Pedro Gonzalez............	2.00	.90	.25
☐ 98	Bob Miller..................	2.00	.90	.25
☐ 99	Gil Hodges MG.............	7.00	3.10	.85
☐ 100	Ken Boyer	4.00	1.80	.50
☐ 101	Fred Newman	2.00	.90	.25
☐ 102	Steve Boros	2.00	.90	.25
☐ 103	Harvey Kuenn	2.50	1.10	.30
☐ 104	Checklist 2	10.00	2.00	1.00
☐ 105	Chico Salmon	2.00	.90	.25
☐ 106	Gene Oliver	2.00	.90	.25
☐ 107	Phillies Rookies	3.50	1.55	.45
	Pat Corrales			
	Costen Shockley			
☐ 108	Don Mincher................	2.00	.90	.25
☐ 109	Walt Bond..................	2.00	.90	.25
☐ 110	Ron Santo...................	5.00	2.20	.60
☐ 111	Lee Thomas	2.50	1.10	.30
☐ 112	Derrell Griffith.............	2.00	.90	.25
☐ 113	Steve Barber	2.00	.90	.25
☐ 114	Jim Hickman................	2.50	1.10	.30
☐ 115	Bobby Richardson	5.00	2.20	.60
☐ 116	Cardinals Rookies	2.50	1.10	.30
	Dave Dowling			
	Bob Tolan			
☐ 117	Wes Stock...................	2.00	.90	.25

☐ 118	Hal Lanier	2.50	1.10	.30
☐ 119	John Kennedy	2.00	.90	.25
☐ 120	Frank Robinson	32.00	14.50	4.00
☐ 121	Gene Alley	2.50	1.10	.30
☐ 122	Bill Pleis	2.00	.90	.25
☐ 123	Frank Thomas	2.50	1.10	.30
☐ 124	Tom Satriano	2.00	.90	.25
☐ 125	Juan Pizarro	2.00	.90	.25
☐ 126	Dodgers Team	5.00	2.20	.60
☐ 127	Frank Lary	2.00	.90	.25
☐ 128	Vic Davalillo	2.00	.90	.25
☐ 129	Bennie Daniels	2.00	.90	.25
☐ 130	Al Kaline	32.00	14.50	4.00
☐ 131	Johnny Keane MG	2.00	.90	.25
☐ 132	World Series Game 1.	4.00	1.80	.50
	Cards take opener			
	(Mike Shannon)			
☐ 133	World Series Game 2.	4.00	1.80	.50
	Mel Stottlemyre wins			
☐ 134	World Series Game 3	70.00	32.00	8.75
	Mickey Mantle's homer			
☐ 135	World Series Game 4.	4.00	1.80	.50
	Ken Boyer's grand-slam			
☐ 136	World Series Game 5.	4.00	1.80	.50
	10th inning triumph			
	(Tim McCarver being			
	greeted at home)			
☐ 137	World Series Game 6.	4.00	1.80	.50
	Jim Bouton wins game			
☐ 138	World Series Game 7	12.00	5.50	1.50
	Bob Gibson wins finale			
☐ 139	World Series Summary	4.00	1.80	.50
	Cards celebrate			
☐ 140	Dean Chance	2.50	1.10	.30
☐ 141	Charlie James	2.00	.90	.25
☐ 142	Bill Monbouquette	2.00	.90	.25
☐ 143	Pirates Rookies	2.00	.90	.25
	John Gelnar			
	Jerry May			
☐ 144	Ed Kranepool	2.50	1.10	.30
☐ 145	Luis Tiant	24.00	11.00	3.00
☐ 146	Ron Hansen	2.00	.90	.25
☐ 147	Dennis Bennett	2.00	.90	.25
☐ 148	Willie Kirkland	2.00	.90	.25
☐ 149	Wayne Schurr	2.00	.90	.25
☐ 150	Brooks Robinson	32.00	14.50	4.00
☐ 151	Athletics Team	4.00	1.80	.50
☐ 152	Phil Ortega	2.00	.90	.25
☐ 153	Norm Cash	4.00	1.80	.50
☐ 154	Bob Humphreys	2.00	.90	.25
☐ 155	Roger Maris	50.00	22.00	6.25
☐ 156	Bob Sadowski	2.00	.90	.25
☐ 157	Zoilo Versalles	2.50	1.10	.30
☐ 158	Dick Sisler	2.00	.90	.25
☐ 159	Jim Duffalo	2.00	.90	.25
☐ 160	Bob Clemente UER.	100.00	45.00	12.50
	(1960 Pittsburfh)			
☐ 161	Frank Baumann	2.00	.90	.25
☐ 162	Russ Nixon	2.00	.90	.25
☐ 163	Johnny Briggs	2.00	.90	.25
☐ 164	Al Spangler	2.00	.90	.25
☐ 165	Dick Ellsworth	2.00	.90	.25
☐ 166	Indians Rookies	5.00	2.20	.60
	George Culver			
	Tommie Agee			
☐ 167	Bill Wakefield	2.00	.90	.25
☐ 168	Dick Green	2.00	.90	.25
☐ 169	Dave Vineyard	2.00	.90	.25
☐ 170	Hank Aaron	90.00	40.00	11.00
☐ 171	Jim Roland	2.00	.90	.25
☐ 172	Jim Piersall	2.50	1.10	.30

☐ 173	Detroit Tigers	4.00	1.80	.50
	Team Card			
☐ 174	Joey Jay	2.00	.90	.25
☐ 175	Bob Aspromonte	2.00	.90	.25
☐ 176	Willie McCovey	20.00	9.00	2.50
☐ 177	Pete Mikkelsen	2.00	.90	.25
☐ 178	Dalton Jones	2.00	.90	.25
☐ 179	Hal Woodeshick	2.00	.90	.25
☐ 180	Bob Allison	2.50	1.10	.30
☐ 181	Senators Rookies	2.00	.90	.25
	Don Loun			
	Joe McCabe			
☐ 182	Mike de la Hoz	2.00	.90	.25
☐ 183	Dave Nicholson	2.00	.90	.25
☐ 184	John Boozer	2.00	.90	.25
☐ 185	Max Alvis	2.00	.90	.25
☐ 186	Billy Cowan	2.00	.90	.25
☐ 187	Casey Stengel MG	15.00	6.75	1.85
☐ 188	Sam Bowens	2.00	.90	.25
☐ 189	Checklist 3	10.00	2.00	1.00
☐ 190	Bill White	4.00	1.80	.50
☐ 191	Phil Regan	2.50	1.10	.30
☐ 192	Jim Coker	2.00	.90	.25
☐ 193	Gaylord Perry	18.00	8.00	2.20
☐ 194	Rookie Stars	2.00	.90	.25
	Bill Kelso			
	Rick Reichardt			
☐ 195	Bob Veale	2.50	1.10	.30
☐ 196	Ron Fairly	2.50	1.10	.30
☐ 197	Diego Segui	2.50	1.10	.30
☐ 198	Smoky Burgess	4.00	1.80	.50
☐ 199	Bob Heffner	2.50	1.10	.30
☐ 200	Joe Torre	4.00	1.80	.50
☐ 201	Twins Rookies	4.00	1.80	.50
	Sandy Valdespino			
	Cesar Tovar			
☐ 202	Leo Burke	2.50	1.10	.30
☐ 203	Dallas Green	4.00	1.80	.50
☐ 204	Russ Snyder	2.50	1.10	.30
☐ 205	Warren Spahn	30.00	13.50	3.70
☐ 206	Willie Horton	4.00	1.80	.50
☐ 207	Pete Rose	150.00	70.00	19.00
☐ 208	Tommy John	10.00	4.50	1.25
☐ 209	Pirates Team	5.00	2.20	.60
☐ 210	Jim Fregosi	4.00	1.80	.50
☐ 211	Steve Ridzik	2.50	1.10	.30
☐ 212	Ron Brand	2.50	1.10	.30
☐ 213	Jim Davenport	2.50	1.10	.30
☐ 214	Bob Purkey	2.50	1.10	.30
☐ 215	Pete Ward	2.50	1.10	.30
☐ 216	Al Worthington	2.50	1.10	.30
☐ 217	Walt Alston MG	4.00	1.80	.50
☐ 218	Dick Schofield	2.50	1.10	.30
☐ 219	Bob Meyer	2.50	1.10	.30
☐ 220	Billy Williams	10.00	4.50	1.25
☐ 221	John Tsitouris	2.50	1.10	.30
☐ 222	Bob Tillman	2.50	1.10	.30
☐ 223	Dan Osinski	2.50	1.10	.30
☐ 224	Bob Chance	2.50	1.10	.30
☐ 225	Bo Belinsky	4.00	1.80	.50
☐ 226	Yankees Rookies	2.50	1.10	.30
	Elvio Jimenez			
	Jake Gibbs			
☐ 227	Bobby Klaus	2.50	1.10	.30
☐ 228	Jack Sanford	2.50	1.10	.30
☐ 229	Lou Clinton	2.50	1.10	.30
☐ 230	Ray Sadecki	2.50	1.10	.30
☐ 231	Jerry Adair	2.50	1.10	.30
☐ 232	Steve Blass	4.00	1.80	.50
☐ 233	Don Zimmer	4.00	1.80	.50
☐ 234	White Sox Team	5.00	2.20	.60

☐ 235	Chuck Hinton	2.50	1.10	.30
☐ 236	Denny McLain	30.00	13.50	3.70
☐ 237	Bernie Allen	2.50	1.10	.30
☐ 238	Joe Moeller	2.50	1.10	.30
☐ 239	Doc Edwards	2.50	1.10	.30
☐ 240	Bob Bruce	2.50	1.10	.30
☐ 241	Mack Jones	2.50	1.10	.30
☐ 242	George Brunet	2.50	1.10	.30
☐ 243	Reds Rookies	5.00	2.20	.60
	Ted Davidson			
	Tommy Helms			
☐ 244	Lindy McDaniel	4.00	1.80	.50
☐ 245	Joe Pepitone	4.00	1.80	.50
☐ 246	Tom Butters	4.00	1.80	.50
☐ 247	Wally Moon	4.00	1.80	.50
☐ 248	Gus Triandos	4.00	1.80	.50
☐ 249	Dave McNally	4.00	1.80	.50
☐ 250	Willie Mays	90.00	40.00	11.00
☐ 251	Billy Herman MG	3.50	1.55	.45
☐ 252	Pete Richert	2.50	1.10	.30
☐ 253	Danny Cater	2.50	1.10	.30
☐ 254	Roland Sheldon	2.50	1.10	.30
☐ 255	Camilo Pascual	4.00	1.80	.50
☐ 256	Tito Francona	2.50	1.10	.30
☐ 257	Jim Wynn	4.00	1.80	.50
☐ 258	Larry Bearnarth	2.50	1.10	.30
☐ 259	Tigers Rookies	7.00	3.10	.85
	Jim Northrup			
	Ray Oyler			
☐ 260	Don Drysdale	20.00	9.00	2.50
☐ 261	Duke Carmel	2.50	1.10	.30
☐ 262	Bud Daley	2.50	1.10	.30
☐ 263	Marty Keough	2.50	1.10	.30
☐ 264	Bob Buhl	4.00	1.80	.50
☐ 265	Jim Pagliaroni	2.50	1.10	.30
☐ 266	Bert Campaneris	10.00	4.50	1.25
☐ 267	Senators Team	4.50	2.00	.55
☐ 268	Ken McBride	2.50	1.10	.30
☐ 269	Frank Bolling	2.50	1.10	.30
☐ 270	Milt Pappas	4.00	1.80	.50
☐ 271	Don Wert	2.50	1.10	.30
☐ 272	Chuck Schilling	2.50	1.10	.30
☐ 273	Checklist 4	10.00	2.00	1.00
☐ 274	Lum Harris MG	2.50	1.10	.30
☐ 275	Dick Groat	4.00	1.80	.50
☐ 276	Hoyt Wilhelm	10.00	4.50	1.25
☐ 277	Johnny Lewis	2.50	1.10	.30
☐ 278	Ken Retzer	2.50	1.10	.30
☐ 279	Dick Tracewski	2.50	1.10	.30
☐ 280	Dick Stuart	4.00	1.80	.50
☐ 281	Bill Stafford	2.50	1.10	.30
☐ 282	Giants Rookies	30.00	13.50	3.70
	Dick Estelle			
	Masanori Murakami			
☐ 283	Fred Whitfield	2.50	1.10	.30
☐ 284	Nick Willhite	4.00	1.80	.50
☐ 285	Ron Hunt	4.00	1.80	.50
☐ 286	Athletics Rookies	4.00	1.80	.50
	Jim Dickson			
	Aurelio Monteagudo			
☐ 287	Gary Kolb	4.00	1.80	.50
☐ 288	Jack Hamilton	4.00	1.80	.50
☐ 289	Gordy Coleman	5.00	2.20	.60
☐ 290	Wally Bunker	5.00	2.20	.60
☐ 291	Jerry Lynch	4.00	1.80	.50
☐ 292	Larry Yellen	4.00	1.80	.50
☐ 293	Angels Team	7.00	3.10	.85
☐ 294	Tim McCarver	8.00	3.60	1.00
☐ 295	Dick Radatz	5.00	2.20	.60
☐ 296	Tony Taylor	4.00	1.80	.50
☐ 297	Dave DeBusschere	6.00	2.70	.75
☐ 298	Jim Stewart	4.00	1.80	.50
☐ 299	Jerry Zimmerman	4.00	1.80	.50
☐ 300	Sandy Koufax	120.00	55.00	15.00
☐ 301	Birdie Tebbetts MG	5.00	2.20	.60
☐ 302	Al Stanek	4.00	1.80	.50
☐ 303	John Orsino	4.00	1.80	.50
☐ 304	Dave Stenhouse	4.00	1.80	.50
☐ 305	Rico Carty	5.00	2.20	.60
☐ 306	Bubba Phillips	4.00	1.80	.50
☐ 307	Barry Latman	4.00	1.80	.50
☐ 308	Mets Rookies	8.00	3.60	1.00
	Cleon Jones			
	Tom Parsons			
☐ 309	Steve Hamilton	4.00	1.80	.50
☐ 310	Johnny Callison	5.00	2.20	.60
☐ 311	Orlando Pena	4.00	1.80	.50
☐ 312	Joe Nuxhall	5.00	2.20	.60
☐ 313	Jim Schaffer	4.00	1.80	.50
☐ 314	Sterling Slaughter	4.00	1.80	.50
☐ 315	Frank Malzone	5.00	2.20	.60
☐ 316	Reds Team	7.00	3.10	.85
☐ 317	Don McMahon	4.00	1.80	.50
☐ 318	Matty Alou	5.00	2.20	.60
☐ 319	Ken McMullen	4.00	1.80	.50
☐ 320	Bob Gibson	40.00	18.00	5.00
☐ 321	Rusty Staub	5.00	2.20	.60
☐ 322	Rick Wise	5.00	2.20	.60
☐ 323	Hank Bauer MG	5.00	2.20	.60
☐ 324	Bobby Locke	4.00	1.80	.50
☐ 325	Donn Clendenon	5.00	2.20	.60
☐ 326	Dwight Siebler	4.00	1.80	.50
☐ 327	Denis Menke	4.00	1.80	.50
☐ 328	Eddie Fisher	4.00	1.80	.50
☐ 329	Hawk Taylor	4.00	1.80	.50
☐ 330	Whitey Ford	35.00	16.00	4.40
☐ 331	Dodgers Rookies	5.00	2.20	.60
	Al Ferrara			
	John Purdin			
☐ 332	Ted Abernathy	4.00	1.80	.50
☐ 333	Tom Reynolds	4.00	1.80	.50
☐ 334	Vic Roznovsky	4.00	1.80	.50
☐ 335	Mickey Lolich	8.00	3.60	1.00
☐ 336	Woody Held	4.00	1.80	.50
☐ 337	Mike Cuellar	5.00	2.20	.60
☐ 338	Philadelphia Phillies	7.00	3.10	.85
	Team Card			
☐ 339	Ryne Duren	5.00	2.20	.60
☐ 340	Tony Oliva	18.00	8.00	2.20
☐ 341	Bob Bolin	4.00	1.80	.50
☐ 342	Bob Rodgers	5.00	2.20	.60
☐ 343	Mike McCormick	5.00	2.20	.60
☐ 344	Wes Parker	5.00	2.20	.60
☐ 345	Floyd Robinson	4.00	1.80	.50
☐ 346	Bobby Bragan MG	4.00	1.80	.50
☐ 347	Roy Face	5.00	2.20	.60
☐ 348	George Banks	4.00	1.80	.50
☐ 349	Larry Miller	4.00	1.80	.50
☐ 350	Mickey Mantle	575.00	250.00	70.00
☐ 351	Jim Perry	5.00	2.20	.60
☐ 352	Alex Johnson	5.00	2.20	.60
☐ 353	Jerry Lumpe	4.00	1.80	.50
☐ 354	Cubs Rookies	4.00	1.80	.50
	Billy Ott			
	Jack Warner			
☐ 355	Vada Pinson	5.00	2.20	.60
☐ 356	Bill Spanswick	4.00	1.80	.50
☐ 357	Carl Warwick	4.00	1.80	.50
☐ 358	Albie Pearson	5.00	2.20	.60
☐ 359	Ken Johnson	4.00	1.80	.50
☐ 360	Orlando Cepeda	8.00	3.60	1.00
☐ 361	Checklist 5	12.00	2.40	1.20

☐ 362	Don Schwall	4.00	1.80	.50
☐ 363	Bob Johnson	4.00	1.80	.50
☐ 364	Galen Cisco	4.00	1.80	.50
☐ 365	Jim Gentile	5.00	2.20	.60
☐ 366	Dan Schneider	4.00	1.80	.50
☐ 367	Leon Wagner	4.00	1.80	.50
☐ 368	White Sox Rookies	5.00	2.20	.60
	Ken Berry			
	Joel Gibson			
☐ 369	Phil Linz	5.00	2.20	.60
☐ 370	Tommy Davis	5.00	2.20	.60
☐ 371	Frank Kreutzer	7.00	3.10	.85
☐ 372	Clay Dalrymple	7.00	3.10	.85
☐ 373	Curt Simmons	7.50	3.40	.95
☐ 374	Angels Rookies	8.00	3.60	1.00
	Jose Cardenal			
	Dick Simpson			
☐ 375	Dave Wickersham	7.00	3.10	.85
☐ 376	Jim Landis	7.00	3.10	.85
☐ 377	Willie Stargell	30.00	13.50	3.70
☐ 378	Chuck Estrada	7.00	3.10	.85
☐ 379	Giants Team	10.00	4.50	1.25
☐ 380	Rocky Colavito	15.00	6.75	1.85
☐ 381	Al Jackson	7.00	3.10	.85
☐ 382	J.C. Martin	7.00	3.10	.85
☐ 383	Felipe Alou	7.50	3.40	.95
☐ 384	Johnny Klippstein	7.00	3.10	.85
☐ 385	Carl Yastrzemski	70.00	32.00	8.75
☐ 386	Cubs Rookies	7.00	3.10	.85
	Paul Jaeckel			
	Fred Norman			
☐ 387	Johnny Podres	7.50	3.40	.95
☐ 388	John Blanchard	7.00	3.10	.85
☐ 389	Don Larsen	7.50	3.40	.95
☐ 390	Bill Freehan	8.00	3.60	1.00
☐ 391	Mel McGaha MG	7.00	3.10	.85
☐ 392	Bob Friend	7.50	3.40	.95
☐ 393	Ed Kirkpatrick	7.00	3.10	.85
☐ 394	Jim Hannan	7.00	3.10	.85
☐ 395	Jim Ray Hart	7.50	3.40	.95
☐ 396	Frank Bertaina	7.00	3.10	.85
☐ 397	Jerry Buchek	7.00	3.10	.85
☐ 398	Reds Rookies	7.50	3.40	.95
	Dan Neville			
	Art Shamsky			
☐ 399	Ray Herbert	7.00	3.10	.85
☐ 400	Harmon Killebrew	40.00	18.00	5.00
☐ 401	Carl Willey	7.00	3.10	.85
☐ 402	Joe Amalfitano	7.00	3.10	.85
☐ 403	Boston Red Sox	10.00	4.50	1.25
	Team Card			
☐ 404	Stan Williams	7.50	3.40	.95
	(Listed as Indian			
	but Yankee cap)			
☐ 405	John Roseboro	7.50	3.40	.95
☐ 406	Ralph Terry	7.50	3.40	.95
☐ 407	Lee Maye	7.00	3.10	.85
☐ 408	Larry Sherry	7.50	3.40	.95
☐ 409	Astros Rookies	8.00	3.60	1.00
	Jim Beauchamp			
	Larry Dierker			
☐ 410	Luis Aparicio	12.00	5.50	1.50
☐ 411	Roger Craig	7.50	3.40	.95
☐ 412	Bob Bailey	7.50	3.40	.95
☐ 413	Hal Reniff	7.00	3.10	.85
☐ 414	Al Lopez MG	8.00	3.60	1.00
☐ 415	Curt Flood	10.00	4.50	1.25
☐ 416	Jim Brewer	7.00	3:10	.85
☐ 417	Ed Brinkman	7.00	3.10	.85
☐ 418	Johnny Edwards	7.00	3.10	.85
☐ 419	Ruben Amaro	7.00	3.10	.85
☐ 420	Larry Jackson	7.00	3.10	.85
☐ 421	Twins Rookies	7.00	3.10	.85
	Gary Dotter			
	Jay Ward			
☐ 422	Aubrey Gatewood	7.00	3.10	.85
☐ 423	Jesse Gonder	7.00	3.10	.85
☐ 424	Gary Bell	7.00	3.10	.85
☐ 425	Wayne Causey	7.00	3.10	.85
☐ 426	Braves Team	10.00	4.50	1.25
☐ 427	Bob Saverine	7.00	3.10	.85
☐ 428	Bob Shaw	7.00	3.10	.85
☐ 429	Don Demeter	7.00	3.10	.85
☐ 430	Gary Peters	7.00	3.10	.85
☐ 431	Cards Rookies	8.00	3.60	1.00
	Nelson Briles			
	Wayne Spiezio			
☐ 432	Jim Grant	7.50	3.40	.95
☐ 433	John Bateman	7.00	3.10	.85
☐ 434	Dave Morehead	7.00	3.10	.85
☐ 435	Willie Davis	7.50	3.40	.95
☐ 436	Don Elston	7.00	3.10	.85
☐ 437	Chico Cardenas	7.50	3.40	.95
☐ 438	Harry Walker MG	7.00	3.10	.85
☐ 439	Moe Drabowsky	7.50	3.40	.95
☐ 440	Tom Tresh	7.50	3.40	.95
☐ 441	Denny Lemaster	7.00	3.10	.85
☐ 442	Vic Power	7.50	3.40	.95
☐ 443	Checklist 6	12.00	3.50	1.20
☐ 444	Bob Hendley	7.00	3.10	.85
☐ 445	Don Lock	7.00	3.10	.85
☐ 446	Art Mahaffey	7.00	3.10	.85
☐ 447	Julian Javier	7.50	3.40	.95
☐ 448	Lee Stange	7.00	3.10	.85
☐ 449	Mets Rookies	7.00	3.10	.85
	Jerry Hinsley			
	Gary Kroll			
☐ 450	Elston Howard	8.00	3.60	1.00
☐ 451	Jim Owens	7.00	3.10	.85
☐ 452	Gary Geiger	7.00	3.10	.85
☐ 453	Dodgers Rookies	7.50	3.40	.95
	Willie Crawford			
	John Werhas			
☐ 454	Ed Rakow	7.00	3.10	.85
☐ 455	Norm Siebern	7.00	3.10	.85
☐ 456	Bill Henry	7.00	3.10	.85
☐ 457	Bob Kennedy MG	7.50	3.40	.95
☐ 458	John Buzhardt	7.00	3.10	.85
☐ 459	Frank Kostro	7.00	3.10	.85
☐ 460	Richie Allen	40.00	18.00	5.00
☐ 461	Braves Rookies	50.00	22.00	6.25
	Clay Carroll			
	Phil Niekro			
☐ 462	Lew Krausse UER	7.50	3.40	.95
	(Photo actually			
	Pete Lovrich)			
☐ 463	Manny Mota	7.50	3.40	.95
☐ 464	Ron Piche	7.00	3.10	.85
☐ 465	Tom Haller	7.50	3.40	.95
☐ 466	Senators Rookies	7.00	3.10	.85
	Pete Craig			
	Dick Nen			
☐ 467	Ray Washburn	7.00	3.10	.85
☐ 468	Larry Brown	7.00	3.10	.85
☐ 469	Don Nottebart	7.00	3.10	.85
☐ 470	Yogi Berra P/CO	50.00	22.00	6.25
☐ 471	Billy Hoeft	7.00	3.10	.85
☐ 472	Don Pavletich	7.00	3.10	.85
☐ 473	Orioles Rookies	16.00	7.25	2.00
	Paul Blair			
	Dave Johnson			
☐ 474	Cookie Rojas	7.50	3.40	.95

☐ 475	Clete Boyer	8.00	3.60	1.00
☐ 476	Billy O'Dell	7.00	3.10	.85
☐ 477	Cards Rookies	275.00	125.00	34.00
	Fritz Ackley			
	Steve Carlton			
☐ 478	Wilbur Wood	7.50	3.40	.95
☐ 479	Ken Harrelson	8.00	3.60	1.00
☐ 480	Joel Horlen	7.00	3.10	.85
☐ 481	Cleveland Indians	12.00	5.50	1.50
	Team Card			
☐ 482	Bob Priddy	7.00	3.10	.85
☐ 483	George Smith	7.00	3.10	.85
☐ 484	Ron Perranoski	7.50	3.40	.95
☐ 485	Nellie Fox P/CO	16.00	7.25	2.00
☐ 486	Angels Rookies	7.00	3.10	.85
	Tom Egan			
	Pat Rogan			
☐ 487	Woody Woodward	7.50	3.40	.95
☐ 488	Ted Wills	7.00	3.10	.85
☐ 489	Gene Mauch MG	7.50	3.40	.95
☐ 490	Earl Battey	7.00	3.10	.85
☐ 491	Tracy Stallard	7.00	3.10	.85
☐ 492	Gene Freese	7.00	3.10	.85
☐ 493	Tigers Rookies	7.00	3.10	.85
	Bill Roman			
	Bruce Brubaker			
☐ 494	Jay Ritchie	7.00	3.10	.85
☐ 495	Joe Christopher	7.00	3.10	.85
☐ 496	Joe Cunningham	7.50	3.40	.95
☐ 497	Giants Rookies	7.50	3.40	.95
	Ken Henderson			
	Jack Hiatt			
☐ 498	Gene Stephens	7.00	3.10	.85
☐ 499	Stu Miller	7.50	3.40	.95
☐ 500	Eddie Mathews	32.00	14.50	4.00
☐ 501	Indians Rookies	7.00	3.10	.85
	Ralph Gagliano			
	Jim Rittwage			
☐ 502	Don Cardwell	7.00	3.10	.85
☐ 503	Phil Gagliano	7.00	3.10	.85
☐ 504	Jerry Grote	7.00	3.10	.85
☐ 505	Ray Culp	7.00	3.10	.85
☐ 506	Sam Mele MG	7.00	3.10	.85
☐ 507	Sammy Ellis	7.00	3.10	.85
☐ 508	Checklist 7	12.00	4.00	1.20
☐ 509	Red Sox Rookies	7.00	3.10	.85
	Bob Guindon			
	Gerry Vezendy			
☐ 510	Ernie Banks	80.00	36.00	10.00
☐ 511	Ron Locke	7.00	3.10	.85
☐ 512	Cap Peterson	7.00	3.10	.85
☐ 513	New York Yankees	40.00	18.00	5.00
	Team Card			
☐ 514	Joe Azcue	7.00	3.10	.85
☐ 515	Vern Law	7.50	3.40	.95
☐ 516	Al Weis	7.00	3.10	.85
☐ 517	Angels Rookies	7.50	3.40	.95
	Paul Schaal			
	Jack Warner			
☐ 518	Ken Rowe	7.00	3.10	.85
☐ 519	Bob Uecker UER	32.00	14.50	4.00
	(Posing as a left-			
	handed batter)			
☐ 520	Tony Cloninger	7.00	3.10	.85
☐ 521	Phillies Rookies	7.00	3.10	.85
	Dave Bennett			
	Morrie Stevens			
☐ 522	Hank Aguirre	7.00	3.10	.85
☐ 523	Mike Brumley SP	12.00	5.50	1.50
☐ 524	Dave Giusti SP	12.00	5.50	1.50
☐ 525	Eddie Bressoud	7.00	3.10	.85

☐ 526	Athletics Rookies SP	90.00	40.00	11.00
	Rene Lachemann			
	Johnny Odom			
	Jim Hunter UER			
	("Tim" on back)			
	Skip Lockwood			
☐ 527	Jeff Torborg SP	16.00	7.25	2.00
☐ 528	George Altman	7.00	3.10	.85
☐ 529	Jerry Fosnow SP	12.00	5.50	1.50
☐ 530	Jim Maloney	7.50	3.40	.95
☐ 531	Chuck Hiller	7.00	3.10	.85
☐ 532	Hector Lopez	7.50	3.40	.95
☐ 533	Mets Rookies SP	25.00	11.00	3.10
	Dan Napoleon			
	Ron Swoboda			
	Tug McGraw			
	Jim Bethke			
☐ 534	John Herrnstein	7.00	3.10	.85
☐ 535	Jack Kralick SP	12.00	5.50	1.50
☐ 536	Andre Rodgers SP	12.00	5.50	1.50
☐ 537	Angels Rookies	7.00	3.10	.85
	Marcelino Lopez			
	Phil Roof			
	Rudy May			
☐ 538	Chuck Dressen SP MG	14.00	6.25	1.75
☐ 539	Herm Starrette	7.00	3.10	.85
☐ 540	Lou Brock SP	50.00	22.00	6.25
☐ 541	White Sox Rookies	7.00	3.10	.85
	Greg Bollo			
	Bob Locker			
☐ 542	Lou Klimchock	7.00	3.10	.85
☐ 543	Ed Connolly SP	12.00	5.50	1.50
☐ 544	Howie Reed	7.00	3.10	.85
☐ 545	Jesus Alou SP	12.00	5.50	1.50
☐ 546	Indians Rookies	7.00	3.10	.85
	Bill Davis			
	Mike Hedlund			
	Ray Barker			
	Floyd Weaver			
☐ 547	Jake Wood SP	12.00	5.50	1.50
☐ 548	Dick Stigman	7.00	3.10	.85
☐ 549	Cubs Rookies SP	20.00	9.00	2.50
	Roberto Pena			
	Glenn Beckert			
☐ 550	Mel Stottlemyre SP	30.00	13.50	3.70
☐ 551	New York Mets SP	30.00	13.50	3.70
	Team Card			
☐ 552	Julio Gotay	7.00	3.10	.85
☐ 553	Astros Rookies	7.00	3.10	.85
	Dan Coombs			
	Gene Ratliff			
	Jack McClure			
☐ 554	Chico Ruiz SP	12.00	5.50	1.50
☐ 555	Jack Baldschun SP	12.00	5.50	1.50
☐ 556	Red Schoendienst	24.00	11.00	3.00
	SP MG			
☐ 557	Jose Santiago	7.00	3.10	.85
☐ 558	Tommie Sisk	7.00	3.10	.85
☐ 559	Ed Bailey SP	12.00	5.50	1.50
☐ 560	Boog Powell SP	24.00	11.00	3.00
☐ 561	Dodgers Rookies	10.00	4.50	1.25
	Dennis Daboll			
	Mike Kekich			
	Hector Valle			
	Jim Lefebvre			
☐ 562	Billy Moran	7.00	3.10	.85
☐ 563	Julio Navarro	7.00	3.10	.85
☐ 564	Mel Nelson	7.00	3.10	.85
☐ 565	Ernie Broglio SP	12.00	5.50	1.50
☐ 566	Yankees Rookies SP	12.00	5.50	1.50
	Gil Blanco			

Ross Moschitto
Art Lopez

		NRMT	VG-E	GOOD
☐ 567	Tommie Aaron	7.50	3.40	.95
☐ 568	Ron Taylor SP	12.00	5.50	1.50
☐ 569	Gino Cimoli SP	12.00	5.50	1.50
☐ 570	Claude Osteen SP	12.00	5.50	1.50
☐ 571	Ossie Virgil SP	12.00	5.50	1.50
☐ 572	Baltimore Orioles SP	30.00	13.50	3.70

Team Card

☐ 573	Red Sox Rookies SP	24.00	11.00	3.00

Jim Lonborg
Gerry Moses
Bill Schlesinger
Mike Ryan

☐ 574	Roy Sievers	7.50	3.40	.95
☐ 575	Jose Pagan	7.00	3.10	.85
☐ 576	Terry Fox SP	12.00	5.50	1.50
☐ 577	AL Rookie Stars SP	14.00	6.25	1.75

Darold Knowles
Don Buschhorn
Richie Scheinblum

☐ 578	Camilo Carreon SP	12.00	5.50	1.50
☐ 579	Dick Smith SP	12.00	5.50	1.50
☐ 580	Jimmie Hall SP	12.00	5.50	1.50
☐ 581	NL Rookie Stars SP	90.00	40.00	11.00

Tony Perez
Dave Ricketts
Kevin Collins

☐ 582	Bob Schmidt SP	12.00	5.50	1.50
☐ 583	Wes Covington SP	12.00	5.50	1.50
☐ 584	Harry Bright	7.00	3.10	.85
☐ 585	Hank Fischer	7.00	3.10	.85
☐ 586	Tom McCraw SP	12.00	5.50	1.50
☐ 587	Joe Sparma	7.00	3.10	.85
☐ 588	Lenny Green	7.00	3.10	.85
☐ 589	Giants Rookies SP	12.00	5.50	1.50

Frank Linzy
Bob Schroder

☐ 590	John Wyatt	7.00	3.10	.85
☐ 591	Bob Skinner SP	14.00	6.25	1.75
☐ 592	Frank Bork SP	12.00	5.50	1.50
☐ 593	Tigers Rookies SP	12.00	5.50	1.50

Jackie Moore
John Sullivan

☐ 594	Joe Gaines	7.00	3.10	.85
☐ 595	Don Lee	7.00	3.10	.85
☐ 596	Don Landrum SP	12.00	5.50	1.50
☐ 597	Twins Rookies	7.00	3.10	.85

Joe Nossek
John Sevcik
Dick Reese

☐ 598	Al Downing SP	20.00	6.00	2.00

1966 Topps

The cards in this 598-card set measure 2 1/2" by 3 1/2". There are the same number of cards as in the 1965 set. Once again, the seventh series cards (523 to 598) are considered more difficult to obtain than the cards of any other series in the set. Within this last series there are 43 cards that were printed in lesser quantities than the other cards in that series; these shorter-printed cards are marked by SP in the checklist below. The only featured subset within this set is League Leaders (215-226). Noteworthy Rookie Cards in the set include

Jim Palmer (126), Ferguson Jenkins (254), and Don Sutton (288). Jim Palmer is described in the bio (on his card back) as a left-hander.

	NRMT	VG-E	GOOD
COMPLETE SET (598)	4000.00	1800.00	500.00
COMMON CARD (1-109)	1.50	.70	.19
COMMON CARD (110-283)	2.00	.90	.25
COMMON CARD (284-370)	3.00	1.35	.35
COMMON CARD (371-446)	5.00	2.20	.60
COMMON CARD (447-522)	9.00	4.00	1.10
COMMON CARD (523-598)	15.00	6.75	1.85

		NRMT	VG-E	GOOD
☐ 1	Willie Mays	135.00	42.50	16.00
☐ 2	Ted Abernathy	1.50	.70	.19
☐ 3	Sam Mele MG	1.50	.70	.19
☐ 4	Ray Culp	1.50	.70	.19
☐ 5	Jim Fregosi	2.50	1.10	.30
☐ 6	Chuck Schilling	1.50	.70	.19
☐ 7	Tracy Stallard	1.50	.70	.19
☐ 8	Floyd Robinson	1.50	.70	.19
☐ 9	Clete Boyer	2.50	1.10	.30
☐ 10	Tony Cloninger	1.50	.70	.19
☐ 11	Senators Rookies	1.50	.70	.19

Brant Alyea
Pete Craig

☐ 12	John Tsitouris	1.50	.70	.19
☐ 13	Lou Johnson	2.50	1.10	.30
☐ 14	Norm Siebern	1.50	.70	.19
☐ 15	Vern Law	2.50	1.10	.30
☐ 16	Larry Brown	1.50	.70	.19
☐ 17	John Stephenson	1.50	.70	.19
☐ 18	Roland Sheldon	1.50	.70	.19
☐ 19	San Francisco Giants	4.00	1.80	.50

Team Card

☐ 20	Willie Horton	2.50	1.10	.30
☐ 21	Don Nottebart	1.50	.70	.19
☐ 22	Joe Nossek	1.50	.70	.19
☐ 23	Jack Sanford	1.50	.70	.19
☐ 24	Don Kessinger	5.00	2.20	.60
☐ 25	Pete Ward	1.50	.70	.19
☐ 26	Ray Sadecki	1.50	.70	.19
☐ 27	Orioles Rookies	1.50	.70	.19

Darold Knowles
Andy Etchebarren

☐ 28	Phil Niekro	20.00	9.00	2.50
☐ 29	Mike Brumley	1.50	.70	.19
☐ 30	Pete Rose DP	45.00	20.00	5.50
☐ 31	Jack Cullen	1.50	.70	.19
☐ 32	Adolfo Phillips	1.50	.70	.19
☐ 33	Jim Pagliaroni	1.50	.70	.19
☐ 34	Checklist 1	8.00	1.60	.80
☐ 35	Ron Swoboda	1.50	.70	.19
☐ 36	Jim Hunter UER	20.00	9.00	2.50

(Stats say 1963 and

1964, should be
1963 and 1964)

☐	37	Billy Herman MG	2.50	1.10	.30
☐	38	Ron Nischwitz	1.50	.70	.19
☐	39	Ken Henderson	1.50	.70	.19
☐	40	Jim Grant	1.50	.70	.19
☐	41	Don LeJohn	1.50	.70	.19
☐	42	Aubrey Gatewood	1.50	.70	.19
☐	43A	Don Landrum	2.00	.90	.25
		(Dark button on pants showing)			
☐	43B	Don Landrum	2.00	.90	.25
		(Button on pants partially airbrushed)			
☐	43C	Don Landrum	2.00	.90	.25
		(Button on pants not showing)			
☐	44	Indians Rookies	1.50	.70	.19
		Bill Davis			
		Tom Kelley			
☐	45	Jim Gentile	2.50	1.10	.30
☐	46	Howie Koplitz	1.50	.70	.19
☐	47	J.C. Martin	1.50	.70	.19
☐	48	Paul Blair	2.50	1.10	.30
☐	49	Woody Woodward	2.50	1.10	.30
☐	50	Mickey Mantle DP	225.00	100.00	28.00
☐	51	Gordon Richardson	1.50	.70	.19
☐	52	Power Plus	2.50	1.10	.30
		Wes Covington			
		Johnny Callison			
☐	53	Bob Duliba	1.50	.70	.19
☐	54	Jose Pagan	1.50	.70	.19
☐	55	Ken Harrelson	2.50	1.10	.30
☐	56	Sandy Valdespino	1.50	.70	.19
☐	57	Jim Lefebvre	1.50	.70	.19
☐	58	Dave Wickersham	1.50	.70	.19
☐	59	Reds Team	4.00	1.80	.50
☐	60	Curt Flood	2.50	1.10	.30
☐	61	Bob Bolin	1.50	.70	.19
☐	62A	Merritt Ranew	1.50	.70	.19
		(With sold line)			
☐	62B	Merritt Ranew	40.00	18.00	5.00
		(Without sold line)			
☐	63	Jim Stewart	1.50	.70	.19
☐	64	Bob Bruce	1.50	.70	.19
☐	65	Leon Wagner	1.50	.70	.19
☐	66	Al Weis	1.50	.70	.19
☐	67	Mets Rookies	2.50	1.10	.30
		Cleon Jones			
		Dick Selma			
☐	68	Hal Reniff	1.50	.70	.19
☐	69	Ken Hamlin	1.50	.70	.19
☐	70	Carl Yastrzemski	30.00	13.50	3.70
☐	71	Frank Carpin	1.50	.70	.19
☐	72	Tony Perez	25.00	11.00	3.10
☐	73	Jerry Zimmerman	1.50	.70	.19
☐	74	Don Mossi	2.50	1.10	.30
☐	75	Tommy Davis	2.50	1.10	.30
☐	76	Red Schoendienst MG	4.00	1.80	.50
☐	77	John Orsino	1.50	.70	.19
☐	78	Frank Linzy	1.50	.70	.19
☐	79	Joe Pepitone	2.50	1.10	.30
☐	80	Richie Allen	6.00	2.70	.75
☐	81	Ray Oyler	1.50	.70	.19
☐	82	Bob Hendley	1.50	.70	.19
☐	83	Albie Pearson	2.50	1.10	.30
☐	84	Braves Rookies	1.50	.70	.19
		Jim Beauchamp			
		Dick Kelley			
☐	85	Eddie Fisher	1.50	.70	.19
☐	86	John Bateman	1.50	.70	.19
☐	87	Dan Napoleon	1.50	.70	.19
☐	88	Fred Whitfield	1.50	.70	.19
☐	89	Ted Davidson	1.50	.70	.19
☐	90	Luis Aparicio	6.00	2.70	.75
☐	91A	Bob Uecker TR	12.00	5.50	1.50
☐	91B	Bob Uecker NTR	40.00	18.00	5.00
☐	92	Yankees Team	12.00	5.50	1.50
☐	93	Jim Lonborg	2.50	1.10	.30
☐	94	Matty Alou	2.50	1.10	.30
☐	95	Pete Richert	1.50	.70	.19
☐	96	Felipe Alou	2.50	1.10	.30
☐	97	Jim Merritt	1.50	.70	.19
☐	98	Don Demeter	1.50	.70	.19
☐	99	Buc Belters	6.00	2.70	.75
		Willie Stargell			
		Donn Clendenon			
☐	100	Sandy Koufax	75.00	34.00	9.50
☐	101A	Checklist 2	16.00	3.20	1.60
		(115 W. Spahn) ERR			
☐	101B	Checklist 2	10.00	2.00	1.00
		(115 Bill Henry) COR			
☐	102	Ed Kirkpatrick	1.50	.70	.19
☐	103A	Dick Groat TR	2.50	1.10	.30
☐	103B	Dick Groat NTR	40.00	18.00	5.00
☐	104A	Alex Johnson TR	2.50	1.10	.30
☐	104B	Alex Johnson NTR	40.00	18.00	5.00
☐	105	Milt Pappas	2.50	1.10	.30
☐	106	Rusty Staub	4.00	1.80	.50
☐	107	A's Rookies	1.50	.70	.19
		Larry Stahl			
		Ron Tompkins			
☐	108	Bobby Klaus	1.50	.70	.19
☐	109	Ralph Terry	2.50	1.10	.30
☐	110	Ernie Banks	30.00	13.50	3.70
☐	111	Gary Peters	2.00	.90	.25
☐	112	Manny Mota	3.00	1.35	.35
☐	113	Hank Aguirre	2.00	.90	.25
☐	114	Jim Gosger	2.00	.90	.25
☐	115	Bill Henry	2.00	.90	.25
☐	116	Walt Alston MG	4.00	1.80	.50
☐	117	Jake Gibbs	3.00	1.35	.35
☐	118	Mike McCormick	3.00	1.35	.35
☐	119	Art Shamsky	2.00	.90	.25
☐	120	Harmon Killebrew	16.00	7.25	2.00
☐	121	Ray Herbert	2.00	.90	.25
☐	122	Joe Gaines	2.00	.90	.25
☐	123	Pirates Rookies	2.00	.90	.25
		Frank Bork			
		Jerry May			
☐	124	Tug McGraw	4.00	1.80	.50
☐	125	Lou Brock	20.00	9.00	2.50
☐	126	Jim Palmer UER	125.00	55.00	15.50
		(Described as a lefthander on card back)			
☐	127	Ken Berry	2.00	.90	.25
☐	128	Jim Landis	2.00	.90	.25
☐	129	Jack Kralick	2.00	.90	.25
☐	130	Joe Torre	4.00	1.80	.50
☐	131	Angels Team	5.00	2.20	.60
☐	132	Orlando Cepeda	5.00	2.20	.60
☐	133	Don McMahon	2.00	.90	.25
☐	134	Wes Parker	3.00	1.35	.35
☐	135	Dave Morehead	2.00	.90	.25
☐	136	Woody Held	2.00	.90	.25
☐	137	Pat Corrales	3.00	1.35	.35
☐	138	Roger Repoz	2.00	.90	.25
☐	139	Cubs Rookies	2.00	.90	.25
		Byron Browne			
		Don Young			
☐	140	Jim Maloney	3.00	1.35	.35

☐ 141	Tom McCraw	2.00	.90	.25
☐ 142	Don Dennis	2.00	.90	.25
☐ 143	Jose Tartabull	3.00	1.35	.35
☐ 144	Don Schwall	2.00	.90	.25
☐ 145	Bill Freehan	3.00	1.35	.35
☐ 146	George Altman	2.00	.90	.25
☐ 147	Lum Harris MG	2.00	.90	.25
☐ 148	Bob Johnson	2.00	.90	.25
☐ 149	Dick Nen	2.00	.90	.25
☐ 150	Rocky Colavito	8.00	3.60	1.00
☐ 151	Gary Wagner	2.00	.90	.25
☐ 152	Frank Malzone	3.00	1.35	.35
☐ 153	Rico Carty	3.00	1.35	.35
☐ 154	Chuck Hiller	2.00	.90	.25
☐ 155	Marcelino Lopez	2.00	.90	.25
☐ 156	Double Play Combo	2.00	.90	.25
	Dick Schofield			
	Hal Lanier			
☐ 157	Rene Lachemann	3.00	1.35	.35
☐ 158	Jim Brewer	2.00	.90	.25
☐ 159	Chico Ruiz	2.00	.90	.25
☐ 160	Whitey Ford	25.00	11.00	3.10
☐ 161	Jerry Lumpe	2.00	.90	.25
☐ 162	Lee Maye	2.00	.90	.25
☐ 163	Tito Francona	2.00	.90	.25
☐ 164	White Sox Rookies	3.00	1.35	.35
	Tommie Agee			
	Marv Staehle			
☐ 165	Don Lock	2.00	.90	.25
☐ 166	Chris Krug	2.00	.90	.25
☐ 167	Boog Powell	5.00	2.20	.60
☐ 168	Dan Osinski	2.00	.90	.25
☐ 169	Duke Sims	2.00	.90	.25
☐ 170	Cookie Rojas	3.00	1.35	.35
☐ 171	Nick Willhite	2.00	.90	.25
☐ 172	Mets Team	5.00	2.20	.60
☐ 173	Al Spangler	2.00	.90	.25
☐ 174	Ron Taylor	2.00	.90	.25
☐ 175	Bert Campaneris	3.00	1.35	.35
☐ 176	Jim Davenport	2.00	.90	.25
☐ 177	Hector Lopez	2.00	.90	.25
☐ 178	Bob Tillman	2.00	.90	.25
☐ 179	Cards Rookies	3.00	1.35	.35
	Dennis Aust			
	Bob Tolan			
☐ 180	Vada Pinson	3.00	1.35	.35
☐ 181	Al Worthington	2.00	.90	.25
☐ 182	Jerry Lynch	2.00	.90	.25
☐ 183A	Checklist 3	8.00	1.60	.80
	(Large print			
	on front)			
☐ 183B	Checklist 3	8.00	1.60	.80
	(Small print			
	on front)			
☐ 184	Denis Menke	2.00	.90	.25
☐ 185	Bob Buhl	3.00	1.35	.35
☐ 186	Ruben Amaro	2.00	.90	.25
☐ 187	Chuck Dressen MG	3.00	1.35	.35
☐ 188	Al Luplow	2.00	.90	.25
☐ 189	John Roseboro	3.00	1.35	.35
☐ 190	Jimmie Hall	2.00	.90	.25
☐ 191	Darrell Sutherland	2.00	.90	.25
☐ 192	Vic Power	3.00	1.35	.35
☐ 193	Dave McNally	3.00	1.35	.35
☐ 194	Senators Team	5.00	2.20	.60
☐ 195	Joe Morgan	14.00	6.25	1.75
☐ 196	Don Pavletich	2.00	.90	.25
☐ 197	Sonny Siebert	2.00	.90	.25
☐ 198	Mickey Stanley	4.00	1.80	.50
☐ 199	Chisox Clubbers	3.00	1.35	.35
	Bill Skowron			
	Johnny Romano			
	Floyd Robinson			
☐ 200	Eddie Mathews	14.00	6.25	1.75
☐ 201	Jim Dickson	2.00	.90	.25
☐ 202	Clay Dalrymple	2.00	.90	.25
☐ 203	Jose Santiago	2.00	.90	.25
☐ 204	Cubs Team	5.00	2.20	.60
☐ 205	Tom Tresh	3.00	1.35	.35
☐ 206	Al Jackson	2.00	.90	.25
☐ 207	Frank Quilici	2.00	.90	.25
☐ 208	Bob Miller	2.00	.90	.25
☐ 209	Tigers Rookies	3.50	1.55	.45
	Fritz Fisher			
	John Hiller			
☐ 210	Bill Mazeroski	5.00	2.20	.60
☐ 211	Frank Kreutzer	2.00	.90	.25
☐ 212	Ed Kranepool	3.00	1.35	.35
☐ 213	Fred Newman	2.00	.90	.25
☐ 214	Tommy Harper	3.00	1.35	.35
☐ 215	NL Batting Leaders	40.00	18.00	5.00
	Bob Clemente			
	Hank Aaron			
	Willie Mays			
☐ 216	AL Batting Leaders	6.00	2.70	.75
	Tony Oliva			
	Carl Yastrzemski			
	Vic Davalillo			
☐ 217	NL Home Run Leaders	20.00	9.00	2.50
	Willie Mays			
	Willie McCovey			
	Billy Williams			
☐ 218	AL Home Run Leaders	5.00	2.20	.60
	Tony Conigliaro			
	Norm Cash			
	Willie Horton			
☐ 219	NL RBI Leaders	12.00	5.50	1.50
	Deron Johnson			
	Frank Robinson			
	Willie Mays			
☐ 220	AL RBI Leaders	5.00	2.20	.60
	Rocky Colavito			
	Willie Horton			
	Tony Oliva			
☐ 221	NL ERA Leaders	12.00	5.50	1.50
	Sandy Koufax			
	Juan Marichal			
	Vern Law			
☐ 222	AL ERA Leaders	5.00	2.20	.60
	Sam McDowell			
	Eddie Fisher			
	Sonny Siebert			
☐ 223	NL Pitching Leaders	12.00	5.50	1.50
	Sandy Koufax			
	Tony Cloninger			
	Don Drysdale			
☐ 224	AL Pitching Leaders	5.00	2.20	.60
	Jim Grant			
	Mel Stottlemyre			
	Jim Kaat			
☐ 225	NL Strikeout Leaders	12.00	5.50	1.50
	Sandy Koufax			
	Bob Veale			
	Bob Gibson			
☐ 226	AL Strikeout Leaders	5.00	2.20	.60
	Sam McDowell			
	Mickey Lolich			
	Dennis McLain			
	Sonny Siebert			
☐ 227	Russ Nixon	2.00	.90	.25
☐ 228	Larry Dierker	2.00	.90	.25
☐ 229	Hank Bauer MG	3.00	1.35	.35

☐ 230	Johnny Callison	3.00	1.35	.35
☐ 231	Floyd Weaver	2.00	.90	.25
☐ 232	Glenn Beckert	3.00	1.35	.35
☐ 233	Dom Zanni	2.00	.90	.25
☐ 234	Yankees Rookies	8.00	3.60	1.00
	Rich Beck			
	Roy White			
☐ 235	Don Cardwell	2.00	.90	.25
☐ 236	Mike Hershberger	2.00	.90	.25
☐ 237	Billy O'Dell	2.00	.90	.25
☐ 238	Dodgers Team	5.00	2.20	.60
☐ 239	Orlando Pena	2.00	.90	.25
☐ 240	Earl Battey	2.00	.90	.25
☐ 241	Dennis Ribant	2.00	.90	.25
☐ 242	Jesus Alou	2.00	.90	.25
☐ 243	Nelson Briles	3.00	1.35	.35
☐ 244	Astros Rookies	2.00	.90	.25
	Chuck Harrison			
	Sonny Jackson			
☐ 245	John Buzhardt	2.00	.90	.25
☐ 246	Ed Bailey	2.00	.90	.25
☐ 247	Carl Warwick	2.00	.90	.25
☐ 248	Pete Mikkelsen	2.00	.90	.25
☐ 249	Bill Rigney MG	2.00	.90	.25
☐ 250	Sammy Ellis	2.00	.90	.25
☐ 251	Ed Brinkman	2.00	.90	.25
☐ 252	Denny Lemaster	2.00	.90	.25
☐ 253	Don Wert	2.00	.90	.25
☐ 254	Phillies Rookies	90.00	40.00	11.00
	Ferguson Jenkins			
	Bill Sorrell			
☐ 255	Willie Stargell	20.00	9.00	2.50
☐ 256	Lew Krausse	2.00	.90	.25
☐ 257	Jeff Torborg	3.00	1.35	.35
☐ 258	Dave Giusti	2.00	.90	.25
☐ 259	Boston Red Sox	5.00	2.20	.60
	Team Card			
☐ 260	Bob Shaw	2.00	.90	.25
☐ 261	Ron Hansen	2.00	.90	.25
☐ 262	Jack Hamilton	2.00	.90	.25
☐ 263	Tom Egan	2.00	.90	.25
☐ 264	Twins Rookies	2.00	.90	.25
	Andy Kosco			
	Ted Uhlaender			
☐ 265	Stu Miller	3.00	1.35	.35
☐ 266	Pedro Gonzalez UER	2.00	.90	.25
	(Misspelled Gonzales			
	on card back)			
☐ 267	Joe Sparma	2.00	.90	.25
☐ 268	John Blanchard	2.00	.90	.25
☐ 269	Don Heffner MG	2.00	.90	.25
☐ 270	Claude Osteen	3.00	1.35	.35
☐ 271	Hal Lanier	2.00	.90	.25
☐ 272	Jack Baldschun	2.00	.90	.25
☐ 273	Astro Aces	3.00	1.35	.35
	Bob Aspromonte			
	Rusty Staub			
☐ 274	Buster Narum	2.00	.90	.25
☐ 275	Tim McCarver	5.00	2.20	.60
☐ 276	Jim Bouton	4.00	1.80	.50
☐ 277	George Thomas	2.00	.90	.25
☐ 278	Cal Koonce	2.00	.90	.25
☐ 279A	Checklist 4	8.00	1.60	.80
	(Player's cap black)			
☐ 279B	Checklist 4	8.00	1.60	.80
	(Player's cap red)			
☐ 280	Bobby Knoop	2.00	.90	.25
☐ 281	Bruce Howard	2.00	.90	.25
☐ 282	Johnny Lewis	2.00	.90	.25
☐ 283	Jim Perry	3.00	1.35	.35
☐ 284	Bobby Wine	3.50	1.55	.45
☐ 285	Luis Tiant	4.00	1.80	.50
☐ 286	Gary Geiger	3.00	1.35	.35
☐ 287	Jack Aker	3.00	1.35	.35
☐ 288	Dodgers Rookies	60.00	27.00	7.50
	Bill Singer			
	Don Sutton			
☐ 289	Larry Sherry	3.50	1.55	.45
☐ 290	Ron Santo	6.00	2.70	.75
☐ 291	Moe Drabowsky	3.50	1.55	.45
☐ 292	Jim Coker	3.00	1.35	.35
☐ 293	Mike Shannon	3.50	1.55	.45
☐ 294	Steve Ridzik	3.00	1.35	.35
☐ 295	Jim Ray Hart	3.50	1.55	.45
☐ 296	Johnny Keane MG	3.00	1.35	.35
☐ 297	Jim Owens	3.00	1.35	.35
☐ 298	Rico Petrocelli	3.50	1.55	.45
☐ 299	Lou Burdette	3.50	1.55	.45
☐ 300	Bob Clemente	110.00	50.00	14.00
☐ 301	Greg Bollo	3.00	1.35	.35
☐ 302	Ernie Bowman	3.00	1.35	.35
☐ 303	Cleveland Indians	5.00	2.20	.60
	Team Card			
☐ 304	John Herrnstein	3.00	1.35	.35
☐ 305	Camilo Pascual	3.50	1.55	.45
☐ 306	Ty Cline	3.00	1.35	.35
☐ 307	Clay Carroll	3.50	1.55	.45
☐ 308	Tom Haller	3.50	1.55	.45
☐ 309	Diego Segui	3.00	1.35	.35
☐ 310	Frank Robinson	35.00	16.00	4.40
☐ 311	Reds Rookies	3.50	1.55	.45
	Tommy Helms			
	Dick Simpson			
☐ 312	Bob Saverine	3.00	1.35	.35
☐ 313	Chris Zachary	3.00	1.35	.35
☐ 314	Hector Valle	3.00	1.35	.35
☐ 315	Norm Cash	4.00	1.80	.50
☐ 316	Jack Fisher	3.00	1.35	.35
☐ 317	Dalton Jones	3.00	1.35	.35
☐ 318	Harry Walker MG	3.00	1.35	.35
☐ 319	Gene Freese	3.00	1.35	.35
☐ 320	Bob Gibson	25.00	11.00	3.10
☐ 321	Rick Reichardt	3.00	1.35	.35
☐ 322	Bill Faul	3.00	1.35	.35
☐ 323	Ray Barker	3.00	1.35	.35
☐ 324	John Boozer	3.00	1.35	.35
☐ 325	Vic Davalillo	3.00	1.35	.35
☐ 326	Braves Team	5.00	2.20	.60
☐ 327	Bernie Allen	3.00	1.35	.35
☐ 328	Jerry Grote	3.00	1.35	.35
☐ 329	Pete Charton	3.00	1.35	.35
☐ 330	Ron Fairly	3.50	1.55	.45
☐ 331	Ron Herbel	3.00	1.35	.35
☐ 332	Bill Bryan	3.00	1.35	.35
☐ 333	Senators Rookies	3.00	1.35	.35
	Joe Coleman			
	Jim French			
☐ 334	Marty Keough	3.00	1.35	.35
☐ 335	Juan Pizarro	3.00	1.35	.35
☐ 336	Gene Alley	3.50	1.55	.45
☐ 337	Fred Gladding	3.00	1.35	.35
☐ 338	Dal Maxvill	3.00	1.35	.35
☐ 339	Del Crandall	3.50	1.55	.45
☐ 340	Dean Chance	3.50	1.55	.45
☐ 341	Wes Westrum MG	3.50	1.55	.45
☐ 342	Bob Humphreys	3.00	1.35	.35
☐ 343	Joe Christopher	3.00	1.35	.35
☐ 344	Steve Blass	3.50	1.55	.45
☐ 345	Bob Allison	3.50	1.55	.45
☐ 346	Mike de la Hoz	3.00	1.35	.35
☐ 347	Phil Regan	3.50	1.55	.45
☐ 348	Orioles Team	7.00	3.10	.85

□	349 Cap Peterson	3.00	1.35	.35
□	350 Mel Stottlemyre	5.00	2.20	.60
□	351 Fred Valentine	3.00	1.35	.35
□	352 Bob Aspromonte	3.00	1.35	.35
□	353 Al McBean	3.00	1.35	.35
□	354 Smoky Burgess	3.50	1.55	.45
□	355 Wade Blasingame	3.00	1.35	.35
□	356 Red Sox Rookies	3.00	1.35	.35
	Owen Johnson			
	Ken Sanders			
□	357 Gerry Arrigo	3.00	1.35	.35
□	358 Charlie Smith	3.00	1.35	.35
□	359 Johnny Briggs	3.00	1.35	.35
□	360 Ron Hunt	3.00	1.35	.35
□	361 Tom Satriano	3.00	1.35	.35
□	362 Gates Brown	3.50	1.55	.45
□	363 Checklist 5	10.00	2.00	1.00
□	364 Nate Oliver	3.00	1.35	.35
□	365 Roger Maris	45.00	20.00	5.50
□	366 Wayne Causey	3.00	1.35	.35
□	367 Mel Nelson	3.00	1.35	.35
□	368 Charlie Lau	3.50	1.55	.45
□	369 Jim King	3.00	1.35	.35
□	370 Chico Cardenas	3.00	1.35	.35
□	371 Lee Stange	5.00	2.20	.60
□	372 Harvey Kuenn	5.00	2.20	.60
□	373 Giants Rookies	5.00	2.20	.60
	Jack Hiatt			
	Dick Estelle			
□	374 Bob Locker	5.00	2.20	.60
□	375 Donn Clendenon	5.00	2.20	.60
□	376 Paul Schaal	5.00	2.20	.60
□	377 Turk Farrell	5.00	2.20	.60
□	378 Dick Tracewski	5.00	2.20	.60
□	379 Cardinal Team	10.00	4.50	1.25
□	380 Tony Conigliaro	10.00	4.50	1.25
□	381 Hank Fischer	5.00	2.20	.60
□	382 Phil Roof	5.00	2.20	.60
□	383 Jackie Brandt	5.00	2.20	.60
□	384 Al Downing	5.00	2.20	.60
□	385 Ken Boyer	6.00	2.70	.75
□	386 Gil Hodges MG	8.00	3.60	1.00
□	387 Howie Reed	5.00	2.20	.60
□	388 Don Mincher	5.00	2.20	.60
□	389 Jim O'Toole	5.00	2.20	.60
□	390 Brooks Robinson	45.00	20.00	5.50
□	391 Chuck Hinton	5.00	2.20	.60
□	392 Cubs Rookies	7.00	3.10	.85
	Bill Hands			
	Randy Hundley			
□	393 George Brunet	5.00	2.20	.60
□	394 Ron Brand	5.00	2.20	.60
□	395 Len Gabrielson	5.00	2.20	.60
□	396 Jerry Stephenson	5.00	2.20	.60
□	397 Bill White	5.00	2.20	.60
□	398 Danny Cater	5.00	2.20	.60
□	399 Ray Washburn	5.00	2.20	.60
□	400 Zoilo Versalles	5.00	2.20	.60
□	401 Ken McMullen	5.00	2.20	.60
□	402 Jim Hickman	5.00	2.20	.60
□	403 Fred Talbot	5.00	2.20	.60
□	404 Pittsburgh Pirates	10.00	4.50	1.25
	Team Card			
□	405 Elston Howard	6.00	2.70	.75
□	406 Joey Jay	5.00	2.20	.60
□	407 John Kennedy	5.00	2.20	.60
□	408 Lee Thomas	5.00	2.20	.60
□	409 Billy Hoeft	5.00	2.20	.60
□	410 Al Kaline	35.00	16.00	4.40
□	411 Gene Mauch MG	5.00	2.20	.60
□	412 Sam Bowens	5.00	2.20	.60

□	413 Johnny Romano	5.00	2.20	.60
□	414 Dan Coombs	5.00	2.20	.60
□	415 Max Alvis	5.00	2.20	.60
□	416 Phil Ortega	5.00	2.20	.60
□	417 Angels Rookies	5.00	2.20	.60
	Jim McGlothlin			
	Ed Sukla			
□	418 Phil Gagliano	5.00	2.20	.60
□	419 Mike Ryan	5.00	2.20	.60
□	420 Juan Marichal	14.00	6.25	1.75
□	421 Roy McMillan	5.00	2.20	.60
□	422 Ed Charles	5.00	2.20	.60
□	423 Ernie Broglio	5.00	2.20	.60
□	424 Reds Rookies	10.00	4.50	1.25
	Lee May			
	Darrell Osteen			
□	425 Bob Veale	5.00	2.20	.60
□	426 White Sox Team	10.00	4.50	1.25
□	427 John Miller	5.00	2.20	.60
□	428 Sandy Alomar	5.00	2.20	.60
□	429 Bill Monbouquette	5.00	2.20	.60
□	430 Don Drysdale	20.00	9.00	2.50
□	431 Walt Bond	5.00	2.20	.60
□	432 Bob Heffner	5.00	2.20	.60
□	433 Alvin Dark MG	5.00	2.20	.60
□	434 Willie Kirkland	5.00	2.20	.60
□	435 Jim Bunning	12.00	5.50	1.50
□	436 Julian Javier	5.00	2.20	.60
□	437 Al Stanek	5.00	2.20	.60
□	438 Willie Smith	5.00	2.20	.60
□	439 Pedro Ramos	5.00	2.20	.60
□	440 Deron Johnson	5.00	2.20	.60
□	441 Tommie Sisk	5.00	2.20	.60
□	442 Orioles Rookies	5.00	2.20	.60
	Ed Barnowski			
	Eddie Watt			
□	443 Bill Wakefield	5.00	2.20	.60
□	444 Checklist 6	10.00	2.00	1.00
□	445 Jim Kaat	10.00	4.50	1.25
□	446 Mack Jones	5.00	2.20	.60
□	447 Dick Ellsworth UER	12.00	5.50	1.50
	(Photo actually			
	Ken Hubbs)			
□	448 Eddie Stanky MG	9.00	4.00	1.10
□	449 Joe Moeller	9.00	4.00	1.10
□	450 Tony Oliva	12.00	5.50	1.50
□	451 Barry Latman	9.00	4.00	1.10
□	452 Joe Azcue	9.00	4.00	1.10
□	453 Ron Kline	9.00	4.00	1.10
□	454 Jerry Buchek	9.00	4.00	1.10
□	455 Mickey Lolich	10.00	4.50	1.25
□	456 Red Sox Rookies	9.00	4.00	1.10
	Darrell Brandon			
	Joe Foy			
□	457 Joe Gibbon	9.00	4.00	1.10
□	458 Manny Jiminez	9.00	4.00	1.10
□	459 Bill McCool	9.00	4.00	1.10
□	460 Curt Blefary	9.00	4.00	1.10
□	461 Roy Face	9.00	4.00	1.10
□	462 Bob Rodgers	9.00	4.00	1.10
□	463 Philadelphia Phillies	14.00	6.25	1.75
	Team Card			
□	464 Larry Bearnarth	9.00	4.00	1.10
□	465 Don Buford	9.00	4.00	1.10
□	466 Ken Johnson	9.00	4.00	1.10
□	467 Vic Roznovsky	9.00	4.00	1.10
□	468 Johnny Podres	9.00	4.00	1.10
□	469 Yankees Rookies	25.00	11.00	3.10
	Bobby Murcer			
	Dooley Womack			
□	470 Sam McDowell	9.00	4.00	1.10

□ 471	Bob Skinner	9.00	4.00	1.10
□ 472	Terry Fox	9.00	4.00	1.10
□ 473	Rich Rollins	9.00	4.00	1.10
□ 474	Dick Schofield	9.00	4.00	1.10
□ 475	Dick Radatz	9.00	4.00	1.10
□ 476	Bobby Bragan MG	9.00	4.00	1.10
□ 477	Steve Barber	9.00	4.00	1.10
□ 478	Tony Gonzalez	9.00	4.00	1.10
□ 479	Jim Hannan	9.00	4.00	1.10
□ 480	Dick Stuart	9.00	4.00	1.10
□ 481	Bob Lee	9.00	4.00	1.10
□ 482	Cubs Rookies	9.00	4.00	1.10
	John Boccabella			
	Dave Dowling			
□ 483	Joe Nuxhall	9.00	4.00	1.10
□ 484	Wes Covington	9.00	4.00	1.10
□ 485	Bob Bailey	9.00	4.00	1.10
□ 486	Tommy John	10.00	4.50	1.25
□ 487	Al Ferrara	9.00	4.00	1.10
□ 488	George Banks	9.00	4.00	1.10
□ 489	Curt Simmons	9.00	4.00	1.10
□ 490	Bobby Richardson	12.00	5.50	1.50
□ 491	Dennis Bennett	9.00	4.00	1.10
□ 492	Athletics Team	14.00	6.25	1.75
□ 493	Johnny Klippstein	9.00	4.00	1.10
□ 494	Gordy Coleman	9.00	4.00	1.10
□ 495	Dick McAuliffe	9.00	4.00	1.10
□ 496	Lindy McDaniel	9.00	4.00	1.10
□ 497	Chris Cannizzaro	9.00	4.00	1.10
□ 498	Pirates Rookies	9.00	4.00	1.10
	Luke Walker			
	Woody Fryman			
□ 499	Wally Bunker	9.00	4.00	1.10
□ 500	Hank Aaron	125.00	55.00	15.50
□ 501	John O'Donoghue	9.00	4.00	1.10
□ 502	Lenny Green UER	9.00	4.00	1.10
	(Born: aJn. 6, 1933)			
□ 503	Steve Hamilton	9.00	4.00	1.10
□ 504	Grady Hatton MG	9.00	4.00	1.10
□ 505	Jose Cardenal	9.00	4.00	1.10
□ 506	Bo Belinsky	9.00	4.00	1.10
□ 507	Johnny Edwards	9.00	4.00	1.10
□ 508	Steve Hargan	9.00	4.00	1.10
□ 509	Jake Wood	9.00	4.00	1.10
□ 510	Hoyt Wilhelm	16.00	7.25	2.00
□ 511	Giants Rookies	9.00	4.00	1.10
	Bob Barton			
	Tito Fuentes			
□ 512	Dick Stigman	9.00	4.00	1.10
□ 513	Camilo Carreon	9.00	4.00	1.10
□ 514	Hal Woodeshick	9.00	4.00	1.10
□ 515	Frank Howard	14.00	6.25	1.75
□ 516	Eddie Bressoud	9.00	4.00	1.10
□ 517A	Checklist 7	16.00	3.20	1.60
	529 White Sox Rookies			
	544 Cardinals Rookies			
□ 517B	Checklist 7	16.00	3.20	1.60
	529 W. Sox Rookies			
	544 Cards Rookies			
□ 518	Braves Rookies	9.00	4.00	1.10
	Herb Hippauf			
	Arnie Umbach			
□ 519	Bob Friend	9.00	4.00	1.10
□ 520	Jim Wynn	9.00	4.00	1.10
□ 521	John Wyatt	9.00	4.00	1.10
□ 522	Phil Linz	9.00	4.00	1.10
□ 523	Bob Sadowski	17.50	8.00	2.20
□ 524	Giants Rookies SP	30.00	13.50	3.70
	Ollie Brown			
	Don Mason			
□ 525	Gary Bell SP	30.00	13.50	3.70
□ 526	Twins Team SP	100.00	45.00	12.50
□ 527	Julio Navarro	15.00	6.75	1.85
□ 528	Jesse Gonder SP	30.00	13.50	3.70
□ 529	White Sox Rookies	17.50	8.00	2.20
	Lee Elia			
	Dennis Higgins			
	Bill Voss			
□ 530	Robin Roberts	60.00	27.00	7.50
□ 531	Joe Cunningham	17.50	8.00	2.20
□ 532	Aurelio Monteagudo SP	30.00	013.50	3.70
□ 533	Jerry Adair SP	30.00	13.50	3.70
□ 534	Mets Rookies	15.00	6.75	1.85
	Dave Eilers			
	Rob Gardner			
□ 535	Willie Davis SP	40.00	18.00	5.00
□ 536	Dick Egan	15.00	6.75	1.85
□ 537	Herman Franks MG	15.00	6.75	1.85
□ 538	Bob Allen SP	30.00	13.50	3.70
□ 539	Astros Rookies	15.00	6.75	1.85
	Bill Heath			
	Carroll Sembera			
□ 540	Denny McLain SP	80.00	36.00	10.00
□ 541	Gene Oliver SP	30.00	13.50	3.70
□ 542	George Smith	15.00	6.75	1.85
□ 543	Roger Craig SP	35.00	16.00	4.40
□ 544	Cardinals Rookies SP	30.00	13.50	3.70
	Joe Hoerner			
	George Kernek			
	Jimmy Williams UER			
	(Misspelled Jimmy			
	on card)			
□ 545	Dick Green SP	30.00	13.50	3.70
□ 546	Dwight Siebler	15.00	6.75	1.85
□ 547	Horace Clarke SP	40.00	18.00	5.00
□ 548	Gary Kroll SP	30.00	13.50	3.70
□ 549	Senators Rookies	15.00	6.75	1.85
	Al Closter			
	Casey Cox			
□ 550	Willie McCovey SP.	100.00	45.00	12.50
□ 551	Bob Purkey SP	30.00	13.50	3.70
□ 552	Birdie Tebbetts SP	30.00	13.50	3.70
	MG SP			
□ 553	Rookie Stars	15.00	6.75	1.85
	Pat Garrett			
	Jackie Warner			
□ 554	Jim Northrup SP	30.00	13.50	3.70
□ 555	Ron Perranoski SP	30.00	13.50	3.70
□ 556	Mel Queen SP	30.00	13.50	3.70
□ 557	Felix Mantilla SP	30.00	13.50	3.70
□ 558	Red Sox Rookies	20.00	9.00	2.50
	Guido Grilli			
	Pete Magrini			
	George Scott			
□ 559	Roberto Pena SP	30.00	13.50	3.70
□ 560	Joel Horlen	15.00	6.75	1.85
□ 561	ChooChoo Coleman SP	35.00	16.00	4.40
□ 562	Russ Snyder	15.00	6.75	1.85
□ 563	Twins Rookies	15.00	6.75	1.85
	Pete Cimino			
	Cesar Tovar			
□ 564	Bob Chance SP	30.00	13.50	3.70
□ 565	Jim Piersall SP	40.00	18.00	5.00
□ 566	Mike Cuellar SP	30.00	13.50	3.70
□ 567	Dick Howser SP	40.00	18.00	5.00
□ 568	Athletics Rookies	15.00	6.75	1.85
	Paul Lindblad			
	Ron Stone			
□ 569	Orlando McFarlane SP	30.00	13.50	3.70
□ 570	Art Mahaffey SP	30.00	13.50	3.70
□ 571	Dave Roberts SP	30.00	13.50	3.70
□ 572	Bob Priddy	15.00	6.75	1.85

		NRMT	VG-E	GOOD
☐	573 Derrell Griffith	15.00	6.75	1.85
☐	574 Mets Rookies	15.00	6.75	1.85
	Bill Hepler			
	Bill Murphy			
☐	575 Earl Wilson	17.50	8.00	2.20
☐	576 Dave Nicholson SP	30.00	13.50	3.70
☐	577 Jack Lamabe SP	30.00	13.50	3.70
☐	578 Chi Chi Olivo SP	30.00	13.50	3.70
☐	579 Orioles Rookies	20.00	9.00	2.50
	Frank Bertaina			
	Gene Brabender			
	Dave Johnson			
☐	580 Billy Williams SP	70.00	32.00	8.75
☐	581 Tony Martinez	15.00	6.75	1.85
☐	582 Garry Roggenburk	15.00	6.75	1.85
☐	583 Tigers Team SP UER	125.00	55.00	15.50
	(Text on back states Tigers			
	finished third in 1966 instead			
	of fourth.)			
☐	584 Yankees Rookies	15.00	6.75	1.85
	Frank Fernandez			
	Fritz Peterson			
☐	585 Tony Taylor	15.00	6.75	1.85
☐	586 Claude Raymond SP	30.00	13.50	3.70
☐	587 Dick Bertell	15.00	6.75	1.85
☐	588 Athletics Rookies	15.00	6.75	1.85
	Chuck Dobson			
	Ken Suarez			
☐	589 Lou Klimchock SP	30.00	13.50	3.70
☐	590 Bill Skowron SP	40.00	18.00	5.00
☐	591 NL Rookies SP	40.00	18.00	5.00
	Bart Shirley			
	Grant Jackson			
☐	592 Andre Rodgers	15.00	6.75	1.85
☐	593 Doug Camilli SP	30.00	13.50	3.70
☐	594 Chico Salmon	15.00	6.75	1.85
☐	595 Larry Jackson	15.00	6.75	1.85
☐	596 Astros Rookies SP	30.00	13.50	3.70
	Nate Colbert			
	Greg Sims			
☐	597 John Sullivan	15.00	6.75	1.85
☐	598 Gaylord Perry SP	175.00	50.00	15.00

1967 Topps

 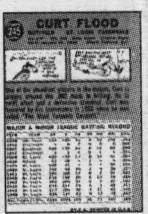

The cards in this 609-card set measure 2 1/2" by 3 1/2". The 1967 Topps series is considered by some collectors to be one of the company's finest accomplishments in baseball card production. Excellent color photographs are combined with easy-to-read backs. Cards 458 to 533 are slightly harder to find than numbers 1 to 457, and the inevitable (difficult to find) high series (534 to 609) exists. Each checklist card features a small circular picture of a popular player included in that series. Printing discrepancies resulted in some high series cards being in shorter supply. The checklist below identifies (by DP) 22 double-printed high numbers; of the 76 cards in the last series, 54 cards were short printed and the other 22 cards are much more plentiful. Featured subsets within this set include World Series cards (151-155) and League Leaders (233-244). Although there are several relatively expensive cards in this popular set, the key cards in the set are undoubtedly the Tom Seaver Rookie Card (581) and the Rod Carew Rookie Card (569). Although rarely seen, there exists a salesman's sample panel of three cards that pictures Earl Battey, Manny Mota, and Gene Brabender with ad information on the back about the "new" Topps cards.

		NRMT	VG-E	GOOD
	COMPLETE SET (609)	4600.00	2100.00	575.00
	COMMON CARD (1-109)	1.50	.70	.19
	COMMON CARD (110-283)	2.00	.90	.25
	COMMON CARD (284-370)	2.50	1.10	.30
	COMMON CARD (371-457)	4.00	1.80	.50
	COMMON CARD (458-533)	6.00	2.70	.75
	COMMON CARD (534-609)	16.00	7.25	2.00
☐	1 The Champs DP	20.00	6.00	2.00
	Frank Robinson			
	Hank Bauer MG			
	Brooks Robinson			
☐	2 Jack Hamilton	1.50	.70	.19
☐	3 Duke Sims	1.50	.70	.19
☐	4 Hal Lanier	1.50	.70	.19
☐	5 Whitey Ford UER	20.00	9.00	2.50
	(1953 listed as			
	1933 in stats on back)			
☐	6 Dick Simpson	1.50	.70	.19
☐	7 Don McMahon	1.50	.70	.19
☐	8 Chuck Harrison	1.50	.70	.19
☐	9 Ron Hansen	1.50	.70	.19
☐	10 Matty Alou	2.00	.90	.25
☐	11 Barry Moore	1.50	.70	.19
☐	12 Dodgers Rookies	2.00	.90	.25
	Jim Campanis			
	Bill Singer			
☐	13 Joe Sparma	1.50	.70	.19
☐	14 Phil Linz	2.00	.90	.25
☐	15 Earl Battey	1.50	.70	.19
☐	16 Bill Hands	1.50	.70	.19
☐	17 Jim Gosger	1.50	.70	.19
☐	18 Gene Oliver	1.50	.70	.19
☐	19 Jim McGlothlin	1.50	.70	.19
☐	20 Orlando Cepeda	6.00	2.70	.75
☐	21 Dave Bristol MG	1.50	.70	.19
☐	22 Gene Brabender	1.50	.70	.19
☐	23 Larry Elliot	1.50	.70	.19
☐	24 Bob Allen	1.50	.70	.19
☐	25 Elston Howard	4.00	1.80	.50
☐	26A Bob Priddy NTR	30.00	13.50	3.70
☐	26B Bob Priddy TR	1.50	.70	.19
☐	27 Bob Saverine	1.50	.70	.19
☐	28 Barry Latman	1.50	.70	.19
☐	29 Tom McCraw	1.50	.70	.19
☐	30 Al Kaline DP	16.00	7.25	2.00
☐	31 Jim Brewer	1.50	.70	.19

☐ 32	Bob Bailey	2.00	.90	.25
☐ 33	Athletic Rookies	5.00	2.20	.60
	Sal Bando			
	Randy Schwartz			
☐ 34	Pete Cimino	1.50	.70	.19
☐ 35	Rico Carty	2.00	.90	.25
☐ 36	Bob Tillman	1.50	.70	.19
☐ 37	Rick Wise	2.00	.90	.25
☐ 38	Bob Johnson	1.50	.70	.19
☐ 39	Curt Simmons	2.00	.90	.25
☐ 40	Rick Reichardt	1.50	.70	.19
☐ 41	Joe Hoerner	1.50	.70	.19
☐ 42	Mets Team	6.00	2.70	.75
☐ 43	Chico Salmon	1.50	.70	.19
☐ 44	Joe Nuxhall	2.00	.90	.25
☐ 45	Roger Maris	35.00	16.00	4.40
☐ 46	Lindy McDaniel	2.00	.90	.25
☐ 47	Ken McMullen	1.50	.70	.19
☐ 48	Bill Freehan	2.00	.90	.25
☐ 49	Roy Face	2.00	.90	.25
☐ 50	Tony Oliva	6.00	2.70	.75
☐ 51	Astros Rookies	1.50	.70	.19
	Dave Adlesh			
	Wes Bales			
☐ 52	Dennis Higgins	1.50	.70	.19
☐ 53	Clay Dalrymple	1.50	.70	.19
☐ 54	Dick Green	1.50	.70	.19
☐ 55	Don Drysdale	16.00	7.25	2.00
☐ 56	Jose Tartabull	2.00	.90	.25
☐ 57	Pat Jarvis	1.50	.70	.19
☐ 58	Paul Schaal	1.50	.70	.19
☐ 59	Ralph Terry	2.00	.90	.25
☐ 60	Luis Aparicio	6.00	2.70	.75
☐ 61	Gordy Coleman	2.00	.90	.25
☐ 62	Checklist 1	7.00	1.40	.70
	Frank Robinson			
☐ 63	Cards' Clubbers	9.00	4.00	1.10
	Lou Brock			
	Curt Flood			
☐ 64	Fred Valentine	1.50	.70	.19
☐ 65	Tom Haller	2.00	.90	.25
☐ 66	Manny Mota	2.00	.90	.25
☐ 67	Ken Berry	1.50	.70	.19
☐ 68	Bob Buhl	2.00	.90	.25
☐ 69	Vic Davalillo	1.50	.70	.19
☐ 70	Ron Santo	4.00	1.80	.50
☐ 71	Camilo Pascual	2.00	.90	.25
☐ 72	Tigers Rookies	1.50	.70	.19
	George Korince			
	(Photo actually			
	James Murray Brown)			
	John (Tom) Matchick			
☐ 73	Rusty Staub	4.00	1.80	.50
☐ 74	Wes Stock	1.50	.70	.19
☐ 75	George Scott	2.00	.90	.25
☐ 76	Jim Barbieri	1.50	.70	.19
☐ 77	Dooley Womack	1.50	.70	.19
☐ 78	Pat Corrales	2.00	.90	.25
☐ 79	Bubba Morton	1.50	.70	.19
☐ 80	Jim Maloney	2.00	.90	.25
☐ 81	Eddie Stanky MG	2.00	.90	.25
☐ 82	Steve Barber	1.50	.70	.19
☐ 83	Ollie Brown	1.50	.70	.19
☐ 84	Tommie Sisk	1.50	.70	.19
☐ 85	Johnny Callison	2.00	.90	.25
☐ 86A	Mike McCormick NTR	30.00	13.50	3.70
	(Senators on front			
	and Senators on back)			
☐ 86B	Mike McCormick TR	2.00	.90	.25
	(Traded line			
	at end of bio;			

	Senators on front,			
	but Giants on back)			
☐ 87	George Altman	1.50	.70	.19
☐ 88	Mickey Lolich	4.00	1.80	.50
☐ 89	Felix Millan	2.00	.90	.25
☐ 90	Jim Nash	1.50	.70	.19
☐ 91	Johnny Lewis	1.50	.70	.19
☐ 92	Ray Washburn	1.50	.70	.19
☐ 93	Yankees Rookies	4.00	1.80	.50
	Stan Bahnsen			
	Bobby Murcer			
☐ 94	Ron Fairly	2.00	.90	.25
☐ 95	Sonny Siebert	1.50	.70	.19
☐ 96	Art Shamsky	1.50	.70	.19
☐ 97	Mike Cuellar	2.00	.90	.25
☐ 98	Rich Rollins	1.50	.70	.19
☐ 99	Lee Stange	1.50	.70	.19
☐ 100	Frank Robinson DP	16.00	7.25	2.00
☐ 101	Ken Johnson	1.50	.70	.19
☐ 102	Philadelphia Phillies	3.00	1.35	.35
	Team Card			
☐ 103	Checklist 2	16.00	3.20	1.60
	Mickey Mantle			
☐ 104	Minnie Rojas	1.50	.70	.19
☐ 105	Ken Boyer	2.00	.90	.25
☐ 106	Randy Hundley	2.00	.90	.25
☐ 107	Joel Horlen	1.50	.70	.19
☐ 108	Alex Johnson	2.00	.90	.25
☐ 109	Tribe Thumpers	5.00	2.20	.60
	Rocky Colavito			
	Leon Wagner			
☐ 110	Jack Aker	3.00	1.35	.35
☐ 111	John Kennedy	2.00	.90	.25
☐ 112	Dave Wickersham	2.00	.90	.25
☐ 113	Dave Nicholson	2.00	.90	.25
☐ 114	Jack Baldschun	2.00	.90	.25
☐ 115	Paul Casanova	2.00	.90	.25
☐ 116	Herman Franks MG	2.00	.90	.25
☐ 117	Darrell Brandon	2.00	.90	.25
☐ 118	Bernie Allen	2.00	.90	.25
☐ 119	Wade Blasingame	2.00	.90	.25
☐ 120	Floyd Robinson	2.00	.90	.25
☐ 121	Eddie Bressoud	2.00	.90	.25
☐ 122	George Brunet	2.00	.90	.25
☐ 123	Pirates Rookies	2.00	.90	.25
	Jim Price			
	Luke Walker			
☐ 124	Jim Stewart	2.00	.90	.25
☐ 125	Moe Drabowsky	3.00	1.35	.35
☐ 126	Tony Taylor	2.00	.90	.25
☐ 127	John O'Donoghue	2.00	.90	.25
☐ 128	Ed Spiezio	2.00	.90	.25
☐ 129	Phil Roof	2.00	.90	.25
☐ 130	Phil Regan	3.00	1.35	.35
☐ 131	Yankees Team	6.00	2.70	.75
☐ 132	Ozzie Virgil	2.00	.90	.25
☐ 133	Ron Kline	2.00	.90	.25
☐ 134	Gates Brown	3.00	1.35	.35
☐ 135	Deron Johnson	3.00	1.35	.35
☐ 136	Carroll Sembera	2.00	.90	.25
☐ 137	Twins Rookies	2.00	.90	.25
	Ron Clark			
	Jim Ollum			
☐ 138	Dick Kelley	2.00	.90	.25
☐ 139	Dalton Jones	3.00	1.35	.35
☐ 140	Willie Stargell	20.00	9.00	2.50
☐ 141	John Miller	2.00	.90	.25
☐ 142	Jackie Brandt	2.00	.90	.25
☐ 143	Sox Sockers	2.00	.90	.25
	Pete Ward			
	Don Buford			

☐ 144	Bill Hepler	2.00	.90	.25
☐ 145	Larry Brown	2.00	.90	.25
☐ 146	Steve Carlton	70.00	32.00	8.75
☐ 147	Tom Egan	2.00	.90	.25
☐ 148	Adolfo Phillips	2.00	.90	.25
☐ 149	Joe Moeller	2.00	.90	.25
☐ 150	Mickey Mantle	325.00	145.00	40.00
☐ 151	World Series Game 1.	4.00	1.80	.50

Moe mows down 11
(Moe Drabowsky)

☐ 152	World Series Game 2.	8.00	3.60	1.00

Jim Palmer blanks
Dodgers

☐ 153	World Series Game 3.	4.00	1.80	.50

Paul Blair's homer
defeats L.A.

☐ 154	World Series Game 4.	4.00	1.80	.50

Orioles 4 straight
(Brooks Robinson
and Dave McNally)

☐ 155	World Series Summary	4.00	1.80	.50

Winners celebrate

☐ 156	Ron Herbel	2.00	.90	.25
☐ 157	Danny Cater	2.00	.90	.25
☐ 158	Jimmie Coker	2.00	.90	.25
☐ 159	Bruce Howard	2.00	.90	.25
☐ 160	Willie Davis	3.00	1.35	.35
☐ 161	Dick Williams MG	3.00	1.35	.35
☐ 162	Billy O'Dell	2.00	.90	.25
☐ 163	Vic Roznovsky	2.00	.90	.25
☐ 164	Dwight Siebler UER	2.00	.90	.25

(Last line of stats
shows 1960 Minnesota)

☐ 165	Cleon Jones	3.00	1.35	.35
☐ 166	Eddie Mathews	16.00	7.25	2.00
☐ 167	Senators Rookies	2.00	.90	.25

Joe Coleman
Tim Cullen

☐ 168	Ray Culp	2.00	.90	.25
☐ 169	Horace Clarke	2.00	.90	.25
☐ 170	Dick McAuliffe	3.00	1.35	.35
☐ 171	Cal Koonce	2.00	.90	.25
☐ 172	Bill Heath	2.00	.90	.25
☐ 173	St. Louis Cardinals	4.00	1.80	.50

Team Card

☐ 174	Dick Radatz	3.00	1.35	.35
☐ 175	Bobby Knoop	2.00	.90	.25
☐ 176	Sammy Ellis	2.00	.90	.25
☐ 177	Tito Fuentes	2.00	.90	.25
☐ 178	John Buzhardt	2.00	.90	.25
☐ 179	Braves Rookies	2.00	.90	.25

Charles Vaughan
Cecil Upshaw

☐ 180	Curt Blefary	2.00	.90	.25
☐ 181	Terry Fox	2.00	.90	.25
☐ 182	Ed Charles	2.00	.90	.25
☐ 183	Jim Pagliaroni	2.00	.90	.25
☐ 184	George Thomas	2.00	.90	.25
☐ 185	Ken Holtzman	4.00	1.80	.50
☐ 186	Mets Maulers	3.00	1.35	.35

Ed Kranepool
Ron Swoboda

☐ 187	Pedro Ramos	2.00	.90	.25
☐ 188	Ken Harrelson	3.00	1.35	.35
☐ 189	Chuck Hinton	2.00	.90	.25
☐ 190	Turk Farrell	2.00	.90	.25
☐ 191A	Checklist 3	8.00	1.60	.80

(214 Tom Kelley)
(Willie Mays)

☐ 191B	Checklist 3	12.00	2.40	1.20

(214 Dick Kelley)

(Willie Mays)

☐ 192	Fred Gladding	2.00	.90	.25
☐ 193	Jose Cardenal	3.00	1.35	.35
☐ 194	Bob Allison	3.00	1.35	.35
☐ 195	Al Jackson	2.00	.90	.25
☐ 196	Johnny Romano	2.00	.90	.25
☐ 197	Ron Perranoski	3.00	1.35	.35
☐ 198	Chuck Hiller	2.00	.90	.25
☐ 199	Billy Hitchcock MG	2.00	.90	.25
☐ 200	Willie Mays UER	90.00	40.00	11.00

('63 Sna Francisco
on card back stats)

☐ 201	Hal Reniff	2.00	.90	.25
☐ 202	Johnny Edwards	2.00	.90	.25
☐ 203	Al McBean	2.00	.90	.25
☐ 204	Orioles Rookies	3.00	1.35	.35

Mike Epstein
Tom Phoebus

☐ 205	Dick Groat	3.00	1.35	.35
☐ 206	Dennis Bennett	2.00	.90	.25
☐ 207	John Orsino	2.00	.90	.25
☐ 208	Jack Lamabe	2.00	.90	.25
☐ 209	Joe Nossek	2.00	.90	.25
☐ 210	Bob Gibson	20.00	9.00	2.50
☐ 211	Twins Team	4.00	1.80	.50
☐ 212	Chris Zachary	2.00	.90	.25
☐ 213	Jay Johnstone	4.00	1.80	.50
☐ 214	Dick Kelley	2.00	.90	.25
☐ 215	Ernie Banks	20.00	9.00	2.50
☐ 216	Bengal Belters	10.00	4.50	1.25

Norm Cash
Al Kaline

☐ 217	Rob Gardner	2.00	.90	.25
☐ 218	Wes Parker	3.00	1.35	.35
☐ 219	Clay Carroll	3.00	1.35	.35
☐ 220	Jim Ray Hart	3.00	1.35	.35
☐ 221	Woody Fryman	3.00	1.35	.35
☐ 222	Reds Rookies	2.00	.90	.25

Darrell Osteen
Lee May

☐ 223	Mike Ryan	2.00	.90	.25
☐ 224	Walt Bond	2.00	.90	.25
☐ 225	Mel Stottlemyre	4.00	1.80	.50
☐ 226	Julian Javier	3.00	1.35	.35
☐ 227	Paul Lindblad	2.00	.90	.25
☐ 228	Gil Hodges MG	5.00	2.20	.60
☐ 229	Larry Jackson	2.00	.90	.25
☐ 230	Boog Powell	6.00	2.70	.75
☐ 231	John Bateman	2.00	.90	.25
☐ 232	Don Buford	2.00	.90	.25
☐ 233	AL ERA Leaders	4.00	1.80	.50

Gary Peters
Joel Horlen
Steve Hargan

☐ 234	NL ERA Leaders	15.00	6.75	1.85

Sandy Koufax
Mike Cuellar
Juan Marichal

☐ 235	AL Pitching Leaders	6.00	2.70	.75

Jim Kaat
Denny McLain
Earl Wilson

☐ 236	NL Pitching Leaders	25.00	11.00	3.10

Sandy Koufax
Juan Marichal
Bob Gibson
Gaylord Perry

☐ 237	AL Strikeout Leaders	6.00	2.70	.75

Sam McDowell
Jim Kaat
Earl Wilson

☐ 238 NL Strikeout Leaders	12.00	5.50	1.50
Sandy Koufax			
Jim Bunning			
Bob Veale			
☐ 239 AL Batting Leaders	9.00	4.00	1.10
Frank Robinson			
Tony Oliva			
Al Kaline			
☐ 240 NL Batting Leaders	6.00	2.70	.75
Matty Alou			
Felipe Alou			
Rico Carty			
☐ 241 AL RBI Leaders	9.00	4.00	1.10
Frank Robinson			
Harmon Killebrew			
Boog Powell			
☐ 242 NL RBI Leaders	20.00	9.00	2.50
Hank Aaron			
Bob Clemente			
Richie Allen			
☐ 243 AL Home Run Leaders	9.00	4.00	1.10
Frank Robinson			
Harmon Killebrew			
Boog Powell			
☐ 244 NL Home Run Leaders	20.00	9.00	2.50
Hank Aaron			
Richie Allen			
Willie Mays			
☐ 245 Curt Flood	3.00	1.35	.35
☐ 246 Jim Perry	3.00	1.35	.35
☐ 247 Jerry Lumpe	2.00	.90	.25
☐ 248 Gene Mauch MG	3.00	1.35	.35
☐ 249 Nick Willhite	2.00	.90	.25
☐ 250 Hank Aaron UER	85.00	38.00	10.50
(Second 1961 in stats should be 1962)			
☐ 251 Woody Held	2.00	.90	.25
☐ 252 Bob Bolin	2.00	.90	.25
☐ 253 Indians Rookies	2.00	.90	.25
Bill Davis			
Gus Gil			
☐ 254 Milt Pappas	3.00	1.35	.35
(No facsimile autograph on card front)			
☐ 255 Frank Howard	4.00	1.80	.50
☐ 256 Bob Hendley	2.00	.90	.25
☐ 257 Charlie Smith	2.00	.90	.25
☐ 258 Lee Maye	2.00	.90	.25
☐ 259 Don Dennis	2.00	.90	.25
☐ 260 Jim Lefebvre	3.00	1.35	.35
☐ 261 John Wyatt	2.00	.90	.25
☐ 262 Athletics Team	4.00	1.80	.50
☐ 263 Hank Aguirre	2.00	.90	.25
☐ 264 Ron Swoboda	3.00	1.35	.35
☐ 265 Lou Burdette	3.00	1.35	.35
☐ 266 Pitt Power	5.00	2.20	.60
Willie Stargell			
Donn Clendenon			
☐ 267 Don Schwall	2.00	.90	.25
☐ 268 Johnny Briggs	2.00	.90	.25
☐ 269 Don Nottebart	2.00	.90	.25
☐ 270 Zoilo Versalles	2.00	.90	.25
☐ 271 Eddie Watt	2.00	.90	.25
☐ 272 Cubs Rookies	3.00	1.35	.35
Bill Connors			
Dave Dowling			
☐ 273 Dick Lines	2.00	.90	.25
☐ 274 Bob Aspromonte	2.00	.90	.25
☐ 275 Fred Whitfield	2.00	.90	.25
☐ 276 Bruce Brubaker	2.00	.90	.25
☐ 277 Steve Whitaker	2.00	.90	.25

☐ 278 Checklist 4	7.00	1.40	.70
Jim Kaat			
☐ 279 Frank Linzy	2.00	.90	.25
☐ 280 Tony Conigliaro	10.00	4.50	1.25
☐ 281 Bob Rodgers	3.00	1.35	.35
☐ 282 John Odom	2.00	.90	.25
☐ 283 Gene Alley	3.00	1.35	.35
☐ 284 Johnny Podres	3.00	1.35	.35
☐ 285 Lou Brock	20.00	9.00	2.50
☐ 286 Wayne Causey	2.50	1.10	.30
☐ 287 Mets Rookies	2.50	1.10	.30
Greg Goossen			
Bart Shirley			
☐ 288 Denny Lemaster	2.50	1.10	.30
☐ 289 Tom Tresh	3.00	1.35	.35
☐ 290 Bill White	3.00	1.35	.35
☐ 291 Jim Hannan	2.50	1.10	.30
☐ 292 Don Pavletich	2.50	1.10	.30
☐ 293 Ed Kirkpatrick	2.50	1.10	.30
☐ 294 Walt Alston MG	4.00	1.80	.50
☐ 295 Sam McDowell	3.00	1.35	.35
☐ 296 Glenn Beckert	3.00	1.35	.35
☐ 297 Dave Morehead	2.50	1.10	.30
☐ 298 Ron Davis	2.50	1.10	.30
☐ 299 Norm Siebern	2.50	1.10	.30
☐ 300 Jim Kaat	6.00	2.70	.75
☐ 301 Jesse Gonder	2.50	1.10	.30
☐ 302 Orioles Team	6.00	2.70	.75
☐ 303 Gil Blanco	2.50	1.10	.30
☐ 304 Phil Gagliano	2.50	1.10	.30
☐ 305 Earl Wilson	3.00	1.35	.35
☐ 306 Bud Harrelson	6.00	2.70	.75
☐ 307 Jim Beauchamp	2.50	1.10	.30
☐ 308 Al Downing	3.00	1.35	.35
☐ 309 Hurlers Beware	3.00	1.35	.35
Johnny Callison			
Richie Allen			
☐ 310 Gary Peters	2.50	1.10	.30
☐ 311 Ed Brinkman	2.50	1.10	.30
☐ 312 Don Mincher	2.50	1.10	.30
☐ 313 Bob Lee	2.50	1.10	.30
☐ 314 Red Sox Rookies	8.00	3.60	1.00
Mike Andrews			
Reggie Smith			
☐ 315 Billy Williams	12.00	5.50	1.50
☐ 316 Jack Kralick	2.50	1.10	.30
☐ 317 Cesar Tovar	3.00	1.35	.35
☐ 318 Dave Giusti	2.50	1.10	.30
☐ 319 Paul Blair	3.00	1.35	.35
☐ 320 Gaylord Perry	14.00	6.25	1.75
☐ 321 Mayo Smith MG	2.50	1.10	.30
☐ 322 Jose Pagan	2.50	1.10	.30
☐ 323 Mike Hershberger	2.50	1.10	.30
☐ 324 Hal Woodeshick	2.50	1.10	.30
☐ 325 Chico Cardenas	3.00	1.35	.35
☐ 326 Bob Uecker	10.00	4.50	1.25
☐ 327 California Angels	6.00	2.70	.75
Team Card			
☐ 328 Clete Boyer UER	3.00	1.35	.35
(Stats only go up through 1965)			
☐ 329 Charlie Lau	3.00	1.35	.35
☐ 330 Claude Osteen	3.00	1.35	.35
☐ 331 Joe Foy	3.00	1.35	.35
☐ 332 Jesus Alou	2.50	1.10	.30
☐ 333 Fergie Jenkins	18.00	8.00	2.20
☐ 334 Twin Terrors	6.00	2.70	.75
Bob Allison			
Harmon Killebrew			
☐ 335 Bob Veale	3.00	1.35	.35
☐ 336 Joe Azcue	2.50	1.10	.30

☐ 337 Joe Morgan	14.00	6.25	1.75
☐ 338 Bob Locker	2.50	1.10	.30
☐ 339 Chico Ruiz	2.50	1.10	.30
☐ 340 Joe Pepitone	3.00	1.35	.35
☐ 341 Giants Rookies	2.50	1.10	.30
Dick Dietz			
Bill Sorrell			
☐ 342 Hank Fischer	2.50	1.10	.30
☐ 343 Tom Satriano	2.50	1.10	.30
☐ 344 Ossie Chavarria	2.50	1.10	.30
☐ 345 Stu Miller	3.00	1.35	.35
☐ 346 Jim Hickman	2.50	1.10	.30
☐ 347 Grady Hatton MG	2.50	1.10	.30
☐ 348 Tug McGraw	4.00	1.80	.50
☐ 349 Bob Chance	2.50	1.10	.30
☐ 350 Joe Torre	4.00	1.80	.50
☐ 351 Vern Law	3.00	1.35	.35
☐ 352 Ray Oyler	2.50	1.10	.30
☐ 353 Bill McCool	2.50	1.10	.30
☐ 354 Cubs Team	6.00	2.70	.75
☐ 355 Carl Yastrzemski	35.00	16.00	4.40
☐ 356 Larry Jaster	2.50	1.10	.30
☐ 357 Bill Skowron	3.00	1.35	.35
☐ 358 Ruben Amaro	2.50	1.10	.30
☐ 359 Dick Ellsworth	2.50	1.10	.30
☐ 360 Leon Wagner	2.50	1.10	.30
☐ 361 Checklist 5	10.00	2.00	1.00
Roberto Clemente			
☐ 362 Darold Knowles	2.50	1.10	.30
☐ 363 Dave Johnson	3.00	1.35	.35
☐ 364 Claude Raymond	2.50	1.10	.30
☐ 365 John Roseboro	3.00	1.35	.35
☐ 366 Andy Kosco	2.50	1.10	.30
☐ 367 Angels Rookies	2.50	1.10	.30
Bill Kelso			
Don Wallace			
☐ 368 Jack Hiatt	2.50	1.10	.30
☐ 369 Jim Hunter	18.00	8.00	2.20
☐ 370 Tommy Davis	3.00	1.35	.35
☐ 371 Jim Lonborg	6.00	2.70	.75
☐ 372 Mike de la Hoz	4.00	1.80	.50
☐ 373 White Sox Rookies DP	4.00	1.80	.50
Duane Josephson			
Fred Klages			
☐ 374A Mel Queen ERR DP	4.00	1.80	.50
(Incomplete stat			
line on back)			
☐ 374B Mel Queen COR DP	4.00	1.80	.50
(Complete stat			
line on back)			
☐ 375 Jake Gibbs	4.00	1.80	.50
☐ 376 Don Lock DP	4.00	1.80	.50
☐ 377 Luis Tiant	6.00	2.70	.75
☐ 378 Detroit Tigers	8.00	3.60	1.00
Team Card UER			
(Willie Horton with			
262 RBI's in 1966)			
☐ 379 Jerry May DP	4.00	1.80	.50
☐ 380 Dean Chance DP	4.00	1.80	.50
☐ 381 Dick Schofield	4.00	1.80	.50
☐ 382 Dave McNally	5.00	2.20	.60
☐ 383 Ken Henderson DP	4.00	1.80	.50
☐ 384 Cardinals Rookies	4.00	1.80	.50
Jim Cosman			
Dick Hughes			
☐ 385 Jim Fregosi	5.00	2.20	.60
(Batting wrong)			
☐ 386 Dick Selma DP	4.00	1.80	.50
☐ 387 Cap Peterson DP	4.00	1.80	.50
☐ 388 Arnold Earley DP	4.00	1.80	.50
☐ 389 Alvin Dark MG DP	5.00	2.20	.60
☐ 390 Jim Wynn DP	5.00	2.20	.60
☐ 391 Wilbur Wood DP	5.00	2.20	.60
☐ 392 Tommy Harper DP	5.00	2.20	.60
☐ 393 Jim Bouton DP	4.00	1.80	.50
☐ 394 Jake Wood DP	4.00	1.80	.50
☐ 395 Chris Short	5.00	2.20	.60
☐ 396 Atlanta Aces	4.00	1.80	.50
Denis Menke			
Tony Cloninger			
☐ 397 Willie Smith DP	4.00	1.80	.50
☐ 398 Jeff Torborg	5.00	2.20	.60
☐ 399 Al Worthington DP	4.00	1.80	.50
☐ 400 Bob Clemente DP	80.00	36.00	10.00
☐ 401 Jim Coates	4.00	1.80	.50
☐ 402 Phillies Rookies DP	5.00	2.20	.60
Grant Jackson			
Billy Wilson			
☐ 403 Dick Nen	4.00	1.80	.50
☐ 404 Nelson Briles	5.00	2.20	.60
☐ 405 Russ Snyder	4.00	1.80	.50
☐ 406 Lee Elia DP	4.00	1.80	.50
☐ 407 Reds Team	8.00	3.60	1.00
☐ 408 Jim Northrup DP	5.00	2.20	.60
☐ 409 Ray Sadecki	4.00	1.80	.50
☐ 410 Lou Johnson DP	4.00	1.80	.50
☐ 411 Dick Howser DP	5.00	2.20	.60
☐ 412 Astros Rookies	5.00	2.20	.60
Norm Miller			
Doug Rader			
☐ 413 Jerry Grote	4.00	1.80	.50
☐ 414 Casey Cox	4.00	1.80	.50
☐ 415 Sonny Jackson	4.00	1.80	.50
☐ 416 Roger Repoz	4.00	1.80	.50
☐ 417A Bob Bruce ERR DP	30.00	13.50	3.70
(RBAVES on back)			
☐ 417B Bob Bruce COR DP	4.00	1.80	.50
☐ 418 Sam Mele MG	4.00	1.80	.50
☐ 419 Don Kessinger DP	5.00	2.20	.60
☐ 420 Denny McLain	6.00	2.70	.75
☐ 421 Dal Maxvill DP	4.00	1.80	.50
☐ 422 Hoyt Wilhelm	8.00	3.60	1.00
☐ 423 Fence Busters DP	25.00	11.00	3.10
Willie Mays			
Willie McCovey			
☐ 424 Pedro Gonzalez	4.00	1.80	.50
☐ 425 Pete Mikkelsen	4.00	1.80	.50
☐ 426 Lou Clinton	4.00	1.80	.50
☐ 427A Ruben Gomez ERR DP	4.00	1.80	.50
(Incomplete stat			
line on back)			
☐ 427B Ruben Gomez COR DP	4.00	1.80	.50
(Complete stat			
line on back)			
☐ 428 Dodgers Rookies DP	5.00	2.20	.60
Tom Hutton			
Gene Michael			
☐ 429 Garry Roggenburk DP	4.00	1.80	.50
☐ 430 Pete Rose	85.00	38.00	10.50
☐ 431 Ted Uhlaender	4.00	1.80	.50
☐ 432 Jimmie Hall DP	4.00	1.80	.50
☐ 433 Al Luplow DP	4.00	1.80	.50
☐ 434 Eddie Fisher DP	4.00	1.80	.50
☐ 435 Mack Jones DP	4.00	1.80	.50
☐ 436 Pete Ward	4.00	1.80	.50
☐ 437 Senators Team	8.00	3.60	1.00
☐ 438 Chuck Dobson	4.00	1.80	.50
☐ 439 Byron Browne	4.00	1.80	.50
☐ 440 Steve Hargan	4.00	1.80	.50
☐ 441 Jim Davenport	4.00	1.80	.50
☐ 442 Yankees Rookies DP	5.00	2.20	.60
Bill Robinson			

Joe Verbanic			
☐ 443 Tito Francona DP	4.00	1.80	.50
☐ 444 George Smith	4.00	1.80	.50
☐ 445 Don Sutton	25.00	11.00	3.10
☐ 446 Russ Nixon DP	4.00	1.80	.50
☐ 447A Bo Belinsky ERR DP	5.00	2.20	.60
(Incomplete stat			
line on back)			
☐ 447B Bo Belinsky COR DP	5.00	2.20	.60
(Complete stat			
line on back)			
☐ 448 Harry Walker DP MG..	4.00	1.80	.50
☐ 449 Orlando Pena	4.00	1.80	.50
☐ 450 Richie Allen	9.00	4.00	1.10
☐ 451 Fred Newman DP	4.00	1.80	.50
☐ 452 Ed Kranepool	5.00	2.20	.60
☐ 453 Aurelio Monteagudo DP	4.00	1.80	.50
☐ 454A Checklist 6 DP	8.00	1.60	.80
Juan Marichal			
(Missing left ear)			
☐ 454B Checklist 6 DP	8.00	1.60	.80
Juan Marichal			
(left ear showing)			
☐ 455 Tommie Agee	5.00	2.20	.60
☐ 456 Phil Niekro	14.00	6.25	1.75
☐ 457 Andy Etchebarren DP.	5.00	2.20	.60
☐ 458 Lee Thomas	7.50	3.40	.95
☐ 459 Senators Rookies	6.00	2.70	.75
Dick Bosman			
Pete Craig			
☐ 460 Harmon Killebrew	50.00	22.00	6.25
☐ 461 Bob Miller	6.00	2.70	.75
☐ 462 Bob Barton	6.00	2.70	.75
☐ 463 Hill Aces	7.50	3.40	.95
Sam McDowell			
Sonny Siebert			
☐ 464 Dan Coombs	6.00	2.70	.75
☐ 465 Willie Horton	7.50	3.40	.95
☐ 466 Bobby Wine	6.00	2.70	.75
☐ 467 Jim O'Toole	7.50	3.40	.95
☐ 468 Ralph Houk MG	7.50	3.40	.95
☐ 469 Len Gabrielson	6.00	2.70	.75
☐ 470 Bob Shaw	6.00	2.70	.75
☐ 471 Rene Lachemann	7.50	3.40	.95
☐ 472 Rookies Pirates	6.00	2.70	.75
John Gelnar			
George Spriggs			
☐ 473 Jose Santiago	7.50	3.40	.95
☐ 474 Bob Tolan	7.50	3.40	.95
☐ 475 Jim Palmer	85.00	38.00	10.50
☐ 476 Tony Perez SP	70.00	32.00	8.75
☐ 477 Braves Team	15.00	6.75	1.85
☐ 478 Bob Humphreys	6.00	2.70	.75
☐ 479 Gary Bell	6.00	2.70	.75
☐ 480 Willie McCovey	35.00	16.00	4.40
☐ 481 Leo Durocher MG	15.00	6.75	1.85
☐ 482 Bill Monbouquette....	6.00	2.70	.75
☐ 483 Jim Landis	6.00	2.70	.75
☐ 484 Jerry Adair	6.00	2.70	.75
☐ 485 Tim McCarver	20.00	9.00	2.50
☐ 486 Twins Rookies	6.00	2.70	.75
Rich Reese			
Bill Whitby			
☐ 487 Tommie Reynolds	6.00	2.70	.75
☐ 488 Gerry Arrigo	6.00	2.70	.75
☐ 489 Doug Clemens	6.00	2.70	.75
☐ 490 Tony Cloninger	6.00	2.70	.75
☐ 491 Sam Bowens	6.00	2.70	.75
☐ 492 Pittsburgh Pirates	15.00	6.75	1.85
Team Card			
☐ 493 Phil Ortega	6.00	2.70	.75

☐ 494 Bill Rigney MG	6.00	2.70	.75
☐ 495 Fritz Peterson	6.00	2.70	.75
☐ 496 Orlando McFarlane....	6.00	2.70	.75
☐ 497 Ron Campbell	6.00	2.70	.75
☐ 498 Larry Dierker	6.00	2.70	.75
☐ 499 Indians Rookies	6.00	2.70	.75
George Culver			
Jose Vidal			
☐ 500 Juan Marichal	25.00	11.00	3.10
☐ 501 Jerry Zimmerman	6.00	2.70	.75
☐ 502 Derrell Griffith	6.00	2.70	.75
☐ 503 Los Angeles Dodgers	15.00	6.75	1.85
Team Card			
☐ 504 Orlando Martinez	6.00	2.70	.75
☐ 505 Tommy Helms	7.50	3.40	.95
☐ 506 Smoky Burgess	7.50	3.40	.95
☐ 507 Orioles Rookies	6.00	2.70	.75
Ed Barnowski			
Larry Haney			
☐ 508 Dick Hall	6.00	2.70	.75
☐ 509 Jim King	6.00	2.70	.75
☐ 510 Bill Mazeroski	15.00	6.75	1.85
☐ 511 Don Wert	6.00	2.70	.75
☐ 512 Red Schoendienst MG	15.00	6.75	1.85
☐ 513 Marcelino Lopez	6.00	2.70	.75
☐ 514 John Werhas	6.00	2.70	.75
☐ 515 Bert Campaneris	9.00	4.00	1.10
☐ 516 Giants Team	15.00	6.75	1.85
☐ 517 Fred Talbot	6.00	2.70	.75
☐ 518 Denis Menke	6.00	2.70	.75
☐ 519 Ted Davidson	6.00	2.70	.75
☐ 520 Max Alvis	6.00	2.70	.75
☐ 521 Bird Bombers	7.50	3.40	.95
Boog Powell			
Curt Blefary			
☐ 522 John Stephenson	6.00	2.70	.75
☐ 523 Jim Merritt	6.00	2.70	.75
☐ 524 Felix Mantilla	6.00	2.70	.75
☐ 525 Ron Hunt	6.00	2.70	.75
☐ 526 Tigers Rookies	6.00	2.70	.75
Pat Dobson			
George Korince			
(See 67T-72)			
☐ 527 Dennis Ribant	6.00	2.70	.75
☐ 528 Rico Petrocelli	10.00	4.50	1.25
☐ 529 Gary Wagner	6.00	2.70	.75
☐ 530 Felipe Alou	7.50	3.40	.95
☐ 531 Checklist 7	14.00	2.80	1.40
Brooks Robinson			
☐ 532 Jim Hicks	6.00	2.70	.75
☐ 533 Jack Fisher	6.00	2.70	.75
☐ 534 Hank Bauer MG DP	9.00	4.00	1.10
☐ 535 Donn Clendenon	17.50	8.00	2.20
☐ 536 Cubs Rookies	35.00	16.00	4.40
Joe Niekro			
Paul Popovich			
☐ 537 Chuck Estrada DP	9.00	4.00	1.10
☐ 538 J.C. Martin	16.00	7.25	2.00
☐ 539 Dick Egan DP	9.00	4.00	1.10
☐ 540 Norm Cash	35.00	16.00	4.40
☐ 541 Joe Gibbon	16.00	7.25	2.00
☐ 542 Athletics Rookies DP	15.00	6.75	1.85
Rick Monday			
Tony Pierce			
☐ 543 Dan Schneider	16.00	7.25	2.00
☐ 544 Cleveland Indians	30.00	13.50	3.70
Team Card			
☐ 545 Jim Grant	16.00	7.25	2.00
☐ 546 Woody Woodward	17.50	8.00	2.20
☐ 547 Red Sox Rookies DP..	9.00	4.00	1.10
Russ Gibson			

		NRMT	VG-E	GOOD
	Bill Rohr			
□ 548	Tony Gonzalez DP	9.00	4.00	1.10
□ 549	Jack Sanford	16.00	7.25	2.00
□ 550	Vada Pinson DP	10.00	4.50	1.25
□ 551	Doug Camilli DP	9.00	4.00	1.10
□ 552	Ted Savage	16.00	7.25	2.00
□ 553	Yankees Rookies	25.00	11.00	3.10
	Mike Hegan			
	Thad Tillotson			
□ 554	Andre Rodgers DP	9.00	4.00	1.10
□ 555	Don Cardwell	17.50	8.00	2.20
□ 556	Al Weis DP	9.00	4.00	1.10
□ 557	Al Ferrara	16.00	7.25	2.00
□ 558	Orioles Rookies	50.00	22.00	6.25
	Mark Belanger			
	Bill Dillman			
□ 559	Dick Tracewski DP	9.00	4.00	1.10
□ 560	Jim Bunning	50.00	22.00	6.25
□ 561	Sandy Alomar	17.50	8.00	2.20
□ 562	Steve Blass DP	10.00	4.50	1.25
□ 563	Joe Adcock	20.00	9.00	2.50
□ 564	Astros Rookies DP	9.00	4.00	1.10
	Alonzo Harris			
	Aaron Pointer			
□ 565	Lew Krausse	16.00	7.25	2.00
□ 566	Gary Geiger DP	9.00	4.00	1.10
□ 567	Steve Hamilton	17.50	8.00	2.20
□ 568	John Sullivan	16.00	7.25	2.00
□ 569	AL Rookies DP	250.00	110.00	31.00
	Rod Carew			
	Hank Allen			
□ 570	Maury Wills	85.00	38.00	10.50
□ 571	Larry Sherry	16.00	7.25	2.00
□ 572	Don Demeter	16.00	7.25	2.00
□ 573	Chicago White Sox	30.00	13.50	3.70
	Team Card UER			
	(Indians team			
	stats on back)			
□ 574	Jerry Buchek	17.50	8.00	2.20
□ 575	Dave Boswell	16.00	7.25	2.00
□ 576	NL Rookies	17.50	8.00	2.20
	Ramon Hernandez			
	Norm Gigon			
□ 577	Bill Short	16.00	7.25	2.00
□ 578	John Boccabella	16.00	7.25	2.00
□ 579	Bill Henry	16.00	7.25	2.00
□ 580	Rocky Colavito	85.00	38.00	10.50
□ 581	Mets Rookies	800.00	350.00	100.00
	Bill Denehy			
	Tom Seaver			
□ 582	Jim Owens DP	9.00	4.00	1.10
□ 583	Ray Barker	16.00	7.25	2.00
□ 584	Jim Piersall	25.00	11.00	3.10
□ 585	Wally Bunker	16.00	7.25	2.00
□ 586	Manny Jimenez	16.00	7.25	2.00
□ 587	NL Rookies	25.00	11.00	3.10
	Don Shaw			
	Gary Sutherland			
□ 588	Johnny Klippstein DP	9.00	4.00	1.10
□ 589	Dave Ricketts DP	9.00	4.00	1.10
□ 590	Pete Richert	16.00	7.25	2.00
□ 591	Ty Cline	16.00	7.25	2.00
□ 592	NL Rookies	17.50	8.00	2.20
	Jim Shellenback			
	Ron Willis			
□ 593	Wes Westrum MG	17.50	8.00	2.20
□ 594	Dan Osinski	17.50	8.00	2.20
□ 595	Cookie Rojas	17.50	8.00	2.20
□ 596	Galen Cisco DP	10.00	4.50	1.25
□ 597	Ted Abernathy	16.00	7.25	2.00
□ 598	White Sox Rookies	17.50	8.00	2.20

		NRMT	VG-E	GOOD
	Walt Williams			
	Ed Stroud			
□ 599	Bob Duliba DP	9.00	4.00	1.10
□ 600	Brooks Robinson	275.00	125.00	34.00
□ 601	Bill Bryan DP	9.00	4.00	1.10
□ 602	Juan Pizarro	16.00	7.25	2.00
□ 603	Athletics Rookies	16.00	7.25	2.00
	Tim Talton			
	Ramon Webster			
□ 604	Red Sox Team	110.00	50.00	14.00
□ 605	Mike Shannon	50.00	22.00	6.25
□ 606	Ron Taylor	16.00	7.25	2.00
□ 607	Mickey Stanley	35.00	16.00	4.40
□ 608	Cubs Rookies DP	9.00	4.00	1.10
	Rich Nye			
	John Upham			
□ 609	Tommy John	70.00	23.00	8.25

1968 Topps

The cards in this 598-card set measure 2 1/2" by 3 1/2". The 1968 Topps set includes Sporting News All-Star Selections as card numbers 361 to 380. Other subsets in the set include League Leaders (1-12) and World Series cards (151-158). The front of each checklist card features a picture of a popular player inside a circle. High numbers 534 to 598 are slightly more difficult to obtain. The first series looks different from the other series, as it has a lighter, wider mesh background on the card front. The later series all had a much darker, finer mesh pattern. Key cards in the set are the Rookie Cards of Johnny Bench (247) and Nolan Ryan (177).

		NRMT	VG-E	GOOD
COMPLETE SET (598)		3000.00	1350.00	375.00
COMMON CARD (1-457)		1.75	.80	.22
COMMON CARD (458-598)		3.50	1.55	.45
□ 1	NL Batting Leaders	25.00	10.00	5.00
	Bob Clemente			
	Tony Gonzalez			
	Matty Alou			
□ 2	AL Batting Leaders	14.00	6.25	1.75
	Carl Yastrzemski			
	Frank Robinson			
	Al Kaline			
□ 3	NL RBI Leaders	16.00	7.25	2.00
	Orlando Cepeda			
	Bob Clemente			

Hank Aaron			
☐ 4 AL RBI Leaders	12.00	5.50	1.50
Carl Yastrzemski			
Harmon Killebrew			
Frank Robinson			
☐ 5 NL Home Run Leaders	8.00	3.60	1.00
Hank Aaron			
Jim Wynn			
Ron Santo			
Willie McCovey			
☐ 6 AL Home Run Leaders	8.00	3.60	1.00
Carl Yastrzemski			
Harmon Killebrew			
Frank Howard			
☐ 7 NL ERA Leaders	3.50	1.55	.45
Phil Niekro			
Jim Bunning			
Chris Short			
☐ 8 AL ERA Leaders	3.50	1.55	.45
Joel Horlen			
Gary Peters			
Sonny Siebert			
☐ 9 NL Pitching Leaders	4.00	1.80	.50
Mike McCormick			
Ferguson Jenkins			
Jim Bunning			
Claude Osteen			
☐ 10A AL Pitching Leaders	4.00	1.80	.50
Jim Lonborg ERR			
(Misspelled Lonberg on card back)			
Earl Wilson			
Dean Chance			
☐ 10B AL Pitching Leaders	4.00	1.80	.50
Jim Lonborg COR			
Earl Wilson			
Dean Chance			
☐ 11 NL Strikeout Leaders	5.00	2.20	.60
Jim Bunning			
Ferguson Jenkins			
Gaylord Perry			
☐ 12 AL Strikeout Leaders	3.50	1.55	.45
Jim Lonborg UER			
(Misspelled Longberg on card back)			
Sam McDowell			
Dean Chance			
☐ 13 Chuck Hartenstein	1.75	.80	.22
☐ 14 Jerry McNertney	1.75	.80	.22
☐ 15 Ron Hunt	1.75	.80	.22
☐ 16 Indians Rookies	4.00	1.80	.50
Lou Piniella			
Richie Scheinblum			
☐ 17 Dick Hall	1.75	.80	.22
☐ 18 Mike Hershberger	1.75	.80	.22
☐ 19 Juan Pizarro	1.75	.80	.22
☐ 20 Brooks Robinson	25.00	11.00	3.10
☐ 21 Ron Davis	1.75	.80	.22
☐ 22 Pat Dobson	2.50	1.10	.30
☐ 23 Chico Cardenas	2.50	1.10	.30
☐ 24 Bobby Locke	1.75	.80	.22
☐ 25 Julian Javier	2.50	1.10	.30
☐ 26 Darrell Brandon	1.75	.80	.22
☐ 27 Gil Hodges MG	8.00	3.60	1.00
☐ 28 Ted Uhlaender	1.75	.80	.22
☐ 29 Joe Verbanic	1.75	.80	.22
☐ 30 Joe Torre	4.00	1.80	.50
☐ 31 Ed Stroud	1.75	.80	.22
☐ 32 Joe Gibbon	1.75	.80	.22
☐ 33 Pete Ward	1.75	.80	.22
☐ 34 Al Ferrara	1.75	.80	.22
☐ 35 Steve Hargan	1.75	.80	.22
☐ 36 Pirates Rookies	2.50	1.10	.30
Bob Moose			
Bob Robertson			
☐ 37 Billy Williams	8.00	3.60	1.00
☐ 38 Tony Pierce	1.75	.80	.22
☐ 39 Cookie Rojas	2.50	1.10	.30
☐ 40 Denny McLain	10.00	4.50	1.25
☐ 41 Julio Gotay	1.75	.80	.22
☐ 42 Larry Haney	1.75	.80	.22
☐ 43 Gary Bell	1.75	.80	.22
☐ 44 Frank Kostro	1.75	.80	.22
☐ 45 Tom Seaver	50.00	22.00	6.25
☐ 46 Dave Ricketts	1.75	.80	.22
☐ 47 Ralph Houk MG	2.50	1.10	.30
☐ 48 Ted Davidson	1.75	.80	.22
☐ 49A Eddie Brinkman	1.75	.80	.22
(White team name)			
☐ 49B Eddie Brinkman	50.00	22.00	6.25
(Yellow team name)			
☐ 50 Willie Mays	65.00	29.00	8.00
☐ 51 Bob Locker	1.75	.80	.22
☐ 52 Hawk Taylor	1.75	.80	.22
☐ 53 Gene Alley	2.50	1.10	.30
☐ 54 Stan Williams	2.50	1.10	.30
☐ 55 Felipe Alou	3.00	1.35	.35
☐ 56 Orioles Rookies	1.75	.80	.22
Dave Leonhard			
Dave May			
☐ 57 Dan Schneider	1.75	.80	.22
☐ 58 Eddie Mathews	16.00	7.25	2.00
☐ 59 Don Lock	1.75	.80	.22
☐ 60 Ken Holtzman	2.50	1.10	.30
☐ 61 Reggie Smith	3.00	1.35	.35
☐ 62 Chuck Dobson	1.75	.80	.22
☐ 63 Dick Kenworthy	1.75	.80	.22
☐ 64 Jim Merritt	1.75	.80	.22
☐ 65 John Roseboro	2.50	1.10	.30
☐ 66A Casey Cox	1.75	.80	.22
(White team name)			
☐ 66B Casey Cox	100.00	45.00	12.50
(Yellow team name)			
☐ 67 Checklist 1	6.00	1.20	.60
Jim Kaat			
☐ 68 Ron Willis	1.75	.80	.22
☐ 69 Tom Tresh	2.50	1.10	.30
☐ 70 Bob Veale	2.50	1.10	.30
☐ 71 Vern Fuller	1.75	.80	.22
☐ 72 Tommy John	5.00	2.20	.60
☐ 73 Jim Ray Hart	2.50	1.10	.30
☐ 74 Milt Pappas	2.50	1.10	.30
☐ 75 Don Mincher	1.75	.80	.22
☐ 76 Braves Rookies	2.50	1.10	.30
Jim Britton			
Ron Reed			
☐ 77 Don Wilson	2.50	1.10	.30
☐ 78 Jim Northrup	2.50	1.10	.30
☐ 79 Ted Kubiak	1.75	.80	.22
☐ 80 Rod Carew	55.00	25.00	7.00
☐ 81 Larry Jackson	1.75	.80	.22
☐ 82 Sam Bowens	1.75	.80	.22
☐ 83 John Stephenson	1.75	.80	.22
☐ 84 Bob Tolan	2.50	1.10	.30
☐ 85 Gaylord Perry	8.00	3.60	1.00
☐ 86 Willie Stargell	8.00	3.60	1.00
☐ 87 Dick Williams MG	2.50	1.10	.30
☐ 88 Phil Regan	2.50	1.10	.30
☐ 89 Jake Gibbs	1.75	.80	.22
☐ 90 Vada Pinson	3.00	1.35	.35
☐ 91 Jim Ollom	1.75	.80	.22
☐ 92 Ed Kranepool	2.50	1.10	.30

☐ 93 Tony Cloninger	1.75	.80	.22
☐ 94 Lee Maye	1.75	.80	.22
☐ 95 Bob Aspromonte	1.75	.80	.22
☐ 96 Senator Rookies	1.75	.80	.22
Frank Coggins			
Dick Nold			
☐ 97 Tom Phoebus	1.75	.80	.22
☐ 98 Gary Sutherland	1.75	.80	.22
☐ 99 Rocky Colavito	6.00	2.70	.75
☐ 100 Bob Gibson	25.00	11.00	3.10
☐ 101 Glenn Beckert	2.50	1.10	.30
☐ 102 Jose Cardenal	2.50	1.10	.30
☐ 103 Don Sutton	8.00	3.60	1.00
☐ 104 Dick Dietz	1.75	.80	.22
☐ 105 Al Downing	2.50	1.10	.30
☐ 106 Dalton Jones	1.75	.80	.22
☐ 107A Checklist 2	6.00	1.20	.60
Juan Marichal			
(Tan wide mesh)			
☐ 107B Checklist 2	6.00	1.20	.60
Juan Marichal			
(Brown fine mesh)			
☐ 108 Don Pavletich	1.75	.80	.22
☐ 109 Bert Campaneris	2.50	1.10	.30
☐ 110 Hank Aaron	65.00	29.00	8.00
☐ 111 Rich Reese	1.75	.80	.22
☐ 112 Woody Fryman	1.75	.80	.22
☐ 113 Tigers Rookies	2.50	1.10	.30
Tom Matchick			
Daryl Patterson			
☐ 114 Ron Swoboda	2.50	1.10	.30
☐ 115 Sam McDowell	2.50	1.10	.30
☐ 116 Ken McMullen	1.75	.80	.22
☐ 117 Larry Jaster	1.75	.80	.22
☐ 118 Mark Belanger	2.50	1.10	.30
☐ 119 Ted Savage	1.75	.80	.22
☐ 120 Mel Stottlemyre	3.00	1.35	.35
☐ 121 Jimmie Hall	1.75	.80	.22
☐ 122 Gene Mauch MG	2.50	1.10	.30
☐ 123 Jose Santiago	1.75	.80	.22
☐ 124 Nate Oliver	1.75	.80	.22
☐ 125 Joel Horlen	1.75	.80	.22
☐ 126 Bobby Etheridge	1.75	.80	.22
☐ 127 Paul Lindblad	1.75	.80	.22
☐ 128 Astros Rookies	1.75	.80	.22
Tom Dukes			
Alonzo Harris			
☐ 129 Mickey Stanley	4.00	1.80	.50
☐ 130 Tony Perez	8.00	3.60	1.00
☐ 131 Frank Bertaina	1.75	.80	.22
☐ 132 Bud Harrelson	2.50	1.10	.30
☐ 133 Fred Whitfield	1.75	.80	.22
☐ 134 Pat Jarvis	1.75	.80	.22
☐ 135 Paul Blair	2.50	1.10	.30
☐ 136 Randy Hundley	2.50	1.10	.30
☐ 137 Twins Team	3.50	1.55	.45
☐ 138 Ruben Amaro	1.75	.80	.22
☐ 139 Chris Short	1.75	.80	.22
☐ 140 Tony Conigliaro	8.00	3.60	1.00
☐ 141 Dal Maxvill	1.75	.80	.22
☐ 142 White Sox Rookies	1.75	.80	.22
Buddy Bradford			
Bill Voss			
☐ 143 Pete Cimino	1.75	.80	.22
☐ 144 Joe Morgan	12.00	5.50	1.50
☐ 145 Don Drysdale	12.00	5.50	1.50
☐ 146 Sal Bando	2.50	1.10	.30
☐ 147 Frank Linzy	1.75	.80	.22
☐ 148 Dave Bristol MG	1.75	.80	.22
☐ 149 Bob Saverine	1.75	.80	.22
☐ 150 Bob Clemente	70.00	32.00	8.75

☐ 151 World Series Game 1	10.00	4.50	1.25
Lou Brock socks 4			
hits in opener			
☐ 152 World Series Game 2	10.00	4.50	1.25
Carl Yastrzemski			
smashes 2 homers			
☐ 153 World Series Game 3	100.00	45.00	12.50
Nellie Briles			
cools Boston			
☐ 154 World Series Game 4	8.00	3.60	1.00
Bob Gibson hurls			
shutout			
☐ 155 World Series Game 5	100.00	45.00	12.50
Jim Lonborg wins			
again			
☐ 156 World Series Game 6	100.00	45.00	12.50
Rico Petrocelli			
two homers			
☐ 157 World Series Game 7	100.00	45.00	12.50
St. Louis wins it			
☐ 158 World Series Summary	100.00	45.00	12.50
Cardinals celebrate			
☐ 159 Don Kessinger	2.50	1.10	.30
☐ 160 Earl Wilson	2.50	1.10	.30
☐ 161 Norm Miller	1.75	.80	.22
☐ 162 Cards Rookies	2.50	1.10	.30
Hal Gilson			
Mike Torrez			
☐ 163 Gene Brabender	1.75	.80	.22
☐ 164 Ramon Webster	1.75	.80	.22
☐ 165 Tony Oliva	4.00	1.80	.50
☐ 166 Claude Raymond	1.75	.80	.22
☐ 167 Elston Howard	3.00	1.35	.35
☐ 168 Dodgers Team	3.50	1.55	.45
☐ 169 Bob Bolin	1.75	.80	.22
☐ 170 Jim Fregosi	2.50	1.10	.30
☐ 171 Don Nottebart	1.75	.80	.22
☐ 172 Walt Williams	1.75	.80	.22
☐ 173 John Boozer	1.75	.80	.22
☐ 174 Bob Tillman	1.75	.80	.22
☐ 175 Maury Wills	5.00	2.20	.60
☐ 176 Bob Allen	1.75	.80	.22
☐ 177 Mets Rookies	1000.00	450.00	125.00
Jerry Koosman			
Nolan Ryan			
☐ 178 Don Wert	2.50	1.10	.30
☐ 179 Bill Stoneman	1.75	.80	.22
☐ 180 Curt Flood	3.00	1.35	.35
☐ 181 Jerry Zimmerman	1.75	.80	.22
☐ 182 Dave Giusti	1.75	.80	.22
☐ 183 Bob Kennedy MG	2.50	1.10	.30
☐ 184 Lou Johnson	2.50	1.10	.30
☐ 185 Tom Haller	1.75	.80	.22
☐ 186 Eddie Watt	1.75	.80	.22
☐ 187 Sonny Jackson	1.75	.80	.22
☐ 188 Cap Peterson	1.75	.80	.22
☐ 189 Bill Landis	1.75	.80	.22
☐ 190 Bill White	3.00	1.35	.35
☐ 191 Dan Frisella	1.75	.80	.22
☐ 192A Checklist 3	7.50	1.50	.75
Carl Yastrzemski			
(Special Baseball			
Playing Card)			
☐ 192B Checklist 3	7.50	1.50	.75
Carl Yastrzemski			
(Special Baseball			
Playing Card Game)			
☐ 193 Jack Hamilton	1.75	.80	.22
☐ 194 Don Buford	1.75	.80	.22
☐ 195 Joe Pepitone	2.50	1.10	.30
☐ 196 Gary Nolan	2.50	1.10	.30

☐ 197	Larry Brown	1.75	.80	.22	☐	Bill Schlesinger			
☐ 198	Roy Face	2.50	1.10	.30	☐ 259	Ken Boyer	3.00	1.35	.35
☐ 199	A's Rookies	1.75	.80	.22	☐ 260	Jim Wynn	2.50	1.10	.30
	Roberto Rodriguez				☐ 261	Dave Duncan	2.50	1.10	.30
	Darrell Osteen				☐ 262	Rick Wise	2.50	1.10	.30
☐ 200	Orlando Cepeda	5.00	2.20	.60	☐ 263	Horace Clarke	1.75	.80	.22
☐ 201	Mike Marshall	4.00	1.80	.50	☐ 264	Ted Abernathy	1.75	.80	.22
☐ 202	Adolfo Phillips	1.75	.80	.22	☐ 265	Tommy Davis	2.50	1.10	.30
☐ 203	Dick Kelley	1.75	.80	.22	☐ 266	Paul Popovich	1.75	.80	.22
☐ 204	Andy Etchebarren	1.75	.80	.22	☐ 267	Herman Franks MG	1.75	.80	.22
☐ 205	Juan Marichal	8.00	3.60	1.00	☐ 268	Bob Humphreys	1.75	.80	.22
☐ 206	Cal Ermer MG	1.75	.80	.22	☐ 269	Bob Tiefenauer	1.75	.80	.22
☐ 207	Carroll Sembera	1.75	.80	.22	☐ 270	Matty Alou	2.50	1.10	.30
☐ 208	Willie Davis	2.50	1.10	.30	☐ 271	Bobby Knoop	1.75	.80	.22
☐ 209	Tim Cullen	1.75	.80	.22	☐ 272	Ray Culp	1.75	.80	.22
☐ 210	Gary Peters	1.75	.80	.22	☐ 273	Dave Johnson	2.50	1.10	.30
☐ 211	J.C. Martin	1.75	.80	.22	☐ 274	Mike Cuellar	2.50	1.10	.30
☐ 212	Dave Morehead	1.75	.80	.22	☐ 275	Tim McCarver	4.00	1.80	.50
☐ 213	Chico Ruiz	1.75	.80	.22	☐ 276	Jim Roland	1.75	.80	.22
☐ 214	Yankees Rookies	2.50	1.10	.30	☐ 277	Jerry Buchek	1.75	.80	.22
	Stan Bahnsen				☐ 278	Checklist 4	6.00	1.20	.60
	Frank Fernandez					Orlando Cepeda			
☐ 215	Jim Bunning	5.00	2.20	.60	☐ 279	Bill Hands	1.75	.80	.22
☐ 216	Bubba Morton	1.75	.80	.22	☐ 280	Mickey Mantle	275.00	125.00	34.00
☐ 217	Dick Farrell	1.75	.80	.22	☐ 281	Jim Campanis	1.75	.80	.22
☐ 218	Ken Suarez	1.75	.80	.22	☐ 282	Rick Monday	2.50	1.10	.30
☐ 219	Rob Gardner	1.75	.80	.22	☐ 283	Mel Queen	1.75	.80	.22
☐ 220	Harmon Killebrew	14.00	6.25	1.75	☐ 284	Johnny Briggs	1.75	.80	.22
☐ 221	Braves Team	3.50	1.55	.45	☐ 285	Dick McAuliffe	2.50	1.10	.30
☐ 222	Jim Hardin	1.75	.80	.22	☐ 286	Cecil Upshaw	1.75	.80	.22
☐ 223	Ollie Brown	1.75	.80	.22	☐ 287	White Sox Rookies	1.75	.80	.22
☐ 224	Jack Aker	1.75	.80	.22		Mickey Abarbanel			
☐ 225	Richie Allen	5.00	2.20	.60		Cisco Carlos			
☐ 226	Jimmie Price	1.75	.80	.22	☐ 288	Dave Wickersham	1.75	.80	.22
☐ 227	Joe Hoerner	1.75	.80	.22	☐ 289	Woody Held	1.75	.80	.22
☐ 228	Dodgers Rookies	2.50	1.10	.30	☐ 290	Willie McCovey	12.00	5.50	1.50
	Jack Billingham				☐ 291	Dick Lines	1.75	.80	.22
	Jim Fairey				☐ 292	Art Shamsky	1.75	.80	.22
☐ 229	Fred Klages	1.75	.80	.22	☐ 293	Bruce Howard	1.75	.80	.22
☐ 230	Pete Rose	45.00	20.00	5.50	☐ 294	Red Schoendienst MG	4.00	1.80	.50
☐ 231	Dave Baldwin	1.75	.80	.22	☐ 295	Sonny Siebert	1.75	.80	.22
☐ 232	Denis Menke	1.75	.80	.22	☐ 296	Byron Browne	1.75	.80	.22
☐ 233	George Scott	2.50	1.10	.30	☐ 297	Russ Gibson	1.75	.80	.22
☐ 234	Bill Monbouquette	1.75	.80	.22	☐ 298	Jim Brewer	1.75	.80	.22
☐ 235	Ron Santo	5.00	2.20	.60	☐ 299	Gene Michael	2.50	1.10	.30
☐ 236	Tug McGraw	3.00	1.35	.35	☐ 300	Rusty Staub	3.00	1.35	.35
☐ 237	Alvin Dark MG	2.50	1.10	.30	☐ 301	Twins Rookies	1.75	.80	.22
☐ 238	Tom Satriano	1.75	.80	.22		George Mitterwald			
☐ 239	Bill Henry	1.75	.80	.22		Rick Renick			
☐ 240	Al Kaline	25.00	11.00	3.10	☐ 302	Gerry Arrigo	1.75	.80	.22
☐ 241	Felix Millan	1.75	.80	.22	☐ 303	Dick Green	2.50	1.10	.30
☐ 242	Moe Drabowsky	2.50	1.10	.30	☐ 304	Sandy Valdespino	1.75	.80	.22
☐ 243	Rich Rollins	1.75	.80	.22	☐ 305	Minnie Rojas	1.75	.80	.22
☐ 244	John Donaldson	1.75	.80	.22	☐ 306	Mike Ryan	1.75	.80	.22
☐ 245	Tony Gonzalez	1.75	.80	.22	☐ 307	John Hiller	2.50	1.10	.30
☐ 246	Fritz Peterson	1.75	.80	.22	☐ 308	Pirates Team	3.50	1.55	.45
☐ 247	Reds Rookies	125.00	55.00	15.50	☐ 309	Ken Henderson	1.75	.80	.22
	Johnny Bench				☐ 310	Luis Aparicio	5.00	2.20	.60
	Ron Tompkins				☐ 311	Jack Lamabe	1.75	.80	.22
☐ 248	Fred Valentine	1.75	.80	.22	☐ 312	Curt Blefary	1.75	.80	.22
☐ 249	Bill Singer	1.75	.80	.22	☐ 313	Al Weis	1.75	.80	.22
☐ 250	Carl Yastrzemski	30.00	13.50	3.70	☐ 314	Red Sox Rookies	1.75	.80	.22
☐ 251	Manny Sanguillen	6.00	2.70	.75		Bill Rohr			
☐ 252	Angels Team	3.50	1.55	.45		George Spriggs			
☐ 253	Dick Hughes	1.75	.80	.22	☐ 315	Zoilo Versalles	1.75	.80	.22
☐ 254	Cleon Jones	2.50	1.10	.30	☐ 316	Steve Barber	1.75	.80	.22
☐ 255	Dean Chance	2.50	1.10	.30	☐ 317	Ron Brand	1.75	.80	.22
☐ 256	Norm Cash	8.00	3.60	1.00	☐ 318	Chico Salmon	1.75	.80	.22
☐ 257	Phil Niekro	8.00	3.60	1.00	☐ 319	George Culver	1.75	.80	.22
☐ 258	Cubs Rookies	1.75	.80	.22	☐ 320	Frank Howard	3.00	1.35	.35
	Jose Arcia				☐ 321	Leo Durocher MG	4.00	1.80	.50

☐ 322	Dave Boswell	1.75	.80	.22
☐ 323	Deron Johnson	2.50	1.10	.30
☐ 324	Jim Nash	1.75	.80	.22
☐ 325	Manny Mota	2.50	1.10	.30
☐ 326	Dennis Ribant	1.75	.80	.22
☐ 327	Tony Taylor	1.75	.80	.22
☐ 328	Angels Rookies	1.75	.80	.22
	Chuck Vinson			
	Jim Weaver			
☐ 329	Duane Josephson	1.75	.80	.22
☐ 330	Roger Maris	40.00	18.00	5.00
☐ 331	Dan Osinski	1.75	.80	.22
☐ 332	Doug Rader	2.50	1.10	.30
☐ 333	Ron Herbel	1.75	.80	.22
☐ 334	Orioles Team	3.50	1.55	.45
☐ 335	Bob Allison	2.50	1.10	.30
☐ 336	John Purdin	1.75	.80	.22
☐ 337	Bill Robinson	2.50	1.10	.30
☐ 338	Bob Johnson	1.75	.80	.22
☐ 339	Rich Nye	1.75	.80	.22
☐ 340	Max Alvis	1.75	.80	.22
☐ 341	Jim Lemon MG	1.75	.80	.22
☐ 342	Ken Johnson	1.75	.80	.22
☐ 343	Jim Gosger	1.75	.80	.22
☐ 344	Donn Clendenon	2.50	1.10	.30
☐ 345	Bob Hendley	1.75	.80	.22
☐ 346	Jerry Adair	1.75	.80	.22
☐ 347	George Brunet	1.75	.80	.22
☐ 348	Phillies Rookies	1.75	.80	.22
	Larry Colton			
	Dick Thoenen			
☐ 349	Ed Spiezio	1.75	.80	.22
☐ 350	Hoyt Wilhelm	6.00	2.70	.75
☐ 351	Bob Barton	1.75	.80	.22
☐ 352	Jackie Hernandez	1.75	.80	.22
☐ 353	Mack Jones	1.75	.80	.22
☐ 354	Pete Richert	1.75	.80	.22
☐ 355	Ernie Banks	25.00	11.00	3.10
☐ 356A	Checklist 5	6.00	1.20	.60
	Ken Holtzman			
	(Head centered			
	within circle)			
☐ 356B	Checklist 5	6.00	1.20	.60
	Ken Holtzman			
	(Head shifted right			
	within circle)			
☐ 357	Len Gabrielson	1.75	.80	.22
☐ 358	Mike Epstein	1.75	.80	.22
☐ 359	Joe Moeller	1.75	.80	.22
☐ 360	Willie Horton	4.00	1.80	.50
☐ 361	Harmon Killebrew AS	8.00	3.60	1.00
☐ 362	Orlando Cepeda AS	3.50	1.55	.45
☐ 363	Rod Carew AS	8.00	3.60	1.00
☐ 364	Joe Morgan AS	8.00	3.60	1.00
☐ 365	Brooks Robinson AS	8.00	3.60	1.00
☐ 366	Ron Santo AS	3.50	1.55	.45
☐ 367	Jim Fregosi AS	2.50	1.10	.30
☐ 368	Gene Alley AS	2.50	1.10	.30
☐ 369	Carl Yastrzemski AS	10.00	4.50	1.25
☐ 370	Hank Aaron AS	20.00	9.00	2.50
☐ 371	Tony Oliva AS	3.00	1.35	.35
☐ 372	Lou Brock AS	8.00	3.60	1.00
☐ 373	Frank Robinson AS	8.00	3.60	1.00
☐ 374	Bob Clemente AS	25.00	11.00	3.10
☐ 375	Bill Freehan AS	3.00	1.35	.35
☐ 376	Tim McCarver AS	3.00	1.35	.35
☐ 377	Joel Horlen AS	2.50	1.10	.30
☐ 378	Bob Gibson AS	8.00	3.60	1.00
☐ 379	Gary Peters AS	2.50	1.10	.30
☐ 380	Ken Holtzman AS	2.50	1.10	.30
☐ 381	Boog Powell	4.00	1.80	.50
☐ 382	Ramon Hernandez	1.75	.80	.22
☐ 383	Steve Whitaker	1.75	.80	.22
☐ 384	Reds Rookies	7.00	3.10	.85
	Bill Henry			
	Hal McRae			
☐ 385	Jim Hunter	14.00	6.25	1.75
☐ 386	Greg Goossen	1.75	.80	.22
☐ 387	Joe Foy	1.75	.80	.22
☐ 388	Ray Washburn	1.75	.80	.22
☐ 389	Jay Johnstone	2.50	1.10	.30
☐ 390	Bill Mazeroski	4.00	1.80	.50
☐ 391	Bob Priddy	1.75	.80	.22
☐ 392	Grady Hatton MG	1.75	.80	.22
☐ 393	Jim Perry	2.50	1.10	.30
☐ 394	Tommie Aaron	2.50	1.10	.30
☐ 395	Camilo Pascual	2.50	1.10	.30
☐ 396	Bobby Wine	1.75	.80	.22
☐ 397	Vic Davalillo	1.75	.80	.22
☐ 398	Jim Grant	1.75	.80	.22
☐ 399	Ray Oyler	2.50	1.10	.30
☐ 400A	Mike McCormick	2.50	1.10	.30
	(Yellow letters)			
☐ 400B	Mike McCormick	125.00	55.00	15.50
	(Team name in			
	white letters)			
☐ 401	Mets Team	3.50	1.55	.45
☐ 402	Mike Hegan	1.75	.80	.22
☐ 403	John Buzhardt	1.75	.80	.22
☐ 404	Floyd Robinson	1.75	.80	.22
☐ 405	Tommy Helms	2.50	1.10	.30
☐ 406	Dick Ellsworth	1.75	.80	.22
☐ 407	Gary Kolb	1.75	.80	.22
☐ 408	Steve Carlton	30.00	13.50	3.70
☐ 409	Orioles Rookies	1.75	.80	.22
	Frank Peters			
	Ron Stone			
☐ 410	Fergie Jenkins	14.00	6.25	1.75
☐ 411	Ron Hansen	1.75	.80	.22
☐ 412	Clay Carroll	2.50	1.10	.30
☐ 413	Tom McCraw	1.75	.80	.22
☐ 414	Mickey Lolich	8.00	3.60	1.00
☐ 415	Johnny Callison	2.50	1.10	.30
☐ 416	Bill Rigney MG	1.75	.80	.22
☐ 417	Willie Crawford	1.75	.80	.22
☐ 418	Eddie Fisher	1.75	.80	.22
☐ 419	Jack Hiatt	1.75	.80	.22
☐ 420	Cesar Tovar	1.75	.80	.22
☐ 421	Ron Taylor	1.75	.80	.22
☐ 422	Rene Lachemann	2.50	1.10	.30
☐ 423	Fred Gladding	1.75	.80	.22
☐ 424	Chicago White Sox	3.50	1.55	.45
	Team Card			
☐ 425	Jim Maloney	2.50	1.10	.30
☐ 426	Hank Allen	1.75	.80	.22
☐ 427	Dick Calmus	1.75	.80	.22
☐ 428	Vic Roznovsky	1.75	.80	.22
☐ 429	Tommie Sisk	1.75	.80	.22
☐ 430	Rico Petrocelli	2.50	1.10	.30
☐ 431	Dooley Womack	1.75	.80	.22
☐ 432	Indians Rookies	1.75	.80	.22
	Bill Davis			
	Jose Vidal			
☐ 433	Bob Rodgers	2.50	1.10	.30
☐ 434	Ricardo Joseph	1.75	.80	.22
☐ 435	Ron Perranoski	2.50	1.10	.30
☐ 436	Hal Lanier	1.75	.80	.22
☐ 437	Don Cardwell	1.75	.80	.22
☐ 438	Lee Thomas	2.50	1.10	.30
☐ 439	Lum Harris MG	1.75	.80	.22
☐ 440	Claude Osteen	2.50	1.10	.30
☐ 441	Alex Johnson	2.50	1.10	.30

☐ 442	Dick Bosman	1.75	.80	.22
☐ 443	Joe Azcue	1.75	.80	.22
☐ 444	Jack Fisher	1.75	.80	.22
☐ 445	Mike Shannon	2.50	1.10	.30
☐ 446	Ron Kline	1.75	.80	.22
☐ 447	Tigers Rookies	1.75	.80	.22
	George Korince			
	Fred Lasher			
☐ 448	Gary Wagner	1.75	.80	.22
☐ 449	Gene Oliver	1.75	.80	.22
☐ 450	Jim Kaat	5.00	2.20	.60
☐ 451	Al Spangler	1.75	.80	.22
☐ 452	Jesus Alou	1.75	.80	.22
☐ 453	Sammy Ellis	1.75	.80	.22
☐ 454A	Checklist 6	7.50	1.50	.75
	Frank Robinson			
	(Cap complete			
	within circle)			
☐ 454B	Checklist 6	7.50	1.50	.75
	Frank Robinson			
	(Cap partially			
	within circle)			
☐ 455	Rico Carty	2.50	1.10	.30
☐ 456	John O'Donoghue	1.75	.80	.22
☐ 457	Jim Lefebvre	2.50	1.10	.30
☐ 458	Lew Krausse	4.00	1.80	.50
☐ 459	Dick Simpson	3.50	1.55	.45
☐ 460	Jim Lonborg	4.00	1.80	.50
☐ 461	Chuck Hiller	3.50	1.55	.45
☐ 462	Barry Moore	3.50	1.55	.45
☐ 463	Jim Schaffer	3.50	1.55	.45
☐ 464	Don McMahon	3.50	1.55	.45
☐ 465	Tommie Agee	4.00	1.80	.50
☐ 466	Bill Dillman	3.50	1.55	.45
☐ 467	Dick Howser	4.00	1.80	.50
☐ 468	Larry Sherry	3.50	1.55	.45
☐ 469	Ty Cline	3.50	1.55	.45
☐ 470	Bill Freehan	6.00	2.70	.75
☐ 471	Orlando Pena	3.50	1.55	.45
☐ 472	Walt Alston MG	5.00	2.20	.60
☐ 473	Al Worthington	3.50	1.55	.45
☐ 474	Paul Schaal	3.50	1.55	.45
☐ 475	Joe Niekro	3.50	1.55	.45
☐ 476	Woody Woodward	4.00	1.80	.50
☐ 477	Philadelphia Phillies	7.00	3.10	.85
	Team Card			
☐ 478	Dave McNally	4.00	1.80	.50
☐ 479	Phil Gagliano	3.50	1.55	.45
☐ 480	Manager's Dream	70.00	32.00	8.75
	Tony Oliva			
	Chico Cardenas			
	Bob Clemente			
☐ 481	John Wyatt	3.50	1.55	.45
☐ 482	Jose Pagan	3.50	1.55	.45
☐ 483	Darold Knowles	3.50	1.55	.45
☐ 484	Phil Roof	3.50	1.55	.45
☐ 485	Ken Berry	3.50	1.55	.45
☐ 486	Cal Koonce	3.50	1.55	.45
☐ 487	Lee May	4.00	1.80	.50
☐ 488	Dick Tracewski	4.00	1.80	.50
☐ 489	Wally Bunker	3.50	1.55	.45
☐ 490	Super Stars	160.00	70.00	20.00
	Harmon Killebrew			
	Willie Mays			
	Mickey Mantle			
☐ 491	Denny Lemaster	3.50	1.55	.45
☐ 492	Jeff Torborg	4.00	1.80	.50
☐ 493	Jim McGlothlin	3.50	1.55	.45
☐ 494	Ray Sadecki	3.50	1.55	.45
☐ 495	Leon Wagner	3.50	1.55	.45
☐ 496	Steve Hamilton	3.50	1.55	.45
☐ 497	Cardinals Team	7.00	3.10	.85
☐ 498	Bill Bryan	3.50	1.55	.45
☐ 499	Steve Blass	4.00	1.80	.50
☐ 500	Frank Robinson	30.00	13.50	3.70
☐ 501	John Odom	4.00	1.80	.50
☐ 502	Mike Andrews	3.50	1.55	.45
☐ 503	Al Jackson	3.50	1.55	.45
☐ 504	Russ Snyder	3.50	1.55	.45
☐ 505	Joe Sparma	10.00	4.50	1.25
☐ 506	Clarence Jones	3.50	1.55	.45
☐ 507	Wade Blasingame	3.50	1.55	.45
☐ 508	Duke Sims	3.50	1.55	.45
☐ 509	Dennis Higgins	3.50	1.55	.45
☐ 510	Ron Fairly	4.00	1.80	.50
☐ 511	Bill Kelso	3.50	1.55	.45
☐ 512	Grant Jackson	3.50	1.55	.45
☐ 513	Hank Bauer MG	4.00	1.80	.50
☐ 514	Al McBean	3.50	1.55	.45
☐ 515	Russ Nixon	3.50	1.55	.45
☐ 516	Pete Mikkelsen	3.50	1.55	.45
☐ 517	Diego Segui	4.00	1.80	.50
☐ 518A	Checklist 7 ERR	12.00	2.40	1.20
	(539 AL Rookies)			
	(Clete Boyer)			
☐ 518B	Checklist 7 COR	12.00	2.40	1.20
	(539 ML Rookies)			
	(Clete Boyer)			
☐ 519	Jerry Stephenson	3.50	1.55	.45
☐ 520	Lou Brock	25.00	11.00	3.10
☐ 521	Don Shaw	3.50	1.55	.45
☐ 522	Wayne Causey	3.50	1.55	.45
☐ 523	John Tsitouris	3.50	1.55	.45
☐ 524	Andy Kosco	3.50	1.55	.45
☐ 525	Jim Davenport	3.50	1.55	.45
☐ 526	Bill Denehy	3.50	1.55	.45
☐ 527	Tito Francona	3.50	1.55	.45
☐ 528	Tigers Team	70.00	32.00	8.75
☐ 529	Bruce Von Hoff	3.50	1.55	.45
☐ 530	Bird Belters	40.00	18.00	5.00
	Brooks Robinson			
	Frank Robinson			
☐ 531	Chuck Hinton	3.50	1.55	.45
☐ 532	Luis Tiant	6.00	2.70	.75
☐ 533	Wes Parker	4.00	1.80	.50
☐ 534	Bob Miller	3.50	1.55	.45
☐ 535	Danny Cater	4.00	1.80	.50
☐ 536	Bill Short	3.50	1.55	.45
☐ 537	Norm Siebern	3.50	1.55	.45
☐ 538	Manny Jimenez	3.50	1.55	.45
☐ 539	Major League Rookies	3.50	1.55	.45
	Jim Ray			
	Mike Ferraro			
☐ 540	Nelson Briles	4.00	1.80	.50
☐ 541	Sandy Alomar	4.00	1.80	.50
☐ 542	John Boccabella	3.50	1.55	.45
☐ 543	Bob Lee	3.50	1.55	.45
☐ 544	Mayo Smith MG	8.00	3.60	1.00
☐ 545	Lindy McDaniel	4.00	1.80	.50
☐ 546	Roy White	4.00	1.80	.50
☐ 547	Dan Coombs	3.50	1.55	.45
☐ 548	Bernie Allen	3.50	1.55	.45
☐ 549	Orioles Rookies	3.50	1.55	.45
	Curt Motton			
	Roger Nelson			
☐ 550	Clete Boyer	4.00	1.80	.50
☐ 551	Darrell Sutherland	3.50	1.55	.45
☐ 552	Ed Kirkpatrick	3.50	1.55	.45
☐ 553	Hank Aguirre	3.50	1.55	.45
☐ 554	A's Team	8.00	3.60	1.00
☐ 555	Jose Tartabull	4.00	1.80	.50
☐ 556	Dick Selma	3.50	1.55	.45

		NRMT	VG-E	GOOD
☐ 557	Frank Quilici	3.50	1.55	.45
☐ 558	Johnny Edwards	3.50	1.55	.45
☐ 559	Pirates Rookies	3.50	1.55	.45
	Carl Taylor			
	Luke Walker			
☐ 560	Paul Casanova	3.50	1.55	.45
☐ 561	Lee Elia	3.50	1.55	.45
☐ 562	Jim Bouton	5.00	2.20	.60
☐ 563	Ed Charles	3.50	1.55	.45
☐ 564	Eddie Stanky MG	4.00	1.80	.50
☐ 565	Larry Dierker	4.00	1.80	.50
☐ 566	Ken Harrelson	4.00	1.80	.50
☐ 567	Clay Dalrymple	3.50	1.55	.45
☐ 568	Willie Smith	3.50	1.55	.45
☐ 569	NL Rookies	3.50	1.55	.45
	Ivan Murrell			
	Les Rohr			
☐ 570	Rick Reichardt	3.50	1.55	.45
☐ 571	Tony LaRussa	12.00	5.50	1.50
☐ 572	Don Bosch	3.50	1.55	.45
☐ 573	Joe Coleman	3.50	1.55	.45
☐ 574	Cincinnati Reds	8.00	3.60	1.00
	Team Card			
☐ 575	Jim Palmer	40.00	18.00	5.00
☐ 576	Dave Adlesh	3.50	1.55	.45
☐ 577	Fred Talbot	3.50	1.55	.45
☐ 578	Orlando Martinez	3.50	1.55	.45
☐ 579	NL Rookies	7.00	3.10	.85
	Larry Hisle			
	Mike Lum			
☐ 580	Bob Bailey	3.50	1.55	.45
☐ 581	Garry Roggenburk	3.50	1.55	.45
☐ 582	Jerry Grote	3.50	1.55	.45
☐ 583	Gates Brown	8.00	3.60	1.00
☐ 584	Larry Shepard MG	3.50	1.55	.45
☐ 585	Wilbur Wood	4.00	1.80	.50
☐ 586	Jim Pagliaroni	4.00	1.80	.50
☐ 587	Roger Repoz	3.50	1.55	.45
☐ 588	Dick Schofield	3.50	1.55	.45
☐ 589	Twins Rookies	3.50	1.55	.45
	Ron Clark			
	Moe Ogier			
☐ 590	Tommy Harper	4.00	1.80	.50
☐ 591	Dick Nen	3.50	1.55	.45
☐ 592	John Bateman	3.50	1.55	.45
☐ 593	Lee Stange	3.50	1.55	.45
☐ 594	Phil Linz	4.00	1.80	.50
☐ 595	Phil Ortega	3.50	1.55	.45
☐ 596	Charlie Smith	3.50	1.55	.45
☐ 597	Bill McCool	3.50	1.55	.45
☐ 598	Jerry May	5.00	1.55	.45

1969 Topps

The cards in this 664-card set measure 2 1/2" by 3 1/2". The 1969 Topps set includes Sporting News All-Star Selections as card numbers 416 to 435. Other popular subsets within this set include League Leaders (1-12) and World Series cards (162-169). The fifth series contains several variations; the more difficult variety consists of cards with the player's first name, last name, and/or position in white letters instead of lettering in some other color. These are designated in the checklist below by WL (white letters).

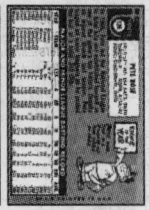

Each checklist card features a different popular player's picture inside a circle on the front of the checklist card. Two different team identifications of Clay Dalrymple and Donn Clendenon exist, as indicated in the checklist. The key Rookie Cards in this set are Rollie Fingers, Reggie Jackson, and Graig Nettles. This was the last year that Topps issued multi-player special star cards, ending a 13-year tradition, which they had begun in 1957. There were cropping differences in checklist cards 57, 214, and 412, due to their each being printed with two different series. The differences are difficult to explain and have not been greatly sought by collectors; hence they are not listed explicitly in the list below. The All-Star cards 426-435, when turned over and placed together, form a puzzle back of Pete Rose.

	NRMT	VG-E	GOOD
COMPLETE SET (664)	2200.00	1000.00	275.00
COMMON CARD (1-218)	1.50	.70	.19
COMMON CARD (219-327)	2.50	1.10	.30
COMMON CARD (328-512)	1.50	.70	.19
COMMON CARD (513-588)	2.00	.90	.25
COMMON CARD (589-664)	3.00	1.35	.35

		NRMT	VG-E	GOOD
☐ 1	AL Batting Leaders	14.00	5.00	2.00
	Carl Yastrzemski			
	Danny Cater			
	Tony Oliva			
☐ 2	NL Batting Leaders	7.00	3.10	.85
	Pete Rose			
	Matty Alou			
	Felipe Alou			
☐ 3	AL RBI Leaders	3.50	1.55	.45
	Ken Harrelson			
	Frank Howard			
	Jim Northrup			
☐ 4	NL RBI Leaders	6.00	2.70	.75
	Willie McCovey			
	Ron Santo			
	Billy Williams			
☐ 5	AL Home Run Leaders	3.50	1.55	.45
	Frank Howard			
	Willie Horton			
	Ken Harrelson			
☐ 6	NL Home Run Leaders	6.00	2.70	.75
	Willie McCovey			
	Richie Allen			
	Ernie Banks			
☐ 7	AL ERA Leaders	3.50	1.55	.45

	Luis Tiant			
	Sam McDowell			
	Dave McNally			
☐ 8	NL ERA Leaders.............	5.00	2.20	.60
	Bob Gibson			
	Bobby Bolin			
	Bob Veale			
☐ 9	AL Pitching Leaders.......	3.50	1.55	.45
	Denny McLain			
	Dave McNally			
	Luis Tiant			
	Mel Stottlemyre			
☐ 10	NL Pitching Leaders.....	7.00	3.10	.85
	Juan Marichal			
	Bob Gibson			
	Fergie Jenkins			
☐ 11	AL Strikeout Leaders ..	3.50	1.55	.45
	Sam McDowell			
	Denny McLain			
	Luis Tiant			
☐ 12	NL Strikeout Leaders ..	4.00	1.80	.50
	Bob Gibson			
	Fergie Jenkins			
	Bill Singer			
☐ 13	Mickey Stanley..............	2.00	.90	.25
☐ 14	Al McBean.....................	1.50	.70	.19
☐ 15	Boog Powell..................	3.50	1.55	.45
☐ 16	Giants Rookies..............	1.50	.70	.19
	Cesar Gutierrez			
	Rich Robertson			
☐ 17	Mike Marshall................	2.00	.90	.25
☐ 18	Dick Schofield	1.50	.70	.19
☐ 19	Ken Suarez	1.50	.70	.19
☐ 20	Ernie Banks..................	18.00	8.00	2.20
☐ 21	Jose Santiago	1.50	.70	.19
☐ 22	Jesus Alou	2.00	.90	.25
☐ 23	Lew Krausse..................	1.50	.70	.19
☐ 24	Walt Alston MG.............	2.50	1.10	.30
☐ 25	Roy White	2.00	.90	.25
☐ 26	Clay Carroll	2.00	.90	.25
☐ 27	Bernie Allen	1.50	.70	.19
☐ 28	Mike Ryan	1.50	.70	.19
☐ 29	Dave Morehead	1.50	.70	.19
☐ 30	Bob Allison	2.00	.90	.25
☐ 31	Mets Rookies................	3.00	1.35	.35
	Gary Gentry			
	Amos Otis			
☐ 32	Sammy Ellis	1.50	.70	.19
☐ 33	Wayne Causey................	1.50	.70	.19
☐ 34	Gary Peters	1.50	.70	.19
☐ 35	Joe Morgan	10.00	4.50	1.25
☐ 36	Luke Walker	1.50	.70	.19
☐ 37	Curt Motton	1.50	.70	.19
☐ 38	Zoilo Versalles	2.00	.90	.25
☐ 39	Dick Hughes	1.50	.70	.19
☐ 40	Mayo Smith MG..............	1.50	.70	.19
☐ 41	Bob Barton	1.50	.70	.19
☐ 42	Tommy Harper................	2.00	.90	.25
☐ 43	Joe Niekro....................	2.00	.90	.25
☐ 44	Danny Cater	1.50	.70	.19
☐ 45	Maury Wills	3.00	1.35	.35
☐ 46	Fritz Peterson	1.50	.70	.19
☐ 47A	Paul Popovich	1.50	.70	.19
	(No helmet emblem)			
☐ 47B	Paul Popovich..........	25.00	11.00	3.10
	(C emblem on helmet)			
☐ 48	Brant Alyea	1.50	.70	.19
☐ 49A	Royals Rookies ERR ..	1.50	.70	.19
	Steve Jones			
	E. Rodriguez "q"			
☐ 49B	Royals Rookies COR	25.00	11.00	3.10
	Steve Jones			
	E. Rodriguez "g"			
☐ 50	Bob Clemente UER.....	50.00	22.00	6.25
	(Bats Right listed twice)			
☐ 51	Woody Fryman	1.50	.70	.19
☐ 52	Mike Andrews	1.50	.70	.19
☐ 53	Sonny Jackson	1.50	.70	.19
☐ 54	Cisco Carlos..................	1.50	.70	.19
☐ 55	Jerry Grote....................	2.00	.90	.25
☐ 56	Rich Reese....................	1.50	.70	.19
☐ 57	Checklist 1	6.00	1.20	.60
	Denny McLain			
☐ 58	Fred Gladding	1.50	.70	.19
☐ 59	Jay Johnstone	2.00	.90	.25
☐ 60	Nelson Briles	2.00	.90	.25
☐ 61	Jimmie Hall	1.50	.70	.19
☐ 62	Chico Salmon	1.50	.70	.19
☐ 63	Jim Hickman	2.00	.90	.25
☐ 64	Bill Monbouquette........	1.50	.70	.19
☐ 65	Willie Davis	2.00	.90	.25
☐ 66	Orioles Rookies............	1.50	.70	.19
	Mike Adamson			
	Merv Rettenmund			
☐ 67	Bill Stoneman	2.00	.90	.25
☐ 68	Dave Duncan..................	2.00	.90	.25
☐ 69	Steve Hamilton	1.50	.70	.19
☐ 70	Tommy Helms	2.00	.90	.25
☐ 71	Steve Whitaker	1.50	.70	.19
☐ 72	Ron Taylor	1.50	.70	.19
☐ 73	Johnny Briggs	1.50	.70	.19
☐ 74	Preston Gomez MG........	2.00	.90	.25
☐ 75	Luis Aparicio	5.00	2.20	.60
☐ 76	Norm Miller....................	1.50	.70	.19
☐ 77A	Ron Perranoski	2.00	.90	.25
	(No emblem on cap)			
☐ 77B	Ron Perranoski	25.00	11.00	3.10
	(LA on cap)			
☐ 78	Tom Satriano	1.50	.70	.19
☐ 79	Milt Pappas	2.00	.90	.25
☐ 80	Norm Cash	3.00	1.35	.35
☐ 81	Mel Queen	1.50	.70	.19
☐ 82	Pirates Rookies..............	12.00	5.50	1.50
	Rich Hebner			
	Al Oliver			
☐ 83	Mike Ferraro	2.00	.90	.25
☐ 84	Bob Humphreys..............	1.50	.70	.19
☐ 85	Lou Brock....................	18.00	8.00	2.20
☐ 86	Pete Richert..................	1.50	.70	.19
☐ 87	Horace Clarke	1.50	.70	.19
☐ 88	Rich Nye	1.50	.70	.19
☐ 89	Russ Gibson	1.50	.70	.19
☐ 90	Jerry Koosman	5.00	2.20	.60
☐ 91	Alvin Dark MG................	2.00	.90	.25
☐ 92	Jack Billingham..............	2.00	.90	.25
☐ 93	Joe Foy	1.50	.70	.19
☐ 94	Hank Aguirre	1.50	.70	.19
☐ 95	Johnny Bench	50.00	22.00	6.25
☐ 96	Denny Lemaster............	1.50	.70	.19
☐ 97	Buddy Bradford	1.50	.70	.19
☐ 98	Dave Giusti	1.50	.70	.19
☐ 99A	Twins Rookies	18.00	8.00	2.20
	Danny Morris			
	Graig Nettles			
	(No loop)			
☐ 99B	Twins Rookies	18.00	8.00	2.20
	Danny Morris			
	Graig Nettles			
	(Errant loop in upper left corner of obverse)			

☐ 100	Hank Aaron	45.00	20.00	5.50
☐ 101	Daryl Patterson	1.50	.70	.19
☐ 102	Jim Davenport	1.50	.70	.19
☐ 103	Roger Repoz	1.50	.70	.19
☐ 104	Steve Blass	2.00	.90	.25
☐ 105	Rick Monday	2.00	.90	.25
☐ 106	Jim Hannan	1.50	.70	.19
☐ 107A	Checklist 2 ERR	6.00	1.20	.60
	(161 Jim Purdin)			
	(Bob Gibson)			
☐ 107B	Checklist 2 COR	7.50	1.50	.75
	(161 John Purdin)			
	(Bob Gibson)			
☐ 108	Tony Taylor	1.50	.70	.19
☐ 109	Jim Lonborg	2.00	.90	.25
☐ 110	Mike Shannon	2.00	.90	.25
☐ 111	Johnny Morris	1.50	.70	.19
☐ 112	J.C. Martin	1.50	.70	.19
☐ 113	Dave May	1.50	.70	.19
☐ 114	Yankees Rookies	1.50	.70	.19
	Alan Closter			
	John Cumberland			
☐ 115	Bill Hands	1.50	.70	.19
☐ 116	Chuck Harrison	1.50	.70	.19
☐ 117	Jim Fairey	1.50	.70	.19
☐ 118	Stan Williams	1.50	.70	.19
☐ 119	Doug Rader	2.00	.90	.25
☐ 120	Pete Rose	25.00	11.00	3.10
☐ 121	Joe Grzenda	1.50	.70	.19
☐ 122	Ron Fairly	2.00	.90	.25
☐ 123	Wilbur Wood	2.00	.90	.25
☐ 124	Hank Bauer MG	2.00	.90	.25
☐ 125	Ray Sadecki	1.50	.70	.19
☐ 126	Dick Tracewski	1.50	.70	.19
☐ 127	Kevin Collins	2.00	.90	.25
☐ 128	Tommie Aaron	2.00	.90	.25
☐ 129	Bill McCool	1.50	.70	.19
☐ 130	Carl Yastrzemski	20.00	9.00	2.50
☐ 131	Chris Cannizzaro	1.50	.70	.19
☐ 132	Dave Baldwin	1.50	.70	.19
☐ 133	Johnny Callison	2.00	.90	.25
☐ 134	Jim Weaver	1.50	.70	.19
☐ 135	Tommy Davis	2.00	.90	.25
☐ 136	Cards Rookies	1.50	.70	.19
	Steve Huntz			
	Mike Torrez			
☐ 137	Wally Bunker	1.50	.70	.19
☐ 138	John Bateman	1.50	.70	.19
☐ 139	Andy Kosco	1.50	.70	.19
☐ 140	Jim Lefebvre	2.00	.90	.25
☐ 141	Bill Dillman	1.50	.70	.19
☐ 142	Woody Woodward	2.00	.90	.25
☐ 143	Joe Nossek	1.50	.70	.19
☐ 144	Bob Hendley	1.50	.70	.19
☐ 145	Max Alvis	1.50	.70	.19
☐ 146	Jim Perry	2.00	.90	.25
☐ 147	Leo Durocher MG	4.00	1.80	.50
☐ 148	Lee Stange	1.50	.70	.19
☐ 149	Ollie Brown	2.00	.90	.25
☐ 150	Denny McLain	4.00	1.80	.50
☐ 151A	Clay Dalrymple	1.50	.70	.19
	(Portrait, Orioles)			
☐ 151B	Clay Dalrymple	16.00	7.25	2.00
	(Catching, Phillies)			
☐ 152	Tommie Sisk	1.50	.70	.19
☐ 153	Ed Brinkman	1.50	.70	.19
☐ 154	Jim Britton	1.50	.70	.19
☐ 155	Pete Ward	1.50	.70	.19
☐ 156	Houston Rookies	1.50	.70	.19
	Hal Gilson			
	Leon McFadden			

☐ 157	Bob Rodgers	2.00	.90	.25
☐ 158	Joe Gibbon	1.50	.70	.19
☐ 159	Jerry Adair	1.50	.70	.19
☐ 160	Vada Pinson	2.50	1.10	.30
☐ 161	John Purdin	1.50	.70	.19
☐ 162	World Series Game 1.	8.00	3.60	1.00
	Bob Gibson fans 17			
☐ 163	World Series Game 2.	5.00	2.20	.60
	Tiger homers			
	deck the Cards			
	(Willie Horton)			
☐ 164	World Series Game 3.	7.00	3.10	.85
	Tim McCarver's homer			
☐ 165	World Series Game 4.	8.00	3.60	1.00
	Lou Brock lead-off			
	homer			
☐ 166	World Series Game 5.	8.00	3.60	1.00
	Al Kaline's key hit			
☐ 167	World Series Game 6.	5.00	2.20	.60
	Jim Northrup grandslam			
☐ 168	World Series Game 7.	8.00	3.60	1.00
	Mickey Lolich outduels			
	Bob Gibson			
☐ 169	World Series Summary	5.00	2.20	.60
	Tigers celebrate			
	(Dick McAuliffe,			
	Denny McLain, and			
	Willie Horton)			
☐ 170	Frank Howard	3.00	1.35	.35
☐ 171	Glenn Beckert	2.00	.90	.25
☐ 172	Jerry Stephenson	1.50	.70	.19
☐ 173	White Sox Rookies	1.50	.70	.19
	Bob Christian			
	Gerry Nyman			
☐ 174	Grant Jackson	1.50	.70	.19
☐ 175	Jim Bunning	4.00	1.80	.50
☐ 176	Joe Azcue	1.50	.70	.19
☐ 177	Ron Reed	1.50	.70	.19
☐ 178	Ray Oyler	2.00	.90	.25
☐ 179	Don Pavletich	1.50	.70	.19
☐ 180	Willie Horton	2.00	.90	.25
☐ 181	Mel Nelson	1.50	.70	.19
☐ 182	Bill Rigney MG	1.50	.70	.19
☐ 183	Don Shaw	1.50	.70	.19
☐ 184	Roberto Pena	1.50	.70	.19
☐ 185	Tom Phoebus	1.50	.70	.19
☐ 186	Johnny Edwards	1.50	.70	.19
☐ 187	Leon Wagner	1.50	.70	.19
☐ 188	Rick Wise	2.00	.90	.25
☐ 189	Red Sox Rookies	1.50	.70	.19
	Joe Lahoud			
	John Thibodeau			
☐ 190	Willie Mays	50.00	22.00	6.25
☐ 191	Lindy McDaniel	2.00	.90	.25
☐ 192	Jose Pagan	1.50	.70	.19
☐ 193	Don Cardwell	1.50	.70	.19
☐ 194	Ted Uhlaender	1.50	.70	.19
☐ 195	John Odom	1.50	.70	.19
☐ 196	Lum Harris MG	1.50	.70	.19
☐ 197	Dick Selma	1.50	.70	.19
☐ 198	Willie Smith	1.50	.70	.19
☐ 199	Jim French	1.50	.70	.19
☐ 200	Bob Gibson	12.00	5.50	1.50
☐ 201	Russ Snyder	1.50	.70	.19
☐ 202	Don Wilson	2.00	.90	.25
☐ 203	Dave Johnson	2.00	.90	.25
☐ 204	Jack Hiatt	1.50	.70	.19
☐ 205	Rick Reichardt	1.50	.70	.19
☐ 206	Phillies Rookies	2.00	.90	.25
	Larry Hisle			
	Barry Lersch			

☐ 207 Roy Face	2.00	.90	.25
☐ 208A Donn Clendenon (Houston)	2.00	.90	.25
☐ 208B Donn Clendenon (Expos)	16.00	7.25	2.00
☐ 209 Larry Haney UER (Reverse negative)	1.50	.70	.19
☐ 210 Felix Millan	1.50	.70	.19
☐ 211 Galen Cisco	1.50	.70	.19
☐ 212 Tom Tresh	2.00	.90	.25
☐ 213 Gerry Arrigo	1.50	.70	.19
☐ 214 Checklist 3 With 69T deckle CL on back (no player)	6.00	1.20	.60
☐ 215 Rico Petrocelli	2.00	.90	.25
☐ 216 Don Sutton	6.00	2.70	.75
☐ 217 John Donaldson	1.50	.70	.19
☐ 218 John Roseboro	2.00	.90	.25
☐ 219 Freddie Patek	3.00	1.35	.35
☐ 220 Sam McDowell	3.00	1.35	.35
☐ 221 Art Shamsky	3.00	1.35	.35
☐ 222 Duane Josephson	2.50	1.10	.30
☐ 223 Tom Dukes	3.00	1.35	.35
☐ 224 Angels Rookies Bill Harrelson Steve Kealey	2.50	1.10	.30
☐ 225 Don Kessinger	3.00	1.35	.35
☐ 226 Bruce Howard	2.50	1.10	.30
☐ 227 Frank Johnson	2.50	1.10	.30
☐ 228 Dave Leonhard	2.50	1.10	.30
☐ 229 Don Lock	2.50	1.10	.30
☐ 230 Rusty Staub	4.00	1.80	.50
☐ 231 Pat Dobson	3.00	1.35	.35
☐ 232 Dave Ricketts	2.50	1.10	.30
☐ 233 Steve Barber	3.00	1.35	.35
☐ 234 Dave Bristol MG	2.50	1.10	.30
☐ 235 Jim Hunter	10.00	4.50	1.25
☐ 236 Manny Mota	3.00	1.35	.35
☐ 237 Bobby Cox	10.00	4.50	1.25
☐ 238 Ken Johnson	2.50	1.10	.30
☐ 239 Bob Taylor	3.00	1.35	.35
☐ 240 Ken Harrelson	3.00	1.35	.35
☐ 241 Jim Brewer	2.50	1.10	.30
☐ 242 Frank Kostro	2.50	1.10	.30
☐ 243 Ron Kline	2.50	1.10	.30
☐ 244 Indians Rookies Ray Fosse George Woodson	6.00	2.70	.75
☐ 245 Ed Charles	3.00	1.35	.35
☐ 246 Joe Coleman	2.50	1.10	.30
☐ 247 Gene Oliver	2.50	1.10	.30
☐ 248 Bob Priddy	2.50	1.10	.30
☐ 249 Ed Spiezio	3.00	1.35	.35
☐ 250 Frank Robinson	30.00	13.50	3.70
☐ 251 Ron Herbel	2.50	1.10	.30
☐ 252 Chuck Cottier	2.50	1.10	.30
☐ 253 Jerry Johnson	2.50	1.10	.30
☐ 254 Joe Schultz MG	3.00	1.35	.35
☐ 255 Steve Carlton	35.00	16.00	4.40
☐ 256 Gates Brown	3.00	1.35	.35
☐ 257 Jim Ray	2.50	1.10	.30
☐ 258 Jackie Hernandez	3.00	1.35	.35
☐ 259 Bill Short	2.50	1.10	.30
☐ 260 Reggie Jackson	375.00	170.00	47.50
☐ 261 Bob Johnson	2.50	1.10	.30
☐ 262 Mike Kekich	2.50	1.10	.30
☐ 263 Jerry May	2.50	1.10	.30
☐ 264 Bill Landis	2.50	1.10	.30
☐ 265 Chico Cardenas	3.00	1.35	.35
☐ 266 Dodger Rookies Tom Hutton	2.50	1.10	.30
☐ 267 Alan Foster Vicente Romo	2.50	1.10	.30
☐ 268 Al Spangler	2.50	1.10	.30
☐ 269 Al Weis	3.00	1.35	.35
☐ 270 Mickey Lolich	4.00	1.80	.50
☐ 271 Larry Stahl	3.00	1.35	.35
☐ 272 Ed Stroud	2.50	1.10	.30
☐ 273 Ron Willis	2.50	1.10	.30
☐ 274 Clyde King MG	2.50	1.10	.30
☐ 275 Vic Davalillo	2.50	1.10	.30
☐ 276 Gary Wagner	2.50	1.10	.30
☐ 277 Elrod Hendricks	2.50	1.10	.30
☐ 278 Gary Geiger UER (Batting wrong)	2.50	1.10	.30
☐ 279 Roger Nelson	3.00	1.35	.35
☐ 280 Alex Johnson	3.00	1.35	.35
☐ 281 Ted Kubiak	2.50	1.10	.30
☐ 282 Pat Jarvis	2.50	1.10	.30
☐ 283 Sandy Alomar	3.00	1.35	.35
☐ 284 Expos Rookies Jerry Robertson Mike Wegener	3.00	1.35	.35
☐ 285 Don Mincher	3.00	1.35	.35
☐ 286 Dock Ellis	4.00	1.80	.50
☐ 287 Jose Tartabull	3.00	1.35	.35
☐ 288 Ken Holtzman	3.00	1.35	.35
☐ 289 Bart Shirley	2.50	1.10	.30
☐ 290 Jim Kaat	5.00	2.20	.60
☐ 291 Vern Fuller	2.50	1.10	.30
☐ 292 Al Downing	3.00	1.35	.35
☐ 293 Dick Dietz	2.50	1.10	.30
☐ 294 Jim Lemon MG	2.50	1.10	.30
☐ 295 Tony Perez	12.00	5.50	1.50
☐ 296 Andy Messersmith	4.00	1.80	.50
☐ 297 Deron Johnson	2.50	1.10	.30
☐ 298 Dave Nicholson	3.00	1.35	.35
☐ 299 Mark Belanger	3.00	1.35	.35
☐ 300 Felipe Alou	4.00	1.80	.50
☐ 301 Darrell Brandon	3.00	1.35	.35
☐ 302 Jim Pagliaroni	2.50	1.10	.30
☐ 303 Cal Koonce	3.00	1.35	.35
☐ 304 Padres Rookies Bill Davis Clarence Gaston	8.00	3.60	1.00
☐ 305 Dick McAuliffe	3.00	1.35	.35
☐ 306 Jim Grant	3.00	1.35	.35
☐ 307 Gary Kolb	2.50	1.10	.30
☐ 308 Wade Blasingame	2.50	1.10	.30
☐ 309 Walt Williams	2.50	1.10	.30
☐ 310 Tom Haller	2.50	1.10	.30
☐ 311 Sparky Lyle	8.00	3.60	1.00
☐ 312 Lee Elia	2.50	1.10	.30
☐ 313 Bill Robinson	3.00	1.35	.35
☐ 314 Checklist 4 Don Drysdale	6.00	1.20	.60
☐ 315 Eddie Fisher	2.50	1.10	.30
☐ 316 Hal Lanier	2.50	1.10	.30
☐ 317 Bruce Look	2.50	1.10	.30
☐ 318 Jack Fisher	2.50	1.10	.30
☐ 319 Ken McMullen UER (Headings on back are for a pitcher)	2.50	1.10	.30
☐ 320 Dal Maxvill	2.50	1.10	.30
☐ 321 Jim McAndrew	3.00	1.35	.35
☐ 322 Jose Vidal	3.00	1.35	.35
☐ 323 Larry Miller	2.50	1.10	.30
☐ 324 Tiger Rookies Les Cain Dave Campbell	2.50	1.10	.30
☐ 325 Jose Cardenal	3.00	1.35	.35
☐ 326 Gary Sutherland	3.00	1.35	.35

☐	327	Willie Crawford	2.50	1.10	.30	☐	390	Bill Freehan	3.00	1.35	.35
☐	328	Joel Horlen	1.50	.70	.19	☐	391	Ray Culp	1.50	.70	.19
☐	329	Rick Joseph	1.50	.70	.19	☐	392	Bob Burda	1.50	.70	.19
☐	330	Tony Conigliaro	5.00	2.20	.60	☐	393	Gene Brabender	2.00	.90	.25
☐	331	Braves Rookies	1.50	.70	.19	☐	394	Pilots Rookies	5.00	2.20	.60
		Gil Garrido						Lou Piniella			
		Tom House						Marv Staehle			
☐	332	Fred Talbot	1.50	.70	.19	☐	395	Chris Short	1.50	.70	.19
☐	333	Ivan Murrell	1.50	.70	.19	☐	396	Jim Campanis	1.50	.70	.19
☐	334	Phil Roof	1.50	.70	.19	☐	397	Chuck Dobson	1.50	.70	.19
☐	335	Bill Mazeroski	3.00	1.35	.35	☐	398	Tito Francona	1.50	.70	.19
☐	336	Jim Roland	1.50	.70	.19	☐	399	Bob Bailey	2.00	.90	.25
☐	337	Marty Martinez	1.50	.70	.19	☐	400	Don Drysdale	15.00	6.75	1.85
☐	338	Del Unser	1.50	.70	.19	☐	401	Jake Gibbs	1.50	.70	.19
☐	339	Reds Rookies	1.50	.70	.19	☐	402	Ken Boswell	2.00	.90	.25
		Steve Mingori						403	Bob Miller	1.50	.70	.19
		Jose Pena				☐	404	Cubs Rookies	1.50	.70	.19
☐	340	Dave McNally	2.00	.90	.25			Vic LaRose			
☐	341	Dave Adlesh	1.50	.70	.19			Gary Ross			
☐	342	Bubba Morton	1.50	.70	.19	☐	405	Lee May	2.00	.90	.25
☐	343	Dan Frisella	1.50	.70	.19	☐	406	Phil Ortega	1.50	.70	.19
☐	344	Tom Matchick	1.50	.70	.19	☐	407	Tom Egan	1.50	.70	.19
☐	345	Frank Linzy	1.50	.70	.19	☐	408	Nate Colbert	1.50	.70	.19
☐	346	Wayne Comer	1.50	.70	.19	☐	409	Bob Moose	1.50	.70	.19
☐	347	Randy Hundley	2.00	.90	.25	☐	410	Al Kaline	20.00	9.00	2.50
☐	348	Steve Hargan	1.50	.70	.19	☐	411	Larry Dierker	1.50	.70	.19
☐	349	Dick Williams MG	2.00	.90	.25	☐	412	Checklist 5 DP	12.00	2.40	1.20
☐	350	Richie Allen	4.00	1.80	.50			Mickey Mantle			
☐	351	Carroll Sembera	1.50	.70	.19	☐	413	Roland Sheldon	1.50	.70	.19
☐	352	Paul Schaal	2.00	.90	.25	☐	414	Duke Sims	1.50	.70	.19
☐	353	Jeff Torborg	2.00	.90	.25	☐	415	Ray Washburn	1.50	.70	.19
☐	354	Nate Oliver	1.50	.70	.19	☐	416	Willie McCovey AS	7.00	3.10	.85
☐	355	Phil Niekro	7.00	3.10	.85	☐	417	Ken Harrelson AS	2.50	1.10	.30
☐	356	Frank Quilici	1.50	.70	.19	☐	418	Tommy Helms AS	2.50	1.10	.30
☐	357	Carl Taylor	1.50	.70	.19	☐	419	Rod Carew AS	10.00	4.50	1.25
☐	358	Athletics Rookies	1.50	.70	.19	☐	420	Ron Santo AS	3.00	1.35	.35
		George Lauzerique				☐	421	Brooks Robinson AS	7.00	3.10	.85
		Roberto Rodriquez				☐	422	Don Kessinger AS	2.50	1.10	.30
☐	359	Dick Kelley	1.50	.70	.19	☐	423	Bert Campaneris AS	2.50	1.10	.30
☐	360	Jim Wynn	2.00	.90	.25	☐	424	Pete Rose AS	15.00	6.75	1.85
☐	361	Gary Holman	1.50	.70	.19	☐	425	Carl Yastrzemski AS	10.00	4.50	1.25
☐	362	Jim Maloney	2.00	.90	.25	☐	426	Curt Flood AS	3.00	1.35	.35
☐	363	Russ Nixon	1.50	.70	.19	☐	427	Tony Oliva AS	3.00	1.35	.35
☐	364	Tommie Agee	2.00	.90	.25	☐	428	Lou Brock AS	6.00	2.70	.75
☐	365	Jim Fregosi	2.00	.90	.25	☐	429	Willie Horton AS	2.50	1.10	.30
☐	366	Bo Belinsky	2.00	.90	.25	☐	430	Johnny Bench AS	10.00	4.50	1.25
☐	367	Lou Johnson	2.00	.90	.25	☐	431	Bill Freehan AS	3.00	1.35	.35
☐	368	Vic Roznovsky	1.50	.70	.19	☐	432	Bob Gibson AS	6.00	2.70	.75
☐	369	Bob Skinner	2.00	.90	.25	☐	433	Denny McLain AS	2.50	1.10	.30
☐	370	Juan Marichal	8.00	3.60	1.00	☐	434	Jerry Koosman AS	3.00	1.35	.35
☐	371	Sal Bando	2.00	.90	.25	☐	435	Sam McDowell AS	2.50	1.10	.30
☐	372	Adolfo Phillips	1.50	.70	.19	☐	436	Gene Alley	2.00	.90	.25
☐	373	Fred Lasher	1.50	.70	.19	☐	437	Luis Alcaraz	1.50	.70	.19
☐	374	Bob Tillman	1.50	.70	.19	☐	438	Gary Waslewski	1.50	.70	.19
☐	375	Harmon Killebrew	18.00	8.00	2.20	☐	439	White Sox Rookies	1.50	.70	.19
☐	376	Royals Rookies	1.50	.70	.19			Ed Herrmann			
		Mike Fiore						Dan Lazar			
		Jim Rooker				☐	440A	Willie McCovey	18.00	8.00	2.20
☐	377	Gary Bell	2.00	.90	.25	☐	440B	Willie McCovey WL	100.00	45.00	12.50
☐	378	Jose Herrera	1.50	.70	.19			(McCovey white)			
☐	379	Ken Boyer	2.50	1.10	.30	☐	441A	Dennis Higgins	1.50	.70	.19
☐	380	Stan Bahnsen	1.50	.70	.19	☐	441B	Dennis Higgins WL	20.00	9.00	2.50
☐	381	Ed Kranepool	2.00	.90	.25			(Higgins white)			
☐	382	Pat Corrales	2.00	.90	.25	☐	442	Ty Cline	1.50	.70	.19
☐	383	Casey Cox	1.50	.70	.19	☐	443	Don Wert	1.50	.70	.19
☐	384	Larry Shepard MG	1.50	.70	.19	☐	444A	Joe Moeller	1.50	.70	.19
☐	385	Orlando Cepeda	3.50	1.55	.45	☐	444B	Joe Moeller WL	20.00	9.00	2.50
☐	386	Jim McGlothlin	1.50	.70	.19			(Moeller white)			
☐	387	Bobby Klaus	1.50	.70	.19	☐	445	Bobby Knoop	1.50	.70	.19
☐	388	Tom McCraw	1.50	.70	.19	☐	446	Claude Raymond	1.50	.70	.19
☐	389	Dan Coombs	1.50	.70	.19	☐	447A	Ralph Houk MG	2.00	.90	.25

☐ 447B Ralph Houk WL	22.00	10.00	2.70
MG (Houk white)			
☐ 448 Bob Tolan	2.00	.90	.25
☐ 449 Paul Lindblad	1.50	.70	.19
☐ 450 Billy Williams	6.00	2.70	.75
☐ 451A Rich Rollins	2.00	.90	.25
☐ 451B Rich Rollins WL	20.00	9.00	2.50
(Rich and 3B white)			
☐ 452A Al Ferrara	1.50	.70	.19
☐ 452B Al Ferrara WL	20.00	9.00	2.50
(Al and OF white)			
☐ 453 Mike Cuellar	2.50	1.10	.30
☐ 454A Phillies Rookies	2.00	.90	.25
Larry Colton			
Don Money			
☐ 454B Phillies Rookies WL	22.00	10.00	2.70
Larry Colton			
Don Money			
(Names in white)			
☐ 455 Sonny Siebert	1.50	.70	.19
☐ 456 Bud Harrelson	2.00	.90	.25
☐ 457 Dalton Jones	1.50	.70	.19
☐ 458 Curt Blefary	1.50	.70	.19
☐ 459 Dave Boswell	1.50	.70	.19
☐ 460 Joe Torre	3.50	1.55	.45
☐ 461A Mike Epstein	1.50	.70	.19
☐ 461B Mike Epstein WL	20.00	9.00	2.50
(Epstein white)			
☐ 462 Red Schoendienst	2.50	1.10	.30
MG			
☐ 463 Dennis Ribant	1.50	.70	.19
☐ 464A Dave Marshall	1.50	.70	.19
☐ 464B Dave Marshall WL	20.00	9.00	2.50
(Marshall white)			
☐ 465 Tommy John	4.00	1.80	.50
☐ 466 John Boccabella	2.00	.90	.25
☐ 467 Tommie Reynolds	1.50	.70	.19
☐ 468A Pirates Rookies	1.50	.70	.19
Bruce Dal Canton			
Bob Robertson			
☐ 468B Pirates Rookies WL	20.00	9.00	2.50
Bruce Dal Canton			
Bob Robertson			
(Names in white)			
☐ 469 Chico Ruiz	1.50	.70	.19
☐ 470A Mel Stottlemyre	2.50	1.10	.30
☐ 470B Mel Stottlemyre WL	30.00	13.50	3.70
(Stottlemyre white)			
☐ 471A Ted Savage	1.50	.70	.19
☐ 471B Ted Savage WL	20.00	9.00	2.50
(Savage white)			
☐ 472 Jim Price	1.50	.70	.19
☐ 473A Jose Arcia	1.50	.70	.19
☐ 473B Jose Arcia WL	20.00	9.00	2.50
(Jose and 2B white)			
☐ 474 Tom Murphy	1.50	.70	.19
☐ 475 Tim McCarver	3.00	1.35	.35
☐ 476A Boston Rookies	3.00	1.35	.35
Ken Brett			
Gerry Moses			
☐ 476B Boston Rookies WL	30.00	13.50	3.70
Ken Brett			
Gerry Moses			
(Names in white)			
☐ 477 Jeff James	1.50	.70	.19
☐ 478 Don Buford	1.50	.70	.19
☐ 479 Richie Scheinblum	1.50	.70	.19
☐ 480 Tom Seaver	80.00	36.00	10.00
☐ 481 Bill Melton	2.00	.90	.25
☐ 482A Jim Gosger	1.50	.70	.19
☐ 482B Jim Gosger WL	20.00	9.00	2.50
(Jim and OF white)			
☐ 483 Ted Abernathy	1.50	.70	.19
☐ 484 Joe Gordon MG	2.00	.90	.25
☐ 485A Gaylord Perry	10.00	4.50	1.25
☐ 485B Gaylord Perry WL	85.00	38.00	10.50
(Perry white)			
☐ 486A Paul Casanova	1.50	.70	.19
☐ 486B Paul Casanova WL	20.00	9.00	2.50
(Casanova white)			
☐ 487 Denis Menke	1.50	.70	.19
☐ 488 Joe Sparma	1.50	.70	.19
☐ 489 Clete Boyer	2.00	.90	.25
☐ 490 Matty Alou	2.00	.90	.25
☐ 491A Twins Rookies	1.50	.70	.19
Jerry Crider			
George Mitterwald			
☐ 491B Twins Rookies WL	20.00	9.00	2.50
Jerry Crider			
George Mitterwald			
(Names in white)			
☐ 492 Tony Cloninger	1.50	.70	.19
☐ 493A Wes Parker	2.00	.90	.25
☐ 493B Wes Parker WL	22.00	10.00	2.70
(Parker white)			
☐ 494 Ken Berry	1.50	.70	.19
☐ 495 Bert Campaneris	2.00	.90	.25
☐ 496 Larry Jaster	1.50	.70	.19
☐ 497 Julian Javier	2.00	.90	.25
☐ 498 Juan Pizarro	2.00	.90	.25
☐ 499 Astro Rookies	1.50	.70	.19
Don Bryant			
Steve Shea			
☐ 500A Mickey Mantle UER	350.00	160.00	45.00
(No Topps copy-			
right on card back)			
☐ 500B Mickey Mantle WL	1000.00	450.00	125.00
(Mantle in white;			
no Topps copyright			
on card back) UER			
☐ 501A Tony Gonzalez	2.00	.90	.25
☐ 501B Tony Gonzalez WL	22.00	10.00	2.70
(Tony and OF white)			
☐ 502 Minnie Rojas	1.50	.70	.19
☐ 503 Larry Brown	1.50	.70	.19
☐ 504 Checklist 6	7.00	1.40	.70
Brooks Robinson			
☐ 505A Bobby Bolin	1.50	.70	.19
☐ 505B Bobby Bolin WL	22.00	10.00	2.70
(Bolin white)			
☐ 506 Paul Blair	2.00	.90	.25
☐ 507 Cookie Rojas	2.00	.90	.25
☐ 508 Moe Drabowsky	2.00	.90	.25
☐ 509 Manny Sanguillen	2.00	.90	.25
☐ 510 Rod Carew	35.00	16.00	4.40
☐ 511A Diego Segui	2.00	.90	.25
☐ 511B Diego Segui WL	22.00	10.00	2.70
(Diego and P white)			
☐ 512 Cleon Jones	2.00	.90	.25
☐ 513 Camilo Pascual	3.00	1.35	.35
☐ 514 Mike Lum	2.00	.90	.25
☐ 515 Dick Green	2.00	.90	.25
☐ 516 Earl Weaver MG	16.00	7.25	2.00
☐ 517 Mike McCormick	3.00	1.35	.35
☐ 518 Fred Whitfield	2.00	.90	.25
☐ 519 Yankees Rookies	2.00	.90	.25
Jerry Kenney			
Len Boehmer			
☐ 520 Bob Veale	3.00	1.35	.35
☐ 521 George Thomas	2.00	.90	.25
☐ 522 Joe Hoerner	2.00	.90	.25
☐ 523 Bob Chance	2.00	.90	.25

☐ 524	Expos Rookies	3.00	1.35	.35
	Jose Laboy			
	Floyd Wicker			
☐ 525	Earl Wilson	3.00	1.35	.35
☐ 526	Hector Torres	2.00	.90	.25
☐ 527	Al Lopez MG	4.00	1.80	.50
☐ 528	Claude Osteen	3.00	1.35	.35
☐ 529	Ed Kirkpatrick	3.00	1.35	.35
☐ 530	Cesar Tovar	2.00	.90	.25
☐ 531	Dick Farrell	2.00	.90	.25
☐ 532	Bird Hill Aces	3.00	1.35	.35
	Tom Phoebus			
	Jim Hardin			
	Dave McNally			
	Mike Cuellar			
☐ 533	Nolan Ryan	450.00	200.00	55.00
☐ 534	Jerry McNertney	3.00	1.35	.35
☐ 535	Phil Regan	3.00	1.35	.35
☐ 536	Padres Rookies	2.00	.90	.25
	Danny Breeden			
	Dave Roberts			
☐ 537	Mike Paul	2.00	.90	.25
☐ 538	Charlie Smith	2.00	.90	.25
☐ 539	Ted Shows How	8.00	3.60	1.00
	Mike Epstein			
	Ted Williams MG			
☐ 540	Curt Flood	3.00	1.35	.35
☐ 541	Joe Verbanic	2.00	.90	.25
☐ 542	Bob Aspromonte	2.00	.90	.25
☐ 543	Fred Newman	2.00	.90	.25
☐ 544	Tigers Rookies	2.00	.90	.25
	Mike Kilkenny			
	Ron Woods			
☐ 545	Willie Stargell	12.00	5.50	1.50
☐ 546	Jim Nash	2.00	.90	.25
☐ 547	Billy Martin MG	6.00	2.70	.75
☐ 548	Bob Locker	2.00	.90	.25
☐ 549	Ron Brand	2.00	.90	.25
☐ 550	Brooks Robinson	30.00	13.50	3.70
☐ 551	Wayne Granger	2.00	.90	.25
☐ 552	Dodgers Rookies	4.00	1.80	.50
	Ted Sizemore			
	Bill Sudakis			
☐ 553	Ron Davis	2.00	.90	.25
☐ 554	Frank Bertaina	2.00	.90	.25
☐ 555	Jim Ray Hart	3.00	1.35	.35
☐ 556	A's Stars	3.00	1.35	.35
	Sal Bando			
	Bert Campaneris			
	Danny Cater			
☐ 557	Frank Fernandez	2.00	.90	.25
☐ 558	Tom Burgmeier	3.00	1.35	.35
☐ 559	Cardinals Rookies	2.00	.90	.25
	Joe Hague			
	Jim Hicks			
☐ 560	Luis Tiant	4.00	1.80	.50
☐ 561	Ron Clark	2.00	.90	.25
☐ 562	Bob Watson	7.00	3.10	.85
☐ 563	Marty Pattin	3.00	1.35	.35
☐ 564	Gil Hodges MG	10.00	4.50	1.25
☐ 565	Hoyt Wilhelm	7.00	3.10	.85
☐ 566	Ron Hansen	2.00	.90	.25
☐ 567	Pirates Rookies	2.00	.90	.25
	Elvio Jimenez			
	Jim Shellenback			
☐ 568	Cecil Upshaw	2.00	.90	.25
☐ 569	Billy Harris	2.00	.90	.25
☐ 570	Ron Santo	7.00	3.10	.85
☐ 571	Cap Peterson	2.00	.90	.25
☐ 572	Giants Heroes	16.00	7.25	2.00
	Willie McCovey			
	Juan Marichal			
☐ 573	Jim Palmer	35.00	16.00	4.40
☐ 574	George Scott	3.00	1.35	.35
☐ 575	Bill Singer	3.00	1.35	.35
☐ 576	Phillies Rookies	2.00	.90	.25
	Ron Stone			
	Bill Wilson			
☐ 577	Mike Hegan	3.00	1.35	.35
☐ 578	Don Bosch	2.00	.90	.25
☐ 579	Dave Nelson	2.00	.90	.25
☐ 580	Jim Northrup	3.00	1.35	.35
☐ 581	Gary Nolan	3.00	1.35	.35
☐ 582A	Checklist 7	6.00	1.20	.60
	(White circle on back)			
	(Tony Oliva)			
☐ 582B	Checklist 7	7.50	1.50	.75
	(Red circle on back)			
	(Tony Oliva)			
☐ 583	Clyde Wright	2.00	.90	.25
☐ 584	Don Mason	2.00	.90	.25
☐ 585	Ron Swoboda	3.00	1.35	.35
☐ 586	Tim Cullen	2.00	.90	.25
☐ 587	Joe Rudi	7.00	3.10	.85
☐ 588	Bill White	3.00	1.35	.35
☐ 589	Joe Pepitone	4.00	1.80	.50
☐ 590	Rico Carty	3.50	1.55	.45
☐ 591	Mike Hedlund	3.00	1.35	.35
☐ 592	Padres Rookies	3.50	1.55	.45
	Rafael Robles			
	Al Santorini			
☐ 593	Don Nottebart	3.00	1.35	.35
☐ 594	Dooley Womack	3.00	1.35	.35
☐ 595	Lee Maye	3.00	1.35	.35
☐ 596	Chuck Hartenstein	3.00	1.35	.35
☐ 597	A.L. Rookies	50.00	22.00	6.25
	Bob Floyd			
	Larry Burchart			
	Rollie Fingers			
☐ 598	Ruben Amaro	3.00	1.35	.35
☐ 599	John Boozer	3.00	1.35	.35
☐ 600	Tony Oliva	7.00	3.10	.85
☐ 601	Tug McGraw	7.00	3.10	.85
☐ 602	Cubs Rookies	3.50	1.55	.45
	Alec Distaso			
	Don Young			
	Jim Qualls			
☐ 603	Joe Keough	3.00	1.35	.35
☐ 604	Bobby Etheridge	3.00	1.35	.35
☐ 605	Dick Ellsworth	3.00	1.35	.35
☐ 606	Gene Mauch MG	3.50	1.55	.45
☐ 607	Dick Bosman	3.00	1.35	.35
☐ 608	Dick Simpson	3.00	1.35	.35
☐ 609	Phil Gagliano	3.00	1.35	.35
☐ 610	Jim Hardin	3.00	1.35	.35
☐ 611	Braves Rookies	4.00	1.80	.50
	Bob Didier			
	Walt Hriniak			
	Gary Neibauer			
☐ 612	Jack Aker	3.50	1.55	.45
☐ 613	Jim Beauchamp	3.00	1.35	.35
☐ 614	Houston Rookies	3.00	1.35	.35
	Tom Griffin			
	Skip Guinn			
☐ 615	Len Gabrielson	3.00	1.35	.35
☐ 616	Don McMahon	3.00	1.35	.35
☐ 617	Jesse Gonder	3.00	1.35	.35
☐ 618	Ramon Webster	3.00	1.35	.35
☐ 619	Royals Rookies	3.50	1.55	.45
	Bill Butler			
	Pat Kelly			
	Juan Rios			

☐ 620	Dean Chance	3.50	1.55	.45
☐ 621	Bill Voss	3.00	1.35	.35
☐ 622	Dan Osinski	3.00	1.35	.35
☐ 623	Hank Allen	3.00	1.35	.35
☐ 624	NL Rookies	3.50	1.55	.45
	Darrel Chaney			
	Duffy Dyer			
	Terry Harmon			
☐ 625	Mack Jones UER	3.50	1.55	.45
	(Batting wrong)			
☐ 626	Gene Michael	3.50	1.55	.45
☐ 627	George Stone	3.00	1.35	.35
☐ 628	Red Sox Rookies	3.50	1.55	.45
	Bill Conigliaro			
	Syd O'Brien			
	Fred Wenz			
☐ 629	Jack Hamilton	3.00	1.35	.35
☐ 630	Bobby Bonds	35.00	16.00	4.40
☐ 631	John Kennedy	3.50	1.55	.45
☐ 632	Jon Warden	3.00	1.35	.35
☐ 633	Harry Walker MG	3.00	1.35	.35
☐ 634	Andy Etchebarren	3.00	1.35	.35
☐ 635	George Culver	3.00	1.35	.35
☐ 636	Woody Held	3.00	1.35	.35
☐ 637	Padres Rookies	3.50	1.55	.45
	Jerry DaVanon			
	Frank Reberger			
	Clay Kirby			
☐ 638	Ed Sprague	3.00	1.35	.35
☐ 639	Barry Moore	3.00	1.35	.35
☐ 640	Fergie Jenkins	20.00	9.00	2.50
☐ 641	NL Rookies	3.50	1.55	.45
	Bobby Darwin			
	John Miller			
	Tommy Dean			
☐ 642	John Hiller	3.00	1.35	.35
☐ 643	Billy Cowan	3.00	1.35	.35
☐ 644	Chuck Hinton	3.00	1.35	.35
☐ 645	George Brunet	3.00	1.35	.35
☐ 646	Expos Rookies	3.50	1.55	.45
	Dan McGinn			
	Carl Morton			
☐ 647	Dave Wickersham	3.00	1.35	.35
☐ 648	Bobby Wine	3.50	1.55	.45
☐ 649	Al Jackson	3.00	1.35	.35
☐ 650	Ted Williams MG	16.00	7.25	2.00
☐ 651	Gus Gil	3.50	1.55	.45
☐ 652	Eddie Watt	3.00	1.35	.35
☐ 653	Aurelio Rodriguez UER	5.00	2.20	.60
	(Photo actually			
	Angels' batboy)			
☐ 654	White Sox Rookies	3.50	1.55	.45
	Carlos May			
	Don Secrist			
	Rich Morales			
☐ 655	Mike Hershberger	3.00	1.35	.35
☐ 656	Dan Schneider	3.00	1.35	.35
☐ 657	Bobby Murcer	6.00	2.70	.75
☐ 658	AL Rookies	3.00	1.35	.35
	Tom Hall			
	Bill Burbach			
	Jim Miles			
☐ 659	Johnny Podres	3.50	1.55	.45
☐ 660	Reggie Smith	6.00	2.70	.75
☐ 661	Jim Merritt	3.00	1.35	.35
☐ 662	Royals Rookies	3.50	1.55	.45
	Dick Drago			
	George Spriggs			
	Bob Oliver			
☐ 663	Dick Radatz	3.50	1.55	.45
☐ 664	Ron Hunt	5.00	1.35	.40

1970 Topps

 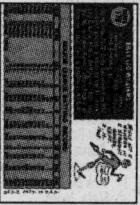

The cards in this 720-card set measure 2 1/2" by 3 1/2". The Topps set for 1970 has color photos surrounded by white frame lines and gray borders. The backs have a blue biographical section and a yellow record section. All-Star selections are featured on cards 450 to 469. Other topical subsets within this set include League Leaders (61-72), Playoffs cards (195-202), and World Series cards (305-310). There are graduations of scarcity, terminating in the high series (634-720), which are outlined in the value summary. The key Rookie Card in this set is Thurman Munson.

	NRMT	VG-E	GOOD
COMPLETE SET (720)	1800.00	800.00	220.00
COMMON CARD (1-372)	1.00	.45	.12
COMMON CARD (373-459)	1.50	.70	.19
COMMON CARD (460-546)	2.00	.90	.25
COMMON CARD (547-633)	4.00	1.80	.50
COMMON CARD (634-720)	10.00	4.50	1.25

☐ 1	New York Mets	16.00	5.00	1.50
	Team Card			
☐ 2	Diego Segui	1.50	.70	.19
☐ 3	Darrel Chaney	1.00	.45	.12
☐ 4	Tom Egan	1.00	.45	.12
☐ 5	Wes Parker	1.50	.70	.19
☐ 6	Grant Jackson	1.00	.45	.12
☐ 7	Indians Rookies	1.00	.45	.12
	Gary Boyd			
	Russ Nagelson			
☐ 8	Jose Martinez	1.00	.45	.12
☐ 9	Checklist 1	12.00	2.40	1.20
☐ 10	Carl Yastrzemski	15.00	6.75	1.85
☐ 11	Nate Colbert	1.00	.45	.12
☐ 12	John Hiller	1.50	.70	.19
☐ 13	Jack Hiatt	1.00	.45	.12
☐ 14	Hank Allen	1.00	.45	.12
☐ 15	Larry Dierker	1.00	.45	.12
☐ 16	Charlie Metro MG	1.00	.45	.12
☐ 17	Hoyt Wilhelm	4.00	1.80	.50
☐ 18	Carlos May	1.50	.70	.19
☐ 19	John Boccabella	1.00	.45	.12
☐ 20	Dave McNally	1.50	.70	.19
☐ 21	A's Rookies	6.00	2.70	.75
	Vida Blue			
	Gene Tenace			
☐ 22	Ray Washburn	1.00	.45	.12
☐ 23	Bill Robinson	1.50	.70	.19
☐ 24	Dick Selma	1.00	.45	.12

☐ 25	Cesar Tovar	1.00	.45	.12
☐ 26	Tug McGraw	1.50	.70	.19
☐ 27	Chuck Hinton	1.00	.45	.12
☐ 28	Billy Wilson	1.00	.45	.12
☐ 29	Sandy Alomar	1.50	.70	.19
☐ 30	Matty Alou	1.50	.70	.19
☐ 31	Marty Pattin	1.50	.70	.19
☐ 32	Harry Walker MG	1.00	.45	.12
☐ 33	Don Wert	1.00	.45	.12
☐ 34	Willie Crawford	1.00	.45	.12
☐ 35	Joel Horlen	1.00	.45	.12
☐ 36	Red Rookies	1.50	.70	.19
	Danny Breeden			
	Bernie Carbo			
☐ 37	Dick Drago	1.00	.45	.12
☐ 38	Mack Jones	1.00	.45	.12
☐ 39	Mike Nagy	1.00	.45	.12
☐ 40	Rich Allen	1.50	.70	.19
☐ 41	George Lauzerique	1.00	.45	.12
☐ 42	Tito Fuentes	1.00	.45	.12
☐ 43	Jack Aker	1.00	.45	.12
☐ 44	Roberto Pena	1.00	.45	.12
☐ 45	Dave Johnson	1.50	.70	.19
☐ 46	Ken Rudolph	1.00	.45	.12
☐ 47	Bob Miller	1.00	.45	.12
☐ 48	Gil Garrido	1.00	.45	.12
☐ 49	Tim Cullen	1.00	.45	.12
☐ 50	Tommie Agee	1.50	.70	.19
☐ 51	Bob Christian	1.00	.45	.12
☐ 52	Bruce Dal Canton	1.00	.45	.12
☐ 53	John Kennedy	1.00	.45	.12
☐ 54	Jeff Torborg	1.50	.70	.19
☐ 55	John Odom	1.00	.45	.12
☐ 56	Phillies Rookies	1.00	.45	.12
	Joe Lis			
	Scott Reid			
☐ 57	Pat Kelly	1.00	.45	.12
☐ 58	Dave Marshall	1.00	.45	.12
☐ 59	Dick Ellsworth	1.00	.45	.12
☐ 60	Jim Wynn	1.50	.70	.19
☐ 61	NL Batting Leaders	10.00	4.50	1.25
	Pete Rose			
	Bob Clemente			
	Cleon Jones			
☐ 62	AL Batting Leaders	3.50	1.55	.45
	Rod Carew			
	Reggie Smith			
	Tony Oliva			
☐ 63	NL RBI Leaders	4.00	1.80	.50
	Willie McCovey			
	Ron Santo			
	Tony Perez			
☐ 64	AL RBI Leaders	6.00	2.70	.75
	Harmon Killebrew			
	Boog Powell			
	Reggie Jackson			
☐ 65	NL Home Run Leaders	6.00	2.70	.75
	Willie McCovey			
	Hank Aaron			
	Lee May			
☐ 66	AL Home Run Leaders	6.00	2.70	.75
	Harmon Killebrew			
	Frank Howard			
	Reggie Jackson			
☐ 67	NL ERA Leaders	7.00	3.10	.85
	Juan Marichal			
	Steve Carlton			
	Bob Gibson			
☐ 68	AL ERA Leaders	3.00	1.35	.35
	Dick Bosman			
	Jim Palmer			
	Mike Cuellar			
☐ 69	NL Pitching Leaders	7.00	3.10	.85
	Tom Seaver			
	Phil Niekro			
	Fergie Jenkins			
	Juan Marichal			
☐ 70	AL Pitching Leaders	2.00	.90	.25
	Dennis McLain			
	Mike Cuellar			
	Dave Boswell			
	Dave McNally			
	Jim Perry			
	Mel Stottlemyre			
☐ 71	NL Strikeout Leaders	4.00	1.80	.50
	Fergie Jenkins			
	Bob Gibson			
	Bill Singer			
☐ 72	AL Strikeout Leaders	2.00	.90	.25
	Sam McDowell			
	Mickey Lolich			
	Andy Messersmith			
☐ 73	Wayne Granger	1.00	.45	.12
☐ 74	Angels Rookies	1.00	.45	.12
	Greg Washburn			
	Wally Wolf			
☐ 75	Jim Kaat	2.00	.90	.25
☐ 76	Carl Taylor	1.00	.45	.12
☐ 77	Frank Linzy	1.00	.45	.12
☐ 78	Joe Lahoud	1.00 *	.45	.12
☐ 79	Clay Kirby	1.00	.45	.12
☐ 80	Don Kessinger	1.50	.70	.19
☐ 81	Dave May	1.00	.45	.12
☐ 82	Frank Fernandez	1.00	.45	.12
☐ 83	Don Cardwell	1.00	.45	.12
☐ 84	Paul Casanova	1.00	.45	.12
☐ 85	Max Alvis	1.00	.45	.12
☐ 86	Lum Harris MG	1.00	.45	.12
☐ 87	Steve Renko	1.00	.45	.12
☐ 88	Pilots Rookies	1.50	.70	.19
	Miguel Fuentes			
	Dick Baney			
☐ 89	Juan Rios	1.00	.45	.12
☐ 90	Tim McCarver	1.50	.70	.19
☐ 91	Rich Morales	1.00	.45	.12
☐ 92	George Culver	1.00	.45	.12
☐ 93	Rick Renick	1.00	.45	.12
☐ 94	Freddie Patek	1.50	.70	.19
☐ 95	Earl Wilson	1.50	.70	.19
☐ 96	Cardinals Rookies	3.00	1.35	.35
	Leron Lee			
	Jerry Reuss			
☐ 97	Joe Moeller	1.00	.45	.12
☐ 98	Gates Brown	1.50	.70	.19
☐ 99	Bobby Pfeil	1.00	.45	.12
☐ 100	Mel Stottlemyre	1.50	.70	.19
☐ 101	Bobby Floyd	1.00	.45	.12
☐ 102	Joe Rudi	1.50	.70	.19
☐ 103	Frank Reberger	1.00	.45	.12
☐ 104	Gerry Moses	1.00	.45	.12
☐ 105	Tony Gonzalez	1.00	.45	.12
☐ 106	Darold Knowles	1.00	.45	.12
☐ 107	Bobby Etheridge	1.00	.45	.12
☐ 108	Tom Burgmeier	1.00	.45	.12
☐ 109	Expos Rookies	1.00	.45	.12
	Garry Jestadt			
	Carl Morton			
☐ 110	Bob Moose	1.00	.45	.12
☐ 111	Mike Hegan	1.50	.70	.19
☐ 112	Dave Nelson	1.00	.45	.12
☐ 113	Jim Ray	1.00	.45	.12
☐ 114	Gene Michael	1.50	.70	.19

☐	115 Alex Johnson	1.50	.70	.19
☐	116 Sparky Lyle	1.50	.70	.19
☐	117 Don Young	1.00	.45	.12
☐	118 George Mitterwald	1.00	.45	.12
☐	119 Chuck Taylor	1.00	.45	.12
☐	120 Sal Bando	1.50	.70	.19
☐	121 Orioles Rookies	1.00	.45	.12
	Fred Beene			
	Terry Crowley			
☐	122 George Stone	1.00	.45	.12
☐	123 Don Gutteridge MG	1.00	.45	.12
☐	124 Larry Jaster	1.00	.45	.12
☐	125 Deron Johnson	1.00	.45	.12
☐	126 Marty Martinez	1.00	.45	.12
☐	127 Joe Coleman	1.00	.45	.12
☐	128A Checklist 2 ERR	6.00	1.20	.60
	(226 R Perranoski)			
☐	128B Checklist 2 COR	6.00	1.20	.60
	(226 R. Perranoski)			
☐	129 Jimmie Price	1.00	.45	.12
☐	130 Ollie Brown	1.00	.45	.12
☐	131 Dodgers Rookies	1.00	.45	.12
	Ray Lamb			
	Bob Stinson			
☐	132 Jim McGlothlin	1.00	.45	.12
☐	133 Clay Carroll	1.00	.45	.12
☐	134 Danny Walton	1.00	.45	.12
☐	135 Dick Dietz	1.00	.45	.12
☐	136 Steve Hargan	1.00	.45	.12
☐	137 Art Shamsky	1.00	.45	.12
☐	138 Joe Foy	1.00	.45	.12
☐	139 Rich Nye	1.00	.45	.12
☐	140 Reggie Jackson	70.00	32.00	8.75
☐	141 Pirates Rookies	1.50	.70	.19
	Dave Cash			
	Johnny Jeter			
☐	142 Fritz Peterson	1.00	.45	.12
☐	143 Phil Gagliano	1.00	.45	.12
☐	144 Ray Culp	1.00	.45	.12
☐	145 Rico Carty	1.50	.70	.19
☐	146 Danny Murphy	1.00	.45	.12
☐	147 Angel Hermoso	1.00	.45	.12
☐	148 Earl Weaver MG	4.00	1.80	.50
☐	149 Billy Champion	1.00	.45	.12
☐	150 Harmon Killebrew	10.00	4.50	1.25
☐	151 Dave Roberts	1.00	.45	.12
☐	152 Ike Brown	1.00	.45	.12
☐	153 Gary Gentry	1.00	.45	.12
☐	154 Senators Rookies	1.00	.45	.12
	Jim Miles			
	Jan Dukes			
☐	155 Denis Menke	1.00	.45	.12
☐	156 Eddie Fisher	1.00	.45	.12
☐	157 Manny Mota	1.50	.70	.19
☐	158 Jerry McNertney	1.50	.70	.19
☐	159 Tommy Helms	1.50	.70	.19
☐	160 Phil Niekro	5.00	2.20	.60
☐	161 Richie Scheinblum	1.00	.45	.12
☐	162 Jerry Johnson	1.00	.45	.12
☐	163 Syd O'Brien	1.00	.45	.12
☐	164 Ty Cline	1.00	.45	.12
☐	165 Ed Kirkpatrick	1.00	.45	.12
☐	166 Al Oliver	2.00	.90	.25
☐	167 Bill Burbach	1.00	.45	.12
☐	168 Dave Watkins	1.00	.45	.12
☐	169 Tom Hall	1.00	.45	.12
☐	170 Billy Williams	6.00	2.70	.75
☐	171 Jim Nash	1.00	.45	.12
☐	172 Braves Rookies	2.50	1.10	.30
	Garry Hill			
	Ralph Garr			

☐	173 Jim Hicks	1.00	.45	.12
☐	174 Ted Sizemore	1.50	.70	.19
☐	175 Dick Bosman	1.00	.45	.12
☐	176 Jim Ray Hart	1.50	.70	.19
☐	177 Jim Northrup	1.50	.70	.19
☐	178 Denny Lemaster	1.00	.45	.12
☐	179 Ivan Murrell	1.00	.45	.12
☐	180 Tommy John	2.50	1.10	.30
☐	181 Sparky Anderson MG	5.00	2.20	.60
☐	182 Dick Hall	1.00	.45	.12
☐	183 Jerry Grote	1.00	.45	.12
☐	184 Ray Fosse	1.00	.45	.12
☐	185 Don Mincher	1.50	.70	.19
☐	186 Rick Joseph	1.00	.45	.12
☐	187 Mike Hedlund	1.00	.45	.12
☐	188 Manny Sanguillen	1.50	.70	.19
☐	189 Yankees Rookies	50.00	22.00	6.25
	Thurman Munson			
	Dave McDonald			
☐	190 Joe Torre	2.00	.90	.25
☐	191 Vicente Romo	1.00	.45	.12
☐	192 Jim Qualls	1.00	.45	.12
☐	193 Mike Wegener	1.00	.45	.12
☐	194 Chuck Manuel	1.00	.45	.12
☐	195 NL Playoff Game 1	15.00	6.75	1.85
	Tom Seaver wins opener			
☐	196 NL Playoff Game 2	2.50	1.10	.30
	Mets show muscle			
	(Ken Boswell)			
☐	197 NL Playoff Game 3	30.00	13.50	3.70
	Nolan Ryan saves			
	the day			
☐	198 NL Playoff Summary	15.00	6.75	1.85
	Mets celebrate			
	(Nolan Ryan)			
☐	199 AL Playoff Game 1	2.50	1.10	.30
	Orioles win squeaker			
	(Mike Cuellar)			
☐	200 AL Playoff Game 2	3.50	1.55	.45
	Boog Powell scores			
	winning run			
☐	201 AL Playoff Game 3	2.50	1.10	.30
	Birds wrap it up			
	(Boog Powell and			
	Andy Etchebarren)			
☐	202 AL Playoff Summary	2.50	1.10	.30
	Orioles celebrate			
☐	203 Rudy May	1.00	.45	.12
☐	204 Len Gabrielson	1.00	.45	.12
☐	205 Bert Campaneris	1.50	.70	.19
☐	206 Clete Boyer	1.50	.70	.19
☐	207 Tigers Rookies	1.00	.45	.12
	Norman McRae			
	Bob Reed			
☐	208 Fred Gladding	1.00	.45	.12
☐	209 Ken Suarez	1.00	.45	.12
☐	210 Juan Marichal	7.00	3.10	.85
☐	211 Ted Williams MG	12.00	5.50	1.50
☐	212 Al Santorini	1.00	.45	.12
☐	213 Andy Etchebarren	1.00	.45	.12
☐	214 Ken Boswell	1.00	.45	.12
☐	215 Reggie Smith	2.00	.90	.25
☐	216 Chuck Hartenstein	1.00	.45	.12
☐	217 Ron Hansen	1.00	.45	.12
☐	218 Ron Stone	1.00	.45	.12
☐	219 Jerry Kenney	1.00	.45	.12
☐	220 Steve Carlton	18.00	8.00	2.20
☐	221 Ron Brand	1.00	.45	.12
☐	222 Jim Rooker	1.50	.70	.19
☐	223 Nate Oliver	1.00	.45	.12
☐	224 Steve Barber	1.50	.70	.19

☐ 225	Lee May	1.50	.70	.19
☐ 226	Ron Perranoski	1.50	.70	.19
☐ 227	Astros Rookies	1.50	.70	.19
	John Mayberry			
	Bob Watkins			
☐ 229	Aurelio Rodriguez	1.50	.70	.19
☐ 230	Rich Robertson	1.00	.45	.12
☐ 230	Brooks Robinson	14.00	6.25	1.75
☐ 231	Luis Tiant	1.50	.70	.19
☐ 232	Bob Didier	1.00	.45	.12
☐ 233	Lew Krausse	1.00	.45	.12
☐ 234	Tommy Dean	1.00	.45	.12
☐ 235	Mike Epstein	1.00	.45	.12
☐ 236	Bob Veale	1.50	.70	.19
☐ 237	Russ Gibson	1.00	.45	.12
☐ 238	Jose Laboy	1.00	.45	.12
☐ 239	Ken Berry	1.00	.45	.12
☐ 240	Fergie Jenkins	7.00	3.10	.85
☐ 241	Royals Rookies	1.00	.45	.12
	Al Fitzmorris			
	Scott Northey			
☐ 242	Walter Alston MG	2.00	.90	.25
☐ 243	Joe Sparma	1.00	.45	.12
☐ 244A	Checklist 3	6.00	1.20	.60
	(Red bat on front)			
☐ 244B	Checklist 3	6.00	1.20	.60
	(Brown bat on front)			
☐ 245	Leo Cardenas	1.00	.45	.12
☐ 246	Jim McAndrew	1.00	.45	.12
☐ 247	Lou Klimchock	1.00	.45	.12
☐ 248	Jesus Alou	1.00	.45	.12
☐ 249	Bob Locker	1.00	.45	.12
☐ 250	Willie McCovey UER	10.00	4.50	1.25
	(1963 San Francisci)			
☐ 251	Dick Schofield	1.00	.45	.12
☐ 252	Lowell Palmer	1.00	.45	.12
☐ 253	Ron Woods	1.00	.45	.12
☐ 254	Camilo Pascual	1.50	.70	.19
☐ 255	Jim Spencer	1.00	.45	.12
☐ 256	Vic Davalillo	1.00	.45	.12
☐ 257	Dennis Higgins	1.00	.45	.12
☐ 258	Paul Popovich	1.00	.45	.12
☐ 259	Tommie Reynolds	1.00	.45	.12
☐ 260	Claude Osteen	1.50	.70	.19
☐ 261	Curt Motton	1.00	.45	.12
☐ 262	Padres Rookies	1.00	.45	.12
	Jerry Morales			
	Jim Williams			
☐ 263	Duane Josephson	1.50	.70	.19
☐ 264	Rich Hebner	1.50	.70	.19
☐ 265	Randy Hundley	1.00	.45	.12
☐ 266	Wally Bunker	1.00	.45	.12
☐ 267	Twins Rookies	1.00	.45	.12
	Herman Hill			
	Paul Ratliff			
☐ 268	Claude Raymond	1.00	.45	.12
☐ 269	Cesar Gutierrez	1.00	.45	.12
☐ 270	Chris Short	1.00	.45	.12
☐ 271	Greg Goossen	1.00	.45	.12
☐ 272	Hector Torres	1.00	.45	.12
☐ 273	Ralph Houk MG	1.50	.70	.19
☐ 274	Gerry Arrigo	1.00	.45	.12
☐ 275	Duke Sims	1.00	.45	.12
☐ 276	Ron Hunt	1.00	.45	.12
☐ 277	Paul Doyle	1.00	.45	.12
☐ 278	Tommie Aaron	1.50	.70	.19
☐ 279	Bill Lee	2.00	.90	.25
☐ 280	Donn Clendenon	1.50	.70	.19
☐ 281	Casey Cox	1.00	.45	.12
☐ 282	Steve Huntz	1.00	.45	.12
☐ 283	Angel Bravo	1.00	.45	.12
☐ 284	Jack Baldschun	1.00	.45	.12
☐ 285	Paul Blair	1.50	.70	.19
☐ 286	Dodgers Rookies	6.00	2.70	.75
	Jack Jenkins			
	Bill Buckner			
☐ 287	Fred Talbot	1.00	.45	.12
☐ 288	Larry Hisle	1.50	.70	.19
☐ 289	Gene Brabender	1.00	.45	.12
☐ 290	Rod Carew	18.00	8.00	2.20
☐ 291	Leo Durocher MG	3.00	1.35	.35
☐ 292	Eddie Leon	1.00	.45	.12
☐ 293	Bob Bailey	1.00	.45	.12
☐ 294	Jose Azcue	1.00	.45	.12
☐ 295	Cecil Upshaw	1.00	.45	.12
☐ 296	Woody Woodward	1.50	.70	.19
☐ 297	Curt Blefary	1.00	.45	.12
☐ 298	Ken Henderson	1.00	.45	.12
☐ 299	Buddy Bradford	1.00	.45	.12
☐ 300	Tom Seaver	40.00	18.00	5.00
☐ 301	Chico Salmon	1.00	.45	.12
☐ 302	Jeff James	1.00	.45	.12
☐ 303	Brant Alyea	1.00	.45	.12
☐ 304	Bill Russell	5.00	2.20	.60
☐ 305	World Series Game 1.	3.00	1.35	.35
	Don Buford leadoff			
	homer			
☐ 306	World Series Game 2.	3.00	1.35	.35
	Donn Clendenon's			
	homer breaks ice			
☐ 307	World Series Game 3.	3.00	1.35	.35
	Tommie Agee's catch			
	saves the day			
☐ 308	World Series Game 4.	3.00	1.35	.35
	J.C. Martin's bunt			
	ends deadlock			
☐ 309	World Series Game 5.	3.50	1.55	.45
	Jerry Koosman			
	shuts door			
☐ 310	World Series Summary	5.00	2.20	.60
	Mets whoop it up			
☐ 311	Dick Green	1.00	.45	.12
☐ 312	Mike Torrez	1.50	.70	.19
☐ 313	Mayo Smith MG	1.00	.45	.12
☐ 314	Bill McCool	1.00	.45	.12
☐ 315	Luis Aparicio	4.00	1.80	.50
☐ 316	Skip Guinn	1.00	.45	.12
☐ 317	Red Sox Rookies	1.50	.70	.19
	Billy Conigliaro			
	Luis Alvarado			
☐ 318	Willie Smith	1.00	.45	.12
☐ 319	Clay Dalrymple	1.00	.45	.12
☐ 320	Jim Maloney	1.50	.70	.19
☐ 321	Lou Piniella	3.00	1.35	.35
☐ 322	Luke Walker	1.00	.45	.12
☐ 323	Wayne Comer	1.00	.45	.12
☐ 324	Tony Taylor	1.00	.45	.12
☐ 325	Dave Boswell	1.00	.45	.12
☐ 326	Bill Voss	1.00	.45	.12
☐ 327	Hal King	1.00	.45	.12
☐ 328	George Brunet	1.00	.45	.12
☐ 329	Chris Cannizzaro	1.00	.45	.12
☐ 330	Lou Brock	10.00	4.50	1.25
☐ 331	Chuck Dobson	1.00	.45	.12
☐ 332	Bobby Wine	1.00	.45	.12
☐ 333	Bobby Murcer	2.00	.90	.25
☐ 334	Phil Regan	1.50	.70	.19
☐ 335	Bill Freehan	1.50	.70	.19
☐ 336	Del Unser	1.00	.45	.12
☐ 337	Mike McCormick	1.50	.70	.19
☐ 338	Paul Schaal	1.00	.45	.12
☐ 339	Johnny Edwards	1.00	.45	.12

☐ 340	Tony Conigliaro	3.00 •	1.35	.35
☐ 341	Bill Sudakis	1.00	.45	.12
☐ 342	Wilbur Wood	1.50	.70	.19
☐ 343A	Checklist 4 (Red bat on front)	6.00	1.20	.60
☐ 343B	Checklist 4 (Brown bat on front)	6.00	1.20	.60
☐ 344	Marcelino Lopez	1.00	.45	.12
☐ 345	Al Ferrara	1.00	.45	.12
☐ 346	Red Schoendienst MG	2.00	.90	.25
☐ 347	Russ Snyder	1.00	.45	.12
☐ 348	Mets Rookies	1.50	.70	.19
	Mike Jorgensen			
	Jesse Hudson			
☐ 349	Steve Hamilton	1.00	.45	.12
☐ 350	Roberto Clemente	60.00	27.00	7.50
☐ 351	Tom Murphy	1.00	.45	.12
☐ 352	Bob Barton	1.00	.45	.12
☐ 353	Stan Williams	1.00	.45	.12
☐ 354	Amos Otis	1.50	.70	.19
☐ 355	Doug Rader	1.50	.70	.19
☐ 356	Fred Lasher	1.00	.45	.12
☐ 357	Bob Burda	1.00	.45	.12
☐ 358	Pedro Borbon	1.50	.70	.19
☐ 359	Phil Roof	1.00	.45	.12
☐ 360	Curt Flood	.50	.23	.06
☐ 361	Ray Jarvis	1.00	.45	.12
☐ 362	Joe Hague	1.00	.45	.12
☐ 363	Tom Shopay	1.00	.45	.12
☐ 364	Dan McGinn	1.00	.45	.12
☐ 365	Zoilo Versalles	1.00	.45	.12
☐ 366	Barry Moore	1.00	.45	.12
☐ 367	Mike Lum	1.00	.45	.12
☐ 368	Ed Herrmann	1.00	.45	.12
☐ 369	Alan Foster	1.00	.45	.12
☐ 370	Tommy Harper	1.50	.70	.19
☐ 371	Rod Gaspar	1.00	.45	.12
☐ 372	Dave Giusti	1.50	.70	.19
☐ 373	Roy White	1.75	.80	.22
☐ 374	Tommie Sisk	1.50	.70	.19
☐ 375	Johnny Callison	1.75	.80	.22
☐ 376	Lefty Phillips MG	1.50	.70	.19
☐ 377	Bill Butler	1.50	.70	.19
☐ 378	Jim Davenport	1.50	.70	.19
☐ 379	Tom Tischinski	1.50	.70	.19
☐ 380	Tony Perez	7.00	3.10	.85
☐ 381	Athletics Rookies	1.50	.70	.19
	Bobby Brooks			
	Mike Olivo			
☐ 382	Jack DiLauro	1.50	.70	.19
☐ 383	Mickey Stanley	1.75	.80	.22
☐ 384	Gary Neibauer	1.50	.70	.19
☐ 385	George Scott	1.75	.80	.22
☐ 386	Bill Dillman	1.50	.70	.19
☐ 387	Baltimore Orioles Team Card	3.00	1.35	.35
☐ 388	Byron Browne	1.50	.70	.19
☐ 389	Jim Shellenback	1.50	.70	.19
☐ 390	Willie Davis	1.75	.80	.22
☐ 391	Larry Brown	1.50	.70	.19
☐ 392	Walt Hriniak	1.50	.70	.19
☐ 393	John Gelnar	1.50	.70	.19
☐ 394	Gil Hodges MG	4.00	1.80	.50
☐ 395	Walt Williams	1.50	.70	.19
☐ 396	Steve Blass	1.75	.80	.22
☐ 397	Roger Repoz	1.50	.70	.19
☐ 398	Bill Stoneman	1.50	.70	.19
☐ 399	New York Yankees Team Card	3.00	1.35	.35
☐ 400	Denny McLain	2.00	.90	.25
☐ 401	Giants Rookies	1.50	.70	.19
	John Harrell			
	Bernie Williams			
☐ 402	Ellie Rodriguez	1.50	.70	.19
☐ 403	Jim Bunning	2.50	1.10	.30
☐ 404	Rich Reese	1.50	.70	.19
☐ 405	Bill Hands	1.50	.70	.19
☐ 406	Mike Andrews	1.50	.70	.19
☐ 407	Bob Watson	1.75	.80	.22
☐ 408	Paul Lindblad	1.50	.70	.19
☐ 409	Bob Tolan	1.75	.80	.22
☐ 410	Boog Powell	4.00	1.80	.50
☐ 411	Los Angeles Dodgers. Team Card	3.00	1.35	.35
☐ 412	Larry Burchart	1.50	.70	.19
☐ 413	Sonny Jackson	1.50	.70	.19
☐ 414	Paul Edmondson	1.50	.70	.19
☐ 415	Julian Javier	1.75	.80	.22
☐ 416	Joe Verbanic	1.50	.70	.19
☐ 417	John Bateman	1.50	.70	.19
☐ 418	John Donaldson	1.50	.70	.19
☐ 419	Ron Taylor	1.50	.70	.19
☐ 420	Ken McMullen	1.75	.80	.22
☐ 421	Pat Dobson	1.75	.80	.22
☐ 422	Royals Team	3.00	1.35	.35
☐ 423	Jerry May	1.50	.70	.19
☐ 424	Mike Kilkenny (Inconsistent design, card number in white circle)	1.50	.70	.19
☐ 425	Bobby Bonds	6.00	2.70	.75
☐ 426	Bill Rigney MG	1.50	.70	.19
☐ 427	Fred Norman	1.50	.70	.19
☐ 428	Don Buford	1.50	.70	.19
☐ 429	Cubs Rookies	1.50	.70	.19
	Randy Bobb			
	Jim Cosman			
☐ 430	Andy Messersmith	1.75	.80	.22
☐ 431	Ron Swoboda	1.75	.80	.22
☐ 432A	Checklist 5 ("Baseball" in yellow letters)	6.00	1.20	.60
☐ 432B	Checklist 5 ("Baseball" in white letters)	6.00	1.20	.60
☐ 433	Ron Bryant	1.50	.70	.19
☐ 434	Felipe Alou	1.75	.80	.22
☐ 435	Nelson Briles	1.75	.80	.22
☐ 436	Philadelphia Phillies Team Card	3.00	1.35	.35
☐ 437	Danny Cater	1.50	.70	.19
☐ 438	Pat Jarvis	1.50	.70	.19
☐ 439	Lee Maye	1.50	.70	.19
☐ 440	Bill Mazeroski	3.00	1.35	.35
☐ 441	John O'Donoghue	1.50	.70	.19
☐ 442	Gene Mauch MG	1.75	.80	.22
☐ 443	Al Jackson	1.50	.70	.19
☐ 444	White Sox Rookies	1.50	.70	.19
	Billy Farmer			
	John Matias			
☐ 445	Vada Pinson	1.75	.80	.22
☐ 446	Billy Grabarkewitz	1.50	.70	.19
☐ 447	Lee Stange	1.50	.70	.19
☐ 448	Houston Astros Team Card	3.00	1.35	.35
☐ 449	Jim Palmer	14.00	6.25	1.75
☐ 450	Willie McCovey AS	7.00	3.10	.85
☐ 451	Boog Powell AS	2.50	1.10	.30
☐ 452	Felix Millan AS	2.00	.90	.25
☐ 453	Rod Carew AS	7.00	3.10	.85
☐ 454	Ron Santo AS	2.50	1.10	.30
☐ 455	Brooks Robinson AS	7.00	3.10	.85

☐ 456	Don Kessinger AS	2.00	.90	.25
☐ 457	Rico Petrocelli AS	2.50	1.10	.30
☐ 458	Pete Rose AS	14.00	6.25	1.75
☐ 459	Reggie Jackson AS ..	14.00	6.25	1.75
☐ 460	Matty Alou AS	2.50	1.10	.30
☐ 461	Carl Yastrzemski AS	10.00	4.50	1.25
☐ 462	Hank Aaron AS	15.00	6.75	1.85
☐ 463	Frank Robinson AS	7.00	3.10	.85
☐ 464	Johnny Bench AS	14.00	6.25	1.75
☐ 465	Bill Freehan AS	3.00	1.35	.35
☐ 466	Juan Marichal AS	4.00	1.80	.50
☐ 467	Denny McLain AS	3.00	1.35	.35
☐ 468	Jerry Koosman AS	3.00	1.35	.35
☐ 469	Sam McDowell AS	2.50	1.10	.30
☐ 470	Willie Stargell AS	10.00	4.50	1.25
☐ 471	Chris Zachary	2.00	.90	.25
☐ 472	Braves Team	3.50	1.55	.45
☐ 473	Don Bryant	2.00	.90	.25
☐ 474	Dick Kelley	2.00	.90	.25
☐ 475	Dick McAuliffe	2.50	1.10	.30
☐ 476	Don Shaw	2.00	.90	.25
☐ 477	Orioles Rookies	2.00	.90	.25
	Al Severinsen			
	Roger Freed			
☐ 478	Bobby Heise	2.00	.90	.25
☐ 479	Dick Woodson	2.00	.90	.25
☐ 480	Glenn Beckert	2.50	1.10	.30
☐ 481	Jose Tartabull	2.50	1.10	.30
☐ 482	Tom Hilgendorf	2.00	.90	.25
☐ 483	Gail Hopkins	2.00	.90	.25
☐ 484	Gary Nolan	2.50	1.10	.30
☐ 485	Jay Johnstone	2.50	1.10	.30
☐ 486	Terry Harmon	2.00	.90	.25
☐ 487	Cisco Carlos	2.00	.90	.25
☐ 488	J.C. Martin	2.00	.90	.25
☐ 489	Eddie Kasko MG	2.00	.90	.25
☐ 490	Bill Singer	2.50	1.10	.30
☐ 491	Graig Nettles	6.00	2.70	.75
☐ 492	Astros Rookies	2.00	.90	.25
	Keith Lampard			
	Scipio Spinks			
☐ 493	Lindy McDaniel	2.50	1.10	.30
☐ 494	Larry Stahl	2.00	.90	.25
☐ 495	Dave Morehead	2.00	.90	.25
☐ 496	Steve Whitaker	2.00	.90	.25
☐ 497	Eddie Watt	2.00	.90	.25
☐ 498	Al Weis	2.00	.90	.25
☐ 499	Skip Lockwood	2.00	.90	.25
☐ 500	Hank Aaron	55.00	25.00	7.00
☐ 501	Chicago White Sox	3.50	1.55	.45
	Team Card			
☐ 502	Rollie Fingers	10.00	4.50	1.25
☐ 503	Dal Maxvill	2.00	.90	.25
☐ 504	Don Pavletich	2.00	.90	.25
☐ 505	Ken Holtzman	2.50	1.10	.30
☐ 506	Ed Stroud	2.00	.90	.25
☐ 507	Pat Corrales	2.50	1.10	.30
☐ 508	Joe Niekro	2.50	1.10	.30
☐ 509	Montreal Expos	3.50	1.55	.45
	Team Card			
☐ 510	Tony Oliva	3.00	1.35	.35
☐ 511	Joe Hoerner	2.00	.90	.25
☐ 512	Billy Harris	2.00	.90	.25
☐ 513	Preston Gomez MG	2.00	.90	.25
☐ 514	Steve Hovley	2.00	.90	.25
☐ 515	Don Wilson	2.50	1.10	.30
☐ 516	Yankees Rookies	2.00	.90	.25
	John Ellis			
	Jim Lyttle			
☐ 517	Joe Gibbon	2.00	.90	.25
☐ 518	Bill Melton	2.00	.90	.25

☐ 519	Don McMahon	2.00	.90	.25
☐ 520	Willie Horton	2.50	1.10	.30
☐ 521	Cal Koonce	2.00	.90	.25
☐ 522	Angels Team	3.50	1.55	.45
☐ 523	Jose Pena	2.00	.90	.25
☐ 524	Alvin Dark MG	2.50	1.10	.30
☐ 525	Jerry Adair	2.00	.90	.25
☐ 526	Ron Herbel	2.00	.90	.25
☐ 527	Don Bosch	2.00	.90	.25
☐ 528	Elrod Hendricks	2.00	.90	.25
☐ 529	Bob Aspromonte	2.00	.90	.25
☐ 530	Bob Gibson	14.00	6.25	1.75
☐ 531	Ron Clark	2.00	.90	.25
☐ 532	Danny Murtaugh MG	2.50	1.10	.30
☐ 533	Buzz Stephen	2.00	.90	.25
☐ 534	Minnesota Twins	3.50	1.55	.45
	Team Card			
☐ 535	Andy Kosco	2.00	.90	.25
☐ 536	Mike Kekich	2.00	.90	.25
☐ 537	Joe Morgan	10.00	4.50	1.25
☐ 538	Bob Humphreys	2.00	.90	.25
☐ 539	Phillies Rookies	6.00	2.70	.75
	Denny Doyle			
	Larry Bowa			
☐ 540	Gary Peters	2.00	.90	.25
☐ 541	Bill Heath	2.00	.90	.25
☐ 542	Checklist 6	6.00	1.20	.60
☐ 543	Clyde Wright	2.00	.90	.25
☐ 544	Cincinnati Reds	3.50	1.55	.45
	Team Card			
☐ 545	Ken Harrelson	2.50	1.10	.30
☐ 546	Ron Reed	2.00	.90	.25
☐ 547	Rick Monday	5.00	2.20	.60
☐ 548	Howie Reed	4.00	1.80	.50
☐ 549	St. Louis Cardinals	6.00	2.70	.75
	Team Card			
☐ 550	Frank Howard	5.00	2.20	.60
☐ 551	Dock Ellis	5.00	2.20	.60
☐ 552	Royals Rookies	4.00	1.80	.50
	Don O'Riley			
	Dennis Paepke			
	Fred Rico			
☐ 553	Jim Lefebvre	5.00	2.20	.60
☐ 554	Tom Timmermann	4.00	1.80	.50
☐ 555	Orlando Cepeda	6.00	2.70	.75
☐ 556	Dave Bristol MG	5.00	2.20	.60
☐ 557	Ed Kranepool	5.00	2.20	.60
☐ 558	Vern Fuller	4.00	1.80	.50
☐ 559	Tommy Davis	5.00	2.20	.60
☐ 560	Gaylord Perry	10.00	4.50	1.25
☐ 561	Tom McCraw	4.00	1.80	.50
☐ 562	Ted Abernathy	4.00	1.80	.50
☐ 563	Boston Red Sox	6.00	2.70	.75
	Team Card			
☐ 564	Johnny Briggs	4.00	1.80	.50
☐ 565	Jim Hunter	10.00	4.50	1.25
☐ 566	Gene Alley	5.00	2.20	.60
☐ 567	Bob Oliver	4.00	1.80	.50
☐ 568	Stan Bahnsen	5.00	2.20	.60
☐ 569	Cookie Rojas	5.00	2.20	.60
☐ 570	Jim Fregosi	5.00	2.20	.60
☐ 571	Jim Brewer	4.00	1.80	.50
☐ 572	Frank Quilici MG	4.00	1.80	.50
☐ 573	Padres Rookies	4.00	1.80	.50
	Mike Corkins			
	Rafael Robles			
	Ron Slocum			
☐ 574	Bobby Bolin	5.00	2.20	.60
☐ 575	Cleon Jones	5.00	2.20	.60
☐ 576	Milt Pappas	5.00	2.20	.60
☐ 577	Bernie Allen	4.00	1.80	.50

☐ 578	Tom Griffin	4.00	1.80	.50
☐ 579	Detroit Tigers Team Card	6.00	2.70	.75
☐ 580	Pete Rose	50.00	22.00	6.25
☐ 581	Tom Satriano	4.00	1.80	.50
☐ 582	Mike Paul	4.00	1.80	.50
☐ 583	Hal Lanier	4.00	1.80	.50
☐ 584	Al Downing	5.00	2.20	.60
☐ 585	Rusty Staub	5.00	2.20	.60
☐ 586	Rickey Clark	4.00	1.80	.50
☐ 587	Jose Arcia	4.00	1.80	.50
☐ 588A	Checklist 7 ERR (666 Adolfo)	8.00	1.60	.80
☐ 588B	Checklist 7 COR (666 Adolpho)	6.00	1.80	.60
☐ 589	Joe Keough	4.00	1.80	.50
☐ 590	Mike Cuellar	5.00	2.20	.60
☐ 591	Mike Ryan UER (Pitching Record header on card back)	4.00	1.80	.50
☐ 592	Daryl Patterson	4.00	1.80	.50
☐ 593	Chicago Cubs Team Card	6.00	2.70	.75
☐ 594	Jake Gibbs	4.00	1.80	.50
☐ 595	Maury Wills	5.00	2.20	.60
☐ 596	Mike Hershberger	5.00	2.20	.60
☐ 597	Sonny Siebert	4.00	1.80	.50
☐ 598	Joe Pepitone	5.00	2.20	.60
☐ 599	Senators Rookies Dick Stelmaszek Gene Martin Dick Such	4.00	1.80	.50
☐ 600	Willie Mays	70.00	32.00	8.75
☐ 601	Pete Richert	4.00	1.80	.50
☐ 602	Ted Savage	4.00	1.80	.50
☐ 603	Ray Oyler	4.00	1.80	.50
☐ 604	Clarence Gaston	5.00	2.20	.60
☐ 605	Rick Wise	5.00	2.20	.60
☐ 606	Chico Ruiz	4.00	1.80	.50
☐ 607	Gary Waslewski	4.00	1.80	.50
☐ 608	Pittsburgh Pirates Team Card	6.00	2.70	.75
☐ 609	Buck Martinez (Inconsistent design, card number in white circle)	5.00	2.20	.60
☐ 610	Jerry Koosman	5.00	2.20	.60
☐ 611	Norm Cash	5.00	2.20	.60
☐ 612	Jim Hickman	5.00	2.20	.60
☐ 613	Dave Baldwin	5.00	2.20	.60
☐ 614	Mike Shannon	5.00	2.20	.60
☐ 615	Mark Belanger	5.00	2.20	.60
☐ 616	Jim Merritt	4.00	1.80	.50
☐ 617	Jim French	4.00	1.80	.50
☐ 618	Billy Wynne	4.00	1.80	.50
☐ 619	Norm Miller	4.00	1.80	.50
☐ 620	Jim Perry	5.00	2.20	.60
☐ 621	Braves Rookies Mike McQueen Darrell Evans Rick Kester	10.00	4.50	1.25
☐ 622	Don Sutton	10.00	4.50	1.25
☐ 623	Horace Clarke	4.00	1.80	.50
☐ 624	Clyde King MG	4.00	1.80	.50
☐ 625	Dean Chance	4.00	1.80	.50
☐ 626	Dave Ricketts	4.00	1.80	.50
☐ 627	Gary Wagner	4.00	1.80	.50
☐ 628	Wayne Garrett	4.00	1.80	.50
☐ 629	Merv Rettenmund	4.00	1.80	.50
☐ 630	Ernie Banks	60.00	27.00	7.50
☐ 631	Oakland Athletics Team Card	6.00	2.70	.75
☐ 632	Gary Sutherland	4.00	1.80	.50
☐ 633	Roger Nelson	4.00	1.80	.50
☐ 634	Bud Harrelson	11.00	4.90	1.35
☐ 635	Bob Allison	11.00	4.90	1.35
☐ 636	Jim Stewart	10.00	4.50	1.25
☐ 637	Cleveland Indians Team Card	12.00	5.50	1.50
☐ 638	Frank Bertaina	10.00	4.50	1.25
☐ 639	Dave Campbell	10.00	4.50	1.25
☐ 640	Al Kaline	50.00	22.00	6.25
☐ 641	Al McBean	10.00	4.50	1.25
☐ 642	Angels Rookies Greg Garrett Gordon Lund Jarvis Tatum	10.00	4.50	1.25
☐ 643	Jose Pagan	10.00	4.50	1.25
☐ 644	Gerry Nyman	10.00	4.50	1.25
☐ 645	Don Money	11.00	4.90	1.35
☐ 646	Jim Britton	10.00	4.50	1.25
☐ 647	Tom Matchick	10.00	4.50	1.25
☐ 648	Larry Haney	10.00	4.50	1.25
☐ 649	Jimmie Hall	10.00	4.50	1.25
☐ 650	Sam McDowell	11.00	4.90	1.35
☐ 651	Jim Gosger	10.00	4.50	1.25
☐ 652	Rich Rollins	11.00	4.90	1.35
☐ 653	Moe Drabowsky	10.00	4.50	1.25
☐ 654	NL Rookies Oscar Gamble Boots Day Angel Mangual	12.00	5.50	1.50
☐ 655	John Roseboro	11.00	4.90	1.35
☐ 656	Jim Hardin	10.00	4.50	1.25
☐ 657	San Diego Padres Team Card	12.00	5.50	1.50
☐ 658	Ken Tatum	10.00	4.50	1.25
☐ 659	Pete Ward	10.00	4.50	1.25
☐ 660	Johnny Bench	100.00	45.00	12.50
☐ 661	Jerry Robertson	10.00	4.50	1.25
☐ 662	Frank Lucchesi MG	10.00	4.50	1.25
☐ 663	Tito Francona	10.00	4.50	1.25
☐ 664	Bob Robertson	10.00	4.50	1.25
☐ 665	Jim Lonborg	11.00	4.90	1.35
☐ 666	Adolpho Phillips	10.00	4.50	1.25
☐ 667	Bob Meyer	11.00	4.90	1.35
☐ 668	Bob Tillman	10.00	4.50	1.25
☐ 669	White Sox Rookies Bart Johnson Dan Lazar Mickey Scott	10.00	4.50	1.25
☐ 670	Ron Santo	12.00	5.50	1.50
☐ 671	Jim Campanis	10.00	4.50	1.25
☐ 672	Leon McFadden	10.00	4.50	1.25
☐ 673	Ted Uhlaender	10.00	4.50	1.25
☐ 674	Dave Leonhard	10.00	4.50	1.25
☐ 675	Jose Cardenal	11.00	4.90	1.35
☐ 676	Washington Senators Team Card	12.00	5.50	1.50
☐ 677	Woodie Fryman	10.00	4.50	1.25
☐ 678	Dave Duncan	11.00	4.90	1.35
☐ 679	Ray Sadecki	10.00	4.50	1.25
☐ 680	Rico Petrocelli	11.00	4.90	1.35
☐ 681	Bob Garibaldi	10.00	4.50	1.25
☐ 682	Dalton Jones	10.00	4.50	1.25
☐ 683	Reds Rookies Vern Geishert Hal McRae Wayne Simpson	10.00	4.50	1.25
☐ 684	Jack Fisher	10.00	4.50	1.25
☐ 685	Tom Haller	10.00	4.50	1.25
☐ 686	Jackie Hernandez	10.00	4.50	1.25

		NRMT	VG-E	GOOD
☐ 687	Bob Priddy	10.00	4.50	1.25
☐ 688	Ted Kubiak	11.00	4.90	1.35
☐ 689	Frank Tepedino	10.00	4.50	1.25
☐ 690	Ron Fairly	11.00	4.90	1.35
☐ 691	Joe Grzenda	10.00	4.50	1.25
☐ 692	Duffy Dyer	10.00	4.50	1.25
☐ 693	Bob Johnson	10.00	4.50	1.25
☐ 694	Gary Ross	10.00	4.50	1.25
☐ 695	Bobby Knoop	10.00	4.50	1.25
☐ 696	San Francisco Giants	12.00	5.50	1.50
	Team Card			
☐ 697	Jim Hannan	10.00	4.50	1.25
☐ 698	Tom Tresh	11.00	4.90	1.35
☐ 699	Hank Aguirre	10.00	4.50	1.25
☐ 700	Frank Robinson	50.00	22.00	6.25
☐ 701	Jack Billingham	10.00	4.50	1.25
☐ 702	AL Rookies	10.00	4.50	1.25
	Bob Johnson			
	Ron Klimkowski			
	Bill Zepp			
☐ 703	Lou Marone	10.00	4.50	1.25
☐ 704	Frank Baker	10.00	4.50	1.25
☐ 705	Tony Cloninger UER.	10.00	4.50	1.25
	(Batter headings			
	on card back)			
☐ 706	John McNamara MG	10.00	4.50	1.25
☐ 707	Kevin Collins	10.00	4.50	1.25
☐ 708	Jose Santiago	10.00	4.50	1.25
☐ 709	Mike Fiore	10.00	4.50	1.25
☐ 710	Felix Millan	10.00	4.50	1.25
☐ 711	Ed Brinkman	10.00	4.50	1.25
☐ 712	Nolan Ryan	425.00	190.00	52.50
☐ 713	Seattle Pilots	25.00	11.00	3.10
	Team Card			
☐ 714	Al Spangler	10.00	4.50	1.25
☐ 715	Mickey Lolich	11.00	4.90	1.35
☐ 716	Cardinals Rookies	11.00	4.90	1.35
	Sal Campisi			
	Reggie Cleveland			
	Santiago Guzman			
☐ 717	Tom Phoebus	10.00	4.50	1.25
☐ 718	Ed Spiezio	10.00	4.50	1.25
☐ 719	Jim Roland	10.00	4.50	1.25
☐ 720	Rick Reichardt	14.00	4.70	1.35

1971 Topps

The cards in this 752-card set measure 2 1/2" by 3 1/2". The 1971 Topps set is a challenge to complete in strict mint condition because the black obverse border is easily scratched and damaged. An unusual feature of this set is that the player is also pictured in black and white on the back of the card. Featured subsets within this set include League Leaders (61-72), Playoffs cards (195-202), and World Series cards (327-332). Cards 524-643 and the last series (644-752) are somewhat scarce. The last series was printed in two sheets of 132. On the printing sheets 44 cards were printed in 50 percent greater quantity than the other 66 cards. These 66 (slightly) shorter-printed numbers are identified in the checklist below by SP. The key Rookie Cards in this set are the multi-player Rookie Card of Dusty Baker and Don Baylor and the individual cards of Bert Blyleven, Dave Concepcion, Steve Garvey, and Ted Simmons.

		NRMT	VG-E	GOOD
COMPLETE SET (752)		2000.00	900.00	250.00
COMMON CARD (1-393)		1.75	.80	.22
COMMON CARD (394-523)		2.50	1.10	.30
COMMON CARD (524-643)		4.00	1.80	.50
COMMON CARD (644-752)		8.00	3.60	1.00
☐ 1	Baltimore Orioles	15.00	5.00	2.00
	Team Card			
☐ 2	Dock Ellis	2.50	1.10	.30
☐ 3	Dick McAuliffe	2.50	1.10	.30
☐ 4	Vic Davalillo	1.75	.80	.22
☐ 5	Thurman Munson	18.00	8.00	2.20
☐ 6	Ed Spiezio	1.75	.80	.22
☐ 7	Jim Holt	1.75	.80	.22
☐ 8	Mike McQueen	1.75	.80	.22
☐ 9	George Scott	2.50	1.10	.30
☐ 10	Claude Osteen	2.50	1.10	.30
☐ 11	Elliott Maddox	2.50	1.10	.30
☐ 12	Johnny Callison	2.50	1.10	.30
☐ 13	White Sox Rookies	1.75	.80	.22
	Charlie Brinkman			
	Dick Moloney			
☐ 14	Dave Concepcion	18.00	8.00	2.20
☐ 15	Andy Messersmith	2.50	1.10	.30
☐ 16	Ken Singleton	4.00	1.80	.50
☐ 17	Billy Sorrell	1.75	.80	.22
☐ 18	Norm Miller	1.75	.80	.22
☐ 19	Skip Pitlock	1.75	.80	.22
☐ 20	Reggie Jackson	40.00	18.00	5.00
☐ 21	Dan McGinn	1.75	.80	.22
☐ 22	Phil Roof	1.75	.80	.22
☐ 23	Oscar Gamble	2.50	1.10	.30
☐ 24	Rich Hand	1.75	.80	.22
☐ 25	Clarence Gaston	3.00	1.35	.35
☐ 26	Bert Blyleven	8.00	3.60	1.00
☐ 27	Pirates Rookies	1.75	.80	.22
	Fred Cambria			
	Gene Clines			
☐ 28	Ron Klimkowski	1.75	.80	.22
☐ 29	Don Buford	1.75	.80	.22
☐ 30	Phil Niekro	5.00	2.20	.60
☐ 31	Eddie Kasko MG	1.75	.80	.22
☐ 32	Jerry DaVanon	1.75	.80	.22
☐ 33	Del Unser	1.75	.80	.22
☐ 34	Sandy Vance	1.75	.80	.22
☐ 35	Lou Piniella	2.50	1.10	.30
☐ 36	Dean Chance	1.75	.80	.22
☐ 37	Rich McKinney	1.75	.80	.22
☐ 38	Jim Colborn	1.75	.80	.22
☐ 39	Tiger Rookies	1.75	.80	.22
	Lerrin LaGrow			
	Gene Lamont			

☐ 40	Lee May	2.50	1.10	.30
☐ 41	Rick Austin	1.75	.80	.22
☐ 42	Boots Day	1.75	.80	.22
☐ 43	Steve Kealey	1.75	.80	.22
☐ 44	Johnny Edwards	1.75	.80	.22
☐ 45	Jim Hunter	7.00	3.10	.85
☐ 46	Dave Campbell	1.75	.80	.22
☐ 47	Johnny Jeter	1.75	.80	.22
☐ 48	Dave Baldwin	1.75	.80	.22
☐ 49	Don Money	1.75	.80	.22
☐ 50	Willie McCovey	8.00	3.60	1.00
☐ 51	Steve Kline	1.75	.80	.22
☐ 52	Braves Rookies	1.75	.80	.22
	Oscar Brown			
	Earl Williams			
☐ 53	Paul Blair	2.50	1.10	.30
☐ 54	Checklist 1	6.00	1.20	.60
☐ 55	Steve Carlton	18.00	8.00	2.20
☐ 56	Duane Josephson	1.75	.80	.22
☐ 57	Von Joshua	1.75	.80	.22
☐ 58	Bill Lee	2.50	1.10	.30
☐ 59	Gene Mauch MG	2.50	1.10	.30
☐ 60	Dick Bosman	1.75	.80	.22
☐ 61	AL Batting Leaders	3.50	1.55	.45
	Alex Johnson			
	Carl Yastrzemski			
	Tony Oliva			
☐ 62	NL Batting Leaders	2.50	1.10	.30
	Rico Carty			
	Joe Torre			
	Manny Sanguillen			
☐ 63	AL RBI Leaders	2.50	1.10	.30
	Frank Howard			
	Tony Conigliaro			
	Boog Powell			
☐ 64	NL RBI Leaders	5.00	2.20	.60
	Johnny Bench			
	Tony Perez			
	Billy Williams			
☐ 65	AL HR Leaders	4.00	1.80	.50
	Frank Howard			
	Harmon Killebrew			
	Carl Yastrzemski			
☐ 66	NL HR Leaders	6.00	2.70	.75
	Johnny Bench			
	Billy Williams			
	Tony Perez			
☐ 67	AL ERA Leaders	3.50	1.55	.45
	Diego Segui			
	Jim Palmer			
	Clyde Wright			
☐ 68	NL ERA Leaders	3.50	1.55	.45
	Tom Seaver			
	Wayne Simpson			
	Luke Walker			
☐ 69	AL Pitching Leaders	2.50	1.10	.30
	Mike Cuellar			
	Dave McNally			
	Jim Perry			
☐ 70	NL Pitching Leaders	6.00	2.70	.75
	Bob Gibson			
	Gaylord Perry			
	Fergie Jenkins			
☐ 71	AL Strikeout Leaders	2.50	1.10	.30
	Sam McDowell			
	Mickey Lolich			
	Bob Johnson			
☐ 72	NL Strikeout Leaders	7.00	3.10	.85
	Tom Seaver			
	Bob Gibson			
	Fergie Jenkins			

☐ 73	George Brunet	1.75	.80	.22
☐ 74	Twins Rookies	1.75	.80	.22
	Pete Hamm			
	Jim Nettles			
☐ 75	Gary Nolan	2.50	1.10	.30
☐ 76	Ted Savage	1.75	.80	.22
☐ 77	Mike Compton	1.75	.80	.22
☐ 78	Jim Spencer	1.75	.80	.22
☐ 79	Wade Blasingame	1.75	.80	.22
☐ 80	Bill Melton	1.75	.80	.22
☐ 81	Felix Millan	1.75	.80	.22
☐ 82	Casey Cox	1.75	.80	.22
☐ 83	Met Rookies	1.75	.80	.22
	Tim Foli			
	Randy Bobb			
☐ 84	Marcel Lachemann	2.50	1.10	.30
☐ 85	Billy Grabarkewitz	1.75	.80	.22
☐ 86	Mike Kilkenny	1.75	.80	.22
☐ 87	Jack Heidemann	1.75	.80	.22
☐ 88	Hal King	1.75	.80	.22
☐ 89	Ken Brett	1.75	.80	.22
☐ 90	Joe Pepitone	2.50	1.10	.30
☐ 91	Bob Lemon MG	2.50	1.10	.30
☐ 92	Fred Wenz	1.75	.80	.22
☐ 93	Senators Rookies	1.75	.80	.22
	Norm McRae			
	Denny Riddleberger			
☐ 94	Don Hahn	1.75	.80	.22
☐ 95	Luis Tiant	2.50	1.10	.30
☐ 96	Joe Hague	1.75	.80	.22
☐ 97	Floyd Wicker	1.75	.80	.22
☐ 98	Joe Decker	1.75	.80	.22
☐ 99	Mark Belanger	2.50	1.10	.30
☐ 100	Pete Rose	40.00	18.00	5.00
☐ 101	Les Cain	1.75	.80	.22
☐ 102	Astros Rookies	2.50	1.10	.30
	Ken Forsch			
	Larry Howard			
☐ 103	Rich Severson	1.75	.80	.22
☐ 104	Dan Frisella	1.75	.80	.22
☐ 105	Tony Conigliaro	3.00	1.35	.35
☐ 106	Tom Dukes	1.75	.80	.22
☐ 107	Roy Foster	1.75	.80	.22
☐ 108	John Cumberland	1.75	.80	.22
☐ 109	Steve Hovley	1.75	.80	.22
☐ 110	Bill Mazeroski	2.50	1.10	.30
☐ 111	Yankee Rookies	1.75	.80	.22
	Loyd Colson			
	Bobby Mitchell			
☐ 112	Manny Mota	2.50	1.10	.30
☐ 113	Jerry Crider	1.75	.80	.22
☐ 114	Billy Conigliaro	2.50	1.10	.30
☐ 115	Donn Clendenon	2.50	1.10	.30
☐ 116	Ken Sanders	1.75	.80	.22
☐ 117	Ted Simmons	14.00	6.25	1.75
☐ 118	Cookie Rojas	2.50	1.10	.30
☐ 119	Frank Lucchesi MG	1.75	.80	.22
☐ 120	Willie Horton	2.50	1.10	.30
☐ 121	Cubs Rookies	1.75	.80	.22
	Jim Dunegan			
	Roe Skidmore			
☐ 122	Eddie Watt	1.75	.80	.22
☐ 123A	Checklist 2	6.00	1.20	.60
	(Card number			
	at bottom right)			
☐ 123B	Checklist 2	6.00	1.20	.60
	(Card number			
	centered)			
☐ 124	Don Gullett	2.50	1.10	.30
☐ 125	Ray Fosse	2.50	1.10	.30
☐ 126	Danny Coombs	1.75	.80	.22

☐ 127	Danny Thompson	2.50	1.10	.30
☐ 128	Frank Johnson	1.75	.80	.22
☐ 129	Aurelio Monteagudo	1.75	.80	.22
☐ 130	Denis Menke	1.75	.80	.22
☐ 131	Curt Blefary	1.75	.80	.22
☐ 132	Jose Laboy	1.75	.80	.22
☐ 133	Mickey Lolich	2.50	1.10	.30
☐ 134	Jose Arcia	1.75	.80	.22
☐ 135	Rick Monday	2.50	1.10	.30
☐ 136	Duffy Dyer	1.75	.80	.22
☐ 137	Marcelino Lopez	1.75	.80	.22
☐ 138	Phillies Rookies	2.50	1.10	.30
	Joe Lis			
	Willie Montanez			
☐ 139	Paul Casanova	1.75	.80	.22
☐ 140	Gaylord Perry	8.00	3.60	1.00
☐ 141	Frank Quilici	1.75	.80	.22
☐ 142	Mack Jones	1.75	.80	.22
☐ 143	Steve Blass	2.50	1.10	.30
☐ 144	Jackie Hernandez	1.75	.80	.22
☐ 145	Bill Singer	2.50	1.10	.30
☐ 146	Ralph Houk MG	2.50	1.10	.30
☐ 147	Bob Priddy	1.75	.80	.22
☐ 148	John Mayberry	2.50	1.10	.30
☐ 149	Mike Hershberger	1.75	.80	.22
☐ 150	Sam McDowell	2.50	1.10	.30
☐ 151	Tommy Davis	2.50	1.10	.30
☐ 152	Angels Rookies	1.75	.80	.22
	Lloyd Allen			
	Winston Llenas			
☐ 153	Gary Ross	1.75	.80	.22
☐ 154	Cesar Gutierrez	1.75	.80	.22
☐ 155	Ken Henderson	1.75	.80	.22
☐ 156	Bart Johnson	1.75	.80	.22
☐ 157	Bob Bailey	1.75	.80	.22
☐ 158	Jerry Reuss	2.50	1.10	.30
☐ 159	Jarvis Tatum	1.75	.80	.22
☐ 160	Tom Seaver	20.00	9.00	2.50
☐ 161	Coin Checklist	6.00	2.70	.75
☐ 162	Jack Billingham	1.75	.80	.22
☐ 163	Buck Martinez	1.75	.80	.22
☐ 164	Reds Rookies	2.50	1.10	.30
	Frank Duffy			
	Milt Wilcox			
☐ 165	Cesar Tovar	1.75	.80	.22
☐ 166	Joe Hoerner	1.75	.80	.22
☐ 167	Tom Grieve	2.50	1.10	.30
☐ 168	Bruce Dal Canton	1.75	.80	.22
☐ 169	Ed Herrmann	1.75	.80	.22
☐ 170	Mike Cuellar	2.50	1.10	.30
☐ 171	Bobby Wine	1.75	.80	.22
☐ 172	Duke Sims	1.75	.80	.22
☐ 173	Gil Garrido	1.75	.80	.22
☐ 174	Dave LaRoche	1.75	.80	.22
☐ 175	Jim Hickman	1.75	.80	.22
☐ 176	Red Sox Rookies	2.50	1.10	.30
	Bob Montgomery			
	Doug Griffin			
☐ 177	Hal McRae	2.50	1.10	.30
☐ 178	Dave Duncan	1.75	.80	.22
☐ 179	Mike Corkins	1.75	.80	.22
☐ 180	Al Kaline UER	18.00	8.00	2.20
	(Home instead			
	of Birth)			
☐ 181	Hal Lanier	1.75	.80	.22
☐ 182	Al Downing	2.50	1.10	.30
☐ 183	Gil Hodges MG	4.00	1.80	.50
☐ 184	Stan Bahnsen	1.75	.80	.22
☐ 185	Julian Javier	2.50	1.10	.30
☐ 186	Bob Spence	1.75	.80	.22
☐ 187	Ted Abernathy	1.75	.80	.22
☐ 188	Dodgers Rookies	3.00	1.35	.35
	Bob Valentine			
	Mike Strahler			
☐ 189	George Mitterwald	1.75	.80	.22
☐ 190	Bob Tolan	2.50	1.10	.30
☐ 191	Mike Andrews	1.75	.80	.22
☐ 192	Billy Wilson	1.75	.80	.22
☐ 193	Bob Grich	4.00	1.80	.50
☐ 194	Mike Lum	1.75	.80	.22
☐ 195	AL Playoff Game 1	2.50	1.10	.30
	Boog Powell muscles			
	Twins			
☐ 196	AL Playoff Game 2	2.50	1.10	.30
	Dave McNally makes			
	it two straight			
☐ 197	AL Playoff Game 3	5.00	2.20	.60
	Jim Palmer mows 'em down			
☐ 198	AL Playoff Summary	2.50	1.10	.30
	Orioles celebrate			
☐ 199	NL Playoff Game 1	2.50	1.10	.30
	Ty Cline pinch-triple			
	decides it			
☐ 200	NL Playoff Game 2	2.50	1.10	.30
	Bobby Tolan scores			
	for third time			
☐ 201	NL Playoff Game 3	2.50	1.10	.30
	Ty Cline scores			
	winning run			
☐ 202	NL Playoff Summary	2.50	1.10	.30
	Reds celebrate			
☐ 203	Larry Gura	1.75	.80	.22
☐ 204	Brewers Rookies	1.75	.80	.22
	Bernie Smith			
	George Kopacz			
☐ 205	Gerry Moses	1.75	.80	.22
☐ 206	Checklist 3	6.00	1.20	.60
☐ 207	Alan Foster	1.75	.80	.22
☐ 208	Billy Martin MG	4.00	1.80	.50
☐ 209	Steve Renko	1.75	.80	.22
☐ 210	Rod Carew	18.00	8.00	2.20
☐ 211	Phil Hennigan	1.75	.80	.22
☐ 212	Rich Hebner	2.50	1.10	.30
☐ 213	Frank Baker	1.75	.80	.22
☐ 214	Al Ferrara	1.75	.80	.22
☐ 215	Diego Segui	1.75	.80	.22
☐ 216	Cards Rookies	1.75	.80	.22
	Reggie Cleveland			
	Luis Melendez			
☐ 217	Ed Stroud	1.75	.80	.22
☐ 218	Tony Cloninger	1.75	.80	.22
☐ 219	Elrod Hendricks	1.75	.80	.22
☐ 220	Ron Santo	2.50	1.10	.30
☐ 221	Dave Morehead	1.75	.80	.22
☐ 222	Bob Watson	2.50	1.10	.30
☐ 223	Cecil Upshaw	1.75	.80	.22
☐ 224	Alan Gallagher	1.75	.80	.22
☐ 225	Gary Peters	1.75	.80	.22
☐ 226	Bill Russell	3.00	1.35	.35
☐ 227	Floyd Weaver	1.75	.80	.22
☐ 228	Wayne Garrett	1.75	.80	.22
☐ 229	Jim Hannan	1.75	.80	.22
☐ 230	Willie Stargell	8.00	3.60	1.00
☐ 231	Indians Rookies	1.75	.80	.22
	Vince Colbert			
	John Lowenstein			
☐ 232	John Strohmayer	1.75	.80	.22
☐ 233	Larry Bowa	2.50	1.10	.30
☐ 234	Jim Lyttle	1.75	.80	.22
☐ 235	Nate Colbert	1.75	.80	.22
☐ 236	Bob Humphreys	1.75	.80	.22
☐ 237	Cesar Cedeno	3.00	1.35	.35

☐	238 Chuck Dobson	1.75	.80	.22
☐	239 Red Schoendienst MG	2.50	1.10	.30
☐	240 Clyde Wright	1.75	.80	.22
☐	241 Dave Nelson	1.75	.80	.22
☐	242 Jim Ray	1.75	.80	.22
☐	243 Carlos May	2.50	1.10	.30
☐	244 Bob Tillman	1.75	.80	.22
☐	245 Jim Kaat	2.50	1.10	.30
☐	246 Tony Taylor	1.75	.80	.22
☐	247 Royals Rookies	2.50	1.10	.30
	Jerry Cram			
	Paul Splittorff			
☐	248 Hoyt Wilhelm	4.00	1.80	.50
☐	249 Chico Salmon	1.75	.80	.22
☐	250 Johnny Bench	20.00	9.00	2.50
☐	251 Frank Reberger	1.75	.80	.22
☐	252 Eddie Leon	1.75	.80	.22
☐	253 Bill Sudakis	1.75	.80	.22
☐	254 Cal Koonce	1.75	.80	.22
☐	255 Bob Robertson	2.50	1.10	.30
☐	256 Tony Gonzalez	1.75	.80	.22
☐	257 Nelson Briles	1.75	.80	.22
☐	258 Dick Green	1.75	.80	.22
☐	259 Dave Marshall	1.75	.80	.22
☐	260 Tommy Harper	2.50	1.10	.30
☐	261 Darold Knowles	1.75	.80	.22
☐	262 Padres Rookies	1.75	.80	.22
	Jim Williams			
	Dave Robinson			
☐	263 John Ellis	2.50	1.10	.30
☐	264 Joe Morgan	7.00	3.10	.85
☐	265 Jim Northrup	2.50	1.10	.30
☐	266 Bill Stoneman	1.75	.80	.22
☐	267 Rich Morales	1.75	.80	.22
☐	268 Philadelphia Phillies	3.00	1.35	.35
	Team Card			
☐	269 Gail Hopkins	1.75	.80	.22
☐	270 Rico Carty	2.50	1.10	.30
☐	271 Bill Zepp	1.75	.80	.22
☐	272 Tommy Helms	2.50	1.10	.30
☐	273 Pete Richert	1.75	.80	.22
☐	274 Ron Slocum	1.75	.80	.22
☐	275 Vada Pinson	2.50	1.10	.30
☐	276 Giants Rookies	8.00	3.60	1.00
	Mike Davison			
	George Foster			
☐	277 Gary Waslewski	1.75	.80	.22
☐	278 Jerry Grote	1.75	.80	.22
☐	279 Lefty Phillips MG	1.75	.80	.22
☐	280 Fergie Jenkins	8.00	3.60	1.00
☐	281 Danny Walton	1.75	.80	.22
☐	282 Jose Pagan	1.75	.80	.22
☐	283 Dick Such	1.75	.80	.22
☐	284 Jim Gosger	1.75	.80	.22
☐	285 Sal Bando	2.50	1.10	.30
☐	286 Jerry McNertney	1.75	.80	.22
☐	287 Mike Fiore	1.75	.80	.22
☐	288 Joe Moeller	1.75	.80	.22
☐	289 Chicago White Sox	3.00	1.35	.35
	Team Card			
☐	290 Tony Oliva	3.00	1.35	.35
☐	291 George Culver	1.75	.80	.22
☐	292 Jay Johnstone	2.50	1.10	.30
☐	293 Pat Corrales	2.50	1.10	.30
☐	294 Steve Dunning	1.75	.80	.22
☐	295 Bobby Bonds	5.00	2.20	.60
☐	296 Tom Timmermann	1.75	.80	.22
☐	297 Johnny Briggs	1.75	.80	.22
☐	298 Jim Nelson	1.75	.80	.22
☐	299 Ed Kirkpatrick	1.75	.80	.22
☐	300 Brooks Robinson	18.00	8.00	2.20
☐	301 Earl Wilson	1.75	.80	.22
☐	302 Phil Gagliano	1.75	.80	.22
☐	303 Lindy McDaniel	2.50	1.10	.30
☐	304 Ron Brand	1.75	.80	.22
☐	305 Reggie Smith	3.00	1.35	.35
☐	306 Jim Nash	1.75	.80	.22
☐	307 Don Wert	1.75	.80	.22
☐	308 St. Louis Cardinals	3.00	1.35	.35
	Team Card			
☐	309 Dick Ellsworth	1.75	.80	.22
☐	310 Tommie Agee	2.50	1.10	.30
☐	311 Lee Stange	1.75	.80	.22
☐	312 Harry Walker MG	1.75	.80	.22
☐	313 Tom Hall	1.75	.80	.22
☐	314 Jeff Torborg	2.50	1.10	.30
☐	315 Ron Fairly	2.50	1.10	.30
☐	316 Fred Scherman	1.75	.80	.22
☐	317 Athletic Rookies	1.75	.80	.22
	Jim Driscoll			
	Angel Mangual			
☐	318 Rudy May	1.75	.80	.22
☐	319 Ty Cline	1.75	.80	.22
☐	320 Dave McNally	2.50	1.10	.30
☐	321 Tom Matchick	1.75	.80	.22
☐	322 Jim Beauchamp	1.75	.80	.22
☐	323 Billy Champion	1.75	.80	.22
☐	324 Graig Nettles	3.00	1.35	.35
☐	325 Juan Marichal	6.00	2.70	.75
☐	326 Richie Scheinblum	1.75	.80	.22
☐	327 World Series Game 1.	2.50	1.10	.30
	Boog Powell homers			
	to opposite field			
☐	328 World Series Game 2.	2.50	1.10	.30
	(Don Buford)			
☐	329 World Series Game 3.	5.00	2.20	.60
	Frank Robinson			
	shows muscle			
☐	330 World Series Game 4.	2.50	1.10	.30
	Reds stay alive			
☐	331 World Series Game 5.	6.00	2.70	.75
	Brooks Robinson			
	commits robbery			
☐	332 World Series Summary	2.50	1.10	.30
	Orioles celebrate			
☐	333 Clay Kirby	1.75	.80	.22
☐	334 Roberto Pena	1.75	.80	.22
☐	335 Jerry Koosman	3.00	1.35	.35
☐	336 Detroit Tigers	3.00	1.35	.35
	Team Card			
☐	337 Jesus Alou	1.75	.80	.22
☐	338 Gene Tenace	2.50	1.10	.30
☐	339 Wayne Simpson	1.75	.80	.22
☐	340 Rico Petrocelli	2.50	1.10	.30
☐	341 Steve Garvey	25.00	11.00	3.10
☐	342 Frank Tepedino	1.75	.80	.22
☐	343 Pirates Rookies	1.75	.80	.22
	Ed Acosta			
	Milt May			
☐	344 Ellie Rodriguez	1.75	.80	.22
☐	345 Joel Horlen	1.75	.80	.22
☐	346 Lum Harris MG	1.75	.80	.22
☐	347 Ted Uhlaender	1.75	.80	.22
☐	348 Fred Norman	1.75	.80	.22
☐	349 Rich Reese	1.75	.80	.22
☐	350 Billy Williams	6.00	2.70	.75
☐	351 Jim Shellenback	1.75	.80	.22
☐	352 Denny Doyle	1.75	.80	.22
☐	353 Carl Taylor	1.75	.80	.22
☐	354 Don McMahon	1.75	.80	.22
☐	355 Bud Harrelson	3.50	1.55	.45
	(Nolan Ryan in photo)			

☐ 356 Bob Locker	1.75	.80	.22
☐ 357 Cincinnati Reds	3.00	1.35	.35
Team Card			
☐ 358 Danny Cater	1.75	.80	.22
☐ 359 Ron Reed	1.75	.80	.22
☐ 360 Jim Fregosi	2.50	1.10	.30
☐ 361 Don Sutton	7.00	3.10	.85
☐ 362 Orioles Rookies	1.75	.80	.22
Mike Adamson			
Roger Freed			
☐ 363 Mike Nagy	1.75	.80	.22
☐ 364 Tommy Dean	1.75	.80	.22
☐ 365 Bob Johnson	1.75	.80	.22
☐ 366 Ron Stone	1.75	.80	.22
☐ 367 Dalton Jones	1.75	.80	.22
☐ 368 Bob Veale	2.50	1.10	.30
☐ 369 Checklist 4	6.00	1.20	.60
☐ 370 Joe Torre	3.00	1.35	.35
☐ 371 Jack Hiatt	1.75	.80	.22
☐ 372 Lew Krausse	1.75	.80	.22
☐ 373 Tom McCraw	1.75	.80	.22
☐ 374 Clete Boyer	2.50	1.10	.30
☐ 375 Steve Hargan	1.75	.80	.22
☐ 376 Expos Rookies	1.75	.80	.22
Clyde Mashore			
Ernie McAnally			
☐ 377 Greg Garrett	1.75	.80	.22
☐ 378 Tito Fuentes	1.75	.80	.22
☐ 379 Wayne Granger	1.75	.80	.22
☐ 380 Ted Williams MG	10.00	4.50	1.25
☐ 381 Fred Gladding	1.75	.80	.22
☐ 382 Jake Gibbs	1.75	.80	.22
☐ 383 Rod Gaspar	1.75	.80	.22
☐ 384 Rollie Fingers	6.00	2.70	.75
☐ 385 Maury Wills	3.00	1.35	.35
☐ 386 Boston Red Sox	3.00	1.35	.35
Team Card			
☐ 387 Ron Herbel	1.75	.80	.22
☐ 388 Al Oliver	3.00	1.35	.35
☐ 389 Ed Brinkman	1.75	.80	.22
☐ 390 Glenn Beckert	2.50	1.10	.30
☐ 391 Twins Rookies	1.75	.80	.22
Steve Brye			
Cotton Nash			
☐ 392 Grant Jackson	1.75	.80	.22
☐ 393 Merv Rettenmund	2.50	1.10	.30
☐ 394 Clay Carroll	2.50	1.10	.30
☐ 395 Roy White	2.50	1.10	.30
☐ 396 Dick Schofield	2.50	1.10	.30
☐ 397 Alvin Dark MG	2.50	1.10	.30
☐ 398 Howie Reed	2.50	1.10	.30
☐ 399 Jim French	2.50	1.10	.30
☐ 400 Hank Aaron	55.00	25.00	7.00
☐ 401 Tom Murphy	2.50	1.10	.30
☐ 402 Los Angeles Dodgers	5.00	2.20	.60
Team Card			
☐ 403 Joe Coleman	2.50	1.10	.30
☐ 404 Astros Rookies	2.50	1.10	.30
Buddy Harris			
Roger Metzger			
☐ 405 Leo Cardenas	2.50	1.10	.30
☐ 406 Ray Sadecki	2.50	1.10	.30
☐ 407 Joe Rudi	2.50	1.10	.30
☐ 408 Rafael Robles	2.50	1.10	.30
☐ 409 Don Pavletich	2.50	1.10	.30
☐ 410 Ken Holtzman	2.50	1.10	.30
☐ 411 George Spriggs	2.50	1.10	.30
☐ 412 Jerry Johnson	2.50	1.10	.30
☐ 413 Pat Kelly	2.50	1.10	.30
☐ 414 Woodie Fryman	2.50	1.10	.30
☐ 415 Mike Hegan	2.50	1.10	.30
☐ 416 Gene Alley	2.50	1.10	.30
☐ 417 Dick Hall	2.50	1.10	.30
☐ 418 Adolfo Phillips	2.50	1.10	.30
☐ 419 Ron Hansen	2.50	1.10	.30
☐ 420 Jim Merritt	2.50	1.10	.30
☐ 421 John Stephenson	2.50	1.10	.30
☐ 422 Frank Bertaina	2.50	1.10	.30
☐ 423 Tigers Rookies	2.50	1.10	.30
Dennis Saunders			
Tim Marting			
☐ 424 Roberto Rodriquez	2.50	1.10	.30
☐ 425 Doug Rader	2.50	1.10	.30
☐ 426 Chris Cannizzaro	2.50	1.10	.30
☐ 427 Bernie Allen	2.50	1.10	.30
☐ 428 Jim McAndrew	2.50	1.10	.30
☐ 429 Chuck Hinton	2.50	1.10	.30
☐ 430 Wes Parker	2.50	1.10	.30
☐ 431 Tom Burgmeier	2.50	1.10	.30
☐ 432 Bob Didier	2.50	1.10	.30
☐ 433 Skip Lockwood	2.50	1.10	.30
☐ 434 Gary Sutherland	2.50	1.10	.30
☐ 435 Jose Cardenal	2.50	1.10	.30
☐ 436 Wilbur Wood	2.50	1.10	.30
☐ 437 Danny Murtaugh MG	2.50	1.10	.30
☐ 438 Mike McCormick	2.50	1.10	.30
☐ 439 Phillies Rookies	6.00	2.70	.75
Greg Luzinski			
Scott Reid			
☐ 440 Bert Campaneris	2.50	1.10	.30
☐ 441 Milt Pappas	2.50	1.10	.30
☐ 442 California Angels	5.00	2.20	.60
Team Card			
☐ 443 Rich Robertson	2.50	1.10	.30
☐ 444 Jimmie Price	2.50	1.10	.30
☐ 445 Art Shamsky	2.50	1.10	.30
☐ 446 Bobby Bolin	2.50	1.10	.30
☐ 447 Cesar Geronimo	2.50	1.10	.30
☐ 448 Dave Roberts	2.50	1.10	.30
☐ 449 Brant Alyea	2.50	1.10	.30
☐ 450 Bob Gibson	18.00	8.00	2.20
☐ 451 Joe Keough	2.50	1.10	.30
☐ 452 John Boccabella	2.50	1.10	.30
☐ 453 Terry Crowley	2.50	1.10	.30
☐ 454 Mike Paul	2.50	1.10	.30
☐ 455 Don Kessinger	2.50	1.10	.30
☐ 456 Bob Meyer	2.50	1.10	.30
☐ 457 Willie Smith	2.50	1.10	.30
☐ 458 White Sox Rookies	2.50	1.10	.30
Ron Lolich			
Dave Lemonds			
☐ 459 Jim Lefebvre	2.50	1.10	.30
☐ 460 Fritz Peterson	2.50	1.10	.30
☐ 461 Jim Ray Hart	2.50	1.10	.30
☐ 462 Washington Senators	5.00	2.20	.60
Team Card			
☐ 463 Tom Kelley	2.50	1.10	.30
☐ 464 Aurelio Rodriguez	2.50	1.10	.30
☐ 465 Tim McCarver	3.00	1.35	.35
☐ 466 Ken Berry	2.50	1.10	.30
☐ 467 Al Santorini	2.50	1.10	.30
☐ 468 Frank Fernandez	2.50	1.10	.30
☐ 469 Bob Aspromonte	2.50	1.10	.30
☐ 470 Bob Oliver	2.50	1.10	.30
☐ 471 Tom Griffin	2.50	1.10	.30
☐ 472 Ken Rudolph	2.50	1.10	.30
☐ 473 Gary Wagner	2.50	1.10	.30
☐ 474 Jim Fairey	2.50	1.10	.30
☐ 475 Ron Perranoski	2.50	1.10	.30
☐ 476 Dal Maxvill	2.50	1.10	.30
☐ 477 Earl Weaver MG	4.00	1.80	.50
☐ 478 Bernie Carbo	2.50	1.10	.30

479	Dennis Higgins	2.50	1.10	.30
480	Manny Sanguillen	2.50	1.10	.30
481	Daryl Patterson	2.50	1.10	.30
482	San Diego Padres Team Card	5.00	2.20	.60
483	Gene Michael	2.50	1.10	.30
484	Don Wilson	2.50	1.10	.30
485	Ken McMullen	2.50	1.10	.30
486	Steve Huntz	2.50	1.10	.30
487	Paul Schaal	2.50	1.10	.30
488	Jerry Stephenson	2.50	1.10	.30
489	Luis Alvarado	2.50	1.10	.30
490	Deron Johnson	2.50	1.10	.30
491	Jim Hardin	2.50	1.10	.30
492	Ken Boswell	2.50	1.10	.30
493	Dave May	2.50	1.10	.30
494	Braves Rookies Ralph Garr Rick Kester	2.50	1.10	.30
495	Felipe Alou	2.50	1.10	.30
496	Woody Woodward	2.50	1.10	.30
497	Horacio Pina	2.50	1.10	.30
498	John Kennedy	2.50	1.10	.30
499	Checklist 5	6.00	1.20	.60
500	Jim Perry	2.50	1.10	.30
501	Andy Etchebarren	2.50	1.10	.30
502	Chicago Cubs Team Card	5.00	2.20	.60
503	Gates Brown	2.50	1.10	.30
504	Ken Wright	2.50	1.10	.30
505	Ollie Brown	2.50	1.10	.30
506	Bobby Knoop	2.50	1.10	.30
507	George Stone	2.50	1.10	.30
508	Roger Repoz	2.50	1.10	.30
509	Jim Grant	2.50	1.10	.30
510	Ken Harrelson	2.50	1.10	.30
511	Chris Short (Pete Rose leading off second)	3.00	1.35	.35
512	Red Sox Rookies Dick Mills Mike Garman	2.50	1.10	.30
513	Nolan Ryan	250.00	110.00	31.00
514	Ron Woods	2.50	1.10	.30
515	Carl Morton	2.50	1.10	.30
516	Ted Kubiak	2.50	1.10	.30
517	Charlie Fox MG	2.50	1.10	.30
518	Joe Grzenda	2.50	1.10	.30
519	Willie Crawford	2.50	1.10	.30
520	Tommy John	5.00	2.20	.60
521	Leron Lee	2.50	1.10	.30
522	Minnesota Twins Team Card	5.00	2.20	.60
523	John Odom	2.50	1.10	.30
524	Mickey Stanley	5.00	2.20	.60
525	Ernie Banks	55.00	25.00	7.00
526	Ray Jarvis	4.00	1.80	.50
527	Cleon Jones	5.00	2.20	.60
528	Wally Bunker	4.00	1.80	.50
529	NL Rookie Infielders Enzo Hernandez Bill Buckner Marty Perez	5.00	2.20	.60
530	Carl Yastrzemski	40.00	18.00	5.00
531	Mike Torrez	5.00	2.20	.60
532	Bill Rigney MG	4.00	1.80	.50
533	Mike Ryan	4.00	1.80	.50
534	Luke Walker	4.00	1.80	.50
535	Curt Flood	5.00	2.20	.60
536	Claude Raymond	5.00	2.20	.60
537	Tom Egan	4.00	1.80	.50
538	Angel Bravo	4.00	1.80	.50
539	Larry Brown	4.00	1.80	.50
540	Larry Dierker	4.00	1.80	.50
541	Bob Burda	4.00	1.80	.50
542	Bob Miller	4.00	1.80	.50
543	New York Yankees Team Card	8.00	3.60	1.00
544	Vida Blue	6.00	2.70	.75
545	Dick Dietz	4.00	1.80	.50
546	John Matias	4.00	1.80	.50
547	Pat Dobson	5.00	2.20	.60
548	Don Mason	4.00	1.80	.50
549	Jim Brewer	5.00	2.20	.60
550	Harmon Killebrew	25.00	11.00	3.10
551	Frank Linzy	4.00	1.80	.50
552	Buddy Bradford	4.00	1.80	.50
553	Kevin Collins	4.00	1.80	.50
554	Lowell Palmer	4.00	1.80	.50
555	Walt Williams	4.00	1.80	.50
556	Jim McGlothlin	4.00	1.80	.50
557	Tom Satriano	4.00	1.80	.50
558	Hector Torres	4.00	1.80	.50
559	AL Rookie Pitchers Terry Cox Bill Gogolewski Gary Jones	4.00	1.80	.50
560	Rusty Staub	5.00	2.20	.60
561	Syd O'Brien	4.00	1.80	.50
562	Dave Giusti	4.00	1.80	.50
563	San Francisco Giants Team Card	8.00	3.60	1.00
564	Al Fitzmorris	4.00	1.80	.50
565	Jim Wynn	5.00	2.20	.60
566	Tim Cullen	4.00	1.80	.50
567	Walt Alston MG	6.00	2.70	.75
568	Sal Campisi	4.00	1.80	.50
569	Ivan Murrell	4.00	1.80	.50
570	Jim Palmer	30.00	13.50	3.70
571	Ted Sizemore	4.00	1.80	.50
572	Jerry Kenney	4.00	1.80	.50
573	Ed Kranepool	5.00	2.20	.60
574	Jim Bunning	5.00	2.20	.60
575	Bill Freehan	5.00	2.20	.60
576	Cubs Rookies Adrian Garrett Brock Davis Garry Jestadt	4.00	1.80	.50
577	Jim Lonborg	5.00	2.20	.60
578	Ron Hunt	4.00	1.80	.50
579	Marty Pattin	4.00	1.80	.50
580	Tony Perez	18.00	8.00	2.20
581	Roger Nelson	4.00	1.80	.50
582	Dave Cash	5.00	2.20	.60
583	Ron Cook	4.00	1.80	.50
584	Cleveland Indians Team Card	8.00	3.60	1.00
585	Willie Davis	5.00	2.20	.60
586	Dick Woodson	4.00	1.80	.50
587	Sonny Jackson	4.00	1.80	.50
588	Tom Bradley	4.00	1.80	.50
589	Bob Barton	4.00	1.80	.50
590	Alex Johnson	5.00	2.20	.60
591	Jackie Brown	4.00	1.80	.50
592	Randy Hundley	4.00	1.80	.50
593	Jack Aker	4.00	1.80	.50
594	Cards Rookies Bob Chlupsa Bob Stinson Al Hrabosky	5.00	2.20	.60
595	Dave Johnson	5.00	2.20	.60
596	Mike Jorgensen	4.00	1.80	.50
597	Ken Suarez	4.00	1.80	.50

☐ 598 Rick Wise	5.00	2.20	.60
☐ 599 Norm Cash	5.00	2.20	.60
☐ 600 Willie Mays	100.00	45.00	12.50
☐ 601 Ken Tatum	4.00	1.80	.50
☐ 602 Marty Martinez	4.00	1.80	.50
☐ 603 Pittsburgh Pirates Team Card	8.00	3.60	1.00
☐ 604 John Gelnar	4.00	1.80	.50
☐ 605 Orlando Cepeda	6.00	2.70	.75
☐ 606 Chuck Taylor	4.00	1.80	.50
☐ 607 Paul Ratliff	4.00	1.80	.50
☐ 608 Mike Wegener	4.00	1.80	.50
☐ 609 Leo Durocher MG	7.00	3.10	.85
☐ 610 Amos Otis	5.00	2.20	.60
☐ 611 Tom Phoebus	4.00	1.80	.50
☐ 612 Indians Rookies Lou Camilli Ted Ford Steve Mingori	4.00	1.80	.50
☐ 613 Pedro Borbon	4.00	1.80	.50
☐ 614 Billy Cowan	4.00	1.80	.50
☐ 615 Mel Stottlemyre	5.00	2.20	.60
☐ 616 Larry Hisle	5.00	2.20	.60
☐ 617 Clay Dalrymple	4.00	1.80	.50
☐ 618 Tug McGraw	5.00	2.20	.60
☐ 619A Checklist 6 ERR (No copyright)	6.00	1.80	.60
☐ 619B Checklist 6 COR (Copyright on back)	10.00	2.00	1.00
☐ 620 Frank Howard	5.00	2.20	.60
☐ 621 Ron Bryant	4.00	1.80	.50
☐ 622 Joe Lahoud	4.00	1.80	.50
☐ 623 Pat Jarvis	4.00	1.80	.50
☐ 624 Oakland Athletics Team Card	8.00	3.60	1.00
☐ 625 Lou Brock	30.00	13.50	3.70
☐ 626 Freddie Patek	5.00	2.20	.60
☐ 627 Steve Hamilton	4.00	1.80	.50
☐ 628 John Bateman	4.00	1.80	.50
☐ 629 John Hiller	5.00	2.20	.60
☐ 630 Roberto Clemente	90.00	40.00	11.00
☐ 631 Eddie Fisher	4.00	1.80	.50
☐ 632 Darrel Chaney	4.00	1.80	.50
☐ 633 AL Rookie Outfielders Bobby Brooks Pete Koegel Scott Northey	4.00	1.80	.50
☐ 634 Phil Regan	5.00	2.20	.60
☐ 635 Bobby Murcer	5.00	2.20	.60
☐ 636 Denny Lemaster	4.00	1.80	.50
☐ 637 Dave Bristol MG	4.00	1.80	.50
☐ 638 Stan Williams	4.00	1.80	.50
☐ 639 Tom Haller	4.00	1.80	.50
☐ 640 Frank Robinson	40.00	18.00	5.00
☐ 641 New York Mets Team Card	14.00	6.25	1.75
☐ 642 Jim Roland	4.00	1.80	.50
☐ 643 Rick Reichardt	5.00	2.20	.60
☐ 644 Jim Stewart SP	12.00	5.50	1.50
☐ 645 Jim Maloney SP	14.00	6.25	1.75
☐ 646 Bobby Floyd SP	12.00	5.50	1.50
☐ 647 Juan Pizarro	8.00	3.60	1.00
☐ 648 Mets Rookies SP Rich Folkers Ted Martinez John Matlack	20.00	9.00	2.50
☐ 649 Sparky Lyle SP	16.00	7.25	2.00
☐ 650 Rich Allen SP	40.00	18.00	5.00
☐ 651 Jerry Robertson SP	12.00	5.50	1.50
☐ 652 Atlanta Braves Team Card	12.00	5.50	1.50
☐ 653 Russ Snyder SP	12.00	5.50	1.50
☐ 654 Don Shaw SP	12.00	5.50	1.50
☐ 655 Mike Epstein SP	12.00	5.50	1.50
☐ 656 Gerry Nyman SP	12.00	5.50	1.50
☐ 657 Jose Azcue	8.00	3.60	1.00
☐ 658 Paul Lindblad SP	12.00	5.50	1.50
☐ 659 Byron Browne SP	12.00	5.50	1.50
☐ 660 Ray Culp	8.00	3.60	1.00
☐ 661 Chuck Tanner MG SP	12.00	5.50	1.50
☐ 662 Mike Hedlund SP	12.00	5.50	1.50
☐ 663 Marv Staehle	8.00	3.60	1.00
☐ 664 Rookie Pitchers SP Archie Reynolds Bob Reynolds Ken Reynolds	12.00	5.50	1.50
☐ 665 Ron Swoboda SP	16.00	7.25	2.00
☐ 666 Gene Brabender SP	12.00	5.50	1.50
☐ 667 Pete Ward	8.00	3.60	1.00
☐ 668 Gary Neibauer	8.00	3.60	1.00
☐ 669 Ike Brown SP	12.00	5.50	1.50
☐ 670 Bill Hands	8.00	3.60	1.00
☐ 671 Bill Voss SP	12.00	5.50	1.50
☐ 672 Ed Crosby SP	12.00	5.50	1.50
☐ 673 Gerry Janeski SP	12.00	5.50	1.50
☐ 674 Montreal Expos Team Card	12.00	5.50	1.50
☐ 675 Dave Boswell	8.00	3.60	1.00
☐ 676 Tommie Reynolds	8.00	3.60	1.00
☐ 677 Jack DiLauro SP	12.00	5.50	1.50
☐ 678 George Thomas	8.00	3.60	1.00
☐ 679 Don O'Riley	8.00	3.60	1.00
☐ 680 Don Mincher SP	12.00	5.50	1.50
☐ 681 Bill Butler	8.00	3.60	1.00
☐ 682 Terry Harmon	8.00	3.60	1.00
☐ 683 Bill Burbach SP	12.00	5.50	1.50
☐ 684 Curt Motton	8.00	3.60	1.00
☐ 685 Moe Drabowsky	8.00	3.60	1.00
☐ 686 Chico Ruiz SP	12.00	5.50	1.50
☐ 687 Ron Taylor SP	12.00	5.50	1.50
☐ 688 Sparky Anderson MG SP	40.00	18.00	5.00
☐ 689 Frank Baker	8.00	3.60	1.00
☐ 690 Bob Moose	8.00	3.60	1.00
☐ 691 Bobby Heise	8.00	3.60	1.00
☐ 692 AL Rookie Pitchers SP Hal Haydel Rogelio Moret Wayne Twitchell	12.00	5.50	1.50
☐ 693 Jose Pena SP	12.00	5.50	1.50
☐ 694 Rick Renick SP	12.00	5.50	1.50
☐ 695 Joe Niekro	10.00	4.50	1.25
☐ 696 Jerry Morales	8.00	3.60	1.00
☐ 697 Rickey Clark SP	12.00	5.50	1.50
☐ 698 Milwaukee Brewers SP Team Card	20.00	9.00	2.50
☐ 699 Jim Britton	8.00	3.60	1.00
☐ 700 Boog Powell SP	25.00	11.00	3.10
☐ 701 Bob Garibaldi	8.00	3.60	1.00
☐ 702 Milt Ramirez	8.00	3.60	1.00
☐ 703 Mike Kekich	8.00	3.60	1.00
☐ 704 J.C. Martin SP	12.00	5.50	1.50
☐ 705 Dick Selma SP	12.00	5.50	1.50
☐ 706 Joe Foy SP	12.00	5.50	1.50
☐ 707 Fred Lasher	8.00	3.60	1.00
☐ 708 Russ Nagelson SP	12.00	5.50	1.50
☐ 709 Rookie Outfielders SP Dusty Baker Don Baylor Tom Paciorek	90.00	40.00	11.00
☐ 710 Sonny Siebert	8.00	3.60	1.00
☐ 711 Larry Stahl SP	12.00	5.50	1.50
☐ 712 Jose Martinez	8.00	3.60	1.00

		NRMT	VG-E	GOOD
☐ 713	Mike Marshall SP	12.00	5.50	1.50
☐ 714	Dick Williams MG SP	12.00	5.50	1.50
☐ 715	Horace Clarke SP	12.00	5.50	1.50
☐ 716	Dave Leonhard	8.00	3.60	1.00
☐ 717	Tommie Aaron SP	12.00	5.50	1.50
☐ 718	Billy Wynne	8.00	3.60	1.00
☐ 719	Jerry May SP	12.00	5.50	1.50
☐ 720	Matty Alou	10.00	4.50	1.25
☐ 721	John Morris	8.00	3.60	1.00
☐ 722	Houston Astros SP	20.00	9.00	2.50
	Team Card			
☐ 723	Vicente Romo SP	12.00	5.50	1.50
☐ 724	Tom Tischinski SP	12.00	5.50	1.50
☐ 725	Gary Gentry SP	12.00	5.50	1.50
☐ 726	Paul Popovich	8.00	3.60	1.00
☐ 727	Ray Lamb SP	12.00	5.50	1.50
☐ 728	NL Rookie Outfielders	8.00	3.60	1.00
	Wayne Redmond			
	Keith Lampard			
	Bernie Williams			
☐ 729	Dick Billings	8.00	3.60	1.00
☐ 730	Jim Rooker	8.00	3.60	1.00
☐ 731	Jim Qualls SP	12.00	5.50	1.50
☐ 732	Bob Reed	8.00	3.60	1.00
☐ 733	Lee Maye SP	12.00	5.50	1.50
☐ 734	Rob Gardner SP	12.00	5.50	1.50
☐ 735	Mike Shannon SP	12.00	5.50	1.50
☐ 736	Mel Queen SP	12.00	5.50	1.50
☐ 737	Preston Gomez SP MG	12.00	5.50	1.50
☐ 738	Russ Gibson SP	12.00	5.50	1.50
☐ 739	Barry Lersch SP	12.00	5.50	1.50
☐ 740	Luis Aparicio SP UER	25.00	11.00	3.10
	(Led AL in steals			
	from 1965 to 1964,			
	should be 1956 to 1964)			
☐ 741	Skip Guinn	8.00	3.60	1.00
☐ 742	Kansas City Royals	12.00	5.50	1.50
	Team Card			
☐ 743	John O'Donoghue SP	12.00	5.50	1.50
☐ 744	Chuck Manuel SP	12.00	5.50	1.50
☐ 745	Sandy Alomar SP	12.00	5.50	1.50
☐ 746	Andy Kosco	8.00	3.60	1.00
☐ 747	NL Rookie Pitchers	8.00	3.60	1.00
	Al Severinsen			
	Scipio Spinks			
	Balor Moore			
☐ 748	John Purdin SP	12.00	5.50	1.50
☐ 749	Ken Szotkiewicz	8.00	3.60	1.00
☐ 750	Denny McLain SP	20.00	9.00	2.50
☐ 751	Al Weis SP	14.00	6.25	1.75
☐ 752	Dick Drago	10.00	2.40	.80

1972 Topps

The cards in this 787-card set measure 2 1/2" by 3 1/2". The 1972 Topps set contained the most cards ever for a Topps set to that point in time. Features appearing for the first time were "Boyhood Photos" (KP: 341-348 and 491-498), Awards and Trophy cards (621-626), "In Action" (distributed throughout the set), and "Traded Cards" (TR: 751-757). Other subsets included League Leaders (85-96), Playoffs cards (221-222), and World Series cards (223-230). The curved lines of the color picture are a departure from the rectangular

designs of other years. There is a series of intermediate scarcity (526-656) and the usual high numbers (657-787). The key Rookie Card in this set is Carlton Fisk.

		NRMT	VG-E	GOOD
COMPLETE SET (787)		1800.00	800.00	220.00
COMMON CARD (1-132)		.60	.25	.07
COMMON CARD (133-263)		1.00	.45	.12
COMMON CARD (264-394)		1.25	.55	.16
COMMON CARD (395-525)		1.50	.70	.19
COMMON CARD (526-656)		4.00	1.80	.50
COMMON CARD (657-787)		12.00	5.50	1.50
☐ 1	Pittsburgh Pirates	7.00	2.50	1.00
	Team Card			
☐ 2	Ray Culp	.60	.25	.07
☐ 3	Bob Tolan	.60	.25	.07
☐ 4	Checklist 1-132	4.00	.80	.40
☐ 5	John Bateman	.60	.25	.07
☐ 6	Fred Scherman	.60	.25	.07
☐ 7	Enzo Hernandez	.60	.25	.07
☐ 8	Ron Swoboda	1.00	.45	.12
☐ 9	Stan Williams	.60	.25	.07
☐ 10	Amos Otis	1.00	.45	.12
☐ 11	Bobby Valentine	.60	.25	.07
☐ 12	Jose Cardenal	.60	.25	.07
☐ 13	Joe Grzenda	.60	.25	.07
☐ 14	Phillies Rookies	.60	.25	.07
	Pete Koegel			
	Mike Anderson			
	Wayne Twitchell			
☐ 15	Walt Williams	.60	.25	.07
☐ 16	Mike Jorgensen	.60	.25	.07
☐ 17	Dave Duncan	.60	.25	.07
☐ 18A	Juan Pizarro	.60	.25	.07
	(Yellow underline			
	C and S of Cubs)			
☐ 18B	Juan Pizarro	5.00	2.20	.60
	(Green underline			
	C and S of Cubs)			
☐ 19	Billy Cowan	.60	.25	.07
☐ 20	Don Wilson	.60	.25	.07
☐ 21	Atlanta Braves	1.50	.70	.19
	Team Card			
☐ 22	Rob Gardner	.60	.25	.07
☐ 23	Ted Kubiak	.60	.25	.07
☐ 24	Ted Ford	.60	.25	.07
☐ 25	Bill Singer	.60	.25	.07
☐ 26	Andy Etchebarren	.60	.25	.07
☐ 27	Bob Johnson	.60	.25	.07
☐ 28	Twins Rookies	.60	.25	.07
	Bob Gebhard			
	Steve Brye			
	Hal Haydel			
☐ 29A	Bill Bonham	.60	.25	.07

	(Yellow underline C and S of Cubs)			
☐ 29B	Bill Bonham	5.00	2.20	.60
	(Green underline C and S of Cubs)			
☐ 30	Rico Petrocelli	1.00	.45	.12
☐ 31	Cleon Jones	1.00	.45	.12
☐ 32	Cleon Jones IA	.60	.25	.07
☐ 33	Billy Martin MG	4.00	1.80	.50
☐ 34	Billy Martin IA	2.00	.90	.25
☐ 35	Jerry Johnson	.60	.25	.07
☐ 36	Jerry Johnson IA	.60	.25	.07
☐ 37	Carl Yastrzemski	12.00	5.50	1.50
☐ 38	Carl Yastrzemski IA	6.00	2.70	.75
☐ 39	Bob Barton	.60	.25	.07
☐ 40	Bob Barton IA	.60	.25	.07
☐ 41	Tommy Davis	1.00	.45	.12
☐ 42	Tommy Davis IA	.60	.25	.07
☐ 43	Rick Wise	1.00	.45	.12
☐ 44	Rick Wise IA	.60	.25	.07
☐ 45A	Glenn Beckert	1.00	.45	.12
	(Yellow underline C and S of Cubs)			
☐ 45B	Glenn Beckert	5.00	2.20	.60
	(Green underline C and S of Cubs)			
☐ 46	Glenn Beckert IA	.60	.25	.07
☐ 47	John Ellis	.60	.25	.07
☐ 48	John Ellis IA	.60	.25	.07
☐ 49	Willie Mays	25.00	11.00	3.10
☐ 50	Willie Mays IA	12.00	5.50	1.50
☐ 51	Harmon Killebrew	7.00	3.10	.85
☐ 52	Harmon Killebrew IA	3.50	1.55	.45
☐ 53	Bud Harrelson	1.00	.45	.12
☐ 54	Bud Harrelson IA	.60	.25	.07
☐ 55	Clyde Wright	.60	.25	.07
☐ 56	Rich Chiles	.60	.25	.07
☐ 57	Bob Oliver	.60	.25	.07
☐ 58	Ernie McAnally	.60	.25	.07
☐ 59	Fred Stanley	.60	.25	.07
☐ 60	Manny Sanguillen	1.00	.45	.12
☐ 61	Cubs Rookies	1.00	.45	.12
	Burt Hooton			
	Gene Hiser			
	Earl Stephenson			
☐ 62	Angel Mangual	.60	.25	.07
☐ 63	Duke Sims	.60	.25	.07
☐ 64	Pete Broberg	.60	.25	.07
☐ 65	Cesar Cedeno	1.00	.45	.12
☐ 66	Ray Corbin	.60	.25	.07
☐ 67	Red Schoendienst MG	1.00	.45	.12
☐ 68	Jim York	.60	.25	.07
☐ 69	Roger Freed	.60	.25	.07
☐ 70	Mike Cuellar	1.00	.45	.12
☐ 71	California Angels	1.50	.70	.19
	Team Card			
☐ 72	Bruce Kison	.60	.25	.07
☐ 73	Steve Huntz	.60	.25	.07
☐ 74	Cecil Upshaw	.60	.25	.07
☐ 75	Bert Campaneris	1.00	.45	.12
☐ 76	Don Carrithers	.60	.25	.07
☐ 77	Ron Theobald	.60	.25	.07
☐ 78	Steve Arlin	.60	.25	.07
☐ 79	Red Sox Rookies	70.00	32.00	8.75
	Mike Garman			
	Cecil Cooper			
	Carlton Fisk			
☐ 80	Tony Perez	4.00	1.80	.50
☐ 81	Mike Hedlund	.60	.25	.07
☐ 82	Ron Woods	.60	.25	.07
☐ 83	Dalton Jones	.60	.25	.07
☐ 84	Vince Colbert	.60	.25	.07
☐ 85	NL Batting Leaders	1.75	.80	.22
	Joe Torre			
	Ralph Garr			
	Glenn Beckert			
☐ 86	AL Batting Leaders	1.75	.80	.22
	Tony Oliva			
	Bobby Murcer			
	Merv Rettenmund			
☐ 87	NL RBI Leaders	3.50	1.55	.45
	Joe Torre			
	Willie Stargell			
	Hank Aaron			
☐ 88	AL RBI Leaders	3.00	1.35	.35
	Harmon Killebrew			
	Frank Robinson			
	Reggie Smith			
☐ 89	NL Home Run Leaders	3.00	1.35	.35
	Willie Stargell			
	Hank Aaron			
	Lee May			
☐ 90	AL Home Run Leaders	2.50	1.10	.30
	Bill Melton			
	Norm Cash			
	Reggie Jackson			
☐ 91	NL ERA Leaders	2.50	1.10	.30
	Tom Seaver			
	Dave Roberts UER			
	(Photo actually			
	Danny Coombs)			
	Don Wilson			
☐ 92	AL ERA Leaders	2.50	1.10	.30
	Vida Blue			
	Wilbur Wood			
	Jim Palmer			
☐ 93	NL Pitching Leaders	4.00	1.80	.50
	Fergie Jenkins			
	Steve Carlton			
	Al Downing			
	Tom Seaver			
☐ 94	AL Pitching Leaders	1.75	.80	.22
	Mickey Lolich			
	Vida Blue			
	Wilbur Wood			
☐ 95	NL Strikeout Leaders	3.00	1.35	.35
	Tom Seaver			
	Fergie Jenkins			
	Bill Stoneman			
☐ 96	AL Strikeout Leaders	1.75	.80	.22
	Mickey Lolich			
	Vida Blue			
	Joe Coleman			
☐ 97	Tom Kelley	.60	.25	.07
☐ 98	Chuck Tanner MG	.60	.45	.12
☐ 99	Ross Grimsley	.60	.25	.07
☐ 100	Frank Robinson	8.00	3.60	1.00
☐ 101	Astros Rookies	3.00	1.35	.35
	Bill Greif			
	J.R. Richard			
	Ray Busse			
☐ 102	Lloyd Allen	.60	.25	.07
☐ 103	Checklist 133-263	4.00	.80	.40
☐ 104	Toby Harrah	2.00	.90	.25
☐ 105	Gary Gentry	.60	.25	.07
☐ 106	Milwaukee Brewers	1.50	.70	.19
	Team Card			
☐ 107	Jose Cruz	2.00	.90	.25
☐ 108	Gary Waslewski	.60	.25	.07
☐ 109	Jerry May	.60	.25	.07
☐ 110	Ron Hunt	.60	.25	.07
☐ 111	Jim Grant	.60	.25	.07

☐ 112	Greg Luzinski	2.00	.90	.25
☐ 113	Rogelio Moret	.60	.25	.07
☐ 114	Bill Buckner	1.50	.70	.19
☐ 115	Jim Fregosi	1.00	.45	.12
☐ 116	Ed Farmer	.60	.25	.07
☐ 117A	Cleo James	.60	.25	.07
	(Yellow underline C and S of Cubs)			
☐ 117B	Cleo James	5.00	2.20	.60
	(Green underline C and S of Cubs)			
☐ 118	Skip Lockwood	.60	.25	.07
☐ 119	Marty Perez	.60	.25	.07
☐ 120	Bill Freehan	1.00	.45	.12
☐ 121	Ed Sprague	.60	.25	.07
☐ 122	Larry Biittner	.60	.25	.07
☐ 123	Ed Acosta	.60	.25	.07
☐ 124	Yankees Rookies	.60	.25	.07
	Alan Closter			
	Rusty Torres			
	Roger Hambright			
☐ 125	Dave Cash	1.00	.45	.12
☐ 126	Bart Johnson	.60	.25	.07
☐ 127	Duffy Dyer	.60	.25	.07
☐ 128	Eddie Watt	.60	.25	.07
☐ 129	Charlie Fox MG	.60	.25	.07
☐ 130	Bob Gibson	8.00	3.60	1.00
☐ 131	Jim Nettles	.60	.25	.07
☐ 132	Joe Morgan	6.00	2.70	.75
☐ 133	Joe Keough	1.00	.45	.12
☐ 134	Carl Morton	1.00	.45	.12
☐ 135	Vada Pinson	1.25	.55	.16
☐ 136	Darrel Chaney	1.00	.45	.12
☐ 137	Dick Williams MG	1.25	.55	.16
☐ 138	Mike Kekich	1.00	.45	.12
☐ 139	Tim McCarver	1.25	.55	.16
☐ 140	Pat Dobson	1.25	.55	.16
☐ 141	Mets Rookies	1.25	.55	.16
	Buzz Capra			
	Lee Stanton			
	Jon Matlack			
☐ 142	Chris Chambliss	5.00	2.20	.60
☐ 143	Garry Jestadt	1.00	.45	.12
☐ 144	Marty Pattin	1.00	.45	.12
☐ 145	Don Kessinger	1.25	.55	.16
☐ 146	Steve Kealey	1.00	.45	.12
☐ 147	Dave Kingman	5.00	2.20	.60
☐ 148	Dick Billings	1.00	.45	.12
☐ 149	Gary Neibauer	1.00	.45	.12
☐ 150	Norm Cash	1.25	.55	.16
☐ 151	Jim Brewer	1.00	.45	.12
☐ 152	Gene Clines	1.00	.45	.12
☐ 153	Rick Auerbach	1.00	.45	.12
☐ 154	Ted Simmons	3.00	1.35	.35
☐ 155	Larry Dierker	1.00	.45	.12
☐ 156	Minnesota Twins	1.50	.70	.19
	Team Card			
☐ 157	Don Gullett	1.00	.45	.12
☐ 158	Jerry Kenney	1.00	.45	.12
☐ 159	John Boccabella	1.00	.45	.12
☐ 160	Andy Messersmith	1.25	.55	.16
☐ 161	Brock Davis	1.00	.45	.12
☐ 162	Brewers Rookies UER	1.25	.55	.16
	Jerry Bell			
	Darrell Porter			
	Bob Reynolds			
	(Porter and Bell photos switched)			
☐ 163	Tug McGraw	1.25	.55	.16
☐ 164	Tug McGraw IA	1.25	.55	.16
☐ 165	Chris Speier	1.25	.55	.16

☐ 166	Chris Speier IA	1.25	.55	.16
☐ 167	Deron Johnson	1.00	.45	.12
☐ 168	Deron Johnson IA	1.00	.45	.12
☐ 169	Vida Blue	1.50	.70	.19
☐ 170	Vida Blue IA	1.25	.55	.16
☐ 171	Darrell Evans	2.00	.90	.25
☐ 172	Darrell Evans IA	1.25	.55	.16
☐ 173	Clay Kirby	1.00	.45	.12
☐ 174	Clay Kirby IA	1.00	.45	.12
☐ 175	Tom Haller	1.00	.45	.12
☐ 176	Tom Haller IA	1.00	.45	.12
☐ 177	Paul Schaal	1.00	.45	.12
☐ 178	Paul Schaal IA	1.00	.45	.12
☐ 179	Dock Ellis	1.00	.45	.12
☐ 180	Dock Ellis IA	1.00	.45	.12
☐ 181	Ed Kranepool	1.00	.45	.12
☐ 182	Ed Kranepool IA	1.00	.45	.12
☐ 183	Bill Melton	1.00	.45	.12
☐ 184	Bill Melton IA	1.00	.45	.12
☐ 185	Ron Bryant	1.00	.45	.12
☐ 186	Ron Bryant IA	1.00	.45	.12
☐ 187	Gates Brown	1.25	.55	.16
☐ 188	Frank Lucchesi MG	1.00	.45	.12
☐ 189	Gene Tenace	1.25	.55	.16
☐ 190	Dave Giusti	1.00	.45	.12
☐ 191	Jeff Burroughs	1.50	.70	.19
☐ 192	Chicago Cubs	1.50	.70	.19
	Team Card			
☐ 193	Kurt Bevacqua	1.00	.45	.12
☐ 194	Fred Norman	1.00	.45	.12
☐ 195	Orlando Cepeda	3.00	1.35	.35
☐ 196	Mel Queen	1.00	.45	.12
☐ 197	Johnny Briggs	1.00	.45	.12
☐ 198	Dodgers Rookies	5.00	2.20	.60
	Charlie Hough			
	Bob O'Brien			
	Mike Strahler			
☐ 199	Mike Fiore	1.00	.45	.12
☐ 200	Lou Brock	7.00	3.10	.85
☐ 201	Phil Roof	1.00	.45	.12
☐ 202	Scipio Spinks	1.00	.45	.12
☐ 203	Ron Blomberg	1.00	.45	.12
☐ 204	Tommy Helms	1.00	.45	.12
☐ 205	Dick Drago	1.00	.45	.12
☐ 206	Dal Maxvill	1.00	.45	.12
☐ 207	Tom Egan	1.00	.45	.12
☐ 208	Milt Pappas	1.25	.55	.16
☐ 209	Joe Rudi	1.25	.55	.16
☐ 210	Denny McLain	1.25	.55	.16
☐ 211	Gary Sutherland	1.00	.45	.12
☐ 212	Grant Jackson	1.00	.45	.12
☐ 213	Angels Rookies	1.00	.45	.12
	Billy Parker			
	Art Kusnyer			
	Tom Silverio			
☐ 214	Mike McQueen	1.00	.45	.12
☐ 215	Alex Johnson	1.25	.55	.16
☐ 216	Joe Niekro	1.25	.55	.16
☐ 217	Roger Metzger	1.00	.45	.12
☐ 218	Eddie Kasko MG	1.00	.45	.12
☐ 219	Rennie Stennett	1.25	.55	.16
☐ 220	Jim Perry	1.25	.55	.16
☐ 221	NL Playoffs	1.50	.70	.19
	Bucs champs			
☐ 222	AL Playoffs	3.00	1.35	.35
	Orioles champs			
	(Brooks Robinson)			
☐ 223	World Series Game 1.	1.75	.80	.22
	(Dave McNally pitching)			
☐ 224	World Series Game 2.	1.75	.80	.22
	(Dave Johnson and			

Mark Belanger)

☐ 225	World Series Game 3. (Manny Sanguillen scoring)	1.75	.80	.22
☐ 226	World Series Game 4. (Roberto Clemente on second)	6.00	2.70	.75
☐ 227	World Series Game 5. (Nellie Briles pitching)	1.75	.80	.22
☐ 228	World Series Game 6. (Frank Robinson and Manny Sanguillen)	1.75	.80	.22
☐ 229	World Series Game 7. (Steve Blass pitching)	1.75	.80	.22
☐ 230	World Series Summary (Pirates celebrate)	1.75	.80	.22
☐ 231	Casey Cox	1.00	.45	.12
☐ 232	Giants Rookies Chris Arnold Jim Barr Dave Rader	1.00	.45	.12
☐ 233	Jay Johnstone	1.25	.55	.16
☐ 234	Ron Taylor	1.00	.45	.12
☐ 235	Merv Rettenmund	1.00	.45	.12
☐ 236	Jim McGlothlin	1.00	.45	.12
☐ 237	New York Yankees Team Card	1.50	.70	.19
☐ 238	Leron Lee	1.00	.45	.12
☐ 239	Tom Timmermann	1.00	.45	.12
☐ 240	Rich Allen	2.50	1.10	.30
☐ 241	Rollie Fingers	6.00	2.70	.75
☐ 242	Don Mincher	1.25	.55	.16
☐ 243	Frank Linzy	1.00	.45	.12
☐ 244	Steve Braun	1.00	.45	.12
☐ 245	Tommie Agee	1.25	.55	.16
☐ 246	Tom Burgmeier	1.00	.45	.12
☐ 247	Milt May	1.00	.45	.12
☐ 248	Tom Bradley	1.00	.45	.12
☐ 249	Harry Walker MG	1.00	.45	.12
☐ 250	Boog Powell	2.00	.90	.25
☐ 251	Checklist 264-394	4.00	.80	.40
☐ 252	Ken Reynolds	1.00	.45	.12
☐ 253	Sandy Alomar	1.25	.55	.16
☐ 254	Boots Day	1.00	.45	.12
☐ 255	Jim Lonborg	1.25	.55	.16
☐ 256	George Foster	2.50	1.10	.30
☐ 257	Tigers Rookies Jim Foor Tim Hosley Paul Jata	1.00	.45	.12
☐ 258	Randy Hundley	1.00	.45	.12
☐ 259	Sparky Lyle	1.25	.55	.16
☐ 260	Ralph Garr	1.25	.55	.16
☐ 261	Steve Mingori	1.00	.45	.12
☐ 262	San Diego Padres Team Card	1.50	.70	.19
☐ 263	Felipe Alou	1.50	.70	.19
☐ 264	Tommy John	2.50	1.10	.30
☐ 265	Wes Parker	1.50	.70	.19
☐ 266	Bobby Bolin	1.25	.55	.16
☐ 267	Dave Concepcion	3.00	1.35	.35
☐ 268	A's Rookies Dwain Anderson Chris Floethe	1.25	.55	.16
☐ 269	Don Hahn	1.25	.55	.16
☐ 270	Jim Palmer	10.00	4.50	1.25
☐ 271	Ken Rudolph	1.25	.55	.16
☐ 272	Mickey Rivers	2.00	.90	.25
☐ 273	Bobby Floyd	1.25	.55	.16
☐ 274	Al Severinsen	1.25	.55	.16
☐ 275	Cesar Tovar	1.25	.55	.16
☐ 276	Gene Mauch MG	1.50	.70	.19
☐ 277	Elliott Maddox	1.25	.55	.16
☐ 278	Dennis Higgins	1.25	.55	.16
☐ 279	Larry Brown	1.25	.55	.16
☐ 280	Willie McCovey	7.00	3.10	.85
☐ 281	Bill Parsons	1.25	.55	.16
☐ 282	Houston Astros Team Card	2.00	.90	.25
☐ 283	Darrell Brandon	1.25	.55	.16
☐ 284	Ike Brown	1.25	.55	.16
☐ 285	Gaylord Perry	6.00	2.70	.75
☐ 286	Gene Alley	1.50	.70	.19
☐ 287	Jim Hardin	1.25	.55	.16
☐ 288	Johnny Jeter	1.25	.55	.16
☐ 289	Syd O'Brien	1.25	.55	.16
☐ 290	Sonny Siebert	1.25	.55	.16
☐ 291	Hal McRae	1.50	.70	.19
☐ 292	Hal McRae IA	1.50	.70	.19
☐ 293	Dan Frisella	1.25	.55	.16
☐ 294	Dan Frisella IA	1.25	.55	.16
☐ 295	Dick Dietz	1.25	.55	.16
☐ 296	Dick Dietz IA	1.25	.55	.16
☐ 297	Claude Osteen	1.50	.70	.19
☐ 298	Claude Osteen IA	1.25	.55	.16
☐ 299	Hank Aaron	40.00	18.00	5.00
☐ 300	Hank Aaron IA	20.00	9.00	2.50
☐ 301	George Mitterwald	1.25	.55	.16
☐ 302	George Mitterwald IA.	1.25	.55	.16
☐ 303	Joe Pepitone	1.50	.70	.19
☐ 304	Joe Pepitone IA	1.25	.55	.16
☐ 305	Ken Boswell	1.25	.55	.16
☐ 306	Ken Boswell IA	1.25	.55	.16
☐ 307	Steve Renko	1.25	.55	.16
☐ 308	Steve Renko IA	1.25	.55	.16
☐ 309	Roberto Clemente	45.00	20.00	5.50
☐ 310	Roberto Clemente IA	25.00	11.00	3.10
☐ 311	Clay Carroll	1.25	.55	.16
☐ 312	Clay Carroll IA	1.25	.55	.16
☐ 313	Luis Aparicio	3.50	1.55	.45
☐ 314	Luis Aparicio IA	1.75	.80	.22
☐ 315	Paul Splittorff	1.25	.55	.16
☐ 316	Cardinals Rookies Jim Bibby Jorge Roque Santiago Guzman	1.50	.70	.19
☐ 317	Rich Hand	1.25	.55	.16
☐ 318	Sonny Jackson	1.25	.55	.16
☐ 319	Aurelio Rodriguez	1.25	.55	.16
☐ 320	Steve Blass	1.50	.70	.19
☐ 321	Joe Lahoud	1.25	.55	.16
☐ 322	Jose Pena	1.25	.55	.16
☐ 323	Earl Weaver MG	2.00	.90	.25
☐ 324	Mike Ryan	1.25	.55	.16
☐ 325	Mel Stottlemyre	1.50	.70	.19
☐ 326	Pat Kelly	1.25	.55	.16
☐ 327	Steve Stone	3.50	1.55	.45
☐ 328	Boston Red Sox Team Card	2.00	.90	.25
☐ 329	Roy Foster	1.25	.55	.16
☐ 330	Jim Hunter	4.00	1.80	.50
☐ 331	Stan Swanson	1.25	.55	.16
☐ 332	Buck Martinez	1.25	.55	.16
☐ 333	Steve Barber	1.25	.55	.16
☐ 334	Rangers Rookies Bill Fahey Jim Mason Tom Ragland	1.25	.55	.16
☐ 335	Bill Hands	1.25	.55	.16
☐ 336	Marty Martinez	1.25	.55	.16
☐ 337	Mike Kilkenny	1.25	.55	.16

338	Bob Grich	2.00	.90	.25
339	Ron Cook	1.25	.55	.16
340	Roy White	1.50	.70	.19
341	Joe Torre KP	1.25	.55	.16
342	Wilbur Wood KP	1.25	.55	.16
343	Willie Stargell KP	1.50	.70	.19
344	Dave McNally KP	1.25	.55	.16
345	Rick Wise KP	1.25	.55	.16
346	Jim Fregosi KP	1.25	.55	.16
347	Tom Seaver KP	3.00	1.35	.35
348	Sal Bando KP	1.25	.55	.16
349	Al Fitzmorris	1.25	.55	.16
350	Frank Howard	1.50	.70	.19
351	Braves Rookies	1.25	.55	.16
	Tom House			
	Rick Kester			
	Jimmy Britton			
352	Dave LaRoche	1.25	.55	.16
353	Art Shamsky	1.25	.55	.16
354	Tom Murphy	1.25	.55	.16
355	Bob Watson	1.50	.70	.19
356	Gerry Moses	1.25	.55	.16
357	Woody Fryman	1.25	.55	.16
358	Sparky Anderson MG	3.00	1.35	.35
359	Don Pavletich	1.25	.55	.16
360	Dave Roberts	1.25	.55	.16
361	Mike Andrews	1.25	.55	.16
362	New York Mets	2.00	.90	.25
	Team Card			
363	Ron Klimkowski	1.25	.55	.16
364	Johnny Callison	1.50	.70	.19
365	Dick Bosman	1.50	.70	.19
366	Jimmy Rosario	1.25	.55	.16
367	Ron Perranoski	1.50	.70	.19
368	Danny Thompson	1.25	.55	.16
369	Jim Lefebvre	1.50	.70	.19
370	Don Buford	1.25	.55	.16
371	Denny Lemaster	1.25	.55	.16
372	Royals Rookies	1.25	.55	.16
	Lance Clemons			
	Monty Montgomery			
373	John Mayberry	1.50	.70	.19
374	Jack Heidemann	1.25	.55	.16
375	Reggie Cleveland	1.25	.55	.16
376	Andy Kosco	1.25	.55	.16
377	Terry Harmon	1.25	.55	.16
378	Checklist 395-525	4.00	.80	.40
379	Ken Berry	1.25	.55	.16
380	Earl Williams	1.25	.55	.16
381	Chicago White Sox	2.00	.90	.25
	Team Card			
382	Joe Gibbon	1.25	.55	.16
383	Brant Alyea	1.25	.55	.16
384	Dave Campbell	1.25	.55	.16
385	Mickey Stanley	1.50	.70	.19
386	Jim Colborn	1.25	.55	.16
387	Horace Clarke	1.25	.55	.16
388	Charlie Williams	1.25	.55	.16
389	Bill Rigney MG	1.25	.55	.16
390	Willie Davis	1.50	.70	.19
391	Ken Sanders	1.25	.55	.16
392	Pirates Rookies	1.50	.70	.19
	Fred Cambria			
	Richie Zisk			
393	Curt Motton	1.25	.55	.16
394	Ken Forsch	1.50	.70	.19
395	Matty Alou	1.75	.80	.22
396	Paul Lindblad	1.50	.70	.19
397	Philadelphia Phillies	3.00	1.35	.35
	Team Card			
398	Larry Hisle	1.75	.80	.22
399	Milt Wilcox	1.50	.70	.19
400	Tony Oliva	2.00	.90	.25
401	Jim Nash	1.50	.70	.19
402	Bobby Heise	1.50	.70	.19
403	John Cumberland	1.50	.70	.19
404	Jeff Torborg	1.75	.80	.22
405	Ron Fairly	1.75	.80	.22
406	George Hendrick	2.00	.90	.25
407	Chuck Taylor	1.50	.70	.19
408	Jim Northrup	1.75	.80	.22
409	Frank Baker	1.50	.70	.19
410	Fergie Jenkins	6.00	2.70	.75
411	Bob Montgomery	1.50	.70	.19
412	Dick Kelley	1.50	.70	.19
413	White Sox Rookies	1.50	.70	.19
	Don Eddy			
	Dave Lemonds			
414	Bob Miller	1.50	.70	.19
415	Cookie Rojas	1.75	.80	.22
416	Johnny Edwards	1.50	.70	.19
417	Tom Hall	1.50	.70	.19
418	Tom Shopay	1.50	.70	.19
419	Jim Spencer	1.50	.70	.19
420	Steve Carlton	18.00	8.00	2.20
421	Ellie Rodriguez	1.50	.70	.19
422	Ray Lamb	1.50	.70	.19
423	Oscar Gamble	1.75	.80	.22
424	Bill Gogolewski	1.50	.70	.19
425	Ken Singleton	1.75	.80	.22
426	Ken Singleton IA	1.50	.70	.19
427	Tito Fuentes	1.50	.70	.19
428	Tito Fuentes IA	1.50	.70	.19
429	Bob Robertson	1.50	.70	.19
430	Bob Robertson IA	1.50	.70	.19
431	Clarence Gaston	2.50	1.10	.30
432	Clarence Gaston IA	1.75	.80	.22
433	Johnny Bench	25.00	11.00	3.10
434	Johnny Bench IA	14.00	6.25	1.75
435	Reggie Jackson	25.00	11.00	3.10
436	Reggie Jackson IA	14.00	6.25	1.75
437	Maury Wills	2.00	.90	.25
438	Maury Wills IA	1.75	.80	.22
439	Billy Williams	5.00	2.20	.60
440	Billy Williams IA	2.50	1.10	.30
441	Thurman Munson	14.00	6.25	1.75
442	Thurman Munson IA	7.00	3.10	.85
443	Ken Henderson	1.50	.70	.19
444	Ken Henderson IA	1.50	.70	.19
445	Tom Seaver	30.00	13.50	3.70
446	Tom Seaver IA	15.00	6.75	1.85
447	Willie Stargell	6.00	2.70	.75
448	Willie Stargell IA	3.00	1.35	.35
449	Bob Lemon MG	1.75	.80	.22
450	Mickey Lolich	2.50	1.10	.30
451	Tony LaRussa	3.00	1.35	.35
452	Ed Herrmann	1.50	.70	.19
453	Barry Lersch	1.50	.70	.19
454	Oakland A's	3.00	1.35	.35
	Team Card			
455	Tommy Harper	1.75	.80	.22
456	Mark Belanger	1.75	.80	.22
457	Padres Rookies	1.50	.70	.19
	Darcy Fast			
	Derrel Thomas			
	Mike Ivie			
458	Aurelio Monteagudo	1.50	.70	.19
459	Rick Renick	1.50	.70	.19
460	Al Downing	1.50	.70	.19
461	Tim Cullen	1.50	.70	.19
462	Rickey Clark	1.50	.70	.19
463	Bernie Carbo	1.50	.70	.19

☐ 464	Jim Roland	1.50	.70	.19
☐ 465	Gil Hodges MG	4.00	1.80	.50
☐ 466	Norm Miller	1.50	.70	.19
☐ 467	Steve Kline	1.50	.70	.19
☐ 468	Richie Scheinblum	1.50	.70	.19
☐ 469	Ron Herbel	1.50	.70	.19
☐ 470	Ray Fosse	1.50	.70	.19
☐ 471	Luke Walker	1.50	.70	.19
☐ 472	Phil Gagliano	1.50	.70	.19
☐ 473	Dan McGinn	1.50	.70	.19
☐ 474	Orioles Rookies	15.00	6.75	1.85
	Don Baylor			
	Roric Harrison			
	Johnny Oates			
☐ 475	Gary Nolan	1.75	.80	.22
☐ 476	Lee Richard	1.50	.70	.19
☐ 477	Tom Phoebus	1.50	.70	.19
☐ 478	Checklist 526-656	4.00	.80	.40
☐ 479	Don Shaw	1.50	.70	.19
☐ 480	Lee May	1.75	.80	.22
☐ 481	Billy Conigliaro	1.75	.80	.22
☐ 482	Joe Hoerner	1.50	.70	.19
☐ 483	Ken Suarez	1.50	.70	.19
☐ 484	Lum Harris MG	1.50	.70	.19
☐ 485	Phil Regan	1.75	.80	.22
☐ 486	John Lowenstein	1.50	.70	.19
☐ 487	Detroit Tigers	3.00	1.35	.35
	Team Card			
☐ 488	Mike Nagy	1.50	.70	.19
☐ 489	Expos Rookies	1.50	.70	.19
	Terry Humphrey			
	Keith Lampard			
☐ 490	Dave McNally	1.75	.80	.22
☐ 491	Lou Piniella KP	2.00	.90	.25
☐ 492	Mel Stottlemyre KP	1.75	.80	.22
☐ 493	Bob Bailey KP	1.75	.80	.22
☐ 494	Willie Horton KP	1.75	.80	.22
☐ 495	Bill Melton KP	1.75	.80	.22
☐ 496	Bud Harrelson KP	1.75	.80	.22
☐ 497	Jim Perry KP	1.75	.80	.22
☐ 498	Brooks Robinson KP	3.00	1.35	.35
☐ 499	Vicente Romo	1.50	.70	.19
☐ 500	Joe Torre	2.50	1.10	.30
☐ 501	Pete Hamm	1.50	.70	.19
☐ 502	Jackie Hernandez	1.50	.70	.19
☐ 503	Gary Peters	1.50	.70	.19
☐ 504	Ed Spiezio	1.50	.70	.19
☐ 505	Mike Marshall	1.75	.80	.22
☐ 506	Indians Rookies	1.50	.70	.19
	Terry Ley			
	Jim Moyer			
	Dick Tidrow			
☐ 507	Fred Gladding	1.50	.70	.19
☐ 508	Elrod Hendricks	1.50	.70	.19
☐ 509	Don McMahon	1.50	.70	.19
☐ 510	Ted Williams MG	10.00	4.50	1.25
☐ 511	Tony Taylor	1.50	.70	.19
☐ 512	Paul Popovich	1.50	.70	.19
☐ 513	Lindy McDaniel	1.75	.80	.22
☐ 514	Ted Sizemore	1.50	.70	.19
☐ 515	Bert Blyleven	4.00	1.80	.50
☐ 516	Oscar Brown	1.50	.70	.19
☐ 517	Ken Brett	1.50	.70	.19
☐ 518	Wayne Garrett	1.50	.70	.19
☐ 519	Ted Abernathy	1.50	.70	.19
☐ 520	Larry Bowa	2.50	1.10	.30
☐ 521	Alan Foster	1.50	.70	.19
☐ 522	Los Angeles Dodgers	3.00	1.35	.35
	Team Card			
☐ 523	Chuck Dobson	1.50	.70	.19
☐ 524	Reds Rookies	1.50	.70	.19
	Ed Armbrister			
	Mel Behney			
☐ 525	Carlos May	1.75	.80	.22
☐ 526	Bob Bailey	4.50	2.00	.55
☐ 527	Dave Leonhard	4.00	1.80	.50
☐ 528	Ron Stone	4.00	1.80	.50
☐ 529	Dave Nelson	4.50	2.00	.55
☐ 530	Don Sutton	7.00	3.10	.85
☐ 531	Freddie Patek	4.50	2.00	.55
☐ 532	Fred Kendall	4.00	1.80	.50
☐ 533	Ralph Houk MG	4.50	2.00	.55
☐ 534	Jim Hickman	4.50	2.00	.55
☐ 535	Ed Brinkman	4.00	1.80	.50
☐ 536	Doug Rader	4.50	2.00	.55
☐ 537	Bob Locker	4.00	1.80	.50
☐ 538	Charlie Sands	4.00	1.80	.50
☐ 539	Terry Forster	5.00	2.20	.60
☐ 540	Felix Millan	4.00	1.80	.50
☐ 541	Roger Repoz	4.00	1.80	.50
☐ 542	Jack Billingham	4.00	1.80	.50
☐ 543	Duane Josephson	4.00	1.80	.50
☐ 544	Ted Martinez	4.00	1.80	.50
☐ 545	Wayne Granger	4.00	1.80	.50
☐ 546	Joe Hague	4.00	1.80	.50
☐ 547	Cleveland Indians	7.00	3.10	.85
	Team Card			
☐ 548	Frank Reberger	4.00	1.80	.50
☐ 549	Dave May	4.00	1.80	.50
☐ 550	Brooks Robinson	25.00	11.00	3.10
☐ 551	Ollie Brown	4.00	1.80	.50
☐ 552	Ollie Brown IA	4.00	1.80	.50
☐ 553	Wilbur Wood	4.50	2.00	.55
☐ 554	Wilbur Wood IA	4.00	1.80	.50
☐ 555	Ron Santo	5.00	2.20	.60
☐ 556	Ron Santo IA	4.50	2.00	.55
☐ 557	John Odom	4.00	1.80	.50
☐ 558	John Odom IA	4.00	1.80	.50
☐ 559	Pete Rose	40.00	18.00	5.00
☐ 560	Pete Rose IA	20.00	9.00	2.50
☐ 561	Leo Cardenas	4.00	1.80	.50
☐ 562	Leo Cardenas IA	4.00	1.80	.50
☐ 563	Ray Sadecki	4.00	1.80	.50
☐ 564	Ray Sadecki IA	4.00	1.80	.50
☐ 565	Reggie Smith	4.50	2.00	.55
☐ 566	Reggie Smith IA	4.00	1.80	.50
☐ 567	Juan Marichal	12.00	5.50	1.50
☐ 568	Juan Marichal IA	6.00	2.70	.75
☐ 569	Ed Kirkpatrick	4.00	1.80	.50
☐ 570	Ed Kirkpatrick IA	4.00	1.80	.50
☐ 571	Nate Colbert	4.00	1.80	.50
☐ 572	Nate Colbert IA	4.00	1.80	.50
☐ 573	Fritz Peterson	4.00	1.80	.50
☐ 574	Fritz Peterson IA	4.00	1.80	.50
☐ 575	Al Oliver	5.00	2.20	.60
☐ 576	Leo Durocher MG	5.00	2.20	.60
☐ 577	Mike Paul	4.50	2.00	.55
☐ 578	Billy Grabarkewitz	4.00	1.80	.50
☐ 579	Doyle Alexander	5.00	2.20	.60
☐ 580	Lou Piniella	5.00	2.20	.60
☐ 581	Wade Blasingame	4.00	1.80	.50
☐ 582	Montreal Expos	7.00	3.10	.85
	Team Card			
☐ 583	Darold Knowles	4.00	1.80	.50
☐ 584	Jerry McNertney	4.00	1.80	.50
☐ 585	George Scott	4.50	2.00	.55
☐ 586	Denis Menke	4.00	1.80	.50
☐ 587	Billy Wilson	4.00	1.80	.50
☐ 588	Jim Holt	4.00	1.80	.50
☐ 589	Hal Lanier	4.00	1.80	.50
☐ 590	Graig Nettles	5.00	2.20	.60
☐ 591	Paul Casanova	4.00	1.80	.50

☐ 592	Lew Krausse	4.00	1.80	.50
☐ 593	Rich Morales	4.00	1.80	.50
☐ 594	Jim Beauchamp	4.00	1.80	.50
☐ 595	Nolan Ryan	225.00	100.00	28.00
☐ 596	Manny Mota	4.50	2.00	.55
☐ 597	Jim Magnuson	4.00	1.80	.50
☐ 598	Hal King	4.50	2.00	.50
☐ 599	Billy Champion	4.00	1.80	.50
☐ 600	Al Kaline	25.00	11.00	3.10
☐ 601	George Stone	4.00	1.80	.50
☐ 602	Dave Bristol MG	4.00	1.80	.50
☐ 603	Jim Ray	4.00	1.80	.50
☐ 604A	Checklist 657-787..	10.00	2.00	1.00
	(Copyright on back bottom right)			
☐ 604B	Checklist 657-787..	10.00	2.00	1.00
	(Copyright on back bottom left)			
☐ 605	Nelson Briles	4.50	2.00	.55
☐ 606	Luis Melendez	4.00	1.80	.50
☐ 607	Frank Duffy	4.00	1.80	.50
☐ 608	Mike Corkins	4.00	1.80	.50
☐ 609	Tom Grieve	4.50	2.00	.55
☐ 610	Bill Stoneman	4.50	2.00	.55
☐ 611	Rich Reese	4.00	1.80	.50
☐ 612	Joe Decker	4.00	1.80	.50
☐ 613	Mike Ferraro	4.00	1.80	.50
☐ 614	Ted Uhlaender	4.00	1.80	.50
☐ 615	Steve Hargan	4.00	1.80	.50
☐ 616	Joe Ferguson	4.00	1.80	.50
☐ 617	Kansas City Royals	7.00	3.10	.85
	Team Card			
☐ 618	Rich Robertson	4.00	1.80	.50
☐ 619	Rich McKinney	4.00	1.80	.50
☐ 620	Phil Niekro	10.00	4.50	1.25
☐ 621	Commissioners Award	5.00	2.20	.60
☐ 622	MVP Award	5.00	2.20	.60
☐ 623	Cy Young Award	5.00	2.20	.60
☐ 624	Minor League Player ..	5.00	2.20	.60
	of the Year			
☐ 625	Rookie of the Year	5.00	2.20	.60
☐ 626	Babe Ruth Award	5.00	2.20	.60
☐ 627	Moe Drabowsky	4.00	1.80	.50
☐ 628	Terry Crowley	4.00	1.80	.50
☐ 629	Paul Doyle	4.00	1.80	.50
☐ 630	Rich Hebner	4.50	2.00	.55
☐ 631	John Strohmayer	4.00	1.80	.50
☐ 632	Mike Hegan	4.00	1.80	.50
☐ 633	Jack Hiatt	4.00	1.80	.50
☐ 634	Dick Woodson	4.00	1.80	.50
☐ 635	Don Money	4.50	2.00	.55
☐ 636	Bill Lee	4.50	2.00	.55
☐ 637	Preston Gomez MG....	4.00	1.80	.50
☐ 638	Ken Wright	4.00	1.80	.50
☐ 639	J.C. Martin	4.00	1.80	.50
☐ 640	Joe Coleman	4.00	1.80	.50
☐ 641	Mike Lum	4.00	1.80	.50
☐ 642	Dennis Riddleberger ..	4.00	1.80	.50
☐ 643	Russ Gibson	4.00	1.80	.50
☐ 644	Bernie Allen	4.00	1.80	.50
☐ 645	Jim Maloney	4.50	2.00	.55
☐ 646	Chico Salmon	4.00	1.80	.50
☐ 647	Bob Moose	4.00	1.80	.50
☐ 648	Jim Lyttle	4.00	1.80	.50
☐ 649	Pete Richert	4.00	1.80	.50
☐ 650	Sal Bando	4.50	2.00	.55
☐ 651	Cincinnati Reds	7.00	3.10	.85
	Team Card			
☐ 652	Marcelino Lopez	4.00	1.80	.50
☐ 653	Jim Fairey	4.00	1.80	.50
☐ 654	Horacio Pina	4.50	2.00	.55

☐ 655	Jerry Grote	4.00	1.80	.50
☐ 656	Rudy May	4.00	1.80	.50
☐ 657	Bobby Wine	12.00	5.50	1.50
☐ 658	Steve Dunning	12.00	5.50	1.50
☐ 659	Bob Aspromonte	12.00	5.50	1.50
☐ 660	Paul Blair	14.00	6.25	1.75
☐ 661	Bill Virdon MG	14.00	6.25	1.75
☐ 662	Stan Bahnsen	12.00	5.50	1.50
☐ 663	Fran Healy	14.00	6.25	1.75
☐ 664	Bobby Knoop	12.00	5.50	1.50
☐ 665	Chris Short	12.00	5.50	1.50
☐ 666	Hector Torres	12.00	5.50	1.50
☐ 667	Ray Newman	12.00	5.50	1.50
☐ 668	Texas Rangers	25.00	11.00	3.10
	Team Card			
☐ 669	Willie Crawford	12.00	5.50	1.50
☐ 670	Ken Holtzman	14.00	6.25	1.75
☐ 671	Donn Clendenon	14.00	6.25	1.75
☐ 672	Archie Reynolds	12.00	5.50	1.50
☐ 673	Dave Marshall	12.00	5.50	1.50
☐ 674	John Kennedy	12.00	5.50	1.50
☐ 675	Pat Jarvis	12.00	5.50	1.50
☐ 676	Danny Cater	12.00	5.50	1.50
☐ 677	Ivan Murrell	12.00	5.50	1.50
☐ 678	Steve Luebber	12.00	5.50	1.50
☐ 679	Astros Rookies	12.00	5.50	1.50
	Bob Fenwick			
	Bob Stinson			
☐ 680	Dave Johnson	14.00	6.25	1.75
☐ 681	Bobby Pfeil	12.00	5.50	1.50
☐ 682	Mike McCormick	14.00	6.25	1.75
☐ 683	Steve Hovley	12.00	5.50	1.50
☐ 684	Hal Breeden	12.00	5.50	1.50
☐ 685	Joel Horlen	12.00	5.50	1.50
☐ 686	Steve Garvey	40.00	18.00	5.00
☐ 687	Del Unser	12.00	5.50	1.50
☐ 688	St. Louis Cardinals ...	20.00	9.00	2.50
	Team Card			
☐ 689	Eddie Fisher	12.00	5.50	1.50
☐ 690	Willie Montanez	14.00	6.25	1.75
☐ 691	Curt Blefary	12.00	5.50	1.50
☐ 692	Curt Blefary IA	12.00	5.50	1.50
☐ 693	Alan Gallagher	12.00	5.50	1.50
☐ 694	Alan Gallagher IA	12.00	5.50	1.50
☐ 695	Rod Carew	70.00	32.00	8.75
☐ 696	Rod Carew IA	35.00	16.00	4.40
☐ 697	Jerry Koosman	15.00	6.75	1.85
☐ 698	Jerry Koosman IA	14.00	6.25	1.75
☐ 699	Bobby Murcer	15.00	6.75	1.85
☐ 700	Bobby Murcer IA	14.00	6.25	1.75
☐ 701	Jose Pagan	12.00	5.50	1.50
☐ 702	Jose Pagan IA	12.00	5.50	1.50
☐ 703	Doug Griffin	12.00	5.50	1.50
☐ 704	Doug Griffin IA	12.00	5.50	1.50
☐ 705	Pat Corrales	14.00	6.25	1.75
☐ 706	Pat Corrales IA	12.00	5.50	1.50
☐ 707	Tim Foli	12.00	5.50	1.50
☐ 708	Tim Foli IA	12.00	5.50	1.50
☐ 709	Jim Kaat	16.00	7.25	2.00
☐ 710	Jim Kaat IA	14.00	6.25	1.75
☐ 711	Bobby Bonds	20.00	9.00	2.50
☐ 712	Bobby Bonds IA	14.00	6.25	1.75
☐ 713	Gene Michael	12.00	5.50	1.50
☐ 714	Gene Michael IA	12.00	5.50	1.50
☐ 715	Mike Epstein	12.00	5.50	1.50
☐ 716	Jesus Alou	12.00	5.50	1.50
☐ 717	Bruce Dal Canton	12.00	5.50	1.50
☐ 718	Del Rice MG	12.00	5.50	1.50
☐ 719	Cesar Geronimo	12.00	5.50	1.50
☐ 720	Sam McDowell	14.00	6.25	1.75
☐ 721	Eddie Leon	12.00	5.50	1.50

☐ 722	Bill Sudakis	12.00	5.50	1.50
☐ 723	Al Santorini	12.00	5.50	1.50
☐ 724	AL Rookie Pitchers	12.00	5.50	1.50
	John Curtis			
	Rich Hinton			
	Mickey Scott			
☐ 725	Dick McAuliffe	14.00	6.25	1.75
☐ 726	Dick Selma	12.00	5.50	1.50
☐ 727	Jose Laboy	12.00	5.50	1.50
☐ 728	Gail Hopkins	12.00	5.50	1.50
☐ 729	Bob Veale	14.00	6.25	1.75
☐ 730	Rick Monday	14.00	6.25	1.75
☐ 731	Baltimore Orioles	20.00	9.00	2.50
	Team Card			
☐ 732	George Culver	12.00	5.50	1.50
☐ 733	Jim Ray Hart	14.00	6.25	1.75
☐ 734	Bob Burda	12.00	5.50	1.50
☐ 735	Diego Segui	12.00	5.50	1.50
☐ 736	Bill Russell	14.00	6.25	1.75
☐ 737	Len Randle	14.00	6.25	1.75
☐ 738	Jim Merritt	12.00	5.50	1.50
☐ 739	Don Mason	12.00	5.50	1.50
☐ 740	Rico Carty	14.00	6.25	1.75
☐ 741	Rookie First Basemen	14.00	6.25	1.75
	Tom Hutton			
	John Milner			
	Rick Miller			
☐ 742	Jim Rooker	12.00	5.50	1.50
☐ 743	Cesar Gutierrez	12.00	5.50	1.50
☐ 744	Jim Slaton	12.00	5.50	1.50
☐ 745	Julian Javier	14.00	6.25	1.75
☐ 746	Lowell Palmer	12.00	5.50	1.50
☐ 747	Jim Stewart	12.00	5.50	1.50
☐ 748	Phil Hennigan	12.00	5.50	1.50
☐ 749	Walter Alston MG	14.00	6.25	1.75
☐ 750	Willie Horton	14.00	6.25	1.75
☐ 751	Steve Carlton TR	50.00	22.00	6.25
☐ 752	Joe Morgan TR	45.00	20.00	5.50
☐ 753	Denny McLain TR	20.00	9.00	2.50
☐ 754	Frank Robinson TR	45.00	20.00	5.50
☐ 755	Jim Fregosi TR	14.00	6.25	1.75
☐ 756	Rick Wise TR	14.00	6.25	1.75
☐ 757	Jose Cardenal TR	12.00	5.50	1.50
☐ 758	Gil Garrido	12.00	5.50	1.50
☐ 759	Chris Cannizzaro	12.00	5.50	1.50
☐ 760	Bill Mazeroski	18.00	8.00	2.20
☐ 761	Rookie Outfielders	25.00	11.00	3.10
	Ben Oglivie			
	Ron Cey			
	Bernie Williams			
☐ 762	Wayne Simpson	12.00	5.50	1.50
☐ 763	Ron Hansen	12.00	5.50	1.50
☐ 764	Dusty Baker	20.00	9.00	2.50
☐ 765	Ken McMullen	12.00	5.50	1.50
☐ 766	Steve Hamilton	12.00	5.50	1.50
☐ 767	Tom McCraw	14.00	6.25	1.75
☐ 768	Denny Doyle	12.00	5.50	1.50
☐ 769	Jack Aker	12.00	5.50	1.50
☐ 770	Jim Wynn	14.00	6.25	1.75
☐ 771	San Francisco Giants	20.00	9.00	2.50
	Team Card			
☐ 772	Ken Tatum	12.00	5.50	1.50
☐ 773	Ron Brand	12.00	5.50	1.50
☐ 774	Luis Alvarado	12.00	5.50	1.50
☐ 775	Jerry Reuss	14.00	6.25	1.75
☐ 776	Bill Voss	12.00	5.50	1.50
☐ 777	Hoyt Wilhelm	25.00	11.00	3.10
☐ 778	Twins Rookies	18.00	8.00	2.20
	Vic Albury			
	Rick Dempsey			
	Jim Strickland			
☐ 779	Tony Cloninger	12.00	5.50	1.50
☐ 780	Dick Green	12.00	5.50	1.50
☐ 781	Jim McAndrew	12.00	5.50	1.50
☐ 782	Larry Stahl	12.00	5.50	1.50
☐ 783	Les Cain	12.00	5.50	1.50
☐ 784	Ken Aspromonte	12.00	5.50	1.50
☐ 785	Vic Davalillo	12.00	5.50	1.50
☐ 786	Chuck Brinkman	12.00	5.50	1.50
☐ 787	Ron Reed	16.00	5.50	1.50

1973 Topps

The cards in this 660-card set measure 2 1/2" by 3 1/2". The 1973 Topps set marked the last year in which Topps marketed baseball cards in consecutive series. The last series (529-660) is more difficult to obtain. In some parts of the country, however, all five series were distributed together. Beginning in 1974, all Topps cards were printed at the same time, thus eliminating the "high number" factor. The set features team leader cards with small individual pictures of the coaching staff members and a larger picture of the manager. The "background" variations below with respect to these leader cards are subtle and are best understood after a side-by-side comparison of the two varieties. An "All-Time Leaders" series (471-478) appeared for the first time in this set. Kid Pictures appeared again for the second year in a row (341-346). Other topical subsets within the set included League Leaders (61-68), Playoffs cards (201-202), World Series cards (203-210), and Rookie Prospects (601-616). The key Rookie Cards in this set are all in the Rookie Prospect series: Bob Boone, Dwight Evans, and Mike Schmidt.

	NRMT	VG-E	GOOD
COMPLETE SET (660)	750.00	350.00	95.00
COMMON CARD (1-264)	.50	.23	.06
COMMON CARD (265-396)	.75	.35	.09
COMMON CARD (397-528)	1.25	.55	.16
COMMON CARD (529-660)	3.50	1.55	.45
☐ 1 All-Time HR Leaders	35.00	10.00	3.50
Babe Ruth 714			
Hank Aaron 673			
Willie Mays 654			
☐ 2 Rich Hebner	.75	.35	.09

☐ 3 Jim Lonborg	.75	.35	.09
☐ 4 John Milner	.50	.23	.06
☐ 5 Ed Brinkman	.50	.23	.06
☐ 6 Mac Scarce	.50	.23	.06
☐ 7 Texas Rangers	1.25	.55	.16
Team Card			
☐ 8 Tom Hall	.50	.23	.06
☐ 9 Johnny Oates	.50	.23	.06
☐ 10 Don Sutton	2.00	.90	.25
☐ 11 Chris Chambliss	1.25	.55	.16
☐ 12A Padres Leaders	.75	.35	.09
Don Zimmer MG			
Dave Garcia CO			
Johnny Podres CO			
Bob Skinner CO			
Whitey Wietelmann CO			
(Padres no right ear)			
☐ 12B Padres Leaders	1.50	.70	.19
(Padres has right ear)			
☐ 13 George Hendrick	.75	.35	.09
☐ 14 Sonny Siebert	.50	.23	.06
☐ 15 Ralph Garr	.75	.35	.09
☐ 16 Steve Braun	.50	.23	.06
☐ 17 Fred Gladding	.50	.23	.06
☐ 18 Leroy Stanton	.50	.23	.06
☐ 19 Tim Foli	.50	.23	.06
☐ 20 Stan Bahnsen	.50	.23	.06
☐ 21 Randy Hundley	.50	.23	.06
☐ 22 Ted Abernathy	.50	.23	.06
☐ 23 Dave Kingman	1.25	.55	.16
☐ 24 Al Santorini	.50	.23	.06
☐ 25 Roy White	.75	.35	.09
☐ 26 Pittsburgh Pirates	1.25	.55	.16
Team Card			
☐ 27 Bill Gogolewski	.50	.23	.06
☐ 28 Hal McRae	1.25	.55	.16
☐ 29 Tony Taylor	.50	.23	.06
☐ 30 Tug McGraw	.75	.35	.09
☐ 31 Buddy Bell	3.00	1.35	.35
☐ 32 Fred Norman	.50	.23	.06
☐ 33 Jim Breazeale	.50	.23	.06
☐ 34 Pat Dobson	.50	.23	.06
☐ 35 Willie Davis	.75	.35	.09
☐ 36 Steve Barber	.50	.23	.06
☐ 37 Bill Robinson	.75	.35	.09
☐ 38 Mike Epstein	.50	.23	.06
☐ 39 Dave Roberts	.50	.23	.06
☐ 40 Reggie Smith	.75	.35	.09
☐ 41 Tom Walker	.50	.23	.06
☐ 42 Mike Andrews	.50	.23	.06
☐ 43 Randy Moffitt	.50	.23	.06
☐ 44 Rick Monday	.75	.35	.09
☐ 45 Ellie Rodriguez UER	.50	.23	.06
(Photo actually			
John Felske)			
☐ 46 Lindy McDaniel	.75	.35	.09
☐ 47 Luis Melendez	.50	.23	.06
☐ 48 Paul Splittorff	.50	.23	.06
☐ 49A Twins Leaders	.75	.35	.09
Frank Quilici MG			
Vern Morgan CO			
Bob Rodgers CO			
Ralph Rowe CO			
Al Worthington CO			
(Solid backgrounds)			
☐ 49B Twins Leaders	1.50	.70	.19
(Natural backgrounds)			
☐ 50 Roberto Clemente	45.00	20.00	5.50
☐ 51 Chuck Seelbach	.50	.23	.06
☐ 52 Denis Menke	.50	.23	.06
☐ 53 Steve Dunning	.50	.23	.06
☐ 54 Checklist 1-132	3.00	.60	.30
☐ 55 Jon Matlack	.75	.35	.09
☐ 56 Merv Rettenmund	.50	.23	.06
☐ 57 Derrel Thomas	.50	.23	.06
☐ 58 Mike Paul	.50	.23	.06
☐ 59 Steve Yeager	1.50	.70	.19
☐ 60 Ken Holtzman	.75	.35	.09
☐ 61 Batting Leaders	3.00	1.35	.35
Billy Williams			
Rod Carew			
☐ 62 Home Run Leaders	2.50	1.10	.30
Johnny Bench			
Dick Allen			
☐ 63 RBI Leaders	2.50	1.10	.30
Johnny Bench			
Dick Allen			
☐ 64 Stolen Base Leaders	2.00	.90	.25
Lou Brock			
Bert Campaneris			
☐ 65 ERA Leaders	2.00	.90	.25
Steve Carlton			
Luis Tiant			
☐ 66 Victory Leaders	2.00	.90	.25
Steve Carlton			
Gaylord Perry			
Wilbur Wood			
☐ 67 Strikeout Leaders	30.00	13.50	3.70
Steve Carlton			
Nolan Ryan			
☐ 68 Leading Firemen	1.00	.45	.12
Clay Carroll			
Sparky Lyle			
☐ 69 Phil Gagliano	.50	.23	.06
☐ 70 Milt Pappas	.75	.35	.09
☐ 71 Johnny Briggs	.50	.23	.06
☐ 72 Ron Reed	.50	.23	.06
☐ 73 Ed Herrmann	.50	.23	.06
☐ 74 Billy Champion	.50	.23	.06
☐ 75 Vada Pinson	.75	.35	.09
☐ 76 Doug Rader	.50	.23	.06
☐ 77 Mike Torrez	.75	.35	.09
☐ 78 Richie Scheinblum	.50	.23	.06
☐ 79 Jim Willoughby	.50	.23	.06
☐ 80 Tony Oliva UER	1.50	.70	.19
(Minnseota on front)			
☐ 81A Cubs Leaders	1.50	.70	.19
Whitey Lockman MG			
Hank Aguirre CO			
Ernie Banks CO			
Larry Jansen CO			
Pete Reiser CO			
(Solid backgrounds)			
☐ 81B Cubs Leaders	2.00	.90	.25
(Natural backgrounds)			
☐ 82 Fritz Peterson	.50	.23	.06
☐ 83 Leron Lee	.50	.23	.06
☐ 84 Rollie Fingers	5.00	2.20	.60
☐ 85 Ted Simmons	2.00	.90	.25
☐ 86 Tom McCraw	.50	.23	.06
☐ 87 Ken Boswell	.50	.23	.06
☐ 88 Mickey Stanley	.75	.35	.09
☐ 89 Jack Billingham	.50	.23	.06
☐ 90 Brooks Robinson	8.00	3.60	1.00
☐ 91 Los Angeles Dodgers	1.25	.55	.16
Team Card			
☐ 92 Jerry Bell	.50	.23	.06
☐ 93 Jesus Alou	.50	.23	.06
☐ 94 Dick Billings	.50	.23	.06
☐ 95 Steve Blass	.75	.35	.09
☐ 96 Doug Griffin	.50	.23	.06
☐ 97 Willie Montanez	.75	.35	.09

☐ 98	Dick Woodson	.50	.23	.06
☐ 99	Carl Taylor	.50	.23	.06
☐ 100	Hank Aaron	30.00	13.50	3.70
☐ 101	Ken Henderson	.50	.23	.06
☐ 102	Rudy May	.50	.23	.06
☐ 103	Celerino Sanchez	.50	.23	.06
☐ 104	Reggie Cleveland	.50	.23	.06
☐ 105	Carlos May	.50	.23	.06
☐ 106	Terry Humphrey	.50	.23	.06
☐ 107	Phil Hennigan	.50	.23	.06
☐ 108	Bill Russell	.75	.35	.09
☐ 109	Doyle Alexander	.75	.35	.09
☐ 110	Bob Watson	.75	.35	.09
☐ 111	Dave Nelson	.50	.23	.06
☐ 112	Gary Ross	.50	.23	.06
☐ 113	Jerry Grote	.50	.23	.06
☐ 114	Lynn McGlothen	.50	.23	.06
☐ 115	Ron Santo	.75	.35	.09
☐ 116A	Yankees Leaders	.75	.35	.09

Ralph Houk MG
Jim Hegan CO
Elston Howard CO
Dick Howser CO
Jim Turner CO
(Solid backgrounds)

☐ 116B	Yankees Leaders	1.50	.70	.19

(Natural backgrounds)

☐ 117	Ramon Hernandez	.50	.23	.06
☐ 118	John Mayberry	.75	.35	.09
☐ 119	Larry Bowa	.75	.35	.09
☐ 120	Joe Coleman	.50	.23	.06
☐ 121	Dave Rader	.50	.23	.06
☐ 122	Jim Strickland	.50	.23	.06
☐ 123	Sandy Alomar	.75	.35	.09
☐ 124	Jim Hardin	.50	.23	.06
☐ 125	Ron Fairly	.75	.35	.09
☐ 126	Jim Brewer	.50	.23	.06
☐ 127	Milwaukee Brewers	1.25	.55	.16

Team Card

☐ 128	Ted Sizemore	.50	.23	.06
☐ 129	Terry Forster	.75	.35	.09
☐ 130	Pete Rose	20.00	9.00	2.50
☐ 131A	Red Sox Leaders	.75	.35	.09

Eddie Kasko MG
Doug Camilli CO
Don Lenhardt CO
Eddie Popowski CO
(No right ear)
Lee Stange CO

☐ 131B	Red Sox Leaders	1.50	.70	.19

(Popowski has right
ear showing)

☐ 132	Matty Alou	.75	.35	.09
☐ 133	Dave Roberts	.50	.23	.06
☐ 134	Milt Wilcox	.50	.23	.06
☐ 135	Lee May UER	.75	.35	.09

(Career average .000)

☐ 136A	Orioles Leaders	2.00	.90	.25

Earl Weaver MG
George Bamberger CO
Jim Frey CO
Billy Hunter CO
George Staller CO
(Orange backgrounds)

☐ 136B	Orioles Leaders	2.50	1.10	.30

(Dark pale
backgrounds)

☐ 137	Jim Beauchamp	.50	.23	.06
☐ 138	Horacio Pina	.50	.23	.06
☐ 139	Carmen Fanzone	.50	.23	.06
☐ 140	Lou Piniella	1.00	.45	.12
☐ 141	Bruce Kison	.50	.23	.06
☐ 142	Thurman Munson	6.00	2.70	.75
☐ 143	John Curtis	.50	.23	.06
☐ 144	Marty Perez	.50	.23	.06
☐ 145	Bobby Bonds	2.00	.90	.25
☐ 146	Woodie Fryman	.50	.23	.06
☐ 147	Mike Anderson	.50	.23	.06
☐ 148	Dave Goltz	.50	.23	.06
☐ 149	Ron Hunt	.50	.23	.06
☐ 150	Wilbur Wood	.75	.35	.09
☐ 151	Wes Parker	.75	.35	.09
☐ 152	Dave May	.50	.23	.06
☐ 153	Al Hrabosky	.75	.35	.09
☐ 154	Jeff Torborg	.75	.35	.09
☐ 155	Sal Bando	.75	.35	.09
☐ 156	Cesar Geronimo	.50	.23	.06
☐ 157	Denny Riddleberger	.50	.23	.06
☐ 158	Houston Astros	1.25	.55	.16

Team Card

☐ 159	Clarence Gaston	1.00	.45	.12
☐ 160	Jim Palmer	8.00	3.60	1.00
☐ 161	Ted Martinez	.50	.23	.06
☐ 162	Pete Broberg	.50	.23	.06
☐ 163	Vic Davalillo	.50	.23	.06
☐ 164	Monty Montgomery	.50	.23	.06
☐ 165	Luis Aparicio	3.00	1.35	.35
☐ 166	Terry Harmon	.50	.23	.06
☐ 167	Steve Stone	.75	.35	.09
☐ 168	Jim Northrup	.75	.35	.09
☐ 169	Ron Schueler	.50	.23	.06
☐ 170	Harmon Killebrew	5.00	2.20	.60
☐ 171	Bernie Carbo	.50	.23	.06
☐ 172	Steve Kline	.50	.23	.06
☐ 173	Hal Breeden	.50	.23	.06
☐ 174	Rich Gossage	8.00	3.60	1.00
☐ 175	Frank Robinson	8.00	3.60	1.00
☐ 176	Chuck Taylor	.50	.23	.06
☐ 177	Bill Plummer	.50	.23	.06
☐ 178	Don Rose	.50	.23	.06
☐ 179A	A's Leaders	.75	.35	.09

Dick Williams MG
Jerry Adair CO
Vern Hoscheit CO
Irv Noren CO
Wes Stock CO
(Hoscheit left ear
showing)

☐ 179B	A's Leaders	1.50	.70	.19

(Hoscheit left ear
not showing)

☐ 180	Fergie Jenkins	5.00	2.20	.60
☐ 181	Jack Brohamer	.50	.23	.06
☐ 182	Mike Caldwell	.50	.23	.06
☐ 183	Don Buford	.50	.23	.06
☐ 184	Jerry Koosman	.75	.35	.09
☐ 185	Jim Wynn	.75	.35	.09
☐ 186	Bill Fahey	.50	.23	.06
☐ 187	Luke Walker	.50	.23	.06
☐ 188	Cookie Rojas	.75	.35	.09
☐ 189	Greg Luzinski	1.25	.55	.16
☐ 190	Bob Gibson	7.00	3.10	.85
☐ 191	Detroit Tigers	1.25	.55	.16

Team Card

☐ 192	Pat Jarvis	.50	.23	.06
☐ 193	Carlton Fisk	14.00	6.25	1.75
☐ 194	Jorge Orta	.50	.23	.06
☐ 195	Clay Carroll	.50	.23	.06
☐ 196	Ken McMullen	.50	.23	.06
☐ 197	Ed Goodson	.50	.23	.06
☐ 198	Horace Clarke	.50	.23	.06
☐ 199	Bert Blyleven	2.00	.90	.25

☐ 200 Billy Williams	4.00	1.80	.50
☐ 201 A.L. Playoffs	1.00	.45	.12
A's over Tigers; George Hendrick scores winning run			
☐ 202 N.L. Playoffs	1.00	.45	.12
Reds over Pirates George Foster's run decides			
☐ 203 World Series Game 1.	1.00	.45	.12
Gene Tenace the Menace			
☐ 204 World Series Game 2.	1.00	.45	.12
A's two straight			
☐ 205 World Series Game 3.	1.00	.45	.12
Reds win squeeker (Tony Perez)			
☐ 206 World Series Game 4.	1.00	.45	.12
Gene Tenace singles in ninth			
☐ 207 World Series Game 5.	1.00	.45	.12
Blue Moon Odom out at plate			
☐ 208 World Series Game 6.	1.00	.45	.12
Reds' slugging ties series (Johnny Bench)			
☐ 209 World Series Game 7.	1.00	.45	.12
Bert Campaneris starts winning rally			
☐ 210 World Series Summary	1.00	.45	.12
World champions: A's Win			
☐ 211 Balor Moore	.50	.23	.06
☐ 212 Joe Lahoud	.50	.23	.06
☐ 213 Steve Garvey	6.00	2.70	.75
☐ 214 Steve Hamilton	.50	.23	.06
☐ 215 Dusty Baker	2.00	.90	.25
☐ 216 Toby Harrah	.75	.35	.09
☐ 217 Don Wilson	.50	.23	.06
☐ 218 Aurelio Rodriguez	.50	.23	.06
☐ 219 St. Louis Cardinals	1.25	.55	.16
Team Card			
☐ 220 Nolan Ryan	100.00	45.00	12.50
☐ 221 Fred Kendall	.50	.23	.06
☐ 222 Rob Gardner	.50	.23	.06
☐ 223 Bud Harrelson	.75	.35	.09
☐ 224 Bill Lee	.75	.35	.09
☐ 225 Al Oliver	1.50	.70	.19
☐ 226 Ray Fosse	.50	.23	.06
☐ 227 Wayne Twitchell	.50	.23	.06
☐ 228 Bobby Darwin	.50	.23	.06
☐ 229 Roric Harrison	.50	.23	.06
☐ 230 Joe Morgan	6.00	2.70	.75
☐ 231 Bill Parsons	.50	.23	.06
☐ 232 Ken Singleton	.75	.35	.09
☐ 233 Ed Kirkpatrick	.50	.23	.06
☐ 234 Bill North	.50	.23	.06
☐ 235 Jim Hunter	4.00	1.80	.50
☐ 236 Tito Fuentes	.50	.23	.06
☐ 237A Braves Leaders	1.50	.70	.19
Eddie Mathews MG Lew Burdette CO Jim Busby CO Roy Hartsfield CO Ken Silvestri CO (Burdette right ear showing)			
☐ 237B Braves Leaders	3.00	1.35	.35
(Burdette right ear not showing)			
☐ 238 Tony Muser	.50	.23	.06
☐ 239 Pete Richert	.50	.23	.06
☐ 240 Bobby Murcer	.75	.35	.09
☐ 241 Dwain Anderson	.50	.23	.06
☐ 242 George Culver	.50	.23	.06
☐ 243 California Angels	1.25	.55	.16
Team Card			
☐ 244 Ed Acosta	.50	.23	.06
☐ 245 Carl Yastrzemski	10.00	4.50	1.25
☐ 246 Ken Sanders	.50	.23	.06
☐ 247 Del Unser	.50	.23	.06
☐ 248 Jerry Johnson	.50	.23	.06
☐ 249 Larry Biittner	.50	.23	.06
☐ 250 Manny Sanguillen	.75	.35	.09
☐ 251 Roger Nelson	.50	.23	.06
☐ 252A Giants Leaders	.75	.35	.09
Charlie Fox MG Joe Amalfitano CO Andy Gilbert CO Don McMahon CO John McNamara CO (Orange backgrounds)			
☐ 252B Giants Leaders	1.50	.70	.19
(Dark pale backgrounds)			
☐ 253 Mark Belanger	.75	.35	.09
☐ 254 Bill Stoneman	.50	.23	.06
☐ 255 Reggie Jackson	20.00	9.00	2.50
☐ 256 Chris Zachary	.50	.23	.06
☐ 257A Mets Leaders	2.50	1.10	.30
Yogi Berra MG Roy McMillan CO Joe Pignatano CO Rube Walker CO Eddie Yost CO (Orange backgrounds)			
☐ 257B Mets Leaders	5.00	2.20	.60
(Dark pale backgrounds)			
☐ 258 Tommy John	1.25	.55	.16
☐ 259 Jim Holt	.50	.23	.06
☐ 260 Gary Nolan	.75	.35	.09
☐ 261 Pat Kelly	.50	.23	.06
☐ 262 Jack Aker	.50	.23	.06
☐ 263 George Scott	.75	.35	.09
☐ 264 Checklist 133-264	3.00	.60	.30
☐ 265 Gene Michael	.75	.35	.09
☐ 266 Mike Lum	.75	.35	.09
☐ 267 Lloyd Allen	.75	.35	.09
☐ 268 Jerry Morales	.75	.35	.09
☐ 269 Tim McCarver	1.00	.45	.12
☐ 270 Luis Tiant	.75	.35	.09
☐ 271 Tom Hutton	.75	.35	.09
☐ 272 Ed Farmer	.75	.35	.09
☐ 273 Chris Speier	.75	.35	.09
☐ 274 Darold Knowles	.75	.35	.09
☐ 275 Tony Perez	4.00	1.80	.50
☐ 276 Joe Lovitto	.75	.35	.09
☐ 277 Bob Miller	.75	.35	.09
☐ 278 Baltimore Orioles	1.50	.70	.19
Team Card			
☐ 279 Mike Strahler	.75	.35	.09
☐ 280 Al Kaline	7.00	3.10	.85
☐ 281 Mike Jorgensen	.75	.35	.09
☐ 282 Steve Hovley	.75	.35	.09
☐ 283 Ray Sadecki	.75	.35	.09
☐ 284 Glenn Borgmann	.75	.35	.09
☐ 285 Don Kessinger	.75	.35	.09
☐ 286 Frank Linzy	.75	.35	.09
☐ 287 Eddie Leon	.75	.35	.09
☐ 288 Gary Gentry	.75	.35	.09
☐ 289 Bob Oliver	.75	.35	.09

☐	290	Cesar Cedeno	.75	.35	.09
☐	291	Rogelio Moret	.75	.35	.09
☐	292	Jose Cruz	.75	.35	.09
☐	293	Bernie Allen	.75	.35	.09
☐	294	Steve Arlin	.75	.35	.09
☐	295	Bert Campaneris	.75	.35	.09
☐	296	Reds Leaders	2.50	1.10	.30
		Sparky Anderson MG			
		Alex Grammas CO			
		Ted Kluszewski CO			
		George Scherger CO			
		Larry Shepard CO			
☐	297	Walt Williams	.75	.35	.09
☐	298	Ron Bryant	.75	.35	.09
☐	299	Ted Ford	.75	.35	.09
☐	300	Steve Carlton	12.00	5.50	1.50
☐	301	Billy Grabarkewitz	.75	.35	.09
☐	302	Terry Crowley	.75	.35	.09
☐	303	Nelson Briles	.75	.35	.09
☐	304	Duke Sims	.75	.35	.09
☐	305	Willie Mays	40.00	18.00	5.00
☐	306	Tom Burgmeier	.75	.35	.09
☐	307	Boots Day	.75	.35	.09
☐	308	Skip Lockwood	.75	.35	.09
☐	309	Paul Popovich	.75	.35	.09
☐	310	Dick Allen	1.50	.70	.19
☐	311	Joe Decker	.75	.35	.09
☐	312	Oscar Brown	.75	.35	.09
☐	313	Jim Ray	.75	.35	.09
☐	314	Ron Swoboda	.75	.35	.09
☐	315	John Odom	.75	.35	.09
☐	316	San Diego Padres	1.50	.70	.19
		Team Card			
☐	317	Danny Cater	.75	.35	.09
☐	318	Jim McGlothlin	.75	.35	.09
☐	319	Jim Spencer	.75	.35	.09
☐	320	Lou Brock	6.00	2.70	.75
☐	321	Rich Hinton	.75	.35	.09
☐	322	Garry Maddox	3.00	1.35	.35
☐	323	Tigers Leaders	1.50	.70	.19
		Billy Martin MG			
		Art Fowler CO			
		Charlie Silvera CO			
		Dick Tracewski CO			
☐	324	Al Downing	.75	.35	.09
☐	325	Boog Powell	1.00	.45	.12
☐	326	Darrel Brandon	.75	.35	.09
☐	327	John Lowenstein	.75	.35	.09
☐	328	Bill Bonham	.75	.35	.09
☐	329	Ed Kranepool	.75	.35	.09
☐	330	Rod Carew	8.00	3.60	1.00
☐	331	Carl Morton	.75	.35	.09
☐	332	John Felske	.75	.35	.09
☐	333	Gene Clines	.75	.35	.09
☐	334	Freddie Patek	.75	.35	.09
☐	335	Bob Tolan	.75	.35	.09
☐	336	Tom Bradley	.75	.35	.09
☐	337	Dave Duncan	.75	.35	.09
☐	338	Checklist 265-396	3.00	.60	.30
☐	339	Dick Tidrow	.75	.35	.09
☐	340	Nate Colbert	.75	.35	.09
☐	341	Jim Palmer KP	1.50	.70	.19
☐	342	Sam McDowell KP	.75	.35	.09
☐	343	Bobby Murcer KP	.75	.35	.09
☐	344	Jim Hunter KP	1.50	.70	.19
☐	345	Chris Speier KP	.75	.35	.09
☐	346	Gaylord Perry KP	1.50	.70	.19
☐	347	Kansas City Royals	1.50	.70	.19
		Team Card			
☐	348	Rennie Stennett	.75	.35	.09
☐	349	Dick McAuliffe	.75	.35	.09
☐	350	Tom Seaver	14.00	6.25	1.75
☐	351	Jimmy Stewart	.75	.35	.09
☐	352	Don Stanhouse	.75	.35	.09
☐	353	Steve Brye	.75	.35	.09
☐	354	Billy Parker	.75	.35	.09
☐	355	Mike Marshall	.75	.35	.09
☐	356	White Sox Leaders	.75	.35	.09
		Chuck Tanner MG			
		Joe Lonnett CO			
		Jim Mahoney CO			
		Al Monchak CO			
		Johnny Sain CO			
☐	357	Ross Grimsley	.75	.35	.09
☐	358	Jim Nettles	.75	.35	.09
☐	359	Cecil Upshaw	.75	.35	.09
☐	360	Joe Rudi UER	.75	.85	.09
		(Photo actually			
		Gene Tenace)			
☐	361	Fran Healy	.75	.35	.09
☐	362	Eddie Watt	.75	.35	.09
☐	363	Jackie Hernandez	.75	.35	.09
☐	364	Rick Wise	.75	.35	.09
☐	365	Rico Petrocelli	.75	.35	.09
☐	366	Brock Davis	.75	.35	.09
☐	367	Burt Hooton	.75	.35	.09
☐	368	Bill Buckner	.75	.35	.09
☐	369	Lerrin LaGrow	.75	.35	.09
☐	370	Willie Stargell	5.00	2.20	.60
☐	371	Mike Kekich	.75	.35	.09
☐	372	Oscar Gamble	.75	.35	.09
☐	373	Clyde Wright	.75	.35	.09
☐	374	Darrell Evans	.75	.35	.09
☐	375	Larry Dierker	.75	.35	.09
☐	376	Frank Duffy	.75	.35	.09
☐	377	Expos Leaders	.75	.35	.09
		Gene Mauch MG			
		Dave Bristol CO			
		Larry Doby CO			
		Cal McLish CO			
		Jerry Zimmerman CO			
☐	378	Len Randle	.75	.35	.09
☐	379	Cy Acosta	.75	.35	.09
☐	380	Johnny Bench	8.00	3.60	1.00
☐	381	Vicente Romo	.75	.35	.09
☐	382	Mike Hegan	.75	.35	.09
☐	383	Diego Segui	.75	.35	.09
☐	384	Don Baylor	4.00	1.80	.50
☐	385	Jim Perry	.75	.35	.09
☐	386	Don Money	.75	.35	.09
☐	387	Jim Barr	.75	.35	.09
☐	388	Ben Oglivie	.75	.35	.09
☐	389	New York Mets	3.00	1.35	.35
		Team Card			
☐	390	Mickey Lolich	.75	.35	.09
☐	391	Lee Lacy	.75	.35	.09
☐	392	Dick Drago	.75	.35	.09
☐	393	Jose Cardenal	.75	.35	.09
☐	394	Sparky Lyle	.75	.35	.09
☐	395	Roger Metzger	.75	.35	.09
☐	396	Grant Jackson	.75	.35	.09
☐	397	Dave Cash	1.25	.55	.16
☐	398	Rich Hand	1.25	.55	.16
☐	399	George Foster	2.00	.90	.25
☐	400	Gaylord Perry	5.00	2.20	.60
☐	401	Clyde Mashore	1.25	.55	.16
☐	402	Jack Hiatt	1.25	.55	.16
☐	403	Sonny Jackson	1.25	.55	.16
☐	404	Chuck Brinkman	1.25	.55	.16
☐	405	Cesar Tovar	1.25	.55	.16
☐	406	Paul Lindblad	1.25	.55	.16
☐	407	Felix Millan	1.25	.55	.16

☐ 408 Jim Colborn	1.25	.55	.16
☐ 409 Ivan Murrell	1.25	.55	.16
☐ 410 Willie McCovey	6.00	2.70	.75
(Bench behind plate)			
☐ 411 Ray Corbin	1.25	.55	.16
☐ 412 Manny Mota	1.25	.55	.16
☐ 413 Tom Timmermann	1.25	.55	.16
☐ 414 Ken Rudolph	1.25	.55	.16
☐ 415 Marty Pattin	1.25	.55	.16
☐ 416 Paul Schaal	1.25	.55	.16
☐ 417 Scipio Spinks	1.25	.55	.16
☐ 418 Bob Grich	1.25	.55	.16
☐ 419 Casey Cox	1.25	.55	.16
☐ 420 Tommie Agee	1.25	.55	.16
☐ 421A Angels Leaders	1.50	.70	.19
Bobby Winkles MG			
Tom Morgan CO			
Salty Parker CO			
Jimmie Reese CO			
John Roseboro CO			
(Orange backgrounds)			
☐ 421B Angels Leaders	3.00	1.35	.35
(Dark pale			
backgrounds)			
☐ 422 Bob Robertson	1.25	.55	.16
☐ 423 Johnny Jeter	1.25	.55	.16
☐ 424 Denny Doyle	1.25	.55	.16
☐ 425 Alex Johnson	1.25	.55	.16
☐ 426 Dave LaRoche	1.25	.55	.16
☐ 427 Rick Auerbach	1.25	.55	.16
☐ 428 Wayne Simpson	1.25	.55	.16
☐ 429 Jim Fairey	1.25	.55	.16
☐ 430 Vida Blue	1.50	.70	.19
☐ 431 Gerry Moses	1.25	.55	.16
☐ 432 Dan Frisella	1.25	.55	.16
☐ 433 Willie Horton	1.25	.55	.16
☐ 434 San Francisco Giants	2.50	1.10	.30
Team Card			
☐ 435 Rico Carty	1.25	.55	.16
☐ 436 Jim McAndrew	1.25	.55	.16
☐ 437 John Kennedy	1.25	.55	.16
☐ 438 Enzo Hernandez	1.25	.55	.16
☐ 439 Eddie Fisher	1.25	.55	.16
☐ 440 Glenn Beckert	1.25	.55	.16
☐ 441 Gail Hopkins	1.25	.55	.16
☐ 442 Dick Dietz	1.25	.55	.16
☐ 443 Danny Thompson	1.25	.55	.16
☐ 444 Ken Brett	1.25	.55	.16
☐ 445 Ken Berry	1.25	.55	.16
☐ 446 Jerry Reuss	1.25	.55	.16
☐ 447 Joe Hague	1.25	.55	.16
☐ 448 Jim Hiller	1.25	.55	.16
☐ 449A Indians Leaders	4.00	1.80	.50
Ken Aspromonte MG			
Rocky Colavito CO			
Joe Lutz CO			
Warren Spahn CO			
(Spahn's right			
ear pointed)			
☐ 449B Indians Leaders	4.00	1.80	.50
(Spahn's right			
ear round)			
☐ 450 Joe Torre	1.50	.70	.19
☐ 451 John Vukovich	1.25	.55	.16
☐ 452 Paul Casanova	1.25	.55	.16
☐ 453 Checklist 397-528	3.00	.60	.30
☐ 454 Tom Haller	1.25	.55	.16
☐ 455 Bill Melton	1.25	.55	.16
☐ 456 Dick Green	1.25	.55	.16
☐ 457 John Strohmayer	1.25	.55	.16
☐ 458 Jim Mason	1.25	.55	.16

☐ 459 Jimmy Howarth	1.25	.55	.16
☐ 460 Bill Freehan	1.25	.55	.16
☐ 461 Mike Corkins	1.25	.55	.16
☐ 462 Ron Blomberg	1.25	.55	.16
☐ 463 Ken Tatum	1.25	.55	.16
☐ 464 Chicago Cubs	2.50	1.10	.30
Team Card			
☐ 465 Dave Giusti	1.25	.55	.16
☐ 466 Jose Arcia	1.25	.55	.16
☐ 467 Mike Ryan	1.25	.55	.16
☐ 468 Tom Griffin	1.25	.55	.16
☐ 469 Dan Monzon	1.25	.55	.16
☐ 470 Mike Cuellar	1.25	.55	.16
☐ 471 Ty Cobb ATL	8.00	3.60	1.00
4191 Hits			
☐ 472 Lou Gehrig ATL	14.00	6.25	1.75
23 Grand Slams			
☐ 473 Hank Aaron ATL	10.00	4.50	1.25
6172 Total Bases			
☐ 474 Babe Ruth ATL	16.00	7.25	2.00
2209 RBI			
☐ 475 Ty Cobb ATL	8.00	3.60	1.00
.367 Batting Average			
☐ 476 Walter Johnson ATL	3.00	1.35	.35
113 Shutouts			
☐ 477 Cy Young ATL	3.00	1.35	.35
511 Victories			
☐ 478 Walter Johnson ATL	3.00	1.35	.35
3508 Strikeouts			
☐ 479 Hal Lanier	1.25	.55	.16
☐ 480 Juan Marichal	5.00	2.20	.60
☐ 481 Chicago White Sox	2.50	1.10	.30
Team Card			
☐ 482 Rick Reuschel	3.00	1.35	.35
☐ 483 Dal Maxvill	1.25	.55	.16
☐ 484 Ernie McAnally	1.25	.55	.16
☐ 485 Norm Cash	1.25	.55	.16
☐ 486A Phillies Leaders	1.50	.70	.19
Danny Ozark MG			
Carroll Beringer CO			
Billy DeMars CO			
Ray Rippelmeyer CO			
Bobby Wine CO			
(Orange backgrounds)			
☐ 486B Phillies Leaders	3.00	1.35	.35
(Dark pale			
backgrounds)			
☐ 487 Bruce Dal Canton	1.25	.55	.16
☐ 488 Dave Campbell	1.25	.55	.16
☐ 489 Jeff Burroughs	1.25	.55	.16
☐ 490 Claude Osteen	1.25	.55	.16
☐ 491 Bob Montgomery	1.25	.55	.16
☐ 492 Pedro Borbon	1.25	.55	.16
☐ 493 Duffy Dyer	1.25	.55	.16
☐ 494 Rich Morales	1.25	.55	.16
☐ 495 Tommy Helms	1.25	.55	.16
☐ 496 Ray Lamb	1.25	.55	.16
☐ 497A Cardinals Leaders	2.00	.90	.25
Red Schoendienst MG			
Vern Benson CO			
George Kissell CO			
Barney Schultz CO			
(Orange backgrounds)			
☐ 497B Cardinals Leaders	4.00	1.80	.50
(Dark pale			
backgrounds)			
☐ 498 Graig Nettles	2.50	1.10	.30
☐ 499 Bob Moose	1.25	.55	.16
☐ 500 Oakland A's	2.50	1.10	.30
Team Card			
☐ 501 Larry Gura	1.25	.55	.16

☐ 502	Bobby Valentine	1.25	.55	.16
☐ 503	Phil Niekro	5.00	2.20	.60
☐ 504	Earl Williams	1.25	.55	.16
☐ 505	Bob Bailey	1.25	.55	.16
☐ 506	Bart Johnson	1.25	.55	.16
☐ 507	Darrel Chaney	1.25	.55	.16
☐ 508	Gates Brown	1.25	.55	.16
☐ 509	Jim Nash	1.25	.55	.16
☐ 510	Amos Otis	1.25	.55	.16
☐ 511	Sam McDowell	1.25	.55	.16
☐ 512	Dalton Jones	1.25	.55	.16
☐ 513	Dave Marshall	1.25	.55	.16
☐ 514	Jerry Kenney	1.25	.55	.16
☐ 515	Andy Messersmith	1.25	.55	.16
☐ 516	Danny Walton	1.25	.55	.16
☐ 517A	Pirates Leaders	1.50	.70	.19
	Bill Virdon MG			
	Don Leppert CO			
	Bill Mazeroski CO			
	Dave Ricketts CO			
	Mel Wright CO			
	(Mazeroski has			
	no right ear)			
☐ 517B	Pirates Leaders	3.00	1.35	.35
	(Mazeroski has			
	right ear)			
☐ 518	Bob Veale	1.25	.55	.16
☐ 519	Johnny Edwards	1.25	.55	.16
☐ 520	Mel Stottlemyre	1.25	.55	.16
☐ 521	Atlanta Braves	2.50	1.10	.30
	Team Card			
☐ 522	Leo Cardenas	1.25	.55	.16
☐ 523	Wayne Granger	1.25	.55	.16
☐ 524	Gene Tenace	1.25	.55	.16
☐ 525	Jim Fregosi	1.25	.55	.16
☐ 526	Ollie Brown	1.25	.55	.16
☐ 527	Dan McGinn	1.25	.55	.16
☐ 528	Paul Blair	1.25	.55	.16
☐ 529	Milt May	3.50	1.55	.45
☐ 530	Jim Kaat	5.00	2.20	.60
☐ 531	Ron Woods	3.50	1.55	.45
☐ 532	Steve Mingori	3.50	1.55	.45
☐ 533	Larry Stahl	3.50	1.55	.45
☐ 534	Dave Lemonds	3.50	1.55	.45
☐ 535	Johnny Callison	4.00	1.80	.50
☐ 536	Philadelphia Phillies	6.00	2.70	.75
	Team Card			
☐ 537	Bill Slayback	3.50	1.55	.45
☐ 538	Jim Ray Hart	4.00	1.80	.50
☐ 539	Tom Murphy	3.50	1.55	.45
☐ 540	Cleon Jones	4.00	1.80	.50
☐ 541	Bob Bolin	3.50	1.55	.45
☐ 542	Pat Corrales	4.00	1.80	.50
☐ 543	Alan Foster	3.50	1.55	.45
☐ 544	Von Joshua	3.50	1.55	.45
☐ 545	Orlando Cepeda	5.00	2.20	.60
☐ 546	Jim York	3.50	1.55	.45
☐ 547	Bobby Heise	3.50	1.55	.45
☐ 548	Don Durham	3.50	1.55	.45
☐ 549	Rangers Leaders	5.00	2.20	.60
	Whitey Herzog MG			
	Chuck Estrada CO			
	Chuck Hiller CO			
	Jackie Moore CO			
☐ 550	Dave Johnson	4.00	1.80	.50
☐ 551	Mike Kilkenny	3.50	1.55	.45
☐ 552	J.C. Martin	3.50	1.55	.45
☐ 553	Mickey Scott	3.50	1.55	.45
☐ 554	Dave Concepcion	5.00	2.20	.60
☐ 555	Bill Hands	3.50	1.55	.45
☐ 556	New York Yankees	8.00	3.60	1.00
	Team Card			
☐ 557	Bernie Williams	3.50	1.55	.45
☐ 558	Jerry May	3.50	1.55	.45
☐ 559	Barry Lersch	3.50	1.55	.45
☐ 560	Frank Howard	4.00	1.80	.50
☐ 561	Jim Geddes	3.50	1.55	.45
☐ 562	Wayne Garrett	3.50	1.55	.45
☐ 563	Larry Haney	3.50	1.55	.45
☐ 564	Mike Thompson	3.50	1.55	.45
☐ 565	Jim Hickman	3.50	1.55	.45
☐ 566	Lew Krausse	3.50	1.55	.45
☐ 567	Bob Fenwick	3.50	1.55	.45
☐ 568	Ray Newman	3.50	1.55	.45
☐ 569	Dodgers Leaders	5.00	2.20	.60
	Walt Alston MG			
	Red Adams CO			
	Monty Basgall CO			
	Jim Gilliam CO			
	Tom Lasorda CO			
☐ 570	Bill Singer	4.00	1.80	.50
☐ 571	Rusty Torres	3.50	1.55	.45
☐ 572	Gary Sutherland	3.50	1.55	.45
☐ 573	Fred Beene	3.50	1.55	.45
☐ 574	Bob Didier	3.50	1.55	.45
☐ 575	Dock Ellis	3.50	1.55	.45
☐ 576	Montreal Expos	6.00	2.70	.75
	Team Card			
☐ 577	Eric Soderholm	3.50	1.55	.45
☐ 578	Ken Wright	3.50	1.55	.45
☐ 579	Tom Grieve	4.00	1.80	.50
☐ 580	Joe Pepitone	4.00	1.80	.50
☐ 581	Steve Kealey	3.50	1.55	.45
☐ 582	Darrell Porter	4.00	1.80	.50
☐ 583	Bill Grief	3.50	1.55	.45
☐ 584	Chris Arnold	3.50	1.55	.45
☐ 585	Joe Niekro	4.00	1.80	.50
☐ 586	Bill Sudakis	3.50	1.55	.45
☐ 587	Rich McKinney	3.50	1.55	.45
☐ 588	Checklist 529-660	24.00	4.80	2.40
☐ 589	Ken Forsch	3.50	1.55	.45
☐ 590	Deron Johnson	3.50	1.55	.45
☐ 591	Mike Hedlund	3.50	1.55	.45
☐ 592	John Boccabella	3.50	1.55	.45
☐ 593	Royals Leaders	3.50	1.55	.45
	Jack McKeon MG			
	Galen Cisco CO			
	Harry Dunlop CO			
	Charlie Lau CO			
☐ 594	Vic Harris	3.50	1.55	.45
☐ 595	Don Gullett	4.00	1.80	.50
☐ 596	Boston Red Sox	6.00	2.70	.75
	Team Card			
☐ 597	Mickey Rivers	4.00	1.80	.50
☐ 598	Phil Roof	3.50	1.55	.45
☐ 599	Ed Crosby	3.50	1.55	.45
☐ 600	Dave McNally	4.00	1.80	.50
☐ 601	Rookie Catchers	4.00	1.80	.50
	Sergio Robles			
	George Pena			
	Rick Stelmaszek			
☐ 602	Rookie Pitchers	4.00	1.80	.50
	Mel Behney			
	Ralph Garcia			
	Doug Rau			
☐ 603	Rookie 3rd Basemen	4.00	1.80	.50
	Terry Hughes			
	Bill McNulty			
	Ken Reitz			
☐ 604	Rookie Pitchers	4.00	1.80	.50
	Jesse Jefferson			
	Dennis O'Toole			

	Bob Strampe			
☐ 605	Rookie 1st Basemen ..	5.00	2.20	.60
	Enos Cabell			
	Pat Bourque			
	Gonzalo Marquez			
☐ 606	Rookie Outfielders	5.00	2.20	.60
	Gary Matthews			
	Tom Paciorek			
	Jorge Roque			
☐ 607	Rookie Shortstops	4.00	1.80	.50
	Pepe Frias			
	Ray Busse			
	Mario Guerrero			
☐ 608	Rookie Pitchers	5.00	2.20	.60
	Steve Busby			
	Dick Colpaert			
	George Medich			
☐ 609	Rookie 2nd Basemen	6.00	2.70	.75
	Larvell Blanks			
	Pedro Garcia			
	Dave Lopes			
☐ 610	Rookie Pitchers	5.00	2.20	.60
	Jimmy Freeman			
	Charlie Hough			
	Hank Webb			
☐ 611	Rookie Outfielders	4.00	1.80	.50
	Rich Coggins			
	Jim Wohlford			
	Richie Zisk			
☐ 612	Rookie Pitchers	4.00	1.80	.50
	Steve Lawson			
	Bob Reynolds			
	Brent Strom			
☐ 613	Rookie Catchers	25.00	11.00	3.10
	Bob Boone			
	Skip Jutze			
	Mike Ivie			
☐ 614	Rookie Outfielders	25.00	11.00	3.10
	Al Bumbry			
	Dwight Evans			
	Charlie Spikes			
☐ 615	Rookie 3rd Basemen	350.00	160.00	45.00
	Ron Cey			
	John Hilton			
	Mike Schmidt			
☐ 616	Rookie Pitchers	4.00	1.80	.50
	Norm Angelini			
	Steve Blateric			
	Mike Garman			
☐ 617	Rich Chiles	3.50	1.55	.45
☐ 618	Andy Etchebarren	3.50	1.55	.45
☐ 619	Billy Wilson	3.50	1.55	.45
☐ 620	Tommy Harper	4.00	1.80	.50
☐ 621	Joe Ferguson	4.00	1.80	.50
☐ 622	Larry Hisle	4.00	1.80	.50
☐ 623	Steve Renko	3.50	1.55	.45
☐ 624	Astros Leaders	6.00	2.70	.75
	Leo Durocher MG			
	Preston Gomez CO			
	Grady Hatton CO			
	Hub Kittle CO			
	Jim Owens CO			
☐ 625	Angel Mangual	3.50	1.55	.45
☐ 626	Bob Barton	3.50	1.55	.45
☐ 627	Luis Alvarado	3.50	1.55	.45
☐ 628	Jim Slaton	3.50	1.55	.45
☐ 629	Cleveland Indians	6.00	2.70	.75
	Team Card			
☐ 630	Denny McLain	5.00	2.20	.60
☐ 631	Tom Matchick	3.50	1.55	.45
☐ 632	Dick Selma	3.50	1.55	.45

☐ 633	Ike Brown	3.50	1.55	.45
☐ 634	Alan Closter	3.50	1.55	.45
☐ 635	Gene Alley	4.00	1.80	.50
☐ 636	Rickey Clark	3.50	1.55	.45
☐ 637	Norm Miller	3.50	1.55	.45
☐ 638	Ken Reynolds	3.50	1.55	.45
☐ 639	Willie Crawford	3.50	1.55	.45
☐ 640	Dick Bosman	3.50	1.55	.45
☐ 641	Cincinnati Reds	6.00	2.70	.75
	Team Card			
☐ 642	Jose Laboy	3.50	1.55	.45
☐ 643	Al Fitzmorris	3.50	1.55	.45
☐ 644	Jack Heidemann	3.50	1.55	.45
☐ 645	Bob Locker	3.50	1.55	.45
☐ 646	Brewers Leaders	3.50	1.55	.45
	Del Crandall MG			
	Harvey Kuenn CO			
	Joe Nossek CO			
	Bob Shaw CO			
	Jim Walton CO			
☐ 647	George Stone	3.50	1.55	.45
☐ 648	Tom Egan	3.50	1.55	.45
☐ 649	Rich Folkers	3.50	1.55	.45
☐ 650	Felipe Alou	4.00	1.80	.50
☐ 651	Don Carrithers	3.50	1.55	.45
☐ 652	Ted Kubiak	3.50	1.55	.45
☐ 653	Joe Hoerner	3.50	1.55	.45
☐ 654	Minnesota Twins	6.00	2.70	.75
	Team Card			
☐ 655	Clay Kirby	3.50	1.55	.45
☐ 656	John Ellis	3.50	1.55	.45
☐ 657	Bob Johnson	3.50	1.55	.45
☐ 658	Elliott Maddox	3.50	1.55	.45
☐ 659	Jose Pagan	3.50	1.55	.45
☐ 660	Fred Scherman	4.00	1.55	.45

1974 Topps

The cards in this 660-card set measure 2 1/2" by 3 1/2". This year marked the first time Topps issued all the cards of its base-ball set at the same time rather than in series. Some interesting variations were created by the rumored move of the San Diego Padres to Washington. Fifteen cards (13 players, the team card, and the rookie card (599) of the Padres were printed either as "San Diego" (SD) or "Washington." The latter are the scarcer variety and are denot-ed in the checklist below by WAS. Each team's manager and his coaches again have a combined card with small pictures of each coach below the larger photo of the

team's manager. The first six cards in the set (1-6) feature Hank Aaron and his illustrious career. Other topical subsets included in the set are League Leaders (201-208), All-Star selections (331-339), Playoffs cards (470-471), World Series cards (472-479), and Rookie Prospects (596-608). The card backs for the All-Stars (331-339) have no statistics, but form a picture puzzle of Bobby Bonds, the 1973 All-Star Game MVP. The key Rookie Cards in this set are Ken Griffey Sr., Dave Parker, and Dave Winfield.

	NRMT-MT	EXC	G-VG
COMPLETE SET (660)	600.00	275.00	75.00
COMPLETE FACT.SET (660)	600.00	275.00	75.00
COMMON CARD (1-660)	.50	.23	.06
☐ 1 Hank Aaron	40.00	12.00	5.00
All-Time Home Run King			
(Complete ML record)			
☐ 2 Aaron Special 54-57	7.00	3.10	.85
(Records on back)			
☐ 3 Aaron Special 58-61	7.00	3.10	.85
(Memorable homers)			
☐ 4 Aaron Special 62-65	7.00	3.10	.85
(Life in ML's 1954-63)			
☐ 5 Aaron Special 66-69	7.00	3.10	.85
(Life in ML's 1964-73)			
☐ 6 Aaron Special 70-73	7.00	3.10	.85
(Milestone homers)			
☐ 7 Jim Hunter	3.00	1.35	.35
☐ 8 George Theodore	.50	.23	.06
☐ 9 Mickey Lolich	.75	.35	.09
☐ 10 Johnny Bench	12.00	5.50	1.50
☐ 11 Jim Bibby	.50	.23	.06
☐ 12 Dave May	.50	.23	.06
☐ 13 Tom Hilgendorf	.50	.23	.06
☐ 14 Paul Popovich	.50	.23	.06
☐ 15 Joe Torre	1.00	.45	.12
☐ 16 Baltimore Orioles	1.50	.70	.19
Team Card			
☐ 17 Doug Bird	.50	.23	.06
☐ 18 Gary Thomasson	.50	.23	.06
☐ 19 Gerry Moses	.50	.23	.06
☐ 20 Nolan Ryan	75.00	34.00	9.50
☐ 21 Bob Gallagher	.50	.23	.06
☐ 22 Cy Acosta	.50	.23	.06
☐ 23 Craig Robinson	.50	.23	.06
☐ 24 John Hiller	.75	.35	.09
☐ 25 Ken Singleton	.75	.35	.09
☐ 26 Bill Campbell	.50	.23	.06
☐ 27 George Scott	.75	.35	.09
☐ 28 Manny Sanguillen	.75	.35	.09
☐ 29 Phil Niekro	2.50	1.10	.30
☐ 30 Bobby Bonds	2.00	.90	.25
☐ 31 Astros Leaders	.75	.35	.09
Preston Gomez MG			
Roger Craig CO			
Hub Kittle CO			
Grady Hatton CO			
Bob Lillis CO			
☐ 32A Johnny Grubb SD	.75	.35	.09
☐ 32B Johnny Grubb WAS	7.00	3.10	.85
☐ 33 Don Newhauser	.50	.23	.06
☐ 34 Andy Kosco	.50	.23	.06
☐ 35 Gaylord Perry	3.00	1.35	.35
☐ 36 St. Louis Cardinals	1.50	.70	.19
Team Card			
☐ 37 Dave Sells	.50	.23	.06
☐ 38 Don Kessinger	.75	.35	.09
☐ 39 Ken Suarez	.50	.23	.06
☐ 40 Jim Palmer	5.00	2.20	.60
☐ 41 Bobby Floyd	.50	.23	.06
☐ 42 Claude Osteen	.75	.35	.09
☐ 43 Jim Wynn	.75	.35	.09
☐ 44 Mel Stottlemyre	.75	.35	.09
☐ 45 Dave Johnson	.75	.35	.09
☐ 46 Pat Kelly	.50	.23	.06
☐ 47 Dick Ruthven	.50	.23	.06
☐ 48 Dick Sharon	.50	.23	.06
☐ 49 Steve Renko	.50	.23	.06
☐ 50 Rod Carew	5.00	2.20	.60
☐ 51 Bobby Heise	.50	.23	.06
☐ 52 Al Oliver	.50	.23	.06
☐ 53A Fred Kendall SD	.75	.35	.09
☐ 53B Fred Kendall WAS	7.00	3.10	.85
☐ 54 Elias Sosa	.50	.23	.06
☐ 55 Frank Robinson	7.00	3.10	.85
☐ 56 New York Mets	1.50	.70	.19
Team Card			
☐ 57 Darold Knowles	.50	.23	.06
☐ 58 Charlie Spikes	.50	.23	.06
☐ 59 Ross Grimsley	.50	.23	.06
☐ 60 Lou Brock	5.00	2.20	.60
☐ 61 Luis Aparicio	3.00	1.35	.35
☐ 62 Bob Locker	.50	.23	.06
☐ 63 Bill Sudakis	.50	.23	.06
☐ 64 Doug Rau	.50	.23	.06
☐ 65 Amos Otis	.75	.35	.09
☐ 66 Sparky Lyle	.75	.35	.09
☐ 67 Tommy Helms	.75	.23	.06
☐ 68 Grant Jackson	.50	.23	.06
☐ 69 Del Unser	.50	.23	.06
☐ 70 Dick Allen	1.00	.45	.12
☐ 71 Dan Frisella	.50	.23	.06
☐ 72 Aurelio Rodriguez	.50	.23	.06
☐ 73 Mike Marshall	.50	.23	.06
☐ 74 Minnesota Twins	1.50	.70	.19
Team Card			
☐ 75 Jim Colborn	.50	.23	.06
☐ 76 Mickey Rivers	.75	.35	.09
☐ 77A Rich Troedson SD	.75	.35	.09
☐ 77B Rich Troedson WAS	7.00	3.10	.85
☐ 78 Giants Leaders	.75	.35	.09
Charlie Fox MG			
John McNamara CO			
Joe Amalfitano CO			
Andy Gilbert CO			
Don McMahon CO			
☐ 79 Gene Tenace	.75	.35	.09
☐ 80 Tom Seaver	12.00	5.50	1.50
☐ 81 Frank Duffy	.50	.23	.06
☐ 82 Dave Giusti	.50	.23	.06
☐ 83 Orlando Cepeda	1.50	.70	.19
☐ 84 Rick Wise	.50	.23	.06
☐ 85 Joe Morgan	5.00	2.20	.60
☐ 86 Joe Ferguson	.75	.35	.09
☐ 87 Fergie Jenkins	3.00	1.35	.35
☐ 88 Freddie Patek	.75	.35	.09
☐ 89 Jackie Brown	.50	.23	.06
☐ 90 Bobby Murcer	.75	.35	.09
☐ 91 Ken Forsch	.50	.23	.06
☐ 92 Paul Blair	.75	.35	.09
☐ 93 Rod Gilbreath	.50	.23	.06
☐ 94 Detroit Tigers	1.50	.70	.19
Team Card			
☐ 95 Steve Carlton	7.00	3.10	.85
☐ 96 Jerry Hairston	.50	.23	.06
☐ 97 Bob Bailey	.50	.23	.06
☐ 98 Bert Blyleven	1.00	.45	.12

☐ 99	Brewers Leaders .... .75	.35	.09
	Del Crandall MG		
	Harvey Kuenn CO		
	Joe Nossek CO		
	Jim Walton CO		
	Al Widmar CO		
☐ 100	Willie Stargell.............. 4.00	1.80	.50
☐ 101	Bobby Valentine .... .75	.35	.09
☐ 102A	Bill Greif SD .... .75	.35	.09
☐ 102B	Bill Greif WAS 7.00	3.10	.85
☐ 103	Sal Bando .... .75	.35	.09
☐ 104	Ron Bryant................ .50	.23	.06
☐ 105	Carlton Fisk 14.00	6.25	1.75
☐ 106	Harry Parker .... .50	.23	.06
☐ 107	Alex Johnson .... .50	.23	.06
☐ 108	Al Hrabosky .... .75	.35	.09
☐ 109	Bob Grich .... .75	.35	.09
☐ 110	Billy Williams........... 4.00	1.80	.50
☐ 111	Clay Carroll .... .50	.23	.06
☐ 112	Dave Lopes 1.00	.45	.12
☐ 113	Dick Drago .... .50	.23	.06
☐ 114	Angels Team 1.50	.70	.19
☐ 115	Willie Horton .... .75	.35	.09
☐ 116	Jerry Reuss .... .75	.35	.09
☐ 117	Ron Blomberg .... .50	.23	.06
☐ 118	Bill Lee .... .75	.35	.09
☐ 119	Phillies Leaders .... .75	.35	.09
	Danny Ozark MG		
	Ray Ripplemeyer CO		
	Bobby Wine CO		
	Carroll Beringer CO		
	Billy DeMars CO		
☐ 120	Wilbur Wood............... .50	.23	.06
☐ 121	Larry Lintz................ .50	.23	.06
☐ 122	Jim Holt .... .50	.23	.06
☐ 123	Nelson Briles............. .75	.35	.09
☐ 124	Bobby Coluccio .... .50	.23	.06
☐ 125A	Nate Colbert SD .... .75	.35	.09
☐ 125B	Nate Colbert WAS 7.00	3.10	.85
☐ 126	Checklist 1-132 .... 2.50	.50	.25
☐ 127	Tom Paciorek............. .75	.35	.09
☐ 128	John Ellis .... .50	.23	.06
☐ 129	Chris Speier .... .50	.23	.06
☐ 130	Reggie Jackson......... 18.00	8.00	2.20
☐ 131	Bob Boone 2.00	.90	.25
☐ 132	Felix Millan .... .50	.23	.06
☐ 133	David Clyde............... .75	.35	.09
☐ 134	Denis Menke .... .50	.23	.06
☐ 135	Roy White .... .75	.35	.09
☐ 136	Rick Reuschel .... .50	.23	.06
☐ 137	Al Bumbry................. .75	.35	.09
☐ 138	Eddie Brinkman.......... .50	.23	.06
☐ 139	Aurelio Monteagudo ... .50	.23	.06
☐ 140	Darrell Evans .... .75	.35	.09
☐ 141	Pat Bourque .... .50	.23	.06
☐ 142	Pedro Garcia .... .50	.23	.06
☐ 143	Dick Woodson .... .50	.23	.06
☐ 144	Dodgers Leaders....... 1.25	.55	.16
	Walter Alston MG		
	Tom Lasorda CO		
	Jim Gilliam CO		
	Red Adams CO		
	Monty Basgall CO		
☐ 145	Dock Ellis .... .50	.23	.06
☐ 146	Ron Fairly .... .75	.35	.09
☐ 147	Bart Johnson .... .50	.23	.06
☐ 148A	Dave Hilton SD .... .75	.35	.09
☐ 148B	Dave Hilton WAS 7.00	3.10	.85
☐ 149	Mac Scarce .... .50	.23	.06
☐ 150	John Mayberry............ .75	.35	.09
☐ 151	Diego Segui .... .50	.23	.06

☐ 152	Oscar Gamble .... .75	.35	.09
☐ 153	Jon Matlack............... .75	.35	.09
☐ 154	Houston Astros 1.50	.70	.19
	Team Card		
☐ 155	Bert Campaneris .... .75	.35	.09
☐ 156	Randy Moffitt............. .50	.23	.06
☐ 157	Vic Harris .... .50	.23	.06
☐ 158	Jack Billingham.......... .50	.23	.06
☐ 159	Jim Ray Hart .... .75	.35	.09
☐ 160	Brooks Robinson 7.00	3.10	.85
☐ 161	Ray Burris UER .... .75	.35	.09
	(Card number is		
	printed sideways)		
☐ 162	Bill Freehan .... .75	.35	.09
☐ 163	Ken Berry .... .50	.23	.06
☐ 164	Tom House .... .50	.23	.06
☐ 165	Willie Davis .... .75	.35	.09
☐ 166	Royals Leaders .... .75	.35	.09
	Jack McKeon MG		
	Charlie Lau CO		
	Harry Dunlop CO		
	Galen Cisco CO		
☐ 167	Luis Tiant .... .75	.35	.09
☐ 168	Danny Thompson .... .50	.23	.06
☐ 169	Steve Rogers .... .75	.35	.09
☐ 170	Bill Melton .... .50	.23	.06
☐ 171	Eduardo Rodriguez ..... .50	.23	.06
☐ 172	Gene Clines............... .50	.23	.06
☐ 173A	Randy Jones SD 1.00	.45	.12
☐ 173B	Randy Jones WAS. 10.00	4.50	1.25
☐ 174	Bill Robinson .... .75	.35	.09
☐ 175	Reggie Cleveland .... .50	.23	.06
☐ 176	John Lowenstein......... .50	.23	.06
☐ 177	Dave Roberts .... .50	.23	.06
☐ 178	Garry Maddox .... .75	.35	.09
☐ 179	Mets Leaders 2.00	.90	.25
	Yogi Berra MG		
	Rube Walker CO		
	Eddie Yost CO		
	Roy McMillan CO		
	Joe Pignatano CO		
☐ 180	Ken Holtzman .... .75	.35	.09
☐ 181	Cesar Geronimo .... .50	.23	.06
☐ 182	Lindy McDaniel........... .75	.35	.09
☐ 183	Johnny Oates............. .75	.35	.09
☐ 184	Texas Rangers 1.50	.70	.19
	Team Card		
☐ 185	Jose Cardenal .... .50	.23	.06
☐ 186	Fred Scherman .... .50	.23	.06
☐ 187	Don Baylor 3.00	1.35	.35
☐ 188	Rudy Meoli .... .50	.23	.06
☐ 189	Jim Brewer .... .50	.23	.06
☐ 190	Tony Oliva 1.00	.45	.12
☐ 191	Al Fitzmorris............. .50	.23	.06
☐ 192	Mario Guerrero .... .50	.23	.06
☐ 193	Tom Walker .... .50	.23	.06
☐ 194	Darrell Porter .... .75	.35	.09
☐ 195	Carlos May .... .50	.23	.06
☐ 196	Jim Fregosi .... .75	.35	.09
☐ 197A	Vicente Romo SD .... .75	.35	.09
☐ 197B	Vicente Romo WAS . 7.00	3.10	.85
☐ 198	Dave Cash .... .50	.23	.06
☐ 199	Mike Kekich .... .50	.23	.06
☐ 200	Cesar Cedeno .... .75	.35	.09
☐ 201	Batting Leaders 5.00	2.20	.60
	Rod Carew		
	Pete Rose		
☐ 202	Home Run Leaders 5.00	2.20	.60
	Reggie Jackson		
	Willie Stargell		
☐ 203	RBI Leaders 5.00	2.20	.60

Reggie Jackson
Willie Stargell

☐ 204 Stolen Base Leaders ..	1.25	.55	.16

Tommy Harper
Lou Brock

☐ 205 Victory Leaders...........	1.00	.45	.12

Wilbur Wood
Ron Bryant

☐ 206 ERA Leaders	5.00	2.20	.60

Jim Palmer
Tom Seaver

☐ 207 Strikeout Leaders.....	20.00	9.00	2.50

Nolan Ryan
Tom Seaver

☐ 208 Leading Firemen	1.00	.45	.12

John Hiller
Mike Marshall

☐ 209 Ted Sizemore............	.50	.23	.06
☐ 210 Bill Singer	.50	.23	.06
☐ 211 Chicago Cubs Team ...	1.50	.70	.19
☐ 212 Rollie Fingers...........	3.00	1.35	.35
☐ 213 Dave Rader	.50	.23	.06
☐ 214 Billy Grabarkewitz.....	.50	.23	.06
☐ 215 Al Kaline UER	5.00	2.20	.60

(No copyright on back)

☐ 216 Ray Sadecki..............	.50	.23	.06
☐ 217 Tim Foli	.50	.23	.06
☐ 218 Johnny Briggs............	.50	.23	.06
☐ 219 Doug Griffin	.50	.23	.06
☐ 220 Don Sutton	2.50	1.10	.30
☐ 221 White Sox Leaders.......	.75	.35	.09

Chuck Tanner MG
Jim Mahoney CO
Alex Monchak CO
Johnny Sain CO
Joe Lonnett CO

☐ 222 Ramon Hernandez	.50	.23	.06
☐ 223 Jeff Burroughs...........	.75	.35	.09
☐ 224 Roger Metzger	.50	.23	.06
☐ 225 Paul Splittorff...........	.50	.23	.06
☐ 226A Padres Team SD........	1.50	.70	.19
☐ 226B Padres Team WAS.....	9.00	4.00	1.10
☐ 227 Mike Lum	.50	.23	.06
☐ 228 Ted Kubiak	.50	.23	.06
☐ 229 Fritz Peterson...........	.50	.23	.06
☐ 230 Tony Perez	3.00	1.35	.35
☐ 231 Dick Tidrow.............	.50	.23	.06
☐ 232 Steve Brye	.50	.23	.06
☐ 233 Jim Barr	.50	.23	.06
☐ 234 John Milner..............	.50	.23	.06
☐ 235 Dave McNally...........	.75	.35	.09
☐ 236 Cardinals Leaders	.75	.35	.09

Red Schoendienst MG
Barney Schultz CO
George Kissell CO
Johnny Lewis CO
Vern Benson CO

☐ 237 Ken Brett................	.50	.23	.06
☐ 238 Fran Healy HOR	.75	.35	.09

(Munson sliding
in background)

☐ 239 Bill Russell	.75	.35	.09
☐ 240 Joe Coleman	.50	.23	.06
☐ 241A Glenn Beckert SD.......	.75	.35	.09
☐ 241B Glenn Beckert WAS...	7.00	3.10	.85
☐ 242 Bill Gogolewski	.50	.23	.06
☐ 243 Bob Oliver	.50	.23	.06
☐ 244 Carl Morton.............	.50	.23	.06
☐ 245 Cleon Jones	.75	.35	.09
☐ 246 Oakland Athletics	1.25	.55	.16

Team Card

☐ 247 Rick Miller................	.50	.23	.06
☐ 248 Tom Hall	.50	.23	.06
☐ 249 George Mitterwald	.50	.23	.06
☐ 250A Willie McCovey SD ..	6.00	2.70	.75
☐ 250B Willie McCovey WAS	30.00	13.50	3.70
☐ 251 Graig Nettles	2.00	.90	.25
☐ 252 Dave Parker	10.00	4.50	1.25
☐ 253 John Boccabella.........	.50	.23	.06
☐ 254 Stan Bahnsen...........	.50	.23	.06
☐ 255 Larry Bowa	.75	.35	.09
☐ 256 Tom Griffin	.50	.23	.06
☐ 257 Buddy Bell...............	1.00	.45	.12
☐ 258 Jerry Morales............	.50	.23	.06
☐ 259 Bob Reynolds	.50	.23	.06
☐ 260 Ted Simmons	1.50	.70	.19
☐ 261 Jerry Bell................	.50	.23	.06
☐ 262 Ed Kirkpatrick...........	.50	.23	.06
☐ 263 Checklist 133-264	2.50	.50	.25
☐ 264 Joe Rudi	.75	.35	.09
☐ 265 Tug McGraw	1.00	.45	.12
☐ 266 Jim Northrup............	.75	.35	.09
☐ 267 Andy Messersmith......	.75	.35	.09
☐ 268 Tom Grieve	.75	.35	.09
☐ 269 Bob Johnson............	.50	.23	.06
☐ 270 Ron Santo	1.00	.45	.12
☐ 271 Bill Hands	.50	.23	.06
☐ 272 Paul Casanova	.50	.23	.06
☐ 273 Checklist 265-396....	2.50	.50	.25
☐ 274 Fred Beene	.50	.23	.06
☐ 275 Ron Hunt	.50	.23	.06
☐ 276 Angels Leaders........	.75	.35	.09

Bobby Winkles MG
John Roseboro CO
Tom Morgan CO
Jimmie Reese CO
Salty Parker CO

☐ 277 Gary Nolan...............	.75	.35	.09
☐ 278 Cookie Rojas............	.75	.35	.09
☐ 279 Jim Crawford...........	.50	.23	.06
☐ 280 Carl Yastrzemski	6.00	2.70	.75
☐ 281 San Francisco Giants .	1.50	.70	.19

Team Card

☐ 282 Doyle Alexander	.75	.35	.09
☐ 283 Mike Schmidt	65.00	29.00	8.00
☐ 284 Dave Duncan	.50	.23	.06
☐ 285 Reggie Smith	.75	.35	.09
☐ 286 Tony Muser	.50	.23	.06
☐ 287 Clay Kirby	.50	.23	.06
☐ 288 Gorman Thomas	1.50	.70	.19
☐ 289 Rick Auerbach...........	.50	.23	.06
☐ 290 Vida Blue	.75	.35	.09
☐ 291 Don Hahn	.50	.23	.06
☐ 292 Chuck Seelbach.........	.50	.23	.06
☐ 293 Milt May	.50	.23	.06
☐ 294 Steve Foucault	.50	.23	.06
☐ 295 Rick Monday	.75	.35	.09
☐ 296 Ray Corbin..............	.50	.23	.06
☐ 297 Hal Breeden	.50	.23	.06
☐ 298 Roric Harrison	.50	.23	.06
☐ 299 Gene Michael	.75	.35	.09
☐ 300 Pete Rose	16.00	7.25	2.00
☐ 301 Bob Montgomery.......	.50	.23	.06
☐ 302 Rudy May	.50	.23	.06
☐ 303 George Hendrick	.75	.35	.09
☐ 304 Don Wilson	.50	.23	.06
☐ 305 Tito Fuentes	.50	.23	.06
☐ 306 Orioles Leaders........	1.50	.70	.19

Earl Weaver MG
Jim Frey CO
George Bamberger CO
Billy Hunter CO

George Staller CO

☐ 307	Luis Melendez	.50	.23	.06
☐ 308	Bruce Dal Canton	.50	.23	.06
☐ 309A	Dave Roberts SD	.75	.35	.09
☐ 309B	Dave Roberts WAS	9.00	4.00	1.10
☐ 310	Terry Forster	.75	.35	.09
☐ 311	Jerry Grote	.50	.23	.06
☐ 312	Deron Johnson	.50	.23	.06
☐ 313	Barry Lersch	.50	.23	.06
☐ 314	Milwaukee Brewers	1.50	.70	.19

Team Card

☐ 315	Ron Cey	1.00	.45	.12
☐ 316	Jim Perry	.75	.35	.09
☐ 317	Richie Zisk	.75	.35	.09
☐ 318	Jim Merritt	.50	.23	.06
☐ 319	Randy Hundley	.50	.23	.06
☐ 320	Dusty Baker	2.00	.90	.25
☐ 321	Steve Braun	.50	.23	.06
☐ 322	Ernie McAnally	.50	.23	.06
☐ 323	Richie Scheinblum	.50	.23	.06
☐ 324	Steve Kline	.50	.23	.06
☐ 325	Tommy Harper	.75	.35	.09
☐ 326	Reds Leaders	2.50	1.10	.30

Sparky Anderson MG
Larry Shepard CO
George Scherger CO
Alex Grammas CO
Ted Kluszewski CO

☐ 327	Tom Timmermann	.50	.23	.06
☐ 328	Skip Jutze	.50	.23	.06
☐ 329	Mark Belanger	.75	.35	.09
☐ 330	Juan Marichal	3.00	1.35	.35
☐ 331	All-Star Catchers	5.00	2.20	.60

Carlton Fisk
Johnny Bench

☐ 332	All-Star 1B	5.00	2.20	.60

Dick Allen
Hank Aaron

☐ 333	All-Star 2B	2.50	1.10	.30

Rod Carew
Joe Morgan

☐ 334	All-Star 3B	2.50	1.10	.30

Brooks Robinson
Ron Santo

☐ 335	All-Star SS	.75	.35	.09

Bert Campaneris
Chris Speier

☐ 336	All-Star LF	3.00	1.35	.35

Bobby Murcer
Pete Rose

☐ 337	All-Star CF	1.00	.45	.12

Amos Otis
Cesar Cedeno

☐ 338	All-Star RF	5.00	2.20	.60

Reggie Jackson
Billy Williams

☐ 339	All-Star Pitchers	1.25	.55	.16

Jim Hunter
Rick Wise

☐ 340	Thurman Munson	6.00	2.70	.75
☐ 341	Dan Driessen	1.00	.45	.12
☐ 342	Jim Lonborg	.75	.35	.09
☐ 343	Royals Team	1.50	.70	.19
☐ 344	Mike Caldwell	.50	.23	.06
☐ 345	Bill North	.50	.23	.06
☐ 346	Ron Reed	.50	.23	.06
☐ 347	Sandy Alomar	.75	.35	.09
☐ 348	Pete Richert	.50	.23	.06
☐ 349	John Vukovich	.50	.23	.06
☐ 350	Bob Gibson	5.00	2.20	.60
☐ 351	Dwight Evans	3.00	1.35	.35

☐ 352	Bill Stoneman	.50	.23	.06
☐ 353	Rich Coggins	.50	.23	.06
☐ 354	Cubs Leaders	.75	.35	.09

Whitey Lockman MG
J.C. Martin CO
Hank Aguirre CO
Al Spangler CO
Jim Marshall CO

☐ 355	Dave Nelson	.50	.23	.06
☐ 356	Jerry Koosman	.75	.35	.09
☐ 357	Buddy Bradford	.50	.23	.06
☐ 358	Dal Maxvill	.50	.23	.06
☐ 359	Brent Strom	.50	.23	.06
☐ 360	Greg Luzinski	1.00	.45	.12
☐ 361	Don Carrithers	.50	.23	.06
☐ 362	Hal King	.50	.23	.06
☐ 363	New York Yankees	1.50	.70	.19

Team Card

☐ 364A	Cito Gaston SD	1.25	.55	.16
☐ 364B	Cito Gaston WAS	10.00	4.50	1.25
☐ 365	Steve Busby	.75	.35	.09
☐ 366	Larry Hisle	.75	.35	.09
☐ 367	Norm Cash	1.00	.45	.12
☐ 368	Manny Mota	.75	.35	.09
☐ 369	Paul Lindblad	.50	.23	.06
☐ 370	Bob Watson	.75	.35	.09
☐ 371	Jim Slaton	.50	.23	.06
☐ 372	Ken Reitz	.50	.23	.06
☐ 373	John Curtis	.50	.23	.06
☐ 374	Marty Perez	.50	.23	.06
☐ 375	Earl Williams	.50	.23	.06
☐ 376	Jorge Orta	.50	.23	.06
☐ 377	Ron Woods	.50	.23	.06
☐ 378	Burt Hooton	.75	.35	.09
☐ 379	Rangers Leaders	1.00	.45	.12

Billy Martin MG
Frank Lucchesi CO
Art Fowler CO
Charlie Silvera CO
Jackie Moore CO

☐ 380	Bud Harrelson	.75	.35	.09
☐ 381	Charlie Sands	.50	.23	.06
☐ 382	Bob Moose	.50	.23	.06
☐ 383	Philadelphia Phillies	1.50	.70	.19

Team Card

☐ 384	Chris Chambliss	.75	.35	.09
☐ 385	Don Gullett	.75	.35	.09
☐ 386	Gary Matthews	.75	.35	.09
☐ 387A	Rich Morales SD	.75	.35	.09
☐ 387B	Rich Morales WAS	9.00	4.00	1.10
☐ 388	Phil Roof	.50	.23	.06
☐ 389	Gates Brown	.50	.23	.06
☐ 390	Lou Piniella	1.25	.55	.16
☐ 391	Billy Champion	.50	.23	.06
☐ 392	Dick Green	.50	.23	.06
☐ 393	Orlando Pena	.50	.23	.06
☐ 394	Ken Henderson	.50	.23	.06
☐ 395	Doug Rader	.50	.23	.06
☐ 396	Tommy Davis	.75	.35	.09
☐ 397	George Stone	.50	.23	.06
☐ 398	Duke Sims	.50	.23	.06
☐ 399	Mike Paul	.50	.23	.06
☐ 400	Harmon Killebrew	5.00	2.20	.60
☐ 401	Elliott Maddox	.50	.23	.06
☐ 402	Jim Rooker	.50	.23	.06
☐ 403	Red Sox Leaders	.75	.35	.09

Darrell Johnson MG
Eddie Popowski CO
Lee Stange CO
Don Zimmer CO
Don Bryant CO

☐ 404 Jim Howarth	.50	.23	.06
☐ 405 Ellie Rodriguez	.50	.23	.06
☐ 406 Steve Arlin	.50	.23	.06
☐ 407 Jim Wohlford	.50	.23	.06
☐ 408 Charlie Hough	1.00	.45	.12
☐ 409 Ike Brown	.50	.23	.06
☐ 410 Pedro Borbon	.50	.23	.06
☐ 411 Frank Baker	.50	.23	.06
☐ 412 Chuck Taylor	.50	.23	.06
☐ 413 Don Money	.75	.35	.09
☐ 414 Checklist 397-528	2.50	.50	.25
☐ 415 Gary Gentry	.50	.23	.06
☐ 416 Chicago White Sox	1.50	.70	.19
Team Card			
☐ 417 Rich Folkers	.50	.23	.06
☐ 418 Walt Williams	.50	.23	.06
☐ 419 Wayne Twitchell	.50	.23	.06
☐ 420 Ray Fosse	.50	.23	.06
☐ 421 Dan Fife	.50	.23	.06
☐ 422 Gonzalo Marquez	.50	.23	.06
☐ 423 Fred Stanley	.50	.23	.06
☐ 424 Jim Beauchamp	.50	.23	.06
☐ 425 Pete Broberg	.50	.23	.06
☐ 426 Rennie Stennett	.50	.23	.06
☐ 427 Bobby Bolin	.50	.23	.06
☐ 428 Gary Sutherland	.50	.23	.06
☐ 429 Dick Lange	.50	.23	.06
☐ 430 Matty Alou	.75	.35	.09
☐ 431 Gene Garber	1.00	.45	.12
☐ 432 Chris Arnold	.50	.23	.06
☐ 433 Lerrin LaGrow	.50	.23	.06
☐ 434 Ken McMullen	.50	.23	.06
☐ 435 Dave Concepcion	2.50	1.10	.30
☐ 436 Don Hood	.50	.23	.06
☐ 437 Jim Lyttle	.50	.23	.06
☐ 438 Ed Herrmann	.50	.23	.06
☐ 439 Norm Miller	.50	.23	.06
☐ 440 Jim Kaat	1.50	.70	.19
☐ 441 Tom Ragland	.50	.23	.06
☐ 442 Alan Foster	.50	.23	.06
☐ 443 Tom Hutton	.50	.23	.06
☐ 444 Vic Davalillo	.50	.23	.06
☐ 445 George Medich	.50	.23	.06
☐ 446 Len Randle	.50	.23	.06
☐ 447 Twins Leaders	.75	.35	.09
Frank Quilici MG			
Ralph Rowe CO			
Bob Rodgers CO			
Vern Morgan CO			
☐ 448 Ron Hodges	.50	.23	.06
☐ 449 Tom McCraw	.50	.23	.06
☐ 450 Rich Hebner	.75	.35	.09
☐ 451 Tommy John	1.50	.70	.19
☐ 452 Gene Hiser	.50	.23	.06
☐ 453 Balor Moore	.50	.23	.06
☐ 454 Kurt Bevacqua	.50	.23	.06
☐ 455 Tom Bradley	.50	.23	.06
☐ 456 Dave Winfield	150.00	70.00	19.00
☐ 457 Chuck Goggin	.50	.23	.06
☐ 458 Jim Ray	.50	.23	.06
☐ 459 Cincinnati Reds	1.50	.70	.19
Team Card			
☐ 460 Boog Powell	1.00	.45	.12
☐ 461 John Odom	.50	.23	.06
☐ 462 Luis Alvarado	.50	.23	.06
☐ 463 Pat Dobson	.50	.23	.06
☐ 464 Jose Cruz	.75	.35	.09
☐ 465 Dick Bosman	.50	.23	.06
☐ 466 Dick Billings	.50	.23	.06
☐ 467 Winston Llenas	.50	.23	.06
☐ 468 Pepe Frias	.50	.23	.06

☐ 469 Joe Decker	.50	.23	.06
☐ 470 AL Playoffs	6.00	2.70	.75
A's over Orioles			
(Reggie Jackson)			
☐ 471 NL Playoffs	1.00	.45	.12
Mets over Reds			
(Jon Matlack pitching)			
☐ 472 World Series Game 1.	1.00	.45	.12
(Darold Knowles			
pitching)			
☐ 473 World Series Game 2.	7.00	3.10	.85
(Willie Mays batting)			
☐ 474 World Series Game 3.	1.00	.45	.12
(Bert Campaneris			
stealing)			
☐ 475 World Series Game 4.	1.00	.45	.12
(Rusty Staub batting)			
☐ 476 World Series Game 5.	1.00	.45	.12
(Cleon Jones scoring)			
☐ 477 World Series Game 6.	6.00	2.70	.75
(Reggie Jackson)			
☐ 478 World Series Game 7.	1.00	.45	.12
(Bert Campaneris			
batting)			
☐ 479 World Series Summary	1.00	.45	.12
A's celebrate; win			
2nd consecutive			
championship			
☐ 480 Willie Crawford	.50	.23	.06
☐ 481 Jerry Terrell	.50	.23	.06
☐ 482 Bob Didier	.50	.23	.06
☐ 483 Atlanta Braves	1.50	.70	.19
Team Card			
☐ 484 Carmen Fanzone	.50	.23	.06
☐ 485 Felipe Alou	1.00	.45	.12
☐ 486 Steve Stone	.75	.35	.09
☐ 487 Ted Martinez	.50	.23	.06
☐ 488 Andy Etchebarren	.50	.23	.06
☐ 489 Pirates Leaders	1.00	.45	.12
Danny Murtaugh MG			
Don Osborn CO			
Don Leppert CO			
Bill Mazeroski CO			
Bob Skinner CO			
☐ 490 Vada Pinson	1.00	.45	.12
☐ 491 Roger Nelson	.50	.23	.06
☐ 492 Mike Rogodzinski	.50	.23	.06
☐ 493 Joe Hoerner	.50	.23	.06
☐ 494 Ed Goodson	.50	.23	.06
☐ 495 Dick McAuliffe	.75	.35	.09
☐ 496 Tom Murphy	.50	.23	.06
☐ 497 Bobby Mitchell	.50	.23	.06
☐ 498 Pat Corrales	.75	.35	.09
☐ 499 Rusty Torres	.50	.23	.06
☐ 500 Lee May	.75	.35	.09
☐ 501 Eddie Leon	.50	.23	.06
☐ 502 Dave LaRoche	.50	.23	.06
☐ 503 Eric Soderholm	.50	.23	.06
☐ 504 Joe Niekro	.75	.35	.09
☐ 505 Bill Buckner	1.00	.45	.12
☐ 506 Ed Farmer	.50	.23	.06
☐ 507 Larry Stahl	.50	.23	.06
☐ 508 Montreal Expos	1.50	.70	.19
Team Card			
☐ 509 Jesse Jefferson	.50	.23	.06
☐ 510 Wayne Garrett	.50	.23	.06
☐ 511 Toby Harrah	.75	.35	.09
☐ 512 Joe Lahoud	.50	.23	.06
☐ 513 Jim Campanis	.50	.23	.06
☐ 514 Paul Schaal	.50	.23	.06
☐ 515 Willie Montanez	.50	.23	.06

☐ 516 Horacio Pina	.50	.23	.06
☐ 517 Mike Hegan	.50	.23	.06
☐ 518 Derrel Thomas	.50	.23	.06
☐ 519 Bill Sharp	.50	.23	.06
☐ 520 Tim McCarver	1.00	.45	.12
☐ 521 Indians Leaders	.75	.35	.09
Ken Aspromonte MG			
Clay Bryant CO			
Tony Pacheco CO			
☐ 522 J.R. Richard	.75	.35	.09
☐ 523 Cecil Cooper	1.00	.45	.12
☐ 524 Bill Plummer	.50	.23	.06
☐ 525 Clyde Wright	.50	.23	.06
☐ 526 Frank Tepedino	.50	.23	.06
☐ 527 Bobby Darwin	.50	.23	.06
☐ 528 Bill Bonham	.50	.23	.06
☐ 529 Horace Clarke	.50	.23	.06
☐ 530 Mickey Stanley	.75	.35	.09
☐ 531 Expos Leaders	.75	.35	.09
Gene Mauch MG			
Dave Bristol CO			
Cal McLish CO			
Larry Doby CO			
Jerry Zimmerman CO			
☐ 532 Skip Lockwood	.50	.23	.06
☐ 533 Mike Phillips	.50	.23	.06
☐ 534 Eddie Watt	.50	.23	.06
☐ 535 Bob Tolan	.50	.23	.06
☐ 536 Duffy Dyer	.50	.23	.06
☐ 537 Steve Mingori	.50	.23	.06
☐ 538 Cesar Tovar	.50	.23	.06
☐ 539 Lloyd Allen	.50	.23	.06
☐ 540 Bob Robertson	.50	.23	.06
☐ 541 Cleveland Indians	1.50	.70	.19
Team Card			
☐ 542 Rich Gossage	3.00	1.35	.35
☐ 543 Danny Cater	.50	.23	.06
☐ 544 Ron Schueler	.50	.23	.06
☐ 545 Billy Conigliaro	.75	.35	.09
☐ 546 Mike Corkins	.50	.23	.06
☐ 547 Glenn Borgmann	.50	.23	.06
☐ 548 Sonny Siebert	.50	.23	.06
☐ 549 Mike Jorgensen	.50	.23	.06
☐ 550 Sam McDowell	.75	.35	.09
☐ 551 Von Joshua	.50	.23	.06
☐ 552 Denny Doyle	.50	.23	.06
☐ 553 Jim Willoughby	.50	.23	.06
☐ 554 Tim Johnson	.50	.23	.06
☐ 555 Woodie Fryman	.50	.23	.06
☐ 556 Dave Campbell	.50	.23	.06
☐ 557 Jim McGlothlin	.50	.23	.06
☐ 558 Bill Fahey	.50	.23	.06
☐ 559 Darrel Chaney	.50	.23	.06
☐ 560 Mike Cuellar	.75	.35	.09
☐ 561 Ed Kranepool	.50	.23	.06
☐ 562 Jack Aker	.50	.23	.06
☐ 563 Hal McRae	1.00	.45	.12
☐ 564 Mike Ryan	.50	.23	.06
☐ 565 Milt Wilcox	.50	.23	.06
☐ 566 Jackie Hernandez	.50	.23	.06
☐ 567 Boston Red Sox	1.50	.70	.19
Team Card			
☐ 568 Mike Torrez	.75	.35	.09
☐ 569 Rick Dempsey	.50	.23	.06
☐ 570 Ralph Garr	.75	.35	.09
☐ 571 Rich Hand	.50	.23	.06
☐ 572 Enzo Hernandez	.50	.23	.06
☐ 573 Mike Adams	.50	.23	.06
☐ 574 Bill Parsons	.50	.23	.06
☐ 575 Steve Garvey	5.00	2.20	.60
☐ 576 Scipio Spinks	.50	.23	.06
☐ 577 Mike Sadek	.50	.23	.06
☐ 578 Ralph Houk MG	.75	.35	.09
☐ 579 Cecil Upshaw	.50	.23	.06
☐ 580 Jim Spencer	.50	.23	.06
☐ 581 Fred Norman	.50	.23	.06
☐ 582 Bucky Dent	2.00	.90	.25
☐ 583 Marty Pattin	.50	.23	.06
☐ 584 Ken Rudolph	.50	.23	.06
☐ 585 Merv Rettenmund	.50	.23	.06
☐ 586 Jack Brohamer	.50	.23	.06
☐ 587 Larry Christenson	.50	.23	.06
☐ 588 Hal Lanier	.50	.23	.06
☐ 589 Boots Day	.50	.23	.06
☐ 590 Roger Moret	.50	.23	.06
☐ 591 Sonny Jackson	.50	.23	.06
☐ 592 Ed Bane	.50	.23	.06
☐ 593 Steve Yeager	.75	.35	.09
☐ 594 Leroy Stanton	.50	.23	.06
☐ 595 Steve Blass	.75	.35	.09
☐ 596 Rookie Pitchers	.50	.23	.06
Wayne Garland			
Fred Holdsworth			
Mark Littell			
Dick Pole			
☐ 597 Rookie Shortstops	.75	.35	.09
Dave Chalk			
John Gamble			
Pete MacKanin			
Manny Trillo			
☐ 598 Rookie Outfielders	16.00	7.25	2.00
Dave Augustine			
Ken Griffey			
Steve Ontiveros			
Jim Tyrone			
☐ 599A Rookie Pitchers WAS	1.25	.55	.16
Ron Diorio			
Dave Freisleben			
Frank Riccelli			
Greg Shanahan			
☐ 599B Rookie Pitchers SD..	4.00	1.80	.50
(SD in large print)			
☐ 599C Rookie Pitchers SD..	6.00	2.70	.75
(SD in small print)			
☐ 600 Rookie Infielders	5.00	2.20	.60
Ron Cash			
Jim Cox			
Bill Madlock			
Reggie Sanders			
☐ 601 Rookie Outfielders	3.00	1.35	.35
Ed Armbrister			
Rich Bladt			
Brian Downing			
Bake McBride			
☐ 602 Rookie Pitchers	.75	.35	.09
Glen Abbott			
Rick Henninger			
Craig Swan			
Dan Vossler			
☐ 603 Rookie Catchers	.75	.35	.09
Barry Foote			
Tom Lundstedt			
Charlie Moore			
Sergio Robles			
☐ 604 Rookie Infielders	5.00	2.20	.60
Terry Hughes			
John Knox			
Andre Thornton			
Frank White			
☐ 605 Rookie Pitchers	5.00	2.20	.60
Vic Albury			
Ken Frailing			

Kevin Kobel
Frank Tanana
☐ 606	Rookie Outfielders	.75	.35	.09

Jim Fuller
Wilbur Howard
Tommy Smith
Otto Velez

☐ 607	Rookie Shortstops	.75	.35	.09

Leo Foster
Tom Heintzelman
Dave Rosello
Frank Taveras

☐ 608A	Rookie Pitchers: ERR	2.00	.90	.25

Bob Apodaco (sic)
Dick Baney
John D'Acquisto
Mike Wallace

☐ 608B	Rookie Pitchers: COR	.75	.35	.09

Bob Apodaca
Dick Baney
John D'Acquisto
Mike Wallace

☐ 609	Rico Petrocelli	.75	.35	.09
☐ 610	Dave Kingman	1.00	.45	.12
☐ 611	Rich Stelmaszek	.50	.23	.06
☐ 612	Luke Walker	.50	.23	.06
☐ 613	Dan Monzon	.50	.23	.06
☐ 614	Adrian Devine	.50	.23	.06
☐ 615	Johnny Jeter UER	.50	.23	.06
	(Misspelled Johnnie on card back)			
☐ 616	Larry Gura	.50	.23	.06
☐ 617	Ted Ford	.50	.23	.06
☐ 618	Jim Mason	.50	.23	.06
☐ 619	Mike Anderson	.50	.23	.06
☐ 620	Al Downing	.50	.23	.06
☐ 621	Bernie Carbo	.50	.23	.06
☐ 622	Phil Gagliano	.50	.23	.06
☐ 623	Celerino Sanchez	.50	.23	.06
☐ 624	Bob Miller	.50	.23	.06
☐ 625	Ollie Brown	.50	.23	.06
☐ 626	Pittsburgh Pirates	1.50	.70	.19
	Team Card			
☐ 627	Carl Taylor	.50	.23	.06
☐ 628	Ivan Murrell	.50	.23	.06
☐ 629	Rusty Staub	1.00	.45	.12
☐ 630	Tommie Agee	.75	.35	.09
☐ 631	Steve Barber	.50	.23	.06
☐ 632	George Culver	.50	.23	.06
☐ 633	Dave Hamilton	.50	.23	.06
☐ 634	Braves Leaders	1.00	.45	.12
	Eddie Mathews MG			
	Herm Starrette CO			
	Connie Ryan CO			
	Jim Busby CO			
	Ken Silvestri CO			
☐ 635	Johnny Edwards	.50	.23	.06
☐ 636	Dave Goltz	.50	.23	.06
☐ 637	Checklist 529-660	2.50	.50	.25
☐ 638	Ken Sanders	.50	.23	.06
☐ 639	Joe Lovitto	.50	.23	.06
☐ 640	Milt Pappas	.75	.35	.09
☐ 641	Chuck Brinkman	.50	.23	.06
☐ 642	Terry Harmon	.50	.23	.06
☐ 643	Dodgers Team	1.50	.70	.19
☐ 644	Wayne Granger	.50	.23	.06
☐ 645	Ken Boswell	.50	.23	.06
☐ 646	George Foster	1.50	.70	.19
☐ 647	Juan Beniquez	.50	.23	.06
☐ 648	Terry Crowley	.50	.23	.06
☐ 649	Fernando Gonzalez	.50	.23	.06
☐ 650	Mike Epstein	.50	.23	.06
☐ 651	Leron Lee	.50	.23	.06
☐ 652	Gail Hopkins	.50	.23	.06
☐ 653	Bob Stinson	.50	.23	.06
☐ 654A	Jesus Alou ERR	.75	.35	.09
	(No position)			
☐ 654B	Jesus Alou COR	7.00	3.10	.85
	(Outfield)			
☐ 655	Mike Tyson	.50	.23	.06
☐ 656	Adrian Garrett	.50	.23	.06
☐ 657	Jim Shellenback	.50	.23	.06
☐ 658	Lee Lacy	.50	.23	.06
☐ 659	Joe Lis	.50	.23	.06
☐ 660	Larry Dierker	1.00	.23	.06

1975 Topps

The cards in the 1975 Topps set were issued in two different sizes: a regular standard size (2 1/2" by 3 1/2") and a mini size (2 1/2" by 3 1/8") which was issued as a test in certain areas of the country. The 660-card Topps baseball set for 1975 was radically different in appearance from sets of the preceding years. The most prominent change was the use of a two-color frame surrounding the picture area rather than a single, subdued color. A facsimile autograph appears on the picture, and the backs are printed in red and green on gray. Cards 189-212 depict the MVP's of both leagues from 1951 through 1974. The first seven cards (1-7) feature players (listed in alphabetical order) breaking records or achieving milestones during the previous season. Cards 306-313 picture league leaders in various statistical categories. Cards 459-466 depict the results of post-season action. Team cards feature a checklist back for players on that team and show a small inset photo of the manager on the front. The following players' regular issue cards are explicitly denoted as All-Stars, 1, 50, 80, 140, 170, 180, 260, 320, 350, 390, 400, 420, 440, 470, 530, 570, and 600. This set is quite popular with collectors, at least in part due to the fact that the Rookie Cards of Robin Yount, George Brett, Gary Carter, Jim Rice, Fred Lynn, and Keith Hernandez are all in the set. Topps minis have the same checklist and are valued from approximately 1.25 times to double the prices listed below.

		NRMT-MT	EXC	G-VG
	COMPLETE SET (660)	800.00	350.00	100.00
	COMMON CARD (1-660)	.50	.23	.06
☐ 1	RB: Hank Aaron	30.00	10.00	5.00
	Sets Homer Mark			
☐ 2	RB: Lou Brock	3.50	1.55	.45
	118 Stolen Bases			
☐ 3	RB: Bob Gibson	3.50	1.55	.45
	3000th Strikeout			
☐ 4	RB: Al Kaline	4.00	1.80	.50
	3000 Hit Club			
☐ 5	RB: Nolan Ryan	30.00	13.50	3.70
	Fans 300 for			
	3rd Year in a Row			
☐ 6	RB: Mike Marshall	.75	.35	.09
	Hurls 106 Games			
☐ 7	No Hitters	12.00	5.50	1.50
	Steve Busby			
	Dick Bosman			
	Nolan Ryan			
☐ 8	Rogelio Moret	.50	.23	.06
☐ 9	Frank Tepedino	.50	.23	.06
☐ 10	Willie Davis	.75	.35	.09
☐ 11	Bill Melton	.50	.23	.06
☐ 12	David Clyde	.50	.23	.06
☐ 13	Gene Locklear	.75	.35	.09
☐ 14	Milt Wilcox	.50	.23	.06
☐ 15	Jose Cardenal	.50	.23	.06
☐ 16	Frank Tanana	2.00	.90	.25
☐ 17	Dave Concepcion	2.00	.90	.25
☐ 18	Tigers: Team/Mgr.	2.25	.45	.23
	Ralph Houk			
	(Checklist back)			
☐ 19	Jerry Koosman	.75	.35	.09
☐ 20	Thurman Munson	6.00	2.70	.75
☐ 21	Rollie Fingers	3.00	1.35	.35
☐ 22	Dave Cash	.50	.23	.06
☐ 23	Bill Russell	.75	.35	.09
☐ 24	Al Fitzmorris	.50	.23	.06
☐ 25	Lee May	.75	.35	.09
☐ 26	Dave McNally	.75	.35	.09
☐ 27	Ken Reitz	.50	.23	.06
☐ 28	Tom Murphy	.50	.23	.06
☐ 29	Dave Parker	4.00	1.80	.50
☐ 30	Bert Blyleven	1.00	.45	.12
☐ 31	Dave Rader	.50	.23	.06
☐ 32	Reggie Cleveland	.50	.23	.06
☐ 33	Dusty Baker	2.00	.90	.25
☐ 34	Steve Renko	.50	.23	.06
☐ 35	Ron Santo	1.00	.45	.12
☐ 36	Joe Lovitto	.50	.23	.06
☐ 37	Dave Freisleben	.50	.23	.06
☐ 38	Buddy Bell	1.00	.45	.12
☐ 39	Andre Thornton	.75	.35	.09
☐ 40	Bill Singer	.50	.23	.06
☐ 41	Cesar Geronimo	.75	.35	.09
☐ 42	Joe Coleman	.50	.23	.06
☐ 43	Cleon Jones	.75	.35	.09
☐ 44	Pat Dobson	.50	.23	.06
☐ 45	Joe Rudi	.75	.35	.09
☐ 46	Phillies: Team/Mgr.	2.25	.45	.23
	Danny Ozark UER			
	(Checklist back)			
	(Terry Harmon listed as 339			
	instead of 399)			
☐ 47	Tommy John	1.50	.70	.19
☐ 48	Freddie Patek	.75	.35	.09
☐ 49	Larry Dierker	.50	.23	.06
☐ 50	Brooks Robinson	6.00	2.70	.75
☐ 51	Bob Forsch	.50	.23	.06
☐ 52	Darrell Porter	.75	.35	.09
☐ 53	Dave Giusti	.50	.23	.06
☐ 54	Eric Soderholm	.50	.23	.06
☐ 55	Bobby Bonds	2.00	.90	.25
☐ 56	Rick Wise	.75	.35	.09
☐ 57	Dave Johnson	.75	.35	.09
☐ 58	Chuck Taylor	.50	.23	.06
☐ 59	Ken Henderson	.50	.23	.06
☐ 60	Fergie Jenkins	3.00	1.35	.35
☐ 61	Dave Winfield	50.00	22.00	6.25
☐ 62	Fritz Peterson	.50	.23	.06
☐ 63	Steve Swisher	.50	.23	.06
☐ 64	Dave Chalk	.50	.23	.06
☐ 65	Don Gullett	.75	.35	.09
☐ 66	Willie Horton	.75	.35	.09
☐ 67	Tug McGraw	.75	.35	.09
☐ 68	Ron Blomberg	.50	.23	.06
☐ 69	John Odom	.50	.23	.06
☐ 70	Mike Schmidt	50.00	22.00	6.25
☐ 71	Charlie Hough	1.00	.45	.12
☐ 72	Royals: Team/Mgr.	2.25	.45	.23
	Jack McKeon			
	(Checklist back)			
☐ 73	J.R. Richard	.75	.35	.09
☐ 74	Mark Belanger	.75	.35	.09
☐ 75	Ted Simmons	1.00	.45	.12
☐ 76	Ed Sprague	.50	.23	.06
☐ 77	Richie Zisk	.75	.35	.09
☐ 78	Ray Corbin	.50	.23	.06
☐ 79	Gary Matthews	.75	.35	.09
☐ 80	Carlton Fisk	12.00	5.50	1.50
☐ 81	Ron Reed	.50	.23	.06
☐ 82	Pat Kelly	.50	.23	.06
☐ 83	Jim Merritt	.50	.23	.06
☐ 84	Enzo Hernandez	.50	.23	.06
☐ 85	Bill Bonham	.50	.23	.06
☐ 86	Joe Lis	.50	.23	.06
☐ 87	George Foster	1.50	.70	.19
☐ 88	Tom Egan	.50	.23	.06
☐ 89	Jim Ray	.50	.23	.06
☐ 90	Rusty Staub	1.00	.45	.12
☐ 91	Dick Green	.50	.23	.06
☐ 92	Cecil Upshaw	.50	.23	.06
☐ 93	Dave Lopes	1.00	.45	.12
☐ 94	Jim Lonborg	.75	.35	.09
☐ 95	John Mayberry	.75	.35	.09
☐ 96	Mike Cosgrove	.50	.23	.06
☐ 97	Earl Williams	.50	.23	.06
☐ 98	Rich Folkers	.50	.23	.06
☐ 99	Mike Hegan	.50	.23	.06
☐ 100	Willie Stargell	4.00	1.80	.50
☐ 101	Expos: Team/Mgr.	2.25	.45	.23
	Gene Mauch			
	(Checklist back)			
☐ 102	Joe Decker	.50	.23	.06
☐ 103	Rick Miller	.50	.23	.06
☐ 104	Bill Madlock	1.00	.45	.12
☐ 105	Buzz Capra	.50	.23	.06
☐ 106	Mike Hargrove	3.00	1.35	.35
☐ 107	Jim Barr	.50	.23	.06
☐ 108	Tom Hall	.50	.23	.06
☐ 109	George Hendrick	.75	.35	.09
☐ 110	Wilbur Wood	.50	.23	.06
☐ 111	Wayne Garrett	.50	.23	.06
☐ 112	Larry Hardy	.50	.23	.06
☐ 113	Elliott Maddox	.50	.23	.06
☐ 114	Dick Lange	.50	.23	.06
☐ 115	Joe Ferguson	.50	.23	.06
☐ 116	Lerrin LaGrow	.50	.23	.06
☐ 117	Orioles: Team/Mgr.	2.25	.45	.23
	Earl Weaver			

(Checklist back)

☐ 118	Mike Anderson	.50	.23	.06
☐ 119	Tommy Helms	.50	.23	.06
☐ 120	Steve Busby UER	.75	.35	.09
	(Photo actually			
	Fran Healy)			
☐ 121	Bill North	.50	.23	.06
☐ 122	Al Hrabosky	.75	.35	.09
☐ 123	Johnny Briggs	.50	.23	.06
☐ 124	Jerry Reuss	.75	.35	.09
☐ 125	Ken Singleton	.75	.35	.09
☐ 126	Checklist 1-132	2.25	.45	.23
☐ 127	Glenn Borgmann	.50	.23	.06
☐ 128	Bill Lee	.75	.35	.09
☐ 129	Rick Monday	.75	.35	.09
☐ 130	Phil Niekro	2.50	1.10	.30
☐ 131	Toby Harrah	.75	.35	.09
☐ 132	Randy Moffitt	.50	.23	.06
☐ 133	Dan Driessen	.75	.35	.09
☐ 134	Ron Hodges	.50	.23	.06
☐ 135	Charlie Spikes	.50	.23	.06
☐ 136	Jim Mason	.50	.23	.06
☐ 137	Terry Forster	.75	.35	.09
☐ 138	Del Unser	.50	.23	.06
☐ 139	Horacio Pina	.50	.23	.06
☐ 140	Steve Garvey	5.00	2.20	.60
☐ 141	Mickey Stanley	.75	.35	.09
☐ 142	Bob Reynolds	.50	.23	.06
☐ 143	Cliff Johnson	.75	.35	.09
☐ 144	Jim Wohlford	.50	.23	.06
☐ 145	Ken Holtzman	.75	.35	.09
☐ 146	Padres: Team/Mgr.	2.25	.45	.23
	John McNamara			
	(Checklist back)			
☐ 147	Pedro Garcia	.50	.23	.06
☐ 148	Jim Rooker	.50	.23	.06
☐ 149	Tim Foli	.50	.23	.06
☐ 150	Bob Gibson	5.00	2.20	.60
☐ 151	Steve Brye	.50	.23	.06
☐ 152	Mario Guerrero	.50	.23	.06
☐ 153	Rick Reuschel	.75	.35	.09
☐ 154	Mike Lum	.50	.23	.06
☐ 155	Jim Bibby	.50	.23	.06
☐ 156	Dave Kingman	1.00	.45	.12
☐ 157	Pedro Borbon	.75	.35	.09
☐ 158	Jerry Grote	.50	.23	.06
☐ 159	Steve Arlin	.50	.23	.06
☐ 160	Graig Nettles	2.00	.90	.25
☐ 161	Stan Bahnsen	.50	.23	.06
☐ 162	Willie Montanez	.50	.23	.06
☐ 163	Jim Brewer	.50	.23	.06
☐ 164	Mickey Rivers	.75	.35	.09
☐ 165	Doug Rader	.75	.35	.09
☐ 166	Woodie Fryman	.50	.23	.06
☐ 167	Rich Coggins	.50	.23	.06
☐ 168	Bill Greif	.50	.23	.06
☐ 169	Cookie Rojas	.75	.35	.09
☐ 170	Bert Campaneris	.75	.35	.09
☐ 171	Ed Kirkpatrick	.50	.23	.06
☐ 172	Red Sox: Team/Mgr.	2.25	.45	.23
	Darrell Johnson			
	(Checklist back)			
☐ 173	Steve Rogers	.75	.35	.09
☐ 174	Bake McBride	.75	.35	.09
☐ 175	Don Money	.75	.35	.09
☐ 176	Burt Hooton	.75	.35	.09
☐ 177	Vic Correll	.50	.23	.06
☐ 178	Cesar Tovar	.50	.23	.06
☐ 179	Tom Bradley	.50	.23	.06
☐ 180	Joe Morgan	5.00	2.20	.60
☐ 181	Fred Beene	.50	.23	.06
☐ 182	Don Hahn	.50	.23	.06
☐ 183	Mel Stottlemyre	.75	.35	.09
☐ 184	Jorge Orta	.50	.23	.06
☐ 185	Steve Carlton	7.00	3.10	.85
☐ 186	Willie Crawford	.50	.23	.06
☐ 187	Denny Doyle	.50	.23	.06
☐ 188	Tom Griffin	.50	.23	.06
☐ 189	1951 MVP's	3.50	1.55	.45
	Larry (Yogi) Berra			
	Roy Campanella			
	(Campy never issued)			
☐ 190	1952 MVP's	.75	.35	.09
	Bobby Shantz			
	Hank Sauer			
☐ 191	1953 MVP's	1.75	.80	.22
	Al Rosen			
	Roy Campanella			
☐ 192	1954 MVP's	4.00	1.80	.50
	Yogi Berra			
	Willie Mays			
☐ 193	1955 MVP's UER	3.50	1.55	.45
	Yogi Berra			
	Roy Campanella			
	(Campy card never			
	issued, pictured			
	with LA cap, sic)			
☐ 194	1956 MVP's	14.00	6.25	1.75
	Mickey Mantle			
	Don Newcombe			
☐ 195	1957 MVP's	25.00	11.00	3.10
	Mickey Mantle			
	Hank Aaron			
☐ 196	1958 MVP's	1.25	.55	.16
	Jackie Jensen			
	Ernie Banks			
☐ 197	1959 MVP's	1.50	.70	.19
	Nellie Fox			
	Ernie Banks			
☐ 198	1960 MVP's	1.25	.55	.16
	Roger Maris			
	Dick Groat			
☐ 199	1961 MVP's	3.00	1.35	.35
	Roger Maris			
	Frank Robinson			
☐ 200	1962 MVP's	14.00	6.25	1.75
	Mickey Mantle			
	Maury Wills			
	(Wills never issued)			
☐ 201	1963 MVP's	1.50	.70	.19
	Elston Howard			
	Sandy Koufax			
☐ 202	1964 MVP's	1.50	.70	.19
	Brooks Robinson			
	Ken Boyer			
☐ 203	1965 MVP's	1.50	.70	.19
	Zoilo Versalles			
	Willie Mays			
☐ 204	1966 MVP's	6.00	2.70	.75
	Frank Robinson			
	Bob Clemente			
☐ 205	1967 MVP's	1.50	.70	.19
	Carl Yastrzemski			
	Orlando Cepeda			
☐ 206	1968 MVP's	1.50	.70	.19
	Denny McLain			
	Bob Gibson			
☐ 207	1969 MVP's	1.50	.70	.19
	Harmon Killebrew			
	Willie McCovey			
☐ 208	1970 MVP's	1.50	.70	.19
	Boog Powell			

	Johnny Bench			
☐ 209	1971 MVP's	.75	.35	.09
	Vida Blue			
	Joe Torre			
☐ 210	1972 MVP's	1.50	.70	.19
	Rich Allen			
	Johnny Bench			
☐ 211	1973 MVP's	6.00	2.70	.75
	Reggie Jackson			
	Pete Rose			
☐ 212	1974 MVP's	.75	.35	.09
	Jeff Burroughs			
	Steve Garvey			
☐ 213	Oscar Gamble	.75	.35	.09
☐ 214	Harry Parker	.50	.23	.06
☐ 215	Bobby Valentine	.50	.23	.06
☐ 216	Giants: Team/Mgr.	2.25	.45	.23
	Wes Westrum			
	(Checklist back)			
☐ 217	Lou Piniella	1.25	.55	.16
☐ 218	Jerry Johnson	.50	.23	.06
☐ 219	Ed Herrmann	.50	.23	.06
☐ 220	Don Sutton	2.50	1.10	.30
☐ 221	Aurelio Rodriguez	.50	.23	.06
☐ 222	Dan Spillner	.50	.23	.06
☐ 223	Robin Yount	125.00	55.00	15.50
☐ 224	Ramon Hernandez	.50	.23	.06
☐ 225	Bob Grich	.75	.35	.09
☐ 226	Bill Campbell	.50	.23	.06
☐ 227	Bob Watson	.75	.35	.09
☐ 228	George Brett	225.00	100.00	28.00
☐ 229	Barry Foote	.50	.23	.06
☐ 230	Jim Hunter	3.00	1.35	.35
☐ 231	Mike Tyson	.50	.23	.06
☐ 232	Diego Segui	.50	.23	.06
☐ 233	Billy Grabarkewitz	.50	.23	.06
☐ 234	Tom Grieve	.75	.35	.09
☐ 235	Jack Billingham	.75	.35	.09
☐ 236	Angels: Team/Mgr.	2.25	.45	.23
	Dick Williams			
	(Checklist back)			
☐ 237	Carl Morton	.50	.23	.06
☐ 238	Dave Duncan	.50	.23	.06
☐ 239	George Stone	.50	.23	.06
☐ 240	Garry Maddox	.75	.35	.09
☐ 241	Dick Tidrow	.50	.23	.06
☐ 242	Jay Johnstone	.75	.35	.09
☐ 243	Jim Kaat	1.00	.45	.12
☐ 244	Bill Buckner	.75	.35	.09
☐ 245	Mickey Lolich	.75	.35	.09
☐ 246	Cardinals: Team/Mgr.	2.25	.45	.23
	Red Schoendienst			
	(Checklist back)			
☐ 247	Enos Cabell	.50	.23	.06
☐ 248	Randy Jones	.75	.35	.09
☐ 249	Danny Thompson	.50	.23	.06
☐ 250	Ken Brett	.50	.23	.06
☐ 251	Fran Healy	.50	.23	.06
☐ 252	Fred Scherman	.50	.23	.06
☐ 253	Jesus Alou	.50	.23	.06
☐ 254	Mike Torrez	.75	.35	.09
☐ 255	Dwight Evans	2.00	.90	.25
☐ 256	Billy Champion	.50	.23	.06
☐ 257	Checklist: 133-264	2.25	.45	.23
☐ 258	Dave LaRoche	.50	.23	.06
☐ 259	Len Randle	.50	.23	.06
☐ 260	Johnny Bench	12.00	5.50	1.50
☐ 261	Andy Hassler	.50	.23	.06
☐ 262	Rowland Office	.50	.23	.06
☐ 263	Jim Perry	.75	.35	.09
☐ 264	John Milner	.50	.23	.06

☐ 265	Ron Bryant	.50	.23	.06
☐ 266	Sandy Alomar	.75	.35	.09
☐ 267	Dick Ruthven	.50	.23	.06
☐ 268	Hal McRae	1.00	.45	.12
☐ 269	Doug Rau	.50	.23	.06
☐ 270	Ron Fairly	.75	.35	.09
☐ 271	Gerry Moses	.50	.23	.06
☐ 272	Lynn McGlothen	.50	.23	.06
☐ 273	Steve Braun	.50	.23	.06
☐ 274	Vicente Romo	.50	.23	.06
☐ 275	Paul Blair	.75	.35	.09
☐ 276	White Sox Team/Mgr.	2.25	.45	.23
	Chuck Tanner			
	(Checklist back)			
☐ 277	Frank Taveras	.50	.23	.06
☐ 278	Paul Lindblad	.50	.23	.06
☐ 279	Milt May	.50	.23	.06
☐ 280	Carl Yastrzemski	6.00	2.70	.75
☐ 281	Jim Slaton	.50	.23	.06
☐ 282	Jerry Morales	.50	.23	.06
☐ 283	Steve Foucault	.50	.23	.06
☐ 284	Ken Griffey	5.00	2.20	.60
☐ 285	Ellie Rodriguez	.50	.23	.06
☐ 286	Mike Jorgensen	.50	.23	.06
☐ 287	Roric Harrison	.50	.23	.06
☐ 288	Bruce Ellingsen	.50	.23	.06
☐ 289	Ken Rudolph	.50	.23	.06
☐ 290	Jon Matlack	.50	.23	.06
☐ 291	Bill Sudakis	.50	.23	.06
☐ 292	Ron Schueler	.50	.23	.06
☐ 293	Dick Sharon	.50	.23	.06
☐ 294	Geoff Zahn	.50	.23	.06
☐ 295	Vada Pinson	1.00	.45	.12
☐ 296	Alan Foster	.50	.23	.06
☐ 297	Craig Kusick	.50	.23	.06
☐ 298	Johnny Grubb	.50	.23	.06
☐ 299	Bucky Dent	.75	.35	.09
☐ 300	Reggie Jackson	20.00	9.00	2.50
☐ 301	Dave Roberts	.50	.23	.06
☐ 302	Rick Burleson	1.00	.45	.12
☐ 303	Grant Jackson	.50	.23	.06
☐ 304	Pirates: Team/Mgr.	2.25	.45	.23
	Danny Murtaugh			
	(Checklist back)			
☐ 305	Jim Colborn	.50	.23	.06
☐ 306	Batting Leaders	1.50	.70	.19
	Rod Carew			
	Ralph Garr			
☐ 307	Home Run Leaders	3.50	1.55	.45
	Dick Allen			
	Mike Schmidt			
☐ 308	RBI Leaders	1.50	.70	.19
	Jeff Burroughs			
	Johnny Bench			
☐ 309	Stolen Base Leaders	1.50	.70	.19
	Bill North			
	Lou Brock			
☐ 310	Victory Leaders	1.50	.70	.19
	Jim Hunter			
	Fergie Jenkins			
	Andy Messersmith			
	Phil Niekro			
☐ 311	ERA Leaders	1.50	.70	.19
	Jim Hunter			
	Buzz Capra			
☐ 312	Strikeout Leaders	20.00	9.00	2.50
	Nolan Ryan			
	Steve Carlton			
☐ 313	Leading Firemen	.75	.35	.09
	Terry Forster			
	Mike Marshall			

☐ 314	Buck Martinez	.50	.23	.06
☐ 315	Don Kessinger	.75	.35	.09
☐ 316	Jackie Brown	.50	.23	.06
☐ 317	Joe Lahoud	.50	.23	.06
☐ 318	Ernie McAnally	.50	.23	.06
☐ 319	Johnny Oates	.75	.35	.09
☐ 320	Pete Rose	20.00	9.00	2.50
☐ 321	Rudy May	.50	.23	.06
☐ 322	Ed Goodson	.50	.23	.06
☐ 323	Fred Holdsworth	.50	.23	.06
☐ 324	Ed Kranepool	.50	.23	.06
☐ 325	Tony Oliva	1.00	.45	.12
☐ 326	Wayne Twitchell	.50	.23	.06
☐ 327	Jerry Hairston	.50	.23	.06
☐ 328	Sonny Siebert	.50	.23	.06
☐ 329	Ted Kubiak	.50	.23	.06
☐ 330	Mike Marshall	.75	.35	.09
☐ 331	Indians: Team/Mgr.	2.25	.45	.23
	Frank Robinson			
	(Checklist back)			
☐ 332	Fred Kendall	.50	.23	.06
☐ 333	Dick Drago	.50	.23	.06
☐ 334	Greg Gross	.50	.23	.06
☐ 335	Jim Palmer	5.00	2.20	.60
☐ 336	Rennie Stennett	.50	.23	.06
☐ 337	Kevin Kobel	.50	.23	.06
☐ 338	Rich Stelmaszek	.50	.23	.06
☐ 339	Jim Fregosi	.75	.35	.09
☐ 340	Paul Splittorff	.50	.23	.06
☐ 341	Hal Breeden	.50	.23	.06
☐ 342	Leroy Stanton	.50	.23	.06
☐ 343	Danny Frisella	.50	.23	.06
☐ 344	Ben Oglivie	.75	.35	.09
☐ 345	Clay Carroll	.75	.35	.09
☐ 346	Bobby Darwin	.50	.23	.06
☐ 347	Mike Caldwell	.50	.23	.06
☐ 348	Tony Muser	.50	.23	.06
☐ 349	Ray Sadecki	.50	.23	.06
☐ 350	Bobby Murcer	1.00	.45	.12
☐ 351	Bob Boone	1.50	.70	.19
☐ 352	Darold Knowles	.50	.23	.06
☐ 353	Luis Melendez	.50	.23	.06
☐ 354	Dick Bosman	.50	.23	.06
☐ 355	Chris Cannizzaro	.50	.23	.06
☐ 356	Rico Petrocelli	.75	.35	.09
☐ 357	Ken Forsch	.50	.23	.06
☐ 358	Al Bumbry	.75	.35	.09
☐ 359	Paul Popovich	.50	.23	.06
☐ 360	George Scott	.75	.35	.09
☐ 361	Dodgers: Team/Mgr.	2.25	.45	.23
	Walter Alston			
	(Checklist back)			
☐ 362	Steve Hargan	.50	.23	.06
☐ 363	Carmen Fanzone	.50	.23	.06
☐ 364	Doug Bird	.50	.23	.06
☐ 365	Bob Bailey	.50	.23	.06
☐ 366	Ken Sanders	.50	.23	.06
☐ 367	Craig Robinson	.50	.23	.06
☐ 368	Vic Albury	.50	.23	.06
☐ 369	Merv Rettenmund	.50	.23	.06
☐ 370	Tom Seaver	12.00	5.50	1.50
☐ 371	Gates Brown	.50	.23	.06
☐ 372	John D'Acquisto	.50	.23	.06
☐ 373	Bill Sharp	.50	.23	.06
☐ 374	Eddie Watt	.50	.23	.06
☐ 375	Roy White	.75	.35	.09
☐ 376	Steve Yeager	.75	.35	.09
☐ 377	Tom Hilgendorf	.50	.23	.06
☐ 378	Derrel Thomas	.50	.23	.06
☐ 379	Bernie Carbo	.50	.23	.06
☐ 380	Sal Bando	.75	.35	.09

☐ 381	John Curtis	.50	.23	.06
☐ 382	Don Baylor	3.00	1.35	.35
☐ 383	Jim York	.50	.23	.06
☐ 384	Brewers: Team/Mgr.	2.25	.45	.23
	Del Crandall			
	(Checklist back)			
☐ 385	Dock Ellis	.50	.23	.06
☐ 386	Checklist: 265-396	2.25	.45	.23
☐ 387	Jim Spencer	.50	.23	.06
☐ 388	Steve Stone	.75	.35	.09
☐ 389	Tony Solaita	.50	.23	.06
☐ 390	Ron Cey	1.00	.45	.12
☐ 391	Don DeMola	.50	.23	.06
☐ 392	Bruce Bochte	.50	.23	.06
☐ 393	Gary Gentry	.50	.23	.06
☐ 394	Larvell Blanks	.50	.23	.06
☐ 395	Bud Harrelson	.75	.35	.09
☐ 396	Fred Norman	.75	.35	.09
☐ 397	Bill Freehan	.75	.35	.09
☐ 398	Elias Sosa	.50	.23	.06
☐ 399	Terry Harmon	.50	.23	.06
☐ 400	Dick Allen	1.00	.45	.12
☐ 401	Mike Wallace	.50	.23	.06
☐ 402	Bob Tolan	.50	.23	.06
☐ 403	Tom Buskey	.50	.23	.06
☐ 404	Ted Sizemore	.50	.23	.06
☐ 405	John Montague	.50	.23	.06
☐ 406	Bob Gallagher	.50	.23	.06
☐ 407	Herb Washington	1.00	.45	.12
☐ 408	Clyde Wright	.50	.23	.06
☐ 409	Bob Robertson	.50	.23	.06
☐ 410	Mike Cueller UER	.75	.35	.09
	(Sic, Cuellar)			
☐ 411	George Mitterwald	.50	.23	.06
☐ 412	Bill Hands	.50	.23	.06
☐ 413	Marty Pattin	.50	.23	.06
☐ 414	Manny Mota	.75	.35	.09
☐ 415	John Hiller	.75	.35	.09
☐ 416	Larry Lintz	.50	.23	.06
☐ 417	Skip Lockwood	.50	.23	.06
☐ 418	Leo Foster	.50	.23	.06
☐ 419	Dave Goltz	.50	.23	.06
☐ 420	Larry Bowa	1.00	.45	.12
☐ 421	Mets: Team/Mgr.	2.25	.45	.23
	Yogi Berra			
	(Checklist back)			
☐ 422	Brian Downing	1.00	.45	.12
☐ 423	Clay Kirby	.50	.23	.06
☐ 424	John Lowenstein	.50	.23	.06
☐ 425	Tito Fuentes	.50	.23	.06
☐ 426	George Medich	.50	.23	.06
☐ 427	Clarence Gaston	.75	.35	.09
☐ 428	Dave Hamilton	.50	.23	.06
☐ 429	Jim Dwyer	.50	.23	.06
☐ 430	Luis Tiant	.75	.35	.09
☐ 431	Rod Gilbreath	.50	.23	.06
☐ 432	Ken Berry	.50	.23	.06
☐ 433	Larry Demery	.50	.23	.06
☐ 434	Bob Locker	.50	.23	.06
☐ 435	Dave Nelson	.50	.23	.06
☐ 436	Ken Frailing	.50	.23	.06
☐ 437	Al Cowens	.75	.35	.09
☐ 438	Don Carrithers	.50	.23	.06
☐ 439	Ed Brinkman	.50	.23	.06
☐ 440	Andy Messersmith	.75	.35	.09
☐ 441	Bobby Heise	.50	.23	.06
☐ 442	Maximino Leon	.50	.23	.06
☐ 443	Twins: Team/Mgr.	2.25	.45	.23
	Frank Quilici			
	(Checklist back)			
☐ 444	Gene Garber	.75	.35	.09

☐ 445	Felix Millan	.50	.23	.06
☐ 446	Bart Johnson	.50	.23	.06
☐ 447	Terry Crowley	.50	.23	.06
☐ 448	Frank Duffy	.50	.23	.06
☐ 449	Charlie Williams	.50	.23	.06
☐ 450	Willie McCovey	5.00	2.20	.60
☐ 451	Rick Dempsey	.75	.35	.09
☐ 452	Angel Mangual	.50	.23	.06
☐ 453	Claude Osteen	.75	.35	.09
☐ 454	Doug Griffin	.50	.23	.06
☐ 455	Don Wilson	.50	.23	.06
☐ 456	Bob Coluccio	.50	.23	.06
☐ 457	Mario Mendoza	.50	.23	.06
☐ 458	Ross Grimsley	.50	.23	.06
☐ 459	1974 AL Champs A's over Orioles (Second base action pictured)	1.00	.45	.12
☐ 460	1974 NL Champs Dodgers over Pirates (Frank Taveras and Steve Garvey at second)	1.50	.70	.19
☐ 461	World Series Game 1. (Reggie Jackson)	4.00	1.80	.50
☐ 462	World Series Game 2. (Dodger dugout)	1.00	.45	.12
☐ 463	World Series Game 3. (Rollie Fingers pitching)	1.25	.55	.16
☐ 464	World Series Game 4. (A's batter)	1.00	.45	.12
☐ 465	World Series Game 5. (Joe Rudi rounding third)	1.00	.45	.12
☐ 466	World Series Summary A's do it again; win third straight (A's group picture)	1.50	.70	.19
☐ 467	Ed Halicki	.50	.23	.06
☐ 468	Bobby Mitchell	.50	.23	.06
☐ 469	Tom Dettore	.50	.23	.06
☐ 470	Jeff Burroughs	.75	.35	.09
☐ 471	Bob Stinson	.50	.23	.06
☐ 472	Bruce Dal Canton	.50	.23	.06
☐ 473	Ken McMullen	.50	.23	.06
☐ 474	Luke Walker	.50	.23	.06
☐ 475	Darrell Evans	.75	.35	.09
☐ 476	Ed Figueroa	.50	.23	.06
☐ 477	Tom Hutton	.50	.23	.06
☐ 478	Tom Burgmeier	.50	.23	.06
☐ 479	Ken Boswell	.50	.23	.06
☐ 480	Carlos May	.50	.23	.06
☐ 481	Will McEnaney	.75	.35	.09
☐ 482	Tom McCraw	.50	.23	.06
☐ 483	Steve Ontiveros	.50	.23	.06
☐ 484	Glenn Beckert	.75	.35	.09
☐ 485	Sparky Lyle	1.00	.45	.12
☐ 486	Ray Fosse	.50	.23	.06
☐ 487	Astros: Team/Mgr. Preston Gomez (Checklist back)	2.25	.45	.23
☐ 488	Bill Travers	.50	.23	.06
☐ 489	Cecil Cooper	1.00	.45	.12
☐ 490	Reggie Smith	.75	.35	.09
☐ 491	Doyle Alexander	.75	.35	.09
☐ 492	Rich Hebner	.75	.35	.09
☐ 493	Don Stanhouse	.50	.23	.06
☐ 494	Pete LaCock	.50	.23	.06
☐ 495	Nelson Briles	.75	.35	.09
☐ 496	Pepe Frias	.50	.23	.06
☐ 497	Jim Nettles	.50	.23	.06
☐ 498	Al Downing	.50	.23	.06
☐ 499	Marty Perez	.50	.23	.06
☐ 500	Nolan Ryan	75.00	34.00	9.50
☐ 501	Bill Robinson	.75	.35	.09
☐ 502	Pat Bourque	.50	.23	.06
☐ 503	Fred Stanley	.50	.23	.06
☐ 504	Buddy Bradford	.50	.23	.06
☐ 505	Chris Speier	.50	.23	.06
☐ 506	Leron Lee	.50	.23	.06
☐ 507	Tom Carroll	.50	.23	.06
☐ 508	Bob Hansen	.50	.23	.06
☐ 509	Dave Hilton	.50	.23	.06
☐ 510	Vida Blue	.75	.35	.09
☐ 511	Rangers: Team/Mgr. Billy Martin (Checklist back)	2.25	.45	.23
☐ 512	Larry Milbourne	.50	.23	.06
☐ 513	Dick Pole	.50	.23	.06
☐ 514	Jose Cruz	.75	.35	.09
☐ 515	Manny Sanguillen	.75	.35	.09
☐ 516	Don Hood	.50	.23	.06
☐ 517	Checklist: 397-528	2.25	.45	.23
☐ 518	Leo Cardenas	.50	.23	.06
☐ 519	Jim Todd	.50	.23	.06
☐ 520	Amos Otis	.75	.35	.09
☐ 521	Dennis Blair	.50	.23	.06
☐ 522	Gary Sutherland	.50	.23	.06
☐ 523	Tom Paciorek	.75	.35	.09
☐ 524	John Doherty	.50	.23	.06
☐ 525	Tom House	.50	.23	.06
☐ 526	Larry Hisle	.75	.35	.09
☐ 527	Mac Scarce	.50	.23	.06
☐ 528	Eddie Leon	.50	.23	.06
☐ 529	Gary Thomasson	.50	.23	.06
☐ 530	Gaylord Perry	3.00	1.35	.35
☐ 531	Reds: Team/Mgr. Sparky Anderson (Checklist back)	4.00	.80	.40
☐ 532	Gorman Thomas	.75	.35	.09
☐ 533	Rudy Meoli	.50	.23	.06
☐ 534	Alex Johnson	.50	.23	.06
☐ 535	Gene Tenace	.75	.35	.09
☐ 536	Bob Moose	.50	.23	.06
☐ 537	Tommy Harper	.75	.35	.09
☐ 538	Duffy Dyer	.50	.23	.06
☐ 539	Jesse Jefferson	.50	.23	.06
☐ 540	Lou Brock	5.00	2.20	.60
☐ 541	Roger Metzger	.50	.23	.06
☐ 542	Pete Broberg	.50	.23	.06
☐ 543	Larry Biittner	.50	.23	.06
☐ 544	Steve Mingori	.50	.23	.06
☐ 545	Billy Williams	3.50	1.55	.45
☐ 546	John Knox	.50	.23	.06
☐ 547	Von Joshua	.50	.23	.06
☐ 548	Charlie Sands	.50	.23	.06
☐ 549	Bill Butler	.50	.23	.06
☐ 550	Ralph Garr	.75	.35	.09
☐ 551	Larry Christenson	.50	.23	.06
☐ 552	Jack Brohamer	.50	.23	.06
☐ 553	John Boccabella	.50	.23	.06
☐ 554	Rich Gossage	2.00	.90	.25
☐ 555	Al Oliver	1.00	.45	.12
☐ 556	Tim Johnson	.50	.23	.06
☐ 557	Larry Gura	.50	.23	.06
☐ 558	Dave Roberts	.50	.23	.06
☐ 559	Bob Montgomery	.50	.23	.06
☐ 560	Tony Perez	3.00	1.35	.35
☐ 561	A's: Team/Mgr. Alvin Dark (Checklist back)	2.25	.45	.23
☐ 562	Gary Nolan	.75	.35	.09

☐ 563	Wilbur Howard	.50	.23	.06
☐ 564	Tommy Davis	.75	.35	.09
☐ 565	Joe Torre	1.00	.45	.12
☐ 566	Ray Burris	.50	.23	.06
☐ 567	Jim Sundberg	1.25	.55	.16
☐ 568	Dale Murray	.50	.23	.06
☐ 569	Frank White	1.00	.45	.12
☐ 570	Jim Wynn	.75	.35	.09
☐ 571	Dave Lemanczyk	.50	.23	.06
☐ 572	Roger Nelson	.50	.23	.06
☐ 573	Orlando Pena	.50	.23	.06
☐ 574	Tony Taylor	.50	.23	.06
☐ 575	Gene Clines	.50	.23	.06
☐ 576	Phil Roof	.50	.23	.06
☐ 577	John Morris	.50	.23	.06
☐ 578	Dave Tomlin	.50	.23	.06
☐ 579	Skip Pitlock	.50	.23	.06
☐ 580	Frank Robinson	6.00	2.70	.75
☐ 581	Darrel Chaney	.50	.23	.06
☐ 582	Eduardo Rodriguez	.50	.23	.06
☐ 583	Andy Etchebarren	.50	.23	.06
☐ 584	Mike Garman	.50	.23	.06
☐ 585	Chris Chambliss	.75	.35	.09
☐ 586	Tim McCarver	1.00	.45	.12
☐ 587	Chris Ward	.50	.23	.06
☐ 588	Rick Auerbach	.50	.23	.06
☐ 589	Braves: Team/Mgr.	2.25	.45	.23
	Clyde King			
	(Checklist back)			
☐ 590	Cesar Cedeno	.75	.35	.09
☐ 591	Glenn Abbott	.50	.23	.06
☐ 592	Balor Moore	.50	.23	.06
☐ 593	Gene Lamont	.50	.23	.06
☐ 594	Jim Fuller	.50	.23	.06
☐ 595	Joe Niekro	.75	.35	.09
☐ 596	Ollie Brown	.50	.23	.06
☐ 597	Winston Llenas	.50	.23	.06
☐ 598	Bruce Kison	.50	.23	.06
☐ 599	Nate Colbert	.50	.23	.06
☐ 600	Rod Carew	5.00	2.20	.60
☐ 601	Juan Beniquez	.50	.23	.06
☐ 602	John Vukovich	.50	.23	.06
☐ 603	Lew Krausse	.50	.23	.06
☐ 604	Oscar Zamora	.50	.23	.06
☐ 605	John Ellis	.50	.23	.06
☐ 606	Bruce Miller	.50	.23	.06
☐ 607	Jim Holt	.50	.23	.06
☐ 608	Gene Michael	.75	.35	.09
☐ 609	Elrod Hendricks	.50	.23	.06
☐ 610	Ron Hunt	.50	.23	.06
☐ 611	Yankees: Team/Mgr.	2.25	.45	.23
	Bill Virdon			
	(Checklist back)			
☐ 612	Terry Hughes	.50	.23	.06
☐ 613	Bill Parsons	.50	.23	.06
☐ 614	Rookie Pitchers	.75	.35	.09
	Jack Kucek			
	Dyar Miller			
	Vern Ruhle			
	Paul Siebert			
☐ 615	Rookie Pitchers	1.00	.45	.12
	Pat Darcy			
	Dennis Leonard			
	Tom Underwood			
	Hank Webb			
☐ 616	Rookie Outfielders	14.00	6.25	1.75
	Dave Augustine			
	Pepe Mangual			
	Jim Rice			
	John Scott			
☐ 617	Rookie Infielders	2.50	1.10	.30

	Mike Cubbage			
	Doug DeCinces			
	Reggie Sanders			
	Manny Trillo			
☐ 618	Rookie Pitchers	1.00	.45	.12
	Jamie Easterly			
	Tom Johnson			
	Scott McGregor			
	Rick Rhoden			
☐ 619	Rookie Outfielders	.75	.35	.09
	Benny Ayala			
	Nyls Nyman			
	Tommy Smith			
	Jerry Turner			
☐ 620	Rookie Catcher/OF	30.00	13.50	3.70
	Gary Carter			
	Marc Hill			
	Danny Meyer			
	Leon Roberts			
☐ 621	Rookie Pitchers	1.00	.45	.12
	John Denny			
	Rawly Eastwick			
	Jim Kern			
	Juan Veintidos			
☐ 622	Rookie Outfielders	6.00	2.70	.75
	Ed Armbrister			
	Fred Lynn			
	Tom Poquette			
	Terry Whitfield UER			
	(Listed as Ney York)			
☐ 623	Rookie Infielders	6.00	2.70	.75
	Phil Garner			
	Keith Hernandez UER			
	(Sic, bats right)			
	Bob Sheldon			
	Tom Veryzer			
☐ 624	Rookie Pitchers	.75	.35	.09
	Doug Konieczny			
	Gary Lavelle			
	Jim Otten			
	Eddie Solomon			
☐ 625	Boog Powell	1.00	.45	.12
☐ 626	Larry Haney UER	.50	.23	.06
	(Photo actually			
	Dave Duncan)			
☐ 627	Tom Walker	.50	.23	.06
☐ 628	Ron LeFlore	1.00	.45	.12
☐ 629	Joe Hoerner	.50	.23	.06
☐ 630	Greg Luzinski	1.00	.45	.12
☐ 631	Lee Lacy	.50	.23	.06
☐ 632	Morris Nettles	.50	.23	.06
☐ 633	Paul Casanova	.50	.23	.06
☐ 634	Cy Acosta	.50	.23	.06
☐ 635	Chuck Dobson	.50	.23	.06
☐ 636	Charlie Moore	.50	.23	.06
☐ 637	Ted Martinez	.50	.23	.06
☐ 638	Cubs: Team/Mgr.	2.25	.45	.23
	Jim Marshall			
	(Checklist back)			
☐ 639	Steve Kline	.50	.23	.06
☐ 640	Harmon Killebrew	5.00	2.20	.60
☐ 641	Jim Northrup	.50	.23	.06
☐ 642	Mike Phillips	.50	.23	.06
☐ 643	Brent Strom	.50	.23	.06
☐ 644	Bill Fahey	.50	.23	.06
☐ 645	Danny Cater	.50	.23	.06
☐ 646	Checklist: 529-660	2.25	.45	.23
☐ 647	Claudell Washington	1.00	.45	.12
☐ 648	Dave Pagan	.50	.23	.06
☐ 649	Jack Heidemann	.50	.23	.06
☐ 650	Dave May	.50	.23	.06

		NRMT-MT	EXC	G-VG
☐ 651	John Morlan	.50	.23	.06
☐ 652	Lindy McDaniel	.75	.35	.09
☐ 653	Lee Richard UER	.50	.23	.06
	(Listed as Richards on card front)			
☐ 654	Jerry Terrell	.50	.23	.06
☐ 655	Rico Carty	.75	.35	.09
☐ 656	Bill Plummer	.50	.23	.06
☐ 657	Bob Oliver	.50	.23	.06
☐ 658	Vic Harris	.50	.23	.06
☐ 659	Bob Apodaca	.50	.23	.06
☐ 660	Hank Aaron	32.00	9.50	6.50

1976 Topps

The 1976 Topps set of 660 cards (measuring 2 1/2" by 3 1/2") is known for its sharp color photographs and interesting presentation of subjects. Team cards feature a checklist back for players on that team and show a small inset photo of the manager on the front. A "Father and Son" series (66-70) spotlights five Major Leaguers whose fathers also made the "Big Show." Other subseries include "All Time All Stars" (341-350), "Record Breakers" from the previous season (1-6), League Leaders (191-205), Post-season cards (461-462), and Rookie Prospects (589-599). The following players' regular issue cards are explicitly denoted as All-Stars, 10, 48, 60, 140, 150, 165, 169, 240, 300, 370, 380, 395, 400, 420, 475, 500, 580, and 650. The key Rookie Cards in this set are Dennis Eckersley, Ron Guidry, and Willie Randolph.

		NRMT-MT	EXC	G-VG
	COMPLETE SET (660)	400.00	180.00	50.00
	COMMON CARD (1-660)	.30	.14	.04
☐ 1	RB: Hank Aaron	16.00	5.00	2.00
	Most RBI's, 2262			
☐ 2	RB: Bobby Bonds	1.00	.45	.12
	Most leadoff HR's 32; plus three seasons 30 homers/30 steals			
☐ 3	RB: Mickey Lolich	.75	.35	.09
	Lefthander, Most Strikeouts, 2679			
☐ 4	RB: Dave Lopes	.75	.35	.09
	Most Consecutive SB attempts, 38			
☐ 5	RB: Tom Seaver	4.00	1.80	.50
	Most Cons. seasons with 200 SO's, 8			
☐ 6	RB: Rennie Stennett	.30	.14	.04
	Most Hits in a 9 inning game, 7			
☐ 7	Jim Umbarger	.30	.14	.04
☐ 8	Tito Fuentes	.30	.14	.04
☐ 9	Paul Lindblad	.30	.14	.04
☐ 10	Lou Brock	4.00	1.80	.50
☐ 11	Jim Hughes	.30	.14	.04
☐ 12	Richie Zisk	.50	.23	.06
☐ 13	John Wockenfuss	.30	.14	.04
☐ 14	Gene Garber	.30	.14	.04
☐ 15	George Scott	.50	.23	.06
☐ 16	Bob Apodaca	.30	.14	.04
☐ 17	New York Yankees	1.50	.30	.15
	Team Card; Billy Martin MG (Checklist back)			
☐ 18	Dale Murray	.30	.14	.04
☐ 19	George Brett	65.00	29.00	8.00
☐ 20	Bob Watson	.50	.23	.06
☐ 21	Dave LaRoche	.30	.14	.04
☐ 22	Bill Russell	.50	.23	.06
☐ 23	Brian Downing	.30	.14	.04
☐ 24	Cesar Geronimo	.50	.23	.06
☐ 25	Mike Torrez	.50	.23	.06
☐ 26	Andre Thornton	.50	.23	.06
☐ 27	Ed Figueroa	.30	.14	.04
☐ 28	Dusty Baker	1.25	.55	.16
☐ 29	Rick Burleson	.50	.23	.06
☐ 30	John Montefusco	.50	.23	.06
☐ 31	Len Randle	.30	.14	.04
☐ 32	Danny Frisella	.30	.14	.04
☐ 33	Bill North	.30	.14	.04
☐ 34	Mike Garman	.30	.14	.04
☐ 35	Tony Oliva	.75	.35	.09
☐ 36	Frank Taveras	.30	.14	.04
☐ 37	John Hiller	.50	.23	.06
☐ 38	Garry Maddox	.50	.23	.06
☐ 39	Pete Broberg	.30	.14	.04
☐ 40	Dave Kingman	.75	.35	.09
☐ 41	Tippy Martinez	.75	.35	.09
☐ 42	Barry Foote	.30	.14	.04
☐ 43	Paul Splittorff	.30	.14	.04
☐ 44	Doug Rader	.50	.23	.06
☐ 45	Boog Powell	.75	.35	.09
☐ 46	Los Angeles Dodgers	1.50	.30	.15
	Team Card; Walter Alston MG (Checklist back)			
☐ 47	Jesse Jefferson	.30	.14	.04
☐ 48	Dave Concepcion	1.25	.55	.16
☐ 49	Dave Duncan	.30	.14	.04
☐ 50	Fred Lynn	1.50	.70	.19
☐ 51	Ray Burris	.30	.14	.04
☐ 52	Dave Chalk	.30	.14	.04
☐ 53	Mike Beard	.30	.14	.04
☐ 54	Dave Rader	.30	.14	.04
☐ 55	Gaylord Perry	2.50	1.10	.30
☐ 56	Bob Tolan	.30	.14	.04
☐ 57	Phil Garner	.75	.35	.09
☐ 58	Ron Reed	.30	.14	.04
☐ 59	Larry Hisle	.50	.23	.06
☐ 60	Jerry Reuss	.50	.23	.06
☐ 61	Ron LeFlore	.50	.23	.06
☐ 62	Johnny Oates	.50	.23	.06
☐ 63	Bobby Darwin	.30	.14	.04
☐ 64	Jerry Koosman	.50	.23	.06
☐ 65	Chris Chambliss	.50	.23	.06

☐ 66	Father and Son Gus Bell Buddy Bell	.50	.23	.06
☐ 67	Father and Son Ray Boone Bob Boone	.50	.23	.06
☐ 68	Father and Son Joe Coleman Joe Coleman Jr.	.30	.14	.04
☐ 69	Father and Son Jim Hegan Mike Hegan	.30	.14	.04
☐ 70	Father and Son Roy Smalley Roy Smalley Jr.	.50	.23	.06
☐ 71	Steve Rogers	.50	.23	.06
☐ 72	Hal McRae	.75	.35	.09
☐ 73	Baltimore Orioles Team Card; Earl Weaver MG (Checklist back)	1.50	.30	.15
☐ 74	Oscar Gamble	.50	.23	.06
☐ 75	Larry Dierker	.30	.14	.04
☐ 76	Willie Crawford	.30	.14	.04
☐ 77	Pedro Borbon	.30	.23	.06
☐ 78	Cecil Cooper	.50	.23	.06
☐ 79	Jerry Morales	.30	.14	.04
☐ 80	Jim Kaat	.75	.35	.09
☐ 81	Darrell Evans	.50	.23	.06
☐ 82	Von Joshua	.30	.14	.04
☐ 83	Jim Spencer	.30	.14	.04
☐ 84	Brent Strom	.30	.14	.04
☐ 85	Mickey Rivers	.50	.23	.06
☐ 86	Mike Tyson	.30	.14	.04
☐ 87	Tom Burgmeier	.30	.14	.04
☐ 88	Duffy Dyer	.30	.14	.04
☐ 89	Vern Ruhle	.30	.14	.04
☐ 90	Sal Bando	.50	.23	.06
☐ 91	Tom Hutton	.30	.14	.04
☐ 92	Eduardo Rodriguez	.30	.14	.04
☐ 93	Mike Phillips	.30	.14	.04
☐ 94	Jim Dwyer	.30	.14	.04
☐ 95	Brooks Robinson	6.00	2.70	.75
☐ 96	Doug Bird	.30	.14	.04
☐ 97	Wilbur Howard	.30	.14	.04
☐ 98	Dennis Eckersley	40.00	18.00	5.00
☐ 99	Lee Lacy	.30	.14	.04
☐ 100	Jim Hunter	2.50	1.10	.30
☐ 101	Pete LaCock	.30	.14	.04
☐ 102	Jim Willoughby	.30	.14	.04
☐ 103	Biff Pocoroba	.30	.14	.04
☐ 104	Cincinnati Reds Team Card; Sparky Anderson MG (Checklist back)	3.00	.60	.30
☐ 105	Gary Lavelle	.30	.14	.04
☐ 106	Tom Grieve	.50	.23	.06
☐ 107	Dave Roberts	.30	.14	.04
☐ 108	Don Kirkwood	.30	.14	.04
☐ 109	Larry Lintz	.30	.14	.04
☐ 110	Carlos May	.30	.14	.04
☐ 111	Danny Thompson	.30	.14	.04
☐ 112	Kent Tekulve	1.50	.70	.19
☐ 113	Gary Sutherland	.30	.14	.04
☐ 114	Jay Johnstone	.50	.23	.06
☐ 115	Ken Holtzman	.50	.23	.06
☐ 116	Charlie Moore	.30	.14	.04
☐ 117	Mike Jorgensen	.30	.14	.04
☐ 118	Boston Red Sox Team Card; Darrell Johnson MG	1.50	.30	.15

	(Checklist back)			
☐ 119	Checklist 1-132	1.50	.30	.15
☐ 120	Rusty Staub	.50	.23	.06
☐ 121	Tony Solaita	.30	.14	.04
☐ 122	Mike Cosgrove	.30	.14	.04
☐ 123	Walt Williams	.30	.14	.04
☐ 124	Doug Rau	.30	.14	.04
☐ 125	Don Baylor	2.00	.90	.25
☐ 126	Tom Dettore	.30	.14	.04
☐ 127	Larvell Blanks	.30	.14	.04
☐ 128	Ken Griffey	2.50	1.10	.30
☐ 129	Andy Etchebarren	.30	.14	.04
☐ 130	Luis Tiant	.50	.23	.06
☐ 131	Bill Stein	.30	.14	.04
☐ 132	Don Hood	.30	.14	.04
☐ 133	Gary Matthews	.50	.23	.06
☐ 134	Mike Ivie	.30	.14	.04
☐ 135	Bake McBride	.50	.23	.06
☐ 136	Dave Goltz	.30	.14	.04
☐ 137	Bill Robinson	.50	.23	.06
☐ 138	Lerrin LaGrow	.30	.14	.04
☐ 139	Gorman Thomas	.50	.23	.06
☐ 140	Vida Blue	.50	.23	.06
☐ 141	Larry Parrish	.75	.35	.09
☐ 142	Dick Drago	.30	.14	.04
☐ 143	Jerry Grote	.30	.14	.04
☐ 144	Al Fitzmorris	.30	.14	.04
☐ 145	Larry Bowa	.30	.14	.04
☐ 146	George Medich	.30	.14	.04
☐ 147	Houston Astros Team Card; Bill Virdon MG (Checklist back)	1.50	.30	.15
☐ 148	Stan Thomas	.30	.14	.04
☐ 149	Tommy Davis	.50	.23	.06
☐ 150	Steve Garvey	4.00	1.80	.50
☐ 151	Bill Bonham	.30	.14	.04
☐ 152	Leroy Stanton	.30	.14	.04
☐ 153	Buzz Capra	.30	.14	.04
☐ 154	Bucky Dent	.30	.14	.04
☐ 155	Jack Billingham	.50	.23	.06
☐ 156	Rico Carty	.50	.23	.06
☐ 157	Mike Caldwell	.30	.14	.04
☐ 158	Ken Reitz	.30	.14	.04
☐ 159	Jerry Terrell	.30	.14	.04
☐ 160	Dave Winfield	25.00	11.00	3.10
☐ 161	Bruce Kison	.30	.14	.04
☐ 162	Jack Pierce	.30	.14	.04
☐ 163	Jim Slaton	.30	.14	.04
☐ 164	Pepe Mangual	.30	.14	.04
☐ 165	Gene Tenace	.50	.23	.06
☐ 166	Skip Lockwood	.30	.14	.04
☐ 167	Freddie Patek	.50	.23	.06
☐ 168	Tom Hilgendorf	.30	.14	.04
☐ 169	Graig Nettles	.75	.35	.09
☐ 170	Rick Wise	.30	.14	.04
☐ 171	Greg Gross	.30	.14	.04
☐ 172	Texas Rangers Team Card; Frank Lucchesi MG (Checklist back)	1.50	.30	.15
☐ 173	Steve Swisher	.30	.14	.04
☐ 174	Charlie Hough	.75	.35	.09
☐ 175	Ken Singleton	.50	.23	.06
☐ 176	Dick Lange	.30	.14	.04
☐ 177	Marty Perez	.30	.14	.04
☐ 178	Tom Buskey	.30	.14	.04
☐ 179	George Foster	1.00	.45	.12
☐ 180	Rich Gossage	2.00	.90	.25
☐ 181	Willie Montanez	.30	.14	.04
☐ 182	Harry Rasmussen	.30	.14	.04

☐ 183	Steve Braun	.30	.14	.04
☐ 184	Bill Greif	.30	.14	.04
☐ 185	Dave Parker	2.00	.90	.25
☐ 186	Tom Walker	.30	.14	.04
☐ 187	Pedro Garcia	.30	.14	.04
☐ 188	Fred Scherman	.30	.14	.04
☐ 189	Claudell Washington	.50	.23	.06
☐ 190	Jon Matlack	.30	.14	.04
☐ 191	NL Batting Leaders	.75	.35	.09
	Bill Madlock			
	Ted Simmons			
	Manny Sanguillen			
☐ 192	AL Batting Leaders	2.00	.90	.25
	Rod Carew			
	Fred Lynn			
	Thurman Munson			
☐ 193	NL Home Run Leaders	3.00	1.35	.35
	Mike Schmidt			
	Dave Kingman			
	Greg Luzinski			
☐ 194	AL Home Run Leaders	2.50	1.10	.30
	Reggie Jackson			
	George Scott			
	John Mayberry			
☐ 195	NL RBI Leaders	1.50	.70	.19
	Greg Luzinski			
	Johnny Bench			
	Tony Perez			
☐ 196	AL RBI Leaders	.75	.35	.09
	George Scott			
	John Mayberry			
	Fred Lynn			
☐ 197	NL Steals Leaders	1.50	.70	.19
	Dave Lopes			
	Joe Morgan			
	Lou Brock			
☐ 198	AL Steals Leaders	.75	.35	.09
	Mickey Rivers			
	Claudell Washington			
	Amos Otis			
☐ 199	NL Victory Leaders	1.50	.70	.19
	Tom Seaver			
	Randy Jones			
	Andy Messersmith			
☐ 200	AL Victory Leaders	1.50	.70	.19
	Jim Hunter			
	Jim Palmer			
	Vida Blue			
☐ 201	NL ERA Leaders	1.50	.70	.19
	Randy Jones			
	Andy Messersmith			
	Tom Seaver			
☐ 202	AL ERA Leaders	5.00	2.20	.60
	Jim Palmer			
	Jim Hunter			
	Dennis Eckersley			
☐ 203	NL Strikeout Leaders	1.50	.70	.19
	Tom Seaver			
	John Montefusco			
	Andy Messersmith			
☐ 204	AL Strikeout Leaders	1.00	.45	.12
	Frank Tanana			
	Bert Blyleven			
	Gaylord Perry			
☐ 205	Leading Firemen	.75	.35	.09
	Al Hrabosky			
	Rich Gossage			
☐ 206	Manny Trillo	.30	.14	.04
☐ 207	Andy Hassler	.30	.14	.04
☐ 208	Mike Lum	.30	.14	.04
☐ 209	Alan Ashby	.50	.23	.06
☐ 210	Lee May	.50	.23	.06
☐ 211	Clay Carroll	.50	.23	.06
☐ 212	Pat Kelly	.30	.14	.04
☐ 213	Dave Heaverlo	.30	.14	.04
☐ 214	Eric Soderholm	.30	.14	.04
☐ 215	Reggie Smith	.50	.23	.06
☐ 216	Montreal Expos	1.50	.30	.15
	Team Card;			
	Karl Kuehl MG			
	(Checklist back)			
☐ 217	Dave Freisleben	.30	.14	.04
☐ 218	John Knox	.30	.14	.04
☐ 219	Tom Murphy	.30	.14	.04
☐ 220	Manny Sanguillen	.50	.23	.06
☐ 221	Jim Todd	.30	.14	.04
☐ 222	Wayne Garrett	.30	.14	.04
☐ 223	Ollie Brown	.30	.14	.04
☐ 224	Jim York	.30	.14	.04
☐ 225	Roy White	.50	.23	.06
☐ 226	Jim Sundberg	.50	.23	.06
☐ 227	Oscar Zamora	.30	.14	.04
☐ 228	John Hale	.30	.14	.04
☐ 229	Jerry Remy	.30	.14	.04
☐ 230	Carl Yastrzemski	5.00	2.20	.60
☐ 231	Tom House	.30	.14	.04
☐ 232	Frank Duffy	.30	.14	.04
☐ 233	Grant Jackson	.30	.14	.04
☐ 234	Mike Sadek	.30	.14	.04
☐ 235	Bert Blyleven	.75	.35	.09
☐ 236	Kansas City Royals	1.50	.30	.15
	Team Card;			
	Whitey Herzog MG			
	(Checklist back)			
☐ 237	Dave Hamilton	.30	.14	.04
☐ 238	Larry Biittner	.30	.14	.04
☐ 239	John Curtis	.30	.14	.04
☐ 240	Pete Rose	14.00	6.25	1.75
☐ 241	Hector Torres	.30	.14	.04
☐ 242	Dan Meyer	.30	.14	.04
☐ 243	Jim Rooker	.30	.14	.04
☐ 244	Bill Sharp	.30	.14	.04
☐ 245	Felix Millan	.30	.14	.04
☐ 246	Cesar Tovar	.30	.14	.04
☐ 247	Terry Harmon	.30	.14	.04
☐ 248	Dick Tidrow	.30	.14	.04
☐ 249	Cliff Johnson	.50	.23	.06
☐ 250	Fergie Jenkins	2.50	1.10	.30
☐ 251	Rick Monday	.50	.23	.06
☐ 252	Tim Nordbrook	.30	.14	.04
☐ 253	Bill Buckner	.50	.23	.06
☐ 254	Rudy Meoli	.30	.14	.04
☐ 255	Fritz Peterson	.30	.14	.04
☐ 256	Rowland Office	.30	.14	.04
☐ 257	Ross Grimsley	.30	.14	.04
☐ 258	Nyls Nyman	.30	.14	.04
☐ 259	Darrel Chaney	.30	.14	.04
☐ 260	Steve Busby	.30	.14	.04
☐ 261	Gary Thomasson	.30	.14	.04
☐ 262	Checklist 133-264	1.50	.30	.15
☐ 263	Lyman Bostock	1.00	.45	.12
☐ 264	Steve Renko	.30	.14	.04
☐ 265	Willie Davis	.50	.23	.06
☐ 266	Alan Foster	.30	.14	.04
☐ 267	Aurelio Rodriguez	.30	.14	.04
☐ 268	Del Unser	.30	.14	.04
☐ 269	Rick Austin	.30	.14	.04
☐ 270	Willie Stargell	3.00	1.35	.35
☐ 271	Jim Lonborg	.50	.23	.06
☐ 272	Rick Dempsey	.50	.23	.06
☐ 273	Joe Niekro	.50	.23	.06
☐ 274	Tommy Harper	.50	.23	.06

☐ 275	Rick Manning	.30	.14	.04
☐ 276	Mickey Scott	.30	.14	.04
☐ 277	Chicago Cubs Team Card; Jim Marshall MG (Checklist back)	1.50	.30	.15
☐ 278	Bernie Carbo	.30	.14	.04
☐ 279	Roy Howell	.30	.14	.04
☐ 280	Burt Hooton	.50	.23	.06
☐ 281	Dave May	.30	.14	.04
☐ 282	Dan Osborn	.30	.14	.04
☐ 283	Merv Rettenmund	.30	.14	.04
☐ 284	Steve Ontiveros	.30	.14	.04
☐ 285	Mike Cuellar	.50	.23	.06
☐ 286	Jim Wohlford	.30	.14	.04
☐ 287	Pete Mackanin	.30	.14	.04
☐ 288	Bill Campbell	.30	.14	.04
☐ 289	Enzo Hernandez	.30	.14	.04
☐ 290	Ted Simmons	.75	.35	.09
☐ 291	Ken Sanders	.30	.14	.04
☐ 292	Leon Roberts	.30	.14	.04
☐ 293	Bill Castro	.30	.14	.04
☐ 294	Ed Kirkpatrick	.30	.14	.04
☐ 295	Dave Cash	.30	.14	.04
☐ 296	Pat Dobson	.30	.14	.04
☐ 297	Roger Metzger	.30	.14	.04
☐ 298	Dick Bosman	.30	.14	.04
☐ 299	Champ Summers	.30	.14	.04
☐ 300	Johnny Bench	7.00	3.10	.85
☐ 301	Jackie Brown	.30	.14	.04
☐ 302	Rick Miller	.30	.14	.04
☐ 303	Steve Foucault	.30	.14	.04
☐ 304	California Angels Team Card; Dick Williams MG (Checklist back)	1.50	.30	.15
☐ 305	Andy Messersmith	.50	.23	.06
☐ 306	Rod Gilbreath	.30	.14	.04
☐ 307	Al Bumbry	.50	.23	.06
☐ 308	Jim Barr	.30	.14	.04
☐ 309	Bill Melton	.30	.14	.04
☐ 310	Randy Jones	.50	.23	.06
☐ 311	Cookie Rojas	.50	.23	.06
☐ 312	Don Carrithers	.30	.14	.04
☐ 313	Dan Ford	.30	.14	.04
☐ 314	Ed Kranepool	.30	.14	.04
☐ 315	Al Hrabosky	.50	.23	.06
☐ 316	Robin Yount	30.00	13.50	3.70
☐ 317	John Candelaria	2.00	.90	.25
☐ 318	Bob Boone	.75	.35	.09
☐ 319	Larry Gura	.30	.14	.04
☐ 320	Willie Horton	.50	.23	.06
☐ 321	Jose Cruz	.50	.23	.06
☐ 322	Glenn Abbott	.30	.14	.04
☐ 323	Rob Sperring	.30	.14	.04
☐ 324	Jim Bibby	.30	.14	.04
☐ 325	Tony Perez	2.00	.90	.25
☐ 326	Dick Pole	.30	.14	.04
☐ 327	Dave Moates	.30	.14	.04
☐ 328	Carl Morton	.30	.14	.04
☐ 329	Joe Ferguson	.30	.14	.04
☐ 330	Nolan Ryan	70.00	32.00	8.75
☐ 331	San Diego Padres Team Card; John McNamara MG (Checklist back)	1.50	.30	.15
☐ 332	Charlie Williams	.30	.14	.04
☐ 333	Bob Coluccio	.30	.14	.04
☐ 334	Dennis Leonard	.50	.23	.06
☐ 335	Bob Grich	.50	.23	.06
☐ 336	Vic Albury	.30	.14	.04
☐ 337	Bud Harrelson	.50	.23	.06
☐ 338	Bob Bailey	.30	.14	.04
☐ 339	John Denny	.50	.23	.06
☐ 340	Jim Rice	5.00	2.20	.60
☐ 341	Lou Gehrig All-Time 1B	12.00	5.50	1.50
☐ 342	Rogers Hornsby All-Time 2B	3.00	1.35	.35
☐ 343	Pie Traynor All-Time 3B	1.00	.45	.12
☐ 344	Honus Wagner All-Time SS	5.00	2.20	.60
☐ 345	Babe Ruth All-Time OF	15.00	6.75	1.85
☐ 346	Ty Cobb All-Time OF	8.00	3.60	1.00
☐ 347	Ted Williams All-Time OF	10.00	4.50	1.25
☐ 348	Mickey Cochrane All-Time C	1.00	.45	.12
☐ 349	Walter Johnson All-Time RHP	3.00	1.35	.35
☐ 350	Lefty Grove All-Time LHP	1.00	.45	.12
☐ 351	Randy Hundley	.30	.14	.04
☐ 352	Dave Giusti	.30	.14	.04
☐ 353	Sixto Lezcano	.50	.23	.06
☐ 354	Ron Blomberg	.30	.14	.04
☐ 355	Steve Carlton	6.00	2.70	.75
☐ 356	Ted Martinez	.30	.14	.04
☐ 357	Ken Forsch	.30	.14	.04
☐ 358	Buddy Bell	.50	.23	.06
☐ 359	Rick Reuschel	.50	.23	.06
☐ 360	Jeff Burroughs	.50	.23	.06
☐ 361	Detroit Tigers Team Card; Ralph Houk MG (Checklist back)	1.50	.30	.15
☐ 362	Will McEnaney	.50	.23	.06
☐ 363	Dave Collins	.50	.23	.06
☐ 364	Elias Sosa	.30	.14	.04
☐ 365	Carlton Fisk	7.00	3.10	.85
☐ 366	Bobby Valentine	.30	.14	.04
☐ 367	Bruce Miller	.30	.14	.04
☐ 368	Wilbur Wood	.30	.14	.04
☐ 369	Frank White	.50	.23	.06
☐ 370	Ron Cey	.50	.23	.06
☐ 371	Elrod Hendricks	.30	.14	.04
☐ 372	Rick Baldwin	.30	.14	.04
☐ 373	Johnny Briggs	.30	.14	.04
☐ 374	Dan Warthen	.30	.14	.04
☐ 375	Ron Fairly	.30	.14	.04
☐ 376	Rich Hebner	.50	.23	.06
☐ 377	Mike Hegan	.30	.14	.04
☐ 378	Steve Stone	.50	.23	.06
☐ 379	Ken Boswell	.30	.14	.04
☐ 380	Bobby Bonds	1.50	.70	.19
☐ 381	Denny Doyle	.30	.14	.04
☐ 382	Matt Alexander	.30	.14	.04
☐ 383	John Ellis	.30	.14	.04
☐ 384	Philadelphia Phillies Team Card; Danny Ozark MG (Checklist back)	1.50	.30	.15
☐ 385	Mickey Lolich	.50	.23	.06
☐ 386	Ed Goodson	.30	.14	.04
☐ 387	Mike Miley	.30	.14	.04
☐ 388	Stan Perzanowski	.30	.14	.04
☐ 389	Glenn Adams	.30	.14	.04
☐ 390	Don Gullett	.50	.23	.06
☐ 391	Jerry Hairston	.30	.14	.04

☐ 392	Checklist 265-396	1.50	.30	.15
☐ 393	Paul Mitchell	.30	.14	.04
☐ 394	Fran Healy	.30	.14	.04
☐ 395	Jim Wynn	.50	.23	.06
☐ 396	Bill Lee	.30	.14	.04
☐ 397	Tim Foli	.30	.14	.04
☐ 398	Dave Tomlin	.30	.14	.04
☐ 399	Luis Melendez	.30	.14	.04
☐ 400	Rod Carew	4.00	1.80	.50
☐ 401	Ken Brett	.30	.14	.04
☐ 402	Don Money	.50	.23	.06
☐ 403	Geoff Zahn	.30	.14	.04
☐ 404	Enos Cabell	.30	.14	.04
☐ 405	Rollie Fingers	2.50	1.10	.30
☐ 406	Ed Herrmann	.30	.14	.04
☐ 407	Tom Underwood	.30	.14	.04
☐ 408	Charlie Spikes	.30	.14	.04
☐ 409	Dave Lemanczyk	.30	.14	.04
☐ 410	Ralph Garr	.50	.23	.06
☐ 411	Bill Singer	.30	.14	.04
☐ 412	Toby Harrah	.50	.23	.06
☐ 413	Pete Varney	.30	.14	.04
☐ 414	Wayne Garland	.30	.14	.04
☐ 415	Vada Pinson	.75	.35	.09
☐ 416	Tommy John	.75	.35	.09
☐ 417	Gene Clines	.30	.14	.04
☐ 418	Jose Morales	.30	.14	.04
☐ 419	Reggie Cleveland	.30	.14	.04
☐ 420	Joe Morgan	4.00	1.80	.50
☐ 421	Oakland A's; Team Card; (No MG on front; checklist back)	1.50	.30	.15
☐ 422	Johnny Grubb	.30	.14	.04
☐ 423	Ed Halicki	.30	.14	.04
☐ 424	Phil Roof	.30	.14	.04
☐ 425	Rennie Stennett	.30	.14	.04
☐ 426	Bob Forsch	.30	.14	.04
☐ 427	Kurt Bevacqua	.30	.14	.04
☐ 428	Jim Crawford	.30	.14	.04
☐ 429	Fred Stanley	.30	.14	.04
☐ 430	Jose Cardenal	.30	.14	.04
☐ 431	Dick Ruthven	.30	.14	.04
☐ 432	Tom Veryzer	.30	.14	.04
☐ 433	Rick Waits	.30	.14	.04
☐ 434	Morris Nettles	.30	.14	.04
☐ 435	Phil Niekro	2.00	.90	.25
☐ 436	Bill Fahey	.30	.14	.04
☐ 437	Terry Forster	.30	.14	.04
☐ 438	Doug DeCinces	.30	.14	.04
☐ 439	Rick Rhoden	.50	.23	.06
☐ 440	John Mayberry	.50	.23	.06
☐ 441	Gary Carter	7.00	3.10	.85
☐ 442	Hank Webb	.30	.14	.04
☐ 443	San Francisco Giants; Team Card; (No MG on front; checklist back)	1.50	.30	.15
☐ 444	Gary Nolan	.50	.23	.06
☐ 445	Rico Petrocelli	.50	.23	.06
☐ 446	Larry Haney	.30	.14	.04
☐ 447	Gene Locklear	.50	.23	.06
☐ 448	Tom Johnson	.30	.14	.04
☐ 449	Bob Robertson	.30	.14	.04
☐ 450	Jim Palmer	4.00	1.80	.50
☐ 451	Buddy Bradford	.30	.14	.04
☐ 452	Tom Hausman	.30	.14	.04
☐ 453	Lou Piniella	1.00	.45	.12
☐ 454	Tom Griffin	.30	.14	.04
☐ 455	Dick Allen	.75	.35	.09
☐ 456	Joe Coleman	.30	.14	.04
☐ 457	Ed Crosby	.30	.14	.04
☐ 458	Earl Williams	.30	.14	.04
☐ 459	Jim Brewer	.30	.14	.04
☐ 460	Cesar Cedeno	.50	.23	.06
☐ 461	NL and AL Champs; Reds sweep Bucs, Bosox surprise A's	.75	.35	.09
☐ 462	'75 World Series; Reds Champs	.75	.35	.09
☐ 463	Steve Hargan	.30	.14	.04
☐ 464	Ken Henderson	.30	.14	.04
☐ 465	Mike Marshall	.50	.23	.06
☐ 466	Bob Stinson	.30	.14	.04
☐ 467	Woodie Fryman	.30	.14	.04
☐ 468	Jesus Alou	.30	.14	.04
☐ 469	Rawly Eastwick	.50	.23	.06
☐ 470	Bobby Murcer	.50	.23	.06
☐ 471	Jim Burton	.30	.14	.04
☐ 472	Bob Davis	.30	.14	.04
☐ 473	Paul Blair	.50	.23	.06
☐ 474	Ray Corbin	.30	.14	.04
☐ 475	Joe Rudi	.50	.23	.06
☐ 476	Bob Moose	.30	.14	.04
☐ 477	Cleveland Indians; Team Card; Frank Robinson MG (Checklist back)	1.50	.30	.15
☐ 478	Lynn McGlothen	.30	.14	.04
☐ 479	Bobby Mitchell	.30	.14	.04
☐ 480	Mike Schmidt	25.00	11.00	3.10
☐ 481	Rudy May	.30	.14	.04
☐ 482	Tim Hosley	.30	.14	.04
☐ 483	Mickey Stanley	.30	.14	.04
☐ 484	Eric Raich	.30	.14	.04
☐ 485	Mike Hargrove	.50	.23	.06
☐ 486	Bruce Dal Canton	.30	.14	.04
☐ 487	Leron Lee	.30	.14	.04
☐ 488	Claude Osteen	.50	.23	.06
☐ 489	Skip Jutze	.30	.14	.04
☐ 490	Frank Tanana	.75	.35	.09
☐ 491	Terry Crowley	.30	.14	.04
☐ 492	Marty Pattin	.30	.14	.04
☐ 493	Derrel Thomas	.30	.14	.04
☐ 494	Craig Swan	.50	.23	.06
☐ 495	Nate Colbert	.30	.14	.04
☐ 496	Juan Beniquez	.30	.14	.04
☐ 497	Joe McIntosh	.30	.14	.04
☐ 498	Glenn Borgmann	.30	.14	.04
☐ 499	Mario Guerrero	.30	.14	.04
☐ 500	Reggie Jackson	14.00	6.25	1.75
☐ 501	Billy Champion	.30	.14	.04
☐ 502	Tim McCarver	.50	.23	.06
☐ 503	Elliott Maddox	.30	.14	.04
☐ 504	Pittsburgh Pirates; Team Card; Danny Murtaugh MG (Checklist back)	1.50	.30	.15
☐ 505	Mark Belanger	.50	.23	.06
☐ 506	George Mitterwald	.30	.14	.04
☐ 507	Ray Bare	.30	.14	.04
☐ 508	Duane Kuiper	.30	.14	.04
☐ 509	Bill Hands	.30	.14	.04
☐ 510	Amos Otis	.50	.23	.06
☐ 511	Jamie Easterley	.30	.14	.04
☐ 512	Ellie Rodriguez	.30	.14	.04
☐ 513	Bart Johnson	.30	.14	.04
☐ 514	Dan Driessen	.50	.23	.06
☐ 515	Steve Yeager	.50	.23	.06
☐ 516	Wayne Granger	.30	.14	.04
☐ 517	John Milner	.30	.14	.04
☐ 518	Doug Flynn	.30	.14	.04

☐ 519	Steve Brye	.30	.14	.04
☐ 520	Willie McCovey	4.00	1.80	.50
☐ 521	Jim Colborn	.30	.14	.04
☐ 522	Ted Sizemore	.30	.14	.04
☐ 523	Bob Montgomery	.30	.14	.04
☐ 524	Pete Falcone	.30	.14	.04
☐ 525	Billy Williams	2.50	1.10	.30
☐ 526	Checklist 397-528	1.50	.30	.15
☐ 527	Mike Anderson	.30	.14	.04
☐ 528	Dock Ellis	.30	.14	.04
☐ 529	Deron Johnson	.30	.14	.04
☐ 530	Don Sutton	1.50	.70	.19
☐ 531	New York Mets	1.50	.30	.15
	Team Card;			
	Joe Frazier MG			
	(Checklist back)			
☐ 532	Milt May	.30	.14	.04
☐ 533	Lee Richard	.30	.14	.04
☐ 534	Stan Bahnsen	.30	.14	.04
☐ 535	Dave Nelson	.30	.14	.04
☐ 536	Mike Thompson	.30	.14	.04
☐ 537	Tony Muser	.30	.14	.04
☐ 538	Pat Darcy	.30	.14	.04
☐ 539	John Balaz	.50	.23	.06
☐ 540	Bill Freehan	.50	.23	.06
☐ 541	Steve Mingori	.30	.14	.04
☐ 542	Keith Hernandez	1.50	.70	.19
☐ 543	Wayne Twitchell	.30	.14	.04
☐ 544	Pepe Frias	.30	.14	.04
☐ 545	Sparky Lyle	.50	.23	.06
☐ 546	Dave Rosello	.30	.14	.04
☐ 547	Roric Harrison	.30	.14	.04
☐ 548	Manny Mota	.50	.23	.06
☐ 549	Randy Tate	.30	.14	.04
☐ 550	Hank Aaron	25.00	11.00	3.10
☐ 551	Jerry DaVanon	.30	.14	.04
☐ 552	Terry Humphrey	.30	.14	.04
☐ 553	Randy Moffitt	.30	.14	.04
☐ 554	Ray Fosse	.30	.14	.04
☐ 555	Dyar Miller	.30	.14	.04
☐ 556	Minnesota Twins	1.50	.30	.15
	Team Card;			
	Gene Mauch MG			
	(Checklist back)			
☐ 557	Dan Spillner	.30	.14	.04
☐ 558	Clarence Gaston	.50	.23	.06
☐ 559	Clyde Wright	.30	.14	.04
☐ 560	Jorge Orta	.30	.14	.04
☐ 561	Tom Carroll	.30	.14	.04
☐ 562	Adrian Garrett	.30	.14	.04
☐ 563	Larry Demery	.30	.14	.04
☐ 564	Bubble Gum Champ	.75	.35	.09
	Kurt Bevacqua			
☐ 565	Tug McGraw	.50	.23	.06
☐ 566	Ken McMullen	.30	.14	.04
☐ 567	George Stone	.30	.14	.04
☐ 568	Rob Andrews	.30	.14	.04
☐ 569	Nelson Briles	.50	.23	.06
☐ 570	George Hendrick	.50	.23	.06
☐ 571	Don DeMola	.30	.14	.04
☐ 572	Rich Coggins	.30	.14	.04
☐ 573	Bill Travers	.30	.14	.04
☐ 574	Don Kessinger	.50	.23	.06
☐ 575	Dwight Evans	1.50	.70	.19
☐ 576	Maximino Leon	.30	.14	.04
☐ 577	Marc Hill	.30	.14	.04
☐ 578	Ted Kubiak	.30	.14	.04
☐ 579	Clay Kirby	.30	.14	.04
☐ 580	Bert Campaneris	.50	.23	.06
☐ 581	St. Louis Cardinals	1.50	.30	.15
	Team Card;			

	Red Schoendienst MG			
	(Checklist back)			
☐ 582	Mike Kekich	.30	.14	.04
☐ 583	Tommy Helms	.30	.14	.04
☐ 584	Stan Wall	.30	.14	.04
☐ 585	Joe Torre	.75	.35	.09
☐ 586	Ron Schueler	.30	.14	.04
☐ 587	Leo Cardenas	.30	.14	.04
☐ 588	Kevin Kobel	.30	.14	.04
☐ 589	Rookie Pitchers	1.50	.70	.19
	Santo Alcala			
	Mike Flanagan			
	Joe Pactwa			
	Pablo Torrealba			
☐ 590	Rookie Outfielders	.75	.35	.09
	Henry Cruz			
	Chet Lemon			
	Ellis Valentine			
	Terry Whitfield			
☐ 591	Rookie Pitchers	.50	.23	.06
	Steve Grilli			
	Craig Mitchell			
	Jose Sosa			
	George Throop			
☐ 592	Rookie Infielders	6.00	2.70	.75
	Willie Randolph			
	Dave McKay			
	Jerry Royster			
	Roy Staiger			
☐ 593	Rookie Pitchers	.50	.23	.06
	Larry Anderson			
	Ken Crosby			
	Mark Littell			
	Butch Metzger			
☐ 594	Rookie Catchers/OF	.50	.23	.06
	Andy Merchant			
	Ed Ott			
	Royle Stillman			
	Jerry White			
☐ 595	Rookie Pitchers	.50	.23	.06
	Art DeFillipis			
	Randy Lerch			
	Sid Monge			
	Steve Barr			
☐ 596	Rookie Infielders	.50	.23	.06
	Craig Reynolds			
	Lamar Johnson			
	Johnnie LeMaster			
	Jerry Manuel			
☐ 597	Rookie Pitchers	.50	.23	.06
	Don Aase			
	Jack Kucek			
	Frank LaCorte			
	Mike Pazik			
☐ 598	Rookie Outfielders	.50	.23	.06
	Hector Cruz			
	Jamie Quirk			
	Jerry Turner			
	Joe Wallis			
☐ 599	Rookie Pitchers	6.00	2.70	.75
	Rob Dressler			
	Ron Guidry			
	Bob McClure			
	Pat Zachry			
☐ 600	Tom Seaver	7.00	3.10	.85
☐ 601	Ken Rudolph	.30	.14	.04
☐ 602	Doug Konieczny	.30	.14	.04
☐ 603	Jim Holt	.30	.14	.04
☐ 604	Joe Lovitto	.30	.14	.04
☐ 605	Al Downing	.30	.14	.04
☐ 606	Milwaukee Brewers	1.50	.30	.15

	Team Card;		
	Alex Grammas MG		
	(Checklist back)		
☐ 607	Rich Hinton	.30	.14	.04
☐ 608	Vic Correll	.30	.14	.04
☐ 609	Fred Norman	.50	.23	.06
☐ 610	Greg Luzinski	.30	.14	.04
☐ 611	Rich Folkers	.30	.14	.04
☐ 612	Joe Lahoud	.30	.14	.04
☐ 613	Tim Johnson	.30	.14	.04
☐ 614	Fernando Arroyo	.30	.14	.04
☐ 615	Mike Cubbage	.30	.14	.04
☐ 616	Buck Martinez	.30	.14	.04
☐ 617	Darold Knowles	.30	.14	.04
☐ 618	Jack Brohamer	.30	.14	.04
☐ 619	Bill Butler	.30	.14	.04
☐ 620	Al Oliver	.50	.23	.06
☐ 621	Tom Hall	.30	.14	.04
☐ 622	Rick Auerbach	.30	.14	.04
☐ 623	Bob Allietta	.30	.14	.04
☐ 624	Tony Taylor	.30	.14	.04
☐ 625	J.R. Richard	.50	.23	.06
☐ 626	Bob Sheldon	.30	.14	.04
☐ 627	Bill Plummer	.30	.14	.04
☐ 628	John D'Acquisto	.30	.14	.04
☐ 629	Sandy Alomar	.50	.23	.06
☐ 630	Chris Speier	.30	.14	.04
☐ 631	Atlanta Braves	1.50	.30	.15
	Team Card;		
	Dave Bristol MG		
	(Checklist back)		
☐ 632	Rogelio Moret	.30	.14	.04
☐ 633	John Stearns	.50	.23	.06
☐ 634	Larry Christenson	.30	.14	.04
☐ 635	Jim Fregosi	.50	.23	.06
☐ 636	Joe Decker	.30	.14	.04
☐ 637	Bruce Bochte	.30	.14	.04
☐ 638	Doyle Alexander	.50	.23	.06
☐ 639	Fred Kendall	.30	.14	.04
☐ 640	Bill Madlock	.75	.35	.09
☐ 641	Tom Paciorek	.50	.23	.06
☐ 642	Dennis Blair	.30	.14	.04
☐ 643	Checklist 529-660	1.50	.30	.15
☐ 644	Tom Bradley	.30	.14	.04
☐ 645	Darrell Porter	.50	.23	.06
☐ 646	John Lowenstein	.30	.14	.04
☐ 647	Ramon Hernandez	.30	.14	.04
☐ 648	Al Cowens	.30	.14	.04
☐ 649	Dave Roberts	.30	.14	.04
☐ 650	Thurman Munson	4.00	1.80	.50
☐ 651	John Odom	.30	.14	.04
☐ 652	Ed Armbrister	.30	.14	.04
☐ 653	Mike Norris	.50	.23	.06
☐ 654	Doug Griffin	.30	.14	.04
☐ 655	Mike Vail	.30	.14	.04
☐ 656	Chicago White Sox	1.50	.30	.15
	Team Card;		
	Chuck Tanner MG		
	(Checklist back)		
☐ 657	Roy Smalley	.50	.23	.06
☐ 658	Jerry Johnson	.30	.14	.04
☐ 659	Ben Oglivie	.50	.23	.06
☐ 660	Dave Lopes	1.00	.45	.12

1977 Topps

*The cards in this 660-card set measure 2
1/2" by 3 1/2". In 1977 for the fifth consecutive year, Topps produced a 660-card base
ball set. The player's name, team affiliation,
and his position are compactly arranged
over the picture area and a facsimile autograph appears on the photo. Team cards
feature a checklist of that team's players in
the set and a small picture of the manager
on the front of the card. Appearing for the
first time are the series "Brothers" (631-
634) and "Turn Back the Clock" (433-437).
Other subseries in the set are League
Leaders (1-8), Record Breakers (231-234),
Playoffs cards (276-277), World Series
cards (411-413), and Rookie Prospects
(472-479 and 487-494). The following players' regular issue cards are explicitly denoted as All-Stars, 30, 70, 100, 120, 170, 210,
240, 265, 301, 347, 400, 420, 450, 500,
521, 550, 560, and 580. The key cards in
the set are the Rookie Cards of Dale
Murphy (476) and Andre Dawson (473).
Other notable Rookie Cards in the set
include Jack Clark, Dennis Martinez, and
Bruce Sutter. Cards numbered 23 or lower,
that feature Yankees and do not follow the
numbering checklisted below, are not necessarily error cards. They are undoubtedly
Burger King cards, a separate set with its
own pricing and mass distribution. Burger
King cards are indistinguishable from the
corresponding Topps cards except for the
card numbering difference and the fact that
Burger King cards do not have a printing
sheet designation (such as A through F like
the regular Topps) anywhere on the card
back in very small print. There was an alu-
minum version of the Dale Murphy rookie
card number 476 produced (legally) in the
early '80s; proceeds from the sales (originally priced at 10.00) of this "card" went to
the Huntington's Disease Foundation.*

		NRMT-MT	EXC	G-VG
COMPLETE SET (660)		400.00	180.00	50.00
COMMON CARD (1-660)		.25	.11	.03
☐ 1	Batting Leaders	7.00	2.00	.75
	George Brett			
	Bill Madlock			
☐ 2	Home Run Leaders	1.75	.80	.22
	Graig Nettles			
	Mike Schmidt			
☐ 3	RBI Leaders	.60	.25	.07
	Lee May			
	George Foster			
☐ 4	Stolen Base Leaders	.40	.18	.05
	Bill North			

	Dave Lopes		
☐ 5	Victory Leaders	.75	.35	.09
	Jim Palmer		
	Randy Jones		
☐ 6	Strikeout Leaders	15.00	6.75	1.85
	Nolan Ryan		
	Tom Seaver		
☐ 7	ERA Leaders	.40	.18	.05
	Mark Fidrych		
	John Denny		
☐ 8	Leading Firemen	.40	.18	.05
	Bill Campbell		
	Rawly Eastwick		
☐ 9	Doug Rader	.25	.11	.03
☐ 10	Reggie Jackson	10.00	4.50	1.25
☐ 11	Rob Dressler	.25	.11	.03
☐ 12	Larry Haney	.25	.11	.03
☐ 13	Luis Gomez	.25	.11	.03
☐ 14	Tommy Smith	.25	.11	.03
☐ 15	Don Gullett	.40	.18	.05
☐ 16	Bob Jones	.25	.11	.03
☐ 17	Steve Stone	.40	.18	.05
☐ 18	Indians Team/Mgr.	1.25	.25	.12
	Frank Robinson		
	(Checklist back)		
☐ 19	John D'Acquisto	.25	.11	.03
☐ 20	Graig Nettles	.60	.25	.07
☐ 21	Ken Forsch	.25	.11	.03
☐ 22	Bill Freehan	.40	.18	.05
☐ 23	Dan Driessen	.25	.11	.03
☐ 24	Carl Morton	.25	.11	.03
☐ 25	Dwight Evans	1.00	.45	.12
☐ 26	Ray Sadecki	.25	.11	.03
☐ 27	Bill Buckner	.40	.18	.05
☐ 28	Woodie Fryman	.25	.11	.03
☐ 29	Bucky Dent	.25	.11	.03
☐ 30	Greg Luzinski	.60	.25	.07
☐ 31	Jim Todd	.25	.11	.03
☐ 32	Checklist 1-132	1.25	.25	.12
☐ 33	Wayne Garland	.25	.11	.03
☐ 34	Angels Team/Mgr.	1.25	.25	.12
	Norm Sherry		
	(Checklist back)		
☐ 35	Rennie Stennett	.25	.11	.03
☐ 36	John Ellis	.25	.11	.03
☐ 37	Steve Hargan	.25	.11	.03
☐ 38	Craig Kusick	.25	.11	.03
☐ 39	Tom Griffin	.25	.11	.03
☐ 40	Bobby Murcer	.40	.18	.05
☐ 41	Jim Kern	.25	.11	.03
☐ 42	Jose Cruz	.40	.18	.05
☐ 43	Ray Bare	.25	.11	.03
☐ 44	Bud Harrelson	.40	.18	.05
☐ 45	Rawly Eastwick	.25	.11	.03
☐ 46	Buck Martinez	.25	.11	.03
☐ 47	Lynn McGlothen	.25	.11	.03
☐ 48	Tom Paciorek	.40	.18	.05
☐ 49	Grant Jackson	.25	.11	.03
☐ 50	Ron Cey	.40	.18	.05
☐ 51	Brewers Team/Mgr.	1.25	.25	.12
	Alex Grammas		
	(Checklist back)		
☐ 52	Ellis Valentine	.25	.11	.03
☐ 53	Paul Mitchell	.25	.11	.03
☐ 54	Sandy Alomar	.40	.18	.05
☐ 55	Jeff Burroughs	.40	.18	.05
☐ 56	Rudy May	.25	.11	.03
☐ 57	Marc Hill	.25	.11	.03
☐ 58	Chet Lemon	.40	.18	.05
☐ 59	Larry Christenson	.25	.11	.03
☐ 60	Jim Rice	3.00	1.35	.35
☐ 61	Manny Sanguillen	.40	.18	.05
☐ 62	Eric Raich	.25	.11	.03
☐ 63	Tito Fuentes	.25	.11	.03
☐ 64	Larry Biittner	.25	.11	.03
☐ 65	Skip Lockwood	.25	.11	.03
☐ 66	Roy Smalley	.40	.18	.05
☐ 67	Joaquin Andujar	.40	.18	.05
☐ 68	Bruce Bochte	.25	.11	.03
☐ 69	Jim Crawford	.25	.11	.03
☐ 70	Johnny Bench	6.00	2.70	.75
☐ 71	Dock Ellis	.25	.11	.03
☐ 72	Mike Anderson	.25	.11	.03
☐ 73	Charlie Williams	.25	.11	.03
☐ 74	A's Team/Mgr.	1.25	.25	.12
	Jack McKeon		
	(Checklist back)		
☐ 75	Dennis Leonard	.40	.18	.05
☐ 76	Tim Foli	.25	.11	.03
☐ 77	Dyar Miller	.25	.11	.03
☐ 78	Bob Davis	.25	.11	.03
☐ 79	Don Money	.25	.11	.05
☐ 80	Andy Messersmith	.40	.18	.05
☐ 81	Juan Beniquez	.25	.11	.03
☐ 82	Jim Rooker	.25	.11	.03
☐ 83	Kevin Bell	.25	.11	.03
☐ 84	Ollie Brown	.25	.11	.03
☐ 85	Duane Kuiper	.25	.11	.03
☐ 86	Pat Zachry	.25	.11	.03
☐ 87	Glenn Borgmann	.25	.11	.03
☐ 88	Stan Wall	.25	.11	.03
☐ 89	Butch Hobson	.60	.25	.07
☐ 90	Cesar Cedeno	.40	.18	.05
☐ 91	John Verhoeven	.25	.11	.03
☐ 92	Dave Rosello	.25	.11	.03
☐ 93	Tom Poquette	.25	.11	.03
☐ 94	Craig Swan	.25	.11	.03
☐ 95	Keith Hernandez	.60	.25	.07
☐ 96	Lou Piniella	.60	.25	.07
☐ 97	Dave Heaverlo	.25	.11	.03
☐ 98	Milt May	.25	.11	.03
☐ 99	Tom Hausman	.25	.11	.03
☐ 100	Joe Morgan	3.00	1.35	.35
☐ 101	Dick Bosman	.25	.11	.03
☐ 102	Jose Morales	.25	.11	.03
☐ 103	Mike Bacsik	.25	.11	.03
☐ 104	Omar Moreno	.40	.18	.05
☐ 105	Steve Yeager	.40	.18	.05
☐ 106	Mike Flanagan	.40	.18	.05
☐ 107	Bill Melton	.25	.11	.03
☐ 108	Alan Foster	.25	.11	.03
☐ 109	Jorge Orta	.25	.11	.03
☐ 110	Steve Carlton	5.00	2.20	.60
☐ 111	Rico Petrocelli	.40	.18	.05
☐ 112	Bill Greif	.25	.11	.03
☐ 113	Blue Jays Leaders	1.25	.25	.12
	Roy Hartsfield MG		
	Don Leppert CO		
	Bob Miller CO		
	Jackie Moore CO		
	Harry Warner CO		
	(Checklist back)		
☐ 114	Bruce Dal Canton	.25	.11	.03
☐ 115	Rick Manning	.25	.11	.03
☐ 116	Joe Niekro	.40	.18	.05
☐ 117	Frank White	.40	.18	.05
☐ 118	Rick Jones	.25	.11	.03
☐ 119	John Stearns	.25	.11	.03
☐ 120	Rod Carew	3.00	1.35	.35
☐ 121	Gary Nolan	.25	.11	.03
☐ 122	Ben Oglivie	.40	.18	.05
☐ 123	Fred Stanley	.25	.11	.03

☐ 124	George Mitterwald	.25	.11	.03
☐ 125	Bill Travers	.25	.11	.03
☐ 126	Rod Gilbreath	.25	.11	.03
☐ 127	Ron Fairly	.40	.18	.05
☐ 128	Tommy John	.60	.25	.07
☐ 129	Mike Sadek	.25	.11	.03
☐ 130	Al Oliver	.40	.18	.05
☐ 131	Orlando Ramirez	.25	.11	.03
☐ 132	Chip Lang	.25	.11	.03
☐ 133	Ralph Garr	.40	.18	.05
☐ 134	Padres Team/Mgr.	1.25	.25	.12
	John McNamara			
	(Checklist back)			
☐ 135	Mark Belanger	.40	.18	.05
☐ 136	Jerry Mumphrey	.25	.11	.03
☐ 137	Jeff Terpko	.25	.11	.03
☐ 138	Bob Stinson	.25	.11	.03
☐ 139	Fred Norman	.25	.11	.03
☐ 140	Mike Schmidt	16.00	7.25	2.00
☐ 141	Mark Littell	.25	.11	.03
☐ 142	Steve Dillard	.25	.11	.03
☐ 143	Ed Herrmann	.25	.11	.03
☐ 144	Bruce Sutter	2.50	1.10	.30
☐ 145	Tom Veryzer	.25	.11	.03
☐ 146	Dusty Baker	.60	.25	.07
☐ 147	Jackie Brown	.25	.11	.03
☐ 148	Fran Healy	.25	.11	.03
☐ 149	Mike Cubbage	.25	.11	.03
☐ 150	Tom Seaver	5.00	2.20	.60
☐ 151	Johnny LeMaster	.25	.11	.03
☐ 152	Gaylord Perry	2.00	.90	.25
☐ 153	Ron Jackson	.25	.11	.03
☐ 154	Dave Giusti	.25	.11	.03
☐ 155	Joe Rudi	.40	.18	.05
☐ 156	Pete Mackanin	.25	.11	.03
☐ 157	Ken Brett	.25	.11	.03
☐ 158	Ted Kubiak	.25	.11	.03
☐ 159	Bernie Carbo	.25	.11	.03
☐ 160	Will McEnaney	.25	.11	.03
☐ 161	Garry Templeton	1.00	.45	.12
☐ 162	Mike Cuellar	.40	.18	.05
☐ 163	Dave Hilton	.25	.11	.03
☐ 164	Tug McGraw	.40	.18	.05
☐ 165	Jim Wynn	.40	.18	.05
☐ 166	Bill Campbell	.25	.11	.03
☐ 167	Rich Hebner	.40	.18	.05
☐ 168	Charlie Spikes	.25	.11	.03
☐ 169	Darold Knowles	.25	.11	.03
☐ 170	Thurman Munson	4.00	1.80	.50
☐ 171	Ken Sanders	.25	.11	.03
☐ 172	John Milner	.25	.11	.03
☐ 173	Chuck Scrivener	.25	.11	.03
☐ 174	Nelson Briles	.40	.18	.05
☐ 175	Butch Wynegar	.40	.18	.05
☐ 176	Bob Robertson	.25	.11	.03
☐ 177	Bart Johnson	.25	.11	.03
☐ 178	Bombo Rivera	.25	.11	.03
☐ 179	Paul Hartzell	.25	.11	.03
☐ 180	Dave Lopes	.40	.18	.05
☐ 181	Ken McMullen	.25	.11	.03
☐ 182	Dan Spillner	.25	.11	.03
☐ 183	Cardinals Team/Mgr.	1.25	.25	.12
	Vern Rapp			
	(Checklist back)			
☐ 184	Bo McLaughlin	.25	.11	.03
☐ 185	Sixto Lezcano	.25	.11	.03
☐ 186	Doug Flynn	.25	.11	.03
☐ 187	Dick Pole	.25	.11	.03
☐ 188	Bob Tolan	.25	.11	.03
☐ 189	Rick Dempsey	.40	.18	.05
☐ 190	Ray Burris	.25	.11	.03
☐ 191	Doug Griffin	.25	.11	.03
☐ 192	Clarence Gaston	.40	.18	.05
☐ 193	Larry Gura	.25	.11	.03
☐ 194	Gary Matthews	.40	.18	.05
☐ 195	Ed Figueroa	.25	.11	.03
☐ 196	Len Randle	.25	.11	.03
☐ 197	Ed Ott	.25	.11	.03
☐ 198	Wilbur Wood	.25	.11	.03
☐ 199	Pepe Frias	.25	.11	.03
☐ 200	Frank Tanana	.60	.25	.07
☐ 201	Ed Kranepool	.25	.11	.03
☐ 202	Tom Johnson	.25	.11	.03
☐ 203	Ed Armbrister	.25	.11	.03
☐ 204	Jeff Newman	.25	.11	.03
☐ 205	Pete Falcone	.25	.11	.03
☐ 206	Boog Powell	.40	.18	.05
☐ 207	Glenn Abbott	.25	.11	.03
☐ 208	Checklist 133-264	1.25	.25	.12
☐ 209	Rob Andrews	.25	.11	.03
☐ 210	Fred Lynn	1.25	.25	.12
☐ 211	Giants Team/Mgr.	1.25	.55	.16
	Joe Altobelli			
	(Checklist back)			
☐ 212	Jim Mason	.25	.11	.03
☐ 213	Maximino Leon	.25	.11	.03
☐ 214	Darrell Porter	.40	.18	.05
☐ 215	Butch Metzger	.40	.18	.05
☐ 216	Doug DeCinces	.40	.18	.05
☐ 217	Tom Underwood	.25	.11	.03
☐ 218	John Wathan	.25	.11	.03
☐ 219	Joe Coleman	.25	.11	.03
☐ 220	Chris Chambliss	.40	.18	.05
☐ 221	Bob Bailey	.25	.11	.03
☐ 222	Francisco Barrios	.25	.11	.03
☐ 223	Earl Williams	.25	.11	.03
☐ 224	Rusty Torres	.25	.11	.03
☐ 225	Bob Apodaca	.25	.11	.03
☐ 226	Leroy Stanton	.40	.18	.05
☐ 227	Joe Sambito	.25	.11	.03
☐ 228	Twins Team/Mgr.	1.25	.25	.12
	Gene Mauch			
	(Checklist back)			
☐ 229	Don Kessinger	.40	.18	.05
☐ 230	Vida Blue	.40	.18	.05
☐ 231	RB: George Brett	12.00	5.50	1.50
	Most cons. games			
	with 3 or more hits			
☐ 232	RB: Minnie Minoso	.40	.18	.05
	Oldest to hit safely			
☐ 233	RB: Jose Morales, Most	.25	.11	.03
	pinch-hits, season			
☐ 234	RB: Nolan Ryan	18.00	8.00	2.20
	Most seasons, 300			
	or more strikeouts			
☐ 235	Cecil Cooper	.40	.18	.05
☐ 236	Tom Buskey	.25	.11	.03
☐ 237	Gene Clines	.25	.11	.03
☐ 238	Tippy Martinez	.40	.18	.05
☐ 239	Bill Plummer	.25	.11	.03
☐ 240	Ron LeFlore	.40	.18	.05
☐ 241	Dave Tomlin	.25	.11	.03
☐ 242	Ken Henderson	.25	.11	.03
☐ 243	Ron Reed	.25	.11	.03
☐ 244	John Mayberry	.60	.25	.07
	(Cartoon mentions			
	T206 Wagner)			
☐ 245	Rick Rhoden	.40	.18	.05
☐ 246	Mike Vail	.25	.11	.03
☐ 247	Chris Knapp	.25	.11	.03
☐ 248	Wilbur Howard	.25	.11	.03
☐ 249	Pete Redfern	.25	.11	.03

☐ 250	Bill Madlock	.40	.18	.05
☐ 251	Tony Muser	.25	.11	.03
☐ 252	Dale Murray	.25	.11	.03
☐ 253	John Hale	.25	.11	.03
☐ 254	Doyle Alexander	.25	.11	.03
☐ 255	George Scott	.40	.18	.05
☐ 256	Joe Hoerner	.25	.11	.03
☐ 257	Mike Miley	.25	.11	.03
☐ 258	Luis Tiant	.40	.18	.05
☐ 259	Mets Team/Mgr.	1.25	.25	.12
	Joe Frazier			
	(Checklist back)			
☐ 260	J.R. Richard	.40	.18	.05
☐ 261	Phil Garner	.40	.18	.05
☐ 262	Al Cowens	.25	.11	.03
☐ 263	Mike Marshall	.40	.18	.05
☐ 264	Tom Hutton	.25	.11	.03
☐ 265	Mark Fidrych	5.00	2.20	.60
☐ 266	Derrel Thomas	.25	.11	.03
☐ 267	Ray Fosse	.25	.11	.03
☐ 268	Rick Sawyer	.25	.11	.03
☐ 269	Joe Lis	.25	.11	.03
☐ 270	Dave Parker	1.50	.70	.19
☐ 271	Terry Forster	.25	.11	.03
☐ 272	Lee Lacy	.25	.11	.03
☐ 273	Eric Soderholm	.25	.11	.03
☐ 274	Don Stanhouse	.25	.11	.03
☐ 275	Mike Hargrove	.40	.18	.05
☐ 276	AL Champs	.40	.18	.05
	Chris Chambliss'			
	homer decides it			
☐ 277	NL Champs	2.00	.90	.25
	Reds sweep Phillies			
☐ 278	Danny Frisella	.25	.11	.03
☐ 279	Joe Wallis	.25	.11	.03
☐ 280	Jim Hunter	2.00	.90	.25
☐ 281	Roy Staiger	.25	.11	.03
☐ 282	Sid Monge	.25	.11	.03
☐ 283	Jerry DaVanon	.25	.11	.03
☐ 284	Mike Norris	.25	.11	.03
☐ 285	Brooks Robinson	4.00	1.80	.50
☐ 286	Johnny Grubb	.25	.05	.03
☐ 287	Reds Team/Mgr.	1.25	.55	.16
	Sparky Anderson			
	(Checklist back)			
☐ 288	Bob Montgomery	.25	.11	.03
☐ 289	Gene Garber	.25	.11	.03
☐ 290	Amos Otis	.40	.18	.05
☐ 291	Jason Thompson	.25	.11	.03
☐ 292	Rogelio Moret	.25	.11	.03
☐ 293	Jack Brohamer	.25	.11	.03
☐ 294	George Medich	.25	.11	.03
☐ 295	Gary Carter	4.00	1.80	.50
☐ 296	Don Hood	.25	.11	.03
☐ 297	Ken Reitz	.25	.11	.03
☐ 298	Charlie Hough	.60	.25	.07
☐ 299	Otto Velez	.40	.18	.05
☐ 300	Jerry Koosman	.40	.18	.05
☐ 301	Toby Harrah	.40	.18	.05
☐ 302	Mike Garman	.25	.11	.03
☐ 303	Gene Tenace	.40	.18	.05
☐ 304	Jim Hughes	.25	.11	.03
☐ 305	Mickey Rivers	.40	.18	.05
☐ 306	Rick Waits	.25	.11	.03
☐ 307	Gary Sutherland	.25	.11	.03
☐ 308	Gene Pentz	.25	.11	.03
☐ 309	Red Sox Team/Mgr.	1.25	.25	.12
	Don Zimmer			
	(Checklist back)			
☐ 310	Larry Bowa	.60	.25	.07
☐ 311	Vern Ruhle	.25	.11	.03

☐ 312	Rob Belloir	.25	.11	.03
☐ 313	Paul Blair	.40	.18	.05
☐ 314	Steve Mingori	.25	.11	.03
☐ 315	Dave Chalk	.25	.11	.03
☐ 316	Steve Rogers	.25	.11	.03
☐ 317	Kurt Bevacqua	.25	.11	.03
☐ 318	Duffy Dyer	.25	.11	.03
☐ 319	Rich Gossage	1.00	.45	.12
☐ 320	Ken Griffey	1.50	.70	.19
☐ 321	Dave Goltz	.25	.11	.03
☐ 322	Bill Russell	.40	.18	.05
☐ 323	Larry Lintz	.25	.11	.03
☐ 324	John Curtis	.25	.11	.03
☐ 325	Mike Ivie	.25	.11	.03
☐ 326	Jesse Jefferson	.25	.11	.03
☐ 327	Astros Team/Mgr.	1.25	.25	.12
	Bill Virdon			
	(Checklist back)			
☐ 328	Tommy Boggs	.25	.11	.03
☐ 329	Ron Hodges	.25	.11	.03
☐ 330	George Hendrick	.40	.18	.05
☐ 331	Jim Colborn	.25	.11	.03
☐ 332	Elliott Maddox	.25	.11	.03
☐ 333	Paul Reuschel	.25	.11	.03
☐ 334	Bill Stein	.25	.11	.03
☐ 335	Bill Robinson	.40	.18	.05
☐ 336	Denny Doyle	.25	.11	.03
☐ 337	Ron Schueler	.25	.11	.03
☐ 338	Dave Duncan	.25	.11	.03
☐ 339	Adrian Devine	.25	.11	.03
☐ 340	Hal McRae	.60	.25	.07
☐ 341	Joe Kerrigan	.25	.11	.03
☐ 342	Jerry Remy	.25	.11	.03
☐ 343	Ed Halicki	.25	.11	.03
☐ 344	Brian Downing	.40	.18	.05
☐ 345	Reggie Smith	.40	.18	.05
☐ 346	Bill Singer	.25	.11	.03
☐ 347	George Foster	.75	.35	.09
☐ 348	Brent Strom	.25	.11	.03
☐ 349	Jim Holt	.25	.11	.03
☐ 350	Larry Dierker	.25	.11	.03
☐ 351	Jim Sundberg	.40	.18	.05
☐ 352	Mike Phillips	.25	.11	.03
☐ 353	Stan Thomas	.25	.11	.03
☐ 354	Pirates Team/Mgr.	1.25	.25	.12
	Chuck Tanner			
	(Checklist back)			
☐ 355	Lou Brock	3.00	1.35	.35
☐ 356	Checklist 265-396	1.25	.25	.12
☐ 357	Tim McCarver	.40	.18	.05
☐ 358	Tom House	.25	.11	.03
☐ 359	Willie Randolph	2.00	.90	.25
☐ 360	Rick Monday	.40	.18	.05
☐ 361	Eduardo Rodriguez	.25	.11	.03
☐ 362	Tommy Davis	.40	.18	.05
☐ 363	Dave Roberts	.25	.11	.03
☐ 364	Vic Correll	.25	.11	.03
☐ 365	Mike Torrez	.40	.18	.05
☐ 366	Ted Sizemore	.25	.11	.03
☐ 367	Dave Hamilton	.25	.11	.03
☐ 368	Mike Jorgensen	.25	.11	.03
☐ 369	Terry Humphrey	.25	.11	.03
☐ 370	John Montefusco	.25	.11	.03
☐ 371	Royals Team/Mgr.	1.25	.25	.12
	Whitey Herzog			
	(Checklist back)			
☐ 372	Rich Folkers	.25	.11	.03
☐ 373	Bert Campaneris	.40	.18	.05
☐ 374	Kent Tekulve	.60	.25	.07
☐ 375	Larry Hisle	.40	.18	.05
☐ 376	Nino Espinosa	.25	.11	.03

☐	377	Dave McKay	.25	.11	.03
☐	378	Jim Umbarger	.25	.11	.03
☐	379	Larry Cox	.25	.11	.03
☐	380	Lee May	.40	.18	.05
☐	381	Bob Forsch	.25	.11	.03
☐	382	Charlie Moore	.25	.11	.03
☐	383	Stan Bahnsen	.25	.11	.03
☐	384	Darrel Chaney	.25	.11	.03
☐	385	Dave LaRoche	.25	.11	.03
☐	386	Manny Mota	.40	.18	.05
☐	387	Yankees Team/Mgr.	1.75	.35	.17
		Billy Martin			
		(Checklist back)			
☐	388	Terry Harmon	.25	.11	.03
☐	389	Ken Kravec	.25	.11	.03
☐	390	Dave Winfield	18.00	8.00	2.20
☐	391	Dan Warthen	.25	.11	.03
☐	392	Phil Roof	.25	.11	.03
☐	393	John Lowenstein	.25	.11	.03
☐	394	Bill Laxton	.25	.11	.03
☐	395	Manny Trillo	.25	.11	.03
☐	396	Tom Murphy	.25	.11	.03
☐	397	Larry Herndon	.25	.11	.03
☐	398	Tom Burgmeier	.25	.11	.03
☐	399	Bruce Boisclair	.25	.11	.03
☐	400	Steve Garvey	2.50	1.10	.30
☐	401	Mickey Scott	.25	.11	.03
☐	402	Tommy Helms	.25	.11	.03
☐	403	Tom Grieve	.40	.18	.05
☐	404	Eric Rasmussen	.25	.11	.03
☐	405	Claudell Washington	.40	.18	.05
☐	406	Tim Johnson	.25	.11	.03
☐	407	Dave Freisleben	.25	.11	.03
☐	408	Cesar Tovar	.25	.11	.03
☐	409	Pete Broberg	.25	.11	.03
☐	410	Willie Montanez	.25	.11	.03
☐	411	W.S. Games 1 and 2 ..	1.75	.80	.22
		Joe Morgan homers			
		in opener;			
		Johnny Bench stars as			
		Reds take 2nd game			
☐	412	W.S. Games 3 and 4 ..	1.75	.80	.22
		Reds stop Yankees;			
		Johnny Bench's two			
		homers wrap it up			
☐	413	World Series Summary	.60	.25	.07
		Cincy wins 2nd			
		straight series			
☐	414	Tommy Harper	.40	.18	.05
☐	415	Jay Johnstone	.40	.18	.05
☐	416	Chuck Hartenstein	.25	.11	.03
☐	417	Wayne Garrett	.25	.11	.03
☐	418	White Sox Team/Mgr.	1.25	.25	.12
		Bob Lemon			
		(Checklist back)			
☐	419	Steve Swisher	.25	.11	.03
☐	420	Rusty Staub	.60	.25	.07
☐	421	Doug Rau	.25	.11	.03
☐	422	Freddie Patek	.40	.18	.05
☐	423	Gary Lavelle	.25	.11	.03
☐	424	Steve Brye	.25	.11	.03
☐	425	Joe Torre	.40	.18	.05
☐	426	Dick Drago	.25	.11	.03
☐	427	Dave Rader	.25	.11	.03
☐	428	Rangers Team/Mgr.	1.25	.25	.12
		Frank Lucchesi			
		(Checklist back)			
☐	429	Ken Boswell	.25	.11	.03
☐	430	Fergie Jenkins	2.00	.90	.25
☐	431	Dave Collins UER	.40	.18	.05
		(Photo actually			

		Bobby Jones)			
☐	432	Buzz Capra	.25	.11	.03
☐	433	Nate Colbert TBC '72	.25	.11	.03
		(5 HR, 13 RBI)			
☐	434	Carl Yastrzemski TBC.	1.50	.70	.19
		'67 Triple Crown			
☐	435	Maury Wills TBC '62	.40	.18	.05
		104 steals			
☐	436	Bob Keegan TBC '57	.25	.11	.03
		Majors' only no-hitter			
☐	437	Ralph Kiner TBC '52	.50	.23	.06
		Leads NL in HR's			
		7th straight year			
☐	438	Marty Perez	.25	.11	.03
☐	439	Gorman Thomas	.40	.18	.05
☐	440	Jon Matlack	.25	.11	.03
☐	441	Larvell Blanks	.25	.11	.03
☐	442	Braves Team/Mgr.	1.25	.25	.12
		Dave Bristol			
		(Checklist back)			
☐	443	Lamar Johnson	.25	.11	.03
☐	444	Wayne Twitchell	.25	.11	.03
☐	445	Ken Singleton	.40	.18	.05
☐	446	Bill Bonham	.25	.11	.03
☐	447	Jerry Turner	.25	.11	.03
☐	448	Ellie Rodriguez	.25	.11	.03
☐	449	Al Fitzmorris	.25	.11	.03
☐	450	Pete Rose	10.00	4.50	1.25
☐	451	Checklist 397-528	1.25	.25	.12
☐	452	Mike Caldwell	.25	.11	.03
☐	453	Pedro Garcia	.25	.11	.03
☐	454	Andy Etchebarren	.25	.11	.03
☐	455	Rick Wise	.25	.11	.03
☐	456	Leon Roberts	.25	.11	.03
☐	457	Steve Luebber	.25	.11	.03
☐	458	Leo Foster	.25	.11	.03
☐	459	Steve Foucault	.25	.11	.03
☐	460	Willie Stargell	2.50	1.10	.30
☐	461	Dick Tidrow	.25	.11	.03
☐	462	Don Baylor	1.25	.55	.16
☐	463	Jamie Quirk	.25	.11	.03
☐	464	Randy Moffitt	.25	.11	.03
☐	465	Rico Carty	.40	.18	.05
☐	466	Fred Holdsworth	.25	.11	.03
☐	467	Phillies Team/Mgr.	1.25	.25	.12
		Danny Ozark			
		(Checklist back)			
☐	468	Ramon Hernandez	.25	.11	.03
☐	469	Pat Kelly	.25	.11	.03
☐	470	Ted Simmons	.25	.11	.03
☐	471	Del Unser	.25	.11	.03
☐	472	Rookie Pitchers	.25	.11	.03
		Don Aase			
		Bob McClure			
		Gil Patterson			
		Dave Wehrmeister			
☐	473	Rookie Outfielders	60.00	27.00	7.50
		Andre Dawson			
		Gene Richards			
		John Scott			
		Denny Walling			
☐	474	Rookie Shortstops	.40	.18	.05
		Bob Bailor			
		Kiko Garcia			
		Craig Reynolds			
		Alex Taveras			
☐	475	Rookie Pitchers	.60	.25	.07
		Chris Batton			
		Rick Camp			
		Scott McGregor			
		Manny Sarmiento			

☐ 476 Rookie Catchers.......	25.00	11.00	3.10
Gary Alexander			
Rick Cerone			
Dale Murphy			
Kevin Pasley			
☐ 477 Rookie Infielders..........	.60	.25	.07
Doug Ault			
Rich Dauer			
Orlando Gonzalez			
Phil Mankowski			
☐ 478 Rookie Pitchers.............	.40	.18	.05
Jim Gideon			
Leon Hooten			
Dave Johnson			
Mark Lemongello			
☐ 479 Rookie Outfielders	.60	.25	.07
Brian Asselstine			
Wayne Gross			
Sam Mejias			
Alvis Woods			
☐ 480 Carl Yastrzemski..........	4.00	1.80	.50
☐ 481 Roger Metzger..............	.25	.11	.03
☐ 482 Tony Solaita.................	.25	.11	.03
☐ 483 Richie Zisk..................	.25	.11	.03
☐ 484 Burt Hooton.................	.40	.18	.05
☐ 485 Roy White....................	.40	.18	.05
☐ 486 Ed Bane......................	.25	.11	.03
☐ 487 Rookie Pitchers.............	.40	.18	.05
Larry Anderson			
Ed Glynn			
Joe Henderson			
Greg Terlecky			
☐ 488 Rookie Outfielders	5.00	2.20	.60
Jack Clark			
Ruppert Jones			
Lee Mazzilli			
Dan Thomas			
☐ 489 Rookie Pitchers.............	.60	.25	.07
Len Barker			
Randy Lerch			
Greg Minton			
Mike Overy			
☐ 490 Rookie Shortstops	.40	.18	.05
Billy Almon			
Mickey Klutts			
Tommy McMillan			
Mark Wagner			
☐ 491 Rookie Pitchers.............	6.00	2.70	.75
Mike Dupree			
Dennis Martinez			
Craig Mitchell			
Bob Sykes			
☐ 492 Rookie Outfielders	.60	.25	.07
Tony Armas			
Steve Kemp			
Carlos Lopez			
Gary Woods			
☐ 493 Rookie Pitchers.............	.40	.18	.05
Mike Krukow			
Jim Otten			
Gary Wheelock			
Mike Willis			
☐ 494 Rookie Infielders..........	2.00	.90	.25
Juan Bernhardt			
Mike Champion			
Jim Gantner			
Bump Wills			
☐ 495 Al Hrabosky................	.25	.11	.03
☐ 496 Gary Thomasson..........	.25	.11	.03
☐ 497 Clay Carroll................	.25	.11	.03
☐ 498 Sal Bando	.40	.18	.05

☐ 499 Pablo Torrealba...........	.25	.11	.03
☐ 500 Dave Kingman.............	.40	.18	.05
☐ 501 Jim Bibby...................	.25	.11	.03
☐ 502 Randy Hundley	.25	.11	.03
☐ 503 Bill Lee.....................	.25	.11	.03
☐ 504 Dodgers Team/Mgr.....	1.25	.25	.12
Tom Lasorda			
(Checklist back)			
☐ 505 Oscar Gamble.............	.40	.18	.05
☐ 506 Steve Grilli................	.25	.11	.03
☐ 507 Mike Hegan...............	.25	.11	.03
☐ 508 Dave Pagan...............	.25	.11	.03
☐ 509 Cookie Rojas..............	.40	.18	.05
☐ 510 John Candelaria	.25	.11	.03
☐ 511 Bill Fahey..................	.25	.11	.03
☐ 512 Jack Billingham...........	.25	.11	.03
☐ 513 Jerry Terrell...............	.25	.11	.03
☐ 514 Cliff Johnson..............	.25	.11	.03
☐ 515 Chris Speier...............	.25	.11	.03
☐ 516 Bake McBride.............	.40	.18	.05
☐ 517 Pete Vuckovich............	.40	.18	.05
☐ 518 Cubs Team/Mgr..........	1.25	.25	.12
Herman Franks			
(Checklist back)			
☐ 519 Don Kirkwood.............	.25	.11	.03
☐ 520 Garry Maddox.............	.25	.11	.03
☐ 521 Bob Grich..................	.40	.18	.05
☐ 522 Enzo Hernandez	.25	.11	.03
☐ 523 Rollie Fingers.............	2.00	.90	.25
☐ 524 Rowland Office	.25	.11	.03
☐ 525 Dennis Eckersley.........	6.00	2.70	.75
☐ 526 Larry Parrish..............	.40	.18	.05
☐ 527 Dan Meyer.................	.40	.18	.05
☐ 528 Bill Castro.................	.25	.11	.03
☐ 529 Jim Essian.................	.25	.11	.03
☐ 530 Rick Reuschel.............	.40	.18	.05
☐ 531 Lyman Bostock............	.40	.18	.05
☐ 532 Jim Willoughby............	.25	.11	.03
☐ 533 Mickey Stanley	.25	.11	.03
☐ 534 Paul Splittorff.............	.25	.11	.03
☐ 535 Cesar Geronimo..........	.25	.11	.03
☐ 536 Vic Albury.................	.25	.11	.03
☐ 537 Dave Roberts..............	.25	.11	.03
☐ 538 Frank Taveras.............	.25	.11	.03
☐ 539 Mike Wallace..............	.25	.11	.03
☐ 540 Bob Watson................	.40	.18	.05
☐ 541 John Denny................	.40	.18	.05
☐ 542 Frank Duffy................	.25	.11	.03
☐ 543 Ron Blomberg.............	.25	.11	.03
☐ 544 Gary Ross..................	.25	.11	.03
☐ 545 Bob Boone.................	.60	.25	.07
☐ 546 Orioles Team/Mgr........	1.25	.25	.12
Earl Weaver			
(Checklist back)			
☐ 547 Willie McCovey............	3.00	1.35	.35
☐ 548 Joel Youngblood..........	.25	.11	.03
☐ 549 Jerry Royster..............	.25	.11	.03
☐ 550 Randy Jones...............	.25	.11	.03
☐ 551 Bill North..................	.25	.11	.03
☐ 552 Pepe Mangual.............	.25	.11	.03
☐ 553 Jack Heidemann...........	.25	.11	.03
☐ 554 Bruce Kimm...............	.25	.11	.03
☐ 555 Dan Ford..................	.25	.11	.03
☐ 556 Doug Bird.................	.25	.11	.03
☐ 557 Jerry White................	.25	.11	.03
☐ 558 Elias Sosa.................	.25	.11	.03
☐ 559 Alan Bannister............	.25	.11	.03
☐ 560 Dave Concepcion..........	.75	.35	.09
☐ 561 Pete LaCock...............	.25	.11	.03
☐ 562 Checklist 529-660....	1.25	.25	.12
☐ 563 Bruce Kison................	.25	.11	.03

☐ 564	Alan Ashby	.40	.18	.05
☐ 565	Mickey Lolich	.40	.18	.05
☐ 566	Rick Miller	.25	.11	.03
☐ 567	Enos Cabell	.25	.11	.03
☐ 568	Carlos May	.25	.11	.03
☐ 569	Jim Lonborg	.40	.18	.05
☐ 570	Bobby Bonds	.60	.25	.07
☐ 571	Darrell Evans	.40	.18	.05
☐ 572	Ross Grimsley	.25	.11	.03
☐ 573	Joe Ferguson	.25	.11	.03
☐ 574	Aurelio Rodriguez	.25	.11	.03
☐ 575	Dick Ruthven	.25	.11	.03
☐ 576	Fred Kendall	.25	.11	.03
☐ 577	Jerry Augustine	.25	.11	.03
☐ 578	Bob Randall	.25	.11	.03
☐ 579	Don Carrithers	.25	.11	.03
☐ 580	George Brett	40.00	18.00	5.00
☐ 581	Pedro Borbon	.25	.11	.03
☐ 582	Ed Kirkpatrick	.25	.11	.03
☐ 583	Paul Lindblad	.25	.11	.03
☐ 584	Ed Goodson	.25	.11	.03
☐ 585	Rick Burleson	.40	.18	.05
☐ 586	Steve Renko	.25	.11	.03
☐ 587	Rick Baldwin	.25	.11	.03
☐ 588	Dave Moates	.25	.11	.03
☐ 589	Mike Cosgrove	.25	.11	.03
☐ 590	Buddy Bell	.40	.18	.05
☐ 591	Chris Arnold	.25	.11	.03
☐ 592	Dan Briggs	.25	.11	.03
☐ 593	Dennis Blair	.25	.11	.03
☐ 594	Biff Pocoroba	.25	.11	.03
☐ 595	John Hiller	.25	.11	.03
☐ 596	Jerry Martin	.25	.11	.03
☐ 597	Mariners Leaders	1.25	.25	.12
	Darrell Johnson MG			
	Don Bryant CO			
	Jim Busby CO			
	Vada Pinson CO			
	Wes Stock CO			
	(Checklist back)			
☐ 598	Sparky Lyle	.40	.18	.05
☐ 599	Mike Tyson	.25	.11	.03
☐ 600	Jim Palmer	3.00	1.35	.35
☐ 601	Mike Lum	.25	.11	.03
☐ 602	Andy Hassler	.25	.11	.03
☐ 603	Willie Davis	.40	.18	.05
☐ 604	Jim Slaton	.25	.11	.03
☐ 605	Felix Millan	.25	.11	.03
☐ 606	Steve Braun	.25	.11	.03
☐ 607	Larry Demery	.25	.11	.03
☐ 608	Roy Howell	.25	.11	.03
☐ 609	Jim Barr	.25	.11	.03
☐ 610	Jose Cardenal	.25	.11	.03
☐ 611	Dave Lemanczyk	.25	.11	.03
☐ 612	Barry Foote	.25	.11	.03
☐ 613	Reggie Cleveland	.25	.11	.03
☐ 614	Greg Gross	.25	.11	.03
☐ 615	Phil Niekro	1.50	.70	.19
☐ 616	Tommy Sandt	.25	.11	.03
☐ 617	Bobby Darwin	.25	.11	.03
☐ 618	Pat Dobson	.25	.11	.03
☐ 619	Johnny Oates	.25	.11	.03
☐ 620	Don Sutton	1.00	.45	.12
☐ 621	Tigers Team/Mgr.	1.25	.25	.12
	Ralph Houk			
	(Checklist back)			
☐ 622	Jim Wohlford	.25	.11	.03
☐ 623	Jack Kucek	.25	.11	.03
☐ 624	Hector Cruz	.25	.11	.03
☐ 625	Ken Holtzman	.40	.18	.05
☐ 626	Al Bumbry	.40	.18	.05
☐ 627	Bob Myrick	.25	.11	.03
☐ 628	Mario Guerrero	.25	.11	.03
☐ 629	Bobby Valentine	.25	.11	.03
☐ 630	Bert Blyleven	.60	.25	.07
☐ 631	Big League Brothers	8.00	3.60	1.00
	George Brett			
	Ken Brett			
☐ 632	Big League Brothers	.40	.18	.05
	Bob Forsch			
	Ken Forsch			
☐ 633	Big League Brothers	.40	.18	.05
	Lee May			
	Carlos May			
☐ 634	Big League Brothers	.40	.18	.05
	Paul Reuschel			
	Rick Reuschel UER			
	(Photos switched)			
☐ 635	Robin Yount	25.00	11.00	3.10
☐ 636	Santo Alcala	.25	.11	.03
☐ 637	Alex Johnson	.25	.11	.03
☐ 638	Jim Kaat	.60	.25	.07
☐ 639	Jerry Morales	.25	.11	.03
☐ 640	Carlton Fisk	5.00	2.20	.60
☐ 641	Dan Larson	.25	.11	.03
☐ 642	Willie Crawford	.25	.11	.03
☐ 643	Mike Pazik	.25	.11	.03
☐ 644	Matt Alexander	.25	.11	.03
☐ 645	Jerry Reuss	.40	.18	.05
☐ 646	Andres Mora	.25	.11	.03
☐ 647	Expos Team/Mgr.	1.25	.25	.12
	Dick Williams			
	(Checklist back)			
☐ 648	Jim Spencer	.25	.11	.03
☐ 649	Dave Cash	.25	.11	.03
☐ 650	Nolan Ryan	50.00	22.00	6.25
☐ 651	Von Joshua	.25	.11	.03
☐ 652	Tom Walker	.25	.11	.03
☐ 653	Diego Segui	.40	.18	.05
☐ 654	Ron Pruitt	.25	.11	.03
☐ 655	Tony Perez	1.50	.70	.19
☐ 656	Ron Guidry	1.00	.45	.12
☐ 657	Mick Kelleher	.25	.11	.03
☐ 658	Marty Pattin	.25	.11	.03
☐ 659	Merv Rettenmund	.25	.11	.03
☐ 660	Willie Horton	.60	.25	.07

1978 Topps

The cards in this 726-card set measure 2 1/2" by 3 1/2". The 1978 Topps set experienced an increase in number of cards from the previous five regular issue sets of 660. Card numbers 1 through 7 feature Record

Breakers (RB) of the 1977 season. Other subsets within this set include League Leaders (201-208), Post-season cards (411-413), and Rookie Prospects (701-711). The key Rookie Cards in this set are the multi-player Rookie Card of Paul Molitor and Alan Trammell, Jack Morris, Eddie Murray, Lance Parrish, and Lou Whitaker. The manager cards in the set feature a "then and now" format on the card front showing the manager as he looked many years before, e.g., during his playing days. While no scarcities exist, 66 of the cards are more abundant in supply, as they were "double printed." These 66 double-printed cards are noted in the checklist by DP. Team cards again feature a checklist of that team's players in the set on the back. Cards numbered 23 or lower, that feature Astros, Rangers, Tigers, or Yankees and do not follow the numbering checklisted below, are not necessarily error cards. They are undoubtedly Burger King cards, a separate set with its own pricing and mass distribution. Burger King cards are indistinguishable from the corresponding Topps cards except for the card numbering difference and the fact that Burger King cards do not have a printing sheet designation (such as A through F like the regular Topps) anywhere on the card back in very small print.

	NRMT-MT	EXC	G-VG
COMPLETE SET (726)	300.00	135.00	38.00
COMMON CARD (1-726)	.25	.11	.03
COMMON CARD DP	.15	.07	.02
☐ 1 RB: Lou Brock	2.50	.75	.25
Most steals, lifetime			
☐ 2 RB: Sparky Lyle	.40	.18	.05
Most games, pure relief, lifetime			
☐ 3 RB: Willie McCovey	1.50	.70	.19
Most times, 2 HR's in inning, lifetime			
☐ 4 RB: Brooks Robinson	2.00	.90	.25
Most consecutive seasons with one club			
☐ 5 RB: Pete Rose	3.50	1.55	.45
Most hits, switch hitter, lifetime			
☐ 6 RB: Nolan Ryan	15.00	6.75	1.85
Most games with 10 or more strikeouts, lifetime			
☐ 7 RB: Reggie Jackson	3.50	1.55	.45
Most homers, one World Series			
☐ 8 Mike Sadek	.25	.11	.03
☐ 9 Doug DeCinces	.40	.18	.05
☐ 10 Phil Niekro	1.00	.45	.12
☐ 11 Rick Manning	.25	.11	.03
☐ 12 Don Aase	.25	.11	.03
☐ 13 Art Howe	.40	.18	.05
☐ 14 Lerrin LaGrow	.25	.11	.03
☐ 15 Tony Perez DP	.75	.35	.09
☐ 16 Roy White	.40	.18	.05
☐ 17 Mike Krukow	.25	.11	.03
☐ 18 Bob Grich	.40	.18	.05
☐ 19 Darrell Porter	.40	.18	.05
☐ 20 Pete Rose DP	5.00	2.20	.60
☐ 21 Steve Kemp	.25	.11	.03
☐ 22 Charlie Hough	.40	.18	.05
☐ 23 Bump Wills	.25	.11	.03
☐ 24 Don Money DP	.15	.07	.02
☐ 25 Jon Matlack	.25	.11	.03
☐ 26 Rich Hebner	.25	.11	.03
☐ 27 Geoff Zahn	.25	.11	.03
☐ 28 Ed Ott	.25	.11	.03
☐ 29 Bob Lacey	.25	.11	.03
☐ 30 George Hendrick	.40	.18	.05
☐ 31 Glenn Abbott	.25	.11	.03
☐ 32 Garry Templeton	.60	.25	.07
☐ 33 Dave Lemanczyk	.25	.11	.03
☐ 34 Willie McCovey	2.50	1.10	.30
☐ 35 Sparky Lyle	.40	.18	.05
☐ 36 Eddie Murray	110.00	50.00	14.00
☐ 37 Rick Waits	.25	.11	.03
☐ 38 Willie Montanez	.25	.11	.03
☐ 39 Floyd Bannister	.25	.11	.03
☐ 40 Carl Yastrzemski	3.00	1.35	.35
☐ 41 Burt Hooton	.25	.18	.05
☐ 42 Jorge Orta	.25	.11	.03
☐ 43 Bill Atkinson	.25	.11	.03
☐ 44 Toby Harrah	.40	.18	.05
☐ 45 Mark Fidrych	1.50	.70	.19
☐ 46 Al Cowens	.25	.11	.03
☐ 47 Jack Billingham	.25	.11	.03
☐ 48 Don Baylor	.75	.35	.09
☐ 49 Ed Kranepool	.25	.11	.03
☐ 50 Rick Reuschel	.40	.18	.05
☐ 51 Charlie Moore DP	.15	.07	.02
☐ 52 Jim Lonborg	.25	.11	.03
☐ 53 Phil Garner DP	.25	.11	.03
☐ 54 Tom Johnson	.25	.11	.03
☐ 55 Mitchell Page	.25	.11	.03
☐ 56 Randy Jones	.25	.11	.03
☐ 57 Dan Meyer	.25	.11	.03
☐ 58 Bob Forsch	.25	.11	.03
☐ 59 Otto Velez	.25	.11	.03
☐ 60 Thurman Munson	3.00	1.35	.35
☐ 61 Larvell Blanks	.25	.11	.03
☐ 62 Jim Barr	.25	.11	.03
☐ 63 Don Zimmer MG	.40	.18	.05
☐ 64 Gene Pentz	.25	.11	.03
☐ 65 Ken Singleton	.40	.18	.05
☐ 66 Chicago White Sox	1.25	.25	.12
Team Card (Checklist back)			
☐ 67 Claudell Washington	.40	.18	.05
☐ 68 Steve Foucault DP	.15	.07	.02
☐ 69 Mike Vail	.25	.11	.03
☐ 70 Rich Gossage	.75	.35	.09
☐ 71 Terry Humphrey	.25	.11	.03
☐ 72 Andre Dawson	15.00	6.75	1.85
☐ 73 Andy Hassler	.25	.11	.03
☐ 74 Checklist 1-121	1.25	.25	.12
☐ 75 Dick Ruthven	.25	.11	.03
☐ 76 Steve Ontiveros	.25	.11	.03
☐ 77 Ed Kirkpatrick	.25	.11	.03
☐ 78 Pablo Torrealba	.25	.11	.03
☐ 79 Darrell Johnson DP MG	.15	.07	.02
☐ 80 Ken Griffey	1.00	.45	.12
☐ 81 Pete Redfern	.25	.11	.03
☐ 82 San Francisco Giants	1.25	.25	.12
Team Card (Checklist back)			
☐ 83 Bob Montgomery	.25	.11	.03
☐ 84 Kent Tekulve	.40	.18	.05
☐ 85 Ron Fairly	.40	.18	.05
☐ 86 Dave Tomlin	.25	.11	.03
☐ 87 John Lowenstein	.25	.11	.03

☐ 88	Mike Phillips	.25	.11	.03
☐ 89	Ken Clay	.25	.11	.03
☐ 90	Larry Bowa	.60	.25	.07
☐ 91	Oscar Zamora	.25	.11	.03
☐ 92	Adrian Devine	.25	.11	.03
☐ 93	Bobby Cox DP	.25	.11	.03
☐ 94	Chuck Scrivener	.25	.11	.03
☐ 95	Jamie Quirk	.25	.11	.03
☐ 96	Baltimore Orioles	1.25	.25	.12
	Team Card			
	(Checklist back)			
☐ 97	Stan Bahnsen	.25	.11	.03
☐ 98	Jim Essian	.40	.18	.05
☐ 99	Willie Hernandez	.50	.23	.06
☐ 100	George Brett	25.00	11.00	3.10
☐ 101	Sid Monge	.25	.11	.03
☐ 102	Matt Alexander	.25	.11	.03
☐ 103	Tom Murphy	.25	.11	.03
☐ 104	Lee Lacy	.25	.11	.03
☐ 105	Reggie Cleveland	.25	.11	.03
☐ 106	Bill Plummer	.25	.11	.03
☐ 107	Ed Halicki	.25	.11	.03
☐ 108	Von Joshua	.25	.11	.03
☐ 109	Joe Torre MG	.40	.18	.05
☐ 110	Richie Zisk	.25	.11	.03
☐ 111	Mike Tyson	.25	.11	.03
☐ 112	Houston Astros	1.25	.25	.12
	Team Card			
	(Checklist back)			
☐ 113	Don Carrithers	.25	.11	.03
☐ 114	Paul Blair	.40	.18	.05
☐ 115	Gary Nolan	.25	.11	.03
☐ 116	Tucker Ashford	.25	.11	.03
☐ 117	John Montague	.25	.11	.03
☐ 118	Terry Harmon	.25	.11	.03
☐ 119	Dennis Martinez	2.00	.90	.25
☐ 120	Gary Carter	2.50	1.10	.30
☐ 121	Alvis Woods	.25	.11	.03
☐ 122	Dennis Eckersley	4.00	1.80	.50
☐ 123	Manny Trillo	.25	.11	.03
☐ 124	Dave Rozema	.25	.11	.03
☐ 125	George Scott	.40	.18	.05
☐ 126	Paul Moskau	.25	.11	.03
☐ 127	Chet Lemon	.40	.18	.05
☐ 128	Bill Russell	.40	.18	.05
☐ 129	Jim Colborn	.25	.11	.03
☐ 130	Jeff Burroughs	.40	.18	.05
☐ 131	Bert Blyleven	.60	.25	.07
☐ 132	Enos Cabell	.25	.11	.03
☐ 133	Jerry Augustine	.25	.11	.03
☐ 134	Steve Henderson	.25	.11	.03
☐ 135	Ron Guidry DP	.75	.35	.09
☐ 136	Ted Sizemore	.25	.11	.03
☐ 137	Craig Kusick	.25	.11	.03
☐ 138	Larry Demery	.25	.11	.03
☐ 139	Wayne Gross	.25	.11	.03
☐ 140	Rollie Fingers	1.50	.70	.19
☐ 141	Ruppert Jones	.25	.11	.03
☐ 142	John Montefusco	.25	.11	.03
☐ 143	Keith Hernandez	.60	.25	.07
☐ 144	Jesse Jefferson	.25	.11	.03
☐ 145	Rick Monday	.40	.18	.05
☐ 146	Doyle Alexander	.25	.11	.03
☐ 147	Lee Mazzilli	.25	.11	.03
☐ 148	Andre Thornton	.40	.18	.05
☐ 149	Dale Murray	.25	.11	.03
☐ 150	Bobby Bonds	.60	.25	.07
☐ 151	Milt Wilcox	.25	.11	.03
☐ 152	Ivan DeJesus	.25	.11	.03
☐ 153	Steve Stone	.40	.18	.05
☐ 154	Cecil Cooper DP	.25	.11	.03
☐ 155	Butch Hobson	.40	.18	.05
☐ 156	Andy Messersmith	.40	.18	.05
☐ 157	Pete LaCock DP	.15	.07	.02
☐ 158	Joaquin Andujar	.40	.18	.05
☐ 159	Lou Piniella	.25	.11	.03
☐ 160	Jim Palmer	2.50	1.10	.30
☐ 161	Bob Boone	.60	.25	.07
☐ 162	Paul Thormodsgard	.25	.11	.03
☐ 163	Bill North	.25	.11	.03
☐ 164	Bob Owchinko	.25	.11	.03
☐ 165	Rennie Stennett	.25	.11	.03
☐ 166	Carlos Lopez	.25	.11	.03
☐ 167	Tim Foli	.25	.11	.03
☐ 168	Reggie Smith	.40	.18	.05
☐ 169	Jerry Johnson	.25	.11	.03
☐ 170	Lou Brock	2.50	1.10	.30
☐ 171	Pat Zachry	.25	.11	.03
☐ 172	Mike Hargrove	.40	.18	.05
☐ 173	Robin Yount UER	14.00	6.25	1.75
	(Played for Newark			
	in 1973, not 1971)			
☐ 174	Wayne Garland	.25	.11	.03
☐ 175	Jerry Morales	.25	.11	.03
☐ 176	Milt May	.25	.11	.03
☐ 177	Gene Garber DP	.15	.07	.02
☐ 178	Dave Chalk	.25	.11	.03
☐ 179	Dick Tidrow	.25	.11	.03
☐ 180	Dave Concepcion	.60	.25	.07
☐ 181	Ken Forsch	.25	.11	.03
☐ 182	Jim Spencer	.25	.11	.03
☐ 183	Doug Bird	.25	.11	.03
☐ 184	Checklist 122-242	1.25	.25	.12
☐ 185	Ellis Valentine	.25	.11	.03
☐ 186	Bob Stanley DP	.25	.11	.03
☐ 187	Jerry Royster DP	.15	.07	.02
☐ 188	Al Bumbry	.40	.18	.05
☐ 189	Tom Lasorda MG	.60	.25	.07
☐ 190	John Candelaria	.40	.18	.05
☐ 191	Rodney Scott	.25	.11	.03
☐ 192	San Diego Padres	1.25	.25	.12
	Team Card			
	(Checklist back)			
☐ 193	Rich Chiles	.25	.11	.03
☐ 194	Derrel Thomas	.25	.11	.03
☐ 195	Larry Dierker	.25	.11	.03
☐ 196	Bob Bailor	.25	.11	.03
☐ 197	Nino Espinosa	.25	.11	.03
☐ 198	Ron Pruitt	.25	.11	.03
☐ 199	Craig Reynolds	.25	.11	.03
☐ 200	Reggie Jackson	8.00	3.60	1.00
☐ 201	Batting Leaders	1.00	.45	.12
	Dave Parker			
	Rod Carew			
☐ 202	Home Run Leaders DP	.40	.18	.05
	George Foster			
	Jim Rice			
☐ 203	RBI Leaders	.40	.18	.05
	George Foster			
	Larry Hisle			
☐ 204	Steals Leaders DP	.25	.11	.03
	Frank Taveras			
	Freddie Patek			
☐ 205	Victory Leaders	1.50	.70	.19
	Steve Carlton			
	Dave Goltz			
	Dennis Leonard			
	Jim Palmer			
☐ 206	Strikeout Leaders DP	5.00	2.20	.60
	Phil Niekro			
	Nolan Ryan			
☐ 207	ERA Leaders DP	.35	.16	.04

John Candelaria
Frank Tanana
- [ ] 208 Top Firemen.................. .75 .35 .09
Rollie Fingers
Bill Campbell
- [ ] 209 Dock Ellis...................... .25 .11 .03
- [ ] 210 Jose Cardenal .... .25 .11 .03
- [ ] 211 Earl Weaver MG DP .... .30 .14 .04
- [ ] 212 Mike Caldwell............... .25 .11 .03
- [ ] 213 Alan Bannister............... .25 .11 .03
- [ ] 214 California Angels......... 1.25 .25 .12
Team Card
(Checklist back)
- [ ] 215 Darrell Evans............... .60 .25 .07
- [ ] 216 Mike Paxton .... .25 .11 .03
- [ ] 217 Rod Gilbreath .... .25 .11 .03
- [ ] 218 Marty Pattin .... .25 .11 .03
- [ ] 219 Mike Cubbage .... .25 .11 .03
- [ ] 220 Pedro Borbon .... .25 .11 .03
- [ ] 221 Chris Speier................. .25 .11 .03
- [ ] 222 Jerry Martin .... .25 .11 .03
- [ ] 223 Bruce Kison .... .25 .11 .03
- [ ] 224 Jerry Tabb................... .25 .11 .03
- [ ] 225 Don Gullett DP .... .40 .18 .05
- [ ] 226 Joe Ferguson .... .25 .11 .03
- [ ] 227 Al Fitzmorris .... .25 .11 .03
- [ ] 228 Manny Mota DP .... .25 .11 .03
- [ ] 229 Leo Foster .... .25 .11 .03
- [ ] 230 Al Hrabosky .... .25 .11 .03
- [ ] 231 Wayne Nordhagen .... .25 .11 .03
- [ ] 232 Mickey Stanley.............. .25 .11 .03
- [ ] 233 Dick Pole .... .25 .11 .03
- [ ] 234 Herman Franks MG .... .25 .11 .03
- [ ] 235 Tim McCarver................ .40 .18 .05
- [ ] 236 Terry Whitfield............. .25 .11 .03
- [ ] 237 Rich Dauer.................. .25 .11 .03
- [ ] 238 Juan Beniquez............... .25 .11 .03
- [ ] 239 Dyar Miller .... .25 .11 .03
- [ ] 240 Gene Tenace .... .40 .18 .05
- [ ] 241 Pete Vuckovich .... .40 .18 .05
- [ ] 242 Barry Bonnell DP .... .15 .07 .02
- [ ] 243 Bob McClure................. .25 .11 .03
- [ ] 244 Montreal Expos............. .75 .15 .07
Team Card DP
(Checklist back)
- [ ] 245 Rick Burleson .... .40 .18 .05
- [ ] 246 Dan Driessen .... .25 .11 .03
- [ ] 247 Larry Christenson .... .25 .11 .03
- [ ] 248 Frank White DP .... .40 .18 .05
- [ ] 249 Dave Goltz DP .... .15 .07 .02
- [ ] 250 Graig Nettles DP .... .40 .18 .05
- [ ] 251 Don Kirkwood .... .25 .11 .03
- [ ] 252 Steve Swisher DP .... .15 .07 .02
- [ ] 253 Jim Kern .... .25 .11 .03
- [ ] 254 Dave Collins .... .40 .18 .05
- [ ] 255 Jerry Reuss.................. .40 .18 .05
- [ ] 256 Joe Altobelli MG........... .25 .11 .03
- [ ] 257 Hector Cruz................. .25 .11 .03
- [ ] 258 John Hiller .... .25 .11 .03
- [ ] 259 Los Angeles Dodgers. 1.25 .25 .12
Team Card
(Checklist back)
- [ ] 260 Bert Campaneris .... .40 .18 .05
- [ ] 261 Tim Hosley................... .25 .11 .03
- [ ] 262 Rudy May .... .25 .11 .03
- [ ] 263 Danny Walton .... .25 .11 .03
- [ ] 264 Jamie Easterly .... .25 .11 .03
- [ ] 265 Sal Bando DP .... .40 .18 .05
- [ ] 266 Bob Shirley .... .25 .11 .03
- [ ] 267 Doug Ault.................... .25 .11 .03
- [ ] 268 Gil Flores.................... .25 .11 .03
- [ ] 269 Wayne Twitchell............ .25 .11 .03
- [ ] 270 Carlton Fisk............... 3.00 1.35 .35
- [ ] 271 Randy Lerch DP .... .15 .07 .02
- [ ] 272 Royle Stillman.............. .25 .11 .03
- [ ] 273 Fred Norman................ .25 .11 .03
- [ ] 274 Freddie Patek............... .40 .18 .05
- [ ] 275 Dan Ford .... .25 .11 .03
- [ ] 276 Bill Bonham DP .... .15 .07 .02
- [ ] 277 Bruce Boisclair .... .25 .11 .03
- [ ] 278 Enrique Romo............... .25 .11 .03
- [ ] 279 Bill Virdon MG .... .25 .11 .03
- [ ] 280 Buddy Bell .... .40 .18 .05
- [ ] 281 Eric Rasmussen DP .... .15 .07 .02
- [ ] 282 New York Yankees .... 1.50 .30 .15
Team Card
(Checklist back)
- [ ] 283 Omar Moreno .... .25 .11 .03
- [ ] 284 Randy Moffitt .... .25 .11 .03
- [ ] 285 Steve Yeager DP .... .40 .18 .05
- [ ] 286 Ben Oglivie................. .40 .18 .05
- [ ] 287 Kiko Garcia .... .25 .11 .03
- [ ] 288 Dave Hamilton .... .25 .11 .03
- [ ] 289 Checklist 243-363........ 1.25 .25 .12
- [ ] 290 Willie Horton .... .40 .18 .05
- [ ] 291 Gary Ross .... .25 .11 .03
- [ ] 292 Gene Richards .... .25 .11 .03
- [ ] 293 Mike Willis .... .25 .11 .03
- [ ] 294 Larry Parrish .... .40 .18 .05
- [ ] 295 Bill Lee .... .25 .11 .03
- [ ] 296 Biff Pocoroba .... .25 .11 .03
- [ ] 297 Warren Brusstar DP .... .15 .07 .02
- [ ] 298 Tony Armas .... .40 .18 .05
- [ ] 299 Whitey Herzog MG .... .40 .18 .05
- [ ] 300 Joe Morgan................ 2.50 1.10 .30
- [ ] 301 Buddy Schultz .... .25 .11 .03
- [ ] 302 Chicago Cubs .... 1.25 .25 .12
Team Card
(Checklist back)
- [ ] 303 Sam Hinds .... .25 .11 .03
- [ ] 304 John Milner.................. .25 .11 .03
- [ ] 305 Rico Carty .... .40 .18 .05
- [ ] 306 Joe Niekro................... .40 .18 .05
- [ ] 307 Glenn Borgmann............ .25 .11 .03
- [ ] 308 Jim Rooker .... .25 .11 .03
- [ ] 309 Cliff Johnson .... .25 .11 .03
- [ ] 310 Don Sutton .... .75 .35 .09
- [ ] 311 Jose Baez DP .... .15 .07 .02
- [ ] 312 Greg Minton................. .25 .11 .03
- [ ] 313 Andy Etchebarren .... .25 .11 .03
- [ ] 314 Paul Lindblad .... .25 .11 .03
- [ ] 315 Mark Belanger............... .40 .18 .05
- [ ] 316 Henry Cruz DP .... .15 .07 .02
- [ ] 317 Dave Johnson .... .25 .11 .03
- [ ] 318 Tom Griffin .... .25 .11 .03
- [ ] 319 Alan Ashby .... .25 .11 .03
- [ ] 320 Fred Lynn .... 1.00 .45 .12
- [ ] 321 Santo Alcala................. .25 .11 .03
- [ ] 322 Tom Paciorek................ .40 .18 .05
- [ ] 323 Jim Fregosi DP .... .25 .11 .03
- [ ] 324 Vern Rapp MG .... .25 .11 .03
- [ ] 325 Bruce Sutter................. .60 .25 .07
- [ ] 326 Mike Lum DP .... .15 .07 .02
- [ ] 327 Rick Langford DP .... .15 .07 .02
- [ ] 328 Milwaukee Brewers .... 1.25 .25 .12
Team Card
(Checklist back)
- [ ] 329 John Verhoeven .... .25 .11 .03
- [ ] 330 Bob Watson .... .40 .18 .05
- [ ] 331 Mark Littell.................. .25 .11 .03
- [ ] 332 Duane Kuiper .... .25 .11 .03
- [ ] 333 Jim Todd..................... .25 .11 .03

☐ 334	John Stearns	.25	.11	.03
☐ 335	Bucky Dent	.60	.25	.07
☐ 336	Steve Busby	.25	.11	.03
☐ 337	Tom Grieve	.40	.18	.05
☐ 338	Dave Heaverlo	.25	.11	.03
☐ 339	Mario Guerrero	.25	.11	.03
☐ 340	Bake McBride	.40	.18	.05
☐ 341	Mike Flanagan	.25	.11	.03
☐ 342	Aurelio Rodriguez	.25	.11	.03
☐ 343	John Wathan DP	.15	.07	.02
☐ 344	Sam Ewing	.25	.11	.03
☐ 345	Luis Tiant	.40	.18	.05
☐ 346	Larry Biittner	.25	.11	.03
☐ 347	Terry Forster	.25	.11	.03
☐ 348	Del Unser	.25	.11	.03
☐ 349	Rick Camp DP	.15	.07	.02
☐ 350	Steve Garvey	1.50	.70	.19
☐ 351	Jeff Torborg	.40	.18	.05
☐ 352	Tony Scott	.25	.11	.03
☐ 353	Doug Bair	.25	.11	.03
☐ 354	Cesar Geronimo	.25	.11	.03
☐ 355	Bill Travers	.25	.11	.03
☐ 356	New York Mets	1.25	.25	.12
	Team Card			
	(Checklist back)			
☐ 357	Tom Poquette	.25	.11	.03
☐ 358	Mark Lemongello	.25	.11	.03
☐ 359	Marc Hill	.25	.11	.03
☐ 360	Mike Schmidt	12.00	5.50	1.50
☐ 361	Chris Knapp	.25	.11	.03
☐ 362	Dave May	.25	.11	.03
☐ 363	Bob Randall	.25	.11	.03
☐ 364	Jerry Turner	.25	.11	.03
☐ 365	Ed Figueroa	.25	.11	.03
☐ 366	Larry Milbourne DP	.15	.07	.02
☐ 367	Rick Dempsey	.40	.18	.05
☐ 368	Balor Moore	.25	.11	.03
☐ 369	Tim Nordbrook	.25	.11	.03
☐ 370	Rusty Staub	.60	.25	.07
☐ 371	Ray Burris	.25	.11	.03
☐ 372	Brian Asselstine	.25	.11	.03
☐ 373	Jim Willoughby	.25	.11	.03
☐ 374	Jose Morales	.25	.11	.03
☐ 375	Tommy John	.60	.25	.07
☐ 376	Jim Wohlford	.25	.11	.03
☐ 377	Manny Sarmiento	.25	.11	.03
☐ 378	Bobby Winkles MG	.25	.11	.03
☐ 379	Skip Lockwood	.25	.11	.03
☐ 380	Ted Simmons	.40	.18	.05
☐ 381	Philadelphia Phillies	1.25	.25	.12
	Team Card			
	(Checklist back)			
☐ 382	Joe Lahoud	.25	.11	.03
☐ 383	Mario Mendoza	.25	.11	.03
☐ 384	Jack Clark	.60	.25	.07
☐ 385	Tito Fuentes	.25	.11	.03
☐ 386	Bob Gorinski	.25	.11	.03
☐ 387	Ken Holtzman	.25	.11	.03
☐ 388	Bill Fahey DP	.15	.07	.02
☐ 389	Julio Gonzalez	.25	.11	.03
☐ 390	Oscar Gamble	.40	.18	.05
☐ 391	Larry Haney	.25	.11	.03
☐ 392	Billy Almon	.25	.11	.03
☐ 393	Tippy Martinez	.40	.18	.05
☐ 394	Roy Howell DP	.15	.07	.02
☐ 395	Jim Hughes	.25	.11	.03
☐ 396	Bob Stinson DP	.15	.07	.02
☐ 397	Greg Gross	.25	.11	.03
☐ 398	Don Hood	.25	.11	.03
☐ 399	Pete Mackanin	.25	.11	.03
☐ 400	Nolan Ryan	35.00	16.00	4.40
☐ 401	Sparky Anderson MG	.40	.18	.05
☐ 402	Dave Campbell	.25	.11	.03
☐ 403	Bud Harrelson	.25	.11	.03
☐ 404	Detroit Tigers	1.25	.25	.12
	Team Card			
	(Checklist back)			
☐ 405	Rawly Eastwick	.25	.11	.03
☐ 406	Mike Jorgensen	.25	.11	.03
☐ 407	Odell Jones	.25	.11	.03
☐ 408	Joe Zdeb	.25	.11	.03
☐ 409	Ron Schueler	.25	.11	.03
☐ 410	Bill Madlock	.40	.18	.05
☐ 411	AL Champs	.50	.23	.06
	Yankees rally to			
	defeat Royals			
	(Willie Randolph sliding)			
☐ 412	NL Champs	.50	.23	.06
	Dodgers overpower			
	Phillies in four			
☐ 413	World Series	3.00	1.35	.35
	Reggie Jackson and			
	Yankees reign supreme			
	(Davey Lopes batting)			
☐ 414	Darold Knowles DP	.15	.07	.02
☐ 415	Ray Fosse	.25	.11	.03
☐ 416	Jack Brohamer	.25	.11	.03
☐ 417	Mike Garman DP	.15	.07	.02
☐ 418	Tony Muser	.25	.11	.03
☐ 419	Jerry Garvin	.25	.11	.03
☐ 420	Greg Luzinski	.60	.25	.07
☐ 421	Junior Moore	.25	.11	.03
☐ 422	Steve Braun	.25	.11	.03
☐ 423	Dave Rosello	.25	.11	.03
☐ 424	Boston Red Sox	1.25	.25	.12
	Team Card			
	(Checklist back)			
☐ 425	Steve Rogers DP	.20	.09	.03
☐ 426	Fred Kendall	.25	.11	.03
☐ 427	Mario Soto	.40	.18	.05
☐ 428	Joel Youngblood	.25	.11	.03
☐ 429	Mike Barlow	.25	.11	.03
☐ 430	Al Oliver	.40	.18	.05
☐ 431	Butch Metzger	.25	.11	.03
☐ 432	Terry Bulling	.25	.11	.03
☐ 433	Fernando Gonzalez	.25	.11	.03
☐ 434	Mike Norris	.25	.11	.03
☐ 435	Checklist 364-484	1.25	.25	.12
☐ 436	Vic Harris DP	.15	.07	.02
☐ 437	Bo McLaughlin	.25	.11	.03
☐ 438	John Ellis	.25	.11	.03
☐ 439	Ken Kravec	.25	.11	.03
☐ 440	Dave Lopes	.40	.18	.05
☐ 441	Larry Gura	.25	.11	.03
☐ 442	Elliott Maddox	.25	.11	.03
☐ 443	Darrel Chaney	.25	.11	.03
☐ 444	Roy Hartsfield MG	.25	.11	.03
☐ 445	Mike Ivie	.25	.11	.03
☐ 446	Tug McGraw	.40	.18	.05
☐ 447	Leroy Stanton	.25	.11	.03
☐ 448	Bill Castro	.25	.11	.03
☐ 449	Tim Blackwell DP	.15	.07	.02
☐ 450	Tom Seaver	4.00	1.80	.50
☐ 451	Minnesota Twins	1.25	.25	.12
	Team Card			
	(Checklist back)			
☐ 452	Jerry Mumphrey	.25	.11	.03
☐ 453	Doug Flynn	.25	.11	.03
☐ 454	Dave LaRoche	.25	.11	.03
☐ 455	Bill Robinson	.40	.18	.05
☐ 456	Vern Ruhle	.25	.11	.03
☐ 457	Bob Bailey	.25	.11	.03

☐ 458	Jeff Newman	.25	.11	.03
☐ 459	Charlie Spikes	.25	.11	.03
☐ 460	Jim Hunter	1.50	.70	.19
☐ 461	Rob Andrews DP	.15	.07	.02
☐ 462	Rogelio Moret	.25	.11	.03
☐ 463	Kevin Bell	.25	.11	.03
☐ 464	Jerry Grote	.25	.11	.03
☐ 465	Hal McRae	.60	.25	.07
☐ 466	Dennis Blair	.25	.11	.03
☐ 467	Alvin Dark MG	.25	.11	.03
☐ 468	Warren Cromartie	.40	.18	.05
☐ 469	Rick Cerone	.40	.18	.05
☐ 470	J.R. Richard	.40	.18	.05
☐ 471	Roy Smalley	.40	.18	.05
☐ 472	Ron Reed	.25	.11	.03
☐ 473	Bill Buckner	.60	.25	.07
☐ 474	Jim Slaton	.25	.11	.03
☐ 475	Gary Matthews	.40	.18	.05
☐ 476	Bill Stein	.25	.11	.03
☐ 477	Doug Capilla	.25	.11	.03
☐ 478	Jerry Remy	.25	.11	.03
☐ 479	St. Louis Cardinals.... Team Card (Checklist back)	1.25	.25	.12
☐ 480	Ron LeFlore	.40	.18	.05
☐ 481	Jackson Todd	.25	.11	.03
☐ 482	Rick Miller	.25	.11	.03
☐ 483	Ken Macha	.25	.11	.03
☐ 484	Jim Norris	.25	.11	.03
☐ 485	Chris Chambliss	.40	.18	.05
☐ 486	John Curtis	.25	.11	.03
☐ 487	Jim Tyrone	.25	.11	.03
☐ 488	Dan Spillner	.25	.11	.03
☐ 489	Rudy Meoli	.25	.11	.03
☐ 490	Amos Otis	.40	.18	.05
☐ 491	Scott McGregor	.40	.18	.05
☐ 492	Jim Sundberg	.40	.18	.05
☐ 493	Steve Renko	.25	.11	.03
☐ 494	Chuck Tanner MG	.40	.18	.05
☐ 495	Dave Cash	.25	.11	.03
☐ 496	Jim Clancy DP	.15	.07	.02
☐ 497	Glenn Adams	.25	.11	.03
☐ 498	Joe Sambito	.25	.11	.03
☐ 499	Seattle Mariners Team Card (Checklist back)	1.25	.25	.12
☐ 500	George Foster	.60	.25	.07
☐ 501	Dave Roberts	.25	.11	.03
☐ 502	Pat Rockett	.25	.11	.03
☐ 503	Ike Hampton	.25	.11	.03
☐ 504	Roger Freed	.25	.11	.03
☐ 505	Felix Millan	.25	.11	.03
☐ 506	Ron Blomberg	.25	.11	.03
☐ 507	Willie Crawford	.25	.11	.03
☐ 508	Johnny Oates	.25	.11	.03
☐ 509	Brent Strom	.25	.11	.03
☐ 510	Willie Stargell	2.00	.90	.25
☐ 511	Frank Duffy	.25	.11	.03
☐ 512	Larry Herndon	.25	.11	.03
☐ 513	Barry Foote	.25	.11	.03
☐ 514	Rob Sperring	.25	.11	.03
☐ 515	Tim Corcoran	.25	.11	.03
☐ 516	Gary Beare	.25	.11	.03
☐ 517	Andres Mora	.25	.11	.03
☐ 518	Tommy Boggs DP	.15	.07	.02
☐ 519	Brian Downing	.40	.18	.05
☐ 520	Larry Hisle	.25	.11	.03
☐ 521	Steve Staggs	.25	.11	.03
☐ 522	Dick Williams MG	.40	.18	.05
☐ 523	Donnie Moore	.25	.11	.03
☐ 524	Bernie Carbo	.25	.11	.03

☐ 525	Jerry Terrell	.25	.11	.03
☐ 526	Cincinnati Reds Team Card (Checklist back)	1.25	.25	.12
☐ 527	Vic Correll	.25	.11	.03
☐ 528	Rob Picciolo	.25	.11	.03
☐ 529	Paul Hartzell	.25	.11	.03
☐ 530	Dave Winfield	12.00	5.50	1.50
☐ 531	Tom Underwood	.25	.11	.03
☐ 532	Skip Jutze	.25	.11	.03
☐ 533	Sandy Alomar	.40	.18	.05
☐ 534	Wilbur Howard	.25	.11	.03
☐ 535	Checklist 485-605.....	1.25	.25	.12
☐ 536	Roric Harrison	.25	.11	.03
☐ 537	Bruce Bochte	.25	.11	.03
☐ 538	Johnny LeMaster	.25	.11	.03
☐ 539	Vic Davalillo DP	.15	.07	.02
☐ 540	Steve Carlton	3.00	1.35	.35
☐ 541	Larry Cox	.25	.11	.03
☐ 542	Tim Johnson	.25	.11	.03
☐ 543	Larry Harlow DP	.15	.07	.02
☐ 544	Len Randle DP	.15	.07	.02
☐ 545	Bill Campbell	.25	.11	.03
☐ 546	Ted Martinez	.25	.11	.03
☐ 547	John Scott	.25	.11	.03
☐ 548	Billy Hunter DP MG	.15	.07	.02
☐ 549	Joe Kerrigan	.25	.11	.03
☐ 550	John Mayberry	.40	.18	.05
☐ 551	Atlanta Braves Team Card (Checklist back)	1.25	.25	.12
☐ 552	Francisco Barrios	.25	.11	.03
☐ 553	Terry Puhl	.60	.25	.07
☐ 554	Joe Coleman	.25	.11	.03
☐ 555	Butch Wynegar	.25	.11	.03
☐ 556	Ed Armbrister	.25	.11	.03
☐ 557	Tony Solaita	.25	.11	.03
☐ 558	Paul Mitchell	.25	.11	.03
☐ 559	Phil Mankowski	.25	.11	.03
☐ 560	Dave Parker	1.00	.45	.12
☐ 561	Charlie Williams	.25	.11	.03
☐ 562	Glenn Burke	.25	.11	.03
☐ 563	Dave Rader	.25	.11	.03
☐ 564	Mick Kelleher	.25	.11	.03
☐ 565	Jerry Koosman	.40	.18	.05
☐ 566	Merv Rettenmund	.25	.11	.03
☐ 567	Dick Drago	.25	.11	.03
☐ 568	Tom Hutton	.25	.11	.03
☐ 569	Lary Sorensen	.25	.11	.03
☐ 570	Dave Kingman	.40	.18	.05
☐ 571	Buck Martinez	.25	.11	.03
☐ 572	Rick Wise	.25	.11	.03
☐ 573	Luis Gomez	.25	.11	.03
☐ 574	Bob Lemon MG	.40	.18	.05
☐ 575	Pat Dobson	.25	.11	.03
☐ 576	Sam Mejias	.25	.11	.03
☐ 577	Oakland A's Team Card (Checklist back)	1.25	.25	.12
☐ 578	Buzz Capra	.25	.11	.03
☐ 579	Rance Mulliniks	.25	.11	.03
☐ 580	Rod Carew	2.50	1.10	.30
☐ 581	Lynn McGlothen	.25	.11	.03
☐ 582	Fran Healy	.25	.11	.03
☐ 583	George Medich	.25	.11	.03
☐ 584	John Hale	.25	.11	.03
☐ 585	Woodie Fryman DP	.15	.07	.02
☐ 586	Ed Goodson	.25	.11	.03
☐ 587	John Urrea	.25	.11	.03
☐ 588	Jim Mason	.25	.11	.03
☐ 589	Bob Knepper	.25	.11	.03

☐ 590	Bobby Murcer	.40	.18	.05
☐ 591	George Zeber	.25	.11	.03
☐ 592	Bob Apodaca	.25	.11	.03
☐ 593	Dave Skaggs	.25	.11	.03
☐ 594	Dave Freisleben	.25	.11	.03
☐ 595	Sixto Lezcano	.25	.11	.03
☐ 596	Gary Wheelock	.25	.11	.03
☐ 597	Steve Dillard	.25	.11	.03
☐ 598	Eddie Solomon	.25	.11	.03
☐ 599	Gary Woods	.25	.11	.03
☐ 600	Frank Tanana	.25	.11	.03
☐ 601	Gene Mauch MG	.40	.18	.05
☐ 602	Eric Soderholm	.25	.11	.03
☐ 603	Will McEnaney	.25	.11	.03
☐ 604	Earl Williams	.25	.11	.03
☐ 605	Rick Rhoden	.40	.18	.05
☐ 606	Pittsburgh Pirates	1.25	.25	.12
	Team Card			
	(Checklist back)			
☐ 607	Fernando Arroyo	.25	.11	.03
☐ 608	Johnny Grubb	.25	.11	.03
☐ 609	John Denny	.25	.11	.03
☐ 610	Garry Maddox	.40	.18	.05
☐ 611	Pat Scanlon	.25	.11	.03
☐ 612	Ken Henderson	.25	.11	.03
☐ 613	Marty Perez	.25	.11	.03
☐ 614	Joe Wallis	.25	.11	.03
☐ 615	Clay Carroll	.25	.11	.03
☐ 616	Pat Kelly	.25	.11	.03
☐ 617	Joe Nolan	.25	.11	.03
☐ 618	Tommy Helms	.25	.11	.03
☐ 619	Thad Bosley DP	.15	.07	.02
☐ 620	Willie Randolph	.60	.25	.07
☐ 621	Craig Swan DP	.15	.07	.02
☐ 622	Champ Summers	.25	.11	.03
☐ 623	Eduardo Rodriguez	.25	.11	.03
☐ 624	Gary Alexander DP	.15	.07	.02
☐ 625	Jose Cruz	.40	.18	.05
☐ 626	Toronto Blue Jays	.75	.15	.07
	Team Card DP			
	(Checklist back)			
☐ 627	David Johnson	.25	.11	.03
☐ 628	Ralph Garr	.40	.18	.05
☐ 629	Don Stanhouse	.25	.11	.03
☐ 630	Ron Cey	.60	.25	.07
☐ 631	Danny Ozark MG	.25	.11	.03
☐ 632	Rowland Office	.25	.11	.03
☐ 633	Tom Veryzer	.25	.11	.03
☐ 634	Len Barker	.25	.11	.03
☐ 635	Joe Rudi	.40	.18	.05
☐ 636	Jim Bibby	.25	.11	.03
☐ 637	Duffy Dyer	.25	.11	.03
☐ 638	Paul Splittorff	.25	.11	.03
☐ 639	Gene Clines	.25	.11	.03
☐ 640	Lee May DP	.25	.11	.03
☐ 641	Doug Rau	.25	.11	.03
☐ 642	Denny Doyle	.25	.11	.03
☐ 643	Tom House	.25	.11	.03
☐ 644	Jim Dwyer	.25	.11	.03
☐ 645	Mike Torrez	.40	.18	.05
☐ 646	Rick Auerbach DP	.15	.07	.02
☐ 647	Steve Dunning	.25	.11	.03
☐ 648	Gary Thomasson	.25	.11	.03
☐ 649	Moose Haas	.25	.11	.03
☐ 650	Cesar Cedeno	.40	.18	.05
☐ 651	Doug Rader	.25	.11	.03
☐ 652	Checklist 606-726	1.25	.25	.12
☐ 653	Ron Hodges DP	.15	.07	.02
☐ 654	Pepe Frias	.25	.11	.03
☐ 655	Lyman Bostock	.40	.18	.05
☐ 656	Dave Garcia MG	.25	.11	.03
☐ 657	Bombo Rivera	.25	.11	.03
☐ 658	Manny Sanguillen	.40	.18	.05
☐ 659	Texas Rangers	1.25	.25	.12
	Team Card			
	(Checklist back)			
☐ 660	Jason Thompson	.40	.18	.05
☐ 661	Grant Jackson	.25	.11	.03
☐ 662	Paul Dade	.25	.11	.03
☐ 663	Paul Reuschel	.25	.11	.03
☐ 664	Fred Stanley	.25	.11	.03
☐ 665	Dennis Leonard	.40	.18	.05
☐ 666	Billy Smith	.25	.11	.03
☐ 667	Jeff Byrd	.25	.11	.03
☐ 668	Dusty Baker	.60	.25	.07
☐ 669	Pete Falcone	.25	.11	.03
☐ 670	Jim Rice	2.00	.90	.25
☐ 671	Gary Lavelle	.25	.11	.03
☐ 672	Don Kessinger	.40	.18	.05
☐ 673	Steve Brye	.25	.11	.03
☐ 674	Ray Knight	2.50	1.10	.30
☐ 675	Jay Johnstone	.60	.25	.07
☐ 676	Bob Myrick	.25	.11	.03
☐ 677	Ed Herrmann	.25	.11	.03
☐ 678	Tom Burgmeier	.25	.11	.03
☐ 679	Wayne Garrett	.25	.11	.03
☐ 680	Vida Blue	.40	.18	.05
☐ 681	Rob Belloir	.25	.11	.03
☐ 682	Ken Brett	.25	.11	.03
☐ 683	Mike Champion	.25	.11	.03
☐ 684	Ralph Houk MG	.40	.18	.05
☐ 685	Frank Taveras	.25	.11	.03
☐ 686	Gaylord Perry	1.50	.70	.19
☐ 687	Julio Cruz	.25	.11	.03
☐ 688	George Mitterwald	.25	.11	.03
☐ 689	Cleveland Indians	1.25	.25	.12
	Team Card			
	(Checklist back)			
☐ 690	Mickey Rivers	.40	.18	.05
☐ 691	Ross Grimsley	.25	.11	.03
☐ 692	Ken Reitz	.25	.11	.03
☐ 693	Lamar Johnson	.25	.11	.03
☐ 694	Elias Sosa	.25	.11	.03
☐ 695	Dwight Evans	.60	.25	.07
☐ 696	Steve Mingori	.25	.11	.03
☐ 697	Roger Metzger	.25	.11	.03
☐ 698	Juan Bernhardt	.25	.11	.03
☐ 699	Jackie Brown	.25	.11	.03
☐ 700	Johnny Bench	3.00	1.35	.35
☐ 701	Rookie Pitchers	.40	.18	.05
	Tom Hume			
	Larry Landreth			
	Steve McCatty			
	Bruce Taylor			
☐ 702	Rookie Catchers	.40	.18	.05
	Bill Nahorodny			
	Kevin Pasley			
	Rick Sweet			
	Don Werner			
☐ 703	Rookie Pitchers DP	5.00	2.20	.60
	Larry Andersen			
	Tim Jones			
	Mickey Mahler			
	Jack Morris			
☐ 704	Rookie 2nd Basemen	24.00	11.00	3.00
	Garth Iorg			
	Dave Oliver			
	Sam Perlozzo			
	Lou Whitaker			
☐ 705	Rookie Outfielders	.60	.25	.07
	Dave Bergman			
	Miguel Dilone			

Clint Hurdle
Willie Norwood
☐ 706 Rookie 1st Basemen .... .40 .18 .05
Wayne Cage
Ted Cox
Pat Putnam
Dave Revering
☐ 707 Rookie Shortstops ... 90.00 40.00 11.00
Mickey Klutts
Paul Molitor
Alan Trammell
U.L. Washington
☐ 708 Rookie Catchers....... 10.00 4.50 1.25
Bo Diaz
Dale Murphy
Lance Parrish
Ernie Whitt
☐ 709 Rookie Pitchers............ .40 .18 .05
Steve Burke
Matt Keough
Lance Rautzhan
Dan Schatzeder
☐ 710 Rookie Outfielders .... .60 .25 .07
Dell Alston
Rick Bosetti
Mike Easler
Keith Smith
☐ 711 Rookie Pitchers DP ...... .25 .11 .03
Cardell Camper
Dennis Lamp
Craig Mitchell
Roy Thomas
☐ 712 Bobby Valentine............ .25 .11 .03
☐ 713 Bob Davis .... .25 .11 .03
☐ 714 Mike Anderson............. .25 .11 .03
☐ 715 Jim Kaat...................... .60 .25 .07
☐ 716 Clarence Gaston........... .40 .18 .05
☐ 717 Nelson Briles............... .25 .11 .03
☐ 718 Ron Jackson................ .25 .11 .03
☐ 719 Randy Elliott................. .25 .11 .03
☐ 720 Fergie Jenkins.............. 1.50 .70 .19
☐ 721 Billy Martin MG............. .60 .25 .07
☐ 722 Pete Broberg................ .25 .11 .03
☐ 723 John Wockenfuss.......... .25 .11 .03
☐ 724 Kansas City Royals .... 1.25 .25 .12
Team Card
(Checklist back)
☐ 725 Kurt Bevacqua.............. .25 .11 .03
☐ 726 Wilbur Wood................. .50 .11 .03

1979 Topps

The cards in this 726-card set measure 2
1/2" by 3 1/2". Topps continued with the
same number of cards as in 1978. Various
series spotlight League Leaders (1-8),
"Season and Career Record Holders" (411-
418), "Record Breakers of 1978" (201-206),
and one "Prospects" card for each team
(701-726). Team cards feature a checklist
on back of that team's players in the set
and a small picture of the manager on the
front of the card. There are 66 cards that
were double printed and these are noted in
the checklist by the abbreviation DP. Bump
Wills (369) was initially depicted in a
Ranger uniform but with a Blue Jays affiliation; later printings correctly labeled him
with Texas. The set price listed does not
include the scarcer Wills (Rangers) card.
The key Rookie Cards in this set are Pedro
Guerrero, Carney Lansford, Ozzie Smith,
and Bob Welch. Cards numbered 23 or
lower, which feature Phillies or Yankees
and do not follow the numbering checklisted below, are not necessarily error cards.
They are undoubtedly Burger King cards,
separate sets for each team each with its
own pricing and mass distribution. Burger
King cards are indistinguishable from the
corresponding Topps cards except for the
card numbering difference and the fact that
Burger King cards do not have a printing
sheet designation (such as A through F like
the regular Topps) anywhere on the card
back in very small print.

	NRMT-MT	EXC	G-VG
COMPLETE SET (726)	200.00	90.00	25.00
COMMON CARD (1-726).........	.20	.09	.03
COMMON CARD DP..............	.10	.05	.01
☐ 1 Batting Leaders...............	2.50	.50	.25
Rod Carew			
Dave Parker			
☐ 2 Home Run Leaders...........	.40	.18	.05
Jim Rice			
George Foster			
☐ 3 RBI Leaders...................	.40	.18	.05
Jim Rice			
George Foster			
☐ 4 Stolen Base Leaders.........	.35	.16	.04
Ron LeFlore			
Omar Moreno			
☐ 5 Victory Leaders................	.40	.18	.05
Ron Guidry			
Gaylord Perry			
☐ 6 Strikeout Leaders............	6.00	2.70	.75
Nolan Ryan			
J.R. Richard			
☐ 7 ERA Leaders	.35	.16	.04
Ron Guidry			
Craig Swan			
☐ 8 Leading Firemen	.40	.18	.05
Rich Gossage			
Rollie Fingers			
☐ 9 Dave Campbell.................	.20	.09	.03
☐ 10 Lee May	.35	.16	.04
☐ 11 Marc Hill.......................	.20	.09	.03
☐ 12 Dick Drago....................	.20	.09	.03
☐ 13 Paul Dade.....................	.20	.09	.03
☐ 14 Rafael Landestoy	.20	.09	.03
☐ 15 Ross Grimsley................	.20	.09	.03
☐ 16 Fred Stanley..................	.20	.09	.03
☐ 17 Donnie Moore................	.20	.09	.03

☐	18	Tony Solaita	.20	.09	.03
☐	19	Larry Gura DP	.10	.05	.01
☐	20	Joe Morgan DP	1.00	.45	.12
☐	21	Kevin Kobel	.20	.09	.03
☐	22	Mike Jorgensen	.20	.09	.03
☐	23	Terry Forster	.20	.09	.03
☐	24	Paul Molitor	20.00	9.00	2.50
☐	25	Steve Carlton	2.50	1.10	.30
☐	26	Jamie Quirk	.20	.09	.03
☐	27	Dave Goltz	.20	.09	.03
☐	28	Steve Brye	.20	.09	.03
☐	29	Rick Langford	.20	.09	.03
☐	30	Dave Winfield	8.00	3.60	1.00
☐	31	Tom House DP	.10	.05	.01
☐	32	Jerry Mumphrey	.20	.09	.03
☐	33	Dave Rozema	.20	.09	.03
☐	34	Rob Andrews	.20	.09	.03
☐	35	Ed Figueroa	.20	.09	.03
☐	36	Alan Ashby	.20	.09	.03
☐	37	Joe Kerrigan DP	.10	.05	.01
☐	38	Bernie Carbo	.20	.09	.03
☐	39	Dale Murphy	5.00	2.20	.60
☐	40	Dennis Eckersley	2.00	.90	.25
☐	41	Twins Team/Mgr. Gene Mauch (Checklist back)	1.00	.20	.10
☐	42	Ron Blomberg	.20	.09	.03
☐	43	Wayne Twitchell	.20	.09	.03
☐	44	Kurt Bevacqua	.20	.09	.03
☐	45	Al Hrabosky	.20	.09	.03
☐	46	Ron Hodges	.20	.09	.03
☐	47	Fred Norman	.20	.09	.03
☐	48	Merv Rettenmund	.20	.09	.03
☐	49	Vern Ruhle	.20	.09	.03
☐	50	Steve Garvey DP	.75	.35	.09
☐	51	Ray Fosse DP	.10	.05	.01
☐	52	Randy Lerch	.20	.09	.03
☐	53	Mick Kelleher	.20	.09	.03
☐	54	Dell Alston DP	.10	.05	.01
☐	55	Willie Stargell	1.50	.70	.19
☐	56	John Hale	.20	.09	.03
☐	57	Eric Rasmussen	.20	.09	.03
☐	58	Bob Randall DP	.10	.05	.01
☐	59	John Denny DP	.15	.07	.02
☐	60	Mickey Rivers	.35	.16	.04
☐	61	Bo Diaz	.20	.09	.03
☐	62	Randy Moffitt	.20	.09	.03
☐	63	Jack Brohamer	.20	.09	.03
☐	64	Tom Underwood	.20	.09	.03
☐	65	Mark Belanger	.35	.16	.04
☐	66	Tigers Team/Mgr. Les Moss (Checklist back)	1.00	.20	.10
☐	67	Jim Mason DP	.10	.05	.01
☐	68	Joe Niekro DP	.20	.09	.03
☐	69	Elliott Maddox	.20	.09	.03
☐	70	John Candelaria	.35	.16	.04
☐	71	Brian Downing	.35	.16	.04
☐	72	Steve Mingori	.20	.09	.03
☐	73	Ken Henderson	.20	.09	.03
☐	74	Shane Rawley	.20	.09	.03
☐	75	Steve Yeager	.35	.16	.04
☐	76	Warren Cromartie	.35	.16	.04
☐	77	Dan Briggs DP	.10	.05	.01
☐	78	Elias Sosa	.20	.09	.03
☐	79	Ted Cox	.20	.09	.03
☐	80	Jason Thompson	.35	.16	.04
☐	81	Roger Erickson	.20	.09	.03
☐	82	Mets Team/Mgr. Joe Torre (Checklist back)	1.00	.20	.10
☐	83	Fred Kendall	.20	.09	.03
☐	84	Greg Minton	.20	.09	.03
☐	85	Gary Matthews	.35	.16	.04
☐	86	Rodney Scott	.20	.09	.03
☐	87	Pete Falcone	.20	.09	.03
☐	88	Bob Molinaro	.20	.09	.03
☐	89	Dick Tidrow	.20	.09	.03
☐	90	Bob Boone	.50	.23	.06
☐	91	Terry Crowley	.20	.09	.03
☐	92	Jim Bibby	.20	.09	.03
☐	93	Phil Mankowski	.20	.09	.03
☐	94	Len Barker	.20	.09	.03
☐	95	Robin Yount	10.00	4.50	1.25
☐	96	Indians Team/Mgr. Jeff Torborg (Checklist back)	1.00	.20	.10
☐	97	Sam Mejias	.20	.09	.03
☐	98	Ray Burris	.20	.09	.03
☐	99	John Wathan	.35	.16	.04
☐	100	Tom Seaver DP	2.00	.90	.25
☐	101	Roy Howell	.20	.09	.03
☐	102	Mike Anderson	.20	.09	.03
☐	103	Jim Todd	.20	.09	.03
☐	104	Johnny Oates DP	.20	.09	.03
☐	105	Rick Camp DP	.10	.05	.01
☐	106	Frank Duffy	.20	.09	.03
☐	107	Jesus Alou DP	.10	.05	.01
☐	108	Eduardo Rodriguez	.20	.09	.03
☐	109	Joel Youngblood	.20	.09	.03
☐	110	Vida Blue	.35	.16	.04
☐	111	Roger Freed	.20	.09	.03
☐	112	Phillies Team/Mgr. Danny Ozark (Checklist back)	1.00	.20	.10
☐	113	Pete Redfern	.20	.09	.03
☐	114	Cliff Johnson	.20	.09	.03
☐	115	Nolan Ryan	30.00	13.50	3.70
☐	116	Ozzie Smith	90.00	40.00	11.00
☐	117	Grant Jackson	.20	.09	.03
☐	118	Bud Harrelson	.20	.09	.03
☐	119	Don Stanhouse	.20	.09	.03
☐	120	Jim Sundberg	.35	.16	.04
☐	121	Checklist 1-121 DP	.60	.12	.06
☐	122	Mike Paxton	.20	.09	.03
☐	123	Lou Whitaker	10.00	4.50	1.25
☐	124	Dan Schatzeder	.20	.09	.03
☐	125	Rick Burleson	.20	.09	.03
☐	126	Doug Bair	.20	.09	.03
☐	127	Thad Bosley	.20	.09	.03
☐	128	Ted Martinez	.20	.09	.03
☐	129	Marty Pattin DP	.10	.05	.01
☐	130	Bob Watson DP	.20	.09	.03
☐	131	Jim Clancy	.20	.09	.03
☐	132	Rowland Office	.20	.09	.03
☐	133	Bill Castro	.20	.09	.03
☐	134	Alan Bannister	.20	.09	.03
☐	135	Bobby Murcer	.35	.16	.04
☐	136	Jim Kaat	.35	.16	.04
☐	137	Larry Wolfe DP	.10	.05	.01
☐	138	Mark Lee	.20	.09	.03
☐	139	Luis Pujols	.20	.09	.03
☐	140	Don Gullett	.35	.16	.04
☐	141	Tom Paciorek	.35	.16	.04
☐	142	Charlie Williams	.20	.09	.03
☐	143	Tony Scott	.20	.09	.03
☐	144	Sandy Alomar	.35	.16	.04
☐	145	Rick Rhoden	.20	.09	.03
☐	146	Duane Kuiper	.20	.09	.03
☐	147	Dave Hamilton	.20	.09	.03
☐	148	Bruce Boisclair	.20	.09	.03
☐	149	Manny Sarmiento	.20	.09	.03

☐ 150	Wayne Cage	.20	.09	.03
☐ 151	John Hiller	.20	.09	.03
☐ 152	Rick Cerone	.20	.09	.03
☐ 153	Dennis Lamp	.20	.09	.03
☐ 154	Jim Gantner DP	.20	.09	.03
☐ 155	Dwight Evans	.50	.23	.06
☐ 156	Buddy Solomon	.20	.09	.03
☐ 157	U.L. Washington UER	.20	.09	.03
	(Sic, bats left, should be right)			
☐ 158	Joe Sambito	.20	.09	.03
☐ 159	Roy White	.35	.16	.04
☐ 160	Mike Flanagan	.50	.23	.06
☐ 161	Barry Foote	.20	.09	.03
☐ 162	Tom Johnson	.20	.09	.03
☐ 163	Glenn Burke	.20	.09	.03
☐ 164	Mickey Lolich	.35	.16	.04
☐ 165	Frank Taveras	.20	.09	.03
☐ 166	Leon Roberts	.20	.09	.03
☐ 167	Roger Metzger DP	.10	.05	.01
☐ 168	Dave Freisleben	.20	.09	.03
☐ 169	Bill Nahorodny	.20	.09	.03
☐ 170	Don Sutton	.60	.25	.07
☐ 171	Gene Clines	.20	.09	.03
☐ 172	Mike Bruhert	.20	.09	.03
☐ 173	John Lowenstein	.20	.09	.03
☐ 174	Rick Auerbach	.20	.09	.03
☐ 175	George Hendrick	.35	.16	.04
☐ 176	Aurelio Rodriguez	.20	.09	.03
☐ 177	Ron Reed	.20	.09	.03
☐ 178	Alvis Woods	.20	.09	.03
☐ 179	Jim Beattie DP	.20	.09	.03
☐ 180	Larry Hisle	.20	.09	.03
☐ 181	Mike Garman	.20	.09	.03
☐ 182	Tim Johnson	.20	.09	.03
☐ 183	Paul Splittorff	.20	.09	.03
☐ 184	Darrel Chaney	.20	.09	.03
☐ 185	Mike Torrez	.35	.16	.04
☐ 186	Eric Soderholm	.20	.09	.03
☐ 187	Mark Lemongello	.20	.09	.03
☐ 188	Pat Kelly	.20	.09	.03
☐ 189	Eddie Whitson	.20	.09	.03
☐ 190	Ron Cey	.35	.16	.04
☐ 191	Mike Norris	.20	.09	.03
☐ 192	Cardinals Team/Mgr..	1.00	.20	.10
	Ken Boyer (Checklist back)			
☐ 193	Glenn Adams	.20	.09	.03
☐ 194	Randy Jones	.20	.09	.03
☐ 195	Bill Madlock	.35	.16	.04
☐ 196	Steve Kemp DP	.15	.07	.02
☐ 197	Bob Apodaca	.20	.09	.03
☐ 198	Johnny Grubb	.20	.09	.03
☐ 199	Larry Milbourne	.20	.09	.03
☐ 200	Johnny Bench DP	2.00	.90	.25
☐ 201	RB: Mike Edwards	.20		.03
	Most unassisted DP's, second basemen			
☐ 202	RB: Ron Guidry, Most..	.50	.23	.06
	strikeouts, lefthander, nine inning game			
☐ 203	RB: J.R. Richard	.20	.09	.03
	Most strikeouts, season, righthander			
☐ 204	RB: Pete Rose	2.00	.90	.25
	Most consecutive games batting safely			
☐ 205	RB: John Stearns	.20	.09	.03
	Most SB's by catcher, season			
☐ 206	RB: Sammy Stewart	.20	.09	.03
	7 straight SO's, first ML game			
☐ 207	Dave Lemanczyk	.20	.09	.03
☐ 208	Clarence Gaston	.35	.16	.04
☐ 209	Reggie Cleveland	.20	.09	.03
☐ 210	Larry Bowa	.35	.16	.04
☐ 211	Denny Martinez	1.50	.70	.19
☐ 212	Carney Lansford	2.00	.90	.25
☐ 213	Bill Travers	.20	.09	.03
☐ 214	Red Sox Team/Mgr....	1.00	.20	.10
	Don Zimmer (Checklist back)			
☐ 215	Willie McCovey	2.00	.90	.25
☐ 216	Wilbur Wood	.20	.09	.03
☐ 217	Steve Dillard	.20	.09	.03
☐ 218	Dennis Leonard	.35	.16	.04
☐ 219	Roy Smalley	.35	.16	.04
☐ 220	Cesar Geronimo	.20	.09	.03
☐ 221	Jesse Jefferson	.20	.09	.03
☐ 222	Bob Beall	.20	.09	.03
☐ 223	Kent Tekulve	.35	.16	.04
☐ 224	Dave Revering	.20	.09	.03
☐ 225	Rich Gossage	.50	.23	.06
☐ 226	Ron Pruitt	.20	.09	.03
☐ 227	Steve Stone	.35	.16	.04
☐ 228	Vic Davalillo	.20	.09	.03
☐ 229	Doug Flynn	.20	.09	.03
☐ 230	Bob Forsch	.20	.09	.03
☐ 231	John Wockenfuss	.20	.09	.03
☐ 232	Jimmy Sexton	.20	.09	.03
☐ 233	Paul Mitchell	.20	.09	.03
☐ 234	Toby Harrah	.35	.16	.04
☐ 235	Steve Rogers	.20	.09	.03
☐ 236	Jim Dwyer	.20	.09	.03
☐ 237	Billy Smith	.20	.09	.03
☐ 238	Balor Moore	.20	.09	.03
☐ 239	Willie Horton	.35	.16	.04
☐ 240	Rick Reuschel	.35	.16	.04
☐ 241	Checklist 122-242 DP ..	.60	.12	.06
☐ 242	Pablo Torrealba	.20	.09	.03
☐ 243	Buck Martinez DP	.10	.05	.01
☐ 244	Pirates Team/Mgr.	.50	.10	.03
	Chuck Tanner (Checklist back)			
☐ 245	Jeff Burroughs	.20	.09	.03
☐ 246	Darrell Jackson	.20	.09	.03
☐ 247	Tucker Ashford DP	.10	.05	.01
☐ 248	Pete LaCock	.20	.09	.03
☐ 249	Paul Thormodsgard	.20	.09	.03
☐ 250	Willie Randolph	.50	.23	.06
☐ 251	Jack Morris	2.00	.90	.25
☐ 252	Bob Stinson	.20	.09	.03
☐ 253	Rick Wise	.20	.09	.03
☐ 254	Luis Gomez	.20	.09	.03
☐ 255	Tommy John	.50	.23	.06
☐ 256	Mike Sadek	.20	.09	.03
☐ 257	Adrian Devine	.20	.09	.03
☐ 258	Mike Phillips	.20	.09	.03
☐ 259	Reds Team/Mgr.	1.00	.20	.10
	Sparky Anderson (Checklist back)			
☐ 260	Richie Zisk	.20	.09	.03
☐ 261	Mario Guerrero	.20	.09	.03
☐ 262	Nelson Briles	.20	.09	.03
☐ 263	Oscar Gamble	.35	.16	.04
☐ 264	Don Robinson	.20	.09	.03
☐ 265	Don Money	.20	.09	.03
☐ 266	Jim Willoughby	.20	.09	.03
☐ 267	Joe Rudi	.35	.16	.04
☐ 268	Julio Gonzalez	.20	.09	.03
☐ 269	Woodie Fryman	.20	.09	.03

☐ 270	Butch Hobson	.35	.16	.04
☐ 271	Rawly Eastwick	.20	.09	.03
☐ 272	Tim Corcoran	.20	.09	.03
☐ 273	Jerry Terrell	.20	.09	.03
☐ 274	Willie Norwood	.20	.09	.03
☐ 275	Junior Moore	.20	.09	.03
☐ 276	Jim Colborn	.20	.09	.03
☐ 277	Tom Grieve	.35	.16	.04
☐ 278	Andy Messersmith	.35	.16	.04
☐ 279	Jerry Grote	.10	.05	.01
☐ 280	Andre Thornton	.35	.16	.04
☐ 281	Vic Correll DP	.10	.05	.01
☐ 282	Blue Jays Team/Mgr.	1.00	.20	.09
	Roy Hartsfield			
	(Checklist back)			
☐ 283	Ken Kravec	.20	.09	.03
☐ 284	Johnnie LeMaster	.20	.09	.03
☐ 285	Bobby Bonds	.50	.23	.06
☐ 286	Duffy Dyer	.20	.09	.03
☐ 287	Andres Mora	.20	.09	.03
☐ 288	Milt Wilcox	.20	.09	.03
☐ 289	Jose Cruz	.35	.16	.04
☐ 290	Dave Lopes	.35	.16	.04
☐ 291	Tom Griffin	.20	.09	.03
☐ 292	Don Reynolds	.20	.09	.03
☐ 293	Jerry Garvin	.20	.09	.03
☐ 294	Pepe Frias	.20	.09	.03
☐ 295	Mitchell Page	.20	.09	.03
☐ 296	Preston Hanna	.20	.09	.03
☐ 297	Ted Sizemore	.20	.09	.03
☐ 298	Rich Gale	.20	.09	.03
☐ 299	Steve Ontiveros	.20	.09	.03
☐ 300	Rod Carew	2.00	.90	.25
☐ 301	Tom Hume	.20	.09	.03
☐ 302	Braves Team/Mgr.	1.00	.20	.10
	Bobby Cox			
	(Checklist back)			
☐ 303	Lary Sorensen DP	.10	.05	.01
☐ 304	Steve Swisher	.20	.09	.03
☐ 305	Willie Montanez	.20	.09	.03
☐ 306	Floyd Bannister	.20	.09	.03
☐ 307	Larvell Blanks	.20	.09	.03
☐ 308	Bert Blyleven	.50	.23	.06
☐ 309	Ralph Garr	.35	.16	.04
☐ 310	Thurman Munson	2.00	.90	.25
☐ 311	Gary Lavelle	.20	.09	.03
☐ 312	Bob Robertson	.20	.09	.03
☐ 313	Dyar Miller	.20	.09	.03
☐ 314	Larry Harlow	.20	.09	.03
☐ 315	Jon Matlack	.20	.09	.03
☐ 316	Milt May	.20	.09	.03
☐ 317	Jose Cardenal	.20	.09	.03
☐ 318	Bob Welch	2.00	.90	.25
☐ 319	Wayne Garrett	.20	.09	.03
☐ 320	Carl Yastrzemski	2.50	1.10	.30
☐ 321	Gaylord Perry	1.00	.45	.12
☐ 322	Danny Goodwin	.20	.09	.03
☐ 323	Lynn McGlothen	.20	.09	.03
☐ 324	Mike Tyson	.20	.09	.03
☐ 325	Cecil Cooper	.35	.16	.04
☐ 326	Pedro Borbon	.20	.09	.03
☐ 327	Art Howe DP	.20	.09	.03
☐ 328	Oakland A's Team/Mgr.	1.00	.20	.10
	Jack McKeon			
	(Checklist back)			
☐ 329	Joe Coleman	.20	.09	.03
☐ 330	George Brett	20.00	9.00	2.50
☐ 331	Mickey Mahler	.20	.09	.03
☐ 332	Gary Alexander	.20	.09	.03
☐ 333	Chet Lemon	.35	.16	.04
☐ 334	Craig Swan	.20	.09	.03
☐ 335	Chris Chambliss	.35	.16	.04
☐ 336	Bobby Thompson	.20	.09	.03
☐ 337	John Montague	.20	.09	.03
☐ 338	Vic Harris	.20	.09	.03
☐ 339	Ron Jackson	.20	.09	.03
☐ 340	Jim Palmer	2.00	.90	.25
☐ 341	Willie Upshaw	.35	.16	.04
☐ 342	Dave Roberts	.20	.09	.03
☐ 343	Ed Glynn	.20	.09	.03
☐ 344	Jerry Royster	.20	.09	.03
☐ 345	Tug McGraw	.35	.16	.04
☐ 346	Bill Buckner	.35	.16	.04
☐ 347	Doug Rau	.20	.09	.03
☐ 348	Andre Dawson	8.00	3.60	1.00
☐ 349	Jim Wright	.20	.09	.03
☐ 350	Garry Templeton	.35	.16	.04
☐ 351	Wayne Nordhagen DP	.10	.05	.01
☐ 352	Steve Renko	.20	.09	.03
☐ 353	Checklist 243-363	1.00	.20	.10
☐ 354	Bill Bonham	.20	.09	.03
☐ 355	Lee Mazzilli	.20	.09	.03
☐ 356	Giants Team/Mgr.	1.00	.20	.10
	Joe Altobelli			
	(Checklist back)			
☐ 357	Jerry Augustine	.20	.09	.03
☐ 358	Alan Trammell	12.00	5.50	1.50
☐ 359	Dan Spillner DP	.10	.05	.01
☐ 360	Amos Otis	.35	.16	.04
☐ 361	Tom Dixon	.20	.09	.03
☐ 362	Mike Cubbage	.20	.09	.03
☐ 363	Craig Skok	.20	.09	.03
☐ 364	Gene Richards	.20	.09	.03
☐ 365	Sparky Lyle	.35	.16	.04
☐ 366	Juan Bernhardt	.20	.09	.03
☐ 367	Dave Skaggs	.20	.09	.03
☐ 368	Don Aase	.20	.09	.03
☐ 369A	Bump Wills ERR	3.00	1.35	.35
	(Blue Jays)			
☐ 369B	Bump Wills COR	3.00	1.35	.35
	(Rangers)			
☐ 370	Dave Kingman	.35	.16	.04
☐ 371	Jeff Holly	.20	.09	.03
☐ 372	Lamar Johnson	.20	.09	.03
☐ 373	Lance Rautzhan	.20	.09	.03
☐ 374	Ed Herrmann	.20	.09	.03
☐ 375	Bill Campbell	.20	.09	.03
☐ 376	Gorman Thomas	.35	.16	.04
☐ 377	Paul Moskau	.20	.09	.03
☐ 378	Rob Picciolo DP	.10	.05	.01
☐ 379	Dale Murray	.20	.09	.03
☐ 380	John Mayberry	.35	.16	.04
☐ 381	Astros Team/Mgr.	1.00	.20	.10
	Bill Virdon			
	(Checklist back)			
☐ 382	Jerry Martin	.20	.09	.03
☐ 383	Phil Garner	.35	.16	.04
☐ 384	Tommy Boggs	.20	.09	.03
☐ 385	Dan Ford	.20	.09	.03
☐ 386	Francisco Barrios	.20	.09	.03
☐ 387	Gary Thomasson	.20	.09	.03
☐ 388	Jack Billingham	.20	.09	.03
☐ 389	Joe Zdeb	.20	.09	.03
☐ 390	Rollie Fingers	1.00	.45	.12
☐ 391	Al Oliver	.35	.16	.04
☐ 392	Doug Ault	.20	.09	.03
☐ 393	Scott McGregor	.35	.16	.04
☐ 394	Randy Stein	.20	.09	.03
☐ 395	Dave Cash	.20	.09	.03
☐ 396	Bill Plummer	.20	.09	.03
☐ 397	Sergio Ferrer	.20	.09	.03
☐ 398	Ivan DeJesus	.20	.09	.03

☐ 399 David Clyde	.20	.09	.03
☐ 400 Jim Rice	1.50	.70	.19
☐ 401 Ray Knight	.50	.23	.06
☐ 402 Paul Hartzell	.20	.09	.03
☐ 403 Tim Foli	.20	.09	.03
☐ 404 White Sox Team/Mgr.	1.00	.20	.10
Don Kessinger			
(Checklist back)			
☐ 405 Butch Wynegar DP	.10	.05	.01
☐ 406 Joe Wallis DP	.10	.05	.01
☐ 407 Pete Vuckovich	.35	.16	.04
☐ 408 Charlie Moore DP	.10	.05	.01
☐ 409 Willie Wilson	2.00	.90	.25
☐ 410 Darrell Evans	.50	.23	.06
☐ 411 Hits Record	.75	.35	.09
Season: George Sisler			
Career: Ty Cobb			
☐ 412 RBI Record	1.00	.45	.12
Season: Hack Wilson			
Career: Hank Aaron			
☐ 413 Home Run Record	1.50	.70	.19
Season: Roger Maris			
Career: Hank Aaron			
☐ 414 Batting Record	1.00	.45	.12
Season: Rogers Hornsby			
Career: Ty Cobb			
☐ 415 Steals Record	.50	.23	.06
Season: Lou Brock			
Career: Lou Brock			
☐ 416 Wins Record	.35	.16	.04
Season: Jack Chesbro			
Career: Cy Young			
☐ 417 Strikeout Record DP	4.00	1.80	.50
Season: Nolan Ryan			
Career: Walter Johnson			
☐ 418 ERA Record DP	.25	.11	.03
Season: Dutch Leonard			
Career: Walter Johnson			
☐ 419 Dick Ruthven	.20	.09	.03
☐ 420 Ken Griffey	.75	.35	.09
☐ 421 Doug DeCinces	.35	.16	.04
☐ 422 Ruppert Jones	.20	.09	.03
☐ 423 Bob Montgomery	.20	.09	.03
☐ 424 Angels Team/Mgr.	1.00	.20	.10
Jim Fregosi			
(Checklist back)			
☐ 425 Rick Manning	.20	.09	.03
☐ 426 Chris Speier	.20	.09	.03
☐ 427 Andy Replogle	.20	.09	.03
☐ 428 Bobby Valentine	.20	.09	.03
☐ 429 John Urrea DP	.10	.05	.01
☐ 430 Dave Parker	.75	.35	.09
☐ 431 Glenn Borgmann	.20	.09	.03
☐ 432 Dave Heaverlo	.20	.09	.03
☐ 433 Larry Biittner	.20	.09	.03
☐ 434 Ken Clay	.20	.09	.03
☐ 435 Gene Tenace	.35	.16	.04
☐ 436 Hector Cruz	.20	.09	.03
☐ 437 Rick Williams	.20	.09	.03
☐ 438 Horace Speed	.20	.09	.03
☐ 439 Frank White	.35	.16	.04
☐ 440 Rusty Staub	.50	.23	.06
☐ 441 Lee Lacy	.20	.09	.03
☐ 442 Doyle Alexander	.20	.09	.03
☐ 443 Bruce Bochte	.20	.09	.03
☐ 444 Aurelio Lopez	.20	.09	.03
☐ 445 Steve Henderson	.20	.09	.03
☐ 446 Jim Lonborg	.35	.16	.04
☐ 447 Manny Sanguillen	.35	.16	.04
☐ 448 Moose Haas	.20	.09	.03
☐ 449 Bombo Rivera	.20	.09	.03

☐ 450 Dave Concepcion	.50	.23	.06
☐ 451 Royals Team/Mgr.	1.00	.20	.10
Whitey Herzog			
(Checklist back)			
☐ 452 Jerry Morales	.20	.09	.03
☐ 453 Chris Knapp	.20	.09	.03
☐ 454 Len Randle	.20	.09	.03
☐ 455 Bill Lee DP	.10	.05	.01
☐ 456 Chuck Baker	.20	.09	.03
☐ 457 Bruce Sutter	.50	.23	.06
☐ 458 Jim Essian	.20	.09	.03
☐ 459 Sid Monge	.20	.09	.03
☐ 460 Graig Nettles	.35	.16	.04
☐ 461 Jim Barr DP	.10	.05	.01
☐ 462 Otto Velez	.20	.09	.03
☐ 463 Steve Comer	.20	.09	.03
☐ 464 Joe Nolan	.20	.09	.03
☐ 465 Reggie Smith	.35	.16	.04
☐ 466 Mark Littell	.20	.09	.03
☐ 467 Don Kessinger DP	.15	.07	.02
☐ 468 Stan Bahnsen DP	.10	.05	.01
☐ 469 Lance Parrish	1.00	.45	.12
☐ 470 Garry Maddox DP	.20	.09	.03
☐ 471 Joaquin Andujar	.35	.16	.04
☐ 472 Craig Kusick	.20	.09	.03
☐ 473 Dave Roberts	.20	.09	.03
☐ 474 Dick Davis	.20	.09	.03
☐ 475 Dan Driessen	.20	.09	.03
☐ 476 Tom Poquette	.20	.09	.03
☐ 477 Bob Grich	.35	.16	.04
☐ 478 Juan Beniquez	.20	.09	.03
☐ 479 Padres Team/Mgr.	1.00	.20	.10
Roger Craig			
(Checklist back)			
☐ 480 Fred Lynn	.50	.23	.06
☐ 481 Skip Lockwood	.20	.09	.03
☐ 482 Craig Reynolds	.20	.09	.03
☐ 483 Checklist 364-484 DP	.60	.12	.06
☐ 484 Rick Waits	.20	.09	.03
☐ 485 Bucky Dent	.35	.16	.04
☐ 486 Bob Knepper	.20	.09	.03
☐ 487 Miguel Dilone	.20	.09	.03
☐ 488 Bob Owchinko	.20	.09	.03
☐ 489 Larry Cox UER	.20	.09	.03
(Photo actually			
Dave Rader)			
☐ 490 Al Cowens	.20	.09	.03
☐ 491 Tippy Martinez	.35	.16	.04
☐ 492 Bob Bailor	.20	.09	.03
☐ 493 Larry Christenson	.20	.09	.03
☐ 494 Jerry White	.20	.09	.03
☐ 495 Tony Perez	1.00	.45	.12
☐ 496 Barry Bonnell DP	.20	.09	.03
☐ 497 Glenn Abbott	.20	.09	.03
☐ 498 Rich Chiles	.20	.04	.02
☐ 499 Rangers Team/Mgr.	1.00	.45	.12
Pat Corrales			
(Checklist back)			
☐ 500 Ron Guidry	.50	.23	.06
☐ 501 Junior Kennedy	.20	.09	.03
☐ 502 Steve Braun	.20	.09	.03
☐ 503 Terry Humphrey	.20	.09	.03
☐ 504 Larry McWilliams	.20	.09	.03
☐ 505 Ed Kranepool	.20	.09	.03
☐ 506 John D'Acquisto	.20	.09	.03
☐ 507 Tony Armas	.20	.09	.03
☐ 508 Charlie Hough	.35	.16	.04
☐ 509 Mario Mendoza UER	.20	.09	.03
(Career BA .278,			
should say .204)			
☐ 510 Ted Simmons	.20	.09	.03

☐ 511	Paul Reuschel DP	.10	.05	.01
☐ 512	Jack Clark	.50	.23	.06
☐ 513	Dave Johnson	.20	.09	.03
☐ 514	Mike Proly	.20	.09	.03
☐ 515	Enos Cabell	.20	.09	.03
☐ 516	Champ Summers DP	.10	.05	.01
☐ 517	Al Bumbry	.35	.16	.04
☐ 518	Jim Umbarger	.20	.09	.03
☐ 519	Ben Oglivie	.35	.16	.04
☐ 520	Gary Carter	2.00	.90	.25
☐ 521	Sam Ewing	.20	.09	.03
☐ 522	Ken Holtzman	.20	.09	.03
☐ 523	John Milner	.20	.09	.03
☐ 524	Tom Burgmeier	.20	.09	.03
☐ 525	Freddie Patek	.20	.09	.03
☐ 526	Dodgers Team/Mgr. Tom Lasorda (Checklist back)	1.00	.20	.10
☐ 527	Lerrin LaGrow	.20	.09	.03
☐ 528	Wayne Gross DP	.10	.05	.01
☐ 529	Brian Asselstine	.20	.09	.03
☐ 530	Frank Tanana	.20	.09	.03
☐ 531	Fernando Gonzalez	.20	.09	.03
☐ 532	Buddy Schultz	.20	.09	.03
☐ 533	Leroy Stanton	.20	.09	.03
☐ 534	Ken Forsch	.20	.09	.03
☐ 535	Ellis Valentine	.20	.09	.03
☐ 536	Jerry Reuss	.35	.16	.04
☐ 537	Tom Veryzer	.20	.09	.03
☐ 538	Mike Ivie DP	.10	.05	.01
☐ 539	John Ellis	.20	.09	.03
☐ 540	Greg Luzinski	.35	.16	.04
☐ 541	Jim Slaton	.20	.09	.03
☐ 542	Rick Bosetti	.20	.09	.03
☐ 543	Kiko Garcia	.20	.09	.03
☐ 544	Fergie Jenkins	1.00	.45	.12
☐ 545	John Stearns	.20	.09	.03
☐ 546	Bill Russell	.35	.16	.04
☐ 547	Clint Hurdle	.20	.09	.03
☐ 548	Enrique Romo	.20	.09	.03
☐ 549	Bob Bailey	.20	.09	.03
☐ 550	Sal Bando	.35	.16	.04
☐ 551	Cubs Team/Mgr. Herman Franks (Checklist back)	1.00	.20	.10
☐ 552	Jose Morales	.20	.09	.03
☐ 553	Denny Walling	.20	.09	.03
☐ 554	Matt Keough	.20	.09	.03
☐ 555	Biff Pocoroba	.20	.09	.03
☐ 556	Mike Lum	.20	.09	.03
☐ 557	Ken Brett	.20	.09	.03
☐ 558	Jay Johnstone	.35	.16	.04
☐ 559	Greg Pryor	.20	.09	.03
☐ 560	John Montefusco	.20	.09	.03
☐ 561	Ed Ott	.20	.09	.03
☐ 562	Dusty Baker	.50	.23	.06
☐ 563	Roy Thomas	.20	.09	.03
☐ 564	Jerry Turner	.20	.09	.03
☐ 565	Rico Carty	.35	.16	.04
☐ 566	Nino Espinosa	.20	.09	.03
☐ 567	Richie Hebner	.20	.09	.03
☐ 568	Carlos Lopez	.20	.09	.03
☐ 569	Bob Sykes	.20	.09	.03
☐ 570	Cesar Cedeno	.35	.16	.04
☐ 571	Darrell Porter	.20	.09	.03
☐ 572	Rod Gilbreath	.20	.09	.03
☐ 573	Jim Kern	.20	.09	.03
☐ 574	Claudell Washington	.35	.16	.04
☐ 575	Luis Tiant	.35	.16	.04
☐ 576	Mike Parrott	.20	.09	.03
☐ 577	Brewers Team/Mgr. George Bamberger (Checklist back)	1.00	.20	.10
☐ 578	Pete Broberg	.20	.09	.03
☐ 579	Greg Gross	.20	.09	.03
☐ 580	Ron Fairly	.35	.16	.04
☐ 581	Darold Knowles	.20	.09	.03
☐ 582	Paul Blair	.35	.16	.04
☐ 583	Julio Cruz	.20	.09	.03
☐ 584	Jim Rooker	.20	.09	.03
☐ 585	Hal McRae	.50	.23	.06
☐ 586	Bob Horner	.50	.23	.06
☐ 587	Ken Reitz	.20	.09	.03
☐ 588	Tom Murphy	.20	.09	.03
☐ 589	Terry Whitfield	.20	.09	.03
☐ 590	J.R. Richard	.35	.16	.04
☐ 591	Mike Hargrove	.35	.16	.04
☐ 592	Mike Krukow	.20	.09	.03
☐ 593	Rick Dempsey	.35	.16	.04
☐ 594	Bob Shirley	.20	.09	.03
☐ 595	Phil Niekro	.60	.25	.07
☐ 596	Jim Wohlford	.20	.09	.03
☐ 597	Bob Stanley	.20	.09	.03
☐ 598	Mark Wagner	.20	.09	.03
☐ 599	Jim Spencer	.20•	.09	.03
☐ 600	George Foster	.35	.16	.04
☐ 601	Dave LaRoche	.20	.09	.03
☐ 602	Checklist 485-605	1.00	.20	.10
☐ 603	Rudy May	.20	.09	.03
☐ 604	Jeff Newman	.20	.09	.03
☐ 605	Rick Monday DP	.15	.07	.02
☐ 606	Expos Team/Mgr. Dick Williams (Checklist back)	1.00	.20	.10
☐ 607	Omar Moreno	.20	.09	.03
☐ 608	Dave McKay	.20	.09	.03
☐ 609	Silvio Martinez	.20	.09	.03
☐ 610	Mike Schmidt	8.00	3.60	1.00
☐ 611	Jim Norris	.20	.09	.03
☐ 612	Rick Honeycutt	.35	.16	.04
☐ 613	Mike Edwards	.20	.09	.03
☐ 614	Willie Hernandez	.35	.16	.04
☐ 615	Ken Singleton	.35	.16	.04
☐ 616	Billy Almon	.20	.09	.03
☐ 617	Terry Puhl	.35	.16	.04
☐ 618	Jerry Remy	.20	.09	.03
☐ 619	Ken Landreaux	.35	.16	.04
☐ 620	Bert Campaneris	.35	.16	.04
☐ 621	Pat Zachry	.20	.09	.03
☐ 622	Dave Collins	.35	.16	.04
☐ 623	Bob McClure	.20	.09	.03
☐ 624	Larry Herndon	.20	.09	.03
☐ 625	Mark Fidrych	.35	.16	.04
☐ 626	Yankees Team/Mgr. Bob Lemon (Checklist back)	1.00	.20	.10
☐ 627	Gary Serum	.20	.09	.03
☐ 628	Del Unser	.20	.09	.03
☐ 629	Gene Garber	.20	.09	.03
☐ 630	Bake McBride	.35	.16	.04
☐ 631	Jorge Orta	.20	.09	.03
☐ 632	Don Kirkwood	.20	.09	.03
☐ 633	Rob Wilfong DP	.10	.05	.01
☐ 634	Paul Lindblad	.20	.09	.03
☐ 635	Don Baylor	.75	.35	.09
☐ 636	Wayne Garland	.20	.09	.03
☐ 637	Bill Robinson	.35	.16	.04
☐ 638	Al Fitzmorris	.20	.09	.03
☐ 639	Manny Trillo	.20	.09	.03
☐ 640	Eddie Murray	30.00	13.50	3.70
☐ 641	Bobby Castillo	.20	.09	.03
☐ 642	Wilbur Howard DP	.10	.05	.01

☐ 643	Tom Hausman	.20	.09	.03
☐ 644	Manny Mota	.35	.16	.04
☐ 645	George Scott DP	.15	.07	.02
☐ 646	Rick Sweet	.20	.09	.03
☐ 647	Bob Lacey	.20	.09	.03
☐ 648	Lou Piniella	.35	.16	.04
☐ 649	John Curtis	.20	.09	.03
☐ 650	Pete Rose	5.00	2.20	.60
☐ 651	Mike Caldwell	.20	.09	.03
☐ 652	Stan Papi	.20	.09	.03
☐ 653	Warren Brusstar DP	.10	.05	.01
☐ 654	Rick Miller	.20	.09	.03
☐ 655	Jerry Koosman	.35	.16	.04
☐ 656	Hosken Powell	.20	.09	.03
☐ 657	George Medich	.20	.09	.03
☐ 658	Taylor Duncan	.20	.09	.03
☐ 659	Mariners Team/Mgr.	1.00	.20	.10
	Darrell Johnson			
	(Checklist back)			
☐ 660	Ron LeFlore DP	.20	.09	.03
☐ 661	Bruce Kison	.20	.09	.03
☐ 662	Kevin Bell	.20	.09	.03
☐ 663	Mike Vail	.20	.09	.03
☐ 664	Doug Bird	.20	.09	.03
☐ 665	Lou Brock	2.00	.90	.25
☐ 666	Rich Dauer	.20	.09	.03
☐ 667	Don Hood	.20	.09	.03
☐ 668	Bill North	.20	.09	.03
☐ 669	Checklist 606-726	1.00	.20	.10
☐ 670	Jim Hunter DP	.75	.35	.09
☐ 671	Joe Ferguson DP	.10	.05	.01
☐ 672	Ed Halicki	.20	.09	.03
☐ 673	Tom Hutton	.20	.09	.03
☐ 674	Dave Tomlin	.20	.09	.03
☐ 675	Tim McCarver	.35	.16	.04
☐ 676	Johnny Sutton	.20	.09	.03
☐ 677	Larry Parrish	.35	.16	.04
☐ 678	Geoff Zahn	.20	.09	.03
☐ 679	Derrel Thomas	.20	.09	.03
☐ 680	Carlton Fisk	2.50	1.10	.30
☐ 681	John Henry Johnson	.20	.09	.03
☐ 682	Dave Chalk	.20	.09	.03
☐ 683	Dan Meyer DP	.10	.05	.01
☐ 684	Jamie Easterly DP	.10	.05	.01
☐ 685	Sixto Lezcano	.20	.09	.03
☐ 686	Ron Schueler DP	.10	.05	.01
☐ 687	Rennie Stennett	.20	.09	.03
☐ 688	Mike Willis	.20	.09	.03
☐ 689	Orioles Team/Mgr.	1.00	.20	.10
	Earl Weaver			
	(Checklist back)			
☐ 690	Buddy Bell DP	.20	.09	.03
☐ 691	Dock Ellis DP	.10	.05	.01
☐ 692	Mickey Stanley	.20	.09	.03
☐ 693	Dave Rader	.20	.09	.03
☐ 694	Burt Hooton	.35	.16	.04
☐ 695	Keith Hernandez	.50	.23	.06
☐ 696	Andy Hassler	.20	.09	.03
☐ 697	Dave Bergman	.20	.09	.03
☐ 698	Bill Stein	.20	.09	.03
☐ 699	Hal Dues	.20	.09	.03
☐ 700	Reggie Jackson DP	2.00	.90	.25
☐ 701	Orioles Prospects	.35	.16	.04
	Mark Corey			
	John Flinn			
	Sammy Stewart			
☐ 702	Red Sox Prospects	.35	.16	.04
	Joel Finch			
	Garry Hancock			
	Allen Ripley			
☐ 703	Angels Prospects	.35	.16	.04
	Jim Anderson			
	Dave Frost			
	Bob Slater			
☐ 704	White Sox Prospects	.35	.16	.04
	Ross Baumgarten			
	Mike Colbern			
	Mike Squires			
☐ 705	Indians Prospects	.50	.23	.06
	Alfredo Griffin			
	Tim Norrid			
	Dave Oliver			
☐ 706	Tigers Prospects	.35	.16	.04
	Dave Stegman			
	Dave Tobik			
	Kip Young			
☐ 707	Royals Prospects	.50	.23	.06
	Randy Bass			
	Jim Gaudet			
	Randy McGilberry			
☐ 708	Brewers Prospects	1.00	.45	.12
	Kevin Bass			
	Eddie Romero			
	Ned Yost			
☐ 709	Twins Prospects	.35	.16	.04
	Sam Perlozzo			
	Rick Sofield			
	Kevin Stanfield			
☐ 710	Yankees Prospects	.35	.16	.04
	Brian Doyle			
	Mike Heath			
	Dave Rajsich			
☐ 711	A's Prospects	.50	.23	.06
	Dwayne Murphy			
	Bruce Robinson			
	Alan Wirth			
☐ 712	Mariners Prospects	.35	.16	.04
	Bud Anderson			
	Greg Biercevicz			
	Byron McLaughlin			
☐ 713	Rangers Prospects	.50	.23	.06
	Danny Darwin			
	Pat Putnam			
	Billy Sample			
☐ 714	Blue Jays Prospects	.35	.16	.04
	Victor Cruz			
	Pat Kelly			
	Ernie Whitt			
☐ 715	Braves Prospects	.50	.23	.06
	Bruce Benedict			
	Glenn Hubbard			
	Larry Whisenton			
☐ 716	Cubs Prospects	.35	.16	.04
	Dave Geisel			
	Karl Pagel			
	Scot Thompson			
☐ 717	Reds Prospects	.35	.16	.04
	Mike LaCoss			
	Ron Oester			
	Harry Spilman			
☐ 718	Astros Prospects	.35	.16	.04
	Bruce Bochy			
	Mike Fischlin			
	Don Pisker			
☐ 719	Dodgers Prospects	2.00	.90	.25
	Pedro Guerrero			
	Rudy Law			
	Joe Simpson			
☐ 720	Expos Prospects	.50	.23	.06
	Jerry Fry			
	Jerry Pirtle			
	Scott Sanderson			

		NRMT-MT	EXC	G-VG
☐ 721	Mets Prospects	.35	.16	.04
	Juan Berenguer			
	Dwight Bernard			
	Dan Norman			
☐ 722	Phillies Prospects	.50	.23	.06
	Jim Morrison			
	Lonnie Smith			
	Jim Wright			
☐ 723	Pirates Prospects	.35	.16	.04
	Dale Berra			
	Eugenio Cotes			
	Ben Wiltbank			
☐ 724	Cardinals Prospects	.50	.23	.06
	Tom Bruno			
	George Frazier			
	Terry Kennedy			
☐ 725	Padres Prospects	.35	.16	.04
	Jim Beswick			
	Steve Mura			
	Broderick Perkins			
☐ 726	Giants Prospects	.35	.16	.04
	Greg Johnston			
	Joe Strain			
	John Tamargo			

1980 Topps

The cards in this 726-card set measure 2 1/2" by 3 1/2". In 1980 Topps released another set of the same size and number of cards as the previous two years. As with those sets, Topps again has produced 66 double-printed cards in the set; they are noted by DP in the checklist below. The player's name appears over the picture and his position and team are found in pennant design. Every card carries a facsimile autograph. Team cards feature a team checklist of players in the set on the back and the manager's name on the front. Cards 1-6 show Highlights (HL) of the 1979 season, cards 201-207 are League Leaders, and cards 661-686 feature American and National League rookie "Future Stars," one card for each team showing three young prospects. The key Rookie Card in this set is Rickey Henderson; other Rookie Cards included in this set are Dave Stieb and Rick Sutcliffe.

	NRMT-MT	EXC	G-VG
COMPLETE SET (726)	150.00	70.00	19.00
COMMON CARD (1-726)	.20	.09	.03
COMMON CARD DP	.10	.05	.01

☐ 1	Lou Brock and	3.00	.60	.30
	Carl Yastrzemski HL			
	Enter 3000 hit circle			
☐ 2	Willie McCovey HL	.75	.35	.09
	512th homer sets new			
	mark for NL lefties			
☐ 3	Manny Mota HL	.35	.16	.04
	All-time pinch-hits, 145			
☐ 4	Pete Rose HL	2.00	.90	.25
	Career Record 10th season			
	with 200 or more hits			
☐ 5	Garry Templeton HL	.35	.16	.04
	First with 100 hits			
	from each side of plate			
☐ 6	Del Unser HL	.35	.16	.04
	Third consecutive			
	pinch homer sets			
	new ML standard			
☐ 7	Mike Lum	.20	.09	.03
☐ 8	Craig Swan	.20	.09	.03
☐ 9	Steve Braun	.20	.09	.03
☐ 10	Dennis Martinez	.75	.35	.09
☐ 11	Jimmy Sexton	.20	.09	.03
☐ 12	John Curtis DP	.10	.05	.01
☐ 13	Ron Pruitt	.20	.09	.03
☐ 14	Dave Cash	.20	.09	.03
☐ 15	Bill Campbell	.20	.09	.03
☐ 16	Jerry Narron	.20	.09	.03
☐ 17	Bruce Sutter	.35	.16	.04
☐ 18	Ron Jackson	.20	.09	.03
☐ 19	Balor Moore	.20	.09	.03
☐ 20	Dan Ford	.20	.09	.03
☐ 21	Manny Sarmiento	.20	.09	.03
☐ 22	Pat Putnam	.20	.09	.03
☐ 23	Derrel Thomas	.20	.09	.03
☐ 24	Jim Slaton	.20	.09	.03
☐ 25	Lee Mazzilli	.20	.09	.03
☐ 26	Marty Pattin	.20	.09	.03
☐ 27	Del Unser	.20	.09	.03
☐ 28	Bruce Kison	.20	.09	.03
☐ 29	Mark Wagner	.20	.09	.03
☐ 30	Vida Blue	.35	.16	.04
☐ 31	Jay Johnstone	.35	.16	.04
☐ 32	Julio Cruz DP	.10	.05	.01
☐ 33	Tony Scott	.20	.09	.03
☐ 34	Jeff Newman DP	.10	.05	.01
☐ 35	Luis Tiant	.35	.16	.04
☐ 36	Rusty Torres	.20	.09	.03
☐ 37	Kiko Garcia	.20	.09	.03
☐ 38	Dan Spillner DP	.10	.05	.01
☐ 39	Rowland Office	.20	.09	.03
☐ 40	Carlton Fisk	2.00	.90	.25
☐ 41	Rangers Team/Mgr.	.75	.15	.07
	Pat Corrales			
	(Checklist back)			
☐ 42	David Palmer	.20	.09	.03
☐ 43	Bombo Rivera	.20	.09	.03
☐ 44	Bill Fahey	.20	.09	.03
☐ 45	Frank White	.35	.16	.04
☐ 46	Rico Carty	.35	.16	.04
☐ 47	Bill Bonham DP	.10	.05	.01
☐ 48	Rick Miller	.20	.09	.03
☐ 49	Mario Guerrero	.20	.09	.03
☐ 50	J.R. Richard	.35	.16	.04
☐ 51	Joe Ferguson DP	.10	.05	.01
☐ 52	Warren Brusstar	.20	.09	.03
☐ 53	Ben Oglivie	.35	.16	.04
☐ 54	Dennis Lamp	.20	.09	.03
☐ 55	Bill Madlock	.35	.16	.04
☐ 56	Bobby Valentine	.20	.09	.03
☐ 57	Pete Vuckovich	.35	.16	.04

□	#	Player			
□	58	Doug Flynn	.20	.09	.03
□	59	Eddy Putman	.20	.09	.03
□	60	Bucky Dent	.35	.16	.04
□	61	Gary Serum	.20	.09	.03
□	62	Mike Ivie	.20	.09	.03
□	63	Bob Stanley	.20	.09	.03
□	64	Joe Nolan	.20	.09	.03
□	65	Al Bumbry	.35	.16	.04
□	66	Royals Team/Mgr.	.75	.15	.07
		Jim Frey			
		(Checklist back)			
□	67	Doyle Alexander	.20	.09	.03
□	68	Larry Harlow	.20	.09	.03
□	69	Rick Williams	.20	.09	.03
□	70	Gary Carter	1.50	.70	.19
□	71	John Milner DP	.10	.05	.01
□	72	Fred Howard DP	.10	.05	.01
□	73	Dave Collins	.20	.09	.03
□	74	Sid Monge	.20	.09	.03
□	75	Bill Russell	.35	.16	.04
□	76	John Stearns	.20	.09	.03
□	77	Dave Stieb	1.50	.70	.19
□	78	Ruppert Jones	.20	.09	.03
□	79	Bob Owchinko	.20	.09	.03
□	80	Ron LeFlore	.35	.16	.04
□	81	Ted Sizemore	.20	.09	.03
□	82	Astros Team/Mgr.	.75	.15	.07
		Bill Virdon			
		(Checklist back)			
□	83	Steve Trout	.20	.09	.03
□	84	Gary Lavelle	.20	.09	.03
□	85	Ted Simmons	.35	.16	.04
□	86	Dave Hamilton	.20	.09	.03
□	87	Pepe Frias	.20	.09	.03
□	88	Ken Landreaux	.20	.09	.03
□	89	Don Hood	.20	.09	.03
□	90	Manny Trillo	.20	.09	.03
□	91	Rick Dempsey	.35	.16	.04
□	92	Rick Rhoden	.20	.09	.03
□	93	Dave Roberts DP	.10	.05	.01
□	94	Neil Allen	.35	.16	.04
□	95	Cecil Cooper	.35	.16	.04
□	96	A's Team/Mgr.	.75	.15	.07
		Jim Marshall			
		(Checklist back)			
□	97	Bill Lee	.20	.09	.03
□	98	Jerry Terrell	.20	.09	.03
□	99	Victor Cruz	.20	.09	.03
□	100	Johnny Bench	3.00	1.35	.35
□	101	Aurelio Lopez	.20	.09	.03
□	102	Rich Dauer	.20	.09	.03
□	103	Bill Caudill	.20	.09	.03
□	104	Manny Mota	.35	.16	.04
□	105	Frank Tanana	.50	.23	.06
□	106	Jeff Leonard	.50	.23	.06
□	107	Francisco Barrios	.20	.09	.03
□	108	Bob Horner	.35	.16	.04
□	109	Bill Travers	.20	.09	.03
□	110	Fred Lynn DP	.20	.09	.03
□	111	Bob Knepper	.20	.09	.03
□	112	White Sox Team/Mgr.	.75	.15	.07
		Tony LaRussa			
		(Checklist back)			
□	113	Geoff Zahn	.20	.09	.03
□	114	Juan Beniquez	.20	.09	.03
□	115	Sparky Lyle	.35	.16	.04
□	116	Larry Cox	.20	.09	.03
□	117	Dock Ellis	.20	.09	.03
□	118	Phil Garner	.35	.16	.04
□	119	Sammy Stewart	.20	.09	.03
□	120	Greg Luzinski	.35	.16	.04
□	121	Checklist 1-121	.75	.15	.07
□	122	Dave Rosello DP	.10	.05	.01
□	123	Lynn Jones	.20	.09	.03
□	124	Dave Lemanczyk	.20	.09	.03
□	125	Tony Perez	.75	.35	.09
□	126	Dave Tomlin	.20	.09	.03
□	127	Gary Thomasson	.20	.09	.03
□	128	Tom Burgmeier	.20	.09	.03
□	129	Craig Reynolds	.20	.09	.03
□	130	Amos Otis	.35	.16	.04
□	131	Paul Mitchell	.20	.09	.03
□	132	Biff Pocoroba	.20	.09	.03
□	133	Jerry Turner	.20	.09	.03
□	134	Matt Keough	.20	.09	.03
□	135	Bill Buckner	.35	.16	.04
□	136	Dick Ruthven	.20	.09	.03
□	137	John Castino	.20	.09	.03
□	138	Ross Baumgarten	.20	.09	.03
□	139	Dane Iorg	.20	.09	.03
□	140	Rich Gossage	.50	.23	.06
□	141	Gary Alexander	.20	.09	.03
□	142	Phil Huffman	.20	.09	.03
□	143	Bruce Bochte DP	.10	.05	.01
□	144	Steve Comer	.20	.09	.03
□	145	Darrell Evans	.35	.16	.04
□	146	Bob Welch	.50	.23	.06
□	147	Terry Puhl	.20	.09	.03
□	148	Manny Sanguillen	.35	.16	.04
□	149	Tom Hume	.20	.09	.03
□	150	Jason Thompson	.35	.16	.04
□	151	Tom Hausman DP	.10	.05	.01
□	152	John Fulgham	.20	.09	.03
□	153	Tim Blackwell	.20	.09	.03
□	154	Lary Sorensen	.20	.09	.03
□	155	Jerry Remy	.20	.09	.03
□	156	Tony Brizzolara	.20	.09	.03
□	157	Willie Wilson DP	.50	.23	.06
□	158	Rob Picciolo DP	.10	.05	.01
□	159	Ken Clay	.20	.09	.03
□	160	Eddie Murray	16.00	7.25	2.00
□	161	Larry Christenson	.20	.09	.03
□	162	Bob Randall	.20	.09	.03
□	163	Steve Swisher	.20	.09	.03
□	164	Greg Pryor	.20	.09	.03
□	165	Omar Moreno	.20	.09	.03
□	166	Glenn Abbott	.20	.09	.03
□	167	Jack Clark	.20	.09	.03
□	168	Rick Waits	.20	.09	.03
□	169	Luis Gomez	.20	.09	.03
□	170	Burt Hooton	.35	.16	.04
□	171	Fernando Gonzalez	.20	.09	.03
□	172	Ron Hodges	.20	.09	.03
□	173	John Henry Johnson	.20	.09	.03
□	174	Ray Knight	.35	.16	.04
□	175	Rick Reuschel	.35	.16	.04
□	176	Champ Summers	.20	.09	.03
□	177	Dave Heaverlo	.20	.09	.03
□	178	Tim McCarver	.50	.23	.06
□	179	Ron Davis	.35	.16	.04
□	180	Warren Cromartie	.20	.09	.03
□	181	Moose Haas	.20	.09	.03
□	182	Ken Reitz	.20	.09	.03
□	183	Jim Anderson DP	.10	.05	.01
□	184	Steve Renko DP	.10	.05	.01
□	185	Hal McRae	.50	.23	.06
□	186	Junior Moore	.20	.09	.03
□	187	Alan Ashby	.20	.09	.03
□	188	Terry Crowley	.20	.09	.03
□	189	Kevin Kobel	.20	.09	.03
□	190	Buddy Bell	.35	.16	.04
□	191	Ted Martinez	.20	.09	.03

☐ 192	Braves Team/Mgr.	.75	.15	.07
	Bobby Cox			
	(Checklist back)			
☐ 193	Dave Goltz	.20	.09	.03
☐ 194	Mike Easler	.20	.09	.03
☐ 195	John Montefusco	.20	.09	.03
☐ 196	Lance Parrish	.50	.23	.06
☐ 197	Byron McLaughlin	.20	.09	.03
☐ 198	Dell Alston DP	.10	.05	.01
☐ 199	Mike LaCoss	.20	.09	.03
☐ 200	Jim Rice	1.00	.45	.12
☐ 201	Batting Leaders	.50	.23	.06
	Keith Hernandez			
	Fred Lynn			
☐ 202	Home Run Leaders	.50	.23	.06
	Dave Kingman			
	Gorman Thomas			
☐ 203	RBI Leaders	1.00	.45	.12
	Dave Winfield			
	Don Baylor			
☐ 204	Stolen Base Leaders	.35	.16	.04
	Omar Moreno			
	Willie Wilson			
☐ 205	Victory Leaders	.50	.23	.06
	Joe Niekro			
	Phil Niekro			
	Mike Flanagan			
☐ 206	Strikeout Leaders	4.00	1.80	.50
	J.R. Richard			
	Nolan Ryan			
☐ 207	ERA Leaders	.50	.23	.06
	J.R. Richard			
	Ron Guidry			
☐ 208	Wayne Cage	.20	.09	.03
☐ 209	Von Joshua	.20	.09	.03
☐ 210	Steve Carlton	2.00	.90	.25
☐ 211	Dave Skaggs DP	.10	.05	.01
☐ 212	Dave Roberts	.20	.09	.03
☐ 213	Mike Jorgensen DP	.10	.05	.01
☐ 214	Angels Team/Mgr.	.75	.15	.07
	Jim Fregosi			
	(Checklist back)			
☐ 215	Sixto Lezcano	.20	.09	.03
☐ 216	Phil Mankowski	.20	.09	.03
☐ 217	Ed Halicki	.20	.09	.03
☐ 218	Jose Morales	.20	.09	.03
☐ 219	Steve Mingori	.20	.09	.03
☐ 220	Dave Concepcion	.50	.23	.06
☐ 221	Joe Cannon	.20	.09	.03
☐ 222	Ron Hassey	.20	.09	.03
☐ 223	Bob Sykes	.20	.09	.03
☐ 224	Willie Montanez	.20	.09	.03
☐ 225	Lou Piniella	.35	.16	.04
☐ 226	Bill Stein	.20	.09	.03
☐ 227	Len Barker	.20	.09	.03
☐ 228	Johnny Oates	.35	.16	.04
☐ 229	Jim Bibby	.20	.09	.03
☐ 230	Dave Winfield	6.00	2.70	.75
☐ 231	Steve McCatty	.20	.09	.03
☐ 232	Alan Trammell	6.00	2.70	.75
☐ 233	LaRue Washington	.20	.09	.03
☐ 234	Vern Ruhle	.20	.09	.03
☐ 235	Andre Dawson	5.00	2.20	.60
☐ 236	Marc Hill	.20	.09	.03
☐ 237	Scott McGregor	.35	.16	.04
☐ 238	Rob Wilfong	.20	.09	.03
☐ 239	Don Aase	.20	.09	.03
☐ 240	Dave Kingman	.35	.16	.04
☐ 241	Checklist 122-242	.75	.15	.07
☐ 242	Lamar Johnson	.20	.09	.03
☐ 243	Jerry Augustine	.20	.09	.03
☐ 244	Cardinals Team/Mgr.	.75	.15	.07
	Ken Boyer			
	(Checklist back)			
☐ 245	Phil Niekro	.50	.23	.06
☐ 246	Tim Foli DP	.10	.05	.01
☐ 247	Frank Riccelli	.20	.09	.03
☐ 248	Jamie Quirk	.20	.09	.03
☐ 249	Jim Clancy	.20	.09	.03
☐ 250	Jim Kaat	.50	.23	.06
☐ 251	Kip Young	.20	.09	.03
☐ 252	Ted Cox	.20	.09	.03
☐ 253	John Montague	.20	.09	.03
☐ 254	Paul Dade DP	.10	.05	.01
☐ 255	Dusty Baker DP	.20	.09	.03
☐ 256	Roger Erickson	.20	.09	.03
☐ 257	Larry Herndon	.20	.09	.03
☐ 258	Paul Moskau	.20	.09	.03
☐ 259	Mets Team/Mgr.	.75	.15	.07
	Joe Torre			
	(Checklist back)			
☐ 260	Al Oliver	.50	.23	.06
☐ 261	Dave Chalk	.20	.09	.03
☐ 262	Benny Ayala	.20	.09	.03
☐ 263	Dave LaRoche DP	.10	.05	.01
☐ 264	Bill Robinson	.35	.16	.04
☐ 265	Robin Yount	8.00	3.60	1.00
☐ 266	Bernie Carbo	.20	.09	.03
☐ 267	Dan Schatzeder	.20	.09	.03
☐ 268	Rafael Landestoy	.20	.09	.03
☐ 269	Dave Tobik	.20	.09	.03
☐ 270	Mike Schmidt DP	3.00	1.35	.35
☐ 271	Dick Drago DP	.10	.05	.01
☐ 272	Ralph Garr	.35	.16	.04
☐ 273	Eduardo Rodriguez	.20	.09	.03
☐ 274	Dale Murphy	2.50	1.10	.30
☐ 275	Jerry Koosman	.35	.16	.04
☐ 276	Tom Veryzer	.20	.09	.03
☐ 277	Rick Bosetti	.20	.09	.03
☐ 278	Jim Spencer	.20	.09	.03
☐ 279	Rob Andrews	.20	.09	.03
☐ 280	Gaylord Perry	.75	.35	.09
☐ 281	Paul Blair	.35	.16	.04
☐ 282	Mariners Team/Mgr.	.75	.15	.07
	Darrell Johnson			
	(Checklist back)			
☐ 283	John Ellis	.20	.09	.03
☐ 284	Larry Murray DP	.10	.05	.01
☐ 285	Don Baylor	.50	.23	.06
☐ 286	Darold Knowles DP	.10	.05	.01
☐ 287	John Lowenstein	.20	.09	.03
☐ 288	Dave Rozema	.20	.09	.03
☐ 289	Bruce Bochy	.20	.09	.03
☐ 290	Steve Garvey	1.25	.55	.16
☐ 291	Randy Scarberry	.20	.09	.03
☐ 292	Dale Berra	.20	.09	.03
☐ 293	Elias Sosa	.20	.09	.03
☐ 294	Charlie Spikes	.20	.09	.03
☐ 295	Larry Gura	.20	.09	.03
☐ 296	Dave Rader	.20	.09	.03
☐ 297	Tim Johnson	.20	.09	.03
☐ 298	Ken Holtzman	.20	.09	.03
☐ 299	Steve Henderson	.20	.09	.03
☐ 300	Ron Guidry	.35	.16	.04
☐ 301	Mike Edwards	.20	.09	.03
☐ 302	Dodgers Team/Mgr.	.75	.15	.07
	Tom Lasorda			
	(Checklist back)			
☐ 303	Bill Castro	.20	.09	.03
☐ 304	Butch Wynegar	.20	.09	.03
☐ 305	Randy Jones	.20	.09	.03
☐ 306	Denny Walling	.20	.09	.03

☐ 307	Rick Honeycutt	.35	.16	.04
☐ 308	Mike Hargrove	.35	.16	.04
☐ 309	Larry McWilliams	.20	.09	.03
☐ 310	Dave Parker	.50	.23	.06
☐ 311	Roger Metzger	.20	.09	.03
☐ 312	Mike Barlow	.20	.09	.03
☐ 313	Johnny Grubb	.20	.09	.03
☐ 314	Tim Stoddard	.20	.09	.03
☐ 315	Steve Kemp	.20	.09	.03
☐ 316	Bob Lacey	.20	.09	.03
☐ 317	Mike Anderson DP	.10	.05	.01
☐ 318	Jerry Reuss	.35	.16	.04
☐ 319	Chris Speier	.20	.09	.03
☐ 320	Dennis Eckersley	1.50	.70	.19
☐ 321	Keith Hernandez	.50	.23	.06
☐ 322	Claudell Washington	.35	.16	.04
☐ 323	Mick Kelleher	.20	.09	.03
☐ 324	Tom Underwood	.20	.09	.03
☐ 325	Dan Driessen	.20	.09	.03
☐ 326	Bo McLaughlin	.20	.09	.03
☐ 327	Ray Fosse DP	.10	.05	.01
☐ 328	Twins Team/Mgr.	.75	.15	.07
	Gene Mauch			
	(Checklist back)			
☐ 329	Bert Roberge	.20	.09	.03
☐ 330	Al Cowens	.20	.09	.03
☐ 331	Richie Hebner	.20	.09	.03
☐ 332	Enrique Romo	.20	.09	.03
☐ 333	Jim Norris DP	.10	.05	.01
☐ 334	Jim Beattie	.35	.16	.04
☐ 335	Willie McCovey	1.50	.70	.19
☐ 336	George Medich	.20	.09	.03
☐ 337	Carney Lansford	.50	.23	.06
☐ 338	John Wockenfuss	.20	.09	.03
☐ 339	John D'Acquisto	.20	.09	.03
☐ 340	Ken Singleton	.35	.16	.04
☐ 341	Jim Essian	.20	.09	.03
☐ 342	Odell Jones	.20	.09	.03
☐ 343	Mike Vail	.20	.09	.03
☐ 344	Randy Lerch	.20	.09	.03
☐ 345	Larry Parrish	.35	.16	.04
☐ 346	Buddy Solomon	.20	.09	.03
☐ 347	Harry Chappas	.20	.09	.03
☐ 348	Checklist 243-363	.75	.15	.07
☐ 349	Jack Brohamer	.20	.09	.03
☐ 350	George Hendrick	.35	.16	.04
☐ 351	Bob Davis	.20	.09	.03
☐ 352	Dan Briggs	.20	.09	.03
☐ 353	Andy Hassler	.20	.09	.03
☐ 354	Rick Auerbach	.20	.09	.03
☐ 355	Gary Matthews	.35	.16	.04
☐ 356	Padres Team/Mgr.	.75	.15	.07
	Jerry Coleman			
	(Checklist back)			
☐ 357	Bob McClure	.20	.09	.03
☐ 358	Lou Whitaker	5.00	2.20	.60
☐ 359	Randy Moffitt	.20	.09	.03
☐ 360	Darrell Porter DP	.20	.09	.03
☐ 361	Wayne Garland	.20	.09	.03
☐ 362	Danny Goodwin	.20	.09	.03
☐ 363	Wayne Gross	.20	.09	.03
☐ 364	Ray Burris	.20	.09	.03
☐ 365	Bobby Murcer	.35	.16	.04
☐ 366	Rob Dressler	.20	.09	.03
☐ 367	Billy Smith	.20	.09	.03
☐ 368	Willie Aikens	.35	.16	.04
☐ 369	Jim Kern	.20	.09	.03
☐ 370	Cesar Cedeno	.35	.16	.04
☐ 371	Jack Morris	1.00	.45	.12
☐ 372	Joel Youngblood	.20	.09	.03
☐ 373	Dan Petry DP			
☐ 374	Jim Gantner	.35	.16	.04
☐ 375	Ross Grimsley	.20	.09	.03
☐ 376	Gary Allenson	.20	.09	.03
☐ 377	Junior Kennedy	.20	.09	.03
☐ 378	Jerry Mumphrey	.20	.09	.03
☐ 379	Kevin Bell	.20	.09	.03
☐ 380	Garry Maddox	.20	.09	.03
☐ 381	Cubs Team/Mgr.	.75	.15	.07
	Preston Gomez			
	(Checklist back)			
☐ 382	Dave Freisleben	.20	.09	.03
☐ 383	Ed Ott	.20	.09	.03
☐ 384	Joey McLaughlin	.20	.09	.03
☐ 385	Enos Cabell	.20	.09	.03
☐ 386	Darrell Jackson	.20	.09	.03
☐ 387A	Fred Stanley YL	2.00	.90	.25
☐ 387B	Fred Stanley	.20	.09	.03
	(Red name on front)			
☐ 388	Mike Paxton	.20	.09	.03
☐ 389	Pete LaCock	.20	.09	.03
☐ 390	Fergie Jenkins	.75	.35	.09
☐ 391	Tony Armas DP	.10	.05	.01
☐ 392	Milt Wilcox	.20	.09	.03
☐ 393	Ozzie Smith	18.00	8.00	2.20
☐ 394	Reggie Cleveland	.20	.09	.03
☐ 395	Ellis Valentine	.20	.09	.03
☐ 396	Dan Meyer	.20	.09	.03
☐ 397	Roy Thomas DP	.10	.05	.01
☐ 398	Barry Foote	.20	.09	.03
☐ 399	Mike Proly DP	.10	.05	.01
☐ 400	George Foster	.35	.16	.04
☐ 401	Pete Falcone	.20	.09	.03
☐ 402	Merv Rettenmund	.20	.09	.03
☐ 403	Pete Redfern DP	.10	.05	.01
☐ 404	Orioles Team/Mgr.	.75	.15	.07
	Earl Weaver			
	(Checklist back)			
☐ 405	Dwight Evans	.50	.23	.06
☐ 406	Paul Molitor	14.00	6.25	1.75
☐ 407	Tony Solaita	.20	.09	.03
☐ 408	Bill North	.20	.09	.03
☐ 409	Paul Splittorff	.20	.09	.03
☐ 410	Bobby Bonds	.50	.23	.06
☐ 411	Frank LaCorte	.20	.09	.03
☐ 412	Thad Bosley	.20	.09	.03
☐ 413	Allen Ripley	.20	.09	.03
☐ 414	George Scott	.35	.16	.04
☐ 415	Bill Atkinson	.20	.09	.03
☐ 416	Tom Brookens	.20	.09	.03
☐ 417	Craig Chamberlain DP	.10	.05	.01
☐ 418	Roger Freed DP	.10	.05	.01
☐ 419	Vic Correll	.20	.09	.03
☐ 420	Butch Hobson	.35	.16	.04
☐ 421	Doug Bird	.20	.09	.03
☐ 422	Larry Milbourne	.20	.09	.03
☐ 423	Dave Frost	.20	.09	.03
☐ 424	Yankees Team/Mgr.	.75	.15	.07
	Dick Howser			
	(Checklist back)			
☐ 425	Mark Belanger	.35	.16	.04
☐ 426	Grant Jackson	.20	.09	.03
☐ 427	Tom Hutton DP	.10	.05	.01
☐ 428	Pat Zachry	.20	.09	.03
☐ 429	Duane Kuiper	.20	.09	.03
☐ 430	Larry Hisle DP	.10	.05	.01
☐ 431	Mike Krukow	.20	.09	.03
☐ 432	Willie Norwood	.20	.09	.03
☐ 433	Rich Gale	.20	.09	.03
☐ 434	Johnnie LeMaster	.20	.09	.03
☐ 435	Don Gullett	.35	.16	.04
☐ 436	Billy Almon	.20	.09	.03

☐ 437	Joe Niekro	.35	.16	.04
☐ 438	Dave Revering	.20	.09	.03
☐ 439	Mike Phillips	.20	.09	.03
☐ 440	Don Sutton	.50	.23	.06
☐ 441	Eric Soderholm	.20	.09	.03
☐ 442	Jorge Orta	.20	.09	.03
☐ 443	Mike Parrott	.20	.09	.03
☐ 444	Alvis Woods	.20	.09	.03
☐ 445	Mark Fidrych	.35	.16	.04
☐ 446	Duffy Dyer	.20	.09	.03
☐ 447	Nino Espinosa	.20	.09	.03
☐ 448	Jim Wohlford	.20	.09	.03
☐ 449	Doug Bair	.20	.09	.03
☐ 450	George Brett	16.00	7.25	2.00
☐ 451	Indians Team/Mgr.	.75	.15	.07
	Dave Garcia			
	(Checklist back)			
☐ 452	Steve Dillard	.20	.09	.03
☐ 453	Mike Bacsik	.20	.09	.03
☐ 454	Tom Donohue	.20	.09	.03
☐ 455	Mike Torrez	.20	.09	.03
☐ 456	Frank Taveras	.20	.09	.03
☐ 457	Bert Blyleven	.50	.23	.06
☐ 458	Billy Sample	.20	.09	.03
☐ 459	Mickey Lolich DP	.20	.09	.03
☐ 460	Willie Randolph	.35	.16	.04
☐ 461	Dwayne Murphy	.20	.09	.03
☐ 462	Mike Sadek DP	.10	.05	.01
☐ 463	Jerry Royster	.20	.09	.03
☐ 464	John Denny	.20	.09	.03
☐ 465	Rick Monday	.35	.16	.04
☐ 466	Mike Squires	.20	.09	.03
☐ 467	Jesse Jefferson	.20	.09	.03
☐ 468	Aurelio Rodriguez	.20	.09	.03
☐ 469	Randy Niemann DP	.10	.05	.01
☐ 470	Bob Boone	.20	.09	.03
☐ 471	Hosken Powell DP	.10	.05	.01
☐ 472	Willie Hernandez	.35	.16	.04
☐ 473	Bump Wills	.20	.09	.03
☐ 474	Steve Busby	.20	.09	.03
☐ 475	Cesar Geronimo	.20	.09	.03
☐ 476	Bob Shirley	.20	.09	.03
☐ 477	Buck Martinez	.20	.09	.03
☐ 478	Gil Flores	.20	.09	.03
☐ 479	Expos Team/Mgr.	.75	.15	.07
	Dick Williams			
	(Checklist back)			
☐ 480	Bob Watson	.35	.16	.04
☐ 481	Tom Paciorek	.35	.16	.04
☐ 482	Rickey Henderson UER	50.00	22.00	6.25
	(7 steals at Modesto,			
	should be at Fresno)			
☐ 483	Bo Diaz	.20	.09	.03
☐ 484	Checklist 364-484	.75	.15	.07
☐ 485	Mickey Rivers	.35	.16	.04
☐ 486	Mike Tyson DP	.10	.05	.01
☐ 487	Wayne Nordhagen	.20	.09	.03
☐ 488	Roy Howell	.20	.09	.03
☐ 489	Preston Hanna DP	.10	.05	.01
☐ 490	Lee May	.35	.16	.04
☐ 491	Steve Mura DP	.10	.05	.01
☐ 492	Todd Cruz	.20	.09	.03
☐ 493	Jerry Martin	.20	.09	.03
☐ 494	Craig Minetto	.20	.09	.03
☐ 495	Bake McBride	.35	.16	.04
☐ 496	Silvio Martinez	.20	.09	.03
☐ 497	Jim Mason	.20	.09	.03
☐ 498	Danny Darwin	.20	.09	.03
☐ 499	Giants Team/Mgr.	.75	.15	.07
	Dave Bristol			
	(Checklist back)			
☐ 500	Tom Seaver	3.00	1.35	.35
☐ 501	Rennie Stennett	.20	.09	.03
☐ 502	Rich Wortham DP	.10	.05	.01
☐ 503	Mike Cubbage	.20	.09	.03
☐ 504	Gene Garber	.20	.09	.03
☐ 505	Bert Campaneris	.35	.16	.04
☐ 506	Tom Buskey	.20	.09	.03
☐ 507	Leon Roberts	.20	.09	.03
☐ 508	U.L. Washington	.20	.09	.03
☐ 509	Ed Glynn	.20	.09	.03
☐ 510	Ron Cey	.35	.16	.04
☐ 511	Eric Wilkins	.20	.09	.03
☐ 512	Jose Cardenal	.20	.09	.03
☐ 513	Tom Dixon DP	.10	.05	.01
☐ 514	Steve Ontiveros	.20	.09	.03
☐ 515	Mike Caldwell UER	.20	.09	.03
	1979 loss total reads			
	96 instead of 6#			
☐ 516	Hector Cruz	.20	.09	.03
☐ 517	Don Stanhouse	.20	.09	.03
☐ 518	Nelson Norman	.20	.09	.03
☐ 519	Steve Nicosia	.20	.09	.03
☐ 520	Steve Rogers	.20	.09	.03
☐ 521	Ken Brett	.20	.09	.03
☐ 522	Jim Morrison	.20	.09	.03
☐ 523	Ken Henderson	.20	.09	.03
☐ 524	Jim Wright DP	.10	.05	.01
☐ 525	Clint Hurdle	.20	.09	.03
☐ 526	Phillies Team/Mgr.	.75	.15	.07
	Dallas Green			
	(Checklist back)			
☐ 527	Doug Rau DP	.10	.05	.01
☐ 528	Adrian Devine	.20	.09	.03
☐ 529	Jim Barr	.20	.09	.03
☐ 530	Jim Sundberg DP	.20	.09	.03
☐ 531	Eric Rasmussen	.20	.09	.03
☐ 532	Willie Horton	.35	.16	.04
☐ 533	Checklist 485-605	.75	.15	.07
☐ 534	Andre Thornton	.35	.16	.04
☐ 535	Bob Forsch	.20	.09	.03
☐ 536	Lee Lacy	.20	.09	.03
☐ 537	Alex Trevino	.20	.09	.03
☐ 538	Joe Strain	.20	.09	.03
☐ 539	Rudy May	.20	.09	.03
☐ 540	Pete Rose	4.00	1.80	.50
☐ 541	Miguel Dilone	.20	.09	.03
☐ 542	Joe Coleman	.20	.09	.03
☐ 543	Pat Kelly	.20	.09	.03
☐ 544	Rick Sutcliffe	2.00	.90	.25
☐ 545	Jeff Burroughs	.20	.09	.03
☐ 546	Rick Langford	.20	.09	.03
☐ 547	John Wathan	.20	.09	.03
☐ 548	Dave Rajsich	.20	.09	.03
☐ 549	Larry Wolfe	.20	.09	.03
☐ 550	Ken Griffey	.50	.23	.06
☐ 551	Pirates Team/Mgr.	.75	.15	.07
	Chuck Tanner			
	(Checklist back)			
☐ 552	Bill Nahorodny	.20	.09	.03
☐ 553	Dick Davis	.20	.09	.03
☐ 554	Art Howe	.35	.16	.04
☐ 555	Ed Figueroa	.20	.09	.03
☐ 556	Joe Rudi	.35	.16	.04
☐ 557	Mark Lee	.20	.09	.03
☐ 558	Alfredo Griffin	.20	.09	.03
☐ 559	Dale Murray	.20	.09	.03
☐ 560	Dave Lopes	.35	.16	.04
☐ 561	Eddie Whitson	.20	.09	.03
☐ 562	Joe Wallis	.20	.09	.03
☐ 563	Will McEnaney	.20	.09	.03
☐ 564	Rick Manning	.20	.09	.03

☐ 565	Dennis Leonard	.35	.16	.04
☐ 566	Bud Harrelson	.20	.09	.03
☐ 567	Skip Lockwood	.20	.09	.03
☐ 568	Gary Roenicke	.20	.09	.03
☐ 569	Terry Kennedy	.35	.16	.04
☐ 570	Roy Smalley	.35	.16	.04
☐ 571	Joe Sambito	.20	.09	.03
☐ 572	Jerry Morales DP	.10	.05	.01
☐ 573	Kent Tekulve	.35	.16	.04
☐ 574	Scot Thompson	.20	.09	.03
☐ 575	Ken Kravec	.20	.09	.03
☐ 576	Jim Dwyer	.20	.09	.03
☐ 577	Blue Jays Team/Mgr.	.75	.15	.07
	Bobby Mattick			
	(Checklist back)			
☐ 578	Scott Sanderson	.35	.16	.04
☐ 579	Charlie Moore	.20	.09	.03
☐ 580	Nolan Ryan	20.00	9.00	2.50
☐ 581	Bob Bailor	.20	.09	.03
☐ 582	Brian Doyle	.20	.09	.03
☐ 583	Bob Stinson	.20	.09	.03
☐ 584	Kurt Bevacqua	.20	.09	.03
☐ 585	Al Hrabosky	.20	.09	.03
☐ 586	Mitchell Page	.20	.09	.03
☐ 587	Garry Templeton	.35	.16	.04
☐ 588	Greg Minton	.20	.09	.03
☐ 589	Chet Lemon	.35	.16	.04
☐ 590	Jim Palmer	1.50	.70	.19
☐ 591	Rick Cerone	.20	.09	.03
☐ 592	Jon Matlack	.20	.09	.03
☐ 593	Jesus Alou	.20	.09	.03
☐ 594	Dick Tidrow	.20	.09	.03
☐ 595	Don Money	.20	.09	.03
☐ 596	Rick Matula	.20	.09	.03
☐ 597	Tom Poquette	.20	.09	.03
☐ 598	Fred Kendall DP	.10	.05	.01
☐ 599	Mike Norris	.20	.09	.03
☐ 600	Reggie Jackson	4.00	1.80	.50
☐ 601	Buddy Schultz	.20	.09	.03
☐ 602	Brian Downing	.35	.16	.04
☐ 603	Jack Billingham DP	.10	.05	.01
☐ 604	Glenn Adams	.20	.09	.03
☐ 605	Terry Forster	.20	.09	.03
☐ 606	Reds Team/Mgr.	.75	.15	.07
	John McNamara			
	(Checklist back)			
☐ 607	Woodie Fryman	.20	.09	.03
☐ 608	Alan Bannister	.20	.09	.03
☐ 609	Ron Reed	.20	.09	.03
☐ 610	Willie Stargell	1.25	.55	.16
☐ 611	Jerry Garvin DP	.10	.05	.01
☐ 612	Cliff Johnson	.20	.09	.03
☐ 613	Randy Stein	.20	.09	.03
☐ 614	John Hiller	.20	.09	.03
☐ 615	Doug DeCinces	.35	.16	.04
☐ 616	Gene Richards	.20	.09	.03
☐ 617	Joaquin Andujar	.35	.16	.04
☐ 618	Bob Montgomery DP	.10	.05	.01
☐ 619	Sergio Ferrer	.20	.09	.03
☐ 620	Richie Zisk	.20	.09	.03
☐ 621	Bob Grich	.35	.16	.04
☐ 622	Mario Soto	.20	.09	.03
☐ 623	Gorman Thomas	.35	.16	.04
☐ 624	Lerrin LaGrow	.20	.09	.03
☐ 625	Chris Chambliss	.35	.16	.04
☐ 626	Tigers Team/Mgr.	.75	.15	.07
	Sparky Anderson			
	(Checklist back)			
☐ 627	Pedro Borbon	.20	.09	.03
☐ 628	Doug Capilla	.20	.09	.03
☐ 629	Jim Todd	.20	.09	.03

☐ 630	Larry Bowa	.35	.16	.04
☐ 631	Mark Littell	.20	.09	.03
☐ 632	Barry Bonnell	.20	.09	.03
☐ 633	Bob Apodaca	.20	.09	.03
☐ 634	Glenn Borgmann DP	.10	.05	.01
☐ 635	John Candelaria	.35	.16	.04
☐ 636	Toby Harrah	.35	.16	.04
☐ 637	Joe Simpson	.20	.09	.03
☐ 638	Mark Clear	.20	.09	.03
☐ 639	Larry Biittner	.20	.09	.03
☐ 640	Mike Flanagan	.35	.16	.04
☐ 641	Ed Kranepool	.20	.09	.03
☐ 642	Ken Forsch DP	.10	.05	.01
☐ 643	John Mayberry	.20	.09	.03
☐ 644	Charlie Hough	.35	.16	.04
☐ 645	Rick Burleson	.20	.09	.03
☐ 646	Checklist 606-726	.75	.15	.07
☐ 647	Milt May	.20	.09	.03
☐ 648	Roy White	.35	.16	.04
☐ 649	Tom Griffin	.20	.09	.03
☐ 650	Joe Morgan	1.50	.70	.19
☐ 651	Rollie Fingers	.75	.35	.09
☐ 652	Mario Mendoza	.20	.09	.03
☐ 653	Stan Bahnsen	.20	.09	.03
☐ 654	Bruce Boisclair DP	.10	.05	.01
☐ 655	Tug McGraw	.35	.16	.04
☐ 656	Larvell Blanks	.20	.09	.03
☐ 657	Dave Edwards	.20	.09	.03
☐ 658	Chris Knapp	.20	.09	.03
☐ 659	Brewers Team/Mgr.	.75	.15	.07
	George Bamberger			
	(Checklist back)			
☐ 660	Rusty Staub	.35	.16	.04
☐ 661	Orioles Rookies	.35	.16	.04
	Mark Corey			
	Dave Ford			
	Wayne Krenchicki			
☐ 662	Red Sox Rookies	.35	.16	.04
	Joel Finch			
	Mike O'Berry			
	Chuck Rainey			
☐ 663	Angels Rookies	.50	.23	.06
	Ralph Botting			
	Bob Clark			
	Dickie Thon			
☐ 664	White Sox Rookies	.35	.16	.04
	Mike Colbern			
	Guy Hoffman			
	Dewey Robinson			
☐ 665	Indians Rookies	.50	.23	.06
	Larry Andersen			
	Bobby Cuellar			
	Sandy Wihtol			
☐ 666	Tigers Rookies	.35	.16	.04
	Mike Chris			
	Al Greene			
	Bruce Robbins			
☐ 667	Royals Rookies	2.00	.90	.25
	Renie Martin			
	Bill Paschall			
	Dan Quisenberry			
☐ 668	Brewers Rookies	.35	.16	.04
	Danny Boitano			
	Willie Mueller			
	Lenn Sakata			
☐ 669	Twins Rookies	.35	.16	.04
	Dan Graham			
	Rick Sofield			
	Gary Ward			
☐ 670	Yankees Rookies	.35	.16	.04
	Bobby Brown			

Brad Gulden
Darryl Jones
☐ 671 A's Rookies............ 1.00 .45 .12
Derek Bryant
Brian Kingman
Mike Morgan
☐ 672 Mariners Rookies......... .35 .16 .04
Charlie Beamon
Rodney Craig
Rafael Vasquez
☐ 673 Rangers Rookies......... .35 .16 .04
Brian Allard
Jerry Don Gleaton
Greg Mahlberg
☐ 674 Blue Jays Rookies...... .35 .16 .04
Butch Edge
Pat Kelly
Ted Wilborn
☐ 675 Braves Rookies.......... .35 .16 .04
Bruce Benedict
Larry Bradford
Eddie Miller
☐ 676 Cubs Rookies............ .35 .16 .04
Dave Geisel
Steve Macko
Karl Pagel
☐ 677 Reds Rookies............ .35 .16 .04
Art DeFreites
Frank Pastore
Harry Spilman
☐ 678 Astros Rookies.......... .35 .16 .04
Reggie Baldwin
Alan Knicely
Pete Ladd
☐ 679 Dodgers Rookies .... .50 .23 .06
Joe Beckwith
Mickey Hatcher
Dave Patterson
☐ 680 Expos Rookies .... .50 .23 .06
Tony Bernazard
Randy Miller
John Tamargo
☐ 681 Mets Rookies............ 1.00 .45 .12
Dan Norman
Jesse Orosco
Mike Scott
☐ 682 Phillies Rookies......... .35 .16 .04
Ramon Aviles
Dickie Noles
Kevin Saucier
☐ 683 Pirates Rookies.......... .35 .16 .04
Dorian Boyland
Alberto Lois
Harry Saferight
☐ 684 Cardinals Rookies........ .50 .23 .06
George Frazier
Tom Herr
Dan O'Brien
☐ 685 Padres Rookies.......... .35 .16 .04
Tim Flannery
Brian Greer
Jim Wilhelm
☐ 686 Giants Rookies........... .35 .16 .04
Greg Johnston
Dennis Littlejohn
Phil Nastu
☐ 687 Mike Heath DP .... .10 .05 .01
☐ 688 Steve Stone.............. .35 .16 .04
☐ 689 Red Sox Team/Mgr...... .75 .15 .07
Don Zimmer
(Checklist back)

☐ 690 Tommy John................ .50 .23 .06
☐ 691 Ivan DeJesus............... .20 .09 .03
☐ 692 Rawly Eastwick DP ...... .10 .05 .01
☐ 693 Craig Kusick................ .20 .09 .03
☐ 694 Jim Rooker .... .20 .09 .03
☐ 695 Reggie Smith.............. .35 .16 .04
☐ 696 Julio Gonzalez .... .20 .09 .03
☐ 697 David Clyde................ .20 .09 .03
☐ 698 Oscar Gamble............. .35 .16 .04
☐ 699 Floyd Bannister .... .20 .09 .03
☐ 700 Rod Carew DP .... 1.00 .45 .12
☐ 701 Ken Oberkfell .... .20 .09 .03
☐ 702 Ed Farmer .... .20 .09 .03
☐ 703 Otto Velez .... .20 .09 .03
☐ 704 Gene Tenace .... .35 .16 .04
☐ 705 Freddie Patek .... .20 .09 .03
☐ 706 Tippy Martinez .... .35 .16 .04
☐ 707 Elliott Maddox .... .20 .09 .03
☐ 708 Bob Tolan .... .20 .09 .03
☐ 709 Pat Underwood .... .20 .09 .03
☐ 710 Graig Nettles .... .35 .16 .04
☐ 711 Bob Galasso .... .20 .09 .03
☐ 712 Rodney Scott .... .20 .09 .03
☐ 713 Terry Whitfield .... .20 .09 .03
☐ 714 Fred Norman .... .20 .09 .03
☐ 715 Sal Bando .... .35 .16 .04
☐ 716 Lynn McGlothen .... .20 .09 .03
☐ 717 Mickey Klutts DP .... .10 .05 .01
☐ 718 Greg Gross .... .20 .09 .03
☐ 719 Don Robinson .... .35 .16 .04
☐ 720 Carl Yastrzemski DP .... 1.50 .70 .19
☐ 721 Paul Hartzell .... .20 .09 .03
☐ 722 Jose Cruz.................. .35 .16 .04
☐ 723 Shane Rawley .... .20 .09 .03
☐ 724 Jerry White .... .20 .09 .03
☐ 725 Rick Wise.................. .20 .09 .03
☐ 726 Steve Yeager............... .35 .09 .03

1981 Topps

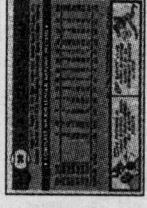

The cards in this 726-card set measure 2 1/2" by 3 1/2". League Leaders (1-8), Record Breakers (201-208), and Post-season cards (401-404) are topical subsets found in this set marketed by Topps in 1981. The team cards are all grouped together (661-686) and feature team checklist backs and a very small photo of the team's manager in the upper right corner of the obverse. The obverses carry the player's position and team in a baseball cap design, and the company name is printed in a small baseball. The backs are red and gray. The 66 double-printed cards are noted in the checklist by DP. The more

notable Rookie Cards in the set include Harold Baines, Kirk Gibson, Bruce Hurst, Tim Raines, Jeff Reardon, and Fernando Valenzuela. Other Rookie Cards in the set are Mike Boddicker, Hubie Brooks, Bill Gullickson, Charlie Leibrandt, Lloyd Moseby, Tony Pena, and John Tudor.

	NRMT-MT	EXC	G-VG
COMPLETE SET (726)	60.00	27.00	7.50
COMMON CARD (1-726)	.15	.07	.02
COMMON CARD DP	.07	.03	.01

☐ 1	Batting Leaders	2.50	1.10	.30
	George Brett			
	Bill Buckner			
☐ 2	Home Run Leaders	1.00	.45	.12
	Reggie Jackson			
	Ben Oglivie			
	Mike Schmidt			
☐ 3	RBI Leaders	.50	.23	.06
	Cecil Cooper			
	Mike Schmidt			
☐ 4	Stolen Base Leaders	1.50	.70	.19
	Rickey Henderson			
	Ron LeFlore			
☐ 5	Victory Leaders	.40	.18	.05
	Steve Stone			
	Steve Carlton			
☐ 6	Strikeout Leaders	.40	.18	.05
	Len Barker			
	Steve Carlton			
☐ 7	ERA Leaders	.40	.18	.05
	Rudy May			
	Don Sutton			
☐ 8	Leading Firemen	.40	.18	.05
	Dan Quisenberry			
	Rollie Fingers			
	Tom Hume			
☐ 9	Pete LaCock DP	.07	.03	.01
☐ 10	Mike Flanagan	.25	.11	.03
☐ 11	Jim Wohlford DP	.07	.03	.01
☐ 12	Mark Clear	.15	.07	.02
☐ 13	Joe Charboneau	.40	.18	.05
☐ 14	John Tudor	.40	.18	.05
☐ 15	Larry Parrish	.15	.07	.02
☐ 16	Ron Davis	.15	.07	.02
☐ 17	Cliff Johnson	.15	.07	.02
☐ 18	Glenn Adams	.15	.07	.02
☐ 19	Jim Clancy	.15	.07	.02
☐ 20	Jeff Burroughs	.15	.07	.02
☐ 21	Ron Oester	.15	.07	.02
☐ 22	Danny Darwin	.25	.11	.03
☐ 23	Alex Trevino	.15	.07	.02
☐ 24	Don Stanhouse	.15	.07	.02
☐ 25	Sixto Lezcano	.15	.07	.02
☐ 26	U.L. Washington	.15	.07	.02
☐ 27	Champ Summers DP	.07	.03	.01
☐ 28	Enrique Romo	.15	.07	.02
☐ 29	Gene Tenace	.25	.11	.03
☐ 30	Jack Clark	.25	.11	.03
☐ 31	Checklist 1-121 DP	.15	.07	.02
☐ 32	Ken Oberkfell	.15	.07	.02
☐ 33	Rick Honeycutt	.15	.07	.02
☐ 34	Aurelio Rodriguez	.15	.07	.02
☐ 35	Mitchell Page	.15	.07	.02
☐ 36	Ed Farmer	.15	.07	.02
☐ 37	Gary Roenicke	.15	.07	.02
☐ 38	Win Remmerswaal	.15	.07	.02
☐ 39	Tom Veryzer	.15	.07	.02
☐ 40	Tug McGraw	.25	.11	.03

☐ 41	Ranger Rookies	.15	.07	.02
	Bob Babcock			
	John Butcher			
	Jerry Don Gleaton			
☐ 42	Jerry White DP	.07	.03	.01
☐ 43	Jose Morales	.15	.07	.02
☐ 44	Larry McWilliams	.15	.07	.02
☐ 45	Enos Cabell	.15	.07	.02
☐ 46	Rick Bosetti	.15	.07	.02
☐ 47	Ken Brett	.15	.07	.02
☐ 48	Dave Skaggs	.15	.07	.02
☐ 49	Bob Shirley	.15	.07	.02
☐ 50	Dave Lopes	.25	.11	.03
☐ 51	Bill Robinson DP	.15	.07	.02
☐ 52	Hector Cruz	.15	.07	.02
☐ 53	Kevin Saucier	.15	.07	.02
☐ 54	Ivan DeJesus	.15	.07	.02
☐ 55	Mike Norris	.15	.07	.02
☐ 56	Buck Martinez	.15	.07	.02
☐ 57	Dave Roberts	.15	.07	.02
☐ 58	Joel Youngblood	.15	.07	.02
☐ 59	Dan Petry	.25	.11	.03
☐ 60	Willie Randolph	.25	.11	.03
☐ 61	Butch Wynegar	.15	.07	.02
☐ 62	Joe Pettini	.15	.07	.02
☐ 63	Steve Renko DP	.07	.03	.01
☐ 64	Brian Asselstine	.15	.07	.02
☐ 65	Scott McGregor	.15	.07	.02
☐ 66	Royals Rookies	.15	.07	.02
	Manny Castillo			
	Tim Ireland			
	Mike Jones			
☐ 67	Ken Kravec	.15	.07	.02
☐ 68	Matt Alexander DP	.07	.03	.01
☐ 69	Ed Halicki	.15	.07	.02
☐ 70	Al Oliver DP	.15	.07	.02
☐ 71	Hal Dues	.15	.07	.02
☐ 72	Barry Evans DP	.07	.03	.01
☐ 73	Doug Bair	.15	.07	.02
☐ 74	Mike Hargrove	.25	.11	.03
☐ 75	Reggie Smith	.25	.11	.03
☐ 76	Mario Mendoza	.15	.07	.02
☐ 77	Mike Barlow	.15	.07	.02
☐ 78	Steve Dillard	.15	.07	.02
☐ 79	Bruce Robbins	.15	.07	.02
☐ 80	Rusty Staub	.25	.11	.03
☐ 81	Dave Stapleton	.15	.07	.02
☐ 82	Astros Rookies DP	.15	.07	.02
	Danny Heep			
	Alan Knicely			
	Bobby Sprowl			
☐ 83	Mike Proly	.15	.07	.02
☐ 84	Johnnie LeMaster	.15	.07	.02
☐ 85	Mike Caldwell	.15	.07	.02
☐ 86	Wayne Gross	.15	.07	.02
☐ 87	Rick Camp	.15	.07	.02
☐ 88	Joe Lefebvre	.15	.07	.02
☐ 89	Darrell Jackson	.15	.07	.02
☐ 90	Bake McBride	.15	.07	.02
☐ 91	Tim Stoddard DP	.07	.03	.01
☐ 92	Mike Easler	.15	.07	.02
☐ 93	Ed Glynn DP	.15	.07	.02
☐ 94	Harry Spilman DP	.07	.03	.01
☐ 95	Jim Sundberg	.25	.11	.03
☐ 96	A's Rookies	.15	.07	.02
	Dave Beard			
	Ernie Camacho			
	Pat Dempsey			
☐ 97	Chris Speier	.15	.07	.02
☐ 98	Clint Hurdle	.15	.07	.02
☐ 99	Eric Wilkins	.15	.07	.02

☐ 100	Rod Carew	1.50	.70	.19
☐ 101	Benny Ayala	.15	.07	.02
☐ 102	Dave Tobik	.15	.07	.02
☐ 103	Jerry Martin	.15	.07	.02
☐ 104	Terry Forster	.15	.07	.02
☐ 105	Jose Cruz	.25	.11	.03
☐ 106	Don Money	.15	.07	.02
☐ 107	Rich Wortham	.15	.07	.02
☐ 108	Bruce Benedict	.15	.07	.02
☐ 109	Mike Scott	.15	.07	.02
☐ 110	Carl Yastrzemski	1.50	.70	.19
☐ 111	Greg Minton	.15	.07	.02
☐ 112	White Sox Rookies	.15	.07	.02
	Rusty Kuntz			
	Fran Mullins			
	Leo Sutherland			
☐ 113	Mike Phillips	.15	.07	.02
☐ 114	Tom Underwood	.15	.07	.02
☐ 115	Roy Smalley	.15	.07	.02
☐ 116	Joe Simpson	.15	.07	.02
☐ 117	Pete Falcone	.15	.07	.02
☐ 118	Kurt Bevacqua	.15	.07	.02
☐ 119	Tippy Martinez	.25	.11	.03
☐ 120	Larry Bowa	.25	.11	.03
☐ 121	Larry Harlow	.15	.07	.02
☐ 122	John Denny	.15	.07	.02
☐ 123	Al Cowens	.15	.07	.02
☐ 124	Jerry Garvin	.15	.07	.02
☐ 125	Andre Dawson	2.00	.90	.25
☐ 126	Charlie Leibrandt	.40	.18	.05
☐ 127	Rudy Law	.15	.07	.02
☐ 128	Gary Allenson DP	.07	.03	.01
☐ 129	Art Howe	.25	.11	.03
☐ 130	Larry Gura	.15	.07	.02
☐ 131	Keith Moreland	.25	.11	.03
☐ 132	Tommy Boggs	.15	.07	.02
☐ 133	Jeff Cox	.15	.07	.02
☐ 134	Steve Mura	.15	.07	.02
☐ 135	Gorman Thomas	.25	.11	.03
☐ 136	Doug Capilla	.15	.07	.02
☐ 137	Hosken Powell	.15	.07	.02
☐ 138	Rich Dotson DP	.25	.11	.03
☐ 139	Oscar Gamble	.15	.07	.02
☐ 140	Bob Forsch	.15	.07	.02
☐ 141	Miguel Dilone	.15	.07	.02
☐ 142	Jackson Todd	.15	.07	.02
☐ 143	Dan Meyer	.15	.07	.02
☐ 144	Allen Ripley	.15	.07	.02
☐ 145	Mickey Rivers	.25	.11	.03
☐ 146	Bobby Castillo	.15	.07	.02
☐ 147	Dale Berra	.15	.07	.02
☐ 148	Randy Niemann	.15	.07	.02
☐ 149	Joe Nolan	.15	.07	.02
☐ 150	Mark Fidrych	.25	.11	.03
☐ 151	Claudell Washington	.15	.07	.02
☐ 152	John Urrea	.15	.07	.02
☐ 153	Tom Poquette	.15	.07	.02
☐ 154	Rick Langford	.15	.07	.02
☐ 155	Chris Chambliss	.25	.11	.03
☐ 156	Bob McClure	.15	.07	.02
☐ 157	John Wathan	.15	.07	.02
☐ 158	Fergie Jenkins	.40	.18	.05
☐ 159	Brian Doyle	.15	.07	.02
☐ 160	Garry Maddox	.15	.07	.02
☐ 161	Dan Graham	.15	.07	.02
☐ 162	Doug Corbett	.15	.07	.02
☐ 163	Bill Almon	.15	.07	.02
☐ 164	LaMarr Hoyt	.25	.11	.03
☐ 165	Tony Scott	.15	.07	.02
☐ 166	Floyd Bannister	.15	.07	.02
☐ 167	Terry Whitfield	.15	.07	.02
☐ 168	Don Robinson DP	.07	.03	.01
☐ 169	John Mayberry	.15	.07	.02
☐ 170	Ross Grimsley	.15	.07	.02
☐ 171	Gene Richards	.15	.07	.02
☐ 172	Gary Woods	.15	.07	.02
☐ 173	Bump Wills	.15	.07	.02
☐ 174	Doug Rau	.15	.07	.02
☐ 175	Dave Collins	.15	.07	.02
☐ 176	Mike Krukow	.15	.07	.02
☐ 177	Rick Peters	.15	.07	.02
☐ 178	Jim Essian DP	.07	.03	.01
☐ 179	Rudy May	.15	.07	.02
☐ 180	Pete Rose	3.00	1.35	.35
☐ 181	Elias Sosa	.15	.07	.02
☐ 182	Bob Grich	.25	.11	.03
☐ 183	Dick Davis DP	.07	.03	.01
☐ 184	Jim Dwyer	.15	.07	.02
☐ 185	Dennis Leonard	.15	.07	.02
☐ 186	Wayne Nordhagen	.15	.07	.02
☐ 187	Mike Parrott	.15	.07	.02
☐ 188	Doug DeCinces	.25	.11	.03
☐ 189	Craig Swan	.15	.07	.02
☐ 190	Cesar Cedeno	.25	.11	.03
☐ 191	Rick Sutcliffe	.40	.18	.05
☐ 192	Braves Rookies	.25	.11	.03
	Terry Harper			
	Ed Miller			
	Rafael Ramirez			
☐ 193	Pete Vuckovich	.25	.11	.03
☐ 194	Rod Scurry	.15	.07	.02
☐ 195	Rich Murray	.15	.07	.02
☐ 196	Duffy Dyer	.15	.07	.02
☐ 197	Jim Kern	.15	.07	.02
☐ 198	Jerry Dybzinski	.15	.07	.02
☐ 199	Chuck Rainey	.15	.07	.02
☐ 200	George Foster	.25	.11	.03
☐ 201	Johnny Bench RB	.75	.35	.09
	Most homers,			
	lifetime, catcher			
☐ 202	Steve Carlton RB	.75	.35	.09
	Most strikeouts,			
	lefthander, lifetime			
☐ 203	Bill Gullickson RB	.40	.18	.05
	Most strikeouts,			
	game, rookie			
☐ 204	Ron LeFlore and	.25	.11	.03
	Rodney Scott RB			
	Most stolen bases,			
	teammates, season			
☐ 205	Pete Rose RB	1.50	.70	.19
	Most cons. seasons			
	600 or more at-bats			
☐ 206	Mike Schmidt RB	1.50	.70	.19
	Most homers, third			
	baseman, season			
☐ 207	Ozzie Smith RB	2.00	.90	.25
	Most assists,			
	season, shortstop			
☐ 208	Willie Wilson RB	.25	.11	.03
	Most at-bats, season			
☐ 209	Dickie Thon DP	.25	.11	.03
☐ 210	Jim Palmer	1.00	.45	.12
☐ 211	Derrel Thomas	.15	.07	.02
☐ 212	Steve Nicosia	.15	.07	.02
☐ 213	Al Holland	.15	.07	.02
☐ 214	Angels Rookies	.15	.07	.02
	Ralph Botting			
	Jim Dorsey			
	John Harris			
☐ 215	Larry Hisle	.15	.07	.02
☐ 216	John Henry Johnson	.15	.07	.02

☐ 217	Rich Hebner	.15	.07	.02
☐ 218	Paul Splittorff	.15	.07	.02
☐ 219	Ken Landreaux	.15	.07	.02
☐ 220	Tom Seaver	2.00	.90	.25
☐ 221	Bob Davis	.15	.07	.02
☐ 222	Jorge Orta	.15	.07	.02
☐ 223	Roy Lee Jackson	.15	.07	.02
☐ 224	Pat Zachry	.15	.07	.02
☐ 225	Ruppert Jones	.15	.07	.02
☐ 226	Manny Sanguillen DP	.07	.03	.01
☐ 227	Fred Martinez	.15	.07	.02
☐ 228	Tom Paciorek	.25	.11	.03
☐ 229	Rollie Fingers	.40	.18	.05
☐ 230	George Hendrick	.25	.11	.03
☐ 231	Joe Beckwith	.15	.07	.02
☐ 232	Mickey Klutts	.15	.07	.02
☐ 233	Skip Lockwood	.15	.07	.02
☐ 234	Lou Whitaker	1.50	.70	.19
☐ 235	Scott Sanderson	.25	.11	.03
☐ 236	Mike Ivie	.15	.07	.02
☐ 237	Charlie Moore	.15	.07	.02
☐ 238	Willie Hernandez	.25	.11	.03
☐ 239	Rick Miller DP	.07	.03	.01
☐ 240	Nolan Ryan	8.00	3.60	1.00
☐ 241	Checklist 122-242 DP	.15	.07	.02
☐ 242	Chet Lemon	.15	.07	.02
☐ 243	Sal Butera	.15	.07	.02
☐ 244	Cardinals Rookies	.15	.07	.02
	Tito Landrum			
	Al Olmsted			
	Andy Rincon			
☐ 245	Ed Figueroa	.15	.07	.02
☐ 246	Ed Ott DP	.07	.03	.01
☐ 247	Glenn Hubbard DP	.07	.03	.01
☐ 248	Joey McLaughlin	.15	.07	.02
☐ 249	Larry Cox	.15	.07	.02
☐ 250	Ron Guidry	.25	.11	.03
☐ 251	Tom Brookens	.15	.07	.02
☐ 252	Victor Cruz	.15	.07	.02
☐ 253	Dave Bergman	.15	.07	.02
☐ 254	Ozzie Smith	5.00	2.20	.60
☐ 255	Mark Littell	.15	.07	.02
☐ 256	Bombo Rivera	.15	.07	.02
☐ 257	Rennie Stennett	.15	.07	.02
☐ 258	Joe Price	.15	.07	.02
☐ 259	Mets Rookies	.40	.18	.05
	Juan Berenguer			
	Hubie Brooks			
	Mookie Wilson			
☐ 260	Ron Cey	.25	.11	.03
☐ 261	Rickey Henderson	6.00	2.70	.75
☐ 262	Sammy Stewart	.15	.07	.02
☐ 263	Brian Downing	.25	.11	.03
☐ 264	Jim Norris	.15	.07	.02
☐ 265	John Candelaria	.25	.11	.03
☐ 266	Tom Herr	.25	.11	.03
☐ 267	Stan Bahnsen	.15	.07	.02
☐ 268	Jerry Royster	.15	.07	.02
☐ 269	Ken Forsch	.15	.07	.02
☐ 270	Greg Luzinski	.25	.11	.03
☐ 271	Bill Castro	.15	.07	.02
☐ 272	Bruce Kimm	.15	.07	.02
☐ 273	Stan Papi	.15	.07	.02
☐ 274	Craig Chamberlain	.15	.07	.02
☐ 275	Dwight Evans	.40	.18	.05
☐ 276	Dan Spillner	.15	.07	.02
☐ 277	Alfredo Griffin	.15	.07	.02
☐ 278	Rick Sofield	.15	.07	.02
☐ 279	Bob Knepper	.15	.07	.02
☐ 280	Ken Griffey	.25	.11	.03
☐ 281	Fred Stanley	.15	.07	.02
☐ 282	Mariners Rookies	.15	.07	.02
	Rick Anderson			
	Greg Biercevicz			
	Rodney Craig			
☐ 283	Billy Sample	.15	.07	.02
☐ 284	Brian Kingman	.15	.07	.02
☐ 285	Jerry Turner	.15	.07	.02
☐ 286	Dave Frost	.15	.07	.02
☐ 287	Lenn Sakata	.15	.07	.02
☐ 288	Bob Clark	.15	.07	.02
☐ 289	Mickey Hatcher	.15	.07	.02
☐ 290	Bob Boone DP	.25	.11	.03
☐ 291	Aurelio Lopez	.15	.07	.02
☐ 292	Mike Squires	.15	.07	.02
☐ 293	Charlie Lea	.15	.07	.02
☐ 294	Mike Tyson DP	.07	.03	.01
☐ 295	Hal McRae	.40	.18	.05
☐ 296	Bill Nahorodny DP	.07	.03	.01
☐ 297	Bob Bailor	.15	.07	.02
☐ 298	Buddy Solomon	.15	.07	.02
☐ 299	Elliott Maddox	.15	.07	.02
☐ 300	Paul Molitor	2.00	.90	.25
☐ 301	Matt Keough	.15	.07	.02
☐ 302	Dodgers Rookies	3.00	1.35	.35
	Jack Perconte			
	Mike Scioscia			
	Fernando Valenzuela			
☐ 303	Johnny Oates	.15	.07	.02
☐ 304	John Castino	.15	.07	.02
☐ 305	Ken Clay	.15	.07	.02
☐ 306	Juan Beniquez DP	.07	.03	.01
☐ 307	Gene Garber	.15	.07	.02
☐ 308	Rick Manning	.15	.07	.02
☐ 309	Luis Salazar	.15	.07	.02
☐ 310	Vida Blue DP	.15	.07	.02
☐ 311	Freddie Patek	.15	.07	.02
☐ 312	Rick Rhoden	.15	.07	.02
☐ 313	Luis Pujols	.15	.07	.02
☐ 314	Rich Dauer	.15	.07	.02
☐ 315	Kirk Gibson	4.00	1.80	.50
☐ 316	Craig Minetto	.15	.07	.02
☐ 317	Lonnie Smith	.15	.07	.02
☐ 318	Steve Yeager	.15	.07	.02
☐ 319	Rowland Office	.15	.07	.02
☐ 320	Tom Burgmeier	.15	.07	.02
☐ 321	Leon Durham	.25	.11	.03
☐ 322	Neil Allen	.15	.07	.02
☐ 323	Jim Morrison DP	.07	.03	.01
☐ 324	Mike Willis	.15	.07	.02
☐ 325	Ray Knight	.25	.11	.03
☐ 326	Biff Pocoroba	.15	.07	.02
☐ 327	Moose Haas	.15	.07	.02
☐ 328	Twins Rookies	.15	.07	.02
	Dave Engle			
	Greg Johnston			
	Gary Ward			
☐ 329	Joaquin Andujar	.25	.11	.03
☐ 330	Frank White	.25	.11	.03
☐ 331	Dennis Lamp	.15	.07	.02
☐ 332	Lee Lacy DP	.07	.03	.01
☐ 333	Sid Monge	.15	.07	.02
☐ 334	Dane Iorg	.15	.07	.02
☐ 335	Rick Cerone	.15	.07	.02
☐ 336	Eddie Whitson	.15	.07	.02
☐ 337	Lynn Jones	.15	.07	.02
☐ 338	Checklist 243-363	.40	.18	.05
☐ 339	John Ellis	.15	.07	.02
☐ 340	Bruce Kison	.15	.07	.02
☐ 341	Dwayne Murphy	.15	.07	.02
☐ 342	Eric Rasmussen DP	.07	.03	.01
☐ 343	Frank Taveras	.15	.07	.02

☐ 344 Byron McLaughlin	.15	.07	.02
☐ 345 Warren Cromartie	.15	.07	.02
☐ 346 Larry Christenson DP	.07	.03	.01
☐ 347 Harold Baines	4.00	1.80	.50
☐ 348 Bob Sykes	.15	.07	.02
☐ 349 Glenn Hoffman	.15	.07	.02
☐ 350 J.R. Richard	.25	.11	.03
☐ 351 Otto Velez	.15	.07	.02
☐ 352 Dick Tidrow DP	.07	.03	.01
☐ 353 Terry Kennedy	.15	.07	.02
☐ 354 Mario Soto	.15	.07	.02
☐ 355 Bob Horner	.25	.11	.03
☐ 356 Padres Rookies	.15	.07	.02
George Stablein			
Craig Stimac			
Tom Tellmann			
☐ 357 Jim Slaton	.15	.07	.02
☐ 358 Mark Wagner	.15	.07	.02
☐ 359 Tom Hausman	.15	.07	.02
☐ 360 Willie Wilson	.15	.07	.02
☐ 361 Joe Strain	.15	.07	.02
☐ 362 Bo Diaz	.15	.07	.02
☐ 363 Geoff Zahn	.15	.07	.02
☐ 364 Mike Davis	.15	.07	.02
☐ 365 Graig Nettles DP	.25	.11	.03
☐ 366 Mike Ramsey	.15	.07	.02
☐ 367 Dennis Martinez	.25	.11	.03
☐ 368 Leon Roberts	.15	.07	.02
☐ 369 Frank Tanana	.25	.11	.03
☐ 370 Dave Winfield	3.50	1.55	.45
☐ 371 Charlie Hough	.25	.11	.03
☐ 372 Jay Johnstone	.25	.11	.03
☐ 373 Pat Underwood	.15	.07	.02
☐ 374 Tommy Hutton	.15	.07	.02
☐ 375 Dave Concepcion	.25	.11	.03
☐ 376 Ron Reed	.15	.07	.02
☐ 377 Jerry Morales	.15	.07	.02
☐ 378 Dave Rader	.15	.07	.02
☐ 379 Lary Sorensen	.15	.07	.02
☐ 380 Willie Stargell	1.00	.45	.12
☐ 381 Cubs Rookies	.15	.07	.02
Carlos Lezcano			
Steve Macko			
Randy Martz			
☐ 382 Paul Mirabella	.15	.07	.02
☐ 383 Eric Soderholm DP	.07	.03	.01
☐ 384 Mike Sadek	.15	.07	.02
☐ 385 Joe Sambito	.15	.07	.02
☐ 386 Dave Edwards	.15	.07	.02
☐ 387 Phil Niekro	.60	.25	.07
☐ 388 Andre Thornton	.25	.11	.03
☐ 389 Marty Pattin	.15	.07	.02
☐ 390 Cesar Geronimo	.15	.07	.02
☐ 391 Dave Lemanczyk DP	.07	.03	.01
☐ 392 Lance Parrish	.40	.18	.05
☐ 393 Broderick Perkins	.15	.07	.02
☐ 394 Woodie Fryman	.15	.07	.02
☐ 395 Scot Thompson	.15	.07	.02
☐ 396 Bill Campbell	.15	.07	.02
☐ 397 Julio Cruz	.15	.07	.02
☐ 398 Ross Baumgarten	.15	.07	.02
☐ 399 Orioles Rookies	.40	.18	.05
Mike Boddicker			
Mark Corey			
Floyd Rayford			
☐ 400 Reggie Jackson	3.00	1.35	.35
☐ 401 AL Champs	2.00	.90	.25
Royals sweep Yanks			
(George Brett swinging)			
☐ 402 NL Champs	.40	.18	.05
Phillies squeak			

past Astros			
(Phillies celebrating)			
☐ 403 1980 World Series	.40	.18	.05
Phillies beat			
Royals in six			
(Larry Bowa sliding)			
☐ 404 1980 World Series	.40	.18	.05
Phillies win first			
World Series			
(Tug McGraw)			
☐ 405 Nino Espinosa	.15	.07	.02
☐ 406 Dickie Noles	.15	.07	.02
☐ 407 Ernie Whitt	.15	.07	.02
☐ 408 Fernando Arroyo	.15	.07	.02
☐ 409 Larry Herndon	.15	.07	.02
☐ 410 Bert Campaneris	.25	.11	.03
☐ 411 Terry Puhl	.15	.07	.02
☐ 412 Britt Burns	.25	.11	.03
☐ 413 Tony Bernazard	.15	.07	.02
☐ 414 John Pacella DP	.07	.03	.01
☐ 415 Ben Oglivie	.25	.11	.03
☐ 416 Gary Alexander	.15	.07	.02
☐ 417 Dan Schatzeder	.15	.07	.02
☐ 418 Bobby Brown	.15	.07	.02
☐ 419 Tom Hume	.15	.07	.02
☐ 420 Keith Hernandez	.40	.18	.05
☐ 421 Bob Stanley	.15	.07	.02
☐ 422 Dan Ford	.15	.07	.02
☐ 423 Shane Rawley	.15	.07	.02
☐ 424 Yankees Rookies	.15	.07	.02
Tim Lollar			
Bruce Robinson			
Dennis Werth			
☐ 425 Al Bumbry	.25	.11	.03
☐ 426 Warren Brusstar	.15	.07	.02
☐ 427 John D'Acquisto	.15	.07	.02
☐ 428 John Stearns	.15	.07	.02
☐ 429 Mick Kelleher	.15	.07	.02
☐ 430 Jim Bibby	.15	.07	.02
☐ 431 Dave Roberts	.15	.07	.02
☐ 432 Len Barker	.15	.07	.02
☐ 433 Rance Mulliniks	.15	.07	.02
☐ 434 Roger Erickson	.15	.07	.02
☐ 435 Jim Spencer	.15	.07	.02
☐ 436 Gary Lucas	.15	.07	.02
☐ 437 Mike Heath DP	.07	.03	.01
☐ 438 John Montefusco	.15	.07	.02
☐ 439 Denny Walling	.15	.07	.02
☐ 440 Jerry Reuss	.25	.11	.03
☐ 441 Ken Reitz	.15	.07	.02
☐ 442 Ron Pruitt	.15	.07	.02
☐ 443 Jim Beattie DP	.07	.03	.01
☐ 444 Garth Iorg	.15	.07	.02
☐ 445 Ellis Valentine	.15	.07	.02
☐ 446 Checklist 364-484	.40	.18	.05
☐ 447 Junior Kennedy DP	.07	.03	.01
☐ 448 Tim Corcoran	.15	.07	.02
☐ 449 Paul Mitchell	.15	.07	.02
☐ 450 Dave Kingman DP	.25	.11	.03
☐ 451 Indians Rookies	.15	.07	.02
Chris Bando			
Tom Brennan			
Sandy Wihtol			
☐ 452 Renie Martin	.15	.07	.02
☐ 453 Rob Wilfong DP	.07	.03	.01
☐ 454 Andy Hassler	.15	.07	.02
☐ 455 Rick Burleson	.15	.07	.02
☐ 456 Jeff Reardon	2.00	.90	.25
☐ 457 Mike Lum	.15	.07	.02
☐ 458 Randy Jones	.15	.07	.02
☐ 459 Greg Gross	.15	.07	.02

☐ 460 Rich Gossage	.40	.18	.05
☐ 461 Dave McKay	.15	.07	.02
☐ 462 Jack Brohamer	.15	.07	.02
☐ 463 Milt May	.15	.07	.02
☐ 464 Adrian Devine	.15	.07	.02
☐ 465 Bill Russell	.25	.11	.03
☐ 466 Bob Molinaro	.15	.07	.02
☐ 467 Dave Stieb	.25	.11	.03
☐ 468 John Wockenfuss	.15	.07	.02
☐ 469 Jeff Leonard	.25	.11	.03
☐ 470 Manny Trillo	.15	.07	.02
☐ 471 Mike Vail	.15	.07	.02
☐ 472 Dyar Miller DP	.07	.03	.01
☐ 473 Jose Cardenal	.15	.07	.02
☐ 474 Mike LaCoss	.15	.07	.02
☐ 475 Buddy Bell	.25	.11	.03
☐ 476 Jerry Koosman	.25	.11	.03
☐ 477 Luis Gomez	.15	.07	.02
☐ 478 Juan Eichelberger	.15	.07	.02
☐ 479 Expos Rookies	6.00	2.70	.75
Tim Raines			
Roberto Ramos			
Bobby Pate			
☐ 480 Carlton Fisk	2.00	.90	.25
☐ 481 Bob Lacey DP	.07	.03	.01
☐ 482 Jim Gantner	.25	.11	.03
☐ 483 Mike Griffin	.15	.07	.02
☐ 484 Max Venable DP	.07	.03	.01
☐ 485 Garry Templeton	.25	.11	.03
☐ 486 Marc Hill	.15	.07	.02
☐ 487 Dewey Robinson	.15	.07	.02
☐ 488 Damaso Garcia	.25	.11	.03
☐ 489 John Littlefield	.15	.07	.02
☐ 490 Eddie Murray	6.00	2.70	.75
☐ 491 Gordy Pladson	.15	.07	.02
☐ 492 Barry Foote	.15	.07	.02
☐ 493 Dan Quisenberry	.40	.18	.05
☐ 494 Bob Walk	.40	.18	.05
☐ 495 Dusty Baker	.40	.18	.05
☐ 496 Paul Dade	.15	.07	.02
☐ 497 Fred Norman	.15	.07	.02
☐ 498 Pat Putnam	.15	.07	.02
☐ 499 Frank Pastore	.15	.07	.02
☐ 500 Jim Rice	.40	.18	.05
☐ 501 Tim Foli DP	.07	.03	.01
☐ 502 Giants Rookies	.15	.07	.02
Chris Bourjos			
Al Hargesheimer			
Mike Rowland			
☐ 503 Steve McCatty	.15	.07	.02
☐ 504 Dale Murphy	1.25	.55	.16
☐ 505 Jason Thompson	.15	.07	.02
☐ 506 Phil Huffman	.15	.07	.02
☐ 507 Jamie Quirk	.15	.07	.02
☐ 508 Rob Dressler	.15	.07	.02
☐ 509 Pete Mackanin	.15	.07	.02
☐ 510 Lee Mazzilli	.15	.07	.02
☐ 511 Wayne Garland	.15	.07	.02
☐ 512 Gary Thomasson	.15	.07	.02
☐ 513 Frank LaCorte	.15	.07	.02
☐ 514 George Riley	.15	.07	.02
☐ 515 Robin Yount	3.50	1.55	.45
☐ 516 Doug Bird	.15	.07	.02
☐ 517 Richie Zisk	.15	.07	.02
☐ 518 Grant Jackson	.15	.07	.02
☐ 519 John Tamargo DP	.07	.03	.01
☐ 520 Steve Stone	.25	.11	.03
☐ 521 Sam Mejias	.15	.07	.02
☐ 522 Mike Colbern	.15	.07	.02
☐ 523 John Fulgham	.15	.07	.02
☐ 524 Willie Aikens	.15	.07	.02

☐ 525 Mike Torrez	.15	.07	.02
☐ 526 Phillies Rookies	.15	.07	.02
Marty Bystrom			
Jay Loviglio			
Jim Wright			
☐ 527 Danny Goodwin	.15	.07	.02
☐ 528 Gary Matthews	.25	.11	.03
☐ 529 Dave LaRoche	.15	.07	.02
☐ 530 Steve Garvey	.40	.18	.05
☐ 531 John Curtis	.15	.07	.02
☐ 532 Bill Stein	.15	.07	.02
☐ 533 Jesus Figueroa	.15	.07	.02
☐ 534 Dave Smith	.25	.11	.03
☐ 535 Omar Moreno	.15	.07	.02
☐ 536 Bob Owchinko DP	.07	.03	.01
☐ 537 Ron Hodges	.15	.07	.02
☐ 538 Tom Griffin	.15	.07	.02
☐ 539 Rodney Scott	.15	.07	.02
☐ 540 Mike Schmidt DP	2.00	.90	.25
☐ 541 Steve Swisher	.15	.07	.02
☐ 542 Larry Bradford DP	.07	.03	.01
☐ 543 Terry Crowley	.15	.07	.02
☐ 544 Rich Gale	.15	.07	.02
☐ 545 Johnny Grubb	.15	.07	.02
☐ 546 Paul Moskau	.15	.07	.02
☐ 547 Mario Guerrero	.15	.07	.02
☐ 548 Dave Goltz	.15	.07	.02
☐ 549 Jerry Remy	.15	.07	.02
☐ 550 Tommy John	.40	.18	.05
☐ 551 Pirates Rookies	.40	.18	.05
Vance Law			
Tony Pena			
Pascual Perez			
☐ 552 Steve Trout	.15	.07	.02
☐ 553 Tim Blackwell	.15	.07	.02
☐ 554 Bert Blyleven UER	.40	.18	.05
(1 is missing from			
1980 on card back)			
☐ 555 Cecil Cooper	.25	.11	.03
☐ 556 Jerry Mumphrey	.15	.07	.02
☐ 557 Chris Knapp	.15	.07	.02
☐ 558 Barry Bonnell	.15	.07	.02
☐ 559 Willie Montanez	.15	.07	.02
☐ 560 Joe Morgan	.75	.35	.09
☐ 561 Dennis Littlejohn	.15	.07	.02
☐ 562 Checklist 485-605	.40	.18	.05
☐ 563 Jim Kaat	.25	.11	.03
☐ 564 Ron Hassey DP	.07	.03	.01
☐ 565 Burt Hooton	.15	.07	.02
☐ 566 Del Unser	.15	.07	.02
☐ 567 Mark Bomback	.15	.07	.02
☐ 568 Dave Revering	.15	.07	.02
☐ 569 Al Williams DP	.07	.03	.01
☐ 570 Ken Singleton	.25	.11	.03
☐ 571 Todd Cruz	.15	.07	.02
☐ 572 Jack Morris	.40	.18	.05
☐ 573 Phil Garner	.25	.11	.03
☐ 574 Bill Caudill	.15	.07	.02
☐ 575 Tony Perez	.40	.18	.05
☐ 576 Reggie Cleveland	.15	.07	.02
☐ 577 Blue Jays Rookies	.15	.07	.02
Luis Leal			
Brian Milner			
Ken Schrom			
☐ 578 Bill Gullickson	.40	.18	.05
☐ 579 Tim Flannery	.15	.07	.02
☐ 580 Don Baylor	.40	.18	.05
☐ 581 Roy Howell	.15	.07	.02
☐ 582 Gaylord Perry	.40	.18	.05
☐ 583 Larry Milbourne	.15	.07	.02
☐ 584 Randy Lerch	.15	.07	.02

☐ 585	Amos Otis	.25	.11	.03
☐ 586	Silvio Martinez	.15	.07	.02
☐ 587	Jeff Newman	.15	.07	.02
☐ 588	Gary Lavelle	.15	.07	.02
☐ 589	Lamar Johnson	.15	.07	.02
☐ 590	Bruce Sutter	.25	.11	.03
☐ 591	John Lowenstein	.15	.07	.02
☐ 592	Steve Comer	.15	.07	.02
☐ 593	Steve Kemp	.15	.07	.02
☐ 594	Preston Hanna DP	.07	.03	.01
☐ 595	Butch Hobson	.25	.11	.03
☐ 596	Jerry Augustine	.15	.07	.02
☐ 597	Rafael Landestoy	.15	.07	.02
☐ 598	George Vukovich DP	.07	.03	.01
☐ 599	Dennis Kinney	.15	.07	.02
☐ 600	Johnny Bench	2.00	.90	.25
☐ 601	Don Aase	.15	.07	.02
☐ 602	Bobby Murcer	.25	.11	.03
☐ 603	John Verhoeven	.15	.07	.02
☐ 604	Rob Picciolo	.15	.07	.02
☐ 605	Don Sutton	.40	.18	.05
☐ 606	Reds Rookies DP	.15	.07	.02
	Bruce Berenyi			
	Geoff Combe			
	Paul Householder			
☐ 607	David Palmer	.15	.07	.02
☐ 608	Greg Pryor	.15	.07	.02
☐ 609	Lynn McGlothen	.15	.07	.02
☐ 610	Darrell Porter	.15	.07	.02
☐ 611	Rick Matula DP	.07	.03	.01
☐ 612	Duane Kuiper	.15	.07	.02
☐ 613	Jim Anderson	.15	.07	.02
☐ 614	Dave Rozema	.15	.07	.02
☐ 615	Rick Dempsey	.25	.11	.03
☐ 616	Rick Wise	.15	.07	.02
☐ 617	Craig Reynolds	.15	.07	.02
☐ 618	John Milner	.15	.07	.02
☐ 619	Steve Henderson	.15	.07	.02
☐ 620	Dennis Eckersley	1.25	.55	.16
☐ 621	Tom Donohue	.15	.07	.02
☐ 622	Randy Moffitt	.15	.07	.02
☐ 623	Sal Bando	.25	.11	.03
☐ 624	Bob Welch	.25	.11	.03
☐ 625	Bill Buckner	.25	.11	.03
☐ 626	Tigers Rookies	.15	.07	.02
	Dave Steffen			
	Jerry Ujdur			
	Roger Weaver			
☐ 627	Luis Tiant	.25	.11	.03
☐ 628	Vic Correll	.15	.07	.02
☐ 629	Tony Armas	.25	.11	.03
☐ 630	Steve Carlton	2.00	.90	.25
☐ 631	Ron Jackson	.15	.07	.02
☐ 632	Alan Bannister	.15	.07	.02
☐ 633	Bill Lee	.15	.07	.02
☐ 634	Doug Flynn	.15	.07	.02
☐ 635	Bobby Bonds	.25	.11	.03
☐ 636	Al Hrabosky	.15	.07	.02
☐ 637	Jerry Narron	.15	.07	.02
☐ 638	Checklist 606-726	.40	.18	.05
☐ 639	Carney Lansford	.25	.11	.03
☐ 640	Dave Parker	.40	.18	.05
☐ 641	Mark Belanger	.25	.11	.03
☐ 642	Vern Ruhle	.15	.07	.02
☐ 643	Lloyd Moseby	.25	.11	.03
☐ 644	Ramon Aviles DP	.07	.03	.01
☐ 645	Rick Reuschel	.25	.11	.03
☐ 646	Marvis Foley	.15	.07	.02
☐ 647	Dick Drago	.15	.07	.02
☐ 648	Darrell Evans	.25	.11	.03
☐ 649	Manny Sarmiento	.15	.07	.02

☐ 650	Bucky Dent	.25	.11	.03
☐ 651	Pedro Guerrero	.15	.07	.02
☐ 652	John Montague	.15	.07	.02
☐ 653	Bill Fahey	.15	.07	.02
☐ 654	Ray Burris	.15	.07	.02
☐ 655	Dan Driessen	.15	.07	.02
☐ 656	Jon Matlack	.15	.07	.02
☐ 657	Mike Cubbage DP	.07	.03	.01
☐ 658	Milt Wilcox	.15	.07	.02
☐ 659	Brewers Rookies	.15	.07	.02
	John Flinn			
	Ed Romero			
	Ned Yost			
☐ 660	Gary Carter	.75	.35	.09
☐ 661	Orioles Team/Mgr.	.40	.18	.05
	Earl Weaver			
	(Checklist back)			
☐ 662	Red Sox Team/Mgr.	.40	.18	.05
	Ralph Houk			
	(Checklist back)			
☐ 663	Angels Team/Mgr.	.40	.18	.05
	Jim Fregosi			
	(Checklist back)			
☐ 664	White Sox Team/Mgr.	.40	.18	.05
	Tony LaRussa			
	(Checklist back)			
☐ 665	Indians Team/Mgr.	.40	.18	.05
	Dave Garcia			
	(Checklist back)			
☐ 666	Tigers Team/Mgr.	.40	.18	.05
	Sparky Anderson			
	(Checklist back)			
☐ 667	Royals Team/Mgr.	.40	.18	.05
	Jim Frey			
	(Checklist back)			
☐ 668	Brewers Team/Mgr.	.40	.18	.05
	Bob Rodgers			
	(Checklist back)			
☐ 669	Twins Team/Mgr.	.40	.18	.05
	John Goryl			
	(Checklist back)			
☐ 670	Yankees Team/Mgr.	.40	.18	.05
	Gene Michael			
	(Checklist back)			
☐ 671	A's Team/Mgr.	.40	.18	.05
	Billy Martin			
	(Checklist back)			
☐ 672	Mariners Team/Mgr.	.40	.18	.05
	Maury Wills			
	(Checklist back)			
☐ 673	Rangers Team/Mgr.	.40	.18	.05
	Don Zimmer			
	(Checklist back)			
☐ 674	Blue Jays Team/Mgr.	.40	.18	.05
	Bobby Mattick			
	(Checklist back)			
☐ 675	Braves Team/Mgr.	.40	.18	.05
	Bobby Cox			
	(Checklist back)			
☐ 676	Cubs Team/Mgr.	.40	.18	.05
	Joe Amalfitano			
	(Checklist back)			
☐ 677	Reds Team/Mgr.	.40	.18	.05
	John McNamara			
	(Checklist back)			
☐ 678	Astros Team/Mgr.	.40	.18	.05
	Bill Virdon			
	(Checklist back)			
☐ 679	Dodgers Team/Mgr.	.40	.18	.05
	Tom Lasorda			
	(Checklist back)			

☐ 680	Expos Team/Mgr. Dick Williams (Checklist back)	.40	.18	.05
☐ 681	Mets Team/Mgr. Joe Torre (Checklist back)	.40	.18	.05
☐ 682	Phillies Team/Mgr. Dallas Green (Checklist back)	.40	.18	.05
☐ 683	Pirates Team/Mgr. Chuck Tanner (Checklist back)	.40	.18	.05
☐ 684	Cardinals Team/Mgr. Whitey Herzog (Checklist back)	.40	.18	.05
☐ 685	Padres Team/Mgr. Frank Howard (Checklist back)	.40	.18	.05
☐ 686	Giants Team/Mgr. Dave Bristol (Checklist back)	.40	.18	.05
☐ 687	Jeff Jones	.15	.07	.02
☐ 688	Kiko Garcia	.15	.07	.02
☐ 689	Red Sox Rookies Bruce Hurst Keith MacWhorter Reid Nichols	.40	.18	.05
☐ 690	Bob Watson	.25	.11	.03
☐ 691	Dick Ruthven	.15	.07	.02
☐ 692	Lenny Randle	.15	.07	.02
☐ 693	Steve Howe	.25	.11	.03
☐ 694	Bud Harrelson DP	.07	.03	.01
☐ 695	Kent Tekulve	.25	.11	.03
☐ 696	Alan Ashby	.15	.07	.02
☐ 697	Rick Waits	.15	.07	.02
☐ 698	Mike Jorgensen	.15	.07	.02
☐ 699	Glenn Abbott	.15	.07	.02
☐ 700	George Brett	6.00	2.70	.75
☐ 701	Joe Rudi	.25	.11	.03
☐ 702	George Medich	.15	.07	.02
☐ 703	Alvis Woods	.15	.07	.02
☐ 704	Bill Travers DP	.07	.03	.01
☐ 705	Ted Simmons	.25	.11	.03
☐ 706	Dave Ford	.15	.07	.02
☐ 707	Dave Cash	.15	.07	.02
☐ 708	Doyle Alexander	.15	.07	.02
☐ 709	Alan Trammell DP	1.50	.70	.19
☐ 710	Ron LeFlore DP	.07	.03	.01
☐ 711	Joe Ferguson	.15	.07	.02
☐ 712	Bill Bonham	.15	.07	.02
☐ 713	Bill North	.15	.07	.02
☐ 714	Pete Redfern	.15	.07	.02
☐ 715	Bill Madlock	.25	.11	.03
☐ 716	Glenn Borgmann	.15	.07	.02
☐ 717	Jim Barr DP	.07	.03	.01
☐ 718	Larry Biittner	.15	.07	.02
☐ 719	Sparky Lyle	.25	.11	.03
☐ 720	Fred Lynn	.25	.11	.03
☐ 721	Toby Harrah	.25	.11	.03
☐ 722	Joe Niekro	.25	.11	.03
☐ 723	Bruce Bochte	.15	.07	.02
☐ 724	Lou Piniella	.25	.11	.03
☐ 725	Steve Rogers	.15	.07	.02
☐ 726	Rick Monday	.25	.11	.03

1981 Topps Traded

Topps issued a "traded" set in 1981. Unlike the small traded sets of 1974 and 1976, this set contains a larger number of cards and was sequentially numbered, alphabetically, from 727 to 858. Thus, this set gives the impression it is a continuation of their regular issue of this year. The sets were issued only through hobby card dealers and were boxed in complete sets of 132 cards. There are no key Rookie Cards in this set although Tim Raines, Jeff Reardon, and Fernando Valenzuela are depicted in their rookie cards for cards. The key extended Rookie Card in the set is Danny Ainge.

		NRMT-MT	EXC	G-VG
	COMPLETE SET (132)	30.00	13.50	3.70
	COMPLETE FACT.SET (132)	32.00	14.50	4.00
	COMMON CARD (727-858)	.25	.11	.03
☐ 727	Danny Ainge	6.00	2.70	.75
☐ 728	Doyle Alexander	.25	.11	.03
☐ 729	Gary Alexander	.25	.11	.03
☐ 730	Bill Almon	.25	.11	.03
☐ 731	Joaquin Andujar	.35	.16	.04
☐ 732	Bob Bailor	.25	.11	.03
☐ 733	Juan Beniquez	.25	.11	.03
☐ 734	Dave Bergman	.25	.11	.03
☐ 735	Tony Bernazard	.25	.11	.03
☐ 736	Larry Biittner	.25	.11	.03
☐ 737	Doug Bird	.25	.11	.03
☐ 738	Bert Blyleven	.50	.23	.06
☐ 739	Mark Bomback	.25	.11	.03
☐ 740	Bobby Bonds	.50	.23	.06
☐ 741	Rick Bosetti	.25	.11	.03
☐ 742	Hubie Brooks	.35	.16	.04
☐ 743	Rick Burleson	.25	.11	.03
☐ 744	Ray Burris	.25	.11	.03
☐ 745	Jeff Burroughs	.25	.11	.03
☐ 746	Enos Cabell	.25	.11	.03
☐ 747	Ken Clay	.25	.11	.03
☐ 748	Mark Clear	.25	.11	.03
☐ 749	Larry Cox	.25	.11	.03
☐ 750	Hector Cruz	.25	.11	.03
☐ 751	Victor Cruz	.25	.11	.03
☐ 752	Mike Cubbage	.25	.11	.03
☐ 753	Dick Davis	.25	.11	.03
☐ 754	Brian Doyle	.25	.11	.03
☐ 755	Dick Drago	.25	.11	.03
☐ 756	Leon Durham	.35	.16	.04
☐ 757	Jim Dwyer	.25	.11	.03
☐ 758	Dave Edwards UER No birthdate on card	.25	.11	.03
☐ 759	Jim Essian	.25	.11	.03
☐ 760	Bill Fahey	.25	.11	.03
☐ 761	Rollie Fingers	1.25	.55	.16

The cards in this 132-card set measure 2 1/2" by 3 1/2". For the first time since 1976,

☐ 762	Carlton Fisk	4.00	1.80	.50
☐ 763	Barry Foote	.25	.11	.03
☐ 764	Ken Forsch	.25	.11	.03
☐ 765	Kiko Garcia	.25	.11	.03
☐ 766	Cesar Geronimo	.25	.11	.03
☐ 767	Gary Gray	.25	.11	.03
☐ 768	Mickey Hatcher	.25	.11	.03
☐ 769	Steve Henderson	.25	.11	.03
☐ 770	Marc Hill	.25	.11	.03
☐ 771	Butch Hobson	.35	.16	.04
☐ 772	Rick Honeycutt	.25	.11	.03
☐ 773	Roy Howell	.25	.11	.03
☐ 774	Mike Ivie	.25	.11	.03
☐ 775	Roy Lee Jackson	.25	.11	.03
☐ 776	Cliff Johnson	.25	.11	.03
☐ 777	Randy Jones	.25	.11	.03
☐ 778	Ruppert Jones	.25	.11	.03
☐ 779	Mick Kelleher	.25	.11	.03
☐ 780	Terry Kennedy	.25	.11	.03
☐ 781	Dave Kingman	.35	.16	.04
☐ 782	Bob Knepper	.25	.11	.03
☐ 783	Ken Kravec	.25	.11	.03
☐ 784	Bob Lacey	.25	.11	.03
☐ 785	Dennis Lamp	.25	.11	.03
☐ 786	Rafael Landestoy	.25	.11	.03
☐ 787	Ken Landreaux	.25	.11	.03
☐ 788	Carney Lansford	.50	.23	.06
☐ 789	Dave LaRoche	.25	.11	.03
☐ 790	Joe Lefebvre	.25	.11	.03
☐ 791	Ron LeFlore	.35	.16	.04
☐ 792	Randy Lerch	.25	.11	.03
☐ 793	Sixto Lezcano	.25	.11	.03
☐ 794	John Littlefield	.25	.11	.03
☐ 795	Mike Lum	.25	.11	.03
☐ 796	Greg Luzinski	.35	.16	.04
☐ 797	Fred Lynn	.35	.16	.04
☐ 798	Jerry Martin	.25	.11	.03
☐ 799	Buck Martinez	.25	.11	.03
☐ 800	Gary Matthews	.35	.16	.04
☐ 801	Mario Mendoza	.25	.11	.03
☐ 802	Larry Milbourne	.25	.11	.03
☐ 803	Rick Miller	.25	.11	.03
☐ 804	John Montefusco	.25	.11	.03
☐ 805	Jerry Morales	.25	.11	.03
☐ 806	Jose Morales	.25	.11	.03
☐ 807	Joe Morgan	3.00	1.35	.35
☐ 808	Jerry Mumphrey	.25	.11	.03
☐ 809	Gene Nelson	.25	.11	.03
☐ 810	Ed Ott	.25	.11	.03
☐ 811	Bob Owchinko	.25	.11	.03
☐ 812	Gaylord Perry	1.25	.55	.16
☐ 813	Mike Phillips	.25	.11	.03
☐ 814	Darrell Porter	.25	.11	.03
☐ 815	Mike Proly	.25	.11	.03
☐ 816	Tim Raines	10.00	4.50	1.25
☐ 817	Lenny Randle	.25	.11	.03
☐ 818	Doug Rau	.25	.11	.03
☐ 819	Jeff Reardon	3.00	1.35	.35
☐ 820	Ken Reitz	.25	.11	.03
☐ 821	Steve Renko	.25	.11	.03
☐ 822	Rick Reuschel	.35	.16	.04
☐ 823	Dave Revering	.25	.11	.03
☐ 824	Dave Roberts	.25	.11	.03
☐ 825	Leon Roberts	.25	.11	.03
☐ 826	Joe Rudi	.35	.16	.04
☐ 827	Kevin Saucier	.25	.11	.03
☐ 828	Tony Scott	.25	.11	.03
☐ 829	Bob Shirley	.25	.11	.03
☐ 830	Ted Simmons	.35	.16	.04
☐ 831	Lary Sorensen	.25	.11	.03
☐ 832	Jim Spencer	.25	.11	.03

☐ 833	Harry Spilman	.25	.11	.03
☐ 834	Fred Stanley	.25	.11	.03
☐ 835	Rusty Staub	.35	.16	.04
☐ 836	Bill Stein	.25	.11	.03
☐ 837	Joe Strain	.25	.11	.03
☐ 838	Bruce Sutter	.35	.16	.04
☐ 839	Don Sutton	.50	.23	.06
☐ 840	Steve Swisher	.25	.11	.03
☐ 841	Frank Tanana	.35	.16	.04
☐ 842	Gene Tenace	.25	.11	.03
☐ 843	Jason Thompson	.25	.11	.03
☐ 844	Dickie Thon	.35	.16	.04
☐ 845	Bill Travers	.25	.11	.03
☐ 846	Tom Underwood	.25	.11	.03
☐ 847	John Urrea	.25	.11	.03
☐ 848	Mike Vail	.25	.11	.03
☐ 849	Ellis Valentine	.25	.11	.03
☐ 850	Fernando Valenzuela	2.50	1.10	.30
☐ 851	Pete Vuckovich	.35	.16	.04
☐ 852	Mark Wagner	.25	.11	.03
☐ 853	Bob Walk	.25	.11	.03
☐ 854	Claudell Washington	.25	.11	.03
☐ 855	Dave Winfield	8.00	3.60	1.00
☐ 856	Geoff Zahn	.25	.11	.03
☐ 857	Richie Zisk	.25	.11	.03
☐ 858	Checklist 727-858	.25	.11	.03

1982 Topps

The cards in this 792-card set measure 2 1/2" by 3 1/2". The 1982 baseball series was the first of the largest sets Topps issued at one printing. The 66-card increase from the previous year's total eliminated the "double print" practice, that had occurred in every regular issue since 1978. Cards 1-6 depict Highlights (HL) of the 1981 season, cards 161-168 picture League Leaders, and there are mini-series of AL (547-557) and NL (337-347) All-Stars (AS). The abbreviation "SA" in the checklist is given for the 40 "Super Action" cards introduced in this set. The team cards are actually Team Leader (TL) cards picturing the batting (BA: batting average) and pitching leader for that team with a checklist back. All 26 cards were available from Topps on a perforated sheet through an offer on wax pack wrappers. The key Rookie Cards in this set are Steve Bedrosian, George Bell, Brett Butler, Chili Davis, Kent Hrbek, Cal Ripken, Steve Sax, Lee Smith, and Dave Stewart.

	NRMT-MT	EXC	G-VG
COMPLETE SET (792)	125.00	55.00	15.50
COMMON CARD (1-792)	.10	.05	.01
☐ 1 Steve Carlton HL	1.00	.45	.12
Sets new NL			
strikeout record			
☐ 2 Ron Davis HL	.20	.09	.03
Fans 8 straight			
in relief			
☐ 3 Tim Raines HL	.60	.25	.07
Swipes 71 bases			
as rookie			
☐ 4 Pete Rose HL	1.00	.45	.12
Sets NL career			
hits mark			
☐ 5 Nolan Ryan HL	3.00	1.35	.35
Pitches fifth			
career no-hitter			
☐ 6 Fernando Valenzuela HL	.20	.09	.03
8 shutouts as rookie			
☐ 7 Scott Sanderson	.20	.09	.03
☐ 8 Rich Dauer	.10	.05	.01
☐ 9 Ron Guidry	.20	.09	.03
☐ 10 Ron Guidry SA	.10	.05	.01
☐ 11 Gary Alexander	.10	.05	.01
☐ 12 Moose Haas	.10	.05	.01
☐ 13 Lamar Johnson	.10	.05	.01
☐ 14 Steve Howe	.10	.05	.01
☐ 15 Ellis Valentine	.10	.05	.01
☐ 16 Steve Comer	.10	.05	.01
☐ 17 Darrell Evans	.20	.09	.03
☐ 18 Fernando Arroyo	.10	.05	.01
☐ 19 Ernie Whitt	.10	.05	.01
☐ 20 Garry Maddox	.10	.05	.01
☐ 21 Orioles Rookies	80.00	36.00	10.00
Bob Bonner			
Cal Ripken			
Jeff Schneider			
☐ 22 Jim Beattie	.10	.05	.01
☐ 23 Willie Hernandez	.20	.09	.03
☐ 24 Dave Frost	.10	.05	.01
☐ 25 Jerry Remy	.10	.05	.01
☐ 26 Jorge Orta	.10	.05	.01
☐ 27 Tom Herr	.20	.09	.03
☐ 28 John Urrea	.10	.05	.01
☐ 29 Dwayne Murphy	.10	.05	.01
☐ 30 Tom Seaver	1.50	.70	.19
☐ 31 Tom Seaver SA	.75	.35	.09
☐ 32 Gene Garber	.10	.05	.01
☐ 33 Jerry Morales	.10	.05	.01
☐ 34 Joe Sambito	.10	.05	.01
☐ 35 Willie Aikens	.10	.05	.01
☐ 36 Rangers TL	.40	.18	.05
BA: Al Oliver			
Pitching: Doc Medich			
(Checklist on back)			
☐ 37 Dan Graham	.10	.05	.01
☐ 38 Charlie Lea	.10	.05	.01
☐ 39 Lou Whitaker	1.00	.45	.12
☐ 40 Dave Parker	.40	.18	.05
☐ 41 Dave Parker SA	.20	.09	.03
☐ 42 Rick Sofield	.10	.05	.01
☐ 43 Mike Cubbage	.10	.05	.01
☐ 44 Britt Burns	.10	.05	.01
☐ 45 Rick Cerone	.10	.05	.01
☐ 46 Jerry Augustine	.10	.05	.01
☐ 47 Jeff Leonard	.10	.05	.01
☐ 48 Bobby Castillo	.10	.05	.01
☐ 49 Alvis Woods	.10	.05	.01
☐ 50 Buddy Bell	.20	.09	.03
☐ 51 Cubs Rookies	.40	.18	.05
Jay Howell			
Carlos Lezcano			
Ty Waller			
☐ 52 Larry Andersen	.10	.05	.01
☐ 53 Greg Gross	.10	.05	.01
☐ 54 Ron Hassey	.10	.05	.01
☐ 55 Rick Burleson	.10	.05	.01
☐ 56 Mark Littell	.10	.05	.01
☐ 57 Craig Reynolds	.10	.05	.01
☐ 58 John D'Acquisto	.10	.05	.01
☐ 59 Rich Gedman	.20	.09	.03
☐ 60 Tony Armas	.10	.05	.01
☐ 61 Tommy Boggs	.10	.05	.01
☐ 62 Mike Tyson	.10	.05	.01
☐ 63 Mario Soto	.10	.05	.01
☐ 64 Lynn Jones	.10	.05	.01
☐ 65 Terry Kennedy	.10	.05	.01
☐ 66 Astros TL	2.00	.90	.25
BA: Art Howe			
Pitching: Nolan Ryan			
(Checklist on back)			
☐ 67 Rich Gale	.10	.05	.01
☐ 68 Roy Howell	.10	.05	.01
☐ 69 Al Williams	.10	.05	.01
☐ 70 Tim Raines	2.50	1.10	.30
☐ 71 Roy Lee Jackson	.10	.05	.01
☐ 72 Rick Auerbach	.10	.05	.01
☐ 73 Buddy Solomon	.10	.05	.01
☐ 74 Bob Clark	.10	.05	.01
☐ 75 Tommy John	.40	.18	.05
☐ 76 Greg Pryor	.10	.05	.01
☐ 77 Miguel Dilone	.10	.05	.01
☐ 78 George Medich	.10	.05	.01
☐ 79 Bob Bailor	.10	.05	.01
☐ 80 Jim Palmer	.75	.35	.09
☐ 81 Jim Palmer SA	.50	.23	.06
☐ 82 Bob Welch	.20	.09	.03
☐ 83 Yankees Rookies	.40	.18	.05
Steve Balboni			
Andy McGaffigan			
Andre Robertson			
☐ 84 Rennie Stennett	.10	.05	.01
☐ 85 Lynn McGlothen	.10	.05	.01
☐ 86 Dane Iorg	.10	.05	.01
☐ 87 Matt Keough	.10	.05	.01
☐ 88 Biff Pocoroba	.10	.05	.01
☐ 89 Steve Henderson	.10	.05	.01
☐ 90 Nolan Ryan	8.00	3.60	1.00
☐ 91 Carney Lansford	.20	.09	.03
☐ 92 Brad Havens	.10	.05	.01
☐ 93 Larry Hisle	.10	.05	.01
☐ 94 Andy Hassler	.10	.05	.01
☐ 95 Ozzie Smith	4.00	1.80	.50
☐ 96 Royals TL	.60	.25	.07
BA: George Brett			
Pitching: Larry Gura			
(Checklist on back)			
☐ 97 Paul Moskau	.10	.05	.01
☐ 98 Terry Bulling	.10	.05	.01
☐ 99 Barry Bonnell	.10	.05	.01
☐ 100 Mike Schmidt	3.00	1.35	.35
☐ 101 Mike Schmidt SA	1.50	.70	.19
☐ 102 Dan Briggs	.10	.05	.01
☐ 103 Bob Lacey	.10	.05	.01
☐ 104 Rance Mulliniks	.10	.05	.01
☐ 105 Kirk Gibson	1.00	.45	.12
☐ 106 Enrique Romo	.10	.05	.01
☐ 107 Wayne Krenchicki	.10	.05	.01
☐ 108 Bob Sykes	.10	.05	.01
☐ 109 Dave Revering	.10	.05	.01

☐	110 Carlton Fisk	1.50	.70	.19
☐	111 Carlton Fisk SA	.75	.35	.09
☐	112 Billy Sample	.10	.05	.01
☐	113 Steve McCatty	.10	.05	.01
☐	114 Ken Landreaux	.10	.05	.01
☐	115 Gaylord Perry	.40	.18	.05
☐	116 Jim Wohlford	.10	.05	.01
☐	117 Rawly Eastwick	.10	.05	.01
☐	118 Expos Rookies	.20	.09	.03
	Terry Francona			
	Brad Mills			
	Bryn Smith			
☐	119 Joe Pittman	.10	.05	.01
☐	120 Gary Lucas	.10	.05	.01
☐	121 Ed Lynch	.10	.05	.01
☐	122 Jamie Easterly UER	.10	.05	.01
	(Photo actually			
	Reggie Cleveland)			
☒	123 Danny Goodwin	.10	.05	.01
☐	124 Reid Nichols	.10	.05	.01
☐	125 Danny Ainge	2.00	.90	.25
☐	126 Braves TL	.40	.18	.05
	BA: Claudell Washington			
	Pitching: Rick Mahler			
	(Checklist on back)			
☐	127 Lonnie Smith	.20	.09	.03
☐	128 Frank Pastore	.10	.05	.01
☐	129 Checklist 1-132	.40	.18	.05
☐	130 Julio Cruz	.10	.05	.01
☐	131 Stan Bahnsen	.10	.05	.01
☐	132 Lee May	.20	.09	.03
☐	133 Pat Underwood	.10	.05	.01
☐	134 Dan Ford	.10	.05	.01
☐	135 Andy Rincon	.10	.05	.01
☐	136 Lenn Sakata	.10	.05	.01
☐	137 George Cappuzzello	.10	.05	.01
☐	138 Tony Pena	.20	.09	.03
☐	139 Jeff Jones	.10	.05	.01
☐	140 Ron LeFlore	.20	.09	.03
☐	141 Indians Rookies	.20	.09	.03
	Chris Bando			
	Tom Brennan			
	Von Hayes			
☐	142 Dave LaRoche	.10	.05	.01
☐	143 Mookie Wilson	.20	.09	.03
☐	144 Fred Breining	.10	.05	.01
☐	145 Bob Horner	.20	.09	.03
☐	146 Mike Griffin	.10	.05	.01
☐	147 Denny Walling	.10	.05	.01
☐	148 Mickey Klutts	.10	.05	.01
☐	149 Pat Putnam	.10	.05	.01
☐	150 Ted Simmons	.20	.09	.03
☐	151 Dave Edwards	.10	.05	.01
☐	152 Ramon Aviles	.10	.05	.01
☐	153 Roger Erickson	.10	.05	.01
☐	154 Dennis Werth	.10	.05	.01
☐	155 Otto Velez	.10	.05	.01
☐	156 Oakland A's TL	.75	.35	.09
	BA: Rickey Henderson			
	Pitching: Steve McCatty			
	(Checklist on back)			
☐	157 Steve Crawford	.10	.05	.01
☐	158 Brian Downing	.20	.09	.03
☐	159 Larry Biittner	.10	.05	.01
☐	160 Luis Tiant	.20	.09	.03
☐	161 Batting Leaders	.20	.09	.03
	Bill Madlock			
	Carney Lansford			
☐	162 Home Run Leaders	.75	.35	.09
	Mike Schmidt			
	Tony Armas			

	Dwight Evans			
	Bobby Grich			
	Eddie Murray			
☐	163 RBI Leaders	.75	.35	.09
	Mike Schmidt			
	Eddie Murray			
☐	164 Stolen Base Leaders	1.00	.45	.12
	Tim Raines			
	Rickey Henderson			
☐	165 Victory Leaders	.60	.25	.07
	Tom Seaver			
	Denny Martinez			
	Steve McCatty			
	Jack Morris			
	Pete Vuckovich			
☐	166 Strikeout Leaders	.20	.09	.03
	Fernando Valenzuela			
	Len Barker			
☐	167 ERA Leaders	2.00	.90	.25
	Nolan Ryan			
	Steve McCatty			
☐	168 Leading Firemen	.40	.18	.05
	Bruce Sutter			
	Rollie Fingers			
☐	169 Charlie Leibrandt	.20	.09	.03
☐	170 Jim Bibby	.10	.05	.01
☐	171 Giants Rookies	2.50	1.10	.30
	Bob Brenly			
	Chili Davis			
	Bob Tufts			
☐	172 Bill Gullickson	.20	.09	.03
☐	173 Jamie Quirk	.10	.05	.01
☐	174 Dave Ford	.10	.05	.01
☐	175 Jerry Mumphrey	.10	.05	.01
☐	176 Dewey Robinson	.10	.05	.01
☐	177 John Ellis	.10	.05	.01
☐	178 Dyar Miller	.10	.05	.01
☐	179 Steve Garvey	.40	.18	.05
☐	180 Steve Garvey SA	.20	.09	.03
☐	181 Silvio Martinez	.10	.05	.01
☐	182 Larry Herndon	.10	.05	.01
☐	183 Mike Proly	.10	.05	.01
☐	184 Mick Kelleher	.10	.05	.01
☐	185 Phil Niekro	.40	.18	.05
☐	186 Cardinals TL	.40	.18	.05
	BA: Keith Hernandez			
	Pitching: Bob Forsch			
	(Checklist on back)			
☐	187 Jeff Newman	.10	.05	.01
☐	188 Randy Martz	.10	.05	.01
☐	189 Glenn Hoffman	.10	.05	.01
☐	190 J.R. Richard	.20	.09	.03
☐	191 Tim Wallach	1.00	.45	.12
☐	192 Broderick Perkins	.10	.05	.01
☐	193 Darrell Jackson	.10	.05	.01
☐	194 Mike Vail	.10	.05	.01
☐	195 Paul Molitor	1.50	.70	.19
☐	196 Willie Upshaw	.10	.05	.01
☐	197 Shane Rawley	.10	.05	.01
☐	198 Chris Speier	.10	.05	.01
☐	199 Don Aase	.10	.05	.01
☐	200 George Brett	5.00	2.20	.60
☐	201 George Brett SA	2.50	1.10	.30
☐	202 Rick Manning	.10	.05	.01
☐	203 Blue Jays Rookies	.40	.18	.05
	Jesse Barfield			
	Brian Milner			
	Boomer Wells			
☐	204 Gary Roenicke	.10	.05	.01
☐	205 Neil Allen	.10	.05	.01
☐	206 Tony Bernazard	.10	.05	.01

☐ 207	Rod Scurry	.10	.05	.01
☐ 208	Bobby Murcer	.20	.09	.03
☐ 209	Gary Lavelle	.10	.05	.01
☐ 210	Keith Hernandez	.40	.18	.05
☐ 211	Dan Petry	.10	.05	.01
☐ 212	Mario Mendoza	.10	.05	.01
☐ 213	Dave Stewart	2.50	1.10	.30
☐ 214	Brian Asselstine	.10	.05	.01
☐ 215	Mike Krukow	.10	.05	.01
☐ 216	White Sox TL	.40	.18	.05
	BA: Chet Lemon			
	Pitching: Dennis Lamp			
	(Checklist on back)			
☐ 217	Bo McLaughlin	.10	.05	.01
☐ 218	Dave Roberts	.10	.05	.01
☐ 219	John Curtis	.10	.05	.01
☐ 220	Manny Trillo	.10	.05	.01
☐ 221	Jim Slaton	.10	.05	.01
☐ 222	Butch Wynegar	.10	.05	.01
☐ 223	Lloyd Moseby	.10	.05	.01
☐ 224	Bruce Bochte	.10	.05	.01
☐ 225	Mike Torrez	.10	.05	.01
☐ 226	Checklist 133-264	.40	.18	.05
☐ 227	Ray Burris	.10	.05	.01
☐ 228	Sam Mejias	.10	.05	.01
☐ 229	Geoff Zahn	.10	.05	.01
☐ 230	Willie Wilson	.20	.09	.03
☐ 231	Phillies Rookies	.40	.18	.05
	Mark Davis			
	Bob Dernier			
	Ozzie Virgil			
☐ 232	Terry Crowley	.10	.05	.01
☐ 233	Duane Kuiper	.10	.05	.01
☐ 234	Ron Hodges	.10	.05	.01
☐ 235	Mike Easler	.10	.05	.01
☐ 236	John Martin	.10	.05	.01
☐ 237	Rusty Kuntz	.10	.05	.01
☐ 238	Kevin Saucier	.10	.05	.01
☐ 239	Jon Matlack	.10	.05	.01
☐ 240	Bucky Dent	.20	.09	.03
☐ 241	Bucky Dent SA	.10	.05	.01
☐ 242	Milt May	.10	.05	.01
☐ 243	Bob Owchinko	.10	.05	.01
☐ 244	Rufino Linares	.10	.05	.01
☐ 245	Ken Reitz	.10	.05	.01
☐ 246	New York Mets TL	.40	.18	.05
	BA: Hubie Brooks			
	Pitching: Mike Scott			
	(Checklist on back)			
☐ 247	Pedro Guerrero	.20	.09	.03
☐ 248	Frank LaCorte	.10	.05	.01
☐ 249	Tim Flannery	.10	.05	.01
☐ 250	Tug McGraw	.20	.09	.03
☐ 251	Fred Lynn	.20	.09	.03
☐ 252	Fred Lynn SA	.10	.05	.01
☐ 253	Chuck Baker	.10	.05	.01
☐ 254	Jorge Bell	1.00	.45	.12
☐ 255	Tony Perez	.40	.18	.05
☐ 256	Tony Perez SA	.20	.09	.03
☐ 257	Larry Harlow	.10	.05	.01
☐ 258	Bo Diaz	.10	.05	.01
☐ 259	Rodney Scott	.10	.05	.01
☐ 260	Bruce Sutter	.20	.09	.03
☐ 261	Tigers Rookies UER	.10	.05	.01
	Howard Bailey			
	Marty Castillo			
	Dave Rucker			
	(Rucker photo act-			
	ally Roger Weaver)			
☐ 262	Doug Bair	.10	.05	.01
☐ 263	Victor Cruz	.10	.05	.01

☐ 264	Dan Quisenberry	.20	.09	.03
☐ 265	Al Bumbry	.20	.09	.03
☐ 266	Rick Leach	.20	.09	.03
☐ 267	Kurt Bevacqua	.10	.05	.01
☐ 268	Rickey Keeton	.10	.05	.01
☐ 269	Jim Essian	.10	.05	.01
☐ 270	Rusty Staub	.20	.09	.03
☐ 271	Larry Bradford	.10	.05	.01
☐ 272	Bump Wills	.10	.05	.01
☐ 273	Doug Bird	.10	.05	.01
☐ 274	Bob Ojeda	.40	.18	.05
☐ 275	Bob Watson	.20	.09	.03
☐ 276	Angels TL	.40	.18	.05
	BA: Rod Carew			
	Pitching: Ken Forsch			
	(Checklist on back)			
☐ 277	Terry Puhl	.10	.05	.01
☐ 278	John Littlefield	.10	.05	.01
☐ 279	Bill Russell	.20	.09	.03
☐ 280	Ben Oglivie	.20	.09	.03
☐ 281	John Verhoeven	.10	.05	.01
☐ 282	Ken Macha	.10	.05	.01
☐ 283	Brian Allard	.10	.05	.01
☐ 284	Bob Grich	.20	.09	.03
☐ 285	Sparky Lyle	.20	.09	.03
☐ 286	Bill Fahey	.10	.05	.01
☐ 287	Alan Bannister	.10	.05	.01
☐ 288	Garry Templeton	.20	.09	.03
☐ 289	Bob Stanley	.10	.05	.01
☐ 290	Ken Singleton	.20	.09	.03
☐ 291	Pirates Rookies	.20	.09	.03
	Vance Law			
	Bob Long			
	Johnny Ray			
☐ 292	David Palmer	.10	.05	.01
☐ 293	Rob Picciolo	.10	.05	.01
☐ 294	Mike LaCoss	.10	.05	.01
☐ 295	Jason Thompson	.10	.05	.01
☐ 296	Bob Walk	.10	.05	.01
☐ 297	Clint Hurdle	.10	.05	.01
☐ 298	Danny Darwin	.10	.05	.01
☐ 299	Steve Trout	.10	.05	.01
☐ 300	Reggie Jackson	1.50	.70	.19
☐ 301	Reggie Jackson SA	.75	.35	.09
☐ 302	Doug Flynn	.10	.05	.01
☐ 303	Bill Caudill	.10	.05	.01
☐ 304	Johnnie LeMaster	.10	.05	.01
☐ 305	Don Sutton	.40	.18	.05
☐ 306	Don Sutton SA	.20	.09	.03
☐ 307	Randy Bass	.10	.05	.01
☐ 308	Charlie Moore	.10	.05	.01
☐ 309	Pete Redfern	.10	.05	.01
☐ 310	Mike Hargrove	.20	.09	.03
☐ 311	Dodgers TL	.40	.18	.05
	BA: Dusty Baker			
	Pitching: Burt Hooton			
	(Checklist on back)			
☐ 312	Lenny Randle	.10	.05	.01
☐ 313	John Harris	.10	.05	.01
☐ 314	Buck Martinez	.10	.05	.01
☐ 315	Burt Hooton	.10	.05	.01
☐ 316	Steve Braun	.10	.05	.01
☐ 317	Dick Ruthven	.10	.05	.01
☐ 318	Mike Heath	.10	.05	.01
☐ 319	Dave Rozema	.10	.05	.01
☐ 320	Chris Chambliss	.20	.09	.03
☐ 321	Chris Chambliss SA	.10	.05	.01
☐ 322	Garry Hancock	.10	.05	.01
☐ 323	Bill Lee	.10	.05	.01
☐ 324	Steve Dillard	.10	.05	.01
☐ 325	Jose Cruz	.20	.09	.03

☐ 326 Pete Falcone	.10	.05	.01
☐ 327 Joe Nolan	.10	.05	.01
☐ 328 Ed Farmer	.10	.05	.01
☐ 329 U.L. Washington	.10	.05	.01
☐ 330 Rick Wise	.10	.05	.01
☐ 331 Benny Ayala	.10	.05	.01
☐ 332 Don Robinson	.10	.05	.01
☐ 333 Brewers Rookies	.10	.05	.01
Frank DiPino			
Marshall Edwards			
Chuck Porter			
☐ 334 Aurelio Rodriguez	.10	.05	.01
☐ 335 Jim Sundberg	.20	.09	.03
☐ 336 Mariners TL	.40	.18	.05
BA: Tom Paciorek			
Pitching: Glenn Abbott			
(Checklist on back)			
☐ 337 Pete Rose AS	1.00	.45	.12
☐ 338 Dave Lopes AS	.20	.09	.03
☐ 339 Mike Schmidt AS	.75	.35	.09
☐ 340 Dave Concepcion AS	.20	.09	.03
☐ 341 Andre Dawson AS	.60	.25	.07
☐ 342A George Foster AS	.20	.09	.03
(With autograph)			
☐ 342B George Foster AS	1.00	.45	.12
(W/o autograph)			
☐ 343 Dave Parker AS	.20	.09	.03
☐ 344 Gary Carter AS	.40	.18	.05
☐ 345 Fernando Valenzuela AS	.20	.09	.03
☐ 346A Tom Seaver AS ERR	1.25	.55	.16
("ted")			
☐ 346B Tom Seaver AS COR	.75	.35	.09
("tied")			
☐ 347 Bruce Sutter AS	.20	.09	.03
☐ 348 Derrel Thomas	.10	.05	.01
☐ 349 George Frazier	.10	.05	.01
☐ 350 Thad Bosley	.10	.05	.01
☐ 351 Reds Rookies	.10	.05	.01
Scott Brown			
Geoff Combe			
Paul Householder			
☐ 352 Dick Davis	.10	.05	.01
☐ 353 Jack O'Connor	.10	.05	.01
☐ 354 Roberto Ramos	.10	.05	.01
☐ 355 Dwight Evans	.40	.18	.05
☐ 356 Denny Lewallyn	.10	.05	.01
☐ 357 Butch Hobson	.20	.09	.03
☐ 358 Mike Parrott	.10	.05	.01
☐ 359 Jim Dwyer	.10	.05	.01
☐ 360 Len Barker	.10	.05	.01
☐ 361 Rafael Landestoy	.10	.05	.01
☐ 362 Jim Wright UER	.10	.05	.01
(Wrong Jim Wright			
pictured)			
☐ 363 Bob Molinaro	.10	.05	.01
☐ 364 Doyle Alexander	.10	.05	.01
☐ 365 Bill Madlock	.20	.09	.03
☐ 366 Padres TL	.40	.18	.05
BA: Luis Salazar			
Pitching: Juan			
Eichelberger			
(Checklist on back)			
☐ 367 Jim Kaat	.20	.09	.03
☐ 368 Alex Trevino	.10	.05	.01
☐ 369 Champ Summers	.10	.05	.01
☐ 370 Mike Norris	.10	.05	.01
☐ 371 Jerry Don Gleaton	.10	.05	.01
☐ 372 Luis Gomez	.10	.05	.01
☐ 373 Gene Nelson	.10	.05	.01
☐ 374 Tim Blackwell	.10	.05	.01
☐ 375 Dusty Baker	.40	.18	.05
☐ 376 Chris Welsh	.10	.05	.01
☐ 377 Kiko Garcia	.10	.05	.01
☐ 378 Mike Caldwell	.10	.05	.01
☐ 379 Rob Wilfong	.10	.05	.01
☐ 380 Dave Stieb	.20	.09	.03
☐ 381 Red Sox Rookies	.20	.09	.03
Bruce Hurst			
Dave Schmidt			
Julio Valdez			
☐ 382 Joe Simpson	.10	.05	.01
☐ 383A Pascual Perez ERR	10.00	4.50	1.25
(No position			
on front)			
☐ 383B Pascual Perez COR	.10	.05	.01
☐ 384 Keith Moreland	.10	.05	.01
☐ 385 Ken Forsch	.10	.05	.01
☐ 386 Jerry White	.10	.05	.01
☐ 387 Tom Veryzer	.10	.05	.01
☐ 388 Joe Rudi	.10	.05	.01
☐ 389 George Vukovich	.10	.05	.01
☐ 390 Eddie Murray	3.00	1.35	.35
☐ 391 Dave Tobik	.10	.05	.01
☐ 392 Rick Bosetti	.10	.05	.01
☐ 393 Al Hrabosky	.10	.05	.01
☐ 394 Checklist 265-396	.40	.18	.05
☐ 395 Omar Moreno	.10	.05	.01
☐ 396 Twins TL	.40	.18	.05
BA: John Castino			
Pitching: Fernando			
Arroyo			
(Checklist on back)			
☐ 397 Ken Brett	.10	.05	.01
☐ 398 Mike Squires	.10	.05	.01
☐ 399 Pat Zachry	.10	.05	.01
☐ 400 Johnny Bench	1.50	.70	.19
☐ 401 Johnny Bench SA	.75	.35	.09
☐ 402 Bill Stein	.10	.05	.01
☐ 403 Jim Tracy	.10	.05	.01
☐ 404 Dickie Thon	.10	.05	.01
☐ 405 Rick Reuschel	.20	.09	.03
☐ 406 Al Holland	.10	.05	.01
☐ 407 Danny Boone	.10	.05	.01
☐ 408 Ed Romero	.10	.05	.01
☐ 409 Don Cooper	.10	.05	.01
☐ 410 Ron Cey	.20	.09	.03
☐ 411 Ron Cey SA	.10	.05	.01
☐ 412 Luis Leal	.10	.05	.01
☐ 413 Dan Meyer	.10	.05	.01
☐ 414 Elias Sosa	.10	.05	.01
☐ 415 Don Baylor	.40	.18	.05
☐ 416 Marty Bystrom	.10	.05	.01
☐ 417 Pat Kelly	.10	.05	.01
☐ 418 Rangers Rookies	.10	.05	.01
John Butcher			
Bobby Johnson			
Dave Schmidt			
☐ 419 Steve Stone	.20	.09	.03
☐ 420 George Hendrick	.20	.09	.03
☐ 421 Mark Clear	.10	.05	.01
☐ 422 Cliff Johnson	.10	.05	.01
☐ 423 Stan Papi	.10	.05	.01
☐ 424 Bruce Benedict	.10	.05	.01
☐ 425 John Candelaria	.10	.05	.01
☐ 426 Orioles TL	.50	.23	.06
BA: Eddie Murray			
Pitching: Sammy Stewart			
(Checklist on back)			
☐ 427 Ron Oester	.10	.05	.01
☐ 428 LaMarr Hoyt	.10	.05	.01
☐ 429 John Wathan	.10	.05	.01
☐ 430 Vida Blue	.20	.09	.03

☐ 431 Vida Blue SA	.10	.05	.01
☐ 432 Mike Scott	.20	.09	.03
☐ 433 Alan Ashby	.10	.05	.01
☐ 434 Joe Lefebvre	.10	.05	.01
☐ 435 Robin Yount	2.00	.90	.25
☐ 436 Joe Strain	.10	.05	.01
☐ 437 Juan Berenguer	.10	.05	.01
☐ 438 Pete Mackanin	.10	.05	.01
☐ 439 Dave Righetti	.40	.18	.05
☐ 440 Jeff Burroughs	.10	.05	.01
☐ 441 Astros Rookies	.10	.05	.01
Danny Heep			
Billy Smith			
Bobby Sprowl			
☐ 442 Bruce Kison	.10	.05	.01
☐ 443 Mark Wagner	.10	.05	.01
☐ 444 Terry Forster	.10	.05	.01
☐ 445 Larry Parrish	.10	.05	.01
☐ 446 Wayne Garland	.10	.05	.01
☐ 447 Darrell Porter	.10	.05	.01
☐ 448 Darrell Porter SA	.10	.05	.01
☐ 449 Luis Aguayo	.10	.05	.01
☐ 450 Jack Morris	.40	.18	.05
☐ 451 Ed Miller	.10	.05	.01
☐ 452 Lee Smith	8.00	3.60	1.00
☐ 453 Art Howe	.10	.05	.01
☐ 454 Rick Langford	.10	.05	.01
☐ 455 Tom Burgmeier	.10	.05	.01
☐ 456 Chicago Cubs TL	.40	.18	.05
BA: Bill Buckner			
Pitching: Randy Martz			
(Checklist on back)			
☐ 457 Tim Stoddard	.10	.05	.01
☐ 458 Willie Montanez	.10	.05	.01
☐ 459 Bruce Berenyi	.10	.05	.01
☐ 460 Jack Clark	.20	.09	.03
☐ 461 Rich Dotson	.10	.05	.01
☐ 462 Dave Chalk	.10	.05	.01
☐ 463 Jim Kern	.10	.05	.01
☐ 464 Juan Bonilla	.10	.05	.01
☐ 465 Lee Mazzilli	.10	.05	.01
☐ 466 Randy Lerch	.10	.05	.01
☐ 467 Mickey Hatcher	.10	.05	.01
☐ 468 Floyd Bannister	.10	.05	.01
☐ 469 Ed Ott	.10	.05	.01
☐ 470 John Mayberry	.10	.05	.01
☐ 471 Royals Rookies	.10	.05	.01
Atlee Hammaker			
Mike Jones			
Darryl Motley			
☐ 472 Oscar Gamble	.10	.05	.01
☐ 473 Mike Stanton	.10	.05	.01
☐ 474 Ken Oberkfell	.10	.05	.01
☐ 475 Alan Trammell	1.25	.55	.16
☐ 476 Brian Kingman	.10	.05	.01
☐ 477 Steve Yeager	.10	.05	.01
☐ 478 Ray Searage	.10	.05	.01
☐ 479 Rowland Office	.10	.05	.01
☐ 480 Steve Carlton	1.25	.55	.16
☐ 481 Steve Carlton SA	.60	.25	.07
☐ 482 Glenn Hubbard	.10	.05	.01
☐ 483 Gary Woods	.10	.05	.01
☐ 484 Ivan DeJesus	.10	.05	.01
☐ 485 Kent Tekulve	.20	.09	.03
☐ 486 Yankees TL	.20	.09	.03
BA: Jerry Mumphrey			
Pitching: Tommy John			
(Checklist on back)			
☐ 487 Bob McClure	.10	.05	.01
☐ 488 Ron Jackson	.10	.05	.01
☐ 489 Rick Dempsey	.20	.09	.03

☐ 490 Dennis Eckersley	.75	.35	.09
☐ 491 Checklist 397-528	.40	.18	.05
☐ 492 Joe Price	.10	.05	.01
☐ 493 Chet Lemon	.10	.05	.01
☐ 494 Hubie Brooks	.20	.09	.03
☐ 495 Dennis Leonard	.10	.05	.01
☐ 496 Johnny Grubb	.10	.05	.01
☐ 497 Jim Anderson	.10	.05	.01
☐ 498 Dave Bergman	.10	.05	.01
☐ 499 Paul Mirabella	.10	.05	.01
☐ 500 Rod Carew	1.00	.45	.12
☐ 501 Rod Carew SA	.50	.23	.06
☐ 502 Braves Rookies	3.00	1.35	.35
Steve Bedrosian UER			
(Photo actually			
Larry Owen)			
Brett Butler			
Larry Owen			
☐ 503 Julio Gonzalez	.10	.05	.01
☐ 504 Rick Peters	.10	.05	.01
☐ 505 Graig Nettles	.20	.09	.03
☐ 506 Graig Nettles SA	.10	.05	.01
☐ 507 Terry Harper	.10	.05	.01
☐ 508 Jody Davis	.10	.05	.01
☐ 509 Harry Spilman	.10	.05	.01
☐ 510 Fernando Valenzuela	.40	.18	.05
☐ 511 Ruppert Jones	.10	.05	.01
☐ 512 Jerry Dybzinski	.10	.05	.01
☐ 513 Rick Rhoden	.10	.05	.01
☐ 514 Joe Ferguson	.10	.05	.01
☐ 515 Larry Bowa	.20	.09	.03
☐ 516 Larry Bowa SA	.10	.05	.01
☐ 517 Mark Brouhard	.10	.05	.01
☐ 518 Garth Iorg	.10	.05	.01
☐ 519 Glenn Adams	.10	.05	.01
☐ 520 Mike Flanagan	.20	.09	.03
☐ 521 Bill Almon	.10	.05	.01
☐ 522 Chuck Rainey	.10	.05	.01
☐ 523 Gary Gray	.10	.05	.01
☐ 524 Tom Hausman	.10	.05	.01
☐ 525 Ray Knight	.20	.09	.03
☐ 526 Expos TL	.40	.18	.05
BA: Warren Cromartie			
Pitching: Bill Gullickson			
(Checklist on back)			
☐ 527 John Henry Johnson	.10	.05	.01
☐ 528 Matt Alexander	.10	.05	.01
☐ 529 Allen Ripley	.10	.05	.01
☐ 530 Dickie Noles	.10	.05	.01
☐ 531 A's Rookies	.10	.05	.01
Rich Bordi			
Mark Budaska			
Kelvin Moore			
☐ 532 Toby Harrah	.20	.09	.03
☐ 533 Joaquin Andujar	.20	.09	.03
☐ 534 Dave McKay	.10	.05	.01
☐ 535 Lance Parrish	.40	.18	.05
☐ 536 Rafael Ramirez	.10	.05	.01
☐ 537 Doug Capilla	.10	.05	.01
☐ 538 Lou Piniella	.20	.09	.03
☐ 539 Vern Ruhle	.10	.05	.01
☐ 540 Andre Dawson	1.50	.70	.19
☐ 541 Barry Evans	.10	.05	.01
☐ 542 Ned Yost	.10	.05	.01
☐ 543 Bill Robinson	.20	.09	.03
☐ 544 Larry Christenson	.10	.05	.01
☐ 545 Reggie Smith	.20	.09	.03
☐ 546 Reggie Smith SA	.10	.05	.01
☐ 547 Rod Carew AS	.50	.23	.06
☐ 548 Willie Randolph AS	.20	.09	.03
☐ 549 George Brett AS	2.50	1.10	.30

550	Bucky Dent AS	.20	.09	.03
551	Reggie Jackson AS	.75	.35	.09
552	Ken Singleton AS	.20	.09	.03
553	Dave Winfield AS	1.25	.55	.16
554	Carlton Fisk AS	.40	.18	.05
555	Scott McGregor AS	.20	.09	.03
556	Jack Morris AS	.40	.18	.05
557	Rich Gossage AS	.20	.09	.03
558	John Tudor	.20	.09	.03
559	Indians TL	.20	.09	.03
	BA: Mike Hargrove			
	Pitching: Bert Blyleven			
	(Checklist on back)			
560	Doug Corbett	.10	.05	.01
561	Cardinals Rookies	.10	.05	.01
	Glenn Brummer			
	Luis DeLeon			
	Gene Roof			
562	Mike O'Berry	.10	.05	.01
563	Ross Baumgarten	.10	.05	.01
564	Doug DeCinces	.20	.09	.03
565	Jackson Todd	.10	.05	.01
566	Mike Jorgensen	.10	.05	.01
567	Bob Babcock	.10	.05	.01
568	Joe Pettini	.10	.05	.01
569	Willie Randolph	.20	.09	.03
570	Willie Randolph SA	.10	.05	.01
571	Glenn Abbott	.10	.05	.01
572	Juan Beniquez	.10	.05	.01
573	Rick Waits	.10	.05	.01
574	Mike Ramsey	.10	.05	.01
575	Al Cowens	.10	.05	.01
576	Giants TL	.40	.18	.05
	BA: Milt May			
	Pitching: Vida Blue			
	(Checklist on back)			
577	Rick Monday	.10	.05	.01
578	Shooty Babitt	.10	.05	.01
579	Rick Mahler	.10	.05	.01
580	Bobby Bonds	.20	.09	.03
581	Ron Reed	.20	.09	.03
582	Luis Pujols	.10	.05	.01
583	Tippy Martinez	.10	.05	.01
584	Hosken Powell	.10	.05	.01
585	Rollie Fingers	.40	.18	.05
586	Rollie Fingers SA	.20	.09	.03
587	Tim Lollar	.10	.05	.01
588	Dale Berra	.10	.05	.01
589	Dave Stapleton	.10	.05	.01
590	Al Oliver	.20	.09	.03
591	Al Oliver SA	.10	.05	.01
592	Craig Swan	.10	.05	.01
593	Billy Smith	.10	.05	.01
594	Renie Martin	.10	.05	.01
595	Dave Collins	.10	.05	.01
596	Damaso Garcia	.10	.05	.01
597	Wayne Nordhagen	.10	.05	.01
598	Bob Galasso	.10	.05	.01
599	White Sox Rookies	.10	.05	.01
	Jay Loviglio			
	Reggie Patterson			
	Leo Sutherland			
600	Dave Winfield	2.50	1.10	.30
601	Sid Monge	.10	.05	.01
602	Freddie Patek	.10	.05	.01
603	Rich Hebner	.10	.05	.01
604	Orlando Sanchez	.10	.05	.01
605	Steve Rogers	.10	.05	.01
606	Blue Jays TL	.40	.18	.05
	BA: John Mayberry			
	Pitching: Dave Stieb			
	(Checklist on back)			
607	Leon Durham	.10	.05	.01
608	Jerry Royster	.10	.05	.01
609	Rick Sutcliffe	.20	.09	.03
610	Rickey Henderson	4.00	1.80	.50
611	Joe Niekro	.20	.09	.03
612	Gary Ward	.10	.05	.01
613	Jim Gantner	.20	.09	.03
614	Juan Eichelberger	.10	.05	.01
615	Bob Boone	.20	.09	.03
616	Bob Boone SA	.10	.05	.01
617	Scott McGregor	.10	.05	.01
618	Tim Foli	.10	.05	.01
619	Bill Campbell	.10	.05	.01
620	Ken Griffey	.20	.09	.03
621	Ken Griffey SA	.10	.05	.01
622	Dennis Lamp	.10	.05	.01
623	Mets Rookies	.40	.18	.05
	Ron Gardenhire			
	Terry Leach			
	Tim Leary			
624	Fergie Jenkins	.40	.18	.05
625	Hal McRae	.40	.18	.05
626	Randy Jones	.10	.05	.01
627	Enos Cabell	.10	.05	.01
628	Bill Travers	.10	.05	.01
629	John Wockenfuss	.10	.05	.01
630	Joe Charboneau	.20	.09	.03
631	Gene Tenace	.10	.05	.01
632	Bryan Clark	.10	.05	.01
633	Mitchell Page	.10	.05	.01
634	Checklist 529-660	.40	.18	.05
635	Ron Davis	.10	.05	.01
636	Phillies TL	.40	.18	.05
	BA: Pete Rose			
	Pitching: Steve Carlton			
	(Checklist on back)			
637	Rick Camp	.10	.05	.01
638	John Milner	.10	.05	.01
639	Ken Kravec	.10	.05	.01
640	Cesar Cedeno	.20	.09	.03
641	Steve Mura	.10	.05	.01
642	Mike Scioscia	.20	.09	.03
643	Pete Vuckovich	.20	.09	.03
644	John Castino	.10	.05	.01
645	Frank White	.20	.09	.03
646	Frank White SA	.10	.05	.01
647	Warren Brusstar	.10	.05	.01
648	Jose Morales	.10	.05	.01
649	Ken Clay	.10	.05	.01
650	Carl Yastrzemski	1.25	.55	.16
651	Carl Yastrzemski SA	.60	.25	.07
652	Steve Nicosia	.10	.05	.01
653	Angels Rookies	.40	.18	.05
	Tom Brunansky			
	Luis Sanchez			
	Daryl Sconiers			
654	Jim Morrison	.10	.05	.01
655	Joel Youngblood	.10	.05	.01
656	Eddie Whitson	.10	.05	.01
657	Tom Poquette	.10	.05	.01
658	Tito Landrum	.10	.05	.01
659	Fred Martinez	.10	.05	.01
660	Dave Concepcion	.20	.09	.03
661	Dave Concepcion SA	.10	.05	.01
662	Luis Salazar	.10	.05	.01
663	Hector Cruz	.10	.05	.01
664	Dan Spiller	.10	.05	.01
665	Jim Clancy	.10	.05	.01
666	Tigers TL	.40	.18	.05
	BA: Steve Kemp			

Pitching: Dan Petry
(Checklist on back)

☐	667	Jeff Reardon	.75	.35	.09
☐	668	Dale Murphy	1.00	.45	.12
☐	669	Larry Milbourne	.10	.05	.01
☐	670	Steve Kemp	.10	.05	.01
☐	671	Mike Davis	.10	.05	.01
☐	672	Bob Knepper	.10	.05	.01
☐	673	Keith Drumwright	.10	.05	.01
☐	674	Dave Goltz	.10	.05	.01
☐	675	Cecil Cooper	.20	.09	.03
☐	676	Sal Butera	.10	.05	.01
☐	677	Alfredo Griffin	.10	.05	.01
☐	678	Tom Paciorek	.20	.09	.03
☐	679	Sammy Stewart	.10	.05	.01
☐	680	Gary Matthews	.20	.09	.03
☐	681	Dodgers Rookies	.75	.35	.09
		Mike Marshall			
		Ron Roenicke			
		Steve Sax			
☐	682	Jesse Jefferson	.10	.05	.01
☐	683	Phil Garner	.20	.09	.03
☐	684	Harold Baines	1.00	.45	.12
☐	685	Bert Blyleven	.40	.18	.05
☐	686	Gary Allenson	.10	.05	.01
☐	687	Greg Minton	.10	.05	.01
☐	688	Leon Roberts	.10	.05	.01
☐	689	Lary Sorensen	.10	.05	.01
☐	690	Dave Kingman	.20	.09	.03
☐	691	Dan Schatzeder	.10	.05	.01
☐	692	Wayne Gross	.10	.05	.01
☐	693	Cesar Geronimo	.10	.05	.01
☐	694	Dave Wehrmeister	.10	.05	.01
☐	695	Warren Cromartie	.10	.05	.01
☐	696	Pirates TL	.40	.18	.05
		BA: Bill Madlock			
		Pitching: Eddie Solomon			
		(Checklist on back)			
☐	697	John Montefusco	.10	.05	.01
☐	698	Tony Scott	.10	.05	.01
☐	699	Dick Tidrow	.10	.05	.01
☐	700	George Foster	.20	.09	.03
☐	701	George Foster SA	.10	.05	.01
☐	702	Steve Renko	.10	.05	.01
☐	703	Brewers TL	.40	.18	.05
		BA: Cecil Cooper			
		Pitching: Pete Vuckovich			
		(Checklist on back)			
☐	704	Mickey Rivers	.10	.05	.01
☐	705	Mickey Rivers SA	.10	.05	.01
☐	706	Barry Foote	.10	.05	.01
☐	707	Mark Bomback	.10	.05	.01
☐	708	Gene Richards	.10	.05	.01
☐	709	Don Money	.10	.05	.01
☐	710	Jerry Reuss	.10	.05	.01
☐	711	Mariners Rookies	.75	.35	.09
		Dave Edler			
		Dave Henderson			
		Reggie Walton			
☐	712	Dennis Martinez	.20	.09	.03
☐	713	Del Unser	.10	.05	.01
☐	714	Jerry Koosman	.20	.09	.03
☐	715	Willie Stargell	.75	.35	.09
☐	716	Willie Stargell SA	.35	.16	.04
☐	717	Rick Miller	.10	.05	.01
☐	718	Charlie Hough	.20	.09	.03
☐	719	Jerry Narron	.10	.05	.01
☐	720	Greg Luzinski	.20	.09	.03
☐	721	Greg Luzinski SA	.10	.05	.01
☐	722	Jerry Martin	.10	.05	.01
☐	723	Junior Kennedy	.10	.05	.01
☐	724	Dave Rosello	.10	.05	.01
☐	725	Amos Otis	.20	.09	.03
☐	726	Amos Otis SA	.10	.05	.01
☐	727	Sixto Lezcano	.10	.05	.01
☐	728	Aurelio Lopez	.10	.05	.01
☐	729	Jim Spencer	.10	.05	.01
☐	730	Gary Carter	.60	.25	.07
☐	731	Padres Rookies	.10	.05	.01
		Mike Armstrong			
		Doug Gwosdz			
		Fred Kuhaulua			
☐	732	Mike Lum	.10	.05	.01
☐	733	Larry McWilliams	.10	.05	.01
☐	734	Mike Ivie	.10	.05	.01
☐	735	Rudy May	.10	.05	.01
☐	736	Jerry Turner	.10	.05	.01
☐	737	Reggie Cleveland	.10	.05	.01
☐	738	Dave Engle	.10	.05	.01
☐	739	Joey McLaughlin	.10	.05	.01
☐	740	Dave Lopes	.20	.09	.03
☐	741	Dave Lopes SA	.10	.05	.01
☐	742	Dick Drago	.10	.05	.01
☐	743	John Stearns	.10	.05	.01
☐	744	Mike Witt	.10	.05	.01
☐	745	Bake McBride	.10	.05	.01
☐	746	Andre Thornton	.20	.09	.03
☐	747	John Lowenstein	.10	.05	.01
☐	748	Marc Hill	.10	.05	.01
☐	749	Bob Shirley	.10	.05	.01
☐	750	Jim Rice	.40	.18	.05
☐	751	Rick Honeycutt	.10	.05	.01
☐	752	Lee Lacy	.10	.05	.01
☐	753	Tom Brookens	.10	.05	.01
☐	754	Joe Morgan	.75	.35	.09
☐	755	Joe Morgan SA	.35	.16	.04
☐	756	Reds TL	.30	.14	.04
		BA: Ken Griffey			
		Pitching: Tom Seaver			
		(Checklist on back)			
☐	757	Tom Underwood	.10	.05	.01
☐	758	Claudell Washington	.10	.05	.01
☐	759	Paul Splittorff	.10	.05	.01
☐	760	Bill Buckner	.20	.09	.03
☐	761	Dave Smith	.10	.05	.01
☐	762	Mike Phillips	.10	.05	.01
☐	763	Tom Hume	.10	.05	.01
☐	764	Steve Swisher	.10	.05	.01
☐	765	Gorman Thomas	.20	.09	.03
☐	766	Twins Rookies	3.00	1.35	.35
		Lenny Faedo			
		Kent Hrbek			
		Tim Laudner			
☐	767	Roy Smalley	.10	.05	.01
☐	768	Jerry Garvin	.10	.05	.01
☐	769	Richie Zisk	.10	.05	.01
☐	770	Rich Gossage	.40	.18	.05
☐	771	Rich Gossage SA	.20	.09	.03
☐	772	Bert Campaneris	.20	.09	.03
☐	773	John Denny	.10	.05	.01
☐	774	Jay Johnstone	.20	.09	.03
☐	775	Bob Forsch	.10	.05	.01
☐	776	Mark Belanger	.20	.09	.03
☐	777	Tom Griffin	.10	.05	.01
☐	778	Kevin Hickey	.10	.05	.01
☐	779	Grant Jackson	.10	.05	.01
☐	780	Pete Rose	2.00	.90	.25
☐	781	Pete Rose SA	1.00	.45	.12
☐	782	Frank Taveras	.10	.05	.01
☐	783	Greg Harris	.10	.05	.01
☐	784	Milt Wilcox	.10	.05	.01
☐	785	Dan Driessen	.10	.05	.01

		NRMT-MT	EXC	G-VG
☐ 786	Red Sox TL	.40	.18	.05
	BA: Carney Lansford			
	Pitching: Mike Torrez			
	(Checklist on back)			
☐ 787	Fred Stanley	.10	.05	.01
☐ 788	Woodie Fryman	.10	.05	.01
☐ 789	Checklist 661-792	.40	.18	.05
☐ 790	Larry Gura	.10	.05	.01
☐ 791	Bobby Brown	.10	.05	.01
☐ 792	Frank Tanana	.20	.09	.03

1982 Topps Traded

 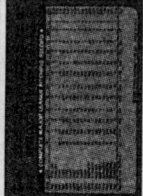

The cards in this 132-card set measure 2 1/2" by 3 1/2". The 1982 Topps Traded or extended series is distinguished by a "T" printed after the number (located on the reverse). This was the first time Topps began a tradition of newly numbering (and alphabetizing) their traded series from 1T to 132T. Of the total cards, 70 players represent the American League and 61 represent the National League, with the remaining card a numbered checklist (132T). The Cubs lead the pack with 12 changes, while the Red Sox are the only team in either league to have no new additions. All 131 player photos used in the set are completely new. Of this total, 112 individuals are seen in the uniform of their new team, 11 others have been elevated to single card status from "Future Stars" cards, and eight more are entirely new to the 1982 Topps lineup. The backs are almost completely red in color with black print. There are no key rookie cards in this set. Although the Cal Ripken card is this set's most valuable card, it is not his Rookie Card since he had already been included in the 1982 regular set, albeit on a multi-player card.

		NRMT-MT	EXC	G-VG
COMPLETE FACT.SET (132)		350.00	160.00	45.00
COMMON CARD (1T-132T)		.35	.16	.04
☐ 1T	Doyle Alexander	.35	.16	.04
☐ 2T	Jesse Barfield	.60	.25	.07
☐ 3T	Ross Baumgarten	.35	.16	.04
☐ 4T	Steve Bedrosian	.60	.25	.07
☐ 5T	Mark Belanger	.50	.23	.06
☐ 6T	Kurt Bevacqua	.35	.16	.04
☐ 7T	Tim Blackwell	.35	.16	.04
☐ 8T	Vida Blue	.50	.23	.06
☐ 9T	Bob Boone	.50	.23	.06
☐ 10T	Larry Bowa	.50	.23	.06
☐ 11T	Dan Briggs	.35	.16	.04
☐ 12T	Bobby Brown	.35	.16	.04
☐ 13T	Tom Brunansky	.50	.23	.06
☐ 14T	Jeff Burroughs	.35	.16	.04
☐ 15T	Enos Cabell	.35	.16	.04
☐ 16T	Bill Campbell	.35	.16	.04
☐ 17T	Bobby Castillo	.35	.16	.04
☐ 18T	Bill Caudill	.35	.16	.04
☐ 19T	Cesar Cedeno	.50	.23	.06
☐ 20T	Dave Collins	.35	.16	.04
☐ 21T	Doug Corbett	.35	.16	.04
☐ 22T	Al Cowens	.35	.16	.04
☐ 23T	Chili Davis	6.00	2.70	.75
☐ 24T	Dick Davis	.35	.16	.04
☐ 25T	Ron Davis	.35	.16	.04
☐ 26T	Doug DeCinces	.50	.23	.06
☐ 27T	Ivan DeJesus	.35	.16	.04
☐ 28T	Bob Dernier	.35	.16	.04
☐ 29T	Bo Diaz	.35	.16	.04
☐ 30T	Roger Erickson	.35	.16	.04
☐ 31T	Jim Essian	.35	.16	.04
☐ 32T	Ed Farmer	.35	.16	.04
☐ 33T	Doug Flynn	.35	.16	.04
☐ 34T	Tim Foli	.35	.16	.04
☐ 35T	Dan Ford	.35	.16	.04
☐ 36T	George Foster	.50	.23	.06
☐ 37T	Dave Frost	.35	.16	.04
☐ 38T	Rich Gale	.35	.16	.04
☐ 39T	Ron Gardenhire	.35	.16	.04
☐ 40T	Ken Griffey	.60	.25	.07
☐ 41T	Greg Harris	.50	.23	.06
☐ 42T	Von Hayes	.50	.23	.06
☐ 43T	Larry Herndon	.35	.16	.04
☐ 44T	Kent Hrbek	4.00	1.80	.50
☐ 45T	Mike Ivie	.35	.16	.04
☐ 46T	Grant Jackson	.35	.16	.04
☐ 47T	Reggie Jackson	10.00	4.50	1.25
☐ 48T	Ron Jackson	.35	.16	.04
☐ 49T	Fergie Jenkins	1.00	.45	.12
☐ 50T	Lamar Johnson	.35	.16	.04
☐ 51T	Randy Johnson	.35	.16	.04
☐ 52T	Jay Johnstone	.50	.23	.06
☐ 53T	Mick Kelleher	.35	.16	.04
☐ 54T	Steve Kemp	.35	.16	.04
☐ 55T	Junior Kennedy	.35	.16	.04
☐ 56T	Jim Kern	.35	.16	.04
☐ 57T	Ray Knight	.50	.23	.06
☐ 58T	Wayne Krenchicki	.35	.16	.04
☐ 59T	Mike Krukow	.35	.16	.04
☐ 60T	Duane Kuiper	.35	.16	.04
☐ 61T	Mike LaCoss	.35	.16	.04
☐ 62T	Chet Lemon	.35	.16	.04
☐ 63T	Sixto Lezcano	.35	.16	.04
☐ 64T	Dave Lopes	.50	.23	.06
☐ 65T	Jerry Martin	.35	.16	.04
☐ 66T	Renie Martin	.35	.16	.04
☐ 67T	John Mayberry	.35	.16	.04
☐ 68T	Lee Mazzilli	.35	.16	.04
☐ 69T	Bake McBride	.35	.16	.04
☐ 70T	Dan Meyer	.35	.16	.04
☐ 71T	Larry Milbourne	.35	.16	.04
☐ 72T	Eddie Milner	.35	.16	.04
☐ 73T	Sid Monge	.35	.16	.04
☐ 74T	John Montefusco	.35	.16	.04
☐ 75T	Jose Morales	.35	.16	.04
☐ 76T	Keith Moreland	.35	.16	.04
☐ 77T	Jim Morrison	.35	.16	.04
☐ 78T	Rance Mulliniks	.35	.16	.04

☐ 79T	Steve Mura	.35	.16	.04
☐ 80T	Gene Nelson	.35	.16	.04
☐ 81T	Joe Nolan	.35	.16	.04
☐ 82T	Dickie Noles	.35	.16	.04
☐ 83T	Al Oliver	.50	.23	.06
☐ 84T	Jorge Orta	.35	.16	.04
☐ 85T	Tom Paciorek	.50	.23	.06
☐ 86T	Larry Parrish	.35	.16	.04
☐ 87T	Jack Perconte	.35	.16	.04
☐ 88T	Gaylord Perry	1.00	.45	.12
☐ 89T	Rob Picciolo	.35	.16	.04
☐ 90T	Joe Pittman	.35	.16	.04
☐ 91T	Hosken Powell	.35	.16	.04
☐ 92T	Mike Proly	.35	.16	.04
☐ 93T	Greg Pryor	.35	.16	.04
☐ 94T	Charlie Puleo	.35	.16	.04
☐ 95T	Shane Rawley	.35	.16	.04
☐ 96T	Johnny Ray	.50	.23	.06
☐ 97T	Dave Revering	.35	.16	.04
☐ 98T	Cal Ripken	325.00	145.00	40.00
☐ 99T	Allen Ripley	.35	.16	.04
☐ 100T	Bill Robinson	.50	.23	.06
☐ 101T	Aurelio Rodriguez	.35	.16	.04
☐ 102T	Joe Rudi	.35	.16	.04
☐ 103T	Steve Sax	1.00	.45	.12
☐ 104T	Dan Schatzeder	.35	.16	.04
☐ 105T	Bob Shirley	.35	.16	.04
☐ 106T	Eric Show	.50	.23	.06
☐ 107T	Roy Smalley	.35	.16	.04
☐ 108T	Lonnie Smith	.50	.23	.06
☐ 109T	Ozzie Smith	25.00	11.00	3.10
☐ 110T	Reggie Smith	.50	.23	.06
☐ 111T	Lary Sorensen	.35	.16	.04
☐ 112T	Elias Sosa	.35	.16	.04
☐ 113T	Mike Stanton	.35	.16	.04
☐ 114T	Steve Stroughter	.35	.16	.04
☐ 115T	Champ Summers	.35	.16	.04
☐ 116T	Rick Sutcliffe	.50	.23	.06
☐ 117T	Frank Tanana	.50	.23	.06
☐ 118T	Frank Taveras	.35	.16	.04
☐ 119T	Garry Templeton	.50	.23	.06
☐ 120T	Alex Trevino	.35	.16	.04
☐ 121T	Jerry Turner	.35	.16	.04
☐ 122T	Ed VandeBerg	.35	.16	.04
☐ 123T	Tom Veryzer	.35	.16	.04
☐ 124T	Ron Washington	.35	.16	.04
☐ 125T	Bob Watson	.50	.23	.06
☐ 126T	Dennis Werth	.35	.16	.04
☐ 127T	Eddie Whitson	.35	.16	.04
☐ 128T	Rob Wilfong	.35	.16	.04
☐ 129T	Bump Wills	.35	.16	.04
☐ 130T	Gary Woods	.35	.16	.04
☐ 131T	Butch Wynegar	.35	.16	.04
☐ 132T	Checklist: 1-132	.35	.16	.04

1983 Topps

The cards in this 792-card set measure 2 1/2" by 3 1/2". Each regular card of the Topps set for 1983 features a large action shot of a player with a small cameo portrait at bottom right. There are special series for AL and NL All Stars (386-407), League Leaders (701-708), and Record Breakers (1-6). In addition, there are 34 "Super Veteran" (SV) cards and six numbered checklist cards. The Super Veteran cards

are oriented horizontally and show two pictures of the featured player, a recent picture and a picture showing the player as a rookie when he broke in. The cards are numbered on the reverse at the upper left corner. The team cards are actually Team Leader (TL) cards picturing the batting (BA: batting average) and pitching leader for that team with a checklist back. The key Rookie Cards in this set are Wade Boggs, Tony Gwynn, Willie McGee, Ryne Sandberg, and Frank Viola.

	NRMT-MT	EXC	G-VG
COMPLETE SET (792)	130.00	57.50	16.00
COMMON CARD (1-792)	.10	.05	.01
☐ 1 Tony Armas RB	.40	.18	.05
11 putouts by rightfielder			
☐ 2 Rickey Henderson RB	1.00	.45	.12
Sets modern record for steals, season			
☐ 3 Greg Minton RB	.10	.05	.01
269 1/3 homerless innings streak			
☐ 4 Lance Parrish RB	.20	.09	.03
Threw out three baserunners in All-Star game			
☐ 5 Manny Trillo RB	.20	.09	.03
479 consecutive errorless chances, second baseman			
☐ 6 John Wathan RB	.10	.05	.01
ML steals record for catchers, 31			
☐ 7 Gene Richards	.10	.05	.01
☐ 8 Steve Balboni	.10	.05	.01
☐ 9 Joey McLaughlin	.10	.05	.01
☐ 10 Gorman Thomas	.10	.05	.01
☐ 11 Billy Gardner MG	.10	.05	.01
☐ 12 Paul Mirabella	.10	.05	.01
☐ 13 Larry Herndon	.10	.05	.01
☐ 14 Frank LaCorte	.10	.05	.01
☐ 15 Ron Cey	.20	.09	.03
☐ 16 George Vukovich	.10	.05	.01
☐ 17 Kent Tekulve	.20	.09	.03
☐ 18 Kent Tekulve SV	.10	.05	.01
☐ 19 Oscar Gamble	.10	.05	.01
☐ 20 Carlton Fisk	1.00	.45	.12
☐ 21 Baltimore Orioles TL	.40	.18	.05
BA: Eddie Murray ERA: Jim Palmer (Checklist on back)			
☐ 22 Randy Martz	.10	.05	.01

☐ 23	Mike Heath	.10	.05	.01
☐ 24	Steve Mura	.10	.05	.01
☐ 25	Hal McRae	.40	.18	.05
☐ 26	Jerry Royster	.10	.05	.01
☐ 27	Doug Corbett	.10	.05	.01
☐ 28	Bruce Bochte	.10	.05	.01
☐ 29	Randy Jones	.10	.05	.01
☐ 30	Jim Rice	.40	.18	.05
☐ 31	Bill Gullickson	.20	.09	.03
☐ 32	Dave Bergman	.10	.05	.01
☐ 33	Jack O'Connor	.10	.05	.01
☐ 34	Paul Householder	.10	.05	.01
☐ 35	Rollie Fingers	.40	.18	.05
☐ 36	Rollie Fingers SV	.20	.09	.03
☐ 37	Darrell Johnson MG	.10	.05	.01
☐ 38	Tim Flannery	.10	.05	.01
☐ 39	Terry Puhl	.10	.05	.01
☐ 40	Fernando Valenzuela	.20	.09	.03
☐ 41	Jerry Turner	.10	.05	.01
☐ 42	Dale Murray	.10	.05	.01
☐ 43	Bob Dernier	.10	.05	.01
☐ 44	Don Robinson	.10	.05	.01
☐ 45	John Mayberry	.10	.05	.01
☐ 46	Richard Dotson	.10	.05	.01
☐ 47	Dave McKay	.10	.05	.01
☐ 48	Lary Sorensen	.10	.05	.01
☐ 49	Willie McGee	1.00	.45	.12
☐ 50	Bob Horner UER	.20	.09	.03
	('82 RBI total 7)			
☐ 51	Chicago Cubs TL	.20	.09	.03
	BA: Leon Durham			
	ERA: Fergie Jenkins			
	(Checklist on back)			
☐ 52	Onix Concepcion	.10	.05	.01
☐ 53	Mike Witt	.10	.05	.01
☐ 54	Jim Maler	.10	.05	.01
☐ 55	Mookie Wilson	.20	.09	.03
☐ 56	Chuck Rainey	.10	.05	.01
☐ 57	Tim Blackwell	.10	.05	.01
☐ 58	Al Holland	.10	.05	.01
☐ 59	Benny Ayala	.10	.05	.01
☐ 60	Johnny Bench	1.00	.45	.12
☐ 61	Johnny Bench SV	.50	.23	.06
☐ 62	Bob McClure	.10	.05	.01
☐ 63	Rick Monday	.10	.05	.01
☐ 64	Bill Stein	.10	.05	.01
☐ 65	Jack Morris	.40	.18	.05
☐ 66	Bob Lillis MG	.10	.05	.01
☐ 67	Sal Butera	.10	.05	.01
☐ 68	Eric Show	.20	.09	.03
☐ 69	Lee Lacy	.10	.05	.01
☐ 70	Steve Carlton	1.00	.45	.12
☐ 71	Steve Carlton SV	.50	.23	.06
☐ 72	Tom Paciorek	.20	.09	.03
☐ 73	Allen Ripley	.10	.05	.01
☐ 74	Julio Gonzalez	.10	.05	.01
☐ 75	Amos Otis	.20	.09	.03
☐ 76	Rick Mahler	.10	.05	.01
☐ 77	Hosken Powell	.10	.05	.01
☐ 78	Bill Caudill	.10	.05	.01
☐ 79	Mick Kelleher	.10	.05	.01
☐ 80	George Foster	.20	.09	.03
☐ 81	Yankees TL	.20	.09	.03
	BA: Jerry Mumphrey			
	ERA: Dave Righetti			
	(Checklist on back)			
☐ 82	Bruce Hurst	.20	.09	.03
☐ 83	Ryne Sandberg	30.00	13.50	3.70
☐ 84	Milt May	.10	.05	.01
☐ 85	Ken Singleton	.20	.09	.03
☐ 86	Tom Hume	.10	.05	.01
☐ 87	Joe Rudi	.10	.05	.01
☐ 88	Jim Gantner	.20	.09	.03
☐ 89	Leon Roberts	.10	.05	.01
☐ 90	Jerry Reuss	.20	.09	.03
☐ 91	Larry Milbourne	.10	.05	.01
☐ 92	Mike LaCoss	.10	.05	.01
☐ 93	John Castino	.10	.05	.01
☐ 94	Dave Edwards	.10	.05	.01
☐ 95	Alan Trammell	1.25	.55	.16
☐ 96	Dick Howser MG	.10	.05	.01
☐ 97	Ross Baumgarten	.10	.05	.01
☐ 98	Vance Law	.10	.05	.01
☐ 99	Dickie Noles	.10	.05	.01
☐ 100	Pete Rose	2.00	.90	.25
☐ 101	Pete Rose SV	1.00	.45	.12
☐ 102	Dave Beard	.10	.05	.01
☐ 103	Darrell Porter	.10	.05	.01
☐ 104	Bob Walk	.10	.05	.01
☐ 105	Don Baylor	.40	.18	.05
☐ 106	Gene Nelson	.10	.05	.01
☐ 107	Mike Jorgensen	.10	.05	.01
☐ 108	Glenn Hoffman	.10	.05	.01
☐ 109	Luis Leal	.10	.05	.01
☐ 110	Ken Griffey	.20	.09	.03
☐ 111	Montreal Expos TL	.20	.09	.03
	BA: Al Oliver			
	ERA: Steve Rogers			
	(Checklist on back)			
☐ 112	Bob Shirley	.10	.05	.01
☐ 113	Ron Roenicke	.10	.05	.01
☐ 114	Jim Slaton	.10	.05	.01
☐ 115	Chili Davis	.75	.35	.09
☐ 116	Dave Schmidt	.10	.05	.01
☐ 117	Alan Knicely	.10	.05	.01
☐ 118	Chris Welsh	.10	.05	.01
☐ 119	Tom Brookens	.10	.05	.01
☐ 120	Len Barker	.10	.05	.01
☐ 121	Mickey Hatcher	.10	.05	.01
☐ 122	Jimmy Smith	.10	.05	.01
☐ 123	George Frazier	.10	.05	.01
☐ 124	Marc Hill	.10	.05	.01
☐ 125	Leon Durham	.10	.05	.01
☐ 126	Joe Torre MG	.20	.09	.03
☐ 127	Preston Hanna	.10	.05	.01
☐ 128	Mike Ramsey	.10	.05	.01
☐ 129	Checklist: 1-132	.20	.09	.03
☐ 130	Dave Stieb	.20	.09	.03
☐ 131	Ed Ott	.10	.05	.01
☐ 132	Todd Cruz	.10	.05	.01
☐ 133	Jim Barr	.10	.05	.01
☐ 134	Hubie Brooks	.20	.09	.03
☐ 135	Dwight Evans	.20	.09	.03
☐ 136	Willie Aikens	.10	.05	.01
☐ 137	Woodie Fryman	.10	.05	.01
☐ 138	Rick Dempsey	.20	.09	.03
☐ 139	Bruce Berenyi	.10	.05	.01
☐ 140	Willie Randolph	.20	.09	.03
☐ 141	Indians TL	.20	.09	.03
	BA: Toby Harrah			
	ERA: Rick Sutcliffe			
	(Checklist on back)			
☐ 142	Mike Caldwell	.10	.05	.01
☐ 143	Joe Pettini	.10	.05	.01
☐ 144	Mark Wagner	.10	.05	.01
☐ 145	Don Sutton	.40	.18	.05
☐ 146	Don Sutton SV	.20	.09	.03
☐ 147	Rick Leach	.10	.05	.01
☐ 148	Dave Roberts	.10	.05	.01
☐ 149	Johnny Ray	.10	.05	.01
☐ 150	Bruce Sutter	.20	.09	.03
☐ 151	Bruce Sutter SV	.10	.05	.01

☐ 152 Jay Johnstone	.20	.09	.03
☐ 153 Jerry Koosman	.20	.09	.03
☐ 154 Johnnie LeMaster	.10	.05	.01
☐ 155 Dan Quisenberry	.20	.09	.03
☐ 156 Billy Martin MG	.20	.09	.03
☐ 157 Steve Bedrosian	.20	.09	.03
☐ 158 Rob Wilfong	.10	.05	.01
☐ 159 Mike Stanton	.10	.05	.01
☐ 160 Dave Kingman	.20	.09	.03
☐ 161 Dave Kingman SV	.10	.05	.01
☐ 162 Mark Clear	.10	.05	.01
☐ 163 Cal Ripken	20.00	9.00	2.50
☐ 164 David Palmer	.10	.05	.01
☐ 165 Dan Driessen	.10	.05	.01
☐ 166 John Pacella	.10	.05	.01
☐ 167 Mark Brouhard	.10	.05	.01
☐ 168 Juan Eichelberger	.10	.05	.01
☐ 169 Doug Flynn	.10	.05	.01
☐ 170 Steve Howe	.10	.05	.01
☐ 171 Giants TL	.40	.18	.05
BA: Joe Morgan			
ERA: Bill Laskey			
(Checklist on back)			
☐ 172 Vern Ruhle	.10	.05	.01
☐ 173 Jim Morrison	.10	.05	.01
☐ 174 Jerry Ujdur	.10	.05	.01
☐ 175 Bo Diaz	.10	.05	.01
☐ 176 Dave Righetti	.20	.09	.03
☐ 177 Harold Baines	.40	.18	.05
☐ 178 Luis Tiant	.20	.09	.03
☐ 179 Luis Tiant SV	.10	.05	.01
☐ 180 Rickey Henderson	2.50	1.10	.30
☐ 181 Terry Felton	.10	.05	.01
☐ 182 Mike Fischlin	.10	.05	.01
☐ 183 Ed VandeBerg	.10	.05	.01
☐ 184 Bob Clark	.10	.05	.01
☐ 185 Tim Lollar	.10	.05	.01
☐ 186 Whitey Herzog MG	.20	.09	.03
☐ 187 Terry Leach	.10	.05	.01
☐ 188 Rick Miller	.10	.05	.01
☐ 189 Dan Schatzeder	.10	.05	.01
☐ 190 Cecil Cooper	.20	.09	.03
☐ 191 Joe Price	.10	.05	.01
☐ 192 Floyd Rayford	.10	.05	.01
☐ 193 Harry Spilman	.10	.05	.01
☐ 194 Cesar Geronimo	.10	.05	.01
☐ 195 Bob Stoddard	.10	.05	.01
☐ 196 Bill Fahey	.10	.05	.01
☐ 197 Jim Eisenreich	1.00	.45	.12
☐ 198 Kiko Garcia	.10	.05	.01
☐ 199 Marty Bystrom	.10	.05	.01
☐ 200 Rod Carew	.75	.35	.09
☐ 201 Rod Carew SV	.40	.18	.05
☐ 202 Blue Jays TL	.20	.09	.03
BA: Damaso Garcia			
ERA: Dave Stieb			
(Checklist on back)			
☐ 203 Mike Morgan	.10	.05	.01
☐ 204 Junior Kennedy	.10	.05	.01
☐ 205 Dave Parker	.40	.18	.05
☐ 206 Ken Oberkfell	.10	.05	.01
☐ 207 Rick Camp	.10	.05	.01
☐ 208 Dan Meyer	.10	.05	.01
☐ 209 Mike Moore	.20	.09	.03
☐ 210 Jack Clark	.20	.09	.03
☐ 211 John Denny	.10	.05	.01
☐ 212 John Stearns	.10	.05	.01
☐ 213 Tom Burgmeier	.10	.05	.01
☐ 214 Jerry White	.10	.05	.01
☐ 215 Mario Soto	.10	.05	.01
☐ 216 Tony LaRussa MG	.20	.09	.03

☐ 217 Tim Stoddard	.10	.05	.01
☐ 218 Roy Howell	.10	.05	.01
☐ 219 Mike Armstrong	.10	.05	.01
☐ 220 Dusty Baker	.40	.18	.05
☐ 221 Joe Niekro	.20	.09	.03
☐ 222 Damaso Garcia	.10	.05	.01
☐ 223 John Montefusco	.10	.05	.01
☐ 224 Mickey Rivers	.10	.05	.01
☐ 225 Enos Cabell	.10	.05	.01
☐ 226 Enrique Romo	.10	.05	.01
☐ 227 Chris Bando	.10	.05	.01
☐ 228 Joaquin Andujar	.10	.05	.01
☐ 229 Phillies TL	.40	.18	.05
BA: Bo Diaz			
ERA: Steve Carlton			
(Checklist on back)			
☐ 230 Fergie Jenkins	.40	.18	.05
☐ 231 Fergie Jenkins SV	.20	.09	.03
☐ 232 Tom Brunansky	.20	.09	.03
☐ 233 Wayne Gross	.10	.05	.01
☐ 234 Larry Andersen	.10	.05	.01
☐ 235 Claudell Washington	.10	.05	.01
☐ 236 Steve Renko	.10	.05	.01
☐ 237 Dan Norman	.10	.05	.01
☐ 238 Bud Black	.20	.09	.03
☐ 239 Dave Stapleton	.10	.05	.01
☐ 240 Rich Gossage	.40	.18	.05
☐ 241 Rich Gossage SV	.20	.09	.03
☐ 242 Joe Nolan	.10	.05	.01
☐ 243 Duane Walker	.10	.05	.01
☐ 244 Dwight Bernard	.10	.05	.01
☐ 245 Steve Sax	.20	.09	.03
☐ 246 George Bamberger MG	.10	.05	.01
☐ 247 Dave Smith	.10	.05	.01
☐ 248 Bake McBride	.10	.05	.01
☐ 249 Checklist: 133-264	.20	.09	.03
☐ 250 Bill Buckner	.20	.09	.03
☐ 251 Alan Wiggins	.10	.05	.01
☐ 252 Luis Aguayo	.10	.05	.01
☐ 253 Larry McWilliams	.10	.05	.01
☐ 254 Rick Cerone	.10	.05	.01
☐ 255 Gene Garber	.10	.05	.01
☐ 256 Gene Garber SV	.10	.05	.01
☐ 257 Jesse Barfield	.20	.09	.03
☐ 258 Manny Castillo	.10	.05	.01
☐ 259 Jeff Jones	.10	.05	.01
☐ 260 Steve Kemp	.10	.05	.01
☐ 261 Tigers TL	.20	.09	.03
BA: Larry Herndon			
ERA: Dan Petry			
(Checklist on back)			
☐ 262 Ron Jackson	.10	.05	.01
☐ 263 Renie Martin	.10	.05	.01
☐ 264 Jamie Quirk	.10	.05	.01
☐ 265 Joel Youngblood	.10	.05	.01
☐ 266 Paul Boris	.10	.05	.01
☐ 267 Terry Francona	.10	.05	.01
☐ 268 Storm Davis	.10	.05	.01
☐ 269 Ron Oester	.10	.05	.01
☐ 270 Dennis Eckersley	.75	.35	.09
☐ 271 Ed Romero	.10	.05	.01
☐ 272 Frank Tanana	.20	.09	.03
☐ 273 Mark Belanger	.10	.05	.01
☐ 274 Terry Kennedy	.10	.05	.01
☐ 275 Ray Knight	.20	.09	.03
☐ 276 Gene Mauch MG	.10	.05	.01
☐ 277 Rance Mulliniks	.10	.05	.01
☐ 278 Kevin Hickey	.10	.05	.01
☐ 279 Greg Gross	.10	.05	.01
☐ 280 Bert Blyleven	.40	.18	.05
☐ 281 Andre Robertson	.10	.05	.01

☐ 282	Reggie Smith (Ryne Sandberg ducking back)	.60	.25	.07
☐ 283	Reggie Smith SV	.10	.05	.01
☐ 284	Jeff Lahti	.10	.05	.01
☐ 285	Lance Parrish	.20	.09	.03
☐ 286	Rick Langford	.10	.05	.01
☐ 287	Bobby Brown	.10	.05	.01
☐ 288	Joe Cowley	.10	.05	.01
☐ 289	Jerry Dybzinski	.10	.05	.01
☐ 290	Jeff Reardon	.40	.18	.05
☐ 291	Pirates TL BA: Bill Madlock ERA: John Candelaria (Checklist on back)	.20	.09	.03
☐ 292	Craig Swan	.10	.05	.01
☐ 293	Glenn Gulliver	.10	.05	.01
☐ 294	Dave Engle	.10	.05	.01
☐ 295	Jerry Remy	.10	.05	.01
☐ 296	Greg Harris	.10	.05	.01
☐ 297	Ned Yost	.10	.05	.01
☐ 298	Floyd Chiffer	.10	.05	.01
☐ 299	George Wright	.10	.05	.01
☐ 300	Mike Schmidt	2.00	.90	.25
☐ 301	Mike Schmidt SV	1.00	.45	.12
☐ 302	Ernie Whitt	.10	.05	.01
☐ 303	Miguel Dilone	.10	.05	.01
☐ 304	Dave Rucker	.10	.05	.01
☐ 305	Larry Bowa	.20	.09	.03
☐ 306	Tom Lasorda MG	.20	.09	.03
☐ 307	Lou Piniella	.20	.09	.03
☐ 308	Jesus Vega	.10	.05	.01
☐ 309	Jeff Leonard	.10	.05	.01
☐ 310	Greg Luzinski	.20	.09	.03
☐ 311	Glenn Brummer	.10	.05	.01
☐ 312	Brian Kingman	.10	.05	.01
☐ 313	Gary Gray	.10	.05	.01
☐ 314	Ken Dayley	.10	.05	.01
☐ 315	Rick Burleson	.10	.05	.01
☐ 316	Paul Splittorff	.10	.05	.01
☐ 317	Gary Rajsich	.10	.05	.01
☐ 318	John Tudor	.20	.09	.03
☐ 319	Lenn Sakata	.10	.05	.01
☐ 320	Steve Rogers	.10	.05	.01
☐ 321	Brewers TL BA: Robin Yount ERA: Pete Vuckovich (Checklist on back)	.40	.18	.05
☐ 322	Dave Van Gorder	.10	.05	.01
☐ 323	Luis DeLeon	.10	.05	.01
☐ 324	Mike Marshall	.10	.05	.01
☐ 325	Von Hayes	.20	.09	.03
☐ 326	Garth Iorg	.10	.05	.01
☐ 327	Bobby Castillo	.10	.05	.01
☐ 328	Craig Reynolds	.10	.05	.01
☐ 329	Randy Niemann	.10	.05	.01
☐ 330	Buddy Bell	.20	.09	.03
☐ 331	Mike Krukow	.10	.05	.01
☐ 332	Glenn Wilson	.20	.09	.03
☐ 333	Dave LaRoche	.10	.05	.01
☐ 334	Dave LaRoche SV	.10	.05	.01
☐ 335	Steve Henderson	.10	.05	.01
☐ 336	Rene Lachemann MG	.10	.05	.01
☐ 337	Tito Landrum	.10	.05	.01
☐ 338	Bob Owchinko	.10	.05	.01
☐ 339	Terry Harper	.10	.05	.01
☐ 340	Larry Gura	.10	.05	.01
☐ 341	Doug DeCinces	.20	.09	.03
☐ 342	Atlee Hammaker	.10	.05	.01
☐ 343	Bob Bailor	.10	.05	.01
☐ 344	Roger LaFrancois	.10	.05	.01
☐ 345	Jim Clancy	.10	.05	.01
☐ 346	Joe Pittman	.10	.05	.01
☐ 347	Sammy Stewart	.10	.05	.01
☐ 348	Alan Bannister	.10	.05	.01
☐ 349	Checklist: 265-396	.20	.09	.03
☐ 350	Robin Yount	2.00	.90	.25
☐ 351	Reds TL BA: Cesar Cedeno ERA: Mario Soto (Checklist on back)	.20	.09	.03
☐ 352	Mike Scioscia	.20	.09	.03
☐ 353	Steve Comer	.10	.05	.01
☐ 354	Randy Johnson	.10	.05	.01
☐ 355	Jim Bibby	.10	.05	.01
☐ 356	Gary Woods	.10	.05	.01
☐ 357	Len Matuszek	.10	.05	.01
☐ 358	Jerry Garvin	.10	.05	.01
☐ 359	Dave Collins	.10	.05	.01
☐ 360	Nolan Ryan	7.00	3.10	.85
☐ 361	Nolan Ryan SV	4.00	1.80	.50
☐ 362	Bill Almon	.10	.05	.01
☐ 363	John Stuper	.10	.05	.01
☐ 364	Brett Butler	.75	.35	.09
☐ 365	Dave Lopes	.20	.09	.03
☐ 366	Dick Williams MG	.10	.05	.01
☐ 367	Bud Anderson	.10	.05	.01
☐ 368	Richie Zisk	.10	.05	.01
☐ 369	Jesse Orosco	.10	.05	.01
☐ 370	Gary Carter	.60	.25	.07
☐ 371	Mike Richardt	.10	.05	.01
☐ 372	Terry Crowley	.10	.05	.01
☐ 373	Kevin Saucier	.10	.05	.01
☐ 374	Wayne Krenchicki	.10	.05	.01
☐ 375	Pete Vuckovich	.10	.05	.01
☐ 376	Ken Landreaux	.10	.05	.01
☐ 377	Lee May	.20	.09	.03
☐ 378	Lee May SV	.10	.05	.01
☐ 379	Guy Sularz	.10	.05	.01
☐ 380	Ron Davis	.10	.05	.01
☐ 381	Red Sox TL BA: Jim Rice ERA: Bob Stanley (Checklist on back)	.20	.09	.03
☐ 382	Bob Knepper	.10	.05	.01
☐ 383	Ozzie Virgil	.10	.05	.01
☐ 384	Dave Dravecky	.75	.35	.09
☐ 385	Mike Easler	.10	.05	.01
☐ 386	Rod Carew AS	.40	.18	.05
☐ 387	Bob Grich AS	.20	.09	.03
☐ 388	George Brett AS	1.75	.80	.22
☐ 389	Robin Yount AS	1.25	.55	.16
☐ 390	Reggie Jackson AS	.75	.35	.09
☐ 391	Rickey Henderson AS	1.00	.45	.12
☐ 392	Fred Lynn AS	.20	.09	.03
☐ 393	Carlton Fisk AS	.40	.18	.05
☐ 394	Pete Vuckovich AS	.10	.05	.01
☐ 395	Larry Gura AS	.10	.05	.01
☐ 396	Dan Quisenberry AS	.20	.09	.03
☐ 397	Pete Rose AS	1.00	.45	.12
☐ 398	Manny Trillo AS	.10	.05	.01
☐ 399	Mike Schmidt AS	1.00	.45	.12
☐ 400	Dave Concepcion AS	.20	.09	.03
☐ 401	Dale Murphy AS	.40	.18	.05
☐ 402	Andre Dawson AS	.60	.25	.07
☐ 403	Tim Raines AS	.40	.18	.05
☐ 404	Gary Carter AS	.40	.18	.05
☐ 405	Steve Rogers AS	.20	.09	.03
☐ 406	Steve Carlton AS	.60	.25	.07
☐ 407	Bruce Sutter AS	.20	.09	.03
☐ 408	Rudy May	.10	.05	.01
☐ 409	Marvis Foley	.10	.05	.01

☐ 410 Phil Niekro	.40	.18	.05
☐ 411 Phil Niekro SV	.20	.09	.03
☐ 412 Rangers TL	.20	.09	.03
BA: Buddy Bell			
ERA: Charlie Hough			
(Checklist on back)			
☐ 413 Matt Keough	.10	.05	.01
☐ 414 Julio Cruz	.10	.05	.01
☐ 415 Bob Forsch	.10	.05	.01
☐ 416 Joe Ferguson	.10	.05	.01
☐ 417 Tom Hausman	.10	.05	.01
☐ 418 Greg Pryor	.10	.05	.01
☐ 419 Steve Crawford	.10	.05	.01
☐ 420 Al Oliver	.20	.09	.03
☐ 421 Al Oliver SV	.10	.05	.01
☐ 422 George Cappuzzello	.10	.05	.01
☐ 423 Tom Lawless	.10	.05	.01
☐ 424 Jerry Augustine	.10	.05	.01
☐ 425 Pedro Guerrero	.20	.09	.03
☐ 426 Earl Weaver MG	.20	.09	.03
☐ 427 Roy Lee Jackson	.10	.05	.01
☐ 428 Champ Summers	.10	.05	.01
☐ 429 Eddie Whitson	.10	.05	.01
☐ 430 Kirk Gibson	1.00	.45	.12
☐ 431 Gary Gaetti	1.25	.55	.16
☐ 432 Porfirio Altamirano	.10	.05	.01
☐ 433 Dale Berra	.10	.05	.01
☐ 434 Dennis Lamp	.10	.05	.01
☐ 435 Tony Armas	.10	.05	.01
☐ 436 Bill Campbell	.10	.05	.01
☐ 437 Rick Sweet	.10	.05	.01
☐ 438 Dave LaPoint	.10	.05	.01
☐ 439 Rafael Ramirez	.10	.05	.01
☐ 440 Ron Guidry	.20	.09	.03
☐ 441 Astros TL	.20	.09	.03
BA: Ray Knight			
ERA: Joe Niekro			
(Checklist on back)			
☐ 442 Brian Downing	.20	.09	.03
☐ 443 Don Hood	.10	.05	.01
☐ 444 Wally Backman	.10	.05	.01
☐ 445 Mike Flanagan	.20	.09	.03
☐ 446 Reid Nichols	.10	.05	.01
☐ 447 Bryn Smith	.10	.05	.01
☐ 448 Darrell Evans	.20	.09	.03
☐ 449 Eddie Milner	.10	.05	.01
☐ 450 Ted Simmons	.20	.09	.03
☐ 451 Ted Simmons SV	.10	.05	.01
☐ 452 Lloyd Moseby	.10	.05	.01
☐ 453 Lamar Johnson	.10	.05	.01
☐ 454 Bob Welch	.20	.09	.03
☐ 455 Sixto Lezcano	.10	.05	.01
☐ 456 Lee Elia MG	.10	.05	.01
☐ 457 Milt Wilcox	.10	.05	.01
☐ 458 Ron Washington	.10	.05	.01
☐ 459 Ed Farmer	.10	.05	.01
☐ 460 Roy Smalley	.10	.05	.01
☐ 461 Steve Trout	.10	.05	.01
☐ 462 Steve Nicosia	.10	.05	.01
☐ 463 Gaylord Perry	.40	.18	.05
☐ 464 Gaylord Perry SV	.20	.09	.03
☐ 465 Lonnie Smith	.20	.09	.03
☐ 466 Tom Underwood	.10	.05	.01
☐ 467 Rufino Linares	.10	.05	.01
☐ 468 Dave Goltz	.10	.05	.01
☐ 469 Ron Gardenhire	.10	.05	.01
☐ 470 Greg Minton	.10	.05	.01
☐ 471 Kansas City Royals TL	.20	.09	.03
BA: Willie Wilson			
ERA: Vida Blue			
(Checklist on back)			
☐ 472 Gary Allenson	.10	.05	.01
☐ 473 John Lowenstein	.10	.05	.01
☐ 474 Ray Burris	.10	.05	.01
☐ 475 Cesar Cedeno	.20	.09	.03
☐ 476 Rob Picciolo	.10	.05	.01
☐ 477 Tom Niedenfuer	.10	.05	.01
☐ 478 Phil Garner	.20	.09	.03
☐ 479 Charlie Hough	.20	.09	.03
☐ 480 Toby Harrah	.10	.05	.01
☐ 481 Scot Thompson	.10	.05	.01
☐ 482 Tony Gwynn UER	32.00	14.50	4.00
(No Topps logo under			
card number on back)			
☐ 483 Lynn Jones	.10	.05	.01
☐ 484 Dick Ruthven	.10	.05	.01
☐ 485 Omar Moreno	.10	.05	.01
☐ 486 Clyde King MG	.10	.05	.01
☐ 487 Jerry Hairston	.10	.05	.01
☐ 488 Alfredo Griffin	.10	.05	.01
☐ 489 Tom Herr	.20	.09	.03
☐ 490 Jim Palmer	.75	.35	.09
☐ 491 Jim Palmer SV	.40	.18	.05
☐ 492 Paul Serna	.10	.05	.01
☐ 493 Steve McCatty	.10	.05	.01
☐ 494 Bob Brenly	.10	.05	.01
☐ 495 Warren Cromartie	.10	.05	.01
☐ 496 Tom Veryzer	.10	.05	.01
☐ 497 Rick Sutcliffe	.20	.09	.03
☐ 498 Wade Boggs	20.00	9.00	2.50
☐ 499 Jeff Little	.10	.05	.01
☐ 500 Reggie Jackson	1.50	.70	.19
☐ 501 Reggie Jackson SV	.75	.35	.09
☐ 502 Atlanta Braves TL	.20	.09	.03
BA: Dale Murphy			
ERA: Phil Niekro			
(Checklist on back)			
☐ 503 Moose Haas	.10	.05	.01
☐ 504 Don Werner	.10	.05	.01
☐ 505 Garry Templeton	.10	.05	.01
☐ 506 Jim Gott	.20	.09	.03
☐ 507 Tony Scott	.10	.05	.01
☐ 508 Tom Filer	.10	.05	.01
☐ 509 Lou Whitaker	.60	.25	.07
☐ 510 Tug McGraw	.20	.09	.03
☐ 511 Tug McGraw SV	.10	.05	.01
☐ 512 Doyle Alexander	.10	.05	.01
☐ 513 Fred Stanley	.10	.05	.01
☐ 514 Rudy Law	.10	.05	.01
☐ 515 Gene Tenace	.10	.05	.01
☐ 516 Bill Virdon MG	.10	.05	.01
☐ 517 Gary Ward	.10	.05	.01
☐ 518 Bill Laskey	.10	.05	.01
☐ 519 Terry Bulling	.10	.05	.01
☐ 520 Fred Lynn	.20	.09	.03
☐ 521 Bruce Benedict	.10	.05	.01
☐ 522 Pat Zachry	.10	.05	.01
☐ 523 Carney Lansford	.20	.09	.03
☐ 524 Tom Brennan	.10	.05	.01
☐ 525 Frank White	.20	.09	.03
☐ 526 Checklist: 397-528	.20	.09	.03
☐ 527 Larry Biittner	.10	.05	.01
☐ 528 Jamie Easterly	.10	.05	.01
☐ 529 Tim Laudner	.10	.05	.01
☐ 530 Eddie Murray	2.50	1.10	.30
☐ 531 Oakland A's TL	.40	.18	.05
BA: Rickey Henderson			
ERA: Rick Langford			
(Checklist on back)			
☐ 532 Dave Stewart	.40	.18	.05
☐ 533 Luis Salazar	.10	.05	.01
☐ 534 John Butcher	.10	.05	.01

535	Manny Trillo	.10	.05	.01
536	John Wockenfuss	.10	.05	.01
537	Rod Scurry	.10	.05	.01
538	Danny Heep	.10	.05	.01
539	Roger Erickson	.10	.05	.01
540	Ozzie Smith	3.00	1.35	.35
541	Britt Burns	.10	.05	.01
542	Jody Davis	.10	.05	.01
543	Alan Fowlkes	.10	.05	.01
544	Larry Whisenton	.10	.05	.01
545	Floyd Bannister	.10	.05	.01
546	Dave Garcia MG	.10	.05	.01
547	Geoff Zahn	.10	.05	.01
548	Brian Giles	.10	.05	.01
549	Charlie Puleo	.10	.05	.01
550	Carl Yastrzemski	1.00	.45	.12
551	Carl Yastrzemski SV	.50	.23	.06
552	Tim Wallach	.40	.18	.05
553	Dennis Martinez	.20	.09	.03
554	Mike Vail	.10	.05	.01
555	Steve Yeager	.10	.05	.01
556	Willie Upshaw	.10	.05	.01
557	Rick Honeycutt	.10	.05	.01
558	Dickie Thon	.10	.05	.01
559	Pete Redfern	.10	.05	.01
560	Ron LeFlore	.20	.09	.03
561	Cardinals TL	.20	.09	.03
	BA: Lonnie Smith			
	ERA: Joaquin Andujar			
	(Checklist on back)			
562	Dave Rozema	.10	.05	.01
563	Juan Bonilla	.10	.05	.01
564	Sid Monge	.10	.05	.01
565	Bucky Dent	.20	.09	.03
566	Manny Sarmiento	.10	.05	.01
567	Joe Simpson	.10	.05	.01
568	Willie Hernandez	.20	.09	.03
569	Jack Perconte	.10	.05	.01
570	Vida Blue	.20	.09	.03
571	Mickey Klutts	.10	.05	.01
572	Bob Watson	.20	.09	.03
573	Andy Hassler	.10	.05	.01
574	Glenn Adams	.10	.05	.01
575	Neil Allen	.10	.05	.01
576	Frank Robinson MG	.40	.18	.05
577	Luis Aponte	.10	.05	.01
578	David Green	.10	.05	.01
579	Rich Dauer	.10	.05	.01
580	Tom Seaver	1.00	.45	.12
581	Tom Seaver SV	.50	.23	.06
582	Marshall Edwards	.10	.05	.01
583	Terry Forster	.10	.05	.01
584	Dave Hostetler	.10	.05	.01
585	Jose Cruz	.20	.09	.03
586	Frank Viola	1.00	.45	.12
587	Ivan DeJesus	.10	.05	.01
588	Pat Underwood	.10	.05	.01
589	Alvis Woods	.10	.05	.01
590	Tony Pena	.20	.09	.03
591	White Sox TL	.20	.09	.03
	BA: Greg Luzinski			
	ERA: LaMarr Hoyt			
	(Checklist on back)			
592	Shane Rawley	.10	.05	.01
593	Broderick Perkins	.10	.05	.01
594	Eric Rasmussen	.10	.05	.01
595	Tim Raines	.75	.35	.09
596	Randy Johnson	.10	.05	.01
597	Mike Proly	.10	.05	.01
598	Dwayne Murphy	.10	.05	.01
599	Don Aase	.10	.05	.01
600	George Brett	4.00	1.80	.50
601	Ed Lynch	.10	.05	.01
602	Rich Gedman	.10	.05	.01
603	Joe Morgan	.60	.25	.07
604	Joe Morgan SV	.40	.18	.05
605	Gary Roenicke	.10	.05	.01
606	Bobby Cox MG	.20	.09	.03
607	Charlie Leibrandt	.20	.09	.03
608	Don Money	.10	.05	.01
609	Danny Darwin	.10	.05	.01
610	Steve Garvey	.40	.18	.05
611	Bert Roberge	.10	.05	.01
612	Steve Swisher	.10	.05	.01
613	Mike Ivie	.10	.05	.01
614	Ed Glynn	.10	.05	.01
615	Garry Maddox	.10	.05	.01
616	Bill Nahorodny	.10	.05	.01
617	Butch Wynegar	.10	.05	.01
618	LaMarr Hoyt	.10	.05	.01
619	Keith Moreland	.10	.05	.01
620	Mike Norris	.10	.05	.01
621	New York Mets TL	.20	.09	.03
	BA: Mookie Wilson			
	ERA: Craig Swan			
	(Checklist on back)			
622	Dave Edler	.10	.05	.01
623	Luis Sanchez	.10	.05	.01
624	Glenn Hubbard	.10	.05	.01
625	Ken Forsch	.10	.05	.01
626	Jerry Martin	.10	.05	.01
627	Doug Bair	.10	.05	.01
628	Julio Valdez	.10	.05	.01
629	Charlie Lea	.10	.05	.01
630	Paul Molitor	1.00	.45	.12
631	Tippy Martinez	.10	.05	.01
632	Alex Trevino	.10	.05	.01
633	Vicente Romo	.10	.05	.01
634	Max Venable	.10	.05	.01
635	Graig Nettles	.20	.09	.03
636	Graig Nettles SV	.10	.05	.01
637	Pat Corrales MG	.10	.05	.01
638	Dan Petry	.10	.05	.01
639	Art Howe	.10	.05	.01
640	Andre Thornton	.10	.05	.01
641	Billy Sample	.10	.05	.01
642	Checklist: 529-660	.20	.09	.03
643	Bump Wills	.10	.05	.01
644	Joe Lefebvre	.10	.05	.01
645	Bill Madlock	.20	.09	.03
646	Jim Essian	.10	.05	.01
647	Bobby Mitchell	.10	.05	.01
648	Jeff Burroughs	.10	.05	.01
649	Tommy Boggs	.10	.05	.01
650	George Hendrick	.10	.05	.01
651	Angels TL	.40	.18	.05
	BA: Rod Carew			
	ERA: Mike Witt			
	(Checklist on back)			
652	Butch Hobson	.20	.09	.03
653	Ellis Valentine	.10	.05	.01
654	Bob Ojeda	.20	.09	.03
655	Al Bumbry	.20	.09	.03
656	Dave Frost	.10	.05	.01
657	Mike Gates	.10	.05	.01
658	Frank Pastore	.10	.05	.01
659	Charlie Moore	.10	.05	.01
660	Mike Hargrove	.20	.09	.03
661	Bill Russell	.20	.09	.03
662	Joe Sambito	.10	.05	.01
663	Tom O'Malley	.10	.05	.01
664	Bob Molinaro	.10	.05	.01

☐ 665 Jim Sundberg	.20	.09	.03
☐ 666 Sparky Anderson MG	.20	.09	.03
☐ 667 Dick Davis	.10	.05	.01
☐ 668 Larry Christenson	.10	.05	.01
☐ 669 Mike Squires	.10	.05	.01
☐ 670 Jerry Mumphrey	.10	.05	.01
☐ 671 Lenny Faedo	.10	.05	.01
☐ 672 Jim Kaat	.20	.09	.03
☐ 673 Jim Kaat SV	.10	.05	.01
☐ 674 Kurt Bevacqua	.10	.05	.01
☐ 675 Jim Beattie	.10	.05	.01
☐ 676 Biff Pocoroba	.10	.05	.01
☐ 677 Dave Revering	.10	.05	.01
☐ 678 Juan Beniquez	.10	.05	.01
☐ 679 Mike Scott	.20	.09	.03
☐ 680 Andre Dawson	1.00	.45	.12
☐ 681 Dodgers Leaders	.20	.09	.03
BA: Pedro Guerrero			
ERA: Fernando Valenzuela			
(Checklist on back)			
☐ 682 Bob Stanley	.10	.05	.01
☐ 683 Dan Ford	.10	.05	.01
☐ 684 Rafael Landestoy	.10	.05	.01
☐ 685 Lee Mazzilli	.10	.05	.01
☐ 686 Randy Lerch	.10	.05	.01
☐ 687 U.L. Washington	.10	.05	.01
☐ 688 Jim Wohlford	.10	.05	.01
☐ 689 Ron Hassey	.10	.05	.01
☐ 690 Kent Hrbek	.40	.18	.05
☐ 691 Dave Tobik	.10	.05	.01
☐ 692 Denny Walling	.10	.05	.01
☐ 693 Sparky Lyle	.20	.09	.03
☐ 694 Sparky Lyle SV	.10	.05	.01
☐ 695 Ruppert Jones	.10	.05	.01
☐ 696 Chuck Tanner MG	.20	.09	.03
☐ 697 Barry Foote	.10	.05	.01
☐ 698 Tony Bernazard	.10	.05	.01
☐ 699 Lee Smith	2.50	1.10	.30
☐ 700 Keith Hernandez	.40	.18	.05
☐ 701 Batting Leaders	.20	.09	.03
AL: Willie Wilson			
NL: Al Oliver			
☐ 702 Home Run Leaders	.40	.18	.05
AL: Reggie Jackson			
AL: Gorman Thomas			
NL: Dave Kingman			
☐ 703 RBI Leaders	.20	.09	.03
AL: Hal McRae			
NL: Dale Murphy			
NL: Al Oliver			
☐ 704 SB Leaders	1.00	.45	.12
AL: Rickey Henderson			
NL: Tim Raines			
☐ 705 Victory Leaders	.40	.18	.05
AL: LaMarr Hoyt			
NL: Steve Carlton			
☐ 706 Strikeout Leaders	.40	.18	.05
AL: Floyd Bannister			
NL: Steve Carlton			
☐ 707 ERA Leaders	.20	.09	.03
AL: Rick Sutcliffe			
NL: Steve Rogers			
☐ 708 Leading Firemen	.20	.09	.03
AL: Dan Quisenberry			
NL: Bruce Sutter			
☐ 709 Jimmy Sexton	.10	.05	.01
☐ 710 Willie Wilson	.20	.09	.03
☐ 711 Mariners TL	.20	.09	.03
BA: Bruce Bochte			
ERA: Jim Beattie			
(Checklist on back)			
☐ 712 Bruce Kison	.10	.05	.01
☐ 713 Ron Hodges	.10	.05	.01
☐ 714 Wayne Nordhagen	.10	.05	.01
☐ 715 Tony Perez	.40	.18	.05
☐ 716 Tony Perez SV	.20	.09	.03
☐ 717 Scott Sanderson	.10	.05	.01
☐ 718 Jim Dwyer	.10	.05	.01
☐ 719 Rich Gale	.10	.05	.01
☐ 720 Dave Concepcion	.20	.09	.03
☐ 721 John Martin	.10	.05	.01
☐ 722 Jorge Orta	.10	.05	.01
☐ 723 Randy Moffitt	.10	.05	.01
☐ 724 Johnny Grubb	.10	.05	.01
☐ 725 Dan Spillner	.10	.05	.01
☐ 726 Harvey Kuenn MG	.20	.09	.03
☐ 727 Chet Lemon	.10	.05	.01
☐ 728 Ron Reed	.10	.05	.01
☐ 729 Jerry Morales	.10	.05	.01
☐ 730 Jason Thompson	.10	.05	.01
☐ 731 Al Williams	.10	.05	.01
☐ 732 Dave Henderson	.20	.09	.03
☐ 733 Buck Martinez	.10	.05	.01
☐ 734 Steve Braun	.10	.05	.01
☐ 735 Tommy John	.40	.18	.05
☐ 736 Tommy John SV	.20	.09	.03
☐ 737 Mitchell Page	.10	.05	.01
☐ 738 Tim Foli	.10	.05	.01
☐ 739 Rick Ownbey	.10	.05	.01
☐ 740 Rusty Staub	.20	.09	.03
☐ 741 Rusty Staub SV	.10	.05	.01
☐ 742 Padres TL	.20	.09	.03
BA: Terry Kennedy			
ERA: Tim Lollar			
(Checklist on back)			
☐ 743 Mike Torrez	.10	.05	.01
☐ 744 Brad Mills	.10	.05	.01
☐ 745 Scott McGregor	.10	.05	.01
☐ 746 John Wathan	.10	.05	.01
☐ 747 Fred Breining	.10	.05	.01
☐ 748 Derrel Thomas	.10	.05	.01
☐ 749 Jon Matlack	.10	.05	.01
☐ 750 Ben Oglivie	.10	.05	.01
☐ 751 Brad Havens	.10	.05	.01
☐ 752 Luis Pujols	.10	.05	.01
☐ 753 Elias Sosa	.10	.05	.01
☐ 754 Bill Robinson	.20	.09	.03
☐ 755 John Candelaria	.10	.05	.01
☐ 756 Russ Nixon MG	.10	.05	.01
☐ 757 Rick Manning	.10	.05	.01
☐ 758 Aurelio Rodriguez	.10	.05	.01
☐ 759 Doug Bird	.10	.05	.01
☐ 760 Dale Murphy	.75	.35	.09
☐ 761 Gary Lucas	.10	.05	.01
☐ 762 Cliff Johnson	.10	.05	.01
☐ 763 Al Cowens	.10	.05	.01
☐ 764 Pete Falcone	.10	.05	.01
☐ 765 Bob Boone	.20	.09	.03
☐ 766 Barry Bonnell	.10	.05	.01
☐ 767 Duane Kuiper	.10	.05	.01
☐ 768 Chris Speier	.10	.05	.01
☐ 769 Checklist: 661-792	.20	.09	.03
☐ 770 Dave Winfield	2.00	.90	.25
☐ 771 Twins TL	.20	.09	.03
BA: Kent Hrbek			
ERA: Bobby Castillo			
(Checklist on back)			
☐ 772 Jim Kern	.10	.05	.01
☐ 773 Larry Hisle	.10	.05	.01
☐ 774 Alan Ashby	.10	.05	.01
☐ 775 Burt Hooton	.10	.05	.01
☐ 776 Larry Parrish	.10	.05	.01

		NRMT-MT	EXC	G-VG
☐	777 John Curtis	.10	.05	.01
☐	778 Rich Hebner	.10	.05	.01
☐	779 Rick Waits	.10	.05	.01
☐	780 Gary Matthews	.20	.09	.03
☐	781 Rick Rhoden	.10	.05	.01
☐	782 Bobby Murcer	.20	.09	.03
☐	783 Bobby Murcer SV	.10	.05	.01
☐	784 Jeff Newman	.10	.05	.01
☐	785 Dennis Leonard	.10	.05	.01
☐	786 Ralph Houk MG	.10	.05	.01
☐	787 Dick Tidrow	.10	.05	.01
☐	788 Dane Iorg	.10	.05	.01
☐	789 Bryan Clark	.10	.05	.01
☐	790 Bob Grich	.20	.09	.03
☐	791 Gary Lavelle	.10	.05	.01
☐	792 Chris Chambliss	.20	.09	.03

1983 Topps Traded

The cards in this 132-card set measure 2 1/2" by 3 1/2". For the third year in a row, Topps issued a 132-card Traded (or extended) set featuring some of the year's top rookies and players who had changed teams during the year, but were featured with their old team in the Topps regular issue of 1983. The cards were available through hobby dealers only and were printed in Ireland by the Topps affiliate in that country. The set is numbered alphabetically by the last name of the player of the card. The Darryl Strawberry card number 108 can be found with either one or two asterisks (in the lower left corner of the reverse). The key (extended) Rookie Cards in this set are Tony Phillips and Darryl Strawberry. Also noteworthy is Julio Franco's first Topps (extended) card.

		NRMT-MT	EXC	G-VG
	COMPLETE FACT.SET (132)	35.00	16.00	4.40
	COMMON CARD (1T-132T)	.25	.11	.03
☐	1T Neil Allen	.25	.11	.03
☐	2T Bill Almon	.25	.11	.03
☐	3T Joe Altobelli MG	.25	.11	.03
☐	4T Tony Armas	.25	.11	.03
☐	5T Doug Bair	.25	.11	.03
☐	6T Steve Baker	.25	.11	.03
☐	7T Floyd Bannister	.25	.11	.03
☐	8T Don Baylor	.50	.23	.06
☐	9T Tony Bernazard	.25	.11	.03

☐	10T Larry Biittner	.25	.11	.03
☐	11T Dann Bilardello	.25	.11	.03
☐	12T Doug Bird	.25	.11	.03
☐	13T Steve Boros MG	.25	.11	.03
☐	14T Greg Brock	.25	.11	.03
☐	15T Mike C. Brown	.25	.11	.03
☐	16T Tom Burgmeier	.25	.11	.03
☐	17T Randy Bush	.25	.11	.03
☐	18T Bert Campaneris	.35	.16	.04
☐	19T Ron Cey	.35	.16	.04
☐	20T Chris Codiroli	.25	.11	.03
☐	21T Dave Collins	.25	.11	.03
☐	22T Terry Crowley	.25	.11	.03
☐	23T Julio Cruz	.25	.11	.03
☐	24T Mike Davis	.25	.11	.03
☐	25T Frank DiPino	.25	.11	.03
☐	26T Bill Doran	.35	.16	.04
☐	27T Jerry Dybzinski	.25	.11	.03
☐	28T Jamie Easterly	.25	.11	.03
☐	29T Juan Eichelberger	.25	.11	.03
☐	30T Jim Essian	.25	.11	.03
☐	31T Pete Falcone	.25	.11	.03
☐	32T Mike Ferraro MG	.25	.11	.03
☐	33T Terry Forster	.25	.11	.03
☐	34T Julio Franco	2.00	.90	.25
☐	35T Rich Gale	.25	.11	.03
☐	36T Kiko Garcia	.25	.11	.03
☐	37T Steve Garvey	.50	.23	.06
☐	38T Johnny Grubb	.25	.11	.03
☐	39T Mel Hall	.35	.16	.04
☐	40T Von Hayes	.35	.16	.04
☐	41T Danny Heep	.25	.11	.03
☐	42T Steve Henderson	.25	.11	.03
☐	43T Keith Hernandez	.50	.23	.06
☐	44T Leo Hernandez	.25	.11	.03
☐	45T Willie Hernandez	.35	.16	.04
☐	46T Al Holland	.25	.11	.03
☐	47T Frank Howard MG	.35	.16	.04
☐	48T Bobby Johnson	.25	.11	.03
☐	49T Cliff Johnson	.25	.11	.03
☐	50T Odell Jones	.25	.11	.03
☐	51T Mike Jorgensen	.25	.11	.03
☐	52T Bob Kearney	.25	.11	.03
☐	53T Steve Kemp	.25	.11	.03
☐	54T Matt Keough	.25	.11	.03
☐	55T Ron Kittle	.35	.16	.04
☐	56T Mickey Klutts	.25	.11	.03
☐	57T Alan Knicely	.25	.11	.03
☐	58T Mike Krukow	.25	.11	.03
☐	59T Rafael Landestoy	.25	.11	.03
☐	60T Carney Lansford	.35	.16	.04
☐	61T Joe Lefebvre	.25	.11	.03
☐	62T Bryan Little	.25	.11	.03
☐	63T Aurelio Lopez	.25	.11	.03
☐	64T Mike Madden	.25	.11	.03
☐	65T Rick Manning	.25	.11	.03
☐	66T Billy Martin MG	.35	.16	.04
☐	67T Lee Mazzilli	.25	.11	.03
☐	68T Andy McGaffigan	.25	.11	.03
☐	69T Craig McMurtry	.25	.11	.03
☐	70T John McNamara MG	.25	.11	.03
☐	71T Orlando Mercado	.25	.11	.03
☐	72T Larry Milbourne	.25	.11	.03
☐	73T Randy Moffitt	.25	.11	.03
☐	74T Sid Monge	.25	.11	.03
☐	75T Jose Morales	.25	.11	.03
☐	76T Omar Moreno	.25	.11	.03
☐	77T Joe Morgan	2.00	.90	.25
☐	78T Mike Morgan	.25	.11	.03
☐	79T Dale Murray	.25	.11	.03
☐	80T Jeff Newman	.25	.11	.03

		NRMT-MT	EXC	G-VG
☐ 81T	Pete O'Brien	.35	.16	.04
☐ 82T	Jorge Orta	.25	.11	.03
☐ 83T	Alejandro Pena	.35	.16	.04
☐ 84T	Pascual Perez	.25	.11	.03
☐ 85T	Tony Perez	1.00	.45	.12
☐ 86T	Broderick Perkins	.25	.11	.03
☐ 87T	Tony Phillips	6.00	2.70	.75
☐ 88T	Charlie Puleo	.25	.11	.03
☐ 89T	Pat Putnam	.25	.11	.03
☐ 90T	Jamie Quirk	.25	.11	.03
☐ 91T	Doug Rader MG	.25	.11	.03
☐ 92T	Chuck Rainey	.25	.11	.03
☐ 93T	Bobby Ramos	.25	.11	.03
☐ 94T	Gary Redus	.35	.16	.03
☐ 95T	Steve Renko	.25	.11	.03
☐ 96T	Leon Roberts	.25	.11	.03
☐ 97T	Aurelio Rodriguez	.25	.11	.03
☐ 98T	Dick Ruthven	.25	.11	.03
☐ 99T	Daryl Sconiers	.25	.11	.03
☐ 100T	Mike Scott	.35	.16	.04
☐ 101T	Tom Seaver	5.00	2.20	.60
☐ 102T	John Shelby	.25	.11	.03
☐ 103T	Bob Shirley	.25	.11	.03
☐ 104T	Joe Simpson	.25	.11	.03
☐ 105T	Doug Sisk	.25	.11	.03
☐ 106T	Mike Smithson	.25	.11	.03
☐ 107T	Elias Sosa	.25	.11	.03
☐ 108T	Darryl Strawberry	10.00	4.50	1.25
☐ 109T	Tom Tellmann	.25	.11	.03
☐ 110T	Gene Tenace	.35	.16	.04
☐ 111T	Gorman Thomas	.25	.11	.03
☐ 112T	Dick Tidrow	.25	.11	.03
☐ 113T	Dave Tobik	.25	.11	.03
☐ 114T	Wayne Tolleson	.25	.11	.03
☐ 115T	Mike Torrez	.25	.11	.03
☐ 116T	Manny Trillo	.25	.11	.03
☐ 117T	Steve Trout	.25	.11	.03
☐ 118T	Lee Tunnell	.25	.11	.03
☐ 119T	Mike Vail	.25	.11	.03
☐ 120T	Ellis Valentine	.25	.11	.03
☐ 121T	Tom Veryzer	.25	.11	.03
☐ 122T	George Vukovich	.25	.11	.03
☐ 123T	Rick Waits	.25	.11	.03
☐ 124T	Greg Walker	.25	.11	.03
☐ 125T	Chris Welsh	.25	.11	.03
☐ 126T	Len Whitehouse	.25	.11	.03
☐ 127T	Eddie Whitson	.25	.11	.03
☐ 128T	Jim Wohlford	.25	.11	.03
☐ 129T	Matt Young	.25	.11	.03
☐ 130T	Joel Youngblood	.25	.11	.03
☐ 131T	Pat Zachry	.25	.11	.03
☐ 132T	Checklist 1T-132T	.25	.11	.03

1984 Topps

The cards in this 792-card set measure 2 1/2" by 3 1/2". For the second year in a row, Topps utilized a dual picture on the front of the card. A portrait is shown in a square insert and an action shot is featured in the main photo. Card numbers 1-6 feature 1983 Highlights (HL), cards 131-138 depict League Leaders, card numbers 386-407 feature All-Stars, and card numbers 701-718 feature active Major League career leaders in various statistical categories. Each team leader (TL) card features the

team's leading hitter and pitcher pictured on the front with a team checklist back. There are six numerical checklist cards in the set. The player cards feature team logos in the upper right corner of the reverse. The key Rookie Cards in this set are Don Mattingly, Darryl Strawberry, and Andy Van Slyke. Topps also produced a specially boxed "glossy" edition, frequently referred to as the Topps Tiffany set. There were supposedly only 10,000 sets of the Tiffany cards produced; they were marketed to hobby dealers. The checklist of cards (792 regular and 132 Traded) is identical to that of the normal non-glossy cards. There are two primary distinguishing features of the Tiffany cards, white card stock reverses and high gloss obverses. These Tiffany cards are valued approximately from five to ten times the values listed below. Topps tested a special send-in offer in Michigan and a few other states whereby collectors could obtain direct from Topps ten cards of their choice. Needless to say most people ordered the key (most valuable) players necessitating the printing of a special sheet to keep up with the demand. The special sheet had five cards of Darryl Strawberry, three cards of Don Mattingly, etc. The test was apparently a failure in Topps' eyes as they have never tried it again.

	NRMT-MT	EXC	G-VG
COMPLETE SET (792)	60.00	27.00	7.50
COMMON CARD (1-792)	.08	.04	.01
☐ 1 Steve Carlton HL 300th win and all-time SO king	.50	.23	.06
☐ 2 Rickey Henderson HL 100 stolen bases, three times	.75	.35	.09
☐ 3 Dan Quisenberry HL Sets save record	.15	.07	.02
☐ 4 Nolan Ryan, Steve Carlton, and Gaylord Perry HL (All surpass Johnson)	1.00	.45	.12
☐ 5 Dave Righetti, Bob Forsch, and Mike Warren HL (All pitch no-hitters)	.15	.07	.02
☐ 6 Johnny Bench, Gaylord Perry, and Carl Yastrzemski HL (Superstars retire)	.50	.23	.06

☐ 7 Gary Lucas	.08	.04	.01
☐ 8 Don Mattingly	12.00	5.50	1.50
☐ 9 Jim Gott	.08	.04	.01
☐ 10 Robin Yount	1.00	.45	.12
☐ 11 Minnesota Twins TL	.15	.07	.02

Kent Hrbek
Ken Schrom
(Checklist on back)

☐ 12 Billy Sample	.08	.04	.01
☐ 13 Scott Holman	.08	.04	.01
☐ 14 Tom Brookens	.08	.04	.01
☐ 15 Burt Hooton	.08	.04	.01
☐ 16 Omar Moreno	.08	.04	.01
☐ 17 John Denny	.08	.04	.01
☐ 18 Dale Berra	.08	.04	.01
☐ 19 Ray Fontenot	.08	.04	.01
☐ 20 Greg Luzinski	.15	.07	.02
☐ 21 Joe Altobelli MG	.08	.04	.01
☐ 22 Bryan Clark	.08	.04	.01
☐ 23 Keith Moreland	.08	.04	.01
☐ 24 John Martin	.08	.04	.01
☐ 25 Glenn Hubbard	.08	.04	.01
☐ 26 Bud Black	.08	.04	.01
☐ 27 Daryl Sconiers	.08	.04	.01
☐ 28 Frank Viola	.15	.07	.02
☐ 29 Danny Heep	.08	.04	.01
☐ 30 Wade Boggs	1.25	.55	.16
☐ 31 Andy McGaffigan	.08	.04	.01
☐ 32 Bobby Ramos	.08	.04	.01
☐ 33 Tom Burgmeier	.08	.04	.01
☐ 34 Eddie Milner	.08	.04	.01
☐ 35 Don Sutton	.30	.14	.04
☐ 36 Denny Walling	.08	.04	.01
☐ 37 Texas Rangers TL	.15	.07	.02

Buddy Bell
Rick Honeycutt
(Checklist on back)

☐ 38 Luis DeLeon	.08	.04	.01
☐ 39 Garth Iorg	.08	.04	.01
☐ 40 Dusty Baker	.30	.14	.04
☐ 41 Tony Bernazard	.08	.04	.01
☐ 42 Johnny Grubb	.08	.04	.01
☐ 43 Ron Reed	.08	.04	.01
☐ 44 Jim Morrison	.08	.04	.01
☐ 45 Jerry Mumphrey	.08	.04	.01
☐ 46 Ray Smith	.08	.04	.01
☐ 47 Rudy Law	.08	.04	.01
☐ 48 Julio Franco	.30	.14	.04
☐ 49 John Stuper	.08	.04	.01
☐ 50 Chris Chambliss	.15	.07	.02
☐ 51 Jim Frey MG	.08	.04	.01
☐ 52 Paul Splittorff	.08	.04	.01
☐ 53 Juan Beniquez	.08	.04	.01
☐ 54 Jesse Orosco	.08	.04	.01
☐ 55 Dave Concepcion	.15	.07	.02
☐ 56 Gary Allenson	.08	.04	.01
☐ 57 Dan Schatzeder	.08	.04	.01
☐ 58 Max Venable	.08	.04	.01
☐ 59 Sammy Stewart	.08	.04	.01
☐ 60 Paul Molitor UER	.75	.35	.09

('83 stats .272, 613,
167; should be .270,
608, 164)

☐ 61 Chris Codiroli	.08	.04	.01
☐ 62 Dave Hostetler	.08	.04	.01
☐ 63 Ed VandeBerg	.08	.04	.01
☐ 64 Mike Scioscia	.08	.04	.01
☐ 65 Kirk Gibson	.40	.18	.05
☐ 66 Houston Astros TL	.75	.35	.09

Jose Cruz
Nolan Ryan

(Checklist on back)

☐ 67 Gary Ward	.08	.04	.01
☐ 68 Luis Salazar	.08	.04	.01
☐ 69 Rod Scurry	.08	.04	.01
☐ 70 Gary Matthews	.15	.07	.02
☐ 71 Leo Hernandez	.08	.04	.01
☐ 72 Mike Squires	.08	.04	.01
☐ 73 Jody Davis	.08	.04	.01
☐ 74 Jerry Martin	.08	.04	.01
☐ 75 Bob Forsch	.08	.04	.01
☐ 76 Alfredo Griffin	.08	.04	.01
☐ 77 Brett Butler	.30	.14	.04
☐ 78 Mike Torrez	.08	.04	.01
☐ 79 Rob Wilfong	.08	.04	.01
☐ 80 Steve Rogers	.08	.04	.01
☐ 81 Billy Martin MG	.15	.07	.02
☐ 82 Doug Bird	.08	.04	.01
☐ 83 Richie Zisk	.08	.04	.01
☐ 84 Lenny Faedo	.08	.04	.01
☐ 85 Atlee Hammaker	.08	.04	.01
☐ 86 John Shelby	.08	.04	.01
☐ 87 Frank Pastore	.08	.04	.01
☐ 88 Rob Picciolo	.08	.04	.01
☐ 89 Mike Smithson	.08	.04	.01
☐ 90 Pedro Guerrero	.15	.07	.02
☐ 91 Dan Spillner	.08	.04	.01
☐ 92 Lloyd Moseby	.08	.04	.01
☐ 93 Bob Knepper	.08	.04	.01
☐ 94 Mario Ramirez	.08	.04	.01
☐ 95 Aurelio Lopez	.08	.04	.01
☐ 96 Kansas City Royals TL	.30	.14	.04

Hal McRae
Larry Gura
(Checklist on back)

☐ 97 LaMarr Hoyt	.08	.04	.01
☐ 98 Steve Nicosia	.08	.04	.01
☐ 99 Craig Lefferts	.08	.04	.01
☐ 100 Reggie Jackson	.75	.35	.09
☐ 101 Porfirio Altamirano	.08	.04	.01
☐ 102 Ken Oberkfell	.08	.04	.01
☐ 103 Dwayne Murphy	.08	.04	.01
☐ 104 Ken Dayley	.08	.04	.01
☐ 105 Tony Armas	.08	.04	.01
☐ 106 Tim Stoddard	.08	.04	.01
☐ 107 Ned Yost	.08	.04	.01
☐ 108 Randy Moffitt	.08	.04	.01
☐ 109 Brad Wellman	.08	.04	.01
☐ 110 Ron Guidry	.15	.07	.02
☐ 111 Bill Virdon MG	.08	.04	.01
☐ 112 Tom Niedenfuer	.08	.04	.01
☐ 113 Kelly Paris	.08	.04	.01
☐ 114 Checklist 1-132	.15	.07	.02
☐ 115 Andre Thornton	.08	.04	.01
☐ 116 George Bjorkman	.08	.04	.01
☐ 117 Tom Veryzer	.08	.04	.01
☐ 118 Charlie Hough	.15	.07	.02
☐ 119 John Wockenfuss	.08	.04	.01
☐ 120 Keith Hernandez	.30	.14	.04
☐ 121 Pat Sheridan	.08	.04	.01
☐ 122 Cecilio Guante	.08	.04	.01
☐ 123 Butch Wynegar	.08	.04	.01
☐ 124 Damaso Garcia	.08	.04	.01
☐ 125 Britt Burns	.08	.04	.01
☐ 126 Atlanta Braves TL	.30	.14	.04

Dale Murphy
Craig McMurtry
(Checklist on back)

☐ 127 Mike Madden	.08	.04	.01
☐ 128 Rick Manning	.08	.04	.01
☐ 129 Bill Laskey	.08	.04	.01
☐ 130 Ozzie Smith	1.25	.55	.16

☐ 131	Batting Leaders	.50	.23	.06
	Bill Madlock			
	Wade Boggs			
☐ 132	Home Run Leaders	.30	.14	.04
	Mike Schmidt			
	Jim Rice			
☐ 133	RBI Leaders	.30	.14	.04
	Dale Murphy			
	Cecil Cooper			
	Jim Rice			
☐ 134	Stolen Base Leaders	.75	.35	.09
	Tim Raines			
	Rickey Henderson			
☐ 135	Victory Leaders	.30	.14	.04
	John Denny			
	LaMarr Hoyt			
☐ 136	Strikeout Leaders	.30	.14	.04
	Steve Carlton			
	Jack Morris			
☐ 137	ERA Leaders	.30	.14	.04
	Atlee Hammaker			
	Rick Honeycutt			
☐ 138	Leading Firemen	.30	.14	.04
	Al Holland			
	Dan Quisenberry			
☐ 139	Bert Campaneris	.15	.07	.02
☐ 140	Storm Davis	.08	.04	.01
☐ 141	Pat Corrales MG	.08	.04	.01
☐ 142	Rich Gale	.08	.04	.01
☐ 143	Jose Morales	.08	.04	.01
☐ 144	Brian Harper	.40	.18	.05
☐ 145	Gary Lavelle	.08	.04	.01
☐ 146	Ed Romero	.08	.04	.01
☐ 147	Dan Petry	.08	.04	.01
☐ 148	Joe Lefebvre	.08	.04	.01
☐ 149	Jon Matlack	.08	.04	.01
☐ 150	Dale Murphy	.40	.18	.05
☐ 151	Steve Trout	.08	.04	.01
☐ 152	Glenn Brummer	.08	.04	.01
☐ 153	Dick Tidrow	.08	.04	.01
☐ 154	Dave Henderson	.15	.07	.02
☐ 155	Frank White	.15	.07	.02
☐ 156	Oakland A's TL	.25	.11	.03
	Rickey Henderson			
	Tim Conroy			
	(Checklist on back)			
☐ 157	Gary Gaetti	.30	.14	.04
☐ 158	John Curtis	.08	.04	.01
☐ 159	Darryl Cias	.08	.04	.01
☐ 160	Mario Soto	.08	.04	.01
☐ 161	Junior Ortiz	.08	.04	.01
☐ 162	Bob Ojeda	.15	.07	.02
☐ 163	Lorenzo Gray	.08	.04	.01
☐ 164	Scott Sanderson	.08	.04	.01
☐ 165	Ken Singleton	.15	.07	.02
☐ 166	Jamie Nelson	.08	.04	.01
☐ 167	Marshall Edwards	.08	.04	.01
☐ 168	Juan Bonilla	.08	.04	.01
☐ 169	Larry Parrish	.08	.04	.01
☐ 170	Jerry Reuss	.15	.07	.02
☐ 171	Frank Robinson MG	.30	.14	.04
☐ 172	Frank DiPino	.08	.04	.01
☐ 173	Marvell Wynne	.08	.04	.01
☐ 174	Juan Berenguer	.08	.04	.01
☐ 175	Graig Nettles	.15	.07	.02
☐ 176	Lee Smith	.75	.35	.09
☐ 177	Jerry Hairston	.08	.04	.01
☐ 178	Bill Krueger	.08	.04	.01
☐ 179	Buck Martinez	.08	.04	.01
☐ 180	Manny Trillo	.08	.04	.01
☐ 181	Roy Thomas	.08	.04	.01

☐ 182	Darryl Strawberry	2.00	.90	.25
☐ 183	Al Williams	.08	.04	.01
☐ 184	Mike O'Berry	.08	.04	.01
☐ 185	Sixto Lezcano	.08	.04	.01
☐ 186	Cardinal TL	.15	.07	.02
	Lonnie Smith			
	John Stuper			
	(Checklist on back)			
☐ 187	Luis Aponte	.08	.04	.01
☐ 188	Bryan Little	.08	.04	.01
☐ 189	Tim Conroy	.08	.04	.01
☐ 190	Ben Oglivie	.08	.04	.01
☐ 191	Mike Boddicker	.08	.04	.01
☐ 192	Nick Esasky	.08	.04	.01
☐ 193	Darrell Brown	.08	.04	.01
☐ 194	Domingo Ramos	.08	.04	.01
☐ 195	Jack Morris	.30	.14	.04
☐ 196	Don Slaught	.08	.04	.01
☐ 197	Garry Hancock	.08	.04	.01
☐ 198	Bill Doran	.15	.07	.02
☐ 199	Willie Hernandez	.15	.07	.02
☐ 200	Andre Dawson	.75	.35	.09
☐ 201	Bruce Kison	.08	.04	.01
☐ 202	Bobby Cox MG	.15	.07	.02
☐ 203	Matt Keough	.08	.04	.01
☐ 204	Bobby Meacham	.08	.04	.01
☐ 205	Greg Minton	.08	.04	.01
☐ 206	Andy Van Slyke	.75	.35	.09
☐ 207	Donnie Moore	.08	.04	.01
☐ 208	Jose Oquendo	.15	.07	.02
☐ 209	Manny Sarmiento	.08	.04	.01
☐ 210	Joe Morgan	.40	.18	.05
☐ 211	Rick Sweet	.08	.04	.01
☐ 212	Broderick Perkins	.08	.04	.01
☐ 213	Bruce Hurst	.15	.07	.02
☐ 214	Paul Householder	.08	.04	.01
☐ 215	Tippy Martinez	.08	.04	.01
☐ 216	White Sox TL	.30	.14	.04
	Carlton Fisk			
	Richard Dotson			
	(Checklist on back)			
☐ 217	Alan Ashby	.08	.04	.01
☐ 218	Rick Waits	.08	.04	.01
☐ 219	Joe Simpson	.08	.04	.01
☐ 220	Fernando Valenzuela	.15	.07	.02
☐ 221	Cliff Johnson	.08	.04	.01
☐ 222	Rick Honeycutt	.08	.04	.01
☐ 223	Wayne Krenchicki	.08	.04	.01
☐ 224	Sid Monge	.08	.04	.01
☐ 225	Lee Mazzilli	.08	.04	.01
☐ 226	Juan Eichelberger	.08	.04	.01
☐ 227	Steve Braun	.08	.04	.01
☐ 228	John Rabb	.08	.04	.01
☐ 229	Paul Owens MG	.08	.04	.01
☐ 230	Rickey Henderson	1.00	.45	.12
☐ 231	Gary Woods	.08	.04	.01
☐ 232	Tim Wallach	.15	.07	.02
☐ 233	Checklist 133-264	.15	.07	.02
☐ 234	Rafael Ramirez	.08	.04	.01
☐ 235	Matt Young	.08	.04	.01
☐ 236	Ellis Valentine	.08	.04	.01
☐ 237	John Castino	.08	.04	.01
☐ 238	Reid Nichols	.08	.04	.01
☐ 239	Jay Howell	.15	.07	.02
☐ 240	Eddie Murray	1.50	.70	.19
☐ 241	Bill Almon	.08	.04	.01
☐ 242	Alex Trevino	.08	.04	.01
☐ 243	Pete Ladd	.08	.04	.01
☐ 244	Candy Maldonado	.08	.04	.01
☐ 245	Rick Sutcliffe	.15	.07	.02
☐ 246	New York Mets TL	.25	.11	.03

	Mookie Wilson		
	Tom Seaver		
	(Checklist on back)		
☐ 247	Onix Concepcion	.08	.04	.01
☐ 248	Bill Dawley	.08	.04	.01
☐ 249	Jay Johnstone	.15	.07	.02
☐ 250	Bill Madlock	.15	.07	.02
☐ 251	Tony Gwynn	4.00	1.80	.50
☐ 252	Larry Christenson	.08	.04	.01
☐ 253	Jim Wohlford	.08	.04	.01
☐ 254	Shane Rawley	.08	.04	.01
☐ 255	Bruce Benedict	.08	.04	.01
☐ 256	Dave Geisel	.08	.04	.01
☐ 257	Julio Cruz	.08	.04	.01
☐ 258	Luis Sanchez	.08	.04	.01
☐ 259	Sparky Anderson MG	.15	.07	.02
☐ 260	Scott McGregor	.08	.04	.01
☐ 261	Bobby Brown	.08	.04	.01
☐ 262	Tom Candiotti	.40	.18	.05
☐ 263	Jack Fimple	.08	.04	.01
☐ 264	Doug Frobel	.08	.04	.01
☐ 265	Donnie Hill	.08	.04	.01
☐ 266	Steve Lubratich	.08	.04	.01
☐ 267	Carmelo Martinez	.08	.04	.01
☐ 268	Jack O'Connor	.08	.04	.01
☐ 269	Aurelio Rodriguez	.08	.04	.01
☐ 270	Jeff Russell	.30	.14	.04
☐ 271	Moose Haas	.08	.04	.01
☐ 272	Rick Dempsey	.15	.07	.02
☐ 273	Charlie Puleo	.08	.04	.01
☐ 274	Rick Monday	.08	.04	.01
☐ 275	Len Matuszek	.08	.04	.01
☐ 276	Angels TL	.30	.14	.04
	Rod Carew		
	Geoff Zahn		
	(Checklist on back)		
☐ 277	Eddie Whitson	.08	.04	.01
☐ 278	Jorge Bell	.15	.07	.02
☐ 279	Ivan DeJesus	.08	.04	.01
☐ 280	Floyd Bannister	.08	.04	.01
☐ 281	Larry Milbourne	.08	.04	.01
☐ 282	Jim Barr	.08	.04	.01
☐ 283	Larry Biittner	.08	.04	.01
☐ 284	Howard Bailey	.08	.04	.01
☐ 285	Darrell Porter	.08	.04	.01
☐ 286	Lary Sorensen	.08	.04	.01
☐ 287	Warren Cromartie	.08	.04	.01
☐ 288	Jim Beattie	.08	.04	.01
☐ 289	Randy Johnson	.08	.04	.01
☐ 290	Dave Dravecky	.08	.04	.01
☐ 291	Chuck Tanner MG	.08	.04	.01
☐ 292	Tony Scott	.08	.04	.01
☐ 293	Ed Lynch	.08	.04	.01
☐ 294	U.L. Washington	.08	.04	.01
☐ 295	Mike Flanagan	.08	.04	.01
☐ 296	Jeff Newman	.08	.04	.01
☐ 297	Bruce Berenyi	.08	.04	.01
☐ 298	Jim Gantner	.15	.07	.02
☐ 299	John Butcher	.08	.04	.01
☐ 300	Pete Rose	1.00	.45	.12
☐ 301	Frank LaCorte	.08	.04	.01
☐ 302	Barry Bonnell	.08	.04	.01
☐ 303	Marty Castillo	.08	.04	.01
☐ 304	Warren Brusstar	.08	.04	.01
☐ 305	Roy Smalley	.08	.04	.01
☐ 306	Dodgers TL	.15	.07	.02
	Pedro Guerrero		
	Bob Welch		
	(Checklist on back)		
☐ 307	Bobby Mitchell	.08	.04	.01
☐ 308	Ron Hassey	.08	.04	.01
☐ 309	Tony Phillips	1.00	.45	.12
☐ 310	Willie McGee	.15	.07	.02
☐ 311	Jerry Koosman	.15	.07	.02
☐ 312	Jorge Orta	.08	.04	.01
☐ 313	Mike Jorgensen	.08	.04	.01
☐ 314	Orlando Mercado	.08	.04	.01
☐ 315	Bob Grich	.15	.07	.02
☐ 316	Mark Bradley	.08	.04	.01
☐ 317	Greg Pryor	.08	.04	.01
☐ 318	Bill Gullickson	.15	.07	.02
☐ 319	Al Bumbry	.15	.07	.02
☐ 320	Bob Stanley	.08	.04	.01
☐ 321	Harvey Kuenn MG	.15	.07	.02
☐ 322	Ken Schrom	.08	.04	.01
☐ 323	Alan Knicely	.08	.04	.01
☐ 324	Alejandro Pena	.15	.07	.02
☐ 325	Darrell Evans	.15	.07	.02
☐ 326	Bob Kearney	.08	.04	.01
☐ 327	Ruppert Jones	.08	.04	.01
☐ 328	Vern Ruhle	.08	.04	.01
☐ 329	Pat Tabler	.08	.04	.01
☐ 330	John Candelaria	.08	.04	.01
☐ 331	Bucky Dent	.15	.07	.02
☐ 332	Kevin Gross	.15	.07	.02
☐ 333	Larry Herndon	.08	.04	.01
☐ 334	Chuck Rainey	.08	.04	.01
☐ 335	Don Baylor	.30	.14	.04
☐ 336	Seattle Mariners TL	.15	.07	.02
	Pat Putnam		
	Matt Young		
	(Checklist on back)		
☐ 337	Kevin Hagen	.08	.04	.01
☐ 338	Mike Warren	.08	.04	.01
☐ 339	Roy Lee Jackson	.08	.04	.01
☐ 340	Hal McRae	.30	.14	.04
☐ 341	Dave Tobik	.08	.04	.01
☐ 342	Tim Foli	.08	.04	.01
☐ 343	Mark Davis	.08	.04	.01
☐ 344	Rick Miller	.08	.04	.01
☐ 345	Kent Hrbek	.30	.14	.04
☐ 346	Kurt Bevacqua	.08	.04	.01
☐ 347	Allan Ramirez	.08	.04	.01
☐ 348	Toby Harrah	.08	.04	.01
☐ 349	Bob L. Gibson	.08	.04	.01
☐ 350	George Foster	.15	.07	.02
☐ 351	Russ Nixon MG	.08	.04	.01
☐ 352	Dave Stewart	.30	.14	.04
☐ 353	Jim Anderson	.08	.04	.01
☐ 354	Jeff Burroughs	.08	.04	.01
☐ 355	Jason Thompson	.08	.04	.01
☐ 356	Glenn Abbott	.08	.04	.01
☐ 357	Ron Cey	.15	.07	.02
☐ 358	Bob Dernier	.08	.04	.01
☐ 359	Jim Acker	.08	.04	.01
☐ 360	Willie Randolph	.15	.07	.02
☐ 361	Dave Smith	.08	.04	.01
☐ 362	David Green	.08	.04	.01
☐ 363	Tim Laudner	.08	.04	.01
☐ 364	Scott Fletcher	.08	.04	.01
☐ 365	Steve Bedrosian	.15	.07	.02
☐ 366	Padres TL	.15	.07	.02
	Terry Kennedy		
	Dave Dravecky		
	(Checklist on back)		
☐ 367	Jamie Easterly	.08	.04	.01
☐ 368	Hubie Brooks	.15	.07	.02
☐ 369	Steve McCatty	.08	.04	.01
☐ 370	Tim Raines	.50	.23	.06
☐ 371	Dave Gumpert	.08	.04	.01
☐ 372	Gary Roenicke	.08	.04	.01
☐ 373	Bill Scherrer	.08	.04	.01

☐ 374	Don Money	.08	.04	.01
☐ 375	Dennis Leonard	.08	.04	.01
☐ 376	Dave Anderson	.08	.04	.01
☐ 377	Danny Darwin	.08	.04	.01
☐ 378	Bob Brenly	.08	.04	.01
☐ 379	Checklist 265-396	.15	.07	.02
☐ 380	Steve Garvey	.30	.14	.04
☐ 381	Ralph Houk MG	.15	.07	.02
☐ 382	Chris Nyman	.08	.04	.01
☐ 383	Terry Puhl	.08	.04	.01
☐ 384	Lee Tunnell	.08	.04	.01
☐ 385	Tony Perez	.30	.14	.04
☐ 386	George Hendrick AS	.08	.04	.01
☐ 387	Johnny Ray AS	.08	.04	.01
☐ 388	Mike Schmidt AS	.50	.23	.06
☐ 389	Ozzie Smith AS	.60	.25	.07
☐ 390	Tim Raines AS	.30	.14	.04
☐ 391	Dale Murphy AS	.30	.14	.04
☐ 392	Andre Dawson AS	.50	.23	.06
☐ 393	Gary Carter AS	.15	.07	.02
☐ 394	Steve Rogers AS	.08	.04	.01
☐ 395	Steve Carlton AS	.50	.23	.06
☐ 396	Jesse Orosco AS	.08	.04	.01
☐ 397	Eddie Murray AS	.50	.23	.06
☐ 398	Lou Whitaker AS	.30	.14	.04
☐ 399	George Brett AS	1.00	.45	.12
☐ 400	Cal Ripken AS	2.00	.90	.25
☐ 401	Jim Rice AS	.15	.07	.02
☐ 402	Dave Winfield AS	.60	.25	.07
☐ 403	Lloyd Moseby AS	.08	.04	.01
☐ 404	Ted Simmons AS	.15	.07	.02
☐ 405	LaMarr Hoyt AS	.08	.04	.01
☐ 406	Ron Guidry AS	.15	.07	.02
☐ 407	Dan Quisenberry AS	.15	.07	.02
☐ 408	Lou Piniella	.15	.07	.02
☐ 409	Juan Agosto	.08	.04	.01
☐ 410	Claudell Washington	.08	.04	.01
☐ 411	Houston Jimenez	.08	.04	.01
☐ 412	Doug Rader MG	.08	.04	.01
☐ 413	Spike Owen	.15	.07	.02
☐ 414	Mitchell Page	.08	.04	.01
☐ 415	Tommy John	.30	.14	.04
☐ 416	Dane Iorg	.08	.04	.01
☐ 417	Mike Armstrong	.08	.04	.01
☐ 418	Ron Hodges	.08	.04	.01
☐ 419	John Henry Johnson	.08	.04	.01
☐ 420	Cecil Cooper	.15	.07	.02
☐ 421	Charlie Lea	.08	.04	.01
☐ 422	Jose Cruz	.15	.07	.02
☐ 423	Mike Morgan	.15	.07	.02
☐ 424	Dann Bilardello	.08	.04	.01
☐ 425	Steve Howe	.08	.04	.01
☐ 426	Orioles TL	1.50	.70	.19
	Cal Ripken			
	Mike Boddicker			
	(Checklist on back)			
☐ 427	Rick Leach	.08	.04	.01
☐ 428	Fred Breining	.08	.04	.01
☐ 429	Randy Bush	.08	.04	.01
☐ 430	Rusty Staub	.15	.07	.02
☐ 431	Chris Bando	.08	.04	.01
☐ 432	Charles Hudson	.08	.04	.01
☐ 433	Rich Hebner	.08	.04	.01
☐ 434	Harold Baines	.30	.14	.04
☐ 435	Neil Allen	.08	.04	.01
☐ 436	Rick Peters	.08	.04	.01
☐ 437	Mike Proly	.08	.04	.01
☐ 438	Biff Pocoroba	.08	.04	.01
☐ 439	Bob Stoddard	.08	.04	.01
☐ 440	Steve Kemp	.08	.04	.01
☐ 441	Bob Lillis MG	.08	.04	.01
☐ 442	Byron McLaughlin	.08	.04	.01
☐ 443	Benny Ayala	.08	.04	.01
☐ 444	Steve Renko	.08	.04	.01
☐ 445	Jerry Remy	.08	.04	.01
☐ 446	Luis Pujols	.08	.04	.01
☐ 447	Tom Brunansky	.08	.04	.01
☐ 448	Ben Hayes	.08	.04	.01
☐ 449	Joe Pettini	.08	.04	.01
☐ 450	Gary Carter	.30	.14	.04
☐ 451	Bob Jones	.08	.04	.01
☐ 452	Chuck Porter	.08	.04	.01
☐ 453	Willie Upshaw	.08	.04	.01
☐ 454	Joe Beckwith	.08	.04	.01
☐ 455	Terry Kennedy	.08	.04	.01
☐ 456	Chicago Cubs TL	.30	.14	.04
	Keith Moreland			
	Fergie Jenkins			
	(Checklist on back)			
☐ 457	Dave Rozema	.08	.04	.01
☐ 458	Kiko Garcia	.08	.04	.01
☐ 459	Kevin Hickey	.08	.04	.01
☐ 460	Dave Winfield	1.00	.45	.12
☐ 461	Jim Maler	.08	.04	.01
☐ 462	Lee Lacy	.08	.04	.01
☐ 463	Dave Engle	.08	.04	.01
☐ 464	Jeff A. Jones	.08	.04	.01
☐ 465	Mookie Wilson	.15	.07	.02
☐ 466	Gene Garber	.08	.04	.01
☐ 467	Mike Ramsey	.08	.04	.01
☐ 468	Geoff Zahn	.08	.04	.01
☐ 469	Tom O'Malley	.08	.04	.01
☐ 470	Nolan Ryan	5.00	2.20	.60
☐ 471	Dick Howser MG	.08	.04	.01
☐ 472	Mike G. Brown	.08	.04	.01
☐ 473	Jim Dwyer	.08	.04	.01
☐ 474	Greg Bargar	.08	.04	.01
☐ 475	Gary Redus	.08	.04	.01
☐ 476	Tom Tellmann	.08	.04	.01
☐ 477	Rafael Landestoy	.08	.04	.01
☐ 478	Alan Bannister	.08	.04	.01
☐ 479	Frank Tanana	.15	.07	.02
☐ 480	Ron Kittle	.08	.04	.01
☐ 481	Mark Thurmond	.08	.04	.01
☐ 482	Enos Cabell	.08	.04	.01
☐ 483	Fergie Jenkins	.30	.14	.04
☐ 484	Ozzie Virgil	.08	.04	.01
☐ 485	Rick Rhoden	.08	.04	.01
☐ 486	N.Y. Yankees TL	.30	.14	.04
	Don Baylor			
	Ron Guidry			
	(Checklist on back)			
☐ 487	Ricky Adams	.08	.04	.01
☐ 488	Jesse Barfield	.15	.07	.02
☐ 489	Dave Von Ohlen	.08	.04	.01
☐ 490	Cal Ripken	6.00	2.70	.75
☐ 491	Bobby Castillo	.08	.04	.01
☐ 492	Tucker Ashford	.08	.04	.01
☐ 493	Mike Norris	.08	.04	.01
☐ 494	Chili Davis	.30	.14	.04
☐ 495	Rollie Fingers	.30	.14	.04
☐ 496	Terry Francona	.08	.04	.01
☐ 497	Bud Anderson	.08	.04	.01
☐ 498	Rich Gedman	.08	.04	.01
☐ 499	Mike Witt	.08	.04	.01
☐ 500	George Brett	2.50	1.10	.30
☐ 501	Steve Henderson	.08	.04	.01
☐ 502	Joe Torre MG	.15	.07	.02
☐ 503	Elias Sosa	.08	.04	.01
☐ 504	Mickey Rivers	.08	.04	.01
☐ 505	Pete Vuckovich	.08	.04	.01
☐ 506	Ernie Whitt	.08	.04	.01

☐ 507	Mike LaCoss	.08	.04	.01
☐ 508	Mel Hall	.15	.07	.02
☐ 509	Brad Havens	.08	.04	.01
☐ 510	Alan Trammell	.50	.23	.06
☐ 511	Marty Bystrom	.08	.04	.01
☐ 512	Oscar Gamble	.08	.04	.01
☐ 513	Dave Beard	.08	.04	.01
☐ 514	Floyd Rayford	.08	.04	.01
☐ 515	Gorman Thomas	.08	.04	.01
☐ 516	Montreal Expos TL	.15	.07	.02
	Al Oliver			
	Charlie Lea			
	(Checklist on back)			
☐ 517	John Moses	.08	.04	.01
☐ 518	Greg Walker	.08	.04	.01
☐ 519	Ron Davis	.08	.04	.01
☐ 520	Bob Boone	.15	.07	.02
☐ 521	Pete Falcone	.08	.04	.01
☐ 522	Dave Bergman	.08	.04	.01
☐ 523	Glenn Hoffman	.08	.04	.01
☐ 524	Carlos Diaz	.08	.04	.01
☐ 525	Willie Wilson	.15	.07	.02
☐ 526	Ron Oester	.08	.04	.01
☐ 527	Checklist 397-528	.15	.07	.02
☐ 528	Mark Brouhard	.08	.04	.01
☐ 529	Keith Atherton	.08	.04	.01
☐ 530	Dan Ford	.08	.04	.01
☐ 531	Steve Boros MG	.08	.04	.01
☐ 532	Eric Show	.08	.04	.01
☐ 533	Ken Landreaux	.08	.04	.01
☐ 534	Pete O'Brien	.30	.14	.04
☐ 535	Bo Diaz	.08	.04	.01
☐ 536	Doug Bair	.08	.04	.01
☐ 537	Johnny Ray	.08	.04	.01
☐ 538	Kevin Bass	.08	.04	.01
☐ 539	George Frazier	.08	.04	.01
☐ 540	George Hendrick	.08	.04	.01
☐ 541	Dennis Lamp	.06	.04	.01
☐ 542	Duane Kuiper	.08	.04	.01
☐ 543	Craig McMurtry	.08	.04	.01
☐ 544	Cesar Geronimo	.08	.04	.01
☐ 545	Bill Buckner	.15	.07	.02
☐ 546	Indians TL	.15	.07	.02
	Mike Hargrove			
	Lary Sorensen			
	(Checklist on back)			
☐ 547	Mike Moore	.15	.07	.02
☐ 548	Ron Jackson	.08	.04	.01
☐ 549	Walt Terrell	.08	.04	.01
☐ 550	Jim Rice	.30	.14	.04
☐ 551	Scott Ullger	.08	.04	.01
☐ 552	Ray Burris	.08	.04	.01
☐ 553	Joe Nolan	.08	.04	.01
☐ 554	Ted Power	.08	.04	.01
☐ 555	Greg Brock	.08	.04	.01
☐ 556	Joey McLaughlin	.08	.04	.01
☐ 557	Wayne Tolleson	.08	.04	.01
☐ 558	Mike Davis	.08	.04	.01
☐ 559	Mike Scott	.15	.07	.02
☐ 560	Carlton Fisk	.75	.35	.09
☐ 561	Whitey Herzog MG	.15	.07	.02
☐ 562	Manny Castillo	.08	.04	.01
☐ 563	Glenn Wilson	.08	.04	.01
☐ 564	Al Holland	.08	.04	.01
☐ 565	Leon Durham	.08	.04	.01
☐ 566	Jim Bibby	.08	.04	.01
☐ 567	Mike Heath	.08	.04	.01
☐ 568	Pete Filson	.08	.04	.01
☐ 569	Bake McBride	.08	.04	.01
☐ 570	Dan Quisenberry	.15	.07	.02
☐ 571	Bruce Bochy	.08	.04	.01
☐ 572	Jerry Royster	.08	.04	.01
☐ 573	Dave Kingman	.15	.07	.02
☐ 574	Brian Downing	.15	.07	.02
☐ 575	Jim Clancy	.08	.04	.01
☐ 576	Giants TL	.15	.07	.02
	Jeff Leonard			
	Atlee Hammaker			
	(Checklist on back)			
☐ 577	Mark Clear	.08	.04	.01
☐ 578	Lenn Sakata	.08	.04	.01
☐ 579	Bob James	.08	.04	.01
☐ 580	Lonnie Smith	.15	.07	.02
☐ 581	Jose DeLeon	.15	.07	.02
☐ 582	Bob McClure	.08	.04	.01
☐ 583	Derrel Thomas	.08	.04	.01
☐ 584	Dave Schmidt	.08	.04	.01
☐ 585	Dan Driessen	.08	.04	.01
☐ 586	Joe Niekro	.15	.07	.02
☐ 587	Von Hayes	.08	.04	.01
☐ 588	Milt Wilcox	.08	.04	.01
☐ 589	Mike Easler	.08	.04	.01
☐ 590	Dave Stieb	.15	.07	.02
☐ 591	Tony LaRussa MG	.15	.07	.02
☐ 592	Andre Robertson	.08	.04	.01
☐ 593	Jeff Lahti	.08	.04	.01
☐ 594	Gene Richards	.08	.04	.01
☐ 595	Jeff Reardon	.30	.14	.04
☐ 596	Ryne Sandberg	4.00	1.80	.50
☐ 597	Rick Camp	.08	.04	.01
☐ 598	Rusty Kuntz	.08	.04	.01
☐ 599	Doug Sisk	.08	.04	.01
☐ 600	Rod Carew	.60	.25	.07
☐ 601	John Tudor	.15	.07	.02
☐ 602	John Wathan	.08	.04	.01
☐ 603	Renie Martin	.08	.04	.01
☐ 604	John Lowenstein	.08	.04	.01
☐ 605	Mike Caldwell	.08	.04	.01
☐ 606	Blue Jays TL	.15	.07	.02
	Lloyd Moseby			
	Dave Stieb			
	(Checklist on back)			
☐ 607	Tom Hume	.08	.04	.01
☐ 608	Bobby Johnson	.08	.04	.01
☐ 609	Dan Meyer	.08	.04	.01
☐ 610	Steve Sax	.15	.07	.02
☐ 611	Chet Lemon	.08	.04	.01
☐ 612	Harry Spilman	.08	.04	.01
☐ 613	Greg Gross	.08	.04	.01
☐ 614	Len Barker	.08	.04	.01
☐ 615	Garry Templeton	.08	.04	.01
☐ 616	Don Robinson	.08	.04	.01
☐ 617	Rick Cerone	.08	.04	.01
☐ 618	Dickie Noles	.08	.04	.01
☐ 619	Jerry Dybzinski	.08	.04	.01
☐ 620	Al Oliver	.15	.07	.02
☐ 621	Frank Howard MG	.15	.07	.02
☐ 622	Al Cowens	.08	.04	.01
☐ 623	Ron Washington	.08	.04	.01
☐ 624	Terry Harper	.08	.04	.01
☐ 625	Larry Gura	.08	.04	.01
☐ 626	Bob Clark	.08	.04	.01
☐ 627	Dave LaPoint	.08	.04	.01
☐ 628	Ed Jurak	.08	.04	.01
☐ 629	Rick Langford	.08	.04	.01
☐ 630	Ted Simmons	.15	.07	.02
☐ 631	Dennis Martinez	.15	.07	.02
☐ 632	Tom Foley	.08	.04	.01
☐ 633	Mike Krukow	.08	.04	.01
☐ 634	Mike Marshall	.08	.04	.01
☐ 635	Dave Righetti	.15	.07	.02
☐ 636	Pat Putnam	.08	.04	.01

☐ 637	Phillies TL	.15	.07	.02
	Gary Matthews			
	John Denny			
	(Checklist on back)			
☐ 638	George Vukovich	.08	.04	.01
☐ 639	Rick Lysander	.08	.04	.01
☐ 640	Lance Parrish	.15	.07	.02
☐ 641	Mike Richardt	.08	.04	.01
☐ 642	Tom Underwood	.08	.04	.01
☐ 643	Mike C. Brown	.08	.04	.01
☐ 644	Tim Lollar	.08	.04	.01
☐ 645	Tony Pena	.15	.07	.02
☐ 646	Checklist 529-660	.15	.07	.02
☐ 647	Ron Roenicke	.08	.04	.01
☐ 648	Len Whitehouse	.08	.04	.01
☐ 649	Tom Herr	.15	.07	.02
☐ 650	Phil Niekro	.30	.14	.04
☐ 651	John McNamara MG	.08	.04	.01
☐ 652	Rudy May	.08	.04	.01
☐ 653	Dave Stapleton	.08	.04	.01
☐ 654	Bob Bailor	.08	.04	.01
☐ 655	Amos Otis	.15	.07	.02
☐ 656	Bryn Smith	.08	.04	.01
☐ 657	Thad Bosley	.08	.04	.01
☐ 658	Jerry Augustine	.08	.04	.01
☐ 659	Duane Walker	.08	.04	.01
☐ 660	Ray Knight	.15	.07	.02
☐ 661	Steve Yeager	.08	.04	.01
☐ 662	Tom Brennan	.08	.04	.01
☐ 663	Johnnie LeMaster	.08	.04	.01
☐ 664	Dave Stegman	.08	.04	.01
☐ 665	Buddy Bell	.15	.07	.02
☐ 666	Detroit Tigers TL	.30	.14	.04
	Lou Whitaker			
	Jack Morris			
	(Checklist on back)			
☐ 667	Vance Law	.08	.04	.01
☐ 668	Larry McWilliams	.08	.04	.01
☐ 669	Dave Lopes	.15	.07	.02
☐ 670	Rich Gossage	.30	.14	.04
☐ 671	Jamie Quirk	.08	.04	.01
☐ 672	Ricky Nelson	.08	.04	.01
☐ 673	Mike Walters	.08	.04	.01
☐ 674	Tim Flannery	.08	.04	.01
☐ 675	Pascual Perez	.08	.04	.01
☐ 676	Brian Giles	.08	.04	.01
☐ 677	Doyle Alexander	.08	.04	.01
☐ 678	Chris Speier	.08	.04	.01
☐ 679	Art Howe	.08	.04	.01
☐ 680	Fred Lynn	.15	.07	.02
☐ 681	Tom Lasorda MG	.15	.07	.02
☐ 682	Dan Morogiello	.08	.04	.01
☐ 683	Marty Barrett	.15	.07	.02
☐ 684	Bob Shirley	.08	.04	.01
☐ 685	Willie Aikens	.08	.04	.01
☐ 686	Joe Price	.08	.04	.01
☐ 687	Roy Howell	.08	.04	.01
☐ 688	George Wright	.08	.04	.01
☐ 689	Mike Fischlin	.08	.04	.01
☐ 690	Jack Clark	.15	.07	.02
☐ 691	Steve Lake	.08	.04	.01
☐ 692	Dickie Thon	.08	.04	.01
☐ 693	Alan Wiggins	.08	.04	.01
☐ 694	Mike Stanton	.08	.04	.01
☐ 695	Lou Whitaker	.40	.18	.05
☐ 696	Pirates TL	.15	.07	.02
	Bill Madlock			
	Rick Rhoden			
	(Checklist on back)			
☐ 697	Dale Murray	.08	.04	.01
☐ 698	Marc Hill	.08	.04	.01
☐ 699	Dave Rucker	.08	.04	.01
☐ 700	Mike Schmidt	2.00	.90	.25
☐ 701	NL Active Batting	.30	.14	.04
	Bill Madlock			
	Pete Rose			
	Dave Parker			
☐ 702	NL Active Hits	.30	.14	.04
	Pete Rose			
	Rusty Staub			
	Tony Perez			
☐ 703	NL Active Home Run	.30	.14	.04
	Mike Schmidt			
	Tony Perez			
	Dave Kingman			
☐ 704	NL Active RBI	.30	.14	.04
	Tony Perez			
	Rusty Staub			
	Al Oliver			
☐ 705	NL Active Steals	.30	.14	.04
	Joe Morgan			
	Cesar Cedeno			
	Larry Bowa			
☐ 706	NL Active Victory	.40	.18	.05
	Steve Carlton			
	Fergie Jenkins			
	Tom Seaver			
☐ 707	NL Active Strikeout	1.50	.70	.19
	Steve Carlton			
	Nolan Ryan			
	Tom Seaver			
☐ 708	NL Active ERA	.35	.16	.04
	Tom Seaver			
	Steve Carlton			
	Steve Rogers			
☐ 709	NL Active Save	.15	.07	.02
	Bruce Sutter			
	Tug McGraw			
	Gene Garber			
☐ 710	AL Active Batting	.30	.14	.04
	Rod Carew			
	George Brett			
	Cecil Cooper			
☐ 711	AL Active Hits	.30	.14	.04
	Rod Carew			
	Bert Campaneris			
	Reggie Jackson			
☐ 712	AL Active Home Run	.30	.14	.04
	Reggie Jackson			
	Graig Nettles			
	Greg Luzinski			
☐ 713	AL Active RBI	.30	.14	.04
	Reggie Jackson			
	Ted Simmons			
	Graig Nettles			
☐ 714	AL Active Steals	.15	.07	.02
	Bert Campaneris			
	Dave Lopes			
	Omar Moreno			
☐ 715	AL Active Victory	.30	.14	.04
	Jim Palmer			
	Don Sutton			
	Tommy John			
☐ 716	AL Active Strikeout	.30	.14	.04
	Don Sutton			
	Bert Blyleven			
	Jerry Koosman			
☐ 717	AL Active ERA	.30	.14	.04
	Jim Palmer			
	Rollie Fingers			
	Ron Guidry			
☐ 718	AL Active Save	.30	.14	.04

		Rollie Fingers			
		Rich Gossage			
		Dan Quisenberry			
☐	719	Andy Hassler	.08	.04	.01
☐	720	Dwight Evans	.15	.07	.02
☐	721	Del Crandall MG	.08	.04	.01
☐	722	Bob Welch	.15	.07	.02
☐	723	Rich Dauer	.08	.04	.01
☐	724	Eric Rasmussen	.08	.04	.01
☐	725	Cesar Cedeno	.15	.07	.02
☐	726	Brewers TL	.15	.07	.02
		Ted Simmons			
		Moose Haas			
		(Checklist on back)			
☐	727	Joel Youngblood	.08	.04	.01
☐	728	Tug McGraw	.15	.07	.02
☐	729	Gene Tenace	.08	.04	.01
☐	730	Bruce Sutter	.15	.07	.02
☐	731	Lynn Jones	.08	.04	.01
☐	732	Terry Crowley	.08	.04	.01
☐	733	Dave Collins	.08	.04	.01
☐	734	Odell Jones	.08	.04	.01
☐	735	Rick Burleson	.08	.04	.01
☐	736	Dick Ruthven	.08	.04	.01
☐	737	Jim Essian	.08	.04	.01
☐	738	Bill Schroeder	.08	.04	.01
☐	739	Bob Watson	.15	.07	.02
☐	740	Tom Seaver	.75	.35	.09
☐	741	Wayne Gross	.08	.04	.01
☐	742	Dick Williams MG	.15	.07	.02
☐	743	Don Hood	.08	.04	.01
☐	744	Jamie Allen	.08	.04	.01
☐	745	Dennis Eckersley	.50	.23	.06
☐	746	Mickey Hatcher	.08	.04	.01
☐	747	Pat Zachry	.08	.04	.01
☐	748	Jeff Leonard	.08	.04	.01
☐	749	Doug Flynn	.08	.04	.01
☐	750	Jim Palmer	.75	.35	.09
☐	751	Charlie Moore	.08	.04	.01
☐	752	Phil Garner	.15	.07	.02
☐	753	Doug Gwosdz	.08	.04	.01
☐	754	Kent Tekulve	.15	.07	.02
☐	755	Garry Maddox	.08	.04	.01
☐	756	Reds TL	.15	.07	.02
		Ron Oester			
		Mario Soto			
		(Checklist on back)			
☐	757	Larry Bowa	.15	.07	.02
☐	758	Bill Stein	.08	.04	.01
☐	759	Richard Dotson	.08	.04	.01
☐	760	Bob Horner	.15	.07	.02
☐	761	John Montefusco	.08	.04	.01
☐	762	Rance Mulliniks	.08	.04	.01
☐	763	Craig Swan	.08	.04	.01
☐	764	Mike Hargrove	.15	.07	.02
☐	765	Ken Forsch	.08	.04	.01
☐	766	Mike Vail	.08	.04	.01
☐	767	Carney Lansford	.15	.07	.02
☐	768	Champ Summers	.08	.04	.01
☐	769	Bill Caudill	.08	.04	.01
☐	770	Ken Griffey	.15	.07	.02
☐	771	Billy Gardner MG	.08	.04	.01
☐	772	Jim Slaton	.08	.04	.01
☐	773	Todd Cruz	.08	.04	.01
☐	774	Tom Gorman	.08	.04	.01
☐	775	Dave Parker	.30	.14	.04
☐	776	Craig Reynolds	.08	.04	.01
☐	777	Tom Paciorek	.15	.07	.02
☐	778	Andy Hawkins	.08	.04	.01
☐	779	Jim Sundberg	.15	.07	.02
☐	780	Steve Carlton	.75	.35	.09

☐	781	Checklist 661-792	.15	.07	.02
☐	782	Steve Balboni	.08	.04	.01
☐	783	Luis Leal	.08	.04	.01
☐	784	Leon Roberts	.08	.04	.01
☐	785	Joaquin Andujar	.08	.04	.01
☐	786	Red Sox TL	.40	.18	.05
		Wade Boggs			
		Bob Ojeda			
		(Checklist on back)			
☐	787	Bill Campbell	.08	.04	.01
☐	788	Milt May	.08	.04	.01
☐	789	Bert Blyleven	.30	.14	.04
☐	790	Doug DeCinces	.08	.04	.01
☐	791	Terry Forster	.08	.04	.01
☐	792	Bill Russell	.15	.07	.02

1984 Topps Traded

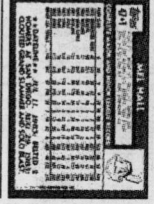

The cards in this 132-card set measure 2 1/2" by 3 1/2". In its now standard procedure, Topps issued its Traded (or extended) set for the fourth year in a row. Because all photos and statistics of its regular set were developed during the fall and winter months of the preceding year, players who changed teams during the fall, winter, and spring months are portrayed with the teams they were with in 1983. The Traded set updates the shortcomings of the regular set by presenting the players with their proper teams for the current year. Several of 1984's top rookies not contained in the regular set are pictured in the Traded set. The (extended) rookie cards in this set are Alvin Davis, Dwight Gooden, Jimmy Key, Mark Langston, Jose Rijo, and Bret Saberhagen. Again this year, the Topps affiliate in Ireland printed the cards, and the cards were available through hobby channels only. Topps also produced a specially boxed "glossy" edition, frequently referred to as the Topps Traded Tiffany set. There were supposedly 10,000 sets of the Tiffany cards produced; they were marketed to hobby dealers. The checklist of cards is identical to that of the normal non-glossy cards. There are two primary distinguishing features of the Tiffany cards, white card stock reverses and high gloss obverses. These Tiffany cards are

valued approximately from five to ten times the values listed below. The set numbering is in alphabetical order by player's name.

	NRMT-MT	EXC	G-VG
COMPLETE FACT.SET (132) ..	50.00	22.00	6.25
COMMON CARD (1T-132T)	.25	.11	.03

	NRMT-MT	EXC	G-VG
☐ 1T Willie Aikens	.25	.11	.03
☐ 2T Luis Aponte	.25	.11	.03
☐ 3T Mike Armstrong	.25	.11	.03
☐ 4T Bob Bailor	.25	.11	.03
☐ 5T Dusty Baker	.60	.25	.07
☐ 6T Steve Balboni	.25	.11	.03
☐ 7T Alan Bannister	.25	.11	.03
☐ 8T Dave Beard	.25	.11	.03
☐ 9T Joe Beckwith.................	.25	.11	.03
☐ 10T Bruce Berenyi	.25	.11	.03
☐ 11T Dave Bergman	.25	.11	.03
☐ 12T Tony Bernazard	.25	.11	.03
☐ 13T Yogi Berra MG	.75	.35	.09
☐ 14T Barry Bonnell	.25	.11	.03
☐ 15T Phil Bradley.................	.40	.18	.05
☐ 16T Fred Breining	.25	.11	.03
☐ 17T Bill Buckner	.40	.18	.05
☐ 18T Ray Burris	.25	.11	.03
☐ 19T John Butcher	.25	.11	.03
☐ 20T Brett Butler	.60	.25	.07
☐ 21T Enos Cabell	.25	.11	.03
☐ 22T Bill Campbell	.25	.11	.03
☐ 23T Bill Caudill..................	.25	.11	.03
☐ 24T Bob Clark	.25	.11	.03
☐ 25T Bryan Clark	.25	.11	.03
☐ 26T Jaime Cocanower	.25	.11	.03
☐ 27T Ron Darling.................	.60	.25	.07
☐ 28T Alvin Davis	.40	.18	.05
☐ 29T Ken Dayley	.25	.11	.03
☐ 30T Jeff Dedmon	.25	.11	.03
☐ 31T Bob Dernier	.25	.11	.03
☐ 32T Carlos Diaz	.25	.11	.03
☐ 33T Mike Easler	.25	.11	.03
☐ 34T Dennis Eckersley........	3.00	1.35	.35
☐ 35T Jim Essian	.25	.11	.03
☐ 36T Darrell Evans..............	.40	.18	.05
☐ 37T Mike Fitzgerald	.25	.11	.03
☐ 38T Tim Foli	.25	.11	.03
☐ 39T George Frazier............	.25	.11	.03
☐ 40T Rich Gale	.25	.11	.03
☐ 41T Barbaro Garbey...........	.25	.11	.03
☐ 42T Dwight Gooden	3.00	1.35	.35
☐ 43T Rich Gossage.............	.60	.25	.07
☐ 44T Wayne Gross	.25	.11	.03
☐ 45T Mark Gubicza	.60	.25	.07
☐ 46T Jackie Gutierrez	.25	.11	.03
☐ 47T Mel Hall	.40	.18	.05
☐ 48T Toby Harrah	.25	.11	.03
☐ 49T Ron Hassey	.25	.11	.03
☐ 50T Rich Hebner................	.25	.11	.03
☐ 51T Willie Hernandez	.40	.18	.05
☐ 52T Ricky Horton	.25	.11	.03
☐ 53T Art Howe.....................	.40	.18	.05
☐ 54T Dane Iorg	.25	.11	.03
☐ 55T Brook Jacoby..............	.40	.18	.05
☐ 56T Mike Jeffcoat..............	.25	.11	.03
☐ 57T Dave Johnson MG	.40	.18	.05
☐ 58T Lynn Jones	.25	.11	.03
☐ 59T Ruppert Jones	.25	.11	.03
☐ 60T Mike Jorgensen	.25	.11	.03
☐ 61T Bob Kearney...............	.25	.11	.03
☐ 62T Jimmy Key..................	4.00	1.80	.50
☐ 63T Dave Kingman.............	.40	.18	.05
☐ 64T Jerry Koosman	.40	.18	.05
☐ 65T Wayne Krenchicki	.25	.11	.03
☐ 66T Rusty Kuntz	.25	.11	.03
☐ 67T Rene Lachemann MG ...	.25	.11	.03
☐ 68T Frank LaCorte	.25	.11	.03
☐ 69T Dennis Lamp..............	.25	.11	.03
☐ 70T Mark Langston............	6.00	2.70	.75
☐ 71T Rick Leach	.25	.11	.03
☐ 72T Craig Lefferts	.40	.18	.05
☐ 73T Gary Lucas.................	.25	.11	.03
☐ 74T Jerry Martin	.25	.11	.03
☐ 75T Carmelo Martinez........	.40	.18	.05
☐ 76T Mike Mason	.25	.11	.03
☐ 77T Gary Matthews............	.40	.18	.05
☐ 78T Andy McGaffigan	.25	.11	.03
☐ 79T Larry Milbourne...........	.25	.11	.03
☐ 80T Sid Monge	.25	.11	.03
☐ 81T Jackie Moore MG	.25	.11	.03
☐ 82T Joe Morgan.................	3.00	1.35	.35
☐ 83T Graig Nettles	.60	.25	.07
☐ 84T Phil Niekro	.75	.35	.09
☐ 85T Ken Oberkfell	.25	.11	.03
☐ 86T Mike O'Berry...............	.25	.11	.03
☐ 87T Al Oliver	.40	.18	.05
☐ 88T Jorge Orta	.25	.11	.03
☐ 89T Amos Otis..................	.40	.18	.05
☐ 90T Dave Parker	.60	.25	.07
☐ 91T Tony Perez..................	1.00	.45	.12
☐ 92T Gerald Perry	.40	.18	.05
☐ 93T Gary Pettis.................	.25	.11	.03
☐ 94T Rob Picciolo	.25	.11	.03
☐ 95T Vern Rapp MG	.25	.11	.03
☐ 96T Floyd Rayford	.25	.11	.03
☐ 97T Randy Ready...............	.40	.18	.05
☐ 98T Ron Reed	.25	.11	.03
☐ 99T Gene Richards............	.25	.11	.03
☐ 100T Jose Rijo	5.00	2.20	.60
☐ 101T Jeff D. Robinson	.25	.11	.03
☐ 102T Ron Romanick	.25	.11	.03
☐ 103T Pete Rose	8.00	3.60	1.00
☐ 104T Bret Saberhagen	8.00	3.60	1.00
☐ 105T Juan Samuel	.60	.25	.07
☐ 106T Scott Sanderson	.25	.11	.03
☐ 107T Dick Schofield	.40	.18	.05
☐ 108T Tom Seaver	4.00	1.80	.50
☐ 109T Jim Slaton	.25	.11	.03
☐ 110T Mike Smithson	.25	.11	.03
☐ 111T Lary Sorensen...........	.25	.11	.03
☐ 112T Tim Stoddard	.25	.11	.03
☐ 113T Champ Summers	.25	.11	.03
☐ 114T Jim Sundberg	.40	.18	.05
☐ 115T Rick Sutcliffe	.40	.18	.05
☐ 116T Craig Swan	.25	.11	.03
☐ 117T Tim Teufel	.25	.11	.03
☐ 118T Derrel Thomas	.25	.11	.03
☐ 119T Gorman Thomas........	.25	.11	.03
☐ 120T Alex Trevino	.25	.11	.03
☐ 121T Manny Trillo	.25	.11	.03
☐ 122T John Tudor	.40	.18	.05
☐ 123T Tom Underwood	.25	.11	.03
☐ 124T Mike Vail	.25	.11	.03
☐ 125T Tom Waddell.............	.25	.11	.03
☐ 126T Gary Ward	.25	.11	.03
☐ 127T Curt Wilkerson	.25	.11	.03
☐ 128T Frank Williams	.25	.11	.03
☐ 129T Glenn Wilson	.25	.11	.03
☐ 130T John Wockenfuss	.25	.11	.03
☐ 131T Ned Yost.................	.25	.11	.03
☐ 132T Checklist 1T-132T......	.25	.11	.03

1985 Topps

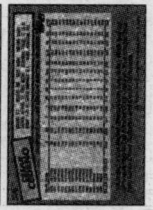

The cards in this 792-card set measure 2 1/2" by 3 1/2". The 1985 Topps set contains full color cards. The fronts feature both the Topps and team logos along with the team name, player's name, and his position. The backs feature player statistics with ink colors of light green and maroon on a gray stock. A trivia quiz is included on the lower portion of the backs. The first ten cards (1-10) are Record Breakers (RB), cards 131-143 are Father and Son (FS) cards, and cards 701 to 722 portray All-Star selections (AS). Cards 271 to 282 represent "First Draft Picks" still active in professional baseball and cards 389-404 feature the coach and eligible (not returning to college) players on the 1984 U.S. Olympic Baseball Team. The manager cards in the set are important in that they contain the checklist of that team's players on the back. The key Rookie Cards in this set are Roger Clemens, Eric Davis, Shawon Dunston, Dwight Gooden, Orel Hershiser, Jimmy Key, Mark Langston, Shane Mack, Mark McGwire, Terry Pendleton, Kirby Puckett, Jose Rijo, Bret Saberhagen, and Bill Swift. Topps also produced a specially boxed "glossy" edition, frequently referred to as the Topps Tiffany set. There were supposedly only 8,000 sets of the Tiffany cards produced; they were marketed to hobby dealers. The checklist of cards (792 regular and 132 Traded) is identical to that of the normal non-glossy cards. There are two primary distinguishing features of the Tiffany cards, white card stock reverses and high gloss obverses. These Tiffany cards are valued approximately from five to ten times the values listed below.

	NRMT-MT	EXC	G-VG
COMPLETE SET (792)	60.00	27.00	7.50
COMMON CARD (1-792)	.08	.04	.01
☐ 1 Carlton Fisk RB .... Longest game by catcher	.30	.14	.04
☐ 2 Steve Garvey RB .... Consecutive error-less games, 1B	.25	.11	.03
☐ 3 Dwight Gooden RB .... Most strikeouts, rookie, season	.25	.11	.03
☐ 4 Cliff Johnson RB .... Most pinch homers, lifetime	.08	.04	.01
☐ 5 Joe Morgan RB .... Most homers, 2B, lifetime	.25	.11	.03
☐ 6 Pete Rose RB .... Most singles, lifetime	.40	.18	.05
☐ 7 Nolan Ryan RB .... Most strikeouts, lifetime	1.50	.70	.19
☐ 8 Juan Samuel RB .... Most stolen bases, rookie, season	.08	.04	.01
☐ 9 Bruce Sutter RB .... Most saves, season, NL	.15	.07	.02
☐ 10 Don Sutton RB .... Most seasons, 100 or more K's	.15	.07	.02
☐ 11 Ralph Houk MG .... (Checklist back)	.08	.04	.01
☐ 12 Dave Lopes .... (Now with Cubs on card front)	.15	.07	.02
☐ 13 Tim Lollar	.08	.04	.01
☐ 14 Chris Bando	.08	.04	.01
☐ 15 Jerry Koosman	.15	.07	.02
☐ 16 Bobby Meacham	.08	.04	.01
☐ 17 Mike Scott	.15	.07	.02
☐ 18 Mickey Hatcher	.08	.04	.01
☐ 19 George Frazier	.08	.04	.01
☐ 20 Chet Lemon	.08	.04	.01
☐ 21 Lee Tunnell	.08	.04	.01
☐ 22 Duane Kuiper	.08	.04	.01
☐ 23 Bret Saberhagen	1.50	.70	.19
☐ 24 Jesse Barfield	.08	.04	.01
☐ 25 Steve Bedrosian	.08	.04	.01
☐ 26 Roy Smalley	.08	.04	.01
☐ 27 Bruce Berenyi	.08	.04	.01
☐ 28 Dann Bilardello	.08	.04	.01
☐ 29 Odell Jones	.08	.04	.01
☐ 30 Cal Ripken	3.00	1.35	.35
☐ 31 Terry Whitfield	.08	.04	.01
☐ 32 Chuck Porter	.08	.04	.01
☐ 33 Tito Landrum	.08	.04	.01
☐ 34 Ed Nunez	.08	.04	.01
☐ 35 Graig Nettles	.15	.07	.02
☐ 36 Fred Breining	.08	.04	.01
☐ 37 Reid Nichols	.08	.04	.01
☐ 38 Jackie Moore MG .... (Checklist back)	.15	.07	.02
☐ 39 John Wockenfuss	.08	.04	.01
☐ 40 Phil Niekro	.25	.11	.03
☐ 41 Mike Fischlin	.08	.04	.01
☐ 42 Luis Sanchez	.08	.04	.01
☐ 43 Andre David	.08	.04	.01
☐ 44 Dickie Thon	.08	.04	.01
☐ 45 Greg Minton	.08	.04	.01
☐ 46 Gary Woods	.08	.04	.01
☐ 47 Dave Rozema	.08	.04	.01
☐ 48 Tony Fernandez	.15	.07	.02
☐ 49 Butch Davis	.08	.04	.01
☐ 50 John Candelaria	.08	.04	.01
☐ 51 Bob Watson	.15	.07	.02
☐ 52 Jerry Dybzinski	.08	.04	.01
☐ 53 Tom Gorman	.08	.04	.01
☐ 54 Cesar Cedeno	.15	.07	.02
☐ 55 Frank Tanana	.15	.07	.02

☐ 56 Jim Dwyer	.08	.04	.01
☐ 57 Pat Zachry	.08	.04	.01
☐ 58 Orlando Mercado	.08	.04	.01
☐ 59 Rick Waits	.08	.04	.01
☐ 60 George Hendrick	.08	.04	.01
☐ 61 Curt Kaufman	.08	.04	.01
☐ 62 Mike Ramsey	.08	.04	.01
☐ 63 Steve McCatty	.08	.04	.01
☐ 64 Mark Bailey	.08	.04	.01
☐ 65 Bill Buckner	.15	.07	.02
☐ 66 Dick Williams MG	.15	.07	.02
(Checklist back)			
☐ 67 Rafael Santana	.08	.04	.01
☐ 68 Von Hayes	.08	.04	.01
☐ 69 Jim Winn	.08	.04	.01
☐ 70 Don Baylor	.25	.11	.03
☐ 71 Tim Laudner	.08	.04	.01
☐ 72 Rick Sutcliffe	.15	.07	.02
☐ 73 Rusty Kuntz	.08	.04	.01
☐ 74 Mike Krukow	.08	.04	.01
☐ 75 Willie Upshaw	.08	.04	.01
☐ 76 Alan Bannister	.08	.04	.01
☐ 77 Joe Beckwith	.08	.04	.01
☐ 78 Scott Fletcher	.08	.04	.01
☐ 79 Rick Mahler	.08	.04	.01
☐ 80 Keith Hernandez	.25	.11	.03
☐ 81 Lenn Sakata	.08	.04	.01
☐ 82 Joe Price	.08	.04	.01
☐ 83 Charlie Moore	.08	.04	.01
☐ 84 Spike Owen	.08	.04	.01
☐ 85 Mike Marshall	.08	.04	.01
☐ 86 Don Aase	.08	.04	.01
☐ 87 David Green	.08	.04	.01
☐ 88 Bryn Smith	.08	.04	.01
☐ 89 Jackie Gutierrez	.08	.04	.01
☐ 90 Rich Gossage	.25	.11	.03
☐ 91 Jeff Burroughs	.08	.04	.01
☐ 92 Paul Owens MG	.15	.07	.02
(Checklist back)			
☐ 93 Don Schulze	.08	.04	.01
☐ 94 Toby Harrah	.08	.04	.01
☐ 95 Jose Cruz	.15	.07	.02
☐ 96 Johnny Ray	.08	.04	.01
☐ 97 Pete Filson	.08	.04	.01
☐ 98 Steve Lake	.08	.04	.01
☐ 99 Milt Wilcox	.08	.04	.01
☐ 100 George Brett	1.50	.70	.19
☐ 101 Jim Acker	.08	.04	.01
☐ 102 Tommy Dunbar	.08	.04	.01
☐ 103 Randy Lerch	.08	.04	.01
☐ 104 Mike Fitzgerald	.08	.04	.01
☐ 105 Ron Kittle	.08	.04	.01
☐ 106 Pascual Perez	.08	.04	.01
☐ 107 Tom Foley	.08	.04	.01
☐ 108 Darnell Coles	.08	.04	.01
☐ 109 Gary Roenicke	.08	.04	.01
☐ 110 Alejandro Pena	.08	.04	.01
☐ 111 Doug DeCinces	.08	.04	.01
☐ 112 Tom Tellmann	.08	.04	.01
☐ 113 Tom Herr	.15	.07	.02
☐ 114 Bob James	.08	.04	.01
☐ 115 Rickey Henderson	.60	.25	.07
☐ 116 Dennis Boyd	.08	.04	.01
☐ 117 Greg Gross	.08	.04	.01
☐ 118 Eric Show	.08	.04	.01
☐ 119 Pat Corrales MG	.15	.07	.02
(Checklist back)			
☐ 120 Steve Kemp	.08	.04	.01
☐ 121 Checklist: 1-132	.15	.07	.02
☐ 122 Tom Brunansky	.08	.04	.01
☐ 123 Dave Smith	.08	.04	.01
☐ 124 Rich Hebner	.08	.04	.01
☐ 125 Kent Tekulve	.08	.04	.01
☐ 126 Ruppert Jones	.08	.04	.01
☐ 127 Mark Gubicza	.25	.11	.03
☐ 128 Ernie Whitt	.08	.04	.01
☐ 129 Gene Garber	.08	.04	.01
☐ 130 Al Oliver	.15	.07	.02
☐ 131 Buddy/Gus Bell FS	.15	.07	.02
☐ 132 Dale/Yogi Berra FS	.15	.07	.02
☐ 133 Bob/Ray Boone FS	.15	.07	.02
☐ 134 Terry/Tito Francona FS	.15	.07	.02
☐ 135 Terry/Bob Kennedy FS	.15	.07	.02
☐ 136 Jeff/Bill Kunkel FS	.15	.07	.02
☐ 137 Vance/Vern Law FS	.15	.07	.02
☐ 138 Dick/Dick Schofield FS	.08	.04	.01
☐ 139 Joel/Bob Skinner FS	.08	.04	.01
☐ 140 Roy/Roy Smalley FS	.15	.07	.02
☐ 141 Mike/Dave Stenhouse FS	.08	.04	.01
☐ 142 Steve/Dizzy Trout FS	.15	.07	.02
☐ 143 Ozzie/Ossie Virgil FS	.08	.04	.01
☐ 144 Ron Gardenhire	.08	.04	.01
☐ 145 Alvin Davis	.15	.07	.02
☐ 146 Gary Redus	.08	.04	.01
☐ 147 Bill Swaggerty	.08	.04	.01
☐ 148 Steve Yeager	.08	.04	.01
☐ 149 Dickie Noles	.08	.04	.01
☐ 150 Jim Rice	.25	.11	.03
☐ 151 Moose Haas	.08	.04	.01
☐ 152 Steve Braun	.08	.04	.01
☐ 153 Frank LaCorte	.08	.04	.01
☐ 154 Argenis Salazar	.08	.04	.01
☐ 155 Yogi Berra MG	.25	.11	.03
(Checklist back)			
☐ 156 Craig Reynolds	.08	.04	.01
☐ 157 Tug McGraw	.15	.07	.02
☐ 158 Pat Tabler	.08	.04	.01
☐ 159 Carlos Diaz	.08	.04	.01
☐ 160 Lance Parrish	.15	.07	.02
☐ 161 Ken Schrom	.08	.04	.01
☐ 162 Benny Distefano	.08	.04	.01
☐ 163 Dennis Eckersley	.25	.11	.03
☐ 164 Jorge Orta	.08	.04	.01
☐ 165 Dusty Baker	.25	.11	.03
☐ 166 Keith Atherton	.08	.04	.01
☐ 167 Rufino Linares	.08	.04	.01
☐ 168 Garth Iorg	.08	.04	.01
☐ 169 Dan Spillner	.08	.04	.01
☐ 170 George Foster	.15	.07	.02
☐ 171 Bill Stein	.08	.04	.01
☐ 172 Jack Perconte	.08	.04	.01
☐ 173 Mike Young	.08	.04	.01
☐ 174 Rick Honeycutt	.08	.04	.01
☐ 175 Dave Parker	.25	.11	.03
☐ 176 Bill Schroeder	.08	.04	.01
☐ 177 Dave Von Ohlen	.08	.04	.01
☐ 178 Miguel Dilone	.08	.04	.01
☐ 179 Tommy John	.25	.11	.03
☐ 180 Dave Winfield	.60	.25	.07
☐ 181 Roger Clemens	8.00	3.60	1.00
☐ 182 Tim Flannery	.08	.04	.01
☐ 183 Larry McWilliams	.08	.04	.01
☐ 184 Carmen Castillo	.08	.04	.01
☐ 185 Al Holland	.08	.04	.01
☐ 186 Bob Lillis MG	.15	.07	.02
(Checklist back)			
☐ 187 Mike Walters	.08	.04	.01
☐ 188 Greg Pryor	.08	.04	.01
☐ 189 Warren Brusstar	.08	.04	.01
☐ 190 Rusty Staub	.15	.07	.02
☐ 191 Steve Nicosia	.08	.04	.01
☐ 192 Howard Johnson	.15	.07	.02

☐ 193	Jimmy Key	.60	.25	.07
☐ 194	Dave Stegman	.08	.04	.01
☐ 195	Glenn Hubbard	.08	.04	.01
☐ 196	Pete O'Brien	.15	.07	.02
☐ 197	Mike Warren	.08	.04	.01
☐ 198	Eddie Milner	.08	.04	.01
☐ 199	Dennis Martinez	.15	.07	.02
☐ 200	Reggie Jackson	.60	.25	.07
☐ 201	Burt Hooton	.08	.04	.01
☐ 202	Gorman Thomas	.08	.04	.01
☐ 203	Bob McClure	.08	.04	.01
☐ 204	Art Howe	.15	.07	.02
☐ 205	Steve Rogers	.08	.04	.01
☐ 206	Phil Garner	.15	.07	.02
☐ 207	Mark Clear	.08	.04	.01
☐ 208	Champ Summers	.08	.04	.01
☐ 209	Bill Campbell	.08	.04	.01
☐ 210	Gary Matthews	.08	.04	.01
☐ 211	Clay Christiansen	.08	.04	.01
☐ 212	George Vukovich	.08	.04	.01
☐ 213	Billy Gardner MG	.15	.07	.02
	(Checklist back)			
☐ 214	John Tudor	.15	.07	.02
☐ 215	Bob Brenly	.08	.04	.01
☐ 216	Jerry Don Gleaton	.08	.04	.01
☐ 217	Leon Roberts	.08	.04	.01
☐ 218	Doyle Alexander	.08	.04	.01
☐ 219	Gerald Perry	.08	.04	.01
☐ 220	Fred Lynn	.15	.07	.02
☐ 221	Ron Reed	.08	.04	.01
☐ 222	Hubie Brooks	.15	.07	.02
☐ 223	Tom Hume	.08	.04	.01
☐ 224	Al Cowens	.08	.04	.01
☐ 225	Mike Boddicker	.08	.04	.01
☐ 226	Juan Beniquez	.08	.04	.01
☐ 227	Danny Darwin	.08	.04	.01
☐ 228	Dion James	.08	.04	.01
☐ 229	Dave LaPoint	.08	.04	.01
☐ 230	Gary Carter	.25	.11	.03
☐ 231	Dwayne Murphy	.08	.04	.01
☐ 232	Dave Beard	.08	.04	.01
☐ 233	Ed Jurak	.08	.04	.01
☐ 234	Jerry Narron	.08	.04	.01
☐ 235	Garry Maddox	.08	.04	.01
☐ 236	Mark Thurmond	.08	.04	.01
☐ 237	Julio Franco	.25	.11	.03
☐ 238	Jose Rijo	.75	.35	.09
☐ 239	Tim Teufel	.08	.04	.01
☐ 240	Dave Stieb	.15	.07	.02
☐ 241	Jim Frey MG	.15	.07	.02
	(Checklist back)			
☐ 242	Greg Harris	.08	.04	.01
☐ 243	Barbaro Garbey	.08	.04	.01
☐ 244	Mike Jones	.08	.04	.01
☐ 245	Chili Davis	.15	.07	.02
☐ 246	Mike Norris	.08	.04	.01
☐ 247	Wayne Tolleson	.08	.04	.01
☐ 248	Terry Forster	.08	.04	.01
☐ 249	Harold Baines	.25	.11	.03
☐ 250	Jesse Orosco	.08	.04	.01
☐ 251	Brad Gulden	.08	.04	.01
☐ 252	Dan Ford	.08	.04	.01
☐ 253	Sid Bream	.15	.07	.02
☐ 254	Pete Vuckovich	.08	.04	.01
☐ 255	Lonnie Smith	.08	.04	.01
☐ 256	Mike Stanton	.08	.04	.01
☐ 257	Bryan Little UER	.08	.04	.01
	Name spelled Brian on front			
☐ 258	Mike C. Brown	.08	.04	.01
☐ 259	Gary Allenson	.08	.04	.01
☐ 260	Dave Righetti	.15	.07	.02
☐ 261	Checklist: 133-264	.15	.07	.02
☐ 262	Greg Booker	.08	.04	.01
☐ 263	Mel Hall	.08	.04	.01
☐ 264	Joe Sambito	.08	.04	.01
☐ 265	Juan Samuel	.15	.07	.02
☐ 266	Frank Viola	.15	.07	.02
☐ 267	Henry Cotto	.08	.04	.01
☐ 268	Chuck Tanner MG	.15	.07	.02
	(Checklist back)			
☐ 269	Doug Baker	.08	.04	.01
☐ 270	Dan Quisenberry	.15	.07	.02
☐ 271	Tim Foli FDP68	.08	.04	.01
☐ 272	Jeff Burroughs FDP69	.08	.04	.01
☐ 273	Bill Almon FDP74	.08	.04	.01
☐ 274	Floyd Bannister FDP76	.08	.04	.01
☐ 275	Harold Baines FDP77	.25	.11	.03
☐ 276	Bob Horner FDP78	.15	.07	.02
☐ 277	Al Chambers FDP79	.08	.04	.01
☐ 278	Darryl Strawberry FDP80	.15	.07	.02
☐ 279	Mike Moore FDP81	.08	.04	.01
☐ 280	Shawon Dunston FDP82	.60	.25	.07
☐ 281	Tim Belcher FDP83	.15	.07	.02
☐ 282	Shawn Abner FDP84	.08	.04	.01
☐ 283	Fran Mullins	.08	.04	.01
☐ 284	Marty Bystrom	.08	.04	.01
☐ 285	Dan Driessen	.08	.04	.01
☐ 286	Rudy Law	.08	.04	.01
☐ 287	Walt Terrell	.08	.04	.01
☐ 288	Jeff Kunkel	.08	.04	.01
☐ 289	Tom Underwood	.08	.04	.01
☐ 290	Cecil Cooper	.15	.07	.02
☐ 291	Bob Welch	.15	.07	.02
☐ 292	Brad Komminsk	.08	.04	.01
☐ 293	Curt Young	.08	.04	.01
☐ 294	Tom Nieto	.08	.04	.01
☐ 295	Joe Niekro	.15	.07	.02
☐ 296	Ricky Nelson	.08	.04	.01
☐ 297	Gary Lucas	.08	.04	.01
☐ 298	Marty Barrett	.08	.04	.01
☐ 299	Andy Hawkins	.08	.04	.01
☐ 300	Rod Carew	.50	.23	.06
☐ 301	John Montefusco	.08	.04	.01
☐ 302	Tim Corcoran	.08	.04	.01
☐ 303	Mike Jeffcoat	.08	.04	.01
☐ 304	Gary Gaetti	.15	.07	.02
☐ 305	Dale Berra	.08	.04	.01
☐ 306	Rick Reuschel	.15	.07	.02
☐ 307	Sparky Anderson MG	.25	.11	.03
	(Checklist back)			
☐ 308	John Wathan	.08	.04	.01
☐ 309	Mike Witt	.08	.04	.01
☐ 310	Manny Trillo	.08	.04	.01
☐ 311	Jim Gott	.08	.04	.01
☐ 312	Marc Hill	.08	.04	.01
☐ 313	Dave Schmidt	.08	.04	.01
☐ 314	Ron Oester	.08	.04	.01
☐ 315	Doug Sisk	.08	.04	.01
☐ 316	John Lowenstein	.08	.04	.01
☐ 317	Jack Lazorko	.08	.04	.01
☐ 318	Ted Simmons	.15	.07	.02
☐ 319	Jeff Jones	.08	.04	.01
☐ 320	Dale Murphy	.25	.11	.03
☐ 321	Ricky Horton	.08	.04	.01
☐ 322	Dave Stapleton	.08	.04	.01
☐ 323	Andy McGaffigan	.08	.04	.01
☐ 324	Bruce Bochy	.08	.04	.01
☐ 325	John Denny	.08	.04	.01
☐ 326	Kevin Bass	.08	.04	.01
☐ 327	Brook Jacoby	.08	.04	.01
☐ 328	Bob Shirley	.08	.04	.01

☐ 329 Ron Washington	.08	.04	.01
☐ 330 Leon Durham	.08	.04	.01
☐ 331 Bill Laskey	.08	.04	.01
☐ 332 Brian Harper	.15	.07	.02
☐ 333 Willie Hernandez	.08	.04	.01
☐ 334 Dick Howser MG	.15	.07	.02
(Checklist back)			
☐ 335 Bruce Benedict	.08	.04	.01
☐ 336 Rance Mulliniks	.08	.04	.01
☐ 337 Billy Sample	.08	.04	.01
☐ 338 Britt Burns	.08	.04	.01
☐ 339 Danny Heep	.08	.04	.01
☐ 340 Robin Yount	.75	.35	.09
☐ 341 Floyd Rayford	.08	.04	.01
☐ 342 Ted Power	.08	.04	.01
☐ 343 Bill Russell	.15	.07	.02
☐ 344 Dave Henderson	.15	.07	.02
☐ 345 Charlie Lea	.08	.04	.01
☐ 346 Terry Pendleton	.75	.35	.09
☐ 347 Rick Langford	.08	.04	.01
☐ 348 Bob Boone	.15	.07	.02
☐ 349 Domingo Ramos	.08	.04	.01
☐ 350 Wade Boggs	1.00	.45	.12
☐ 351 Juan Agosto	.08	.04	.01
☐ 352 Joe Morgan	.25	.11	.03
☐ 353 Julio Solano	.08	.04	.01
☐ 354 Andre Robertson	.08	.04	.01
☐ 355 Bert Blyleven	.25	.11	.03
☐ 356 Dave Meier	.08	.04	.01
☐ 357 Rich Bordi	.08	.04	.01
☐ 358 Tony Pena	.08	.04	.01
☐ 359 Pat Sheridan	.08	.04	.01
☐ 360 Steve Carlton	.40	.18	.05
☐ 361 Alfredo Griffin	.08	.04	.01
☐ 362 Craig McMurtry	.08	.04	.01
☐ 363 Ron Hodges	.08	.04	.01
☐ 364 Richard Dotson	.08	.04	.01
☐ 365 Danny Ozark MG	.15	.07	.02
(Checklist back)			
☐ 366 Todd Cruz	.08	.04	.01
☐ 367 Keefe Cato	.08	.04	.01
☐ 368 Dave Bergman	.08	.04	.01
☐ 369 R.J. Reynolds	.08	.04	.01
☐ 370 Bruce Sutter	.15	.07	.02
☐ 371 Mickey Rivers	.08	.04	.01
☐ 372 Roy Howell	.08	.04	.01
☐ 373 Mike Moore	.15	.07	.02
☐ 374 Brian Downing	.15	.07	.02
☐ 375 Jeff Reardon	.25	.11	.03
☐ 376 Jeff Newman	.08	.04	.01
☐ 377 Checklist: 265-396	.15	.07	.02
☐ 378 Alan Wiggins	.08	.04	.01
☐ 379 Charles Hudson	.08	.04	.01
☐ 380 Ken Griffey	.15	.07	.02
☐ 381 Roy Smith	.08	.04	.01
☐ 382 Denny Walling	.08	.04	.01
☐ 383 Rick Lysander	.08	.04	.01
☐ 384 Jody Davis	.08	.04	.01
☐ 385 Jose DeLeon	.08	.04	.01
☐ 386 Dan Gladden	.15	.07	.02
☐ 387 Buddy Biancalana	.08	.04	.01
☐ 388 Bert Roberge	.08	.04	.01
☐ 389 Rod Dedeaux OLY CO	.15	.07	.02
☐ 390 Sid Akins OLY	.08	.04	.01
☐ 391 Flavio Alfaro OLY	.15	.07	.02
☐ 392 Don August OLY	.15	.07	.02
☐ 393 Scott Bankhead OLY	.15	.07	.02
☐ 394 Bob Caffrey OLY	.08	.04	.01
☐ 395 Mike Dunne OLY	.15	.07	.02
☐ 396 Gary Green OLY	.15	.07	.02
☐ 397 John Hoover OLY	.08	.04	.01

☐ 398 Shane Mack OLY	.25	.11	.03
☐ 399 John Marzano OLY	.08	.04	.01
☐ 400 Oddibe McDowell OLY	.15	.07	.02
☐ 401 Mark McGwire OLY	8.00	3.60	1.00
☐ 402 Pat Pacillo OLY	.08	.04	.01
☐ 403 Cory Snyder OLY	.25	.11	.03
☐ 404 Billy Swift OLY	1.00	.45	.12
☐ 405 Tom Veryzer	.08	.04	.01
☐ 406 Len Whitehouse	.08	.04	.01
☐ 407 Bobby Ramos	.08	.04	.01
☐ 408 Sid Monge	.08	.04	.01
☐ 409 Brad Wellman	.08	.04	.01
☐ 410 Bob Horner	.08	.04	.01
☐ 411 Bobby Cox MG	.15	.07	.02
(Checklist back)			
☐ 412 Bud Black	.08	.04	.01
☐ 413 Vance Law	.08	.04	.01
☐ 414 Gary Ward	.08	.04	.01
☐ 415 Ron Darling UER	.15	.07	.02
(No trivia answer)			
☐ 416 Wayne Gross	.08	.04	.01
☐ 417 John Franco	.50	.23	.06
☐ 418 Ken Landreaux	.08	.04	.01
☐ 419 Mike Caldwell	.08	.04	.01
☐ 420 Andre Dawson	.60	.25	.07
☐ 421 Dave Rucker	.08	.04	.01
☐ 422 Carney Lansford	.15	.07	.02
☐ 423 Barry Bonnell	.08	.04	.01
☐ 424 Al Nipper	.08	.04	.01
☐ 425 Mike Hargrove	.15	.07	.02
☐ 426 Vern Ruhle	.08	.04	.01
☐ 427 Mario Ramirez	.08	.04	.01
☐ 428 Larry Andersen	.08	.04	.01
☐ 429 Rick Cerone	.08	.04	.01
☐ 430 Ron Davis	.08	.04	.01
☐ 431 U.L. Washington	.08	.04	.01
☐ 432 Thad Bosley	.08	.04	.01
☐ 433 Jim Morrison	.08	.04	.01
☐ 434 Gene Richards	.08	.04	.01
☐ 435 Dan Petry	.08	.04	.01
☐ 436 Willie Aikens	.08	.04	.01
☐ 437 Al Jones	.08	.04	.01
☐ 438 Joe Torre MG	.15	.07	.02
(Checklist back)			
☐ 439 Junior Ortiz	.08	.04	.01
☐ 440 Fernando Valenzuela	.15	.07	.02
☐ 441 Duane Walker	.08	.04	.01
☐ 442 Ken Forsch	.08	.04	.01
☐ 443 George Wright	.08	.04	.01
☐ 444 Tony Phillips	.25	.11	.03
☐ 445 Tippy Martinez	.08	.04	.01
☐ 446 Jim Sundberg	.15	.07	.02
☐ 447 Jeff Lahti	.08	.04	.01
☐ 448 Derrel Thomas	.08	.04	.01
☐ 449 Phil Bradley	.15	.07	.02
☐ 450 Steve Garvey	.25	.11	.03
☐ 451 Bruce Hurst	.15	.07	.02
☐ 452 John Castino	.08	.04	.01
☐ 453 Tom Waddell	.08	.04	.01
☐ 454 Glenn Wilson	.08	.04	.01
☐ 455 Bob Knepper	.08	.04	.01
☐ 456 Tim Foli	.08	.04	.01
☐ 457 Cecilio Guante	.08	.04	.01
☐ 458 Randy Johnson	.08	.04	.01
☐ 459 Charlie Leibrandt	.08	.04	.01
☐ 460 Ryne Sandberg	2.00	.90	.25
☐ 461 Marty Castillo	.08	.04	.01
☐ 462 Gary Lavelle	.08	.04	.01
☐ 463 Dave Collins	.08	.04	.01
☐ 464 Mike Mason	.08	.04	.01
☐ 465 Bob Grich	.15	.07	.02

☐ 466	Tony LaRussa MG (Checklist back)	.15	.07	.02
☐ 467	Ed Lynch	.08	.04	.01
☐ 468	Wayne Krenchicki	.08	.04	.01
☐ 469	Sammy Stewart	.08	.04	.01
☐ 470	Steve Sax	.15	.07	.02
☐ 471	Pete Ladd	.08	.04	.01
☐ 472	Jim Essian	.08	.04	.01
☐ 473	Tim Wallach	.15	.07	.02
☐ 474	Kurt Kepshire	.08	.04	.01
☐ 475	Andre Thornton	.08	.04	.01
☐ 476	Jeff Stone	.08	.04	.01
☐ 477	Bob Ojeda	.15	.07	.02
☐ 478	Kurt Bevacqua	.08	.04	.01
☐ 479	Mike Madden	.08	.04	.01
☐ 480	Lou Whitaker	.25	.11	.03
☐ 481	Dale Murray	.08	.04	.01
☐ 482	Harry Spilman	.08	.04	.01
☐ 483	Mike Smithson	.08	.04	.01
☐ 484	Larry Bowa	.15	.07	.02
☐ 485	Matt Young	.08	.04	.01
☐ 486	Steve Balboni	.08	.04	.01
☐ 487	Frank Williams	.08	.04	.01
☐ 488	Joel Skinner	.08	.04	.01
☐ 489	Bryan Clark	.08	.04	.01
☐ 490	Jason Thompson	.08	.04	.01
☐ 491	Rick Camp	.08	.04	.01
☐ 492	Dave Johnson MG (Checklist back)	.15	.07	.02
☐ 493	Orel Hershiser	1.50	.70	.19
☐ 494	Rich Dauer	.08	.04	.01
☐ 495	Mario Soto	.08	.04	.01
☐ 496	Donnie Scott	.08	.04	.01
☐ 497	Gary Pettis UER (Photo actually Gary's little brother, Lynn)	.08	.04	.01
☐ 498	Ed Romero	.08	.04	.01
☐ 499	Danny Cox	.08	.04	.01
☐ 500	Mike Schmidt	1.00	.45	.12
☐ 501	Dan Schatzeder	.08	.04	.01
☐ 502	Rick Miller	.08	.04	.01
☐ 503	Tim Conroy	.08	.04	.01
☐ 504	Jerry Willard	.08	.04	.01
☐ 505	Jim Beattie	.08	.04	.01
☐ 506	Franklin Stubbs	.08	.04	.01
☐ 507	Ray Fontenot	.08	.04	.01
☐ 508	John Shelby	.08	.04	.01
☐ 509	Milt May	.08	.04	.01
☐ 510	Kent Hrbek	.25	.11	.03
☐ 511	Lee Smith	.25	.11	.03
☐ 512	Tom Brookens	.08	.04	.01
☐ 513	Lynn Jones	.08	.04	.01
☐ 514	Jeff Cornell	.08	.04	.01
☐ 515	Dave Concepcion	.15	.07	.02
☐ 516	Roy Lee Jackson	.08	.04	.01
☐ 517	Jerry Martin	.08	.04	.01
☐ 518	Chris Chambliss	.15	.07	.02
☐ 519	Doug Rader MG (Checklist back)	.15	.07	.02
☐ 520	LaMarr Hoyt	.08	.04	.01
☐ 521	Rick Dempsey	.08	.04	.01
☐ 522	Paul Molitor	.50	.23	.06
☐ 523	Candy Maldonado	.08	.04	.01
☐ 524	Rob Wilfong	.08	.04	.01
☐ 525	Darrell Porter	.08	.04	.01
☐ 526	David Palmer	.08	.04	.01
☐ 527	Checklist: 397-528	.15	.07	.02
☐ 528	Bill Krueger	.08	.04	.01
☐ 529	Rich Gedman	.08	.04	.01
☐ 530	Dave Dravecky	.15	.07	.02
☐ 531	Joe Lefebvre	.08	.04	.01
☐ 532	Frank DiPino	.08	.04	.01
☐ 533	Tony Bernazard	.08	.04	.01
☐ 534	Brian Dayett	.08	.04	.01
☐ 535	Pat Putnam	.08	.04	.01
☐ 536	Kirby Puckett	12.00	5.50	1.50
☐ 537	Don Robinson	.08	.04	.01
☐ 538	Keith Moreland	.08	.04	.01
☐ 539	Aurelio Lopez	.08	.04	.01
☐ 540	Claudell Washington	.08	.04	.01
☐ 541	Mark Davis	.08	.04	.01
☐ 542	Don Slaught	.08	.04	.01
☐ 543	Mike Squires	.08	.04	.01
☐ 544	Bruce Kison	.08	.04	.01
☐ 545	Lloyd Moseby	.08	.04	.01
☐ 546	Brent Gaff	.08	.04	.01
☐ 547	Pete Rose MG (Checklist back)	.50	.23	.06
☐ 548	Larry Parrish	.08	.04	.01
☐ 549	Mike Scioscia	.08	.04	.01
☐ 550	Scott McGregor	.08	.04	.01
☐ 551	Andy Van Slyke	.15	.07	.02
☐ 552	Chris Codiroli	.08	.04	.01
☐ 553	Bob Clark	.08	.04	.01
☐ 554	Doug Flynn	.08	.04	.01
☐ 555	Bob Stanley	.08	.04	.01
☐ 556	Sixto Lezcano	.08	.04	.01
☐ 557	Len Barker	.08	.04	.01
☐ 558	Carmelo Martinez	.08	.04	.01
☐ 559	Jay Howell	.15	.07	.02
☐ 560	Bill Madlock	.15	.07	.02
☐ 561	Darryl Motley	.08	.04	.01
☐ 562	Houston Jimenez	.08	.04	.01
☐ 563	Dick Ruthven	.08	.04	.01
☐ 564	Alan Ashby	.08	.04	.01
☐ 565	Kirk Gibson	.25	.11	.03
☐ 566	Ed VandeBerg	.08	.04	.01
☐ 567	Joel Youngblood	.08	.04	.01
☐ 568	Cliff Johnson	.08	.04	.01
☐ 569	Ken Oberkfell	.08	.04	.01
☐ 570	Darryl Strawberry	.25	.11	.03
☐ 571	Charlie Hough	.15	.07	.02
☐ 572	Tom Paciorek	.15	.07	.02
☐ 573	Jay Tibbs	.08	.04	.01
☐ 574	Joe Altobelli MG (Checklist back)	.15	.07	.02
☐ 575	Pedro Guerrero	.15	.07	.02
☐ 576	Jaime Cocanower	.08	.04	.01
☐ 577	Chris Speier	.08	.04	.01
☐ 578	Terry Francona	.08	.04	.01
☐ 579	Ron Romanick	.08	.04	.01
☐ 580	Dwight Evans	.15	.07	.02
☐ 581	Mark Wagner	.08	.04	.01
☐ 582	Ken Phelps	.08	.04	.01
☐ 583	Bobby Brown	.08	.04	.01
☐ 584	Kevin Gross	.08	.04	.01
☐ 585	Butch Wynegar	.08	.04	.01
☐ 586	Bill Scherrer	.08	.04	.01
☐ 587	Doug Frobel	.08	.04	.01
☐ 588	Bobby Castillo	.08	.04	.01
☐ 589	Bob Dernier	.08	.04	.01
☐ 590	Ray Knight	.15	.07	.02
☐ 591	Larry Herndon	.08	.04	.01
☐ 592	Jeff D. Robinson	.08	.04	.01
☐ 593	Rick Leach	.08	.04	.01
☐ 594	Curt Wilkerson	.08	.04	.01
☐ 595	Larry Gura	.08	.04	.01
☐ 596	Jerry Hairston	.08	.04	.01
☐ 597	Brad Lesley	.08	.04	.01
☐ 598	Jose Oquendo	.08	.04	.01
☐ 599	Storm Davis	.08	.04	.01

☐	600	Pete Rose	.75	.35	.09
☐	601	Tom Lasorda MG (Checklist back)	.25	.11	.03
☐	602	Jeff Dedmon	.08	.04	.01
☐	603	Rick Manning	.08	.04	.01
☐	604	Daryl Sconiers	.08	.04	.01
☐	605	Ozzie Smith	1.00	.45	.12
☐	606	Rich Gale	.08	.04	.01
☐	607	Bill Almon	.08	.04	.01
☐	608	Craig Lefferts	.15	.07	.02
☐	609	Broderick Perkins	.08	.04	.01
☐	610	Jack Morris	.25	.11	.03
☐	611	Ozzie Virgil	.08	.04	.01
☐	612	Mike Armstrong	.08	.04	.01
☐	613	Terry Puhl	.08	.04	.01
☐	614	Al Williams	.08	.04	.01
☐	615	Marvell Wynne	.08	.04	.01
☐	616	Scott Sanderson	.08	.04	.01
☐	617	Willie Wilson	.15	.07	.02
☐	618	Pete Falcone	.08	.04	.01
☐	619	Jeff Leonard	.08	.04	.01
☐	620	Dwight Gooden	.40	.18	.05
☐	621	Marvis Foley	.08	.04	.01
☐	622	Luis Leal	.08	.04	.01
☐	623	Greg Walker	.08	.04	.01
☐	624	Benny Ayala	.08	.04	.01
☐	625	Mark Langston	1.25	.55	.16
☐	626	German Rivera	.08	.04	.01
☐	627	Eric Davis	.50	.23	.06
☐	628	Rene Lachemann MG (Checklist back)	.15	.07	.02
☐	629	Dick Schofield	.08	.04	.01
☐	630	Tim Raines	.25	.11	.03
☐	631	Bob Forsch	.08	.04	.01
☐	632	Bruce Bochte	.08	.04	.01
☐	633	Glenn Hoffman	.08	.04	.01
☐	634	Bill Dawley	.08	.04	.01
☐	635	Terry Kennedy	.08	.04	.01
☐	636	Shane Rawley	.08	.04	.01
☐	637	Brett Butler	.25	.11	.03
☐	638	Mike Pagliarulo	.08	.04	.01
☐	639	Ed Hodge	.08	.04	.01
☐	640	Steve Henderson	.08	.04	.01
☐	641	Rod Scurry	.08	.04	.01
☐	642	Dave Owen	.08	.04	.01
☐	643	Johnny Grubb	.08	.04	.01
☐	644	Mark Huismann	.08	.04	.01
☐	645	Damaso Garcia	.08	.04	.01
☐	646	Scot Thompson	.08	.04	.01
☐	647	Rafael Ramirez	.08	.04	.01
☐	648	Bob Jones	.08	.04	.01
☐	649	Sid Fernandez	.25	.11	.03
☐	650	Greg Luzinski	.15	.07	.02
☐	651	Jeff Russell	.15	.07	.02
☐	652	Joe Nolan	.08	.04	.01
☐	653	Mark Brouhard	.08	.04	.01
☐	654	Dave Anderson	.08	.04	.01
☐	655	Joaquin Andujar	.08	.04	.01
☐	656	Chuck Cottier MG (Checklist back)	.15	.07	.02
☐	657	Jim Slaton	.08	.04	.01
☐	658	Mike Stenhouse	.08	.04	.01
☐	659	Checklist: 529-660	.15	.07	.02
☐	660	Tony Gwynn	2.00	.90	.25
☐	661	Steve Crawford	.08	.04	.01
☐	662	Mike Heath	.08	.04	.01
☐	663	Luis Aguayo	.08	.04	.01
☐	664	Steve Farr	.15	.07	.02
☐	665	Don Mattingly	3.00	1.35	.35
☐	666	Mike LaCoss	.08	.04	.01
☐	667	Dave Engle	.08	.04	.01
☐	668	Steve Trout	.08	.04	.01
☐	669	Lee Lacy	.08	.04	.01
☐	670	Tom Seaver	.40	.18	.05
☐	671	Dane Iorg	.08	.04	.01
☐	672	Juan Berenguer	.08	.04	.01
☐	673	Buck Martinez	.08	.04	.01
☐	674	Atlee Hammaker	.08	.04	.01
☐	675	Tony Perez	.25	.11	.03
☐	676	Albert Hall	.08	.04	.01
☐	677	Wally Backman	.08	.04	.01
☐	678	Joey McLaughlin	.08	.04	.01
☐	679	Bob Kearney	.08	.04	.01
☐	680	Jerry Reuss	.15	.07	.02
☐	681	Ben Oglivie	.08	.04	.01
☐	682	Doug Corbett	.08	.04	.01
☐	683	Whitey Herzog MG (Checklist back)	.15	.07	.02
☐	684	Bill Doran	.08	.04	.01
☐	685	Bill Caudill	.08	.04	.01
☐	686	Mike Easler	.08	.04	.01
☐	687	Bill Gullickson	.15	.07	.02
☐	688	Len Matuszek	.08	.04	.01
☐	689	Luis DeLeon	.08	.04	.01
☐	690	Alan Trammell	.30	.14	.04
☐	691	Dennis Rasmussen	.08	.04	.01
☐	692	Randy Bush	.08	.04	.01
☐	693	Tim Stoddard	.08	.04	.01
☐	694	Joe Carter	2.50	1.10	.30
☐	695	Rick Rhoden	.08	.04	.01
☐	696	John Rabb	.08	.04	.01
☐	697	Onix Concepcion	.08	.04	.01
☐	698	Jorge Bell	.15	.07	.02
☐	699	Donnie Moore	.08	.04	.01
☐	700	Eddie Murray	1.00	.45	.12
☐	701	Eddie Murray AS	.30	.14	.04
☐	702	Damaso Garcia AS	.08	.04	.01
☐	703	George Brett AS	.75	.35	.09
☐	704	Cal Ripken AS	1.50	.70	.19
☐	705	Dave Winfield AS	.25	.11	.03
☐	706	Rickey Henderson AS	.25	.11	.03
☐	707	Tony Armas AS	.08	.04	.01
☐	708	Lance Parrish AS	.15	.07	.02
☐	709	Mike Boddicker AS	.08	.04	.01
☐	710	Frank Viola AS	.15	.07	.02
☐	711	Dan Quisenberry AS	.15	.07	.02
☐	712	Keith Hernandez AS	.15	.07	.02
☐	713	Ryne Sandberg AS	.75	.35	.09
☐	714	Mike Schmidt AS	.35	.16	.04
☐	715	Ozzie Smith AS	.50	.23	.06
☐	716	Dale Murphy AS	.15	.07	.02
☐	717	Tony Gwynn AS	.75	.35	.09
☐	718	Jeff Leonard AS	.08	.04	.01
☐	719	Gary Carter AS	.15	.07	.02
☐	720	Rick Sutcliffe AS	.15	.07	.02
☐	721	Bob Knepper AS	.08	.04	.01
☐	722	Bruce Sutter AS	.15	.07	.02
☐	723	Dave Stewart	.25	.11	.03
☐	724	Oscar Gamble	.08	.04	.01
☐	725	Floyd Bannister	.08	.04	.01
☐	726	Al Bumbry	.15	.07	.02
☐	727	Frank Pastore	.08	.04	.01
☐	728	Bob Bailor	.08	.04	.01
☐	729	Don Sutton	.25	.11	.03
☐	730	Dave Kingman	.15	.07	.02
☐	731	Neil Allen	.08	.04	.01
☐	732	John McNamara MG (Checklist back)	.15	.07	.02
☐	733	Tony Scott	.08	.04	.01
☐	734	John Henry Johnson	.08	.04	.01
☐	735	Garry Templeton	.08	.04	.01
☐	736	Jerry Mumphrey	.08	.04	.01

		NRMT-MT	EXC	G-VG
☐ 737	Bo Diaz	.08	.04	.01
☐ 738	Omar Moreno	.08	.04	.01
☐ 739	Ernie Camacho	.08	.04	.01
☐ 740	Jack Clark	.15	.07	.02
☐ 741	John Butcher	.08	.04	.01
☐ 742	Ron Hassey	.08	.04	.01
☐ 743	Frank White	.15	.07	.02
☐ 744	Doug Bair	.08	.04	.01
☐ 745	Buddy Bell	.15	.07	.02
☐ 746	Jim Clancy	.08	.04	.01
☐ 747	Alex Trevino	.08	.04	.01
☐ 748	Lee Mazzilli	.08	.04	.01
☐ 749	Julio Cruz	.08	.04	.01
☐ 750	Rollie Fingers	.25	.11	.03
☐ 751	Kelvin Chapman	.08	.04	.01
☐ 752	Bob Owchinko	.08	.04	.01
☐ 753	Greg Brock	.08	.04	.01
☐ 754	Larry Milbourne	.08	.04	.01
☐ 755	Ken Singleton	.15	.07	.02
☐ 756	Rob Picciolo	.08	.04	.01
☐ 757	Willie McGee	.15	.07	.02
☐ 758	Ray Burris	.08	.04	.01
☐ 759	Jim Fanning MG	.15	.07	.02
	(Checklist back)			
☐ 760	Nolan Ryan	4.00	1.80	.50
☐ 761	Jerry Remy	.08	.04	.01
☐ 762	Eddie Whitson	.08	.04	.01
☐ 763	Kiko Garcia	.08	.04	.01
☐ 764	Jamie Easterly	.08	.04	.01
☐ 765	Willie Randolph	.15	.07	.02
☐ 766	Paul Mirabella	.08	.04	.01
☐ 767	Darrell Brown	.08	.04	.01
☐ 768	Ron Cey	.15	.07	.02
☐ 769	Joe Cowley	.08	.04	.01
☐ 770	Carlton Fisk	.40	.18	.05
☐ 771	Geoff Zahn	.08	.04	.01
☐ 772	Johnnie LeMaster	.08	.04	.01
☐ 773	Hal McRae	.25	.11	.03
☐ 774	Dennis Lamp	.08	.04	.01
☐ 775	Mookie Wilson	.15	.07	.02
☐ 776	Jerry Royster	.08	.04	.01
☐ 777	Ned Yost	.08	.04	.01
☐ 778	Mike Davis	.08	.04	.01
☐ 779	Nick Esasky	.08	.04	.01
☐ 780	Mike Flanagan	.08	.04	.01
☐ 781	Jim Gantner	.15	.07	.02
☐ 782	Tom Niedenfuer	.08	.04	.01
☐ 783	Mike Jorgensen	.08	.04	.01
☐ 784	Checklist: 661-792	.15	.07	.02
☐ 785	Tony Armas	.08	.04	.01
☐ 786	Enos Cabell	.08	.04	.01
☐ 787	Jim Wohlford	.08	.04	.01
☐ 788	Steve Comer	.08	.04	.01
☐ 789	Luis Salazar	.08	.04	.01
☐ 790	Ron Guidry	.15	.07	.02
☐ 791	Ivan DeJesus	.08	.04	.01
☐ 792	Darrell Evans	.15	.07	.02

1985 Topps Traded

The cards in this 132-card set measure 2 1/2" by 3 1/2". In its now standard procedure, Topps issued its Traded (or extended) set for the fifth year in a row. Topps did however test on a limited basis the issuance of these Traded cards in wax packs. Because all photos and statistics of

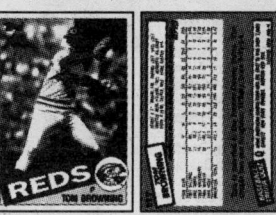

its regular set for the year were developed during the fall and winter months of the preceding year, players who changed teams during the fall, winter, and spring months are portrayed in the 1985 regular issue set with the teams they were with in 1984. The Traded set updates the shortcomings of the regular set by presenting the players with their proper teams for the current year. Most of 1985's top rookies not contained in the regular set are picked up in the Traded set. The key (extended) Rookie Cards in this set are Vince Coleman, Mariano Duncan, Ozzie Guillen, and Mickey Tettleton. Again this year, the Topps affiliate in Ireland printed the cards, and the cards were available through hobby channels only. Topps also produced a specially boxed "glossy" edition, frequently referred to as the Topps Traded Tiffany set. There were supposedly only 8,000 sets of the Tiffany cards produced; they were marketed to hobby dealers. The checklist of cards is identical to that of the normal non-glossy cards. There are two primary distinguishing features of the Tiffany cards, white card stock reverses and high gloss obverses. These Tiffany cards are valued from approximately five to ten times the values listed below. The set numbering is in alphabetical order by player's name.

		NRMT-MT	EXC	G-VG
COMPLETE FACT.SET (132)		18.00	8.00	2.20
COMMON CARD (1T-132T)		.15	.07	.02
☐ 1T	Don Aase	.15	.07	.02
☐ 2T	Bill Almon	.15	.07	.02
☐ 3T	Benny Ayala	.15	.07	.02
☐ 4T	Dusty Baker	.25	.11	.03
☐ 5T	George Bamberger MG	.15	.07	.02
☐ 6T	Dale Berra	.15	.07	.02
☐ 7T	Rich Bordi	.15	.07	.02
☐ 8T	Daryl Boston	.20	.09	.03
☐ 9T	Hubie Brooks	.20	.09	.03
☐ 10T	Chris Brown	.15	.07	.02
☐ 11T	Tom Browning	.25	.11	.03
☐ 12T	Al Bumbry	.15	.07	.02
☐ 13T	Ray Burris	.15	.07	.02
☐ 14T	Jeff Burroughs	.15	.07	.02
☐ 15T	Bill Campbell	.15	.07	.02
☐ 16T	Don Carman	.15	.07	.02
☐ 17T	Gary Carter	.25	.11	.03
☐ 18T	Bobby Castillo	.15	.07	.02
☐ 19T	Bill Caudill	.15	.07	.02
☐ 20T	Rick Cerone	.15	.07	.02

☐ 21T Bryan Clark	.15	.07	.02
☐ 22T Jack Clark	.20	.09	.03
☐ 23T Pat Clements	.15	.07	.02
☐ 24T Vince Coleman	1.50	.70	.19
☐ 25T Dave Collins	.15	.07	.02
☐ 26T Danny Darwin	.15	.07	.02
☐ 27T Jim Davenport MG	.15	.07	.02
☐ 28T Jerry Davis	.15	.07	.02
☐ 29T Brian Dayett	.15	.07	.02
☐ 30T Ivan DeJesus	.15	.07	.02
☐ 31T Ken Dixon	.15	.07	.02
☐ 32T Mariano Duncan	1.00	.45	.12
☐ 33T John Felske MG	.15	.07	.02
☐ 34T Mike Fitzgerald	.15	.07	.02
☐ 35T Ray Fontenot	.15	.07	.02
☐ 36T Greg Gagne	.20	.09	.03
☐ 37T Oscar Gamble	.15	.07	.02
☐ 38T Scott Garrelts	.15	.07	.02
☐ 39T Bob L. Gibson	.15	.07	.02
☐ 40T Jim Gott	.15	.07	.02
☐ 41T David Green	.15	.07	.02
☐ 42T Alfredo Griffin	.15	.07	.02
☐ 43T Ozzie Guillen	2.00	.90	.25
☐ 44T Eddie Haas MG	.15	.07	.02
☐ 45T Terry Harper	.15	.07	.02
☐ 46T Toby Harrah	.15	.07	.02
☐ 47T Greg Harris	.15	.07	.02
☐ 48T Ron Hassey	.15	.07	.02
☐ 49T Rickey Henderson	1.50	.70	.19
☐ 50T Steve Henderson	.15	.07	.02
☐ 51T George Hendrick	.15	.07	.02
☐ 52T Joe Hesketh	.15	.07	.02
☐ 53T Teddy Higuera	.20	.09	.03
☐ 54T Donnie Hill	.15	.07	.02
☐ 55T Al Holland	.15	.07	.02
☐ 56T Burt Hooton	.15	.07	.02
☐ 57T Jay Howell	.15	.07	.02
☐ 58T Ken Howell	.15	.07	.02
☐ 59T LaMarr Hoyt	.15	.07	.02
☐ 60T Tim Hulett	.20	.09	.03
☐ 61T Bob James	.15	.07	.02
☐ 62T Steve Jeltz	.15	.07	.02
☐ 63T Cliff Johnson	.15	.07	.02
☐ 64T Howard Johnson	.20	.09	.03
☐ 65T Ruppert Jones	.15	.07	.02
☐ 66T Steve Kemp	.15	.07	.02
☐ 67T Bruce Kison	.15	.07	.02
☐ 68T Alan Knicely	.15	.07	.02
☐ 69T Mike LaCoss	.15	.07	.02
☐ 70T Lee Lacy	.15	.07	.02
☐ 71T Dave LaPoint	.15	.07	.02
☐ 72T Gary Lavelle	.15	.07	.02
☐ 73T Vance Law	.15	.07	.02
☐ 74T Johnnie LeMaster	.15	.07	.02
☐ 75T Sixto Lezcano	.15	.07	.02
☐ 76T Tim Lollar	.15	.07	.02
☐ 77T Fred Lynn	.20	.09	.03
☐ 78T Billy Martin MG	.20	.09	.03
☐ 79T Ron Mathis	.15	.07	.02
☐ 80T Len Matuszek	.15	.07	.02
☐ 81T Gene Mauch MG	.15	.07	.02
☐ 82T Oddibe McDowell	.15	.07	.02
☐ 83T Roger McDowell	.20	.09	.03
☐ 84T John McNamara MG	.15	.07	.02
☐ 85T Donnie Moore	.15	.07	.02
☐ 86T Gene Nelson	.15	.07	.02
☐ 87T Steve Nicosia	.15	.07	.02
☐ 88T Al Oliver	.20	.09	.03
☐ 89T Joe Orsulak	.25	.11	.03
☐ 90T Rob Picciolo	.15	.07	.02
☐ 91T Chris Pittaro	.15	.07	.02

☐ 92T Jim Presley	.20	.09	.03
☐ 93T Rick Reuschel	.20	.09	.03
☐ 94T Bert Roberge	.15	.07	.02
☐ 95T Bob Rodgers MG	.15	.07	.02
☐ 96T Jerry Royster	.15	.07	.02
☐ 97T Dave Rozema	.15	.07	.02
☐ 98T Dave Rucker	.15	.07	.02
☐ 99T Vern Ruhle	.15	.07	.02
☐ 100T Paul Runge	.15	.07	.02
☐ 101T Mark Salas	.15	.07	.02
☐ 102T Luis Salazar	.15	.07	.02
☐ 103T Joe Sambito	.15	.07	.02
☐ 104T Rick Schu	.15	.07	.02
☐ 105T Donnie Scott	.15	.07	.02
☐ 106T Larry Sheets	.15	.07	.02
☐ 107T Don Slaught	.15	.07	.02
☐ 108T Roy Smalley	.15	.07	.02
☐ 109T Lonnie Smith	.15	.07	.02
☐ 110T Nate Snell UER	.15	.07	.02
(Headings on back			
for a batter)			
☐ 111T Chris Speier	.15	.07	.02
☐ 112T Mike Stenhouse	.15	.07	.02
☐ 113T Tim Stoddard	.15	.07	.02
☐ 114T Jim Sundberg	.20	.09	.03
☐ 115T Bruce Sutter	.15	.07	.02
☐ 116T Don Sutton	.25	.11	.03
☐ 117T Kent Tekulve	.15	.07	.02
☐ 118T Tom Tellmann	.15	.07	.02
☐ 119T Walt Terrell	.15	.07	.02
☐ 120T Mickey Tettleton	4.00	1.80	.50
☐ 121T Derrel Thomas	.15	.07	.02
☐ 122T Rich Thompson	.15	.07	.02
☐ 123T Alex Trevino	.15	.07	.02
☐ 124T John Tudor	.20	.09	.03
☐ 125T Jose Uribe	.15	.07	.02
☐ 126T Bobby Valentine MG	.15	.07	.02
☐ 127T Dave Von Ohlen	.15	.07	.02
☐ 128T U.L. Washington	.15	.07	.02
☐ 129T Earl Weaver MG	.25	.11	.03
☐ 130T Eddie Whitson	.15	.07	.02
☐ 131T Herm Winningham	.15	.07	.02
☐ 132T Checklist 1-132	.15	.07	.02

1986 Topps

The cards in this 792-card set are standard-size (2 1/2" by 3 1/2"). The first seven cards are a tribute to Pete Rose and his career. Card numbers 2-7 show small photos of Pete's Topps cards of the given years on the front with biographical information pertaining to those years on the back. The team leader cards were done differently with a simple player action shot on a white background; the player pictured is dubbed the "Dean" of that team, i.e., the player with the longest continuous service with that team. Topps again features a "Turn Back the Clock" series (401-405). Record breakers of the previous year are acknowledged on card numbers 201 to 207. Card numbers 701-722 feature All-Star selections from each league. Manager cards feature the team checklist on the reverse. Ryne Sandberg (690) is the only player card in the set without a Topps logo on the front of the card; this omission was never corrected by Topps. There are two other uncorrected errors involving misnumbered cards; see card numbers 51, 57, 141, and 171 in the checklist below. The backs of all the cards have a distinctive red background. The key Rookie Cards in this set are Vince Coleman, Darren Daulton, Len Dykstra, Cecil Fielder, and Mickey Tettleton. Topps also produced a specially boxed "glossy" edition, frequently referred to as the Topps Tiffany set. There were supposedly only 5,000 sets of the Tiffany cards produced; they were marketed to hobby dealers. The checklist (792 regular and 132 Traded) is identical to that of the normal non-glossy cards. There are two primary distinguishing features of the Tiffany cards, white card stock reverses and high gloss obverses. These Tiffany cards are valued approximately from five to ten times the values listed below.

	MINT	NRMT	EXC
COMPLETE SET (792)	25.00	11.00	3.10
COMPLETE FACT.SET (792)	30.00	13.50	3.70
COMMON CARD (1-792)	.05	.02	.01
☐ 1 Pete Rose	1.00	.45	.12
☐ 2 Rose Special: '63-'66	.30	.14	.04
☐ 3 Rose Special: '67-'70	.30	.14	.04
☐ 4 Rose Special: '71-'74	.30	.14	.04
☐ 5 Rose Special: '75-'78	.30	.14	.04
☐ 6 Rose Special: '79-'82	.30	.14	.04
☐ 7 Rose Special: '83-'85	.30	.14	.04
☐ 8 Dwayne Murphy	.05	.02	.01
☐ 9 Roy Smith	.05	.02	.01
☐ 10 Tony Gwynn	1.00	.45	.12
☐ 11 Bob Ojeda	.10	.05	.01
☐ 12 Jose Uribe	.05	.02	.01
☐ 13 Bob Kearney	.05	.02	.01
☐ 14 Julio Cruz	.05	.02	.01
☐ 15 Eddie Whitson	.05	.02	.01
☐ 16 Rick Schu	.05	.02	.01
☐ 17 Mike Stenhouse	.05	.02	.01
☐ 18 Brent Gaff	.05	.02	.01
☐ 19 Rich Hebner	.05	.02	.01
☐ 20 Lou Whitaker	.15	.07	.02
☐ 21 George Bamberger MG	.10	.05	.01
(Checklist back)			
☐ 22 Duane Walker	.05	.02	.01
☐ 23 Manny Lee	.05	.02	.01
☐ 24 Len Barker	.05	.02	.01
☐ 25 Willie Wilson	.05	.02	.01
☐ 26 Frank DiPino	.05	.02	.01
☐ 27 Ray Knight	.10	.05	.01
☐ 28 Eric Davis	.15	.07	.02
☐ 29 Tony Phillips	.15	.07	.02
☐ 30 Eddie Murray	.50	.23	.06
☐ 31 Jamie Easterly	.05	.02	.01
☐ 32 Steve Yeager	.05	.02	.01
☐ 33 Jeff Lahti	.05	.02	.01
☐ 34 Ken Phelps	.05	.02	.01
☐ 35 Jeff Reardon	.15	.07	.02
☐ 36 Tigers Leaders	.10	.05	.01
Lance Parrish			
☐ 37 Mark Thurmond	.05	.02	.01
☐ 38 Glenn Hoffman	.05	.02	.01
☐ 39 Dave Rucker	.05	.02	.01
☐ 40 Ken Griffey	.10	.05	.01
☐ 41 Brad Wellman	.05	.02	.01
☐ 42 Geoff Zahn	.05	.02	.01
☐ 43 Dave Engle	.05	.02	.01
☐ 44 Lance McCullers	.05	.02	.01
☐ 45 Damaso Garcia	.05	.02	.01
☐ 46 Billy Hatcher	.05	.02	.01
☐ 47 Juan Berenguer	.05	.02	.01
☐ 48 Bill Almon	.05	.02	.01
☐ 49 Rick Manning	.05	.02	.01
☐ 50 Dan Quisenberry	.10	.05	.01
☐ 51 Bobby Wine MG ERR	.10	.05	.01
(Checklist back)			
(Number of card on			
back is actually 57)			
☐ 52 Chris Welsh	.05	.02	.01
☐ 53 Len Dykstra	.75	.35	.09
☐ 54 John Franco	.10	.05	.01
☐ 55 Fred Lynn	.10	.05	.01
☐ 56 Tom Niedenfuer	.05	.02	.01
☐ 57 Bill Doran	.05	.02	.01
(See also 51)			
☐ 58 Bill Krueger	.05	.02	.01
☐ 59 Andre Thornton	.05	.02	.01
☐ 60 Dwight Evans	.10	.05	.01
☐ 61 Karl Best	.05	.02	.01
☐ 62 Bob Boone	.10	.05	.01
☐ 63 Ron Roenicke	.05	.02	.01
☐ 64 Floyd Bannister	.05	.02	.01
☐ 65 Dan Driessen	.05	.02	.01
☐ 66 Cardinals Leaders	.10	.05	.01
Bob Forsch			
☐ 67 Carmelo Martinez	.05	.02	.01
☐ 68 Ed Lynch	.05	.02	.01
☐ 69 Luis Aguayo	.05	.02	.01
☐ 70 Dave Winfield	.30	.14	.04
☐ 71 Ken Schrom	.05	.02	.01
☐ 72 Shawon Dunston	.10	.05	.01
☐ 73 Randy O'Neal	.05	.02	.01
☐ 74 Rance Mulliniks	.05	.02	.01
☐ 75 Jose DeLeon	.05	.02	.01
☐ 76 Dion James	.05	.02	.01
☐ 77 Charlie Leibrandt	.05	.02	.01
☐ 78 Bruce Benedict	.05	.02	.01
☐ 79 Dave Schmidt	.05	.02	.01
☐ 80 Darryl Strawberry	.15	.07	.02
☐ 81 Gene Mauch MG	.10	.05	.01
(Checklist back)			
☐ 82 Tippy Martinez	.05	.02	.01
☐ 83 Phil Garner	.10	.05	.01
☐ 84 Curt Young	.05	.02	.01
☐ 85 Tony Perez	.15	.07	.02
(Eric Davis also			
shown on card)			
☐ 86 Tom Waddell	.05	.02	.01
☐ 87 Candy Maldonado	.05	.02	.01
☐ 88 Tom Nieto	.05	.02	.01
☐ 89 Randy St.Claire	.05	.02	.01
☐ 90 Garry Templeton	.05	.02	.01

☐ 91	Steve Crawford	.05	.02	.01
☐ 92	Al Cowens	.05	.02	.01
☐ 93	Scot Thompson	.05	.02	.01
☐ 94	Rich Bordi	.05	.02	.01
☐ 95	Ozzie Virgil	.05	.02	.01
☐ 96	Blue Jays Leaders	.10	.05	.01
	Jim Clancy			
☐ 97	Gary Gaetti	.15	.07	.02
☐ 98	Dick Ruthven	.05	.02	.01
☐ 99	Buddy Biancalana	.05	.02	.01
☐ 100	Nolan Ryan	2.00	.90	.25
☐ 101	Dave Bergman	.05	.02	.01
☐ 102	Joe Orsulak	.10	.05	.01
☐ 103	Luis Salazar	.05	.02	.01
☐ 104	Sid Fernandez	.10	.05	.01
☐ 105	Gary Ward	.05	.02	.01
☐ 106	Ray Burris	.05	.02	.01
☐ 107	Rafael Ramirez	.05	.02	.01
☐ 108	Ted Power	.05	.02	.01
☐ 109	Len Matuszek	.05	.02	.01
☐ 110	Scott McGregor	.05	.02	.01
☐ 111	Roger Craig MG	.10	.05	.01
	(Checklist back)			
☐ 112	Bill Campbell	.05	.02	.01
☐ 113	U.L. Washington	.05	.02	.01
☐ 114	Mike C. Brown	.05	.02	.01
☐ 115	Jay Howell	.05	.02	.01
☐ 116	Brook Jacoby	.05	.02	.01
☐ 117	Bruce Kison	.05	.02	.01
☐ 118	Jerry Royster	.05	.02	.01
☐ 119	Barry Bonnell	.05	.02	.01
☐ 120	Steve Carlton	.20	.09	.03
☐ 121	Nelson Simmons	.05	.02	.01
☐ 122	Pete Filson	.05	.02	.01
☐ 123	Greg Walker	.05	.02	.01
☐ 124	Luis Sanchez	.05	.02	.01
☐ 125	Dave Lopes	.10	.05	.01
☐ 126	Mets Leaders	.15	.07	.02
	Mookie Wilson			
☐ 127	Jack Howell	.05	.02	.01
☐ 128	John Wathan	.05	.02	.01
☐ 129	Jeff Dedmon	.05	.02	.01
☐ 130	Alan Trammell	.15	.07	.02
☐ 131	Checklist: 1-132	.10	.05	.01
☐ 132	Razor Shines	.05	.02	.01
☐ 133	Andy McGaffigan	.05	.02	.01
☐ 134	Carney Lansford	.10	.05	.01
☐ 135	Joe Niekro	.10	.05	.01
☐ 136	Mike Hargrove	.10	.05	.01
☐ 137	Charlie Moore	.05	.02	.01
☐ 138	Mark Davis	.05	.02	.01
☐ 139	Daryl Boston	.05	.02	.01
☐ 140	John Candelaria	.05	.02	.01
☐ 141	Chuck Cottier MG	.10	.05	.01
	(Checklist back)			
	(See also 171)			
☐ 142	Bob Jones	.05	.02	.01
☐ 143	Dave Van Gorder	.05	.02	.01
☐ 144	Doug Sisk	.05	.02	.01
☐ 145	Pedro Guerrero	.10	.05	.01
☐ 146	Jack Perconte	.05	.02	.01
☐ 147	Larry Sheets	.05	.02	.01
☐ 148	Mike Heath	.05	.02	.01
☐ 149	Brett Butler	.15	.07	.02
☐ 150	Joaquin Andujar	.05	.02	.01
☐ 151	Dave Stapleton	.05	.02	.01
☐ 152	Mike Morgan	.05	.02	.01
☐ 153	Ricky Adams	.05	.02	.01
☐ 154	Bert Roberge	.05	.02	.01
☐ 155	Bob Grich	.10	.05	.01
☐ 156	White Sox Leaders	.10	.05	.01
	Richard Dotson			
☐ 157	Ron Hassey	.05	.02	.01
☐ 158	Derrel Thomas	.05	.02	.01
☐ 159	Orel Hershiser UER	.15	.07	.02
	(82 Alburquerque)			
☐ 160	Chet Lemon	.05	.02	.01
☐ 161	Lee Tunnell	.05	.02	.01
☐ 162	Greg Gagne	.10	.05	.01
☐ 163	Pete Ladd	.05	.02	.01
☐ 164	Steve Balboni	.05	.02	.01
☐ 165	Mike Davis	.05	.02	.01
☐ 166	Dickie Thon	.05	.02	.01
☐ 167	Zane Smith	.05	.02	.01
☐ 168	Jeff Burroughs	.05	.02	.01
☐ 169	George Wright	.05	.02	.01
☐ 170	Gary Carter	.15	.07	.02
☐ 171	Bob Rodgers MG ERR	.10	.05	.01
	(Checklist back)			
	(Number of card on			
	back actually 141)			
☐ 172	Jerry Reed	.05	.02	.01
☐ 173	Wayne Gross	.05	.02	.01
☐ 174	Brian Snyder	.05	.02	.01
☐ 175	Steve Sax	.05	.02	.01
☐ 176	Jay Tibbs	.05	.02	.01
☐ 177	Joel Youngblood	.05	.02	.01
☐ 178	Ivan DeJesus	.05	.02	.01
☐ 179	Stu Cliburn	.05	.02	.01
☐ 180	Don Mattingly	1.00	.45	.12
☐ 181	Al Nipper	.05	.02	.01
☐ 182	Bobby Brown	.05	.02	.01
☐ 183	Larry Andersen	.05	.02	.01
☐ 184	Tim Laudner	.05	.02	.01
☐ 185	Rollie Fingers	.15	.07	.02
☐ 186	Astros Leaders	.10	.05	.01
	Jose Cruz			
☐ 187	Scott Fletcher	.05	.02	.01
☐ 188	Bob Dernier	.05	.02	.01
☐ 189	Mike Mason	.05	.02	.01
☐ 190	George Hendrick	.05	.02	.01
☐ 191	Wally Backman	.05	.02	.01
☐ 192	Milt Wilcox	.05	.02	.01
☐ 193	Daryl Sconiers	.05	.02	.01
☐ 194	Craig McMurtry	.05	.02	.01
☐ 195	Dave Concepcion	.10	.05	.01
☐ 196	Doyle Alexander	.05	.02	.01
☐ 197	Enos Cabell	.05	.02	.01
☐ 198	Ken Dixon	.05	.02	.01
☐ 199	Dick Howser MG	.10	.05	.01
	(Checklist back)			
☐ 200	Mike Schmidt	.40	.18	.05
☐ 201	Vince Coleman RB	.10	.05	.01
	Most stolen bases,			
	season, rookie			
☐ 202	Dwight Gooden RB	.10	.05	.01
	Youngest 20 game			
	winner			
☐ 203	Keith Hernandez RB	.10	.05	.01
	Most game-winning			
	RBI's			
☐ 204	Phil Niekro RB	.10	.05	.01
	Oldest shutout pitcher			
☐ 205	Tony Perez RB	.10	.05	.01
	Oldest grand slammer			
☐ 206	Pete Rose RB	.35	.16	.04
	Most hits, lifetime			
☐ 207	Fernando Valenzuela RB	.10	.05	.01
	Most cons. innings,			
	start of season,			
	no earned runs			
☐ 208	Ramon Romero	.05	.02	.01

☐	209 Randy Ready	.05	.02	.01
☐	210 Calvin Schiraldi	.05	.02	.01
☐	211 Ed Wojna	.05	.02	.01
☐	212 Chris Speier	.05	.02	.01
☐	213 Bob Shirley	.05	.02	.01
☐	214 Randy Bush	.05	.02	.01
☐	215 Frank White	.10	.05	.01
☐	216 A's Leaders	.10	.05	.01
	Dwayne Murphy			
☐	217 Bill Scherrer	.05	.02	.01
☐	218 Randy Hunt	.05	.02	.01
☐	219 Dennis Lamp	.05	.02	.01
☐	220 Bob Horner	.05	.02	.01
☐	221 Dave Henderson	.05	.02	.01
☐	222 Craig Gerber	.05	.02	.01
☐	223 Atlee Hammaker	.05	.02	.01
☐	224 Cesar Cedeno	.10	.05	.01
☐	225 Ron Darling	.10	.05	.01
☐	226 Lee Lacy	.05	.02	.01
☐	227 Al Jones	.05	.02	.01
☐	228 Tom Lawless	.05	.02	.01
☐	229 Bill Gullickson	.10	.05	.01
☐	230 Terry Kennedy	.05	.02	.01
☐	231 Jim Frey MG	.10	.05	.01
	(Checklist back)			
☐	232 Rick Rhoden	.05	.02	.01
☐	233 Steve Lyons	.05	.02	.01
☐	234 Doug Corbett	.05	.02	.01
☐	235 Butch Wynegar	.05	.02	.01
☐	236 Frank Eufemia	.05	.02	.01
☐	237 Ted Simmons	.10	.05	.01
☐	238 Larry Parrish	.05	.02	.01
☐	239 Joel Skinner	.05	.02	.01
☐	240 Tommy John	.15	.07	.02
☐	241 Tony Fernandez	.10	.05	.01
☐	242 Rich Thompson	.05	.02	.01
☐	243 Johnny Grubb	.05	.02	.01
☐	244 Craig Lefferts	.05	.02	.01
☐	245 Jim Sundberg	.05	.02	.01
☐	246 Phillies Leaders	.10	.05	.01
	Steve Carlton			
☐	247 Terry Harper	.05	.02	.01
☐	248 Spike Owen	.05	.02	.01
☐	249 Rob Deer	.10	.05	.01
☐	250 Dwight Gooden	.15	.07	.02
☐	251 Rich Dauer	.05	.02	.01
☐	252 Bobby Castillo	.05	.02	.01
☐	253 Dann Bilardello	.05	.02	.01
☐	254 Ozzie Guillen	.30	.14	.04
☐	255 Tony Armas	.05	.02	.01
☐	256 Kurt Kepshire	.05	.02	.01
☐	257 Doug DeCinces	.05	.02	.01
☐	258 Tim Burke	.05	.02	.01
☐	259 Dan Pasqua	.05	.02	.01
☐	260 Tony Pena	.05	.02	.01
☐	261 Bobby Valentine MG	.10	.05	.01
	(Checklist back)			
☐	262 Mario Ramirez	.05	.02	.01
☐	263 Checklist: 133-264	.10	.05	.01
☐	264 Darren Daulton	1.00	.45	.12
☐	265 Ron Davis	.05	.02	.01
☐	266 Keith Moreland	.05	.02	.01
☐	267 Paul Molitor	.20	.09	.03
☐	268 Mike Scott	.05	.02	.01
☐	269 Dane Iorg	.05	.02	.01
☐	270 Jack Morris	.15	.07	.02
☐	271 Dave Collins	.05	.02	.01
☐	272 Tim Tolman	.05	.02	.01
☐	273 Jerry Willard	.05	.02	.01
☐	274 Ron Gardenhire	.05	.02	.01
☐	275 Charlie Hough	.10	.05	.01

☐	276 Yankees Leaders	.10	.05	.01
	Willie Randolph			
☐	277 Jaime Cocanower	.05	.02	.01
☐	278 Sixto Lezcano	.05	.02	.01
☐	279 Al Pardo	.05	.02	.01
☐	280 Tim Raines	.15	.07	.02
☐	281 Steve Mura	.05	.02	.01
☐	282 Jerry Mumphrey	.05	.02	.01
☐	283 Mike Fischlin	.05	.02	.01
☐	284 Brian Dayett	.05	.02	.01
☐	285 Buddy Bell	.10	.05	.01
☐	286 Luis DeLeon	.05	.02	.01
☐	287 John Christensen	.05	.02	.01
☐	288 Don Aase	.05	.02	.01
☐	289 Johnnie LeMaster	.05	.02	.01
☐	290 Carlton Fisk	.30	.14	.04
☐	291 Tom Lasorda MG	.10	.05	.01
	(Checklist back)			
☐	292 Chuck Porter	.05	.02	.01
☐	293 Chris Chambliss	.10	.05	.01
☐	294 Danny Cox	.05	.02	.01
☐	295 Kirk Gibson	.15	.07	.02
☐	296 Geno Petralli	.05	.02	.01
☐	297 Tim Lollar	.05	.02	.01
☐	298 Craig Reynolds	.05	.02	.01
☐	299 Bryn Smith	.05	.02	.01
☐	300 George Brett	1.00	.45	.12
☐	301 Dennis Rasmussen	.05	.02	.01
☐	302 Greg Gross	.05	.02	.01
☐	303 Curt Wardle	.05	.02	.01
☐	304 Mike Gallego	.10	.05	.01
☐	305 Phil Bradley	.05	.02	.01
☐	306 Padres Leaders	.10	.05	.01
	Terry Kennedy			
☐	307 Dave Sax	.05	.02	.01
☐	308 Ray Fontenot	.05	.02	.01
☐	309 John Shelby	.05	.02	.01
☐	310 Greg Minton	.05	.02	.01
☐	311 Dick Schofield	.05	.02	.01
☐	312 Tom Filer	.05	.02	.01
☐	313 Joe DeSa	.05	.02	.01
☐	314 Frank Pastore	.05	.02	.01
☐	315 Mookie Wilson	.10	.05	.01
☐	316 Sammy Khalifa	.05	.02	.04
☐	317 Ed Romero	.05	.02	.01
☐	318 Terry Whitfield	.05	.02	.01
☐	319 Rick Camp	.05	.02	.01
☐	320 Jim Rice	.15	.07	.02
☐	321 Earl Weaver MG	.10	.05	.01
	(Checklist back)			
☐	322 Bob Forsch	.05	.02	.01
☐	323 Jerry Davis	.05	.02	.01
☐	324 Dan Schatzeder	.05	.02	.01
☐	325 Juan Beniquez	.05	.02	.01
☐	326 Kent Tekulve	.05	.02	.01
☐	327 Mike Pagliarulo	.05	.02	.01
☐	328 Pete O'Brien	.05	.02	.01
☐	329 Kirby Puckett	2.00	.90	.25
☐	330 Rick Sutcliffe	.10	.05	.01
☐	331 Alan Ashby	.05	.02	.01
☐	332 Darryl Motley	.05	.02	.01
☐	333 Tom Henke	.10	.05	.01
☐	334 Ken Oberkfell	.05	.02	.01
☐	335 Don Sutton	.15	.07	.02
☐	336 Indians Leaders	.10	.05	.01
	Andre Thornton			
☐	337 Darnell Coles	.05	.02	.01
☐	338 Jorge Bell	.10	.05	.01
☐	339 Bruce Berenyi	.05	.02	.01
☐	340 Cal Ripken	2.00	.90	.25
☐	341 Frank Williams	.05	.02	.01

☐ 342	Gary Redus	.05	.02	.01
☐ 343	Carlos Diaz	.05	.02	.01
☐ 344	Jim Wohlford	.05	.02	.01
☐ 345	Donnie Moore	.05	.02	.01
☐ 346	Bryan Little	.05	.02	.01
☐ 347	Teddy Higuera	.10	.05	.01
☐ 348	Cliff Johnson	.05	.02	.01
☐ 349	Mark Clear	.05	.02	.01
☐ 350	Jack Clark	.10	.05	.01
☐ 351	Chuck Tanner MG (Checklist back)	.10	.05	.01
☐ 352	Harry Spilman	.05	.02	.01
☐ 353	Keith Atherton	.05	.02	.01
☐ 354	Tony Bernazard	.05	.02	.01
☐ 355	Lee Smith	.15	.07	.02
☐ 356	Mickey Hatcher	.05	.02	.01
☐ 357	Ed VandeBerg	.05	.02	.01
☐ 358	Rick Dempsey	.10	.05	.01
☐ 359	Mike LaCoss	.05	.02	.01
☐ 360	Lloyd Moseby	.05	.02	.01
☐ 361	Shane Rawley	.05	.02	.01
☐ 362	Tom Paciorek	.10	.05	.01
☐ 363	Terry Forster	.05	.02	.01
☐ 364	Reid Nichols	.05	.02	.01
☐ 365	Mike Flanagan	.05	.02	.01
☐ 366	Reds Leaders Dave Concepcion	.10	.05	.01
☐ 367	Aurelio Lopez	.05	.02	.01
☐ 368	Greg Brock	.05	.02	.01
☐ 369	Al Holland	.05	.02	.01
☐ 370	Vince Coleman	.25	.11	.03
☐ 371	Bill Stein	.05	.02	.01
☐ 372	Ben Oglivie	.05	.02	.01
☐ 373	Urbano Lugo	.05	.02	.01
☐ 374	Terry Francona	.05	.02	.01
☐ 375	Rich Gedman	.05	.02	.01
☐ 376	Bill Dawley	.05	.02	.01
☐ 377	Joe Carter	1.00	.45	.12
☐ 378	Bruce Bochte	.05	.02	.01
☐ 379	Bobby Meacham	.05	.02	.01
☐ 380	LaMarr Hoyt	.05	.02	.01
☐ 381	Ray Miller MG (Checklist back)	.10	.05	.01
☐ 382	Ivan Calderon	.10	.05	.01
☐ 383	Chris Brown	.05	.02	.01
☐ 384	Steve Trout	.05	.02	.01
☐ 385	Cecil Cooper	.10	.05	.01
☐ 386	Cecil Fielder	2.00	.90	.25
☐ 387	Steve Kemp	.05	.02	.01
☐ 388	Dickie Noles	.05	.02	.01
☐ 389	Glenn Davis	.05	.02	.01
☐ 390	Tom Seaver	.20	.09	.03
☐ 391	Julio Franco	.15	.07	.02
☐ 392	John Russell	.05	.02	.01
☐ 393	Chris Pittaro	.05	.02	.01
☐ 394	Checklist: 265-396	.10	.05	.01
☐ 395	Scott Garrelts	.05	.02	.01
☐ 396	Red Sox Leaders Dwight Evans	.10	.05	.01
☐ 397	Steve Buechele	.10	.05	.01
☐ 398	Earnie Riles	.05	.02	.01
☐ 399	Bill Swift	.10	.05	.01
☐ 400	Rod Carew	.20	.09	.03
☐ 401	Fernando Valenzuela TBC '81	.10	.05	.01
☐ 402	Tom Seaver TBC '76	.10	.05	.01
☐ 403	Willie Mays TBC '71	.10	.05	.01
☐ 404	Frank Robinson TBC '66	.10	.05	.01
☐ 405	Roger Maris TBC '61	.10	.05	.01
☐ 406	Scott Sanderson	.05	.02	.01
☐ 407	Sal Butera	.05	.02	.01
☐ 408	Dave Smith	.05	.02	.01
☐ 409	Paul Runge	.05	.02	.01
☐ 410	Dave Kingman	.10	.05	.01
☐ 411	Sparky Anderson MG (Checklist back)	.10	.05	.01
☐ 412	Jim Clancy	.05	.02	.01
☐ 413	Tim Flannery	.05	.02	.01
☐ 414	Tom Gorman	.05	.02	.01
☐ 415	Hal McRae	.15	.07	.02
☐ 416	Dennis Martinez	.10	.05	.01
☐ 417	R.J. Reynolds	.05	.02	.01
☐ 418	Alan Knicely	.05	.02	.01
☐ 419	Frank Wills	.05	.02	.01
☐ 420	Von Hayes	.05	.02	.01
☐ 421	David Palmer	.05	.02	.01
☐ 422	Mike Jorgensen	.05	.02	.01
☐ 423	Dan Spillner	.05	.02	.01
☐ 424	Rick Miller	.05	.02	.01
☐ 425	Larry McWilliams	.05	.02	.01
☐ 426	Brewers Leaders Charlie Moore	.10	.05	.01
☐ 427	Joe Cowley	.05	.02	.01
☐ 428	Max Venable	.05	.02	.01
☐ 429	Greg Booker	.05	.02	.01
☐ 430	Kent Hrbek	.10	.05	.01
☐ 431	George Frazier	.05	.02	.01
☐ 432	Mark Bailey	.05	.02	.01
☐ 433	Chris Codiroli	.05	.02	.01
☐ 434	Curt Wilkerson	.05	.02	.01
☐ 435	Bill Caudill	.05	.02	.01
☐ 436	Doug Flynn	.05	.02	.01
☐ 437	Rick Mahler	.05	.02	.01
☐ 438	Clint Hurdle	.05	.02	.01
☐ 439	Rick Honeycutt	.05	.02	.01
☐ 440	Alvin Davis	.05	.02	.01
☐ 441	Whitey Herzog MG (Checklist back)	.10	.05	.01
☐ 442	Ron Robinson	.05	.02	.01
☐ 443	Bill Buckner	.10	.05	.01
☐ 444	Alex Trevino	.05	.02	.01
☐ 445	Bert Blyleven	.15	.07	.02
☐ 446	Lenn Sakata	.05	.02	.01
☐ 447	Jerry Don Gleaton	.05	.02	.01
☐ 448	Herm Winningham	.05	.02	.01
☐ 449	Rod Scurry	.05	.02	.01
☐ 450	Graig Nettles	.10	.05	.01
☐ 451	Mark Brown	.05	.02	.01
☐ 452	Bob Clark	.05	.02	.01
☐ 453	Steve Jeltz	.05	.02	.01
☐ 454	Burt Hooton	.05	.02	.01
☐ 455	Willie Randolph	.10	.05	.01
☐ 456	Braves Leaders Dale Murphy	.10	.05	.01
☐ 457	Mickey Tettleton	.60	.25	.07
☐ 458	Kevin Bass	.05	.02	.01
☐ 459	Luis Leal	.05	.02	.01
☐ 460	Leon Durham	.05	.02	.01
☐ 461	Walt Terrell	.05	.02	.01
☐ 462	Domingo Ramos	.05	.02	.01
☐ 463	Jim Gott	.05	.02	.01
☐ 464	Ruppert Jones	.05	.02	.01
☐ 465	Jesse Orosco	.05	.02	.01
☐ 466	Tom Foley	.05	.02	.01
☐ 467	Bob James	.05	.02	.01
☐ 468	Mike Scioscia	.05	.02	.01
☐ 469	Storm Davis	.05	.02	.01
☐ 470	Bill Madlock	.10	.05	.01
☐ 471	Bobby Cox MG (Checklist back)	.10	.05	.01
☐ 472	Joe Hesketh	.05	.02	.01

473	Mark Brouhard	.05	.02	.01
474	John Tudor	.10	.05	.01
475	Juan Samuel	.05	.02	.01
476	Ron Mathis	.05	.02	.01
477	Mike Easler	.05	.02	.01
478	Andy Hawkins	.05	.02	.01
479	Bob Melvin	.05	.02	.01
480	Oddibe McDowell	.05	.02	.01
481	Scott Bradley	.05	.02	.01
482	Rick Lysander	.05	.02	.01
483	George Vukovich	.05	.02	.01
484	Donnie Hill	.05	.02	.01
485	Gary Matthews	.05	.02	.01
486	Angels Leaders Bobby Grich	.10	.05	.01
487	Bret Saberhagen	.20	.09	.03
488	Lou Thornton	.05	.02	.01
489	Jim Winn	.05	.02	.01
490	Jeff Leonard	.05	.02	.01
491	Pascual Perez	.05	.02	.01
492	Kelvin Chapman	.05	.02	.01
493	Gene Nelson	.05	.02	.01
494	Gary Roenicke	.05	.02	.01
495	Mark Langston	.15	.07	.02
496	Jay Johnstone	.10	.05	.01
497	John Stuper	.05	.02	.01
498	Tito Landrum	.05	.02	.01
499	Bob L. Gibson	.05	.02	.01
500	Rickey Henderson	.30	.14	.04
501	Dave Johnson MG (Checklist back)	.10	.05	.01
502	Glen Cook	.05	.02	.01
503	Mike Fitzgerald	.05	.02	.01
504	Denny Walling	.05	.02	.01
505	Jerry Koosman	.10	.05	.01
506	Bill Russell	.10	.05	.01
507	Steve Ontiveros	.30	.14	.04
508	Alan Wiggins	.05	.02	.01
509	Ernie Camacho	.05	.02	.01
510	Wade Boggs	.40	.18	.05
511	Ed Nunez	.05	.02	.01
512	Thad Bosley	.05	.02	.01
513	Ron Washington	.05	.02	.01
514	Mike Jones	.05	.02	.01
515	Darrell Evans	.10	.05	.01
516	Giants Leaders Greg Minton	.10	.05	.01
517	Milt Thompson	.10	.05	.01
518	Buck Martinez	.05	.02	.01
519	Danny Darwin	.05	.02	.01
520	Keith Hernandez	.10	.05	.01
521	Nate Snell	.05	.02	.01
522	Bob Bailor	.05	.02	.01
523	Joe Price	.05	.02	.01
524	Darrell Miller	.05	.02	.01
525	Marvell Wynne	.05	.02	.01
526	Charlie Lea	.05	.02	.01
527	Checklist: 397-528	.10	.05	.01
528	Terry Pendleton	.15	.07	.02
529	Marc Sullivan	.05	.02	.01
530	Rich Gossage	.15	.07	.02
531	Tony LaRussa MG (Checklist back)	.10	.05	.01
532	Don Carman	.05	.02	.01
533	Billy Sample	.05	.02	.01
534	Jeff Calhoun	.05	.02	.01
535	Toby Harrah	.05	.02	.01
536	Jose Rijo	.15	.07	.02
537	Mark Salas	.05	.02	.01
538	Dennis Eckersley	.15	.07	.02
539	Glenn Hubbard	.05	.02	.01
540	Dan Petry	.05	.02	.01
541	Jorge Orta	.05	.02	.01
542	Don Schulze	.05	.02	.01
543	Jerry Narron	.05	.02	.01
544	Eddie Milner	.05	.02	.01
545	Jimmy Key	.15	.07	.02
546	Mariners Leaders Dave Henderson	.10	.05	.01
547	Roger McDowell	.10	.05	.01
548	Mike Young	.05	.02	.01
549	Bob Welch	.10	.05	.01
550	Tom Herr	.05	.02	.01
551	Dave LaPoint	.05	.02	.01
552	Marc Hill	.05	.02	.01
553	Jim Morrison	.05	.02	.01
554	Paul Householder	.05	.02	.01
555	Hubie Brooks	.05	.02	.01
556	John Denny	.05	.02	.01
557	Gerald Perry	.05	.02	.01
558	Tim Stoddard	.05	.02	.01
559	Tommy Dunbar	.05	.02	.01
560	Dave Righetti	.10	.05	.01
561	Bob Lillis MG (Checklist back)	.10	.05	.01
562	Joe Beckwith	.05	.02	.01
563	Alejandro Sanchez	.05	.02	.01
564	Warren Brusstar	.05	.02	.01
565	Tom Brunansky	.10	.05	.01
566	Alfredo Griffin	.05	.02	.01
567	Jeff Barkley	.05	.02	.01
568	Donnie Scott	.05	.02	.01
569	Jim Acker	.05	.02	.01
570	Rusty Staub	.10	.05	.01
571	Mike Jeffcoat	.05	.02	.01
572	Paul Zuvella	.05	.02	.01
573	Tom Hume	.05	.02	.01
574	Ron Kittle	.05	.02	.01
575	Mike Boddicker	.05	.02	.01
576	Expos Leaders Andre Dawson	.10	.05	.01
577	Jerry Reuss	.05	.02	.01
578	Lee Mazzilli	.05	.02	.01
579	Jim Slaton	.05	.02	.01
580	Willie McGee	.10	.05	.01
581	Bruce Hurst	.10	.05	.01
582	Jim Gantner	.05	.02	.01
583	Al Bumbry	.05	.02	.01
584	Brian Fisher	.05	.02	.01
585	Garry Maddox	.05	.02	.01
586	Greg Harris	.05	.02	.01
587	Rafael Santana	.05	.02	.01
588	Steve Lake	.05	.02	.01
589	Sid Bream	.10	.05	.01
590	Bob Knepper	.05	.02	.01
591	Jackie Moore MG (Checklist back)	.10	.05	.01
592	Frank Tanana	.10	.05	.01
593	Jesse Barfield	.05	.02	.01
594	Chris Bando	.05	.02	.01
595	Dave Parker	.15	.07	.02
596	Onix Concepcion	.05	.02	.01
597	Sammy Stewart	.05	.02	.01
598	Jim Presley	.05	.02	.01
599	Rick Aguilera	.50	.23	.06
600	Dale Murphy	.15	.07	.02
601	Gary Lucas	.05	.02	.01
602	Mariano Duncan	.10	.05	.01
603	Bill Laskey	.05	.02	.01
604	Gary Pettis	.05	.02	.01
605	Dennis Boyd	.05	.02	.01
606	Royals Leaders	.10	.05	.01

Hal McRae

☐ 607 Ken Dayley	.05	.02	.01
☐ 608 Bruce Bochy	.05	.02	.01
☐ 609 Barbaro Garbey	.05	.02	.01
☐ 610 Ron Guidry	.10	.05	.01
☐ 611 Gary Woods	.05	.02	.01
☐ 612 Richard Dotson	.05	.02	.01
☐ 613 Roy Smalley	.05	.02	.01
☐ 614 Rick Waits	.05	.02	.01
☐ 615 Johnny Ray	.05	.02	.01
☐ 616 Glenn Brummer	.05	.02	.01
☐ 617 Lonnie Smith	.05	.02	.01
☐ 618 Jim Pankovits	.05	.02	.01
☐ 619 Danny Heep	.05	.02	.01
☐ 620 Bruce Sutter	.10	.05	.01
☐ 621 John Felske MG	.10	.05	.01
(Checklist back)			
☐ 622 Gary Lavelle	.05	.02	.01
☐ 623 Floyd Rayford	.05	.02	.01
☐ 624 Steve McCatty	.05	.02	.01
☐ 625 Bob Brenly	.05	.02	.01
☐ 626 Roy Thomas	.05	.02	.01
☐ 627 Ron Oester	.05	.02	.01
☐ 628 Kirk McCaskill	.10	.05	.01
☐ 629 Mitch Webster	.05	.02	.01
☐ 630 Fernando Valenzuela	.10	.05	.01
☐ 631 Steve Braun	.05	.02	.01
☐ 632 Dave Von Ohlen	.05	.02	.01
☐ 633 Jackie Gutierrez	.05	.02	.01
☐ 634 Roy Lee Jackson	.05	.02	.01
☐ 635 Jason Thompson	.05	.02	.01
☐ 636 Cubs Leaders	.10	.05	.01
Lee Smith			
☐ 637 Rudy Law	.05	.02	.01
☐ 638 John Butcher	.05	.02	.01
☐ 639 Bo Diaz	.05	.02	.01
☐ 640 Jose Cruz	.05	.02	.01
☐ 641 Wayne Tolleson	.05	.02	.01
☐ 642 Ray Searage	.05	.02	.01
☐ 643 Tom Brookens	.05	.02	.01
☐ 644 Mark Gubicza	.10	.05	.01
☐ 645 Dusty Baker	.15	.07	.02
☐ 646 Mike Moore	.05	.02	.01
☐ 647 Mel Hall	.05	.02	.01
☐ 648 Steve Bedrosian	.05	.02	.01
☐ 649 Ronn Reynolds	.05	.02	.01
☐ 650 Dave Stieb	.10	.05	.01
☐ 651 Billy Martin MG	.10	.05	.01
(Checklist back)			
☐ 652 Tom Browning	.10	.05	.01
☐ 653 Jim Dwyer	.05	.02	.01
☐ 654 Ken Howell	.05	.02	.01
☐ 655 Manny Trillo	.05	.02	.01
☐ 656 Brian Harper	.10	.05	.01
☐ 657 Juan Agosto	.05	.02	.01
☐ 658 Rob Wilfong	.05	.02	.01
☐ 659 Checklist: 529-660	.05	.01	.01
☐ 660 Steve Garvey	.15	.07	.02
☐ 661 Roger Clemens	1.00	.45	.12
☐ 662 Bill Schroeder	.05	.02	.01
☐ 663 Neil Allen	.05	.02	.01
☐ 664 Tim Corcoran	.05	.02	.01
☐ 665 Alejandro Pena	.05	.02	.01
☐ 666 Rangers Leaders	.10	.05	.01
Charlie Hough			
☐ 667 Tim Teufel	.05	.02	.01
☐ 668 Cecilio Guante	.05	.02	.01
☐ 669 Ron Cey	.10	.05	.01
☐ 670 Willie Hernandez	.05	.02	.01
☐ 671 Lynn Jones	.05	.02	.01
☐ 672 Rob Picciolo	.05	.02	.01

☐ 673 Ernie Whitt	.05	.02	.01
☐ 674 Pat Tabler	.05	.02	.01
☐ 675 Claudell Washington	.05	.02	.01
☐ 676 Matt Young	.05	.02	.01
☐ 677 Nick Esasky	.05	.02	.01
☐ 678 Dan Gladden	.05	.02	.01
☐ 679 Britt Burns	.05	.02	.01
☐ 680 George Foster	.10	.05	.01
☐ 681 Dick Williams MG	.10	.05	.01
(Checklist back)			
☐ 682 Junior Ortiz	.05	.02	.01
☐ 683 Andy Van Slyke	.10	.05	.01
☐ 684 Bob McClure	.05	.02	.01
☐ 685 Tim Wallach	.10	.05	.01
☐ 686 Jeff Stone	.05	.02	.01
☐ 687 Mike Trujillo	.05	.02	.01
☐ 688 Larry Herndon	.05	.02	.01
☐ 689 Dave Stewart	.15	.07	.02
☐ 690 Ryne Sandberg UER	1.00	.45	.12
(No Topps logo on front)			
☐ 691 Mike Madden	.05	.02	.01
☐ 692 Dale Berra	.05	.02	.01
☐ 693 Tom Tellmann	.05	.02	.01
☐ 694 Garth Iorg	.05	.02	.01
☐ 695 Mike Smithson	.05	.02	.01
☐ 696 Dodgers Leaders	.10	.05	.01
Bill Russell			
☐ 697 Bud Black	.05	.02	.01
☐ 698 Brad Komminsk	.05	.02	.01
☐ 699 Pat Corrales MG	.10	.05	.01
(Checklist back)			
☐ 700 Reggie Jackson	.30	.14	.04
☐ 701 Keith Hernandez AS	.10	.05	.01
☐ 702 Tom Herr AS	30.00	13.50	3.70
☐ 703 Tim Wallach AS	.10	.05	.01
☐ 704 Ozzie Smith AS	.15	.07	.02
☐ 705 Dale Murphy AS	.10	.05	.01
☐ 706 Pedro Guerrero AS	.10	.05	.01
☐ 707 Willie McGee AS	.10	.05	.01
☐ 708 Gary Carter AS	.10	.05	.01
☐ 709 Dwight Gooden AS	.10	.05	.01
☐ 710 John Tudor AS	30.00	13.50	3.70
☐ 711 Jeff Reardon AS	.10	.05	.01
☐ 712 Don Mattingly AS	.50	.23	.06
☐ 713 Damaso Garcia AS	30.00	13.50	3.70
☐ 714 George Brett AS	.50	.23	.06
☐ 715 Cal Ripken AS	1.00	.45	.12
☐ 716 Rickey Henderson AS	.15	.07	.02
☐ 717 Dave Winfield AS	.15	.07	.02
☐ 718 George Bell AS	.10	.05	.01
☐ 719 Carlton Fisk AS	.10	.05	.01
☐ 720 Bret Saberhagen AS	.10	.05	.01
☐ 721 Ron Guidry AS	.10	.05	.01
☐ 722 Dan Quisenberry AS	.10	.05	.01
☐ 723 Marty Bystrom	.05	.02	.01
☐ 724 Tim Hulett	.05	.02	.01
☐ 725 Mario Soto	.05	.02	.01
☐ 726 Orioles Leaders	.10	.05	.01
Rick Dempsey			
☐ 727 David Green	.05	.02	.01
☐ 728 Mike Marshall	.05	.02	.01
☐ 729 Jim Beattie	.05	.02	.01
☐ 730 Ozzie Smith	.50	.23	.06
☐ 731 Don Robinson	.05	.02	.01
☐ 732 Floyd Youmans	.05	.02	.01
☐ 733 Ron Romanick	.05	.02	.01
☐ 734 Marty Barrett	.05	.02	.01
☐ 735 Dave Dravecky	.10	.05	.01
☐ 736 Glenn Wilson	.05	.02	.01
☐ 737 Pete Vuckovich	.05	.02	.01

☐	738	Andre Robertson	.05	.02	.01
☐	739	Dave Rozema	.05	.02	.01
☐	740	Lance Parrish	.10	.05	.01
☐	741	Pete Rose MG	.25	.11	.03
		(Checklist back)			
☐	742	Frank Viola	.10	.05	.01
☐	743	Pat Sheridan	.05	.02	.01
☐	744	Lary Sorensen	.05	.02	.01
☐	745	Willie Upshaw	.05	.02	.01
☐	746	Denny Gonzalez	.05	.02	.01
☐	747	Rick Cerone	.05	.02	.01
☐	748	Steve Henderson	.05	.02	.01
☐	749	Ed Jurak	.05	.02	.01
☐	750	Gorman Thomas	.05	.02	.01
☐	751	Howard Johnson	.10	.05	.01
☐	752	Mike Krukow	.05	.02	.01
☐	753	Dan Ford	.05	.02	.01
☐	754	Pat Clements	.05	.02	.01
☐	755	Harold Baines	.15	.07	.02
☐	756	Pirates Leaders	.10	.05	.01
		Rick Rhoden			
☐	757	Darrell Porter	.05	.02	.01
☐	758	Dave Anderson	.05	.02	.01
☐	759	Moose Haas	.05	.02	.01
☐	760	Andre Dawson	.20	.09	.03
☐	761	Don Slaught	.05	.02	.01
☐	762	Eric Show	.05	.02	.01
☐	763	Terry Puhl	.05	.02	.01
☐	764	Kevin Gross	.05	.02	.01
☐	765	Don Baylor	.15	.07	.02
☐	766	Rick Langford	.05	.02	.01
☐	767	Jody Davis	.05	.02	.01
☐	768	Vern Ruhle	.05	.02	.01
☐	769	Harold Reynolds	.10	.05	.01
☐	770	Vida Blue	.10	.05	.01
☐	771	John McNamara MG	.10	.05	.01
		(Checklist back)			
☐	772	Brian Downing	.10	.05	.01
☐	773	Greg Pryor	.05	.02	.01
☐	774	Terry Leach	.05	.02	.01
☐	775	Al Oliver	.10	.05	.01
☐	776	Gene Garber	.05	.02	.01
☐	777	Wayne Krenchicki	.05	.02	.01
☐	778	Jerry Hairston	.05	.02	.01
☐	779	Rick Reuschel	.10	.05	.01
☐	780	Robin Yount	.40	.18	.05
☐	781	Joe Nolan	.05	.02	.01
☐	782	Ken Landreaux	.05	.02	.01
☐	783	Ricky Horton	.05	.02	.01
☐	784	Alan Bannister	.05	.02	.01
☐	785	Bob Stanley	.05	.02	.01
☐	786	Twins Leaders	.10	.05	.01
		Mickey Hatcher			
☐	787	Vance Law	.05	.02	.01
☐	788	Marty Castillo	.05	.02	.01
☐	789	Kurt Bevacqua	.05	.02	.01
☐	790	Phil Niekro	.15	.07	.02
☐	791	Checklist: 661-792	.10	.05	.01
☐	792	Charles Hudson	.10	.05	.01

1986 Topps Traded

This 132-card Traded or extended set was distributed by Topps to dealers in a special red and white box as a complete set. The card fronts are identical in style to the Topps regular issue and are also 2 1/2" by

3 1/2". The backs are printed in red and black on white card stock. Cards are numbered (with a T suffix) alphabetically according to the name of the player. The key (extended) Rookie Cards in this set are Barry Bonds, Bobby Bonilla, Jose Canseco, Will Clark, Andres Galarraga, Bo Jackson, Wally Joyner, John Kruk, Kevin Mitchell, and Robby Thompson. Topps also produced a specially boxed "glossy" edition frequently referred to as the Topps Traded Tiffany set. There were supposedly only 5,000 sets of the Tiffany cards produced; they were marketed to hobby dealers. The checklist of cards is identical to that of the normal non-glossy cards. There are two primary distinguishing features of the Tiffany cards, white card stock reverses and high gloss obverses. These Tiffany cards are valued approximately from five to ten times the values listed below.

			MINT	NRMT	EXC
COMPLETE FACT.SET (132)			12.00	5.50	1.50
COMMON CARD (1T-132T)			.05	.02	.01
☐	1T	Andy Allanson	.05	.02	.01
☐	2T	Neil Allen	.05	.02	.01
☐	3T	Joaquin Andujar	.05	.02	.01
☐	4T	Paul Assenmacher	.05	.02	.01
☐	5T	Scott Bailes	.05	.02	.01
☐	6T	Don Baylor	.10	.05	.01
☐	7T	Steve Bedrosian	.05	.02	.01
☐	8T	Juan Beniquez	.05	.02	.01
☐	9T	Juan Berenguer	.05	.02	.01
☐	10T	Mike Bielecki	.05	.02	.01
☐	11T	Barry Bonds	3.00	1.35	.35
☐	12T	Bobby Bonilla	.75	.35	.09
☐	13T	Juan Bonilla	.05	.02	.01
☐	14T	Rich Bordi	.05	.02	.01
☐	15T	Steve Boros MG	.05	.02	.01
☐	16T	Rick Burleson	.05	.02	.01
☐	17T	Bill Campbell	.05	.02	.01
☐	18T	Tom Candiotti	.08	.04	.01
☐	19T	John Cangelosi	.08	.04	.01
☐	20T	Jose Canseco	2.00	.90	.25
☐	21T	Carmen Castillo	.05	.02	.01
☐	22T	Rick Cerone	.05	.02	.01
☐	23T	John Cerutti	.05	.02	.01
☐	24T	Will Clark	2.00	.90	.25
☐	25T	Mark Clear	.05	.02	.01
☐	26T	Darnell Coles	.05	.02	.01
☐	27T	Dave Collins	.05	.02	.01
☐	28T	Tim Conroy	.05	.02	.01
☐	29T	Joe Cowley	.05	.02	.01
☐	30T	Joel Davis	.05	.02	.01

☐ 31T Rob Deer	.08	.04	.01
☐ 32T John Denny	.05	.02	.01
☐ 33T Mike Easler	.05	.02	.01
☐ 34T Mark Eichhorn	.05	.02	.01
☐ 35T Steve Farr	.08	.04	.01
☐ 36T Scott Fletcher	.05	.02	.01
☐ 37T Terry Forster	.05	.02	.01
☐ 38T Terry Francona	.05	.02	.01
☐ 39T Jim Fregosi MG	.05	.02	.01
☐ 40T Andres Galarraga	1.00	.45	.12
☐ 41T Ken Griffey	.10	.05	.01
☐ 42T Bill Gullickson	.08	.04	.01
☐ 43T Jose Guzman	.10	.05	.01
☐ 44T Moose Haas	.05	.02	.01
☐ 45T Billy Hatcher	.08	.04	.01
☐ 46T Mike Heath	.05	.02	.01
☐ 47T Tom Hume	.05	.02	.01
☐ 48T Pete Incaviglia	.10	.05	.01
☐ 49T Dane Iorg	.05	.02	.01
☐ 50T Bo Jackson	.75	.35	.09
☐ 51T Wally Joyner	.40	.18	.05
☐ 52T Charlie Kerfeld	.05	.02	.01
☐ 53T Eric King	.05	.02	.01
☐ 54T Bob Kipper	.05	.02	.01
☐ 55T Wayne Krenchicki	.05	.02	.01
☐ 56T John Kruk	.40	.18	.05
☐ 57T Mike LaCoss	.05	.02	.01
☐ 58T Pete Ladd	.05	.02	.01
☐ 59T Mike Laga	.05	.02	.01
☐ 60T Hal Lanier MG	.05	.02	.01
☐ 61T Dave LaPoint	.05	.02	.01
☐ 62T Rudy Law	.05	.02	.01
☐ 63T Rick Leach	.05	.02	.01
☐ 64T Tim Leary	.05	.02	.01
☐ 65T Dennis Leonard	.05	.02	.01
☐ 66T Jim Leyland MG	.05	.02	.01
☐ 67T Steve Lyons	.05	.02	.01
☐ 68T Mickey Mahler	.05	.02	.01
☐ 69T Candy Maldonado	.05	.02	.01
☐ 70T Roger Mason	.05	.02	.01
☐ 71T Bob McClure	.05	.02	.01
☐ 72T Andy McGaffigan	.05	.02	.01
☐ 73T Gene Michael MG	.05	.02	.01
☐ 74T Kevin Mitchell	.25	.11	.03
☐ 75T Omar Moreno	.05	.02	.01
☐ 76T Jerry Mumphrey	.05	.02	.01
☐ 77T Phil Niekro	.10	.05	.01
☐ 78T Randy Niemann	.05	.02	.01
☐ 79T Juan Nieves	.05	.02	.01
☐ 80T Otis Nixon	.40	.18	.05
☐ 81T Bob Ojeda	.08	.04	.01
☐ 82T Jose Oquendo	.05	.02	.01
☐ 83T Tom Paciorek	.08	.04	.01
☐ 84T David Palmer	.05	.02	.01
☐ 85T Frank Pastore	.05	.02	.01
☐ 86T Lou Piniella MG	.08	.04	.01
☐ 87T Dan Plesac	.05	.02	.01
☐ 88T Darrell Porter	.05	.02	.01
☐ 89T Rey Quinones	.05	.02	.01
☐ 90T Gary Redus	.05	.02	.01
☐ 91T Bip Roberts	.30	.14	.04
☐ 92T Billy Joe Robidoux	.05	.02	.01
☐ 93T Jeff D. Robinson	.05	.02	.01
☐ 94T Gary Roenicke	.05	.02	.01
☐ 95T Ed Romero	.05	.02	.01
☐ 96T Argenis Salazar	.05	.02	.01
☐ 97T Joe Sambito	.05	.02	.01
☐ 98T Billy Sample	.05	.02	.01
☐ 99T Dave Schmidt	.05	.02	.01
☐ 100T Ken Schrom	.05	.02	.01
☐ 101T Tom Seaver	.20	.09	.03

☐ 102T Ted Simmons	.08	.04	.01
☐ 103T Sammy Stewart	.05	.02	.01
☐ 104T Kurt Stillwell	.05	.02	.01
☐ 105T Franklin Stubbs	.05	.02	.01
☐ 106T Dale Sveum	.05	.02	.01
☐ 107T Chuck Tanner MG	.08	.04	.01
☐ 108T Danny Tartabull	.10	.05	.01
☐ 109T Tim Teufel	.05	.02	.01
☐ 110T Bob Tewksbury	.08	.04	.01
☐ 111T Andres Thomas	.05	.02	.01
☐ 112T Milt Thompson	.05	.02	.01
☐ 113T Robby Thompson	.10	.05	.01
☐ 114T Jay Tibbs	.05	.02	.01
☐ 115T Wayne Tolleson	.05	.02	.01
☐ 116T Alex Trevino	.05	.02	.01
☐ 117T Manny Trillo	.05	.02	.01
☐ 118T Ed VandeBerg	.05	.02	.01
☐ 119T Ozzie Virgil	.05	.02	.01
☐ 120T Bob Walk	.05	.02	.01
☐ 121T Gene Walter	.05	.02	.01
☐ 122T Claudell Washington	.05	.02	.01
☐ 123T Bill Wegman	.05	.02	.01
☐ 124T Dick Williams MG	.08	.04	.01
☐ 125T Mitch Williams	.08	.04	.01
☐ 126T Bobby Witt	.08	.04	.01
☐ 127T Todd Worrell	.10	.05	.01
☐ 128T George Wright	.05	.02	.01
☐ 129T Ricky Wright	.05	.02	.01
☐ 130T Steve Yeager	.05	.02	.01
☐ 131T Paul Zuvella	.05	.02	.01
☐ 132T Checklist 1T-132T	.05	.02	.01

1987 Topps

This 792-card set is reminiscent of the 1962 Topps baseball cards with their simulated wood grain borders. The backs are printed in yellow and blue on gray card stock. The manager cards contain a checklist of the respective team's players on the back. Subsets in the set include Record Breakers (1-7), Turn Back the Clock (311-315), and All-Star selections (595-616). The Team Leader cards typically show players conferring on the mound inside a white cloud. The wax pack wrapper gives details of "Spring Fever Baseball" where a lucky collector can win a trip for four to Spring Training. The key Rookie Cards in this set are Barry Bonds, Bobby Bonilla, Will Clark, Doug Drabek, Mike Greenwell, Bo Jackson, Wally Joyner, John Kruk, Barry Larkin, Dave Magadan, Kevin Mitchell, Rafael

Palmiero, Ruben Sierra, Duane Ward, and Devon White. Topps also produced a specially boxed "glossy" edition, frequently referred to as the Topps Tiffany set. This year Topps did not disclose the number of sets they produced or sold. It is apparent from the availability that there were many more sets produced this year compared to the 1984-86 Tiffany sets, perhaps 30,000 sets, more than three times as many. The checklist of cards (792 regular and 132 Traded) is identical to that of the normal non-glossy cards. There are two primary distinguishing features of the Tiffany cards, white card stock reverses and high gloss obverses. These Tiffany cards are valued approximately from three to five times the values listed below.

	MINT	NRMT	EXC
COMPLETE SET (792)	15.00	6.75	1.85
COMPLETE FACT.SET (792)	15.00	6.75	1.85
COMMON CARD (1-792)	.05	.02	.01
☐ 1 Roger Clemens RB	.20	.09	.03
Most strikeouts, nine inning game			
☐ 2 Jim Deshaies RB	.05	.02	.01
Most cons. K's, start of game			
☐ 3 Dwight Evans RB	.10	.05	.01
Earliest home run, season			
☐ 4 Davey Lopes RB	.05	.02	.01
Most steals, season, 40-year-old			
☐ 5 Dave Righetti RB	.05	.02	.01
Most saves, season			
☐ 6 Ruben Sierra RB	.15	.07	.02
Youngest player to switch hit homers in game			
☐ 7 Todd Worrell RB	.10	.05	.01
Most saves, season, rookie			
☐ 8 Terry Pendleton	.15	.07	.02
☐ 9 Jay Tibbs	.05	.02	.01
☐ 10 Cecil Cooper	.10	.05	.01
☐ 11 Indians Team	.05	.02	.01
(Mound conference)			
☐ 12 Jeff Sellers	.05	.02	.01
☐ 13 Nick Esasky	.05	.02	.01
☐ 14 Dave Stewart	.15	.07	.02
☐ 15 Claudell Washington	.05	.02	.01
☐ 16 Pat Clements	.05	.02	.01
☐ 17 Pete O'Brien	.05	.02	.01
☐ 18 Dick Howser MG	.10	.05	.01
(Checklist back)			
☐ 19 Matt Young	.05	.02	.01
☐ 20 Gary Carter	.15	.07	.02
☐ 21 Mark Davis	.05	.02	.01
☐ 22 Doug DeCinces	.05	.02	.01
☐ 23 Lee Smith	.15	.07	.02
☐ 24 Tony Walker	.05	.02	.01
☐ 25 Bert Blyleven	.15	.07	.02
☐ 26 Greg Brock	.05	.02	.01
☐ 27 Joe Cowley	.05	.02	.01
☐ 28 Rick Dempsey	.05	.02	.01
☐ 29 Jimmy Key	.10	.05	.01
☐ 30 Tim Raines	.15	.07	.02
☐ 31 Braves Team	.05	.02	.01

(Glenn Hubbard and Rafael Ramirez)			
☐ 32 Tim Leary	.05	.02	.01
☐ 33 Andy Van Slyke	.10	.05	.01
☐ 34 Jose Rijo	.15	.07	.02
☐ 35 Sid Bream	.05	.02	.01
☐ 36 Eric King	.05	.02	.01
☐ 37 Marvell Wynne	.05	.02	.01
☐ 38 Dennis Leonard	.05	.02	.01
☐ 39 Marty Barrett	.05	.02	.01
☐ 40 Dave Righetti	.10	.05	.01
☐ 41 Bo Diaz	.05	.02	.01
☐ 42 Gary Redus	.05	.02	.01
☐ 43 Gene Michael MG	.10	.05	.01
(Checklist back)			
☐ 44 Greg Harris	.05	.02	.01
☐ 45 Jim Presley	.05	.02	.01
☐ 46 Dan Gladden	.05	.02	.01
☐ 47 Dennis Powell	.05	.02	.01
☐ 48 Wally Backman	.05	.02	.01
☐ 49 Terry Harper	.05	.02	.01
☐ 50 Dave Smith	.05	.02	.01
☐ 51 Mel Hall	.05	.02	.01
☐ 52 Keith Atherton	.05	.02	.01
☐ 53 Ruppert Jones	.05	.02	.01
☐ 54 Bill Dawley	.05	.02	.01
☐ 55 Tim Wallach	.10	.05	.01
☐ 56 Brewers Team	.05	.02	.01
(Mound conference)			
☐ 57 Scott Nielsen	.05	.02	.01
☐ 58 Thad Bosley	.05	.02	.01
☐ 59 Ken Dayley	.05	.02	.01
☐ 60 Tony Pena	.05	.02	.01
☐ 61 Bobby Thigpen	.10	.05	.01
☐ 62 Bobby Meacham	.05	.02	.01
☐ 63 Fred Toliver	.05	.02	.01
☐ 64 Harry Spilman	.05	.02	.01
☐ 65 Tom Browning	.05	.02	.01
☐ 66 Marc Sullivan	.05	.02	.01
☐ 67 Bill Swift	.10	.05	.01
☐ 68 Tony LaRussa MG	.10	.05	.01
(Checklist back)			
☐ 69 Lonnie Smith	.05	.02	.01
☐ 70 Charlie Hough	.10	.05	.01
☐ 71 Mike Aldrete	.10	.05	.01
☐ 72 Walt Terrell	.05	.02	.01
☐ 73 Dave Anderson	.05	.02	.01
☐ 74 Dan Pasqua	.05	.02	.01
☐ 75 Ron Darling	.10	.05	.01
☐ 76 Rafael Ramirez	.05	.02	.01
☐ 77 Bryan Oelkers	.05	.02	.01
☐ 78 Tom Foley	.05	.02	.01
☐ 79 Juan Nieves	.05	.02	.01
☐ 80 Wally Joyner	.20	.09	.03
☐ 81 Padres Team	.05	.02	.01
(Andy Hawkins and Terry Kennedy)			
☐ 82 Rob Murphy	.05	.02	.01
☐ 83 Mike Davis	.05	.02	.01
☐ 84 Steve Lake	.05	.02	.01
☐ 85 Kevin Bass	.05	.02	.01
☐ 86 Nate Snell	.05	.02	.01
☐ 87 Mark Salas	.05	.02	.01
☐ 88 Ed Wojna	.05	.02	.01
☐ 89 Ozzie Guillen	.15	.07	.02
☐ 90 Dave Stieb	.10	.05	.01
☐ 91 Harold Reynolds	.05	.02	.01
☐ 92A Urbano Lugo	.05	.02	.01
ERR (no trademark)			
☐ 92B Urbano Lugo COR	.05	.02	.01
☐ 93 Jim Leyland MG	.10	.05	.01

(Checklist back)

☐ 94	Calvin Schiraldi	.05	.02	.01
☐ 95	Oddibe McDowell	.05	.02	.01
☐ 96	Frank Williams	.05	.02	.01
☐ 97	Glenn Wilson	.05	.02	.01
☐ 98	Bill Scherrer	.05	.02	.01
☐ 99	Darryl Motley	.05	.02	.01

(Now with Braves on card front)

☐ 100	Steve Garvey	.15	.07	.02
☐ 101	Carl Willis	.05	.02	.01
☐ 102	Paul Zuvella	.05	.02	.01
☐ 103	Rick Aguilera	.10	.05	.01
☐ 104	Billy Sample	.05	.02	.01
☐ 105	Floyd Youmans	.05	.02	.01
☐ 106	Blue Jays Team	.05	.02	.01

(George Bell and Jesse Barfield)

☐ 107	John Butcher	.05	.02	.01
☐ 108	Jim Gantner UER	.05	.02	.01

(Brewers logo reversed)

☐ 109	R.J. Reynolds	.05	.02	.01
☐ 110	John Tudor	.05	.02	.01
☐ 111	Alfredo Griffin	.05	.02	.01
☐ 112	Alan Ashby	.05	.02	.01
☐ 113	Neil Allen	.05	.02	.01
☐ 114	Billy Beane	.05	.02	.01
☐ 115	Donnie Moore	.05	.02	.01
☐ 116	Bill Russell	.10	.05	.01
☐ 117	Jim Beattie	.05	.02	.01
☐ 118	Bobby Valentine MG	.10	.05	.01

(Checklist back)

☐ 119	Ron Robinson	.05	.02	.01
☐ 120	Eddie Murray	.25	.11	.03
☐ 121	Kevin Romine	.05	.02	.01
☐ 122	Jim Clancy	.05	.02	.01
☐ 123	John Kruk	.20	.09	.03
☐ 124	Ray Fontenot	.05	.02	.01
☐ 125	Bob Brenly	.05	.02	.01
☐ 126	Mike Loynd	.05	.02	.01
☐ 127	Vance Law	.05	.02	.01
☐ 128	Checklist 1-132	.10	.05	.01
☐ 129	Rick Cerone	.05	.02	.01
☐ 130	Dwight Gooden	.10	.05	.01
☐ 131	Pirates Team	.05	.02	.01

(Sid Bream and Tony Pena)

☐ 132	Paul Assenmacher	.05	.02	.01
☐ 133	Jose Oquendo	.05	.02	.01
☐ 134	Rich Yett	.05	.02	.01
☐ 135	Mike Easler	.05	.02	.01
☐ 136	Ron Romanick	.05	.02	.01
☐ 137	Jerry Willard	.05	.02	.01
☐ 138	Roy Lee Jackson	.05	.02	.01
☐ 139	Devon White	.50	.23	.06
☐ 140	Bret Saberhagen	.15	.07	.02
☐ 141	Herm Winningham	.05	.02	.01
☐ 142	Rick Sutcliffe	.10	.05	.01
☐ 143	Steve Boros MG	.10	.05	.01

(Checklist back)

☐ 144	Mike Scioscia	.05	.02	.01
☐ 145	Charlie Kerfeld	.05	.02	.01
☐ 146	Tracy Jones	.10	.05	.01
☐ 147	Randy Niemann	.05	.02	.01
☐ 148	Dave Collins	.05	.02	.01
☐ 149	Ray Searage	.05	.02	.01
☐ 150	Wade Boggs	.15	.07	.02
☐ 151	Mike LaCoss	.05	.02	.01
☐ 152	Toby Harrah	.05	.02	.01
☐ 153	Duane Ward	.10	.05	.01

☐ 154	Tom O'Malley	.05	.02	.01
☐ 155	Eddie Whitson	.05	.02	.01
☐ 156	Mariners Team	.05	.02	.01

(Mound conference)

☐ 157	Danny Darwin	.05	.02	.01
☐ 158	Tim Teufel	.05	.02	.01
☐ 159	Ed Olwine	.05	.02	.01
☐ 160	Julio Franco	.10	.05	.01
☐ 161	Steve Ontiveros	.05	.02	.01
☐ 162	Mike LaValliere	.05	.02	.01
☐ 163	Kevin Gross	.05	.02	.01
☐ 164	Sammy Khalifa	.05	.02	.01
☐ 165	Jeff Reardon	.15	.07	.02
☐ 166	Bob Boone	.10	.05	.01
☐ 167	Jim Deshaies	.05	.02	.01
☐ 168	Lou Piniella MG	.10	.05	.01

(Checklist back)

☐ 169	Ron Washington	.05	.02	.01
☐ 170	Bo Jackson	.50	.23	.06
☐ 171	Chuck Cary	.05	.02	.01
☐ 172	Ron Oester	.05	.02	.01
☐ 173	Alex Trevino	.05	.02	.01
☐ 174	Henry Cotto	.05	.02	.01
☐ 175	Bob Stanley	.05	.02	.01
☐ 176	Steve Buechele	.05	.02	.01
☐ 177	Keith Moreland	.05	.02	.01
☐ 178	Cecil Fielder	.40	.18	.05
☐ 179	Bill Wegman	.05	.02	.01
☐ 180	Chris Brown	.05	.02	.01
☐ 181	Cardinals Team	.05	.02	.01

(Mound conference)

☐ 182	Lee Lacy	.05	.02	.01
☐ 183	Andy Hawkins	.05	.02	.01
☐ 184	Bobby Bonilla	.40	.18	.05
☐ 185	Roger McDowell	.05	.02	.01
☐ 186	Bruce Benedict	.05	.02	.01
☐ 187	Mark Huismann	.05	.02	.01
☐ 188	Tony Phillips	.15	.07	.02
☐ 189	Joe Hesketh	.05	.02	.01
☐ 190	Jim Sundberg	.05	.02	.01
☐ 191	Charles Hudson	.05	.02	.01
☐ 192	Cory Snyder	.05	.02	.01
☐ 193	Roger Craig MG	.10	.05	.01

(Checklist back)

☐ 194	Kirk McCaskill	.05	.02	.01
☐ 195	Mike Pagliarulo	.05	.02	.01
☐ 196	Randy O'Neal UER	.05	.02	.01

(Wrong ML career W-L totals)

☐ 197	Mark Bailey	.05	.02	.01
☐ 198	Lee Mazzilli	.05	.02	.01
☐ 199	Mariano Duncan	.05	.02	.01
☐ 200	Pete Rose	.30	.14	.04
☐ 201	John Cangelosi	.05	.02	.01
☐ 202	Ricky Wright	.05	.02	.01
☐ 203	Mike Kingery	.15	.07	.02
☐ 204	Sammy Stewart	.05	.02	.01
☐ 205	Graig Nettles	.10	.05	.01
☐ 206	Twins Team	.05	.02	.01

(Frank Viola and Tim Laudner)

☐ 207	George Frazier	.05	.02	.01
☐ 208	John Shelby	.05	.02	.01
☐ 209	Rick Schu	.05	.02	.01
☐ 210	Lloyd Moseby	.05	.02	.01
☐ 211	John Morris	.05	.02	.01
☐ 212	Mike Fitzgerald	.05	.02	.01
☐ 213	Randy Myers	.20	.09	.03
☐ 214	Omar Moreno	.05	.02	.01
☐ 215	Mark Langston	.15	.07	.02
☐ 216	B.J. Surhoff	.15	.07	.02

☐ 217 Chris Codiroli	.05	.02	.01
☐ 218 Sparky Anderson MG (Checklist back)	.10	.05	.01
☐ 219 Cecilio Guante	.05	.02	.01
☐ 220 Joe Carter	.30	.14	.04
☐ 221 Vern Ruhle	.05	.02	.01
☐ 222 Denny Walling	.05	.02	.01
☐ 223 Charlie Leibrandt	.05	.02	.01
☐ 224 Wayne Tolleson	.05	.02	.01
☐ 225 Mike Smithson	.05	.02	.01
☐ 226 Max Venable	.05	.02	.01
☐ 227 Jamie Moyer	.10	.05	.01
☐ 228 Curt Wilkerson	.05	.02	.01
☐ 229 Mike Birkbeck	.05	.02	.01
☐ 230 Don Baylor	.15	.07	.02
☐ 231 Giants Team (Bob Brenly and Jim Gott)	.05	.02	.01
☐ 232 Reggie Williams	.05	.02	.01
☐ 233 Russ Morman	.05	.02	.01
☐ 234 Pat Sheridan	.05	.02	.01
☐ 235 Alvin Davis	.05	.02	.01
☐ 236 Tommy John	.15	.07	.02
☐ 237 Jim Morrison	.05	.02	.01
☐ 238 Bill Krueger	.05	.02	.01
☐ 239 Juan Espino	.05	.02	.01
☐ 240 Steve Balboni	.05	.02	.01
☐ 241 Danny Heep	.05	.02	.01
☐ 242 Rick Mahler	.05	.02	.01
☐ 243 Whitey Herzog MG (Checklist back)	.10	.05	.01
☐ 244 Dickie Noles	.05	.02	.01
☐ 245 Willie Upshaw	.05	.02	.01
☐ 246 Jim Dwyer	.05	.02	.01
☐ 247 Jeff Reed	.05	.02	.01
☐ 248 Gene Walter	.05	.02	.01
☐ 249 Jim Pankovits	.05	.02	.01
☐ 250 Teddy Higuera	.05	.02	.01
☐ 251 Rob Wilfong	.05	.02	.01
☐ 252 Dennis Martinez	.10	.05	.01
☐ 253 Eddie Milner	.05	.02	.01
☐ 254 Bob Tewksbury	.10	.05	.01
☐ 255 Juan Samuel	.05	.02	.01
☐ 256 Royals Team (George Brett and Frank White)	.15	.07	.02
☐ 257 Bob Forsch	.05	.02	.01
☐ 258 Steve Yeager	.05	.02	.01
☐ 259 Mike Greenwell	.20	.09	.03
☐ 260 Vida Blue	.10	.05	.01
☐ 261 Ruben Sierra	.60	.25	.07
☐ 262 Jim Winn	.05	.02	.01
☐ 263 Stan Javier	.05	.02	.01
☐ 264 Checklist 133-264	.10	.02	.01
☐ 265 Darrell Evans	.10	.05	.01
☐ 266 Jeff Hamilton	.05	.02	.01
☐ 267 Howard Johnson	.10	.05	.01
☐ 268 Pat Corrales MG (Checklist back)	.10	.05	.01
☐ 269 Cliff Speck	.05	.02	.01
☐ 270 Jody Davis	.05	.02	.01
☐ 271 Mike G. Brown	.05	.02	.01
☐ 272 Andres Galarraga	.30	.14	.04
☐ 273 Gene Nelson	.05	.02	.01
☐ 274 Jeff Hearron UER (Duplicate 1986 stat line on back)	.05	.02	.01
☐ 275 LaMarr Hoyt	.05	.02	.01
☐ 276 Jackie Gutierrez	.05	.02	.01
☐ 277 Juan Agosto	.05	.02	.01
☐ 278 Gary Pettis	.05	.02	.01
☐ 279 Dan Plesac	.05	.02	.01
☐ 280 Jeff Leonard	.05	.02	.01
☐ 281 Reds Team (Pete Rose, Bo Diaz, and Bill Gullickson)	.15	.07	.02
☐ 282 Jeff Calhoun	.05	.02	.01
☐ 283 Doug Drabek	.20	.09	.03
☐ 284 John Moses	.05	.02	.01
☐ 285 Dennis Boyd	.05	.02	.01
☐ 286 Mike Woodard	.05	.02	.01
☐ 287 Dave Von Ohlen	.05	.02	.01
☐ 288 Tito Landrum	.05	.02	.01
☐ 289 Bob Kipper	.05	.02	.01
☐ 290 Leon Durham	.05	.02	.01
☐ 291 Mitch Williams	.10	.05	.01
☐ 292 Franklin Stubbs	.05	.02	.01
☐ 293 Bob Rodgers MG (Checklist back, inconsistent design on card back)	.10	.05	.01
☐ 294 Steve Jeltz	.05	.02	.01
☐ 295 Len Dykstra	.15	.07	.02
☐ 296 Andres Thomas	.05	.02	.01
☐ 297 Don Schulze	.05	.02	.01
☐ 298 Larry Herndon	.05	.02	.01
☐ 299 Joel Davis	.05	.02	.01
☐ 300 Reggie Jackson	.20	.09	.03
☐ 301 Luis Aquino UER (No trademark, never corrected)	.05	.02	.01
☐ 302 Bill Schroeder	.05	.02	.01
☐ 303 Juan Berenguer	.05	.02	.01
☐ 304 Phil Garner	.10	.05	.01
☐ 305 John Franco	.10	.05	.01
☐ 306 Red Sox Team (Tom Seaver, John McNamara MG, and Rich Gedman)	.15	.07	.02
☐ 307 Lee Guetterman	.05	.02	.01
☐ 308 Don Slaught	.05	.02	.01
☐ 309 Mike Young	.05	.02	.01
☐ 310 Frank Viola	.10	.05	.01
☐ 311 Rickey Henderson TBC '82	.10	.05	.01
☐ 312 Reggie Jackson TBC '77	.10	.05	.01
☐ 313 Roberto Clemente TBC '72	.20	.09	.03
☐ 314 Carl Yastrzemski UER TBC '67 (Sic, 112 RBI's on back)	.10	.05	.01
☐ 315 Maury Wills TBC '62	.05	.02	.01
☐ 316 Brian Fisher	.05	.02	.01
☐ 317 Clint Hurdle	.05	.02	.01
☐ 318 Jim Fregosi MG (Checklist back)	.10	.05	.01
☐ 319 Greg Swindell	.20	.09	.03
☐ 320 Barry Bonds	1.25	.55	.16
☐ 321 Mike Laga	.05	.02	.01
☐ 322 Chris Bando	.05	.02	.01
☐ 323 Al Newman	.05	.02	.01
☐ 324 David Palmer	.05	.02	.01
☐ 325 Garry Templeton	.05	.02	.01
☐ 326 Mark Gubicza	.05	.02	.01
☐ 327 Dale Sveum	.05	.02	.01
☐ 328 Bob Welch	.10	.05	.01
☐ 329 Ron Roenicke	.05	.02	.01
☐ 330 Mike Scott	.05	.02	.01
☐ 331 Mets Team (Gary Carter and Darryl Strawberry)	.10	.05	.01

☐ 332 Joe Price	.05	.02	.01
☐ 333 Ken Phelps	.05	.02	.01
☐ 334 Ed Correa	.05	.02	.01
☐ 335 Candy Maldonado	.05	.02	.01
☐ 336 Allan Anderson	.05	.02	.01
☐ 337 Darrell Miller	.05	.02	.01
☐ 338 Tim Conroy	.05	.02	.01
☐ 339 Donnie Hill	.05	.02	.01
☐ 340 Roger Clemens	.40	.18	.05
☐ 341 Mike C. Brown	.05	.02	.01
☐ 342 Bob James	.05	.02	.01
☐ 343 Hal Lanier MG	.10	.05	.01
(Checklist back)			
☐ 344A Joe Niekro	.10	.05	.01
(Copyright inside			
righthand border)			
☐ 344B Joe Niekro	.10	.05	.01
(Copyright outside			
righthand border)			
☐ 345 Andre Dawson	.15	.07	.02
☐ 346 Shawon Dunston	.10	.05	.01
☐ 347 Mickey Brantley	.05	.02	.01
☐ 348 Carmelo Martinez	.05	.02	.01
☐ 349 Storm Davis	.05	.02	.01
☐ 350 Keith Hernandez	.10	.05	.01
☐ 351 Gene Garber	.05	.02	.01
☐ 352 Mike Felder	.05	.02	.01
☐ 353 Ernie Camacho	.05	.02	.01
☐ 354 Jamie Quirk	.05	.02	.01
☐ 355 Don Carman	.05	.02	.01
☐ 356 White Sox Team	.05	.02	.01
(Mound conference)			
☐ 357 Steve Fireovid	.05	.02	.01
☐ 358 Sal Butera	.05	.02	.01
☐ 359 Doug Corbett	.05	.02	.01
☐ 360 Pedro Guerrero	.10	.05	.01
☐ 361 Mark Thurmond	.05	.02	.01
☐ 362 Luis Quinones	.05	.02	.01
☐ 363 Jose Guzman	.10	.05	.01
☐ 364 Randy Bush	.05	.02	.01
☐ 365 Rick Rhoden	.05	.02	.01
☐ 366 Mark McGwire	.75	.35	.09
☐ 367 Jeff Lahti	.05	.02	.01
☐ 368 John McNamara MG	.10	.05	.01
(Checklist back)			
☐ 369 Brian Dayett	.05	.02	.01
☐ 370 Fred Lynn	.10	.05	.01
☐ 371 Mark Eichhorn	.05	.02	.01
☐ 372 Jerry Mumphrey	.05	.02	.01
☐ 373 Jeff Dedmon	.05	.02	.01
☐ 374 Glenn Hoffman	.05	.02	.01
☐ 375 Ron Guidry	.10	.05	.01
☐ 376 Scott Bradley	.05	.02	.01
☐ 377 John Henry Johnson	.05	.02	.01
☐ 378 Rafael Santana	.05	.02	.01
☐ 379 John Russell	.05	.02	.01
☐ 380 Rich Gossage	.15	.07	.02
☐ 381 Expos Team	.05	.02	.01
(Mound conference)			
☐ 382 Rudy Law	.05	.02	.01
☐ 383 Ron Davis	.05	.02	.01
☐ 384 Johnny Grubb	.05	.02	.01
☐ 385 Orel Hershiser	.15	.07	.02
☐ 386 Dickie Thon	.05	.02	.01
☐ 387 T.R. Bryden	.05	.02	.01
☐ 388 Geno Petralli	.05	.02	.01
☐ 389 Jeff D. Robinson	.05	.02	.01
☐ 390 Gary Matthews	.05	.02	.01
☐ 391 Jay Howell	.05	.02	.01
☐ 392 Checklist 265-396	.10	.05	.01
☐ 393 Pete Rose MG	.25	.11	.03

(Checklist back)			
☐ 394 Mike Bielecki	.05	.02	.01
☐ 395 Damaso Garcia	.05	.02	.01
☐ 396 Tim Lollar	.05	.02	.01
☐ 397 Greg Walker	.05	.02	.01
☐ 398 Brad Havens	.05	.02	.01
☐ 399 Curt Ford	.05	.02	.01
☐ 400 George Brett	.50	.23	.06
☐ 401 Billy Joe Robidoux	.05	.02	.01
☐ 402 Mike Trujillo	.05	.02	.01
☐ 403 Jerry Royster	.05	.02	.01
☐ 404 Doug Sisk	.05	.02	.01
☐ 405 Brook Jacoby	.05	.02	.01
☐ 406 Yankees Team	.15	.07	.02
(Rickey Henderson and			
Don Mattingly)			
☐ 407 Jim Acker	.05	.02	.01
☐ 408 John Mizerock	.05	.02	.01
☐ 409 Milt Thompson	.05	.02	.01
☐ 410 Fernando Valenzuela	.05	.02	.01
☐ 411 Darnell Coles	.05	.02	.01
☐ 412 Eric Davis	.15	.07	.02
☐ 413 Moose Haas	.05	.02	.01
☐ 414 Joe Orsulak	.05	.02	.01
☐ 415 Bobby Witt	.10	.05	.01
☐ 416 Tom Nieto	.05	.02	.01
☐ 417 Pat Perry	.05	.02	.01
☐ 418 Dick Williams MG	.10	.05	.01
(Checklist back)			
☐ 419 Mark Portugal	.20	.09	.03
☐ 420 Will Clark	1.00	.45	.12
☐ 421 Jose DeLeon	.05	.02	.01
☐ 422 Jack Howell	.05	.02	.01
☐ 423 Jaime Cocanower	.05	.02	.01
☐ 424 Chris Speier	.05	.02	.01
☐ 425 Tom Seaver	.20	.09	.03
☐ 426 Floyd Rayford	.05	.02	.01
☐ 427 Edwin Nunez	.05	.02	.01
☐ 428 Bruce Bochy	.05	.02	.01
☐ 429 Tim Pyznarski	.05	.02	.01
☐ 430 Mike Schmidt	.20	.09	.03
☐ 431 Dodgers Team	.05	.02	.01
(Mound conference)			
☐ 432 Jim Slaton	.05	.02	.01
☐ 433 Ed Hearn	.05	.02	.01
☐ 434 Mike Fischlin	.05	.02	.01
☐ 435 Bruce Sutter	.10	.05	.01
☐ 436 Andy Allanson	.05	.02	.01
☐ 437 Ted Power	.05	.02	.01
☐ 438 Kelly Downs	.05	.02	.01
☐ 439 Karl Best	.05	.02	.01
☐ 440 Willie McGee	.10	.05	.01
☐ 441 Dave Leiper	.05	.02	.01
☐ 442 Mitch Webster	.05	.02	.01
☐ 443 John Felske MG	.10	.05	.01
(Checklist back)			
☐ 444 Jeff Russell	.05	.02	.01
☐ 445 Dave Lopes	.10	.05	.01
☐ 446 Chuck Finley	.20	.09	.03
☐ 447 Bill Almon	.05	.02	.01
☐ 448 Chris Bosio	.15	.07	.02
☐ 449 Pat Dodson	.05	.02	.01
☐ 450 Kirby Puckett	.75	.35	.09
☐ 451 Joe Sambito	.05	.02	.01
☐ 452 Dave Henderson	.05	.02	.01
☐ 453 Scott Terry	.05	.02	.01
☐ 454 Luis Salazar	.05	.02	.01
☐ 455 Mike Boddicker	.05	.02	.01
☐ 456 A's Team	.05	.02	.01
(Mound conference)			
☐ 457 Len Matuszek	.05	.02	.01

☐ 458	Kelly Gruber	.05	.02	.01
☐ 459	Dennis Eckersley	.15	.07	.02
☐ 460	Darryl Strawberry	.15	.07	.02
☐ 461	Craig McMurtry	.05	.02	.01
☐ 462	Scott Fletcher	.05	.02	.01
☐ 463	Tom Candiotti	.10	.05	.01
☐ 464	Butch Wynegar	.05	.02	.01
☐ 465	Todd Worrell	.10	.05	.01
☐ 466	Kal Daniels	.05	.02	.01
☐ 467	Randy St.Claire	.05	.02	.01
☐ 468	George Bamberger MG	.10	.05	.01
	(Checklist back)			
☐ 469	Mike Diaz	.05	.02	.01
☐ 470	Dave Dravecky	.10	.05	.01
☐ 471	Ronn Reynolds	.05	.02	.01
☐ 472	Bill Doran	.05	.02	.01
☐ 473	Steve Farr	.05	.02	.01
☐ 474	Jerry Narron	.05	.02	.01
☐ 475	Scott Garrelts	.05	.02	.01
☐ 476	Danny Tartabull	.10	.05	.01
☐ 477	Ken Howell	.05	.02	.01
☐ 478	Tim Laudner	.05	.02	.01
☐ 479	Bob Sebra	.05	.02	.01
☐ 480	Jim Rice	.15	.07	.02
☐ 481	Phillies Team	.05	.02	.01
	(Glenn Wilson,			
	Juan Samuel, and			
	Von Hayes)			
☐ 482	Daryl Boston	.05	.02	.01
☐ 483	Dwight Lowry	.05	.02	.01
☐ 484	Jim Traber	.05	.02	.01
☐ 485	Tony Fernandez	.10	.05	.01
☐ 486	Otis Nixon	.05	.02	.01
☐ 487	Dave Gumpert	.05	.02	.01
☐ 488	Ray Knight	.10	.05	.01
☐ 489	Bill Gullickson	.05	.02	.01
☐ 490	Dale Murphy	.15	.07	.02
☐ 491	Ron Karkovice	.10	.05	.01
☐ 492	Mike Heath	.05	.02	.01
☐ 493	Tom Lasorda MG	.10	.05	.01
	(Checklist back)			
☐ 494	Barry Jones	.05	.02	.01
☐ 495	Gorman Thomas	.05	.02	.01
☐ 496	Bruce Bochte	.05	.02	.01
☐ 497	Dale Mohorcic	.05	.02	.01
☐ 498	Bob Kearney	.05	.02	.01
☐ 499	Bruce Ruffin	.10	.05	.01
☐ 500	Don Mattingly	.50	.23	.06
☐ 501	Craig Lefferts	.05	.02	.01
☐ 502	Dick Schofield	.05	.02	.01
☐ 503	Larry Andersen	.05	.02	.01
☐ 504	Mickey Hatcher	.05	.02	.01
☐ 505	Bryn Smith	.05	.02	.01
☐ 506	Orioles Team	.05	.02	.01
	(Mound conference)			
☐ 507	Dave L. Stapleton	.05	.02	.01
☐ 508	Scott Bankhead	.05	.02	.01
☐ 509	Enos Cabell	.05	.02	.01
☐ 510	Tom Henke	.10	.05	.01
☐ 511	Steve Lyons	.05	.02	.01
☐ 512	Dave Magadan	.10	.05	.01
☐ 513	Carmen Castillo	.05	.02	.01
☐ 514	Orlando Mercado	.05	.02	.01
☐ 515	Willie Hernandez	.05	.02	.01
☐ 516	Ted Simmons	.10	.05	.01
☐ 517	Mario Soto	.05	.02	.01
☐ 518	Gene Mauch MG	.10	.05	.01
	(Checklist back)			
☐ 519	Curt Young	.05	.02	.01
☐ 520	Jack Clark	.10	.05	.01
☐ 521	Rick Reuschel	.05	.02	.01
☐ 522	Checklist 397-528	.10	.05	.01
☐ 523	Earnie Riles	.05	.02	.01
☐ 524	Bob Shirley	.05	.02	.01
☐ 525	Phil Bradley	.05	.02	.01
☐ 526	Roger Mason	.05	.02	.01
☐ 527	Jim Wohlford	.05	.02	.01
☐ 528	Ken Dixon	.05	.02	.01
☐ 529	Alvaro Espinoza	.05	.02	.01
☐ 530	Tony Gwynn	.50	.23	.06
☐ 531	Astros Team	.10	.05	.01
	(Yogi Berra conference)			
☐ 532	Jeff Stone	.05	.02	.01
☐ 533	Argenis Salazar	.05	.02	.01
☐ 534	Scott Sanderson	.05	.02	.01
☐ 535	Tony Armas	.05	.02	.01
☐ 536	Terry Mulholland	.10	.05	.01
☐ 537	Rance Mulliniks	.05	.02	.01
☐ 538	Tom Niedenfuer	.05	.02	.01
☐ 539	Reid Nichols	.05	.02	.01
☐ 540	Terry Kennedy	.05	.02	.01
☐ 541	Rafael Belliard	.05	.02	.01
☐ 542	Ricky Horton	.05	.02	.01
☐ 543	Dave Johnson MG	.10	.05	.01
	(Checklist back)			
☐ 544	Zane Smith	.05	.02	.01
☐ 545	Buddy Bell	.10	.05	.01
☐ 546	Mike Morgan	.05	.02	.01
☐ 547	Rob Deer	.05	.02	.01
☐ 548	Bill Mooneyham	.05	.02	.01
☐ 549	Bob Melvin	.05	.02	.01
☐ 550	Pete Incaviglia	.15	.07	.02
☐ 551	Frank Wills	.05	.02	.01
☐ 552	Larry Sheets	.05	.02	.01
☐ 553	Mike Maddux	.05	.02	.01
☐ 554	Buddy Biancalana	.05	.02	.01
☐ 555	Dennis Rasmussen	.05	.02	.01
☐ 556	Angels Team	.05	.02	.01
	(Rene Lachemann CO,			
	Mike Witt, and			
	Bob Boone)			
☐ 557	John Cerutti	.05	.02	.01
☐ 558	Greg Gagne	.10	.05	.01
☐ 559	Lance McCullers	.05	.02	.01
☐ 560	Glenn Davis	.05	.02	.01
☐ 561	Rey Quinones	.05	.02	.01
☐ 562	Bryan Clutterbuck	.05	.02	.01
☐ 563	John Stefero	.05	.02	.01
☐ 564	Larry McWilliams	.05	.02	.01
☐ 565	Dusty Baker	.15	.07	.02
☐ 566	Tim Hulett	.05	.02	.01
☐ 567	Greg Mathews	.05	.02	.01
☐ 568	Earl Weaver MG	.10	.05	.01
	(Checklist back)			
☐ 569	Wade Rowdon	.05	.02	.01
☐ 570	Sid Fernandez	.10	.05	.01
☐ 571	Ozzie Virgil	.05	.02	.01
☐ 572	Pete Ladd	.05	.02	.01
☐ 573	Hal McRae	.15	.07	.02
☐ 574	Manny Lee	.05	.02	.01
☐ 575	Pat Tabler	.05	.02	.01
☐ 576	Frank Pastore	.05	.02	.01
☐ 577	Dann Bilardello	.05	.02	.01
☐ 578	Billy Hatcher	.05	.02	.01
☐ 579	Rick Burleson	.05	.02	.01
☐ 580	Mike Krukow	.05	.02	.01
☐ 581	Cubs Team	.05	.02	.01
	(Ron Cey and			
	Steve Trout)			
☐ 582	Bruce Berenyi	.05	.02	.01
☐ 583	Junior Ortiz	.05	.02	.01
☐ 584	Ron Kittle	.05	.02	.01

☐ 585	Scott Bailes	.05	.02	.01
☐ 586	Ben Oglivie	.05	.02	.01
☐ 587	Eric Plunk	.05	.02	.01
☐ 588	Wallace Johnson	.05	.02	.01
☐ 589	Steve Crawford	.05	.02	.01
☐ 590	Vince Coleman	.10	.05	.01
☐ 591	Spike Owen	.05	.02	.01
☐ 592	Chris Welsh	.05	.02	.01
☐ 593	Chuck Tanner MG (Checklist back)	.10	.05	.01
☐ 594	Rick Anderson	.05	.02	.01
☐ 595	Keith Hernandez AS	.10	.05	.01
☐ 596	Steve Sax AS	.05	.02	.01
☐ 597	Mike Schmidt AS	.15	.07	.02
☐ 598	Ozzie Smith AS	.15	.07	.02
☐ 599	Tony Gwynn AS	.25	.11	.03
☐ 600	Dave Parker AS	.10	.05	.01
☐ 601	Darryl Strawberry AS	.10	.05	.01
☐ 602	Gary Carter AS	.10	.05	.01
☐ 603A	Dwight Gooden AS ERR (no trademark)	.10	.05	.01
☐ 603B	Dwight Gooden AS COR	.10	.05	.01
☐ 604	Fernando Valenzuela AS	.05	.02	.01
☐ 605	Todd Worrell AS	.05	.02	.01
☐ 606A	Don Mattingly AS ERR (no trademark)	.75	.35	.09
☐ 606B	Don Mattingly AS COR	.25	.11	.03
☐ 607	Tony Bernazard AS	.05	.02	.01
☐ 608	Wade Boggs AS	.15	.07	.02
☐ 609	Cal Ripken AS	.50	.23	.06
☐ 610	Jim Rice AS	.10	.05	.01
☐ 611	Kirby Puckett AS	.35	.16	.04
☐ 612	George Bell AS	.05	.02	.01
☐ 613	Lance Parrish AS UER (Pitcher heading on back)	.10	.05	.01
☐ 614	Roger Clemens AS	.20	.09	.03
☐ 615	Teddy Higuera AS	.05	.02	.01
☐ 616	Dave Righetti AS	.05	.02	.01
☐ 617	Al Nipper AS	.05	.02	.01
☐ 618	Tom Kelly MG (Checklist back)	.10	.05	.01
☐ 619	Jerry Reed	.05	.02	.01
☐ 620	Jose Canseco	1.00	.45	.12
☐ 621	Danny Cox	.05	.02	.01
☐ 622	Glenn Braggs	.05	.02	.01
☐ 623	Kurt Stillwell	.05	.02	.01
☐ 624	Tim Burke	.05	.02	.01
☐ 625	Mookie Wilson	.10	.05	.01
☐ 626	Joel Skinner	.05	.02	.01
☐ 627	Ken Oberkfell	.05	.02	.01
☐ 628	Bob Walk	.05	.02	.01
☐ 629	Larry Parrish	.05	.02	.01
☐ 630	John Candelaria	.05	.02	.01
☐ 631	Tigers Team (Mound conference)	.05	.02	.01
☐ 632	Rob Woodward	.05	.02	.01
☐ 633	Jose Uribe	.05	.02	.01
☐ 634	Rafael Palmeiro	1.00	.45	.12
☐ 635	Ken Schrom	.05	.02	.01
☐ 636	Darren Daulton	.15	.07	.02
☐ 637	Bip Roberts	.20	.09	.03
☐ 638	Rich Bordi	.05	.02	.01
☐ 639	Gerald Perry	.05	.02	.01
☐ 640	Mark Clear	.05	.02	.01
☐ 641	Domingo Ramos	.05	.02	.01
☐ 642	Al Pulido	.05	.02	.01
☐ 643	Ron Shepherd	.05	.02	.01
☐ 644	John Denny	.05	.02	.01
☐ 645	Dwight Evans	.10	.05	.01
☐ 646	Mike Mason	.05	.02	.01
☐ 647	Tom Lawless	.05	.02	.01
☐ 648	Barry Larkin	1.00	.45	.12
☐ 649	Mickey Tettleton	.10	.05	.01
☐ 650	Hubie Brooks	.05	.02	.01
☐ 651	Benny Distefano	.05	.02	.01
☐ 652	Terry Forster	.05	.02	.01
☐ 653	Kevin Mitchell	.15	.07	.02
☐ 654	Checklist 529-660	.10	.05	.01
☐ 655	Jesse Barfield	.05	.02	.01
☐ 656	Rangers Team (Bobby Valentine MG and Ricky Wright)	.05	.02	.01
☐ 657	Tom Waddell	.05	.02	.01
☐ 658	Robby Thompson	.15	.07	.02
☐ 659	Aurelio Lopez	.05	.02	.01
☐ 660	Bob Horner	.05	.02	.01
☐ 661	Lou Whitaker	.15	.07	.02
☐ 662	Frank DiPino	.05	.02	.01
☐ 663	Cliff Johnson	.05	.02	.01
☐ 664	Mike Marshall	.05	.02	.01
☐ 665	Rod Scurry	.05	.02	.01
☐ 666	Von Hayes	.05	.02	.01
☐ 667	Ron Hassey	.05	.02	.01
☐ 668	Juan Bonilla	.05	.02	.01
☐ 669	Bud Black	.05	.02	.01
☐ 670	Jose Cruz	.05	.02	.01
☐ 671A	Ray Soff ERR (No D* before copyright line)	.05	.02	.01
☐ 671B	Ray Soff COR (D* before copyright line)	.05	.02	.01
☐ 672	Chili Davis	.15	.07	.02
☐ 673	Don Sutton	.15	.07	.02
☐ 674	Bill Campbell	.05	.02	.01
☐ 675	Ed Romero	.05	.02	.01
☐ 676	Charlie Moore	.05	.02	.01
☐ 677	Bob Grich	.10	.05	.01
☐ 678	Carney Lansford	.10	.05	.01
☐ 679	Kent Hrbek	.15	.07	.02
☐ 680	Ryne Sandberg	.40	.18	.05
☐ 681	George Bell	.10	.05	.01
☐ 682	Jerry Reuss	.05	.02	.01
☐ 683	Gary Roenicke	.05	.02	.01
☐ 684	Kent Tekulve	.05	.02	.01
☐ 685	Jerry Hairston	.05	.02	.01
☐ 686	Doyle Alexander	.05	.02	.01
☐ 687	Alan Trammell	.15	.07	.02
☐ 688	Juan Beniquez	.05	.02	.01
☐ 689	Darrell Porter	.05	.02	.01
☐ 690	Dane Iorg	.05	.02	.01
☐ 691	Dave Parker	.15	.07	.02
☐ 692	Frank White	.10	.05	.01
☐ 693	Terry Puhl	.05	.02	.01
☐ 694	Phil Niekro	.15	.07	.02
☐ 695	Chico Walker	.05	.02	.01
☐ 696	Gary Lucas	.05	.02	.01
☐ 697	Ed Lynch	.05	.02	.01
☐ 698	Ernie Whitt	.05	.02	.01
☐ 699	Ken Landreaux	.05	.02	.01
☐ 700	Dave Bergman	.05	.02	.01
☐ 701	Willie Randolph	.10	.05	.01
☐ 702	Greg Gross	.05	.02	.01
☐ 703	Dave Schmidt	.05	.02	.01
☐ 704	Jesse Orosco	.05	.02	.01
☐ 705	Bruce Hurst	.05	.02	.01
☐ 706	Rick Manning	.05	.02	.01
☐ 707	Bob McClure	.05	.02	.01
☐ 708	Scott McGregor	.05	.02	.01
☐ 709	Dave Kingman	.10	.05	.01
☐ 710	Gary Gaetti	.05	.02	.01

☐ 711	Ken Griffey	.10	.05	.01
☐ 712	Don Robinson	.05	.02	.01
☐ 713	Tom Brookens	.05	.02	.01
☐ 714	Dan Quisenberry	.10	.05	.01
☐ 715	Bob Dernier	.05	.02	.01
☐ 716	Rick Leach	.05	.02	.01
☐ 717	Ed VandeBerg	.05	.02	.01
☐ 718	Steve Carlton	.15	.07	.02
☐ 719	Tom Hume	.05	.02	.01
☐ 720	Richard Dotson	.05	.02	.01
☐ 721	Tom Herr	.05	.02	.01
☐ 722	Bob Knepper	.05	.02	.01
☐ 723	Brett Butler	.15	.07	.02
☐ 724	Greg Minton	.05	.02	.01
☐ 725	George Hendrick	.05	.02	.01
☐ 726	Frank Tanana	.10	.05	.01
☐ 727	Mike Moore	.05	.02	.01
☐ 728	Tippy Martinez	.05	.02	.01
☐ 729	Tom Paciorek	.10	.05	.01
☐ 730	Eric Show	.05	.02	.01
☐ 731	Dave Concepcion	.10	.05	.01
☐ 732	Manny Trillo	.05	.02	.01
☐ 733	Bill Caudill	.05	.02	.01
☐ 734	Bill Madlock	.10	.05	.01
☐ 735	Rickey Henderson	.15	.07	.02
☐ 736	Steve Bedrosian	.05	.02	.01
☐ 737	Floyd Bannister	.05	.02	.01
☐ 738	Jorge Orta	.05	.02	.01
☐ 739	Chet Lemon	.05	.02	.01
☐ 740	Rich Gedman	.05	.02	.01
☐ 741	Paul Molitor	.20	.09	.03
☐ 742	Andy McGaffigan	.05	.02	.01
☐ 743	Dwayne Murphy	.05	.02	.01
☐ 744	Roy Smalley	.05	.02	.01
☐ 745	Glenn Hubbard	.05	.02	.01
☐ 746	Bob Ojeda	.05	.02	.01
☐ 747	Johnny Ray	.05	.02	.01
☐ 748	Mike Flanagan	.05	.02	.01
☐ 749	Ozzie Smith	.35	.16	.04
☐ 750	Steve Trout	.05	.02	.01
☐ 751	Garth Iorg	.05	.02	.01
☐ 752	Dan Petry	.05	.02	.01
☐ 753	Rick Honeycutt	.05	.02	.01
☐ 754	Dave LaPoint	.05	.02	.01
☐ 755	Luis Aguayo	.05	.02	.01
☐ 756	Carlton Fisk	.15	.07	.02
☐ 757	Nolan Ryan	.75	.35	.09
☐ 758	Tony Bernazard	.05	.02	.01
☐ 759	Joel Youngblood	.05	.02	.01
☐ 760	Mike Witt	.05	.02	.01
☐ 761	Greg Pryor	.05	.02	.01
☐ 762	Gary Ward	.05	.02	.01
☐ 763	Tim Flannery	.05	.02	.01
☐ 764	Bill Buckner	.10	.05	.01
☐ 765	Kirk Gibson	.15	.07	.02
☐ 766	Don Aase	.05	.02	.01
☐ 767	Ron Cey	.10	.05	.01
☐ 768	Dennis Lamp	.05	.02	.01
☐ 769	Steve Sax	.05	.02	.01
☐ 770	Dave Winfield	.15	.07	.02
☐ 771	Shane Rawley	.05	.02	.01
☐ 772	Harold Baines	.15	.07	.02
☐ 773	Robin Yount	.20	.09	.03
☐ 774	Wayne Krenchicki	.05	.02	.01
☐ 775	Joaquin Andujar	.05	.02	.01
☐ 776	Tom Brunansky	.05	.02	.01
☐ 777	Chris Chambliss	.10	.05	.01
☐ 778	Jack Morris	.15	.07	.02
☐ 779	Craig Reynolds	.05	.02	.01
☐ 780	Andre Thornton	.05	.02	.01
☐ 781	Atlee Hammaker	.05	.02	.01

☐ 782	Brian Downing	.10	.05	.01
☐ 783	Willie Wilson	.05	.02	.01
☐ 784	Cal Ripken	1.00	.45	.12
☐ 785	Terry Francona	.05	.02	.01
☐ 786	Jimy Williams MG (Checklist back)	.10	.05	.01
☐ 787	Alejandro Pena	.05	.02	.01
☐ 788	Tim Stoddard	.05	.02	.01
☐ 789	Dan Schatzeder	.05	.02	.01
☐ 790	Julio Cruz	.05	.02	.01
☐ 791	Lance Parrish UER (No trademark, never corrected)	.10	.05	.01
☐ 792	Checklist 661-792	.10	.05	.01

1987 Topps Traded

This 132-card Traded or extended set was distributed by Topps to dealers in a special green and white box as a complete set. The card fronts are identical in style to the Topps regular issue and are also 2 1/2" by 3 1/2". The backs are printed in yellow and blue on white card stock. Cards are numbered (with a T suffix) alphabetically according to the name of the player. The key (extended) Rookie Cards in this set (without any prior cards) are Ellis Burks and Matt Williams. Extended Rookie Cards in this set (with prior cards but not from Topps) are David Cone, Greg Maddux, and Fred McGriff. Topps also produced a specially boxed "glossy" edition, frequently referred to as the Topps Traded Tiffany set. This year Topps did not disclose the number of sets they produced or sold. It is apparent from the availability that there were many more sets produced this year compared to the 1984-86 Tiffany sets, perhaps 30,000 sets, more than three times as many. The checklist of cards is identical to that of the normal non-glossy cards. There are two primary distinguishing features of the Tiffany cards, white card stock reverses and high gloss obverses. These Tiffany cards are valued approximately from three to five times the values listed below.

	MINT	NRMT	EXC
COMPLETE FACT.SET (132)	8.00	3.60	1.00
COMMON CARD (1T-132T)	.05	.02	.01
☐ 1T Bill Almon	.05	.02	.01
☐ 2T Scott Bankhead	.05	.02	.01

☐ 3T Eric Bell	.05	.02	.01
☐ 4T Juan Beniquez	.05	.02	.01
☐ 5T Juan Berenguer	.05	.02	.01
☐ 6T Greg Booker	.05	.02	.01
☐ 7T Thad Bosley	.05	.02	.01
☐ 8T Larry Bowa MG	.08	.04	.01
☐ 9T Greg Brock	.05	.02	.01
☐ 10T Bob Brower	.05	.02	.01
☐ 11T Jerry Browne	.05	.02	.01
☐ 12T Ralph Bryant	.05	.02	.01
☐ 13T DeWayne Buice	.05	.02	.01
☐ 14T Ellis Burks	.25	.11	.03
☐ 15T Ivan Calderon	.05	.02	.01
☐ 16T Jeff Calhoun	.05	.02	.01
☐ 17T Casey Candaele	.05	.02	.01
☐ 18T John Cangelosi	.05	.02	.01
☐ 19T Steve Carlton	.10	.05	.01
☐ 20T Juan Castillo	.05	.02	.01
☐ 21T Rick Cerone	.05	.02	.01
☐ 22T Ron Cey	.08	.04	.01
☐ 23T John Christensen	.05	.02	.01
☐ 24T David Cone	.75	.35	.09
☐ 25T Chuck Crim	.05	.02	.01
☐ 26T Storm Davis	.05	.02	.01
☐ 27T Andre Dawson	.10	.05	.01
☐ 28T Rick Dempsey	.08	.04	.01
☐ 29T Doug Drabek	.25	.11	.03
☐ 30T Mike Dunne	.05	.02	.01
☐ 31T Dennis Eckersley	.10	.05	.01
☐ 32T Lee Elia MG	.05	.02	.01
☐ 33T Brian Fisher	.05	.02	.01
☐ 34T Terry Francona	.05	.02	.01
☐ 35T Willie Fraser	.05	.02	.01
☐ 36T Billy Gardner MG	.05	.02	.01
☐ 37T Ken Gerhart	.05	.02	.01
☐ 38T Dan Gladden	.05	.02	.01
☐ 39T Jim Gott	.05	.02	.01
☐ 40T Cecilio Guante	.05	.02	.01
☐ 41T Albert Hall	.05	.02	.01
☐ 42T Terry Harper	.05	.02	.01
☐ 43T Mickey Hatcher	.05	.02	.01
☐ 44T Brad Havens	.05	.02	.01
☐ 45T Neal Heaton	.05	.02	.01
☐ 46T Mike Henneman	.15	.07	.02
☐ 47T Donnie Hill	.05	.02	.01
☐ 48T Guy Hoffman	.05	.02	.01
☐ 49T Brian Holton	.05	.02	.01
☐ 50T Charles Hudson	.05	.02	.01
☐ 51T Danny Jackson	.08	.04	.01
☐ 52T Reggie Jackson	.20	.09	.03
☐ 53T Chris James	.05	.02	.01
☐ 54T Dion James	.05	.02	.01
☐ 55T Stan Jefferson	.05	.02	.01
☐ 56T Joe Johnson	.05	.02	.01
☐ 57T Terry Kennedy	.05	.02	.01
☐ 58T Mike Kingery	.08	.04	.01
☐ 59T Ray Knight	.08	.04	.01
☐ 60T Gene Larkin	.08	.04	.01
☐ 61T Mike LaValliere	.05	.02	.01
☐ 62T Jack Lazorko	.05	.02	.01
☐ 63T Terry Leach	.05	.02	.01
☐ 64T Tim Leary	.05	.02	.01
☐ 65T Jim Lindeman	.05	.02	.01
☐ 66T Steve Lombardozzi	.05	.02	.01
☐ 67T Bill Long	.05	.02	.01
☐ 68T Barry Lyons	.05	.02	.01
☐ 69T Shane Mack	.08	.04	.01
☐ 70T Greg Maddux	5.00	2.20	.60
☐ 71T Bill Madlock	.08	.04	.01
☐ 72T Joe Magrane	.05	.02	.01
☐ 73T Dave Martinez	.08	.04	.01
☐ 74T Fred McGriff	1.00	.45	.12
☐ 75T Mark McLemore	.05	.02	.01
☐ 76T Kevin McReynolds	.08	.04	.01
☐ 77T Dave Meads	.05	.02	.01
☐ 78T Eddie Milner	.05	.02	.01
☐ 79T Greg Minton	.05	.02	.01
☐ 80T John Mitchell	.05	.02	.01
☐ 81T Kevin Mitchell	.10	.05	.01
☐ 82T Charlie Moore	.05	.02	.01
☐ 83T Jeff Musselman	.05	.02	.01
☐ 84T Gene Nelson	.05	.02	.01
☐ 85T Graig Nettles	.08	.04	.01
☐ 86T Al Newman	.05	.02	.01
☐ 87T Reid Nichols	.05	.02	.01
☐ 88T Tom Niedenfuer	.05	.02	.01
☐ 89T Joe Niekro	.08	.04	.01
☐ 90T Tom Nieto	.05	.02	.01
☐ 91T Matt Nokes	.08	.04	.01
☐ 92T Dickie Noles	.05	.02	.01
☐ 93T Pat Pacillo	.05	.02	.01
☐ 94T Lance Parrish	.08	.04	.01
☐ 95T Tony Pena	.05	.02	.01
☐ 96T Luis Polonia	.25	.11	.03
☐ 97T Randy Ready	.05	.02	.01
☐ 98T Jeff Reardon	.10	.05	.01
☐ 99T Gary Redus	.05	.02	.01
☐ 100T Jeff Reed	.05	.02	.01
☐ 101T Rick Rhoden	.05	.02	.01
☐ 102T Cal Ripken Sr. MG	.08	.04	.01
☐ 103T Wally Ritchie	.05	.02	.01
☐ 104T Jeff M. Robinson	.05	.02	.01
☐ 105T Gary Roenicke	.05	.02	.01
☐ 106T Jerry Royster	.05	.02	.01
☐ 107T Mark Salas	.05	.02	.01
☐ 108T Luis Salazar	.05	.02	.01
☐ 109T Benny Santiago	.08	.04	.01
☐ 110T Dave Schmidt	.05	.02	.01
☐ 111T Kevin Seitzer	.08	.04	.01
☐ 112T John Shelby	.05	.02	.01
☐ 113T Steve Shields	.05	.02	.01
☐ 114T John Smiley	.15	.07	.02
☐ 115T Chris Speier	.05	.02	.01
☐ 116T Mike Stanley	.20	.09	.03
☐ 117T Terry Steinbach	.20	.09	.03
☐ 118T Les Straker	.05	.02	.01
☐ 119T Jim Sundberg	.05	.02	.01
☐ 120T Danny Tartabull	.08	.04	.01
☐ 121T Tom Trebelhorn MG	.05	.02	.01
☐ 122T Dave Valle	.05	.02	.01
☐ 123T Ed VandeBerg	.05	.02	.01
☐ 124T Andy Van Slyke	.08	.04	.01
☐ 125T Gary Ward	.05	.02	.01
☐ 126T Alan Wiggins	.05	.02	.01
☐ 127T Bill Wilkinson	.05	.02	.01
☐ 128T Frank Williams	.05	.02	.01
☐ 129T Matt Williams	2.00	.90	.25
☐ 130T Jim Winn	.05	.02	.01
☐ 131T Matt Young	.05	.02	.01
☐ 132T Checklist 1T-132T	.05	.02	.01

1988 Topps

This 792-card set features backs that are printed in orange and black on light gray card stock. The manager cards contain a checklist of the respective team's players on the back. Subsets in the set include

Record Breakers (1-7), Turn Back the Clock (661-665), and All-Star selections (386-407). The Team Leader cards typically show two players together inside a white cloud. The key Rookie Cards in this set are Ellis Burks, Tom Glavine, Jeff Montgomery, and Matt Williams. Topps also produced a specially boxed "glossy" edition, frequently referred to as the Topps Tiffany set. This year, again, Topps did not disclose the number of Tiffany sets they produced or sold. It is apparent from the availability that there were many more sets produced this year compared to the 1984-86 Tiffany sets, perhaps 25,000 sets. The checklist of cards (792 regular and 132 Traded) is identical to that of the normal non-glossy cards. There are two primary distinguishing features of the Tiffany cards, white card stock reverses and high gloss obverses. These Tiffany cards are valued approximately from three to five times the values listed below.

	MINT	NRMT	EXC
COMPLETE SET (792)	12.00	5.50	1.50
COMPLETE FACT.SET (792)	12.00	5.50	1.50
COMMON CARD (1-792)	.05	.02	.01
☐ 1 Vince Coleman RB	.10	.05	.01
100 Steals for Third Cons. Season			
☐ 2 Don Mattingly RB	.15	.07	.02
Six Grand Slams			
☐ 3A Mark McGwire RB	.15	.07	.02
Rookie Homer Record (White spot behind left foot)			
☐ 3B Mark McGwire RB	.10	.05	.01
Rookie Homer Record (No white spot)			
☐ 4A Eddie Murray RB	.40	.18	.05
Switch Home Runs, Two Straight Games (Caption in box on card front)			
☐ 4B Eddie Murray RB	.20	.09	.03
Switch Home Runs, Two Straight Games (No caption on front)			
☐ 5 Phil/Joe Niekro RB	.10	.05	.01
Brothers Win Record			
☐ 6 Nolan Ryan RB	.40	.18	.05
11th Season with 200 Strikeouts			
☐ 7 Benito Santiago RB	.05	.02	.01
34-Game Hitting Streak,			
Rookie Record			
☐ 8 Kevin Elster	.05	.02	.01
☐ 9 Andy Hawkins	.05	.02	.01
☐ 10 Ryne Sandberg	.30	.14	.04
☐ 11 Mike Young	.05	.02	.01
☐ 12 Bill Schroeder	.05	.02	.01
☐ 13 Andres Thomas	.05	.02	.01
☐ 14 Sparky Anderson MG	.10	.05	.01
(Checklist back)			
☐ 15 Chili Davis	.15	.07	.02
☐ 16 Kirk McCaskill	.05	.02	.01
☐ 17 Ron Oester	.05	.02	.01
☐ 18A Al Leiter ERR	.15	.07	.02
(Photo actually Steve George, right ear visible)			
☐ 18B Al Leiter COR	.10	.05	.01
(Left ear visible)			
☐ 19 Mark Davidson	.05	.02	.01
☐ 20 Kevin Gross	.05	.02	.01
☐ 21 Red Sox TL	.10	.05	.01
Wade Boggs and Spike Owen			
☐ 22 Greg Swindell	.10	.05	.01
☐ 23 Ken Landreaux	.05	.02	.01
☐ 24 Jim Deshaies	.05	.02	.01
☐ 25 Andres Galarraga	.15	.07	.02
☐ 26 Mitch Williams	.10	.05	.01
☐ 27 R.J. Reynolds	.05	.02	.01
☐ 28 Jose Nunez	.05	.02	.01
☐ 29 Argenis Salazar	.05	.02	.01
☐ 30 Sid Fernandez	.10	.05	.01
☐ 31 Bruce Bochy	.05	.02	.01
☐ 32 Mike Morgan	.05	.02	.01
☐ 33 Rob Deer	.05	.02	.01
☐ 34 Ricky Horton	.05	.02	.01
☐ 35 Harold Baines	.15	.07	.02
☐ 36 Jamie Moyer	.05	.02	.01
☐ 37 Ed Romero	.05	.02	.01
☐ 38 Jeff Calhoun	.05	.02	.01
☐ 39 Gerald Perry	.05	.02	.01
☐ 40 Orel Hershiser	.15	.07	.02
☐ 41 Bob Melvin	.05	.02	.01
☐ 42 Bill Landrum	.05	.02	.01
☐ 43 Dick Schofield	.05	.02	.01
☐ 44 Lou Piniella MG	.10	.05	.01
(Checklist back)			
☐ 45 Kent Hrbek	.15	.07	.02
☐ 46 Darnell Coles	.05	.02	.01
☐ 47 Joaquin Andujar	.05	.02	.01
☐ 48 Alan Ashby	.05	.02	.01
☐ 49 Dave Clark	.05	.02	.01
☐ 50 Hubie Brooks	.05	.02	.01
☐ 51 Orioles TL	.40	.18	.05
Eddie Murray and Cal Ripken			
☐ 52 Don Robinson	.05	.02	.01
☐ 53 Curt Wilkerson	.05	.02	.01
☐ 54 Jim Clancy	.05	.02	.01
☐ 55 Phil Bradley	.05	.02	.01
☐ 56 Ed Hearn	.05	.02	.01
☐ 57 Tim Crews	.05	.02	.01
☐ 58 Dave Magadan	.10	.05	.01
☐ 59 Danny Cox	.05	.02	.01
☐ 60 Rickey Henderson	.15	.07	.02
☐ 61 Mark Knudson	.05	.02	.01
☐ 62 Jeff Hamilton	.05	.02	.01
☐ 63 Jimmy Jones	.05	.02	.01
☐ 64 Ken Caminiti	.50	.23	.06
☐ 65 Leon Durham	.05	.02	.01
☐ 66 Shane Rawley	.05	.02	.01

☐	67	Ken Oberkfell	.05	.02	.01
☐	68	Dave Dravecky	.10	.05	.01
☐	69	Mike Hart	.05	.02	.01
☐	70	Roger Clemens	.25	.11	.03
☐	71	Gary Pettis	.05	.02	.01
☐	72	Dennis Eckersley	.15	.07	.02
☐	73	Randy Bush	.05	.02	.01
☐	74	Tom Lasorda MG (Checklist back)	.10	.05	.01
☐	75	Joe Carter	.15	.07	.02
☐	76	Dennis Martinez	.10	.05	.01
☐	77	Tom O'Malley	.05	.02	.01
☐	78	Dan Petry	.05	.02	.01
☐	79	Ernie Whitt	.05	.02	.01
☐	80	Mark Langston	.15	.07	.02
☐	81	Reds TL Ron Robinson and John Franco	.05	.02	.01
☐	82	Darrel Akerfelds	.05	.02	.01
☐	83	Jose Oquendo	.05	.02	.01
☐	84	Cecilio Guante	.05	.02	.01
☐	85	Howard Johnson	.10	.05	.01
☐	86	Ron Karkovice	.05	.02	.01
☐	87	Mike Mason	.05	.02	.01
☐	88	Earnie Riles	.05	.02	.01
☐	89	Gary Thurman	.05	.02	.01
☐	90	Dale Murphy	.15	.07	.02
☐	91	Joey Cora	.15	.07	.02
☐	92	Len Matuszek	.05	.02	.01
☐	93	Bob Sebra	.05	.02	.01
☐	94	Chuck Jackson	.05	.02	.01
☐	95	Lance Parrish	.10	.05	.01
☐	96	Todd Benzinger	.10	.05	.01
☐	97	Scott Garrelts	.05	.02	.01
☐	98	Rene Gonzales	.05	.02	.01
☐	99	Chuck Finley	.10	.05	.01
☐	100	Jack Clark	.10	.05	.01
☐	101	Allan Anderson	.05	.02	.01
☐	102	Barry Larkin	.30	.14	.04
☐	103	Curt Young	.05	.02	.01
☐	104	Dick Williams MG (Checklist back)	.10	.05	.01
☐	105	Jesse Orosco	.05	.02	.01
☐	106	Jim Walewander	.05	.02	.01
☐	107	Scott Bailes	.05	.02	.01
☐	108	Steve Lyons	.05	.02	.01
☐	109	Joel Skinner	.05	.02	.01
☐	110	Teddy Higuera	.05	.02	.01
☐	111	Expos TL Hubie Brooks and Vance Law	.05	.02	.01
☐	112	Les Lancaster	.05	.02	.01
☐	113	Kelly Gruber	.05	.02	.01
☐	114	Jeff Russell	.05	.02	.01
☐	115	Johnny Ray	.05	.02	.01
☐	116	Jerry Don Gleaton	.05	.02	.01
☐	117	James Steels	.05	.02	.01
☐	118	Bob Welch	.10	.05	.01
☐	119	Robbie Wine	.05	.02	.01
☐	120	Kirby Puckett	.40	.18	.05
☐	121	Checklist 1-132	.10	.05	.01
☐	122	Tony Bernazard	.05	.02	.01
☐	123	Tom Candiotti	.05	.02	.01
☐	124	Ray Knight	.10	.05	.01
☐	125	Bruce Hurst	.05	.02	.01
☐	126	Steve Jeltz	.05	.02	.01
☐	127	Jim Gott	.05	.02	.01
☐	128	Johnny Grubb	.05	.02	.01
☐	129	Greg Minton	.05	.02	.01
☐	130	Buddy Bell	.10	.05	.01
☐	131	Don Schulze	.05	.02	.01
☐	132	Donnie Hill	.05	.02	.01
☐	133	Greg Mathews	.05	.02	.01
☐	134	Chuck Tanner MG (Checklist back)	.10	.05	.01
☐	135	Dennis Rasmussen	.05	.02	.01
☐	136	Brian Dayett	.05	.02	.01
☐	137	Chris Bosio	.10	.05	.01
☐	138	Mitch Webster	.05	.02	.01
☐	139	Jerry Browne	.05	.02	.01
☐	140	Jesse Barfield	.05	.02	.01
☐	141	Royals TL George Brett and Bret Saberhagen	.15	.07	.02
☐	142	Andy Van Slyke	.10	.05	.01
☐	143	Mickey Tettleton	.10	.05	.01
☐	144	Don Gordon	.05	.02	.01
☐	145	Bill Madlock	.10	.05	.01
☐	146	Donell Nixon	.05	.02	.01
☐	147	Bill Buckner	.10	.05	.01
☐	148	Carmelo Martinez	.05	.02	.01
☐	149	Ken Howell	.05	.02	.01
☐	150	Eric Davis	.10	.05	.01
☐	151	Bob Knepper	.05	.02	.01
☐	152	Jody Reed	.10	.05	.01
☐	153	John Habyan	.05	.02	.01
☐	154	Jeff Stone	.05	.02	.01
☐	155	Bruce Sutter	.10	.05	.01
☐	156	Gary Matthews	.05	.02	.01
☐	157	Atlee Hammaker	.05	.02	.01
☐	158	Tim Hulett	.05	.02	.01
☐	159	Brad Arnsberg	.05	.02	.01
☐	160	Willie McGee	.10	.05	.01
☐	161	Bryn Smith	.05	.02	.01
☐	162	Mark McLemore	.05	.02	.01
☐	163	Dale Mohorcic	.05	.02	.01
☐	164	Dave Johnson MG (Checklist back)	.10	.05	.01
☐	165	Robin Yount	.20	.09	.03
☐	166	Rick Rodriquez	.05	.02	.01
☐	167	Rance Mulliniks	.05	.02	.01
☐	168	Barry Jones	.05	.02	.01
☐	169	Ross Jones	.05	.02	.01
☐	170	Rich Gossage	.15	.07	.02
☐	171	Cubs TL Shawon Dunston and Manny Trillo	.05	.02	.01
☐	172	Lloyd McClendon	.05	.02	.01
☐	173	Eric Plunk	.05	.02	.01
☐	174	Phil Garner	.10	.05	.01
☐	175	Kevin Bass	.05	.02	.01
☐	176	Jeff Reed	.05	.02	.01
☐	177	Frank Tanana	.10	.05	.01
☐	178	Dwayne Henry	.05	.02	.01
☐	179	Charlie Puleo	.05	.02	.01
☐	180	Terry Kennedy	.05	.02	.01
☐	181	David Cone	.35	.16	.04
☐	182	Ken Phelps	.05	.02	.01
☐	183	Tom Lawless	.05	.02	.01
☐	184	Ivan Calderon	.05	.02	.01
☐	185	Rick Rhoden	.05	.02	.01
☐	186	Rafael Palmeiro	.40	.18	.05
☐	187	Steve Kiefer	.05	.02	.01
☐	188	John Russell	.05	.02	.01
☐	189	Wes Gardner	.05	.02	.01
☐	190	Candy Maldonado	.05	.02	.01
☐	191	John Cerutti	.05	.02	.01
☐	192	Devon White	.15	.07	.02
☐	193	Brian Fisher	.05	.02	.01
☐	194	Tom Kelly MG (Checklist back)	.10	.05	.01
☐	195	Dan Quisenberry	.10	.05	.01

☐ 196	Dave Engle	.05	.02	.01
☐ 197	Lance McCullers	.05	.02	.01
☐ 198	Franklin Stubbs	.05	.02	.01
☐ 199	Dave Meads	.05	.02	.01
☐ 200	Wade Boggs	.15	.07	.02
☐ 201	Rangers TL	.05	.02	.01
	Bobby Valentine MG,			
	Pete O'Brien,			
	Pete Incaviglia, and			
	Steve Buechele			
☐ 202	Glenn Hoffman	.05	.02	.01
☐ 203	Fred Toliver	.05	.02	.01
☐ 204	Paul O'Neill	.15	.07	.02
☐ 205	Nelson Liriano	.10	.05	.01
☐ 206	Domingo Ramos	.05	.02	.01
☐ 207	John Mitchell	.05	.02	.01
☐ 208	Steve Lake	.05	.02	.01
☐ 209	Richard Dotson	.05	.02	.01
☑ 210	Willie Randolph	.10	.05	.01
☑ 211	Frank DiPino	.05	.02	.01
☑ 212	Greg Brock	.05	.02	.01
☑ 213	Albert Hall	.05	.02	.01
☐ 214	Dave Schmidt	.05	.02	.01
☐ 215	Von Hayes	.05	.02	.01
☐ 216	Jerry Reuss	.10	.05	.01
☐ 217	Harry Spilman	.05	.02	.01
☐ 218	Dan Schatzeder	.05	.02	.01
☐ 219	Mike Stanley	.10	.05	.01
☐ 220	Tom Henke	.10	.05	.01
☐ 221	Rafael Belliard	.05	.02	.01
☐ 222	Steve Farr	.05	.02	.01
☐ 223	Stan Jefferson	.05	.02	.01
☐ 224	Tom Trebelhorn MG	.10	.05	.01
	(Checklist back)			
☐ 225	Mike Scioscia	.05	.02	.01
☐ 226	Dave Lopes	.10	.05	.01
☐ 227	Ed Correa	.05	.02	.01
☐ 228	Wallace Johnson	.05	.02	.01
☐ 229	Jeff Musselman	.05	.02	.01
☐ 230	Pat Tabler	.05	.02	.01
☐ 231	Pirates TL	.15	.07	.02
	Barry Bonds and			
	Bobby Bonilla			
☐ 232	Bob James	.05	.02	.01
☐ 233	Rafael Santana	.05	.02	.01
☐ 234	Ken Dayley	.05	.02	.01
☐ 235	Gary Ward	.05	.02	.01
☐ 236	Ted Power	.05	.02	.01
☐ 237	Mike Heath	.05	.02	.01
☐ 238	Luis Polonia	.20	.09	.03
☐ 239	Roy Smalley	.05	.02	.01
☐ 240	Lee Smith	.15	.07	.02
☐ 241	Damaso Garcia	.05	.02	.01
☐ 242	Tom Niedenfuer	.05	.02	.01
☐ 243	Mark Ryal	.05	.02	.01
☐ 244	Jeff D. Robinson	.05	.02	.01
☐ 245	Rich Gedman	.05	.02	.01
☐ 246	Mike Campbell	.05	.02	.01
☐ 247	Thad Bosley	.05	.02	.01
☐ 248	Storm Davis	.05	.02	.01
☐ 249	Mike Marshall	.05	.02	.01
☐ 250	Nolan Ryan	.75	.35	.09
☐ 251	Tom Foley	.05	.02	.01
☐ 252	Bob Brower	.05	.02	.01
☐ 253	Checklist 133-264	.10	.01	.01
☐ 254	Lee Elia MG	.10	.05	.01
	(Checklist back)			
☐ 255	Mookie Wilson	.10	.05	.01
☐ 256	Ken Schrom	.05	.02	.01
☐ 257	Jerry Royster	.05	.02	.01
☐ 258	Ed Nunez	.05	.02	.01
☐ 259	Ron Kittle	.05	.02	.01
☐ 260	Vince Coleman	.10	.05	.01
☐ 261	Giants TL	.05	.02	.01
	(Five players)			
☐ 262	Drew Hall	.05	.02	.01
☐ 263	Glenn Braggs	.05	.02	.01
☐ 264	Les Straker	.05	.02	.01
☐ 265	Bo Diaz	.05	.02	.01
☐ 266	Paul Assenmacher	.05	.02	.01
☐ 267	Billy Bean	.05	.02	.01
☐ 268	Bruce Ruffin	.05	.02	.01
☐ 269	Ellis Burks	.15	.07	.02
☐ 270	Mike Witt	.05	.02	.01
☐ 271	Ken Gerhart	.05	.02	.01
☐ 272	Steve Ontiveros	.05	.02	.01
☐ 273	Garth Iorg	.05	.02	.01
☐ 274	Junior Ortiz	.05	.02	.01
☐ 275	Kevin Seitzer	.10	.05	.01
☐ 276	Luis Salazar	.05	.02	.01
☐ 277	Alejandro Pena	.05	.02	.01
☐ 278	Jose Cruz	.05	.02	.01
☐ 279	Randy St.Claire	.05	.02	.01
☐ 280	Pete Incaviglia	.10	.05	.01
☐ 281	Jerry Hairston	.05	.02	.01
☐ 282	Pat Perry	.05	.02	.01
☐ 283	Phil Lombardi	.05	.02	.01
☐ 284	Larry Bowa MG	.10	.05	.01
	(Checklist back)			
☐ 285	Jim Presley	.05	.02	.01
☐ 286	Chuck Crim	.05	.02	.01
☐ 287	Manny Trillo	.05	.02	.01
☐ 288	Pat Pacillo	.05	.02	.01
	(Chris Sabo in			
	background of photo)			
☐ 289	Dave Bergman	.05	.02	.01
☐ 290	Tony Fernandez	.10	.05	.01
☐ 291	Astros TL	.05	.02	.01
	Billy Hatcher			
	and Kevin Bass			
☐ 292	Carney Lansford	.10	.05	.01
☐ 293	Doug Jones	.10	.05	.01
☐ 294	Al Pedrique	.05	.02	.01
☐ 295	Bert Blyleven	.15	.07	.02
☐ 296	Floyd Rayford	.05	.02	.01
☐ 297	Zane Smith	.05	.02	.01
☐ 298	Milt Thompson	.05	.02	.01
☐ 299	Steve Crawford	.05	.02	.01
☐ 300	Don Mattingly	.40	.18	.05
☐ 301	Bud Black	.05	.02	.01
☐ 302	Jose Uribe	.05	.02	.01
☐ 303	Eric Show	.05	.02	.01
☐ 304	George Hendrick	.05	.02	.01
☐ 305	Steve Sax	.10	.05	.01
☐ 306	Billy Hatcher	.05	.02	.01
☐ 307	Mike Trujillo	.05	.02	.01
☐ 308	Lee Mazzilli	.05	.02	.01
☐ 309	Bill Long	.05	.02	.01
☐ 310	Tom Herr	.05	.02	.01
☐ 311	Scott Sanderson	.05	.02	.01
☐ 312	Joey Meyer	.05	.02	.01
☐ 313	Bob McClure	.05	.02	.01
☐ 314	Jimy Williams MG	.05	.02	.01
	(Checklist back)			
☐ 315	Dave Parker	.15	.07	.02
☐ 316	Jose Rijo	.15	.07	.02
☐ 317	Tom Nieto	.05	.02	.01
☐ 318	Mel Hall	.05	.02	.01
☐ 319	Mike Loynd	.05	.02	.01
☐ 320	Alan Trammell	.15	.07	.02
☐ 321	White Sox TL	.10	.05	.01
	Harold Baines and			

Carlton Fisk

☐ 322	Vicente Palacios	.05	.02	.01
☐ 323	Rick Leach	.05	.02	.01
☐ 324	Danny Jackson	.05	.02	.01
☐ 325	Glenn Hubbard	.05	.02	.01
☐ 326	Al Nipper	.05	.02	.01
☐ 327	Larry Sheets	.05	.02	.01
☐ 328	Greg Cadaret	.05	.02	.01
☐ 329	Chris Speier	.05	.02	.01
☐ 330	Eddie Whitson	.05	.02	.01
☐ 331	Brian Downing	.05	.02	.01
☐ 332	Jerry Reed	.05	.02	.01
☐ 333	Wally Backman	.05	.02	.01
☐ 334	Dave LaPoint	.05	.02	.01
☐ 335	Claudell Washington	.05	.02	.01
☐ 336	Ed Lynch	.05	.02	.01
☐ 337	Jim Gantner	.05	.02	.01
☐ 338	Brian Holton UER	.05	.02	.01
	(1987 ERA .389, should be 3.89)			
☐ 339	Kurt Stillwell	.05	.02	.01
☐ 340	Jack Morris	.15	.07	.02
☐ 341	Carmen Castillo	.05	.02	.01
☐ 342	Larry Andersen	.05	.02	.01
☐ 343	Greg Gagne	.05	.02	.01
☐ 344	Tony LaRussa MG	.10	.05	.01
	(Checklist back)			
☐ 345	Scott Fletcher	.05	.02	.01
☐ 346	Vance Law	.05	.02	.01
☐ 347	Joe Johnson	.05	.02	.01
☐ 348	Jim Eisenreich	.10	.05	.01
☐ 349	Bob Walk	.05	.02	.01
☐ 350	Will Clark	.30	.14	.04
☐ 351	Cardinals TL	.05	.02	.01
	Red Schoendienst CO and Tony Pena			
☐ 352	Billy Ripken	.05	.02	.01
☐ 353	Ed Olwine	.05	.02	.01
☐ 354	Marc Sullivan	.05	.02	.01
☐ 355	Roger McDowell	.05	.02	.01
☐ 356	Luis Aguayo	.05	.02	.01
☐ 357	Floyd Bannister	.05	.02	.01
☐ 358	Rey Quinones	.05	.02	.01
☐ 359	Tim Stoddard	.05	.02	.01
☐ 360	Tony Gwynn	.30	.14	.04
☐ 361	Greg Maddux	1.25	.55	.16
☐ 362	Juan Castillo	.05	.02	.01
☐ 363	Willie Fraser	.05	.02	.01
☐ 364	Nick Esasky	.05	.02	.01
☐ 365	Floyd Youmans	.05	.02	.01
☐ 366	Chet Lemon	.05	.02	.01
☐ 367	Tim Leary	.05	.02	.01
☐ 368	Gerald Young	.05	.02	.01
☐ 369	Greg Harris	.05	.02	.01
☐ 370	Jose Canseco	.50	.23	.06
☐ 371	Joe Hesketh	.05	.02	.01
☐ 372	Matt Williams	1.25	.55	.16
☐ 373	Checklist 265-396	.10	.05	.01
☐ 374	Doc Edwards MG	.10	.05	.01
	(Checklist back)			
☐ 375	Tom Brunansky	.05	.02	.01
☐ 376	Bill Wilkinson	.05	.02	.01
☐ 377	Sam Horn	.05	.02	.01
☐ 378	Todd Frohwirth	.05	.02	.01
☐ 379	Rafael Ramirez	.05	.02	.01
☐ 380	Joe Magrane	.05	.02	.01
☐ 381	Angels TL	.05	.02	.01
	Wally Joyner and Jack Howell			
☐ 382	Keith A. Miller	.05	.02	.01
☐ 383	Eric Bell	.05	.02	.01

☐ 384	Neil Allen	.05	.02	.01
☐ 385	Carlton Fisk	.15	.07	.02
☐ 386	Don Mattingly AS	.20	.09	.03
☐ 387	Willie Randolph AS	.05	.02	.01
☐ 388	Wade Boggs AS	.15	.07	.02
☐ 389	Alan Trammell AS	.10	.05	.01
☐ 390	George Bell AS	.05	.02	.01
☐ 391	Kirby Puckett AS	.25	.11	.03
☐ 392	Dave Winfield AS	.15	.07	.02
☐ 393	Matt Nokes AS	.05	.02	.01
☐ 394	Roger Clemens AS	.15	.07	.02
☐ 395	Jimmy Key AS	.10	.05	.01
☐ 396	Tom Henke AS	.05	.02	.01
☐ 397	Jack Clark AS	.05	.02	.01
☐ 398	Juan Samuel AS	.05	.02	.01
☐ 399	Tim Wallach AS	.05	.02	.01
☐ 400	Ozzie Smith AS	.15	.07	.02
☐ 401	Andre Dawson AS	.10	.05	.01
☐ 402	Tony Gwynn AS	.15	.07	.02
☐ 403	Tim Raines AS	.10	.05	.01
☐ 404	Benny Santiago AS	.05	.02	.01
☐ 405	Dwight Gooden AS	.10	.05	.01
☐ 406	Shane Rawley AS	.05	.02	.01
☐ 407	Steve Bedrosian AS	.05	.02	.01
☐ 408	Dion James	.05	.02	.01
☐ 409	Joel McKeon	.05	.02	.01
☐ 410	Tony Pena	.05	.02	.01
☐ 411	Wayne Tolleson	.05	.02	.01
☐ 412	Randy Myers	.15	.07	.02
☐ 413	John Christensen	.05	.02	.01
☐ 414	John McNamara MG	.10	.05	.01
	(Checklist back)			
☐ 415	Don Carman	.05	.02	.01
☐ 416	Keith Moreland	.05	.02	.01
☐ 417	Mark Ciardi	.05	.02	.01
☐ 418	Joel Youngblood	.05	.02	.01
☐ 419	Scott McGregor	.05	.02	.01
☐ 420	Wally Joyner	.10	.05	.01
☐ 421	Ed VandeBerg	.05	.02	.01
☐ 422	Dave Concepcion	.10	.05	.01
☐ 423	John Smiley	.20	.09	.03
☐ 424	Dwayne Murphy	.05	.02	.01
☐ 425	Jeff Reardon	.15	.07	.02
☐ 426	Randy Ready	.05	.02	.01
☐ 427	Paul Kilgus	.05	.02	.01
☐ 428	John Shelby	.05	.02	.01
☐ 429	Tigers TL	.10	.05	.01
	Alan Trammell and Kirk Gibson			
☐ 430	Glenn Davis	.05	.02	.01
☐ 431	Casey Candaele	.05	.02	.01
☐ 432	Mike Moore	.05	.02	.01
☐ 433	Bill Pecota	.05	.02	.01
☐ 434	Rick Aguilera	.15	.07	.02
☐ 435	Mike Pagliarulo	.05	.02	.01
☐ 436	Mike Bielecki	.05	.02	.01
☐ 437	Fred Manrique	.05	.02	.01
☐ 438	Rob Ducey	.05	.02	.01
☐ 439	Dave Martinez	.05	.02	.01
☐ 440	Steve Bedrosian	.05	.02	.01
☐ 441	Rick Manning	.05	.02	.01
☐ 442	Tom Bolton	.05	.02	.01
☐ 443	Ken Griffey	.10	.05	.01
☐ 444	Cal Ripken, Sr. MG	.10	.05	.01
	(Checklist back) UER (two copyrights)			
☐ 445	Mike Krukow	.05	.02	.01
☐ 446	Doug DeCinces	.05	.02	.01
	(Now with Cardinals on card front)			
☐ 447	Jeff Montgomery	.20	.09	.03

☐ 448 Mike Davis	.05	.02	.01
☐ 449 Jeff M. Robinson	.05	.02	.01
☐ 450 Barry Bonds	.60	.25	.07
☐ 451 Keith Atherton	.05	.02	.01
☐ 452 Willie Wilson	.05	.02	.01
☐ 453 Dennis Powell	.05	.02	.01
☐ 454 Marvell Wynne	.05	.02	.01
☐ 455 Shawn Hillegas	.05	.02	.01
☐ 456 Dave Anderson	.05	.02	.01
☐ 457 Terry Leach	.05	.02	.01
☐ 458 Ron Hassey	.05	.02	.01
☐ 459 Yankees TL	.10	.05	.01
Dave Winfield and			
Willie Randolph			
☐ 460 Ozzie Smith	.30	.14	.04
☐ 461 Danny Darwin	.05	.02	.01
☐ 462 Don Slaught	.05	.02	.01
☐ 463 Fred McGriff	.40	.18	.05
☐ 464 Jay Tibbs	.05	.02	.01
☐ 465 Paul Molitor	.15	.07	.02
☐ 466 Jerry Mumphrey	.05	.02	.01
☐ 467 Don Aase	.05	.02	.01
☐ 468 Darren Daulton	.15	.07	.02
☐ 469 Jeff Dedmon	.05	.02	.01
☐ 470 Dwight Evans	.10	.05	.01
☐ 471 Donnie Moore	.05	.02	.01
☐ 472 Robby Thompson	.10	.05	.01
☐ 473 Joe Niekro	.10	.05	.01
☐ 474 Tom Brookens	.05	.02	.01
☐ 475 Pete Rose MG	.20	.09	.03
(Checklist back)			
☐ 476 Dave Stewart	.15	.07	.02
☐ 477 Jamie Quirk	.05	.02	.01
☐ 478 Sid Bream	.05	.02	.01
☐ 479 Brett Butler	.15	.07	.02
☐ 480 Dwight Gooden	.10	.05	.01
☐ 481 Mariano Duncan	.05	.02	.01
☐ 482 Mark Davis	.05	.02	.01
☐ 483 Rod Booker	.05	.02	.01
☐ 484 Pat Clements	.05	.02	.01
☐ 485 Harold Reynolds	.05	.02	.01
☐ 486 Pat Keedy	.05	.02	.01
☐ 487 Jim Pankovits	.05	.02	.01
☐ 488 Andy McGaffigan	.05	.02	.01
☐ 489 Dodgers TL	.05	.02	.01
Pedro Guerrero and			
Fernando Valenzuela			
☐ 490 Larry Parrish	.05	.02	.01
☐ 491 B.J. Surhoff	.10	.05	.01
☐ 492 Doyle Alexander	.05	.02	.01
☐ 493 Mike Greenwell	.15	.07	.02
☐ 494 Wally Ritchie	.05	.02	.01
☐ 495 Eddie Murray	.25	.11	.03
☐ 496 Guy Hoffman	.05	.02	.01
☐ 497 Kevin Mitchell	.10	.05	.01
☐ 498 Bob Boone	.10	.05	.01
☐ 499 Eric King	.05	.02	.01
☐ 500 Andre Dawson	.15	.07	.02
☐ 501 Tim Birtsas	.05	.02	.01
☐ 502 Dan Gladden	.05	.02	.01
☐ 503 Junior Noboa	.05	.02	.01
☐ 504 Bob Rodgers MG	.10	.05	.01
(Checklist back)			
☐ 505 Willie Upshaw	.05	.02	.01
☐ 506 John Cangelosi	.05	.02	.01
☐ 507 Mark Gubicza	.05	.02	.01
☐ 508 Tim Teufel	.05	.02	.01
☐ 509 Bill Dawley	.05	.02	.01
☐ 510 Dave Winfield	.15	.07	.02
☐ 511 Joel Davis	.05	.02	.01
☐ 512 Alex Trevino	.05	.02	.01

☐ 513 Tim Flannery	.05	.02	.01
☐ 514 Pat Sheridan	.05	.02	.01
☐ 515 Juan Nieves	.05	.02	.01
☐ 516 Jim Sundberg	.05	.02	.01
☐ 517 Ron Robinson	.05	.02	.01
☐ 518 Greg Gross	.05	.02	.01
☐ 519 Mariners TL	.05	.02	.01
Harold Reynolds and			
Phil Bradley			
☐ 520 Dave Smith	.05	.02	.01
☐ 521 Jim Dwyer	.05	.02	.01
☐ 522 Bob Patterson	.05	.02	.01
☐ 523 Gary Roenicke	.05	.02	.01
☐ 524 Gary Lucas	.05	.02	.01
☐ 525 Marty Barrett	.05	.02	.01
☐ 526 Juan Berenguer	.05	.02	.01
☐ 527 Steve Henderson	.05	.02	.01
☐ 528A Checklist 397-528	.10	.05	.01
ERR (455 S. Carlton)			
☐ 528B Checklist 397-528	.10	.05	.01
COR (455 S. Hillegas)			
☐ 529 Tim Burke	.05	.02	.01
☐ 530 Gary Carter	.15	.07	.02
☐ 531 Rich Yett	.05	.02	.01
☐ 532 Mike Kingery	.05	.02	.01
☐ 533 John Farrell	.05	.02	.01
☐ 534 John Wathan MG	.10	.05	.01
(Checklist back)			
☐ 535 Ron Guidry	.10	.05	.01
☐ 536 John Morris	.05	.02	.01
☐ 537 Steve Buechele	.05	.02	.01
☐ 538 Bill Wegman	.05	.02	.01
☐ 539 Mike LaValliere	.05	.02	.01
☐ 540 Bret Saberhagen	.15	.07	.02
☐ 541 Juan Beniquez	.05	.02	.01
☐ 542 Paul Noce	.05	.02	.01
☐ 543 Kent Tekulve	.05	.02	.01
☐ 544 Jim Traber	.05	.02	.01
☐ 545 Don Baylor	.15	.07	.02
☐ 546 John Candelaria	.05	.02	.01
☐ 547 Felix Fermin	.05	.02	.01
☐ 548 Shane Mack	.10	.05	.01
☐ 549 Braves TL	.05	.02	.01
Albert Hall,			
Dale Murphy,			
Ken Griffey,			
and Dion James			
☐ 550 Pedro Guerrero	.10	.05	.01
☐ 551 Terry Steinbach	.10	.05	.01
☐ 552 Mark Thurmond	.05	.02	.01
☐ 553 Tracy Jones	.05	.02	.01
☐ 554 Mike Smithson	.05	.02	.01
☐ 555 Brook Jacoby	.05	.02	.01
☐ 556 Stan Clarke	.05	.02	.01
☐ 557 Craig Reynolds	.05	.02	.01
☐ 558 Bob Ojeda	.05	.02	.01
☐ 559 Ken Williams	.05	.02	.01
☐ 560 Tim Wallach	.10	.05	.01
☐ 561 Rick Cerone	.05	.02	.01
☐ 562 Jim Lindeman	.05	.02	.01
☐ 563 Jose Guzman	.05	.02	.01
☐ 564 Frank Lucchesi MG	.10	.05	.01
(Checklist back)			
☐ 565 Lloyd Moseby	.05	.02	.01
☐ 566 Charlie O'Brien	.05	.02	.01
☐ 567 Mike Diaz	.05	.02	.01
☐ 568 Chris Brown	.05	.02	.01
☐ 569 Charlie Leibrandt	.05	.02	.01
☐ 570 Jeffrey Leonard	.05	.02	.01
☐ 571 Mark Williamson	.05	.02	.01
☐ 572 Chris James	.05	.02	.01

573	Bob Stanley	.05	.02	.01
574	Graig Nettles	.10	.05	.01
575	Don Sutton	.15	.07	.02
576	Tommy Hinzo	.05	.02	.01
577	Tom Browning	.05	.02	.01
578	Gary Gaetti	.10	.05	.01
579	Mets TL Gary Carter and Kevin McReynolds	.10	.05	.01
580	Mark McGwire	.40	.18	.05
581	Tito Landrum	.05	.02	.01
582	Mike Henneman	.15	.07	.02
583	Dave Valle	.05	.02	.01
584	Steve Trout	.05	.02	.01
585	Ozzie Guillen	.10	.05	.01
586	Bob Forsch	.05	.02	.01
587	Terry Puhl	.05	.02	.01
588	Jeff Parrett	.05	.02	.01
589	Geno Petralli	.05	.02	.01
590	George Bell	.05	.02	.01
591	Doug Drabek	.15	.07	.02
592	Dale Sveum	.05	.02	.01
593	Bob Tewksbury	.10	.05	.01
594	Bobby Valentine MG (Checklist back)	.10	.05	.01
595	Frank White	.10	.05	.01
596	John Kruk	.15	.07	.02
597	Gene Garber	.05	.02	.01
598	Lee Lacy	.05	.02	.01
599	Calvin Schiraldi	.05	.02	.01
600	Mike Schmidt	.25	.11	.03
601	Jack Lazorko	.05	.02	.01
602	Mike Aldrete	.05	.02	.01
603	Rob Murphy	.05	.02	.01
604	Chris Bando	.05	.02	.01
605	Kirk Gibson	.15	.07	.02
606	Moose Haas	.05	.02	.01
607	Mickey Hatcher	.05	.02	.01
608	Charlie Kerfeld	.05	.02	.01
609	Twins TL Gary Gaetti and Kent Hrbek	.05	.02	.01
610	Keith Hernandez	.10	.05	.01
611	Tommy John	.15	.07	.02
612	Curt Ford	.05	.02	.01
613	Bobby Thigpen	.05	.02	.01
614	Herm Winningham	.05	.02	.01
615	Jody Davis	.05	.02	.01
616	Jay Aldrich	.05	.02	.01
617	Oddibe McDowell	.05	.02	.01
618	Cecil Fielder	.15	.07	.02
619	Mike Dunne (Inconsistent design, black name on front)	.05	.02	.01
620	Cory Snyder	.05	.02	.01
621	Gene Nelson	.05	.02	.01
622	Kal Daniels	.05	.02	.01
623	Mike Flanagan	.05	.02	.01
624	Jim Leyland MG (Checklist back)	.10	.05	.01
625	Frank Viola	.10	.05	.01
626	Glenn Wilson	.05	.02	.01
627	Joe Boever	.05	.02	.01
628	Dave Henderson	.10	.05	.01
629	Kelly Downs	.05	.02	.01
630	Darrell Evans	.10	.05	.01
631	Jack Howell	.05	.02	.01
632	Steve Shields	.05	.02	.01
633	Barry Lyons	.05	.02	.01
634	Jose DeLeon	.05	.02	.01
635	Terry Pendleton	.15	.07	.02
636	Charles Hudson	.05	.02	.01
637	Jay Bell	.30	.14	.04
638	Steve Balboni	.05	.02	.01
639	Brewers TL Glenn Braggs and Tony Muser CO	.05	.02	.01
640	Garry Templeton (Inconsistent design, green border)	.05	.02	.01
641	Rick Honeycutt	.05	.02	.01
642	Bob Dernier	.05	.02	.01
643	Rocky Childress	.05	.02	.01
644	Terry McGriff	.05	.02	.01
645	Matt Nokes	.05	.02	.01
646	Checklist 529-660	.10	.05	.01
647	Pascual Perez	.05	.02	.01
648	Al Newman	.05	.02	.01
649	DeWayne Buice	.05	.02	.01
650	Cal Ripken	.75	.35	.09
651	Mike Jackson	.10	.05	.01
652	Bruce Benedict	.05	.02	.01
653	Jeff Sellers	.05	.02	.01
654	Roger Craig MG (Checklist back)	.10	.05	.01
655	Len Dykstra	.15	.07	.02
656	Lee Guetterman	.05	.02	.01
657	Gary Redus	.05	.02	.01
658	Tim Conroy (Inconsistent design, name in white)	.05	.02	.01
659	Bobby Meacham	.05	.02	.01
660	Rick Reuschel	.05	.02	.01
661	Nolan Ryan TBC '83	.35	.16	.04
662	Jim Rice TBC '78	.10	.05	.01
663	Ron Blomberg TBC '73	.05	.02	.01
664	Bob Gibson TBC '68	.10	.05	.01
665	Stan Musial TBC '63	.10	.05	.01
666	Mario Soto	.05	.02	.01
667	Luis Quinones	.05	.02	.01
668	Walt Terrell	.05	.02	.01
669	Phillies TL Lance Parrish and Mike Ryan CO	.05	.02	.01
670	Dan Plesac	.05	.02	.01
671	Tim Laudner	.05	.02	.01
672	John Davis	.05	.02	.01
673	Tony Phillips	.15	.07	.02
674	Mike Fitzgerald	.05	.02	.01
675	Jim Rice	.15	.07	.02
676	Ken Dixon	.05	.02	.01
677	Eddie Milner	.05	.02	.01
678	Jim Acker	.05	.02	.01
679	Darrell Miller	.05	.02	.01
680	Charlie Hough	.10	.05	.01
681	Bobby Bonilla	.15	.07	.02
682	Jimmy Key	.15	.07	.02
683	Julio Franco	.10	.05	.01
684	Hal Lanier MG (Checklist back)	.10	.05	.01
685	Ron Darling	.10	.05	.01
686	Terry Francona	.05	.02	.01
687	Mickey Brantley	.05	.02	.01
688	Jim Winn	.05	.02	.01
689	Tom Pagnozzi	.10	.05	.01
690	Jay Howell	.05	.02	.01
691	Dan Pasqua	.05	.02	.01
692	Mike Birkbeck	.05	.02	.01
693	Benito Santiago	.10	.05	.01
694	Eric Nolte	.05	.02	.01
695	Shawon Dunston	.10	.05	.01
696	Duane Ward	.10	.05	.01

□	697	Steve Lombardozzi	.05	.02	.01
□	698	Brad Havens	.05	.02	.01
□	699	Padres TL	.10	.05	.01
		Benito Santiago			
		and Tony Gwynn			
□	700	George Brett	.40	.18	.05
□	701	Sammy Stewart	.05	.02	.01
□	702	Mike Gallego	.05	.02	.01
□	703	Bob Brenly	.05	.02	.01
□	704	Dennis Boyd	.05	.02	.01
□	705	Juan Samuel	.05	.02	.01
□	706	Rick Mahler	.05	.02	.01
□	707	Fred Lynn	.10	.05	.01
□	708	Gus Polidor	.05	.02	.01
□	709	George Frazier	.05	.02	.01
□	710	Darryl Strawberry	.15	.07	.02
□	711	Bill Gullickson	.05	.02	.01
□	712	John Moses	.05	.02	.01
□	713	Willie Hernandez	.05	.02	.01
□	714	Jim Fregosi MG	.10	.05	.01
		(Checklist back)			
□	715	Todd Worrell	.05	.02	.01
□	716	Lenn Sakata	.05	.02	.01
□	717	Jay Baller	.05	.02	.01
□	718	Mike Felder	.05	.02	.01
□	719	Denny Walling	.05	.02	.01
□	720	Tim Raines	.15	.07	.02
□	721	Pete O'Brien	.05	.02	.01
□	722	Manny Lee	.05	.02	.01
□	723	Bob Kipper	.05	.02	.01
□	724	Danny Tartabull	.10	.05	.01
□	725	Mike Boddicker	.05	.02	.01
□	726	Alfredo Griffin	.05	.02	.01
□	727	Greg Booker	.05	.02	.01
□	728	Andy Allanson	.05	.02	.01
□	729	Blue Jays TL	.10	.05	.01
		George Bell and			
		Fred McGriff			
□	730	John Franco	.10	.05	.01
□	731	Rick Schu	.05	.02	.01
□	732	David Palmer	.05	.02	.01
□	733	Spike Owen	.05	.02	.01
□	734	Craig Lefferts	.05	.02	.01
□	735	Kevin McReynolds	.05	.02	.01
□	736	Matt Young	.05	.02	.01
□	737	Butch Wynegar	.05	.02	.01
□	738	Scott Bankhead	.05	.02	.01
□	739	Daryl Boston	.05	.02	.01
□	740	Rick Sutcliffe	.10	.05	.01
□	741	Mike Easler	.05	.02	.01
□	742	Mark Clear	.05	.02	.01
□	743	Larry Herndon	.05	.02	.01
□	744	Whitey Herzog MG	.10	.05	.01
		(Checklist back)			
□	745	Bill Doran	.05	.02	.01
□	746	Gene Larkin	.05	.02	.01
□	747	Bobby Witt	.10	.05	.01
□	748	Reid Nichols	.05	.02	.01
□	749	Mark Eichhorn	.05	.02	.01
□	750	Bo Jackson	.25	.11	.03
□	751	Jim Morrison	.05	.02	.01
□	752	Mark Grant	.05	.02	.01
□	753	Danny Heep	.05	.02	.01
□	754	Mike LaCoss	.05	.02	.01
□	755	Ozzie Virgil	.05	.02	.01
□	756	Mike Maddux	.05	.02	.01
□	757	John Marzano	.05	.02	.01
□	758	Eddie Williams	.10	.05	.01
□	759	A's TL UER	.25	.11	.03
		Mark McGwire			
		and Jose Canseco			

		(two copyrights)			
□	760	Mike Scott	.05	.02	.01
□	761	Tony Armas	.05	.02	.01
□	762	Scott Bradley	.05	.02	.01
□	763	Doug Sisk	.05	.02	.01
□	764	Greg Walker	.05	.02	.01
□	765	Neal Heaton	.05	.02	.01
□	766	Henry Cotto	.05	.02	.01
□	767	Jose Lind	.05	.02	.01
□	768	Dickie Noles	.05	.02	.01
		(Now with Tigers			
		on card front)			
□	769	Cecil Cooper	.10	.05	.01
□	770	Lou Whitaker	.15	.07	.02
□	771	Ruben Sierra	.25	.11	.03
□	772	Sal Butera	.05	.02	.01
□	773	Frank Williams	.05	.02	.01
□	774	Gene Mauch MG	.10	.05	.01
		(Checklist back)			
□	775	Dave Stieb	.10	.05	.01
□	776	Checklist 661-792	.10	.05	.01
□	777	Lonnie Smith	.05	.02	.01
□	778A	Keith Comstock ERR	2.00	.90	.25
		(White "Padres")			
□	778B	Keith Comstock COR	.05	.02	.01
		(Blue "Padres")			
□	779	Tom Glavine	1.25	.55	.16
□	780	Fernando Valenzuela	.05	.02	.01
□	781	Keith Hughes	.05	.02	.01
□	782	Jeff Ballard	.05	.02	.01
□	783	Ron Roenicke	.05	.02	.01
□	784	Joe Sambito	.05	.02	.01
□	785	Alvin Davis	.05	.02	.01
□	786	Joe Price	.05	.02	.01
		(Inconsistent design,			
		orange team name)			
□	787	Bill Almon	.05	.02	.01
□	788	Ray Searage	.05	.02	.01
□	789	Indians' TL	.10	.05	.01
		Joe Carter and			
		Cory Snyder			
□	790	Dave Righetti	.05	.02	.01
□	791	Ted Simmons	.10	.05	.01
□	792	John Tudor	.05	.02	.01

1988 Topps Traded

This 132-card Traded or extended set was distributed by Topps to dealers in a special blue and white box as a complete set. The card fronts are identical in style to the Topps regular issue and are also 2 1/2" by 3 1/2". The backs are printed in orange and black on white card stock. Cards are numbered (with a T suffix) alphabetically according to the name of the player. This set has generated additional interest due to the inclusion of the 1988 U.S. Olympic baseball team members. These Olympians are indicated in the checklist below by OLY. The key (extended) Rookie Cards in this set are Jim Abbott, Roberto Alomar, Brady Anderson, Andy Benes, Jay Buhner, Ron Gant, Mark Grace, Bryan Harvey, Roberto Kelly, Tino Martinez, Jack McDowell, Charles Nagy, Chris Sabo, Robin Ventura, and Walt Weiss. Topps also produced a specially boxed "glossy" edition, frequently referred to as the Topps Traded Tiffany set. This year, again, Topps did not disclose the number of Tiffany sets they produced or sold. It is apparent from the availability that there were many more sets produced this year compared to the 1984-86 Tiffany sets, perhaps 25,000 sets. The checklist of cards is identical to that of the normal non-glossy cards. There are two primary distinguishing features of the Tiffany cards, white card stock reverses and high gloss obverses. These Tiffany cards are valued approximately from three to five times the values listed below.

	MINT	NRMT	EXC
COMPLETE FACT.SET (132) ..	12.00	5.50	1.50
COMMON CARD (1T-132T)	.05	.02	.01

		MINT	NRMT	EXC
☐ 1T	Jim Abbott OLY	.60	.25	.07
☐ 2T	Juan Agosto	.05	.02	.01
☐ 3T	Luis Alicea	.08	.04	.01
☐ 4T	Roberto Alomar	4.00	1.80	.50
☐ 5T	Brady Anderson	1.00	.45	.12
☐ 6T	Jack Armstrong	.05	.02	.01
☐ 7T	Don August	.05	.02	.01
☐ 8T	Floyd Bannister	.05	.02	.01
☐ 9T	Bret Barberie OLY	.08	.04	.01
☐ 10T	Jose Bautista	.05	.02	.01
☐ 11T	Don Baylor	.10	.05	.01
☐ 12T	Tim Belcher	.05	.02	.01
☐ 13T	Buddy Bell	.08	.04	.01
☐ 14T	Andy Benes OLY	.60	.25	.07
☐ 15T	Damon Berryhill	.05	.02	.01
☐ 16T	Bud Black	.05	.02	.01
☐ 17T	Pat Borders	.08	.04	.01
☐ 18T	Phil Bradley	.05	.02	.01
☐ 19T	Jeff Branson OLY	.08	.04	.01
☐ 20T	Tom Brunansky	.05	.02	.01
☐ 21T	Jay Buhner	1.00	.45	.12
☐ 22T	Brett Butler	.10	.05	.01
☐ 23T	Jim Campanis OLY	.05	.02	.01
☐ 24T	Sil Campusano	.05	.02	.01
☐ 25T	John Candelaria	.05	.02	.01
☐ 26T	Jose Cecena	.05	.02	.01
☐ 27T	Rick Cerone	.05	.02	.01
☐ 28T	Jack Clark	.08	.04	.01
☐ 29T	Kevin Coffman	.05	.02	.01
☐ 30T	Pat Combs OLY	.05	.02	.01
☐ 31T	Henry Cotto	.05	.02	.01
☐ 32T	Chili Davis	.10	.05	.01
☐ 33T	Mike Davis	.05	.02	.01
☐ 34T	Jose DeLeon	.05	.02	.01
☐ 35T	Richard Dotson	.05	.02	.01
☐ 36T	Cecil Espy	.05	.02	.01
☐ 37T	Tom Filer	.05	.02	.01
☐ 38T	Mike Fiore OLY	.05	.02	.01
☐ 39T	Ron Gant	1.50	.70	.19
☐ 40T	Kirk Gibson	.10	.05	.01
☐ 41T	Rich Gossage	.10	.05	.01
☐ 42T	Mark Grace	1.00	.45	.12
☐ 43T	Alfredo Griffin	.05	.02	.01
☐ 44T	Ty Griffin OLY	.05	.02	.01
☐ 45T	Bryan Harvey	.10	.05	.01
☐ 46T	Ron Hassey	.05	.02	.01
☐ 47T	Ray Hayward	.05	.02	.01
☐ 48T	Dave Henderson	.05	.02	.01
☐ 49T	Tom Herr	.05	.02	.01
☐ 50T	Bob Horner	.05	.02	.01
☐ 51T	Ricky Horton	.05	.02	.01
☐ 52T	Jay Howell	.05	.02	.01
☐ 53T	Glenn Hubbard	.05	.02	.01
☐ 54T	Jeff Innis	.05	.02	.01
☐ 55T	Danny Jackson	.05	.02	.01
☐ 56T	Darrin Jackson	.08	.04	.01
☐ 57T	Roberto Kelly	.30	.14	.04
☐ 58T	Ron Kittle	.05	.02	.01
☐ 59T	Ray Knight	.08	.04	.01
☐ 60T	Vance Law	.05	.02	.01
☐ 61T	Jeffrey Leonard	.05	.02	.01
☐ 62T	Mike Macfarlane	.25	.11	.03
☐ 63T	Scotti Madison	.05	.02	.01
☐ 64T	Kirt Manwaring	.05	.02	.01
☐ 65T	Mark Marquess OLY CO	.05	.02	.01
☐ 66T	Tino Martinez OLY	2.00	.90	.25
☐ 67T	Billy Masse OLY	.05	.02	.01
☐ 68T	Jack McDowell	.75	.35	.09
☐ 69T	Jack McKeon MG	.05	.02	.01
☐ 70T	Larry McWilliams	.05	.02	.01
☐ 71T	Mickey Morandini OLY	.40	.18	.05
☐ 72T	Keith Moreland	.05	.02	.01
☐ 73T	Mike Morgan	.05	.02	.01
☐ 74T	Charles Nagy OLY	1.25	.55	.16
☐ 75T	Al Nipper	.05	.02	.01
☐ 76T	Russ Nixon MG	.05	.02	.01
☐ 77T	Jesse Orosco	.05	.02	.01
☐ 78T	Joe Orsulak	.05	.02	.01
☐ 79T	Dave Palmer	.05	.02	.01
☐ 80T	Mark Parent	.05	.02	.01
☐ 81T	Dave Parker	.10	.05	.01
☐ 82T	Dan Pasqua	.05	.02	.01
☐ 83T	Melido Perez	.08	.04	.01
☐ 84T	Steve Peters	.05	.02	.01
☐ 85T	Dan Petry	.05	.02	.01
☐ 86T	Gary Pettis	.05	.02	.01
☐ 87T	Jeff Pico	.05	.02	.01
☐ 88T	Jim Poole OLY	.08	.04	.01
☐ 89T	Ted Power	.05	.02	.01
☐ 90T	Rafael Ramirez	.05	.02	.01
☐ 91T	Dennis Rasmussen	.05	.02	.01
☐ 92T	Jose Rijo	.10	.05	.01
☐ 93T	Ernie Riles	.05	.02	.01
☐ 94T	Luis Rivera	.05	.02	.01
☐ 95T	Doug Robbins OLY	.05	.02	.01
☐ 96T	Frank Robinson MG	.08	.04	.01
☐ 97T	Cookie Rojas MG	.05	.02	.01
☐ 98T	Chris Sabo	.08	.04	.01
☐ 99T	Mark Salas	.05	.02	.01
☐ 100T	Luis Salazar	.05	.02	.01
☐ 101T	Rafael Santana	.05	.02	.01
☐ 102T	Nelson Santovenia	.05	.02	.01
☐ 103T	Mackey Sasser	.05	.02	.01
☐ 104T	Calvin Schiraldi	.05	.02	.01
☐ 105T	Mike Schooler	.05	.02	.01
☐ 106T	Scott Servais OLY	.08	.04	.01
☐ 107T	Dave Silvestri OLY	.05	.02	.01
☐ 108T	Don Slaught	.05	.02	.01

			MINT	NRMT	EXC
☐ 109T	Joe Slusarski OLY	.05	.02	.01
☐ 110T	Lee Smith	.10	.02	.01
☐ 111T	Pete Smith	.05	.02	.01
☐ 112T	Jim Snyder MG	.05	.02	.01
☐ 113T	Ed Sprague OLY	.50	.23	.06
☐ 114T	Pete Stanicek	.05	.02	.01
☐ 115T	Kurt Stillwell	.05	.02	.01
☐ 116T	Todd Stottlemyre	.50	.23	.06
☐ 117T	Bill Swift	.08	.04	.01
☐ 118T	Pat Tabler	.05	.02	.01
☐ 119T	Scott Terry	.05	.02	.01
☐ 120T	Mickey Tettleton	.08	.04	.01
☐ 121T	Dickie Thon	.05	.02	.01
☐ 122T	Jeff Treadway	.05	.02	.01
☐ 123T	Willie Upshaw	.05	.02	.01
☐ 124T	Robin Ventura OLY	2.00	.90	.25
☐ 125T	Ron Washington	.05	.02	.01
☐ 126T	Walt Weiss	.08	.04	.01
☐ 127T	Bob Welch	.08	.04	.01
☐ 128T	David Wells	.30	.14	.04
☐ 129T	Glenn Wilson	.05	.02	.01
☐ 130T	Ted Wood OLY	.05	.02	.01
☐ 131T	Don Zimmer MG	.08	.04	.01
☐ 132T	Checklist 1T-132T	.05	.02	.01

1989 Topps

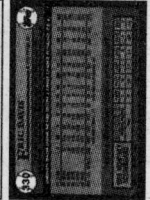

This 792-card set features backs that are printed in pink and black on gray card stock. The manager cards contain a checklist of the respective team's players on the back. Subsets in the set include Record Breakers (1-7), Turn Back the Clock (661-665), and All-Star selections (386-407). The bonus cards distributed throughout the set, which are indicated on the Topps checklist cards, are actually Team Leader (TL) cards. Also sprinkled throughout the set are Future Stars (FS) and First Draft Picks (FDP). There are subtle variations found in the Future Stars cards with respect to the placement of print and type on the card; in fact, each card has at least two varieties but they are difficult to detect (requiring precise measurement) as well as difficult to explain. The key Rookie Cards in this set are Jim Abbott, Sandy Alomar Jr., Brady Anderson, Steve Avery, Andy Benes, Craig Biggio, Bryan Harvey, Randy Johnson, Ramon Martinez, Gregg Olson, Gary Sheffield, John Smoltz, and Robin Ventura. Topps also produced a specially boxed "glossy" edition, frequently referred to as

the Topps Tiffany set. This year, again, Topps did not disclose the number of Tiffany sets they produced or sold but it seems that production quantities were roughly similar (or slightly smaller, approximately 15,000 sets) to the previous two years. The checklist of cards (792 regular and 132 Traded) is identical to that of the normal non-glossy cards. There are two primary distinguishing features of the Tiffany cards, white card stock reverses and high gloss obverses. These Tiffany cards are valued approximately from three to five times the values listed below.

		MINT	NRMT	EXC
COMPLETE SET (792)		10.00	4.50	1.25
COMPLETE FACT.SET (792)		10.00	4.50	1.25
COMMON CARD (1-792)		.05	.02	.01

			MINT	NRMT	EXC
☐ 1	George Bell RB Slams 3 HR on Opening Day		.10	.05	.01
☐ 2	Wade Boggs RB Gets 200 Hits 6th Straight Season		.15	.07	.02
☐ 3	Gary Carter RB Sets Record for Career Putouts		.10	.05	.01
☐ 4	Andre Dawson RB Logs Double Figures in HR and SB		.10	.05	.01
☐ 5	Orel Hershiser RB Pitches 59 Scoreless Innings		.10	.05	.01
☐ 6	Doug Jones RB UER Earns His 15th Straight Save (Photo actually Chris Codiroli)		.05	.02	.01
☐ 7	Kevin McReynolds RB Steals 21 Without Being Caught		.05	.02	.01
☐ 8	Dave Eiland		.05	.02	.01
☐ 9	Tim Teufel		.05	.02	.01
☐ 10	Andre Dawson		.15	.07	.02
☐ 11	Bruce Sutter		.10	.05	.01
☐ 12	Dale Sveum		.05	.02	.01
☐ 13	Doug Sisk		.05	.02	.01
☐ 14	Tom Kelly MG (Team checklist back)		.05	.02	.01
☐ 15	Robby Thompson		.10	.05	.01
☐ 16	Ron Robinson		.05	.02	.01
☐ 17	Brian Downing		.05	.02	.01
☐ 18	Rick Rhoden		.05	.02	.01
☐ 19	Greg Gagne		.05	.02	.01
☐ 20	Steve Bedrosian		.05	.02	.01
☐ 21	Chicago White Sox TL Greg Walker		.05	.02	.01
☐ 22	Tim Crews		.05	.02	.01
☐ 23	Mike Fitzgerald		.05	.02	.01
☐ 24	Larry Andersen		.05	.02	.01
☐ 25	Frank White		.10	.05	.01
☐ 26	Dale Mohorcic		.05	.02	.01
☐ 27A	Orestes Destrade (F* next to copyright)		.05	.02	.01
☐ 27B	Orestes Destrade (E*F* next to copyright)		.05	.02	.01
☐ 28	Mike Moore		.05	.02	.01
☐ 29	Kelly Gruber		.05	.02	.01

☐ 30	Dwight Gooden	.10	.05	.01
☐ 31	Terry Francona	.05	.02	.01
☐ 32	Dennis Rasmussen	.05	.02	.01
☐ 33	B.J. Surhoff	.10	.05	.01
☐ 34	Ken Williams	.05	.02	.01
☐ 35	John Tudor UER	.05	.02	.01
	(With Red Sox in '84,should be Pirates)			
☐ 36	Mitch Webster	.05	.02	.01
☐ 37	Bob Stanley	.05	.02	.01
☐ 38	Paul Runge	.05	.02	.01
☐ 39	Mike Maddux	.05	.02	.01
☐ 40	Steve Sax	.05	.02	.01
☐ 41	Terry Mulholland	.10	.05	.01
☐ 42	Jim Eppard	.05	.02	.01
☐ 43	Guillermo Hernandez	.05	.02	.01
☐ 44	Jim Snyder MG	.05	.02	.01
	(Team checklist back)			
☐ 45	Kal Daniels	.05	.02	.01
☐ 46	Mark Portugal	.10	.05	.01
☐ 47	Carney Lansford	.10	.05	.01
☐ 48	Tim Burke	.05	.02	.01
☐ 49	Craig Biggio	.60	.25	.07
☐ 50	George Bell	.05	.02	.01
☐ 51	California Angels TL	.05	.02	.01
	Mark McLemore			
☐ 52	Bob Brenly	.05	.02	.01
☐ 53	Ruben Sierra	.15	.07	.02
☐ 54	Steve Trout	.05	.02	.01
☐ 55	Julio Franco	.10	.05	.01
☐ 56	Pat Tabler	.05	.02	.01
☐ 57	Alejandro Pena	.05	.02	.01
☐ 58	Lee Mazzilli	.05	.02	.01
☐ 59	Mark Davis	.05	.02	.01
☐ 60	Tom Brunansky	.05	.02	.01
☐ 61	Neil Allen	.05	.02	.01
☐ 62	Alfredo Griffin	.05	.02	.01
☐ 63	Mark Clear	.05	.02	.01
☐ 64	Alex Trevino	.05	.02	.01
☐ 65	Rick Reuschel	.05	.02	.01
☐ 66	Manny Trillo	.05	.02	.01
☐ 67	Dave Palmer	.05	.02	.01
☐ 68	Darrell Miller	.05	.02	.01
☐ 69	Jeff Ballard	.05	.02	.01
☐ 70	Mark McGwire	.15	.07	.02
☐ 71	Mike Boddicker	.05	.02	.01
☐ 72	John Moses	.05	.02	.01
☐ 73	Pascual Perez	.05	.02	.01
☐ 74	Nick Leyva MG	.05	.02	.01
	(Team checklist back)			
☐ 75	Tom Henke	.10	.05	.01
☐ 76	Terry Blocker	.05	.02	.01
☐ 77	Doyle Alexander	.05	.02	.01
☐ 78	Jim Sundberg	.05	.02	.01
☐ 79	Scott Bankhead	.05	.02	.01
☐ 80	Cory Snyder	.05	.02	.01
☐ 81	Montreal Expos TL	.10	.05	.01
	Tim Raines			
☐ 82	Dave Leiper	.05	.02	.01
☐ 83	Jeff Blauser	.15	.07	.02
☐ 84	Bill Bene FDP	.05	.02	.01
☐ 85	Kevin McReynolds	.05	.02	.01
☐ 86	Al Nipper	.05	.02	.01
☐ 87	Larry Owen	.05	.02	.01
☐ 88	Darryl Hamilton	.10	.05	.01
☐ 89	Dave LaPoint	.05	.02	.01
☐ 90	Vince Coleman UER	.10	.05	.01
	(Wrong birth year)			
☐ 91	Floyd Youmans	.05	.02	.01
☐ 92	Jeff Kunkel	.05	.02	.01
☐ 93	Ken Howell	.05	.02	.01
☐ 94	Chris Speier	.05	.02	.01

☐ 95	Gerald Young	.05	.02	.01
☐ 96	Rick Cerone	.05	.02	.01
	(Ellis Burks in			
	background of photo)			
☐ 97	Greg Mathews	.05	.02	.01
☐ 98	Larry Sheets	.05	.02	.01
☐ 99	Sherman Corbett	.05	.02	.01
☐ 100	Mike Schmidt	.25	.11	.03
☐ 101	Les Straker	.05	.02	.01
☐ 102	Mike Gallego	.05	.02	.01
☐ 103	Tim Birtsas	.05	.02	.01
☐ 104	Dallas Green MG	.05	.02	.01
	(Team checklist back)			
☐ 105	Ron Darling	.10	.05	.01
☐ 106	Willie Upshaw	.05	.02	.01
☐ 107	Jose DeLeon	.05	.02	.01
☐ 108	Fred Manrique	.05	.02	.01
☐ 109	Hipolito Pena	.05	.02	.01
☐ 110	Paul Molitor	.15	.07	.02
☐ 111	Cincinnati Reds TL	.05	.02	.01
	Eric Davis			
	(Swinging bat)			
☐ 112	Jim Presley	.05	.02	.01
☐ 113	Lloyd Moseby	.05	.02	.01
☐ 114	Bob Kipper	.05	.02	.01
☐ 115	Jody Davis	.05	.02	.01
☐ 116	Jeff Montgomery	.10	.05	.01
☐ 117	Dave Anderson	.05	.02	.01
☐ 118	Checklist 1-132	.05	.02	.01
☐ 119	Terry Puhl	.05	.02	.01
☐ 120	Frank Viola	.10	.05	.01
☐ 121	Garry Templeton	.05	.02	.01
☐ 122	Lance Johnson	.10	.05	.01
☐ 123	Spike Owen	.05	.02	.01
☐ 124	Jim Traber	.05	.02	.01
☐ 125	Mike Krukow	.05	.02	.01
☐ 126	Sid Bream	.05	.02	.01
☐ 127	Walt Terrell	.05	.02	.01
☐ 128	Milt Thompson	.05	.02	.01
☐ 129	Terry Clark	.05	.02	.01
☐ 130	Gerald Perry	.05	.02	.01
☐ 131	Dave Otto	.05	.02	.01
☐ 132	Curt Ford	.05	.02	.01
☐ 133	Bill Long	.05	.02	.01
☐ 134	Don Zimmer MG	.05	.02	.01
	(Team checklist back)			
☐ 135	Jose Rijo	.15	.07	.02
☐ 136	Joey Meyer	.05	.02	.01
☐ 137	Geno Petralli	.05	.02	.01
☐ 138	Wallace Johnson	.05	.02	.01
☐ 139	Mike Flanagan	.05	.02	.01
☐ 140	Shawon Dunston	.10	.05	.01
☐ 141	Cleveland Indians TL	.05	.02	.01
	Brook Jacoby			
☐ 142	Mike Diaz	.05	.02	.01
☐ 143	Mike Campbell	.05	.02	.01
☐ 144	Jay Bell	.15	.07	.02
☐ 145	Dave Stewart	.15	.07	.02
☐ 146	Gary Pettis	.05	.02	.01
☐ 147	DeWayne Buice	.05	.02	.01
☐ 148	Bill Pecota	.05	.02	.01
☐ 149	Doug Dascenzo	.05	.02	.01
☐ 150	Fernando Valenzuela	.10	.05	.01
☐ 151	Terry McGriff	.05	.02	.01
☐ 152	Mark Thurmond	.05	.02	.01
☐ 153	Jim Pankovits	.05	.02	.01
☐ 154	Don Carman	.05	.02	.01
☐ 155	Marty Barrett	.05	.02	.01
☐ 156	Dave Gallagher	.05	.02	.01
☐ 157	Tom Glavine	.40	.18	.05
☐ 158	Mike Aldrete	.05	.02	.01

☐ 159	Pat Clements	.05	.02	.01
☐ 160	Jeffrey Leonard	.05	.02	.01
☐ 161	Gregg Olson FDP UER	.15	.07	.02
	(Born Scribner, NE, should be Omaha, NE)			
☐ 162	John Davis	.05	.02	.01
☐ 163	Bob Forsch	.05	.02	.01
☐ 164	Hal Lanier MG	.05	.02	.01
	(Team checklist back)			
☐ 165	Mike Dunne	.05	.02	.01
☐ 166	Doug Jennings	.05	.02	.01
☐ 167	Steve Searcy FS	.05	.02	.01
☐ 168	Willie Wilson	.05	.02	.01
☐ 169	Mike Jackson	.05	.02	.01
☐ 170	Tony Fernandez	.10	.05	.01
☐ 171	Atlanta Braves TL	.05	.02	.01
	Andres Thomas			
☐ 172	Frank Williams	.05	.02	.01
☐ 173	Mel Hall	.05	.02	.01
☐ 174	Todd Burns	.05	.02	.01
☐ 175	John Shelby	.05	.02	.01
☐ 176	Jeff Parrett	.05	.02	.01
☐ 177	Monty Fariss FDP	.05	.02	.01
☐ 178	Mark Grant	.05	.02	.01
☐ 179	Ozzie Virgil	.05	.02	.01
☐ 180	Mike Scott	.05	.02	.01
☐ 181	Craig Worthington	.05	.02	.01
☐ 182	Bob McClure	.05	.02	.01
☐ 183	Oddibe McDowell	.05	.02	.01
☐ 184	John Costello	.05	.02	.01
☐ 185	Claudell Washington	.05	.02	.01
☐ 186	Pat Perry	.05	.02	.01
☐ 187	Darren Daulton	.15	.07	.02
☐ 188	Dennis Lamp	.05	.02	.01
☐ 189	Kevin Mitchell	.10	.05	.01
☐ 190	Mike Witt	.05	.02	.01
☐ 191	Sil Campusano	.05	.02	.01
☐ 192	Paul Mirabella	.05	.02	.01
☐ 193	Sparky Anderson MG	.10	.05	.01
	(Team checklist back) UER (553 Salazer)			
☐ 194	Greg W. Harris	.05	.02	.01
☐ 195	Ozzie Guillen	.10	.05	.01
☐ 196	Denny Walling	.05	.02	.01
☐ 197	Neal Heaton	.05	.02	.01
☐ 198	Danny Heep	.05	.02	.01
☐ 199	Mike Schooler	.05	.02	.01
☐ 200	George Brett	.40	.18	.05
☐ 201	Blue Jays TL	.05	.02	.01
	Kelly Gruber			
☐ 202	Brad Moore	.05	.02	.01
☐ 203	Rob Ducey	.05	.02	.01
☐ 204	Brad Havens	.05	.02	.01
☐ 205	Dwight Evans	.10	.05	.01
☐ 206	Roberto Alomar	.50	.23	.06
☐ 207	Terry Leach	.05	.02	.01
☐ 208	Tom Pagnozzi	.05	.02	.01
☐ 209	Jeff Bittiger	.05	.02	.01
☐ 210	Dale Murphy	.15	.07	.02
☐ 211	Mike Pagliarulo	.05	.02	.01
☐ 212	Scott Sanderson	.05	.02	.01
☐ 213	Rene Gonzales	.05	.02	.01
☐ 214	Charlie O'Brien	.05	.02	.01
☐ 215	Kevin Gross	.05	.02	.01
☐ 216	Jack Howell	.05	.02	.01
☐ 217	Joe Price	.05	.02	.01
☐ 218	Mike LaValliere	.05	.02	.01
☐ 219	Jim Clancy	.05	.02	.01
☐ 220	Gary Gaetti	.10	.05	.01
☐ 221	Cecil Espy	.05	.02	.01
☐ 222	Mark Lewis FDP	.10	.05	.01
☐ 223	Jay Buhner	.15	.07	.02
☐ 224	Tony LaRussa MG	.10	.05	.01
	(Team checklist back)			
☐ 225	Ramon Martinez	.30	.14	.04
☐ 226	Bill Doran	.05	.02	.01
☐ 227	John Farrell	.05	.02	.01
☐ 228	Nelson Santovenia	.05	.02	.01
☐ 229	Jimmy Key	.15	.07	.02
☐ 230	Ozzie Smith	.30	.14	.04
☐ 231	San Diego Padres TL	.15	.07	.02
	Roberto Alomar			
	(Gary Carter at plate)			
☐ 232	Ricky Horton	.05	.02	.01
☐ 233	Gregg Jefferies FS	.20	.09	.03
☐ 234	Tom Browning	.05	.02	.01
☐ 235	John Kruk	.15	.07	.02
☐ 236	Charles Hudson	.05	.02	.01
☐ 237	Glenn Hubbard	.05	.02	.01
☐ 238	Eric King	.05	.02	.01
☐ 239	Tim Laudner	.05	.02	.01
☐ 240	Greg Maddux	.75	.35	.09
☐ 241	Brett Butler	.15	.07	.02
☐ 242	Ed VandeBerg	.05	.02	.01
☐ 243	Bob Boone	.10	.05	.01
☐ 244	Jim Acker	.05	.02	.01
☐ 245	Jim Rice	.15	.07	.02
☐ 246	Rey Quinones	.05	.02	.01
☐ 247	Shawn Hillegas	.05	.02	.01
☐ 248	Tony Phillips	.15	.07	.02
☐ 249	Tim Leary	.05	.02	.01
☐ 250	Cal Ripken	.75	.35	.09
☐ 251	John Dopson	.05	.02	.01
☐ 252	Billy Hatcher	.05	.02	.01
☐ 253	Jose Alvarez	.05	.02	.01
☐ 254	Tom Lasorda MG	.10	.05	.01
	(Team checklist back)			
☐ 255	Ron Guidry	.10	.05	.01
☐ 256	Benny Santiago	.10	.05	.01
☐ 257	Rick Aguilera	.15	.07	.02
☐ 258	Checklist 133-264	.05	.02	.01
☐ 259	Larry McWilliams	.05	.02	.01
☐ 260	Dave Winfield	.15	.07	.02
☐ 261	St.Louis Cardinals TL	.05	.02	.01
	Tom Brunansky			
	(With Luis Alicea)			
☐ 262	Jeff Pico	.05	.02	.01
☐ 263	Mike Felder	.05	.02	.01
☐ 264	Rob Dibble	.10	.05	.01
☐ 265	Kent Hrbek	.05	.02	.01
☐ 266	Luis Aquino	.05	.02	.01
☐ 267	Jeff M. Robinson	.05	.02	.01
☐ 268	N. Keith Miller	.05	.02	.01
☐ 269	Tom Bolton	.05	.02	.01
☐ 270	Wally Joyner	.10	.05	.01
☐ 271	Jay Tibbs	.05	.02	.01
☐ 272	Ron Hassey	.05	.02	.01
☐ 273	Jose Lind	.05	.02	.01
☐ 274	Mark Eichhorn	.05	.02	.01
☐ 275	Danny Tartabull UER	.10	.05	.01
	(Born San Juan, PR should be Miami, FL)			
☐ 276	Paul Kilgus	.05	.02	.01
☐ 277	Mike Davis	.05	.02	.01
☐ 278	Andy McGaffigan	.05	.02	.01
☐ 279	Scott Bradley	.05	.02	.01
☐ 280	Bob Knepper	.05	.02	.01
☐ 281	Gary Redus	.05	.02	.01
☐ 282	Cris Carpenter	.05	.02	.01
☐ 283	Andy Allanson	.05	.02	.01
☐ 284	Jim Leyland MG	.05	.02	.01
	(Team checklist back)			

☐ 285	John Candelaria	.05	.02	.01
☐ 286	Darrin Jackson	.05	.02	.01
☐ 287	Juan Nieves	.05	.02	.01
☐ 288	Pat Sheridan	.05	.02	.01
☐ 289	Ernie Whitt	.05	.02	.01
☐ 290	John Franco	.10	.05	.01
☐ 291	New York Mets TL	.10	.05	.01
	Darryl Strawberry			
	(With Keith Hernandez			
	and Kevin McReynolds)			
☐ 292	Jim Corsi	.05	.02	.01
☐ 293	Glenn Wilson	.05	.02	.01
☐ 294	Juan Berenguer	.05	.02	.01
☐ 295	Scott Fletcher	.05	.02	.01
☐ 296	Ron Gant	.25	.11	.03
☐ 297	Oswald Peraza	.05	.02	.01
☐ 298	Chris James	.05	.02	.01
☐ 299	Steve Ellsworth	.05	.02	.01
☐ 300	Darryl Strawberry	.15	.07	.02
☐ 301	Charlie Leibrandt	.05	.02	.01
☐ 302	Gary Ward	.05	.02	.01
☐ 303	Felix Fermin	.05	.02	.01
☐ 304	Joel Youngblood	.05	.02	.01
☐ 305	Dave Smith	.05	.02	.01
☐ 306	Tracy Woodson	.05	.02	.01
☐ 307	Lance McCullers	.05	.02	.01
☐ 308	Ron Karkovice	.05	.02	.01
☐ 309	Mario Diaz	.05	.02	.01
☐ 310	Rafael Palmeiro	.25	.11	.03
☐ 311	Chris Bosio	.05	.02	.01
☐ 312	Tom Lawless	.05	.02	.01
☐ 313	Dennis Martinez	.10	.05	.01
☐ 314	Bobby Valentine MG	.05	.02	.01
	(Team checklist back)			
☐ 315	Greg Swindell	.10	.05	.01
☐ 316	Walt Weiss	.10	.05	.01
☐ 317	Jack Armstrong	.05	.02	.01
☐ 318	Gene Larkin	.05	.02	.01
☐ 319	Greg Booker	.05	.02	.01
☐ 320	Lou Whitaker	.15	.07	.02
☐ 321	Boston Red Sox TL	.05	.02	.01
	Jody Reed			
☐ 322	John Smiley	.05	.02	.01
☐ 323	Gary Thurman	.05	.02	.01
☐ 324	Bob Milacki	.05	.02	.01
☐ 325	Jesse Barfield	.05	.02	.01
☐ 326	Dennis Boyd	.05	.02	.01
☐ 327	Mark Lemke	.10	.05	.01
☐ 328	Rick Honeycutt	.05	.02	.01
☐ 329	Bob Melvin	.05	.02	.01
☐ 330	Eric Davis	.10	.05	.01
☐ 331	Curt Wilkerson	.05	.02	.01
☐ 332	Tony Armas	.05	.02	.01
☐ 333	Bob Ojeda	.05	.02	.01
☐ 334	Steve Lyons	.05	.02	.01
☐ 335	Dave Righetti	.05	.02	.01
☐ 336	Steve Balboni	.05	.02	.01
☐ 337	Calvin Schiraldi	.05	.02	.01
☐ 338	Jim Adduci	.05	.02	.01
☐ 339	Scott Bailes	.05	.02	.01
☐ 340	Kirk Gibson	.15	.07	.02
☐ 341	Jim Deshaies	.05	.02	.01
☐ 342	Tom Brookens	.05	.02	.01
☐ 343	Gary Sheffield FS	.60	.25	.07
☐ 344	Tom Trebelhorn MG	.05	.02	.01
	(Team checklist back)			
☐ 345	Charlie Hough	.10	.05	.01
☐ 346	Rex Hudler	.05	.02	.01
☐ 347	John Cerutti	.05	.02	.01
☐ 348	Ed Hearn	.05	.02	.01
☐ 349	Ron Jones	.05	.02	.01

☐ 350	Andy Van Slyke	.10	.05	.01
☐ 351	San Fran. Giants TL	.05	.02	.01
	Bob Melvin			
	(With Bill Fahey CO)			
☐ 352	Rick Schu	.05	.02	.01
☐ 353	Marvell Wynne	.05	.02	.01
☐ 354	Larry Parrish	.05	.02	.01
☐ 355	Mark Langston	.15	.07	.02
☐ 356	Kevin Elster	.05	.02	.01
☐ 357	Jerry Reuss	.10	.05	.01
☐ 358	Ricky Jordan	.05	.02	.01
☐ 359	Tommy John	.15	.07	.02
☐ 360	Ryne Sandberg	.30	.14	.04
☐ 361	Kelly Downs	.05	.02	.01
☐ 362	Jack Lazorko	.05	.02	.01
☐ 363	Rich Yett	.05	.02	.01
☐ 364	Rob Deer	.05	.02	.01
☐ 365	Mike Henneman	.10	.05	.01
☐ 366	Herm Winningham	.05	.02	.01
☐ 367	Johnny Paredes	.05	.02	.01
☐ 368	Brian Holton	.05	.02	.01
☐ 369	Ken Caminiti	.15	.07	.02
☐ 370	Dennis Eckersley	.15	.07	.02
☐ 371	Manny Lee	.05	.02	.01
☐ 372	Craig Lefferts	.05	.02	.01
☐ 373	Tracy Jones	.05	.02	.01
☐ 374	John Wathan MG	.05	.02	.01
	(Team checklist back)			
☐ 375	Terry Pendleton	.15	.07	.02
☐ 376	Steve Lombardozzi	.05	.02	.01
☐ 377	Mike Smithson	.05	.02	.01
☐ 378	Checklist 265-396	.05	.02	.01
☐ 379	Tim Flannery	.05	.02	.01
☐ 380	Rickey Henderson	.15	.07	.02
☐ 381	Baltimore Orioles TL	.05	.02	.01
	Larry Sheets			
☐ 382	John Smoltz	.40	.18	.05
☐ 383	Howard Johnson	.10	.05	.01
☐ 384	Mark Salas	.05	.02	.01
☐ 385	Von Hayes	.05	.02	.01
☐ 386	Andres Galarraga AS	.15	.07	.02
☐ 387	Ryne Sandberg AS	.15	.07	.02
☐ 388	Bobby Bonilla AS	.10	.05	.01
☐ 389	Ozzie Smith AS	.15	.07	.02
☐ 390	Darryl Strawberry AS	.10	.05	.01
☐ 391	Andre Dawson AS	.10	.05	.01
☐ 392	Andy Van Slyke AS	.05	.02	.01
☐ 393	Gary Carter AS	.10	.05	.01
☐ 394	Orel Hershiser AS	.10	.05	.01
☐ 395	Danny Jackson AS	.05	.02	.01
☐ 396	Kirk Gibson AS	.10	.05	.01
☐ 397	Don Mattingly AS	.20	.09	.03
☐ 398	Julio Franco AS	.05	.02	.01
☐ 399	Wade Boggs AS	.15	.07	.02
☐ 400	Alan Trammell AS	.10	.05	.01
☐ 401	Jose Canseco AS	.15	.07	.02
☐ 402	Mike Greenwell AS	.10	.05	.01
☐ 403	Kirby Puckett AS	.20	.09	.03
☐ 404	Bob Boone AS	.05	.02	.01
☐ 405	Roger Clemens AS	.15	.07	.02
☐ 406	Frank Viola AS	.05	.02	.01
☐ 407	Dave Winfield AS	.15	.07	.02
☐ 408	Greg Walker	.05	.02	.01
☐ 409	Ken Dayley	.05	.02	.01
☐ 410	Jack Clark	.10	.05	.01
☐ 411	Mitch Williams	.10	.05	.01
☐ 412	Barry Lyons	.05	.02	.01
☐ 413	Mike Kingery	.05	.02	.01
☐ 414	Jim Fregosi MG	.05	.02	.01
	(Team checklist back)			
☐ 415	Rich Gossage	.15	.07	.02

☐ 416	Fred Lynn	.10	.05	.01
☐ 417	Mike LaCoss	.05	.02	.01
☐ 418	Bob Dernier	.05	.02	.01
☐ 419	Tom Filer	.05	.02	.01
☐ 420	Joe Carter	.20	.09	.03
☐ 421	Kirk McCaskill	.05	.02	.01
☐ 422	Bo Diaz	.05	.02	.01
☐ 423	Brian Fisher	.05	.02	.01
☐ 424	Luis Polonia UER	.10	.05	.01
	(Wrong birthdate)			
☐ 425	Jay Howell	.05	.02	.01
☐ 426	Dan Gladden	.05	.02	.01
☐ 427	Eric Show	.05	.02	.01
☐ 428	Craig Reynolds	.05	.02	.01
☐ 429	Minnesota Twins TL	.05	.02	.01
	Greg Gagne			
	(Taking throw at 2nd)			
☐ 430	Mark Gubicza	.05	.02	.01
☐ 431	Luis Rivera	.05	.02	.01
☐ 432	Chad Kreuter	.05	.02	.01
☐ 433	Albert Hall	.05	.02	.01
☐ 434	Ken Patterson	.05	.02	.01
☐ 435	Len Dykstra	.15	.07	.02
☐ 436	Bobby Meacham	.05	.02	.01
☐ 437	Andy Benes FDP	.25	.11	.03
☐ 438	Greg Gross	.05	.02	.01
☐ 439	Frank DiPino	.05	.02	.01
☐ 440	Bobby Bonilla	.15	.07	.02
☐ 441	Jerry Reed	.05	.02	.01
☐ 442	Jose Oquendo	.05	.02	.01
☐ 443	Rod Nichols	.05	.02	.01
☐ 444	Moose Stubing MG	.05	.02	.01
	(Team checklist back)			
☐ 445	Matt Nokes	.05	.02	.01
☐ 446	Rob Murphy	.05	.02	.01
☐ 447	Donell Nixon	.05	.02	.01
☐ 448	Eric Plunk	.05	.02	.01
☐ 449	Carmelo Martinez	.05	.02	.01
☐ 450	Roger Clemens	.20	.09	.03
☐ 451	Mark Davidson	.05	.02	.01
☐ 452	Israel Sanchez	.05	.02	.01
☐ 453	Tom Prince	.05	.02	.01
☐ 454	Paul Assenmacher	.05	.02	.01
☐ 455	Johnny Ray	.05	.02	.01
☐ 456	Tim Belcher	.05	.02	.01
☐ 457	Mackey Sasser	.05	.02	.01
☐ 458	Donn Pall	.05	.02	.01
☐ 459	Seattle Mariners TL	.05	.02	.01
	Dave Valle			
☐ 460	Dave Stieb	.10	.05	.01
☐ 461	Buddy Bell	.10	.05	.01
☐ 462	Jose Guzman	.05	.02	.01
☐ 463	Steve Lake	.05	.02	.01
☐ 464	Bryn Smith	.05	.02	.01
☐ 465	Mark Grace	.15	.07	.02
☐ 466	Chuck Crim	.05	.02	.01
☐ 467	Jim Walewander	.05	.02	.01
☐ 468	Henry Cotto	.05	.02	.01
☐ 469	Jose Bautista	.05	.02	.01
☐ 470	Lance Parrish	.10	.05	.01
☐ 471	Steve Curry	.05	.02	.01
☐ 472	Brian Harper	.10	.05	.01
☐ 473	Don Robinson	.05	.02	.01
☐ 474	Bob Rodgers MG	.05	.02	.01
	(Team checklist back)			
☐ 475	Dave Parker	.15	.07	.02
☐ 476	Jon Perlman	.05	.02	.01
☐ 477	Dick Schofield	.05	.02	.01
☐ 478	Doug Drabek	.15	.07	.02
☐ 479	Mike Macfarlane	.10	.05	.01
☐ 480	Keith Hernandez	.10	.05	.01
☐ 481	Chris Brown	.05	.02	.01
☐ 482	Steve Peters	.05	.02	.01
☐ 483	Mickey Hatcher	.05	.02	.01
☐ 484	Steve Shields	.05	.02	.01
☐ 485	Hubie Brooks	.05	.02	.01
☐ 486	Jack McDowell	.15	.07	.02
☐ 487	Scott Lusader	.05	.02	.01
☐ 488	Kevin Coffman	.05	.02	.01
	("Now with Cubs")			
☐ 489	Phila. Phillies TL	.10	.05	.01
	Mike Schmidt			
☐ 490	Chris Sabo	.10	.05	.01
☐ 491	Mike Birkbeck	.05	.02	.01
☐ 492	Alan Ashby	.05	.02	.01
☐ 493	Todd Benzinger	.05	.02	.01
☐ 494	Shane Rawley	.05	.02	.01
☐ 495	Candy Maldonado	.05	.02	.01
☐ 496	Dwayne Henry	.05	.02	.01
☐ 497	Pete Stanicek	.05	.02	.01
☐ 498	Dave Valle	.05	.02	.01
☐ 499	Don Heinkel	.05	.02	.01
☐ 500	Jose Canseco	.30	.14	.04
☐ 501	Vance Law	.05	.02	.01
☐ 502	Duane Ward	.10	.05	.01
☐ 503	Al Newman	.05	.02	.01
☐ 504	Bob Walk	.05	.02	.01
☐ 505	Pete Rose MG	.20	.09	.03
	(Team checklist back)			
☐ 506	Kirt Manwaring	.05	.02	.01
☐ 507	Steve Farr	.05	.02	.01
☐ 508	Wally Backman	.05	.02	.01
☐ 509	Bud Black	.05	.02	.01
☐ 510	Bob Horner	.05	.02	.01
☐ 511	Richard Dotson	.05	.02	.01
☐ 512	Donnie Hill	.05	.02	.01
☐ 513	Jesse Orosco	.05	.02	.01
☐ 514	Chet Lemon	.05	.02	.01
☐ 515	Barry Larkin	.20	.09	.03
☐ 516	Eddie Whitson	.05	.02	.01
☐ 517	Greg Brock	.05	.02	.01
☐ 518	Bruce Ruffin	.05	.02	.01
☐ 519	New York Yankees TL	.05	.02	.01
	Willie Randolph			
☐ 520	Rick Sutcliffe	.10	.05	.01
☐ 521	Mickey Tettleton	.10	.05	.01
☐ 522	Randy Kramer	.05	.02	.01
☐ 523	Andres Thomas	.05	.02	.01
☐ 524	Checklist 397-528	.05	.02	.01
☐ 525	Chili Davis	.15	.07	.02
☐ 526	Wes Gardner	.05	.02	.01
☐ 527	Dave Henderson	.05	.02	.01
☐ 528	Luis Medina	.05	.02	.01
	(Lower left front			
	has white triangle)			
☐ 529	Tom Foley	.05	.02	.01
☐ 530	Nolan Ryan	.75	.35	.09
☐ 531	Dave Hengel	.05	.02	.01
☐ 532	Jerry Browne	.05	.02	.01
☐ 533	Andy Hawkins	.05	.02	.01
☐ 534	Doc Edwards MG	.05	.02	.01
	(Team checklist back)			
☐ 535	Todd Worrell UER	.10	.05	.01
	(4 wins in '88,			
	should be 5)			
☐ 536	Joel Skinner	.05	.02	.01
☐ 537	Pete Smith	.05	.02	.01
☐ 538	Juan Castillo	.05	.02	.01
☐ 539	Barry Jones	.05	.02	.01
☐ 540	Bo Jackson	.15	.07	.02
☐ 541	Cecil Fielder	.15	.07	.02
☐ 542	Todd Frohwirth	.05	.02	.01

☐ 543	Damon Berryhill	.05	.02	.01
☐ 544	Jeff Sellers	.05	.02	.01
☐ 545	Mookie Wilson	.10	.05	.01
☐ 546	Mark Williamson	.05	.02	.01
☐ 547	Mark McLemore	.05	.02	.01
☐ 548	Bobby Witt	.10	.05	.01
☐ 549	Chicago Cubs TL	.05	.02	.01
	Jamie Moyer			
	(Pitching)			
☐ 550	Orel Hershiser	.15	.07	.02
☐ 551	Randy Ready	.05	.02	.01
☐ 552	Greg Cadaret	.05	.02	.01
☐ 553	Luis Salazar	.05	.02	.01
☐ 554	Nick Esasky	.05	.02	.01
☐ 555	Bert Blyleven	.15	.07	.02
☐ 556	Bruce Fields	.05	.02	.01
☐ 557	Keith A. Miller	.05	.02	.01
☐ 558	Dan Pasqua	.05	.02	.01
☐ 559	Juan Agosto	.05	.02	.01
☐ 560	Tim Raines	.15	.07	.02
☐ 561	Luis Aguayo	.05	.02	.01
☐ 562	Danny Cox	.05	.02	.01
☐ 563	Bill Schroeder	.05	.02	.01
☐ 564	Russ Nixon MG	.05	.02	.01
	(Team checklist back)			
☐ 565	Jeff Russell	.05	.02	.01
☐ 566	Al Pedrique	.05	.02	.01
☐ 567	David Wells UER	.05	.02	.01
	(Complete Pitching			
	Recor)			
☐ 568	Mickey Brantley	.05	.02	.01
☐ 569	German Jimenez	.05	.02	.01
☐ 570	Tony Gwynn UER	.30	.14	.04
	('88 average should			
	be italicized as			
	league leader)			
☐ 571	Billy Ripken	.05	.02	.01
☐ 572	Atlee Hammaker	.05	.02	.01
☐ 573	Jim Abbott FDP	.30	.14	.04
☐ 574	Dave Clark	.05	.02	.01
☐ 575	Juan Samuel	.05	.02	.01
☐ 576	Greg Minton	.05	.02	.01
☐ 577	Randy Bush	.05	.02	.01
☐ 578	John Morris	.05	.02	.01
☐ 579	Houston Astros TL	.05	.02	.01
	Glenn Davis			
	(Batting stance)			
☐ 580	Harold Reynolds	.05	.02	.01
☐ 581	Gene Nelson	.05	.02	.01
☐ 582	Mike Marshall	.05	.02	.01
☐ 583	Paul Gibson	.05	.02	.01
☐ 584	Randy Velarde UER	.05	.02	.01
	(Signed 1935,			
	should be 1985)			
☐ 585	Harold Baines	.15	.07	.02
☐ 586	Joe Boever	.05	.02	.01
☐ 587	Mike Stanley	.10	.05	.01
☐ 588	Luis Alicea	.05	.02	.01
☐ 589	Dave Meads	.05	.02	.01
☐ 590	Andres Galarraga	.15	.07	.02
☐ 591	Jeff Musselman	.05	.02	.01
☐ 592	John Cangelosi	.05	.02	.01
☐ 593	Drew Hall	.05	.02	.01
☐ 594	Jimy Williams MG	.05	.02	.01
	(Team checklist back)			
☐ 595	Teddy Higuera	.05	.02	.01
☐ 596	Kurt Stillwell	.05	.02	.01
☐ 597	Terry Taylor	.05	.02	.01
☐ 598	Ken Oberkfell	.05	.02	.01
☐ 599	Tom Candiotti	.05	.02	.01
☐ 600	Wade Boggs	.15	.07	.02

☐ 601	Dave Dravecky	.10	.05	.01
☐ 602	Devon White	.15	.07	.02
☐ 603	Frank Tanana	.05	.02	.01
☐ 604	Paul O'Neill	.15	.07	.02
☐ 605A	Bob Welch ERR	2.00	.90	.25
	(Missing line on back,			
	"Complete M.L.			
	Pitching Record")			
☐ 605B	Bob Welch COR	.10	.05	.01
☐ 606	Rick Dempsey	.05	.02	.01
☐ 607	Willie Ansley FDP	.05	.02	.01
☐ 608	Phil Bradley	.05	.02	.01
☐ 609	Detroit Tigers TL	.05	.02	.01
	Frank Tanana			
	(With Alan Trammell			
	and Mike Heath)			
☐ 610	Randy Myers	.15	.07	.02
☐ 611	Don Slaught	.05	.02	.01
☐ 612	Dan Quisenberry	.10	.05	.01
☐ 613	Gary Varsho	.05	.02	.01
☐ 614	Joe Hesketh	.05	.02	.01
☐ 615	Robin Yount	.20	.09	.03
☐ 616	Steve Rosenberg	.05	.02	.01
☐ 617	Mark Parent	.05	.02	.01
☐ 618	Rance Mulliniks	.05	.02	.01
☐ 619	Checklist 529-660	.05	.02	.01
☐ 620	Barry Bonds	.40	.18	.05
☐ 621	Rick Mahler	.05	.02	.01
☐ 622	Stan Javier	.05	.02	.01
☐ 623	Fred Toliver	.05	.02	.01
☐ 624	Jack McKeon MG	.05	.02	.01
	(Team checklist back)			
☐ 625	Eddie Murray	.20	.09	.03
☐ 626	Jeff Reed	.05	.02	.01
☐ 627	Greg A. Harris	.05	.02	.01
☐ 628	Matt Williams	.50	.23	.06
☐ 629	Pete O'Brien	.05	.02	.01
☐ 630	Mike Greenwell	.10	.05	.01
☐ 631	Dave Bergman	.05	.02	.01
☐ 632	Bryan Harvey	.10	.05	.01
☐ 633	Daryl Boston	.05	.02	.01
☐ 634	Marvin Freeman	.05	.02	.01
☐ 635	Willie Randolph	.10	.05	.01
☐ 636	Bill Wilkinson	.05	.02	.01
☐ 637	Carmen Castillo	.05	.02	.01
☐ 638	Floyd Bannister	.05	.02	.01
☐ 639	Oakland A's TL	.05	.02	.01
	Walt Weiss			
☐ 640	Willie McGee	.10	.05	.01
☐ 641	Curt Young	.05	.02	.01
☐ 642	Argenis Salazar	.05	.02	.01
☐ 643	Louie Meadows	.05	.02	.01
☐ 644	Lloyd McClendon	.05	.02	.01
☐ 645	Jack Morris	.15	.07	.02
☐ 646	Kevin Bass	.05	.02	.01
☐ 647	Randy Johnson	1.00	.45	.12
☐ 648	Sandy Alomar FS	.20	.09	.03
☐ 649	Stewart Cliburn	.05	.02	.01
☐ 650	Kirby Puckett	.40	.18	.05
☐ 651	Tom Niedenfuer	.05	.02	.01
☐ 652	Rich Gedman	.05	.02	.01
☐ 653	Tommy Barrett	.05	.02	.01
☐ 654	Whitey Herzog MG	.10	.05	.01
	(Team checklist back)			
☐ 655	Dave Magadan	.05	.02	.01
☐ 656	Ivan Calderon	.05	.02	.01
☐ 657	Joe Magrane	.05	.02	.01
☐ 658	R.J. Reynolds	.05	.02	.01
☐ 659	Al Leiter	.05	.02	.01
☐ 660	Will Clark	.20	.09	.03
☐ 661	Dwight Gooden TBC84	.10	.05	.01

☐ 662	Lou Brock TBC79	.10	.05	.01
☐ 663	Hank Aaron TBC74	.20	.09	.03
☐ 664	Gil Hodges TBC69	.10	.05	.01
☐ 665A	Tony Oliva TBC64 ERR (fabricated card is enlarged version of Oliva's 64T card; Topps copyright missing)	2.00	.90	.25
☐ 665B	Tony Oliva TBC64 COR (fabricated card)	.10	.05	.01
☐ 666	Randy St.Claire	.05	.02	.01
☐ 667	Dwayne Murphy	.05	.02	.01
☐ 668	Mike Bielecki	.05	.02	.01
☐ 669	L.A. Dodgers TL Orel Hershiser (Mound conference with Mike Scioscia)	.10	.05	.01
☐ 670	Kevin Seitzer	.05	.02	.01
☐ 671	Jim Gantner	.05	.02	.01
☐ 672	Allan Anderson	.05	.02	.01
☐ 673	Don Baylor	.15	.07	.02
☐ 674	Otis Nixon	.05	.02	.01
☐ 675	Bruce Hurst	.05	.02	.01
☐ 676	Ernie Riles	.05	.02	.01
☐ 677	Dave Schmidt	.05	.02	.01
☐ 678	Dion James	.05	.02	.01
☐ 679	Willie Fraser	.05	.02	.01
☐ 680	Gary Carter	.15	.07	.02
☐ 681	Jeff D. Robinson	.05	.02	.01
☐ 682	Rick Leach	.05	.02	.01
☐ 683	Jose Cecena	.05	.02	.01
☐ 684	Dave Johnson MG (Team checklist back)	.05	.02	.01
☐ 685	Jeff Treadway	.05	.02	.01
☐ 686	Scott Terry	.05	.02	.01
☐ 687	Alvin Davis	.05	.02	.01
☐ 688	Zane Smith	.05	.02	.01
☐ 689A	Stan Jefferson (Pink triangle on front bottom left)	.05	.02	.01
☐ 689B	Stan Jefferson (Violet triangle on front bottom left)	.05	.02	.01
☐ 690	Doug Jones	.10	.05	.01
☐ 691	Roberto Kelly UER (83 Oneonta)	.10	.05	.01
☐ 692	Steve Ontiveros	.05	.02	.01
☐ 693	Pat Borders	.10	.05	.01
☐ 694	Les Lancaster	.05	.02	.01
☐ 695	Carlton Fisk	.15	.07	.02
☐ 696	Don August	.05	.02	.01
☐ 697A	Franklin Stubbs (Team name on front in white)	.05	.02	.01
☐ 697B	Franklin Stubbs (Team name on front in gray)	.05	.02	.01
☐ 698	Keith Atherton	.05	.02	.01
☐ 699	Pittsburgh Pirates TL Al Pedrique (Tony Gwynn sliding)	.05	.02	.01
☐ 700	Don Mattingly	.40	.18	.05
☐ 701	Storm Davis	.05	.02	.01
☐ 702	Jamie Quirk	.05	.02	.01
☐ 703	Scott Garrelts	.05	.02	.01
☐ 704	Carlos Quintana	.05	.02	.01
☐ 705	Terry Kennedy	.05	.02	.01
☐ 706	Pete Incaviglia	.10	.05	.01
☐ 707	Steve Jeltz	.05	.02	.01
☐ 708	Chuck Finley	.10	.05	.01
☐ 709	Tom Herr	.05	.02	.01
☐ 710	David Cone	.15	.07	.02
☐ 711	Candy Sierra	.05	.02	.01
☐ 712	Bill Swift	.10	.05	.01
☐ 713	Ty Griffin FDP	.05	.02	.01
☐ 714	Joe Morgan MG (Team checklist back)	.05	.02	.01
☐ 715	Tony Pena	.05	.02	.01
☐ 716	Wayne Tolleson	.05	.02	.01
☐ 717	Jamie Moyer	.05	.02	.01
☐ 718	Glenn Braggs	.05	.02	.01
☐ 719	Danny Darwin	.05	.02	.01
☐ 720	Tim Wallach	.05	.02	.01
☐ 721	Ron Tingley	.05	.02	.01
☐ 722	Todd Stottlemyre	.10	.05	.01
☐ 723	Rafael Belliard	.05	.02	.01
☐ 724	Jerry Don Gleaton	.05	.02	.01
☐ 725	Terry Steinbach	.10	.05	.01
☐ 726	Dickie Thon	.05	.02	.01
☐ 727	Joe Orsulak	.05	.02	.01
☐ 728	Charlie Puleo	.05	.02	.01
☐ 729	Texas Rangers TL Steve Buechele (Inconsistent design, team name on front surrounded by black, should be white)	.05	.02	.01
☐ 730	Danny Jackson	.05	.02	.01
☐ 731	Mike Young	.05	.02	.01
☐ 732	Steve Buechele	.05	.02	.01
☐ 733	Randy Bockus	.05	.02	.01
☐ 734	Jody Reed	.05	.02	.01
☐ 735	Roger McDowell	.05	.02	.01
☐ 736	Jeff Hamilton	.05	.02	.01
☐ 737	Norm Charlton	.10	.05	.01
☐ 738	Darnell Coles	.05	.02	.01
☐ 739	Brook Jacoby	.05	.02	.01
☐ 740	Dan Plesac	.05	.02	.01
☐ 741	Ken Phelps	.05	.02	.01
☐ 742	Mike Harkey FS	.05	.02	.01
☐ 743	Mike Heath	.05	.02	.01
☐ 744	Roger Craig MG (Team checklist back)	.05	.02	.01
☐ 745	Fred McGriff	.25	.11	.03
☐ 746	German Gonzalez UER (Wrong birthdate)	.05	.02	.01
☐ 747	Wil Tejada	.05	.02	.01
☐ 748	Jimmy Jones	.05	.02	.01
☐ 749	Rafael Ramirez	.05	.02	.01
☐ 750	Bret Saberhagen	.15	.07	.02
☐ 751	Ken Oberkfell	.05	.02	.01
☐ 752	Jim Gott	.05	.02	.01
☐ 753	Jose Uribe	.05	.02	.01
☐ 754	Bob Brower	.05	.02	.01
☐ 755	Mike Scioscia	.05	.02	.01
☐ 756	Scott Medvin	.05	.02	.01
☐ 757	Brady Anderson	.40	.18	.05
☐ 758	Gene Walter	.05	.02	.01
☐ 759	Milwaukee Brewers TL Rob Deer	.05	.02	.01
☐ 760	Lee Smith	.15	.07	.02
☐ 761	Dante Bichette	.75	.35	.09
☐ 762	Bobby Thigpen	.05	.02	.01
☐ 763	Dave Martinez	.05	.02	.01
☐ 764	Robin Ventura FDP	.50	.23	.06
☐ 765	Glenn Davis	.05	.02	.01
☐ 766	Cecilio Guante	.05	.02	.01
☐ 767	Mike Capel	.05	.02	.01
☐ 768	Bill Wegman	.05	.02	.01
☐ 769	Junior Ortiz	.05	.02	.01

		MINT	NRMT	EXC
☐ 770	Alan Trammell	.15	.07	.02
☐ 771	Ron Kittle	.05	.02	.01
☐ 772	Ron Oester	.05	.02	.01
☐ 773	Keith Moreland	.05	.02	.01
☐ 774	Frank Robinson MG (Team checklist back)	.15	.07	.02
☐ 775	Jeff Reardon	.15	.07	.02
☐ 776	Nelson Liriano	.05	.02	.01
☐ 777	Ted Power	.05	.02	.01
☐ 778	Bruce Benedict	.05	.02	.01
☐ 779	Craig McMurtry	.05	.02	.01
☐ 780	Pedro Guerrero	.10	.05	.01
☐ 781	Greg Briley	.05	.02	.01
☐ 782	Checklist 661-792	.05	.02	.01
☐ 783	Trevor Wilson	.05	.02	.01
☐ 784	Steve Avery FDP	.50	.23	.06
☐ 785	Ellis Burks	.15	.07	.02
☐ 786	Melido Perez	.05	.02	.01
☐ 787	Dave West	.10	.05	.01
☐ 788	Mike Morgan	.05	.02	.01
☐ 789	Kansas City Royals TL. Bo Jackson (Throwing)	.15	.07	.02
☐ 790	Sid Fernandez	.10	.05	.01
☐ 791	Jim Lindeman	.05	.02	.01
☐ 792	Rafael Santana	.05	.02	.01

1989 Topps Traded

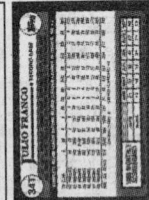

The 1989 Topps Traded set contains 132 standard-size (2 1/2" by 3 1/2") cards. The fronts have white borders; the horizontally oriented backs are red and pink. From the front the cards' style is indistinguishable from the 1989 Topps regular issue. The cards were distributed as a boxed set. Rookie Cards in this set include Ken Griffey Jr., Ken Hill, Deion Sanders, and Jerome Walton. Topps also produced a specially boxed "glossy" edition frequently referred to as the Topps Traded Tiffany set. This year, again, Topps did not disclose the number of Tiffany sets they produced or sold but it seems that production quantities were roughly similar (or slightly smaller, 15,000 sets) to the previous two years. The checklist of cards is identical to that of the normal non-glossy cards. There are two primary distinguishing features of the Tiffany cards, white card stock reverses and high gloss obverses. These Tiffany cards are valued approximately from three to five times the values listed below.

		MINT	NRMT	EXC
COMPLETE FACT.SET (132)		6.00	2.70	.75
COMMON CARD (1T-132T)		.05	.02	.01
☐ 1T	Don Aase	.05	.02	.01
☐ 2T	Jim Abbott	.25	.11	.03
☐ 3T	Kent Anderson	.05	.02	.01
☐ 4T	Keith Atherton	.05	.02	.01
☐ 5T	Wally Backman	.05	.02	.01
☐ 6T	Steve Balboni	.05	.02	.01
☐ 7T	Jesse Barfield	.05	.02	.01
☐ 8T	Steve Bedrosian	.05	.02	.01
☐ 9T	Todd Benzinger	.05	.02	.01
☐ 10T	Geronimo Berroa	.08	.04	.01
☐ 11T	Bert Blyleven	.10	.05	.01
☐ 12T	Bob Boone	.08	.04	.01
☐ 13T	Phil Bradley	.05	.02	.01
☐ 14T	Jeff Brantley	.05	.02	.01
☐ 15T	Kevin Brown	.08	.04	.01
☐ 16T	Jerry Browne	.05	.02	.01
☐ 17T	Chuck Cary	.05	.02	.01
☐ 18T	Carmen Castillo	.05	.02	.01
☐ 19T	Jim Clancy	.05	.02	.01
☐ 20T	Jack Clark	.08	.04	.01
☐ 21T	Bryan Clutterbuck	.05	.02	.01
☐ 22T	Jody Davis	.05	.02	.01
☐ 23T	Mike Devereaux	.05	.02	.01
☐ 24T	Frank DiPino	.05	.02	.01
☐ 25T	Benny Distefano	.05	.02	.01
☐ 26T	John Dopson	.05	.02	.01
☐ 27T	Len Dykstra	.10	.05	.01
☐ 28T	Jim Eisenreich	.05	.02	.01
☐ 29T	Nick Esasky	.05	.02	.01
☐ 30T	Alvaro Espinoza	.05	.02	.01
☐ 31T	Darrell Evans UER (Stat headings on back are for a pitcher)	.08	.04	.01
☐ 32T	Junior Felix	.05	.02	.01
☐ 33T	Felix Fermin	.05	.02	.01
☐ 34T	Julio Franco	.08	.04	.01
☐ 35T	Terry Francona	.05	.02	.01
☐ 36T	Cito Gaston MG	.08	.04	.01
☐ 37T	Bob Geren UER (Photo actually Mike Fennell)	.05	.02	.01
☐ 38T	Tom Gordon	.15	.07	.02
☐ 39T	Tommy Gregg	.05	.02	.01
☐ 40T	Ken Griffey Sr.	.08	.04	.01
☐ 41T	Ken Griffey Jr.	4.00	1.80	.50
☐ 42T	Kevin Gross	.05	.02	.01
☐ 43T	Lee Guetterman	.05	.02	.01
☐ 44T	Mel Hall	.05	.02	.01
☐ 45T	Erik Hanson	.25	.11	.03
☐ 46T	Gene Harris	.05	.02	.01
☐ 47T	Andy Hawkins	.05	.02	.01
☐ 48T	Rickey Henderson	.10	.05	.01
☐ 49T	Tom Herr	.05	.02	.01
☐ 50T	Ken Hill	.40	.18	.05
☐ 51T	Brian Holman	.05	.02	.01
☐ 52T	Brian Holton	.05	.02	.01
☐ 53T	Art Howe MG	.05	.02	.01
☐ 54T	Ken Howell	.05	.02	.01
☐ 55T	Bruce Hurst	.05	.02	.01
☐ 56T	Chris James	.05	.02	.01
☐ 57T	Randy Johnson	.75	.35	.09
☐ 58T	Jimmy Jones	.05	.02	.01
☐ 59T	Terry Kennedy	.05	.02	.01
☐ 60T	Paul Kilgus	.05	.02	.01
☐ 61T	Eric King	.05	.02	.01
☐ 62T	Ron Kittle	.05	.02	.01
☐ 63T	John Kruk	.10	.05	.01

☐	64T	Randy Kutcher	.05	.02	.01
☐	65T	Steve Lake	.05	.02	.01
☐	66T	Mark Langston	.10	.05	.01
☐	67T	Dave LaPoint	.05	.02	.01
☐	68T	Rick Leach	.05	.02	.01
☐	69T	Terry Leach	.05	.02	.01
☐	70T	Jim Lefebvre MG	.05	.02	.01
☐	71T	Al Leiter	.05	.02	.01
☐	72T	Jeffrey Leonard	.05	.02	.01
☐	73T	Derek Lilliquist	.05	.02	.01
☐	74T	Rick Mahler	.05	.02	.01
☐	75T	Tom McCarthy	.05	.02	.01
☐	76T	Lloyd McClendon	.05	.02	.01
☐	77T	Lance McCullers	.05	.02	.01
☐	78T	Oddibe McDowell	.05	.02	.01
☐	79T	Roger McDowell	.05	.02	.01
☐	80T	Larry McWilliams	.05	.02	.01
☐	81T	Randy Milligan	.05	.02	.01
☐	82T	Mike Moore	.05	.02	.01
☐	83T	Keith Moreland	.05	.02	.01
☐	84T	Mike Morgan	.05	.02	.01
☐	85T	Jamie Moyer	.05	.02	.01
☐	86T	Rob Murphy	.05	.02	.01
☐	87T	Eddie Murray	.20	.09	.03
☐	88T	Pete O'Brien	.05	.02	.01
☐	89T	Gregg Olson	.05	.02	.01
☐	90T	Steve Ontiveros	.05	.02	.01
☐	91T	Jesse Orosco	.05	.02	.01
☐	92T	Spike Owen	.05	.02	.01
☐	93T	Rafael Palmeiro	.25	.11	.03
☐	94T	Clay Parker	.05	.02	.01
☐	95T	Jeff Parrett	.05	.02	.01
☐	96T	Lance Parrish	.08	.04	.01
☐	97T	Dennis Powell	.05	.02	.01
☐	98T	Rey Quinones	.05	.02	.01
☐	99T	Doug Rader MG	.05	.02	.01
☐	100T	Willie Randolph	.08	.04	.01
☐	101T	Shane Rawley	.05	.02	.01
☐	102T	Randy Ready	.05	.02	.01
☐	103T	Bip Roberts	.08	.04	.01
☐	104T	Kenny Rogers	.30	.14	.04
☐	105T	Ed Romero	.05	.02	.01
☐	106T	Nolan Ryan	1.25	.55	.16
☐	107T	Luis Salazar	.05	.02	.01
☐	108T	Juan Samuel	.05	.02	.01
☐	109T	Alex Sanchez	.05	.02	.01
☐	110T	Deion Sanders	1.50	.70	.19
☐	111T	Steve Sax	.05	.02	.01
☐	112T	Rick Schu	.05	.02	.01
☐	113T	Dwight Smith	.05	.02	.01
☐	114T	Lonnie Smith	.05	.02	.01
☐	115T	Billy Spiers	.05	.02	.01
☐	116T	Kent Tekulve	.05	.02	.01
☐	117T	Walt Terrell	.05	.02	.01
☐	118T	Milt Thompson	.05	.02	.01
☐	119T	Dickie Thon	.05	.02	.01
☐	120T	Jeff Torborg MG	.05	.02	.01
☐	121T	Jeff Treadway	.05	.02	.01
☐	122T	Omar Vizquel	.25	.11	.03
☐	123T	Jerome Walton	.08	.04	.01
☐	124T	Gary Ward	.05	.02	.01
☐	125T	Claudell Washington	.05	.02	.01
☐	126T	Curt Wilkerson	.05	.02	.01
☐	127T	Eddie Williams	.05	.02	.01
☐	128T	Frank Williams	.05	.02	.01
☐	129T	Ken Williams	.05	.02	.01
☐	130T	Mitch Williams	.08	.04	.01
☐	131T	Steve Wilson	.05	.02	.01
☐	132T	Checklist 1T-132T	.05	.02	.01

1990 Topps

The 1990 Topps set contains 792 standard-size (2 1/2" by 3 1/2") cards. The front borders are various colors with the player's name at the bottom and team name at top. The horizontally oriented backs are yellowish green and contain statistics and highlights. Subsets include All-Stars (385-407) and Turn Back the Clock (661-665). The checklist cards are oriented alphabetically by team name and player name. The key Rookie Cards in this set are Delino DeShields, Juan Gonzalez, Marquis Grissom, Ben McDonald, Sammy Sosa, Frank Thomas, and Larry Walker. The Thomas card (414A) was printed without his name on front creating a scarce variation. The card is rarely seen and, for a newer issue, has experienced unprecedented growth as far as value. Topps also produced a specially boxed "glossy" edition frequently referred to as the Topps Tiffany set. This year, again, Topps did not disclose the number of Tiffany sets they produced or sold but it seems that production quantities were roughly similar (approximately 15,000 sets) to the previous year. The checklist of cards is identical to that of the normal non-glossy cards. There are two primary distinguishing features of the Tiffany cards, white card stock reverses and high gloss obverses. These Tiffany cards are valued approximately from three to five times the values listed below.in, Topps did not disclose the number of Tiffany sets they produced or sold but it seems that production quantities were roughly similar (approximately 15,000 sets) to the previous year. The checklist of cards is identical to that of the normal non-glossy cards. There are two primary distinguishing features of the Tiffany cards, white card stock reverses and high gloss obverses. These Tiffany cards are valued approximately from three to five times the values listed below.

	MINT	NRMT	EXC
COMPLETE SET (792)	15.00	6.75	1.85
COMPLETE FACT.SET (792)	15.00	6.75	1.85
COMMON CARD (1-792)	.05	.02	.01

BEWARE COUNTERFEIT THOMAS NNOF

☐ 1 Nolan Ryan	.75	.35	.09
☐ 2 Nolan Ryan Salute	.40	.18	.05
New York Mets			
☐ 3 Nolan Ryan Salute	.40	.18	.05
California Angels			
☐ 4 Nolan Ryan Salute	.40	.18	.05
Houston Astros			
☐ 5 Nolan Ryan Salute	.40	.18	.05
Texas Rangers UER			
(Says Texas Stadium			
rather than			
Arlington Stadium)			
☐ 6 Vince Coleman RB	.05	.02	.01
(50 consecutive			
stolen bases)			
☐ 7 Rickey Henderson RB	.10	.05	.01
(40 career leadoff			
home runs)			
☐ 8 Cal Ripken RB	.40	.18	.05
(20 or more homers for			
8 consecutive years,			
record for shortstops)			
☐ 9 Eric Plunk	.05	.02	.01
☐ 10 Barry Larkin	.20	.09	.03
☐ 11 Paul Gibson	.05	.02	.01
☐ 12 Joe Girardi	.05	.02	.01
☐ 13 Mark Williamson	.05	.02	.01
☐ 14 Mike Fetters	.05	.02	.01
☐ 15 Teddy Higuera	.05	.02	.01
☐ 16 Kent Anderson	.05	.02	.01
☐ 17 Kelly Downs	.05	.02	.01
☐ 18 Carlos Quintana	.05	.02	.01
☐ 19 Al Newman	.05	.02	.01
☐ 20 Mark Gubicza	.05	.02	.01
☐ 21 Jeff Torborg MG	.05	.02	.01
☐ 22 Bruce Ruffin	.05	.02	.01
☐ 23 Randy Velarde	.05	.02	.01
☐ 24 Joe Hesketh	.05	.02	.01
☐ 25 Willie Randolph	.10	.05	.01
☐ 26 Don Slaught	.05	.02	.01
☐ 27 Rick Leach	.05	.02	.01
☐ 28 Duane Ward	.05	.02	.01
☐ 29 John Cangelosi	.05	.02	:01
☐ 30 David Cone	.15	.07	.02
☐ 31 Henry Cotto	.05	.02	.01
☐ 32 John Farrell	.05	.02	.01
☐ 33 Greg Walker	.05	.02	.01
☐ 34 Tony Fossas	.05	.02	.01
☐ 35 Benito Santiago	.10	.05	.01
☐ 36 John Costello	.05	.02	.01
☐ 37 Domingo Ramos	.05	.02	.01
☐ 38 Wes Gardner	.05	.02	.01
☐ 39 Curt Ford	.05	.02	.01
☐ 40 Jay Howell	.05	.02	.01
☐ 41 Matt Williams	.30	.14	.04
☐ 42 Jeff M. Robinson	.05	.02	.01
☐ 43 Dante Bichette	.30	.14	.04
☐ 44 Roger Salkeld FDP	.05	.02	.01
☐ 45 Dave Parker UER	.10	.05	.01
(Born in Jackson,			
not Calhoun)			
☐ 46 Rob Dibble	.10	.05	.01
☐ 47 Brian Harper	.05	.02	.01
☐ 48 Zane Smith	.05	.02	.01
☐ 49 Tom Lawless	.05	.02	.01
☐ 50 Glenn Davis	.05	.02	.01
☐ 51 Doug Rader MG	.05	.02	.01
☐ 52 Jack Daugherty	.05	.02	.01
☐ 53 Mike LaCoss	.05	.02	.01
☐ 54 Joel Skinner	.05	.02	.01
☐ 55 Darrell Evans UER	.10	.05	.01

(HR total should be			
414, not 424)			
☐ 56 Franklin Stubbs	.05	.02	.01
☐ 57 Greg Vaughn	.10	.05	.01
☐ 58 Keith Miller	.05	.02	.01
☐ 59 Ted Power	.05	.02	.01
☐ 60 George Brett	.40	.18	.05
☐ 61 Deion Sanders	.50	.23	.06
☐ 62 Ramon Martinez	.15	.07	.02
☐ 63 Mike Pagliarulo	.05	.02	.01
☐ 64 Danny Darwin	.05	.02	.01
☐ 65 Devon White	.15	.07	.02
☐ 66 Greg Litton	.05	.02	.01
☐ 67 Scott Sanderson	.05	.02	.01
☐ 68 Dave Henderson	.05	.02	.01
☐ 69 Todd Frohwirth	.05	.02	.01
☐ 70 Mike Greenwell	.15	.07	.02
☐ 71 Allan Anderson	.05	.02	.01
☐ 72 Jeff Huson	.05	.02	.01
☐ 73 Bob Milacki	.05	.02	.01
☐ 74 Jeff Jackson FDP	.05	.02	.01
☐ 75 Doug Jones	.05	.02	.01
☐ 76 Dave Valle	.05	.02	.01
☐ 77 Dave Bergman	.05	.02	.01
☐ 78 Mike Flanagan	.05	.02	.01
☐ 79 Ron Kittle	.05	.02	.01
☐ 80 Jeff Russell	.05	.02	.01
☐ 81 Bob Rodgers MG	.05	.02	.01
☐ 82 Scott Terry	.05	.02	.01
☐ 83 Hensley Meulens	.05	.02	.01
☐ 84 Ray Searage	.05	.02	.01
☐ 85 Juan Samuel	.05	.02	.01
☐ 86 Paul Kilgus	.05	.02	.01
☐ 87 Rick Luecken	.05	.02	.01
☐ 88 Glenn Braggs	.05	.02	.01
☐ 89 Clint Zavaras	.05	.02	.01
☐ 90 Jack Clark	.10	.05	.01
☐ 91 Steve Frey	.05	.02	.01
☐ 92 Mike Stanley	.10	.05	.01
☐ 93 Shawn Hillegas	.05	.02	.01
☐ 94 Herm Winningham	.05	.02	.01
☐ 95 Todd Worrell	.05	.02	.01
☐ 96 Jody Reed	.05	.02	.01
☐ 97 Curt Schilling	.05	.02	.01
☐ 98 Jose Gonzalez	.05	.02	.01
☐ 99 Rich Monteleone	.05	.02	.01
☐ 100 Will Clark	.20	.09	.03
☐ 101 Shane Rawley	.05	.02	.01
☐ 102 Stan Javier	.05	.02	.01
☐ 103 Marvin Freeman	.05	.02	.01
☐ 104 Bob Knepper	.05	.02	.01
☐ 105 Randy Myers	.15	.07	.02
☐ 106 Charlie O'Brien	.05	.02	.01
☐ 107 Fred Lynn	.10	.05	.01
☐ 108 Rod Nichols	.05	.02	.01
☐ 109 Roberto Kelly	.10	.05	.01
☐ 110 Tommy Helms MG	.05	.02	.01
☐ 111 Ed Whited	.05	.02	.01
☐ 112 Glenn Wilson	.05	.02	.01
☐ 113 Manny Lee	.05	.02	.01
☐ 114 Mike Bielecki	.05	.02	.01
☐ 115 Tony Pena	.05	.02	.01
☐ 116 Floyd Bannister	.05	.02	.01
☐ 117 Mike Sharperson	.05	.02	.01
☐ 118 Erik Hanson	.10	.05	.01
☐ 119 Billy Hatcher	.05	.02	.01
☐ 120 John Franco	.15	.07	.02
☐ 121 Robin Ventura	.25	.11	.03
☐ 122 Shawn Abner	.05	.02	.01
☐ 123 Rich Gedman	.05	.02	.01
☐ 124 Dave Dravecky	.10	.05	.01

☐ 125	Kent Hrbek	.10	.05	.01	☐ 196	Gerald Young	.05	.02	.01
☐ 126	Randy Kramer	.05	.02	.01	☐ 197	Doug Drabek	.10	.05	.01
☐ 127	Mike Devereaux	.10	.05	.01	☐ 198	Mike Marshall	.05	.02	.01
☐ 128	Checklist 1	.05	.02	.01	☐ 199	Sergio Valdez	.05	.02	.01
☐ 129	Ron Jones	.05	.02	.01	☐ 200	Don Mattingly	.40	.18	.05
☐ 130	Bert Blyleven	.15	.07	.02	☐ 201	Cito Gaston MG	.10	.05	.01
☐ 131	Matt Nokes	.05	.02	.01	☐ 202	Mike Macfarlane	.05	.02	.01
☐ 132	Lance Blankenship	.05	.02	.01	☐ 203	Mike Roesler	.05	.02	.01
☐ 133	Ricky Horton	.05	.02	.01	☐ 204	Bob Dernier	.05	.02	.01
☐ 134	Earl Cunningham FDP	.05	.02	.01	☐ 205	Mark Davis	.05	.02	.01
☐ 135	Dave Magadan	.05	.02	.01	☐ 206	Nick Esasky	.05	.02	.01
☐ 136	Kevin Brown	.10	.05	.01	☐ 207	Bob Ojeda	.05	.02	.01
☐ 137	Marty Pevey	.05	.02	.01	☐ 208	Brook Jacoby	.05	.02	.01
☐ 138	Al Leiter	.05	.02	.01	☐ 209	Greg Mathews	.05	.02	.01
☐ 139	Greg Brock	.05	.02	.01	☐ 210	Ryne Sandberg	.30	.14	.04
☐ 140	Andre Dawson	.15	.07	.02	☐ 211	John Cerutti	.05	.02	.01
☐ 141	John Hart MG	.05	.02	.01	☐ 212	Joe Orsulak	.05	.02	.01
☐ 142	Jeff Wetherby	.05	.02	.01	☐ 213	Scott Bankhead	.05	.02	.01
☐ 143	Rafael Belliard	.05	.02	.01	☐ 214	Terry Francona	.05	.02	.01
☐ 144	Bud Black	.05	.02	.01	☐ 215	Kirk McCaskill	.05	.02	.01
☐ 145	Terry Steinbach	.10	.05	.01	☐ 216	Ricky Jordan	.05	.02	.01
☐ 146	Rob Richie	.05	.02	.01	☐ 217	Don Robinson	.05	.02	.01
☐ 147	Chuck Finley	.10	.05	.01	☐ 218	Wally Backman	.05	.02	.01
☐ 148	Edgar Martinez	.15	.07	.02	☐ 219	Donn Pall	.05	.02	.01
☐ 149	Steve Farr	.05	.02	.01	☐ 220	Barry Bonds	.30	.14	.04
☐ 150	Kirk Gibson	.15	.07	.02	☐ 221	Gary Mielke	.05	.02	.01
☐ 151	Rick Mahler	.05	.02	.01	☐ 222	Kurt Stillwell UER	.05	.02	.01
☐ 152	Lonnie Smith	.05	.02	.01		(Graduate misspelled			
☐ 153	Randy Milligan	.05	.02	.01		as gradute)			
☐ 154	Mike Maddux	.05	.02	.01	☐ 223	Tommy Gregg	.05	.02	.01
☐ 155	Ellis Burks	.10	.05	.01	☐ 224	Delino DeShields	.15	.07	.02
☐ 156	Ken Patterson	.05	.02	.01	☐ 225	Jim Deshaies	.05	.02	.01
☐ 157	Craig Biggio	.15	.07	.02	☐ 226	Mickey Hatcher	.05	.02	.01
☐ 158	Craig Lefferts	.05	.02	.01	☐ 227	Kevin Tapani	.15	.07	.02
☐ 159	Mike Felder	.05	.02	.01	☐ 228	Dave Martinez	.05	.02	.01
☐ 160	Dave Righetti	.05	.02	.01	☐ 229	David Wells	.05	.02	.01
☐ 161	Harold Reynolds	.05	.02	.01	☐ 230	Keith Hernandez	.10	.05	.01
☐ 162	Todd Zeile	.10	.05	.01	☐ 231	Jack McKeon MG	.05	.02	.01
☐ 163	Phil Bradley	.05	.02	.01	☐ 232	Darnell Coles	.05	.02	.01
☐ 164	Jeff Juden FDP	.05	.02	.01	☐ 233	Ken Hill	.15	.07	.02
☐ 165	Walt Weiss	.05	.02	.01	☐ 234	Mariano Duncan	.05	.02	.01
☐ 166	Bobby Witt	.05	.02	.01	☐ 235	Jeff Reardon	.15	.07	.02
☐ 167	Kevin Appier	.25	.11	.03	☐ 236	Hal Morris	.10	.05	.01
☐ 168	Jose Lind	.05	.02	.01	☐ 237	Kevin Ritz	.05	.02	.01
☐ 169	Richard Dotson	.05	.02	.01	☐ 238	Felix Jose	.05	.02	.01
☐ 170	George Bell	.05	.02	.01	☐ 239	Eric Show	.05	.02	.01
☐ 171	Russ Nixon MG	.05	.02	.01	☐ 240	Mark Grace	.15	.07	.02
☐ 172	Tom Lampkin	.05	.02	.01	☐ 241	Mike Krukow	.05	.02	.01
☐ 173	Tim Belcher	.05	.02	.01	☐ 242	Fred Manrique	.05	.02	.01
☐ 174	Jeff Kunkel	.05	.02	.01	☐ 243	Barry Jones	.05	.02	.01
☐ 175	Mike Moore	.05	.02	.01	☐ 244	Bill Schroeder	.05	.02	.01
☐ 176	Luis Quinones	.05	.02	.01	☐ 245	Roger Clemens	.15	.07	.02
☐ 177	Mike Henneman	.05	.02	.01	☐ 246	Jim Eisenreich	.05	.02	.01
☐ 178	Chris James	.05	.02	.01	☐ 247	Jerry Reed	.05	.02	.01
☐ 179	Brian Holton	.05	.02	.01	☐ 248	Dave Anderson	.05	.02	.01
☐ 180	Tim Raines	.15	.07	.02	☐ 249	Mike(Texas) Smith	.05	.02	.01
☐ 181	Juan Agosto	.05	.02	.01	☐ 250	Jose Canseco	.20	.09	.03
☐ 182	Mookie Wilson	.10	.05	.01	☐ 251	Jeff Blauser	.10	.05	.01
☐ 183	Steve Lake	.05	.02	.01	☐ 252	Otis Nixon	.05	.02	.01
☐ 184	Danny Cox	.05	.02	.01	☐ 253	Mark Portugal	.05	.02	.01
☐ 185	Ruben Sierra	.15	.07	.02	☐ 254	Francisco Cabrera	.05	.02	.01
☐ 186	Dave LaPoint	.05	.02	.01	☐ 255	Bobby Thigpen	.05	.02	.01
☐ 187	Rick Wrona	.05	.02	.01	☐ 256	Marvell Wynne	.05	.02	.01
☐ 188	Mike Smithson	.05	.02	.01	☐ 257	Jose DeLeon	.05	.02	.01
☐ 189	Dick Schofield	.05	.02	.01	☐ 258	Barry Lyons	.05	.02	.01
☐ 190	Rick Reuschel	.10	.05	.01	☐ 259	Lance McCullers	.05	.02	.01
☐ 191	Pat Borders	.05	.02	.01	☐ 260	Eric Davis	.10	.05	.01
☐ 192	Don August	.05	.02	.01	☐ 261	Whitey Herzog MG	.10	.05	.01
☐ 193	Andy Benes	.10	.05	.01	☐ 262	Checklist 2	.05	.02	.01
☐ 194	Glenallen Hill	.10	.05	.01	☐ 263	Mel Stottlemyre Jr.	.05	.02	.01
☐ 195	Tim Burke	.05	.02	.01	☐ 264	Bryan Clutterbuck	.05	.02	.01

☐ 265	Pete O'Brien	.05	.02	.01
☐ 266	German Gonzalez	.05	.02	.01
☐ 267	Mark Davidson	.05	.02	.01
☐ 268	Rob Murphy	.05	.02	.01
☐ 269	Dickie Thon	.05	.02	.01
☐ 270	Dave Stewart	.15	.07	.02
☐ 271	Chet Lemon	.05	.02	.01
☐ 272	Bryan Harvey	.10	.05	.01
☐ 273	Bobby Bonilla	.15	.07	.02
☐ 274	Mauro Gozzo	.05	.02	.01
☐ 275	Mickey Tettleton	.10	.05	.01
☐ 276	Gary Thurman	.05	.02	.01
☐ 277	Lenny Harris	.05	.02	.01
☐ 278	Pascual Perez	.05	.02	.01
☐ 279	Steve Buechele	.05	.02	.01
☐ 280	Lou Whitaker	.15	.07	.02
☐ 281	Kevin Bass	.05	.02	.01
☐ 282	Derek Lilliquist	.05	.02	.01
☐ 283	Joey Belle	1.00	.45	.12
☐ 284	Mark Gardner	.05	.02	.01
☐ 285	Willie McGee	.10	.05	.01
☐ 286	Lee Guetterman	.05	.02	.01
☐ 287	Vance Law	.05	.02	.01
☐ 288	Greg Briley	.05	.02	.01
☐ 289	Norm Charlton	.10	.05	.01
☐ 290	Robin Yount	.20	.09	.03
☐ 291	Dave Johnson MG	.10	.05	.01
☐ 292	Jim Gott	.05	.02	.01
☐ 293	Mike Gallego	.05	.02	.01
☐ 294	Craig McMurtry	.05	.02	.01
☐ 295	Fred McGriff	.20	.09	.03
☐ 296	Jeff Ballard	.05	.02	.01
☐ 297	Tommy Herr	.05	.02	.01
☐ 298	Dan Gladden	.05	.02	.01
☐ 299	Adam Peterson	.05	.02	.01
☐ 300	Bo Jackson	.15	.07	.02
☐ 301	Don Aase	.05	.02	.01
☐ 302	Marcus Lawton	.05	.02	.01
☐ 303	Rick Cerone	.05	.02	.01
☐ 304	Marty Clary	.05	.02	.01
☐ 305	Eddie Murray	.25	.11	.03
☐ 306	Tom Niedenfuer	.05	.02	.01
☐ 307	Bip Roberts	.10	.05	.01
☐ 308	Jose Guzman	.05	.02	.01
☐ 309	Eric Yelding	.05	.02	.01
☐ 310	Steve Bedrosian	.05	.02	.01
☐ 311	Dwight Smith	.05	.02	.01
☐ 312	Dan Quisenberry	.05	.02	.01
☐ 313	Gus Polidor	.05	.02	.01
☐ 314	Donald Harris FDP	.05	.02	.01
☐ 315	Bruce Hurst	.05	.02	.01
☐ 316	Carney Lansford	.10	.05	.01
☐ 317	Mark Guthrie	.05	.02	.01
☐ 318	Wallace Johnson	.05	.02	.01
☐ 319	Dion James	.05	.02	.01
☐ 320	Dave Stieb	.10	.05	.01
☐ 321	Joe Morgan MG	.05	.02	.01
☐ 322	Junior Ortiz	.05	.02	.01
☐ 323	Willie Wilson	.05	.02	.01
☐ 324	Pete Harnisch	.05	.02	.01
☐ 325	Robby Thompson	.10	.05	.01
☐ 326	Tom McCarthy	.05	.02	.01
☐ 327	Ken Williams	.05	.02	.01
☐ 328	Curt Young	.05	.02	.01
☐ 329	Oddibe McDowell	.05	.02	.01
☐ 330	Ron Darling	.05	.02	.01
☐ 331	Juan Gonzalez	1.25	.55	.16
☐ 332	Paul O'Neill	.15	.07	.02
☐ 333	Bill Wegman	.05	.02	.01
☐ 334	Johnny Ray	.05	.02	.01
☐ 335	Andy Hawkins	.05	.02	.01
☐ 336	Ken Griffey Jr.	2.00	.90	.25
☐ 337	Lloyd McClendon	.05	.02	.01
☐ 338	Dennis Lamp	.05	.02	.01
☐ 339	Dave Clark	.05	.02	.01
☐ 340	Fernando Valenzuela	.10	.05	.01
☐ 341	Tom Foley	.05	.02	.01
☐ 342	Alex Trevino	.05	.02	.01
☐ 343	Frank Tanana	.05	.02	.01
☐ 344	George Canale	.05	.02	.01
☐ 345	Harold Baines	.15	.07	.02
☐ 346	Jim Presley	.05	.02	.01
☐ 347	Junior Felix	.05	.02	.01
☐ 348	Gary Wayne	.05	.02	.01
☐ 349	Steve Finley	.10	.05	.01
☐ 350	Bret Saberhagen	.15	.07	.02
☐ 351	Roger Craig MG	.05	.02	.01
☐ 352	Bryn Smith	.05	.02	.01
☐ 353	Sandy Alomar Jr.	.10	.05	.01
	(Not listed as Jr. on card front)			
☐ 354	Stan Belinda	.05	.02	.01
☐ 355	Marty Barrett	.05	.02	.01
☐ 356	Randy Ready	.05	.02	.01
☐ 357	Dave West	.05	.02	.01
☐ 358	Andres Thomas	.05	.02	.01
☐ 359	Jimmy Jones	.05	.02	.01
☐ 360	Paul Molitor	.15	.07	.02
☐ 361	Randy McCament	.05	.02	.01
☐ 362	Damon Berryhill	.05	.02	.01
☐ 363	Dan Petry	.05	.02	.01
☐ 364	Rolando Roomes	.05	.02	.01
☐ 365	Ozzie Guillen	.10	.05	.01
☐ 366	Mike Heath	.05	.02	.01
☐ 367	Mike Morgan	.05	.02	.01
☐ 368	Bill Doran	.05	.02	.01
☐ 369	Todd Burns	.05	.02	.01
☐ 370	Tim Wallach	.05	.02	.01
☐ 371	Jimmy Key	.10	.05	.01
☐ 372	Terry Kennedy	.05	.02	.01
☐ 373	Alvin Davis	.05	.02	.01
☐ 374	Steve Cummings	.05	.02	.01
☐ 375	Dwight Evans	.10	.05	.01
☐ 376	Checklist 3 UER	.05	.02	.01
	(Higuera misalphabet- ized in Brewer list)			
☐ 377	Mickey Weston	.05	.02	.01
☐ 378	Luis Salazar	.05	.02	.01
☐ 379	Steve Rosenberg	.05	.02	.01
☐ 380	Dave Winfield	.15	.07	.02
☐ 381	Frank Robinson MG	.10	.05	.01
☐ 382	Jeff Musselman	.05	.02	.01
☐ 383	John Morris	.05	.02	.01
☐ 384	Pat Combs	.05	.02	.01
☐ 385	Fred McGriff AS	.10	.05	.01
☐ 386	Julio Franco AS	.05	.02	.01
☐ 387	Wade Boggs AS	.15	.07	.02
☐ 388	Cal Ripken AS	.40	.18	.05
☐ 389	Robin Yount AS	.10	.05	.01
☐ 390	Ruben Sierra AS	.10	.05	.01
☐ 391	Kirby Puckett AS	.20	.09	.03
☐ 392	Carlton Fisk AS	.10	.05	.01
☐ 393	Bret Saberhagen AS	.10	.05	.01
☐ 394	Jeff Ballard AS	.05	.02	.01
☐ 395	Jeff Russell AS	.05	.02	.01
☐ 396	A.Bartlett Giamatti	.20	.09	.03
	COMM MEM			
☐ 397	Will Clark AS	.15	.07	.02
☐ 398	Ryne Sandberg AS	.20	.09	.03
☐ 399	Howard Johnson AS	.05	.02	.01
☐ 400	Ozzie Smith AS	.15	.07	.02
☐ 401	Kevin Mitchell AS	.05	.02	.01

☐ 402 Eric Davis AS	.05	.02	.01
☐ 403 Tony Gwynn AS	.20	.09	.03
☐ 404 Craig Biggio AS	.15	.07	.02
☐ 405 Mike Scott AS	.05	.02	.01
☐ 406 Joe Magrane AS	.05	.02	.01
☐ 407 Mark Davis AS	.05	.02	.01
☐ 408 Trevor Wilson	.05	.02	.01
☐ 409 Tom Brunansky	.05	.02	.01
☐ 410 Joe Boever	.05	.02	.01
☐ 411 Ken Phelps	.05	.02	.01
☐ 412 Jamie Moyer	.05	.02	.01
☐ 413 Brian DuBois	.05	.02	.01
☐ 414A Frank Thomas FDP	1800.00	800.00	220.00
ERR (Name missing on card front)			
☐ 414B Frank Thomas FDP COR	4.00	1.80	.50
☐ 415 Shawon Dunston	.05	.02	.01
☐ 416 Dave Johnson (P)	.05	.02	.01
☐ 417 Jim Gantner	.05	.02	.01
☐ 418 Tom Browning	.05	.02	.01
☐ 419 Beau Allred	.05	.02	.01
☐ 420 Carlton Fisk	.15	.07	.02
☐ 421 Greg Minton	.05	.02	.01
☐ 422 Pat Sheridan	.05	.02	.01
☐ 423 Fred Toliver	.05	.02	.01
☐ 424 Jerry Reuss	.10	.05	.01
☐ 425 Bill Landrum	.05	.02	.01
☐ 426 Jeff Hamilton UER	.05	.02	.01
(Stats say he fanned 197 times in 1987, but he had 147 at bats)			
☐ 427 Carmen Castillo	.05	.02	.01
☐ 428 Steve Davis	.05	.02	.01
☐ 429 Tom Kelly MG	.05	.02	.01
☐ 430 Pete Incaviglia	.05	.02	.01
☐ 431 Randy Johnson	.40	.18	.05
☐ 432 Damaso Garcia	.05	.02	.01
☐ 433 Steve Olin	.05	.02	.01
☐ 434 Mark Carreon	.05	.02	.01
☐ 435 Kevin Seitzer	.05	.02	.01
☐ 436 Mel Hall	.05	.02	.01
☐ 437 Les Lancaster	.05	.02	.01
☐ 438 Greg Myers	.05	.02	.01
☐ 439 Jeff Parrett	.05	.02	.01
☐ 440 Alan Trammell	.15	.07	.02
☐ 441 Bob Kipper	.05	.02	.01
☐ 442 Jerry Browne	.05	.02	.01
☐ 443 Cris Carpenter	.05	.02	.01
☐ 444 Kyle Abbott FDP	.05	.02	.01
☐ 445 Danny Jackson	.05	.02	.01
☐ 446 Dan Pasqua	.05	.02	.01
☐ 447 Atlee Hammaker	.05	.02	.01
☐ 448 Greg Gagne	.05	.02	.01
☐ 449 Dennis Rasmussen	.05	.02	.01
☐ 450 Rickey Henderson	.15	.07	.02
☐ 451 Mark Lemke	.10	.05	.01
☐ 452 Luis DeLosSantos	.05	.02	.01
☐ 453 Jody Davis	.05	.02	.01
☐ 454 Jeff King	.10	.05	.01
☐ 455 Jeffrey Leonard	.05	.02	.01
☐ 456 Chris Gwynn	.05	.02	.01
☐ 457 Gregg Jefferies	.15	.07	.02
☐ 458 Bob McClure	.05	.02	.01
☐ 459 Jim Lefebvre MG	.05	.02	.01
☐ 460 Mike Scott	.05	.02	.01
☐ 461 Carlos Martinez	.05	.02	.01
☐ 462 Denny Walling	.05	.02	.01
☐ 463 Drew Hall	.05	.02	.01
☐ 464 Jerome Walton	.05	.02	.01
☐ 465 Kevin Gross	.05	.02	.01
☐ 466 Rance Mulliniks	.05	.02	.01

☐ 467 Juan Nieves	.05	.02	.01
☐ 468 Bill Ripken	.05	.02	.01
☐ 469 John Kruk	.15	.07	.02
☐ 470 Frank Viola	.10	.05	.01
☐ 471 Mike Brumley	.05	.02	.01
☐ 472 Jose Uribe	.05	.02	.01
☐ 473 Joe Price	.05	.02	.01
☐ 474 Rich Thompson	.05	.02	.01
☐ 475 Bob Welch	.10	.05	.01
☐ 476 Brad Komminsk	.05	.02	.01
☐ 477 Willie Fraser	.05	.02	.01
☐ 478 Mike LaValliere	.05	.02	.01
☐ 479 Frank White	.10	.05	.01
☐ 480 Sid Fernandez	.10	.05	.01
☐ 481 Garry Templeton	.05	.02	.01
☐ 482 Steve Carter	.05	.02	.01
☐ 483 Alejandro Pena	.05	.02	.01
☐ 484 Mike Fitzgerald	.05	.02	.01
☐ 485 John Candelaria	.05	.02	.01
☐ 486 Jeff Treadway	.05	.02	.01
☐ 487 Steve Searcy	.05	.02	.01
☐ 488 Ken Oberkfell	.05	.02	.01
☐ 489 Nick Leyva MG	.05	.02	.01
☐ 490 Dan Plesac	.05	.02	.01
☐ 491 Dave Cochrane	.05	.02	.01
☐ 492 Ron Oester	.05	.02	.01
☐ 493 Jason Grimsley	.05	.02	.01
☐ 494 Terry Puhl	.05	.02	.01
☐ 495 Lee Smith	.15	.07	.02
☐ 496 Cecil Espy UER	.05	.02	.01
('88 stats have 3 SB's, should be 33)			
☐ 497 Dave Schmidt	.05	.02	.01
☐ 498 Rick Schu	.05	.02	.01
☐ 499 Bill Long	.05	.02	.01
☐ 500 Kevin Mitchell	.10	.05	.01
☐ 501 Matt Young	.05	.02	.01
☐ 502 Mitch Webster	.05	.02	.01
☐ 503 Randy St.Claire	.05	.02	.01
☐ 504 Tom O'Malley	.05	.02	.01
☐ 505 Kelly Gruber	.05	.02	.01
☐ 506 Tom Glavine	.25	.11	.03
☐ 507 Gary Redus	.05	.02	.01
☐ 508 Terry Leach	.05	.02	.01
☐ 509 Tom Pagnozzi	.05	.02	.01
☐ 510 Dwight Gooden	.10	.05	.01
☐ 511 Clay Parker	.05	.02	.01
☐ 512 Gary Pettis	.05	.02	.01
☐ 513 Mark Eichhorn	.05	.02	.01
☐ 514 Andy Allanson	.05	.02	.01
☐ 515 Len Dykstra	.15	.07	.02
☐ 516 Tim Leary	.05	.02	.01
☐ 517 Roberto Alomar	.30	.14	.04
☐ 518 Bill Krueger	.05	.02	.01
☐ 519 Bucky Dent MG	.05	.02	.01
☐ 520 Mitch Williams	.10	.05	.01
☐ 521 Craig Worthington	.05	.02	.01
☐ 522 Mike Dunne	.05	.02	.01
☐ 523 Jay Bell	.10	.05	.01
☐ 524 Daryl Boston	.05	.02	.01
☐ 525 Wally Joyner	.15	.07	.02
☐ 526 Checklist 4	.05	.02	.01
☐ 527 Ron Hassey	.05	.02	.01
☐ 528 Kevin Wickander UER	.05	.02	.01
(Monthly scoreboard strikeout total was 2.2, that was his innings pitched total)			
☐ 529 Greg A. Harris	.05	.02	.01
☐ 530 Mark Langston	.15	.07	.02
☐ 531 Ken Caminiti	.15	.07	.02

☐ 532	Cecilio Guante	.05	.02	.01
☐ 533	Tim Jones	.05	.02	.01
☐ 534	Louie Meadows	.05	.02	.01
☐ 535	John Smoltz	.15	.07	.02
☐ 536	Bob Geren	.05	.02	.01
☐ 537	Mark Grant	.05	.02	.01
☐ 538	Bill Spiers UER	.05	.02	.01
	(Photo actually George Canale)			
☐ 539	Neal Heaton	.05	.02	.01
☐ 540	Danny Tartabull	.10	.05	.01
☐ 541	Pat Perry	.05	.02	.01
☐ 542	Darren Daulton	.15	.07	.02
☐ 543	Nelson Liriano	.05	.02	.01
☐ 544	Dennis Boyd	.05	.02	.01
☐ 545	Kevin McReynolds	.05	.02	.01
☐ 546	Kevin Hickey	.05	.02	.01
☐ 547	Jack Howell	.05	.02	.01
☐ 548	Pat Clements	.05	.02	.01
☐ 549	Don Zimmer MG	.05	.02	.01
☐ 550	Julio Franco	.10	.05	.01
☐ 551	Tim Crews	.10	.05	.01
☐ 552	Mike(Miss.) Smith	.05	.02	.01
☐ 553	Scott Scudder UER	.05	.02	.01
	(Cedar Rap1ds)			
☐ 554	Jay Buhner	.15	.07	.02
☐ 555	Jack Morris	.15	.07	.02
☐ 556	Gene Larkin	.05	.02	.01
☐ 557	Jeff Innis	.05	.02	.01
☐ 558	Rafael Ramirez	.05	.02	.01
☐ 559	Andy McGaffigan	.05	.02	.01
☐ 560	Steve Sax	.05	.02	.01
☐ 561	Ken Dayley	.05	.02	.01
☐ 562	Chad Kreuter	.05	.02	.01
☐ 563	Alex Sanchez	.05	.02	.01
☐ 564	Tyler Houston FDP	.05	.02	.01
☐ 565	Scott Fletcher	.05	.02	.01
☐ 566	Mark Knudson	.05	.02	.01
☐ 567	Ron Gant	.15	.07	.02
☐ 568	John Smiley	.05	.02	.01
☐ 569	Ivan Calderon	.05	.02	.01
☐ 570	Cal Ripken	.75	.35	.09
☐ 571	Brett Butler	.15	.07	.02
☐ 572	Greg W. Harris	.05	.02	.01
☐ 573	Danny Heep	.05	.02	.01
☐ 574	Bill Swift	.05	.02	.01
☐ 575	Lance Parrish	.10	.05	.01
☐ 576	Mike Dyer	.05	.02	.01
☐ 577	Charlie Hayes	.10	.05	.01
☐ 578	Joe Magrane	.05	.02	.01
☐ 579	Art Howe MG	.05	.02	.01
☐ 580	Joe Carter	.15	.07	.02
☐ 581	Ken Griffey Sr.	.10	.05	.01
☐ 582	Rick Honeycutt	.05	.02	.01
☐ 583	Bruce Benedict	.05	.02	.01
☐ 584	Phil Stephenson	.05	.02	.01
☐ 585	Kal Daniels	.05	.02	.01
☐ 586	Edwin Nunez	.05	.02	.01
☐ 587	Lance Johnson	.10	.05	.01
☐ 588	Rick Rhoden	.05	.02	.01
☐ 589	Mike Aldrete	.05	.02	.01
☐ 590	Ozzie Smith	.20	.09	.03
☐ 591	Todd Stottlemyre	.10	.05	.01
☐ 592	R.J. Reynolds	.05	.02	.01
☐ 593	Scott Bradley	.05	.02	.01
☐ 594	Luis Sojo	.05	.02	.01
☐ 595	Greg Swindell	.10	.05	.01
☐ 596	Jose DeJesus	.05	.02	.01
☐ 597	Chris Bosio	.05	.02	.01
☐ 598	Brady Anderson	.10	.05	.01
☐ 599	Frank Williams	.05	.02	.01
☐ 600	Darryl Strawberry	.10	.05	.01
☐ 601	Luis Rivera	.05	.02	.01
☐ 602	Scott Garrelts	.05	.02	.01
☐ 603	Tony Armas	.05	.02	.01
☐ 604	Ron Robinson	.05	.02	.01
☐ 605	Mike Scioscia	.05	.02	.01
☐ 606	Storm Davis	.05	.02	.01
☐ 607	Steve Jeltz	.05	.02	.01
☐ 608	Eric Anthony	.05	.02	.01
☐ 609	Sparky Anderson MG	.10	.05	.01
☐ 610	Pedro Guerrero	.10	.05	.01
☐ 611	Walt Terrell	.05	.02	.01
☐ 612	Dave Gallagher	.05	.02	.01
☐ 613	Jeff Pico	.05	.02	.01
☐ 614	Nelson Santovenia	.05	.02	.01
☐ 615	Rob Deer	.05	.02	.01
☐ 616	Brian Holman	.05	.02	.01
☐ 617	Geronimo Berroa	.10	.05	.01
☐ 618	Ed Whitson	.05	.02	.01
☐ 619	Rob Ducey	.05	.02	.01
☐ 620	Tony Castillo	.05	.02	.01
☐ 621	Melido Perez	.05	.02	.01
☐ 622	Sid Bream	.05	.02	.01
☐ 623	Jim Corsi	.05	.02	.01
☐ 624	Darrin Jackson	.05	.02	.01
☐ 625	Roger McDowell	.05	.02	.01
☐ 626	Bob Melvin	.05	.02	.01
☐ 627	Jose Rijo	.10	.05	.01
☐ 628	Candy Maldonado	.05	.02	.01
☐ 629	Eric Hetzel	.05	.02	.01
☐ 630	Gary Gaetti	.10	.05	.01
☐ 631	John Wetteland	.10	.05	.01
☐ 632	Scott Lusader	.05	.02	.01
☐ 633	Dennis Cook	.05	.02	.01
☐ 634	Luis Polonia	.10	.05	.01
☐ 635	Brian Downing	.05	.02	.01
☐ 636	Jesse Orosco	.05	.02	.01
☐ 637	Craig Reynolds	.05	.02	.01
☐ 638	Jeff Montgomery	.10	.05	.01
☐ 639	Tony LaRussa MG	.10	.05	.01
☐ 640	Rick Sutcliffe	.05	.02	.01
☐ 641	Doug Strange	.05	.02	.01
☐ 642	Jack Armstrong	.05	.02	.01
☐ 643	Alfredo Griffin	.05	.02	.01
☐ 644	Paul Assenmacher	.05	.02	.01
☐ 645	Jose Oquendo	.05	.02	.01
☐ 646	Checklist 5	.05	.02	.01
☐ 647	Rex Hudler	.05	.02	.01
☐ 648	Jim Clancy	.05	.02	.01
☐ 649	Dan Murphy	.05	.02	.01
☐ 650	Mike Witt	.05	.02	.01
☐ 651	Rafael Santana	.05	.02	.01
☐ 652	Mike Boddicker	.05	.02	.01
☐ 653	John Moses	.05	.02	.01
☐ 654	Paul Coleman FDP	.05	.02	.01
☐ 655	Gregg Olson	.05	.02	.01
☐ 656	Mackey Sasser	.05	.02	.01
☐ 657	Terry Mulholland	.05	.02	.01
☐ 658	Donell Nixon	.05	.02	.01
☐ 659	Greg Cadaret	.05	.02	.01
☐ 660	Vince Coleman	.10	.05	.01
☐ 661	Dick Howser TBC'85	.05	.02	.01
	UER (Seaver's 300th on 7/11/85, should be 8/4/85)			
☐ 662	Mike Schmidt TBC'80	.15	.07	.02
☐ 663	Fred Lynn TBC'75	.05	.02	.01
☐ 664	Johnny Bench TBC'70	.10	.05	.01
☐ 665	Sandy Koufax TBC'65	.20	.09	.03
☐ 666	Brian Fisher	.05	.02	.01
☐ 667	Curt Wilkerson	.05	.02	.01

☐ 668	Joe Oliver	.05	.02 .01
☐ 669	Tom Lasorda MG	.10	.05 .01
☐ 670	Dennis Eckersley	.15	.07 .02
☐ 671	Bob Boone	.10	.05 .01
☐ 672	Roy Smith	.05	.02 .01
☐ 673	Joey Meyer	.05	.02 .01
☐ 674	Spike Owen	.05	.02 .01
☐ 675	Jim Abbott	.15	.07 .02
☐ 676	Randy Kutcher	.05	.02 .01
☐ 677	Jay Tibbs	.05	.02 .01
☐ 678	Kirt Manwaring UER	.05	.02 .01
	('88 Phoenix stats repeated)		
☐ 679	Gary Ward	.05	.02 .01
☐ 680	Howard Johnson	.10	.05 .01
☐ 681	Mike Schooler	.05	.02 .01
☐ 682	Dann Bilardello	.05	.02 .01
☐ 683	Kenny Rogers	.05	.02 .01
☐ 684	Julio Machado	.05	.02 .01
☐ 685	Tony Fernandez	.10	.05 .01
☐ 686	Carmelo Martinez	.05	.02 .01
☐ 687	Tim Birtsas	.05	.02 .01
☐ 688	Milt Thompson	.05	.02 .01
☐ 689	Rich Yett	.05	.02 .01
☐ 690	Mark McGwire	.15	.07 .02
☐ 691	Chuck Cary	.05	.02 .01
☐ 692	Sammy Sosa	.75	.35 .09
☐ 693	Calvin Schiraldi	.05	.02 .01
☐ 694	Mike Stanton	.05	.02 .01
☐ 695	Tom Henke	.10	.05 .01
☐ 696	B.J. Surhoff	.10	.05 .01
☐ 697	Mike Davis	.05	.02 .01
☐ 698	Omar Vizquel	.05	.02 .01
☐ 699	Jim Leyland MG	.05	.02 .01
☐ 700	Kirby Puckett	.30	.14 .04
☐ 701	Bernie Williams	.30	.14 .04
☐ 702	Tony Phillips	.15	.07 .02
☐ 703	Jeff Brantley	.05	.02 .01
☐ 704	Chip Hale	.05	.02 .01
☐ 705	Claudell Washington	.05	.02 .01
☐ 706	Geno Petralli	.05	.02 .01
☐ 707	Luis Aquino	.05	.02 .01
☐ 708	Larry Sheets	.05	.02 .01
☐ 709	Juan Berenguer	.05	.02 .01
☐ 710	Von Hayes	.05	.02 .01
☐ 711	Rick Aguilera	.10	.05 .01
☐ 712	Todd Benzinger	.05	.02 .01
☐ 713	Tim Drummond	.05	.02 .01
☐ 714	Marquis Grissom	.60	.25 .07
☐ 715	Greg Maddux	.60	.25 .07
☐ 716	Steve Balboni	.05	.02 .01
☐ 717	Ron Karkovice	.05	.02 .01
☐ 718	Gary Sheffield	.20	.09 .03
☐ 719	Wally Whitehurst	.05	.02 .01
☐ 720	Andres Galarraga	.15	.07 .02
☐ 721	Lee Mazzilli	.05	.02 .01
☐ 722	Felix Fermin	.05	.02 .01
☐ 723	Jeff D. Robinson	.05	.02 .01
☐ 724	Juan Bell	.05	.02 .01
☐ 725	Terry Pendleton	.15	.07 .02
☐ 726	Gene Nelson	.05	.02 .01
☐ 727	Pat Tabler	.05	.02 .01
☐ 728	Jim Acker	.05	.02 .01
☐ 729	Bobby Valentine MG	.05	.02 .01
☐ 730	Tony Gwynn	.30	.14 .04
☐ 731	Don Carman	.05	.02 .01
☐ 732	Ernest Riles	.05	.02 .01
☐ 733	John Dopson	.05	.02 .01
☐ 734	Kevin Elster	.05	.02 .01
☐ 735	Charlie Hough	.10	.05 .01
☐ 736	Rick Dempsey	.05	.02 .01
☐ 737	Chris Sabo	.05	.02 .01
☐ 738	Gene Harris	.05	.02 .01
☐ 739	Dale Sveum	.05	.02 .01
☐ 740	Jesse Barfield	.05	.02 .01
☐ 741	Steve Wilson	.05	.02 .01
☐ 742	Ernie Whitt	.05	.02 .01
☐ 743	Tom Candiotti	.05	.02 .01
☐ 744	Kelly Mann	.05	.02 .01
☐ 745	Hubie Brooks	.05	.02 .01
☐ 746	Dave Smith	.05	.02 .01
☐ 747	Randy Bush	.05	.02 .01
☐ 748	Doyle Alexander	.05	.02 .01
☐ 749	Mark Parent UER	.05	.02 .01
	('87 BA .80, should be .080)		
☐ 750	Dale Murphy	.15	.07 .02
☐ 751	Steve Lyons	.05	.02 .01
☐ 752	Tom Gordon	.10	.05 .01
☐ 753	Chris Speier	.05	.02 .01
☐ 754	Bob Walk	.05	.02 .01
☐ 755	Rafael Palmeiro	.15	.07 .02
☐ 756	Ken Howell	.05	.02 .01
☐ 757	Larry Walker	.75	.35 .09
☐ 758	Mark Thurmond	.05	.02 .01
☐ 759	Tom Trebelhorn MG	.05	.02 .01
☐ 760	Wade Boggs	.15	.07 .02
☐ 761	Mike Jackson	.05	.02 .01
☐ 762	Doug Dascenzo	.05	.02 .01
☐ 763	Dennis Martinez	.10	.05 .01
☐ 764	Tim Teufel	.05	.02 .01
☐ 765	Chili Davis	.15	.07 .02
☐ 766	Brian Meyer	.05	.02 .01
☐ 767	Tracy Jones	.05	.02 .01
☐ 768	Chuck Crim	.05	.02 .01
☐ 769	Greg Hibbard	.05	.02 .01
☐ 770	Cory Snyder	.05	.02 .01
☐ 771	Pete Smith	.05	.02 .01
☐ 772	Jeff Reed	.05	.02 .01
☐ 773	Dave Leiper	.05	.02 .01
☐ 774	Ben McDonald	.15	.07 .02
☐ 775	Andy Van Slyke	.10	.05 .01
☐ 776	Charlie Leibrandt	.05	.02 .01
☐ 777	Tim Laudner	.05	.02 .01
☐ 778	Mike Jeffcoat	.05	.02 .01
☐ 779	Lloyd Moseby	.05	.02 .01
☐ 780	Orel Hershiser	.15	.07 .02
☐ 781	Mario Diaz	.05	.02 .01
☐ 782	Jose Alvarez	.05	.02 .01
☐ 783	Checklist 6	.05	.02 .01
☐ 784	Scott Bailes	.05	.02 .01
☐ 785	Jim Rice	.15	.07 .02
☐ 786	Eric King	.05	.02 .01
☐ 787	Rene Gonzales	.05	.02 .01
☐ 788	Frank DiPino	.05	.02 .01
☐ 789	John Wathan MG	.05	.02 .01
☐ 790	Gary Carter	.15	.07 .02
☐ 791	Alvaro Espinoza	.05	.02 .01
☐ 792	Gerald Perry	.05	.02 .01

1990 Topps Traded

The 1990 Topps Traded Set was the tenth consecutive year Topps issued a set at the end of the year. This 132-card standard size (2 1/2" by 3 1/2") set was arranged alphabetically by player and includes a mix of traded players and rookies for whom

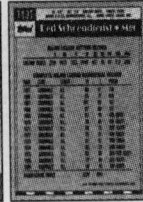

Topps did not include a card in the regular set. The key Rookie Cards in this set are Carlos Baerga, Scott Erickson, Travis Fryman, Dave Hollins, Dave Justice, Kevin Maas, and John Olerud. Also for the first time, Topps not only issued the set in a special collector boxes (made in Ireland) but distributed (on a significant basis) the set via their own wax packs. The wax pack cards were produced Topps' Duryea, Pennsylvania plant. There were seven cards in the packs and the wrapper highlighted the set as containing promising rookies, players who changed teams, and new managers. The cards differ in that the Irish-made cards have the whiter-type backs typical of the cards made in Ireland while the American cards have the typical Topps gray-type card stock on the back. Topps also produced a specially boxed "glossy" edition frequently referred to as the Topps Traded Tiffany set. This year, again, Topps did not disclose the number of Tiffany sets they produced or sold but it seems that production quantities were roughly similar (approximately 15,000 sets) to the previous year. The checklist of cards is identical to that of the normal non-glossy cards. There are two primary distinguishing features of the Tiffany cards, white card stock reverses and high gloss obverses. These Tiffany cards are valued approximately from three to five times the values listed below.

	MINT	NRMT	EXC
COMPLETE SET (132)	4.00	1.80	.50
COMPLETE FACT.SET (132)	4.00	1.80	.50
COMMON CARD (1T-132T)	.05	.02	.01
*GRAY AND WHITE BACKS: SAME VALUE			

☐ 1T	Darrel Akerfelds	.05	.02	.01
☐ 2T	Sandy Alomar Jr.	.10	.05	.01
☐ 3T	Brad Arnsberg	.05	.02	.01
☐ 4T	Steve Avery	.20	.09	.03
☐ 5T	Wally Backman	.05	.02	.01
☐ 6T	Carlos Baerga	1.50	.70	.19
☐ 7T	Kevin Bass	.05	.02	.01
☐ 8T	Willie Blair	.05	.02	.01
☐ 9T	Mike Blowers	.20	.09	.03
☐ 10T	Shawn Boskie	.05	.02	.01
☐ 11T	Daryl Boston	.05	.02	.01
☐ 12T	Dennis Boyd	.05	.02	.01
☐ 13T	Glenn Braggs	.05	.02	.01
☐ 14T	Hubie Brooks	.05	.02	.01
☐ 15T	Tom Brunansky	.05	.02	.01
☐ 16T	John Burkett	.05	.02	.01
☐ 17T	Casey Candaele	.05	.02	.01
☐ 18T	John Candelaria	.05	.02	.01
☐ 19T	Gary Carter	.15	.07	.02
☐ 20T	Joe Carter	.15	.07	.02
☐ 21T	Rick Cerone	.05	.02	.01
☐ 22T	Scott Coolbaugh	.05	.02	.01
☐ 23T	Bobby Cox MG	.05	.02	.01
☐ 24T	Mark Davis	.05	.02	.01
☐ 25T	Storm Davis	.05	.02	.01
☐ 26T	Edgar Diaz	.05	.02	.01
☐ 27T	Wayne Edwards	.05	.02	.01
☐ 28T	Mark Eichhorn	.05	.02	.01
☐ 29T	Scott Erickson	.15	.07	.02
☐ 30T	Nick Esasky	.05	.02	.01
☐ 31T	Cecil Fielder	.15	.07	.02
☐ 32T	John Franco	.10	.05	.01
☐ 33T	Travis Fryman	.50	.23	.06
☐ 34T	Bill Gullickson	.05	.02	.01
☐ 35T	Darryl Hamilton	.10	.05	.01
☐ 36T	Mike Harkey	.05	.02	.01
☐ 37T	Bud Harrelson MG	.05	.02	.01
☐ 38T	Billy Hatcher	.05	.02	.01
☐ 39T	Keith Hernandez	.10	.05	.01
☐ 40T	Joe Hesketh	.05	.02	.01
☐ 41T	Dave Hollins	.15	.07	.02
☐ 42T	Sam Horn	.05	.02	.01
☐ 43T	Steve Howard	.05	.02	.01
☐ 44T	Todd Hundley	.15	.07	.02
☐ 45T	Jeff Huson	.05	.02	.01
☐ 46T	Chris James	.05	.02	.01
☐ 47T	Stan Javier	.05	.02	.01
☐ 48T	Dave Justice	.75	.35	.09
☐ 49T	Jeff Kaiser	.05	.02	.01
☐ 50T	Dana Kiecker	.05	.02	.01
☐ 51T	Joe Klink	.05	.02	.01
☐ 52T	Brent Knackert	.05	.02	.01
☐ 53T	Brad Komminsk	.05	.02	.01
☐ 54T	Mark Langston	.15	.07	.02
☐ 55T	Tim Layana	.05	.02	.01
☐ 56T	Rick Leach	.05	.02	.01
☐ 57T	Terry Leach	.05	.02	.01
☐ 58T	Tim Leary	.05	.02	.01
☐ 59T	Craig Lefferts	.05	.02	.01
☐ 60T	Charlie Leibrandt	.05	.02	.01
☐ 61T	Jim Leyritz	.05	.02	.01
☐ 62T	Fred Lynn	.10	.05	.01
☐ 63T	Kevin Maas	.10	.05	.01
☐ 64T	Shane Mack	.05	.02	.01
☐ 65T	Candy Maldonado	.05	.02	.01
☐ 66T	Fred Manrique	.05	.02	.01
☐ 67T	Mike Marshall	.05	.02	.01
☐ 68T	Carmelo Martinez	.05	.02	.01
☐ 69T	John Marzano	.05	.02	.01
☐ 70T	Ben McDonald	.10	.05	.01
☐ 71T	Jack McDowell	.15	.07	.02
☐ 72T	John McNamara MG	.05	.02	.01
☐ 73T	Orlando Mercado	.05	.02	.01
☐ 74T	Stump Merrill MG	.05	.02	.01
☐ 75T	Alan Mills	.05	.02	.01
☐ 76T	Hal Morris	.10	.05	.01
☐ 77T	Lloyd Moseby	.05	.02	.01
☐ 78T	Randy Myers	.15	.07	.02
☐ 79T	Tim Naehring	.30	.14	.04
☐ 80T	Junior Noboa	.05	.02	.01
☐ 81T	Matt Nokes	.05	.02	.01
☐ 82T	Pete O'Brien	.05	.02	.01
☐ 83T	John Olerud	.20	.09	.03
☐ 84T	Greg Olson	.05	.02	.01
☐ 85T	Junior Ortiz	.05	.02	.01
☐ 86T	Dave Parker	.10	.05	.01

☐ 87T	Rick Parker	.05	.02	.01
☐ 88T	Bob Patterson	.05	.02	.01
☐ 89T	Alejandro Pena	.05	.02	.01
☐ 90T	Tony Pena	.05	.02	.01
☐ 91T	Pascual Perez	.05	.02	.01
☐ 92T	Gerald Perry	.05	.02	.01
☐ 93T	Dan Petry	.05	.02	.01
☐ 94T	Gary Pettis	.05	.02	.01
☐ 95T	Tony Phillips	.15	.07	.02
☐ 96T	Lou Piniella MG	.10	.05	.01
☐ 97T	Luis Polonia	.10	.05	.01
☐ 98T	Jim Presley	.05	.02	.01
☐ 99T	Scott Radinsky	.10	.05	.01
☐ 100T	Willie Randolph	.10	.05	.01
☐ 101T	Jeff Reardon	.15	.07	.02
☐ 102T	Greg Riddoch MG	.05	.02	.01
☐ 103T	Jeff Robinson	.05	.02	.01
☐ 104T	Ron Robinson	.05	.02	.01
☐ 105T	Kevin Romine	.05	.02	.01
☐ 106T	Scott Ruskin	.05	.02	.01
☐ 107T	John Russell	.05	.02	.01
☐ 108T	Bill Sampen	.05	.02	.01
☐ 109T	Juan Samuel	.05	.02	.01
☐ 110T	Scott Sanderson	.05	.02	.01
☐ 111T	Jack Savage	.05	.02	.01
☐ 112T	Dave Schmidt	.05	.02	.01
☐ 113T	Red Schoendienst MG	.10	.05	.01
☐ 114T	Terry Shumpert	.05	.02	.01
☐ 115T	Matt Sinatro	.05	.02	.01
☐ 116T	Don Slaught	.05	.02	.01
☐ 117T	Bryn Smith	.05	.02	.01
☐ 118T	Lee Smith	.15	.07	.02
☐ 119T	Paul Sorrento	.20	.09	.03
☐ 120T	Franklin Stubbs UER..	.05	.02	.01
	('84 says '99 and has			
	the same stats as '89,			
	'83 stats are missing)			
☐ 121T	Russ Swan	.05	.02	.01
☐ 122T	Bob Tewksbury	.05	.02	.01
☐ 123T	Wayne Tolleson	.05	.02	.01
☐ 124T	John Tudor	.05	.02	.01
☐ 125T	Randy Veres	.05	.02	.01
☐ 126T	Hector Villanueva	.05	.02	.01
☐ 127T	Mitch Webster	.05	.02	.01
☐ 128T	Ernie Whitt	.05	.02	.01
☐ 129T	Frank Wills	.05	.02	.01
☐ 130T	Dave Winfield	.15	.07	.02
☐ 131T	Matt Young	.05	.02	.01
☐ 132T	Checklist 1T-132T	.05	.02	.01

1991 Topps

The 1991 Topps Set consists of 792 cards in the now standard size of 2 1/2" by 3 1/2".

This set marks Topps tenth consecutive year of issuing a 792-card set. Topps also commemorated their fortieth anniversary by including a "Topps 40" logo on the front and back of each card. Virtually all of the cards have been discovered without the 40th logo on the back. As a special promotion Topps inserted (randomly) into their wax packs one of every previous card they ever issued. Topps again issued their checklists in team order (and alphabetically within team) and included a special 22-card All-Star set (386-407). There are five players listed as Future Stars, 114 Lance Dickson, 211 Brian Barnes, 561 Tim McIntosh, 587 Jose Offerman, and 594 Rich Garces. There are nine players listed as First Draft Picks, 74 Shane Andrews, 103 Tim Costo, 113 Carl Everett, 278 Alex Fernandez, 471 Mike Lieberthal, 491 Kurt Miller, 529 Marc Newfield, 596 Ronnie Walden, and 767 Dan Wilson. The key Rookie Cards in this set are Wes Chamberlain, Carl Everett, Chipper Jones, Brian McRae, Marc Newfield, and Phil Plantier. The complete 1991 Topps set was also issued as a factory set of micro baseball cards with cards measuring approximately one-fourth the size of the regular size cards but identical in other respects. The micro set and its cards are valued at approximately half the values listed below for the regular size cards. The set was also issued with a gold "Operation Desert Shield" emblem stamped on the cards. It has been reported that Topps sent wax cases (equivalent to 6,313 sets) as gifts to U.S. troops stationed in the Persian Gulf. These Desert Shield cards are quite valuable in comparison to the regular issue of Topps; but one must be careful as counterfeits of these cards are known. These counterfeit Desert Shield cards can typically be detected by the shape of the gold shield stamped on the card. The bottom of the shield on the original is rounded, almost flat; the known forgeries come to a point. Due to the scarcity of these Desert Shield cards, they are usually sold at one hundred times the value of the corresponding regular card. Topps also produced a specially boxed glossy edition frequently referred to as the Topps Tiffany set. This year, again, Topps did not disclose the number of Tiffany sets they produced or sold. The checklist of cards is identical to that of the normal non-glossy cards. There are two primary distinguishing features of the Tiffany cards, white card stock reverses and high gloss obverses. These Tiffany cards are valued approximately from three to five times the values listed below.

	MINT	NRMT	EXC
COMPLETE SET (792)	12.00	5.50	1.50
COMPLETE FACT.SET (792) ..	15.00	6.75	1.85
COMMON CARD (1-792)	.05	.02	.01
☐ 1 Nolan Ryan	.75	.35	.09
☐ 2 George Brett RB	.20	.09	.03
☐ 3 Carlton Fisk RB	.10	.05	.01
☐ 4 Kevin Maas RB	.05	.02	.01

☐ 5	Cal Ripken RB	.40	.18	.05
☐ 6	Nolan Ryan RB	.40	.18	.05
☐ 7	Ryne Sandberg RB	.15	.07	.02
☐ 8	Bobby Thigpen RB	.05	.02	.01
☐ 9	Darrin Fletcher	.05	.02	.01
☐ 10	Gregg Olson	.05	.02	.01
☐ 11	Roberto Kelly	.10	.05	.01
☐ 12	Paul Assenmacher	.05	.02	.01
☐ 13	Mariano Duncan	.05	.02	.01
☐ 14	Dennis Lamp	.05	.02	.01
☐ 15	Von Hayes	.05	.02	.01
☐ 16	Mike Heath	.05	.02	.01
☐ 17	Jeff Brantley	.05	.02	.01
☐ 18	Nelson Liriano	.05	.02	.01
☐ 19	Jeff D. Robinson	.05	.02	.01
☐ 20	Pedro Guerrero	.10	.05	.01
☐ 21	Joe Morgan MG	.05	.02	.01
☐ 22	Storm Davis	.05	.02	.01
☐ 23	Jim Gantner	.05	.02	.01
☐ 24	Dave Martinez	.05	.02	.01
☐ 25	Tim Belcher	.05	.02	.01
☐ 26	Luis Sojo UER	.05	.02	.01
	(Born in Barquisimento, not Carquis)			
☐ 27	Bobby Witt	.05	.02	.01
☐ 28	Alvaro Espinoza	.05	.02	.01
☐ 29	Bob Walk	.05	.02	.01
☐ 30	Gregg Jefferies	.15	.07	.02
☐ 31	Colby Ward	.05	.02	.01
☐ 32	Mike Simms	.05	.02	.01
☐ 33	Barry Jones	.05	.02	.01
☐ 34	Atlee Hammaker	.05	.02	.01
☐ 35	Greg Maddux	.60	.25	.07
☐ 36	Donnie Hill	.05	.02	.01
☐ 37	Tom Bolton	.05	.02	.01
☐ 38	Scott Bradley	.05	.02	.01
☐ 39	Jim Neidlinger	.05	.02	.01
☐ 40	Kevin Mitchell	.10	.05	.01
☐ 41	Ken Dayley	.05	.02	.01
☐ 42	Chris Hoiles	.10	.05	.01
☐ 43	Roger McDowell	.05	.02	.01
☐ 44	Mike Felder	.05	.02	.01
☐ 45	Chris Sabo	.05	.02	.01
☐ 46	Tim Drummond	.05	.02	.01
☐ 47	Brook Jacoby	.05	.02	.01
☐ 48	Dennis Boyd	.05	.02	.01
☐ 49A	Pat Borders ERR	.05	.02	.01
	(40 steals at Kinston in '86)			
☐ 49B	Pat Borders COR	.05	.02	.01
	(0 steals at Kinston in '86)			
☐ 50	Bob Welch	.05	.02	.01
☐ 51	Art Howe MG	.05	.02	.01
☐ 52	Francisco Oliveras	.05	.02	.01
☐ 53	Mike Sharperson UER	.05	.02	.01
	(Born in 1961, not 1960)			
☐ 54	Gary Mielke	.05	.02	.01
☐ 55	Jeffrey Leonard	.05	.02	.01
☐ 56	Jeff Parrett	.05	.02	.01
☐ 57	Jack Howell	.05	.02	.01
☐ 58	Mel Stottlemyre Jr.	.05	.02	.01
☐ 59	Eric Yelding	.05	.02	.01
☐ 60	Frank Viola	.10	.05	.01
☐ 61	Stan Javier	.05	.02	.01
☐ 62	Lee Guetterman	.05	.02	.01
☐ 63	Milt Thompson	.05	.02	.01
☐ 64	Tom Herr	.05	.02	.01
☐ 65	Bruce Hurst	.05	.02	.01
☐ 66	Terry Kennedy	.05	.02	.01
☐ 67	Rick Honeycutt	.05	.02	.01
☐ 68	Gary Sheffield	.15	.07	.02
☐ 69	Steve Wilson	.05	.02	.01
☐ 70	Ellis Burks	.10	.05	.01
☐ 71	Jim Acker	.05	.02	.01
☐ 72	Junior Ortiz	.05	.02	.01
☐ 73	Craig Worthington	.05	.02	.01
☐ 74	Shane Andrews	.10	.05	.01
☐ 75	Jack Morris	.15	.07	.02
☐ 76	Jerry Browne	.05	.02	.01
☐ 77	Drew Hall	.05	.02	.01
☐ 78	Geno Petralli	.05	.02	.01
☐ 79	Frank Thomas	2.00	.90	.25
☐ 80A	Fernando Valenzuela ERR	.10	.05	.01
	(104 earned runs in '90 tied for league lead)			
☐ 80B	Fernando Valenzuela COR	.05	.02	.01
	(104 earned runs in '90 led league, 20 CG's in 1986 now italicized)			
☐ 81	Cito Gaston MG	.05	.02	.01
☐ 82	Tom Glavine	.20	.09	.03
☐ 83	Daryl Boston	.05	.02	.01
☐ 84	Bob McClure	.05	.02	.01
☐ 85	Jesse Barfield	.05	.02	.01
☐ 86	Les Lancaster	.05	.02	.01
☐ 87	Tracy Jones	.05	.02	.01
☐ 88	Bob Tewksbury	.10	.05	.01
☐ 89	Darren Daulton	.15	.07	.02
☐ 90	Danny Tartabull	.10	.05	.01
☐ 91	Greg Colbrunn	.20	.09	.03
☐ 92	Danny Jackson	.05	.02	.01
☐ 93	Ivan Calderon	.05	.02	.01
☐ 94	John Dopson	.05	.02	.01
☐ 95	Paul Molitor	.15	.07	.02
☐ 96	Trevor Wilson	.05	.02	.01
☐ 97A	Brady Anderson ERR	.15	.07	.02
	(September, 2 RBI and 3 hits, should be 3 RBI and 14 hits			
☐ 97B	Brady Anderson COR	.08	.04	.01
☐ 98	Sergio Valdez	.05	.02	.01
☐ 99	Chris Gwynn	.05	.02	.01
☐ 100A	Don Mattingly ERR	.75	.35	.09
	(10 hits in 1990)			
☐ 100B	Don Mattingly COR	.40	.18	.05
	(101 hits in 1990)			
☐ 101	Rob Ducey	.05	.02	.01
☐ 102	Gene Larkin	.05	.02	.01
☐ 103	Tim Costo	.05	.02	.01
☐ 104	Don Robinson	.05	.02	.01
☐ 105	Kevin McReynolds	.05	.02	.01
☐ 106	Ed Nunez	.05	.02	.01
☐ 107	Luis Polonia	.05	.02	.01
☐ 108	Matt Young	.05	.02	.01
☐ 109	Greg Riddoch MG	.05	.02	.01
☐ 110	Tom Henke	.10	.05	.01
☐ 111	Andres Thomas	.05	.02	.01
☐ 112	Frank DiPino	.05	.02	.01
☐ 113	Carl Everett	.25	.11	.03
☐ 114	Lance Dickson	.05	.02	.01
☐ 115	Hubie Brooks	.05	.02	.01
☐ 116	Mark Davis	.05	.02	.01
☐ 117	Dion James	.05	.02	.01
☐ 118	Tom Edens	.05	.02	.01
☐ 119	Carl Nichols	.05	.02	.01
☐ 120	Joe Carter	.15	.07	.02
☐ 121	Eric King	.05	.02	.01
☐ 122	Paul O'Neill	.15	.07	.02
☐ 123	Greg A. Harris	.05	.02	.01

☐ 124 Randy Bush	.05	.02	.01
☐ 125 Steve Bedrosian	.05	.02	.01
☐ 126 Bernard Gilkey	.10	.05	.01
☐ 127 Joe Price	.05	.02	.01
☐ 128 Travis Fryman	.20	.09	.03
(Front has SS,			
back has SS-3B)			
☐ 129 Mark Eichhorn	.05	.02	.01
☐ 130 Ozzie Smith	.20	.09	.03
☐ 131A Checklist 1 ERR	.05	.02	.01
727 Phil Bradley			
☐ 131B Checklist 1 COR	.05	.02	.01
717 Phil Bradley			
☐ 132 Jamie Quirk	.05	.02	.01
☐ 133 Greg Briley	.05	.02	.01
☐ 134 Kevin Elster	.05	.02	.01
☐ 135 Jerome Walton	.05	.02	.01
☐ 136 Dave Schmidt	.05	.02	.01
☐ 137 Randy Ready	.05	.02	.01
☐ 138 Jamie Moyer	.05	.02	.01
☐ 139 Jeff Treadway	.05	.02	.01
☐ 140 Fred McGriff	.15	.07	.02
☐ 141 Nick Leyva MG	.05	.02	.01
☐ 142 Curt Wilkerson	.05	.02	.01
☐ 143 John Smiley	.05	.02	.01
☐ 144 Dave Henderson	.05	.02	.01
☐ 145 Lou Whitaker	.10	.05	.01
☐ 146 Dan Plesac	.05	.02	.01
☐ 147 Carlos Baerga	.40	.18	.05
☐ 148 Rey Palacios	.05	.02	.01
☐ 149 Al Osuna UER	.05	.02	.01
(Shown throwing right,			
but bio says lefty)			
☐ 150 Cal Ripken	.75	.35	.09
☐ 151 Tom Browning	.05	.02	.01
☐ 152 Mickey Hatcher	.05	.02	.01
☐ 153 Bryan Harvey	.05	.02	.01
☐ 154 Jay Buhner	.15	.07	.02
☐ 155A Dwight Evans ERR	.10	.05	.01
(Led league with			
162 games in '82)			
☐ 155B Dwight Evans COR	.08	.04	.01
(Tied for lead with			
162 games in '82)			
☐ 156 Carlos Martinez	.05	.02	.01
☐ 157 John Smoltz	.15	.07	.02
☐ 158 Jose Uribe	.05	.02	.01
☐ 159 Joe Boever	.05	.02	.01
☐ 160 Vince Coleman UER	.05	.02	.01
(Wrong birth year,			
born 9/22/60)			
☐ 161 Tim Leary	.05	.02	.01
☐ 162 Ozzie Canseco	.05	.02	.01
☐ 163 Dave Johnson	.05	.02	.01
☐ 164 Edgar Diaz	.05	.02	.01
☐ 165 Sandy Alomar Jr.	.10	.05	.01
☐ 166 Harold Baines	.15	.07	.02
☐ 167A Randy Tomlin ERR	.05	.02	.01
(Harriburg)			
☐ 167B Randy Tomlin COR	.05	.02	.01
(Harrisburg)			
☐ 168 John Olerud	.10	.05	.01
☐ 169 Luis Aquino	.05	.02	.01
☐ 170 Carlton Fisk	.15	.07	.02
☐ 171 Tony LaRussa MG	.10	.05	.01
☐ 172 Pete Incaviglia	.05	.02	.01
☐ 173 Jason Grimsley	.05	.02	.01
☐ 174 Ken Caminiti	.15	.07	.02
☐ 175 Jack Armstrong	.05	.02	.01
☐ 176 John Orton	.05	.02	.01
☐ 177 Reggie Harris	.05	.02	.01

☐ 178 Dave Valle	.05	.02	.01
☐ 179 Pete Harnisch	.05	.02	.01
☐ 180 Tony Gwynn	.30	.14	.04
☐ 181 Duane Ward	.05	.02	.01
☐ 182 Junior Noboa	.05	.02	.01
☐ 183 Clay Parker	.05	.02	.01
☐ 184 Gary Green	.05	.02	.01
☐ 185 Joe Magrane	.05	.02	.01
☐ 186 Rod Booker	.05	.02	.01
☐ 187 Greg Cadaret	.05	.02	.01
☐ 188 Damon Berryhill	.05	.02	.01
☐ 189 Daryl Irvine	.05	.02	.01
☐ 190 Matt Williams	.20	.09	.03
☐ 191 Willie Blair	.05	.02	.01
☐ 192 Rob Deer	.05	.02	.01
☐ 193 Felix Fermin	.05	.02	.01
☐ 194 Xavier Hernandez	.05	.02	.01
☐ 195 Wally Joyner	.15	.07	.02
☐ 196 Jim Vatcher	.05	.02	.01
☐ 197 Chris Nabholz	.05	.02	.01
☐ 198 R.J. Reynolds	.05	.02	.01
☐ 199 Mike Hartley	.05	.02	.01
☐ 200 Darryl Strawberry	.10	.05	.01
☐ 201 Tom Kelly MG	.05	.02	.01
☐ 202 Jim Leyritz	.05	.02	.01
☐ 203 Gene Harris	.05	.02	.01
☐ 204 Herm Winningham	.05	.02	.01
☐ 205 Mike Perez	.05	.02	.01
☐ 206 Carlos Quintana	.05	.02	.01
☐ 207 Gary Wayne	.05	.02	.01
☐ 208 Willie Wilson	.05	.02	.01
☐ 209 Ken Howell	.05	.02	.01
☐ 210 Lance Parrish	.10	.05	.01
☐ 211 Brian Barnes	.05	.02	.01
☐ 212 Steve Finley	.05	.02	.01
☐ 213 Frank Wills	.05	.02	.01
☐ 214 Joe Girardi	.05	.02	.01
☐ 215 Dave Smith	.05	.02	.01
☐ 216 Greg Gagne	.05	.02	.01
☐ 217 Chris Bosio	.05	.02	.01
☐ 218 Rick Parker	.05	.02	.01
☐ 219 Jack McDowell	.15	.07	.02
☐ 220 Tim Wallach	.05	.02	.01
☐ 221 Don Slaught	.05	.02	.01
☐ 222 Brian McRae	.30	.14	.04
☐ 223 Allan Anderson	.05	.02	.01
☐ 224 Juan Gonzalez	.50	.23	.06
☐ 225 Randy Johnson	.25	.11	.03
☐ 226 Alfredo Griffin	.05	.02	.01
☐ 227 Steve Avery UER	.15	.07	.02
(Pitched 13 games for			
Durham in 1989, not 2)			
☐ 228 Rex Hudler	.05	.02	.01
☐ 229 Rance Mulliniks	.05	.02	.01
☐ 230 Sid Fernandez	.10	.05	.01
☐ 231 Doug Rader MG	.05	.02	.01
☐ 232 Jose DeJesus	.05	.02	.01
☐ 233 Al Leiter	.05	.02	.01
☐ 234 Scott Erickson	.10	.05	.01
☐ 235 Dave Parker	.10	.05	.01
☐ 236A Frank Tanana ERR	.15	.07	.02
(Tied for lead with			
269 K's in '75)			
☐ 236B Frank Tanana COR	.05	.02	.01
(Led league with			
269 K's in '75)			
☐ 237 Rick Cerone	.05	.02	.01
☐ 238 Mike Dunne	.05	.02	.01
☐ 239 Darren Lewis	.10	.05	.01
☐ 240 Mike Scott	.05	.02	.01
☐ 241 Dave Clark UER	.05	.02	.01

(Career totals 19 HR
and 5 3B, should
be 22 and 3)

☐ 242	Mike LaCoss	.05	.02	.01
☐ 243	Lance Johnson	.05	.02	.01
☐ 244	Mike Jeffcoat	.05	.02	.01
☐ 245	Kal Daniels	.05	.02	.01
☐ 246	Kevin Wickander	.05	.02	.01
☐ 247	Jody Reed	.05	.02	.01
☐ 248	Tom Gordon	.10	.05	.01
☐ 249	Bob Melvin	.05	.02	.01
☐ 250	Dennis Eckersley	.15	.07	.02
☐ 251	Mark Lemke	.10	.05	.01
☐ 252	Mel Rojas	.10	.05	.01
☐ 253	Garry Templeton	.05	.02	.01
☐ 254	Shawn Boskie	.05	.02	.01
☐ 255	Brian Downing	.05	.02	.01
☐ 256	Greg Hibbard	.05	.02	.01
☐ 257	Tom O'Malley	.05	.02	.01
☐ 258	Chris Hammond	.05	.02	.01
☐ 259	Hensley Meulens	.05	.02	.01
☐ 260	Harold Reynolds	.05	.02	.01
☐ 261	Bud Harrelson MG	.05	.02	.01
☐ 262	Tim Jones	.05	.02	.01
☐ 263	Checklist 2	.05	.02	.01
☐ 264	Dave Hollins	.05	.02	.01
☐ 265	Mark Gubicza	.05	.02	.01
☐ 266	Carmelo Castillo	.05	.02	.01
☐ 267	Mark Knudson	.05	.02	.01
☐ 268	Tom Brookens	.05	.02	.01
☐ 269	Joe Hesketh	.05	.02	.01
☐ 270A	Mark McGwire ERR	.20	.09	.03
	(1987 Slugging Pctg. listed as 618)			
☐ 270B	Mark McGwire COR	.15	.07	.02
	(1987 Slugging Pctg. listed as .618)			
☐ 271	Omar Olivares	.05	.02	.01
☐ 272	Jeff King	.05	.02	.01
☐ 273	Johnny Ray	.05	.02	.01
☐ 274	Ken Williams	.05	.02	.01
☐ 275	Alan Trammell	.15	.07	.02
☐ 276	Bill Swift	.05	.02	.01
☐ 277	Scott Coolbaugh	.05	.02	.01
☐ 278	Alex Fernandez UER	.15	.07	.02
	(No '90 White Sox stats)			
☐ 279A	Jose Gonzalez ERR	.05	.02	.01
	(Photo actually Billy Bean)			
☐ 279B	Jose Gonzalez COR	.05	.02	.01
☐ 280	Bret Saberhagen	.15	.07	.02
☐ 281	Larry Sheets	.05	.02	.01
☐ 282	Don Carman	.05	.02	.01
☐ 283	Marquis Grissom	.20	.09	.03
☐ 284	Billy Spiers	.05	.02	.01
☐ 285	Jim Abbott	.15	.07	.02
☐ 286	Ken Oberkfell	.05	.02	.01
☐ 287	Mark Grant	.05	.02	.01
☐ 288	Derrick May	.10	.05	.01
☐ 289	Tim Birtsas	.05	.02	.01
☐ 290	Steve Sax	.05	.02	.01
☐ 291	John Wathan MG	.05	.02	.01
☐ 292	Bud Black	.05	.02	.01
☐ 293	Jay Bell	.10	.05	.01
☐ 294	Mike Moore	.05	.02	.01
☐ 295	Rafael Palmeiro	.15	.07	.02
☐ 296	Mark Williamson	.05	.02	.01
☐ 297	Manny Lee	.05	.02	.01
☐ 298	Omar Vizquel	.10	.05	.01
☐ 299	Scott Radinsky	.05	.02	.01
☐ 300	Kirby Puckett	.30	.14	.04
☐ 301	Steve Farr	.05	.02	.01
☐ 302	Tim Teufel	.05	.02	.01
☐ 303	Mike Boddicker	.05	.02	.01
☐ 304	Kevin Reimer	.05	.02	.01
☐ 305	Mike Scioscia	.05	.02	.01
☐ 306A	Lonnie Smith ERR	.05	.02	.01
	(136 games in '90)			
☐ 306B	Lonnie Smith COR	.05	.02	.01
	(135 games in '90)			
☐ 307	Andy Benes	.10	.05	.01
☐ 308	Tom Pagnozzi	.05	.02	.01
☐ 309	Norm Charlton	.05	.02	.01
☐ 310	Gary Carter	.15	.07	.02
☐ 311	Jeff Pico	.05	.02	.01
☐ 312	Charlie Hayes	.10	.05	.01
☐ 313	Ron Robinson	.05	.02	.01
☐ 314	Gary Pettis	.05	.02	.01
☐ 315	Roberto Alomar	.25	.11	.03
☐ 316	Gene Nelson	.05	.02	.01
☐ 317	Mike Fitzgerald	.05	.02	.01
☐ 318	Rick Aguilera	.10	.05	.01
☐ 319	Jeff McKnight	.05	.02	.01
☐ 320	Tony Fernandez	.05	.02	.01
☐ 321	Bob Rodgers MG	.05	.02	.01
☐ 322	Terry Shumpert	.05	.02	.01
☐ 323	Cory Snyder	.05	.02	.01
☐ 324A	Ron Kittle ERR	.05	.02	.01
	(Set another standard ...)			
☐ 324B	Ron Kittle COR	.05	.02	.01
	(Tied another standard ...)			
☐ 325	Brett Butler	.15	.07	.02
☐ 326	Ken Patterson	.05	.02	.01
☐ 327	Ron Hassey	.05	.02	.01
☐ 328	Walt Terrell	.05	.02	.01
☐ 329	Dave Justice ROY	.20	.09	.03
	(Drafted third round on card, should say fourth pick)			
☐ 330	Dwight Gooden	.10	.05	.01
☐ 331	Eric Anthony	.05	.02	.01
☐ 332	Kenny Rogers	.10	.05	.01
☐ 333	Chipper Jones FDP	3.00	1.35	.35
☐ 334	Todd Benzinger	.05	.02	.01
☐ 335	Mitch Williams	.10	.05	.01
☐ 336	Matt Nokes	.05	.02	.01
☐ 337A	Keith Comstock ERR	.05	.02	.01
	(Cubs logo on front)			
☐ 337B	Keith Comstock COR	.05	.02	.01
	(Mariners logo on front)			
☐ 338	Luis Rivera	.05	.02	.01
☐ 339	Larry Walker	.25	.11	.03
☐ 340	Ramon Martinez	.15	.07	.02
☐ 341	John Moses	.05	.02	.01
☐ 342	Mickey Morandini	.05	.02	.01
☐ 343	Jose Oquendo	.05	.02	.01
☐ 344	Jeff Russell	.05	.02	.01
☐ 345	Len Dykstra	.15	.07	.02
☐ 346	Jesse Orosco	.05	.02	.01
☐ 347	Greg Vaughn	.05	.02	.01
☐ 348	Todd Stottlemyre	.05	.02	.01
☐ 349	Dave Gallagher	.05	.02	.01
☐ 350	Glenn Davis	.05	.02	.01
☐ 351	Joe Torre MG	.10	.05	.01
☐ 352	Frank White	.10	.05	.01
☐ 353	Tony Castillo	.05	.02	.01
☐ 354	Sid Bream	.05	.02	.01
☐ 355	Chili Davis	.15	.07	.02
☐ 356	Mike Marshall	.05	.02	.01
☐ 357	Jack Savage	.05	.02	.01

☐ 358 Mark Parent	.05	.02	.01
☐ 359 Chuck Cary	.05	.02	.01
☐ 360 Tim Raines	.15	.07	.02
☐ 361 Scott Garrelts	.05	.02	.01
☐ 362 Hector Villenueva	.05	.02	.01
☐ 363 Rick Mahler	.05	.02	.01
☐ 364 Dan Pasqua	.05	.02	.01
☐ 365 Mike Schooler	.05	.02	.01
☐ 366A Checklist 3 ERR	.05	.02	.01
19 Carl Nichols			
☐ 366B Checklist 3 COR	.05	.02	.01
119 Carl Nichols			
☐ 367 Dave Walsh	.05	.02	.01
☐ 368 Felix Jose	.05	.02	.01
☐ 369 Steve Searcy	.05	.02	.01
☐ 370 Kelly Gruber	.05	.02	.01
☐ 371 Jeff Montgomery	.10	.05	.01
☐ 372 Spike Owen	.05	.02	.01
☐ 373 Darrin Jackson	.05	.02	.01
☐ 374 Larry Casian	.05	.02	.01
☐ 375 Tony Pena	.05	.02	.01
☐ 376 Mike Harkey	.05	.02	.01
☐ 377 Rene Gonzales	.05	.02	.01
☐ 378A Wilson Alvarez ERR	.50	.23	.06
('89 Port Charlotte and '90 Birmingham stat lines omitted)			
☐ 378B Wilson Alvarez COR	.15	.07	.02
(Text still says 143 K's in 1988, whereas stats say 134)			
☐ 379 Randy Velarde	.05	.02	.01
☐ 380 Willie McGee	.10	.05	.01
☐ 381 Jim Leyland MG	.05	.02	.01
☐ 382 Mackey Sasser	.05	.02	.01
☐ 383 Pete Smith	.05	.02	.01
☐ 384 Gerald Perry	.05	.02	.01
☐ 385 Mickey Tettleton	.10	.05	.01
☐ 386 Cecil Fielder AS	.10	.05	.01
☐ 387 Julio Franco AS	.05	.02	.01
☐ 388 Kelly Gruber AS	.05	.02	.01
☐ 389 Alan Trammell AS	.10	.05	.01
☐ 390 Jose Canseco AS	.15	.07	.02
☐ 391 Rickey Henderson AS	.15	.07	.02
☐ 392 Ken Griffey Jr. AS	.75	.35	.09
☐ 393 Carlton Fisk AS	.10	.05	.01
☐ 394 Bob Welch AS	.05	.02	.01
☐ 395 Chuck Finley AS	.05	.02	.01
☐ 396 Bobby Thigpen AS	.05	.02	.01
☐ 397 Eddie Murray AS	.15	.07	.02
☐ 398 Ryne Sandberg AS	.15	.07	.02
☐ 399 Matt Williams AS	.15	.07	.02
☐ 400 Barry Larkin AS	.15	.07	.02
☐ 401 Barry Bonds AS	.15	.07	.02
☐ 402 Darryl Strawbery AS	.10	.05	.01
☐ 403 Bobby Bonilla AS	.15	.07	.02
☐ 404 Mike Scioscia AS	.05	.02	.01
☐ 405 Doug Drabek AS	.10	.05	.01
☐ 406 Frank Viola AS	.05	.02	.01
☐ 407 John Franco AS	.10	.05	.01
☐ 408 Earnie Riles	.05	.02	.01
☐ 409 Mike Stanley	.10	.05	.01
☐ 410 Dave Righetti	.05	.02	.01
☐ 411 Lance Blankenship	.05	.02	.01
☐ 412 Dave Bergman	.05	.02	.01
☐ 413 Terry Mulholland	.05	.02	.01
☐ 414 Sammy Sosa	.25	.11	.03
☐ 415 Rick Sutcliffe	.10	.05	.01
☐ 416 Randy Milligan	.05	.02	.01
☐ 417 Bill Krueger	.05	.02	.01
☐ 418 Nick Esasky	.05	.02	.01
☐ 419 Jeff Reed	.05	.02	.01
☐ 420 Bobby Thigpen	.05	.02	.01
☐ 421 Alex Cole	.05	.02	.01
☐ 422 Rick Reuschel	.05	.02	.01
☐ 423 Rafael Ramirez UER	.05	.02	.01
(Born 1959, not 1958)			
☐ 424 Calvin Schiraldi	.05	.02	.01
☐ 425 Andy Van Slyke	.10	.05	.01
☐ 426 Joe Grahe	.05	.02	.01
☐ 427 Rick Dempsey	.05	.02	.01
☐ 428 John Barfield	.05	.02	.01
☐ 429 Stump Merrill MG	.05	.02	.01
☐ 430 Gary Gaetti	.10	.05	.01
☐ 431 Paul Gibson	.05	.02	.01
☐ 432 Delino DeShields	.10	.05	.01
☐ 433 Pat Tabler	.05	.02	.01
☐ 434 Julio Machado	.05	.02	.01
☐ 435 Kevin Maas	.05	.02	.01
☐ 436 Scott Bankhead	.05	.02	.01
☐ 437 Doug Dascenzo	.05	.02	.01
☐ 438 Vicente Palacios	.05	.02	.01
☐ 439 Dickie Thon	.05	.02	.01
☐ 440 George Bell	.05	.02	.01
☐ 441 Zane Smith	.05	.02	.01
☐ 442 Charlie O'Brien	.05	.02	.01
☐ 443 Jeff Innis	.05	.02	.01
☐ 444 Glenn Braggs	.05	.02	.01
☐ 445 Greg Swindell	.05	.02	.01
☐ 446 Craig Grebeck	.05	.02	.01
☐ 447 John Burkett	.05	.02	.01
☐ 448 Craig Lefferts	.05	.02	.01
☐ 449 Juan Berenguer	.05	.02	.01
☐ 450 Wade Boggs	.15	.07	.02
☐ 451 Neal Heaton	.05	.02	.01
☐ 452 Bill Schroeder	.05	.02	.01
☐ 453 Lenny Harris	.05	.02	.01
☐ 454A Kevin Appier ERR	.15	.07	.02
('90 Omaha stat line omitted)			
☐ 454B Kevin Appier COR	.08	.04	.01
☐ 455 Walt Weiss	.05	.02	.01
☐ 456 Charlie Leibrandt	.05	.02	.01
☐ 457 Todd Hundley	.10	.05	.01
☐ 458 Brian Holman	.05	.02	.01
☐ 459 Tom Trebelhorn MG UER	.05	.02	.01
(Pitching and batting columns switched)			
☐ 460 Dave Stieb	.10	.05	.01
☐ 461 Robin Ventura	.15	.07	.02
☐ 462 Steve Frey	.05	.02	.01
☐ 463 Dwight Smith	.05	.02	.01
☐ 464 Steve Buechele	.05	.02	.01
☐ 465 Ken Griffey Sr.	.10	.05	.01
☐ 466 Charles Nagy	.10	.05	.01
☐ 467 Dennis Cook	.05	.02	.01
☐ 468 Tim Hulett	.05	.02	.01
☐ 469 Chet Lemon	.05	.02	.01
☐ 470 Howard Johnson	.10	.05	.01
☐ 471 Mike Lieberthal	.05	.02	.01
☐ 472 Kirt Manwaring	.05	.02	.01
☐ 473 Curt Young	.05	.02	.01
☐ 474 Phil Plantier	.15	.07	.02
☐ 475 Teddy Higuera	.05	.02	.01
☐ 476 Glenn Wilson	.05	.02	.01
☐ 477 Mike Fetters	.05	.02	.01
☐ 478 Kurt Stillwell	.05	.02	.01
☐ 479 Bob Patterson UER	.05	.02	.01
(Has a decimal point between 7 and 9)			
☐ 480 Dave Magadan	.05	.02	.01
☐ 481 Eddie Whitson	.05	.02	.01

☐ 482 Tino Martinez	.15	.07	.02
☐ 483 Mike Aldrete	.05	.02	.01
☐ 484 Dave LaPoint	.05	.02	.01
☐ 485 Terry Pendleton	.15	.07	.02
☐ 486 Tommy Greene	.05	.02	.01
☐ 487 Rafael Belliard	.05	.02	.01
☐ 488 Jeff Manto	.05	.02	.01
☐ 489 Bobby Valentine MG	.05	.02	.01
☐ 490 Kirk Gibson	.15	.07	.02
☐ 491 Kurt Miller	.10	.05	.01
☐ 492 Ernie Whitt	.05	.02	.01
☐ 493 Jose Rijo	.10	.05	.01
☐ 494 Chris James	.05	.02	.01
☐ 495 Charlie Hough	.10	.05	.01
☐ 496 Marty Barrett	.05	.02	.01
☐ 497 Ben McDonald	.10	.05	.01
☐ 498 Mark Salas	.05	.02	.01
☐ 499 Melido Perez	.05	.02	.01
☐ 500 Will Clark	.15	.07	.02
☐ 501 Mike Bielecki	.05	.02	.01
☐ 502 Carney Lansford	.10	.05	.01
☐ 503 Roy Smith	.05	.02	.01
☐ 504 Julio Valera	.05	.02	.01
☐ 505 Chuck Finley	.10	.05	.01
☐ 506 Darnell Coles	.05	.02	.01
☐ 507 Steve Jeltz	.05	.02	.01
☐ 508 Mike York	.05	.02	.01
☐ 509 Glenallen Hill	.10	.05	.01
☐ 510 John Franco	.15	.07	.02
☐ 511 Steve Balboni	.05	.02	.01
☐ 512 Jose Mesa	.10	.05	.01
☐ 513 Jerald Clark	.05	.02	.01
☐ 514 Mike Stanton	.05	.02	.01
☐ 515 Alvin Davis	.05	.02	.01
☐ 516 Karl Rhodes	.05	.02	.01
☐ 517 Joe Oliver	.05	.02	.01
☐ 518 Cris Carpenter	.05	.02	.01
☐ 519 Sparky Anderson MG	.10	.05	.01
☐ 520 Mark Grace	.15	.07	.02
☐ 521 Joe Orsulak	.05	.02	.01
☐ 522 Stan Belinda	.05	.02	.01
☐ 523 Rodney McCray	.05	.02	.01
☐ 524 Darrel Akerfelds	.05	.02	.01
☐ 525 Willie Randolph	.10	.05	.01
☐ 526A Moises Alou ERR	.75	.35	.09
(37 runs in 2 games			
for '90 Pirates)			
☐ 526B Moises Alou COR	.15	.07	.02
(0 runs in 2 games			
for '90 Pirates)			
☐ 527A Checklist 4 ERR	.05	.02	.01
105 Keith Miller			
719 Kevin McReynolds			
☐ 527B Checklist 4 COR	.05	.02	.01
105 Keith Miller			
719 Kevin McReynolds			
☐ 528 Denny Martinez	.10	.05	.01
☐ 529 Marc Newfield	.20	.09	.03
☐ 530 Roger Clemens	.15	.07	.02
☐ 531 Dave Rohde	.05	.02	.01
☐ 532 Kirk McCaskill	.05	.02	.01
☐ 533 Oddibe McDowell	.05	.02	.01
☐ 534 Mike Jackson	.05	.02	.01
☐ 535 Ruben Sierra UER	.15	.07	.02
(Back reads 100 Runs			
amd 100 RBI's)			
☐ 536 Mike Witt	.05	.02	.01
☐ 537 Jose Lind	.05	.02	.01
☐ 538 Bip Roberts	.10	.05	.01
☐ 539 Scott Terry	.05	.02	.01
☐ 540 George Brett	.40	.18	.05
☐ 541 Domingo Ramos	.05	.02	.01
☐ 542 Rob Murphy	.05	.02	.01
☐ 543 Junior Felix	.05	.02	.01
☐ 544 Alejandro Pena	.05	.02	.01
☐ 545 Dale Murphy	.15	.07	.02
☐ 546 Jeff Ballard	.05	.02	.01
☐ 547 Mike Pagliarulo	.05	.02	.01
☐ 548 Jaime Navarro	.05	.02	.01
☐ 549 John McNamara MG	.05	.02	.01
☐ 550 Eric Davis	.10	.05	.01
☐ 551 Bob Kipper	.05	.02	.01
☐ 552 Jeff Hamilton	.05	.02	.01
☐ 553 Joe Klink	.05	.02	.01
☐ 554 Brian Harper	.05	.02	.01
☐ 555 Turner Ward	.05	.02	.01
☐ 556 Gary Ward	.05	.02	.01
☐ 557 Wally Whitehurst	.05	.02	.01
☐ 558 Otis Nixon	.05	.02	.01
☐ 559 Adam Peterson	.05	.02	.01
☐ 560 Greg Smith	.05	.02	.01
☐ 561 Tim McIntosh	.05	.02	.01
☐ 562 Jeff Kunkel	.05	.02	.01
☐ 563 Brent Knackert	.05	.02	.01
☐ 564 Dante Bichette	.20	.09	.03
☐ 565 Craig Biggio	.15	.07	.02
☐ 566 Craig Wilson	.05	.02	.01
☐ 567 Dwayne Henry	.05	.02	.01
☐ 568 Ron Karkovice	.05	.02	.01
☐ 569 Curt Schilling	.05	.02	.01
☐ 570 Barry Bonds	.30	.14	.04
☐ 571 Pat Combs	.05	.02	.01
☐ 572 Dave Anderson	.05	.02	.01
☐ 573 Rich Rodriguez UER	.05	.02	.01
(Stats say drafted 4th,			
but bio says 9th round)			
☐ 574 John Marzano	.05	.02	.01
☐ 575 Robin Yount	.15	.07	.02
☐ 576 Jeff Kaiser	.05	.02	.01
☐ 577 Bill Doran	.05	.02	.01
☐ 578 Dave West	.05	.02	.01
☐ 579 Roger Craig MG	.05	.02	.01
☐ 580 Dave Stewart	.15	.07	.02
☐ 581 Luis Quinones	.05	.02	.01
☐ 582 Marty Clary	.05	.02	.01
☐ 583 Tony Phillips	.15	.07	.02
☐ 584 Kevin Brown	.10	.05	.01
☐ 585 Pete O'Brien	.05	.02	.01
☐ 586 Fred Lynn	.10	.05	.01
☐ 587 Jose Offerman UER	.05	.02	.01
(Text says he signed			
7/24/86, but bio			
says 1988)			
☐ 588 Mark Whiten	.10	.05	.01
☐ 589 Scott Ruskin	.05	.02	.01
☐ 590 Eddie Murray	.20	.09	.03
☐ 591 Ken Hill	.15	.07	.02
☐ 592 B.J. Surhoff	.10	.05	.01
☐ 593A Mike Walker ERR	.05	.02	.01
('90 Canton-Akron			
stat line omitted)			
☐ 593B Mike Walker COR	.05	.02	.01
☐ 594 Rich Garces	.05	.02	.01
☐ 595 Bill Landrum	.05	.02	.01
☐ 596 Ronnie Walden	.05	.02	.01
☐ 597 Jerry Don Gleaton	.05	.02	.01
☐ 598 Sam Horn	.05	.02	.01
☐ 599A Greg Myers ERR	.05	.02	.01
('90 Syracuse			
stat line omitted)			
☐ 599B Greg Myers COR	.05	.02	.01
☐ 600 Bo Jackson	.15	.07	.02

☐ 601	Bob Ojeda	.05	.02	.01
☐ 602	Casey Candaele	.05	.02	.01
☐ 603A	Wes Chamberlain ERR (Photo actually Louie Meadows)	.05	.02	.01
☐ 603B	Wes Chamberlain COR	.05	.02	.01
☐ 604	Billy Hatcher	.05	.02	.01
☐ 605	Jeff Reardon	.10	.05	.01
☐ 606	Jim Gott	.05	.02	.01
☐ 607	Edgar Martinez	.15	.07	.02
☐ 608	Todd Burns	.05	.02	.01
☐ 609	Jeff Torborg MG	.05	.02	.01
☐ 610	Andres Galarraga	.15	.07	.02
☐ 611	Dave Eiland	.05	.02	.01
☐ 612	Steve Lyons	.05	.02	.01
☐ 613	Eric Show	.05	.02	.01
☐ 614	Luis Salazar	.05	.02	.01
☐ 615	Bert Blyleven	.15	.07	.02
☐ 616	Todd Zeile	.10	.05	.01
☐ 617	Bill Wegman	.05	.02	.01
☐ 618	Sil Campusano	.05	.02	.01
☐ 619	David Wells	.05	.02	.01
☐ 620	Ozzie Guillen	.10	.05	.01
☐ 621	Ted Power	.05	.02	.01
☐ 622	Jack Daugherty	.05	.02	.01
☐ 623	Jeff Blauser	.10	.05	.01
☐ 624	Tom Candiotti	.05	.02	.01
☐ 625	Terry Steinbach	.10	.05	.01
☐ 626	Gerald Young	.05	.02	.01
☐ 627	Tim Layana	.05	.02	.01
☐ 628	Greg Litton	.05	.02	.01
☐ 629	Wes Gardner	.05	.02	.01
☐ 630	Dave Winfield	.15	.07	.02
☐ 631	Mike Morgan	.05	.02	.01
☐ 632	Lloyd Moseby	.05	.02	.01
☐ 633	Kevin Tapani	.10	.05	.01
☐ 634	Henry Cotto	.05	.02	.01
☐ 635	Andy Hawkins	.05	.02	.01
☐ 636	Geronimo Pena	.05	.02	.01
☐ 637	Bruce Ruffin	.05	.02	.01
☐ 638	Mike Macfarlane	.05	.02	.01
☐ 639	Frank Robinson MG	.10	.05	.01
☐ 640	Andre Dawson	.15	.07	.02
☐ 641	Mike Henneman	.05	.02	.01
☐ 642	Hal Morris	.10	.05	.01
☐ 643	Jim Presley	.05	.02	.01
☐ 644	Chuck Crim	.05	.02	.01
☐ 645	Juan Samuel	.05	.02	.01
☐ 646	Andujar Cedeno	.05	.02	.01
☐ 647	Mark Portugal	.05	.02	.01
☐ 648	Lee Stevens	.05	.02	.01
☐ 649	Bill Sampen	.05	.02	.01
☐ 650	Jack Clark	.10	.05	.01
☐ 651	Alan Mills	.05	.02	.01
☐ 652	Kevin Romine	.05	.02	.01
☐ 653	Anthony Telford	.05	.02	.01
☐ 654	Paul Sorrento	.10	.05	.01
☐ 655	Erik Hanson	.05	.02	.01
☐ 656A	Checklist 5 ERR 348 Vicente Palacios 381 Jose Lind 537 Mike LaValliere 665 Jim Leyland	.05	.02	.01
☐ 656B	Checklist 5 ERR 433 Vicente Palacios (Palacios should be 438) 537 Jose Lind 665 Mike LaValliere 381 Jim Leyland	.05	.02	.01
☐ 656C	Checklist 5 COR 438 Vicente Palacios	.05	.02	.01

537 Jose Lind
665 Mike LaValliere
381 Jim Leyland

☐ 657	Mike Kingery	.05	.02	.01
☐ 658	Scott Aldred	.05	.02	.01
☐ 659	Oscar Azocar	.05	.02	.01
☐ 660	Lee Smith	.15	.07	.02
☐ 661	Steve Lake	.05	.02	.01
☐ 662	Ron Dibble	.10	.05	.01
☐ 663	Greg Brock	.05	.02	.01
☐ 664	John Farrell	.05	.02	.01
☐ 665	Mike LaValliere	.05	.02	.01
☐ 666	Danny Darwin	.05	.02	.01
☐ 667	Kent Anderson	.05	.02	.01
☐ 668	Bill Long	.05	.02	.01
☐ 669	Lou Piniella MG	.05	.02	.01
☐ 670	Rickey Henderson	.15	.07	.02
☐ 671	Andy McGaffigan	.05	.02	.01
☐ 672	Shane Mack	.05	.02	.01
☐ 673	Greg Olson UER (6 RBI in '88 at Tidewater and 2 RBI in '87, should be 48 and 15)	.05	.02	.01
☐ 674A	Kevin Gross ERR (89 BB with Phillies in '88 tied for league lead)	.05	.02	.01
☐ 674B	Kevin Gross COR (89 BB with Phillies in '88 led league)	.05	.02	.01
☐ 675	Tom Brunansky	.05	.02	.01
☐ 676	Scott Chiamparino	.05	.02	.01
☐ 677	Billy Ripken	.05	.02	.01
☐ 678	Mark Davidson	.05	.02	.01
☐ 679	Bill Bathe	.05	.02	.01
☐ 680	David Cone	.15	.07	.02
☐ 681	Jeff Schaefer	.05	.02	.01
☐ 682	Ray Lankford	.15	.07	.02
☐ 683	Derek Lilliquist	.05	.02	.01
☐ 684	Milt Cuyler	.05	.02	.01
☐ 685	Doug Drabek	.10	.05	.01
☐ 686	Mike Gallego	.05	.02	.01
☐ 687A	John Cerutti ERR (4.46 ERA in '90)	.05	.02	.01
☐ 687B	John Cerutti COR (4.76 ERA in '90)	.05	.02	.01
☐ 688	Rosario Rodriguez	.05	.02	.01
☐ 689	John Kruk	.15	.07	.02
☐ 690	Orel Hershiser	.15	.07	.02
☐ 691	Mike Blowers	.10	.05	.01
☐ 692A	Efrain Valdez ERR (Born 6/11/66) *	.05	.02	.01
☐ 692B	Efrain Valdez COR (Born 7/11/66 and two lines of text added)	.05	.02	.01
☐ 693	Francisco Cabrera	.05	.02	.01
☐ 694	Randy Veres	.05	.02	.01
☐ 695	Kevin Seitzer	.05	.02	.01
☐ 696	Steve Olin	.05	.02	.01
☐ 697	Shawn Abner	.05	.02	.01
☐ 698	Mark Guthrie	.05	.02	.01
☐ 699	Jim Lefebvre MG	.05	.02	.01
☐ 700	Jose Canseco	.15	.07	.02
☐ 701	Pascual Perez	.05	.02	.01
☐ 702	Tim Naehring	.05	.02	.01
☐ 703	Juan Agosto	.05	.02	.01
☐ 704	Devon White	.10	.05	.01
☐ 705	Robby Thompson	.10	.05	.01
☐ 706A	Brad Arnsberg ERR (68.2 IP in '90)	.05	.02	.01
☐ 706B	Brad Arnsberg COR	.05	.02	.01

(62.2 IP in '90)

☐ 707	Jim Eisenreich	.05	.02	.01
☐ 708	John Mitchell	.05	.02	.01
☐ 709	Matt Sinatro	.05	.02	.01
☐ 710	Kent Hrbek	.10	.05	.01
☐ 711	Jose DeLeon	.05	.02	.01
☐ 712	Ricky Jordan	.05	.02	.01
☐ 713	Scott Scudder	.05	.02	.01
☐ 714	Marvell Wynne	.05	.02	.01
☐ 715	Tim Burke	.05	.02	.01
☐ 716	Bob Geren	.05	.02	.01
☐ 717	Phil Bradley	.05	.02	.01
☐ 718	Steve Crawford	.05	.02	.01
☐ 719	Keith Miller	.05	.02	.01
☐ 720	Cecil Fielder	.15	.07	.02
☐ 721	Mark Lee	.05	.02	.01
☐ 722	Wally Backman	.05	.02	.01
☐ 723	Candy Maldonado	.05	.02	.01
☐ 724	David Segui	.10	.05	.01
☐ 725	Ron Gant	.15	.07	.02
☐ 726	Phil Stephenson	.05	.02	.01
☐ 727	Mookie Wilson	.10	.05	.01
☐ 728	Scott Sanderson	.05	.02	.01
☐ 729	Don Zimmer MG	.05	.02	.01
☐ 730	Barry Larkin	.15	.07	.02
☐ 731	Jeff Gray	.05	.02	.01
☐ 732	Franklin Stubbs	.05	.02	.01
☐ 733	Kelly Downs	.05	.02	.01
☐ 734	John Russell	.05	.02	.01
☐ 735	Ron Darling	.05	.02	.01
☐ 736	Dick Schofield	.05	.02	.01
☐ 737	Tim Crews	.05	.02	.01
☐ 738	Mel Hall	.05	.02	.01
☐ 739	Russ Swan	.05	.02	.01
☐ 740	Ryne Sandberg	.30	.14	.04
☐ 741	Jimmy Key	.10	.05	.01
☐ 742	Tommy Gregg	.05	.02	.01
☐ 743	Bryn Smith	.05	.02	.01
☐ 744	Nelson Santovenia	.05	.02	.01
☐ 745	Doug Jones	.05	.02	.01
☐ 746	John Shelby	.05	.02	.01
☐ 747	Tony Fossas	.05	.02	.01
☐ 748	Al Newman	.05	.02	.01
☐ 749	Greg W. Harris	.05	.02	.01
☐ 750	Bobby Bonilla	.15	.07	.02
☐ 751	Wayne Edwards	.05	.02	.01
☐ 752	Kevin Bass	.05	.02	.01
☐ 753	Paul Marak UER	.05	.02	.01

(Stats say drafted in
Jan., but bio says May)

☐ 754	Bill Pecota	.05	.02	.01
☐ 755	Mark Langston	.15	.07	.02
☐ 756	Jeff Huson	.05	.02	.01
☐ 757	Mark Gardner	.05	.02	.01
☐ 758	Mike Devereaux	.05	.02	.01
☐ 759	Bobby Cox MG	.05	.02	.01
☐ 760	Benny Santiago	.10	.05	.01
☐ 761	Larry Andersen	.05	.02	.01
☐ 762	Mitch Webster	.05	.02	.01
☐ 763	Dana Kiecker	.05	.02	.01
☐ 764	Mark Carreon	.05	.02	.01
☐ 765	Shawon Dunston	.05	.02	.01
☐ 766	Jeff Robinson	.05	.02	.01
☐ 767	Dan Wilson	.15	.07	.02
☐ 768	Don Pall	.05	.02	.01
☐ 769	Tim Sherrill	.05	.02	.01
☐ 770	Jay Howell	.05	.02	.01
☐ 771	Gary Redus UER	.05	.02	.01

(Born in Tanner,
should say Athens)

☐ 772	Kent Mercker	.10	.05	.01

(Born in Indianapolis,
should say Dublin, Ohio)

☐ 773	Tom Foley	.05	.02	.01
☐ 774	Dennis Rasmussen	.05	.02	.01
☐ 775	Julio Franco	.10	.05	.01
☐ 776	Brent Mayne	.05	.02	.01
☐ 777	John Candelaria	.05	.02	.01
☐ 778	Dan Gladden	.05	.02	.01
☐ 779	Carmelo Martinez	.05	.02	.01
☐ 780A	Randy Myers ERR	.15	.07	.02

(15 career losses)

☐ 780B	Randy Myers COR	.10	.05	.01

(19 career losses)

☐ 781	Darryl Hamilton	.10	.05	.01
☐ 782	Jim Deshaies	.05	.02	.01
☐ 783	Joel Skinner	.05	.02	.01
☐ 784	Willie Fraser	.05	.02	.01
☐ 785	Scott Fletcher	.05	.02	.01
☐ 786	Eric Plunk	.05	.02	.01
☐ 787	Checklist 6	.05	.02	.01
☐ 788	Bob Milacki	.05	.02	.01
☐ 789	Tom Lasorda MG	.10	.05	.01
☐ 790	Ken Griffey Jr.	1.50	.70	.19
☐ 791	Mike Benjamin	.05	.02	.01
☐ 792	Mike Greenwell	.15	.07	.02

1991 Topps Traded

*The 1991 Topps Traded set contains 132
standard-size cards. The set includes a
Team U.S.A. subset, featuring 25 of
America's top collegiate players; these
players are indicated in the checklist below
by USA. The cards were sold in wax packs
as well as factory sets. The cards in the
wax packs (gray backs) and collated factory sets (white backs) are from different card
stock. The fronts have color action player
photos, with two different color borders on a
white card face. The player's position and
name are given in the thicker border below
the picture. In blue print on a pink and gray
background, the horizontally oriented backs
have biographical information and statistics.
The cards are numbered on the back in the
upper left corner; the set numbering corresponds to alphabetical order. The key
Rookie Cards in this set are Jeff Bagwell,
Darren Dreifort, Todd Greene, Jeffrey
Hammonds, Charles Johnson, Phil Nevin,
and Ivan Rodriguez.*

	MINT	NRMT	EXC
COMPLETE SET (132)	5.00	2.20	.60
COMPLETE FACT.SET (132)	5.00	2.20	.60
COMMON CARD (1T-132T)	.05	.02	.01
*GRAY AND WHITE BACKS: SAME VALUE			

		MINT	NRMT	EXC
☐ 1T	Juan Agosto	.05	.02	.01
☐ 2T	Roberto Alomar	.25	.11	.03
☐ 3T	Wally Backman	.05	.02	.01
☐ 4T	Jeff Bagwell	2.00	.90	.25
☐ 5T	Skeeter Barnes	.05	.02	.01
☐ 6T	Steve Bedrosian	.05	.02	.01
☐ 7T	Derek Bell	.15	.07	.02
☐ 8T	George Bell	.05	.02	.01
☐ 9T	Rafael Belliard	.05	.02	.01
☐ 10T	Dante Bichette	.20	.09	.03
☐ 11T	Bud Black	.05	.02	.01
☐ 12T	Mike Boddicker	.05	.02	.01
☐ 13T	Sid Bream	.05	.02	.01
☐ 14T	Hubie Brooks	.05	.02	.01
☐ 15T	Brett Butler	.15	.07	.02
☐ 16T	Ivan Calderon	.05	.02	.01
☐ 17T	John Candelaria	.05	.02	.01
☐ 18T	Tom Candiotti	.05	.02	.01
☐ 19T	Gary Carter	.15	.07	.02
☐ 20T	Joe Carter	.15	.07	.02
☐ 21T	Rick Cerone	.05	.02	.01
☐ 22T	Jack Clark	.10	.05	.01
☐ 23T	Vince Coleman	.05	.02	.01
☐ 24T	Scott Coolbaugh	.05	.02	.01
☐ 25T	Danny Cox	.05	.02	.01
☐ 26T	Danny Darwin	.05	.02	.01
☐ 27T	Chili Davis	.15	.07	.02
☐ 28T	Glenn Davis	.05	.02	.01
☐ 29T	Steve Decker	.05	.02	.01
☐ 30T	Rob Deer	.05	.02	.01
☐ 31T	Rich DeLucia	.05	.02	.01
☐ 32T	John Dettmer USA	.10	.05	.01
☐ 33T	Brian Downing	.05	.02	.01
☐ 34T	Darren Dreifort USA	.15	.07	.02
☐ 35T	Kirk Dressendorfer	.05	.02	.01
☐ 36T	Jim Essian MG	.05	.02	.01
☐ 37T	Dwight Evans	.10	.05	.01
☐ 38T	Steve Farr	.05	.02	.01
☐ 39T	Jeff Fassero	.10	.05	.01
☐ 40T	Junior Felix	.05	.02	.01
☐ 41T	Tony Fernandez	.05	.02	.01
☐ 42T	Steve Finley	.10	.05	.01
☐ 43T	Jim Fregosi MG	.05	.02	.01
☐ 44T	Gary Gaetti	.10	.05	.01
☐ 45T	Jason Giambi USA	.50	.23	.06
☐ 46T	Kirk Gibson	.15	.07	.02
☐ 47T	Leo Gomez	.05	.02	.01
☐ 48T	Luis Gonzalez	.15	.07	.02
☐ 49T	Jeff Granger USA	.15	.07	.02
☐ 50T	Todd Greene USA	1.25	.55	.16
☐ 51T	Jeffrey Hammonds USA	.40	.18	.05
☐ 52T	Mike Hargrove MG	.05	.02	.01
☐ 53T	Pete Harnisch	.05	.02	.01
☐ 54T	Rick Helling USA UER	.10	.05	.01
	(Misspelled Hellings on card back)			
☐ 55T	Glenallen Hill	.10	.05	.01
☐ 56T	Charlie Hough	.10	.05	.01
☐ 57T	Pete Incaviglia	.05	.02	.01
☐ 58T	Bo Jackson	.15	.07	.02
☐ 59T	Danny Jackson	.05	.02	.01
☐ 60T	Reggie Jefferson	.10	.05	.01
☐ 61T	Charles Johnson USA	.75	.35	.09
☐ 62T	Jeff Johnson	.05	.02	.01
☐ 63T	Todd Johnson USA	.05	.02	.01
☐ 64T	Barry Jones	.05	.02	.01
☐ 65T	Chris Jones	.05	.02	.01
☐ 66T	Scott Kamieniecki	.05	.02	.01
☐ 67T	Pat Kelly	.10	.05	.01
☐ 68T	Darryl Kile	.05	.02	.01
☐ 69T	Chuck Knoblauch	.25	.11	.03
☐ 70T	Bill Krueger	.05	.02	.01
☐ 71T	Scott Leius	.05	.02	.01
☐ 72T	Donnie Leshnock USA	.05	.02	.01
☐ 73T	Mark Lewis	.05	.02	.01
☐ 74T	Candy Maldonado	.05	.02	.01
☐ 75T	Jason McDonald USA	.25	.11	.03
☐ 76T	Willie McGee	.10	.05	.01
☐ 77T	Fred McGriff	.15	.07	.02
☐ 78T	Billy McMillon USA	.25	.11	.03
☐ 79T	Hal McRae MG	.05	.02	.01
☐ 80T	Dan Melendez USA	.05	.02	.01
☐ 81T	Orlando Merced	.15	.07	.02
☐ 82T	Jack Morris	.15	.07	.02
☐ 83T	Phil Nevin USA	.15	.07	.02
☐ 84T	Otis Nixon	.05	.02	.01
☐ 85T	Johnny Oates MG	.05	.02	.01
☐ 86T	Bob Ojeda	.05	.02	.01
☐ 87T	Mike Pagliarulo	.05	.02	.01
☐ 88T	Dean Palmer	.10	.05	.01
☐ 89T	Dave Parker	.10	.05	.01
☐ 90T	Terry Pendleton	.15	.07	.02
☐ 91T	Tony Phillips (P) USA	.05	.02	.01
☐ 92T	Doug Piatt	.05	.02	.01
☐ 93T	Ron Polk USA CO	.10	.05	.01
☐ 94T	Tim Raines	.15	.07	.02
☐ 95T	Willie Randolph	.10	.05	.01
☐ 96T	Dave Righetti	.05	.02	.01
☐ 97T	Ernie Riles	.05	.02	.01
☐ 98T	Chris Roberts USA	.15	.07	.02
☐ 99T	Jeff D. Robinson	.05	.02	.01
☐ 100T	Jeff M. Robinson	.05	.02	.01
☐ 101T	Ivan Rodriguez	.50	.23	.06
☐ 102T	Steve Rodriguez USA	.05	.02	.01
☐ 103T	Tom Runnells MG	.05	.02	.01
☐ 104T	Scott Sanderson	.05	.02	.01
☐ 105T	Bob Scanlan	.05	.02	.01
☐ 106T	Pete Schourek	.40	.18	.05
☐ 107T	Gary Scott	.05	.02	.01
☐ 108T	Paul Shuey USA	.15	.07	.02
☐ 109T	Doug Simons	.05	.02	.01
☐ 110T	Dave Smith	.05	.02	.01
☐ 111T	Cory Snyder	.05	.02	.01
☐ 112T	Luis Sojo	.05	.02	.01
☐ 113T	Kennie Steenstra USA	.05	.02	.01
☐ 114T	Darryl Strawberry	.10	.05	.01
☐ 115T	Franklin Stubbs	.05	.02	.01
☐ 116T	Todd Taylor USA	.05	.02	.01
☐ 117T	Wade Taylor	.05	.02	.01
☐ 118T	Garry Templeton	.05	.02	.01
☐ 119T	Mickey Tettleton	.10	.05	.01
☐ 120T	Tim Teufel	.05	.02	.01
☐ 121T	Mike Timlin	.05	.02	.01
☐ 122T	David Tuttle USA	.05	.02	.01
☐ 123T	Mo Vaughn	.50	.23	.06
☐ 124T	Jeff Ware USA	.10	.05	.01
☐ 125T	Devon White	.10	.05	.01
☐ 126T	Mark Whiten	.10	.05	.01
☐ 127T	Mitch Williams	.10	.05	.01
☐ 128T	Craig Wilson USA	.05	.02	.01
☐ 129T	Willie Wilson	.05	.02	.01
☐ 130T	Chris Wimmer USA	.05	.02	.01
☐ 131T	Ivan Zweig USA	.05	.02	.01
☐ 132T	Checklist 1T-132T	.05	.02	.01

1992 Topps

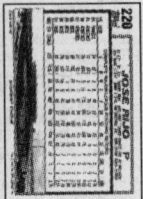

The 1992 Topps set contains 792 cards measuring the standard size (2 1/2" by 3 1/2"). The fronts have either posed or action color player photos on a white card face. Different color stripes frame the pictures, and the player's name and team name appear in two short color stripes respectively at the bottom. In a horizontal format, the backs have biography and complete career batting or pitching record. In addition, some of the cards have a picture of a baseball field and stadium on the back. Special subsets included are Record Breakers (2-5), Prospects (58, 126, 179, 473, 551, 591, 618, 656, 676), and All-Stars (386-407). These cards were not issued with bubble gum and feature white card stock. The key Rookie Cards in this set are Cliff Floyd, Shawn Green, Manny Ramirez, Aaron Sele, and Brien Taylor. The complete 1992 Topps set was also issued as a factory set of micro baseball cards with cards measuring approximately one-fourth the size of the regular size cards but identical in other respects. The micro set and its cards are valued at approximately half the values listed below for the regular size cards.

	MINT	NRMT	EXC
COMPLETE SET (792)	20.00	9.00	2.50
COMPLETE FACT.SET (802)	30.00	13.50	3.70
COMPLETE HOLIDAY SET (811)	35.00	16.00	4.40
1993 PREPRODUCTION SET (9)	6.00	2.70	.75
COMMON CARD (1-792)	.05	.02	.01
COMPLETE GOLD SET (792)	175.00	80.00	22.00
COMP. GOLD FACT. SET (793)	200.00	90.00	25.00
GOLD COMMON CARDS (1-792)	.25	.11	.03
GOLD SEMISTARS	.50	.23	.06
*GOLD VETERAN STARS: 9X TO 15X BASIC CARDS
*GOLD YOUNG STARS: 6X TO 12X BASIC CARDS
*GOLD RC'S: 4X TO 8X BASIC CARDS
COMPLETE GOLD WIN. SET (792)	60.00	27.00	7.50
GOLD WIN. COM. CARDS (1-792)	.10	.05	.01
GOLD WIN. SEMISTARS	.20	.09	.03
*GOLD WIN .VETERAN STARS: 2.5X TO 5X BASIC CARDS
*GOLD WIN. YOUNG STARS: 2X TO 4X BASIC CARDS
*GOLD WIN. RC'S: 1.25X TO 2.5X BASIC CARDS

☐ 1 Nolan Ryan	.75	.35	.09
☐ 2 Ricky Henderson RB	.15	.07	.02

(Some cards have print marks that show 1.991 on the front)

☐ 3 Jeff Reardon RB	.05	.02	.01
☐ 4 Nolan Ryan RB	.40	.18	.05
☐ 5 Dave Winfield RB	.15	.07	.02
☐ 6 Brien Taylor	.15	.07	.02
☐ 7 Jim Olander	.05	.02	.01
☐ 8 Bryan Hickerson	.05	.02	.01
☐ 9 Jon Farrell	.05	.02	.01
☐ 10 Wade Boggs	.15	.07	.02
☐ 11 Jack McDowell	.15	.07	.02
☐ 12 Luis Gonzalez	.10	.05	.01
☐ 13 Mike Scioscia	.05	.02	.01
☐ 14 Wes Chamberlain	.05	.02	.01
☐ 15 Dennis Martinez	.10	.05	.01
☐ 16 Jeff Montgomery	.10	.05	.01
☐ 17 Randy Milligan	.05	.02	.01
☐ 18 Greg Cadaret	.05	.02	.01
☐ 19 Jamie Quirk	.05	.02	.01
☐ 20 Bip Roberts	.05	.02	.01
☐ 21 Buck Rogers MG	.05	.02	.01
☐ 22 Bill Wegman	.05	.02	.01
☐ 23 Chuck Knoblauch	.15	.07	.02
☐ 24 Randy Myers	.15	.07	.02
☐ 25 Ron Gant	.15	.07	.02
☐ 26 Mike Bielecki	.05	.02	.01
☐ 27 Juan Gonzalez	.40	.18	.05
☐ 28 Mike Schooler	.05	.02	.01
☐ 29 Mickey Tettleton	.10	.05	.01
☐ 30 John Kruk	.15	.07	.02
☐ 31 Bryn Smith	.05	.02	.01
☐ 32 Chris Nabholz	.05	.02	.01
☐ 33 Carlos Baerga	.30	.14	.04
☐ 34 Jeff Juden	.05	.02	.01
☐ 35 Dave Righetti	.05	.02	.01
☐ 36 Scott Ruffcorn	.05	.02	.01
☐ 37 Luis Polonia	.05	.02	.01
☐ 38 Tom Candiotti	.05	.02	.01
☐ 39 Greg Olson	.05	.02	.01
☐ 40 Cal Ripken	2.50	1.10	.30
☐ 41 Craig Lefferts	.05	.02	.01
☐ 42 Mike Macfarlane	.05	.02	.01
☐ 43 Jose Lind	.05	.02	.01
☐ 44 Rick Aguilera	.10	.05	.01
☐ 45 Gary Carter	.15	.07	.02
☐ 46 Steve Farr	.05	.02	.01
☐ 47 Rex Hudler	.05	.02	.01
☐ 48 Scott Scudder	.05	.02	.01
☐ 49 Damon Berryhill	.05	.02	.01
☐ 50 Ken Griffey Jr.	1.50	.70	.19
☐ 51 Tom Runnells MG	.05	.02	.01
☐ 52 Juan Bell	.05	.02	.01
☐ 53 Tommy Gregg	.05	.02	.01
☐ 54 David Wells	.05	.02	.01
☐ 55 Rafael Palmeiro	.15	.07	.02
☐ 56 Charlie O'Brien	.05	.02	.01
☐ 57 Donn Pall	.05	.02	.01
☐ 58 1992 Prospects C	.15	.07	.02
Brad Ausmus
Jim Campanis Jr.
Dave Nilsson
Doug Robbins
☐ 59 Mo Vaughn	.40	.18	.05
☐ 60 Tony Fernandez	.05	.02	.01
☐ 61 Paul O'Neill	.15	.07	.02
☐ 62 Gene Nelson	.05	.02	.01
☐ 63 Randy Ready	.05	.02	.01
☐ 64 Bob Kipper	.05	.02	.01
☐ 65 Willie McGee	.10	.05	.01
☐ 66 Scott Stahoviak	.05	.02	.01

67	Luis Salazar	.05	.02	.01
68	Marvin Freeman	.05	.02	.01
69	Kenny Lofton	1.00	.45	.12
70	Gary Gaetti	.10	.05	.01
71	Erik Hanson	.05	.02	.01
72	Eddie Zosky	.05	.02	.01
73	Brian Barnes	.05	.02	.01
74	Scott Leius	.05	.02	.01
75	Bret Saberhagen	.15	.07	.02
76	Mike Gallego	.05	.02	.01
77	Jack Armstrong	.05	.02	.01
78	Ivan Rodriguez	.15	.07	.02
79	Jesse Orosco	.05	.02	.01
80	David Justice	.15	.07	.02
81	Ced Landrum	.05	.02	.01
82	Doug Simons	.05	.02	.01
83	Tommy Greene	.05	.02	.01
84	Leo Gomez	.05	.02	.01
85	Jose DeLeon	.05	.02	.01
86	Steve Finley	.10	.05	.01
87	Bob MacDonald	.05	.02	.01
88	Darrin Jackson	.05	.02	.01
89	Neal Heaton	.05	.02	.01
90	Robin Yount	.15	.07	.02
91	Jeff Reed	.05	.02	.01
92	Lenny Harris	.05	.02	.01
93	Reggie Jefferson	.05	.02	.01
94	Sammy Sosa	.15	.07	.02
95	Scott Bailes	.05	.02	.01
96	Tom McKinnon	.05	.02	.01
97	Luis Rivera	.05	.02	.01
98	Mike Harkey	.05	.02	.01
99	Jeff Treadway	.05	.02	.01
100	Jose Canseco	.15	.07	.02
101	Omar Vizquel	.10	.05	.01
102	Scott Kamieniecki	.05	.02	.01
103	Ricky Jordan	.05	.02	.01
104	Jeff Ballard	.05	.02	.01
105	Felix Jose	.05	.02	.01
106	Mike Boddicker	.05	.02	.01
107	Dan Pasqua	.05	.02	.01
108	Mike Timlin	.05	.02	.01
109	Roger Craig MG	.05	.02	.01
110	Ryne Sandberg	.25	.11	.03
111	Mark Carreon	.05	.02	.01
112	Oscar Azocar	.05	.02	.01
113	Mike Greenwell	.15	.07	.02
114	Mark Portugal	.05	.02	.01
115	Terry Pendleton	.15	.07	.02
116	Willie Randolph	.10	.05	.01
117	Scott Terry	.05	.02	.01
118	Chili Davis	.15	.07	.02
119	Mark Gardner	.05	.02	.01
120	Alan Trammell	.15	.07	.02
121	Derek Bell	.10	.05	.01
122	Gary Varsho	.05	.02	.01
123	Bob Ojeda	.05	.02	.01
124	Shawn Livsey	.05	.02	.01
125	Chris Hoiles	.10	.05	.01
126	1992 Prospects 1B	.75	.35	.09
	Ryan Klesko			
	John Jaha			
	Rico Brogna			
	Dave Staton			
127	Carlos Quintana	.05	.02	.01
128	Kurt Stillwell	.05	.02	.01
129	Melido Perez	.05	.02	.01
130	Alvin Davis	.05	.02	.01
131	Checklist 1-132	.05	.02	.01
132	Eric Show	.05	.02	.01
133	Rance Mulliniks	.05	.02	.01
134	Darryl Kile	.05	.02	.01
135	Von Hayes	.05	.02	.01
136	Bill Doran	.05	.02	.01
137	Jeff D. Robinson	.05	.02	.01
138	Monty Fariss	.05	.02	.01
139	Jeff Innis	.05	.02	.01
140	Mark Grace UER	.15	.07	.02
	(Home Calie., should be Calif.)			
141	Jim Leyland MG UER	.05	.02	.01
	(No closed parenthesis after East in 1991)			
142	Todd Van Poppel	.10	.05	.01
143	Paul Gibson	.05	.02	.01
144	Bill Swift	.05	.02	.01
145	Danny Tartabull	.10	.05	.01
146	Al Newman	.05	.02	.01
147	Cris Carpenter	.05	.02	.01
148	Anthony Young	.05	.02	.01
149	Brian Bohanon	.05	.02	.01
150	Roger Clemens UER	.15	.07	.02
	(League leading ERA in 1990 not italicized)			
151	Jeff Hamilton	.05	.02	.01
152	Charlie Leibrandt	.05	.02	.01
153	Ron Karkovice	.05	.02	.01
154	Hensley Meulens	.05	.02	.01
155	Scott Bankhead	.05	.02	.01
156	Manny Ramirez	3.00	1.35	.35
157	Keith Miller	.05	.02	.01
158	Todd Frohwirth	.05	.02	.01
159	Darrin Fletcher	.05	.02	.01
160	Bobby Bonilla	.15	.07	.02
161	Casey Candaele	.05	.02	.01
162	Paul Faries	.05	.02	.01
163	Dana Kiecker	.05	.02	.01
164	Shane Mack	.05	.02	.01
165	Mark Langston	.15	.07	.02
166	Geronimo Pena	.05	.02	.01
167	Andy Allanson	.05	.02	.01
168	Dwight Smith	.05	.02	.01
169	Chuck Crim	.05	.02	.01
170	Alex Cole	.05	.02	.01
171	Bill Plummer MG	.05	.02	.01
172	Juan Berenguer	.05	.02	.01
173	Brian Downing	.05	.02	.01
174	Steve Frey	.05	.02	.01
175	Orel Hershiser	.15	.07	.02
176	Ramon Garcia	.05	.02	.01
177	Dan Gladden	.05	.02	.01
178	Jim Acker	.05	.02	.01
179	1992 Prospects 2B	.05	.02	.01
	Bobby DeJardin			
	Cesar Bernhardt			
	Armando Moreno			
	Andy Stankiewicz			
180	Kevin Mitchell	.10	.05	.01
181	Hector Villanueva	.05	.02	.01
182	Jeff Reardon	.10	.05	.01
183	Brent Mayne	.05	.02	.01
184	Jimmy Jones	.05	.02	.01
185	Benito Santiago	.05	.02	.01
186	Cliff Floyd	.40	.18	.05
187	Ernie Riles	.05	.02	.01
188	Jose Guzman	.05	.02	.01
189	Junior Felix	.05	.02	.01
190	Glenn Davis	.05	.02	.01
191	Charlie Hough	.10	.05	.01
192	Dave Fleming	.05	.02	.01
193	Omar Olivares	.05	.02	.01
194	Eric Karros	.20	.09	.03

☐ 195 David Cone	.15	.07	.02
☐ 196 Frank Castillo	.05	.02	.01
☐ 197 Glenn Braggs	.05	.02	.01
☐ 198 Scott Aldred	.05	.02	.01
☐ 199 Jeff Blauser	.10	.05	.01
☐ 200 Len Dykstra	.15	.07	.02
☐ 201 Buck Showalter MG	.05	.02	.01
☐ 202 Rick Honeycutt	.05	.02	.01
☐ 203 Greg Myers	.05	.02	.01
☐ 204 Trevor Wilson	.05	.02	.01
☐ 205 Jay Howell	.05	.02	.01
☐ 206 Luis Sojo	.05	.02	.01
☐ 207 Jack Clark	.10	.05	.01
☐ 208 Julio Machado	.05	.02	.01
☐ 209 Lloyd McClendon	.05	.02	.01
☐ 210 Ozzie Guillen	.10	.05	.01
☐ 211 Jeremy Hernandez	.05	.02	.01
☐ 212 Randy Velarde	.05	.02	.01
☐ 213 Les Lancaster	.05	.02	.01
☐ 214 Andy Mota	.05	.02	.01
☐ 215 Rich Gossage	.10	.05	.01
☐ 216 Brent Gates	.10	.05	.01
☐ 217 Brian Harper	.05	.02	.01
☐ 218 Mike Flanagan	.05	.02	.01
☐ 219 Jerry Browne	.05	.02	.01
☐ 220 Jose Rijo	.10	.05	.01
☐ 221 Skeeter Barnes	.05	.02	.01
☐ 222 Jaime Navarro	.05	.02	.01
☐ 223 Mel Hall	.05	.02	.01
☐ 224 Bret Barberie	.05	.02	.01
☐ 225 Roberto Alomar	.20	.09	.03
☐ 226 Pete Smith	.05	.02	.01
☐ 227 Daryl Boston	.05	.02	.01
☐ 228 Eddie Whitson	.05	.02	.01
☐ 229 Shawn Boskie	.05	.02	.01
☐ 230 Dick Schofield	.05	.02	.01
☐ 231 Brian Drahman	.05	.02	.01
☐ 232 John Smiley	.05	.02	.01
☐ 233 Mitch Webster	.05	.02	.01
☐ 234 Terry Steinbach	.10	.05	.01
☐ 235 Jack Morris	.15	.07	.02
☐ 236 Bill Pecota	.05	.02	.01
☐ 237 Jose Hernandez	.05	.02	.01
☐ 238 Greg Litton	.05	.02	.01
☐ 239 Brian Holman	.05	.02	.01
☐ 240 Andres Galarraga	.15	.07	.02
☐ 241 Gerald Young	.05	.02	.01
☐ 242 Mike Mussina	.25	.11	.03
☐ 243 Alvaro Espinoza	.05	.02	.01
☐ 244 Darren Daulton	.15	.07	.02
☐ 245 John Smoltz	.15	.07	.02
☐ 246 Jason Pruitt	.05	.02	.01
☐ 247 Chuck Finley	.05	.02	.01
☐ 248 Jim Gantner	.05	.02	.01
☐ 249 Tony Fossas	.05	.02	.01
☐ 250 Ken Griffey Sr.	.10	.05	.01
☐ 251 Kevin Elster	.05	.02	.01
☐ 252 Dennis Rasmussen	.05	.02	.01
☐ 253 Terry Kennedy	.05	.02	.01
☐ 254 Ryan Bowen	.05	.02	.01
☐ 255 Robin Ventura	.15	.07	.02
☐ 256 Mike Aldrete	.05	.02	.01
☐ 257 Jeff Russell	.05	.02	.01
☐ 258 Jim Lindeman	.05	.02	.01
☐ 259 Ron Darling	.05	.02	.01
☐ 260 Devon White	.10	.05	.01
☐ 261 Tom Lasorda MG	.10	.05	.01
☐ 262 Terry Lee	.05	.02	.01
☐ 263 Bob Patterson	.05	.02	.01
☐ 264 Checklist 133-264	.05	.02	.01
☐ 265 Teddy Higuera	.05	.02	.01

☐ 266 Roberto Kelly	.10	.05	.01
☐ 267 Steve Bedrosian	.05	.02	.01
☐ 268 Brady Anderson	.10	.05	.01
☐ 269 Ruben Amaro Jr.	.05	.02	.01
☐ 270 Tony Gwynn	.30	.14	.04
☐ 271 Tracy Jones	.05	.02	.01
☐ 272 Jerry Don Gleaton	.05	.02	.01
☐ 273 Craig Grebeck	.05	.02	.01
☐ 274 Bob Scanlan	.05	.02	.01
☐ 275 Todd Zeile	.05	.05	.01
☐ 276 Shawn Green	1.00	.45	.12
☐ 277 Scott Chiamparino	.05	.02	.01
☐ 278 Darryl Hamilton	.10	.05	.01
☐ 279 Jim Clancy	.05	.02	.01
☐ 280 Carlos Martinez	.05	.02	.01
☐ 281 Kevin Appier	.10	.05	.01
☐ 282 John Wehner	.05	.02	.01
☐ 283 Reggie Sanders	.20	.09	.03
☐ 284 Gene Larkin	.05	.02	.01
☐ 285 Bob Welch	.10	.05	.01
☐ 286 Gilberto Reyes	.05	.02	.01
☐ 287 Pete Schourek	.15	.07	.02
☐ 288 Andujar Cedeno	.05	.02	.01
☐ 289 Mike Morgan	.05	.02	.01
☐ 290 Bo Jackson	.15	.07	.02
☐ 291 Phil Garner MG	.05	.02	.01
☐ 292 Ray Lankford	.15	.07	.02
☐ 293 Mike Henneman	.05	.02	.01
☐ 294 Dave Valle	.05	.02	.01
☐ 295 Alonzo Powell	.05	.02	.01
☐ 296 Tom Brunansky	.05	.02	.01
☐ 297 Kevin Brown	.10	.05	.01
☐ 298 Kelly Gruber	.05	.02	.01
☐ 299 Charles Nagy	.10	.05	.01
☐ 300 Don Mattingly	.50	.23	.06
☐ 301 Kirk McCaskill	.05	.02	.01
☐ 302 Joey Cora	.05	.02	.01
☐ 303 Dan Plesac	.05	.02	.01
☐ 304 Joe Oliver	.05	.02	.01
☐ 305 Tom Glavine	.15	.07	.02
☐ 306 Al Shirley	.15	.07	.02
☐ 307 Bruce Ruffin	.05	.02	.01
☐ 308 Craig Shipley	.05	.02	.01
☐ 309 Dave Martinez	.05	.02	.01
☐ 310 Jose Mesa	.05	.02	.01
☐ 311 Henry Cotto	.05	.02	.01
☐ 312 Mike LaValliere	.05	.02	.01
☐ 313 Kevin Tapani	.05	.02	.01
☐ 314 Jeff Huson	.05	.02	.01
(Shows Jose Canseco sliding into second)				
☐ 315 Juan Samuel	.05	.02	.01
☐ 316 Curt Schilling	.05	.02	.01
☐ 317 Mike Bordick	.05	.02	.01
☐ 318 Steve Howe	.05	.02	.01
☐ 319 Tony Phillips	.15	.07	.02
☐ 320 George Bell	.05	.02	.01
☐ 321 Lou Piniella MG	.10	.05	.01
☐ 322 Tim Burke	.05	.02	.01
☐ 323 Milt Thompson	.05	.02	.01
☐ 324 Danny Darwin	.05	.02	.01
☐ 325 Joe Orsulak	.05	.02	.01
☐ 326 Eric King	.05	.02	.01
☐ 327 Jay Buhner	.15	.07	.02
☐ 328 Joel Johnston	.05	.02	.01
☐ 329 Franklin Stubbs	.05	.02	.01
☐ 330 Will Clark	.15	.07	.02
☐ 331 Steve Lake	.05	.02	.01
☐ 332 Chris Jones	.05	.02	.01
☐ 333 Pat Tabler	.05	.02	.01
☐ 334 Kevin Gross	.05	.02	.01

☐ 335	Dave Henderson	.05	.02	.01
☐ 336	Greg Anthony	.05	.02	.01
☐ 337	Alejandro Pena	.05	.02	.01
☐ 338	Shawn Abner	.05	.02	.01
☐ 339	Tom Browning	.05	.02	.01
☐ 340	Otis Nixon	.05	.02	.01
☐ 341	Bob Geren	.05	.02	.01
☐ 342	Tim Spehr	.05	.02	.01
☐ 343	John Vander Wal	.05	.02	.01
☐ 344	Jack Daugherty	.05	.02	.01
☐ 345	Zane Smith	.05	.02	.01
☐ 346	Rheal Cormier	.05	.02	.01
☐ 347	Kent Hrbek	.10	.05	.01
☐ 348	Rick Wilkins	.05	.02	.01
☐ 349	Steve Lyons	.05	.02	.01
☐ 350	Gregg Olson	.05	.02	.01
☐ 351	Greg Riddoch MG	.05	.02	.01
☐ 352	Ed Nunez	.05	.02	.01
☐ 353	Braulio Castillo	.05	.02	.01
☐ 354	Dave Bergman	.05	.02	.01
☐ 355	Warren Newson	.05	.02	.01
☐ 356	Luis Quinones	.05	.02	.01
☐ 357	Mike Witt	.05	.02	.01
☐ 358	Ted Wood	.05	.02	.01
☐ 359	Mike Moore	.05	.02	.01
☐ 360	Lance Parrish	.10	.05	.01
☐ 361	Barry Jones	.05	.02	.01
☐ 362	Javier Ortiz	.05	.02	.01
☐ 363	John Candelaria	.05	.02	.01
☐ 364	Glenallen Hill	.10	.05	.01
☐ 365	Duane Ward	.05	.02	.01
☐ 366	Checklist 265-396	.05	.02	.01
☐ 367	Rafael Belliard	.05	.02	.01
☐ 368	Bill Krueger	.05	.02	.01
☐ 369	Steve Whitaker	.05	.02	.01
☐ 370	Shawon Dunston	.05	.02	.01
☐ 371	Dante Bichette	.20	.09	.03
☐ 372	Kip Gross	.05	.02	.01
☐ 373	Don Robinson	.05	.02	.01
☐ 374	Bernie Williams	.15	.07	.02
☐ 375	Bert Blyleven	.15	.07	.02
☐ 376	Chris Donnels	.05	.02	.01
☐ 377	Bob Zupcic	.05	.02	.01
☐ 378	Joel Skinner	.05	.02	.01
☐ 379	Steve Chitren	.05	.02	.01
☐ 380	Barry Bonds	.25	.11	.03
☐ 381	Sparky Anderson MG	.10	.05	.01
☐ 382	Sid Fernandez	.10	.05	.01
☐ 383	Dave Hollins	.05	.02	.01
☐ 384	Mark Lee	.05	.02	.01
☐ 385	Tim Wallach	.05	.02	.01
☐ 386	Will Clark AS	.15	.07	.02
☐ 387	Ryne Sandberg AS	.15	.07	.02
☐ 388	Howard Johnson AS	.05	.02	.01
☐ 389	Barry Larkin AS	.15	.07	.02
☐ 390	Barry Bonds AS	.15	.07	.02
☐ 391	Ron Gant AS	.10	.05	.01
☐ 392	Bobby Bonilla AS	.10	.05	.01
☐ 393	Craig Biggio AS	.10	.05	.01
☐ 394	Dennis Martinez AS	.05	.02	.01
☐ 395	Tom Glavine AS	.10	.05	.01
☐ 396	Lee Smith AS	.10	.05	.01
☐ 397	Cecil Fielder AS	.15	.07	.02
☐ 398	Julio Franco AS	.05	.02	.01
☐ 399	Wade Boggs AS	.15	.07	.02
☐ 400	Cal Ripken AS	.50	.23	.06
☐ 401	Jose Canseco AS	.15	.07	.02
☐ 402	Joe Carter AS	.15	.07	.02
☐ 403	Ruben Sierra AS	.10	.05	.01
☐ 404	Matt Nokes AS	.05	.02	.01
☐ 405	Roger Clemens AS	.15	.07	.02
☐ 406	Jim Abbott AS	.10	.05	.01
☐ 407	Bryan Harvey AS	.05	.02	.01
☐ 408	Bob Milacki	.05	.02	.01
☐ 409	Geno Petralli	.05	.02	.01
☐ 410	Dave Stewart	.15	.07	.02
☐ 411	Mike Jackson	.05	.02	.01
☐ 412	Luis Aquino	.05	.02	.01
☐ 413	Tim Teufel	.05	.02	.01
☐ 414	Jeff Ware	.05	.02	.01
☐ 415	Jim Deshaies	.05	.02	.01
☐ 416	Ellis Burks	.10	.05	.01
☐ 417	Allan Anderson	.05	.02	.01
☐ 418	Alfredo Griffin	.05	.02	.01
☐ 419	Wally Whitehurst	.05	.02	.01
☐ 420	Sandy Alomar Jr.	.10	.05	.01
☐ 421	Juan Agosto	.05	.02	.01
☐ 422	Sam Horn	.05	.02	.01
☐ 423	Jeff Fassero	.10	.05	.01
☐ 424	Paul McClellan	.05	.02	.01
☐ 425	Cecil Fielder	.15	.07	.02
☐ 426	Tim Raines	.15	.07	.02
☐ 427	Eddie Taubensee	.05	.02	.01
☐ 428	Dennis Boyd	.05	.02	.01
☐ 429	Tony LaRussa MG	.10	.05	.01
☐ 430	Steve Sax	.05	.02	.01
☐ 431	Tom Gordon	.10	.05	.01
☐ 432	Billy Hatcher	.05	.02	.01
☐ 433	Cal Eldred	.05	.02	.01
☐ 434	Wally Backman	.05	.02	.01
☐ 435	Mark Eichhorn	.05	.02	.01
☐ 436	Mookie Wilson	.10	.05	.01
☐ 437	Scott Servais	.05	.02	.01
☐ 438	Mike Maddux	.05	.02	.01
☐ 439	Chico Walker	.05	.02	.01
☐ 440	Doug Drabek	.10	.05	.01
☐ 441	Rob Deer	.05	.02	.01
☐ 442	Dave West	.05	.02	.01
☐ 443	Spike Owen	.05	.02	.01
☐ 444	Tyrone Hill	.05	.02	.01
☐ 445	Matt Williams	.20	.09	.03
☐ 446	Mark Lewis	.05	.02	.01
☐ 447	David Segui	.05	.02	.01
☐ 448	Tom Pagnozzi	.05	.02	.01
☐ 449	Jeff Johnson	.05	.02	.01
☐ 450	Mark McGwire	.15	.07	.02
☐ 451	Tom Henke	.10	.05	.01
☐ 452	Wilson Alvarez	.15	.07	.02
☐ 453	Gary Redus	.05	.02	.01
☐ 454	Darren Holmes	.05	.02	.01
☐ 455	Pete O'Brien	.05	.02	.01
☐ 456	Pat Combs	.05	.02	.01
☐ 457	Hubie Brooks	.05	.02	.01
☐ 458	Frank Tanana	.05	.02	.01
☐ 459	Tom Kelly MG	.05	.02	.01
☐ 460	Andre Dawson	.15	.07	.02
☐ 461	Doug Jones	.05	.02	.01
☐ 462	Rich Rodriguez	.05	.02	.01
☐ 463	Mike Simms	.05	.02	.01
☐ 464	Mike Jeffcoat	.05	.02	.01
☐ 465	Barry Larkin	.15	.07	.02
☐ 466	Stan Belinda	.05	.02	.01
☐ 467	Lonnie Smith	.05	.02	.01
☐ 468	Greg Harris	.05	.02	.01
☐ 469	Jim Eisenreich	.05	.02	.01
☐ 470	Pedro Guerrero	.05	.02	.01
☐ 471	Jose DeJesus	.05	.02	.01
☐ 472	Rich Rowland	.05	.02	.01
☐ 473	1992 Prospects 3B UER	.15	.07	.02
	Frank Bolick			
	Craig Paquette			
	Tom Redington			

Paul Russo
(Line around top border)

☐ 474	Mike Rossiter	.05	.02	.01
☐ 475	Robby Thompson	.10	.05	.01
☐ 476	Randy Bush	.05	.02	.01
☐ 477	Greg Hibbard	.05	.02	.01
☐ 478	Dale Sveum	.05	.02	.01
☐ 479	Chito Martinez	.05	.02	.01
☐ 480	Scott Sanderson	.05	.02	.01
☐ 481	Tino Martinez	.15	.07	.02
☐ 482	Jimmy Key	.10	.05	.01
☐ 483	Terry Shumpert	.05	.02	.01
☐ 484	Mike Hartley	.05	.02	.01
☐ 485	Chris Sabo	.05	.02	.01
☐ 486	Bob Walk	.05	.02	.01
☐ 487	John Cerutti	.05	.02	.01
☐ 488	Scott Cooper	.05	.02	.01
☐ 489	Bobby Cox MG	.05	.02	.01
☐ 490	Julio Franco	.10	.05	.01
☐ 491	Jeff Brantley	.05	.02	.01
☐ 492	Mike Devereaux	.10	.05	.01
☐ 493	Jose Offerman	.05	.02	.01
☐ 494	Gary Thurman	.05	.02	.01
☐ 495	Carney Lansford	.10	.05	.01
☐ 496	Joe Grahe	.05	.02	.01
☐ 497	Andy Ashby	.05	.02	.01
☐ 498	Gerald Perry	.05	.02	.01
☐ 499	Dave Otto	.05	.02	.01
☐ 500	Vince Coleman	.05	.02	.01
☐ 501	Rob Mallicoat	.05	.02	.01
☐ 502	Greg Briley	.05	.02	.01
☐ 503	Pascual Perez	.05	.02	.01
☐ 504	Aaron Sele	.30	.14	.04
☐ 505	Bobby Thigpen	.05	.02	.01
☐ 506	Todd Benzinger	.05	.02	.01
☐ 507	Candy Maldonado	.05	.02	.01
☐ 508	Bill Gullickson	.05	.02	.01
☐ 509	Doug Dascenzo	.05	.02	.01
☐ 510	Frank Viola	.05	.02	.01
☐ 511	Kenny Rogers	.10	.05	.01
☐ 512	Mike Heath	.05	.02	.01
☐ 513	Kevin Bass	.05	.02	.01
☐ 514	Kim Batiste	.05	.02	.01
☐ 515	Delino DeShields	.15	.07	.02
☐ 516	Ed Sprague Jr.	.10	.05	.01
☐ 517	Jim Gott	.05	.02	.01
☐ 518	Jose Melendez	.05	.02	.01
☐ 519	Hal McRae MG	.05	.02	.01
☐ 520	Jeff Bagwell	.50	.23	.06
☐ 521	Joe Hesketh	.05	.02	.01
☐ 522	Milt Cuyler	.05	.02	.01
☐ 523	Shawn Hillegas	.05	.02	.01
☐ 524	Don Slaught	.05	.02	.01
☐ 525	Randy Johnson	.25	.11	.03
☐ 526	Doug Piatt	.05	.02	.01
☐ 527	Checklist 397-528	.05	.02	.01
☐ 528	Steve Foster	.05	.02	.01
☐ 529	Joe Girardi	.05	.02	.01
☐ 530	Jim Abbott	.15	.07	.02
☐ 531	Larry Walker	.15	.07	.02
☐ 532	Mike Huff	.05	.02	.01
☐ 533	Mackey Sasser	.05	.02	.01
☐ 534	Benji Gil	.25	.11	.03
☐ 535	Dave Stieb	.05	.02	.01
☐ 536	Willie Wilson	.05	.02	.01
☐ 537	Mark Leiter	.05	.02	.01
☐ 538	Jose Uribe	.05	.02	.01
☐ 539	Thomas Howard	.05	.02	.01
☐ 540	Ben McDonald	.10	.05	.01
☐ 541	Jose Tolentino	.05	.02	.01
☐ 542	Keith Mitchell	.05	.02	.01
☐ 543	Jerome Walton	.05	.02	.01
☐ 544	Cliff Brantley	.05	.02	.01
☐ 545	Andy Van Slyke	.10	.05	.01
☐ 546	Paul Sorrento	.05	.02	.01
☐ 547	Herm Winningham	.05	.02	.01
☐ 548	Mark Guthrie	.05	.02	.01
☐ 549	Joe Torre MG	.10	.05	.01
☐ 550	Darryl Strawberry	.05	.02	.01
☐ 551	1992 Prospects SS UER	1.50	.70	.19

Wilfredo Cordero
Chipper Jones
Manny Alexander
Alex Arias
(No line around
top border)

☐ 552	Dave Gallagher	.05	.02	.01
☐ 553	Edgar Martinez	.15	.07	.02
☐ 554	Donald Harris	.05	.02	.01
☐ 555	Frank Thomas	1.50	.70	.19
☐ 556	Storm Davis	.05	.02	.01
☐ 557	Dickie Thon	.05	.02	.01
☐ 558	Scott Garrelts	.05	.02	.01
☐ 559	Steve Olin	.05	.02	.01
☐ 560	Rickey Henderson	.15	.07	.02
☐ 561	Jose Vizcaino	.05	.02	.01
☐ 562	Wade Taylor	.05	.02	.01
☐ 563	Pat Borders	.05	.02	.01
☐ 564	Jimmy Gonzalez	.05	.02	.01
☐ 565	Lee Smith	.15	.07	.02
☐ 566	Bill Sampen	.05	.02	.01
☐ 567	Dean Palmer	.10	.05	.01
☐ 568	Bryan Harvey	.05	.02	.01
☐ 569	Tony Pena	.05	.02	.01
☐ 570	Lou Whitaker	.15	.07	.02
☐ 571	Randy Tomlin	.05	.02	.01
☐ 572	Greg Vaughn	.10	.05	.01
☐ 573	Kelly Downs	.05	.02	.01
☐ 574	Steve Avery UER	.15	.07	.02

(Should be 13 games
for Durham in 1989)

☐ 575	Kirby Puckett	.30	.14	.04
☐ 576	Heathcliff Slocumb	.10	.05	.01
☐ 577	Kevin Seitzer	.05	.02	.01
☐ 578	Lee Guetterman	.05	.02	.01
☐ 579	Johnny Oates MG	.05	.02	.01
☐ 580	Greg Maddux	.75	.35	.09
☐ 581	Stan Javier	.05	.02	.01
☐ 582	Vicente Palacios	.05	.02	.01
☐ 583	Mel Rojas	.10	.05	.01
☐ 584	Wayne Rosenthal	.05	.02	.01
☐ 585	Lenny Webster	.05	.02	.01
☐ 586	Rod Nichols	.05	.02	.01
☐ 587	Mickey Morandini	.05	.02	.01
☐ 588	Russ Swan	.05	.02	.01
☐ 589	Mariano Duncan	.05	.02	.01
☐ 590	Howard Johnson	.05	.02	.01
☐ 591	1992 Prospects OF	.10	.05	.01

Jeromy Burnitz
Jacob Brumfield
Alan Cockrell
D.J. Dozier

☐ 592	Denny Neagle	.10	.05	.01
☐ 593	Steve Decker	.05	.02	.01
☐ 594	Brian Barber	.15	.07	.02
☐ 595	Bruce Hurst	.05	.02	.01
☐ 596	Kent Mercker	.05	.02	.01
☐ 597	Mike Magnante	.05	.02	.01
☐ 598	Jody Reed	.05	.02	.01
☐ 599	Steve Searcy	.05	.02	.01
☐ 600	Paul Molitor	.15	.07	.02
☐ 601	Dave Smith	.05	.02	.01

☐ 602	Mike Fetters	.05	.02	.01
☐ 603	Luis Mercedes	.05	.02	.01
☐ 604	Chris Gwynn	.05	.02	.01
☐ 605	Scott Erickson	.10	.05	.01
☐ 606	Brook Jacoby	.05	.02	.01
☐ 607	Todd Stottlemyre	.05	.02	.01
☐ 608	Scott Bradley	.05	.02	.01
☐ 609	Mike Hargrove MG	.05	.02	.01
☐ 610	Eric Davis	.10	.05	.01
☐ 611	Brian Hunter	.05	.02	.01
☐ 612	Pat Kelly	.05	.02	.01
☐ 613	Pedro Munoz	.10	.05	.01
☐ 614	Al Osuna	.05	.02	.01
☐ 615	Matt Merullo	.05	.02	.01
☐ 616	Larry Andersen	.05	.02	.01
☐ 617	Junior Ortiz	.05	.02	.01
☐ 618	1992 Prospects OF	.05	.02	.01
	Cesar Hernandez			
	Steve Hosey			
	Jeff McNeely			
	Dan Peltier			
☐ 619	Danny Jackson	.05	.02	.01
☐ 620	George Brett	.40	.18	.05
☐ 621	Dan Gakeler	.05	.02	.01
☐ 622	Steve Buechele	.05	.02	.01
☐ 623	Bob Tewksbury	.05	.02	.01
☐ 624	Shawn Estes	.15	.07	.02
☐ 625	Kevin McReynolds	.05	.02	.01
☐ 626	Chris Haney	.05	.02	.01
☐ 627	Mike Sharperson	.05	.02	.01
☐ 628	Mark Williamson	.05	.02	.01
☐ 629	Wally Joyner	.15	.07	.02
☐ 630	Carlton Fisk	.15	.07	.02
☐ 631	Armando Reynoso	.05	.02	.01
☐ 632	Felix Fermin	.05	.02	.01
☐ 633	Mitch Williams	.10	.05	.01
☐ 634	Manuel Lee	.05	.02	.01
☐ 635	Harold Baines	.15	.07	.02
☐ 636	Greg Harris	.05	.02	.01
☐ 637	Orlando Merced	.05	.02	.01
☐ 638	Chris Bosio	.05	.02	.01
☐ 639	Wayne Housie	.05	.02	.01
☐ 640	Xavier Hernandez	.05	.02	.01
☐ 641	David Howard	.05	.02	.01
☐ 642	Tim Crews	.05	.02	.01
☐ 643	Rick Cerone	.05	.02	.01
☐ 644	Terry Leach	.05	.02	.01
☐ 645	Deion Sanders	.20	.09	.03
☐ 646	Craig Wilson	.05	.02	.01
☐ 647	Marquis Grissom	.15	.07	.02
☐ 648	Scott Fletcher	.05	.02	.01
☐ 649	Norm Charlton	.05	.02	.01
☐ 650	Jesse Barfield	.05	.02	.01
☐ 651	Joe Slusarski	.05	.02	.01
☐ 652	Bobby Rose	.05	.02	.01
☐ 653	Dennis Lamp	.05	.02	.01
☐ 654	Allen Watson	.15	.07	.02
☐ 655	Brett Butler	.15	.07	.02
☐ 656	1992 Prospects OF	.15	.07	.02
	Rudy Pemberton			
	Henry Rodriguez			
	Lee Tinsley			
	Gerald Williams			
☐ 657	Dave Johnson	.05	.02	.01
☐ 658	Checklist 529-660	.05	.02	.01
☐ 659	Brian McRae	.15	.07	.02
☐ 660	Fred McGriff	.15	.07	.02
☐ 661	Bill Landrum	.05	.02	.01
☐ 662	Juan Guzman	.10	.05	.01
☐ 663	Greg Gagne	.05	.02	.01
☐ 664	Ken Hill	.15	.07	.02
☐ 665	Dave Haas	.05	.02	.01
☐ 666	Tom Foley	.05	.02	.01
☐ 667	Roberto Hernandez	.10	.05	.01
☐ 668	Dwayne Henry	.05	.02	.01
☐ 669	Jim Fregosi MG	.05	.02	.01
☐ 670	Harold Reynolds	.05	.02	.01
☐ 671	Mark Whiten	.10	.05	.01
☐ 672	Eric Plunk	.05	.02	.01
☐ 673	Todd Hundley	.05	.02	.01
☐ 674	Mo Sanford	.05	.02	.01
☐ 675	Bobby Witt	.05	.02	.01
☐ 676	1992 Prospects P	.10	.05	.01
	Sam Militello			
	Pat Mahomes			
	Turk Wendell			
	Roger Salkeld			
☐ 677	John Marzano	.05	.02	.01
☐ 678	Joe Klink	.05	.02	.01
☐ 679	Pete Incaviglia	.05	.02	.01
☐ 680	Dale Murphy	.15	.07	.02
☐ 681	Rene Gonzales	.05	.02	.01
☐ 682	Andy Benes	.10	.05	.01
☐ 683	Jim Poole	.05	.02	.01
☐ 684	Trever Miller	.05	.02	.01
☐ 685	Scott Livingstone	.05	.02	.01
☐ 686	Rich DeLucia	.05	.02	.01
☐ 687	Harvey Pulliam	.05	.02	.01
☐ 688	Tim Belcher	.05	.02	.01
☐ 689	Mark Lemke	.10	.05	.01
☐ 690	John Franco	.15	.07	.02
☐ 691	Walt Weiss	.05	.02	.01
☐ 692	Scott Ruskin	.05	.02	.01
☐ 693	Jeff King	.10	.05	.01
☐ 694	Mike Gardiner	.05	.02	.01
☐ 695	Gary Sheffield	.15	.07	.02
☐ 696	Joe Boever	.05	.02	.01
☐ 697	Mike Felder	.05	.02	.01
☐ 698	John Habyan	.05	.02	.01
☐ 699	Cito Gaston MG	.05	.02	.01
☐ 700	Ruben Sierra	.15	.07	.02
☐ 701	Scott Radinsky	.05	.02	.01
☐ 702	Lee Stevens	.05	.02	.01
☐ 703	Mark Wohlers	.10	.05	.01
☐ 704	Curt Young	.05	.02	.01
☐ 705	Dwight Evans	.10	.05	.01
☐ 706	Rob Murphy	.05	.02	.01
☐ 707	Gregg Jefferies	.15	.07	.02
☐ 708	Tom Bolton	.05	.02	.01
☐ 709	Chris James	.05	.02	.01
☐ 710	Kevin Maas	.05	.02	.01
☐ 711	Ricky Bones	.05	.02	.01
☐ 712	Curt Wilkerson	.05	.02	.01
☐ 713	Roger McDowell	.05	.02	.01
☐ 714	Calvin Reese	.25	.11	.03
☐ 715	Craig Biggio	.15	.07	.02
☐ 716	Kirk Dressendorfer	.05	.02	.01
☐ 717	Ken Dayley	.05	.02	.01
☐ 718	B.J. Surhoff	.10	.05	.01
☐ 719	Terry Mulholland	.05	.02	.01
☐ 720	Kirk Gibson	.15	.07	.02
☐ 721	Mike Pagliarulo	.05	.02	.01
☐ 722	Walt Terrell	.05	.02	.01
☐ 723	Jose Oquendo	.05	.02	.01
☐ 724	Kevin Morton	.05	.02	.01
☐ 725	Dwight Gooden	.10	.05	.01
☐ 726	Kirt Manwaring	.05	.02	.01
☐ 727	Chuck McElroy	.05	.02	.01
☐ 728	Dave Burba	.05	.02	.01
☐ 729	Art Howe MG	.05	.02	.01
☐ 730	Ramon Martinez	.15	.07	.02
☐ 731	Donnie Hill	.05	.02	.01

☐ 732	Nelson Santovenia	.05	.02	.01
☐ 733	Bob Melvin	.05	.02	.01
☐ 734	Scott Hatteberg	.05	.02	.01
☐ 735	Greg Swindell	.05	.02	.01
☐ 736	Lance Johnson	.05	.02	.01
☐ 737	Kevin Reimer	.05	.02	.01
☐ 738	Dennis Eckersley	.15	.07	.02
☐ 739	Rob Ducey	.05	.02	.01
☐ 740	Ken Caminiti	.15	.07	.02
☐ 741	Mark Gubicza	.05	.02	.01
☐ 742	Billy Spiers	.05	.02	.01
☐ 743	Darren Lewis	.10	.05	.01
☐ 744	Chris Hammond	.05	.02	.01
☐ 745	Dave Magadan	.05	.02	.01
☐ 746	Bernard Gilkey	.10	.05	.01
☐ 747	Willie Banks	.05	.02	.01
☐ 748	Matt Nokes	.05	.02	.01
☐ 749	Jerald Clark	.05	.02	.01
☐ 750	Travis Fryman	.15	.07	.02
☐ 751	Steve Wilson	.05	.02	.01
☐ 752	Billy Ripken	.05	.02	.01
☐ 753	Paul Assenmacher	.05	.02	.01
☐ 754	Charlie Hayes	.10	.05	.01
☐ 755	Alex Fernandez	.15	.07	.02
☐ 756	Gary Pettis	.05	.02	.01
☐ 757	Rob Dibble	.05	.02	.01
☐ 758	Tim Naehring	.05	.02	.01
☐ 759	Jeff Torborg MG	.05	.02	.01
☐ 760	Ozzie Smith	.20	.09	.03
☐ 761	Mike Fitzgerald	.05	.02	.01
☐ 762	John Burkett	.05	.02	.01
☐ 763	Kyle Abbott	.05	.02	.01
☐ 764	Tyler Green	.10	.05	.01
☐ 765	Pete Harnisch	.05	.02	.01
☐ 766	Mark Davis	.05	.02	.01
☐ 767	Kal Daniels	.05	.02	.01
☐ 768	Jim Thome	.75	.35	.09
☐ 769	Jack Howell	.05	.02	.01
☐ 770	Sid Bream	.05	.02	.01
☐ 771	Arthur Rhodes	.05	.02	.01
☐ 772	Garry Templeton UER	.05	.02	.01
	(Stat heading in for pitchers)			
☐ 773	Hal Morris	.10	.05	.01
☐ 774	Bud Black	.05	.02	.01
☐ 775	Ivan Calderon	.05	.02	.01
☐ 776	Doug Henry	.05	.02	.01
☐ 777	John Olerud	.10	.05	.01
☐ 778	Tim Leary	.05	.02	.01
☐ 779	Jay Bell	.10	.05	.01
☐ 780	Eddie Murray	.15	.07	.02
☐ 781	Paul Abbott	.05	.02	.01
☐ 782	Phil Plantier	.10	.05	.01
☐ 783	Joe Magrane	.05	.02	.01
☐ 784	Ken Patterson	.05	.02	.01
☐ 785	Albert Belle	.50	.23	.06
☐ 786	Royce Clayton	.10	.05	.01
☐ 787	Checklist 661-792	.05	.02	.01
☐ 788	Mike Stanton	.05	.02	.01
☐ 789	Bobby Valentine MG	.05	.02	.01
☐ 790	Joe Carter	.15	.07	.02
☐ 791	Danny Cox	.05	.02	.01
☐ 792	Dave Winfield	.15	.07	.02
☐ 793	Brien Taylor AU/12000	20.00	9.00	2.50

1992 Topps Traded

The 1992 Topps Traded set comprises 132 cards, each measuring the standard size (2

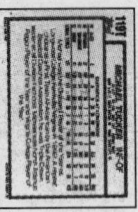

1/2" by 3 1/2"). As in past editions, the set focuses on promising rookies, new managers, and players who changed teams. The set also includes a Team U.S.A. subset, featuring 25 of America's top college players and the Team U.S.A. coach. Inside a white outer border, the fronts display color action photos that have two-color (white and another color) picture frames. The player's name appears in a short color bar at the lower left corner while the team name is given in a different color bar at the lower right corner. In a horizontal format, the backs carry biography, statistics, player summary, or a small color picture of the team's stadium . The cards are arranged in alphabetical order by player's last name and numbered on the back. The key Rookie Cards in this set are Jeff Alkire, Chad Curtis, Tim Davis, Nomar Garciaparra, Pat Listach, Jason Moler, Calvin Murray, Michael Tucker, Jason Varitek, and B.J. Wallace.

	MINT	NRMT	EXC
COMPLETE FACT.SET (132) ..	15.00	6.75	1.85
COMMON CARD (1T-132T)	.10	.05	.01
COMP. GOLD FACT. SET (132)	30.00	13.50	3.70
GOLD COMMON CARDS (1-132)	.15	.07	.02
GOLD SEMISTARS	.40	.18	.05
*GOLD STARS: 1.25X to 2X BASIC CARDS			

☐ 1T	Willie Adams USA	.10	.05	.01
☐ 2T	Jeff Alkire USA	.10	.05	.01
☐ 3T	Felipe Alou MG	.10	.05	.01
☐ 4T	Moises Alou	.15	.07	.02
☐ 5T	Ruben Amaro	.10	.05	.01
☐ 6T	Jack Armstrong	.10	.05	.01
☐ 7T	Scott Bankhead	.10	.05	.01
☐ 8T	Tim Belcher	.10	.05	.01
☐ 9T	George Bell	.15	.07	.02
☐ 10T	Freddie Benavides	.10	.05	.01
☐ 11T	Todd Benzinger	.10	.05	.01
☐ 12T	Joe Boever	.10	.05	.01
☐ 13T	Ricky Bones	.10	.05	.01
☐ 14T	Bobby Bonilla	.20	.09	.03
☐ 15T	Hubie Brooks	.10	.05	.01
☐ 16T	Jerry Browne	.10	.05	.01
☐ 17T	Jim Bullinger	.10	.05	.01
☐ 18T	Dave Burba	.10	.05	.01
☐ 19T	Kevin Campbell	.10	.05	.01
☐ 20T	Tom Candiotti	.10	.05	.01
☐ 21T	Mark Carreon	.10	.05	.01
☐ 22T	Gary Carter	.20	.09	.03
☐ 23T	Archi Cianfrocco	.10	.05	.01
☐ 24T	Phil Clark	.10	.05	.01

☐ 25T	Chad Curtis	.20	.09	.03
☐ 26T	Eric Davis	.15	.07	.02
☐ 27T	Tim Davis USA	.10	.05	.01
☐ 28T	Gary DiSarcina	.10	.05	.01
☐ 29T	Darren Dreifort USA	.15	.07	.02
☐ 30T	Mariano Duncan	.10	.05	.01
☐ 31T	Mike Fitzgerald	.10	.05	.01
☐ 32T	John Flaherty	.15	.07	.02
☐ 33T	Darrin Fletcher	.10	.05	.01
☐ 34T	Scott Fletcher	.10	.05	.01
☐ 35T	Ron Fraser CO USA	.15	.07	.02
☐ 36T	Andres Galarraga	.20	.09	.03
☐ 37T	Dave Gallagher	.10	.05	.01
☐ 38T	Mike Gallego	.10	.05	.01
☐ 39T	Nomar Garciaparra USA	1.00	.45	.12
☐ 40T	Jason Giambi USA	.75	.35	.09
☐ 41T	Danny Gladden	.10	.05	.01
☐ 42T	Rene Gonzales	.10	.05	.01
☐ 43T	Jeff Granger USA	.15	.07	.02
☐ 44T	Rick Greene USA	.10	.05	.01
☐ 45T	Jeffrey Hammonds USA	.40	.18	.05
☐ 46T	Charlie Hayes	.15	.07	.02
☐ 47T	Von Hayes	.10	.05	.01
☐ 48T	Rick Helling USA	.10	.05	.01
☐ 49T	Butch Henry	.10	.05	.01
☐ 50T	Carlos Hernandez	.10	.05	.01
☐ 51T	Ken Hill	.15	.07	.02
☐ 52T	Butch Hobson	.10	.05	.01
☐ 53T	Vince Horsman	.10	.05	.01
☐ 54T	Pete Incaviglia	.10	.05	.01
☐ 55T	Gregg Jefferies	.20	.09	.03
☐ 56T	Charles Johnson USA	.75	.35	.09
☐ 57T	Doug Jones	.10	.05	.01
☐ 58T	Brian Jordan	.25	.11	.03
☐ 59T	Wally Joyner	.15	.07	.02
☐ 60T	Daron Kirkreit USA	.15	.07	.02
☐ 61T	Bill Krueger	.10	.05	.01
☐ 62T	Gene Lamont MG	.10	.05	.01
☐ 63T	Jim Lefebvre MG	.10	.05	.01
☐ 64T	Danny Leon	.10	.05	.01
☐ 65T	Pat Listach	.15	.07	.02
☐ 66T	Kenny Lofton	2.00	.90	.25
☐ 67T	Dave Martinez	.10	.05	.01
☐ 68T	Derrick May	.15	.07	.02
☐ 69T	Kirk McCaskill	.10	.05	.01
☐ 70T	Chad McConnell USA	.15	.07	.02
☐ 71T	Kevin McReynolds	.10	.05	.01
☐ 72T	Rusty Meacham	.10	.05	.01
☐ 73T	Keith Miller	.10	.05	.01
☐ 74T	Kevin Mitchell	.15	.07	.02
☐ 75T	Jason Moler USA	.10	.05	.01
☐ 76T	Mike Morgan	.10	.05	.01
☐ 77T	Jack Morris	.20	.09	.03
☐ 78T	Calvin Murray USA	.10	.05	.01
☐ 79T	Eddie Murray	.25	.11	.03
☐ 80T	Randy Myers	.20	.09	.03
☐ 81T	Denny Neagle	.15	.07	.02
☐ 82T	Phil Nevin USA	.15	.07	.02
☐ 83T	Dave Nilsson	.15	.07	.02
☐ 84T	Junior Ortiz	.10	.05	.01
☐ 85T	Donovan Osborne	.10	.05	.01
☐ 86T	Bill Pecota	.10	.05	.01
☐ 87T	Melido Perez	.10	.05	.01
☐ 88T	Mike Perez	.10	.05	.01
☐ 89T	Hipolito Pichardo	.10	.05	.01
☐ 90T	Willie Randolph	.15	.07	.02
☐ 91T	Darren Reed	.10	.05	.01
☐ 92T	Bip Roberts	.10	.05	.01
☐ 93T	Chris Roberts USA	.15	.07	.02
☐ 94T	Steve Rodriguez USA	.10	.05	.01
☐ 95T	Bruce Ruffin	.10	.05	.01

☐ 96T	Scott Ruskin	.10	.05	.01
☐ 97T	Bret Saberhagen	.20	.09	.03
☐ 98T	Rey Sanchez	.10	.05	.01
☐ 99T	Steve Sax	.10	.05	.01
☐ 100T	Curt Schilling	.10	.05	.01
☐ 101T	Dick Schofield	.10	.05	.01
☐ 102T	Gary Scott	.10	.05	.01
☐ 103T	Kevin Seitzer	.10	.05	.01
☐ 104T	Frank Seminara	.15	.07	.02
☐ 105T	Gary Sheffield	.20	.09	.03
☐ 106T	John Smiley	.10	.05	.01
☐ 107T	Cory Snyder	.10	.05	.01
☐ 108T	Paul Sorrento	.10	.05	.01
☐ 109T	Sammy Sosa	.25	.11	.03
☐ 110T	Matt Stairs	.10	.05	.01
☐ 111T	Andy Stankiewicz	.10	.05	.01
☐ 112T	Kurt Stillwell	.10	.05	.01
☐ 113T	Rick Sutcliffe	.15	.07	.02
☐ 114T	Bill Swift	.15	.07	.02
☐ 115T	Jeff Tackett	.10	.05	.01
☐ 116T	Danny Tartabull	.15	.07	.02
☐ 117T	Eddie Taubensee	.15	.07	.02
☐ 118T	Dickie Thon	.10	.05	.01
☐ 119T	Michael Tucker USA	.50	.23	.06
☐ 120T	Scooter Tucker	.10	.05	.01
☐ 121T	Marc Valdes USA	.25	.11	.03
☐ 122T	Julio Valera	.10	.05	.01
☐ 123T	Jason Varitek USA	.75	.35	.09
☐ 124T	Ron Villone USA	.15	.07	.02
☐ 125T	Frank Viola	.15	.07	.02
☐ 126T	B.J. Wallace USA	.15	.07	.02
☐ 127T	Dan Walters	.10	.05	.01
☐ 128T	Craig Wilson USA	.10	.05	.01
☐ 129T	Chris Wimmer USA	.10	.05	.01
☐ 130T	Dave Winfield	.20	.09	.03
☐ 131T	Herm Winningham	.10	.05	.01
☐ 132T	Checklist 1T-132T	.10	.05	.01

1993 Topps

The 1993 Topps baseball set consists of two series of 396 and 429 cards measuring the standard size (2 1/2" by 3 1/2"). A Topps Gold card was inserted in every 15-card pack, and Topps Black Gold cards were randomly inserted throughout the packs. The fronts feature color action player photos with white borders. The player's name appears in a stripe at the bottom of the picture, and this stripe and two short diagonal stripes at the bottom corners of the picture are team color-coded. The *backs are colorful and carry a color head shot, biography, complete statistical information, with a career highlight if space permitted. The cards are numbered on the back. Cards 401-411 comprise an All-Star subset. Rookie Cards in this set include Derek Jeter, Chad Mottola, J.T. Snow, and Preston Wilson. For the Colorado Rockies and the Florida Marlins, Topps also produced cards gold-foil stamped factory complete sets on the front with the inaugural team's logo. Five thousand complete factory sets with the Rockies' logo and four thousand complete factory sets with the Marlins' logo were initially printed, and each team has the option of having a maximum of 10,000 special sets produced. The Rockies' sets were distributed through the four team-owned stores and at Mile High Stadium. The Marlins' sets were distributed from FMI and Joe Robbie Stadium. The complete 1993 Topps set was also issued as a factory set of micro baseball cards with cards measuring approximately one-fourth the size of the regular size cards but identical in other respects. The micro set and its cards are valued at approximately half the values listed below for the regular size cards.*

	MINT	NRMT	EXC
COMPLETE SET (825)	30.00	13.50	3.70
COMPLETE RETAIL SET (838)	40.00	18.00	5.00
COMPLETE HOBBY SET (847)	45.00	20.00	5.50
COMP.1994 PREPROD. (9)	7.00	3.10	.85
COMPLETE SERIES 1 (396)	15.00	6.75	1.85
COMPLETE SERIES 2 (429)	15.00	6.75	1.85
COMMON CARD (1-396)	.05	.02	.01
COMMON CARD (397-825)	.05	.02	.01
COMPLETE GOLD SET (825)	80.00	36.00	10.00
GOLD COMMON CARDS (1-825)	.10	.05	.01
GOLD SEMISTARS	.20	.09	.03
GOLD STARS	.30	.14	.04
*GOLD VETERAN STARS: 2X TO 4X BASIC CARDS			
*GOLD YOUNG STARS: 1.5X TO 3X BASIC CARDS			
*GOLD RC'S: 1.25X TO 2.5X BASIC CARDS			

☐	1 Robin Yount	.25	.11	.03
☐	2 Barry Bonds	.50	.23	.06
☐	3 Ryne Sandberg	.50	.23	.06
☐	4 Roger Clemens	.30	.14	.04
☐	5 Tony Gwynn	.60	.25	.07
☐	6 Jeff Tackett	.05	.02	.01
☐	7 Pete Incaviglia	.05	.02	.01
☐	8 Mark Wohlers	.10	.05	.01
☐	9 Kent Hrbek	.10	.05	.01
☐	10 Will Clark	.25	.11	.03
☐	11 Eric Karros	.15	.07	.02
☐	12 Lee Smith	.15	.07	.02
☐	13 Esteban Beltre	.05	.02	.01
☐	14 Greg Briley	.05	.02	.01
☐	15 Marquis Grissom	.15	.07	.02
☐	16 Dan Plesac	.05	.02	.01
☐	17 Dave Hollins	.05	.02	.01
☐	18 Terry Steinbach	.10	.05	.01
☐	19 Ed Nunez	.05	.02	.01
☐	20 Tim Salmon	.60	.25	.07
☐	21 Luis Salazar	.05	.02	.01
☐	22 Jim Eisenreich	.05	.02	.01
☐	23 Todd Stottlemyre	.05	.02	.01
☐	24 Tim Naehring	.05	.02	.01
☐	25 John Franco	.10	.05	.01
☐	26 Skeeter Barnes	.05	.02	.01
☐	27 Carlos Garcia	.10	.05	.01
☐	28 Joe Orsulak	.05	.02	.01
☐	29 Dwayne Henry	.05	.02	.01
☐	30 Fred McGriff	.25	.11	.03
☐	31 Derek Lilliquist	.05	.02	.01
☐	32 Don Mattingly	1.00	.45	.12
☐	33 B.J. Wallace	.05	.02	.01
☐	34 Juan Gonzalez	.40	.18	.05
☐	35 John Smoltz	.10	.05	.01
☐	36 Scott Servais	.05	.02	.01
☐	37 Lenny Webster	.05	.02	.01
☐	38 Chris James	.05	.02	.01
☐	39 Roger McDowell	.05	.02	.01
☐	40 Ozzie Smith	.40	.18	.05
☐	41 Alex Fernandez	.15	.07	.02
☐	42 Spike Owen	.05	.02	.01
☐	43 Ruben Amaro	.05	.02	.01
☐	44 Kevin Seitzer	.05	.02	.01
☐	45 Dave Fleming	.05	.02	.01
☐	46 Eric Fox	.05	.02	.01
☐	47 Bob Scanlan	.05	.02	.01
☐	48 Bert Blyleven	.15	.07	.02
☐	49 Brian McRae	.15	.07	.02
☐	50 Roberto Alomar	.40	.18	.05
☐	51 Mo Vaughn	.30	.14	.04
☐	52 Bobby Bonilla	.15	.07	.02
☐	53 Frank Tanana	.05	.02	.01
☐	54 Mike LaValliere	.05	.02	.01
☐	55 Mark McLemore	.05	.02	.01
☐	56 Chad Mottola	.15	.07	.02
☐	57 Norm Charlton	.05	.02	.01
☐	58 Jose Melendez	.05	.02	.01
☐	59 Carlos Martinez	.05	.02	.01
☐	60 Roberto Kelly	.10	.05	.01
☐	61 Gene Larkin	.05	.02	.01
☐	62 Rafael Belliard	.05	.02	.01
☐	63 Al Osuna	.05	.02	.01
☐	64 Scott Chiamparino	.05	.02	.01
☐	65 Brett Butler	.10	.05	.01
☐	66 John Burkett	.05	.02	.01
☐	67 Felix Jose	.05	.02	.01
☐	68 Omar Vizquel	.05	.02	.01
☐	69 John Vander Wal	.05	.02	.01
☐	70 Roberto Hernandez	.10	.05	.01
☐	71 Ricky Bones	.05	.02	.01
☐	72 Jeff Grotewold	.05	.02	.01
☐	73 Mike Moore	.05	.02	.01
☐	74 Steve Buechele	.05	.02	.01
☐	75 Juan Guzman	.10	.05	.01
☐	76 Kevin Appier	.10	.05	.01
☐	77 Junior Felix	.05	.02	.01
☐	78 Greg W. Harris	.05	.02	.01
☐	79 Dick Schofield	.05	.02	.01
☐	80 Cecil Fielder	.15	.07	.02
☐	81 Lloyd McClendon	.05	.02	.01
☐	82 David Segui	.05	.02	.01
☐	83 Reggie Sanders	.15	.07	.02
☐	84 Kurt Stillwell	.05	.02	.01
☐	85 Sandy Alomar	.10	.05	.01
☐	86 John Habyan	.05	.02	.01
☐	87 Kevin Reimer	.05	.02	.01
☐	88 Mike Stanton	.05	.02	.01
☐	89 Eric Anthony	.05	.02	.01
☐	90 Scott Erickson	.10	.05	.01
☐	91 Craig Colbert	.05	.02	.01
☐	92 Tom Pagnozzi	.05	.02	.01
☐	93 Pedro Astacio	.05	.02	.01
☐	94 Lance Johnson	.05	.02	.01
☐	95 Larry Walker	.25	.11	.03

☐ 96 Russ Swan	.05	.02	.01
☐ 97 Scott Fletcher	.05	.02	.01
☐ 98 Derek Jeter	1.50	.70	.19
☐ 99 Mike Williams	.05	.02	.01
☐ 100 Mark McGwire	.15	.07	.02
☐ 101 Jim Bullinger	.05	.02	.01
☐ 102 Brian Hunter	.05	.02	.01
☐ 103 Jody Reed	.05	.02	.01
☐ 104 Mike Butcher	.05	.02	.01
☐ 105 Gregg Jefferies	.15	.07	.02
☐ 106 Howard Johnson	.05	.02	.01
☐ 107 John Kiely	.05	.02	.01
☐ 108 Jose Lind	.05	.02	.01
☐ 109 Sam Horn	.05	.02	.01
☐ 110 Barry Larkin	.25	.11	.03
☐ 111 Bruce Hurst	.05	.02	.01
☐ 112 Brian Barnes	.05	.02	.01
☐ 113 Thomas Howard	.05	.02	.01
☐ 114 Mel Hall	.05	.02	.01
☐ 115 Robby Thompson	.05	.02	.01
☐ 116 Mark Lemke	.10	.05	.01
☐ 117 Eddie Taubensee	.05	.02	.01
☐ 118 David Hulse	.05	.02	.01
☐ 119 Pedro Munoz	.10	.05	.01
☐ 120 Ramon Martinez	.10	.05	.01
☐ 121 Todd Worrell	.05	.02	.01
☐ 122 Joey Cora	.05	.02	.01
☐ 123 Moises Alou	.15	.07	.02
☐ 124 Franklin Stubbs	.05	.02	.01
☐ 125 Pete O'Brien	.05	.02	.01
☐ 126 Bob Ayrault	.05	.02	.01
☐ 127 Carney Lansford	.05	.02	.01
☐ 128 Kal Daniels	.05	.02	.01
☐ 129 Joe Grahe	.05	.02	.01
☐ 130 Jeff Montgomery	.10	.05	.01
☐ 131 Dave Winfield	.15	.07	.02
☐ 132 Preston Wilson	.30	.14	.04
☐ 133 Steve Wilson	.05	.02	.01
☐ 134 Lee Guetterman	.05	.02	.01
☐ 135 Mickey Tettleton	.10	.05	.01
☐ 136 Jeff King	.05	.02	.01
☐ 137 Alan Mills	.05	.02	.01
☐ 138 Joe Oliver	.05	.02	.01
☐ 139 Gary Gaetti	.10	.05	.01
☐ 140 Gary Sheffield	.15	.07	.02
☐ 141 Dennis Cook	.05	.02	.01
☐ 142 Charlie Hayes	.10	.05	.01
☐ 143 Jeff Huson	.05	.02	.01
☐ 144 Kent Mercker	.05	.02	.01
☐ 145 Eric Young	.10	.05	.01
☐ 146 Scott Leius	.05	.02	.01
☐ 147 Bryan Hickerson	.05	.02	.01
☐ 148 Steve Finley	.10	.05	.01
☐ 149 Rheal Cormier	.05	.02	.01
☐ 150 Frank Thomas UER	2.00	.90	.25
(Categories leading league are italicized but not printed in red)			
☐ 151 Archi Cianfrocco	.05	.02	.01
☐ 152 Rich DeLucia	.05	.02	.01
☐ 153 Greg Vaughn	.05	.02	.01
☐ 154 Wes Chamberlain	.05	.02	.01
☐ 155 Dennis Eckersley	.15	.07	.02
☐ 156 Sammy Sosa	.15	.07	.02
☐ 157 Gary DiSarcina	.05	.02	.01
☐ 158 Kevin Koslofski	.05	.02	.01
☐ 159 Doug Linton	.05	.02	.01
☐ 160 Lou Whitaker	.15	.07	.02
☐ 161 Chad McConnell	.05	.02	.01
☐ 162 Joe Hesketh	.05	.02	.01
☐ 163 Tim Wakefield	.15	.07	.02
☐ 164 Leo Gomez	.05	.02	.01
☐ 165 Jose Rijo	.10	.05	.01
☐ 166 Tim Scott	.05	.02	.01
☐ 167 Steve Olin UER	.05	.02	.01
(Born 10/4/65, should say 10/10/65)			
☐ 168 Kevin Maas	.05	.02	.01
☐ 169 Kenny Rogers	.05	.02	.01
☐ 170 David Justice	.25	.11	.03
☐ 171 Doug Jones	.05	.02	.01
☐ 172 Jeff Reboulet	.05	.02	.01
☐ 173 Andres Galarraga	.15	.07	.02
☐ 174 Randy Velarde	.05	.02	.01
☐ 175 Kirk McCaskill	.05	.02	.01
☐ 176 Darren Lewis	.05	.02	.01
☐ 177 Lenny Harris	.05	.02	.01
☐ 178 Jeff Fassero	.05	.02	.01
☐ 179 Ken Griffey Jr.	2.00	.90	.25
☐ 180 Darren Daulton	.15	.07	.02
☐ 181 John Jaha	.10	.05	.01
☐ 182 Ron Darling	.05	.02	.01
☐ 183 Greg Maddux	2.00	.90	.25
☐ 184 Damion Easley	.10	.05	.01
☐ 185 Jack Morris	.15	.07	.02
☐ 186 Mike Magnante	.05	.02	.01
☐ 187 John Dopson	.05	.02	.01
☐ 188 Sid Fernandez	.05	.02	.01
☐ 189 Tony Phillips	.05	.02	.01
☐ 190 Doug Drabek	.10	.05	.01
☐ 191 Sean Lowe	.05	.02	.01
☐ 192 Bob Milacki	.05	.02	.01
☐ 193 Steve Foster	.05	.02	.01
☐ 194 Jerald Clark	.05	.02	.01
☐ 195 Pete Harnisch	.05	.02	.01
☐ 196 Pat Kelly	.05	.02	.01
☐ 197 Jeff Frye	.05	.02	.01
☐ 198 Alejandro Pena	.05	.02	.01
☐ 199 Junior Ortiz	.05	.02	.01
☐ 200 Kirby Puckett	.60	.25	.07
☐ 201 Jose Uribe	.05	.02	.01
☐ 202 Mike Scioscia	.05	.02	.01
☐ 203 Bernard Gilkey	.10	.05	.01
☐ 204 Dan Pasqua	.05	.02	.01
☐ 205 Gary Carter	.15	.07	.02
☐ 206 Henry Cotto	.05	.02	.01
☐ 207 Paul Molitor	.15	.07	.02
☐ 208 Mike Hartley	.05	.02	.01
☐ 209 Jeff Parrett	.05	.02	.01
☐ 210 Mark Langston	.15	.07	.02
☐ 211 Doug Dascenzo	.05	.02	.01
☐ 212 Rick Reed	.05	.02	.01
☐ 213 Candy Maldonado	.05	.02	.01
☐ 214 Danny Darwin	.05	.02	.01
☐ 215 Pat Howell	.05	.02	.01
☐ 216 Mark Leiter	.05	.02	.01
☐ 217 Kevin Mitchell	.10	.05	.01
☐ 218 Ben McDonald	.05	.02	.01
☐ 219 Bip Roberts	.05	.02	.01
☐ 220 Benny Santiago	.05	.02	.01
☐ 221 Carlos Baerga	.40	.18	.05
☐ 222 Bernie Williams	.10	.05	.01
☐ 223 Roger Pavlik	.05	.02	.01
☐ 224 Sid Bream	.05	.02	.01
☐ 225 Matt Williams	.30	.14	.04
☐ 226 Willie Banks	.05	.02	.01
☐ 227 Jeff Bagwell	.75	.35	.09
☐ 228 Tom Goodwin	.05	.02	.01
☐ 229 Mike Perez	.05	.02	.01
☐ 230 Carlton Fisk	.15	.07	.02
☐ 231 John Wetteland	.10	.05	.01
☐ 232 Tino Martinez	.15	.07	.02

☐ 233	Rick Greene	.05	.02	.01	☐ 303	Brook Jacoby	.05	.02	.01
☐ 234	Tim McIntosh	.05	.02	.01	☐ 304	Melido Perez	.05	.02	.01
☐ 235	Mitch Williams	.10	.05	.01	☐ 305	Rafael Palmeiro	.15	.07	.02
☐ 236	Kevin Campbell	.05	.02	.01	☐ 306	Damon Berryhill	.05	.02	.01
☐ 237	Jose Vizcaino	.05	.02	.01	☐ 307	Dan Serafini	.30	.14	.04
☐ 238	Chris Donnels	.05	.02	.01	☐ 308	Darryl Kile	.05	.02	.01
☐ 239	Mike Boddicker	.05	.02	.01	☐ 309	J.T. Bruett	.05	.02	.01
☐ 240	John Olerud	.10	.05	.01	☐ 310	Dave Righetti	.05	.02	.01
☐ 241	Mike Gardiner	.05	.02	.01	☐ 311	Jay Howell	.05	.02	.01
☐ 242	Charlie O'Brien	.05	.02	.01	☐ 312	Geronimo Pena	.05	.02	.01
☐ 243	Rob Deer	.05	.02	.01	☐ 313	Greg Hibbard	.05	.02	.01
☐ 244	Denny Neagle	.05	.02	.01	☐ 314	Mark Gardner	.05	.02	.01
☐ 245	Chris Sabo	.05	.02	.01	☐ 315	Edgar Martinez	.15	.07	.02
☐ 246	Gregg Olson	.05	.02	.01	☐ 316	Dave Nilsson	.10	.05	.01
☐ 247	Frank Seminara UER	.05	.02	.01	☐ 317	Kyle Abbott	.05	.02	.01
	(Acquired 12/3/98)				☐ 318	Willie Wilson	.05	.02	.01
☐ 248	Scott Scudder	.05	.02	.01	☐ 319	Paul Assenmacher	.05	.02	.01
☐ 249	Tim Burke	.05	.02	.01	☐ 320	Tim Fortugno	.05	.02	.01
☐ 250	Chuck Knoblauch	.15	.07	.02	☐ 321	Rusty Meacham	.05	.02	.01
☐ 251	Mike Bielecki	.05	.02	.01	☐ 322	Pat Borders	.05	.02	.01
☐ 252	Xavier Hernandez	.05	.02	.01	☐ 323	Mike Greenwell	.10	.05	.01
☐ 253	Jose Guzman	.05	.02	.01	☐ 324	Willie Randolph	.10	.05	.01
☐ 254	Cory Snyder	.05	.02	.01	☐ 325	Bill Gullickson	.05	.02	.01
☐ 255	Orel Hershiser	.10	.05	.01	☐ 326	Gary Varsho	.05	.02	.01
☐ 256	Wil Cordero	.10	.05	.01	☐ 327	Tim Hulett	.05	.02	.01
☐ 257	Luis Alicea	.05	.02	.01	☐ 328	Scott Ruskin	.05	.02	.01
☐ 258	Mike Schooler	.05	.02	.01	☐ 329	Mike Maddux	.05	.02	.01
☐ 259	Craig Grebeck	.05	.02	.01	☐ 330	Danny Tartabull	.10	.05	.01
☐ 260	Duane Ward	.05	.02	.01	☐ 331	Kenny Lofton	.60	.25	.07
☐ 261	Bill Wegman	.05	.02	.01	☐ 332	Geno Petralli	.05	.02	.01
☐ 262	Mickey Morandini	.05	.02	.01	☐ 333	Otis Nixon	.05	.02	.01
☐ 263	Vince Horsman	.05	.02	.01	☐ 334	Jason Kendall	.60	.25	.07
☐ 264	Paul Sorrento	.05	.02	.01	☐ 335	Mark Portugal	.05	.02	.01
☐ 265	Andre Dawson	.15	.07	.02	☐ 336	Mike Pagliarulo	.05	.02	.01
☐ 266	Rene Gonzales	.05	.02	.01	☐ 337	Kirt Manwaring	.05	.02	.01
☐ 267	Keith Miller	.05	.02	.01	☐ 338	Bob Ojeda	.05	.02	.01
☐ 268	Derek Bell	.15	.07	.02	☐ 339	Mark Clark	.05	.02	.01
☐ 269	Todd Steverson	.05	.02	.01	☐ 340	John Kruk	.15	.07	.02
☐ 270	Frank Viola	.10	.05	.01	☐ 341	Mel Rojas	.10	.05	.01
☐ 271	Wally Whitehurst	.05	.02	.01	☐ 342	Erik Hanson	.05	.02	.01
☐ 272	Kurt Knudsen	.05	.02	.01	☐ 343	Doug Henry	.05	.02	.01
☐ 273	Dan Walters	.05	.02	.01	☐ 344	Jack McDowell	.15	.07	.02
☐ 274	Rick Sutcliffe	.10	.05	.01	☐ 345	Harold Baines	.10	.05	.01
☐ 275	Andy Van Slyke	.10	.05	.01	☐ 346	Chuck McElroy	.05	.02	.01
☐ 276	Paul O'Neill	.10	.05	.01	☐ 347	Luis Sojo	.05	.02	.01
☐ 277	Mark Whiten	.10	.05	.01	☐ 348	Andy Stankiewicz	.05	.02	.01
☐ 278	Chris Nabholz	.05	.02	.01	☐ 349	Hipolito Pichardo	.05	.02	.01
☐ 279	Todd Burns	.05	.02	.01	☐ 350	Joe Carter	.15	.07	.02
☐ 280	Tom Glavine	.15	.07	.02	☐ 351	Ellis Burks	.10	.05	.01
☐ 281	Butch Henry	.05	.02	.01	☐ 352	Pete Schourek	.15	.07	.02
☐ 282	Shane Mack	.05	.02	.01	☐ 353	Bubby Groom	.05	.02	.01
☐ 283	Mike Jackson	.05	.02	.01	☐ 354	Jay Bell	.10	.05	.01
☐ 284	Henry Rodriguez	.05	.02	.01	☐ 355	Brady Anderson	.10	.05	.01
☐ 285	Bob Tewksbury	.05	.02	.01	☐ 356	Freddie Benavides	.05	.02	.01
☐ 286	Ron Karkovice	.05	.02	.01	☐ 357	Phil Stephenson	.05	.02	.01
☐ 287	Mike Gallego	.05	.02	.01	☐ 358	Kevin Wickander	.05	.02	.01
☐ 288	Dave Cochrane	.05	.02	.01	☐ 359	Mike Stanley	.10	.05	.01
☐ 289	Jesse Orosco	.05	.02	.01	☐ 360	Ivan Rodriguez	.15	.07	.02
☐ 290	Dave Stewart	.10	.05	.01	☐ 361	Scott Bankhead	.05	.02	.01
☐ 291	Tommy Greene	.05	.02	.01	☐ 362	Luis Gonzalez	.10	.05	.01
☐ 292	Rey Sanchez	.05	.02	.01	☐ 363	John Smiley	.05	.02	.01
☐ 293	Rob Ducey	.05	.02	.01	☐ 364	Trevor Wilson	.05	.02	.01
☐ 294	Brent Mayne	.05	.02	.01	☐ 365	Tom Candiotti	.05	.02	.01
☐ 295	Dave Stieb	.05	.02	.01	☐ 366	Craig Wilson	.05	.02	.01
☐ 296	Luis Rivera	.05	.02	.01	☐ 367	Steve Sax	.05	.02	.01
☐ 297	Jeff Innis	.05	.02	.01	☐ 368	Delino DeShields	.10	.05	.01
☐ 298	Scott Livingstone	.05	.02	.01	☐ 369	Jaime Navarro	.05	.02	.01
☐ 299	Bob Patterson	.05	.02	.01	☐ 370	Dave Valle	.05	.02	.01
☐ 300	Cal Ripken	2.00	.90	.25	☐ 371	Mariano Duncan	.05	.02	.01
☐ 301	Cesar Hernandez	.05	.02	.01	☐ 372	Rod Nichols	.05	.02	.01
☐ 302	Randy Myers	.10	.05	.01	☐ 373	Mike Morgan	.05	.02	.01

☐ 374 Julio Valera	.05	.02	.01
☐ 375 Wally Joyner	.10	.05	.01
☐ 376 Tom Henke	.10	.05	.01
☐ 377 Herm Winningham	.05	.02	.01
☐ 378 Orlando Merced	.10	.05	.01
☐ 379 Mike Munoz	.05	.02	.01
☐ 380 Todd Hundley	.10	.05	.01
☐ 381 Mike Flanagan	.05	.02	.01
☐ 382 Tim Belcher	.05	.02	.01
☐ 383 Jerry Browne	.05	.02	.01
☐ 384 Mike Benjamin	.05	.02	.01
☐ 385 Jim Leyritz	.05	.02	.01
☐ 386 Ray Lankford	.15	.07	.02
☐ 387 Devon White	.10	.05	.01
☐ 388 Jeremy Hernandez	.05	.02	.01
☐ 389 Brian Harper	.05	.02	.01
☐ 390 Wade Boggs	.15	.07	.02
☐ 391 Derrick May	.10	.05	.01
☐ 392 Travis Fryman	.15	.07	.02
☐ 393 Ron Gant	.15	.07	.02
☐ 394 Checklist 1-132	.05	.02	.01
☐ 395 Checklist 133-264 UER	.05	.02	.01
(Eckerlsey)			
☐ 396 Checklist 265-396	.05	.02	.01
☐ 397 George Brett	.75	.35	.09
☐ 398 Bobby Witt	.05	.02	.01
☐ 399 Daryl Boston	.05	.02	.01
☐ 400 Bo Jackson	.15	.07	.02
☐ 401 Fred McGriff	.50	.23	.06
Frank Thomas			
☐ 402 Ryne Sandberg	.10	.05	.01
Carlos Baerga			
☐ 403 Gary Sheffield	.10	.05	.01
Edgar Martinez			
☐ 404 Barry Larkin	.10	.05	.01
Travis Fryman			
☐ 405 Andy Van Slyke	.50	.23	.06
Ken Griffey Jr.			
☐ 406 Larry Walker	.15	.07	.02
Kirby Puckett			
☐ 407 Barry Bonds	.10	.05	.01
Joe Carter			
☐ 408 Darren Daulton	.05	.02	.01
Brian Harper			
☐ 409 Greg Maddux	.50	.23	.06
Roger Clemens			
☐ 410 Tom Glavine	.05	.02	.01
Dave Fleming			
☐ 411 Lee Smith	.10	.05	.01
Dennis Eckersley			
☐ 412 Jamie McAndrew	.05	.02	.01
☐ 413 Pete Smith	.05	.02	.01
☐ 414 Juan Guerrero	.05	.02	.01
☐ 415 Todd Frohwirth	.05	.02	.01
☐ 416 Randy Tomlin	.05	.02	.01
☐ 417 B.J. Surhoff	.10	.05	.01
☐ 418 Jim Gott	.05	.02	.01
☐ 419 Mark Thompson	.05	.02	.01
☐ 420 Kevin Tapani	.05	.02	.01
☐ 421 Curt Schilling	.05	.02	.01
☐ 422 J.T. Snow	.60	.25	.07
☐ 423 1993 Prospects	.75	.35	.09
Ryan Klesko			
Ivan Cruz			
Bubba Smith			
Larry Sutton			
☐ 424 John Valentin	.15	.07	.02
☐ 425 Joe Girardi	.05	.02	.01
☐ 426 Nigel Wilson	.10	.05	.01
☐ 427 Bob MacDonald	.05	.02	.01
☐ 428 Todd Zeile	.10	.05	.01
☐ 429 Milt Cuyler	.05	.02	.01
☐ 430 Eddie Murray	.30	.14	.04
☐ 431 Rich Amaral	.05	.02	.01
☐ 432 Pete Young	.05	.02	.01
☐ 433 Roger Bailey and	.15	.07	.02
Tom Schmidt			
☐ 434 Jack Armstrong	.05	.02	.01
☐ 435 Willie McGee	.10	.05	.01
☐ 436 Greg W. Harris	.05	.02	.01
☐ 437 Chris Hammond	.05	.02	.01
☐ 438 Ritchie Moody	.05	.02	.01
☐ 439 Bryan Harvey	.10	.05	.01
☐ 440 Ruben Sierra	.15	.07	.02
☐ 441 Don Lemon and	.10	.05	.01
Todd Pridy			
☐ 442 Kevin McReynolds	.05	.02	.01
☐ 443 Terry Leach	.05	.02	.01
☐ 444 David Nied	.10	.05	.01
☐ 445 Dale Murphy	.15	.07	.02
☐ 446 Luis Mercedes	.05	.02	.01
☐ 447 Keith Shepherd	.05	.02	.01
☐ 448 Ken Caminiti	.10	.05	.01
☐ 449 James Austin	.05	.02	.01
☐ 450 Darryl Strawberry	.10	.05	.01
☐ 451 1993 Prospects	.10	.05	.01
Ramon Caraballo			
Jon Shave			
Brent Gates			
Quinton McCracken			
☐ 452 Bob Wickman	.05	.02	.01
☐ 453 Victor Cole	.05	.02	.01
☐ 454 John Johnstone	.05	.02	.01
☐ 455 Chili Davis	.10	.05	.01
☐ 456 Scott Taylor	.05	.02	.01
☐ 457 Tracy Woodson	.05	.02	.01
☐ 458 David Wells	.05	.02	.01
☐ 459 Derek Wallace	.05	.02	.01
☐ 460 Randy Johnson	.40	.18	.05
☐ 461 Steve Reed	.05	.02	.01
☐ 462 Felix Fermin	.05	.02	.01
☐ 463 Scott Aldred	.05	.02	.01
☐ 464 Greg Colbrunn	.15	.07	.02
☐ 465 Tony Fernandez	.05	.02	.01
☐ 466 Mike Felder	.05	.02	.01
☐ 467 Lee Stevens	.05	.02	.01
☐ 468 Matt Whiteside	.05	.02	.01
☐ 469 Dave Hansen	.05	.02	.01
☐ 470 Rob Dibble	.05	.02	.01
☐ 471 Dave Gallagher	.05	.02	.01
☐ 472 Chris Gwynn	.05	.02	.01
☐ 473 Dave Henderson	.05	.02	.01
☐ 474 Ozzie Guillen	.05	.02	.01
☐ 475 Jeff Reardon	.10	.05	.01
☐ 476 Mark Voisard and	.10	.05	.01
Will Scalzitti			
☐ 477 Jimmy Jones	.05	.02	.01
☐ 478 Greg Cadaret	.05	.02	.01
☐ 479 Todd Pratt	.05	.02	.01
☐ 480 Pat Listach	.05	.02	.01
☐ 481 Ryan Luzinski	.15	.07	.02
☐ 482 Darren Reed	.05	.02	.01
☐ 483 Brian Griffiths	.05	.02	.01
☐ 484 John Wehner	.05	.02	.01
☐ 485 Glenn Davis	.05	.02	.01
☐ 486 Eric Wedge	.05	.02	.01
☐ 487 Jesse Hollins	.05	.02	.01
☐ 488 Manuel Lee	.05	.02	.01
☐ 489 Scott Fredrickson	.05	.02	.01
☐ 490 Omar Olivares	.05	.02	.01
☐ 491 Shawn Hare	.05	.02	.01
☐ 492 Tom Lampkin	.05	.02	.01

☐ 493	Jeff Nelson	.05	.02	.01
☐ 494	1993 Prospects	.10	.05	.01
	Kevin Young			
	Adell Davenport			
	Eduardo Perez			
	Lou Lucca			
☐ 495	Ken Hill	.10	.05	.01
☐ 496	Reggie Jefferson	.05	.02	.01
☐ 497	Matt Petersen and	.10	.05	.01
	Willie Brown			
☐ 498	Bud Black	.05	.02	.01
☐ 499	Chuck Crim	.05	.02	.01
☐ 500	Jose Canseco	.30	.14	.04
☐ 501	Johnny Oates MG	.05	.02	.01
	Bobby Cox MG			
☐ 502	Butch Hobson MG	.05	.02	.01
	Jim Lefebvre MG			
☐ 503	Buck Rodgers MG	.10	.05	.01
	Tony Perez MG			
☐ 504	Gene Lamont MG	.10	.05	.01
	Don Baylor MG			
☐ 505	Mike Hargrove MG	.10	.05	.01
	Rene Lachemann MG			
☐ 506	Sparky Anderson MG	.10	.05	.01
	Art Howe MG			
☐ 507	Hal McRae MG	.10	.05	.01
	Tom Lasorda MG			
☐ 508	Phil Garner MG	.05	.02	.01
	Felipe Alou MG			
☐ 509	Tom Kelly MG	.05	.02	.01
	Jeff Torborg MG			
☐ 510	Buck Showalter MG	.05	.02	.01
	Jim Fregosi MG			
☐ 511	Tony LaRussa MG	.10	.05	.01
	Jim Leyland MG			
☐ 512	Lou Piniella MG	.10	.05	.01
	Joe Torre MG			
☐ 513	Kevin Kennedy MG	.05	.02	.01
	Jim Riggleman MG			
☐ 514	Cito Gaston MG	.10	.05	.01
	Dusty Baker MG			
☐ 515	Greg Swindell	.05	.02	.01
☐ 516	Alex Arias	.05	.02	.01
☐ 517	Bill Pecota	.05	.02	.01
☐ 518	Benji Grigsby UER	.05	.02	.01
	(Misspelled Bengi on card front)			
☐ 519	David Howard	.05	.02	.01
☐ 520	Charlie Hough	.10	.05	.01
☐ 521	Kevin Flora	.05	.02	.01
☐ 522	Shane Reynolds	.10	.05	.01
☐ 523	Doug Bochtler	.05	.02	.01
☐ 524	Chris Hoiles	.10	.05	.01
☐ 525	Scott Sanderson	.05	.02	.01
☐ 526	Mike Sharperson	.05	.02	.01
☐ 527	Mike Fetters	.05	.02	.01
☐ 528	Paul Quantrill	.05	.02	.01
☐ 529	1993 Prospects	2.00	.90	.25
	Dave Silvestri			
	Chipper Jones			
	Benji Gil			
	Jeff Patzke			
☐ 530	Sterling Hitchcock	.20	.09	.03
☐ 531	Joe Millette	.05	.02	.01
☐ 532	Tom Brunansky	.05	.02	.01
☐ 533	Frank Castillo	.05	.02	.01
☐ 534	Randy Knorr	.05	.02	.01
☐ 535	Jose Oquendo	.05	.02	.01
☐ 536	Dave Haas	.05	.02	.01
☐ 537	Jason Hutchins and	.10	.05	.01
	Ryan Turner			
☐ 538	Jimmy Baron	.05	.02	.01
☐ 539	Kerry Woodson	.05	.02	.01
☐ 540	Ivan Calderon	.05	.02	.01
☐ 541	Denis Boucher	.05	.02	.01
☐ 542	Royce Clayton	.10	.05	.01
☐ 543	Reggie Williams	.05	.02	.01
☐ 544	Steve Decker	.05	.02	.01
☐ 545	Dean Palmer	.10	.05	.01
☐ 546	Hal Morris	.10	.05	.01
☐ 547	Ryan Thompson	.10	.05	.01
☐ 548	Lance Blankenship	.05	.02	.01
☐ 549	Hensley Meulens	.05	.02	.01
☐ 550	Scott Radinsky	.05	.02	.01
☐ 551	Eric Young	.10	.05	.01
☐ 552	Jeff Blauser	.10	.05	.01
☐ 553	Andujar Cedeno	.05	.02	.01
☐ 554	Arthur Rhodes	.10	.05	.01
☐ 555	Terry Mulholland	.05	.02	.01
☐ 556	Darryl Hamilton	.05	.02	.01
☐ 557	Pedro Martinez	.15	.07	.02
☐ 558	Ryan Whitman and	.10	.05	.01
	Mark Skeels			
☐ 559	Jamie Arnold	.05	.02	.01
☐ 560	Zane Smith	.05	.02	.01
☐ 561	Matt Nokes	.05	.02	.01
☐ 562	Bob Zupcic	.05	.02	.01
☐ 563	Shawn Boskie	.05	.02	.01
☐ 564	Mike Timlin	.05	.02	.01
☐ 565	Jerald Clark	.05	.02	.01
☐ 566	Rod Brewer	.05	.02	.01
☐ 567	Mark Carreon	.05	.02	.01
☐ 568	Andy Benes	.10	.05	.01
☐ 569	Shawn Barton	.05	.02	.01
☐ 570	Tim Wallach	.05	.02	.01
☐ 571	Dave Mlicki	.05	.02	.01
☐ 572	Trevor Hoffman	.10	.05	.01
☐ 573	John Patterson	.05	.02	.01
☐ 574	De Shawn Warren	.20	.09	.03
☐ 575	Monty Fariss	.05	.02	.01
☐ 576	1993 Prospects	.10	.05	.01
	Darrell Sherman			
	Damon Buford			
	Cliff Floyd			
	Michael Moore			
☐ 577	Tim Costo	.05	.02	.01
☐ 578	Dave Magadan	.05	.02	.01
☐ 579	Neil Garret and	.25	.11	.03
	Jason Bates			
☐ 580	Walt Weiss	.05	.02	.01
☐ 581	Chris Haney	.05	.02	.01
☐ 582	Shawn Abner	.05	.02	.01
☐ 583	Marvin Freeman	.05	.02	.01
☐ 584	Casey Candaele	.05	.02	.01
☐ 585	Ricky Jordan	.05	.02	.01
☐ 586	Jeff Tabaka	.05	.02	.01
☐ 587	Manny Alexander	.05	.02	.01
☐ 588	Mike Trombley	.05	.02	.01
☐ 589	Carlos Hernandez	.05	.02	.01
☐ 590	Cal Eldred	.05	.02	.01
☐ 591	Alex Cole	.05	.02	.01
☐ 592	Phil Plantier	.05	.02	.01
☐ 593	Brett Merriman	.05	.02	.01
☐ 594	Jerry Nielsen	.05	.02	.01
☐ 595	Shawon Dunston	.05	.02	.01
☐ 596	Jimmy Key	.10	.05	.01
☐ 597	Gerald Perry	.05	.02	.01
☐ 598	Rico Brogna	.15	.07	.02
☐ 599	Clemente Nunez and	.10	.05	.01
	Daniel Robinson			
☐ 600	Bret Saberhagen	.10	.05	.01
☐ 601	Craig Shipley	.05	.02	.01

602	Henry Mercedes	.05	.02	.01
603	Jim Thome	.75	.35	.09
604	Rod Beck	.15	.07	.02
605	Chuck Finley	.05	.02	.01
606	J. Owens	.05	.02	.01
607	Dan Smith	.05	.02	.01
608	Bill Doran	.05	.02	.01
609	Lance Parrish	.10	.05	.01
610	Denny Martinez	.10	.05	.01
611	Tom Gordon	.05	.02	.01
612	Byron Mathews	.05	.02	.01
613	Joel Adamson	.05	.02	.01
614	Brian Williams	.05	.02	.01
615	Steve Avery	.15	.07	.02
616	1993 Prospects	.30	.14	.04

Matt Mieske
Tracy Sanders
Midre Cummings
Ryan Freeburg

617	Craig Lefferts	.05	.02	.01
618	Tony Pena	.05	.02	.01
619	Billy Spiers	.05	.02	.01
620	Todd Benzinger	.05	.02	.01
621	Mike Kotarski and	.10	.05	.01

Greg Boyd

622	Ben Rivera	.05	.02	.01
623	Al Martin	.10	.05	.01
624	Sam Militello UER	.05	.02	.01

(Profile says drafted
in 1988, bio says
drafted in 1990)

625	Rick Aguilera	.10	.05	.01
626	Dan Gladden	.05	.02	.01
627	Andres Berumen	.05	.02	.01
628	Kelly Gruber	.05	.02	.01
629	Cris Carpenter	.05	.02	.01
630	Mark Grace	.15	.07	.02
631	Jeff Brantley	.05	.02	.01
632	Chris Widger	.05	.02	.01
633	Three Russians UER	.05	.02	.01

(Ilya Bogatyrev is
shortstop, but he has
pitching stats header)

634	Mo Sanford	.05	.02	.01
635	Albert Belle	.75	.35	.09
636	Tim Teufel	.05	.02	.01
637	Greg Myers	.05	.02	.01
638	Brian Bohanon	.05	.02	.01
639	Mike Bordick	.05	.02	.01
640	Dwight Gooden	.10	.05	.01
641	Pat Leahy and	.20	.09	.03

Gavin Baugh

642	Milt Hill	.05	.02	.01
643	Luis Aquino	.05	.02	.01
644	Dante Bichette	.25	.11	.03
645	Bobby Thigpen	.05	.02	.01
646	Rich Scheid	.05	.02	.01
647	Brian Sackinsky	.05	.02	.01
648	Ryan Hawblitzel	.05	.02	.01
649	Tom Marsh	.05	.02	.01
650	Terry Pendleton	.10	.05	.01
651	Rafael Bournigal	.05	.02	.01
652	Dave West	.05	.02	.01
653	Steve Hosey	.05	.02	.01
654	Gerald Williams	.05	.02	.01
655	Scott Cooper	.05	.02	.01
656	Gary Scott	.05	.02	.01
657	Mike Harkey	.05	.02	.01
658	1993 Prospects	.20	.09	.03

Jeromy Burnitz
Melvin Nieves
Rich Becker
Shon Walker

659	Ed Sprague	.05	.02	.01
660	Alan Trammell	.15	.07	.02
661	Garvin Alston and	.10	.05	.01

Michael Case

662	Donovan Osborne	.05	.02	.01
663	Jeff Gardner	.05	.02	.01
664	Calvin Jones	.05	.02	.01
665	Darrin Fletcher	.05	.02	.01
666	Glenallen Hill	.05	.02	.01
667	Jim Rosenbohm	.15	.07	.02
668	Scott Lewis	.05	.02	.01
669	Kip Yaughn	.05	.02	.01
670	Julio Franco	.10	.05	.01
671	Dave Martinez	.05	.02	.01
672	Kevin Bass	.05	.02	.01
673	Todd Van Poppel	.10	.05	.01
674	Mark Gubicza	.05	.02	.01
675	Tim Raines	.15	.07	.02
676	Rudy Seanez	.05	.02	.01
677	Charlie Leibrandt	.05	.02	.01
678	Randy Milligan	.05	.02	.01
679	Kim Batiste	.05	.02	.01
680	Craig Biggio	.15	.07	.02
681	Darren Holmes	.10	.05	.01
682	John Candelaria	.05	.02	.01
683	Jerry Stafford and	.10	.05	.01

Eddie Christian

684	Pat Mahomes	.05	.02	.01
685	Bob Walk	.05	.02	.01
686	Russ Springer	.05	.02	.01
687	Tony Sheffield	.05	.02	.01
688	Dwight Smith	.05	.02	.01
689	Eddie Zosky	.05	.02	.01
690	Bien Figueroa	.05	.02	.01
691	Jim Tatum	.05	.02	.01
692	Chad Kreuter	.05	.02	.01
693	Rich Rodriguez	.05	.02	.01
694	Shane Turner	.05	.02	.01
695	Kent Bottenfield	.05	.02	.01
696	Jose Mesa	.10	.05	.01
697	Darrell Whitmore	.05	.02	.01
698	Ted Wood	.05	.02	.01
699	Chad Curtis	.10	.05	.01
700	Nolan Ryan	2.00	.90	.25
701	1993 Prospects	1.50	.70	.19

Mike Piazza
Brook Fordyce
Carlos Delgado
Donnie Leshnock

702	Tim Pugh	.05	.02	.01
703	Jeff Kent	.15	.07	.02
704	Jon Goodrich and	.15	.07	.02

Danny Figueroa

705	Bob Welch	.05	.02	.01
706	Sherard Clinkscales	.05	.02	.01
707	Donn Pall	.05	.02	.01
708	Greg Olson	.05	.02	.01
709	Jeff Juden	.05	.02	.01
710	Mike Mussina	.30	.14	.04
711	Scott Chiamparino	.05	.02	.01
712	Stan Javier	.05	.02	.01
713	John Doherty	.05	.02	.01
714	Kevin Gross	.05	.02	.01
715	Greg Gagne	.05	.02	.01
716	Steve Cooke	.05	.02	.01
717	Steve Farr	.05	.02	.01
718	Jay Buhner	.15	.07	.02
719	Butch Henry	.05	.02	.01
720	David Cone	.15	.07	.02

☐ 721	Rick Wilkins	.05	.02	.01
☐ 722	Chuck Carr	.05	.02	.01
☐ 723	Kenny Felder	.05	.02	.01
☐ 724	Guillermo Velasquez	.05	.02	.01
☐ 725	Billy Hatcher	.05	.02	.01
☐ 726	Mike Veneziale and	.10	.05	.01
	Ken Kendrena			
☐ 727	Jonathan Hurst	.05	.02	.01
☐ 728	Steve Frey	.05	.02	.01
☐ 729	Mark Leonard	.05	.02	.01
☐ 730	Charles Nagy	.10	.05	.01
☐ 731	Donald Harris	.05	.02	.01
☐ 732	Travis Buckley	.05	.02	.01
☐ 733	Tom Browning	.05	.02	.01
☐ 734	Anthony Young	.05	.02	.01
☐ 735	Steve Shifflett	.05	.02	.01
☐ 736	Jeff Russell	.05	.02	.01
☐ 737	Wilson Alvarez	.15	.07	.02
☐ 738	Lance Painter	.05	.02	.01
☐ 739	Dave Weathers	.05	.02	.01
☐ 740	Len Dykstra	.15	.07	.02
☐ 741	Mike Devereaux	.10	.05	.01
☐ 742	1993 Prospects	.10	.05	.01
	Rene Arocha			
	Alan Embree			
	Brien Taylor			
	Tim Crabtree			
☐ 743	Dave Landaker	.05	.02	.01
☐ 744	Chris George	.05	.02	.01
☐ 745	Eric Davis	.05	.02	.01
☐ 746	Mark Strittmatter and	.10	.05	.01
	Lamarr Rogers			
☐ 747	Carl Willis	.05	.02	.01
☐ 748	Stan Belinda	.05	.02	.01
☐ 749	Scott Kamieniecki	.05	.02	.01
☐ 750	Rickey Henderson	.15	.07	.02
☐ 751	Eric Hillman	.05	.02	.01
☐ 752	Pat Hentgen	.10	.05	.01
☐ 753	Jim Corsi	.05	.02	.01
☐ 754	Brian Jordan	.15	.07	.02
☐ 755	Bill Swift	.05	.02	.01
☐ 756	Mike Henneman	.05	.02	.01
☐ 757	Harold Reynolds	.05	.02	.01
☐ 758	Sean Berry	.05	.02	.01
☐ 759	Charlie Hayes	.10	.05	.01
☐ 760	Luis Polonia	.05	.02	.01
☐ 761	Darrin Jackson	.05	.02	.01
☐ 762	Mark Lewis	.05	.02	.01
☐ 763	Rob Maurer	.05	.02	.01
☐ 764	Willie Greene	.10	.05	.01
☐ 765	Vince Coleman	.05	.02	.01
☐ 766	Todd Revenig	.05	.02	.01
☐ 767	Rich Ireland	.05	.02	.01
☐ 768	Mike Macfarlane	.05	.02	.01
☐ 769	Francisco Cabrera	.05	.02	.01
☐ 770	Robin Ventura	.15	.07	.02
☐ 771	Kevin Ritz	.05	.02	.01
☐ 772	Chito Martinez	.05	.02	.01
☐ 773	Cliff Brantley	.05	.02	.01
☐ 774	Curtis Leskanic	.10	.05	.01
☐ 775	Chris Bosio	.05	.02	.01
☐ 776	Jose Offerman	.05	.02	.01
☐ 777	Mark Guthrie	.05	.02	.01
☐ 778	Don Slaught	.05	.02	.01
☐ 779	Rich Monteleone	.05	.02	.01
☐ 780	Jim Abbott	.15	.07	.02
☐ 781	Jack Clark	.05	.02	.01
☐ 782	Reynol Mendoza and	.10	.05	.01
	Dan Roman			
☐ 783	Heathcliff Slocumb	.05	.02	.01
☐ 784	Jeff Branson	.05	.02	.01

☐ 785	Kevin Brown	.05	.02	.01
☐ 786	1993 Prospects	.10	.05	.01
	Mike Christopher			
	Ken Ryan			
	Aaron Taylor			
	Gus Gandarillas			
☐ 787	Mike Matthews	.15	.07	.02
☐ 788	Mackey Sasser	.05	.02	.01
☐ 789	Jeff Conine UER	.15	.07	.02
	(No inclusion of 1990			
	stats in career total)			
☐ 790	George Bell	.10	.05	.01
☐ 791	Pat Rapp	.10	.05	.01
☐ 792	Joe Boever	.05	.02	.01
☐ 793	Jim Poole	.05	.02	.01
☐ 794	Andy Ashby	.05	.02	.01
☐ 795	Deion Sanders	.40	.18	.05
☐ 796	Scott Brosius	.05	.02	.01
☐ 797	Brad Pennington	.05	.02	.01
☐ 798	Greg Briley	.05	.02	.01
☐ 799	Jim Edmonds	1.25	.55	.16
☐ 800	Shawn Jeter	.05	.02	.01
☐ 801	Jesse Levis	.05	.02	.01
☐ 802	Phil Clark UER	.05	.02	.01
	(Word "a" is missing in			
	sentence beginning			
	with "In 1992 ...")			
☐ 803	Ed Pierce	.05	.02	.01
☐ 804	Jose Valentin	.25	.11	.03
☐ 805	Terry Jorgensen	.05	.02	.01
☐ 806	Mark Hutton	.05	.02	.01
☐ 807	Troy Neel	.05	.02	.01
☐ 808	Bret Boone	.15	.07	.02
☐ 809	Cris Colon	.05	.02	.01
☐ 810	Domingo Martinez	.05	.02	.01
☐ 811	Javier Lopez	.60	.25	.07
☐ 812	Matt Walbeck	.05	.02	.01
☐ 813	Dan Wilson	.10	.05	.01
☐ 814	Scooter Tucker	.05	.02	.01
☐ 815	Billy Ashley	.10	.05	.01
☐ 816	Tim Laker	.05	.02	.01
☐ 817	Bobby Jones	.10	.05	.01
☐ 818	Brad Brink	.05	.02	.01
☐ 819	William Pennyfeather	.05	.02	.01
☐ 820	Stan Royer	.05	.02	.01
☐ 821	Doug Brocail	.05	.02	.01
☐ 822	Kevin Rogers	.05	.02	.01
☐ 823	Checklist 397-540	.05	.02	.01
☐ 824	Checklist 541-691	.05	.02	.01
☐ 825	Checklist 692-825	.05	.02	.01

1993 Topps Traded

This 132-card set focuses on promising rookies, new managers, free agents, and players who changed teams. The set also includes 22 members of Team USA. The standard-size cards carry the same design on the front as the regular 1993 Topps issue. The backs are also the same design and carry a head shot, biography, stats, and career highlights. The cards are numbered on the back. Rookie Cards in this set include Todd Helton, Dante Powell, Todd Walker and Paul Wilson.

	MINT	NRMT	EXC
COMPLETE FACT.SET (132) ..	13.00	5.75	1.60
COMMON CARD (1T-132T)	.05	.02	.01

		MINT	NRMT	EXC
☐ 1T	Barry Bonds	.50	.23	.06
☐ 2T	Rich Renteria	.05	.02	.01
☐ 3T	Aaron Sele	.10	.05	.01
☐ 4T	Carlton Loewer USA	.40	.18	.05
☐ 5T	Erik Pappas	.05	.02	.01
☐ 6T	Greg McMichael	.15	.07	.02
☐ 7T	Freddie Benavides	.05	.02	.01
☐ 8T	Kirk Gibson	.10	.05	.01
☐ 9T	Tony Fernandez	.05	.02	.01
☐ 10T	Jay Gainer	.05	.02	.01
☐ 11T	Orestes Destrade	.05	.02	.01
☐ 12T	A.J. Hinch USA	.50	.23	.06
☐ 13T	Bobby Munoz	.05	.02	.01
☐ 14T	Tom Henke	.10	.05	.01
☐ 15T	Rob Butler	.10	.05	.01
☐ 16T	Gary Wayne	.05	.02	.01
☐ 17T	David McCarty	.05	.02	.01
☐ 18T	Walt Weiss	.10	.05	.01
☐ 19T	Todd Helton USA	3.00	1.35	.35
☐ 20T	Mark Whiten	.10	.05	.01
☐ 21T	Ricky Gutierrez	.05	.02	.01
☐ 22T	Dustin Hermanson USA	.50	.23	.06
☐ 23T	Sherman Obando	.10	.05	.01
☐ 24T	Mike Piazza	1.50	.70	.19
☐ 25T	Jeff Russell	.05	.02	.01
☐ 26T	Jason Bere	.10	.05	.01
☐ 27T	Jack Voigt	.05	.02	.01
☐ 28T	Chris Bosio	.05	.02	.01
☐ 29T	Phil Hiatt	.05	.02	.01
☐ 30T	Matt Beaumont USA	.75	.35	.09
☐ 31T	Andres Galarraga	.15	.07	.02
☐ 32T	Greg Swindell	.05	.02	.01
☐ 33T	Vinny Castilla	.15	.07	.02
☐ 34T	Pat Clougherty USA	.05	.02	.01
☐ 35T	Greg Briley	.05	.02	.01
☐ 36T	Dallas Green MG	.05	.02	.01
	Davey Johnson MG			
☐ 37T	Tyler Green	.05	.02	.01
☐ 38T	Craig Paquette	.05	.02	.01
☐ 39T	Danny Sheaffer	.05	.02	.01
☐ 40T	Jim Converse	.10	.05	.01
☐ 41T	Terry Harvey USA	.05	.02	.01
☐ 42T	Phil Plantier	.05	.02	.01
☐ 43T	Doug Saunders	.05	.02	.01
☐ 44T	Benny Santiago	.05	.02	.01
☐ 45T	Dante Powell USA	1.00	.45	.12
☐ 46T	Jeff Parrett	.05	.02	.01
☐ 47T	Wade Boggs	.15	.07	.02
☐ 48T	Paul Molitor	.15	.07	.02
☐ 49T	Turk Wendell	.10	.05	.01
☐ 50T	David Wells	.05	.02	.01
☐ 51T	Gary Sheffield	.15	.07	.02
☐ 52T	Kevin Young	.05	.02	.01
☐ 53T	Nelson Liriano	.05	.02	.01
☐ 54T	Greg Maddux	2.00	.90	.25
☐ 55T	Derek Bell	.15	.07	.02
☐ 56T	Matt Turner	.05	.02	.01
☐ 57T	Charlie Nelson USA	.05	.02	.01
☐ 58T	Mike Hampton	.05	.02	.01
☐ 59T	Troy O'Leary	.40	.18	.05
☐ 60T	Benji Gil	.10	.05	.01
☐ 61T	Mitch Lyden	.05	.02	.01
☐ 62T	J.T. Snow	.30	.14	.04
☐ 63T	Damon Buford	.05	.02	.01
☐ 64T	Gene Harris	.05	.02	.01
☐ 65T	Randy Myers	.10	.05	.01
☐ 66T	Felix Jose	.05	.02	.01
☐ 67T	Todd Dunn USA	.10	.05	.01
☐ 68T	Jimmy Key	.10	.05	.01
☐ 69T	Pedro Castellano	.05	.02	.01
☐ 70T	Mark Merila USA	.10	.05	.01
☐ 71T	Rich Rodriguez	.05	.02	.01
☐ 72T	Matt Mieske	.10	.05	.01
☐ 73T	Pete Incaviglia	.05	.02	.01
☐ 74T	Carl Everett	.10	.05	.01
☐ 75T	Jim Abbott	.15	.07	.02
☐ 76T	Luis Aquino	.05	.02	.01
☐ 77T	Rene Arocha	.10	.05	.01
☐ 78T	Jon Shave	.05	.02	.01
☐ 79T	Todd Walker USA	2.00	.90	.25
☐ 80T	Jack Armstrong	.05	.02	.01
☐ 81T	Jeff Richardson	.05	.02	.01
☐ 82T	Blas Minor	.05	.02	.01
☐ 83T	Dave Winfield	.15	.07	.02
☐ 84T	Paul O'Neill	.10	.05	.01
☐ 85T	Steve Reich USA	.05	.02	.01
☐ 86T	Chris Hammond	.05	.02	.01
☐ 87T	Hilly Hathaway	.05	.02	.01
☐ 88T	Fred McGriff	.25	.11	.03
☐ 89T	Dave Telgheder	.05	.02	.01
☐ 90T	Richie Lewis	.05	.02	.01
☐ 91T	Brent Gates	.10	.05	.01
☐ 92T	Andre Dawson	.15	.07	.02
☐ 93T	Andy Barkett USA	.10	.05	.01
☐ 94T	Doug Drabek	.15	.07	.02
☐ 95T	Joe Klink	.05	.02	.01
☐ 96T	Willie Blair	.05	.02	.01
☐ 97T	Danny Graves USA	.20	.09	.03
☐ 98T	Pat Meares	.10	.05	.01
☐ 99T	Mike Lansing	.15	.07	.02
☐ 100T	Marcos Armas	.05	.02	.01
☐ 101T	Darren Grass USA	.05	.02	.01
☐ 102T	Chris Jones	.05	.02	.01
☐ 103T	Ken Ryan	.05	.02	.01
☐ 104T	Ellis Burks	.10	.05	.01
☐ 105T	Roberto Kelly	.10	.05	.01
☐ 106T	Dave Magadan	.05	.02	.01
☐ 107T	Paul Wilson USA	1.50	.70	.19
☐ 108T	Rob Natal	.05	.02	.01
☐ 109T	Paul Wagner	.05	.02	.01
☐ 110T	Jeromy Burnitz	.05	.02	.01
☐ 111T	Monty Fariss	.05	.02	.01
☐ 112T	Kevin Mitchell	.10	.05	.01
☐ 113T	Scott Pose	.05	.02	.01
☐ 114T	Dave Stewart	.10	.05	.01
☐ 115T	Russ Johnson USA	.40	.18	.05
☐ 116T	Armando Reynoso	.05	.02	.01
☐ 117T	Geronimo Berroa	.05	.02	.01
☐ 118T	Woody Williams	.05	.02	.01
☐ 119T	Tim Bogar	.05	.02	.01
☐ 120T	Bob Scafa USA	.05	.02	.01
☐ 121T	Henry Cotto	.05	.02	.01
☐ 122T	Gregg Jefferies	.15	.07	.02

☐ 123T Norm Charlton	.05	.02	.01
☐ 124T Bret Wagner USA	.40	.18	.05
☐ 125T David Cone	.15	.07	.02
☐ 126T Daryl Boston	.05	.02	.01
☐ 127T Tim Wallach	.05	.02	.01
☐ 128T Mike Martin USA	.10	.05	.01
☐ 129T John Cummings	.10	.05	.01
☐ 130T Ryan Bowen	.05	.02	.01
☐ 131T John Powell USA	.25	.11	.03
☐ 132T Checklist 1-132	.05	.02	.01

1994 Topps

*These 792 standard-size cards were issued
in two series of 396. Two types of factory
sets were also issued. One features the
792 basic cards, ten Topps Gold, three
Black Gold and three Finest Pre-Production
cards for a total of 808. The other factory
set (Bakers Dozen) includes the 792 basic
cards, ten Topps Gold, three Black Gold,
ten 1995 Topps Pre-Production cards and a
sample pack of three special Topps cards
for a total of 818. In each case, one of the
Pre-Production cards is a Spectralite version of one of the nine players included
among the sample. The sample pack consists of three different Topps brand cards
(Bowman, Finest, Stadium Club) of the
same player. Including those featured in the
special packs are Mo Vaughn, Larry
Walker, Cliff Floyd, Rafael Palmeiro, David
Justice and Ken Griffey Jr. The standard
cards feature glossy color player photos
with white borders on the fronts. The player's name is in white cursive lettering at the
bottom left, with the team name and player's position printed on a team color-coded
bar. There is an inner multicolored border
along the left side that extends obliquely
across the bottom. The horizontal backs
carry an action shot of the player with biography, statistics and highlights. Subsets
include Draft Picks (201-210/739-762), All-
Stars (384-394) and Stat Twins (601-609).
Rookie Cards include Alan Benes, Brooks
Kieschnick, Kirk Presley and Pat Watkins.*

	MINT	NRMT	EXC
COMPLETE SET (792)	30.00	13.50	3.70
COMPLETE FACT.SET (808)	50.00	22.00	6.25
COMP.BAKERS DOZEN (818)	50.00	22.00	6.25

COMPLETE SERIES 1 (396)	15.00	6.75	1.85
COMPLETE SERIES 2 (396)	15.00	6.75	1.85
COMMON CARD (1-396)	.05	.02	.01
COMMON CARD (397-792)	.05	.02	.01
COMPLETE GOLD SET (792)	80.00	36.00	10.00
GOLD COMMON CARDS (1-792)	.10	.05	.01
GOLD SEMISTARS	.25	.11	.03
*GOLD VETERAN STARS: 2X TO4X BASIC CARDS			
*GOLD YOUNG STARS: 1.5X TO 3X BASIC CARDS			
*GOLD RC'S: 1.25X TO 2.5X BASIC CARDS			

☐ 1 Mike Piazza	.75	.35	.09
☐ 2 Bernie Williams	.10	.05	.01
☐ 3 Kevin Rogers	.05	.02	.01
☐ 4 Paul Carey	.05	.02	.01
☐ 5 Ozzie Guillen	.05	.02	.01
☐ 6 Derrick May	.10	.05	.01
☐ 7 Jose Mesa	.05	.02	.01
☐ 8 Todd Hundley	.10	.05	.01
☐ 9 Chris Haney	.05	.02	.01
☐ 10 John Olerud	.15	.07	.02
☐ 11 Andujar Cedeno	.05	.02	.01
☐ 12 John Smiley	.05	.02	.01
☐ 13 Phil Plantier	.10	.05	.01
☐ 14 Willie Banks	.05	.02	.01
☐ 15 Jay Bell	.10	.05	.01
☐ 16 Doug Henry	.05	.02	.01
☐ 17 Lance Blankenship	.05	.02	.01
☐ 18 Greg W. Harris	.05	.02	.01
☐ 19 Scott Livingstone	.05	.02	.01
☐ 20 Bryan Harvey	.05	.02	.01
☐ 21 Wil Cordero	.15	.07	.02
☐ 22 Roger Pavlik	.05	.02	.01
☐ 23 Mark Lemke	.05	.02	.01
☐ 24 Jeff Nelson	.05	.02	.01
☐ 25 Todd Zeile	.10	.05	.01
☐ 26 Billy Hatcher	.05	.02	.01
☐ 27 Joe Magrane	.05	.02	.01
☐ 28 Tony Longmire	.05	.02	.01
☐ 29 Omar Daal	.05	.02	.01
☐ 30 Kirt Manwaring	.05	.02	.01
☐ 31 Melido Perez	.05	.02	.01
☐ 32 Tim Hulett	.05	.02	.01
☐ 33 Jeff Schwartz	.05	.02	.01
☐ 34 Nolan Ryan	2.00	.90	.25
☐ 35 Jose Guzman	.05	.02	.01
☐ 36 Felix Fermin	.05	.02	.01
☐ 37 Jeff Innis	.05	.02	.01
☐ 38 Brett Mayne	.05	.02	.01
☐ 39 Huck Flener	.05	.02	.01
☐ 40 Jeff Bagwell	.60	.25	.07
☐ 41 Kevin Wickander	.05	.02	.01
☐ 42 Ricky Gutierrez	.05	.02	.01
☐ 43 Pat Mahomes	.05	.02	.01
☐ 44 Jeff King	.05	.02	.01
☐ 45 Cal Eldred	.10	.05	.01
☐ 46 Craig Paquette	.05	.02	.01
☐ 47 Richie Lewis	.05	.02	.01
☐ 48 Tony Phillips	.05	.02	.01
☐ 49 Armando Reynoso	.05	.02	.01
☐ 50 Moises Alou	.15	.07	.02
☐ 51 Manuel Lee	.05	.02	.01
☐ 52 Otis Nixon	.05	.02	.01
☐ 53 Billy Ashley	.15	.07	.02
☐ 54 Mark Whiten	.10	.05	.01
☐ 55 Jeff Russell	.05	.02	.01
☐ 56 Chad Curtis	.10	.05	.01
☐ 57 Kevin Stocker	.10	.05	.01
☐ 58 Mike Jackson	.05	.02	.01
☐ 59 Matt Nokes	.05	.02	.01
☐ 60 Chris Bosio	.05	.02	.01

☐ 61	Damon Buford	.05	.02	.01
☐ 62	Tim Belcher	.05	.02	.01
☐ 63	Glenallen Hill	.05	.02	.01
☐ 64	Bill Wertz	.05	.02	.01
☐ 65	Eddie Murray	.25	.11	.03
☐ 66	Tom Gordon	.05	.02	.01
☐ 67	Alex Gonzalez	.15	.07	.02
☐ 68	Eddie Taubensee	.05	.02	.01
☐ 69	Jacob Brumfield	.05	.02	.01
☐ 70	Andy Benes	.10	.05	.01
☐ 71	Rich Becker	.10	.05	.01
☐ 72	Steve Cooke	.05	.02	.01
☐ 73	Billy Spiers	.05	.02	.01
☐ 74	Scott Brosius	.05	.02	.01
☐ 75	Alan Trammell	.15	.07	.02
☐ 76	Luis Aquino	.05	.02	.01
☐ 77	Jerald Clark	.05	.02	.01
☐ 78	Mel Rojas	.05	.02	.01
☐ 79	Outfield Prospects	.25	.11	.03
	Billy Masse			
	Stanton Cameron			
	Tim Clark			
	Craig McClure			
☐ 80	Jose Canseco	.30	.14	.04
☐ 81	Greg McMichael	.05	.02	.01
☐ 82	Brian Turang	.05	.02	.01
☐ 83	Tom Urbani	.05	.02	.01
☐ 84	Garret Anderson	.60	.25	.07
☐ 85	Tony Pena	.05	.02	.01
☐ 86	Ricky Jordan	.05	.02	.01
☐ 87	Jim Gott	.05	.02	.01
☐ 88	Pat Kelly	.05	.02	.01
☐ 89	Bud Black	.05	.02	.01
☐ 90	Robin Ventura	.10	.05	.01
☐ 91	Rick Sutcliffe	.05	.02	.01
☐ 92	Jose Bautista	.05	.02	.01
☐ 93	Bob Ojeda	.05	.02	.01
☐ 94	Phil Hiatt	.10	.05	.01
☐ 95	Tim Pugh	.05	.02	.01
☐ 96	Randy Knorr	.05	.02	.01
☐ 97	Todd Jones	.05	.02	.01
☐ 98	Ryan Thompson	.10	.05	.01
☐ 99	Tim Mauser	.05	.02	.01
☐ 100	Kirby Puckett	.60	.25	.07
☐ 101	Mark Dewey	.05	.02	.01
☐ 102	B.J. Surhoff	.05	.02	.01
☐ 103	Sterling Hitchcock	.10	.05	.01
☐ 104	Alex Arias	.05	.02	.01
☐ 105	David Wells	.05	.02	.01
☐ 106	Daryl Boston	.05	.02	.01
☐ 107	Mike Stanton	.05	.02	.01
☐ 108	Gary Redus	.05	.02	.01
☐ 109	Delino DeShields	.10	.05	.01
☐ 110	Lee Smith	.15	.07	.02
☐ 111	Greg Litton	.05	.02	.01
☐ 112	Frankie Rodriguez	.15	.07	.02
☐ 113	Russ Springer	.05	.02	.01
☐ 114	Mitch Williams	.05	.02	.01
☐ 115	Eric Karros	.10	.05	.01
☐ 116	Jeff Brantley	.05	.02	.01
☐ 117	Jack Voigt	.05	.02	.01
☐ 118	Jason Bere	.15	.07	.02
☐ 119	Kevin Roberson	.05	.02	.01
☐ 120	Jimmy Key	.10	.05	.01
☐ 121	Reggie Jefferson	.05	.02	.01
☐ 122	Jeromy Burnitz	.05	.02	.01
☐ 123	Billy Brewer	.05	.02	.01
☐ 124	Willie Canate	.05	.02	.01
☐ 125	Greg Swindell	.05	.02	.01
☐ 126	Hal Morris	.10	.05	.01
☐ 127	Brad Ausmus	.05	.02	.01
☐ 128	George Tsamis	.05	.02	.01
☐ 129	Denny Neagle	.10	.05	.01
☐ 130	Pat Listach	.05	.02	.01
☐ 131	Steve Karsay	.05	.02	.01
☐ 132	Bret Barberie	.05	.02	.01
☐ 133	Mark Leiter	.05	.02	.01
☐ 134	Greg Colbrunn	.05	.02	.01
☐ 135	David Nied	.10	.05	.01
☐ 136	Dean Palmer	.10	.05	.01
☐ 137	Steve Avery	.15	.07	.02
☐ 138	Bill Haselman	.05	.02	.01
☐ 139	Tripp Cromer	.05	.02	.01
☐ 140	Frank Viola	.05	.02	.01
☐ 141	Rene Gonzales	.05	.02	.01
☐ 142	Curt Schilling	.05	.02	.01
☐ 143	Tim Wallach	.05	.02	.01
☐ 144	Bobby Munoz	.05	.02	.01
☐ 145	Brady Anderson	.10	.05	.01
☐ 146	Rod Beck	.10	.05	.01
☐ 147	Mike LaValliere	.05	.02	.01
☐ 148	Greg Hibbard	.05	.02	.01
☐ 149	Kenny Lofton	.60	.25	.07
☐ 150	Doc Gooden	.05	.02	.01
☐ 151	Greg Gagne	.05	.02	.01
☐ 152	Ray McDavid	.10	.05	.01
☐ 153	Chris Donnels	.05	.02	.01
☐ 154	Dan Wilson	.05	.02	.01
☐ 155	Todd Stottlemyre	.05	.02	.01
☐ 156	David McCarty	.05	.02	.01
☐ 157	Paul Wagner	.05	.02	.01
☐ 158	Shortstop Prospects	.50	.23	.06
	Orlando Miller			
	Brandon Wilson			
	Derek Jeter			
	Mike Neal			
☐ 159	Mike Fetters	.05	.02	.01
☐ 160	Scott Lydy	.05	.02	.01
☐ 161	Darrell Whitmore	.10	.05	.01
☐ 162	Bob MacDonald	.05	.02	.01
☐ 163	Vinny Castilla	.10	.05	.01
☐ 164	Denis Boucher	.05	.02	.01
☐ 165	Ivan Rodriguez	.15	.07	.02
☐ 166	Ron Gant	.10	.05	.01
☐ 167	Tim Davis	.05	.02	.01
☐ 168	Steve Dixon	.05	.02	.01
☐ 169	Scott Fletcher	.05	.02	.01
☐ 170	Terry Mulholland	.05	.02	.01
☐ 171	Greg Myers	.05	.02	.01
☐ 172	Brett Butler	.10	.05	.01
☐ 173	Bob Wickman	.05	.02	.01
☐ 174	Dave Martinez	.05	.02	.01
☐ 175	Fernando Valenzuela	.05	.02	.01
☐ 176	Craig Grebeck	.05	.02	.01
☐ 177	Shawn Boskie	.05	.02	.01
☐ 178	Albie Lopez	.15	.07	.02
☐ 179	Butch Huskey	.10	.05	.01
☐ 180	George Brett	.75	.35	.09
☐ 181	Juan Guzman	.10	.05	.01
☐ 182	Eric Anthony	.05	.02	.01
☐ 183	Rob Dibble	.05	.02	.01
☐ 184	Craig Shipley	.05	.02	.01
☐ 185	Kevin Tapani	.05	.02	.01
☐ 186	Marcus Moore	.05	.02	.01
☐ 187	Graeme Lloyd	.05	.02	.01
☐ 188	Mike Bordick	.05	.02	.01
☐ 189	Chris Hammond	.05	.02	.01
☐ 190	Cecil Fielder	.15	.07	.02
☐ 191	Curtis Leskanic	.05	.02	.01
☐ 192	Lou Frazier	.05	.02	.01
☐ 193	Steve Dreyer	.05	.02	.01
☐ 194	Javier Lopez	.30	.14	.04

☐ 195	Edgar Martinez	.10	.05	.01
☐ 196	Allen Watson	.05	.02	.01
☐ 197	John Flaherty	.05	.02	.01
☐ 198	Kurt Stillwell	.05	.02	.01
☐ 199	Danny Jackson	.05	.02	.01
☐ 200	Cal Ripken	2.00	.90	.25
☐ 201	Mike Bell FDP	.15	.07	.02
☐ 202	Alan Benes FDP	.60	.25	.07
☐ 203	Matt Farner FDP	.25	.11	.03
☐ 204	Jeff Granger FDP	.10	.05	.01
☐ 205	Brooks Kieschnick FDP	1.50	.70	.19
☐ 206	Jeremy Lee FDP	.20	.09	.03
☐ 207	Charles Peterson FDP	.30	.14	.04
☐ 208	Alan Rice FDP	.20	.09	.03
☐ 209	Billy Wagner FDP	.40	.18	.05
☐ 210	Kelly Wunsch FDP	.20	.09	.03
☐ 211	Tom Candiotti	.05	.02	.01
☐ 212	Domingo Jean	.05	.02	.01
☐ 213	John Burkett	.10	.05	.01
☐ 214	George Bell	.10	.05	.01
☐ 215	Dan Plesac	.05	.02	.01
☐ 216	Manny Ramirez	1.00	.45	.12
☐ 217	Mike Maddux	.05	.02	.01
☐ 218	Kevin McReynolds	.05	.02	.01
☐ 219	Pat Borders	.05	.02	.01
☐ 220	Doug Drabek	.15	.07	.02
☐ 221	Larry Luebbers	.05	.02	.01
☐ 222	Trevor Hoffman	.05	.02	.01
☐ 223	Pat Meares	.05	.02	.01
☐ 224	Danny Miceli	.05	.02	.01
☐ 225	Greg Vaughn	.10	.05	.01
☐ 226	Scott Hemond	.05	.02	.01
☐ 227	Pat Rapp	.05	.02	.01
☐ 228	Kirk Gibson	.10	.05	.01
☐ 229	Lance Painter	.05	.02	.01
☐ 230	Larry Walker	.25	.11	.03
☐ 231	Benji Gil	.10	.05	.01
☐ 232	Mark Wohlers	.05	.02	.01
☐ 233	Rich Amaral	.05	.02	.01
☐ 234	Eric Pappas	.05	.02	.01
☐ 235	Scott Cooper	.10	.05	.01
☐ 236	Mike Butcher	.05	.02	.01
☐ 237	Outfield Prospects	.25	.11	.03
	Curtis Pride			
	Shawn Green			
	Mark Sweeney			
	Eddie Davis			
☐ 238	Kim Batiste	.05	.02	.01
☐ 239	Paul Assenmacher	.05	.02	.01
☐ 240	Will Clark	.25	.11	.03
☐ 241	Jose Offerman	.10	.05	.01
☐ 242	Todd Frohwirth	.05	.02	.01
☐ 243	Tim Raines	.15	.07	.02
☐ 244	Rick Wilkins	.05	.02	.01
☐ 245	Bret Saberhagen	.10	.05	.01
☐ 246	Thomas Howard	.05	.02	.01
☐ 247	Stan Belinda	.05	.02	.01
☐ 248	Rickey Henderson	.15	.07	.02
☐ 249	Brian Williams	.05	.02	.01
☐ 250	Barry Larkin	.25	.11	.03
☐ 251	Jose Valentin	.05	.02	.01
☐ 252	Lenny Webster	.05	.02	.01
☐ 253	Blas Minor	.05	.02	.01
☐ 254	Tim Teufel	.05	.02	.01
☐ 255	Bobby Witt	.05	.02	.01
☐ 256	Walt Weiss	.05	.02	.01
☐ 257	Chad Kreuter	.05	.02	.01
☐ 258	Roberto Mejia	.05	.02	.01
☐ 259	Cliff Floyd	.15	.07	.02
☐ 260	Julio Franco	.10	.05	.01
☐ 261	Rafael Belliard	.05	.02	.01
☐ 262	Marc Newfield	.15	.07	.02
☐ 263	Gerald Perry	.05	.02	.01
☐ 264	Ken Ryan	.05	.02	.01
☐ 265	Chili Davis	.10	.05	.01
☐ 266	Dave West	.05	.02	.01
☐ 267	Royce Clayton	.10	.05	.01
☐ 268	Pedro Martinez	.15	.07	.02
☐ 269	Mark Hutton	.05	.02	.01
☐ 270	Frank Thomas	2.00	.90	.25
☐ 271	Brad Pennington	.05	.02	.01
☐ 272	Mike Harkey	.05	.02	.01
☐ 273	Sandy Alomar	.10	.05	.01
☐ 274	Dave Gallagher	.05	.02	.01
☐ 275	Wally Joyner	.10	.05	.01
☐ 276	Ricky Trlicek	.05	.02	.01
☐ 277	Al Osuna	.05	.02	.01
☐ 278	Calvin Reese	.10	.05	.01
☐ 279	Kevin Higgins	.05	.02	.01
☐ 280	Rick Aguilera	.10	.05	.01
☐ 281	Orlando Merced	.10	.05	.01
☐ 282	Mike Mohler	.05	.02	.01
☐ 283	John Jaha	.05	.02	.01
☐ 284	Robb Nen	.05	.02	.01
☐ 285	Travis Fryman	.15	.07	.02
☐ 286	Mark Thompson	.10	.05	.01
☐ 287	Mike Lansing	.10	.05	.01
☐ 288	Craig Lefferts	.05	.02	.01
☐ 289	Damon Berryhill	.05	.02	.01
☐ 290	Randy Johnson	.40	.18	.05
☐ 291	Jeff Reed	.05	.02	.01
☐ 292	Danny Darwin	.05	.02	.01
☐ 293	J.T. Snow	.10	.05	.01
☐ 294	Tyler Green	.05	.02	.01
☐ 295	Chris Hoiles	.10	.05	.01
☐ 296	Roger McDowell	.05	.02	.01
☐ 297	Spike Owen	.05	.02	.01
☐ 298	Salomon Torres	.10	.05	.01
☐ 299	Wilson Alvarez	.15	.07	.02
☐ 300	Ryne Sandberg	.50	.23	.06
☐ 301	Derek Lilliquist	.05	.02	.01
☐ 302	Howard Johnson	.05	.02	.01
☐ 303	Greg Cadaret	.05	.02	.01
☐ 304	Pat Hentgen	.10	.05	.01
☐ 305	Craig Biggio	.10	.05	.01
☐ 306	Scott Service	.05	.02	.01
☐ 307	Melvin Nieves	.15	.07	.02
☐ 308	Mike Trombley	.05	.02	.01
☐ 309	Carlos Garcia	.05	.02	.01
☐ 310	Robin Yount UER	.25	.11	.03
	(listed with 111 triples in			
	1988; should be 11)			
☐ 311	Marcos Armas	.05	.02	.01
☐ 312	Rich Rodriguez	.05	.02	.01
☐ 313	Justin Thompson	.05	.02	.01
☐ 314	Danny Sheaffer	.05	.02	.01
☐ 315	Ken Hill	.10	.05	.01
☐ 316	Pitching Prospects	.25	.11	.03
	Chad Ogea			
	Duff Brumley			
	Terrell Wade			
	Chris Michalak			
☐ 317	Cris Carpenter	.05	.02	.01
☐ 318	Jeff Blauser	.10	.05	.01
☐ 319	Ted Power	.05	.02	.01
☐ 320	Ozzie Smith	.40	.18	.05
☐ 321	John Dopson	.05	.02	.01
☐ 322	Chris Turner	.05	.02	.01
☐ 323	Pete Incaviglia	.05	.02	.01
☐ 324	Alan Mills	.05	.02	.01
☐ 325	Jody Reed	.05	.02	.01
☐ 326	Rich Monteleone	.05	.02	.01

327	Mark Carreon	.05	.02	.01
328	Donn Pall	.05	.02	.01
329	Matt Walbeck	.05	.02	.01
330	Charley Nagy	.10	.05	.01
331	Jeff McKnight	.05	.02	.01
332	Jose Lind	.05	.02	.01
333	Mike Timlin	.05	.02	.01
334	Doug Jones	.05	.02	.01
335	Kevin Mitchell	.10	.05	.01
336	Luis Lopez	.05	.02	.01
337	Shane Mack	.10	.05	.01
338	Randy Tomlin	.05	.02	.01
339	Matt Mieske	.05	.02	.01
340	Mark McGwire	.15	.07	.02
341	Nigel Wilson	.05	.02	.01
342	Danny Gladden	.05	.02	.01
343	Mo Sanford	.05	.02	.01
344	Sean Berry	.05	.02	.01
345	Kevin Brown	.05	.02	.01
346	Greg Olson	.05	.02	.01
347	Dave Magadan	.05	.02	.01
348	Rene Arocha	.10	.05	.01
349	Carlos Quintana	.05	.02	.01
350	Jim Abbott	.15	.07	.02
351	Gary DiSarcina	.05	.02	.01
352	Ben Rivera	.05	.02	.01
353	Carlos Hernandez	.05	.02	.01
354	Darren Lewis	.05	.02	.01
355	Harold Reynolds	.05	.02	.01
356	Scott Ruffcorn	.10	.05	.01
357	Mark Gubicza	.05	.02	.01
358	Paul Sorrento	.05	.02	.01
359	Anthony Young	.05	.02	.01
360	Mark Grace	.15	.07	.02
361	Rob Butler	.05	.02	.01
362	Kevin Bass	.05	.02	.01
363	Eric Helfand	.05	.02	.01
364	Derek Bell	.10	.05	.01
365	Scott Erickson	.05	.02	.01
366	Al Martin	.05	.02	.01
367	Ricky Bones	.05	.02	.01
368	Jeff Branson	.05	.02	.01
369	Third Base Prospects	.75	.35	.09
	Luis Ortiz			
	David Bell			
	Jason Giambi			
	George Arias			
370	Benito Santiago	.05	.02	.01
	(See also 379)			
371	John Doherty	.05	.02	.01
372	Joe Girardi	.05	.02	.01
373	Tim Scott	.05	.02	.01
374	Marvin Freeman	.05	.02	.01
375	Deion Sanders	.40	.18	.05
376	Roger Salkeld	.05	.02	.01
377	Berard Gilkey	.10	.05	.01
378	Tony Fossas	.05	.02	.01
379	Mark McLemore UER	.05	.02	.01
	(Card number is 370)			
380	Darren Daulton	.15	.07	.02
381	Chuck Finley	.05	.02	.01
382	Mitch Webster	.05	.02	.01
383	Gerald Williams	.05	.02	.01
384	Frank Thomas AS	.60	.25	.07
	Fred McGriff			
385	Roberto Alomar AS	.05	.02	.01
	Robby Thompson AS			
386	Wade Boggs AS	.10	.05	.01
	Matt Williams AS			
387	Cal Ripken AS	.60	.25	.07
	Jeff Blauser AS			
388	Ken Griffey Jr. AS	.50	.23	.06
	Len Dykstra AS			
389	Juan Gonzalez AS	.15	.07	.02
	David Justice AS			
390	George Belle AS	.30	.14	.04
	Bobby Bonds AS			
391	Mike Stanley AS	.25	.11	.03
	Mike Piazza AS			
392	Jack McDowell AS	.50	.23	.06
	Greg Maddux AS			
393	Jimmy Key AS	.10	.05	.01
	Tom Glavine AS			
394	Jeff Montgomery AS	.05	.02	.01
	Randy Myers AS			
395	Checklist 1-198	.05	.02	.01
396	Checklist 199-396	.05	.02	.01
397	Tim Salmon	.40	.18	.05
398	Todd Benzinger	.05	.02	.01
399	Frank Castillo	.05	.02	.01
400	Ken Griffey Jr.	2.00	.90	.25
401	John Kruk	.10	.05	.01
402	Dave Telgheder	.05	.02	.01
403	Gary Gaetti	.05	.02	.01
404	Jim Edmonds	.30	.14	.04
405	Don Slaught	.05	.02	.01
406	Jose Oquendo	.05	.02	.01
407	Bruce Ruffin	.05	.02	.01
408	Phil Clark	.05	.02	.01
409	Joe Klink	.05	.02	.01
410	Lou Whitaker	.15	.07	.02
411	Kevin Seitzer	.05	.02	.01
412	Darrin Fletcher	.05	.02	.01
413	Kenny Rogers	.10	.05	.01
414	Bill Pecota	.05	.02	.01
415	Dave Fleming	.05	.02	.01
416	Luis Alicea	.05	.02	.01
417	Paul Quantrill	.05	.02	.01
418	Damion Easley	.05	.02	.01
419	Wes Chamberlain	.05	.02	.01
420	Harold Baines	.10	.05	.01
421	Scott Radinsky	.05	.02	.01
422	Rey Sanchez	.05	.02	.01
423	Junior Ortiz	.05	.02	.01
424	Jeff Kent	.10	.05	.01
425	Brian McRae	.10	.05	.01
426	Ed Sprague	.05	.02	.01
427	Tom Edens	.05	.02	.01
428	Willie Greene	.10	.05	.01
429	Bryan Hickerson	.05	.02	.01
430	Dave Winfield	.15	.07	.02
431	Pedro Astacio	.10	.05	.01
432	Mike Gallego	.05	.02	.01
433	Dave Burba	.05	.02	.01
434	Bob Walk	.05	.02	.01
435	Darryl Hamilton	.05	.02	.01
436	Vince Horsman	.05	.02	.01
437	Bob Natal	.05	.02	.01
438	Mike Henneman	.05	.02	.01
439	Willie Blair	.05	.02	.01
440	Denny Martinez	.10	.05	.01
441	Dan Peltier	.05	.02	.01
442	Tony Tarasco	.15	.07	.02
443	John Cummings	.05	.02	.01
444	Geronimo Pena	.05	.02	.01
445	Aaron Sele	.15	.07	.02
446	Stan Javier	.05	.02	.01
447	Mike Williams	.05	.02	.01
448	First Basemen	.15	.07	.02
	Prospects			
	Greg Pirkl			
	Roberto Petagine			

D.J.Boston
Shawn Wooten

☐ 449	Jim Poole	.05	.02	.01
☐ 450	Carlos Baerga	.40	.18	.05
☐ 451	Bob Scanlan	.05	.02	.01
☐ 452	Lance Johnson	.05	.02	.01
☐ 453	Eric Hillman	.05	.02	.01
☐ 454	Keith Miller	.05	.02	.01
☐ 455	Dave Stewart	.10	.05	.01
☐ 456	Pete Harnisch	.05	.02	.01
☐ 457	Roberto Kelly	.05	.02	.01
☐ 458	Tim Worrell	.05	.02	.01
☐ 459	Pedro Munoz	.05	.02	.01
☐ 460	Orel Hershiser	.05	.02	.01
☐ 461	Randy Velarde	.05	.02	.01
☐ 462	Trevor Wilson	.05	.02	.01
☐ 463	Jerry Goff	.05	.02	.01
☐ 464	Bill Wegman	.05	.02	.01
☐ 465	Dennis Eckersley	.15	.07	.02
☐ 466	Jeff Conine	.15	.07	.02
☐ 467	Joe Boever	.05	.02	.01
☐ 468	Dante Bichette	.25	.11	.03
☐ 469	Jeff Shaw	.05	.02	.01
☐ 470	Rafael Palmeiro	.15	.07	.02
☐ 471	Phil Leftwich	.05	.02	.01
☐ 472	Jay Buhner	.10	.05	.01
☐ 473	Bob Tewksbury	.05	.02	.01
☐ 474	Tim Naehring	.05	.02	.01
☐ 475	Tom Glavine	.15	.07	.02
☐ 476	Dave Hollins	.15	.07	.02
☐ 477	Arthur Rhodes	.05	.02	.01
☐ 478	Joey Cora	.05	.02	.01
☐ 479	Mike Morgan	.05	.02	.01
☐ 480	Albert Belle	.75	.35	.09
☐ 481	John Franco	.05	.02	.01
☐ 482	Hipolito Pichardo	.05	.02	.01
☐ 483	Duane Ward	.05	.02	.01
☐ 484	Luis Gonzalez	.05	.02	.01
☐ 485	Joe Oliver	.05	.02	.01
☐ 486	Wally Whitehurst	.05	.02	.01
☐ 487	Mike Benjamin	.05	.02	.01
☐ 488	Eric Davis	.05	.02	.01
☐ 489	Scott Kamieniecki	.05	.02	.01
☐ 490	Kent Hrbek	.10	.05	.01
☐ 491	John Hope	.05	.02	.01
☐ 492	Jesse Orosco	.05	.02	.01
☐ 493	Troy Neel	.05	.02	.01
☐ 494	Ryan Bowen	.05	.02	.01
☐ 495	Mickey Tettleton	.05	.02	.01
☐ 496	Chris Jones	.05	.02	.01
☐ 497	John Wetteland	.05	.02	.01
☐ 498	David Hulse	.05	.02	.01
☐ 499	Greg Maddux	2.00	.90	.25
☐ 500	Bo Jackson	.15	.07	.02
☐ 501	Donovan Osborne	.05	.02	.01
☐ 502	Mike Greenwell	.10	.05	.01
☐ 503	Steve Frey	.05	.02	.01
☐ 504	Jim Eisenreich	.05	.02	.01
☐ 505	Robby Thompson	.05	.02	.01
☐ 506	Leo Gomez	.05	.02	.01
☐ 507	Dave Staton	.05	.02	.01
☐ 508	Wayne Kirby	.05	.02	.01
☐ 509	Tim Bogar	.05	.02	.01
☐ 510	David Cone	.15	.07	.02
☐ 511	Devon White	.05	.02	.01
☐ 512	Xavier Hernandez	.05	.02	.01
☐ 513	Tim Costo	.05	.02	.01
☐ 514	Gene Harris	.05	.02	.01
☐ 515	Jack McDowell	.15	.07	.02
☐ 516	Kevin Gross	.05	.02	.01
☐ 517	Scott Leius	.05	.02	.01
☐ 518	Lloyd McClendon	.05	.02	.01
☐ 519	Alex Diaz	.05	.02	.01
☐ 520	Wade Boggs	.15	.07	.02
☐ 521	Bob Welch	.05	.02	.01
☐ 522	Henry Cotto	.05	.02	.01
☐ 523	Mike Moore	.05	.02	.01
☐ 524	Tim Laker	.05	.02	.01
☐ 525	Andres Galarraga	.15	.07	.02
☐ 526	Jamie Moyer	.05	.02	.01
☐ 527	Second Baseman	.10	.05	.01

Prospects
Norberto Martin
Ruben Santana
Jason Hardtke
Chris Sexton

☐ 528	Sid Bream	.05	.02	.01
☐ 529	Erik Hanson	.05	.02	.01
☐ 530	Ray Lankford	.15	.07	.02
☐ 531	Rob Deer	.05	.02	.01
☐ 532	Rod Correia	.05	.02	.01
☐ 533	Roger Mason	.05	.02	.01
☐ 534	Mike Devereaux	.10	.05	.01
☐ 535	Jeff Montgomery	.10	.05	.01
☐ 536	Dwight Smith	.05	.02	.01
☐ 537	Jeremy Hernandez	.05	.02	.01
☐ 538	Ellis Burks	.10	.05	.01
☐ 539	Bobby Jones	.15	.07	.02
☐ 540	Paul Molitor	.15	.07	.02
☐ 541	Jeff Juden	.05	.02	.01
☐ 542	Chris Sabo	.05	.02	.01
☐ 543	Larry Casian	.05	.02	.01
☐ 544	Jeff Gardner	.05	.02	.01
☐ 545	Ramon Martinez	.10	.05	.01
☐ 546	Paul O'Neill	.10	.05	.01
☐ 547	Steve Hosey	.05	.02	.01
☐ 548	Dave Nilsson	.05	.02	.01
☐ 549	Ron Darling	.05	.02	.01
☐ 550	Matt Williams	.30	.14	.04
☐ 551	Jack Armstrong	.05	.02	.01
☐ 552	Bill Krueger	.05	.02	.01
☐ 553	Freddie Benavides	.05	.02	.01
☐ 554	Jeff Fassero	.05	.02	.01
☐ 555	Chuck Knoblauch	.15	.07	.02
☐ 556	Guillermo Velasquez	.05	.02	.01
☐ 557	Joel Johnston	.05	.02	.01
☐ 558	Tom Lampkin	.05	.02	.01
☐ 559	Todd Van Poppel	.10	.05	.01
☐ 560	Gary Sheffield	.15	.07	.02
☐ 561	Skeeter Barnes	.05	.02	.01
☐ 562	Darren Holmes	.05	.02	.01
☐ 563	John Vander Wal	.05	.02	.01
☐ 564	Mike Ignasiak	.05	.02	.01
☐ 565	Fred McGriff	.25	.11	.03
☐ 566	Luis Polonia	.05	.02	.01
☐ 567	Mike Perez	.05	.02	.01
☐ 568	John Valentin	.10	.05	.01
☐ 569	Mike Felder	.05	.02	.01
☐ 570	Tommy Greene	.05	.02	.01
☐ 571	David Segui	.05	.02	.01
☐ 572	Roberto Hernandez	.05	.02	.01
☐ 573	Steve Wilson	.05	.02	.01
☐ 574	Willie McGee	.05	.02	.01
☐ 575	Randy Myers	.05	.02	.01
☐ 576	Darrin Jackson	.05	.02	.01
☐ 577	Eric Plunk	.05	.02	.01
☐ 578	Mike Macfarlane	.05	.02	.01
☐ 579	Doug Brocail	.05	.02	.01
☐ 580	Steve Finley	.05	.02	.01
☐ 581	John Roper	.10	.05	.01
☐ 582	Danny Cox	.05	.02	.01
☐ 583	Chip Hale	.05	.02	.01

☐ 584 Scott Bullett	.05	.02	.01
☐ 585 Kevin Reimer	.05	.02	.01
☐ 586 Brent Gates	.10	.05	.01
☐ 587 Matt Turner	.05	.02	.01
☐ 588 Rich Rowland	.05	.02	.01
☐ 589 Kent Bottenfield	.05	.02	.01
☐ 590 Marquis Grissom	.15	.07	.02
☐ 591 Doug Strange	.05	.02	.01
☐ 592 Jay Howell	.05	.02	.01
☐ 593 Omar Vizquel	.05	.02	.01
☐ 594 Rheal Cormier	.05	.02	.01
☐ 595 Andre Dawson	.15	.07	.02
☐ 596 Hilly Hathaway	.05	.02	.01
☐ 597 Todd Pratt	.05	.02	.01
☐ 598 Mike Mussina	.25	.11	.03
☐ 599 Alex Fernandez	.15	.07	.02
☐ 600 Don Mattingly	1.00	.45	.12
☐ 601 Frank Thomas ST	1.00	.45	.12
☐ 602 Ryne Sandberg ST	.25	.11	.03
☐ 603 Wade Boggs ST	.15	.07	.02
☐ 604 Cal Ripken ST	1.00	.45	.12
☐ 605 Barry Bonds ST	.25	.11	.03
☐ 606 Ken Griffey Jr. ST	1.00	.45	.12
☐ 607 Kirby Puckett ST	.30	.14	.04
☐ 608 Darren Daulton ST	.15	.07	.02
☐ 609 Paul Molitor ST	.15	.07	.02
☐ 610 Terry Steinbach	.10	.05	.01
☐ 611 Todd Worrell	.05	.02	.01
☐ 612 Jim Thome	.40	.18	.05
☐ 613 Chuck McElroy	.05	.02	.01
☐ 614 John Habyan	.05	.02	.01
☐ 615 Sid Fernandez	.05	.02	.01
☐ 616 Outfield	.15	.07	.02
Prospects			
Eddie Zambrano			
Glenn Murray			
Chad Mottola			
Jermaine Allensworth			
☐ 617 Steve Bedrosian	.05	.02	.01
☐ 618 Rob Ducey	.05	.02	.01
☐ 619 Tom Browning	.05	.02	.01
☐ 620 Tony Gwynn	.60	.25	.07
☐ 621 Carl Willis	.05	.02	.01
☐ 622 Kevin Young	.05	.02	.01
☐ 623 Rafael Novoa	.05	.02	.01
☐ 624 Jerry Browne	.05	.02	.01
☐ 625 Charlie Hough	.10	.05	.01
☐ 626 Chris Gomez	.15	.07	.02
☐ 627 Steve Reed	.05	.02	.01
☐ 628 Kirk Rueter	.05	.02	.01
☐ 629 Matt Whiteside	.05	.02	.01
☐ 630 David Justice	.25	.11	.03
☐ 631 Brad Holman	.05	.02	.01
☐ 632 Brian Jordan	.10	.05	.01
☐ 633 Scott Bankhead	.05	.02	.01
☐ 634 Torey Lovullo	.05	.02	.01
☐ 635 Len Dykstra	.15	.07	.02
☐ 636 Ben McDonald	.10	.05	.01
☐ 637 Steve Howe	.05	.02	.01
☐ 638 Jose Vizcaino	.05	.02	.01
☐ 639 Bill Swift	.05	.02	.01
☐ 640 Darryl Strawberry	.10	.05	.01
☐ 641 Steve Farr	.05	.02	.01
☐ 642 Tom Kramer	.05	.02	.01
☐ 643 Joe Orsulak	.05	.02	.01
☐ 644 Tom Henke	.05	.02	.01
☐ 645 Joe Carter	.15	.07	.02
☐ 646 Ken Caminiti	.10	.05	.01
☐ 647 Reggie Sanders	.15	.07	.02
☐ 648 Andy Ashby	.05	.02	.01
☐ 649 Derek Parks	.05	.02	.01

☐ 650 Andy Van Slyke	.15	.07	.02
☐ 651 Juan Bell	.05	.02	.01
☐ 652 Roger Smithberg	.05	.02	.01
☐ 653 Chuck Carr	.05	.02	.01
☐ 654 Bill Gullickson	.05	.02	.01
☐ 655 Charlie Hayes	.10	.05	.01
☐ 656 Chris Nabholz	.05	.02	.01
☐ 657 Karl Rhodes	.05	.02	.01
☐ 658 Pete Smith	.05	.02	.01
☐ 659 Bret Boone	.15	.07	.02
☐ 660 Gregg Jefferies	.15	.07	.02
☐ 661 Bob Zupcic	.05	.02	.01
☐ 662 Steve Sax	.05	.02	.01
☐ 663 Mariano Duncan	.05	.02	.01
☐ 664 Jeff Tackett	.05	.02	.01
☐ 665 Mark Langston	.15	.07	.02
☐ 666 Steve Buechele	.05	.02	.01
☐ 667 Candy Maldonado	.05	.02	.01
☐ 668 Woody Williams	.05	.02	.01
☐ 669 Tim Wakefield	.10	.05	.01
☐ 670 Danny Tartabull	.10	.05	.01
☐ 671 Charlie O'Brien	.05	.02	.01
☐ 672 Felix Jose	.05	.02	.01
☐ 673 Bobby Ayala	.05	.02	.01
☐ 674 Scott Servais	.05	.02	.01
☐ 675 Roberto Alomar	.40	.18	.05
☐ 676 Pedro Martinez	.15	.07	.02
☐ 677 Eddie Guardado	.05	.02	.01
☐ 678 Mark Lewis	.05	.02	.01
☐ 679 Jaime Navarro	.05	.02	.01
☐ 680 Ruben Sierrra	.15	.07	.02
☐ 681 Rick Renteria	.05	.02	.01
☐ 682 Storm Davis	.05	.02	.01
☐ 683 Cory Snyder	.05	.02	.01
☐ 684 Ron Karkovice	.05	.02	.01
☐ 685 Juan Gonzalez	.50	.23	.06
☐ 686 Catchers	.25	.11	.03
Prospects			
Chris Howard			
Carlos Delgado			
Jason Kendall			
Paul Bako			
☐ 687 John Smoltz	.10	.05	.01
☐ 688 Brian Dorsett	.05	.02	.01
☐ 689 Omar Olivares	.05	.02	.01
☐ 690 Mo Vaughn	.30	.14	.04
☐ 691 Joe Grahe	.05	.02	.01
☐ 692 Mickey Morandini	.05	.02	.01
☐ 693 Tino Martinez	.10	.05	.01
☐ 694 Brian Barnes	.05	.02	.01
☐ 695 Mike Stanley	.05	.02	.01
☐ 696 Mark Clark	.05	.02	.01
☐ 697 Dave Hansen	.05	.02	.01
☐ 698 Willie Wilson	.05	.02	.01
☐ 699 Pete Schourek	.10	.05	.01
☐ 700 Barry Bonds	.50	.23	.06
☐ 701 Kevin Appier	.05	.02	.01
☐ 702 Tony Fernandez	.05	.02	.01
☐ 703 Darryl Kile	.10	.05	.01
☐ 704 Archi Cianfrocco	.05	.02	.01
☐ 705 Jose Rijo	.10	.05	.01
☐ 706 Brian Harper	.05	.02	.01
☐ 707 Zane Smith	.05	.02	.01
☐ 708 Dave Henderson	.05	.02	.01
☐ 709 Angel Miranda	.05	.02	.01
☐ 710 Orestes Destrade	.05	.02	.01
☐ 711 Greg Gohr	.05	.02	.01
☐ 712 Eric Young	.10	.05	.01
☐ 713 Relief Pitchers	.10	.05	.01
Prospects			
Todd Williams			

Ron Watson
Kirk Bullinger
Mike Welch

☐ 714	Tim Spehr	.05	.02	.01
☐ 715	Hank Aaron	.50	.23	.06
☐ 716	Nate Minchey	.10	.05	.01
☐ 717	Mike Blowers	.10	.05	.01
☐ 718	Kent Mercker	.05	.02	.01
☐ 719	Tom Pagnozzi	.05	.02	.01
☐ 720	Roger Clemens	.30	.14	.04
☐ 721	Eduardo Perez	.05	.02	.01
☐ 722	Milt Thompson	.05	.02	.01
☐ 723	Gregg Olson	.05	.02	.01
☐ 724	Kirk McCaskill	.05	.02	.01
☐ 725	Sammy Sosa	.15	.07	.02
☐ 726	Alvaro Espinoza	.05	.02	.01
☐ 727	Henry Rodriguez	.05	.02	.01
☐ 728	Jim Leyritz	.05	.02	.01
☐ 729	Steve Scarsone	.05	.02	.01
☐ 730	Bobby Bonilla	.15	.07	.02
☐ 731	Chris Gwynn	.05	.02	.01
☐ 732	Al Leiter	.05	.02	.01
☐ 733	Bip Roberts	.05	.02	.01
☐ 734	Mark Portugal	.05	.02	.01
☐ 735	Terry Pendleton	.05	.02	.01
☐ 736	Dave Valle	.05	.02	.01
☐ 737	Paul Kilgus	.05	.02	.01
☐ 738	Greg A. Harris	.05	.02	.01
☐ 739	Jon Ratliff DP	.10	.05	.01
☐ 740	Kirk Presley DP	.20	.09	.03
☐ 741	Josue Estrada DP	.20	.09	.03
☐ 742	Wayne Gomes DP	.25	.11	.03
☐ 743	Pat Watkins DP	.50	.23	.06
☐ 744	Jamey Wright DP	.20	.09	.03
☐ 745	Jay Powell DP	.20	.09	.03
☐ 746	Ryan McGuire DP	.10	.05	.01
☐ 747	Marc Barcelo DP	.20	.09	.03
☐ 748	Sloan Smith DP	.20	.09	.03
☐ 749	John Wasdin DP	.40	.18	.05
☐ 750	Marc Vlades DP	.10	.05	.01
☐ 751	Dan Ehler DP	.25	.11	.03
☐ 752	Andre King DP	.15	.07	.02
☐ 753	Greg Keagle DP	.10	.05	.01
☐ 754	Jason Myers DP	.20	.09	.03
☐ 755	Dax Winslett DP	.25	.11	.03
☐ 756	Casey Whitten DP	.20	.09	.03
☐ 757	Tony Fuduric DP	.20	.09	.03
☐ 758	Greg Norton DP	.10	.05	.01
☐ 759	Jeff D'Amico DP	.50	.23	.06
☐ 760	Ryan Hancock DP	.10	.05	.01
☐ 761	David Cooper DP	.15	.07	.02
☐ 762	Kevin Orie DP	.15	.07	.02
☐ 763	John O'Donoghue	.05	.02	.01
	Mike Oquist			
☐ 764	Cory Bailey	.05	.02	.01
	Scott Hatteberg			
☐ 765	Mark Holzemer	.05	.02	.01
	Paul Swingle			
☐ 766	James Baldwin	.10	.05	.01
	Rod Bolton			
☐ 767	Jerry Di Poto	.40	.18	.05
	Julian Tavarez			
☐ 768	Danny Bautista	.10	.05	.01
	Sean Bergman			
☐ 769	Bob Hamelin	.10	.05	.01
	Joe Vitiello			
☐ 770	Mark Kiefer	.10	.05	.01
	Troy O'Leary			
☐ 771	Denny Hocking	.05	.02	.01
	Oscar Munoz			
☐ 772	Russ Davis	.10	.05	.01

Brien Taylor

☐ 773	Kyle Abbott	.15	.07	.02
	Miguel Jimenez			
☐ 774	Kevin King	.05	.02	.01
	Eric Plantenberg			
☐ 775	Jon Shave	.05	.02	.01
	Desi Wilson			
☐ 776	Domingo Cedeno	.05	.02	.01
	Paul Spoljaric			
☐ 777	Chipper Jones	1.50	.70	.19
	Ryan Klesko			
☐ 778	Steve Trachsel	.10	.05	.01
	Turk Wendell			
☐ 779	Johnny Ruffin	.05	.02	.01
	Jerry Spradlin			
☐ 780	Jason Bates	.10	.05	.01
	John Burke			
☐ 781	Carl Everett	.10	.05	.01
	Dave Weathers			
☐ 782	Gary Mota	.10	.05	.01
	James Mouton			
☐ 783	Raul Mondesi	.60	.25	.07
	Ben Van Ryn			
☐ 784	Gabe White	.15	.07	.02
	Rondell White			
☐ 785	Brook Fordyce	.30	.14	.04
	Bill Pulsipher			
☐ 786	Kevin Foster	.10	.05	.01
	Gene Schall			
☐ 787	Rich Aude	.10	.05	.01
	Midre Cummings			
☐ 788	Brian Barber	.10	.05	.01
	Rich Batchelor			
☐ 789	Brian Johnson	.10	.05	.01
	Scott Sanders			
☐ 790	Ricky Faneyte	.10	.05	.01
	J.R. Phillips			
☐ 791	Checklist 3	.05	.02	.01
☐ 792	Checklist 4	.05	.02	.01

1994 Topps Traded

This set consists of 132 color cards featuring traded players in their new uniforms, rookies and draft choices. Factory sets consisted of 140 cards including a set of eight Topps Finest cards. Card fronts feature a player photo with the player's name, team and position at the bottom. The horizontal backs have a player photo to the left with complete career statisics and highlights. The cards are numbered with a "T" suffix. Rookie Cards include Brian Anderson, John

Hudek, Terrance Long, Doug Million, Chan
Ho Park, Mac Suzuki and Terrell Wade.

	MINT	NRMT	EXC
COMPLETE FACT.SET (140) ..	40.00	18.00	5.00
COMPLETE SET (132)	6.00	2.70	.75
COMMON CARD (1T-132T)	.05	.02	.01

		MINT	NRMT	EXC
☐	1T Paul Wilson	.75	.35	.09
☐	2T Bill Taylor	.05	.02	.01
☐	3T Dan Wilson	.10	.05	.01
☐	4T Mark Smith	.05	.02	.01
☐	5T Toby Borland	.05	.02	.01
☐	6T Dave Clark	.05	.02	.01
☐	7T Denny Martinez	.10	.05	.01
☐	8T Dave Gallagher	.05	.02	.01
☐	9T Josias Manzanillo	.05	.02	.01
☐	10T Brian Anderson	.15	.07	.02
☐	11T Damon Berryhill	.05	.02	.01
☐	12T Alex Cole	.05	.02	.01
☐	13T Jacob Shumate	.25	.11	.03
☐	14T Oddibe McDowell	.05	.02	.01
☐	15T Willie Banks	.05	.02	.01
☐	16T Jerry Browne	.05	.02	.01
☐	17T Donnie Elliott	.05	.02	.01
☐	18T Ellis Burks	.10	.05	.01
☐	19T Chuck McElroy	.05	.02	.01
☐	20T Luis Polonia	.05	.02	.01
☐	21T Brian Harper	.05	.02	.01
☐	22T Mark Portugal	.05	.02	.01
☐	23T Dave Henderson	.05	.02	.01
☐	24T Mark Acre	.05	.02	.01
☐	25T Julio Franco	.10	.05	.01
☐	26T Darren Hall	.05	.02	.01
☐	27T Eric Anthony	.05	.02	.01
☐	28T Sid Fernandez	.05	.02	.01
☐	29T Rusty Greer	.30	.14	.04
☐	30T Riccardo Ingram	.05	.02	.01
☐	31T Gabe White	.05	.02	.01
☐	32T Tim Belcher	.05	.02	.01
☐	33T Terrence Long	.40	.18	.05
☐	34T Mark Dalesandro	.05	.02	.01
☐	35T Mike Kelly	.05	.02	.01
☐	36T Jack Morris	.15	.07	.02
☐	37T Jeff Brantley	.05	.02	.01
☐	38T Larry Barnes	.20	.09	.03
☐	39T Brian R. Hunter	.05	.02	.01
☐	40T Otis Nixon	.05	.02	.01
☐	41T Bret Wagner	.15	.07	.02
☐	42T Anatomy of a Trade	.05	.02	.01
	Pedro Martinez			
	Delino DeShields			
☐	43T Heathcliff Slocumb	.05	.02	.01
☐	44T Ben Grieve	2.00	.90	.25
☐	45T John Hudek	.05	.02	.01
☐	46T Shawon Dunston	.05	.02	.01
☐	47T Greg Colbrunn	.10	.05	.01
☐	48T Joey Hamilton	.15	.07	.02
☐	49T Marvin Freeman	.05	.02	.01
☐	50T Terry Mulholland	.05	.02	.01
☐	51T Keith Mitchell	.05	.02	.01
☐	52T Dwight Smith	.05	.02	.01
☐	53T Shawn Boskie	.05	.02	.01
☐	54T Kevin Witt	.50	.23	.06
☐	55T Ron Gant	.10	.05	.01
☐	56T 1994 Prospects	.50	.23	.06
	Trenidad Hubbard			
	Jason Schmidt			
	Larry Sutton			
	Stephen Larkin			
☐	57T Jody Reed	.05	.02	.01
☐	58T Rick Helling	.05	.02	.01
☐	59T John Powell	.10	.05	.01
☐	60T Eddie Murray	.25	.11	.03
☐	61T Joe Hall	.05	.02	.01
☐	62T Jorge Fabregas	.05	.02	.01
☐	63T Mike Mordecai	.05	.02	.01
☐	64T Ed Vosberg	.05	.02	.01
☐	65T Rickey Henderson	.15	.07	.02
☐	66T Tim Grieve	.10	.05	.01
☐	67T Jon Lieber	.05	.02	.01
☐	68T Chris Howard	.05	.02	.01
☐	69T Matt Walbeck	.05	.02	.01
☐	70T Chan Ho Park	.20	.09	.03
☐	71T Bryan Eversgerd	.05	.02	.01
☐	72T John Dettmer	.05	.02	.01
☐	73T Erik Hanson	.05	.02	.01
☐	74T Mike Thurman	.20	.09	.03
☐	75T Bobby Ayala	.05	.02	.01
☐	76T Rafael Palmeiro	.15	.07	.02
☐	77T Bret Boone	.15	.07	.02
☐	78T Paul Shuey	.10	.05	.01
☐	79T Kevin Foster	.05	.02	.01
☐	80T Dave Magadan	.05	.02	.01
☐	81T Bip Roberts	.05	.02	.01
☐	82T Howard Johnson	.05	.02	.01
☐	83T Xavier Hernandez	.05	.02	.01
☐	84T Ross Powell	.05	.02	.01
☐	85T Doug Million	.50	.23	.06
☐	86T Geronimo Berroa	.05	.02	.01
☐	87T Mark Farris	.25	.11	.03
☐	88T Butch Henry	.05	.02	.01
☐	89T Junior Felix	.05	.02	.01
☐	90T Bo Jackson	.15	.07	.02
☐	91T Hector Carrasco	.05	.02	.01
☐	92T Charlie O'Brien	.05	.02	.01
☐	93T Omar Vizquel	.10	.05	.01
☐	94T David Segui	.10	.05	.01
☐	95T Dustin Hermanson	.25	.11	.03
☐	96T Gar Finnvold	.05	.02	.01
☐	97T Dave Stevens	.05	.02	.01
☐	98T Corey Pointer	.25	.11	.03
☐	99T Felix Fermin	.05	.02	.01
☐	100T Lee Smith	.15	.07	.02
☐	101T Reid Ryan	.75	.35	.09
☐	102T Bobby Munoz	.05	.02	.01
☐	103T Anatomy of a Trade	.30	.14	.04
	Deion Sanders			
	Roberto Kelly			
☐	104T Turner Ward	.05	.02	.01
☐	105T W.VanLandingham	.20	.09	.03
☐	106T Vince Coleman	.05	.02	.01
☐	107T Stan Javier	.05	.02	.01
☐	108T Darrin Jackson	.05	.02	.01
☐	109T C.J. Nitkowski	.40	.18	.05
☐	110T Anthony Young	.05	.02	.01
☐	111T Kurt Miller	.05	.02	.01
☐	112T Paul Konerko	.75	.35	.09
☐	113T Walt Weiss	.05	.02	.01
☐	114T Daryl Boston	.05	.02	.01
☐	115T Will Clark	.25	.11	.03
☐	116T Matt Smith	.40	.18	.05
☐	117T Mark Leiter	.05	.02	.01
☐	118T Gregg Olson	.05	.02	.01
☐	119T Tony Pena	.05	.02	.01
☐	120T Jose Vizcaino	.05	.02	.01
☐	121T Rick White	.05	.02	.01
☐	122T Rich Rowland	.05	.02	.01
☐	123T Jeff Reboulet	.05	.02	.01
☐	124T Greg Hibbard	.05	.02	.01
☐	125T Chris Sabo	.05	.02	.01
☐	126T Doug Jones	.05	.02	.01

		MINT	NRMT	EXC
☐	127T Tony Fernandez	.05	.02	.01
☐	128T Carlos Reyes	.05	.02	.01
☐	129T Kevin Brown	.30	.14	.04
☐	130T Ryne Sandberg Farewell	1.00	.45	.12
☐	131T Ryne Sandberg Farewell	1.00	.45	.12
☐	132T Checklist 1-132	.05	.02	.01

1994 Topps Traded Finest

Issued one set per Topps Traded factory set, these eight cards showcase top young talent. The metallic cards feature a rainbow colored front with a color player photo and the backs also carry a color player photo with 1994 monthly statistics through July 10. The backs also have a write-up about the first half of the season. There are six MVP candidate and two Rookie of the Year candidate cards.

	MINT	NRMT	EXC
COMPLETE SET (8)	35.00	16.00	4.40
COMMON CARD (1-8)	1.50	.70	.19

		MINT	NRMT	EXC
☐	1 Greg Maddux NL MVP Candidate	10.00	4.50	1.25
☐	2 Mike Piazza NL MVP Candidate	4.00	1.80	.50
☐	3 Matt Williams NL MVP Candidate	1.50	.70	.19
☐	4 Raul Mondesi NL ROY Candidate	2.50	1.10	.30
☐	5 Ken Griffey Jr. AL MVP Candidate	10.00	4.50	1.25
☐	6 Kenny Lofton AL MVP Candidate	3.00	1.35	.35
☐	7 Frank Thomas AL MVP Candidate	10.00	4.50	1.25
☐	8 Manny Ramirez AL ROY Candidate	4.00	1.80	.50

1995 Topps

These 660 standard-size cards feature color action player photos with white

borders on the fronts. This set was released in two series. The first series contained 396 cards while the second series had 264 cards. The player's name in gold-foil appears below the photo, with his position and team name underneath. The horizontal backs carry a color player close-up with a color player cut-out superimposed over it. Player biography, statistics and career highlights complete the backs. One "Own The Game" instant winner card has been inserted in every 120 packs. Rookie cards in this set include Jacob Cruz, Tommy Davis, Scott Elarton, Jay Payton and Carlos Perez.

	MINT	NRMT	EXC
COMP.HOB.FACT.SET (677)	55.00	25.00	7.00
COMP.RET.FACT.SET (677)	50.00	22.00	6.25
COMPLETE SET (660)	45.00	20.00	5.50
COMPLETE SERIES 1 (396)	25.00	11.00	3.10
COMPLETE SERIES 2 (264)	20.00	9.00	2.50
COMMON CARD (1-396)	.10	.05	.01
COMMON CARD (397-660)	.10	.05	.01

		MINT	NRMT	EXC
☐	1 Frank Thomas	3.00	1.35	.35
☐	2 Mickey Morandini	.10	.05	.01
☐	3 Babe Ruth	2.00	.90	.25
☐	4 Scott Cooper	.10	.05	.01
☐	5 David Cone	.30	.14	.04
☐	6 Jacob Shumate	.20	.09	.03
☐	7 Trevor Hoffman	.20	.09	.03
☐	8 Shane Mack	.10	.05	.01
☐	9 Delino DeShields	.20	.09	.03
☐	10 Matt Williams	.50	.23	.06
☐	11 Sammy Sosa	.30	.14	.04
☐	12 Gary DiSarcina	.10	.05	.01
☐	13 Kenny Rogers	.10	.05	.01
☐	14 Jose Vizcaino	.10	.05	.01
☐	15 Lou Whitaker	.30	.14	.04
☐	16 Ron Darling	.10	.05	.01
☐	17 Dave Nilsson	.20	.09	.03
☐	18 Chris Hammond	.10	.05	.01
☐	19 Sid Bream	.10	.05	.01
☐	20 Denny Martinez	.20	.09	.03
☐	21 Orlando Merced	.10	.05	.01
☐	22 John Wetteland	.20	.09	.03
☐	23 Mike Devereaux	.20	.09	.03
☐	24 Rene Arocha	.10	.05	.01
☐	25 Jay Buhner	.30	.14	.04
☐	26 Darren Holmes	.20	.09	.03
☐	27 Hal Morris	.20	.09	.03
☐	28 Brian Buchanan	.25	.11	.03
☐	29 Keith Miller	.10	.05	.01
☐	30 Paul Molitor	.30	.14	.04
☐	31 Dave West	.10	.05	.01

□	32	Tony Tarasco	.20	.09	.03
□	33	Scott Sanders	.10	.05	.01
□	34	Eddie Zambrano	.10	.05	.01
□	35	Ricky Bones	.10	.05	.01
□	36	John Valentin	.30	.14	.04
□	37	Kevin Tapani	.10	.05	.01
□	38	Tim Wallach	.10	.05	.01
□	39	Darren Lewis	.10	.05	.01
□	40	Travis Fryman	.30	.14	.04
□	41	Mark Leiter	.10	.05	.01
□	42	Jose Bautista	.10	.05	.01
□	43	Pete Smith	.10	.05	.01
□	44	Bret Barberie	.10	.05	.01
□	45	Dennis Eckersley	.30	.14	.04
□	46	Ken Hill	.20	.09	.03
□	47	Chad Ogea	.20	.09	.03
□	48	Pete Harnisch	.10	.05	.01
□	49	James Baldwin	.10	.05	.01
□	50	Mike Mussina	.40	.18	.05
□	51	Al Martin	.20	.09	.03
□	52	Mark Thompson	.20	.09	.03
□	53	Matt Smith	.10	.05	.01
□	54	Joey Hamilton	.20	.09	.03
□	55	Edgar Martinez	.30	.14	.04
□	56	John Smiley	.10	.05	.01
□	57	Rey Sanchez	.10	.05	.01
□	58	Mike Timlin	.10	.05	.01
□	59	Ricky Bottalico	.10	.05	.01
□	60	Jim Abbott	.30	.14	.04
□	61	Mike Kelly	.20	.09	.03
□	62	Brian Jordan	.30	.14	.04
□	63	Ken Ryan	.10	.05	.01
□	64	Matt Mieske	.10	.05	.01
□	65	Rick Aguilera	.20	.09	.03
□	66	Ismael Valdes	.10	.05	.01
□	67	Royce Clayton	.20	.09	.03
□	68	Junior Felix	.10	.05	.01
□	69	Harold Reynolds	.10	.05	.01
□	70	Juan Gonzalez	.75	.35	.09
□	71	Kelly Stinnett	.10	.05	.01
□	72	Carlos Reyes	.10	.05	.01
□	73	Dave Weathers	.10	.05	.01
□	74	Mel Rojas	.20	.09	.03
□	75	Doug Drabek	.20	.09	.03
□	76	Charles Nagy	.20	.09	.03
□	77	Tim Raines	.30	.14	.04
□	78	Midre Cummings	.20	.09	.03
□	79	First Base Prospects	.50	.23	.06
		Gene Schall			
		Scott Talanoa			
		Harold Williams			
		Ray Brown			
□	80	Rafael Palmeiro	.30	.14	.04
□	81	Charlie Hayes	.20	.09	.03
□	82	Ray Lankford	.30	.14	.04
□	83	Tim Davis	.10	.05	.01
□	84	C.J. Nitkowski	.10	.05	.01
□	85	Andy Ashby	.10	.05	.01
□	86	Gerald Williams	.10	.05	.01
□	87	Terry Shumpert	.10	.05	.01
□	88	Heathcliff Slocumb	.10	.05	.01
□	89	Domingo Cedeno	.10	.05	.01
□	90	Mark Grace	.30	.14	.04
□	91	Brad Woodall	.10	.05	.01
□	92	Gar Finnvold	.10	.05	.01
□	93	Jaime Navarro	.10	.05	.01
□	94	Carlos Hernandez	.10	.05	.01
□	95	Mark Langston	.30	.14	.04
□	96	Chuck Carr	.10	.05	.01
□	97	Mike Gardiner	.10	.05	.01
□	98	Dave McCarty	.10	.05	.01
□	99	Cris Carpenter	.10	.05	.01
□	100	Barry Bonds	.75	.35	.09
□	101	David Segui	.10	.05	.01
□	102	Scott Brosius	.10	.05	.01
□	103	Mariano Duncan	.10	.05	.01
□	104	Kenny Lofton	1.00	.45	.12
□	105	Ken Caminiti	.20	.09	.03
□	106	Darrin Jackson	.10	.05	.01
□	107	Jim Poole	.10	.05	.01
□	108	Wil Cordero	.20	.09	.03
□	109	Danny Miceli	.10	.05	.01
□	110	Walt Weiss	.20	.09	.03
□	111	Tom Pagnozzi	.10	.05	.01
□	112	Terrence Long	.20	.09	.03
□	113	Bret Boone	.30	.14	.04
□	114	Daryl Boston	.10	.05	.01
□	115	Wally Joyner	.20	.09	.03
□	116	Rob Butler	.10	.05	.01
□	117	Rafael Belliard	.10	.05	.01
□	118	Luis Lopez	.10	.05	.01
□	119	Tony Fossas	.10	.05	.01
□	120	Len Dykstra	.30	.14	.04
□	121	Mike Morgan	.10	.05	.01
□	122	Denny Hocking	.10	.05	.01
□	123	Kevin Gross	.10	.05	.01
□	124	Todd Benzinger	.10	.05	.01
□	125	John Doherty	.10	.05	.01
□	126	Eduardo Perez	.10	.05	.01
□	127	Dan Smith	.10	.05	.01
□	128	Joe Orsulak	.10	.05	.01
□	129	Brent Gates	.20	.09	.03
□	130	Jeff Conine	.30	.14	.04
□	131	Doug Henry	.10	.05	.01
□	132	Paul Sorrento	.10	.05	.01
□	133	Mike Hampton	.10	.05	.01
□	134	Tim Spehr	.10	.05	.01
□	135	Julio Franco	.20	.09	.03
□	136	Mike Dyer	.10	.05	.01
□	137	Chris Sabo	.10	.05	.01
□	138	Rheal Cormier	.10	.05	.01
□	139	Paul Konerko	.30	.14	.04
□	140	Dante Bichette	.40	.18	.05
□	141	Chuck McElroy	.10	.05	.01
□	142	Mike Stanley	.20	.09	.03
□	143	Bob Hamelin	.10	.05	.01
□	144	Tommy Greene	.10	.05	.01
□	145	John Smoltz	.20	.09	.03
□	146	Ed Sprague	.10	.05	.01
□	147	Ray McDavid	.20	.09	.03
□	148	Otis Nixon	.10	.05	.01
□	149	Turk Wendell	.10	.05	.01
□	150	Chris James	.10	.05	.01
□	151	Derek Parks	.10	.05	.01
□	152	Jose Offerman	.10	.05	.01
□	153	Tony Clark	.10	.05	.01
□	154	Chad Curtis	.20	.09	.03
□	155	Mark Portugal	.10	.05	.01
□	156	Bill Pulsipher	.30	.14	.04
□	157	Troy Neel	.10	.05	.01
□	158	Dave Winfield	.30	.14	.04
□	159	Bill Wegman	.10	.05	.01
□	160	Benito Santiago	.10	.05	.01
□	161	Jose Mesa	.20	.09	.03
□	162	Luis Gonzalez	.20	.09	.03
□	163	Alex Fernandez	.30	.14	.04
□	164	Freddie Benavides	.10	.05	.01
□	165	Ben McDonald	.10	.05	.01
□	166	Blas Minor	.10	.05	.01
□	167	Bret Wagner	.10	.05	.01
□	168	Mac Suzuki	.20	.09	.03
□	169	Roberto Mejia	.20	.09	.03

170	Wade Boggs	.30	.14	.04
171	Calvin Reese	.20	.09	.03
172	Hipolito Pichardo	.10	.05	.01
173	Kim Batiste	.10	.05	.01
174	Darren Hall	.10	.05	.01
175	Tom Glavine	.30	.14	.04
176	Phil Plantier	.10	.05	.01
177	Chris Howard	.10	.05	.01
178	Karl Rhodes	.10	.05	.01
179	LaTroy Hawkins	.10	.05	.01
180	Raul Mondesi	.75	.35	.09
181	Jeff Reed	.10	.05	.01
182	Milt Cuyler	.10	.05	.01
183	Jim Edmonds	.40	.18	.05
184	Hector Fajardo	.10	.05	.01
185	Jeff Kent	.20	.09	.03
186	Wilson Alvarez	.30	.14	.04
187	Geronimo Berroa	.10	.05	.01
188	Billy Spiers	.10	.05	.01
189	Derek Lilliquist	.10	.05	.01
190	Craig Biggio	.30	.14	.04
191	Roberto Hernandez	.20	.09	.03
192	Bob Natal	.10	.05	.01
193	Bobby Ayala	.10	.05	.01
194	Travis Miller	.30	.14	.04
195	Bob Tewksbury	.10	.05	.01
196	Rondell White	.30	.14	.04
197	Steve Cooke	.10	.05	.01
198	Jeff Branson	.10	.05	.01
199	Derek Jeter	.50	.23	.06
200	Tim Salmon	.50	.23	.06
201	Steve Frey	.10	.05	.01
202	Kent Mercker	.10	.05	.01
203	Randy Johnson	.60	.25	.07
204	Todd Worrell	.10	.05	.01
205	Mo Vaughn	.50	.23	.06
206	Howard Johnson	.10	.05	.01
207	John Wasdin	.10	.05	.01
208	Eddie Williams	.10	.05	.01
209	Tim Belcher	.10	.05	.01
210	Jeff Montgomery	.20	.09	.03
211	Kirt Manwaring	.10	.05	.01
212	Ben Grieve	.75	.35	.09
213	Pat Hentgen	.20	.09	.03
214	Shawon Dunston	.10	.05	.01
215	Mike Greenwell	.20	.09	.03
216	Alex Diaz	.10	.05	.01
217	Pat Mahomes	.10	.05	.01
218	Dave Hansen	.10	.05	.01
219	Kevin Rogers	.10	.05	.01
220	Cecil Fielder	.30	.14	.04
221	Andrew Lorraine	.10	.05	.01
222	Jack Armstrong	.10	.05	.01
223	Todd Hundley	.20	.09	.03
224	Mark Acre	.10	.05	.01
225	Darrell Whitmore	.10	.05	.01
226	Randy Milligan	.10	.05	.01
227	Wayne Kirby	.10	.05	.01
228	Darryl Kile	.10	.05	.01
229	Bob Zupcic	.10	.05	.01
230	Jay Bell	.20	.09	.03
231	Dustin Hermanson	.10	.05	.01
232	Harold Baines	.20	.09	.03
233	Alan Benes	.30	.14	.04
234	Felix Fermin	.10	.05	.01
235	Ellis Burks	.20	.09	.03
236	Jeff Brantley	.10	.05	.01
237	Outfield Prospects	1.50	.70	.19
	Brian Hunter			
	Jose Malave			
	Karim Garcia			
	Shane Pullen			
238	Matt Nokes	.10	.05	.01
239	Ben Rivera	.10	.05	.01
240	Joe Carter	.30	.14	.04
241	Jeff Granger	.10	.05	.01
242	Terry Pendleton	.20	.09	.03
243	Melvin Nieves	.30	.14	.04
244	Frankie Rodriguez	.20	.09	.03
245	Darryl Hamilton	.10	.05	.01
246	Brooks Kieschnick	.60	.25	.07
247	Todd Hollandsworth	.10	.05	.01
248	Joe Rosselli	.10	.05	.01
249	Bill Gullickson	.10	.05	.01
250	Chuck Knoblauch	.30	.14	.04
251	Kurt Miller	.10	.05	.01
252	Bobby Jones	.30	.14	.04
253	Lance Blankenship	.10	.05	.01
254	Matt Whiteside	.10	.05	.01
255	Darrin Fletcher	.10	.05	.01
256	Eric Plunk	.10	.05	.01
257	Shane Reynolds	.10	.05	.01
258	Norberto Martin	.10	.05	.01
259	Mike Thurman	.10	.05	.01
260	Andy Van Slyke	.20	.09	.03
261	Dwight Smith	.10	.05	.01
262	Allen Watson	.20	.09	.03
263	Dan Wilson	.20	.09	.03
264	Brent Mayne	.10	.05	.01
265	Bip Roberts	.10	.05	.01
266	Sterling Hitchcock	.20	.09	.03
267	Alex Gonzalez	.20	.09	.03
268	Greg Harris	.10	.05	.01
269	Ricky Jordan	.10	.05	.01
270	Johnny Ruffin	.10	.05	.01
271	Mike Stanton	.10	.05	.01
272	Rich Rowland	.10	.05	.01
273	Steve Trachsel	.10	.05	.01
274	Pedro Munoz	.20	.09	.03
275	Ramon Martinez	.20	.09	.03
276	Dave Henderson	.10	.05	.01
277	Chris Gomez	.20	.09	.03
278	Joe Grahe	.10	.05	.01
279	Rusty Greer	.10	.05	.01
280	John Franco	.20	.09	.03
281	Mike Bordick	.10	.05	.01
282	Jeff D'Amico	.20	.09	.03
283	Dave Magadan	.10	.05	.01
284	Tony Pena	.10	.05	.01
285	Greg Swindell	.10	.05	.01
286	Doug Million	.20	.09	.03
287	Gabe White	.10	.05	.01
288	Trey Beamon	.30	.14	.04
289	Arthur Rhodes	.10	.05	.01
290	Juan Guzman	.20	.09	.03
291	Jose Oquendo	.10	.05	.01
292	Willie Blair	.10	.05	.01
293	Eddie Taubensee	.10	.05	.01
294	Steve Howe	.10	.05	.01
295	Greg Maddux	3.00	1.35	.35
296	Mike Macfarlane	.10	.05	.01
297	Curt Schilling	.10	.05	.01
298	Phil Clark	.10	.05	.01
299	Woody Williams	.10	.05	.01
300	Jose Canseco	.50	.23	.06
301	Aaron Sele	.20	.09	.03
302	Carl Willis	.10	.05	.01
303	Steve Buechele	.10	.05	.01
304	Dave Burba	.10	.05	.01
305	Orel Hershiser	.20	.09	.03
306	Damion Easley	.10	.05	.01
307	Mike Henneman	.10	.05	.01

☐ 308	Josias Manzanillo	.10	.05	.01
☐ 309	Kevin Seitzer	.10	.05	.01
☐ 310	Ruben Sierra	.30	.14	.04
☐ 311	Bryan Harvey	.20	.09	.03
☐ 312	Jim Thome	.50	.23	.06
☐ 313	Ramon Castro	.40	.18	.05
☐ 314	Lance Johnson	.10	.05	.01
☐ 315	Marquis Grissom	.30	.14	.04
☐ 316	Starting Pitcher	.30	.14	.04
	Prospects			
	Terrell Wade			
	Juan Acevedo			
	Matt Arrandale			
	Eddie Priest			
☐ 317	Paul Wagner	.10	.05	.01
☐ 318	Jamie Moyer	.10	.05	.01
☐ 319	Todd Zeile	.20	.09	.03
☐ 320	Chris Bosio	.10	.05	.01
☐ 321	Steve Reed	.10	.05	.01
☐ 322	Erik Hanson	.20	.09	.03
☐ 323	Luis Polonia	.10	.05	.01
☐ 324	Ryan Klesko	.60	.25	.07
☐ 325	Kevin Appier	.20	.09	.03
☐ 326	Jim Eisenreich	.10	.05	.01
☐ 327	Randy Knorr	.10	.05	.01
☐ 328	Craig Shipley	.10	.05	.01
☐ 329	Tim Naehring	.10	.05	.01
☐ 330	Randy Myers	.20	.09	.03
☐ 331	Alex Cole	.10	.05	.01
☐ 332	Jim Gott	.10	.05	.01
☐ 333	Mike Jackson	.10	.05	.01
☐ 334	John Flaherty	.10	.05	.01
☐ 335	Chili Davis	.20	.09	.03
☐ 336	Benji Gil	.20	.09	.03
☐ 337	Jason Jacome	.10	.05	.01
☐ 338	Stan Javier	.10	.05	.01
☐ 339	Mike Fetters	.10	.05	.01
☐ 340	Rich Renteria	.10	.05	.01
☐ 341	Kevin Witt	.20	.09	.03
☐ 342	Scott Servais	.10	.05	.01
☐ 343	Craig Grebeck	.10	.05	.01
☐ 344	Kirk Rueter	.10	.05	.01
☐ 345	Don Slaught	.10	.05	.01
☐ 346	Armando Benitez	.10	.05	.01
☐ 347	Ozzie Smith	.60	.25	.07
☐ 348	Mike Blowers	.20	.09	.03
☐ 349	Armando Reynoso	.10	.05	.01
☐ 350	Barry Larkin	.40	.18	.05
☐ 351	Mike Williams	.10	.05	.01
☐ 352	Scott Kamieniecki	.10	.05	.01
☐ 353	Gary Gaetti	.20	.09	.03
☐ 354	Todd Stottlemyre	.10	.05	.01
☐ 355	Fred McGriff	.40	.18	.05
☐ 356	Tim Mauser	.10	.05	.01
☐ 357	Chris Gwynn	.10	.05	.01
☐ 358	Frank Castillo	.10	.05	.01
☐ 359	Jeff Reboulet	.10	.05	.01
☐ 360	Roger Clemens	.50	.23	.06
☐ 361	Mark Carreon	.10	.05	.01
☐ 362	Chad Kreuter	.10	.05	.01
☐ 363	Mark Farris	.10	.05	.01
☐ 364	Bob Welch	.20	.09	.03
☐ 365	Dean Palmer	.20	.09	.03
☐ 366	Jeromy Burnitz	.10	.05	.01
☐ 367	B.J. Surhoff	.20	.09	.03
☐ 368	Mike Butcher	.10	.05	.01
☐ 369	Relief Pitcher	.15	.07	.02
	Prospects			
	Brad Clontz			
	Steve Phoenix			
	Scott Gentile			
	Bucky Buckles			
☐ 370	Eddie Murray	.40	.18	.05
☐ 371	Orlando Miller	.20	.09	.03
☐ 372	Ron Karkovice	.10	.05	.01
☐ 373	Richie Lewis	.10	.05	.01
☐ 374	Lenny Webster	.10	.05	.01
☐ 375	Jeff Tackett	.10	.05	.01
☐ 376	Tom Urbani	.10	.05	.01
☐ 377	Tino Martinez	.30	.14	.04
☐ 378	Mark Dewey	.10	.05	.01
☐ 379	Charles O'Brien	.10	.05	.01
☐ 380	Terry Mulholland	.10	.05	.01
☐ 381	Thomas Howard	.10	.05	.01
☐ 382	Chris Haney	.10	.05	.01
☐ 383	Billy Hatcher	.10	.05	.01
☐ 384	Jeff Bagwell AS	.75	.35	.09
	Frank Thomas AS			
☐ 385	Bret Boone AS	.20	.09	.03
	Carlos Baerga AS			
☐ 386	Matt Williams AS	.20	.09	.03
	Wade Boggs AS			
☐ 387	Wil Cordero AS	.60	.25	.07
	Cal Ripken AS			
☐ 388	Barry Bonds AS	.60	.25	.07
	Ken Griffey AS			
☐ 389	Tony Gwynn AS	.50	.23	.06
	Albert Belle AS			
☐ 390	Dante Bichette AS	.30	.14	.04
	Kirby Puckett AS			
☐ 391	Mike Piazza AS	.30	.14	.04
	Mike Stanley AS			
☐ 392	Greg Maddux AS	.50	.23	.06
	David Cone AS			
☐ 393	Danny Jackson AS	.10	.05	.01
	Jimmy Key AS			
☐ 394	John Franco AS	.10	.05	.01
	Lee Smith AS			
☐ 395	Checklist 1-198	.10	.05	.01
☐ 396	Checklist 199-396	.10	.05	.01
☐ 397	Ken Griffey Jr.	3.00	1.35	.35
☐ 398	Rick Heiserman RC	.20	.09	.03
☐ 399	Don Mattingly	1.50	.70	.19
☐ 400	Henry Rodriguez	.10	.05	.01
☐ 401	Lenny Harris	.10	.05	.01
☐ 402	Ryan Thompson	.10	.05	.01
☐ 403	Darren Oliver	.10	.05	.01
☐ 404	Omar Vizquel	.20	.09	.03
☐ 405	Jeff Bagwell	1.00	.45	.12
☐ 406	Doug Webb	.15	.07	.02
☐ 407	Todd Van Poppel	.10	.05	.01
☐ 408	Leo Gomez	.10	.05	.01
☐ 409	Mark Whiten	.10	.05	.01
☐ 410	Pedro Martinez	.10	.05	.01
☐ 411	Reggie Sanders	.30	.14	.04
☐ 412	Kevin Foster	.10	.05	.01
☐ 413	Danny Tartabull	.20	.09	.03
☐ 414	Jeff Blauser	.10	.05	.01
☐ 415	Mike Magnante	.10	.05	.01
☐ 416	Tom Candiotti	.10	.05	.01
☐ 417	Rod Beck	.10	.05	.01
☐ 418	Jody Reed	.10	.05	.01
☐ 419	Vince Coleman	.10	.05	.01
☐ 420	Danny Jackson	.10	.05	.01
☐ 421	Ryan Nye	.40	.18	.05
☐ 422	Larry Walker	.40	.18	.05
☐ 423	Russ Johnson DP	.20	.09	.03
☐ 424	Pat Borders	.10	.05	.01
☐ 425	Lee Smith	.30	.14	.04
☐ 426	Paul O'Neil	.30	.14	.04
☐ 427	Devon White	.20	.09	.03
☐ 428	Jim Bullinger	.10	.05	.01

☐ 429	Starting Pitchers	.20	.09	.03
	Prospects			
	Greg Hansell			
	Brian Sackinsky			
	Carey Paige			
	Rob Welch			
☐ 430	Steve Avery	.20	.09	.03
☐ 431	Tony Gwynn	1.00	.45	.12
☐ 432	Pat Meares	.10	.05	.01
☐ 433	Bill Swift	.10	.05	.01
☐ 434	David Wells	.10	.05	.01
☐ 435	John Briscoe	.10	.05	.01
☐ 436	Roger Pavlik	.10	.05	.01
☐ 437	Jayson Peterson	.30	.14	.04
☐ 438	Roberto Alomar	.60	.25	.07
☐ 439	Billy Brewer	.10	.05	.01
☐ 440	Gary Sheffield	.30	.14	.04
☐ 441	Lou Frazier	.10	.05	.01
☐ 442	Terry Steinbach	.20	.09	.03
☐ 443	Jay Payton	1.50	.70	.19
☐ 444	Jason Bere	.10	.05	.01
☐ 445	Denny Neagle	.20	.09	.03
☐ 446	Andres Galarraga	.30	.14	.04
☐ 447	Hector Carrasco	.10	.05	.01
☐ 448	Bill Risley	.10	.05	.01
☐ 449	Andy Benes	.20	.09	.03
☐ 450	Jim Leyritz	.10	.05	.01
☐ 451	Jose Oliva	.10	.05	.01
☐ 452	Greg Vaughn	.10	.05	.01
☐ 453	Rich Monteleone	.10	.05	.01
☐ 454	Tony Eusebio	.10	.05	.01
☐ 455	Chuck Finley	.20	.09	.03
☐ 456	Kevin Brown	.10	.05	.01
☐ 457	Joe Boever	.10	.05	.01
☐ 458	Bobby Munoz	.10	.05	.01
☐ 459	Bret Saberhagen	.20	.09	.03
☐ 460	Kurt Abbott	.10	.05	.01
☐ 461	Bobby Witt	.10	.05	.01
☐ 462	Cliff Floyd	.30	.14	.04
☐ 463	Mark Clark	.10	.05	.01
☐ 464	Andujar Cedeno	.10	.05	.01
☐ 465	Marvin Freeman	.10	.05	.01
☐ 466	Mike Piazza	1.25	.55	.16
☐ 467	Willie Greene	.10	.05	.01
☐ 468	Pat Kelly	.10	.05	.01
☐ 469	Carlos Delgado	.20	.09	.03
☐ 470	Willie Banks	.10	.05	.01
☐ 471	Matt Walbeck	.10	.05	.01
☐ 472	Mark McGwire	.30	.14	.04
☐ 473	McKay Christensen	.25	.11	.03
☐ 474	Alan Trammell	.30	.14	.04
☐ 475	Tom Gordon	.10	.05	.01
☐ 476	Greg Colbrunn	.30	.14	.04
☐ 477	Darren Daulton	.20	.09	.03
☐ 478	Albie Lopez	.10	.05	.01
☐ 479	Robin Ventura	.30	.14	.04
☐ 480	Catcher Prospects	.25	.11	.03
	Eddie Perez			
	Jason Kendall			
	Einar Diaz			
	Bret Hemphill			
☐ 481	Bryan Eversgerd	.10	.05	.01
☐ 482	Dave Fleming	.10	.05	.01
☐ 483	Scott Livingstone	.10	.05	.01
☐ 484	Pete Schourek	.30	.14	.04
☐ 485	Bernie Williams	.20	.09	.03
☐ 486	Mark Lemke	.20	.09	.03
☐ 487	Eric Karros	.30	.14	.04
☐ 488	Scott Ruffcorn	.10	.05	.01
☐ 489	Billy Ashley	.10	.05	.01
☐ 490	Rico Brogna	.30	.14	.04

☐ 491	John Burkett	.10	.05	.01
☐ 492	Cade Gaspar	.30	.14	.04
☐ 493	Jorge Fabregas	.10	.05	.01
☐ 494	Greg Gagne	.10	.05	.01
☐ 495	Doug Jones	.10	.05	.01
☐ 496	Troy O'Leary	.20	.09	.03
☐ 497	Pat Rapp	.20	.09	.03
☐ 498	Butch Henry	.10	.05	.01
☐ 499	John Olerud	.20	.09	.03
☐ 500	John Hudek	.10	.05	.01
☐ 501	Jeff King	.10	.05	.01
☐ 502	Bobby Bonilla	.30	.14	.04
☐ 503	Albert Belle	1.25	.55	.16
☐ 504	Rick Wilkins	.10	.05	.01
☐ 505	John Jaha	.20	.09	.03
☐ 506	Nigel Wilson	.10	.05	.01
☐ 507	Sid Fernandez	.10	.05	.01
☐ 508	Deion Sanders	.60	.25	.07
☐ 509	Gil Heredia	.10	.05	.01
☐ 510	Scott Elarton	.50	.23	.06
☐ 511	Melido Perez	.10	.05	.01
☐ 512	Greg McMichael	.10	.05	.01
☐ 513	Rusty Meacham	.10	.05	.01
☐ 514	Shawn Green	.30	.14	.04
☐ 515	Carlos Garcia	.10	.05	.01
☐ 516	Dave Stevens	.10	.05	.01
☐ 517	Eric Young	.20	.09	.03
☐ 518	Omar Daal	.10	.05	.01
☐ 519	Kirk Gibson	.20	.09	.03
☐ 520	Spike Owen	.10	.05	.01
☐ 521	Jacob Cruz	.60	.25	.07
☐ 522	Sandy Alomar	.10	.05	.01
☐ 523	Steve Bedrosian	.10	.05	.01
☐ 524	Ricky Gutierrez	.10	.05	.01
☐ 525	Dave Veres	.10	.05	.01
☐ 526	Gregg Jefferies	.30	.14	.04
☐ 527	Jose Valentin	.10	.05	.01
☐ 528	Robb Nen	.20	.09	.03
☐ 529	Jose Rijo	.20	.09	.03
☐ 530	Sean Berry	.10	.05	.01
☐ 531	Mike Gallego	.10	.05	.01
☐ 532	Roberto Kelly	.20	.09	.03
☐ 533	Kevin Stocker	.10	.05	.01
☐ 534	Kirby Puckett	1.00	.45	.12
☐ 535	Chipper Jones	1.25	.55	.16
☐ 536	Russ Davis	.20	.09	.03
☐ 537	Jon Lieber	.10	.05	.01
☐ 538	Trey Moore	.20	.09	.03
☐ 539	Joe Girardi	.10	.05	.01
☐ 540	Second Baseman	.25	.11	.03
	Prospects			
	Quilvio Veras			
	Arquimedez Pozo			
	Miguel Cairo			
	Jason Camilli			
☐ 541	Tony Phillips	.10	.05	.01
☐ 542	Brian Anderson	.10	.05	.01
☐ 543	Ivan Rodriguez	.30	.14	.04
☐ 544	Jeff Cirillo	.20	.09	.03
☐ 545	Joey Cora	.10	.05	.01
☐ 546	Chris Hoiles	.20	.09	.03
☐ 547	Bernard Gilkey	.20	.09	.03
☐ 548	Mike Lansing	.10	.05	.01
☐ 549	Jimmy Key	.10	.05	.01
☐ 550	Mark Wohlers	.10	.05	.01
☐ 551	Chris Clemons	.15	.07	.02
☐ 552	Vinny Castilla	.30	.14	.04
☐ 553	Mark Guthrie	.10	.05	.01
☐ 554	Mike Lieberthal	.10	.05	.01
☐ 555	Tommy Davis	.50	.23	.06
☐ 556	Robby Thompson	.10	.05	.01

☐ 557 Danny Bautista	.10	.05	.01
☐ 558 Will Clark	.40	.18	.05
☐ 559 Rickey Henderson	.30	.14	.04
☐ 560 Todd Jones	.10	.05	.01
☐ 561 Jack McDowell	.30	.14	.04
☐ 562 Carlos Rodriguez	.10	.05	.01
☐ 563 Mark Eichhorn	.10	.05	.01
☐ 564 Jeff Nelson	.10	.05	.01
☐ 565 Eric Anthony	.10	.05	.01
☐ 566 Randy Velarde	.10	.05	.01
☐ 567 Javier Lopez	.40	.18	.05
☐ 568 Kevin Mitchell	.20	.09	.03
☐ 569 Steve Karsay	.10	.05	.01
☐ 570 Brian Meadows	.25	.11	.03
☐ 571 Rey Ordonez	.20	.09	.03
Mike Metcalfe			
☐ 572 John Kruk	.20	.09	.03
☐ 573 Scott Leius	.10	.05	.01
☐ 574 John Patterson	.10	.05	.01
☐ 575 Kevin Brown	.10	.05	.01
☐ 576 Mike Moore	.10	.05	.01
☐ 577 Manny Ramirez	1.25	.55	.16
☐ 578 Jose Lind	.10	.05	.01
☐ 579 Derrick May	.20	.09	.03
☐ 580 Cal Eldred	.10	.05	.01
☐ 581 Third Baseman	.30	.14	.04
Prospects			
David Bell			
Joel Chelmis			
Lino Diaz			
Aaron Boone			
☐ 582 J.T. Snow	.30	.14	.04
☐ 583 Luis Sojo	.10	.05	.01
☐ 584 Moises Alou	.20	.09	.03
☐ 585 Dave Clark	.10	.05	.01
☐ 586 Dave Hollins	.10	.05	.01
☐ 587 Nomar Garciaparra	.30	.14	.04
☐ 588 Cal Ripken	3.00	1.35	.35
☐ 589 Pedro Astacio	.10	.05	.01
☐ 590 J.R. Phillips	.10	.05	.01
☐ 591 Jeff Frye	.10	.05	.01
☐ 592 Bo Jackson	.30	.14	.04
☐ 593 Steve Ontiveros	.10	.05	.01
☐ 594 David Nied	.20	.09	.03
☐ 595 Brad Ausmus	.10	.05	.01
☐ 596 Carlos Baerga	.60	.25	.07
☐ 597 James Mouton	.20	.09	.03
☐ 598 Ozzie Guillen	.10	.05	.01
☐ 599 Outfielders	.75	.35	.09
Prospects			
Ozzie Timmons			
Curtis Goodwin			
Johnny Damon			
Jeff Abbott			
☐ 600 Yorkis Perez	.10	.05	.01
☐ 601 Rich Rodriguez	.10	.05	.01
☐ 602 Mark McLemore	.10	.05	.01
☐ 603 Jeff Fassero	.10	.05	.01
☐ 604 John Roper	.10	.05	.01
☐ 605 Mark Johnson	.30	.14	.04
☐ 606 Wes Chamberlain	.10	.05	.01
☐ 607 Felix Jose	.10	.05	.01
☐ 608 Tony Longmire	.10	.05	.01
☐ 609 Duane Ward	.10	.05	.01
☐ 610 Brett Butler	.20	.09	.03
☐ 611 William VanLandingham	.20	.09	.03
☐ 612 Mickey Tettleton	.20	.09	.03
☐ 613 Brady Anderson	.20	.09	.03
☐ 614 Reggie Jefferson	.10	.05	.01
☐ 615 Mike Kingery	.10	.05	.01
☐ 616 Derek Bell	.30	.14	.04
☐ 617 Scott Erickson	.20	.09	.03
☐ 618 Bob Wickman	.10	.05	.01
☐ 619 Phil Leftwich	.10	.05	.01
☐ 620 David Justice	.40	.18	.05
☐ 621 Paul Wilson	.60	.25	.07
☐ 622 Pedro Martinez	.10	.05	.01
☐ 623 Terry Mathews	.10	.05	.01
☐ 624 Brian McRae	.20	.09	.03
☐ 625 Bruce Ruffin	.10	.05	.01
☐ 626 Steve Finley	.20	.09	.03
☐ 627 Ron Gant	.10	.05	.01
☐ 628 Rafael Bournigal	.10	.05	.01
☐ 629 Darryl Strawberry	.30	.14	.04
☐ 630 Luis Alicea	.10	.05	.01
☐ 631 Orioles Prospects	.20	.09	.03
Mark Smith			
Scott Klingenbeck			
☐ 632 Red Sox Prospects	.20	.09	.03
Cory Bailey			
Scott Hatteberg			
☐ 633 Angels Prospects	.50	.23	.06
Todd Greene			
Troy Percival			
☐ 634 White Sox Prospects	.10	.05	.01
Rod Bolton			
Olmedo Saenz			
☐ 635 Indians Prospects	.20	.09	.03
Steve Kline			
Herb Perry			
☐ 636 Tigers Prospects	.20	.09	.03
Sean Bergman			
Shannon Penn			
☐ 637 Royals Prospects	.20	.09	.03
Joe Randa			
Joe Vitiello			
☐ 638 Brewers Prospects	.20	.09	.03
Jose Mercedes			
Duane Singleton			
☐ 639 Twins Prospects	.50	.23	.06
Marc Barcelo			
Marty Cordova			
☐ 640 Yankees Prospects	2.50	1.10	.30
Andy Pettitte			
Ruben Rivera			
☐ 641 Athletics Prospects	.20	.09	.03
Willie Adams			
Scott Spiezio			
☐ 642 Mariners Prospects	.20	.09	.03
Eddy Diaz			
Desi Relaford			
☐ 643 Rangers Prospects	.10	.05	.01
Terrell Lowery			
Jon Shave			
☐ 644 Blue Jays Prospects	.20	.09	.03
Angel Martinez			
Paul Spoljaric			
☐ 645 Braves Prospects	.30	.14	.04
Tony Graffanino			
Damon Hollins			
☐ 646 Cubs Prospects	.20	.09	.03
Darron Cox			
Doug Glanville			
☐ 647 Reds Prospects	.20	.09	.03
Tim Belk			
Pat Watkins			
☐ 648 Rockies Propsects	.10	.05	.01
Rod Pedraza			
Phil Schneider			
☐ 649 Marlins Prospects	.20	.09	.03
Vic Darensbourg			
Marc Valdes			

		MINT	NRMT	EXC
☐ 650	Astros Prospects	.20	.09	.03
	Rick Huisman			
	Roberto Petagine			
☐ 651	Dodgers Prospects	.30	.14	.04
	Roger Cedeno			
	Ron Coomer			
☐ 652	Expos Prospects	.75	.35	.09
	Shane Andrews			
	Carlos Perez			
☐ 653	Mets Prospects	1.50	.70	.19
	Jason Isringhausen			
	Chris Roberts			
☐ 654	Phillies Prospects	.20	.09	.03
	Wayne Gomes			
	Kevin Jordan			
☐ 655	Pirates Prospects	.20	.09	.03
	Esteban Loiaza			
	Steve Pegues			
☐ 656	Cardinals Prospects	.20	.09	.03
	Terry Bradshaw			
	John Frascatore			
☐ 657	Padres Prospects	.20	.09	.03
	Andres Berumen			
	Bryce Florie			
☐ 658	Giants Prospects	.20	.09	.03
	Dan Carlson			
	Keith Williams			
☐ 659	Checklist	.10	.05	.01
☐ 660	Checklist	.10	.05	.01

		MINT	NRMT	EXC
☐ 4	Frank Thomas	20.00	9.00	2.50
☐ 5	Matt Williams	3.00	1.35	.35
☐ 6	Dante Bichette	2.50	1.10	.30
☐ 7	Barry Bonds	5.00	2.20	.60
☐ 8	Moises Alou	2.00	.90	.25
☐ 9	Andres Galarraga	2.00	.90	.25
☐ 10	Kenny Lofton	6.00	2.70	.75
☐ 11	Rafael Palmeiro	2.00	.90	.25
☐ 12	Tony Gwynn	6.00	2.70	.75
☐ 13	Kirby Puckett	6.00	2.70	.75
☐ 14	Jose Canseco	3.00	1.35	.35
☐ 15	Jeff Conine	2.00	.90	.25

1995 Topps Traded

This set contains 165 cards and was sold in 11-card packs for $1.29. The set features rookies, draft picks and players who had been traded. The fronts contain a photo with a white border. The backs have a player picture in a scoreboard and his statistics and information. Subsets featured are: At the Break (1-10) and All-Stars (156-164).

		MINT	NRMT	EXC
COMPLETE SET (165)		20.00	9.00	2.50
COMMON CARD (1-165)		.05	.02	.01
T PREFIX ON CARD NUMBERS				
☐ 1	Frank Thomas ATB	1.50	.70	.19
☐ 2	Ken Griffey Jr.	1.50	.70	.19
☐ 3	Barry Bonds ATB	.40	.18	.05
☐ 4	Albert Belle ATB	.60	.25	.07
☐ 5	Cal Ripken ATB	1.50	.70	.19
☐ 6	Mike Piazza ATB	.60	.25	.07
☐ 7	Tony Gwynn ATB	.50	.23	.06
☐ 8	Jeff Bagwell ATB	.50	.23	.06
☐ 9	Mo Vaughn ATB	.05	.02	.01
☐ 10	Matt Williams ATB	.10	.05	.01
☐ 11	Ray Durham	.10	.05	.01
☐ 12	Juan LeBron	.30	.14	.04
☐ 13	Shawn Green	.15	.07	.02
☐ 14	Kevin Gross	.05	.02	.01
☐ 15	Jon Nunnally	.10	.05	.01
☐ 16	Brian Maxcy	.05	.02	.01
☐ 17	Mark Kiefer	.05	.02	.01
☐ 18	Carlos Beltran	.25	.11	.03
☐ 19	Mike Mimbs	.20	.09	.03
☐ 20	Larry Walker	.25	.11	.03
☐ 21	Chad Curtis	.05	.02	.01
☐ 22	Jeff Barry	.05	.02	.01
☐ 23	Joe Oliver	.05	.02	.01

1995 Topps Finest

This 15-card standard-size set was inserted one every 36 packs in Topps series two. This set featured the top 15 players in total bases from the 1994 season. The fronts feature a player photo, with his team identification and name on the bottom of the card. The horizontal backs feature another player photo along with a breakdown of how many of each type of hit each player got on the way to their season total. The set is sequenced in order of how they finished in the majors for the 1994 season.

		MINT	NRMT	EXC
COMPLETE SET (15)		75.00	34.00	9.50
COMMON CARD (1-15)		2.00	.90	.25
☐ 1	Jeff Bagwell	6.00	2.70	.75
☐ 2	Albert Belle	8.00	3.60	1.00
☐ 3	Ken Griffey Jr.	20.00	9.00	2.50

24	Tomas Perez	.15	.07	.02
25	Michael Barrett	.25	.11	.03
26	Brian McRae	.05	.02	.01
27	Derek Bell	.10	.05	.01
28	Ray Durham	.15	.07	.02
29	Todd Williams	.05	.02	.01
30	Ryan Jaroncyk	.25	.11	.03
31	Todd Steverson	.05	.02	.01
32	Mike Devereaux	.05	.02	.01
33	Rheal Cormier	.05	.02	.01
34	Benny Santiago	.05	.02	.01
35	Bobby Higginson	.20	.09	.03
36	Jack McDowell	.05	.02	.01
37	Mike Macfarlane	.05	.02	.01
38	Tony McKnight	.25	.11	.03
39	Brian Hunter	.25	.11	.03
40	Hideo Nomo	4.00	1.80	.50
41	Brett Butler	.10	.05	.01
42	Donovan Osborne	.05	.02	.01
43	Scott Karl	.05	.02	.01
44	Tony Phillips	.05	.02	.01
45	Marty Cordova	.30	.14	.04
46	Dave Mlicki	.05	.02	.01
47	Bronson Arroyo	.25	.11	.03
48	John Burkett	.05	.02	.01
49	J.D. Smart	.25	.11	.03
50	Mickey Tettleton	.05	.02	.01
51	Todd Stottlemyre	.05	.02	.01
52	Mike Perez	.05	.02	.01
53	Terry Mulholland	.05	.02	.01
54	Edgardo Alfonzo	.15	.07	.02
55	Zane Smith	.05	.02	.01
56	Jacob Brumfield	.05	.02	.01
57	Andujar Cedeno	.05	.02	.01
58	Jose Parra	.10	.05	.01
59	Manny Alexander	.05	.02	.01
60	Tony Tarasco	.10	.05	.01
61	Orel Hershiser	.10	.05	.01
62	Tim Scott	.05	.02	.01
63	Felix Rodriguez	.20	.09	.03
64	Ken Hill	.05	.02	.01
65	Marquis Grissom	.15	.07	.02
66	Lee Smith	.15	.07	.02
67	Jason Bates	.10	.05	.01
68	Felipe Lira	.10	.05	.01
69	Alex Hernandez	.30	.14	.04
70	Tony Fernandez	.05	.02	.01
71	Scott Radinsky	.05	.02	.01
72	Jose Canseco	.30	.14	.04
73	Mark Grudzielanek	.20	.09	.03
74	Ben Davis	.75	.35	.09
75	Jim Abbott	.05	.02	.01
76	Roger Bailey	.05	.02	.01
77	Gregg Jefferies	.10	.05	.01
78	Erik Hanson	.05	.02	.01
79	Brad Radke	.25	.11	.03
80	Jaime Navarro	.05	.02	.01
81	John Wetteland	.10	.05	.01
82	Chad Fonville	.30	.14	.04
83	John Mabry	.15	.07	.02
84	Glenallen Hill	.10	.05	.01
85	Ken Caminiti	.05	.02	.01
86	Tom Goodwin	.05	.02	.01
87	Darren Bragg	.05	.02	.01
88	Pitching Prospects	.40	.18	.05
	Pat Ahearne			
	Gary Rath			
	Larry Wimberly			
	Robbie Bell			
89	Jeff Russell	.05	.02	.01
90	Dave Gallagher	.05	.02	.01
91	Steve Finley	.05	.02	.01
92	Vaughn Eshelman	.05	.02	.01
93	Kevin Jarvis	.05	.02	.01
94	Mark Gubicza	.05	.02	.01
95	Tim Wakefield	.10	.05	.01
96	Bob Tewksbury	.05	.02	.01
97	Sid Roberson	.05	.02	.01
98	Tom Henke	.10	.05	.01
99	Michael Tucker	.10	.05	.01
100	Jason Bates	.10	.05	.01
101	Otis Nixon	.05	.02	.01
102	Mark Whiten	.05	.02	.01
103	Dilson Torres	.05	.02	.01
104	Melvin Bunch	.10	.05	.01
105	Terry Pendleton	.05	.02	.01
106	Corey Jenkins	.50	.23	.06
107	Glenn Dishman	.25	.11	.03
	Rob Grable			
108	Reggie Taylor	.30	.14	.04
109	Curtis Goodwin	.10	.05	.01
110	David Cone	.15	.07	.02
111	Antonio Osuna	.05	.02	.01
112	Paul Shuey	.05	.02	.01
113	Doug Jones	.05	.02	.01
114	Mark McLemore	.05	.02	.01
115	Kevin Ritz	.05	.02	.01
116	John Kruk	.05	.02	.01
117	Trevor Wilson	.05	.02	.01
118	Jerald Clark	.05	.02	.01
119	Julian Tavarez	.10	.05	.01
120	Tim Pugh	.05	.02	.01
121	Todd Zeile	.05	.02	.01
122	Prospects	.50	.23	.06
	Mark Sweeney UER			
	George Arias			
	Richie Sexson			
	Brian Schneider			
123	Bobby Witt	.05	.02	.01
124	Hideo Nomo	1.50	.70	.19
125	Joey Cora	.05	.02	.01
126	Jim Scharrer	.25	.11	.03
127	Paul Quantrill	.05	.02	.01
128	Chipper Jones	.75	.35	.09
129	Kenny James	.25	.11	.03
130	Lyle Mouton	.10	.05	.01
	Mariano Rivera			
131	Tyler Green	.05	.02	.01
132	Brad Clontz	.05	.02	.01
133	Jon Nunnally	.10	.05	.01
134	Dave Magadan	.05	.02	.01
135	Al Leiter	.05	.02	.01
136	Bret Barberie	.05	.02	.01
137	Bill Swift	.05	.02	.01
138	Scott Cooper	.05	.02	.01
139	Roberto Kelly	.05	.02	.01
140	Charlie Hayes	.05	.02	.01
141	Pete Harnisch	.05	.02	.01
142	Rich Amaral	.05	.02	.01
143	Rudy Seanez	.05	.02	.01
144	Pat Listach	.05	.02	.01
145	Quilvio Veras	.05	.02	.01
146	Jose Olmeda	.25	.11	.03
147	Roberto Petagine	.05	.02	.01
148	Kevin Brown	.05	.02	.01
149	Phil Plantier	.05	.02	.01
150	Carlos Perez	.50	.23	.06
151	Pat Borders	.05	.02	.01
152	Tyler Green	.05	.02	.01
153	Stan Belinda	.05	.02	.01
154	Dave Stewart	.05	.02	.01
155	Andre Dawson	.05	.02	.01

☐ 156	Frank Thomas AS......... .40 Fred McGriff	.18	.05
☐ 157	Carlos Baerga AS .... .10 Craig Biggio	.05	.01
☐ 158	Wade Boggs AS .... .10 Matt Williams	.05	.01
☐ 159	Cal Ripken AS .... .50 Ozzie Smith	.23	.06
☐ 160	Ken Griffey Jr. AS .... .50 Tony Gwynn	.23	.06
☐ 161	Albert Belle AS .... .30 Barry Bonds	.14	.04
☐ 162	Kirby Puckett .... .25 Len Dykstra	.11	.03
☐ 163	Ivan Rodriguez AS .... .25 Mike Piazza	.11	.03
☐ 164	Randy Johnson AS .... 1.50 Hideo Nomo	.70	.19
☐ 165	Checklist .... .05	.02	.01

1995 Topps Traded Power Boosters

This 10-card set was inserted in packs at a rate of one in 36. The set is comprised of parallel cards for the first 10 cards of the regular Topps Traded set which was the "At the Break" subset. The cards are done on extra-thick stock. The fronts have an action photo on a "Power Boosted" background, which is similar to diffraction technology, with the words "at the break" on the left side. The backs have a head shot and player information including his mid-season statistics for 1995 and previous years.

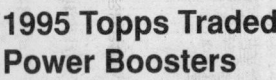

	MINT	NRMT	EXC
COMPLETE SET (10)	125.00	55.00	15.50
COMMON CARD (1-10)	6.00	2.70	.75
☐ 1 Frank Thomas...............	30.00	13.50	3.70
☐ 2 Ken Griffey Jr...............	30.00	13.50	3.70
☐ 3 Barry Bonds.................	8.00	3.60	1.00
☐ 4 Albert Belle.................	12.00	5.50	1.50
☐ 5 Cal Ripken...................	30.00	13.50	3.70
☐ 6 Mike Piazza.................	12.00	5.50	1.50
☐ 7 Tony Gwynn.................	10.00	4.50	1.25
☐ 8 Jeff Bagwell.................	10.00	4.50	1.25
☐ 9 Mo Vaughn..................	6.00	2.70	.75
☐ 10 Matt Williams..............	6.00	2.70	.75

1996 Topps

This first series set consists of 220 cards. These cards were issued in 12-card foil packs with a suggested retail price of $1.29. The fronts feature full-color photos surrounded by a white background. Information on the backs includes a player photo, season and career stats and text. Subsets include Star Power (1-6, 8-12), Draft Picks (13-26), AAA Stars (101-104), and Future Stars (210-219). A special Mickey Mantle card was issued as card #7 (his uniform number) and became the last

card to be issued as card #7 in the Topps brand set. Rookie Cards in this set include Sean Casey and Geoff Jenkins.

	MINT	NRMT	EXC
COMPLETE SERIES 1 (220)...	16.00	7.25	2.00
COMMON CARD (1-220)	.10	.05	.01
☐ 1 Tony Gwynn STP	.50	.23	.06
☐ 2 Mike Piazza STP	.60	.25	.07
☐ 3 Greg Maddux STP	1.50	.70	.19
☐ 4 Jeff Bagwell STP	.50	.23	.06
☐ 5 Larry Walker STP	.10	.05	.01
☐ 6 Barry Larkin STP	.20	.09	.03
☐ 7 Mickey Mantle.................	4.00	1.80	.50
☐ 8 Tom Glavine STP	.10	.05	.01
☐ 9 Craig Biggio STP	.10	.05	.01
☐ 10 Barry Bonds STP	.30	.14	.04
☐ 11 Heathcliff Slocumb STP.	.10	.05	.01
☐ 12 Matt Williams STP	.10	.05	.01
☐ 13 Todd Helton	.30	.14	.04
☐ 14 Mark Redman	.20	.09	.03
☐ 15 Michael Barrett	.10	.05	.01
☐ 16 Ben Davis......................	.40	.18	.05
☐ 17 Juan LeBron	.10	.05	.01
☐ 18 Tony McKnight	.10	.05	.01
☐ 19 Ryan Jaroncyk	.10	.05	.01
☐ 20 Corey Jenkins	.20	.09	.03
☐ 21 Jim Scharrer	.10	.05	.01
☐ 22 Mark Bellhorn	.25	.11	.03
☐ 23 Jarrod Washburn...........	.20	.09	.03
☐ 24 Geoff Jenkins	.40	.18	.05
☐ 25 Sean Casey	.30	.14	.04
☐ 26 Brett Tomko	.20	.09	.03
☐ 27 Tony Fernandez............	.10	.05	.01
☐ 28 Rich Becker..................	.10	.05	.01
☐ 29 Andujar Cedeno	.10	.05	.01
☐ 30 Paul Molitor	.30	.14	.04
☐ 31 Brent Gates	.10	.05	.01
☐ 32 Glenallen Hill	.20	.09	.03
☐ 33 Mike Macfarlane	.10	.05	.01
☐ 34 Manny Alexander	.10	.05	.01
☐ 35 Todd Zeile	.10	.05	.01
☐ 36 Joe Girardi	.10	.05	.01
☐ 37 Tony Tarasco	.20	.09	.03
☐ 38 Tim Belcher.................	.10	.05	.01
☐ 39 Tom Goodwin	.10	.05	.01
☐ 40 Orel Hershiser	.20	.09	.03
☐ 41 Tripp Cromer	.10	.05	.01
☐ 42 Sean Bergman	.10	.05	.01
☐ 43 Troy Percival	.20	.09	.03
☐ 44 Kevin Stocker	.10	.05	.01
☐ 45 Albert Belle	1.25	.55	.16
☐ 46 Tony Eusebio	.10	.05	.01
☐ 47 Sid Roberson...............	.10	.05	.01

48	Todd Hollandsworth	.10	.05	.01
49	Mark Wohlers	.20	.09	.03
50	Kirby Puckett	1.00	.45	.12
51	Darren Holmes	.10	.05	.01
52	Ron Karkovice	.10	.05	.01
53	Al Martin	.20	.09	.03
54	Pat Rapp	.20	.09	.03
55	Mark Grace	.30	.14	.04
56	Greg Gagne	.10	.05	.01
57	Stan Javier	.10	.05	.01
58	Scott Sanders	.10	.05	.01
59	J.T. Snow	.30	.14	.04
60	David Justice	.40	.18	.05
61	Royce Clayton	.10	.05	.01
62	Kevin Foster	.10	.05	.01
63	Tim Naehring	.10	.05	.01
64	Orlando Miller	.20	.09	.03
65	Mike Mussina	.40	.18	.05
66	Jim Eisenreich	.10	.05	.01
67	Felix Fermin	.10	.05	.01
68	Bernie Williams	.20	.09	.03
69	Robb Nen	.10	.05	.01
70	Ron Gant	.30	.14	.04
71	Felipe Lira	.10	.05	.01
72	Jacob Brumfield	.10	.05	.01
73	John Mabry	.20	.09	.03
74	Mark Carreon	.10	.05	.01
75	Carlos Baerga	.60	.25	.07
76	Jim Dougherty	.10	.05	.01
77	Ryan Thompson	.10	.05	.01
78	Scott Leius	.10	.05	.01
79	Roger Pavlik	.10	.05	.01
80	Gary Sheffield	.30	.14	.04
81	Julian Tavarez	.20	.09	.03
82	Andy Ashby	.10	.05	.01
83	Mark Lemke	.20	.09	.03
84	Omar Vizquel	.20	.09	.03
85	Darren Daulton	.20	.09	.03
86	Mike Lansing	.10	.05	.01
87	Rusty Greer	.10	.05	.01
88	Dave Stevens	.10	.05	.01
89	Jose Offerman	.10	.05	.01
90	Tom Henke	.20	.09	.03
91	Troy O'Leary	.10	.05	.01
92	Michael Tucker	.20	.09	.03
93	Marvin Freeman	.10	.05	.01
94	Alex Diaz	.10	.05	.01
95	John Wetteland	.20	.09	.03
96	Cal Ripken 2131	4.00	1.80	.50
97	Mike Mimbs	.10	.05	.01
98	Bobby Higginson	.30	.14	.04
99	Edgardo Alfonzo	.20	.09	.03
100	Frank Thomas	3.00	1.35	.35
101	Steve Gibralter Bob Abreu	.20	.09	.03
102	Brian Givens T.J. Mathews	.10	.05	.01
103	Chris Pritchett Trenidad Hubbard	.10	.05	.01
104	Eric Owens Butch Huskey	.10	.05	.01
105	Doug Drabek	.20	.09	.03
106	Tomas Perez	.20	.09	.03
107	Mark Leiter	.10	.05	.01
108	Joe Oliver	.10	.05	.01
109	Tony Castillo	.10	.05	.01
110	Checklist (1-110)	.10	.05	.01
111	Kevin Seitzer	.10	.05	.01
112	Pete Schourek	.30	.14	.04
113	Sean Berry	.10	.05	.01
114	Todd Stottlemyre	.10	.05	.01
115	Joe Carter	.30	.14	.04
116	Jeff King	.10	.05	.01
117	Dan Wilson	.20	.09	.03
118	Kurt Abbott	.20	.09	.03
119	Lyle Mouton	.20	.09	.03
120	Jose Rijo	.10	.05	.01
121	Curtis Goodwin	.20	.09	.03
122	Jose Valentin	.10	.05	.01
123	Ellis Burks	.20	.09	.03
124	David Cone	.30	.14	.04
125	Eddie Murray	.40	.18	.05
126	Brian Jordan	.30	.14	.04
127	Darrin Fletcher	.10	.05	.01
128	Curt Schilling	.10	.05	.01
129	Ozzie Guillen	.10	.05	.01
130	Kenny Rogers	.10	.05	.01
131	Tom Pagnozzi	.10	.05	.01
132	Garret Anderson	.30	.14	.04
133	Bobby Jones	.10	.05	.01
134	Chris Gomez	.10	.05	.01
135	Mike Stanley	.20	.09	.03
136	Hideo Nomo	1.25	.55	.16
137	Jon Nunnally	.20	.09	.03
138	Tim Wakefield	.10	.05	.01
139	Steve Finley	.20	.09	.03
140	Ivan Rodriguez	.30	.14	.04
141	Quilvio Veras	.20	.09	.03
142	Mike Fetters	.10	.05	.01
143	Mike Greenwell	.10	.05	.01
144	Bill Pulsipher	.30	.14	.04
145	Mark McGwire	.30	.14	.04
146	Frank Castillo	.10	.05	.01
147	Greg Vaughn	.10	.05	.01
148	Pat Hentgen	.20	.09	.03
149	Walt Weiss	.10	.05	.01
150	Randy Johnson	.60	.25	.07
151	David Segui	.10	.05	.01
152	Benji Gil	.10	.05	.01
153	Tom Candiotti	.10	.05	.01
154	Geronimo Berroa	.10	.05	.01
155	John Franco	.20	.09	.03
156	Jay Bell	.20	.09	.03
157	Mark Gubicza	.10	.05	.01
158	Hal Morris	.20	.09	.03
159	Wilson Alvarez	.20	.09	.03
160	Derek Bell	.30	.14	.04
161	Ricky Bottalico	.10	.05	.01
162	Bret Boone	.20	.09	.03
163	Brad Radke	.10	.05	.01
164	John Valentin	.30	.14	.04
165	Steve Avery	.20	.09	.03
166	Mark McLemore	.10	.05	.01
167	Danny Jackson	.10	.05	.01
168	Tino Martinez	.30	.14	.04
169	Shane Reynolds	.10	.05	.01
170	Terry Pendleton	.20	.09	.03
171	Jim Edmonds	.30	.14	.04
172	Esteban Loaiza	.10	.05	.01
173	Ray Durham	.30	.14	.04
174	Carlos Perez	.30	.14	.04
175	Raul Mondesi	.60	.25	.07
176	Steve Ontiveros	.10	.05	.01
177	Chipper Jones	1.25	.55	.16
178	Otis Nixon	.10	.05	.01
179	John Burkett	.10	.05	.01
180	Gregg Jefferies	.30	.14	.04
181	Denny Martinez	.20	.09	.03
182	Ken Caminiti	.10	.05	.01
183	Doug Jones	.10	.05	.01
184	Brian McRae	.20	.09	.03
185	Don Mattingly	1.50	.70	.19

		MINT	NRMT	EXC
☐ 186	Mel Rojas	.20	.09	.03
☐ 187	Marty Cordova	.30	.14	.04
☐ 188	Vinny Castilla	.30	.14	.04
☐ 189	John Smoltz	.20	.09	.03
☐ 190	Travis Fryman	.30	.14	.04
☐ 191	Chris Hoiles	.20	.09	.03
☐ 192	Chuck Finley	.20	.09	.03
☐ 193	Ryan Klesko	.30	.14	.04
☐ 194	Alex Fernandez	.20	.09	.03
☐ 195	Dante Bichette	.40	.18	.05
☐ 196	Eric Karros	.30	.14	.04
☐ 197	Roger Clemens	.50	.23	.06
☐ 198	Randy Myers	.20	.09	.03
☐ 199	Tony Phillips	.10	.05	.01
☐ 200	Cal Ripken	3.00	1.35	.35
☐ 201	Rod Beck	.20	.09	.03
☐ 202	Chad Curtis	.20	.09	.03
☐ 203	Jack McDowell	.30	.14	.04
☐ 204	Gary Gaetti	.20	.09	.03
☐ 205	Ken Griffey Jr.	3.00	1.35	.35
☐ 206	Ramon Martinez	.20	.09	.03
☐ 207	Jeff Kent	.20	.09	.03
☐ 208	Brad Ausmus	.10	.05	.01
☐ 209	Devon White	.10	.05	.01
☐ 210	Jason Giambi	.20	.09	.03
☐ 211	Nomar Garciaparra	.20	.09	.03
☐ 212	Billy Wagner	.20	.09	.03
☐ 213	Todd Greene	.20	.09	.03
☐ 214	Paul Wilson	.20	.09	.03
☐ 215	Johnny Damon	.30	.14	.04
☐ 216	Alan Benes	.10	.05	.01
☐ 217	Karim Garcia	.40	.18	.05
☐ 218	Dustin Hermanson	.10	.05	.01
☐ 219	Derek Jeter	.30	.14	.04
☐ 220	Checklist (111-220)	.10	.05	.01

		MINT	NRMT	EXC
☐ M4	Chipper Jones	10.00	4.50	1.25
☐ M5	Marty Cordova	2.00	.90	.25
☐ M6	Garret Anderson	2.00	.90	.25
☐ M7	Cal Ripken	20.00	9.00	2.50
☐ M8	Kirby Puckett	6.00	2.70	.75
☐ M9	Tony Gwynn	6.00	2.70	.75
☐ M10	Manny Ramirez	8.00	3.60	1.00
☐ M11	Jim Edmonds	2.00	.90	.25
☐ M12	Mike Piazza	8.00	3.60	1.00
☐ M13	Barry Bonds	5.00	2.20	.60
☐ M14	Raul Mondesi	5.00	2.20	.60
☐ M15	Sammy Sosa	2.00	.90	.25
☐ M16	Ken Griffey Jr.	20.00	9.00	2.50
☐ M17	Albert Belle	8.00	3.60	1.00
☐ M18	Dante Bichette	2.50	1.10	.30
☐ M19	Mo Vaughn	3.00	1.35	.35
☐ M20	Jeff Bagwell	6.00	2.70	.75
☐ M21	Frank Thomas	20.00	9.00	2.50
☐ M22	Hideo Nomo	8.00	3.60	1.00
☐ M23	Cal Ripken	20.00	9.00	2.50
☐ M24	Mike Piazza	8.00	3.60	1.00
☐ M25	Ken Griffey Jr.	20.00	9.00	2.50
☐ M26	Frank Thomas	20.00	9.00	2.50

1996 Topps Mantle

Randomly inserted in packs, these cards are reprints of the original Mickey Mantle cards issued from 1951 through 1969. The fronts look the same except for a commemorative stamp, while the backs clearly state that they are "Mickey Mantle Commemorative" cards and have a 1996 copyright date. These cards honor Yankee great Mickey Mantle, who passed away in August 1995 after a gallant battle against cancer.

	MINT	NRMT	EXC
COMPLETE SET (19)	100.00	45.00	12.50
COMMON MANTLE (1-19)	6.00	2.70	.75
☐ 1 1951 Bowman	10.00	4.50	1.25
☐ 2 1952 Topps	10.00	4.50	1.25

1996 Topps Finest

Randomly inserted in packs, this set features a bit of a mystery. The fronts have opaque coating that must be removed before the player can be identified. After the opaque coating is removed, the fronts feature a player photo surrounded by silver borders. The backs feature a choice of players along with a corresponding mystery finest trivia fact.

	MINT	NRMT	EXC
COMPLETE SET (26)	200.00	90.00	25.00
COMMON CARD (M1-M26)	2.00	.90	.25
REFRACTORS: 2.5X TO 4X BASIC CARDS			
☐ M1 Hideo Nomo	8.00	3.60	1.00
☐ M2 Greg Maddux	20.00	9.00	2.50
☐ M3 Randy Johnson	4.00	1.80	.50

1996 Topps Masters of the Game

This 20-card set was randomly inserted into hobby packs. The horizontal fronts comprise of silver foil set against white borders.

The left side of the card has a player photo. The words "Master of the Game" and the player's name are printed on the right. The horizontal backs have a player photo, a brief write-up and some quick important dates in the player's career. The cards are numbered with a "MG" prefix in the lower left corner.

	MINT	NRMT	EXC
COMPLETE SET (20)	40.00	18.00	5.00
COMMON CARD (1-20)	.75	.35	.09

		MINT	NRMT	EXC
☐ 1	Dennis Eckersley	.75	.35	.09
☐ 2	Denny Martinez	.75	.35	.09
☐ 3	Eddie Murray	1.00	.45	.12
☐ 4	Paul Molitor	.75	.35	.09
☐ 5	Ozzie Smith	1.50	.70	.19
☐ 6	Rickey Henderson	.75	.35	.09
☐ 7	Tim Raines	.75	.35	.09
☐ 8	Lee Smith	.75	.35	.09
☐ 9	Cal Ripken	10.00	4.50	1.25
☐ 10	Chili Davis	.75	.35	.09
☐ 11	Wade Boggs	.75	.35	.09
☐ 12	Tony Gwynn	3.00	1.35	.35
☐ 13	Don Mattingly	5.00	2.20	.60
☐ 14	Bret Saberhagen	.75	.35	.09
☐ 15	Kirby Puckett	3.00	1.35	.35
☐ 16	Joe Carter	.75	.35	.09
☐ 17	Roger Clemens	1.25	.55	.16
☐ 18	Barry Bonds	2.00	.90	.25
☐ 19	Greg Maddux	10.00	4.50	1.25
☐ 20	Frank Thomas	10.00	4.50	1.25

1996 Topps Power Boosters

Randomly inserted into packs, these cards are a metallic version of 25 of the first 26 cards from the basic Topps set. Cards #1-6, 8-12 were issued in retail packs, while #13-26 were issued in hobby packs. Inserted in place of two basic cards, they are printed on 28 point stock and the fronts have prismatic foil printing. Card #7, which is Mickey Mantle in the regular set, was not issued in a Power Booster form.

	MINT	NRMT	EXC
COMP. STAR POWER SET (11)	50.00	22.00	6.25
COMP. DRAFT PICKS SET (14)	40.00	18.00	5.00

	MINT	NRMT	EXC
COMMON STAR POWER (1-12)	2.00	.90	.25
COMMON DRAFT PICK (12-26)	3.00	1.35	.35

		MINT	NRMT	EXC
☐ 1	Tony Gwynn	6.00	2.70	.75
☐ 2	Mike Piazza	8.00	3.60	1.00
☐ 3	Greg Maddux	20.00	9.00	2.50
☐ 4	Jeff Bagwell	6.00	2.70	.75
☐ 5	Larry Walker	3.00	1.35	.35
☐ 6	Barry Larkin	3.00	1.35	.35
☐ 8	Tom Glavine	2.50	1.10	.30
☐ 9	Craig Biggio	2.50	1.10	.30
☐ 10	Barry Bonds	4.00	1.80	.50
☐ 11	Heathcliff Slocumb	2.00	.90	.25
☐ 12	Matt Williams	3.00	1.35	.35
☐ 13	Todd Helton	5.00	2.20	.60
☐ 14	Mark Redman	3.00	1.35	.35
☐ 15	Michael Barrett	3.00	1.35	.35
☐ 16	Ben Davis	8.00	3.60	1.00
☐ 17	Juan LeBron	3.00	1.35	.35
☐ 18	Tony McKnight	3.00	1.35	.35
☐ 19	Ryan Jaroncyk	3.00	1.35	.35
☐ 20	Corey Jenkins	4.00	1.80	.50
☐ 21	Jim Scharrer	3.00	1.35	.35
☐ 22	Mark Bellhorn	3.00	1.35	.35
☐ 23	Jarrod Washburn	3.00	1.35	.35
☐ 24	Geoff Jenkins	6.00	2.70	.75
☐ 25	Sean Casey	4.00	1.80	.50
☐ 26	Brett Tomko	3.00	1.35	.35

1996 Topps Profiles

Randomly inserted into packs, this 20-card set features 10 players from each league. Topps spokesmen Kirby Puckett (AL) and Tony Gwynn (NL) give opinions on players within their league. The fronts feature a player photo set against a silver-foil background. The player's name is on the bottom. A photo of either Gwynn or Puckett as well as the words "Profiles by ..." is on the right. The backs feature a player photo, some career data as well as Gwynn's or Puckett's opinion about the featured player. The cards are numbered with either an "AL or NL" prefix on the back depending on the player's league. The cards are sequenced in alphabetical order within league.

	MINT	NRMT	EXC
COMPLETE SET (20)	30.00	13.50	3.70
COMMON CARD (A1-A10)	.50	.23	.06
COMMON CARD (N1-N10)	.50	.23	.06

☐ AL1	Roberto Alomar	1.00	.45	.12
☐ AL2	Carlos Baerga	1.00	.45	.12
☐ AL3	Albert Belle	2.00	.90	.25
☐ AL4	Cecil Fielder	.50	.23	.06
☐ AL5	Ken Griffey Jr.	5.00	2.20	.60
☐ AL6	Randy Johnson	1.00	.45	.12
☐ AL7	Paul O'Neill	.50	.23	.06
☐ AL8	Cal Ripken	5.00	2.20	.60
☐ AL9	Frank Thomas	5.00	2.20	.60
☐ AL10	Mo Vaughn	.75	.35	.09
☐ NL1	Jeff Bagwell	1.50	.70	.19
☐ NL2	Derek Bell	.50	.23	.06
☐ NL3	Barry Bonds	1.25	.55	.16
☐ NL4	Greg Maddux	5.00	2.20	.60
☐ NL5	Fred McGriff	.60	.25	.07
☐ NL6	Raul Mondesi	1.00	.45	.12
☐ NL7	Mike Piazza	2.00	.90	.25
☐ NL8	Reggie Sanders	.50	.23	.06
☐ NL9	Sammy Sosa	.50	.23	.06
☐ NL10	Larry Walker	.60	.25	.07

1991 Ultra

This 400-card standard size (2 1/2" by 3 1/2") set marked Fleer's first entry into the high-end premium card market. The set was released in wax packs and features the best players in the majors along with a good mix of young prospects. The cards feature full color action photography on the fronts and three full-color photos on the backs along with 1990 and career statistics. Fleer claimed in their original press release that there would only be 15 percent of Ultra issued as there was of the regular issue. Fleer also issued the sets in their now traditional alphabetical order as well as the teams in alphabetical order. The card numbering is as follows, Atlanta Braves (1-13), Baltimore Orioles (14-26), Boston Red Sox (27-42), California Angels (43-54), Chicago Cubs (55-71), Chicago White Sox (72-86), Cincinnati Reds (87-103), Cleveland Indians (104-119), Detroit Tigers (120-130), Houston Astros (131-142), Kansas City Royals (143-158), Los Angeles Dodgers (159-171), Milwaukee Brewers (172-184), Minnesota Twins (185-196), Montreal Expos (197-210), New York Mets (211-227), New York Yankees (228-242), Oakland Athletics (243-257), Philadelphia Phillies (258-272), Pittsburgh Pirates (273-287), St. Louis Cardinals (288-299), San

Diego Padres (300-313), San Francisco Giants (314-331), Seattle Mariners (332-345), Texas Rangers (346-357), Toronto Blue Jays (358-372), Major League Prospects (373-390), Elite Performance (391-396), and Checklists (397-400). The key Rookie Cards in this set are Wes Chamberlain, Jeff Conine, Carlos Garcia, Eric Karros, Brian McRae, Orlando Merced, Pedro Munoz, and Phil Plantier.

		MINT	NRMT	EXC
	COMPLETE SET (400)	20.00	9.00	2.50
	COMMON CARD (1-400)	.05	.02	.01
☐ 1	Steve Avery	.20	.09	.03
☐ 2	Jeff Blauser	.10	.05	.01
☐ 3	Francisco Cabrera	.05	.02	.01
☐ 4	Ron Gant	.20	.09	.03
☐ 5	Tom Glavine	.30	.14	.04
☐ 6	Tommy Gregg	.05	.02	.01
☐ 7	Dave Justice	.40	.18	.05
☐ 8	Oddibe McDowell	.05	.02	.01
☐ 9	Greg Olson	.05	.02	.01
☐ 10	Terry Pendleton	.20	.09	.03
☐ 11	Lonnie Smith	.05	.02	.01
☐ 12	John Smoltz	.20	.09	.03
☐ 13	Jeff Treadway	.05	.02	.01
☐ 14	Glenn Davis	.05	.02	.01
☐ 15	Mike Devereaux	.10	.05	.01
☐ 16	Leo Gomez	.05	.02	.01
☐ 17	Chris Hoiles	.10	.05	.01
☐ 18	Dave Johnson	.05	.02	.01
☐ 19	Ben McDonald	.10	.05	.01
☐ 20	Randy Milligan	.05	.02	.01
☐ 21	Gregg Olson	.05	.02	.01
☐ 22	Joe Orsulak	.05	.02	.01
☐ 23	Bill Ripken	.05	.02	.01
☐ 24	Cal Ripken	2.00	.90	.25
☐ 25	David Segui	.10	.05	.01
☐ 26	Craig Worthington	.05	.02	.01
☐ 27	Wade Boggs	.20	.09	.03
☐ 28	Tom Bolton	.05	.02	.01
☐ 29	Tom Brunansky	.05	.02	.01
☐ 30	Ellis Burks	.10	.05	.01
☐ 31	Roger Clemens	.30	.14	.04
☐ 32	Mike Greenwell	.20	.09	.03
☐ 33	Greg A. Harris	.05	.02	.01
☐ 34	Daryl Irvine	.05	.02	.01
☐ 35	Mike Marshall UER	.05	.02	.01
	(1990 in stats is shown as 990)			
☐ 36	Tim Naehring	.10	.05	.01
☐ 37	Tony Pena	.05	.02	.01
☐ 38	Phil Plantier	.30	.14	.04
☐ 39	Carlos Quintana	.05	.02	.01
☐ 40	Jeff Reardon	.10	.05	.01
☐ 41	Jody Reed	.05	.02	.01
☐ 42	Luis Rivera	.05	.02	.01
☐ 43	Jim Abbott	.20	.09	.03
☐ 44	Chuck Finley	.10	.05	.01
☐ 45	Bryan Harvey	.10	.05	.01
☐ 46	Donnie Hill	.05	.02	.01
☐ 47	Jack Howell	.05	.02	.01
☐ 48	Wally Joyner	.10	.05	.01
☐ 49	Mark Langston	.20	.09	.03
☐ 50	Kirk McCaskill	.05	.02	.01
☐ 51	Lance Parrish	.10	.05	.01
☐ 52	Dick Schofield	.05	.02	.01
☐ 53	Lee Stevens	.05	.02	.01
☐ 54	Dave Winfield	.20	.09	.03

☐ 55	George Bell	.05	.02	.01
☐ 56	Damon Berryhill	.05	.02	.01
☐ 57	Mike Bielecki	.05	.02	.01
☐ 58	Andre Dawson	.20	.09	.03
☐ 59	Shawon Dunston	.05	.02	.01
☐ 60	Joe Girardi UER	.05	.02	.01
	(Bats right, LH hitter			
	shown is Doug Dascenzo)			
☐ 61	Mark Grace	.20	.09	.03
☐ 62	Mike Harkey	.05	.02	.01
☐ 63	Les Lancaster	.05	.02	.01
☐ 64	Greg Maddux	1.25	.55	.16
☐ 65	Derrick May	.10	.05	.01
☐ 66	Ryne Sandberg	.60	.25	.07
☐ 67	Luis Salazar	.05	.02	.01
☐ 68	Dwight Smith	.05	.02	.01
☐ 69	Hector Villanueva	.05	.02	.01
☐ 70	Jerome Walton	.05	.02	.01
☐ 71	Mitch Williams	.10	.05	.01
☐ 72	Carlton Fisk	.20	.09	.03
☐ 73	Scott Fletcher	.05	.02	.01
☐ 74	Ozzie Guillen	.10	.05	.01
☐ 75	Greg Hibbard	.05	.02	.01
☐ 76	Lance Johnson	.05	.02	.01
☐ 77	Steve Lyons	.05	.02	.01
☐ 78	Jack McDowell	.20	.09	.03
☐ 79	Dan Pasqua	.05	.02	.01
☐ 80	Melido Perez	.05	.02	.01
☐ 81	Tim Raines	.20	.09	.03
☐ 82	Sammy Sosa	.40	.18	.05
☐ 83	Cory Snyder	.05	.02	.01
☐ 84	Bobby Thigpen	.05	.02	.01
☐ 85	Frank Thomas	4.00	1.80	.50
	(Card says he is			
	an outfielder)			
☐ 86	Robin Ventura	.20	.09	.03
☐ 87	Todd Benzinger	.05	.02	.01
☐ 88	Glenn Braggs	.05	.02	.01
☐ 89	Tom Browning UER	.05	.02	.01
	(Front photo actually			
	Norm Charlton)			
☐ 90	Norm Charlton	.05	.02	.01
☐ 91	Eric Davis	.10	.05	.01
☐ 92	Rob Dibble	.10	.05	.01
☐ 93	Bill Doran	.05	.02	.01
☐ 94	Mariano Duncan UER	.05	.02	.01
	(Right back photo			
	is Billy Hatcher)			
☐ 95	Billy Hatcher	.05	.02	.01
☐ 96	Barry Larkin	.30	.14	.04
☐ 97	Randy Myers	.20	.09	.03
☐ 98	Hal Morris	.10	.05	.01
☐ 99	Joe Oliver	.05	.02	.01
☐ 100	Paul O'Neill	.20	.09	.03
☐ 101	Jeff Reed	.05	.02	.01
	(See also 104)			
☐ 102	Jose Rijo	.10	.05	.01
☐ 103	Chris Sabo	.05	.02	.01
	(See also 106)			
☐ 104	Beau Allred UER	.05	.02	.01
	(Card number is 101)			
☐ 105	Sandy Alomar Jr.	.10	.05	.01
☐ 106	Carlos Baerga UER	.75	.35	.09
	(Card number is 103)			
☐ 107	Albert Belle	1.00	.45	.12
☐ 108	Jerry Browne	.05	.02	.01
☐ 109	Tom Candiotti	.05	.02	.01
☐ 110	Alex Cole	.05	.02	.01
☐ 111	John Farrell	.05	.02	.01
	(See also 114)			
☐ 112	Felix Fermin	.05	.02	.01
☐ 113	Brook Jacoby	.05	.02	.01
☐ 114	Chris James UER	.05	.02	.01
	(Card number is 111)			
☐ 115	Doug Jones	.05	.02	.01
☐ 116	Steve Olin	.05	.02	.01
	(See also 119)			
☐ 117	Greg Swindell	.05	.02	.01
☐ 118	Turner Ward	.05	.02	.01
☐ 119	Mitch Webster UER	.05	.02	.01
	(Card number is 116)			
☐ 120	Dave Bergman	.05	.02	.01
☐ 121	Cecil Fielder	.20	.09	.03
☐ 122	Travis Fryman	.40	.18	.05
☐ 123	Mike Henneman	.05	.02	.01
☐ 124	Lloyd Moseby	.05	.02	.01
☐ 125	Dan Petry	.05	.02	.01
☐ 126	Tony Phillips	.20	.09	.03
☐ 127	Mark Salas	.05	.02	.01
☐ 128	Frank Tanana	.10	.05	.01
☐ 129	Alan Trammell	.20	.09	.03
☐ 130	Lou Whitaker	.20	.09	.03
☐ 131	Eric Anthony	.05	.02	.01
☐ 132	Craig Biggio	.20	.09	.03
☐ 133	Ken Caminiti	.20	.09	.03
☐ 134	Casey Candaele	.05	.02	.01
☐ 135	Andujar Cedeno	.05	.02	.01
☐ 136	Mark Davidson	.05	.02	.01
☐ 137	Jim Deshaies	.05	.02	.01
☐ 138	Mark Portugal	.05	.02	.01
☐ 139	Rafael Ramirez	.05	.02	.01
☐ 140	Mike Scott	.05	.02	.01
☐ 141	Eric Yelding	.05	.02	.01
☐ 142	Gerald Young	.05	.02	.01
☐ 143	Kevin Appier	.10	.05	.01
☐ 144	George Brett	.75	.35	.09
☐ 145	Jeff Conine	1.00	.45	.12
☐ 146	Jim Eisenreich	.05	.02	.01
☐ 147	Tom Gordon	.10	.05	.01
☐ 148	Mark Gubicza	.05	.02	.01
☐ 149	Bo Jackson	.20	.09	.03
☐ 150	Brent Mayne	.05	.02	.01
☐ 151	Mike Macfarlane	.05	.02	.01
☐ 152	Brian McRae	.60	.25	.07
☐ 153	Jeff Montgomery	.10	.05	.01
☐ 154	Bret Saberhagen	.20	.09	.03
☐ 155	Kevin Seitzer	.05	.02	.01
☐ 156	Terry Shumpert	.05	.02	.01
☐ 157	Kurt Stillwell	.05	.02	.01
☐ 158	Danny Tartabull	.10	.05	.01
☐ 159	Tim Belcher	.05	.02	.01
☐ 160	Kal Daniels	.05	.02	.01
☐ 161	Alfredo Griffin	.05	.02	.01
☐ 162	Lenny Harris	.05	.02	.01
☐ 163	Jay Howell	.05	.02	.01
☐ 164	Ramon Martinez	.10	.05	.01
☐ 165	Mike Morgan	.05	.02	.01
☐ 166	Eddie Murray	.40	.18	.05
☐ 167	Jose Offerman	.10	.05	.01
☐ 168	Juan Samuel	.05	.02	.01
☐ 169	Mike Scioscia	.05	.02	.01
☐ 170	Mike Sharperson	.05	.02	.01
☐ 171	Darryl Strawberry	.10	.05	.01
☐ 172	Greg Brock	.05	.02	.01
☐ 173	Chuck Crim	.05	.02	.01
☐ 174	Jim Gantner	.05	.02	.01
☐ 175	Ted Higuera	.05	.02	.01
☐ 176	Mark Knudson	.05	.02	.01
☐ 177	Tim McIntosh	.05	.02	.01
☐ 178	Paul Molitor	.20	.09	.03
☐ 179	Dan Plesac	.05	.02	.01
☐ 180	Gary Sheffield	.20	.09	.03

☐ 181 Bill Spiers	.05	.02	.01
☐ 182 B.J. Surhoff	.10	.05	.01
☐ 183 Greg Vaughn	.05	.02	.01
☐ 184 Robin Yount	.30	.14	.04
☐ 185 Rick Aguilera	.10	.05	.01
☐ 186 Greg Gagne	.05	.02	.01
☐ 187 Dan Gladden	.05	.02	.01
☐ 188 Brian Harper	.05	.02	.01
☐ 189 Kent Hrbek	.10	.05	.01
☐ 190 Gene Larkin	.05	.02	.01
☐ 191 Shane Mack	.05	.02	.01
☐ 192 Pedro Munoz	.10	.05	.01
☐ 193 Al Newman	.05	.02	.01
☐ 194 Junior Ortiz	.05	.02	.01
☐ 195 Kirby Puckett	.60	.25	.07
☐ 196 Kevin Tapani	.10	.05	.01
☐ 197 Dennis Boyd	.05	.02	.01
☐ 198 Tim Burke	.05	.02	.01
☐ 199 Ivan Calderon	.05	.02	.01
☐ 200 Delino DeShields	.10	.05	.01
☐ 201 Mike Fitzgerald	.05	.02	.01
☐ 202 Steve Frey	.05	.02	.01
☐ 203 Andres Galarraga	.20	.09	.03
☐ 204 Marquis Grissom	.35	.16	.04
☐ 205 Dave Martinez	.05	.02	.01
☐ 206 Dennis Martinez	.10	.05	.01
☐ 207 Junior Noboa	.05	.02	.01
☐ 208 Spike Owen	.05	.02	.01
☐ 209 Scott Ruskin	.05	.02	.01
☐ 210 Tim Wallach	.05	.02	.01
☐ 211 Daryl Boston	.05	.02	.01
☐ 212 Vince Coleman	.05	.02	.01
☐ 213 David Cone	.20	.09	.03
☐ 214 Ron Darling	.05	.02	.01
☐ 215 Kevin Elster	.05	.02	.01
☐ 216 Sid Fernandez	.10	.05	.01
☐ 217 John Franco	.20	.09	.03
☐ 218 Dwight Gooden	.10	.05	.01
☐ 219 Tom Herr	.05	.02	.01
☐ 220 Todd Hundley	.10	.05	.01
☐ 221 Gregg Jefferies	.20	.09	.03
☐ 222 Howard Johnson	.05	.02	.01
☐ 223 Dave Magadan	.05	.02	.01
☐ 224 Kevin McReynolds	.05	.02	.01
☐ 225 Keith Miller	.05	.02	.01
☐ 226 Mackey Sasser	.05	.02	.01
☐ 227 Frank Viola	.10	.05	.01
☐ 228 Jesse Barfield	.05	.02	.01
☐ 229 Greg Cadaret	.05	.02	.01
☐ 230 Alvaro Espinoza	.05	.02	.01
☐ 231 Bob Geren	.05	.02	.01
☐ 232 Lee Guetterman	.05	.02	.01
☐ 233 Mel Hall	.05	.02	.01
☐ 234 Andy Hawkins UER	.05	.02	.01
(Back center photo			
is not him)			
☐ 235 Roberto Kelly	.10	.05	.01
☐ 236 Tim Leary	.05	.02	.01
☐ 237 Jim Leyritz	.05	.02	.01
☐ 238 Kevin Maas	.05	.02	.01
☐ 239 Don Mattingly	1.00	.45	.12
☐ 240 Hensley Meulens	.05	.02	.01
☐ 241 Eric Plunk	.05	.02	.01
☐ 242 Steve Sax	.05	.02	.01
☐ 243 Todd Burns	.05	.02	.01
☐ 244 Jose Canseco	.30	.14	.04
☐ 245 Dennis Eckersley	.20	.09	.03
☐ 246 Mike Gallego	.05	.02	.01
☐ 247 Dave Henderson	.05	.02	.01
☐ 248 Rickey Henderson	.20	.09	.03
☐ 249 Rick Honeycutt	.05	.02	.01
☐ 250 Carney Lansford	.10	.05	.01
☐ 251 Mark McGwire	.20	.09	.03
☐ 252 Mike Moore	.05	.02	.01
☐ 253 Terry Steinbach	.10	.05	.01
☐ 254 Dave Stewart	.20	.09	.03
☐ 255 Walt Weiss	.05	.02	.01
☐ 256 Bob Welch	.10	.05	.01
☐ 257 Curt Young	.05	.02	.01
☐ 258 Wes Chamberlain	.05	.02	.01
☐ 259 Pat Combs	.05	.02	.01
☐ 260 Darren Daulton	.20	.09	.03
☐ 261 Jose DeJesus	.05	.02	.01
☐ 262 Len Dykstra	.20	.09	.03
☐ 263 Charlie Hayes	.10	.05	.01
☐ 264 Von Hayes	.05	.02	.01
☐ 265 Ken Howell	.05	.02	.01
☐ 266 John Kruk	.20	.09	.03
☐ 267 Roger McDowell	.05	.02	.01
☐ 268 Mickey Morandini	.05	.02	.01
☐ 269 Terry Mulholland	.05	.02	.01
☐ 270 Dale Murphy	.20	.09	.03
☐ 271 Randy Ready	.05	.02	.01
☐ 272 Dickie Thon	.05	.02	.01
☐ 273 Stan Belinda	.05	.02	.01
☐ 274 Jay Bell	.10	.05	.01
☐ 275 Barry Bonds	.60	.25	.07
☐ 276 Bobby Bonilla	.20	.09	.03
☐ 277 Doug Drabek	.10	.05	.01
☐ 278 Carlos Garcia	.30	.14	.04
☐ 279 Neal Heaton	.05	.02	.01
☐ 280 Jeff King	.10	.05	.01
☐ 281 Bill Landrum	.05	.02	.01
☐ 282 Mike LaValliere	.05	.02	.01
☐ 283 Jose Lind	.05	.02	.01
☐ 284 Orlando Merced	.30	.14	.04
☐ 285 Gary Redus	.05	.02	.01
☐ 286 Don Slaught	.05	.02	.01
☐ 287 Andy Van Slyke	.10	.05	.01
☐ 288 Jose DeLeon	.05	.02	.01
☐ 289 Pedro Guerrero	.10	.05	.01
☐ 290 Ray Lankford	.40	.18	.05
☐ 291 Joe Magrane	.05	.02	.01
☐ 292 Jose Oquendo	.05	.02	.01
☐ 293 Tom Pagnozzi	.05	.02	.01
☐ 294 Bryn Smith	.05	.02	.01
☐ 295 Lee Smith	.20	.09	.03
☐ 296 Ozzie Smith UER	.30	.14	.04
(Born 12-26, 54,			
should have hyphen)			
☐ 297 Milt Thompson	.05	.02	.01
☐ 298 Craig Wilson	.05	.02	.01
☐ 299 Todd Zeile	.10	.05	.01
☐ 300 Shawn Abner	.05	.02	.01
☐ 301 Andy Benes	.10	.05	.01
☐ 302 Paul Faries	.05	.02	.01
☐ 303 Tony Gwynn	.60	.25	.07
☐ 304 Greg W. Harris	.05	.02	.01
☐ 305 Thomas Howard	.05	.02	.01
☐ 306 Bruce Hurst	.05	.02	.01
☐ 307 Craig Lefferts	.05	.02	.01
☐ 308 Fred McGriff	.30	.14	.04
☐ 309 Dennis Rasmussen	.05	.02	.01
☐ 310 Bip Roberts	.10	.05	.01
☐ 311 Benito Santiago	.10	.05	.01
☐ 312 Garry Templeton	.05	.02	.01
☐ 313 Ed Whitson	.05	.02	.01
☐ 314 Dave Anderson	.05	.02	.01
☐ 315 Kevin Bass	.05	.02	.01
☐ 316 Jeff Brantley	.05	.02	.01
☐ 317 John Burkett	.05	.02	.01
☐ 318 Will Clark	.30	.14	.04

☐ 319	Steve Decker	.05	.02	.01
☐ 320	Scott Garrelts	.05	.02	.01
☐ 321	Terry Kennedy	.05	.02	.01
☐ 322	Mark Leonard	.05	.02	.01
☐ 323	Darren Lewis	.10	.05	.01
☐ 324	Greg Litton	.05	.02	.01
☐ 325	Willie McGee	.10	.05	.01
☐ 326	Kevin Mitchell	.10	.05	.01
☐ 327	Don Robinson	.05	.02	.01
☐ 328	Andres Santana	.05	.02	.01
☐ 329	Robby Thompson	.05	.02	.01
☐ 330	Jose Uribe	.05	.02	.01
☐ 331	Matt Williams	.40	.18	.05
☐ 332	Scott Bradley	.05	.02	.01
☐ 333	Henry Cotto	.05	.02	.01
☐ 334	Alvin Davis	.05	.02	.01
☐ 335	Ken Griffey Sr.	.10	.05	.01
☐ 336	Ken Griffey Jr.	3.00	1.35	.35
☐ 337	Erik Hanson	.05	.02	.01
☐ 338	Brian Holman	.05	.02	.01
☐ 339	Randy Johnson	.50	.23	.06
☐ 340	Edgar Martinez UER	.20	.09	.03
	(Listed as playing SS)			
☐ 341	Tino Martinez	.20	.09	.03
☐ 342	Pete O'Brien	.05	.02	.01
☐ 343	Harold Reynolds	.05	.02	.01
☐ 344	Dave Valle	.05	.02	.01
☐ 345	Omar Vizquel	.10	.05	.01
☐ 346	Brad Arnsberg	.05	.02	.01
☐ 347	Kevin Brown	.10	.05	.01
☐ 348	Julio Franco	.10	.05	.01
☐ 349	Jeff Huson	.05	.02	.01
☐ 350	Rafael Palmeiro	.20	.09	.03
☐ 351	Geno Petralli	.05	.02	.01
☐ 352	Gary Pettis	.05	.02	.01
☐ 353	Kenny Rogers	.10	.05	.01
☐ 354	Jeff Russell	.05	.02	.01
☐ 355	Nolan Ryan	1.50	.70	.19
☐ 356	Ruben Sierra	.20	.09	.03
☐ 357	Bobby Witt	.05	.02	.01
☐ 358	Roberto Alomar	.50	.23	.06
☐ 359	Pat Borders	.05	.02	.01
☐ 360	Joe Carter UER	.20	.09	.03
	(Reverse negative			
	on back photo)			
☐ 361	Kelly Gruber	.05	.02	.01
☐ 362	Tom Henke	.10	.05	.01
☐ 363	Glenallen Hill	.05	.02	.01
☐ 364	Jimmy Key	.10	.05	.01
☐ 365	Manny Lee	.05	.02	.01
☐ 366	Rance Mulliniks	.05	.02	.01
☐ 367	John Olerud UER	.10	.05	.01
	(Throwing left on card;			
	back has throws right;			
	he does throw lefty)			
☐ 368	Dave Stieb	.05	.02	.01
☐ 369	Duane Ward	.05	.02	.01
☐ 370	David Wells	.05	.02	.01
☐ 371	Mark Whiten	.10	.05	.01
☐ 372	Mookie Wilson	.10	.05	.01
☐ 373	Willie Banks MLP	.05	.02	.01
☐ 374	Steve Carter MLP	.05	.02	.01
☐ 375	Scott Chiamparino MLP	.05	.02	.01
☐ 376	Steve Chitren MLP	.05	.02	.01
☐ 377	Darrin Fletcher MLP	.05	.02	.01
☐ 378	Rich Garces MLP	.05	.02	.01
☐ 379	Reggie Jefferson MLP	.10	.05	.01
☐ 380	Eric Karros MLP	1.00	.45	.12
☐ 381	Pat Kelly MLP	.10	.05	.01
☐ 382	Chuck Knoblauch MLP	.50	.23	.06
☐ 383	Denny Neagle MLP	.30	.14	.04
☐ 384	Dan Opperman MLP	.05	.02	.01
☐ 385	John Ramos MLP	.05	.02	.01
☐ 386	Henry Rodriguez MLP	.10	.05	.01
☐ 387	Mo Vaughn MLP	1.25	.55	.16
☐ 388	Gerald Williams MLP	.05	.02	.01
☐ 389	Mike York MLP	.05	.02	.01
☐ 390	Eddie Zosky MLP	.05	.02	.01
☐ 391	Barry Bonds EP	.30	.14	.04
☐ 392	Cecil Fielder EP	.10	.05	.01
☐ 393	Rickey Henderson EP	.20	.09	.03
☐ 394	Dave Justice EP	.25	.11	.03
☐ 395	Nolan Ryan EP	.75	.35	.09
☐ 396	Bobby Thigpen EP	.05	.02	.01
☐ 397	Checklist Card	.10	.05	.01
	Gregg Jefferies			
☐ 398	Checklist Card	.05	.02	.01
	Von Hayes			
☐ 399	Checklist Card	.05	.02	.01
	Terry Kennedy			
☐ 400	Checklist Card	.20	.09	.03
	Nolan Ryan			

1991 Ultra Update

The 1991 Ultra Baseball Update factory set
contains 120 cards and 20 team logo stickers. The set includes the year's hottest
rookies and important veteran players traded after the original Ultra series was produced. The cards measure the standard
size. The front has a color action shot,
while the back has a portrait photo and two
full-figure action shots. The cards are numbered (with a U prefix) and checklisted
below alphabetically within and according
to teams for each league as follow:
Baltimore Orioles (1-4), Boston Red Sox (5-
7), California Angels (8-12), Chicago White
Sox (13-18), Cleveland Indians (19-21),
Detroit Tigers (22-24), Kansas City Royals
(25-29), Milwaukee Brewers (30-33),
Minnesota Twins (34-39), New York
Yankees (40-44), Oakland Athletics (45-
48), Seattle Mariners (49-53), Texas
Rangers (54-58), Toronto Blue Jays (59-
64), Atlanta Braves (65-69), Chicago Cubs
(70-75), Cincinnati Reds (76-78), Houston
Astros (79-84), Los Angeles Dodgers (85-
89), Montreal Expos (90-93), New York
Mets (94-97), Philadelphia Phillies (98-101),
Pittsburgh Pirates (102-104), St. Louis
Cardinals (105-109), San Diego Padres
(110-114), and San Francisco Giants (115-

119). The key Rookie Cards in this set are Jeff Bagwell, Juan Guzman, Mike Mussina, and Ivan Rodriguez.

	MINT	NRMT	EXC
COMPLETE FACT.SET (120) ..	32.00	14.50	4.00
COMMON CARD (1-120)	.15	.07	.02

		MINT	NRMT	EXC
☐ 1	Dwight Evans	.30	.14	.04
☐ 2	Chito Martinez	.15	.07	.02
☐ 3	Bob Melvin	.15	.07	.02
☐ 4	Mike Mussina	6.00	2.70	.75
☐ 5	Jack Clark	.30	.14	.04
☐ 6	Dana Kiecker	.15	.07	.02
☐ 7	Steve Lyons	.15	.07	.02
☐ 8	Gary Gaetti	.30	.14	.04
☐ 9	Dave Gallagher	.15	.07	.02
☐ 10	Dave Parker	.30	.14	.04
☐ 11	Luis Polonia	.15	.07	.02
☐ 12	Luis Sojo	.15	.07	.02
☐ 13	Wilson Alvarez	.75	.35	.09
☐ 14	Alex Fernandez	1.50	.70	.19
☐ 15	Craig Grebeck	.15	.07	.02
☐ 16	Ron Karkovice	.15	.07	.02
☐ 17	Warren Newson	.15	.07	.02
☐ 18	Scott Radinsky	.15	.07	.02
☐ 19	Glenallen Hill	.30	.14	.04
☐ 20	Charles Nagy	1.50	.70	.19
☐ 21	Mark Whiten	.30	.14	.04
☐ 22	Milt Cuyler	.15	.07	.02
☐ 23	Paul Gibson	.15	.07	.02
☐ 24	Mickey Tettleton	.30	.14	.04
☐ 25	Todd Benzinger	.15	.07	.02
☐ 26	Storm Davis	.15	.07	.02
☐ 27	Kirk Gibson	.50	.23	.06
☐ 28	Bill Pecota	.15	.07	.02
☐ 29	Gary Thurman	.15	.07	.02
☐ 30	Darryl Hamilton	.30	.14	.04
☐ 31	Jaime Navarro	.15	.07	.02
☐ 32	Willie Randolph	.30	.14	.04
☐ 33	Bill Wegman	.15	.07	.02
☐ 34	Randy Bush	.15	.07	.02
☐ 35	Chili Davis	.50	.23	.06
☐ 36	Scott Erickson	.30	.14	.04
☐ 37	Chuck Knoblauch	2.50	1.10	.30
☐ 38	Scott Leius	.15	.07	.02
☐ 39	Jack Morris	.50	.23	.06
☐ 40	John Habyan	.15	.07	.02
☐ 41	Pat Kelly	.30	.14	.04
☐ 42	Matt Nokes	.15	.07	.02
☐ 43	Scott Sanderson	.15	.07	.02
☐ 44	Bernie Williams	1.50	.70	.19
☐ 45	Harold Baines	.50	.23	.06
☐ 46	Brook Jacoby	.15	.07	.02
☐ 47	Earnest Riles	.15	.07	.02
☐ 48	Willie Wilson	.15	.07	.02
☐ 49	Jay Buhner	1.00	.45	.12
☐ 50	Rich DeLucia	.15	.07	.02
☐ 51	Mike Jackson	.15	.07	.02
☐ 52	Bill Krueger	.15	.07	.02
☐ 53	Bill Swift	.15	.07	.02
☐ 54	Brian Downing	.15	.07	.02
☐ 55	Juan Gonzalez	10.00	4.50	1.25
☐ 56	Dean Palmer	1.00	.45	.12
☐ 57	Kevin Reimer	.15	.07	.02
☐ 58	Ivan Rodriguez	2.50	1.10	.30
☐ 59	Tom Candiotti	.15	.07	.02
☐ 60	Juan Guzman	.75	.35	.09
☐ 61	Mark McDonald	.15	.07	.02
☐ 62	Greg Myers	.15	.07	.02
☐ 63	Ed Sprague	.15	.07	.02
☐ 64	Devon White	.30	.14	.04
☐ 65	Rafael Belliard	.15	.07	.02
☐ 66	Juan Berenguer	.15	.07	.02
☐ 67	Brian R. Hunter	.15	.07	.02
☐ 68	Kent Mercker	.75	.35	.09
☐ 69	Otis Nixon	.15	.07	.02
☐ 70	Danny Jackson	.15	.07	.02
☐ 71	Chuck McElroy	.15	.07	.02
☐ 72	Gary Scott	.15	.07	.02
☐ 73	Heathcliff Slocumb	.75	.35	.09
☐ 74	Chico Walker	.15	.07	.02
☐ 75	Rick Wilkins	.15	.07	.02
☐ 76	Chris Hammond	.15	.07	.02
☐ 77	Luis Quinones	.15	.07	.02
☐ 78	Herm Winningham	.15	.07	.02
☐ 79	Jeff Bagwell	12.00	5.50	1.50
☐ 80	Jim Corsi	.15	.07	.02
☐ 81	Steve Finley	.30	.14	.04
☐ 82	Luis Gonzalez	1.00	.45	.12
☐ 83	Pete Harnisch	.15	.07	.02
☐ 84	Darryl Kile	.15	.07	.02
☐ 85	Brett Butler	.50	.23	.06
☐ 86	Gary Carter	.50	.23	.06
☐ 87	Tim Crews	.15	.07	.02
☐ 88	Orel Hershiser	.50	.23	.06
☐ 89	Bob Ojeda	.15	.07	.02
☐ 90	Bret Barberie	.30	.14	.04
☐ 91	Barry Jones	.15	.07	.02
☐ 92	Gilberto Reyes	.15	.07	.02
☐ 93	Larry Walker	3.00	1.35	.35
☐ 94	Hubie Brooks	.15	.07	.02
☐ 95	Tim Burke	.15	.07	.02
☐ 96	Rick Cerone	.15	.07	.02
☐ 97	Jeff Innis	.15	.07	.02
☐ 98	Wally Backman	.15	.07	.02
☐ 99	Tommy Greene	.15	.07	.02
☐ 100	Ricky Jordan	.15	.07	.02
☐ 101	Mitch Williams	.30	.14	.04
☐ 102	John Smiley	.15	.07	.02
☐ 103	Randy Tomlin	.15	.07	.02
☐ 104	Gary Varsho	.15	.07	.02
☐ 105	Cris Carpenter	.15	.07	.02
☐ 106	Ken Hill	1.00	.45	.12
☐ 107	Felix Jose	.15	.07	.02
☐ 108	Omar Olivares	.15	.07	.02
☐ 109	Gerald Perry	.15	.07	.02
☐ 110	Jerald Clark	.15	.07	.02
☐ 111	Tony Fernandez	.15	.07	.02
☐ 112	Darrin Jackson	.15	.07	.02
☐ 113	Mike Maddux	.15	.07	.02
☐ 114	Tim Teufel	.15	.07	.02
☐ 115	Bud Black	.15	.07	.02
☐ 116	Kelly Downs	.15	.07	.02
☐ 117	Mike Felder	.15	.07	.02
☐ 118	Willie McGee	.30	.14	.04
☐ 119	Trevor Wilson	.15	.07	.02
☐ 120	Checklist 1-120	.15	.07	.02

1992 Ultra

Consisting of 600 cards, the 1992 Fleer Ultra set was issued in two series of 300 cards each. The glossy color action player photos on the fronts are full-bleed except at the bottom where a diagonal gold-foil stripe edges a green marbleized border. The player's name and team appear on the

marble-colored area in bars that are color-coded by team. The horizontal backs display an action and close-up cut-out player photo against a grid shaded with a gradated team color. The grid, team-colored bars containing stats and the player's name, biographical information, and the team logo all rest on a green marbleized background. The cards are numbered on the back and checklisted below alphabetically within and according to teams for each league as follows: Baltimore Orioles (1-11/301-310), Boston Red Sox (12-23/311-320), California Angels (24-31/321-331), Chicago White Sox (32-44/332-343), Cleveland Indians (45-55/344-357), Detroit Tigers (56-65/358-368), Kansas City Royals (66-77/369-377), Milwaukee Brewers (78-87/378-392), Minnesota Twins (88-98/393-403), New York Yankees (99-108/404-417), Oakland Athletics (109-119/418-429), Seattle Mariners (120-130/430-436), Texas Rangers (131-142/437-447), Toronto Blue Jays (143-156/448-454), Atlanta Braves (157-171/455-465), Chicago Cubs (172-184/466-477), Cincinnati Reds (185-197/478-487), Houston Astros (198-208/488-498), Los Angeles Dodgers (209-219/499-510), Montreal Expos (220-226/511-526), New York Mets (227-238/527-539), Philadelphia Phillies (239-249/540-549), Pittsburgh Pirates (250-262/550-561), St. Louis Cardinals (263-273/562-574), San Diego Padres (274-283/575-585) and San Francisco Giants (284-297/586-597). Rookie Cards in the set include Rod Beck, Chad Curtis, Pat Listach, Pat Mahomes, Rey Sanchez, and Brian Williams. Some cards have been found without the word Fleer on the front.

	MINT	NRMT	EXC
COMPLETE SET (600)	40.00	18.00	5.00
COMPLETE SERIES 1 (300)	25.00	11.00	3.10
COMPLETE SERIES 2 (300)	15.00	6.75	1.85
COMMON CARD (1-300)	.10	.05	.01
COMMON CARD (301-600)	.10	.05	.01
☐ 1 Glenn Davis	.10	.05	.01
☐ 2 Mike Devereaux	.15	.07	.02
☐ 3 Dwight Evans	.15	.07	.02
☐ 4 Leo Gomez	.10	.05	.01
☐ 5 Chris Hoiles	.15	.07	.02
☐ 6 Sam Horn	.10	.05	.01
☐ 7 Chito Martinez	.10	.05	.01
☐ 8 Randy Milligan	.10	.05	.01
☐ 9 Mike Mussina	.50	.23	.06
☐ 10 Billy Ripken	.10	.05	.01
☐ 11 Cal Ripken	2.00	.90	.25
☐ 12 Tom Brunansky	.10	.05	.01
☐ 13 Ellis Burks	.15	.07	.02
☐ 14 Jack Clark	.15	.07	.02
☐ 15 Roger Clemens	.30	.14	.04
☐ 16 Mike Greenwell	.25	.11	.03
☐ 17 Joe Hesketh	.10	.05	.01
☐ 18 Tony Pena	.10	.05	.01
☐ 19 Carlos Quintana	.10	.05	.01
☐ 20 Jeff Reardon	.15	.07	.02
☐ 21 Jody Reed	.10	.05	.01
☐ 22 Luis Rivera	.10	.05	.01
☐ 23 Mo Vaughn	.75	.35	.09
☐ 24 Gary DiSarcina	.10	.05	.01
☐ 25 Chuck Finley	.10	.05	.01
☐ 26 Gary Gaetti	.15	.07	.02
☐ 27 Bryan Harvey	.10	.05	.01
☐ 28 Lance Parrish	.15	.07	.02
☐ 29 Luis Polonia	.10	.05	.01
☐ 30 Dick Schofield	.10	.05	.01
☐ 31 Luis Sojo	.10	.05	.01
☐ 32 Wilson Alvarez	.25	.11	.03
☐ 33 Carlton Fisk	.25	.11	.03
☐ 34 Craig Grebeck	.10	.05	.01
☐ 35 Ozzie Guillen	.15	.07	.02
☐ 36 Greg Hibbard	.10	.05	.01
☐ 37 Charlie Hough	.15	.07	.02
☐ 38 Lance Johnson	.10	.05	.01
☐ 39 Ron Karkovice	.10	.05	.01
☐ 40 Jack McDowell	.25	.11	.03
☐ 41 Donn Pall	.10	.05	.01
☐ 42 Melido Perez	.10	.05	.01
☐ 43 Tim Raines	.25	.11	.03
☐ 44 Frank Thomas	3.00	1.35	.35
☐ 45 Sandy Alomar Jr.	.15	.07	.02
☐ 46 Carlos Baerga	.60	.25	.07
☐ 47 Albert Belle	1.00	.45	.12
☐ 48 Jerry Browne UER	.10	.05	.01
(Reversed negative on card back)			
☐ 49 Felix Fermin	.10	.05	.01
☐ 50 Reggie Jefferson UER	.10	.05	.01
(Born 1968, not 1966)			
☐ 51 Mark Lewis	.10	.05	.01
☐ 52 Carlos Martinez	.10	.05	.01
☐ 53 Steve Olin	.10	.05	.01
☐ 54 Jim Thome	1.50	.70	.19
☐ 55 Mark Whiten	.15	.07	.02
☐ 56 Dave Bergman	.10	.05	.01
☐ 57 Milt Cuyler	.10	.05	.01
☐ 58 Rob Deer	.10	.05	.01
☐ 59 Cecil Fielder	.25	.11	.03
☐ 60 Travis Fryman	.25	.11	.03
☐ 61 Scott Livingstone	.10	.05	.01
☐ 62 Tony Phillips	.25	.11	.03
☐ 63 Mickey Tettleton	.15	.07	.02
☐ 64 Alan Trammell	.25	.11	.03
☐ 65 Lou Whitaker	.25	.11	.03
☐ 66 Kevin Appier	.15	.07	.02
☐ 67 Mike Boddicker	.10	.05	.01
☐ 68 George Brett	.75	.35	.09
☐ 69 Jim Eisenreich	.10	.05	.01
☐ 70 Mark Gubicza	.10	.05	.01
☐ 71 David Howard	.10	.05	.01
☐ 72 Joel Johnson	.10	.05	.01
☐ 73 Mike Macfarlane	.10	.05	.01
☐ 74 Brent Mayne	.10	.05	.01
☐ 75 Brian McRae	.25	.11	.03
☐ 76 Jeff Montgomery	.15	.07	.02

77	Danny Tartabull	.15	.07	.02
78	Don August	.10	.05	.01
79	Dante Bichette	.30	.14	.04
80	Ted Higuera	.10	.05	.01
81	Paul Molitor	.25	.11	.03
82	Jaime Navarro	.10	.05	.01
83	Gary Sheffield	.25	.11	.03
84	Bill Spiers	.10	.05	.01
85	B.J. Surhoff	.15	.07	.02
86	Greg Vaughn	.15	.07	.02
87	Robin Yount	.30	.14	.04
88	Rick Aguilera	.15	.07	.02
89	Chili Davis	.25	.11	.03
90	Scott Erickson	.15	.07	.02
91	Brian Harper	.10	.05	.01
92	Kent Hrbek	.15	.07	.02
93	Chuck Knoblauch	.30	.14	.04
94	Scott Leius	.10	.05	.01
95	Shane Mack	.10	.05	.01
96	Mike Pagliarulo	.10	.05	.01
97	Kirby Puckett	.60	.25	.07
98	Kevin Tapani	.10	.05	.01
99	Jesse Barfield	.10	.05	.01
100	Alvaro Espinoza	.10	.05	.01
101	Mel Hall	.10	.05	.01
102	Pat Kelly	.10	.05	.01
103	Roberto Kelly	.15	.07	.02
104	Kevin Maas	.10	.05	.01
105	Don Mattingly	1.00	.45	.12
106	Hensley Meulens	.10	.05	.01
107	Matt Nokes	.10	.05	.01
108	Steve Sax	.10	.05	.01
109	Harold Baines	.25	.11	.03
110	Jose Canseco	.30	.14	.04
111	Ron Darling	.10	.05	.01
112	Mike Gallego	.10	.05	.01
113	Dave Henderson	.10	.05	.01
114	Rickey Henderson	.25	.11	.03
115	Mark McGwire	.25	.11	.03
116	Terry Steinbach	.15	.07	.02
117	Dave Stewart	.25	.11	.03
118	Todd Van Poppel	.15	.07	.02
119	Bob Welch	.15	.07	.02
120	Greg Briley	.10	.05	.01
121	Jay Buhner	.25	.11	.03
122	Rick DeLucia	.10	.05	.01
123	Ken Griffey Jr.	3.00	1.35	.35
124	Erik Hanson	.10	.05	.01
125	Randy Johnson	.50	.23	.06
126	Edgar Martinez	.25	.11	.03
127	Tino Martinez	.25	.11	.03
128	Pete O'Brien	.10	.05	.01
129	Harold Reynolds	.10	.05	.01
130	Dave Valle	.10	.05	.01
131	Julio Franco	.15	.07	.02
132	Juan Gonzalez	.75	.35	.09
133	Jeff Huson	.10	.05	.01
	(Shows Jose Canseco sliding into second)			
134	Mike Jeffcoat	.10	.05	.01
135	Terry Mathews	.10	.05	.01
136	Rafael Palmeiro	.25	.11	.03
137	Dean Palmer	.15	.07	.02
138	Geno Petralli	.10	.05	.01
139	Ivan Rodriguez	.25	.11	.03
140	Jeff Russell	.10	.05	.01
141	Nolan Ryan	1.50	.70	.19
142	Ruben Sierra	.25	.11	.03
143	Roberto Alomar	.40	.18	.05
144	Pat Borders	.10	.05	.01
145	Joe Carter	.25	.11	.03

146	Kelly Gruber	.10	.05	.01
147	Jimmy Key	.15	.07	.02
148	Manny Lee	.10	.05	.01
149	Rance Mulliniks	.10	.05	.01
150	Greg Myers	.10	.05	.01
151	John Olerud	.15	.07	.02
152	Dave Stieb	.10	.05	.01
153	Todd Stottlemyre	.10	.05	.01
154	Duane Ward	.10	.05	.01
155	Devon White			
156	Eddie Zosky	.10	.05	.01
157	Steve Avery	.25	.11	.03
158	Rafael Belliard	.10	.05	.01
159	Jeff Blauser	.15	.07	.02
160	Sid Bream	.10	.05	.01
161	Ron Gant	.25	.11	.03
162	Tom Glavine	.25	.11	.03
163	Brian Hunter	.10	.05	.01
164	Dave Justice	.30	.14	.04
165	Mark Lemke	.15	.07	.02
166	Greg Olson	.10	.05	.01
167	Terry Pendleton	.25	.11	.03
168	Lonnie Smith	.10	.05	.01
169	John Smoltz	.25	.11	.03
170	Mike Stanton	.10	.05	.01
171	Jeff Treadway	.10	.05	.01
172	Paul Assenmacher	.10	.05	.01
173	George Bell	.10	.05	.01
174	Shawon Dunston	.10	.05	.01
175	Mark Grace	.25	.11	.03
176	Danny Jackson	.10	.05	.01
177	Les Lancaster	.10	.05	.01
178	Greg Maddux	1.50	.70	.19
179	Luis Salazar	.10	.05	.01
180	Rey Sanchez	.10	.05	.01
181	Ryne Sandberg	.50	.23	.06
182	Jose Vizcaino	.10	.05	.01
183	Chico Walker	.10	.05	.01
184	Jerome Walton	.10	.05	.01
185	Glenn Braggs	.10	.05	.01
186	Tom Browning	.10	.05	.01
187	Rob Dibble	.10	.05	.01
188	Bill Doran	.10	.05	.01
189	Chris Hammond	.10	.05	.01
190	Billy Hatcher	.10	.05	.01
191	Barry Larkin	.30	.14	.04
192	Hal Morris	.15	.07	.02
193	Joe Oliver	.10	.05	.01
194	Paul O'Neill	.25	.11	.03
195	Jeff Reed	.10	.05	.01
196	Jose Rijo	.15	.07	.02
197	Chris Sabo	.10	.05	.01
198	Jeff Bagwell	1.00	.45	.12
199	Craig Biggio	.25	.11	.03
200	Ken Caminiti	.25	.11	.03
201	Andujar Cedeno	.10	.05	.01
202	Steve Finley	.15	.07	.02
203	Luis Gonzalez	.15	.07	.02
204	Pete Harnisch	.10	.05	.01
205	Xavier Hernandez	.10	.05	.01
206	Darryl Kile	.10	.05	.01
207	Al Osuna	.10	.05	.01
208	Curt Schilling	.10	.05	.01
209	Brett Butler	.25	.11	.03
210	Kal Daniels	.10	.05	.01
211	Lenny Harris	.10	.05	.01
212	Stan Javier	.10	.05	.01
213	Ramon Martinez	.25	.11	.03
214	Roger McDowell	.10	.05	.01
215	Jose Offerman	.10	.05	.01
216	Juan Samuel	.10	.05	.01

☐ 217	Mike Scioscia	.10	.05	.01
☐ 218	Mike Sharperson	.10	.05	.01
☐ 219	Darryl Strawberry	.15	.07	.02
☐ 220	Delino DeShields	.15	.07	.02
☐ 221	Tom Foley	.10	.05	.01
☐ 222	Steve Frey	.10	.05	.01
☐ 223	Dennis Martinez	.15	.07	.02
☐ 224	Spike Owen	.10	.05	.01
☐ 225	Gilberto Reyes	.10	.05	.01
☐ 226	Tim Wallach	.10	.05	.01
☐ 227	Daryl Boston	.10	.05	.01
☐ 228	Tim Burke	.10	.05	.01
☐ 229	Vince Coleman	.10	.05	.01
☐ 230	David Cone	.25	.11	.03
☐ 231	Kevin Elster	.10	.05	.01
☐ 232	Dwight Gooden	.15	.07	.02
☐ 233	Todd Hundley	.15	.07	.02
☐ 234	Jeff Innis	.10	.05	.01
☐ 235	Howard Johnson	.10	.05	.01
☐ 236	Dave Magadan	.10	.05	.01
☐ 237	Mackey Sasser	.10	.05	.01
☐ 238	Anthony Young	.10	.05	.01
☐ 239	Wes Chamberlain	.10	.05	.01
☐ 240	Darren Daulton	.25	.11	.03
☐ 241	Len Dykstra	.25	.11	.03
☐ 242	Tommy Greene	.10	.05	.01
☐ 243	Charlie Hayes	.15	.07	.02
☐ 244	Dave Hollins	.10	.05	.01
☐ 245	Ricky Jordan	.10	.05	.01
☐ 246	John Kruk	.25	.11	.03
☐ 247	Mickey Morandini	.10	.05	.01
☐ 248	Terry Mulholland	.10	.05	.01
☐ 249	Dale Murphy	.25	.11	.03
☐ 250	Jay Bell	.15	.07	.02
☐ 251	Barry Bonds	.50	.23	.06
☐ 252	Steve Buechele	.10	.05	.01
☐ 253	Doug Drabek	.15	.07	.02
☐ 254	Mike LaValliere	.10	.05	.01
☐ 255	Jose Lind	.10	.05	.01
☐ 256	Lloyd McClendon	.10	.05	.01
☐ 257	Orlando Merced	.15	.07	.02
☐ 258	Don Slaught	.10	.05	.01
☐ 259	John Smiley	.10	.05	.01
☐ 260	Zane Smith	.10	.05	.01
☐ 261	Randy Tomlin	.10	.05	.01
☐ 262	Andy Van Slyke	.15	.07	.02
☐ 263	Pedro Guerrero	.10	.05	.01
☐ 264	Felix Jose	.10	.05	.01
☐ 265	Ray Lankford	.25	.11	.03
☐ 266	Omar Olivares	.10	.05	.01
☐ 267	Jose Oquendo	.10	.05	.01
☐ 268	Tom Pagnozzi	.10	.05	.01
☐ 269	Bryn Smith	.10	.05	.01
☐ 270	Lee Smith UER	.25	.11	.03
	(1991 record listed as 61-61)			
☐ 271	Ozzie Smith UER	.40	.18	.05
	(Comma before year of birth on card back)			
☐ 272	Milt Thompson	.10	.05	.01
☐ 273	Todd Zeile	.15	.07	.02
☐ 274	Andy Benes	.15	.07	.02
☐ 275	Jerald Clark	.10	.05	.01
☐ 276	Tony Fernandez	.10	.05	.01
☐ 277	Tony Gwynn	.60	.25	.07
☐ 278	Greg W. Harris	.10	.05	.01
☐ 279	Thomas Howard	.10	.05	.01
☐ 280	Bruce Hurst	.10	.05	.01
☐ 281	Mike Maddux	.10	.05	.01
☐ 282	Fred McGriff	.30	.14	.04
☐ 283	Benito Santiago	.10	.05	.01
☐ 284	Kevin Bass	.10	.05	.01
☐ 285	Jeff Brantley	.10	.05	.01
☐ 286	John Burkett	.10	.05	.01
☐ 287	Will Clark	.30	.14	.04
☐ 288	Royce Clayton	.15	.07	.02
☐ 289	Steve Decker	.10	.05	.01
☐ 290	Kelly Downs	.10	.05	.01
☐ 291	Mike Felder	.10	.05	.01
☐ 292	Darren Lewis	.15	.07	.02
☐ 293	Kirt Manwaring	.10	.05	.01
☐ 294	Willie McGee	.15	.07	.02
☐ 295	Robby Thompson	.10	.05	.01
☐ 296	Matt Williams	.40	.18	.05
☐ 297	Trevor Wilson	.10	.05	.01
☐ 298	Checklist 1-100	.10	.05	.01
☐ 299	Checklist 101-200	.10	.05	.01
☐ 300	Checklist 201-300	.10	.05	.01
☐ 301	Brady Anderson	.15	.07	.02
☐ 302	Todd Frohwirth	.10	.05	.01
☐ 303	Ben McDonald	.15	.07	.02
☐ 304	Mark McLemore	.10	.05	.01
☐ 305	Jose Mesa	.10	.05	.01
☐ 306	Bob Milacki	.10	.05	.01
☐ 307	Gregg Olson	.10	.05	.01
☐ 308	David Segui	.15	.07	.02
☐ 309	Rick Sutcliffe	.15	.07	.02
☐ 310	Jeff Tackett	.10	.05	.01
☐ 311	Wade Boggs	.25	.11	.03
☐ 312	Scott Cooper	.10	.05	.01
☐ 313	John Flaherty	.10	.05	.01
☐ 314	Wayne Housie	.10	.05	.01
☐ 315	Peter Hoy	.10	.05	.01
☐ 316	John Marzano	.10	.05	.01
☐ 317	Tim Naehring	.15	.07	.02
☐ 318	Phil Plantier	.15	.07	.02
☐ 319	Frank Viola	.10	.05	.01
☐ 320	Matt Young	.10	.05	.01
☐ 321	Jim Abbott	.25	.11	.03
☐ 322	Hubie Brooks	.10	.05	.01
☐ 323	Chad Curtis	.40	.18	.05
☐ 324	Alvin Davis	.10	.05	.01
☐ 325	Junior Felix	.10	.05	.01
☐ 326	Von Hayes	.10	.05	.01
☐ 327	Mark Langston	.15	.07	.02
☐ 328	Scott Lewis	.10	.05	.01
☐ 329	Don Robinson	.10	.05	.01
☐ 330	Bobby Rose	.10	.05	.01
☐ 331	Lee Stevens	.10	.05	.01
☐ 332	George Bell	.10	.05	.01
☐ 333	Esteban Beltre	.10	.05	.01
☐ 334	Joey Cora	.10	.05	.01
☐ 335	Alex Fernandez	.15	.07	.02
☐ 336	Roberto Hernandez	.15	.07	.02
☐ 337	Mike Huff	.10	.05	.01
☐ 338	Kirk McCaskill	.10	.05	.01
☐ 339	Dan Pasqua	.10	.05	.01
☐ 340	Scott Radinsky	.10	.05	.01
☐ 341	Steve Sax	.10	.05	.01
☐ 342	Bobby Thigpen	.10	.05	.01
☐ 343	Robin Ventura	.25	.11	.03
☐ 344	Jack Armstrong	.10	.05	.01
☐ 345	Alex Cole	.10	.05	.01
☐ 346	Dennis Cook	.10	.05	.01
☐ 347	Glenallen Hill	.15	.07	.02
☐ 348	Thomas Howard	.10	.05	.01
☐ 349	Brook Jacoby	.10	.05	.01
☐ 350	Kenny Lofton	2.50	1.10	.30
☐ 351	Charles Nagy	.15	.07	.02
☐ 352	Rod Nichols	.10	.05	.01
☐ 353	Junior Ortiz	.10	.05	.01
☐ 354	Dave Otto	.10	.05	.01

☐	355	Tony Perezchica	.10	.05	.01	☐ 426	Gene Nelson	.10	.05	.01
☐	356	Scott Scudder	.10	.05	.01	☐ 427	Randy Ready	.10	.05	.01
☐	357	Paul Sorrento	.15	.07	.02	☐ 428	Bruce Walton	.10	.05	.01
☐	358	Skeeter Barnes	.10	.05	.01	☐ 429	Willie Wilson	.10	.05	.01
☐	359	Mark Carreon	.10	.05	.01	☐ 430	Rich Amaral	.10	.05	.01
☐	360	John Doherty	.10	.05	.01	☐ 431	Dave Cochrane	.10	.05	.01
☐	361	Dan Gladden	.10	.05	.01	☐ 432	Henry Cotto	.10	.05	.01
☐	362	Bill Gullickson	.10	.05	.01	☐ 433	Calvin Jones	.10	.05	.01
☐	363	Shawn Hare	.10	.05	.01	☐ 434	Kevin Mitchell	.15	.07	.02
☐	364	Mike Henneman	.10	.05	.01	☐ 435	Clay Parker	.10	.05	.01
☐	365	Chad Kreuter	.10	.05	.01	☐ 436	Omar Vizquel	.15	.07	.02
☐	366	Mark Leiter	.10	.05	.01	☐ 437	Floyd Bannister	.10	.05	.01
☐	367	Mike Munoz	.10	.05	.01	☐ 438	Kevin Brown	.15	.07	.02
☐	368	Kevin Ritz	.10	.05	.01	☐ 439	John Cangelosi	.10	.05	.01
☐	369	Mark Davis	.10	.05	.01	☐ 440	Brian Downing	.10	.05	.01
☐	370	Tom Gordon	.15	.07	.02	☐ 441	Monty Fariss	.10	.05	.01
☐	371	Chris Gwynn	.10	.05	.01	☐ 442	Jose Guzman	.10	.05	.01
☐	372	Gregg Jefferies	.25	.11	.03	☐ 443	Donald Harris	.10	.05	.01
☐	373	Wally Joyner	.25	.11	.03	☐ 444	Kevin Reimer	.10	.05	.01
☐	374	Kevin McReynolds	.10	.05	.01	☐ 445	Kenny Rogers	.15	.07	.02
☐	375	Keith Miller	.10	.05	.01	☐ 446	Wayne Rosenthal	.10	.05	.01
☐	376	Rico Rossy	.10	.05	.01	☐ 447	Dickie Thon	.10	.05	.01
☐	377	Curtis Wilkerson	.10	.05	.01	☐ 448	Derek Bell	.15	.07	.02
☐	378	Ricky Bones	.10	.05	.01	☐ 449	Juan Guzman	.15	.07	.02
☐	379	Chris Bosio	.10	.05	.01	☐ 450	Tom Henke	.15	.07	.02
☐	380	Cal Eldred	.10	.05	.01	☐ 451	Candy Maldonado	.10	.05	.01
☐	381	Scott Fletcher	.10	.05	.01	☐ 452	Jack Morris	.15	.07	.02
☐	382	Jim Gantner	.10	.05	.01	☐ 453	David Wells	.15	.07	.02
☐	383	Darryl Hamilton	.15	.07	.02	☐ 454	Dave Winfield	.25	.11	.03
☐	384	Doug Henry	.10	.05	.01	☐ 455	Juan Berenguer	.10	.05	.01
☐	385	Pat Listach	.15	.07	.02	☐ 456	Damon Berryhill	.10	.05	.01
☐	386	Tim McIntosh	.10	.05	.01	☐ 457	Mike Bielecki	.10	.05	.01
☐	387	Edwin Nunez	.10	.05	.01	☐ 458	Marvin Freeman	.10	.05	.01
☐	388	Dan Plesac	.10	.05	.01	☐ 459	Charlie Leibrandt	.10	.05	.01
☐	389	Kevin Seitzer	.10	.05	.01	☐ 460	Kent Mercker	.10	.05	.01
☐	390	Franklin Stubbs	.10	.05	.01	☐ 461	Otis Nixon	.10	.05	.01
☐	391	William Suero	.10	.05	.01	☐ 462	Alejandro Pena	.10	.05	.01
☐	392	Bill Wegman	.10	.05	.01	☐ 463	Ben Rivera	.10	.05	.01
☐	393	Willie Banks	.10	.05	.01	☐ 464	Deion Sanders	.40	.18	.05
☐	394	Jarvis Brown	.10	.05	.01	☐ 465	Mark Wohlers	.15	.07	.02
☐	395	Greg Gagne	.10	.05	.01	☐ 466	Shawn Boskie	.10	.05	.01
☐	396	Mark Guthrie	.10	.05	.01	☐ 467	Frank Castillo	.10	.05	.01
☐	397	Bill Krueger	.10	.05	.01	☐ 468	Andre Dawson	.25	.11	.03
☐	398	Pat Mahomes	.10	.05	.01	☐ 469	Joe Girardi	.10	.05	.01
☐	399	Pedro Munoz	.15	.07	.02	☐ 470	Chuck McElroy	.10	.05	.01
☐	400	John Smiley	.10	.05	.01	☐ 471	Mike Morgan	.10	.05	.01
☐	401	Gary Wayne	.10	.05	.01	☐ 472	Ken Patterson	.10	.05	.01
☐	402	Lenny Webster	.10	.05	.01	☐ 473	Bob Scanlan	.10	.05	.01
☐	403	Carl Willis	.10	.05	.01	☐ 474	Gary Scott	.10	.05	.01
☐	404	Greg Cadaret	.10	.05	.01	☐ 475	Dave Smith	.10	.05	.01
☐	405	Steve Farr	.10	.05	.01	☐ 476	Sammy Sosa	.30	.14	.04
☐	406	Mike Gallego	.10	.05	.01	☐ 477	Hector Villanueva	.10	.05	.01
☐	407	Charlie Hayes	.15	.07	.02	☐ 478	Scott Bankhead	.10	.05	.01
☐	408	Steve Howe	.10	.05	.01	☐ 479	Tim Belcher	.10	.05	.01
☐	409	Dion James	.10	.05	.01	☐ 480	Freddie Benavides	.10	.05	.01
☐	410	Jeff Johnson	.10	.05	.01	☐ 481	Jacob Brumfield	.10	.05	.01
☐	411	Tim Leary	.10	.05	.01	☐ 482	Norm Charlton	.10	.05	.01
☐	412	Jim Leyritz	.10	.05	.01	☐ 483	Dwayne Henry	.10	.05	.01
☐	413	Melido Perez	.10	.05	.01	☐ 484	Dave Martinez	.10	.05	.01
☐	414	Scott Sanderson	.10	.05	.01	☐ 485	Bip Roberts	.15	.07	.02
☐	415	Andy Stankiewicz	.10	.05	.01	☐ 486	Reggie Sanders	.40	.18	.05
☐	416	Mike Stanley	.15	.07	.02	☐ 487	Greg Swindell	.10	.05	.01
☐	417	Danny Tartabull	.15	.07	.02	☐ 488	Ryan Bowen	.10	.05	.01
☐	418	Lance Blankenship	.10	.05	.01	☐ 489	Casey Candaele	.10	.05	.01
☐	419	Mike Bordick	.10	.05	.01	☐ 490	Juan Guerrero	.10	.05	.01
☐	420	Scott Brosius	.10	.05	.01	☐ 491	Pete Incaviglia	.10	.05	.01
☐	421	Dennis Eckersley	.25	.11	.03	☐ 492	Jeff Juden	.10	.05	.01
☐	422	Scott Hemond	.10	.05	.01	☐ 493	Rob Murphy	.10	.05	.01
☐	423	Carney Lansford	.15	.07	.02	☐ 494	Mark Portugal	.10	.05	.01
☐	424	Henry Mercedes	.10	.05	.01	☐ 495	Rafael Ramirez	.10	.05	.01
☐	425	Mike Moore	.10	.05	.01	☐ 496	Scott Servais	.10	.05	.01

☐ 497 Ed Taubensee	.10	.05	.01
☐ 498 Brian Williams	.10	.05	.01
☐ 499 Todd Benzinger	.10	.05	.01
☐ 500 John Candelaria	.10	.05	.01
☐ 501 Tom Candiotti	.10	.05	.01
☐ 502 Tim Crews	.10	.05	.01
☐ 503 Eric Davis	.15	.07	.02
☐ 504 Jim Gott	.10	.05	.01
☐ 505 Dave Hansen	.10	.05	.01
☐ 506 Carlos Hernandez	.10	.05	.01
☐ 507 Orel Hershiser	.25	.11	.03
☐ 508 Eric Karros	.50	.23	.06
☐ 509 Bob Ojeda	.10	.05	.01
☐ 510 Steve Wilson	.10	.05	.01
☐ 511 Moises Alou	.25	.11	.03
☐ 512 Bret Barberie	.10	.05	.01
☐ 513 Ivan Calderon	.10	.05	.01
☐ 514 Gary Carter	.25	.11	.03
☐ 515 Archi Cianfrocco	.10	.05	.01
☐ 516 Jeff Fassero	.15	.07	.02
☐ 517 Darrin Fletcher	.10	.05	.01
☐ 518 Marquis Grissom	.25	.11	.03
☐ 519 Chris Haney	.10	.05	.01
☐ 520 Ken Hill	.25	.11	.03
☐ 521 Chris Nabholz	.10	.05	.01
☐ 522 Bill Sampen	.10	.05	.01
☐ 523 John Vander Wal	.10	.05	.01
☐ 524 Dave Wainhouse	.10	.05	.01
☐ 525 Larry Walker	.30	.14	.04
☐ 526 John Wetteland	.15	.07	.02
☐ 527 Bobby Bonilla	.25	.11	.03
☐ 528 Sid Fernandez	.15	.07	.02
☐ 529 John Franco	.25	.11	.03
☐ 530 Dave Gallagher	.10	.05	.01
☐ 531 Paul Gibson	.10	.05	.01
☐ 532 Eddie Murray	.30	.14	.04
☐ 533 Junior Noboa	.10	.05	.01
☐ 534 Charlie O'Brien	.10	.05	.01
☐ 535 Bill Pecota	.10	.05	.01
☐ 536 Willie Randolph	.15	.07	.02
☐ 537 Bret Saberhagen	.25	.11	.03
☐ 538 Dick Schofield	.10	.05	.01
☐ 539 Pete Schourek	.15	.07	.02
☐ 540 Ruben Amaro	.10	.05	.01
☐ 541 Andy Ashby	.10	.05	.01
☐ 542 Kim Batiste	.10	.05	.01
☐ 543 Cliff Brantley	.10	.05	.01
☐ 544 Mariano Duncan	.10	.05	.01
☐ 545 Jeff Grotewold	.10	.05	.01
☐ 546 Barry Jones	.10	.05	.01
☐ 547 Julio Peguero	.10	.05	.01
☐ 548 Curt Schilling	.10	.05	.01
☐ 549 Mitch Williams	.15	.07	.02
☐ 550 Stan Belinda	.10	.05	.01
☐ 551 Scott Bullett	.10	.05	.01
☐ 552 Cecil Espy	.10	.05	.01
☐ 553 Jeff King	.15	.07	.02
☐ 554 Roger Mason	.10	.05	.01
☐ 555 Paul Miller	.10	.05	.01
☐ 556 Denny Neagle	.10	.07	.02
☐ 557 Vicente Palacios	.10	.05	.01
☐ 558 Bob Patterson	.10	.05	.01
☐ 559 Tom Prince	.10	.05	.01
☐ 560 Gary Redus	.10	.05	.01
☐ 561 Gary Varsho	.10	.05	.01
☐ 562 Juan Agosto	.10	.05	.01
☐ 563 Cris Carpenter	.10	.05	.01
☐ 564 Mark Clark	.25	.11	.03
☐ 565 Jose DeLeon	.10	.05	.01
☐ 566 Rich Gedman	.10	.05	.01
☐ 567 Bernard Gilkey	.15	.07	.02

☐ 568 Rex Hudler	.10	.05	.01
☐ 569 Tim Jones	.10	.05	.01
☐ 570 Donovan Osborne	.10	.05	.01
☐ 571 Mike Perez	.10	.05	.01
☐ 572 Gerald Perry	.10	.05	.01
☐ 573 Bob Tewksbury	.10	.05	.01
☐ 574 Todd Worrell	.15	.07	.02
☐ 575 Dave Eiland	.10	.05	.01
☐ 576 Jeremy Hernandez	.10	.05	.01
☐ 577 Craig Lefferts	.10	.05	.01
☐ 578 Jose Melendez	.10	.05	.01
☐ 579 Randy Myers	.25	.11	.03
☐ 580 Gary Pettis	.10	.05	.01
☐ 581 Rich Rodriguez	.10	.05	.01
☐ 582 Gary Sheffield	.25	.11	.03
☐ 583 Craig Shipley	.10	.05	.01
☐ 584 Kurt Stillwell	.10	.05	.01
☐ 585 Tim Teufel	.10	.05	.01
☐ 586 Rod Beck	.50	.23	.06
☐ 587 Dave Burba	.10	.05	.01
☐ 588 Craig Colbert	.10	.05	.01
☐ 589 Bryan Hickerson	.10	.05	.01
☐ 590 Mike Jackson	.10	.05	.01
☐ 591 Mark Leonard	.10	.05	.01
☐ 592 Jim McNamara	.10	.05	.01
☐ 593 John Patterson	.10	.05	.01
☐ 594 Dave Righetti	.10	.05	.01
☐ 595 Cory Snyder	.10	.05	.01
☐ 596 Bill Swift	.10	.05	.01
☐ 597 Ted Wood	.10	.05	.01
☐ 598 Checklist 301-400	.10	.05	.01
☐ 599 Checklist 401-500	.10	.05	.01
☐ 600 Checklist 501-600	.10	.05	.01

1992 Ultra All-Rookies

This ten-card standard-size (2 1/2" by 3 1/2") set was randomly inserted in 1992 Fleer Ultra II foil packs. The fronts feature borderless color action player photos except at the bottom where they are edged by a marbleized black wedge. The words "All-Rookie Team" in gold foil lettering appear in a black marbleized inverted triangle at the lower right corner, with the player's name on a color banner. On a black marbleized background, the backs present a color headshot inside an inverted triangle and career summary on a gray marbleized panel. The cards are numbered on the back.

		MINT	NRMT	EXC
	COMPLETE SET (10)	15.00	6.75	1.85
	COMMON CARD (1-10)	.50	.23	.06
☐ 1	Eric Karros	2.50	1.10	.30
☐ 2	Andy Stankiewicz	.50	.23	.06
☐ 3	Gary DiSarcina	1.00	.45	.12
☐ 4	Archi Cianfrocco	.50	.23	.06
☐ 5	Jim McNamara	.50	.23	.06
☐ 6	Chad Curtis	1.50	.70	.19
☐ 7	Kenny Lofton	10.00	4.50	1.25
☐ 8	Reggie Sanders	2.50	1.10	.30
☐ 9	Pat Mahomes	.50	.23	.06
☐ 10	Donovan Osborne	.50	.23	.06

1992 Ultra All-Stars

Featuring many of the season's current mega-stars, this 20-card standard-size (2 1/2" by 3 1/2") set was randomly inserted in 1992 Fleer Ultra II foil packs. The front design displays color action player photos enclosed by black marbleized borders. The word "All-Star" and the player's name are printed in gold foil lettering in the bottom border. On a gray marbleized background, the backs carry a color headshot (in a circular format) and a summary of the player's recent performance in on a pastel yellow panel. The cards are numbered on the back.

		MINT	NRMT	EXC
	COMPLETE SET (20)	25.00	11.00	3.10
	COMMON CARD (1-20)	.50	.23	.06
☐ 1	Mark McGwire	.75	.35	.09
☐ 2	Roberto Alomar	1.50	.70	.19
☐ 3	Cal Ripken Jr.	8.00	3.60	1.00
☐ 4	Wade Boggs	.75	.35	.09
☐ 5	Mickey Tettleton	.50	.23	.06
☐ 6	Ken Griffey Jr.	10.00	4.50	1.25
☐ 7	Roberto Kelly	.50	.23	.06
☐ 8	Kirby Puckett	2.00	.90	.25
☐ 9	Frank Thomas	10.00	4.50	1.25
☐ 10	Jack McDowell	.75	.35	.09
☐ 11	Will Clark	1.00	.45	.12
☐ 12	Ryne Sandberg	1.50	.70	.19
☐ 13	Barry Larkin	1.00	.45	.12
☐ 14	Gary Sheffield	.75	.35	.09
☐ 15	Tom Pagnozzi	.50	.23	.06
☐ 16	Barry Bonds	2.00	.90	.25
☐ 17	Deion Sanders	1.50	.70	.19

☐ 18	Darryl Strawberry	.75	.35	.09
☐ 19	David Cone	.75	.35	.09
☐ 20	Tom Glavine	1.00	.45	.12

1992 Ultra Award Winners

This 25-card set features 18 Gold Glove winners, both Cy Young Award winners, both Rookies of the Year, both league MVP's, and the World Series MVP. The cards measure the standard size (2 1/2" by 3 1/2") and were randomly inserted in 1992 Fleer Ultra I packs. The fronts carry full-bleed color player photos that have a diagonal blue marbleized border at the bottom. The player's name appears in this bottom border, and a diamond-shaped gold foil seal signifying the award the player won is superimposed at the lower right corner. The backs also have blue marbleized borders and carry player profile on a tan marbleized panel. A head shot of the player appears in a diamond at the upper right corner, with the words "Award Winners" on orange ribbons extending below the diamond. The cards are numbered on the back.

		MINT	NRMT	EXC
	COMPLETE SET (25)	50.00	22.00	6.25
	COMMON CARD (1-25)	.75	.35	.09
☐ 1	Jack Morris	1.00	.45	.12
☐ 2	Chuck Knoblauch	1.25	.55	.16
☐ 3	Jeff Bagwell	7.00	3.10	.85
☐ 4	Terry Pendleton	1.00	.45	.12
☐ 5	Cal Ripken	10.00	4.50	1.25
☐ 6	Roger Clemens	1.50	.70	.19
☐ 7	Tom Glavine	1.25	.55	.16
☐ 8	Tom Pagnozzi	.75	.35	.09
☐ 9	Ozzie Smith	2.00	.90	.25
☐ 10	Andy Van Slyke	1.00	.45	.12
☐ 11	Barry Bonds	3.00	1.35	.35
☐ 12	Tony Gwynn	3.00	1.35	.35
☐ 13	Matt Williams	2.50	1.10	.30
☐ 14	Will Clark	1.50	.70	.19
☐ 15	Robin Ventura	1.00	.45	.12
☐ 16	Mark Langston	1.00	.45	.12
☐ 17	Tony Pena	.75	.35	.09
☐ 18	Devon White	1.00	.45	.12
☐ 19	Don Mattingly	5.00	2.20	.60

		MINT	NRMT	EXC
☐	20 Roberto Alomar	2.00	.90	.25
☐	21A Cal Ripken ERR (Reversed negative on card back)	20.00	9.00	2.50
☐	21B Cal Ripken COR	12.00	5.50	1.50
☐	22 Ken Griffey Jr.	15.00	6.75	1.85
☐	23 Kirby Puckett	3.00	1.35	.35
☐	24 Greg Maddux	10.00	4.50	1.25
☐	25 Ryne Sandberg	2.50	1.10	.30

1993 Ultra

The 1993 Ultra baseball set was issued in two series and totaled 650 cards. A ten-card Dennis Eckersley subset was randomly inserted in the foil packs. The full-bleed color-enhanced action photos are edged at the bottom by a gold foil stripe and a fawn-colored border that is streaked with white for a marbleized effect. On a dimensionalized ball park background, the horizontal backs have an action shot, a portrait, last season statistics, and the player's entire professional career totals. The cards are numbered on the back, grouped alphabetically within teams, and checklisted below alphabetically according to teams for the National and American Leagues as follows: Atlanta Braves (1-13), Chicago Cubs (14-25), Cincinnati Reds (26-36), Houston Astros (37-48), Los Angeles Dodgers (49-60), Montreal Expos (61-71), New York Mets (72-81), Philadelphia Phillies (82-94), Pittsburgh Pirates (95-105), St. Louis Cardinals (106-115), San Diego Padres (116-125), and San Francisco Giants (126-137), Baltimore Orioles (138-147), Boston Red Sox (148-158), California Angels (159-169), Chicago White Sox (170-181), Cleveland Indians (182-193), Detroit Tigers (194-204), Kansas City Royals (205-216), Milwaukee Brewers (217-227), Minnesota Twins (228-239), New York Yankees (240-252), Oakland Athletics (253-264), Seattle Mariners (265-275), Texas Rangers (276-285), and Toronto Blue Jays (286-297). The first series closes with checklist cards (298-300). The second series features 83 Ultra Rookies, 51 Rockies and Marlins, traded veteran players, and other major league veterans not included in the first series. The Rookie cards show a gold foil stamped Rookie "flag" as part of the card design. Randomly inserted in second series packs were a 20-card All-Stars subset, a ten-card All-Rookie Team subset, and a five-card Strikeout Kings subset. Rookie Cards in this set include Rene Arocha, Russ Davis, Greg McMichael, and J.T. Snow.

	MINT	NRMT	EXC
COMPLETE SET (650)	40.00	18.00	5.00
COMPLETE SERIES 1 (300)	20.00	9.00	2.50
COMPLETE SERIES 2 (350)	20.00	9.00	2.50
COMMON CARD (1-300)	.10	.05	.01
COMMON CARD (301-650)	.10	.05	.01

☐	1 Steve Avery	.30	.14	.04
☐	2 Rafael Belliard	.10	.05	.01
☐	3 Damon Berryhill	.10	.05	.01
☐	4 Sid Bream	.10	.05	.01
☐	5 Ron Gant	.30	.14	.04
☐	6 Tom Glavine	.30	.14	.04
☐	7 Ryan Klesko	1.50	.70	.19
☐	8 Mark Lemke	.20	.09	.03
☐	9 Javier Lopez	1.00	.45	.12
☐	10 Greg Olson	.10	.05	.01
☐	11 Terry Pendleton	.30	.14	.04
☐	12 Deion Sanders	.60	.25	.07
☐	13 Mike Stanton	.10	.05	.01
☐	14 Paul Assenmacher	.10	.05	.01
☐	15 Steve Buechele	.10	.05	.01
☐	16 Frank Castillo	.10	.05	.01
☐	17 Shawon Dunston	.10	.05	.01
☐	18 Mark Grace	.30	.14	.04
☐	19 Derrick May	.20	.09	.03
☐	20 Chuck McElroy	.10	.05	.01
☐	21 Mike Morgan	.10	.05	.01
☐	22 Bob Scanlan	.10	.05	.01
☐	23 Dwight Smith	.10	.05	.01
☐	24 Sammy Sosa	.30	.14	.04
☐	25 Rick Wilkins	.10	.05	.01
☐	26 Tim Belcher	.10	.05	.01
☐	27 Jeff Branson	.10	.05	.01
☐	28 Bill Doran	.10	.05	.01
☐	29 Chris Hammond	.10	.05	.01
☐	30 Barry Larkin	.40	.18	.05
☐	31 Hal Morris	.20	.09	.03
☐	32 Joe Oliver	.10	.05	.01
☐	33 Jose Rijo	.20	.09	.03
☐	34 Bip Roberts	.10	.05	.01
☐	35 Chris Sabo	.10	.05	.01
☐	36 Reggie Sanders	.30	.14	.04
☐	37 Craig Biggio	.30	.14	.04
☐	38 Ken Caminiti	.20	.09	.03
☐	39 Steve Finley	.10	.05	.01
☐	40 Luis Gonzalez	.20	.09	.03
☐	41 Juan Guerrero	.10	.05	.01
☐	42 Pete Harnisch	.10	.05	.01
☐	43 Xavier Hernandez	.10	.05	.01
☐	44 Doug Jones	.10	.05	.01
☐	45 Al Osuna	.10	.05	.01
☐	46 Eddie Taubensee	.10	.05	.01
☐	47 Scooter Tucker	.10	.05	.01
☐	48 Brian Williams	.10	.05	.01
☐	49 Pedro Astacio	.10	.05	.01
☐	50 Rafael Bournigal	.10	.05	.01
☐	51 Brett Butler	.20	.09	.03
☐	52 Tom Candiotti	.10	.05	.01
☐	53 Eric Davis	.10	.05	.01
☐	54 Lenny Harris	.10	.05	.01
☐	55 Orel Hershiser	.20	.09	.03
☐	56 Eric Karros	.30	.14	.04

☐ 57	Pedro Martinez	.30	.14	.04
☐ 58	Roger McDowell	.10	.05	.01
☐ 59	Jose Offerman	.10	.05	.01
☐ 60	Mike Piazza	2.50	1.10	.30
☐ 61	Moises Alou	.30	.14	.04
☐ 62	Kent Bottenfield	.10	.05	.01
☐ 63	Archi Cianfrocco	.10	.05	.01
☐ 64	Greg Colbrunn	.30	.14	.04
☐ 65	Wil Cordero	.20	.09	.03
☐ 66	Delino DeShields	.20	.09	.03
☐ 67	Darrin Fletcher	.10	.05	.01
☐ 68	Ken Hill	.20	.09	.03
☐ 69	Chris Nabholz	.10	.05	.01
☐ 70	Mel Rojas	.20	.09	.03
☐ 71	Larry Walker	.40	.18	.05
☐ 72	Sid Fernandez	.10	.05	.01
☐ 73	John Franco	.20	.09	.03
☐ 74	Dave Gallagher	.10	.05	.01
☐ 75	Todd Hundley	.20	.09	.03
☐ 76	Howard Johnson	.10	.05	.01
☐ 77	Jeff Kent	.30	.14	.04
☐ 78	Eddie Murray	.50	.23	.06
☐ 79	Bret Saberhagen	.20	.09	.03
☐ 80	Chico Walker	.10	.05	.01
☐ 81	Anthony Young	.10	.05	.01
☐ 82	Kyle Abbott	.10	.05	.01
☐ 83	Ruben Amaro	.10	.05	.01
☐ 84	Juan Bell	.10	.05	.01
☐ 85	Wes Chamberlain	.10	.05	.01
☐ 86	Darren Daulton	.30	.14	.04
☐ 87	Mariano Duncan	.10	.05	.01
☐ 88	Dave Hollins	.10	.05	.01
☐ 89	Ricky Jordan	.10	.05	.01
☐ 90	John Kruk	.30	.14	.04
☐ 91	Mickey Morandini	.10	.05	.01
☐ 92	Terry Mulholland	.10	.05	.01
☐ 93	Ben Rivera	.10	.05	.01
☐ 94	Mike Williams	.10	.05	.01
☐ 95	Stan Belinda	.10	.05	.01
☐ 96	Jay Bell	.20	.09	.03
☐ 97	Jeff King	.10	.05	.01
☐ 98	Mike LaValliere	.10	.05	.01
☐ 99	Lloyd McClendon	.10	.05	.01
☐ 100	Orlando Merced	.20	.09	.03
☐ 101	Zane Smith	.10	.05	.01
☐ 102	Randy Tomlin	.10	.05	.01
☐ 103	Andy Van Slyke	.20	.09	.03
☐ 104	Tim Wakefield	.30	.14	.04
☐ 105	John Wehner	.10	.05	.01
☐ 106	Bernard Gilkey	.20	.09	.03
☐ 107	Brian Jordan	.30	.14	.04
☐ 108	Ray Lankford	.30	.14	.04
☐ 109	Donovan Osborne	.10	.05	.01
☐ 110	Tom Pagnozzi	.10	.05	.01
☐ 111	Mike Perez	.10	.05	.01
☐ 112	Lee Smith	.30	.14	.04
☐ 113	Ozzie Smith	.60	.25	.07
☐ 114	Bob Tewksbury	.10	.05	.01
☐ 115	Todd Zeile	.20	.09	.03
☐ 116	Andy Benes	.20	.09	.03
☐ 117	Greg W. Harris	.10	.05	.01
☐ 118	Darrin Jackson	.10	.05	.01
☐ 119	Fred McGriff	.40	.18	.05
☐ 120	Rich Rodriguez	.10	.05	.01
☐ 121	Frank Seminara	.10	.05	.01
☐ 122	Gary Sheffield	.30	.14	.04
☐ 123	Craig Shipley	.10	.05	.01
☐ 124	Kurt Stillwell	.10	.05	.01
☐ 125	Dan Walters	.10	.05	.01
☐ 126	Rod Beck	.30	.14	.04
☐ 127	Mike Benjamin	.10	.05	.01

☐ 128	Jeff Brantley	.10	.05	.01
☐ 129	John Burkett	.10	.05	.01
☐ 130	Will Clark	.40	.18	.05
☐ 131	Royce Clayton	.20	.09	.03
☐ 132	Steve Hosey	.10	.05	.01
☐ 133	Mike Jackson	.10	.05	.01
☐ 134	Darren Lewis	.10	.05	.01
☐ 135	Kirt Manwaring	.10	.05	.01
☐ 136	Bill Swift	.10	.05	.01
☐ 137	Robby Thompson	.10	.05	.01
☐ 138	Brady Anderson	.20	.09	.03
☐ 139	Glenn Davis	.10	.05	.01
☐ 140	Leo Gomez	.10	.05	.01
☐ 141	Chito Martinez	.10	.05	.01
☐ 142	Ben McDonald	.10	.05	.01
☐ 143	Alan Mills	.10	.05	.01
☐ 144	Mike Mussina	.50	.23	.06
☐ 145	Gregg Olson	.10	.05	.01
☐ 146	David Segui	.10	.05	.01
☐ 147	Jeff Tackett	.10	.05	.01
☐ 148	Jack Clark	.10	.05	.01
☐ 149	Scott Cooper	.10	.05	.01
☐ 150	Danny Darwin	.10	.05	.01
☐ 151	John Dopson	.10	.05	.01
☐ 152	Mike Greenwell	.20	.09	.03
☐ 153	Tim Naehring	.20	.09	.03
☐ 154	Tony Pena	.10	.05	.01
☐ 155	Paul Quantrill	.10	.05	.01
☐ 156	Mo Vaughn	.50	.23	.06
☐ 157	Frank Viola	.20	.09	.03
☐ 158	Bob Zupcic	.10	.05	.01
☐ 159	Chad Curtis	.20	.09	.03
☐ 160	Gary DiSarcina	.10	.05	.01
☐ 161	Damion Easley	.20	.09	.03
☐ 162	Chuck Finley	.20	.09	.03
☐ 163	Tim Fortugno	.10	.05	.01
☐ 164	Rene Gonzales	.10	.05	.01
☐ 165	Joe Grahe	.10	.05	.01
☐ 166	Mark Langston	.30	.14	.04
☐ 167	John Orton	.10	.05	.01
☐ 168	Luis Polonia	.10	.05	.01
☐ 169	Julio Valera	.10	.05	.01
☐ 170	Wilson Alvarez	.30	.14	.04
☐ 171	George Bell	.20	.09	.03
☐ 172	Joey Cora	.10	.05	.01
☐ 173	Alex Fernandez	.30	.14	.04
☐ 174	Lance Johnson	.10	.05	.01
☐ 175	Ron Karkovice	.10	.05	.01
☐ 176	Jack McDowell	.30	.14	.04
☐ 177	Scott Radinsky	.10	.05	.01
☐ 178	Tim Raines	.30	.14	.04
☐ 179	Steve Sax	.10	.05	.01
☐ 180	Bobby Thigpen	.10	.05	.01
☐ 181	Frank Thomas	3.00	1.35	.35
☐ 182	Sandy Alomar	.20	.09	.03
☐ 183	Carlos Baerga	.60	.25	.07
☐ 184	Felix Fermin	.10	.05	.01
☐ 185	Thomas Howard	.10	.05	.01
☐ 186	Mark Lewis	.10	.05	.01
☐ 187	Derek Lilliquist	.10	.05	.01
☐ 188	Carlos Martinez	.10	.05	.01
☐ 189	Charles Nagy	.20	.09	.03
☐ 190	Scott Scudder	.10	.05	.01
☐ 191	Paul Sorrento	.10	.05	.01
☐ 192	Jim Thome	1.25	.55	.16
☐ 193	Mark Whiten	.20	.09	.03
☐ 194	Milt Cuyler UER	.10	.05	.01
	(Reversed negative on card front)			
☐ 195	Rob Deer	.10	.05	.01
☐ 196	John Doherty	.10	.05	.01

□	#	Player			
□	197	Travis Fryman	.30	.14	.04
□	198	Dan Gladden	.10	.05	.01
□	199	Mike Henneman	.10	.05	.01
□	200	John Kiely	.10	.05	.01
□	201	Chad Kreuter	.10	.05	.01
□	202	Scott Livingstone	.10	.05	.01
□	203	Tony Phillips	.10	.05	.01
□	204	Alan Trammell	.30	.14	.04
□	205	Mike Boddicker	.10	.05	.01
□	206	George Brett	1.25	.55	.16
□	207	Tom Gordon	.10	.05	.01
□	208	Mark Gubicza	.10	.05	.01
□	209	Gregg Jefferies	.30	.14	.04
□	210	Wally Joyner	.20	.09	.03
□	211	Kevin Koslofski	.10	.05	.01
□	212	Brent Mayne	.10	.05	.01
□	213	Brian McRae	.30	.14	.04
□	214	Kevin McReynolds	.10	.05	.01
□	215	Rusty Meacham	.10	.05	.01
□	216	Steve Shifflett	.10	.05	.01
□	217	James Austin	.10	.05	.01
□	218	Cal Eldred	.10	.05	.01
□	219	Darryl Hamilton	.10	.05	.01
□	220	Doug Henry	.10	.05	.01
□	221	John Jaha	.20	.09	.03
□	222	Dave Nilsson	.20	.09	.03
□	223	Jesse Orosco	.10	.05	.01
□	224	B.J. Surhoff	.20	.09	.03
□	225	Greg Vaughn	.10	.05	.01
□	226	Bill Wegman	.10	.05	.01
□	227	Robin Yount UER (Born in Illinois, not in Virginia)	.40	.18	.05
□	228	Rick Aguilera	.20	.09	.03
□	229	J.T. Bruett	.10	.05	.01
□	230	Scott Erickson	.20	.09	.03
□	231	Kent Hrbek	.20	.09	.03
□	232	Terry Jorgensen	.10	.05	.01
□	233	Scott Leius	.10	.05	.01
□	234	Pat Mahomes	.10	.05	.01
□	235	Pedro Munoz	.20	.09	.03
□	236	Kirby Puckett	1.00	.45	.12
□	237	Kevin Tapani	.10	.05	.01
□	238	Lenny Webster	.10	.05	.01
□	239	Carl Willis	.10	.05	.01
□	240	Mike Gallego	.10	.05	.01
□	241	John Habyan	.10	.05	.01
□	242	Pat Kelly	.10	.05	.01
□	243	Kevin Maas	.10	.05	.01
□	244	Don Mattingly	1.50	.70	.19
□	245	Hensley Meulens	.10	.05	.01
□	246	Sam Militello	.10	.05	.01
□	247	Matt Nokes	.10	.05	.01
□	248	Melido Perez	.10	.05	.01
□	249	Andy Stankiewicz	.10	.05	.01
□	250	Randy Velarde	.10	.05	.01
□	251	Bob Wickman	.10	.05	.01
□	252	Bernie Williams	.20	.09	.03
□	253	Lance Blankenship	.10	.05	.01
□	254	Mike Bordick	.10	.05	.01
□	255	Jerry Browne	.10	.05	.01
□	256	Ron Darling	.10	.05	.01
□	257	Dennis Eckersley	.30	.14	.04
□	258	Rickey Henderson	.30	.14	.04
□	259	Vince Horsman	.10	.05	.01
□	260	Troy Neel	.10	.05	.01
□	261	Jeff Parrett	.10	.05	.01
□	262	Terry Steinbach	.20	.09	.03
□	263	Bob Welch	.10	.05	.01
□	264	Bobby Witt	.10	.05	.01
□	265	Rich Amaral	.10	.05	.01
□	266	Bret Boone	.30	.14	.04
□	267	Jay Buhner	.30	.14	.04
□	268	Dave Fleming	.10	.05	.01
□	269	Randy Johnson	.60	.25	.07
□	270	Edgar Martinez	.30	.14	.04
□	271	Mike Schooler	.10	.05	.01
□	272	Russ Swan	.10	.05	.01
□	273	Dave Valle	.10	.05	.01
□	274	Omar Vizquel	.20	.09	.03
□	275	Kerry Woodson	.10	.05	.01
□	276	Kevin Brown	.10	.05	.01
□	277	Julio Franco	.20	.09	.03
□	278	Jeff Frye	.10	.05	.01
□	279	Juan Gonzalez	.60	.25	.07
□	280	Jeff Huson	.10	.05	.01
□	281	Rafael Palmeiro	.30	.14	.04
□	282	Dean Palmer	.20	.09	.03
□	283	Roger Pavlik	.10	.05	.01
□	284	Ivan Rodriguez	.30	.14	.04
□	285	Kenny Rogers	.10	.05	.01
□	286	Derek Bell	.30	.14	.04
□	287	Pat Borders	.10	.05	.01
□	288	Joe Carter	.30	.14	.04
□	289	Bob MacDonald	.10	.05	.01
□	290	Jack Morris	.30	.14	.04
□	291	John Olerud	.20	.09	.03
□	292	Ed Sprague	.10	.05	.01
□	293	Todd Stottlemyre	.10	.05	.01
□	294	Mike Timlin	.10	.05	.01
□	295	Duane Ward	.10	.05	.01
□	296	David Wells	.10	.05	.01
□	297	Devon White	.20	.09	.03
□	298	Checklist 1-94 Ray Lankford	.10	.05	.01
□	299	Checklist 95-193 Bobby Witt	.10	.05	.01
□	300	Checklist 194-300 Mike Piazza	.30	.14	.04
□	301	Steve Bedrosian	.10	.05	.01
□	302	Jeff Blauser	.20	.09	.03
□	303	Francisco Cabrera	.10	.05	.01
□	304	Marvin Freeman	.10	.05	.01
□	305	Brian Hunter	.10	.05	.01
□	306	David Justice	.40	.18	.05
□	307	Greg Maddux	3.00	1.35	.35
□	308	Greg McMichael	.20	.09	.03
□	309	Kent Mercker	.10	.05	.01
□	310	Otis Nixon	.10	.05	.01
□	311	Pete Smith	.10	.05	.01
□	312	John Smoltz	.20	.09	.03
□	313	Jose Guzman	.10	.05	.01
□	314	Mike Harkey	.10	.05	.01
□	315	Greg Hibbard	.10	.05	.01
□	316	Candy Maldonado	.10	.05	.01
□	317	Randy Myers	.20	.09	.03
□	318	Dan Plesac	.10	.05	.01
□	319	Rey Sanchez	.10	.05	.01
□	320	Ryne Sandberg	.75	.35	.09
□	321	Tommy Shields	.10	.05	.01
□	322	Jose Vizcaino	.10	.05	.01
□	323	Matt Walbeck	.20	.09	.03
□	324	Willie Wilson	.10	.05	.01
□	325	Tom Browning	.10	.05	.01
□	326	Tim Costo	.10	.05	.01
□	327	Rob Dibble	.10	.05	.01
□	328	Steve Foster	.10	.05	.01
□	329	Roberto Kelly	.20	.09	.03
□	330	Randy Milligan	.10	.05	.01
□	331	Kevin Mitchell	.20	.09	.03
□	332	Tim Pugh	.10	.05	.01
□	333	Jeff Reardon	.20	.09	.03

☐	334	John Roper	.20	.09	.03				
☐	335	Juan Samuel	.10	.05	.01				
☐	336	John Smiley	.10	.05	.01				
☐	337	Dan Wilson	.20	.09	.03				
☐	338	Scott Aldred	.10	.05	.01				
☐	339	Andy Ashby	.10	.05	.01				
☐	340	Freddie Benavides	.10	.05	.01				
☐	341	Dante Bichette	.40	.18	.05				
☐	342	Willie Blair	.10	.05	.01				
☐	343	Daryl Boston	.10	.05	.01				
☐	344	Vinny Castilla	.30	.14	.04				
☐	345	Jerald Clark	.10	.05	.01				
☐	346	Alex Cole	.10	.05	.01				
☐	347	Andres Galarraga	.30	.14	.04				
☐	348	Joe Girardi	.10	.05	.01				
☐	349	Ryan Hawblitzel	.10	.05	.01				
☐	350	Charlie Hayes	.20	.09	.03				
☐	351	Butch Henry	.10	.05	.01				
☐	352	Darren Holmes	.20	.09	.03				
☐	353	Dale Murphy	.30	.14	.04				
☐	354	David Nied	.20	.09	.03				
☐	355	Jeff Parrett	.10	.05	.01				
☐	356	Steve Reed	.10	.05	.01				
☐	357	Bruce Ruffin	.10	.05	.01				
☐	358	Danny Sheaffer	.10	.05	.01				
☐	359	Bryn Smith	.10	.05	.01				
☐	360	Jim Tatum	.10	.05	.01				
☐	361	Eric Young	.20	.09	.03				
☐	362	Gerald Young	.10	.05	.01				
☐	363	Luis Aquino	.10	.05	.01				
☐	364	Alex Arias	.10	.05	.01				
☐	365	Jack Armstrong	.10	.05	.01				
☐	366	Bret Barberie	.10	.05	.01				
☐	367	Ryan Bowen	.10	.05	.01				
☐	368	Greg Briley	.10	.05	.01				
☐	369	Cris Carpenter	.10	.05	.01				
☐	370	Chuck Carr	.10	.05	.01				
☐	371	Jeff Conine	.30	.14	.04				
☐	372	Steve Decker	.10	.05	.01				
☐	373	Orestes Destrade	.10	.05	.01				
☐	374	Monty Fariss	.10	.05	.01				
☐	375	Junior Felix	.10	.05	.01				
☐	376	Chris Hammond	.10	.05	.01				
☐	377	Bryan Harvey	.20	.09	.03				
☐	378	Trevor Hoffman	.20	.09	.03				
☐	379	Charlie Hough	.20	.09	.03				
☐	380	Joe Klink	.10	.05	.01				
☐	381	Richie Lewis	.10	.05	.01				
☐	382	Dave Magadan	.10	.05	.01				
☐	383	Bob McClure	.10	.05	.01				
☐	384	Scott Pose	.10	.05	.01				
☐	385	Rich Renteria	.10	.05	.01				
☐	386	Benito Santiago	.10	.05	.01				
☐	387	Walt Weiss	.10	.05	.01				
☐	388	Nigel Wilson	.20	.09	.03				
☐	389	Eric Anthony	.10	.05	.01				
☐	390	Jeff Bagwell	1.25	.55	.16				
☐	391	Andujar Cedeno	.10	.05	.01				
☐	392	Doug Drabek	.20	.09	.03				
☐	393	Darryl Kile	.10	.05	.01				
☐	394	Mark Portugal	.10	.05	.01				
☐	395	Karl Rhodes	.10	.05	.01				
☐	396	Scott Servais	.10	.05	.01				
☐	397	Greg Swindell	.10	.05	.01				
☐	398	Tom Goodwin	.10	.05	.01				
☐	399	Kevin Gross	.10	.05	.01				
☐	400	Carlos Hernandez	.10	.05	.01				
☐	401	Ramon Martinez	.20	.09	.03				
☐	402	Raul Mondesi	2.00	.90	.25				
☐	403	Jody Reed	.10	.05	.01				
☐	404	Mike Sharperson	.10	.05	.01				

☐	405	Cory Snyder	.10	.05	.01
☐	406	Darryl Strawberry	.20	.09	.03
☐	407	Rick Trlicek	.10	.05	.01
☐	408	Tim Wallach	.10	.05	.01
☐	409	Todd Worrell	.10	.05	.01
☐	410	Tavo Alvarez	.10	.05	.01
☐	411	Sean Berry	.10	.05	.01
☐	412	Frank Bolick	.10	.05	.01
☐	413	Cliff Floyd	.30	.14	.04
☐	414	Mike Gardiner	.10	.05	.01
☐	415	Marquis Grissom	.30	.14	.04
☐	416	Tim Laker	.10	.05	.01
☐	417	Mike Lansing	.20	.09	.03
☐	418	Dennis Martinez	.20	.09	.03
☐	419	John Vander Wal	.10	.05	.01
☐	420	John Wetteland	.20	.09	.03
☐	421	Rondell White	.75	.35	.09
☐	422	Bobby Bonilla	.30	.14	.04
☐	423	Jeromy Burnitz	.20	.09	.03
☐	424	Vince Coleman	.10	.05	.01
☐	425	Mike Draper	.10	.05	.01
☐	426	Tony Fernandez	.10	.05	.01
☐	427	Dwight Gooden	.20	.09	.03
☐	428	Jeff Innis	.10	.05	.01
☐	429	Bobby Jones	.20	.09	.03
☐	430	Mike Maddux	.10	.05	.01
☐	431	Charlie O'Brien	.10	.05	.01
☐	432	Joe Orsulak	.10	.05	.01
☐	433	Pete Schourek	.30	.14	.04
☐	434	Frank Tanana	.10	.05	.01
☐	435	Ryan Thompson	.20	.09	.03
☐	436	Kim Batiste	.10	.05	.01
☐	437	Mark Davis	.10	.05	.01
☐	438	Jose DeLeon	.10	.05	.01
☐	439	Len Dykstra	.30	.14	.04
☐	440	Jim Eisenreich	.10	.05	.01
☐	441	Tommy Greene	.10	.05	.01
☐	442	Pete Incaviglia	.10	.05	.01
☐	443	Danny Jackson	.10	.05	.01
☐	444	Todd Pratt	.10	.05	.01
☐	445	Curt Schilling	.10	.05	.01
☐	446	Milt Thompson	.10	.05	.01
☐	447	David West	.10	.05	.01
☐	448	Mitch Williams	.20	.09	.03
☐	449	Steve Cooke	.10	.05	.01
☐	450	Carlos Garcia	.20	.09	.03
☐	451	Al Martin	.20	.09	.03
☐	452	Blas Minor	.10	.05	.01
☐	453	Dennis Moeller	.10	.05	.01
☐	454	Denny Neagle	.10	.05	.01
☐	455	Don Slaught	.10	.05	.01
☐	456	Lonnie Smith	.10	.05	.01
☐	457	Paul Wagner	.10	.05	.01
☐	458	Bob Walk	.10	.05	.01
☐	459	Kevin Young	.10	.05	.01
☐	460	Rene Arocha	.20	.09	.03
☐	461	Brian Barber	.10	.05	.01
☐	462	Rheal Cormier	.10	.05	.01
☐	463	Gregg Jefferies	.30	.14	.04
☐	464	Joe Magrane	.10	.05	.01
☐	465	Omar Olivares	.10	.05	.01
☐	466	Geronimo Pena	.10	.05	.01
☐	467	Allen Watson	.10	.05	.01
☐	468	Mark Whiten	.20	.09	.03
☐	469	Derek Bell	.30	.14	.04
☐	470	Phil Clark	.10	.05	.01
☐	471	Pat Gomez	.10	.05	.01
☐	472	Tony Gwynn	1.00	.45	.12
☐	473	Jeremy Hernandez	.10	.05	.01
☐	474	Bruce Hurst	.10	.05	.01
☐	475	Phil Plantier	.10	.05	.01

□	#	Player			
□	476	Scott Sanders	.25	.11	.03
□	477	Tim Scott	.10	.05	.01
□	478	Darrell Sherman	.10	.05	.01
□	479	Guillermo Velasquez	.10	.05	.01
□	480	Tim Worrell	.10	.05	.01
□	481	Todd Benzinger	.10	.05	.01
□	482	Bud Black	.10	.05	.01
□	483	Barry Bonds	.75	.35	.09
□	484	Dave Burba	.10	.05	.01
□	485	Bryan Hickerson	.10	.05	.01
□	486	Dave Martinez	.10	.05	.01
□	487	Willie McGee	.20	.09	.03
□	488	Jeff Reed	.10	.05	.01
□	489	Kevin Rogers	.10	.05	.01
□	490	Matt Williams	.50	.23	.06
□	491	Trevor Wilson	.10	.05	.01
□	492	Harold Baines	.20	.09	.03
□	493	Mike Devereaux	.20	.09	.03
□	494	Todd Frohwirth	.10	.05	.01
□	495	Chris Hoiles	.20	.09	.03
□	496	Luis Mercedes	.10	.05	.01
□	497	Sherman Obando	.20	.09	.03
□	498	Brad Pennington	.10	.05	.01
□	499	Harold Reynolds	.10	.05	.01
□	500	Arthur Rhodes	.10	.05	.01
□	501	Cal Ripken	3.00	1.35	.35
□	502	Rick Sutcliffe	.20	.09	.03
□	503	Fernando Valenzuela	.20	.09	.03
□	504	Mark Williamson	.10	.05	.01
□	505	Scott Bankhead	.10	.05	.01
□	506	Greg Blosser	.10	.05	.01
□	507	Ivan Calderon	.10	.05	.01
□	508	Roger Clemens	.50	.23	.06
□	509	Andre Dawson	.30	.14	.04
□	510	Scott Fletcher	.10	.05	.01
□	511	Greg A. Harris	.10	.05	.01
□	512	Billy Hatcher	.10	.05	.01
□	513	Bob Melvin	.10	.05	.01
□	514	Carlos Quintana	.10	.05	.01
□	515	Luis Rivera	.10	.05	.01
□	516	Jeff Russell	.10	.05	.01
□	517	Ken Ryan	.10	.05	.01
□	518	Chili Davis	.20	.09	.03
□	519	Jim Edmonds	2.00	.90	.25
□	520	Gary Gaetti	.20	.09	.03
□	521	Torey Lovullo	.10	.05	.01
□	522	Troy Percival	.20	.09	.03
□	523	Tim Salmon	1.00	.45	.12
□	524	Scott Sanderson	.10	.05	.01
□	525	J.T. Snow	1.00	.45	.12
□	526	Jerome Walton	.10	.05	.01
□	527	Jason Bere	.20	.09	.03
□	528	Rod Bolton	.10	.05	.01
□	529	Ellis Burks	.20	.09	.03
□	530	Carlton Fisk	.30	.14	.04
□	531	Craig Grebeck	.10	.05	.01
□	532	Ozzie Guillen	.10	.05	.01
□	533	Roberto Hernandez	.20	.09	.03
□	534	Bo Jackson	.30	.14	.04
□	535	Kirk McCaskill	.10	.05	.01
□	536	Dave Stieb	.10	.05	.01
□	537	Robin Ventura	.30	.14	.04
□	538	Albert Belle	1.25	.55	.16
□	539	Mike Bielecki	.10	.05	.01
□	540	Glenallen Hill	.10	.05	.01
□	541	Reggie Jefferson	.10	.05	.01
□	542	Kenny Lofton	1.00	.45	.12
□	543	Jeff Mutis	.10	.05	.01
□	544	Junior Ortiz	.10	.05	.01
□	545	Manny Ramirez	2.50	1.10	.30
□	546	Jeff Treadway	.10	.05	.01
□	547	Kevin Wickander	.10	.05	.01
□	548	Cecil Fielder	.30	.14	.04
□	549	Kirk Gibson	.20	.09	.03
□	550	Greg Gohr	.10	.05	.01
□	551	David Haas	.10	.05	.01
□	552	Bill Krueger	.10	.05	.01
□	553	Mike Moore	.10	.05	.01
□	554	Mickey Tettleton	.20	.09	.03
□	555	Lou Whitaker	.30	.14	.04
□	556	Kevin Appier	.20	.09	.03
□	557	Billy Brewer	.10	.05	.01
□	558	David Cone	.30	.14	.04
□	559	Greg Gagne	.10	.05	.01
□	560	Mark Gardner	.10	.05	.01
□	561	Phil Hiatt	.10	.05	.01
□	562	Felix Jose	.10	.05	.01
□	563	Jose Lind	.10	.05	.01
□	564	Mike Macfarlane	.10	.05	.01
□	565	Keith Miller	.10	.05	.01
□	566	Jeff Montgomery	.20	.09	.03
□	567	Hipolito Pichardo	.10	.05	.01
□	568	Ricky Bones	.10	.05	.01
□	569	Tom Brunansky	.10	.05	.01
□	570	Joe Kmak	.10	.05	.01
□	571	Pat Listach	.10	.05	.01
□	572	Graeme Lloyd	.10	.05	.01
□	573	Carlos Maldonado	.10	.05	.01
□	574	Josias Manzanillo	.10	.05	.01
□	575	Matt Mieske	.20	.09	.03
□	576	Kevin Reimer	.10	.05	.01
□	577	Bill Spiers	.10	.05	.01
□	578	Dickie Thon	.10	.05	.01
□	579	Willie Banks	.10	.05	.01
□	580	Jim Deshaies	.10	.05	.01
□	581	Mark Guthrie	.10	.05	.01
□	582	Brian Harper	.10	.05	.01
□	583	Chuck Knoblauch	.30	.14	.04
□	584	Gene Larkin	.10	.05	.01
□	585	Shane Mack	.10	.05	.01
□	586	David McCarty	.10	.05	.01
□	587	Mike Pagliarulo	.10	.05	.01
□	588	Mike Trombley	.10	.05	.01
□	589	Dave Winfield	.30	.14	.04
□	590	Jim Abbott	.30	.14	.04
□	591	Wade Boggs	.30	.14	.04
□	592	Russ Davis	.30	.14	.04
□	593	Steve Farr	.10	.05	.01
□	594	Steve Howe	.10	.05	.01
□	595	Mike Humphreys	.10	.05	.01
□	596	Jimmy Key	.20	.09	.03
□	597	Jim Leyritz	.10	.05	.01
□	598	Bobby Munoz	.10	.05	.01
□	599	Paul O'Neill	.20	.09	.03
□	600	Spike Owen	.10	.05	.01
□	601	Mike Stanley	.10	.05	.01
□	602	Danny Tartabull	.20	.09	.03
□	603	Scott Brosius	.10	.05	.01
□	604	Storm Davis	.10	.05	.01
□	605	Eric Fox	.10	.05	.01
□	606	Rich Gossage	.30	.14	.04
□	607	Scott Hemond	.10	.05	.01
□	608	Dave Henderson	.10	.05	.01
□	609	Mark McGwire	.30	.14	.04
□	610	Mike Mohler	.10	.05	.01
□	611	Edwin Nunez	.10	.05	.01
□	612	Kevin Seitzer	.10	.05	.01
□	613	Ruben Sierra	.30	.14	.04
□	614	Chris Bosio	.10	.05	.01
□	615	Norm Charlton	.10	.05	.01
□	616	Jim Converse	.20	.09	.03
□	617	John Cummings	.20	.09	.03

			MINT	NRMT	EXC
☐ 618	Mike Felder		.10	.05	.01
☐ 619	Ken Griffey Jr.		3.00	1.35	.35
☐ 620	Mike Hampton		.10	.05	.01
☐ 621	Erik Hanson		.10	.05	.01
☐ 622	Bill Haselman		.10	.05	.01
☐ 623	Tino Martinez		.30	.14	.04
☐ 624	Lee Tinsley		.20	.09	.03
☐ 625	Fernando Vina		.10	.05	.01
☐ 626	David Wainhouse		.10	.05	.01
☐ 627	Jose Canseco		.50	.23	.06
☐ 628	Benji Gil		.20	.09	.03
☐ 629	Tom Henke		.20	.09	.03
☐ 630	David Hulse		.10	.05	.01
☐ 631	Manuel Lee		.10	.05	.01
☐ 632	Craig Lefferts		.10	.05	.01
☐ 633	Robb Nen		.10	.05	.01
☐ 634	Gary Redus		.10	.05	.01
☐ 635	Bill Ripken		.10	.05	.01
☐ 636	Nolan Ryan		2.50	1.10	.30
☐ 637	Dan Smith		.10	.05	.01
☐ 638	Matt Whiteside		.10	.05	.01
☐ 639	Roberto Alomar		.60	.25	.07
☐ 640	Juan Guzman		.20	.09	.03
☐ 641	Pat Hentgen		.20	.09	.03
☐ 642	Darrin Jackson		.10	.05	.01
☐ 643	Randy Knorr		.10	.05	.01
☐ 644	Domingo Martinez		.10	.05	.01
☐ 645	Paul Molitor		.30	.14	.04
☐ 646	Dick Schofield		.10	.05	.01
☐ 647	Dave Stewart		.20	.09	.03
☐ 648	Checklist 301-421 Rey Sanchez		.10	.05	.01
☐ 649	Checklist 422-537 Jeremy Hernandez		.10	.05	.01
☐ 650	Checklist 538-650 Junior Ortiz		.10	.05	.01

1993 Ultra All-Rookies

Randomly inserted into series II packs, this ten-card standard-size (2 1/2" by 3 1/2") set features cutout color player action shots that are superposed upon a black background, which carries the player's uniform number, position, team name, and the set's title in multicolored lettering. The player's name appears in gold foil at the bottom. A posed color cutout player shot adorns the back, and is also projected upon a black background. The set's title appears at the top printed in gold foil and red lettering, and the player's name in gold foil precedes his career highlights, printed in white. The cards are numbered on the back in gold foil. The key cards in this set are Mike Piazza and Tim Salmon.

		MINT	NRMT	EXC
COMPLETE SET (10)		15.00	6.75	1.85
COMMON CARD (1-10)		.50	.23	.06
☐ 1	Rene Arocha	.50	.23	.06
☐ 2	Jeff Conine	2.50	1.10	.30
☐ 3	Phil Hiatt	.50	.23	.06
☐ 4	Mike Lansing	1.00	.45	.12
☐ 5	Al Martin	1.00	.45	.12
☐ 6	David Nied	1.00	.45	.12
☐ 7	Mike Piazza	10.00	4.50	1.25
☐ 8	Tim Salmon	5.00	2.20	.60
☐ 9	J.T. Snow	3.00	1.35	.35
☐ 10	Kevin Young	.50	.23	.06

1993 Ultra All-Stars

Randomly inserted into series II packs, this 20-card subset features National League (1-10) and American League (11-20) All-Stars. The gray-bordered fronts carry color player action shots that are cutout and superposed upon their original, but faded and shifted, backgrounds. The player's name and the set's title are printed in gold foil upon simulated flames that issue from a baseball icon in the lower right. That same design of the player's name, the set's title, and flaming baseball icon appears again at the top of the gray-bordered back. The player's career highlights follow below. The cards are numbered on the back in gold foil.

		MINT	NRMT	EXC
COMPLETE SET (20)		50.00	22.00	6.25
COMMON CARD (1-20)		.50	.23	.06
☐ 1	Darren Daulton	.50	.23	.06
☐ 2	Will Clark	1.50	.70	.19
☐ 3	Ryne Sandberg	4.00	1.80	.50
☐ 4	Barry Larkin	2.00	.90	.25
☐ 5	Gary Sheffield	1.00	.45	.12
☐ 6	Barry Bonds	4.00	1.80	.50
☐ 7	Ray Lankford	.50	.23	.06
☐ 8	Larry Walker	2.00	.90	.25

		MINT	NRMT	EXC
☐ 9	Greg Maddux	15.00	6.75	1.85
☐ 10	Lee Smith	1.00	.45	.12
☐ 11	Ivan Rodriguez	1.00	.45	.12
☐ 12	Mark McGwire	1.00	.45	.12
☐ 13	Carlos Baerga	3.00	1.35	.35
☐ 14	Cal Ripken	16.00	7.25	2.00
☐ 15	Edgar Martinez	1.00	.45	.12
☐ 16	Juan Gonzalez	3.00	1.35	.35
☐ 17	Ken Griffey Jr.	15.00	6.75	1.85
☐ 18	Kirby Puckett	5.00	2.20	.60
☐ 19	Frank Thomas	15.00	6.75	1.85
☐ 20	Mike Mussina	2.50	1.10	.30

1993 Ultra
Award Winners

*Randomly inserted in first series packs, this
first series of 1993 Ultra Award Winners
presents the Top Glove for the National (1-
9) and American (10-18) Leagues and
other major league award winners (19-25).
The 25 standard-size (2 1/2" by 3 1/2")
cards comprising this set feature horizontal
black-marbleized card designs and carry
two color player photos: an action shot on
the left and a posed photo on the right. The
player's name appears in gold-foil cursive
lettering near the bottom left. The category
of award is shown in gold foil below. A gold-
foil line highlights the card's lower edge.
The horizontal and black-marbleized design
continues on the back. A color player head
shot appears on the left side. The player's
name reappears in gold-foil cursive lettering near the top. Below is the player's
award category in gold foil above a gold-foil
underline. The player's career highlights are
shown in white lettering below. The cards
are numbered on the back.*

		MINT	NRMT	EXC
	COMPLETE SET (25)	50.00	22.00	6.25
	COMMON CARD (1-25)	.50	.23	.06
☐ 1	Greg Maddux	15.00	6.75	1.85
☐ 2	Tom Pagnozzi	.50	.23	.06
☐ 3	Mark Grace	1.00	.45	.12
☐ 4	Jose Lind	.50	.23	.06
☐ 5	Terry Pendleton	1.00	.45	.12
☐ 6	Ozzie Smith	3.00	1.35	.35
☐ 7	Barry Bonds	4.00	1.80	.50

		MINT	NRMT	EXC
☐ 8	Andy Van Slyke	.50	.23	.06
☐ 9	Larry Walker	2.00	.90	.25
☐ 10	Mark Langston	.50	.23	.06
☐ 11	Ivan Rodriguez	1.00	.45	.12
☐ 12	Don Mattingly	8.00	3.60	1.00
☐ 13	Roberto Alomar	3.00	1.35	.35
☐ 14	Robin Ventura	1.00	.45	.12
☐ 15	Cal Ripken	16.00	7.25	2.00
☐ 16	Ken Griffey	15.00	6.75	1.85
☐ 17	Kirby Puckett	5.00	2.20	.60
☐ 18	Devon White	.50	.23	.06
☐ 19	Pat Listach	.50	.23	.06
	AL ROY			
☐ 20	Eric Karros	2.00	.90	.25
	NL ROY			
☐ 21	Pat Borders	.50	.23	.06
	World Series MVP			
☐ 22	Greg Maddux	15.00	6.75	1.85
	NL Cy Young			
☐ 23	Dennis Eckersley	1.00	.45	.12
	AL MVP and Cy Young			
☐ 24	Barry Bonds	4.00	1.80	.50
	NL MVP			
☐ 25	Gary Sheffield	1.00	.45	.12
	Ultra POY			

1993 Ultra
Home Run Kings

*Randomly inserted into all 1993 Ultra
packs, this ten-card standard-size (2 1/2"
by 3 1/2") set features the best long ball hitters in baseball. The borderless cards carry
cutout color action player photos that are
superposed upon an outer space scene,
which includes a baseball "planet" and
background stars. The player's name and
team, along with the set's logo, are printed
in gold foil and rest at the bottom. The horizontal black-and-stellar back carries a color
player close-up on the left side, and the
player's name, nickname, and career highlights in white lettering on the right side.
The set's logo, printed in gold foil at the
upper right, rounds out the card. The cards
are numbered on the back in gold foil.*

	MINT	NRMT	EXC
COMPLETE SET (10)	25.00	11.00	3.10
COMMON CARD (1-10)	.75	.35	.09

		MINT	NRMT	EXC
☐ 1	Juan Gonzalez	3.00	1.35	.35
☐ 2	Mark McGwire	1.50	.70	.19
☐ 3	Cecil Fielder	1.50	.70	.19
☐ 4	Fred McGriff	2.00	.90	.25
☐ 5	Albert Belle	6.00	2.70	.75
☐ 6	Barry Bonds	4.00	1.80	.50
☐ 7	Joe Carter	1.50	.70	.19
☐ 8	Gary Sheffield	1.50	.70	.19
☐ 9	Darren Daulton	.75	.35	.09
☐ 10	Dave Hollins	.75	.35	.09

1993 Ultra Strikeout Kings

Randomly inserted into series II packs, this five-card set showcases outstanding pitchers from both leagues. The color cutout action player photo on the front of each card shows a pitcher on the mound superposed upon a background of stars and a metallic baseball. The player's name appears in gold foil at the bottom. The gold foil-stamped set logo also appears on the front. Upon a metallic-baseball-and-stellar background, the horizontal back carries a posed color player photo on the left side, and the player's career highlights in yellow lettering on the right side. The player's name and team, as well as the set's logo, appear in gold foil at the top.

		MINT	NRMT	EXC
COMPLETE SET (5)		20.00	9.00	2.50
COMMON CARD (1-5)		.50	.23	.06
☐ 1	Roger Clemens	2.50	1.10	.30
☐ 2	Juan Guzman	.50	.23	.06
☐ 3	Randy Johnson	3.00	1.35	.35
☐ 4	Nolan Ryan	15.00	6.75	1.85
☐ 5	John Smoltz	1.50	.70	.19

1994 Ultra

The 1994 Ultra baseball set consists of 600 standard-size cards that were issued in two series of 300. The front features a full-bleed color action player photo at the bottom, where a gold foil strip edges the picture. The player's name, his position, team name, and company logo are gold foil stamped across the bottom of the front. The horizontal back has a montage of three different player cutouts on a action scene with a team color-coded border. Biography and statistics on a thin panel toward the bottom round out the back. The cards are numbered on the back, grouped alphabetically within teams, and checklisted below alphabetically according to teams for each league as follows: Baltimore Orioles (1-10/301-311), Boston Red Sox (11-19/312-319), California Angels (20-29/320-331), Chicago White Sox (30-39/332-341), Cleveland Indians (40-50/342-351), Detroit Tigers (51-60/352-358), Kansas City Royals (61-71/359-368), Milwaukee Brewers (72-82/369-381), Minnesota Twins (83-92/382-393), New York Yankees (93-103/394-401), Oakland Athletics (104-115/402-412), Seattle Mariners (116-125/413-424), Texas Rangers (126-134/425-433), Toronto Blue Jays (135-146/434-442), Atlanta Braves (147-158/443-453), Chicago Cubs (159-169/454-466), Cincinnati Reds (170-179/467-476), Colorado Rockies (180-190/477-488), Florida Marlins (191-201/489-498), Houston Astros (202-211/499-512), Los Angeles Dodgers (212-221/513-522), Montreal Expos (222-233/523-528), New York Mets (234-241/529-540), Philadelphia Phillies (242-253/541-554), Pittsburgh Pirates (254-263/555-560), St. Louis Cardinals (264-274/561-570), San Diego Padres (275-284/571-585) and San Francisco Giants (285-296/586-595). Rookie Cards include Brian Anderson, Ray Durham, LaTroy Hawkins, Brooks Kieschnick, Chan Ho Park, Mac Suzuki and Terrell Wade.

		MINT	NRMT	EXC
COMPLETE SET (600)		50.00	22.00	6.25
COMPLETE SERIES 1 (300)		25.00	11.00	3.10
COMPLETE SERIES 2 (300)		25.00	11.00	3.10
COMMON CARD (1-300)		.10	.05	.01
COMMON CARD (301-600)		.10	.05	.01
ONE INSERT PER PACK				
HOT PACKS CONTAIN INSERTS ONLY				
☐ 1	Jeffrey Hammonds	.30	.14	.04
☐ 2	Chris Hoiles	.20	.09	.03
☐ 3	Ben McDonald	.20	.09	.03
☐ 4	Mark McLemore	.10	.05	.01

☐ 5 Alan Mills	.10	.05	.01	☐ 74 Darryl Hamilton	.10	.05	.01

☐ 5	Alan Mills	.10	.05	.01	☐ 74	Darryl Hamilton	.10	.05	.01
☐ 6	Jamie Moyer	.10	.05	.01	☐ 75	Doug Henry	.10	.05	.01
☐ 7	Brad Pennington	.10	.05	.01	☐ 76	Mike Ignasiak	.10	.05	.01
☐ 8	Jim Poole	.10	.05	.01	☐ 77	John Jaha	.10	.05	.01
☐ 9	Cal Ripken Jr.	3.00	1.35	.35	☐ 78	Graeme Lloyd	.10	.05	.01
☐ 10	Jack Voigt	.10	.05	.01	☐ 79	Angel Miranda	.10	.05	.01
☐ 11	Roger Clemens	.50	.23	.06	☐ 80	Dave Nilsson	.10	.05	.01
☐ 12	Danny Darwin	.10	.05	.01	☐ 81	Troy O'Leary	.20	.09	.03
☐ 13	Andre Dawson	.30	.14	.04	☐ 82	Kevin Reimer	.10	.05	.01
☐ 14	Scott Fletcher	.10	.05	.01	☐ 83	Willie Banks	.10	.05	.01
☐ 15	Greg A Harris	.10	.05	.01	☐ 84	Larry Casian	.10	.05	.01
☐ 16	Billy Hatcher	.10	.05	.01	☐ 85	Scott Erickson	.10	.05	.01
☐ 17	Jeff Russell	.10	.05	.01	☐ 86	Eddie Guardado	.10	.05	.01
☐ 18	Aaron Sele	.30	.14	.04	☐ 87	Kent Hrbek	.10	.05	.01
☐ 19	Mo Vaughn	.50	.23	.06	☐ 88	Terry Jorgensen	.10	.05	.01
☐ 20	Mike Butcher	.10	.05	.01	☐ 89	Chuck Knoblauch	.30	.14	.04
☐ 21	Rod Correia	.10	.05	.01	☐ 90	Pat Meares	.10	.05	.01
☐ 22	Steve Frey	.10	.05	.01	☐ 91	Mike Trombley	.10	.05	.01
☐ 23	Phil Leftwich	.10	.05	.01	☐ 92	Dave Winfield	.30	.14	.04
☐ 24	Torey Lovullo	.10	.05	.01	☐ 93	Wade Boggs	.30	.14	.04
☐ 25	Ken Patterson	.10	.05	.01	☐ 94	Scott Kamieniecki	.10	.05	.01
☐ 26	Eduardo Perez UER	.10	.05	.01	☐ 95	Pat Kelly	.10	.05	.01
	(listed as a Twin instead				☐ 96	Jimmy Key	.20	.09	.03
	of Angel)				☐ 97	Jim Leyritz	.10	.05	.01
☐ 27	Tim Salmon	.60	.25	.07	☐ 98	Bobby Munoz	.10	.05	.01
☐ 28	J.T. Snow	.20	.09	.03	☐ 99	Paul O'Neill	.10	.05	.01
☐ 29	Chris Turner	.10	.05	.01	☐ 100	Melido Perez	.10	.05	.01
☐ 30	Wilson Alvarez	.30	.14	.04	☐ 101	Mike Stanley	.10	.05	.01
☐ 31	Jason Bere	.30	.14	.04	☐ 102	Danny Tartabull	.20	.09	.03
☐ 32	Joey Cora	.10	.05	.01	☐ 103	Bernie Williams	.20	.09	.03
☐ 33	Alex Fernandez	.30	.14	.04	☐ 104	Kurt Abbott	.25	.11	.03
☐ 34	Roberto Hernandez	.10	.05	.01	☐ 105	Mike Bordick	.10	.05	.01
☐ 35	Lance Johnson	.10	.05	.01	☐ 106	Ron Darling	.10	.05	.01
☐ 36	Ron Karkovice	.10	.05	.01	☐ 107	Brent Gates	.20	.09	.03
☐ 37	Kirk McCaskill	.10	.05	.01	☐ 108	Miguel Jimenez	.10	.05	.01
☐ 38	Jeff Schwarz	.10	.05	.01	☐ 109	Steve Karsay	.20	.09	.03
☐ 39	Frank Thomas	3.00	1.35	.35	☐ 110	Scott Lydy	.10	.05	.01
☐ 40	Sandy Alomar Jr.	.20	.09	.03	☐ 111	Mark McGwire	.30	.14	.04
☐ 41	Albert Belle	1.25	.55	.16	☐ 112	Troy Neel	.10	.05	.01
☐ 42	Felix Fermin	.10	.05	.01	☐ 113	Craig Paquette	.10	.05	.01
☐ 43	Wayne Kirby	.20	.09	.03	☐ 114	Bob Welch	.10	.05	.01
☐ 44	Tom Kramer	.10	.05	.01	☐ 115	Bobby Witt	.10	.05	.01
☐ 45	Kenny Lofton	1.00	.45	.12	☐ 116	Rich Amaral	.10	.05	.01
☐ 46	Jose Mesa	.10	.05	.01	☐ 117	Mike Blowers	.20	.09	.03
☐ 47	Eric Plunk	.10	.05	.01	☐ 118	Jay Buhner	.20	.09	.03
☐ 48	Paul Sorrento	.10	.05	.01	☐ 119	Dave Fleming	.10	.05	.01
☐ 49	Jim Thome	.60	.25	.07	☐ 120	Ken Griffey Jr.	3.00	1.35	.35
☐ 50	Bill Wertz	.10	.05	.01	☐ 121	Tino Martinez	.20	.09	.03
☐ 51	John Doherty	.10	.05	.01	☐ 122	Marc Newfield	.30	.14	.04
☐ 52	Cecil Fielder	.30	.14	.04	☐ 123	Ted Power	.10	.05	.01
☐ 53	Travis Fryman	.30	.14	.04	☐ 124	Mackey Sasser	.10	.05	.01
☐ 54	Chris Gomez	.30	.14	.04	☐ 125	Omar Vizquel	.10	.05	.01
☐ 55	Mike Henneman	.10	.05	.01	☐ 126	Kevin Brown	.10	.05	.01
☐ 56	Chad Kreuter	.10	.05	.01	☐ 127	Juan Gonzalez	.75	.35	.09
☐ 57	Bob MacDonald	.10	.05	.01	☐ 128	Tom Henke	.10	.05	.01
☐ 58	Mike Moore	.10	.05	.01	☐ 129	David Hulse	.10	.05	.01
☐ 59	Tony Phillips	.10	.05	.01	☐ 130	Dean Palmer	.20	.09	.03
☐ 60	Lou Whitaker	.30	.14	.04	☐ 131	Roger Pavlik	.10	.05	.01
☐ 61	Kevin Appier	.20	.09	.03	☐ 132	Ivan Rodriguez	.30	.14	.04
☐ 62	Greg Gagne	.10	.05	.01	☐ 133	Kenny Rogers	.10	.05	.01
☐ 63	Chris Gwynn	.10	.05	.01	☐ 134	Doug Strange	.10	.05	.01
☐ 64	Bob Hamelin	.20	.09	.03	☐ 135	Pat Borders	.10	.05	.01
☐ 65	Chris Haney	.10	.05	.01	☐ 136	Joe Carter	.30	.14	.04
☐ 66	Phil Hiatt	.20	.09	.03	☐ 137	Darnell Coles	.10	.05	.01
☐ 67	Felix Jose	.10	.05	.01	☐ 138	Pat Hentgen	.20	.09	.03
☐ 68	Jose Lind	.10	.05	.01	☐ 139	Al Leiter	.10	.05	.01
☐ 69	Mike Macfarlane	.10	.05	.01	☐ 140	Paul Molitor	.30	.14	.04
☐ 70	Jeff Montgomery	.20	.09	.03	☐ 141	John Olerud	.30	.14	.04
☐ 71	Hipolito Pichardo	.10	.05	.01	☐ 142	Ed Sprague	.10	.05	.01
☐ 72	Juan Bell	.10	.05	.01	☐ 143	Dave Stewart	.10	.05	.01
☐ 73	Cal Eldred	.20	.09	.03	☐ 144	Mike Timlin	.10	.05	.01

☐	145	Duane Ward	.10	.05	.01			
☐	146	Devon White	.20	.09	.03			
☐	147	Steve Avery	.30	.14	.04			
☐	148	Steve Bedrosian	.10	.05	.01			
☐	149	Damon Berryhill	.10	.05	.01			
☐	150	Jeff Blauser	.10	.05	.01			
☐	151	Tom Glavine	.30	.14	.04			
☐	152	Chipper Jones	1.50	.70	.19			
☐	153	Mark Lemke	.10	.05	.01			
☐	154	Fred McGriff	.40	.18	.05			
☐	155	Greg McMichael	.10	.05	.01			
☐	156	Deion Sanders	.60	.25	.07			
☐	157	John Smoltz	.20	.09	.03			
☐	158	Mark Wohlers	.10	.05	.01			
☐	159	Jose Bautista	.10	.05	.01			
☐	160	Steve Buechele	.10	.05	.01			
☐	161	Mike Harkey	.10	.05	.01			
☐	162	Greg Hibbard	.10	.05	.01			
☐	163	Chuck McElroy	.10	.05	.01			
☐	164	Mike Morgan	.10	.05	.01			
☐	165	Kevin Roberson	.10	.05	.01			
☐	166	Ryne Sandberg	.75	.35	.09			
☐	167	Jose Vizcaino	.10	.05	.01			
☐	168	Rick Wilkins	.10	.05	.01			
☐	169	Willie Wilson	.10	.05	.01			
☐	170	Willie Greene	.20	.09	.03			
☐	171	Roberto Kelly	.20	.09	.03			
☐	172	Larry Luebbers	.10	.05	.01			
☐	173	Kevin Mitchell	.20	.09	.03			
☐	174	Joe Oliver	.10	.05	.01			
☐	175	John Roper	.10	.05	.01			
☐	176	Johnny Ruffin	.10	.05	.01			
☐	177	Reggie Sanders	.30	.14	.04			
☐	178	John Smiley	.10	.05	.01			
☐	179	Jerry Spradlin	.10	.05	.01			
☐	180	Freddie Benavides	.10	.05	.01			
☐	181	Dante Bichette	.40	.18	.05			
☐	182	Willie Blair	.10	.05	.01			
☐	183	Kent Bottenfield	.10	.05	.01			
☐	184	Jerald Clark	.10	.05	.01			
☐	185	Joe Girardi	.10	.05	.01			
☐	186	Roberto Mejia	.10	.05	.01			
☐	187	Steve Reed	.10	.05	.01			
☐	188	Armando Reynoso	.10	.05	.01			
☐	189	Bruce Ruffin	.10	.05	.01			
☐	190	Eric Young	.10	.05	.01			
☐	191	Luis Aquino	.10	.05	.01			
☐	192	Bret Barberie	.10	.05	.01			
☐	193	Ryan Bowen	.10	.05	.01			
☐	194	Chuck Carr	.10	.05	.01			
☐	195	Orestes Destrade	.10	.05	.01			
☐	196	Richie Lewis	.10	.05	.01			
☐	197	Dave Magadan	.10	.05	.01			
☐	198	Bob Natal	.10	.05	.01			
☐	199	Gary Sheffield	.30	.14	.04			
☐	200	Matt Turner	.10	.05	.01			
☐	201	Darrell Whitmore	.10	.05	.01			
☐	202	Eric Anthony	.10	.05	.01			
☐	203	Jeff Bagwell	1.00	.45	.12			
☐	204	Andujar Cedeno	.10	.05	.01			
☐	205	Luis Gonzalez	.10	.05	.01			
☐	206	Xavier Hernandez	.10	.05	.01			
☐	207	Doug Jones	.10	.05	.01			
☐	208	Darryl Kile	.20	.09	.03			
☐	209	Scott Servais	.10	.05	.01			
☐	210	Greg Swindell	.10	.05	.01			
☐	211	Brian Williams	.10	.05	.01			
☐	212	Pedro Astacio	.20	.09	.03			
☐	213	Brett Butler	.20	.09	.03			
☐	214	Omar Daal	.10	.05	.01			
☐	215	Jim Gott	.10	.05	.01			

☐	216	Raul Mondesi	1.00	.45	.12
☐	217	Jose Offerman	.20	.09	.03
☐	218	Mike Piazza	1.25	.55	.16
☐	219	Cory Snyder	.10	.05	.01
☐	220	Tim Wallach	.10	.05	.01
☐	221	Todd Worrell	.10	.05	.01
☐	222	Moises Alou	.30	.14	.04
☐	223	Sean Berry	.10	.05	.01
☐	224	Wil Cordero	.30	.14	.04
☐	225	Jeff Fassero	.10	.05	.01
☐	226	Darrin Fletcher	.10	.05	.01
☐	227	Cliff Floyd	.30	.14	.04
☐	228	Marquis Grissom	.30	.14	.04
☐	229	Ken Hill	.20	.09	.03
☐	230	Mike Lansing	.20	.09	.03
☐	231	Kirk Rueter	.10	.05	.01
☐	232	John Wetteland	.10	.05	.01
☐	233	Rondell White	.30	.14	.04
☐	234	Tim Bogar	.10	.05	.01
☐	235	Jeromy Burnitz	.10	.05	.01
☐	236	Dwight Gooden	.10	.05	.01
☐	237	Todd Hundley	.20	.09	.03
☐	238	Jeff Kent	.20	.09	.03
☐	239	Josias Manzanillo	.10	.05	.01
☐	240	Joe Orsulak	.10	.05	.01
☐	241	Ryan Thompson	.20	.09	.03
☐	242	Kim Batiste	.10	.05	.01
☐	243	Darren Daulton	.30	.14	.04
☐	244	Tommy Greene	.10	.05	.01
☐	245	Dave Hollins	.20	.09	.03
☐	246	Pete Incaviglia	.10	.05	.01
☐	247	Danny Jackson	.10	.05	.01
☐	248	Ricky Jordan	.10	.05	.01
☐	249	John Kruk	.20	.09	.03
☐	250	Mickey Morandini	.10	.05	.01
☐	251	Terry Mulholland	.10	.05	.01
☐	252	Ben Rivera	.10	.05	.01
☐	253	Kevin Stocker	.10	.05	.01
☐	254	Jay Bell	.10	.05	.01
☐	255	Steve Cooke	.10	.05	.01
☐	256	Jeff King	.10	.05	.01
☐	257	Al Martin	.10	.05	.01
☐	258	Danny Miceli	.10	.05	.01
☐	259	Blas Minor	.10	.05	.01
☐	260	Don Slaught	.10	.05	.01
☐	261	Paul Wagner	.10	.05	.01
☐	262	Tim Wakefield	.20	.09	.03
☐	263	Kevin Young	.10	.05	.01
☐	264	Rene Arocha	.10	.05	.01
☐	265	Richard Batchelor	.10	.05	.01
☐	266	Gregg Jefferies	.30	.14	.04
☐	267	Brian Jordan	.20	.09	.03
☐	268	Jose Oquendo	.10	.05	.01
☐	269	Donovan Osborne	.10	.05	.01
☐	270	Erik Pappas	.10	.05	.01
☐	271	Mike Perez	.10	.05	.01
☐	272	Bob Tewksbury	.10	.05	.01
☐	273	Mark Whiten	.10	.05	.01
☐	274	Todd Zeile	.20	.09	.03
☐	275	Andy Ashby	.10	.05	.01
☐	276	Brad Ausmus	.10	.05	.01
☐	277	Phil Clark	.10	.05	.01
☐	278	Jeff Gardner	.10	.05	.01
☐	279	Ricky Gutierrez	.10	.05	.01
☐	280	Tony Gwynn	1.00	.45	.12
☐	281	Tim Mauser	.10	.05	.01
☐	282	Scott Sanders	.20	.09	.03
☐	283	Frank Seminara	.10	.05	.01
☐	284	Wally Whitehurst	.10	.05	.01
☐	285	Rod Beck	.20	.09	.03
☐	286	Barry Bonds	.75	.35	.09

☐ 287	Dave Burba	.10	.05	.01
☐ 288	Mark Carreon	.10	.05	.01
☐ 289	Royce Clayton	.20	.09	.03
☐ 290	Mike Jackson	.10	.05	.01
☐ 291	Darren Lewis	.10	.05	.01
☐ 292	Kirt Manwaring	.10	.05	.01
☐ 293	Dave Martinez	.10	.05	.01
☐ 294	Billy Swift	.10	.05	.01
☐ 295	Salomon Torres	.20	.09	.03
☐ 296	Matt Williams	.50	.23	.06
☐ 297	Checklist 1-75	.10	.05	.01
☐ 298	Checklist 76-150	.10	.05	.01
☐ 299	Checklist 151-225	.10	.05	.01
☐ 300	Checklist 226-300	.10	.05	.01
☐ 301	Brady Anderson	.20	.09	.03
☐ 302	Harold Baines	.20	.09	.03
☐ 303	Damon Buford	.10	.05	.01
☐ 304	Mike Devereaux	.10	.05	.01
☐ 305	Sid Fernandez	.10	.05	.01
☐ 306	Rick Krivda	.20	.09	.03
☐ 307	Mike Mussina	.40	.18	.05
☐ 308	Rafael Palmeiro	.30	.14	.04
☐ 309	Arthur Rhodes	.10	.05	.01
☐ 310	Chris Sabo	.10	.05	.01
☐ 311	Lee Smith	.30	.14	.04
☐ 312	Gregg Zaun	.20	.09	.03
☐ 313	Scott Cooper	.20	.09	.03
☐ 314	Mike Greenwell	.20	.09	.03
☐ 315	Tim Naehring	.20	.09	.03
☐ 316	Otis Nixon	.10	.05	.01
☐ 317	Paul Quantrill	.10	.05	.01
☐ 318	John Valentin	.30	.14	.04
☐ 319	Dave Valle	.10	.05	.01
☐ 320	Frank Viola	.10	.05	.01
☐ 321	Brian Anderson	.30	.14	.04
☐ 322	Garret Anderson	1.00	.45	.12
☐ 323	Chad Curtis	.20	.09	.03
☐ 324	Chili Davis	.20	.09	.03
☐ 325	Gary DiSarcina	.10	.05	.01
☐ 326	Damion Easley	.10	.05	.01
☐ 327	Jim Edmonds	.50	.23	.06
☐ 328	Chuck Finley	.10	.05	.01
☐ 329	Joe Grahe	.10	.05	.01
☐ 330	Bo Jackson	.30	.14	.04
☐ 331	Mark Langston	.30	.14	.04
☐ 332	Harold Reynolds	.10	.05	.01
☐ 333	James Baldwin	.30	.14	.04
☐ 334	Ray Durham	.75	.35	.09
☐ 335	Julio Franco	.20	.09	.03
☐ 336	Craig Grebeck	.10	.05	.01
☐ 337	Ozzie Guillen	.10	.05	.01
☐ 338	Joe Hall	.10	.05	.01
☐ 339	Darrin Jackson	.10	.05	.01
☐ 340	Jack McDowell	.30	.14	.04
☐ 341	Tim Raines	.30	.14	.04
☐ 342	Robin Ventura	.20	.09	.03
☐ 343	Carlos Baerga	.60	.25	.07
☐ 344	Derek Lilliquist	.10	.05	.01
☐ 345	Dennis Martinez	.20	.09	.03
☐ 346	Jack Morris	.20	.09	.03
☐ 347	Eddie Murray	.40	.18	.05
☐ 348	Chris Nabholz	.10	.05	.01
☐ 349	Charles Nagy	.20	.09	.03
☐ 350	Chad Ogea	.20	.09	.03
☐ 351	Manny Ramirez	1.50	.70	.19
☐ 352	Omar Vizquel	.10	.05	.01
☐ 353	Tim Belcher	.10	.05	.01
☐ 354	Eric Davis	.10	.05	.01
☐ 355	Kirk Gibson	.20	.09	.03
☐ 356	Rick Greene	.20	.09	.03
☐ 357	Mickey Tettleton	.20	.09	.03
☐ 358	Alan Trammell	.30	.14	.04
☐ 359	David Wells	.10	.05	.01
☐ 360	Stan Belinda	.10	.05	.01
☐ 361	Vince Coleman	.10	.05	.01
☐ 362	David Cone	.30	.14	.04
☐ 363	Gary Gaetti	.10	.05	.01
☐ 364	Tom Gordon	.10	.05	.01
☐ 365	Dave Henderson	.10	.05	.01
☐ 366	Wally Joyner	.20	.09	.03
☐ 367	Brent Mayne	.10	.05	.01
☐ 368	Brian McRae	.20	.09	.03
☐ 369	Michael Tucker	.30	.14	.04
☐ 370	Ricky Bones	.10	.05	.01
☐ 371	Brian Harper	.10	.05	.01
☐ 372	Tyrone Hill	.20	.09	.03
☐ 373	Mark Kiefer	.10	.05	.01
☐ 374	Pat Listach	.10	.05	.01
☐ 375	Mike Matheny	.10	.05	.01
☐ 376	Jose Mercedes	.10	.05	.01
☐ 377	Jody Reed	.10	.05	.01
☐ 378	Kevin Seitzer	.10	.05	.01
☐ 379	B.J. Surhoff	.10	.05	.01
☐ 380	Greg Vaughn	.20	.09	.03
☐ 381	Turner Ward	.10	.05	.01
☐ 382	Wes Weger	.10	.05	.01
☐ 383	Bill Wegman	.10	.05	.01
☐ 384	Rick Aguilera	.20	.09	.03
☐ 385	Rich Becker	.20	.09	.03
☐ 386	Alex Cole	.10	.05	.01
☐ 387	Steve Dunn	.10	.05	.01
☐ 388	Keith Garagozzo	.10	.05	.01
☐ 389	LaTroy Hawkins	.30	.14	.04
☐ 390	Shane Mack	.10	.05	.01
☐ 391	David McCarty	.10	.05	.01
☐ 392	Pedro Munoz	.10	.05	.01
☐ 393	Derek Parks	.10	.05	.01
☐ 394	Kirby Puckett	1.00	.45	.12
☐ 395	Kevin Tapani	.10	.05	.01
☐ 396	Matt Walbeck	.10	.05	.01
☐ 397	Jim Abbott	.30	.14	.04
☐ 398	Mike Gallego	.10	.05	.01
☐ 399	Xavier Hernandez	.10	.05	.01
☐ 400	Don Mattingly	1.50	.70	.19
☐ 401	Terry Mulholland	.10	.05	.01
☐ 402	Matt Nokes	.10	.05	.01
☐ 403	Luis Polonia	.10	.05	.01
☐ 404	Bob Wickman	.10	.05	.01
☐ 405	Mark Acre	.10	.05	.01
☐ 406	Fausto Cruz	.10	.05	.01
☐ 407	Dennis Eckersley	.30	.14	.04
☐ 408	Rickey Henderson	.30	.14	.04
☐ 409	Stan Javier	.10	.05	.01
☐ 410	Carlos Reyes	.10	.05	.01
☐ 411	Ruben Sierra	.30	.14	.04
☐ 412	Terry Steinbach	.20	.09	.03
☐ 413	Bill Taylor	.10	.05	.01
☐ 414	Todd Van Poppel	.20	.09	.03
☐ 415	Eric Anthony	.10	.05	.01
☐ 416	Bobby Ayala	.10	.05	.01
☐ 417	Chris Bosio	.10	.05	.01
☐ 418	Tim Davis	.10	.05	.01
☐ 419	Randy Johnson	.60	.25	.07
☐ 420	Kevin King	.10	.05	.01
☐ 421	Anthony Manahan	.10	.05	.01
☐ 422	Edgar Martinez	.20	.09	.03
☐ 423	Keith Mitchell	.10	.05	.01
☐ 424	Roger Salkeld	.10	.05	.01
☐ 425	Mac Suzuki	.30	.14	.04
☐ 426	Dan Wilson	.10	.05	.01
☐ 427	Duff Brumley	.10	.05	.01
☐ 428	Jose Canseco	.50	.23	.06

☐ 429	Will Clark	.40	.18	.05
☐ 430	Steve Dreyer	.10	.05	.01
☐ 431	Rick Helling	.10	.05	.01
☐ 432	Chris James	.10	.05	.01
☐ 433	Matt Whiteside	.10	.05	.01
☐ 434	Roberto Alomar	.60	.25	.07
☐ 435	Scott Brow	.10	.05	.01
☐ 436	Domingo Cedeno	.10	.05	.01
☐ 437	Carlos Delgado	.30	.14	.04
☐ 438	Juan Guzman	.20	.09	.03
☐ 439	Paul Spoljaric	.10	.05	.01
☐ 440	Todd Stottlemyre	.10	.05	.01
☐ 441	Woody Williams	.10	.05	.01
☐ 442	David Justice	.40	.18	.05
☐ 443	Mike Kelly	.20	.09	.03
☐ 444	Ryan Klesko	.75	.35	.09
☐ 445	Javier Lopez	.50	.23	.06
☐ 446	Greg Maddux	3.00	1.35	.35
☐ 447	Kent Mercker	.10	.05	.01
☐ 448	Charlie O'Brien	.10	.05	.01
☐ 449	Terry Pendleton	.10	.05	.01
☐ 450	Mike Stanton	.10	.05	.01
☐ 451	Tony Tarasco	.30	.14	.04
☐ 452	Terrell Wade	.40	.18	.05
☐ 453	Willie Banks	.10	.05	.01
☐ 454	Shawon Dunston	.10	.05	.01
☐ 455	Mark Grace	.30	.14	.04
☐ 456	Jose Guzman	.10	.05	.01
☐ 457	Jose Hernandez	.10	.05	.01
☐ 458	Glenallen Hill	.10	.05	.01
☐ 459	Blaise Ilsley	.10	.05	.01
☐ 460	Brooks Kieschnick	2.50	1.10	.30
☐ 461	Derrick May	.10	.05	.01
☐ 462	Randy Myers	.10	.05	.01
☐ 463	Karl Rhodes	.10	.05	.01
☐ 464	Sammy Sosa	.30	.14	.04
☐ 465	Steve Trachsel	.30	.14	.04
☐ 466	Anthony Young	.10	.05	.01
☐ 467	Eddie Zambrano	.10	.05	.01
☐ 468	Bret Boone	.30	.14	.04
☐ 469	Tom Browning	.10	.05	.01
☐ 470	Hector Carrasco	.10	.05	.01
☐ 471	Rob Dibble	.10	.05	.01
☐ 472	Erik Hanson	.10	.05	.01
☐ 473	Thomas Howard	.10	.05	.01
☐ 474	Barry Larkin	.40	.18	.05
☐ 475	Hal Morris	.20	.09	.03
☐ 476	Jose Rijo	.20	.09	.03
☐ 477	John Burke	.10	.05	.01
☐ 478	Ellis Burks	.20	.09	.03
☐ 479	Marvin Freeman	.10	.05	.01
☐ 480	Andres Galarraga	.30	.14	.04
☐ 481	Greg W. Harris	.10	.05	.01
☐ 482	Charlie Hayes	.20	.09	.03
☐ 483	Darren Holmes	.10	.05	.01
☐ 484	Howard Johnson	.10	.05	.01
☐ 485	Marcus Moore	.10	.05	.01
☐ 486	David Nied	.30	.14	.04
☐ 487	Mark Thompson	.20	.09	.03
☐ 488	Walt Weiss	.10	.05	.01
☐ 489	Kurt Abbott	.20	.09	.03
☐ 490	Matias Carrillo	.10	.05	.01
☐ 491	Jeff Conine	.30	.14	.04
☐ 492	Chris Hammond	.10	.05	.01
☐ 493	Bryan Harvey	.10	.05	.01
☐ 494	Charlie Hough	.10	.05	.01
☐ 495	Yorkis Perez	.10	.05	.01
☐ 496	Pat Rapp	.10	.05	.01
☐ 497	Benito Santiago	.10	.05	.01
☐ 498	David Weathers	.10	.05	.01
☐ 499	Craig Biggio	.20	.09	.03
☐ 500	Ken Caminiti	.20	.09	.03
☐ 501	Doug Drabek	.20	.09	.03
☐ 502	Tony Eusebio	.10	.05	.01
☐ 503	Steve Finley	.10	.05	.01
☐ 504	Pete Harnisch	.10	.05	.01
☐ 505	Brian Hunter	.75	.35	.09
☐ 506	Domingo Jean	.10	.05	.01
☐ 507	Todd Jones	.10	.05	.01
☐ 508	Orlando Miller	.20	.09	.03
☐ 509	James Mouton	.20	.09	.03
☐ 510	Roberto Petagine	.20	.09	.03
☐ 511	Shane Reynolds	.10	.05	.01
☐ 512	Mitch Williams	.10	.05	.01
☐ 513	Billy Ashley	.30	.14	.04
☐ 514	Tom Candiotti	.10	.05	.01
☐ 515	Delino DeShields	.20	.09	.03
☐ 516	Kevin Gross	.10	.05	.01
☐ 517	Orel Hershiser	.20	.09	.03
☐ 518	Eric Karros	.20	.09	.03
☐ 519	Ramon Martinez	.20	.09	.03
☐ 520	Chan Ho Park	.30	.14	.04
☐ 521	Henry Rodriguez	.10	.05	.01
☐ 522	Joey Eischen	.20	.09	.03
☐ 523	Rod Henderson	.10	.05	.01
☐ 524	Pedro J. Martinez	.30	.14	.04
☐ 525	Mel Rojas	.10	.05	.01
☐ 526	Larry Walker	.40	.18	.05
☐ 527	Gabe White	.10	.05	.01
☐ 528	Bobby Bonilla	.30	.14	.04
☐ 529	Jonathan Hurst	.10	.05	.01
☐ 530	Bobby Jones	.30	.14	.04
☐ 531	Kevin McReynolds	.10	.05	.01
☐ 532	Bill Pulsipher	.50	.23	.06
☐ 533	Bret Saberhagen	.20	.09	.03
☐ 534	David Segui	.10	.05	.01
☐ 535	Pete Smith	.10	.05	.01
☐ 536	Kelly Stinnett	.10	.05	.01
☐ 537	Dave Telgheder	.10	.05	.01
☐ 538	Quilvio Veras	.20	.09	.03
☐ 539	Jose Vizcaino	.10	.05	.01
☐ 540	Pete Walker	.10	.05	.01
☐ 541	Ricky Bottalico	.20	.09	.03
☐ 542	Wes Chamberlain	.10	.05	.01
☐ 543	Mariano Duncan	.10	.05	.01
☐ 544	Lenny Dykstra	.30	.14	.04
☐ 545	Jim Eisenreich	.10	.05	.01
☐ 546	Phil Geisler	.20	.09	.03
☐ 547	Wayne Gomes	.40	.18	.05
☐ 548	Doug Jones	.10	.05	.01
☐ 549	Jeff Juden	.10	.05	.01
☐ 550	Mike Lieberthal	.10	.05	.01
☐ 551	Tony Longmire	.10	.05	.01
☐ 552	Tom Marsh	.10	.05	.01
☐ 553	Bobby Munoz	.10	.05	.01
☐ 554	Curt Schilling	.10	.05	.01
☐ 555	Carlos Garcia	.10	.05	.01
☐ 556	Ravelo Manzanillo	.10	.05	.01
☐ 557	Orlando Merced	.20	.09	.03
☐ 558	Will Pennyfeather	.10	.05	.01
☐ 559	Zane Smith	.10	.05	.01
☐ 560	Andy Van Slyke	.20	.09	.03
☐ 561	Rick White	.10	.05	.01
☐ 562	Luis Alicea	.10	.05	.01
☐ 563	Brian Barber	.20	.09	.03
☐ 564	Clint Davis	.10	.05	.01
☐ 565	Bernard Gilkey	.20	.09	.03
☐ 566	Ray Lankford	.30	.14	.04
☐ 567	Tom Pagnozzi	.10	.05	.01
☐ 568	Ozzie Smith	.60	.25	.07
☐ 569	Rick Sutcliffe	.20	.09	.03
☐ 570	Allen Watson	.20	.09	.03

☐ 571	Dmitri Young	.20	.09	.03
☐ 572	Derek Bell	.20	.09	.03
☐ 573	Andy Benes	.20	.09	.03
☐ 574	Archi Cianfrocco	.10	.05	.01
☐ 575	Joey Hamilton	.30	.14	.04
☐ 576	Gene Harris	.10	.05	.01
☐ 577	Trevor Hoffman	.10	.05	.01
☐ 578	Tim Hyers	.10	.05	.01
☐ 579	Brian Johnson	.10	.05	.01
☐ 580	Keith Lockhart	.10	.05	.01
☐ 581	Pedro A. Martinez	.10	.05	.01
☐ 582	Ray McDavid	.20	.09	.03
☐ 583	Phil Plantier	.20	.09	.03
☐ 584	Bip Roberts	.10	.05	.01
☐ 585	Dave Staton	.10	.05	.01
☐ 586	Todd Benzinger	.10	.05	.01
☐ 587	John Burkett	.20	.09	.03
☐ 588	Bryan Hickerson	.10	.05	.01
☐ 589	Willie McGee	.10	.05	.01
☐ 590	John Patterson	.10	.05	.01
☐ 591	Mark Portugal	.10	.05	.01
☐ 592	Kevin Rogers	.10	.05	.01
☐ 593	Joe Rosselli	.10	.05	.01
☐ 594	Steve Soderstrom	.30	.14	.04
☐ 595	Robby Thompson	.10	.05	.01
☐ 596	125th Anniversary Card	.10	.05	.01
☐ 597	Checklist	.10	.05	.01
☐ 598	Checklist	.10	.05	.01
☐ 599	Checklist	.10	.05	.01
☐ 600	Checklist	.10	.05	.01

		MINT	NRMT	EXC
COMPLETE SET (10)		12.00	5.50	1.50
COMMON CARD (1-10)		.50	.23	.06
☐ 1	Kurt Abbott	.50	.23	.06
☐ 2	Carlos Delgado	1.25	.55	.16
☐ 3	Cliff Floyd	1.00	.45	.12
☐ 4	Jeffrey Hammonds	1.00	.45	.12
☐ 5	Ryan Klesko	3.00	1.35	.35
☐ 6	Javier Lopez	2.00	.90	.25
☐ 7	Raul Mondesi	4.00	1.80	.50
☐ 8	James Mouton	.50	.23	.06
☐ 9	Chan Ho Park	1.00	.45	.12
☐ 10	Dave Staton	.50	.23	.06

1994 Ultra All-Stars

Randomly inserted in second series foil and jumbo packs at a rate of one in three, this 20-card set contains top major league stars. The fronts have a color player photo superimposed over a bright red (American League players) or dark blue (National League) background. The backs are much the same except they include highlights from 1993.

		MINT	NRMT	EXC
COMPLETE SET (20)		18.00	8.00	2.20
COMMON CARD (1-20)		.25	.11	.03
☐ 1	Chris Hoiles	.25	.11	.03
☐ 2	Frank Thomas	5.00	2.20	.60
☐ 3	Roberto Alomar	1.00	.45	.12
☐ 4	Cal Ripken Jr.	5.00	2.20	.60
☐ 5	Robin Ventura	.40	.18	.05
☐ 6	Albert Belle	2.00	.90	.25
☐ 7	Juan Gonzalez	1.25	.55	.16
☐ 8	Ken Griffey Jr.	5.00	2.20	.60
☐ 9	John Olerud	.40	.18	.05
☐ 10	Jack McDowell	.40	.18	.05
☐ 11	Mike Piazza	2.00	.90	.25
☐ 12	Fred McGriff	.60	.25	.07
☐ 13	Ryne Sandberg	1.25	.55	.16
☐ 14	Jay Bell	.25	.11	.03
☐ 15	Matt Williams	.75	.35	.09
☐ 16	Barry Bonds	1.25	.55	.16
☐ 17	Lenny Dykstra	.40	.18	.05
☐ 18	David Justice	.60	.25	.07
☐ 19	Tom Glavine	.40	.18	.05
☐ 20	Greg Maddux	5.00	2.20	.60

1994 Ultra All-Rookies

This 10-card set features top rookies of 1994. Randomly inserted in second series jumbo and foil packs at a rate of one in 10, these cards measure the standard size. Card fronts have a color player photo cutout over a computer generated background that resembles volcanic activity. The player's name and All-Rookie Team logo appear in gold foil at the bottom. On the backs, the player cut-out appears toward the right with text on the left. The background is much the same as the front. Every seciond series Ultra hobby case included this set in jumbo (3 1/2" by 5") form. These jumbo versions are priced up to twice the values below.

1994 Ultra
Award Winners

Randomly inserted in all first series packs at a rate of one in three, this 25-card standard-size set features three MVP's, two Rookies of the Year, and 18 Top Glove defensive standouts. The set is divided into American League Top Gloves (1-9), National League Top Gloves (10-18), and Award Winners (19-25). A horizontal design includes a color player cut-out over a gold background on front. Also on front, is a gold foil logo that indicates the honor. The backs have a small photo and text.

	MINT	NRMT	EXC
COMPLETE SET (25)	18.00	8.00	2.20
COMMON CARD (1-25)	.25	.11	.03
☐ 1 Ivan Rodriguez	.40	.18	.05
☐ 2 Don Mattingly	2.50	1.10	.30
☐ 3 Roberto Alomar	1.00	.45	.12
☐ 4 Robin Ventura	.40	.18	.05
☐ 5 Omar Vizquel	.25	.11	.03
☐ 6 Ken Griffey Jr.	5.00	2.20	.60
☐ 7 Kenny Lofton	1.50	.70	.19
☐ 8 Devon White	.40	.18	.05
☐ 9 Mark Langston	.40	.18	.05
☐ 10 Kirt Manwaring	.25	.11	.03
☐ 11 Mark Grace	.40	.18	.05
☐ 12 Robby Thompson	.25	.11	.03
☐ 13 Matt Williams	.75	.35	.09
☐ 14 Jay Bell	.25	.11	.03
☐ 15 Barry Bonds	1.25	.55	.16
☐ 16 Marquis Grissom	.40	.18	.05
☐ 17 Larry Walker	.60	.25	.07
☐ 18 Greg Maddux	5.00	2.20	.60
☐ 19 Frank Thomas	5.00	2.20	.60
AL MVP			
☐ 20 Barry Bonds	1.25	.55	.16
NL MVP			
☐ 21 Paul Molitor	.40	.18	.05
World Series MVP			
☐ 22 Jack McDowell	.40	.18	.05
☐ 23 Greg Maddux	5.00	2.20	.60
AL POY			
☐ 24 Tim Salmon	1.00	.45	.12
AL ROY			
☐ 25 Mike Piazza	2.00	.90	.25
NL ROY			

1994 Ultra Career
Achievement

Randomly inserted in all first series packs at a rate of one in 21, this five card set highlights veteran stars and milestones they have reached during their brilliant careers. Horizontally designed cards have fronts that feature a color player photo superimposed over solid color background that contains another player photo. A photo of the player earlier in his career is on back along with text.

	MINT	NRMT	EXC
COMPLETE SET (5)	15.00	6.75	1.85
COMMON CARD (1-5)	1.00	.45	.12
☐ 1 Joe Carter	1.00	.45	.12
☐ 2 Paul Molitor	1.00	.45	.12
☐ 3 Cal Ripken Jr.	10.00	4.50	1.25
☐ 4 Ryne Sandberg	2.00	.90	.25
☐ 5 Dave Winfield	1.00	.45	.12

1994 Ultra Hitting
Machines

Randomly inserted in all second series packs at a rate of one in five, this 10-card horizontally designed set features top hitters from 1993. The fronts have a color player cut-out over a "Hitting Machines" background. The back has a smaller player cut-out and text.

	MINT	NRMT	EXC
COMPLETE SET (10)	12.00	5.50	1.50
COMMON CARD (1-10)	.50	.23	.06
☐ 1 Roberto Alomar	1.00	.45	.12
☐ 2 Carlos Baerga	1.00	.45	.12
☐ 3 Barry Bonds	1.25	.55	.16
☐ 4 Andres Galarraga	.50	.23	.06
☐ 5 Juan Gonzalez	1.25	.55	.16
☐ 6 Tony Gwynn	1.50	.70	.19
☐ 7 Paul Molitor	.50	.23	.06
☐ 8 John Olerud	.50	.23	.06
☐ 9 Mike Piazza	2.00	.90	.25
☐ 10 Frank Thomas	5.00	2.20	.60

1994 Ultra
Home Run Kings

Randomly inserted exclusively in foil packs at a rate of one in 36, these 12 standard-size cards highlight home run hitters by an etched metalized look. Cards 1-6 feature American League Home Run Kings while cards 7-12 present National League Home Run Kings.

	MINT	NRMT	EXC
COMPLETE SET (12)	85.00	38.00	10.50
COMMON CARD (1-12)	2.50	1.10	.30
☐ 1 Juan Gonzalez	6.00	2.70	.75
☐ 2 Ken Griffey Jr.	25.00	11.00	3.10
☐ 3 Frank Thomas	25.00	11.00	3.10
☐ 4 Albert Belle	10.00	4.50	1.25
☐ 5 Rafael Palmeiro	2.50	1.10	.30
☐ 6 Joe Carter	2.50	1.10	.30
☐ 7 Barry Bonds	6.00	2.70	.75
☐ 8 David Justice	3.00	1.35	.35
☐ 9 Matt Williams	4.00	1.80	.50
☐ 10 Fred McGriff	3.00	1.35	.35
☐ 11 Ron Gant	2.50	1.10	.30
☐ 12 Mike Piazza	10.00	4.50	1.25

1994 Ultra
League Leaders

Randomly inserted in all packs at a rate of one in 11, this ten-card standard-size set features ten of 1993's most impressive hitters, runners, and pitchers. The fronts feature borderless color player action shots,

with a color-screening that shades from being imperceptible at the top to washing out the photos' true colors at the bottom. The player's name in gold foil appears across the card face. The borderless back carries a color player head shot in a lower corner with his career highlights appearing above, all on a monochrome background that shades from dark to light, from top to bottom. The set is arranged according to American League (1-5) and National League (6-10) players.

	MINT	NRMT	EXC
COMPLETE SET (10)	5.00	2.20	.60
COMMON CARD (1-10)	.25	.11	.03
☐ 1 John Olerud AL Batting Average Leader	.25	.11	.03
☐ 2 Rafael Palmeiro AL Runs Scored Leader	.50	.23	.06
☐ 3 Kenny Lofton AL Stolen Base Leader	2.00	.90	.25
☐ 4 Jack McDowell AL Winningest Pitcher	.50	.23	.06
☐ 5 Randy Johnson AL Strikeout Leader	1.25	.55	.16
☐ 6 Andres Galarraga NL Batting Average Leader	.50	.23	.06
☐ 7 Lenny Dykstra NL Runs Scored Leader	.50	.23	.06
☐ 8 Chuck Carr NL Stolen Base Leader	.25	.11	.03
☐ 9 Tom Glavine NL Winningest Pitcher	.50	.23	.06
☐ 10 Jose Rijo NL Strikeout Leader	.25	.11	.03

1994 Ultra
On-Base Leaders

Randomly inserted in jumbo packs at a rate of one in 36, this 12-card set features those

that were among the Major League leaders in on-base percentage. Card fronts have the player superimposed over a metallic background that simulates statistics from a sports page. The backs have a player cutout and text over a statistical background that is not metallic.

	MINT	NRMT	EXC
COMPLETE SET (12)	200.00	90.00	25.00
COMMON CARD (1-12)	6.00	2.70	.75
☐ 1 Roberto Alomar	15.00	6.75	1.85
☐ 2 Barry Bonds	20.00	9.00	2.50
☐ 3 Lenny Dykstra	8.00	3.60	1.00
☐ 4 Andres Galarraga	8.00	3.60	1.00
☐ 5 Mark Grace	8.00	3.60	1.00
☐ 6 Ken Griffey Jr.	75.00	34.00	9.50
☐ 7 Gregg Jefferies	8.00	3.60	1.00
☐ 8 Orlando Merced	6.00	2.70	.75
☐ 9 Paul Molitor	8.00	3.60	1.00
☐ 10 John Olerud	6.00	2.70	.75
☐ 11 Tony Phillips	6.00	2.70	.75
☐ 12 Frank Thomas	75.00	34.00	9.50

1994 Ultra RBI Kings

Randomly inserted in first series jumbo packs at a rate of one in 36, this 12-card standard-size set features RBI leaders. These horizontal, metallized cards have a color player photo on front that superimposes a player image. The backs have a write-up and a small color player photo. Cards 1-6 feature American League RBI Kings while cards 7-12 present National League RBI Kings.

	MINT	NRMT	EXC
COMPLETE SET (12)	200.00	90.00	25.00
COMMON CARD (1-12)	8.00	3.60	1.00
☐ 1 Albert Belle	30.00	13.50	3.70
☐ 2 Frank Thomas	75.00	34.00	9.50
☐ 3 Joe Carter	8.00	3.60	1.00
☐ 4 Juan Gonzalez	20.00	9.00	2.50
☐ 5 Cecil Fielder	8.00	3.60	1.00
☐ 6 Carlos Baerga	15.00	6.75	1.85
☐ 7 Barry Bonds	20.00	9.00	2.50
☐ 8 David Justice	10.00	4.50	1.25
☐ 9 Ron Gant	8.00	3.60	1.00
☐ 10 Mike Piazza	30.00	13.50	3.70
☐ 11 Matt Williams	12.00	5.50	1.50
☐ 12 Darren Daulton	8.00	3.60	1.00

1994 Ultra Rising Stars

Randomly inserted in second series foil packs and jumbo packs at a rate of one in 36, this 12-card set spotlights top young major league stars. Metallic fronts have the player superimposed over icons resembling outer space. The backs feature the player in the same format along with text.

	MINT	NRMT	EXC
COMPLETE SET (12)	150.00	70.00	19.00
COMMON CARD (1-12)	5.00	2.20	.60
☐ 1 Carlos Baerga	15.00	6.75	1.85
☐ 2 Jeff Bagwell	25.00	11.00	3.10
☐ 3 Albert Belle	30.00	13.50	3.70
☐ 4 Cliff Floyd	8.00	3.60	1.00
☐ 5 Travis Fryman	8.00	3.60	1.00
☐ 6 Marquis Grissom	8.00	3.60	1.00
☐ 7 Kenny Lofton	25.00	11.00	3.10
☐ 8 John Olerud	5.00	2.20	.60
☐ 9 Mike Piazza	30.00	13.50	3.70
☐ 10 Kirk Rueter	5.00	2.20	.60
☐ 11 Tim Salmon	15.00	6.75	1.85
☐ 12 Aaron Sele	5.00	2.20	.60

1994 Ultra Second Year Standouts

Randomly inserted in all first series packs at a rate of one in 11, this 10-card standard-size set included 10 1993 outstanding

rookies who are destined to become future stars. The fronts feature two color player action cutouts superimposed upon borderless team-colored backgrounds. The player's name appears in gold foil at the bottom. The back carries a color player head shot in a lower corner with his career highlights appearing alongside, all on a borderless team color-coded background. The set is arranged according to American League (1-5) and National League (6-10) players.

	MINT	NRMT	EXC
COMPLETE SET (10)	15.00	6.75	1.85
COMMON CARD (1-10)	.50	.23	.06
☐ 1 Jason Bere	1.00	.45	.12
☐ 2 Brent Gates	.50	.23	.06
☐ 3 Jeffrey Hammonds	1.00	.45	.12
☐ 4 Tim Salmon	4.00	1.80	.50
☐ 5 Aaron Sele	1.00	.45	.12
☐ 6 Chuck Carr	.50	.23	.06
☐ 7 Jeff Conine	2.00	.90	.25
☐ 8 Greg McMichael	.50	.23	.06
☐ 9 Mike Piazza	8.00	3.60	1.00
☐ 10 Kevin Stocker	.50	.23	.06

1994 Ultra Strikeout Kings

Randomly inserted in all second series packs at a rate of one in seven, this five-card standard-size set features top strikeout artists. Full-bleed fronts offer triple exposure photos and a gold foil Strikeout King logo. The backs contain a photo and write-up with the Strikeout King logo as background.

	MINT	NRMT	EXC
COMPLETE SET (5)	6.00	2.70	.75
COMMON CARD (1-5)	.25	.11	.03
☐ 1 Randy Johnson	1.00	.45	.12
☐ 2 Mark Langston	.50	.23	.06
☐ 3 Greg Maddux	5.00	2.20	.60
☐ 4 Jose Rijo	.25	.11	.03
☐ 5 John Smoltz	.50	.23	.06

1995 Ultra

This 450-card was issued in two series. The first series contained 250 cards while the second series consisted of 200 cards. They were issued in 12-card packs (either hobby or retail) with a suggested retail price of $1.99. Also, 15-card pre-priced packs with a suggested retail of $2.69. The full-bleed fronts feature the player's photo with the team name and player's name at the bottom. The "95 Fleer Ultra" logo is in the upper right corner. The backs have a two-photo design; one of which is a full-size duotone shot with the other being a full-color action shot. Personal bio, seasonal and career information are also included on the back. In each series the cards were grouped alphabetically within teams and checklisted alphabetically according to teams for each league as follows: Baltimore Orioles (1-8, 251-258), Boston Red Sox (9-17, 259-264), California Angels (18-25, 265-272), Chicago White Sox (26-34, 273-277), Cleveland Indians (35-43, 278-283), Detroit Tigers (44-52, 284-287), Kansas City Royals (53-61, 288-293), Milwaukee Brewers (62-70, 294-300), Minnesota Twins (71-79, 301-306), New York Yankees (80-88, 307-314), Oakland Athletics (89-97, 315-323), Seattle Mariners (98-106, 324-331), Texas Rangers (107-115, 332-336), Toronto Blue Jays (116-124, 337-344), Atlanta Braves (125-133, 345-356), Chicago Cubs (134-141, 357-362), Cincinnati Reds (142-150, 363-372), Colorado Rockies (151-159, 373-377), Florida Marlins (160-168, 3378-383), Houston Astros (169-177, 384-391), Los

Angeles Dodgers (178-185, 392-401), Montreal Expos (186-194, 402-410), New York Mets (195-202, 411-416), Philadelphia Phillies (203-211, 417-422), Pittsburgh Pirates (212-220, 423-428), St. Louis Cardinals (221-229, 429-434), San Diego Padres (230-238, 435-441) and San Francisco Giants (239-247, 442-447).

	MINT	NRMT	EXC
COMPLETE SET (450)	30.00	13.50	3.70
COMPLETE SERIES 1 (250)	18.00	8.00	2.20
COMPLETE SERIES 2 (200)	12.00	5.50	1.50
COMMON CARD (1-250)	.10	.05	.01
COMMON CARD (251-450)	.10	.05	.01
CHECKLISTS (248-250)	.10	.05	.01
CHECKLISTS (448-450)	.10	.05	.01
ONE INSERT PER PACK			
HOT PACKS CONTAIN INSERTS ONLY			
COMP. GOLD MED. SET (450)	120.00	55.00	15.00
GOLD MED. COMM. CARDS (1-450)	.25	.11	.03
GOLD MED. SEMISTARS	.50	.23	.06

*GOLD MED VETERAN STARS: 2X TO 4X BASIC CARDS
*GOLD MED YOUNG STARS: 1.5X TO 3X BASIC CARDS

☐ 1	Brady Anderson	.20	.09	.03
☐ 2	Sid Fernandez	.10	.05	.01
☐ 3	Jeffrey Hammonds	.10	.05	.01
☐ 4	Chris Hoiles	.10	.05	.01
☐ 5	Ben McDonald	.10	.05	.01
☐ 6	Mike Mussina	.40	.18	.05
☐ 7	Rafael Palmeiro	.30	.14	.04
☐ 8	Jack Voigt	.10	.05	.01
☐ 9	Wes Chamberlain	.10	.05	.01
☐ 10	Roger Clemens	.50	.23	.06
☐ 11	Chris Howard	.10	.05	.01
☐ 12	Tim Naehring	.20	.09	.03
☐ 13	Otis Nixon	.10	.05	.01
☐ 14	Rich Rowland	.10	.05	.01
☐ 15	Ken Ryan	.10	.05	.01
☐ 16	John Valentin	.30	.14	.04
☐ 17	Mo Vaughn	.50	.23	.06
☐ 18	Brian Anderson	.10	.05	.01
☐ 19	Chili Davis	.20	.09	.03
☐ 20	Damion Easley	.10	.05	.01
☐ 21	Jim Edmonds	.40	.18	.05
☐ 22	Mark Langston	.10	.05	.01
☐ 23	Tim Salmon	.50	.23	.06
☐ 24	J.T. Snow	.30	.14	.04
☐ 25	Chris Turner	.10	.05	.01
☐ 26	Wilson Alvarez	.20	.09	.03
☐ 27	Joey Cora	.10	.05	.01
☐ 28	Alex Fernandez	.20	.09	.03
☐ 29	Roberto Hernandez	.20	.09	.03
☐ 30	Lance Johnson	.10	.05	.01
☐ 31	Ron Karkovice	.10	.05	.01
☐ 32	Kirk McCaskill	.10	.05	.01
☐ 33	Tim Raines	.30	.14	.04
☐ 34	Frank Thomas	3.00	1.35	.35
☐ 35	Sandy Alomar Jr.	.10	.05	.01
☐ 36	Albert Belle	1.25	.55	.16
☐ 37	Mark Clark	.10	.05	.01
☐ 38	Kenny Lofton	1.00	.45	.12
☐ 39	Eddie Murray	.40	.18	.05
☐ 40	Eric Plunk	.10	.05	.01
☐ 41	Manny Ramirez	1.25	.55	.16
☐ 42	Jim Thome	.50	.23	.06
☐ 43	Omar Vizquel	.20	.09	.03
☐ 44	Danny Bautista	.10	.05	.01
☐ 45	Junior Felix	.10	.05	.01
☐ 46	Cecil Fielder	.30	.14	.04
☐ 47	Chris Gomez	.10	.05	.01
☐ 48	Chad Kreuter	.10	.05	.01
☐ 49	Mike Moore	.10	.05	.01
☐ 50	Tony Phillips	.10	.05	.01
☐ 51	Alan Trammell	.20	.09	.03
☐ 52	David Wells	.10	.05	.01
☐ 53	Kevin Appier	.20	.09	.03
☐ 54	Billy Brewer	.10	.05	.01
☐ 55	David Cone	.30	.14	.04
☐ 56	Greg Gagne	.10	.05	.01
☐ 57	Bob Hamelin	.10	.05	.01
☐ 58	Jose Lind	.10	.05	.01
☐ 59	Brent Mayne	.10	.05	.01
☐ 60	Brian McRae	.20	.09	.03
☐ 61	Terry Shumpert	.10	.05	.01
☐ 62	Ricky Bones	.10	.05	.01
☐ 63	Mike Fetters	.10	.05	.01
☐ 64	Darryl Hamilton	.10	.05	.01
☐ 65	John Jaha	.20	.09	.03
☐ 66	Graeme Lloyd	.10	.05	.01
☐ 67	Matt Mieske	.10	.05	.01
☐ 68	Kevin Seitzer	.10	.05	.01
☐ 69	Jose Valentin	.10	.05	.01
☐ 70	Turner Ward	.10	.05	.01
☐ 71	Rick Aguilera	.20	.09	.03
☐ 72	Rich Becker	.10	.05	.01
☐ 73	Alex Cole	.10	.05	.01
☐ 74	Scott Leius	.10	.05	.01
☐ 75	Pat Meares	.10	.05	.01
☐ 76	Kirby Puckett	1.00	.45	.12
☐ 77	Dave Stevens	.10	.05	.01
☐ 78	Kevin Tapani	.10	.05	.01
☐ 79	Matt Walbeck	.10	.05	.01
☐ 80	Wade Boggs	.30	.14	.04
☐ 81	Scott Kamieniecki	.10	.05	.01
☐ 82	Pat Kelly	.10	.05	.01
☐ 83	Jimmy Key	.20	.09	.03
☐ 84	Paul O'Neill	.20	.09	.03
☐ 85	Luis Polonia	.10	.05	.01
☐ 86	Mike Stanley	.20	.09	.03
☐ 87	Danny Tartabull	.10	.05	.01
☐ 88	Bob Wickman	.10	.05	.01
☐ 89	Mark Acre	.10	.05	.01
☐ 90	Geronimo Berroa	.10	.05	.01
☐ 91	Mike Bordick	.10	.05	.01
☐ 92	Ron Darling	.10	.05	.01
☐ 93	Stan Javier	.10	.05	.01
☐ 94	Mark McGwire	.30	.14	.04
☐ 95	Troy Neel	.10	.05	.01
☐ 96	Ruben Sierra	.30	.14	.04
☐ 97	Terry Steinbach	.10	.05	.01
☐ 98	Eric Anthony	.10	.05	.01
☐ 99	Chris Bosio	.10	.05	.01
☐ 100	Dave Fleming	.10	.05	.01
☐ 101	Ken Griffey Jr.	3.00	1.35	.35
☐ 102	Reggie Jefferson	.10	.05	.01
☐ 103	Randy Johnson	.60	.25	.07
☐ 104	Edgar Martinez	.30	.14	.04
☐ 105	Bill Risley	.10	.05	.01
☐ 106	Dan Wilson	.20	.09	.03
☐ 107	Cris Carpenter	.10	.05	.01
☐ 108	Will Clark	.40	.18	.05
☐ 109	Juan Gonzalez	.75	.35	.09
☐ 110	Rusty Greer	.10	.05	.01
☐ 111	David Hulse	.10	.05	.01
☐ 112	Roger Pavlik	.10	.05	.01
☐ 113	Ivan Rodriguez	.30	.14	.04
☐ 114	Doug Strange	.10	.05	.01
☐ 115	Matt Whiteside	.10	.05	.01
☐ 116	Roberto Alomar	.60	.25	.07
☐ 117	Brad Cornett	.10	.05	.01

☐ 118	Carlos Delgado	.20	.09	.03
☐ 119	Alex Gonzalez	.20	.09	.03
☐ 120	Darren Hall	.10	.05	.01
☐ 121	Pat Hentgen	.20	.09	.03
☐ 122	Paul Molitor	.30	.14	.04
☐ 123	Ed Sprague	.10	.05	.01
☐ 124	Devon White	.10	.05	.01
☐ 125	Tom Glavine	.30	.14	.04
☐ 126	David Justice	.40	.18	.05
☐ 127	Roberto Kelly	.20	.09	.03
☐ 128	Mark Lemke	.20	.09	.03
☐ 129	Greg Maddux	3.00	1.35	.35
☐ 130	Greg McMichael	.10	.05	.01
☐ 131	Kent Mercker	.10	.05	.01
☐ 132	Charlie O'Brien	.10	.05	.01
☐ 133	John Smoltz	.10	.05	.01
☐ 134	Willie Banks	.10	.05	.01
☐ 135	Steve Buechele	.10	.05	.01
☐ 136	Kevin Foster	.10	.05	.01
☐ 137	Glenallen Hill	.10	.05	.01
☐ 138	Rey Sanchez	.10	.05	.01
☐ 139	Sammy Sosa	.30	.14	.04
☐ 140	Steve Trachsel	.10	.05	.01
☐ 141	Rick Wilkins	.10	.05	.01
☐ 142	Jeff Brantley	.10	.05	.01
☐ 143	Hector Carrasco	.10	.05	.01
☐ 144	Kevin Jarvis	.10	.05	.01
☐ 145	Barry Larkin	.40	.18	.05
☐ 146	Chuck McElroy	.10	.05	.01
☐ 147	Jose Rijo	.10	.05	.01
☐ 148	Johnny Ruffin	.10	.05	.01
☐ 149	Deion Sanders	.60	.25	.07
☐ 150	Eddie Taubensee	.10	.05	.01
☐ 151	Dante Bichette	.40	.18	.05
☐ 152	Ellis Burks	.20	.09	.03
☐ 153	Joe Girardi	.10	.05	.01
☐ 154	Charlie Hayes	.20	.09	.03
☐ 155	Mike Kingery	.10	.05	.01
☐ 156	Steve Reed	.10	.05	.01
☐ 157	Kevin Ritz	.10	.05	.01
☐ 158	Bruce Ruffin	.10	.05	.01
☐ 159	Eric Young	.20	.09	.03
☐ 160	Kurt Abbott	.20	.09	.03
☐ 161	Chuck Carr	.10	.05	.01
☐ 162	Chris Hammond	.10	.05	.01
☐ 163	Bryan Harvey	.20	.09	.03
☐ 164	Terry Mathews	.10	.05	.01
☐ 165	Yorkis Perez	.10	.05	.01
☐ 166	Pat Rapp	.20	.09	.03
☐ 167	Gary Sheffield	.20	.09	.03
☐ 168	Dave Weathers	.10	.05	.01
☐ 169	Jeff Bagwell	1.00	.45	.12
☐ 170	Ken Caminiti	.10	.05	.01
☐ 171	Doug Drabek	.20	.09	.03
☐ 172	Steve Finley	.20	.09	.03
☐ 173	John Hudek	.10	.05	.01
☐ 174	Todd Jones	.10	.05	.01
☐ 175	James Mouton	.20	.09	.03
☐ 176	Shane Reynolds	.20	.09	.03
☐ 177	Scott Servais	.10	.05	.01
☐ 178	Tom Candiotti	.10	.05	.01
☐ 179	Omar Daal	.10	.05	.01
☐ 180	Darren Dreifort	.10	.05	.01
☐ 181	Eric Karros	.30	.14	.04
☐ 182	Ramon J.Martinez	.20	.09	.03
☐ 183	Raul Mondesi	.75	.35	.09
☐ 184	Henry Rodriguez	.10	.05	.01
☐ 185	Todd Worrell	.10	.05	.01
☐ 186	Moises Alou	.20	.09	.03
☐ 187	Sean Berry	.10	.05	.01
☐ 188	Wil Cordero	.20	.09	.03
☐ 189	Jeff Fassero	.20	.09	.03
☐ 190	Darrin Fletcher	.10	.05	.01
☐ 191	Butch Henry	.10	.05	.01
☐ 192	Ken Hill	.10	.05	.01
☐ 193	Mel Rojas	.20	.09	.03
☐ 194	John Wetteland	.20	.09	.03
☐ 195	Bobby Bonilla	.30	.14	.04
☐ 196	Rico Brogna	.30	.14	.04
☐ 197	Bobby Jones	.20	.09	.03
☐ 198	Jeff Kent	.20	.09	.03
☐ 199	Josias Manzanillo	.10	.05	.01
☐ 200	Kelly Stinnett	.10	.05	.01
☐ 201	Ryan Thompson	.10	.05	.01
☐ 202	Jose Vizcaino	.10	.05	.01
☐ 203	Lenny Dykstra	.20	.09	.03
☐ 204	Jim Eisenreich	.10	.05	.01
☐ 205	Dave Hollins	.10	.05	.01
☐ 206	Mike Lieberthal	.10	.05	.01
☐ 207	Mickey Morandini	.10	.05	.01
☐ 208	Bobby Munoz	.10	.05	.01
☐ 209	Curt Schilling	.10	.05	.01
☐ 210	Heathcliff Slocumb	.10	.05	.01
☐ 211	David West	.10	.05	.01
☐ 212	Dave Clark	.10	.05	.01
☐ 213	Steve Cooke	.10	.05	.01
☐ 214	Midre Cummings	.20	.09	.03
☐ 215	Carlos Garcia	.20	.09	.03
☐ 216	Jeff King	.10	.05	.01
☐ 217	Jon Lieber	.10	.05	.01
☐ 218	Orlando Merced	.20	.09	.03
☐ 219	Don Slaught	.10	.05	.01
☐ 220	Rick White	.10	.05	.01
☐ 221	Rene Arocha	.10	.05	.01
☐ 222	Bernard Gilkey	.20	.09	.03
☐ 223	Brian Jordan	.30	.14	.04
☐ 224	Tom Pagnozzi	.10	.05	.01
☐ 225	Vicente Palacios	.10	.05	.01
☐ 226	Geronimo Pena	.10	.05	.01
☐ 227	Ozzie Smith	.60	.25	.07
☐ 228	Allen Watson	.20	.09	.03
☐ 229	Mark Whiten	.10	.05	.01
☐ 230	Brad Ausmus	.10	.05	.01
☐ 231	Derek Bell	.30	.14	.04
☐ 232	Andy Benes	.20	.09	.03
☐ 233	Tony Gwynn	1.00	.45	.12
☐ 234	Joey Hamilton	.20	.09	.03
☐ 235	Luis Lopez	.10	.05	.01
☐ 236	Pedro A.Martinez	.10	.05	.01
☐ 237	Scott Sanders	.10	.05	.01
☐ 238	Eddie Williams	.10	.05	.01
☐ 239	Rod Beck	.20	.09	.03
☐ 240	Dave Burba	.10	.05	.01
☐ 241	Darren Lewis	.10	.05	.01
☐ 242	Kirt Manwaring	.10	.05	.01
☐ 243	Mark Portugal	.10	.05	.01
☐ 244	Darryl Strawberry	.20	.09	.03
☐ 245	Robby Thompson	.10	.05	.01
☐ 246	Wm.VanLandingham	.20	.09	.03
☐ 247	Matt Williams	.50	.23	.06
☐ 248	Checklist	.10	.05	.01
☐ 249	Checklist	.10	.05	.01
☐ 250	Checklist	.10	.05	.01
☐ 251	Harold Baines	.20	.09	.03
☐ 252	Bret Barberie	.10	.05	.01
☐ 253	Armando Benitez	.10	.05	.01
☐ 254	Mike Devereaux	.10	.05	.01
☐ 255	Leo Gomez	.10	.05	.01
☐ 256	Jamie Moyer	.10	.05	.01
☐ 257	Arthur Rhodes	.10	.05	.01
☐ 258	Cal Ripken	3.00	1.35	.35
☐ 259	Luis Alicea	.10	.05	.01

☐ 260 Jose Canseco	.50	.23	.06
☐ 261 Scott Cooper	.10	.05	.01
☐ 262 Andre Dawson	.30	.14	.04
☐ 263 Mike Greenwell	.20	.09	.03
☐ 264 Aaron Sele	.20	.09	.03
☐ 265 Garret Anderson	.60	.25	.07
☐ 266 Chad Curtis	.20	.09	.03
☐ 267 Gary DiSarcina	.10	.05	.01
☐ 268 Chuck Finley	.20	.09	.03
☐ 269 Rex Hudler	.10	.05	.01
☐ 270 Andrew Lorraine	.10	.05	.01
☐ 271 Spike Owen	.10	.05	.01
☐ 272 Lee Smith	.30	.14	.04
☐ 273 Jason Bere	.10	.05	.01
☐ 274 Ozzie Guillen	.10	.05	.01
☐ 275 Norberto Martin	.10	.05	.01
☐ 276 Scott Ruffcorn	.10	.05	.01
☐ 277 Robin Ventura	.30	.14	.04
☐ 278 Carlos Baerga	.60	.25	.07
☐ 279 Jason Grimsley	.10	.05	.01
☐ 280 Dennis Martinez	.20	.09	.03
☐ 281 Charles Nagy	.20	.09	.03
☐ 282 Paul Sorrento	.10	.05	.01
☐ 283 Dave Winfield	.30	.14	.04
☐ 284 John Doherty	.10	.05	.01
☐ 285 Travis Fryman	.30	.14	.04
☐ 286 Kirk Gibson	.20	.09	.03
☐ 287 Lou Whitaker	.30	.14	.04
☐ 288 Gary Gaetti	.20	.09	.03
☐ 289 Tom Gordon	.10	.05	.01
☐ 290 Mark Gubicza	.10	.05	.01
☐ 291 Wally Joyner	.20	.09	.03
☐ 292 Mike Macfarlane	.10	.05	.01
☐ 293 Jeff Montgomery	.20	.09	.03
☐ 294 Jeff Cirillo	.20	.09	.03
☐ 295 Cal Eldred	.10	.05	.01
☐ 296 Pat Listach	.10	.05	.01
☐ 297 Jose Mercedes	.10	.05	.01
☐ 298 Dave Nilsson	.20	.09	.03
☐ 299 Duane Singleton	.10	.05	.01
☐ 300 Greg Vaughn	.10	.05	.01
☐ 301 Scott Erickson	.20	.09	.03
☐ 302 Denny Hocking	.10	.05	.01
☐ 303 Chuck Knoblauch	.30	.14	.04
☐ 304 Pat Mahomes	.10	.05	.01
☐ 305 Pedro Munoz	.20	.09	.03
☐ 306 Erik Schullstrom	.10	.05	.01
☐ 307 Jim Abbott	.30	.14	.04
☐ 308 Tony Fernandez	.10	.05	.01
☐ 309 Sterling Hitchcock	.20	.09	.03
☐ 310 Jim Leyritz	.10	.05	.01
☐ 311 Don Mattingly	1.50	.70	.19
☐ 312 Jack McDowell	.30	.14	.04
☐ 313 Melido Perez	.10	.05	.01
☐ 314 Bernie Williams	.20	.09	.03
☐ 315 Scott Brosius	.10	.05	.01
☐ 316 Dennis Eckersley	.30	.14	.04
☐ 317 Brent Gates	.20	.09	.03
☐ 318 Rickey Henderson	.30	.14	.04
☐ 319 Steve Karsay	.10	.05	.01
☐ 320 Steve Ontiveros	.10	.05	.01
☐ 321 Bill Taylor	.10	.05	.01
☐ 322 Todd Van Poppel	.10	.05	.01
☐ 323 Bob Welch	.20	.09	.03
☐ 324 Bobby Ayala	.10	.05	.01
☐ 325 Mike Blowers	.20	.09	.03
☐ 326 Jay Buhner	.30	.14	.04
☐ 327 Felix Fermin	.10	.05	.01
☐ 328 Tino Martinez	.30	.14	.04
☐ 329 Marc Newfield	.10	.05	.01
☐ 330 Greg Pirkl	.10	.05	.01
☐ 331 Alex Rodriguez	.60	.25	.07
☐ 332 Kevin Brown	.10	.05	.01
☐ 333 John Burkett	.10	.05	.01
☐ 334 Jeff Frye	.10	.05	.01
☐ 335 Kevin Gross	.10	.05	.01
☐ 336 Dean Palmer	.10	.05	.01
☐ 337 Joe Carter	.30	.14	.04
☐ 338 Shawn Green	.30	.14	.04
☐ 339 Juan Guzman	.10	.05	.01
☐ 340 Mike Huff	.10	.05	.01
☐ 341 Al Leiter	.10	.05	.01
☐ 342 John Olerud	.10	.05	.01
☐ 343 Dave Stewart	.20	.09	.03
☐ 344 Todd Stottlemyre	.10	.05	.01
☐ 345 Steve Avery	.20	.09	.03
☐ 346 Jeff Blauser	.10	.05	.01
☐ 347 Chipper Jones	1.25	.55	.16
☐ 348 Mike Kelly	.10	.05	.01
☐ 349 Ryan Klesko	.60	.25	.07
☐ 350 Javier Lopez	.40	.18	.05
☐ 351 Fred McGriff	.40	.18	.05
☐ 352 Jose Oliva	.10	.05	.01
☐ 353 Terry Pendleton	.20	.09	.03
☐ 354 Mike Stanton	.10	.05	.01
☐ 355 Tony Tarasco	.20	.09	.03
☐ 356 Mark Wohlers	.20	.09	.03
☐ 357 Jim Bullinger	.10	.05	.01
☐ 358 Shawon Dunston	.10	.05	.01
☐ 359 Mark Grace	.30	.14	.04
☐ 360 Derrick May	.20	.09	.03
☐ 361 Randy Myers	.20	.09	.03
☐ 362 Karl Rhodes	.10	.05	.01
☐ 363 Bret Boone	.30	.14	.04
☐ 364 Brian Dorsett	.10	.05	.01
☐ 365 Ron Gant	.30	.14	.04
☐ 366 Brian A.Hunter	.10	.05	.01
☐ 367 Hal Morris	.20	.09	.03
☐ 368 Jack Morris	.20	.09	.03
☐ 369 John Roper	.10	.05	.01
☐ 370 Reggie Sanders	.30	.14	.04
☐ 371 Pete Schourek	.30	.14	.04
☐ 372 John Smiley	.10	.05	.01
☐ 373 Marvin Freeman	.10	.05	.01
☐ 374 Andres Galarraga	.30	.14	.04
☐ 375 Mike Munoz	.10	.05	.01
☐ 376 David Nied	.10	.05	.01
☐ 377 Walt Weiss	.20	.09	.03
☐ 378 Greg Colbrunn	.30	.14	.04
☐ 379 Jeff Conine	.30	.14	.04
☐ 380 Charles Johnson	.30	.14	.04
☐ 381 Kurt Miller	.10	.05	.01
☐ 382 Robb Nen	.20	.09	.03
☐ 383 Benito Santiago	.20	.09	.03
☐ 384 Craig Biggio	.30	.14	.04
☐ 385 Tony Eusebio	.10	.05	.01
☐ 386 Luis Gonzalez	.20	.09	.03
☐ 387 Brian L.Hunter	.40	.18	.05
☐ 388 Darryl Kile	.10	.05	.01
☐ 389 Orlando Miller	.20	.09	.03
☐ 390 Phil Plantier	.10	.05	.01
☐ 391 Greg Swindell	.10	.05	.01
☐ 392 Billy Ashley	.10	.05	.01
☐ 393 Pedro Astacio	.10	.05	.01
☐ 394 Brett Butler	.20	.09	.03
☐ 395 Delino DeShields	.20	.09	.03
☐ 396 Orel Hershiser	.20	.09	.03
☐ 397 Garey Ingram	.10	.05	.01
☐ 398 Chan Ho Park	.20	.09	.03
☐ 399 Mike Piazza	1.25	.55	.16
☐ 400 Ismael Valdes	.10	.05	.01
☐ 401 Tim Wallach	.10	.05	.01

☐ 402	Cliff Floyd	.30	.14	.04
☐ 403	Marquis Grissom	.30	.14	.04
☐ 404	Mike Lansing	.10	.05	.01
☐ 405	Pedro J.Martinez	.10	.09	.03
☐ 406	Kirk Rueter	.10	.05	.01
☐ 407	Tim Scott	.10	.05	.01
☐ 408	Jeff Shaw	.10	.05	.01
☐ 409	Larry Walker	.40	.18	.05
☐ 410	Rondell White	.30	.14	.04
☐ 411	John Franco	.20	.09	.03
☐ 412	Todd Hundley	.20	.09	.03
☐ 413	Jason Jacome	.10	.05	.01
☐ 414	Joe Orsulak	.10	.05	.01
☐ 415	Bret Saberhagen	.20	.09	.03
☐ 416	David Segui	.10	.05	.01
☐ 417	Darren Daulton	.20	.09	.03
☐ 418	Mariano Duncan	.10	.05	.01
☐ 419	Tommy Greene	.10	.05	.01
☐ 420	Gregg Jefferies	.30	.14	.04
☐ 421	John Kruk	.20	.09	.03
☐ 422	Kevin Stocker	.10	.05	.01
☐ 423	Jay Bell	.20	.09	.03
☐ 424	Al Martin	.20	.09	.03
☐ 425	Denny Neagle	.10	.05	.01
☐ 426	Zane Smith	.10	.05	.01
☐ 427	Andy Van Slyke	.20	.09	.03
☐ 428	Paul Wagner	.10	.05	.01
☐ 429	Tom Henke	.20	.09	.03
☐ 430	Danny Jackson	.10	.05	.01
☐ 431	Ray Lankford	.30	.14	.04
☐ 432	John Mabry	.20	.09	.03
☐ 433	Bob Tewksbury	.10	.05	.01
☐ 434	Todd Zeile	.10	.05	.01
☐ 435	Andy Ashby	.10	.05	.01
☐ 436	Andujar Cedeno	.10	.05	.01
☐ 437	Donnie Elliott	.10	.05	.01
☐ 438	Bryce Florie	.10	.05	.01
☐ 439	Trevor Hoffman	.20	.09	.03
☐ 440	Melvin Nieves	.10	.05	.01
☐ 441	Bip Roberts	.10	.05	.01
☐ 442	Barry Bonds	.75	.35	.09
☐ 443	Royce Clayton	.10	.05	.01
☐ 444	Mike Jackson	.10	.05	.01
☐ 445	John Patterson	.10	.05	.01
☐ 446	J.R. Phillips	.10	.05	.01
☐ 447	Bill Swift	.10	.05	.01
☐ 448	Checklist	.10	.05	.01
☐ 449	Checklist	.10	.05	.01
☐ 450	Checklist	.10	.05	.01

1995 Ultra All-Rookies

This 10-card set features rookies who emerged with an impact in 1994. These cards were inserted one in every five second series packs. The fronts feature a player's photo in the middle of the card with each corner devoted to a close-up of part of that action shot. The horizontal backs feature some player information as well as a photo. That same photo is also included in the background as a duotone photo as well. The cards are numbered in the lower left as "X" of 10 and are sequenced in alphabetical order. The tougher to find Gold Medallion

versions are valued at two to three times these prices.

	MINT	NRMT	EXC
COMPLETE SET (10)	6.00	2.70	.75
COMMON CARD (1-10)	.25	.11	.03
*GOLD MEDALLION: 2X TO 3X BASIC CARDS			

☐ 1	Cliff Floyd	.50	.23	.06
☐ 2	Chris Gomez	.25	.11	.03
☐ 3	Rusty Greer	.25	.11	.03
☐ 4	Bob Hamelin	.25	.11	.03
☐ 5	Joey Hamilton	.25	.11	.03
☐ 6	John Hudek	.25	.11	.03
☐ 7	Ryan Klesko	1.50	.70	.19
☐ 8	Raul Mondesi	2.00	.90	.25
☐ 9	Manny Ramirez	3.00	1.35	.35
☐ 10	Steve Trachsel	.25	.11	.03

1995 Ultra All-Stars

This 20-card standard-size set feature players who are considered to be the top players in the game. Cards were inserted one in every four second series packs. The fronts feature two photos. One photo is in full-color while the other is a shaded black and white shot. The player's name, "All-Star" and his team name are at the bottom. The back is split between a player photo and career highlights. The cards are numbered in the bottom left as "X" of 20 and are sequenced in alphabetical order. The tougher to find Gold Medallion versions are valued at two to three times these prices.

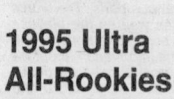

	MINT	NRMT	EXC
COMPLETE SET (20)	20.00	9.00	2.50
COMMON CARD (1-20)	.25	.11	.03
*GOLD MEDALLION: 2X TO 3X BASIC CARDS			

		MINT	NRMT	EXC
☐ 1	Moises Alou	.25	.11	.03
☐ 2	Albert Belle	2.00	.90	.25
☐ 3	Craig Biggio	.40	.18	.05
☐ 4	Wade Boggs	.40	.18	.05
☐ 5	Barry Bonds	1.25	.55	.16
☐ 6	David Cone	.40	.18	.05
☐ 7	Ken Griffey Jr.	5.00	2.20	.60
☐ 8	Tony Gwynn	1.50	.70	.19
☐ 9	Chuck Knoblauch	.40	.18	.05
☐ 10	Barry Larkin	.60	.25	.07
☐ 11	Kenny Lofton	1.50	.70	.19
☐ 12	Greg Maddux	5.00	2.20	.60
☐ 13	Fred McGriff	.60	.25	.07
☐ 14	Paul O'Neill	.25	.11	.03
☐ 15	Mike Piazza	2.00	.90	.25
☐ 16	Kirby Puckett	1.50	.70	.19
☐ 17	Cal Ripken	5.00	2.20	.60
☐ 18	Ivan Rodriguez	.40	.18	.05
☐ 19	Frank Thomas	5.00	2.20	.60
☐ 20	Matt Williams	.75	.35	.09

1995 Ultra Award Winners

Featuring players who won major awards in 1994, this 25-card standard-size set was inserted one in four packs. The horizontal fronts feature a full-color photo as well as a "stretched" duotone photo. The award the player won is indicated at the top while the player's name is on the bottom. The backs feature two more photos as well as reasons for the player winning the given award. The cards are numbered as "X" of 25. The tougher to find Gold Medallion versions are valued at two to three times these prices.

	MINT	NRMT	EXC
COMPLETE SET (25)	20.00	9.00	2.50
COMMON CARD (1-25)	.25	.11	.03
*GOLD MEDALLION: 2X TO 3X BASIC CARDS			

		MINT	NRMT	EXC
☐ 1	Ivan Rodriguez	.40	.18	.05
☐ 2	Don Mattingly	2.50	1.10	.30
☐ 3	Roberto Alomar	1.00	.45	.12
☐ 4	Wade Boggs	.40	.18	.05

		MINT	NRMT	EXC
☐ 5	Omar Vizquel	.25	.11	.03
☐ 6	Ken Griffey Jr.	5.00	2.20	.60
☐ 7	Kenny Lofton	1.50	.70	.19
☐ 8	Devon White	.25	.11	.03
☐ 9	Mark Langston	.25	.11	.03
☐ 10	Tom Pagnozzi	.25	.11	.03
☐ 11	Jeff Bagwell	1.50	.70	.19
☐ 12	Craig Biggio	.40	.18	.05
☐ 13	Matt Williams	.75	.35	.09
☐ 14	Barry Larkin	.60	.25	.07
☐ 15	Barry Bonds	1.25	.55	.16
☐ 16	Marquis Grissom	.40	.18	.05
☐ 17	Darren Lewis	.25	.11	.03
☐ 18	Greg Maddux	5.00	2.20	.60
☐ 19	Frank Thomas	5.00	2.20	.60
☐ 20	Jeff Bagwell	1.50	.70	.19
☐ 21	David Cone	.40	.18	.05
☐ 22	Greg Maddux	5.00	2.20	.60
☐ 23	Bob Hamelin	.25	.11	.03
☐ 24	Raul Mondesi	1.25	.55	.16
☐ 25	Moises Alou	.25	.11	.03

1995 Ultra Golden Prospects

Inserted one every eight first series hobby packs, this 10-card set features potential impact players. The horizontal fronts feature the same photo with multiple view-points giving the impression the photo has been "cut up" into various parts. The words "Golden Prospect" as well as the player's name and team are across the bottom. The horizontal backs have information about his career as well as a normal full-color photo. The cards are numbered as "X" of 10 and are sequenced alphabetically. The tougher to find Gold Medallion versions are valued at two to three times these prices.

	MINT	NRMT	EXC
COMPLETE SET (10)	10.00	4.50	1.25
COMMON CARD (1-10)	.75	.35	.09
*GOLD MEDALLION: 2X TO 3X BASIC CARDS			

		MINT	NRMT	EXC
☐ 1	James Baldwin	.75	.35	.09
☐ 2	Alan Benes	1.25	.55	.16
☐ 3	Armando Benitez	.75	.35	.09
☐ 4	Ray Durham	1.25	.55	.16
☐ 5	LaTroy Hawkins	.75	.35	.09
☐ 6	Brian L.Hunter	2.00	.90	.25

		MINT	NRMT	EXC
☐ 7	Derek Jeter	2.00	.90	.25
☐ 8	Charles Johnson	1.50	.70	.19
☐ 9	Alex Rodriguez	2.50	1.10	.30
☐ 10	Michael Tucker	.75	.35	.09

1995 Ultra Hitting Machines

This 10-card set features some of baseball's leading batters. Inserted one in every eight second-series retail packs, these horizontal cards have the player's photo against a background of the words "Hitting Machine." The player's name and team are identified on the bottom. The horizontal backs feature another player photo and reasons why they are great batters. The cards are numbered as "X" of 10 in the upper right. The tougher to find Gold Medallion versions are valued at two to three times these prices.

		MINT	NRMT	EXC
COMPLETE SET (10)		15.00	6.75	1.85
COMMON CARD (1-10)		.60	.25	.07
*GOLD MEDALLION: 2X TO 3X BASIC CARDS				
☐ 1	Jeff Bagwell	1.50	.70	.19
☐ 2	Albert Belle	2.00	.90	.25
☐ 3	Dante Bichette	.60	.25	.07
☐ 4	Barry Bonds	1.25	.55	.16
☐ 5	Jose Canseco	.75	.35	.09
☐ 6	Ken Griffey Jr.	5.00	2.20	.60
☐ 7	Tony Gwynn	1.50	.70	.19
☐ 8	Fred McGriff	.60	.25	.07
☐ 9	Mike Piazza	2.00	.90	.25
☐ 10	Frank Thomas	5.00	2.20	.60

1995 Ultra Home Run Kings

This 10-card set featured the five leading home run hitters in each league. These cards were issued one every eight first series retail packs. These cards have a player photo on one side with the letters

HRK on the other side. The player is identified vertically in the middle. The backs have information about the player's home run prowess as well as another action photo. The cards are numbered as "X" of 10 and are sequenced by league according to 1994's home run standings. The tougher to find Gold Medallion versions are valued at two to three times these prices.

		MINT	NRMT	EXC
COMPLETE SET (10)		35.00	16.00	4.40
COMMON CARD (1-10)		1.00	.45	.12
*GOLD MEDALLION: 2X TO 3X BASIC CARDS				
☐ 1	Ken Griffey Jr.	12.00	5.50	1.50
☐ 2	Frank Thomas	12.00	5.50	1.50
☐ 3	Albert Belle	5.00	2.20	.60
☐ 4	Jose Canseco	2.00	.90	.25
☐ 5	Cecil Fielder	1.00	.45	.12
☐ 6	Matt Williams	2.00	.90	.25
☐ 7	Jeff Bagwell	4.00	1.80	.50
☐ 8	Barry Bonds	3.00	1.35	.35
☐ 9	Fred McGriff	1.50	.70	.19
☐ 10	Andres Galarraga	1.00	.45	.12

1995 Ultra League Leaders

This 10-card set was inserted one in three first series packs. The horizontal fronts feature a player photo against a background of his league's logo. He is identified in one corner and the category he led the league in is featured in the other corner. The horizontal backs have a player photo as well as explaining more about the stat with which he paced the field. The tougher to find Gold Medallion versions are valued at two to three times these prices.

	MINT	NRMT	EXC
COMPLETE SET (10)	7.00	3.10	.85
COMMON CARD (1-10)	.25	.11	.03
*GOLD MEDALLION: 2X TO 3X BASIC CARDS			

		MINT	NRMT	EXC
☐ 1	Paul O'Neill	.25	.11	.03
☐ 2	Kenny Lofton	1.25	.55	.16
☐ 3	Jimmy Key	.25	.11	.03
☐ 4	Randy Johnson	.75	.35	.09
☐ 5	Lee Smith	.50	.23	.06
☐ 6	Tony Gwynn	1.25	.55	.16
☐ 7	Craig Biggio	.50	.23	.06
☐ 8	Greg Maddux	5.00	2.20	.60
☐ 9	Andy Benes	.25	.11	.03
☐ 10	John Franco	.25	.11	.03

1995 Ultra
On-Base Leaders

This 10-card set features ten players who are constantly reaching base safely. These cards were inserted one in every eight pre-priced jumbo packs. The fronts have an action photo against a background of several smaller action photos. The words "On-Base Leaders" are featured in the upper right corner along with the player's name. The horizontal backs contain the player's team, some information on how often they get on base and a player photo. The cards are numbered in the upper right corner as "X" of 10 and are sequenced in alphabetical order. The tougher to find Gold Medallion versions are valued at two to three times these prices.

	MINT	NRMT	EXC
COMPLETE SET (10)	45.00	20.00	5.50
COMMON CARD (1-10)	2.00	.90	.25
*GOLD MEDALLION: 2X TO 3X BASIC CARDS			

		MINT	NRMT	EXC
☐ 1	Jeff Bagwell	6.00	2.70	.75
☐ 2	Albert Belle	8.00	3.60	1.00
☐ 3	Craig Biggio	2.00	.90	.25
☐ 4	Wade Boggs	2.00	.90	.25
☐ 5	Barry Bonds	5.00	2.20	.60

		MINT	NRMT	EXC
☐ 6	Will Clark	3.00	1.35	.35
☐ 7	Tony Gwynn	6.00	2.70	.75
☐ 8	David Justice	3.00	1.35	.35
☐ 9	Paul O'Neill	2.00	.90	.25
☐ 10	Frank Thomas	20.00	9.00	2.50

1995 Ultra
Power Plus

This six-card set was inserted one in every 37 first series packs. The six players portrayed are not only sluggers, but also excel at another part of the game. Unlike the 1995 Ultra cards and the other insert sets, these cards are 100 percent foil. The fronts have a player photo against a background that has the words "Power Plus" spelled in various size letters. The player and his team are identified on the bottom in gold foil. The backs have a player photo and some player information. The cards are numbered on the bottom right as "X" of 6 and are sequenced in alphabetical order by league. The tougher to find Gold Medallion versions are valued at two to three times these prices.

	MINT	NRMT	EXC
COMPLETE SET (6)	50.00	22.00	6.25
COMMON CARD (1-6)	4.00	1.80	.50
*GOLD MEDALLION: 2X TO 3X BASIC CARDS			

		MINT	NRMT	EXC
☐ 1	Albert Belle	8.00	3.60	1.00
☐ 2	Ken Griffey Jr.	20.00	9.00	2.50
☐ 3	Frank Thomas	20.00	9.00	2.50
☐ 4	Jeff Bagwell	6.00	2.70	.75
☐ 5	Barry Bonds	5.00	2.20	.60
☐ 6	Matt Williams	4.00	1.80	.50

1995 Ultra
RBI Kings

This 10-card set was inserted into series one jumbo packs at a rate of one every 11. The cards feature a player photo against a multi-colored background. The player's

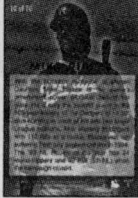

name, the words "RBI King" as well as his team identity are printed in gold foil in the middle. The backs have a player photo as well as some information about the players batting prowess. The cards are numbered in the upper left as "X" of 10 and are sequenced in order by league. The tougher to find Gold Medallion versions are valued at two to three times these prices.

	MINT	NRMT	EXC
COMPLETE SET (10)	50.00	22.00	6.25
COMMON CARD (1-10)	2.00	.90	.25
*GOLD MEDALLION: 2X TO 3X BASIC CARDS			
☐ 1 Kirby Puckett	6.00	2.70	.75
☐ 2 Joe Carter	2.00	.90	.25
☐ 3 Albert Belle	8.00	3.60	1.00
☐ 4 Frank Thomas	20.00	9.00	2.50
☐ 5 Julio Franco	2.00	.90	.25
☐ 6 Jeff Bagwell	6.00	2.70	.75
☐ 7 Matt Williams	4.00	1.80	.50
☐ 8 Dante Bichette	3.00	1.35	.35
☐ 9 Fred McGriff	3.00	1.35	.35
☐ 10 Mike Piazza	8.00	3.60	1.00

1995 Ultra Rising Stars

This nine-card set was inserted one every 37 second series packs. Horizontal fronts feature two photos with the words "Rising Stars" as well as the player's name and team on the bottom left. This front design is set against a shiny background. The backs contain player information as well as a player photo. The cards are numbered "X" of 9 and are sequenced in alphabetical order. The tougher to find Gold Medallion versions are valued at two to three times these prices.

	MINT	NRMT	EXC
COMPLETE SET (9)	90.00	40.00	11.00
COMMON CARD (1-9)	4.00	1.80	.50
*GOLD MEDALLION: 2X TO 3X BASIC CARDS			
☐ 1 Moises Alou	4.00	1.80	.50
☐ 2 Jeff Bagwell	12.00	5.50	1.50
☐ 3 Albert Belle	15.00	6.75	1.85
☐ 4 Juan Gonzalez	10.00	4.50	1.25
☐ 5 Chuck Knoblauch	6.00	2.70	.75
☐ 6 Kenny Lofton	12.00	5.50	1.50
☐ 7 Raul Mondesi	10.00	4.50	1.25
☐ 8 Mike Piazza	15.00	6.75	1.85
☐ 9 Frank Thomas	35.00	16.00	4.40

1995 Ultra Second Year Standouts

This 15-card set was inserted into first series packs at a rate of not greater than one in six packs. The players in this set were all rookies in 1994 whom big things were expected from in 1995. The horizontal fronts feature the player's photo against a yellowish background. The player, his team's identification as well as the team logo are all printed in gold foil in the middle. The horizontal backs have another player photo as well as information about the player's 1994 season. The cards are numbered in the lower right as "X" of 15 and are sequenced in alphabetical order. The tougher to find Gold Medallion versions are valued at two to three times these prices.

	MINT	NRMT	EXC
COMPLETE SET (15)	10.00	4.50	1.25
COMMON CARD (1-15)	.40	.18	.05
*GOLD MEDALLION: 2X TO 3X BASIC CARDS			
☐ 1 Cliff Floyd	.75	.35	.09
☐ 2 Chris Gomez	.40	.18	.05
☐ 3 Rusty Greer	.40	.18	.05
☐ 4 Darren Hall	.40	.18	.05
☐ 5 Bob Hamelin	.40	.18	.05

☐ 6	Joey Hamilton	.40	.18	.05
☐ 7	Jeffrey Hammonds	.40	.18	.05
☐ 8	John Hudek	.40	.18	.05
☐ 9	Ryan Klesko	2.50	1.10	.30
☐ 10	Raul Mondesi	3.00	1.35	.35
☐ 11	Manny Ramirez	5.00	2.20	.60
☐ 12	Bill Risley	.40	.18	.05
☐ 13	Steve Trachsel	.40	.18	.05
☐ 14	W.VanLandingham	.40	.18	.05
☐ 15	Rondell White	.75	.35	.09

1995 Ultra Strikeout Kings

This six-card set was inserted one every five second series packs. The fronts have a player photo as well as photos of grips for four major pitches. The player's name as well as the words "Strikeout King" is printed in a bottom corner. The horizontal backs feature a player photo, a brief blurb as well as a team logo. The cards are numbered as "X" of 6 and are sequenced in alphabetical order. The tougher to find Gold Medallion versions are valued at two to three times these prices.

	MINT	NRMT	EXC
COMPLETE SET (6)	7.00	3.10	.85
COMMON CARD (1-6)	.25	.11	.03
*GOLD MEDALLION: 2X TO 3X BASIC CARDS			

☐ 1	Andy Benes	.25	.11	.03
☐ 2	Roger Clemens	1.00	.45	.12
☐ 3	Randy Johnson	1.25	.55	.16
☐ 4	Greg Maddux	5.00	2.20	.60
☐ 5	Pedro Martinez	.25	.11	.03
☐ 6	Jose Rijo	.25	.11	.03

1996 Ultra

The 1996 Ultra first series consists of 300 cards. The cards were distributed in packs that included two inserts. The cards are thicker than their 1995 counterparts and the fronts feature the player in an action shot in full-bleed color. Player's name and team are emblazoned across the bottom in silver foil. Backs show the players in two action shots and one pose. The backs are full-bleed color and include biography and player 1995 statistics in gold print across the bottom. The cards are sequenced in alphabetical order within league and team order and are arranged as follows: Baltimore Orioles (1-11), Boston Red Sox (12-23), California Angels (24-34), Chicago White Sox (35-44), Cleveland Indians (45-56), Detroit Tigers (57-66), Kansas City Royals (67-76), Milwaukee Brewers (77-87), Minnesota Twins (88-97), New York Yankees (98-109), Oakland Athletics (110-120), Seattle Mariners (121-131), Texas Rangers (132-141), Toronto Blue Jays (142-151), Atlanta Braves (152-162), Chicago Cubs (163-173), Cincinnati Reds (174-184), Colorado Rockies (185-194), Florida Marlins (195-204), Houston Astros (205-215), Los Angeles Dodgers (216-227), Montreal Expos (228-238), New York Mets (239-248), Philadelphia Phillies (249-259), Pittsburgh Pirates (260-269), St. Louis Cardinals (270-279), San Diego Padres (280-289), and San Francisco Giants (290-300).

	MINT	NRMT	EXC
COMPLETE SERIES 1 (300)	20.00	9.00	2.50
COMMON CARD (1-300)	.10	.05	.01
COMP. GOLD MED. SER. 1 (300)	75.00	34.00	9.50
GOLD MED. COMMON (1-300)	.25	.11	.03
GOLD MED. SEMISTARS	.50	.23	.06
*GOLD MED. VETERAN STARS: 2X TO 4X BASIC CARDS			
*GOLD MED. YOUNG STARS: 1.5X TO 3X BASIC CARDS			

☐ 1	Manny Alexander	.10	.05	.01
☐ 2	Brady Anderson	.20	.09	.03
☐ 3	Bobby Bonilla	.30	.14	.04
☐ 4	Scott Erickson	.20	.09	.03
☐ 5	Curtis Goodwin	.20	.09	.03
☐ 6	Chris Hoiles	.20	.09	.03
☐ 7	Doug Jones	.10	.05	.01
☐ 8	Jeff Manto	.10	.05	.01
☐ 9	Mike Mussina	.40	.18	.05
☐ 10	Rafael Palmeiro	.30	.14	.04
☐ 11	Cal Ripken	3.00	1.35	.35
☐ 12	Rick Aguilera	.20	.09	.03
☐ 13	Luis Alicea	.10	.05	.01
☐ 14	Stan Belinda	.10	.05	.01
☐ 15	Jose Canseco	.50	.23	.06
☐ 16	Roger Clemens	.50	.23	.06

☐	17	Mike Greenwell	.20	.09	.03
☐	18	Mike Macfarlane	.10	.05	.01
☐	19	Tim Naehring	.20	.09	.03
☐	20	Troy O'Leary	.20	.09	.03
☐	21	John Valentin	.30	.14	.04
☐	22	Mo Vaughn	.50	.23	.06
☐	23	Tim Wakefield	.20	.09	.03
☐	24	Brian Anderson	.10	.05	.01
☐	25	Garret Anderson	.30	.14	.04
☐	26	Chili Davis	.20	.09	.03
☐	27	Gary DiSarcina	.10	.05	.01
☐	28	Jim Edmonds	.30	.14	.04
☐	29	Jorge Fabregas	.10	.05	.01
☐	30	Chuck Finley	.20	.09	.03
☐	31	Mark Langston	.20	.09	.03
☐	32	Troy Percival	.20	.09	.03
☐	33	Tim Salmon	.40	.18	.05
☐	34	Lee Smith	.30	.14	.04
☐	35	Wilson Alvarez	.20	.09	.03
☐	36	Ray Durham	.30	.14	.04
☐	37	Alex Fernandez	.20	.09	.03
☐	38	Ozzie Guillen	.10	.05	.01
☐	39	Roberto Hernandez	.20	.09	.03
☐	40	Lance Johnson	.10	.05	.01
☐	41	Ron Karkovice	.10	.05	.01
☐	42	Lyle Mouton	.20	.09	.03
☐	43	Tim Raines	.30	.14	.04
☐	44	Frank Thomas	3.00	1.35	.35
☐	45	Carlos Baerga	.60	.25	.07
☐	46	Albert Belle	1.25	.55	.16
☐	47	Orel Hershiser	.20	.09	.03
☐	48	Kenny Lofton	1.00	.45	.12
☐	49	Dennis Martinez	.20	.09	.03
☐	50	Jose Mesa	.20	.09	.03
☐	51	Eddie Murray	.40	.18	.05
☐	52	Chad Ogea	.20	.09	.03
☐	53	Manny Ramirez	1.25	.55	.16
☐	54	Jim Thome	.30	.14	.04
☐	55	Omar Vizquel	.20	.09	.03
☐	56	Dave Winfield	.30	.14	.04
☐	57	Chad Curtis	.20	.09	.03
☐	58	Cecil Fielder	.30	.14	.04
☐	59	John Flaherty	.10	.05	.01
☐	60	Travis Fryman	.30	.14	.04
☐	61	Chris Gomez	.10	.05	.01
☐	62	Bob Higginson	.30	.14	.04
☐	63	Felipe Lira	.10	.05	.01
☐	64	Brian Maxcy	.10	.05	.01
☐	65	Alan Trammell	.30	.14	.04
☐	66	Lou Whitaker	.30	.14	.04
☐	67	Kevin Appier	.20	.09	.03
☐	68	Gary Gaetti	.20	.09	.03
☐	69	Tom Goodwin	.10	.05	.01
☐	70	Tom Gordon	.10	.05	.01
☐	71	Jason Jacome	.10	.05	.01
☐	72	Wally Joyner	.20	.09	.03
☐	73	Brent Mayne	.10	.05	.01
☐	74	Jeff Montgomery	.20	.09	.03
☐	75	Jon Nunnally	.20	.09	.03
☐	76	Joe Vitiello	.10	.05	.01
☐	77	Ricky Bones	.10	.05	.01
☐	78	Jeff Cirillo	.20	.09	.03
☐	79	Mike Fetters	.10	.05	.01
☐	80	Darryl Hamilton	.10	.05	.01
☐	81	David Hulse	.10	.05	.01
☐	82	Dave Nilsson	.20	.09	.03
☐	83	Kevin Seitzer	.10	.05	.01
☐	84	Steve Sparks	.10	.05	.01
☐	85	B.J. Surhoff	.20	.09	.03
☐	86	Jose Valentin	.10	.05	.01
☐	87	Greg Vaughn	.10	.05	.01
☐	88	Marty Cordova	.20	.09	.03
☐	89	Chuck Knoblauch	.30	.14	.04
☐	90	Pat Meares	.10	.05	.01
☐	91	Pedro Munoz	.20	.09	.03
☐	92	Kirby Puckett	1.00	.45	.12
☐	93	Brad Radke	.10	.05	.01
☐	94	Scott Stahoviak	.10	.05	.01
☐	95	Dave Stevens	.10	.05	.01
☐	96	Mike Trombley	.10	.05	.01
☐	97	Matt Walbeck	.10	.05	.01
☐	98	Wade Boggs	.30	.14	.04
☐	99	Russ Davis	.20	.09	.03
☐	100	Jim Leyritz	.10	.05	.01
☐	101	Don Mattingly	1.50	.70	.19
☐	102	Jack McDowell	.30	.14	.04
☐	103	Paul O'Neill	.20	.09	.03
☐	104	Andy Pettitte	.30	.14	.04
☐	105	Mariano Rivera	.20	.09	.03
☐	106	Ruben Sierra	.20	.09	.03
☐	107	Darryl Strawberry	.20	.09	.03
☐	108	John Wetteland	.20	.09	.03
☐	109	Bernie Williams	.20	.09	.03
☐	110	Geronimo Berroa	.10	.05	.01
☐	111	Scott Brosius	.10	.05	.01
☐	112	Dennis Eckersley	.30	.14	.04
☐	113	Brent Gates	.10	.05	.01
☐	114	Rickey Henderson	.30	.14	.04
☐	115	Mark McGwire	.30	.14	.04
☐	116	Ariel Prieto	.10	.05	.01
☐	117	Terry Steinbach	.20	.09	.03
☐	118	Todd Stottlemyre	.10	.05	.01
☐	119	Todd Van Poppel	.10	.05	.01
☐	120	Steve Wojciechowski	.10	.05	.01
☐	121	Rich Amaral	.10	.05	.01
☐	122	Bobby Ayala	.10	.05	.01
☐	123	Mike Blowers	.20	.09	.03
☐	124	Chris Bosio	.10	.05	.01
☐	125	Joey Cora	.10	.05	.01
☐	126	Ken Griffey Jr.	3.00	1.35	.35
☐	127	Randy Johnson	.60	.25	.07
☐	128	Edgar Martinez	.30	.14	.04
☐	129	Tino Martinez	.30	.14	.04
☐	130	Alex Rodriguez	.30	.14	.04
☐	131	Dan Wilson	.20	.09	.03
☐	132	Will Clark	.40	.18	.05
☐	133	Jeff Frye	.10	.05	.01
☐	134	Benji Gil	.10	.05	.01
☐	135	Juan Gonzalez	.75	.35	.09
☐	136	Rusty Greer	.10	.05	.01
☐	137	Mark McLemore	.10	.05	.01
☐	138	Roger Pavlik	.10	.05	.01
☐	139	Ivan Rodriguez	.30	.14	.04
☐	140	Kenny Rogers	.10	.05	.01
☐	141	Mickey Tettleton	.20	.09	.03
☐	142	Roberto Alomar	.60	.25	.07
☐	143	Joe Carter	.30	.14	.04
☐	144	Tony Castillo	.10	.05	.01
☐	145	Alex Gonzalez	.20	.09	.03
☐	146	Shawn Green	.30	.14	.04
☐	147	Pat Hentgen	.20	.09	.03
☐	148	Sandy Martinez	.20	.09	.03
☐	149	Paul Molitor	.30	.14	.04
☐	150	John Olerud	.30	.14	.04
☐	151	Ed Sprague	.10	.05	.01
☐	152	Jeff Blauser	.10	.05	.01
☐	153	Brad Clontz	.10	.05	.01
☐	154	Tom Glavine	.30	.14	.04
☐	155	Marquis Grissom	.30	.14	.04
☐	156	Chipper Jones	1.25	.55	.16
☐	157	David Justice	.40	.18	.05
☐	158	Ryan Klesko	.30	.14	.04

☐ 159	Javier Lopez	.30	.14	.04	☐ 230	Jeff Fassero	.10	.05	.01
☐ 160	Greg Maddux	3.00	1.35	.35	☐ 231	Darrin Fletcher	.10	.05	.01
☐ 161	John Smoltz	.20	.09	.03	☐ 232	Mike Lansing	.10	.05	.01
☐ 162	Mark Wohlers	.20	.09	.03	☐ 233	Pedro J.Martinez	.20	.09	.03
☐ 163	Jim Bullinger	.10	.05	.01	☐ 234	Carlos Perez	.30	.14	.04
☐ 164	Frank Castillo	.10	.05	.01	☐ 235	Mel Rojas	.20	.09	.03
☐ 165	Shawon Dunston	.10	.05	.01	☐ 236	David Segui	.10	.05	.01
☐ 166	Kevin Foster	.10	.05	.01	☐ 237	Tony Tarasco	.20	.09	.03
☐ 167	Luis Gonzalez	.10	.05	.01	☐ 238	Rondell White	.30	.14	.04
☐ 168	Mark Grace	.30	.14	.04	☐ 239	Edgardo Alfonzo	.20	.09	.03
☐ 169	Rey Sanchez	.10	.05	.01	☐ 240	Rico Brogna	.30	.14	.04
☐ 170	Scott Servais	.10	.05	.01	☐ 241	Carl Everett	.20	.09	.03
☐ 171	Sammy Sosa	.30	.14	.04	☐ 242	Todd Hundley	.20	.09	.03
☐ 172	Ozzie Timmons	.20	.09	.03	☐ 243	Butch Huskey	.20	.09	.03
☐ 173	Steve Trachsel	.10	.05	.01	☐ 244	Jason Isringhausen	.40	.18	.05
☐ 174	Bret Boone	.30	.14	.04	☐ 245	Bobby Jones	.20	.09	.03
☐ 175	Jeff Branson	.10	.05	.01	☐ 246	Jeff Kent	.20	.09	.03
☐ 176	Jeff Brantley	.10	.05	.01	☐ 247	Bill Pulsipher	.30	.14	.04
☐ 177	Dave Burba	.10	.05	.01	☐ 248	Jose Vizcaino	.10	.05	.01
☐ 178	Ron Gant	.30	.14	.04	☐ 249	Ricky Bottalico	.10	.05	.01
☐ 179	Barry Larkin	.40	.18	.05	☐ 250	Darren Daulton	.10	.05	.01
☐ 180	Darren Lewis	.10	.05	.01	☐ 251	Jim Eisenreich	.10	.05	.01
☐ 181	Mark Portugal	.10	.05	.01	☐ 252	Tyler Green	.10	.05	.01
☐ 182	Reggie Sanders	.30	.14	.04	☐ 253	Charlie Hayes	.10	.05	.01
☐ 183	Pete Schourek	.30	.14	.04	☐ 254	Gregg Jefferies	.30	.14	.04
☐ 184	John Smiley	.10	.05	.01	☐ 255	Tony Longmire	.10	.05	.01
☐ 185	Jason Bates	.20	.09	.03	☐ 256	Michael Mimbs	.10	.05	.01
☐ 186	Dante Bichette	.40	.18	.05	☐ 257	Mickey Morandini	.10	.05	.01
☐ 187	Ellis Burks	.20	.09	.03	☐ 258	Paul Quantrill	.10	.05	.01
☐ 188	Vinny Castilla	.30	.14	.04	☐ 259	Heathcliff Slocumb	.10	.05	.01
☐ 189	Andres Galarraga	.30	.14	.04	☐ 260	Jay Bell	.20	.09	.03
☐ 190	Darren Holmes	.20	.09	.03	☐ 261	Jacob Brumfield	.10	.05	.01
☐ 191	Armando Reynoso	.10	.05	.01	☐ 262	Angelo Encarnacion	.25	.11	.03
☐ 192	Kevin Ritz	.10	.05	.01	☐ 263	John Ericks	.10	.05	.01
☐ 193	Bill Swift	.10	.05	.01	☐ 264	Mark Johnson	.10	.05	.01
☐ 194	Larry Walker	.40	.18	.05	☐ 265	Esteban Loaiza	.10	.05	.01
☐ 195	Kurt Abbott	.20	.09	.03	☐ 266	Al Martin	.20	.09	.03
☐ 196	John Burkett	.10	.05	.01	☐ 267	Orlando Merced	.20	.09	.03
☐ 197	Greg Colbrunn	.30	.14	.04	☐ 268	Dan Miceli	.10	.05	.01
☐ 198	Jeff Conine	.30	.14	.04	☐ 269	Denny Neagle	.20	.09	.03
☐ 199	Andre Dawson	.30	.14	.04	☐ 270	Brian Barber	.10	.05	.01
☐ 200	Chris Hammond	.10	.05	.01	☐ 271	Scott Cooper	.10	.05	.01
☐ 201	Charles Johnson	.20	.09	.03	☐ 272	Tripp Cromer	.10	.05	.01
☐ 202	Robb Nen	.20	.09	.03	☐ 273	Bernard Gilkey	.20	.09	.03
☐ 203	Terry Pendleton	.20	.09	.03	☐ 274	Tom Henke	.20	.09	.03
☐ 204	Quilvio Veras	.20	.09	.03	☐ 275	Brian Jordan	.30	.14	.04
☐ 205	Jeff Bagwell	1.00	.45	.12	☐ 276	John Mabry	.10	.05	.01
☐ 206	Derek Bell	.20	.09	.03	☐ 277	Tom Pagnozzi	.10	.05	.01
☐ 207	Doug Drabek	.20	.09	.03	☐ 278	Mark Petkovsek	.10	.05	.01
☐ 208	Tony Eusebio	.10	.05	.01	☐ 279	Ozzie Smith	.60	.25	.07
☐ 209	Mike Hampton	.10	.05	.01	☐ 280	Andy Ashby	.10	.05	.01
☐ 210	Brian L. Hunter	.30	.14	.04	☐ 281	Brad Ausmus	.10	.05	.01
☐ 211	Todd Jones	.10	.05	.01	☐ 282	Ken Caminiti	.20	.09	.03
☐ 212	Orlando Miller	.20	.09	.03	☐ 283	Glenn Dishman	.20	.09	.03
☐ 213	James Mouton	.20	.09	.03	☐ 284	Tony Gwynn	1.00	.45	.12
☐ 214	Shane Reynolds	.20	.09	.03	☐ 285	Joey Hamilton	.20	.09	.03
☐ 215	Dave Veres	.10	.05	.01	☐ 286	Trevor Hoffman	.20	.09	.03
☐ 216	Billy Ashley	.10	.05	.01	☐ 287	Phil Plantier	.10	.05	.01
☐ 217	Brett Butler	.20	.09	.03	☐ 288	Jody Reed	.10	.05	.01
☐ 218	Chad Fonville	.20	.09	.03	☐ 289	Eddie Williams	.10	.05	.01
☐ 219	Todd Hollandsworth	.10	.05	.01	☐ 290	Barry Bonds	.75	.35	.09
☐ 220	Eric Karros	.30	.14	.04	☐ 291	Jamie Brewington	.10	.05	.01
☐ 221	Ramon Martinez	.20	.09	.03	☐ 292	Mark Carreon	.10	.05	.01
☐ 222	Raul Mondesi	.60	.25	.07	☐ 293	Royce Clayton	.20	.09	.03
☐ 223	Hideo Nomo	1.25	.55	.16	☐ 294	Glenallen Hill	.20	.09	.03
☐ 224	Mike Piazza	1.25	.55	.16	☐ 295	Mark Leiter	.10	.05	.01
☐ 225	Kevin Tapani	.10	.05	.01	☐ 296	Kirt Manwaring	.10	.05	.01
☐ 226	Ismael Valdes	.10	.05	.01	☐ 297	J.R. Phillips	.10	.05	.01
☐ 227	Todd Worrell	.10	.05	.01	☐ 298	Deion Sanders	.60	.25	.07
☐ 228	Moises Alou	.20	.09	.03	☐ 299	Wm. VanLandingham	.20	.09	.03
☐ 229	Wil Cordero	.20	.09	.03	☐ 300	Matt Williams	.50	.23	.06

1996 Ultra Diamond Producers

This 12-card set highlights the achievements of Major League stars. The cards were randomly inserted at a rate of one in 20. The horizontal fronts show the player close-up and an action photo on a metallic-silver paper. "Diamond Producers" and the player's name are printed in silver foil at the bottom of the card. The backs feature the player in an action shot on the left half and a white on black description of the player's career achievements. The cards are sequenced in alphabetical order and there are also gold medallion versions of these cards. The gold medallion versions are valued at two to three times the regular cards.

	MINT	NRMT	EXC
COMPLETE SET (12)	75.00	34.00	9.50
COMMON CARD (1-12)	3.00	1.35	.35
*GOLD MEDALLION: 2X TO 3X BASIC CARDS			
☐ 1 Albert Belle	6.00	2.70	.75
☐ 2 Barry Bonds	4.00	1.80	.50
☐ 3 Ken Griffey Jr.	15.00	6.75	1.85
☐ 4 Tony Gwynn	5.00	2.20	.60
☐ 5 Greg Maddux	15.00	6.75	1.85
☐ 6 Hideo Nomo	6.00	2.70	.75
☐ 7 Mike Piazza	6.00	2.70	.75
☐ 8 Kirby Puckett	5.00	2.20	.60
☐ 9 Cal Ripken	15.00	6.75	1.85
☐ 10 Frank Thomas	15.00	6.75	1.85
☐ 11 Mo Vaughn	3.00	1.35	.35
☐ 12 Matt Williams	2.50	1.10	.30

1996 Ultra Home Run Kings

This 12-card set features leading power hitters. These cards were randomly inserted at a rate of one in 75 packs. The card fronts are thin wood with a color cut out of the player and HR KING printed diagonally in copper foil down the left side. The Fleer company was not happy with the final look of the card because of the transfer of the

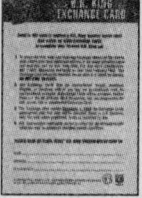

copper foil. Therefore all cards were made redemption cards. Backs of the cards have information about how to redeem the cards for replacement. The exchange offer expires on December 1, 1996. The cards are sequenced in alphabetical order.

	MINT	NRMT	EXC
COMPLETE SET (12)	175.00	80.00	22.00
COMMON CARD (1-12)	6.00	2.70	.75
*GOLD MEDALLION: 2X TO 3X BASIC CARDS			
☐ 1 Albert Belle	20.00	9.00	2.50
☐ 2 Dante Bichette	8.00	3.60	1.00
☐ 3 Barry Bonds	12.00	5.50	1.50
☐ 4 Jose Canseco	10.00	4.50	1.25
☐ 5 Juan Gonzalez	12.00	5.50	1.50
☐ 6 Ken Griffey Jr.	50.00	22.00	6.25
☐ 7 Mark McGwire	6.00	2.70	.75
☐ 8 Manny Ramirez	20.00	9.00	2.50
☐ 9 Tim Salmon	8.00	3.60	1.00
☐ 10 Frank Thomas	50.00	22.00	6.25
☐ 11 Mo Vaughn	10.00	4.50	1.25
☐ 12 Matt Williams	10.00	4.50	1.25

1996 Ultra Power Plus

Randomly inserted at a rate of one in ten packs, this 12-card set features top all-around players. The horizontal fronts feature the player in two cut-out action photos against a multi-colored prismatic wheel background. The player's name and "Power Plus" are stamped in foil across the bottom. The backs are split between a full-

color close-up shot of the player and player information printed in white type against a multi-colored circular background. The cards are sequenced in alphabetical order and gold medallion versions of these cards were also issued. The gold medallion versions are valued at two to three times the regular cards.

	MINT	NRMT	EXC
COMPLETE SET (12)	32.00	14.50	4.00
COMMON CARD (1-12)	1.00	.45	.12
*GOLD MEDALLION: 2X TO 3X BASIC CARDS			

		MINT	NRMT	EXC
☐ 1	Jeff Bagwell	3.00	1.35	.35
☐ 2	Barry Bonds	2.50	1.10	.30
☐ 3	Ken Griffey Jr.	10.00	4.50	1.25
☐ 4	Raul Mondesi	2.00	.90	.25
☐ 5	Rafael Palmeiro	1.00	.45	.12
☐ 6	Mike Piazza	4.00	1.80	.50
☐ 7	Manny Ramirez	4.00	1.80	.50
☐ 8	Tim Salmon	1.50	.70	.19
☐ 9	Reggie Sanders	1.00	.45	.12
☐ 10	Frank Thomas	10.00	4.50	1.25
☐ 11	Larry Walker	1.50	.70	.19
☐ 12	Matt Williams	1.50	.70	.19

1996 Ultra
Prime Leather

Eighteen outstanding defensive players are featured in this set which is inserted approximately one in every eight packs. The horizontal fronts feature a color cut-out shot of the player against an embossed leather-like background. The player's name and team are embossed across the bottom with a black shadow effect. The backs have player's achievements noted in black type with a red outline against a glossy leather background. The other half of the back is a full color shot of the player. The cards are sequenced in alphabetical order and gold medallion versions of these cards were also issued. The gold medallion versions are valued at two to three times the regular cards.

	MINT	NRMT	EXC
COMPLETE SET (18)	45.00	20.00	5.50
COMMON CARD (1-18)	1.00	.45	.12
*GOLD MEDALLION: 2X TO 3X BASIC CARDS			

		MINT	NRMT	EXC
☐ 1	Ivan Rodriguez	1.00	.45	.12
☐ 2	Will Clark	1.50	.70	.19
☐ 3	Roberto Alomar	2.50	1.10	.30
☐ 4	Cal Ripken	12.00	5.50	1.50
☐ 5	Wade Boggs	1.00	.45	.12
☐ 6	Ken Griffey Jr.	12.00	5.50	1.50
☐ 7	Kenny Lofton	4.00	1.80	.50
☐ 8	Kirby Puckett	4.00	1.80	.50
☐ 9	Tim Salmon	1.50	.70	.19
☐ 10	Mike Piazza	5.00	2.20	.60
☐ 11	Mark Grace	1.00	.45	.12
☐ 12	Craig Biggio	1.00	.45	.12
☐ 13	Barry Larkin	1.50	.70	.19
☐ 14	Matt Williams	2.00	.90	.25
☐ 15	Barry Bonds	3.00	1.35	.35
☐ 16	Tony Gwynn	4.00	1.80	.50
☐ 17	Brian McRae	1.00	.45	.12
☐ 18	Raul Mondesi	2.50	1.10	.30

1996 Ultra
Season Crowns

This set features ten award winners and stat leaders. The cards were randomly inserted at a rate of one in ten. The clear acetate cards feature a full-color player cutout against a background of colored foliage and laurels. Backs include the player's 1995 statistics and other facts on a multi-colored background. The cards are sequenced in alphabetical order and gold medallion versions of these cards were also issued. The gold medallion versions are valued at two to three times the regular cards.

	MINT	NRMT	EXC
COMPLETE SET (10)	35.00	16.00	4.40
COMMON CARD (1-10)	.60	.25	.07
*GOLD MEDALLION: 2X TO 3X BASIC CARDS			

		MINT	NRMT	EXC
☐ 1	Barry Bonds	2.50	1.10	.30
☐ 2	Tony Gwynn	3.00	1.35	.35
☐ 3	Randy Johnson	2.00	.90	.25
☐ 4	Kenny Lofton	3.00	1.35	.35
☐ 5	Greg Maddux	10.00	4.50	1.25
☐ 6	Edgar Martinez	1.00	.45	.12
☐ 7	Hideo Nomo	4.00	1.80	.50
☐ 8	Cal Ripken	10.00	4.50	1.25
☐ 9	Frank Thomas	10.00	4.50	1.25
☐ 10	Tim Wakefield	.60	.25	.07

1989 Upper Deck

This attractive 800-card set was introduced in 1989 as an additional fully licensed major card set. The cards feature full color on both the front and the back and are distinguished by the fact that each card has a hologram on the reverse, thus making the cards essentially copy proof. The cards measure standard size, 2 1/2" by 3 1/2". Cards 668-693 feature a "Collector's Choice" (CC) colorful drawing of a player (by artist Vernon Wells) on the card front and a checklist of that team on the card back. Cards 1-26 are designated as "Rookie Stars" by Upper Deck. On many cards "Rookie" and team logos can be found with either a "TM" or (R). Cards with missing or duplicate holograms appear to be relatively common and hence there is little, if any, premium value on these "variations." The more significant variations involving changed photos or changed type are listed below. According to the company, the Murphy and Sheridan cards were corrected very early, after only two percent of the cards had been produced. This means, for example, that out of 1,000,000 Dale Murphy '89 Upper Deck cards produced, there are only 20,000 Murphy error cards. Similarly, the Sheffield was corrected after 15 percent had been printed; Varsho, Gallego, and Schroeder were corrected after 20 percent; and Holton, Manrique, and Winningham were corrected 30 percent of the way through. Collectors should also note that many dealers consider that Upper Deck's "planned" production of 1,000,000 of each player was increased (perhaps even doubled) later in the year due to the explosion in popularity of the Upper Deck cards. Rookie Cards in the set include Jim Abbott, Sandy Alomar Jr., Dante Bichette, Norm Charlton, Junior Felix, Steve Finley, Ken Griffey Jr., Erik Hanson, Pete Harnisch, Charlie Hayes, Randy Johnson, Felix Jose, Ramon Martinez, Gregg Olson, Gary Sheffield, John Smoltz, Jerome Walton, and Todd Zeile. The high number cards (701-800) were made available three different ways: as part of the 800-card factory set, as a separate boxed set of 100 cards in a custom blue box, and in special high number foil packs.

	MINT	NRMT	EXC
COMPLETE SET (800)	100.00	45.00	12.50
COMPLETE FACT.SET (800)	100.00	45.00	12.50
COMPLETE LO SET (700)	90.00	40.00	11.00
COMPLETE HI SET (100)	8.00	3.60	1.00
COMPLETE HI FACT.SET (100)	8.00	3.60	1.00
COMMON CARD (1-800)	.10	.05	.01
☐ 1 Ken Griffey Jr.	75.00	34.00	9.50
☐ 2 Luis Medina	.10	.05	.01
☐ 3 Tony Chance	.10	.05	.01
☐ 4 Dave Otto	.10	.05	.01
☐ 5 Sandy Alomar Jr. UER	.60	.25	.07
(Born 6/16/66, should be 6/18/66)			
☐ 6 Rolando Roomes	.10	.05	.01
☐ 7 Dave West	.20	.09	.03
☐ 8 Cris Carpenter	.10	.05	.01
☐ 9 Gregg Jefferies	.75	.35	.09
☐ 10 Doug Dascenzo	.10	.05	.01
☐ 11 Ron Jones	.10	.05	.01
☐ 12 Luis DeLosSantos	.10	.05	.01
☐ 13A Gary Sheffield ERR	2.50	1.10	.30
(SS upside down on card front)			
☐ 13B Gary Sheffield COR	2.50	1.10	.30
☐ 14 Mike Harkey	.10	.05	.01
☐ 15 Lance Blankenship	.10	.05	.01
☐ 16 William Brennan	.10	.05	.01
☐ 17 John Smoltz	1.00	.45	.12
☐ 18 Ramon Martinez	1.00	.45	.12
☐ 19 Mark Lemke	.20	.09	.03
☐ 20 Juan Bell	.10	.05	.01
☐ 21 Rey Palacios	.10	.05	.01
☐ 22 Felix Jose	.20	.09	.03
☐ 23 Van Snider	.10	.05	.01
☐ 24 Dante Bichette	4.00	1.80	.50
☐ 25 Randy Johnson	5.00	2.20	.60
☐ 26 Carlos Quintana	.10	.05	.01
☐ 27 Star Rookie CL	.10	.05	.01
☐ 28 Mike Schooler	.10	.05	.01
☐ 29 Randy St.Claire	.10	.05	.01
☐ 30 Jerald Clark	.10	.05	.01
☐ 31 Kevin Gross	.10	.05	.01
☐ 32 Dan Firova	.10	.05	.01
☐ 33 Jeff Calhoun	.10	.05	.01
☐ 34 Tommy Hinzo	.10	.05	.01
☐ 35 Ricky Jordan	.10	.05	.01
☐ 36 Larry Parrish	.10	.05	.01
☐ 37 Bret Saberhagen UER	.30	.14	.04
(Hit total 931, should be 1031)			
☐ 38 Mike Smithson	.10	.05	.01
☐ 39 Dave Dravecky	.20	.09	.03
☐ 40 Ed Romero	.10	.05	.01
☐ 41 Jeff Musselman	.10	.05	.01
☐ 42 Ed Hearn	.10	.05	.01
☐ 43 Rance Mulliniks	.10	.05	.01
☐ 44 Jim Eisenreich	.20	.09	.03
☐ 45 Sil Campusano	.10	.05	.01
☐ 46 Mike Krukow	.10	.05	.01
☐ 47 Paul Gibson	.10	.05	.01
☐ 48 Mike LaCoss	.10	.05	.01
☐ 49 Larry Herndon	.10	.05	.01
☐ 50 Scott Garrelts	.10	.05	.01
☐ 51 Dwayne Henry	.10	.05	.01
☐ 52 Jim Acker	.10	.05	.01
☐ 53 Steve Sax	.10	.05	.01
☐ 54 Pete O'Brien	.10	.05	.01
☐ 55 Paul Runge	.10	.05	.01
☐ 56 Rick Rhoden	.10	.05	.01

☐ 57 John Dopson	.10	.05	.01	
☐ 58 Casey Cangelosi UER	.10	.05	.01	
(No stats for Astros for '88 season)				
☐ 59 Dave Righetti	.10	.05	.01	
☐ 60 Joe Hesketh	.10	.05	.01	
☐ 61 Frank DiPino	.10	.05	.01	
☐ 62 Tim Laudner	.10	.05	.01	
☐ 63 Jamie Moyer	.10	.05	.01	
☐ 64 Fred Toliver	.10	.05	.01	
☐ 65 Mitch Webster	.10	.05	.01	
☐ 66 John Tudor	.10	.05	.01	
☐ 67 John Cangelosi	.10	.05	.01	
☐ 68 Mike Devereaux	.20	.09	.03	
☐ 69 Brian Fisher	.10	.05	.01	
☐ 70 Mike Marshall	.10	.05	.01	
☐ 71 Zane Smith	.10	.05	.01	
☐ 72A Brian Holton ERR	1.00	.45	.12	
(Photo actually Shawn Hillegas)				
☐ 72B Brian Holton COR	.10	.05	.01	
☐ 73 Jose Guzman	.10	.05	.01	
☐ 74 Rick Mahler	.10	.05	.01	
☐ 75 John Shelby	.10	.05	.01	
☐ 76 Jim Deshaies	.10	.05	.01	
☐ 77 Bobby Meacham	.10	.05	.01	
☐ 78 Bryn Smith	.10	.05	.01	
☐ 79 Joaquin Andujar	.10	.05	.01	
☐ 80 Richard Dotson	.10	.05	.01	
☐ 81 Charlie Lea	.10	.05	.01	
☐ 82 Calvin Schiraldi	.10	.05	.01	
☐ 83 Les Straker	.10	.05	.01	
☐ 84 Les Lancaster	.10	.05	.01	
☐ 85 Allan Anderson	.10	.05	.01	
☐ 86 Junior Ortiz	.10	.05	.01	
☐ 87 Jesse Orosco	.10	.05	.01	
☐ 88 Felix Fermin	.10	.05	.01	
☐ 89 Dave Anderson	.10	.05	.01	
☐ 90 Rafael Belliard UER	.10	.05	.01	
(Born '61, not '51)				
☐ 91 Franklin Stubbs	.10	.05	.01	
☐ 92 Cecil Espy	.10	.05	.01	
☐ 93 Albert Hall	.10	.05	.01	
☐ 94 Tim Leary	.10	.05	.01	
☐ 95 Mitch Williams	.20	.09	.03	
☐ 96 Tracy Jones	.10	.05	.01	
☐ 97 Danny Darwin	.10	.05	.01	
☐ 98 Gary Ward	.10	.05	.01	
☐ 99 Neal Heaton	.10	.05	.01	
☐ 100 Jim Pankovits	.10	.05	.01	
☐ 101 Bill Doran	.10	.05	.01	
☐ 102 Tim Wallach	.20	.09	.03	
☐ 103 Joe Magrane	.10	.05	.01	
☐ 104 Ozzie Virgil	.10	.05	.01	
☐ 105 Alvin Davis	.10	.05	.01	
☐ 106 Tom Brookens	.10	.05	.01	
☐ 107 Shawon Dunston	.20	.09	.03	
☐ 108 Tracy Woodson	.10	.05	.01	
☐ 109 Nelson Liriano	.10	.05	.01	
☐ 110 Devon White UER	.30	.14	.04	
(Doubles total 46, should be 56)				
☐ 111 Steve Balboni	.10	.05	.01	
☐ 112 Buddy Bell	.20	.09	.03	
☐ 113 German Jimenez	.10	.05	.01	
☐ 114 Ken Dayley	.10	.05	.01	
☐ 115 Andres Galarraga	.40	.18	.05	
☐ 116 Mike Scioscia	.10	.05	.01	
☐ 117 Gary Pettis	.10	.05	.01	
☐ 118 Ernie Whitt	.10	.05	.01	
☐ 119 Bob Boone	.20	.09	.03	
☐ 120 Ryne Sandberg	1.00	.45	.12	
☐ 121 Bruce Benedict	.10	.05	.01	
☐ 122 Hubie Brooks	.10	.05	.01	
☐ 123 Mike Moore	.10	.05	.01	
☐ 124 Wallace Johnson	.10	.05	.01	
☐ 125 Bob Horner	.10	.05	.01	
☐ 126 Chili Davis	.30	.14	.04	
☐ 127 Manny Trillo	.10	.05	.01	
☐ 128 Chet Lemon	.10	.05	.01	
☐ 129 John Cerutti	.10	.05	.01	
☐ 130 Orel Hershiser	.30	.14	.04	
☐ 131 Terry Pendleton	.20	.09	.03	
☐ 132 Jeff Blauser	.30	.14	.04	
☐ 133 Mike Fitzgerald	.10	.05	.01	
☐ 134 Henry Cotto	.10	.05	.01	
☐ 135 Gerald Young	.10	.05	.01	
☐ 136 Luis Salazar	.10	.05	.01	
☐ 137 Alejandro Pena	.10	.05	.01	
☐ 138 Jack Howell	.10	.05	.01	
☐ 139 Tony Fernandez	.20	.09	.03	
☐ 140 Mark Grace	.60	.25	.07	
☐ 141 Ken Caminiti	.30	.14	.04	
☐ 142 Mike Jackson	.10	.05	.01	
☐ 143 Larry McWilliams	.10	.05	.01	
☐ 144 Andres Thomas	.10	.05	.01	
☐ 145 Nolan Ryan 3X	3.00	1.35	.35	
☐ 146 Mike Davis	.10	.05	.01	
☐ 147 DeWayne Buice	.10	.05	.01	
☐ 148 Jody Davis	.10	.05	.01	
☐ 149 Jesse Barfield	.10	.05	.01	
☐ 150 Matt Nokes	.10	.05	.01	
☐ 151 Jerry Reuss	.20	.09	.03	
☐ 152 Rick Cerone	.10	.05	.01	
☐ 153 Storm Davis	.10	.05	.01	
☐ 154 Marvell Wynne	.10	.05	.01	
☐ 155 Will Clark	.75	.35	.09	
☐ 156 Luis Aguayo	.10	.05	.01	
☐ 157 Willie Upshaw	.10	.05	.01	
☐ 158 Randy Bush	.10	.05	.01	
☐ 159 Ron Darling	.20	.09	.03	
☐ 160 Kal Daniels	.10	.05	.01	
☐ 161 Spike Owen	.10	.05	.01	
☐ 162 Luis Polonia	.20	.09	.03	
☐ 163 Kevin Mitchell UER	.20	.09	.03	
('88/total HR's 18/52, should be 19/53)				
☐ 164 Dave Gallagher	.10	.05	.01	
☐ 165 Benito Santiago	.20	.09	.03	
☐ 166 Greg Gagne	.10	.05	.01	
☐ 167 Ken Phelps	.10	.05	.01	
☐ 168 Sid Fernandez	.20	.09	.03	
☐ 169 Bo Diaz	.10	.05	.01	
☐ 170 Cory Snyder	.10	.05	.01	
☐ 171 Eric Show	.10	.05	.01	
☐ 172 Robby Thompson	.20	.09	.03	
☐ 173 Marty Barrett	.10	.05	.01	
☐ 174 Dave Henderson	.10	.05	.01	
☐ 175 Ozzie Guillen	.20	.09	.03	
☐ 176 Barry Lyons	.10	.05	.01	
☐ 177 Kelvin Torve	.10	.05	.01	
☐ 178 Don Slaught	.10	.05	.01	
☐ 179 Steve Lombardozzi	.10	.05	.01	
☐ 180 Chris Sabo	.20	.09	.03	
☐ 181 Jose Uribe	.10	.05	.01	
☐ 182 Shane Mack	.20	.09	.03	
☐ 183 Ron Karkovice	.10	.05	.01	
☐ 184 Todd Benzinger	.10	.05	.01	
☐ 185 Dave Stewart	.30	.14	.04	
☐ 186 Julio Franco	.20	.09	.03	
☐ 187 Ron Robinson	.10	.05	.01	
☐ 188 Wally Backman	.10	.05	.01	

☐	189	Randy Velarde	.10	.05	.01			
☐	190	Joe Carter	.75	.35	.09			
☐	191	Bob Welch	.20	.09	.03			
☐	192	Kelly Paris	.10	.05	.01			
☐	193	Chris Brown	.10	.05	.01			
☐	194	Rick Reuschel	.20	.09	.03			
☐	195	Roger Clemens	.75	.35	.09			
☐	196	Dave Concepcion	.20	.09	.03			
☐	197	Al Newman	.10	.05	.01			
☐	198	Brook Jacoby	.10	.05	.01			
☐	199	Mookie Wilson	.20	.09	.03			
☐	200	Don Mattingly	1.50	.70	.19			
☐	201	Dick Schofield	.10	.05	.01			
☐	202	Mark Gubicza	.20	.09	.03			
☐	203	Gary Gaetti	.10	.05	.01			
☐	204	Dan Pasqua	.10	.05	.01			
☐	205	Andre Dawson	.30	.14	.04			
☐	206	Chris Speier	.10	.05	.01			
☐	207	Kent Tekulve	.10	.05	.01			
☐	208	Rod Scurry	.10	.05	.01			
☐	209	Scott Bailes	.10	.05	.01			
☐	210	Rickey Henderson UER	.75	.35	.09			
		(Throws Right)						
☐	211	Harold Baines	.30	.14	.04			
☐	212	Tony Armas	.10	.05	.01			
☐	213	Kent Hrbek	.30	.14	.04			
☐	214	Darrin Jackson	.10	.05	.01			
☐	215	George Brett	1.50	.70	.19			
☐	216	Rafael Santana	.10	.05	.01			
☐	217	Andy Allanson	.10	.05	.01			
☐	218	Brett Butler	.30	.14	.04			
☐	219	Steve Jeltz	.10	.05	.01			
☐	220	Jay Buhner	.75	.35	.09			
☐	221	Bo Jackson	.50	.23	.06			
☐	222	Angel Salazar	.10	.05	.01			
☐	223	Kirk McCaskill	.10	.05	.01			
☐	224	Steve Lyons	.10	.05	.01			
☐	225	Bert Blyleven	.30	.14	.04			
☐	226	Scott Bradley	.10	.05	.01			
☐	227	Bob Melvin	.10	.05	.01			
☐	228	Ron Kittle	.10	.05	.01			
☐	229	Phil Bradley	.10	.05	.01			
☐	230	Tommy John	.30	.14	.04			
☐	231	Greg Walker	.10	.05	.01			
☐	232	Juan Berenguer	.10	.05	.01			
☐	233	Pat Tabler	.10	.05	.01			
☐	234	Terry Clark	.10	.05	.01			
☐	235	Rafael Palmeiro	1.00	.45	.12			
☐	236	Paul Zuvella	.10	.05	.01			
☐	237	Willie Randolph	.20	.09	.03			
☐	238	Bruce Fields	.10	.05	.01			
☐	239	Mike Aldrete	.10	.05	.01			
☐	240	Lance Parrish	.20	.09	.03			
☐	241	Greg Maddux	5.00	2.20	.60			
☐	242	John Moses	.10	.05	.01			
☐	243	Melido Perez	.10	.05	.01			
☐	244	Willie Wilson	.10	.05	.01			
☐	245	Mark McLemore	.10	.05	.01			
☐	246	Von Hayes	.10	.05	.01			
☐	247	Matt Williams	2.00	.90	.25			
☐	248	John Candelaria UER	.10	.05	.01			
		(Listed as Yankee for						
		part of '87,						
		should be Mets)						
☐	249	Harold Reynolds	.10	.05	.01			
☐	250	Greg Swindell	.20	.09	.03			
☐	251	Juan Agosto	.10	.05	.01			
☐	252	Mike Felder	.10	.05	.01			
☐	253	Vince Coleman	.20	.09	.03			
☐	254	Larry Sheets	.10	.05	.01			
☐	255	George Bell	.10	.05	.01			

☐	256	Terry Steinbach	.20	.09	.03			
☐	257	Jack Armstrong	.10	.05	.01			
☐	258	Dickie Thon	.10	.05	.01			
☐	259	Ray Knight	.20	.09	.03			
☐	260	Darryl Strawberry	.30	.14	.04			
☐	261	Doug Sisk	.10	.05	.01			
☐	262	Alex Trevino	.10	.05	.01			
☐	263	Jeffrey Leonard	.10	.05	.01			
☐	264	Tom Henke	.20	.09	.03			
☐	265	Ozzie Smith	.75	.35	.09			
☐	266	Dave Bergman	.10	.05	.01			
☐	267	Tony Phillips	.30	.14	.04			
☐	268	Mark Davis	.10	.05	.01			
☐	269	Kevin Elster	.10	.05	.01			
☐	270	Barry Larkin	.75	.35	.09			
☐	271	Manny Lee	.10	.05	.01			
☐	272	Tom Brunansky	.10	.05	.01			
☐	273	Craig Biggio	2.50	1.10	.30			
☐	274	Jim Gantner	.20	.09	.03			
☐	275	Eddie Murray	.60	.25	.07			
☐	276	Jeff Reed	.10	.05	.01			
☐	277	Tim Teufel	.10	.05	.01			
☐	278	Rick Honeycutt	.10	.05	.01			
☐	279	Guillermo Hernandez	.10	.05	.01			
☐	280	John Kruk	.30	.14	.04			
☐	281	Luis Alicea	.10	.05	.01			
☐	282	Jim Clancy	.10	.05	.01			
☐	283	Billy Ripken	.10	.05	.01			
☐	284	Craig Reynolds	.10	.05	.01			
☐	285	Robin Yount	.60	.25	.07			
☐	286	Jimmy Jones	.10	.05	.01			
☐	287	Ron Oester	.10	.05	.01			
☐	288	Terry Leach	.10	.05	.01			
☐	289	Dennis Eckersley	.30	.14	.04			
☐	290	Alan Trammell	.30	.14	.04			
☐	291	Jimmy Key	.30	.14	.04			
☐	292	Chris Bosio	.10	.05	.01			
☐	293	Jose DeLeon	.10	.05	.01			
☐	294	Jim Traber	.10	.05	.01			
☐	295	Mike Scott	.10	.05	.01			
☐	296	Roger McDowell	.10	.05	.01			
☐	297	Garry Templeton	.10	.05	.01			
☐	298	Doyle Alexander	.10	.05	.01			
☐	299	Nick Esasky	.10	.05	.01			
☐	300	Mark McGwire UER	1.00	.45	.12			
		(Doubles total 52,						
		should be 51)						
☐	301	Darryl Hamilton	.20	.09	.03			
☐	302	Dave Smith	.10	.05	.01			
☐	303	Rick Sutcliffe	.20	.09	.03			
☐	304	Dave Stapleton	.10	.05	.01			
☐	305	Alan Ashby	.10	.05	.01			
☐	306	Pedro Guerrero	.20	.09	.03			
☐	307	Ron Guidry	.20	.09	.03			
☐	308	Steve Farr	.10	.05	.01			
☐	309	Curt Ford	.10	.05	.01			
☐	310	Claudell Washington	.10	.05	.01			
☐	311	Tom Prince	.10	.05	.01			
☐	312	Chad Kreuter	.10	.05	.01			
☐	313	Ken Oberkfell	.10	.05	.01			
☐	314	Jerry Browne	.10	.05	.01			
☐	315	R.J. Reynolds	.10	.05	.01			
☐	316	Scott Bankhead	.10	.05	.01			
☐	317	Milt Thompson	.10	.05	.01			
☐	318	Mario Diaz	.10	.05	.01			
☐	319	Bruce Ruffin	.10	.05	.01			
☐	320	Dave Valle	.10	.05	.01			
☐	321A	Gary Varsho ERR	2.00	.90	.25			
		(Back photo actually						
		Mike Bielecki bunting)						
☐	321B	Gary Varsho COR	.10	.05	.01			

(In road uniform)

☐ 322 Paul Mirabella	.10	.05	.01
☐ 323 Chuck Jackson	.10	.05	.01
☐ 324 Drew Hall	.10	.05	.01
☐ 325 Don August	.10	.05	.01
☐ 326 Israel Sanchez	.10	.05	.01
☐ 327 Denny Walling	.10	.05	.01
☐ 328 Joel Skinner	.10	.05	.01
☐ 329 Danny Tartabull	.20	.09	.03
☐ 330 Tony Pena	.10	.05	.01
☐ 331 Jim Sundberg	.10	.05	.01
☐ 332 Jeff D. Robinson	.10	.05	.01
☐ 333 Oddibe McDowell	.10	.05	.01
☐ 334 Jose Lind	.10	.05	.01
☐ 335 Paul Kilgus	.10	.05	.01
☐ 336 Juan Samuel	.10	.05	.01
☐ 337 Mike Campbell	.10	.05	.01
☐ 338 Mike Maddux	.10	.05	.01
☐ 339 Darnell Coles	.10	.05	.01
☐ 340 Bob Dernier	.10	.05	.01
☐ 341 Rafael Ramirez	.10	.05	.01
☐ 342 Scott Sanderson	.10	.05	.01
☐ 343 B.J. Surhoff	.20	.09	.03
☐ 344 Billy Hatcher	.10	.05	.01
☐ 345 Pat Perry	.10	.05	.01
☐ 346 Jack Clark	.20	.09	.03
☐ 347 Gary Thurman	.10	.05	.01
☐ 348 Tim Jones	.10	.05	.01
☐ 349 Dave Winfield	.40	.18	.05
☐ 350 Frank White	.20	.09	.03
☐ 351 Dave Collins	.10	.05	.01
☐ 352 Jack Morris	.30	.14	.04
☐ 353 Eric Plunk	.10	.05	.01
☐ 354 Leon Durham	.10	.05	.01
☐ 355 Ivan DeJesus	.10	.05	.01
☐ 356 Brian Holman	.10	.05	.01
☐ 357A Dale Murphy ERR	25.00	11.00	3.10
(Front has			
reverse negative)			
☐ 357B Dale Murphy COR	.20	.09	.03
☐ 358 Mark Portugal	.20	.09	.03
☐ 359 Andy McGaffigan	.10	.05	.01
☐ 360 Tom Glavine	1.25	.55	.16
☐ 361 Keith Moreland	.10	.05	.01
☐ 362 Todd Stottlemyre	.20	.09	.03
☐ 363 Dave Leiper	.10	.05	.01
☐ 364 Cecil Fielder	.60	.25	.07
☐ 365 Carmelo Martinez	.10	.05	.01
☐ 366 Dwight Evans	.20	.09	.03
☐ 367 Kevin McReynolds	.10	.05	.01
☐ 368 Rich Gedman	.10	.05	.01
☐ 369 Len Dykstra	.30	.14	.04
☐ 370 Jody Reed	.10	.05	.01
☐ 371 Jose Canseco UER	1.00	.45	.12
(Strikeout total 391,			
should be 491)			
☐ 372 Rob Murphy	.10	.05	.01
☐ 373 Mike Henneman	.20	.09	.03
☐ 374 Walt Weiss	.20	.09	.03
☐ 375 Rob Dibble	.20	.09	.03
☐ 376 Kirby Puckett	1.25	.55	.16
(Mark McGwire			
in background)			
☐ 377 Dennis Martinez	.20	.09	.03
☐ 378 Ron Gant	1.00	.45	.12
☐ 379 Brian Harper	.20	.09	.03
☐ 380 Nelson Santovenia	.10	.05	.01
☐ 381 Lloyd Moseby	.10	.05	.01
☐ 382 Lance McCullers	.10	.05	.01
☐ 383 Dave Stieb	.20	.09	.03
☐ 384 Tony Gwynn	1.00	.45	.12

☐ 385 Mike Flanagan	.10	.05	.01
☐ 386 Bob Ojeda	.10	.05	.01
☐ 387 Bruce Hurst	.10	.05	.01
☐ 388 Dave Magadan	.10	.05	.01
☐ 389 Wade Boggs	.60	.25	.07
☐ 390 Gary Carter	.30	.14	.04
☐ 391 Frank Tanana	.10	.05	.01
☐ 392 Curt Young	.10	.05	.01
☐ 393 Jeff Treadway	.10	.05	.01
☐ 394 Darrell Evans	.20	.09	.03
☐ 395 Glenn Hubbard	.10	.05	.01
☐ 396 Chuck Cary	.10	.05	.01
☐ 397 Frank Viola	.20	.09	.03
☐ 398 Jeff Parrett	.10	.05	.01
☐ 399 Terry Blocker	.10	.05	.01
☐ 400 Dan Gladden	.10	.05	.01
☐ 401 Louie Meadows	.10	.05	.01
☐ 402 Tim Raines	.30	.14	.04
☐ 403 Joey Meyer	.10	.05	.01
☐ 404 Larry Andersen	.10	.05	.01
☐ 405 Rex Hudler	.10	.05	.01
☐ 406 Mike Schmidt	1.00	.45	.12
☐ 407 John Franco	.20	.09	.03
☐ 408 Brady Anderson	1.00	.45	.12
☐ 409 Don Carman	.10	.05	.01
☐ 410 Eric Davis	.20	.09	.03
☐ 411 Bob Stanley	.10	.05	.01
☐ 412 Pete Smith	.10	.05	.01
☐ 413 Jim Rice	.30	.14	.04
☐ 414 Bruce Sutter	.20	.09	.03
☐ 415 Oil Can Boyd	.10	.05	.01
☐ 416 Ruben Sierra	.50	.23	.06
☐ 417 Mike LaValliere	.10	.05	.01
☐ 418 Steve Buechele	.10	.05	.01
☐ 419 Gary Redus	.10	.05	.01
☐ 420 Scott Fletcher	.10	.05	.01
☐ 421 Dale Sveum	.10	.05	.01
☐ 422 Bob Knepper	.10	.05	.01
☐ 423 Luis Rivera	.10	.05	.01
☐ 424 Ted Higuera	.10	.05	.01
☐ 425 Kevin Bass	.10	.05	.01
☐ 426 Ken Gerhart	.10	.05	.01
☐ 427 Shane Rawley	.10	.05	.01
☐ 428 Paul O'Neill	.30	.14	.04
☐ 429 Joe Orsulak	.10	.05	.01
☐ 430 Jackie Gutierrez	.10	.05	.01
☐ 431 Gerald Perry	.10	.05	.01
☐ 432 Mike Greenwell	.30	.14	.04
☐ 433 Jerry Royster	.10	.05	.01
☐ 434 Ellis Burks	.30	.14	.04
☐ 435 Ed Olwine	.10	.05	.01
☐ 436 Dave Rucker	.10	.05	.01
☐ 437 Charlie Hough	.20	.09	.03
☐ 438 Bob Walk	.10	.05	.01
☐ 439 Bob Brower	.10	.05	.01
☐ 440 Barry Bonds	1.50	.70	.19
☐ 441 Tom Foley	.10	.05	.01
☐ 442 Rob Deer	.10	.05	.01
☐ 443 Glenn Davis	.10	.05	.01
☐ 444 Dave Martinez	.10	.05	.01
☐ 445 Bill Wegman	.10	.05	.01
☐ 446 Lloyd McClendon	.10	.05	.01
☐ 447 Dave Schmidt	.10	.05	.01
☐ 448 Darren Daulton	.30	.14	.04
☐ 449 Frank Williams	.10	.05	.01
☐ 450 Don Aase	.10	.05	.01
☐ 451 Lou Whitaker	.30	.14	.04
☐ 452 Goose Gossage	.30	.14	.04
☐ 453 Ed Whitson	.10	.05	.01
☐ 454 Jim Walewander	.10	.05	.01
☐ 455 Damon Berryhill	.10	.05	.01

☐ 456	Tim Burke	.10	.05	.01
☐ 457	Barry Jones	.10	.05	.01
☐ 458	Joel Youngblood	.10	.05	.01
☐ 459	Floyd Youmans	.10	.05	.01
☐ 460	Mark Salas	.10	.05	.01
☐ 461	Jeff Russell	.10	.05	.01
☐ 462	Darrell Miller	.10	.05	.01
☐ 463	Jeff Kunkel	.10	.05	.01
☐ 464	Sherman Corbett	.10	.05	.01
☐ 465	Curtis Wilkerson	.10	.05	.01
☐ 466	Bud Black	.10	.05	.01
☐ 467	Cal Ripken	3.00	1.35	.35
☐ 468	John Farrell	.10	.05	.01
☐ 469	Terry Kennedy	.10	.05	.01
☐ 470	Tom Candiotti	.10	.05	.01
☐ 471	Roberto Alomar	2.50	1.10	.30
☐ 472	Jeff M. Robinson	.10	.05	.01
☐ 473	Vance Law	.10	.05	.01
☐ 474	Randy Ready UER	.10	.05	.01
	(Strikeout total 136,			
	should be 115)			
☐ 475	Walt Terrell	.10	.05	.01
☐ 476	Kelly Downs	.10	.05	.01
☐ 477	Johnny Paredes	.10	.05	.01
☐ 478	Shawn Hillegas	.10	.05	.01
☐ 479	Bob Brenly	.10	.05	.01
☐ 480	Otis Nixon	.10	.05	.01
☐ 481	Johnny Ray	.10	.05	.01
☐ 482	Geno Petralli	.10	.05	.01
☐ 483	Stu Cliburn	.10	.05	.01
☐ 484	Pat Incaviglia	.20	.09	.03
☐ 485	Brian Downing	.10	.05	.01
☐ 486	Jeff Stone	.10	.05	.01
☐ 487	Carmen Castillo	.10	.05	.01
☐ 488	Tom Niedenfuer	.10	.05	.01
☐ 489	Jay Bell	.30	.14	.04
☐ 490	Rick Schu	.10	.05	.01
☐ 491	Jeff Pico	.10	.05	.01
☐ 492	Mark Parent	.10	.05	.01
☐ 493	Eric King	.10	.05	.01
☐ 494	Al Nipper	.10	.05	.01
☐ 495	Andy Hawkins	.10	.05	.01
☐ 496	Daryl Boston	.10	.05	.01
☐ 497	Ernie Riles	.10	.05	.01
☐ 498	Pascual Perez	.10	.05	.01
☐ 499	Bill Long UER	.10	.05	.01
	(Games started total			
	70, should be 44)			
☐ 500	Kirt Manwaring	.10	.05	.01
☐ 501	Chuck Crim	.10	.05	.01
☐ 502	Candy Maldonado	.10	.05	.01
☐ 503	Dennis Lamp	.10	.05	.01
☐ 504	Glenn Braggs	.10	.05	.01
☐ 505	Joe Price	.10	.05	.01
☐ 506	Ken Williams	.10	.05	.01
☐ 507	Bill Pecota	.10	.05	.01
☐ 508	Rey Quinones	.10	.05	.01
☐ 509	Jeff Bittiger	.10	.05	.01
☐ 510	Kevin Seitzer	.10	.05	.01
☐ 511	Steve Bedrosian	.10	.05	.01
☐ 512	Todd Worrell	.20	.09	.03
☐ 513	Chris James	.10	.05	.01
☐ 514	Jose Oquendo	.10	.05	.01
☐ 515	David Palmer	.10	.05	.01
☐ 516	John Smiley	.10	.05	.01
☐ 517	Dave Clark	.10	.05	.01
☐ 518	Mike Dunne	.10	.05	.01
☐ 519	Ron Washington	.10	.05	.01
☐ 520	Bob Kipper	.10	.05	.01
☐ 521	Lee Smith	.30	.14	.04
☐ 522	Juan Castillo	.10	.05	.01
☐ 523	Don Robinson	.10	.05	.01
☐ 524	Kevin Romine	.10	.05	.01
☐ 525	Paul Molitor	.40	.18	.05
☐ 526	Mark Langston	.30	.14	.04
☐ 527	Donnie Hill	.10	.05	.01
☐ 528	Larry Owen	.10	.05	.01
☐ 529	Jerry Reed	.10	.05	.01
☐ 530	Jack McDowell	.60	.25	.07
☐ 531	Greg Mathews	.10	.05	.01
☐ 532	John Russell	.10	.05	.01
☐ 533	Dan Quisenberry	.20	.09	.03
☐ 534	Greg Gross	.10	.05	.01
☐ 535	Danny Cox	.10	.05	.01
☐ 536	Terry Francona	.10	.05	.01
☐ 537	Andy Van Slyke	.20	.09	.03
☐ 538	Mel Hall	.10	.05	.01
☐ 539	Jim Gott	.10	.05	.01
☐ 540	Doug Jones	.20	.09	.03
☐ 541	Craig Lefferts	.10	.05	.01
☐ 542	Mike Boddicker	.10	.05	.01
☐ 543	Greg Brock	.10	.05	.01
☐ 544	Atlee Hammaker	.10	.05	.01
☐ 545	Tom Bolton	.10	.05	.01
☐ 546	Mike Macfarlane	.40	.18	.05
☐ 547	Rich Renteria	.10	.05	.01
☐ 548	John Davis	.10	.05	.01
☐ 549	Floyd Bannister	.10	.05	.01
☐ 550	Mickey Brantley	.10	.05	.01
☐ 551	Duane Ward	.20	.09	.03
☐ 552	Dan Petry	.10	.05	.01
☐ 553	Mickey Tettleton UER	.20	.09	.03
	(Walks total 175,			
	should be 136)			
☐ 554	Rick Leach	.10	.05	.01
☐ 555	Mike Witt	.10	.05	.01
☐ 556	Sid Bream	.10	.05	.01
☐ 557	Bobby Witt	.20	.09	.03
☐ 558	Tommy Herr	.10	.05	.01
☐ 559	Randy Milligan	.10	.05	.01
☐ 560	Jose Cecena	.10	.05	.01
☐ 561	Mackey Sasser	.10	.05	.01
☐ 562	Carney Lansford	.20	.09	.03
☐ 563	Rick Aguilera	.30	.14	.04
☐ 564	Ron Hassey	.10	.05	.01
☐ 565	Dwight Gooden	.30	.09	.03
☐ 566	Paul Assenmacher	.10	.05	.01
☐ 567	Neil Allen	.10	.05	.01
☐ 568	Jim Morrison	.10	.05	.01
☐ 569	Mike Pagliarulo	.10	.05	.01
☐ 570	Ted Simmons	.20	.09	.03
☐ 571	Mark Thurmond	.10	.05	.01
☐ 572	Fred McGriff	1.00	.45	.12
☐ 573	Wally Joyner	.20	.09	.03
☐ 574	Jose Bautista	.10	.05	.01
☐ 575	Kelly Gruber	.10	.05	.01
☐ 576	Cecilio Guante	.10	.05	.01
☐ 577	Mark Davidson	.10	.05	.01
☐ 578	Bobby Bonilla UER	.30	.14	.04
	(Total steals 2 in '87,			
	should be 3)			
☐ 579	Mike Stanley	.20	.09	.03
☐ 580	Gene Larkin	.10	.05	.01
☐ 581	Stan Javier	.10	.05	.01
☐ 582	Howard Johnson	.20	.09	.03
☐ 583A	Mike Gallego ERR	1.00	.45	.12
	(Front reversed			
	negative)			
☐ 583B	Mike Gallego COR	.10	.05	.01
☐ 584	David Cone	.75	.35	.09
☐ 585	Doug Jennings	.10	.05	.01
☐ 586	Charles Hudson	.10	.05	.01

☐ 587	Dion James	.10	.05	.01
☐ 588	Al Leiter	.10	.05	.01
☐ 589	Charlie Puleo	.10	.05	.01
☐ 590	Roberto Kelly	.20	.09	.03
☐ 591	Thad Bosley	.10	.05	.01
☐ 592	Pete Stanicek	.10	.05	.01
☐ 593	Pat Borders	.20	.09	.03
☐ 594	Bryan Harvey	.30	.14	.04
☐ 595	Jeff Ballard	.10	.05	.01
☐ 596	Jeff Reardon	.30	.14	.04
☐ 597	Doug Drabek	.30	.14	.04
☐ 598	Edwin Correa	.10	.05	.01
☐ 599	Keith Atherton	.10	.05	.01
☐ 600	Dave LaPoint	.10	.05	.01
☐ 601	Don Baylor	.30	.14	.04
☐ 602	Tom Pagnozzi	.10	.05	.01
☐ 603	Tim Flannery	.10	.05	.01
☐ 604	Gene Walter	.10	.05	.01
☐ 605	Dave Parker	.30	.14	.04
☐ 606	Mike Diaz	.10	.05	.01
☐ 607	Chris Gwynn	.10	.05	.01
☐ 608	Odell Jones	.10	.05	.01
☐ 609	Carlton Fisk	.30	.14	.04
☐ 610	Jay Howell	.10	.05	.01
☐ 611	Tim Crews	.10	.05	.01
☐ 612	Keith Hernandez	.20	.09	.03
☐ 613	Willie Fraser	.10	.05	.01
☐ 614	Jim Eppard	.10	.05	.01
☐ 615	Jeff Hamilton	.10	.05	.01
☐ 616	Kurt Stillwell	.10	.05	.01
☐ 617	Tom Browning	.10	.05	.01
☐ 618	Jeff Montgomery	.20	.09	.03
☐ 619	Jose Rijo	.30	.14	.04
☐ 620	Jamie Quirk	.10	.05	.01
☐ 621	Willie McGee	.20	.09	.03
☐ 622	Mark Grant UER	.10	.05	.01
	(Glove on wrong hand)			
☐ 623	Bill Swift	.20	.09	.03
☐ 624	Orlando Mercado	.10	.05	.01
☐ 625	John Costello	.10	.05	.01
☐ 626	Jose Gonzalez	.10	.05	.01
☐ 627A	Bill Schroeder ERR	1.00	.45	.12
	(Back photo actually Ronn Reynolds buckling shin guards)			
☐ 627B	Bill Schroeder COR	.10	.05	.01
☐ 628A	Fred Manrique ERR	.15	.07	.02
	(Back photo actually Ozzie Guillen throwing)			
☐ 628B	Fred Manrique COR	.10	.05	.01
	(Swinging bat on back)			
☐ 629	Ricky Horton	.10	.05	.01
☐ 630	Dan Plesac	.10	.05	.01
☐ 631	Alfredo Griffin	.10	.05	.01
☐ 632	Chuck Finley	.20	.09	.03
☐ 633	Kirk Gibson	.30	.14	.04
☐ 634	Randy Myers	.30	.14	.04
☐ 635	Greg Minton	.10	.05	.01
☐ 636A	Herm Winningham ERR (W1nningham on back)	.10	.05	.01
☐ 636B	Herm Winningham COR	.10	.05	.01
☐ 637	Charlie Leibrandt	.10	.05	.01
☐ 638	Tim Birtsas	.10	.05	.01
☐ 639	Bill Buckner	.20	.09	.03
☐ 640	Danny Jackson	.10	.05	.01
☐ 641	Greg Booker	.10	.05	.01
☐ 642	Jim Presley	.10	.05	.01
☐ 643	Gene Nelson	.10	.05	.01
☐ 644	Rod Booker	.10	.05	.01
☐ 645	Dennis Rasmussen	.10	.05	.01

☐ 646	Juan Nieves	.10	.05	.01
☐ 647	Bobby Thigpen	.10	.05	.01
☐ 648	Tim Belcher	.10	.05	.01
☐ 649	Mike Young	.10	.05	.01
☐ 650	Ivan Calderon	.10	.05	.01
☐ 651	Oswaldo Peraza	.10	.05	.01
☐ 652A	Pat Sheridan ERR	8.00	3.60	1.00
	(No position on front)			
☐ 652B	Pat Sheridan COR	.10	.05	.01
☐ 653	Mike Morgan	.10	.05	.01
☐ 654	Mike Heath	.10	.05	.01
☐ 655	Jay Tibbs	.10	.05	.01
☐ 656	Fernando Valenzuela	.20	.09	.03
☐ 657	Lee Mazzilli	.10	.05	.01
☐ 658	Frank Viola ALCS	.20	.09	.03
☐ 659A	Jose Canseco AL MVP	.60	.25	.07
	(Eagle logo in black)			
☐ 659B	Jose Canseco AL MVP	.60	.25	.07
	(Eagle logo in blue)			
☐ 660	Walt Weiss AL ROY	.20	.09	.03
☐ 661	Orel Hershiser NL CY	.20	.09	.03
☐ 662	Kirk Gibson NL MVP	.20	.09	.03
☐ 663	Chris Sabo NL ROY	.10	.05	.01
☐ 664	D.Eckersley ALCS MVP	.20	.09	.03
☐ 665	O.Hershiser NLCS MVP	.20	.09	.03
☐ 666	Great WS Moment	.30	.14	.04
	(Kirk Gibson's homer)			
☐ 667	Orel Hershiser WS MVP	.20	.09	.03
☐ 668	Wally Joyner TC	.20	.09	.03
☐ 669	Nolan Ryan TC	.75	.35	.09
☐ 670	Jose Canseco TC	.35	.16	.04
☐ 671	Fred McGriff TC	.35	.16	.04
☐ 672	Dale Murphy TC	.20	.09	.03
☐ 673	Paul Molitor TC	.30	.14	.04
☐ 674	Ozzie Smith TC	.30	.14	.04
☐ 675	Ryne Sandberg TC	.30	.14	.04
☐ 676	Kirk Gibson TC	.20	.09	.03
☐ 677	Andres Galarraga TC	.20	.09	.03
☐ 678	Will Clark TC	.30	.14	.04
☐ 679	Cory Snyder TC	.10	.05	.01
☐ 680	Alvin Davis TC	.10	.05	.01
☐ 681	Darryl Strawberry TC	.20	.09	.03
☐ 682	Cal Ripken TC	.75	.35	.09
☐ 683	Tony Gwynn TC	.30	.14	.04
☐ 684	Mike Schmidt TC	.50	.23	.06
☐ 685	Andy Van Slyke TC UER	.10	.05	.01
	(96 Junior Ortiz)			
☐ 686	Ruben Sierra TC	.30	.14	.04
☐ 687	Wade Boggs TC	.30	.14	.04
☐ 688	Eric Davis TC	.20	.09	.03
☐ 689	George Brett TC	.40	.18	.05
☐ 690	Alan Trammell TC	.20	.09	.03
☐ 691	Frank Viola TC	.10	.05	.01
☐ 692	Harold Baines TC	.20	.09	.03
☐ 693	Don Mattingly TC	.40	.18	.05
☐ 694	Checklist 1-100	.10	.05	.01
☐ 695	Checklist 101-200	.10	.05	.01
☐ 696	Checklist 201-300	.10	.05	.01
☐ 697	Checklist 301-400	.10	.05	.01
☐ 698	Checklist 401-500 UER	.10	.05	.01
	(467 Cal Ripken Jr.)			
☐ 699	Checklist 501-600 UER	.10	.05	.01
	(543 Greg Booker)			
☐ 700	Checklist 601-700	.10	.05	.01
☐ 701	Checklist 701-800	.10	.05	.01
☐ 702	Jesse Barfield	.10	.05	.01
☐ 703	Walt Terrell	.10	.05	.01
☐ 704	Dickie Thon	.10	.05	.01
☐ 705	Al Leiter	.10	.05	.01
☐ 706	Dave LaPoint	.10	.05	.01
☐ 707	Charlie Hayes	.60	.25	.07

☐ 708	Andy Hawkins	.10	.05	.01
☐ 709	Mickey Hatcher	.10	.05	.01
☐ 710	Lance McCullers	.10	.05	.01
☐ 711	Ron Kittle	.10	.05	.01
☐ 712	Bert Blyleven	.30	.14	.04
☐ 713	Rick Dempsey	.10	.05	.01
☐ 714	Ken Williams	.10	.05	.01
☐ 715	Steve Rosenberg	.10	.05	.01
☐ 716	Joe Skalski	.10	.05	.01
☐ 717	Spike Owen	.10	.05	.01
☐ 718	Todd Burns	.10	.05	.01
☐ 719	Kevin Gross	.10	.05	.01
☐ 720	Tommy Herr	.10	.05	.01
☐ 721	Rob Ducey	.10	.05	.01
☐ 722	Gary Green	.10	.05	.01
☐ 723	Gregg Olson	.20	.09	.03
☐ 724	Greg W. Harris	.10	.05	.01
☐ 725	Craig Worthington	.10	.05	.01
☐ 726	Tom Howard	.10	.05	.01
☐ 727	Dale Mohorcic	.10	.05	.01
☐ 728	Rich Yett	.10	.05	.01
☐ 729	Mel Hall	.10	.05	.01
☐ 730	Floyd Youmans	.10	.05	.01
☐ 731	Lonnie Smith	.10	.05	.01
☐ 732	Wally Backman	.10	.05	.01
☐ 733	Trevor Wilson	.10	.05	.01
☐ 734	Jose Alvarez	.10	.05	.01
☐ 735	Bob Milacki	.10	.05	.01
☐ 736	Tom Gordon	.40	.18	.05
☐ 737	Wally Whitehurst	.10	.05	.01
☐ 738	Mike Aldrete	.10	.05	.01
☐ 739	Keith Miller	.10	.05	.01
☐ 740	Randy Milligan	.10	.05	.01
☐ 741	Jeff Parrett	.10	.05	.01
☐ 742	Steve Finley	.50	.23	.06
☐ 743	Junior Felix	.10	.05	.01
☐ 744	Pete Harnisch	.20	.09	.03
☐ 745	Bill Spiers	.10	.05	.01
☐ 746	Hensley Meulens	.10	.05	.01
☐ 747	Juan Bell	.10	.05	.01
☐ 748	Steve Sax	.10	.05	.01
☐ 749	Phil Bradley	.10	.05	.01
☐ 750	Rey Quinones	.10	.05	.01
☐ 751	Tommy Gregg	.10	.05	.01
☐ 752	Kevin Brown	.20	.09	.03
☐ 753	Derek Lilliquist	.10	.05	.01
☐ 754	Todd Zeile	.75	.35	.09
☐ 755	Jim Abbott (Triple exposure)	1.00	.45	.12
☐ 756	Ozzie Canseco	.10	.05	.01
☐ 757	Nick Esasky	.10	.05	.01
☐ 758	Mike Moore	.10	.05	.01
☐ 759	Rob Murphy	.10	.05	.01
☐ 760	Rick Mahler	.10	.05	.01
☐ 761	Fred Lynn	.20	.09	.03
☐ 762	Kevin Blankenship	.10	.05	.01
☐ 763	Eddie Murray	.60	.25	.07
☐ 764	Steve Searcy	.10	.05	.01
☐ 765	Jerome Walton	.30	.14	.04
☐ 766	Erik Hanson	.75	.35	.09
☐ 767	Bob Boone	.20	.09	.03
☐ 768	Edgar Martinez	1.00	.45	.12
☐ 769	Jose DeJesus	.10	.05	.01
☐ 770	Greg Briley	.10	.05	.01
☐ 771	Steve Peters	.10	.05	.01
☐ 772	Rafael Palmeiro	1.00	.45	.12
☐ 773	Jack Clark	.20	.09	.03
☐ 774	Nolan Ryan (Throwing football)	3.00	1.35	.35
☐ 775	Lance Parrish	.20	.09	.03
☐ 776	Joe Girardi	.20	.09	.03

☐ 777	Willie Randolph	.20	.09	.03
☐ 778	Mitch Williams	.20	.09	.03
☐ 779	Dennis Cook	.10	.05	.01
☐ 780	Dwight Smith	.10	.05	.01
☐ 781	Lenny Harris	.10	.05	.01
☐ 782	Torey Lovullo	.10	.05	.01
☐ 783	Norm Charlton	.30	.14	.04
☐ 784	Chris Brown	.10	.05	.01
☐ 785	Todd Benzinger	.10	.05	.01
☐ 786	Shane Rawley	.10	.05	.01
☐ 787	Omar Vizquel	.75	.35	.09
☐ 788	LaVel Freeman	.10	.05	.01
☐ 789	Jeffrey Leonard	.10	.05	.01
☐ 790	Eddie Williams	.10	.05	.01
☐ 791	Jamie Moyer	.10	.05	.01
☐ 792	Bruce Hurst UER (Workd Series)	.10	.05	.01
☐ 793	Julio Franco	.20	.09	.03
☐ 794	Claudell Washington	.10	.05	.01
☐ 795	Jody Davis	.10	.05	.01
☐ 796	Oddibe McDowell	.10	.05	.01
☐ 797	Paul Kilgus	.10	.05	.01
☐ 798	Tracy Jones	.10	.05	.01
☐ 799	Steve Wilson	.10	.05	.01
☐ 800	Pete O'Brien	.10	.05	.01

1990 Upper Deck

Kevin Maas

The 1990 Upper Deck set contains 800 standard-size (2 1/2" by 3 1/2") cards issued in two series, low numbers (1-700) and high numbers (701-800). The front and back borders are white, and both sides feature full-color photos. The horizontally oriented backs have recent stats and anti-counterfeiting holograms. Unlike the 1989 Upper Deck set, the team checklist cards are not grouped numerically at the end of the set, but are mixed in with the first 100 cards. Cards 101 through 199 have two minor varieties in that the cards either show or omit "Copyright 1990 Upper Deck Co. Printed in USA below the two licensing logos. Those without are considered minor errors; they were found in the High Number foil packs. The 1990 Upper Deck Extended Set (of high numbers) was issued in July 1990. The cards were in the same style as the first 700 cards of the 1990 Upper Deck set and were issued either as a separate set in its own collectors box, as part of the complete 1-800 factory set, as well as mixed in with the earlier numbered Upper

Deck cards in late-season wax packs. The series also contains a Nolan Ryan variation; all cards produced before August 12th only discuss Ryan's sixth no-hitter while the later-issue cards include a stripe honoring Ryan's 300th victory. Rookie Cards in the set include Wilson Alvarez, Carlos Baerga, Alex Cole, Delino DeShields, Juan Gonzalez, Marquis Grissom, Bob Hamelin, Dave Hollins, David Justice, Ray Lankford, Derrick May, Ben McDonald, John Olerud, Dean Palmer, Sammy Sosa, and Larry Walker. Card 702 was originally scheduled to be Mike Witt. A few Witt cards with 702 on back and checklist cards showing 702 Witt escaped into early packs; they are characterized by a black rectangle covering much of the card's back.

	MINT	NRMT	EXC
COMPLETE SET (800)	24.00	11.00	3.00
COMPLETE FACT.SET (800)	24.00	11.00	3.00
COMPLETE LO SET (700)	20.00	9.00	2.50
COMPLETE HI SET (100)	4.00	1.80	.50
COMPLETE HI FACT.SET (100)	4.00	1.80	.50
COMMON CARD (1-800)	.05	.02	.01
☐ 1 Star Rookie Checklist	.05	.02	.01
☐ 2 Randy Nosek	.05	.02	.01
☐ 3 Tom Drees UER	.05	.02	.01
(11th line, hurled, should be hurled)			
☐ 4 Curt Young	.05	.02	.01
☐ 5 Devon White TC	.10	.05	.01
☐ 6 Luis Salazar	.05	.02	.01
☐ 7 Von Hayes TC	.05	.02	.01
☐ 8 Jose Bautista	.05	.02	.01
☐ 9 Marquis Grissom	1.25	.55	.16
☐ 10 Orel Hershiser TC	.10	.05	.01
☐ 11 Rick Aguilera	.10	.05	.01
☐ 12 Benito Santiago TC	.05	.02	.01
☐ 13 Deion Sanders	1.00	.45	.12
☐ 14 Marvell Wynne	.05	.02	.01
☐ 15 Dave West	.05	.02	.01
☐ 16 Bobby Bonilla TC	.10	.05	.01
☐ 17 Sammy Sosa	1.50	.70	.19
☐ 18 Steve Sax TC	.05	.02	.01
☐ 19 Jack Howell	.05	.02	.01
☐ 20 Mike Schmidt Special	.50	.23	.06
UER (Suprising, should be surprising)			
☐ 21 Robin Ventura UER	.50	.23	.06
(Samta Maria)			
☐ 22 Brian Meyer	.05	.02	.01
☐ 23 Blaine Beatty	.05	.02	.01
☐ 24 Ken Griffey Jr. TC	1.00	.45	.12
☐ 25 Greg Vaughn UER	.10	.05	.01
(Association misspelled as assiocation)			
☐ 26 Xavier Hernandez	.05	.02	.01
☐ 27 Jason Grimsley	.05	.02	.01
☐ 28 Eric Anthony UER	.05	.02	.01
(Ashville, should be Asheville)			
☐ 29 Tim Raines TC UER	.20	.09	.03
(Wallach listed before Walker)			
☐ 30 David Wells	.05	.02	.01
☐ 31 Hal Morris	.10	.05	.01
☐ 32 Bo Jackson TC	.20	.09	.03
☐ 33 Kelly Mann	.05	.02	.01
☐ 34 Nolan Ryan Special	.75	.35	.09
☐ 35 Scott Service UER	.05	.02	.01
(Born Cincinatti on 7/27/67, should be Cincinnati 2/27)			
☐ 36 Mark McGwire TC	.10	.05	.01
☐ 37 Tino Martinez	.40	.18	.05
☐ 38 Chili Davis	.20	.09	.03
☐ 39 Scott Sanderson	.05	.02	.01
☐ 40 Kevin Mitchell TC	.05	.02	.01
☐ 41 Lou Whitaker TC	.10	.05	.01
Detroit Tigers			
☐ 42 Scott Coolbaugh UER	.05	.02	.01
(Definately)			
☐ 43 Jose Cano UER	.05	.02	.01
(Born 9/7/62, should be 3/7/62)			
☐ 44 Jose Vizcaino	.05	.02	.01
☐ 45 Bob Hamelin	.20	.09	.03
☐ 46 Jose Offerman UER	.10	.05	.01
(Posesses)			
☐ 47 Kevin Blankenship	.05	.02	.01
☐ 48 Kirby Puckett TC	.30	.14	.04
☐ 49 Tommy Greene UER	.20	.09	.03
(Livest, should be liveliest)			
☐ 50 Will Clark Special	.20	.09	.03
UER (Perenial, should be perennial)			
☐ 51 Rob Nelson	.05	.02	.01
☐ 52 Chris Hammond UER	.10	.05	.01
(Chatanooga)			
☐ 53 Joe Carter TC	.10	.05	.01
☐ 54A Ben McDonald ERR	8.00	3.60	1.00
(No Rookie designation on card front)			
☐ 54B Ben McDonald COR	.30	.14	.04
☐ 55 Andy Benes UER	.10	.05	.01
(Whichita)			
☐ 56 John Olerud	.40	.18	.05
☐ 57 Roger Clemens TC	.20	.09	.03
☐ 58 Tony Armas	.05	.02	.01
☐ 59 George Canale	.05	.02	.01
☐ 60A Mickey Tettleton TC	2.00	.90	.25
ERR (683 Jamie Weston)			
☐ 60B Mickey Tettleton TC	.05	.02	.01
COR (683 Mickey Weston)			
☐ 61 Mike Stanton	.05	.02	.01
☐ 62 Dwight Gooden TC	.05	.02	.01
☐ 63 Kent Mercker UER	.40	.18	.05
(Albuguerque)			
☐ 64 Francisco Cabrera	.05	.02	.01
☐ 65 Steve Avery UER	.40	.18	.05
(Born NJ, should be MI, Merker should be Mercker)			
☐ 66 Jose Canseco	.40	.18	.05
☐ 67 Matt Merullo	.05	.02	.01
☐ 68 Vince Coleman TC UER	.05	.02	.01
(Guererro)			
☐ 69 Ron Karkovice	.05	.02	.01
☐ 70 Kevin Maas	.10	.05	.01
☐ 71 Dennis Cook UER	.05	.02	.01
(Shown with righty glove on card back)			
☐ 72 Juan Gonzalez UER	2.50	1.10	.30
(135 games for Tulsa in '89, should be 133)			
☐ 73 Andre Dawson TC	.10	.05	.01
☐ 74 Dean Palmer UER	.40	.18	.05
(Permanent misspelled as perminant)			
☐ 75 Bo Jackson Special	.20	.09	.03

	UER (Monsterous, should be monstrous)			
☐ 76	Rob Richie	.05	.02	.01
☐ 77	Bobby Rose UER (Pickin, should be pick in)	.05	.02	.01
☐ 78	Brian DuBois UER (Commiting)	.05	.02	.01
☐ 79	Ozzie Guillen TC	.05	.02	.01
☐ 80	Gene Nelson	.05	.02	.01
☐ 81	Bob McClure	.05	.02	.01
☐ 82	Julio Franco TC	.05	.02	.01
☐ 83	Greg Minton	.05	.02	.01
☐ 84	John Smoltz TC UER (Oddibe not Odibbe)	.10	.05	.01
☐ 85	Willie Fraser	.05	.02	.01
☐ 86	Neal Heaton	.05	.02	.01
☐ 87	Kevin Tapani UER (24th line has excpet, should be except)	.25	.11	.03
☐ 88	Mike Scott TC	.05	.02	.01
☐ 89A	Jim Gott ERR (Photo actually Rick Reed)	2.50	1.10	.30
☐ 89B	Jim Gott COR	.05	.02	.01
☐ 90	Lance Johnson	.10	.05	.01
☐ 91	Robin Yount TC UER (Checklist on back has 178 Rob Deer and 176 Mike Felder)	.20	.09	.03
☐ 92	Jeff Parrett	.05	.02	.01
☐ 93	Julio Machado UER (Valenzulan, should be Venezuelan)	.05	.02	.01
☐ 94	Ron Jones	.05	.02	.01
☐ 95	George Bell TC	.05	.02	.01
☐ 96	Jerry Reuss	.10	.05	.01
☐ 97	Brian Fisher	.05	.02	.01
☐ 98	Kevin Ritz UER (Amercian)	.05	.02	.01
☐ 99	Barry Larkin TC	.20	.09	.03
☐ 100	Checklist 1-100	.05	.02	.01
☐ 101	Gerald Perry	.05	.02	.01
☐ 102	Kevin Appier	.50	.23	.06
☐ 103	Julio Franco	.10	.05	.01
☐ 104	Craig Biggio	.25	.11	.03
☐ 105	Bo Jackson UER ('89 BA wrong, should be .256)	.20	.09	.03
☐ 106	Junior Felix	.05	.02	.01
☐ 107	Mike Harkey	.05	.02	.01
☐ 108	Fred McGriff	.40	.18	.05
☐ 109	Rick Sutcliffe	.10	.05	.01
☐ 110	Pete O'Brien	.05	.02	.01
☐ 111	Kelly Gruber	.05	.02	.01
☐ 112	Dwight Evans	.10	.05	.01
☐ 113	Pat Borders	.05	.02	.01
☐ 114	Dwight Gooden	.10	.05	.01
☐ 115	Kevin Batiste	.05	.02	.01
☐ 116	Eric Davis	.10	.05	.01
☐ 117	Kevin Mitchell UER (Career HR total 99, should be 100)	.10	.05	.01
☐ 118	Ron Oester	.05	.02	.01
☐ 119	Brett Butler	.20	.09	.03
☐ 120	Danny Jackson	.05	.02	.01
☐ 121	Tommy Gregg	.05	.02	.01
☐ 122	Ken Caminiti	.20	.09	.03
☐ 123	Kevin Brown	.10	.05	.01
☐ 124	George Brett UER (133 runs, should be 1300)	.75	.35	.09
☐ 125	Mike Scott	.05	.02	.01
☐ 126	Cory Snyder	.05	.02	.01
☐ 127	George Bell	.05	.02	.01
☐ 128	Mark Grace	.20	.09	.03
☐ 129	Devon White	.10	.05	.01
☐ 130	Tony Fernandez	.10	.05	.01
☐ 131	Don Aase	.05	.02	.01
☐ 132	Rance Mulliniks	.05	.02	.01
☐ 133	Marty Barrett	.05	.02	.01
☐ 134	Nelson Liriano	.05	.02	.01
☐ 135	Mark Carreon	.05	.02	.01
☐ 136	Candy Maldonado	.05	.02	.01
☐ 137	Tim Birtsas	.05	.02	.01
☐ 138	Tom Brookens	.05	.02	.01
☐ 139	John Franco	.20	.09	.03
☐ 140	Mike LaCoss	.05	.02	.01
☐ 141	Jeff Treadway	.05	.02	.01
☐ 142	Pat Tabler	.05	.02	.01
☐ 143	Darrell Evans	.10	.05	.01
☐ 144	Rafael Ramirez	.05	.02	.01
☐ 145	Oddibe McDowell UER (Misspelled Odibbe)	.05	.02	.01
☐ 146	Brian Downing	.05	.02	.01
☐ 147	Curt Wilkerson	.05	.02	.01
☐ 148	Ernie Whitt	.05	.02	.01
☐ 149	Bill Schroeder	.05	.02	.01
☐ 150	Domingo Ramos UER (Says throws right, but shows him throwing lefty)	.05	.02	.01
☐ 151	Rick Honeycutt	.05	.02	.01
☐ 152	Don Slaught	.05	.02	.01
☐ 153	Mitch Webster	.05	.02	.01
☐ 154	Tony Phillips	.20	.09	.03
☐ 155	Paul Kilgus	.05	.02	.01
☐ 156	Ken Griffey Jr. UER (Simultaniously)	4.00	1.80	.50
☐ 157	Gary Sheffield	.30	.14	.04
☐ 158	Wally Backman	.05	.02	.01
☐ 159	B.J. Surhoff	.10	.05	.01
☐ 160	Louie Meadows	.05	.02	.01
☐ 161	Paul O'Neill	.20	.09	.03
☐ 162	Jeff McKnight	.05	.02	.01
☐ 163	Alvaro Espinoza	.05	.02	.01
☐ 164	Scott Scudder	.05	.02	.01
☐ 165	Jeff Reed	.05	.02	.01
☐ 166	Gregg Jefferies	.20	.09	.03
☐ 167	Barry Larkin	.40	.18	.05
☐ 168	Gary Carter	.20	.09	.03
☐ 169	Robby Thompson	.10	.05	.01
☐ 170	Rolando Roomes	.05	.02	.01
☐ 171	Mark McGwire UER (Total games 427 and hits 479, should be 467 and 427)	.20	.09	.03
☐ 172	Steve Sax	.05	.02	.01
☐ 173	Mark Williamson	.05	.02	.01
☐ 174	Mitch Williams	.10	.05	.01
☐ 175	Brian Holton	.05	.02	.01
☐ 176	Rob Deer	.05	.02	.01
☐ 177	Tim Raines	.20	.09	.03
☐ 178	Mike Felder	.05	.02	.01
☐ 179	Harold Reynolds	.05	.02	.01
☐ 180	Terry Francona	.05	.02	.01
☐ 181	Chris Sabo	.05	.02	.01
☐ 182	Darryl Strawberry	.10	.05	.01
☐ 183	Willie Randolph	.10	.05	.01
☐ 184	Bill Ripken	.05	.02	.01
☐ 185	Mackey Sasser	.05	.02	.01
☐ 186	Todd Benzinger	.05	.02	.01

☐ 187	Kevin Elster UER (16 homers in 1989, should be 10)	.05	.02	.01
☐ 188	Jose Uribe	.05	.02	.01
☐ 189	Tom Browning	.05	.02	.01
☐ 190	Keith Miller	.05	.02	.01
☐ 191	Don Mattingly	.75	.35	.09
☐ 192	Dave Parker	.10	.05	.01
☐ 193	Roberto Kelly UER (96 RBI, should be 62)	.10	.05	.01
☐ 194	Phil Bradley	.05	.02	.01
☐ 195	Ron Hassey	.05	.02	.01
☐ 196	Gerald Young	.05	.02	.01
☐ 197	Hubie Brooks	.05	.02	.01
☐ 198	Bill Doran	.05	.02	.01
☐ 199	Al Newman	.05	.02	.01
☐ 200	Checklist 101-200	.05	.02	.01
☐ 201	Terry Puhl	.05	.02	.01
☐ 202	Frank DiPino	.05	.02	.01
☐ 203	Jim Clancy	.05	.02	.01
☐ 204	Bob Ojeda	.05	.02	.01
☐ 205	Alex Trevino	.05	.02	.01
☐ 206	Dave Henderson	.05	.02	.01
☐ 207	Henry Cotto	.05	.02	.01
☐ 208	Rafael Belliard UER (Born 1961, not 1951)	.05	.02	.01
☐ 209	Stan Javier	.05	.02	.01
☐ 210	Jerry Reed	.05	.02	.01
☐ 211	Doug Dascenzo	.05	.02	.01
☐ 212	Andres Thomas	.05	.02	.01
☐ 213	Greg Maddux	1.25	.55	.16
☐ 214	Mike Schooler	.05	.02	.01
☐ 215	Lonnie Smith	.05	.02	.01
☐ 216	Jose Rijo	.10	.05	.01
☐ 217	Greg Gagne	.05	.02	.01
☐ 218	Jim Gantner	.05	.02	.01
☐ 219	Allan Anderson	.05	.02	.01
☐ 220	Rick Mahler	.05	.02	.01
☐ 221	Jim Deshaies	.05	.02	.01
☐ 222	Keith Hernandez	.10	.05	.01
☐ 223	Vince Coleman	.10	.05	.01
☐ 224	David Cone	.20	.09	.03
☐ 225	Ozzie Smith	.40	.18	.05
☐ 226	Matt Nokes	.05	.02	.01
☐ 227	Barry Bonds	.60	.25	.07
☐ 228	Felix Jose	.05	.02	.01
☐ 229	Dennis Powell	.05	.02	.01
☐ 230	Mike Gallego	.05	.02	.01
☐ 231	Shawon Dunston UER ('89 stats are Andre Dawson's)	.05	.02	.01
☐ 232	Ron Gant	.20	.09	.03
☐ 233	Omar Vizquel	.10	.05	.01
☐ 234	Derek Lilliquist	.05	.02	.01
☐ 235	Erik Hanson	.05	.02	.01
☐ 236	Kirby Puckett UER (824 games, should be 924)	.60	.25	.07
☐ 237	Bill Spiers	.05	.02	.01
☐ 238	Dan Gladden	.05	.02	.01
☐ 239	Bryan Clutterbuck	.05	.02	.01
☐ 240	John Moses	.05	.02	.01
☐ 241	Ron Darling	.05	.02	.01
☐ 242	Joe Magrane	.05	.02	.01
☐ 243	Dave Magadan	.05	.02	.01
☐ 244	Pedro Guerrero UER (Misspelled Guererro)	.10	.05	.01
☐ 245	Glenn Davis	.05	.02	.01
☐ 246	Terry Steinbach	.10	.05	.01
☐ 247	Fred Lynn	.10	.05	.01
☐ 248	Gary Redus	.05	.02	.01
☐ 249	Ken Williams	.05	.02	.01
☐ 250	Sid Bream	.05	.02	.01
☐ 251	Bob Welch UER (2587 career strike-outs, should be 1587)	.05	.02	.01
☐ 252	Bill Buckner	.10	.05	.01
☐ 253	Carney Lansford	.10	.05	.01
☐ 254	Paul Molitor	.20	.09	.03
☐ 255	Jose DeJesus	.05	.02	.01
☐ 256	Orel Hershiser	.20	.09	.03
☐ 257	Tom Brunansky	.05	.02	.01
☐ 258	Mike Davis	.05	.02	.01
☐ 259	Jeff Ballard	.05	.02	.01
☐ 260	Scott Terry	.05	.02	.01
☐ 261	Sid Fernandez	.10	.05	.01
☐ 262	Mike Marshall	.05	.02	.01
☐ 263	Howard Johnson UER (192 SO, should be 592)	.10	.05	.01
☐ 264	Kirk Gibson UER (659 runs, should be 669)	.20	.09	.03
☐ 265	Kevin McReynolds	.05	.02	.01
☐ 266	Cal Ripken	1.50	.70	.19
☐ 267	Ozzie Guillen UER (Career triples 27, should be 29)	.10	.05	.01
☐ 268	Jim Traber	.05	.02	.01
☐ 269	Bobby Thigpen UER (31 saves in 1989, should be 34)	.05	.02	.01
☐ 270	Joe Orsulak	.05	.02	.01
☐ 271	Bob Boone	.10	.05	.01
☐ 272	Dave Stewart UER (Totals wrong due to omission of '86 stats)	.20	.09	.03
☐ 273	Tim Wallach	.05	.02	.01
☐ 274	Luis Aquino UER (Says throws lefty, but shows him throwing righty)	.05	.02	.01
☐ 275	Mike Moore	.05	.02	.01
☐ 276	Tony Pena	.05	.02	.01
☐ 277	Eddie Murray UER (Several typos in career total stats)	.50	.23	.06
☐ 278	Milt Thompson	.05	.02	.01
☐ 279	Alejandro Pena	.05	.02	.01
☐ 280	Ken Dayley	.05	.02	.01
☐ 281	Carmen Castillo	.05	.02	.01
☐ 282	Tom Henke	.10	.05	.01
☐ 283	Mickey Hatcher	.05	.02	.01
☐ 284	Roy Smith	.05	.02	.01
☐ 285	Manny Lee	.05	.02	.01
☐ 286	Dan Pasqua	.05	.02	.01
☐ 287	Larry Sheets	.05	.02	.01
☐ 288	Garry Templeton	.05	.02	.01
☐ 289	Eddie Williams	.05	.02	.01
☐ 290	Brady Anderson UER (Home: Silver Springs, not Siver Springs)	.10	.05	.01
☐ 291	Spike Owen	.05	.02	.01
☐ 292	Storm Davis	.05	.02	.01
☐ 293	Chris Bosio	.05	.02	.01
☐ 294	Jim Eisenreich	.05	.02	.01
☐ 295	Don August	.05	.02	.01
☐ 296	Jeff Hamilton	.05	.02	.01
☐ 297	Mickey Tettleton	.10	.05	.01
☐ 298	Mike Scioscia	.05	.02	.01
☐ 299	Kevin Hickey	.05	.02	.01
☐ 300	Checklist 201-300	.05	.02	.01
☐ 301	Shawn Abner	.05	.02	.01

☐ 302	Kevin Bass	.05	.02	.01
☐ 303	Bip Roberts	.10	.05	.01
☐ 304	Joe Girardi	.05	.02	.01
☐ 305	Danny Darwin	.05	.02	.01
☐ 306	Mike Heath	.05	.02	.01
☐ 307	Mike Macfarlane	.05	.02	.01
☐ 308	Ed Whitson	.05	.02	.01
☐ 309	Tracy Jones	.05	.02	.01
☐ 310	Scott Fletcher	.05	.02	.01
☐ 311	Darnell Coles	.05	.02	.01
☐ 312	Mike Brumley	.05	.02	.01
☐ 313	Bill Swift	.05	.02	.01
☐ 314	Charlie Hough	.10	.05	.01
☐ 315	Jim Presley	.05	.02	.01
☐ 316	Luis Polonia	.10	.05	.01
☐ 317	Mike Morgan	.05	.02	.01
☐ 318	Lee Guetterman	.05	.02	.01
☐ 319	Jose Oquendo	.05	.02	.01
☐ 320	Wayne Tolleson	.05	.02	.01
☐ 321	Jody Reed	.05	.02	.01
☐ 322	Damon Berryhill	.05	.02	.01
☐ 323	Roger Clemens	.30	.14	.04
☐ 324	Ryne Sandberg	.60	.25	.07
☐ 325	Benito Santiago UER	.10	.05	.01
	(Misspelled Santago on card back)			
☐ 326	Bret Saberhagen UER	.20	.09	.03
	(1140 hits, should be 1240; 56 CG, should be 52)			
☐ 327	Lou Whitaker	.20	.09	.03
☐ 328	Dave Gallagher	.05	.02	.01
☐ 329	Mike Pagliarulo	.05	.02	.01
☐ 330	Doyle Alexander	.05	.02	.01
☐ 331	Jeffrey Leonard	.05	.02	.01
☐ 332	Torey Lovullo	.05	.02	.01
☐ 333	Pete Incaviglia	.05	.02	.01
☐ 334	Rickey Henderson	.20	.09	.03
☐ 335	Rafael Palmeiro	.30	.14	.04
☐ 336	Ken Hill	.25	.11	.03
☐ 337	Dave Winfield UER	.20	.09	.03
	(1418 RBI, should be 1438)			
☐ 338	Alfredo Griffin	.05	.02	.01
☐ 339	Andy Hawkins	.05	.02	.01
☐ 340	Ted Power	.05	.02	.01
☐ 341	Steve Wilson	.05	.02	.01
☐ 342	Jack Clark UER	.10	.05	.01
	(916 BB, should be 1006; 1142 SO, should be 1130)			
☐ 343	Ellis Burks	.10	.05	.01
☐ 344	Tony Gwynn UER	.60	.25	.07
	(Doubles stats on card back are wrong)			
☐ 345	Jerome Walton UER	.05	.02	.01
	(Total At Bats 476, should be 475)			
☐ 346	Roberto Alomar UER	.60	.25	.07
	(61 doubles, should be 51)			
☐ 347	Carlos Martinez UER	.05	.02	.01
	(Born 8/11/64, should be 8/11/65)			
☐ 348	Chet Lemon	.05	.02	.01
☐ 349	Willie Wilson	.05	.02	.01
☐ 350	Greg Walker	.05	.02	.01
☐ 351	Tom Bolton	.05	.02	.01
☐ 352	German Gonzalez	.05	.02	.01
☐ 353	Harold Baines	.20	.09	.03
☐ 354	Mike Greenwell	.20	.09	.03
☐ 355	Ruben Sierra	.20	.09	.03
☐ 356	Andres Galarraga	.20	.09	.03
☐ 357	Andre Dawson	.20	.09	.03
☐ 358	Jeff Brantley	.05	.02	.01
☐ 359	Mike Bielecki	.05	.02	.01
☐ 360	Ken Oberkfell	.05	.02	.01
☐ 361	Kurt Stillwell	.05	.02	.01
☐ 362	Brian Holman	.05	.02	.01
☐ 363	Kevin Seitzer UER	.05	.02	.01
	(Career triples total does not add up)			
☐ 364	Alvin Davis	.05	.02	.01
☐ 365	Tom Gordon	.10	.05	.01
☐ 366	Bobby Bonilla UER	.20	.09	.03
	(Two steals in 1987, should be 3)			
☐ 367	Carlton Fisk	.20	.09	.03
☐ 368	Steve Carter UER	.05	.02	.01
	(Charlottesville)			
☐ 369	Joel Skinner	.05	.02	.01
☐ 370	John Cangelosi	.05	.02	.01
☐ 371	Cecil Espy	.05	.02	.01
☐ 372	Gary Wayne	.05	.02	.01
☐ 373	Jim Rice	.20	.09	.03
☐ 374	Mike Dyer	.05	.02	.01
☐ 375	Joe Carter	.20	.09	.03
☐ 376	Dwight Smith	.05	.02	.01
☐ 377	John Wetteland	.10	.05	.01
☐ 378	Earnie Riles	.05	.02	.01
☐ 379	Otis Nixon	.10	.05	.01
☐ 380	Vance Law	.05	.02	.01
☐ 381	Dave Bergman	.05	.02	.01
☐ 382	Frank White	.10	.05	.01
☐ 383	Scott Bradley	.05	.02	.01
☐ 384	Israel Sanchez UER	.05	.02	.01
	(Totals don't include '89 stats)			
☐ 385	Gary Pettis	.05	.02	.01
☐ 386	Donn Pall	.05	.02	.01
☐ 387	John Smiley	.05	.02	.01
☐ 388	Tom Candiotti	.05	.02	.01
☐ 389	Junior Ortiz	.05	.02	.01
☐ 390	Steve Lyons	.05	.02	.01
☐ 391	Brian Harper	.05	.02	.01
☐ 392	Fred Manrique	.05	.02	.01
☐ 393	Lee Smith	.20	.09	.03
☐ 394	Jeff Kunkel	.05	.02	.01
☐ 395	Claudell Washington	.05	.02	.01
☐ 396	John Tudor	.05	.02	.01
☐ 397	Terry Kennedy UER	.05	.02	.01
	(Career totals all wrong)			
☐ 398	Lloyd McClendon	.05	.02	.01
☐ 399	Craig Lefferts	.05	.02	.01
☐ 400	Checklist 301-400	.05	.02	.01
☐ 401	Keith Moreland	.05	.02	.01
☐ 402	Rich Gedman	.05	.02	.01
☐ 403	Jeff D. Robinson	.05	.02	.01
☐ 404	Randy Ready	.05	.02	.01
☐ 405	Rick Cerone	.05	.02	.01
☐ 406	Jeff Blauser	.10	.05	.01
☐ 407	Larry Andersen	.05	.02	.01
☐ 408	Joe Boever	.05	.02	.01
☐ 409	Felix Fermin	.05	.02	.01
☐ 410	Glenn Wilson	.05	.02	.01
☐ 411	Rex Hudler	.05	.02	.01
☐ 412	Mark Grant	.05	.02	.01
☐ 413	Dennis Martinez	.10	.05	.01
☐ 414	Darrin Jackson	.05	.02	.01
☐ 415	Mike Aldrete	.05	.02	.01
☐ 416	Roger McDowell	.05	.02	.01

☐ 417	Jeff Reardon	.20	.09	.03
☐ 418	Darren Daulton	.20	.09	.03
☐ 419	Tim Laudner	.05	.02	.01
☐ 420	Don Carman	.05	.02	.01
☐ 421	Lloyd Moseby	.05	.02	.01
☐ 422	Doug Drabek	.10	.05	.01
☐ 423	Lenny Harris UER	.05	.02	.01
	(Walks 2 in '89, should be 20)			
☐ 424	Jose Lind	.05	.02	.01
☐ 425	Dave Johnson (P)	.05	.02	.01
☐ 426	Jerry Browne	.05	.02	.01
☐ 427	Eric Yelding	.05	.02	.01
☐ 428	Brad Komminsk	.05	.02	.01
☐ 429	Jody Davis	.05	.02	.01
☐ 430	Mariano Duncan	.05	.02	.01
☐ 431	Mark Davis	.05	.02	.01
☐ 432	Nelson Santovenia	.05	.02	.01
☐ 433	Bruce Hurst	.05	.02	.01
☐ 434	Jeff Huson	.05	.02	.01
☐ 435	Chris James	.05	.02	.01
☐ 436	Mark Guthrie	.05	.02	.01
☐ 437	Charlie Hayes	.10	.05	.01
☐ 438	Shane Rawley	.05	.02	.01
☐ 439	Dickie Thon	.05	.02	.01
☐ 440	Juan Berenguer	.05	.02	.01
☐ 441	Kevin Romine	.05	.02	.01
☐ 442	Bill Landrum	.05	.02	.01
☐ 443	Todd Frohwirth	.05	.02	.01
☐ 444	Craig Worthington	.05	.02	.01
☐ 445	Fernando Valenzuela	.05	.02	.01
☐ 446	Joey Belle	2.00	.90	.25
☐ 447	Ed Whited UER	.05	.02	.01
	(Ashville, should be Asheville)			
☐ 448	Dave Smith	.05	.02	.01
☐ 449	Dave Clark	.05	.02	.01
☐ 450	Juan Agosto	.05	.02	.01
☐ 451	Dave Valle	.05	.02	.01
☐ 452	Kent Hrbek	.10	.05	.01
☐ 453	Von Hayes	.05	.02	.01
☐ 454	Gary Gaetti	.05	.02	.01
☐ 455	Greg Briley	.05	.02	.01
☐ 456	Glenn Braggs	.05	.02	.01
☐ 457	Kirt Manwaring	.05	.02	.01
☐ 458	Mel Hall	.05	.02	.01
☐ 459	Brook Jacoby	.05	.02	.01
☐ 460	Pat Sheridan	.05	.02	.01
☐ 461	Rob Murphy	.05	.02	.01
☐ 462	Jimmy Key	.10	.05	.01
☐ 463	Nick Esasky	.05	.02	.01
☐ 464	Rob Ducey	.05	.02	.01
☐ 465	Carlos Quintana UER	.05	.02	.01
	(Internatinoal)			
☐ 466	Larry Walker	1.50	.70	.19
☐ 467	Todd Worrell	.05	.02	.01
☐ 468	Kevin Gross	.05	.02	.01
☐ 469	Terry Pendleton	.20	.09	.03
☐ 470	Dave Martinez	.05	.02	.01
☐ 471	Gene Larkin	.05	.02	.01
☐ 472	Len Dykstra UER	.20	.09	.03
	('89 and total runs understated by 10)			
☐ 473	Barry Lyons	.05	.02	.01
☐ 474	Terry Mulholland	.10	.05	.01
☐ 475	Chip Hale	.05	.02	.01
☐ 476	Jesse Barfield	.05	.02	.01
☐ 477	Dan Plesac	.05	.02	.01
☐ 478A	Scott Garrelts ERR	2.00	.90	.25
	(Photo actually Bill Bathe)			
☐ 478B	Scott Garrelts COR	.05	.02	.01
☐ 479	Dave Righetti	.05	.02	.01
☐ 480	Gus Polidor UER	.05	.02	.01
	(Wearing 14 on front, but 10 on back)			
☐ 481	Mookie Wilson	.05	.02	.01
☐ 482	Luis Rivera	.05	.02	.01
☐ 483	Mike Flanagan	.05	.02	.01
☐ 484	Dennis Boyd	.05	.02	.01
☐ 485	John Cerutti	.05	.02	.01
☐ 486	John Costello	.05	.02	.01
☐ 487	Pascual Perez	.05	.02	.01
☐ 488	Tommy Herr	.05	.02	.01
☐ 489	Tom Foley	.05	.02	.01
☐ 490	Curt Ford	.05	.02	.01
☐ 491	Steve Lake	.05	.02	.01
☐ 492	Tim Teufel	.05	.02	.01
☐ 493	Randy Bush	.05	.02	.01
☐ 494	Mike Jackson	.05	.02	.01
☐ 495	Steve Jeltz	.05	.02	.01
☐ 496	Paul Gibson	.05	.02	.01
☐ 497	Steve Balboni	.05	.02	.01
☐ 498	Bud Black	.05	.02	.01
☐ 499	Dale Sveum	.05	.02	.01
☐ 500	Checklist 401-500	.05	.02	.01
☐ 501	Tim Jones	.05	.02	.01
☐ 502	Mark Portugal	.05	.02	.01
☐ 503	Ivan Calderon	.05	.02	.01
☐ 504	Rick Rhoden	.05	.02	.01
☐ 505	Willie McGee	.10	.05	.01
☐ 506	Kirk McCaskill	.05	.02	.01
☐ 507	Dave LaPoint	.05	.02	.01
☐ 508	Jay Howell	.05	.02	.01
☐ 509	Johnny Ray	.05	.02	.01
☐ 510	Dave Anderson	.05	.02	.01
☐ 511	Chuck Crim	.05	.02	.01
☐ 512	Joe Hesketh	.05	.02	.01
☐ 513	Dennis Eckersley	.20	.09	.03
☐ 514	Greg Brock	.05	.02	.01
☐ 515	Tim Burke	.05	.02	.01
☐ 516	Frank Tanana	.05	.02	.01
☐ 517	Jay Bell	.10	.05	.01
☐ 518	Guillermo Hernandez	.05	.02	.01
☐ 519	Randy Kramer UER	.05	.02	.01
	(Codiroli misspelled as Codoroli)			
☐ 520	Charles Hudson	.05	.02	.01
☐ 521	Jim Corsi	.05	.02	.01
	(Word "originally" is misspelled on back)			
☐ 522	Steve Rosenberg	.05	.02	.01
☐ 523	Cris Carpenter	.05	.02	.01
☐ 524	Matt Winters	.05	.02	.01
☐ 525	Melido Perez	.05	.02	.01
☐ 526	Chris Gwynn UER	.05	.02	.01
	(Albequergue)			
☐ 527	Bert Blyleven UER	.20	.09	.03
	(Games career total is wrong, should be 644)			
☐ 528	Chuck Cary	.05	.02	.01
☐ 529	Daryl Boston	.05	.02	.01
☐ 530	Dale Mohorcic	.05	.02	.01
☐ 531	Geronimo Berroa	.10	.05	.01
☐ 532	Edgar Martinez	.20	.09	.03
☐ 533	Dale Murphy	.20	.09	.03
☐ 534	Jay Buhner	.20	.09	.03
☐ 535	John Smoltz UER	.20	.09	.03
	(HEA Stadium)			
☐ 536	Andy Van Slyke	.10	.05	.01
☐ 537	Mike Henneman	.05	.02	.01
☐ 538	Miguel Garcia	.05	.02	.01

☐ 539	Frank Williams	.05	.02	.01
☐ 540	R.J. Reynolds	.05	.02	.01
☐ 541	Shawn Hillegas	.05	.02	.01
☐ 542	Walt Weiss	.10	.05	.01
☐ 543	Greg Hibbard	.05	.02	.01
☐ 544	Nolan Ryan	1.50	.70	.19
☐ 545	Todd Zeile	.10	.05	.01
☐ 546	Hensley Meulens	.05	.02	.01
☐ 547	Tim Belcher	.05	.02	.01
☐ 548	Mike Witt	.05	.02	.01
☐ 549	Greg Cadaret UER	.05	.02	.01
	(Aquiring, should			
	be Acquiring)			
☐ 550	Franklin Stubbs	.05	.02	.01
☐ 551	Tony Castillo	.05	.02	.01
☐ 552	Jeff M. Robinson	.05	.02	.01
☐ 553	Steve Olin	.10	.05	.01
☐ 554	Alan Trammell	.20	.09	.03
☐ 555	Wade Boggs 4X	.20	.09	.03
	(Bo Jackson			
	in background)			
☐ 556	Will Clark	.40	.18	.05
☐ 557	Jeff King	.10	.05	.01
☐ 558	Mike Fitzgerald	.05	.02	.01
☐ 559	Ken Howell	.05	.02	.01
☐ 560	Bob Kipper	.05	.02	.01
☐ 561	Scott Bankhead	.05	.02	.01
☐ 562A	Jeff Innis ERR	2.00	.90	.25
	(Photo actually			
	David West)			
☐ 562B	Jeff Innis COR	.05	.02	.01
☐ 563	Randy Johnson	.75	.35	.09
☐ 564	Wally Whitehurst	.05	.02	.01
☐ 565	Gene Harris	.05	.02	.01
☐ 566	Norm Charlton	.10	.05	.01
☐ 567	Robin Yount UER	.40	.18	.05
	(7602 career hits,			
	should be 2606)			
☐ 568	Joe Oliver UER	.05	.02	.01
	(Fl.orida)			
☐ 569	Mark Parent	.05	.02	.01
☐ 570	John Farrell UER	.05	.02	.01
	(Loss total added wrong)			
☐ 571	Tom Glavine	.50	.23	.06
☐ 572	Rod Nichols	.05	.02	.01
☐ 573	Jack Morris	.20	.09	.03
☐ 574	Greg Swindell	.10	.05	.01
☐ 575	Steve Searcy	.05	.02	.01
☐ 576	Ricky Jordan	.05	.02	.01
☐ 577	Matt Williams	.60	.25	.07
☐ 578	Mike LaValliere	.05	.02	.01
☐ 579	Bryn Smith	.05	.02	.01
☐ 580	Bruce Ruffin	.05	.02	.01
☐ 581	Randy Myers	.20	.09	.03
☐ 582	Rick Wrona	.05	.02	.01
☐ 583	Juan Samuel	.05	.02	.01
☐ 584	Les Lancaster	.05	.02	.01
☐ 585	Jeff Musselman	.05	.02	.01
☐ 586	Rob Dibble	.10	.05	.01
☐ 587	Eric Show	.05	.02	.01
☐ 588	Jesse Orosco	.05	.02	.01
☐ 589	Herm Winningham	.05	.02	.01
☐ 590	Andy Allanson	.05	.02	.01
☐ 591	Dion James	.05	.02	.01
☐ 592	Carmelo Martinez	.05	.02	.01
☐ 593	Luis Quinones	.05	.02	.01
☐ 594	Dennis Rasmussen	.05	.02	.01
☐ 595	Rich Yett	.05	.02	.01
☐ 596	Bob Walk	.05	.02	.01
☐ 597A	Andy McGaffigan ERR	.15	.07	.02
	(Photo actually			

	Rich Thompson)			
☐ 597B	Andy McGaffigan COR	.05	.02	.01
☐ 598	Billy Hatcher	.05	.02	.01
☐ 599	Bob Knepper	.05	.02	.01
☐ 600	Checklist 501-600 UER	.05	.02	.01
	(599 Bob Kneppers)			
☐ 601	Joey Cora	.10	.05	.01
☐ 602	Steve Finley	.10	.05	.01
☐ 603	Kal Daniels UER	.05	.02	.01
	(12 hits in '87, should			
	be 123; 335 runs,			
	should be 235)			
☐ 604	Gregg Olson	.05	.02	.01
☐ 605	Dave Stieb	.10	.05	.01
☐ 606	Kenny Rogers	.05	.02	.01
	(Shown catching			
	football)			
☐ 607	Zane Smith	.05	.02	.01
☐ 608	Bob Geren UER	.05	.02	.01
	(Originally)			
☐ 609	Chad Kreuter	.05	.02	.01
☐ 610	Mike Smithson	.05	.02	.01
☐ 611	Jeff Wetherby	.05	.02	.01
☐ 612	Gary Mielke	.05	.02	.01
☐ 613	Pete Smith	.05	.02	.01
☐ 614	Jack Daugherty UER	.05	.02	.01
	(Born 7/30/60, should			
	be 7/3/60; originally)			
☐ 615	Lance McCullers	.05	.02	.01
☐ 616	Don Robinson	.05	.02	.01
☐ 617	Jose Guzman	.05	.02	.01
☐ 618	Steve Bedrosian	.05	.02	.01
☐ 619	Jamie Moyer	.05	.02	.01
☐ 620	Atlee Hammaker	.05	.02	.01
☐ 621	Rick Luecken UER	.05	.02	.01
	(Innings pitched wrong)			
☐ 622	Greg W. Harris	.05	.02	.01
☐ 623	Pete Harnisch	.10	.05	.01
☐ 624	Jerald Clark	.05	.02	.01
☐ 625	Jack McDowell UER	.20	.09	.03
	(Career totals for Games			
	and GS don't include			
	1987 season)			
☐ 626	Frank Viola	.10	.05	.01
☐ 627	Teddy Higuera	.05	.02	.01
☐ 628	Marty Pevey	.05	.02	.01
☐ 629	Bill Wegman	.05	.02	.01
☐ 630	Eric Plunk	.05	.02	.01
☐ 631	Drew Hall	.05	.02	.01
☐ 632	Doug Jones	.05	.02	.01
☐ 633	Geno Petralli UER	.05	.02	.01
	(Sacremento)			
☐ 634	Jose Alvarez	.05	.02	.01
☐ 635	Bob Milacki	.05	.02	.01
☐ 636	Bobby Witt	.05	.02	.01
☐ 637	Trevor Wilson	.05	.02	.01
☐ 638	Jeff Russell UER	.05	.02	.01
	(Shutout stats wrong)			
☐ 639	Mike Krukow	.05	.02	.01
☐ 640	Rick Leach	.05	.02	.01
☐ 641	Dave Schmidt	.05	.02	.01
☐ 642	Terry Leach	.05	.02	.01
☐ 643	Calvin Schiraldi	.05	.02	.01
☐ 644	Bob Melvin	.05	.02	.01
☐ 645	Jim Abbott	.20	.09	.03
☐ 646	Jaime Navarro	.05	.02	.01
☐ 647	Mark Langston UER	.20	.09	.03
	(Several errors in			
	stats totals)			
☐ 648	Juan Nieves	.05	.02	.01
☐ 649	Damaso Garcia	.05	.02	.01

☐ 650	Charlie O'Brien	.05	.02	.01
☐ 651	Eric King	.05	.02	.01
☐ 652	Mike Boddicker	.05	.02	.01
☐ 653	Duane Ward	.05	.02	.01
☐ 654	Bob Stanley	.05	.02	.01
☐ 655	Sandy Alomar Jr.	.10	.05	.01
☐ 656	Danny Tartabull UER	.10	.05	.01
	(395 BB, should be 295)			
☐ 657	Randy McCament	.05	.02	.01
☐ 658	Charlie Leibrandt	.05	.02	.01
☐ 659	Dan Quisenberry	.05	.02	.01
☐ 660	Paul Assenmacher	.05	.02	.01
☐ 661	Walt Terrell	.05	.02	.01
☐ 662	Tim Leary	.05	.02	.01
☐ 663	Randy Milligan	.05	.02	.01
☐ 664	Bo Diaz	.05	.02	.01
☐ 665	Mark Lemke UER	.10	.05	.01
	(Richmond misspelled as Richomond)			
☐ 666	Jose Gonzalez	.05	.02	.01
☐ 667	Chuck Finley UER	.10	.05	.01
	(Born 11/16/62, should be 11/26/62)			
☐ 668	John Kruk	.20	.09	.03
☐ 669	Dick Schofield	.05	.02	.01
☐ 670	Tim Crews	.05	.02	.01
☐ 671	John Dopson	.05	.02	.01
☐ 672	John Orton	.05	.02	.01
☐ 673	Eric Hetzel	.05	.02	.01
☐ 674	Lance Parrish	.10	.05	.01
☐ 675	Ramon Martinez	.20	.09	.03
☐ 676	Mark Gubicza	.05	.02	.01
☐ 677	Greg Litton	.05	.02	.01
☐ 678	Greg Mathews	.05	.02	.01
☐ 679	Dave Dravecky	.10	.05	.01
☐ 680	Steve Farr	.05	.02	.01
☐ 681	Mike Devereaux	.10	.05	.01
☐ 682	Ken Griffey Sr.	.10	.05	.01
☐ 683A	Mickey Weston ERR	2.00	.90	.25
	(Listed as Jamie on card)			
☐ 683B	Mickey Weston COR	.05	.02	.01
	(Technically still an error as birthdate is listed as 3/26/81)			
☐ 684	Jack Armstrong	.05	.02	.01
☐ 685	Steve Buechele	.05	.02	.01
☐ 686	Bryan Harvey	.10	.05	.01
☐ 687	Lance Blankenship	.05	.02	.01
☐ 688	Dante Bichette	.60	.25	.07
☐ 689	Todd Burns	.05	.02	.01
☐ 690	Dan Petry	.05	.02	.01
☐ 691	Kent Anderson	.05	.02	.01
☐ 692	Todd Stottlemyre	.10	.05	.01
☐ 693	Wally Joyner UER	.20	.09	.03
	(Several stats errors)			
☐ 694	Mike Rochford	.05	.02	.01
☐ 695	Floyd Bannister	.05	.02	.01
☐ 696	Rick Reuschel	.05	.02	.01
☐ 697	Jose DeLeon	.05	.02	.01
☐ 698	Jeff Montgomery	.10	.05	.01
☐ 699	Kelly Downs	.05	.02	.01
☐ 700A	Checklist 601-700	2.00	.90	.25
	(683 Jamie Weston)			
☐ 700B	Checklist 601-700	.05	.02	.01
	(683 Mickey Weston)			
☐ 701	Jim Gott	.05	.02	.01
☐ 702	Rookie Threats	.75	.35	.09
	Delino DeShields			
	Marquis Grissom			
	Larry Walker			
☐ 703	Alejandro Pena	.05	.02	.01
☐ 704	Willie Randolph	.10	.05	.01
☐ 705	Tim Leary	.05	.02	.01
☐ 706	Chuck McElroy	.05	.02	.01
☐ 707	Gerald Perry	.05	.02	.01
☐ 708	Tom Brunansky	.05	.02	.01
☐ 709	John Franco	.20	.09	.03
☐ 710	Mark Davis	.05	.02	.01
☐ 711	David Justice	1.50	.70	.19
☐ 712	Storm Davis	.05	.02	.01
☐ 713	Scott Ruskin	.05	.02	.01
☐ 714	Glenn Braggs	.05	.02	.01
☐ 715	Kevin Bearse	.05	.02	.01
☐ 716	Jose Nunez	.05	.02	.01
☐ 717	Tim Layana	.05	.02	.01
☐ 718	Greg Myers	.05	.02	.01
☐ 719	Pete O'Brien	.05	.02	.01
☐ 720	John Candelaria	.05	.02	.01
☐ 721	Craig Grebeck	.05	.02	.01
☐ 722	Shawn Boskie	.05	.02	.01
☐ 723	Jim Leyritz	.05	.02	.01
☐ 724	Bill Sampen	.05	.02	.01
☐ 725	Scott Radinsky	.10	.05	.01
☐ 726	Todd Hundley	.10	.05	.01
☐ 727	Scott Hemond	.05	.02	.01
☐ 728	Lenny Webster	.05	.02	.01
☐ 729	Jeff Reardon	.20	.09	.03
☐ 730	Mitch Webster	.05	.02	.01
☐ 731	Brian Bohanon	.05	.02	.01
☐ 732	Rick Parker	.05	.02	.01
☐ 733	Terry Shumpert	.05	.02	.01
☐ 734A	Ryan's 6th No-Hitter	5.00	2.20	.60
	(No stripe on front)			
☐ 734B	Ryan's 6th No-Hitter	.75	.35	.09
	(stripe added on card front for 300th win)			
☐ 735	John Burkett	.10	.05	.01
☐ 736	Derrick May	.20	.09	.03
☐ 737	Carlos Baerga	3.00	1.35	.35
☐ 738	Greg Smith	.05	.02	.01
☐ 739	Scott Sanderson	.05	.02	.01
☐ 740	Joe Kraemer	.05	.02	.01
☐ 741	Hector Villanueva	.05	.02	.01
☐ 742	Mike Fetters	.05	.02	.01
☐ 743	Mark Gardner	.05	.02	.01
☐ 744	Matt Nokes	.05	.02	.01
☐ 745	Dave Winfield	.20	.09	.03
☐ 746	Delino DeShields	.25	.11	.03
☐ 747	Dann Howitt	.05	.02	.01
☐ 748	Tony Pena	.05	.02	.01
☐ 749	Oil Can Boyd	.05	.02	.01
☐ 750	Mike Benjamin	.05	.02	.01
☐ 751	Alex Cole	.05	.02	.01
☐ 752	Eric Gunderson	.05	.02	.01
☐ 753	Howard Farmer	.05	.02	.01
☐ 754	Joe Carter	.30	.14	.04
☐ 755	Ray Lankford	1.00	.45	.12
☐ 756	Sandy Alomar Jr.	.10	.05	.01
☐ 757	Alex Sanchez	.05	.02	.01
☐ 758	Nick Esasky	.05	.02	.01
☐ 759	Stan Belinda	.05	.02	.01
☐ 760	Jim Presley	.05	.02	.01
☐ 761	Gary DiSarcina	.30	.14	.04
☐ 762	Wayne Edwards	.05	.02	.01
☐ 763	Pat Combs	.05	.02	.01
☐ 764	Mickey Pina	.05	.02	.01
☐ 765	Wilson Alvarez	.30	.14	.04
☐ 766	Dave Parker	.10	.05	.01
☐ 767	Mike Blowers	.40	.18	.05
☐ 768	Tony Phillips	.20	.09	.03
☐ 769	Pascual Perez	.05	.02	.01

☐ 770	Gary Pettis	.05	.02	.01
☐ 771	Fred Lynn	.10	.05	.01
☐ 772	Mel Rojas	.20	.09	.03
☐ 773	David Segui	.20	.09	.03
☐ 774	Gary Carter	.20	.09	.03
☐ 775	Rafael Valdez	.05	.02	.01
☐ 776	Glenallen Hill	.05	.02	.01
☐ 777	Keith Hernandez	.10	.05	.01
☐ 778	Billy Hatcher	.05	.02	.01
☐ 779	Marty Clary	.05	.02	.01
☐ 780	Candy Maldonado	.05	.02	.01
☐ 781	Mike Marshall	.05	.02	.01
☐ 782	Billy Joe Robidoux	.05	.02	.01
☐ 783	Mark Langston	.20	.09	.03
☐ 784	Paul Sorrento	.40	.18	.05
☐ 785	Dave Hollins	.20	.09	.03
☐ 786	Cecil Fielder	.20	.09	.03
☐ 787	Matt Young	.05	.02	.01
☐ 788	Jeff Huson	.05	.02	.01
☐ 789	Lloyd Moseby	.05	.02	.01
☐ 790	Ron Kittle	.05	.02	.01
☐ 791	Hubie Brooks	.05	.02	.01
☐ 792	Craig Lefferts	.05	.02	.01
☐ 793	Kevin Bass	.05	.02	.01
☐ 794	Bryn Smith	.05	.02	.01
☐ 795	Juan Samuel	.05	.02	.01
☐ 796	Sam Horn	.05	.02	.01
☐ 797	Randy Myers	.20	.09	.03
☐ 798	Chris James	.05	.02	.01
☐ 799	Bill Gullickson	.05	.02	.01
☐ 800	Checklist 701-800	.05	.02	.01

1991 Upper Deck

This set marked the third year Upper Deck has issued a 700-card set in January. The cards measure 2 1/2" by 3 1/2". The set features 26 star rookies to lead off the set as well as other special cards featuring multi-players. The set is made on the typical Upper Deck card stock and features full-color photos on both the front and the back. The team checklist (TC) cards in the set feature an attractive Vernon Wells drawing of a featured player for that particular team. A special Michael Jordan card (numbered SP1) was randomly included in packs on a somewhat limited basis; this Jordan card is not included in the set price below. The Hank Aaron hologram card was randomly inserted in the 1991 Upper Deck high number foil packs. The 100-card extended or high-number series was issued by Upper

Deck several months after the release of their first series. The extended series features rookie players as well as players who switched teams between seasons. In the extended wax packs were low number cards, special cards featuring Hank Aaron as the next featured player in their baseball heroes series, and a special card honoring the May 1st exploits of Rickey Henderson and Nolan Ryan. For the first time in Upper Deck's three-year history, they did not issue a factory Extended set. Rookie Cards in this set include Jeff Bagwell, Wes Chamberlain, Jeff Conine, Wilfredo Cordero, Luis Gonzalez, Chipper Jones, Eric Karros, Brian McRae, Orlando Merced, Pedro Munoz, Mike Mussina, Phil Plantier, Reggie Sanders, and Todd Van Poppel.

	MINT	NRMT	EXC
COMPLETE SET (800)	20.00	9.00	2.50
COMPLETE FACT.SET (800)	20.00	9.00	2.50
COMPLETE LO SET (700)	16.00	7.25	2.00
COMPLETE HI SET (100)	4.00	1.80	.50
COMMON CARD (1-800)	.05	.02	.01

☐ 1	Star Rookie Checklist	.05	.02	.01
☐ 2	Phil Plantier	.20	.09	.03
☐ 3	D.J. Dozier	.05	.02	.01
☐ 4	Dave Hansen	.05	.02	.01
☐ 5	Maurice Vaughn	.60	.25	.07
☐ 6	Leo Gomez	.05	.02	.01
☐ 7	Scott Aldred	.05	.02	.01
☐ 8	Scott Chiamparino	.05	.02	.01
☐ 9	Lance Dickson	.05	.02	.01
☐ 10	Sean Berry	.10	.05	.01
☐ 11	Bernie Williams	.15	.07	.02
☐ 12	Brian Barnes UER	.05	.02	.01
	(Photo either not him			
	or in wrong jersey)			
☐ 13	Narciso Elvira	.05	.02	.01
☐ 14	Mike Gardiner	.05	.02	.01
☐ 15	Greg Colbrunn	.25	.11	.03
☐ 16	Bernard Gilkey	.10	.05	.01
☐ 17	Mark Lewis	.05	.02	.01
☐ 18	Mickey Morandini	.05	.02	.01
☐ 19	Charles Nagy	.10	.05	.01
☐ 20	Geronimo Pena	.05	.02	.01
☐ 21	Henry Rodriguez	.10	.05	.01
☐ 22	Scott Cooper	.05	.02	.01
☐ 23	Andujar Cedeno UER	.05	.02	.01
	(Shown batting left,			
	back says right)			
☐ 24	Eric Karros	.75	.35	.09
☐ 25	Steve Decker UER	.05	.02	.01
	(Lewis-Clark State			
	College, not Lewis			
	and Clark)			
☐ 26	Kevin Belcher	.05	.02	.01
☐ 27	Jeff Conine	.75	.35	.09
☐ 28	Dave Stewart TC	.10	.05	.01
☐ 29	Carlton Fisk TC	.10	.05	.01
☐ 30	Rafael Palmeiro TC	.10	.05	.01
☐ 31	Chuck Finley TC	.05	.02	.01
☐ 32	Harold Reynolds TC	.05	.02	.01
☐ 33	Bret Saberhagen TC	.10	.05	.01
☐ 34	Gary Gaetti TC	.05	.02	.01
☐ 35	Scott Leius	.05	.02	.01
☐ 36	Neal Heaton	.05	.02	.01
☐ 37	Terry Lee	.05	.02	.01
☐ 38	Gary Redus	.05	.02	.01

☐ 39	Barry Jones	.05	.02	.01
☐ 40	Chuck Knoblauch	.30	.14	.04
☐ 41	Larry Andersen	.05	.02	.01
☐ 42	Darryl Hamilton	.10	.05	.01
☐ 43	Mike Greenwell TC	.10	.05	.01
☐ 44	Kelly Gruber TC	.05	.02	.01
☐ 45	Jack Morris TC	.10	.05	.01
☐ 46	Sandy Alomar Jr. TC	.05	.02	.01
☐ 47	Gregg Olson TC	.05	.02	.01
☐ 48	Dave Parker TC	.05	.02	.01
☐ 49	Roberto Kelly TC	.05	.02	.01
☐ 50	Top Prospect Checklist	.05	.02	.01
☐ 51	Kyle Abbott	.05	.02	.01
☐ 52	Jeff Juden	.05	.02	.01
☐ 53	Todd Van Poppel UER	.10	.05	.01
	(Born Arlington and			
	attended John Martin HS,			
	should say Hinsdale and			
	James Martin HS)			
☐ 54	Steve Karsay	.10	.05	.01
☐ 55	Chipper Jones	4.00	1.80	.50
☐ 56	Chris Johnson UER	.05	.02	.01
	(Called Tim on back)			
☐ 57	John Ericks	.05	.02	.01
☐ 58	Gary Scott	.05	.02	.01
☐ 59	Kiki Jones	.05	.02	.01
☐ 60	Wil Cordero	.50	.23	.06
☐ 61	Royce Clayton	.10	.05	.01
☐ 62	Tim Costo	.05	.02	.01
☐ 63	Roger Salkeld	.05	.02	.01
☐ 64	Brook Fordyce	.05	.02	.01
☐ 65	Mike Mussina	1.25	.55	.16
☐ 66	Dave Staton	.05	.02	.01
☐ 67	Mike Lieberthal	.10	.05	.01
☐ 68	Kurt Miller	.05	.02	.01
☐ 69	Dan Peltier	.05	.02	.01
☐ 70	Greg Blosser	.05	.02	.01
☐ 71	Reggie Sanders	.75	.35	.09
☐ 72	Brent Mayne	.05	.02	.01
☐ 73	Rico Brogna	.15	.07	.02
☐ 74	Willie Banks	.05	.02	.01
☐ 75	Len Brutcher	.05	.02	.01
☐ 76	Pat Kelly	.10	.05	.01
☐ 77	Chris Sabo TC	.05	.02	.01
☐ 78	Ramon Martinez TC	.10	.05	.01
☐ 79	Matt Williams TC	.10	.05	.01
☐ 80	Roberto Alomar TC	.10	.05	.01
☐ 81	Glenn Davis TC	.05	.02	.01
☐ 82	Ron Gant TC	.10	.05	.01
☐ 83	Fielder's Feat	.10	.05	.01
	Cecil Fielder			
☐ 84	Orlando Merced	.20	.09	.03
☐ 85	Domingo Ramos	.05	.02	.01
☐ 86	Tom Bolton	.05	.02	.01
☐ 87	Andres Santana	.05	.02	.01
☐ 88	John Dopson	.05	.02	.01
☐ 89	Kenny Williams	.05	.02	.01
☐ 90	Marty Barrett	.05	.02	.01
☐ 91	Tom Pagnozzi	.05	.02	.01
☐ 92	Carmelo Martinez	.05	.02	.01
☐ 93	Bobby Thigpen	.05	.02	.01
	(Save Master)			
☐ 94	Barry Bonds TC	.20	.09	.03
☐ 95	Gregg Jefferies TC	.10	.05	.01
☐ 96	Tim Wallach TC	.05	.02	.01
☐ 97	Len Dykstra TC	.10	.05	.01
☐ 98	Pedro Guerrero TC	.05	.02	.01
☐ 99	Mark Grace TC	.15	.07	.02
☐ 100	Checklist 1-100	.05	.02	.01
☐ 101	Kevin Elster	.05	.02	.01
☐ 102	Tom Brookens	.05	.02	.01
☐ 103	Mackey Sasser	.05	.02	.01
☐ 104	Felix Fermin	.05	.02	.01
☐ 105	Kevin McReynolds	.05	.02	.01
☐ 106	Dave Stieb	.10	.05	.01
☐ 107	Jeffrey Leonard	.05	.02	.01
☐ 108	Dave Henderson	.05	.02	.01
☐ 109	Sid Bream	.05	.02	.01
☐ 110	Henry Cotto	.05	.02	.01
☐ 111	Shawon Dunston	.05	.02	.01
☐ 112	Mariano Duncan	.05	.02	.01
☐ 113	Joe Girardi	.05	.02	.01
☐ 114	Billy Hatcher	.05	.02	.01
☐ 115	Greg Maddux	.75	.35	.09
☐ 116	Jerry Browne	.05	.02	.01
☐ 117	Juan Samuel	.05	.02	.01
☐ 118	Steve Olin	.05	.02	.01
☐ 119	Alfredo Griffin	.05	.02	.01
☐ 120	Mitch Webster	.05	.02	.01
☐ 121	Joel Skinner	.05	.02	.01
☐ 122	Frank Viola	.05	.02	.01
☐ 123	Cory Snyder	.05	.02	.01
☐ 124	Howard Johnson	.05	.02	.01
☐ 125	Carlos Baerga	.50	.23	.06
☐ 126	Tony Fernandez	.05	.02	.01
☐ 127	Dave Stewart	.15	.07	.02
☐ 128	Jay Buhner	.15	.07	.02
☐ 129	Mike LaValliere	.05	.02	.01
☐ 130	Scott Bradley	.05	.02	.01
☐ 131	Tony Phillips	.15	.07	.02
☐ 132	Ryne Sandberg	.40	.18	.05
☐ 133	Paul O'Neill	.15	.07	.02
☐ 134	Mark Grace	.15	.07	.02
☐ 135	Chris Sabo	.05	.02	.01
☐ 136	Ramon Martinez	.10	.05	.01
☐ 137	Brook Jacoby	.05	.02	.01
☐ 138	Candy Maldonado	.05	.02	.01
☐ 139	Mike Scioscia	.05	.02	.01
☐ 140	Chris James	.05	.02	.01
☐ 141	Craig Worthington	.05	.02	.01
☐ 142	Manny Lee	.05	.02	.01
☐ 143	Tim Raines	.15	.07	.02
☐ 144	Sandy Alomar Jr.	.10	.05	.01
☐ 145	John Olerud	.10	.05	.01
☐ 146	Ozzie Canseco	.10	.05	.01
	(With Jose)			
☐ 147	Pat Borders	.05	.02	.01
☐ 148	Harold Reynolds	.05	.02	.01
☐ 149	Tom Henke	.10	.05	.01
☐ 150	R.J. Reynolds	.05	.02	.01
☐ 151	Mike Gallego	.05	.02	.01
☐ 152	Bobby Bonilla	.15	.07	.02
☐ 153	Terry Steinbach	.10	.05	.01
☐ 154	Barry Bonds	.40	.18	.05
☐ 155	Jose Canseco	.25	.11	.03
☐ 156	Gregg Jefferies	.15	.07	.02
☐ 157	Matt Williams	.40	.18	.05
☐ 158	Craig Biggio	.15	.07	.02
☐ 159	Daryl Boston	.05	.02	.01
☐ 160	Ricky Jordan	.05	.02	.01
☐ 161	Stan Belinda	.05	.02	.01
☐ 162	Ozzie Smith	.25	.11	.03
☐ 163	Tom Brunansky	.05	.02	.01
☐ 164	Todd Zeile	.10	.05	.01
☐ 165	Mike Greenwell	.15	.07	.02
☐ 166	Kal Daniels	.05	.02	.01
☐ 167	Kent Hrbek	.10	.05	.01
☐ 168	Franklin Stubbs	.05	.02	.01
☐ 169	Dick Schofield	.05	.02	.01
☐ 170	Junior Ortiz	.05	.02	.01
☐ 171	Hector Villanueva	.05	.02	.01
☐ 172	Dennis Eckersley	.15	.07	.02

☐ 173 Mitch Williams	.10	.05	.01
☐ 174 Mark McGwire	.15	.07	.02
☐ 175 Fernando Valenzuela 3X	.10	.05	.01
☐ 176 Gary Carter	.15	.07	.02
☐ 177 Dave Magadan	.05	.02	.01
☐ 178 Robby Thompson	.05	.02	.01
☐ 179 Bob Ojeda	.05	.02	.01
☐ 180 Ken Caminiti	.15	.07	.02
☐ 181 Don Slaught	.05	.02	.01
☐ 182 Luis Rivera	.05	.02	.01
☐ 183 Jay Bell	.10	.05	.01
☐ 184 Jody Reed	.05	.02	.01
☐ 185 Wally Backman	.05	.02	.01
☐ 186 Dave Martinez	.05	.02	.01
☐ 187 Luis Polonia	.05	.02	.01
☐ 188 Shane Mack	.05	.02	.01
☐ 189 Spike Owen	.05	.02	.01
☐ 190 Scott Bailes	.05	.02	.01
☐ 191 John Russell	.05	.02	.01
☐ 192 Walt Weiss	.05	.02	.01
☐ 193 Jose Oquendo	.05	.02	.01
☐ 194 Carney Lansford	.10	.05	.01
☐ 195 Jeff Huson	.05	.02	.01
☐ 196 Keith Miller	.05	.02	.01
☐ 197 Eric Yelding	.05	.02	.01
☐ 198 Ron Darling	.05	.02	.01
☐ 199 John Kruk	.15	.07	.02
☐ 200 Checklist 101-200	.05	.02	.01
☐ 201 John Shelby	.05	.02	.01
☐ 202 Bob Geren	.05	.02	.01
☐ 203 Lance McCullers	.05	.02	.01
☐ 204 Alvaro Espinoza	.05	.02	.01
☐ 205 Mark Salas	.05	.02	.01
☐ 206 Mike Pagliarulo	.05	.02	.01
☐ 207 Jose Uribe	.05	.02	.01
☐ 208 Jim Deshaies	.05	.02	.01
☐ 209 Ron Karkovice	.05	.02	.01
☐ 210 Rafael Ramirez	.05	.02	.01
☐ 211 Donnie Hill	.05	.02	.01
☐ 212 Brian Harper	.05	.02	.01
☐ 213 Jack Howell	.05	.02	.01
☐ 214 Wes Gardner	.05	.02	.01
☐ 215 Tim Burke	.05	.02	.01
☐ 216 Doug Jones	.05	.02	.01
☐ 217 Hubie Brooks	.05	.02	.01
☐ 218 Tom Candiotti	.05	.02	.01
☐ 219 Gerald Perry	.05	.02	.01
☐ 220 Jose DeLeon	.05	.02	.01
☐ 221 Wally Whitehurst	.05	.02	.01
☐ 222 Alan Mills	.05	.02	.01
☐ 223 Alan Trammell	.15	.07	.02
☐ 224 Dwight Gooden	.10	.05	.01
☐ 225 Travis Fryman	.30	.14	.04
☐ 226 Joe Carter	.15	.07	.02
☐ 227 Julio Franco	.10	.05	.01
☐ 228 Craig Lefferts	.05	.02	.01
☐ 229 Gary Pettis	.05	.02	.01
☐ 230 Dennis Rasmussen	.05	.02	.01
☐ 231A Brian Downing ERR	.10	.05	.01
(No position on front)			
☐ 231B Brian Downing COR	.15	.07	.02
(DH on front)			
☐ 232 Carlos Quintana	.05	.02	.01
☐ 233 Gary Gaetti	.10	.05	.01
☐ 234 Mark Langston	.15	.07	.02
☐ 235 Tim Wallach	.05	.02	.01
☐ 236 Greg Swindell	.05	.02	.01
☐ 237 Eddie Murray	.30	.14	.04
☐ 238 Jeff Manto	.05	.02	.01
☐ 239 Lenny Harris	.05	.02	.01
☐ 240 Jesse Orosco	.05	.02	.01

☐ 241 Scott Lusader	.05	.02	.01
☐ 242 Sid Fernandez	.10	.05	.01
☐ 243 Jim Leyritz	.05	.02	.01
☐ 244 Cecil Fielder	.15	.07	.02
☐ 245 Darryl Strawberry	.10	.05	.01
☐ 246 Frank Thomas UER	2.50	1.10	.30
(Comiskey Park			
misspelled Comiscky)			
☐ 247 Kevin Mitchell	.10	.05	.01
☐ 248 Lance Johnson	.05	.02	.01
☐ 249 Rick Reuschel	.10	.05	.01
☐ 250 Mark Portugal	.05	.02	.01
☐ 251 Derek Lilliquist	.05	.02	.01
☐ 252 Brian Holman	.05	.02	.01
☐ 253 Rafael Valdez UER	.05	.02	.01
(Born 4/17/68,			
should be 12/17/67)			
☐ 254 B.J. Surhoff	.10	.05	.01
☐ 255 Tony Gwynn	.40	.18	.05
☐ 256 Andy Van Slyke	.10	.05	.01
☐ 257 Todd Stottlemyre	.05	.02	.01
☐ 258 Jose Lind	.05	.02	.01
☐ 259 Greg Myers	.05	.02	.01
☐ 260 Jeff Ballard	.05	.02	.01
☐ 261 Bobby Thigpen	.05	.02	.01
☐ 262 Jimmy Kremers	.05	.02	.01
☐ 263 Robin Ventura	.15	.07	.02
☐ 264 John Smoltz	.15	.07	.02
☐ 265 Sammy Sosa	.30	.14	.04
☐ 266 Gary Sheffield	.15	.07	.02
☐ 267 Len Dykstra	.15	.07	.02
☐ 268 Bill Spiers	.05	.02	.01
☐ 269 Charlie Hayes	.10	.05	.01
☐ 270 Brett Butler	.15	.07	.02
☐ 271 Bip Roberts	.10	.05	.01
☐ 272 Rob Deer	.10	.05	.01
☐ 273 Fred Lynn	.10	.05	.01
☐ 274 Dave Parker	.10	.05	.01
☐ 275 Andy Benes	.10	.05	.01
☐ 276 Glenallen Hill	.10	.05	.01
☐ 277 Steve Howard	.05	.02	.01
☐ 278 Doug Drabek	.10	.05	.01
☐ 279 Joe Oliver	.05	.02	.01
☐ 280 Todd Benzinger	.05	.02	.01
☐ 281 Eric King	.05	.02	.01
☐ 282 Jim Presley	.05	.02	.01
☐ 283 Ken Patterson	.05	.02	.01
☐ 284 Jack Daugherty	.05	.02	.01
☐ 285 Ivan Calderon	.05	.02	.01
☐ 286 Edgar Diaz	.05	.02	.01
☐ 287 Kevin Bass	.05	.02	.01
☐ 288 Don Carman	.05	.02	.01
☐ 289 Greg Brock	.05	.02	.01
☐ 290 John Franco	.15	.07	.02
☐ 291 Joey Cora	.05	.02	.01
☐ 292 Bill Wegman	.05	.02	.01
☐ 293 Eric Show	.05	.02	.01
☐ 294 Scott Bankhead	.05	.02	.01
☐ 295 Garry Templeton	.05	.02	.01
☐ 296 Mickey Tettleton	.10	.05	.01
☐ 297 Luis Sojo	.05	.02	.01
☐ 298 Jose Rijo	.10	.05	.01
☐ 299 Dave Johnson	.05	.02	.01
☐ 300 Checklist 201-300	.05	.02	.01
☐ 301 Mark Grant	.05	.02	.01
☐ 302 Pete Harnisch	.05	.02	.01
☐ 303 Greg Olson	.05	.02	.01
☐ 304 Anthony Telford	.05	.02	.01
☐ 305 Lonnie Smith	.05	.02	.01
☐ 306 Chris Hoiles	.10	.05	.01
☐ 307 Bryn Smith	.05	.02	.01

☐ 308 Mike Devereaux	.10	.05	.01
☐ 309A Milt Thompson ERR	.05	.02	.01
(Under yr information has print dot)			
☐ 309B Milt Thompson COR	.05	.02	.01
(Under yr information says 86)			
☐ 310 Bob Melvin	.05	.02	.01
☐ 311 Luis Salazar	.05	.02	.01
☐ 312 Ed Whitson	.05	.02	.01
☐ 313 Charlie Hough	.10	.05	.01
☐ 314 Dave Clark	.05	.02	.01
☐ 315 Eric Gunderson	.05	.02	.01
☐ 316 Dan Petry	.05	.02	.01
☐ 317 Dante Bichette UER	.25	.11	.03
(Assists misspelled as assissts)			
☐ 318 Mike Heath	.05	.02	.01
☐ 319 Damon Berryhill	.05	.02	.01
☐ 320 Walt Terrell	.05	.02	.01
☐ 321 Scott Fletcher	.05	.02	.01
☐ 322 Dan Plesac	.05	.02	.01
☐ 323 Jack McDowell	.15	.07	.02
☐ 324 Paul Molitor	.15	.07	.02
☐ 325 Ozzie Guillen	.10	.05	.01
☐ 326 Gregg Olson	.05	.02	.01
☐ 327 Pedro Guerrero	.10	.05	.01
☐ 328 Bob Milacki	.05	.02	.01
☐ 329 John Tudor UER	.05	.02	.01
('90 Cardinals, should be '90 Dodgers)			
☐ 330 Steve Finley UER	.10	.05	.01
(Born 3/12/65, should be 5/12)			
☐ 331 Jack Clark	.10	.05	.01
☐ 332 Jerome Walton	.05	.02	.01
☐ 333 Andy Hawkins	.05	.02	.01
☐ 334 Derrick May	.10	.05	.01
☐ 335 Roberto Alomar	.30	.14	.04
☐ 336 Jack Morris	.15	.07	.02
☐ 337 Dave Winfield	.15	.07	.02
☐ 338 Steve Searcy	.05	.02	.01
☐ 339 Chili Davis	.15	.07	.02
☐ 340 Larry Sheets	.05	.02	.01
☐ 341 Ted Higuera	.05	.02	.01
☐ 342 David Segui	.10	.05	.01
☐ 343 Greg Cadaret	.05	.02	.01
☐ 344 Robin Yount	.20	.09	.03
☐ 345 Nolan Ryan	1.00	.45	.12
☐ 346 Ray Lankford	.10	.05	.01
☐ 347 Cal Ripken	1.00	.45	.12
☐ 348 Lee Smith	.15	.07	.02
☐ 349 Brady Anderson	.10	.05	.01
☐ 350 Frank DiPino	.05	.02	.01
☐ 351 Hal Morris	.10	.05	.01
☐ 352 Deion Sanders	.30	.14	.04
☐ 353 Barry Larkin	.20	.09	.03
☐ 354 Don Mattingly	.50	.23	.06
☐ 355 Eric Davis	.10	.05	.01
☐ 356 Jose Offerman	.10	.05	.01
☐ 357 Mel Rojas	.10	.05	.01
☐ 358 Rudy Seanez	.05	.02	.01
☐ 359 Oil Can Boyd	.05	.02	.01
☐ 360 Nelson Liriano	.05	.02	.01
☐ 361 Ron Gant	.15	.07	.02
☐ 362 Howard Farmer	.05	.02	.01
☐ 363 David Justice	.30	.14	.04
☐ 364 Delino DeShields	.10	.05	.01
☐ 365 Steve Avery	.15	.07	.02
☐ 366 David Cone	.15	.07	.02
☐ 367 Lou Whitaker	.15	.07	.02
☐ 368 Von Hayes	.05	.02	.01
☐ 369 Frank Tanana	.05	.02	.01
☐ 370 Tim Teufel	.05	.02	.01
☐ 371 Randy Myers	.15	.07	.02
☐ 372 Roberto Kelly	.10	.05	.01
☐ 373 Jack Armstrong	.05	.02	.01
☐ 374 Kelly Gruber	.05	.02	.01
☐ 375 Kevin Maas	.05	.02	.01
☐ 376 Randy Johnson	.30	.14	.04
☐ 377 David West	.05	.02	.01
☐ 378 Brent Knackert	.05	.02	.01
☐ 379 Rick Honeycutt	.05	.02	.01
☐ 380 Kevin Gross	.05	.02	.01
☐ 381 Tom Foley	.05	.02	.01
☐ 382 Jeff Blauser	.10	.05	.01
☐ 383 Scott Ruskin	.05	.02	.01
☐ 384 Andres Thomas	.05	.02	.01
☐ 385 Dennis Martinez	.10	.05	.01
☐ 386 Mike Henneman	.05	.02	.01
☐ 387 Felix Jose	.05	.02	.01
☐ 388 Alejandro Pena	.05	.02	.01
☐ 389 Chet Lemon	.05	.02	.01
☐ 390 Craig Wilson	.05	.02	.01
☐ 391 Chuck Crim	.05	.02	.01
☐ 392 Mel Hall	.05	.02	.01
☐ 393 Mark Knudson	.05	.02	.01
☐ 394 Norm Charlton	.05	.02	.01
☐ 395 Mike Felder	.05	.02	.01
☐ 396 Tim Layana	.05	.02	.01
☐ 397 Steve Frey	.05	.02	.01
☐ 398 Bill Doran	.05	.02	.01
☐ 399 Dion James	.05	.02	.01
☐ 400 Checklist 301-400	.05	.02	.01
☐ 401 Ron Hassey	.05	.02	.01
☐ 402 Don Robinson	.05	.02	.01
☐ 403 Gene Nelson	.05	.02	.01
☐ 404 Terry Kennedy	.05	.02	.01
☐ 405 Todd Burns	.05	.02	.01
☐ 406 Roger McDowell	.05	.02	.01
☐ 407 Bob Kipper	.05	.02	.01
☐ 408 Darren Daulton	.15	.07	.02
☐ 409 Chuck Cary	.05	.02	.01
☐ 410 Bruce Ruffin	.05	.02	.01
☐ 411 Juan Berenguer	.05	.02	.01
☐ 412 Gary Ward	.05	.02	.01
☐ 413 Al Newman	.05	.02	.01
☐ 414 Danny Jackson	.05	.02	.01
☐ 415 Greg Gagne	.05	.02	.01
☐ 416 Tom Herr	.05	.02	.01
☐ 417 Jeff Parrett	.05	.02	.01
☐ 418 Jeff Reardon	.10	.05	.01
☐ 419 Mark Lemke	.05	.02	.01
☐ 420 Charlie O'Brien	.05	.02	.01
☐ 421 Willie Randolph	.10	.05	.01
☐ 422 Steve Bedrosian	.05	.02	.01
☐ 423 Mike Moore	.05	.02	.01
☐ 424 Jeff Brantley	.05	.02	.01
☐ 425 Bob Welch	.05	.02	.01
☐ 426 Terry Mulholland	.05	.02	.01
☐ 427 Willie Blair	.05	.02	.01
☐ 428 Darrin Fletcher	.05	.02	.01
☐ 429 Mike Witt	.05	.02	.01
☐ 430 Joe Boever	.05	.02	.01
☐ 431 Tom Gordon	.10	.05	.01
☐ 432 Pedro Munoz	.10	.05	.01
☐ 433 Kevin Seitzer	.05	.02	.01
☐ 434 Kevin Tapani	.10	.05	.01
☐ 435 Bret Saberhagen	.15	.07	.02
☐ 436 Ellis Burks	.10	.05	.01
☐ 437 Chuck Finley	.10	.05	.01
☐ 438 Mike Boddicker	.05	.02	.01

☐ 439 Francisco Cabrera	.05	.02	.01
☐ 440 Todd Hundley	.10	.05	.01
☐ 441 Kelly Downs	.05	.02	.01
☐ 442 Dann Howitt	.05	.02	.01
☐ 443 Scott Garrelts	.05	.02	.01
☐ 444 Rickey Henderson 3X	.15	.07	.02
☐ 445 Will Clark	.20	.09	.03
☐ 446 Ben McDonald	.10	.05	.01
☐ 447 Dale Murphy	.15	.07	.02
☐ 448 Dave Righetti	.05	.02	.01
☐ 449 Dickie Thon	.05	.02	.01
☐ 450 Ted Power	.05	.02	.01
☐ 451 Scott Coolbaugh	.05	.02	.01
☐ 452 Dwight Smith	.05	.02	.01
☐ 453 Pete Incaviglia	.05	.02	.01
☐ 454 Andre Dawson	.15	.07	.02
☐ 455 Ruben Sierra	.15	.07	.02
☐ 456 Andres Galarraga	.15	.07	.02
☐ 457 Alvin Davis	.05	.02	.01
☐ 458 Tony Castillo	.05	.02	.01
☐ 459 Pete O'Brien	.05	.02	.01
☐ 460 Charlie Leibrandt	.05	.02	.01
☐ 461 Vince Coleman	.05	.02	.01
☐ 462 Steve Sax	.05	.02	.01
☐ 463 Omar Olivares	.05	.02	.01
☐ 464 Oscar Azocar	.05	.02	.01
☐ 465 Joe Magrane	.05	.02	.01
☐ 466 Karl Rhodes	.05	.02	.01
☐ 467 Benito Santiago	.05	.02	.01
☐ 468 Joe Klink	.05	.02	.01
☐ 469 Sil Campusano	.05	.02	.01
☐ 470 Mark Parent	.05	.02	.01
☐ 471 Shawn Boskie UER	.05	.02	.01
(Depleted misspelled as depleated)			
☐ 472 Kevin Brown	.10	.05	.01
☐ 473 Rick Sutcliffe	.10	.05	.01
☐ 474 Rafael Palmeiro	.15	.07	.02
☐ 475 Mike Harkey	.05	.02	.01
☐ 476 Jaime Navarro	.05	.02	.01
☐ 477 Marquis Grissom UER	.25	.11	.03
(DeShields misspelled as DeSheilds)			
☐ 478 Marty Clary	.05	.02	.01
☐ 479 Greg Briley	.05	.02	.01
☐ 480 Tom Glavine	.25	.11	.03
☐ 481 Lee Guetterman	.05	.02	.01
☐ 482 Rex Hudler	.05	.02	.01
☐ 483 Dave LaPoint	.05	.02	.01
☐ 484 Terry Pendleton	.15	.07	.02
☐ 485 Jesse Barfield	.05	.02	.01
☐ 486 Jose DeJesus	.05	.02	.01
☐ 487 Paul Abbott	.05	.02	.01
☐ 488 Ken Howell	.05	.02	.01
☐ 489 Greg W. Harris	.05	.02	.01
☐ 490 Roy Smith	.05	.02	.01
☐ 491 Paul Assenmacher	.05	.02	.01
☐ 492 Geno Petralli	.05	.02	.01
☐ 493 Steve Wilson	.05	.02	.01
☐ 494 Kevin Reimer	.05	.02	.01
☐ 495 Bill Long	.05	.02	.01
☐ 496 Mike Jackson	.05	.02	.01
☐ 497 Oddibe McDowell	.05	.02	.01
☐ 498 Bill Swift	.05	.02	.01
☐ 499 Jeff Treadway	.05	.02	.01
☐ 500 Checklist 401-500	.05	.02	.01
☐ 501 Gene Larkin	.05	.02	.01
☐ 502 Bob Boone	.10	.05	.01
☐ 503 Allan Anderson	.05	.02	.01
☐ 504 Luis Aquino	.05	.02	.01
☐ 505 Mark Guthrie	.05	.02	.01
☐ 506 Joe Orsulak	.05	.02	.01
☐ 507 Dana Kiecker	.05	.02	.01
☐ 508 Dave Gallagher	.05	.02	.01
☐ 509 Greg A. Harris	.05	.02	.01
☐ 510 Mark Williamson	.05	.02	.01
☐ 511 Casey Candaele	.05	.02	.01
☐ 512 Mookie Wilson	.10	.05	.01
☐ 513 Dave Smith	.05	.02	.01
☐ 514 Chuck Carr	.15	.07	.02
☐ 515 Glenn Wilson	.05	.02	.01
☐ 516 Mike Fitzgerald	.05	.02	.01
☐ 517 Devon White	.10	.05	.01
☐ 518 Dave Hollins	.05	.02	.01
☐ 519 Mark Eichhorn	.05	.02	.01
☐ 520 Otis Nixon	.10	.05	.01
☐ 521 Terry Shumpert	.05	.02	.01
☐ 522 Scott Erickson	.10	.05	.01
☐ 523 Danny Tartabull	.10	.05	.01
☐ 524 Orel Hershiser	.15	.07	.02
☐ 525 George Brett	.50	.23	.06
☐ 526 Greg Vaughn	.10	.05	.01
☐ 527 Tim Naehring	.10	.05	.01
☐ 528 Curt Schilling	.05	.02	.01
☐ 529 Chris Bosio	.05	.02	.01
☐ 530 Sam Horn	.05	.02	.01
☐ 531 Mike Scott	.05	.02	.01
☐ 532 George Bell	.05	.02	.01
☐ 533 Eric Anthony	.10	.05	.01
☐ 534 Julio Valera	.05	.02	.01
☐ 535 Glenn Davis	.05	.02	.01
☐ 536 Larry Walker UER	.30	.14	.04
(Should have comma after Expos in text)			
☐ 537 Pat Combs	.05	.02	.01
☐ 538 Chris Nabholz	.05	.02	.01
☐ 539 Kirk McCaskill	.05	.02	.01
☐ 540 Randy Ready	.05	.02	.01
☐ 541 Mark Gubicza	.05	.02	.01
☐ 542 Rick Aguilera	.10	.05	.01
☐ 543 Brian McRae	.40	.18	.05
☐ 544 Kirby Puckett	.40	.18	.05
☐ 545 Bo Jackson	.15	.07	.02
☐ 546 Wade Boggs	.15	.07	.02
☐ 547 Tim McIntosh	.05	.02	.01
☐ 548 Randy Milligan	.05	.02	.01
☐ 549 Dwight Evans	.10	.05	.01
☐ 550 Billy Ripken	.05	.02	.01
☐ 551 Erik Hanson	.05	.02	.01
☐ 552 Lance Parrish	.10	.05	.01
☐ 553 Tino Martinez	.15	.07	.02
☐ 554 Jim Abbott	.15	.07	.02
☐ 555 Ken Griffey Jr. UER	2.00	.90	.25
(Second most votes for 1991 All-Star Game)			
☐ 556 Milt Cuyler	.05	.02	.01
☐ 557 Mark Leonard	.05	.02	.01
☐ 558 Jay Howell	.05	.02	.01
☐ 559 Lloyd Moseby	.05	.02	.01
☐ 560 Chris Gwynn	.05	.02	.01
☐ 561 Mark Whiten	.10	.05	.01
☐ 562 Harold Baines	.15	.07	.02
☐ 563 Junior Felix	.05	.02	.01
☐ 564 Darren Lewis	.10	.05	.01
☐ 565 Fred McGriff	.25	.11	.03
☐ 566 Kevin Appier	.10	.05	.01
☐ 567 Luis Gonzalez	.20	.09	.03
☐ 568 Frank White	.10	.05	.01
☐ 569 Juan Agosto	.05	.02	.01
☐ 570 Mike Macfarlane	.05	.02	.01
☐ 571 Bert Blyleven	.15	.07	.02
☐ 572 Ken Griffey Sr.	.50	.23	.06

Ken Griffey Jr.

☐ 573	Lee Stevens	.05	.02	.01
☐ 574	Edgar Martinez	.15	.07	.02
☐ 575	Wally Joyner	.10	.05	.01
☐ 576	Tim Belcher	.05	.02	.01
☐ 577	John Burkett	.05	.02	.01
☐ 578	Mike Morgan	.05	.02	.01
☐ 579	Paul Gibson	.05	.02	.01
☐ 580	Jose Vizcaino	.05	.02	.01
☐ 581	Duane Ward	.05	.02	.01
☐ 582	Scott Sanderson	.05	.02	.01
☐ 583	David Wells	.05	.02	.01
☐ 584	Willie McGee	.10	.05	.01
☐ 585	John Cerutti	.05	.02	.01
☐ 586	Danny Darwin	.05	.02	.01
☐ 587	Kurt Stillwell	.05	.02	.01
☐ 588	Rich Gedman	.05	.02	.01
☐ 589	Mark Davis	.05	.02	.01
☐ 590	Bill Gullickson	.05	.02	.01
☐ 591	Matt Young	.05	.02	.01
☐ 592	Bryan Harvey	.05	.02	.01
☐ 593	Omar Vizquel	.10	.05	.01
☐ 594	Scott Lewis	.05	.02	.01
☐ 595	Dave Valle	.05	.02	.01
☐ 596	Tim Crews	.05	.02	.01
☐ 597	Mike Bielecki	.05	.02	.01
☐ 598	Mike Sharperson	.05	.02	.01
☐ 599	Dave Bergman	.05	.02	.01
☐ 600	Checklist 501-600	.05	.02	.01
☐ 601	Steve Lyons	.05	.02	.01
☐ 602	Bruce Hurst	.05	.02	.01
☐ 603	Donn Pall	.05	.02	.01
☐ 604	Jim Vatcher	.05	.02	.01
☐ 605	Dan Pasqua	.05	.02	.01
☐ 606	Kenny Rogers	.05	.02	.01
☐ 607	Jeff Schulz	.05	.02	.01
☐ 608	Brad Arnsberg	.05	.02	.01
☐ 609	Willie Wilson	.05	.02	.01
☐ 610	Jamie Moyer	.05	.02	.01
☐ 611	Ron Oester	.05	.02	.01
☐ 612	Dennis Cook	.05	.02	.01
☐ 613	Rick Mahler	.05	.02	.01
☐ 614	Bill Landrum	.05	.02	.01
☐ 615	Scott Scudder	.05	.02	.01
☐ 616	Tom Edens	.05	.02	.01
☐ 617	1917 Revisited	.10	.05	.01
	(White Sox in vintage uniforms)			
☐ 618	Jim Gantner	.05	.02	.01
☐ 619	Darrel Akerfelds	.05	.02	.01
☐ 620	Ron Robinson	.05	.02	.01
☐ 621	Scott Radinsky	.05	.02	.01
☐ 622	Pete Smith	.05	.02	.01
☐ 623	Melido Perez	.05	.02	.01
☐ 624	Jerald Clark	.05	.02	.01
☐ 625	Carlos Martinez	.05	.02	.01
☐ 626	Wes Chamberlain	.05	.02	.01
☐ 627	Bobby Witt	.05	.02	.01
☐ 628	Ken Dayley	.05	.02	.01
☐ 629	John Barfield	.05	.02	.01
☐ 630	Bob Tewksbury	.05	.02	.01
☐ 631	Glenn Braggs	.05	.02	.01
☐ 632	Jim Neidlinger	.05	.02	.01
☐ 633	Tom Browning	.05	.02	.01
☐ 634	Kirk Gibson	.15	.07	.02
☐ 635	Rob Dibble	.10	.05	.01
☐ 636A	Stolen Base Leaders	.25	.11	.03
	(Rickey Henderson and Lou Brock in tuxedos and no date on card)			
☐ 636B	Stolen Base Leaders	.50	.23	.06
☐ 637	(Dated May 1, 1991 on card front) Jeff Montgomery	.10	.05	.01
☐ 638	Mike Schooler	.05	.02	.01
☐ 639	Storm Davis	.05	.02	.01
☐ 640	Rich Rodriguez	.05	.02	.01
☐ 641	Phil Bradley	.05	.02	.01
☐ 642	Kent Mercker	.05	.02	.01
☐ 643	Carlton Fisk	.15	.07	.02
☐ 644	Mike Bell	.05	.02	.01
☐ 645	Alex Fernandez	.15	.07	.02
☐ 646	Juan Gonzalez	.60	.25	.07
☐ 647	Ken Hill	.15	.07	.02
☐ 648	Jeff Russell	.05	.02	.01
☐ 649	Chuck Malone	.05	.02	.01
☐ 650	Steve Buechele	.05	.02	.01
☐ 651	Mike Benjamin	.05	.02	.01
☐ 652	Tony Pena	.05	.02	.01
☐ 653	Trevor Wilson	.05	.02	.01
☐ 654	Alex Cole	.05	.02	.01
☐ 655	Roger Clemens	.20	.09	.03
☐ 656	Mark McGwire	.15	.07	.02
	(The Bashing Years)			
☐ 657	Joe Grahe	.05	.02	.01
☐ 658	Jim Eisenreich	.05	.02	.01
☐ 659	Dan Gladden	.05	.02	.01
☐ 660	Steve Farr	.05	.02	.01
☐ 661	Bill Sampen	.05	.02	.01
☐ 662	Dave Rohde	.05	.02	.01
☐ 663	Mark Gardner	.05	.02	.01
☐ 664	Mike Simms	.05	.02	.01
☐ 665	Moises Alou	.15	.07	.02
☐ 666	Mickey Hatcher	.05	.02	.01
☐ 667	Jimmy Key	.10	.05	.01
☐ 668	John Wetteland	.10	.05	.01
☐ 669	John Smiley	.05	.02	.01
☐ 670	Jim Acker	.05	.02	.01
☐ 671	Pascual Perez	.05	.02	.01
☐ 672	Reggie Harris UER	.05	.02	.01
	(Opportunity misspelled as oppurtinty)			
☐ 673	Matt Nokes	.05	.02	.01
☐ 674	Rafael Novoa	.05	.02	.01
☐ 675	Hensley Meulens	.05	.02	.01
☐ 676	Jeff M. Robinson	.05	.02	.01
☐ 677	Ground Breaking	.10	.05	.01
	(New Comiskey Park; Carlton Fisk and Robin Ventura)			
☐ 678	Johnny Ray	.05	.02	.01
☐ 679	Greg Hibbard	.05	.02	.01
☐ 680	Paul Sorrento	.10	.05	.01
☐ 681	Mike Marshall	.05	.02	.01
☐ 682	Jim Clancy	.05	.02	.01
☐ 683	Rob Murphy	.05	.02	.01
☐ 684	Dave Schmidt	.05	.02	.01
☐ 685	Jeff Gray	.05	.02	.01
☐ 686	Mike Hartley	.05	.02	.01
☐ 687	Jeff King	.05	.02	.01
☐ 688	Stan Javier	.05	.02	.01
☐ 689	Bob Walk	.05	.02	.01
☐ 690	Jim Gott	.05	.02	.01
☐ 691	Mike LaCoss	.05	.02	.01
☐ 692	John Farrell	.05	.02	.01
☐ 693	Tim Leary	.05	.02	.01
☐ 694	Mike Walker	.05	.02	.01
☐ 695	Eric Plunk	.05	.02	.01
☐ 696	Mike Fetters	.05	.02	.01
☐ 697	Wayne Edwards	.05	.02	.01
☐ 698	Tim Drummond	.05	.02	.01
☐ 699	Willie Fraser	.05	.02	.01

☐ 700	Checklist 601-700	.05	.02	.01
☐ 701	Mike Heath	.05	.02	.01
☐ 702	Rookie Threats	.75	.35	.09
	Luis Gonzalez			
	Karl Rhodes			
	Jeff Bagwell			
☐ 703	Jose Mesa	.10	.05	.01
☐ 704	Dave Smith	.05	.02	.01
☐ 705	Danny Darwin	.05	.02	.01
☐ 706	Rafael Belliard	.05	.02	.01
☐ 707	Rob Murphy	.05	.02	.01
☐ 708	Terry Pendleton	.15	.07	.02
☐ 709	Mike Pagliarulo	.05	.02	.01
☐ 710	Sid Bream	.05	.02	.01
☐ 711	Junior Felix	.05	.02	.01
☐ 712	Dante Bichette	.25	.11	.03
☐ 713	Kevin Gross	.05	.02	.01
☐ 714	Luis Sojo	.05	.02	.01
☐ 715	Bob Ojeda	.05	.02	.01
☐ 716	Julio Machado	.05	.02	.01
☐ 717	Steve Farr	.05	.02	.01
☐ 718	Franklin Stubbs	.05	.02	.01
☐ 719	Mike Boddicker	.05	.02	.01
☐ 720	Willie Randolph	.10	.05	.01
☐ 721	Willie McGee	.10	.05	.01
☐ 722	Chili Davis	.15	.07	.02
☐ 723	Danny Jackson	.05	.02	.01
☐ 724	Cory Snyder	.05	.02	.01
☐ 725	MVP Lineup	.15	.07	.02
	Andre Dawson			
	George Bell			
	Ryne Sandberg			
☐ 726	Rob Deer	.05	.02	.01
☐ 727	Rich DeLucia	.05	.02	.01
☐ 728	Mike Perez	.05	.02	.01
☐ 729	Mickey Tettleton	.10	.05	.01
☐ 730	Mike Blowers	.10	.05	.01
☐ 731	Gary Gaetti	.10	.05	.01
☐ 732	Brett Butler	.15	.07	.02
☐ 733	Dave Parker	.10	.05	.01
☐ 734	Eddie Zosky	.05	.02	.01
☐ 735	Jack Clark	.10	.05	.01
☐ 736	Jack Morris	.15	.07	.02
☐ 737	Kirk Gibson	.05	.02	.01
☐ 738	Steve Bedrosian	.05	.02	.01
☐ 739	Candy Maldonado	.05	.02	.01
☐ 740	Matt Young	.05	.02	.01
☐ 741	Rich Garces	.05	.02	.01
☐ 742	George Bell	.05	.02	.01
☐ 743	Deion Sanders	.30	.14	.04
☐ 744	Bo Jackson	.15	.07	.02
☐ 745	Luis Mercedes	.05	.02	.01
☐ 746	Reggie Jefferson UER	.10	.05	.01
	(Throwing left on card; back has throws right)			
☐ 747	Pete Incaviglia	.05	.02	.01
☐ 748	Chris Hammond	.10	.05	.01
☐ 749	Mike Stanton	.05	.02	.01
☐ 750	Scott Sanderson	.05	.02	.01
☐ 751	Paul Faries	.05	.02	.01
☐ 752	Al Osuna	.05	.02	.01
☐ 753	Steve Chitren	.05	.02	.01
☐ 754	Tony Fernandez	.05	.02	.01
☐ 755	Jeff Bagwell UER	2.50	1.10	.30
	(Strikeout and walk totals reversed)			
☐ 756	Kirk Dressendorfer	.05	.02	.01
☐ 757	Glenn Davis	.05	.02	.01
☐ 758	Gary Carter	.15	.07	.02
☐ 759	Zane Smith	.05	.02	.01
☐ 760	Vance Law	.05	.02	.01

☐ 761	Denis Boucher	.05	.02	.01
☐ 762	Turner Ward	.05	.02	.01
☐ 763	Roberto Alomar	.30	.14	.04
☐ 764	Albert Belle	.60	.25	.07
☐ 765	Joe Carter	.15	.07	.02
☐ 766	Pete Schourek	.50	.23	.06
☐ 767	Heathcliff Slocumb	.20	.09	.03
☐ 768	Vince Coleman	.05	.02	.01
☐ 769	Mitch Williams	.10	.05	.01
☐ 770	Brian Downing	.05	.02	.01
☐ 771	Dana Allison	.05	.02	.01
☐ 772	Pete Harnisch	.05	.02	.01
☐ 773	Tim Raines	.15	.07	.02
☐ 774	Darryl Kile	.05	.02	.01
☐ 775	Fred McGriff	.20	.09	.03
☐ 776	Dwight Evans	.10	.05	.01
☐ 777	Joe Slusarski	.05	.02	.01
☐ 778	Dave Righetti	.05	.02	.01
☐ 779	Jeff Hamilton	.05	.02	.01
☐ 780	Ernest Riles	.05	.02	.01
☐ 781	Ken Dayley	.05	.02	.01
☐ 782	Eric King	.05	.02	.01
☐ 783	Devon White	.10	.05	.01
☐ 784	Beau Allred	.05	.02	.01
☐ 785	Mike Timlin	.05	.02	.01
☐ 786	Ivan Calderon	.05	.02	.01
☐ 787	Hubie Brooks	.05	.02	.01
☐ 788	Juan Agosto	.05	.02	.01
☐ 789	Barry Jones	.05	.02	.01
☐ 790	Wally Backman	.05	.02	.01
☐ 791	Jim Presley	.05	.02	.01
☐ 792	Charlie Hough	.10	.05	.01
☐ 793	Larry Andersen	.05	.02	.01
☐ 794	Steve Finley	.05	.02	.01
☐ 795	Shawn Abner	.05	.02	.01
☐ 796	Jeff M. Robinson	.05	.02	.01
☐ 797	Joe Bitker	.05	.02	.01
☐ 798	Eric Show	.05	.02	.01
☐ 799	Bud Black	.05	.02	.01
☐ 800	Checklist 701-800	.05	.02	.01
☐ HH1	Hank Aaron Hologram	2.50	1.10	.30
☐ SP1	Michael Jordan SP	18.00	8.00	2.20
	(Shown batting in White Sox uniform)			
☐ SP2	Henderson/Ryan	3.00	1.35	.35
	(Rickey and Nolan) (Commemorating 5/1/91 record breaking)			

1991 Upper Deck Final Edition

The 1991 Upper Deck Final Edition boxed set contains 100 cards and showcases players who made major contributions during their team's late-season pennant drive. In addition to the late season traded and impact rookie cards (22-78), the set includes two special subsets: Diamond Skills cards (1-21), depicting the best Minor League prospects, and All-Star cards (80-99). Six assorted hologram cards were issued with each set. The cards measure the standard size (2 1/2" by 3 1/2"). The fronts feature posed or action color player photos on a white card face, with the upper

left corner of the picture cut out to provide space for the Upper Deck logo. The pictures are bordered in green on the left, with the player's name in a tan border below the picture. Two-thirds of the back are occupied by another color action photo, with biography, statistics, and career highlights in a horizontally oriented red rectangle to the left of the picture. The cards are numbered on the back with an F suffix. Among the outstanding Rookie Cards in this set are Ryan Klesko, Kenny Lofton, Pedro Martinez, Marc Newfield, Frankie Rodriguez, Ivan Rodriguez, Jim Thome, Rondell White, Rick Wilkins, and Dmitri Young.

	MINT	NRMT	EXC
COMPLETE FACT.SET (100)	4.00	1.80	.50
COMMON CARD (1F-100F)	.05	.02	.01

		MINT	NRMT	EXC
☐ 1F	Diamond Skills Checklist Card (Ryan Klesko and Reggie Sanders)	.30	.14	.04
☐ 2F	Pedro Martinez	.40	.18	.05
☐ 3F	Lance Dickson	.05	.02	.01
☐ 4F	Royce Clayton	.10	.05	.01
☐ 5F	Scott Bryant	.05	.02	.01
☐ 6F	Dan Wilson	.15	.07	.02
☐ 7F	Dmitri Young	.20	.09	.03
☐ 8F	Ryan Klesko	1.50	.70	.19
☐ 9F	Tom Goodwin	.10	.05	.01
☐ 10F	Rondell White	1.00	.45	.12
☐ 11F	Reggie Sanders	.30	.14	.04
☐ 12F	Todd Van Poppel	.10	.05	.01
☐ 13F	Arthur Rhodes	.05	.02	.01
☐ 14F	Eddie Zosky	.10	.05	.01
☐ 15F	Gerald Williams	.05	.02	.01
☐ 16F	Robert Eenhoorn	.05	.02	.01
☐ 17F	Jim Thome	1.50	.70	.19
☐ 18F	Marc Newfield	.20	.09	.03
☐ 19F	Kerwin Moore	.05	.02	.01
☐ 20F	Jeff McNeely	.05	.02	.01
☐ 21F	Frankie Rodriguez	.15	.07	.02
☐ 22F	Andy Mota	.05	.02	.01
☐ 23F	Chris Haney	.05	.02	.01
☐ 24F	Kenny Lofton	2.00	.90	.25
☐ 25F	Dave Nilsson	.15	.07	.02
☐ 26F	Derek Bell	.15	.07	.02
☐ 27F	Frank Castillo	.15	.07	.02
☐ 28F	Candy Maldonado	.05	.02	.01
☐ 29F	Chuck McElroy	.05	.02	.01
☐ 30F	Chito Martinez	.05	.02	.01
☐ 31F	Steve Howe	.05	.02	.01
☐ 32F	Freddie Benavides	.05	.02	.01
☐ 33F	Scott Kamieniecki	.05	.02	.01
☐ 34F	Denny Neagle	.20	.09	.03
☐ 35F	Mike Humphreys	.05	.02	.01
☐ 36F	Mike Remlinger	.05	.02	.01
☐ 37F	Scott Coolbaugh	.05	.02	.01
☐ 38F	Darren Lewis	.10	.05	.01
☐ 39F	Thomas Howard	.05	.02	.01
☐ 40F	John Candelaria	.05	.02	.01
☐ 41F	Todd Benzinger	.05	.02	.01
☐ 42F	Wilson Alvarez	.15	.07	.02
☐ 43F	Patrick Lennon	.05	.02	.01
☐ 44F	Rusty Meacham	.05	.02	.01
☐ 45F	Ryan Bowen	.05	.02	.01
☐ 46F	Rick Wilkins	.05	.02	.01
☐ 47F	Ed Sprague	.05	.02	.01
☐ 48F	Bob Scanlan	.05	.02	.01
☐ 49F	Tom Candiotti	.05	.02	.01
☐ 50F	Dennis Martinez (Perfecto)	.10	.05	.01
☐ 51F	Oil Can Boyd	.05	.02	.01
☐ 52F	Glenallen Hill	.10	.05	.01
☐ 53F	Scott Livingstone	.05	.02	.01
☐ 54F	Brian R. Hunter	.05	.02	.01
☐ 55F	Ivan Rodriguez	.50	.23	.06
☐ 56F	Keith Mitchell	.05	.02	.01
☐ 57F	Roger McDowell	.05	.02	.01
☐ 58F	Otis Nixon	.05	.02	.01
☐ 59F	Juan Bell	.05	.02	.01
☐ 60F	Bill Krueger	.05	.02	.01
☐ 61F	Chris Donnels	.05	.02	.01
☐ 62F	Tommy Greene	.10	.05	.01
☐ 63F	Doug Simons	.05	.02	.01
☐ 64F	Andy Ashby	.10	.05	.01
☐ 65F	Anthony Young	.05	.02	.01
☐ 66F	Kevin Morton	.05	.02	.01
☐ 67F	Bret Barberie	.10	.05	.01
☐ 68F	Scott Servais	.05	.02	.01
☐ 69F	Ron Darling	.05	.02	.01
☐ 70F	Tim Burke	.05	.02	.01
☐ 71F	Vicente Palacios	.05	.02	.01
☐ 72F	Gerald Alexander	.05	.02	.01
☐ 73F	Reggie Jefferson	.10	.05	.01
☐ 74F	Dean Palmer	.10	.05	.01
☐ 75F	Mark Whiten	.10	.05	.01
☐ 76F	Randy Tomlin	.05	.02	.01
☐ 77F	Mark Wohlers	.40	.18	.05
☐ 78F	Brook Jacoby	.05	.02	.01
☐ 79F	All-Star Checklist (Ken Griffey Jr. and Ryne Sandberg)	.40	.18	.05
☐ 80F	Jack Morris AS	.10	.05	.01
☐ 81F	Sandy Alomar Jr. AS	.05	.02	.01
☐ 82F	Cecil Fielder AS	.15	.07	.02
☐ 83F	Roberto Alomar AS	.15	.07	.02
☐ 84F	Wade Boggs AS	.15	.07	.02
☐ 85F	Cal Ripken AS	.50	.23	.06
☐ 86F	Rickey Henderson AS	.15	.07	.02
☐ 87F	Ken Griffey Jr. AS	.75	.35	.09
☐ 88F	Dave Henderson AS	.05	.02	.01
☐ 89F	Danny Tartabull AS	.10	.05	.01
☐ 90F	Tom Glavine AS	.15	.07	.02
☐ 91F	Benito Santiago AS	.05	.02	.01
☐ 92F	Will Clark AS	.15	.07	.02
☐ 93F	Ryne Sandberg AS	.20	.09	.03
☐ 94F	Chris Sabo AS	.05	.02	.01
☐ 95F	Ozzie Smith AS	.10	.05	.01
☐ 96F	Ivan Calderon AS	.05	.02	.01
☐ 97F	Tony Gwynn AS	.20	.09	.03
☐ 98F	Andre Dawson AS	.15	.07	.02
☐ 99F	Bobby Bonilla AS	.10	.05	.01
☐ 100F	Checklist 1-100	.05	.02	.01

1992 Upper Deck

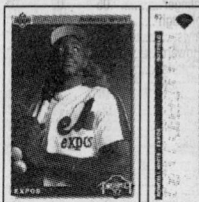

The 1992 Upper Deck set contains 800 standard-size (2 1/2" by 3 1/2") cards. The set was produced in two series: a low-number series of 700 cards and a high-number series of 100 cards later in the season. Special subsets included in the set are Star Rookies (1-27; SR), Team Checklists (29-40, 86-99; TC), with player portraits by Vernon Wells; Top Prospects (52-77; TP); Bloodlines (79-85), and Diamond Skills (640-650; DS). Moreover, a nine-card Baseball Heroes subset (randomly inserted in packs) focuses on the career of Ted Williams. He autographed and numbered 2,500 cards, which were randomly inserted in low series foil packs. The cards are numbered on the back. By mailing in 15 1992 Upper Deck low number foil wrappers, a completed order form, and a handling fee, the collector could receive an 8 1/2" by 11" numbered, black and white lithograph picturing Ted Williams in his batting swing. A standard-size Ted Williams hologram card was randomly inserted in 1992 low number foil packs. The front design of the Williams hologram is horizontally oriented and features the artwork of Vernon Wells showing Williams in three different poses. The horizontally oriented back has a full-bleed sepia-tone photo of Williams and career highlights printed in black over the photo. Factory sets feature a unique gold-foil hologram on the card backs (in contrast to the silver hologram on foil pack cards). In addition to traded players and called-up rookies, the extended series features a National League Diamond Skills subset (711-721), a Diamond Debuts subset (771-780), two expansion-team player cards (701 Clemente Nunez and 710 Ryan Turner), and two commemorative cards highlighting Eddie Murray's 400th home run (728) and Rickey Henderson's 1,000th stolen base (782). Randomly inserted into high number foil packs were a 20-card Ted Williams' Best Hitters subset, a three-card hologram subset featuring College Player of the Year winners for 1989 through 1991, a ten-card Baseball Heroes subset highlighting the careers of Joe Morgan and Johnny Bench and featuring 2,500 dual autographed checklist cards. and a special card picturing Tom Selleck and Frank Thomas and com-

memorating the movie "Mr. Baseball." The fronts features shadow-bordered action color player photos on a white card face. The player's name appears above the photo, with the team name superimposed at the lower right corner. The backs include color action player photos and biography and statistics. The cards are numbered on the back. Rookie Cards in the set include Chad Curtis, Shawn Green, Tyler Green, Joey Hamilton, Mike Kelly, Pat Listach, David McCarty, Clemente Nunez, Eduardo Perez, Manny Ramirez, Mark Smith, Ryan Turner, Joe Vitiello, and Brian Williams.

		MINT	NRMT	EXC
	COMPLETE SET (800)	15.00	6.75	1.85
	COMPLETE FACT.SET (800)	20.00	9.00	2.50
	COMPLETE LO SET (700)	12.00	5.50	1.50
	COMPLETE HI SET (100)	3.00	1.35	.35
	COLLEGE POY HOLOGRAM SET (3)	2.00	.90	.25
	COMMON CARD (1-700)	.05	.02	.01
	COMMON CARD (701-800)	.05	.02	.01
☐ 1	Star Rookie Checklist	.75	.35	.09
	Ryan Klesko			
	Jim Thome			
☐ 2	Royce Clayton SR	.10	.05	.01
☐ 3	Brian Jordan SR	.25	.11	.03
☐ 4	Dave Fleming SR	.05	.02	.01
☐ 5	Jim Thome SR	.75	.35	.09
☐ 6	Jeff Juden SR	.05	.02	.01
☐ 7	Roberto Hernandez SR	.10	.05	.01
☐ 8	Kyle Abbott SR	.05	.02	.01
☐ 9	Chris George SR	.05	.02	.01
☐ 10	Rob Maurer SR	.05	.02	.01
☐ 11	Donald Harris SR	.05	.02	.01
☐ 12	Ted Wood SR	.05	.02	.01
☐ 13	Patrick Lennon SR	.05	.02	.01
☐ 14	Willie Banks SR	.05	.02	.01
☐ 15	Roger Salkeld SR UER	.05	.02	.01
	(Bill was his grand-father, not his father)			
☐ 16	Wil Cordero SR	.20	.09	.03
☐ 17	Arthur Rhodes SR	.05	.02	.01
☐ 18	Pedro Martinez SR	.25	.11	.03
☐ 19	Andy Ashby SR	.05	.02	.01
☐ 20	Tom Goodwin SR	.10	.05	.01
☐ 21	Braulio Castillo SR	.05	.02	.01
☐ 22	Todd Van Poppel SR	.10	.05	.01
☐ 23	Brian Williams SR	.05	.02	.01
☐ 24	Ryan Klesko SR	.75	.35	.09
☐ 25	Kenny Lofton SR	1.00	.45	.12
☐ 26	Derek Bell SR	.10	.05	.01
☐ 27	Reggie Sanders SR	.20	.09	.03
☐ 28	Dave Winfield's 400th	.15	.07	.02
☐ 29	David Justice TC	.10	.05	.01
☐ 30	Rob Dibble TC	.05	.02	.01
☐ 31	Craig Biggio TC	.10	.05	.01
☐ 32	Eddie Murray TC	.15	.07	.02
☐ 33	Fred McGriff TC	.15	.07	.02
☐ 34	Willie McGee TC	.05	.02	.01
☐ 35	Shawon Dunston TC	.05	.02	.01
☐ 36	Delino DeShields TC	.05	.02	.01
☐ 37	Howard Johnson TC	.05	.02	.01
☐ 38	John Kruk TC	.10	.05	.01
☐ 39	Doug Drabek TC	.05	.02	.01
☐ 40	Todd Zeile TC	.05	.02	.01
☐ 41	Steve Avery	.10	.05	.01
	Playoff Perfection			
☐ 42	Jeremy Hernandez	.05	.02	.01

☐ 43 Doug Henry	.05	.02	.01
☐ 44 Chris Donnels	.05	.02	.01
☐ 45 Mo Sanford	.05	.02	.01
☐ 46 Scott Kamieniecki	.05	.02	.01
☐ 47 Mark Lemke	.10	.05	.01
☐ 48 Steve Farr	.05	.02	.01
☐ 49 Francisco Oliveras	.05	.02	.01
☐ 50 Ced Landrum	.05	.02	.01
☐ 51 Top Prospect Checklist	.15	.07	.02
Rondell White			
Craig Griffey			
☐ 52 Eduardo Perez TP	.05	.02	.01
☐ 53 Tom Nevers TP	.05	.02	.01
☐ 54 David Zancanaro TP	.05	.02	.01
☐ 55 Shawn Green TP	1.00	.45	.12
☐ 56 Mark Wohlers TP	.10	.05	.01
☐ 57 Dave Nilsson TP	.05	.02	.01
☐ 58 Dmitri Young TP	.10	.05	.01
☐ 59 Ryan Hawblitzel TP	.05	.02	.01
☐ 60 Raul Mondesi TP	1.00	.45	.12
☐ 61 Rondell White TP	.40	.18	.05
☐ 62 Steve Hosey TP	.05	.02	.01
☐ 63 Manny Ramirez TP	3.00	1.35	.35
☐ 64 Marc Newfield TP	.10	.05	.01
☐ 65 Jeromy Burnitz TP	.05	.02	.01
☐ 66 Mark Smith TP	.05	.02	.01
☐ 67 Joey Hamilton TP	.75	.35	.09
☐ 68 Tyler Green TP	.10	.05	.01
☐ 69 Jon Farrell TP	.05	.02	.01
☐ 70 Kurt Miller TP	.05	.02	.01
☐ 71 Jeff Plympton TP	.05	.02	.01
☐ 72 Dan Wilson TP	.10	.05	.01
☐ 73 Joe Vitiello TP	.30	.14	.04
☐ 74 Rico Brogna TP	.10	.05	.01
☐ 75 David McCarty TP	.05	.02	.01
☐ 76 Bob Wickman TP	.05	.02	.01
☐ 77 Carlos Rodriguez TP	.05	.02	.01
☐ 78 Jim Abbott	.10	.05	.01
Stay In School			
☐ 79 Ramon Martinez	.15	.07	.02
Pedro Martinez			
☐ 80 Kevin Mitchell	.05	.02	.01
Keith Mitchell			
☐ 81 Sandy Alomar Jr.	.10	.05	.01
Roberto Alomar			
☐ 82 Cal Ripken	.50	.23	.06
Billy Ripken			
☐ 83 Tony Gwynn	.15	.07	.02
Chris Gwynn			
☐ 84 Dwight Gooden	.10	.05	.01
Gary Sheffield			
☐ 85 Ken Griffey Sr.	.75	.35	.09
Ken Griffey Jr.			
Craig Griffey			
☐ 86 Jim Abbott TC	.10	.05	.01
☐ 87 Frank Thomas TC	.75	.35	.09
☐ 88 Danny Tartabull TC	.05	.02	.01
☐ 89 Scott Erickson TC	.05	.02	.01
☐ 90 Rickey Henderson TC	.15	.07	.02
☐ 91 Edgar Martinez TC	.05	.02	.01
☐ 92 Nolan Ryan TC	.40	.18	.05
☐ 93 Ben McDonald TC	.05	.02	.01
☐ 94 Ellis Burks TC	.10	.05	.01
☐ 95 Greg Swindell TC	.05	.02	.01
☐ 96 Cecil Fielder TC	.15	.07	.02
☐ 97 Greg Vaughn TC	.05	.02	.01
☐ 98 Kevin Maas TC	.05	.02	.01
☐ 99 Dave Stieb TC	.05	.02	.01
☐ 100 Checklist 1-100	.05	.02	.01
☐ 101 Joe Oliver	.05	.02	.01
☐ 102 Hector Villanueva	.05	.02	.01
☐ 103 Ed Whitson	.05	.02	.01
☐ 104 Danny Jackson	.05	.02	.01
☐ 105 Chris Hammond	.05	.02	.01
☐ 106 Ricky Jordan	.05	.02	.01
☐ 107 Kevin Bass	.05	.02	.01
☐ 108 Darrin Fletcher	.05	.02	.01
☐ 109 Junior Ortiz	.05	.02	.01
☐ 110 Tom Bolton	.05	.02	.01
☐ 111 Jeff King	.10	.05	.01
☐ 112 Dave Magadan	.05	.02	.01
☐ 113 Mike LaValliere	.05	.02	.01
☐ 114 Hubie Brooks	.05	.02	.01
☐ 115 Jay Bell	.10	.05	.01
☐ 116 David Wells	.10	.05	.01
☐ 117 Jim Leyritz	.05	.02	.01
☐ 118 Manuel Lee	.05	.02	.01
☐ 119 Alvaro Espinoza	.05	.02	.01
☐ 120 B.J. Surhoff	.10	.05	.01
☐ 121 Hal Morris	.10	.05	.01
☐ 122 Shawon Dawson	.05	.02	.01
☐ 123 Chris Sabo	.05	.02	.01
☐ 124 Andre Dawson	.15	.07	.02
☐ 125 Eric Davis	.10	.05	.01
☐ 126 Chili Davis	.15	.07	.02
☐ 127 Dale Murphy	.15	.07	.02
☐ 128 Kirk McCaskill	.05	.02	.01
☐ 129 Terry Mulholland	.05	.02	.01
☐ 130 Rick Aguilera	.10	.05	.01
☐ 131 Vince Coleman	.05	.02	.01
☐ 132 Andy Van Slyke	.10	.05	.01
☐ 133 Gregg Jefferies	.15	.07	.02
☐ 134 Barry Bonds	.25	.11	.03
☐ 135 Dwight Gooden	.10	.05	.01
☐ 136 Dave Stieb	.05	.02	.01
☐ 137 Albert Belle	.50	.23	.06
☐ 138 Teddy Higuera	.05	.02	.01
☐ 139 Jesse Barfield	.05	.02	.01
☐ 140 Pat Borders	.05	.02	.01
☐ 141 Bip Roberts	.10	.05	.01
☐ 142 Rob Dibble	.05	.02	.01
☐ 143 Mark Grace	.15	.07	.02
☐ 144 Barry Larkin	.15	.07	.02
☐ 145 Ryne Sandberg	.25	.11	.03
☐ 146 Scott Erickson	.10	.05	.01
☐ 147 Luis Polonia	.05	.02	.01
☐ 148 John Burkett	.05	.02	.01
☐ 149 Luis Sojo	.05	.02	.01
☐ 150 Dickie Thon	.05	.02	.01
☐ 151 Walt Weiss	.05	.02	.01
☐ 152 Mike Scioscia	.05	.02	.01
☐ 153 Mark McGwire	.15	.07	.02
☐ 154 Matt Williams	.20	.09	.03
☐ 155 Rickey Henderson	.15	.07	.02
☐ 156 Sandy Alomar Jr.	.10	.05	.01
☐ 157 Brian McRae	.15	.07	.02
☐ 158 Harold Baines	.15	.07	.02
☐ 159 Kevin Appier	.10	.05	.01
☐ 160 Felix Fermin	.05	.02	.01
☐ 161 Leo Gomez	.05	.02	.01
☐ 162 Craig Biggio	.15	.07	.02
☐ 163 Ben McDonald	.10	.05	.01
☐ 164 Randy Johnson	.25	.11	.03
☐ 165 Cal Ripken	1.00	.45	.12
☐ 166 Frank Thomas	1.50	.70	.19
☐ 167 Delino DeShields	.10	.05	.01
☐ 168 Greg Gagne	.05	.02	.01
☐ 169 Ron Karkovice	.05	.02	.01
☐ 170 Charlie Leibrandt	.05	.02	.01
☐ 171 Dave Righetti	.05	.02	.01
☐ 172 Dave Henderson	.05	.02	.01
☐ 173 Steve Decker	.05	.02	.01

☐ 174 Darryl Strawberry	.10	.05	.01
☐ 175 Will Clark	.15	.07	.02
☐ 176 Ruben Sierra	.15	.07	.02
☐ 177 Ozzie Smith	.20	.09	.03
☐ 178 Charles Nagy	.10	.05	.01
☐ 179 Gary Pettis	.05	.02	.01
☐ 180 Kirk Gibson	.15	.07	.02
☐ 181 Randy Milligan	.05	.02	.01
☐ 182 Dave Valle	.05	.02	.01
☐ 183 Chris Hoiles	.10	.05	.01
☐ 184 Tony Phillips	.15	.07	.02
☐ 185 Brady Anderson	.10	.05	.01
☐ 186 Scott Fletcher	.05	.02	.01
☐ 187 Gene Larkin	.05	.02	.01
☐ 188 Lance Johnson	.05	.02	.01
☐ 189 Greg Olson	.05	.02	.01
☐ 190 Melido Perez	.05	.02	.01
☐ 191 Lenny Harris	.05	.02	.01
☐ 192 Terry Kennedy	.05	.02	.01
☐ 193 Mike Gallego	.05	.02	.01
☐ 194 Willie McGee	.10	.05	.01
☐ 195 Juan Samuel	.05	.02	.01
☐ 196 Jeff Huson	.10	.05	.01
(Shows Jose Canseco sliding into second)			
☐ 197 Alex Cole	.05	.02	.01
☐ 198 Ron Robinson	.05	.02	.01
☐ 199 Joel Skinner	.05	.02	.01
☐ 200 Checklist 101-200	.05	.02	.01
☐ 201 Kevin Reimer	.05	.02	.01
☐ 202 Stan Belinda	.05	.02	.01
☐ 203 Pat Tabler	.05	.02	.01
☐ 204 Jose Guzman	.05	.02	.01
☐ 205 Jose Lind	.05	.02	.01
☐ 206 Spike Owen	.05	.02	.01
☐ 207 Joe Orsulak	.05	.02	.01
☐ 208 Charlie Hayes	.10	.05	.01
☐ 209 Mike Devereaux	.10	.05	.01
☐ 210 Mike Fitzgerald	.05	.02	.01
☐ 211 Willie Randolph	.10	.05	.01
☐ 212 Rod Nichols	.05	.02	.01
☐ 213 Mike Boddicker	.05	.02	.01
☐ 214 Bill Spiers	.05	.02	.01
☐ 215 Steve Olin	.05	.02	.01
☐ 216 David Howard	.05	.02	.01
☐ 217 Gary Varsho	.05	.02	.01
☐ 218 Mike Harkey	.05	.02	.01
☐ 219 Luis Aquino	.05	.02	.01
☐ 220 Chuck McElroy	.05	.02	.01
☐ 221 Doug Drabek	.10	.05	.01
☐ 222 Dave Winfield	.15	.07	.02
☐ 223 Rafael Palmeiro	.15	.07	.02
☐ 224 Joe Carter	.15	.07	.02
☐ 225 Bobby Bonilla	.15	.07	.02
☐ 226 Ivan Calderon	.05	.02	.01
☐ 227 Gregg Olson	.05	.02	.01
☐ 228 Tim Wallach	.05	.02	.01
☐ 229 Terry Pendleton	.15	.07	.02
☐ 230 Gilberto Reyes	.05	.02	.01
☐ 231 Carlos Baerga	.30	.14	.04
☐ 232 Greg Vaughn	.05	.02	.01
☐ 233 Bret Saberhagen	.15	.07	.02
☐ 234 Gary Sheffield	.15	.07	.02
☐ 235 Mark Lewis	.05	.02	.01
☐ 236 George Bell	.05	.02	.01
☐ 237 Danny Tartabull	.10	.05	.01
☐ 238 Willie Wilson	.05	.02	.01
☐ 239 Doug Dascenzo	.05	.02	.01
☐ 240 Bill Pecota	.05	.02	.01
☐ 241 Julio Franco	.10	.05	.01
☐ 242 Ed Sprague	.10	.05	.01
☐ 243 Juan Gonzalez	.40	.18	.05
☐ 244 Chuck Finley	.05	.02	.01
☐ 245 Ivan Rodriguez	.15	.07	.02
☐ 246 Len Dykstra	.15	.07	.02
☐ 247 Deion Sanders	.20	.09	.03
☐ 248 Dwight Evans	.10	.05	.01
☐ 249 Larry Walker	.15	.07	.02
☐ 250 Billy Ripken	.05	.02	.01
☐ 251 Mickey Tettleton	.10	.05	.01
☐ 252 Tony Pena	.05	.02	.01
☐ 253 Benito Santiago	.05	.02	.01
☐ 254 Kirby Puckett	.30	.14	.04
☐ 255 Cecil Fielder	.15	.07	.02
☐ 256 Howard Johnson	.05	.02	.01
☐ 257 Andujar Cedeno	.05	.02	.01
☐ 258 Jose Rijo	.10	.05	.01
☐ 259 Al Osuna	.05	.02	.01
☐ 260 Todd Hundley	.10	.05	.01
☐ 261 Orel Hershiser	.15	.07	.02
☐ 262 Ray Lankford	.15	.07	.02
☐ 263 Robin Ventura	.15	.07	.02
☐ 264 Felix Jose	.05	.02	.01
☐ 265 Eddie Murray	.15	.07	.02
☐ 266 Kevin Mitchell	.10	.05	.01
☐ 267 Gary Carter	.15	.07	.02
☐ 268 Mike Benjamin	.05	.02	.01
☐ 269 Dick Schofield	.05	.02	.01
☐ 270 Jose Uribe	.05	.02	.01
☐ 271 Pete Incaviglia	.05	.02	.01
☐ 272 Tony Fernandez	.05	.02	.01
☐ 273 Alan Trammell	.15	.07	.02
☐ 274 Tony Gwynn	.30	.14	.04
☐ 275 Mike Greenwell	.15	.07	.02
☐ 276 Jeff Bagwell	.50	.23	.06
☐ 277 Frank Viola	.05	.02	.01
☐ 278 Randy Myers	.05	.02	.01
☐ 279 Ken Caminiti	.15	.07	.02
☐ 280 Bill Doran	.05	.02	.01
☐ 281 Dan Pasqua	.05	.02	.01
☐ 282 Alfredo Griffin	.05	.02	.01
☐ 283 Jose Oquendo	.05	.02	.01
☐ 284 Kal Daniels	.05	.02	.01
☐ 285 Bobby Thigpen	.05	.02	.01
☐ 286 Robby Thompson	.10	.05	.01
☐ 287 Mark Eichhorn	.05	.02	.01
☐ 288 Mike Felder	.05	.02	.01
☐ 289 Dave Gallagher	.05	.02	.01
☐ 290 Dave Anderson	.05	.02	.01
☐ 291 Mel Hall	.05	.02	.01
☐ 292 Jerald Clark	.05	.02	.01
☐ 293 Al Newman	.05	.02	.01
☐ 294 Rob Deer	.05	.02	.01
☐ 295 Matt Nokes	.05	.02	.01
☐ 296 Jack Armstrong	.05	.02	.01
☐ 297 Jim Deshaies	.05	.02	.01
☐ 298 Jeff Innis	.05	.02	.01
☐ 299 Jeff Reed	.05	.02	.01
☐ 300 Checklist 201-300	.05	.02	.01
☐ 301 Lonnie Smith	.05	.02	.01
☐ 302 Jimmy Key	.10	.05	.01
☐ 303 Junior Felix	.05	.02	.01
☐ 304 Mike Heath	.05	.02	.01
☐ 305 Mark Langston	.10	.05	.01
☐ 306 Greg W. Harris	.05	.02	.01
☐ 307 Brett Butler	.15	.07	.02
☐ 308 Luis Rivera	.05	.02	.01
☐ 309 Bruce Ruffin	.05	.02	.01
☐ 310 Paul Faries	.05	.02	.01
☐ 311 Terry Leach	.05	.02	.01
☐ 312 Scott Brosius	.05	.02	.01
☐ 313 Scott Leius	.05	.02	.01

□	#	Name			
□	314	Harold Reynolds	.05	.02	.01
□	315	Jack Morris	.10	.05	.01
□	316	David Segui	.10	.05	.01
□	317	Bill Gullickson	.05	.02	.01
□	318	Todd Frohwirth	.05	.02	.01
□	319	Mark Leiter	.05	.02	.01
□	320	Jeff M. Robinson	.05	.02	.01
□	321	Gary Gaetti	.10	.05	.01
□	322	John Smoltz	.15	.07	.02
□	323	Andy Benes	.10	.05	.01
□	324	Kelly Gruber	.05	.02	.01
□	325	Jim Abbott	.15	.07	.02
□	326	John Kruk	.15	.07	.02
□	327	Kevin Seitzer	.05	.02	.01
□	328	Darrin Jackson	.05	.02	.01
□	329	Kurt Stillwell	.05	.02	.01
□	330	Mike Maddux	.05	.02	.01
□	331	Dennis Eckersley	.15	.07	.02
□	332	Dan Gladden	.05	.02	.01
□	333	Jose Canseco	.15	.07	.02
□	334	Kent Hrbek	.10	.05	.01
□	335	Ken Griffey Sr.	.10	.05	.01
□	336	Greg Swindell	.05	.02	.01
□	337	Trevor Wilson	.05	.02	.01
□	338	Sam Horn	.05	.02	.01
□	339	Mike Henneman	.05	.02	.01
□	340	Jerry Browne	.05	.02	.01
□	341	Glenn Braggs	.05	.02	.01
□	342	Tom Glavine	.15	.07	.02
□	343	Wally Joyner	.15	.07	.02
□	344	Fred McGriff	.15	.07	.02
□	345	Ron Gant	.15	.07	.02
□	346	Ramon Martinez	.15	.07	.02
□	347	Wes Chamberlain	.05	.02	.01
□	348	Terry Shumpert	.05	.02	.01
□	349	Tim Teufel	.05	.02	.01
□	350	Wally Backman	.05	.02	.01
□	351	Joe Girardi	.05	.02	.01
□	352	Devon White	.05	.02	.01
□	353	Greg Maddux	.75	.35	.09
□	354	Ryan Bowen	.05	.02	.01
□	355	Roberto Alomar	.20	.09	.03
□	356	Don Mattingly	.50	.23	.06
□	357	Pedro Guerrero	.05	.02	.01
□	358	Steve Sax	.05	.02	.01
□	359	Joey Cora	.05	.02	.01
□	360	Jim Gantner	.10	.05	.01
□	361	Brian Barnes	.05	.02	.01
□	362	Kevin McReynolds	.05	.02	.01
□	363	Bret Barberie	.05	.02	.01
□	364	David Cone	.15	.07	.02
□	365	Dennis Martinez	.10	.05	.01
□	366	Brian Hunter	.05	.02	.01
□	367	Edgar Martinez	.15	.07	.02
□	368	Steve Finley	.10	.05	.01
□	369	Greg Briley	.05	.02	.01
□	370	Jeff Blauser	.10	.05	.01
□	371	Todd Stottlemyre	.05	.02	.01
□	372	Luis Gonzalez	.10	.05	.01
□	373	Rick Wilkins	.05	.02	.01
□	374	Darryl Kile	.05	.02	.01
□	375	John Olerud	.10	.05	.01
□	376	Lee Smith	.15	.07	.02
□	377	Kevin Maas	.05	.02	.01
□	378	Dante Bichette	.20	.09	.03
□	379	Tom Pagnozzi	.05	.02	.01
□	380	Mike Flanagan	.05	.02	.01
□	381	Charlie O'Brien	.05	.02	.01
□	382	Dave Martinez	.05	.02	.01
□	383	Keith Miller	.05	.02	.01
□	384	Scott Ruskin	.05	.02	.01
□	385	Kevin Elster	.05	.02	.01
□	386	Alvin Davis	.05	.02	.01
□	387	Casey Candaele	.05	.02	.01
□	388	Pete O'Brien	.05	.02	.01
□	389	Jeff Treadway	.05	.02	.01
□	390	Scott Bradley	.05	.02	.01
□	391	Mookie Wilson	.10	.05	.01
□	392	Jimmy Jones	.05	.02	.01
□	393	Candy Maldonado	.05	.02	.01
□	394	Eric Yelding	.05	.02	.01
□	395	Tom Henke	.10	.05	.01
□	396	Franklin Stubbs	.05	.02	.01
□	397	Milt Thompson	.05	.02	.01
□	398	Mark Carreon	.05	.02	.01
□	399	Randy Velarde	.05	.02	.01
□	400	Checklist 301-400	.05	.02	.01
□	401	Omar Vizquel	.10	.05	.01
□	402	Joe Boever	.05	.02	.01
□	403	Bill Krueger	.05	.02	.01
□	404	Jody Reed	.05	.02	.01
□	405	Mike Schooler	.05	.02	.01
□	406	Jason Grimsley	.05	.02	.01
□	407	Greg Myers	.05	.02	.01
□	408	Randy Ready	.05	.02	.01
□	409	Mike Timlin	.05	.02	.01
□	410	Mitch Williams	.10	.05	.01
□	411	Garry Templeton	.05	.02	.01
□	412	Greg Cadaret	.05	.02	.01
□	413	Donnie Hill	.05	.02	.01
□	414	Wally Whitehurst	.05	.02	.01
□	415	Scott Sanderson	.05	.02	.01
□	416	Thomas Howard	.05	.02	.01
□	417	Neal Heaton	.05	.02	.01
□	418	Charlie Hough	.10	.05	.01
□	419	Jack Howell	.05	.02	.01
□	420	Greg Hibbard	.05	.02	.01
□	421	Carlos Quintana	.05	.02	.01
□	422	Kim Batiste	.05	.02	.01
□	423	Paul Molitor	.15	.07	.02
□	424	Ken Griffey Jr.	1.50	.70	.19
□	425	Phil Plantier	.10	.05	.01
□	426	Denny Neagle	.10	.05	.01
□	427	Von Hayes	.05	.02	.01
□	428	Shane Mack	.05	.02	.01
□	429	Darren Daulton	.15	.07	.02
□	430	Dwayne Henry	.05	.02	.01
□	431	Lance Parrish	.10	.05	.01
□	432	Mike Humphreys	.05	.02	.01
□	433	Tim Burke	.05	.02	.01
□	434	Bryan Harvey	.05	.02	.01
□	435	Pat Kelly	.05	.02	.01
□	436	Ozzie Guillen	.10	.05	.01
□	437	Bruce Hurst	.05	.02	.01
□	438	Sammy Sosa	.15	.07	.02
□	439	Dennis Rasmussen	.05	.02	.01
□	440	Ken Patterson	.05	.02	.01
□	441	Jay Buhner	.15	.07	.02
□	442	Pat Combs	.05	.02	.01
□	443	Wade Boggs	.15	.07	.02
□	444	George Brett	.40	.18	.05
□	445	Mo Vaughn	.40	.18	.05
□	446	Chuck Knoblauch	.15	.07	.02
□	447	Tom Candiotti	.05	.02	.01
□	448	Mark Portugal	.05	.02	.01
□	449	Mickey Morandini	.05	.02	.01
□	450	Duane Ward	.05	.02	.01
□	451	Otis Nixon	.05	.02	.01
□	452	Bob Welch	.05	.02	.01
□	453	Rusty Meacham	.05	.02	.01
□	454	Keith Mitchell	.05	.02	.01
□	455	Marquis Grissom	.15	.07	.02

☐ 456 Robin Yount	.15	.07	.02
☐ 457 Harvey Pulliam	.05	.02	.01
☐ 458 Jose DeLeon	.05	.02	.01
☐ 459 Mark Gubicza	.05	.02	.01
☐ 460 Darryl Hamilton	.10	.05	.01
☐ 461 Tom Browning	.05	.02	.01
☐ 462 Monty Fariss	.05	.02	.01
☐ 463 Jerome Walton	.05	.02	.01
☐ 464 Paul O'Neill	.15	.07	.02
☐ 465 Dean Palmer	.10	.05	.01
☐ 466 Travis Fryman	.15	.07	.02
☐ 467 John Smiley	.05	.02	.01
☐ 468 Lloyd Moseby	.05	.02	.01
☐ 469 John Wehner	.05	.02	.01
☐ 470 Skeeter Barnes	.05	.02	.01
☐ 471 Steve Chitren	.05	.02	.01
☐ 472 Kent Mercker	.05	.02	.01
☐ 473 Terry Steinbach	.10	.05	.01
☐ 474 Andres Galarraga	.15	.07	.02
☐ 475 Steve Avery	.15	.07	.02
☐ 476 Tom Gordon	.10	.05	.01
☐ 477 Cal Eldred	.05	.02	.01
☐ 478 Omar Olivares	.05	.02	.01
☐ 479 Julio Machado	.05	.02	.01
☐ 480 Bob Milacki	.05	.02	.01
☐ 481 Les Lancaster	.05	.02	.01
☐ 482 John Candelaria	.05	.02	.01
☐ 483 Brian Downing	.05	.02	.01
☐ 484 Roger McDowell	.05	.02	.01
☐ 485 Scott Scudder	.05	.02	.01
☐ 486 Zane Smith	.05	.02	.01
☐ 487 John Cerutti	.05	.02	.01
☐ 488 Steve Buechele	.05	.02	.01
☐ 489 Paul Gibson	.05	.02	.01
☐ 490 Curtis Wilkerson	.05	.02	.01
☐ 491 Marvin Freeman	.05	.02	.01
☐ 492 Tom Foley	.05	.02	.01
☐ 493 Juan Berenguer	.05	.02	.01
☐ 494 Ernest Riles	.05	.02	.01
☐ 495 Sid Bream	.05	.02	.01
☐ 496 Chuck Crim	.05	.02	.01
☐ 497 Mike Macfarlane	.05	.02	.01
☐ 498 Dale Sveum	.05	.02	.01
☐ 499 Storm Davis	.05	.02	.01
☐ 500 Checklist 401-500	.05	.02	.01
☐ 501 Jeff Reardon	.10	.05	.01
☐ 502 Shawn Abner	.05	.02	.01
☐ 503 Tony Fossas	.05	.02	.01
☐ 504 Cory Snyder	.05	.02	.01
☐ 505 Matt Young	.05	.02	.01
☐ 506 Allan Anderson	.05	.02	.01
☐ 507 Mark Lee	.05	.02	.01
☐ 508 Gene Nelson	.05	.02	.01
☐ 509 Mike Pagliarulo	.05	.02	.01
☐ 510 Rafael Belliard	.05	.02	.01
☐ 511 Jay Howell	.05	.02	.01
☐ 512 Bob Tewksbury	.05	.02	.01
☐ 513 Mike Morgan	.05	.02	.01
☐ 514 John Franco	.15	.07	.02
☐ 515 Kevin Gross	.05	.02	.01
☐ 516 Lou Whitaker	.15	.07	.02
☐ 517 Orlando Merced	.05	.02	.01
☐ 518 Todd Benzinger	.05	.02	.01
☐ 519 Gary Redus	.05	.02	.01
☐ 520 Walt Terrell	.05	.02	.01
☐ 521 Jack Clark	.10	.05	.01
☐ 522 Dave Parker	.10	.05	.01
☐ 523 Tim Naehring	.05	.02	.01
☐ 524 Mark Whiten	.10	.05	.01
☐ 525 Ellis Burks	.10	.05	.01
☐ 526 Frank Castillo	.05	.02	.01

☐ 527 Brian Harper	.05	.02	.01
☐ 528 Brook Jacoby	.05	.02	.01
☐ 529 Rick Sutcliffe	.10	.05	.01
☐ 530 Joe Klink	.05	.02	.01
☐ 531 Terry Bross	.05	.02	.01
☐ 532 Jose Offerman	.05	.02	.01
☐ 533 Todd Zeile	.10	.05	.01
☐ 534 Eric Karros	.20	.09	.03
☐ 535 Anthony Young	.05	.02	.01
☐ 536 Milt Cuyler	.05	.02	.01
☐ 537 Randy Tomlin	.05	.02	.01
☐ 538 Scott Livingstone	.05	.02	.01
☐ 539 Jim Eisenreich	.05	.02	.01
☐ 540 Don Slaught	.05	.02	.01
☐ 541 Scott Cooper	.05	.02	.01
☐ 542 Joe Grahe	.05	.02	.01
☐ 543 Tom Brunansky	.05	.02	.01
☐ 544 Eddie Zosky	.05	.02	.01
☐ 545 Roger Clemens	.20	.09	.03
☐ 546 David Justice	.15	.07	.02
☐ 547 Dave Stewart	.15	.07	.02
☐ 548 David West	.05	.02	.01
☐ 549 Dave Smith	.05	.02	.01
☐ 550 Dan Plesac	.05	.02	.01
☐ 551 Alex Fernandez	.15	.07	.02
☐ 552 Bernard Gilkey	.10	.05	.01
☐ 553 Jack McDowell	.15	.07	.02
☐ 554 Tino Martinez	.15	.07	.02
☐ 555 Bo Jackson	.15	.07	.02
☐ 556 Bernie Williams	.15	.07	.02
☐ 557 Mark Gardner	.05	.02	.01
☐ 558 Glenallen Hill	.10	.05	.01
☐ 559 Oil Can Boyd	.05	.02	.01
☐ 560 Chris James	.05	.02	.01
☐ 561 Scott Servais	.05	.02	.01
☐ 562 Rey Sanchez	.05	.02	.01
☐ 563 Paul McClellan	.05	.02	.01
☐ 564 Andy Mota	.05	.02	.01
☐ 565 Darren Lewis	.10	.05	.01
☐ 566 Jose Melendez	.05	.02	.01
☐ 567 Tommy Greene	.05	.02	.01
☐ 568 Rich Rodriguez	.05	.02	.01
☐ 569 Heathcliff Slocumb	.10	.05	.01
☐ 570 Joe Hesketh	.05	.02	.01
☐ 571 Carlton Fisk	.15	.07	.02
☐ 572 Erik Hanson	.05	.02	.01
☐ 573 Wilson Alvarez	.15	.07	.02
☐ 574 Rheal Cormier	.05	.02	.01
☐ 575 Tim Raines	.15	.07	.02
☐ 576 Bobby Witt	.05	.02	.01
☐ 577 Roberto Kelly	.10	.05	.01
☐ 578 Kevin Brown	.10	.05	.01
☐ 579 Chris Nabholz	.05	.02	.01
☐ 580 Jesse Orosco	.05	.02	.01
☐ 581 Jeff Brantley	.05	.02	.01
☐ 582 Rafael Ramirez	.05	.02	.01
☐ 583 Kelly Downs	.05	.02	.01
☐ 584 Mike Simms	.05	.02	.01
☐ 585 Mike Remlinger	.05	.02	.01
☐ 586 Dave Hollins	.05	.02	.01
☐ 587 Larry Andersen	.05	.02	.01
☐ 588 Mike Gardiner	.05	.02	.01
☐ 589 Craig Lefferts	.05	.02	.01
☐ 590 Paul Assenmacher	.05	.02	.01
☐ 591 Bryn Smith	.05	.02	.01
☐ 592 Donn Pall	.05	.02	.01
☐ 593 Mike Jackson	.05	.02	.01
☐ 594 Scott Radinsky	.05	.02	.01
☐ 595 Brian Holman	.05	.02	.01
☐ 596 Geronimo Pena	.05	.02	.01
☐ 597 Mike Jeffcoat	.05	.02	.01

#	Name			
☐ 598	Carlos Martinez	.05	.02	.01
☐ 599	Geno Petralli	.05	.02	.01
☐ 600	Checklist 501-600	.05	.02	.01
☐ 601	Jerry Don Gleaton	.05	.02	.01
☐ 602	Adam Peterson	.05	.02	.01
☐ 603	Craig Grebeck	.05	.02	.01
☐ 604	Mark Guthrie	.05	.02	.01
☐ 605	Frank Tanana	.05	.02	.01
☐ 606	Hensley Meulens	.05	.02	.01
☐ 607	Mark Davis	.05	.02	.01
☐ 608	Eric Plunk	.05	.02	.01
☐ 609	Mark Williamson	.05	.02	.01
☐ 610	Lee Guetterman	.05	.02	.01
☐ 611	Bobby Rose	.05	.02	.01
☐ 612	Bill Wegman	.05	.02	.01
☐ 613	Mike Hartley	.05	.02	.01
☐ 614	Chris Beasley	.05	.02	.01
☐ 615	Chris Bosio	.05	.02	.01
☐ 616	Henry Cotto	.05	.02	.01
☐ 617	Chico Walker	.05	.02	.01
☐ 618	Russ Swan	.05	.02	.01
☐ 619	Bob Walk	.05	.02	.01
☐ 620	Billy Swift	.05	.02	.01
☐ 621	Warren Newson	.05	.02	.01
☐ 622	Steve Bedrosian	.05	.02	.01
☐ 623	Ricky Bones	.05	.02	.01
☐ 624	Kevin Tapani	.05	.02	.01
☐ 625	Juan Guzman	.10	.05	.01
☐ 626	Jeff Johnson	.05	.02	.01
☐ 627	Jeff Montgomery	.10	.05	.01
☐ 628	Ken Hill	.15	.07	.02
☐ 629	Gary Thurman	.05	.02	.01
☐ 630	Steve Howe	.05	.02	.01
☐ 631	Jose DeJesus	.05	.02	.01
☐ 632	Kirk Dressendorfer	.05	.02	.01
☐ 633	Jaime Navarro	.05	.02	.01
☐ 634	Lee Stevens	.05	.02	.01
☐ 635	Pete Harnisch	.05	.02	.01
☐ 636	Bill Landrum	.05	.02	.01
☐ 637	Rich DeLucia	.05	.02	.01
☐ 638	Luis Salazar	.05	.02	.01
☐ 639	Rob Murphy	.05	.02	.01
☐ 640	Diamond Skills	.15	.07	.02
	Checklist			
	Jose Canseco			
	Rickey Henderson			
☐ 641	Roger Clemens DS	.15	.07	.02
☐ 642	Jim Abbott DS	.10	.05	.01
☐ 643	Travis Fryman DS	.15	.07	.02
☐ 644	Jesse Barfield DS	.05	.02	.01
☐ 645	Cal Ripken DS	.50	.23	.06
☐ 646	Wade Boggs DS	.15	.07	.02
☐ 647	Cecil Fielder DS	.10	.05	.01
☐ 648	Rickey Henderson DS	.15	.07	.02
☐ 649	Jose Canseco DS	.15	.07	.02
☐ 650	Ken Griffey Jr. DS	.75	.35	.09
☐ 651	Kenny Rogers	.05	.02	.01
☐ 652	Luis Mercedes	.05	.02	.01
☐ 653	Mike Stanton	.05	.02	.01
☐ 654	Glenn Davis	.05	.02	.01
☐ 655	Nolan Ryan	.75	.35	.09
☐ 656	Reggie Jefferson	.05	.02	.01
☐ 657	Javier Ortiz	.05	.02	.01
☐ 658	Greg A. Harris	.05	.02	.01
☐ 659	Mariano Duncan	.05	.02	.01
☐ 660	Jeff Shaw	.05	.02	.01
☐ 661	Mike Moore	.05	.02	.01
☐ 662	Chris Haney	.05	.02	.01
☐ 663	Joe Slusarski	.05	.02	.01
☐ 664	Wayne Housie	.05	.02	.01
☐ 665	Carlos Garcia	.10	.05	.01
☐ 666	Bob Ojeda	.05	.02	.01
☐ 667	Bryan Hickerson	.05	.02	.01
☐ 668	Tim Belcher	.05	.02	.01
☐ 669	Ron Darling	.05	.02	.01
☐ 670	Rex Hudler	.05	.02	.01
☐ 671	Sid Fernandez	.10	.05	.01
☐ 672	Chito Martinez	.05	.02	.01
☐ 673	Pete Schourek	.10	.05	.01
☐ 674	Armando Reynoso	.05	.02	.01
☐ 675	Mike Mussina	.25	.11	.03
☐ 676	Kevin Morton	.05	.02	.01
☐ 677	Norm Charlton	.05	.02	.01
☐ 678	Danny Darwin	.05	.02	.01
☐ 679	Eric King	.05	.02	.01
☐ 680	Ted Power	.05	.02	.01
☐ 681	Barry Jones	.05	.02	.01
☐ 682	Carney Lansford	.10	.05	.01
☐ 683	Mel Rojas	.10	.05	.01
☐ 684	Rick Honeycutt	.05	.02	.01
☐ 685	Jeff Fassero	.10	.05	.01
☐ 686	Cris Carpenter	.05	.02	.01
☐ 687	Tim Crews	.05	.02	.01
☐ 688	Scott Terry	.05	.02	.01
☐ 689	Chris Gwynn	.05	.02	.01
☐ 690	Gerald Perry	.05	.02	.01
☐ 691	John Barfield	.05	.02	.01
☐ 692	Bob Melvin	.05	.02	.01
☐ 693	Juan Agosto	.05	.02	.01
☐ 694	Alejandro Pena	.05	.02	.01
☐ 695	Jeff Russell	.05	.02	.01
☐ 696	Carmelo Martinez	.05	.02	.01
☐ 697	Bud Black	.05	.02	.01
☐ 698	Dave Otto	.05	.02	.01
☐ 699	Billy Hatcher	.05	.02	.01
☐ 700	Checklist 601-700	.05	.02	.01
☐ 701	Clemente Nunez	.30	.14	.04
☐ 702	Rookie Threats	.05	.02	.01
	Mark Clark			
	Donovan Osborne			
	Brian Jordan			
☐ 703	Mike Morgan	.05	.02	.01
☐ 704	Keith Miller	.05	.02	.01
☐ 705	Kurt Stillwell	.05	.02	.01
☐ 706	Damon Berryhill	.05	.02	.01
☐ 707	Von Hayes	.05	.02	.01
☐ 708	Rick Sutcliffe	.10	.05	.01
☐ 709	Hubie Brooks	.05	.02	.01
☐ 710	Ryan Turner	.15	.07	.02
☐ 711	Diamond Skills	.15	.07	.02
	Checklist			
	Barry Bonds			
	Andy Van Slyke			
☐ 712	Jose Rijo DS	.05	.02	.01
☐ 713	Tom Glavine DS	.10	.05	.01
☐ 714	Shawon Dunston DS	.05	.02	.01
☐ 715	Andy Van Slyke DS	.05	.02	.01
☐ 716	Ozzie Smith DS	.15	.07	.02
☐ 717	Tony Gwynn DS	.15	.07	.02
☐ 718	Will Clark DS	.10	.05	.01
☐ 719	Marquis Grissom DS	.10	.05	.01
☐ 720	Howard Johnson DS	.05	.02	.01
☐ 721	Barry Bonds DS	.15	.07	.02
☐ 722	Kirk McCaskill	.05	.02	.01
☐ 723	Sammy Sosa	.15	.07	.02
☐ 724	George Bell	.05	.02	.01
☐ 725	Gregg Jefferies	.15	.07	.02
☐ 726	Gary DiSarcina	.05	.02	.01
☐ 727	Mike Bordick	.05	.02	.01
☐ 728	Eddie Murray	.15	.07	.02
	400 Home Run Club			
☐ 729	Rene Gonzales	.05	.02	.01

☐ 730	Mike Bielecki	.05	.02	.01
☐ 731	Calvin Jones	.05	.02	.01
☐ 732	Jack Morris	.15	.07	.02
☐ 733	Frank Viola	.05	.02	.01
☐ 734	Dave Winfield	.15	.07	.02
☐ 735	Kevin Mitchell	.10	.05	.01
☐ 736	Bill Swift	.05	.02	.01
☐ 737	Dan Gladden	.05	.02	.01
☐ 738	Mike Jackson	.05	.02	.01
☐ 739	Mark Carreon	.05	.02	.01
☐ 740	Kirt Manwaring	.05	.02	.01
☐ 741	Randy Myers	.15	.07	.02
☐ 742	Kevin McReynolds	.05	.02	.01
☐ 743	Steve Sax	.05	.02	.01
☐ 744	Wally Joyner	.15	.07	.02
☐ 745	Gary Sheffield	.15	.07	.02
☐ 746	Danny Tartabull	.10	.05	.01
☐ 747	Julio Valera	.05	.02	.01
☐ 748	Denny Neagle	.10	.05	.01
☐ 749	Lance Blankenship	.05	.02	.01
☐ 750	Mike Gallego	.05	.02	.01
☐ 751	Bret Saberhagen	.15	.07	.02
☐ 752	Ruben Amaro	.05	.02	.01
☐ 753	Eddie Murray	.15	.07	.02
☐ 754	Kyle Abbott	.05	.02	.01
☐ 755	Bobby Bonilla	.15	.07	.02
☐ 756	Eric Davis	.10	.05	.01
☐ 757	Eddie Taubensee	.10	.05	.01
☐ 758	Andres Galarraga	.15	.07	.02
☐ 759	Pete Incaviglia	.05	.02	.01
☐ 760	Tom Candiotti	.05	.02	.01
☐ 761	Tim Belcher	.05	.02	.01
☐ 762	Ricky Bones	.05	.02	.01
☐ 763	Bip Roberts	.05	.02	.01
☐ 764	Pedro Munoz	.10	.05	.01
☐ 765	Greg Swindell	.05	.02	.01
☐ 766	Kenny Lofton	1.00	.45	.12
☐ 767	Gary Carter	.15	.07	.02
☐ 768	Charlie Hayes	.10	.05	.01
☐ 769	Dickie Thon	.05	.02	.01
☐ 770	Donovan Osborne DD CL	.05	.02	.01
☐ 771	Bret Boone DD	.20	.09	.03
☐ 772	Archi Cianfrocco DD	.05	.02	.01
☐ 773	Mark Clark DD	.15	.07	.02
☐ 774	Chad Curtis DD	.20	.09	.03
☐ 775	Pat Listach DD	.05	.02	.01
☐ 776	Pat Mahomes DD	.05	.02	.01
☐ 777	Donovan Osborne DD	.05	.02	.01
☐ 778	John Patterson DD	.05	.02	.01
☐ 779	Andy Stankiewicz DD	.05	.02	.01
☐ 780	Turk Wendell DD	.10	.05	.01
☐ 781	Bill Krueger	.05	.02	.01
☐ 782	Rickey Henderson	.15	.07	.02
	Grand Theft			
☐ 783	Kevin Seitzer	.05	.02	.01
☐ 784	Dave Martinez	.05	.02	.01
☐ 785	John Smiley	.05	.02	.01
☐ 786	Matt Stairs	.05	.02	.01
☐ 787	Scott Scudder	.05	.02	.01
☐ 788	John Wetteland	.10	.05	.01
☐ 789	Jack Armstrong	.05	.02	.01
☐ 790	Ken Hill	.15	.07	.02
☐ 791	Dick Schofield	.05	.02	.01
☐ 792	Mariano Duncan	.05	.02	.01
☐ 793	Bill Pecota	.05	.02	.01
☐ 794	Mike Kelly	.05	.02	.01
☐ 795	Willie Randolph	.10	.05	.01
☐ 796	Butch Henry	.05	.02	.01
☐ 797	Carlos Hernandez	.05	.02	.01
☐ 798	Doug Jones	.05	.02	.01
☐ 799	Melido Perez	.05	.02	.01

☐ 800	Checklist 701-800	.05	.02	.01
☐ HH2	Ted Williams Hologram	2.00	.90	.25
	(Top left corner says,			
	91 Upper Deck 92)			
☐ SP3	Deion Sanders FB/BB	3.00	1.35	.35
☐ SP4	Tom Selleck and	5.00	2.20	.60
	Frank Thomas SP			
	(Mr. Baseball)			

1992 Upper Deck Scouting Report

Randomly inserted one per high series jumbo pack, this 25-card set features outstanding prospects in baseball. The cards measure the standard size (2 1/2" by 3 1/2"). The fronts carry color action player photos that are full-bleed on the top and right, bordered below by a black stripe with the player's name, and by a black jagged left border that resembles torn paper. The words "Scouting Report" are printed vertically in silver lettering in the left border. The back design features a clipboard with three items held fast by the clamp: 1) a color player photo; 2) a 4" by 6" index card with major league rating in five categories (average, power, speed, fielding, and arm), and an 8 1/2" by 11" piece of paper typed with a player profile. The cards are numbered on the back with an SR prefix. The card numbering follows alphabetical order by player's name.

	MINT	NRMT	EXC
COMPLETE SET (25)	15.00	6.75	1.85
COMMON CARD (SR1-SR25)	.25	.11	.03

☐ SR1	Andy Ashby	.35	.16	.04
☐ SR2	Willie Banks	.25	.11	.03
☐ SR3	Kim Batiste	.25	.11	.03
☐ SR4	Derek Bell	.75	.35	.09
☐ SR5	Archi Cianfrocco	.25	.11	.03
☐ SR6	Royce Clayton	.35	.16	.04
☐ SR7	Gary DiSarcina	.25	.11	.03
☐ SR8	Dave Fleming	.35	.16	.04
☐ SR9	Butch Henry	.25	.11	.03
☐ SR10	Todd Hundley	.35	.16	.04
☐ SR11	Brian Jordan	.75	.35	.09
☐ SR12	Eric Karros	2.00	.90	.25
☐ SR13	Pat Listach	.35	.16	.04

		MINT	NRMT	EXC
☐	SR14 Scott Livingstone	.25	.11	.03
☐	SR15 Kenny Lofton	8.00	3.60	1.00
☐	SR16 Pat Mahomes	.25	.11	.03
☐	SR17 Denny Neagle	.75	.35	.09
☐	SR18 Dave Nilsson	.50	.23	.06
☐	SR19 Donovan Osborne	.25	.11	.03
☐	SR20 Reggie Sanders	2.00	.90	.25
☐	SR21 Andy Stankiewicz	.25	.11	.03
☐	SR22 Jim Thome	6.00	2.70	.75
☐	SR23 Julio Valera	.25	.11	.03
☐	SR24 Mark Wohlers	.75	.35	.09
☐	SR25 Anthony Young	.25	.11	.03

☐	T12 Jeff Bagwell	2.50	1.10	.30
☐	T13 Albert Belle	2.00	.90	.25
☐	T14 Juan Gonzalez	2.00	.90	.25
☐	T15 Ken Griffey Jr	8.00	3.60	1.00
☐	T16 Chris Hoiles	.50	.23	.06
☐	T17 David Justice	1.00	.45	.12
☐	T18 Phil Plantier	.50	.23	.06
☐	T19 Frank Thomas	8.00	3.60	1.00
☐	T20 Robin Ventura	.75	.35	.09

1993 Upper Deck

1992 Upper Deck Williams Best

 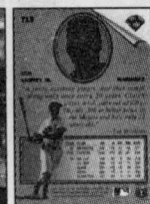

This 20-card set contains Ted Williams' choices of best current and future hitters in the game. The standard size cards (2 1/2" by 3 1/2") were randomly inserted in Upper Deck high number foil packs. The fronts feature full-bleed color action photos with the player's name in a black field separated from the picture by Ted Williams' gold-stamped signature. The back design displays a color close-up of the player in a purple and gold bordered oval on a gray cement-textured background. The upper right corner appears peeled back to reveal the Upper Deck hologram. A Ted Williams' quote about the player is included below the photo. Player's statistics in a purple and gold bordered box round out the back. The cards are numbered on the back with a "T" prefix.

	MINT	NRMT	EXC
COMPLETE SET (20)	30.00	13.50	3.70
COMMON CARD (T1-T20)	.50	.23	.06

		MINT	NRMT	EXC
☐	T1 Wade Boggs	.75	.35	.09
☐	T2 Barry Bonds	1.50	.70	.19
☐	T3 Jose Canseco	1.00	.45	.12
☐	T4 Will Clark	1.00	.45	.12
☐	T5 Cecil Fielder	.75	.35	.09
☐	T6 Tony Gwynn	1.50	.70	.19
☐	T7 Rickey Henderson	.75	.35	.09
☐	T8 Fred McGriff	1.00	.45	.12
☐	T9 Kirby Puckett	1.50	.70	.19
☐	T10 Ruben Sierra	.75	.35	.09
☐	T11 Roberto Alomar	1.25	.55	.16

The 1993 Upper Deck set consists of two series of 420 cards each measuring the standard size, 2 1/2" by 3 1/2". The first series inserts included a ten-card hobby-only insert set featuring Triple Crown Contenders while a 26-card Walter Iooss Collection was found in retail foil packs only. A ten-card Baseball Heroes insert set pays tribute to Willie Mays. Also a nine-card "Then And Now" hologram set was randomly inserted in foil packs and one card of a 28-card insert set was featured exclusively in each jumbo foil pack. A special card (SP5) was randomly inserted in first series packs to commemorate the 3,000th hit of Brett and Yount. Randomly inserted into second series foil packs were ten Future Heroes cards, a special card (SP6) commemorating Nolan Ryan's last season, a second nine-card Then and Now hologram subset, a 15-card Fifth Anniversary subset (hobby only), a 20-card Reggie Jackson's Clutch Performers subset (retail only), and a 25-card On Deck subset (jumbo packs only). The front designs features color action player photos bordered in white. The company name is printed along the photo surface of the card top. The player's name appears in script in a color stripe cutting across the bottom of the picture while the team name and his position appear in another color stripe immediately below. The backs have a color close-up photo on the upper portion and biography, statistics, and career highlights on the lower portion. Special subsets featured include Star Rookies (1-29), Community Heroes (30-40), and American League Teammates (41-55), Top Prospects (421-449), Inside the Numbers (450-470), Team Stars (471-485), Award Winners (486-499), and

Diamond Debuts (500-510). The cards are numbered on the back. Rookie Cards in this set include Midre Cummings, Derek Jeter, Ray McDavid, Michael Moore, Chad Mottola, J.T. Snow, and Tony Tarasco.

	MINT	NRMT	EXC
COMPLETE SET (840)	40.00	18.00	5.00
COMPLETE FACT.SET (840)	45.00	20.00	5.50
COMPLETE SERIES 1 (420)	20.00	9.00	2.50
COMPLETE SERIES 2 (420)	20.00	9.00	2.50
COMMON CARD (1-420)	.05	.02	.01
COMMON CARD (421-840)	.05	.02	.01
*GOLD HOLOGRAM: 1.5X VALUE			

		MINT	NRMT	EXC
☐ 1	Star Rookie CL	.30	.14	.04
	Tim Salmon			
☐ 2	Mike Piazza SR	1.50	.70	.19
☐ 3	Rene Arocha SR	.10	.05	.01
☐ 4	Willie Greene SR	.10	.05	.01
☐ 5	Manny Alexander SR	.05	.02	.01
☐ 6	Dan Wilson SR	.10	.05	.01
☐ 7	Dan Smith SR	.05	.02	.01
☐ 8	Kevin Rogers SR	.05	.02	.01
☐ 9	Kurt Miller SR	.05	.02	.01
☐ 10	Joe Vitko SR	.05	.02	.01
☐ 11	Tim Costo SR	.05	.02	.01
☐ 12	Alan Embree SR	.05	.02	.01
☐ 13	Jim Tatum SR	.05	.02	.01
☐ 14	Cris Colon SR	.05	.02	.01
☐ 15	Steve Hosey SR	.05	.02	.01
☐ 16	Sterling Hitchcock SR	.20	.09	.03
☐ 17	Dave Mlicki SR	.05	.02	.01
☐ 18	Jessie Hollins SR	.05	.02	.01
☐ 19	Bobby Jones SR	.10	.05	.01
☐ 20	Kurt Miller SR	.05	.02	.01
☐ 21	Melvin Nieves SR	.15	.07	.02
☐ 22	Billy Ashley SR	.10	.05	.01
☐ 23	J.T. Snow SR	.60	.25	.07
☐ 24	Chipper Jones SR	2.00	.90	.25
☐ 25	Tim Salmon SR	.60	.25	.07
☐ 26	Tim Pugh SR	.05	.02	.01
☐ 27	David Nied SR	.10	.05	.01
☐ 28	Mike Trombley SR	.05	.02	.01
☐ 29	Javier Lopez SR	.60	.25	.07
☐ 30	Community Heroes CL	.05	.02	.01
	Jim Abbott			
☐ 31	Jim Abbott CH	.10	.05	.01
☐ 32	Dale Murphy CH	.10	.05	.01
☐ 33	Tony Pena CH	.05	.02	.01
☐ 34	Kirby Puckett CH	.30	.14	.04
☐ 35	Harold Reynolds CH	.05	.02	.01
☐ 36	Cal Ripken CH	1.00	.45	.12
☐ 37	Nolan Ryan CH	1.00	.45	.12
☐ 38	Ryne Sandberg CH	.25	.11	.03
☐ 39	Dave Stewart CH	.05	.02	.01
☐ 40	Dave Winfield CH	.10	.05	.01
☐ 41	Teammates CL	.10	.05	.01
	Joe Carter			
	Mark McGwire			
☐ 42	Blockbuster Trade	.10	.05	.01
	Joe Carter			
	Roberto Alomar			
☐ 43	Brew Crew	.10	.05	.01
	Paul Molitor			
	Pat Listach			
	Robin Yount			
☐ 44	Iron and Steel	.50	.23	.06
	Cal Ripken			
	Brady Anderson			
☐ 45	Youthful Tribe	.75	.35	.09
	Albert Belle			
	Sandy Alomar Jr.			
	Jim Thome			
	Carlos Baerga			
	Kenny Lofton			
☐ 46	Motown Mashers	.05	.02	.01
	Cecil Fielder			
	Mickey Tettleton			
☐ 47	Yankee Pride	.25	.11	.03
	Roberto Kelly			
	Don Mattingly			
☐ 48	Boston Cy Sox	.10	.05	.01
	Frank Viola			
	Roger Clemens			
☐ 49	Bash Brothers	.05	.02	.01
	Ruben Sierra			
	Mark McGwire			
☐ 50	Twin Titles	.15	.07	.02
	Kent Hrbek			
	Kirby Puckett			
☐ 51	Southside Sluggers	.50	.23	.06
	Robin Ventura			
	Frank Thomas			
☐ 52	Latin Stars	.20	.09	.03
	Juan Gonzalez			
	Jose Canseco			
	Ivan Rodriguez			
	Rafael Palmeiro			
☐ 53	Lethal Lefties	.05	.02	.01
	Mark Langston			
	Jim Abbott			
	Chuck Finley			
☐ 54	Royal Family	.20	.09	.03
	Wally Joyner			
	Gregg Jefferies			
	George Brett			
☐ 55	Pacific Sock Exchange	.50	.23	.06
	Kevin Mitchell			
	Ken Griffey Jr.			
	Jay Buhner			
☐ 56	George Brett	.75	.35	.09
☐ 57	Scott Cooper	.05	.02	.01
☐ 58	Mike Maddux	.05	.02	.01
☐ 59	Rusty Meacham	.05	.02	.01
☐ 60	Wil Cordero	.10	.05	.01
☐ 61	Tim Teufel	.05	.02	.01
☐ 62	Jeff Montgomery	.05	.02	.01
☐ 63	Scott Livingstone	.05	.02	.01
☐ 64	Doug Dascenzo	.05	.02	.01
☐ 65	Bret Boone	.15	.07	.02
☐ 66	Tim Wakefield	.15	.07	.02
☐ 67	Curt Schilling	.15	.07	.02
☐ 68	Frank Tanana	.05	.02	.01
☐ 69	Len Dykstra	.15	.07	.02
☐ 70	Derek Lilliquist	.05	.02	.01
☐ 71	Anthony Young	.05	.02	.01
☐ 72	Hipolito Pichardo	.05	.02	.01
☐ 73	Rod Beck	.15	.07	.02
☐ 74	Kent Hrbek	.10	.05	.01
☐ 75	Tom Glavine	.15	.07	.02
☐ 76	Kevin Brown	.05	.02	.01
☐ 77	Chuck Finley	.10	.05	.01
☐ 78	Bob Walk	.05	.02	.01
☐ 79	Rheal Cormier UER	.05	.02	.01
	(Born in New Brunswick,			
	not British Columbia)			
☐ 80	Rick Sutcliffe	.10	.05	.01
☐ 81	Harold Baines	.10	.05	.01
☐ 82	Lee Smith	.15	.07	.02
☐ 83	Geno Petralli	.05	.02	.01
☐ 84	Jose Oquendo	.05	.02	.01

☐ 85 Mark Gubicza	.05	.02	.01
☐ 86 Mickey Tettleton	.10	.05	.01
☐ 87 Bobby Witt	.05	.02	.01
☐ 88 Mark Lewis	.05	.02	.01
☐ 89 Kevin Appier	.10	.05	.01
☐ 90 Mike Stanton	.05	.02	.01
☐ 91 Rafael Belliard	.05	.02	.01
☐ 92 Kenny Rogers	.05	.02	.01
☐ 93 Randy Velarde	.05	.02	.01
☐ 94 Luis Sojo	.05	.02	.01
☐ 95 Mark Leiter	.05	.02	.01
☐ 96 Jody Reed	.05	.02	.01
☐ 97 Pete Harnisch	.05	.02	.01
☐ 98 Tom Candiotti	.05	.02	.01
☐ 99 Mark Portugal	.05	.02	.01
☐ 100 Dave Valle	.05	.02	.01
☐ 101 Shawon Dunston	.05	.02	.01
☐ 102 B.J. Surhoff	.10	.05	.01
☐ 103 Jay Bell	.10	.05	.01
☐ 104 Sid Bream	.05	.02	.01
☐ 105 Checklist 1-105	.15	.07	.02
Frank Thomas			
☐ 106 Mike Morgan	.05	.02	.01
☐ 107 Bill Doran	.05	.02	.01
☐ 108 Lance Blankenship	.05	.02	.01
☐ 109 Mark Lemke	.10	.05	.01
☐ 110 Brian Harper	.05	.02	.01
☐ 111 Brady Anderson	.10	.05	.01
☐ 112 Bip Roberts	.05	.02	.01
☐ 113 Mitch Williams	.10	.05	.01
☐ 114 Craig Biggio	.15	.07	.02
☐ 115 Eddie Murray	.30	.14	.04
☐ 116 Matt Nokes	.05	.02	.01
☐ 117 Lance Parrish	.10	.05	.01
☐ 118 Bill Swift	.05	.02	.01
☐ 119 Jeff Innis	.05	.02	.01
☐ 120 Mike LaValliere	.05	.02	.01
☐ 121 Hal Morris	.10	.05	.01
☐ 122 Walt Weiss	.05	.02	.01
☐ 123 Ivan Rodriguez	.15	.07	.02
☐ 124 Andy Van Slyke	.15	.07	.02
☐ 125 Roberto Alomar	.40	.18	.05
☐ 126 Robby Thompson	.05	.02	.01
☐ 127 Sammy Sosa	.15	.07	.02
☐ 128 Mark Langston	.15	.07	.02
☐ 129 Jerry Browne	.05	.02	.01
☐ 130 Chuck McElroy	.05	.02	.01
☐ 131 Frank Viola	.10	.05	.01
☐ 132 Leo Gomez	.05	.02	.01
☐ 133 Ramon Martinez	.10	.05	.01
☐ 134 Don Mattingly	1.00	.45	.12
☐ 135 Roger Clemens	.30	.14	.04
☐ 136 Rickey Henderson	.15	.07	.02
☐ 137 Darren Daulton	.15	.07	.02
☐ 138 Ken Hill	.10	.05	.01
☐ 139 Ozzie Guillen	.05	.02	.01
☐ 140 Jerald Clark	.05	.02	.01
☐ 141 Dave Fleming	.05	.02	.01
☐ 142 Delino DeShields	.10	.05	.01
☐ 143 Matt Williams	.30	.14	.04
☐ 144 Larry Walker	.25	.11	.03
☐ 145 Ruben Sierra	.15	.07	.02
☐ 146 Ozzie Smith	.40	.18	.05
☐ 147 Chris Sabo	.05	.02	.01
☐ 148 Carlos Hernandez	.05	.02	.01
☐ 149 Pat Borders	.05	.02	.01
☐ 150 Orlando Merced	.10	.05	.01
☐ 151 Royce Clayton	.10	.05	.01
☐ 152 Kurt Stillwell	.05	.02	.01
☐ 153 Dave Hollins	.05	.02	.01
☐ 154 Mike Greenwell	.10	.05	.01
☐ 155 Nolan Ryan	2.00	.90	.25
☐ 156 Felix Jose	.05	.02	.01
☐ 157 Junior Felix	.05	.02	.01
☐ 158 Derek Bell	.15	.07	.02
☐ 159 Steve Buechele	.05	.02	.01
☐ 160 John Burkett	.05	.02	.01
☐ 161 Pat Howell	.05	.02	.01
☐ 162 Milt Cuyler	.05	.02	.01
☐ 163 Terry Pendleton	.10	.05	.01
☐ 164 Jack Morris	.15	.07	.02
☐ 165 Tony Gwynn	.60	.25	.07
☐ 166 Deion Sanders	.40	.18	.05
☐ 167 Mike Devereaux	.10	.05	.01
☐ 168 Ron Darling	.05	.02	.01
☐ 169 Orel Hershiser	.10	.05	.01
☐ 170 Mike Jackson	.05	.02	.01
☐ 171 Doug Jones	.05	.02	.01
☐ 172 Dan Walters	.05	.02	.01
☐ 173 Darren Lewis	.05	.02	.01
☐ 174 Carlos Baerga	.40	.18	.05
☐ 175 Ryne Sandberg	.50	.23	.06
☐ 176 Gregg Jefferies	.15	.07	.02
☐ 177 John Jaha	.10	.05	.01
☐ 178 Luis Polonia	.05	.02	.01
☐ 179 Kirt Manwaring	.05	.02	.01
☐ 180 Mike Magnante	.05	.02	.01
☐ 181 Billy Ripken	.05	.02	.01
☐ 182 Mike Moore	.05	.02	.01
☐ 183 Eric Anthony	.05	.02	.01
☐ 184 Lenny Harris	.05	.02	.01
☐ 185 Tony Pena	.05	.02	.01
☐ 186 Mike Felder	.05	.02	.01
☐ 187 Greg Olson	.05	.02	.01
☐ 188 Rene Gonzales	.05	.02	.01
☐ 189 Mike Bordick	.05	.02	.01
☐ 190 Mel Rojas	.10	.05	.01
☐ 191 Todd Frohwirth	.05	.02	.01
☐ 192 Darryl Hamilton	.05	.02	.01
☐ 193 Mike Fetters	.05	.02	.01
☐ 194 Omar Olivares	.05	.02	.01
☐ 195 Tony Phillips	.05	.02	.01
☐ 196 Paul Sorrento	.05	.02	.01
☐ 197 Trevor Wilson	.05	.02	.01
☐ 198 Kevin Gross	.05	.02	.01
☐ 199 Ron Karkovice	.05	.02	.01
☐ 200 Brook Jacoby	.05	.02	.01
☐ 201 Mariano Duncan	.05	.02	.01
☐ 202 Dennis Cook	.05	.02	.01
☐ 203 Daryl Boston	.05	.02	.01
☐ 204 Mike Perez	.05	.02	.01
☐ 205 Manuel Lee	.05	.02	.01
☐ 206 Steve Olin	.05	.02	.01
☐ 207 Charlie Hough	.10	.05	.01
☐ 208 Scott Scudder	.05	.02	.01
☐ 209 Charlie O'Brien	.05	.02	.01
☐ 210 Checklist 106-210	.15	.07	.02
Barry Bonds			
☐ 211 Jose Vizcaino	.05	.02	.01
☐ 212 Scott Leius	.05	.02	.01
☐ 213 Kevin Mitchell	.10	.05	.01
☐ 214 Brian Barnes	.05	.02	.01
☐ 215 Pat Kelly	.05	.02	.01
☐ 216 Chris Hammond	.05	.02	.01
☐ 217 Rob Deer	.05	.02	.01
☐ 218 Cory Snyder	.05	.02	.01
☐ 219 Gary Carter	.15	.07	.02
☐ 220 Danny Darwin	.05	.02	.01
☐ 221 Tom Gordon	.05	.02	.01
☐ 222 Gary Sheffield	.15	.07	.02
☐ 223 Joe Carter	.15	.07	.02
☐ 224 Jay Buhner	.15	.07	.02

☐ 225 Jose Offerman	.05	.02	.01
☐ 226 Jose Rijo	.10	.05	.01
☐ 227 Mark Whiten	.10	.05	.01
☐ 228 Randy Milligan	.05	.02	.01
☐ 229 Bud Black	.05	.02	.01
☐ 230 Gary DiSarcina	.05	.02	.01
☐ 231 Steve Finley	.05	.02	.01
☐ 232 Dennis Martinez	.10	.05	.01
☐ 233 Mike Mussina	.15	.07	.02
☐ 234 Joe Oliver	.05	.02	.01
☐ 235 Chad Curtis	.10	.05	.01
☐ 236 Shane Mack	.05	.02	.01
☐ 237 Jaime Navarro	.05	.02	.01
☐ 238 Brian McRae	.15	.07	.02
☐ 239 Chili Davis	.10	.05	.01
☐ 240 Jeff King	.05	.02	.01
☐ 241 Dean Palmer	.10	.05	.01
☐ 242 Danny Tartabull	.10	.05	.01
☐ 243 Charles Nagy	.10	.05	.01
☐ 244 Ray Lankford	.15	.07	.02
☐ 245 Barry Larkin	.25	.11	.03
☐ 246 Steve Avery	.15	.07	.02
☐ 247 John Kruk	.15	.07	.02
☐ 248 Derrick May	.10	.05	.01
☐ 249 Stan Javier	.05	.02	.01
☐ 250 Roger McDowell	.05	.02	.01
☐ 251 Dan Gladden	.05	.02	.01
☐ 252 Wally Joyner	.10	.05	.01
☐ 253 Pat Listach	.05	.02	.01
☐ 254 Chuck Knoblauch	.15	.07	.02
☐ 255 Sandy Alomar Jr.	.10	.05	.01
☐ 256 Jeff Bagwell	.75	.35	.09
☐ 257 Andy Stankiewicz	.05	.02	.01
☐ 258 Darrin Jackson	.05	.02	.01
☐ 259 Brett Butler	.10	.05	.01
☐ 260 Joe Orsulak	.05	.02	.01
☐ 261 Andy Benes	.10	.05	.01
☐ 262 Kenny Lofton	.60	.25	.07
☐ 263 Robin Ventura	.15	.07	.02
☐ 264 Ron Gant	.15	.07	.02
☐ 265 Ellis Burks	.10	.05	.01
☐ 266 Juan Guzman	.10	.05	.01
☐ 267 Wes Chamberlain	.05	.02	.01
☐ 268 John Smiley	.05	.02	.01
☐ 269 Franklin Stubbs	.05	.02	.01
☐ 270 Tom Browning	.05	.02	.01
☐ 271 Dennis Eckersley	.15	.07	.02
☐ 272 Carlton Fisk	.15	.07	.02
☐ 273 Lou Whitaker	.15	.07	.02
☐ 274 Phil Plantier	.05	.02	.01
☐ 275 Bobby Bonilla	.15	.07	.02
☐ 276 Ben McDonald	.05	.02	.01
☐ 277 Bob Zupcic	.05	.02	.01
☐ 278 Terry Steinbach	.10	.05	.01
☐ 279 Terry Mulholland	.05	.02	.01
☐ 280 Lance Johnson	.05	.02	.01
☐ 281 Willie McGee	.10	.05	.01
☐ 282 Bret Saberhagen	.10	.05	.01
☐ 283 Randy Myers	.10	.05	.01
☐ 284 Randy Tomlin	.05	.02	.01
☐ 285 Mickey Morandini	.05	.02	.01
☐ 286 Brian Williams	.05	.02	.01
☐ 287 Tino Martinez	.15	.07	.02
☐ 288 Jose Melendez	.05	.02	.01
☐ 289 Jeff Huson	.05	.02	.01
☐ 290 Joe Grahe	.05	.02	.01
☐ 291 Mel Hall	.05	.02	.01
☐ 292 Otis Nixon	.05	.02	.01
☐ 293 Todd Hundley	.05	.02	.01
☐ 294 Casey Candaele	.05	.02	.01
☐ 295 Kevin Seitzer	.05	.02	.01
☐ 296 Eddie Taubensee	.05	.02	.01
☐ 297 Moises Alou	.15	.07	.02
☐ 298 Scott Radinsky	.05	.02	.01
☐ 299 Thomas Howard	.05	.02	.01
☐ 300 Kyle Abbott	.05	.02	.01
☐ 301 Omar Vizquel	.10	.05	.01
☐ 302 Keith Miller	.05	.02	.01
☐ 303 Rick Aguilera	.10	.05	.01
☐ 304 Bruce Hurst	.05	.02	.01
☐ 305 Ken Caminiti	.10	.05	.01
☐ 306 Mike Pagliarulo	.05	.02	.01
☐ 307 Frank Seminara	.05	.02	.01
☐ 308 Andre Dawson	.15	.07	.02
☐ 309 Jose Lind	.05	.02	.01
☐ 310 Joe Boever	.05	.02	.01
☐ 311 Jeff Parrett	.05	.02	.01
☐ 312 Alan Mills	.05	.02	.01
☐ 313 Kevin Tapani	.05	.02	.01
☐ 314 Darryl Kile	.05	.02	.01
☐ 315 Checklist 211-315	.10	.05	.01
Will Clark			
☐ 316 Mike Sharperson	.05	.02	.01
☐ 317 John Orton	.05	.02	.01
☐ 318 Bob Tewksbury	.05	.02	.01
☐ 319 Xavier Hernandez	.05	.02	.01
☐ 320 Paul Assenmacher	.05	.02	.01
☐ 321 John Franco	.10	.05	.01
☐ 322 Mike Timlin	.05	.02	.01
☐ 323 Jose Guzman	.05	.02	.01
☐ 324 Pedro Martinez	.15	.07	.02
☐ 325 Bill Spiers	.05	.02	.01
☐ 326 Melido Perez	.05	.02	.01
☐ 327 Mike Macfarlane	.05	.02	.01
☐ 328 Ricky Bones	.05	.02	.01
☐ 329 Scott Bankhead	.05	.02	.01
☐ 330 Rich Rodriguez	.05	.02	.01
☐ 331 Geronimo Pena	.05	.02	.01
☐ 332 Bernie Williams	.10	.05	.01
☐ 333 Paul Molitor	.15	.07	.02
☐ 334 Carlos Garcia	.10	.05	.01
☐ 335 David Cone	.15	.07	.02
☐ 336 Randy Johnson	.40	.18	.05
☐ 337 Pat Mahomes	.05	.02	.01
☐ 338 Erik Hanson	.05	.02	.01
☐ 339 Duane Ward	.05	.02	.01
☐ 340 Al Martin	.10	.05	.01
☐ 341 Pedro Munoz	.10	.05	.01
☐ 342 Greg Colbrunn	.15	.07	.02
☐ 343 Julio Valera	.05	.02	.01
☐ 344 John Olerud	.15	.07	.02
☐ 345 George Bell	.10	.05	.01
☐ 346 Devon White	.10	.05	.01
☐ 347 Donovan Osborne	.05	.02	.01
☐ 348 Mark Gardner	.05	.02	.01
☐ 349 Zane Smith	.05	.02	.01
☐ 350 Wilson Alvarez	.15	.07	.02
☐ 351 Kevin Koslofski	.05	.02	.01
☐ 352 Roberto Hernandez	.10	.05	.01
☐ 353 Glenn Davis	.05	.02	.01
☐ 354 Reggie Sanders	.15	.07	.02
☐ 355 Ken Griffey Jr.	2.00	.90	.25
☐ 356 Marquis Grissom	.15	.07	.02
☐ 357 Jack McDowell	.15	.07	.02
☐ 358 Jimmy Key	.10	.05	.01
☐ 359 Stan Belinda	.05	.02	.01
☐ 360 Gerald Williams	.05	.02	.01
☐ 361 Sid Fernandez	.05	.02	.01
☐ 362 Alex Fernandez	.15	.07	.02
☐ 363 John Smoltz	.10	.05	.01
☐ 364 Travis Fryman	.15	.07	.02
☐ 365 Jose Canseco	.30	.14	.04

☐ 366	David Justice	.25	.11	.03
☐ 367	Pedro Astacio	.05	.02	.01
☐ 368	Tim Belcher	.05	.02	.01
☐ 369	Steve Sax	.05	.02	.01
☐ 370	Gary Gaetti	.10	.05	.01
☐ 371	Jeff Frye	.05	.02	.01
☐ 372	Bob Wickman	.05	.02	.01
☐ 373	Ryan Thompson	.10	.05	.01
☐ 374	David Hulse	.05	.02	.01
☐ 375	Cal Eldred	.05	.02	.01
☐ 376	Ryan Klesko	1.00	.45	.12
☐ 377	Damion Easley	.10	.05	.01
☐ 378	John Kiely	.05	.02	.01
☐ 379	Jim Bullinger	.05	.02	.01
☐ 380	Brian Bohanon	.05	.02	.01
☐ 381	Rod Brewer	.05	.02	.01
☐ 382	Fernando Ramsey	.05	.02	.01
☐ 383	Sam Militello	.05	.02	.01
☐ 384	Arthur Rhodes	.05	.02	.01
☐ 385	Eric Karros	.15	.07	.02
☐ 386	Rico Brogna	.15	.07	.02
☐ 387	John Valentin	.15	.07	.02
☐ 388	Kerry Woodson	.05	.02	.01
☐ 389	Ben Rivera	.05	.02	.01
☐ 390	Matt Whiteside	.05	.02	.01
☐ 391	Henry Rodriguez	.05	.02	.01
☐ 392	John Wetteland	.10	.05	.01
☐ 393	Kent Mercker	.05	.02	.01
☐ 394	Bernard Gilkey	.10	.05	.01
☐ 395	Doug Henry	.05	.02	.01
☐ 396	Mo Vaughn	.30	.14	.04
☐ 397	Scott Erickson	.10	.05	.01
☐ 398	Bill Gullickson	.05	.02	.01
☐ 399	Mark Guthrie	.05	.02	.01
☐ 400	Dave Martinez	.05	.02	.01
☐ 401	Jeff Kent	.15	.07	.02
☐ 402	Chris Hoiles	.10	.05	.01
☐ 403	Mike Henneman	.05	.02	.01
☐ 404	Chris Nabholz	.05	.02	.01
☐ 405	Tom Pagnozzi	.05	.02	.01
☐ 406	Kelly Gruber	.05	.02	.01
☐ 407	Bob Welch	.10	.05	.01
☐ 408	Frank Castillo	.05	.02	.01
☐ 409	John Dopson	.05	.02	.01
☐ 410	Steve Farr	.05	.02	.01
☐ 411	Henry Cotto	.05	.02	.01
☐ 412	Bob Patterson	.05	.02	.01
☐ 413	Todd Stottlemyre	.05	.02	.01
☐ 414	Greg A. Harris	.05	.02	.01
☐ 415	Denny Neagle	.05	.02	.01
☐ 416	Bill Wegman	.05	.02	.01
☐ 417	Willie Wilson	.05	.02	.01
☐ 418	Terry Leach	.05	.02	.01
☐ 419	Willie Randolph	.10	.05	.01
☐ 420	Checklist 316-420	.10	.05	.01
	Mark McGwire			
☐ 421	Top Prospect CL	.05	.02	.01
	Calvin Murray			
☐ 422	Pete Janicki TP	.05	.02	.01
☐ 423	Todd Jones TP	.05	.02	.01
☐ 424	Mike Neill TP	.05	.02	.01
☐ 425	Carlos Delgado TP	.40	.18	.05
☐ 426	Jose Oliva TP	.05	.02	.01
☐ 427	Tyrone Hill TP	.05	.02	.01
☐ 428	Dmitri Young TP	.15	.07	.02
☐ 429	Derek Wallace TP	.05	.02	.01
☐ 430	Michael Moore TP	.05	.02	.01
☐ 431	Cliff Floyd TP	.15	.07	.02
☐ 432	Calvin Murray TP	.05	.02	.01
☐ 433	Manny Ramirez TP	1.50	.70	.19
☐ 434	Marc Newfield TP	.10	.05	.01
☐ 435	Charles Johnson TP	.40	.18	.05
☐ 436	Butch Huskey TP	.10	.05	.01
☐ 437	Brad Pennington TP	.05	.02	.01
☐ 438	Ray McDavid TP	.10	.05	.01
☐ 439	Chad McConnell TP	.05	.02	.01
☐ 440	Midre Cummings TP	.30	.14	.04
☐ 441	Benji Gil TP	.10	.05	.01
☐ 442	Frankie Rodriguez TP	.10	.05	.01
☐ 443	Chad Mottola TP	.15	.07	.02
☐ 444	John Burke TP	.05	.02	.01
☐ 445	Michael Tucker TP	.15	.07	.02
☐ 446	Rick Greene TP	.05	.02	.01
☐ 447	Rich Becker TP	.10	.05	.01
☐ 448	Mike Robertson TP	.05	.02	.01
☐ 449	Derek Jeter TP	1.50	.70	.19
☐ 450	Inside the Numbers CL	.05	.02	.01
	Ivan Rodriguez			
	David McCarty			
☐ 451	Jim Abbott IN	.10	.05	.01
☐ 452	Jeff Bagwell IN	.40	.18	.05
☐ 453	Jason Bere IN	.05	.02	.01
☐ 454	Delino DeShields IN	.05	.02	.01
☐ 455	Travis Fryman IN	.10	.05	.01
☐ 456	Alex Gonzalez IN	.05	.02	.01
☐ 457	Phil Hiatt IN	.05	.02	.01
☐ 458	Dave Hollins IN	.05	.02	.01
☐ 459	Chipper Jones IN	1.00	.45	.12
☐ 460	David Justice IN	.10	.05	.01
☐ 461	Ray Lankford IN	.10	.05	.01
☐ 462	David McCarty IN	.05	.02	.01
☐ 463	Mike Mussina IN	.05	.02	.01
☐ 464	Jose Offerman IN	.05	.02	.01
☐ 465	Dean Palmer IN	.05	.02	.01
☐ 466	Geronimo Pena IN	.05	.02	.01
☐ 467	Eduardo Perez IN	.05	.02	.01
☐ 468	Ivan Rodriguez IN	.10	.05	.01
☐ 469	Reggie Sanders IN	.10	.05	.01
☐ 470	Bernie Williams IN	.05	.02	.01
☐ 471	Team Stars Checklist	.20	.09	.03
☐ 472	Strike Force	.60	.25	.07
	Greg Maddux			
	Steve Avery			
	John Smoltz			
	Tom Glavine			
☐ 473	Red October	.05	.02	.01
	Jose Rijo			
	Rob Dibble			
	Roberto Kelly			
	Reggie Sanders			
	Barry Larkin			
☐ 474	Four Corners	.15	.07	.02
	Gary Sheffield			
	Phil Plantier			
	Tony Gwynn			
	Fred McGriff			
☐ 475	Shooting Stars	.10	.05	.01
	Doug Drabek			
	Craig Biggio			
	Jeff Bagwell			
☐ 476	Giant Sticks	.20	.09	.03
	Will Clark			
	Barry Bonds			
	Matt Williams			
☐ 477	Boyhood Friends	.05	.02	.01
	Eric Davis			
	Darryl Strawberry			
☐ 478	Rock Solid Foundation	.25	.11	.03
	Dante Bichette			
	David Nied			
	Andres Galarraga			
☐ 479	Inaugural Catch	.05	.02	.01

	Dave Magadan		
	Orestes Destrade		
	Bret Barberie		
	Jeff Conine		
☐ 480	Steel City Champions... .05	.02	.01
	Tim Wakefield		
	Andy Van Slyke		
	Jay Bell		
☐ 481	Les Grandes Etoiles .... .10	.05	.01
	Marquis Grissom		
	Delino DeShields		
	Dennis Martinez		
	Larry Walker		
☐ 482	Runnin' Redbirds......... .10	.05	.01
	Geronimo Pena		
	Ray Lankford		
	Ozzie Smith		
	Bernard Gilkey		
☐ 483	Ivy Leaguers .... .10	.05	.01
	Randy Myers		
	Ryne Sandberg		
	Mark Grace		
☐ 484	Big Apple Power Switch .10	.05	.01
	Eddie Murray		
	Howard Johnson		
	Bobby Bonilla		
☐ 485	Hammers and Nails ..... .05	.02	.01
	John Kruk		
	Dave Hollins		
	Darren Daulton		
	Len Dykstra		
☐ 486	Barry Bonds AW .... .25	.11	.03
☐ 487	Dennis Eckersley AW .10	.05	.01
☐ 488	Greg Maddux AW....... 1.00	.45	.12
☐ 489	Dennis Eckersley AW ... .10	.05	.01
☐ 490	Eric Karros AW .... .10	.05	.01
☐ 491	Pat Listach AW .... .05	.02	.01
☐ 492	Gary Sheffield AW ...... .10	.05	.01
☐ 493	Mark McGwire AW ...... .10	.05	.01
☐ 494	Gary Sheffield AW ...... .10	.05	.01
☐ 495	Edgar Martinez AW ..... .10	.05	.01
☐ 496	Fred McGriff AW .... .10	.05	.01
☐ 497	Juan Gonzalez AW ...... .10	.05	.01
☐ 498	Darren Daulton AW ..... .10	.05	.01
☐ 499	Cecil Fielder AW .... .10	.05	.01
☐ 500	Diamond Debuts CL ..... .05	.02	.01
	Brent Gates		
☐ 501	Tavo Alvarez DD........... .05	.02	.01
☐ 502	Rod Bolton DD............. .05	.02	.01
☐ 503	John Cummings DD....... .05	.02	.01
☐ 504	Brent Gates DD .... .10	.05	.01
☐ 505	Tyler Green DD .... .05	.02	.01
☐ 506	Jose Martinez DD......... .05	.02	.01
☐ 507	Troy Percival DD .... .05	.02	.01
☐ 508	Kevin Stocker DD......... .05	.02	.01
☐ 509	Matt Walbeck DD .... .05	.02	.01
☐ 510	Rondell White DD .... .50	.23	.06
☐ 511	Billy Ripken............... .05	.02	.01
☐ 512	Mike Moore................ .05	.02	.01
☐ 513	Jose Lind .... .05	.02	.01
☐ 514	Chito Martinez............ .05	.02	.01
☐ 515	Jose Guzman .... .05	.02	.01
☐ 516	Kim Batiste .... .05	.02	.01
☐ 517	Jeff Tackett............... .05	.02	.01
☐ 518	Charlie Hough .... .10	.05	.01
☐ 519	Marvin Freeman.......... .05	.02	.01
☐ 520	Carlos Martinez.......... .05	.02	.01
☐ 521	Eric Young .... .10	.05	.01
☐ 522	Pete Incaviglia .... .05	.02	.01
☐ 523	Scott Fletcher............. .05	.02	.01
☐ 524	Orestes Destrade .... .05	.02	.01

☐ 525	Checklist 421-525........ .15	.07	.02
	Ken Griffey Jr.		
☐ 526	Ellis Burks................. .10	.05	.01
☐ 527	Juan Samuel .... .05	.02	.01
☐ 528	Dave Magadan .... .05	.02	.01
☐ 529	Jeff Parrett................ .05	.02	.01
☐ 530	Bill Krueger............... .05	.02	.01
☐ 531	Frank Bolick .... .05	.02	.01
☐ 532	Alan Trammell............ .15	.07	.02
☐ 533	Walt Weiss................ .10	.05	.01
☐ 534	David Cone .... .15	.07	.02
☐ 535	Greg Maddux............ 2.00	.90	.25
☐ 536	Kevin Young .... .05	.02	.01
☐ 537	Dave Hansen.............. .05	.02	.01
☐ 538	Alex Cole .... .05	.02	.01
☐ 539	Greg Hibbard .... .05	.02	.01
☐ 540	Gene Larkin............... .05	.02	.01
☐ 541	Jeff Reardon.............. .10	.05	.01
☐ 542	Felix Jose .... .05	.02	.01
☐ 543	Jimmy Key .... .10	.05	.01
☐ 544	Reggie Jefferson.......... .05	.02	.01
☐ 545	Gregg Jefferies .... .15	.07	.02
☐ 546	Dave Stewart .... .10	.05	.01
☐ 547	Tim Wallach .... .05	.02	.01
☐ 548	Spike Owen .... .05	.02	.01
☐ 549	Tommy Greene .... .05	.02	.01
☐ 550	Fernando Valenzuela .... .10	.05	.01
☐ 551	Rich Amaral .... .05	.02	.01
☐ 552	Bret Barberie .... .05	.02	.01
☐ 553	Edgar Martinez .... .15	.07	.02
☐ 554	Jim Abbott................. .15	.07	.02
☐ 555	Frank Thomas............ 2.00	.90	.25
☐ 556	Wade Boggs............... .15	.07	.02
☐ 557	Tom Henke .... .10	.05	.01
☐ 558	Milt Thompson............ .05	.02	.01
☐ 559	Lloyd McClendon.......... .05	.02	.01
☐ 560	Vinny Castilla .... .15	.07	.02
☐ 561	Ricky Jordan.............. .05	.02	.01
☐ 562	Andujar Cedeno .... .05	.02	.01
☐ 563	Greg Vaughn.............. .05	.02	.01
☐ 564	Cecil Fielder .... .15	.07	.02
☐ 565	Kirby Puckett............. .60	.25	.07
☐ 566	Mark McGwire .... .15	.07	.02
☐ 567	Barry Bonds .... .50	.23	.06
☐ 568	Jody Reed .... .05	.02	.01
☐ 569	Todd Zeile .... .10	.05	.01
☐ 570	Mark Carreon............. .05	.02	.01
☐ 571	Joe Girardi .... .05	.02	.01
☐ 572	Luis Gonzalez .... .10	.05	.01
☐ 573	Mark Grace .... .15	.07	.02
☐ 574	Rafael Palmeiro .... .15	.07	.02
☐ 575	Darryl Strawberry .... .10	.05	.01
☐ 576	Will Clark .... .25	.11	.03
☐ 577	Fred McGriff.............. .25	.11	.03
☐ 578	Kevin Reimer .... .05	.02	.01
☐ 579	Dave Righetti .... .05	.02	.01
☐ 580	Juan Bell .... .05	.02	.01
☐ 581	Jeff Brantley.............. .05	.02	.01
☐ 582	Brian Hunter .... .05	.02	.01
☐ 583	Tim Naehring............. .05	.02	.01
☐ 584	Glenallen Hill .... .05	.02	.01
☐ 585	Cal Ripken............... 2.00	.90	.25
☐ 586	Albert Belle............... .75	.35	.09
☐ 587	Robin Yount .... .25	.11	.03
☐ 588	Chris Bosio .... .05	.02	.01
☐ 589	Pete Smith .... .05	.02	.01
☐ 590	Chuck Carr................ .05	.02	.01
☐ 591	Jeff Blauser............... .10	.05	.01
☐ 592	Kevin McReynolds .... .05	.02	.01
☐ 593	Andres Galarraga .... .15	.07	.02
☐ 594	Kevin Maas .... .05	.02	.01

☐ 595 Eric Davis	.05	.02	.01
☐ 596 Brian Jordan	.15	.07	.02
☐ 597 Tim Raines	.15	.07	.02
☐ 598 Rick Wilkins	.05	.02	.01
☐ 599 Steve Cooke	.05	.02	.01
☐ 600 Mike Gallego	.05	.02	.01
☐ 601 Mike Munoz	.05	.02	.01
☐ 602 Luis Rivera	.05	.02	.01
☐ 603 Junior Ortiz	.05	.02	.01
☐ 604 Brent Mayne	.05	.02	.01
☐ 605 Luis Alicea	.05	.02	.01
☐ 606 Damon Berryhill	.05	.02	.01
☐ 607 Dave Henderson	.05	.02	.01
☐ 608 Kirk McCaskill	.05	.02	.01
☐ 609 Jeff Fassero	.05	.02	.01
☐ 610 Mike Harkey	.05	.02	.01
☐ 611 Francisco Cabrera	.05	.02	.01
☐ 612 Rey Sanchez	.05	.02	.01
☐ 613 Scott Servais	.05	.02	.01
☐ 614 Darrin Fletcher	.05	.02	.01
☐ 615 Felix Fermin	.05	.02	.01
☐ 616 Kevin Seitzer	.05	.02	.01
☐ 617 Bob Scanlan	.05	.02	.01
☐ 618 Billy Hatcher	.05	.02	.01
☐ 619 John Vander Wal	.05	.02	.01
☐ 620 Joe Hesketh	.05	.02	.01
☐ 621 Hector Villanueva	.05	.02	.01
☐ 622 Randy Milligan	.05	.02	.01
☐ 623 Tony Tarasco	.25	.11	.03
☐ 624 Russ Swan	.05	.02	.01
☐ 625 Willie Wilson	.05	.02	.01
☐ 626 Frank Tanana	.05	.02	.01
☐ 627 Pete O'Brien	.05	.02	.01
☐ 628 Lenny Webster	.05	.02	.01
☐ 629 Mark Clark	.05	.02	.01
☐ 630 Checklist 526-630	.10	.05	.01
Roger Clemens			
☐ 631 Alex Arias	.05	.02	.01
☐ 632 Chris Gwynn	.05	.02	.01
☐ 633 Tom Bolton	.05	.02	.01
☐ 634 Greg Briley	.05	.02	.01
☐ 635 Kent Bottenfield	.05	.02	.01
☐ 636 Kelly Downs	.05	.02	.01
☐ 637 Manuel Lee	.05	.02	.01
☐ 638 Al Leiter	.05	.02	.01
☐ 639 Jeff Gardner	.05	.02	.01
☐ 640 Mike Gardiner	.05	.02	.01
☐ 641 Mark Gardner	.05	.02	.01
☐ 642 Jeff Branson	.05	.02	.01
☐ 643 Paul Wagner	.05	.02	.01
☐ 644 Sean Berry	.05	.02	.01
☐ 645 Phil Hiatt	.05	.02	.01
☐ 646 Kevin Mitchell	.10	.05	.01
☐ 647 Charlie Hayes	.10	.05	.01
☐ 648 Jim Deshaies	.05	.02	.01
☐ 649 Dan Pasqua	.05	.02	.01
☐ 650 Mike Maddux	.05	.02	.01
☐ 651 Domingo Martinez	.05	.02	.01
☐ 652 Greg McMichael	.10	.05	.01
☐ 653 Eric Wedge	.05	.02	.01
☐ 654 Mark Whiten	.10	.05	.01
☐ 655 Roberto Kelly	.10	.05	.01
☐ 656 Julio Franco	.10	.05	.01
☐ 657 Gene Harris	.05	.02	.01
☐ 658 Pete Schourek	.05	.02	.01
☐ 659 Mike Bielecki	.05	.02	.01
☐ 660 Ricky Gutierrez	.05	.02	.01
☐ 661 Chris Hammond	.05	.02	.01
☐ 662 Tim Scott	.05	.02	.01
☐ 663 Norm Charlton	.05	.02	.01
☐ 664 Doug Drabek	.15	.07	.02

☐ 665 Dwight Gooden	.10	.05	.01
☐ 666 Jim Gott	.05	.02	.01
☐ 667 Randy Myers	.10	.05	.01
☐ 668 Darren Holmes	.05	.02	.01
☐ 669 Tim Spehr	.05	.02	.01
☐ 670 Bruce Ruffin	.05	.02	.01
☐ 671 Bobby Thigpen	.05	.02	.01
☐ 672 Tony Fernandez	.05	.02	.01
☐ 673 Darrin Jackson	.05	.02	.01
☐ 674 Gregg Olson	.05	.02	.01
☐ 675 Rob Dibble	.05	.02	.01
☐ 676 Howard Johnson	.05	.02	.01
☐ 677 Mike Lansing	.15	.07	.02
☐ 678 Charlie Leibrandt	.05	.02	.01
☐ 679 Kevin Bass	.05	.02	.01
☐ 680 Hubie Brooks	.05	.02	.01
☐ 681 Scott Brosius	.05	.02	.01
☐ 682 Randy Knorr	.05	.02	.01
☐ 683 Dante Bichette	.25	.11	.03
☐ 684 Bryan Harvey	.10	.05	.01
☐ 685 Greg Gohr	.05	.02	.01
☐ 686 Willie Banks	.05	.02	.01
☐ 687 Robb Nen	.05	.02	.01
☐ 688 Mike Sciosia	.05	.02	.01
☐ 689 John Farrell	.05	.02	.01
☐ 690 John Candelaria	.05	.02	.01
☐ 691 Damon Buford	.05	.02	.01
☐ 692 Todd Worrell	.05	.02	.01
☐ 693 Pat Hentgen	.10	.05	.01
☐ 694 John Smiley	.05	.02	.01
☐ 695 Greg Swindell	.05	.02	.01
☐ 696 Derek Bell	.15	.07	.02
☐ 697 Terry Jorgensen	.05	.02	.01
☐ 698 Jimmy Jones	.05	.02	.01
☐ 699 David Wells	.05	.02	.01
☐ 700 Dave Martinez	.05	.02	.01
☐ 701 Steve Bedrosian	.05	.02	.01
☐ 702 Jeff Russell	.05	.02	.01
☐ 703 Joe Magrane	.05	.02	.01
☐ 704 Matt Mieske	.10	.05	.01
☐ 705 Paul Molitor	.15	.07	.02
☐ 706 Dale Murphy	.15	.07	.02
☐ 707 Steve Howe	.05	.02	.01
☐ 708 Greg Gagne	.05	.02	.01
☐ 709 Dave Eiland	.05	.02	.01
☐ 710 David West	.05	.02	.01
☐ 711 Luis Aquino	.05	.02	.01
☐ 712 Joe Orsulak	.05	.02	.01
☐ 713 Eric Plunk	.05	.02	.01
☐ 714 Mike Felder	.05	.02	.01
☐ 715 Joe Klink	.05	.02	.01
☐ 716 Lonnie Smith	.05	.02	.01
☐ 717 Monty Fariss	.05	.02	.01
☐ 718 Craig Lefferts	.05	.02	.01
☐ 719 John Habyan	.05	.02	.01
☐ 720 Willie Blair	.05	.02	.01
☐ 721 Darnell Coles	.05	.02	.01
☐ 722 Mark Williamson	.05	.02	.01
☐ 723 Bryn Smith	.05	.02	.01
☐ 724 Greg W. Harris	.05	.02	.01
☐ 725 Graeme Lloyd	.05	.02	.01
☐ 726 Cris Carpenter	.05	.02	.01
☐ 727 Chico Walker	.05	.02	.01
☐ 728 Tracy Woodson	.05	.02	.01
☐ 729 Jose Uribe	.05	.02	.01
☐ 730 Stan Javier	.05	.02	.01
☐ 731 Jay Howell	.05	.02	.01
☐ 732 Freddie Benavides	.05	.02	.01
☐ 733 Jeff Reboulet	.05	.02	.01
☐ 734 Scott Sanderson	.05	.02	.01
☐ 735 Checklist 631-735	.15	.07	.02

Ryne Sandberg

☐ 736 Archi Cianfrocco	.05	.02	.01
☐ 737 Daryl Boston	.05	.02	.01
☐ 738 Craig Grebeck	.05	.02	.01
☐ 739 Doug Dascenzo	.05	.02	.01
☐ 740 Gerald Young	.05	.02	.01
☐ 741 Candy Maldonado	.05	.02	.01
☐ 742 Joey Cora	.05	.02	.01
☐ 743 Don Slaught	.05	.02	.01
☐ 744 Steve Decker	.05	.02	.01
☐ 745 Blas Minor	.05	.02	.01
☐ 746 Storm Davis	.05	.02	.01
☐ 747 Carlos Quintana	.05	.02	.01
☐ 748 Vince Coleman	.05	.02	.01
☐ 749 Todd Burns	.05	.02	.01
☐ 750 Steve Frey	.05	.02	.01
☐ 751 Ivan Calderon	.05	.02	.01
☐ 752 Steve Reed	.05	.02	.01
☐ 753 Danny Jackson	.05	.02	.01
☐ 754 Jeff Conine	.15	.07	.02
☐ 755 Juan Gonzalez	.40	.18	.05
☐ 756 Mike Kelly	.10	.05	.01
☐ 757 John Doherty	.05	.02	.01
☐ 758 Jack Armstrong	.05	.02	.01
☐ 759 John Wehner	.05	.02	.01
☐ 760 Scott Bankhead	.05	.02	.01
☐ 761 Jim Tatum	.05	.02	.01
☐ 762 Scott Pose	.05	.02	.01
☐ 763 Andy Ashby	.05	.02	.01
☐ 764 Ed Sprague	.05	.02	.01
☐ 765 Harold Baines	.10	.05	.01
☐ 766 Kirk Gibson	.10	.05	.01
☐ 767 Troy Neel	.05	.02	.01
☐ 768 Dick Schofield	.05	.02	.01
☐ 769 Dickie Thon	.05	.02	.01
☐ 770 Butch Henry	.05	.02	.01
☐ 771 Junior Felix	.05	.02	.01
☐ 772 Ken Ryan	.05	.02	.01
☐ 773 Trevor Hoffman	.10	.05	.01
☐ 774 Phil Plantier	.05	.02	.01
☐ 775 Bo Jackson	.15	.07	.02
☐ 776 Benito Santiago	.05	.02	.01
☐ 777 Andre Dawson	.15	.07	.02
☐ 778 Bryan Hickerson	.05	.02	.01
☐ 779 Dennis Moeller	.05	.02	.01
☐ 780 Ryan Bowen	.05	.02	.01
☐ 781 Eric Fox	.05	.02	.01
☐ 782 Joe Kmak	.05	.02	.01
☐ 783 Mike Hampton	.05	.02	.01
☐ 784 Darrell Sherman	.05	.02	.01
☐ 785 J.T. Snow	.30	.14	.04
☐ 786 Dave Winfield	.15	.07	.02
☐ 787 Jim Austin	.05	.02	.01
☐ 788 Craig Shipley	.05	.02	.01
☐ 789 Greg Myers	.05	.02	.01
☐ 790 Todd Benzinger	.05	.02	.01
☐ 791 Cory Snyder	.05	.02	.01
☐ 792 David Segui	.05	.02	.01
☐ 793 Armando Reynoso	.05	.02	.01
☐ 794 Chili Davis	.10	.05	.01
☐ 795 Dave Nilsson	.10	.05	.01
☐ 796 Paul O'Neill	.10	.05	.01
☐ 797 Jerald Clark	.05	.02	.01
☐ 798 Jose Mesa	.10	.05	.01
☐ 799 Brain Holman	.05	.02	.01
☐ 800 Jim Eisenreich	.05	.02	.01
☐ 801 Mark McLemore	.05	.02	.01
☐ 802 Luis Sojo	.05	.02	.01
☐ 803 Harold Reynolds	.05	.02	.01
☐ 804 Dan Plesac	.05	.02	.01
☐ 805 Dave Stieb	.05	.02	.01

☐ 806 Tom Brunansky	.05	.02	.01
☐ 807 Kelly Gruber	.05	.02	.01
☐ 808 Bob Ojeda	.05	.02	.01
☐ 809 Dave Burba	.05	.02	.01
☐ 810 Joe Boever	.05	.02	.01
☐ 811 Jeremy Hernandez	.05	.02	.01
☐ 812 Tim Salmon TC	.30	.14	.04
☐ 813 Jeff Bagwell TC	.40	.18	.05
☐ 814 Dennis Eckersley TC	.10	.05	.01
☐ 815 Roberto Alomar TC	.10	.05	.01
☐ 816 Steve Avery TC	.10	.05	.01
☐ 817 Pat Listach TC	.05	.02	.01
☐ 818 Gregg Jefferies TC	.10	.05	.01
☐ 819 Sammy Sosa TC	.10	.05	.01
☐ 820 Darryl Strawberry TC	.10	.05	.01
☐ 821 Dennis Martinez TC	.05	.02	.01
☐ 822 Robby Thompson TC	.05	.02	.01
☐ 823 Albert Belle TC	.40	.18	.05
☐ 824 Randy Johnson TC	.10	.05	.01
☐ 825 Nigel Wilson TC	.10	.05	.01
☐ 826 Bobby Bonilla TC	.10	.05	.01
☐ 827 Glenn Davis TC	.05	.02	.01
☐ 828 Gary Sheffield TC	.10	.05	.01
☐ 829 Darren Daulton TC	.10	.05	.01
☐ 830 Jay Bell TC	.05	.02	.01
☐ 831 Juan Gonzalez TC	.10	.05	.01
☐ 832 Andre Dawson TC	.10	.05	.01
☐ 833 Hal Morris TC	.05	.02	.01
☐ 834 David Nied TC	.10	.05	.01
☐ 835 Felix Jose TC	.05	.02	.01
☐ 836 Travis Fryman TC	.10	.05	.01
☐ 837 Shane Mack TC	.05	.02	.01
☐ 838 Robin Ventura TC	.10	.05	.01
☐ 839 Danny Tartabull TC	.10	.05	.01
☐ 840 Checklist 736-840	.10	.05	.01
Roberto Alomar			
☐ SP5 George Brett and	1.50	.70	.19
Robin Yount			
(Commemorating			
3,000th Hit)			
☐ SP6 Nolan Ryan	4.00	1.80	.50

1993 Upper Deck Fifth Anniversary

This 15-card set celebrates Upper Deck's five years in the sports card business. The cards are essentially reprinted versions of some of Upper Deck's most popular cards in the last five years. The standard-size (2 1/2" by 3 1/2") cards were randomly insert-

ed in second series hobby packs. The black-bordered fronts feature player photos that previously appeared on an Upper Deck card. The Five-Year Anniversary logo is located in one of the corners and the player's name is printed in gold-foil along the lower black border. The black backs carry a picture of the original card on the left side with narrative historical information on Upper Deck and a brief career summary of the player. The gold-colored year of issue of the original card is prominently displayed in the middle of the text. The cards are numbered on the back with an A prefix. One over-sized (3 1/2" by 5") version of each of these cards was initially inserted into retail blister repacks, which contained one foil pack each of 1993 Upper Deck Series I and II. These cards are individually numbered out of 10,000 and were later inserted into various forms of repackaging. These over-sized cards are valued up to 2X the prices listed below.

	MINT	NRMT	EXC
COMPLETE SET (15)	20.00	9.00	2.50
COMMON CARD (A1-A15)	.25	.11	.03
☐ A1 Ken Griffey Jr.	8.00	3.60	1.00
☐ A2 Gary Sheffield	.50	.23	.06
☐ A3 Roberto Alomar	1.00	.45	.12
☐ A4 Jim Abbott	.50	.23	.06
☐ A5 Nolan Ryan	5.00	2.20	.60
☐ A6 Juan Gonzalez	1.00	.45	.12
☐ A7 David Justice	.60	.25	.07
☐ A8 Carlos Baerga	1.00	.45	.12
☐ A9 Reggie Jackson	.75	.35	.09
☐ A10 Eric Karros	.50	.23	.06
☐ A11 Chipper Jones	3.00	1.35	.35
☐ A12 Ivan Rodriguez	.50	.23	.06
☐ A13 Pat Listach	.25	.11	.03
☐ A14 Frank Thomas	5.00	2.20	.60
☐ A15 Tim Salmon	1.00	.45	.12

1993 Upper Deck Future Heroes

Randomly inserted in second series foil packs and continuing the Heroes insert set begun in the 1990 Upper Deck high-number set, this ten-card standard-size (2 1/2" by 3 1/2") set features eight different "Future Heroes" along with a checklist and header card. The fronts feature borderless color player action shots that bear the player's simulated autograph in gold foil in an upper corner. His name appears within a black stripe formed by the simulated tearing away of a piece of the photo. His team's name appears below. The back carries the player's name vertically within a black "tearaway" stripe along the right edge. Career highlights are displayed within a white, gray, and tan panel on the left. The cards are numbered on the back.

	MINT	NRMT	EXC
COMPLETE SET (10)	15.00	6.75	1.85
COMMON CARD (55-63)	.25	.11	.03
☐ 55 Roberto Alomar	1.00	.45	.12
☐ 56 Barry Bonds	1.25	.55	.16
☐ 57 Roger Clemens	.75	.35	.09
☐ 58 Juan Gonzalez	1.00	.45	.12
☐ 59 Ken Griffey Jr.	5.00	2.20	.60
☐ 60 Mark McGwire	.50	.23	.06
☐ 61 Kirby Puckett	1.50	.70	.19
☐ 62 Frank Thomas	5.00	2.20	.60
☐ 63 Checklist	.25	.11	.03
☐ NNO Header Card SP	.75	.35	.09

1993 Upper Deck Iooss Collection

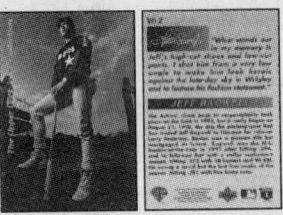

This 27-card standard-size (2 1/2" by 3 1/2") set spotlights the work of famous sports photographer Walter Iooss Jr. by presenting 26 of the game's current greats in a candid photo set. The cards were randomly inserted in series I foil packs purchased from major retail outlets only. The posed color player photos on the fronts are full-bleed and either horizontally or vertically oriented. The words "The Upper Deck Iooss Collection" are printed in gold foil. The back carries a quote from Iooss about the shoot and the player's career highlights. The text blocks on the card backs are separated by a gradated bars of varying colors. The cards are numbered on the back with a "WI" prefix. One over-sized version of each of these cards were initially inserted into retail blister repacks containing one foil pack each of 1993 Upper Deck Series I and II. These over-sized (3 1/2" by 5") cards are individually numbered out of 10,000 and were later inserted in various forms of repackaging. They are valued up to 2X the prices below.

	MINT	NRMT	EXC
COMPLETE SET (27)	25.00	11.00	3.10
COMMON CARD (WI1-WI26)	.30	.14	.04
☐ WI1 Tim Salmon	1.25	.55	.16
☐ WI2 Jeff Bagwell	2.50	1.10	.30
☐ WI3 Mark McGwire	.60	.25	.07
☐ WI4 Roberto Alomar	1.25	.55	.16
☐ WI5 Steve Avery	.60	.25	.07
☐ WI6 Paul Molitor	.60	.25	.07
☐ WI7 Ozzie Smith	1.25	.55	.16
☐ WI8 Mark Grace	.60	.25	.07
☐ WI9 Eric Karros	.60	.25	.07
☐ WI10 Delino DeShields	.60	.25	.07
☐ WI11 Will Clark	.75	.35	.09
☐ WI12 Albert Belle	2.50	1.10	.30
☐ WI13 Ken Griffey Jr.	6.00	2.70	.75
☐ WI14 Howard Johnson	.30	.14	.04
☐ WI15 Cal Ripken Jr.	6.00	2.70	.75
☐ WI16 Fred McGriff	.75	.35	.09
☐ WI17 Darren Daulton	.60	.25	.07
☐ WI18 Andy Van Slyke	.30	.14	.04
☐ WI19 Nolan Ryan	6.00	2.70	.75
☐ WI20 Wade Boggs	.60	.25	.07
☐ WI21 Barry Larkin	.75	.35	.09
☐ WI22 George Brett	2.50	1.10	.30
☐ WI23 Cecil Fielder	.60	.25	.07
☐ WI24 Kirby Puckett	2.00	.90	.25
☐ WI25 Frank Thomas	6.00	2.70	.75
☐ WI26 Don Mattingly	3.00	1.35	.35
☐ NNO Title Card	.75	.35	.09
Iooss Header			

1993 Upper Deck Then And Now

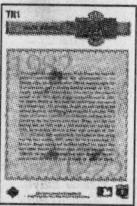

This 18-card, standard-size (2 1/2" by 3 1/2") hologram set highlights 18 veteran stars in their rookie year and today, reflecting on how they and the game have changed. Cards 1-9 were randomly inserted in series I foil packs; cards 10-18 were randomly inserted in series II foil packs.

The cards are numbered on the back with a "TN" prefix. The nine lithogram cards in the second series feature one card each of Hall of Famers Reggie Jackson, Mickey Mantle, and Willie Mays, as well as six active players. The second series cards are numbered on the back in continuation of the Then And Now Lithograms found in the 1993 Upper Deck first series baseball set. The horizontal fronts have a color close-up photo cutout and superimposed at the left corner of a full-bleed hologram portraying the player in an action scene. The skyline of the player's city serves as the background for the holograms. The player's name and the manufacturer's name form a right angle at the upper right corner. At the upper left corner, a "Then And Now" logo which includes the length of the player's career in years rounds out the front. On a sand-colored panel that resembles a postage stamp, the backs present career summary. The cards are numbered on the back with a "TN" prefix and arranged alphabetically within subgroup according to player's last name.

	MINT	NRMT	EXC
COMPLETE SET (18)	50.00	22.00	6.25
COMPLETE SERIES 1 (9)	25.00	11.00	3.10
COMPLETE SERIES 2 (9)	25.00	11.00	3.10
COMMON CARD (TN1-TN9)	.50	.23	.06
COMMON CARD (TN10-TN18)	.50	.23	.06
☐ TN1 Wade Boggs	1.00	.45	.12
☐ TN2 George Brett	4.00	1.80	.50
☐ TN3 Rickey Henderson	1.00	.45	.12
☐ TN4 Cal Ripken	10.00	4.50	1.25
☐ TN5 Nolan Ryan	10.00	4.50	1.25
☐ TN6 Ryne Sandberg	2.50	1.10	.30
☐ TN7 Ozzie Smith	2.00	.90	.25
☐ TN8 Darryl Strawberry	.50	.23	.06
☐ TN9 Dave Winfield	1.00	.45	.12
☐ TN10 Dennis Eckersley	1.00	.45	.12
☐ TN11 Tony Gwynn	3.00	1.35	.35
☐ TN12 Howard Johnson	.50	.23	.06
☐ TN13 Don Mattingly	5.00	2.20	.60
☐ TN14 Eddie Murray	1.50	.70	.19
☐ TN15 Robin Yount	1.25	.55	.16
☐ TN16 Reggie Jackson	2.50	1.10	.30
☐ TN17 Mickey Mantle	15.00	6.75	1.85
☐ TN18 Willie Mays	8.00	3.60	1.00

1993 Upper Deck Triple Crown

This ten-card, standard-size (2 1/2" by 3 1/2") subset highlights ten players who were selected by Upper Deck as having the best shot at winning Major League Baseball's Triple Crown. The cards were randomly inserted in series I foil packs sold by hobby dealers only. The fronts display glossy full-bleed color player photos. At the bottom, a purple ribbon edged in gold foil carries the words "Triple Crown Contenders," while the player's name

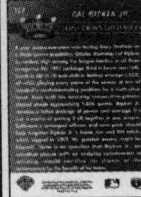

appears in gold foil lettering immediately below on a gradated black background. A crown overlays the ribbon at the lower left corner and rounds out the front. On a gradated black background, the backs summarize the player's performance in home runs, RBIs, and batting average. The cards are numbered on the back with a "TC" prefix and arranged alphabetically by player's last name.

	MINT	NRMT	EXC
COMPLETE SET (10)	30.00	13.50	3.70
COMMON CARD (TC1-TC10)	1.00	.45	.12

		MINT	NRMT	EXC
☐	TC1 Barry Bonds..............	2.50	1.10	.30
☐	TC2 Jose Canseco	1.50	.70	.19
☐	TC3 Will Clark	1.25	.55	.16
☐	TC4 Ken Griffey Jr.	10.00	4.50	1.25
☐	TC5 Fred McGriff	1.25	.55	.16
☐	TC6 Kirby Puckett	3.00	1.35	.35
☐	TC7 Cal Ripken Jr.	10.00	4.50	1.25
☐	TC8 Gary Sheffield	1.00	.45	.12
☐	TC9 Frank Thomas	10.00	4.50	1.25
☐	TC10 Larry Walker	1.25	.55	.16

1994 Upper Deck

The 1994 Upper Deck set was issued in two series of 280 and 270 cards for a total of 550. Card fronts feature a color photo of the player with a smaller version of the same photo along the left-hand border. The player's name appears in a black box in the upper left-hand corner. There are a number of subsets including Star Rookies (1-30), Fantasy Team (31-40), The Future is Now (41-55), Home Field Advantage (267-294), Upper Deck Classic Alumni (295-299), Diamond Debuts (511-522) and Top Prospects (523-550). Three autograph cards were randomly inserted in first series retail packs. They are Ken Griffey, Jr. (KG), Mickey Mantle (MM) and Griffey/Mantle (GM). An Alex Rodriguez (298A) autograph card was randomly inserted in second series retail packs. Rookie Cards include Brian Anderson, Alan Benes, John Hudek, Michael Jordan, Brooks Kieschnick, Chan Ho Park, Alex Rodriguez and Will VanLandingham.

	MINT	NRMT	EXC
COMPLETE SET (550)	50.00	22.00	6.25
COMPLETE SERIES 1 (280)	30.00	13.50	3.70
COMPLETE SERIES 2 (270)	20.00	9.00	2.50
COMMON CARD (1-280)	.10	.05	.01
COMMON CARD (281-550) ..	.10	.05	.01
COMP. ELEC. DIAM. SET (550)	125.00	55.00	15.50
ELECTRIC DIAM. COMM. (1-550)	.15	.07	.02
ELEC. DIAM. SEMISTARS....	.30	.14	.04
*ELEC. DIAM. VETERAN STARS: 2X TO 4X BASIC CARDS			
*ELEC. DIAM. YOUNG STARS: 1.5X TO 3X BASIC CARDS			
*ELEC DIAM RC'S: 1.25X TO 2.5X BASIC CARDS			

		MINT	NRMT	EXC
☐	1 Brian Anderson.........	.30	.14	.04
☐	2 Shane Andrews.........	.20	.09	.03
☐	3 James Baldwin..........	.20	.09	.03
☐	4 Rich Becker.............	.20	.09	.03
☐	5 Greg Blosser	.10	.05	.01
☐	6 Ricky Bottalico.........	.20	.09	.03
☐	7 Midre Cummings	.20	.09	.03
☐	8 Carlos Delgado	.30	.14	.04
☐	9 Steve Dreyer	.10	.05	.01
☐	10 Joey Eischen..........	.20	.09	.03
☐	11 Carl Everett...........	.20	.09	.03
☐	12 Cliff Floyd UER.......	.30	.14	.04
	(text indicates he throws left; should be right)			
☐	13 Alex Gonzalez........	.30	.14	.04
☐	14 Jeff Granger..........	.20	.09	.03
☐	15 Shawn Green	.40	.18	.05
☐	16 Brian Hunter	.75	.35	.09
☐	17 Butch Huskey.........	.20	.09	.03
☐	18 Mark Hutton	.10	.05	.01
☐	19 Michael Jordan	12.00	5.50	1.50
☐	20 Steve Karsay..........	.20	.09	.03
☐	21 Jeff McNeely..........	.10	.05	.01
☐	22 Marc Newfield	.30	.14	.04
☐	23 Manny Ramirez........	1.50	.70	.19
☐	24 Alex Rodriguez........	2.50	1.10	.30
☐	25 Scott Ruffcorn UER...	.30	.14	.04
	(photo on back is Robert Ellis)			
☐	26 Paul Spoljaric........	.10	.05	.01
☐	27 Salomon Torres	.20	.09	.03
☐	28 Steve Trachsel	.20	.09	.03
☐	29 Chris Turner..........	.10	.05	.01
☐	30 Gabe White	.10	.05	.01
☐	31 Randy Johnson FT....	.20	.09	.03
☐	32 John Wetteland FT....	.10	.05	.01
☐	33 Mike Piazza FT........	.60	.25	.07
☐	34 Rafael Palmeiro FT...	.20	.09	.03
☐	35 Roberto Alomar FT....	.20	.09	.03
☐	36 Matt Williams FT......	.20	.09	.03
☐	37 Travis Fryman FT......	.20	.09	.03

☐ 38	Barry Bonds FT	.40	.18	.05
☐ 39	Marquis Grissom FT	.20	.09	.03
☐ 40	Albert Belle FT	.60	.25	.07
☐ 41	Steve Avery FUT	.30	.14	.04
☐ 42	Jason Bere FUT	.30	.14	.04
☐ 43	Alex Fernandez FUT	.20	.09	.03
☐ 44	Mike Mussina FUT	.30	.14	.04
☐ 45	Aaron Sele FUT	.30	.14	.04
☐ 46	Rod Beck FUT	.20	.09	.03
☐ 47	Mike Piazza FUT	.60	.25	.07
☐ 48	John Olerud FUT	.20	.09	.03
☐ 49	Carlos Baerga FUT	.30	.14	.04
☐ 50	Gary Sheffield FUT	.20	.09	.03
☐ 51	Travis Fryman FUT	.20	.09	.03
☐ 52	Juan Gonzalez FUT	.30	.14	.04
☐ 53	Ken Griffey Jr. FUT	1.50	.70	.19
☐ 54	Tim Salmon FUT	.30	.14	.04
☐ 55	Frank Thomas FUT	1.50	.70	.19
☐ 56	Tony Phillips	.10	.05	.01
☐ 57	Julio Franco	.20	.09	.03
☐ 58	Kevin Mitchell	.20	.09	.03
☐ 59	Raul Mondesi	1.00	.45	.12
☐ 60	Rickey Henderson	.30	.14	.04
☐ 61	Jay Buhner	.30	.14	.04
☐ 62	Bill Swift	.10	.05	.01
☐ 63	Brady Anderson	.20	.09	.03
☐ 64	Ryan Klesko	.75	.35	.09
☐ 65	Darren Daulton	.30	.14	.04
☐ 66	Damion Easley	.10	.05	.01
☐ 67	Mark McGwire	.30	.14	.04
☐ 68	John Roper	.10	.05	.01
☐ 69	Dave Telgheder	.10	.05	.01
☐ 70	Dave Nied	.20	.09	.03
☐ 71	Mo Vaughn	.50	.23	.06
☐ 72	Tyler Green	.20	.09	.03
☐ 73	Dave Magadan	.10	.05	.01
☐ 74	Chili Davis	.20	.09	.03
☐ 75	Archi Cianfrocco	.10	.05	.01
☐ 76	Joe Girardi	.10	.05	.01
☐ 77	Chris Hoiles	.20	.09	.03
☐ 78	Ryan Bowen	.10	.05	.01
☐ 79	Greg Gagne	.10	.05	.01
☐ 80	Aaron Sele	.30	.14	.04
☐ 81	Dave Winfield	.30	.14	.04
☐ 82	Chad Curtis	.20	.09	.03
☐ 83	Andy Van Slyke	.20	.09	.03
☐ 84	Kevin Stocker	.20	.09	.03
☐ 85	Deion Sanders	.60	.25	.07
☐ 86	Bernie Williams	.20	.09	.03
☐ 87	John Smoltz	.20	.09	.03
☐ 88	Ruben Santana	.10	.05	.01
☐ 89	Dave Stewart	.10	.05	.01
☐ 90	Don Mattingly	1.50	.70	.19
☐ 91	Joe Carter	.30	.14	.04
☐ 92	Ryne Sandberg	.75	.35	.09
☐ 93	Chris Gomez	.20	.09	.03
☐ 94	Tino Martinez	.10	.05	.01
☐ 95	Terry Pendleton	.10	.05	.01
☐ 96	Andre Dawson	.30	.14	.04
☐ 97	Wil Cordero	.30	.14	.04
☐ 98	Kent Hrbek	.10	.05	.01
☐ 99	John Olerud	.30	.14	.04
☐ 100	Kirt Manwaring	.10	.05	.01
☐ 101	Tim Bogar	.10	.05	.01
☐ 102	Mike Mussina	.40	.18	.05
☐ 103	Nigel Wilson	.20	.09	.03
☐ 104	Ricky Gutierrez	.10	.05	.01
☐ 105	Roberto Mejia	.10	.05	.01
☐ 106	Tom Pagnozzi	.10	.05	.01
☐ 107	Mike Macfarlane	.10	.05	.01
☐ 108	Jose Bautista	.10	.05	.01
☐ 109	Luis Ortiz	.10	.05	.01
☐ 110	Brent Gates	.20	.09	.03
☐ 111	Tim Salmon	.60	.25	.07
☐ 112	Wade Boggs	.30	.14	.04
☐ 113	Tripp Cromer	.10	.05	.01
☐ 114	Denny Hocking	.10	.05	.01
☐ 115	Carlos Baerga	.60	.25	.07
☐ 116	J.R. Phillips	.20	.09	.03
☐ 117	Bo Jackson	.30	.14	.04
☐ 118	Lance Johnson	.10	.05	.01
☐ 119	Bobby Jones	.30	.14	.04
☐ 120	Bobby Witt	.10	.05	.01
☐ 121	Ron Karkovice	.10	.05	.01
☐ 122	Jose Vizcaino	.10	.05	.01
☐ 123	Danny Darwin	.10	.05	.01
☐ 124	Eduardo Perez	.10	.05	.01
☐ 125	Brian Looney	.10	.05	.01
☐ 126	Pat Hentgen	.20	.09	.03
☐ 127	Frank Viola	.10	.05	.01
☐ 128	Darren Holmes	.10	.05	.01
☐ 129	Wally Whitehurst	.10	.05	.01
☐ 130	Matt Walbeck	.10	.05	.01
☐ 131	Albert Belle	1.25	.55	.16
☐ 132	Steve Cooke	.10	.05	.01
☐ 133	Kevin Appier	.20	.09	.03
☐ 134	Joe Oliver	.10	.05	.01
☐ 135	Benji Gil	.20	.09	.03
☐ 136	Steve Buechele	.10	.05	.01
☐ 137	Devon White	.10	.05	.01
☐ 138	Sterling Hitchcock UER (two losses for career; should be four)	.20	.09	.03
☐ 139	Phil Leftwich	.10	.05	.01
☐ 140	Jose Canseco	.50	.23	.06
☐ 141	Rick Aguilera	.20	.09	.03
☐ 142	Rod Beck	.20	.09	.03
☐ 143	Jose Rijo	.20	.09	.03
☐ 144	Tom Glavine	.30	.14	.04
☐ 145	Phil Plantier	.20	.09	.03
☐ 146	Jason Bere	.30	.14	.04
☐ 147	Jamie Moyer	.10	.05	.01
☐ 148	Wes Chamberlain	.10	.05	.01
☐ 149	Glenallen Hill	.10	.05	.01
☐ 150	Mark Whiten	.10	.05	.01
☐ 151	Bret Barberie	.10	.05	.01
☐ 152	Chuck Knoblauch	.30	.14	.04
☐ 153	Trevor Hoffman	.10	.05	.01
☐ 154	Rick Wilkins	.10	.05	.01
☐ 155	Juan Gonzalez	.75	.35	.09
☐ 156	Ozzie Guillen	.10	.05	.01
☐ 157	Jim Eisenreich	.10	.05	.01
☐ 158	Pedro Astacio	.10	.05	.01
☐ 159	Joe Magrane	.10	.05	.01
☐ 160	Ryan Thompson	.20	.09	.03
☐ 161	Jose Lind	.10	.05	.01
☐ 162	Jeff Conine	.30	.14	.04
☐ 163	Todd Benzinger	.10	.05	.01
☐ 164	Roger Salkeld	.10	.05	.01
☐ 165	Gary DiSarcina	.10	.05	.01
☐ 166	Kevin Gross	.10	.05	.01
☐ 167	Charlie Hayes	.20	.09	.03
☐ 168	Tim Costo	.10	.05	.01
☐ 169	Wally Joyner	.20	.09	.03
☐ 170	Johnny Ruffin	.10	.05	.01
☐ 171	Kirk Rueter	.10	.05	.01
☐ 172	Lenny Dykstra	.30	.14	.04
☐ 173	Ken Hill	.20	.09	.03
☐ 174	Mike Bordick	.10	.05	.01
☐ 175	Billy Hall	.10	.05	.01
☐ 176	Rob Butler	.10	.05	.01
☐ 177	Jay Bell	.20	.09	.03

☐ 178	Jeff Kent	.20	.09	.03
☐ 179	David Wells	.10	.05	.01
☐ 180	Dean Palmer	.20	.09	.03
☐ 181	Mariano Duncan	.10	.05	.01
☐ 182	Orlando Merced	.20	.09	.03
☐ 183	Brett Butler	.20	.09	.03
☐ 184	Milt Thompson	.10	.05	.01
☐ 185	Chipper Jones	1.50	.70	.19
☐ 186	Paul O'Neill	.20	.09	.03
☐ 187	Mike Greenwell	.20	.09	.03
☐ 188	Harold Baines	.20	.09	.03
☐ 189	Todd Stottlemyre	.10	.05	.01
☐ 190	Jeromy Burnitz	.10	.05	.01
☐ 191	Rene Arocha	.10	.05	.01
☐ 192	Jeff Fassero	.10	.05	.01
☐ 193	Robby Thompson	.10	.05	.01
☐ 194	Greg W. Harris	.10	.05	.01
☐ 195	Todd Van Poppel	.20	.09	.03
☐ 196	Jose Guzman	.10	.05	.01
☐ 197	Shane Mack	.10	.05	.01
☐ 198	Carlos Garcia	.10	.05	.01
☐ 199	Kevin Roberson	.10	.05	.01
☐ 200	David McCarty	.10	.05	.01
☐ 201	Alan Trammell	.30	.14	.04
☐ 202	Chuck Carr	.10	.05	.01
☐ 203	Tommy Greene	.10	.05	.01
☐ 204	Wilson Alvarez	.30	.14	.04
☐ 205	Dwight Gooden	.10	.05	.01
☐ 206	Tony Tarasco	.30	.14	.04
☐ 207	Darren Lewis	.10	.05	.01
☐ 208	Eric Karros	.20	.09	.03
☐ 209	Chris Hammond	.10	.05	.01
☐ 210	Jeffrey Hammonds	.30	.14	.04
☐ 211	Rich Amaral	.10	.05	.01
☐ 212	Danny Tartabull	.20	.09	.03
☐ 213	Jeff Russell	.10	.05	.01
☐ 214	Dave Staton	.10	.05	.01
☐ 215	Kenny Lofton	1.00	.45	.12
☐ 216	Manuel Lee	.10	.05	.01
☐ 217	Brian Koelling	.10	.05	.01
☐ 218	Scott Lydy	.10	.05	.01
☐ 219	Tony Gwynn	1.00	.45	.12
☐ 220	Cecil Fielder	.30	.14	.04
☐ 221	Royce Clayton	.20	.09	.03
☐ 222	Reggie Sanders	.30	.14	.04
☐ 223	Brian Jordan	.20	.09	.03
☐ 224	Ken Griffey Jr.	3.00	1.35	.35
☐ 225	Fred McGriff	.40	.18	.05
☐ 226	Felix Jose	.10	.05	.01
☐ 227	Brad Pennington	.10	.05	.01
☐ 228	Chris Bosio	.10	.05	.01
☐ 229	Mike Stanley	.10	.05	.01
☐ 230	Willie Greene	.10	.05	.01
☐ 231	Alex Fernandez	.30	.14	.04
☐ 232	Brad Ausmus	.10	.05	.01
☐ 233	Darrell Whitmore	.10	.05	.01
☐ 234	Marcus Moore	.10	.05	.01
☐ 235	Allen Watson	.10	.05	.01
☐ 236	Jose Offerman	.10	.05	.01
☐ 237	Rondell White	.30	.14	.04
☐ 238	Jeff King	.10	.05	.01
☐ 239	Luis Alicea	.10	.05	.01
☐ 240	Dan Wilson	.10	.05	.01
☐ 241	Ed Sprague	.10	.05	.01
☐ 242	Todd Hundley	.20	.09	.03
☐ 243	Al Martin	.10	.05	.01
☐ 244	Mike Lansing	.20	.09	.03
☐ 245	Ivan Rodriguez	.30	.14	.04
☐ 246	Dave Fleming	.10	.05	.01
☐ 247	John Doherty	.10	.05	.01
☐ 248	Mark McLemore	.10	.05	.01

☐ 249	Bob Hamelin	.20	.09	.03
☐ 250	Curtis Pride	.20	.09	.03
☐ 251	Zane Smith	.10	.05	.01
☐ 252	Eric Young	.10	.05	.01
☐ 253	Brian McRae	.20	.09	.03
☐ 254	Tim Raines	.30	.14	.04
☐ 255	Javier Lopez	.50	.23	.06
☐ 256	Melvin Nieves	.30	.14	.04
☐ 257	Randy Myers	.10	.05	.01
☐ 258	Willie McGee	.10	.05	.01
☐ 259	Jimmy Key UER	.20	.09	.03
	(birthdate missing on back)			
☐ 260	Tom Candiotti	.10	.05	.01
☐ 261	Eric Davis	.10	.05	.01
☐ 262	Craig Paquette	.10	.05	.01
☐ 263	Robin Ventura	.20	.09	.03
☐ 264	Pat Kelly	.10	.05	.01
☐ 265	Gregg Jefferies	.30	.14	.04
☐ 266	Cory Snyder	.10	.05	.01
☐ 267	David Justice HFA	.30	.14	.04
☐ 268	Sammy Sosa HFA	.20	.09	.03
☐ 269	Barry Larkin HFA	.20	.09	.03
☐ 270	Andres Galarraga HFA	.20	.09	.03
☐ 271	Gary Sheffield HFA	.20	.09	.03
☐ 272	Jeff Bagwell HFA	.50	.23	.06
☐ 273	Mike Piazza HFA	.60	.25	.07
☐ 274	Larry Walker HFA	.20	.09	.03
☐ 275	Bobby Bonilla HFA	.30	.14	.04
☐ 276	John Kruk HFA	.20	.09	.03
☐ 277	Jay Bell HFA	.10	.05	.01
☐ 278	Ozzie Smith HFA	.30	.14	.04
☐ 279	Tony Gwynn HFA	.50	.23	.06
☐ 280	Barry Bonds HFA	.40	.18	.05
☐ 281	Cal Ripken Jr. HFA	1.50	.70	.19
☐ 282	Mo Vaughn HFA	.30	.14	.04
☐ 283	Tim Salmon HFA	.30	.14	.04
☐ 284	Frank Thomas HFA	1.50	.70	.19
☐ 285	Albert Belle HFA	.60	.25	.07
☐ 286	Cecil Fielder HFA	.20	.09	.03
☐ 287	Wally Joyner HFA	.10	.05	.01
☐ 288	Greg Vaughn HFA	.20	.09	.03
☐ 289	Kirby Puckett HFA	.50	.23	.06
☐ 290	Don Mattingly HFA	.75	.35	.09
☐ 291	Terry Steinbach HFA	.10	.05	.01
☐ 292	Ken Griffey Jr. HFA	1.50	.70	.19
☐ 293	Juan Gonzalez HFA	.30	.14	.04
☐ 294	Paul Molitor HFA	.30	.14	.04
☐ 295	Tavo Alvarez UDC	.10	.05	.01
☐ 296	Matt Brunson UDC	.20	.09	.03
☐ 297	Shawn Green UDC	.20	.09	.03
☐ 298	Alex Rodriguez UDC	1.00	.45	.12
☐ 299	Shannon Stewart UDC	.10	.05	.01
☐ 300	Frank Thomas	3.00	1.35	.35
☐ 301	Mickey Tettleton	.20	.09	.03
☐ 302	Pedro Munoz	.10	.05	.01
☐ 303	Jose Valentin	.10	.05	.01
☐ 304	Orestes Destrade	.10	.05	.01
☐ 305	Pat Listach	.10	.05	.01
☐ 306	Scott Brosius	.10	.05	.01
☐ 307	Kurt Miller	.10	.05	.01
☐ 308	Rob Dibble	.10	.05	.01
☐ 309	Mike Blowers	.20	.09	.03
☐ 310	Jim Abbott	.30	.14	.04
☐ 311	Mike Jackson	.10	.05	.01
☐ 312	Craig Biggio	.20	.09	.03
☐ 313	Kurt Abbott	.25	.11	.03
☐ 314	Chuck Finley	.10	.05	.01
☐ 315	Andres Galarraga	.30	.14	.04
☐ 316	Mike Moore	.10	.05	.01
☐ 317	Doug Strange	.10	.05	.01
☐ 318	Pedro J. Martinez	.30	.14	.04

☐ 319	Kevin McReynolds	.10	.05	.01
☐ 320	Greg Maddux	3.00	1.35	.35
☐ 321	Mike Henneman	.10	.05	.01
☐ 322	Scott Leius	.10	.05	.01
☐ 323	John Franco	.10	.05	.01
☐ 324	Jeff Blauser	.20	.09	.03
☐ 325	Kirby Puckett	1.00	.45	.12
☐ 326	Darryl Hamilton	.10	.05	.01
☐ 327	John Smiley	.10	.05	.01
☐ 328	Derrick May	.10	.05	.01
☐ 329	Jose Vizcaino	.10	.05	.01
☐ 330	Randy Johnson	.60	.25	.07
☐ 331	Jack Morris	.20	.09	.03
☐ 332	Graeme Lloyd	.10	.05	.01
☐ 333	Dave Valle	.10	.05	.01
☐ 334	Greg Myers	.10	.05	.01
☐ 335	John Wetteland	.20	.09	.03
☐ 336	Jim Gott	.10	.05	.01
☐ 337	Tim Naehring	.20	.09	.03
☐ 338	Mike Kelly	.20	.09	.03
☐ 339	Jeff Montgomery	.20	.09	.03
☐ 340	Rafael Palmeiro	.30	.14	.04
☐ 341	Eddie Murray	.40	.18	.05
☐ 342	Xavier Hernandez	.10	.05	.01
☐ 343	Bobby Munoz	.10	.05	.01
☐ 344	Bobby Bonilla	.30	.14	.04
☐ 345	Travis Fryman	.30	.14	.04
☐ 346	Steve Finley	.10	.05	.01
☐ 347	Chris Sabo	.10	.05	.01
☐ 348	Armando Reynoso	.10	.05	.01
☐ 349	Ramon Martinez	.20	.09	.03
☐ 350	Will Clark	.40	.18	.05
☐ 351	Moises Alou	.30	.14	.04
☐ 352	Jim Thome	.60	.25	.07
☐ 353	Bob Tewksbury	.10	.05	.01
☐ 354	Andujar Cedeno	.10	.05	.01
☐ 355	Orel Hershiser	.20	.09	.03
☐ 356	Mike Devereaux	.10	.05	.01
☐ 357	Mike Perez	.10	.05	.01
☐ 358	Dennis Martinez	.20	.09	.03
☐ 359	Dave Nilsson	.10	.05	.01
☐ 360	Ozzie Smith	.60	.25	.07
☐ 361	Eric Anthony	.10	.05	.01
☐ 362	Scott Sanders	.10	.05	.01
☐ 363	Paul Sorrento	.10	.05	.01
☐ 364	Tim Belcher	.10	.05	.01
☐ 365	Dennis Eckersley	.30	.14	.04
☐ 366	Mel Rojas	.10	.05	.01
☐ 367	Tom Henke	.10	.05	.01
☐ 368	Randy Tomlin	.10	.05	.01
☐ 369	B.J. Surhoff	.10	.05	.01
☐ 370	Larry Walker	.40	.18	.05
☐ 371	Joey Cora	.10	.05	.01
☐ 372	Mike Harkey	.10	.05	.01
☐ 373	John Valentin	.30	.14	.04
☐ 374	Doug Jones	.10	.05	.01
☐ 375	David Justice	.40	.18	.05
☐ 376	Vince Coleman	.10	.05	.01
☐ 377	David Hulse	.10	.05	.01
☐ 378	Kevin Seitzer	.10	.05	.01
☐ 379	Pete Harnisch	.10	.05	.01
☐ 380	Ruben Sierra	.30	.14	.04
☐ 381	Mark Lewis	.10	.05	.01
☐ 382	Bip Roberts	.10	.05	.01
☐ 383	Paul Wagner	.10	.05	.01
☐ 384	Stan Javier	.10	.05	.01
☐ 385	Barry Larkin	.40	.18	.05
☐ 386	Mark Portugal	.10	.05	.01
☐ 387	Roberto Kelly	.10	.05	.01
☐ 388	Andy Benes	.20	.09	.03
☐ 389	Felix Fermin	.10	.05	.01
☐ 390	Marquis Grissom	.30	.14	.04
☐ 391	Troy Neel	.10	.05	.01
☐ 392	Chad Kreuter	.10	.05	.01
☐ 393	Gregg Olson	.10	.05	.01
☐ 394	Charles Nagy	.20	.09	.03
☐ 395	Jack McDowell	.30	.14	.04
☐ 396	Luis Gonzalez	.10	.05	.01
☐ 397	Benito Santiago	.10	.05	.01
☐ 398	Chris James	.10	.05	.01
☐ 399	Terry Mulholland	.10	.05	.01
☐ 400	Barry Bonds	.75	.35	.09
☐ 401	Joe Grahe	.10	.05	.01
☐ 402	Duane Ward	.10	.05	.01
☐ 403	John Burkett	.20	.09	.03
☐ 404	Scott Servais	.10	.05	.01
☐ 405	Bryan Harvey	.10	.05	.01
☐ 406	Bernard Gilkey	.20	.09	.03
☐ 407	Greg McMichael	.10	.05	.01
☐ 408	Tim Wallach	.10	.05	.01
☐ 409	Ken Caminiti	.20	.09	.03
☐ 410	John Kruk	.20	.09	.03
☐ 411	Darrin Jackson	.10	.05	.01
☐ 412	Mike Gallego	.10	.05	.01
☐ 413	David Cone	.30	.14	.04
☐ 414	Lou Whitaker	.30	.14	.04
☐ 415	Sandy Alomar Jr.	.20	.09	.03
☐ 416	Bill Wegman	.10	.05	.01
☐ 417	Pat Borders	.10	.05	.01
☐ 418	Roger Pavlik	.10	.05	.01
☐ 419	Pete Smith	.10	.05	.01
☐ 420	Steve Avery	.30	.14	.04
☐ 421	David Segui	.10	.05	.01
☐ 422	Rheal Cormier	.10	.05	.01
☐ 423	Harold Reynolds	.10	.05	.01
☐ 424	Edgar Martinez	.20	.09	.03
☐ 425	Cal Ripken Jr.	3.00	1.35	.35
☐ 426	Jaime Navarro	.10	.05	.01
☐ 427	Sean Berry	.10	.05	.01
☐ 428	Bret Saberhagen	.20	.09	.03
☐ 429	Bob Welch	.10	.05	.01
☐ 430	Juan Guzman	.20	.09	.03
☐ 431	Cal Eldred	.20	.09	.03
☐ 432	Dave Hollins	.30	.14	.04
☐ 433	Sid Fernandez	.10	.05	.01
☐ 434	Willie Banks	.10	.05	.01
☐ 435	Darryl Kile	.20	.09	.03
☐ 436	Henry Rodriguez	.10	.05	.01
☐ 437	Tony Fernandez	.10	.05	.01
☐ 438	Walt Weiss	.10	.05	.01
☐ 439	Kevin Tapani	.10	.05	.01
☐ 440	Mark Grace	.30	.14	.04
☐ 441	Brian Harper	.10	.05	.01
☐ 442	Kent Mercker	.10	.05	.01
☐ 443	Anthony Young	.10	.05	.01
☐ 444	Todd Zeile	.20	.09	.03
☐ 445	Greg Vaughn	.20	.09	.03
☐ 446	Ray Lankford	.30	.14	.04
☐ 447	Dave Weathers	.10	.05	.01
☐ 448	Bret Boone	.30	.14	.04
☐ 449	Charlie Hough	.20	.09	.03
☐ 450	Roger Clemens	.50	.23	.06
☐ 451	Mike Morgan	.10	.05	.01
☐ 452	Doug Drabek	.20	.09	.03
☐ 453	Danny Jackson	.10	.05	.01
☐ 454	Dante Bichette	.40	.18	.05
☐ 455	Roberto Alomar	.60	.25	.07
☐ 456	Ben McDonald	.20	.09	.03
☐ 457	Kenny Rogers	.20	.09	.03
☐ 458	Bill Gullickson	.10	.05	.01
☐ 459	Darrin Fletcher	.10	.05	.01
☐ 460	Curt Schilling	.10	.05	.01

☐ 461 Billy Hatcher	.10	.05	.01
☐ 462 Howard Johnson	.10	.05	.01
☐ 463 Mickey Morandini	.10	.05	.01
☐ 464 Frank Castillo	.10	.05	.01
☐ 465 Delino DeShields	.20	.09	.03
☐ 466 Gary Gaetti	.10	.05	.01
☐ 467 Steve Farr	.10	.05	.01
☐ 468 Roberto Hernandez	.10	.05	.01
☐ 469 Jack Armstrong	.10	.05	.01
☐ 470 Paul Molitor	.30	.14	.04
☐ 471 Melido Perez	.10	.05	.01
☐ 472 Greg Hibbard	.10	.05	.01
☐ 473 Jody Reed	.10	.05	.01
☐ 474 Tom Gordon	.10	.05	.01
☐ 475 Gary Sheffield	.30	.14	.04
☐ 476 John Jaha	.10	.05	.01
☐ 477 Shawon Dunston	.10	.05	.01
☐ 478 Reggie Jefferson	.10	.05	.01
☐ 479 Don Slaught	.10	.05	.01
☐ 480 Jeff Bagwell	1.00	.45	.12
☐ 481 Tim Pugh	.10	.05	.01
☐ 482 Kevin Young	.10	.05	.01
☐ 483 Ellis Burks	.20	.09	.03
☐ 484 Greg Swindell	.10	.05	.01
☐ 485 Mark Langston	.30	.14	.04
☐ 486 Omar Vizquel	.10	.05	.01
☐ 487 Kevin Brown	.10	.05	.01
☐ 488 Terry Steinbach	.20	.09	.03
☐ 489 Mark Lemke	.10	.05	.01
☐ 490 Matt Williams	.50	.23	.06
☐ 491 Pete Incaviglia	.10	.05	.01
☐ 492 Karl Rhodes	.10	.05	.01
☐ 493 Shawn Green	.40	.18	.05
☐ 494 Hal Morris	.20	.09	.03
☐ 495 Derek Bell	.20	.09	.03
☐ 496 Luis Polonia	.10	.05	.01
☐ 497 Otis Nixon	.10	.05	.01
☐ 498 Ron Darling	.10	.05	.01
☐ 499 Mitch Williams	.10	.05	.01
☐ 500 Mike Piazza	1.25	.55	.16
☐ 501 Pat Meares	.10	.05	.01
☐ 502 Scott Cooper	.20	.09	.03
☐ 503 Scott Erickson	.10	.05	.01
☐ 504 Jeff Juden	.10	.05	.01
☐ 505 Lee Smith	.30	.14	.04
☐ 506 Bobby Ayala	.10	.05	.01
☐ 507 Dave Henderson	.10	.05	.01
☐ 508 Erik Hanson	.10	.05	.01
☐ 509 Bob Wickman	.10	.05	.01
☐ 510 Sammy Sosa	.30	.14	.04
☐ 511 Hector Carrasco DD	.10	.05	.01
☐ 512 Tim Davis DD	.10	.05	.01
☐ 513 Joey Hamilton DD	.20	.09	.03
☐ 514 Robert Eenhoorn DD	.10	.05	.01
☐ 515 Jorge Fabregas DD	.10	.05	.01
☐ 516 Tim Hyers DD	.10	.05	.01
☐ 517 John Hudek DD	.20	.09	.03
☐ 518 James Mouton DD	.20	.09	.03
☐ 519 Herbert Perry DD	.30	.14	.04
☐ 520 Chan Ho Park DD	.30	.14	.04
☐ 521 W.Van Landingham DD	.30	.14	.04
☐ 522 Paul Shuey DD	.20	.09	.03
☐ 523 Ryan Hancock TP	.20	.09	.03
☐ 524 Billy Wagner TP	.60	.25	.07
☐ 525 Jason Giambi TP	.30	.09	.03
☐ 526 Jose Silva TP	.40	.18	.05
☐ 527 Terrell Wade TP	.40	.18	.05
☐ 528 Todd Dunn TP	.10	.05	.01
☐ 529 Alan Benes TP	1.00	.45	.12
☐ 530 Brooks Kieschnick TP	2.50	1.10	.30
☐ 531 Todd Hollandsworth TP	.30	.14	.04

☐ 532 Brad Fullmer TP	.30	.14	.04
☐ 533 Steve Soderstrom TP	.30	.14	.04
☐ 534 Daron Kirkreit TP	.20	.09	.03
☐ 535 Arquimedez Pozo TP	.40	.18	.05
☐ 536 Charles Johnson TP	.30	.14	.04
☐ 537 Preston Wilson TP	.30	.14	.04
☐ 538 Alex Ochoa TP	.20	.09	.03
☐ 539 Derrek Lee TP	1.25	.55	.16
☐ 540 Wayne Gomes TP	.40	.18	.05
☐ 541 Jermaine Allensworth TP	.25	.11	.03
☐ 542 Mike Bell TP	.25	.11	.03
☐ 543 Trot Nixon TP	.75	.35	.09
☐ 544 Pokey Reese TP	.20	.09	.03
☐ 545 Neifi Perez TP	.25	.11	.03
☐ 546 Johnny Damon TP	1.50	.70	.19
☐ 547 Matt Brunson TP	.25	.11	.03
☐ 548 LaTroy Hawkins TP	.30	.14	.04
☐ 549 Eddie Pearson TP	.25	.11	.03
☐ 550 Derek Jeter TP	.75	.35	.09
☐ A298 Alex Rodriguez AU	80.00	36.00	10.00
☐ GM Griffey/Mantle AU	1000.00	450.00	125.00
☐ KG Ken Griffey AU	1000 250.00	110.00	31.00
☐ MM Mickey Mantle AU	600.00	275.00	75.00

1994 Upper Deck Diamond Collection

This 30-card set was inserted regionally in first series hobby packs at a rate of one in 18. The three regions are Central (C1-C10), East (E1-E10) and West (W1-W10). While each card has the same horizontal format, the color scheme differs by region. The Central cards have a blue background, the East green and the West a deep shade of red. Color player photos are superimposed over the backgrounds. Each card has, "The Upper Deck Diamond Collection" as part of the background. The backs have a small photo and career highlights.

	MINT	NRMT	EXC
COMPLETE SET (30)	375.00	170.00	47.50
COMPLETE CENTRAL (10)	175.00	80.00	22.00
COMPLETE EAST (10)	80.00	36.00	10.00
COMPLETE WEST (10)	120.00	55.00	15.00
COMMON CARD	2.00	.90	.25

☐ C1 Jeff Bagwell	15.00	6.75	1.85
☐ C2 Michael Jordan	50.00	22.00	6.25
☐ C3 Barry Larkin	5.00	2.20	.60

		MINT	NRMT	EXC
☐ C4	Kirby Puckett	15.00	6.75	1.85
☐ C5	Manny Ramirez	25.00	11.00	3.10
☐ C6	Ryne Sandberg	12.00	5.50	1.50
☐ C7	Ozzie Smith	10.00	4.50	1.25
☐ C8	Frank Thomas	50.00	22.00	6.25
☐ C9	Andy Van Slyke	2.00	.90	.25
☐ C10	Robin Yount	6.00	2.70	.75
☐ E1	Roberto Alomar	8.00	3.60	1.00
☐ E2	Roger Clemens	6.00	2.70	.75
☐ E3	Lenny Dykstra	3.00	1.35	.35
☐ E4	Cecil Fielder	3.00	1.35	.35
☐ E5	Cliff Floyd	3.00	1.35	.35
☐ E6	Dwight Gooden	2.00	.90	.25
☐ E7	David Justice	5.00	2.20	.60
☐ E8	Don Mattingly	20.00	9.00	2.50
☐ E9	Cal Ripken Jr.	40.00	18.00	5.00
☐ E10	Gary Sheffield	3.00	1.35	.35
☐ W1	Barry Bonds	12.00	5.50	1.50
☐ W2	Andres Galarraga	3.00	1.35	.35
☐ W3	Juan Gonzalez	12.00	5.50	1.50
☐ W4	Ken Griffey Jr.	50.00	22.00	6.25
☐ W5	Tony Gwynn	15.00	6.75	1.85
☐ W6	Rickey Henderson	3.00	1.35	.35
☐ W7	Bo Jackson	3.00	1.35	.35
☐ W8	Mark McGwire	3.00	1.35	.35
☐ W9	Mike Piazza	20.00	9.00	2.50
☐ W10	Tim Salmon	10.00	4.50	1.25

numbers. The cards are numbered on the back with a "MM" prefix.

		MINT	NRMT	EXC
COMPLETE SET (21)		50.00	22.00	6.25
COMMON CARD (MM1-MM21)		.50	.23	.06
*ELECTRIC DIAMOND VERSIONS: 1.25X VALUE				

		MINT	NRMT	EXC
☐ MM1	Jeff Bagwell	3.00	1.35	.35
☐ MM2	Albert Belle	4.00	1.80	.50
☐ MM3	Barry Bonds	2.50	1.10	.30
☐ MM4	Jose Canseco	1.50	.70	.19
☐ MM5	Joe Carter	1.00	.45	.12
☐ MM6	Carlos Delgado	.50	.23	.06
☐ MM7	Cecil Fielder	1.00	.45	.12
☐ MM8	Cliff Floyd	1.00	.45	.12
☐ MM9	Juan Gonzalez	2.50	1.10	.30
☐ MM10	Ken Griffey Jr	10.00	4.50	1.25
☐ MM11	David Justice	1.25	.55	.16
☐ MM12	Fred McGriff	1.25	.55	.16
☐ MM13	Mark McGwire	1.00	.45	.12
☐ MM14	Dean Palmer	.50	.23	.06
☐ MM15	Mike Piazza	4.00	1.80	.50
☐ MM16	Manny Ramirez	5.00	2.20	.60
☐ MM17	Tim Salmon	2.00	.90	.25
☐ MM18	Frank Thomas	10.00	4.50	1.25
☐ MM19	Mo Vaughn	1.50	.70	.19
☐ MM20	Matt Williams	1.50	.70	.19
☐ MM21	Mickey Mantle	15.00	6.75	1.85
☐ NNO	Mantle ED LS Tr. Blue	12.00	5.50	1.50
☐ NNO	Mantle LS Trade Silver	6.00	2.70	.75

1994 Upper Deck Mantle's Long Shots

Randomly inserted in first series retail packs at a rate of one in 18, this 21-card silver foil set features top longball hitters as selected by Mickey Mantle. Two trade cards, were also random inserts and were redeemable (expiration: December 31, 1994) for either the basic silver foil set version (Silver Trade card) or the Electric Diamond version (blue Trade card). The Electric Diamond set and singles command up to 1.25X the values below. The only way to obtain the Electric Diamond version was through the trade card. These cards differ in that they have an Electric Diamond logo on front. Card fronts are horizontal with a color player photo standing out from a dulled holographic image. The backs have a vertical format with a player photo at the top, a small photo of Mickey Mantle, a quote from The Mick and career power

1994 Upper Deck Next Generation

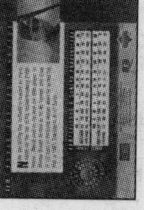

Randomly inserted in second series retail packs at a rate of one in 35, this 18-card set spotlights young established stars and promising prospects. Metallic fronts feature a color player photo on solid background. A small player hologram is halfway up the card on the right and comes between the player's first and last name. The Next Generation logo is at bottom left. Horizontal backs contain statistical comparisons, where applicable, to Hall of Famers and brief write-up noting the comparisons. A Next Generation Electric Diamond Trade Card and a Next Generation Trade Card were randomly in second series hobby packs. Each card could be redeemed for that set. Expiration date for redemption was October 31, 1994. The Electric Diamond versions are priced at 1.25X the values below.

	MINT	NRMT	EXC
COMPLETE SET (18)	100.00	45.00	12.50
COMMON CARD (1-18)	1.00	.45	.12

*ELECTRIC DIAMOND VERSIONS: 1.25X VALUE

		MINT	NRMT	EXC
☐ 1	Roberto Alomar	4.00	1.80	.50
☐ 2	Carlos Delgado	2.00	.90	.25
☐ 3	Cliff Floyd	2.00	.90	.25
☐ 4	Alex Gonzalez	1.00	.45	.12
☐ 5	Juan Gonzalez	5.00	2.20	.60
☐ 6	Ken Griffey Jr.	25.00	11.00	3.10
☐ 7	Jeffrey Hammonds	2.00	.90	.25
☐ 8	Michael Jordan	30.00	13.50	3.70
☐ 9	David Justice	2.50	1.10	.30
☐ 10	Ryan Klesko	4.00	1.80	.50
☐ 11	Javier Lopez	3.00	1.35	.35
☐ 12	Raul Mondesi	5.00	2.20	.60
☐ 13	Mike Piazza	10.00	4.50	1.25
☐ 14	Kirby Puckett	8.00	3.60	1.00
☐ 15	Manny Ramirez	10.00	4.50	1.25
☐ 16	Alex Rodriguez	6.00	2.70	.75
☐ 17	Tim Salmon	4.00	1.80	.50
☐ 18	Gary Sheffield	2.00	.90	.25
☐ NNO	Expired NG Trade Card	4.00	1.80	.50
☐ NNO	Expired NG Trade Card	4.00	1.80	.50

1995 Upper Deck

The 1995 Upper Deck baseball set was issued in two series of 225 cards for a total of 450. Autographed jumbo cards (Roger Clemens for series one, Alex Rodriguez for either series) were available through a wrapper redemption offer. The cards were distributed in 12-card packs (36 per box) with a suggested retail price of $1.99. The fronts display full-bleed color action photos, with the player's name in copper foil across the bottom. The backs carry another photo, biography, and season and career statistics. Second series packs contained trade cards for autographed cards of these players: Roger Clemens, Reggie Jackson, Willie Mays, Raul Mondesi and Frank

Robinson. Subsets include Top Prospect (1-15, 251-265), 90's Midpoint (101-110), Star Rookie (211-240), and Diamond Debuts (241-250). Rookie Cards in this set include Raul Casanova, Karim Garcia, Hideo Nomo and Carlos Perez.

	MINT	NRMT	EXC
COMPLETE SET (450)	50.00	22.00	6.25
COMPLETE SERIES 1 (225)	25.00	11.00	3.10
COMPLETE SET (225)	25.00	11.00	3.10
COMMON CARD (1-225)	.10	.05	.01
COMMON CARD (226-450)	.10	.05	.01
FIVE-CARD TRADE SET	5.00	2.20	.60
TRADE CARDS EXPIRED 2/1/96			
COMP. ELEC. DIAM. SET (450)	110.00	50.00	14.00
ELEC. DIAMOND COMM. (1-450)	.15	.07	.02
ELEC. DIAM. SEMISTARS	.30	.14	.04

*ELEC. DIAM. VETERAN STARS: 2X TO 4X BASIC CARDS
*ELEC. DIAM. YOUNG STARS: 1.5X TO 3X BASIC CARDS
*ELEC. DIAM. RC'S: 1.25X TO 2.5X BASIC CARDS

		MINT	NRMT	EXC
☐ 1	Ruben Rivera	2.00	.90	.25
☐ 2	Bill Pulsipher	.30	.14	.04
☐ 3	Ben Grieve	.75	.35	.09
☐ 4	Curtis Goodwin	.20	.09	.03
☐ 5	Damon Hollins	.20	.09	.03
☐ 6	Todd Greene	.50	.23	.06
☐ 7	Glenn Williams	.30	.14	.04
☐ 8	Bret Wagner	.20	.09	.03
☐ 9	Karim Garcia	2.50	1.10	.30
☐ 10	Nomar Garciaparra	.30	.14	.04
☐ 11	Raul Casanova	.75	.35	.09
☐ 12	Matt Smith	.20	.09	.03
☐ 13	Paul Wilson	.60	.25	.07
☐ 14	Jason Isringhausen	1.50	.70	.19
☐ 15	Reid Ryan	.30	.14	.04
☐ 16	Lee Smith	.30	.14	.04
☐ 17	Chili Davis	.20	.09	.03
☐ 18	Brian Anderson	.10	.05	.01
☐ 19	Gary DiSarcina	.20	.09	.03
☐ 20	Bo Jackson	.30	.14	.04
☐ 21	Chuck Finley	.20	.09	.03
☐ 22	Darryl Kile	.10	.05	.01
☐ 23	Shane Reynolds	.20	.09	.03
☐ 24	Tony Eusebio	.10	.05	.01
☐ 25	Craig Biggio	.30	.14	.04
☐ 26	Doug Drabek	.20	.09	.03
☐ 27	Brian L. Hunter	.40	.18	.05
☐ 28	James Mouton	.20	.09	.03
☐ 29	Geronimo Berroa	.10	.05	.01
☐ 30	Rickey Henderson	.30	.14	.04
☐ 31	Steve Karsay	.10	.05	.01
☐ 32	Steve Ontiveros	.10	.05	.01
☐ 33	Ernie Young	.10	.05	.01
☐ 34	Dennis Eckersley	.30	.14	.04
☐ 35	Mark McGwire	.30	.14	.04
☐ 36	Dave Stewart	.20	.09	.03
☐ 37	Pat Hentgen	.20	.09	.03
☐ 38	Carlos Delgado	.20	.09	.03
☐ 39	Joe Carter	.30	.14	.04
☐ 40	Roberto Alomar	.60	.25	.07
☐ 41	John Olerud	.20	.09	.03
☐ 42	Devon White	.20	.09	.03
☐ 43	Roberto Kelly	.20	.09	.03
☐ 44	Jeff Blauser	.20	.09	.03
☐ 45	Fred McGriff	.40	.18	.05
☐ 46	Tom Glavine	.30	.14	.04
☐ 47	Mike Kelly	.10	.05	.01
☐ 48	Javier Lopez	.40	.18	.05

☐ 49	Greg Maddux	3.00	1.35	.35
☐ 50	Matt Mieske	.10	.05	.01
☐ 51	Troy O'Leary	.20	.09	.03
☐ 52	Jeff Cirillo	.20	.09	.03
☐ 53	Cal Eldred	.10	.05	.01
☐ 54	Pat Listach	.10	.05	.01
☐ 55	Jose Valentin	.10	.05	.01
☐ 56	John Mabry	.20	.09	.03
☐ 57	Bob Tewksbury	.10	.05	.01
☐ 58	Brian Jordan	.30	.14	.04
☐ 59	Gregg Jefferies	.30	.14	.04
☐ 60	Ozzie Smith	.60	.25	.07
☐ 61	Geronimo Pena	.10	.05	.01
☐ 62	Mark Whiten	.10	.05	.01
☐ 63	Rey Sanchez	.10	.05	.01
☐ 64	Willie Banks	.10	.05	.01
☐ 65	Mark Grace	.30	.14	.04
☐ 66	Randy Myers	.10	.05	.01
☐ 67	Steve Trachsel	.10	.05	.01
☐ 68	Derrick May	.20	.09	.03
☐ 69	Brett Butler	.20	.09	.03
☐ 70	Eric Karros	.20	.09	.03
☐ 71	Tim Wallach	.10	.05	.01
☐ 72	Delino DeShields	.20	.09	.03
☐ 73	Darren Dreifort	.10	.05	.01
☐ 74	Orel Hershiser	.20	.09	.03
☐ 75	Billy Ashley	.20	.09	.03
☐ 76	Sean Berry	.10	.05	.01
☐ 77	Ken Hill	.20	.09	.03
☐ 78	John Wetteland	.20	.09	.03
☐ 79	Moises Alou	.20	.09	.03
☐ 80	Cliff Floyd	.30	.14	.04
☐ 81	Marquis Grissom	.30	.14	.04
☐ 82	Larry Walker	.40	.18	.05
☐ 83	Rondell White	.30	.14	.04
☐ 84	William VanLandingham	.20	.09	.03
☐ 85	Matt Williams	.50	.23	.06
☐ 86	Rod Beck	.20	.09	.03
☐ 87	Darren Lewis	.10	.05	.01
☐ 88	Robby Thompson	.10	.05	.01
☐ 89	Darryl Strawberry	.20	.09	.03
☐ 90	Kenny Lofton	1.00	.45	.12
☐ 91	Charles Nagy	.20	.09	.03
☐ 92	Sandy Alomar Jr.	.20	.09	.03
☐ 93	Mark Clark	.10	.05	.01
☐ 94	Dennis Martinez	.20	.09	.03
☐ 95	Dave Winfield	.30	.14	.04
☐ 96	Jim Thome	.50	.23	.06
☐ 97	Manny Ramirez	1.25	.55	.16
☐ 98	Goose Gossage	.20	.09	.03
☐ 99	Tino Martinez	.30	.14	.04
☐ 100	Ken Griffey Jr.	3.00	1.35	.35
☐ 101	Greg Maddux ANA	1.50	.70	.19
☐ 102	Randy Johnson ANA	.30	.14	.04
☐ 103	Barry Bonds ANA	.40	.18	.05
☐ 104	Juan Gonzalez ANA	.30	.14	.04
☐ 105	Frank Thomas ANA	1.50	.70	.19
☐ 106	Matt Williams ANA	.30	.14	.04
☐ 107	Paul Molitor ANA	.10	.05	.01
☐ 108	Fred McGriff ANA	.10	.05	.01
☐ 109	Carlos Baerga ANA	.10	.05	.01
☐ 110	Ken Griffey Jr. ANA	1.50	.70	.19
☐ 111	Reggie Jefferson	.10	.05	.01
☐ 112	Randy Johnson	.60	.25	.07
☐ 113	Marc Newfield	.20	.09	.03
☐ 114	Robb Nen	.20	.09	.03
☐ 115	Jeff Conine	.20	.09	.03
☐ 116	Kurt Abbott	.20	.09	.03
☐ 117	Charlie Hough	.20	.09	.03
☐ 118	Dave Weathers	.10	.05	.01
☐ 119	Juan Castillo	.10	.05	.01
☐ 120	Bret Saberhagen	.20	.09	.03
☐ 121	Rico Brogna	.30	.14	.04
☐ 122	John Franco	.20	.09	.03
☐ 123	Todd Hundley	.20	.09	.03
☐ 124	Jason Jacome	.10	.05	.01
☐ 125	Bobby Jones	.20	.09	.03
☐ 126	Bret Barberie	.10	.05	.01
☐ 127	Ben McDonald	.10	.05	.01
☐ 128	Harold Baines	.20	.09	.03
☐ 129	Jeffrey Hammonds	.20	.09	.03
☐ 130	Mike Mussina	.40	.18	.05
☐ 131	Chris Hoiles	.20	.09	.03
☐ 132	Brady Anderson	.20	.09	.03
☐ 133	Eddie Williams	.10	.05	.01
☐ 134	Andy Benes	.20	.09	.03
☐ 135	Tony Gwynn	1.00	.45	.12
☐ 136	Bip Roberts	.10	.05	.01
☐ 137	Joey Hamilton	.20	.09	.03
☐ 138	Luis Lopez	.10	.05	.01
☐ 139	Ray McDavid	.20	.09	.03
☐ 140	Lenny Dykstra	.20	.09	.03
☐ 141	Mariano Duncan	.10	.05	.01
☐ 142	Fernando Valenzuela	.20	.09	.03
☐ 143	Bobby Munoz	.10	.05	.01
☐ 144	Kevin Stocker	.10	.05	.01
☐ 145	John Kruk	.20	.09	.03
☐ 146	Jon Lieber	.10	.05	.01
☐ 147	Zane Smith	.10	.05	.01
☐ 148	Steve Cooke	.10	.05	.01
☐ 149	Andy Van Slyke	.20	.09	.03
☐ 150	Jay Bell	.20	.09	.03
☐ 151	Carlos Garcia	.20	.09	.03
☐ 152	John Dettmer	.10	.05	.01
☐ 153	Darren Oliver	.10	.05	.01
☐ 154	Dean Palmer	.20	.09	.03
☐ 155	Otis Nixon	.10	.05	.01
☐ 156	Rusty Greer	.10	.05	.01
☐ 157	Rick Helling	.10	.05	.01
☐ 158	Jose Canseco	.50	.23	.06
☐ 159	Roger Clemens	.50	.23	.06
☐ 160	Andre Dawson	.30	.14	.04
☐ 161	Mo Vaughn	.50	.23	.06
☐ 162	Aaron Sele	.10	.05	.01
☐ 163	John Valentin	.30	.14	.04
☐ 164	Brian R. Hunter	.10	.05	.01
☐ 165	Bret Boone	.30	.14	.04
☐ 166	Hector Carrasco	.10	.05	.01
☐ 167	Pete Schourek	.30	.14	.04
☐ 168	Willie Greene	.10	.05	.01
☐ 169	Kevin Mitchell	.20	.09	.03
☐ 170	Deion Sanders	.60	.25	.07
☐ 171	John Roper	.10	.05	.01
☐ 172	Charlie Hayes	.20	.09	.03
☐ 173	David Nied	.20	.09	.03
☐ 174	Ellis Burks	.20	.09	.03
☐ 175	Dante Bichette	.40	.18	.05
☐ 176	Marvin Freeman	.10	.05	.01
☐ 177	Eric Young	.20	.09	.03
☐ 178	David Cone	.30	.14	.04
☐ 179	Greg Gagne	.10	.05	.01
☐ 180	Bob Hamelin	.10	.05	.01
☐ 181	Wally Joyner	.20	.09	.03
☐ 182	Jeff Montgomery	.20	.09	.03
☐ 183	Jose Lind	.10	.05	.01
☐ 184	Chris Gomez	.10	.05	.01
☐ 185	Travis Fryman	.30	.14	.04
☐ 186	Kirk Gibson	.20	.09	.03
☐ 187	Mike Moore	.10	.05	.01
☐ 188	Lou Whitaker	.30	.14	.04
☐ 189	Sean Bergman	.10	.05	.01
☐ 190	Shane Mack	.10	.05	.01

☐ 191 Rick Aguilera	.20	.09	.03
☐ 192 Denny Hocking	.10	.05	.01
☐ 193 Chuck Knoblauch	.30	.14	.04
☐ 194 Kevin Tapani	.10	.05	.01
☐ 195 Kent Hrbek	.10	.05	.01
☐ 196 Ozzie Guillen	.10	.05	.01
☐ 197 Wilson Alvarez	.20	.09	.03
☐ 198 Tim Raines	.30	.14	.04
☐ 199 Scott Ruffcorn	.10	.05	.01
☐ 200 Michael Jordan	4.00	1.80	.50
☐ 201 Robin Ventura	.30	.14	.04
☐ 202 Jason Bere	.20	.09	.03
☐ 203 Darrin Jackson	.10	.05	.01
☐ 204 Russ Davis	.20	.09	.03
☐ 205 Jimmy Key	.20	.09	.03
☐ 206 Jack McDowell	.30	.14	.04
☐ 207 Jim Abbott	.30	.14	.04
☐ 208 Paul O'Neill	.20	.09	.03
☐ 209 Bernie Williams	.20	.09	.03
☐ 210 Don Mattingly	1.50	.70	.19
☐ 211 Orlando Miller	.20	.09	.03
☐ 212 Alex Gonzalez	.20	.09	.03
☐ 213 Terrell Wade	.20	.09	.03
☐ 214 Jose Oliva	.10	.05	.01
☐ 215 Alex Rodriguez	.60	.25	.07
☐ 216 Garret Anderson	.60	.25	.07
☐ 217 Alan Benes	.30	.14	.04
☐ 218 Armando Benitez	.10	.05	.01
☐ 219 Dustin Hermanson	.10	.05	.01
☐ 220 Charles Johnson	.30	.14	.04
☐ 221 Julian Tavarez	.20	.09	.03
☐ 222 Jason Giambi	.20	.09	.03
☐ 223 LaTroy Hawkins	.10	.05	.01
☐ 224 Todd Hollandsworth	.10	.05	.01
☐ 225 Derek Jeter	.50	.23	.06
☐ 226 Hideo Nomo	6.00	2.70	.75
☐ 227 Tony Clark	.20	.09	.03
☐ 228 Roger Cedeno	.30	.14	.04
☐ 229 Scott Stahoviak	.10	.05	.01
☐ 230 Michael Tucker	.20	.09	.03
☐ 231 Joe Rosselli	.10	.05	.01
☐ 232 Antonio Osuna	.10	.05	.01
☐ 233 Bobby Higginson	.30	.14	.04
☐ 234 Mark Grudzielanek	.20	.09	.03
☐ 235 Ray Durham	.30	.14	.04
☐ 236 Frank Rodriguez	.20	.09	.03
☐ 237 Quilvio Veras	.20	.09	.03
☐ 238 Darren Bragg	.10	.05	.01
☐ 239 Ugueth Urbina	.20	.09	.03
☐ 240 Jason Bates	.20	.09	.03
☐ 241 David Bell	.20	.09	.03
☐ 242 Ron Villone	.10	.05	.01
☐ 243 Joe Randa	.10	.05	.01
☐ 244 Carlos Perez	.75	.35	.09
☐ 245 Brad Clontz	.10	.05	.01
☐ 246 Steve Rodriguez	.10	.05	.01
☐ 247 Joe Vitiello	.10	.05	.01
☐ 248 Ozzie Timmons	.20	.09	.03
☐ 249 Rudy Pemberton	.10	.05	.01
☐ 250 Marty Cordova	.50	.23	.06
☐ 251 Tony Graffanino	.10	.05	.01
☐ 252 Mark Johnson	.10	.05	.01
☐ 253 Tomas Perez	.25	.11	.03
☐ 254 Jimmy Hurst	.10	.05	.01
☐ 255 Edgardo Alfonzo	.20	.09	.03
☐ 256 Jose Malave	.10	.05	.01
☐ 257 Brad Radke	.30	.14	.04
☐ 258 Jon Nunnally	.20	.09	.03
☐ 259 Dilson Torres	.10	.05	.01
☐ 260 Esteban Loaiza	.20	.09	.03
☐ 261 Freddy Garcia	.20	.09	.03

☐ 262 Don Wengert	.10	.05	.01
☐ 263 Robert Person	.10	.05	.01
☐ 264 Tim Unroe	.25	.11	.03
☐ 265 Juan Acevedo	.10	.05	.01
☐ 266 Eduardo Perez	.10	.05	.01
☐ 267 Tony Phillips	.10	.05	.01
☐ 268 Jim Edmonds	.40	.18	.05
☐ 269 Jorge Fabregas	.10	.05	.01
☐ 270 Tim Salmon	.50	.23	.06
☐ 271 Mark Langston	.20	.09	.03
☐ 272 J.T. Snow	.30	.14	.04
☐ 273 Phil Plantier	.10	.05	.01
☐ 274 Derek Bell	.30	.14	.04
☐ 275 Jeff Bagwell	1.00	.45	.12
☐ 276 Luis Gonzalez	.20	.09	.03
☐ 277 John Hudek	.10	.05	.01
☐ 278 Todd Stottlemyre	.10	.05	.01
☐ 279 Mark Acre	.10	.05	.01
☐ 280 Ruben Sierra	.30	.14	.04
☐ 281 Mike Bordick	.10	.05	.01
☐ 282 Ron Darling	.10	.05	.01
☐ 283 Brent Gates	.20	.09	.03
☐ 284 Todd Van Poppel	.10	.05	.01
☐ 285 Paul Molitor	.30	.14	.04
☐ 286 Ed Sprague	.10	.05	.01
☐ 287 Juan Guzman	.10	.05	.01
☐ 288 David Cone	.30	.14	.04
☐ 289 Shawn Green	.30	.14	.04
☐ 290 Marquis Grissom	.30	.14	.04
☐ 291 Kent Mercker	.10	.05	.01
☐ 292 Steve Avery	.20	.09	.03
☐ 293 Chipper Jones	1.25	.55	.16
☐ 294 John Smoltz	.20	.09	.03
☐ 295 David Justice	.40	.18	.05
☐ 296 Ryan Klesko	.60	.25	.07
☐ 297 Joe Oliver	.10	.05	.01
☐ 298 Ricky Bones	.10	.05	.01
☐ 299 John Jaha	.20	.09	.03
☐ 300 Greg Vaughn	.10	.05	.01
☐ 301 Dave Nilsson	.20	.09	.03
☐ 302 Kevin Seitzer	.10	.05	.01
☐ 303 Bernard Gilkey	.20	.09	.03
☐ 304 Allen Battle	.10	.05	.01
☐ 305 Ray Lankford	.30	.14	.04
☐ 306 Tom Pagnozzi	.10	.05	.01
☐ 307 Allen Watson	.20	.09	.03
☐ 308 Danny Jackson	.10	.05	.01
☐ 309 Ken Hill	.20	.09	.03
☐ 310 Todd Zeile	.20	.09	.03
☐ 311 Kevin Roberson	.10	.05	.01
☐ 312 Steve Buechele	.10	.05	.01
☐ 313 Rick Wilkins	.10	.05	.01
☐ 314 Kevin Foster	.10	.05	.01
☐ 315 Sammy Sosa	.30	.14	.04
☐ 316 Howard Johnson	.10	.05	.01
☐ 317 Greg Hansell	.10	.05	.01
☐ 318 Pedro Astacio	.10	.05	.01
☐ 319 Rafael Bournigal	.10	.05	.01
☐ 320 Mike Piazza	1.25	.55	.16
☐ 321 Ramon Martinez	.20	.09	.03
☐ 322 Raul Mondesi	.75	.35	.09
☐ 323 Ismael Valdes	.10	.05	.01
☐ 324 Wil Cordero	.20	.09	.03
☐ 325 Tony Tarasco	.20	.09	.03
☐ 326 Roberto Kelly	.20	.09	.03
☐ 327 Jeff Fassero	.20	.09	.03
☐ 328 Mike Lansing	.10	.05	.01
☐ 329 Pedro J. Martinez	.20	.09	.03
☐ 330 Kirk Rueter	.10	.05	.01
☐ 331 Glenallen Hill	.10	.05	.01
☐ 332 Kirt Manwaring	.10	.05	.01

☐ 333 Royce Clayton	.10	.05	.01
☐ 334 J.R. Phillips	.10	.05	.01
☐ 335 Barry Bonds	.75	.35	.09
☐ 336 Mark Portugal	.10	.05	.01
☐ 337 Terry Mulholland	.10	.05	.01
☐ 338 Omar Vizquel	.20	.09	.03
☐ 339 Carlos Baerga	.60	.25	.07
☐ 340 Albert Belle	1.25	.55	.16
☐ 341 Eddie Murray	.40	.18	.05
☐ 342 Wayne Kirby	.10	.05	.01
☐ 343 Chad Ogea	.20	.09	.03
☐ 344 Tim Davis	.10	.05	.01
☐ 345 Jay Buhner	.30	.14	.04
☐ 346 Bobby Ayala	.10	.05	.01
☐ 347 Mike Blowers	.20	.09	.03
☐ 348 Dave Fleming	.10	.05	.01
☐ 349 Edgar Martinez	.30	.14	.04
☐ 350 Andre Dawson	.30	.14	.04
☐ 351 Darrell Whitmore	.10	.05	.01
☐ 352 Chuck Carr	.10	.05	.01
☐ 353 John Burkett	.10	.05	.01
☐ 354 Chris Hammond	.10	.05	.01
☐ 355 Gary Sheffield	.30	.14	.04
☐ 356 Pat Rapp	.20	.09	.03
☐ 357 Greg Colbrunn	.30	.14	.04
☐ 358 David Segui	.10	.05	.01
☐ 359 Jeff Kent	.20	.09	.03
☐ 360 Bobby Bonilla	.30	.14	.04
☐ 361 Pete Harnisch	.10	.05	.01
☐ 362 Ryan Thompson	.10	.05	.01
☐ 363 Jose Vizcaino	.10	.05	.01
☐ 364 Brett Butler	.20	.09	.03
☐ 365 Cal Ripken Jr.	3.00	1.35	.35
☐ 366 Rafael Palmeiro	.30	.14	.04
☐ 367 Leo Gomez	.10	.05	.01
☐ 368 Andy Van Slyke	.20	.09	.03
☐ 369 Arthur Rhodes	.10	.05	.01
☐ 370 Ken Caminiti	.20	.09	.03
☐ 371 Steve Finley	.20	.09	.03
☐ 372 Melvin Nieves	.20	.09	.03
☐ 373 Andujar Cedeno	.10	.05	.01
☐ 374 Trevor Hoffman	.20	.09	.03
☐ 375 Fernando Valenzuela	.20	.09	.03
☐ 376 Ricky Bottalico	.10	.05	.01
☐ 377 Tommy Greene	.10	.05	.01
☐ 378 Charlie Hayes	.20	.09	.03
☐ 379 Tommy Greene	.10	.05	.01
☐ 380 Darren Daulton	.20	.09	.03
☐ 381 Curt Schilling	.10	.05	.01
☐ 382 Midre Cummings	.20	.09	.03
☐ 383 Al Martin	.20	.09	.03
☐ 384 Jeff King	.10	.05	.01
☐ 385 Orlando Merced	.20	.09	.03
☐ 386 Denny Neagle	.10	.05	.01
☐ 387 Don Slaught	.10	.05	.01
☐ 388 Dave Clark	.10	.05	.01
☐ 389 Kevin Gross	.10	.05	.01
☐ 390 Will Clark	.40	.18	.05
☐ 391 Ivan Rodriguez	.30	.14	.04
☐ 392 Benji Gil	.10	.05	.01
☐ 393 Jeff Frye	.10	.05	.01
☐ 394 Kenny Rogers	.10	.05	.01
☐ 395 Juan Gonzalez	.75	.35	.09
☐ 396 Mike Macfarlane	.10	.05	.01
☐ 397 Lee Tinsley	.20	.09	.03
☐ 398 Tim Naehring	.20	.09	.03
☐ 399 Tim Vanegmond	.10	.05	.01
☐ 400 Mike Greenwell	.10	.05	.01
☐ 401 Ken Ryan	.10	.05	.01
☐ 402 John Smiley	.10	.05	.01
☐ 403 Tim Pugh	.10	.05	.01
☐ 404 Reggie Sanders	.30	.14	.04
☐ 405 Barry Larkin	.40	.18	.05
☐ 406 Hal Morris	.20	.09	.03
☐ 407 Jose Rijo	.10	.05	.01
☐ 408 Lance Painter	.10	.05	.01
☐ 409 Joe Girardi	.10	.05	.01
☐ 410 Andres Galarraga	.30	.14	.04
☐ 411 Mike Kingery	.10	.05	.01
☐ 412 Roberto Mejia	.10	.05	.01
☐ 413 Walt Weiss	.20	.09	.03
☐ 414 Bill Swift	.10	.05	.01
☐ 415 Larry Walker	.40	.18	.05
☐ 416 Billy Brewer	.10	.05	.01
☐ 417 Pat Borders	.10	.05	.01
☐ 418 Tom Gordon	.10	.05	.01
☐ 419 Kevin Appier	.20	.09	.03
☐ 420 Gary Gaetti	.20	.09	.03
☐ 421 Greg Gohr	.10	.05	.01
☐ 422 Felipe Lira	.10	.05	.01
☐ 423 John Doherty	.10	.05	.01
☐ 424 Chad Curtis	.20	.09	.03
☐ 425 Cecil Fielder	.30	.14	.04
☐ 426 Alan Trammell	.30	.14	.04
☐ 427 David McCarty	.10	.05	.01
☐ 428 Scott Erickson	.10	.05	.01
☐ 429 Pat Mahomes	.10	.05	.01
☐ 430 Kirby Puckett	1.00	.45	.12
☐ 431 Dave Stevens	.10	.05	.01
☐ 432 Pedro Munoz	.20	.09	.03
☐ 433 Chris Sabo	.10	.05	.01
☐ 434 Alex Fernandez	.20	.09	.03
☐ 435 Frank Thomas	3.00	1.35	.35
☐ 436 Roberto Hernandez	.20	.09	.03
☐ 437 Lance Johnson	.10	.05	.01
☐ 438 Jim Abbott	.20	.09	.03
☐ 439 John Wetteland	.20	.09	.03
☐ 440 Melido Perez	.10	.05	.01
☐ 441 Tony Fernandez	.10	.05	.01
☐ 442 Pat Kelly	.10	.05	.01
☐ 443 Mike Stanley	.20	.09	.03
☐ 444 Danny Tartabull	.20	.09	.03
☐ 445 Wade Boggs	.30	.14	.04
☐ 446 Robin Yount	.40	.18	.05
☐ 447 Ryne Sandberg	.60	.25	.07
☐ 448 Nolan Ryan	2.50	1.10	.30
☐ 449 George Brett	1.00	.45	.12
☐ 450 Mike Schmidt	.60	.25	.07
☐ J159 R. Clemens Jumbo AU	20.00	9.00	2.50
☐ J215 A. Rodriguez Jumbo AU	15.00	6.75	1.85
☐ NNO R. Clemens AU Trade	20.00	9.00	2.50
☐ NNO R. Jackson AU Trade	20.00	9.00	2.50
☐ NNO W. Mays AU Trade..	50.00	22.00	6.25
☐ NNO R. Mondesi AU Trade	40.00	18.00	5.00
☐ NNO F. Robinson AU Trade	30.00	13.50	3.70

1995 Upper Deck Electric Diamond Gold

This 450-card parallel set was randomly inserted in retail and mini-jumbo packs. These cards are identical to the Electric Diamond series except for the special gold foil treatment.

	MINT	NRMT	EXC
COMPLETE SET (450)	1400.00	650.00	180.00
COMPLETE SERIES 1 (225)	650.00	300.00	80.00
COMPLETE SERIES 2 (225)	750.00	350.00	95.00
COMMON CARD (1-225)	3.00	1.35	.35
COMMON CARD (226-450)	3.00	1.35	.35
SEMISTARS	6.00	2.70	.75

*VETERAN STARS: 18X TO 30X BASIC CARDS
*YOUNG STARS: 15X TO 25X BASIC CARDS
*RCs: 10X TO 20X BASIC CARDS

☐ 1	Ruben Rivera	40.00	18.00	5.00
☐ 49	Greg Maddux	100.00	45.00	12.50
☐ 90	Kenny Lofton	30.00	13.50	3.70
☐ 97	Manny Ramirez	40.00	18.00	5.00
☐ 100	Ken Griffey Jr.	100.00	45.00	12.50
☐ 101	Greg Maddux ANA	50.00	22.00	6.25
☐ 105	Frank Thomas ANA	50.00	22.00	6.25
☐ 110	Ken Griffey Jr. ANA	50.00	22.00	6.25
☐ 135	Tony Gwynn	30.00	13.50	3.70
☐ 200	Michael Jordan	125.00	55.00	15.50
☐ 210	Don Mattingly	50.00	22.00	6.25
☐ 226	Hideo Nomo	80.00	36.00	10.00
☐ 275	Jeff Bagwell	30.00	13.50	3.70
☐ 293	Chipper Jones	50.00	22.00	6.25
☐ 320	Mike Piazza	40.00	18.00	5.00
☐ 340	Albert Belle	40.00	18.00	5.00
☐ 365	Cal Ripken	125.00	55.00	15.50
☐ 430	Kirby Puckett	30.00	13.50	3.70
☐ 435	Frank Thomas	100.00	45.00	12.50
☐ 448	Nolan Ryan TRIB	100.00	45.00	12.50
☐ 449	George Brett TRIB	40.00	18.00	5.00

1995 Upper Deck Checklists

Each card of these 10 cards features a star player on its front and a checklist on the back. The cards were randomly inserted in hobby and retail packs at a rate of one in 17. The horizontal fronts feature a player photo along with a sentence about the player's 1994 highlight. He is identified on the right side. The card is numbered as "X" of 5 in the upper left.

	MINT	NRMT	EXC
COMPLETE SET (5)	25.00	11.00	3.10
COMPLETE SERIES 1 (5)	10.00	4.50	1.25
COMPLETE SERIES 2 (5)	15.00	6.75	1.85
COMMON CARD (1-5)	1.00	.45	.12
COMMON CARD (1B-5B)	1.50	.70	.19

☐ 1A	Montreal Expos	1.00	.45	.12
☐ 2A	Fred McGriff	1.25	.55	.16
☐ 3A	John Valentin	1.00	.45	.12
☐ 4A	Kenny Rogers	1.00	.45	.12
☐ 5A	Greg Maddux CY	10.00	4.50	1.25
☐ 1B	Cecil Fielder	1.50	.70	.19
☐ 2B	Tony Gwynn	3.00	1.35	.35
☐ 3B	Greg Maddux	10.00	4.50	1.25
☐ 4B	Randy Johnson	2.00	.90	.25
☐ 5B	Mike Schmidt	2.50	1.10	.30

1995 Upper Deck Special Edition

Randomly inserted at a rate of one per pack, this 135-card set features full color action shots of players on a silver foil background. The back highlights the player's previous performance, including 1994 and career statistics. Another player photo is also featured on the back.

	MINT	NRMT	EXC
COMPLETE SET (270)	200.00	90.00	25.00
COMPLETE SET (135)	90.00	40.00	11.00
COMPLETE SERIES 2 (135)	110.00	50.00	14.00
COMMON CARD (1-135)	.30	.14	.04
COMMON CARD (136-270)	.30	.14	.04

☐ 1	Cliff Floyd	.50	.23	.06
☐ 2	Wil Cordero	.30	.14	.04
☐ 3	Pedro J. Martinez	.50	.23	.06
☐ 4	Larry Walker	1.25	.55	.16
☐ 5	Derek Jeter	1.50	.70	.19
☐ 6	Mike Stanley	.30	.14	.04
☐ 7	Melido Perez	.30	.14	.04
☐ 8	Jim Leyritz	.30	.14	.04
☐ 9	Danny Tartabull	.30	.14	.04
☐ 10	Wade Boggs	.75	.35	.09
☐ 11	Ryan Klesko	2.00	.90	.25
☐ 12	Steve Avery	.30	.14	.04
☐ 13	Damon Hollins	.75	.35	.09
☐ 14	Chipper Jones	4.00	1.80	.50
☐ 15	David Justice	1.25	.55	.16
☐ 16	Glenn Williams	.75	.35	.09
☐ 17	Jose Oliva	.30	.14	.04
☐ 18	Terrell Wade	.30	.14	.04
☐ 19	Alex Fernandez	.30	.14	.04
☐ 20	Frank Thomas	10.00	4.50	1.25
☐ 21	Ozzie Guillen	.30	.14	.04
☐ 22	Roberto Hernandez	.30	.14	.04

☐ 23 Albie Lopez	.30	.14	.04	☐ 94 Rene Arocha	.30	.14	.04
☐ 24 Eddie Murray	1.25	.55	.16	☐ 95 Cecil Fielder	.75	.35	.09
☐ 25 Albert Belle	4.00	1.80	.50	☐ 96 Alan Trammell	.75	.35	.09
☐ 26 Omar Vizquel	.30	.14	.04	☐ 97 Tony Phillips	.30	.14	.04
☐ 27 Carlos Baerga	2.00	.90	.25	☐ 98 Junior Felix	.30	.14	.04
☐ 28 Jose Rijo	.30	.14	.04	☐ 99 Brian Harper	.30	.14	.04
☐ 29 Hal Morris	.30	.14	.04	☐ 100 Greg Vaughn	.30	.14	.04
☐ 30 Reggie Sanders	.75	.35	.09	☐ 101 Ricky Bones	.30	.14	.04
☐ 31 Jack Morris	.75	.35	.09	☐ 102 Walt Weiss	.30	.23	.06
☐ 32 Raul Mondesi	2.50	1.10	.30	☐ 103 Lance Painter	.30	.14	.04
☐ 33 Karim Garcia	6.00	2.70	.75	☐ 104 Roberto Mejia	.30	.14	.04
☐ 34 Todd Hollandsworth	.30	.14	.04	☐ 105 Andres Galarraga	.75	.35	.09
☐ 35 Mike Piazza	4.00	1.80	.50	☐ 106 Todd Van Poppel	.30	.14	.04
☐ 36 Chan Ho Park	.50	.23	.06	☐ 107 Ben Grieve	2.50	1.10	.30
☐ 37 Ramon Martinez	.50	.23	.06	☐ 108 Brent Gates	.30	.14	.04
☐ 38 Kenny Rogers	.30	.14	.04	☐ 109 Jason Giambi	.30	.14	.04
☐ 39 Will Clark	1.25	.55	.16	☐ 110 Ruben Sierra	.50	.23	.06
☐ 40 Juan Gonzalez	2.50	1.10	.30	☐ 111 Terry Steinbach	.30	.14	.04
☐ 41 Ivan Rodriguez	.75	.35	.09	☐ 112 Chris Hammond	.30	.14	.04
☐ 42 Orlando Miller	.30	.14	.04	☐ 113 Charles Johnson	.50	.23	.06
☐ 43 John Hudek	.30	.14	.04	☐ 114 Jesus Tavarez	.30	.14	.04
☐ 44 Luis Gonzalez	.30	.14	.04	☐ 115 Gary Sheffield	.75	.35	.09
☐ 45 Jeff Bagwell	3.00	1.35	.35	☐ 116 Chuck Carr	.30	.14	.04
☐ 46 Cal Ripken	10.00	4.50	1.25	☐ 117 Bobby Ayala	.30	.14	.04
☐ 47 Mike Oquist	.30	.14	.04	☐ 118 Randy Johnson	2.00	.90	.25
☐ 48 Armando Benitez	.30	.14	.04	☐ 119 Edgar Martinez	.75	.35	.09
☐ 49 Ben McDonald	.30	.14	.04	☐ 120 Alex Rodriguez	2.00	.90	.25
☐ 50 Rafael Palmeiro	.75	.35	.09	☐ 121 Kevin Foster	.30	.14	.04
☐ 51 Curtis Goodwin	.30	.14	.04	☐ 122 Kevin Roberson	.30	.14	.04
☐ 52 Vince Coleman	.30	.14	.04	☐ 123 Sammy Sosa	.75	.35	.09
☐ 53 Tom Gordon	.30	.14	.04	☐ 124 Steve Trachsel	.30	.14	.04
☐ 54 Mike Macfarlane	.30	.14	.04	☐ 125 Eduardo Perez	.30	.14	.04
☐ 55 Brian McRae	.30	.14	.04	☐ 126 Tim Salmon	1.50	.70	.19
☐ 56 Matt Smith	.30	.14	.04	☐ 127 Todd Greene	1.50	.70	.19
☐ 57 David Segui	.30	.14	.04	☐ 128 Jorge Fabregas	.30	.14	.04
☐ 58 Paul Wilson	2.00	.90	.25	☐ 129 Mark Langston	.30	.14	.04
☐ 59 Bill Pulsipher	.75	.35	.09	☐ 130 Mitch Williams	.30	.14	.04
☐ 60 Bobby Bonilla	.75	.35	.09	☐ 131 Raul Casanova	2.00	.90	.25
☐ 61 Jeff Kent	.30	.14	.04	☐ 132 Mel Nieves	.30	.14	.04
☐ 62 Ryan Thompson	.30	.14	.04	☐ 133 Andy Benes	.30	.14	.04
☐ 63 Jason Isringhausen	4.00	1.80	.50	☐ 134 Dustin Hermanson	.30	.14	.04
☐ 64 Ed Sprague	.30	.14	.04	☐ 135 Trevor Hoffman	.30	.14	.04
☐ 65 Paul Molitor	.75	.35	.09	☐ 136 Mark Grudzielanek	.75	.35	.09
☐ 66 Juan Guzman	.30	.14	.04	☐ 137 Ugueth Urbina	.30	.14	.04
☐ 67 Alex Gonzalez	.30	.14	.04	☐ 138 Moises Alou	.30	.14	.04
☐ 68 Shawn Green	.75	.35	.09	☐ 139 Roberto Kelly	.30	.14	.04
☐ 69 Mark Portugal	.30	.14	.04	☐ 140 Rondell White	.50	.23	.06
☐ 70 Barry Bonds	2.50	1.10	.30	☐ 141 Paul O'Neill	.50	.23	.06
☐ 71 Robby Thompson	.30	.14	.04	☐ 142 Jimmy Key	.30	.14	.04
☐ 72 Royce Clayton	.30	.14	.04	☐ 143 Jack McDowell	.50	.23	.06
☐ 73 Ricky Bottalico	.30	.14	.04	☐ 144 Ruben Rivera	6.00	2.70	.75
☐ 74 Doug Jones	.30	.14	.04	☐ 145 Don Mattingly	5.00	2.20	.60
☐ 75 Darren Daulton	.50	.23	.06	☐ 146 John Wetteland	.30	.14	.04
☐ 76 Gregg Jefferies	.50	.23	.06	☐ 147 Tom Glavine	.75	.35	.09
☐ 77 Scott Cooper	.30	.14	.04	☐ 148 Marquis Grissom	.75	.35	.09
☐ 78 Nomar Garciaparra	1.25	.55	.16	☐ 149 Javier Lopez	1.25	.55	.16
☐ 79 Ken Ryan	.30	.14	.04	☐ 150 Fred McGriff	1.25	.55	.16
☐ 80 Mike Greenwell	.30	.14	.04	☐ 151 Greg Maddux	10.00	4.50	1.25
☐ 81 LaTroy Hawkins	.30	.14	.04	☐ 152 Chris Sabo	.30	.14	.04
☐ 82 Rich Becker	.30	.14	.04	☐ 153 Ray Durham	.50	.23	.06
☐ 83 Scott Erickson	.30	.14	.04	☐ 154 Robin Ventura	.50	.23	.06
☐ 84 Pedro Munoz	.30	.14	.04	☐ 155 Jim Abbott	.75	.35	.09
☐ 85 Kirby Puckett	3.00	1.35	.35	☐ 156 Jimmy Hurst	.30	.14	.04
☐ 86 Orlando Merced	.30	.14	.04	☐ 157 Tim Raines	.50	.23	.06
☐ 87 Jeff King	.30	.14	.04	☐ 158 Dennis Martinez	.50	.23	.06
☐ 88 Midre Cummings	.50	.23	.06	☐ 159 Kenny Lofton	3.00	1.35	.35
☐ 89 Bernard Gilkey	.30	.14	.04	☐ 160 Dave Winfield	.75	.35	.09
☐ 90 Ray Lankford	.50	.23	.06	☐ 161 Manny Ramirez	4.00	1.80	.50
☐ 91 Todd Zeile	.30	.14	.04	☐ 162 Jim Thome	1.50	.70	.19
☐ 92 Alan Benes	.30	.14	.04	☐ 163 Barry Larkin	1.25	.55	.16
☐ 93 Bret Wagner	.30	.14	.04	☐ 164 Bret Boone	.50	.23	.06

		MINT	NRMT	EXC
☐ 165	Deion Sanders	2.00	.90	.25
☐ 166	Ron Gant	.75	.35	.09
☐ 167	Benito Santiago	.30	.14	.04
☐ 168	Hideo Nomo	20.00	9.00	2.50
☐ 169	Billy Ashley	.30	.14	.04
☐ 170	Roger Cedeno	.75	.35	.09
☐ 171	Ismael Valdes	.30	.14	.04
☐ 172	Eric Karros	.50	.23	.06
☐ 173	Rusty Greer	.30	.14	.04
☐ 174	Rick Helling	.30	.14	.04
☐ 175	Nolan Ryan	10.00	4.50	1.25
☐ 176	Dean Palmer	.30	.14	.04
☐ 177	Phil Plantier	.30	.14	.04
☐ 178	Darryl Kile	.30	.14	.04
☐ 179	Derek Bell	.30	.14	.04
☐ 180	Doug Drabek	.30	.14	.04
☐ 181	Craig Biggio	.75	.35	.09
☐ 182	Kevin Brown	.30	.14	.04
☐ 183	Harold Baines	.50	.23	.06
☐ 184	Jeffrey Hammonds	.30	.14	.04
☐ 185	Chris Hoiles	.30	.14	.04
☐ 186	Mike Mussina	1.25	.55	.16
☐ 187	Bob Hamelin	.30	.14	.04
☐ 188	Jeff Montgomery	.30	.14	.04
☐ 189	Michael Tucker	.30	.14	.04
☐ 190	George Brett	4.00	1.80	.50
☐ 191	Edgardo Alfonzo	.30	.14	.04
☐ 192	Brett Butler	.30	.14	.04
☐ 193	Bobby Jones	.30	.14	.04
☐ 194	Todd Hundley	.30	.14	.04
☐ 195	Bret Saberhagen	.30	.14	.04
☐ 196	Pat Hentgen	.30	.14	.04
☐ 197	Roberto Alomar	2.00	.90	.25
☐ 198	David Cone	.50	.23	.06
☐ 199	Carlos Delgado	.30	.14	.04
☐ 200	Joe Carter	.75	.35	.09
☐ 201	Wm. VanLandingham	.30	.14	.04
☐ 202	Rod Beck	.30	.14	.04
☐ 203	J.R. Phillips	.30	.14	.04
☐ 204	Darren Lewis	.30	.14	.04
☐ 205	Matt Williams	1.50	.70	.19
☐ 206	Lenny Dykstra	.50	.23	.06
☐ 207	Dave Hollins	.30	.14	.04
☐ 208	Mike Schmidt	2.50	1.10	.30
☐ 209	Charlie Hayes	.30	.14	.04
☐ 210	Mo Vaughn	1.50	.70	.19
☐ 211	Jose Malave	.30	.14	.04
☐ 212	Roger Clemens	1.50	.70	.19
☐ 213	Jose Canseco	1.50	.70	.19
☐ 214	Mark Whiten	.30	.14	.04
☐ 215	Marty Cordova	1.50	.70	.19
☐ 216	Rick Aguilera	.30	.14	.04
☐ 217	Kevin Tapani	.30	.14	.04
☐ 218	Chuck Knoblauch	.75	.35	.09
☐ 219	Al Martin	.30	.14	.04
☐ 220	Jay Bell	.30	.14	.04
☐ 221	Carlos Garcia	.30	.14	.04
☐ 222	Freddy Garcia	.30	.14	.04
☐ 223	Jon Lieber	.30	.14	.04
☐ 224	Danny Jackson	.30	.14	.04
☐ 225	Ozzie Smith	2.00	.90	.25
☐ 226	Brian Jordan	.30	.14	.04
☐ 227	Ken Hill	.30	.14	.04
☐ 228	Scott Cooper	.30	.14	.04
☐ 229	Chad Curtis	.30	.14	.04
☐ 230	Lou Whitaker	.75	.35	.09
☐ 231	Kirk Gibson	.50	.23	.06
☐ 232	Travis Fryman	.75	.35	.09
☐ 233	Jose Valentin	.30	.14	.04
☐ 234	Dave Nilsson	.30	.14	.04
☐ 235	Cal Eldred	.30	.14	.04
☐ 236	Matt Mieske	.30	.14	.04
☐ 237	Bill Swift	.30	.14	.04
☐ 238	Marvin Freeman	.30	.14	.04
☐ 239	Jason Bates	.30	.14	.04
☐ 240	Larry Walker	1.25	.55	.16
☐ 241	Dave Nied	.30	.14	.04
☐ 242	Dante Bichette	1.25	.55	.16
☐ 243	Dennis Eckersley	.75	.35	.09
☐ 244	Todd Stottlemyre	.30	.14	.04
☐ 245	Rickey Henderson	.75	.35	.09
☐ 246	Geronimo Berroa	.30	.14	.04
☐ 247	Mark McGwire	.75	.35	.09
☐ 248	Quilvio Veras	.30	.14	.04
☐ 249	Terry Pendleton	.50	.23	.06
☐ 250	Andre Dawson	.75	.35	.09
☐ 251	Jeff Conine	.75	.35	.09
☐ 252	Kurt Abbott	.30	.14	.04
☐ 253	Jay Buhner	.75	.35	.09
☐ 254	Darren Bragg	.30	.14	.04
☐ 255	Ken Griffey Jr.	10.00	4.50	1.25
☐ 256	Tino Martinez	.75	.35	.09
☐ 257	Mark Grace	.75	.35	.09
☐ 258	Ryne Sandberg	2.50	1.10	.30
☐ 259	Randy Myers	.50	.23	.06
☐ 260	Howard Johnson	.30	.14	.04
☐ 261	Lee Smith	.75	.35	.09
☐ 262	J.T. Snow	.75	.35	.09
☐ 263	Chili Davis	.30	.14	.04
☐ 264	Chuck Finley	.30	.14	.04
☐ 265	Eddie Williams	.30	.14	.04
☐ 266	Joey Hamilton	.30	.14	.04
☐ 267	Ken Caminiti	.30	.14	.04
☐ 268	Andujar Cedeno	.30	.14	.04
☐ 269	Steve Finley	.30	.14	.04
☐ 270	Tony Gwynn	3.00	1.35	.35

1995 Upper Deck Special Edition Gold

The Gold set parallels the basic Special Edition set and features the player in a full color photo on gold foil paper. Backs include the player's close-up photo and outstanding achievements. Season and career statistics are featured at the bottom of the cards.

	MINT	NRMT	EXC
COMPLETE SET (270)	2600.00	1150.00	325.00
COMPLETE SERIES 1 (135)	1200.00	550.00	150.00
COMPLETE SERIES 2 (135)	1400.00	650.00	180.00
COMMON CARD (1-135)	4.00	1.80	.50
COMMON CARD (136-270)	4.00	1.80	.50
SEMISTARS	8.00	3.60	1.00
*VETERAN STARS: 12X TO 20X BASIC CARDS			
*YOUNG STARS: 9X TO 15X BASIC CARDS			
*RCs: 6X TO 12X BASIC CARDS			

		MINT	NRMT	EXC
☐ 14	Chipper Jones	60.00	27.00	7.50
☐ 20	Frank Thomas	125.00	55.00	15.50
☐ 25	Albert Belle	50.00	22.00	6.25
☐ 35	Mike Piazza	50.00	22.00	6.25
☐ 45	Jeff Bagwell	40.00	18.00	5.00
☐ 46	Cal Ripken	140.00	65.00	17.50
☐ 85	Kirby Puckett	40.00	18.00	5.00
☐ 144	Ruben Rivera	50.00	22.00	6.25
☐ 145	Don Mattingly	60.00	27.00	7.50

		MINT	NRMT	EXC
☐ 151	Greg Maddux	125.00	55.00	15.50
☐ 159	Kenny Lofton	40.00	18.00	5.00
☐ 161	Manny Ramirez	50.00	22.00	6.25
☐ 168	Hideo Nomo	100.00	45.00	12.50
☐ 175	Nolan Ryan TRIB	125.00	55.00	15.50
☐ 190	George Brett TRIB	50.00	22.00	6.25
☐ 255	Ken Griffey Jr.	125.00	55.00	15.50
☐ 270	Tony Gwynn	40.00	18.00	5.00

1995 Upper Deck Steal of a Deal

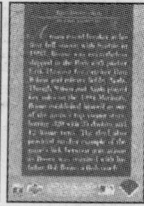

This set was inserted in hobby and retail packs at a rate of approximately one in 34. This 15-card set focuses on players who were acquired through, according to Upper Deck, "astute trades" or low round draft picks. The horizontal fronts feature a player cutout on a green background with a bronze seal. Backs feature information of how the player was acquired and past performance. The cards are numbered in the upper left with an "SD" prefix.

		MINT	NRMT	EXC
COMPLETE SET (15)		110.00	50.00	14.00
COMMON CARD (SD1-SD15)		2.00	.90	.25
☐ SD1	Mike Piazza	15.00	6.75	1.85
☐ SD2	Fred McGriff	5.00	2.20	.60
☐ SD3	Kenny Lofton	12.00	5.50	1.50
☐ SD4	Jose Oliva	2.00	.90	.25
☐ SD5	Jeff Bagwell	12.00	5.50	1.50
☐ SD6	R.Alomar/J.Carter	8.00	3.60	1.00
☐ SD7	Steve Karsay	2.00	.90	.25
☐ SD8	Ozzie Smith	8.00	3.60	1.00
☐ SD9	Dennis Eckersley	4.00	1.80	.50
☐ SD10	Jose Canseco	6.00	2.70	.75
☐ SD11	Carlos Baerga	8.00	3.60	1.00
☐ SD12	Cecil Fielder	4.00	1.80	.50
☐ SD13	Don Mattingly	20.00	9.00	2.50
☐ SD14	Bret Boone	4.00	1.80	.50
☐ SD15	Michael Jordan	40.00	18.00	5.00

1995 Zenith

The complete 1995 Zenith set consists of 150 cards. The cards are made of thick stock and are borderless. The fronts have an action photo with a pyramid design serving as background. The player's name appears vertically up the left side with the Pinnacle logo in the upper right-hand corner. The backs have a head shot and statistical information such as pitcher's strike frequency and what part of the field batters have the tendency to go to most. Included is a subset of 50 Rookies (111-150). The regular issued cards are in alphabetical order by first name.

		MINT	NRMT	EXC
COMPLETE SET (150)		50.00	22.00	6.25
COMMON CARD (1-150)		.25	.11	.03
☐ 1	Albert Belle	2.00	.90	.25
☐ 2	Alex Fernandez	.25	.11	.03
☐ 3	Andy Benes	.25	.11	.03
☐ 4	Barry Larkin	.60	.25	.07
☐ 5	Barry Bonds	1.25	.55	.16
☐ 6	Ben McDonald	.25	.11	.03
☐ 7	Bernard Gilkey	.25	.11	.03
☐ 8	Billy Ashley	.25	.11	.03
☐ 9	Bobby Bonilla	.40	.18	.05
☐ 10	Bret Saberhagen	.25	.11	.03
☐ 11	Brian Jordan	.25	.11	.03
☐ 12	Cal Ripken	5.00	2.20	.60
☐ 13	Carlos Baerga	1.00	.45	.12
☐ 14	Carlos Delgado	.25	.11	.03
☐ 15	Cecil Fielder	.40	.18	.05
☐ 16	Chili Davis	.25	.11	.03
☐ 17	Chuck Knoblauch	.40	.18	.05
☐ 18	Craig Biggio	.40	.18	.05
☐ 19	Danny Tartabull	.25	.11	.03
☐ 20	Dante Bichette	.60	.25	.07
☐ 21	Darren Daulton	.40	.18	.05
☐ 22	David Justice	.60	.25	.07
☐ 23	Dave Winfield	.40	.18	.05
☐ 24	David Cone	.40	.18	.05
☐ 25	Dean Palmer	.25	.11	.03
☐ 26	Deion Sanders	1.00	.45	.12
☐ 27	Dennis Eckersley	.40	.18	.05
☐ 28	Derek Bell	.25	.11	.03
☐ 29	Don Mattingly	2.50	1.10	.30
☐ 30	Edgar Martinez	.40	.18	.05
☐ 31	Eric Karros	.25	.11	.03
☐ 32	James Mouton	.25	.11	.03
☐ 33	Frank Thomas	5.00	2.20	.60
☐ 34	Fred McGriff	.60	.25	.07
☐ 35	Gary Sheffield	.40	.18	.05
☐ 36	Gary Gaetti	.25	.11	.03
☐ 37	Greg Maddux	5.00	2.20	.60
☐ 38	Gregg Jefferies	.25	.11	.03
☐ 39	Ivan Rodriguez	.40	.18	.05
☐ 40	Kenny Rogers	.25	.11	.03

☐ 41	J.T. Snow	.25	.11	.03
☐ 42	Hal Morris	.25	.11	.03
☐ 43	Eddie Murray 3000th Hit	.60	.25	.07
☐ 44	Javier Lopez	.60	.25	.07
☐ 45	Jay Bell	.25	.11	.03
☐ 46	Jeff Conine	.40	.18	.05
☐ 47	Jeff Bagwell	1.50	.70	.19
☐ 48	Hideo Nomo Japanese	8.00	3.60	1.00
☐ 49	Jeff Kent	.25	.11	.03
☐ 50	Jeff King	.25	.11	.03
☐ 51	Jim Thome	.60	.25	.07
☐ 52	Jimmy Key	.25	.11	.03
☐ 53	Joe Carter	.40	.18	.05
☐ 54	John Valentin	.40	.18	.05
☐ 55	John Olerud	.25	.11	.03
☐ 56	Jose Canseco	.75	.35	.09
☐ 57	Jose Rijo	.25	.11	.03
☐ 58	Jose Offerman	.25	.11	.03
☐ 59	Juan Gonzalez	1.25	.55	.16
☐ 60	Ken Caminiti	.25	.11	.03
☐ 61	Ken Griffey Jr.	5.00	2.20	.60
☐ 62	Kenny Lofton	1.50	.70	.19
☐ 63	Kevin Appier	.25	.11	.03
☐ 64	Kevin Seitzer	.25	.11	.03
☐ 65	Kirby Puckett	1.50	.70	.19
☐ 66	Kirk Gibson	.40	.18	.05
☐ 67	Larry Walker	.60	.25	.07
☐ 68	Lenny Dykstra	.40	.18	.05
☐ 69	Manny Ramirez	2.00	.90	.25
☐ 70	Mark Grace	.40	.18	.05
☐ 71	Mark McGwire	.40	.18	.05
☐ 72	Marquis Grissom	.40	.18	.05
☐ 73	Jim Edmonds	.60	.25	.07
☐ 74	Matt Williams	1.00	.45	.12
☐ 75	Mike Mussina	.60	.25	.07
☐ 76	Mike Piazza	2.00	.90	.25
☐ 77	Mo Vaughn	.75	.35	.09
☐ 78	Moises Alou	.25	.11	.03
☐ 79	Ozzie Smith	1.00	.45	.12
☐ 80	Paul O'Neill	.25	.11	.03
☐ 81	Paul Molitor	.40	.18	.05
☐ 82	Rafael Palmeiro	.40	.18	.05
☐ 83	Randy Johnson	1.00	.45	.12
☐ 84	Raul Mondesi	1.25	.55	.16
☐ 85	Ray Lankford	.25	.11	.03
☐ 86	Reggie Sanders	.40	.18	.05
☐ 87	Rickey Henderson	.40	.18	.05
☐ 88	Rico Brogna	.25	.11	.03
☐ 89	Roberto Alomar	1.00	.45	.12
☐ 90	Robin Ventura	.40	.18	.05
☐ 91	Roger Clemens	.75	.35	.09
☐ 92	Ron Gant	.40	.18	.05
☐ 93	Rondell White	.25	.11	.03
☐ 94	Royce Clayton	.25	.11	.03
☐ 95	Ruben Sierra	.25	.11	.03
☐ 96	Rusty Greer	.25	.11	.03
☐ 97	Ryan Klesko	1.00	.45	.12
☐ 98	Sammy Sosa	.40	.18	.05
☐ 99	Shawon Dunston	.25	.11	.03
☐ 100	Steve Ontiveros	.25	.11	.03
☐ 101	Tim Naehring	.25	.11	.03
☐ 102	Tim Salmon	.75	.35	.09
☐ 103	Tino Martinez	.40	.18	.05
☐ 104	Tony Gwynn	1.50	.70	.19
☐ 105	Travis Fryman	.40	.18	.05
☐ 106	Vinny Castilla	.40	.18	.05
☐ 107	Wade Boggs	.40	.18	.05
☐ 108	Wally Joyner	.25	.11	.03
☐ 109	Wil Cordero	.25	.11	.03
☐ 110	Will Clark	.60	.25	.07
☐ 111	Chipper Jones	2.00	.90	.25
☐ 112	Armando Benitez	.25	.11	.03
☐ 113	Curtis Goodwin	.25	.11	.03
☐ 114	Gabe White	.25	.11	.03
☐ 115	Vaughn Eshelman	.25	.11	.03
☐ 116	Marty Cordova	.75	.35	.09
☐ 117	Dustin Hermanson	.25	.11	.03
☐ 118	Rich Becker	.25	.11	.03
☐ 119	Ray Durham	.40	.18	.05
☐ 120	Shane Andrews	.25	.11	.03
☐ 121	Scott Ruffcorn	.25	.11	.03
☐ 122	Mark Grudzielanek	.50	.23	.06
☐ 123	James Baldwin	.25	.11	.03
☐ 124	Carlos Perez	1.25	.55	.16
☐ 125	Julian Tavarez	.25	.11	.03
☐ 126	Joe Vitiello	.25	.11	.03
☐ 127	Jason Bates	.25	.11	.03
☐ 128	Edgardo Alfonzo	.25	.11	.03
☐ 129	Juan Acevedo	.25	.11	.03
☐ 130	Bill Pulsipher	.25	.11	.03
☐ 131	Bob Higginson	.75	.35	.09
☐ 132	Russ Davis	.25	.11	.03
☐ 133	Charles Johnson	.25	.11	.03
☐ 134	Derek Jeter	.60	.25	.07
☐ 135	Orlando Miller	.25	.11	.03
☐ 136	LaTroy Hawkins	.25	.11	.03
☐ 137	Brian L.Hunter	.60	.25	.07
☐ 138	Roberto Petagine	.25	.11	.03
☐ 139	Midre Cummings	.25	.11	.03
☐ 140	Garret Anderson	1.00	.45	.12
☐ 141	Ugueth Urbina	.25	.11	.03
☐ 142	Antonio Osuna	.25	.11	.03
☐ 143	Michael Tucker	.25	.11	.03
☐ 144	Benji Gil	.25	.11	.03
☐ 145	Jon Nunnally	.25	.11	.03
☐ 146	Alex Rodriguez	1.00	.45	.12
☐ 147	Todd Hollandsworth	.25	.11	.03
☐ 148	Alex Gonzalez	.25	.11	.03
☐ 149	Hideo Nomo	8.00	3.60	1.00
☐ 150	Shawn Green	.40	.18	.05

1995 Zenith
All-Star Salute

This 18-card set was randomly inserted in packs at a rate of one in six. The set commemorates many of the memorable plays of the 1995 All-Star Game played in Arlington, TX. The fronts have an action photo set out against the background of the game giving it a 3D look. The words "All-Star Salute" are in gold on the left with the player's name at the bottom. The backs *have a color photo with personal All-Star Game tidbits. The cards are numbered "X of 18."*

	MINT	NRMT	EXC
COMPLETE SET (18)	70.00	32.00	8.75
COMMON CARD (1-18)	1.00	.45	.12

		MINT	NRMT	EXC
☐ 1	Cal Ripken	10.00	4.50	1.25
☐ 2	Frank Thomas	10.00	4.50	1.25
☐ 3	Mike Piazza	4.00	1.80	.50
☐ 4	Kirby Puckett	3.00	1.35	.35
☐ 5	Manny Ramirez	4.00	1.80	.50
☐ 6	Tony Gwynn	3.00	1.35	.35
☐ 7	Hideo Nomo	12.00	5.50	1.50
☐ 8	Matt Williams	1.50	.70	.19
☐ 9	Randy Johnson	2.00	.90	.25
☐ 10	Raul Mondesi	2.50	1.10	.30
☐ 11	Albert Belle	4.00	1.80	.50
☐ 12	Ivan Rodriguez	1.00	.45	.12
☐ 13	Barry Bonds	2.50	1.10	.30
☐ 14	Carlos Baerga	2.00	.90	.25
☐ 15	Ken Griffey Jr.	10.00	4.50	1.25
☐ 16	Jeff Conine	1.00	.45	.12
☐ 17	Frank Thomas	10.00	4.50	1.25
☐ 18	Cal Ripken	8.00	3.60	1.00
	Barry Bonds			

1995 Zenith Rookie Roll Call

This 18-card, Dufex-designed set was randomly inserted in packs at a rate of one in 24. The set is comprised of 18 top rookies from 1995. The fronts have two photos and a colorful star in the background with which rays of color emanate. The backs are laid out horizontally with a color photo on a multi-color foil background. Player information of previous accomplishments is also on the back and the cards are numbered "X of 18."

		MINT	NRMT	EXC
COMPLETE SET (18)		400.00	180.00	50.00
COMMON CARD (1-18)		12.00	5.50	1.50

		MINT	NRMT	EXC
☐ 1	Alex Rodriguez	30.00	13.50	3.70
☐ 2	Derek Jeter	25.00	11.00	3.10
☐ 3	Chipper Jones	60.00	27.00	7.50
☐ 4	Shawn Green	20.00	9.00	2.50
☐ 5	Todd Hollandsworth	15.00	6.75	1.85

		MINT	NRMT	EXC
☐ 6	Bill Pulsipher	20.00	9.00	2.50
☐ 7	Hideo Nomo	50.00	22.00	6.25
☐ 8	Ray Durham	15.00	6.75	1.85
☐ 9	Curtis Goodwin	15.00	6.75	1.85
☐ 10	Brian L.Hunter	25.00	11.00	3.10
☐ 11	Julian Tavarez	15.00	6.75	1.85
☐ 12	Marty Cordova UER	30.00	13.50	3.70
	Kevin Maas pictured			
☐ 13	Michael Tucker	15.00	6.75	1.85
☐ 14	Edgardo Alfonzo	12.00	5.50	1.50
☐ 15	LaTroy Hawkins	12.00	5.50	1.50
☐ 16	Carlos Perez	25.00	11.00	3.10
☐ 17	Charles Johnson	20.00	9.00	2.50
☐ 18	Benji Gil	12.00	5.50	1.50

1995 Zenith Z-Team

This 18-card set was randomly inserted in packs at a rate of one in 72. The set is comprised of the best players in baseball and is done in 3-D Dufex. The fronts have a player action photo positioned on home plate which has the words "Z Team". There are multi-colored rays coming out of the card background. The back is laid out horizontally with a color head shot and a stadium crowd background. The back also has player information and a "Z Team" emblem.

		MINT	NRMT	EXC
COMPLETE SET (18)		1200.00	550.00	150.00
COMMON CARD (1-18)		25.00	11.00	3.10

		MINT	NRMT	EXC
☐ 1	Cal Ripken	200.00	90.00	25.00
☐ 2	Ken Griffey Jr.	175.00	80.00	22.00
☐ 3	Frank Thomas	175.00	80.00	22.00
☐ 4	Matt Williams	35.00	16.00	4.40
☐ 5	Mike Piazza UER	70.00	32.00	8.75
	(Card says started at first base Piazza is a catcher)			
☐ 6	Barry Bonds	45.00	20.00	5.50
☐ 7	Raul Mondesi	45.00	20.00	5.50
☐ 8	Greg Maddux	175.00	80.00	22.00
☐ 9	Jeff Bagwell	60.00	27.00	7.50
☐ 10	Manny Ramirez	70.00	32.00	8.75
☐ 11	Larry Walker	30.00	13.50	3.70
☐ 12	Tony Gwynn	60.00	27.00	7.50
☐ 13	Will Clark	30.00	13.50	3.70
☐ 14	Albert Belle	70.00	32.00	8.75
☐ 15	Kenny Lofton	60.00	27.00	7.50
☐ 16	Rafael Palmeiro	25.00	11.00	3.10
☐ 17	Don Mattingly	75.00	34.00	9.50
☐ 18	Carlos Baerga	40.00	18.00	5.00

Acknowledgments

Each year we refine the process of developing the most accurate and up-to-date information for this book. I believe this year's Price Guide is our best yet. Thanks again to all the contributors nationwide (listed below) as well as our staff here in Dallas.

Those who have worked closely with us on this and many other books have again proven themselves invaluable — Chris Benjamin, Levi Bleam, Peter Brennan, Ray Bright, Card Collectors Co., Cartophilium (Andrew Pywowarczuk), Classic (Elaine McConnell), Barry Colla, Bill and Diane Dodge, David Festberg, Fleer (Rich Bradley and Ted Taylor), Steve Freedman, Gervise Ford, Larry and Jeff Fritsch, Tony Galovich, Georgia Music and Sports (Dick DeCourcey), Dick Gilkeson, Steve Gold (AU Sports), Bill Goodwin (St. Louis Baseball Cards), Mike and Howard Gordon, George Grauer, John Greenwald, Wayne Grove, Bill Haber, Bill Henderson, Jerry and Etta Hersh, Mike Hersh, Neil Hoppenworth, Jay and Mary Kasper, David Kohler (SportsCards Plus), Leaf (Traci Santiago), Paul Lewicki, Lew Lipset, Mike Livingston (University Trading Cards), Mark Macrae, Bill Madden, Michael McDonald (The Sports Page), Megacards (Dawn Ridgeway, Rick Starks), Mid-Atlantic Sports Cards (Bill Bossert), John Miller, Gary Mills, Brian Morris, Mike Mosier (Columbia City Collectibles Co.), B.A. Murry, Ralph Nozaki, Mike O'Brien, Oldies and Goodies (Nigel Spill), Pacific Trading Cards (Mike Cramer and Mike Monson), Pinnacle (Kurt Iverson), Jack Pollard, Jeff Prillaman, Gavin Riley, Alan Rosen (Mr. Mint), Clifton Rouse, John Rumierz, San Diego Sport Collectibles (Bill Goepner and Nacho Arredondo), Kevin Savage (Sports Gallery), Gary Sawatski, Mike Schechter, Signature Rookies (Tim Johnson), Barry Sloate, John E. Spalding, Phil Spector (Scoreboard, Inc.), Sports Collectors Store, Frank Steele, Murvin Sterling, Lee Temanson, Topps (Marty Appel, Sy Berger and Melisa Rosen), Treat (Harold Anderson), Ed Twombly (New England Bullpen), Upper Deck (Marilyn Van Dyke), Wayne Varner, Bill Vizas, Bill Wesslund (Portland Sports Card Co.), Kit Young, Ted Zanidakis, and Bill Zimpleman. Finally we give a special acknowledgment to the late Dennis W. Eckes, "Mr. Sport Americana." The success of the Beckett Price Guides has always been the result of a team effort.

It is very difficult to be "accurate" — one can only do one's best. But this job is especially difficult since we're shooting at a moving target: Prices are fluctuating all the time. Having several full-time pricing experts has definitely proven to be better than just one, and I thank all of them for working together to provide you, our readers, with the most accurate prices possible.

Many people have provided price input, illustrative material, checklist verifications, errata, and/or background information. We should like to individually thank AbD Cards (Dale Wesolewski), Action Card Sales, Jerry Adamic, Johnny and Sandy Adams, Alex's MVP Cards & Comics, Doug Allen (Round Tripper Sportscards), Will Allison, Dennis Anderson, Ed Anderson, Shane Anderson, Bruce W. Andrews, Ellis Anmuth, Tom Antonowicz, Ric Apter, Jason Arasate, Clyde Archer, Matt Argento, Burl Armstrong, Neil Armstrong (World Series Cards), Todd Armstrong, B and J Sportscards, Dave Bailey, Shawn Bailey, Ball Four Cards (Frank and Steve Pemper), Frank and Vivian Barning, Bob Bartosz, Nathan Basford, Carl Berg, David Berman, Beulah Sports (Jeff Blatt), Brian Bigelow, George Birsic, B.J. Sportscollectables, David Boedicker (The Wild Pitch Inc.), Bob Boffa, Tim Bond (Tim's Cards & Comics), Brian W. Bottles, Bill Brandt, Jeff Breitenfield, John Brigandi, Chuck Brooks, Dan Bruner, Lesha Bundrick, Michael Bunker, John E. Burick, Ed Burkey Jr., Bubba Burnett, Virgil Burns, California Card Co., Capital Cards, Danny Cariseo, Carl

Carlson (C.T.S.), Jim Carr, Patrick Carroll, Carves Cards, Ira Cetron, Don Chaffee, Michael Chan, Sandy Chan, Ric Chandgie, Dwight Chapin, Ray Cherry, Bigg Wayne Christian, Dick Cianciotto, Derrick F. Clark, Bill Cochran, Don Coe, Tom Cohoon (Cardboard Dreams), Collection de Sport AZ (Ronald Villaneuve), Gary Collett, Andrew T. Collier, Charles A. Collins, Curt Cooter, Steven Cooter, Pedro Cortes, Rick Cosmen (RC Card Co.), Lou Costanzo (Champion Sports), Mike Coyne, Paul and Ryan Crabb, Kevin Crane, Taylor Crane, Chad Cripe, Brian Cunningham, Allen Custer, Donald L. Cutler, Eugene C. Dalager, Dave Dame, Brett Daniel, Tony Daniele III, Roy Datema, John Davidson, Travis Deaton, Dee's Baseball Cards (Dee Robinson), Tim DelVecchio, Steve Dempski, John Derossett, Mark Diamond, Gilberto Diaz Jr., Ken Dinerman (California Cruizers), Discount Dorothy, Walter J. Dodds Sr., Bill Dodson, Richard Dolloff (Dolloff Coin Center), Ron Dorsey, Double Play Baseball Cards, Richard Duglin (Baseball Cards-N-More), The Dugout, Kyle Dunbar, B.M. Dungan, Ken Edick (Home Plate of Utah), Randall Edwards, Rick Einhorn, Mark Ely, Todd Entenman, Doak Ewing, Bryan Failing, R.J. Faletti, John Fedak, Stephen A. Ferradino, Tom Ferrara, Louis Fineberg, Jay Finglass, L.V. Fischer, Fremont Fong, Perry Fong, Craig Frank, Mark Franke, Walter Franklin, Richard Galasso, Ray Garner, David Garza, David Gaumer, Georgetown Card Exchange, Richard Gibson Jr., Glenn A. Giesey, Dick Goddard, Dr. John R. Goldberg, Alvin Goldblum, Brian Goldner, Jeff Goldstein, Ron Gomez, Greg's Cards, Mike Grimm, Neil Gubitz (What-A-Card), Hall's Nostalgia, Hershell Hanks, Gregg Hara, Zac Hargis, Floyd Haynes (H and H Baseball Cards), Ben Heckert, Kevin Heimbigner, Dennis Heitland, Joel Hellman, Arthur W. Henkel, Hit and Run Cards (Jon, David, and Kirk Peterson), Gary Holcomb, Lyle Holcomb, Rich Hovorka, John Howard, Mark Hromalik, H.P. Hubert, Dennis Hughes, Harold Hull, Johnny Hustle Card Co., Tom Imboden, Chris Imbriaco, Vern Isenberg, Robert A. Ivanjack (Kit Young Cards), Dale Jackson, Hal Jarvis, Paul Jastrzembski, Jeff's Sports Cards, David Jenkins, Donn Jennings Cards, George Johnson, Robe Johnson, Stephen Jones, Steven L. Judd, Al Julian, Dave Jurgensmeier, John Just, Robert Just, Frank J. Katen, Jerry Katz (Bottom of the Ninth), Mark Kauffman, Allan Kaye, Rick Keplinger, Sam Kessler, Kevin's Kards, Larry B. Killian, Kingdom Collectibles, Inc., Philip C. Klutts, Steven Koenigsberg, Blake Krier, Neil Krohn, Scott Ku, Thomas Kunnecke, Gary Lambert, Matthew Lancaster (MC's Card and Hobby), Jason Lassic, Allan Latawiec, Gerald A. Lavelle, Dan Lavin, Richard S. Lawrence, William Lawrence, W.H. Lee, Morley Leeking, Ronald Lenhardt, Brian Lentz, Tom Leon, Leo's Sports Collectibles, Irv Lerner, Lisa Licitra, James Litopoulos, Larry Loeschen (A and J Sportscards), Allan Lowenberg, Kendall Loyd (Orlando Sportscards South), Robert Luce, David Macaray, Jim Macie, Joe Maddigan, David Madison, Rob Maerten, Pierre Marceau, Paul Marchant, Rich Markus, Bob Marquette, Brad L. Marten, Ronald L. Martin, Frank J. Masi, Bill Mastro, Duane Matthes, James S. Maxwell Jr., Dr. William McAvoy, Michael McCormick, Paul McCormick, McDag Productions Inc., Branson H. McKay, Tony McLaughlin, Mendal Mearkle, Ken Melanson, William Mendel, Eric Meredith, Blake Meyer (Lone Star Sportscards), Joe Michalowicz, Lee Milazzo, Jimmy Milburn, Cary S. Miller, David (Otis) Miller, Eldon Miller, George Miller, Wayne Miller, Dick Millerd, Mitchell's Baseball Cards, Perry Miyashita, Douglas Mo, William Munn, Mark Murphy, John Musacchio, National Sportscard Exchange, Bud Obermeyer, Francisco Ochoa, John O'Hara, Mike Orth, Ron Oser, Luther Owen, Earle Parrish, Clay Pasternack, Mickey Payne, Michael Perrotta, Doug and Zachary Perry, Tom Pfirrmann, Bob Pirro, George Pollitt, Don Prestia, Coy Priest, Bob Ragonese, Richard H. Ranck, Robert M. Ray, R.W. Ray, Phil

Regli, Tom Reid, Glenn Renick, Rob Resnick, John Revell, Bill Rodman, Craig Roehrig, David H. Rogers, Michael H. Rosen, Martin Rotunno, Michael Runyan, Mark Rush, George Rusnak, Mark Russell, Terry Sack, Joe Sak, Jennifer Salems, Barry Sanders, Everett Sands, Jon Sands, Dave Schau (Baseball Cards), Bruce M. Schwartz, Keith A. Schwartz, Charlie Seaver, Tom Shanyfelt, Steven C. Sharek, Art Smith, Ben Smith, Michael Smith, Jerry Sorice, Carl Specht, Sports Card Fan-Attic, The Sport Hobbyist, Dauer Stackpole, Norm Stapleton, Bill Steinberg, Bob Stern, Bill Stone, Tim Strandberg (East Texas Sports Cards), Edward Strauss, Strike Three, Richard Strobino, Superior Sport Card, Dr. Richard Swales, Paul Taglione, George Tahinos, Ian Taylor, Lyle Telfer, The Thirdhand Shoppe, Scott A. Thomas, Paul Thornton, Carl N. Thrower, Jim Thurtell, Bud Tompkins (Minnesota Connection), Philip J. Tremont, Ralph Triplette, Mike Trotta, Umpire's Choice Inc., Eric Unglaub, Nathan Voss, Steven Wagman, Jonathan Waldman, Terry Walker, T. Wall, Gary A. Walter, Mark Weber, Joe and John Weisenburger (The Wise Guys), Richard West, Mike Wheat, Richard Wiercinski, Don Williams (Robin's Nest of Dolls), Jeff Williams, Kent Williams, Craig Williamson, Opry Winston, Brandon Witz, John Wolf Jr., Jay Wolt (Cavalcade of Sports), Carl Womack, Pete Wooten, Peter Yee, Wes Young, Robert Zanze (Z-Cards and Sports), Dean Zindler, Tom Zmuda (Koinz & Kardz), and Tim Zwick.

Every year we make active solicitations for expert input. We are particularly appreciative of help (however extensive or cursory) provided for this volume. We receive many inquiries, comments and questions regarding material within this book. In fact, each and every one is read and digested. Time constraints, however, prevent us from personally replying. But keep sharing your knowledge. Your letters and input are part of the "big picture" of hobby information we can pass along to readers in our books and magazines. Even though we cannot respond to each letter, you are making significant contributions to the hobby through your interest and comments.

The effort to continually refine and improve this book also involves a growing number of people and types of expertise on our home team. Our company boasts a substantial Technical Services team, which strengthens our ability to provide comprehensive analysis of the marketplace. Technical Services capably handled numerous technical details and provided able assistance in the preparation of this edition.

Our baseball analysts played a major part in compiling this year's book, travelling thousands of miles during the past year to attend sports card shows and visit card shops around the United States and Canada. The Beckett baseball specialists are Theo Chen (Assistant Manager, Hobby Information), Ben Ecklar, Mike Jaspersen (Product Information Coordinator), Eddie Kelly, Rich Klein, Tom Layberger and Grant Sandground (Assistant Manager, Pricing Analysis). Their pricing analysis and careful proofreading were key contributions to the accuracy of this annual.

Theo Chen's coordination and reconciling of prices as *Beckett Baseball Card Monthly* title analyst helped immeasurably, as did Tom Layberger's editing and proofing of set and pricing information. Rich Klein, as research analyst, contributed detailed pricing analysis and hours of proofing.

The effort was led by Director of Technical Services Jay Johnson. He was ably assisted by the rest of the Price Guide analysts: Randy Barning, Pat Blandford, Dan Hitt, Allan Muir and Rob Springs. Also contributing to Technical Services functions was the card librarian Gabriel Rangel.

The price gathering and analytical talents of this fine group of hobbyists have helped make our Beckett team stronger, while making this guide and its companion monthly Price Guide more widely recognized as the hobby's most reliable and relied upon sources of pricing information.

Scott Layton, Assistant Manager of Database Production, was a key person in the organization of both technological and people resources for the book. He set up initial schedules and ensured that all deadlines were met, while looking for all the fine points to improve our process and presentation throughout the cycle. He was ably assisted by Jeany Finch and Beverly Mills who helped enter new sets, ensured the proper administration of our contributor Price Guide surveys and performed various other tasks.

The IS (Information Services) department, ably headed by Mark Harwell, played a critical role in technology. Working with software designed by assistant manager David Schneider, Eric Best and Greg Flaming spent countless hours programming, testing, and implementing it to simplify the handling of thousands of prices that must be checked and updated for each edition.

In the Production Department, Paul Kerutis was responsible for the typesetting and for the card photos you see throughout the book. He was ably assisted by Rob Barry and Lisa O'Neill.

Loretta Gibbs and Carrie Ehrhardt spent tireless hours on the phone attending to the wishes of our dealer advertisers. Once the ad specifications were delivered to our offices, Dawn Ciaccio used her computer skills to turn raw copy into attractive display advertisements.

In the years since this guide debuted, Beckett Publications has grown beyond any rational expectation. A great many talented and hard working individuals have been instrumental in this growth and success. Our whole team is to be congratulated for what we together have accomplished. Our Beckett Publications team is led by Executive Vice President Jeff Amano, Vice Presidents Claire Backus, Joe Galindo and Fred Reed, Directors Mark Harwell, Jay Johnson and Reed Poole, and Senior Managers Jeff Anthony, Beth Harwell and Pepper Hastings. They are ably assisted by Dana Alecknavage, Theresa Anderson, Kelly Atkins, Kaye Ball, Airey Baringer, Barbara Barry, James R. Beane, Therese Bellar, Louise Bird, Cathryn Black, Amy Brougher, Bob Brown, Chris Calandro, Randall Calvert, Emily Camp, Mary Campana, Susan Catka, Jud Chappell, Albert Chavez, Marty Click, Cindy Cockroft, Laura Corley, Andy Costilla, Randy Cummings, Brandon Davis, Marlon DePaula, Julie Dussair, Marcelo Gomez DeSouza, Gail Docekal, Barbara Faraldo, Craig Ferris, Gean Paul Figari, Kim Ford, Gayle Gasperin, Steve Genusa, Rosanna Gonzalez-Olaechea, Jeff Greer, Mary Gregory, Jenifer Grellhesl, Julie Grove, Tracy Hackler, Leslie Harris, Joanna Hayden, Chris Hellem, Tracy Hinton, E.J. Hradek, Tim Jaksa, Wendy Kizer, Rudy Klancnik, Brian Kosley, Jane Ann Layton, Sara Leeman, Benedito Leme, Lori Lindsey, Stanley Lira, Kirk Lockhart, Lisa Lujan, Sara Maneval, Louis Marroquin, Mike McAllister, Omar Mediano, Lisa McQuilkin Monaghan, Sherry Monday, Rob Moore, Mila Morante, Daniel Moscoso Jr., Mike Moss, Randy Mosty, Hugh Murphy, Shawn Murphy, Steve Naughton, Mike Obert, Stacy Olivieri, Mike Pagel, Wendy Pallugna, Laura Patterson, Mike Payne, Diego Picon, Tim Polzer, Fran Poole, Will Pry, Bob Richardson, Tina Riojas, Susan Sainz, Gary Santaniello, Elaine Simmons, Dave Sliepka, Judi Smalling, Sheri Smith, Jeff Stanton, Margaret Steele, Marcia Stoesz, Doree Tate, Jim Tereschuk, Lawrence Treachler, Carol Weaver, Steve Wilson and Mark Zeske. The whole Beckett Publications team has my thanks for jobs well done. Thank you, everyone.

I also thank my family, especially my wife, Patti, and our daughters, Christina, Rebecca, and Melissa, for putting up with me again.

Weather Update

"Expert Beckett Analysts Report Current Conditions – Hot Players and Trends – In Beckett Basketball Monthly."

- List Of Hot Players!
- Prices On All Popular Card Sets
- Explanations Of Significant Monthly Price Changes
- Illustrative Card Photos For Each Set Listed
- Much More!

Subscribe To
Beckett Basketball Monthly **Today!**

Health Watch

"Get A Steady Diet Of Superstar Players And Card Hobby News In *Beckett Hockey Monthly*."

- Up-To-Date Prices On All Popular Card Sets
- Comprehensive Card Condition Guide
- Player Interviews
- List Of Hot Players
- Much More!

Subscribe To *Beckett Hockey Monthly* Today!

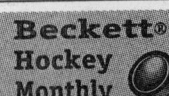

Notes